AutoCAD for Architecture

AutoCAD *for Architecture*

Tuna Saka

Pennsylvania College of Technology—Williamsport, PA

Prentice Hall, Inc.
Upper Saddle River, NJ 07458

Library of Congress Cataloging-in-Publication Data

Saka, Tuna
    AutoCAD for architecture / Tuna Saka.
       p. cm.
    Includes index.
    ISBN 0-13-091436-3
    1. Architectural drawing—Computer-aided design. 2. AutoCAD. I. Title.

NA2728.S25 2001
720'.285"5369—dc21   2001021417

Vice President and Editorial Director, ECS: *Marcia J. Horton*
Executive Editor: *Eric Svendsen*
Vice President and Director of Production and Manufacturing, ESM: *David W. Riccardi*
Executive Managing Editor: *Vince O'Brien*
Managing Editor: *David A. George*
Production Editor: *Lynn Steines*
Director of Creative Services: *Paul Belfanti*
Creative Director: *Carole Anson*
Art Director: *Jayne Conte*
Art Editor: *Adam Velthaus*
Cover Designer: *Bruce Kenselaar*
Manufacturing Manager: *Trudy Pisciotti*
Manufacturing Buyer: *Lynn Castillo*
Marketing Manager: *Holly Stark*
Marketing Assistant: *Karen Moon*

© 2002 by Prentice Hall
Prentice-Hall, Inc.
Upper Saddle River, New Jersey 07458

The author and publisher of this book have used their best efforts in preparing this book. These efforts include the development, research, and testing of the theories and programs to determine their effectiveness. The author and publisher make no warranty of any kind, expressed or implied, with regard to these programs or the documentation contained in this book. The author and publisher shall not be liable in any event for incidental or consequential damages in connection with, or arising out of, the furnishing, performance, or use of these programs.

AutoCAD, and the AutoCAD and Autodesk logos are registered trademarks of Autodesk, Inc., 111 McInnis Parkway, San Rafael, CA 94903.

Printed in the United States of America.

10 9 8 7 6 5 4 3 2 1

ISBN 0-13-091436-3

Prentice-Hall International (UK) Limited, *London*
Prentice-Hall of Australia Pty. Limited, *Sydney*
Prentice-Hall Canada Inc., *Toronto*
Prentice-Hall Hispanoamericana, S.A., *Mexico City*
Prentice-Hall of India Private Limited, *New Delhi*
Prentice-Hall of Japan, Inc., *Tokyo*
Pearson Education Asia Pte. Ltd., *Singapore*
Editora Prentice-Hall do Brasil, Ltda., *Rio de Janeiro*

This book is dedicated to my wife Fulya,
my son Serkan, and my daughter Selin,
whose support and encouragement made this book a reality.

Contents

CHAPTER 20   *Creating Architectural Graphic Patterns*   656

CHAPTER 21   *Assigning Attributes to Symbols*   695

CHAPTER 23   Printing and Plotting   761

CHAPTER 24   Externally Referenced Drawings   783

Preface

This book provides detailed and systematic explanation of the commands, system variables, tools, procedures, processes, and techniques of AutoCAD for creating architectural and construction-related drawings. It is a practical and comprehensive learning tool, text, and work-book that teaches basic and advanced AutoCAD skills to architects, interior designers, facilities planners, building contractors, architectural drafters, and students of architecture, interior design, and construction. It includes step-by-step exercises for hands-on practical applications that provide the know-how to create basic drawings used in architectural working drawings and construction documents. Commands and procedures are presented in a logical sequence that is easy to read and understand. The primary objective of this book is to provide enough tools that relate to architectural applications of AutoCAD and not to cover every command and procedure. It is a textbook, not an encyclopedia. Other specific features of this book include the following:

- Fundamentals of AutoCAD commands and procedures with hands-on, step-by-step exercises to produce basic two-dimensional architectural drawings.

- Explanation of how AutoCAD procedures relate to what an architect or an interior designer might do when creating drawings.

- Show and tell approach to what an architect, an interior designer, or a student should know in AutoCAD to create and print architectural drawings accurately and precisely.

- A full range of AutoCAD commands and features specific to the process of creating architectural drawings that you will use on a daily basis in your profession or in the classroom.

- Contents structured to teach the skills required to practice and master the two-dimensional drawing commands and procedures that allow you to create architectural working drawings and construction related documents.

- Concepts and commands that are correlated with architectural examples so that you can apply them immediately to your drawings and identify the appropriate commands and procedures to create the required drawings.

- Step-by-step exercises to reinforce and apply options and command procedures.

- Useful tips, notes, and cautions that will increase your productivity without sacrificing accuracy. The shortcuts and tricks definitely increase drawing efficiency.

- Hands-on system of learning with a *show-me-how-it's-done* approach supported by practical drawing exercises.

- Tables and charts to make the learning process easier and faster.

- Advanced commands, procedures and Express Tools to boost productivity.

In addition, each chapter and exercise is built around the concept of "tool and apparatus," where I explain a command, option, or a procedure as a tool and then you execute it with an exercise as an apparatus. As you complete the exercises, I am with you every step of the way with explanations and suggestions. This will give you a real sense of progression as you master commands and procedures. Each chapter is written and presented in a pedagogical format in which fundamental commands and concepts are explained first, followed by step-by-step exercises, and advanced features including many of the express tools, ending with review questions and chapter problems. Commands and procedures are presented in a logical sequence and each chapter is created on the skills presented in the previous chapter. Files for chapter exercise can be downloaded from the http://www.prenhall.com/saka web site.

I have given special attention to commands that are specific to architecture and procedures that an architect or an interior designer may apply when creating architectural drawings. For example, I have included an in-depth coverage and explanation of the MULTILINE command in a separate chapter. I have included the AIA CAD Layer guidelines as part of the architectural layer standards in a separate chapter and the actual layers in the Appendix. As you build your knowledge from one chapter to the next, you will progress to become at ease with easy-to-understand commands and procedures. I have included chapter tests for review of commands and key AutoCAD concepts. I have also created a *test bank* available for instructors and CAD Managers. The test bank can be used to create an AutoCAD exam to assess skills learned in a semester or to test the skill level of a future employee in a firm.

TYPESTYLE CONVENTIONS

Throughout the book you are requested to access and select commands and respond to commands and their options in the command line using your keyboard or your mouse. The words *select, pick, click, left-click, and right-click* refer to accessing a command or performing a procedure using the buttons on your mouse. The words *enter* and *type* refer to typing a command or a system variable at the command line using your keyboard. The word *cursor* refers to the pick box on the screen and the act of moving the mouse to perform such tasks as picking a point, drawing a line, or accessing a command. Different typefaces are used throughout the book to define procedures and identify AutoCAD commands. The typestyle conventions of the book are as follows:

Text	Style Example
Commands and System Variables at keyboard entry	**MLINE**
Command options or values at keyboard entry	**@2',7'**
Commands and System Variables as defined	CHAMFER
Important terms and file names	*defpoints*
Command line prompt procedures	*(move your cursor to Point A)*
Tips (shortcuts and tricks)	**Tips:**
Note (additional information)	**Note:**
Caution (attention and warning)	*Caution:*
Steps used to calculate, draw, or perform a task as part of Exercise	**Step#1:**

Once the command is entered, pressing the Enter or Return key is required and will be presented by the ~Enter Key~ symbol. AutoCAD is not case sensitive therefore you can enter at the command line either using lower case or upper case. In most exercises, command entries are shown as typed instead of accessed from a pull-down menu or a toolbar.

HOW TO USE THIS BOOK

The first chapter of this book provides an overview of the new features of AutoCAD 2000i as well as Internet features of both versions 2000 and 2000i. Features that are new in AutoCAD 2000i that pertain to a specific chapter and section are referenced as ***AutoCAD 2000i Update****:* followed by the description of the new feature throughout the text. Chapters 2 through 24 are based on the use of AutoCAD2000 and include the updates. If you just started working with AutoCAD 2000 or AutoCAD2000i, each chapter in this book will teach you important concepts and include step-by-step exercises that show you how to use both versions of AutoCAD effectively and efficiently. Exercises provide key elements necessary to complete a specific task. The text is organized around the procedures that an architect or designer might typically follow when performing a similar task. The following guidelines will help you get the most out of this book:

- Read the chapter objectives at the beginning of each chapter and understand what tasks you should be able to perform.

- Read the concepts and key terms in each chapter to understand the application of commands and procedures into the drawing processes.
- Reread essential features that apply to all types of architectural design and drawing tasks.
- Review key terms and processes before executing exercises.
- Complete all exercises to apply AutoCAD features to drawing tasks.
- When using the step-by-step exercises, review each step to understand what you did for what particular reason.
- After completing an exercise, ask yourself if you can complete the same exercise without following the steps from the book. If so, move on to the next concept. If not, repeat each exercise until you become comfortable performing the exercise on your own.
- Pay close attention to tips, notes, and cautions. These allow you to incorporate a different procedure, present an alternate point of view, warn you about things you should not do, or provide a shortcut that you may use to save drawing time.
- After completing a chapter, answer the Review Questions to assess what you have learned.
- After the Review Questions, complete the Problems at the end of each chapter.
- Don't give up if you become frustrated. Practice over and over again until you understand the procedures related to each objective.
- Don't be afraid to experiment. There is a lot of room for self-exploration and self-discovery. With patience and practice, AutoCAD will grow on you.

This book can also be used as a reference and training manual in the office and in the studio. With many tools to create company standards to facilitate productivity, it can also be used as the office or studio companion with major architectural CAD concepts and applications that you need to produce and manage construction documents. Whether you are a professional or a student learning AutoCAD on your own or through an instructor-led course, you can use this text as a guide that will provide the know-how you need to increase and boost productivity and efficiency at work or in the classroom. Whether you are a novice or a seasoned AutoCAD user, this text will lead you through the basics as well as the advanced features of AutoCAD.

The successful application of AutoCAD to architectural drawings requires only a basic understanding of the architectural drawing processes, time, patience, and practice. This may be a lot to ask at first, but envision yourself as the person able to create wonderful architectural drawings that some day will transform into a skyscraper or an opera house.

◆ ABOUT THE AUTHOR

Tuna Saka is an Associate Professor with the Architectural Technology program, Pennsylvania College of Technology, Williamsport, PA. He received the Associate in Applied Science degree in civil engineering technology from Hudson Valley Community College in 1983 and the Bachelor of Professional Studies and Masters degrees in architecture from the State University of New York at Buffalo in 1986 and 1988, respectively. He is an Autodesk Certified Instructor in the Autodesk Training Center at the Pennsylvania College of Technology and has extensive training in architectural applications of AutoCAD. In addition to teaching, he provides AutoCAD productivity consulting to AEC firms around the globe. Mr. Saka was the recipient of the and the R. Buckminster Fuller scholarship award from the State University of New York at Buffalo and the American Institute of Architects (AIA) foundation scholarship award in 1986 and 1987, respectively. His research interests include the integration of computer technology in architecture and the utilization of computer-aided architectural design in education and practice. He has been teaching AutoCAD at the college level since 1994. He is married and has two children.

Acknowledgments

I would like to thank the following individuals:

Lester Wertheimer, AIA at Architecture License Seminars (ALS) for giving me permission to use design drawings for a Commercial Office Building from the Graphic Planning and Design course, which was copyrighted by ALS in 1982, and allowing me to recreate it with AutoCAD for this book. These drawings appear throughout the book and in COM1-Plan and Elevation Exercises.

My students Leonard A. Nolt, Tony Austin, David E. Klacik, and Jamie Bierly for allowing me to use their drawings, which appear throughout the book and in COM1-drawing Exercises. These drawings were created as part of the ACH 234 Working Drawings-Commercial course in the Fall 1999 semester at the Pennsylvania College of Technology.

David E. Klacik for allowing me to use his drawings, which appear throughout the text and in RES2-drawing Exercises.

David W. Daneker at Tiadaghton Contractors, Inc. for giving me permission to use his working drawings, which appear throughout the text and in RES1-Exercises.

Ralph Horne and Richard Mason for letting me join the Autodesk Authorized Training Center (ATC) at the Pennsylvania College of Technology, which allowed me to excel in AutoCAD.

Kathy Walker and David Probst, members of the CAD faculty at the Pennsylvania College of Technology, for being there to answer my AutoCAD questions.

Eric Svendsen, Executive Editor at Prentice Hall for trusting and believing in my AutoCAD teaching skills enough to publish this book.

Lynn Steines, my production editor at Carlisle Communications for editing the entire book with care and diligence.

CHAPTER

1

Introduction to AutoCAD 2000i and AutoCAD 2000

After successful completion of this chapter you should be able to:

▲ Describe the role of CAD in architecture, engineering, and construction (AEC) firms.

▲ Describe the role of CAD in architecture schools.

▲ Gain increase awareness of digital-design technology.

▲ Understand the fundamental difference between AutoCAD 2000i and AutoCAD 2000.

▲ Talk about some of the common features of both versions.

▲ Launch AutoCAD 2000i and use the AutoCAD Today dialog box.

▲ Use Active Assistance dialog box to access command related information.

▲ Launch AutoCAD 2000 and describe the components of the AutoCAD 2000 graphics window.

▲ Access, dock, float, and resize AutoCAD toolbars.

▲ Understand and use right-click shortcut menus.

▲ Use the right-click customization dialog box to customize right-click operations.

▲ Understand and use Microsoft IntelliMouse functions in AutoCAD.

▲ Understand and use AutoCAD 2000i's Internet functions.

▲ Use the Publish to Web dialog box in AutoCAD 2000i to publish drawings to the Web or to company intranet.

▲ Use the i-drop feature in AutoCAD 2000i to drag and drop objects from manufacturer's Web pages for use in drawings.

▲ Use the Meet Now feature in AutoCAD 2000i to communicate in real time with clients, colleagues, suppliers, vendors, and the project team, no matter where they are in the world.

▲ Use the Create Transmittal dialog box in AutoCAD 2000i to transmit drawings with all associated files and externally referenced drawings (xrefs) as a single set of digital information to clients, suppliers, and the project team.

▲ Use the File Navigation feature in AutoCAD 2000i to design and save projects across intranet and Internet sites and publish drawings through integrated user interface. Use the file transfer protocol (FTP) browser to save a list of favorite FTP sites through Web or intranet folders with your login and password.

▲ Use the Internet function of AutoCAD 2000.

▲ Access the Internet.

▲ Open and save files from the Internet.

▲ Save files to the Internet.

▲ Load applications into AutoCAD.

▲ Insert blocks and xrefs from the Internet.

▲ Publish drawing Web format (DWF) files on the Internet.

▲ View DWF files on the Internet.

▲ Use AutoCad 2000i's USC Icon, Purge, and Array dialog boxes.

▲ Use AutoCAD 2000i's plotting enhancement features.

▲ Understand and use the additional features of AutoCAD 2000i.

▲ Access useful CAD-related Web sites.

▲ Understand the ergonomics of the CAD workstation.

1.1 THE ARCHITECT'S TOOLS OF CAD

Many advances in computer and information technology have altered the landscape of AEC (architecture, engineering, and construction) fields. The conversion from T-squares, to parallel rules, to CAD workstations is not new, but the fact that it has spread so quickly and so consistently during the past 20 years is bewildering. Computers utilized as desktops and laptops are now part of many individuals' daily activities in most AEC firms. Although not widespread, the hand-held personal computer (PC) is beginning to emerge as the small computer that fits into our pocket. The technology, features, and applications of CAD (computer aided design/drafting) enable architects, designers, and engineers to create conceptual design, design development, and construction documentation work. Some CAD packages are better suited for design work, and some are better for production work. AutoCAD is in the forefront of those packages, bringing unsurpassed benefits, features, and efficiency to the AEC industry. AutoCAD provides the tools necessary to create architecture specific applications such as computer aided architectural design (CAAD) as well as engineering specific applications such as computer aided manufacturing (CAM). AutoCAD has changed the way architects, interior designers, engineers, and contractors conduct business from designing to sharing data through Internet. Very soon the Internet and the World Wide Web will become a giant drawing file for AEC professionals to save, access, and share their electronic drawing files. As we embark into the twenty-first century, many AEC firms will be hiring individuals with efficient and solid AutoCAD skills. To become a productive member of a growing AEC firm you must bring with you proved design and production skills using AutoCAD. The tools of CAD are the major means of producing construction documents in the architecture firm today. Computer technology is advancing faster than we can learn it. But the only way to understand and use this technology efficiently and effectively is to learn it. AutoCAD is only one part of this ever-changing technology. You are about to learn the most sophisticated and most widely used CAD software in the AEC field today.

1.1.1   CAD in the AEC Firm

AutoCAD is, by every objective measure, the most widely used design and drafting software on the market. It is a comprehensive and sophisticated drawing/design/production tool. According to the 1997 American Institute of Architects (AIA) Firm Survey Report, over 85 percent of the architecture firms with 10 or more employees use AutoCAD. The report also states that over 87 percent of the firms with 10 or more employees use AutoCAD to produce two-dimensional drawings, while 69 percent of the same group use AutoCAD to produce three-dimensional drawings. If this AIA Firm Survey Report is any indication of where AutoCAD is headed, the percentage of architecture firms with 10 or more employees using AutoCAD in 2002 will be over 90 percent. As more architecture firms plan to create project-specific Web sites, Internet access in firms with 50 or more employees is close to 100 percent. Internet access for research is an important component of Web use. The AEC market uses Internet on a daily basis to access vital information related to business, design, and construction. As Internet access and World Wide Web becomes a major part of project implementation and management, AutoCAD brings to the market a more powerful architecture that allows users to transform designs through the power of the Internet.

Some potential clients of architects now require that the architecture firm they hire use AutoCAD for their projects. This has not only transformed the architect/designer into Auto-CAD architect but has also created a fairly new profession called *CAD manager.* It is not surprising to see hundreds of AutoCAD-related job opportunities in the AIA Web site and in major metropolitan newspapers. With so much technology and so many CAD tools available to the architect and designer, it is not surprising to see these individuals with laptops working on the job site and at home. AutoCAD provides two major tools to the AEC firm:

1. A fast and efficient means for producing construction documents in construction and management of buildings and structures.
2. A consistent platform to exchange data (drawing files) between all parties involved.

One of the strongest arguments to back this up is based on this fact: The power and potential of AutoCAD can only be realized when the ability to reuse, recreate, redesign, and share drawing files and information is used to connect individuals to teams, consultants, contractors, or the client through a set of expanded features.

In every AEC firm a standard organization of CAD apparatus is essential for accurate and efficient work and communication. AutoCAD delivers on this platform with improved productivity and efficiency. AutoCAD is also user-friendly and can be customized to suit many requirements. For the AEC firm this translates to *profitability,* and for many potential users this translates to *marketability.* To work efficiently and accurately with AutoCAD, you must acquire a solid foundation. You must learn hands-on the intricate mesh between command and options, the details of concepts and procedures that will help you create drawings quickly and with precision. This book is designed to give you that solid foundation and hands-on skills. In the real world, what matters most is not just what you know about AutoCAD but also how well you customize it to create templates and reusable content to get the project out the door to the contractor, yesterday.

1.1.2 CAD in the Architecture Schools

With the majority of the AEC firms utilizing AutoCAD, it is no wonder that the typical job advertised for an architect, CAD manager, project manager, or CAD operator includes the phrase "must know AutoCAD" or "must be proficient with AutoCAD" as one of the requirements. Most of the two-year architectural technology curriculums offered at community or technical colleges have enough CAD courses to meet or exceed the general CAD requirements put forth by architecture firms. The two-year architectural technology education is based on learning the computer technology and CAD along with the basic introduction of other architectural core classes such as design, working drawings, graphics, structures, environmental systems, estimating, specifications, codes, and history. The emphasis in this curriculum is the training of proficient CAD operators and CAD managers who are equipped with enough CAD knowledge to tackle day-to-day activities of producing and managing architectural projects using CAD. A typical two-year architectural technology student receives the degree of AAS (Associate of Applied Science) in Architectural Technology.

There are also four-year technology-based architecture schools. These schools provide more education and more training than their two-year technology counterparts. They incorporate more computer science courses into their curriculums. A four-year architectural engineering technology curriculum might offer more advanced CAD classes along with information technology (IT), information systems (IS), and information and project management courses. Some of these curriculums are accredited by the Accrediting Board for Engineering Technologies (ABET) and grant the degree of Bachelor of Engineering Technology in Architecture.

The role of the traditional schools of architecture remains as strongly committed to educating students to become registered architects today as in the past. Most of the five-year traditional schools of architecture have adapted well to the technological changes. There are more

CAD-based courses both in design studios and in classrooms than ever before. There are many architecture schools with digital and paperless studios to train and educate architects with strong CAD-based knowledge. Although traditional architecture curriculums are heavily concentrated on teaching design and other core architecture courses, there are many schools that integrate computer technology into the design studio. Most of the five-year architecture schools grant the degree of Bachelor of Architecture that is required to become a registered architect. If your ultimate goal is to become a registered architect, make sure the architecture degree offered at the institution is a professional degree and accredited by the National Architectural Accrediting Board (NAAB). The National Council of Architectural Registration Boards (NCARB) has established standards and criteria which licensing boards have adopted as their standard for admission to licensing examinations. For more information, you can read the "Guide to Architecture Schools" published by the Association of Collegiate Schools of Architecture or log-on to www.ncarb.org and www.naab.org. You can also get architecture related information by visiting www.aiaonline.com.

1.2 THE DIGITAL DESIGNFORCE

Technology today allows AEC professionals and students to connect to the Internet from a PC desktop, a laptop, a palm device, a pocket PC, a personal digital assistant (PDA), and wireless phone. These devices are all used to send and receive e-mail, browse Internet sites, and receive vital information. The result of this technology is a wireless and digital workforce where Internet connects individuals with design and product information, with colleagues, and with the world. The Wireless Application Protocol (WAP) initiatives for Web sites will soon enable Internet access through portable devices from pagers and mobile phones to wireless modems. This is good news to the AutoCAD user because more information will be accessed through more devices. It is a fascinating revolution because the concept of "connect everywhere" will allow architects, engineers, designers, contractors, and clients to communicate ideas in a written and graphic format in a more effective and efficient manner. The kind of information you want whenever you want and wherever you are is available through the Internet. Used correctly, technology will enable better communications and more efficient businesses within the AEC. With e-business growing steadily and with all the advances in Information Technology (IT) and Information Systems (IS), we are reminded that the pace of development continues to accelerate.

1.3 AutoCAD 2000i AND AutoCAD 2000

By transforming AutoCAD 2000 into the twenty-first century Internet platform, Autodesk has put the *"i"* in the Internet into AutoCAD 2000i. By building an Internet-driven design portal directly inside AutoCAD, Autodesk has harnessed the power of the Internet. AutoCAD 2000i provides you with the tools to compete in the global Internet-based design and production marketplace. With AutoCAD 2000i you can quickly and efficiently connect to project Web sites, receive up-to-date information from your design team, and exchange ideas from colleagues around the globe. In addition to direct browser access, object hyperlinks, database connectivity, ePlot, and drawing Web format (DWF) features found already in AutoCAD 2000, AutoCAD 2000i provides you with a window to the Internet/intranet design environment. AutoCAD 2000i is the AutoCAD 2000 transformed into an Internet design platform. As far as drawing and production of construction documents (without an Internet platform) are concerned, there are no major differences between AutoCAD 2000i and AutoCAD 2000. There are a few new dialog boxes and enhancements to improve overall production in AutoCAD 2000i, and they are explained in this chapter and throughout the text. The fundamental difference comes in the way a user interacts with Internet functions in AutoCAD 2000i. With AutoCAD 2000i, the initial user interface is expanded with Internet functions such as AutoCAD Today and access to Autodesk Point A, which is the Internet design portal. After the initial interface, both versions contain the same drawing start up and production features. AutoCAD 2000i is backward compatible with applications and scripts written for AutoCAD 2000. All ARX and LISP routines currently running on AutoCAD 2000 will continue to run on AutoCAD 2000i. AutoCAD 2000i help system now includes an HTML-based format as opposed to WinHelp format found in AutoCAD 2000.

AutoCAD 2000 is still the powerhouse for drawing and producing working drawings. It harnesses the power of maximizing productivity and increasing drawing efficiency. This makes AutoCAD 2000 an invaluable design and production tool. Unlike AutoCAD 2000i, AutoCAD 2000 does not have the Internet-driven portal built inside but has the Web publishing capabilities to create DWF files.

This chapter covers AutoCAD start up procedures common to both versions, the AutoCAD 2000i initial screen with Internet platform, the Internet specific functions available in both versions, and the new dialog boxes and features in AutoCAD 2000i. The remaining chapters are based on the use of AutoCAD 2000. Features that are specific to AutoCAD 2000i are included throughout the text and appear as *AutoCAD 2000i Update:* followed by the explanation of the new features.

> *Note: To use the Internet functions of AutoCAD 2000i and AutoCAD 2000, you must have access to the Internet either through an Internet service provider (ISP) or through a company server. You must also have an Internet browser in your computer. The two most common browsers are Internet Explorer and Netscape Navigator. The speed with which you connect to the Internet determines how fast or slow you work with the new Internet features of AutoCAD 2000i. Internet-specific features for both versions are discussed later in the chapter.*

The following are some of the production features common to both versions of AutoCAD (excluding Internet functions):

- One of the most impressive features of AutoCAD is its graphical user interface (GUI), which provides effective visual cues before performing special tasks. Toolbars, standard menus, and shortcut menus allow easy access to commands and procedures at the click of a button. For example, creating and managing dimension styles with the Dimension Style Manager dialog box and plotting through Paper Space Layouts provide a quick, on-the-fly, "what you see is what you get" (WYSIWYG) format.

- The production-oriented features allow you to view, edit, and plot with a streamlined operation. For example, the Layout feature allows you to preview exactly what will be plotted out, specify plot parameters such as plot device, paper size, plot scale, plot orientation, and plot area in one single dialog box. With layouts, you are in charge of your drawing output.

- The accuracy, efficiency, and speed features allow you to create and position object geometry without ever having to touch the keyboard. For example, the AutoSnap and AutoTracking features allow you to see temporary alignment paths with the move of the cursor when creating objects in relation to other objects. This is a real timesaver because you don't need to create construction lines to track points. Polar Snap and Polar Tracking allow you to establish lengths by moving the cursor.

- The Multiple Design Environment (MDE) feature streamlines the transfer of data, objects, and properties between drawings in a single session. This feature is incorporated into the Windows environment, providing you with an intelligent environment to perform multitask operations. You can open multiple sessions of AutoCAD and cut, copy, and paste objects between drawings.

- Increased productivity is achieved by a smarter design and production environment through AutoCAD DesignCenter (ADC). This feature allows you to list drawing content from a source drawing and copy or insert specific content into the destination drawing by simple drag-and-drop operation.

- An effective use of AutoCAD is to have project standards that would eliminate redundancy and bring consistency to the project cycle. The Ease of Customization feature allows you to customize toolbars and create custom templates and profiles to meet a wide variety of company drawing standards and personal drawing habits. Right-click operation allows access to shortcut menus with editing options that can be performed right on the spot. Right-click customization allows different selection options.

- Object association allows a link between an object and its associative dimensions and hatching. The Associative feature of dimensioning and hatching allows you to edit objects while the dimensions and hatching are updated.

- The Architecture Friendly Interface provides quick creation or customization of specific features. For example, the Find feature provides a quick and easy method for finding text, attributes, dimension annotations, and hyperlink/URL names. The Multiline command allows you to create many different wall styles with quick setup and editing.

- The Quick Select feature allows you to customize how you filter object information for editing and selection purposes. With the Quick Select feature, you can intuitively and easily create a filtering selection set based on object color, type, layer, linetype, or lineweight.

- You can share AutoCAD drawing files with other CAD applications using the DXF file format. You can import external data into a drawing or export the current drawing to files that can be used in other programs. You can save an entire drawing or just a few objects as a DXF file. You can also save AutoCAD 2000i or AutoCAD 2000 drawings in Release 13 and 14 format.

When you are ready to explore other related programs, such as 3D Studio Max and Architectural Desktop, the skills you have gained in both versions of AutoCAD will carry over. Architectural Desktop provides massing and space planning tools as well as conceptual modeling, design development, and construction documentation tools. I strongly recommend learning AutoCAD before venturing into this highly sophisticated software. 3D Studio Max provides advanced rendering and animation techniques including, but not limited to, building walkthroughs.

1.4 LAUNCHING AutoCAD 2000i

You cannot have AutoCAD 2000i and AutoCAD 2000 both installed on the same computer. If you already have AutoCAD 2000 installed in your computer you must remove it before you can install AutoCAD 2000i. The following describes the process and procedures for launching AutoCAD 2000i. The procedure is identical for the other versions.

When you turn on your computer, the system components communicate with each other. The blinking lights and beeping sounds are indications that the computer is checking installed drives and configurations. It basically performs a system check. When the system check is complete, your operating system (O/S) takes over so that you may run your programs. After the O/S kicks in, the Windows desktop appears on your screen. To start AutoCAD, double-click on the AutoCAD 2000i icon on the Windows desktop. The desktop is the screen area where program icons and shortcut program menu icons are displayed as shown in Figure 1–1. An icon is a picture that identifies a program that is installed in your computer. When you install a program in your computer, you are asked during the installation process if you want an icon to be placed on your desktop as a shortcut menu. Double-click on the icon to start the application. You can also start AutoCAD by selecting the Start button at the lower-left corner of the Windows desktop. This will display the Start menu. Select Programs and move your cursor to AutoCAD 2000i. This will display all items in the AutoCAD 2000i program folder. Click on AutoCAD 2000i as shown in Figure 1–2.

1.4.1 AutoCAD Today

When you launch AutoCAD 2000i the first time, AutoCAD Today and Active Assistance dialog boxes will be displayed as shown in Figure 1–3. This is your first AutoCAD 2000i screen that includes many Internet features and options, and this is where the two versions differ from each other. Active Assistance dialog box is discussed in section 1.4.2. You can use AutoCAD Today to open drawings you have edited most recently with the MRU (most recently used) list, create new drawings immediately, or access Autodesk Point A, which is the industry-specific Autodesk Internet Design portal. The option to open existing drawings or create new drawings is not new, but incorporating these options directly into the initial AutoCAD Today dialog box certainly creates a significant separation between AutoCAD 2000i and AutoCAD 2000. Basically, the AutoCAD Today in AutoCAD 2000i replaces the Startup dialog box in AutoCAD 2000 that is used

FIGURE 1–1 Double-click on the AutoCAD 2000i icon on the desktop to start AutoCAD.

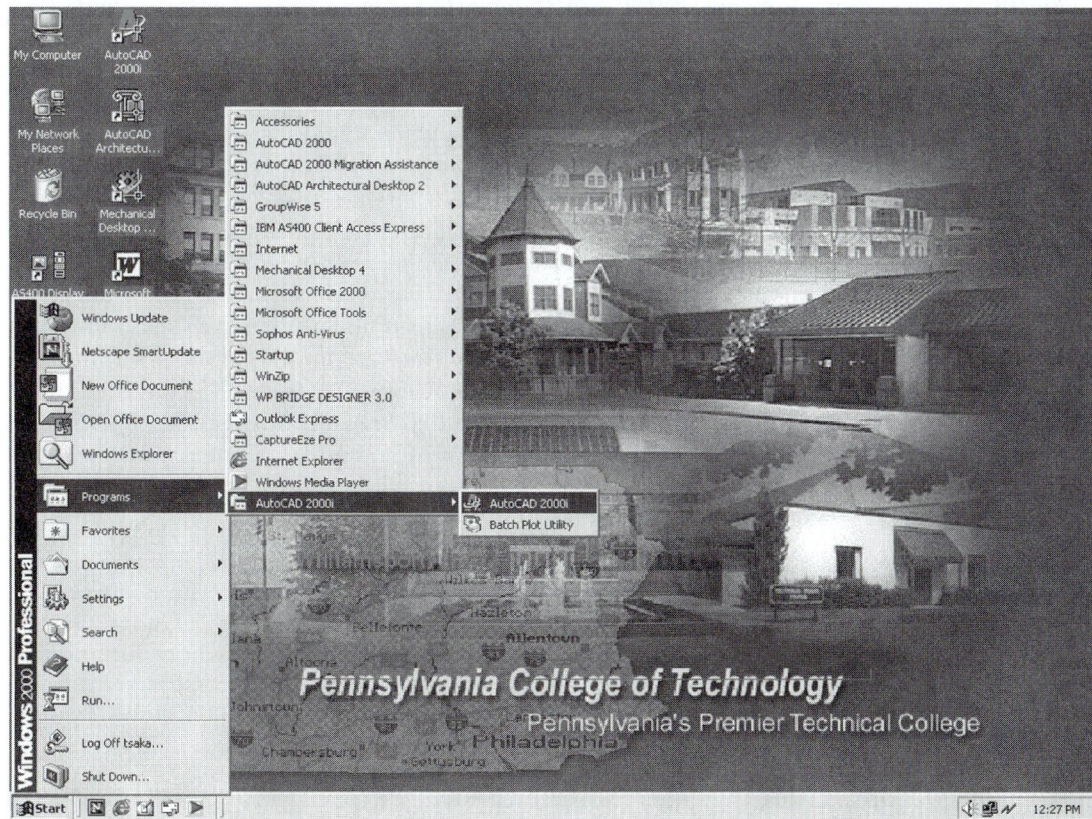

FIGURE 1–2 Select AutoCAD 2000i from the Programs menu to start AutoCAD.

FIGURE 1–3 The AutoCAD Today is both an integrated feature of AutoCAD and a window into Internet through Autodesk Point A.

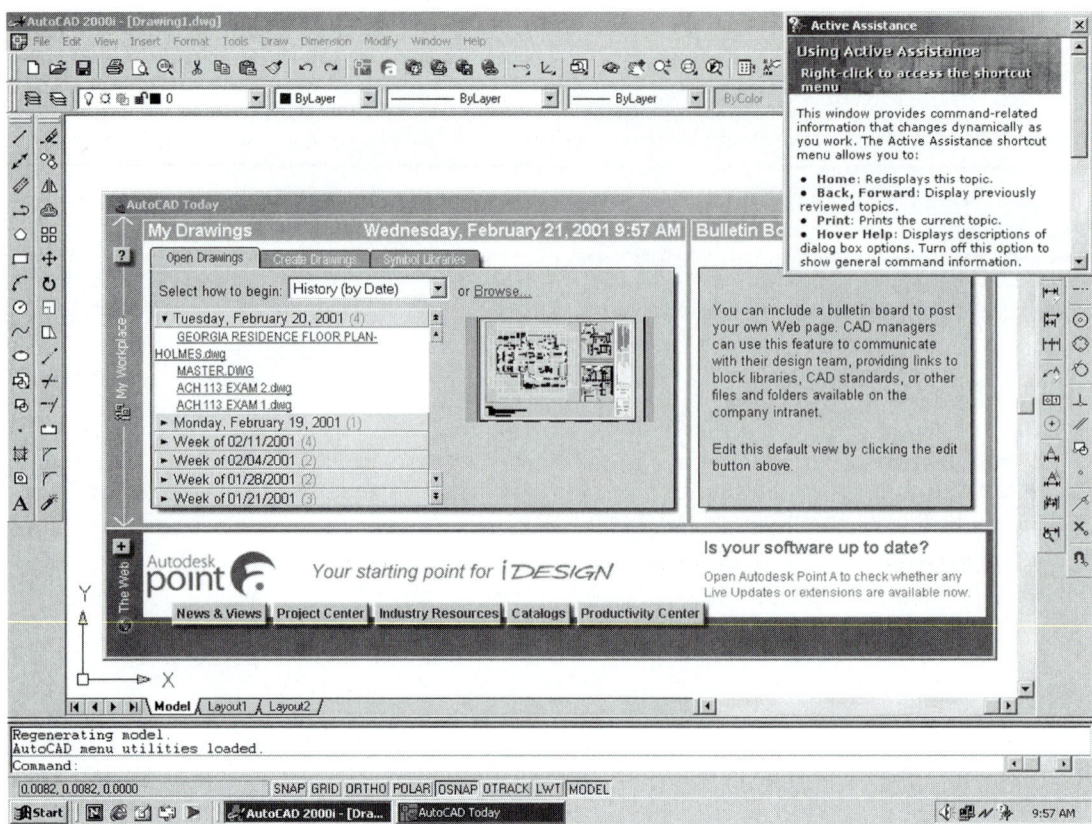

for opening and creating drawings. AutoCAD Today acts as a central station for viewing and accessing drawings in addition to providing many Internet features. You can minimize Auto-CAD Today by clicking on the minus (−) sign box located at the upper right corner, or you can close it by clicking on the (×) sign box. When you minimize AutoCAD Today, you are placing all the Internet functions on hold. To access AutoCAD Today when it is minimized, click on the Au-toCAD Today box in the Taskbar located at the bottom of your screen. When you close Auto-CAD Today, you are removing all the Internet functions temporarily. To access AutoCAD To-day when it is closed, move your cursor to the Standard Toolbar and click on the *Today* button. This is the 13th button from the left in the Standard Toolbar in AutoCAD 2000i. Toolbars are discussed in AutoCAD Graphics Window section 1.6. You can also enter TODAY at the com-mand line or select Today from the Tools pull-down menu to access AutoCAD Today. Pull-down menus are discussed in section 1.6. When you close or exit AutoCAD Today without setting any-thing up, you can work on existing drawings or create new drawings using the New and Open buttons in the Standard Toolbar. However, if you use AutoCAD 2000i for Internet functional-ity (which you should do), you may want to configure AutoCAD Today to meet your personal Internet design and project requirements. AutoCAD Today includes three main areas that pro-vide easy access to drawings and to the Internet.

- **MY DRAWINGS:** This area can be used to open existing drawings, create new drawings, or ac-cess the AutoCAD DesignCenter for symbol libraries. AutoCAD DesignCenter is discussed in Chapter 10 and 19. The Open Drawings tab allows you to open an existing drawing from a list of most recently edited drawings and has a built-in preview window. There are four op-tions under the Select how to begin: list box. To view the options, click on the down arrow. To select an option, click on it. The Most Recently Used option displays the most recently used and edited AutoCAD files before the current session. The History (by Date) option dis-plays, in reverse-chronological order, the most recently used files. The History (by Filename) option displays in alphabetical order the most recently used files. The History (by Location) option displays in drive location in alphabetical order, the most recently used files such as C:\AutoCAD 2000i\AutoCAD Drawings\Saka Residence\Front Elevation.dwg. Move your cursor over the list of drawing files to display the preview images. To open a drawing, single-click on the drawing file. You can click on the Browse . . . to search for a file to open. This will display the Select File dialog box as shown in Figure 1–26. You can use this dialog box to navigate through your computer to locate files to open or use its integrated Internet tools to connect to the Internet. The Select File dialog box in AutoCAD 2000i is discussed later in the chapter. The Create Drawings tab allows you to start a drawing according to your personal and project requirements. This is similar to the Startup dialog box in AutoCAD 2000. There are three different startup options under the Select how to begin: list box. The Template, Start from Scratch, and Wizards options are discussed in detail in Chapter 3. The Symbol Libraries tab displays the available symbols in the DesignCenter Symbol Libraries. There are 15 symbol libraries that are included in your installation. The first one is House Designer and the second one is Kitchens. When you click on the House Designer symbol library, AutoCAD will display the AutoCAD DesignCenter with the symbols displayed as blocks that can be used in architectural drawings. These are blocks under the C:\Program Files\AutoCAD 2000i\Design Center\House Blocks Designer.dwg file. Architectural symbols and Blocks are discussed in Chapter 19.

- **BULLETIN BOARD:** The Bulletin Board provides an area for CAD managers to communicate with project teams on the company intranet. This area is also known as the CAD manager's corner. You can post project information, a calendar of events, meetings, company project standards, and news to keep everyone involved and up-to-date on specific issues. You can also use the Bulletin Board to post messages or your own Web page. The Bulletin Board is your personal corner for accessing a wealth of information. Remember to check information regularly. To edit the Bulletin Board, click on the Edit button. Click on the Browse button, then select the appropriate directory in the Choose File dialog box. Click on CAD Manager.htm and click on the Open button. In the Bulletin Board, click on the Save Path button, and the CAD Manager's Web page will be displayed. Click on the desired item to view its content.

- **AUTODESK POINT A:** This is the new Autodesk Internet Driven Design portal that displays an HTML-based window inside AutoCAD. It is content-rich and industry-specific. It provides up-to-date content and industry-specific links for all your project needs and requirements. In the Autodesk Point A area, click on the plus (+) sign to expand it and when done, click on the minus (−) sign to collapse it. You can use Autodesk Point A to access all the resources of the Internet or intranet directly within AutoCAD. Autodesk Point A is your starting point for iDesign. You can access information from News and Views, Project Center, Industry Resources, Catalogs, and Productivity Center. Autodesk Point A is shown in Figure 1–4. With Autodesk Point A, you can access all the resources of the Internet/intranet without leaving AutoCAD. It is created as a forum to share information with architects, designers, and colleagues around the globe. With AutoCAD 2000i, Internet is at your fingertips, so let your "mouse do the walking." You can access Autodesk Point A as a separate window by clicking on the Autodesk Point A button in the Standard Toolbar. You can also access it from the Tools pull-down menu. Use the back, forward, and home buttons to navigate through Autodesk Point A.

The initial Autodesk Point A includes six buttons that provide page links. These are News and View, Project Center, Industry Resources, Catalogs, Productivity Center, and Industry Center. These are your links to the Internet with content-rich and industry-specific information. You can register for a free account with Autodesk Point A by clicking on Login and Register. Provide the required information including your name, password, e-mail address, and industry. You can then personalize your view of Autodesk Point A by clicking on Personalize. Select the column you want to edit and then select the services you want to add.

Here are some of the links you can click on:

Highlights: This area provides product information under the Product Zone and What's Hot categories. Click on the links to access information relating to new products and services. You can also click on the Personalize this Site link to customize links that meet your individual requirements.

FIGURE 1–4 Autodesk Point A is a content-rich and industry-specific Internet portal.

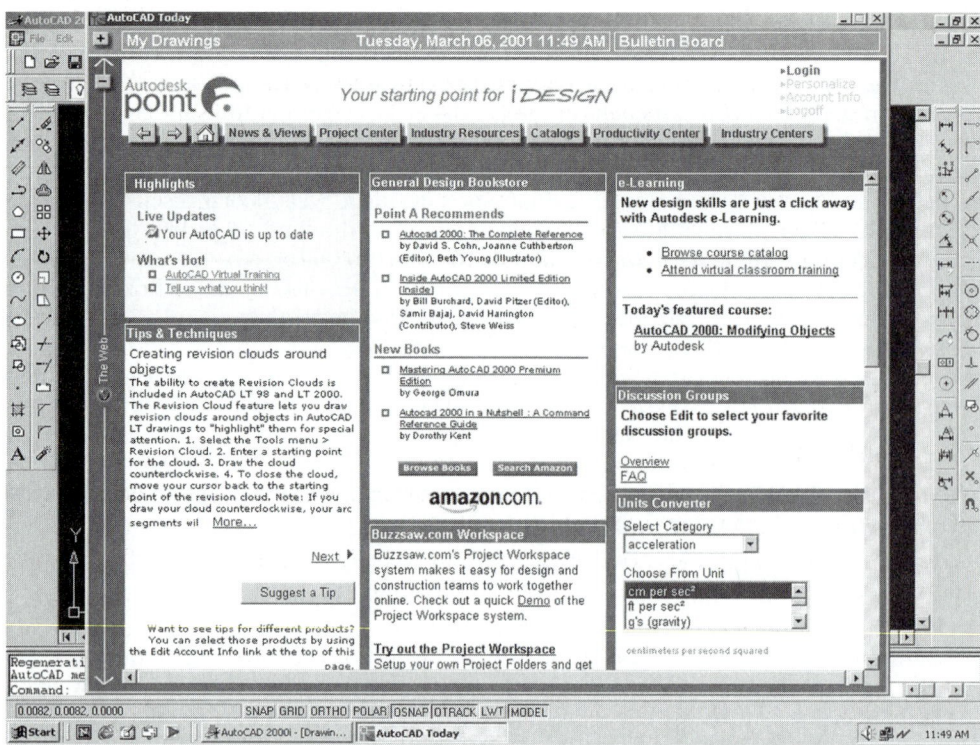

Symbols Library: This area allows you to download over 15,000 symbols for free. You can use the Quick Search box to search for a specific symbol to download. Simply enter the name of the symbol and click on the Search button. You can also click on the predefined search categories such as Architectural or Space Planner to view the symbols specific to those areas.

Architecture Links: This area allows you to access information specific to the architecture profession. For example, under Codes and Standards you can click on the [BOCA—Building Officials and Code Administrators] link to access the BOCA Web site. Under Professional Associations, you can click on the [AIA—American Institute of Architects] to access the AIA Web site.

News: General Design, AEC, and Manufacturing: This area allows you to access news and information specific to the AEC industries. The Business Wire links allow access to specific business categories. Current news headlines are available through Autodesk Point A. News providers have live links that provide up-to-date information. You now have a real-time interface that will keep you current with your profession without leaving AutoCAD 2000i.

Tips and Techniques: This area displays tips and techniques on how to use AutoCAD 2000i. You can upload your own tips and techniques directly to the Autodesk Point A database. You can suggest tips by clicking on the Suggest a Tip button, and your clients can quickly and easily find solutions to user problems.

Building Services Links: This area provides links to associations dealing with construction and building services. For example, under Codes and Standards you can link to the American National Standards Institute (ANSI) Web site.

Discussion Groups: This area allows you to access discussion groups. It is a large network of AutoCAD 2000i users who work with the software on a daily basis. You can choose a category to read messages or to post questions.

Tips: Use the Add to Favorites *button to bookmark your favorite Web site as opposed to setting CAD favorites in a separate browser.*

Tips: The AutoCAD and IS managers can control the Live Updates *feature of Autodesk Point A by having automatic updates occur and choosing which updates and patches are relevant for download. This will maintain consistent configurations across your company.*

Tips: Use the System tab in the Options dialog box to customize AutoCAD startup. The traditional Startup dialog box is displayed in AutoCAD 2000 when it is launched. The AutoCAD Today is displayed when AutoCAD 2000i is launched. In AutoCAD 2000i, access the Options dialog box and select the System tab. Inside the Startup: box, select one of the following options: Show TODAY startup dialog, Show traditional startup dialog, or Do not show a startup dialog.

Note: The Options dialog box is discussed throughout the text. Refer to Chapter 15 for more information about the Options dialog box.

Note: It is possible to launch more than one session of AutoCAD at the same time, however, each additional AutoCAD session will demand more system resources. You can make better use of your computer system resources by launching a single session of Auto-CAD. You can open multiple drawings in the same session using the Multiple Design Environment feature. This feature is discussed in Chapter 10.

1.4.2 Active Assistance

In addition to the AutoCAD Today window, the Active Assistance window will also be displayed at the initial startup of AutoCAD 2000i. This is shown in Figure 1–3. You can customize the Active Assistance window so that it does not display each time you launch AutoCAD 2000i. Active Assistance provides instant, automatic, and on-demand command, system variable, and procedural information while using AutoCAD. In addition to the Active Assistance window, the Active Assistance icon is displayed in the Windows system tray at the lower right corner of the screen. Each time you access a command, a system variable, or a feature, the Active Assistance will display infomation in context-sensitive format. To access the Active Assistance window, single-click on the Active Assistance button in the Standard Toolbar, double-click on the Active Assistance icon in the system tray, or enter ASSIST at the command line. You can close the Active Assistance by clicking on the (x) button, but it will be displayed again next time you access a command, a system variable, or a feature. You can control how and when Active Assistance is displayed by using the Active Assistance Settings dialog box. You can access the Active Assistance Settings dialog box by right clicking on the Active Assistance icon in the system tray and left clicking on Settings . . . in the shortcut menu. Place a check mark in Show on start check box if you want Active Assistance to start automatically when you launch AutoCAD 2000i. If you remove this check mark, you can select an alternate method to start Active Assistance. Place a check mark in Hover Help to display details about specific dialog box button features when you move your cursor over them. With this option, as you move your cursor around a dialog box, the Active Assistance window will display information about dialog box options related to the buttons. The information changes as you move your cursor to a different position (button). The Activation area allows you to specify when to display Active Assistance window. The default setting is set to On Demand. To display Active Assistance when you start a command, click on the All commands radio button. To display Active Assistance when you start a command that is new or changed in AutoCAD 2000i, click on the New and enhanced commands radio button. To display Active Assistance when you access a dialog box, click on the Dialogs only radio button. To display Active Assistance as needed, click on the On demand radio button.

Tips: As a beginner, the information and guidance you get from the Active Assistance window is just enough to get you started with unfamiliar commands or hard to learn tasks. Set it to All commands activation to learn commands and procedures as you work with AutoCAD throughout the book. If you used AutoCAD 2000 before, set it to New and enhanced commands activation.

▐▌5 AutoCAD 2000 STARTUP FEATURE

When you launch AutoCAD 2000, the Startup dialog box will be displayed as shown in Figure 1–5. This dialog box allows you to open existing drawings or create new drawings using three different methods. The drawing startup options are discussed in detail in Chapter 3. Whether you use AutoCAD 2000i or AutoCAD 2000, the tools provided by both versions allow you to increase

FIGURE 1–5 The Startup dialog box is displayed when you start AutoCAD 2000.

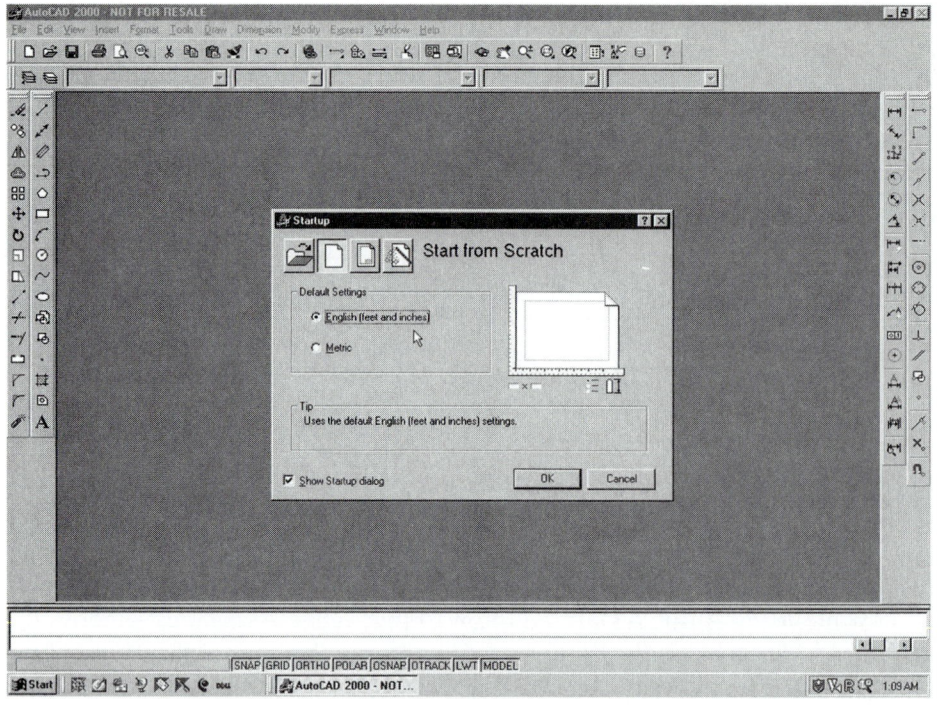

productivity, improve speed and accuracy, plot and present drawings accurately in a visually impressive manner, and use Internet to facilitate connection to new technology.

1.6 AutoCAD 2000 GRAPHICS WINDOW

AutoCAD graphics window is where the user interfaces with the program. It consists of toolbars, buttons, menus, and a drawing area. The standard AutoCAD 2000 screen layout provides a drawing area as shown in Figure 1–6. When you move your cursor inside the drawing area it turns into a pickbox. The square is the pickbox, and the vertical and a horizontal line form the crosshairs. The size of the pickbox and the crosshairs can be adjusted to meet individual drawing habits. When you move your cursor outside the drawing area it turns into an arrow similar to a pointing device. You use the pickbox and the pointing device to single-click, double-click, left-click, or right-click on the toolbars, buttons, and menu items. Most tasks in AutoCAD involve commands that are accessed by selecting an option from a menu, selecting a button from a toolbar, or typing at the command line. For example, you can left-click on the Draw pull-down menu and then select Line or you can left-click on the Draw button in the Draw toolbar or type LINE at the command line to access the LINE command. In some cases, you need to respond to prompts by selecting an object with the pickbox. In other cases, you must specify a point by left clicking when your crosshairs are in the desired position. You can also type commands and system variables at the command line to access them. You might even type information such as the length of a line or the sides of a polygon at the keyboard. For some users it is convenient to type commands and system variables at the command line to access them, for some it is more convenient to select buttons. Use the option that best suits your needs.

AutoCAD 2000i graphics window is very similar to the AutoCAD 2000 graphics window. The AutoCAD Graphics Window shown in Figure 1–6 has the following components:

1.6.1   Title Bar

The Title Bar is the first horizontal bar on top of the graphics window and has the control icon used to access the window control menu, the AutoCAD 2000—NOT FOR RESALE—(Drawing 1) text, and the three small buttons on the right side. The first button on the right side with the (−) sign is the Minimize button. When you click on this button, AutoCAD will be minimized (put on hold), and the AutoCAD 2000 icon will be placed on the taskbar.

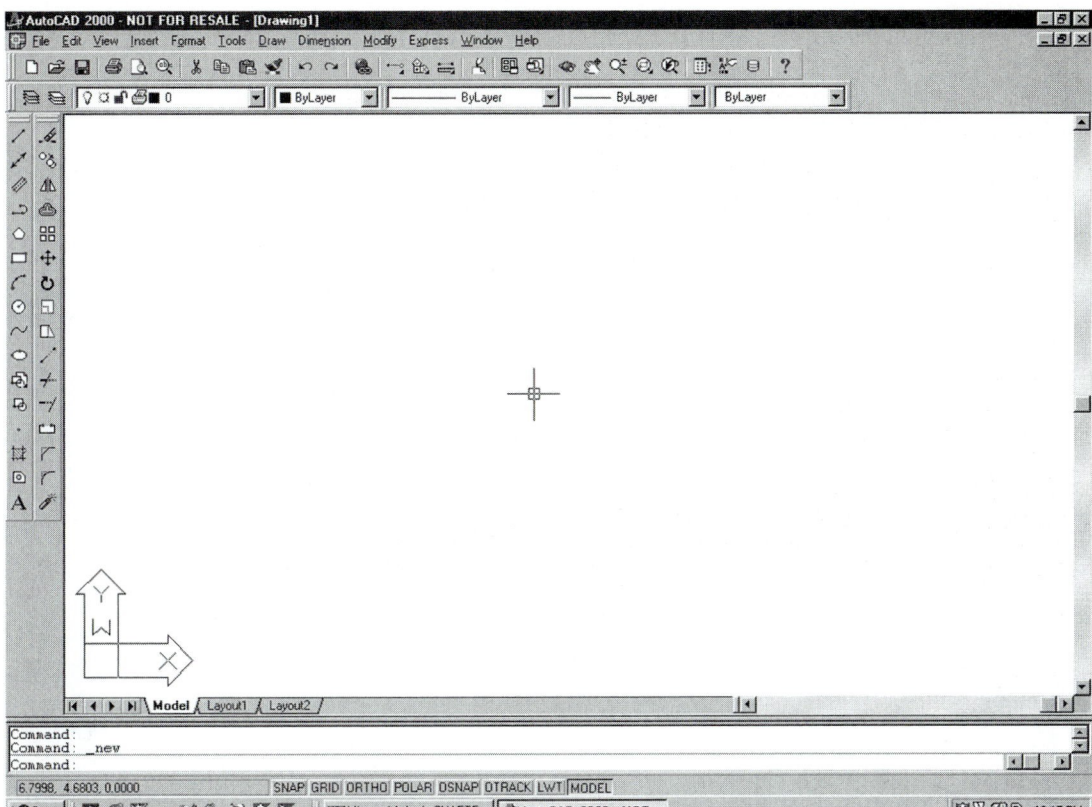

FIGURE 1–6 The AutoCAD 2000 user interface drawing window.

Taskbar is the horizontal bar at the very bottom of the screen (the Start button is located on the left side of the taskbar). To bring AutoCAD up on the screen, select the AutoCAD 2000—NOT FOR RESALE—button on the taskbar. The second button is the Restore button. This button will display a smaller size AutoCAD graphics window in its entirety inside the other program you are running as shown in Figure 1–7. When you restore a program, you can bring it back to its original state by selecting the middle button. The middle button after restoring a program becomes the Maximize button. To bring AutoCAD up on the full screen, click on the Maximize button to maximize the AutoCAD graphics window. The third button with the (×) sign is the Close button. Selecting this button will close AutoCAD and exit the program. Make sure that you save your work before selecting this button. Saving drawings is discussed in Chapter 8.

In AutoCAD, you can display drawings in their own separate windows or you can maximize them to fill the entire AutoCAD graphics window by using the three additional small buttons located directly below the Minimize, Restore, and Close buttons that were described above. These buttons are also called Minimize, Restore, and Close. The Minimize button will minimize the current drawing inside the inactive (grayed-out) AutoCAD graphics window, but all menus will be available. At this point, you can either create a new drawing by selecting New ... from the File pull-down menu or open an existing drawing by selecting Open ... from the File pull-down menu (see section 1.6.2). You can also click on the New button or click on the Open button located in the Standard Toolbar (see section 1.6.3) to achieve the same results. A minimized drawing can be brought back to fill the entire AutoCAD drawing area by selecting the Restore or the Maximize button. The Restore button will display the drawing in its own separate window in a floating position as shown in Figure 1–8. You can work inside this window or close it to work inside the graphics window. In either case, you are still working with AutoCAD.

Tips: You can right-click on the blue title bar and select Restore, Minimize, and Close from the shortcut menu. Right-click shortcut menus and right-click customization are discussed later in the chapter.

Note: AutoCAD will remain running even after closing all drawings until you exit AutoCAD.

FIGURE 1–7   Restoring the AutoCAD graphics window. Click on the Restore button. You can also select and hold the left mouse button on the title bar to move the window anywhere on the screen.

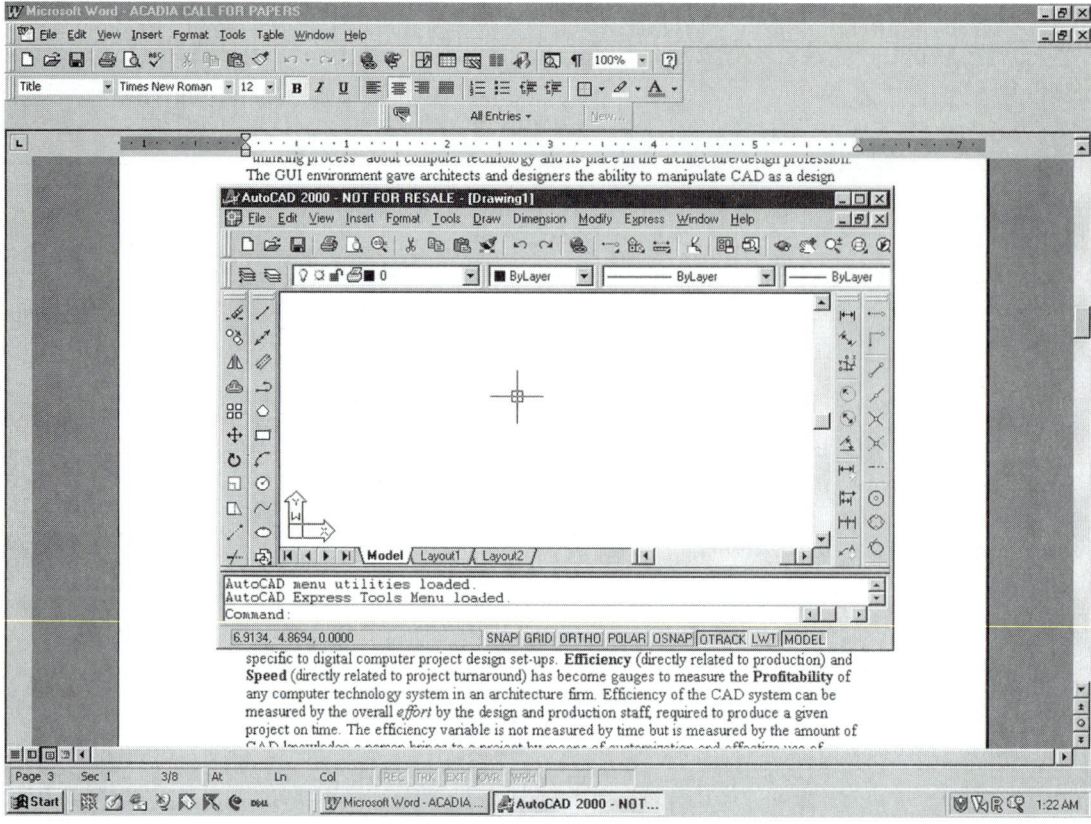

FIGURE 1–8   The AutoCAD drawing window displayed in its own separate window.

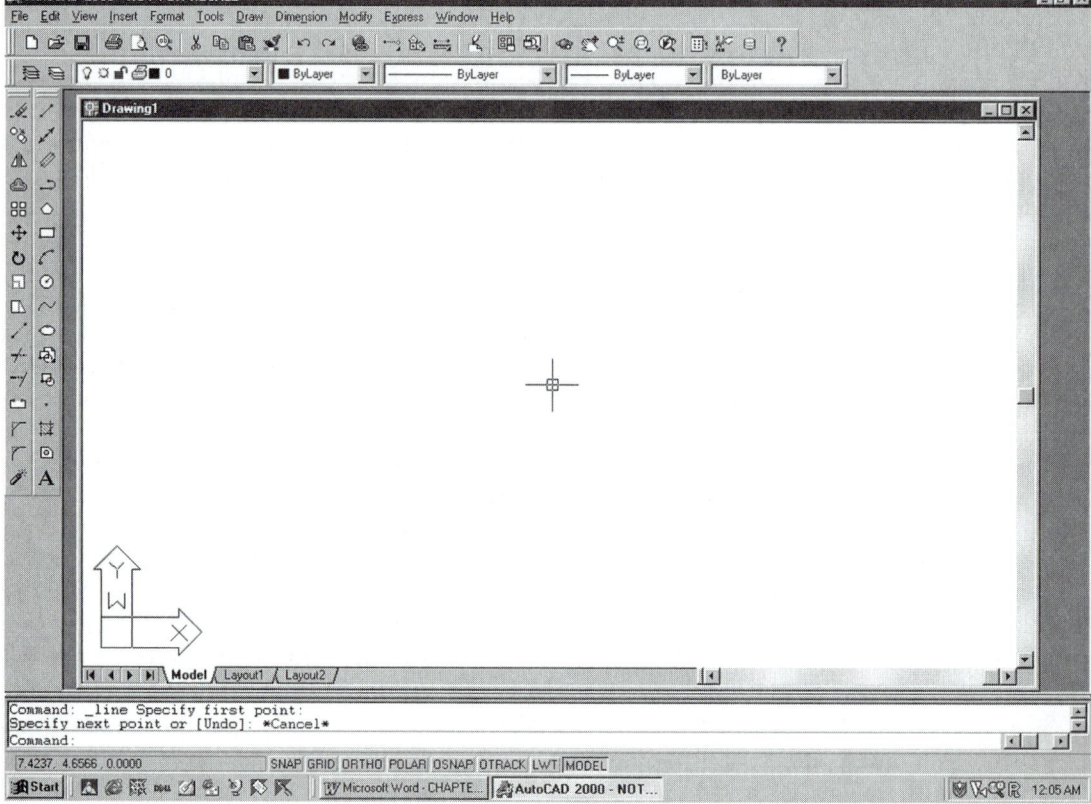

1.6.2 Pull-Down Menus

The second horizontal bar from the top is the pull-down menu bar. There are 12 pull-down menus in AutoCAD 2000 and 11 pull-down menus in AutoCAD 2000i with full installation of the software. The Express pull-down menu is removed from AutoCAD 2000i. Each pull-down menu offers a command, a dialog box, or a command option through a cascading menu. A cascading menu displays more options associated with the selected item and is indicated by a small triangle located on the right of the option. Moving the cursor over the cascading menu will display more options, as shown in Figure 1–9. When you select an option followed by an ellipsis (. . .), a dialog box will be displayed. A dialog box is a rectangular display containing many options associated with a specific command or function. Many features of AutoCAD display dialog boxes for specific settings to perform specific tasks. For example, the Layer Properties Manager dialog box allows you to create and manage layer settings.

Note: Most of the pull-down menus will disappear when you close all drawings, but you can still use the File pull-down menu and the New or Open buttons.

AutoCAD 2000i Update: *The File pull-down menu includes eTransmit and Publish to Web options. The View pull-down menu includes the Properties option in the UCS Icon cascading menu in the Display area. The Insert pull-down menu includes the Markup option. The Tools pull-down menu includes the Today, Autodesk Point A, and Meet Now options. The Window pull-down menu includes the Close All option. The Help pull-down menu includes the Active Assistance and Today options.*

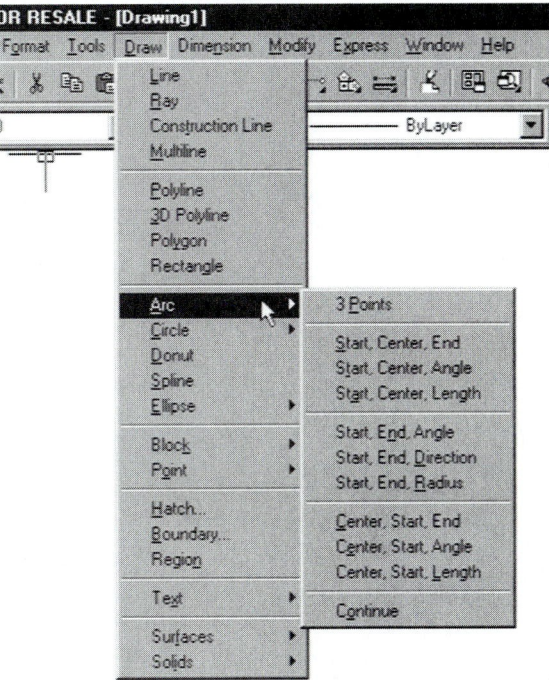

FIGURE 1–9 The Draw pull-down menu contains commands that are associated with the drawing function of AutoCAD. Notice the ARC cascading menu displaying many more options relating to the ARC command.

1.6.3 Standard Toolbar

The third horizontal bar from the top is called the Standard toolbar. A toolbar is a re-sizeable, floatable, movable box that provides access to commands. The name of each toolbar is identified only when the toolbar is dragged and floated on the drawing screen. The default state for Standard toolbar is docked below the Pull-Down Menus on top as shown in Figure 1–6. A docked toolbar is like parking the toolbar in a visible location for easy access. Each toolbar has grab bars indicated by two thin bars located at the top or left edge of a docked toolbar. To float a toolbar you must move it from its docked position. To move a docked toolbar, move your cursor on the grab bars, left-click, hold, and drag the toolbar onto the drawing area. Remember to keep your finger on the left-button when dragging the toolbar. Release your finger from the left-button when you have moved the toolbar into a new position on the screen. Figure 1–10 shows the Draw toolbar moved and floated on the drawing area. You can also double-click on the grab bars to float a toolbar on the screen.

When you move your cursor over the grab bar, the name of the toolbar is displayed on the lower-left corner of the screen, just above the Start button. This is a convenient way to find out the name of the toolbar. When you move your cursor over a button on any toolbar, the description of the button is displayed on the lower-left corner of the screen, just above the Start button. The top of a toolbar contains its title and has a blue surface. Each toolbar contains command buttons associated with the name of the toolbar. For example, the Draw toolbar consists of command buttons that allow you to draw many objects and shapes. When you move your cursor over a flat button, a three-dimensional border is displayed. A bar placed between buttons is called a separator. This allows separation for grouping of buttons in the toolbar. The name of the button is associated with the command it accesses and is displayed by a tooltip when you move your cursor over a button. Figure 1–11 shows the Line button on the Draw toolbar used to access the LINE command.

FIGURE 1–10   The Draw toolbar moved and floated on the drawing screen.

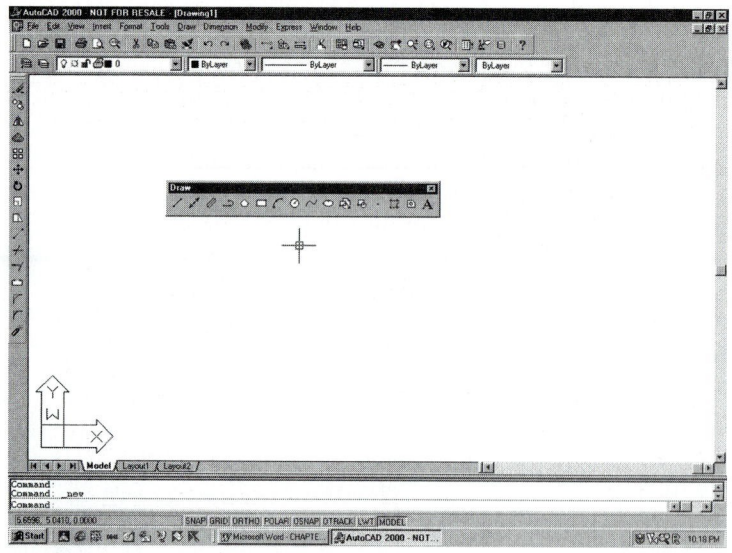

FIGURE 1–11   Each toolbar contains buttons that provide access to commands. The first button on the Draw toolbar is the Line button and is used to access the LINE command.

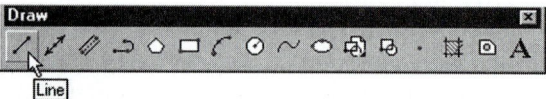

To move a toolbar on the screen, move your cursor over the blue title bar and drag the toolbar while holding the left button on the mouse. You can dock a toolbar using two different methods:

1. Double-click on the title bar of the toolbar. This will dock the toolbar on the top border of the drawing area.

2. Move your cursor over the title bar (blue surface) of the toolbar. While holding down the left button, slowly drag the toolbar to the left, right, top, or bottom side of the drawing border. As you approach the very edge of the drawing area, the toolbar will automatically snap, and the outline of the toolbar will turn into a dotted line. Release the left button to dock the toolbar. When a toolbar is docked, it loses its border and the title bar and becomes a part of the graphics window.

FIGURE 1–12   To access any of the toolbars, right-click on any toolbar and select the name of the toolbar.

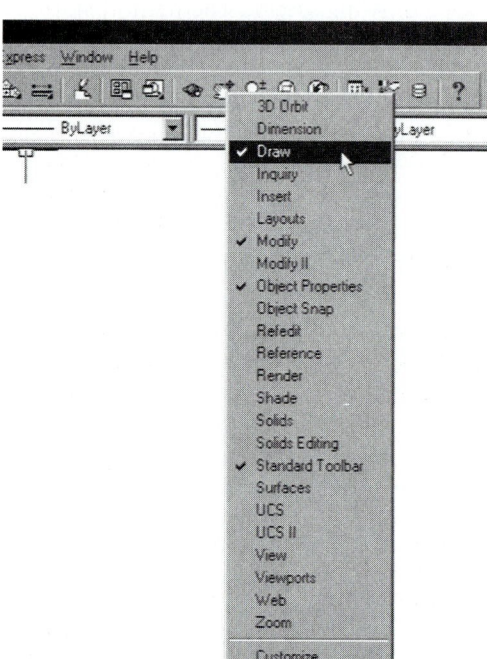

To remove a toolbar from the graphics window, left-click on the X button located on the upper-right corner of the toolbar. You can bring back a removed toolbar or access a toolbar not displayed on the screen using two different methods:

1. Right-click on any toolbar. Left-click on the name of the toolbar you want to access, as shown in Figure 1–12. A check mark in front of the toolbar indicates that it is already displayed on the screen. If it is not displayed, check to see if it is under another toolbar.

2. Click on the View pull-down menu and select Toolbars . . . The Toolbars dialog box will be displayed as shown in Figure 1–13. Select the box in front of the toolbar you wish to display. A check mark inside the

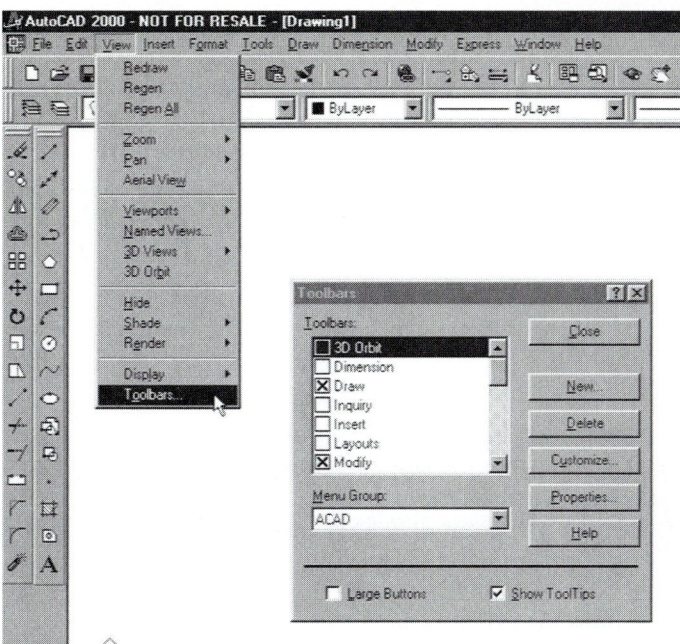

FIGURE 1–13 Selecting Toolbars . . . from the View pull-down menu will display the Toolbars dialog box, where you can access one or more toolbars to be displayed as well as create custom toolbars.

checkbox in front of the toolbar indicates that the toolbar is already displayed on the screen either docked or floating. To close the dialog box, click on the Close button.

The Toolbars dialog box allows you to access Express toolbars in addition to standard ACAD toolbars. This is shown in the Menu Group: down-arrow in the dialog box. You can also create custom toolbars with this dialog box.

Note: The right-click operation is on by default. If you are unable to access shortcut menus with right-click, you need to use the Right-Click Customization dialog box.

AutoCAD 2000i Update: *The Standard Toolbar includes Today, Autodesk Point A, Meet Now, Publish to Web, eTransmit, UCS, and Active Assistance buttons. The Active Assistance button is located at the end of the Standard Toolbar while the Today, Autodesk Point A, Meet Now, Publish to Web, and eTransmit buttons are located in the middle of the Standard Toolbar on the left side of the Redo button.*

AutoCAD 2000i Update: *The Customize dialog box will be displayed when you select Toolbars . . . from the View pull-down menu. This dialog box provides an easy-to-use interface for customizing toolbars, command buttons, and shortcut keys. The Commands tab allows you to add command buttons to the default toolbars, remove buttons you hardly use, and create your own toolbars. The Toolbars tab allows you to display or modify the properties of any button on a toolbar. The Keyboard tab allows you to assign keyboard shortcuts to commands.*

Note: Customizing toolbars is beyond the scope of this book. You can sign up for customization courses at your local community or technical college that teach AutoCAD Customization courses. You can also locate the nearest Autodesk Training Center (ATC) that teaches customization courses by visiting www.autodesk.com.

1.6.4 Object Properties Toolbar

The fourth horizontal bar from the top is called the Object Properties toolbar. The default state for the Object Properties toolbar is docked below the Standard toolbar on top as shown in Figure 1–6. This toolbar contains buttons and control boxes for setting and adjusting the properties of objects. The first two buttons relate to Layers. The five control boxes with down-arrows allow you to change object properties. The Object Properties Toolbar is discussed in detail in

Chapter 9. The default AutoCAD drawing area is bordered by the Object Properties toolbars at the top, Draw and Modify toolbars on the left, Scroll Bar on the right, and by the Model, Layout1, and Layout2 tabs and a Scroll Bar on the bottom. The default docked Draw and Modify toolbars on the left side of the AutoCAD drawing area are conveniently located for easy access to common drawing and editing commands.

> ***AutoCAD 2000i Update:***   *In the Object Properties Toolbar, the Layer Control box includes the Freeze or Thaw in Current Viewport option, but the Make layer plottable or non-plottable icon has been removed. The Lineweight Control box includes a list to display the current lineweight. The Plot Style Control box includes a list to display available plot styles.*

1.6.5 Coordinate System Icon

This is the icon for the user coordinate system. It is located at the lower left corner of the screen. It describes the current coordinate system based on the X, Y, and Z coordinates. AutoCAD uses two coordinate systems, a fixed world coordinate system (WCS) and a moveable user coordinate system (UCS). A plus (+) sign is displayed on the icon when it is positioned at the origin of the current UCS. If the icon is positioned on the origin of the World Coordinate System, a W is displayed on the 2D icon, and a square is displayed on the 3D icon. If you are using AutoCAD 2000i, you can change the look and feel of the AutoCAD UCS Icon with the UCS Icon dialog box.

> ***AutoCAD 2000i Update:***   *The UCS Icon dialog box can be used to change the style, size, and color properties of the UCS icon. See section 1.13.*

1.6.6 Scroll Bars

Scroll bars located on the right and the lower-right corner of the drawing area allow you to adjust the view of your drawing. These are the blank buttons located between the arrow buttons on the opposite sides similar to a down arrow found in a dialog box or a control box. You simply use these buttons to scroll up or down. When you scroll up, your drawing moves down, and when you scroll down, your drawing moves up. The scroll arrow buttons allow you to scroll in small increments. The blank scroll arrow allows you to scroll faster. If needed, the scroll bars can be removed from the screen using the Options dialog box. See Chapter 15.

> *Tips: Use the Microsoft IntelliMouse rotating wheel as real-time zoom and pan to zoom in and out and scroll up or down your drawing.*

1.6.7 Command Window

This is the area where you communicate with AutoCAD using the keyboard and where you type information or enter a command name. As a default, it is docked at the bottom of the graphics window. It displays the Command: prompt and command options. Always read the command line window for information regarding your entries. Everything you type at the keyboard in response to command line prompts will appear on the command line. There may be more than one option for a command after a command is running. In this case, AutoCAD will prompt you for a response. Command options are listed on the command line inside [square brackets] and you must type all capitalized letters of the desired option to use that option. For example, to use the STyle option of the MLINE (multiline) command, type ST or st after accessing the multiline command. Notice that entering S will access the Scale option of the same command. You must press the ~EnterKey~ after you type the desired option. When an option appears inside <angled brackets> you can access that option by pressing the ~EnterKey~. For example, you can press the ~EnterKey~ after accessing the ZOOM command to use the <real time> option. You can also select options inside [square brackets] from a shortcut menu instead of typing keyword letters. See section 1.8 for right-click customization. You can also type the abbreviated letter(s) of a command instead of typing the entire command name. For example, you can type S at the command line to access the STRETCH command.

1.6.8 Coordinate Display

The Coordinate Display is located on the left side of the Status Bar and displays the XYZ cursor location and descriptions for toolbars and command buttons. Refer to Section 5.10 for a discussion on the coordinate display and the COORDS system variable.

1.6.9 Status Bar

This area contains eight buttons related to the specific drawing control features. These buttons can be toggled on or off by a single-click. You can also right-click on a button in the Status Bar to establish settings associated with that button. For example, you can display the Object Snap modes inside the Drafting Settings dialog box by right clicking on the OSNAP button and left clicking on the Settings . . . These buttons will disappear temporarily when a description of a command is displayed.

Note: The Express pull-down menu offers increased productivity and time-saving features. It is only available if a complete installation of AutoCAD 2000 is performed. Express toolbars are discussed throughout the text. There is no Express pull-down menu in AutoCAD 2000i (see section 1.8.5).

1.7 RESIZING A FLOATING TOOLBAR

Sometimes it is necessary to change the size and geometry of the horizontal or vertical toolbar. This is especially true when you want to float toolbars in a clustered area. You can resize a floating toolbar as follows:

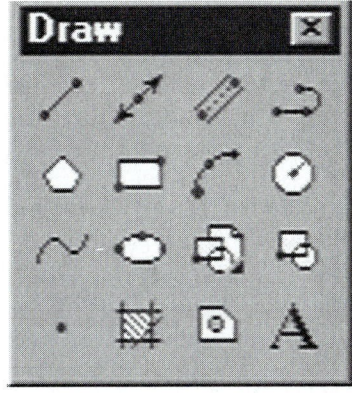

FIGURE 1–14 The resized floating toolbar.

1. Move your cursor to one of the edges of the toolbar. The cursor will turn into a double arrow.

2. While pressing on the left button, drag the cursor up, down, left, or right depending on which corner you hold the cursor.

3. Release the button when you are satisfied with the new shape. Figure 1–14 shows a resized toolbar.

Tips: You can resize dialog boxes in a similar way. However, there is a minimum size requirement for dialog boxes since all information must be visible for proper selection.

1.8 RIGHT-CLICK SHORTCUT MENU

The use of the right-click shortcut menu provides quick access to the options available for tasks or commands currently underway. For example, while dimensioning a floor plan, the right-click shortcut menu will display a series of options that will allow you to edit dimension text on the spot. Different shortcut menus are displayed at different times. The following are the right-click shortcut menu options.

1.8.1 Default Mode

With no command running and no selection set available, right-click in the drawing area. This will display the shortcut menu as shown in Figure 1–15. The first option is the repeat of the last command. To select an option, move the cursor over the option and left-click. Standard Windows cut-and-paste options are also available.

1.8.2 Command Mode

With a command running but no point selected, the right-click shortcut menu will display options related to the command in progress along with other options. For example, click on the Circle button in the Draw toolbar, then right-click inside the drawing area. This will display a shortcut menu with three different sections with a total of seven options as shown in Figure 1–16. The

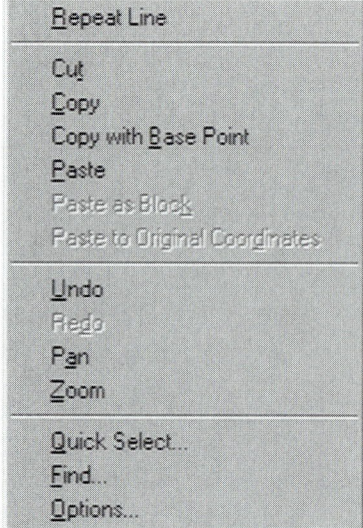

FIGURE 1–15   Right-click shortcut menu default mode.

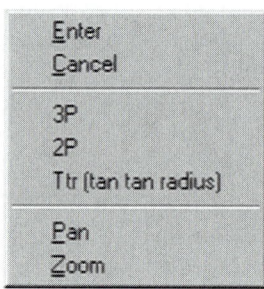

FIGURE 1–16   Right-click shortcut menu command mode.

first section has the Enter and Cancel options. The second section has three options specific to the command as its options. The third section has two options as Pan and Zoom, which are discussed in Chapter 11. To select an option, move the cursor over the option and left-click. For the Circle button, the Enter shortcut menu option will display the *Point or option keyword required* message displayed at the command line. This is the same as pressing the ~EnterKey~ on the keyboard. This is because a center point or one of the command options has not been specified. The Cancel option will cancel the command in process. Selecting any of the 3P, 2P, or Ttr (tan tan radius) options will allow you to draw a circle in three different ways. The CIRCLE command and its options are discussed in Chapter 6. More or fewer options may be displayed, depending on the command or method.

1.8.3   Edit Mode

When you select an object with left-click, but no command in progress, the right-click shortcut menu will display editing options related to the object selected. With this mode, you can edit objects on the spot without a need to access the editing command as well as access the previous command. Depending on the object selected, more or fewer options will be displayed. For example, when you select an existing rectangle the shortcut menu will be displayed as shown in Figure 1–17. When you select an existing dimension and then right-click, editing options with cascading menu options will be displayed inside the shortcut menu as shown in Figure 1–18.

1.8.4   Recent Commands Mode

When you right-click on the Command: line, the shortcut menu will display the six most recent commands used along with other options as shown in Figure 1–19. This is extremely useful because it eliminates typing or finding any of the six recent commands used.

1.8.5   Express Tools Mode

Express tools allow advanced editing operations relating to commands or procedures. For example, the Express Layer tools allow you to streamline layer management tasks. To access the Express tools, right-click on the empty space to the right of the

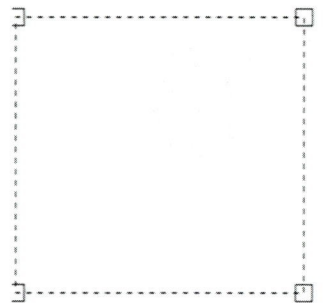

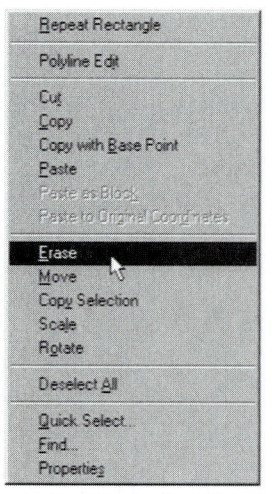

FIGURE 1–17   When you left-click on the object and then right-click, a shortcut menu is displayed, allowing you to edit the object or repeat the last command.

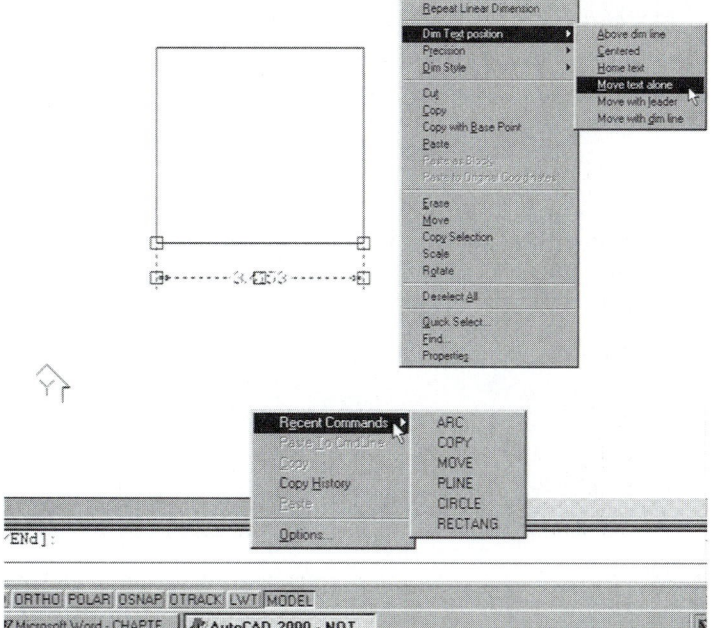

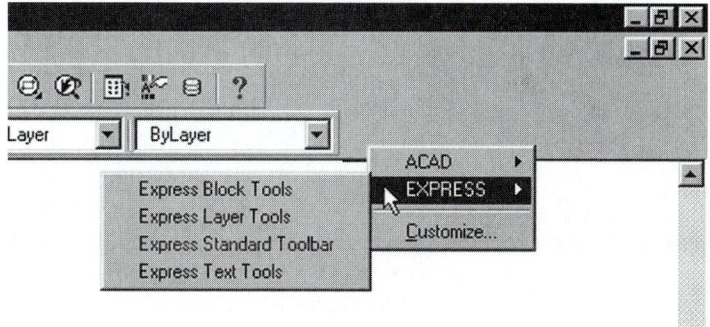

Standard or the Objects properties toolbar. Then click on the Express cascading menu and select the desired Express Toolbar, as shown in Figure 1–20. The ACAD cascading menu will display the Standard Toolbars. Express tools can also be accessed by selecting the desired tool from the Express pull-down menu. There are eight express tools that you can use for layers, blocks, text, dimension, selection, modify, draw, and tools. If you install AutoCAD using the Full option, a sample collection of Free Express Tools is automatically loaded in your computer. If you did not install express tools initially, you can rerun the AutoCAD installation, select Add and then select Express Tools. The last three tools at the bottom of the Express pull-down menu allows you to access additional information about express tools such as Web Links, FAQ, and Help. The Express Tools Web site can be found at http://www.autodesk.com/expresstools and the Express Tools newsgroup can be found at news://adesknews.autodesk.com/autodesk.expresstools.

Caution: All Express Tools can select objects even if they are on layers that are frozen or turned off. See Chapter 9 for Layers.

AutoCAD 2000i Update: *AutoCAD 2000i delivers Express Tools in the form of Extensions. Therefore, there is no Express pull-down menu in AutoCAD 2000i. Extensions are bundled collections of new features and tools that plug into the new AutoCAD platform. When upgrading from AutoCAD 2000, 2000i will preserve your existing installation of Express Tools. If you are upgrading but performing a clean installation, the instructions for installing Express Tools with AutoCAD 2000i can be found on the product support site.*

Note: Many of the AutoCAD 2000 Express Tools to increase productivity are discussed throughout the text .

▣ RIGHT-CLICK CUSTOMIZATION

You can customize the way you use right-click in AutoCAD. To access the Right-Click Customization dialog box, click on the Tools pull-down menu and select Options . . . This will display the Options dialog box. Select the User Preferences tab as shown in Figure 1–21. You can also right-click on the drawing area and select Options . . . from the shortcut menu as shown in Figure 1–15.

FIGURE 1–21 The User Preferences tab of the Options dialog box allows you to customize the way you use right-click in AutoCAD.

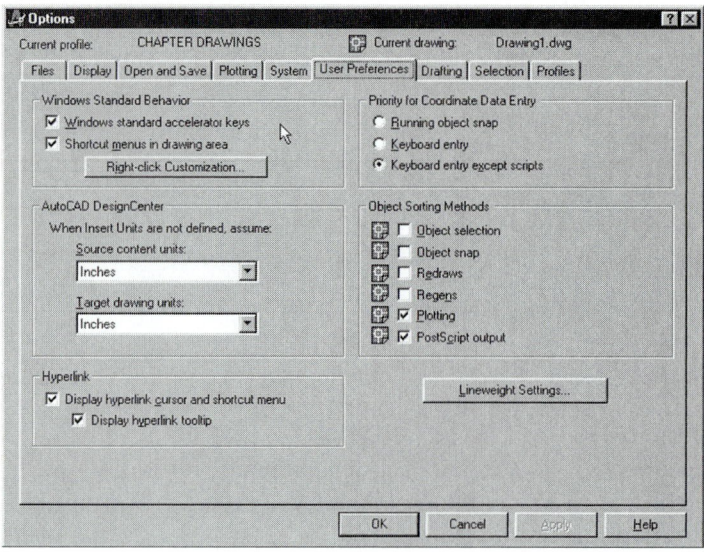

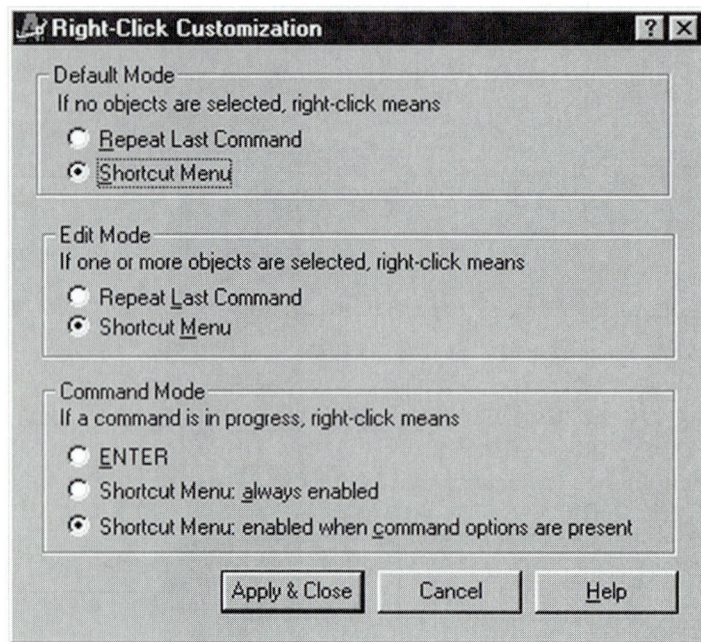

FIGURE 1–22 The Right-click Customization dialog box is used to customize the way you use right-click.

Inside the Windows Standard Behavior category, there are two check boxes and the Right-click Customization . . . box. The two check boxes are explained as follows:

Windows standard accelerator keys: This check box is on by default. It allows you to use Windows' keyboard accelerators. If you remove this checkmark, this option will be turned off. When this feature is off, you can use DOS-based AutoCAD keyboard accelerators.

Shortcut menus in drawing area: This check box is on by default. This will display a shortcut menu when you right-click in the drawing area. When this feature is off, right-click is equal to pressing the ~EnterKey~.

Right-click Customization . . . : This button will display the Right-Click Customization dialog box, as shown in Figure 1–22.

The Right-click Customization dialog box has three categories as follows:

DEFAULT MODE: This category has two radio buttons as two options. In the default mode, if no objects are selected, right-click means either Repeat Last Command or Display Shortcut Menu. Click on the desired option radio button to make it active.

EDIT MODE: This category has two options. In edit mode, if one or more objects are selected, right-click means either Repeat Last Command or Display Shortcut Menu. Click on the desired option.

COMMAND MODE: This category has three options. In command mode, if a command is in progress, right-click means either ENTER, Display Shortcut Menu (always enabled), or Display Shortcut Menu (enabled when command options are present). Click on the desired option.

Caution: When you change settings in the Options dialog box, you must click on the Apply & Close button in the sub-dialog box and then click on the Apply button in the Options dialog box.

1.10 MS INTELLIMOUSE FUNCTIONS

IntelliMouse is a function of the mouse that allows you to zoom in, zoom out, and pan (move drawing around) using the rotating wheel of the IntelliMouse. AutoCAD 2000 supports Microsoft IntelliMouse. This mouse has a rotating wheel between the two buttons. The IntelliMouse has the following functions:

- When you rotate the wheel away from you, the objects on the screen will become larger. This is the Zoom-in function of the IntelliMouse.
- When you rotate the wheel toward you, the objects on the screen will become smaller. This is the Zoom-out function of the IntelliMouse.
- When you press and drag the wheel the objects will move on the screen. The cursor will turn into a hand icon. This is the real-time Pan function of the IntelliMouse.
- When you double-click on the wheel, the objects will be displayed at their maximum magnification to fill the entire screen. This is the Zoom-Extents function of the IntelliMouse.
- When you press the ~CtrlKey~ and then press the wheel and move the mouse, the objects will move at certain increments on the screen. The cursor will turn into a dot and arrow. The arrow will point to the direction of the cursor movement. This is the Panning function of the IntelliMouse.

The ZOOMFACTOR system variable controls the speed of zoom level of the IntelliMouse rotating wheel. The default ZOOMFACTOR is 10. The valid values range between 3 and 100. For example, you can change the speed of the zoom level at the Command line via IntelliMouse rotating wheel as follows:

```
Command: ZOOMFACTOR ~EnterKey~
Enter new value for ZOOMFACTOR <10>: 100 ~EnterKey~
```

This will change the speed of the zoom function of the IntelliMouse from 10 to 100. This means that when you use the rotating wheel, zoom-in and zoom-out will be at maximum speeds.

The MBUTTONPAN system variable determines the behavior of the rotating wheel on IntelliMouse. By default, the MBUTTONPAN is set to 1 (On). This means that all functions described above using the IntelliMouse is possible. When the MBUTTOMPAN is set to 0 (off), the zooming and panning via IntelliMouse is still possible, but when you press on the wheel, the Object Snap modes settings shortcut menu will be displayed. The ZOOM and PAN commands are discussed in Chapter 11. The Object Snap modes are discussed in Chapter 7.

1.11 INTERNET FUNCTIONS OF AutoCAD 2000i

The Internet functions and tools of AutoCAD 2000i allow architects, designers, and building professionals to communicate and connect to projects and other users around the globe. With Auto-CAD 2000i, AutoCAD is now Web aware. New file navigation dialog boxes include a more intuitive interface and more functionality, including direct access to the Internet. The Internet tools allow you to browse Web sites for DWG, DXF, DWF, and other AutoCAD files. In addition to AutoCAD Today and Autodesk Point A, AutoCAD 2000i offers the following Internet functions.

1.11.1 Publish to Web

AutoCAD 2000i's Publish to Web feature allows you to publish drawing(s) to the Web or company intranet in HTML format using a wizard with predefined templates. You don't need a web expert to set-up, maintain, or update your Web site. Click on the Publish to Web button in the Standard Toolbar or select the Publish to Web . . . in the File pull-down menu to display the Publish to Web dialog box. The Publish to Web dialog box is shown in Figure 1–23 and starts with the Begin page. The wizard allows you to create a Web page that displays images from one or more drawing files in DWF or JPEG image format.

FIGURE 1–23 The Publish to Web wizard in AutoCAD 2000i allows you to create, preview, and post a Web page that includes an image of your drawing(s).

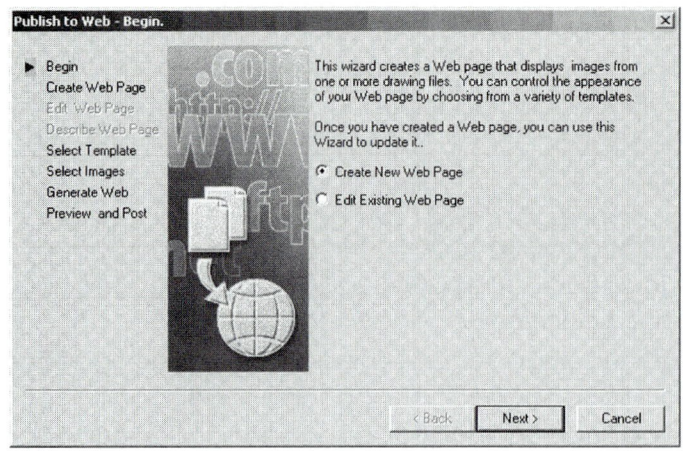

Once you create a Web page you can use this wizard to update it. The following are the pages inside the Publish to Web wizard:

BEGIN: This page allows you to either create a new Web page or edit an existing Web page. Select the Create New Web Page radio button to create a new Web page. Select the Edit Existing Web Page radio button to edit an existing Web page. Selecting the Next> button will display the next page appropriate to the selected option. When you select the first radio button, the following pages will appear:

CREATE WEB PAGE: This page allows you to enter a title for your Web page and a description to appear on your Web page. Selecting the Next> button will display the next page.

SELECT TEMPLATE: This page allows you to select one of two templates for your Web site. The DWF template translates and publishes selected DWG files in DWF format. The DWF files can be viewed with either Volo View Express or the WHIP! plug-in. You can download any one of the plug-ins free of charge from the autodesk.com Web site. The JPEG & Thumbnail image template translates and publishes your selected files to a thumbnail and raster image in either medium or large JPEG or PNG file format. You do not need any specific plug-in for viewing these files. Any standard browser (Internet Explorer 4.0 or higher or Netscape 4.0 or higher) will allow you to view JPEG and PNG files. When you select a template from the list, the preview image will show how the selected template will affect the layout of drawing images in your Web page. Selecting the Next> button will display the next page.

Note: JPEG files do not display sharp images as DWF files, but do not require the use of the DWF viewing plug-in.

SELECT IMAGES: This page allows you to add an image to your Web page after selecting the template. From the Drawing: drop-down, select the file or click on the (…) button to browse and search for the file. After selecting the drawing, pick one of the layouts from the Layout drop-down list. Next, enter a label for the layout inside the Label text box. The label can be a short name such as Hospital or Museum. Next, enter a description for the label inside the Description text box. Next, click on the Add-> button to add the label to the image list. The new name will appear inside the Image list box. You can delete an image from the list by selecting the image from the Image list box and clicking on the Remove button. If you specify new settings, select the image from the list and click on the Update-> button. To choose a different image, use the Move Up or Move Down buttons. Selecting the Next> button will display the next page.

GENERATE WEB: This page allows you to preview or post your finished Web page. It displays the path of the directory of the image. The Preview button will display the contents of the image with a list of all the images. Select the image you wish to preview and the newly created Web page will be displayed using your Web browser. You can use the Microsoft Intellimouse rotating wheel to pan and zoom in real time around your drawings. Use the right-click shortcut menu to change Layers, Named Views, and Location of the drawings. The Post Now button displays the Posting Web dialog box and allows you to post your Web page.

Note: You can move content to the Web or company intranet by specifying the server lo-
cation and configuration, where uploads will generate automatically.

Once you post your finished Web page, you can update it by selecting the Edit Existing Web
Page radio button in the Begin page of the Publish to Web dialog box.

1.11.2 i-Drop

The i-drop ActiveX control allows manufacturers and design professionals to publish design
data using standard Web pages. The i-drop in AutoCAD 2000i is an XML-based architecture
that allows content developers (such as furniture manufacturers) to post design drawings on the
Web. These can be in the form of DWG, VIZ, or MAX drawing objects. Web pages that contain
i-drop objects behave exactly like a standard Web page in a standard Web browser. When you
display the Web pages that contain these objects using any of AutoCAD's new Web-enabled
desktop design tools, you can drag the i-drop object from the manufacturer's Web page and drop
it into AutoCAD 2000i for use in a specific design project. Autodesk is currently working with
major manufacturers to accomplish the goal of a global network of pre-built design data available free over the Internet. For example, furniture manufacturers can place an entire block library of recent office furniture on the Web. With i-drop, you can drag furniture designs that can
be used in your projects, not only to scale but also with attributes. It is necessary to have HTML
knowledge to create the i-drop document files.

The Web drag-and-drop operations allow you to insert AutoCAD drawing files into an existing or new drawing file by dragging the file from a Web browser. AutoCAD 2000i recognizes
Web file formats to be read and inserted in this fashion. With Web drag and drop, you can search
and use different design content. This gives the AEC professional an extra edge in the design
content search.

1.11.3 Meet Now

The Meet Now feature allows you to communicate in real time with clients, colleagues, suppliers, vendors, and the project team, no matter where they are in the world. You can even
train staff online from a remote location. Meet Now uses Microsoft's Net Meeting technology for hosting meetings on Autodesk's own ILS server or to a company intranet, both of
which can be accessed within AutoCAD 2000i. This simplifies collaboration on design in consultation with other individuals. This is also a great way for CAD managers to train and teach
new tools to a wide number of users from their desktop or laptop. The automatic-application-
sharing feature allows everyone's PC to display the same information once connected. This
feature also allows principals and CAD managers to explain design changes to designers and
production personnel. To access Meet Now, click on the Meet Now button in the Standard
Toolbar, select Meet Now from the Tools pull-down menu or enter MEETNOW at the command line. The first time you launch Meet Now, the Microsoft NetMeeting configuration wizard will be displayed, similar to the NetMeeting dialog box as shown in Figure 1–24. This wizard allows you to communicate with others over the Internet, use video to see others, share
applications and documents with others, create drawings with others in a shared Whiteboard,
and send messages to others in a chat room. To display the next page of the NetMeeting wizard, click on the Next> button. Enter information about yourself for use with NetMeeting
and click on the Next> button. You will now be prompted to enter a directory server name.
A directory server is needed to identify participants and enable them to connect to each
other. Autodesk provides a server named Meetnow.autodesk.com for its customers. When
NetMeeting starts, click on Log on to a directory server check box and click on the Next>
button. On the next page, identify the speed of your network connection and click on the
Next> button. If you have a Cable, DSL, or ISDN connection, be sure to check the correct
box. On the next page, specify whether you want a NewMeeting shortcut on your desktop
and on the Quick Launch bar in your Start menu, and then click on the Next> button. The
next step allows you to set audio settings, but you may skip this if you do not plan to use audio. You can change NetMeeting configuration settings at a later time by starting NetMeeting and selecting Options on the Tools menu.

FIGURE 1–24 The NetMeeting dialog box allows you to collaborate in real time with the individuals you wish to communicate.

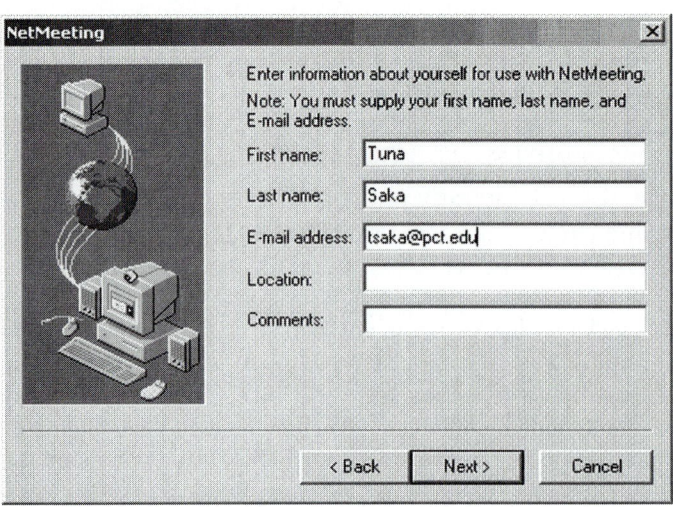

The Online Meeting toolbar has the following features:

MEET NOW INSIDE AUTOCAD: This automatically starts the NetMeeting program inside AutoCAD and establishes the meeting.

AUTOMATIC APPLICATION SHARING: Once a meeting is established, this feature automatically enables the AutoCAD session to be shared with other individuals. When other guests establish a connection, the AutoCAD session automatically displays the connection. This is a great advantage in the learning and training of the project team.

AUTODESK ILS SERVER: This feature registers the AutoCAD user and adds his or her name to the list of users already connected to the Online Meeting. The Autodesk ILS server helps AutoCAD users find and connect to each other easily.

NetMeeting provides other features such as chat and a shared whiteboard. Whiteboard is a feature where everyone in a meeting draws and types simultaneously.

1.11.4   eTransmit

This feature allows you to transmit drawings with all associated files and external references (xrefs) as a single set of digital information to clients, suppliers, and the project team. This tool allows you to compress and transmit DWG files with all associated content and xrefs as a complete digital packet. With eTransmit there are no lost materials, no confusion about updates, no time spent organizing and arranging for delivery of hard-copy equivalents, and no delivery charges. You can post the data to your company Web site or intranet or send it to a host server such as Buzzsaw.com or RedSpark.com. You can also generate a log report for easy tracking, and your transmittal is password protected. You can also post transmittals as AutoCAD Release 14 files for clients and suppliers who are not yet using AutoCAD 2000i.

Click on the eTransmit button in the standard toolbar, select eTransmit from the File pull-down menu, or enter ETRANSMIT at the command line to display the Create Transmittal dialog box as shown in Figure 1–25. Inside the General tab, type the required information inside the Notes: text box. Select the file compression type inside the Type: drop-down list. Select either EXE (self-extracting executable) or ZIP file format. Compression reduces the file size so that it can be delivered electronically. For added security you can click on the Password button to password-protect your transmittal. Use the Location: drop-down list to locate the file or change the location. You can also use the Browse button to browse for a different folder or file. Use the Convert drawing to: drop-down list to create transmittals in AutoCAD R14 or AutoCAD 2000 file format. Use the Send e-mail with Transmittal check box to Send e-mail notification to the receiving party. This is an excellent way to inform the receiver about the transmittal location and password. The Files tab allows you to find specific files inside the directory structure. The Report tab provides complete log information about the transmittal. If you click

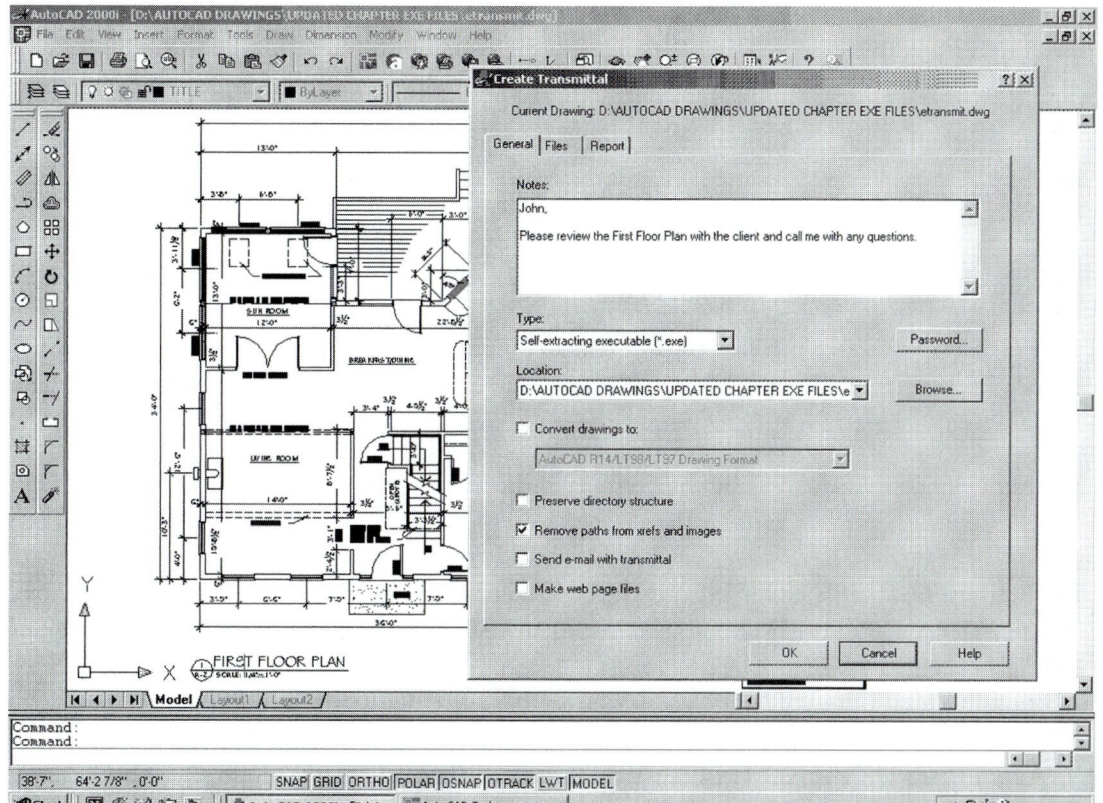

FIGURE 1–25 The Create Transmittal dialog box allows you to create an electronic transmittal.

on the Send e-mail with transmittal check box, your e-mail application will be launched after the transmittal is created.

1.11.5 File Navigation

The new Select File dialog box (or any other dialog box with new file navigation feature), as shown in Figure 1–26, has a more intuitive user interface and greater functionality with integrated Internet connectivity. With the integrated file navigation feature, you can design and save projects across intranet and Internet sites and publish drawings through integrated user interface. This interface has the same look and feel as Microsoft Office 2000. The startup feature automatically loads frequently used applications created in Visual Basic, Visual Lisp, and ObjectARX. The FTP browser allows you to save a list of favorite FTP sites through Web or intranet folders with your login and password. The Web folders allow you to use the Internet as an extension of your file system. You can access files from remote locations, share them with your project team, or create an intranet file location that is easily accessed from within AutoCAD. The Places list on the left side provides quick access to the following file locations:

History: This will list the shortcuts to files most recently accessed from the dialog box.

Desktop: This will display the contents of your desktop.

Personal/My Documents: This will display the contents of the Personal or My Documents folder.

Favorites: This will display the contents of the Favorites folder. This is the folder containing shortcuts to files or folders added to Favorites using the Tools Add to Favorites option of the dialog box. The Tools down arrow is located in the upper right corner of the Select File dialog box.

Buzzsaw: This will provide access to projects hosted by Buzzsaw.com. It is a B2B (business-to-business) marketplace for building design and construction industry.

FIGURE 1–26 The Select File dialog box in AutoCAD 2000i includes integrated Internet connectivity.

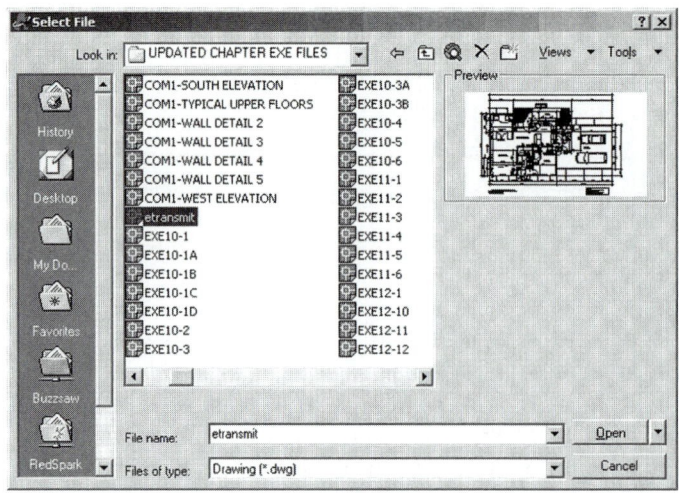

RedSpark: This will provide access to projects hosted by RedSpark.com. It is a B2B (business-to-business) marketplace for building design and construction industry.

FTP: FTP stands for File Transfer Protocol. This will display the FTP sites that are available for browsing.

Tips: You can reorganize the icons on the Places list by dragging them to a new location.

1.12 INTERNET FUNCTIONS OF AutoCAD 2000

Even without the Internet Design portal built directly inside, AutoCAD 2000 provides enough tools that allow Internet functionality. These tools include direct access to the Web using dialog boxes, AutoCAD Web browser, automatic recognition of URLs, ability to hyperlink AutoCAD objects to files in DWG format, and electronic plotting and publishing of compressed DWG files to the Web. This kind of technology allows design information to be created and accessed in real time to everyone involved in the building process. Many AEC firms are using AutoCAD and the Internet to communicate and collaborate on projects.

There are millions of people using the Internet to access and exchange information. AutoCAD 2000 also allows you to access and store drawing files on the Internet. You can open and save AutoCAD drawings to an Internet location from your computer or across a network. You can attach hyperlinks to drawings so that other users can access a variety of related documents. With an Internet browser and connection, you can use AutoCAD 2000 to publish DWF files that can be opened and plotted by anyone with an Internet browser and the free Autodesk WHIP! (Windows HIgh Performance) 4.0 plug-in, even if they don't have AutoCAD installed in their computers. The free WHIP! 4.0 plug-in is included with the full installation of AutoCAD. You can also download and install the required plug-in from http://www.autodesk.com/whip. If you have the WHIP! 3.0 plug-in, you can use AutoCAD to create legacy DWF files. However, legacy DWF files have limitations that are not compatible with DWF files created for WHIP! 4.0. With the required files installed you can use the Internet to:

- Open drawing files from Internet sites.
- Insert xrefs and blocks from Internet sites.
- Access information from the manufacturer site that will update the xref when modifications are made.
- Create and save drawing files to an Internet site.
- Load DWG, DXF, DWF, ARX, LSP, SCR, and MNU files to update applications.

There are three terms associated with Internet access:

URL: The Uniform Resource Locator is an address that points to a directory on an Internet server. It allows you to locate a Web page on the Internet. It is the universal file-naming system used on the Internet. A typical URL for accessing the Autodesk Web site would be www. Autodesk.com. The prefix http:// is typically not required.

HYPERLINK: This term is now being used instead of URL. The HYPERLINK command is used to link a drawing with other files on your computer or the Internet.

HTML: This is the Hypertext Markup Language.

1.12.1 Opening and Saving Files from the Internet

You can launch a Web browser from within AutoCAD using the BROWSER command or the three buttons located in the upper right corner of the Select File dialog box. The two most common browsers are the Microsoft Internet Explorer and Netscape Communicator. To use the AutoCAD Internet features, certain components of Microsoft Internet Explorer must be installed in your computer. Usually these are automatically installed in your computer when Internet Explorer 4.0 or higher is installed in your computer. You can get more information about installing the latest version of the two browsers by visiting www.microsoft.com and www.netscape.com and clicking on the Download button. You can use the BROWSER command to launch a Web browser as follows:

```
Command: BROWSER ~EnterKey~
Enter Web location (URL) <C:\PROGRAM FILES\ACAD 2000\Home.htm>:
~EnterKey~
```

This will launch the default Web browser with the Autodesk Internet Features Home Page as shown in Figure 1–27. Notice that in Figure 1–27 the Internet Service Provider (ISP) is Compuserve, with Microsoft Internet Explorer as the default Web browser.

You can enter a URL address inside the Address list area to access a Web site. For example, when you enter www.autodesk.com the Web browser will contact the Web site and display the first page of the Autodesk's Web site. You must have an Internet connection to access a Web page.

You can also use the Select File dialog box to access the Web Browser through three buttons that are specifically for use with the Internet, as shown in Figure 1–28.

FIGURE 1–27 The default Web browser with the Autodesk Internet Features Home Page.

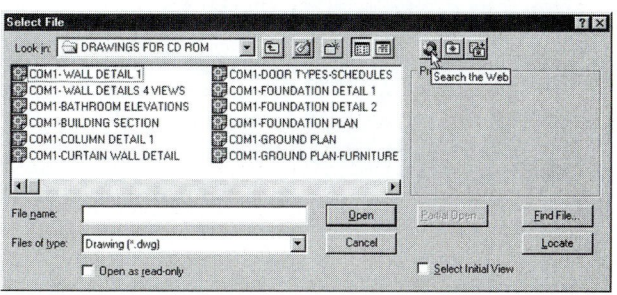

FIGURE 1–28 The Select File dialog box has three buttons that will allow you to use the Internet.

The three buttons from left to right are:

SEARCH THE WEB: This button will display the Browse the Web–Open dialog box as shown in Figure 1–29. This is the simplified Web browser. This dialog box displays information about AutoCAD's Internet features and can be used to browse files at a Web site. The default URL is an HTML file added to your computer. The URL is actually Autodesk's own Web site that is stored in the INETLOCATION system variable. You can change the default Web site from within AutoCAD as follows:

```
Command: INETLOCATION ~EnterKey~
Enter new value for INETLOCATION <"C:\PROGRAM FILES\ACAD
2000\Home.htm">: (enter a URL address)
```

LOOK IN FAVORITES: This button will display the Favorites folder in the Look in: drop-down list inside the Select File dialog box. Think of this folder as a bookmark that stores Internet Web sites.

ADD TO FAVORITES: This button will allow you to add a specific Web site to the Favorites folder or add selected items to the Favorites folder.

The Browse the Web dialog box has six buttons across the top to help you work with the current Web site as follows:

BACK: This button is used to go back to the previous Web page.

FORWARD: This button is used to go forward to the next Web page.

STOP: This button is used to stop the display of the Web page. It is useful when the Internet connection is too slow or the Web page is too large.

REFRESH: This button will re-display the current Web page.

HOME: This button will take you back to the Home Web page location specified by the INETLOCATION system variable.

FAVORITES: This button will display the stored Web sites or bookmarks.

You can enter the URL inside the Look in: drop-down list box to access a Web site. You can also click on the down arrow to select a previously accessed destination. If you store Web sites in the Favorites folder, select the URL from that list.

Note: The Locate and Find File . . . buttons in the Select File dialog box do not locate files on the Internet. They allow you to find and locate a file inside your hard drive.

FIGURE 1–29 The Browse the Web dialog box displays the contents of the URL stored in the INETLOCATION system variable.

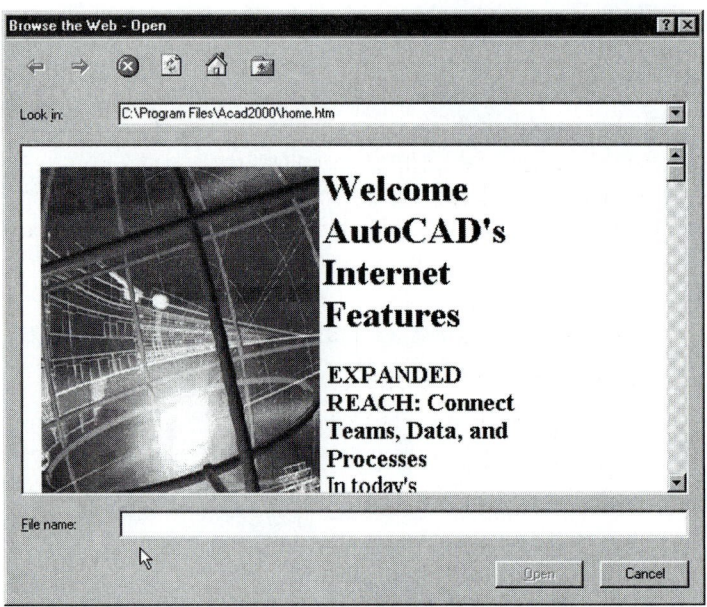

1.12.2 Opening AutoCAD Files from the Internet

You can use the Browse the Web dialog box to navigate to a specific Web site to open an Auto-CAD file. When you open a drawing from the Internet, the actual time to open the file depends on the type of Internet connection your computer has.

To open a drawing from the Internet use the following guidelines:

1. Start AutoCAD.
2. Access the Internet using one of the methods described above.
3. Access the Select File dialog box.
4. Click on the Search the Web button. This will display the Browse the Web–Open dialog box as shown in Figure 1–29.
5. Inside the Look in: drop-down list type the URL and press the ~EnterKey~.
6. Locate the file that you want to open and click on the Open button.
7. As an alternate to step 6, inside the File name: text box enter the file name and press the ~EnterKey~.

AutoCAD will download the file.

1.12.3 Saving AutoCAD Files to the Internet

You can use the Browse the Web dialog box to navigate to a specific Web site to save an Auto-CAD file. To save files to an Internet location, you must have access rights to the directory where the files are stored. Contact your network administrator or ISP to gain access rights. If you connect to the Internet from your company's network, you might need to setup proxy server configuration to create security barriers.

To save a drawing to an Internet location use the following guidelines:

1. From the File pull-down menu, select Save As. . . .
2. Access the Internet using one of the methods described previously.
3. In the Save Drawing As dialog box, click on the Search the Web button. This will display the Browse the Web - Save dialog box similar to the one shown in Figure 1–29.
4. Inside the Look in: drop-down list type the URL and press the ~EnterKey~.
5. Navigate to the location at which you want to save the file.
6. Click on the Save button.

With this method, you can only save AutoCAD files using the PTF protocol.

1.12.4 Loading Applications into AutoCAD

You can use the Web Browser dialog box to load specific applications into AutoCAD to boost drawing productivity, such as an ObjectARX routine or an AutoLisp routine. For example, you can access a specific Web site and select a file name from the list of ObjectARX files to download the routine into your active session. To load an ObjectARX routine or a specific application use the following guidelines:

1. From the Tools pull-down menu, click on Load Application . . . This will display the Load/Unload Applications dialog box as shown in Figure 1–30.
2. Click on the Search the Web button to display the Web Browser.
3. Inside the Look in: drop-down list type the Web address (URL) and press the ~EnterKey~.
4. Select the file name from the list of ObjectARX files. The file name will be displayed in the File name: area.
5. Click on the Load button to download the ObjectARX routine into your active session. The routine will be added to the Loaded Applications list.

FIGURE 1–30   The
Load/Unload
Applications dialog box.

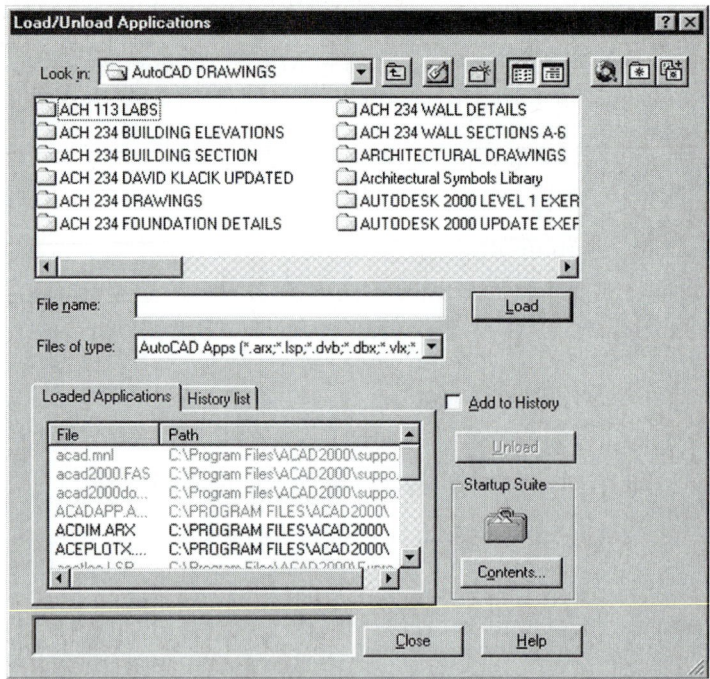

1.12.5   Inserting Blocks from the Internet

You can use the INSERT command to insert a block (symbol) that is available on the Internet. To insert a block from the Internet use the following guidelines:

1. Access the Insert dialog box.
2. Click on the Browse button. This will display the Select File dialog box.
3. Use the Search the Web button to access the Web site.
4. Locate the file for the symbol and download.

The process is identical for accessing external references (xref) and raster image files. Creating Blocks is discussed in Chapter 19. Externally referenced drawings are discussed in Chapter 24.

1.12.6   Using Dialog Boxes to Access Other Files from the Internet

You can use the Internet to store project specific standards. You can use the specific dialog boxes to access LIN or PAT files over the Internet as follows:

Linetypes: From the Format pull-down menu, select Linetype. . . . Inside the Linetype Manager dialog box, click on the Load . . . button. Inside the Load or Reload Linetypes dialog box, click on the File . . . button. Inside the Select Linetype File dialog box, click on the Search the Web button. Follow the procedures described earlier to download the files.

Hatch Patterns: You can use the AutoCAD Web browser to copy .PAT files from the Internet.

Multiline Styles: From the Format pull-down menu, select Multiline Style . . . Inside the Multiline Styles dialog box click on the Load . . . button. Inside the Load Multiline Styles dialog box click on the File . . . button. Inside the Load Multiline Style From File dialog box, click on the Search the Web button. Follow the procedures described earlier to download the files.

Layer Names: From the Express pull-down menu, select Layer and Layer Manager. . . . Inside the Layer Manager dialog box click on the Import . . . button. Inside the Import file name dialog box click on the Search the Web button. Follow the procedures described earlier to download the files.

Scripts: From the Tools pull-down menu, select Run Script.... Inside the Select Script File dialog box, click on Search the Web button. Follow the procedures described earlier to download the files.

Menus: From the Tools pull-down menu select Customize Menus.... Inside the Menu Customization dialog box, click on the Browse ... button. Inside the Select Menu File dialog box click on the Search the Web button. Follow the procedures described earlier to download the files.

Images: From the Tools pull-down menu and from the Display Image select View.... Inside the Replay dialog box click on the Search the Web button. Follow the procedures described earlier to download the files.

Note: You cannot access text files, text fonts, color settings, lineweights, dimension styles, or plot styles through the Internet.

1.12.7   Publishing DWF Files on the Internet

In order to display AutoCAD 2000 drawings on the Internet you must convert the DWG file into a DWF file format. The DWF files are generated in a vector-based format and are compressed. Compression of DWF files allows faster transmission time over the Internet than DWG files. The compression does not result in any loss of data. The vector-based format allows proper resolution during zoom operations. DWF files are an increasingly popular way to share AutoCAD files with others that don't have AutoCAD. The DWF files are not displayed as original drawings, so are more secure over the Internet. Other users cannot edit the DWF files. However, the DWF file format has the following drawbacks:

- You must go through extra steps to convert a DWG file into a DWF file format.
- You cannot convert rendered or shaded drawings into a DWF file format.
- DWF files are strictly in two-dimensional format and cannot be displayed as three-dimensional data.
- You cannot display DWF files inside AutoCAD.
- You cannot convert DWF files back to DWG format without using third-party file conversion software.

AutoCAD includes a DWF driver and an ePlot feature that will allow you to publish electronic drawing files to the Internet. In other words, you can plot AutoCAD DWG files as DWF files to a local file, a network, or a specific Internet location as virtual electronic plots. With ePlot, you can control pen settings, paper size, and rotation just as you would with regular Plot. In order to open, view, and plot DWF files, you must have an Internet browser and the latest WHIP! plug-in. AutoCAD has two ePlot pc3 plotter configuration files that you can use to create DWF files:

DWF EPLOT.PC3:   This file creates DWF files with white background and paper boundary.

DWF CLASSIC.PC3:   This file creates DWF files that resemble AutoCAD R14 DWF files with a black background.

Tips: Use the Add-a-Plotter wizard to create additional DWF plotter configuration files.
You can plot a DWF file as follows:

1. Create the drawing in AutoCAD 2000.
2. Click on the Plot button. This will display the Plot dialog box.
3. Select the Plot Device tab. In the Plotter Configuration category and in the Name: drop-down list, select DWF ePlot.pc3.
4. Click on the Properties ... button next to the Name: drop-down list. This will display the Plotter Configuration Editor–DWF ePlot.pc3 dialog box. Select the Device and Document Settings tab.
5. Click on the Custom Properties in the tree view as shown in Figure 1–31.

FIGURE 1–31 The Plotter Configuration Editor dialog box is used to set the ePlot custom properties.

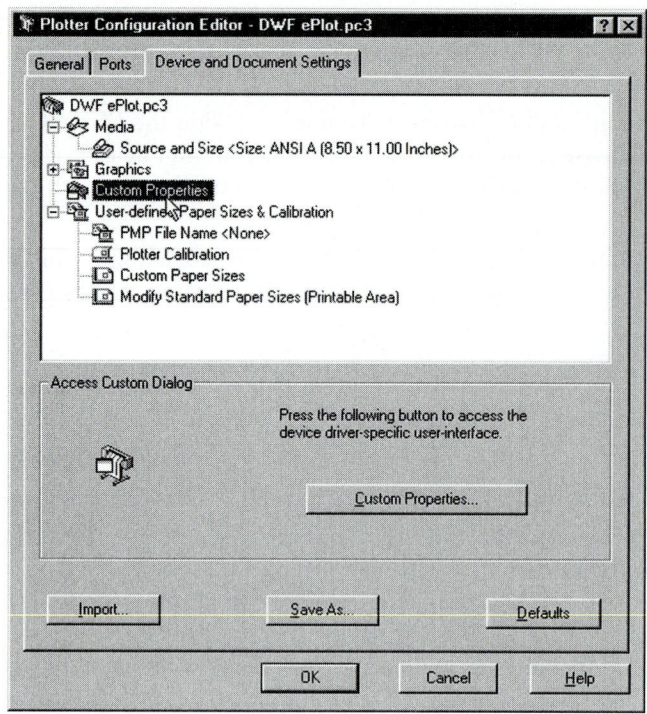

6. Inside the Access Custom Dialog category click on the Custom Properties ... button. This will display the DWF Properties dialog box as shown in Figure 1–32.

The DWF Properties dialog box has the following categories:

RESOLUTION: This category allows you to specify the resolution of the DWF files that you create. High resolution will provide greater precision but with larger file size. For most DWF files, a medium resolution setting is appropriate. However, if you create DWF files of large geometry, such as a regional map, use a higher resolution setting.

FORMAT: This category allows you to specify the DWF file compression. Compression reduces the size of the DWF files and is the recommended format for most DWF files. As an option, you can also create uncompressed binary or uncompressed text files.

BACKGROUND COLOR SHOWN IN VIEWER: This category allows you to specify the background color for the DWF files when viewed in an external browser.

INCLUDE LAYER INFORMATION: This check box allows you to include layer information in the DWF file.

INCLUDE SCALE AND MEASUREMENT INFORMATION: This check box allows you to include scale and measurement information in the DWF file.

SHOW PAPER BOUNDARIES: This check box allows you to include a paper boundary in the DWF file similar to what is displayed in a layout tab.

CONVERT .DWG HYPERLINK EXTENSIONS TO .DWF: This check box allows you to convert all .dwg hyperlink extensions to .dwf extensions.

7. Click on the OK button to exit the DWF Properties dialog box.

8. Click on the OK button to exit the Plotter Configuration Editor–DWF ePlot.pc3 dialog box.

9. If you made changes, the Changes to a Printer Configuration File dialog box will appear. Select Apply Changes for the current plot-only radio button to specify a one-time override that is not saved to the ePlot configuration file as shown in Figure 1–33. Select Save changes to the following file: radio button to save the configuration changes to the ePlot configuration file. Click on the OK button to exit the dialog box.

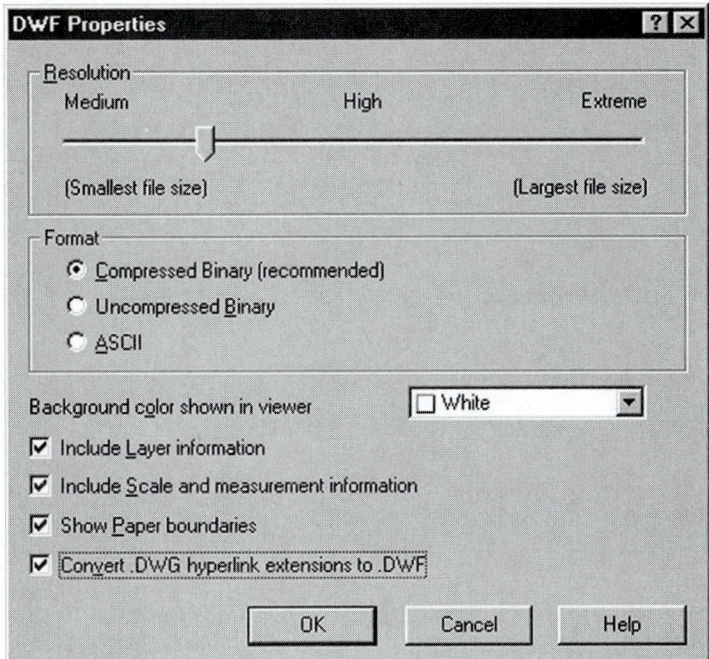

FIGURE 1–32 The DWF Properties dialog box is used to edit the resolution, format, and background color of the DWF files.

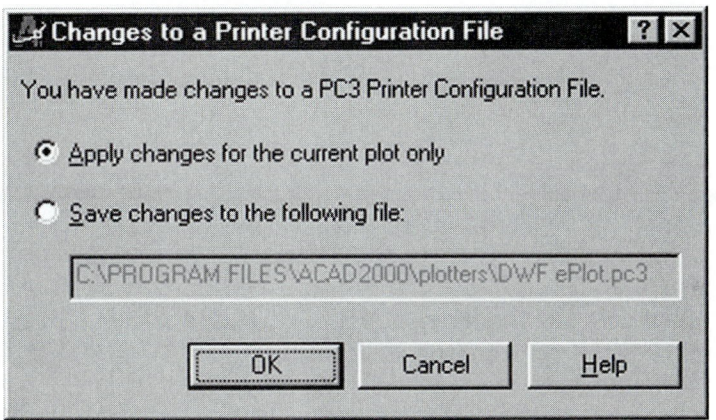

FIGURE 1–33 The Changes to a Printer Configuration File dialog box allows you to save the changes.

10. In the Plot dialog box (Plot device tab), take a look at the Plot to File category. Inside the File Name: text box, accept the DWF file name or enter a new name. In Figure 1–34 the DWF file name is shown as EXE18-20-Model.dwf. This means that the EXE18-20.dwg file has been converted to a DWF file with the same name in Model Space.

11. In the Location: drop-down list box, enter the location of a local or network folder to plot the file to. You can also browse for a specific folder by selecting the (...) button next to the Location: drop-down list box. This will display the Browse for Folder dialog box. Select the appropriate folder and click on the OK button. You can also enter an Internet or intranet URL to plot the file to.

12. Click on the OK button.

Note: You can use the SAVE command to save a drawing file to a server on the Internet. If a drawing of the same name already exists on that specific Web site, AutoCAD will display a warning message. If you inserted a drawing file from the Internet using the INSERT command and want to save it to the Internet, you must first save the drawing to the hard drive.

FIGURE 1–34
Specifying a plotting
location for the DWF
file.

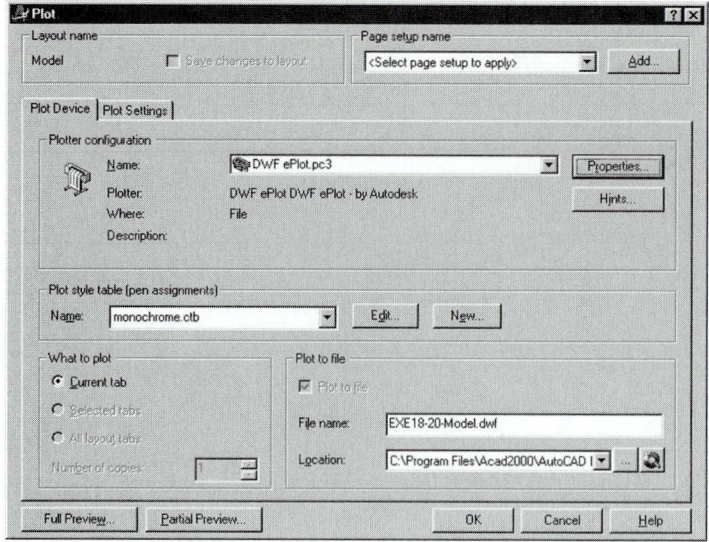

1.12.8   Viewing DWF Files Using an External Browser

If you have installed the latest version of the WHIP! plug-in, you can view DWF files using Internet Explorer or Netscape Communicator. If the DWF file includes layers or named view, you can control their display directly inside the browser. To check to see whether the DWF plug-in is installed in your Web browser, select the Help pull-down menu and select About Plug-ins in the browser. Scroll down the list of plug-ins to find the WHIP! plug-in similar to Figure 1–35.

FIGURE 1–35   The
WHIP! plug-in in the
Netscape Web browser.

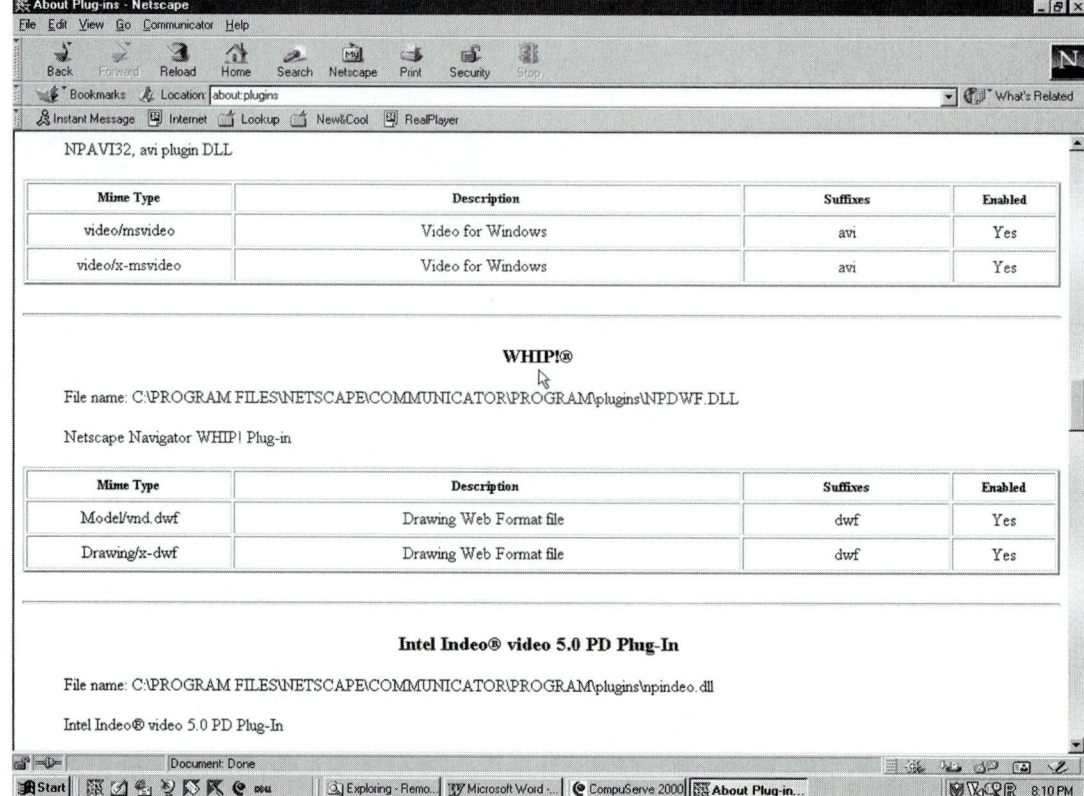

You can control the display of Layers in a DWF file as follows:

1. Open a DWF file using an Internet browser.
2. Right-click in the DWF file area and select Layers . . . from the shortcut menu. Only DWF files created with the Include Layer Information option selected can have layer control option.
3. Select the Layers you want to turn off and click on the light bulb icon to turn them off.
4. To turn the Layers back on, click on the light bulb icon again.

You can activate a named view in a DWF file as follows:

1. Open a DWF file using an Internet browser.
2. Right-click in the DWF file area and select Named Views . . . from the shortcut menu.
3. Select the view you want to display.

The following restrictions apply when you activate a named view in a DWF file:

- Only the named views applicable to the current UCS are written to the DWF file.
- If you plot a DWF file in model space, only model space–named views are written to the DWF file.
- If you plot a DWF file in paper space, only paper space–named views are written to the DWF file.
- Named views outside the plotted limits of a DWF file are not included in the DWF file.

1.12.9 Drag-and-Drop Functions

The WHIP! plug-in allows you to perform the following drag-and-drop functions:

1. You can drag a DWF file from Windows Explorer into a Web browser.
2. You can drag and drop a DWF file from Windows Explorer into AutoCAD. For this function to work, you must have another software program that allows the viewing of DWF files in AutoCAD.

1.12.10 Other DWF Viewing Options

Autodesk provides two other options for viewing DWF files in addition to the WHIP! plug-in. The CADViewer Light can be used to view DWF files and works with all operating systems. The only requirement is that your computer has access to Java. The Volo View Express can be used as a stand-alone DWF viewer that views and plots DWG, DWF, and DXF files. You can download both products free from the Autodesk Web site.

Note: The Internet tools in AutoCAD 2000i and AutoCAD 2000 allow design professionals, consultants, contractors, and suppliers to work on projects more easily, more quickly, and with less cost even when they are in different locations. Using the Internet architects can now connect to project hosting Web sites or communicate more directly with suppliers. For example, architects can post designs on the Internet using 3D Studio VIZ from Autodesk for clients to look at photo-realistic renderings and walkthroughs during the design phase of a project using the Asset Browser. In the e-business category, Autodesk has created the buzzsaw.com Web site as the portal for the design industry. It is the building industry's most comprehensive business-to-business (B2B) e-commerce hub. This Web site brings a broad array of services from project hosting to bid management and aims to streamline design and building collaboration. For more information visit their Web site at www.buzzsaw.com.

1.13 WHAT ELSE IS NEW IN AutoCAD 2000i?

In addition to Internet Design platform feature, AutoCAD 2000i has the following features not available in AutoCAD 2000. Refer to these features if you are using AutoCAD 2000i.

1.13.1 UCS Icon Dialog Box

The User Coordinate System (UCS) icon dialog box in AutoCAD 2000i is shown in Figure 1–36. It allows you to change the look and feel of the AutoCAD UCS Icon. To access the UCS Icon

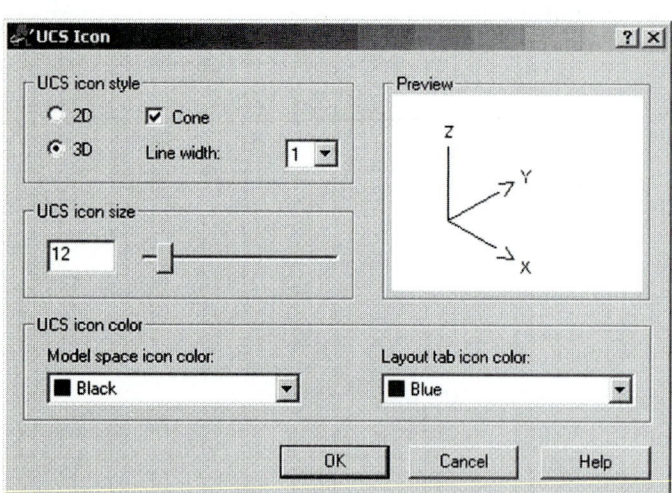

dialog box, click on the UCS button in the Standard Toolbar, click on the View pull-down menu and select Properties . . . from the UCS Icon cascading menu of the Display option, or enter UCSICON at the command line. The UCS icon style area has two-dimensional, three-dimensional, and cone options as radio buttons. Select the style you desire. You can also assign a line width to the Icon by selecting a number from the Line Width: drop-down list. There are three settings available. The default setting is at 1 pixel. This is similar to assigning a lineweight to an object. The UCS icon size area allows you to change the size of the UCS icon as a percentage of the screen area. The default size is 12 and the range is 5 to 95. The UCS icon color area allows you to change the color of the UCS icon in model space and/or in layout. The Preview area allows you to see the changes made to the UCS Icon.

FIGURE 1–36 The UCS Icon dialog box allows you to change the look and feel of the UCS Icon.

1.13.2 Drag-and-Drop Hatching

The new drag-and-drop hatch feature allows you to drag and drop hatch patterns between drawings using the AutoCAD DesignCenter. The AutoCAD DesignCenter is discussed in detail in Chapters 10 and 19. After accessing the DesignCenter window, click on the Desktop button to display the contents of your computer. Locate the Support folder and either click on the acad.pat or acadiso.pat file. The hatch patterns will be displayed in the palette area. Select the hatch pattern and drag and drop it inside the object in the drawing. During this process, the pickbox will display a preview of the selected pattern. You can adjust the hatch pattern settings before drag-and-drop by right clicking the hatch pattern and selecting BHATCH . . . from the short cut menu in the palette area. This will display the Boundary Hatch dialog box. This dialog box is discussed in Chapter 20. You can now add hatch patterns to the drawing content list that can be copied from the source drawing through the AutoCAD DesignCenter. See Chapter 10 for DesignCenter and Chapter 20 for creating hatch patterns.

1.13.3 The Purge Dialog Box

The Purge dialog box in AutoCAD 2000i, as shown in Figure 1–37, allows you to purge all nested objects quickly and efficiently. The Purge dialog box eliminates the need to use multiple purge commands when removing unused items such as Blocks, Dimension styles, Layers, Linetypes, Mline styles, Plot styles, Shapes, and Text styles from the drawing. You can either view items you can purge or view items you cannot purge by selecting the appropriate radio button. When viewing items you can purge, select the item you wish to purge from the list. The View items you can purge option will display items that have been deleted from the drawing and are available for purging. The View items you cannot purge option will display the reason an item cannot be purged when the item is selected. The reason will appear in the bottom of the dialog box. You can also have AutoCAD confirm each item to be purged or purge nested items. Select the appropriate check box at the bottom of the dialog box. Click on the Purge button to purge a single item or click on the Purge All button to purge all items in the drawing. See Chapter 19 for the PURGE command.

1.13.4 The Array Dialog Box

The Array dialog box can be accessed by entering ARRAY at the command line or selecting the Array button in the Modify toolbar and is shown in Figure 1–38. It provides an easy-to-use user interface and allows you to preview and modify the objects being arrayed prior to executing the

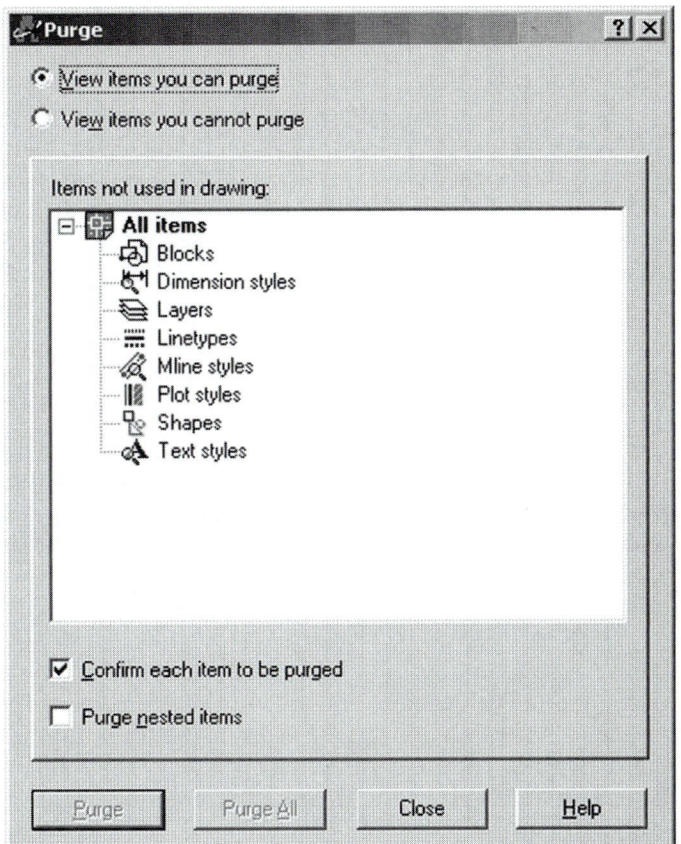

FIGURE 1–37 The Purge dialog box allows you to purge all nested objects.

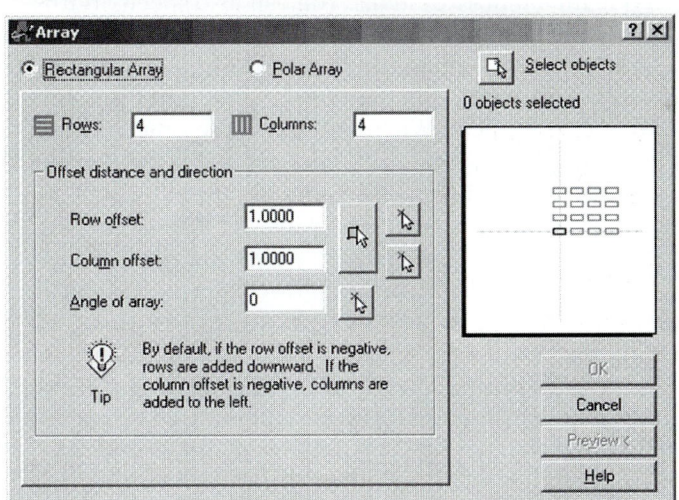

FIGURE 1–38 The Array dialog box allows you to array objects with an easy to use interface.

command. The Rectangular Array radio button allows you to array objects on a rectangular format and the Polar Array radio button allows you to array objects on a circular format.

Rectangular Array: When this radio button is checked, you will be required to enter the number of rows you wish to have inside the Rows text box and the number of columns you wish to have inside the Columns text box. The Offset distance and direction area allows you to enter offset distances for the Row and the Column including an angle for the rectangular array. The angle of array for rectangular array is normally 0, so the rows and columns are orthogonal with respect to x and y drawing axes. The Row and Column offsets can also be selected on the screen by selecting the Pick Both Offsets button or the Pick Row Offset or Pick Column Offset buttons. If the row offset is a negative number, rows will be added downward. If the column offset is a negative number, columns will be added to the left. After setting offset distance and direction, click on the Select objects button to select the object(s) to array. The dialog box will temporarily disappear. When you select the object(s) on the screen press the ~EnterKey~ and the dialog box will return. Check for correctness and click on the OK button to finalize the array operation. You can also click on the Preview< button to preview the rectangular array. This will display the Array confirmation dialog box. Click on the Accept button to finalize the array operation. If the array is not what you expected it to be, click on the Modify button. This will take you back to the Array dialog box where you can modify the required items.

Polar Array: When this radio button is checked you will be required to select the center point for the array. If you know the coordinates of the center point, enter it in the Center point: X and Y boxes. Otherwise click on the Pick Center Point button. The Array dialog box will temporarily disappear, and AutoCAD will prompt you to select the center point of the object. When you select the center point the Array dialog box will return. Next, select the method and values for the polar array. There are three different array methods to select from. The *Total number of items & Angle to fill* option allows you to enter a number in the Total number of items: box and the angle in the Angle to fill: box. For example, 6 chairs around the circle table arrayed 360 degrees. You can also specify an angle on the screen by selecting the Pick Angle to Fill button. If this is the case, you will be required to move your cursor and select a point that specifies the angle to fill on screen. The *Total number of items & Angle between items* option allows you to enter the total number of items and the angle between the items. With this method, AutoCAD will array the total number of items based on the angle between the items in a counterclockwise direction. This may not necessarily cover the entire 360 degrees. You can also specify the angle between items on the screen by selecting the Pick Angle Between Items box. The *Angle to fill & Angle between items* option allows you to specify angle to fill and angle between items. This allows you to array up to 360 degrees without specifying the number of items. You can also specify both angles by selecting the appropriate buttons next to it. Next, place a checkmark in the Rotate items as copied check box to rotate the objects selected along the edge of the object as they are copied. Next, click on the Select Objects button located in the upper right corner to select the object(s). The dialog box will temporarily disappear. When you select the object(s) on the screen, press the ~EnterKey~ and the dialog box will return. Check for correctness and click on the OK button to finalize the array operation. You can also click on the Preview< button to preview the polar array similar to the rectangular array. The More/Less button will turn the display of additional options in the Array dialog box on or off. When you click on the More button, additional options are displayed, and the name of the button changes to Less. The Object base point area allows you to specify a new reference (base) point relative to the selected objects that will remain at a constant distance from the center point of the array as the objects are arrayed. In the case of polar array, AutoCAD determines the distance from the array's center point to a base point on the last object selected. The base point used depends on the object type as follows:

Object type	Default base point
Line, Mline, Polyline, Donut, Ray, Spline	Starting point
Circle, Arc, Ellipse	Center point
Polygon, Rectangle	First corner
Block, Single-Line Text, MText	Insertion point
Construction Lines	Midpoint

When the Set to object's default checkbox is checked, AutoCAD uses the default base point of the object to display the arrayed object. You can manually set the base point by removing the checkmark. This will allow you to enter the X and Y coordinates of the base point or you can click on the Pick Base Point button to select the base point on the screen. Refer to Chapter 13 for the ARRAY command.

> *Note: If you select multiple objects, the base point of the last selected object will be used to create the array.*

1.13.5 Plotting Enhancements

The new plotting tools in AutoCAD 2000i include *Merge Control, Device Filters, Paper Size Filters, Plot Stamp,* and *True Color in Plot Styles.* See Chapter 23 for printing and plotting.

Setting Plot Merge Control   The Plot Merge Control feature allows you to plot overlapping objects as you merge objects or have them overwrite one another based on their drawing order. This feature is available for both Heidi Device Interface (HDI) and Windows-based printing devices. The Merge Control <Lines Overwrite> can be accessed by clicking on the Properties . . . button in the Plotter Configuration area of the Plot Device tab in the Plot dialog box. This will display the Plotter Configuration Editor dialog box. You can select the Merge Control <Lines Overwrite> from the Device and Document Settings tab. There are two settings for merge Control, Lines Overwrite and Lines Merge. If you select the Lines Overwrite radio button, the last plotted line will hide any lines underneath. Only the top line will be visible on the plot. If you select the Lines Merge radio button, the colors of all lines at the intersections will be merged. Merge control has no effect if the object output is black. You can also access the Plotter Configuration Editor dialog box by selecting the Plotter Manager . . . from the File pull-down menu and double-clicking on the desired plotter from the icons.

Filtering Windows System Printers   You can filter the Windows system printers from the Plot and Page Setup dialog boxes or from the Options dialog box. After accessing the Plot dialog box, select the Plot Device tab and click on the Properties . . . button. Form the Device and Document Settings tab of the Plotter Configuration Editor dialog box, click on the desired device and select Hide system printers. After accessing the Options dialog box, select the Plotting tab and place a checkmark in the Hide system printers checkbox located in the lower left corner of the dialog box. This allows you to filter unwanted printers by allowing access to only company standard printer device.

> *Note: Only the system printers that are configured using the AutoCAD Add-a-Plotter wizard will be displayed.*

Filtering Available Paper Sizes   The Paper Size drop-down lists in the Plot dialog box includes *filters* that allows you to manage paper sizes. After accessing the Plot dialog box, select the Plot Device tab and click on the Properties . . . button. From the Device and Document Settings tab of the Plotter Configuration Editor dialog box, click on the plus (+) sign in front of the Media to expand it. Select the Source and Size to review available paper sizes for the selected device. Expand User-defined Paper Sizes and Calibration. Click on Filter Paper Sizes and click Uncheck All. In Size area, place a checkmark for paper sizes that are required by school or company standards and click on the OK button. This allows you to filter unwanted paper sizes and printers by allowing access to only school or company standard paper sizes.

> *Note: You can review the filtered device and paper sizes list from the Page Setup dialog box based on the selections made during the configuration of the plotters and printers.*

Creating a Plot Stamp   You can create and edit a plot stamp that contains data about the plot. This can be added to the plot and saved in a log file. To access the Plot Stamp dialog box, select the Plot Device tab in the Plot dialog box, place a checkmark inside the on checkbox, and click on the Settings . . . button or enter PLOTSTAMP at the command line. The Plot stamp fields area allows you to specify the drawing information for the plot stamp. The available options are Drawing name, Device name, Layout name, Paper size, Date and Time, Plot scale, and Login name. Place a checkmark in the desired checkbox. The Preview area allows you to preview the plot stamp. The User defined fields area allows you to add two fields of optional text that can be added to the plot stamp, sent to a log file, or both. Click on the Add/Edit button to access the User Defined Fields dialog box, click Add, and then type the required entries. A typical application can be a project name, media type, or related information. Click on the OK button to get back to the Plot Stamp dialog box. The Plot stamp parameter file area lists the location of stamp parameter files. These files store plot stamp data with a *.pss* file name extension. This allows multiple users to access the same file and maintain company or school standards for plot stamps. The Advanced button will display the Advanced Options dialog box. The Location and offset area allows you to set the location, orientation, and offset of the plot stamp. You can justify the plot stamp on one of the four drawing corners and can print up to two lines. You can also create a plot stamp upside-down by placing a check mark in the Stamp upside-down check box. You can specify X and Y off-set values relative to printable area or relative to paper border by selecting the appropriate radio button. The Text properties area allows you to set the font, height, and number of lines for the plot stamp. The Plot stamps unit area allows you to set the units for offset and height. You can set the units to inches, millimeters, or pixels. The Log file location allows you to create a log file and the folder where the log file is written when you place a checkmark in Create a log file. You can turn Plot stamp on by placing a checkmark in the On checkbox in the Plot stamp area. Plotting and Printing are discussed in Chapter 23.

Note: Plot stamping will remain active with the most recently entered plot settings until it is specifically turned off. AutoCAD creates a plot stamp at the time of plotting, but the plot stamp is not saved with the drawing.

Applying True Color Values to Plot Styles The new Truecolor Plot Styles feature brings true color plotting capability to plotstyles that include 24-bit Truecolor support for rendered and raster images, significantly increasing the plot quality of the drawings. Presentation drawings now can have a wide range of colors than the standard AutoCAD 255-color palette. To apply true color values to plot styles, access the Plot dialog box and select the Plot Device tab. In the Plot style table (pen assignments) area, click on the Edit . . . button. Inside the Plot Style Table Editor dialog box, select the Form View tab. Select a Plot style from the Plot styles: list box. In the Properties area, select the down arrow in the Color: drop-down list and select True Color. Inside the True Color dialog box, enter values desired color between 0 and 255. Click on OK button and click on the Save & Close button. You can also access the Plot Style Table Editor dialog box by selecting Plot Style Manager . . . from the File pull-down menu and double clicking on the desired plot style.

Note: The Zoom command can now be used on rendered images.

1.13.6 Improved Help Tools

The help system in AutoCAD 2000i incorporates the Natural Language Query engine from AnswerWorks and has been converted from WinHelp to HTML-based help. The new AutoCAD Help dialog box is shown in Figure 1–39. The new Active Assistant automatically displays brief, pertinent, non-intrusive help for current commands and dialog boxes while using a command. It also includes a Search the Web feature and the ability to print user help and learning documents without installing AutoCAD software.

FIGURE 1–39 The Natural Language Query Engine of the Help dialog box allows you to type in a question.

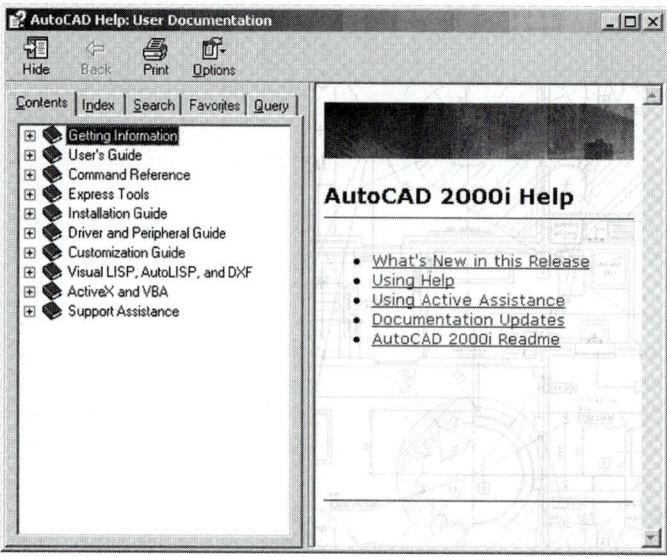

1.13.7 Additional Features

Additional features new in AutoCAD 2000i include the following and are indicated as *AutoCAD 2000i Update:* throughout the text:

- Double-click to edit objects. Controlled by the DBLCLKEDIT system variable. Default set to ON. See Chapter 13.
- Clear grips with a single ~EscKey~. See Chapter 13.
- CLOSEALL command allows you to close all open drawings at once. See Chapter 8 and 10.
- Properties window includes the PICKADD and Select Objects buttons. See Chapter 13.
- Change fillet radius without exiting the FILLET command and change chamfer distance without exiting the CHAMFER command. Use the FILLET and CHAMFER commands with multiple polylines. See Chapter 6.
- RECTANGLE command includes Dimension option. See Chapter 6.
- Edit multiple polylines with a single command. Multiple polylines can be joined even if polylines do not intersect each other. See Chapter 6.
- Trim and extend to objects within blocks. You do not have to explode a block to trim and extend to it. See Chapter 19.
- TRIM and EXTEND commands combined by holding down the ~ShiftKey~. See Chapter 12.
- TEXT and DTEXT commands are combined into a single TEXT command. See Chapter 14.
- The Layer Properties Manager dialog box contains two additional buttons as Save state . . . and Restore state . . . Layer states allow you to take a snapshot of your current layer settings. Layer states can be saved, restored, exported, and imported. See Chapter 9.

1.14 USEFUL CAD WEB SITES

Finding CAD-related information using a search engine could be cumbersome. The following Web sites can deliver the specific CAD information you have been searching for. These sites provide a variety of services ranging from technical help to discussion forums.

www.e-architect.com: This site is an affiliate of the American Institute of Architects Web site. It provides useful information about architects and the architecture profession. The iTALK section provides a discussion group dedicated to CAD and AutoCAD-related subjects.

www.ACADIA.org: This is the site for the Association for Computer Aided Design in Architecture. Its function is to serve the needs of the CAAD profession. You can become a member for approximately $100 per year. This includes becoming a member of the ACADIA list-serve.

www.CAD-Forum.com: This site is the ultimate online resource for the AutoCAD users. It is packed with information and offers a keyword-searchable database from which you can find CAD products, news, jobs, and consultants. The CAD Interact section includes a free DrawingSHARE service allowing CAD community to share and discuss AutoCAD drawings on the Internet. The site also includes user groups, a listing of CAD tips and tricks, downloadable drawings, and a bulletin board.

www.CADontheWeb.com: This site offers information on more than 300 CAD-related software and hardware companies and more than 1,000 products. You can use the keyword search to locate a company by name.

www.CADwire.net: This site provides CAD-related information under four categories: News, Reviews, Articles, and Events. This is a good place to visit if you are looking for CAD-related news on the Internet.

www.caddepot.com: This site offers Autodesk product trials, CAD shareware programs, utilities, patches, and upgrades. It also includes discussion groups and a technical support group composed of volunteers.

www.tenlinks.com: This site offers a comprehensive CAD directory that allows you to locate thousands of CAD-related sites.

1.15 THE ERGONOMICS OF THE CAD WORKSTATION

It is important to purchase the right furniture for the CAD workstation. The amount of desk space, the type and fabric of the chair, the height for the keyboard, and the correct tilt of the monitor are some of the items that you must consider. It is also important to consider how you sit and function in front of the computer. This relates to the ergonomics of a CAD workstation. The latest Occupational Safety and Health Organization (OSHA) figures indicate that a large number of people complained about eye strain, neck and back pain, and joint and posture disorders after working for many years in front of the computer. For your comfort, use the following guidelines each time you use your computer:

- Tilt the monitor slightly lower than the eye level. This will prevent direct glare coming to your eyes.

- Position yourself directly in front of your monitor and keyboard. As you type at the keyboard, you should be able to look up slightly and read your monitor. Your monitor should be set 20 to 25 inches from your eyes. This is a comfortable viewing distance.

- Adjust the lighting around you to minimize reflections and glare on the monitor screen. If you have direct natural light use curtains or blinds. If this is not possible, purchase an anti-glare screen for your monitor. Check your local computer store.

- Adjust the settings of your monitor, especially its brightness and contrast settings.

- Use a chair that provides good lower back support. Adjust your chair's height so that the monitor screen is at or below your eye level.

- When sitting, sit straight with your feet flat on the floor and keep your thighs level. Adjust your posture from time to time and stretch often.

- Your wrists should be relaxed and flat and your forearms horizontal when typing. Your upper arms should hang naturally. You can purchase a wrist support from your local computer store and place it in front of the keyboard.

REVIEW QUESTIONS

1. Discuss the function of AutoCAD in your firm or school.
2. What is the fundamental difference between AutoCAD 2000i and AutoCAD 2000?
3. Discuss at least four production features common to both versions of AutoCAD.
4. What is displayed when you launch AutoCAD 2000i?
5. What is displayed when you launch AutoCAD 2000?
6. What is the function of the Minimize button located on the Title Bar?
7. What is the function of the Pull-Down Menus?
8. What will be displayed when you select an option followed by an ellipsis (...)?
9. What is the function of the Grab Bars located on docked Toolbars?
10. Describe the procedure to dock a floating Toolbar.
11. Describe the procedure to bring back a removed Toolbar.
12. What is the name of the Toolbar that contain buttons and control boxes used to change properties of objects?
13. What is the function of the right-click feature of AutoCAD?
14. Where would you have to right-click to access the six most recent commands used?
15. What is the name of the dialog box used to customize the right-click operations?
16. What is the function of the Microsoft IntelliMouse rotating wheel?
17. What does DWF mean?
18. What is the name of the plug-in needed to create DWF files?
19. What does URL mean?
20. What is the function of the i-drop feature in AutoCAD 2000i?
21. How do you launch a Web browser from within AutoCAD?

22. Name three dialog boxes that have the Search the Web button.
23. What is the function of the Load/Unload Applications dialog box?
24. Can you convert rendered or shaded objects into DWF file format?
25. Can you convert three-dimensional drawings into a DWF file format?
26. What is the function of the ePlot feature of AutoCAD 2000?
27. What are the names of the two DWF plotter configurations?

PROBLEMS

1. Using the Right-Click Customization dialog box, create a right-click customization as follows:

    Default Mode: Repeat Last Command.

    Edit Mode: Shortcut Menu.

    Command Mode: ENTER.

2. Describe, in writing, what will happen when you right-click in the three Modes you have selected for Exercise 1.

3. Create the AutoCAD Graphics Window shown in Figure 1–40.

4. Create the AutoCAD Graphics Window shown in Figure 1–41.

5. Create the AutoCAD Graphics Window shown in Figure 1–42.

6. Verify with two local and one national PC retailer the cost of purchasing and setting up a CAD work-station (desktop computer) with the following requirements (do not include furniture):

    800 MHz Pentium III or faster PC with 256MB of RAM, 20GB hard drive, 19-inch monitor running Windows 2000, Nvidia GeForce 256 graphics card with 32MB of RAM, CD-RW drive, V.90 modem, net-work card, and Zip drive. Make a chart and compare prices for each retailer and vendor.

7. Using the Web sites of Dell Computer Corporation, Gateway, and IBM Corporation custom configure and compare the cost of purchasing a desktop computer with the following requirements:

    1GHz Pentium 4 or faster, 256MB of SDRAM, 256KB L2 cache, 30GB hard drive, 15-inch flat moni-tor, ATI Rage Fury Max graphics card or better with 64MB of RAM, 8X DVD-ROM drive, 4X/4X/32X

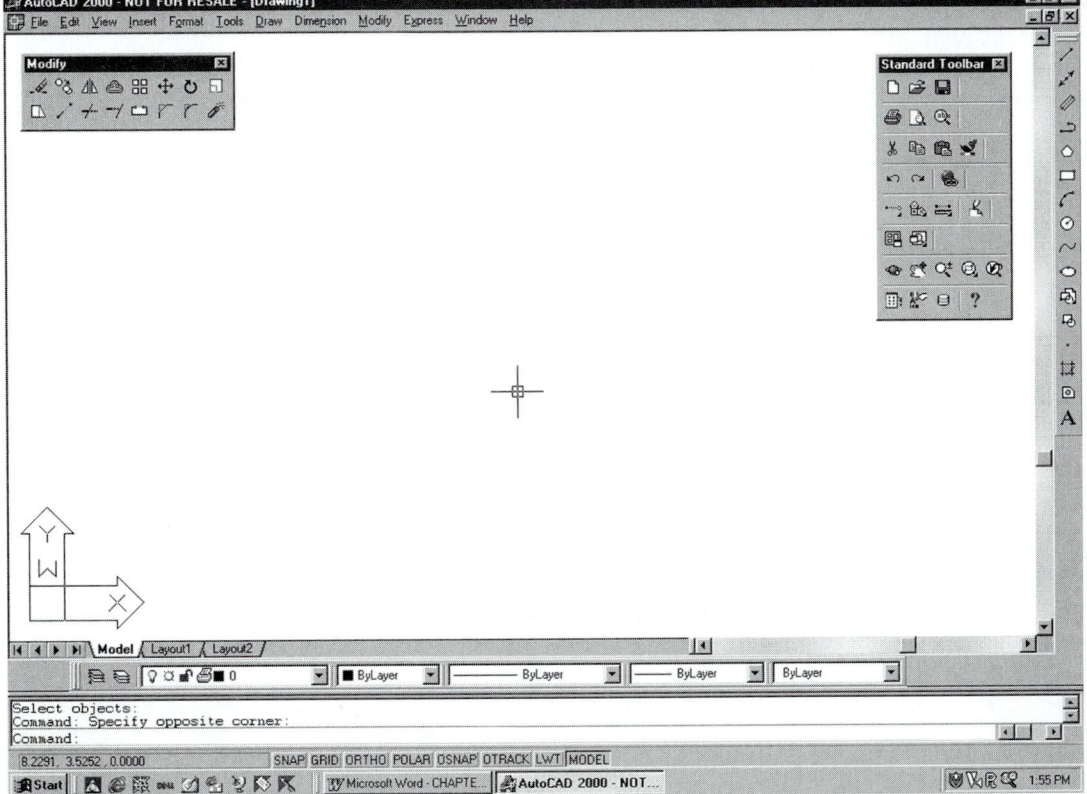

FIGURE 1–40 Problem 1–3.

FIGURE 1—41   Problem
1–4.

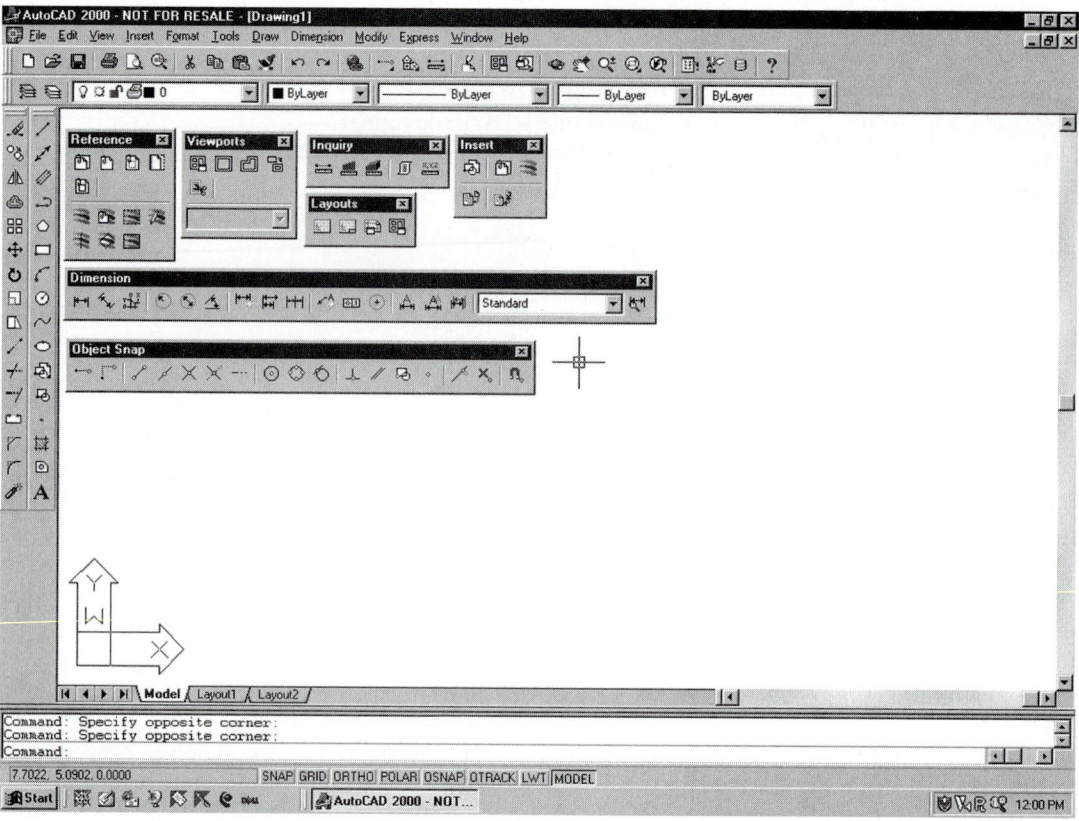

FIGURE 1—42   Problem
1–5.

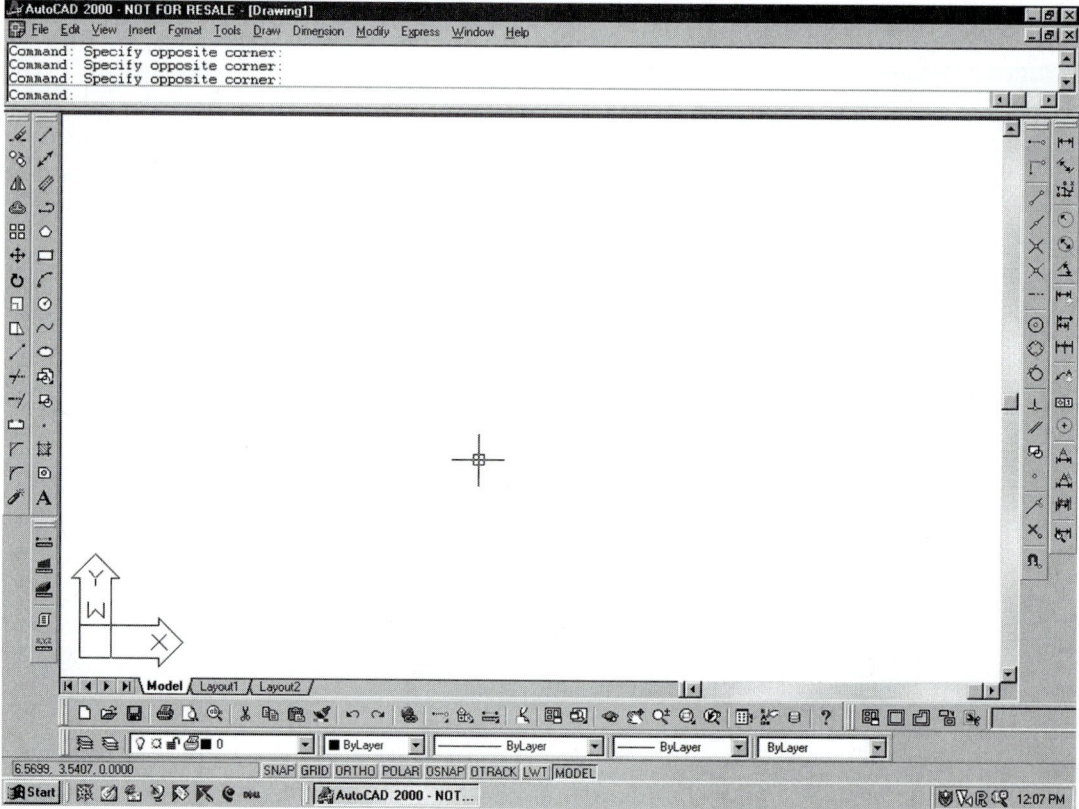

CD-RW drive, V.90 modem, minimum of two open drive bays, and four open slots. Also include a HP DeskJet 970CSE or Epson Stylus 900 inkjet printer. Make a chart and compare prices for each vendor.

8. Using the same Web sites mentioned above, custom configure and compare a laptop computer with the following requirements:

   800 MHz Pentium III or faster, 15-inch active screen, touchpad, 128MB of RAM, 12BG hard drive, 6X DVD-ROM, V.90 modem, LS-120 drive, lithium ion battery, and a carrying case. Make a chart and compare prices for each vendor.

9. Purchase the latest issue of three computer magazines (*PC World, PC Magazine,* and *Laptop Buyer's Guide & Handbook*). Read the major issues concerning desktop and laptop PCs. Discuss the new technology in computers and how it might affect the architecture and design professions.

10. Call a local architecture firm that uses AutoCAD 2000i or AutoCAD 2000. Make an appointment to see their CAD operation. While at the firm, observe the CAD workstations and ask questions about different aspects of hardware and software.

Establishing Drawing Settings

2

After successful completion of this chapter you should be able to:

▲ Organize and plan for AutoCAD drawings.

▲ Understand the concept behind establishing drawing settings.

▲ Execute basic planning decisions before starting a drawing.

▲ Identify the six major AutoCAD drawing elements that affect drawing format.

▲ Understand and establish drawing units and drawing precision.

▲ Utilize the Drawing Units dialog box.

▲ Understand and establish drawing angle format and precision.

▲ Change angle direction and base angle location using the Direction Control dialog box.

▲ Understand and discuss as to how to proceed with creating and plotting drawings and how drawing settings, setup, and scale utilized in the drawing process affect the final outcome of drawings.

▲ Understand and discuss some of the methods you can use to proceed with drawings and methods to prepare the final drawing composition.

▲ Understand the concept behind scale factors.

▲ Calculate scale factors for different drawing scales.

▲ Calculate and establish drawing Limits.

▲ Understand the relation between scale factor, drawing scale, and text height.

▲ Understand how scale factors affect drawing scale and text height.

▲ Read and utilize the Limits and the Text Height charts.

▲ Zoom to the Limits of your drawing.

2.1 ORGANIZING AND PLANNING FOR AUTOCAD DRAWINGS

Before starting a drawing in AutoCAD, certain factors that affect drawing format must be understood and considered. The drawing format involves setting up specific parameters that make up the basic elements of your drawing. Once you gain an understanding of drawing settings, you can establish different settings for different drawings. Understanding the basic elements of a drawing is crucial to designing and producing accurate and precise drawings in AutoCAD. How you begin a new drawing depends on what kind of drawing information you have. If you know the scale, units, and the size of the paper on which the drawing will be printed on, then you need to set-up *Units* and *Limits* for the drawing. Since all drawings in AutoCAD are drawn at Full

Scale, setting up Units and Limits for the drawing will establish the format needed to print or plot drawings to an actual sheet of paper *plotted to scale*. Plotting is discussed in Chapter 23.

2.2 UNDERSTANDING DRAWING SETTINGS

AutoCAD is not just about drawing objects on the screen, it is about understanding the elements and knowing the procedures behind creating and plotting drawings. It is about understanding different settings and methods that will lead you to the final outcome of the drawing. It is about creating settings and choosing the appropriate method that will allow you to plot drawings at the precise scale, unit, and size. A drawing that looks good on the screen is useless if it does not plot at the precise scale and format and if it does not contain correct dimension and text height. If the final outcome is to plot a floor plan on a specific-size sheet at a specific scale and units, with a title block and a borderline, then all the elements and settings that make the plot possible must be created with great care. You must understand that many options and settings are available not only at the drawing and editing phases but also at the printing and plotting phase. Choosing the most appropriate and effective option, setting, and method in a drawing is what will make you stand out in the crowd.

2.2.1 AutoCAD Drawing Elements

There are six major elements that affect the outcome of the final drawing format:

- **DRAWING UNITS:** Determines the *units* of measurement AutoCAD will use while the drawing is created on the screen. This element is set by the user in AutoCAD before starting a drawing and can be changed as required.

- **DRAWING PRECISION:** Determines the *precision* of the unit of measurement when creating objects in relation to distances and lengths of objects in the drawing. Such as in the case of using Polar snap and Polar distance for Polar Tracking. This element is set by the user in AutoCAD and is an integral part of the drawing Units.

- **DRAWING SCALE:** Determines the *scale* of the drawing. The scale of the drawing is used to determine the *Limits* for the drawing. Most of the time, you will know the drawing scale before you start the drawing. If you also know the sheet size that your drawing will plot on, you can then calculate the Limits of your drawing based on the drawing scale and sheet size. This will allow you to start drawing with the correct scale. This element is an integral part of drawing limits.

- **DRAWING SHEET SIZE:** Determines the size of the paper on which the drawing will be printed or plotted. The drawing sheet size along with the drawing scale is used to calculate drawing Limits.

- **DRAWING SCALE FACTOR:** Determines the Scale Factor value to establish drawing Limits based on a given Scale and *Sheet Size*. The scale factor is also used to determine correct text height and to establish size for dimension variables.

- **DRAWING LIMITS:** Determines the boundaries for a drawing based on the Scale Factor and the Sheet Size. This element is entered in AutoCAD before starting a drawing.

Drawing Units, Precision, and Limits are elements that you enter using a dialog box or at the command line when starting a drawing. Drawing Scale and Sheet Size are elements determined by you or the person in charge of the project (project architect/project manager) before you start establishing drawing Units, Precision, and Limits. Drawing Scale Factor is an element you must calculate after you determine what the scale of the drawing is. Drawing Units, Precision, and Limits are usually established using the Start from Scratch or Use a Wizard setup methods found in the Create New Drawing dialog box. Drawing setup methods are discussed in Chapter 3.

2.3 CONSIDERATIONS BEFORE DRAWING

Before establishing drawing settings, try to get as much information as possible about the final outcome of the drawing by gathering data from individuals who will provide you with a sketch or a schematic of the drawing. A sketch is a rough outline of a drawing, usually in a preliminary format. A schematic is a procedural diagram outlining elements of a drawing or a component. A sketch of an elevation of a building or a schematic of a structural diagram evolves by including and determining some or all of the elements mentioned above.

Once the drawing Scale and Sheet Size are obtained, they can be used to create drawing settings in AutoCAD. The six major drawing elements discussed above can also be used to create custom drawing *templates* where the specific elements of the drawing can be stored permanently and can be accessed as many times as needed without altering the original format and composition of the drawing. Drawing templates are discussed in Chapter 3. As with any design and drawing activity, elements of a drawing can change many times before the final outcome is reached. Changes and addendums to drawings are inevitable, and AutoCAD provides the flexibility to change some or all of the elements in the drawing by automated setup dialog box options or by entering the system variables that control these settings at the command line.

2.3.1 Setting Up a Scale Before Drawing

It is possible to set a drawing scale before starting to draw based on the final plot sheet size of your drawing. This is accomplished by entering new Limits for the drawing using the LIMITS command. This requires you to calculate and establish Limits based on the scale factor of your new drawing. A scale factor is used to set scale and annotation-containing text (drawing text and dimension text) to the correct text height based on the final plot size of annotation. The scale factor is also used to calculate drawing Limits. Custom drawing scales and annotation (text) size can be incorporated into drawing templates. Not all drawings start with a specific scale or sheet size. But a drawing must have a specific unit of measurement before it can be put on the AutoCAD screen. Hence, you can start a drawing by simply setting up Units only without setting up Limits. In other words, AutoCAD will allow you to start a drawing with or without knowing the precise scale or the precise plot sheet size.

2.4 UNDERSTANDING DRAWING UNITS

Drawing units allow you to create object geometry with a specific unit format. Object geometry in AutoCAD is created and measured in units at full scale. The value given to the unit of drawing and measurement depends on the type of drawings you create. The drawing unit settings control how AutoCAD determines point location, coordinate, and angle entries you make to create objects. You determine the value of the units before starting a project. For example, if you are creating a floor plan for an architect or an interior designer, a unit drawn should equal feet and fractional inches. If you are creating gear shaft details for a mechanical engineer, a unit might equal inches or millimeters. If you are creating plot plans with property lines for a land surveyor, a unit might equal feet and decimal inches. Most architectural drawings are created with the Units set to Architectural. You can set drawing units by using the Drawing Units dialog box. When you select Units . . . from the Format pull-down menu or enter UNITS at the command line, AutoCAD will display the Drawing Units dialog box as shown in Figure 2–1.

In the Drawing Units dialog box, AutoCAD refers Drawing Units as the *Length Type* used for the drawings. The default length type for drawing units is Decimal. You can set a different unit by clicking on the down arrow next to the Type: drop-down list. Select the drawing units you want from the list and click on the OK button. There are five different Length Types for drawing units to choose from as follows:

2.4.1 Architectural

The Architectural unit format creates object geometry as feet, inches, and fractional inches. It will allow you to enter lengths as inches, fractional inches, feet and inches, or feet and fractional inches. With Architectural Units, each unit drawn represents one inch. To draw in architectural units, click on Architectural under the Type: drop-down list for the Length category in the Drawing Units dialog box and click on the OK button. To draw a line 1'-0" in length, use the LINE command and enter 12 or 1' at the SPECIFY NEXT POINT OR [UNDO]: command prompt. Drawing lines is discussed in Chapter 5. If you enter a length without the feet (') or the inches

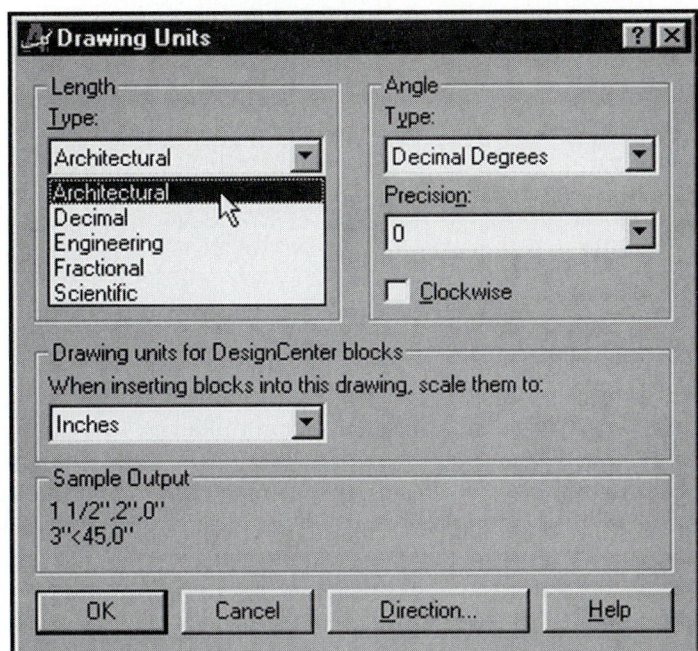

FIGURE 2–1 The Drawing Units dialog box will allow you to set the drawing units for object geometry. The drawing units in this case is set to Architectural with Precision set at 0′-1/16″. The default drawing units is Decimal with Precision set at 0.0000.

(″) mark, AutoCAD will register that length as inches. For example, entering 60 or 5′ at the command line will draw an object 60 inches or 5 feet long. When entering whole numbers as feet and inches, there is no need to enter a dash (-) after the feet. For example, to draw an object 12 feet and 6 inches (12′-6″) in length, you can enter 150 or 12′6 at the command line. It is more convenient and efficient to enter 12′6 as opposed to 150 because you do not have to convert to decimal inches. When drawing objects that include fractional inches, you must separate the inches measurement from the fraction with a dash (-). For example, to draw a line 12 feet 6 and 3/4 inch (12′-6 3/4″) long you must enter 12′6-3/4 at the command line. When the object is dimensioned using the proper dimensioning variables and settings, the length will be displayed as 12′-6 3/4″.

2.4.2 Decimal

The Decimal unit format creates object geometry as inches or fractional inches. One unit drawn is considered to be one inch in length. To draw an object one foot in length in Decimal units, you must enter 12 at the command line. If you enter 1′, AutoCAD will give you the following error message:

```
Point or option keyword required.
```

To draw a 1 foot 2 and 1/2 inches (1′-2 1/2″) length object, you can enter 14.50 or 14-1/2 at the command line.

2.4.3 Engineering

The Engineering unit format creates object geometry as inches, fractional inches, feet and inches, or feet and fractional inches. When creating object geometry, there is no difference between entering in Architectural or Engineering units. The difference comes in when the objects are dimensioned using their respective dimensioning units.

2.4.4 Fractional

The Fractional unit format creates object geometry as inches and fractional inches. One unit drawn is one inch in length. To draw a 1 foot 6 and 1/2 inch (1′-6 1/2″) length object you must enter 18.50 or 18-1/2 at the command line.

TABLE 2–1: Comparison of five different Length Type Drawing Units for a 1'-6 3/4" length object as drawn and dimensioned.

Drawing Units	1'-6 3/4" Length Object	
Length Type	**Entered (drawn) As**	**Dimensioned As**
Architectural	18.75 or 18-3/4 or 1'6-3/4	1'-6 3/4"
Decimal	18.75 or 18-3/4	18.7500
Engineering	18.75 or 18-3/4 or 1'6-3/4	1'-6.7500"
Fractional	18.75 or 18-3/4	18 3/4
Scientific	18.75 or 18-3/4	1.8750E+01

2.4.5 Scientific

The Scientific unit format creates object geometry as inches and fractional inches. The scientific unit is displayed as the base number multiplied by 10 to the first power when the dimensioning unit is set to Scientific.

When you create objects using a specific Drawing Units Length Type you can then create dimensions for the same objects using the same or different Linear Dimension Unit Format. See Chapter 18 for setting units for dimensioning. Table 2–1 shows how a 1'-6 3/4" length object can be drawn using different drawing units and what it would measure if it was dimensioned using the same unit format. The Unit Format for Linear Dimensions is set to the same Drawing Units Length Type. For example, if the Drawing Units Length Type is set to Architectural when drawing objects, then the Unit Format for Linear Dimensions is also set to Architectural when dimensioning like objects.

2.5 UNDERSTANDING DRAWING PRECISION

Drawing Precision allows you to select the number of digits displayed after the decimal point when Decimal, Engineering, and Scientific drawing units are used. In the Drawing Units dialog box as shown in Figure 2–1, AutoCAD refers Drawing Precision as the *Length Precision*. The default length precision value for Decimal units is 0.0000 (four digits), with a maximum of 0.00000000 (eight digits). Table 2–1 shows the Decimal drawing length precision for 1'-6 3/4" as 18.7500, Engineering drawing length precision as 1'-6.7500", and Scientific drawing length precision as 1.8750E+01. For Architectural and Fractional units, the length precision values relate to the smallest desired fractional denominator. The default value for Architectural length precision is 0'-1/16" with a maximum precision value of 0'-1/256". The default value for Fractional length precision is 1/16 with a maximum precision value of 1/256. For architectural drawings, a length precision value of 0'-1/16" would mean that the lengths of the objects will be *dimensioned* at 1/16" fractional denominator providing that the lengths of the objects are *drawn* (entered as) at that precision. However, the Drawing Units Precision does not have to correspond to that precision. For example, you can enter a length as 12'6-5/8 to draw a line 12 feet 6 and 5/8 inches long with a Length Precision value set to 0'-0" (no fractional inches precision). Even though the drawing precision does not match the precision of the actual length of the object, you can create a dimension for the same object displayed as 12'-6 5/8" by setting the Precision of the Linear Dimension to 0'-1/8" using the Dimension Style Manager dialog box. See Chapter 18 for a detailed discussion on this subject. You can set a different drawing length precision by clicking on the down arrow next to the Precision: drop-down list. Select the precision you want and click on the OK button. There are nine length precision values to choose from. Figure 2–2 shows some of the length precision values for the Architectural length type.

Tips: The true Length Precision of an object drawn is not achieved until the object is dimensioned with the corresponding units and precision. This is accomplished by setting the Linear Dimensions Unit Format and Precision to the desired unit and precision using the Primary Units tab in the Dimension Style dialog box. Refer to Chapter 18 for more information. For architectural drawings, it is possible to set the drawing length precision to 0'-0" and still draw with feet and fractional inches. But be careful, since 0'-0" length precision will not allow you to set dimensioning variables at fractional inch values when using the dialog boxes associated with Dimension Style Manager dialog box.

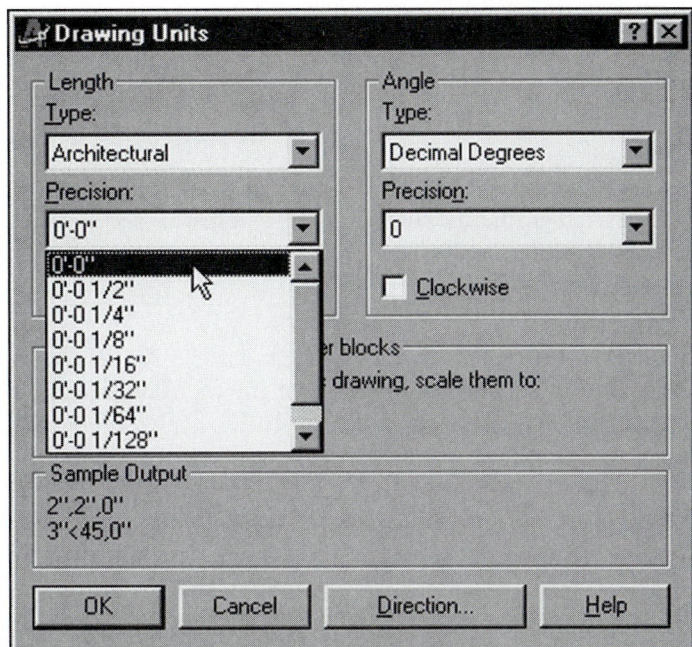

FIGURE 2–2 The Length Precision: drop-down list allows for object length precision control.

The length type and length precision can be changed at any point during the project. To facilitate drawing speed and accuracy, set the length precision as large as possible.

Tips: The Unit Length Precision *may need to be adjusted when using Polar Track, Polar Distance, and Polar Snap settings. This will allow AutoCAD to track lengths at the precision you require. Refer to Chapter 7 for additional information.*

2.6 ANGLE FORMAT

The Drawing Units dialog box can also be used to specify the current angle format and the precision for the current angle. The Angle Type: drop-down list allows you to select the appropriate angle format for the current drawing. The Precision: drop-down list allows you to select angle precision settings. There are five different angle formats to choose from, as shown in Figure 2–3.

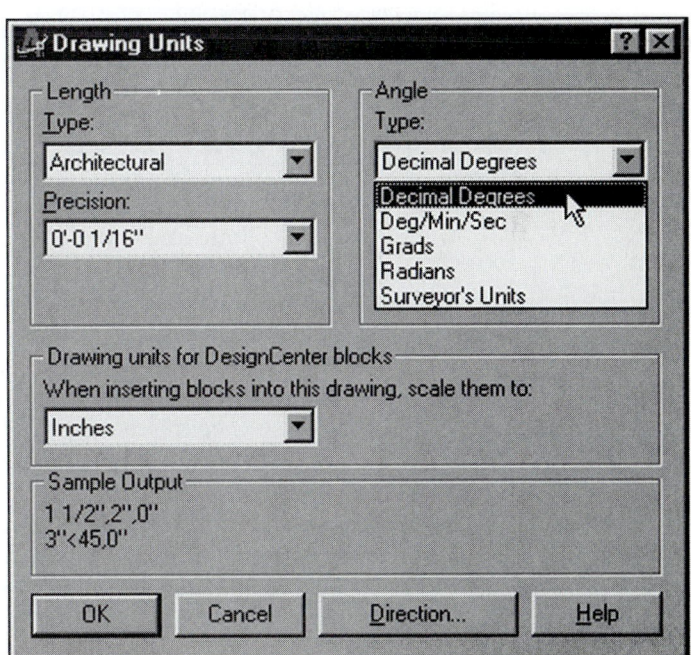

2.6.1 Decimal Degrees

This angle type will allow you to draw angles with decimal degrees. This is the default angle type setting. It is commonly used in mechanical and architectural drafting where degrees and decimal parts of a degree are commonly used for angles. For example, if you draw a line at a 65 degree angle, AutoCAD will create the angle as 65.0000 degrees when the angle Precision: drop-down list is set to 0.0000. If the precision is changed to 0.0, the angle will be created as 65.0 degrees.

2.6.2 Deg/Min/Sec

This angle type will allow you to draw angles with degrees, minutes, and seconds. It is commonly used in plot and plat plans by land surveyors and in architectural drawings to indicate angles of property lines in degrees, minutes, and seconds. There are 60 minutes in one degree and 60 seconds in one minute. This format uses *d* for degrees, ' for minutes, and " for seconds. For example, if you draw a line at a 68.73 degree

FIGURE 2–3 The Angle Type: drop-down list will allow you to select one of five different angle formats.

angle, AutoCAD will create the angle as 68d43′48″ when the angle precision is set to 0d00′00.00″. The Precision: drop-down list is used to select the precision of degrees, minutes, and seconds.

2.6.3 Grads

This angle type uses *gradient* as the unit of angle. There are 100 gradients in 90 degrees. A full circle has 400 gradients. This format uses a lowercase g suffix. For example, the 68.73 degree angle will be created as 76.37g when the angle precision is set to 0.00g.

2.6.4 Radians

This angle type uses *radians* as the unit of angle. There are 2π radians in a full circle. This format uses a lowercase r suffix. For example, the 68.73 degree angle will be created as 1.20r when the angle precision is set to 0.00r.

2.6.5 Surveyor's Unit

This angle type uses angle bearings measured from North (N) or South (S) as degrees, minutes, and seconds going toward East (E) or West (W). The angle is always less than 90 degrees and is created as degrees, minutes, and seconds with an N or S prefix and E or W suffix, depending on the quadrant. For example, the 68.73 degree angle measured from North toward West will be created as N68d43′48″W. If the angle is precisely north, south, east, or west, only the single letter representing the bearing is created.

Tips: The true angle format and precision are not achieved until the object is dimensioned with the corresponding units and precision. This is accomplished by setting the Angular Dimensions Unit Format and Precision to the desired unit and precision using the Primary Units tab in the Dimension Style dialog box. For architectural drawings, set the angle format and precision to decimal degrees and 0.00 and dimension the objects at any angle format and precision. The angle format and precision can be changed at any point during the project.

Tips: Using Polar Angle settings will override the angle format when using Polar Tracking. Refer to Chapter 7 for additional information.

2.7 ANGLE DIRECTION

In AutoCAD angles are measured and created from a base angle going clockwise or counterclockwise. The base angle determines where 0 degrees is in reference to the four quadrants of the circle. The default direction for the 0 (base) angle is at East. Angles are measured from this base angle in a counterclockwise direction. The 90 degrees angle is at North, the 180 degrees angle is at West, and the 270 degrees angle is at South direction. You can change the direction in which AutoCAD measures lines and angles. You can also change the location of the base angle. To change the angle direction from counterclockwise to clockwise, place a check mark in the Clockwise checkbox inside the Drawing Units dialog box. You can create a clockwise direction while using the default counterclockwise direction by entering a minus sign (−) in front of the angle. For example, you can draw a line with a −60 degree angle using default counterclockwise direction that would force the line to be created clockwise. The angle direction affects the rotation of objects and polar coordinates. It is best to keep the angle direction counterclockwise and enter a minus sign in front of the angle to direct it clockwise. Coordinates are discussed in Chapter 5.

The Direction . . . button in the Drawing Units dialog box will allow you to set the direction of the base angle. Selecting this button will display the Direction Control dialog box as shown in Figure 2–4. You can select East, North, West, or South to set the direction for the 0 angle. For example, if you select North as the base angle, this location will become the 0 angle, and all an-

FIGURE 2–4 The Direction Control dialog box.

gles will be measured from North counterclockwise. You can also select Other to set a direction of angle measurement different than 0, 90, 180, and 270. When you select Other, the Angle: text box will be available to enter a new angle. The Pick An Angle button allows you to define the angle on the screen using the mouse. Simply connect two points on an imaginary line to create the angle. AutoCAD will display that angle in the Angle: text box.

Tips: The Use a Wizard button in the Create New Drawing dialog box will also allow you to set drawing Units, Angle, Angle Measure, Angle Direction, and Area (Limits) one step at a time through Quick Setup or Advanced Setup dialog boxes. See Chapter 3.

2.8 UNDERSTANDING DRAWING SCALE IN RELATION TO FINAL OUTCOME OF THE DRAWING

You may be surprised to learn that a scale for the drawing can either be established before you start the drawing or after you finish the drawing. No, there is no magic button in AutoCAD that will enable you to click on a scale to draw at a specific scale before you start drawing. In order to do this you have to establish drawing units and calculate and set drawing limits and then start drawing. The concept of limits will make more sense to you as you proceed with this and other chapters. But there are certain buttons and/or selections in AutoCAD that enable you to click on a scale and paper size to plot at that specific scale and paper size. In order to do this you must use the Plot or the Page Setup dialog box to establish plot settings after you complete the drawing. You can assign or change drawing scale just before you *layout,* or *plot,* a drawing. Layouts and Plotting are discussed in Chapters 22 and 23. The scale and paper size assigned before, during, or after the drawing is completed can always be changed just before you plot the drawing. However, with the latter method you are risking the possibility of plotting text, dimension text, and hatching not consistent with the drawing scale. This is because changing the scale of the drawing after creating notes, dimensions, and hatching will require you to update the height of text and scale factor of hatching to match the new drawing scale. You can avoid this by creating notes, text, dimensions, and hatching just before you plot the drawing. But this may not always be possible. Understanding the intricate relationship between drawing and plotting options will help you understand the concept of scale in a wider context.

There are many options to consider as to how to proceed with creating and plotting drawings and how drawing settings, setup, and scale utilized in the process affect the final outcome of drawings. The following are some of the methods you can use to create drawings and establish the final composition of your projects. As you study the chapters on Layouts, Paper Space, Plotting, and Externally Referenced Drawings you will get a much better sense of these methods.

1. Just before you start drawing assign the proper drawing units and establish drawing Limits based on the scale factor and the final plotted sheet size of your drawing. When you are ready to plot, use the PLOT command to plot the drawing to scale or assign a different plot scale or a different sheet size using the Plot dialog box. Printing and Plotting is discussed in Chapter 23. You can change drawing limits at any time when you want to change the drawing scale and to assign a different size sheet. This is possible for one or more drawings with the same scale composed on one sheet size created and plotted in Model Tab. With this method you start a drawing precisely knowing the scale of the drawing and the precise sheet size that it will be plotted on. You assign the drawing scale and paper size before you start the drawing or during plotting. You can create a borderline and title block in Model Tab and still plot in Model Space.

2. Start a drawing by assigning the proper drawing units. Establish drawing limits not necessarily based on a scale factor or a particular sheet size but on a general drawing size. Just make sure that the entire drawing appears on the screen. When you are ready to plot, use the PLOT command to plot the drawing to scale. Use the Plot dialog box to change the scale and sheet size of your drawing and to assign plot settings. This is also possible for one or more drawings with same scale composed on one sheet size created and plotted in Model Tab.

3. Start a drawing with or without Limits. When you are finished with the drawing, access one of the Layouts. Your drawing will now be displayed in Paper Space. If necessary create the layout from an existing template. Use the Page Setup dialog box to establish plot settings or close this dialog box and use the Plot dialog box to establish plot settings when you are ready to plot. Modify your drawing inside the model of the viewport if required. Use the Viewports dialog box to assign or change the drawing scale in the Model Space of the viewport. If you are plotting two or more drawings with different scales, create individual viewports in Paper Space for each drawing and assign the appropriate scale to each viewport using the Viewports toolbar. Plot your final drawing(s) in Paper Space at 1:1 scale using the Plot dialog box. With this method you start a drawing with or without knowing the precise scale and sheet size and with or without using a template. You assign a 1:1 plot scale and sheet size during plotting in Paper Space. AutoCAD will not allow you to plot in Model Tab with this method.

4. Start a drawing using a template (.dwt file). AutoCAD will automatically switch to a Paper Space layout. Use the default viewport to create a drawing or drawings at the same scale or create different viewports and draw inside the model of the viewports to create multiscale drawings. Assign a scale for the viewport(s) using the Viewports toolbar. Plot drawing(s) in Paper Space using the PLOT command or use the Page Setup dialog box to create plot settings. Template drawings appear in Paper Space Layout with title block and borderline. With this method, you must plot in Paper Space.

5. Create one or more drawings with the required scale and paper size (Limits) in Model Tab (default). Save the drawing(s) with appropriate names. Start a drawing using a template large enough to compose the drawing(s). Create individual floating viewports in Paper Space for each drawing. Use the XREF command to externally reference each drawing into its own viewport inside the Model of the viewports. Assign a scale for each viewport using the Viewports toolbar and plot in Paper Space. Multiple floating viewports and Paper Space Layouts are discussed in Chapter 22.

If you are a seasoned AutoCAD user you may have a different approach or method to the process of creating and plotting drawings than the five methods described above. Or perhaps you have a method that works for you. I realize that there are more methods out there used by many individuals every day. The methods described above are proved to save time and boost productivity, especially in the production of construction documents. If you are not using any of the methods described above or if you are using just one method, try one method and see how it works for you and how it affects your productivity. The most important thing is to use the method(s) that will increase efficiency and productivity at the same time.

2.9 INTRODUCTION TO SCALE FACTOR, SHEET SIZE, AND LIMITS

Even though you can establish a drawing scale at the start or at the end, all drawings in Auto-CAD are created at *full scale*. It is the Limits that will show your drawing at the desired scale and the final plot scale that will plot your drawing at the desired scale. Hence, when you create object geometry in AutoCAD, you draw at full scale. If you draw an object using Decimal Length Type, then you draw the object using inches at *real world size* at full scale. For example, if you draw a line six inches in length using all default values, you will see that line as six inches at full scale in your screen. If you draw another line at 48 inches, you will not be able to see the end-point of that line because it will be off your screen. If you draw an object using Architectural Length Type, then you draw the object using inches, feet and inches, or feet and fractional inches at full scale. For example, if you draw a line 3 feet 8 and 3/4 inches in length, you will not be able to see the endpoint of that line because it will be off your screen. How can you create a house plan or a building façade (elevation) on a sheet of paper in AutoCAD unless the paper is as large as the house plan or elevation at full scale? You actually tell AutoCAD that you will use a sheet of paper a bit larger than the house plan or elevation and you will also tell AutoCAD that you have a scale in mind. That sheet of paper in relation to the drawing scale is the drawing Limits.

There are standard sizes of sheet and scales used in architectural drawings. To determine Limits, that is, what we tell AutoCAD about sheet size and scale, we need to determine how many feet (or inches) will fit into a specific size sheet at a specific scale. Unlike Units and Precision, the drawing scale is not selected from a dialog box or entered at the command line. In manual drafting, the drawing scale is determined by the size of the drawing and the size of the sheet needed to draw the final drawing. In AutoCAD, we need to shrink the sheet to the size of the monitor so that the entire drawing is visible on the screen. This is referred to as the calculation of drawing Limits. The objects that you draw will not be scaled and will not be shown on the screen as in the case of a house plan until the *scale factor* of the drawing is multiplied by the *sheet size* and entered as the drawing *Limits*. To calculate Limits of a drawing, you must understand scale factor and sheet size.

Typical architectural scales used in projects range from 1/16″=1′-0″ (very small scale) to 3″=1′-0″ (very large scale). Large projects require small scales plotted on large sheet sizes, and large detailed work requires large scales plotted on many different sheet sizes. Most of the floor plans are drawn at a scale of 1/4″=1′-0″ or 1/8″=1′-0″. Most of the working drawing details are drawn at a scale of 1″=1′-0″ and up to 3″=1′-0″. Most residential-type wall sections are drawn at a scale of 3/4″=1′-0″. The available 11 architectural scales are shown in Figure 2–6. Some of the architectural drawings use engineering scale. For example, a site plan for a large office building can be created using an engineering scale of 1″=30′, where one inch drawn in real world units is equal to 30 feet at that scale. The available eight engineering scales are shown in Figure 2–7.

2.9.1   Understanding Sheet Size

A sheet size is selected for the final plot. This may or may not be known before the drawing is started. The final drawing may be composed of one or more drawings at different scales placed on the same sheet. Some of the architectural working drawings may require three or more types of drawings at different scales to be composed on a single sheet. When this is the case, the single sheet of paper becomes the *template* drawing, where a borderline and title block is incorporated and made a part of the template. Templates are drawings that have already been set up with the required information such as a borderline, title block, revision block, company logo, and so on. See Chapter 3 for more information on templates. Some drawings, such as a floor plan, may be drawn at a large scale as one drawing to fit on a single sheet. In this case the drawing may not require a template but would simply be printed on a specific-size sheet. Regardless of the drawing composition, the sheet size is the final size of the paper that is being used to plot the final composition of the drawing. Before selecting a sheet size, take into account the scale of the

FIGURE 2–5 D size architectural template with available drawing area when the scale is to be ¼″ = 1′-0″.

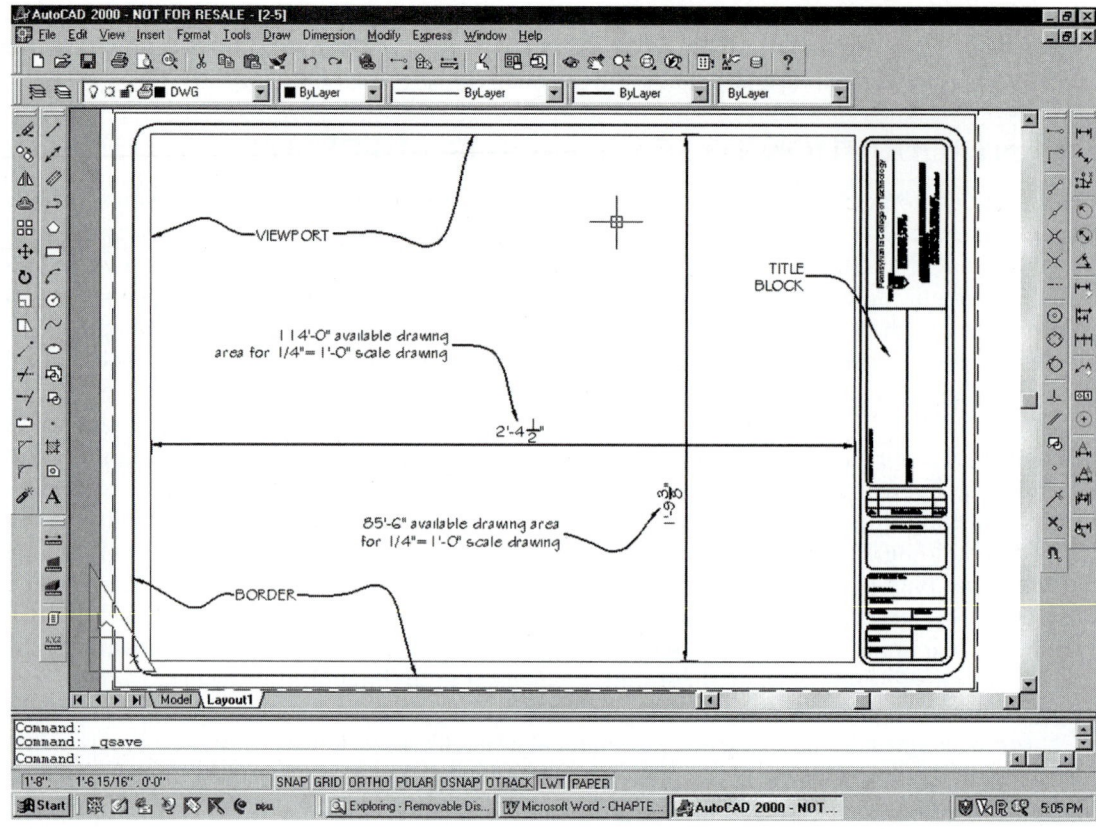

TABLE 2–2: Available standard sheet sizes for architectural drawings.

Size Designation	Size in Horizontal Format
A	11″ × 8 1/2″
B	17″ × 11″
C	24″ × 18″
D	36″ × 24″
E	42″ × 30″
F	48″ × 36″

drawing, the room for dimensions, notes, legends, title block, revision block, and borderlines. The total available space for the drawing must be determined from all these variables so that the drawing intended at a specific scale fits inside the selected sheet size. Figure 2–5 shows a 36″ × 24″ D-size architectural template with borderlines, title block, and revision block. The X and Y dimensions indicate the maximum drawing area for a project at a scale of 1/4″=1′-0″. Similarly, if the scale of the drawing is to be 1/8″=1′-0″, the available drawing area would double.

There are six different standard sheet sizes available for architectural projects as shown in Table 2–2.

Tips: Roll sizes are also available for plotting drawings that require more length. A roll of paper is attached to the plotter.

2.9.2 Understanding the Scale Factor

A scale factor is a unitless multiplier used in conjunction with the scale and the sheet size of the drawing to determine drawing Limits. After determining a drawing scale and selecting a sheet size for the project, the scale factor must be calculated and multiplied by the horizontal and vertical lengths of the sheet size to determine drawing Limits. Remember that all objects regardless of their length type and sheet size are drawn at full scale. When you start a drawing from scratch, AutoCAD provides a default drawing Limits based on "A" size paper that is equal to 12″ × 9″. This default drawing Limits and any other calculated Limits are also referred to as the *drawing area,* which is the default drawing paper without any border or title block. In other words, AutoCAD gives you one blank piece of paper that is 12″ × 9″ in horizontal format to draw on. This default drawing area is great if you are to draw a full-scale detail of a doorknob or a receptacle outlet. Most of us are not so lucky and need to draw floor plans, elevations, and site plans of residential and commercial buildings at different architectural scales using different sizes of sheet. This is where the scale factor comes into play. Remember the 3 feet 8 and 3/4 inch line length example, in which you did not see the endpoint of that line using default drawing area at full scale. In order to see all the objects created for the drawing at a specific drawing scale and sheet size a scale factor must be calculated and multiplied by the actual dimensions of the sheet size. The calculated numbers are referred to as the Limits of the drawing. The Limits of the drawing actually represent the lower-left and the upper-right coordinates of the selected sheet size that we tell AutoCAD in regard to drawing scale and drawing sheet size. To calculate a scale factor, the scale and the sheet size of the project must be known. The following are the steps used to calculate the scale factor:

Step #1: Convert both sides of the drawing scale equation to decimal units.

Step #2: Divide the right side of the equation with the left side. The result is the scale factor for the drawing. The scale factor has no units.

■ **EXERCISE 2–1:** *The following step-by-step exercise will help you calculate the scale factor for a drawing having a scale of 1/8″=1′-0″:*

Step #1: Convert both sides of the drawing scale equation to decimal units as follows:

0.125″ = 12″

Step #2: Divide the right side of the equation with the left side as follows:

12″ / 0.125″ = 96

96 is the Scale Factor for a 1/8″=1′-0″ drawing scale.

■ **EXERCISE 2–2:** *The following step-by-step exercise will help you calculate the scale factor for a drawing having a scale of 3/4″=1′-0″:*

Step #1: Convert both sides of the drawing scale equation to decimal units as follows:

0.75″ = 12″

Step #2: Divide the right side of the equation with the left side as follows:

12″ / 0.75″ = 16

16 is the Scale Factor for a 3/4″=1′-0″ drawing scale.

■ **EXERCISE 2–3:** *The following step-by-step exercise will help you calculate the scale factor for a drawing having a scale of 1″=30′:*

Step #1: Convert both sides of the drawing scale equation to decimal units as follows:

1″ = 360″ (30 × 12)

Step #2: Divide the right side of the equation with the left side as follows:

360″ / 1″ = 360

360 is the Scale Factor for a 1″=30′ drawing scale.

2.9.3 Understanding Limits

After calculating the scale factor, a new sheet size must be entered to change the default drawing area. The drawing area is defined as the Limits of the drawing that specify the coordinates for the lower-left corner and the upper-right corner of the sheet size. The limits of the default drawing area are 0.0000″, 0.0000″ for the lower-left corner and 12″, 9″ for the upper-right corner. Basically this is a rectangular piece of paper used as the drawing area. The limits of the drawing actually represent the maximum drawing area that is the sheet size for the project. The lower-left corner of a drawing is usually set at 0,0 because this is the lower-left corner of the drawing. As the default, the UCS icon is placed on the lower-left corner of the drawing area to give you the maximum exposure to your drawing limits. To calculate the limits for the upper-right corner of a new drawing, the scale factor must be multiplied with the horizontal and the vertical dimensions of the sheet size. This will reconfigure the default drawing limits and change it to a different-size sheet with the scale that you chose. The following steps are used to calculate the limits:

Step #1:   Multiply the scale factor by the sheet size.

Step #2:   Convert the upper-right corner limits to match the current length type. For example, if new limits are in inches, convert to feet and inches for architectural length type.

■   **EXERCISE 2–4:**   *The following step-by-step exercise will help you calculate drawing limits for a 1/8″=1′-0″ scale drawing using a C-size sheet:*

Step #1:   The scale factor is 96. The dimensions for the C-size sheet are 24″ × 18″ with horizontal format. Multiply the scale factor by the sheet size as follows:

96 × 24″ = 2304″
96 × 18″ = 1728″

Step #2:   Convert the upper-right corner limits to match the current length type as follows:

2304″ / 12″ = 192′
1728″ / 12″ = 144′

The new upper-right corner limits for a 1/8″=1′-0″ scale drawing to be plotted on a C-size (24″ × 18″) sheet are **192′, 144′.**

■   **EXERCISE 2–5:**   *The following step-by-step exercise will help you calculate drawing limits for a 3/4″=1′-0″ scale drawing using a D-size sheet.*

Step #1:   The scale factor is 16. The dimensions for the D-size sheet are 36″ × 24″ with horizontal format. Multiply the scale factor by the sheet size as follows:

16 × 36″ = 576″
16 × 24″ = 384″

Step #2:   Convert the upper-right corner limits to match the current length type as follows:

576″ / 12″ = 48′
384″ / 12″ = 32′

The new upper-right corner limits for a 3/4″=1′-0″ scale drawing to be plotted on a D-size (36″ × 24″) sheet are **48′, 32′.**

■   **EXERCISE 2–6:**   *The following step-by-step exercise will help you calculate drawing limits for a 1″=30′ scale drawing using a B-size sheet:*

Step #1:   The scale factor is 360. The dimensions for the B-size sheet are 17″ × 11″ with horizontal format. Multiply the scale factor by the sheet size as follows:

360 × 17″ = 6120″
360 × 11″ = 3960″

Step #2:   Convert the upper-right corner limits to match the current length type as follows:

6120″ / 12″ = 510′
3960″ / 12″ = 330′

The new upper-right corner limits for a 1″=30′ scale drawing to be plotted on a B-size (17″ × 11″) sheet are **510′, 330′.**

As you can see, for each drawing scale plotted on a different sheet size you must calculate Limits for each. This translates to 50 different Limits for the 10 architecture scales using five different sheet sizes and 35 different Limits for the seven engineering scales using five different sheet

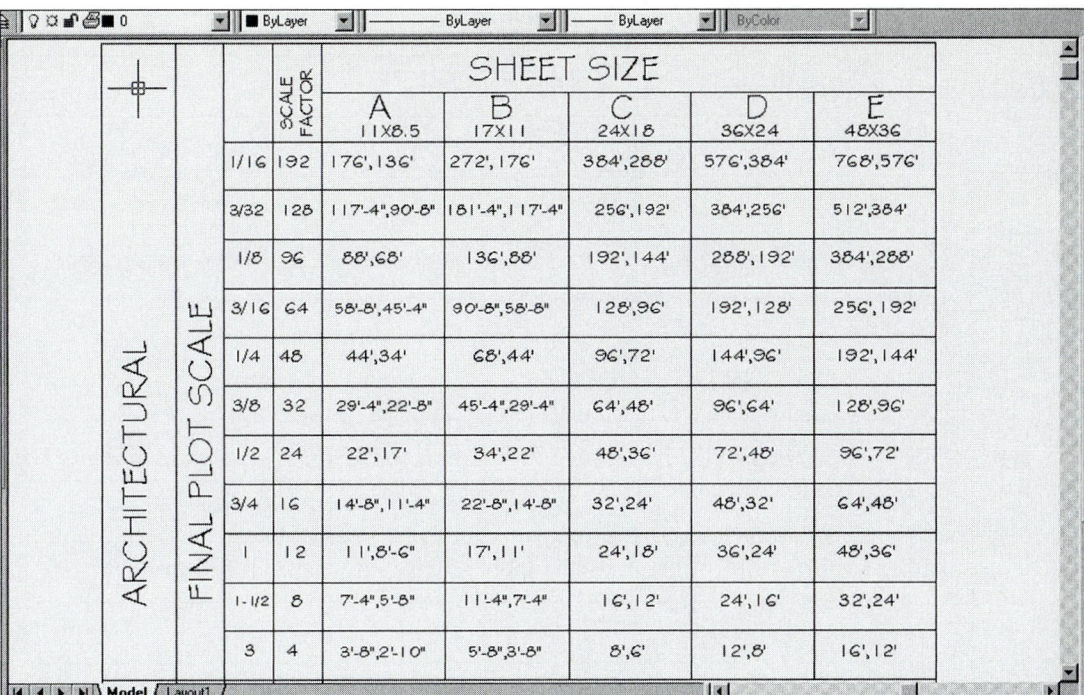

FIGURE 2–6 The Limits Chart as the upper-right corner coordinate values (limits) for 11 architectural scales with five sheet sizes.

sizes. Fortunately, I calculated all 85 Limits and put them on two tables for you. Figure 2–6 shows the upper-right corner limits for 11 architectural scales, and Figure 2–7 shows the upper-right corner limits for eight engineering scales using A, B, C, D, and E size sheets.

Note: It is not absolutely necessary to convert decimal inches to feet and inches. You can enter decimal inches as opposed to feet and inches as the Limits of a new drawing. However, entering feet and inches allows you to visualize the size of the drawing in architectural terms. It also makes more sense to communicate with architects about working drawings using the feet and inches format. For example, you should identify a wall length to the architect as "The wall measures 34 feet and 8 inches," not "The wall measures 416 inches." Besides, objects on drawings are communicated by feet and inches or feet and fractions of inch format.

2.9.4 How to Read the Limits Chart

The drawing scales are listed in the first column (next to Final Plot Scale). This is the scale of the drawing and it may or may not be the final scale to which the drawing will be plotted. You can change the Limits any time during the drawing process. The Scale Factor column lists all the corresponding scale factors for each of the scales. For example, the scale factor for a drawing that will be plotted at a scale of 3/4″=1′-0″ is 16. The sheet sizes are listed on top with A, B, C, D, and E. Each Sheet Size column has a corresponding Limits value for each row of scale. To find the appropriate drawing Limits, place one finger on the Final Plot Scale and place another finger on the Sheet Size. Move both of your fingers until they intersect; this is the corresponding drawing Limits. For example, the Limits for a drawing with final plot scale of 1/8″=1′-0″ plotted on a C-size sheet (24″ × 18″) are 192′, 144′. Remember that these numbers represent the upper-right corner of the drawing.

2.9.5 Entering Limits

After the upper-right corner limits for the drawing are calculated, they are entered in AutoCAD using three different methods as follows:

1. From the Format pull-down menu, left-click on Drawing Limits. Use the following command line procedure to enter Drawing Limits:

```
Command: '_ limits
Reset Model space limits:
```

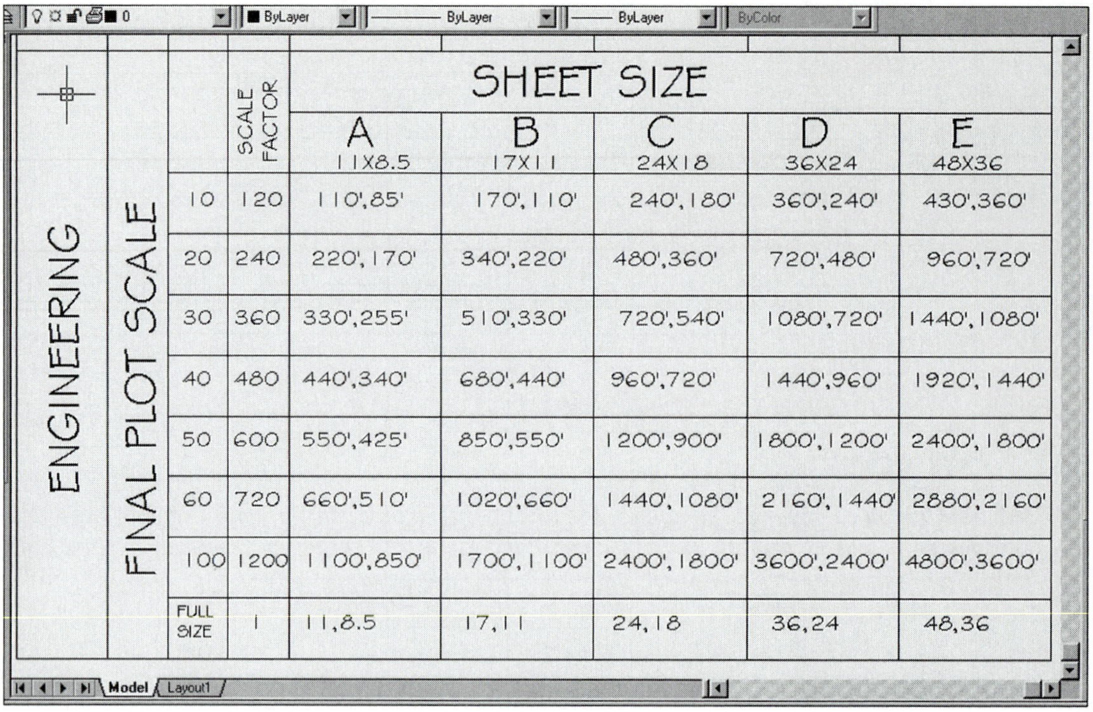

FIGURE 2–7 The Limits Chart as the upper-right corner coordinate values (limits) for 7 engineering scales plus full scale with five sheet sizes.

ENGINEERING — FINAL PLOT SCALE

SCALE FACTOR		SHEET SIZE				
		A 11X8.5	B 17X11	C 24X18	D 36X24	E 48X36
10	120	110',85'	170',110'	240',180'	360',240'	430',360'
20	240	220',170'	340',220'	480',360'	720',480'	960',720'
30	360	330',255'	510',330'	720',540'	1080',720'	1440',1080'
40	480	440',340'	680',440'	960',720'	1440',960'	1920',1440'
50	600	550',425'	850',550'	1200',900'	1800',1200'	2400',1800'
60	720	660',510'	1020',660'	1440',1080'	2160',1440'	2880',2160'
100	1200	1100',850'	1700',1100'	2400',1800'	3600',2400'	4800',3600'
FULL SIZE	1	11,8.5	17,11	24,18	36,24	48,36

```
Specify lower left corner or [ON/OFF] <0.0000,0.0000>: ~EnterKey~
Specify upper right corner <12.0000, 9.0000>: (enter the limits for
your project)
```

2. Enter LIMITS at the command line and set limits for the upper-right corner as shown above.

3. Enter the LIMMAX system variable at the command line as follows:

```
Command: LIMMAX ~EnterKey~
Enter new value for LIMMAX <12.0000, 9.0000>: (enter a new value for
the upper-right corner as the drawing limits)
```

System variables are explained in Chapter 4.

2.9.6　Showing the Limits of the Drawing

When you enter the upper-right corner for the new drawing limits, you are actually resetting the current drawing area or limits. You are basically removing the old sheet and placing the new sheet to setup a new drawing area with a scale. Before you start drawing on the new sheet with the intended scale, however, you must have AutoCAD zoom to the new limits of the new drawing to finalize the new drawing area. By zooming to the limits, AutoCAD will reset the drawing area and fit the new drawing area to size by actually shrinking the drawing area so that you can see the beginning and ending points of the objects created in the new drawing. You are still drawing at full scale. The only difference now is that you set new limits for the upper-right corner by using a scale factor that is derived from new scale and new sheet size. To zoom to the new limits of the drawing, use the Zoom All button in the Standard toolbar. This final procedure must be performed after each new Limits parameter is calculated and set; otherwise you will not be able to see your drawing on the screen or plot at the precise drawing scale.

The following describes the entire procedure for creating new drawing settings, which allows you to start a drawing with a scale to be plotted on a specific sheet size:

• Determine a scale for the drawing. You may at any time change the Limits of the drawing that will change the scale. When your drawing is finished, you may plot the drawing to scale on to the selected sheet of paper or change the scale and sheet according to your requirements.

- Determine the size of the paper on which you intend to plot the final drawing. You may at any time change the paper size.
- Calculate the scale factor for the selected drawing scale. When you change the drawing scale your scale factor changes also.
- Multiply the scale factor by the horizontal and vertical dimensions of the new sheet size. This will be your drawing Limits parameter and represents the coordinate points for the upper-right corner of the selected sheet size.
- Convert the Limits to match the length type.
- Enter the new Limits as the upper-right corner.
- Zoom to the Limits of your drawing by entering Z or ZOOM and then enter A or ALL at the command line.

CAUTION: You can change the Limits of your drawing at any point in your drawing to establish final plot scale and new sheet size for your drawing. AutoCAD will automatically update object geometry to reflect the new scale for the new limits. After setting new limits, you can continue drawing with the new scale of the project. This procedure does not require the object geometry to be changed or rescaled as long as the object geometry is composed of lines, circles, polylines, multilines, and any other entities having linear formats. Objects such as text, dimension text, certain dimensioning variables such as tick marks, and linetypes having a height or width are all affected by the new limits and must be recalculated for correct size.

Note: You may change drawing settings such as Units, Precision, and Limits at any time during the project using commands, system variables, or dialog boxes. It is very common to change sheet size (Limits) to accommodate a new scale or new drawings. However, I do not recommend waiting too long to change drawing settings. Most of the working drawings associated with construction documents will have a final plot scale and a sheet size.

Tips: Select at least a sheet size at the start of a drawing even if you are not sure about the final plot scale. If you decide on a final plot scale after creating the drawing, change the drawing Limits and make appropriate adjustments to other system variables.

2.10 SCALE FACTOR AND TEXT HEIGHT

When creating text, AutoCAD prompts you to enter a height for the text. If the drawing scale is 1″=1″, the text height is entered as full scale. For example, if you want the text to be plotted at 1/4″ height when creating a drawing with a scale of 1″=1″, enter 1/4 or 0.25 as the text height. When using architectural drawing scale, a new text height relative to architectural units must be calculated based on the scale factor of the drawing. When new drawing Limits are entered for the architectural drawings, object geometry with heights must correspond to the new scale. This is accomplished by multiplying the scale factor of the drawing by the desired text height in full scale. The resulting number in inches or feet and inches must be entered as the text height.

- **EXERCISE 2–7:** *The following step-by-step exercise will help you calculate the text height in inches for the following drawing settings:*

> Drawing Scale: 1/4″=1′-0″.
> Required text height in full scale when plotted: 1/8″.

Step #1: Multiply the scale factor of the drawing by the required text height as follows:

> $48 \times 0.125″ = 6″$

Step #2: Enter the new text height at the command line as follows:

> Command: **DTEXT** ~EnterKey~
> Current text style: "Standard" Text height 0.20

Specify start point of text or [Justify/Style]: (*specify a starting point for the text on the screen*)
Specify height: **6** ~EnterKey~

This will allow you to create text at a height of 6″ using a scale of 1/4″=1′-0″ but will create the text at a height of 1/8″ when plotted.

■ **EXERCISE 2–8:**   *The following step-by-step exercise will help you calculate the text height in inches for the following drawing settings:*

Drawing Scale: 3/4″=1′-0″.
Required text height in full scale when plotted: 3/16″.

Step #1:   Multiply the scale factor of the drawing by the required text height as follows:

16 × 0.1875″ = 3″

Step #2:   Enter the new text height at the command line as follows:

Command: **DTEXT** ~EnterKey~
Current text style: "Standard" Text height 0.20
Specify start point of text or [Justify/Style]: (*specify a starting point for the text on the screen*)
Specify height: **3** ~EnterKey~

This will allow you to create text at a height of 3″ using a scale of 3/4″=1′-0″ but will create the text at a height of 3/16″ when plotted.

Note: Exercises 2–7 and 2–8 assumes that you have established drawing units, Limits, and zoomed to the limits of the drawing. Figure 2–8 shows the required text height for the 11 architectural scales when the actual plotted text height is 3/32″, 1/8″, 3/16″, 1/4″, 3/8″, 1/2″, and 1.″ The Text Height Chart in Figure 2–8 can also be used to determine the appropriate radius and diameter of circles in full scale to architectural scale. For example, to calculate the diameter of a circle in feet and inches with a scale of 1/8″=1′-0″ that would be plotted at 1/2″, multiply the scale factor by 0.5″ as follows:

96 × 0.5″ = 48″ = 4′-0″

The diameter of the circle is then entered at the command line as follows:

Command: **C** ~EnterKey~
CIRCLE Specify center point for circle or [3P/2P/Ttr (tan tan radius)]: (*specify the center of the circle on the screen*)
Specify radius of circle or [Diameter]: **D** ~EnterKey~
Specify diameter of circle: **4′** ~EnterKey~

This will draw a circle with a diameter of 4′-0″ that would plot at 1/2″ (diameter) when the drawing is printed at the scale of 1/8″=1′-0″.

2.10.1   How to Read the Text Height Chart

The drawing scales are listed in the first column. This is the final plot scale of the drawing. The Actual Plotted Text Height in Full Scale is listed on top with seven different heights. This is the height of the text you want plotted at full scale. Each column lists the text height you must enter at the command prompt to a corresponding scale. To find the appropriate text height, place one finger on the Final Plot Scale and place another finger on the Actual Plotted Text Height. Move both fingers until they intersect. This is the corresponding text height you must enter at the command prompt. For example, the text height you must enter for a text with an actual plotted text height of 1/2″ having a final plotted scale of 1/2″=1′-0″ is 1′ or 12″.

Tips: When cross-referencing a set of architectural drawings, it is best to create the symbols (i.e. circles for drawing titles, section marks, break marks, elevation marks, and detail marks) as Blocks at 1″=1″ and insert them in Paper Space at full scale. You can also create the symbols directly in Paper Space in Layouts at full scale without worrying about scale conversions. Blocks are discussed in Chapter 19 and Paper Space and Layouts are discussed in Chapter 22.

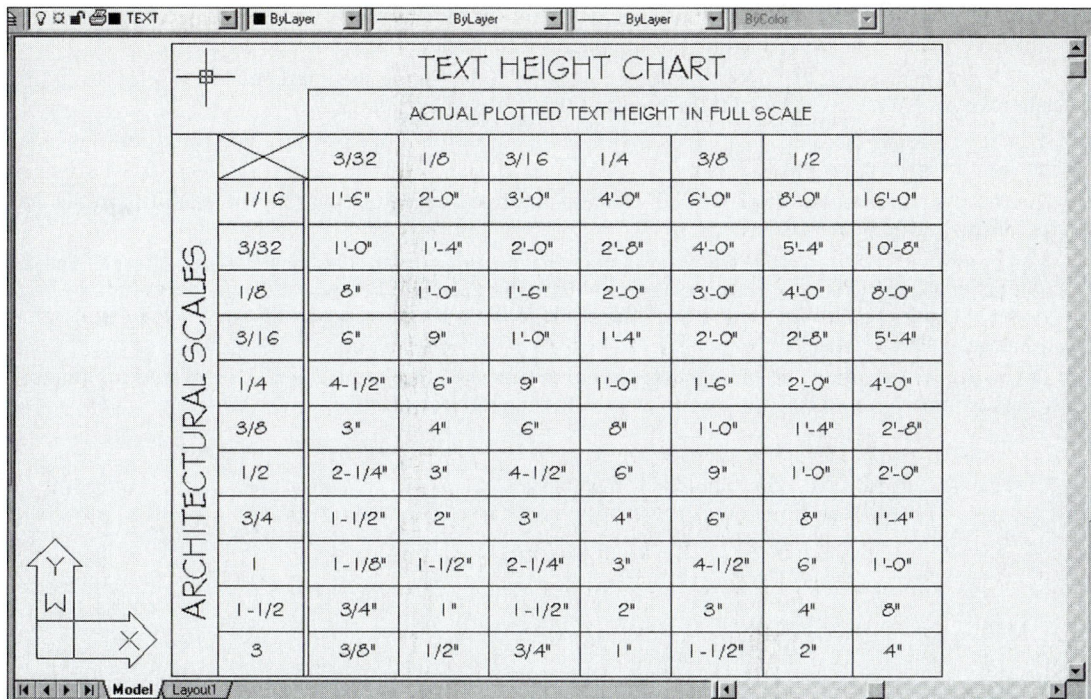

FIGURE 2–8 The Text Height Chart is used to select the appropriate text height for different scales.

REVIEW QUESTIONS

1. What are some of the elements that affect drawing format?
2. Which of the drawing elements are entered in AutoCAD?
3. Which of the drawing elements are established outside AutoCAD?
4. What drawing element must be calculated to establish a new upper-right corner coordinate for the drawing?
5. What are the steps involved in calculating a scale factor for the drawing?
6. What are the default AutoCAD drawing limits?
7. How does drawing object geometry differ from dimensioning object geometry?
8. Using the Fractional Length Type as the drawing units, can you enter a length as 2′8-5/8 to draw a line that is 32.625″ long?
9. What does a Length Precision of 0′-1/32″ mean when using Architectural Length Type?
10. Calculate the scale factor for a drawing having a scale of 1 1/2″=1′-0″.
11. Calculate the upper-right-corner limits for a drawing having a scale of 3/32″=1′-0″ and to be plotted on a C-size sheet.
12. Calculate the size of a circle in diameter to be plotted at 2 1/2″ using a scale of 1″=1′-0″.

PROBLEMS

1. Using the Drawing Units dialog box, establish a drawing with the following settings:

   Use Architectural Units with a Precision of 0′-0″. Assume a final plot scale of 1/4″=1′-0″. Assume that you will plot this drawing on a D-size sheet (36″ × 24″) oriented horizontally. All angles will be measured clockwise with base angle (0°) at North. Do not save this drawing. What did you enter for Drawing Limits?

2. Calculate the Drawing Limits for a drawing with a final plot scale of 3/8″=1′-0″ to be plotted on a C-size sheet oriented vertically. Show all calculations.

3. Calculate the Drawing Limits for a drawing with a final plot scale of 1/8″=1′-0″ to be plotted on a B-size sheet oriented horizontally. Show all calculations.

4. Calculate the text height that must be entered at the command prompt for notes requiring an actual plotted text height of 3/16″ for a drawing with a final plot scale of 1/4″=1′-0″.

5. A floor plan measures 60′ × 80′ at a scale of 1/4″=1′-0″. What blank sheet size must you select to fit this floor plan so that it covers most of the paper at that scale when plotted?

6. A site plan measures 240′ × 460′ at a scale of 1″=30′. What blank sheet size must you select to fit this site plan so that it covers most of the paper at that scale when plotted?

7. You have a paper measuring 24″ × 18″. What is the maximum floor plan size you can fit onto this paper using a scale of 3/8″=1′-0″?

8. You have a paper measuring 30″ × 30″. What is the maximum site plan size you can fit onto this paper using a scale of 1″=10′?

9. You are about to draw a circle for a detail mark inside a floor plan that has a 3/4″=1′-0″ scale. The diameter of the circle is required to measure 1 3/4″ when plotted. You access the circle command, and AutoCAD asks you for the diameter of the circle. What is the corresponding architectural unit value you must enter?

10. Discuss the implications of adding a metric column next to the Limits chart. How would millimeters (mm) be incorporated into the metric scale with metric sheet sizes?

CHAPTER 3
Establishing Drawing Setup

After successful completion of this chapter you should be able to:

▲ Understand Drawing Setup.

▲ Start a new drawing from scratch.

▲ Use a wizard to start a new drawing.

▲ Understand the difference between Quick Setup and Advanced Setup.

▲ Use a template to start a new drawing.

▲ Understand the role of using drawing templates.

▲ Understand AutoCAD default drawing settings.

▲ Open an existing drawing.

▲ Use appropriate setup procedures for different phases of the project.

▲ Change the drawing scale and/or sheet size using the LIMITS command.

▲ Partial Open and Partial Load drawings.

3.1 UNDERSTANDING DRAWING SETUP

After learning how to establish drawing Units and Precision and calculating the Scale Factor and Limits for a new drawing, you are now ready to set up a new drawing based on the required settings. All drawing elements established prior to drawing setup must be applied to your new drawing so that the drawing you are about to create incorporates the proper drawing units, precision, scale, scale factor, limits, and sheet size. In other words, you are ready to start a project based on the six drawing elements you have established in Chapter 2. If the drawing elements are incorrect or if they are incorrectly entered during drawing setup, the final drawing will not be plotted to scale. A project that is not plotted to scale is not precise and is not accurate because it does not represent drawing geometry at the intended scale. You can start a project without establishing or calculating the drawing elements mentioned in Chapter 2, but this will not allow you to create architectural drawings based on a specific architectural scale and sheet size. In order to create and plot architectural drawings based on a scale and plotted sheet size, you must first establish drawing settings and then apply them to AutoCAD using different startup methods.

3.2 STARTING A NEW DRAWING

You can create drawings to be plotted at any scale on any sheet size based on the required drawing elements. However, the appropriate sheet sizes must be configured into the plot settings while the printer or the plotter is configured. Plotting is discussed in Chapter 23. When you first start AutoCAD, the Startup dialog box will be displayed as shown in Figure 3–1. This dialog box will allow you to open an existing drawing or start a new drawing based on your drawing elements using three different startup methods. There are four buttons inside the Startup dialog box: Open a Drawing, Start from Scratch, Use a Template, and Use a Wizard. When the Startup dialog box is displayed, the startup option last used will be shown as the current selection option. The startup options are as follows:

- **OPEN A DRAWING:**   (button). This is the first button in the Startup dialog box. Selecting this button will display the name and location of the last four drawings opened during the previous AutoCAD drawing session. This information is displayed as part of the Startup dialog box. Figure 3–2 shows the listing of the last four previous drawings accessed during a previous drawing session. The names of the four drawings are listed under the File column inside the Select a File: list box. The location of each drawing is listed under the Path column. If you cannot read the complete location listing, simply move your cursor over the drawing path listing and a complete name for the drawing location will be shown. You can adjust the width of the File and Path columns to make each column shorter or longer. To adjust the width of these columns, move your cursor over the separator, left click, and drag the mouse either left or right. You can also adjust the size of the dialog box. The scroll bars on the bottom of the Select a File: list box will allow you to scroll left or right of the File and Path information. Each time a file name is selected, the size of the file and the date the drawing was last modified will be displayed under the Select a File: list box. This information is useful when you want to know the file size or the date that the drawing was last mod-

FIGURE 3–1   The Startup dialog box is the first dialog box AutoCAD will display when it is first launched. It is used to open an existing drawing or start a new drawing based on your drawing elements using three different methods.

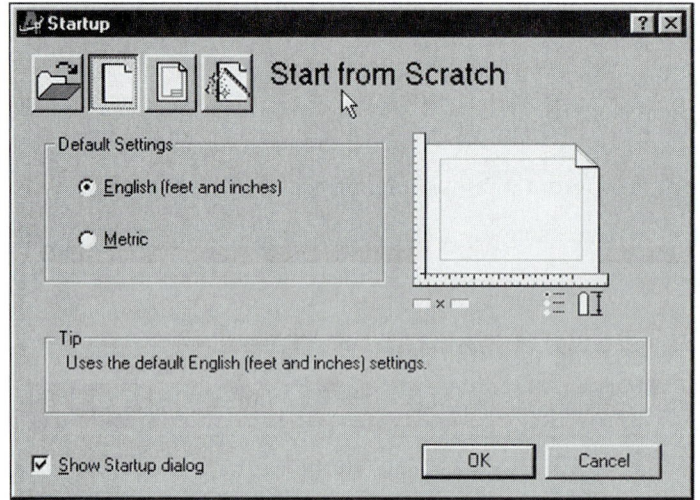

FIGURE 3–2   When you select the Open a Drawing button, the Startup dialog box will display information about the last four drawings accessed during the previous AutoCAD drawing session.

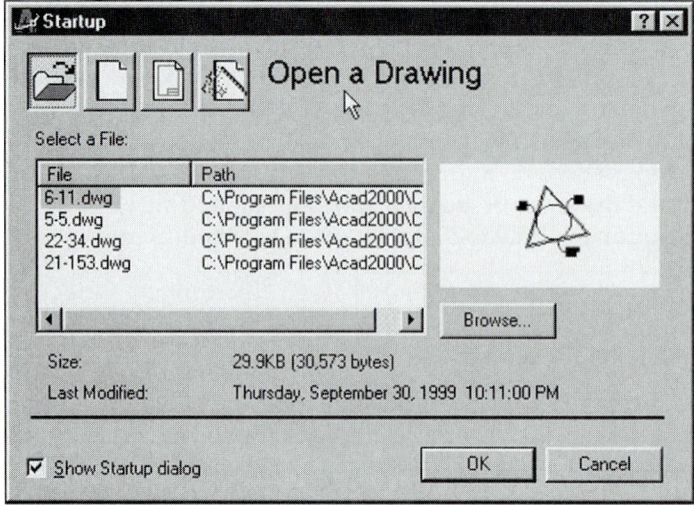

ified. To open an existing file, select the file and click on the OK button. The selected drawing will open. The image window to the right of the Select a File: list box will display a small image of the selected file. This is very helpful when you can't remember the content of the drawing file but can recognize if you saw an image of it.

Tips: You can open multiple drawing files in a single AutoCAD session using the Select File dialog box. This is discussed under the Multiple Design Environment in Chapter 10.

- **BROWSE...:** (button). This button will allow you to select a file not listed in the Select a File: list box. When you click on the Browse... button, the Select File dialog box will be displayed as shown in Figure 3–3. This dialog box will allow you to select, view, and open any drawing file in your computer.

- **SHOW STARTUP DIALOG:** (check box). This check box is on by default. If the check mark is removed, the Startup dialog box will not be displayed when AutoCAD is first started. If this is the case, you can have the Startup dialog box displayed as follows:

1. Right click on the drawing area. A shortcut menu will be displayed.
2. From the shortcut menu, select Options... The Options dialog box will be displayed.
3. Inside the Options dialog box, select the System tab.
4. Inside the System tab and under the General Options category, place a check mark in the Show Startup dialog check box. This dialog box will be discussed later in the textbook.

There are three different methods you can use to start a new drawing. The three buttons next to the Open a Drawing button involve using these three options as follows:

- **START FROM SCRATCH:** (button). This is the second button in the Startup dialog box. Selecting this option will allow you to start a drawing from scratch. This method allows you to establish drawing *units* (length type and length precision), *angle type, angle precision, and angle direction* using the Drawing Units dialog box as explained in Chapter 2. If your drawing involves using a scale other than 1″ = 1″, the Start from Scratch button can be used to define the drawing settings starting from scratch. Don't forget to Zoom to the limits of your drawing after setting new drawing limits. If your drawing involves using a scale of 1″ = 1″ (scale factor of 1) and if you plan to print this project on A-size paper, the Start from Scratch button can be used as the default drawing. If this is the case, you do not have to establish any drawing settings. As the default settings, AutoCAD gives you a 12″ × 9″ size paper and a drawing scale of 1″ = 1″. But more explicitly, AutoCAD gives you the following drawing settings for the default drawing:

1. Drawing Units Length Type: *Decimal.*
2. Length Precision: *0.0000.*
3. Angle Type: *Decimal Degrees.*
4. Angle Precision: *0.*

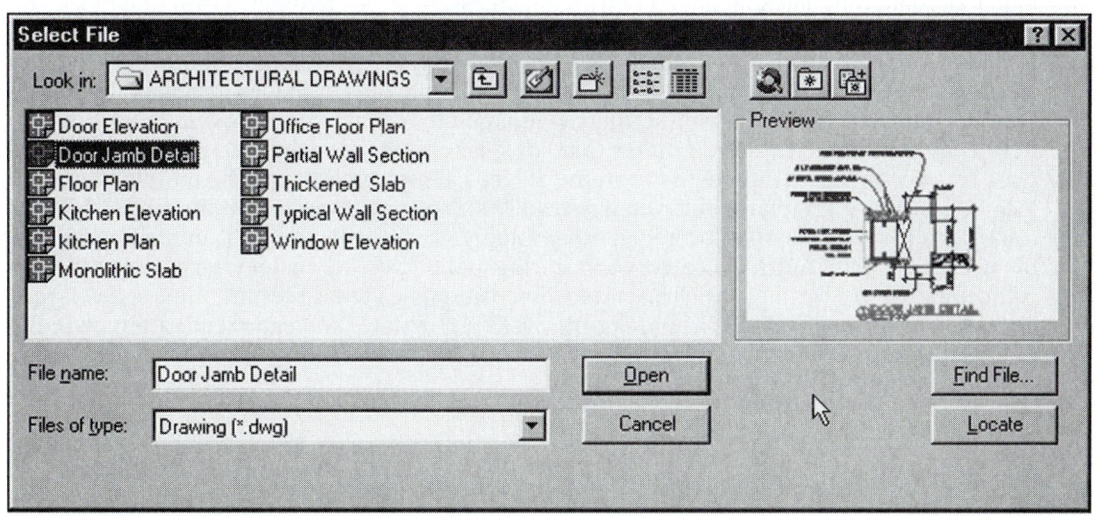

FIGURE 3–3 The Select File dialog box will allow you to select, view, and open any drawing file in your computer as well as search and access the Internet.

5. Base Angle Direction: *Counterclockwise.*

6. Direction for the 0 Base Angle: *East.*

7. Drawing Units for DesignCenter blocks: *Inches.*

8. Drawing Scale: 1″ = 1″ (*this is known from the Limits of the drawing*).

9. Drawing Limits: *Upper-right corner: 12.0000, 9.0000.*

10. Printed Paper Size: *12″ × 9″ (horizontal format).*

3.2.1 Default Settings

This category in the Start from Scratch option will allow you to select either English (feet and inches) or Metric (millimeters) units when drawing. For example, if you draw a line that is five units long using the English default settings, the line will actually measure 5 inches when plotted. On the other hand, if you draw a line that is five units long using the Metric default settings, the line will actually measure 5 mm when plotted. If you select Metric for default settings, the new drawing will be setup appropriately for objects created in millimeters. Metric drawings are similar to drawings created from the Acadiso.dwt template file. The acronym ISO stands for International Standardization Organization that promotes the use of metric system. English drawings are appropriate for objects created in inches and feet and inches and are similar to drawings created from the Acad.dwt template file.

The MEASUREINIT system variable has a default setting of 0 that is set to English. You can change the default setting to Metric by entering 1 after typing MEASUREINIT at the command line. This system variable is saved in the registry and will set the default for default settings until you change it. The MEASUREMENT system variable on the other hand is saved in the new drawing file and is used to set drawing units as English or Metric for the current drawing only. More specifically, the MEASUREMENT system variable controls which hatch pattern and linetype files the existing drawing uses when it is open. When it is set to 0, AutoCAD uses the hatch pattern file and linetype file designated by the ANSI (American National Standards Institute) Hatch and Linetype settings. When it is set to 1, AutoCAD uses the hatch pattern file and linetype file designated by the ISO Hatch and Linetype settings.

Note: The MEASUREMENT setting of a drawing always overrides the MEA-SUREINIT setting.

- **USE A TEMPLATE:** (button). This is the third button in the Startup dialog box. Templates are .dwt files with pre-established drawing settings. You can use a template to create a new drawing based on your own drawing requirements. Once the drawing settings are created, the template drawing can be used as many times as needed. In addition to having specific drawing settings, a template file usually contains standard drawing borders, title block, revision block, firm logo, and drawing information. Most of the templates supplied with AutoCAD are created for a specific sheet size. Some templates may contain a drawing list and a legend. AutoCAD provides many standard templates, including two architectural 24″ × 36″ templates with title block and border. The first template uses Color Dependent Plot Styles and the second one uses Named Plot Styles. Plot Styles are discussed in Chapter 25. Figure 3–4 shows some of the template files listed in the Select a Template: list box. The first two templates in the list are blank templates based on feet and inches drawing settings. Template files are similar to drawing files, but they have a *.dwt* file name extension rather than *.dwg* extension. You can see a preview of a template by selecting the template file from the Select a Template: list box. The template files are located inside the Template folder under Acad2000. You can also click on the Browse... button to look for template files located in other folders in your computer. The architectural templates supplied with AutoCAD are a good starting point to create custom templates with project specific drawing settings. You can create dimension styles, text styles, multiline styles, layers, and add blocks and linetypes as part of the custom template. You can create a template file (*.dwt*) from a drawing (*.dwg*) file that has the proper drawing settings as follows:

1. Click on the Open button in the Standard Toolbar.

2. Inside the Select File dialog box, select the file you want to use as a template and click on the Open button.

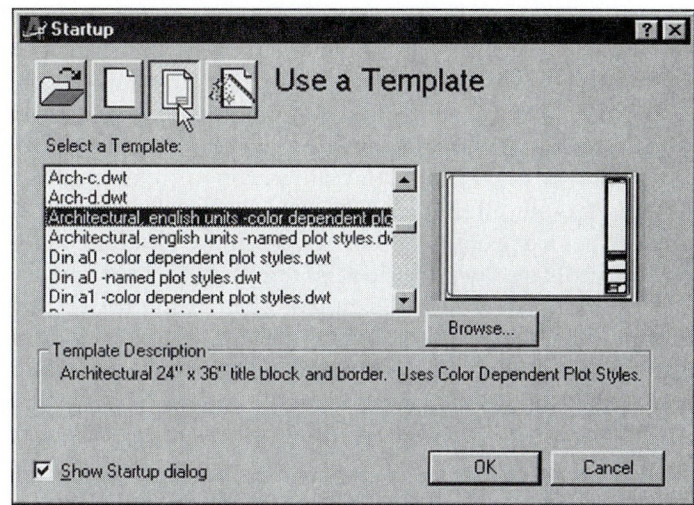

FIGURE 3–4 The Template option in the Startup dialog box will allow you to select a template to start a new drawing.

3. If necessary, modify settings or add additional settings to the drawing.

4. From the File pull-down menu select Save As.... The Save Drawing As dialog box will be displayed.

5. Inside the dialog box under Save as type: list box, select AutoCAD Drawing Template File [*.dwt].

6. Inside the File Name: text box, enter a name for the template and click on the Save button. The Template Description dialog box will be displayed.

7. Inside the Template Description dialog box, enter a brief description of the template and click on the OK button.

The new template will be saved in the template folder. Next time you select this file as the template from the Startup dialog box, the template description will be displayed. You can also create a custom template file (*.dwt*) from an existing or default template file (*.dwt*) using a similar procedure described above.

Note: Template files listed in the Select a Template: list box are created primarily to plot from a Layout tab using Paper Space environment. Layouts usually include templates with title block and borderlines created in Paper Space. Refer to Chapter 22 for a discussion on Layouts and Paper Space.

Tips: When using templates, make sure you select a template that uses the plot style behavior you plan to use. You can use named plot styles *or* color dependent plot styles *but you cannot change it after you create the drawing. See Chapter 23 for a discussion on plot styles.*

Note: When you click on the New button in the Standard toolbar, the Startup dialog box will be displayed. The Open a Drawing option is not available when you access this dialog box in this fashion. You can still start a new drawing from scratch, use a template, or use a wizard.

AutoCAD 2000i Update: *When creating a template file (.dwt) from a drawing (.dwg) file or from an existing template file select the AutoCAD Drawing Template File [*.dwt] from the Files of type: drop-down list and enter a template file name in the File name: list box and then click on the Save button. Follow steps number 6 and 7 above.*

3.2.2 A Brief Introduction to Paper Space and Layouts

When you select the Architectural, English Units-Color Dependent Plot Styles.dwt template from the Select a Template: list box and click on the OK button, AutoCAD will display the template in the Layout with the name "Architectural Title Block" located next to the Model tab. This template with borderlines and title block will appear in Paper Space in the appropriate Layout tab as shown in Figure 3–5. A Layout is a drawing environment that allows you to create and compose the final composition of your project. The Paper Space area in a Layout makes this composition possible by allowing you to create one or more viewports. *Viewports* in a layout are views of the drawing model that show your drawing at the appropriate drawing scale when you plot layouts at a 1:1 plot scale. Multiple drawings at the same or different scales are possible while composing each drawing in a separate viewport using the Paper Space area of the Layout. The Model tab in the Status Bar allows you to create a drawing based on one scale and one sheet size. The Layout tab in the Status Bar allows you to create one or multiple drawings with different scales using one sheet size. Paper Space and Layouts are discussed in Chapter 24. It is possible to create a drawing inside the template by switching to Model Space. The Units and Precision are already set for this template, but you must set the Limits and perform Zoom All to reformat the Model Space drawing area so that you can begin drawing using architectural units at the required scale. The template and the Model Space area are shown in Figure 3–6. Paper Space Layout is also used to externally reference drawing files for multiple drawing composition. Externally referenced drawings (xrefs) are explained in Chapter 24.

> *Note: Templates are created so that specific drawing aids, settings, drawing conventions, and standards can be incorporated into the drawing that remain constant between each project and each member of the project team. These include units, limits, precision, snap*

FIGURE 3–5 The Architectural Title Block Template is displayed in the Paper Space environment inside the Layout. The Layout 1 is actually renamed Architectural Title Block.

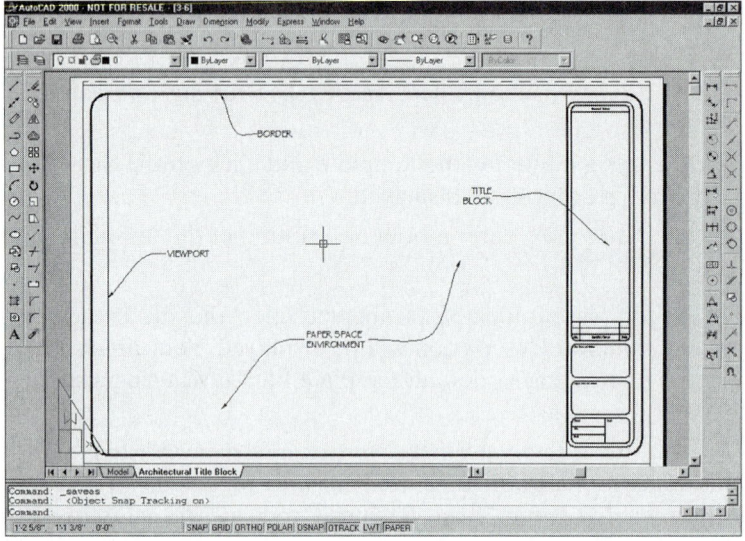

FIGURE 3–6 The same Template in Figure 3–5 showing the Model Space drawing area.

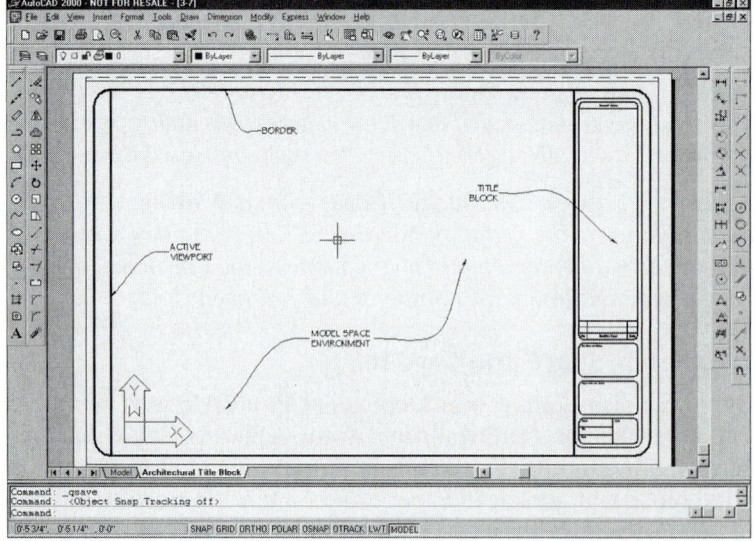

and grid settings, blocks, dimension styles, cross referencing, drawing marks, labeling symbols, text styles, layers, layouts, and linetypes. Customizing drawing settings for different projects is an effective method to create AutoCAD project standards. Drawing Template files provide a method of saving these settings. New drawings can then be created using a specific template drawing file. Every designer/drafter should know and use drawing templates.

Note: Although there no universally accepted drawing conventions and symbols in the AEC industry, the American Institute of Architects recently published CAD Layer Guidelines *as part of* National CAD Standards. *The purpose of the National CAD Standards is voluntary adoption of the CAD Standards by the building and construction industry in order to streamline and simplify the exchange of CAD documents. See Chapter 9 for CAD Layer Guidelines.*

• **Use a Wizard:** (button). This is the fourth button in the Startup dialog box. Selecting this button will allow you to use a wizard to establish drawing settings. The Advanced Setup or the Quick Setup dialog box will guide you through a step-by-step method. When you click on this button, the two wizard setup options are presented inside the Select a Wizard: list box as shown in Figure 3–7. The Quick Setup will allow you to set the drawing units (length type) and drawing limits for your drawing using a more intuitive GUI dialog box as opposed to using the Drawing Units dialog box or the Command: prompt. The Advanced Setup will allow you to use the same dialog box as in the Quick Setup but with more drawing setting options, such as precision, angle measure, angle direction, and limits.

3.2.3 Quick Setup (Wizard option)

The Quick Setup Wizard option will allow you to quickly start a drawing by establish drawing units and area only. The *Area* is the same as *Limits*. When you select this option, a brief description is displayed inside the Wizard Description text area. To proceed, click on the OK button. The Quick Setup contains two pages under the Quick Setup dialog box. The first page allows you to select the unit of measurement as shown in Figure 3–8. The Units page shown with a small triangle marker indicates the active page. You can change the unit of measurement setting by selecting the appropriate radio button. An example of the selected unit of measurement is displayed in the preview image on the right. When you click on the Next> button, the second page will be displayed as shown in Figure 3–9. The second page of the Quick Setup will allow you to enter the Limits for the new drawing. This is called the Area page. The area you want to represent is actually the Limits (coordinates of the upper-right corner) of the sheet you select to plot the drawing. The Width: and the Length: boxes represent the X and Y coordinates of the upper-right corner. For example, if the final plot scale of your drawing is 1/4″ = 1′-0″ plotted on

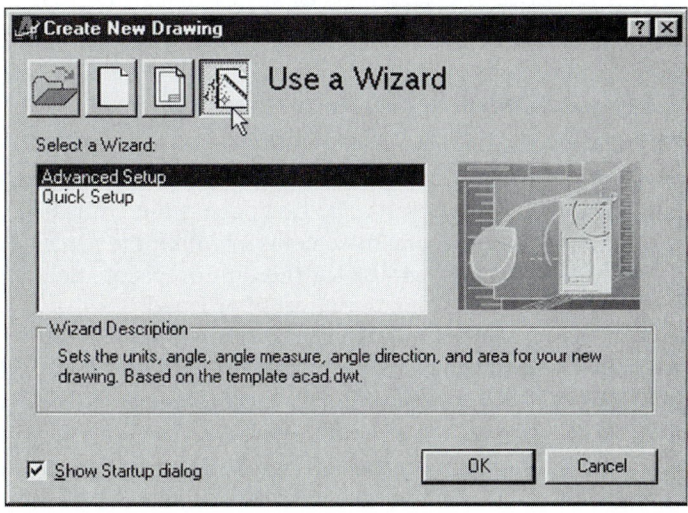

FIGURE 3–7 The Use a Wizard option in the Startup dialog box will allow you to use two different wizards to establish drawing settings.

FIGURE 3–8 The first page of the Quick Setup dialog box is the Units page. It will allow you to set drawing units similar to the Length Type in Drawing Units dialog box.

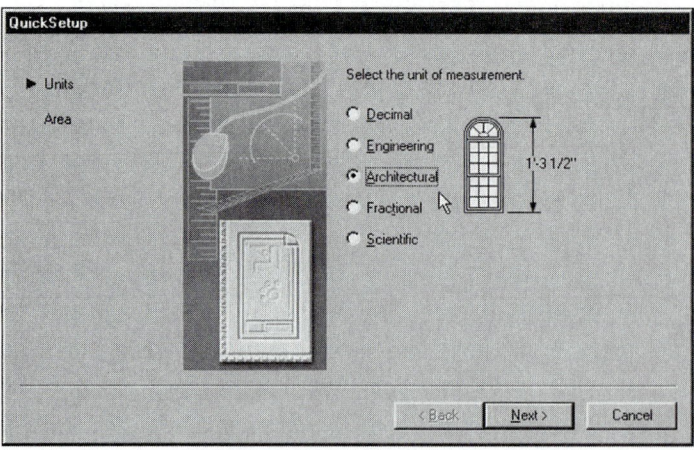

FIGURE 3–9 The second page of the Quick setup dialog box is the Area page. It will allow you to set the Limits of your project based on the scale factor and sheet size.

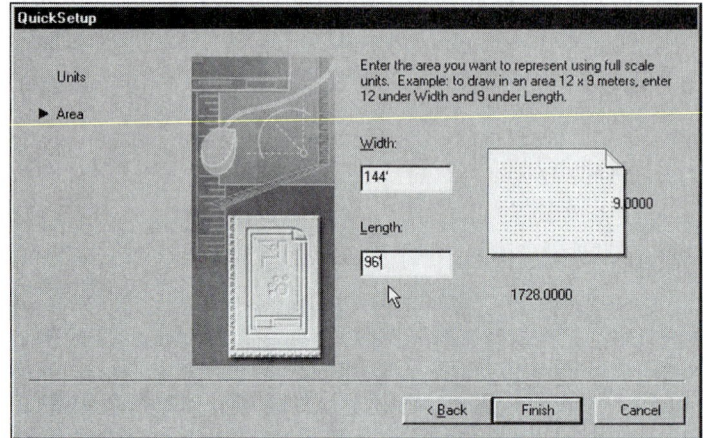

a D-size sheet (36″ × 24″) oriented horizontally, enter 144′ for the width and 96′ for the length. The preview area will show the image of a paper with a width of 1728.0000 and a length of 1152.0000. These numbers represent the Limits of the drawing in *inches unit*. The scale factor for 1/4″ = 1′-0″ scale drawing is 48. The scale factor multiplied by the width and length of the sheet size is 48 × 36″ = 1728″ and 48 × 24″ = 1152″, respectively, and will correspond to 144′ and 96′ if converted to feet. You can click on the <Back button to go back to the previous page to change a setting. When you are done click on the Finish button. **As a final step you must zoom to the limits of your drawing.** If you do not zoom to the limits of your drawing, you will not be able to see the entire drawing fit inside your paper. The Cancel button will cancel the Quick Setup and bring you to the drawing area. This will start a drawing from scratch with default settings.

3.2.4 Advanced Setup (Wizard option)

The advanced setup is similar to the quick setup but provides additional drawing settings such as precision, angle measure, and angle direction. The Advanced Setup dialog box has five pages and is shown in Figure 3–10. The first page is the Units page and contains the five radio buttons for the unit of measurement selection. Unlike the Quick Setup, the Advanced Setup contains the Precision: drop-down list for the unit precision. Select the required unit and the precision and then click on the Next> button to proceed.

The second page of the Advanced Setup dialog box is the Angle page. It contains the five radio buttons for the angle of measurement similar to the Angle Type: drop-down list in the Drawing Units dialog box. You can also set the precision for angles using the Precision: drop-down list. The Angle page is shown in Figure 3–11. The preview image area shows a 90 degree angle with corresponding precision settings. Select the required angle of measurement and the precision and then click on the Next> button to proceed.

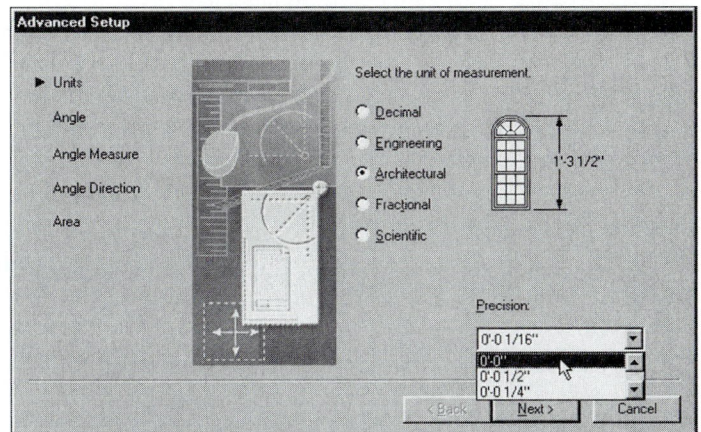

FIGURE 3–10 The first page of the Advanced Setup dialog box is similar to the Quick Setup but adds the Precision: drop-down list.

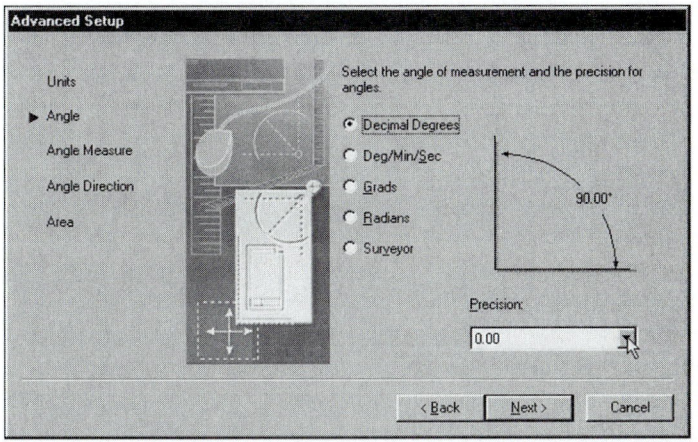

FIGURE 3–11 The second page of the Advanced Setup allows you to set angle of measurement and the precision for angles.

The third page of the Advanced Setup dialog box is the Angle Measure page. It contains the five radio buttons for the direction of angle measurement and is similar to the Direction Control dialog box displayed when selecting the Direction. . . button in the Drawing Units dialog box. The base angle of 0 degrees is set to East as a default direction for angle measurement. Selecting the North radio button will set the base angle of 0 degrees to North. The preview image area shows the orientation of the compass direction where a zero will be displayed at the selected direction. You can enter any angle in the box provided after selecting the Other radio button. The Angle Measure page is shown in Figure 3–12. Select the required direction for angle measurement and click on the Next> button to proceed.

The fourth page of the Advanced Setup dialog box is the Angle Direction page. It contains the two selections for the orientation for angle measurement. The default angle direction is Counter-Clockwise. When the Clockwise radio button is selected, angles are drawn clockwise from East at zero degrees. The Angle Direction page is shown in Figure 3–13. The preview image area shows the direction of angle measurement. Figure 3–14 shows two lines as line A and line B. Line A is drawn at 45 degrees when the angle direction is counterclockwise, and line B is drawn at 45 degrees when the angle direction is clockwise. For both lines the direction for angle measurement is set to East. You can also draw line B when the angle direction is counterclockwise by entering a minus (−) symbol in front of the 45 degrees. Select the required orientation for angle measurement and click on the Next> button to proceed.

Note: The direction and orientation for angle measurement makes more sense when drawing lines using the LINE command. See Chapter 5 for drawing lines using coordinate systems and angle measurement.

The fifth page of the Advanced Setup dialog box is the Area page and is similar to the Area page of the Quick Setup dialog box. Enter the drawing Limits in the Width and Length boxes.

FIGURE 3–12 The third page of the Advanced Setup allows you to set the angle zero direction.

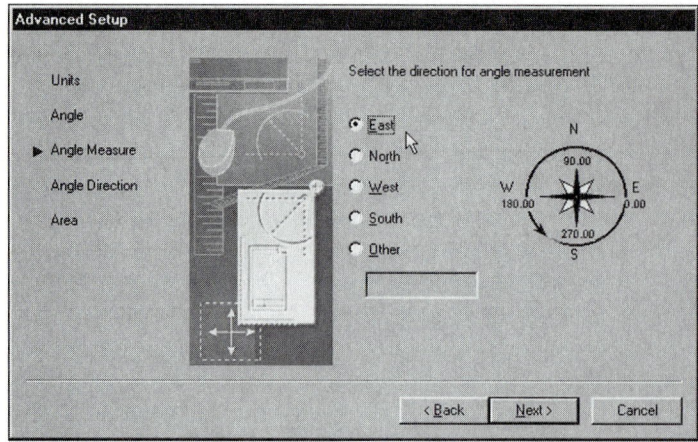

FIGURE 3–13 The fourth page of the Advanced Setup allows you to set the orientation for angle measurement.

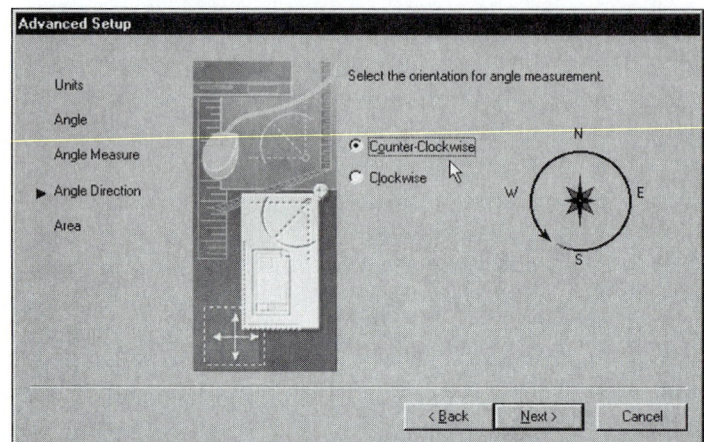

FIGURE 3–14 Line A drawn as 45 degrees counterclockwise and line B drawn as 45 degrees clockwise.

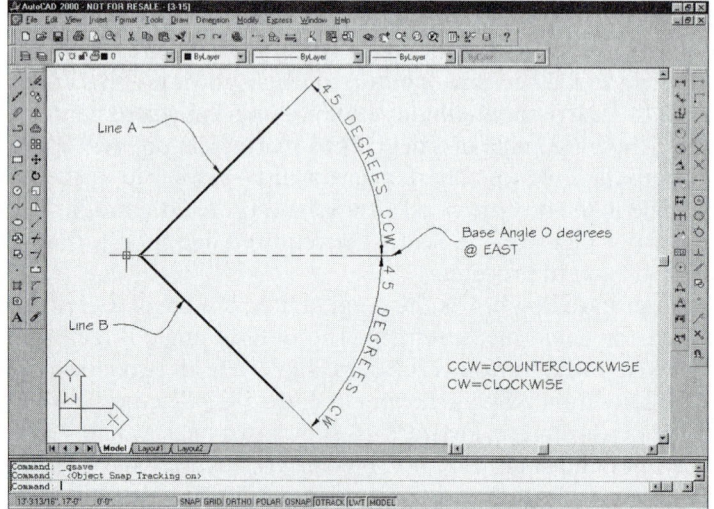

To review individual settings, click on the <Back button to go back to the previous pages. When finished, click on the Finish button to complete the Advanced Setup option of the Wizard.

Tips: Select the best startup method that meets your drawing requirements. When using a Wizard, drawing settings are entered in the dialog boxes provided. When using a template, drawing settings are automatically set. Create a template containing borderline, title block, revision block, and firm logo/graphics or any other information related to the project from default AutoCAD templates. The

Quick and Advanced Setup of the Wizard are based on the template acad.dwt. Using a custom template will help you maintain consistent project standards for all your design and drafting work. Use the template in Layout to either create a drawing(s) with a single scale or create multiple drawings with different scales. Use the Paper Space environment of the Layout to create individual viewports for each drawing. See Chapter 24 for Layouts and Paper Space.

Caution: When using the Wizards, do not press the ~EnterKey~ after you entered the length value in the Area page. Enter the appropriate Limits for the width and length and then click on the Finish button. Otherwise the grid X and Y spacing will not be displayed properly on the screen.

3.3 STARTUP RECOMMENDATIONS

You can set up a drawing to plot from Model tab or you can set up a drawing to plot from a Layout tab. The Start from Scratch and the Wizards setup options allow you to start a drawing to plot from Model tab. The Use a Template option allows you to plot from a Layout tab. Layouts are becoming a standard approach to drawing setup because a drawing is created inside a template that includes a title block and a borderline. In Layouts, you can control drawing scale by setting the appropriate scale in each *layout viewport* (in model space) using the Viewports toolbar. This is explained in detail in Chapters 22 and 23. The following is a list of recommendations as to which startup option to use during the many phases of the project:

- **CONCEPTUAL DESIGN (SKETCH/SCHEMATIC) PHASE:** If you are not sure about the final format and the outcome of the drawings, use the Start from Scratch option. Use the default settings that require no scale and don't be too concerned with setting units, precision, angle measurement, or limits at this point because all object geometry can be sketched first and formatted to your settings (scaled) later.

- **DESIGN DEVELOPMENT (POST-DESIGN/PRELIMINARY DRAWINGS) PHASE:** At this point you should have some ideas about the final format of the drawings. Use Wizards to set up some preliminary drawing settings. Establish Units and Limits. But your Limits do not need to conform to any standard sheet size, only to drawing size. Change Limits at any time when more or less space is required or when changing the final plot scale.

- **CONSTRUCTION DOCUMENTS (WORKING DRAWINGS/PRODUCTION) PHASE:** At this point the drawings are finalized, ready to be plotted. Use Model tab or use custom templates to start the drawings or externally reference (xref) drawings into viewports in Paper Space Layouts. Adjust drawing settings as needed. Custom templates may contain dimension styles, text styles, multiline styles, linetypes, lineweights, xrefs, layers, layouts, and blocks.

Tips: Although you can start a drawing before you know the final drawing scale, you should always establish a target drawing scale early in the drawing process to avoid any extra work later on.

3.4 USING LIMITS TO CHANGE DRAWING SCALE AND PAPER SIZE

When you start a drawing you should follow a certain set of rules and establish settings in a specific order of progression so that you may see the paper size on your screen. Before you start a new drawing, you should perform the following tasks in the given order:

1. Inside the Startup dialog box, decide which option to use to start a drawing.
2. Set drawing units either through the Wizards or using the Drawing Units dialog box.
3. Enter drawing limits at the command line or through the Wizards.
4. Zoom to the limits of your drawing.
5. Establish any other settings that will help you with your drawing, such as grid and snap. See Chapter 4 for establishing grid and snap settings.

To change the sheet size of the drawing during the drawing session will require you to re-establish the Limits based on the new drawing settings. For example, suppose the floor plan you created using a scale of 1/8″ = 1′-0″ to be plotted on a C-size sheet (24″ × 18″) has current Limits of 192′, 144′. You can enter the new Limits of 144′, 96′ using the LIMITS command to change the scale to 1/4″ = 1′-0″ using a D-size sheet as follows:

```
Command: LIMITS ~EnterKey~
Reset Model Space Limits:
Specify lower-left corner or [ON/OFF] <0′-0″, 0′-0>.: ~EnterKey~
Specify upper-right corner <192′-0″, 144′-0″>: 144′, 96′ ~EnterKey~
Command: ZOOM ~EnterKey~
Specify corner of window, enter a scale factor (nX or nXP), or
[All/Center/Dynamic/Extents/Previous/Scale/Window] <real time>: ALL
~EnterKey~
```

AutoCAD will automatically change the sheet size from 24″ × 18″ to 36″ × 24″ (from 192′ × 144′ to 144′ × 96′), and your drawing will be displayed twice as large and the drawing area will appear smaller. Technically speaking, the floor plan is still the same size, but it appears larger because the drawing size decreased according to corresponding limit values. It might be necessary to move the floor plan inside the new drawing area because changing Limits during the drawing process will change the size of the paper, and the floor plan may not cover the original area. At this point you may draw at a new scale of 1/4″ = 1′-0″ on a larger sheet even though the drawing area seems smaller. You may also plot this drawing at a final plot scale of 1/4″ = 1′-0″ or at any scale you wish (conforming to paper size). In other words, if the floor plan objects are drawn using the new Limits, they will have less drawing area but can be plotted at 1/4″ = 1′-0″ scale on a D-size sheet. It is important to remember that the unit length of the objects does not change with the change of Limits, only the size of objects displayed on a different size sheet. When this floor plan drawing is plotted with the new Limits it can be measured using a scale of 1/4″ = 1′-0″. If the drawing contains text, dimension text, linetypes, and hatching the new Limits will not automatically adjust the height and scale of these items to correspond to the new scale. You have to recalculate the proper text height, linetype, and hatch scale by multiplying the new scale factor by the text height. Once you figure out the new text height, linetype, and hatch scale, use the Properties window to assign new values for text, linetype, and hatching. The Properties Window is discussed in Chapter 14.

You can use the Limits command to also prevent drawing outside the drawing area. When you turn the Limits ON, AutoCAD will not allow you to draw outside the boundaries of your drawing limits. When you turn the Limits OFF, you can draw outside the boundaries of your drawing limits. You can turn the Limits on as follows:

```
Command: LIMITS ~EnterKey~
Reset Model Space Limits:
Specify lower-left corner or [ON/OFF] <0′-0″, 0′-0″>: ON
```

Now, when you draw outside the drawing limits AutoCAD will display **Outside Limits message at the Command: line. See Chapter 5 for drawing lines.

Tips: To quickly change the Limits of your drawing, use the LIMMIN and LIMMAX system variables. The LIMMIN system variable allows you to quickly change the lower-left coordinates of the current Limits. The LIMMAX system variable allows you to quickly change the upper-right coordinates of the current Limits.

  Note: Drawing scale affects many parameters, such as text height, linetype scale, hatch scale, dimension feature sizes, and custom block applications (i.e. plumbing fixtures and section marks inserted as blocks). These parameters need to be re-adjusted after changing the scale of the drawing.

3.5 OPENING A DRAWING

The Open a Drawing button in the Startup dialog box allows you to access the last four drawings, and the Browse button allows you to use the Select File dialog box to search for other existing files in AutoCAD. You can click on a drawing name and click on the OK button to open that drawing. You can also double-click on the drawing you wish to open. When you click on the

Open button in the Standard Toolbar or enter OPEN at the command line, the Select File dialog box with the Partial Open . . . button will be displayed as shown in Figure 3–15. When creating and working with large drawing files, you can use the Partial Open and Partial Load features of AutoCAD. The Partial Open option allows you to open a specific view and specific layers within those views of the drawing. The Partial Load option allows you to load additional views after the drawing is partially open.

3.5.1 Opening Partial Drawings

For large drawings you can save loading time by opening a part of the drawing. When you select a file from the Select File dialog box, the Partial Open button will be available for selection. When you click on the Partial Open. . . button, the Partial Open dialog box will be displayed as shown in Figure 3–16. This dialog box allows you to specify what geometry to load into the selected drawing.

You can reduce memory requirements by selecting the minimal amount of geometry you need to load when you open a large drawing. The Partial Open dialog box has four major categories as follows:

- **VIEW GEOMETRY TO LOAD:**   (area). This area will display the view to be selected. The *Extents* is the default and the *Last* is the view of the drawing that was saved last. Only the Model Space views are available for loading. Geometry that is created in Paper Space can be loaded by loading the layer on which the paper space geometry is created. When you select

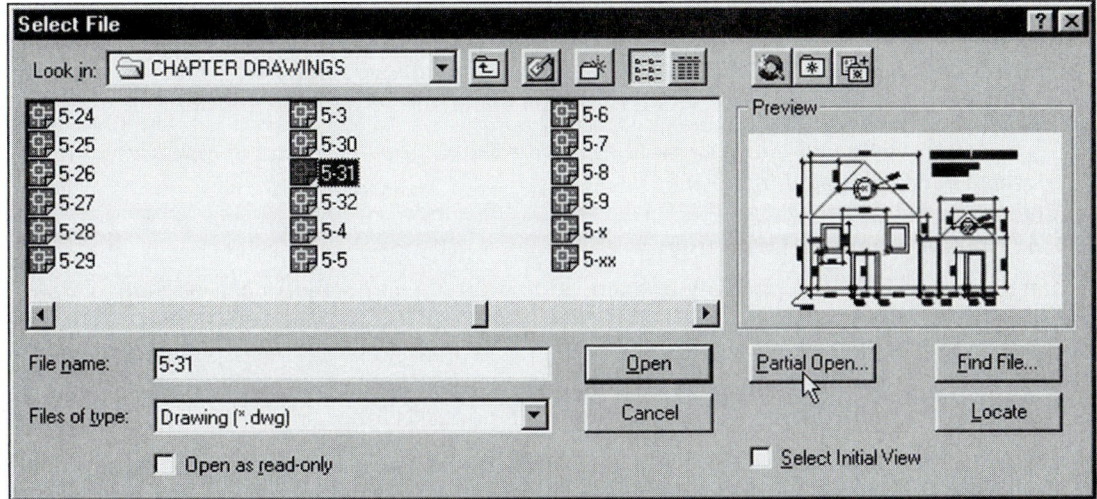

FIGURE 3–15 The Select File dialog box with the Partial Open . . . button.

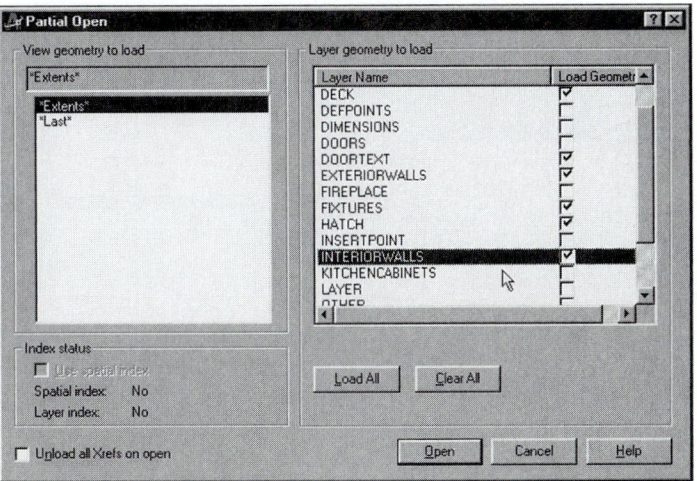

FIGURE 3–16 The Partial Open dialog box will allow you to open only a part of a large drawing file.

a view, the geometry in that view is automatically loaded. When a drawing is partially open, dimension styles, text styles, multiline styles, blocks, linetypes, layers, and layouts are loaded into the file.

- **LAYER GEOMETRY TO LOAD:**   (area). This area will display all the layers available in the selected drawing file. When you select the square next to the layer name, the geometry on those selected layers within the selected view will be loaded. The Layer Name column displays the names of the layers in the selected file. The Load Geometry column loads the geometry from that layer. You can also right-click and use the shortcut menu to load or clear geometry from all layers. The Load All button is used to load geometry from all layers. When the Clear All button is selected, no geometry from any layer is loaded. The title bar will show that a drawing has been partially loaded.

- **INDEX STATUS:**   (area). If the selected drawing file contains a spatial or layer index, this area will show the index status. You can enter the INDEXCTL (index control) system variable at the command line to control whether spatial and layer indexes are saved with the drawing file. A spatial index categorizes object geometry based on their spatial location and minimizes open time. A layer index shows objects that are on each layer. The INDEXCTL values are as follows:

```
0 = no index is created
1 = layer index is created
2 = spatial index is created
3 = layer and spatial index are created
```

- **UNLOAD ALL XREF ON OPEN:**   (check box). If external references are part of the drawing file, placing a check mark here will load all external references when opening the drawing.

When you click on the Open button, AutoCAD will load the geometry from the selected view and layers. You can also use the PARTIALOPEN command to perform above tasks.

Tips: Use the Help pull-down menu to find more information on drawing indexing under the "Using Layer and Spatial Indexes".

3.5.2   Partial Loading Drawings

When a drawing has been partially opened, additional object geometry can be loaded from a view, area, or layers. When you enter PARTIALOAD at the command line or select Partial Load from the File pull-down menu, the Partial Load dialog box will be displayed as shown in Figure 3–17. You cannot unload geometry that is currently loaded in the drawing.

The Partial Load dialog box has three major categories as follows:

- **VIEW GEOMETRY TO LOAD:**   (area). This area will display the selected view and the available views in the drawing. The Pick Window button will allow you to select an area to load and is displayed in the View Geometry To Load List box.

FIGURE 3–17   The Partial Load dialog box allows you to load additional geometry into the partial open drawing.

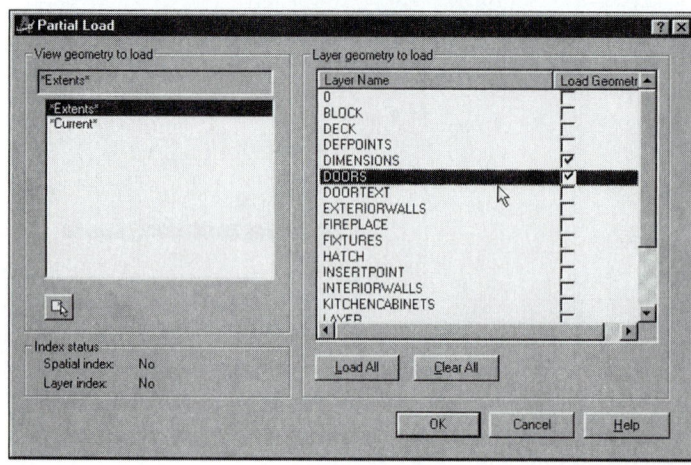

- **LAYER GEOMETRY TO LOAD:** (area). This area will display all the layers available in the selected drawing file. Place a check mark inside the box next to the layer to load.

- **INDEX STATUS:** (area). If the selected drawing file contains a spatial or layer index, this area will show the index status. You can use the INDEXCTL (index control) system variable to control whether spatial and layer indexes are saved with the drawing file.

Note: The Title Bar shows that a drawing has been partially loaded by displaying [Partially loaded] next to the drawing name.

Note: When you save a drawing that has been partially opened, AutoCAD updates the original file. When you reopen the drawing, a warning message gives the option to fully opening the drawing or restoring the last saved partially opened state.

Note: The PARTIALOAD command is only available in drawings that are partially loaded.

Tips: You can save partially opened drawings as DXF files. This will create a new file containing only the geometry that has been loaded into the partially opened drawing.

Caution: You cannot use the PURGE command in a partially opened drawing.

REVIEW QUESTIONS

1. What kind of drawing settings can you change using the Quick Setup dialog box?
2. What is a template file used for?
3. What type of file extension is given to template files?
4. What is the procedure to create a template file from a *.dwg* file?
5. What are the options for setting drawing units in the Units page of the Quick Setup dialog box?
6. What do the Width: and Length: text box areas in the Area page of the Quick Setup dialog box represent?
7. In what way does the direction for angle measurement affect the drawings?
8. What happens when you turn Limits ON?
9. What does AutoCAD refer to as the Drawing Area?
10. How do you partially open a drawing?

PROBLEMS

1. Open *EXE3-1.dwg* file. Zoom to the Limits of this drawing. Using the Format pull-down menu or the LIMMAX system variable, determine the Limits of this drawing. What scale do you think this drawing is drawn at? On what paper size do you think this drawing is meant to print?

2. Using the *EXE3-1.dwg* file and using the LIMITS command, change the final plot scale of this drawing to 1″ = 1′-0″ to be printed on B-size sheet. Zoom to the new Limits of this drawing. Observe what has taken place. What happened to the drawing size? What happened to the drawing sheet indicated by a series of dots? Do not save the changes.

3. Open *EXE3-2.dwg* file. Zoom to the Limits of this drawing. Using the Format pull-down menu or the LIMMAX system variable, determine the Limits of this drawing. What scale do you think this drawing is drawn at? On what paper size do you think this drawing is meant to print?

4. Using the *EXE3-2.dwg* file and using the Format pull-down menu change the final plot scale of this drawing to 1/8″ = 1′-0″ to be plotted on A-size sheet. Zoom to the new Limits of this drawing. Observe what has taken place. What happened to the drawing size? What happened to the drawing sheet indicated by a series of dots? Do not save the changes.

5. Using the Format pull-down menu, set up a new drawing from scratch with the following settings:

   Units: Architectural

   Precision: 0′-0″

   Limits: 34′, 22′

   What is the scale of the drawing that you setup? What is the final plot sheet size?

6. Using the LIMMAX system variable, change the scale of the drawing in Problem 1 to 1 1/2″ = 1-0″ to be printed on C-size sheet. What are the new Limits of the drawing? Do not save the changes.

7. Click on the New button in the Standard toolbar to start a new drawing. In the Startup dialog box click on the Use a Wizard button. Select the Advanced Setup Wizard option and click on the OK button. Using the next five pages of the Advanced Setup dialog box, establish the following setup:

   Units: Decimal

   Angle: Deg/Min/Sec

   Angle Measure: North

   Angle Direction: Clockwise

   Area: 480′, 360′

   What is the final plot scale of this drawing? What is the final plot sheet size? Do not save the drawing.

8. Click on the New button in the Standard toolbar to start a new drawing. In the Startup dialog box, click on the Start from Scratch button and remove the checkmark inside the Show Startup dialog check box. Click on the OK button. Click on the New button again. Notice that the Startup dialog box is not displayed. What must you do to bring this dialog box back?

9. Click on the New button in the Standard toolbar to start a new drawing. In the Startup dialog box, click on the Use a Wizard button. Select the Advanced Setup wizard option and click on the OK button. Using the next five pages of the Advanced Setup dialog box, establish the following setup:

   Units: Architectural

   Angle: Grads

   Angle Measure: West

   Angle Direction: Counterclockwise

   Area: 14′-8″, 22′-8″

   What is the final plot scale of this drawing? What is the final plot sheet size? Is the drawing sheet horizontal or vertical? How will the angles be measured? Do not save this drawing.

10. Click on the new button in the Standard toolbar to start a new drawing. In the Startup dialog box click on the Use a Template button. Select one of the Architectural, English Units templates and click on the OK button. What is displayed on the screen? What does the Architectural Title Block (Layout) mean? What are the Units and Limits for this template? What does the Limits of 2′-11 7/16″, 1′-11 1/2″ mean? Do not save the drawing.

CHAPTER

4

Establishing Drawing Aids

After successful completion of this chapter you should be able to:

▲ Access the Drafting Settings dialog box.

▲ Use the Drafting Settings dialog box to create a grid on the screen.

▲ Use the Drafting Settings dialog box to establish a snap for the grid.

▲ Use the grid and snap to verify the lower-left and the upper-right corners of the drawing limits.

▲ Use the Drafting Settings dialog box to rotate the grid and snap.

▲ Use isometric snap and grid to create isometric setup.

▲ Use the Drafting Settings dialog box to change the base coordinate points of the grid.

▲ Use the Drafting Settings dialog box to change the snap type and style.

▲ Use System Variables at the command line to change grid and snap settings.

▲ Change the size of the crosshairs.

▲ Use the FILEDIA system variable.

▲ Use system variables transparently.

▲ Establish grid and snap at the command line.

4.1 USING DRAWING AIDS

After establishing drawing settings and selecting an option to start a drawing, you are now ready to establish drawing aids. Drawing aids boost productivity by allowing you to control drawing parameters from within a drawing so that you may create accurate drawings. Drawing parameters, drawing settings, and drawing setup can be changed at any time during the drawing process, allowing you the maximum flexibility. The two drawing aids that can assist you are Grid and Snap. AutoCAD provides default grid and snap settings of 0.5000 for the default drawing.

4.2 CREATING A GRID ON THE SCREEN

A grid is a series of dots placed on the drawing that can help you visualize and create predetermined distances for your objects. The grid can help you lay out the composition of a floor plan or a wall section. It can also be used as a reference source for your designs. The dots that define the grid can also define the outside parameters (length and width) of your drawings. In other words, the grid can show the true size of your drawing limits based on the scale and the drawing sheet size you specified. A grid can also be used as a guideline to draw text, dimension references on floor plans, or any other reference. When you create a new drawing and establish the upper-right corner as the limits of your new project, and when you zoom to the limits of your new drawing, it is beneficial to see the sheet size you specified at the scale you established. This is a good way to see the outside edges of your drawing. The grid that you establish on the screen will not plot. When a grid is created, a series of dots are placed at the X and Y directions at the spacing you specify, starting from the lower-left corner to the upper-right corner of the drawing limits. The grid can be created and adjusted using a dialog box or at the command line. The grid can be changed at any time to accommodate different spacing.

Note: Some architectural drawings use a system called Modular Coordination Grid. This system uses a gridwork to create drawings so that a maximal amount of modular building materials can be used. The standard module is a 4″ cube. Ideally, building materials and dimensions are multiples of the basic 4″. A grid size in increments of 4″ can be created for this purpose. For example, you can create a floor plan on a 4′-0″ grid. Nominal sizes of the drawing units will fall directly on the grid lines, and fewer fractional dimensions will be needed. Also, the creation of a grid will allow you to determine many of the wall sizes and spaces quickly by merely counting the grid spaces.

4.3 ESTABLISHING A SNAP FOR THE GRID

After creating the desired grid on the screen, a snap setting can be established to control the accuracy of the points you establish on the screen. Without a snap setting, the cursor movement is dependent on the specific point entry method used to create objects on the screen. To pick points accurately and to allow the cursor to move in exact increments, a snap spacing is established. The snap setting is different from the grid setting. While the grid on the screen is a visual guide, the snap setting controls the precise movement of the cursor, which contains the pickbox and the crosshairs. The snap setting controls an invisible grid that sets the cursor movement to desired increments. The snap setting can be established to snap at every grid dot or it can be independent from the grid. When used together, the grid and snap can greatly increase drawing speed and accuracy.

4.4 ESTABLISHING GRID AND SNAP USING A DIALOG BOX

The Drafting Settings dialog box is used to establish the X and Y spacing of the grid and snap and can also be used to turn the grid and snap on and off. You can access the Drafting Settings dialog box as follows:

1. From the Tools pull-down menu, select Drafting Settings. . .
2. Right-click on the GRID or SNAP button on the Status Bar. Select Settings . . . from the short-cut menu. You can also turn grid and snap on and off from this short-cut menu after you establish a grid and snap on the screen.
3. Enter DS, DSETTINGS, RM, or SE at the command line.
4. Press on the Space Bar of your keyboard. (this will display AutoCAD Help window in AutoCAD 2000i)

The Snap and Grid tab of the Drafting Settings dialog box is shown in Figure 4–1.

- **GRID ON [F7]:** (check box). Placing a checkmark in this check box will turn the grid on. Left-click inside the check box to turn the grid on. You can also press function key F7 or single click on the Grid button on the Status Bar to turn the grid on.

- **GRID X SPACING:** (text box). A value entered in this box specifies the grid dot spacing in the X direction. As a default, the grid X spacing is set to 0.5000 units. For architectural projects the grid X spacing is determined from the limits of the drawing. For example, if the limits for the drawing are 144′, 96′, a value of 1′ entered as the grid X spacing will display 144 dots horizontally or one dot every foot. If the grid X spacing value represents too small a value compared with the horizontal limits value, AutoCAD will display the "*Grid too dense to display*" message at the command line. If this happens, change the grid X spacing to a larger value.

- **GRID Y SPACING:** (text box). This area specifies the grid dot spacing in the Y direction. The default grid Y spacing is set to 0.5000 units. If the limits for the drawing are 144′, 96′, a value

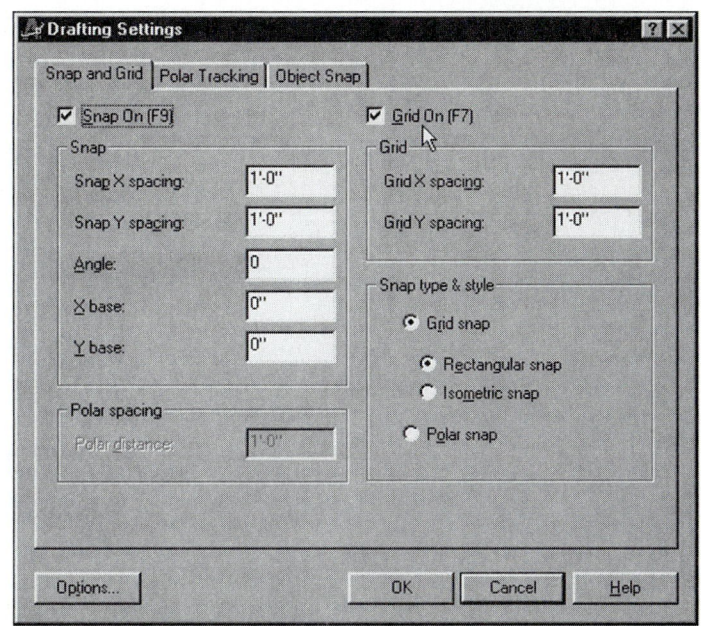

FIGURE 4–1 The Snap and Grid tab of the Drafting Settings dialog box can be used to create a grid and grid snap on the screen.

of 1′ entered as the grid Y spacing will display 96 dots vertically, or one dot every foot. If the grid X and Y spacing is set to 0, the grid will assume the values set for snap X and Y spacing. You can set different values for the grid X and Y spacing.

Figure 4–2 shows a drawing with limits of 44′, 34′ and a grid X and Y spacing of 12″.

- **SNAP ON [F9]:** (check box). Placing a checkmark in this check box will turn the snap on. You can also press function key F9 or single click on the Snap button on the Status Bar to turn the snap on.

- **SNAP X SPACING:** (text box). A value entered in this box specifies the snap spacing in the X direction. The value entered must be a positive number.

- **SNAP Y SPACING:** (text box). A value entered in this box specifies the snap spacing in the Y direction. The value entered must be a positive number. You can set different values for the snap X and Y spacing.

The minimum size of the grid spacing depends on the scale and the plotted sheet size of the drawing. For floor plan and space planning layouts, a large grid spacing value can be used as a visual aid to show the drawing limits. A snap spacing of 4″, 6″, 8″, or 10″ can be used to create exterior and interior walls. Figure 4–3 shows a partial floor plan created using a snap spacing of 6″ to create 12″ exterior and 6″ interior walls.

Tips: One of the best methods used to see the limits of the drawing displayed on the screen is to create a grid and snap setting on the screen. After setting the limits and zooming to the limits of the drawing, it is difficult to comprehend and visualize what has taken place on the screen. To help visualize the transformation of a new drawing area, set a grid and snap of 12″ or 24″ depending on the limits of the drawing. For example, set limits to 144′, 96′ and zoom to the limits of the drawing. Set grid and snap to 24″. Turn grid and snap on. Move the cursor to the first dot located on the lower-left corner and snap to that point. This should display the coordinates of 0′-0″, 0′-0″, 0′-0″. Now move the cursor to the upper-right corner and snap to that point. This should display the coordinates of 144′-0″, 96′-0″, 0′-0″. This is the visual verification of the D (36″ × 24″) size sheet on the screen.

- **ANGLE:** (text box). This area controls the rotation of the snap and grid by the angle specified. The standard grid and snap type displays dots based on horizontal rows and vertical columns. You can specify a rotation angle for the grid and snap using this option. The Angle option is useful when you want to draw pictorial views of objects. To change the snap

FIGURE 4–2 Drawing limits of 44', 34' with X and Y grid spacing of 12". The 6'-0" × 6'-0" square is drawn using the LINE command and snapping to the grids.

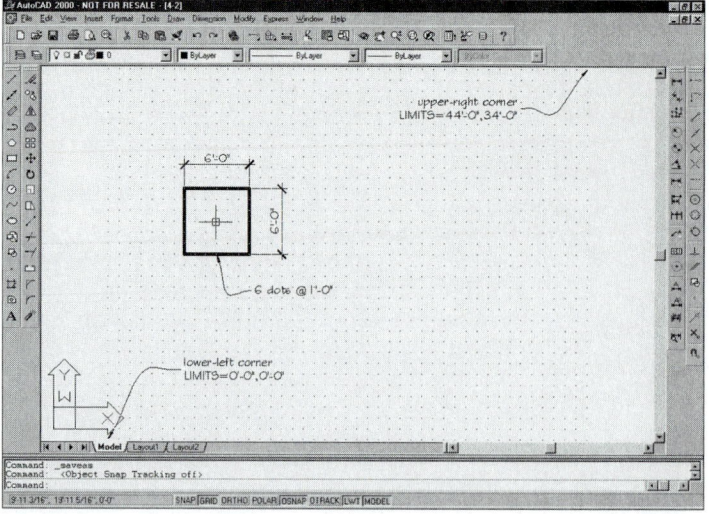

FIGURE 4–3 A partial floor plan created using a snap spacing of 6" and a grid spacing of 24".

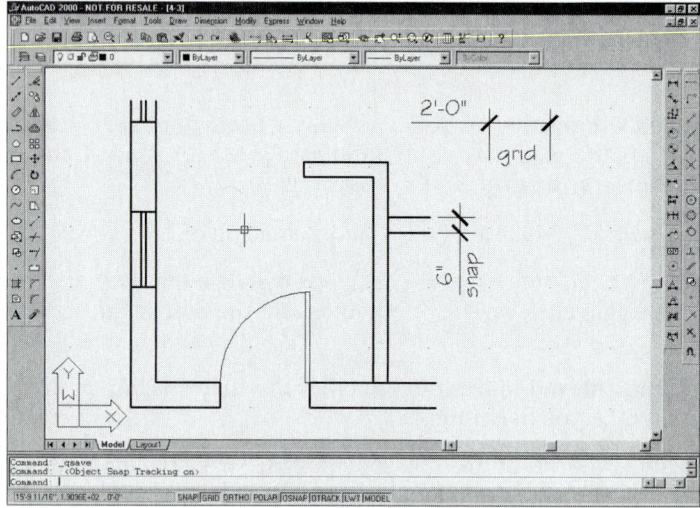

and grid rotation angle, enter the desired angle inside the Angle: text box and click on the OK button. When you change the angle of the snap and grid, the crosshairs will automatically rotate to the specified angle. The angle specified is relative to the UCS icon that is located at the lower-left corner of the drawing. Figure 4–4 shows two objects drawn at a 45 degree rotation with grid and snap X any Y spacing set to 36" using 144', 96' as the drawing Limits.

- **X BASE:** (text box). The base point represents the pivot point for the snap and grid rotation. It is generally located at the lower left corner of the drawing. In some cases, it may be more beneficial to move the base point to a location where the drawing will start. This area controls the X base coordinate point for the grid.

- **BASE:** (text box). This area controls the Y base coordinate point for the grid.

Note: The grid that you establish will be displayed only in the drawing limits area. This will help you work inside the paper size you have specified when establishing limits for the drawing.

Caution: If the space between each dot on the grid is too dense (too small) to display, AutoCAD will not display the grid when you are zoomed out.

4.4.1 Snap Type and Style

There are two different types of snap settings, Grid Snap and Polar Snap.

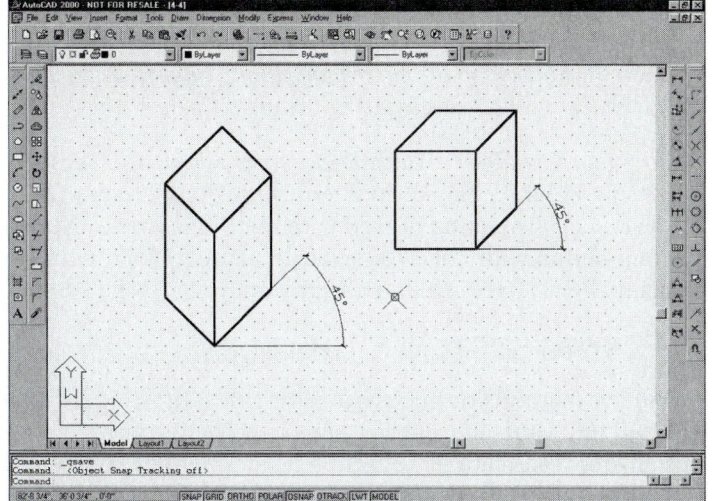

FIGURE 4–4 The two objects are drawn with a 45 degree snap angle rotation with grid and snap X and Y spacing of 36″. The drawing settings are based on a limits of 144′, 96′.

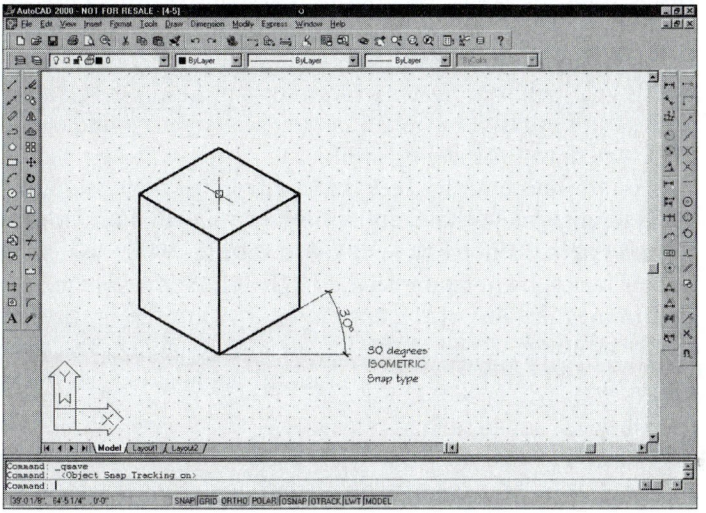

FIGURE 4–5 The object is drawn with isometric grid snap type set to Isometric snap. Notice the 30 degree isometric format.

Grid snap: (radio button). Grid snap allows you to set the snap type to grid where you can set the X and Y values for the grid spacing, as explained previously. There are two grid snap types—Rectangular and Isometric.

- **RECTANGULAR SNAP:** (radio button). This grid snap type is the standard snap mode based on the rectangular format. When this option is checked, AutoCAD will snap to the regular grid on the X and Y coordinates with orthogonal format. When you set the snap type to Grid snap, set the Snap X and Y spacing, and turn Snap On, the cursor will snap to a rectangular snap grid.

- **ISOMETRIC SNAP:** (radio button). This grid snap type will set an isometric snap grid on the screen. This option is used for creating isometric views of objects. When this option is checked, the crosshairs will automatically assume the 30 degree isometric drawing format. The standard grid and snap X spacing text boxes are not available with this option and will display 0.86602540. This value is based on the default snap X and Y spacing of 0.5000 and X spacing = Y spacing divided by tangent 30 degrees. Since X spacing is calculated using the value entered for Y spacing, entering 1 for Y spacing would display 1.73205080 for X spacing (reciprocal of tangent 30 degrees). However, you can set a different angle value using the Angle: text box to create isometric or oblique drawings based on different angles. Figure 4–5 shows an isometric view of an object using the Isometric snap option and a grid based on the same drawing settings of Figure 4–4.

Note: There is no specific command to create isometric dimensions. However, the Aligned Dimension button in the Dimension toolbar or the DIMALIGNED command can be adjusted to the correct obliquing angle to match isometric snap and grid. Isometric Dimensioning is discussed in Chapter 18.

Polar snap: (radio button). Polar snap allows the cursor to snap along polar alignment angles using Polar Angle Settings and snap along precise distances using polar spacing set as polar distance. This option is used with the Polar Tracking tab in the Drafting Settings dialog box in conjunction with Polar Snap. See Chapter 7 for a complete discussion on Polar Snap, Polar Spacing, Polar Tracking, and Object Snap Tracking.

4.5 USING SYSTEM VARIABLES

Whatever method you choose to start a new drawing or whatever drawing settings you specify, you will find yourself using system variables to control certain aspects of AutoCAD to help you design, draw, and plot projects in a faster and more efficient environment. AutoCAD has many functions that can be controlled through dialog boxes. The same functions can also be controlled at the command line by simply entering the name of the system variable and setting the appropriate value. In reality, system variables control how AutoCAD commands work by allowing you to set and control many functions of design, production, and plotting. These variables are recognized as a *mode, format, size,* or *option* to control the way a command works or in general how AutoCAD behaves. System variables can help you turn Snap and Grid on or off, set default scales for dimensioning and hatching scale factors, and change the size of your crosshairs. There are more than 400 system variables in AutoCAD. As a matter of fact, there are more than 60 dimensioning system variables that control just dimensioning settings.

System variables have abbreviated names that are approximately six to ten characters long. Some system variables have on or off settings, while some system variables have numerical value or text settings. For example, the CURSORSIZE system variable set through a numerical value determines the size of the *crosshairs* that are the vertical and horizontal lines attached to the cursor as a percentage of the screen size. To change the size of the crosshairs, enter CURSORSIZE system variable at the command line and enter a value between 1 and 100 as follows:

```
Command: CURSORSIZE ~EnterKey~
Enter a new value for CURSORSIZE <5>:35 ~EnterKey~ (this will set the
size of the crosshairs to 35 percent of the screen size)
```

The initial value in the brackets represents the default value for the size of the crosshairs that is 5 percent of the screen size.

The FILEDIA system variable controls the display of dialog boxes that read and write files. By default it is set to 1 which means that it is on. When the FILEDIA system variable is set to 0 (off), the Select File dialog box (when you click on the Open button in the Standard Toolbar) will not be displayed. If this is the case, you can either enter the file name at the file name prompt or enter ~ (tilde) to display the Select File dialog box or turn the system variable on as follows:

```
Command: FILEDIA ~EnterKey~
Enter new value for FILEDIA <0>: 1 ~EnterKey~
```

4.5.1   Using System Variables Transparently

System variables can be used *transparently* while a specific command is still active. To start a new command or to enter a system variable in AutoCAD, you must in most instances complete or cancel the current command. A *transparent command* will allow you to enter a system variable or some of the display commands while using another command. After the transparent command is completed, the active command will resume. You can check or change the setting of a system variable while a command is running by entering *apostrophe* (') before the system variable. For example, you can turn the grid off using the GRIDMODE system variable at the command line while using the LINE command as follows:

```
Command: LINE ~EnterKey~
Specify first point: (select a point on the screen to start a line)
```

```
Specify next point or [Undo]: (move the cursor and specify the next point for the line)
Specify next point or [Undo]: (move the cursor and specify another point
for the line)
Specify next point or [Close/Undo]: 'GRIDMODE ~EnterKey~
>>Enter new value for GRIDMODE <1>: 0 ~EnterKey~ (the grid will be
turned off)
Specify next point or [Close/Undo]: (continue selecting points for the line)
```

The double greater than symbols (>>) before the prompt indicates that the LINE (for the example above) command has been interrupted and is awaiting the completion of the GRID-MODE system variable. You can also move your cursor on the GRID button located at the status bar and turn it off while using the LINE command. Some of the display commands that can be used transparently are REDRAW, PAN, and ZOOM. The Pan Realtime and the Zoom Realtime buttons in the Standard Toolbar are automatically used transparently.

The SETVAR command can also be used to list or change system variable values. To display all system variables and their values, enter a question mark (?), then an asterisk (*) after the SETVAR command as follows:

```
Command: SETVAR ~EnterKey~
Enter variable name or [?] <GRIDMODE>: ? ~EnterKey~ (you can also enter
a new system variable)
Enter variable(s) to list <*>: ~EnterKey~ (you can also enter the name
of the variable to list its value)
```

This will display all system variables and their values as shown in Figure 4–6. Use the scroll bars to move to the next page.

You can use the SETVAR command transparently to check on the value of a system variable while another command is running. To accomplish this, place an apostrophe (') before the SETVAR.

The System Variables are read-only and cannot be modified directly by the user. A *system variable* remains in effect until it is accessed and changed by the user. When appropriate, each chapter will contain system variables for you to change certain settings either at the command line or using the Options dialog box.

Tips: You can use a variety of system variables to control how AutoCAD behaves. These system variables and preferences can be saved in drawings or saved in the system registry using the Options dialog box. A system variable can also be entered at the command line. System variables saved in drawing files will have the AutoCAD drawing icon next to the description. Other variables and preferences can be saved in the system registry. The Options dialog box is discussed throughout the text.

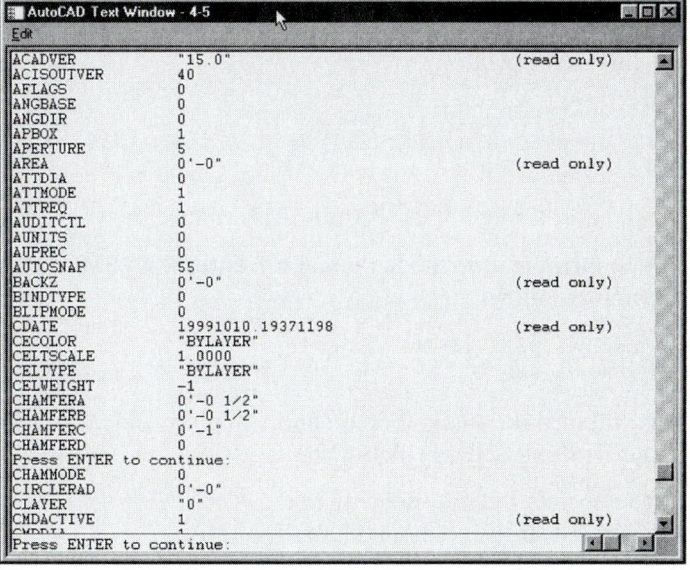

FIGURE 4–6 The AutoCAD Text Window dialog box showing some of the system variables and their values.

Caution: Changing system variables and settings either through the command line or through the Options dialog box without justification can cause AutoCAD to work improperly. Becoming familiar with settings and system variables early in the drawing stage will help you diagnose problems effectively and quickly.

Tips: A system variable stored in the system registry will affect all drawings while a system variable stored in the drawing will affect only the current drawing. A system variable that is not stored will be set as a default value when AutoCAD is loaded.

Tips: Create AutoCAD user settings to personalize drawing aids and system variables using the Options dialog box. Establishing user settings is discussed in Chapter 15.

4.6 ESTABLISHING GRID AND SNAP AT THE COMMAND LINE

The grid and snap settings, spacing, and the snap type and style can also be established at the command line. Some of the procedures are explained below:

- To turn the grid mode on and off, enter GRIDMODE system variable at the command line as follows:

```
Command: GRIDMODE ~EnterKey~
Enter a new value for GRIDMODE <0>: 1 ~EnterKey~
```

This will turn the grid on and will place a check mark inside the Grid On [F7] check box in the Drafting Settings dialog box.

- To establish a horizontal and vertical grid spacing, enter the GRID command at the command line as follows:

```
Command: GRID ~EnterKey~
Specify grid spacing (X) or [ON/OFF/Snap/Aspect] <3'-0">: (enter a grid X
spacing value)
```

If you specify a value followed by X, AutoCAD will set the grid spacing to the specified value times the snap interval. You can also enter ON or OFF to turn the grid mode On or Off. The Snap option will set the grid spacing to the current snap interval established by the SNAP command. The Aspect option will allow you to set the grid to a different X and Y spacing. For example, if you want to set a horizontal grid spacing of 24" and a vertical grid spacing of 36", enter the following:

```
Specify grid spacing (X) or [ON/OFF/Snap/Aspect] <1'-0">: A ~EnterKey~
Specify the horizontal spacing (X) <1'-0">: 2'~EnterKey~
Specify the vertical spacing (Y) <1'-0">: 3' ~EnterKey~
```

- To specify the grid X and Y spacing, enter GRIDUNIT system variable at the command line as follows:

```
Command: GRIDUNIT <EnterKey<
Enter new value for GRIDUNIT <2'-0", 3'-0">: (enter a new grid X and Y
spacing)
```

If you enter a value of 0', 0' AutoCAD will use the value set for snap X and Y spacing.

- To turn the snap mode on and off, enter SNAPMODE system variable at the command line as follows:

```
Command: SNAPMODE ~EnterKey~
Enter a new value for SNAPMODE <0>: 1 ~EnterKey~
```

This will turn the snap mode on and will place a checkmark inside the Snap On [F9] check box in the Drafting Settings dialog box.

- To specify the snap spacing in the X and Y direction, enter the SNAPUNIT system variable at the command line as follows:

```
Command: SNAPUNIT ~EnterKey~
Enter new value for SNAPUNIT <2'-0", 2'-0">: (enter a positive number)
```

- To specify isometric snap as the snap type, enter 1 for the SNAPSTYL system variable as follows:

```
Command: SNAPSTYL ~EnterKey~
Enter new value for SNAPSTYL <0>: 1 ~EnterKey~ (this will display the
isometric snap grid on the screen)
```

The default SNAPSTYL value of zero represents the standard rectangular snap.

- To set the snap and grid rotation angle, enter the SNAPANG system variable at the command line as follows:

```
Command: SNAPANG ~EnterKey~
Enter new value for SNAPANG <0>: (enter a snap grid rotation angle
relative to the current UCS)
```

- To set the snap and grid origin point, enter the SNAPBASE system variable at the command line as follows:

```
Command: SNAPBASE ~EnterKey~
Enter new value for SNAPBASE <0'-0", 0'-0">: (enter the X and Y base
coordinate points for the grid)
```

- To set the snap type to polar snap, enter the SNAPTYPE system variable at the command line as follows:

```
Command: SNAPTYPE ~EnterKey~
Enter new value for SNAPTYPE <0>: 1 (this will set the snap type to
polar snap).
```

The default SNAPSTYLE value of zero represents the standard snap grid.

REVIEW QUESTIONS

1. How many different ways can you access the Drafting Settings dialog box?
2. What is a grid and what is it used for?
3. How do you establish a snap for the grid?
4. What purpose does the snap serve while creating a floor plan on the screen?
5. What does a value of 70 represent inside the Angle: text box?
6. What are the names of the two different types of snap settings?
7. What is a system variable?
8. What is the function of the FILEDIA system variable?
9. What is a transparent command?
10. What command is used to check on the status of a certain system variable?
11. What option of the GRID command is used to enter a different X and Y grid spacing?
12. What system variable is used to specify an isometric snap?

PROBLEMS

1. Using the Start from Scratch option, set up a floor plan with a final plot scale of 1/4″ = 1′-0″ to be plotted on C-size sheet. Create a grid and snap X and Y spacing of 12″. Turn Snap and Grid on. You should see 96 dots placed horizontally and 72 dots placed vertically. Move your cursor to the lower-left corner of the grid and snap to the first dot. You should read 0′-0″,0′-0″,0′-0″ displayed in the Coordinates area. Move your cursor to the upper-right corner of the grid and snap to the dot located in the upper-right corner. What is shown in the coordinate displayed area? Change the grid and snap spacing to 4′. What has changed about the scale or the paper about this drawing? Change the grid and snap spacing to 2″. Why didn't the grid display? Do not save the drawing.

2. Using the Quick Setup Wizard option, set up a site plan with a final plot scale of 1″ = 20′ to be plotted on B- size sheet. Create a grid and snap X and Y spacing of 10′. Turn Snap and grid on. How many

dots do you see in the X and Y direction? Change the final plot scale to 1″ = 50′ to be plotted on C-size sheet. How many dots do you see now? Change the X and Y spacing to 50′. How many dots are displayed horizontally and vertically? How can you verify the size of your drawing sheet? Do not save the drawing.

3. Start a new drawing using the Quick Setup Wizard option and establish the following drawing settings and drawing aids:

   Units: Architectural

   Limits: 192′, 128′

   Grid X spacing: 24″

   Grid Y spacing: 48″

   Snap X and Y spacing: 12″

   Snap type: Grid

   Snap style: Rectangular snap

   What drawing scale can you use this setup for?

4. Start a new drawing using the Quick Setup Wizard option and establish the following drawing settings and drawing aids:

   Units: Architectural

   Limits: 22′-8″, 14′-8″

   Grid X and Y spacing: 8″

   Snap X and Y spacing: 8″

   Snap type: Grid

   Snap style: Isometric snap

   What drawing scale can you use this setup for? What drawing aids must you change to setup a rectangular grid and snap? Do not save the drawing.

5. Open the *EXE4-1.dwg* file. Change the Snap type to Isometric snap and change the snap and grid spacing to 12″. Does the object line up with the isometric grid? Do not save the drawing.

6. Using the *EXE4-1.dwg* file, change the isometric snap angle to 45 degrees. Does the object line up with the new isometric snap angle? Do not save the drawing.

7. Using the same file above, turn the snap mode off at the command line. What system variable did you enter at the command line? Do not save the drawing.

8. Using the same file above, change the isometric snap to rectangular snap at the command line. What system variable did you enter at the command line? Do not save the drawing.

9. Open the *EXE3-1.dwg* file. Change the grid and snap X and Y spacing to 2″. How many dots are displayed horizontally and vertically? Do not save the changes.

10. Open the *EXE3-2.dwg* file. Change the grid and snap X and Y spacing to 1/2″. Why didn't the grid display?

CHAPTER 5

Drawing Lines

After successful completion of this chapter you should be able to:

▲ Draw lines using the LINE command.

▲ Use the LINE command with Snap and Grid spacing.

▲ Use the Close and Undo options of the LINE command.

▲ Understand the Cartesian coordinate system.

▲ Use the absolute coordinate system to draw lines.

▲ Use the relative coordinate system to draw lines.

▲ Use the polar coordinate system to draw lines.

▲ Use the direct distance point entry system to draw lines.

▲ Use the Ortho mode.

▲ Understand COORDS system variable.

▲ Use blipmarks on the screen and use the REDRAW command to remove them.

▲ Use the BLIPMODE system variable.

▲ Use the OFFSET command.

▲ Use the XLINE and the RAY commands to draw construction lines.

▲ Use the U, UNDO, and REDO commands.

5.1 DRAWING LINES WITH AutoCAD

Once you determine the units and the limits of your drawing and establish a grid on the screen, you are ready to draw with AutoCAD. However, you may not always start a drawing with specific limits or a grid on the screen. Drawing is only a small part of the daily activities of document production. Approximately 30 percent of your time will be spent on drawing, but the vast majority of your time will be spent on modifying existing drawings. Modifying or revising a drawing may involve removing or adding objects, inserting symbols, placing text, creating dimensions, applying hatch patterns, and composing the final drawing for plot. Without the basic knowledge of drawing lines and the basic understanding of the *Cartesian coordinate system,* you will be lost in the vast sea of commands and will have a difficult time navigating through intermediate and advanced AutoCAD drawing and editing procedures. Most basic object geometry can be created with the use of the LINE and the CIRCLE commands even though there are hundreds of commands applicable to specific drawing tasks. This chapter covers the use of the LINE, OFFSET, XLINE, and RAY commands as the basic drawing commands. The XRAY and RAY commands can be used as visual line references, however, certain Object Snap modes such as *Snap to Extension* and Object Snap Tracking provide a more efficient means to create line references. Object Snap modes and Object Snap Tracking are discussed in Chapter 7. The use of U, UNDO, REDO, and REDRAW commands are also explained to give you the first drawing manipulation tools. The COORDS and the BLIPMODE system variables are explained so as to help you navigate effectively through your drawings.

5.2 ACCESSING COMMANDS

You can access AutoCAD commands by entering the command name at the command: prompt. However, you can also select a command from the appropriate toolbar or from the pull-down menu. If you are accustomed to typing the entire command name on your keyboard, you should be happy to know that you do not have to type every single letter of the command. Most commands have simple abbreviations, or *aliases*. For example, to draw a line you can either type LINE or L at the command: prompt, to draw a rectangle you can type RECTANGLE, REC-TANG, or REC at the command: prompt. If you make a mistake when entering at the command: prompt, use the Backspace key to retype or press the ~EscKey~ in the upper left corner of your keyboard to return to the command: prompt, where you can start over.

5.3 USING THE LINE COMMAND

The LINE command is the primary command used to create objects involving series of connected straight-line segments. These straight-line segments can be in the form of horizontal, vertical, or slanted lines. The LINE command allows you to create individual line segments by connecting the endpoint of the previous line segment with the beginning point of the next line segment. AutoCAD automatically repeats this process until you decide to cancel or end the LINE command. Since the LINE command creates a series of connected line segments, the object geometry created with the LINE command is considered to be a *multi-entity* object. This means that the individual line segments that make up the composition of the objects are separate objects connected to each other. Although line segments are created in the same Line command, you must realize that each line segment is a separate object. These separate yet connected objects can be edited using any of the editing commands and procedures one line at a time. On the other hand, a *single-entity* object is considered to be geometry composed of interconnected or single object(s) that is a whole unit. This means that the individual objects that make up the whole composition cannot be edited on an individual basis; rather, the entire object as a whole is edited. However, the EXPLODE command can be used to convert a single-entity object into a multi-entity object. See chapter 12. Some of the commands that allow you to create *single-entity* objects are the PLINE (Polyline), SPLINE, RECTANG (Rectangle), MLINE (Multiline), and POLYGON commands. You can access the LINE command in three different ways:

1. Enter L or LINE at the command line.
2. Select LINE from the Draw pull-down menu.
3. Click on the LINE button in the Draw Toolbar.

Whichever method you choose to access the LINE command, AutoCAD will give you the following prompt:

```
Command: _line Specify first point: (select a point on the drawing)
```

Specify first point: is the starting point location for the LINE command. This is the point location where you start drawing a line or line segments. The *first point* can be established in three different ways:

1. Move the cursor to any location on the screen and left click.
2. Enter the X and Y coordinates.
3. Establish grid and snap settings on the screen. Click on the Grid and Snap buttons in the Status Bar to turn the grid and snap on. Move the cursor to the desired grid point location and left-click to snap to that point.

Once you establish the *first point,* AutoCAD will present you the following prompt:

```
Specify next point or [Undo]: (select another point on the drawing)
```

Specify next point is the second point location on the screen that will draw the first line segment. This *next point* can be established using three different methods:

1. Move the cursor to any location on the screen and left-click.
2. Use any of the point entry methods described in section 5.5 of this chapter.
3. Establish Polar Snap, Polar Angle, and Polar Tracking settings using the Drafting Settings dialog box. These settings are discussed in Chapter 7.

In Figure 5–1 the *first point* location is established at point A and the *next point* location is established at Point B. Once you establish the next point, a line will be drawn from point A to point B as shown in Figure 5–1. To draw the second line segment attached to the endpoint of the first line segment, select another point on the screen at the next command prompt as follows:

```
Specify next point or [Undo]: (select Point C)
```

Once you establish the third point, you will have two line segments from point A to point B to point C as shown in Figure 5–1. After two line segments are created on the screen, the following command prompt will be presented:

```
Specify next point or [Close/Undo]:
```

The Close option is presented at the third and consecutive command prompts and is used to connect the endpoint of the last line segment to the start point of the first line segment. It allows you to close the object geometry without having to precisely snap to the start point of the first line segment. The object in Figure 5–1 is drawn as follows:

```
Command: LINE ~EnterKey~
Specify first point: (select Point A)
Specify next point or [Undo]: (select Point B)
Specify next point or [Undo]: (select Point C)
Specify next point or [Close/Undo]: C ~EnterKey~
```

> *Tips: In addition to the LINE command, a few more commands will have the C (Close) option. In cluttered drawing situations closing an object in this fashion is more efficient.*

The Undo option will allow you to remove the previously drawn line segment(s). When you create a series of line segments, you may discover that you made a mistake with one or more

TIPS

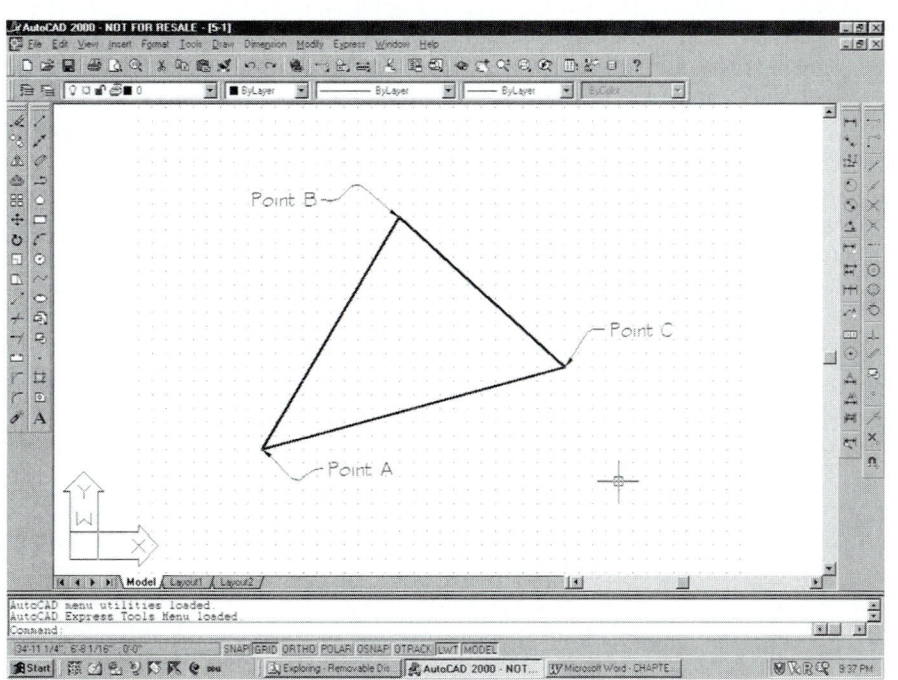

FIGURE 5–1 The three line segments are created using the LINE command. The *first point* is selected at point A, the *next point* is selected at point B, the *next point* is selected at point C, and the *Close* option is used to connect the endpoint of the last line segment with the start point of the first line segment.

previously drawn lines you created. If this is the case, enter U at the command prompt as follows:

```
Specify next point or [Undo]: U ~EnterKey~ (this will delete the last
line segment drawn)
```

You can keep entering U at the command prompt until the lines drawn by error are deleted from the screen. You might have to move the cursor to see the lines being removed each time you enter U at the command prompt.

Caution: The Undo option of the LINE command (or any other command having this option) will remove one previously drawn line segment at a time while the command is still active. If you enter U at the Command: prompt immediately after you complete a command, the entire object geometry will be deleted from the screen. You can bring the object back if you enter REDO at the Command: prompt immediately after the Undo.

You can also use the Undo option repeatedly to continue removing lines until you reach the *Specify first point:* prompt location. When you draw line segments on the screen, a *rubber band* line is attached to the endpoint of the last line segment, allowing you to see the line segment before you pick the point location. When the last line segment is drawn you can finish or discontinue the LINE command in four different ways:

1. Press the ~EnterKey~ at the *Specify next point or [Close/Undo]: prompt.*

2. Right-click at the *Specify next point or [Close/Undo]: prompt* and select Enter or Cancel from the shortcut menu. You can also select Close option from the shortcut menu.

3. Press the ~EscKey~. This can also be used to cancel a command entered in error or stop an active command.

4. Press the space bar.

Note: Only the commands that present specify next point prompt after selecting the first point allow you to finish that command using the ~EnterKey~, ~EscKey~, and pressing the space bar. The LINE, XLINE, MULTILINE, and POLYLINE commands are examples of such commands. The LINE, MULTILINE, and POLYLINE commands present specify next point prompt after specify first point prompt. The XLINE command will present specify through point prompt.

Tips: If you cancel the Line command by mistake you can easily get back to the Line command and continue creating lines from the endpoint of the last line segment by pressing the ~EnterKey~ or ~SpaceBar~ twice. However, this operation must be done immediately after terminating the Line command. This method of continuing creating object segments can be used with any command requiring more than two points. You can get back to any command or system variable you cancelled by mistake by pressing the ~EnterKey~ or ~Space Bar~ once immediately after terminating the command or system variable.

5.4 DRAWING LINES USING GRID AND SNAP SPACING

One of the basic drawing aid tools to help you draw lines precisely at specific lengths and angles is to create a grid on the drawing screen. As you learned in Chapter 4, a grid is a series of dots displayed at specific intervals in the X and Y coordinate direction used as a *visual reference tool.* When the Grid X and Y spacing is used in conjunction with the Snap X and Y spacing, it creates an excellent *visual reference tool.* It allows you to *snap* precisely to the *first* and *next points* of the LINE command, creating a series of connected line segments without the aid of entering distances at the command line or using *object snap modes.* Object Snap Modes are discussed in Chapter 7. This initial learning tool is very beneficial in understanding the concept behind *distance, length, direction, orientation,* and *measurement.* The grid and snap spacing is a precise, effective, and useful tool, especially in the early stages of your design development activities. However, you must understand that as you become an experienced AutoCAD user, the grid and snap spacing may not be an effective or useful tool to consider when creating complex projects. When you master the intricate details of advanced drawing aids, you might consider grid and snap spacing as a *primitive* tool with respect to some of the more advanced drawing precision tools such as the *Polar Snap, Polar Spacing, Polar Tracking, Object Snap Tracking,* and *Object Snap Modes.* Nevertheless, your education and training must start with fundamentals that are crucial in providing you the solid foundation you need to gain all that experience.

> *Note: Learning a complex drawing software such as AutoCAD begins with the understanding of the basic tools. After a while it is normal and acceptable to ask the following question: "Why did we learn this or that method or command before since I now can do the same thing with a new command or method?" Every command and every option has a purpose and serves the needs of many different individuals with different drawing needs. You may learn to do something in a different method and it may very well be a faster and more efficient way to do something, but it is the basic tool that allows you to understand the complex drawing procedures and a method that gives you an individual choice.*

A variety of *point entry* methods are used with the *Cartesian coordinate system* that will be explained next. A point entry method allows you to enter coordinates, distances, and angles that determine the object's *length, direction, orientation,* and *measurement.* However, you can draw lines at precise lengths and angles using the grid and snap spacing settings as opposed to using the Cartesian coordinate system. You can snap to grid points on the screen to draw lines as precisely as any other point entry method.

■ **EXERCISE 5–1:** *The following step-by-step exercise will help you to draw the object in Figure 5–2 using the LINE command and the snap and grid spacing in the Drafting Settings dialog box:*

Step #1: Start a new drawing using the Start from Scratch option.

Step #2: Use the Drawing Units dialog box to set Length Type to *Architectural.*

Step #3: Use the LIMMAX system variable to enter *44', 34'* as the new Limits. Or use the Drawing Limits option in the Format pull-down menu.

Step #4: Zoom to the Limits of the drawing.

Step #5: Using the Drafting Settings dialog box set Grid and Snap X and Y spacing to *24".*

Step #6: Turn Grid and Snap on.

Step #7: Use the LINE command to draw the object as follows:

> Command: **L** ~EnterKey~
>
> Specify first point: 6', 6' *(or move the cursor three grid points in the X and Y direction until the coordinate display reads 6'-0", 6'-0", 0'-0" and click on that coordinate point)*
>
> Specify next point or [Undo]: *(move the cursor up five grid points and snap to that point. This will draw a line 10'-0" in length at 90 degrees)*
>
> Specify next point or [Undo]: *(move the cursor toward East, six grid points and snap to that point. This will draw a line 12'-0" in length at 0 degrees)*
>
> Specify next point or [Close/Undo]: *(move the cursor toward South, five grid points and snap to that point. This will draw a line 10'-0" in length at 270 degrees)*
>
> Specify next point or [Close/Undo]: **C** ~EnterKey~ *(this will close the object)*

Congratulations! You just created a 12' by 10' rectangle using the alias for the LINE command and Snap and Grid spacing of 24" without entering any lengths at the command line.

Using the grid and snap settings in this respect will allow you to quickly draw lines to create objects. This can be useful when creating a quick floor plan that require you to snap at increments of 6" to create interior and exterior walls or 6' to create spaces for conceptual design. Figure 5–3 shows a preliminary floor plan using a snap and grid spacing of 6".

FIGURE 5–2   The 12′ by
10′ rectangle object is
created using the grid
and snap spacing of 24″
and the LINE
command.

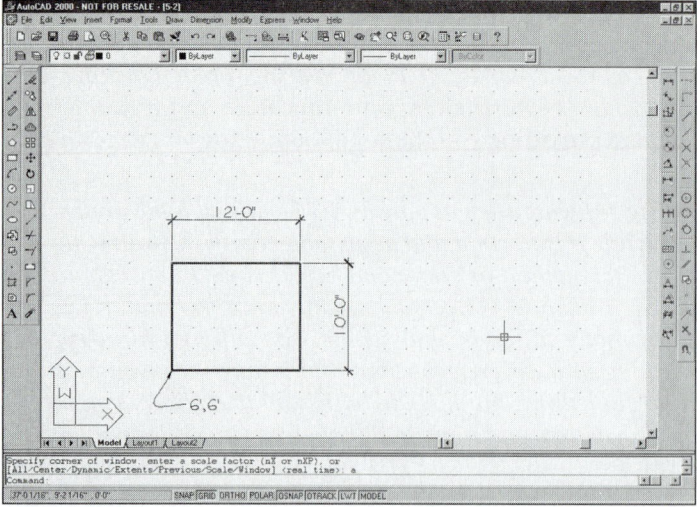

FIGURE 5–3   A
preliminary floor plan
drawn with the LINE
command using only the
grid and snap settings.

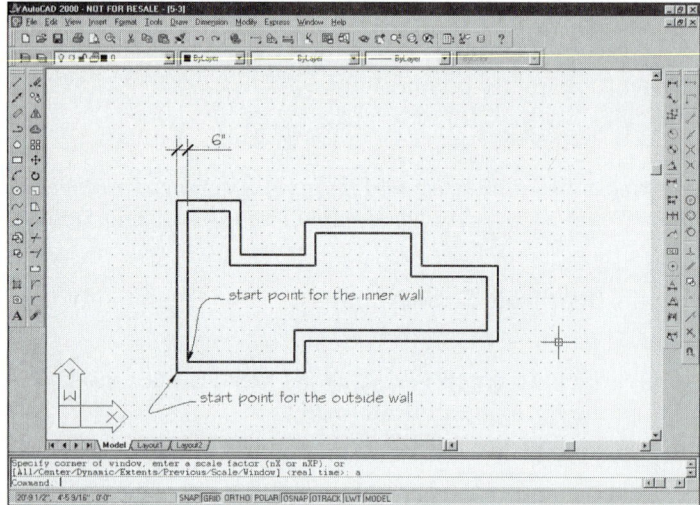

5.5 USING POINT ENTRY SYSTEMS TO DRAW LINES

When creating two-dimensional objects, you can specify X and Y coordinate points similar
to drawing on a grid paper. Individual line segments with precise lengths and angles are created using a point entry system. A point entry system uses the *Cartesian coordinate system*
that is based on specifying distances from the X and Y intersecting axes when creating two-
dimensional drawings. It is extremely important to become familiar with the Cartesian coordinate system and the different point entry methods. Drawing a line from a point of *origin* on
the screen requires the understanding of moving in the plus (+) or minus (−) X and Y directions. The coordinate system is divided into four quadrants in the X and Y plane as shown in Figure 5–4. When points are located in relation to the origin, the X and Y values determine the
length and angle of the lines. The X value specifies horizontal distance and the Y value specifies
vertical distance. The origin in this case is the intersection of the X and Y plane that is at X=0
and Y=0 (0,0). However, when creating two-dimensional drawings, the origin is usually at the
lower-left corner of the screen near the Model Space UCS icon. In Figure 5–4, line A is established by moving 12 units in the −X direction and moving 9 units in the +Y direction.

   There are three different point entry methods in the Cartesian coordinate system: absolute
coordinate system, relative coordinate system, and polar coordinate system.

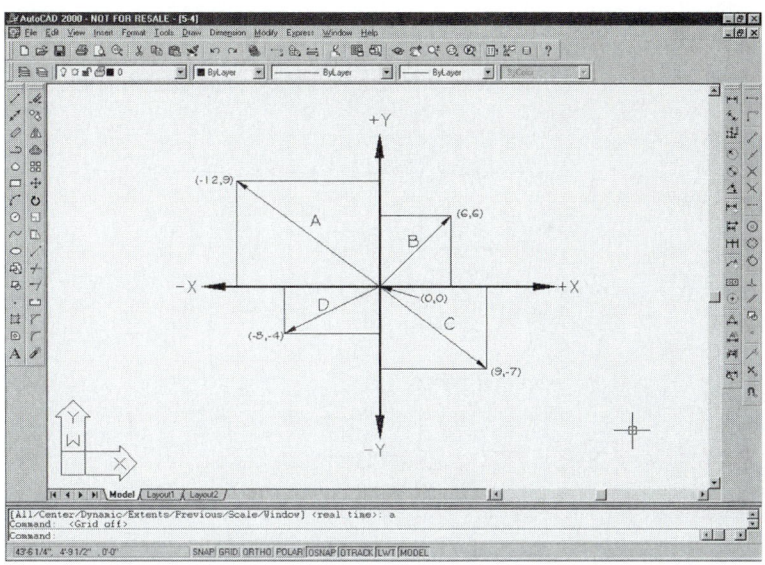

FIGURE 5–4 The Cartesian coordinate system.

5.5.1 Using Absolute Coordinate System

The absolute coordinate method measures points from the origin of 0,0. When determining the X and Y coordinates for the line points, you must either add or subtract the lengths from the starting point coordinates, depending on whether the line is in the plus or in the minus direction. In Figure 5–5 the object is drawn using the first point at 6′, 12′. The drawing settings are as follows:

```
Drawing Units: Architectural
Drawing Limits: 44', 34'
```

All points are determined from 0′, 0′. The first point is at 6′, 12′. The line from point 1 to point 2 is 10′-0″ in length. The rest of the lengths are shown in the drawing.

To draw the next point (the first line segment) using the absolute coordinates, you must enter 6′, 22′. This is calculated as follows:

The line from point 1 to point 2 is 10′ in the + Y direction and has no length in the X direction. The initial value is determined to be (0′, 10′). Since this point is determined from 0′, 0′, the X = 6′ and Y = 12′ must be added to the final calculation (0′ + 6′ = 6′ and 10′ + 12′ = 22′). Hence the absolute coordinates for point 1 to point 2 is entered as 6′, 22′.

■ **EXERCISE 5–2:** *The following step-by-step exercise will help you create the object shown in Figure 5–5 using the LINE command with absolute coordinate system:*

Step #1: Start a new drawing using the Start from Scratch option.

Step #2: Use the Drawing Units dialog box to set Length Type to *Architectural*.

Step #3: Use the LIMMAX system variable to enter *44′, 34′* as the new Limits. Or use the Drawing Limits option in the Format pull-down menu.

Step #4: Zoom to the Limits of the drawing.

Step #5: Use the Drafting Settings dialog box to set Grid X and Y spacing to 12″.

Step #6: Turn only Grid on.

Step #7: Use the LINE command to draw the object as follows:

Command: **LINE** ~EnterKey~

Specify first point: **6′, 12′** ~EnterKey~

Specify next point or [Undo]: **6′, 22′** ~EnterKey~ *(this will draw the line from point 1 to point 2)*

Specify next point or [Undo]: **17′, 22′** ~EnterKey~ *(this will draw the line from point 2 to point 3 as X = 11′ + 6′, Y = no change)*

FIGURE 5–5 Points located with the absolute coordinate system are measured from the origin of 0,0.

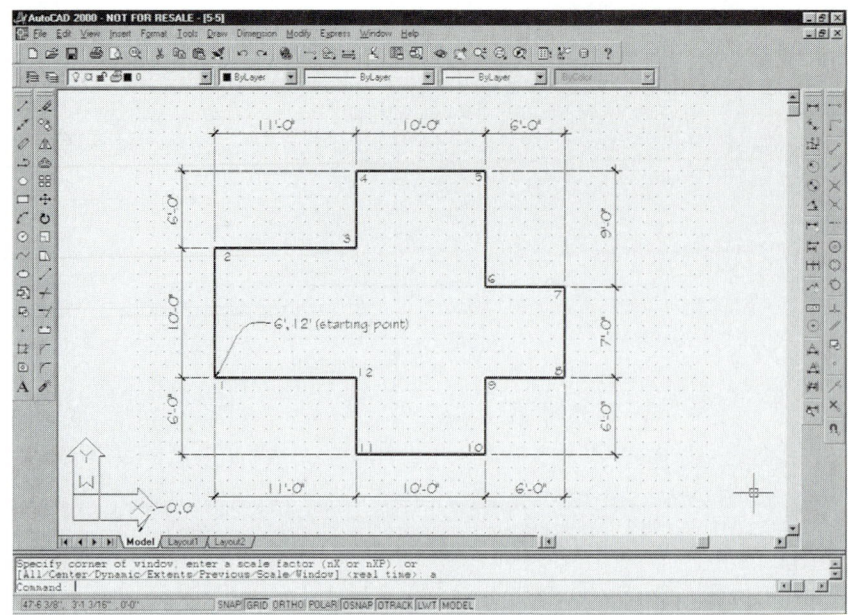

Specify next point or [Close/Undo]: **17′, 28′** ~EnterKey~ *(this will draw the line from point 3 to point 4 as X = no change, Y = 22′ + 6′)*

Specify next point or [Close/Undo]: **27′, 28′** ~EnterKey~ *(this will draw the line from point 4 to point 5 as X = 17′ + 10′, Y = no change)*

Specify next point or [Close/Undo]: **27′, 19′** ~EnterKey~ *(this will draw the line from point 5 to point 6 as X = no change, Y = 28′-9′)*

Specify next point or [Close/Undo]: **33′, 19′** ~EnterKey~ *(this will draw the line from point 6 to point 7 as X = 27′ + 6′, Y = no change)*

Specify next point or [Close/Undo]: **33′, 12′** ~EnterKey~ *(this will draw the line from point 7 to point 8 as X = no change, Y = 19′-7′)*

Specify next point or [Close/Undo]: **27′, 12′** ~EnterKey~ *(this will draw the line from point 8 to point 9 as X = 33′-6′, Y = no change)*

Specify next point or [Close/Undo]: **27′, 6′** ~EnterKey~ *(this will draw the line from point 9 to point 10 as X = no change, Y = 12′-6′)*

Specify next point or [Close/Undo]: **17′, 6′** ~EnterKey~ *(this will draw the line from point 10 to point 11 as X = 27′-10′, Y = no change)*

Specify next point or [Close/Undo]: **17′, 12′** ~EnterKey~ *(this will draw the line from point 11 to point 12 as X = no change, Y = 6′ + 6′)*

Specify next point or [Close/Undo]: **6′, 12′** OR **C**~EnterKey~ *(this will draw the line from point 12 to point 1 as X = 17′-11′, Y = no change or close the object)*

Congratulations! You just created the object shown in Figure 5–5 using the LINE command with absolute coordinate system.

5.5.2 Using Relative Coordinate System

The relative coordinate method measures points from the previous position, as opposed to going back to the 0,0 origin. All points are relative to the last point. To indicate the last point, the @ symbol is used followed by the X and Y coordinates for the point. The @ symbol is entered by holding the ~ShiftKey~ and pressing the number 2 key in the keyboard.

■ **EXERCISE 5–3:** *The following step-by-step exercise will help you create the object shown in Figure 5–6 using the Line button in the Draw toolbar with relative coordinate system:*

Step #1: Start a new drawing using the Start from Scratch option.

Step #2: Use the Drawing Units dialog box to set Length Type to *Architectural*.

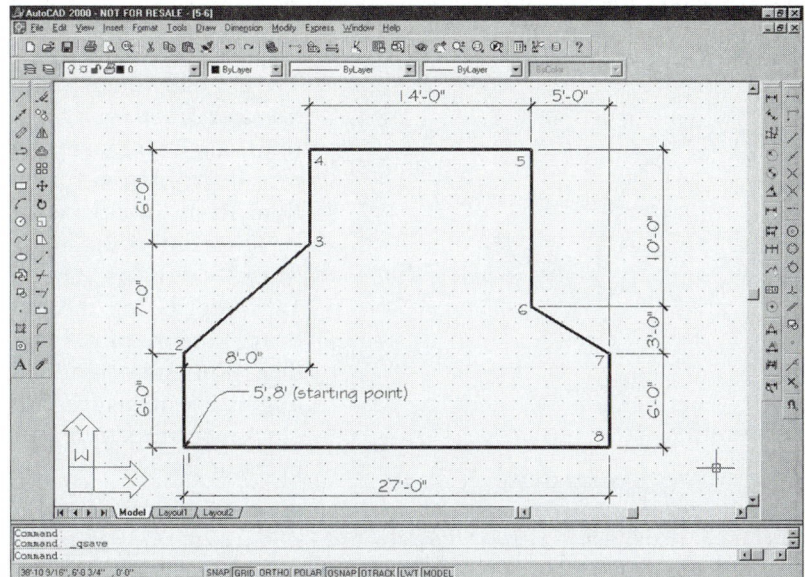

FIGURE 5–6 Points located with the relative coordinate system are measured from the previous point with the @ followed by the X and Y coordinate points.

Step #3: Use the LIMMAX system variable to enter *44′, 34′* as the new Limits. Or use the Drawing Limits option in the Format pull-down menu.

Step #4: Zoom to the Limits of the drawing.

Step #5: Use the Drafting Settings dialog box to set Grid X and Y spacing to 12″.

Step #6: Turn only Grid on.

Step #7: Click on the Line button in the Draw toolbar to use the LINE command to draw the object as follows:

Command: _line Specify first point: **5′, 8′** ~EnterKey~

Specify next point or [Undo]: **@ 0′, 6′** ~EnterKey~ *(this will draw the line from point 1 to point 2)*

Specify next point or [Undo]: **@ 8′, 7′** ~EnterKey~ *(this will draw the line from point 2 to point 3)*

Specify next point or [Close/Undo]: **@ 0′, 6′** ~EnterKey~ *(this will draw the line from point 3 to point 4)*

Specify next point or [Close/Undo]: **@ 14′, 0′** ~EnterKey~ *(this will draw the line from point 4 to point 5)*

Specify next point or [Close/Undo]: **@ 0′, -10′** ~EnterKey~ *(this will draw the line from point 5 to point 6)*

Specify next point or [Close/Undo]: **@ 5′, -3′** ~EnterKey~ *(this will draw the line from point 6 to point 7)*

Specify next point or [Close/Undo]: **@ 0′, -6′** ~EnterKey~ *(this will draw the line from point 7 to point 8)*

Specify next point or [Close/Undo]: **@ -27′, 0′** OR **C** ~EnterKey~ *(this will draw the line from point 8 to point 1 or close the object)*

Congratulations! You just created the object shown in Figure 5–6 using the Line button in the Draw toolbar with relative coordinate system.

5.5.3 Using the Polar Coordinate System

A polar coordinate is entered as a distance and an angle from the last point. The distance and the angle are separated by the less than symbol (<) preceded by the @ symbol. The polar coordinate system is referred to as the *distance<angle* format. For example, to draw a line 5′-6 5/8″ in length from the previous point at an angle of 74 degrees, enter @ 5′6-5/8<74 and

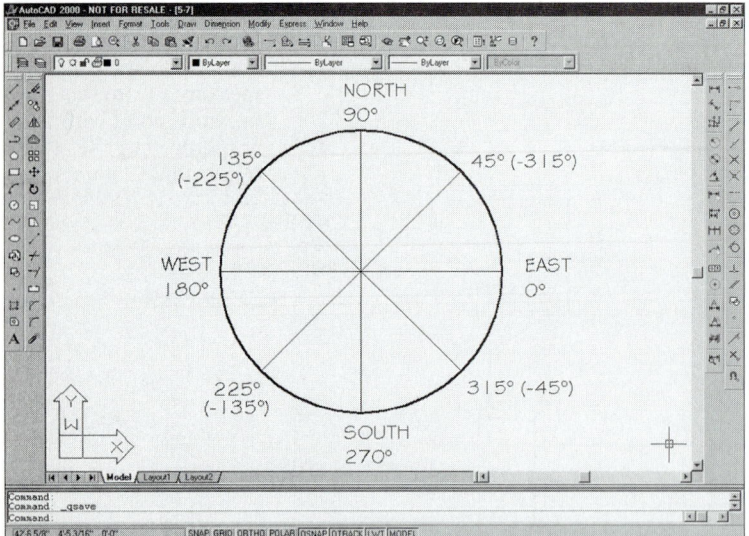

FIGURE 5–7 Points located using the polar coordinate system are based on the angle direction of counterclockwise. Notice the minus (−) angle values represent clockwise angle direction that can also be used.

press ~EnterKey~. If the @ symbol is not included, the point is located relative to the origin. The angular values are determined from the *direction and orientation for angle measurement*. By default, angles are measured from the base angle zero degrees from East at counterclockwise direction. To move clockwise, enter the minus symbol (−) in front of the angle. For example, entering @ 12′<300 is the same as entering @ 12′<−60. Using the polar coordinate system to draw lines requires the understanding of angle direction and orientation. Figure 5–7 shows how angles are measured using the default counterclockwise direction with base angle of zero degrees at East.

■ **EXERCISE 5–4:** *The following step-by-step exercise will help you create the object shown in Figure 5–8 using the Line button in the Draw toolbar with the polar coordinate system:*

Step #1: Start a new drawing using the Start from Scratch option.

Step #2: Use the Drawing Units dialog box to set Length Type to *Architectural.*

Step #3: Use the LIMMAX system variable to enter *44′, 34′* as the new Limits. Or use the Drawing Limits option in the Format pull-down menu.

Step #4: Zoom to the Limits of the drawing.

Step #5: Use the Drafting Settings dialog box to set Grid X and Y spacing to 12″.

Step #6: Turn only Grid on.

Step #7: Click on the Line button in the Draw toolbar to use the LINE command to draw the object as follows:

Command: _line Specify first point: **7′, 7′** ~EnterKey~

Specify next point or [Undo]: **@ 10′<90** ~EnterKey~ (this will draw the 10′ line at 90 degrees from point 1 to point 2)

Specify next point or [Undo]: **@ 11′3-3/4<45** ~EnterKey~ (this will draw the 11′-3 3/4″ line at 45° counterclockwise from point 2 to point 3)

Specify next point or [Close/Undo]: **@ 10′<0** ~EnterKey~ (this will draw the 10′ line at 0 degrees from point 3 to point 4)

Specify next point or [Close/Undo]: **@ 6′<270** ~EnterKey~ (this will draw the 6′ line at 270 degrees from point 4 to point 5)

Specify next point or [Close/Undo]: **@ 8′5-3/4<-45** ~EnterKey~ (this will draw the 8′-5 3/4″ line at 45 degrees clockwise from point 5 to point 6)

Specify next point or [Close/Undo]: **@ 6′<270** ~EnterKey~ (this will draw the 6′ line at 270 degrees from point 6 to point 7)

Specify next point or [Close/Undo]: **@ 24′<180** OR **C** ~EnterKey~ (this will draw the 24′ line at 180 degrees from point 7 to point 1 or close the object)

Congratulations! You just created the object shown in Figure 5–8 using the Line button in the Draw toolbar with polar coordinate system.

You probably noticed that the absolute coordinate system seems to be the most difficult point entry system because all points are measured from 0,0, which passes through the starting point of the drawing. You must remember to add or subtract the X and Y coordinates from the starting point coordinates, depending on the direction on the Cartesian coordinate system. The relative and polar coordinates use the @ symbol at the beginning of the distance entry, which locates points from the previous location and can be used interchangably during the drawing process.

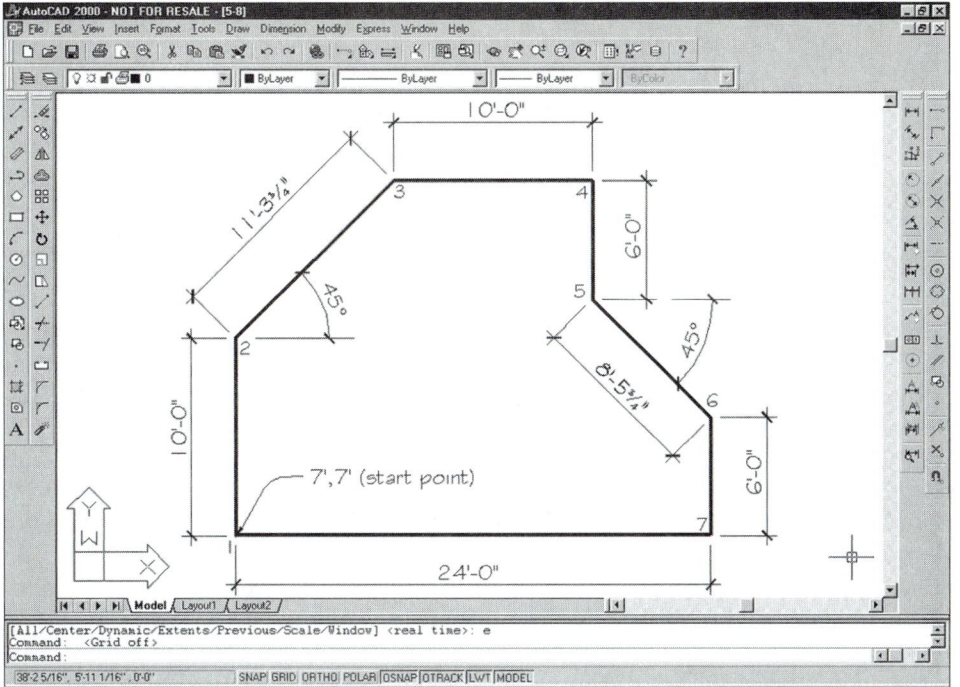

FIGURE 5–8 Points located with the polar coordinate system are measured from the previous point with the @ symbol followed by a distance, the less than symbol (<) and the angle. Notice that the angle direction is counterclockwise.

5.6 DRAWING LINES AT AN ANGLE

A line that is drawn at an angle other than 0, 90, 180, and 270 degrees can be drawn using any of the methods shown above; however, a minimum of two sets of information must be provided to draw the angle as follows:

1. The length of the line and the angle from a reference line must be given as shown in Figure 5–9 A. In this case the line is drawn as follows:

```
Command: L ~EnterKey~
Specify first point: 8',10' ~EnterKey~
Specify next point or [Undo]: @15'<60 ~EnterKey~
```

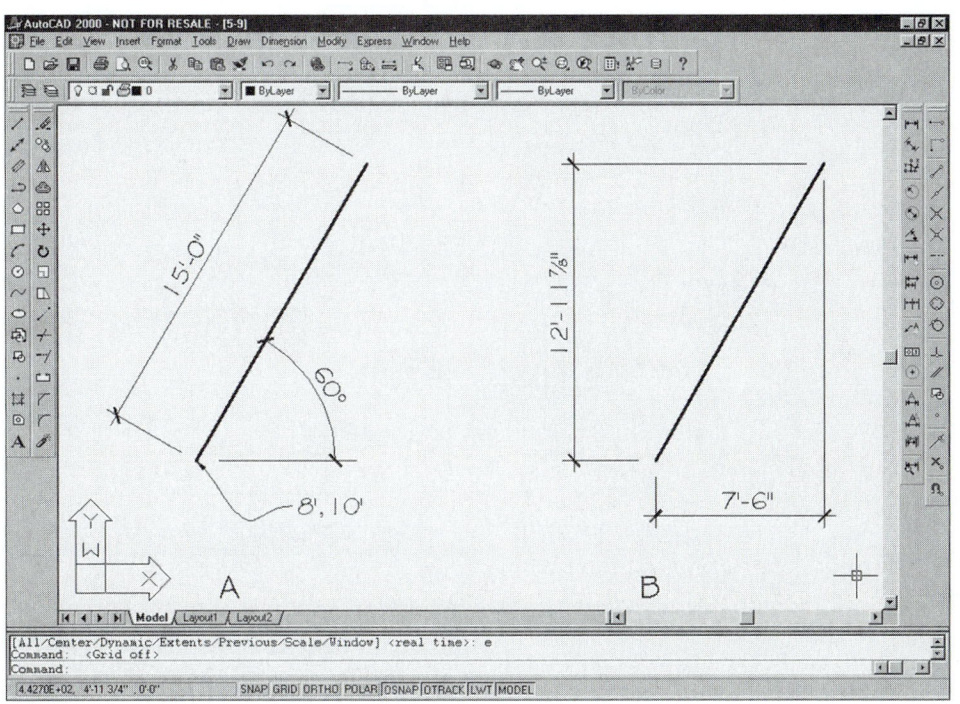

FIGURE 5–9 A: If a line includes the length and angle information, the polar coordinate system is used since no horizontal and vertical distances are given. B: If a line includes the horizontal and the vertical distances but no length and no angle is given, the absolute or relative coordinate system is used.

2. The vertical and the horizontal distances of the line must be given as shown in Figure 5–9 B. In this case the line is drawn as follows:

```
Command: L ~EnterKey~
Specify first point: 8',10' ~EnterKey~
Specify next point or [Undo]: @7'6,12'11-7/8 OR 15'6,22'11-7/8
~EnterKey~
```

5.7 USING THE ORTHO MODE

The orthogonal (Ortho) mode in AutoCAD allows you to draw straight lines in the horizontal and vertical directions. In mathematics, the term orthogonal means "relating to or composed of right angles." When you draw in Ortho mode, AutoCAD forces the lines to be created only horizontally or vertically. You can turn the Ortho mode on by selecting the Ortho button in the status bar, pressing the function key F8, or entering Ortho at the command line. You can also right-click on the Ortho button and use the shortcut menu to turn Ortho mode on or off. The Ortho mode is similar to the concept of setting a grid and snap spacing where horizontal and vertical snap allows for drawing straight lines. When you use the absolute, relative, and polar coordinate systems to draw lines, you do not have to turn the Ortho mode on because the coordinates you enter force AutoCAD to create lines horizontally and vertically or at any other angle. When you use the polar coordinate system to draw lines, it does not matter if you turn the Ortho mode on or off because the 0, 90, 180, or 270 you enter as the direction forces AutoCAD to draw lines that are perfectly horizontal and vertical. You can have the Ortho mode on and still draw a line at an angle other than 0, 90, 180, and 270 degrees. Using the grid and snap spacing will also allow you to draw lines as if the Ortho mode was on. However, when you use the snap spacing to snap to a specific grid point on the screen, you must turn Ortho mode off to snap to a grid point that will give you a specific angle. Turn the Ortho mode on when drawing square and rectangular objects while using the cursor to select points on the screen (when you are not using one of the three coordinate systems). Figure 5–10 shows an object created using the Ortho mode. This object will be created using the polar coordinate system in Exercise 5–5.

FIGURE 5–10 The Ortho mode can be used to draw horizontal and vertical lines when using the LINE command to create the necessary openings in the walls. Start with the outside wall lines, establish the openings, then use the OFFSET command to offset the lines to create the actual wall thickness. This object will be created in Exercise 5–5.

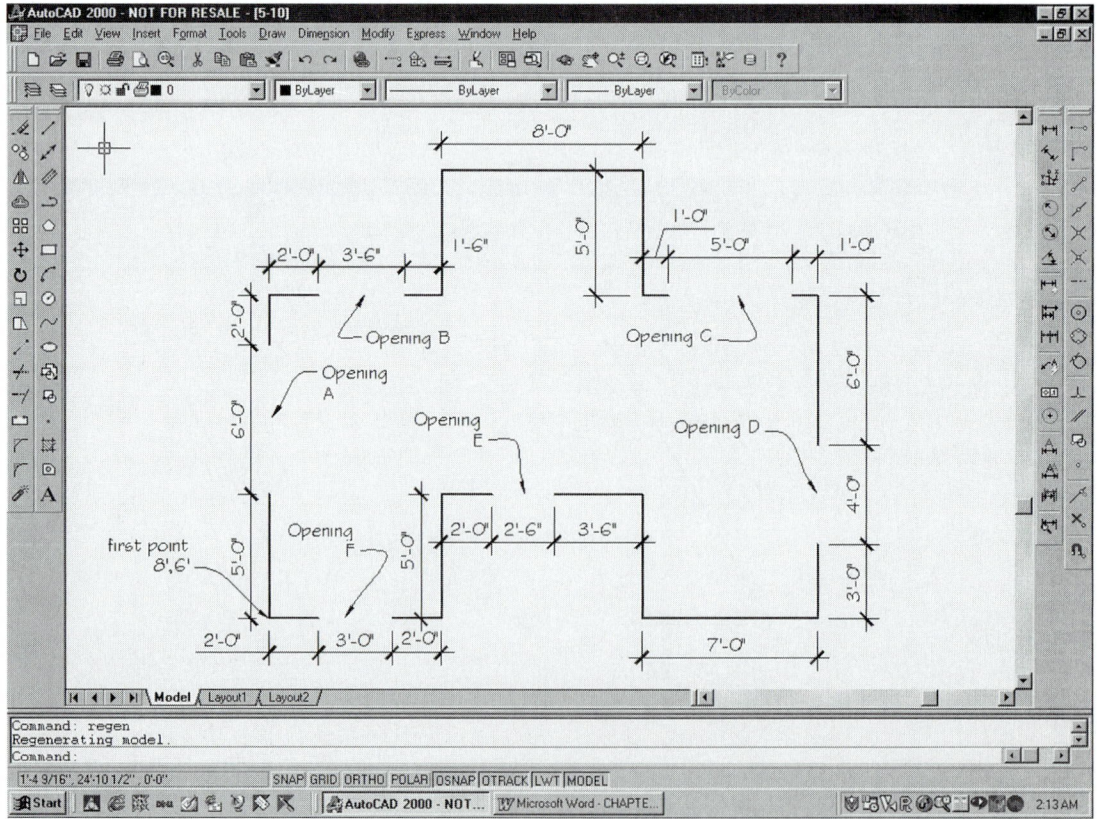

5.8 USING THE DIRECT DISTANCE POINT ENTRY SYSTEM

In addition to the absolute, relative, and polar coordinate point entry systems, AutoCAD provides another point entry system, called direct distance entry. To use this method, simply move the cursor to specify the direction and enter the distance at the keyboard. To draw horizontal and vertical lines with this method, you must turn the Ortho on. For example, to draw the line from point 1 to point 2 in Figure 5–8, use the following command procedure:

```
Command: L ~EnterKey~
Specify first point: 7',7' ~EnterKey~
Specify next point or [Undo]: (turn Ortho on and move the cursor
vertically in the direction of 90 degrees)10' ~EnterKey~
```

To draw lines that are at a specific angle, use the relative or polar coordinate system with or without the Ortho on. To draw with the direct distance point entry system again, turn Ortho on and move the cursor in the direction you want the line drawn. To draw the line from point 3 to point 4 in Figure 5–8, use the following procedure:

```
Specify next point or [Close/Undo]: (turn Ortho on and move the cursor
horizontally in the direction of 0 degrees)10' ~EnterKey~
```

Tips: Using the direct distance point entry system in combination with the Ortho and polar coordinate system increases efficiency and reduces the time it takes to create a drawing.

5.9 CREATING OPENINGS IN FLOOR PLANS

The LINE command can be used to create the appropriate door and window openings in floor plans as well as the walls. This is different than creating the entire perimeter of the floor plan and then using the BREAK or the TRIM commands to cut the door and window openings. To create openings in floor plans using the Line command, you must first draw individual line segments and then exit the LINE command. You must then reissue the LINE command and enter the opening between the first and the next wall segment as a polar coordinate (or another point entry method).

■ **EXERCISE 5–5:** *The following step-by-step exercise will help you create the door and window openings as well as the walls of the floor plan shown in Figure 5–10 using the Line button in the Draw toolbar with the polar coordinate system:*

Step #1: Start a new drawing using the Start from Scratch option.

Step #2: Use the Drawing Units dialog box to set Length Type to *Architectural.*

Step #3: Use the LIMMAX system variable to enter *44', 34'* as the new Limits. Or use the Drawing Limits option in the Format pull-down menu.

Step #4: Zoom to the Limits of the drawing.

Step #5: Use the Drafting Settings dialog box to set Grid X and Y spacing to 12".

Step #6: Turn only Grid on.

Step #7: Click on the Line button in the Draw toolbar to use the LINE command to draw the object as follows:

Command: _line Specify first point: **8', 6'** ~EnterKey~

Specify next point or [Undo]: **@5'<90** ~EnterKey~

Specify next point or [Undo]: ~EnterKey~ *(this will finish the first wall segment)*

Command: ~EnterKey~ *(this will bring back the line command)*

Line specify first point: **@6'<90** ~EnterKey~ *(this will start the next wall segment 6'-0" away from the previous point. This is opening A)*

Specify next point or [Undo]: **@2'<90** ~EnterKey~

Specify next point or [Undo]: **@2′<0** ~EnterKey~

Specify next point or [Undo]: ~EnterKey~ *(this will finish the second wall segment)*

Command: ~EnterKey~ *(this will bring back the line command)*

Line specify first point: **@3′6<0** ~EnterKey~ *(this will start the next wall segment 3′-6″ away from the previous point. This is opening B)*

Specify next point or [Undo]: **@1′6<0** ~EnterKey~

Specify next point or [Undo]: **@5′<90** ~EnterKey~

Specify next point or [Undo]: **@8′<0** ~EnterKey~

Specify next point or [Undo]: **@5′<270** ~EnterKey~

Specify next point or [Undo]: **@1′<0** ~EnterKey~

Specify next point or [Undo]: ~EnterKey~ *(this will finish the third wall segment)*

Command: ~EnterKey~ *(this will bring back the line command)*

Line specify first point: **@5′<0** ~EnterKey~ *(this will start the next wall segment 5′-0″ away from the previous point. This is opening C)*

Specify next point or [Undo]: **@1′<0** ~EnterKey~

Specify next point or [Undo]: **@6′<270** ~EnterKey~

Specify next point or [Undo]: ~EnterKey~ *(this will finish the fourth wall segment)*

Command: ~EnterKey~ *(this will bring back the line command)*

Line specify first point: **@4′<270** ~EnterKey~ *(this will start the next wall segment 4′-0″ away from the previous point. This is opening D)*

Specify next point or [Undo]: **@3′<270** ~EnterKey~

Specify next point or [Undo]: **@7′<180** ~EnterKey~

Specify next point or [Undo]: **@5′<90** ~EnterKey~

Specify next point or [Undo]: **@3′6<180** ~EnterKey~

Specify next point or [Undo]: ~EnterKey~ *(this will finish the fifth wall segment)*

Command: ~EnterKey~ *(this will bring back the line command)*

Line specify first point: **@2′6<180** ~EnterKey~ *(this will start the next wall segment 2′-6″ away from the previous point. This is opening E)*

Specify next point or [Undo]: **@2′<180** ~EnterKey~

Specify next point or [Undo]: **@5′<270** ~EnterKey~

Specify next point or [Undo]: **@2′<180** ~EnterKey~

Specify next point or [Undo]: ~EnterKey~ *(this will finish the sixth wall segment)*

Command: ~EnterKey~ *(this will bring back the line command)*

Line specify first point: **@3′<180** ~EnterKey~ *(this will start the next wall segment 3′-0″ away from the previous point. This is opening F)*

Specify next point or [Undo]: **@2′<180** ~EnterKey~

Step #8: Save this drawing as MYEXE5-9.

Congratulations! You just created the six wall openings for the floor plan shown in Figure 5–10 using the Line button in the Draw toolbar with polar coordinate system. You will add wall thicknesses to lines using the OFFSET command in Exercise 5–6.

Tips: After creating individual line segments with all the openings for a floor plan, use the OFFSET command to offset lines at a specific distance to create actual walls with thickness. You can also use the OFFSET command to offset the closed perimeter of a floor plan or an outline of a building to create a uniform wall thickness.

Note:　You can also use the MLINE (multiline) command to create floor plans. The MLEDIT (multiline edit) command allows you to cut openings in the floor plan. Drawing Multilines is discussed in Chapter 17.

5.10 USING THE COORDS SYSTEM VARIABLE

When you pick points on the screen, AutoCAD displays the current cursor location as a coordinate value in the coordinate display window located in the lower left corner of the screen. This area displays the X, Y, and Z coordinates of the points selected with the cursor. When you move your cursor, the coordinates change to represent the location of your cursor. Every time you move the cursor or select a new point on the screen the coordinates are updated to reflect the new coordinate location. For example, when you set Drawing Units to architectural, Limits to 44′, 34′, and the Grid and Snap X and Y spacing to 12″, the lower-left corner is displayed as 0′-0″, 0′-0″ and the upper-right corner is displayed as 44′-0″, 34′-0″. If you use AutoCAD default drawing settings, the number of decimal places to the right of the decimal point, or, if you use architectural drawing settings, the *length precision,* is controlled by the Drawing Units dialog box. By default, the coordinate display window is on. To turn the coordinate display window off, click on the coordinate display window in the status bar or press the function key F6. With coordinates off, no coordinates are displayed when you move the cursor but the coordinates are updated when points are picked on the screen. When used in combination with the grid and snap settings, the coordinate display window can help you identify the X and Y coordinates of points picked.

The COORDS (coordinate display style) system variable has three coordinate display modes as follows:

- When COORDS is set to 0, the coordinate display will be turned off (grayed out). This is referred to as the *static display.* With this mode the coordinates are updated only when you specify a point on the screen.

- When COORDS is set to 1, the coordinate values are updated as you move the cursor. This is referred to as the *dynamic absolute display.* With this mode the coordinate display will show coordinates based on the absolute coordinate system method such as 14′-8″, 22′-5″, 0′-0″.

- When COORDS is set to 2, the coordinate values are updated with the absolute coordinate system method as you move the cursor. However, when you specify points on the screen using the line command or any other command that prompts you for more than one point, AutoCAD will display the *distance<angle* format as in the case of the polar coordinate system. This is referred to as the *distance and angle display.*

You can also right click on the coordinate display window on the status bar to display options from a shortcut menu.

5.11 USING BLIPS IN DRAWINGS

Blips are temporary markers that appear as small plus (+) signs in the drawing screen every time you select a point, an object, or location. Figure 5–11 shows the display of blips in a drawing. The blips that appear on the drawing are used as a reference and do not plot or print. You can remove *blip marks* by entering REDRAW or REGEN at the command line, or you can click on the Redraw All button in the standard toolbar. However, this does not prevent blip marks from appearing next time you select a point. To prevent blip marks from appearing for the duration of the drawing session, you must turn the BLIPMODE system variable off as follows:

```
Command: BLIPMODE ~EnterKey~
Enter mode [ON/OFF] <ON>: OFF ~EnterKey~
```

The REDRAW and REDRAWALL commands refresh the current display by removing blip marks and pixels left behind while using the draw and editing commands. The REGEN command not only refreshes the current display but also updates the drawing database by converting the floating-point database values to the appropriate screen coordinates. In other words, REGEN command regenerates the entire screen by recalculating every single pixel point on object geometry. Because regeneration can take a long time in complex drawings, using the REDRAW command will save you drawing regeneration time. The REDRAW command can be abbreviated as R and can also be used transparently.

Tips: Use the rotating wheel in the Microsoft Intellimouse to zoom in or out to remove blip marks automatically.

TIPS

FIGURE 5–11 Blip marks are temporary + signs on the screen each time you pick a point, object, or location and are used as a reference.

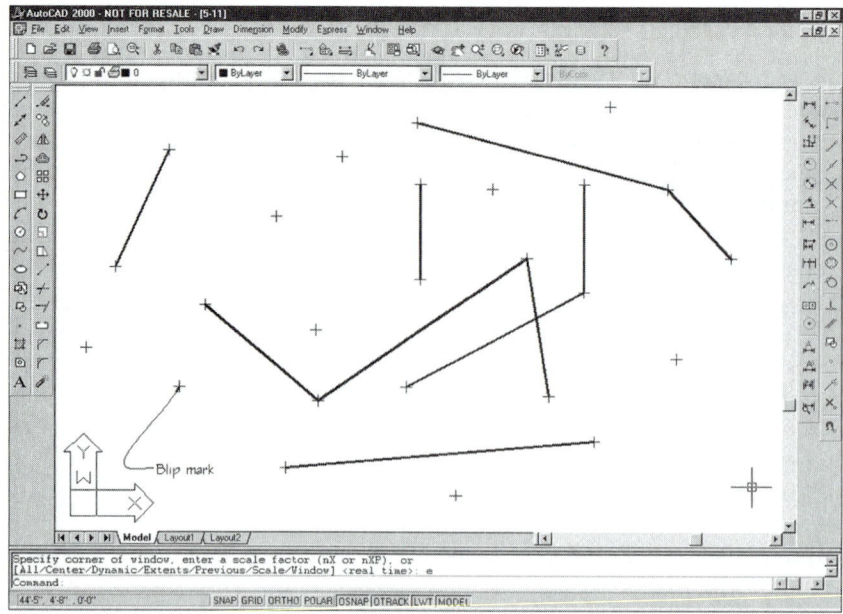

5.12 DRAWING PARALLEL LINES WITH THE OFFSET COMMAND

You already know that you can create the outline of a building using the LINE command. You can also create parallel lines from existing lines at a specified distance using the OFFSET command to represent wall segments in a floor plan. The OFFSET command will allow you to create new objects from existing objects at a distance you specify. You can offset lines, arcs, circles, polylines, ellipses, elliptical arcs, xlines, and splines. When you use the OFFSET command in conjunction with the LINE command, you can create simple and quick floor plans with specific wall thicknesses. You can access the Offset command as follows:

1. Select the Offset button in the Modify toolbar.
2. From the Modify pull-down menu, select Offset.
3. Enter O or OFFSET at the command line.

```
The command prompt is as follows:
Command: O or OFFSET ~EnterKey~
Specify offset distance or [Through] <current>:
```

You can use the Offset command in two different ways:

- Enter a distance in appropriate drawing units to specify the perpendicular distance at which you want AutoCAD to repeat the object. You can also pick two points on the screen to specify the offset distance. This is called the *offset distance* option. The value inside the brackets represents the previous offset distance used.

When you enter an offset distance, the cursor turns into a pickbox, allowing you to select the object to offset. After you select the object, the cursor returns to crosshairs, allowing you to select the side to offset. AutoCAD then repeats the two prompts allowing you to create multiple offset objects. You can end the command by pressing ~EnterKey~ at the *Select object to offset* prompt. The vertical line in Figure 5–12 is to be offset 2′-0″ to the left side to create a wall 24″ thick. The following command line procedure will help you accomplish this using the *offset distance* option:

```
Command: OFFSET ~EnterKey~
Specify offset distance or [Through] <current>: 24 ~EnterKey~
Select object to offset or <exit>: (select the object as shown. The
object will be displayed as dashed lines)
```

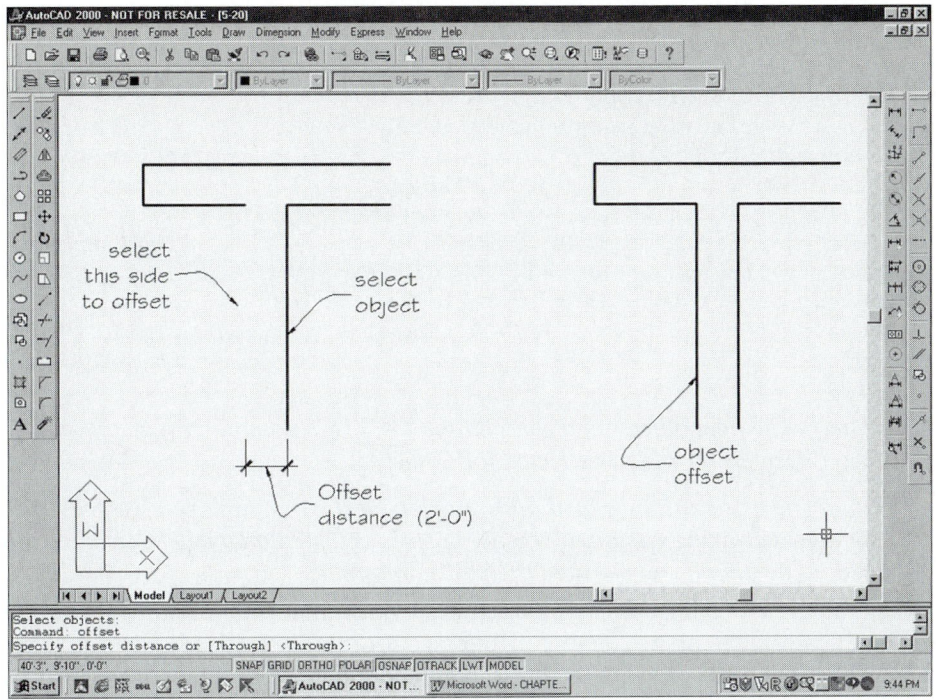

FIGURE 5–12 The *offset distance* option of the OFFSET command can be used to offset a line at a specified distance to create a wall segment.

```
Specify point on side to offset: (click on the left side of the dashed
line)
Select object to offset or <exit>: ~EnterKey~
```

Tips: If the selected object does not become dashed, turn the HIGHLIGHT system variable on.

- Specify a point for the object to pass through. This is called the *through* option. This option is also useful if you do not know the required distance but can specify a point that the new object must pass through. Figure 5–13 shows a wall segment with a door.

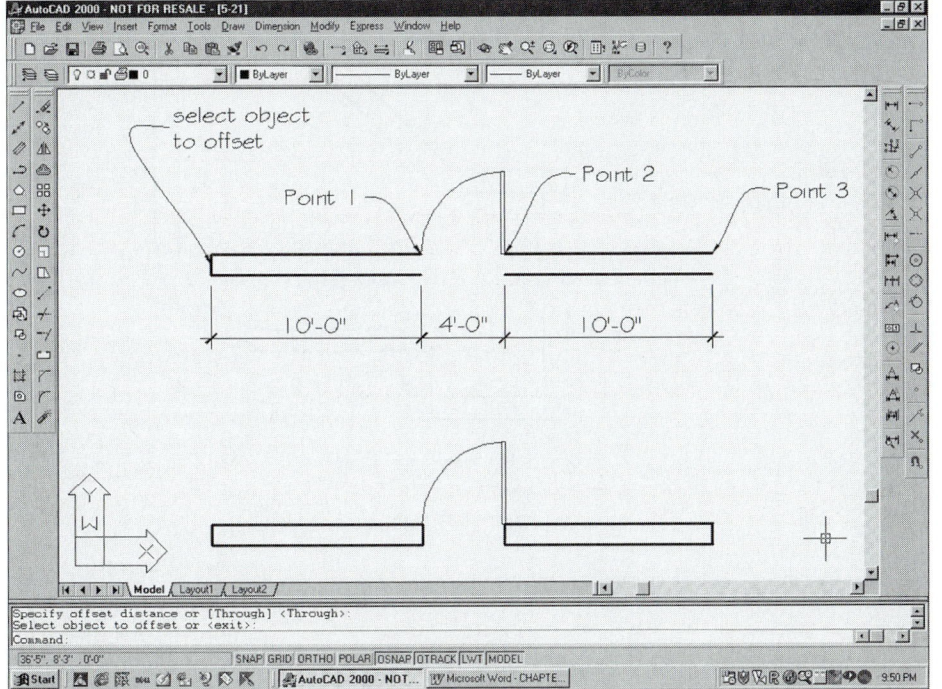

FIGURE 5–13 The *through* option of the OFFSET command can be used to offset an object by specifying a point for the object to pass through.

Points 1, 2, and 3 are missing a wall closure. Use the OFFSET command to offset the line on the left to create the three wall closures as follows:

```
Command: OFFSET ~EnterKey~
Specify offset distance or [through] <current>: T ~EnterKey~
Select object to offset or <exit>: (select the object as shown. The
object will be displayed as dashed lines)
Specify through point: @10'<0 ~EnterKey~(point 1 will be enclosed)
Select object to offset or <exit>: (select the first object again)
Specify through point: @14'<0 ~EnterKey~ (point 2 will be enclosed)
Select object to offset or <exit>: (select the first object again)
Specify through point: @24'<0 ~EnterKey~ (point 3 will be enclosed)
Select object to offset or <exit>: ~EnterKey~ (this will complete the
offset operation)
```

Note: The new objects created with the OFFSET command have the same properties (e.g. Layer) as the objects selected for Offset.

Note: The offset distance method is the default the first time you use the OFFSET command in a drawing session. If you use the through method it will be retained as the default method next time you use the OFFSET command.

When the Offset command is used to create a floor plan from existing lines, the corners do not automatically clean up or completely intersect (join). Figure 5–14 shows an example of an outline of a building created with the LINE command. In this particular drawing, the OFFSET command is then used to create the walls on the inside. As you can see from Figure 5–14, the corners of the building must be modified so that they are perfectly connected and do not overlap. The task of cleaning up the corners and intersections left from the use of the OFFSET command is accomplished by using the TRIM, CHAMFER, and FILLET commands. The TRIM command is a very powerful tool and is discussed in Chapter 12. The CHAMFER and FILLET commands are discussed in Chapter 6. Drawing door swings is accomplished by the use of the ARC command and is discussed in Chapter 6.

FIGURE 5–14   The OFFSET command creates unwanted lines at corners and intersections. These lines can be cleaned up with the TRIM, CHAMFER, and FILLET commands. These commands can also help you finish the corners that are not connected or overlap.

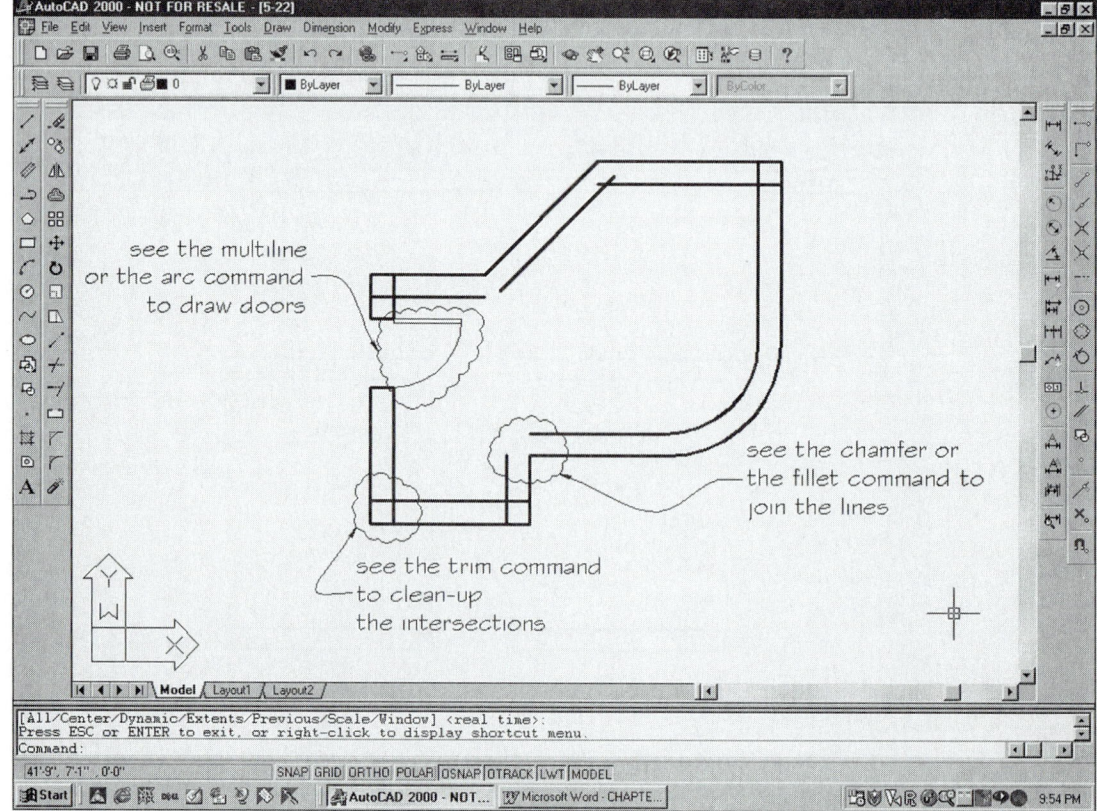

The OFFSETDIST system variable will allow you to set the default offset distance as follows:

```
Command: OFFSETDIST ~EnterKey~
Enter a new value for OFFSETDIST <1'-0">: (enter a default offset
distance value)
```

■ **EXERCISE 5–6:**   *The following step-by-step exercise will help you create a 10" thickness for the drawing created in Exercise 5–5 using Figure 5–10:*

Step #1: Open the MYEXE5-9.dwg file.

Step #2: Use the OFFSET command to create the wall thickness as follows:

```
Command: OFFSET ~EnterKey~
Specify offset distance or [through] <current>: 10 ~EnterKey~
Select object to offset or <exit>: (select one of the walls. The object
will be displayed as dashed lines)
Specify point on side to offset: (click on the inside of the wall)
Select object to offset or <exit>: ~EnterKey~
Select object to offset or <exit>: (select another wall)
Specify point on side to offset: (click on the inside of the wall)
```

Using the selection method shown above select individual walls and offset as required. Use Intellimouse rotating wheel to Pan and Zoom.

Step #3: Save this drawing as MYEXE5-10.

After offsetting all the walls your drawing should look like Figure 5–15.

Congratulations! You just created a floor plan by offsetting existing lines using the OFFSET command.

Note: To add wall caps using the LINE command, you must snap to the endpoints of lines using object snap modes. See chapter 7.

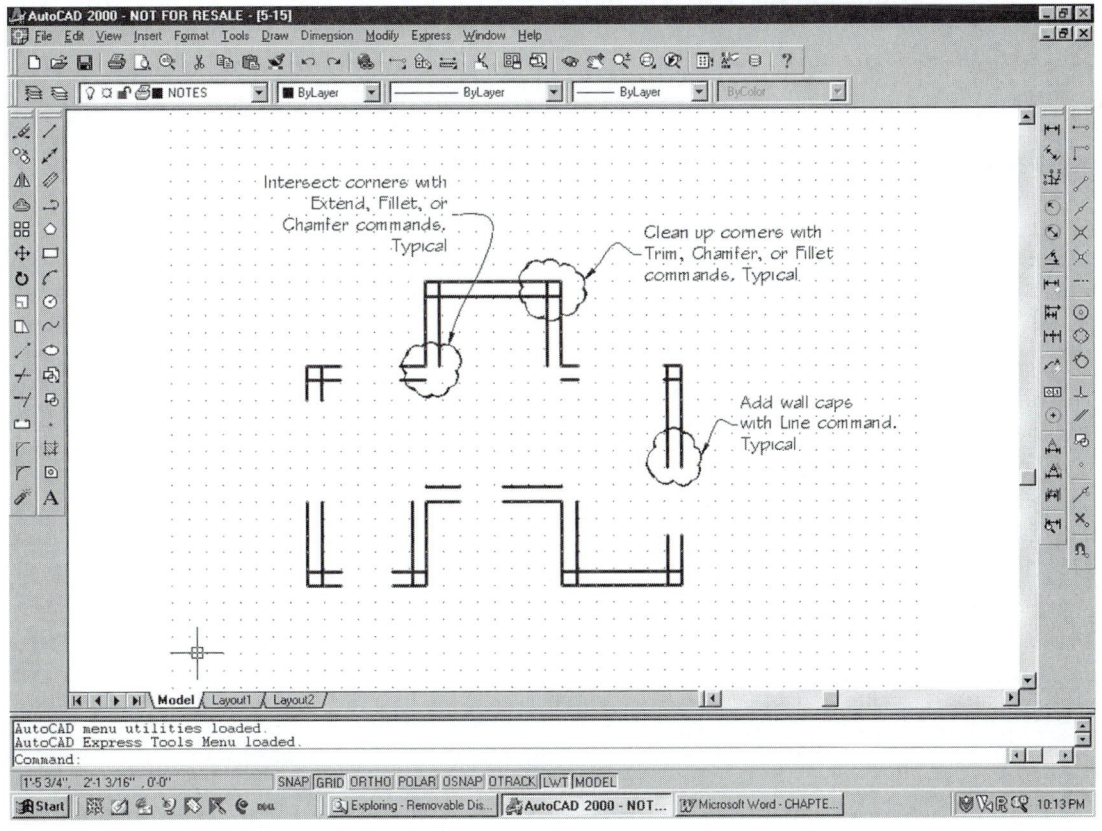

FIGURE 5–15 The lines are offset 10" to create the floor plan. Notice that wall corners must be cleaned up and capped.

5.13 CREATING CONSTRUCTION LINES

In architectural design and drafting, *construction lines* are used for reference purposes similar to using blue lines in manual drafting. These reference lines are created with the XLINE and the RAY commands. The XLINE command will place infinitely long construction lines, while the RAY command will place semi-infinite construction lines.

5.13.1   Using the XLINE Command

You can use the XLINE command to project features between drawings, especially for floor plan and elevations. To use the XLINE command, click on the Construction Line button in the Draw toolbar, enter XL or XLINE at the command line, or select Construction Line from the Draw pull-down menu. Figure 5–16 shows the placement of five construction lines used to generate the elevation from the floor plan. Figure 5–17 shows the elevation created with the help of construction lines.

The command prompt for the XLINE is as follows:

```
Command: XL ~EnterKey~
XLINE specify a point or [Hor/Ver/Ang/Bisect/Offset]: (specify a point or
enter an option)
```

The six options are as follows:

- **POINT:**   (option). This option will specify the location of the construction line using two points where it infinitely will pass through. For example, for Figure 5–16 turn Ortho off and select the building corner as the first point and select a bottom point for the through point.

- **HORIZONTAL (HOR):**   (option). This option will create a horizontal line passing through a single point parallel to the X axis. Enter H or HOR at the option command prompt. After you specify the first point, AutoCAD will keep asking you to specify through point for the second horizontal construction line. Press ~EnterKey~ when you are done.

- **VERTICAL (VER):**   (option). This option will create a vertical line passing through a single point parallel to the Y axis. Enter V or VER at the command prompt. After you specify the first point, AutoCAD will keep asking you to specify through point for the second vertical construction line. Press ~EnterKey~ when you are done.

FIGURE 5–16   The plan on top is used to create an elevation. The XLINE command is used to place infinite vertical lines and two horizontal lines to reference elevation points.

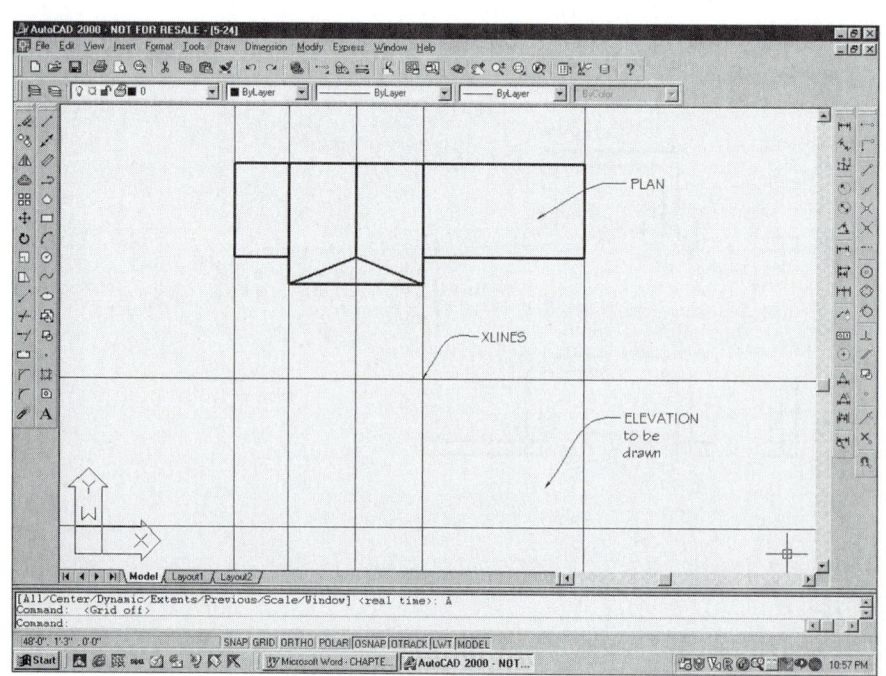

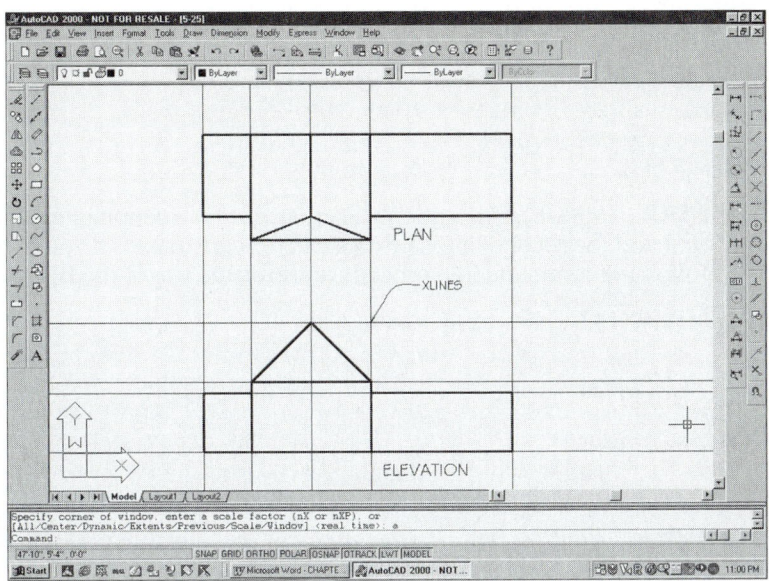

FIGURE 5–17 The elevation is created using the points located by the construction lines.

- **ANGLE (ANG):**   (option). This option will create a construction line at the angle you specify through a single point. Enter A or ANG at the command prompt. After you specify the first point AutoCAD will keep asking you to specify through point for the second construction line. Press ~EnterKey~ when you are done. Figure 5–18 shows a grid and snap spacing of 12″ and a snap angle of 30 degrees. Use the following command prompts to establish the construction lines:

```
Command: XL ~EnterKey~
XLINE Specify a point or
[Hor/Ver/Ang/Bisect/Offset]: A
~EnterKey~
Enter angle of XLINE (0) or
[Reference]: 30 ~EnterKey~
Specify through point: (turn snap on
and select the base point for the
elevation)
Specify through point: (select the
top point for the elevation)
Specify through point: (select the
other point for the elevation)
Specify through point: ~EnterKey~
(or right click to end the command)
Command: ~EnterKey~ (or use the
right click to repeat the command
from the shortcut menu)
XLINE Specify a point or
[Hor/Ver/Ang/Bisect/Offset]: (snap
to the lower left corner of the plan)
Specify through point: (move the cursor and snap to create a
perpendicular xline)
Specify through point: ~EnterKey~ (or right click to end the command)
Command: ~EnterKey~ (or use the right click to repeat the command from
the shortcut menu)
XLINE Specify a point or [Hor/Ver/Ang/Bisect/Offset]: (repeat the same
procedure above to establish other perpendicular xlines)
The [Reference] option could have been used to reference the 30 degrees
construction lines to draw the perpendicular lines at 90 degrees. The
command line procedure would have been as follows:
XLINE Specify a point or [Hor/Ver/Ang/Bisect/Offset]: A ~EnterKey~
```

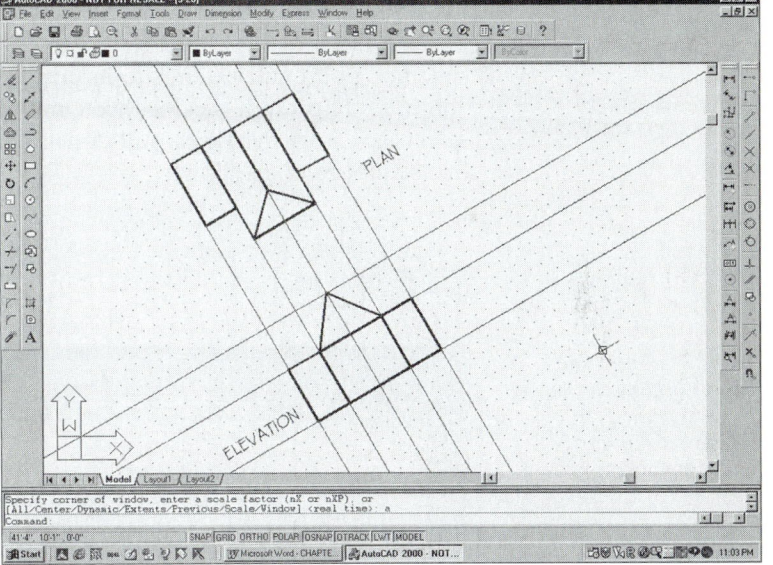

FIGURE 5–18 The Angle option of the XLINE command can be used to create construction lines at the angle you specify.

```
Enter angle of XLINE (0) or [Reference]: R ~EnterKey~
Select a line object: (select one of the construction lines drawn at 30
degrees)
Enter angle of XLINE <0>: 90 ~EnterKey~
Specify through point: (this will allow you to create construction lines
perpendicular to 30 degrees)
```

- **BISECT:** (option). This option will create a construction line that bisects an angle between the first and the second line. The construction line passes through the selected angle vertex. The following command line procedure shows the use of the Bisect option shown in Figure 5–19:

```
Command: XLINE ~EnterKey~
Specify a point or [Hor/Ver/Ang/Bisect/Offset]: B ~EnterKey~
Specify angle vertex point: (select the vertex as shown)
Specify angle start point: (select the angle start point)
Specify angle endpoint: (select the angle end point)
Specify angle end point: (if required, you can draw more xlines)
Specify angle end point: ~EnterKey~
```

- **OFFSET:** (option). This option allows you to create a construction line at a specific distance from a line object similar to the OFFSET command. The sub-options are the same as the OFFSET command.

Tips: Construction lines are object lines that can be modified with the editing commands. Since they are infinite, zooming out has no effect on their display. You can also specify a linetype for the construction lines. Erase construction lines after creating the objects.

Tips: Use Temporary Tracking Point, Object Snap Tracking, and Polar Tracking to avoid creating temporary construction lines. See Chapter 7.

5.13.2 Using the RAY Command

The RAY command will allow you to create semi-infinite construction lines. A ray starts from a specified point and extends to infinity. After you select a starting point for the ray, AutoCAD continues to prompt you for through points to create multiple rays. To use the RAY command, select Ray from the Draw pull-down menu or enter RAY at the command line. The command line sequence is as follows:

```
Command: RAY ~EnterKey~
Specify start point: (specify a starting point)
```

FIGURE 5–19 The Bisect option can be used to draw construction lines bisecting an angle.

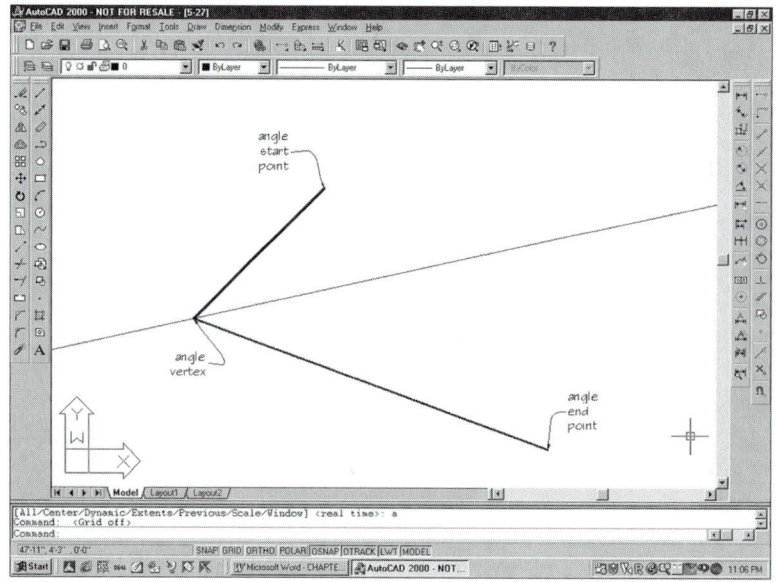

```
Specify through point: (move the cursor and specify a point the ray will
pass through)
Specify through point: (select additional points for the ray to pass
through)
Specify through point: (right click to finish the command)
```

5.14 UNDOING AND REDOING COMMANDS

Objects created in a drawing can be deleted using the ERASE command or by using the U or UNDO commands. Objects that are erased by mistake can be brought back using the REDO command. The ERASE command is explained in Chapter 12. Basically, there are two different commands available in AutoCAD to undo the most recent actions or commands you have performed: The U and the UNDO commands. Each will give you different results.

5.14.1 The U Command

The U command allows you to undo the last command after the command operation has been completed. During some of the command operations, the U option of the command also allows you to undo the last object segment you have created or the last action you have performed on the screen. As previously mentioned, the U option of the LINE command allows you to undo the last line segment. For example, the LINE, MULTILINE, POLYLINE, LENGTHEN, TRIM, and EXTEND are some of the commands that provide you with the U option to undo the previous command actions. To use the U option of a command, enter U during the command operation after you have performed at least one operation using that command.

When you enter U at the command line with no command running, AutoCAD will undo the last command operation as a GROUP. For example, if you create five wall segments using the LINE command and then exit the command to complete the operation, the five wall segments will be displayed on the screen. If you enter U at the command prompt immediately after the LINE command, the five wall segments will be deleted from the drawing. If you repeat the U command, the object(s) created with the previous command(s) will be deleted from the drawing. You can also access the U command by selecting the Undo button from the Standard toolbar or from the shortcut menu as follows:

With no commands running and no objects selected, right-click on the drawing area and select Undo from the shortcut menu. If no shortcut menu is displayed, access the Options dialog box and select the Right-click Customization. . .button to activate the right click shortcut menu.

The following command line sequence shows the undo procedure for the objects created with the MULTILINE, ARC, ELLIPSE, CIRCLE, and LINE commands:

```
Command: U ~EnterKey~
MLINE GROUP
Command: U ~EnterKey~
ARC GROUP
Command: U ~EnterKey~
ELLIPSE GROUP
Command: U ~EnterKey~
CIRCLE GROUP
Command: U ~EnterKey~
LINE GROUP
```

You can technically undo everything on the screen until AutoCAD displays the following message:

```
Everything has been undone
```

You can try the U command again but will get the following message:

```
Nothing to undo
```

5.14.2 The UNDO Command

The UNDO command will allow you to enter the number of operations to undo or select one of the six options associated with the UNDO command. Enter UNDO at the command line as follows:

```
Command: UNDO ~EnterKey~
Enter the number of operations to undo or
[Auto/Control/BEgin/End/Mark/Back] <1>:
```

The default for the number of actions to undo is 1. Enter a number to undo the specified number of actions. For example, to undo the last four actions (commands), enter 4. AutoCAD will display the four commands or system variables that are undone. The U command is equal to entering 1 at the UNDO command. The associated options are as follows:

Auto: (option). The Auto option will display the UNDO Auto mode as follows:

```
Enter the number of operations to undo or
[Auto/Control/BEgin/End/Mark/Back] <1>: A ~EnterKey~
Enter UNDO Auto mode [ON/OFF] <On>:
```

The ON option allows the UNDO command to undo any sub-commands that are part of a command group. You can reverse this action by a single U command. The OFF option allows each sub-command in a command group to be undone individually.

Control: (option). The control option allows you to limit the UNDO command options used as follows:

```
Enter the number of operations to undo or
[Auto/Control/BEgin/End/Mark/Back] <1>: C ~EnterKey~
Enter an UNDO control option [All/None/One] <All>:
```

The All option allows full UNDO command option operations. The None option disables the U command and turns the UNDO command off. When you enter U at the command line, the following message appears:

```
U command disabled. Use UNDO command to turn it on
```

The One option limits the UNDO command to a single undo operation. With this option selected, and when you enter UNDO at the command line the following prompt appears:

```
Command: UNDO ~EnterKey~
Control/<1>: ~EnterKey~
```

BEgin and End: (options). The BEgin option allows you to create a series of undo operations at once. You can put together a group of commands to be treated as a single command. When you create the group, you can use the End option of the UNDO command to undo commands that you entered after the BEgin option.

Mark and Back: (options). With the UNDO command, AutoCAD creates a list of undo operations for the open drawings. This list saves previously used UNDO commands. The Mark option allows you to place a mark in the undo list. The Back option removes all the operations created up to this mark. For example, if you do not want the lines you just drew to be removed by the UNDO command, enter UNDO and Mark option to prevent the lines from being undone. You must enter the Mark option immediately after the command operation. When you try to use the UNDO command after the Mark option, AutoCAD will display the following message:

```
Mark encountered
```

Later, if you decide to remove the *mark,* use the Back option of the UNDO command.

5.14.3 The REDO Command

The REDO command will restore a single U or UNDO command. The REDO command must immediately follow the U or the UNDO command. You can access the REDO command by entering REDO at the command line, selecting the Redo button in the Standard toolbar, or selecting Redo from the Edit pull-down menu.

Project Tutorial The following is a step-by-step tutorial that will reinforce the use of the following commands and procedures learned in Chapters 1 through 5:

1. Creating a drawing using the Start from Scratch option.
2. Using the Drawing Units dialog box to establish drawing units and precision.
3. Using the LIMMAX system variable to establish new drawing limits.
4. Using the Drafting Settings dialog box to establish grid spacing.
5. Using the polar coordinate system with the LINE command.

This Project Tutorial will walk you through the proper command sequence to complete the kitchen cabinet elevation shown in Figure 5–20. Do not create dimensions or text at this time. Only the commands and procedures learned up to this point will be practiced in this tutorial. Figure 5–20 shows the major dimensions (lengths) needed to create the Kitchen Cabinet Elevation. Figure 5–21 shows the coordinate point for the starting point and the coordinate points to be determined for points A, B, C, D, E, and F. Use the following data when creating drawing settings and aids:

```
Drawing Units: Architectural
Drawing Scale: 1 1/2" = 1'-0"
Sheet Size to be plotted: A (8 1/2" × 11")
```

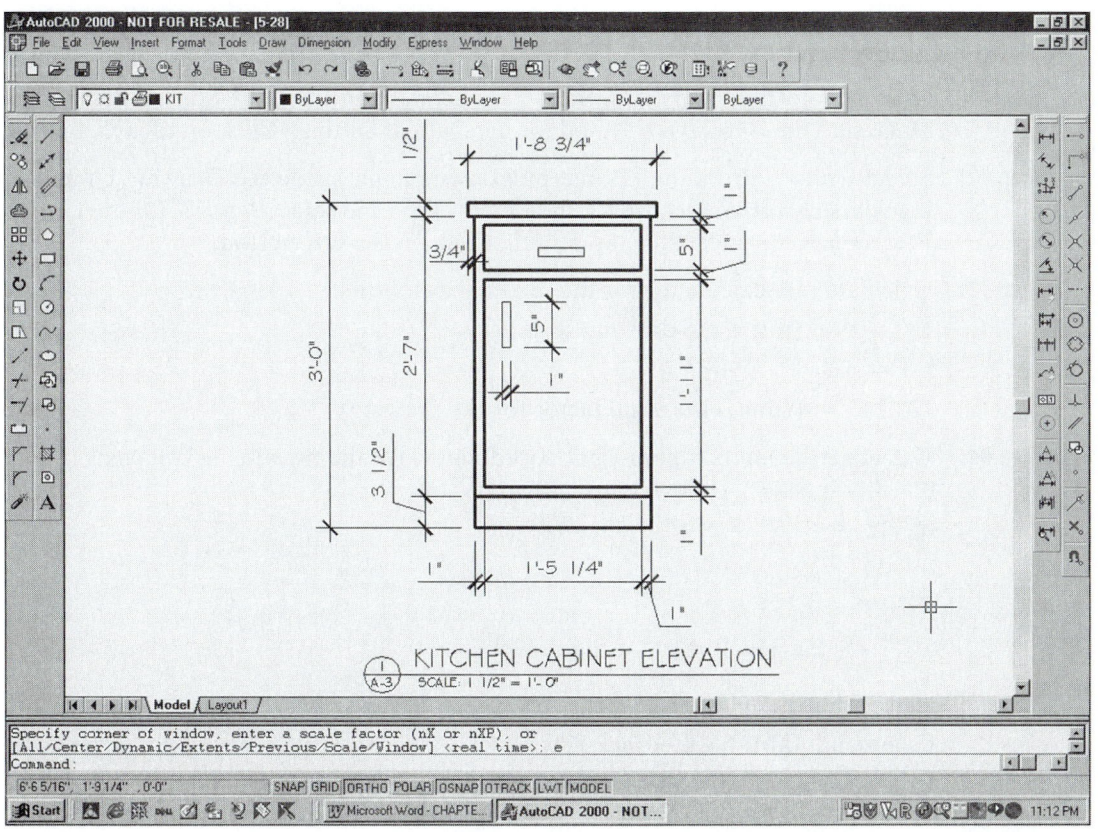

FIGURE 5–20 The kitchen cabinet elevation with dimensions and text.

FIGURE 5–21   The kitchen cabinet elevation with coordinates for points A, B, C, D, E, and F.

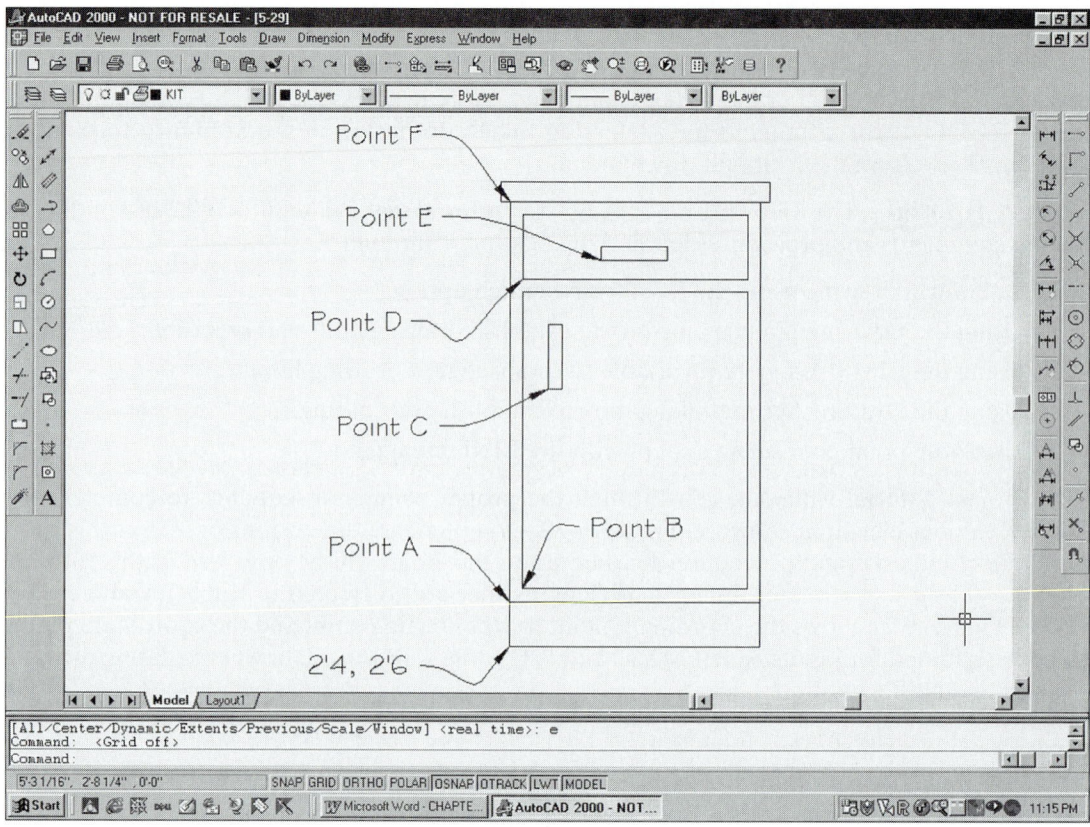

Let's start the project:

Step #1:   Launch AutoCAD and select Start from Scratch button in the Startup dialog box. Make sure the *English* is selected for the Default Settings. Click on the OK button.

Step #2:   Select Units . . . from the Format pull-down menu. Inside the Drawing Units dialog box, select *Architectural* for the Length Type and select *0'-0 1/2"* for the Length Precision. Keep everything as default. Click on the OK button.

Step #3:   Calculate the scale factor for the drawing as follows:

$1\frac{1}{2}"$ = 1'-0" (this is the drawing scale)

1.5" = 12"

12"/1.5" = 8 (this is the scale factor for the drawing)

Step #4:   Calculate the limits (upper-right coordinates) for the drawing as follows:

8 × 8½" = 68"

68"/12" = 5.667' = 5'-8"

8 × 11" = 88"

88"/12" = 7.333' = 7'-4"

5'8, 7'4 is the new Limits for the drawing.

Step #5:   Establish the new Limits for the drawing as follows:

Command: **LIMMAX** ~EnterKey~

Enter new value for LIMMAX <1'-0", 0'-9">: **5'8, 7'4** ~EnterKey~

Step #6:   Zoom to the Limits of the drawing as follows:

Command: **ZOOM** ~EnterKey~

Specify corner of window, enter a scale factor (nX or nXP), or

[All/Center/Dynamic/Extents/Previous/Scale/Window] , real time.: **ALL** ~EnterKey~

Step #7: Establish Grid Spacing as follows:

Right click on the GRID button in the Status bar and select Settings. . . from the shortcut menu. Inside the Drafting Settings dialog box, select the Snap and Grid tab and change Grid X and Y spacing from ½″ to 2″. Place a check mark inside the Grid On [F7] check box and click on the OK button.

Step #8: Create the object as follows:

Command: **LINE** ~EnterKey~

Specify first point: **2′4, 2′6** ~EnterKey~

Specify next point or [Undo]: *(click on the ORTHO button in the Status bar)* **@1′7-1/4<0** ~EnterKey~

Specify next point or [Undo]: **@2′10-1/2<90** ~EnterKey~

Specify next point or [Close/Undo]: **@3/4<0** ~EnterKey~

Specify next point or [Close/Undo]: **@1-1/2<90** ~EnterKey~

Specify next point or [Close/Undo]: **@1′8-3/4<180** ~EnterKey~

Specify next point or [Close/Undo]: **@1-1/2<270** ~EnterKey~

Specify next point or [Close/Undo]: **@3/4<0** ~EnterKey~

Specify next point or [Close/Undo]: **C** ~EnterKey~

Command: ~EnterKey~ *(this will bring back the LINE command)*

LINE Specify first point: **2′4, 2′9-1/2** ~EnterKey~ *(this is the coordinates for point A)*

Specify next point or [Undo]: **@1′7-1/4<0** ~EnterKey~

Specify next point or [Undo]: ~EnterKey~

Command: ~EnterKey~

LINE Specify first point: **2′5, 2′10-1/2** ~EnterKey~ *(this is the coordinates for point B)*

Specify next point or [Undo]: **@1′5-1/4<0** ~EnterKey~

Specify next point or [Undo]: **@1′11<90** ~EnterKey~

Specify next point or [Close/Undo]: **@1′5-1/4<180** ~EnterKey~

Specify next point or [Close/Undo]: **@1′11<270** ~EnterKey~

Specify next point or [Close/Undo]: ~EnterKey~

Command: ~EnterKey~

LINE Specify first point: **2′7, 4′2** ~EnterKey~ *(this is the coordinates for point C)*

Specify next point or [Undo]: **@1<0** ~EnterKey~

Specify next point or [Undo]: **@5<90** ~EnterKey~

Specify next point or [Close/Undo]: **@1<180** ~EnterKey~

Specify next point or [Close/Undo]: **C** ~EnterKey~

Command: ~EnterKey~

LINE Specify first point: **2′5, 4′10-1/2** ~EnterKey~ *(this is the coordinates for Point D)*

Specify next point or [Undo]: **@1′5-1/4<0** ~EnterKey~

Specify next point or [Undo]: **@5<90** ~EnterKey~

Specify next point or [Close/Undo]: **@1′5-1/4<180** ~EnterKey~

Specify next point or [Close/Undo]: **C** ~EnterKey~

Command: ~EnterKey~

LINE Specify first point: **2′11, 5′** ~EnterKey~ *(this is the coordinates for point E)*

Specify next point or [Undo]: **@5<0** ~EnterKey~

Specify next point or [Undo]: **@1<90** ~EnterKey~

Specify next point or [Close/Undo]: **@5<180** ~EnterKey~

Specify next point or [Close/Undo]: **C** ~EnterKey~

Command: ~EnterKey~

LINE Specify first point: **2′4, 5′4-1/2**~EnterKey~ *(this is the coordinates for point F)*

Specify next point or [Undo]: **@1′7-1/2<0** ~EnterKey~

Specify next point or [Undo]: ~EnterKey~

Congratulations! You have successfully completed the Kitchen Cabinet Elevation shown in Figure 5–20. Your final drawing should look like Figure 5–20 without the dimensions and text.

REVIEW QUESTIONS

1. How many different ways can you access the LINE command?
2. What is the difference between entering U while the LINE command is running and entering U after the LINE command is completed?
3. What is the general purpose behind using the grid and snap spacing in conjunction with the LINE command?
4. Briefly describe the three different Cartesian coordinate point entry methods used in AutoCAD.
5. Is the @12′, 15′<180 a valid entry in AutoCAD?
6. Which coordinate point entry method is represented by the following entries:

   3′6, 4′10″ _____

   @27′5-3/4<180 _____

   @9,12 _____

7. When using the direct distance point entry system, is it necessary to turn Ortho mode on?
8. What is the function of the COORDS system variable?
9. How do you remove the blip marks from the screen for the duration of the drawing session?
10. Describe the two options associated with the OFFSET command.
11. What is the function of the XLINE command?
12. What is the difference between the U and the UNDO commands?

PROBLEMS

1. Create the outline of the building shown in Figure 5–22. Establish Limits based on given data. Create a Grid X and Y spacing of 24″. Do not create dimensions or text. The starting point is at 6′, 6′. Use the absolute coordinate system. Save your drawing as MYEXE5-1.
2. Create the elevation shown in Figure 5–23. Establish Limits based on given data. Create a Grid X and Y spacing of 36″. Calculate the coordinates for the points shown with X and start drawing from those locations. The starting point is 10′, 10′. Do not create dimensions and text. Save your drawing as MYEXE5-2.
3. Create the outline of the building shown in Figure 5–24. Establish Limits based on given data. Create a Grid X and Y spacing of 24″. Do not create dimensions or text. The starting point is 14′, 14′. Use the relative coordinate system. Save your drawing as MYEXE5-3.
4. Open the MYEXE5-1.dwg file. Use the OFFSET command and offset the lines 10″ inward. This will give you a floor plan with 6″ thick walls. Save your drawing as MYEXE5-4. You will open this drawing in Chapter 6 and use the CHAMFER and FILLET commands to clean up the intersections created by the OFFSET command.
5. Open the MYEXE5-3.dwg file. Use the OFFSET command and offset the lines 8″ inward. This will give you a floor plan with 8″ thick walls. Save your drawing as MYEXE5-5. You will open this

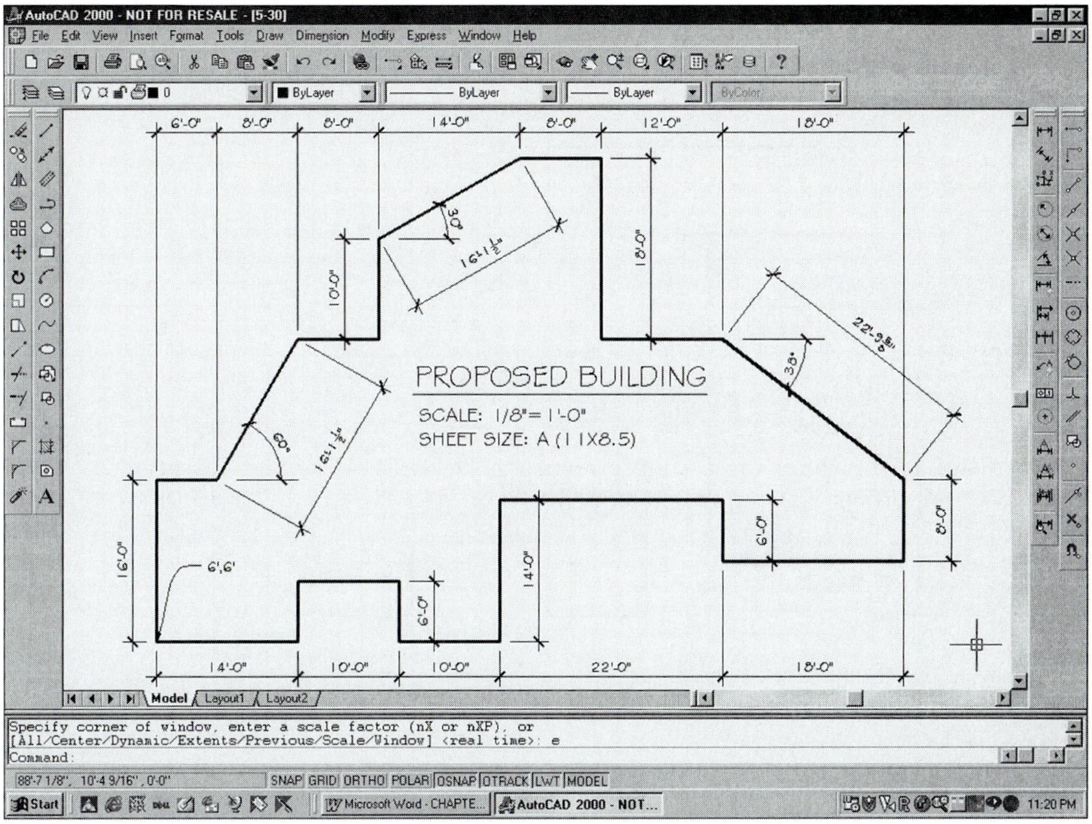

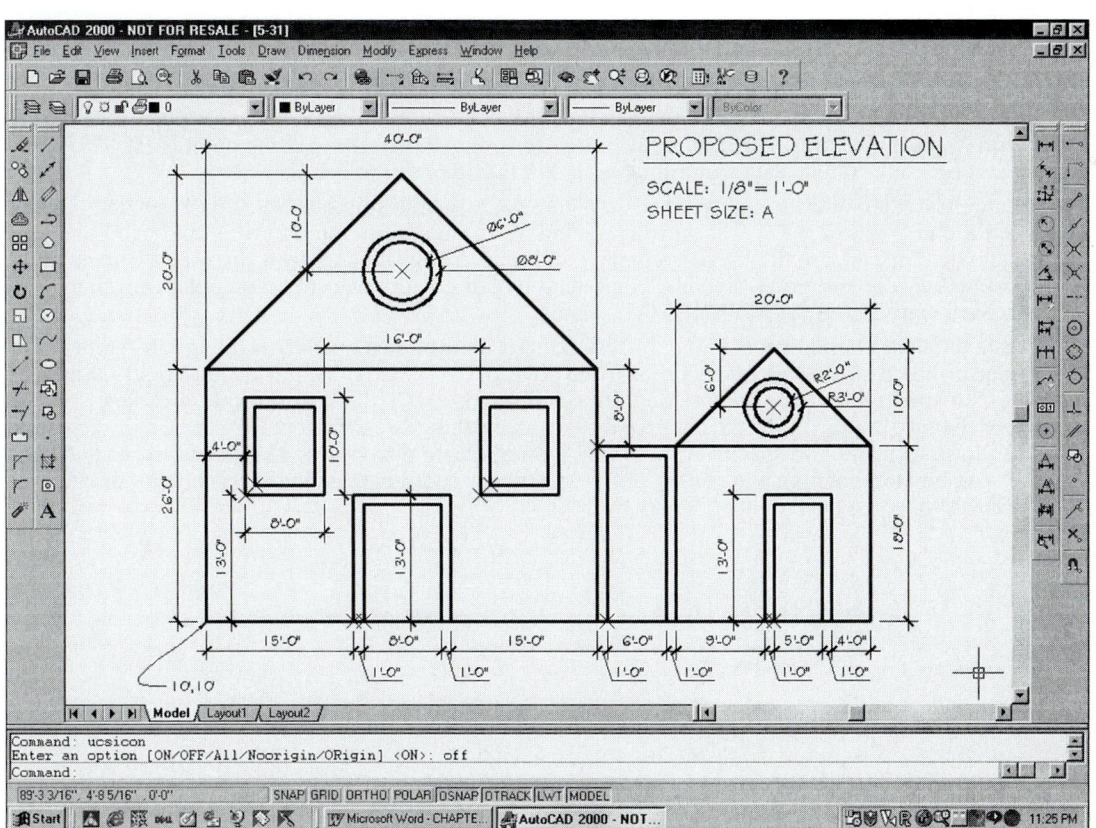

FIGURE 5–22 Problem 5–1.

FIGURE 5–23 Problem 5–2.

FIGURE 5–24 Problem 5–3.

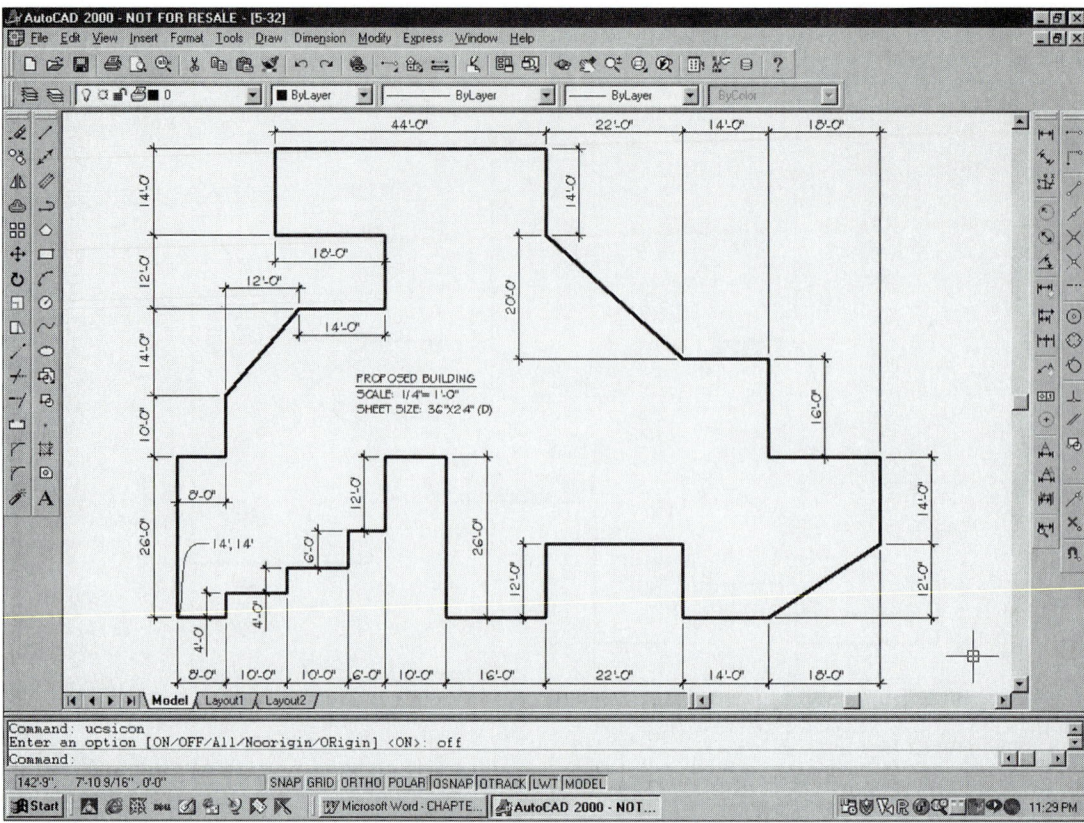

drawing in Chapter 6 and use the CHAMFER and FILLET commands to clean up the intersections created by the OFFSET command.

6. Create the outline of the building shown in Figure 5–25. Establish Limits based on given data. Create a Grid X and Y spacing of 36″. Do not create dimensions or text. The starting point is 15′, 9′. Use the polar coordinate system. Save your drawing as MYEXE5-6.

7. Create the outline of the building shown in Figure 5–26. Establish Limits based on given data. Create a grid X and Y spacing of 6″. The starting point is 4′, 6′. Do not use the OFFSET command to create inside lines. Instead, use the LINE command and snap/grid spacing to draw the wall thickness of 6″. Do not create dimensions or text. Use combination of direct distance entry and polar coordinate system. Save your drawing as MYEXE5-7.

8. Create the floor plan shown in Figure 5–27. Establish Limits based on given data. Create a grid X and Y spacing based on wall thickness. The starting point is 8′, 4′. Create the outside lines first. Adjust grid and snap spacing to create inside lines. Outside brick is 3 1/2″ thick. Total wall thickness is 16″ as shown. Do not use the OFFSET command to create wall thickness. Instead, use the LINE command and adjust snap and grid spacing accordingly. Do not create dimensions, text, furniture, or hatching. Use combination of direct distance entry and polar coordinate system. Save your drawing as MYEXE5-8.

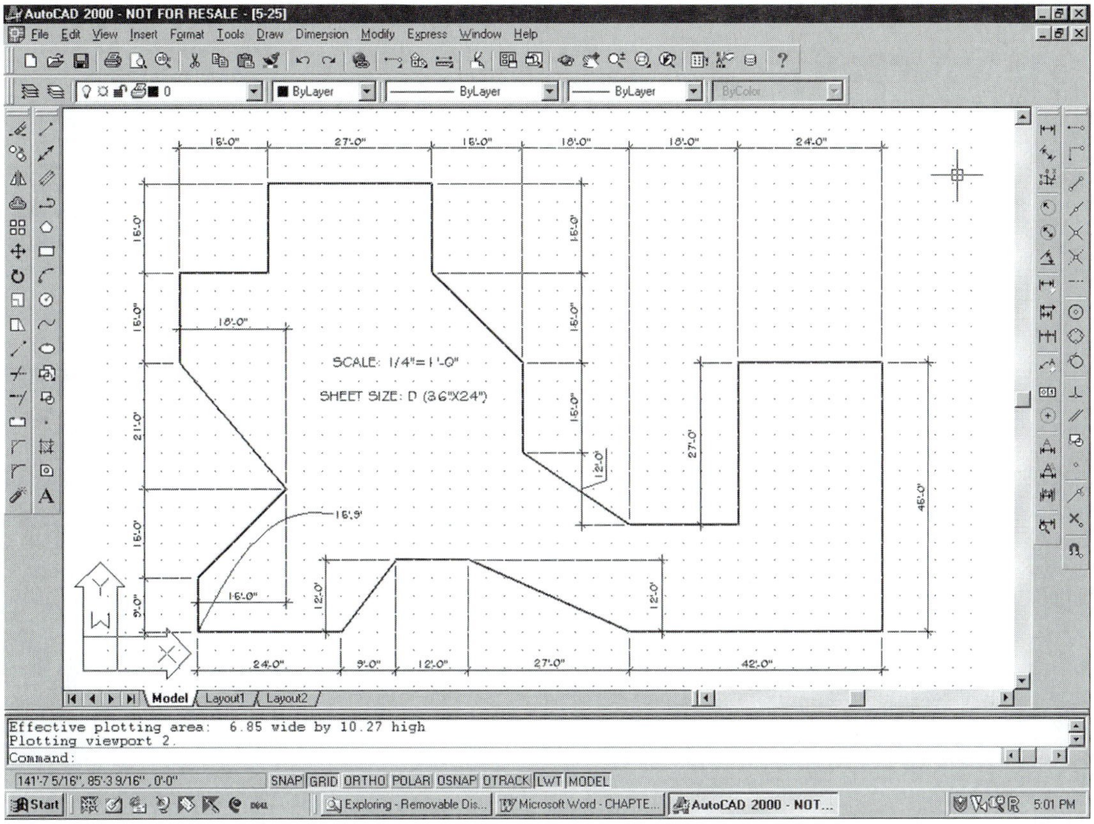

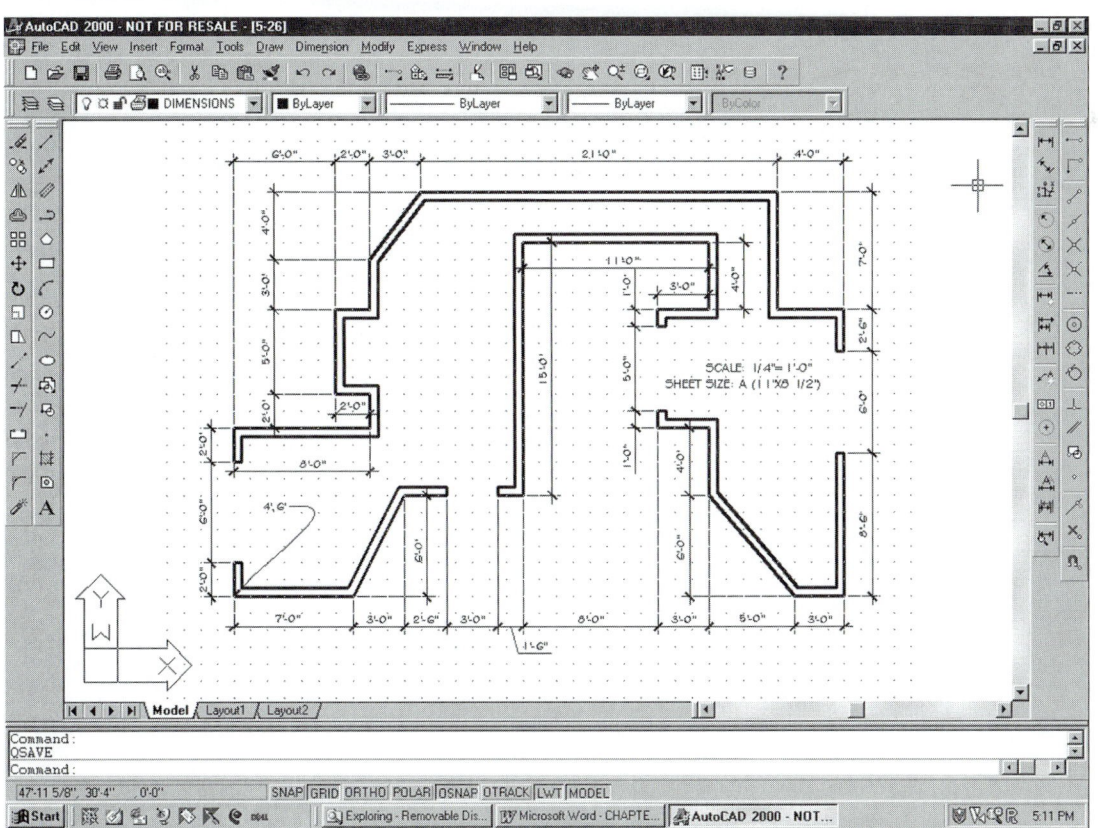

FIGURE 5–25 Problem 5–6.

FIGURE 5–26 Problem 5–7.

FIGURE 5–27   Problem
5–8.

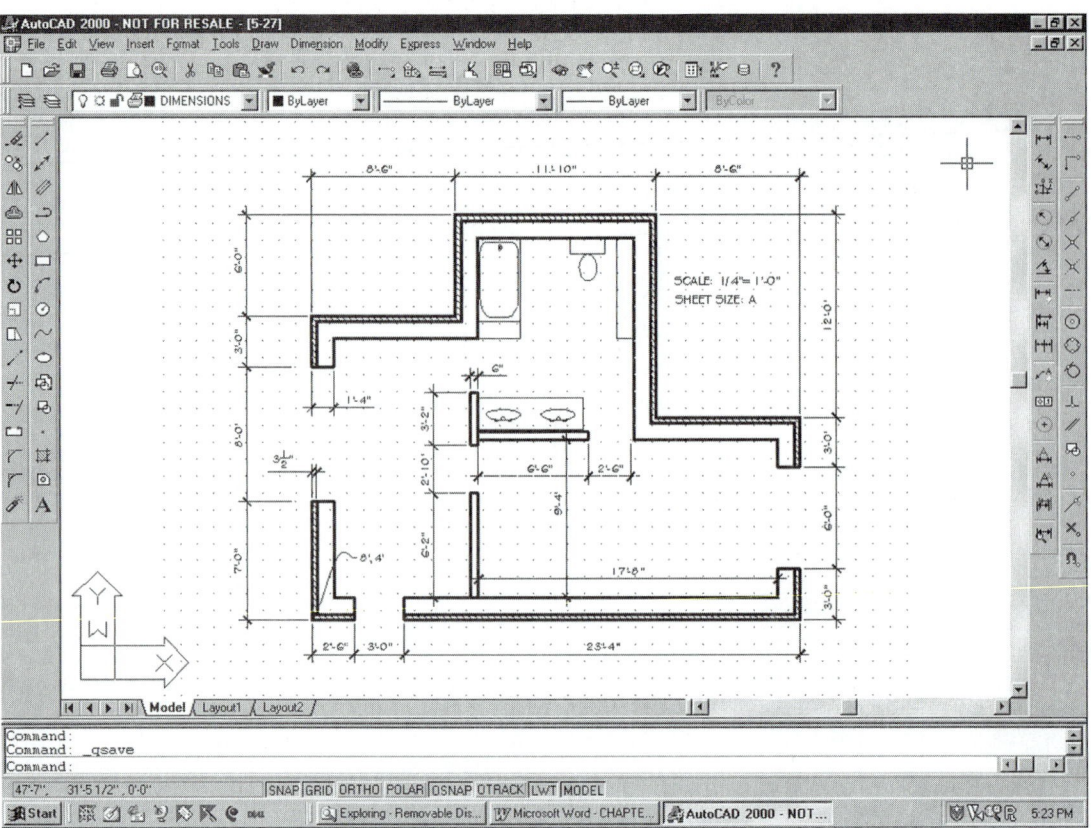

Drawing Basic Objects and Shapes

6

After successful completion of this chapter you should be able to:

▲ Use the DRAGMODE system variable.

▲ Understand the difference between single-entity objects and multi-entity objects.

▲ Use the PLINE command to draw polylines.

▲ Use the three different options of the CIRCLE command to draw circles.

▲ Use the ARC command to draw different arcs.

▲ Use the Center, Start, End option of the ARC command to draw door swings.

▲ Use the ELLIPSE command.

▲ Create elliptical arcs.

▲ Create isometric circles.

▲ Draw circular polylines.

▲ Draw solid circles with the DONUT command.

▲ Use the SOLID command.

▲ Draw rectangles with the RECTANG command.

▲ Draw POLYGONS with different sides.

▲ Use the CHAMFER command to draw angled corners.

▲ Use the FILLET command to draw round corners.

▲ Use the CHAMFER and FILLET commands to trim intersecting lines.

▲ Draw free-hand lines with the SKETCH command.

▲ Use the SPLINE command to draw multipoint curves.

▲ Use the REVCLOUD command to draw revision clouds.

▲ Use the REVCLOUD command to draw trees and bushes for site plans.

▲ Use the ZIGZAG linetype to draw trees.

6.1 THE DRAGGING EFFECT OF OBJECTS

When a new object is created, a physical connection is established between the point selected on the screen, the object itself, and the cursor. The ability to create new objects dynamically and drag them into a new position using the cursor is referred to as the *drag mode* affect. Some of the commands, such as CIRCLE, ARC, POLYGON, ELLIPSE, and RECTANG, will display a rubber band line attached to the cursor and the image of the object attached to the end of the line after establishing the start point. As you drag the cursor, the image of the object evolves and becomes larger or smaller, depending on how far you move the cursor away from the pick point or closer to the pick point. You can then select a point on the screen to finalize the size, shape, or composition of the object being drawn. When an existing object is edited, the same connection is established, and you can drag the objects to a new location using many of the editing commands.

6.1.1   The DRAGMODE System Variable

The DRAGMODE system variable controls the visibility of the object(s) connected to the end-point of the rubber band line and allows you to see the objects drag into place. Enter DRAG-MODE at the command line as follows:

```
Command: DRAGMODE ~EnterKey~
Enter new value [ON/OFF/Auto] <Auto>:
```

There are three options associated with the DRAGMODE system variable.

- **AUTO:**   (option). This option automatically drags objects by connecting the object to the cursor. This will turn on dragging for each command supporting it.

- **ON:**   (option). This option will permit dragging, but only after you enter DRAG during the command sequence.

- **OFF:**   (option). This option will turn Drag mode off. This means that the objects are not visible on the screen until their location is picked with the cursor. Entering DRAG will be ignored.

   Note: When you edit objects, the original object(s) will appear dashed until the editing command is finished. When the DRAGMODE system variable is set to Auto, the object(s) to be edited will be dragged into place.

6.2 SINGLE AND MULTI-ENTITY OBJECTS

In Chapter 5 you learned the basic concept behind single and multi-entity objects. This chapter will cover the concept a bit further. Some commands create a series of connected object segments as a *multi-entity* object. You learned in the previous chapter that the objects created with the LINE command are multi-entity objects. Some commands create an entire object as a *single entity,* such as the RECTANG, PLINE, MLINE, SPLINE, and POLYGON commands. This means that the individual objects that make up the single entity composition cannot be edited on an individual basis; rather the entire object as a whole is edited. Some of the advantages of a single-entity object are as follows:

1. The entire object geometry can be edited by selecting just one common object as opposed to individual selections or placing a window around the object geometry.

2. The entire object geometry can be dimensioned using the QDIM (quick dimension) command by selecting just one common object as opposed to individual selections or placing a window around the object geometry.

3. The entire object geometry can be patterned using the HATCH command by selecting just one common object as opposed to individual selections or placing a window around the object geometry.

A multi-entity object can be turned into a single-entity object using the PEDIT command. A single-entity object can be turned into a multi-entity object using the EXPLODE command. These commands are explained in Chapter 12.

6.3 DRAWING POLYLINES

A polyline is composed of series of connected line and arc segments that is created as a single entity. Because objects created as a polyline are single-entity objects, editing all polyline segments at once is possible. The ability to edit many object segments at once is a great time saver, especially on large projects. Polylines are created with the PLINE command. To draw polylines, enter PL or PLINE at the command line, select Polyline from the Draw pull-down menu, or click on the Polyline button in the Draw toolbar. The PLINE command creates objects similar to the LINE command but has more options relating to the composition, format, and width of the line segments. The PEDIT command is used to edit polylines. The PLINE command has the following advantages:

1. You can draw a polyline with a specific width as opposed to assigning a lineweight to a line.
2. Polylines are single-entity objects; therefore the entire polyline can be selected for editing operations. You can also edit polyline segments singly.
3. Tapered and arc segments can be drawn and made a part of the polylines.
4. You can create polyline arc segments that are automatically attached to the endpoint of the previous polyline segment. You can specify the angle, center point, second point, endpoint, direction, or radius of the polyline arc.
5. You can assign different widths to individual polyline segments.
6. You can change the width of the individual polyline segments using the PEDIT command.
7. You can easily calculate the area and the length of a polyline.
8. Polylines use less memory space and take up less disk space than regular line segments.

Although there are many advantages to the PLINE command, it is nevertheless a very complex command. When you access the PLINE command, you are asked to *specify start point,* similar to the LINE command. When you select a start point for the polyline, you are then given information about the current width of the polyline. This information is useful since you do not have to select the *Width* option to check on the current polyline width status. If the current width of the polyline is not to your specifications, you can use the width option to change it. The command line procedure for the PLINE command is as follows:

```
Command: PLINE ~EnterKey~
Specify start point: (select a starting point for the polyline)
Current line-width is 0'-0" (this represents architectural units and
settings)
Specify next point or [Arc/Close/Halfwidth/Length/Undo/Width]: (specify a
next point or enter an option)
```

If you do not enter any of the six options, you can use the PLINE command exactly as you would use the LINE command. The width of 0'-0" will create a default line width similar to the lines created with the LINE command. The default lineweight is 0.01". Lineweights are discussed in Chapter 9. The six options of the PLINE command are as follows:

- **ARC:** (option). The Arc option allows you to add polyline arcs while using the PLINE command. It is similar to the ARC command but has specific options relating to the polylines. The ARC command is discussed later in the chapter. You can enter the arc option anytime at the *Specify next point* prompt. The arc option is entered as follows:

```
Command: PLINE ~EnterKey~
Specify start point: (select a starting point for the polyline)
Current line -width is 0'-0" (this represents architectural units and
settings)
Specify next point or [Arc/Close/Halfwidth/Length/Undo/Width]: A
~EnterKey~
Specify endpoint of arc or
[Angle/CEnter/CLose/Direction/Halfwidth/Line/Radius/Second
pt/Undo/Width]:
```

The *Specify endpoint of arc* draws an arc segment tangent to the previous point of the polyline segment. The distance specified for the endpoint of the arc determines the diameter for the arc. Once the arc is drawn, AutoCAD repeats the *Specify endpoint of arc or* prompt. You can return to creating polylines by entering the Line option.

Figure 6–1 shows an outline of a building created with the PLINE command and a polyline width of 2″.

■ **EXERCISE 6–1:**   *The following step-by-step exercise will help you create the outline of the building shown in Figure 6–1. The final plot scale is 1/4″ = 1′-0″ to be plotted on "A" size (8 1/2″ × 11″) paper vertically. This corresponds to drawing limits of 34′, 44′. There are two polyline arcs created in this drawing.*

Step #1:   Establish drawing Limits as 34′, 44′.

Step #2:   Use the PLINE command as follows:

Command: **PLINE** ~EnterKey~

Specify start point: (*select the start point shown in Figure 6–1*)

Current line –width is 0′-0″ (*this corresponds to architectural drawing units and settings*)

Specify next point or [Arc/Close/Halfwidth/Length/Undo/Width]: **W** ~EnterKey~

Specify starting width <0′-0″>: **2** ~EnterKey~

Specify ending width <0′-2″>: ~EnterKey~

Specify next point or [Arc/Close/Halfwidth/Length/Undo/Width]: **@11′<0** ~EnterKey~

Specify next point or [Arc/Close/Halfwidth/Length/Undo/Width]: **@7′<270** ~EnterKey~

Specify next point or [Arc/Close/Halfwidth/Length/Undo/Width]: **@6′<0** ~EnterKey~

Specify next point or [Arc/Close/Halfwidth/Length/Undo/Width]: **A** ~EnterKey~

Specify endpoint of arc or

[Angle/CEnter/CLose/Direction/Halfwidth/Line/Radius/Second pt/Undo/Width]: **@9′<270** ~EnterKey~

Specify endpoint of arc or

[Angle/CEnter/CLose/Direction/Halfwidth/Line/Radius/Second pt/Undo/Width]: **L** ~EnterKey~

Specify next point or [Arc/Close/Halfwidth/Length/Undo/Width]: **@5′<270** ~EnterKey~

Specify next point or [Arc/Close/Halfwidth/Length/Undo/Width]: **@6′<180** ~EnterKey~

Specify next point or [Arc/Close/Halfwidth/Length/Undo/Width]: **@5′<90** ~EnterKey~

Specify next point or [Arc/Close/Halfwidth/Length/Undo/Width]: **@11′<180** ~EnterKey~

Specify next point or [Arc/Close/Halfwidth/Length/Undo/Width]: **A** ~EnterKey~

Specify endpoint of arc or

[Angle/CEnter/CLose/Direction/Halfwidth/Line/Radius/Second pt/Undo/Width]: **@6′<90** ~EnterKey~

Specify endpoint of arc or

[Angle/CEnter/CLose/Direction/Halfwidth/Line/Radius/Second pt/Undo/Width]: **L** ~EnterKey~

Specify next point or [Arc/Close/Halfwidth/Length/Undo/Width]: **@10′<270** OR **C** ~EnterKey~

Congratulations! You have created the outline of the building shown in Figure 6–1 using the PLINE command. Specifically, you have used the Width, Arc, and the Line options of the PLINE command.

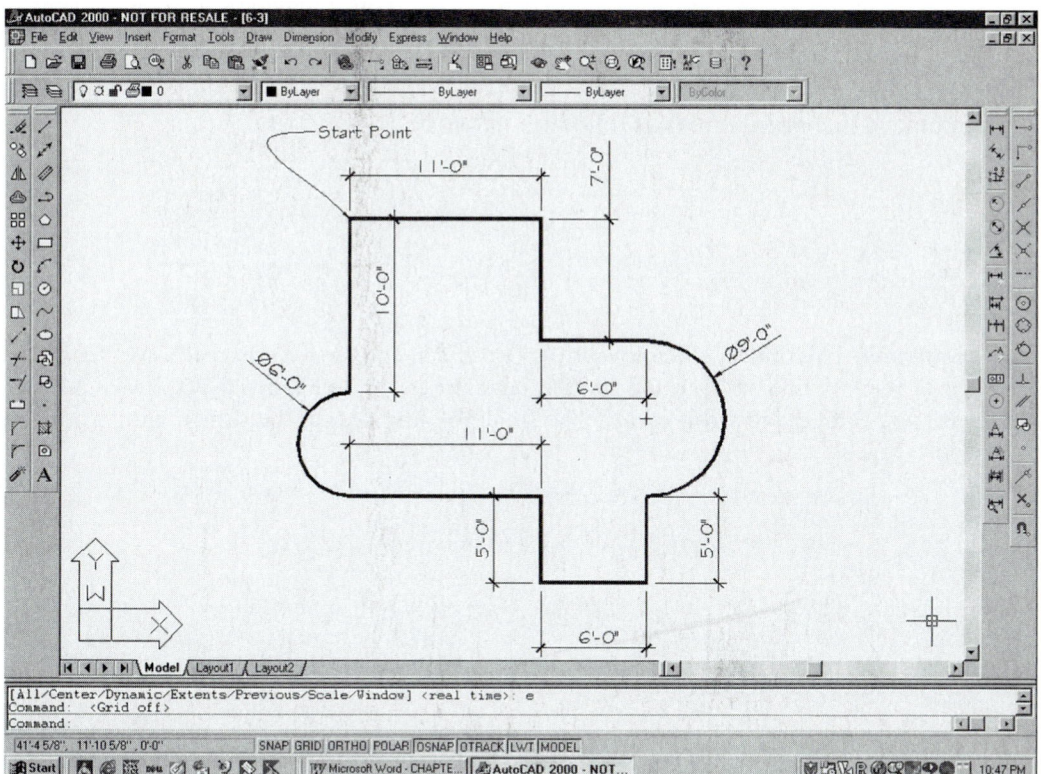

FIGURE 6–1 The object created with the PLINE command using the Width, Arc, and Line options.

The Arc option of the PLINE command has ten sub-options as follows:

1. **Angle:** This option will allow you to create the included angle of the arc segment. You can enter a positive number to create a counterclockwise angle or a negative number to create a clockwise angle. The command line procedure to use this option for Figure 6–1 is as follows:

```
Specify next point or [Arc/Close/Halfwidth/Length/Undo/Width]: A ~EnterKey~
Specify endpoint of arc or
[Angle/CEnter/CLose/Direction/Halfwidth/Line/Radius/Second pt/Undo/Width]:
A ~EnterKey~
Specify included angle: −180 ~EnterKey~ (you must enter the minus
sign because the arc needs to be created clockwise)
Specify endpoint of arc or [CEnter/Radius]: R ~EnterKey~
Specify radius of arc: 4'6 ~EnterKey~
Specify direction of chord for arc <0>: 270 ~EnterKey~
```

After specifying the included angle, you can either enter CE for the center of the arc or enter R to specify the radius of the arc. You must then specify the direction of chord for the arc.

2. **CEnter:** You can specify the center of the arc segment by entering CE at the *Specify endpoint of arc or* prompt. You will then be prompted for more options as follows:

```
Specify next point or [Arc/Close/Halfwidth/Length/Undo/Width]: A ~EnterKey~
Specify endpoint of arc or
[Angle/CEnter/CLose/Direction/Halfwidth/Line/Radius/Second pt/Undo/Width]: CE
~EnterKey~
Specify center point of arc: (specify the center point of arc)
Specify endpoint of arc or [Angle/Length]: (specify the endpoint of
the arc or enter an option)
```

The Angle option allows you to specify the included angle of the arc segment from the last polyline point. The Length option allows you to specify the length of chord of the polyline arc segment.

3. **CLose:** This option will close the polyline with an arc segment. Enter CL to close the polyline. The CL is entered to distinguish the CLose option from the CEnter (CE) option.

4. **Direction:** This option will allow you to specify a starting direction for the arc segment. The command line procedure is as follows:

```
Specify next point or [Arc/Close/Halfwidth/Length/Undo/Width]: A ~EnterKey~
Specify endpoint of arc or
[Angle/CEnter/CLose/Direction/Halfwidth/Line/Radius/Second
pt/Undo/Width]: D ~EnterKey~
Specify the tangent direction for the start point of arc: (select a point)
Specify endpoint of arc: (select a point)
```

5. **Halfwidth:** This option will allow you to enter a specific width that will start from the center of the polyline arc to the opposite side. For example, Figure 6–2 shows a polyline arc with a specified halfwidth of 12″. The final polyline arc can be drawn with a polyline arc width of 2′-0″ as follows:

```
Specify next point or [Arc/Close/Halfwidth/Length/Undo/Width]: A ~EnterKey~
Specify endpoint of arc or
[Angle/CEnter/CLose/Direction/Halfwidth/Line/Radius/Second pt/Undo/Width]:
H ~EnterKey~
Specify starting half-width <0'-0">: 12 ~EnterKey~
Specify ending half-width <1'-0">: ~EnterKey~ (the starting
halfwidth becomes the default ending halfwidth)
Specify endpoint of arc or
[Angle/CEnter/CLose/Direction/Halfwidth/Line/Radius/Second pt/Undo/Width]:
(enter an option to continue)
```

The Halfwidth option is not just arc specific. It applies to the regular polyline segments as well. When you specify the halfwidth option, the ending halfwidth times 2 becomes the starting width

FIGURE 6–2 The halfwidth option.

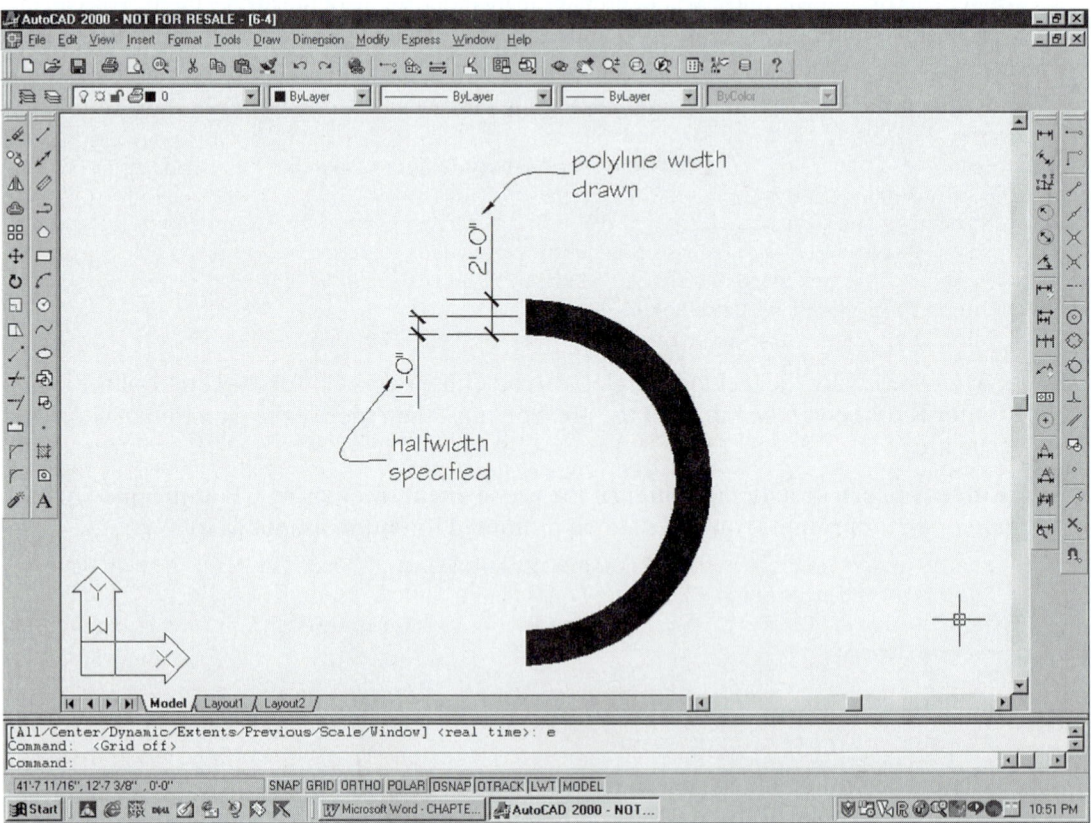

the next time you access the polyline command. In other words, the polyline width will start at twice the halfwidth size. For example, after the arc in Figure 6–2 is drawn, the next PLINE command will show a starting and ending width of 2′-0″.

6. **Length:** Selecting this option will end the polyline Arc option and will allow you to draw regular polylines. Refer to the command line procedure shown in Exercise 6–1 for Figure 6–1.

7. **Radius:** With this option you can specify the radius of the arc segment. You are then asked to specify the endpoint of the arc or the included angle. The command line procedure to use the Radius option for Figure 6–1 is as follows:

```
Specify next point or [Arc/Close/Halfwidth/Length/Undo/Width]:
A ~EnterKey~
Specify endpoint of arc or
[Angle/CEnter/CLose/Direction/Halfwidth/Line/Radius/Second pt/Undo/Width]:
R ~EnterKey~
Specify radius of arc: 4'6 ~EnterKey~
Specify endpoint of arc or [Angle]: A ~EnterKey~
Specify included angle: −180 ~EnterKey~
Specify direction of chord for arc <0>: 270 ~EnterKey~
```

8. **Second pt:** This option will allow you to specify the second point and the endpoint of a three-point arc. This is similar to drawing a three-point arc using the ARC command.

9. **Undo:** Entering U as the option will delete the previous polyline arc segment.

10. **Width:** Entering W will allow you to specify the width of the next polyline arc segment. The starting and ending points of all polyline segments are created from the center of the polyline. For example, if you specify 24″ for the starting and ending width for the polyline, AutoCAD will measure 12″ in both directions from the center of the polyline, giving you a 24″ thick polyline.

• **CLOSE:** (option). This option will draw a polyline segment from the last point to the start point of the polyline, creating a closed polyline. When you complete the polyline object using a number of coordinate point entry methods instead of the Close option, the outside corner where the first and the last polyline segments intersect will not join fully. By default, polylines that are assigned a specific width are created with a solid fill. You can see the structure or the skeleton of the polyline segments having a specific width by turning the FILLMODE system variable off or you can use the FILL command to remove the solid fill to display the *vertices* of the polyline segments. The command line procedure to remove the solid fill from the polylines is as follows:

```
Command: FILL ~EnterKey~
Enter mode [ON/OFF] <ON>: OFF ~EnterKey~
OR
Command: FILLMODE ~EnterKey~
Enter new value for FILLMODE <1>:0 ~EnterKey~
```

Even though this will turn the fill off, AutoCAD will not remove the solid fill from the polylines until you instruct AutoCAD to recalculate every single pixel on the screen and regenerate the polylines without the solid fills. This is accomplished by the REGEN command. After turning the FILLMODE system variable off or the FILL command off, enter REGEN at the command line as follows:

```
Command: REGEN ~EnterKey~
Regenerating model.
```

Figure 6–3 shows the polyline segments with the fill off. Notice the intersection of the start and endpoints when the Close option is not used.

As you can see from Figure 6–3, the intersections of the polyline segments are beveled. These are called *vertices* and can be used when editing polylines with the PEDIT command.

FIGURE 6–3 The skeleton of the polyline segments when the FILLMODE system variable and the FILL command is off.

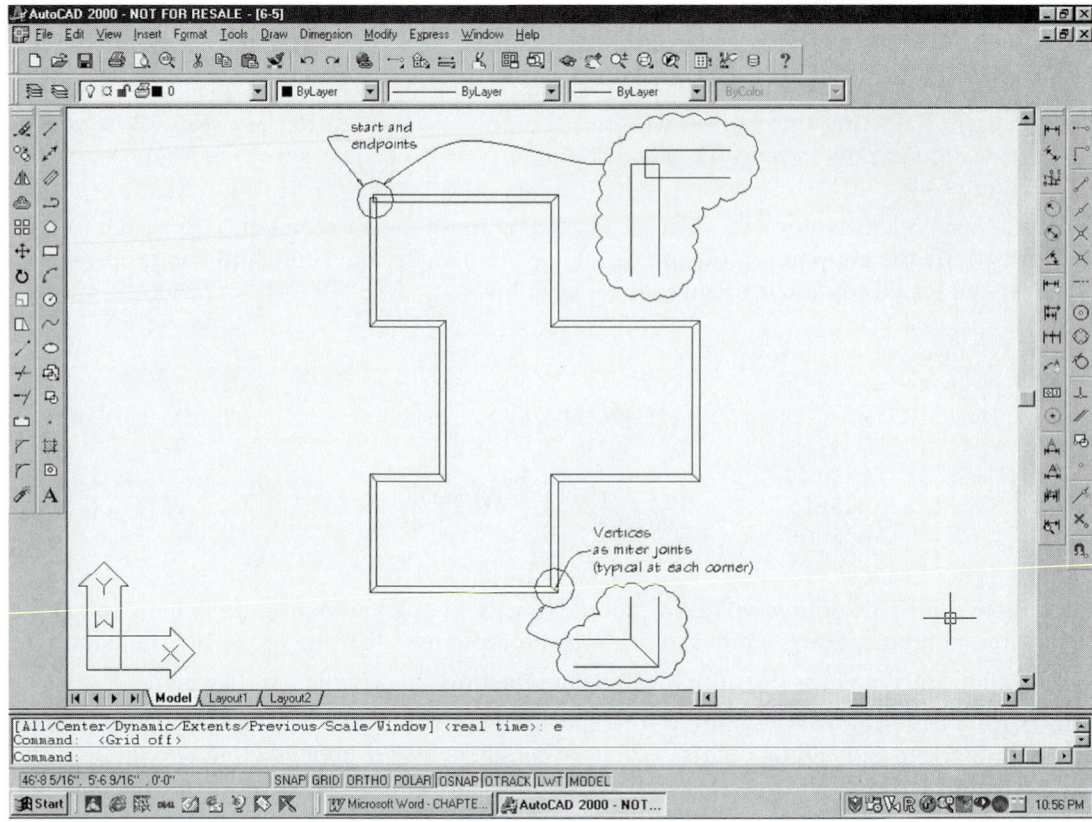

- **HALFWIDTH:** (option). When you create polyline segments you can assign a full width with the Width option. The Halfwidth will specify the width from the center of the polyline to one of its edges. For example, a 6″ halfwidth produces a polyline width of 12″. You can specify a different halfwidth for a starting and ending point. You can create the tapered polyline shown in Figure 6–4 as follows:

```
Command: PLINE ~EnterKey~
Specify start point: (select a starting point)
Current line-width is 0′-0″ (this represents architectural units)
Specify next point or [Arc/Close/Halfwidth/Length/Undo/Width]: H ~EnterKey~
Specify starting halfwidth <0′-0″>: 10 ~EnterKey~ (this will create
a 20″ starting width polyline)
Specify ending width <0′-10″>: 20 ~EnterKey~ (this will create a 40″
ending width polyline)
```

The polyline can then be copied and arrayed around a circle to create a fan symbol that can be turned into a block symbol. Refer to the COPY, ARRAY, and BLOCK commands.

- **LENGTH:** (option). The Length option will allow you to draw polylines as line segments at the length you specify at the same angle and width as the previous polyline segment. If the previous polyline segment is a polyline arc segment, the polyline segment will be drawn tangent to the polyline arc segment. The command line procedure is as follows:

```
Command: PLINE ~EnterKey~
Specify start point: (select a starting point)
Current line-width is 0′-0″ (this represents architectural units)
Specify next point or [Arc/Close/Halfwidth/Length/Undo/Width]: L ~EnterKey~
Specify length of line: (enter a length for the polyline segment)
Specify next point or [Arc/Close/Halfwidth/Length/Undo/Width]:
(specify next point for the polyline or an option)
```

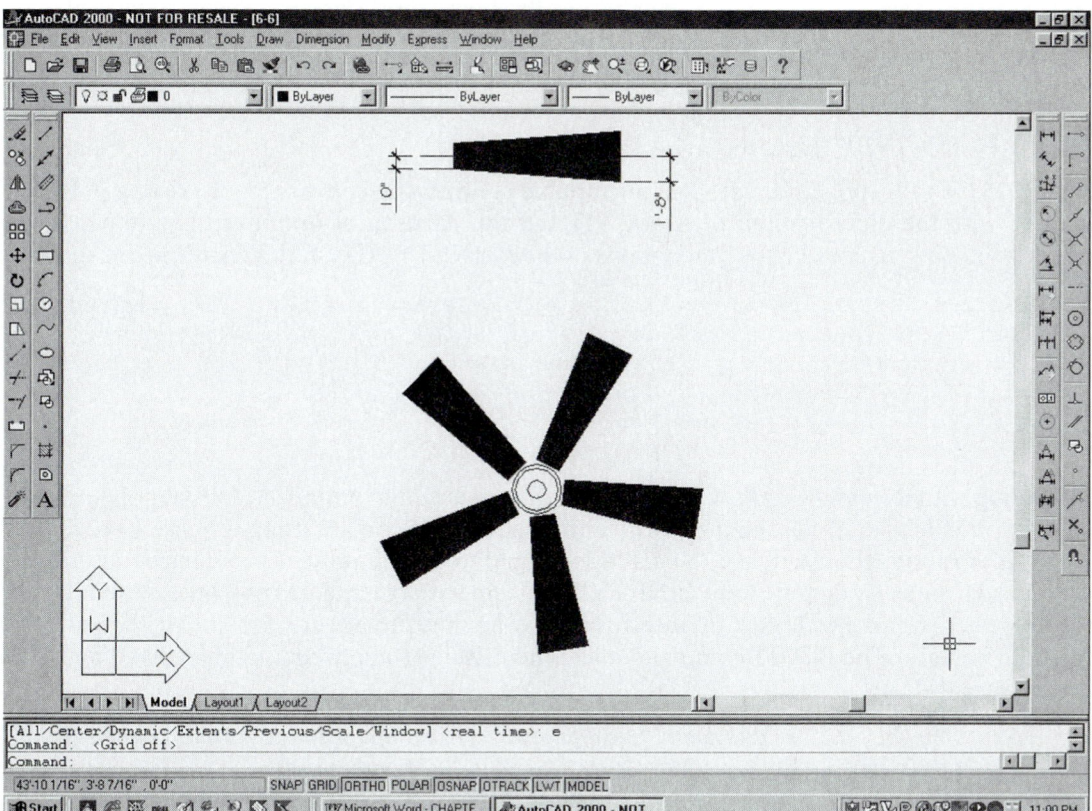

FIGURE 6–4 The starting and ending halfwidth values can be different to create tapered objects.

- **UNDO:** (option). The Undo option will remove the most recent polyline segment. The concept is similar to the U option of the LINE command.

- **WIDTH:** (option). The Width option is similar to the Halfwidth option but allows you to specify the full width of the polyline segments. AutoCAD will ask you to specify the *starting* and the *ending* widths of the polyline. The specified starting width becomes the default ending width, and the ending width becomes the uniform width for all subsequent polyline segments drawn. You can enter **W** at any time during the command sequence that asks you to *specify next point* to change the starting and ending width of the polylines. The actual width of the polyline is determined from the center of the polyline to both edges of the polyline. The command line procedure is as follows:

```
Command: PLINE ~EnterKey~
Specify start point: (select a starting point)
Current line-width is 0'-0" (this represents architectural units)
Specify next point or [Arc/Close/Halfwidth/Length/Undo/Width]: W ~EnterKey~
Specify starting width <0'-0">: (specify a starting width for the polyline)
Specify ending width <current>: (specify an ending width for the
polyline or press ~EnterKey~ to accept a uniform width)
```

6.3.1 PLINEWID System Variable

The PLINEWID (polyline width) system variable allows you to preset a constant starting and ending width for the polyline segments, including polyline arcs. Enter PLINEWID at the command line as follows:

```
Command: PLINEWID ~EnterKey~
Enter new value for PLINEWID <0'-6">: (enter a new constant width for the
polyline. The numbers in the brackets represent the last polyline width
established)
```

The next time you use the PLINE command the width will be constant as set by the PLINEWID system variable until you change it back to zero.

6.3.2   PLINETYPE System Variable

The PLINETYPE (polyline type) system variable controls the conversion of existing polylines created with the older version of AutoCAD and the creation of optimized two-dimensional polylines in the current release. The options of the PLINETYPE system variable are as follows:

```
PLINETYPE: 0 (old-format polylines are created with the PLINE command)
PLINETYPE: 1 (optimized polylines are created with the PLINE command, but
the polylines created with the older versions of AutoCAD are not
converted when opened)
PLINETYPE: 2 (polylines created with the older versions of AutoCAD are
converted to optimized polylines when opened)
```

Beginning with Release 14, AutoCAD creates two-dimensional optimized format polylines and associative hatch patterns, saving memory and disk space. If you are using Release 13 or earlier versions of AutoCAD, use the CONVERT command to update polylines and hatch patterns to optimized format. By default, the PLINETYPE system variable updates polylines automatically when opened in earlier releases; therefore, you may not need to update polylines with the CONVERT command. The PEDIT command makes no distinction between optimized and nonoptimized formats.

Note: The PLINETYPE system variable also controls the polyline format created by the BOUNDARY, DONUT, POLYGON, and SKETCH commands.

6.3.3   PLINEGEN System Variable

The PLINEGEN (poly-linetype generation) system variable controls how different linetypes other than continuous are generated at the vertices of the polyline. This system variable does not affect the tapered polyline segments. By default, the PLINEGEN system variable is set to 0 (off), which generates the linetype in a continuous pattern around the vertices of the polyline. When it is set to 1 (on), the polylines are generated to start and end with a dashed line at the vertices. Figure 6–5 shows a comparison of the polyline object drawn with the *PHANTOM* linetype.

FIGURE 6–5   A comparison of the two polyline objects using two different PLINEGEN settings.

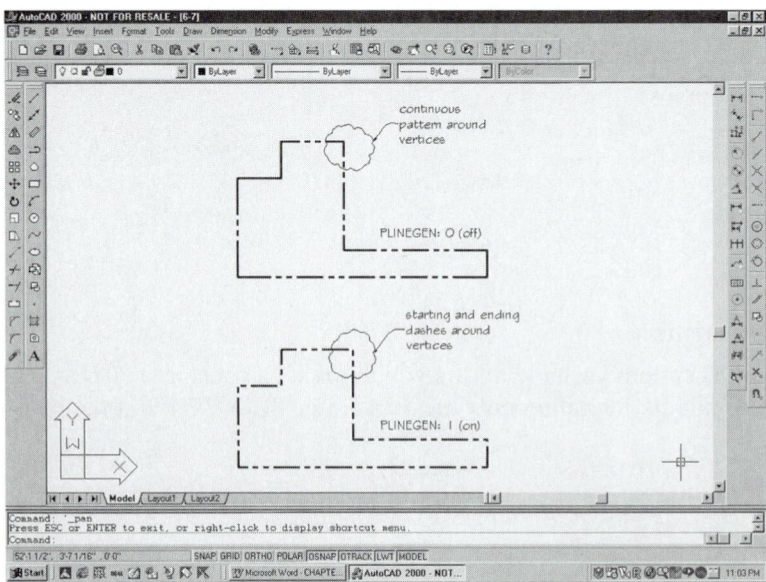

6.4 DRAWING ROUND AND SEMIROUND OBJECTS

The CIRCLE command allows you to draw circular objects, the ARC command allows you to draw arcs, and the ELLIPSE command allows you to draw elliptical objects.

6.4.1 Using the CIRCLE Command

The circle command can be accessed in three different ways:

1. Click on the Circle button in the Draw toolbar.
2. Select Circle from the Draw pull-down menu.
3. Enter C or CIRCLE at the command line.

When you enter C or CIRCLE at the command line, you can draw circles using five different methods as follows:

1. **Radius:** You can create a circle by specifying the center point and the radius. The command line procedure is as follows:

   ```
   Command: C or CIRCLE ~EnterKey~
   Specify center point of circle or [3P/2P/Ttr (tan tan radius)]:
   (enter a coordinate value or select a center point)
   Specify radius of circle or [Diameter]: 5' ~EnterKey~ (this will
   create a circle with a 5' radius)
   ```

2. **Diameter:** You can create a circle by specifying the center point and the diameter. The command line procedure is as follows:

   ```
   Command: C or CIRCLE ~EnterKey~
   Specify center point of circle or [3P/2P/Ttr (tan tan radius)]:
   (enter a coordinate value or select a center point)
   Specify radius of circle or [Diameter] <5'-0">: D ~EnterKey~ (the
   value inside the brackets indicate the last radius value used)
   Specify diameter of circle <10'-
   0">: 5' ~EnterKey~ (this will
   create a circle with a 5'
   diameter or a 2'-6" radius. The
   value inside the brackets
   indicate the diameter equivalent
   of the previous radius value)
   ```

Figures 6–6A and 6–6B shows the two circles created with the radius and diameter options.

3. **Three Points (3P):** You can draw a circle based on the three known points or select three points on the screen. The location of the points will allow AutoCAD to automatically calculate the radius of the circle. The circle in Figure 6–6C can be created as follows:

   ```
   Command: C or CIRCLE ~EnterKey~
   Specify center point of circle
   or [3P/2P/Ttr (tan tan radius)]:
   3P ~EnterKey~
   Specify first point on circle:
   (select point 1)
   Specify second point on circle: (select point 2)
   Specify third point on circle: (select point 3)
   ```

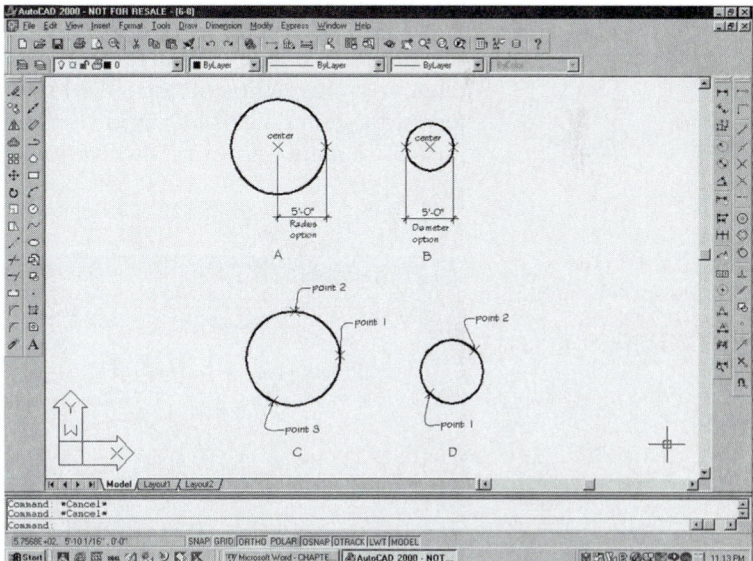

FIGURE 6–6 The Radius (A), Diameter (B), 3P (C), and 2P (D) options of the CIRCLE command.

4. **Two Points (2P):** You can draw a circle based on the two known points or select two points on the screen. The first point selected is the end point of the circle's diameter.

The location of the second point will determine the actual diameter of the circle. The circle in Figure 6–6D can be created as follows:

```
Command: C or CIRCLE ~EnterKey~
Specify center point of circle or [3P/2P/Ttr (tan tan radius)]: 2P
~EnterKey~
Specify first end point of circle's diameter: (select point 1)
Specify second end point of circle's diameter: (select point 2)
```

5. **Tangent to Two Points on Objects with a Radius (TTR):** You can draw a circle tangent to two points selected on the objects and specify the radius of the circle. The two points selected on the objects are *tangent* to the circle and are called *points of tangency*. These two points are selected by *Deferred Tangent* object snap mode by default. Refer to Chapter 7 for object snap modes. When you enter the TTR option, AutoCAD will automatically turn the Tangent object snap mode on. While selecting the points, AutoCAD will display the *"Deferred Tangent"* tooltip. After selecting two points, AutoCAD will ask you to specify the radius of the circle. The circle is drawn with tangent points closest to the selected points. If the radius entered is too small, you will get the following message:

> *Circle does not exist.*

Figure 6–7 shows two circles created with the TTR option. The 7′-0″ radius circle is created as follows:

```
Command: C or CIRCLE ~EnterKey~
Specify center point of circle or [3P/2P/Ttr (tan tan radius)]: TTR
~EnterKey~
Specify point on object for first tangent of circle: (select first
tangent point A)
Specify point on object for second tangent of circle: (select second
tangent point B)
Specify radius of circle: 7' ~EnterKey~
```

To create the 4′-0″ radius circle, follow the procedures described above and select the *first tangent point C* and *second tangent point D*.

When you select the Circle option from the Draw pull-down menu, you can use the Tan, Tan, Tan option to create a circle tangent to three points. The three points selected on the objects are tangent to the circle and are called points of tangency. These three points are selected by Deferred Tangent object snap mode by default. When you select the Tan, Tan, Tan option using the pull-down menu, AutoCAD will automatically turn the Tangent object snap mode on. While se-

FIGURE 6–7   Two circles drawn using the Tangent, Tangent, Radius option.

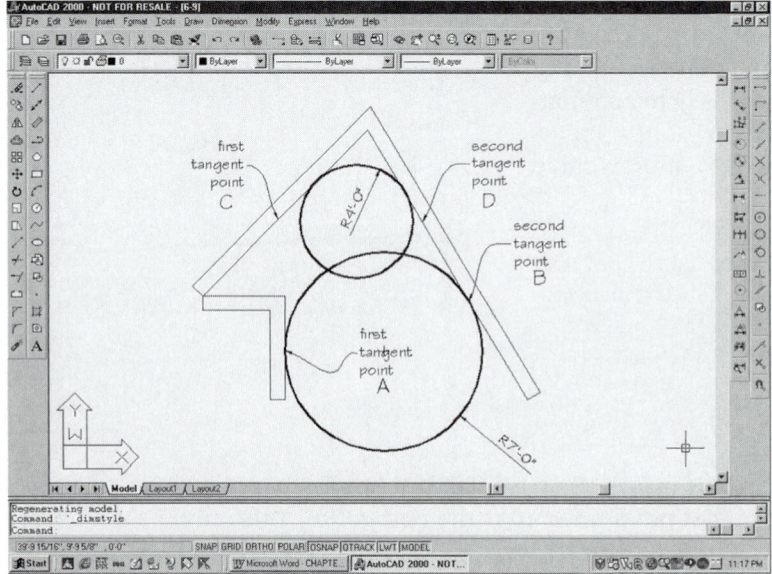

lecting the points, AutoCAD will display the "Deferred Tangent" tooltip. After selecting three points, AutoCAD will draw the circle tangent to three points.

Figure 6–8 shows a circles created with the Tan, Tan, Tan option. This option is not the same as the 3P option because the 3P option does not automatically provide the Deferred Tangent object snap mode. To use the 3P option as the Tan, Tan, Tan option, you must enter TAN object snap mode option at the command line (or select from the objects snap toolbar) before selecting the points.

Note: With the Tan, Tan, Radius option more than one circle placement is possible, depending on the points selected. With the Tan, Tan, Tan option only one circle placement is possible.

You can set the current circle radius by entering the CIRCLERAD system variable at the command line. When you enter CIRCLERAD at the command line, it will display the radius of the previously drawn circle. Enter a value to specify the radius of the next circle as follows:

```
Command: CIRCLERAD ~EnterKey~
Enter new value for CIRCLERAD <current value>: (enter a new value)
```

6.4.2   Using the ARC Command

The ARC command is used to draw a part of a circle or a curve having less than 360 degrees. The ARC command can be accessed by entering A or ARC at the command line, selecting Arc from the Draw pull-down menu, or selecting the Arc button in the Draw toolbar. The Arc cascading menu allows you to draw arcs using 11 different methods. Selecting the Arc button in the Draw toolbar or entering ARC at the command line allows you to select the *start, second,* and *end*points of the arc. This is referred to as the Three Points option that is the default. You can use the CEnter and ENd options of the ARC command with the combination of start and end points to create arcs in 11 different ways similar to the Arc cascading menu in the Draw pull-down menu. The command line arc options are as follows:

Start Second End (SSE):   This is the default three-point arc option. The *start* point indicates the starting point, the *second* indicates the second point selected anywhere along the arc, and the *end* indicates the endpoint of the arc. The arc in Figure 6–9A can be created using the ARC command as follows:

```
Command: A or ARC ~EnterKey~
Specify start point of arc or [CEnter]: (select the start point)
Specify second point of arc or [CEnter/ENd]: (select the second point)
Specify endpoint of arc: (select the endpoint)
```

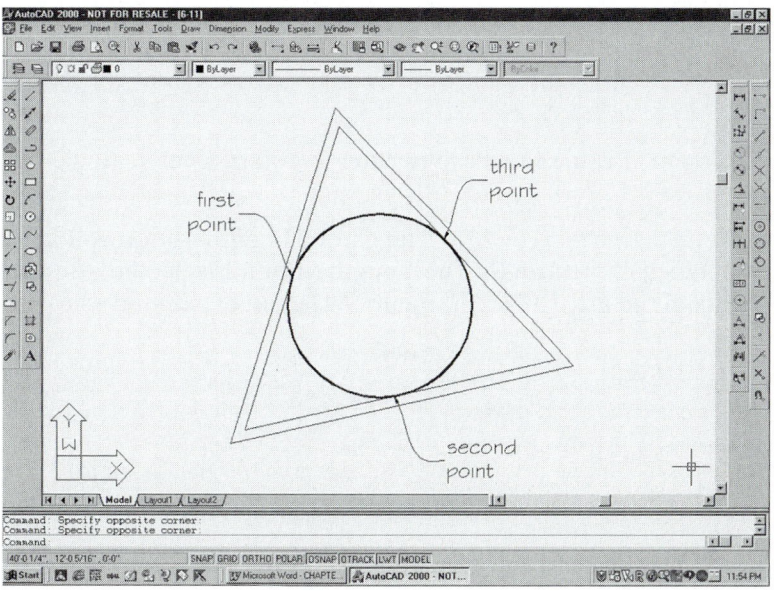

FIGURE 6–8 The circle created tangent to three objects.

FIGURE 6-9 **A:** Using
the Three-Point (3P)
Arc option (Start
Second End) of the
ARC command.
B: Using the Start,
Center, End (Start
Center End) option of
the ARC command.
Notice with the three-
point option, the
locations of the points
determine the direction
of the arc overriding the
counterclockwise
direction.

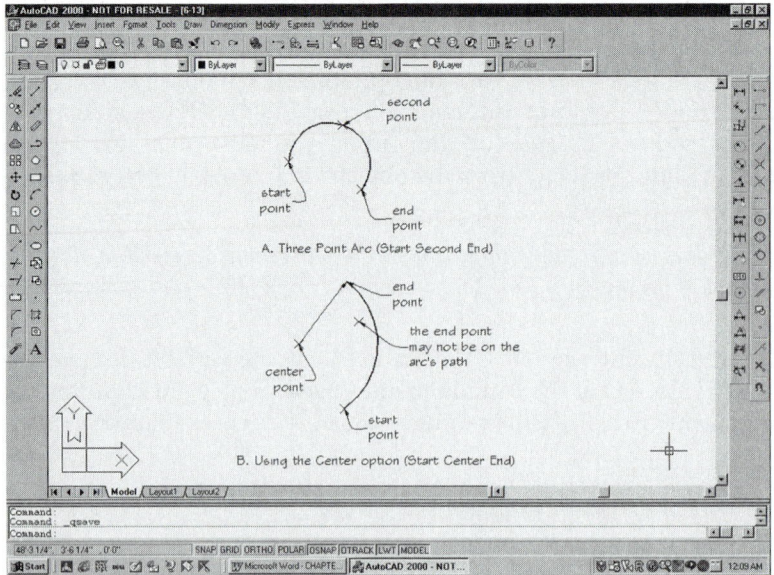

This method is the same as selecting the Three Points option from the Arc cascading menu in the Draw pull-down menu.

Start Center End (SCE):   The CEnter option will allow you to specify the center point of the arc. Select the Center option after you select the start point of the arc. The arc in Figure 6–9B is created using the ARC command as follows:

```
Command: A or ARC ~EnterKey~
Specify start point of arc or [CEnter]: (select the start point)
Specify second point of arc or [CEnter/ENd]: C or CE ~EnterKey~
Specify center point of arc: (select the center point)
Specify endpoint of arc or [Angle/chord length]: (select the endpoint)
```

This method is the same as selecting the Start, Center, End option from the Arc cascading menu.

Start Center Angle (SCA):   The Angle option will allow you to create an arc with a specified angle. The Angle option is selected after selecting the start and center points of the arc. The arc in Figure 6–10 is created as follows:

```
Command: A or ARC ~EnterKey~
Specify start point of arc or [CEnter]: (select the start point)
Specify second point of arc or [CEnter/ENd]: C or CE ~EnterKey~
Specify center point of arc: (select the center point)
Specify endpoint of arc or [Angle/chord Length]: A ~EnterKey~
Specify included angle: 67 ~EnterKey~(notice that the arc is drawn
counterclockwise)
```

This method is the same as selecting the Start, Center, Angle option from the Arc cascading menu.

Start Center Length (SCL):   The Chord Length option will allow you to create an arc with a specified chord length. The Length option is selected after selecting the start and center points of the arc. The arc in Figure 6–11 can be created as follows:

```
Command: A or ARC ~EnterKey~
Specify start point of arc or [CEnter]: (select the start point)
Specify second point of arc or [CEnter/ENd]: C or CE ~EnterKey~
Specify center point of arc: (select the center point)
Specify endpoint of arc or [Angle/chord Length]: L ~EnterKey~
Specify length of chord: 17' ~EnterKey~(notice that the arc is drawn
counterclockwise)
```

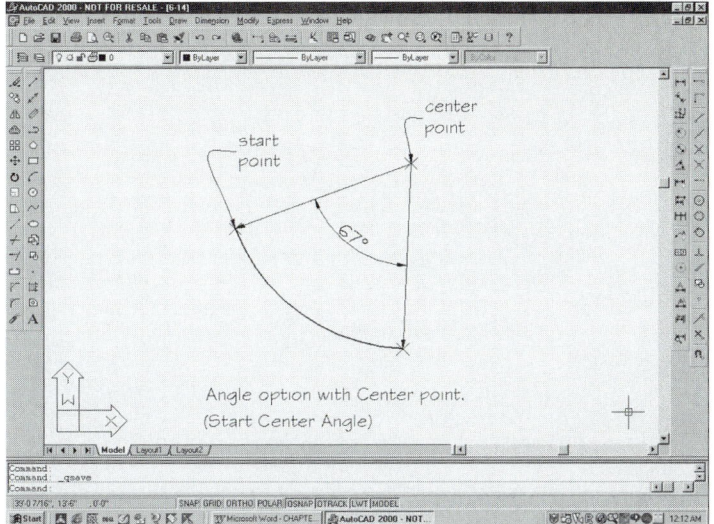

FIGURE 6-10 Using the Center and the Angle (Start Center Angle) option of the ARC command.

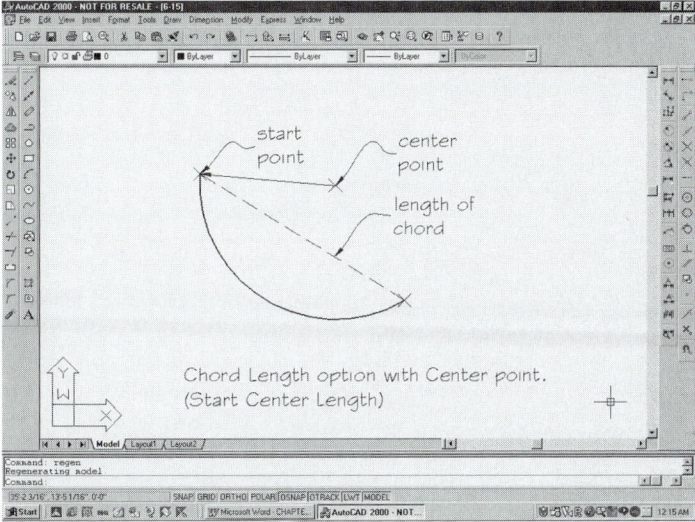

FIGURE 6-11 Using the Center and the chord Length (Start Center Length) option of the ARC command.

This method is the same as selecting the Start, Center, Length option from the Arc cascading menu.

> *Note: A positive chord length will draw the smallest possible arc that is the minor arc. A negative chord length will draw the largest possible arc that is the major arc.*

Start End Angle (SEA):   After selecting the start and endpoint of the arc, you can enter a positive included angle to draw an arc counterclockwise or a negative included angle to draw an arc clockwise. The arc in Figure 6–12A can be created as follows:

```
Command: A or ARC ~EnterKey~
Specify start point of arc or [CEnter]: (select the start point)
Specify second point of arc or [CEnter/ENd]: E or EN ~EnterKey~
Specify endpoint of arc: (select the endpoint)
Specify center point of arc or [Angle/Direction/Radius]: A ~EnterKey~
Specify included angle: 125 ~EnterKey~(notice that the arc is drawn
counterclockwise)
```

To draw the arc in Figure 6–12B, enter –125 as the included angle. This method is the same as selecting the Start End Angle option from the Arc cascading menu.

FIGURE 6–12 Using the Start End Angle option of the Arc command.

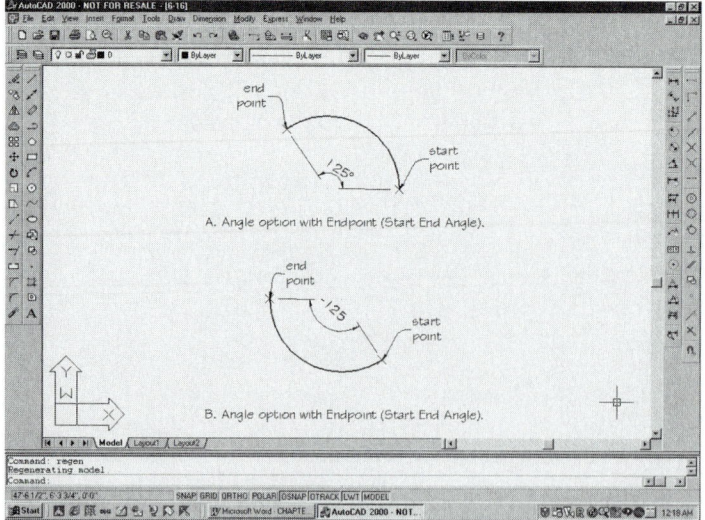

FIGURE 6–13 Using the Start End Direction option of the ARC command.

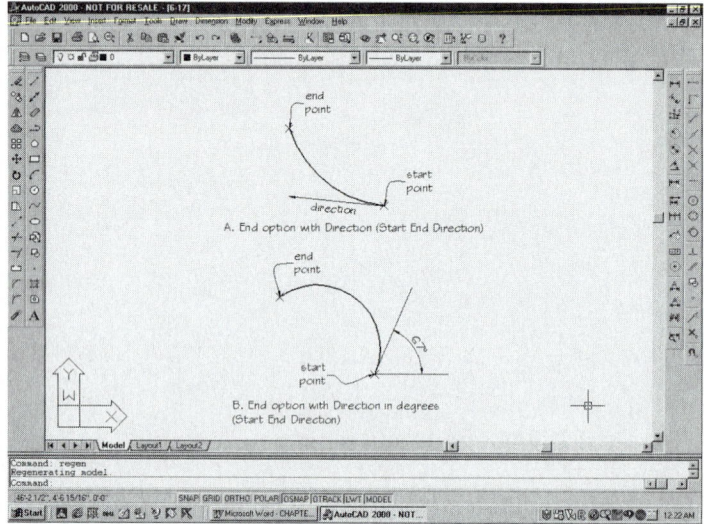

Start End Direction (SED): After selecting the start and endpoint of the arc, you can select a tangent direction from the start point or enter the direction in degrees to create an arc. The arc in Figure 6–13A can be created as follows:

```
Command: A or ARC ~EnterKey~
Specify start point of arc or [CEnter]: (select the start point)
Specify second point of arc or [CEnter/ENd]: E or EN ~EnterKey~
Specify endpoint of arc: (select the endpoint)
Specify center point of arc or [Angle/Direction/Radius]: D ~EnterKey~
Specify tangent direction for the start point of the arc: (select the
direction as shown)
```

To draw the arc in Figure 6–13B, enter 67 as the tangent direction angle. This method is the same as selecting the Start End Direction option from the Arc cascading menu.

Start End Radius (SER): After selecting the start and endpoint of the arc, you can select a radius for the arc. The arc is drawn counterclockwise from the endpoint to the start point. The distance between the start and the endpoint of the arc becomes the diameter of the arc. If you specify a smaller radius, AutoCAD will display the **Invalid** message. The arc in Figure 6–14A can be created as follows:

```
Command: A or ARC ~EnterKey~
Specify start point of arc or [CEnter]:
(select the start point)
Specify second point of arc or
[CEnter/ENd]: E or EN ~EnterKey~
Specify endpoint of arc: (select the
endpoint)
Specify center point of arc or
[Angle/Direction/Radius]: R ~EnterKey~
Specify radius of arc: 5' ~EnterKey~
```

This method is the same as selecting the Start End Radius option from the Arc cascading menu.

Start End Center (SEC):   This option is similar to the Start Center End option of the arc command. Use Start End Center option if it is easier to select the center of the arc last. You can use this option to create the arc in Figure 6–14A clockwise. The arc in Figure 6–14B can be created as follows:

```
Command: A or ARC ~EnterKey~
Specify start point of arc or [CEnter]: (select the start point)
Specify second point of arc or [CEnter/ENd]: E or EN ~EnterKey~
Specify endpoint of arc: (select the endpoint)
Specify center point of arc or [Angle/Direction/Radius]: (select the center point)
```

Center Start End (CSE):   This option can be used to draw an arc as the swing of a door. The center, start, and end points of the arc correspond to the hinge, latch, and endpoints on the door as shown in Figure 6–15. The center, start, and endpoints of the arc are not necessarily selected

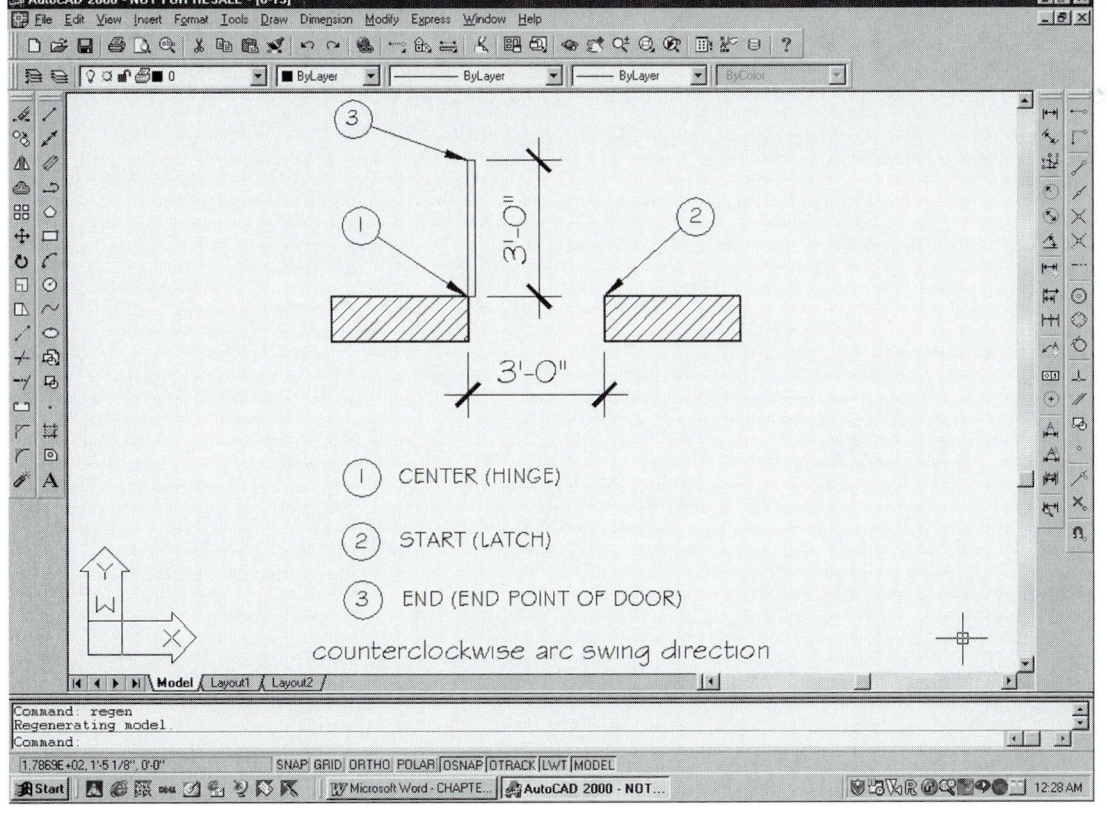

FIGURE 6–14   A: Start End Radius and **B:** Start End Center options of the arc command.

FIGURE 6–15   The Center Start End (CSE) option of the arc command can be used to create the door swing. In this specific door orientation, the center, start, and endpoints of the arc correspond to the hinge, latch, and endpoint on the door. Since the arc is drawn counterclockwise, the three points must be selected in that order.

in the order of hinge, latch, and endpoints on the door. Since the arc is drawn counterclockwise (default), the selection process of these three points must be considered according to the orientation of the door. The door swing in Figure 6–16 is created as follows:

```
Command: A or ARC ~EnterKey~
Specify start point of arc or [CEnter]: C or CE ~EnterKey~
Specify center point of arc: (select point 1. This is the hinge side of
the door)
Specify start point of arc: (select point 2. This is the latch side of
the door)
Specify endpoint of arc or [Angle/chord Length]: (select point 3. This is
the outside endpoint of the door)
```

Figures 6–17 and 6–18 shows four door orientations and their relationship to the three points that must be selected in a specific order to create the counterclockwise door swing direction. Notice the center point that is the hinge point is always selected as the first point. Pay close attention when determining other points.

> *Note: See Chapter 17 Exercise 17–3 for a complete exercise on creating a door and its swing.*

Center Start Angle (CSE):   This option is similar to the Start Center Angle option where the arc begins at the center point rather than at the start point. See Figure 6–10.

Center Start Length (CSL):   This option is similar to the Start Center Length option where the arc begins at the center point rather than at the start point. See Figure 6–11.

6.4.2.1 Arc Continuations   You can continue an arc from a previously drawn arc or a line. When an arc is continued in this fashion, it is drawn tangent to the endpoint of the previous arc or line. To accomplish this, select Continue from the Arc cascading menu in the Draw pull-down menu.

FIGURE 6–16   The actual creation of the door swing in relation to the center, start, and endpoints.

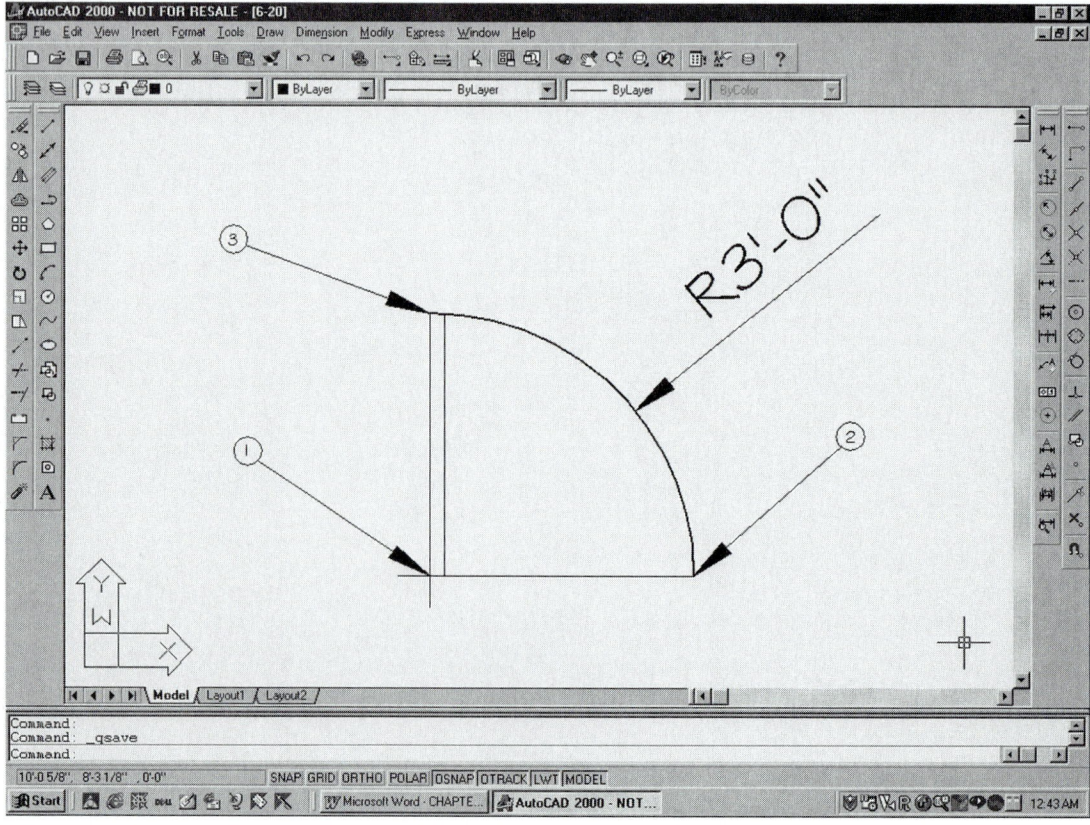

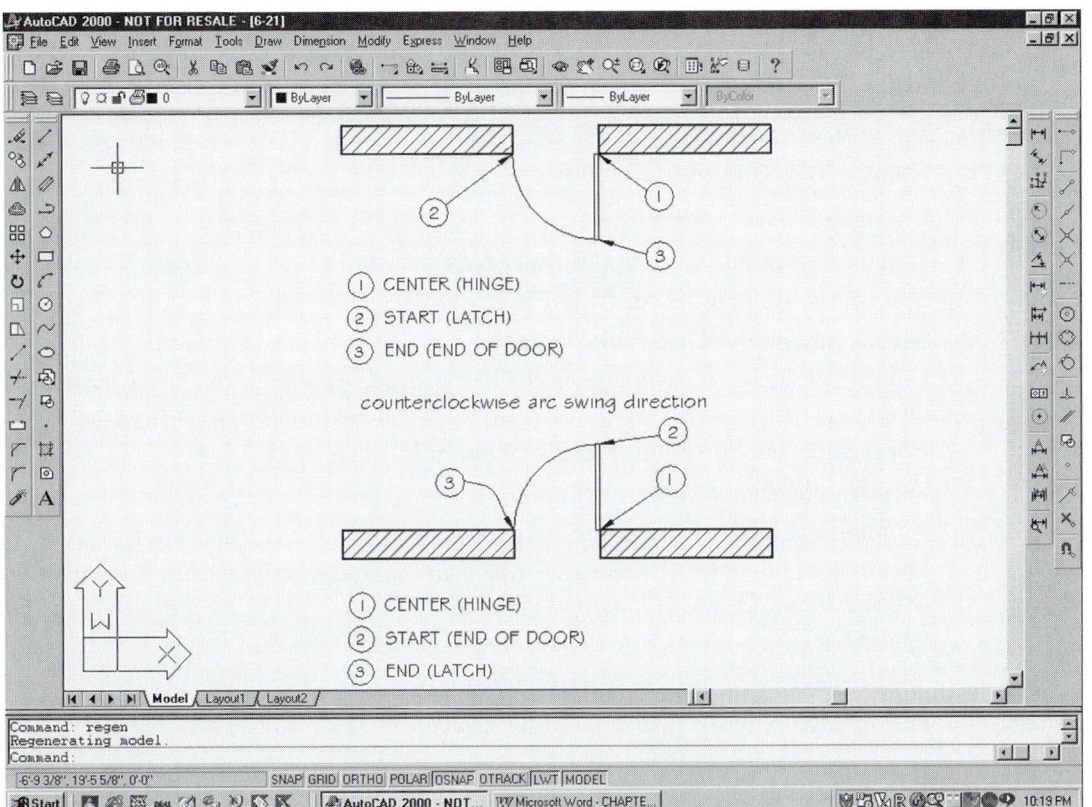

FIGURE 6–17 Two doors oriented differently require different selections for the second and third points. The first point is always the center (hinge) point.

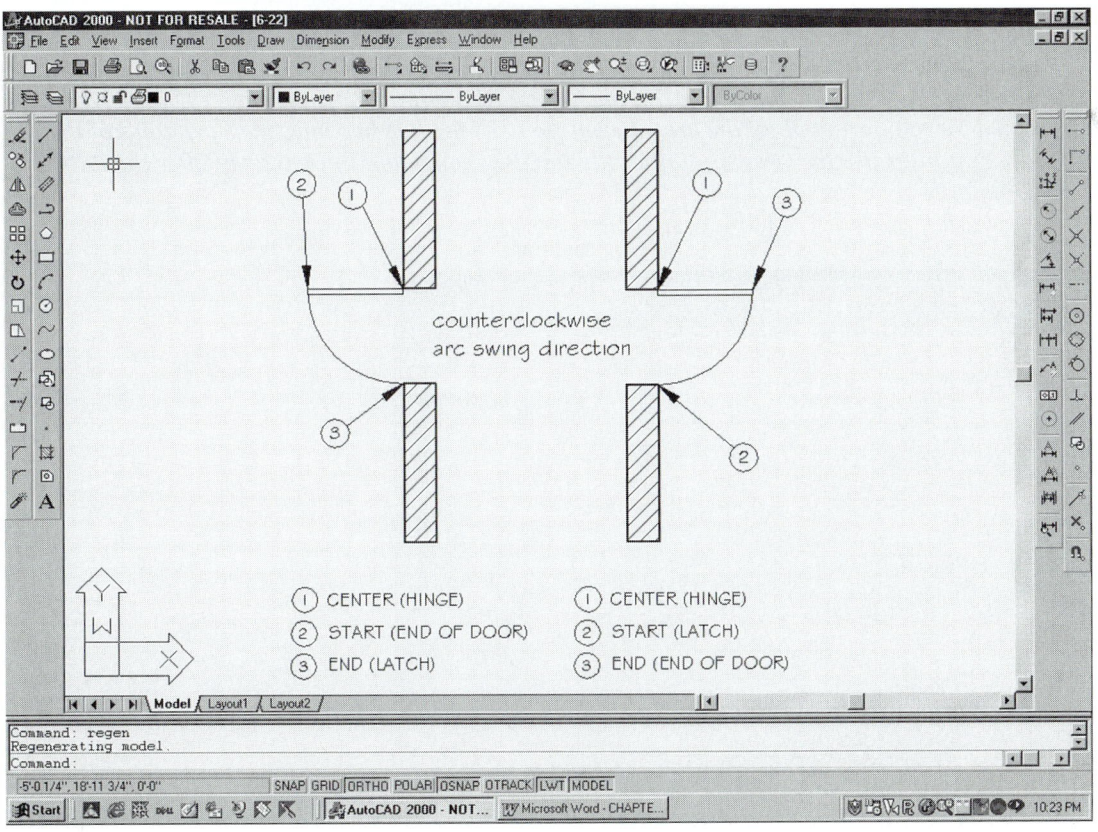

FIGURE 6–18 Two doors oriented differently require different selections for the second and third points. The first point is common to both door swings.

■ **EXERCISE 6–2:** *The following step-by-step exercise will help you create the object as shown in Figure 6–19. The final plot scale is ¼″ = 1′-0″ to be plotted on A = size (8½″ × 11″) paper vertically. This corresponds to drawing limits of 34′, 44′.*

Step #1:   Establish drawing Limits as 34′, 44′.

Step #2:   Use the ARC command as follows:

Command: **ARC** ~EnterKey~

Specify start point of arc or [CEnter]: (*select point 1*)

Specify second point of arc or [CEnter/ENd]: (*select point 2*)

Specify end point of arc: (*select point 3*)

Command: (*select Continue from the Arc cascading menu in the Draw pull-down menu*)

Command: _arc Specify start point of arc or [CEnter]:

Specify end point of arc: (*select point 4*)

Command: **LINE** ~EnterKey~

Specify first point: **@** ~EnterKey~ (*this will start a line from the last known point, which is the end point of the previous arc*)

Specify next point or [Undo]: (*select point 5*)

Specify next point or [Undo]: (*select point 6*)

Specify next point or [Close/Undo]: (*select point 7*)

Specify next point or [Close/Undo]: (*select point 1*)

Specify next point or [Close/Undo]: (*right click and select Enter from the shortcut menu*)

Congratulations! You have created the object shown in Figure 6–19 using the Continue option of the ARC command.

Note: As you learned in Chapter 5, the @ symbol instructs AutoCAD to go to the last point value entered. For example, you can start to draw an arc at the end of the line you just created. Draw the line first then access the ARC command. Enter the @ symbol when asked for the start point of the arc. The endpoint of the line becomes the start point of the arc. You must use the @ symbol after the line is created and immediately after the ARC command.

FIGURE 6–19   An arc can be continued from the previous arc, and the LINE command can be continued from the last arc drawn by entering the @ symbol.

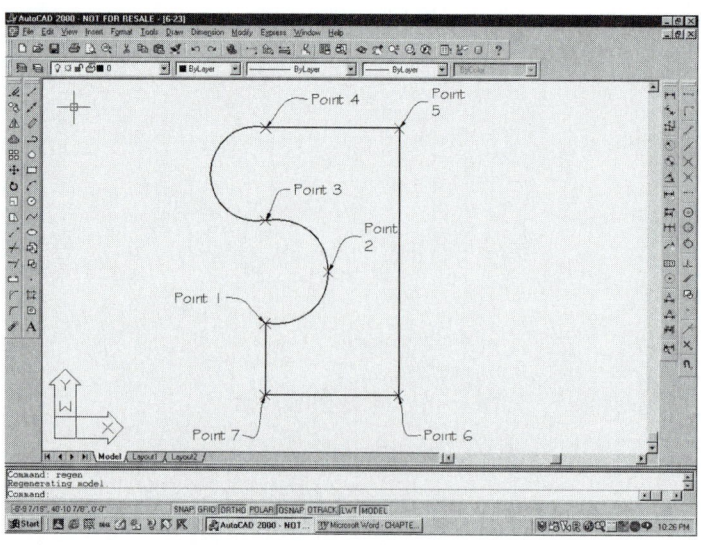

The LASTPOINT system variable allows you to see the last X, Y, and Z coordinates entered. In two-dimensional drawings the Z coordinate is shown as 0.0000. The @ symbol actually retrieves the LASTPOINT coordinate values.

Tips: You can create an arc precisely tangent to the endpoint of the previous arc or line by pressing the ~EnterKey~ at the start point: prompt. If the 11 methods of arc creation give you an overwhelming feeling about the ARC command, use the circle command instead and either BREAK or TRIM the circle to create the desired arc. The BREAK and TRIM commands are discussed in Chapter 12.

6.4.3 Using the ELLIPSE Command

The ELLIPSE command allows you to draw an ellipse by four different methods. You can also use the ELLIPSE command to draw elliptical arcs and isometric circles. The ELLIPSE command can be accessed from the Draw pull-down menu, by selecting Ellipse in the Draw toolbar, or by entering EL or ELLIPSE at the command line. The command line procedure is as follows:

```
Command: EL or ELLIPSE ~EnterKey~
Specify axis endpoint of ellipse or [Arc/Center]: (select the axis endpoint)
Specify other endpoint of axis: (select the other endpoint of the axis)
Specify distance to other axis or [Rotation]: (specify a distance from
the midpoint of the first axis to the second axis or select a rotation)
```

The four methods are as follows:

Endpoint Endpoint Axis (EEA): With this method, the two endpoints define the first axis, and the distance to the other axis defines the second axis. In Figure 6–20, the distance between the axis endpoint 1 and the axis endpoint 2 is the *major axis*. The distance from the midpoint of the major axis and the other axis is the *minor axis*. Whichever axis is longer becomes the *major axis*. The ellipse in Figure 6–20 can be created as follows:

```
Command: EL or ELLIPSE ~EnterKey~
Specify axis endpoint of ellipse or [Arc/Center]: (select axis endpoint 1)
Specify other endpoint of axis: @18'<0 ~EnterKey~
Specify distance to other axis or [Rotation]: @5'<90 ~EnterKey~
```

Endpoint Endpoint Rotation (EER): After selecting the major axis with the first two points, you can enter R for rotation at the Specify distance to other axis or [Rotation]: prompt and enter ellipse rotation angle. The specified angle will rotate the ellipse around the major axis. The rotation is the ratio between the major to minor axis and the rotation of a circle about the first

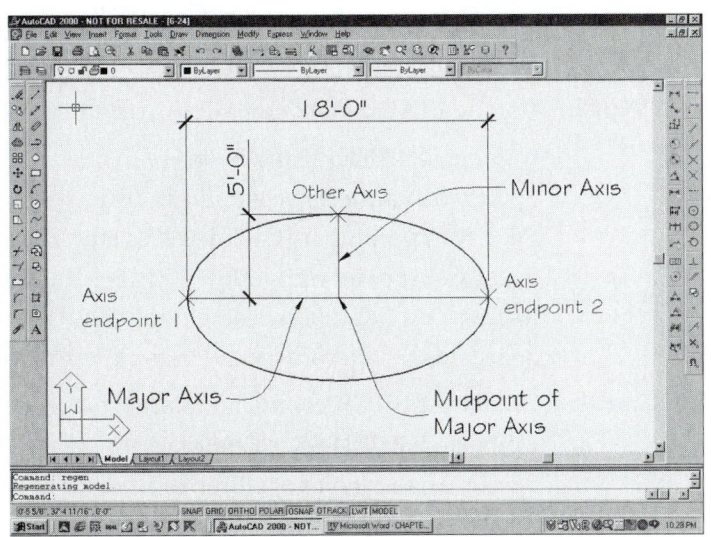

FIGURE 6–20 The major axis of the ellipse is 18'-0" in length, and the minor axis of the ellipse is 5'-0" in length.

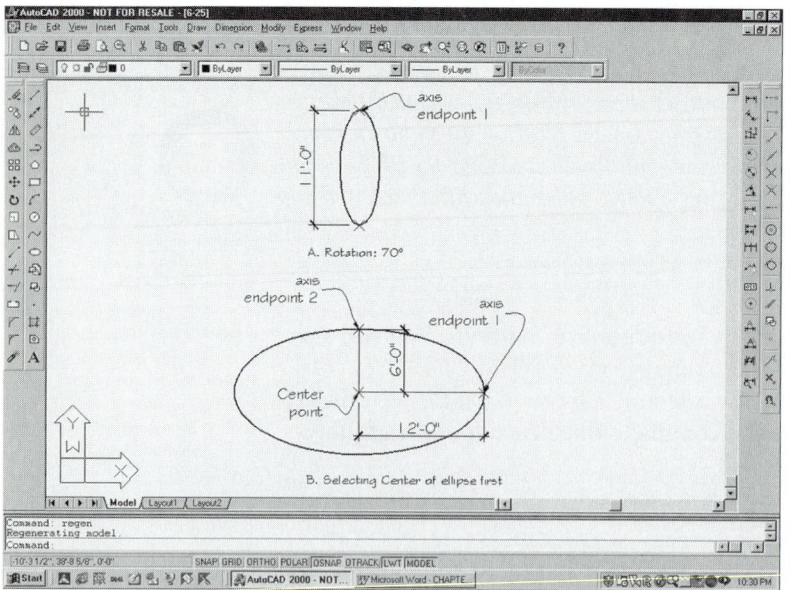

FIGURE 6–21   A: Using the Rotation option of the ELLIPSE command. **B:** Using the Center option of the ELLIPSE command.

(major) axis. The larger the rotation value, the greater the ratio of major to minor axis. A rotation angle of 0 will create a perfect circle, while a rotation angle of 89.4 will create the highest ratio. The ellipse in Figure 6–21A can be created as follows:

```
Command: EL or ELLIPSE ~EnterKey~
Specify axis endpoint of ellipse or
[Arc/Center]: (select axis endpoint 1)
Specify other endpoint of axis:
@11'<270 ~EnterKey~
Specify distance to other axis or
[Rotation]: R ~EnterKey~
Specify rotation around major axis: 70
~EnterKey~
```

Center Endpoint Axis (CEA):   You can create an ellipse by specifying the center point first and one endpoint for each of the two axes. The ellipse in Figure 6–21B can be created as follows:

```
Command: EL or ELLIPSE ~EnterKey~
Specify axis endpoint of ellipse or
[Arc/Center]: C ~EnterKey~
Specify center of ellipse: (select the center point)
Specify endpoint of axis: @12'<0 ~EnterKey~
Specify distance to other axis or [Rotation]: @6'<90 ~EnterKey~
```

Center Axis Rotation (CAR):   This option is a variation of the previous two options. Use Center Axis Rotation to establish the center of the ellipse first, then establish the major axis, and finally set the rotation.

6.4.3.1 Creating a Water Closet with the Ellipse and Line Commands   You can use any of the four methods described above to create an ellipse as part of a Water Closet symbol. Obtain necessary dimensions from the manufacturer's catalog or Architectural Graphic Standards to create the Water Closet symbol. After drawing the symbol, you can create a Block (B) definition or Write Block (W) definition to a file and use it as part of your symbol library. Blocks are discussed in Chapter 19.

■   **EXERCISE 6–3:**   *The following step-by-step exercise will help you create the Water Closet symbol shown in Figure 6–22. Refer to Chapter 19 to create a Block from this symbol.*

Step #1:   Establish drawing Limits or use existing Limits.

Step #2:   Use the LINE command to draw part of the water closet as follows:

Command: **LINE** ~EnterKey~
Specify first point: (*select Point 1*)
Specify next point or [Undo]: **@2'9<90** ~EnterKey~
Specify next point or [Undo]: **@12<0** ~EnterKey~
Specify next point or [Close/Undo]: **@2'9<270** ~EnterKey~
Specify next point or [Close/Undo]: **C** ~EnterKey~

Step #3:   Use the ELLIPSE command to draw the rest of the water closet as follows:
Command: **ELLIPSE** ~EnterKey~
Specify axis endpoint of ellipse or [Arc/Center]: **MID** ~EnterKey~ (*see Chapter 7 for Object Snap Modes*)
mid of (*select Point 2*)

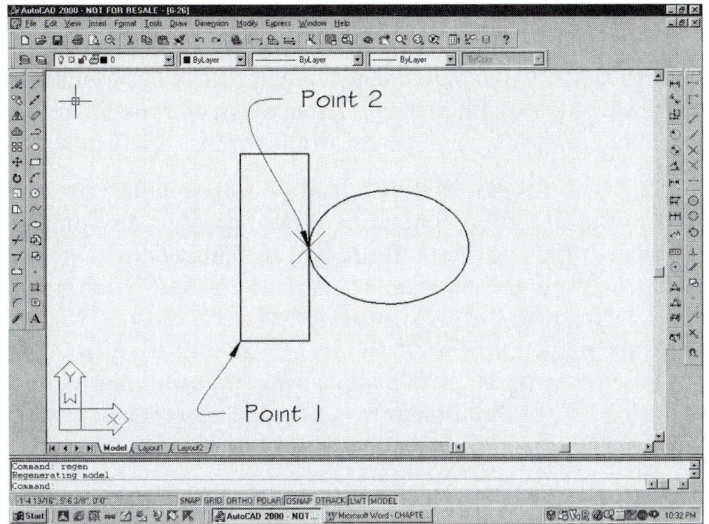

FIGURE 6–22 Drawing a Water Closet using the LINE and ELLIPSE commands.

Specify other endpoint of axis: **@28<0** ~EnterKey~

Specify distance to other axis or [Rotation]: **@10<90** ~EnterKey~

Congratulations! You have created a water closet symbol using the LINE and the ELLIPSE commands as shown in Figure 6–22.

6.4.3.2 Creating Elliptical Arcs
You can use the Arc option of the ELLIPSE command to create elliptical arcs. The angle of the elliptical arc is drawn counterclockwise from the first axis endpoint. The first axis endpoint selected becomes the zero degree as the start angle. If you enter 60 as the start angle, the elliptical arc will be started 60 degrees counterclockwise from the first endpoint location. The elliptical arc in Figure 6–23 can be drawn 180 degrees counterclockwise from the first axis endpoint as follows:

```
Command: EL or ELLIPSE ~EnterKey~
Specify axis endpoint of ellipse or [Arc/Center]: ARC
Specify axis endpoint of elliptical arc or [Center]: (select endpoint 1)
Specify other endpoint of axis: (select endpoint 2)
Specify distance to other axis or [Rotation]: (select second axis point)
Specify start angle or [Parameter]: 0 ~EnterKey~
```

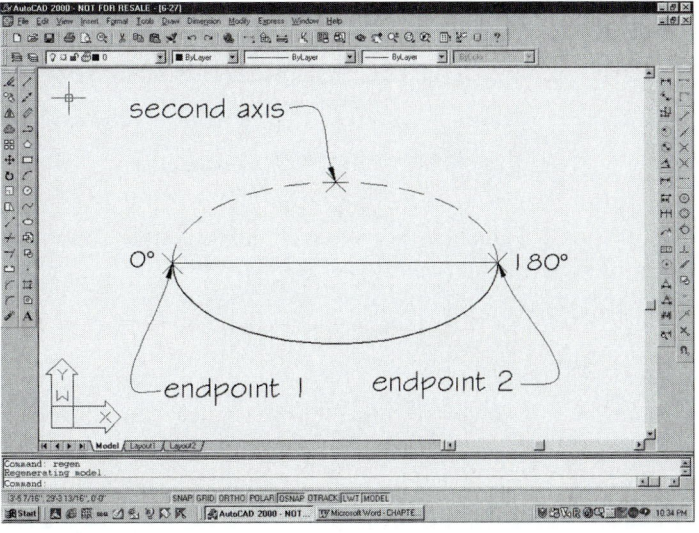

FIGURE 6–23 Creating an elliptical arc. Notice the location of the 0° start angle and the counterclockwise rotation to the 180 degrees end angle.

```
Specify end angle or [Parameter/Included angle]: 180 ~EnterKey~
```
The Parameter option allows you to specify the start angle of the elliptical arc. AutoCAD uses parametric vector equation to create the elliptical arc. The Included Angle option allows you to specify the included angle measured relative to the start angle instead of 0°. You can also use the Rotate option to rotate an elliptical arc around its axis or create an elliptical arc using the Center option.

6.4.3.3 Creating Isometric Circles
An isometric circle can be created using the Isocircle option of the ELLIPSE command. Before creating an isometric circle, you must create an isometric snap grid using the Drafting Settings dialog box. This was discussed in Chapter 4. After creating the isometric snap grid, turn the Snap and Grid on to display the isometric snap and grid. This will change the grid dots on the screen to isometric orientation. When the isometric snap appears on the grid, the crosshairs also change to reflect the proper isometric plane orientation.

When creating isometric circles, the isometric crosshair position must be set to the proper orientation. The orientation must reflect the current isometric plane that the isometric circle is created on. There are three isometric crosshair positions related to the isometric plane:

1. Left isometric plane.
2. Top isometric plane.
3. Right isometric plane.

The isometric positions are referred to as *isoplanes*. To orient the crosshairs to the proper isoplane, press the ~F5Key~. To toggle the isoplane to the next orientation, press the ~F5Key~ again. AutoCAD will display the <Isoplane Left>, <Isoplane Top>, and <Isoplane Right> prompts. You can also use the ISOPLANE command to move to the proper isometric plane as follows:

```
Command: ISOPLANE ~EnterKey~
Current isoplane: Top
Enter isometric plane setting [Left/Top/Right] <current>: (enter L, T, or R)
```

The isometric circles in Figure 6–24 are created as follows (first use the LINE command to create the isometric object):

```
Command: ELLIPSE ~EnterKey~
Specify axis endpoint of ellipse or [Arc/Center/Isocircle]: I ~EnterKey~
Specify center for isocircle: (for each side of the isometric box, make sure
    you are at the correct isoplane and select the center for the isocircle)
Specify radius of isocircle or [Diameter]: (enter a radius value)
Repeat the same procedure for each isoplane.
```

FIGURE 6–24 Creating isometric circles (isocircle) using the ELLIPSE command. This is possible only when Snap Style is set to Isometric snap.

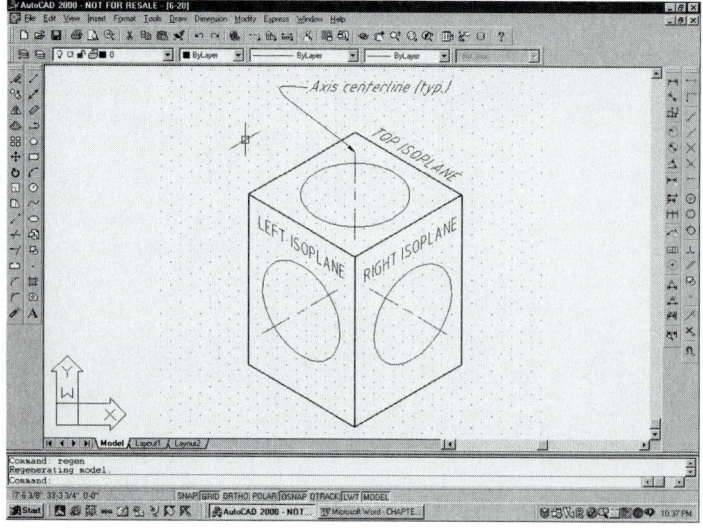

Note: The PELLIPSE system variable allows you to set how an ellipse is drawn. When the PELLIPSE is set to 0 (default), AutoCAD will draw regular ellipse objects, and when it is set to 1 AutoCAD will draw ellipses as a series of polyline arcs. When it is set to 1, the Arc option is not available to use.

Caution: When you edit an isometric circle to change its radius or diameter using the CHANGE command or the Properties window, its angular value will be changed from isocircle to nonisocircle, and it will no longer be isometric. The CHANGE command is discussed in Chapter 12. The Properties window is discussed in Chapter 13.

6.5 DRAWING CIRCULAR POLYLINES

The DONUT or DOUGHNUT command will allow you to draw solid circles. These solid circles are actually polyline arcs with a width. The SOLID command allows you to fill an object solid but is a complicated process. The BHATCH command is used to create hatch patterns that could be solid or otherwise. The BHATCH command is discussed in Chapter 20.

6.5.1 Using the DONUT Command

The DONUT command can be accessed by entering DO, DONUT, DOUGHNUT at the command line or by selecting Donut from the Draw pull-down menu. The command line procedure is as follows:

```
Command: DO, DONUT, or DOUGHNUT ~EnterKey~
Specify inside diameter of donut <current>: (specify inside diameter)
Specify outside diameter of donut <current>: (specify outside diameter)
Specify center of donut or <exit>: (specify center point of donut or
enter E to exit)
```

You can specify as many center points as you like to draw the same size donut until you press the ~EnterKey~ or the ~EscKey~. You can enter a new inside or outside diameter for the donut or accept the current diameter settings inside the brackets by pressing the ~EnterKey~. When you specify different inside and outside diameter values, the donut will not be completely filled solid. This is shown in Figure 6–25A. If the inside diameter of donut is set to zero (0), a complete solid circle without the center hole is drawn according to the specified outside diameter as shown in Figure 6–25B.

AutoCAD fills the interior of the donut based on the current setting of the FILL command or the FILLMODE system variable. When the FILL command is turned off or the FILLMODE

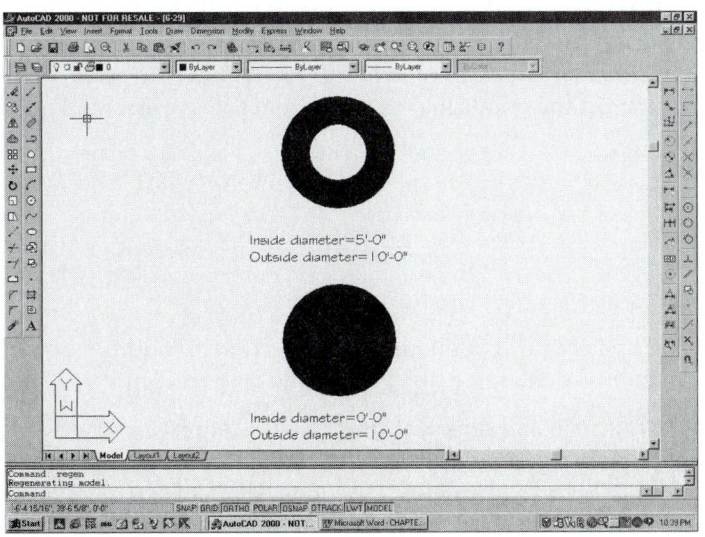

FIGURE 6–25 Two different ways to draw a donut.

FIGURE 6–26 The two donuts in Figure 6–25 with the FILL = off or FILLMODE = 0. Notice how the many pieces of the circle are segmented.

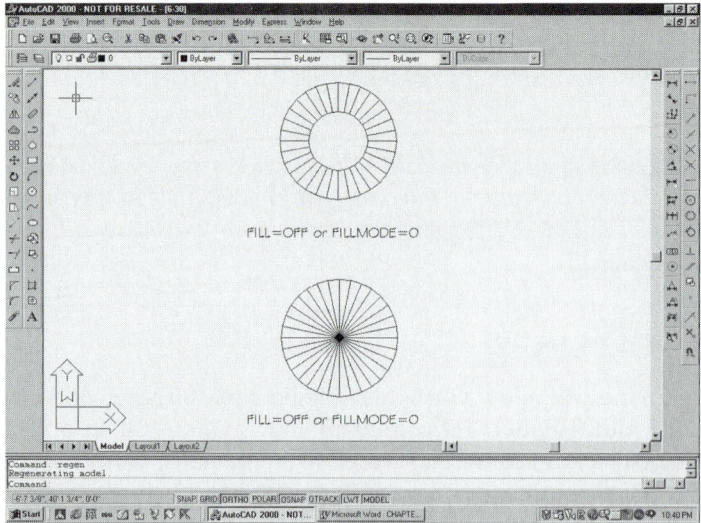

system variable is set to zero, the donut will be displayed as individual segments of the circle as shown in Figure 6–26.

The DONUTID system variable allows you to specify the current inside diameter, and the DONUTOD system variable allows you to specify the current outside diameter of the donut.

Tips: Enter REGEN at the command line after changing the FILL or the FILLMODE values. The FILL command or the FILMODE system variable affects objects created from polylines. These include the DONUT, POLYGON, POLYLINE, and RECTANGLE commands. It will also affect the ELLIPSE command if it is used with PELLIPSE = 1.

6.6 DRAWING SOLID OBJECTS

You can draw solid objects as you create them using the Width option of the PLINE command. This works fine with simple objects and simple floor plans, including polyline circles. But you should not create all your objects using the PLINE command. You can fill an existing closed object solid with the SOLID command or by using the BHATCH command. The solid pattern of the BHATCH command is the simplest and the most efficient and effective way to fill an existing object solid. The BHATCH command is explained in Chapter 20. The SOLID command uses solid triangles and solid quadrilaterals as you select the points on the object. You can access the SOLID command by selecting the 2D Solid button in the Surfaces toolbar, selecting 2D Solid from the Surfaces cascading menu in the Draw pull-down menu, or entering SO or SOLID at the command line. AutoCAD will then ask you to select points on the object. The order in which you select the points makes a difference. The object in Figure 6–27A is filled in solid as follows:

```
Command: SOLID ~EnterKey~
Specify first point: (select point 1)
Specify second point: (select point 2)
Specify third point: (select point 3)
Specify fourth point or <exit>: (select point 1)
Specify third point: ~EnterKey~
```

The Specify third point: prompt is used as an additional point allowing you to fill in additional segments of the same object as in the case of Figure 6–27B and C.

Tips: Solid and dense hatching require long regeneration time, especially in very large projects. To keep the regeneration time to a minimum, create a separate layer for solid and hatched objects and keep that layer frozen until ready to plot. If you are creating check prints, turn FILL off to save plotting time.

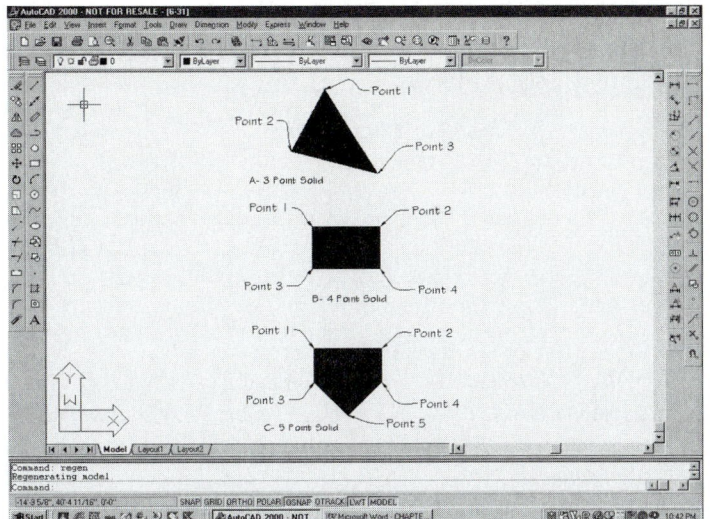

FIGURE 6–27 **A:** Using the SOLID command to triangulate points to fill an object. **B:** Using the second or third point as point 5 to enter the fourth point.

6.7 DRAWING RECTANGLES

The RECTANGLE command allows you to draw rectangles and squares as single-entity objects out of a polyline. This means that you can establish a specific width for the rectangle similar to the PLINE command. You can access the RECTANGLE command by selecting Rectangle from the Draw pull-down menu, selecting the Rectangle button in the Draw toolbar, or by entering REC, RECTANG, or REC-TANGLE at the command line. When drawing rectangles, AutoCAD will ask you to specify the first corner point and the second corner point. You can move your cursor to select these points or enter the coordinates for the points. For example, you can draw the rectangle measuring 15′-8″ × 10′-10″ starting from 7′, 27′ in Figure 6–28A as follows:

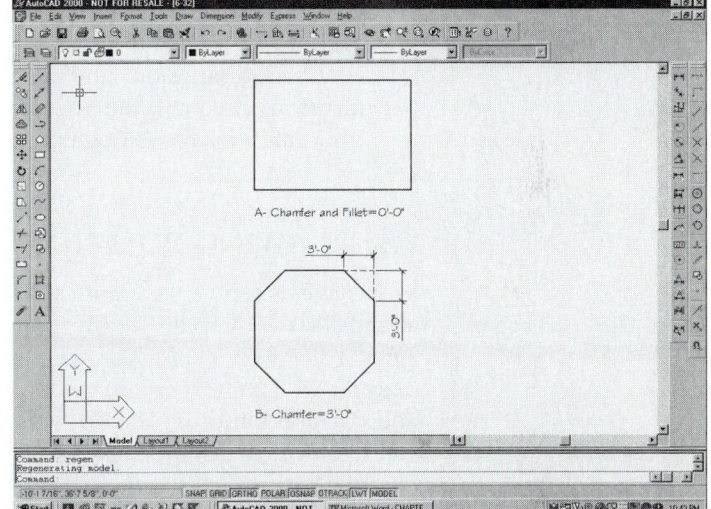

FIGURE 6–28 Using the RECTANGLE command. **A:** A rectangle with straight corners. **B:** A rectangle with angled corners as 3′-0″.

```
Command: REC ~EnterKey~
Specify first corner point or [Chamfer/Elevation/Fillet/Thickness/Width]:
7',27' ~EnterKey~
Specify other corner: @15'8,10'10 ~EnterKey~
```

The @ symbol is needed to establish the second corner from the starting point. To draw a square, enter X and Y coordinates as same value. The command line options are as follows:

CHAMFER: This option allows you to create an angled corner called *chamfer* on all the corners of the square or the rectangle. See the CHAMFER command in this chapter. The default chamfer distance is 0′-0″. Enter C at the command line option.

ELEVATION: This option allows you to set the elevation for the square or the rectangle in the Z direction. This option is used in three-dimensional drawings.

FILLET: This option allows you to create a rounded corner called *fillet* on all the corners of the square or the rectangle. See the FILLET command in this chapter. The default fillet radius is 0′-0″. Enter F at the command line option.

THICKNESS: This option allows you to set the thickness of the rectangle's sides in the Z direction. This option is used in 3D drawings.

WIDTH: This option allows you to set a line width for the rectangle's four sides. This is similar to the width option of the PLINE command. The default width is 0′-0″. Enter W at the command line option.

The values you enter for the Chamfer, Elevation, Fillet, Thickness, and Width options become the default value for the next use of the RECTANGLE command. You can draw the rectangle in Figure 6–28B as follows:

```
Command: RECTANG ~EnterKey~
Specify first corner point or [Chamfer/Elevation/Fillet/Thickness/Width]:
C ~EnterKey~
Specify first chamfer distance for rectangle <0'-0">: 3' ~EnterKey~
Specify second chamfer distance for rectangle <3'-0">: ~EnterKey~
Specify first corner point or [Chamfer/Elevation/Fillet/Thickness/Width]:
(select first corner)
Specify other corner point: @12',12' ~EnterKey~
```

Note: Objects created with the RECTANGLE command are not affected by the CHAMFERA, CHAMFERB, FILLETRAD, and PLINEWID system variables. Since rectangles are drawn from polylines, you can use the PEDIT command to edit an existing rectangle.

AutoCAD 2000i Update: The RECTANGLE command includes a new Dimension option. This option allows you to create a rectangle using the specified points as diagonally opposite corners. After specifying the first corner of the rectangle right click in the drawing area and select the Dimension from the shortcut menu. Enter a number for length (X dimension) and press the ~EnterKey~, then enter a length for width (Y dimension) and press the ~EnterKey~. Move your cursor to display one of the four possible solutions for the rectangle and left click to select the solution.

6.8 DRAWING POLYGONS

A *polygon* is a closed geometrical figure with three or more equal sides. The POLYGON command allows you to draw polygons as single-entity objects. The polygons are created from polylines. You can draw a square using the POLYGON command but not a rectangle. You can access the POLYGON command by selecting Polygon from the Draw pull-down menu, selecting the Polygon button in the Draw toolbar, or by entering POL or POLYGON at the command line. AutoCAD will first ask you to enter the number of sides for the polygon. The value inside the brackets represents the previously entered number for the sides. The number you enter becomes the default number of sides for the next polygon. You are then asked to specify the center of the polygon or the Edge option to select an existing edge for the side of the polygon.

Polygons are created either inside or outside an imaginary circle. With the first method, the polygon is *inscribed* within the circle and is drawn inside the imaginary circle with its corners touching the circle. This is the default method as shown in Figure 6–29A. With the second method, the polygon is *circumscribed* outside of the imaginary circle as shown in Figure 6–29B. You can control the size, direction, and orientation of the polygon with your cursor. The inscribed polygon in Figure 6–29A can be drawn as follows:

```
Command: POL or POLYGON ~EnterKey~
Enter number of sides: 5 ~EnterKey~
Specify center of polygon or [Edge]: (select center point)
Enter an option [Inscribed in circle/Circumscribed about circle] <I>:
~EnterKey~
Specify radius of circle: 5' ~EnterKey~
```

The circumscribed polygon in Figure 6–29B can be drawn as follows:

```
Command: POL or POLYGON ~EnterKey~
Enter number of sides: 7 ~EnterKey~
Specify center of polygon or [Edge]: (select center point)
Enter an option [Inscribed in circle/Circumscribed about circle] <I>: C
~EnterKey~
Specify radius of circle: 5' ~EnterKey~
```

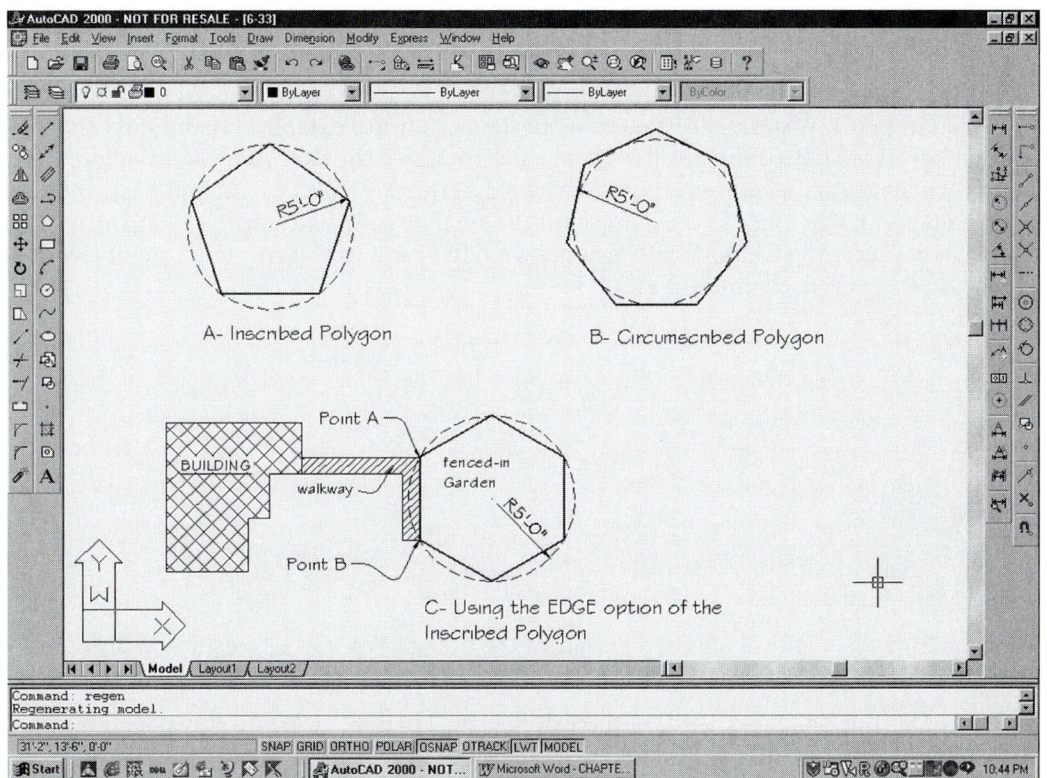

FIGURE 6–29 Using the Inscribed, Circumscribed, and Edge options of the POLYGON command. Notice that the six-sided polygon is created with the Edge option.

The inscribed polygon with the Edge option in Figure 6–29C can be drawn as follows:

```
Command: POL or POLYGON ~EnterKey~
Enter number of sides: 6 ~EnterKey~
Specify center of polygon or [Edge]: E
Specify first endpoint of edge: (select point A)
Specify second endpoint of edge: (select point B)
```

The Edge option uses the selected points (length of one edge) to determine the radius of the imaginary circle for the polygon.

6.9 DRAWING ANGLED AND ROUNDED CORNERS

AutoCAD allows you to create angled and rounded corners with the CHAMFER and the FILLET commands. In AutoCAD, a chamfer is considered to be an angled corner on an object and a fillet is considered to be a rounded corner on an object.

6.9.1 Using The CHAMFER Command

The CHAMFER command allows you to create an angled surface at the intersection of two lines or two polylines. If there is an apparent intersection (when two lines do not intersect), AutoCAD will chamfer the intersection of the two lines. AutoCAD does not chamfer when two polylines do not intersect, and you cannot chamfer Multilines unless the polylines and multilines are exploded. You can chamfer crossing lines, intersecting lines, and nonintersecting lines.

> *AutoCAD 2000i Update: The CHAMFER and FILLET commands can be used on non-intersecting polylines.*

You can access the CHAMFER command by selecting Chamfer from the Modify pull-down menu, selecting the Chamfer button in the Modify toolbar, or entering CHA or CHAMFER at the command line. There are five options associated with the CHAMFER command as follows:

```
Command: CHA or CHAMFER ~EnterKey~
(TRIM mode) Current chamfer Dist1 = 0'-0", Dist2 = 0'-0"
```

```
Select first line or [Polyline/Distance/Angle/Trim/Method]: (select first
line or enter an option)
```

Distance: This option allows you to specify chamfers using two distances measured from the intersection point. When the distances from the corner are established, the next time you access the CHAMFER command the Distance 1 becomes the *first line* you select and the Distance 2 becomes the *second line* you select on the object. In order to actually use the CHAMFER command, you must first establish all the settings associated with the chamfering of the object then access the CHAMFER command again to use it. The corner of the object shown in Figure 6–30A can be chamfered as follows:

```
Command: CHA or CHAMFER ~EnterKey~
(TRIM mode) Current chamfer Dist1 = 0'-0", Dist2 = 0'-0"
Select first line or [Polyline/Distance/Angle/Trim/Method]: D ~EnterKey~
Specify first chamfer distance <0'-0">: 3' ~EnterKey~
Specify second chamfer distance <3'-0">: ~EnterKey~
Command: ~EnterKey~ (this will bring back the CHAMFER command)
CHAMFER
(TRIM mode) Current chamfer Dist1 = 3'-0", Dist2 = 3'-0"
Select first line or [Polyline/Distance/Angle/Trim/Method]: (select Line A)
Select second line: (select Line B)
```

Figure 6–30B shows the chamfered corner of the object. You can also establish different values for chamfer distance 1 and chamfer distance 2.

Angle: This option allows you to establish the first chamfer distance and a chamfer angle applied to determine the second chamfer distance. The corner of the object shown in Figure 6–31A can be established as follows:

```
Command: CHA or CHAMFER ~EnterKey~
(TRIM mode) Current chamfer Dist1 = 3'-0", Dist2 = 3'-0"
```

FIGURE 6–30 A: Object before chamfer and **B:** Object after chamfer.

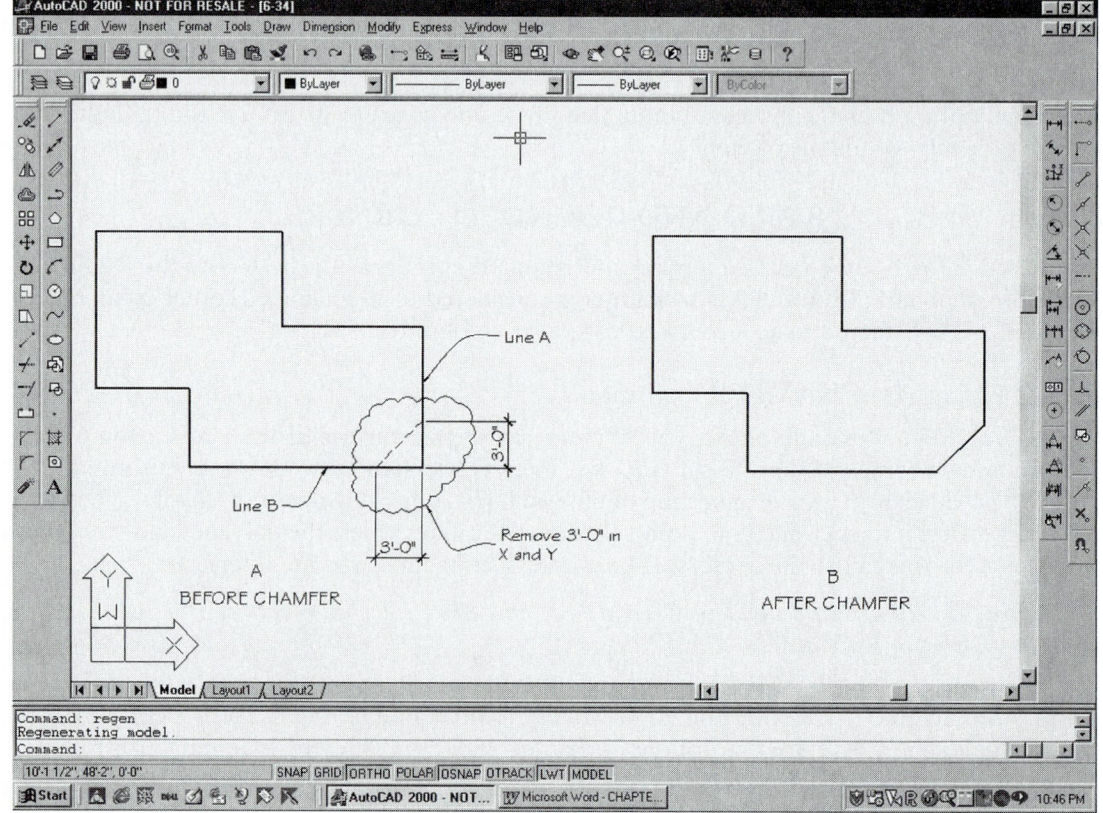

```
Select first line or [Polyline/Distance/Angle/Trim/Method]: A ~EnterKey~
Specify chamfer length on the first line <3'-0">: 0
Specify chamfer angle from the first line <0>: 40 ~EnterKey~
Command: ~EnterKey~ (this will bring back the CHAMFER command)
CHAMFER
(TRIM mode) Current chamfer Length = 0'-0", Angle = 40
Select first line or [Polyline/Distance/Angle/Trim/Method]: (select Line A)
Select second line: (select Line B)
```

Figure 6–31B shows the corner of the object being squared. You can use any angle less than 90 degrees to create the corner shown in Figure 6–31B. However, you cannot use minus angles.

You can enter 0 for the first and second chamfer distance to achieve the same result. The zero (0) chamfer distance option is extremely useful in extending the lines to meet at a corner created by the OFFSET command. For example, the object in Figure 5–14 in Chapter 5 is shown in Figure 6–32A. The inside lines created by the OFFSET command can be cleaned up (crossing lines and nonintersecting lines) using the zero chamfer distance of the CHAMFER command as follows:

```
Command: CHA or CHAMFER ~EnterKey~
(TRIM mode) Current chamfer Dist1 = 3'-0", Dist2 = 3'-0"
Select first line or [Polyline/Distance/Angle/Trim/Method]: D ~EnterKey~
Specify first chamfer distance <3'-0">: 0 ~EnterKey~
Specify second chamfer distance <0'-0">: ~EnterKey~
Command: ~EnterKey~ (this will bring back the CHAMFER command)
CHAMFER
(TRIM mode) Current chamfer Dist1 = 0'-0", Dist2 = 0'-0"
Select first line or [Polyline/Distance/Angle/Trim/Method]: (select line 1)
Select second line: (select line 2)
Right-click on the drawing area and select Repeat CHAMFER from the
shortcut menu. This will bring back the CHAMFER command.
CHAMFER
```

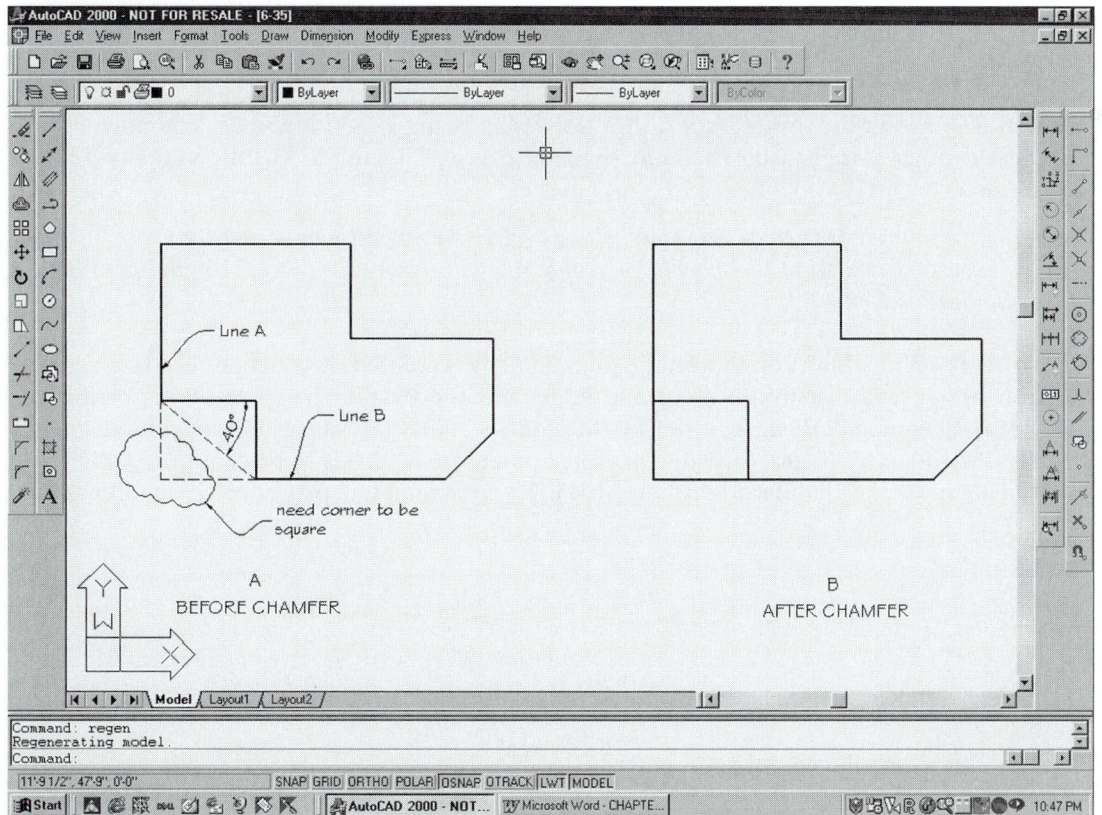

FIGURE 6–31 A: Object corner before chamfer and **B:** Object corner squared after chamfer.

FIGURE 6–32   A: The inside lines of the floor plan created by the OFFSET command need to be joined. **B:** The zero chamfer distance option will join those lines.

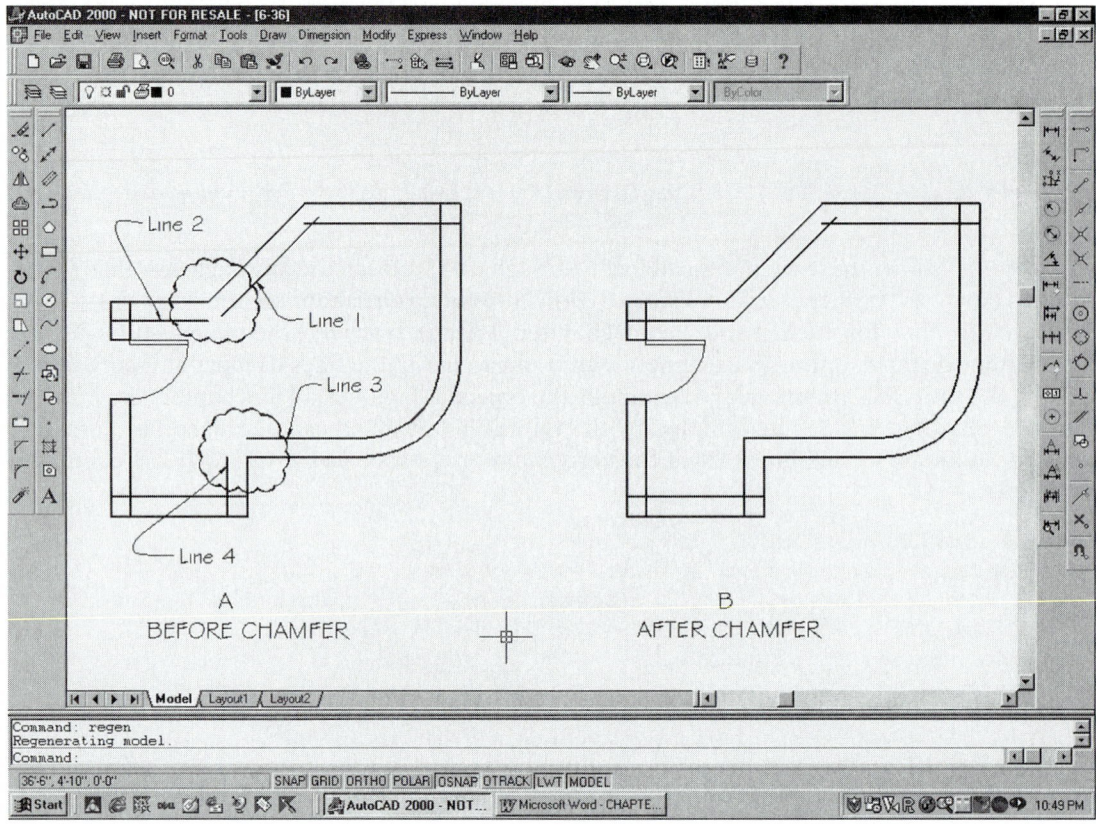

```
(TRIM mode) Current chamfer Dist1 = 0'-0", Dist2 = 0'-0"
Select first line or [Polyline/Distance/Angle/Trim/Method]: (select line 3)
Select second line: (select line 4)
```

Figure 6–32B shows the inside lines of the floor plan being joined together. You may wish to clean up the other corners using the same procedure as well. Figure 6–32B shows the two chamfered corners.

Caution: When selecting lines that cross, always select the longest length, not the short lines that actually cross. If you select the short lines, AutoCAD will remove the longest length lines from the crossing intersection.

Trim: This option allows you to trim the lines and edges created by the chamfered corner. The No Trim option will display the lines and edges created by the chamfered corner after the CHAMFER command. By default the TRIM mode is on. If you want No Trim, you must enter T for TRIM and enter N for No Trim. The object in Figure 6–33A is to be chamfered 4'-0″ with No Trim. First, set the chamfered distance to 4'. The command line procedure is as follows:

```
Command: CHA or CHAMFER ~EnterKey~
(TRIM mode) Current chamfer Dist1 = 4'-0", Dist2 = 4'-0"
Select first line or [Polyline/Distance/Angle/Trim/Method]: T ~EnterKey~
Enter Trim mode option [Trim/No trim] <Trim>: N ~EnterKey~
Select first line or [Polyline/Distance/Angle/Trim/Method]: (select
horizontal line)
Select second line: (select vertical line)
```

Figure 6–33B shows the completed operation.

Note: The TRIM command is discussed in Chapter 12.

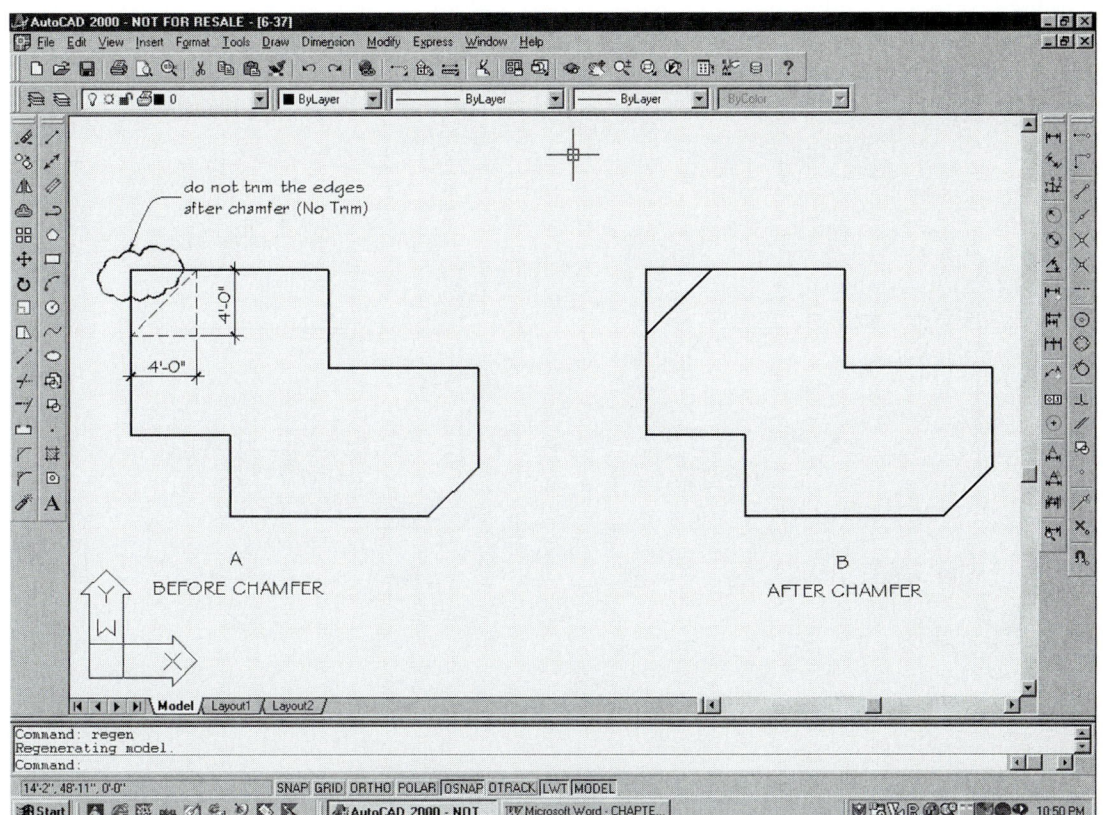

Method: The Method option allows you to set the CHAMFER command to either the Distance or Angle method. In the Distance method, the chamfer is determined by the two specified distances. In the Angle method, the chamfer is determined by the angle and distance you specify. The command line procedure is as follows:

```
Command: CHA or CHAMFER ~EnterKey~
(TRIM mode) Current chamfer Dist1 = 3'-0", Dist2 = 3'-0"
Select first line or [Polyline/Distance/Angle/Trim/Method]: M ~EnterKey~
Enter trim method [Distance/Angle] <Distance>: A ~EnterKey~ (this will
set the Method to Angle)
Select first line or [Polyline/Distance/Angle/Trim/Method]: (you can
continue with the command)
```

Next time you access the CHAMFER command, the Length and Angle values will be shown.

Polyline: This option allows you to chamfer an existing polyline. You can use this option to chamfer objects drawn with the POLYLINE, POLYGON, and RECTANGLE commands. All corners of the polyline object will be chamfered. If the polyline is not closed with the Close option, the first and last segments of the polyline will not be chamfered. Figure 6–34A shows an object created with the Close option of the PLINE command. The corners of the object can be chamfered at a distance of 12″ as follows:

```
Command: CHA or CHAMFER ~EnterKey~
(TRIM mode) Current chamfer Dist1 = 0'-0", Dist2 = 0'-0"
Select first line or [Polyline/Distance/Angle/Trim/Method]: D ~EnterKey~
Specify first chamfer distance <0'-0">: 12 ~EnterKey~
Specify second chamfer distance <1'-0">: ~EnterKey~
Command: ~EnterKey~ (this will bring back the CHAMFER command)
CHAMFER
```

FIGURE 6–34   A: Using the Polyline option of the CHAMFER command when the pline is closed with the Close option. **B:** The same polyline created without using the Close option.

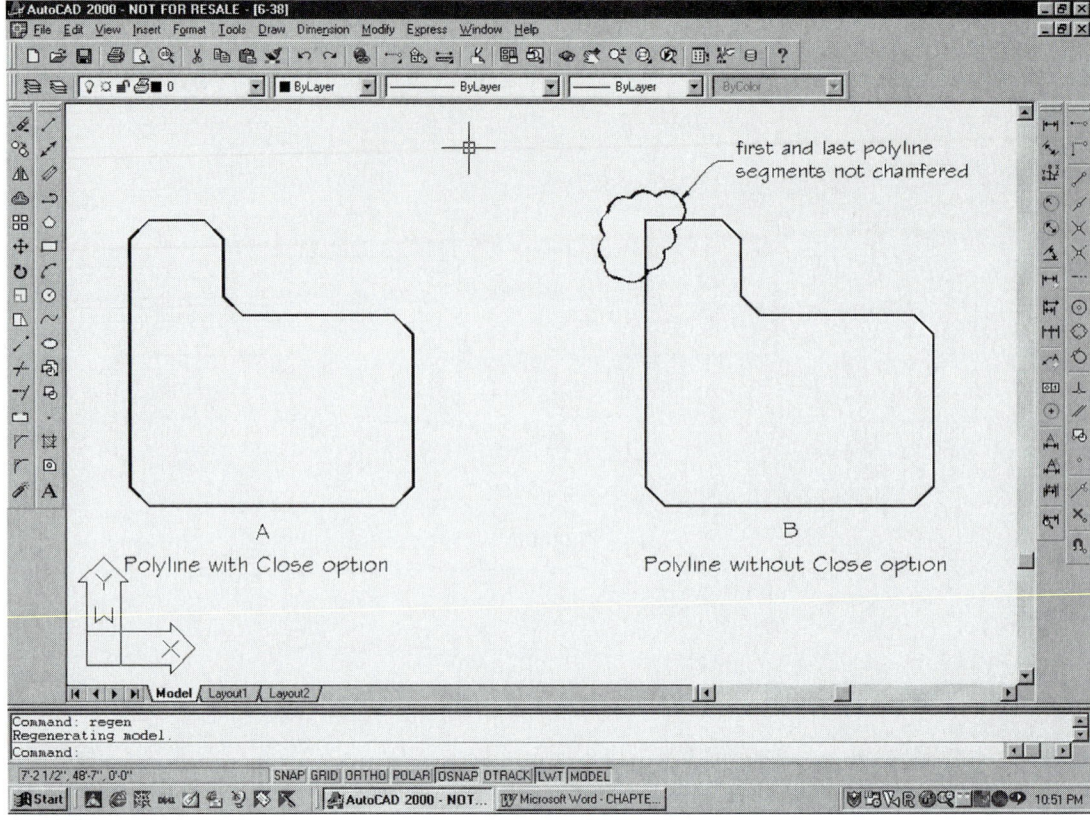

```
(TRIM mode) Current chamfer Dist1 = 1'-0", Dist2 = 1'-0"
Select first line or [Polyline/Distance/Angle/Trim/Method]: P ~EnterKey~
Select 2D polyline: (select any one line of the polyine)
```

The object in Figure 6–34B is created without using the Close option of the PLINE command and chamfered at a distance of 12″.

You can use the CHAMFERC and the CHAMFERD system variables to set the chamfer distance and the chamfer angle.

6.9.2   Using the FILLET Command

The FILLET command allows you to create a rounded corner at the intersection of two lines or two polylines. If there is an apparent intersection (when two lines do not intersect), AutoCAD will fillet the intersection of the two lines. AutoCAD does not fillet when two polylines do not intersect, and you cannot fillet Multilines unless the polylines and multilines are exploded. Similar to the CHAMFER command, you can use the FILLET command (Radius = 0) to trim crossing lines and join nonintersecting lines at an intersection. You can also fillet parallel lines. You can access the FILLET command by selecting Fillet from the Modify pull-down menu, selecting the Fillet button in the Modify toolbar, or by entering F or FILLET at the command line. There are three options associated with the FILLET command as follows:

```
Command: F or FILLET ~EnterKey~
Current settings: Mode = TRIM, Radius = 0'-0"
Select first object or [Polyline/Radius/Trim]: (select object or option)
```

Radius: This option allows you to specify the radius of the corner when using the FILLET command. When the fillet radius is established, you must repeat the FILLET command to actually select the objects to create the rounded corner. The round corners of the object in Figure 6–35A can be created as follows:

```
Command: F or FILLET ~EnterKey~
Current settings: Mode = TRIM, Radius = 0'-0"
Select first object or [Polyline/Radius/Trim]: R ~EnterKey~
```

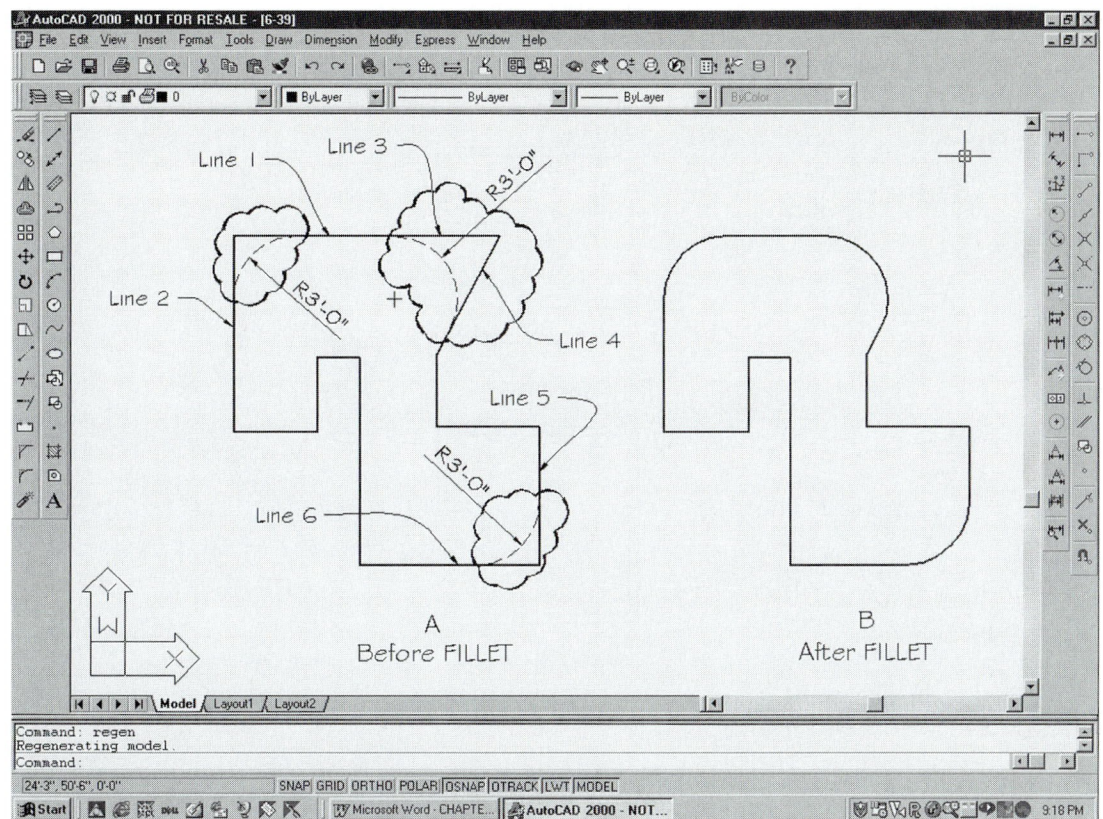

FIGURE 6–35 **A:** The object with three corners to be rounded with a 3'-0" radius. **B:** After the corners are rounded with the FILLET command.

```
Specify fillet radius <0'-0">: 3' ~EnterKey~
Command: ~EnterKey~ (this will bring back the FILLET command after
setting the Radius)
FILLET
Current settings: Mode = TRIM, Radius = 3'-0"
Select first object or [Polyline/Radius/Trim]: (select Line 1)
Select second object: (select Line 2)
Command: ~EnterKey~
```

Repeat the same procedure for lines 3, 4, 5, and 6. Figure 6–35B shows the object after the FILLET operations.

When the Radius is set to zero, the crossing lines are trimmed to an intersection and nonintersecting lines are joined. When rounding parallel lines, you do not have to set a specific radius because AutoCAD automatically establishes the radius as the half the distance of the offset value. Figure 6–36 shows three additional ways to use the FILLET command.

Trim:　*This is the same as the TRIM option of the CHAMFER command.*

Polyline:　This is the same as the POLYLINE option of the CHAMFER command.

You can use the FILLETRAD system variable to set the current fillet radius until it is changed when you enter a new value for the Radius option.

Tips: The CHAMFER and the FILLET commands are extremely useful when creating floor plans with the LINE and the OFFSET commands. You can change the TRIM mode option of the CHAMFER and the FILLET commands by using the TRIMMODE system variable at the command line. Enter 0 for the TRIMMODE to have No Trim.

AutoCAD 2000i Update:　The Fillet and Chamfer radius values can be assigned and changed without exiting the FILLET and the CHAMFER commands.

AutoCAD 2000i Update:　The FILLET and CHAMFER commands can be used with multiple polylines.

FIGURE 6–36 The FILLET command can be used on crossing lines, nonintersecting lines, and parallel lines.

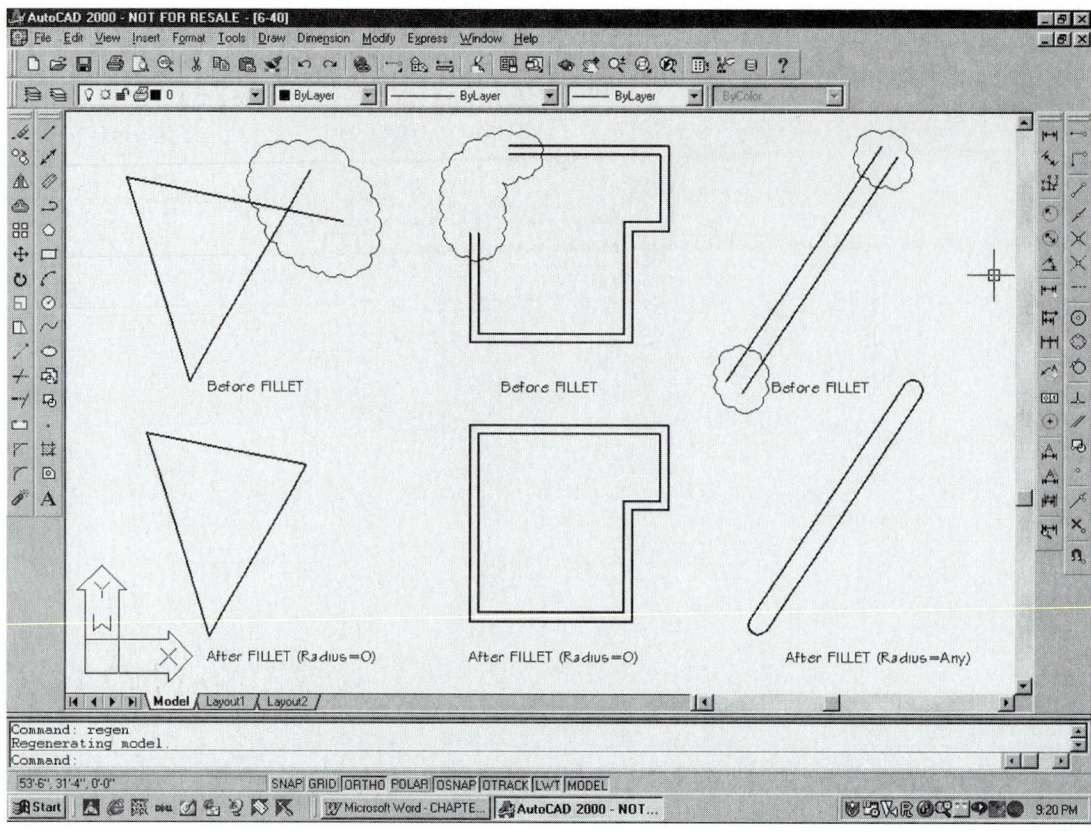

6.10 DRAWING FREEHAND LINES

Just as you would use a pencil and paper to sketch a design or an idea in architectural drawings, AutoCAD allows you to perform *sketching* with the SKETCH command. When using the SKETCH command, be sure to have a free cursor movement by turning the Snap and Ortho off.

6.10.1   Using the SKETCH Command

One of the great benefits of the SKETCH command is the ability to create bubble diagrams and schematics as part of your design process. The most important aspect of the SKETCH command is the *Record increment,* which determines the length of each line element used in sketching. Before using this command, determine the line length you like to use. For example, an increment of 1 creates line segments one unit in length. The command line procedure is as follows:

```
Command: SKETCH ~EnterKey~
Record increment <0'-1">: (enter a value)
Sketch. Pen eXit Quit Record Erase Connect.
(left click to begin sketching)
<Pen down>
(left click again to stop sketching)
<Pen up>
(press ~EnterKey~ to record and exit sketching)
```

AutoCAD will record the lines used with the SKETCH command. You can access a subcommand by entering its corresponding capitalized letter such as X for exit (eXit). Entering P (Pen) toggles the pen up and down. Entering X (eXit) records temporary segments and exits the SKETCH command. Entering Q (Quit) ignores temporary line segments and exits the SKETCH command. Entering R (Record) records line segments to memory. Entering E (Erase) erases temporary line segments. Entering C (Connect) connects to the endpoint of a line segment. Figure 6–37 shows a bubble diagram created with the SKETCH command.

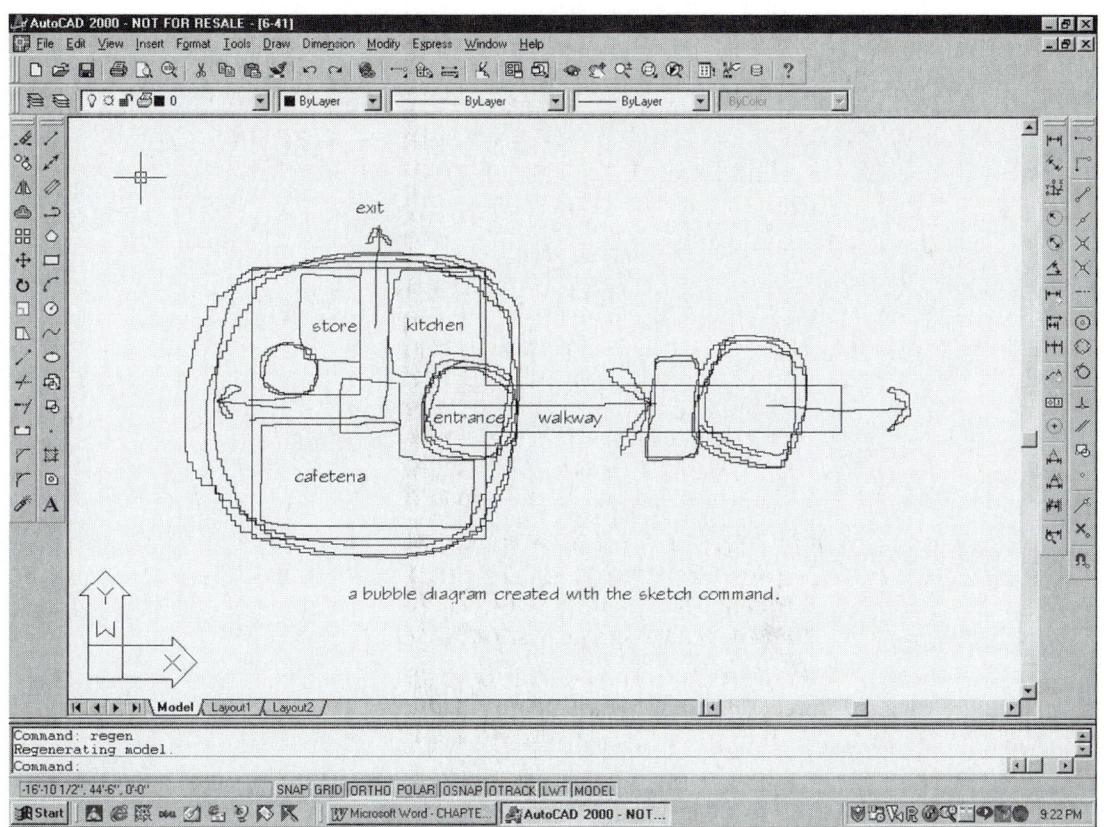

The SKPOLY system variable controls the type of sketching format as follows:

```
SKPOLY = 0 (as a default sketches are recorded as lines).
SKPOLY = 1 (sketches are recorded as polylines).
```

6.11 DRAWING PERFECT CURVES

Sometimes it is necessary to draw long curves connected to several points along a line such as a contour line. The SPLINE command allows you to draw continues curvatures similar to the *French curve* used in manual drafting. The SPLINE command actually draws NURBS (nonuniform rational B-spline).

6.11.1 Using the SPLINE Command

Similar to the LINE command, the SPLINE command allows you to select points on the screen and gives you the Close option to complete the command. You can access the SPLINE command by selecting Spline from the Draw pull-down menu, selecting the Spline button in the Draw toolbar, or by entering SPL or SPLINE at the command line. The contour lines in Figure 6–38 can be drawn as follows:

```
Command: SPL or SPLINE ~EnterKey~
Specify first point or [Object]: (use the Snap to Node Object Snap mode
to snap to the intersection of the X drawn as a point. See Chapter 7 for
the POINT command.)
Specify next point: (select the next point)
Specify next point or [Close/Fit tolerance] <start tangent>: (select the
next point)
Specify next point or [Close/Fit tolerance] <start tangent>: (select the
next point)
Specify next point or [Close/Fit tolerance] <start tangent>: (select the
next point)
```

FIGURE 6–38 The SPLINE command can be used to create contour lines on a site plan.

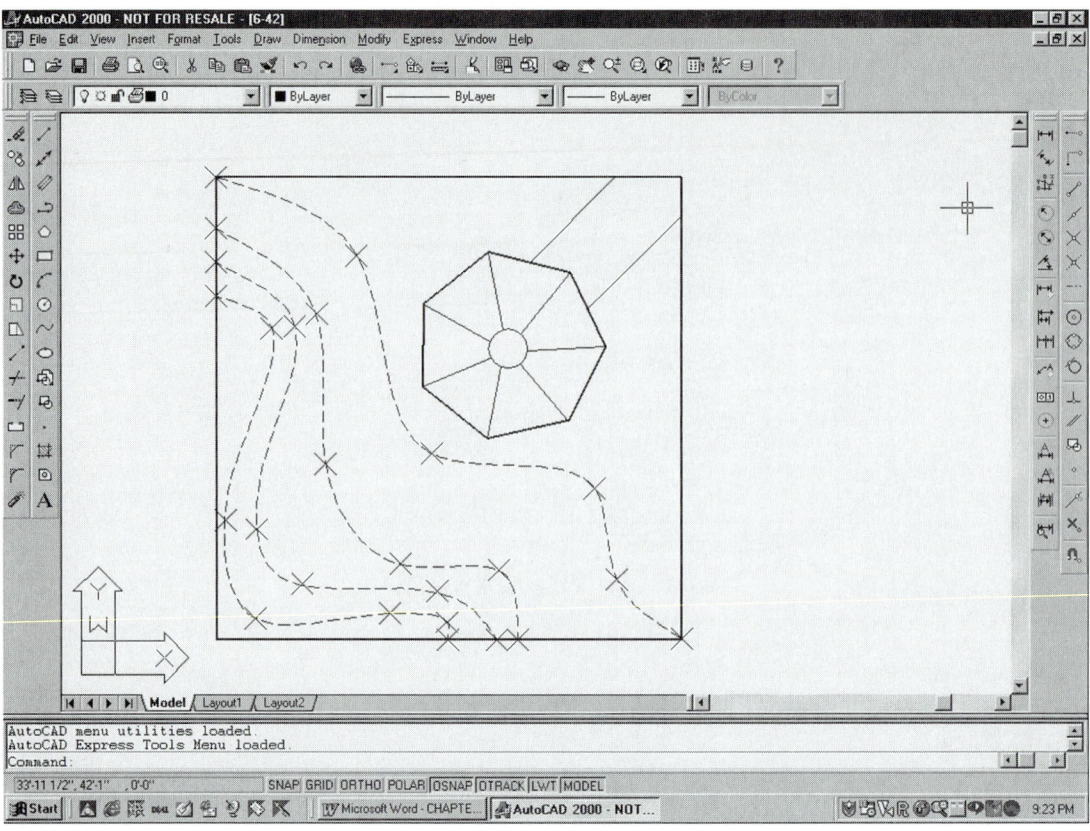

FIGURE 6–39 A site plan with contours created with the SPLINE command.

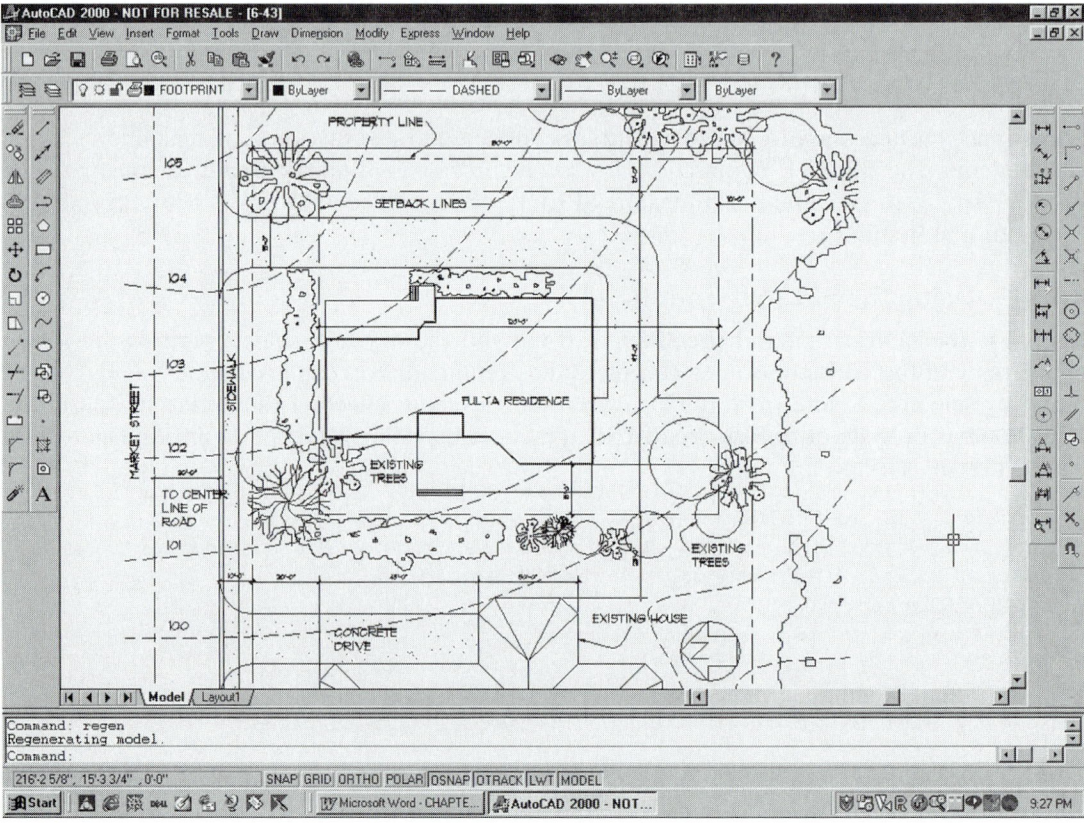

```
Specify next point or [Close/Fit tolerance] <start tangent>: (select the
next point)
Specify next point or [Close/Fit tolerance] <start tangent>: ~EnterKey~
Specify start tangent: ~EnterKey~
Specify end tangent: ~EnterKey~
```

The Object option converts two-dimensional and three-dimensional splined polylines into NURBS. The Close option closes the spline at the starting location. The Fit option allows you to specify a fit tolerance within which the spline curve passes through fit points. The Start tangent option allows you to specify the point of tangency of the starting point. The End tangent option allows you to specify the point of tangency of the endpoint.

Figure 6–39 shows a complete site plan with contour lines created with the SPLINE command.

You can also draw the wood grains on wood furniture using the SPLINE command. Figure 6–40 shows a conference table with wood grains drawn with the SPLINE command. Use the same procedure shown above to create the wood grains. Use Snap to Nearest object snap mode when no specific point is known for the first and the last points.

6.12 DRAWING REVISION CLOUDS

Changes and revisions are a major part of architectural drawings. Even after a project is completed, it is not unusual to make changes to specific drawings. When a change is made to an already completed drawing, a revision cloud is drawn around the change. This revision cloud marks the location of the change. Once the revision cloud is created, a triangle is placed and attached next to the revision cloud to identify the number of the change. The triangle with the revision number inside is then placed in the REVISION/ISSUE section of the Title Block information. Figure 6–41 shows part of a Title Block with REVISION/ISSUE section and the triangle representing revision 1, a brief description, and the date of the revision.

The revision cloud is created with the REVCLOUD command. You can access the REVCLOUD command by selecting Draw and then Revision Cloud from the Express pull-down menu, by selecting Revision Cloud from the Express Standard Toolbar, or by entering

FIGURE 6–41 The Revision Cloud and the REVISION/ISSUE parts of the Title Block with triangle and the revision number.

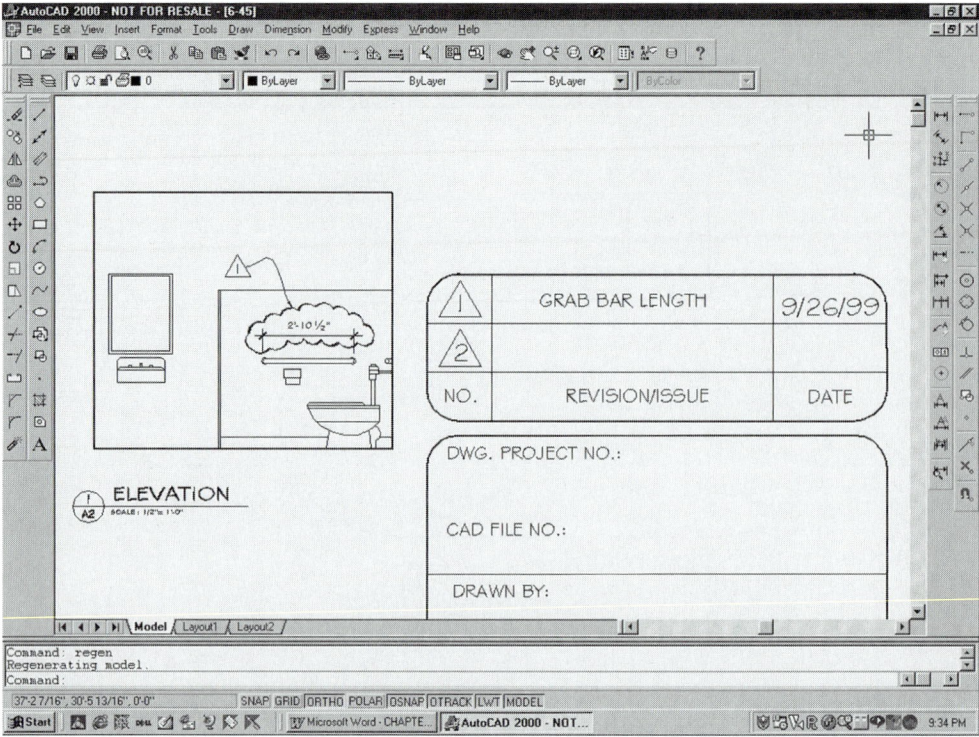

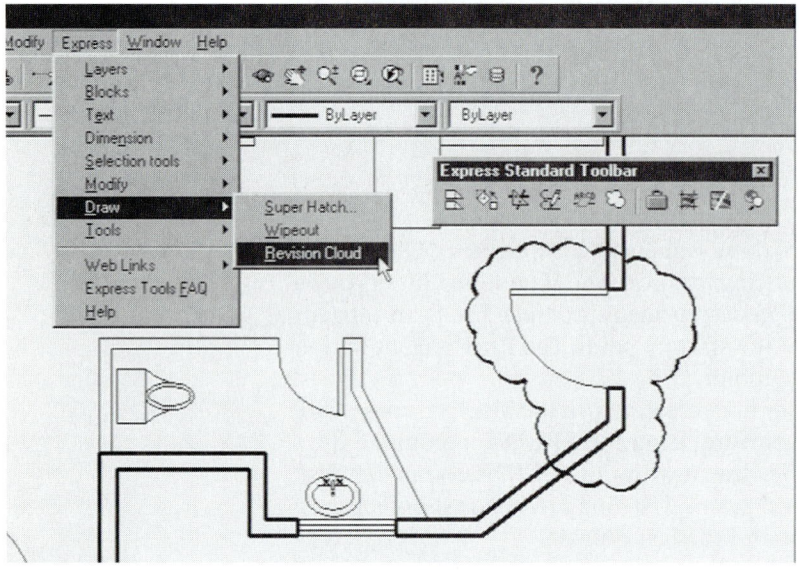

FIGURE 6–42 The Revision Cloud can be accessed from the Express pull-down menu or from the Express Standard Toolbar.

REVCLOUD at the command line. To access the Express Standard Toolbar, right-click on the empty space right side of the Help button on the Standard Toolbar and select Express Standard Toolbar from EXPRESS. The access operation from the Express pull-down menu and the Express Standard Toolbar are shown in Figure 6–42.

A revision cloud is composed of individual arcs joined together. You can draw a revision cloud with a specific arc length and an arc style. The *arc length* determines the individual arc segment lengths that make up the revision cloud. If you want to draw a revision cloud with short arcs, set the arc length to a small number such as 2″. If you want to draw a revision cloud with long arcs, set the arc length to a large number such as 36″. Since the arc length is determined from the actual drawing scale and the current Limits of the drawing, always check your drawing scale and determine the arc length accordingly. The *arc style* allows you to select Normal or Calligraphy for the revision cloud. The Normal option allows you to draw revision clouds with a standard uniform width arc segment. The Calligraphy option allows you to draw revision clouds with a varying width and bold arc segments.

The command line procedure is as follows:

```
Command: REVCLOUD ~EnterKey~
Arc length = 3/16", Arc style = Normal
Specify cloud starting point or [eXit/Options] <eXit>: (specify the
revision cloud starting point or enter O for options to change settings)
If you want to change the arc length and style before starting the
revision cloud enter O as follows:
Specify cloud starting point or [eXit/Options] <eXit>: O ~EnterKey~
```

This will display the Revcloud Options dialog box as shown in Figure 6–43. If you want the Calligraphy Arc Style, click inside the Calligraphy radio button. The preview box will show the new revision cloud arc style as bold. The preview box shows the arc length as X and does not change when you enter different values. If you want to change the current Arc Chord Length, highlight the existing value and enter a new value. You can also click on the Pick<button to select two points on the screen as the arc length. When done, click on the OK button.

After you close the Revcloud Options dialog box, AutoCAD will display the current settings of the revision cloud as follows:

```
Arch length = 4", Arc style = Calligraphy
Specify cloud starting point or [eXit/Options]
<eXit>: (select a starting point)
```

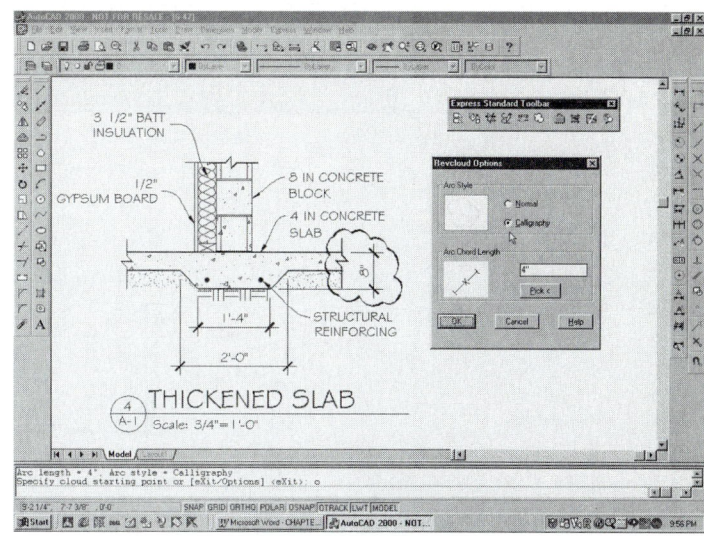

FIGURE 6–43 The Revcloud Options dialog box will allow you to set the Arc Style and the Arc Chord Length of the revision cloud.

Figure 6–44A shows a revision cloud with 4″ arc segments and a Normal arc style. Figure 6–44B shows a revision cloud with 12″ arc segment and a Normal arc style. Figure 6–44C shows a revision cloud with 8″ arc segment and a Calligraphy arc style. Figure 6–44D shows a revision cloud with 16″ arc segment and a Calligraphy arc style. The counterclockwise direction will draw the arcs bending outward while the clockwise direction will draw the arcs bending inward as shown in Figure 6–44E.

After you select the starting point, release your finger from the left button and move the cursor to define the shape and size of the revision cloud. **Do not hold down the left mouse button.** To close the revision cloud, move the cursor back over the starting point. AutoCAD will automatically close the revision cloud. You can also press the ~EnterKey~ or right-click to leave the revision cloud open.

Note: You can stop drawing the revision cloud at any time by pressing the ~EnterKey~ or by right-clicking.

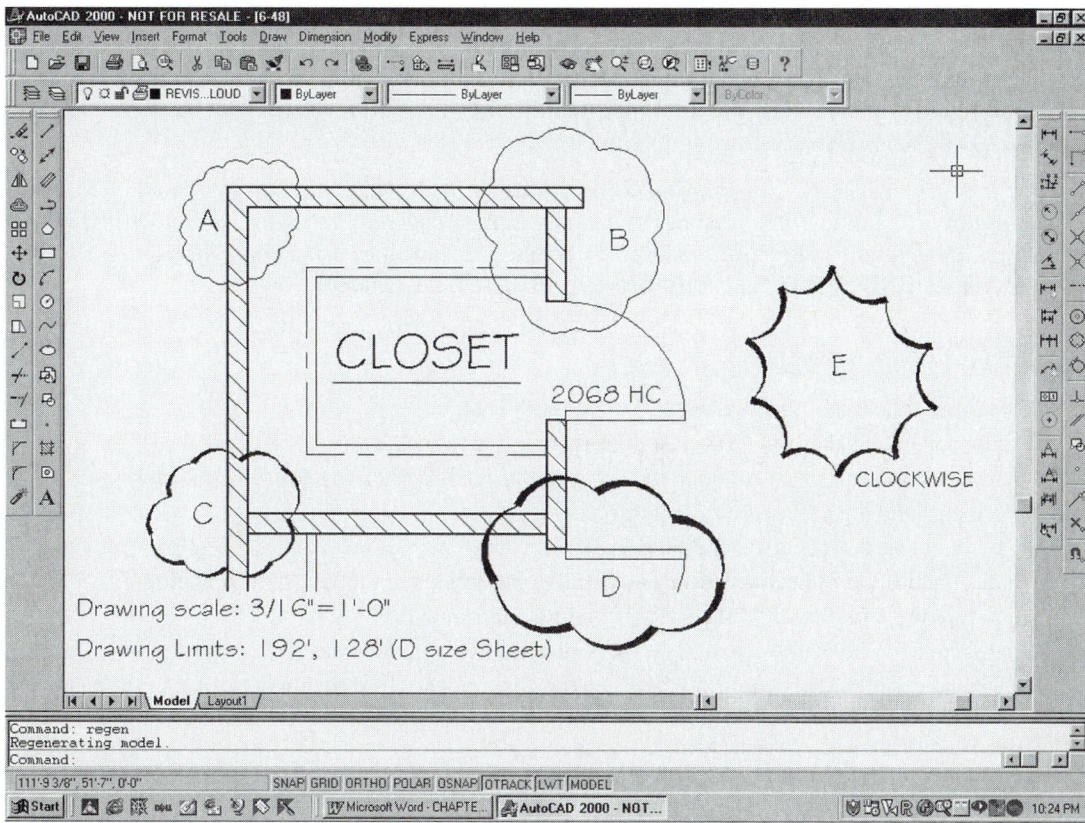

FIGURE 6–44 Different size and style of revision clouds.

FIGURE 6–45 The REVCLOUD command can also be used to create trees and bushes on site plans.

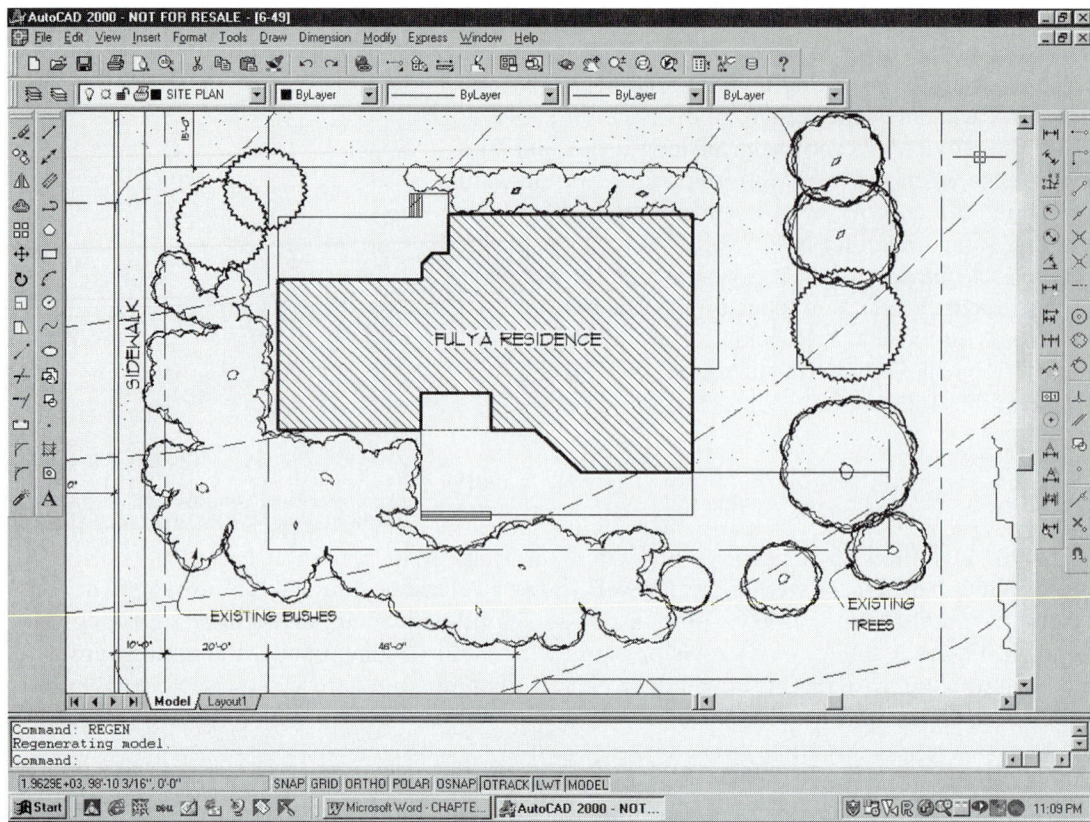

6.12.1 Using the REVCLOUD Command to Draw Trees and Bushes

The REVCLOUD command is a very versatile tool. You can use it to create trees and bushes for site and landscape plans. Use the Calligraphy option of the REVCLOUD command to create the trees and the bushes with varying widths. A site plan with trees and bushes created with the REVCLOUD command is shown in Figure 6–45. Change the Arc Chord length and go over the cloud again. You may use the CIRCLE command as a guide to trace the revision cloud so that the trees come out very close to a true circle.

Tips: Load the ZIGZAG linetype and draw circles with it. This will create different tree types. Change the LTSCALE (linetype scale) system variable (or use the Properties window to change the linetype scale) for different looks and display of trees. The two upper-left trees in Figure 6–45 are created with the ZIGZAG linetype. Linetypes are discussed in Chapter 9.

REVIEW QUESTIONS

1. What is the function of the DRAGMODE system variable?
2. List the commands that will allow you to draw single -entity objects.
3. What option of the PLINE command allows you to specify a thickness for the polyline?
4. Describe briefly the procedure to draw a tapered polyline.
5. What system variable controls the solid fill of polylines?
6. What is the difference between Width and Halfwidth options of the PLINE command?
7. What does the TTR option of the CIRCLE command stand for?
8. What system variable allows you to set the radius for the current circle?
9. Sketch and describe the relationship between the Center, Start, End option of the ARC command and the Hinge, Latch, and Endpoint of a typical door when drawing the door swing.
10. How do you create an elliptical arc?
11. What procedure must be completed before creating isometric circles?

12. Describe the three isometric plane orientations.

13. Describe the procedure to draw a solid circle.

14. What is the command used in lieu of the SOLID command to draw solid objects?

15. Can you draw a square using the RECTANGLE command?

16. Can you draw a rectangle with the POLYGON command?

17. Describe the procedure to trim the intersecting lines created with the offset command when creating a floor plan.

18. What command allows you to draw rounded corners?

19. What command allows you to draw free-hand lines?

20. What command would you use to draw contour lines on the site plan?

21. How do you access the REVCLOUD command?

22. What effect is achieved when you use the REVCLOUD command clockwise?

PROBLEMS

1. Draw the floor plan shown in Figure 6–46 using the LINE command. Use a final plot scale of 1/4" = 1'0" to be plotted on a C-size paper (24" × 18"). Do not create dimensions or text. Save the drawing as *MYEXE6-1*.

2. Using the floor plan you created in Problem 1. Offset all lines and the arc 12" to create the walls. Use the CHAMFER and FILLET commands to trim the intersections. Your finished drawing should look like Figure 6–47. Save the drawing as *MYEXE6-2*.

3. Open the *MYEXE5-10.dwg* file. Clean up the intersections and corners using the CHAMFER and the FILLET commands. Your drawing should now look like Figure 6–48. You will place wall caps using the object snap modes with the LINE command in Chapter 7. Save the drawing as *MYEXE6-3*.

4. Open the *MYEXE5-4.dwg* file. Clean up the intersections and corners using the CHAMFER and the FILLET commands. Your drawing should now look like Figure 6–49. Save the drawing as *MYEXE6-4*.

5. Open the *MYEXE5-5.dwg* file. Clean up the intersections and corners using the CHAMFER and the FILLET commands. Your drawing should now look like Figure 6–50. Save the drawing as *MYEXE6-5*.

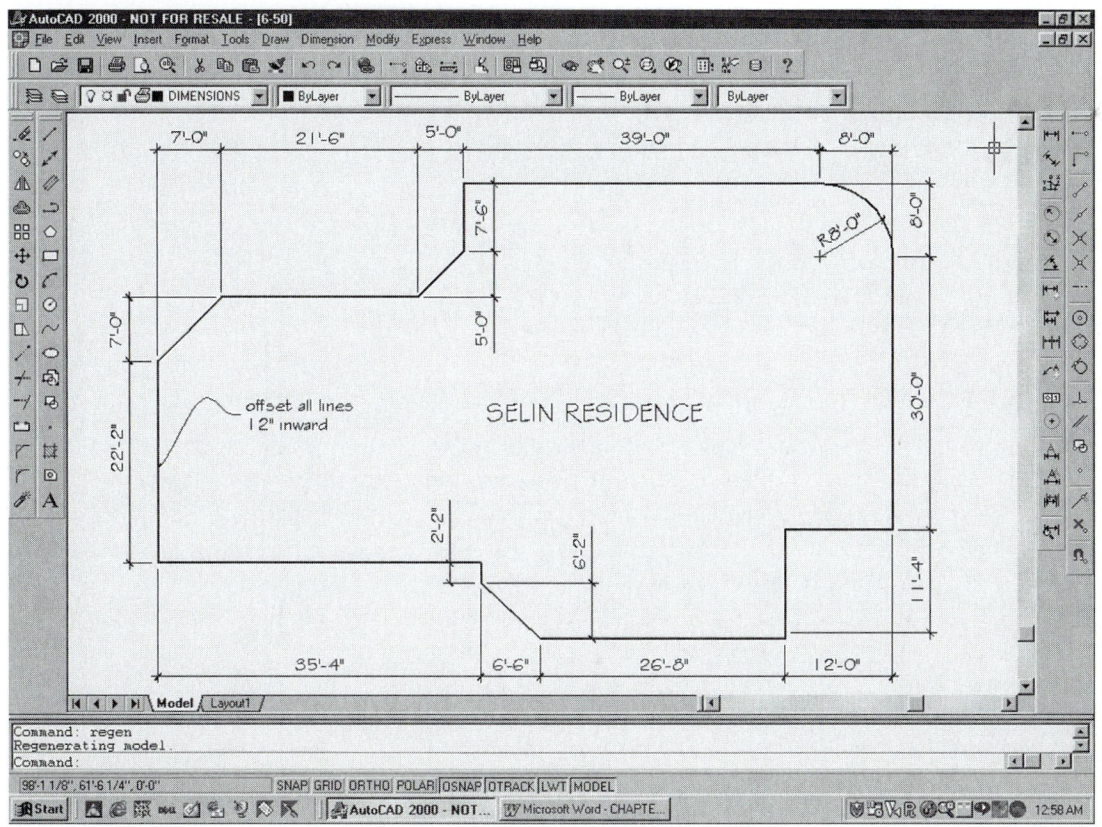

FIGURE 6–46 Problem 6–1.

FIGURE 6–47 Final drawing of Problem 6–2.

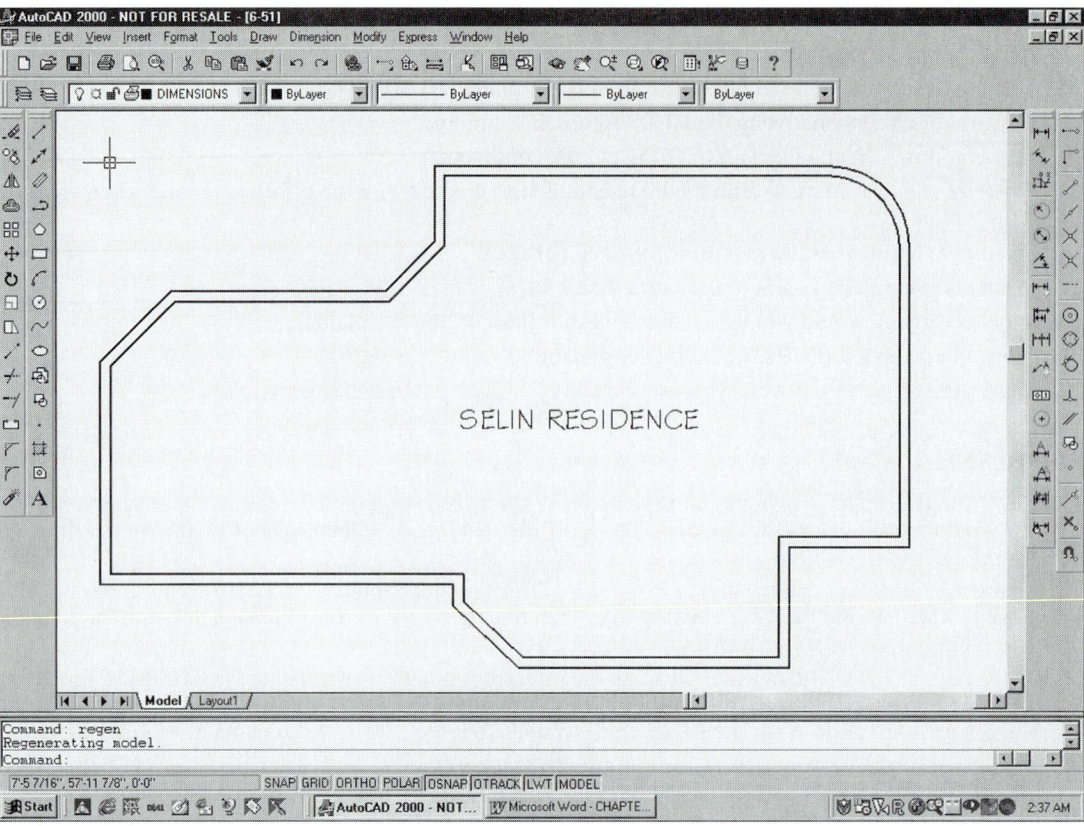

FIGURE 6–48 The floor plan in MYEXE5-10 with trimmed and extended corners. Notice that neither the TRIM or the EXTEND commands are used at this point.

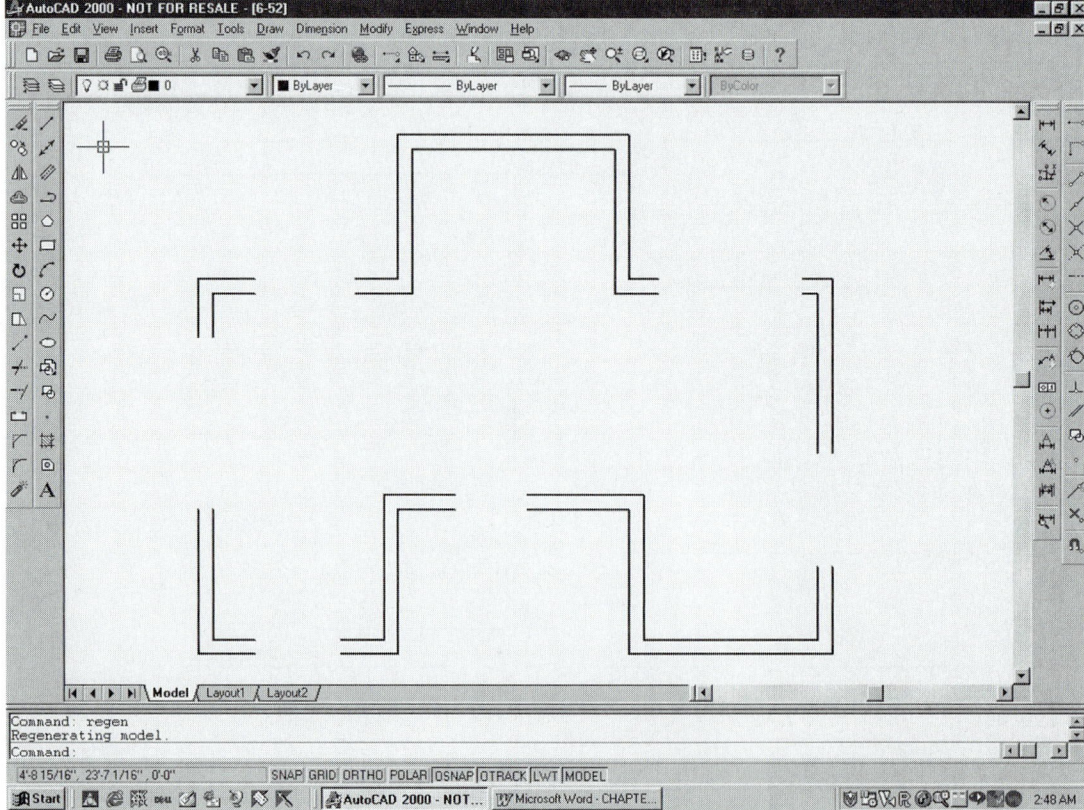

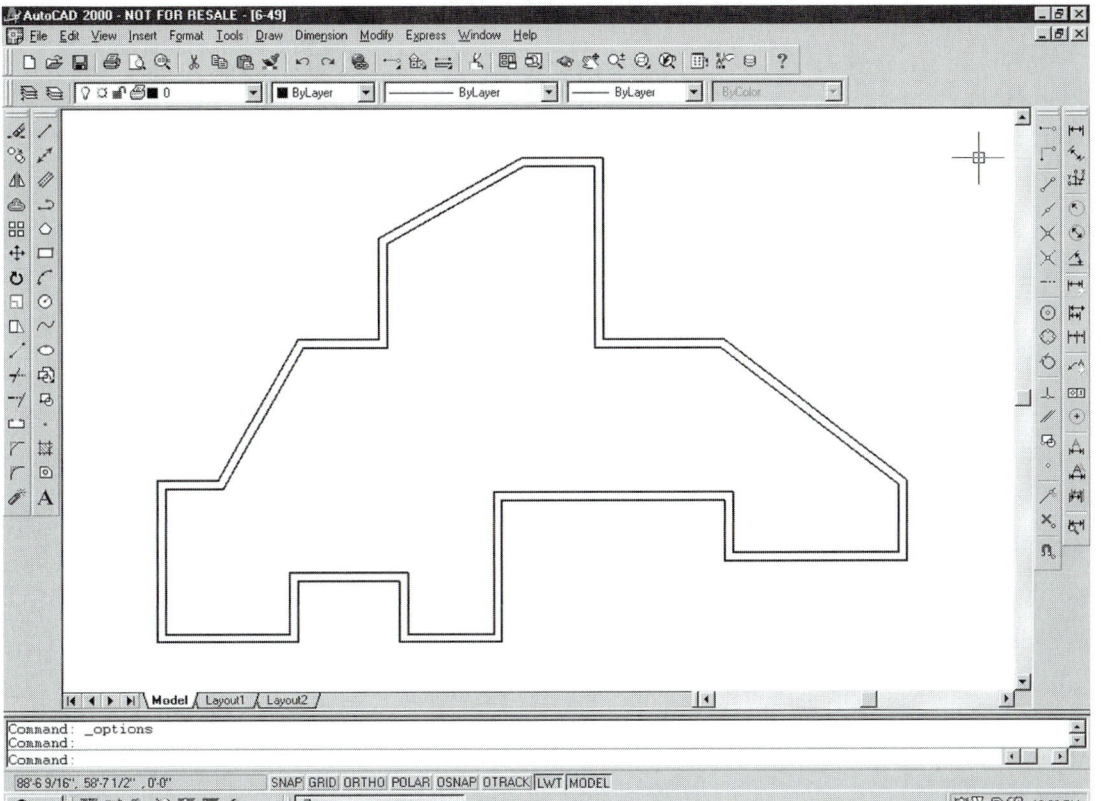

FIGURE 6-49 The floor plan in MYEXE5-4 with trimmed and extended corners. Notice that neither the TRIM or the EXTEND commands are used at this time.

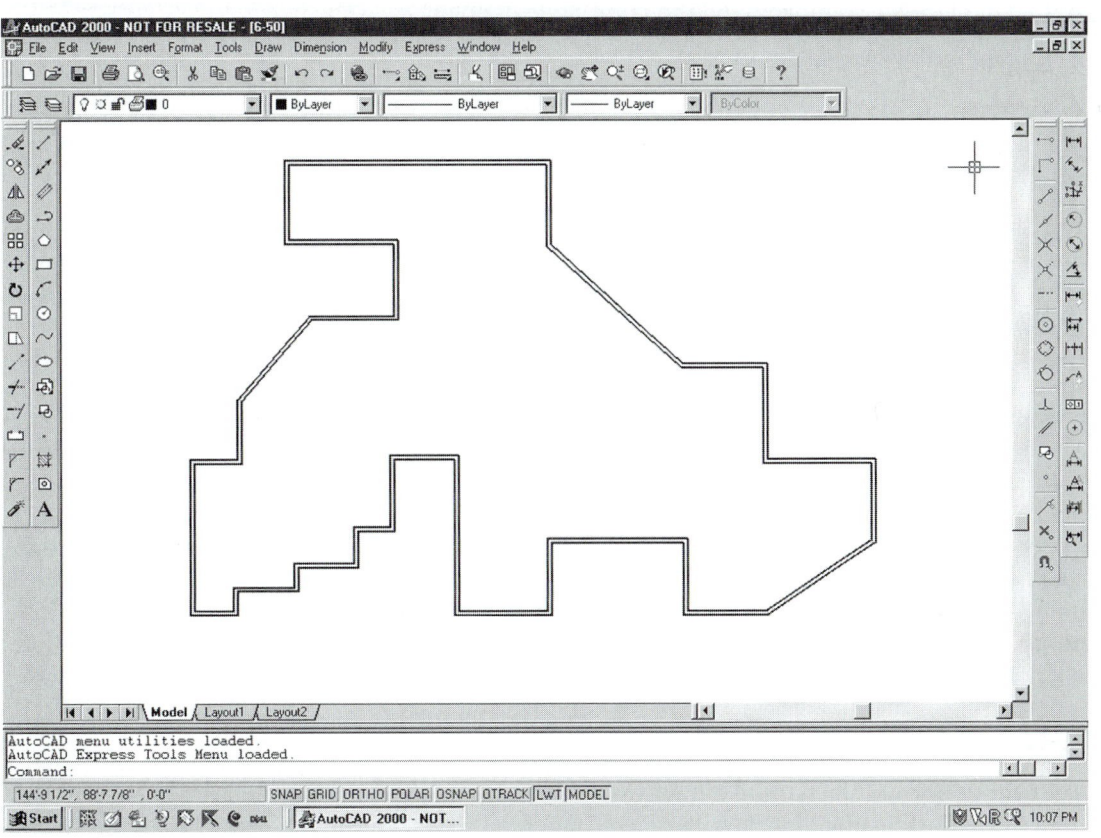

FIGURE 6-50 The floor plan in MYEXE5-5 with trimmed and extended corners.

Creating Precision Points and Segments

CHAPTER

7

After successful completion of this chapter you should be able to:

▲ Use object snap modes to create and edit objects at precise points.

▲ Use AutoTrack Modes to create objects.

▲ Use Polar Tracking, Polar Snap, Polar Angle, and Polar Distance when creating objects.

▲ Understand and use AutoSnap and AutoTrack settings as visual cues.

▲ Set Running Object Snap Modes.

▲ Understand key terms associated with Tracking.

▲ Track points on objects to locate different points.

▲ Understand and use Object Snap Tracking.

▲ Use Temporary Tracking Point.

▲ Use the POINT command and the Point Style dialog box.

▲ Use the DIVIDE command.

▲ Use the MEASURE command.

7.1 THE OBJECT SNAP AND THE AUTOTRACK MODES

In Chapter 5 you learned to create objects using the LINE command with grid and snap settings. Snapping to a grid is one way to precisely locate a point when creating objects but it is not the most efficient method, especially when editing objects. In Chapter 6 you learned to draw basic objects and shapes. The grid and snap are useful tools when creating basic objects. Grid is especially useful to see the limits of your drawing as you create objects inside the actual paper size with a final plot scale. While the grid and snap will guide you through a project, it is not the most efficient way to continue drawing objects. As the drawing size and scale change it becomes very difficult to manage a reasonable-size grid, and adding and edting objects at precise predetermined points becomes very cumbersome. Consider drawing a line starting from the midpoint of an existing line that does not coincide on a grid at that precise point. In this case you want to be able to snap to the precise midpoint of the existing line and draw the new line from that point. Also consider the need to locate new points in relation to one or two existing points. In this case you want to be able to *track* points through tracking lines and lock into a tracking angle and distance from one or two existing points to locate a new point. AutoCAD has two powerful Snap and Track modes to increase drafting precision, speed, performance, and productivity. They are called Object Snap and Autotrack.

7.2 OBJECT SNAP

The Object Snap Mode feature allows you to quickly locate points with precision relative to or directly on the existing object. With object snap modes, you can snap to a precise point to create or edit an object. In AutoCAD terms, OSNAP means Object Snap. With object snap modes you do not have to calculate coordinates to locate points on the drawing; nothing is left to guesswork. For example, you do not have to guess the location of the endpoint, midpoint, or intersecting point of objects. With object snap modes enabled, you can locate those points precisely, and AutoCAD will snap to the desired point automatically; or you can select the appropriate object snap button from the Object Snap toolbar. The predetermined points on objects are controlled by object snap modes settings via visual cues that appear on the screen.

7.2.1 Using the Object Snap Toolbar

Before setting object snap modes you should become familiar with the individual object snap terms. The Object Snap Toolbar shown in Figure 7–1 is used to select the appropriate object snap manually during the course of the drawing. When you move your cursor over a button, a few seconds later the tooltip is displayed with the name of the specific object snap mode. A brief description of that object snap mode is also displayed in the Coordinate display area. You can access the individual object snap modes using six different methods:

1. From the Object Snap toolbar as shown in Figure 7–1. If the Object Snap toolbar is not displayed on the screen, right-click on any toolbar and select Object Snap. If no toolbar is displayed, select Toolbars . . . from the View pull-down menu and select Object Snap from the Toolbars dialog box. Using the Object Snap toolbar is referred to as the *Single Point Mode* method, in which you select a series of single snap modes each time you need to snap to a point on the object. This method is fine if you need one or two snap points to locate. If you need to locate a lot of the same or different snap points, moving back and forth from the object to the Object Snap toolbar can become tedious. If this is the case, you can instruct AutoCAD to select the snap points automatically each time you move your cursor close to the snap points on the objects. This is explained later in the chapter.

2. From the Drafting Settings dialog box as shown in Figure 7–2. Right click on the OSNAP button in the Status Bar and click on Settings. . . . the Drafting Settings dialog box (with Object Snap tab automatically selected) will appear as shown in Figure 7–2 with 13 individual

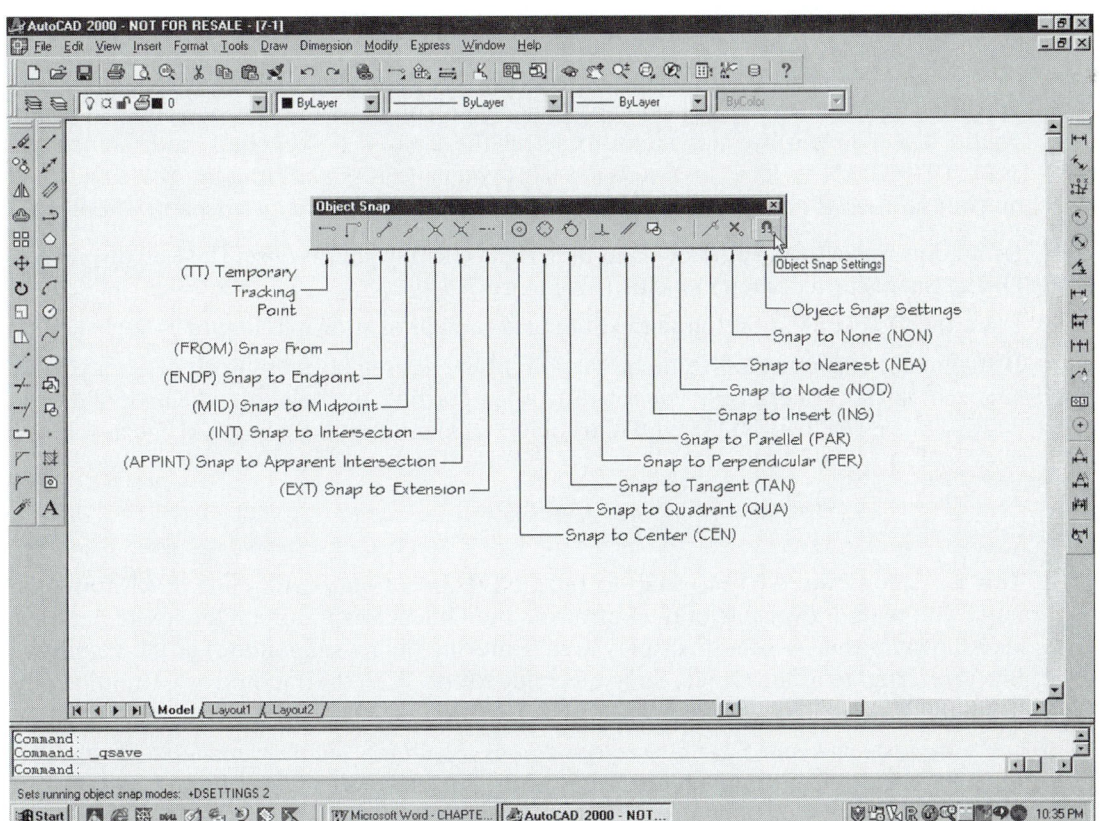

FIGURE 7–1 The Object Snap toolbar allows you to access and manage object snap modes.

FIGURE 7–2 The Object Snap tab of the Drafting Settings dialog box allows you to set individual or several automatic Object Snap modes.

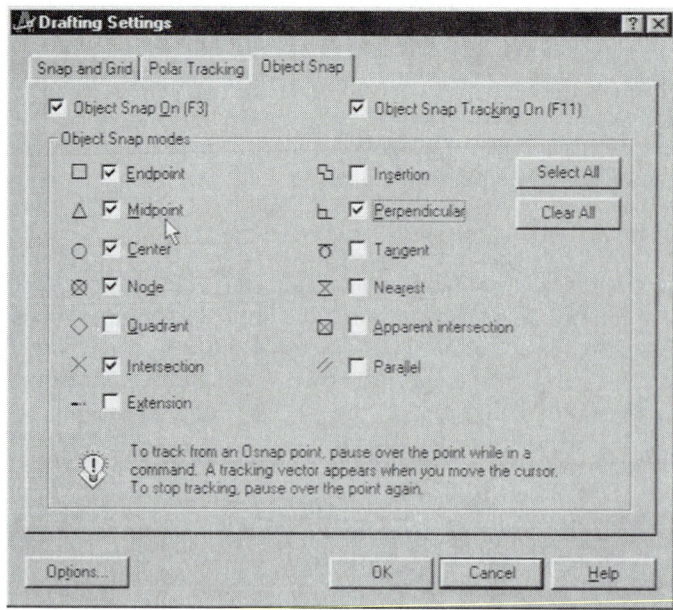

object snap modes to select from. Select the Object Snap tab. Even though you can select an individual object snap mode from the list, this is used to set several object snap modes to be effective for all corresponding snap points that will allow AutoCAD to snap to those points automatically. This is referred to as the Running Object Snap Mode method. You can select all the snap modes by clicking on the Select All button, or you can deselect all of the currently selected modes by clicking on the Clear All button.

3. At the command line as follows:

```
Command: MBUTTONPAN ~EnterKey~
Enter new value for MBUTTONPAN <1>: 0 ~EnterKey~
```

Now, when you press on the rotating wheel of the Microsoft IntelliMouse, the Object Snap shortcut menu listing all available object snap modes will be displayed as shown in Figure 7–3. You can use this menu to select the desired object snap mode. When the MBUTTONPAN system variable is set to 1, you can press and drag the rotating wheel on your mouse for panning of your drawings. Pan and Zoom are discussed in Chapter 11.

4. By holding down the ~ShiftKey~ and then right-clicking your mouse. This will display the Object Snap shortcut menu as shown in Figure 7–3.

5. From the Object Snap button in the Standard toolbar as shown in Figure 7–4.

6. By typing the first three letters (abbreviation) of the desired object snap mode after you access a command. For example, you can draw a line starting precisely from the endpoint of an existing line using the END (ENDPoint) object snap mode at the command line as follows:

```
Command: LINE
Specify first point: END ~EnterKey~
of (move your cursor to the endpoint of the existing line and left-click).
```

This will allow AutoCAD to snap to the ENDPoint of an existing line. Each time you move your cursor over one of the buttons in the Object Snap toolbar, the abbreviation is also shown in the coordinate display area. Entering object snap modes at the command line is referred to as the Object Snap Override Mode. With this method any Running Object Snap Mode will be ignored.

Note: Methods 3, 4, and 5 are also referred to as the Object Snap Override Mode and are active for one snap mode point specification. They will override any previously set

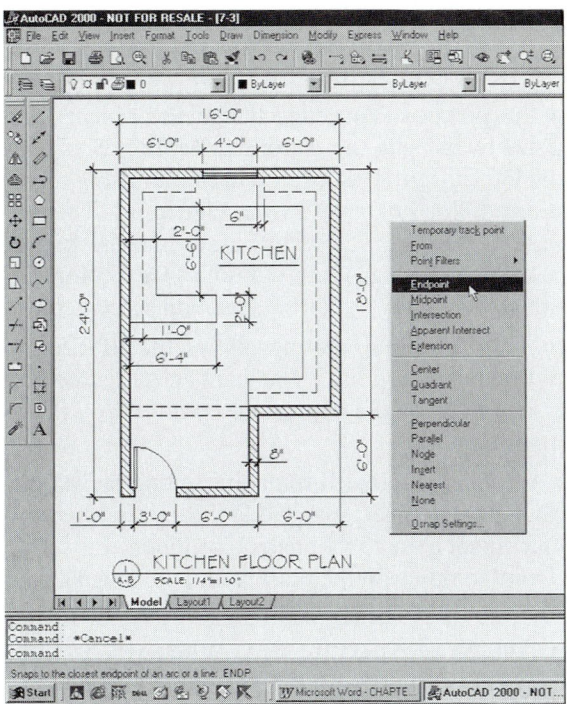

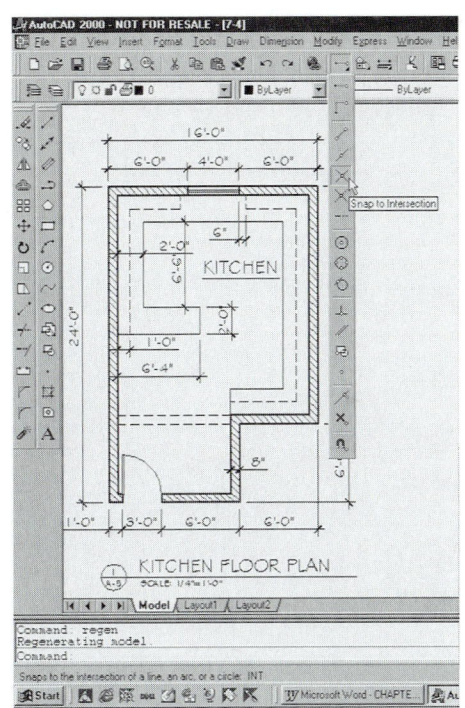

FIGURE 7–3 The Object Snap Modes shortcut menu accessed through the rotating wheel of the Intellimouse.

FIGURE 7–4 The Object Snap modes shortcut menu accessed through the Standard Toolbar.

Object Snap mode for that single entry. Running Object Snap Mode is active for all snap points until an override occurs.

7.2.2 AutoSnap Settings as Visual Cues

The cursor's ability to precisely snap to a point or location on the object is referred to as AutoSnap. AutoSnap is a visual aid that uses a marker and a tooltip to indicate object snap mode type. This feature is on by default and has four settings that can be used as visual aids on the screen. The visual aids will help you get acquainted with the object snap modes because it takes some time to get used to the snapping procedures. When you feel more confident with the object snap operations, you can turn off some or all of the visual aids of the AutoSnap features. The AutoSnap settings can be changed as follows:

1. Right-click on the screen and select Options . . . from the shortcut menu.
2. The Options dialog box will be displayed. Select the Drafting tab and place a checkmark on the desired AutoSnap settings as shown in Figure 7–5.

There are four AutoSnap settings as follows:

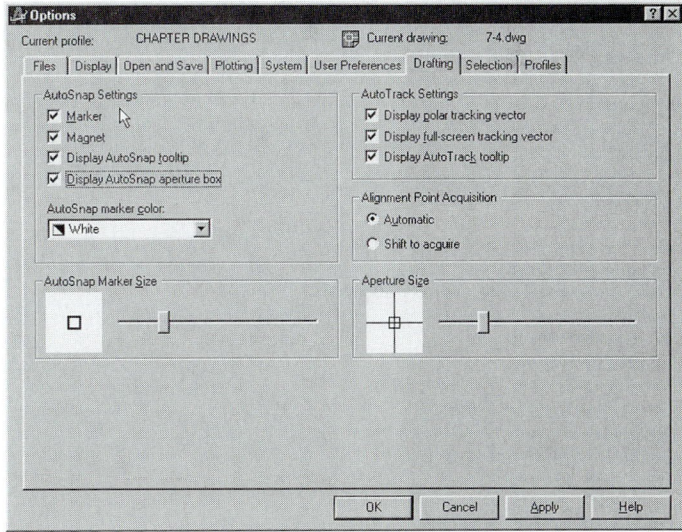

FIGURE 7–5 The Drafting tab of the Options dialog box will allow you to establish AutoSnap settings.

Marker: All object snap modes have AutoSnap settings that allow you to place a marker that snaps to the location as you move your cursor near or on a specific snap point on the object. When the marker is visible, the exact location of the snap point is acquired. To snap to that precise point, click on that point when the marker is visible. For example, the Midpoint object snap

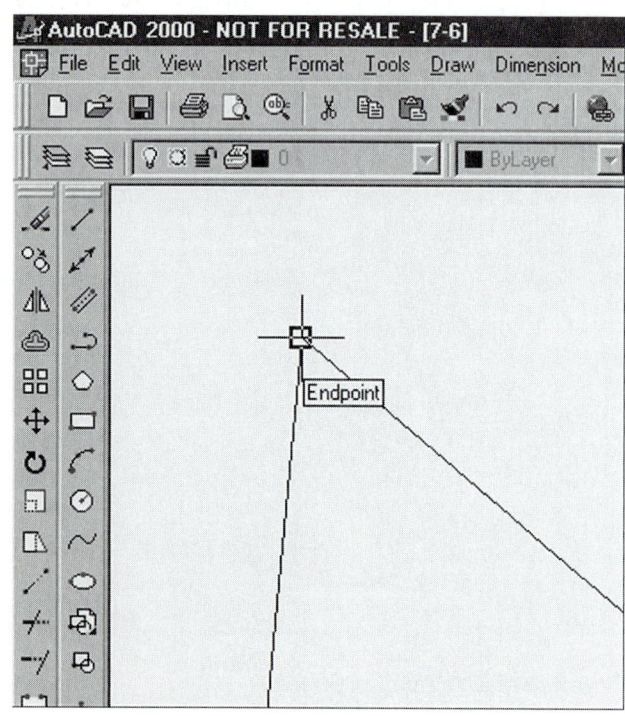

FIGURE 7–6 The triangle as the marker for the Snap to Midpoint object snap mode.

mode has a triangle marker. Figure 7–6 shows the triangle Snap to Midpoint Marker when this check box is turned on. Notice the cursor is turned into a crosshair without the pickbox. You can change the object snap marker size by moving the AutoSnap Marker Size control *slider* left or right. It is located in the Drafting tab of the Options dialog box as shown in Figure 7–5. The AutoSnap marker color is yellow by default that is obvious on a black screen background (default). Use a color that is obvious if you change your background screen color.

Magnet: This AutoSnap setting allows the Marker to snap to the desired point. You can actually see the marker "cling-on" to the object snap point if you move your cursor slowly.

Display AutoSnap Tooltip: Turning this setting on will display the name of the object snap mode as a tooltip when you move your cursor close to the snap point. Figure 7–7 shows the Endpoint tooltip with the marker and the magnet (the square marker is directly on the endpoint of the line).

Display AutoSnap Aperture Box: When you use object snap modes, the crosshairs turn into an aperture box. This aperture box allows you to detect the closest object snap point and snap to it. If the aperture box is large, the object snap point will be detected as you approach to the point. If the aperture box is very small, the object snap point will not be detected until you are directly on that point. Figure 7–8 shows the Endpoint object snap mode with a large aperture box. The Endpoint object snap mode is detected even when the aperture box is not directly on the point. You can change the aperture box size by moving the Aperture

FIGURE 7–7 The Endpoint tooltip with marker and magnet.

FIGURE 7–8 A large aperture box will snap to the object snap point without being directly on it.

Size control *slider* toward left or right in the Drafting tab of the Options dialog box as shown in Figure 7–5.

Note: The TOOLTIPS system variable does not affect the display of AutoSnap tooltips; it only affects the toolbars.

7.3 OBJECT SNAP MODES

There are 13 object snap modes. The first two buttons on the Object Snap toolbar are used for, AutoTrack mode, which is discussed later in the chapter. The last two buttons allow you to turn the Running Object Snap Mode off (the None button) or on (the Object Snap Settings button). See Figure 7–1.

Caution: Object snap modes are not commands. To use an object snap mode, you must first access a command prompting you to specify a point (i.e. start point, first point, end point, center point, etc.) then access the desired object snap mode to be used on that point.

7.3.1 Snap to Endpoint

This object snap mode allows you to snap to the endpoint of an existing line, polyline, multiline, or arc. For example, you can draw the line indicated as "line A" as shown in Figure 7–9 from the endpoint of "point X" and to the endpoint of "point Y" as follows:

```
Command: LINE ~EnterKey~
Specify first point: (click on the Snap to Endpoint button in the Object
Snap toolbar)
Specify first point: _endp of (move your cursor to Point X, wait for the
marker and tooltip to appear, see the aperture box and the magnet snap to
the endpoint and click on Point X)
Specify next point or [Undo]: (click on the Snap to Endpoint button again
in the Object Snap toolbar)
```

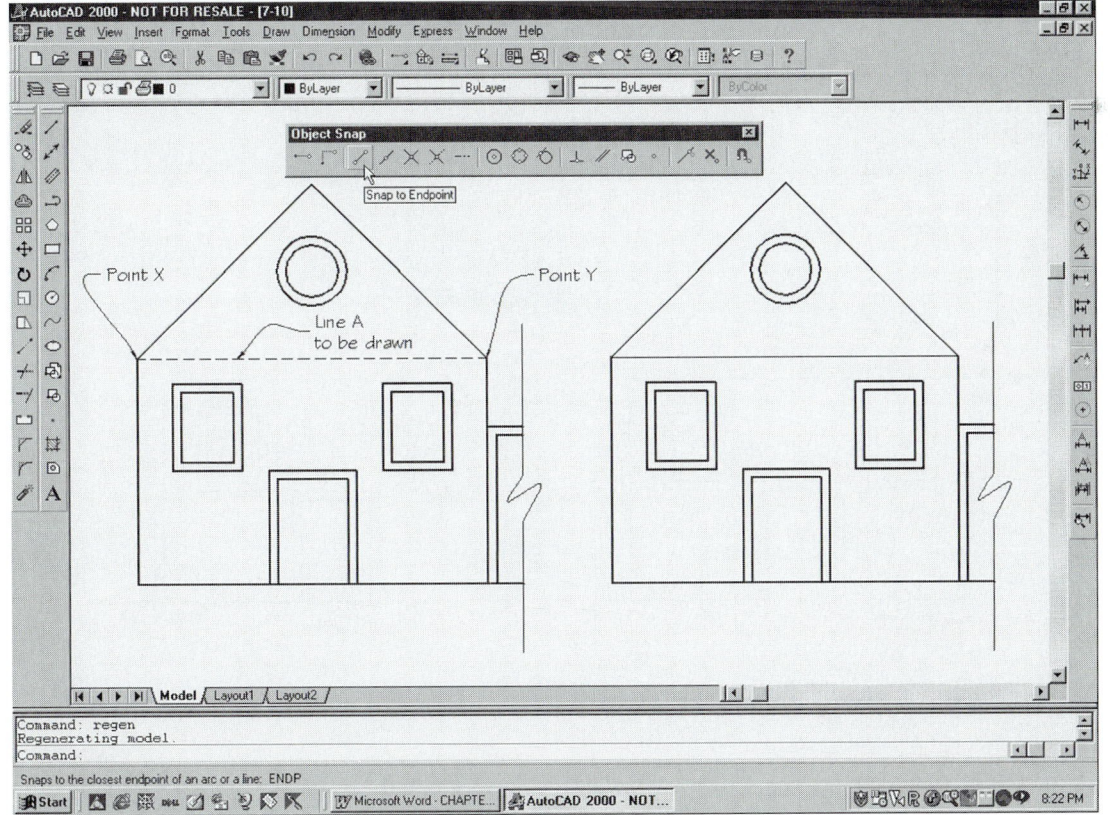

FIGURE 7–9 Using the Snap to Endpoint object snap mode to draw a line.

```
Specify next point or [Undo]: _endp of (move your cursor to Point Y, wait
for the marker and tooltip to appear, see the aperture box and the magnet
snap to the endpoint and click on Point Y)
Specify next point or [Undo]: ~EnterKey~
```

The above procedure uses method 1 as described previously. You can also use methods 2, 3, 4, 5, or 6 to accomplish the same task.

Tips: When you move your cursor to Point X or Y, let the marker and the tooltip guide you when snapping to the endpoint of the line.

7.3.2 Snap to Midpoint

This object snap mode allows you to snap to the midpoint of an existing line, polyline, multiline or arc. For example, you can draw the two circles that are shown in Figure 7–10 from the midpoint of line "A" shown as a reference dashed line as follows:

```
Command: CIRCLE ~EnterKey~
Specify center point for circle or [3P/2P/Ttr (tan tan radius)]: (hold
down the ~ShiftKey~ and right click. While holding down the ~ShiftKey~
left click on Snap to Midpoint)
Specify center point for circle or [3P/2P/Ttr (tan tan radius)]: _mid of
(move your cursor to the mid point of the dashed line, wait for the
marker and tooltip to appear, see the aperture box and the magnet snap to
the midpoint and click on the mid point)
Specify radius of circle or [Diameter]: 3' ~EnterKey~
Command: ~EnterKey~ (this will bring back the CIRCLE command so you can
draw the second circle)
Specify center point for circle or [3P/2P/Ttr (tan tan radius)]: @ (this
will start the center of the circle from the last known point, which is
the midpoint of the dashed line)
Specify radius of circle or [Diameter] <13'-0">: 4' ~EnterKey~
```

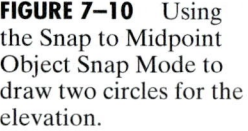

FIGURE 7–10   Using the Snap to Midpoint Object Snap Mode to draw two circles for the elevation.

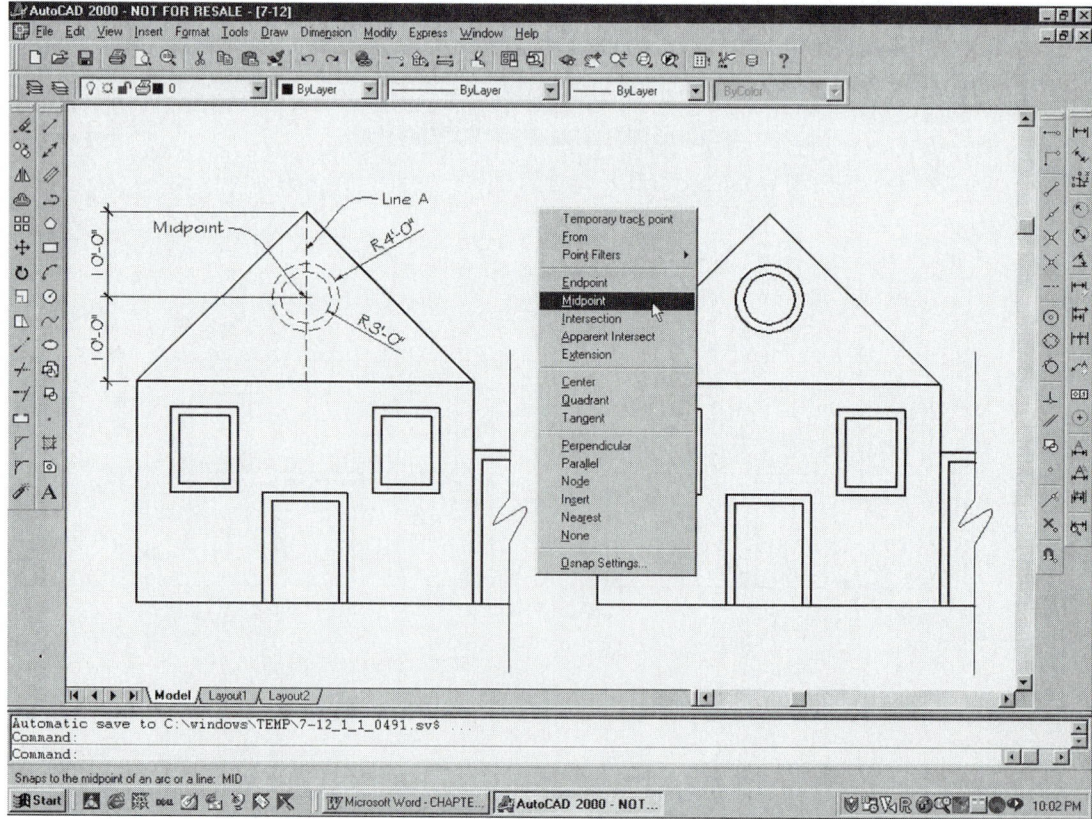

Erase the reference line when done. The above procedure uses method 4 as described previously. You can also use methods 1, 2, 3, 5, or 6 to accomplish the same task.

7.3.3 Snap to Intersection and Perpendicular

The *Intersection* object snap mode allows you to snap to the intersection of two or more objects and the *Perpendicular* object snap mode allows you to draw an object perpendicular to an existing object. For example, you can draw the 4″ thick interior partition wall 6′-8″ in length as shown in Figure 7–11, starting from the intersection of two existing exterior walls as follows:

```
Command: LINE ~EnterKey~
Specify first point: INT ~EnterKey~
Specify first point: _int of (move your cursor to the intersection as
shown, wait for the marker and tooltip to appear, see the aperture box
and the magnet snap to the midpoint and click on the intersection)
Specify next point or [Undo]: @6'8<90 ~EnterKey~
Specify next point or [Undo]: @4<0 ~EnterKey~
Specify next point or [Close/Undo]: PER ~EnterKey~
Specify next point or [Close/Undo]: _per to (move your cursor to the
inside horizontal wall line near the intersection, wait for the marker
and tooltip to appear, see the aperture box and the magnet snap to the
perpendicular, and click on the point)
Specify next point or [Close/Undo]: ~EnterKey~
```

The above procedure uses method 6 as described previously. You can also use methods 1, 2, 3, 4, or 5 to accomplish the same task.

7.3.4 Snap to Apparent Intersection

This object snap mode allows you to snap to the point where two non-intersecting objects would intersect if they were to be extended in space. Figure 7–12 shows an object with line A and line

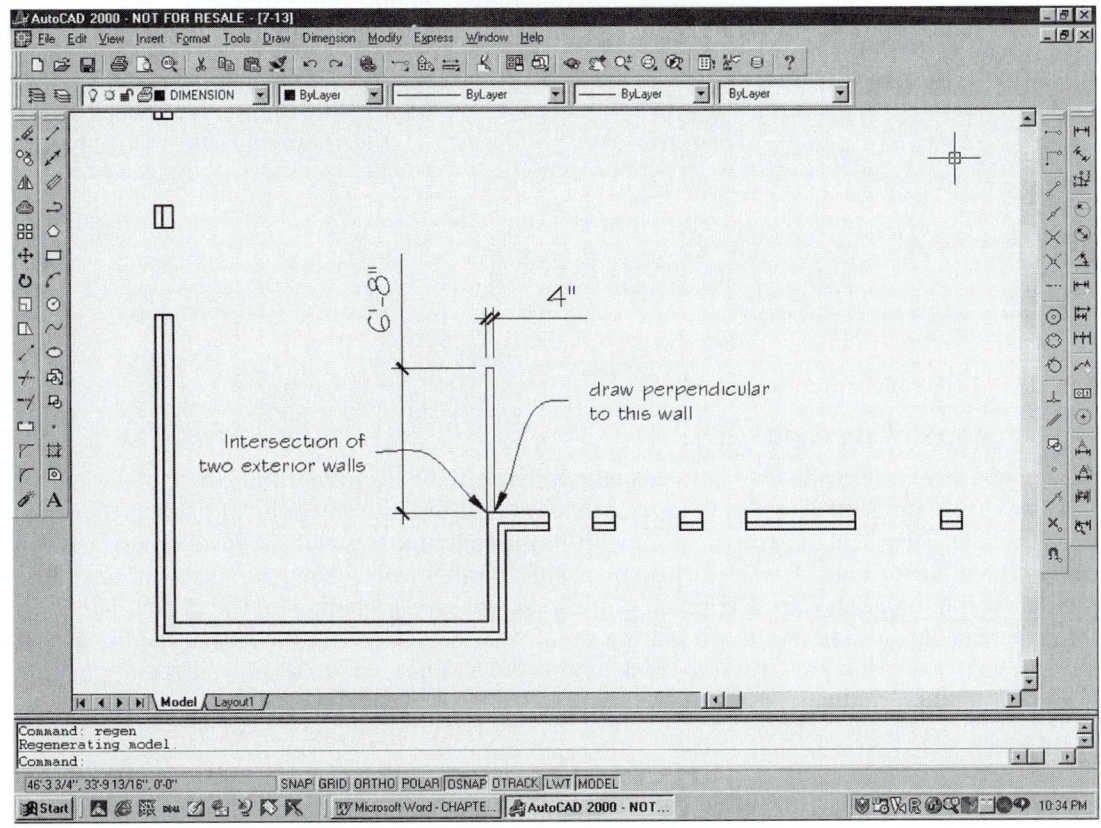

FIGURE 7–11 Using the Intersection and Perpendicular object snap modes.

FIGURE 7–12 Using
the Apparent Intersect
Object Snap Mode.

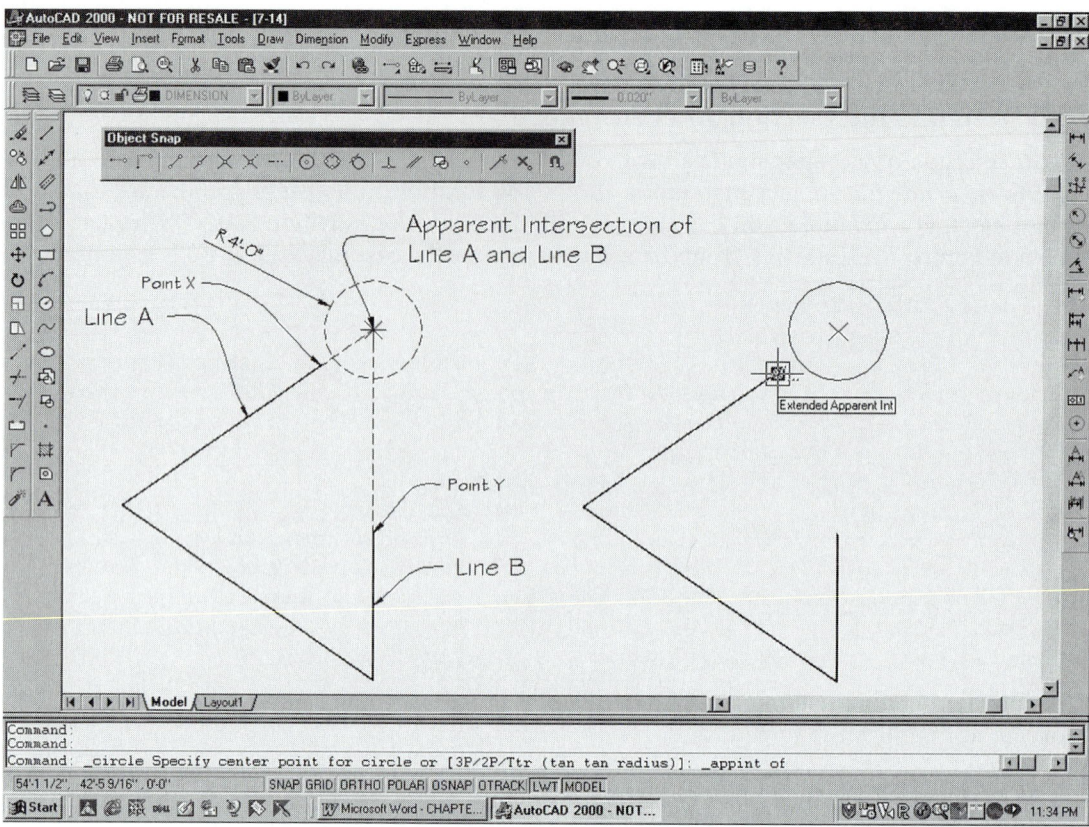

B. The circle with a radius of 4′-0″ can be drawn with the center of the circle precisely at the intersection of lines A and B (apparent intersection of the two lines) as follows:

```
Command: CIRCLE ~EnterKey~
Specify center point for circle or [3P/2P/Ttr (tan tan radius)]: (click
on the Snap to Apparent Intersect button in the Object Snap toolbar)
Specify center point for circle or [3P/2P/Ttr (tan tan radius)]: _appint
of (move your cursor over point X and select. The tooltip should read
Extended Apparent Int)
Specify center point for circle or [3P/2P/Ttr (tan tan radius)]: _appint
of and (as you move your cursor to point Y, a marker with X should appear
at the intersection of line A and line B. When you see this marker,
select point Y. This will start the center of the circle at the apparent
intersection of line A and line B)
Specify radius of circle or [Diameter]: 4′ ~EnterKey~
```

7.3.5　Snap to Extension

This object snap mode allows you to select a point on the extension of an existing line or arc. With Snap to Extension object snap mode, you can track and find any point along the *Alignment Path* of the existing line or arc. An Alignment Path is a temporary dotted line along which you can use your cursor to *track* points. This object snap mode involves the AutoTrack mode, where the cursor follows temporary alignment paths to locate specific points on the object. The Snap to Extension object snap mode will place a small yellow cross (+) at the end of the line or arc being selected as a default. The AutoTrack mode allows AutoCAD to display *Extension tooltip*, which tracks cursor movement along increments of the angle and units of the line.

■　**EXERCISE 7–1:**　*The following step-by-step exercise will help you draw an interior partition wall of the same thickness as the existing wall at a distance of 3′-0″ East of point X and connect it to the perpendicular wall as shown in Figure 7–13. For the Extension tooltip to work best, set drawing unit precision to 0′-0″ and turn Ortho on.*

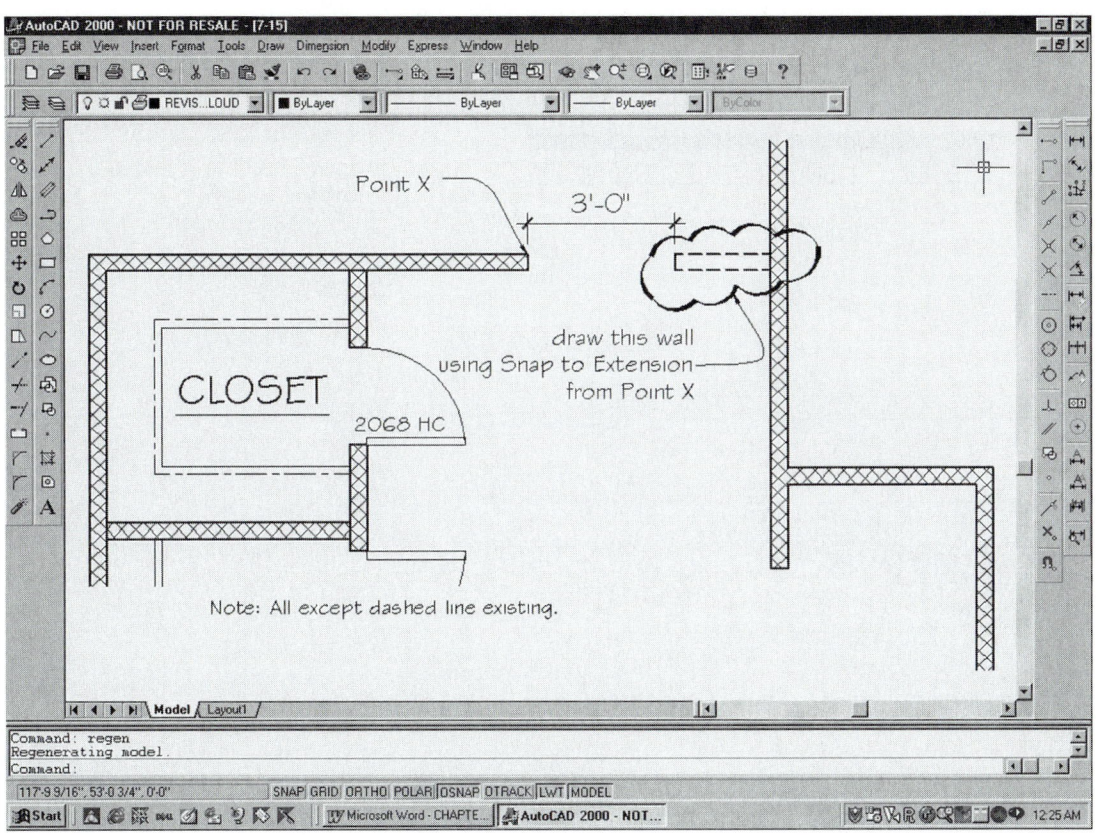

FIGURE 7–13 The wall indicated with dashed lines will be drawn using the Snap to Extension object snap mode.

Step #1: Open the *EXE7-1.dwg* file.

Step #2: Use the following command line procedure to draw the wall:

Command: **LINE** ~EnterKey~

Specify first point: *(select the Snap to Extension button in the Object Snap toolbar)*

Specify first point : _ext of (move your cursor to point X but **do not** select the point. The Extension Tracking of the AutoTrack mode will display the polar coordinates of point X, and the tooltip should read Extension: 0′-0″<0° as shown in Figure 7–14)

Move your cursor along the alignment path at 0 degrees. Stop and left-click when the tooltip reads Extension: 3′-0″<0° as shown in Figure 7–15.

Specify next point or [Undo]: **@4<270** ~EnterKey~

Specify next point or [Undo]: *(select the Snap to Perpendicular button in the Object Snap toolbar)*

Specify next point or [Undo]: _per to *(select and snap to the perpendicular wall)*

Specify next point or [Close/Undo]: ~EnterKey~

Command: **OFFSET** ~EnterKey~

Specify offset distance or [Through] <0′-0″>:**4** ~EnterKey~

Select object to offset or <exit>: *(select the horizontal line you just drew)*

Specify point on side to offset: *(select anywhere on the area above the horizontal line)*

Select object to offset or <exit>: ~EnterKey~

Your drawing should now look like Figure 7–16. Do not draw hatching or text.

Congratulations! You have created a wall from an existing wall using the LINE command and the Snap to Extension object snap mode.

FIGURE 7–14 The Extension Tracking mode of the AutoTrack is displayed when point X is picked.

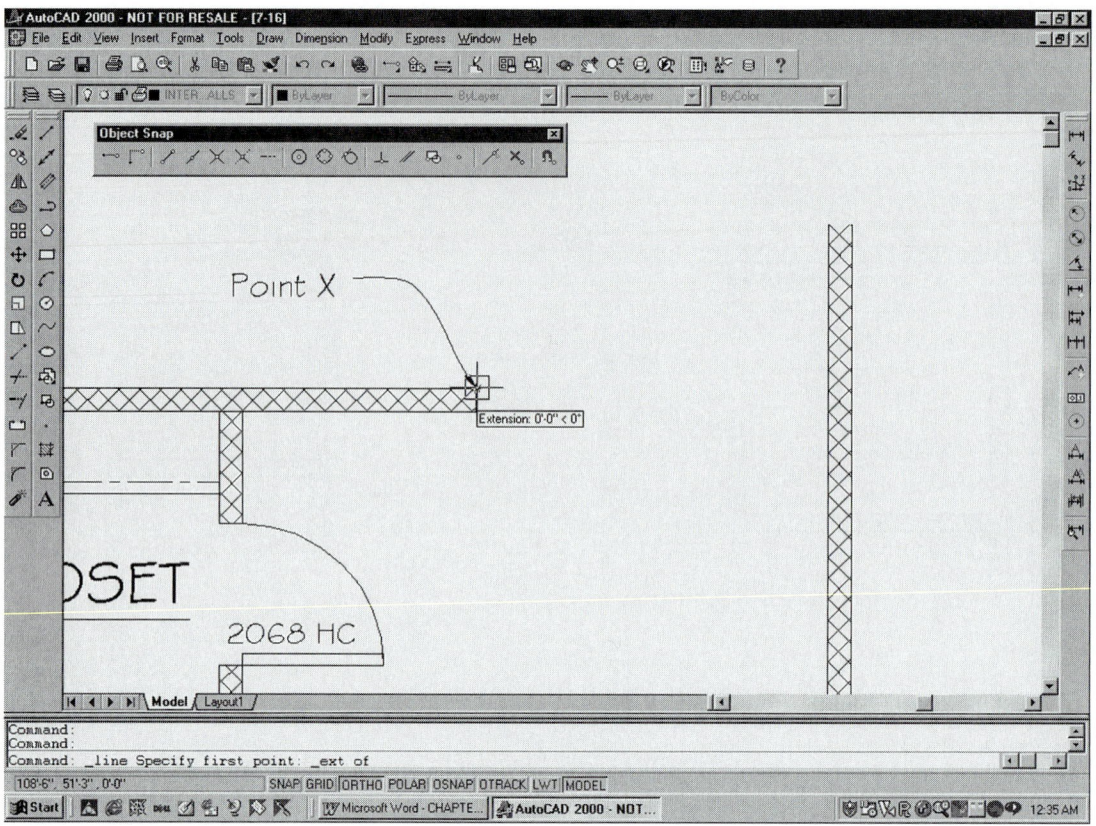

FIGURE 7–15 Tracking cursor movement along increments of 12″ and angle 0 with alignment path.

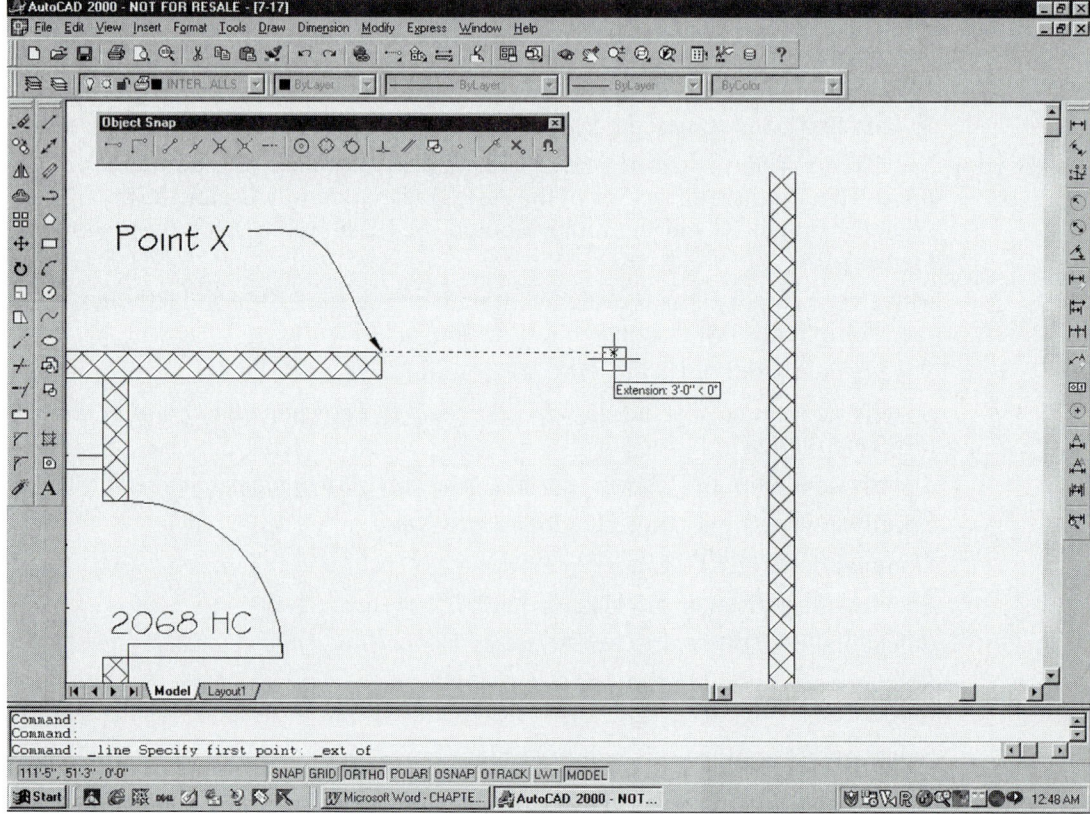

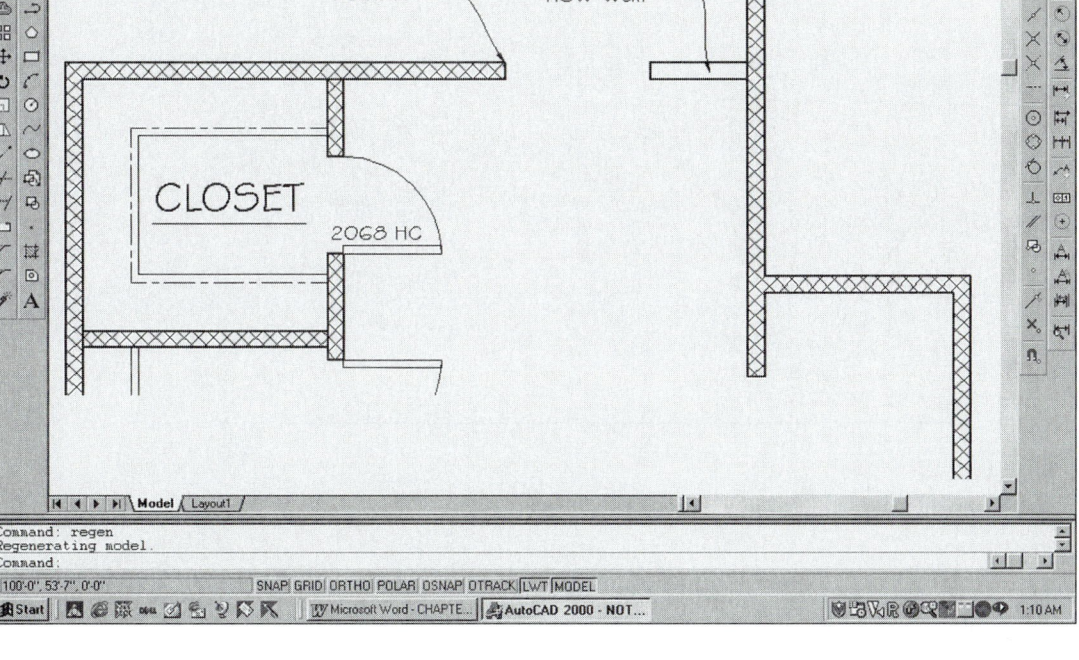

FIGURE 7–16 The completed wall segment for Exercise 7–1.

Note: You can use Snap to Extension to create wall openings with the LINE command when creating a floor plan. For example, all of the drawings having door and window openings as shown in Chapter 6 could be created using the Snap to Extension object snap mode. You can also use Snap to Extension to track along and over an existing line to establish a new point. You can achieve the same result using the Snap From object snap mode but without the tracking and alignment path features. The Object Snap Tracking feature of AutoCAD allows you to locate more than one point in relation to one or two existing points. However, Snap to Extension allows you to locate one point in relation to one existing point.

Tips: Before selecting points on the walls, turn off any layers having a Hatch pattern. This will prevent you from selecting a hatch pattern by mistake.

7.3.6 Snap to Center

This object snap mode allows you to snap to the center of a circle, arc, donut, ellipse, elliptical, or polyline arc. When working with this object snap mode, be sure to select the object perimeter, not the center of the object. Use one of the six methods described above to access this snap mode. Figure 7–17 shows a line drawn from the center of an existing circle at a 90 degree angle to an existing roof intersection. You can draw this line at the command line as follows:

```
Command: LINE ~EnterKey~
Specify first point: CEN ~EnterKey~
Specify first point: cen of (select the perimeter of one of the circles)
Specify next point or [Undo]: INT ~EnterKey~
Specify next point or [Undo]: _int of (select the roof intersection)
Specify next point or [Undo]: ~EnterKey~
Notice that instead of entering INT for the intersection, you could have
entered the polar coordinates for that line as @10'<90 ~EnterKey~ .
```

FIGURE 7–17 Using the Snap to Center object snap mode.

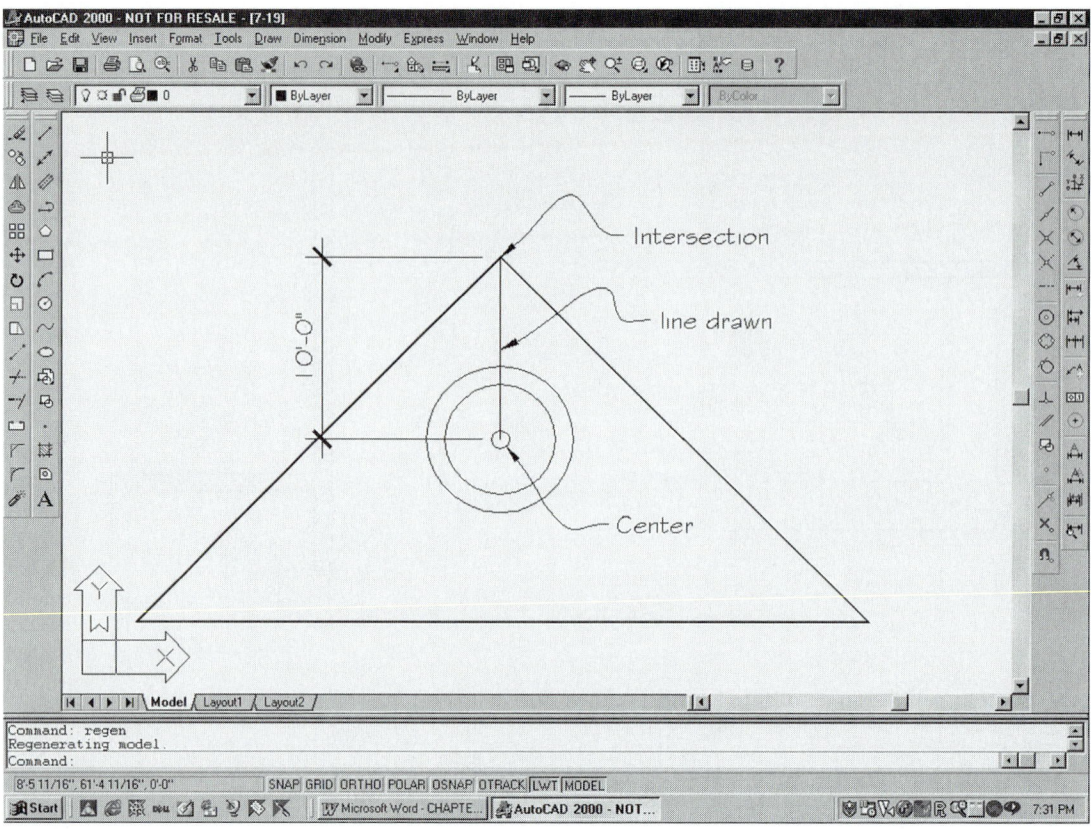

7.3.7 Snap to Quadrant

This object snap mode allows you to snap to one of the four quadrants of a circle, arc, donut, ellipse, elliptical, or polyline arc. When working with this object snap mode, be sure to select the appropriate quadrant of the object. Use one of the six methods described above to access this snap mode. Figure 7–18 shows a drawing title mark as a circle. You can draw the line from the quadrant of the circle as follows:

```
Command: LINE ~EnterKey~
Specify first point: QUA ~EnterKey~
Specify first point : qua of (select the quadrant of the circle as shown)
Specify next point or [Undo]: (with Ortho on, draw the line at the
desired length)
Specify next point or [Undo]: ~EnterKey~
```

7.3.8 Snap to Tangent

This object snap mode allows you to snap to a point of tangency on a circle, arc, donut, ellipse, elliptical, or polyline arc. When working with this object snap mode, move the cursor over to the point of tangency and select. This mode is similar to the concept behind Tan, Tan, Radius option of the CIRCLE command.

■   **EXERCISE 7–2:**   *The following step-by-step exercise will help you draw the two lines tangent to two points on the circle as shown in Figure 7–19. Furthermore, the two lines and the circle will be offset 4″, the line intersections will be cleaned up with the CHAMFER command, and the circle intersections will be cleaned up with the TRIM command to finalize the drawing, as shown in Figure 7–23.*

Step #1:   Open the *EXE7-2.dwg* file.

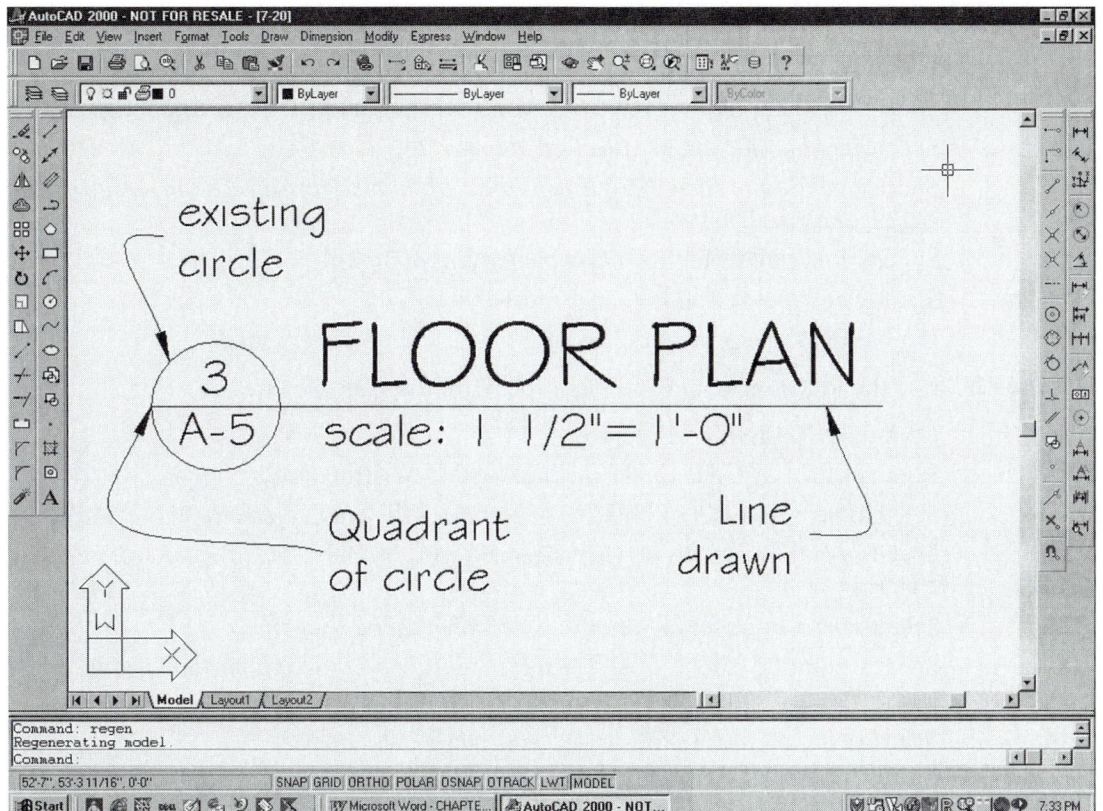

FIGURE 7–18 Using the Snap to Quadrant object snap mode.

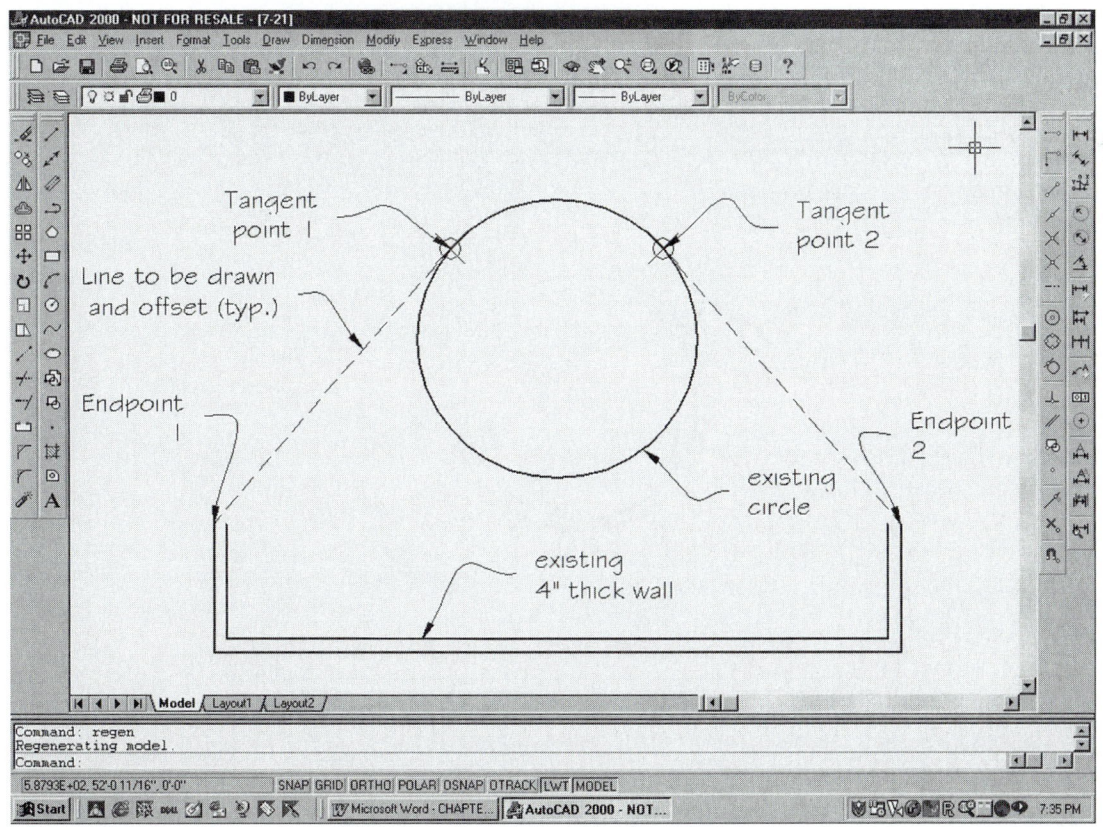

Step #2:   Use the following command line procedure to draw the lines:

Command: **LINE** ~EnterKey~

Specify first point: *(from the Object Snap toolbar, select Snap to Endpoint)*

Specify first point: _endp of *(select endpoint 1)*

Specify next point or [Undo]: *(turn ortho off and select Snap to tangent from the Object Snap toolbar)*

Specify first point: _tan to *(select the tangent point 1)*

Specify next point or [Undo]: ~EnterKey~

Repeat the same procedure for endpoint 2 and tangent point 2.

Step #3:   Use the following command line procedure to offset the lines:

Command: **OFFSET** ~EnterKey~

Specify offset distance or [Through] <0'-0">: **4** ~EnterKey~

Select object to offset or <exit>: *(select one of the lines created)*

Specify point on side to offset: *(select the inside point so that the line will be offset inward)*

Select object to offset or <exit>: *(select the other line created)*

Specify point on side to offset: *(select the inside point so that the line will be offset inward)*

Select object to offset or <exit>: *(select the existing circle)*

Specify point on side to offset: *(select the inside point of the circle so that it is offset inward)*

Your drawing should now look like Figure 7–20.

FIGURE 7–20   After the OFFSET command, the circle and lines can be trimmed using the TRIM command, and the corners can be cleaned up using either the FILLET or the CHAMFER command.

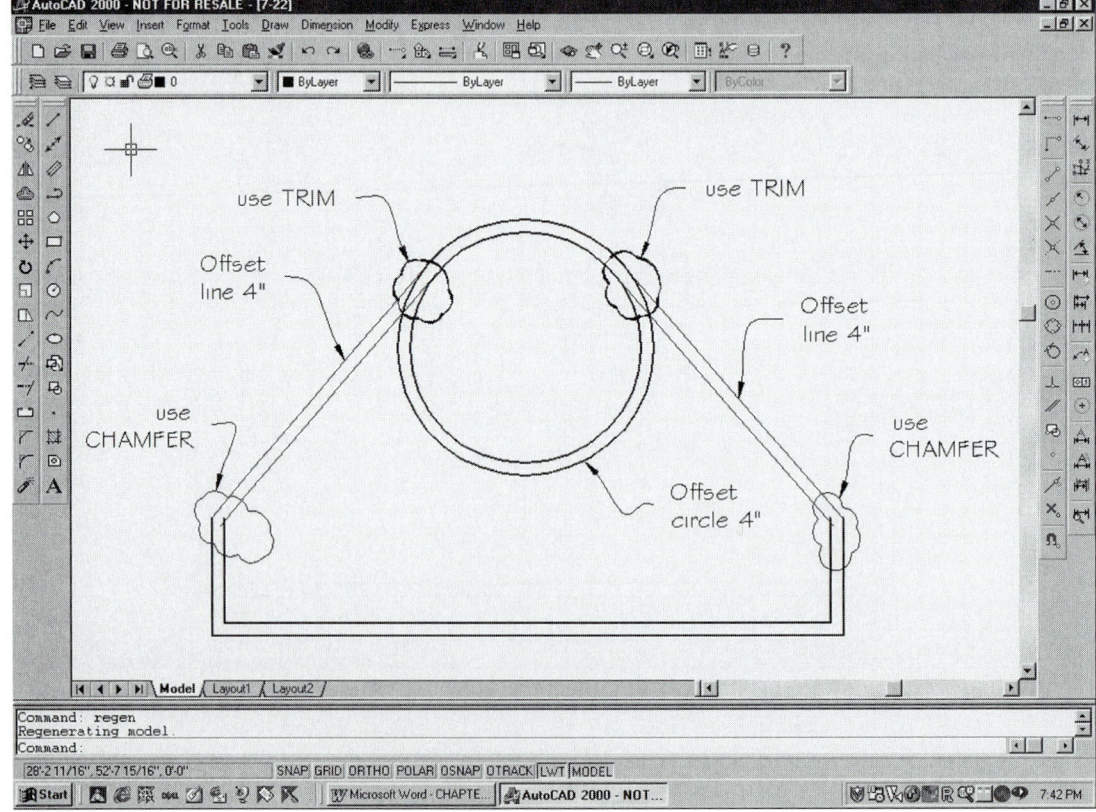

Although the TRIM command is discussed in Chapter 12, it is nevertheless introduced here for the purpose of illustrating the trim operation.

Step #4: Looking at Figure 7–20, perform the TRIM command operation as follows:

Command: **TRIM** ~EnterKey~

Current settings: Projection=UCS Edge=None

Select cutting edge...

Select objects: ~EnterKey~ *(this will bypass the selection of cutting edges procedure and go directly into selecting objects to trim)*

Select object to trim or [Project/Edge/Undo]: *(select circle 1 at the location as shown in Figure 7–21)*

Select object to trim or [Project/Edge/Undo]: *(select circle 2 at the location as shown in Figure 7–21)*

Step #5: Repeat the same TRIM command procedure for circle 1A and circle 2A as shown in Figure 7–21.

Your drawing after the trim operation should now look like Figure 7–22.

Step #6: Use the CHAMFER command you learned in Chapter 6 to clean up the other corners created by the OFFSET command.

Your finished drawing should now look like Figure 7–23.

Congratulations! You created the objects as shown in Figure 7–23 using the Snap to Tangent object snap mode with the LINE, OFFSET, and TRIM commands.

7.3.9 Snap to Parallel

This object snap mode allows you to draw a line parallel to an existing line by using the Auto-Track mode to track the alignment path of the parallel mode to snap to the precise parallel point

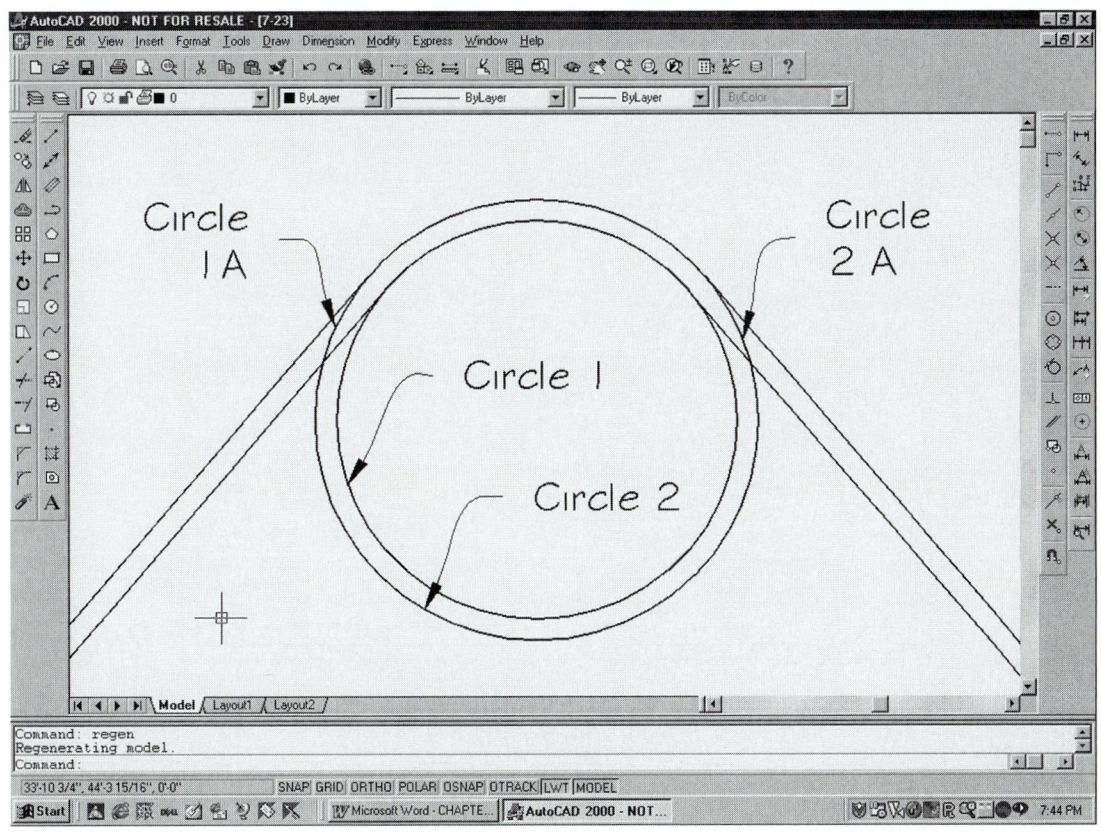

FIGURE 7–21 The circle and the lines after the OFFSET comand operation.

FIGURE 7–22　The circle and the lines after the TRIM command operation.

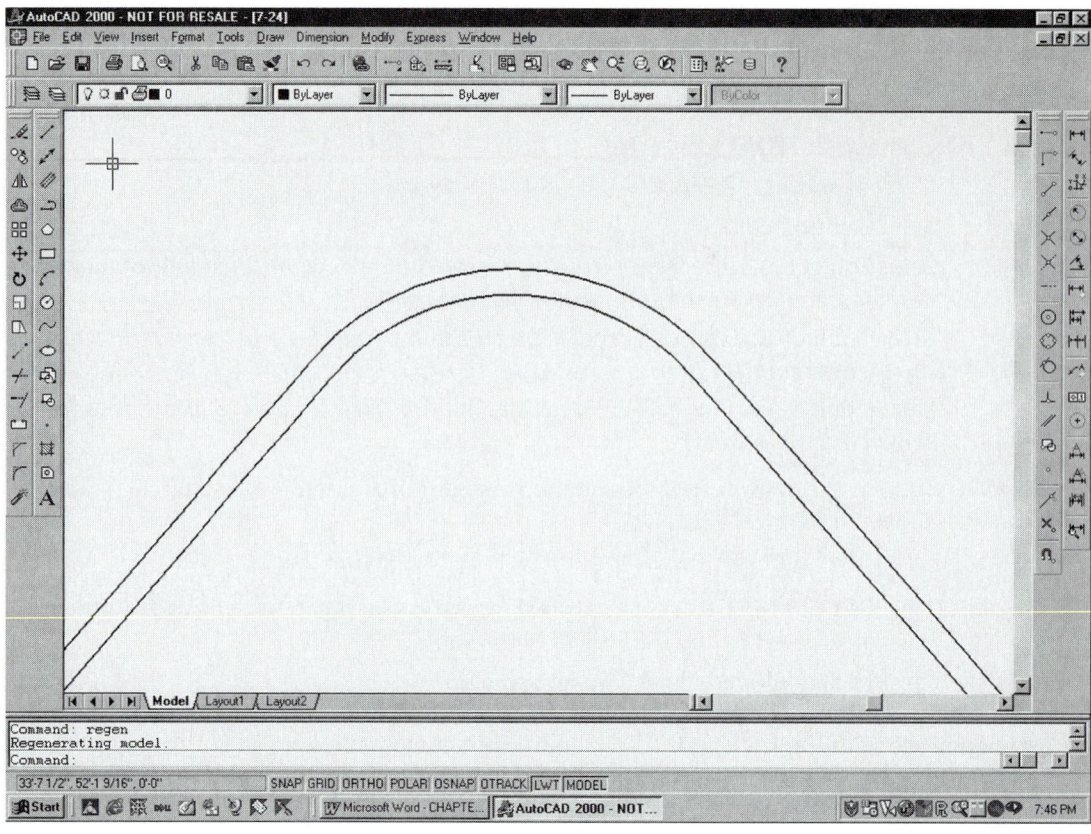

FIGURE 7–23　The completed drawing for Exercise 7–2.

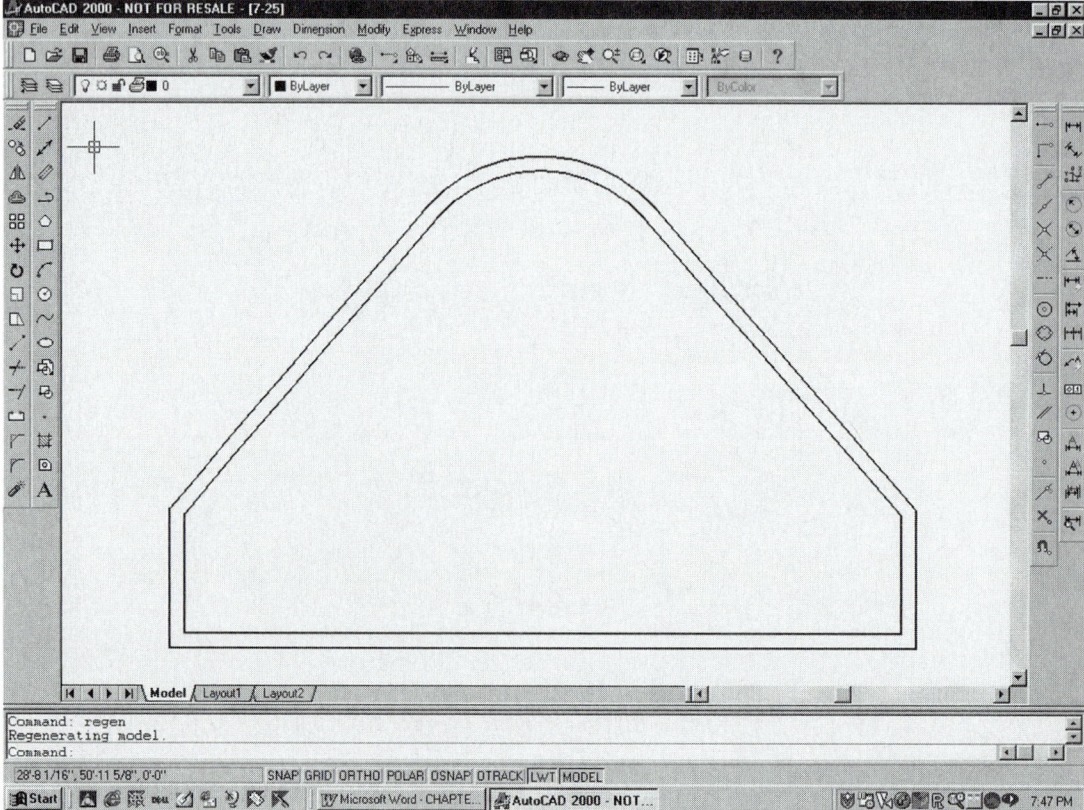

location for the new line. Figure 7–24 shows an existing line and a start point for the new line to be drawn parallel to the existing line. You can use the snap to parallel object snap mode to draw a new line parallel to the existing line as follows:

```
Command: LINE ~EnterKey~
Specify first point: (click on the start point)
Specify next point or [Undo]: (select Snap to Parallel
from the Object Snap toolbar)
Specify next point or [Undo]: _par to (move your cursor
to the existing line and pause over the line. Do not
select the line. Two parallel lines [//] will appear as
the marker for the parallel object snap. The word
Parallel will appear as the tooltip. Move your cursor to
a position that will make the new line approximately
parallel to the existing line. At this time the two
parallel lines will turn into a plus sign on the
existing line. As you move your cursor closer to the
approximate parallel location, AutoCAD will track the
point to the precise position. When the new line is at
the precise parallel location, the tooltip will display
the polar coordinates and the word Parallel. Move your
cursor along the alignment path and select the final
position of the new line. In this example the line is
drawn at 8'-0" at an angle of 54 degrees as shown in
Figure 7-25)
```

7.3.10 Snap to Insert

This object snap mode allows you to find the *insertion point* of text objects and objects inserted as blocks. Placing text is discussed in Chapter 14, and creating blocks is discussed in Chapter 19. For example, when you insert a block, it is inserted with the insertion point that you specify while creating the block. If you want to move, copy, rotate, or use any of the other editing commands, you can select the block by the insertion point when you select the Snap to Insert object snap mode.

FIGURE 7–24 Using the Snap to Parallel object snap mode. Notice the two parallel lines [//] as the marker.

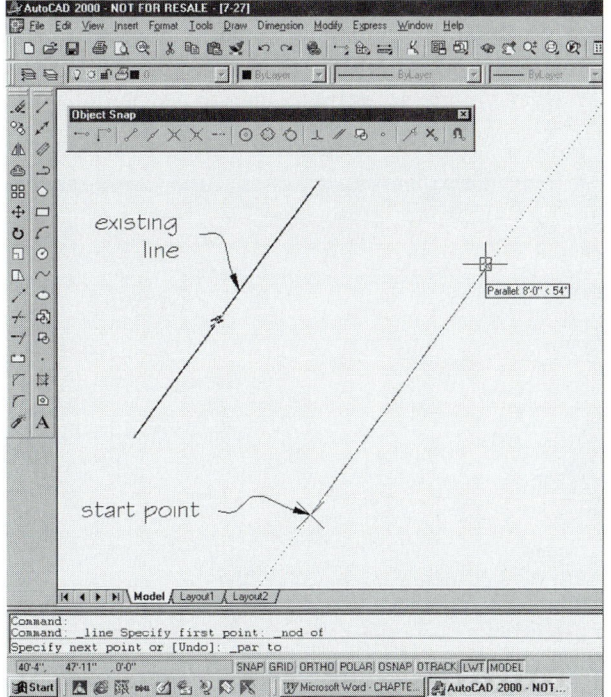

FIGURE 7–25 The alignment path as the temporary line for the parallel tracking. The actual line will be drawn when you left-click.

Although the MOVE command is discussed in Chapter 12, it is nevertheless introduced here for the purpose of illustrating the move operation.

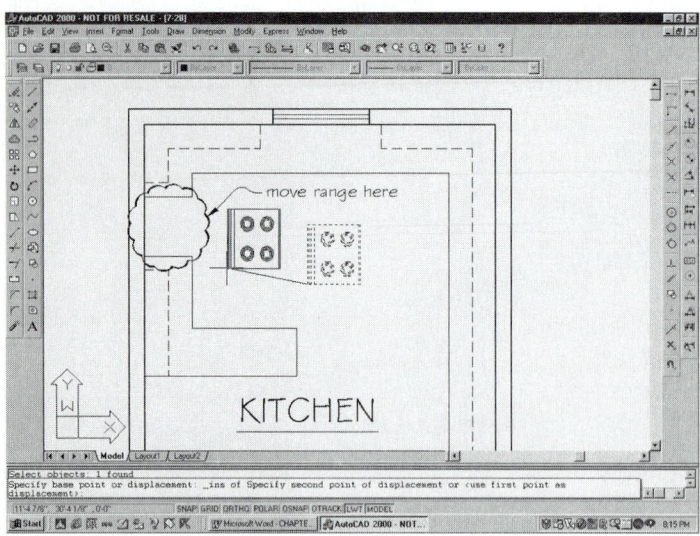

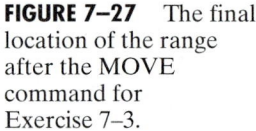

FIGURE 7–26 The Snap to Insert object snap mode allows you to find and snap to the insertion point of a block. The range is shown while being moved to the final location using the Snap to Insert object snap mode.

■ **EXERCISE 7–3:** *Figure 7–26 shows a range inserted as a block into the kitchen plan. The following step-by-step exercise will help you move the range to its proper final location using the MOVE command with the Snap to Insert object snap mode.*

Step #1: Open the *EXE7-3.dwg* file.

Step #2: Use the following command line procedure to move the block:

Command: **MOVE** ~EnterKey~

Select objects: *(select the Range)*

Select objects: ~EnterKey~

Specify base point or displacement: **INS** ~EnterKey~

Specify base point or displacement: ins of *(move your mouse to the range; AutoCAD will automatically locate the insertion point by displaying the double square marker. Click on that point)*

Specify second point of displacement or (use first point as displacement): **INT** ~EnterKey~

int of: *(move your cursor to the intersection of the wall corner and left click)*

The final position of the range in the kitchen plan is shown in Figure 7–27.

Congratulations! You used the Snap to Insert object snap mode to move a block from one location to another location.

7.3.11 Snap to NODE

This object snap mode allows you to snap to the *point object* drawn with the POINT command and is discussed later in this chapter. See section 7.7

7.3.12 Snap to Nearest

This object snap mode allows you to snap to the closest object at the cursor location. This is useful when you do not want to snap to a specified point but rather snap to the nearest point on the

FIGURE 7–27 The final location of the range after the MOVE command for Exercise 7–3.

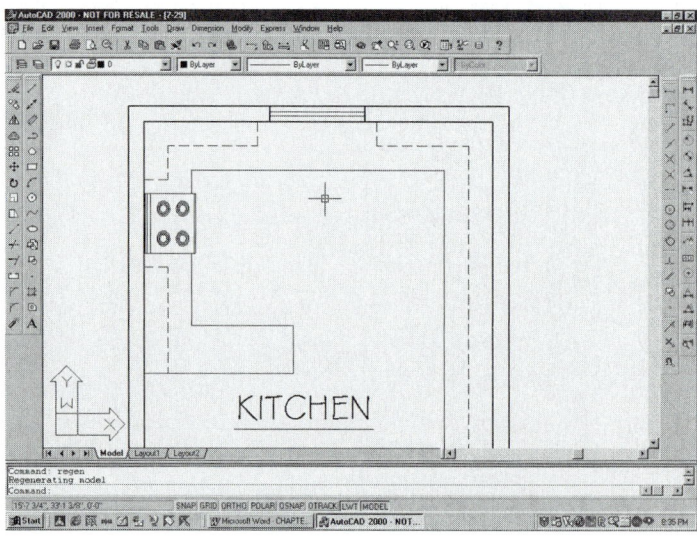

object. For example, you can snap to the perimeter of a circle or arc without snapping to the center, quadrant, or to the tangent by using the Snap to Nearest object snap mode.

Tips: Use Snap to Nearest wisely. This object snap mode should be turned off when using Object Snap Tracking and Polar Tracking. Otherwise all tracking points will snap to nearest as you move your cursor along the alignment path, causing a conflict between tooltip and object snap.

7.3.13 Snap to None

You can establish *Running Object Snap Modes* for AutoCAD to automatically select the snap points. This button in the Object Snap toolbar will turn Running Object Snap Modes off.

7.3.14 Snap From

This object snap mode allows you to draw an object in reference to an existing point. It is considered to be a special override that can be used to establish a temporary reference point. It is usually combined with other object snap modes and one of the *coordinate point entry methods* to specify subsequent location(s). If only one direction is needed (X or Y), use polar coordinates to specify location. If both X and Y directions are needed, use relative coordinates to specify location.

■ **EXERCISE 7–4:** *The following step-by-step exercise will help you draw a new wall from a reference point as shown in Fig 7–28. The location of the new wall is determined to be 5'-0" in the X direction and 3'-7" in the Y direction. Use the Snap From object snap mode with Snap to Intersection and relative coordinates to create the new wall.*

Step #1: Open the *EXE7-4.dwg* file.

Step #2: Use the following command line procedure to draw and locate the new wall:

Command: **LINE** ~EnterKey~

Specify first point: *(select the Snap From button in the Object Snap toolbar)*

Specify first point: _from Base point: *(select the Snap to Intersection button in the Object Snap toolbar)*

Specify first point: _from Base point: _int of *(click on the reference point as shown in Figure 7–28)*

Specify first point: _from Base point: _int of <Offset>: **@5', 3'-7"**, EnterKey.

Specify next point or [Undo]: **@3'<270** ~EnterKey~

Step #3: Use the OFFSET command to offset the wall 4".

Step #4: Use the LINE command with Snap to Endpoint to create wall caps.

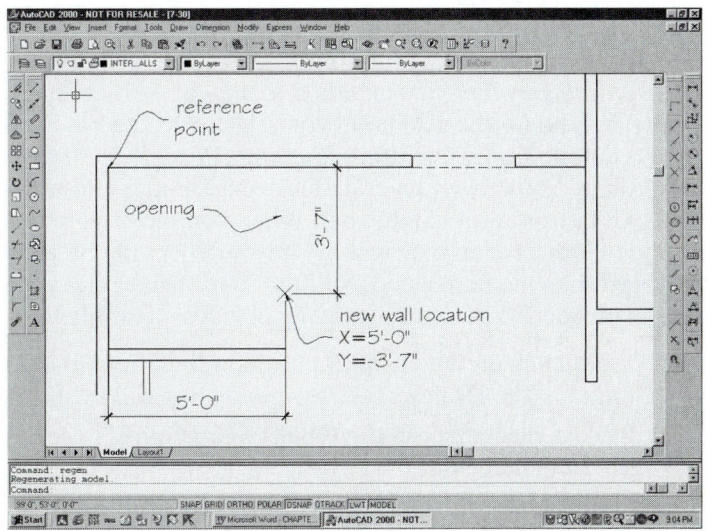

FIGURE 7–28 The Snap From Object Snap Mode is used to establish a temporary base (reference) point to draw an object in reference to the selected base point. It is combined with other object snap modes for maximum efficiency.

FIGURE 7–29 The
new wall is drawn in
reference to the base
point 5'-0" in the X
direction and 3'-7" in
the −Y direction.

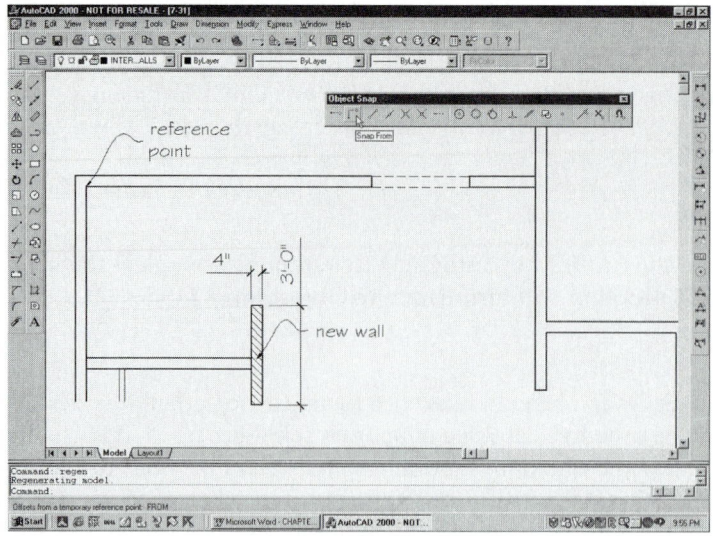

Your drawing should now look like Figure 7–29. Do not draw hatching or text.

Congratulations! You used the Snap From and Snap to Intersection object snap modes to draw a wall in reference to an existing wall in conjunction with the LINE command.

Tips: Snap From is one of the most important and useful object snap modes and can boost productivity and increase drawing efficiency. Use Snap From object snap mode where geometry is located at a given distance from a specific point. For example, you can use Snap From in conjunction with the BREAK command to locate the first break point and the second break point combined with polar coordinates to break a portion of an existing line for a door or a window opening. The BREAK command is discussed in Chapter 12.

Tips: To measure a point on an existing line that is at an unknown angle using the LINE command, use Snap From to snap to the endpoint of the line, then move your cursor to the opposite endpoint of the line and pause it there. At the command line type only the distance, such as 3', and press Enter. Use this method only as a guide not as a drawing aid since this will create a double line from the endpoint of the line. Drawing lines over existing lines is not recommended unless it is for guideline purposes.

Caution: Creating double lines (creating lines over existing lines) to get to a certain point is not an acceptable drawing method.

7.4 SETTING RUNNING OBJECT SNAP MODES

As explained previously, single object snap mode requires the snap mode to be selected for each point as a *single point mode* method that creates object snap overrides. An object snap override is ONLY valid for the next point you select. You can have AutoCAD snap to several object snap modes automatically by setting *Running Object Snap Modes*. This makes object snaps available at all times. You can set several object snap modes and turn them on or off as desired from the OSNAP button in the Status bar. When you move your cursor over the objects, the most appropriate object snap type will be shown depending on the location of the cursor and the type of object snap mode selected. All AutoSnap visual guides can be displayed with the running object snap modes. You can set running object snap modes as follows:

1. Right-click on the OSNAP button in the Status Bar. From the shortcut menu, select Settings. . . . The Drafting Settings dialog box will be displayed.
2. Place a checkmark in the Object Snap On [F3] check box. This will turn the running object snap mode on.
3. Place a checkmark on the object snap modes that you require.
4. Click on the OK button.

After establishing the desired running object snap modes, you can left-click on the OSNAP button to turn all of the object snap modes on or off. When OSNAP button is on and you are prompted for a point on the screen, you can move your cursor over an object to invoke a running object snap mode. You can turn all object snap modes off during a command by selecting the Snap to None button in the Object Snap toolbar.

Tips: Use running object snap modes instead of overrides to use the same object snap modes for more than one point.

Tips: When there are several running object snap modes press the ~TabKey~ to cycle between modes that are currently set. When the desired object snap marker and tooltip appear, left-click to use that object snap mode point.

7.5 AUTOTRACK

As explained previously with the Snap to Extension and Snap to Parallel object snap modes, AutoTrack uses temporary alignment paths to locate specific points on the objects. The AutoTrack mode uses the AutoSnap feature, which allows you to visually preview precise point locations prior to the actual selection of the point. With AutoTrack, you can locate new points in relation to one or two fixed points in the drawing. There are three key terms associated with tracking:

ALIGNMENT PATH: This is a temporary tracking line displayed as a dotted line that the cursor travels along to track points.

TRACKING POINT: This is a temporary point that alignment paths go through. To establish a tracking point, move your cursor over the point and pause for two seconds; do not click on the point. When you pause over the tracking point, AutoCAD will display a small plus sign (+). When the plus sign is displayed on the point, the point becomes *acquired* by Tracking Point. AutoCAD remembers this tracking point when another tracking point is acquired.

EXTENSION PATH: This is an alignment path leading from a line or arc when you use the Snap to Extension object snap mode as described previously.

AutoCAD also allows you to locate a precise point from a reference point and allows you to track a point from several locations through AutoSnap and Object Snap Tracking. You can also instruct AutoCAD to display polar distance and angle as a tooltip while you move your cursor to locate points on the screen using Polar Tracking, Polar Snap, and Polar Angle settings.

7.5.1   Polar Tracking, Polar Snap, Polar Angle, and Polar Distance

Polar Tracking allows you to draw objects without entering distances at the keyboard. It is similar to Ortho and Snap commands, but Polar Tracking adds *polar angles, polar snap,* and *polar distance* features, freeing you from the grid. Polar Tracking has the following features and advantages:

1. It allows you to set angles other than the conventional 0, 90, 180, and 270 degrees. This is called the Polar Angle Settings feature. When you set a specific Polar Angle, AutoCAD tracks cursor movement along alignment paths and increments of the set angle. For example, you can set a Polar Angle of 15 degrees, and AutoCAD will snap to increments of 15 degrees (30, 45, 60, 75, and so on) as you move your cursor. When your cursor approaches one of the polar angles, the Polar Tracking tooltip will display the word *Polar:* followed by the polar coordinates (distance < angle). The alignment path and the tooltip disappear when you move your cursor away from the angle.

2. It allows you to set a Polar Distance that the cursor snaps to along the polar tracking line. You can move the cursor until you get the appropriate distance and angle readout in the tooltip and then select that point.

3. It allows you to override the Grid Snap type and have Polar Snap as the current snap feature that snaps to the Polar Angle and Polar Distance.

Note: Ortho mode and Polar Tracking cannot be active at the same time. AutoCAD will turn Ortho mode off automatically when Polar Tracking is turned on. You can always type polar coordinates or a distance to override Polar Spacing and Polar Angle.

7.5.2   Using Polar Tracking

You can turn Polar Tracking on by left-clicking on the POLAR button on the Status Bar. When you right-click on the POLAR button and select Settings . . ., the Drafting Settings dialog box will be displayed as shown in Figure 7–30. Inside the Polar Tracking tab there are three major categories that will allow you to set Polar Angle Settings, Object Snap Tracking Settings, and Polar Angle measurement.

- **POLAR TRACKING ON [F10]:**   (check box). This will turn Polar Tracking on or off. You can also press the ~F10Key~.

- **POLAR ANGLE SETTINGS:**   (category). This area allows you to select an increment angle for AutoCAD to display along alignment paths. By pressing the down arrow, you can choose from a list of angle increments, including 90, 45, 30, 22.5, 18, 15, 10, and 5 degrees. You can also click on the Additional Angles check box and then click on the New button to enter another angle to use. When you select an increment angle, AutoCAD will snap to that angle and increments of that angle up to 360 degrees. Selecting 90 would be like using the *direct distance entry method* where AutoCAD snaps to 0, 90, 180, and 270 degrees, similar to Ortho mode. The Delete button will allow you to delete the selected Additional Angles from the list.

- **OBJECT SNAP TRACKING SETTINGS:**   (category). This area controls the tracking of available angles used with object snap tracking. If the Track Orthogonally only radio button is checked, only horizontal and vertical alignment paths will be active. If the Track Using All Polar Angle Settings radio button is checked, alignment paths for all polar snap angles will be active.

- **POLAR ANGLE MEASUREMENT:**   (area). If the Absolute radio button is checked, the polar tracking will be relative to the current UCS. If the Relative to Last Segment radio button is checked, polar tracking will be relative to the last segment created.

FIGURE 7–30   The Polar Tracking tab of the Drafting Settings dialog box allows you to set Polar Snap settings.

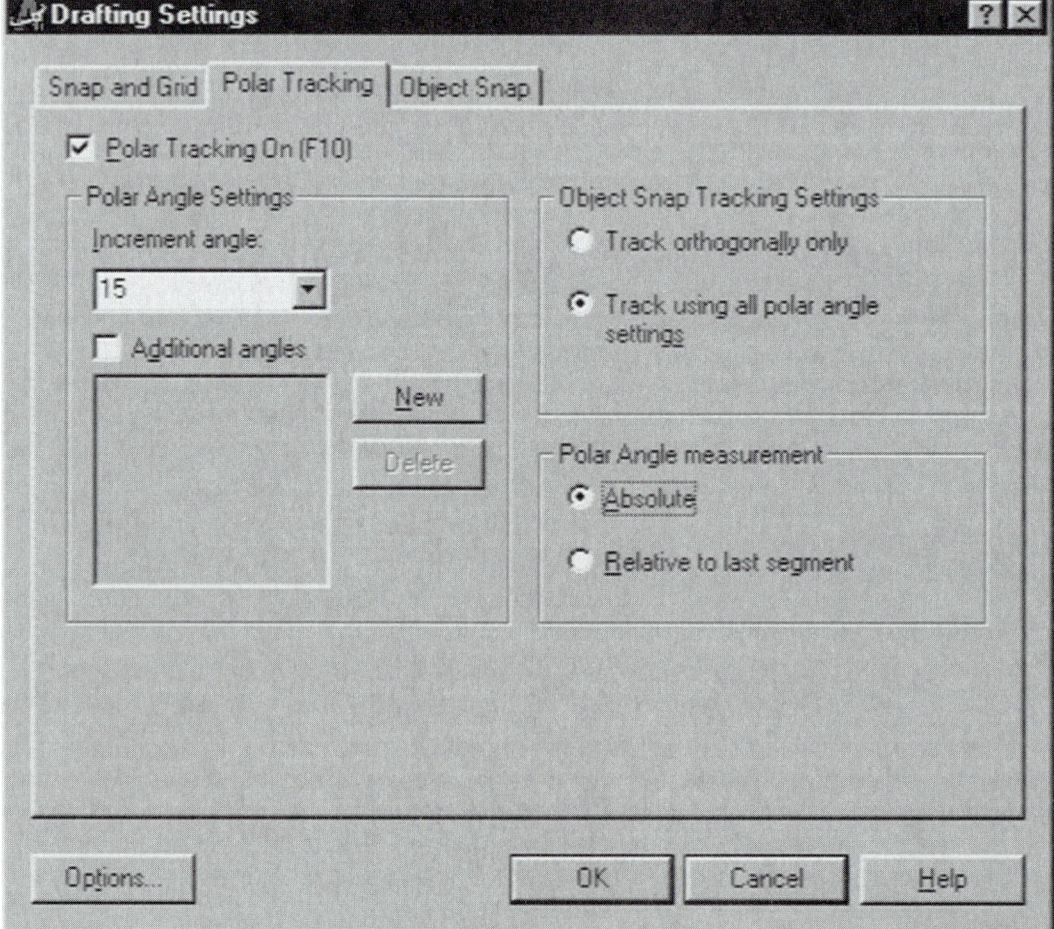

■ **EXERCISE 7–5:**   *The following step-by-step exercise will help you draw a 12'-0" square at an angle of 30 degrees using Polar Tracking and Polar Angle.*

Step #1:   Set drawing Units to *Architectural* and Precision to 0'-0".

Step #2:   Set drawing Limits as 44', 34' and zoom to the Limits of your drawing.

Step #3:   Left-click on the Polar button located in the Status Bar and right-click on Settings..

Step #4:   Inside the Polar Tracking Tab, turn Polar Tracking on.

Step #5:   Inside the increment angle: drop-down list, select 30.

Step #6:   Set Object Snap Tracking settings to Track using all polar angle settings.

Step #7:   Set Polar Angle Measurement to Relative to Last Segment.

Step #8:   Click on the OK button.

Step #9:   Use the following command line procedure to create the square:

Command: **LINE** ~EnterKey~

Specify first point: *(select a starting point)*

Specify next point or [Undo]: *(move the cursor in the direction of 30 degrees. When the correct polar tracking alignment path appears, move the cursor in the direction of the path. When the tooltip reads "Polar: 12'-0"<30°," left click on that point)*

Specify next point or [Undo]: *(move the cursor perpendicular to the first line. When the correct polar tracking alignment path appears move the cursor in the direction of the path. When the tooltip reads "Relative Polar: 12'-0" < 90°," left click on that point. Since the polar angle measurement was set to Relative to Last Segment, the tooltip shows a relative angle of 90 degrees measured from the last line. If the Polar Angle Measurement was set to Absolute, the tooltip would have displayed "Polar: 12'-0"<120°)*

Specify next point or [Close/Undo]: *(move the cursor perpendicular to the previous line. When the correct polar tracking alignment path appears, move the cursor in the direction of the path. When the tooltip reads "Relative Polar: 12'-0"<90°," left-click on that point)*

Specify next point or [Close/Undo]: *(move the cursor to the first point and use snap to endpoint object snap mode to finish the square)*

Congratulations! You have created a 12'-0" square object without entering distances at the command line as shown in Figure 7-31.

> *Note: You can use the POLARMODE system variable to establish polar settings, use POLARANG system variable to specify the increment of polar angle, and POLARADDANG system variable to set up 10 user-defined polar angles.*

7.5.3   Using Polar Snap

When you track along the alignment path using Polar Tracking, you can have the cursor snap to a specific distance using Polar Snap. For example, you can set Polar Tracking and Polar Angle at 90 degrees and a Polar Snap distance of 5'-0" and draw a line 5', 10', 15', 20', etc. in length at angles of 0, 90, 180, and 270 degrees. It is like having Ortho on with Polar Tracking tooltip, and you do not have to type distances at the command line. There are two guidelines you must follow before working with Polar Snap:

1.   You must turn on both Polar and Snap at the Status Bar.

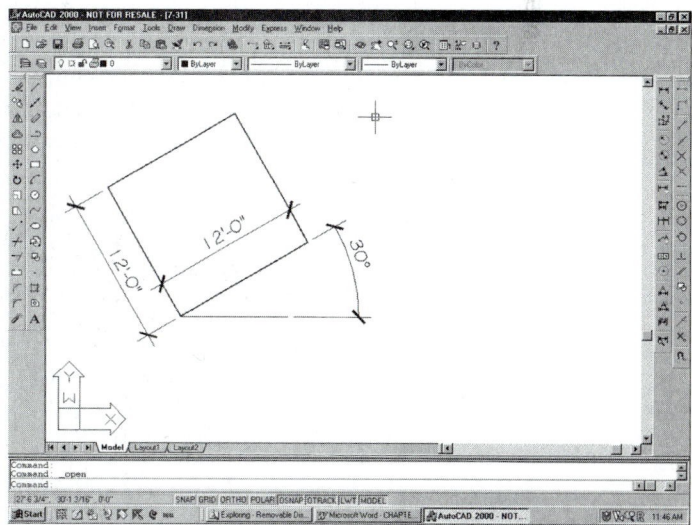

FIGURE 7–31   The square is completed using Polar Tracking and Polar Angle.

2. You must decide on the snap type to be used. There are two snap types available in the Snap and Grid tab of the Drafting Settings dialog box. Grid Snap type is the standard Snap, which allows you to snap to the grid. Polar Snap type allows you to snap to the polar distance and polar angle that you specify through Polar Tracking.

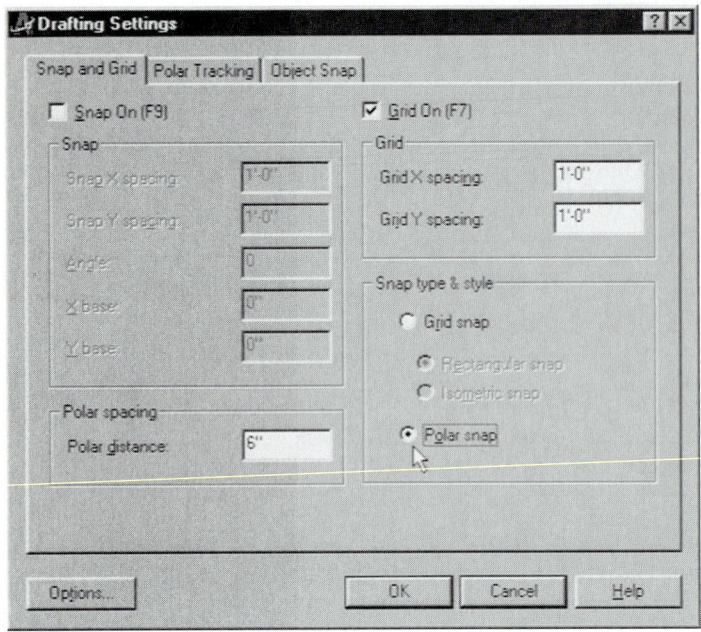

FIGURE 7–32   The Snap and Grid tab of the Drafting Settings dialog box allows you to set Polar Distance with Polar Snap.

The Snap and Grid tab of the Drafting Settings dialog box is shown in Figure 7–32. Placing a checkmark inside the Polar Snap radio button turns Polar Snap on. The Polar Spacing category has the *Polar Distance* text box. When Polar Snap is on, you can enter the increment value the cursor will snap to along the alignment path of Polar Tracking. For example, if you enter a value of 6 inside the Polar Distance text box and turn Polar Snap on, AutoCAD will snap to increments of 6″ along the alignment paths (providing that you have set drawing Units to Architectural and Precision to 0′-0″). If you set a specific Polar Increment angle, AutoCAD will snap to that angle and the distance specified, giving you the flexibility to complete a drawing using Polar Tracking and Polar snap. You can use the SNAPTYPE system variable to set the snap type to Polar (1) or Grid (0).

Note: You can override the polar snap distance by using the direct distance entry method while taking advantage of the polar angle constraint

■   **EXERCISE 7–6:**   *The following step-by-step exercise will help you draw the outline of the building shown in Figure 7–33 using Polar Tracking, Polar Angle, Polar Snap, and Polar Distance.*

Step #1:   Set drawing Units to *Architectural* and Precision to 0′-0″.

Step #2:   Set limits to 34′, 44′ and zoom to the limits of your drawing.

Step #3:   Right-click on the Polar button in the Status Bar and left-click on Settings.... Inside the Drafting Settings dialog box, turn Polar Tracking on. From the Increment Angle select 90. Place a checkmark inside the Additional Angles check box and click on the New button. Inside the text box, enter 60 and set Object Snap Tracking Settings to Track Using All Polar Angle Settings. Set Polar Angle Measurement to Absolute.

Step #4:   Inside the Drafting Settings dialog box, under the Snap and Grid tab, turn Snap on. Under Snap Type and Style, place a checkmark inside the Polar Snap radio button. Inside the Polar Distance text box enter 1′-0″.

Step #5:   Use the following command line procedure to create the object:

Command: **LINE** ~EnterKey~

Specify first point: **5′, 17′** ~EnterKey~ *(this will select the starting point)*

Specify next point or [Undo]: *(move cursor from point 1 to point 2 in the direction of 90 degrees. When the correct Polar Tracking alignment path appears, move the cursor in the direction of the path. When the tooltip reads "Polar: 3′-0″ < 90°," left-click on that point)*

Specify next point or [Undo]: *(move cursor from point 2 to point 3 in the direction of 0 degrees. When the correct Polar Tracking alignment path appears move the cursor in the direction of the path. When the tooltip reads "Polar: 3′-0″ <0°," left-click on that point)*

Specify next point or [Close/Undo]: *(move cursor from point 3 to point 4 in the direction of 90 degrees. When the correct Polar Tracking alignment path appears, move*

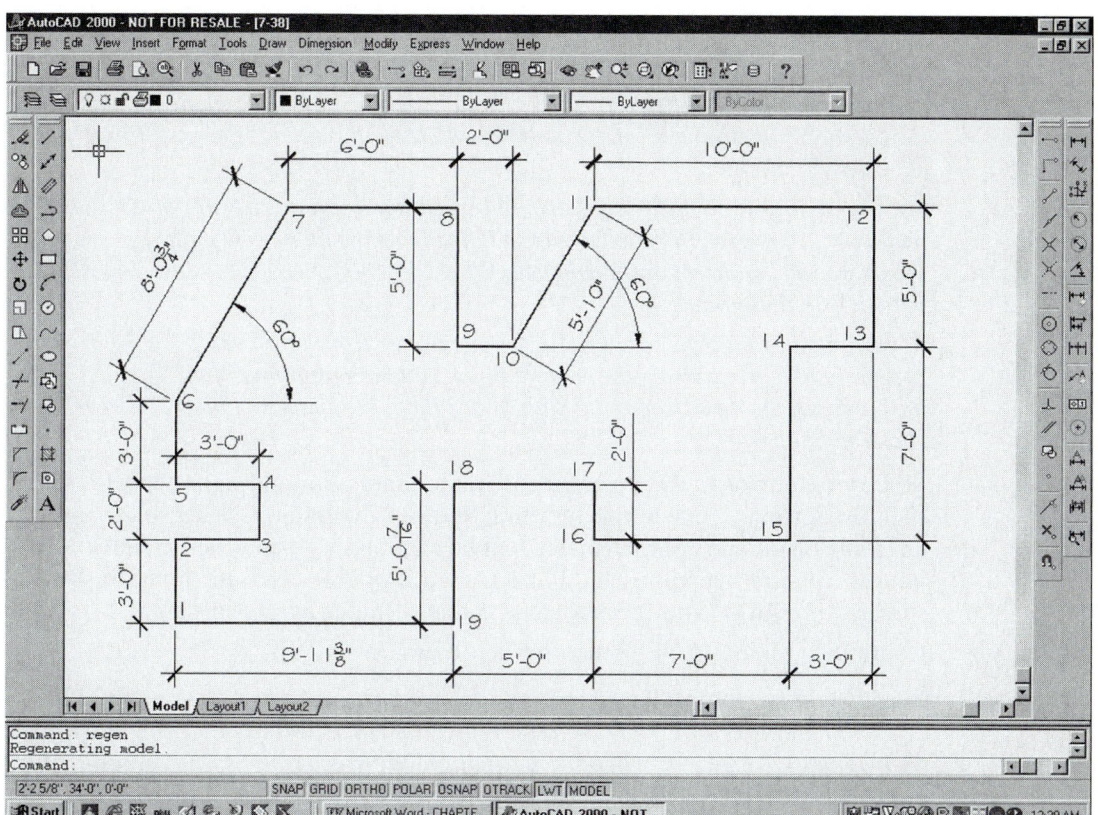

FIGURE 7–33 The building layout for Exercise 7–6. All dimensions and angles are for Polar Tracking and Polar Snap purposes and are not to be created.

the cursor in the direction of the path. When the tooltip reads "Polar: 2'-0"<90°" left-click on that point)

Specify next point or [Close/Undo]: *(move cursor from point 4 to point 5 in the direction of 180 degrees. When the correct Polar Tracking alignment path appears, move the cursor in the direction of the path. When the tooltip reads "Polar: 3'-0"<180°," left-click on that point)*

Specify next point or [Close/Undo]: *(move cursor from point 5 to point 6 in the direction of 90 degrees. When the correct Polar Tracking alignment path appears, move the cursor in the direction of the path. When the tooltip reads "Polar: 3'-0"<90°" left-click on that point)*

Step #6: Move your cursor to the Polar button in the Status Bar and right-click. Left-click on Settings....Inside the Drafting Settings dialog box, select Snap and Grid tab. Inside the Polar distance text box, enter 8'-0 3/4" and click on the OK button. You are overriding the Polar distance of 1'-0" to 8'-0 3/4" temporarily so that AutoCAD can precisely snap to that distance at 60 degrees.

Step #7: Continue with the LINE command as follows:

Specify next point or [Close/Undo]: *(move cursor from point 6 to point 7 in the approximate direction of 60 degrees. When the correct Polar Tracking alignment path appears, AutoCAD will place a small x at the precise point, and the tooltip will read "Polar: 8'-0 3/4"<60°." Left-click on that point)*

Step #8: Move your cursor to the Polar button in the Status Bar and right-click. Left-click on Settings....Inside the Drafting Settings dialog box, select Snap and Grid tab. Inside the Polar distance text box, enter 1'-0" and click on the OK button. You are deleting the override you have just performed.

Step #9:   Continue with the LINE command as follows:

Specify next point or [Close/Undo]: *(move cursor from point 7 to point 8 in the direction of 0 degrees. When the correct Polar Tracking alignment path appears, move the cursor in the direction of the path. When the tooltip reads "Polar: 6'-0″<0°," left-click on that point)*

Specify next point or [Close/Undo]: *(move cursor from point 8 to point 9 in the direction of 270 degrees. When the correct Polar Tracking alignment path appears, move the cursor in the direction of the path. When the tooltip reads "Polar: 5'-0″<270°," left-click on that point)*

Specify next point or [Close/Undo]: *(move cursor from point 9 to point 10 in the direction of 0 degrees. When the correct Polar Tracking alignment path appears, move the cursor in the direction of the path. When the tooltip reads "Polar: 2'-0″<0°," left-click on that point)*

Step #10:   Move your cursor to the Polar button in the Status Bar and right-click. Left-click on Settings....Inside the Drafting Settings dialog box, select Snap and Grid tab. Inside the Polar Distance text box, enter 5'-10″ and click on the OK button. You are overriding the Polar Distance of 1'-0″ to 5'-10″ temporarily so that AutoCAD can precisely snap to that distance at 60 degrees.

Step #11:   Continue with the LINE command as follows:

Specify next point or [Close/Undo]: *(move cursor from point 10 to point 11 in the approximate direction of 60 degrees. When the correct Polar Tracking alignment path appears, AutoCAD will place a small x at the precise point, and the tooltip will read "Polar: 5'-10″<60°." Left-click on that point)*

Step #12:   Move your cursor to the Polar button in the Status Bar and right-click. Left-click on Settings....Inside the Drafting Settings dialog box, select Snap and Grid tab. Inside the Polar distance text box, enter 1' and click on the OK button. You are deleting the override you have just performed.

Step #13:   Continue with the LINE command as follows:

Specify next point or [Close/Undo]: *(move cursor from point 11 to point 12 in the direction of 0 degrees. When the correct Polar Tracking alignment path appears, move the cursor in the direction of the path. When the tooltip reads "Polar: 10'-0″<0°," left-click on that point)*

Step #14:   Continue drawing the lines for points 13, 14, 15, 16, 17, and 18. When drawing the line from point 18 to point 19, set the Polar Distance to 5'-0 7/16″. When drawing the line from point 19 to point 1, you can either enter C for close or snap to the endpoint of the first line.

Step #15:   Save this drawing as MYEXE7-6.

Your drawing should now look like Figure 7–33 without dimensions and text.

Congratulations! You have created the object in Figure 7–33 using Polar Snap, Polar Tracking, and Polar Angle with the LINE command.

7.5.4   AutoTrack Settings (Visual Cues)

Just like AutoSnap settings, the AutoTrack settings have visual cues. The alignment path displayed by dotted lines will also display the Polar Tracking vector at specified angles. The Auto-Track tooltip allows you to visually confirm the distance and angle when creating objects using Polar Tracking. The AutoTrack Settings can be found in the Drafting tab of the Options dialog box, as shown in Figure 7–5.

- **DISPLAY POLAR TRACKING VECTOR:**   (check box). Turning this setting on displays the dotted lines as the Polar Tracking vector. If you turn this setting off, dotted lines will not be displayed, but you can still track.

- **DISPLAY FULL-SCREEN TRACKING VECTOR:** (check box). Turning this setting on will display the tracking vectors.

- **DISPLAY AUTOTRACK TOOLTIP:** (check box). Turning this setting on will display the AutoTrack tooltip.

7.5.5 Alignment Point Acquisition

The Alignment Point Acquisition allows you to change the way you acquire alignment points through tracking vectors.

- **AUTOMATIC:** (radio button). When this option is checked, tracking vectors are automatically displayed when you move your cursor over an object snap.

- **SHIFT TO ACQUIRE:** (radio button). When this option is checked, tracking vectors are displayed when you press ~ShiftKey~ and move your cursor over an object snap.

7.6 OBJECT SNAP TRACKING

Object Snap Tracking allows you to locate one or more points in relation to one or two existing points. The points along the alignment path are automatically tracked. You can turn Object Snap Tracking on by clicking on the OTRACK button in the Status bar or placing a check mark inside the Object Snap Tracking On [F11] check box in the Object Snap tab of the Drafting Settings dialog box, as shown in Figure 7–2.

7.6.1 Object Snap Tracking with One Point

You can locate a specific point from a reference point with Object Snap Tracking. For example, you can locate point A so that you can draw the door 3'-0" west of the reference point as shown in Figure 7–34 as follows:

First, turn OSNAP and OTRACK on at the Status Bar. Make sure the Endpoint running object snap mode is checked and that the Nearest object snap mode is not checked; otherwise AutoCAD will snap to the nearest all the time, causing a conflict between tooltip and object snap. Then, set unit precision to 0'-0" and use the following command line procedure:

```
Command: LINE ~EnterKey~
Specify first point: (move your cursor over reference point but do not
click. A small plus sign (+) will be displayed at the reference point.
Move the cursor away from the point toward west. The alignment path with
tracking tooltip will be displayed. When the cursor snaps on to the
"Endpoint: 3'-0"<180°," left-click.
Specify next point or [Undo]: (click on the Polar button in the Status bar,
move your cursor up, and draw the rest of the door using Polar Tracking)
```

7.6.2 Object Snap Tracking with Two Points

You can locate the intersection of two points with object snap tracking. This is extremely useful in architectural drawings, when locating a specific point to draw an object in relation to two points. AutoCAD will allow you to track with two points to locate the desired point.

■ **EXERCISE 7–7:** *The following step-by-step exercise will help you locate the point where two imaginary lines intersect from the midpoint of the two existing chairs. You will track two points from the midpoint of the two existing chairs, as shown in Figure 7–35. After the point is located, you will draw the circular table. The center of the 1'-6" radius circle is the starting point for the table and is shown as a visual guide as dash lines.*

Step #1: Open the *EXE7-5.dwg* file.

Step #2: Turn OSNAP and OTRACK on at the Status Bar. Make sure the Midpoint running object snap mode is checked and that the Nearest object snap mode is not checked, otherwise AutoCAD will snap to the nearest all the time, causing a conflict between tooltip and object snap.

FIGURE 7–34 Locating point A from a reference point using Object Snap Tracking.

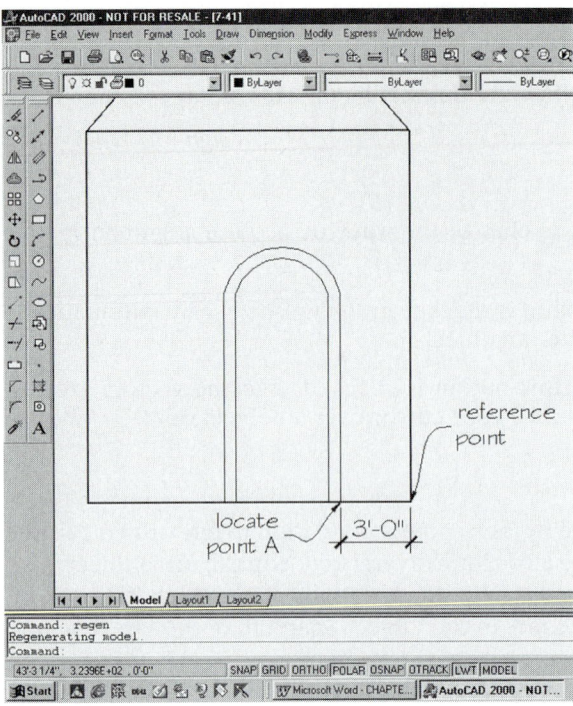

FIGURE 7–35 The Object Snap Tracking can be used to track two points to find their intersection.

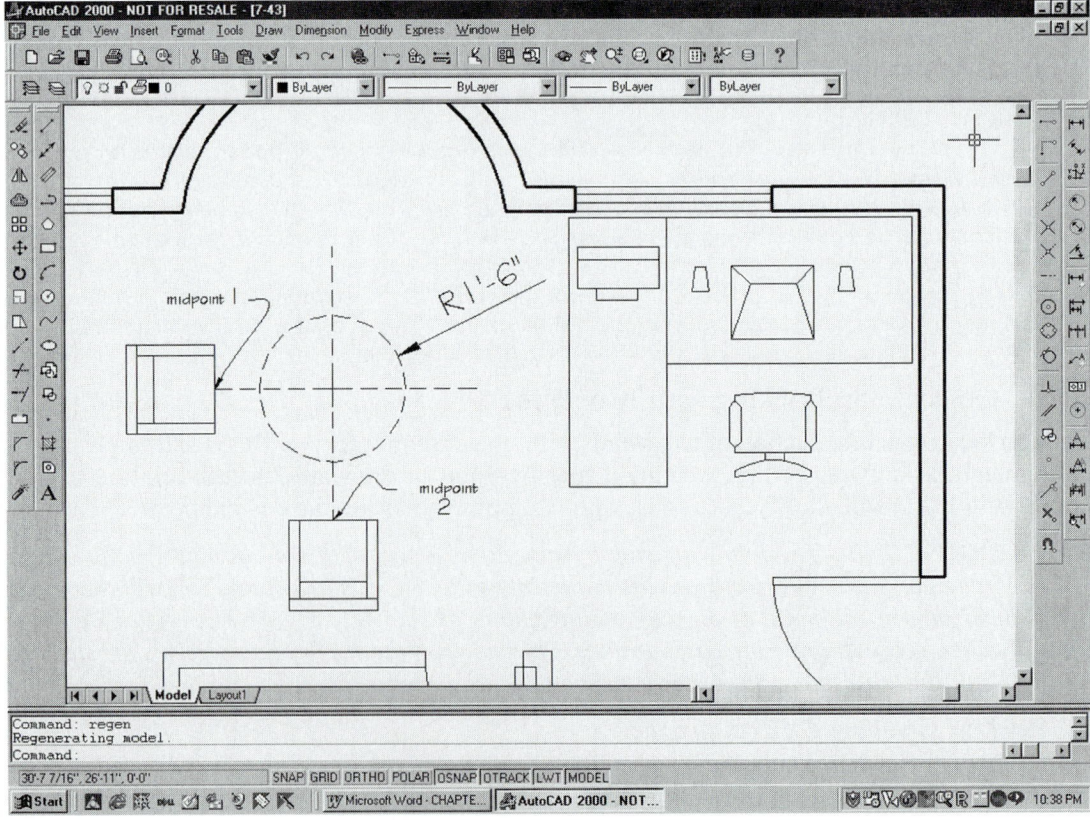

Step #3: Draw the circular table as follows:

Command: **CIRCLE** ~EnterKey~

Specify center point for circle or [3P/2P/Ttr (tan tan radius)]: *(move your cursor over the midpoint 1 of the chair but do not click. A small plus sign (+) will be displayed at the midpoint. Move the cursor over the midpoint 2 of the other chair but do not click. A small plus sign (+) will be displayed at the midpoint. Move your cursor straight up and follow the vertical alignment path until it intersects the horizontal alignment path. When the cursor locks into the intersection, the tooltip will read "Midpoint: <0°, Midpoint: <90°." Left-click to establish the center point of the circle)*

Specify radius of circle or [Diameter]: **1′6** ~EnterKey~

Your drawing should now look like Figure 7–36.

Congratulations! You have created a circular table by tracking two points from the midpoints of the two existing chairs using Object Snap Tracking.

Note: You can perform the same task by using the Temporary Tracking Point button in the Object Snap toolbar (the first button) with OTRACK on. After accessing the CIRCLE command, click on the Temporary Tracking Point and click on the midpoint 1 of the chair. Then move your cursor to midpoint 2 of the other chair but do not click. Repeat the rest of the procedure as shown above.

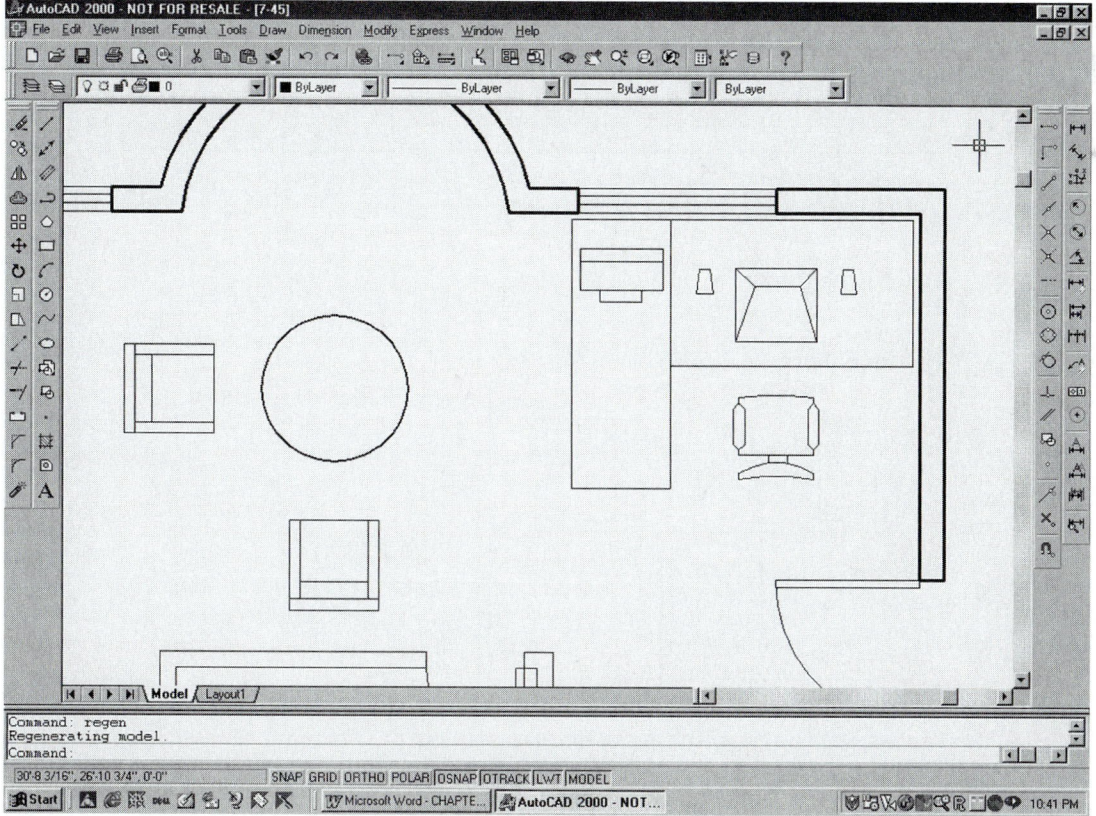

FIGURE 7–36 The table is drawn with the help of two object snap tracking points.

7.6.3   Temporary Tracking Point

This is the first button in the Object Snap toolbar. It allows you to track along an existing object to establish a point either on the X or on the Y coordinates or at any angle established by polar tracking. It is used with the OSNAP button turned on. To track one point, you must click on the reference point after selecting the Temporary Tracking Point or entering TTP at the command line. To track two points, you must acquire the first point along either X or Y coordinate (or any angle) and click on the second point along the other coordinate.

■ **EXERCISE 7–8:**   *The following step-by-step exercise will help you track two points to locate the corner of the window that is 4'-0" over the X coordinate and 13'-0" up the Y coordinate from the reference point using Temporary Tracking Point object snap mode as shown in Figure 7–37 as follows:*

Step #1:   Open the *EXE7-6.dwg* file.

Step #2:   Turn OSNAP and OTRACK on at the Status Bar and set Unit Precision to 0'-0".
Set Intersection as the object snap mode.

Step #3:   Draw the window as follows:

Command: **LINE** ~EnterKey~

Specify first point: *(select the Temporary Tracking Point button in the Object Snap toolbar)*

Specify first point: _tt Specify temporary OTRACK point: *(move your mouse over the reference point but do not click. A small cross will appear at that point, indicating that this point has been acquired. Move your cursor toward East and click when the tooltip reads "Intersection: 4'-0"<0°." Move your cursor straight up and along the alignment path and click when the tooltip reads "Track Point: 13'-0"<90°." Turn ORTHO on and draw the window from this beginning point. Offset the lines and trim.*

FIGURE 7–37   To track two points along the X and Y coordinates, use the Temporary Tracking Point with OSNAP and OTRACK. The corner of the window is located with the Temporary Tracking Point object snap mode.

Your drawing should now look like Figure 7–37.

Congratulations! You have created a window on en existing elevation using the LINE command with temporary tracking point object snap mode.

Tips: When using tracking, know when to click and when to acquire. When you acquire a tracking point, a small plus sign (+) will mark the tracking point. The alignment path will soon appear from the acquired point to indicate default polar alignments (0, 90, 180, and 270). More than two points can be acquired, but you can only track from one or two acquired points. You can clear an acquired point by moving your cursor over the acquired point once more. When you clear an acquired point, make sure the plus sign is removed. When you turn Snap on, the Polar Distance Settings define the distances. If Polar Snap is required with Polar Track, you can set those as well.

7.7 ESTABLISHING POINTS ON SCREEN

Points are established on the screen as a reference mark. AutoCAD uses points when displaying the division and measurement segments created by the DIVIDE and MEASURE commands. When you create points on the screen with the POINT command, you can snap the center location of the point by using the Snap to Node object snap mode. To establish a point on the screen, you must first determine a point style, then a point size before you can use the POINT command.

7.7.1 Setting Point Style and Size

The quickest way to set a point style and point size is to use the Point Style dialog box. To access the Point Style dialog box, select Point Style . . . from the Format pull-down menu. The Point Style dialog box will be displayed as shown in Figure 7–38. There are 20 different point styles to chose from. The current point style is highlighted. To select a different point style, click on the image of the point style. There are two different point sizes to select from. The default point size is 5% of the screen size. When the Set Size Relative to Screen radio button is selected, a point size as a percentage of the screen size can be established. This option allows the point size to change in relation to different display options. For example, when you set the point size relative to screen as a percentage, the point becomes larger or smaller as you zoom in or out. When the Set Size in Absolute Units radio button is selected, you can enter a size relative to the drawing scale inside the Point Size text box. This option will display points at their original size no matter what zoom option is used. This is convenient when you want to have points on the drawing with consistent sizes.

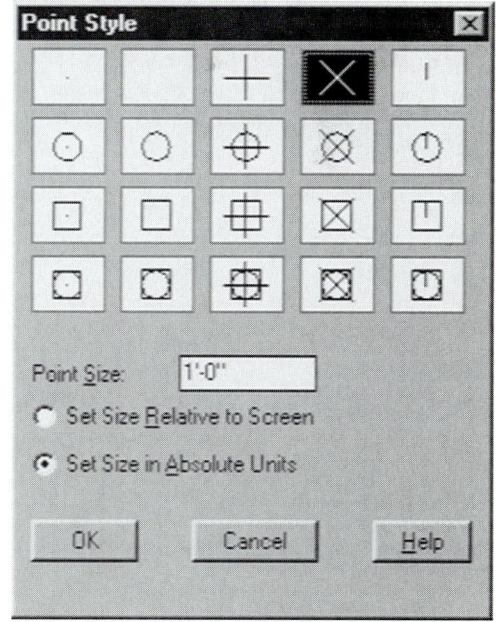

You can use the POINT command to create points on the screen. To access the POINT command, select the Point button from the Draw toolbar, select one of the options from the Point cascading menu in the Draw pull-down menu, or enter PO or POINT at the command line. The command line option is as follows:

```
Command: POINT ~EnterKey~
Current point modes: PDMODE=3 PDSIZE=1'-0"
Specify a point: (enter a coordinate or select a
location for the point)
```

When you use the POINT command, the PDMODE system variable determines the point style. The following numbers correspond to the first point style row in the Point Style dialog box:

```
PDMODE=0 dot
PDMODE=1 nothing
PDMODE=2 +
PDMODE=3 x
PDMODE=4 |
```

FIGURE 7–38 The Point Style dialog box is used to quickly establish the Point Style and Point Size.

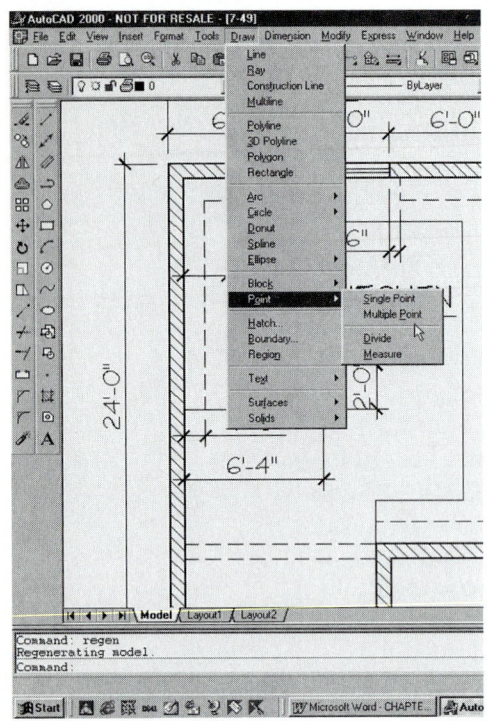

You can change the point style using the PDMODE system variable and adding 32 for a circle, 64 for a square, and 96 for a circle inside a square. For example, if you want to draw a circle with the "x" inside, enter 35 for the PDMODE system variable (32 + 3 = 35). You can also change the point size by using the PDSIZE system variable at the command line. A positive value will set the point size relative to screen. A negative value will set the point size in absolute units.

When you access the POINT command from the Draw pull-down menu, you can select either Single Point or the Multiple Point option as shown in Figure 7–39. The Single Point option will allow you to create a single point on the screen. The Multiple Point option will allow you to create multiple points. You should set a point style and point size either through the dialog box or at the command line before creating points.

You can use the POINT command to establish a reference point on the screen similar to the tracking point established by the X and Y distances of the Temporary Tracking Point. But you must use the POINT command in conjunction with the Snap From object snap mode. For example, you can find the corner of the window shown in Figure 7–37 as follows:

FIGURE 7–39 The Single Point and the Multiple Point options through the Draw pull-down menu.

```
Set the point style to X and point size to Absolute 12".
Command: POINT ~EnterKey~
Specify a point: (select the Snap From button in the Object
Snap toolbar)
Specify a point: _from Base point: (select Snap to Endpoint
button in the Object Snap toolbar)
Specify a point: _endp of (select the reference point shown in Figure 7-37)
Specify a point: _endp of <Offset>: @4',13' ~Enterkey~
```

The point will be drawn as shown in Figure 7–40. You can use the LINE command and Snap to Node object snap mode to snap to that point and then draw the window if you like.

FIGURE 7–40 Using the POINT command with Snap From object snap mode to establish the corner of the window.

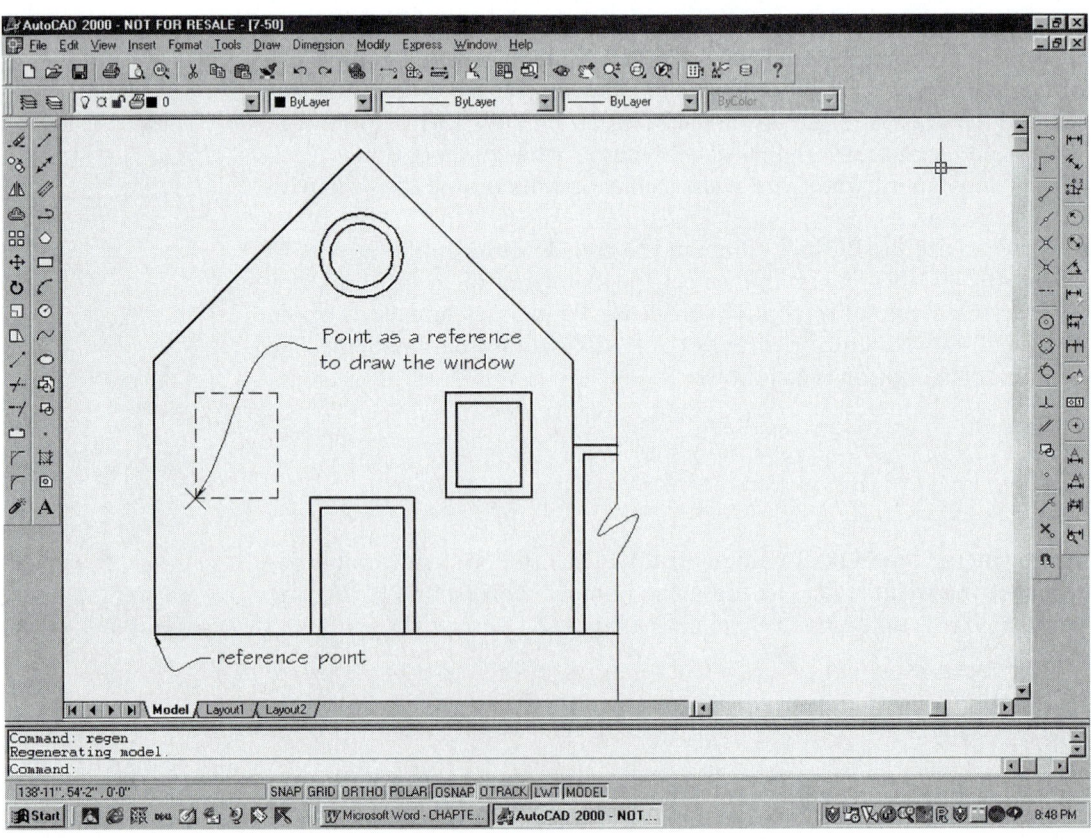

Note: You can also establish points on existing objects using the running object snap modes. For example, you can place points on the endpoints and the midpoint of an existing line or the endpoints and the midpoint of an existing arc or the quadrants and the center of an existing circle. For straight lines, you can also use Object Snap Tracking or Temporary Tracking Point object snap mode in conjunction with the Polar Snap, Polar Angle, and Polar Distance to place points on locations other than the standard object snap points. You can use the alignment paths to track those point locations. However, you can not track on circles, arcs, or objects that are created with the SPLINE command to establish points on locations other than standard object snap points. To establish points on objects created with the ARC, CIRCLE, PLINE ARC, and SPLINE commands use the DIVIDE and MEASURE commands, which are explained next.

7.8 ESTABLISHING POINTS ON OBJECTS

You can establish points on existing straight lines using the POINT command in combination with object snap or AutoTrack modes. You can establish points on existing arcs, circles, and splines using the POINT command in combination with object snap modes but not with Auto-Track mode. However, you can divide a line, circle, spline, arc, or polyline into an equal number of points using the DIVIDE command, and you can divide objects into a specified number of points using the MEASURE command.

7.8.1 Using the DIVIDE Command

The DIVIDE command uses points to divide objects into an equal number of segments. Before using the DIVIDE command, you should establish a point style and a point size as described previously. To start dividing objects, select Divide from the Point cascading menu of the Draw pull-down menu, or enter DIV or DIVIDE at the command line. The points established by the DIVIDE command do not actually break the objects into separate segments. It merely displays the point style of your choice at the locations where the divisions occur. For example, you can divide the line, the circle, the spline, and the rectangle shown in Figure 7–41 into ten equal segments as follows:

Using the Point Style dialog box set the Point Style to circle with "X" inside [second row from top, second column from right or set the PDMODE system variable to 35]. Set Point Size to 8 and check the Set Size in Absolute Units radio button.

```
Command: DIVIDE ~EnterKey~
Select object to divide: (select the spline)
Enter the number of segments or [Block]: 10 ~EnterKey~
Right click and select Repeat Divide from the shortcut menu.
Select object to divide: (select the rectangle)
Enter the number of segments or [Block]: 10 ~EnterKey~
Repeat the same procedure for the circle and the line.
```

For the rectangle, AutoCAD will start the first segment at the intersection and place the points in counterclockwise direction around the perimeter of the rectangle. If you created a special block that you want to place at each division point, use the Block option by entering B at the Enter the number of segments or [Block]: prompt. AutoCAD will ask you if you want the block to be aligned with the selected object. Blocks are discussed in Chapter 19.

You can also place a specific point style proportionately inside a specific wall in a floor plan. For example, in Figure 7–42, four columns are placed inside the 24″ wide wall as follows:

Set the point style to the appropriate style. Set the point size to 24 to match the wall thickness in absolute units. Draw a reference line through the midpoint of the wall. Use the DIVIDE command to divide the reference line into five equal segments and erase the reference after.

7.8.2 Using the MEASURE Command

The MEASURE command will place points a specified distance apart. You can access the MEASURE command by selecting Measure from the Point cascading menu of the Draw

FIGURE 7–41 Using the DIVIDE command to divide objects into an equal number of segments.

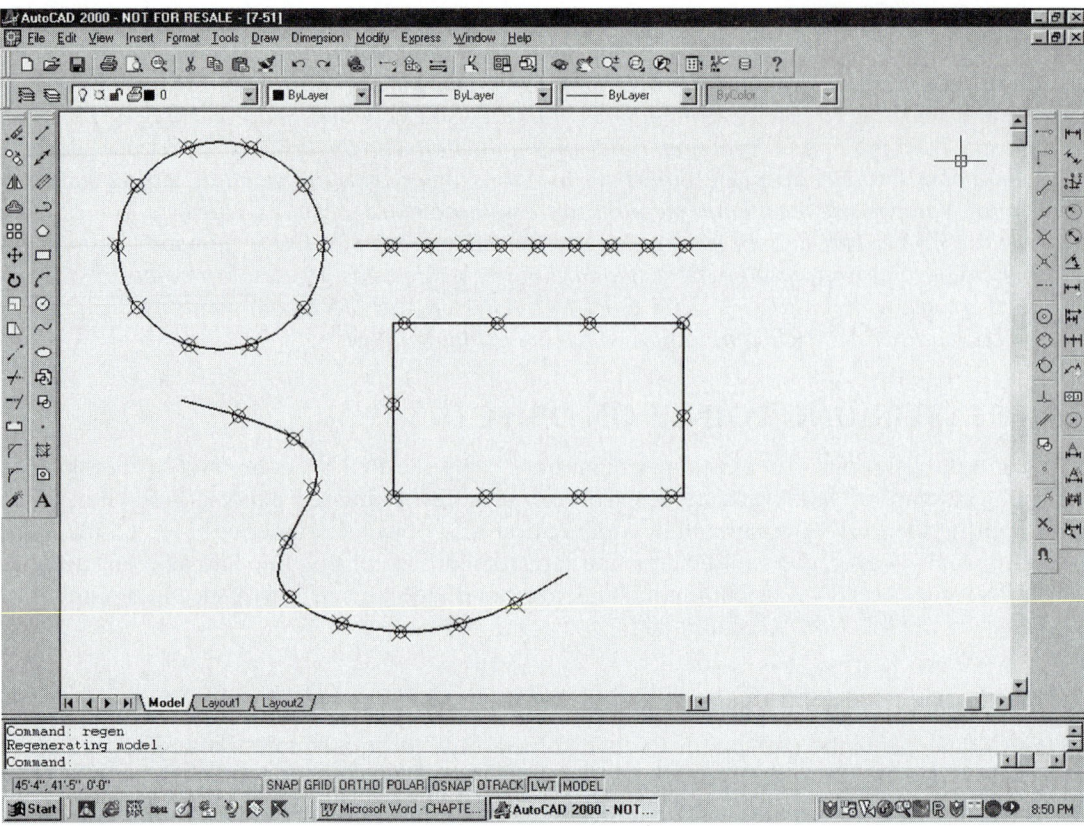

FIGURE 7–42 Using points to display columns inside a wall.

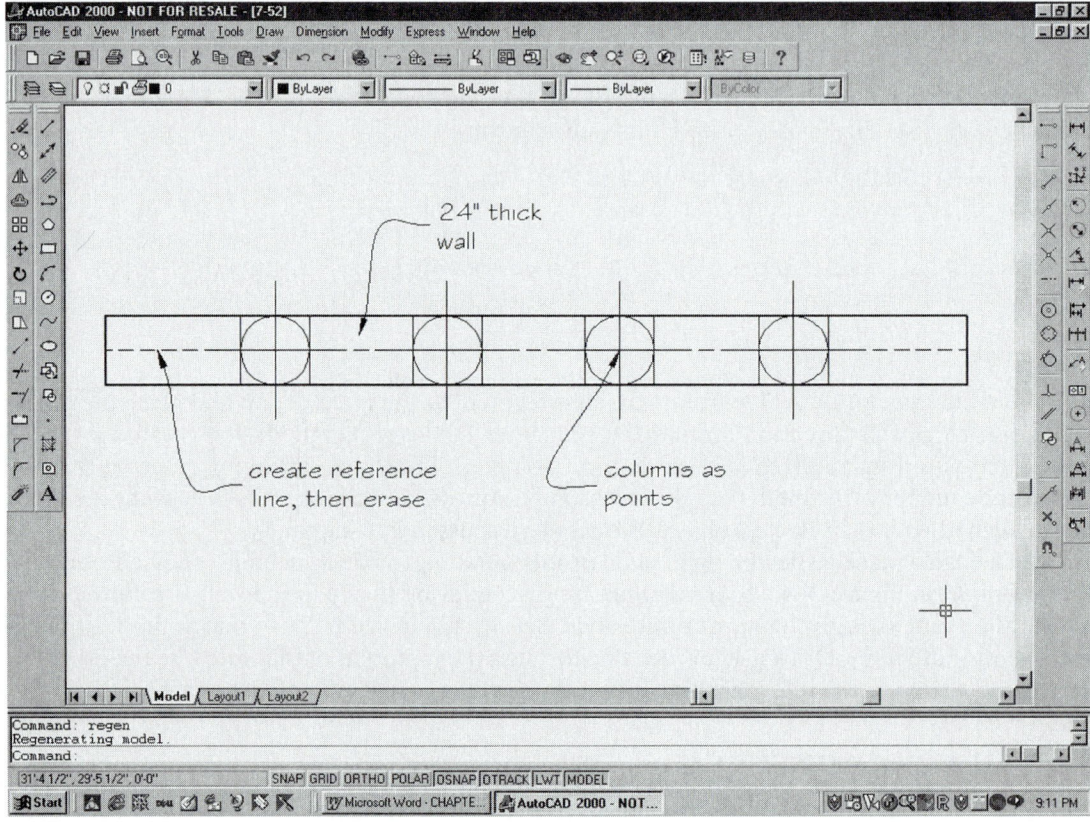

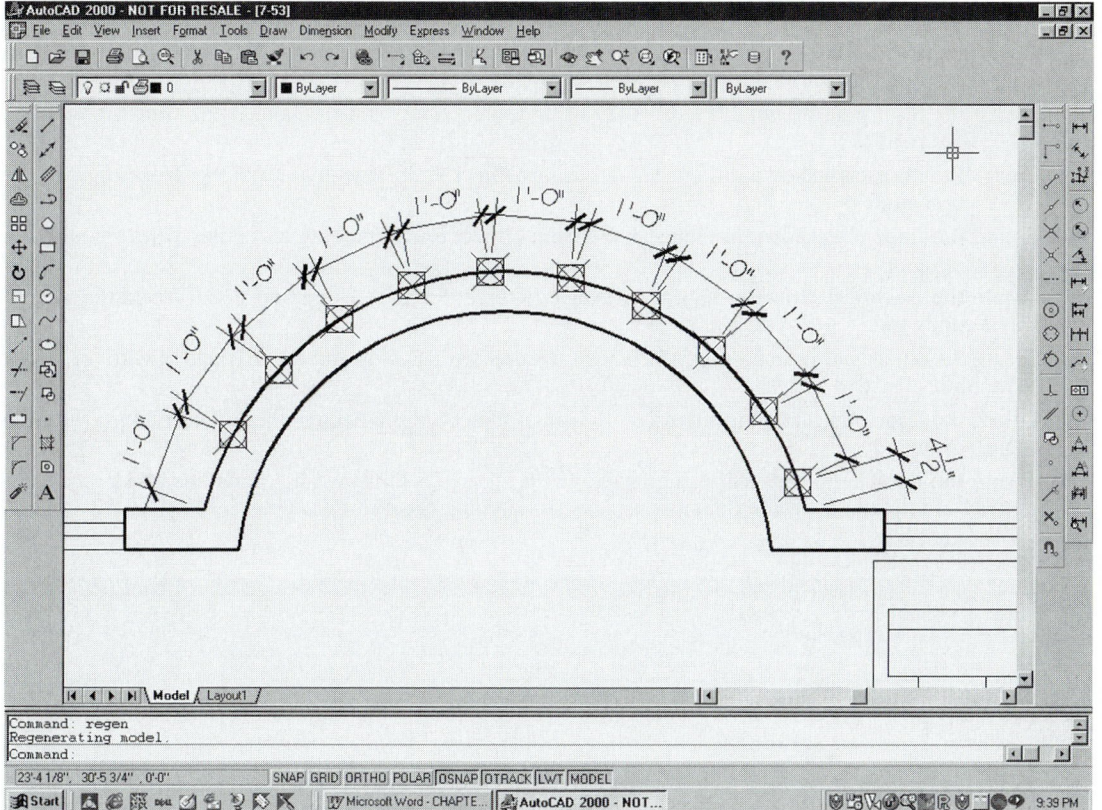

pull-down menu or by entering ME or MEASURE at the command line. AutoCAD will start measuring the object at the endpoint closest to where you selected the object. If the last segment on the object is not equal to the number entered, it will be shorter. Similar to the DIVIDE command, this command also uses point style as the segments on the object. For example, the wall in Figure 7–43 can be divided into 1'-0" segments as follows:

```
Command: MEASURE ~EnterKey~
Select object to measure: (select the arc closer to the lower left
corner)
Specify length of segment or [Block]: 12 ~EnterKey~
```

Caution: By default, AutoCAD uses dots as the point style. These dots may not be visible on the screen or be covered by the thickness of the object. Always check the point style before using the POINT, DIVIDE, and MEASURE commands.

Tips: To change the size or style of existing points on the screen, access the Point Style dialog box and perform the changes. When you click on the OK button, all points on the screen will be updated.

REVIEW QUESTIONS

1. What are the functions of object snap and AutoTrack?
2. Describe at least four different methods to access an object snap.
3. What are the functions of the marker and the magnet in AutoSnap settings?
4. How do you use Extension object snap mode?
5. What is an alignment path associated with AutoTracking?
6. What is Polar Tracking?
7. How do you snap to a Polar Distance?
8. What is Object Snap Tracking?
9. What command would you use to divide an object into specified distances?

PROBLEMS

1. Open the MYEXE6-3.dwg file. Place wall caps using the LINE command and Snap to Endpoint object snap mode. Save your drawing as MYEXE7-1.

2. Create the floor plan shown in Figure 5–27 using Object Snap Tracking and Polar Tracking with the LINE command.

3. Create the floor plan shown in Figure 5–26 using Object Snap Tracking and Polar Tracking with the LINE command.

4. Create the floor plan shown in Figure 5–24 using Object Snap Tracking and Polar Tracking with the LINE command.

5. Create the elevation shown in Figure 5–23 using Object Snap Tracking and Polar Tracking with the LINE command.

6. Create the object shown in Figure 5–22 using Object Snap Tracking and Polar Tracking with the LINE command.

7. Create the floor plan shown in Figure 6–46 using Object Snap Tracking and Polar Tracking with the LINE command.

8. Create the door jamb detail drawing as shown in Figure 7–44 using all commands and procedures learned so far. Do not create dimensions, text, or hatching. Save this drawing as MYEXE7-2.

FIGURE 7–44: Drawing for Problem 8

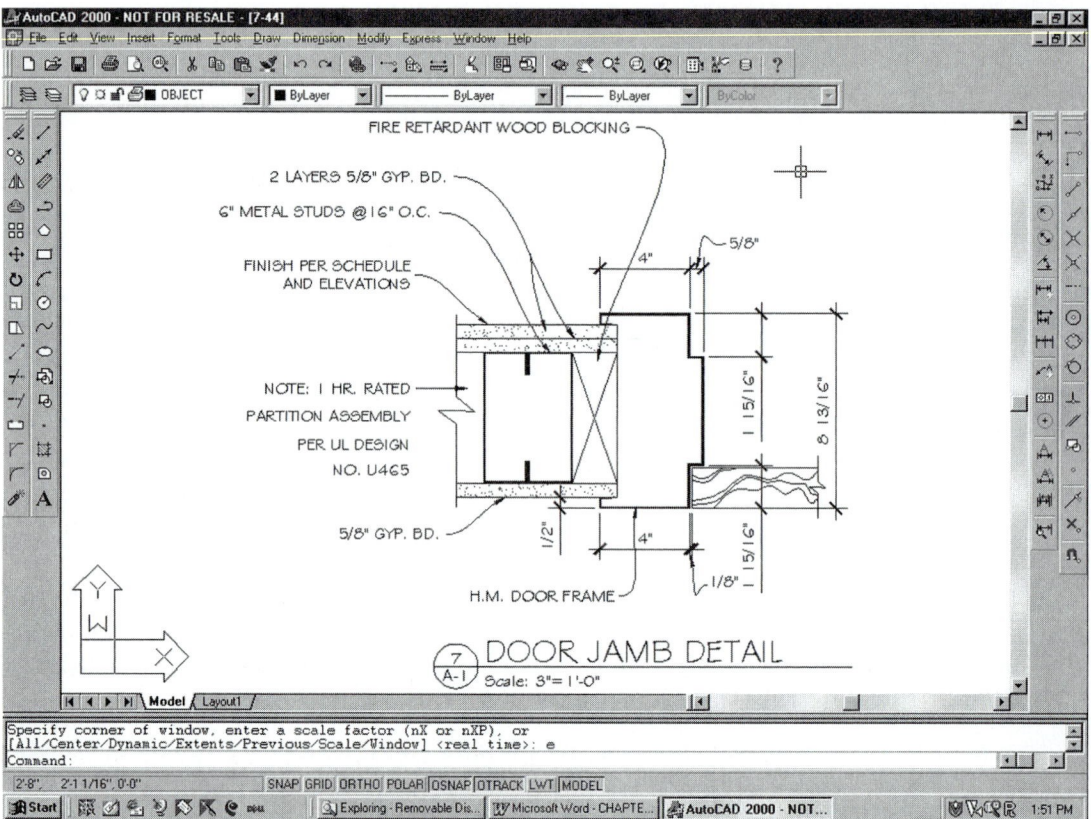

Saving and Ending Drawings

8

After successful completion of this chapter you should be able to:

▲ Name and save drawing files.

▲ Understand the difference between Save and Save As.

▲ Use the Save Drawing As dialog box.

▲ Set a default file format type using the Save as Options dialog box.

▲ Use the SAVE and QSAVE commands.

▲ Use the File pull-down menu for saving and exiting drawings.

▲ Understand the rules and restrictions behind naming drawings.

▲ Use the Open and Save and System tabs of the Options dialog box.

▲ Use drawing properties to store project information to files.

▲ Use the EXIT, CLOSE, and QUIT commands.

8.1 SAVING DRAWINGS

It is a common practice to name a drawing by saving it before putting any information in the drawing. You can also name and save a drawing just before you exit the drawing. However, you need to make sure that the drawing file is saved either by you manually or by AutoCAD automatically just in case there is a power outage or a systems failure. Whether you use the Start from Scratch, Use a Template, or Use a Wizard drawing setup options, AutoCAD will automatically assign a drawing file name each time you start a new drawing. For example, the first drawing that you start will be named [Drawing 1], and when you start another drawing without saving the first one, AutoCAD will name the second drawing as [Drawing 2]. You can read this information on top of the Title Bar just after the AutoCAD 2000—NOT FOR RESALE caption. If you do not intend to print or plot drawings, and if you are simply practicing with AutoCAD, you can keep working without saving drawings. However, if you intend to create a drawing and print or plot it at a precise scale, you should give your drawing a project-specific name and save it accordingly.

8.1.1 Save and Save As

You can save your drawings using three different methods as follows:

1. From the File pull-down menu, select Save. This is shown in Figure 8–1. If the drawing has not been named, AutoCAD will display the Save Drawing As dialog box as shown in Figure 8–2. From the Save in: drop-down list, click on the down arrow and select the folder in which you want to save the drawing. Inside the File name: text box, enter the name you want to assign for the file. Inside the Save as type: drop-down list, click on the down arrow and select the type of file to save. As a default, the drawings will be saved as Auto-CAD 2000 Drawing [*.dwg] file type, but you can change this according to your file-saving

FIGURE 8–1 The File pull-down menu can be used to save a drawing.

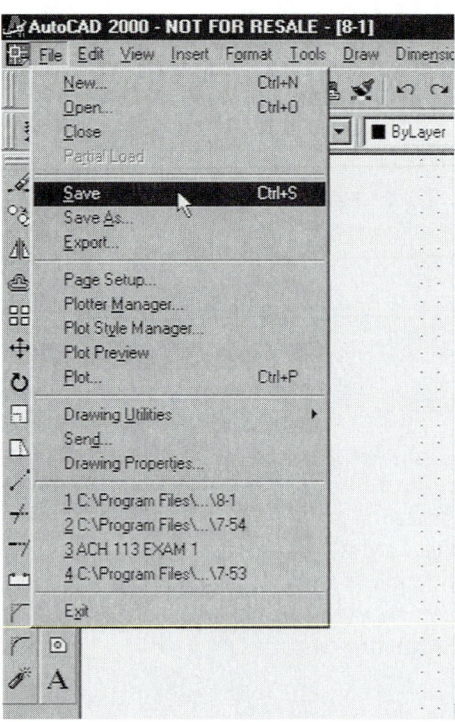

requirements. If you are not working in a mixed-version environment, you should save your drawings as AutoCAD 2000 Drawing format file type. If there is a need, you can save your drawing as an old AutoCAD release in use. You can also save your drawing as AutoCAD Drawing Template File [*.dwt]. This option is used when creating a custom template from an existing template or from an existing drawing. When you select a Save as type, click on the Save button. This will save your drawing to the designated drive or folder in your hard drive. If the drawing has been saved (named) previously, selecting Save from the File pull-down menu will simply save the drawing (as modified) in the folder and drive it was originally assigned. This process is the same as clicking on the Save button in the Standard toolbar. If the drawing has not been named, clicking on the Save button in the Standard toolbar will display the Save Drawing As dialog box.

2. If you want to save an existing drawing with a different name, select Save As . . . from the File pull-down menu. The Save Drawing As dialog box will be displayed as shown in Figure 8–2. Enter the new name over the existing name, select a drawing file type, and click on the Save button. The old drawing will not be altered, but it will be saved as a different file. This is useful when you want to preserve some of the main aspects of a drawing but want to add or change items as a new file using the existing one.

3. Enter SAVE or QSAVE at the command line. AutoCAD will display the Save Drawing As dialog box. You can also enter SAVEAS at the command line to save an existing drawing with a different name.

FIGURE 8–2 The Save Drawing As dialog box will allow you to save the drawing file and select a drawing type.

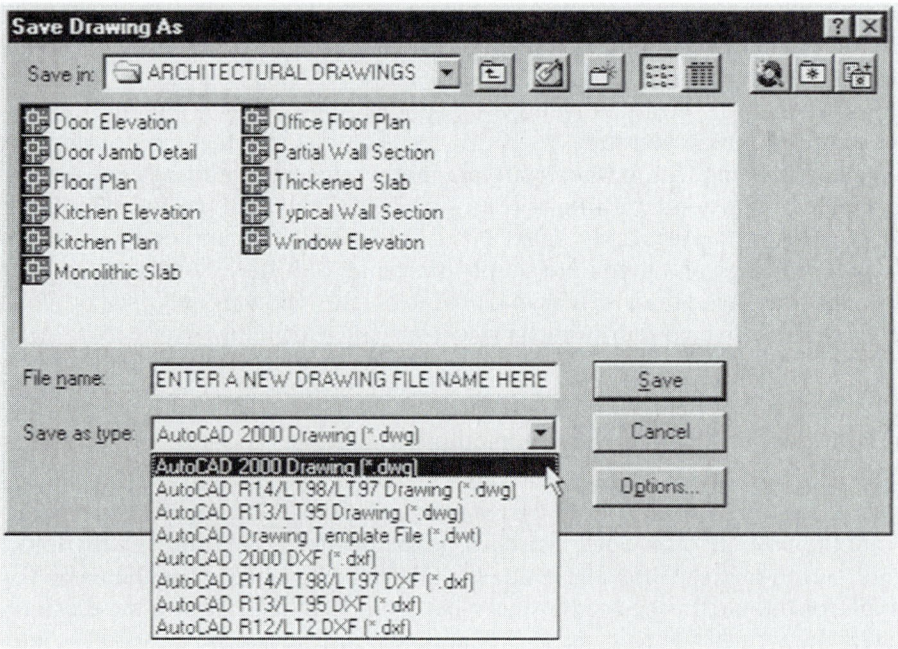

Tips: If the Save Drawing As dialog box is not displayed, turn the FILEDIA system variable on.

Tips: To make upgrading of your software easier, store and save drawing files in folders that are separate from the AutoCAD.

8.1.2 Default Save Format

Instead of using the Save Drawing As dialog box and the Save as type: drop-down list options, you can set a default file format type to save all your drawings by using the Saveas Options dialog box. Inside the Save Drawing As dialog box, click on the Options... button. The Saveas Options dialog box will be displayed as shown in Figure 8–3. Inside the DWG Options tab, click on the Save all drawings as: drop-down list down arrow and select the appropriate drawing type. If you frequently switch from AutoCAD 2000 to one of the previous versions, you may want to set this to the release you are working with. This list will allow you to save your AutoCAD 2000 drawings to a format as far back as R12. To save custom objects created from other software applications, select the Save proxy images of custom objects check box. The Index type: drop-down list includes options for Spatial and Layer Indexing. When finished, click on the OK button.

If you share drawing files with consultants, clients, contractors, or classmates with CAD software other than AutoCAD, the DXF (drawing interchange format) file format can be used to save the drawings. A DXF file is an ASCII text file that identifies the object properties within a specific drawing. An entire drawing or only a portion of the drawing can be selected as a DXF file. Click on the Select objects check box in the DXF Options tab in the Save as Options dialog box. The Options tab is shown in Figure 8–4. A BINARY file allows you to format the DXF file into a binary file format that can reduce the file size as much as 30 percent.

When you close the Save as Options dialog box, the new default drawing format for saving settings will be displayed in the Save as type: drop-down list box inside the Save Drawing As dialog box. This new format will remain until it is changed in the Save as Options dialog box or the Options dialog box.

*Caution: The Save as Options dialog box will save **all** drawings as the selected file type. If you want to save files as another drawing file type only on an as-needed basis, use the Save Drawing As dialog box as shown in Figure 8–2.*

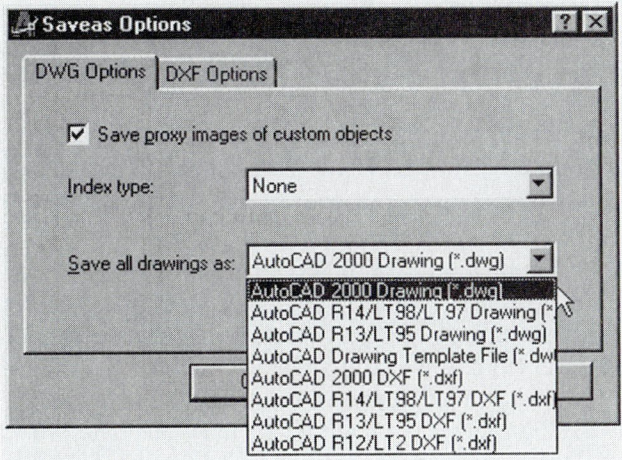

FIGURE 8–3   The Save as Options dialog box with DWG Options tab.

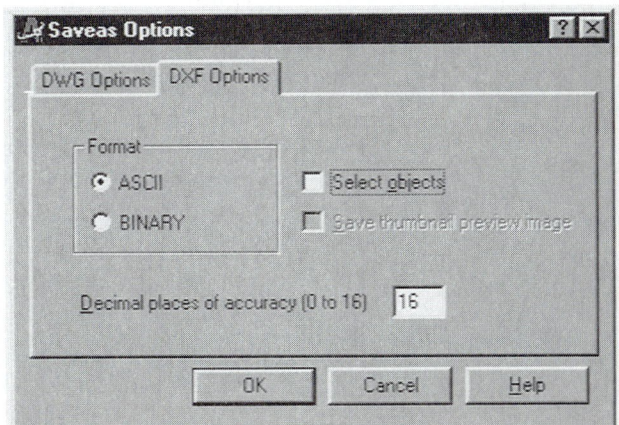

FIGURE 8–4   The DXF Options tab of the Save as Options dialog box.

Note: When you save an AutoCAD 2000 drawing file as a previous-release format and open that file inside the old version of AutoCAD, you will not be able to use the new features of the AutoCAD 2000. Some of the new features that you will not be able to use are Lineweights, Properties Window, Extended File Names, AutoCAD DesignCenter, Multiple Design Environment, Layout tabs, AutoTracking, Object Snap Tracking, and Polar Tracking.

You can also use the Options dialog box to establish file saving settings. The Options dialog box with Open and Save tab is shown in Figure 8–8. Inside the File Save category, select the file type you want to save the drawing as from the Save as: drop-down list. You can also have AutoCAD save a preview image of your drawing. The image of your drawing is displayed when you use the Select File dialog box and select that file from the list. To create a preview image of your drawing, click on the Save a Thumbnail Preview Image check box as shown in Figure 8–8.

Tips: To minimize conflicts and errors through switching between formats, create a User Profile for each of the default drawing file format. Creating User Profiles is discussed in Chapter 15.

Note: When you close a drawing that was saved in a different format, AutoCAD will display a warning message. You are asked to verify the format selection. If you click on the No button, the drawing will retain its old format type. If you click on the Yes button, the drawing will be saved as the new format type.

8.1.3   The QSAVE Command

You can quickly save a drawing in progress by clicking on the Save button in the Standard toolbar, or you can enter QSAVE at the command line. If the current drawing has not been named, the Save Drawing As dialog box will be displayed. Otherwise the QSAVE command quickly updates the drawing and saves it into the appropriate folder of the designated drive. Each time you save a (.dwg) drawing file, AutoCAD will create a back up file from the previous version of the same file with a .bak file name extension. You can rename the .bak file using a .dwg extension if a file is corrupted.

8.2 NAMING DRAWINGS

When choosing a name for the drawing file, consider the contents of the drawing. Your school or company might have a standardized naming system that will help you save time when searching drawing content that is forgotten. A file name consistent with company or school standards will also provide uniform quality and project manageability for all projects. All company standards should be published and made available to personnel working on the projects. If everyone involved in the project uses the same guidelines and standards, projects will flow much smoother and with better efficiency. Establishing *project naming standards* and other standards is crucial to attaining high productivity and uniformity.

The *AIA CAD Guidelines* published by the American Institute of Architects (AIA) contain two distinct categories for CAD standards: Layer Guidelines and File Naming Guidelines. The AIA CAD file-naming guidelines provide a common ground when sharing data between parties involved in design and construction of buildings. The AIA CAD file-naming guidelines consider two different types of CAD files as follows:

1. **Model Files:** Although model space and paper space are discussed in Chapter 22, this is a good place to introduce some of the basic concepts. A model is an environment in AutoCAD in which you design and create the physical geometry of a project that may contain walls, dimensions, text, notes, hatching, columns, electrical symbols, revisions, etc. This environment is the model space and is accessed automatically when you start a drawing in AutoCAD. Model is the environment where you create the *model* of all your projects. The most effective and efficient way to start a project is to create it first in Model. The Model environment is indicated by the Model tab located in the Status Bar and is located directly left of the Layout1 and Layout2 tabs in the Status Bar.

2. **Sheet Files:** A *sheet file* is created in Layout. A *layout* is an environment in AutoCAD where you compose the drawing created in model for the final plot using paper space.

When a drawing is created in Model, it can be scaled or separated into two or more drawings with different scales in a paper space layout. You can access a layout by selecting either the Layout1 or the Layout2 tabs located in the Status Bar of your screen. The layout environment allows you to switch from paper space to model space and vice versa. When in paper space, you can create different views of your model using viewports. When in model space, you can edit the geometry of the drawing. A layout usually contains a template in paper space with title block and borderlines. When you open a template (.dwt) file, AutoCAD will automatically display it in the paper space layout. See Chapter 22 for a detailed discussion of layouts, model space, and paper space.

As per AIA CAD file-naming guidelines, model file names start with the discipline code, followed by a two-letter drawing type, followed by a user-definable field. Some of the discipline codes are as follows: *A* for architectural, *C* for civil, *M* for mechanical, *I* for interiors, *L* for landscape, *S* for structural, and *P* for plumbing.

Some of the drawing type codes are as follows:

`FP` for floor plan, `SP` for site plan, `EL` for elevation, `SC` for section, `SH` for schedules, and `DT` for details.

For example, model file name A-EL3 indicates the drawing as architectural, elevation, third elevation. Sheet file names start with the discipline code, followed by a user-definable numerical field that closely corresponds to the sheet sequence number. For example, sheet file name A-501 means architectural details, sheet 5-1. CAD Layer Guidelines published by the AIA are discussed in Chapter 9.

Naming guidelines affect both the Model and Layout in AutoCAD. The AIA CAD file-naming guidelines recommend the following:

- Each file should include the discipline code, model type code, sheet type code, and sheet sequence identifier. The remainder can be user-definable but should not include project designations such as numbers and/or names.

Although the use of AIA CAD Guidelines is spreading, many firms are still using the project designations as numbers and/or names. For example, drawings can be assigned a reference number such as 018. The month, date, and year the project started can be added to this information. The project reference number can relate to the name of the project. For example, project number 018 can reference a Medical Arts Building project located in Williamsport, PA as follows:

`018-101899-A6:` Williamsport Medical Arts Building sheet A-6 started on October 18, 1999. Always keep a log of project names and reference numbers.

Tips: Create different folders for each project. This will make it easier to back up and archive your projects.

8.2.1 File Name Restrictions

When it comes to naming drawings, the following rules and restrictions apply:

1. You can enter a maximum of 255 characters.

2. You can use spaces, dashes, and most punctuation characters.

3. You cannot use the following characters:

```
< >  less-than and greater-than symbol.
/ \  forward slash and back slash.
:    colon.
;    semicolon.
,    comma.
|    vertical bar (pipe symbol).
*    asterisk.
?    question mark.
"    quotation mark.
```

The same rules apply to naming drawing content, also known as *dependent symbols.* A drawing content is part of a drawing file that contain definitions of objects and entities such as blocks, dimension styles, layers, layouts, linetypes, and text styles in a drawing file. However, multiline styles created with the MLSTYLE (multiline style) command cannot contain more than 31 characters and are governed by items 2 and 3 above. Creating multilines is discussed in Chapter 17.

> *Note: Drawing content (dependent symbol) names and file names are not case sensitive. AutoCAD will retain the file or symbol name as typed, but you can access them by typing either lower or upper case letters. Drawing content that can be used with AutoCAD DesignCenter is discussed in Chapters 10 and 24.*

> *Tips: The EXTNAMES system variable allows you to set AutoCAD so that it recognizes extended file and symbol names when using an older version. When the EXTNAMES is set to 1, AutoCAD 2000 and AutoCAD 2000i format (up to 255 characters) is used. If the EXTNAMES is set to 0, AutoCAD R14 format (up to 31 characters) is used. The advantage of the extended file and symbol names is that you can have a long name for a layer, file, text, dimension style, or a block. The complete name can be accessed even when it is cut off. For example, when a long layer name is accessed through the Layer Properties Manager dialog box, the text field may not display the entire name because of the space limitations. AutoCAD will condense the name and display only the beginning and end of the name with ellipses (...) in the middle as shown in Figure 8–5. When you place your cursor over the text, the tooltip will display the entire name as shown in Figure 8–6.*

> *Note: As the National CAD Standards and the AIA CAD Guidelines become popular and widely used among AEC firms, it is best to start with these standards to establish a uniform CAD platform. See Chapter 1 for Internet addresses for CAD-related Web sites.*

You can control the EXTNAMES system variable using the System tab of the Options dialog box as shown in Figure 8–7. Placing a checkmark inside the Allow long symbol names check box will turn the EXTNAMES system variable on.

8.2.2   How Often Should You Save?

You should save your work periodically while working on the drawing. Saving drawings every 10 minutes assures that in the event of a power loss you would only lose a maximum of 10 minutes of work. You can save drawings manually or automatically. To save drawings manually, click

FIGURE 8–5 A layer with a very long name may not be displayed completely. AutoCAD will condense it.

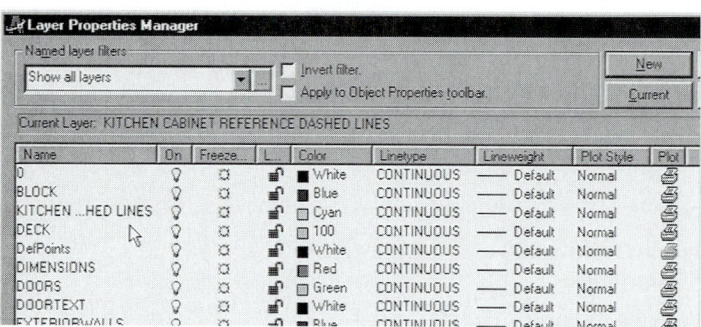

FIGURE 8–6 When you move the cursor over the long name, the complete name will be shown inside the tooltip.

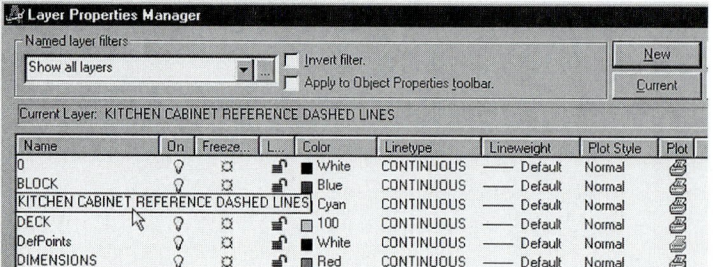

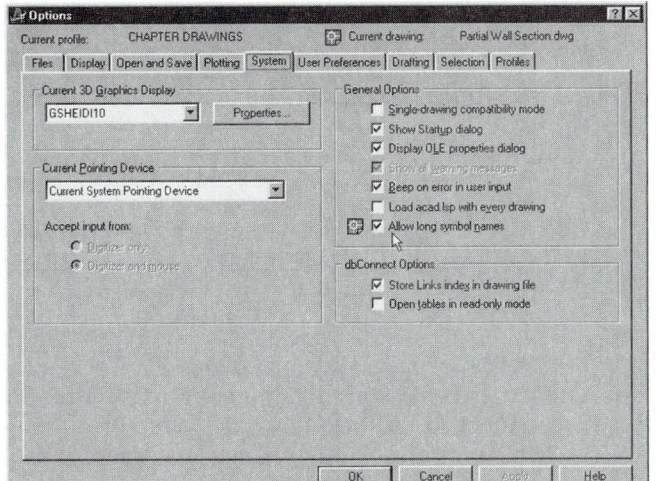

FIGURE 8–7
The System tab of the Options dialog box allows you to control the format for long file names.

on the Save button in the Standard toolbar or enter SAVE, QSAVE, or SAVEAS at the command line. If you can remember to do this every 10 minutes or so, you should be fine. To have AutoCAD save your drawings automatically using a dialog box, you must access the Options dialog box as follows:

Right click in the drawing area and select Options, from the shortcut menu. If you do not have the right click option on, select Options, from the Tools pulldown menu. When the Options dialog box appears, select the Open and Save tab as shown in Figure 8–8. Inside the File Safety Precautions category, enter the amount of time in minutes in the Minutes between saves text box. To activate the automatic save feature, place a checkmark inside the Automatic save check box. You can also have AutoCAD create a backup copy of your drawing (.bak) by placing a checkmark in the Create backup copy with each save check box. You do not have to go back to the Options dialog box to change the number in the Minutes between saves text box. The SAVETIME system variable will change that for you at the command line as follows:

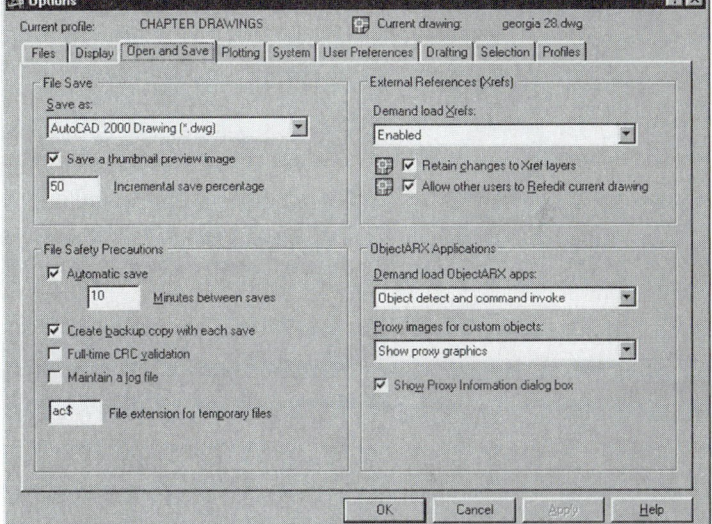

FIGURE 8–8
The Open and Save tab of the Options dialog box can be used to establish file saving and automatic save features.

```
Command: SAVETIME ~EnterKey~

Enter new value for SAVETIME <35>: (enter the amount of time in minutes
you want AutoCAD to save your work automatically. The number in the
brackets indicate the previous amount)
```

Tips: If you are planning to be away from your computer workstation for a while, save your drawing manually before you leave. The automatic save feature starts when you make a change in the drawing, such as drawing a line or erasing a line. But this happens after the automatic save time reaches the number in minutes specified. For example, if you set the automatic save feature to 10 minutes, draw for 8 minutes, and leave for 8 minutes, the automatic save will not be performed until the 16-minute interval, when you come back and draw again.

8.3 DRAWING FILE AND SUMMARY INFORMATION

You can create and store drawing information without writing that information directly onto the file. You can also obtain information within a drawing. The existing drawing Properties dialog box (not to be confused with the Properties window) allows you to customize project information. To access the existing drawing Properties dialog box, select Drawing Properties...from the

File pull-down menu as shown in Figure 8–9. The Drawing Properties dialog box is shown in Figure 8–10. The word *Drawing* in front of the Properties is actually the file name given to your drawing. The four tab options are as follows:

- **THE GENERAL** tab displays information relating to the file type, location, size, and the day-month-year-time the drawing was last modified. It also includes other attributes usually stored in Microsoft Windows Explorer. See Figure 8–10. This information is read-only.

- **THE SUMMARY** tab as shown in Figure 8–11, allows you to enter project information relating to the title, subject, author, and keywords. The keywords can be used to quickly find a file if you cannot remember the file name or it can be found with the Find feature of the AutoCAD DesignCenter. AutoCAD DesignCenter is discussed in Chapter 10.

- **THE STATISTICS** tab as shown in Figure 8–12 displays the same information found in the General tab, but it displays the name of the person who most recently saved the drawing. This is possible with the logon name. It also shows the total editing time. This information is extracted from the drawing file and is automatically updated.

- **THE CUSTOM** tab as shown in Figure 8–13 allows you to enter up to 10 items of information such as Job Number, Revision Date, Completion Status, Office Location, Client, and Consultant information.

You can also enter DWGPROPS at the command line to access the file properties.

Tips: Drawing information that you attach to files can be viewed from Windows Explorer without the use of AutoCAD. Inside Windows Explorer, find the file and right-click on it. Select Properties from the shortcut menu to see the drawing information. This information is read-only. Only information inside the General tab will be displayed unless other data have been attached for the file.

Tips: Create and save custom properties items using a template (.dwt) file. Create a custom template first. You can create a custom template either from a .dwg file or from a .dwt file. This way, all

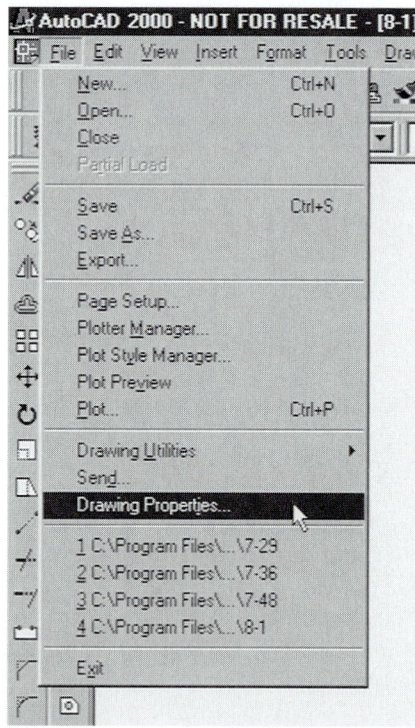

FIGURE 8–9
The Drawing Properties accessed from the File pull-down menu.

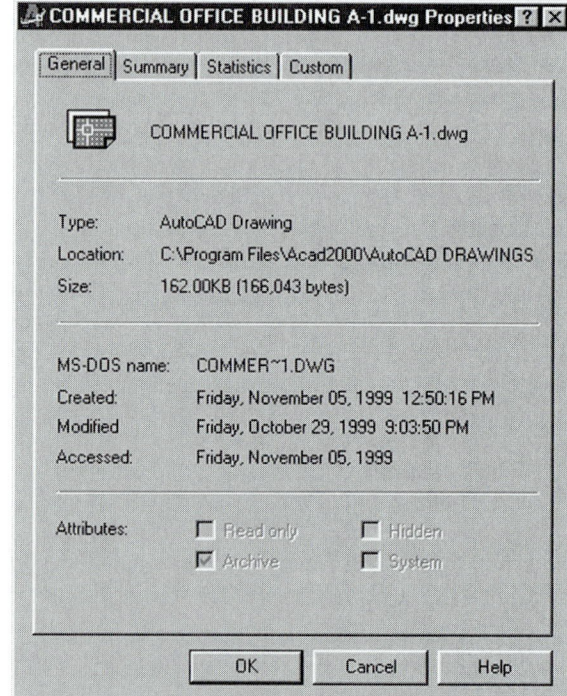

FIGURE 8–10
The General tab of the Commercial Office Building.dwg Properties dialog box.

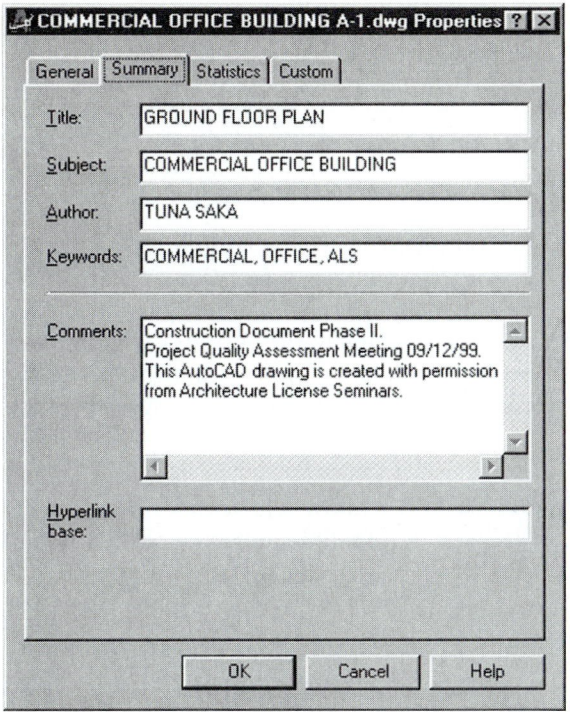

FIGURE 8–11
The Summary tab of the Commercial Office
Building.dwg Properties dialog box.

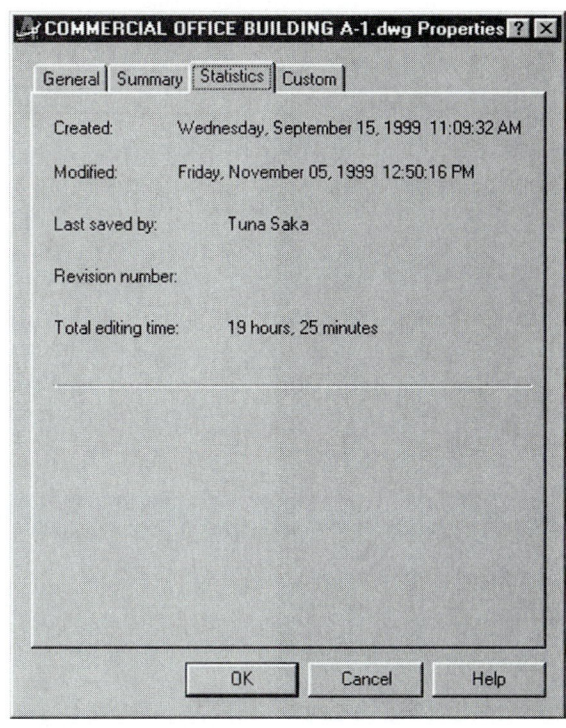

FIGURE 8–12
The Statistics tab of the Commercial Office
Building.dwg Properties dialog box.

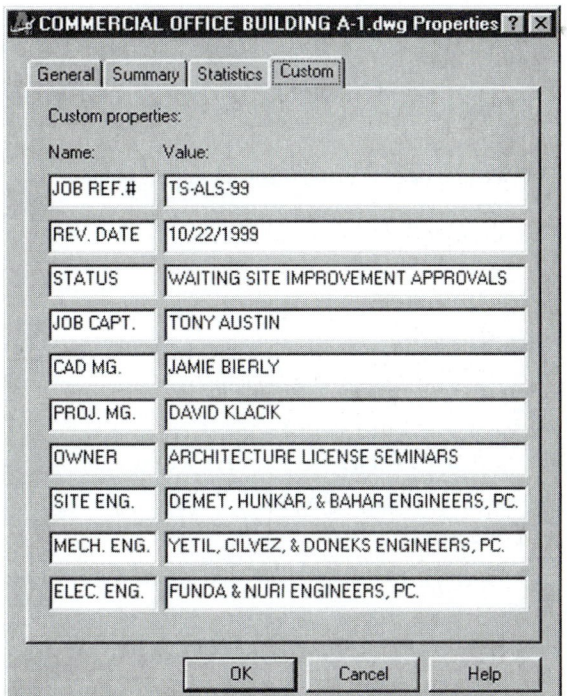

FIGURE 8–13
The Custom tab of the
Commercial Office
Building.dwg Properties
dialog box.

custom properties relating to the project will be retained when the template file is used to plot the projects. To create a custom template (.dwt) file from an existing file (.dwg) or from an existing template (.dwt) file, see Chapter 3.

8.4 EXITING AutoCAD

You can exit AutoCAD in several different ways as follows:

1. Enter CLOSE at the command line. This will exit you out of the drawing without ending the AutoCAD drawing session. You can also select Close from the File pull-down menu. If you close the drawing before saving AutoCAD will display the alert box as shown in Figure 8–14. You can either save the drawing to the current file name or close the drawing. If you click on the Yes button without naming the drawing, the Save Drawing As dialog box will be displayed. If you click on the No button, any changes since the previous save will be discarded.

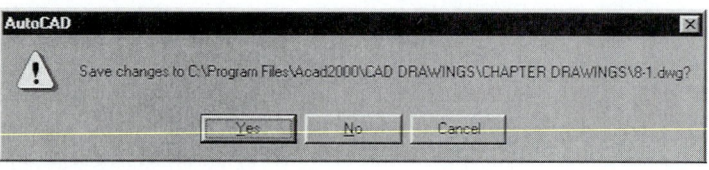

FIGURE 8–14
The AutoCAD alert box will be displayed if you close a drawing file or exit the AutoCAD drawing session without saving the drawing.

2. Enter EXIT at the command line. This will end the AutoCAD session. You can also select Exit from the File pull-down menu. If you exit AutoCAD before saving the drawing, the same alert box in Figure 8–14 will be displayed.

3. Enter QUIT at the command line. The procedure is same as item 2 above.

AutoCAD 2000i Update: The CLOSEALL command allows you to close all open drawings at one time. If drawings need to be saved a message box is displayed for each unsaved drawing so that you can save the changes before closing. You can also select Close All from the Window pull-down menu.

REVIEW QUESTIONS

1. What happens when you select Save from the File pull-down menu?
2. How can you set a default file format type to save all your drawings?
3. Which file format should you save your drawings to if you share drawing files with consultants, clients, contractors, or classmates with CAD software other than AutoCAD?
4. You can quickly save a drawing in progress by clicking on the ——— button in the Standard toolbar or you can enter ——- at the command line.
5. What are some of the characters you can not use when naming drawings?
6. What system variable allows you to change the minutes between automatic save?
7. How can you create and store project information without writing that information directly onto the file?
8. What command will exit you out of the drawing without ending the AutoCAD drawing session?

PROBLEMS

1. Open the *MYEXE7-2.dwg* file. Assign a file and summary information using the Summary tab as follows:

Title: DOOR JAMB DETAIL
Subject: LEARNING TO DRAW WITH PRECISE POINTS
Author: YOUR NAME
Keywords: DOOR, JAMB

2. Open the *MYEXE6-1.dwg* file. Assign a file and summary information using the Summary tab as follows:

Title: PRELIMINARY FLOOR PLAN
Subject: LEARNING TO DRAW WITH POLAR TRACKING
Author: YOUR NAME
Keywords: 6-1, MYEXE

3. Open the *MYEXE6-5.dwg* file. Assign a file and summary information using the Summary tab as follows:

Title: PRELIMINARY FLOOR PLAN
Subject: LEARNING TO DRAW LINES
Author: YOUR NAME
Keywords: 6-5, MYEXE

4. Open the *MYEXE6-3.dwg* file. Assign a file and summary information using the Summary tab as follows:

Title: PRELIMINARY FLOOR PLAN
Subject: LEARNING TO DRAW LINES
Author: YOUR NAME
Keywords: 6-5, MYEXE
Create Custom properties similar to the one shown in Figure 8–13 or as directed.

5. Open the *MYEXE6-2.dwg* file. Assign a file and summary information using the Summary tab as follows:

Title: FLOOR PLAN
Subject: LEARNING TO DRAW FLOOR PLANS
Author: YOUR NAME
Keywords: 6-2, MYEXE
Create Custom properties similar to the one shown in Figure 8–13 or as directed.

6. Open the *COM1-GROUND PLAN A-1.dwg* file. Assign a file and summary information using the Summary tab as follows:

Title: COMMERCIAL BUILDING
Subject: GROUNG FLOOR
Author: YOUR NAME
Keywords: COM1, GROUND, PLAN
Create Custom properties similar to the one shown in Figure 8–13 or as directed.

7. Open the *COM1-CURTAIN WALL DETAIL A-4.dwg* file. Assign a file and summary information using the Summary tab as follows:

Title: COMMERCIAL BUILDING
Subject: CURTAIN WALL
Author: YOUR NAME
Keywords: CURTAIN WALL, DETAIL
Create Custom properties similar to the one shown in Figure 8–13 or as directed.

8. Create a new drawing from scratch. Assign a file and summary information using the Summary tab as follows:

Title: MY BUILDING
Subject: MY PROJECT
Author: YOUR NAME
Keywords: MY BUILDING, PROJECT
Create Custom properties similar to the one shown in Figure 8–13 or as directed.
Save the drawing as MY BUILDING EXERCISE.

Creating Layers, Linetypes, and Lineweights

After successful completion of this chapter you should be able to:

▲ Understand the concept behind creating layers.

▲ Understand and utilize CAD Layer Guidelines published and recommended by the American Institute of Architects (AIA).

▲ Create and manage layers using the Layer Properties Manager dialog box.

▲ Understand the concept behind creating object properties "ByLayer" and "by object."

▲ Use the five control boxes in the Object Properties toolbar to manipulate object properties.

▲ Change status of layers.

▲ Assign Lineweights to objects.

▲ Use the Lineweight Settings dialog box to change and set Lineweight properties.

▲ Create and manage layer filters.

▲ Use shortcut menu to change layer settings.

▲ Load and manage linetypes.

▲ Override object properties using system variables.

▲ Establish and control linetype scale using LTSCALE and CELTSCALE system variables.

▲ Use the Express Layer toolbar to manage layers.

9.1 INTRODUCTION TO LAYERS

The separation of object geometry as it relates to the properties of individual objects in a drawing and the visibility and manipulation of such object geometry is referred to as *layering*. Examples of object geometry include lines, circles, shapes, text, dimensions, hatching, and blocks that you create in Model. Like the overlay system in manual drafting, layering allows graphic information to be separated and grouped for display or plotting purposes. In an overlay system, each individual sheet of drawing is precisely aligned with others. To create this system of overlay, *layers* are properly named and created in AutoCAD. You can assign different color, linetype, lineweight, or plot styles to each layer. This makes it much easier to manage and edit your drawings later on when objects are created on separate layers. Proper and efficient use of layers can increase productivity and improve drawing coordination between consultants. Layers can be turned on or off, locked, or frozen to achieve different configurations of plotted sheets. In AutoCAD, layers are created to manage graphic information.

9.2 WHY USE LAYERS?

The AEC fields involve extensive data and information sharing between consultants. AutoCAD provides a common tool for creating the required drawings for construction and post-construction activities. These activities involve common organizational and project management principles. The flow of information must be consistent and accurate for a successful building design and construction project. One of the most important activities involving shared information comes from the standard organization of layers created for construction documents. A standardized layering system increases efficiency of work and communication in several ways:

- By making it possible to regroup and reuse drawing information per project and owner/consultant requirements.

- By allowing separate consultants for architecture, interior design, electrical engineering, mechanical engineering, structural engineering, and civil engineering to share and reuse information in a consistent manner.

- By creating discipline designations to accommodate others to work and collaborate in design, production, and construction.

- By reproducing different plotted sheets and combining them in any desired format.

- By displaying only the layers you need for the task at hand to make your drawings less cluttered.

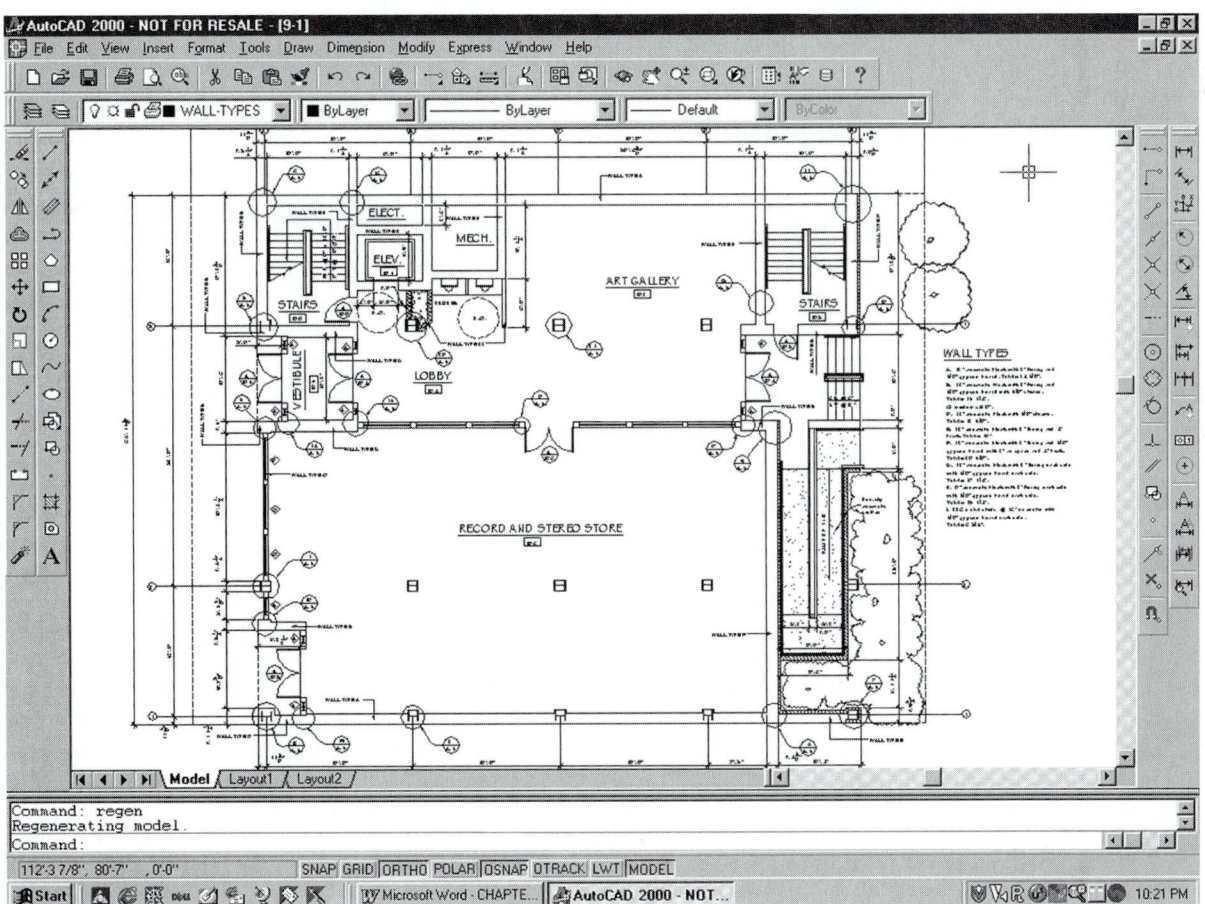

FIGURE 9–1
The ground floor plan drawing, including all object geometry created in Model.
(Drawing created with permission from Architecture License Seminars [ALS]

FIGURE 9–2
The Layer Properties
Manager dialog box
with the Layers created
for the ground floor
plan drawing.

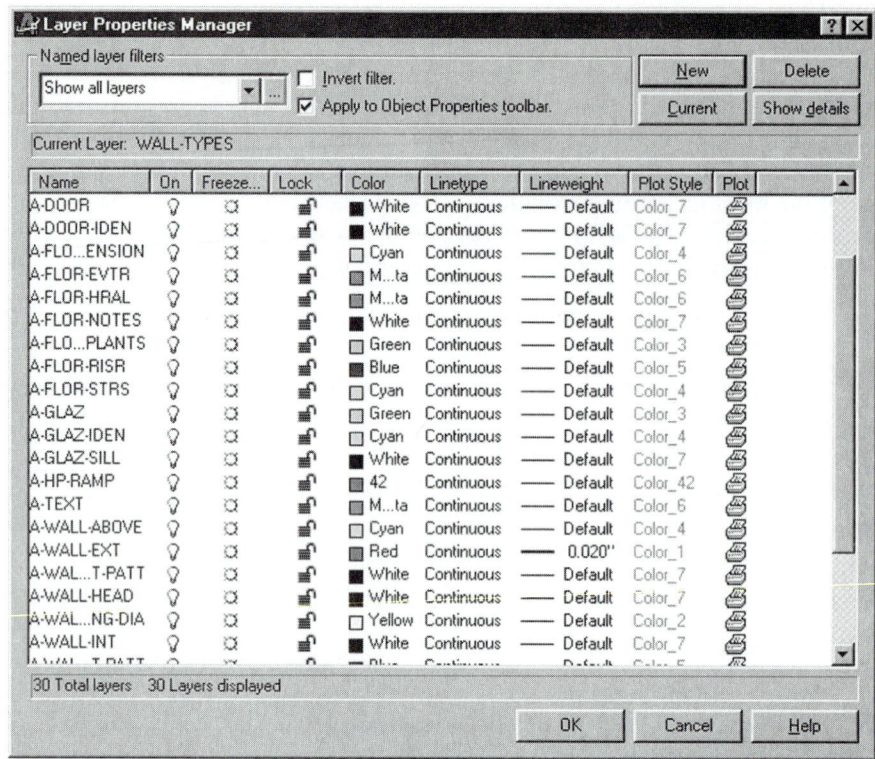

By recognizing the potential for sharing drawing information, the American Institute of Architects (AIA) created and adopted CAD Layer Guidelines in 1997. By creating layers in AutoCAD, you can turn a single drawing file into several plans. For example, the column grid plan, column locations, exterior walls, interior walls, doors, elevator shafts, furniture, and fixtures can all be created in a single file but separated by layers. By manipulating layers from the existing information, a floor plan and a structural framing plan can be plotted by turning off information that is not needed other than for the floor plan and the structural framing plan. Furthermore, assigning different colors, linetypes, and lineweights to different layers can help improve clarity of graphical information. Figure 9–1 shows the ground floor plan for an office building, and Figure 9–2 shows the Layer Properties Manager dialog box with the layers consistent with AIA CAD Layer Guidelines for the floor plan shown in Figure 9–1.

9.3 CREATING OBJECT PROPERTIES ByLayer

Objects created in drawings can be assigned a specific *color, linetype,* and *lineweight.* The color, linetype, and lineweight assigned to objects are referred to as *object properties.* These properties can be assigned to objects immediately before starting a drawing by creating layers. The concept behind assigning object properties while creating layers is called ByLayer. When objects are created ByLayer, each layer is assigned a specific color, linetype, and lineweight. When object properties are assigned to a layer, all objects created on that layer will assume the color, linetype, and lineweight assigned to that layer.

9.4 NAMING LAYERS

Layer names can comprise up to 255 characters and are not case sensitive because AutoCAD considers upper and lower case letters to be the same letter. The file name guidelines discussed in Chapter 7 applies to layers also. You cannot have two layers with the same name in a drawing. Long layer names are concatenated if there is not enough space to display it in the Layer properties Manager dialog box or in the Object Properties drop-down list box. This means that the entire name of the layer will appear in a tooltip only when you hold your cursor over a con-catenated name. You can use the following characters when naming layers.

Allowable Characters	**Example Layer Names**
Upper and lower case letters	DOORS or Doors
Underscore (_)	WALLS_EXTERIOR
Hyphen (-)	A-WALL-PATT
Spaces ( )	DOORS EXISTING
Numbers	ROOM 123

Although any name can be made up for a layer name you should consider looking at some layering standards established by the American Institute of Architects. CAD Layer Guidelines published by the AIA recommends a layer-naming format with major and minor groups starting with a discipline code and separated by dashes (-). The 16 discipline codes are as follows:

Single Character Discipline Codes

A	Architectural	M	Mechanical
C	Civil	P	Plumbing
E	Electrical	Q	Equipment
F	Fire protection	R	Resources
G	General	S	Structural
H	Hazardous materials	T	Telecommunications
I	Interiors	X	Other disciplines
L	Landscape	Z	Contractor/shop drawings

For example, the layer format "A-WALL-DEMO" includes "A" for the architecture as the discipline code, "WALL" as the major group, and "DEMO" for the status field. Hence the objects created in "A-WALL-DEMO" layer contain walls to be demolished. CAD Layer Guidelines consider dimensioning in CAD as annotation and recommend the use of "ANNO" followed by dimensions (DIMS), keynotes (KEYN), revisions (REVS), and text (TEXT). For example, the layer format "A-ANNO-DIMS" would mean the architectural dimensions layer. The CAD Layer Guidelines also allows the minor group field to be defined by the user to accommodate special project requirements but only if a defined layer does not apply to a project. Table 9–1 lists some of the layer names and descriptions defined by the CAD Layer Guidelines published by the AIA in 1997:

For a complete list, refer to the CAD Layer Guidelines published by the American Institute of Architects. Copies can be obtained from the AIA Web site at www.aiaonline.com.

Layer Name	Description
A-WALL-PATT	Wall insulation, hatching and fill
A-DOOR	Doors
A-DOOR-IDEN	Door number, hardware group, etc.
A-GLAZ-FULL	Full-height glazed walls and partitions
A-FLOR	Floor information
A-FLOR-OVHD	Overhead items (skylights, overhangs-usually dashed lines)
A-FURN-PNLS	Furniture system panels
A-CLNG-GRID	Ceiling grid
A-HVAC-RDFF	Return air diffusers
A-AREA-IDEN	Room numbers, tenant identifications, area calculations
A-ELEV	Interior and exterior elevations
C-ROAD-CNTR	Center lines for civil layers
E-POWR-CLNG	Power-ceiling receptacles and devices for electrical layers
F-SPRN	Fire protection sprinkler systems for fire protection layers
I-FURN-STOR	Furniture system storage components for interior layers
L-PLNT-TREE	Trees for landscape layers
M-EXHS-EQPM	Exhaust system equipment for mechanical layers

TABLE 9–1: List of some of the layer names and descriptions published in the CAD Layer Guidelines, AIA 1997

The complete AIA (256 color) Architectural Layer Style based on AIA Format with recommended layer color numbers is included in Appendix B.

9.5 CREATING LAYERS

AutoCAD provides you with a default layer 0. Until you create other layers, objects can be created in layer 0. Layer 0 cannot be renamed, deleted, or purged from the drawing file. Layers are created and managed inside the Layer Properties Manager dialog box as shown in Figure 9–2. To access the Layer Properties Manager dialog box, select the Layers button from the Object Properties toolbar, select Layer... from the Format pull-down menu, or enter LA or LAYER at the command line. When you first access the Layer Properties Manager dialog box, layer 0 will be displayed as the current layer. Current layer is the layer where objects created will be placed on without creating additional layers.

To create a single layer, click on the NEW button in the Layer Properties Manager dialog box. AutoCAD will display Layer1 as the new layer inside a text box. Layer1 will be highlighted, and the blinking cursor will be ready for you to enter a layer name over it. Enter a new layer name, such as A-DOOR, and press the ~EnterKey~. The A-DOOR layer will be created. To create more than one layer without selecting the New button after each layer, press the ~EnterKey~ twice after entering the layer name. The first ~EnterKey~ will create the layer and the second ~EnterKey~ will advance you to the second layer by dropping the Layer1 listing below the previous one. Enter the new name over Layer1 and press the ~EnterKey~ twice. Repeat this procedure until all layers are created. When creating the last layer, press the ~EnterKey~ once. You can always add new layers later by clicking on the New button. When you finish creating layers, all layer names will appear as they are entered but will not be alphabetized. When you click on the OK button to close the Layer Properties Manager dialog box, AutoCAD will alphabetize all layer names when you access the dialog box again.

Tips: If you wish to create many layers one after another without pressing the ~EnterKey~ or using the New button more than once, click on the New button once and enter layer names followed by a comma (,). Press the ~EnterKey~ when done.

Note: When creating a new layer, if no layer is selected, the new layer is placed at the end of the list and scrolls to the end. If one or more layers are selected, the new layer is placed below the last highlighted layer and will take its properties.

9.6 USING THE OBJECT PROPERTIES TOOLBAR

The Object Properties toolbar shown in Figure 9–3 provides a quick reference to layer and object properties management. There are five control boxes in the Object Properties toolbar. These control boxes provide easy access to layers and object properties management. The Layer Control box can be used to quickly display the layers. When you click on the down arrow of the Layer Control box, all layers will be displayed as shown in Figure 9–4. Inside the Layer Control box, you can highlight a layer to make that layer current. You can also turn a layer on, off, freeze, thaw, lock, unlock, and make a layer plottable or nonplottable using this method. However, you cannot change layer color through Layer Control box. The Color Control box can be used to change the color of an object. This is referred to as assigning a color *by object*. When a color is selected from the Color Control box, all new objects will be drawn using the selected color. This means that the objects will be drawn and plotted at the assigned color regardless of the color assigned to that layer. The *by layer* and *by object* concepts are important to understand and are discussed throughout the textbook. The Linetype and Lineweight Control boxes can be used to assign a linetype and a lineweight by object. The Plot Style Control box allows you to assign a Plot Style Table. This is discussed in Chapter 23.

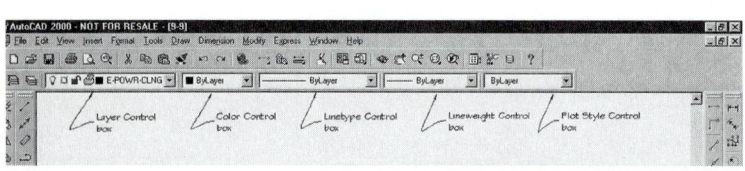

FIGURE 9–3   The five control boxes of the Object Properties toolbar.

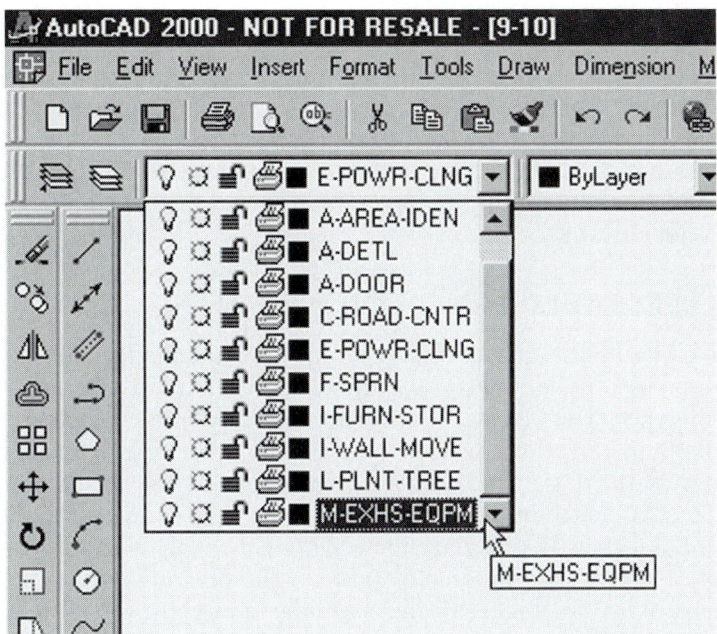

FIGURE 9–4 The Layer Control box allows you to quickly manipulate layer visibility and make a layer current.

Note: The Color, Linetype, and Lineweight Control boxes show the current color, linetype, and lineweight assigned (other than layer ontrol box) to the layer shown in the Layer Control box. If all control boxes display the word ByLayer (other than layer control box), *then all object properties are assigned to their respective layers. You can override ByLayer settings by selecting a different color, linetype, and lineweight independent of the layer assignment. This will only be effective for the objects drawn after the override. This concept is called assigning properties by* object *as opposed to* by layer.

Caution: Assigning object properties explicitly using the by object method is not an effective CAD practice since so much time is lost by not changing object properties ByLayer.

9.7 MAKING A LAYER CURRENT

You can make a layer current using five different methods as follows:

1. To make a layer current inside the Layer Properties Manager dialog box, click on the layer name and select the Current button. The Current Layer: text area will display the selected layer as current.

2. To make a layer current from the Layer Properties Manager dialog box, double click on the layer. The Current Layer: text area will display that layer as current.

3. To make a layer current from the Layer Properties Manager dialog box, right-click on the layer name and select Make Current from the shortcut menu.

4. To make a layer current from the Layer Control box in the Object Properties toolbar, highlight the layer you want to make current.

5. To make a layer current from the Object Properties toolbar, click on the Make Object's Layer Current button (first button). The command line will display the following prompt:

```
Select objects whose layer will become current: (select the object
you want its layer to be current).
```

Tips: You can boost productivity by using the right click shortcut menu for layer manipulations. For example, suppose you have 25 layers and you want to turn off all except Layer X. First, make Layer X current, then right-click on Layer X. A shortcut menu will appear. Click on the Select all but current from the shortcut menu. All layers except Layer X will be highlighted (selected). Click on the light bulb of one of the highlighted layers. All layers except Layer X will be turned off.

9.8 DELETING LAYERS

You cannot delete layer 0, Defpoints layer (dimension definition points, this layer is automatically created when you create dimensions), current layer, xref-dependent layers, and layers containing objects. If you try to do so, AutoCAD will display a dialog box with a warning message. To delete a layer you must first erase all objects created on that layer. Then click on the Delete button in the Layer Properties Manager dialog box and make sure that the layer is not current.

9.9 ESTABLISHING LINEWEIGHTS

Adding lineweight to objects on the screen enhances the visual quality of the drawings and improves the architectural graphic representation of drawings by displaying a width for the linetypes. You can use lineweight to differentiate between thick and thin lines and create depth in elevations, sections, and details. Assigning lineweights to objects is an important aspect of the design and drawing process. Just as you use hard and soft graphite leads with a mechanical pencil in manual drafting, lineweights can be used in AutoCAD to represent different objects with different lineweights. Lineweights can be established for objects or assigned to layers containing specific parts of the drawing. When lineweights are established for objects, only the objects having a specific lineweight value are plotted. When lineweights are assigned to layers, all objects in that layer are plotted with the lineweight assigned to that layer. Objects that are assigned a lineweight plot with the exact width of the lineweight value. You can assign different lineweights to different layers to easily differentiate between new construction, existing construction, and demolition plans. Lineweights for objects can be turned on or off for display purposes.

AutoCAD provides 27 different lineweights based on the industry standard pen sizes. To assign a current lineweight to an object, use the Lineweight Settings dialog box as shown in Figure 9–5. The Lineweight Settings dialog box can be accessed in four different ways as follows:

1. Select Lineweight . . . from the Format pull-down menu.

2. Enter LW or LWEIGHT at the command line.

3. Right click on the LWT button in the Status Bar and select Settings... from the shortcut menu.

4. Select Options . . . from the Tools pull-down menu or right click in the drawing area and select Options . . . from the shortcut menu. Select the User Preferences tab in the Options dialog box and then click on the Lineweight Settings... button. After you establish a lineweight with this option, you must click on the Apply and Close buttons in the Lineweight Settings dialog box and click on the Apply and then Close button in the Options dialog box.

FIGURE 9–5 The Lineweight Settings dialog box can be used to set the current lineweight, the lineweight units, display scale of lineweights, and set the default lineweight value.

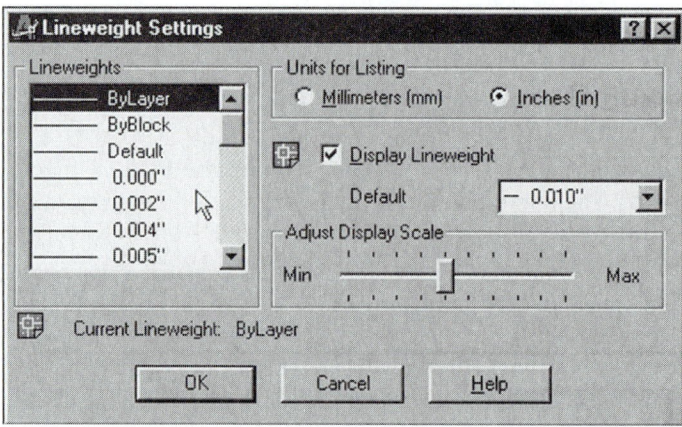

The Lineweight Settings dialog box has the following categories:

- **LINEWEIGHTS:** (display box). This category allows you to select one of the 27 different lineweight settings. The first three consist of the standard ByLayer, ByBlock, and Default lineweight settings. The ByLayer option assigns lineweights on a by-layer basis. When a layer is assigned a lineweight, all objects drawn on that layer will assume the lineweight assigned to that layer. Lineweights assigned as ByLayer behave in the same manner as other layer properties such as linetype and color. The ByBlock option assigns lineweights so that the object inherits the assigned lineweight of any block containing it. Blocks are discussed in Chapter 19. When the ByBlock option is selected, the object's lineweight is determined by the lineweight assigned to the object's block. The Default option assigns a lineweight value of 0.01″ (0.25 mm) in width. All new layers are automatically assigned a setting of Default lineweight value in millimeters. You can use the LWDEFAULT (lineweight default) system variable at the command line to change the default setting. For example, setting a LWDEFAULT value of 40 will set the default lineweight to 0.40 mm. To convert inches to millimeters, multiply inches by 25.4. To convert millimeters to inches divide millimeters by 25.4. For example, 0.40 mm is equal to 0.016″ (0.40/25.4 = 0.016). The CELWEIGHT system variable can be used to set the lineweight of new objects at the command line. Objects created in Model are displayed in relation to pixels. For example, a lineweight value of 0.000″ will be displayed as one pixel and plot at the thinnest lineweight available on the plotting device. All other lineweights will be displayed with a pixel width proportional to the selected lineweight. AutoCAD will display other lineweights using a pixel width proportional to the real-world unit value of the lineweight. The Adjust Display Scale category can be used to vary the proportionality.

- **CURRENT LINEWEIGHT:** (text area). This area will display the current lineweight assigned to the drawing. To set a new lineweight current, select the lineweight from the Lineweights list and click on the OK button.

- **UNITS FOR LISTING:** (category). By default, lineweights are displayed in millimeters. To display the lineweight units in inches, select the Inches (in) radio button. You can also specify whether lineweights are displayed in millimeters or inches by using the LWUNITS system variable at the command line. The initial value of LWUNITS is set to 1 (mm) but can be set to 0 (inches).

- **DISPLAY LINEWEIGHT:** (check box). By default, lineweights are not displayed in the current drawing. If this check box is selected, lineweights will be displayed in model space and paper space. If you are working with a large file containing different lineweights, it is best to turn off lineweight display because AutoCAD regeneration time increases with lineweights having more than one pixel. You can also control the display of lineweights by selecting the LWT button in the status bar. Selecting the LWT button toggles between *<Lineweight On>* and *<Lineweight Off>*. You can also right click on the LWT button to turn lineweight on or off. To control the display of lineweights at the command line, enter the LWDISPLAY system variable and enter 1 for On or 0 for Off.

- **DEFAULT:** (drop-down list). This area controls the lineweight value of the default setting. The default setting is 0.01″ or 0.25 mm and is the default lineweight for layers. The default value is controlled by the LWDEFAULT system variable.

- **ADJUST DISPLAY SCALE:** (slider). When you create objects using the Model tab, lineweights are displayed in pixels. You can adjust the lineweight display scale so that the lineweights are displayed on screen at a smaller or larger scale. To increase the lineweight scale, move the display scale slider toward right. When the Adjust Display Scale slider is at the Max level, the current lineweight will be displayed at the maximum display scale. When you change the lineweight display scale in this fashion, it does not affect the lineweight plotting value.

Note: When you adjust the lineweight display scale, the graphic bar in front of the lineweight value representing the width of the lineweight also changes. Adjusting the display scale to appear objects thicker or thinner in the Model tab does not affect the lineweight plotting value.

Table 9–2 shows the corresponding lineweights in AutoCAD for 2H, H, F, and B lead types used in manual drafting.

TABLE 9-2:
Corresponding
lineweights for various
lead types

Lineweight Value in Millimeters	Lineweight Value in Inches	Lead Type used in Manual Drafting
0.30	0.012	2H or H
0.60	0.024	F or HB
0.70	0.028	B

FIGURE 9-6
The Lineweight Control
box can be used to
assign lineweight by
object.

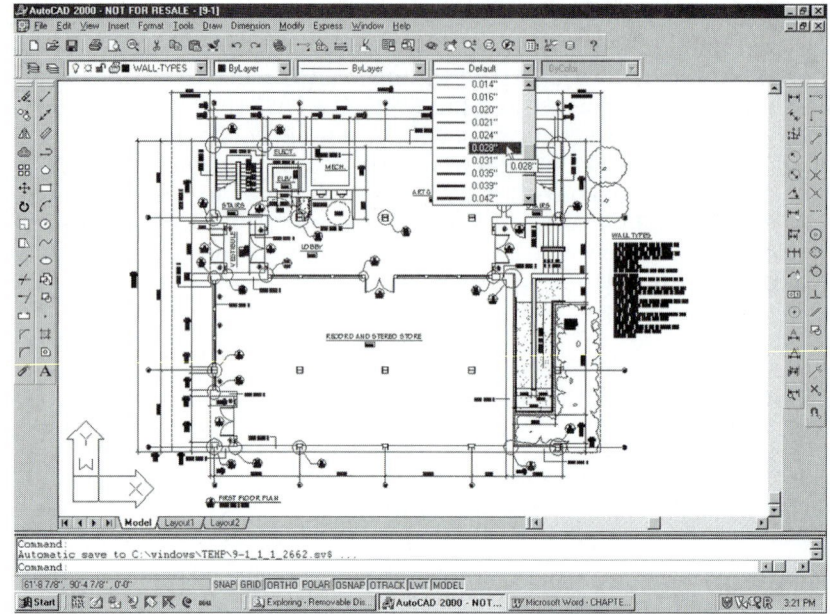

In addition to using the Lineweight Settings dialog box, you can use the Object Properties Toolbar to select a lineweight to draw. The Lineweight Control box can be used to select a lineweight and make it current and is shown in Figure 9–6. When a lineweight is selected, all new objects are drawn using the current lineweight. This means that the lineweight is assigned *by object* not By*Layer*. Not all objects are displayed with the current lineweight. TrueType fonts, raster images, points on the screen created with the POINT command, and two-dimensional solid fills do not display current lineweight.

Tips: Objects created with the PLINE (polyline) command with a specific width will override the current object lineweight.

A lineweight is considered to be an object property similar to color and linetype. When the object's lineweight is assigned as by object, that object will be drawn and plotted at the assigned lineweight regardless of the lineweight assigned to that layer. If the object's lineweight is assigned ByLayer, the object assumes its lineweight from the lineweight assigned to its layer. The Lineweight Control box displays ByLayer, Byblock, Default, and all other available lineweights exactly as it is shown in the Lineweight Settings dialog box. The Lineweight Control box will also display the six most recently used lineweights at the top of the list.

AutoCAD 2000i Update: *The Lineweight Control box in the Object Properties Toolbar displays the current lineweight of an object.*

9.10 MANAGING LINEWEIGHTS

Use the following procedures as guidelines when using and managing lineweights in drawings:
To assign a lineweight for the current object:

• Select the lineweight you want to use from the Lineweight Control box then draw the object. You can also select Lineweight...from the Format pull-down menu and select a lineweight in the Lineweight Settings dialog box and click on the OK button.

To assign a lineweight to a layer:

- Click on the Layers button in the Object Properties toolbar.

- Create a new Layer such as WALLS. Make sure the layer just created is highlighted.

- Move your cursor over the Lineweight column and left-click on the —Default. The Lineweight dialog box will be displayed as shown in Figure 9–7. Inside the Lineweight dialog box select the appropriate lineweight and click on the OK button. The Lineweight column will now show the lineweight assigned to that layer.

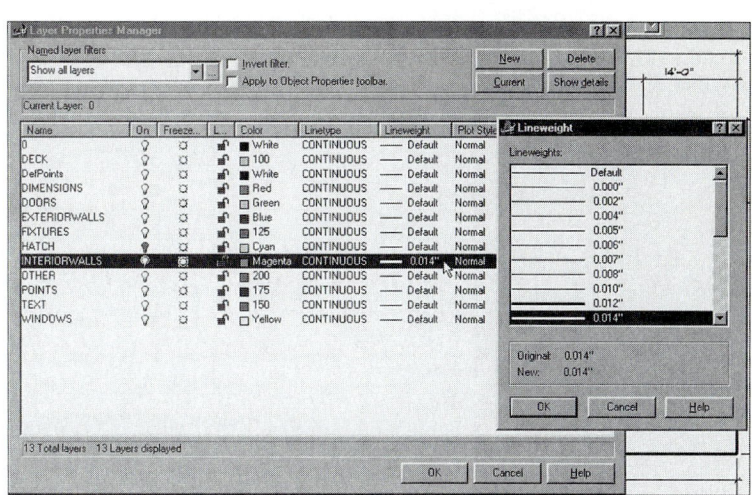

To view the current lineweight of an existing object:

- Left click on the object you want to view lineweight. The Lineweight Control box will display the lineweight of the selected object. If the object is assigned a lineweight as by object, the lineweight bar followed by a value will be displayed. If the object is assigned a lineweight as ByLayer, the lineweight bar followed by ByLayer will be displayed.

- Enter the ~EscKey~ twice (once in AutoCAD 2000i) to set the Lineweight Control box to display the previously displayed layer and lineweight.

FIGURE 9–7 The Lineweight dialog box can be used to assign a lineweight to a layer.

If you select multiple objects, the following conditions apply:

- If selected objects share the same common lineweight, the Lineweight Control box will display that lineweight.

- If selected objects are composed of varying lineweights, the Lineweight Control box will be blank.

- If the selected object lineweight is assigned as ByLayer, the Lineweight Control will display ByLayer.

To change the lineweight of existing objects:

- Left-click on the object whose lineweight you want to change.

- Inside the Lineweight Control box, choose a lineweight. AutoCAD will apply the selected lineweight to all selected objects.

Note: If no object is selected, the Lineweight Control will display the current lineweight. When new objects are created, AutoCAD will apply the current lineweight to those objects.

Note: When you left-click on an existing object it will appear dashed and small blue squares will be displayed. These squares are called Grips and used to edit objects. Grips are discussed in Chapter 13.

9.10.1 Setting the Current Lineweight at the Command Line

You can set the current lineweight at the command line by entering –LWEIGHT as follows:

```
Command: -LWEIGHT ~EnterKey~
Current lineweight: ByLayer (the current lineweight value is displayed)
Enter default lineweight for new objects or [?]: (enter a valid
lineweight, or?)
```

If you enter ?, AutoCAD will list the 27 available lineweights as shown in Figure 9–8. The list includes 24 lineweights plus ByLayer, ByBlock, and Default.

Note: If an AutoCAD 2000 drawing is saved as an earlier release, the drawing preview will display the lineweights but will not support lineweights.

FIGURE 9–8 The command line list of the available lineweights.

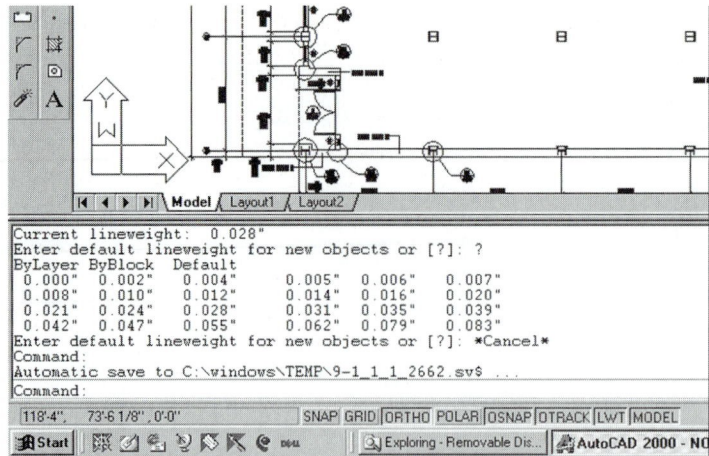

9.11 LINEWEIGHTS IN MODEL AND PAPER SPACE

Lineweights behave differently in model space than they do in paper space layout. In model space, the lineweights are displayed in relation to pixels relative to the screen size and do not represent the object's real-world width. For example, all lineweight values that are less than or equal to 0.01″ are displayed at one pixel. When you zoom out in model space, the lineweight (relative to objects) will increase to impractical widths. In Layout paper space, lineweights are displayed in the exact plotting width specified. When you zoom out the lineweights decrease and when you zoom in lineweights increase in apparent size. You can customize lineweights to plot at non-standard values by using the Plot Style Table Editor. This is discussed in Chapter 23. Lineweights assigned to objects will plot if you check the Plot object lineweights checkbox in the Plot or Page Setup dialog boxes. This checkbox is automatically checked when Plot with plot styles checkbox is checked. Plot and Page Setup dialog boxes are discussed in Chapter 23.

Caution: Do not use lineweights to represent the exact width of an object. For example, do not assign a specific lineweight to a line to draw a solid wall thickness to represent a floor plan. Instead, use the width option of the POLYLINE command or use the MULTILINE command and turn the Fill On. You can also use the offset command in conjunction with the line command to create walls and then hatch them solid.

9.12 STATUS OF LAYERS

The Layer Properties Manager dialog box shown in Figure 9–2 displays nine columns as they relate to layer settings. Each column represents the status relating to the settings of each layer.

Name: This column contains all the layers created for the drawing. If you want to change the name of a layer, highlight the layer, pause for 2 seconds, then select it again. When you select the layer the second time, the layer name will be highlighted with a text box. Enter a new name for the layer and press the ~EnterKey~. If you press the ~EnterKey~ one more time, the Layer1 text box will be displayed for you to enter a new layer. If you press the ~EnterKey~ the second time unintentionally, press the ~EnterKey~ once to accept Layer1, then click on the Delete button to delete it.

On: This column displays a light bulb as the icon for turning a layer on or off. All new layers are created on as default. When the light bulb is yellow, it means the layer is on. When a layer is on, all the objects created on that layer will be displayed and will plot. When you click on the yellow bulb icon, it will turn gray. A gray light bulb icon means the layer is off. When a layer is off, objects on that layer will not be displayed and will not plot.

Freeze: This column displays a sun shining as the icon for freezing and thawing layers. All new layers are created thawed as default. When the sun is shining it means the layer is thawed. When a layer is thawed, all objects created on that layer will be displayed and will plot. When you click on the sun icon, it will turn into a snowflake icon. A snowflake icon means the layer is frozen. When a layer is frozen, objects on that layer will not be displayed and will not plot. The difference between a frozen layer and a layer that is turned off is that the objects on the frozen layer cannot be erased but the objects on a layer that is turned off can be erased. To test this theory, create five circles on a CIRCLES layer and create two rectangles on a RECTANGLES layer. Make Layer 0 current, turn CIRCLES layer off, and freeze the RECTANGLES layer. Even though no objects are displayed because one layer is off and the other one frozen, you can still erase all the circles in the CIRCLES layer. However, none of the rectangles will be erased in the RECTANGLES layer. At the command line, enter ERASE and enter ALL when AutoCAD asks you to select the objects to erase all of the objects. Turn the CIRCLES layer on and thaw the RECTANGLES layer. The two rectangles will be displayed but none of the circles will be displayed because they are erased. This might be useful when you want to erase all the objects in more than one layer to delete those layers. Instead of going into each layer and erasing all objects, freeze all layers except the layer you want to delete, perform erase all as described above, then thaw all layers. All the objects in all the layers other than frozen will be deleted. You can then delete those layers.

Tips: AutoCAD will ignore objects on Frozen layers to increase system resources available for objects on Thawed layers. Layers containing large data and complex drawings should be frozen when it is not needed. This will improve system performance.

Caution: When you Zoom to the Extents of your drawing, AutoCAD displays the area occupied by objects on Thawed layers so the Freeze setting can affect drawing extents.

Lock: This column displays a padlock as the icon for locking and unlocking layers. All new layers are created unlocked as default. When the padlock icon is open, it means the layer is unlocked. When a layer is unlocked, all objects created on that layer will be displayed and will plot. When you click on the open padlock icon, it will turn into a closed padlock. A closed padlock icon means the layer is locked. When a layer is locked, objects on that layer will be displayed but cannot be modified. You can add new objects to a locked layer. This is useful when you do not want others working on the drawing to accidentally delete the objects but you want them to be able to see and add objects.

Color: This column allows you to assign a color to the objects created on that layer as ByLayer. When using the Layer properties Manager dialog box the first time, all new layers are created with color white/black (depending on the background white/black color) as default. To assign a new color to the layer, click on the color swatch (square with the assigned color) or on the color name. The Select Color dialog box will be displayed as shown in Figure 9–9. There are seven standard colors with corresponding numerical values: red (1), yellow (2), green (3), cyan (4), blue (5), magenta (6), and white/black (7). Any color can be selected by clicking on the color. When done, click on the OK button. The color swatch will now show the new color, and the color name will be displayed next to it.

Linetype: This column allows you to assign a new linetype to the objects created on that layer as ByLayer. All new layers are created with the Continuous linetype as default. AutoCAD maintains a wide array of linetypes stored in an external file named *acad.lin*. Before assigning a linetype to a layer, it must be loaded and then selected to become a part of the available linetypes for the current file. It can then be assigned to that layer. The Continuous linetype represents a solid line without dashes. To assign a different linetype, click on the linetype name (Continuous). The Select Linetype dialog box will be displayed as shown in Figure 9–10. If no new linetypes have been loaded, this dialog box will only show the default Continuous linetype. To load one or more linetypes, click on the Load... button. The Load or Reload Linetypes dialog box will be displayed as shown in Figure 9–11. The ACAD_ISO linetypes are used for metric drawings and are governed by the International Standardization Organization(ISO). The available linetypes are multiplied by 25.4 and converted to ISO linetypes from millimeters to inches. Select one or more linetypes from the list. Click on the down arrow to display more linetypes. To select nonconsecutive linetypes, press on the ~CtrlKey~ while selecting different linetypes. When done, click on the OK button. This will take you back to the Select Linetype dialog box.

FIGURE 9–9 The
Select Color dialog box.

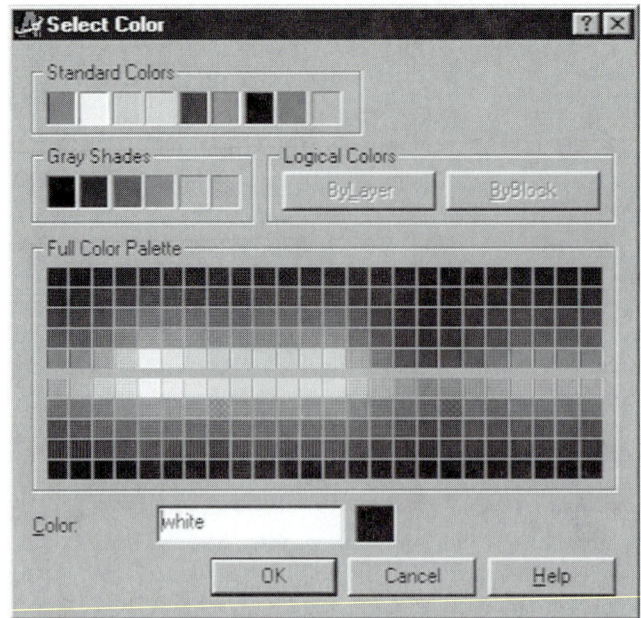

FIGURE 9–10 The
Select Linetype dialog
box.

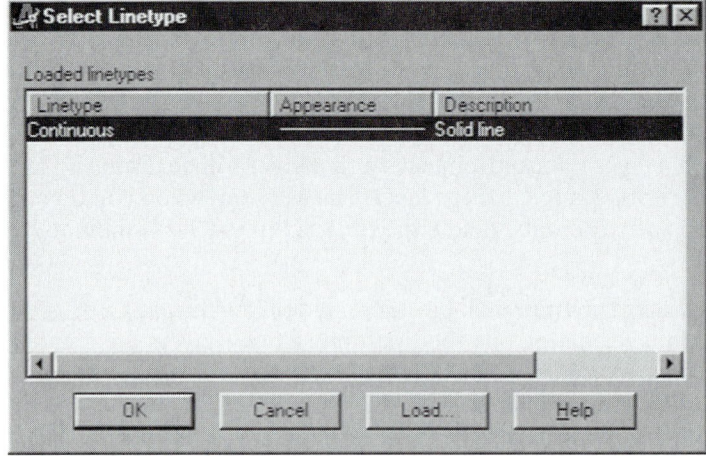

The Select Linetype dialog box shown in Figure 9–12 shows the CENTER, DASHED, PHANTOM, and ZIGZAG linetypes as being loaded. To assign one of the linetypes loaded in Figure 9–12 to the selected layer, click on the linetype and click on the OK button. Other linetypes will be displayed in the Linetype Control box.

> *Note: The AIA CAD Layer Guidelines recommend creating the architectural layers as shown in Appendix B. The A-Grid and A-Grid-Iden layers should be set to Center2 linetype and A-Wall-Fire and A-Grid-Layo layers should be set to Dashed2 linetype.*

Lineweight: This column allows you to assign a lineweight to the objects created on that layer as ByLayer. To assign a new lineweight to the layer, click on the Default lineweight or the existing lineweight. This will display the Lineweight dialog box as shown in Figure 9–7. Select a lineweight and click on the OK button.

> *Tips: When you select the New button in the Layer Properties Manager dialog box after creating layers and assigning properties to layers, the new Layer1 will be created with the same color, linetype, and lineweight as the currently highlighted layer.*

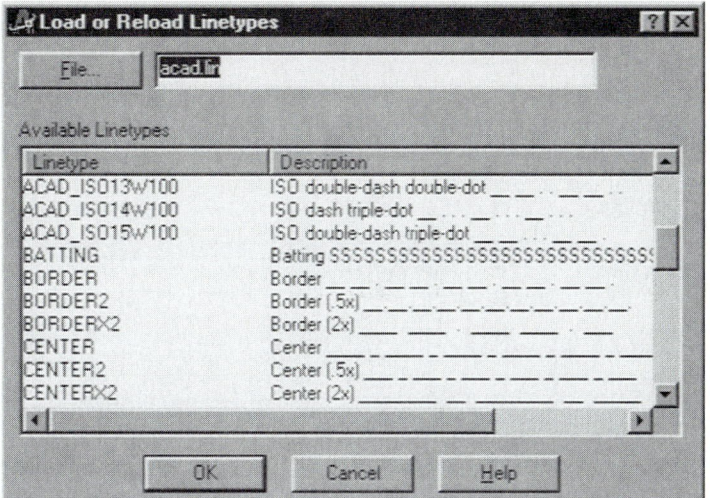

FIGURE 9–11 The Load or Reload Linetypes dialog box.

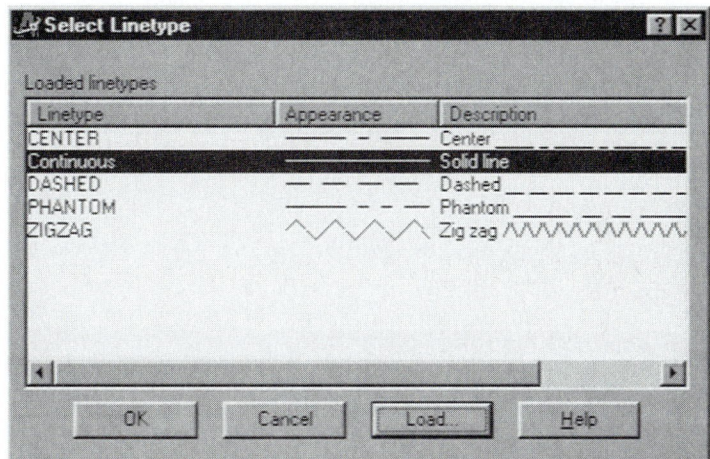

FIGURE 9–12 After loading the required linetypes, the Select Linetype dialog box will display the linetypes loaded.

Plot Style: This column allows you to assign a plot style for all objects on the layer. Plot Styles are discussed in Chapter 23.

Plot: This column allows you to plot or not plot the selected layer. When you click on the plot icon, a red circle with a diagonal line inside will appear. This means that the layer selected will not plot and is considered to be a nonplotting layer. This is useful when you want to see a layer but do not want it plotted. Even if objects are on Layers that are on and thawed they will not plot if the No Plot is selected for those layers.

> *Tips: Select No Plot for the Viewport layers so that the border of viewport objects on Layouts will not plot. Viewports and Layouts are discussed in Chapter 22.*

> ***AutoCAD 2000i Update:*** *The Layer Properties Manager dialog box includes the Freeze Layer by viewport in the Layer list. This is also included in the Layer Control box located in the object Properties Toolbar. This is available only when you work with Layouts.*

9.13 LAYER DETAILS AREA

When you click on the Show details button in the Layer Properties Manager dialog box, a details area will be displayed at the bottom of the dialog box as shown in Figure 9–13. This is a part of the dialog box and not an add-on. To close it, click on the Hide details button in the dialog box. The Details area can be used to create the same settings created in the upper area. When you select a layer name, the details are will list all information related to that layer. You can

FIGURE 9–13 The Layer Details area as the alternate way to assign layer settings.

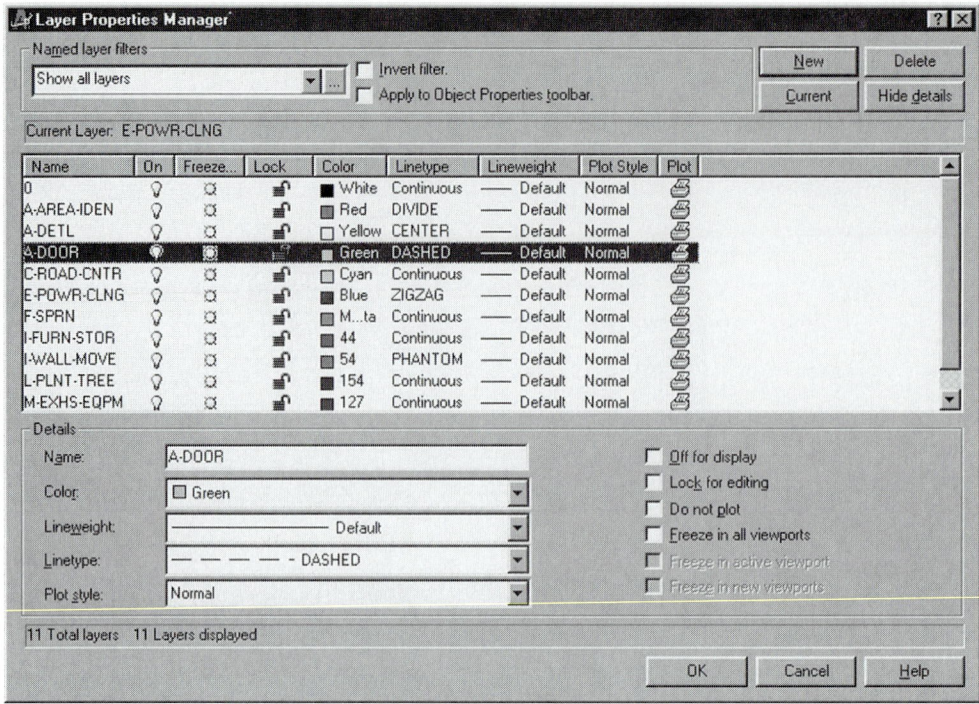

FIGURE 9–14
The two additional columns inside the Layer Properties Manager dilaog box will appear when composing drawings in a Layout.

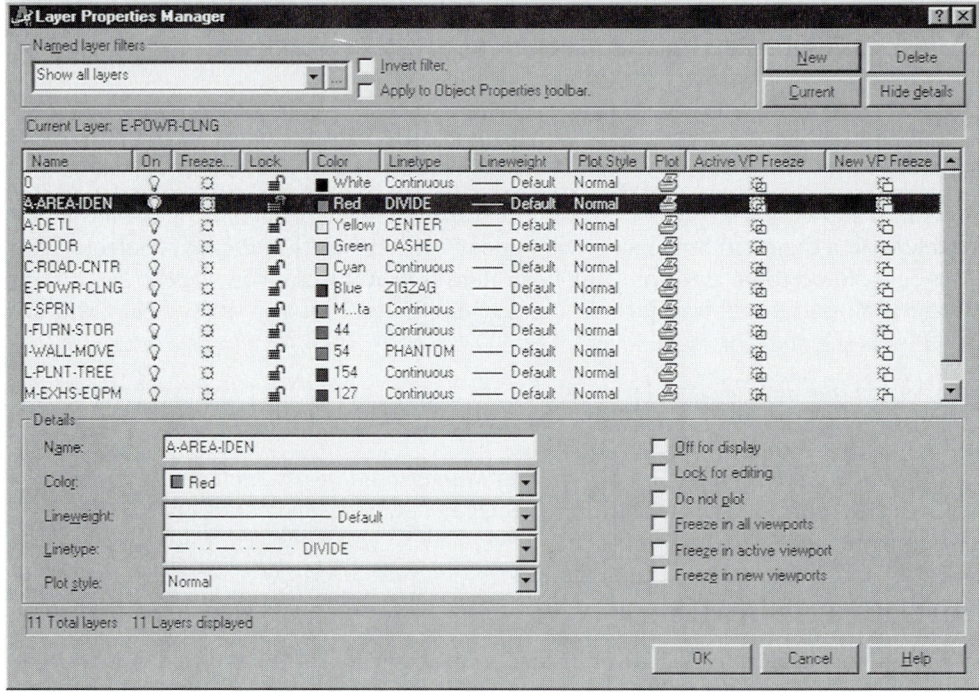

change the name of the selected layer by simply highlighting it and entering the new layer name over it. You can assign color, lineweight, and linetype to the selected layer. Click on the Off for Display check box to turn the selected layer Off. Click on the Lock for Editing check box to lock the selected layer. Click on the Do Not Plot check box to not plot the selected layer. Click on the Freeze in all Viewports check box to freeze the selected layer.

Note: When composing drawings in a layout, AutoCAD displays two additional columns inside the Layer Properties Manager dialog box. These new icons are Active VP (viewport) Freeze and New VP Freeze as shown in Figure 9–14. The Layer Details area shows the two additional check boxes. These two check boxes are not available when working in the Model of your drawing. See AutoCAD 2000i update above. Layouts are discussed in Chapter 22.

9.14 MANAGING LAYERS

The most common method of managing layers is to use the Layer Properties Manager dialog box. You can assign and change color, linetype, and lineweight of objects efficiently and effectively using this dialog box. This is how object properties are specified as ByLayer. You can also use the Layer Control box in the Object Properties toolbar to make an objects layer current, turn layers on, off, freeze, thaw, lock, unlock, and make a layer plotting or nonplotting. Sometimes you may need to assign object properties by referencing a specific layer but with a different color, linetype, or lineweight. In this case you can use the Color Control, Linetype Control, and Lineweight Control boxes in the Object properties toolbar to create object properties by object. When the object's properties are assigned as *by object*, the objects will be created and plotted at the assigned color, linetype, and lineweight regardless of the properties assigned to that layer. In complex drawings, you may not remember the name of the layer you want to make current but you may recognize the objects belonging to that layer. To make the layer of an object on the screen current, click on the Make Object's Layer Current button in the Object Properties toolbar and select the object. To find the name of the layer of an existing object on the screen without making that layer current, left-click on the object and make a note of its layer. Press the ~EscKey~ twice to remove the small boxes, called *grips*, from the object to get back to normal drawing operation.

When there are no objects selected the current layer name will be listed in the Layer Control box in the Objects Properties toolbar. When you select objects when no command is running the layer name of the selected objects will be listed in the Layer Control box. You can select any layer name from the layer list in the Layer Control box to move selected objects to that layer. If you select objects that are on two or more different layers no layer name will be listed in the Layer Control box.

Tips: You can re-size the Layer Properties Manager dialog box by moving your cursor over the border and dragging it. Since layer names along with symbol names are not case sensitive, you do not have to worry about the case of layer names.

9.14.1 Named Layer Filters

When you work on projects with a large number of layers, the management of all layers becomes complicated. To have all layers active at the same time regardless of its use may slow down your progress and make it difficult for you to work with layers. *Layer filters* can be used to filter out layers that are not needed for certain aspects of the project. When layers that are not in use are filtered out, they would not be displayed in the Layer Properties Manager dialog box, therefore making layers more manageable. One of the most powerful aspects of the Layer Properties Manager dialog box is the option to create and save custom layer filters.

■ **EXERCISE 9–1:** *The following step-by-step exercise will help you set up and save a custom-named layer filter for the conditions described below:*

You want only layers that are architectural discipline code (A) to be displayed, and the red and blue colors are thawed and turned on.

Step #1: Create a new drawing and assign layers A-AREA-IDEN (RED), A-DETL (BLUE), A-DOOR (RED), and a few more without the letter A with different layer color.

Step #2: In the Layer Properties Manager dialog box, under the Named layer filters drop-down list, click on the "..." box as shown in Figure 9–15.

Step #3: Inside the Named Layer Filters dialog box enter Architectural Discipline inside the Filter name: text box as shown in Figure 9–16.

Step #4: Inside the Layer name: text box enter A*. This is a wildcard character that will list all the layers that start with letter A (Architectural). See Figure 9–16. Use a single layer name if one layer needs to be filtered out.

Step #5: Inside the On/Off: text box click on the down arrow and select On as shown in Figure 9–16.

Step #6: Inside the Freeze/Thaw: text box click on the down arrow and select Thawed as shown in Figure 9–16.

Step #7: Inside the Color: text box enter red,blue (no space after comma) as shown in Figure 9–16.

Step #8: Click on the Add button to add the new filter name to the list.

Step #9: Click on the Close button.

FIGURE 9–15 The Layer Properties Manager dialog box allows you to create named custom layer filters.

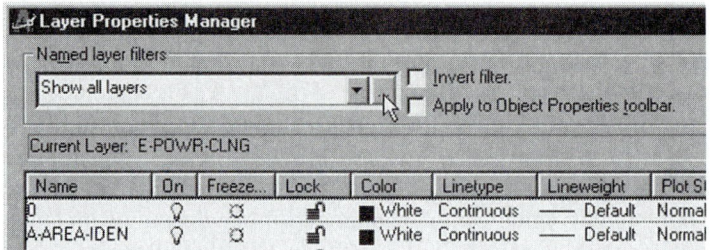

FIGURE 9–16 The Named Layer Filters dialog box is used to establish the layer filtering criteria.

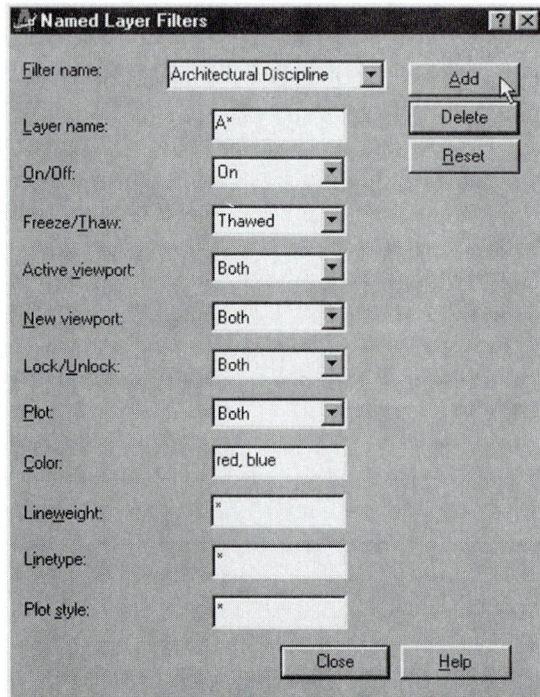

Step #10: Inside the Layer Properties Manager dialog box, click on the down arrow of the Named layer filters: text box as shown in Figure 9–17.

Step #11: Select the Architectural Discipline named layer filter from the list.

The Layer Properties Manager dialog box will now display only the layers starting with letter A (architectural discipline) that have color red and blue as shown in Figure 9–18.

Congratulations! You have created a custom named layer filter based on layer name and color.

Note: For complex projects include as much filtering criteria as possible to manage more aspects of layering requirements.

Tips: When using Layouts to compose multiscale drawings inside viewports and when using external referencing (xref) to reference different files into viewports created in Paper Space, create custom layer filter and use Active viewport and New viewport areas to control viewport visibility. This concept is explained in Chapter 24.

The options in the Named Layer Filters section are as follows:

• **SHOW ALL LAYERS:** This option is the default and displays all created layer names inside the dialog box.

• **SHOW ALL USED LAYERS:** This option displays all layers that contain objects. If there are no objects created in layer 0, it will still be displayed.

• **SHOW ALL XREF DEPENDENT LAYERS:** This option displays all layers of files externally referenced. See Chapter 24.

• **INVERT FILTER:** Placing a checkmark inside this check box reverses the display of layer names. For example, when all used layers are displayed with the Show all used layers option, selecting Invert filter will display all unused layers (layers with no objects).

• **APPLY TO OBJECT PROPERTIES TOOLBAR:** Placing a check mark inside this check box displays only the layers meeting the requirements of the named layer filter selection in the Object Properties toolbar. Use this filtering method to reduce the number of layers listed in the Object Properties Layer drop-down list box. On the Layer Control box, a tooltip is activated when you move your cursor over the layer list. Figure 9–19 shows the A-AREA-IDEN layer meeting the named layer filter selection set requirements.

AutoCAD 2000i Update: The Layer Properties Manager dialog box contains the Save state... and Restore state... buttons for saving and restoring layer states. This allows you to take a snapshot of your current layer states. Selecting save state...button will display the save Layer States dialog box. This dialog box can be used to establish the state and property settings for all layers in a drawing and saved using a layer state name. Enter a layer state name in the New layer state name: list box and select the desired

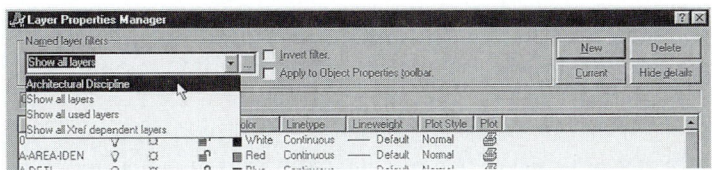

FIGURE 9–17 Once the custom layer filter is created, it is added to the Named layer filters drop-down list box.

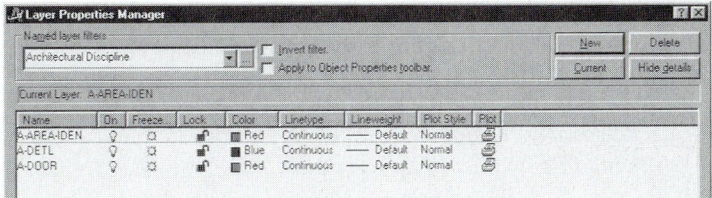

FIGURE 9–18 When the custom Architectural Discipline layer filter is created and selected, only the layers fitting to that filtering criteria are displayed.

FIGURE 9–19 The application of the filter selection set to Object Properties toolbar.

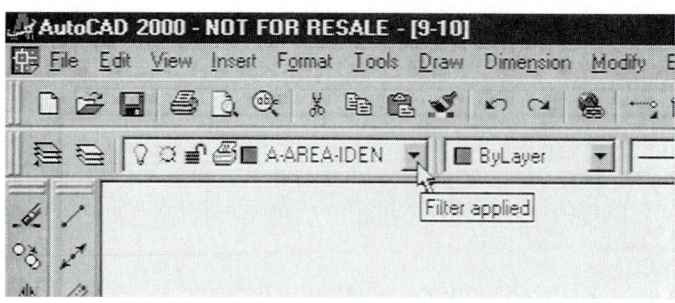

properties from the Layer states and layer properties areas and click on the OK button. To manage named layer states, click on the Restore state...button to display the Layer States Manager dialog box. This dialog box has six options. The restore option allows you to restore previously saved settings. The Edit option will display the Edit layer States dialog box where you can edit the layer states. The Rename option will change the name of a layer state name. The Delete option will delete a layer state name. The Import option allows you to import a layer state by displaying the Import Layer State dialog box. The Export option allows you to export a layer state by displaying the Export Layer Sate dialog box. The exported files are saved with a .las file extension. Linetypes in a saved layer state are not automatically loaded unless the current drawing has the required linetypes loaded.

9.14.2 Using the Shortcut Menu

Shortcut menus can help you save time in a practical way when managing projects. The shortcut menu for layers can be used for more than just making the selected layer current. Right-click inside an empty area in the Layer Properties Manager dialog box (not directly on a layer) to access the shortcut menu as shown in Figure 9–20. The shortcut menu options are as follows:

- **NEW LAYER:** Creates a new layer (Layer1).

- **SELECT ALL:** Selects all layers that are currently displayed in the dialog box.

- **CLEAR ALL:** Clears all layers that are currently highlighted.

- **SELECT ALL BUT CURRENT:** Selects all layers except the current layer.

- **INVERT SELECTION:** Clears selected layers, then reverses the procedure to select layers that were not selected before.

- **INVERT LAYER FILTER:** This is the same as Invert filter explained above.

- **LAYER FILTERS:** This is the same as Named layer filters options described above.

- **NAMED FILTERS:** If you created a custom layer filter, it will be displayed when you select this option. Figure 9–20 shows Architectural Discipline as the available named filter.

Tips: You can select multiple layer names in the Layer Properties Manager dialog box by pressing and holding the ~CtrlKey~ while selecting individual layers that are not listed together. You can also press and hold the ~ShiftKey~ to select all layers between the currently selected layer and the layer that you select next.

  Note: When a drawing is opened the "Show All Layers" preset filter is applied.

Tips: You do not have to create layers for every new drawing you start. The AutoCAD DesignCenter allows you to copy layers, blocks, linetypes, layouts, text, and dimension styles created in one drawing into another drawing. AutoCAD DesignCenter is discussed in Chapter 10.

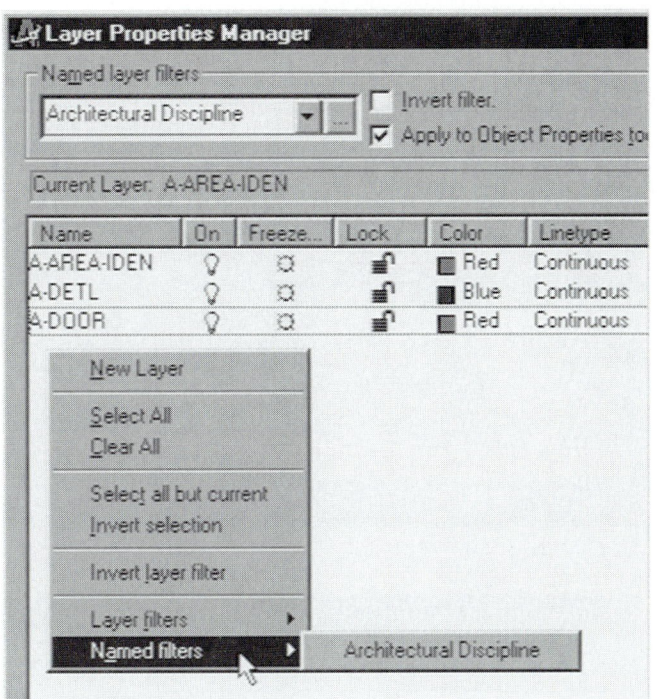

FIGURE 9–20 The right click shortcut menu options.

9.15 MANAGING LINETYPES

Assigning and loading linetypes were introduced previously. A more convenient method to load and manage linetypes is to use the Linetype Manager dialog box. To access this dialog box, select Linetype from the Format pull-down menu, select Other... from the Linetype Control box, or enter LT or LINETYPE at the command line. The Linetype Manager dialog box will be displayed as shown in Figure 9–21. The concept of the Linetype Manager dialog box is very similar to the Layer Properties Manager dialog box. You can manage loaded linetypes through Linetype filters by selecting either Show All Linetypes, Show All Used Linetypes, or Show All Xref-Dependent Linetypes options as shown in Figure 9–22. You can also invert linetype filters much as you would invert layer filters.

The Linetype Manager dialog box displays three columns as it relates to linetype settings as shown in Figure 9–21. Each column represents the status relating to the settings of each linetype.

- **LINETYPE:** This column lists all the loaded linetypes. If no linetypes are loaded, only the ByLayer and ByBlock linetypes are displayed. All new layers are assigned default ByLayer linetype as a Continuous linetype.

- **APPEARANCE:** This column shows how the linetypes will be displayed when used.

- **DESCRIPTION:** This column shows the name and appearance of the linetype.

The Load... button allows you to load linetypes to the current file and will display the Load or Reload Linetypes dialog box as shown in Figure 9–11. AutoCAD stores linetypes in acad.lin file. The Current button will assign the selected linetype to the Linetype Control box in the Object Properties toolbar and override the linetype set ByLayer. This procedure will assign the selected linetype as by object. The Delete button will delete the selected linetype from the drawing but not from the acad.lin file. You cannot delete the following linetypes: ByLayer, ByBlock, Continuous, current linetype, xref-dependent linetypes, and linetypes referenced by layers or objects. The Show details button will display the linetype details area and is explained next.

Once you load linetypes, you can assign a linetype by object. This will override the linetype assigned to the current layer. This will allow you to use a linetype independent from any layer

FIGURE 9–21 The Linetype Manager dialog box.

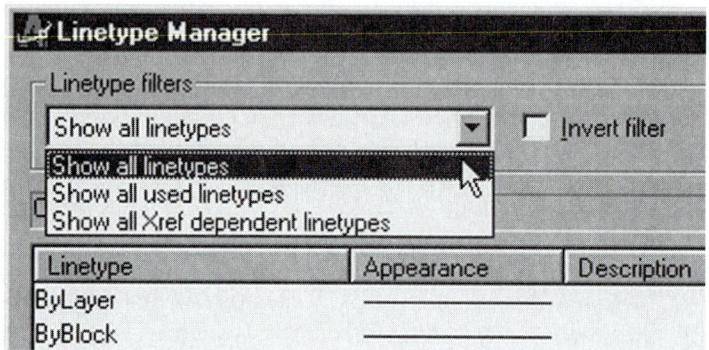

FIGURE 9–22 The Linetype filters.

settings. To assign a linetype by object, select the linetype from the Linetype Control box and create the object.

Tips: Assigning object properties by object will override assigning object properties ByLayer. To keep layer management efficient and consistent, do not mix ByLayer with overrides. Create a separate layer and name it A-WALLS-Overrides.

9.15.1 Linetype Details Area

This area is similar to the layer details area and is shown in Figure 9–23. When you select a linetype from the Linetype column, the name of the linetype will be displayed inside the Name: text box. You can assign a user name by highlighting the linetype name inside the Name: text box and entering the name. You can also assign a user description to the new name by highlighting the linetype inside the Description: text box and entering a new description. For example, the BATTING linetype is primarily used to represent batt insulation in architectural drawings. The Use Paper Space Units for Scaling check box can be turned on to specify the use of paper space linetype scaling. This is the same as using the PSLTSCALE (Paper Space Linetype Scale) system variable. The PSLTSCALE, the global scale factor: and current object scale: areas are discussed in section 9.17

You can also use the –LINETYPE command to manage linetypes. The hyphen (-) must be typed before the LINETYPE. The command line procedure is as follows:

```
Command: -LINETYPE ~EnterKey~
Current line type: "ByLayer"
Enter an option [?/Create/Load/Set]: (enter an option)
```

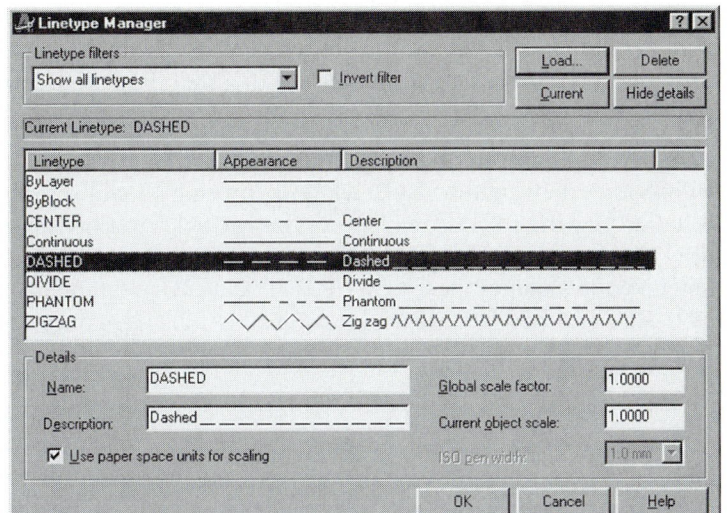

FIGURE 9–23
The linetype details area.

The command line options are as follows:

- **?:**   Entering the ? will display the Select Linetype File dialog box. The file name is *acad.lin*, and the file type is *Linetype [*.lin]*. Click on the Open button to display the AutoCAD Text Window dialog box. This box will display and list all the linetypes available in the acad.lin file. You can make a print of all the linetypes for future reference. Press the ~F2Key~ to close the dialog box.

- **CREATE:**   Entering C will allow you to create a new linetype and store it inside a specified library file.

- **LOAD:**   Entering L will load one or more linetypes from the selected linetype library file.

- **SET:**   Entering S will set a current linetype for newly created objects.

9.16 OVERRIDING OBJECT PROPERTIES USING SYSTEM VARIABLES

You can override the three mostly used object properties (color, linetype, and lineweight) using system variables instead of using their respective Control boxes in the Object Properties toolbar. The three system variables are as follows:

Cecolor: This system variable will override the color of the object independent of the current layer color. The default value for CECOLOR is "ByLayer." To override the color, enter a new color name or number at the command line as follows:

```
Command: CECOLOR ~EnterKey~
Enter new value for CECOLOR <"BYLAYER">: (enter a new color name or
number such as red or 1)
```

The Color Control box will display red color as the new color for the objects to be drawn in the current layer. This will override the original color selected for the current layer.

Celtype: This system variable will override the linetype of the object independent of the current layer linetype. The default value for CELTYPE is "BYLAYER." To override the linetype, enter a new linetype name at the command line as follows:

```
Command: CELTYPE ~EnterKey~
Enter a new value for CELTYPE <"BYLAYER">: (enter a new linetype name
such as dashed)
```

The Linetype Control box will display DASHED, and the dashed linetype as the new linetype for the objects to be drawn in the current layer. This will override the original linetype selected for the current layer. Make sure the linetype you entered is loaded first.

Celweight: This system variable will override the lineweight of the object independent of the current layer lineweight. The default value for CELWEIGHT is –1 (BYLAYER). Entering –2 will set the lineweight to ByBlock and entering –3 will set the lineweight to DEFAULT, which is defined by the LWDEFAULT system variable. To find the correct value as the override, multiply the decimal lineweight by 25.4 and then multiply the result by 100. This will be the millimeter equivalent for the CELWEIGHT value. For example, to override the lineweight of ByLayer by 0.020″, enter 50 (0.020×25.4=0.50×100=50). The command line procedure is as follows:

```
Command: CELWEIGHT ~EnterKey~
Enter a new value for CELWEIGHT <-1>: 50 ~EnterKey~
```

The Lineweight Control box will display 0.020″ as the new lineweight for the objects to be drawn in the current layer. This will override the original lineweight selected for the current layer. To actually see the new lineweight on the screen, turn on the LWT button.

9.17 ESTABLISHING LINETYPE SCALE

Some linetypes are based on dashes, spaces, and dots. For example, the *dashed* linetype has a solid line, a space, a solid line, another space and so on. The length of dashes and spaces are controlled by the LTSCALE (linetype scale) system variable. The LTSCALE system variable is global and affects every linetype (except continuous) on the drawing. The default linetype scale is 1. To change the linetype scale, enter LTS or LTSCALE at the command line. Figure 9–24 shows three different linetypes with dashes and spaces. These linetypes are created using AutoCAD default drawing settings (Units as Decimal, Limits as 12,9, Scale Factor as 1, final plotted scale as 1″=1″). Each linetype has the same spaces between the dashes. The Center and the Phantom linetypes have the same long dashes. When the LTSCALE system variable is changed to 2, the dashes and spaces will be displayed twice as large, as shown in Figure 9–25.

When using linetypes other than continuous in architectural drawings, the linetype scale must be adjusted to meet the visual consistency of dashes and spaces. The rule of thumb is to start the LTSCALE value with half the scale factor value of the drawing and increase or decrease to fine tune it. For example, the floor plan in Figure 9–26 has a drawing scale of 1/4″=1′-0″, drawing limits of 34′, 44′, and a scale factor of 48 and has DASHED and CENTER linetypes. Because the LTSCALE is automatically set to 1 when starting a drawing, no dashes and spaces will be visible with an LTSCALE of 1. To display these linetypes at a visually pleasing format in architec-

FIGURE 9–24 Three different linetypes with LTSCALE system variable as default (1).

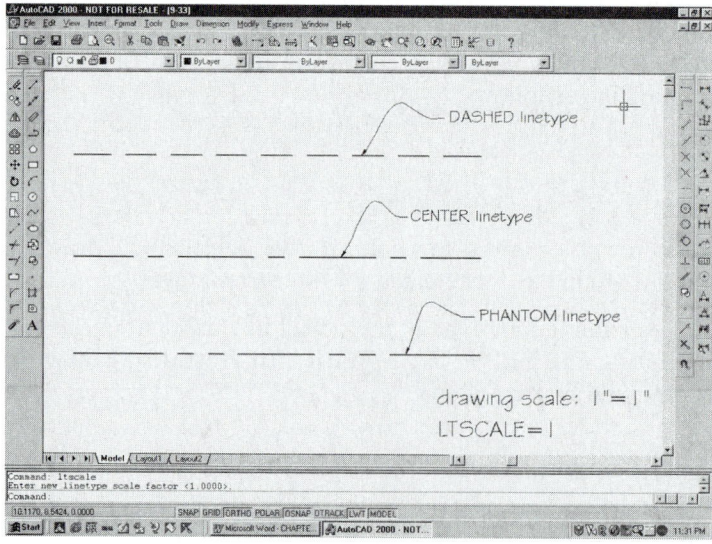

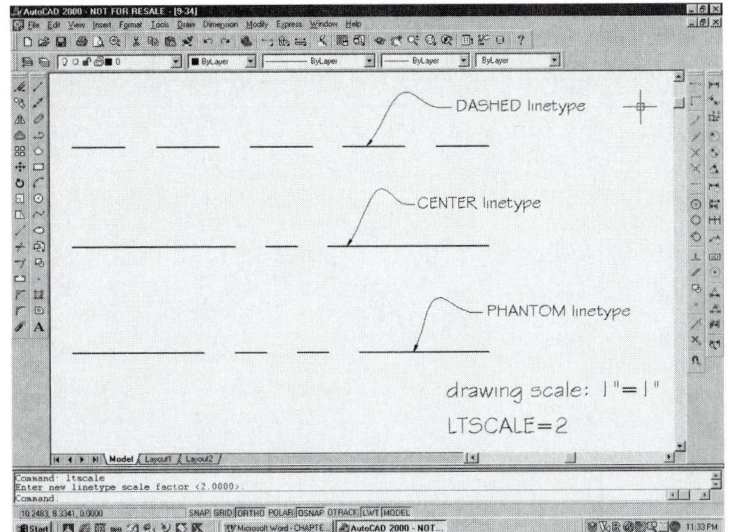

FIGURE 9–25 The three linetypes in Figure 9–24 with LTSCALE set to 2.

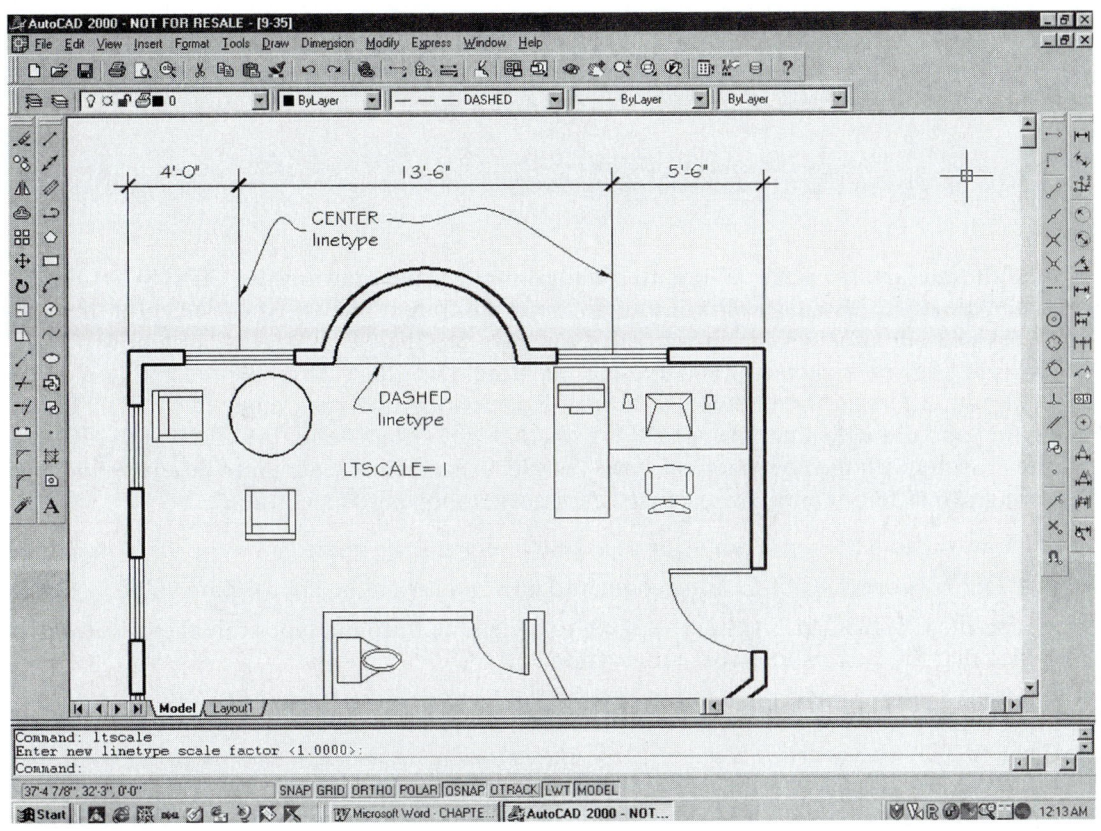

FIGURE 9–26 A floor plan with DASHED and CENTER linetypes. The LTSCALE is at default (1). No dashes or spaces visible.

tural scale, start with an LTSCALE value of half the scale factor. Figure 9–27 shows the same floor plan at an LTSCALE value of 24. You can experiment with different values to come up with your acceptable linetype scale value.

For most of the time, adjusting the LTSCALE to meet linetype scale requirements is not a problem. But what happens when you try to create one unique linetype that requires a fundamentally different linetype scale? Certain linetypes require different linetype scales to be displayed at the same visibility and scale of other linetypes. Changing the LTSCALE system variable to a higher or lower number may work but will affect the existing linetypes. When two or

FIGURE 9–27 The same floor plan with LTSCALE set to half the scale factor (24).

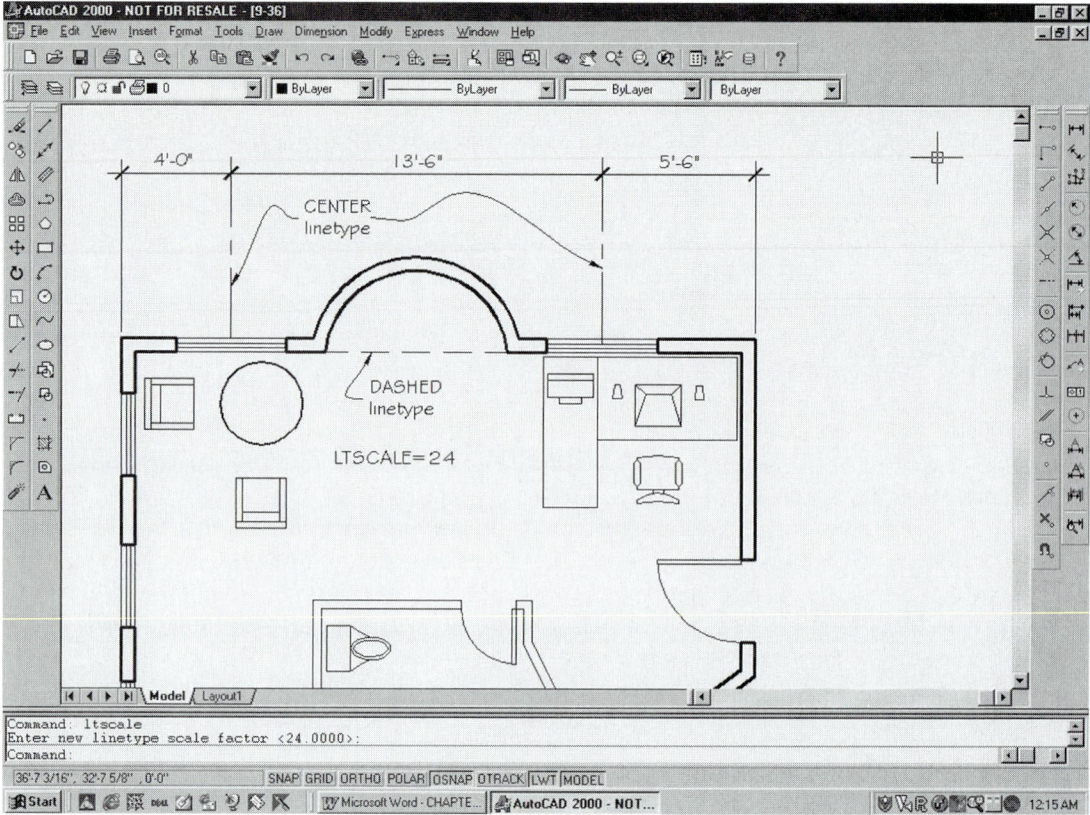

more different linetype scale values are required in the same drawing, the CELTSCALE (current linetype scale) system variable is used to assign a different linetype scale value for the other linetypes without affecting the current LTSCALE value. The CELTSCALE system variable is the current linetype scale factor and does not have a global affect. To create the additional linetype without affecting the linetype scale factor of existing linetypes, enter the CELTSCALE value first and draw the linetype next. It is extremely important to set the CELTSCALE value before drawing with the new linetype. For example, to correctly create three different linetypes requiring two different linetype scale factors, use the following procedure:

1. Draw the two linetypes requiring the same linetype scale value.
2. Enter LTS or LTSCALE at the command line and assign the appropriate value.
3. Use the CELTSCALE system variable to assign the third linetype scale factor value. Notice that the current linetypes are not affected.
4. Use the appropriate command to draw the object using the current linetype.

Caution: The value assigned to the CELTSCALE is used in conjunction with the value assigned to the LTSCALE. The total linetype scale factor value is needed to achieve uniform linetype scale for all different linetypes.

Tips: Remember that there are two different linetype scale factors. The LTSCALE system variable controls the linetype scale of existing linetypes on a global basis. In other words, changing LTSCALE system variable will change the linetype scale of all existing linetypes in the current drawing. The CELTSCALE system variable controls the linetype scale factor on a current (local) basis. This means that the value assigned to CELTSCALE will not affect the linetype scale of current linetypes. You must set a value for CELTSCALE before using the linetype in the current drawing. Although CELTSCALE is another way to enter a linetype scale factor value, it may not correspond to the same LTSCALE values you have been working with.

Instead of entering the LTSCALE and CELTSCALE values at the command line, you can establish them inside the Linetype Manager dialog box. You must first click on the Show Details button. Under the Details area on the right-hand side, the Global Scale Factor represents LTSCALE and the Current Object Scale represents CELTSCALE. Enter the appropriate value inside the edit box and then click on the OK button. You can establish one of the linetype scale factors using the dialog box and the other using the command line if you wish.

If you are plotting from the Model tab you must adjust LTSCALE for all architectural drawings having dashed linetypes with a drawing scale other than 1:1 and not worry about the PSLTSCALE value. If you are plotting from the Layout tab with one viewport having one scale, set the PSLTSCALE to 0 and keep the current LTSCALE value. With this setting when you select the Layout tab to compose your drawing or plot from the Layout tab, all linetypes will display the same linetype scale in Paper Space Viewports as you set in Model tab. If you are plotting from the Layout tab and have multiple viewports at different drawing scales set both LTSCALE and PSLTSCALE to 1. Linetype scale for objects displayed from the Model tab will match objects displayed in Layouts at 1:1 scale. Since LTSCALE is a global linetype scale it will only be ideal for viewports with one drawing scale when PSLTSCALE = 0. When LTSCALE and PSLTSCALE is set to 1 in Layouts with multiple viewports at different drawing scales then linetypes will use reasonably similar (if not same) linetype scale for all drawing scales. When you switch back to the Model tab make sure you change the LTSCALE back to what it was before. Plotting is discussed in Chapter 23. Linetype scales may not reflect the changes you made to LTSCALE and PSLTSCALE until you regenerate the screen and viewports. You can force AutoCAD to display and update changes in all viewports by entering REGENALL at the command line.

Tips: You can assign different linetype scales to individual linetypes without the use of LTSCALE and CELTSCALE system variables by using the Properties window. The Properties window is discussed in Chapter 13. This is a much faster and more efficient way to change current linetype scales.

9.18 EXPRESS LAYER TOOLS

The Express Layer Toolbar allows you to manage layers separate from the regular layer commands and layer dialog boxes. You can access the Express Layer Toolbar as follows:

1. Right-click on the right side (empty space) of the Help button (the button with the question mark) located at the end of the Standard Toolbar. Select the EXPRESS option then select Express Layer Tools as shown in Figure 9–28. The Express Layer Tools toolbar will be displayed as shown in Figure 9–28.

2. From the Express pull-down menu, select Layers then select the appropriate layer express tool as shown in Figure 9–29.

   Note: You must have a full installation of AutoCAD 2000 in order to have the Express pull-down menu and Express Toolbars.

The Express Layer Tools toolbar has the following options:

Layer Manager: This button allows you to save and restore layer settings similar to creating and saving named views. Creating and managing views are covered in Chapter 11. When you select the Layer manager button, the Layer Manager: Save and Restore Layer Settings dialog box will be displayed as shown in Figure 9–30. You can also enter LMAN at the command line to access the same dialog box. You can use the Layer Manager dialog box to save existing views of your drawing with different layers turned on or off. For example, you can save several different layouts of your floor plan to show your client several different schemes using one file. With the Express Layer Manager tool, you can take a snapshot of each floor plan scheme, such as *Scheme A, Scheme B, Scheme C,* and so on. There are seven options in the Layer manager dialog box as follows:

Save: This button will save the layer status. To establish a layer status, use layer settings (on, off, lock, and so on). Then access the Layer Manager dialog box and click on the Save... button. This will display the Layer state name dialog box as shown in Figure 9–31. Enter the name of

FIGURE 9–28 The Express Layer Tools toolbar can be accessed from the EXPRESS option.

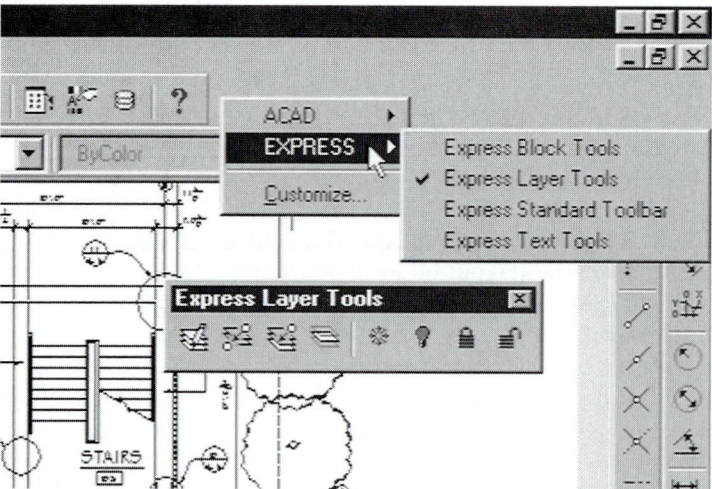

FIGURE 9–29 The Express pull-down menu will provide you with access to express tools such as the Express Layer option.

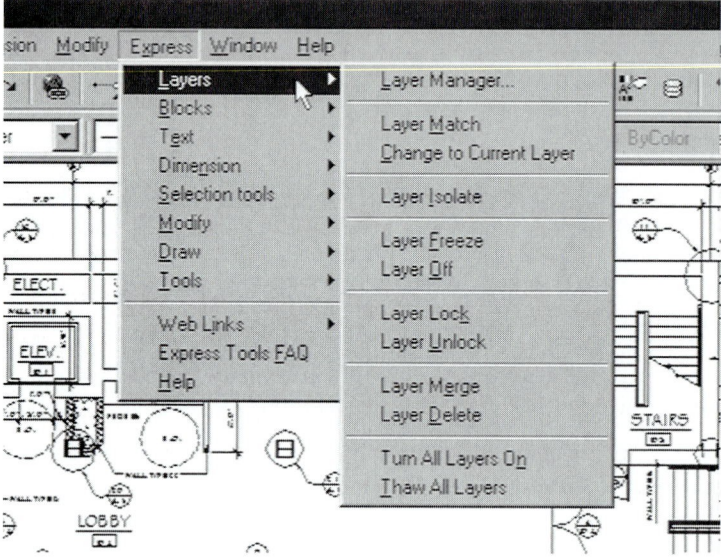

the layer view inside the Save current layer status as: text box. For example, to create a layer status showing only the exterior walls and columns, turn off all layers except the layers containing exterior walls and columns. Enter the current layer status name as *Exterior Walls and Columns* as shown in Figure 9-31. The words *Exterior Walls and Columns* will appear inside the Saved Layer states: list box in the Layer manager dialog box.

Edit: This button is used to edit the existing layer states. Highlight the name of the layer state in the Saved layer states: list box and click on the Edit... button. This will display the Layer Properties Manager dialog box where you can manipulate layers, including changing colors and linetypes.

Rename: This button will allow you to rename the selected layer state name. Fist highlight the name, then click on the Rename... button. This will display the Rename Layer state dialog box and will allow you to enter the new name.

Delete: This button will allow you to delete the highlighted layer state. You can only delete one layer state at a time.

Import: This button will allow you to import layer settings from other drawings. To import, you must first export the layer states of other Saved Layer states to a *.lay file.

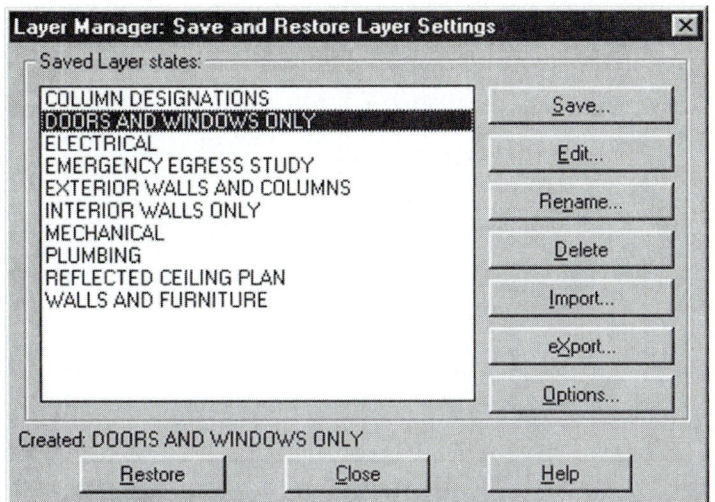

FIGURE 9–30 The Layer Manager: Save and Restore layer Settings dialog box. Notice the 10 layer states created.

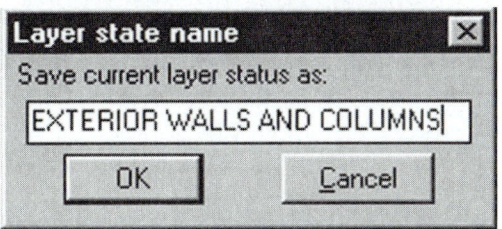

FIGURE 9–31 The Layer state name dialog box.

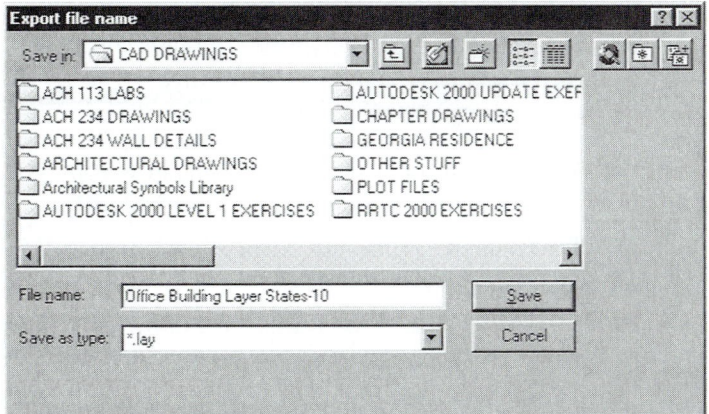

FIGURE 9–32 The Export file name dialog box is used to export saved layer state settings before importing.

Export: This button will allow you to export Saved Layer State settings by displaying the Export file name dialog box as shown in Figure 9–32. Enter the name of the file to be exported to the *.lay. This will allow you to use these layer configuration settings in other drawings.

Options: This button will display the Layer Manager: Restore Options dialog box as shown in Figure 9–33. You can turn off any of the layer properties by removing the checkmark inside the check box.

- **MATCH OBJECT'S LAYER:** The second button in the Express Layer Tools toolbar will allow you to change the layer of selected objects to the layer of a selected destination object. This is similar to the Match Properties button in the Standard Toolbar, where you can copy object properties (color, layer, lineweight, and linetype) from one object to one or more objects. When you click on this button, AutoCAD will ask you to select objects to be changed. After you select the objects, AutoCAD will ask you to select the object for which you want properties to be inherited or type the name of the destination layer. You can also enter LAYMCH at the command line to use the Match Object's Layer tool.

FIGURE 9–33 The Layer Manager: Restore Options dialog box shown all layer properties restored.

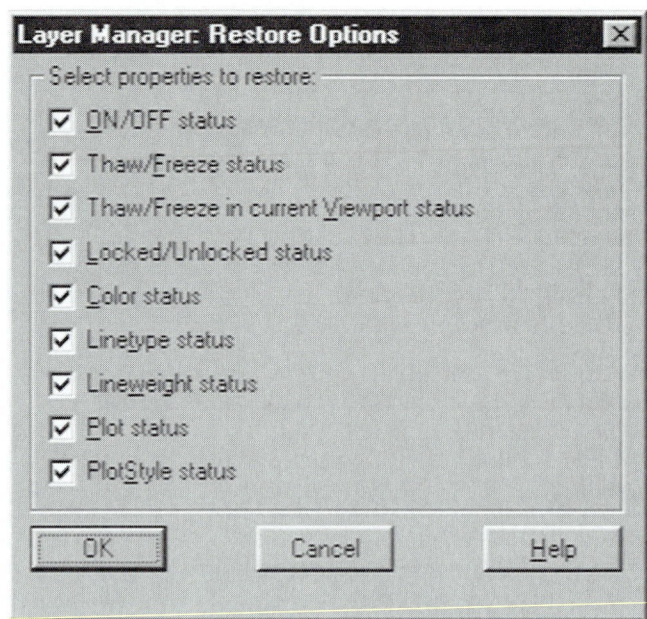

- **CHANGE TO CURRENT LAYER:**   This button will allow you to change the layer of selected objects to the current layer. You can also enter LAYCUR at the command line.

- **ISOLATE OBJECT'S LAYER:**   This button will allow you to isolate the layer of selected objects. You can also enter LAYISO at the command line.

- **FREEZE OBJECT'S LAYER:**   This button will allow you to freeze the layer of selected objects. You can also enter LAYFRZ at the command line.

- **TURN OBJECT'S LAYER OFF:**   This button will allow you to turn off the layer of selected objects. You can also enter LAYOFF at the command line.

- **LOCK OBJECT'S LAYER:**   This button will allow you to lock the layer of selected objects. You can also enter LAYLCK at the command line.

- **UNLOCK OBJECT'S LAYER:**   This button will allow you to unlock the layer of selected objects. You can also enter LAYULK at the command line.

You can perform all of the above functions using the Express pull-down menu under Layers as shown in Figure 9–29.

Layer Merge: This option is found in the Express pull-down menu under Layers. It allows you to incorporate the layers of other drawings that are received outside your firm or school into your layer format. For example, if you receive a drawing from a consultant that has many more layers than what your layer standards call for, use Layer Merge option to move all objects to a specified layer and then delete the unwanted layers. You can also enter LAYMRG at the command line.

Caution: Be careful not to delete the layers you need when using the Layer Merge feature.

REVIEW QUESTIONS

1. Describe the purpose behind using layers in projects
2. Describe the concept behind naming layers recommended by American Institute of Architects using CAD Layer Guidelines.
3. How do you access the Layer Properties Manager dialog box?

4. Why is it important to assign object properties through ByLayer?
5. Describe the difference between a layer that is turned off and a layer that is frozen.
6. Are the objects on the lock layer displayed?
7. Can you delete the layer 0?
8. How do you access the layers detail area in the Layer Properties Manager dialog box?
9. What is the purpose behind creating layer filters?
10. What happens when you right click on a layer name in the Layer Properties Manager dialog box?
11. Describe the process behind loading linetypes.
12. How do you access the Linetype Manager dialog box?
13. What system variables are used to override object properties?
14. What does the LTSCALE system variable do?
15. Describe the difference between LTSCALE and CELTSCALE system variables.
16. How do you access the Express Layer Tools toolbar?

PROBLEMS

1. Draw the wall detail shown in Figure 9–34 using a final plot scale of 1 1/2″=1′-0″ to be printed on "A" size paper. Do not create dimensions, text, or hatching. Create the following layers and properties:

Layer name	Color	Linetype	Lineweight
A-GLAZ	BLUE	CONTINUOUS	DEFAULT
A-COLS	RED	CONTINUOUS	0.012″
A-DETL	GREEN	CONTINUOUS	DEFAULT
A-DETL-PATT	CYAN	CONTINUOUS	DEFAULT
A-ANNO-DIMS	WHITE	CONTINUOUS	DEFAULT
A-ANNO-TEXT	WHITE	CONTINUOUS	DEFAULT
A-DET-MISC	MAGENTA	CONTINUOUS	DEFAULT
A-DET-DASHED	WHITE	DASHED	DEFAULT

Place objects on appropriate layers. Use A-DET-MISC layer for all other objects. Save the drawing as *MYEXE9-1*.

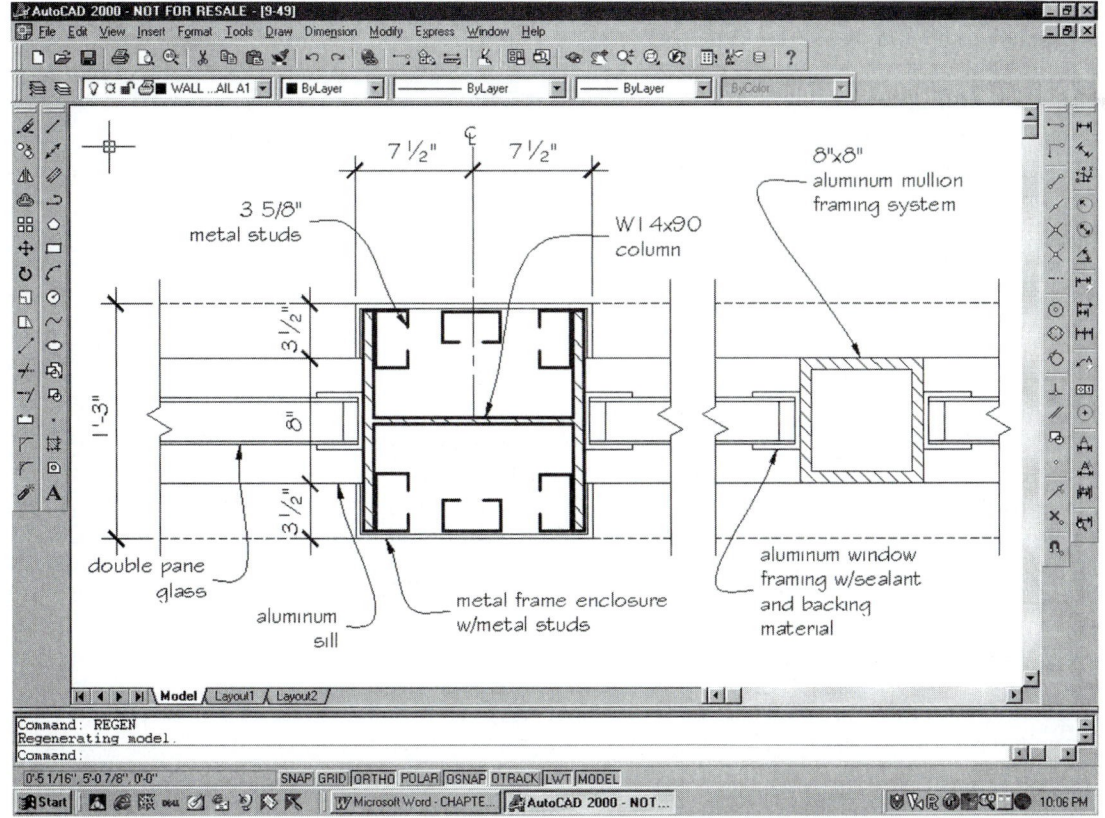

FIGURE 9–34
Wall Detail for
Problem 9–1.

2. Draw the Floor Plan shown in Figure 9–35 and create layers as per AIA CAD Layer Guidelines. Use a final plot scale of 1/4"=1'-0" to be printed on "A" size paper. Exterior walls should be assigned a lineweight of 0.02". Do not create dimensions, fixtures, furniture, or hatching. Save the drawing as *MYEXE9-2.*

3. Open the *MYEXE7-2.dwg* file. Create the following layers and properties:

Layer name	Color	Linetype	Lineweight
DOOR FRAME	*BLUE*	*CONTINUOUS*	*0.02"*
WD BLOCKING	*RED*	*CONTINUOUS*	*DEFAULT*
MTL STUDS	*GREEN*	*CONTINUOUS*	*0.02"*
FINISH	*CYAN*	*CONTINUOUS*	*DEFAULT*
DOOR	*WHITE*	*CONTINUOUS*	*DEFAULT*
DIMENSIONS	*BLUE*	*CONTINUOUS*	*DEFAULT*
HATCHING	*MAGENTA*	*CONTINUOUS*	*DEFAULT*
NOTES	*RED*	*CONTINUOUS*	*DEFAULT*
MISC	*WHITE*	*CONTINUOUS*	*DEFAULT*

4. Open the *MYEXE5-8.dwg* file. Create the following layers and properties:

Layer name	Color	Linetype	Lineweight
EXTERIOR WALS	*BLUE*	*CONTINUOUS*	*0.02"*
INTERIOR WALLS	*RED*	*CONTINUOUS*	*DEFAULT*
FIXTURES	*GREEN*	*CONTINUOUS*	*DEFAULT*
FURNITURE	*CYAN*	*CONTINUOUS*	*DEFAULT*
DOORS	*WHITE*	*CONTINUOUS*	*DEFAULT*
WINDOWS	*BLUE*	*CONTINUOUS*	*DEFAULT*
HATCHING	*MAGENTA*	*CONTINUOUS*	*DEFAULT*
NOTES	*RED*	*CONTINUOUS*	*DEFAULT*
MISC	*WHITE*	*CONTINUOUS*	*DEFAULT*

FIGURE 9–35
Floor Plan for
Problem 9–2.

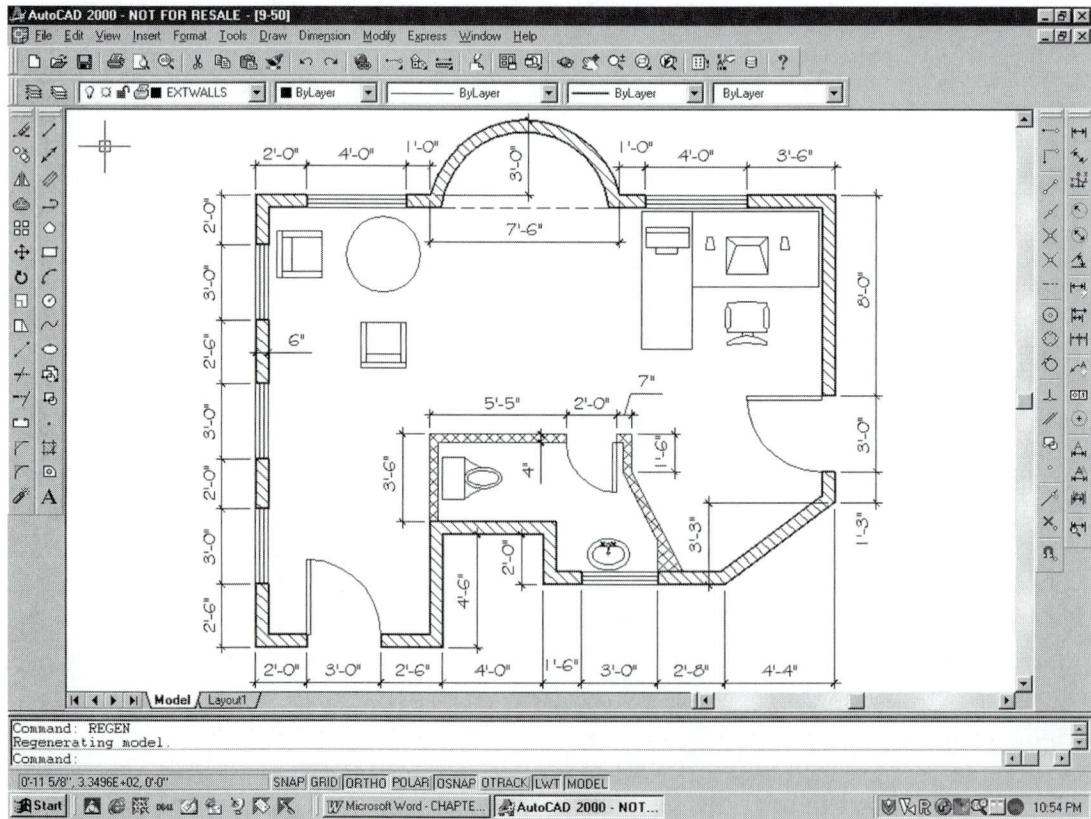

CHAPTER 10

Multiple Design Environment and AutoCAD DesignCenter

After successful completion of this chapter you should be able to:

▲ Use Multiple Design Environment to open multiple drawings in a single AutoCAD session.

▲ Use Windows Explorer to open multiple drawings.

▲ Use Windows clipboard to copy and paste objects between drawings.

▲ Use Windows edit options.

▲ Drag and drop objects between drawings.

▲ Understand left-click and right-click operations.

▲ Use AutoCAD DesignCenter to copy and insert drawing content between drawings.

▲ Utilize DesignCenter toolbar.

10.1 THE MULTIPLE DESIGN ENVIRONMENT (MDE)

In a high-tech architectural design and production environment it is becoming more and more important to increase productivity through faster and improved access to multiple CAD files. AutoCAD by default allows you to view and work with multiple drawings opened in one session through a feature called Multiple Design Environment. Without sacrificing data speed, you can transfer and copy drawing information using traditional Windows editing features in Multiple Design Environment or by utilizing the AutoCAD DesignCenter (ADC). The MDE allows you to perform the following tasks:

- Open multiple drawings in one AutoCAD session.
- Work across open multiple drawings.
- Tile drawing window horizontally or vertically or cascade or arrange icons at the bottom of the window.
- Drag-and-drop files and objects between drawings or from Windows Explorer.
- Cut, copy, and paste objects from one drawing to another as objects or blocks using Windows clipboard. Specify a basepoint or use current coordinate points between drawings.
- Work and switch between drawings without losing the current command.
- Use the Match Properties button in the Standard toolbar to edit properties across drawings progressively. This procedure enables interaction from one drawing to another concurrent drawing window. Match Properties button is discussed in Chapter 13.

You can switch from MDE to Single Document Interface (SDI) using the SDI system variable. By default the SDI system variable is set to 0. When the SDI system variable is set to 1, you can only open one drawing per session. You can also control this feature by using the Options dialog box as follows:

1. From the Tools pull-down menu select Options . . .
2. Inside the Options dialog box select the System tab.
3. In the General Options category, click on the Single-drawing Compatibility mode as shown in Figure 10–1. This will turn SDI on.
4. Click on the Apply button and then click on the OK button.

10.1.1   Opening Multiple Drawings using the Select File Dialog Box

You can select two or more files while holding down the ~CtrlKey~ inside the Select File dialog box as shown in Figure 10–2. When you have selected the files, click on the Open button. AutoCAD will open those files for you one after another. You can also open each file one at a time. These files along with unnamed files (Drawing1, Drawing2, and so on) are listed individually under the Window pull-down menu. To view multiple drawings that are open, click on the Window pull-down menu. Figure 10–3 shows three files open in one AutoCAD session. The drawings that are open are given a number. A checkmark in front of a file indicates the currently viewed file. There are three different ways you can display the three files shown in Figure 10–3.

Cascade: This method will cascade the drawings and stack them on top of each other as shown in Figure 10–4. The drawing with the blue title bar is the active drawing. You can perform normal AutoCAD operations on the active drawing. You can click on the title bar or the drawing area of the inactive file to bring it to the front and make it the active drawing. You can drag the files around the screen and resize the files to suit your needs. To resize the active drawing, move your cursor over to the horizontal or vertical edge of the drawing, wait until the cursor turns into a double arrow, then left-click and drag. There is, however, a minimum size and a maximum size limitation. The maximum size in either direction depends on your monitor size. A 21″ monitor will show more drawing area than a 15″ monitor, and you can only have one drawing current at a time. You can minimize or maximize any or all of the drawings to suit your needs.

FIGURE 10–1   The System tab of the Options dialog box will allow you to switch from MDE to SDI.

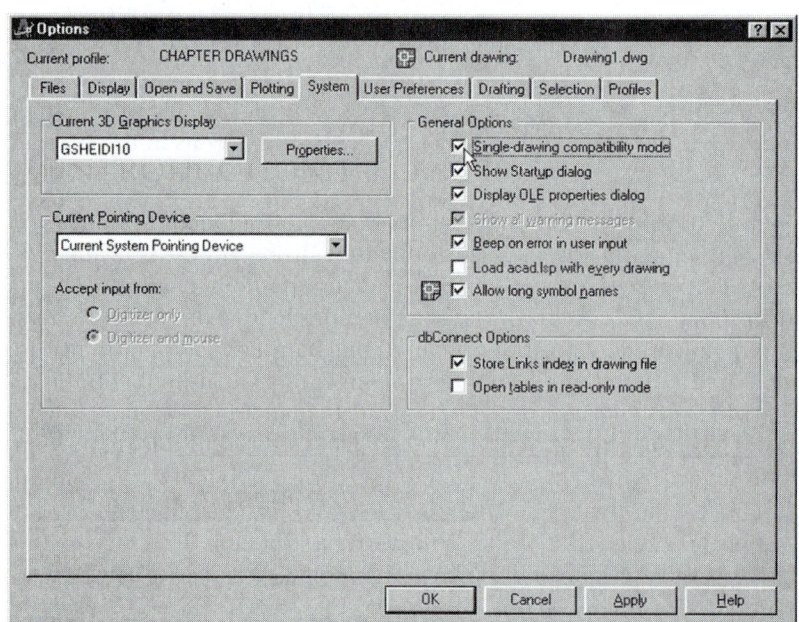

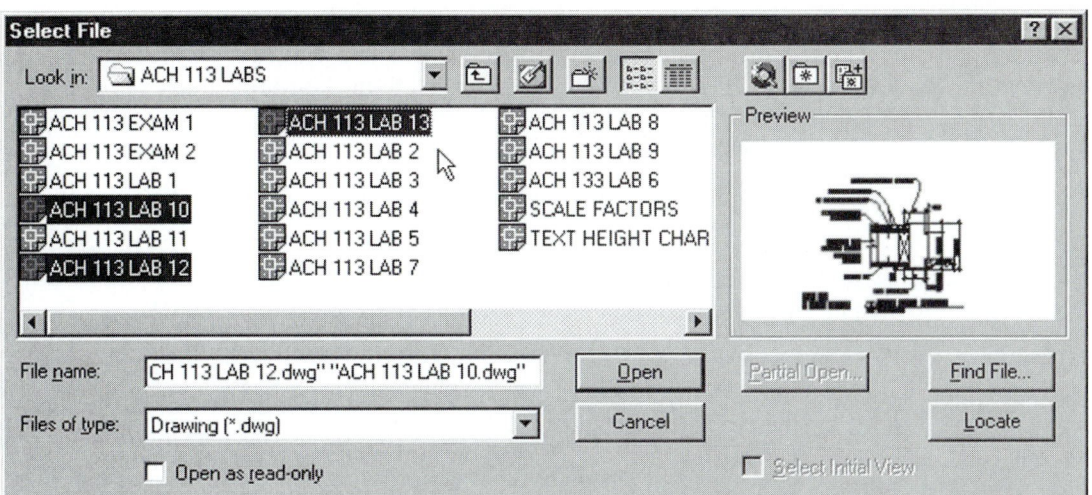

FIGURE 10–2 When using the Select File dialog box, you can select more than one file to open by holding down the ~CtrlKey~.

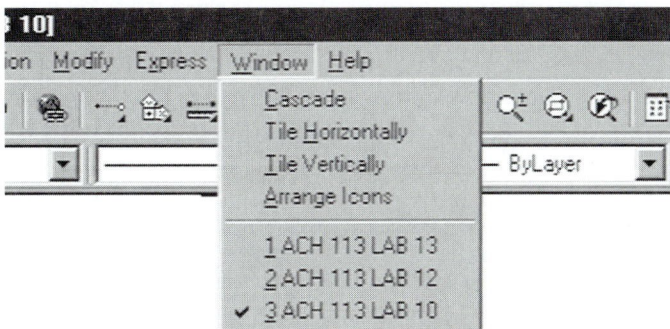

FIGURE 10–3 To view the open drawings, click on the Window pull-down menu.

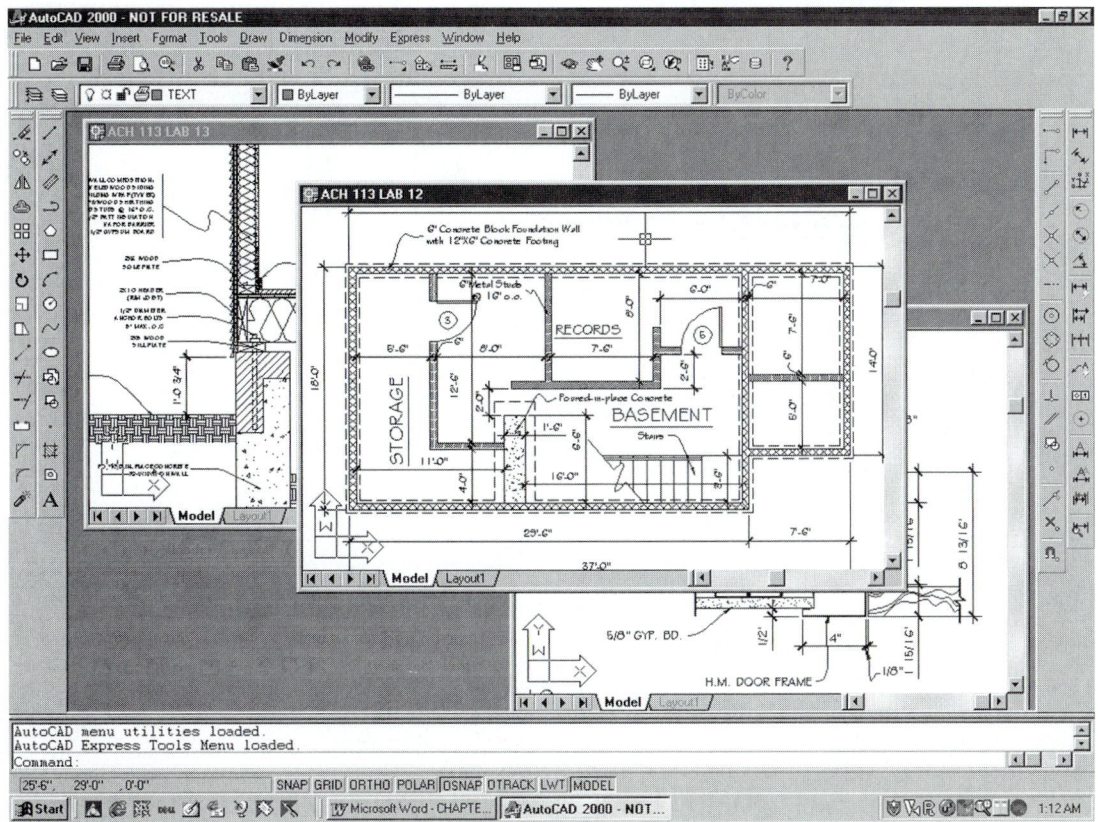

FIGURE 10–4 The Cascade option will stack the drawings. You can move them, resize them, minimize, or maximize.

Tile Horizontally: This method will open the drawings in a horizontal tile format. You can re-arrange files to meet your individual needs. Figure 10–5 shows two drawings on the left side and one drawing made larger on the right side. All file manipulations described above apply to this and other methods also. Notice that each drawing is an individual file containing all of the AutoCAD drawing components.

Tile Vertically: This method will display the drawings vertically next to each other as shown in Figure 10–6.

Tips: You can also switch between drawings by pressing ~CtrlKey~ + ~F6Key~ and ~CtrlKey~ + ~TabKey~. You can also activate the Window pull-down menu by pressing the ~AltKey~ +W.

There are two vocabularies associated with the MDE and the ADC as follows:

- **THE SOURCE DRAWING**   refers to the file where the object selection is performed. In other words the file where objects are selected for inserting or copying. The selected object's file becomes the origin of the source.

- **THE TARGET DRAWING**   refers to the file where the selected objects are moved or copied to. In other words the final destination for the source.

10.1.2   Opening Multiple Documents Using the Windows Explorer

You can open multiple drawings using the Windows Explorer. To access Windows Explorer, click on the Start button found in the lower left corner of your screen. From the Programs area, se-lect Windows Explorer or Windows NT Explorer as shown in Figure 10–7. If the Windows Ex-plorer comes up maximized (full-screen), click on the restore button. The restore button is the button between − (minimize) and × (maximize). You can move and resize Windows Explorer as shown in Figure 10–8.

FIGURE 10–5   A rearranged version of the Tile Horizontally file-viewing method.

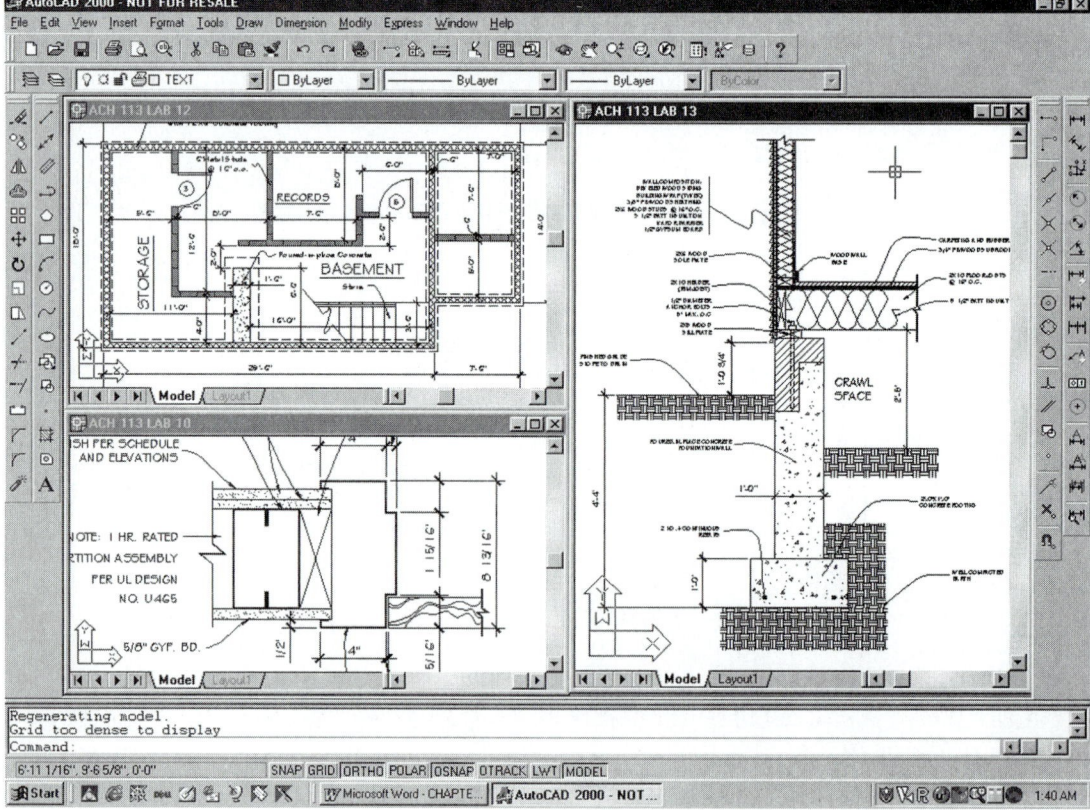

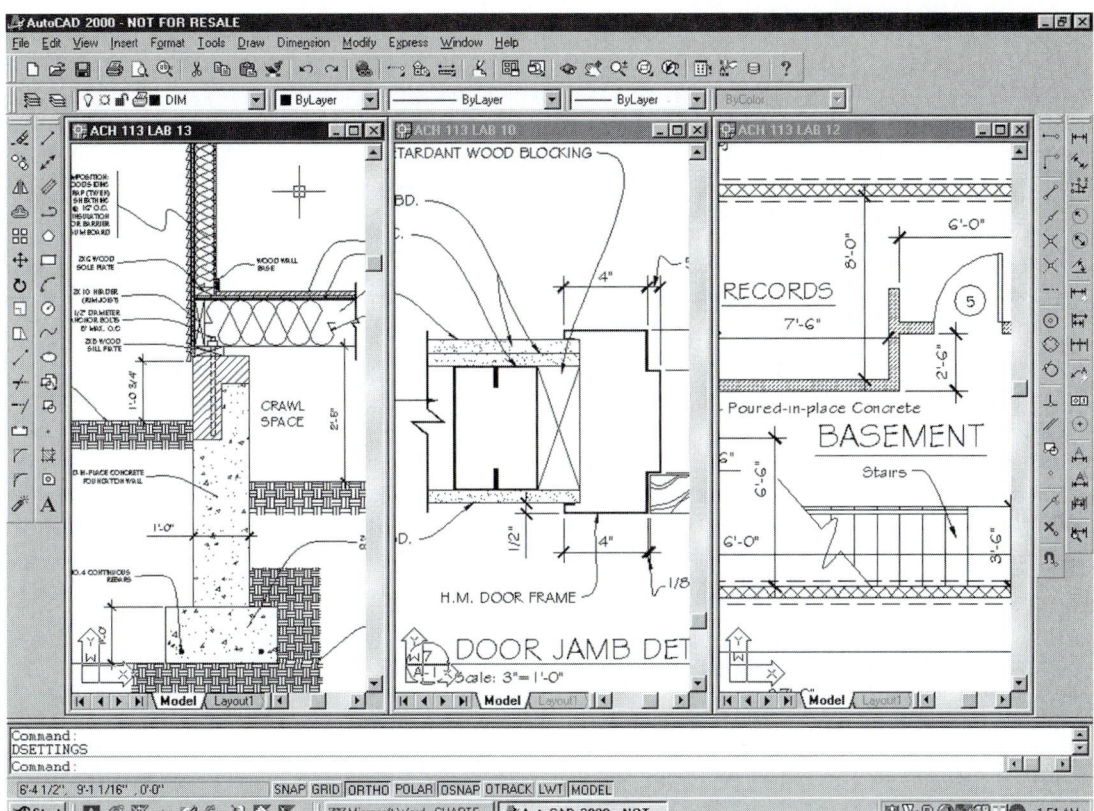

FIGURE 10–6 The Tile Vertically display option.

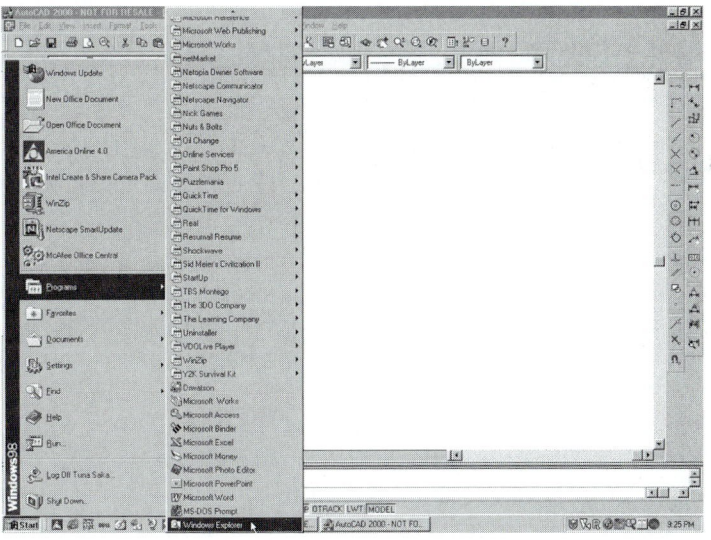

FIGURE 10–7 Accessing Windows Explorer from the Start button. If you have a shortcut icon in your desktop, click on show desktop and select the icon from your desktop.

Inside the *directory tree* area and under All Folders, find the folder containing the drawings you want to open. Click on the folder to show its contents. Creating folders and managing files are discussed in Chapter 15. The contents of the selected folder will appear in the *contents of the current folder* area (right side of the *divider bar*). You can select one or more files and use left or right click to insert or open drawings into the open AutoCAD window. The choices are as follows:

Right-click Single File: First left-click on the file to highlight it, then right-click on the file and drag and drop inside open AutoCAD window. A shortcut menu with five options will appear as

FIGURE 10–8 Resized Windows Explorer with the appropriate folder selected. Notice the contents of the folder are displayed on the right side.

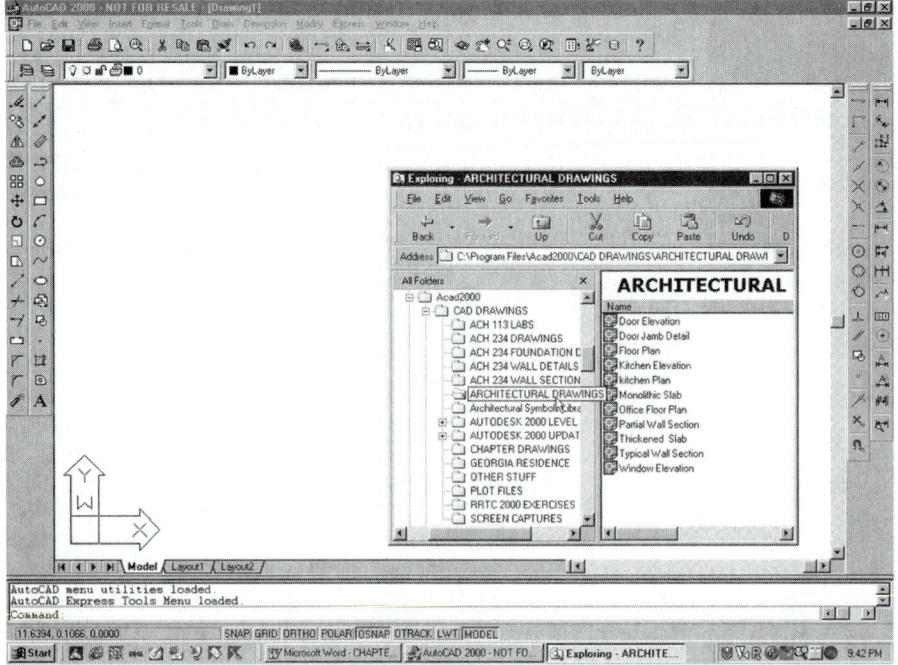

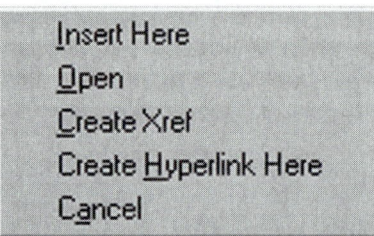

FIGURE 10–9 After you drag and drop a file, the shortcut will appear.

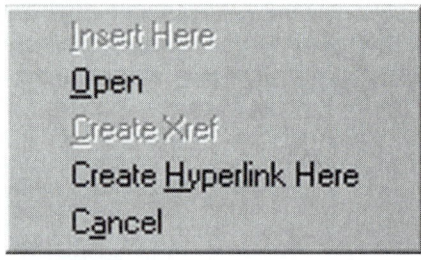

FIGURE 10–10 When you drag and drop multiple files, the shortcut menu options will be limited.

shown in Figure 10–9. The *Insert Here* option will allow you to insert the file as a block. Blocks are discussed in Chapter 19. AutoCAD will ask you for an insertion point, scale, and rotation angle. The *Open* option will allow you to drop and open the file. The *Create xref* option will insert the file as an externally referenced file format (xref). Externally referenced files are discussed in Chapter 24. The *Create Hyperlink Here* option will attach a hyperlink to a selected object. You must have existing objects in the drawing to select. The *Cancel* option will cancel the entire operation. Click on the option of your choice.

Right-click Multiple Files: Select the drawing files by holding down the ~ShiftKey~ or the ~CtrlKey~. The selected drawings will be highlighted. Right-click on one of the drawings and drag and drop these files into the open AutoCAD window. A shortcut menu will appear as shown in Figure 10–10. Notice that with multiple openings, *Insert* and *xref* options are not available. Select the *Open* option and AutoCAD will open all the selected drawings one at a time. The first file selected will be displayed as the current file. To view all opened drawings, select one of the options from the Window pull-down menu as described above.

Left-click Single File: Left-click on one file and drag and drop. This will insert the file as a block definition. Specify the insertion point and X and Y scale factors and specify the rotation angle to open the file. If the file is not visible, enter zoom at the command line, then enter extents.

Left-click of multiple files with drag and drop are not allowed. You can repeat the left-click single file procedure for more than one file to insert many files.

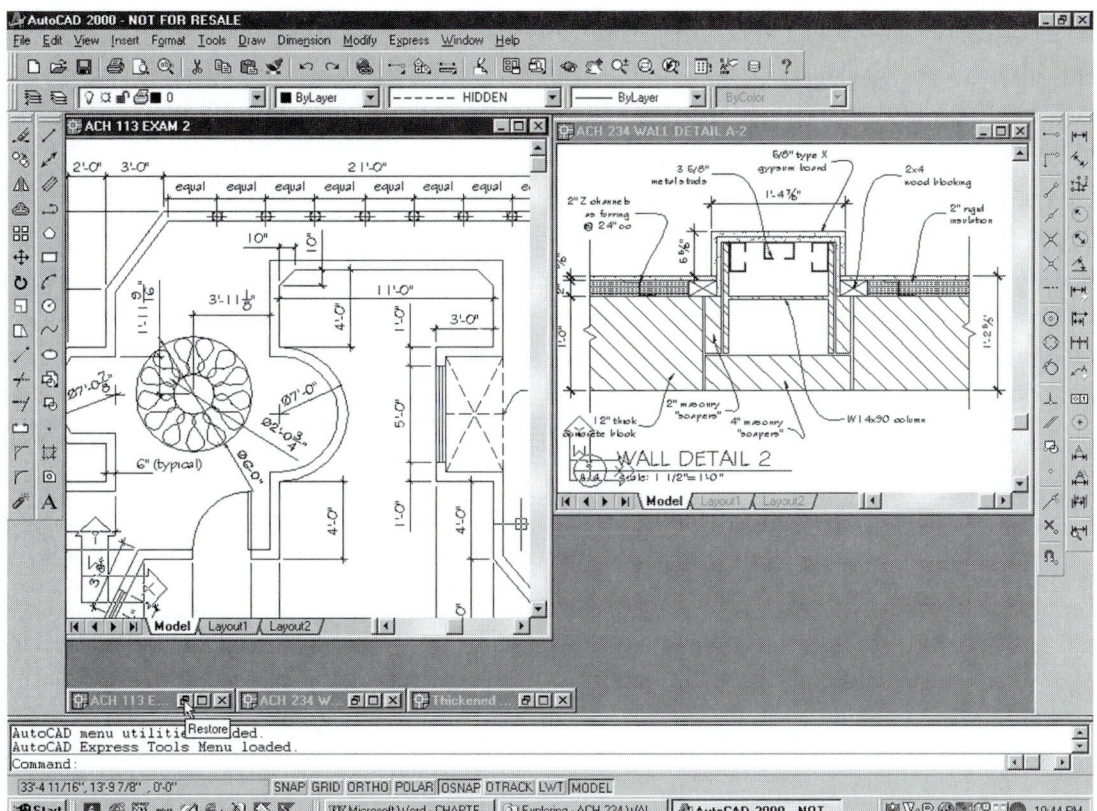

FIGURE 10–11 You can minimize some of the open files to increase window size of other files.

Caution: Inserting files as blocks may not be desirable at certain conditions. When a file is inserted as a block it behaves as a single object. In order to edit individual segments, you have to explode the entire file. Refer to Chapter 19 for more information about Blocks.

Caution: You cannot stack files side-by-side or on top of each other indefinitely. Depending on your monitor size, viewing more than four drawings at once becomes impractical because of their small size.

Tips: You can drag and drop other files into AutoCAD, such as Microsoft Word documents, raster images, etc . . .

You can minimize one or more of the open files to increase the size of one drawing and when you want to put one or more drawings on hold. Minimized drawings are displayed as window icons in the lower section of the drawing as shown in Figure 10–11. You can restore the minimized file to its original position by left clicking on the restore (first control) button.

> **AutoCAD 2000i Update:** *Use the CLOSEALL command to close all your open drawings at once. AutoCAD will prompt you to save when needed.*

10.2 WORK ACROSS DRAWINGS

Each open file is an independent drawing having its own command history. Switching from one drawing to another will not cancel the command you are working with. For example, you can use the LINE command to draw lines in one file, switch to another file without completing the line command use another command in that file, then come back to the first file. The line command will still be active for you to finish. You can use the Match Properties button across drawings to copy the properties of one object to one or more objects. This is explained in Chapter 13.

10.3 COPYING INFORMATION BETWEEN DRAWINGS

Having multiple drawings open makes it convenient to copy and paste objects from one drawing to another. There are two different ways to accomplish this: Copying and Pasting using Windows Clipboard and Drag and Drop Copying.

10.3.1 Copying and Pasting Using Windows Clipboard

You can place information on the Windows clipboard by using the Cut or Copy options from a source drawing. You can then paste that information from the clipboard into a target drawing. Cut, Copy, and Paste operations can be done using the Edit pull-down menu, Standard toolbar, or right-click menu.

- **CUT:**   The Cut option places objects to the clipboard and removes them from the source content. You can use the Cut to Clipboard button located in the Standard toolbar, select Cut from the Edit pull-down menu, right-click on the selected object(s), or enter CUTCLIP at the command line.

- **COPY:**   Copy option leaves the selected objects from the source drawing intact and copies them to the clipboard. AutoCAD uses the lower left corner of the selected object as the base point when copying the object from source drawing to target drawing. You will see the left corner of the object attached to the cursor when copying occurs. You can use the Copy to Clipboard button in the Standard toolbar, select Copy from the Edit pull-down menu, right-click on the selected object(s) and select Copy from the shortcut menu, or enter COPYCLIP at the command line.

- **COPY WITH BASE POINT:**   This option allows you to select the base point of the object from the source drawing after selecting the object. This option gives you more control over the precise location of the base point. You can use the Copy with Base Point from the Edit pull-down menu, right-click on the selected object(s) and select Copy with Base Point, or enter COPYBASE at the command line.

- **PASTE:**   Paste option places the selected object inside the target drawing with the lower left corner of the object at the location you specify. You can use the Paste from Clipboard button in the Standard toolbar, select Paste from the Edit pull-down menu, right-click on the selected object(s) and select Paste from the shortcut menu, or enter PASTECLIP at the command line.

- **PASTE AS BLOCK:**   This option is similar to Paste except the object from the source drawing is inserted into the target drawing as a block. The drawings inserted from one drawing into another in this fashion are assigned an arbitrary name such as A$C4E9426AA. To check the assigned name, enter list at the command line and select the inserted object. You can always rename it later. This option only works when the objects from the source drawing placed on the clipboard are AutoCAD objects. You can select Paste as Block from the Edit pull-down menu, right-click on the selected object(s) and select Paste as Block from the shortcut menu, or enter PASTEBLOCK at the command line.

- **PASTE TO ORIGINAL COORDINATES:**   This option places the objects on the target drawing at the same coordinates as they were in the source drawing. Select this option from the Edit pull-down, right-click on the selected object(s) and select Paste to Original Coordinates from the shortcut menu, or enter PASTEORIG at the command line.

Note: When objects are copied or inserted from the source drawing into the target drawing they retain their original size regardless of the drawing scale and units of the source and the target drawing.

Tips: You can use Paste as Block in the same source drawing to create a new block definition for the object selected. This method of making a Block is faster than using the Block Definition dialog box discussed in Chapter 19, but you may need to rename the block. Use the RENAME command to change the block name.

Tips: You can maximize the source drawing and minimize the target drawing when selecting objects so that the source drawing covers the entire AutoCAD window area. This will make the object selection process more effective. Then you can switch to the source drawing by selecting it from the Window pull-down menu or restore it from its minimized state.

Tips: Place a window around the objects to select or use the pickbox to select individual objects. If you cannot place a window around the objects, make sure that the PICKAUTO system variable is set to on.

Tips: If the objects are not displayed after copying and pasting into the target drawing, zoom to the Limits or to the Extents of the target drawing.

Caution: You cannot use the AutoCAD COPY command to copy objects from source drawing into target drawing.

■ **EXERCISE 10–1:** *The following is a step-by-step exercise that will help you copy the table and two chairs from the source drawing 10–1A to the target drawing 10–1B as shown in Figure 10–12. The right-click shortcut menu procedure will be used for copying and pasting.*

Step #1: Open the *EXE10-1A.dwg* file. This is the *source* drawing.

Step #2: Open the *EXE10-1B.dwg* file. This is the *target* drawing.

Step #3: Using the Windows pull-down menu, tile the two drawings vertically.

Step #4: Make source drawing active. Place a window around two chairs and the table. The selected objects will display small squares, called grips. You can also left-click on the objects to select individually.

Step #5: Right-click in the drawing area and select Copy from the shortcut menu as shown in Figure 10–13.

Step #6: Move your cursor to the target drawing and left-click in the drawing area. This will make the target drawing active.

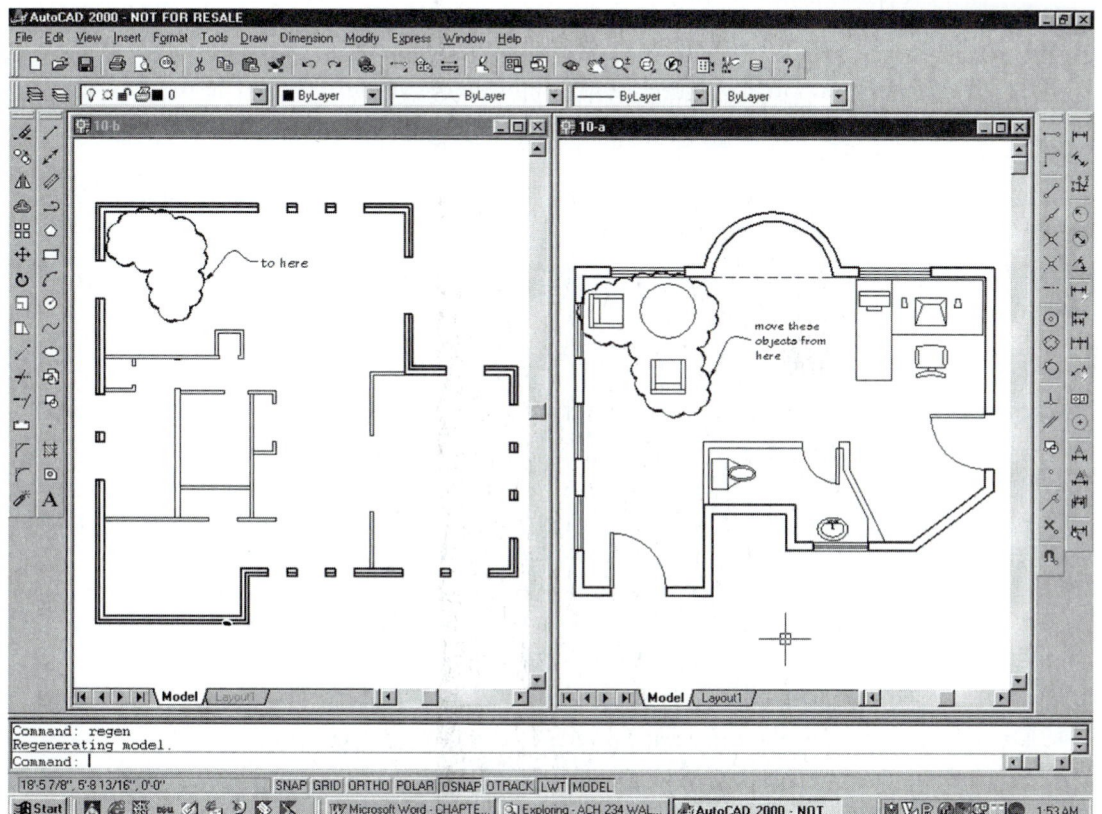

FIGURE 10–12 The table and two chairs from the source drawing (10–12A) will be copied and pasted into the target drawing (10–12B) using the right-click shortcut menu.

FIGURE 10–13
Selecting the objects in the source drawing and using the right-click shortcut menu to copy.

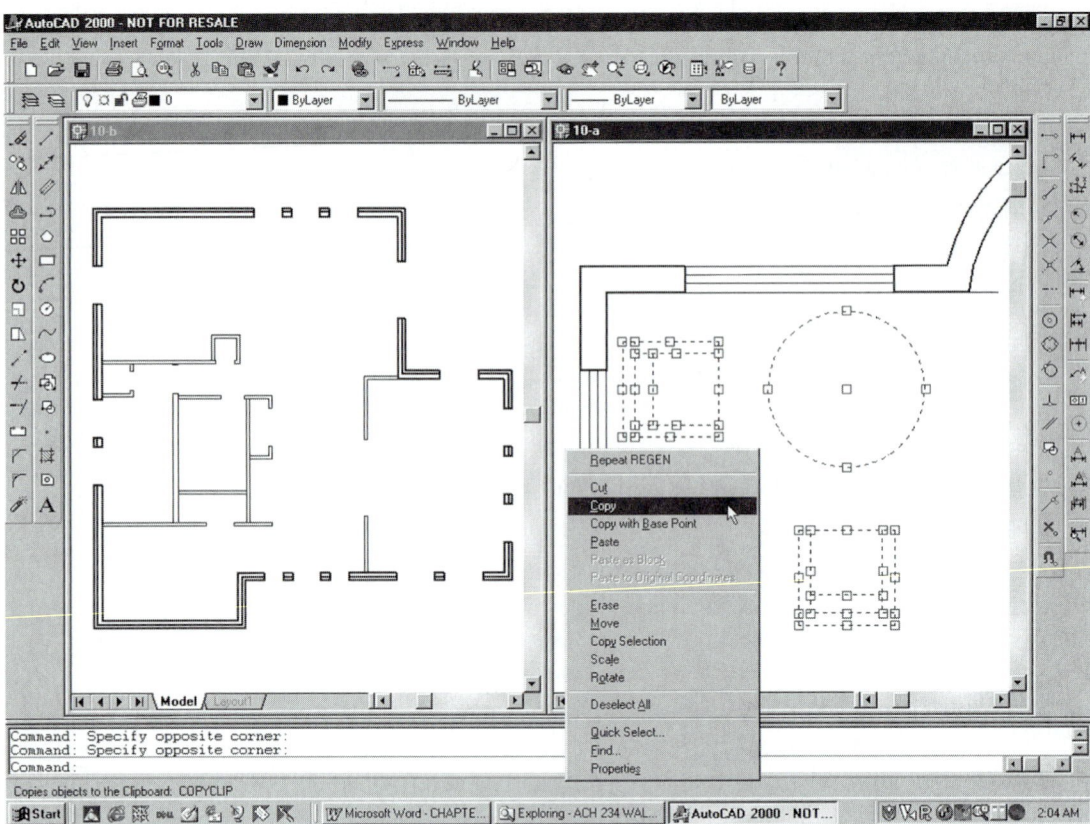

Step #7: Right-click in the target drawing area and select Paste from the shortcut menu as shown in Figure 10–14. The objects will be attached to the cursor. Notice the lower left corner of the window as the insertion point.

Step #8: Move your cursor to the appropriate place and left-click. The objects will be copied from the source drawing to the target drawing as shown in Figure 10–15.

Congratulations! You have successfully used the MDE to copy and paste objects from a source drawing to a target drawing.

Note: You could also use Paste as Block option of the right-click shortcut menu to insert the objects as a Block.

10.3.2   Copying Using Drag-and-Drop

You can also drag-and-drop objects to copy from the source drawing to the target drawing. There are some important rules you must follow for the drag-and-drop operation to work properly as follows:

1. Left-click object(s) to select. All available grips will be displayed as small squares. If an object is a block or consists of many entities, there will be a lot of grips displayed.

2. Hold down the left mouse button and select the object(s) to be copied. Do not select a grip. You might have to zoom in very close to the object so that you do not select one of the small squares (grips) while selecting the object.

3. Drag the object(s) while holding down the left mouse button.

4. Drag the object(s) to the target drawing and release the mouse button.

5. You cannot drop objects into a target drawing that has a command running.

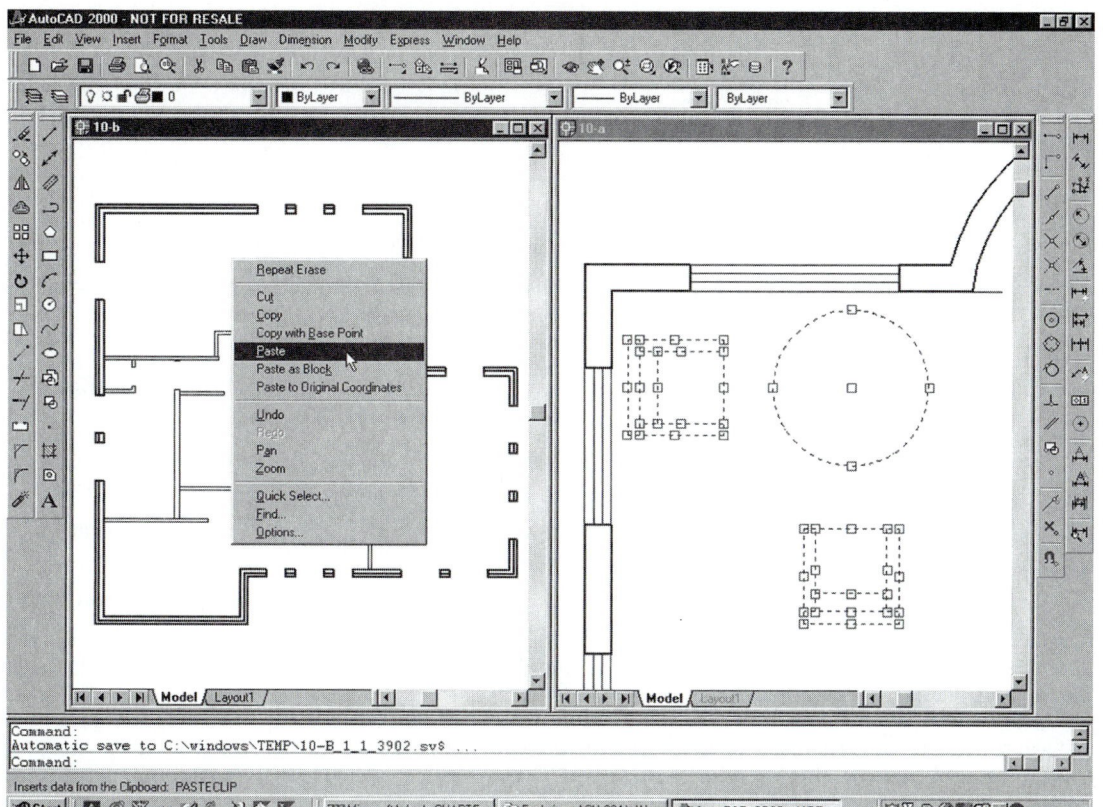

FIGURE 10–14 Right-clicking in the target drawing and using the shortcut menu to paste.

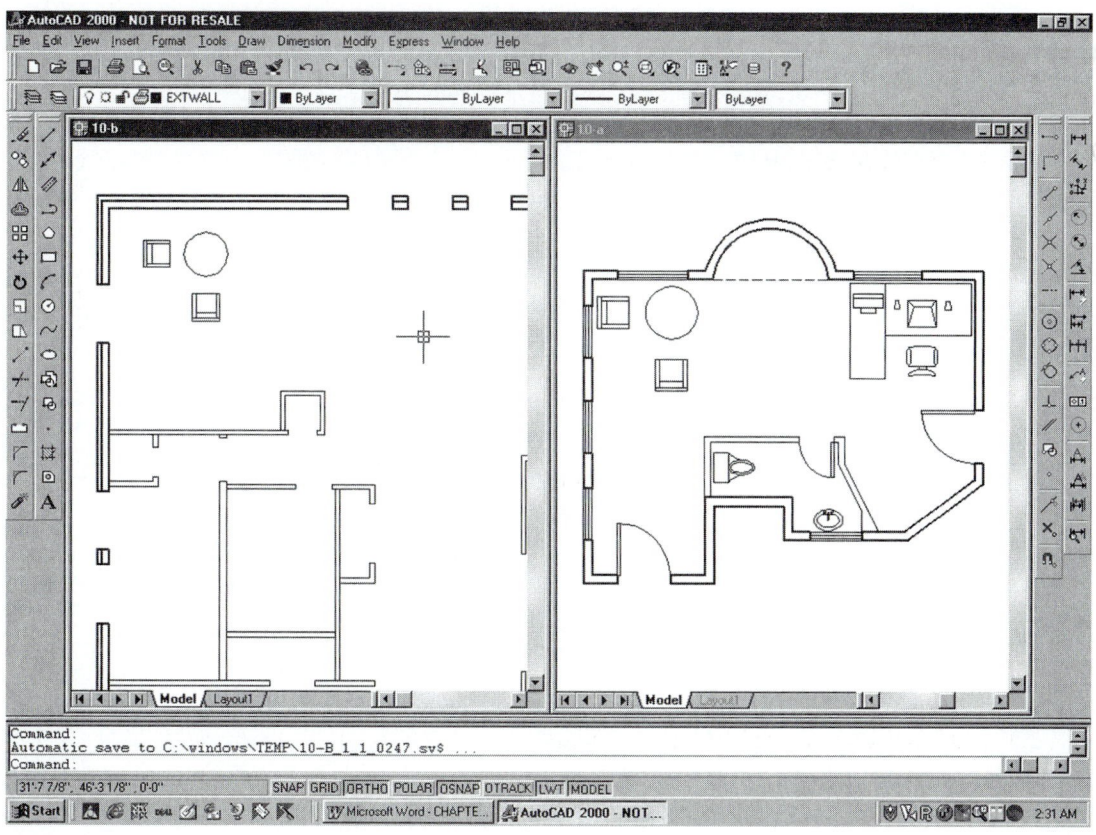

FIGURE 10–15 The table and two chairs are copied from source drawing to target drawing.

■ **EXERCISE 10–2:** *The following is a step-by-step exercise that will help you copy the trees and the bushes from the source drawing 10–1C to the target drawing 10–1D as shown in Figure 10–16. The drag-and-drop method will be used to create the site plan for the proposed SERKAN residence as shown in Figure 10–19.*

Step #1: Open the *EXE10-1C.dwg* file. This is the *source* drawing.

Step #2: Open the *EXE10-1D.dwg* file. This is the *target* drawing.

Step #3: Using the Windows pull-down menu, tile the two drawings vertically.

Step #4: Make source drawing active. Zoom-in close to a group of trees. Select the tree cluster as shown in Figure 10–17. Grips are discussed in Chapter 13. This will display one or more grips as part of a block.

Step #5: Select one of the trees and hold down the left mouse button. Make sure that you do not select the grip.

Step #6: Drag the trees while holding down the left mouse button to the target drawing.

Step #7: Locate the correct placement in the target drawing and release the left mouse button. The trees will be copied as shown in Figure 10–18.

Step #8: Repeat the above procedure to copy more trees and bushes into the target drawing. Figure 10–19 shows the development of the proposed SERKAN residence site plan with trees and bushes dragged and dropped from the source drawing.

Congratulations! You have successfully used the MDE to drag and drop objects from a source drawing to a target drawing.

Note: Refer to Chapter 19 for more exercises on using the MDE with Blocks.

FIGURE 10–16 The trees and bushes in the source drawing (10–1C) will be copied by drag and drop method into the target drawing (10–1D).

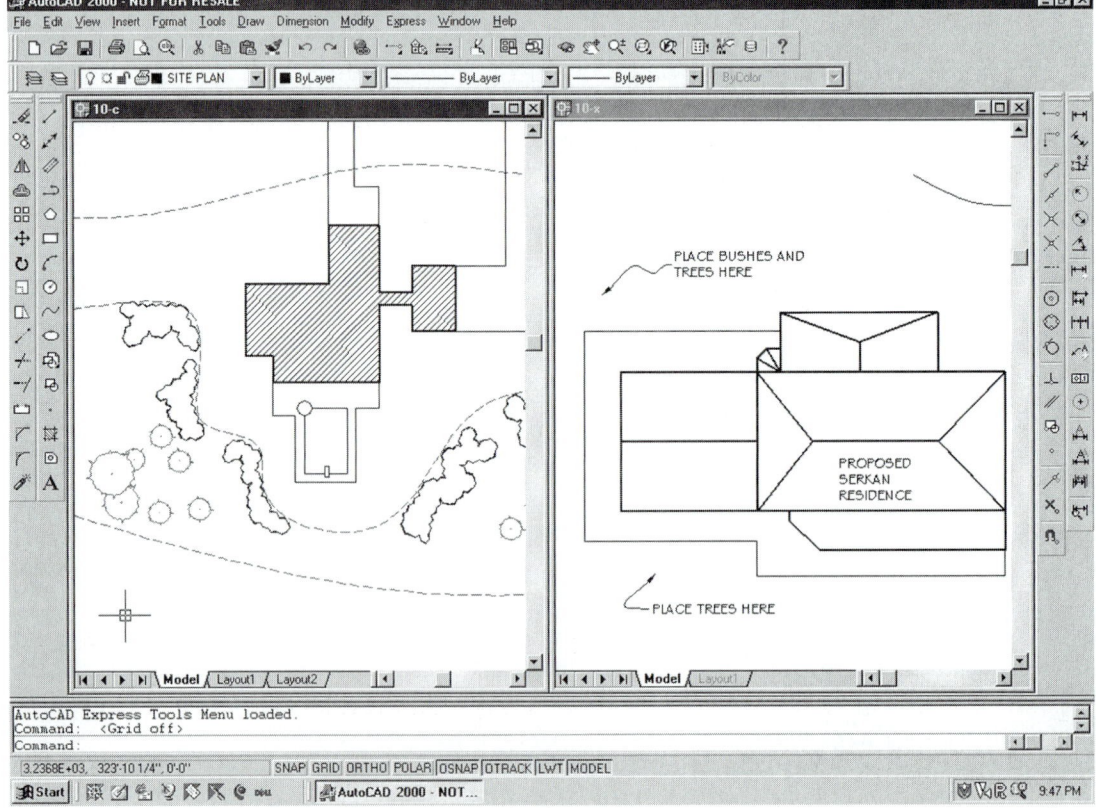

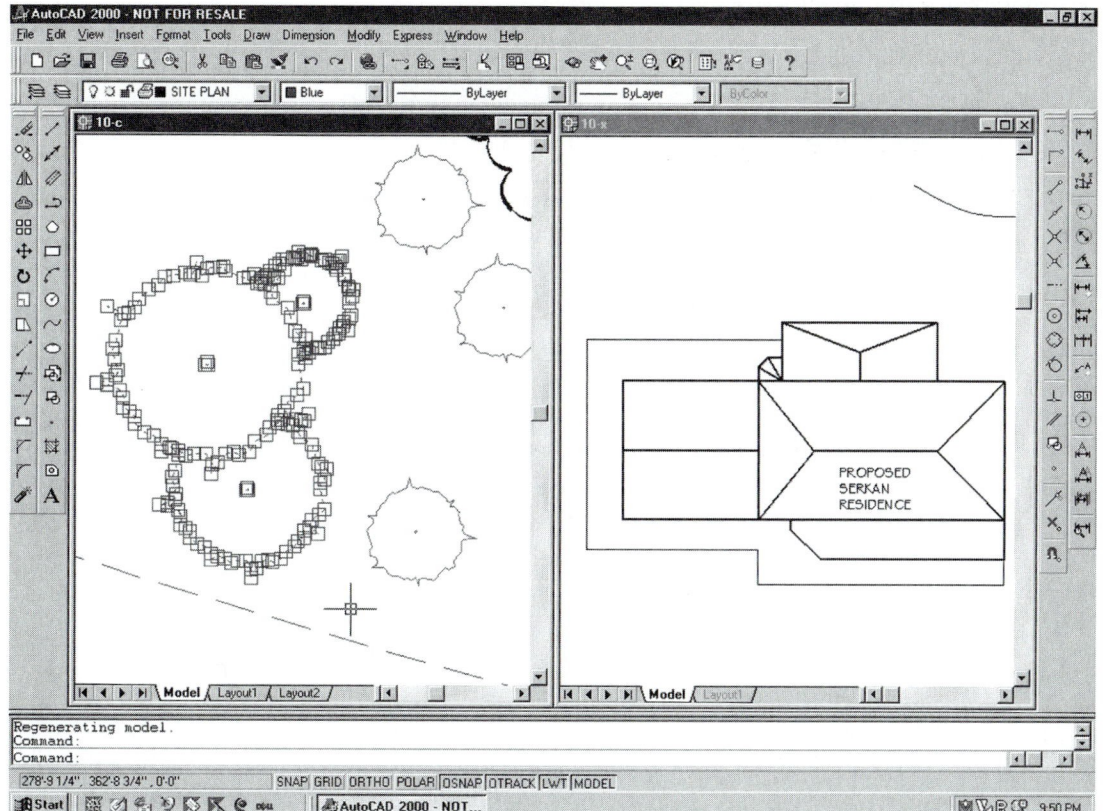

FIGURE 10–17
Selected trees will display many grips. Do not select a grip to drag and drop; select a line entity on the object.

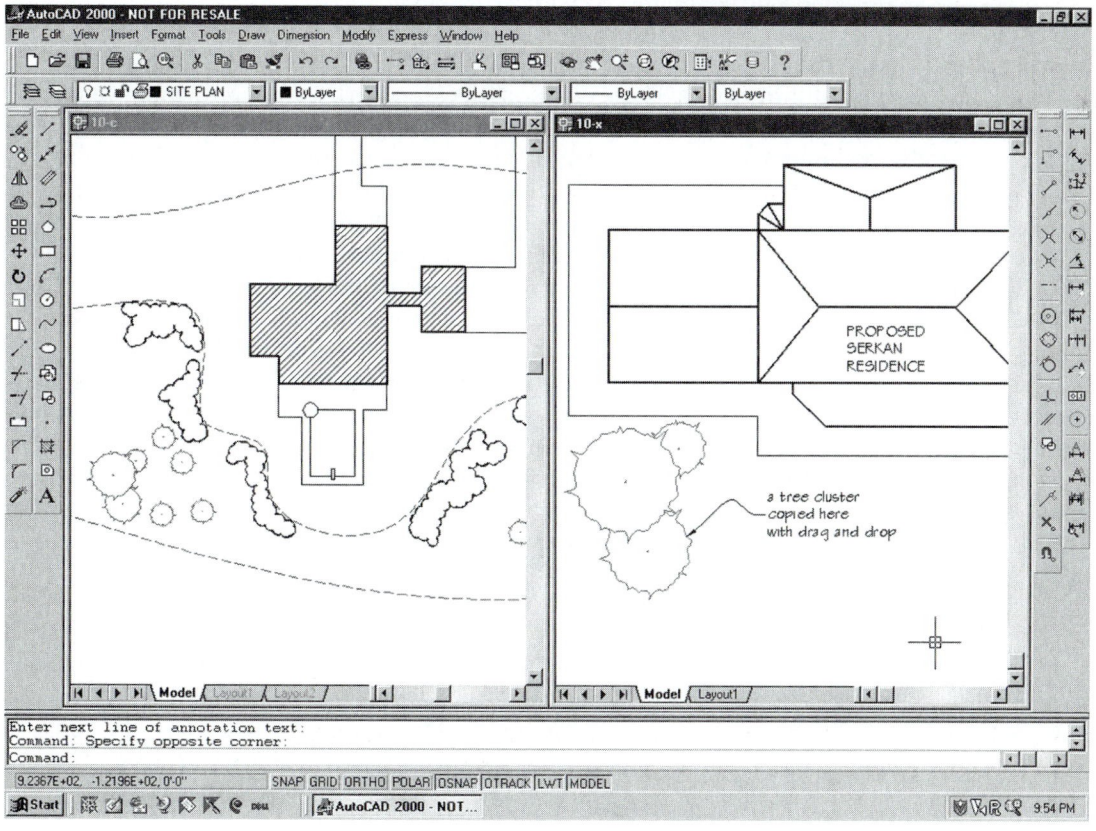

FIGURE 10–18 The selected trees after drag and drop will be copied to the target drawing.

FIGURE 10–19 The site plan for the proposed SERKAN residence. All trees and bushes are copied with drag and drop from the source drawing.

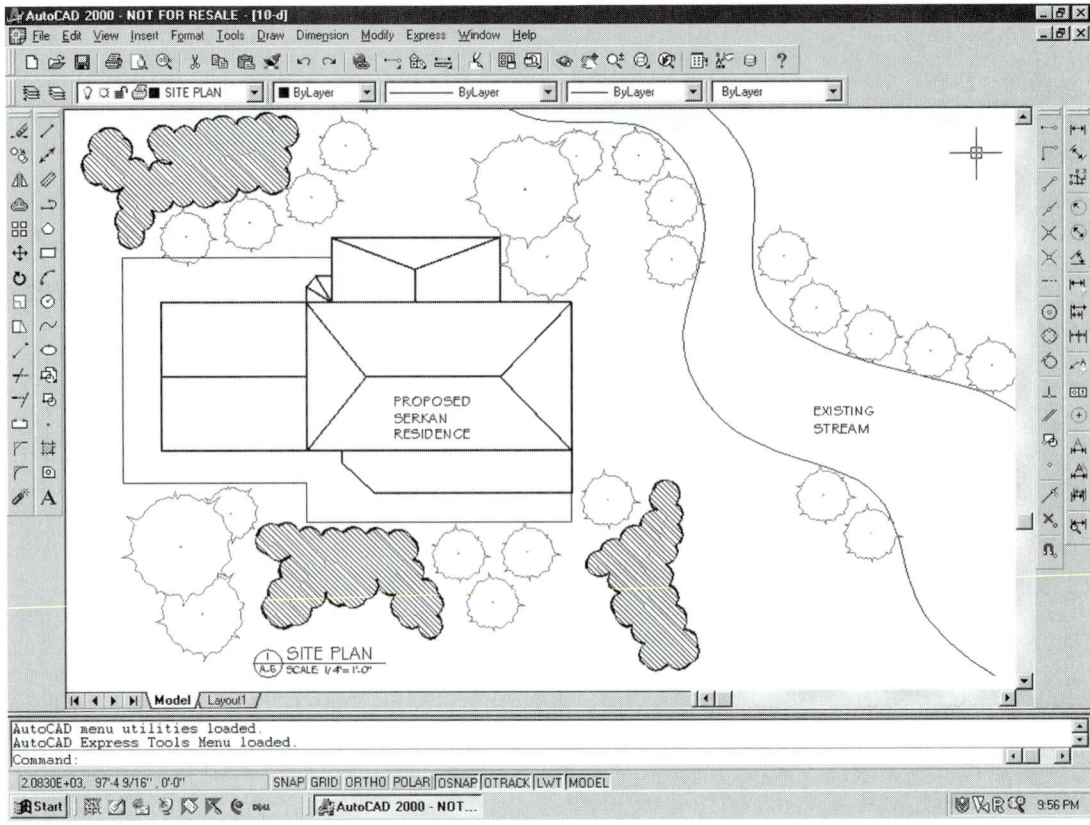

10.4 THE AutoCAD DESIGNCENTER (ADC)

Streamlining information through customization is a significant part of AutoCAD design and drafting tasks. A great deal of time is spent on creating *blocks, dimension styles, layers, layouts, linetypes,* and *text styles* for drawings. These components are referred to as *drawing content* and are also known as *dependent symbols* and reside in the drawing file they are created in. The key to harnessing the maximum potential of AutoCAD is to share these components between drawings. In particular, the time-consuming creation of layers, blocks, and dimension styles take up a significant portion of initial set-up and organization time. When you create individual drawings, you also create specific information and components to identify specific layers, blocks, linetypes, layouts, dimension, and text styles. ADC provides the means to transfer drawing content to other drawings so that you do not have to create them for each new drawing or project. In other words, ADC is a vehicle providing quick access to drawing content. Once accessed, the drawing content can be individually copied into the target drawing that needs the same dimension style, text style, block, layout, layers, and layouts. You no longer have to open Windows Explorer to drag and drop one file into another just so you can use its content. This is one of the most significant tools of AutoCAD that you will be using to increase productivity and streamline design and production procedures.

The easy-to-use interface of ADC gives you the ability to:

1. Access files to copy drawing content to target drawings locally, on network drives, or globally through Internet access.

2. Use find and search to locate text, block descriptions, and/or project summary information. See Chapter 8 for creating drawing properties.

3. Add files and folders to the AutoCAD Favorites folder or create a new favorites folder.

4. Review icons created with block definitions before copying them into target drawing.

5. Access symbol libraries on a Web page.

6. View and attach raster image files.

There are three vocabularies associated with the ADC as follows:

- **DRAWING CONTENTS** include blocks, dimension styles, layers, layouts, linetypes, text styles, and xrefs.

- **TREE VIEW** is the left portion of the ADC used to locate drawing folders and files. This is the interface that provides instant access to drawing content, network, and the Web.

- **PALETTE** is the right portion of the ADC used to view drawing content of the selected file.

To access ADC, click on the AutoCAD DesignCenter button in the Standard toolbar, select DesignCenter from the Tools pull-down menu, enter ADCENTER at the command line, or press ~CtrlKey~ +2. The AutoCAD DesignCenter window will be displayed as shown in Figure 10–20. This is the docked default position of the ADC. You can move and resize ADC window the same way as you move and resize other AutoCAD Window elements. Do not shrink it to a point where it is difficult to see the palette or the tree areas. These areas must have enough visibility to find folders, files, and view content of files.

To float the DesignCenter window, click and drag the grab bar, or right-click on the grab bar and select Allow Docking as shown in Figure 10–21. Once the DesignCenter window is floated, you can resize it to suit your needs. The floating and resized DesignCenter window is shown in Figure 10–22. To dock a floating DesignCenter window, double click on the title bar or click and drag the title bar until it snaps to the side. To hide a docked or floating DesignCenter window, right-click on the title bar and select Hide. Then, click on the AutoCAD DesignCenter button to display it. To close the DesignCenter window, click on the × in the upper right corner of the title-bar or enter ADCCLOSE at the command line.

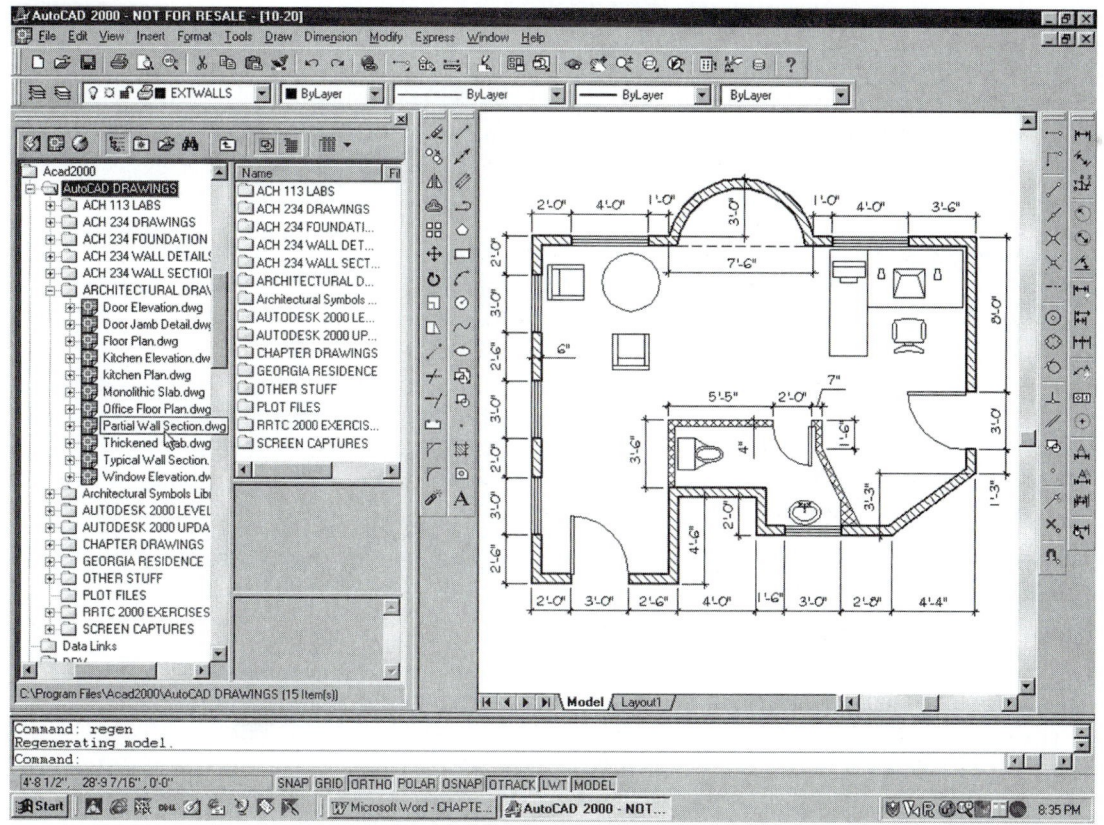

FIGURE 10–20 The AutoCAD DesignCenter window docked on the left side.

FIGURE 10–21   To float and resize DesignCenter, right-click on the grab bars and select Allow Docking. By default this item has a checkmark in front. You are simply removing it to allow docking.

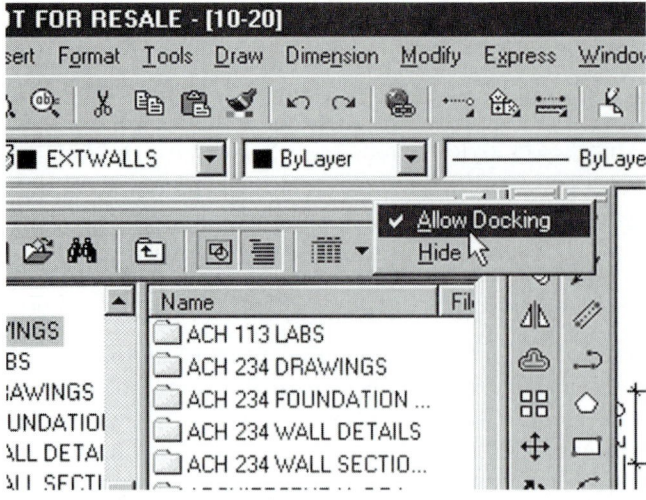

FIGURE 10–22   The DesignCenter can be floating and resized.

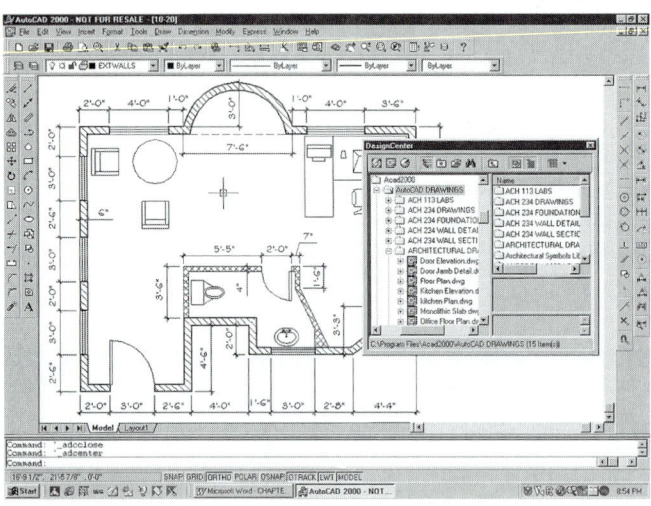

FIGURE 10–23   The 11 buttons of the DesignCenter toolbar.

You can also resize the tree view and the palette areas inside the DesignCenter. Move the vertical slider between the tree view and the palette.

Note: Changes made to the DesignCenter will be retained the next time you use it.

10.4.1   Autocad DesignCenter Toolbar

The DesignCenter toolbar is located across the top of the tree view and palette areas. The 11 buttons are used to control the contents of the DesignCenter and is shown in Figure 10–23.
They are explained as follows:

- **DESKTOP:**   This button will show the full Windows desktop allowing you to access files from anywhere in your computer and network drives. Use the tree view to locate the file and the drawing content you need as follows:

1. Select the + sign in front of the drive you want to search. For example, selecting the + sign in front of [C:] will list all the folders inside the C drive.

2. Select the + sign in front of the folder you want to search. For example, Figure 10–24 shows the Program Files folder as open and all the sub-folders that are under that folder. The − sign means that folder or drive is open and the contents shown below. Figure 10–25 shows the AutoCAD drawings inside the CHAPTER DRAWINGS folder. This folder is located inside another folder called AutoCAD DRAWINGS, which is located inside the Acad2000 folder. To list all drawing content inside a specific drawing, select the + sign in front of the file. For example, Figure 10–26 shows the drawing contents inside the 19-23.dwg file. If you highlight the file, the drawing content will also appear inside the palette as shown in Figure 10–26.

3. Inside the tree view, selecting the desired drawing content will display its contents inside the palette. Figure 10–27 shows the listing of all the blocks inside the palette area for the

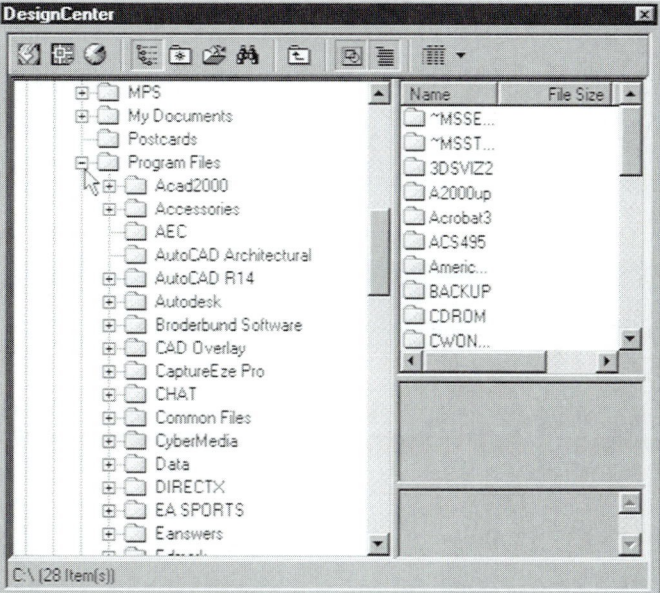

FIGURE 10–24 The tree view showing the hierarchy of the file structure.

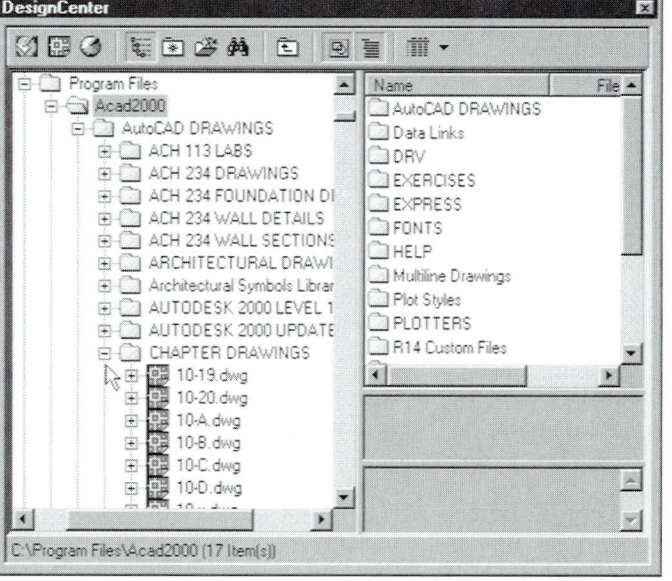

FIGURE 10–25 The AutoCAD drawing files listed under the CHAPTER DRAWINGS folder.

FIGURE 10–26 The drawing contents listed under the 19-23.dwg file. Notice the palette area listing.

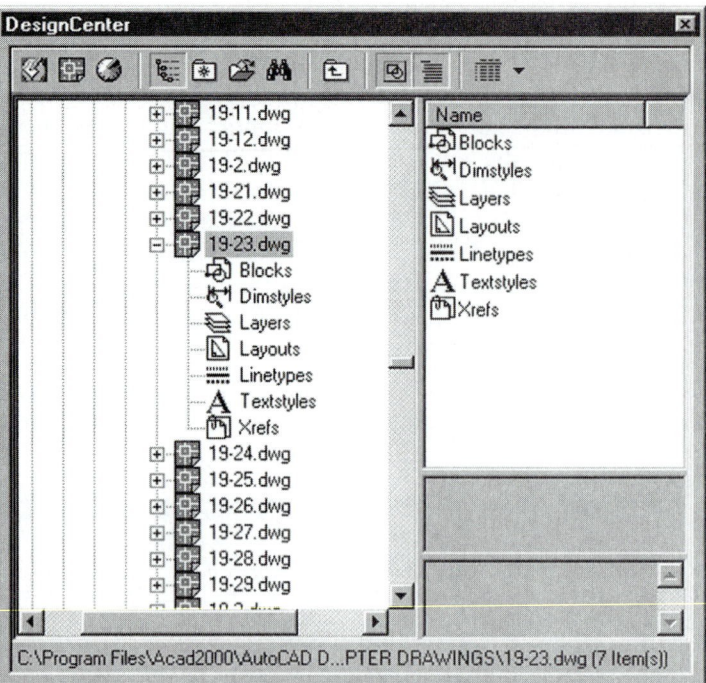

FIGURE 10–27 The listing of all the blocks under the 19-23.dwg file inside the palette area. Notice the door icon and the block description when the DOOR-3' is selected.

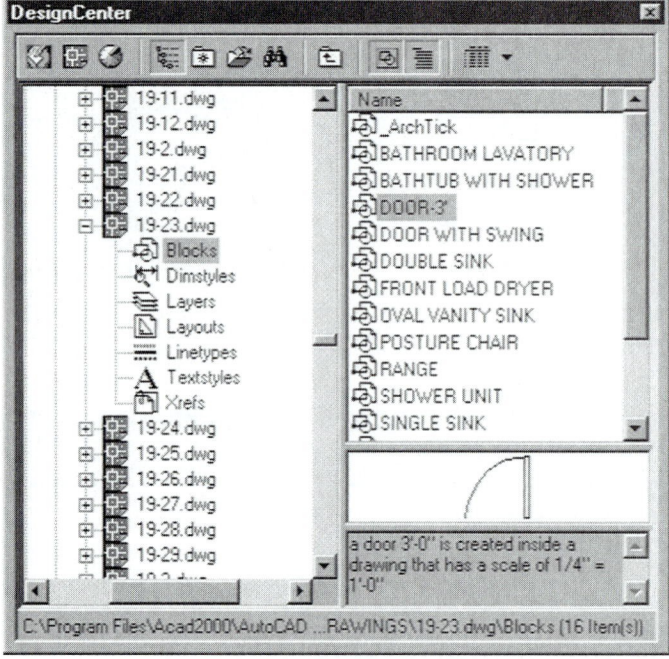

19-23.dwg file. The palette area will also show the icon created for the block and the block description. See Chapter 19 for Blocks.

4. Select the appropriate drawing content to see all the available dimension styles, layers, layouts, linetypes, text styles, and xrefs inside the file. Figure 10–28 lists all the layers created for the ACH 234 A-1 FIRST FLOOR PLAN drawing. Notice that the icon and description area is resized.

- **OPEN DRAWINGS:**   This button will list all drawing files currently open in AutoCAD.

- **HISTORY:**   This button will list all the files accessed throughout ADC operations as shown in Figure 10–29. Notice the palette area is not available with this option.

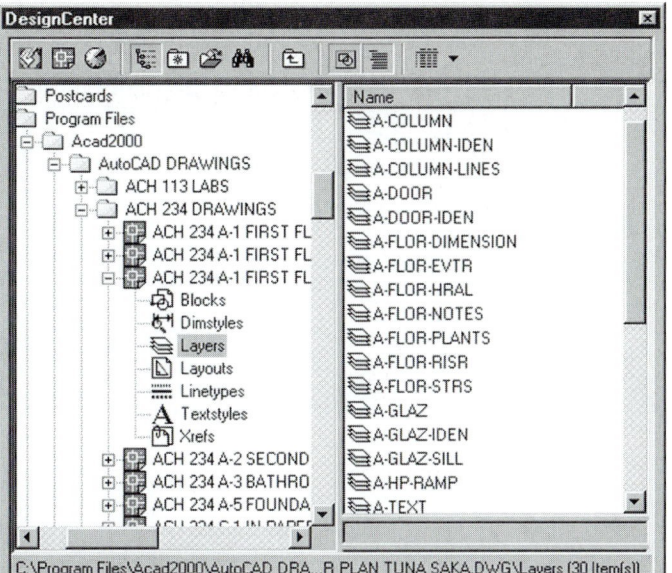

FIGURE 10–28 The listing of layers created for the ACH 234 A-1 FIRST FLOOR PLAN drawing.

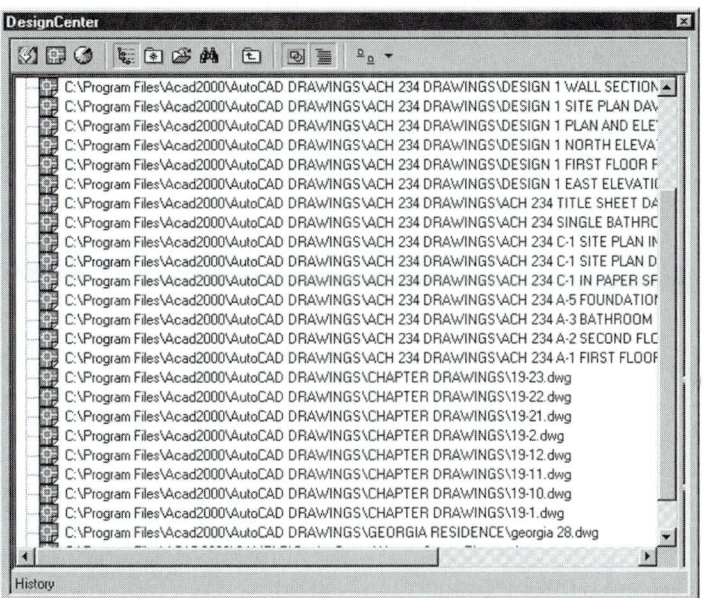

FIGURE 10–29 The History of all DesignCenter operations.

- **TREE TOGGLE VIEW:** This button will display or hide the tree view area.

- **FAVORITES:** This button will display shortcuts to files or folders located in the Favorites folder.

- **LOAD:** This button will display the Load DesignCenter Palette dialog box. Select a file to load into the DesignCenter. When a file is loaded, the tree view will expand to display the file.

- **FIND:** This is one of the most powerful DesignCenter features. It allows you to search for all drawing files or any of the drawing content located in your computer. Selecting this button will display the Find dialog box as shown in Figure 10–30. The default search will be conducted in all drawings. This is shown inside the Look for drop-down list in the Find dialog box. You can click on the Browse . . . button to select a specific drive and folder for the search or use the In drop-down list to search in a specific existing folder and drive. You can narrow your search to find blocks, dimstyles, drawings, drawings and blocks, layers, layouts, linetypes, textstyles, and xrefs by selecting the appropriate item from the down arrow in the Look for drop-down list as shown in Figure 10–31. Depending on what is being searched

FIGURE 10–30 The Find dialog box will help you search for drawings and their contents.

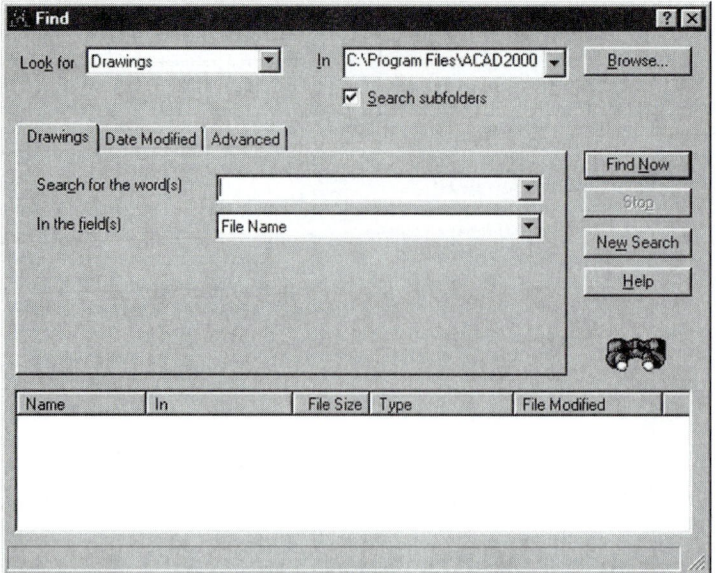

FIGURE 10–31 You can search for any of the available categories.

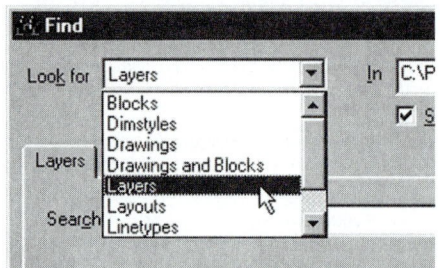

for, you can use one of the three tabs to extend your search criteria to include date last modified, block definition descriptions, and keywords that are included in the Summary tab of the Drawing Properties dialog box.

Drawings: This tab allows you to specify the name or text associated with the category selected under Look for drop-down list. This tab is shown in Figure 10–30. You can use In the field(s) drop-down list to limit the search to File Name, Title, Subject, Author, and Keywords. These fields are items entered in the Drawing Properties dialog box when you start a project. Refer to Chapter 8. For example, entering COMMERCIAL OFFICE BUILDING inside the Search for the word(s) drop-down list and selecting Subject from the In the field(s) drop-down list will search for the file in all the drawings under the specified folder and drive. This is shown in Figure 10–32. To start the search, click on the Find Now button. After the search is completed, the search results appear in the bottom of the Find dialog box as shown in Figure 10–33.

Tips: Right-click on one of the search results and select Load into Palette to load the file into the DesignCenter as shown in Figure 10–34. You can also insert the file as a block or attach as an xref. This is very useful when you are searching for a specific block but don't know the precise file location. You can find the block using the Find dialog box. Right-click on the resulting matching name to load the block into the palette of the DesignCenter.

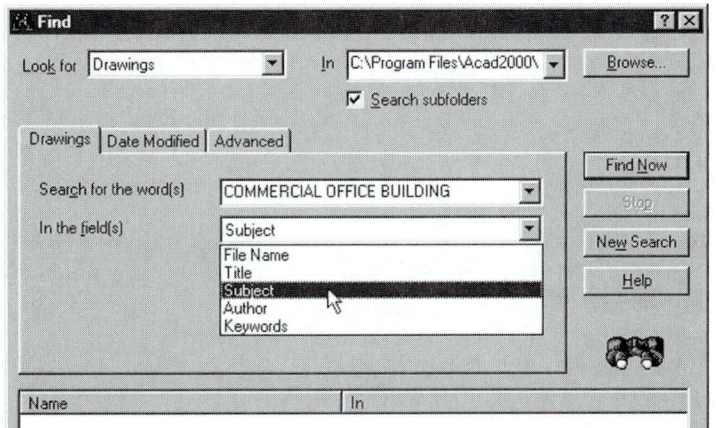

FIGURE 10–32 Searching for Commercial Office Building file under Subject field.

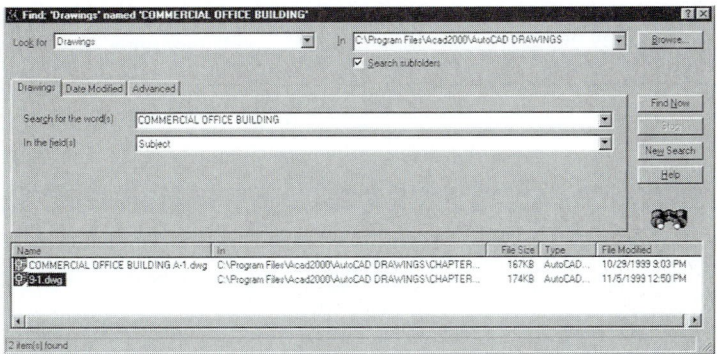

FIGURE 10–33 Two files are found under the search criteria specified. The Commercial Office Building A-1.dwg and 9-1.dwg.

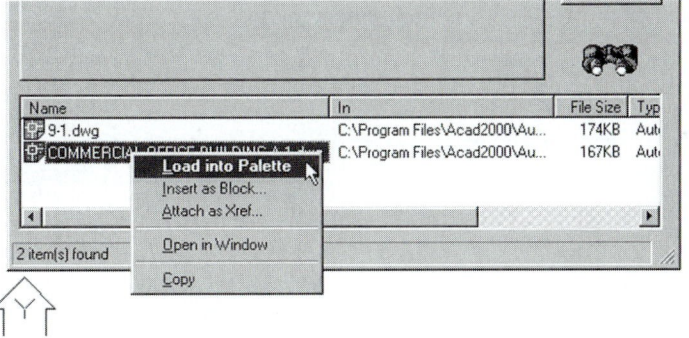

FIGURE 10–34 You can load the selected file into the palette of the DesignCenter using the right-click shortcut menu. Other options include Insert as Block, Attach as xref. . . . Open in Window, and Copy. The ellipses after the option will display a dialog box relating to the specific option.

Date Modified: This tab allows you to search under the specified criteria for the file based on the date that the file was created or last modified. You can search for All files or Find all files created or modified between range of dates, or during the previous days or months as shown in Figure 10–35.

Advanced: This tab allows you to expand your search criteria to include additional search parameters based on text contained in a file or file size. You can conduct a search for a block name, block and drawing description, attribute tag, or attribute value for words containing, but not limited to, a specific word as shown in Figure 10–36. Attributes are discussed in Chapter 21. You can also limit the search to a minimum or maximum file size.

- **UP:** This button will move up one level from the current file location. Use this button if you closed the tree view area.

- **PREVIEW:** This button will display an image of a block object inside a window at the bottom of the palette area. For the image to be displayed, the create icon from block geometry

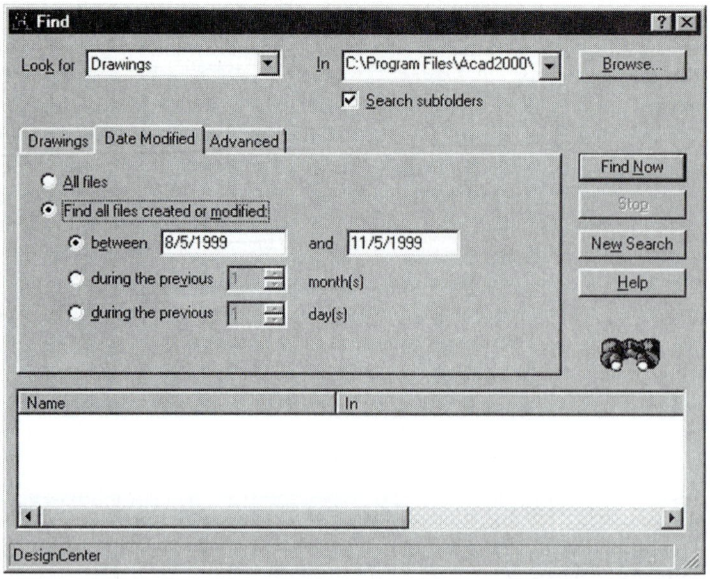

FIGURE 10–35 The Date Modified tab of the Find dialog box.

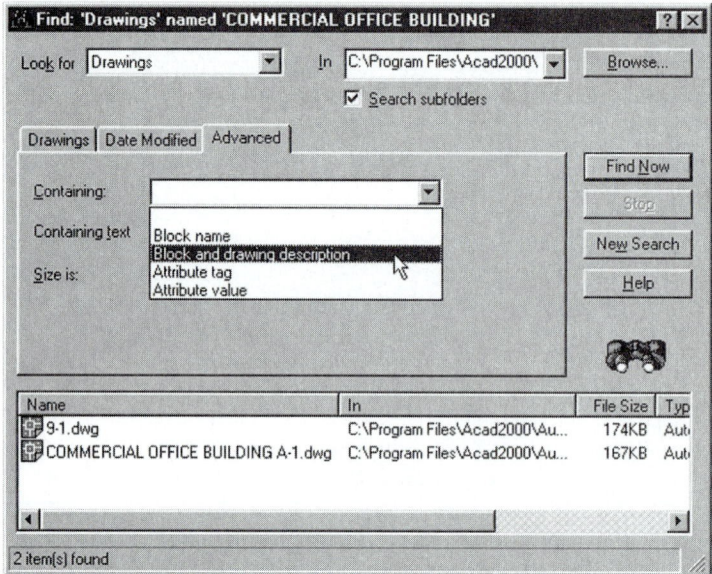

FIGURE 10–36 The Advanced tab of the Find dialog box.

radio button must be checked when using the Block Definition dialog box. Figure 10–37 shows the CAD WORKSTATION block icon inside the preview area.

- **DESCRIPTION:** This button will display the text description of the block object inside a window at the bottom of the palette area. For the text to be displayed, the description text box must include the appropriate text when using the Block Definition dialog box. Figure 10–37 shows the description of the CAD WORKSTATION block.

- **VIEWS:** This button will allow you to select a display format from four different options.

You can also right-click inside the palette area to perform all the tasks associated with the DesignCenter toolbar. The right-click shortcut menu is shown in Figure 10–38.

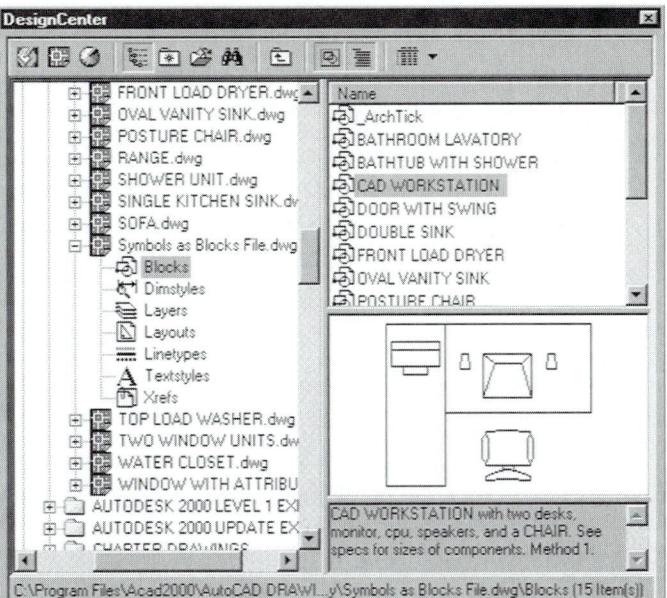

FIGURE 10–37   The preview and description areas of the palette.

FIGURE 10–37   The preview and description areas of the palette.

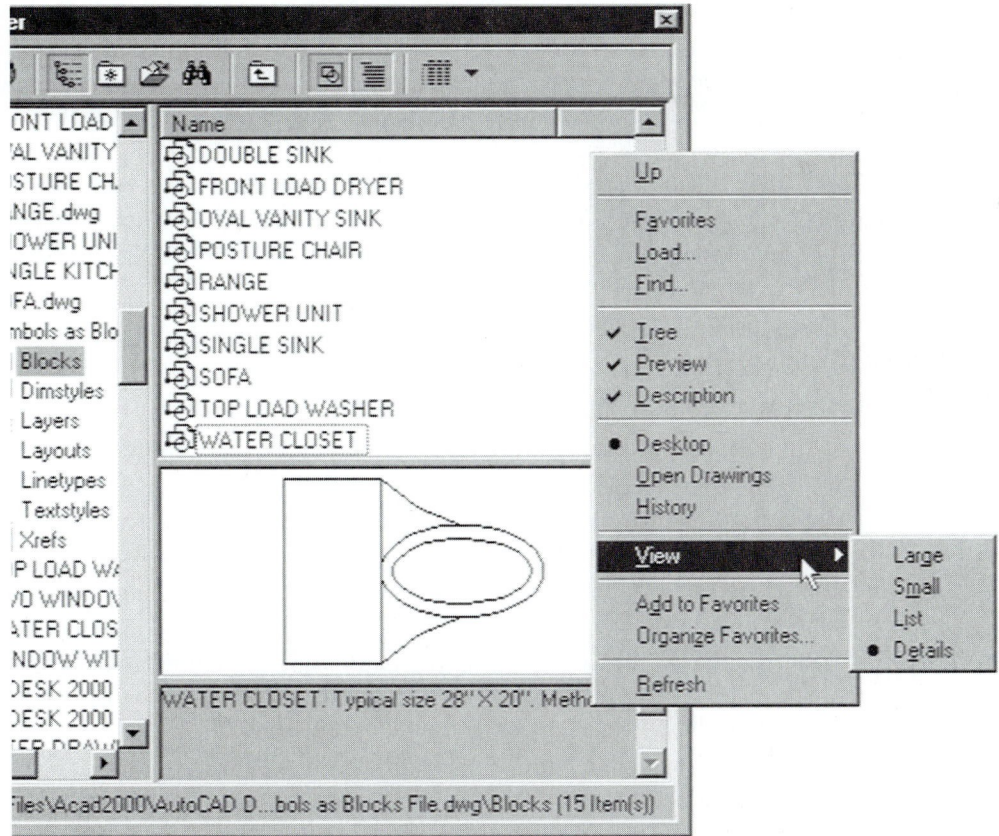

FIGURE 10–38   The right-click shortcut menu inside the palette.

10.5 USING THE AutoCAD DESIGNCENTER

You can use the DesignCenter to copy dimension styles, layers, linetypes, layouts, text styles, and xrefs from the palette area to the target drawing as follows:

- Left-click on the drawing content and drag and drop it into the target drawing. If you right-click on the item and drag and drop, a shortcut menu will appear with several options.
- To select more than one item belonging to drawing content, highlight one and use the shift key to select more, then drag and drop.
- Double click on an item to automatically add it to the target drawing.
- Right-click on an item inside the palette area and select the desired option.

You can use the DesignCenter to copy or insert blocks from the palette area to the target drawing as follows:

- Left-click on the block and drag and drop into the target drawing. This will insert the block.
- Right-click on the block and drag and drop into the target drawing. This will display a shortcut menu. Select either the Insert Block . . . or the Cancel option. The Insert Block option will display the Insert dialog box.
- Right-click on the block inside the palette area and select either the Insert Block . . . or the Copy option.
- Double click on the block inside the palette area. This will display the insert dialog box.

   Note: Refer to Chapter 19 for a complete coverage on inserting blocks using the Auto-CAD DesignCenter, including automatic scaling of blocks and a hands-on exercise.

Tips: The source drawing must be closed and the target drawing must be active for the DesignCenter drag-and-drop operations to work.

AutoCAD 2000i Update: *AutoCAD Design Center provides access to hatch patterns that can be selected from the palette then dragged and dropped to an object in the target drawing. No source drawing need to be opened. Refer to sections 1.13.2 and 20.3 for more information.*

■ **EXERCISE 10–3:**   *The following step-by-step exercise will help you copy the dimension style in drawing EXE10-3A as the source drawing into the EXE10-3B as the target drawing. The target drawing does not contain the architectural dimension style. The ARCHITEC-TURAL dimension style contained in EXE10-3A (FLOOR PLAN) drawing will be used.*

Step #1:   Open the *EXE10-3A.dwg* file. This is the *source* drawing.

Step #2:   Open the *EXE10-3B.dwg* file. This is the *target* drawing.

Step #3:   Using the Windows pull-down menu tile the two drawings vertically.

Step #4:   Close the source drawing and access AutoCAD DesignCenter.

Step #5:   Using the tree view, locate drawing *EXE10-3A.dwg* file. Click on the + sign to display its drawing content and click on the Dimstyles as shown in Figure 10–39. Two existing dimension styles will be displayed in the palette area.

Step #6:   Left-click on the Architectural (dimension style) inside the palette area. Drag and drop it inside the target drawing.

Step #7:   Inside the target drawing, click on the Dimension Style button in the Dimension toolbar. The Dimension Style Manager dialog box should display the Architectural dimension style as shown in Figure 10–40.

Step #8:   Before using the Architectural dimension style, make sure the number inside the *Use overall scale of* under the Scale for Dimension Features category in the Fit tab corresponds to the scale factor of the target drawing. If it does not, simply enter the correct scale factor. This will adjust the dimension scale factor to correspond to the current drawing scale. Dimensioning is discussed in Chapter 18.

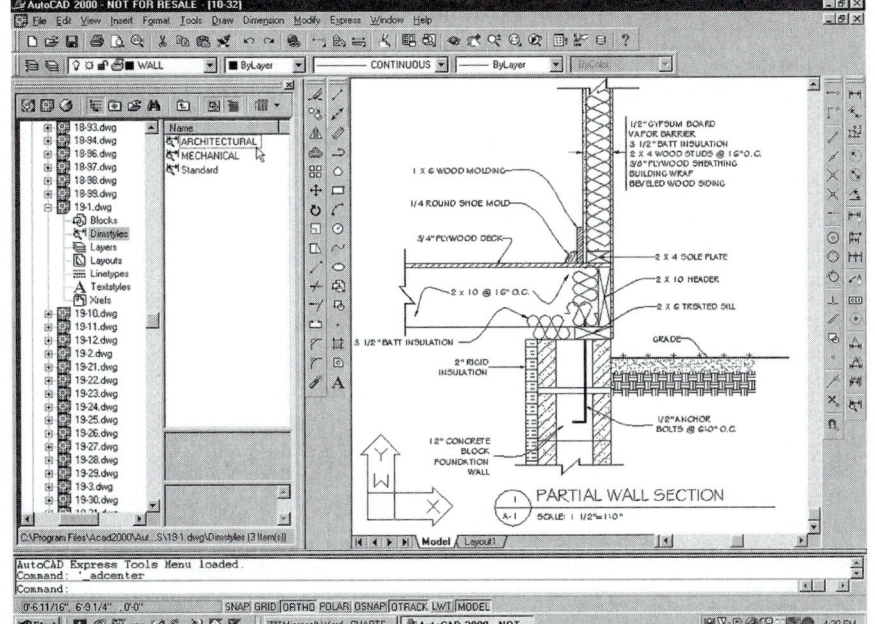

FIGURE 10–39
Drawing EXE10-3A (source drawing) contains an architectural dimension style PARTIAL WALL SECTION (target drawing) needs. ADC will allow you to drag and drop the dimension style needed into the target drawing EXE10-3B.

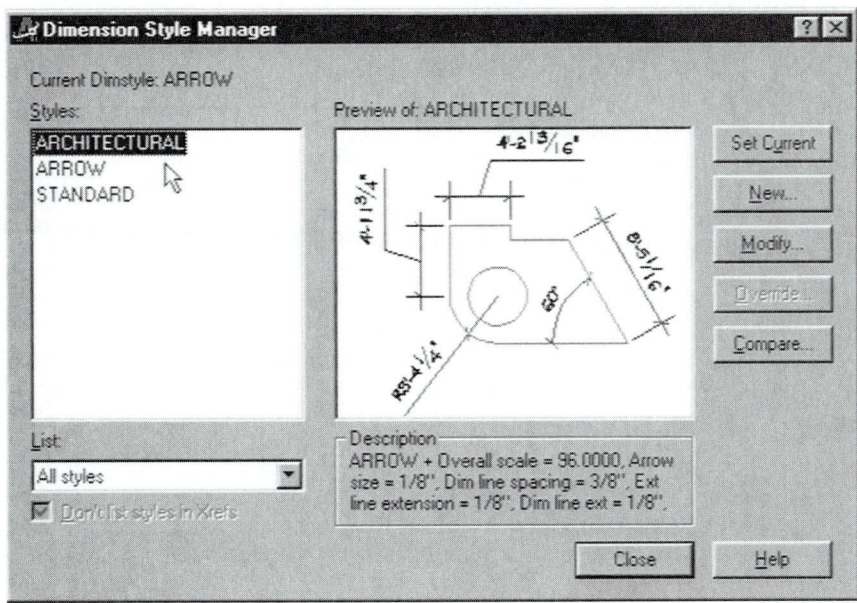

FIGURE 10–40 The architectural dimension style is copied from the source drawing into the target drawing.

Congratulations! You have successfully used the ADC to drag and drop an existing architectural dimension style into a drawing with no architectural dimension style.

REVIEW QUESTIONS

1. Name three tasks that can be performed with the MDE.
2. What is the function of the SDI system variable?
3. How many different ways can you display multiple drawings using the Window pull-down menu?
4. Describe the functions of the source drawing and the target drawing.
5. Describe the process to open multiple drawings from Windows Explorer.
6. Can you drag and drop a word document into an AutoCAD target drawing?

7. In an MDE, can you switch from one drawing to another without canceling the command you are working with?

8. When using Windows clipboard to copy objects in an MDE, what is the difference between Copy and Copy with Base Point?

9. Can you use the COPY command of AutoCAD to copy objects from a source drawing into a target drawing?

10. What is drawing contents or a dependent symbol?

11. List three tasks you can perform with AutoCAD DesignCenter.

12. What is the purpose of the palette area of the DesignCenter?

13. List two methods for accessing the DesignCenter.

14. List two methods for closing the DesignCenter.

15. Inside the tree view area of the DesignCenter, what do the + sign and the − sign mean?

16. How can you make the tree view area larger than the palette area?

17. Describe the History and Find options of the DesignCenter toolbar.

18. What happens when you right-click on Layers item in the palette area?

19. What is the requirement for a block to display an image and a description at the bottom of the palette area?

20. The source and the target drawings are open. Can you drag and drop the Linetypes from the source drawing into the target drawing?

PROBLEMS

1. Open the *EXE10-1.dwg* file. This is the source drawing. Create a new drawing from scratch and set units to Architectural and Limits to 24′, 16′. This is the target drawing. Tile the two drawings horizontally. Using the Windows Clipboard, copy Details 1 and 4 from the source drawing into the target drawing. Close the two drawings without saving.

2. Open the *EXE10-2.dwg* file. This is the target drawing. Open the *EXE10-1C.dwg* drawing. This is the source drawing. Tile the two drawings vertically. Using the right-click shortcut menu and the Windows Clipboard, copy three trees and one bush from the source drawing into the target drawing. Close the two drawings without saving.

3. Open the *EXE10-3.dwg file.* This is the source drawing. Open the *EXE10-1B.dwg* file. This is the target drawing. Tile the two drawings horizontally. Using the Windows Clipboard, copy the water closet, bathtub, and the lavatory from the source drawing into the target drawing. Close the two drawings without saving.

4. Open the *MYEXE6-2.dwg file.* This is the target drawing. Open the *EXE10-2.dwg* file. This is the source drawing. Tile the two drawings vertically. Using the ADC, copy the ARCHITECTURAL dimension style from the source drawing into the target drawing. Close the two drawings and save the changes.

5. Open the *EXE7-5.dwg file.* This is the source drawing. Open the *MYEXE5-7.dwg* file. This is the target drawing. Tile the two drawings vertically. Using the Windows Clipboard, copy the computer workstation including the chair from the source drawing and paste it into the target drawing at a location of your choice. Notice that the computer workstation is a block. Close the source drawing and do not save the changes.

6. Open the *EXE10-4.dwg* file. This is the target drawing. Open the *EXE10-5.dwg* file. This is the source drawing. Tile the two drawings horizontally. Using the Windows Clipboard, copy the two cars from the source drawing inside the garage area of the target drawing. Close the two drawings without saving.

7. Open the *MYEXE6-5.dwg* file. This is the target drawing. Open the *EXE10-6.dwg* file. This is the source drawing. Tile the two drawings vertically. Make the source drawing active. Using the ADC, copy all layers from the source drawing into the target drawing.

CHAPTER 11

Displaying Objects and Creating Views

After successful completion of this chapter you should be able to:

▲ Use the ZOOM command and all of its related options.

▲ Use Zoom Realtime and Pan Realtime.

▲ Use right-click shortcut menu with zoom options.

▲ Use the ZOOM command options transparently.

▲ Understand view display accuracy and set view resolution.

▲ Create, manage, and edit different views of your drawing.

▲ Use the –VIEW command.

▲ Use the Aerial View window and its related options in your drawings.

11.1 GETTING CLOSE TO YOUR WORK

As you proceed with your projects, you will discover that you need to zoom in closer to objects so that you can snap to precise points. This is especially true with AutoSnap and AutoTrack features. Ultimately your drawing precision depends on your ability to precisely select points on the screen for drawing, dimensioning, inserting, hatching, and when using any of the editing commands. For example, when dimensioning a large and complex floor plan you will need to zoom in and select a precise point at one corner of the drawing and then zoom out to see where you are, and then zoom in again into another corner for the second precise point. You will repeat this procedure many times until all dimensioning is complete. Without getting closer to your objects, you will not be able to precisely snap to a specific point. When you work with many small details at a large-scale drawing format, you will need to "zoom in" and "zoom out" to many different parts of the drawing. Zooming in refers to the screen's ability to magnify objects or a portion of the drawing for you to see objects at a large scale. Zooming out refers to the screen's ability to reverse the magnification process so that you can see objects at a small scale. Think of zooming as using a magnifying glass. Every time you zoom you are putting magnifying glasses on. It is important to know that zooming-in and zooming-out do not change the actual scale of the drawing, it merely changes the magnification. One of the greatest additions to AutoCAD zoom feature is the Microsoft Intellimouse rotating wheel. This zooming feature makes zooming in and zooming out very convenient and efficient. Simply rotate the mouse wheel outward to zoom in and inward to zoom out. If you don't have this feature, you can still use the ZOOM command and its options.

11.2 ZOOM OPTIONS

Zoom options can be accessed from the Zoom toolbar, from the View pull-down menu, from the right-click shortcut menu, or by entering ZOOM at the command line. To access the Zoom toolbar,

FIGURE 11–1 The Zoom toolbar with eight zoom option buttons.

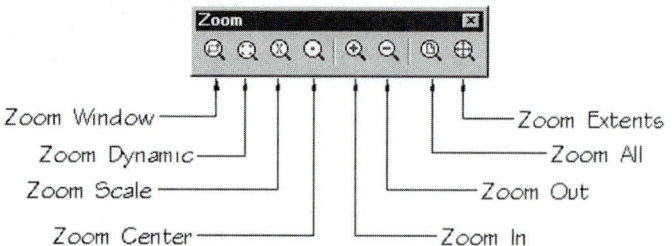

FIGURE 11–2 The Zoom cascading menu accessed from the View pull-down menu.

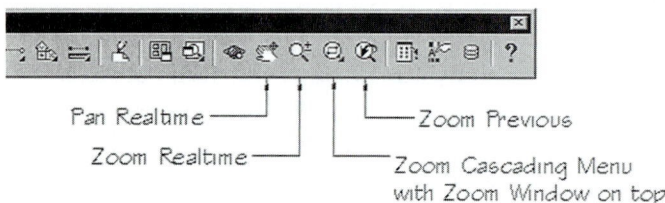

FIGURE 11–3 The four zoom buttons in the Standard toolbar.

right-click on any toolbar and select Zoom. The Zoom toolbar is shown in Figure 11–1. The Zoom cascading menu of the View pull-down menu gives you similar zoom options as shown in Figure 11–2. The four zoom buttons in the Standard toolbar as shown in Figure 11–3 offer a cascading menu for all the zoom options plus the use of the Pan and Zoom Realtime features and a chance to zoom to the previous state. The button with the small triangle in the lower right corner is the zoom cascading menu. When you click on this button, all the zoom option buttons under it will be displayed. To read a description of each button, keep your finger on the left button and move down slowly. A tooltip is displayed for each zoom option. When you release your left finger, the button your finger was last on will be selected and placed on top of the other buttons. For example, Figure 11–3 shows the Zoom Window as the current zoom option. Figure 11–4 shows the cascading zoom buttons.

Let's take a look at the eight zoom options:

11.2.1 Zoom Window

The Zoom Window allows you to place a window around the object to be zoomed-in. Select two opposite corners to zoom in. Figure 11–5 shows a curtain-wall detail. To view the connection between floor joists/slab and the curtain-wall at a larger scale, click on the Zoom Window button

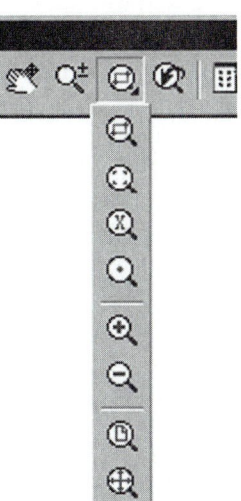

FIGURE 11–4 The eight zoom option buttons can also be accessed from the cascading menu in the Standard toolbar.

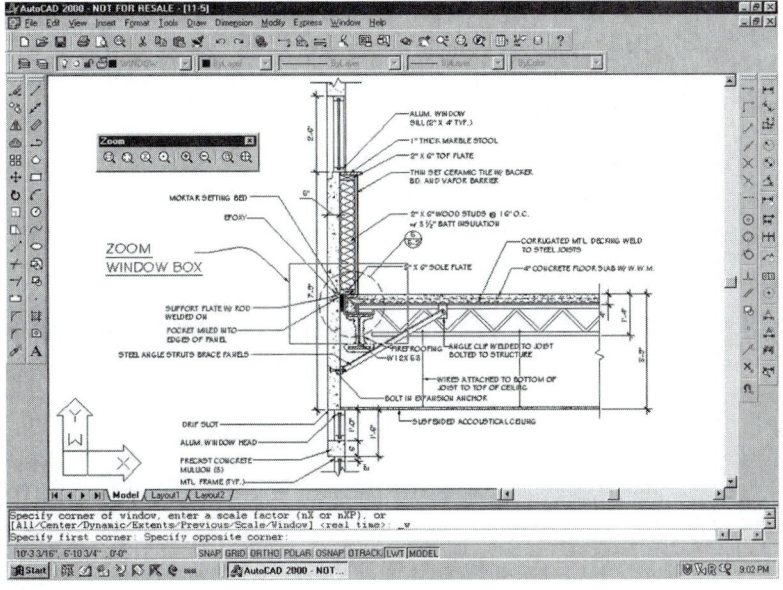

FIGURE 11–5 The zoom magnification or the size of the area to be seen at a larger scale is dependent on the size and location of the Zoom window box.

in the Zoom toolbar or by other methods described previously. Select the first corner (upper-right corner of the Zoom window box) and drag your mouse to the opposite corner and select. The detail will now be displayed as shown in Figure 11–6. The magnification factor is determined by the size of the Zoom window box. The smaller the box, the larger the magnification will be. A larger window box will show more objects, but the magnification will be much smaller. Figure 11–7 shows a Zoom window rectangle larger than the one shown in Figure 11–5. The magnification in this case will be smaller but more of the curtain-wall detail can be seen as shown in Figure 11–8.

11.2.2 Zoom Dynamic

Zoom Dynamic allows you to zoom in to a portion of the drawing by actually creating a *view box*. The view box you create is proportional to the size of the final display area. The final result of the Zoom Dynamic option is the placement of the view area in the center of the drawing screen. This may seem complicated at first, but once you understand the procedure you'll be able to display an area of the drawing precisely centered on your screen.

FIGURE 11–6 The enlarged view of the connection detail. Notice the Zoom window box was originally included the dashed circle, which is now covering almost the entire screen.

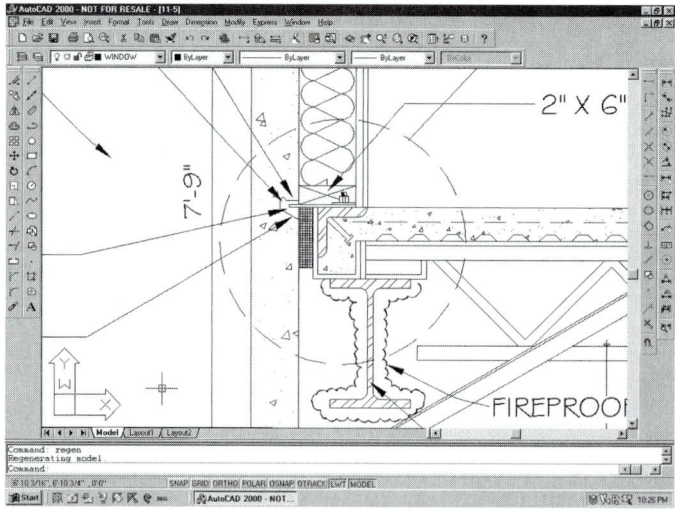

FIGURE 11–7 A larger Zoom window rectangle will result in displaying more of the detail but at a smaller magnification scale.

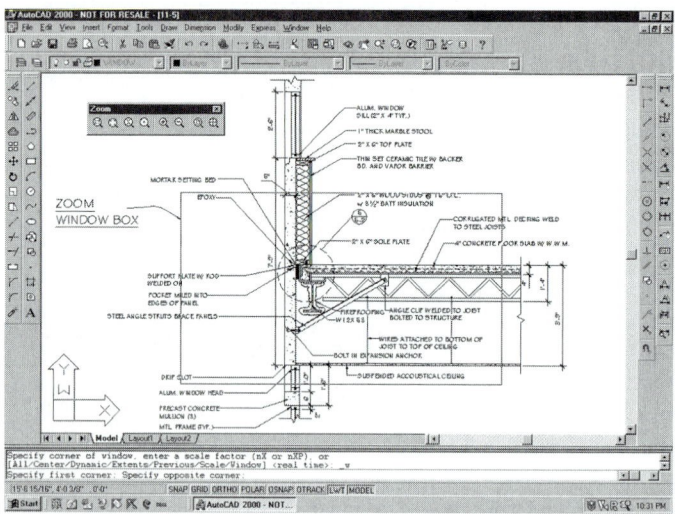

FIGURE 11–8 The result of the Zoom window rectangle of Figure 11–7.

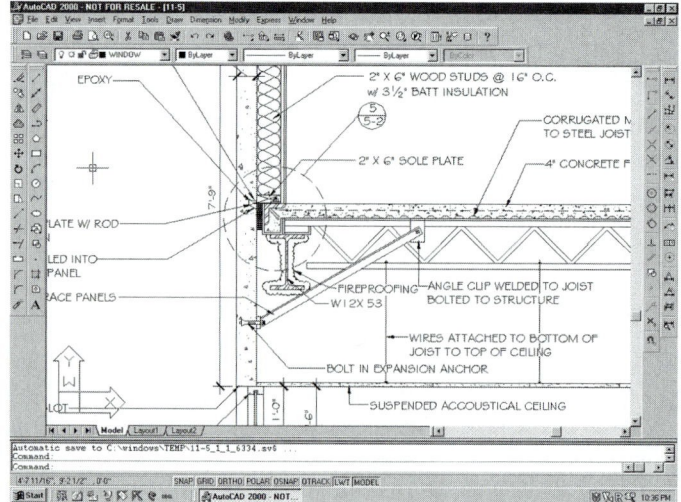

■ **EXERCISE 11–1:** *The following step-by-step exercise will help you use and understand the zoom dynamic option by allowing you to display the top of the anchor bolt at the center of the screen as you zoom in:*

Step #1: Open the *EXE11-1.dwg* file.

Step #2: Select the Zoom Dynamic option. You will see three boxes on the screen as shown in Figure 11–9. The blue dashed lines represent the extents of the drawing. This area is displayed when you use Zoom Extents. It is the maximum size that can be displayed on the screen without cutting any of the objects. The green dotted lines represent the view before you selected the Zoom Dynamic option. This is why the drawing moves from its original display area. The rectangle represented by the "X" in the center is the view box. The X in Figure 11–9 is located inside the 2 × 10 floor joists and the batt insulation. When you move your cursor, the X and the view box move also.

Step #3: Move your cursor so that the X is on top of the anchor bolt (top of sill plate). This means that when dynamic zooming is finalized, the top of the anchor bolt will be at the center of the screen. Left-click when you have placed the X on top of the anchor bolt. The X will now be replaced with an arrow and will move to the right side of the view box as shown in Figure 11–10. At this point you can decrease or increase the area you wish to zoom by moving your cursor left or up and down. Moving the cursor to the left will shrink the view box and moving the cursor to the right will increase the size of the view box. You cannot move the view box itself to the left. Notice that moving the cursor to the left not only shrinks the view box but also moves the box to a blank area.

Step #4: Move your cursor to the left until the arrow coincides with the outside face and upper right corner of the foundation wall as shown in Figure 11–11. Left click and the arrow will now return to the center of the view box as the X.

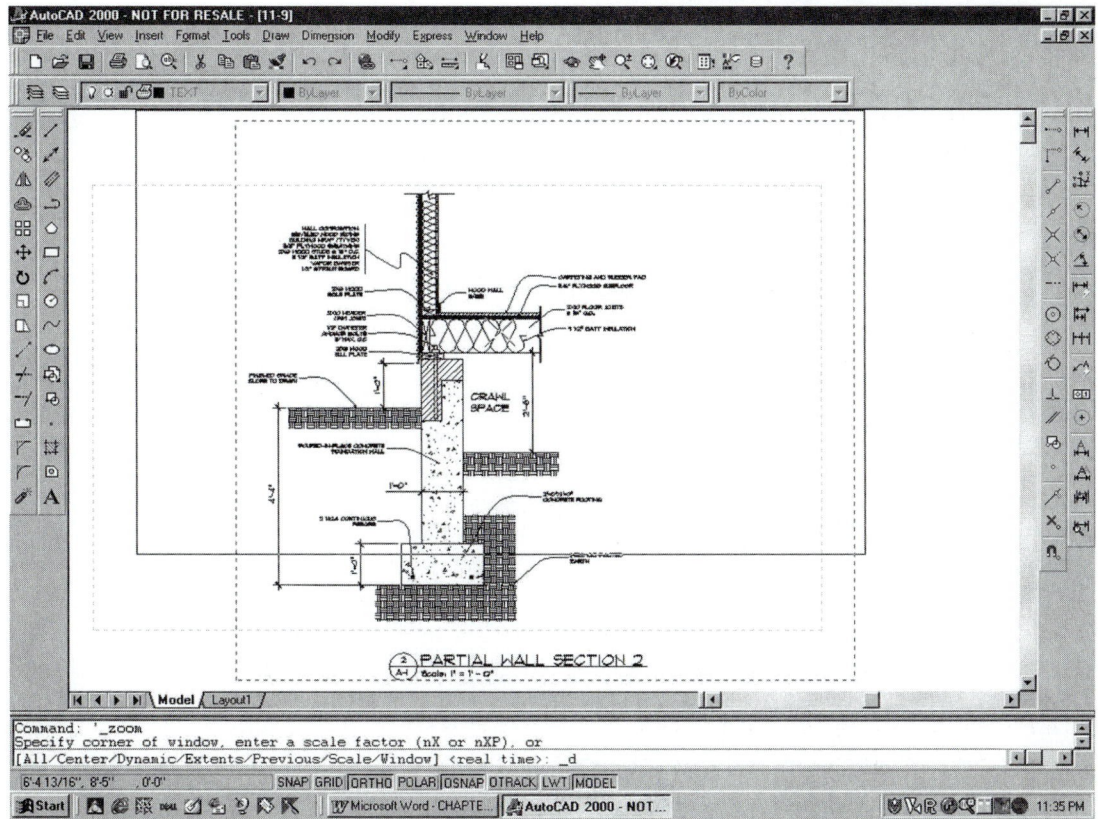

FIGURE 11–9 Three boxes will be displayed when you access the Zoom Dynamic option.

FIGURE 11–10 The X becomes an arrow placed at the inside edge of the right side of the view box. You can resize the view box at this point.

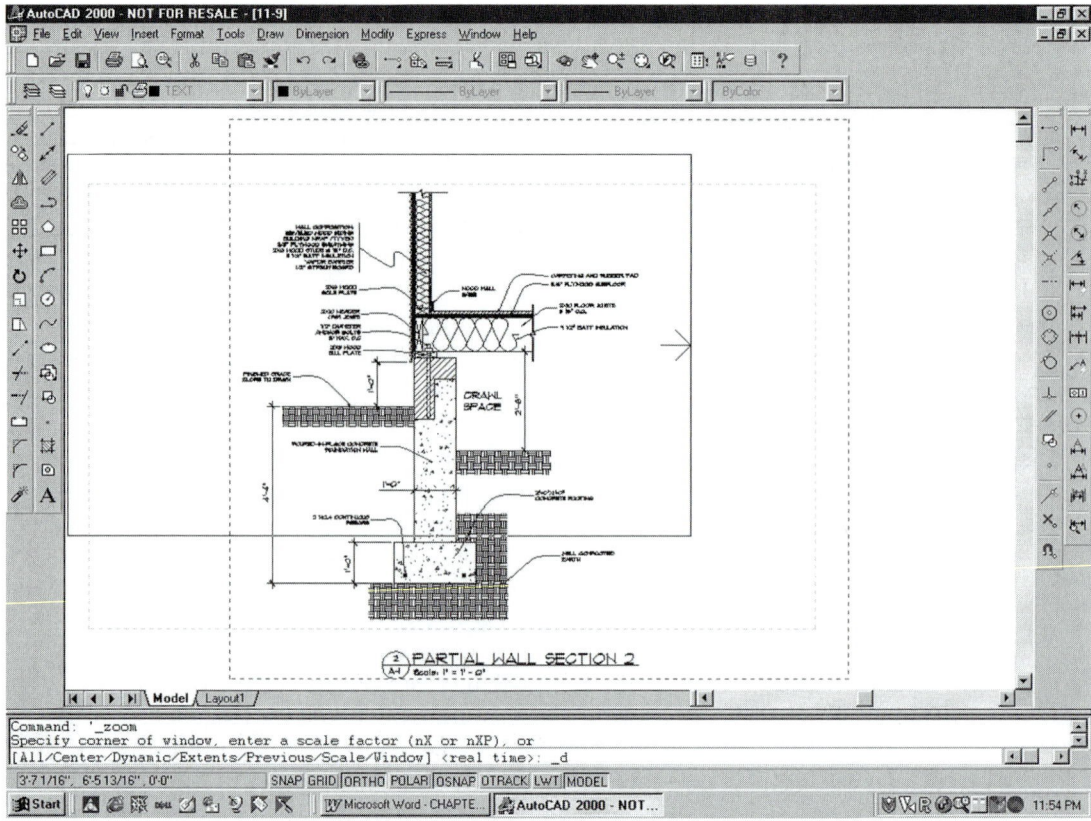

FIGURE 11–11 Moving the view box until it matches the outside corner of the foundation wall in the horizontal direction and centering the box from the anchor bolt in the vertical direction.

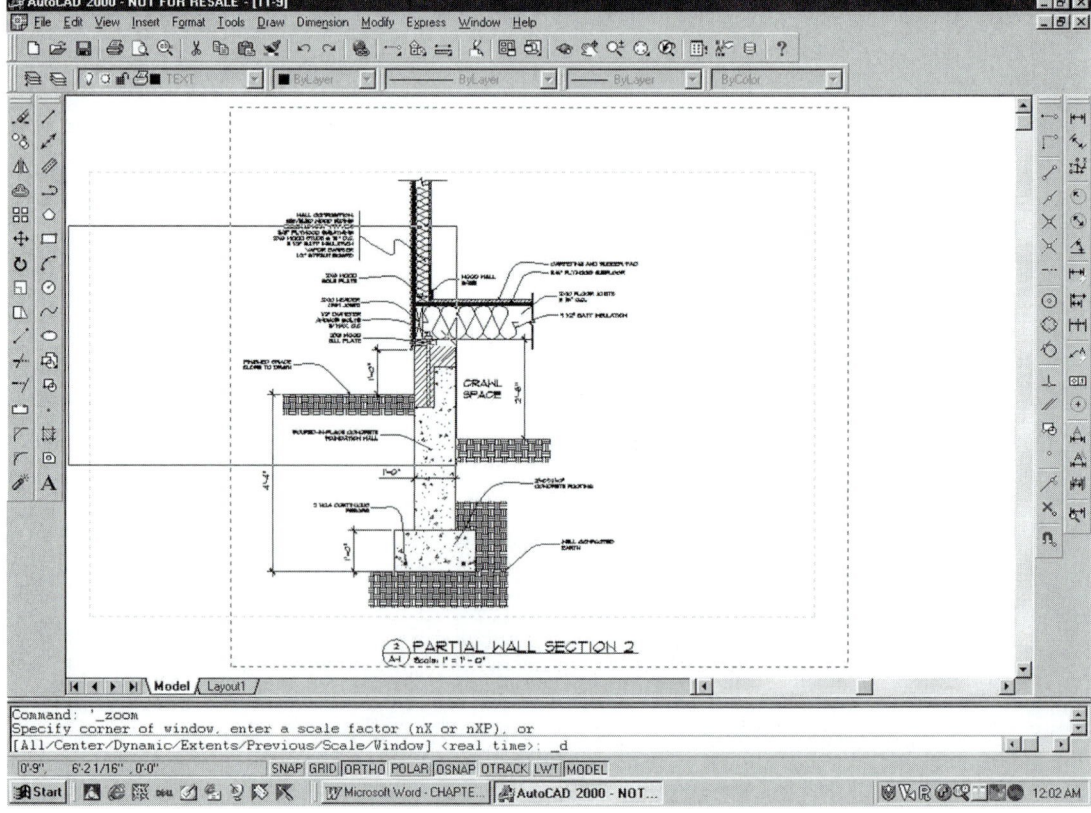

Step #5: Move the X on top of the anchor bolt one more time and repeat the same procedure until the top horizontal line of the view box is approximately on top of the finished floor as shown in Figure 11–12. Remember to have the X on top of the anchor bolt. Right-click and select Enter from the shortcut menu to finalize the Zoom Dynamic operation. The result of the Zoom Dynamic operation is shown in Figure 11–13.

Congratulations! You have successfully displayed a portion of the drawing precisely at the center of the screen by using the zoom dynamic option.

11.2.3 Zoom Scale

This option allows you to enter a scale factor to change the display of the drawing. This does not change the drawing scale. It allows you to change the size of the drawing in relation to the display area. The scale factor can be set relative to full display (n), relative to current display (nX), or relative to Paper Space units (nXP).

- **RELATIVE TO FULL DISPLAY:** This option enlarges or reduces the entire drawing according to the positive number entered at the command line. For example, entering a zoom scale factor of 4 will increase the size of the drawing four times. Entering 0.5 will display the objects half as big as the full display. After selecting the zoom scale button, AutoCAD will display the following command prompt:

Enter a scale factor (nX or nXP): *(enter a positive number such as .5 or 4)* ~EnterKey~

- **RELATIVE TO CURRENT DISPLAY:** If you want the zoom scale option to be relative to the current display (after a zoom window for example), enter a value followed by an "X" at the command line.

The X suffix allows you to scale view magnification relative to the current view magnification. After selecting the zoom scale button, AutoCAD will display the following command prompt:

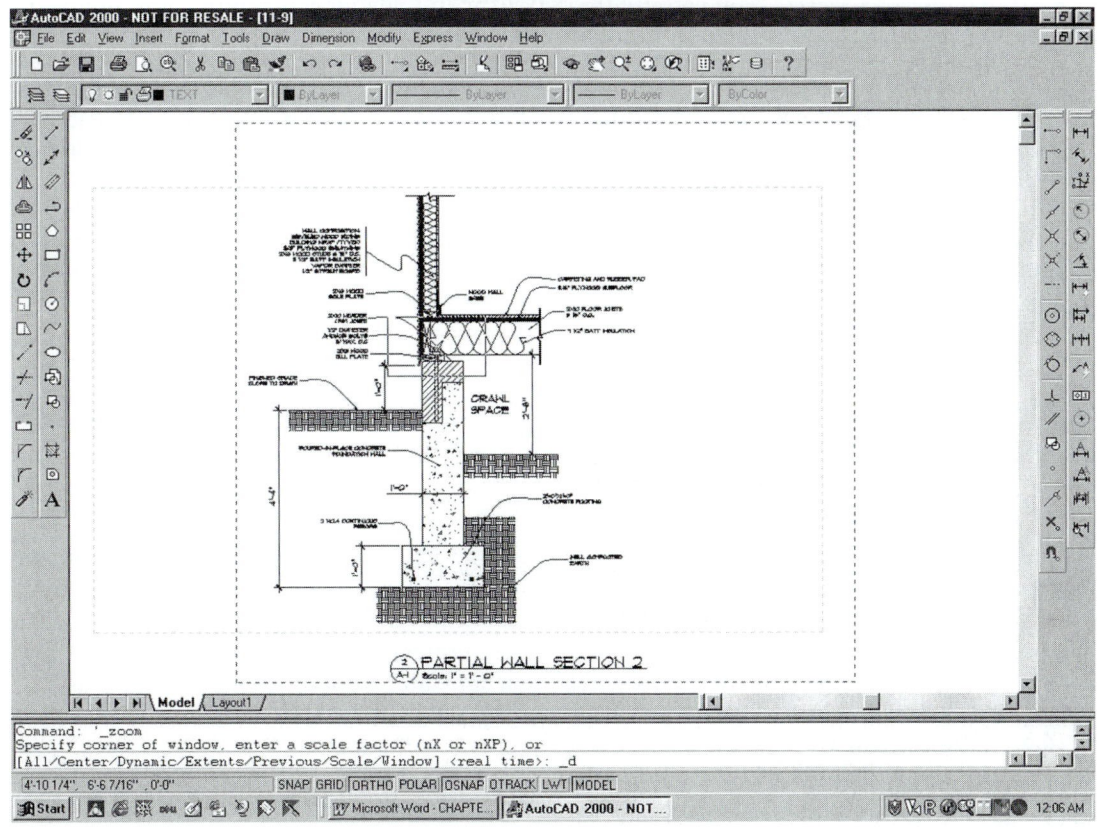

FIGURE 11–12 Moving the view box couple of times until it is small enough to cover the top of the flooring.

FIGURE 11–13 When the Zoom Dynamic operation is completed, the top of the anchor bolt (as indicated previously with X) will be in the center of the screen. Notice the top of flooring (as indicated previously by the upper horizontal line of the view box) at the upper edge of the screen.

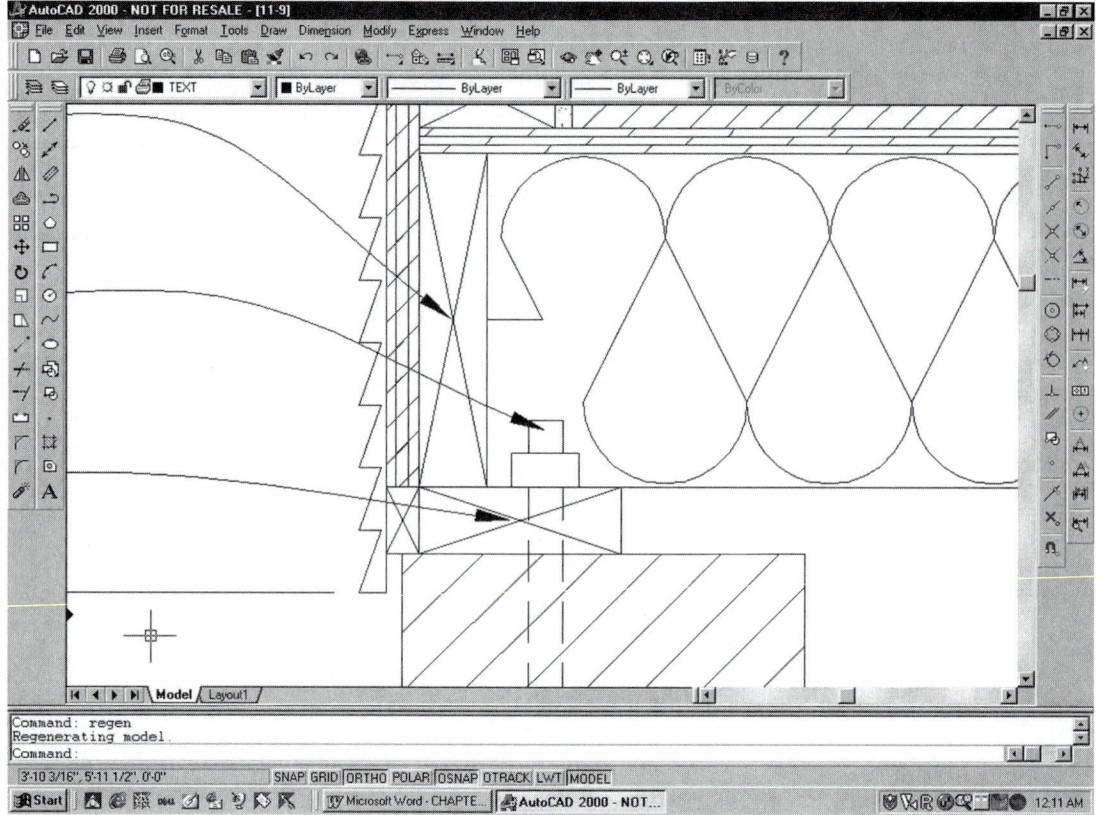

```
Enter a scale factor (nX or nXP): (enter a number followed by X such as
3X)~EnterKey~
```

- **RELATIVE TO PAPER SPACE:** You can use the XP suffix to scale view magnification relative to paper space. This zoom scale option is used in Paper Space and Model Space Layouts. When you create *viewport(s)* in Layouts inside the paper space, you are actually getting ready to compose the final assembly of your drawing(s). Each viewport can represent a different view and a different scale for the drawing. To assign a specific scale to a drawing inside a viewport, you must first access the drawing by switching to model space in a Layout. You can then use the Viewports toolbar to select the scale you want for the drawing from the drop-down list. If the scale you want is not available in the list, enter the *reciprocal* of the scale factor and XP after the command prompt. You must do this in the model space of Layouts. For example, suppose you want the drawing in Layouts to have a scale of 1 1/2″ = 1′-0″ when plotted. While in model space environment of Layouts, access the zoom scale command and enter as follows:

```
Enter a scale factor (nX or nXP):1/8 XP  ~EnterKey~
```

This will assign a scale of 1 1/2″ =1′-0″ to the drawing. Layouts and Paper Space are discussed in Chapter 22. Assigning scale to viewports when plotting is discussed in Chapter 23.

11.2.4　Zoom Center

With the Zoom Center option, you can specify a center point and then enter a magnification or the height of the display. The current height value represents the height of the screen in current drawing units. If you enter a small height value, the drawing will be enlarged. If you enter a large height value, the drawing will be reduced. You can also select two points on the screen to represent the height. Rather than entering a height, you can enter a zoom scale factor such as 2×.

11.2.5　Zoom Extents

This zoom option will display the drawing at its maximum available size based on the size of the screen (monitor size). This is not the limits of your drawing; it is the maximum display size with all the components of the drawing visible. This option is extremely useful when you lose the drawing for some reason or another (it happens to all of us!). If your drawing is lost in model or any other space AutoCAD can throw at you, click on the Zoom Extents button—before you can say *Eureka!* the drawing will appear at its maximum size on the screen based on your monitor size. This depends on the fact that there are no other objects outside your drawing limits.

Tips: Double-click on the Microsoft Rotating Wheel to use Zoom Extents.

*Note: The Zoom Extents of your drawing is defined as the drawing area occupied by objects on layers that are **not** frozen. This means that your drawing extents may change when you add or delete objects and when you freeze or thaw layers containing objects.*

11.2.6 Zoom All

When you establish new limits to the drawing based on the final plot scale and the final plotted sheet size, you must perform this zoom option. With Zoom All, AutoCAD will zoom to the limits of your drawing. By zooming to the limits of your drawing you will be able to see your entire drawing with the boundaries of the sheet size. This will help you plot your drawing at the precise scale at which you based your limits. Refer to Chapter 2 for a detailed discussion on limits, scale, paper size, and scale factors. Figure 11–14 shows a floor plan at a final plot scale of 1/4″ = 1′-0″. The limits are based on the final print paper size of "A" (8 1/2″ × 11″) that is 34′, 44′ (vertical). The drawing is magnified by zooming in. To display the limits of the drawing and to display the drawing at its current scale, click on the Zoom All button in the Zoom toolbar. Figure 11–15 shows the same floor plan zoomed to the limits of its intended print paper size. In other words, what you see in Figure 11–15 is what you will get when this floor plan is printed at a ¼″ = 1′-0″ scale on an A size (8 1/2″ × 11″) sheet. This is referred to as the WYSIWYG (what you see is what you get) feature of AutoCAD. This means that what you see on your screen is what will appear on the final print. What makes this possible is the Limits of 34′, 44′ and Zoom All (along with positioning the drawing inside the limits). The WYSIWYG feature also applies to the Plot dialog box. Plotting is discussed in Chapter 23.

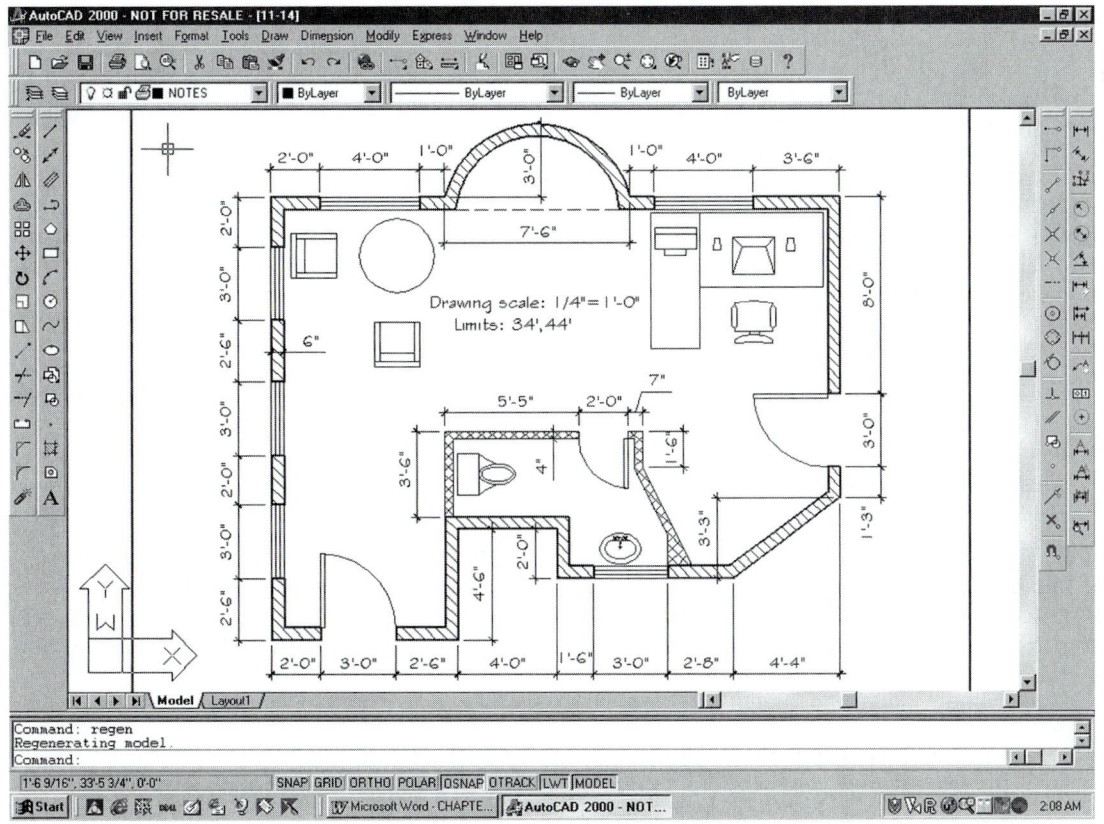

FIGURE 11–14 The floor plan as zoomed in.

FIGURE 11–15 The floor plan after Zoom All. The heavy lines represent the Limits of the drawing at 34′ horizontally and 44′ vertically. At a final plot scale of 1/4″ = 1′ - 0″, this floor plan is designed to fit inside an A size sheet.

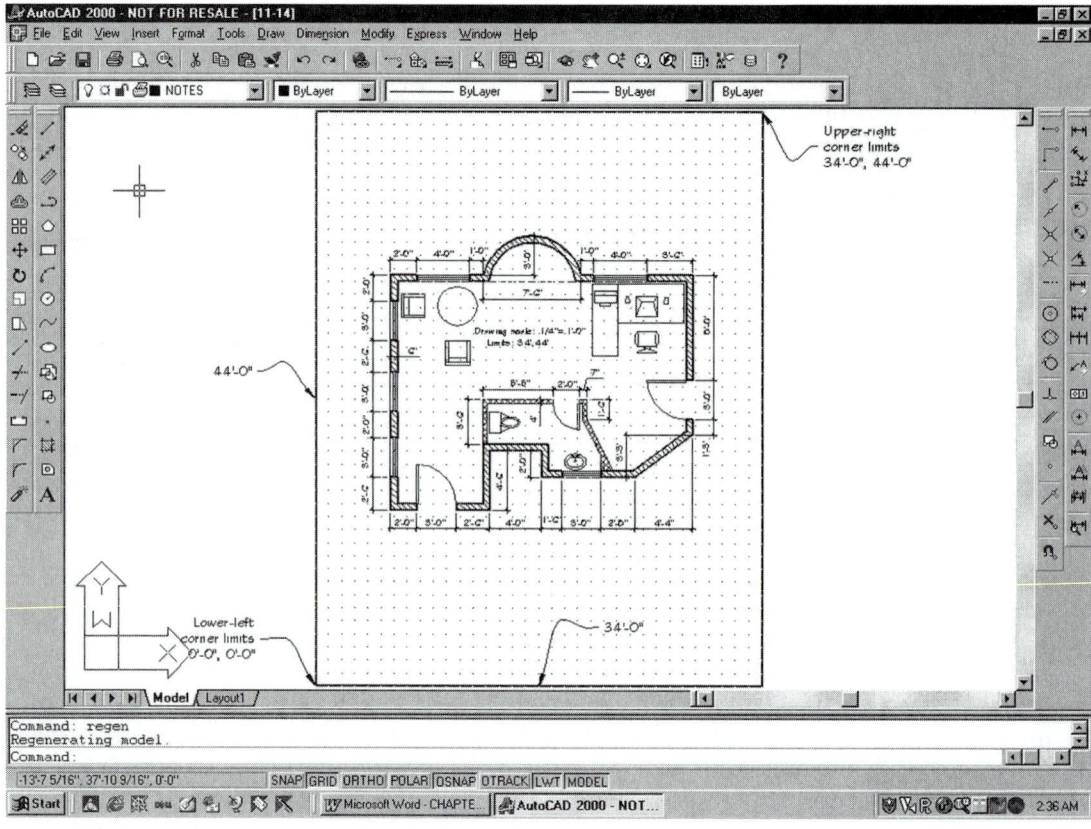

Note: You can always change the final plot scale just before plotting during the final plotting procedure. The Plot dialog box allows you to change the final plot scale using a very intuitive approach. Plotting is discussed in Chapter 23.

11.2.7 Zoom Out

This zoom option automatically performs a 0.5× zoom scale factor. After the zoom out, the drawing size becomes half of its previous size.

11.2.8 Zoom In

This zoom option automatically performs a 2× zoom scale factor. After the zoom in, the drawing size is doubled from its previous size.

11.3 ZOOM REALTIME

There are two other aspects of display magnification that can help increase productivity by allowing you to zoom in, zoom out, and pan around while you watch the display change as you move your cursor. They are called Realtime Zoom and Realtime Pan.

Realtime zooming refers to the screen's ability to move and resize drawings as you move your cursor around the screen. With Realtime Pan and Zoom, you actually see the results of the zooming and panning operations as they occur on the screen. Zoom Realtime is the fastest method for zooming in and zooming out of the drawing. To access Zoom Realtime, click on the Zoom Realtime button in the Standard toolbar, select Realtime from the Zoom cascading menu in the View pull-down menu, enter RTZOOM at the command line, or select the default option of the ZOOM command as follows:

```
Command: ZOOM ~EnterKey~
Specify corner of window, enter a scale factor (nX or nXP), or
[All/Center/Dynamic/Extents/Previous/Scale/Window] <realtime>: ~EnterKey~
```

■ **EXERCISE 11–2:** *The following step-by-step exercise will help you zoom in and out in a drawing using the Zoom Realtime option:*

Step #1: Open the *EXE11-2.dwg* file.

Step #2: Access the Zoom Realtime as described above. The Zoom Realtime cursor as the magnifying glass icon with a plus (+) and minus (−) sign will appear on the screen as shown in Figure 11–16.

Step #3: Zoom in (+) in realtime by holding down the left button in your mouse and move diagonally or vertically from bottom to top.

Step #4: Zoom out (−) in realtime by holding down the left button in your mouse and move diagonally or vertically from top to bottom. Moving the cursor horizontally will not magnify because there has to be some movement vertically or diagonally for Zoom Realtime to work properly.

Step #5: This time, before holding down the left button, move the cursor to the location you want to zoom in. This will give you a better zoom starting point. Figure 11–17 shows how the wall Section will appear if you move your cursor from the starting point (Figure 11–16) diagonally to the upper-left-corner of the screen. When you release the left button, Zoom Realtime does not work but the icon remains on the screen, allowing you to move the cursor to another location for more Zoom Realtime. If the drawing needs more magnification, move the cursor to another location without holding down the left button and then hold down the left button and use the Zoom Realtime again. Every time you want to zoom in again, simply hold down the left button in the mouse and move the cursor as described above.

Step #6: To exit Zoom Realtime, press the ~EnterKey~, ~EscKey~, or right-click and select Exit from the shortcut menu. The right-click shortcut menu options will be discussed later. Notice that in Figure 11–17, the wall section has been

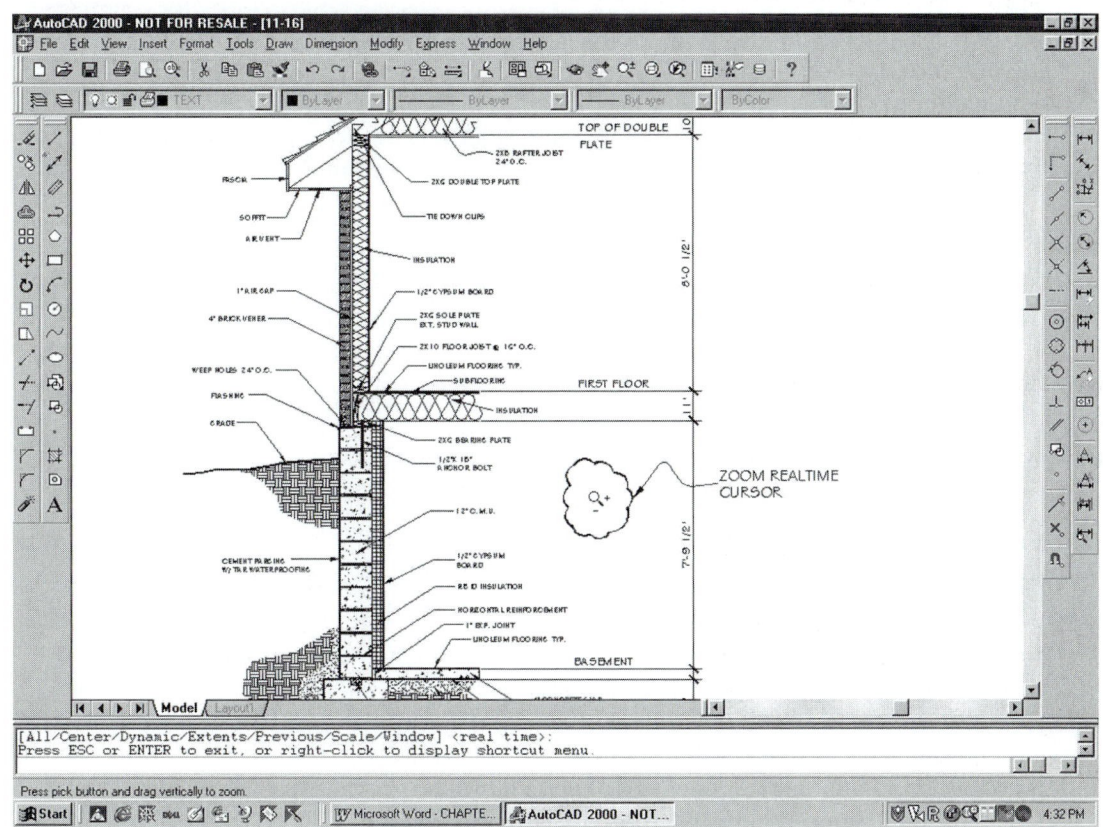

FIGURE 11–16 The Zoom Realtime will allow you to use the Zoom function of AutoCAD in realtime. Move the cursor around to see the magnification effect instantly.

FIGURE 11–17 When you move the cursor from the original point to the upper left corner of the screen the wall section will be moved and magnified. Notice the Zoom Realtime cursor at the upper left corner.

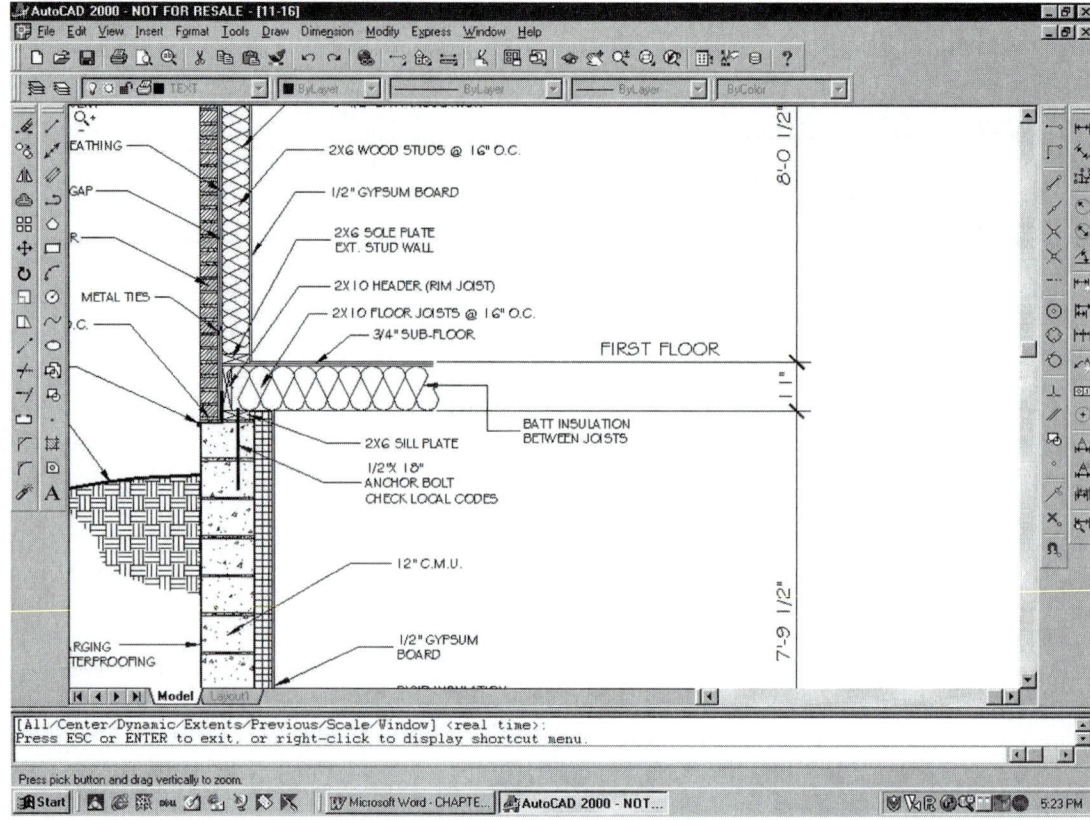

moved almost to the left edge while performing Zoom Realtime. If you keep moving in this fashion the wall section will soon disappear or you will simply run out of moving space.

Congratulations! You have successfully zoomed in and out of a drawing in realtime by using the zoom realtime option.

To move the wall section to the center or toward right side of the screen, you can use the Pan Realtime or any of the other zoom options discussed earlier. The Pan Realtime is discussed next.

11.4 PAN REALTIME

Pan Realtime allows you to pan (move) the objects in realtime so that you can adjust the placement of the objects relative to the screen. It is the fastest method for moving the current drawing view around the screen. To access Pan Realtime, click on the Pan Realtime button in the Standard toolbar, select RealTime from the Pan cascading menu in the View pull-down menu, or enter P, PAN, or RTPAN at the command line.

■ **EXERCISE 11–3:**   *The following step-by-step exercise will help you move around a drawing in realtime by using the Pan Realtime option:*

Step #1:   Open the *EXE11-2.dwg* file.

Step #2:   Access the Pan Realtime as described above. The Pan Realtime cursor as the hand icon will appear on the screen as shown in Figure 11–18.

Step #3:   Pan in realtime by holding down the left button in the mouse and moving vertically or horizontally. Moving vertically from top to bottom will pan the drawing down. Moving horizontally from left to right will pan the drawing to the right side of the screen.

Step #4:   Using Pan Realtime, move your cursor all the way to the right side. Figure 11–19 shows the resulting Pan Realtime operation when the cursor is moved from its original position (Figure 11–18) all the way to the right side.

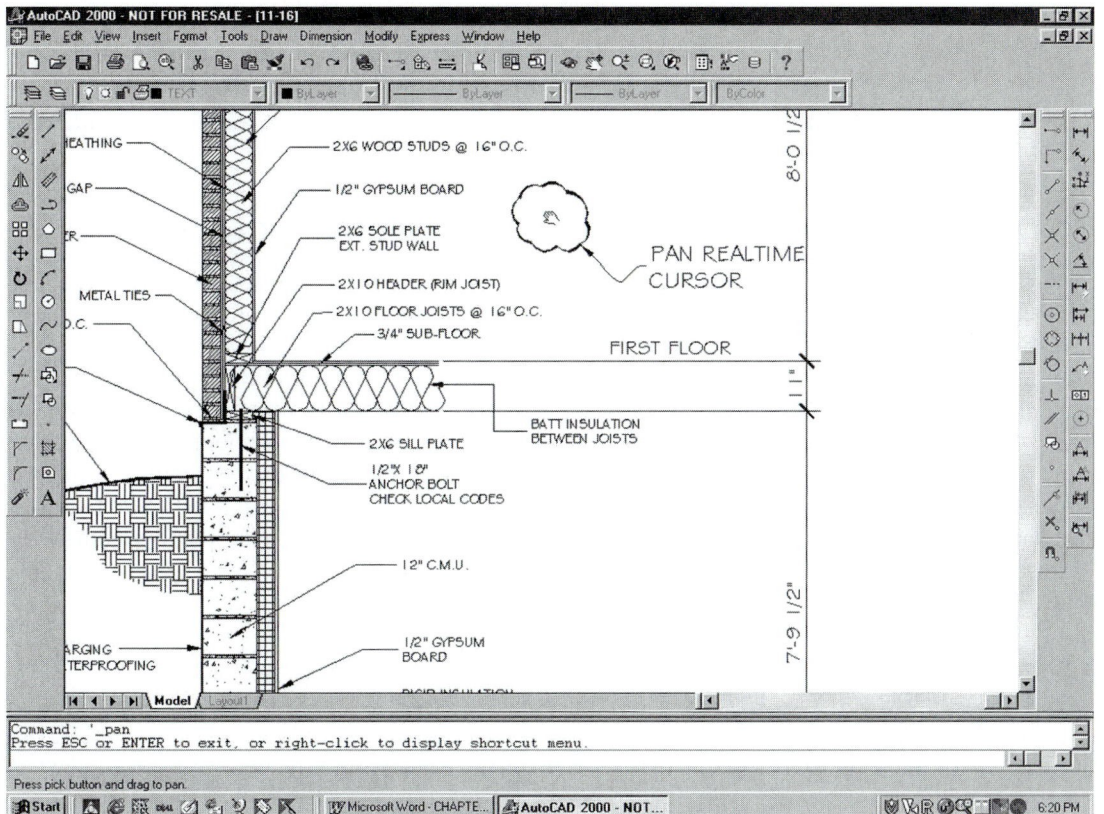

FIGURE 11–18 Pan Realtime will allow you to use the Pan function of AutoCAD in realtime. Move the cursor around to see the panning effect instantly.

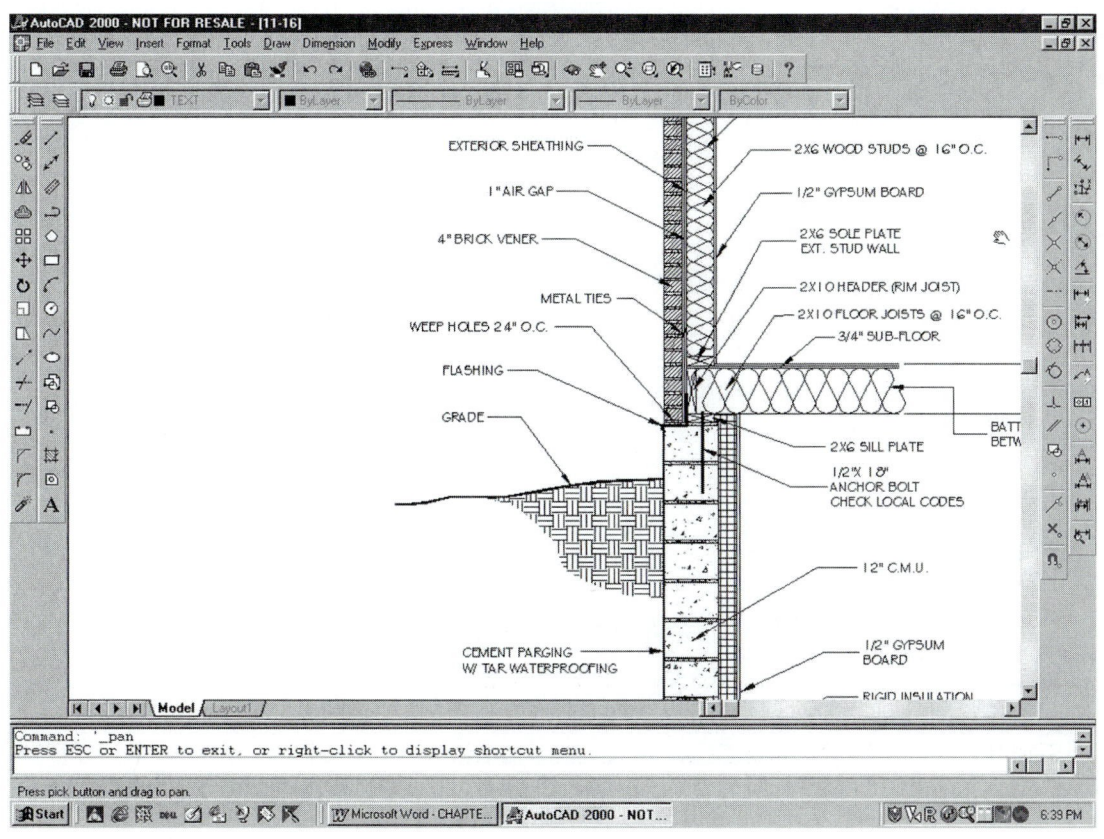

FIGURE 11–19 The wall section is moved in realtime with Pan Realtime. Notice the Pan Realtime icon on the left edge of the screen.

Step #5:   Release the left mouse button. Pan Realtime does not work, but the hand icon remains on the screen, allowing you to pan the drawing to a new location. Hold down the left button on the mouse for additional panning in realtime.

Congratulations! You have successfully moved around a drawing in realtime by using the Pan Realtime option.

11.5 ZOOM AND PAN REALTIME DUO WITH RIGHT-CLICK

One of the greatest benefits of using the Zoom Realtime and Pan Realtime together with the right-click is that you do not have to exit one and access the other to perform many zooming and panning operations. To use Zoom Realtime and Pan Realtime one after another, access either one first. For example, access Zoom Realtime and zoom in or zoom out as required and release the left mouse button. Right-click and select Pan from the shortcut menu as shown in Figure 11–20. The Pan Realtime icon will appear. Pan around as required and release the left mouse button. Right-click and select Zoom from the shortcut menu. Repeat this procedure until the drawing is zoomed and panned as required. This method is extremely useful if you plan to zoom and pan in realtime as one streamlined operation. You can also access Zoom Realtime and Pan Realtime without using either one first. With no command running, right-click on the screen and select Pan or Zoom as shown in Figure 11–21.

FIGURE 11–20   When you right-click after using either Zoom Realtime or Pan Realtime, a shortcut menu will allow you to switch from one to another.

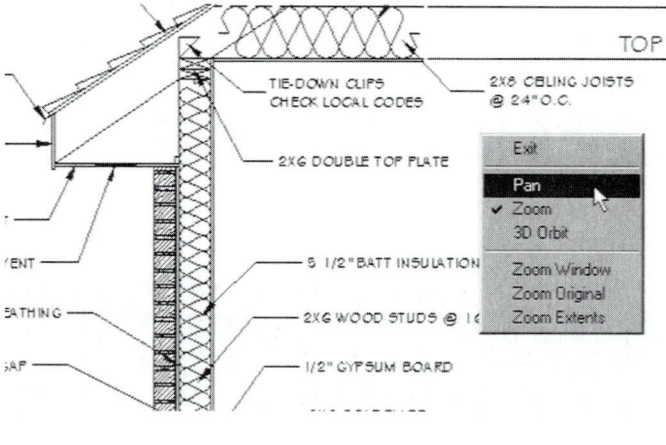

FIGURE 11–21   When you right-click with no command running, you can still access the Zoom and Pan with realtime.

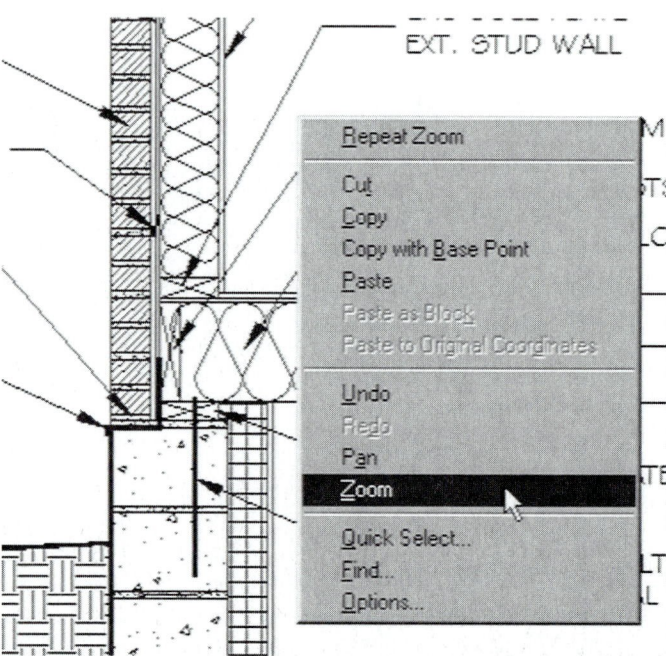

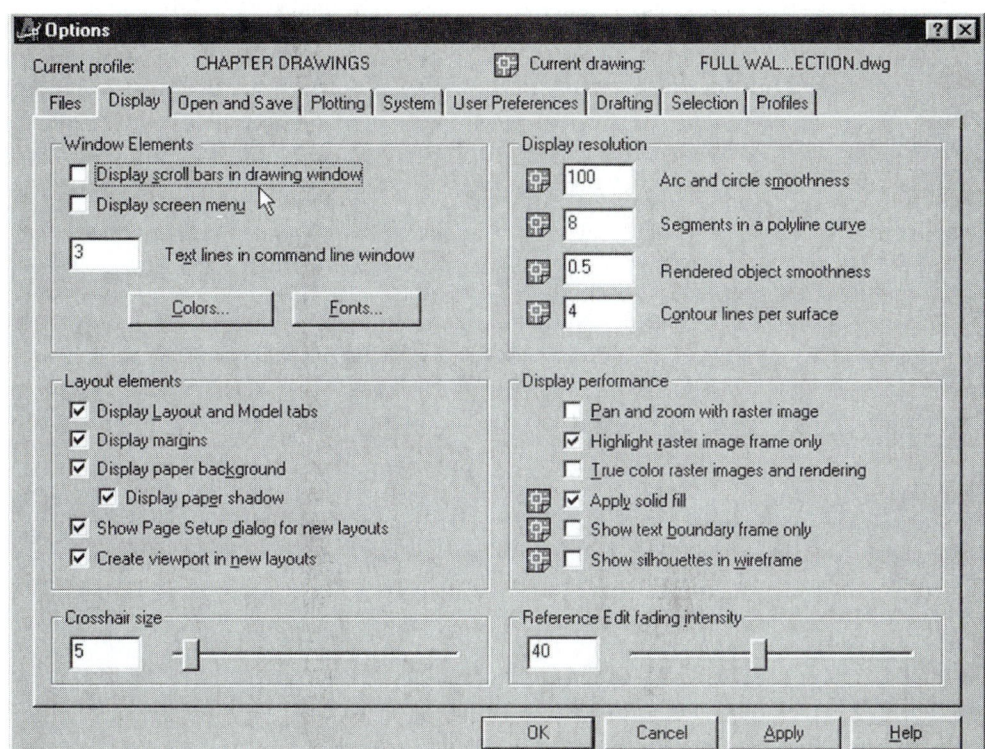

FIGURE 11–22 The scroll bars can be removed from the screen using the Display tab of the Options dialog box. You can also set Display resolution using the same tab and dialog box.

Tips: Toggle between Pan and Zoom to keep the desired area of your drawing near the center of the screen, then use the Zoom options to control the display magnification.

Note: You can also use the scroll bars located at the bottom and at the right side of the drawing screen to pan the drawing. If you do not use scroll bars, you can remove them from the screen by accessing the Options dialog box. Select the Display tab and inside the Window Elements category, remove the checkmark inside the Display scroll bars in drawing window check box as shown in Figure 11–22.

The right-click shortcut menu shown in Figure 11–20 can also be used to access the following options:

Exit: Select this option to complete the command or press the <Esc> key.

3D Orbit: Use this option to view 3D models.

Zoom Window: Use this option to define the desired window to view.

Zoom Original: Use this option to get back to the original view.

Zoom Extents: Use this option to zoom out to the drawing extents.

11.6 USING ZOOM TRANSPARENTLY

You can use any of the zoom options, including Zoom Realtime and Pan Realtime, transparently. Using zoom options transparently means the active command is temporarily interrupted so that a zoom operation can be performed. After the zooming is completed, the initial command that was interrupted resumes. For example, you can start the LINE command, zoom in to a corner for the first precise pick point (using running object snap modes), zoom out to see more of the drawing, and then zoom in to another corner for the second precise pick point. The LINE command will be interrupted each time you use any of the zoomoptions from the toolbar or pull-down menu. This method uses the zoom options transparently and does not require any special action at the command line.

To use a zoom option transparently at the command line, enter an apostrophe (') before entering the zoom command without any spaces. The command sequence for using the Window option of the ZOOM command transparently when using the LINE command is as follows:

(This procedure assumes that the drawing is too small to see and you need to zoom in to a corner for the first point and you need to zoom in again to an opposite corner for the second point.)

```
Command: LINE ~EnterKey~
Specify first point: 'Z ~EnterKey~
>>Specify corner of window, enter a scale factor (nX or nXP), or
[All/Center/Dynamic/Extents/Previous/Scale/Window] <realtime>: W
~EnterKey~
>>Specify first point: (select the first point for the zoom window)
>>Specify opposite corner: (select the opposite corner for the zoom
window)
Resuming LINE command.
Specify first point: (using running object snap modes snap to the desired
point)
Specify next point or [Undo]: 'Z ~EnterKey~
>>Specify corner of window, enter a scale factor (nX or nXP), or
[All/Center/Dynamic/Extents/Previous/Scale/Window] <realtime>: P
~EnterKey~(this will bring the drawing display back to its previous zoom
state in which you still need to zoom in for the next point)
Resuming LINE command. (You should see the line attached to the first
point picked.
Specify next point or [Undo]: 'Z ~EnterKey~
>>Specify corner of window, enter a scale factor (nX or nXP), or
[All/Center/Dynamic/Extents/Previous/Scale/Window] <realtime>: W
~EnterKey~
>>Specify first point: (select the first point for the zoom window)
>>Specify opposite corner: (select the opposite corner for the zoom window)
Resuming LINE command.
Specify next point or [Undo]: (using running object snap modes snap to
the desired point)
```

Note: The double greater than symbol (>>) indicates that the LINE command has been interrupted while you use the ZOOM command transparently. Most of the commands can be interrupted using the ZOOM command transparently.

Note: If you access a display command from a toolbar button or a pull-down menu, it will run transparently by default.

Tips: Use the zoom buttons located in the Zoom toolbar or Standard toolbar or access them from the View pull-down menu for faster and automatic transparent usage. A much faster and efficient method is to use the Microsoft Intellimouse feature when zooming and panning in realtime. The rotating wheel between the two buttons on the mouse can perform zoom and pan in realtime. This is faster than selecting a zoom button or entering 'Z at the command line. Double-click on the rotating wheel for an automatic Zoom Extents.

11.7 DRAWING VIEW DISPLAY ACCURACY

AutoCAD performs zooming and panning extremely fast, but to give you the fastest display, AutoCAD sacrifices view display accuracy. For example, when you zoom in to a circle you just created will appear as a nine-sided figure even though you did not use the POLYGON command with nine sides. To have the highest view display accuracy, you will have to sacrifice zoom and pan speed.

11.7.1   Drawing View Resolution

AutoCAD creates objects by assigning a specific amount of pixels to create them. A line is created with many pixels displayed on the screen, and a circle is created with many line segments joined close to each other. When you create a circle, you do not zoom out to create the circle; instead you zoom in to create it. Once you create the circle its view display accuracy is high enough for you to see the circle perfectly round. It has enough line segments with enough pixels for a perfect display. When you zoom out, most of the line segments that make up the circle use less pixels because the circle at that magnification does not require as many pixels on as many line segments. When you zoom in close to the circle, it no longer has the high display accuracy that it did when it was first created. It will resemble a polygon instead of a smooth circle. This is because AutoCAD performed a very fast zoom without re-adjusting the amount of pixels represented on each line segment to bring the circle at the new magnification display. This accuracy is referred to as the *view resolution*, which is the number of pixels AutoCAD will use to redisplay objects. The view resolution is set to 100 as the default. You can change the view resolution from 1 to 20,000 by using the Options dialog box. The Display tab of the Options dialog box was shown in Figure 11–22. This tab can also be used to adjust the view resolution setting. Inside the *Display resolution* category, highlight the current number in the *Arc and circle smoothness* edit box and enter the desired number. A high view resolution setting will allow the objects to be displayed with more pixels.

11.7.2   Drawing View Regeneration

Without changing the view resolution, you can have AutoCAD redisplay the objects by recalculating and redefining every single pixel composing the objects. This is referred to as *regeneration* and is performed by entering REGEN at the command line. For view display accuracy you have two options as follows:

1. Keep the display resolution at 100. Circular objects will not appear smooth because they will be displayed with fewer pixels. Enter REGEN at the command line after objects are redisplayed. Circular objects will now be displayed as smooth. The fast zooming and panning are not sacrificed.

2. Change the display resolution to 5000 using the Options dialog box and click on the Apply button. AutoCAD will immediately perform a Regen operation. This will display all circular objects smoothly even after you zoom in to a small circle on the screen. From then on, all circular objects will be drawn and redisplayed with a high display resolution scale. Fast zooming and panning are sacrificed, but in return all circular objects are displayed with perfect smoothness.

   Note: The display resolution has no effect on plotted drawings. When a drawing is plotted, the display resolution is selected automatically by the plotter settings.

Let's go back to the Display tab of the Options dialog box. The other options in the *Display resolution* category is as follows:

- **SEGMENTS IN A POLYLINE CURVE:**   This option allows you to specify the number of line segments used to display polyline curves. The default value is 8 with a maximum value of 32767.

- **RENDERED OBJECT SMOOTHNESS:**   This option allows you to set the display smoothness for shaded and rendered objects. The default value is 0.5 and the range is 0.01 to 10.

- **CONTOUR LINES PER SURFACE:**   This option allows you to specify the number of contour lines on three-dimensional objects. The range is from 0 to 2047 with the default value of 4.

The *Display performance* category has the following options:

- **PAN AND ZOOM WITH RASTER IMAGE:**   When working with raster images you can check this option to display raster images while performing realtime pan and zoom.

- **HIGHLIGHT RASTER IMAGE FRAME ONLY:**   Selecting this option will highlight only the frame of the raster image.

- **TRUE COLOR RASTER IMAGES AND RENDERING:**   Selecting this option will render raster images and renderings at True Color format (or at the highest number of colors available in your computer settings).

- **APPLY SOLID FILL:**   This option toggles the displays of solid fills in multilines, solid objects, and wide polylines. This is also controlled with the FILL command or the FILLMODE system variable. For this option to work you must click on the Apply button and then click on the OK button, then use the REGEN command. This option is on as default.

- **SHOW TEXT BOUNDARY FRAME ONLY:**   Selecting this option creates blank rectangles in place of text. This is also controlled by the QTEXT command.

- **SHOW SILHOUETTES IN WIREFRAME:**   Selecting this option displays silhouette curves for three-dimensional solid objects.

11.8 CREATING DRAWING VIEWS

AutoCAD allows you to create views of your drawing so that you can quickly refer to that view without using the ZOOM and PAN commands. This is very convenient if you have a number of separate

FIGURE 11–23
Accessing the View dialog box from the View toolbar.

details in one sheet and want to quickly make one detail appear at a specific magnification so that you can work on it immediately. This concept is similar to using the Layer Manager Express tool to create specific layer settings. With the View dialog box you can take a snapshot of the views you want to create in your drawing. Once you create and name a view, you can have AutoCAD display it at any time during the drawing session. To access the View dialog box click on the Named Views button in the View toolbar, select Named Views from the pull-down menu, click on the Named Views button in the Standard toolbar, or enter V or VIEW at the command line. Figure 11–23 shows the View toolbar, and Figure 11–24 shows the View pull-down menu. The View dialog box is shown in Figure 11–25.

Tips: Create and select a named view as the drawing area before you plot and as the initial view when you open an existing drawing.

FIGURE 11–24   Using the View pull-down menu to access the View dialog box.

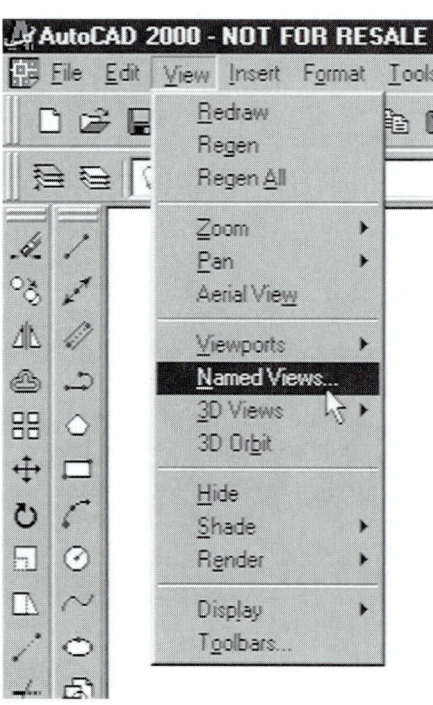

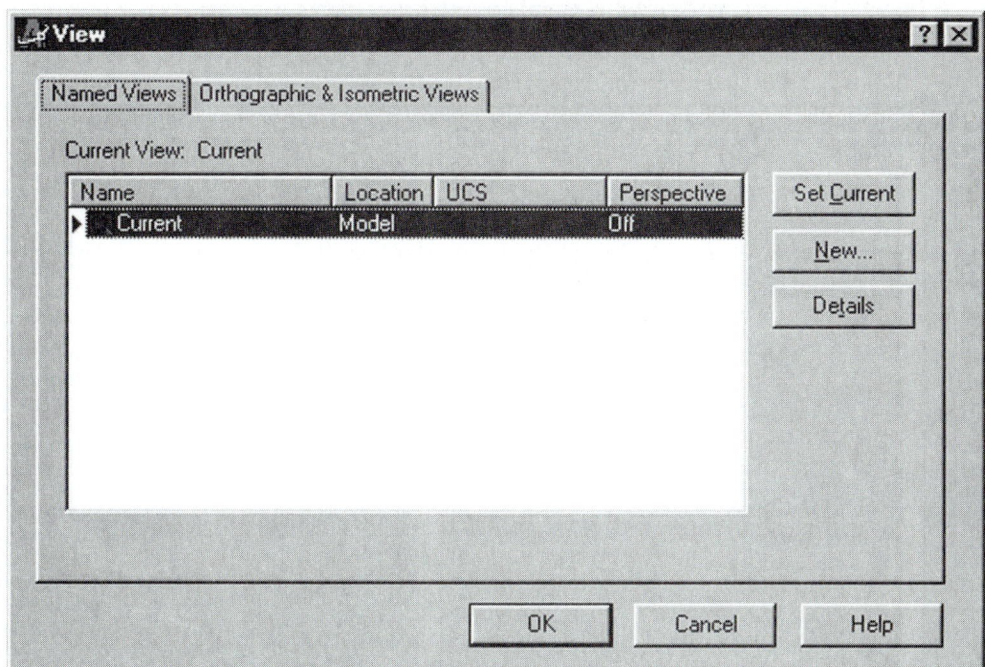

FIGURE 11–25 The View dialog box is used to create named views of your project.

11.8.1 Using the View Dialog Box to Create Views

The View dialog box as shown in Figure 11–25 has two tabs. The *Named Views* tab is used to restore the named views. The Name column lists the names of saved views in the current drawing. In a new drawing, the only view listed is the Current view. The Location column shows the location of the view. If you create a view in Model, the location will display Model. If you create a view in Layout, the location will display Layout. The UCS column shows the name of the UCS saved with the view. The Perspective column indicates whether the view was saved in a perspective format. The *Orthographic and Isometric Views* tab lists the names of the standard orthographic and isometric views of the drawing.

To create and save a view, you can define the view either first or later. If you want to save the current display as a view, select the New... button in the View dialog box. If not, select the New... button and then define the window.

■ **EXERCISE 11–4:** *The following step-by-step exercise will help you to create, name, and save four views of the wall details drawing shown in Figure 11–26. When the views are created, each wall detail can be recalled and displayed for editing purposes. This will eliminate zooming and panning that must be performed to work on each detail.*

Step #1: Open the *EXE11-3.dwg* file.

Step #2: Zoom in to the Wall Detail 1 so that the detail covers the entire screen.

Step #3: Access the View dialog box as discussed above.

Step #4: In the View dialog box, click on the New... button. This will display the New View dialog box as shown in Figure 11–27.

Step #5: In the New View dialog box and inside the View name: text box, enter WALL DETAIL 1 (you can have up to 255 characters) as shown in Figure 11–27. This is your first drawing view name.

Step #6: Select the Current display radio button and click on the OK button. The View dialog box will now display the WALL DETAIL 1 as a named view as shown in Figure 11–28.

FIGURE 11–26 The four wall details occupy the entire drawing. To work on each detail, you must constantly zoom in and zoom out. It is best to create individual views of the four wall details so that each detail can be edited with the largest magnification possible on the screen.

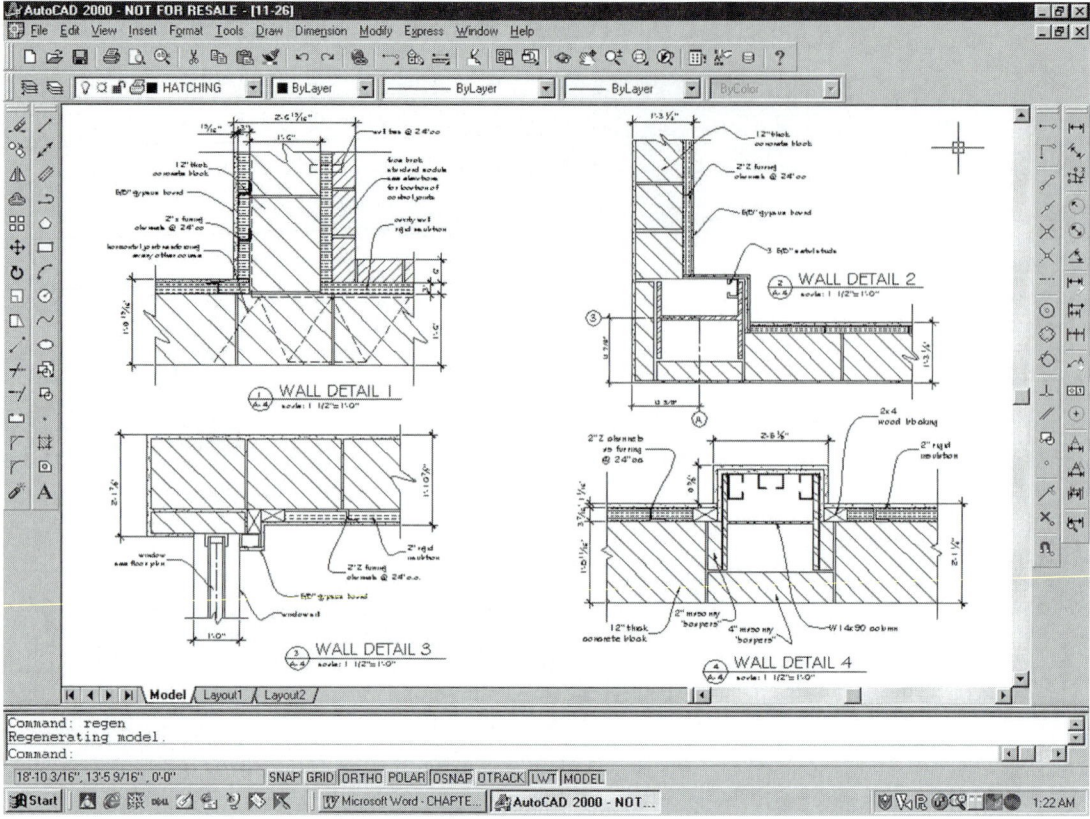

FIGURE 11–27 The New View dialog box is used to name a view, define the new view as the current display, or create a view by going back to the drawing to defining the view.

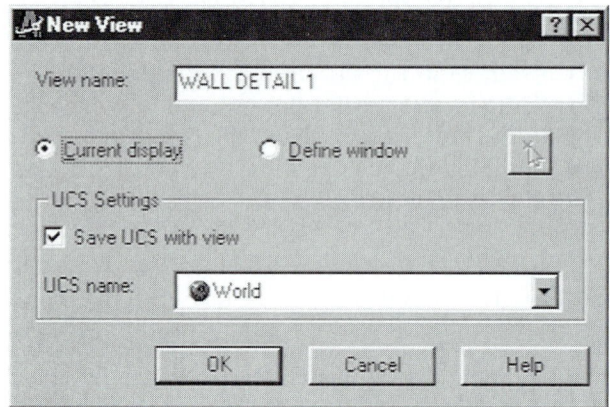

Step #7: In the View dialog box, click on the New... button.

Step #8: In the New View dialog box and inside the View name: text box, enter WALL DETAIL 2 and select the Define window radio button. Click on the Define View Window button as shown in Figure 11–29.

Step #9: Inside the drawing area, you will be prompted to define the first and the second corner of the window. Use ZOOM command options transparently to zoom out of detail 1 and zoom in to WALL DETAIL 2. Define the window around this detail by selecting first and second corner of the window.

Step #10: In the New View dialog box, click on the OK button. The new view will be displayed in the View dialog box as WALL DETAIL 2.

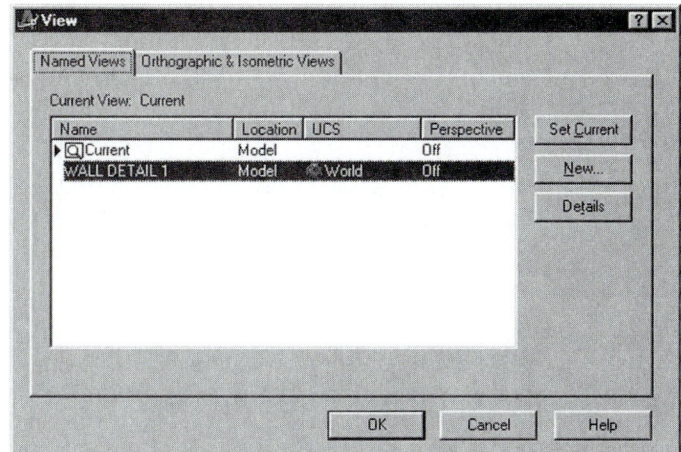

FIGURE 11–28 The View dialog box will now display WALL DETAIL 1 as the named view.

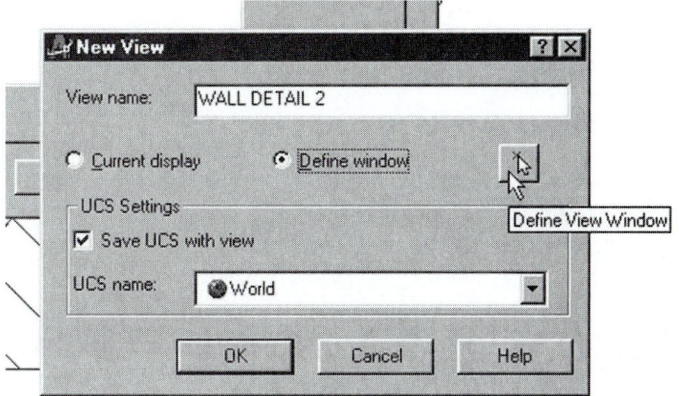

FIGURE 11–29 The Define View Window will allow you to create a window for WALL DETAIL 2.

Step #11: Repeat Steps #7, #8, #9, and #5 to create WALL DETAIL 3 and WALL DE-TAIL 4 views. The View dialog box with four views is shown in Figure 11–30.

Step #12: Click on the OK button when done.

Congratulations! You have successfully used the View and New View dialog boxes to create four views of the current drawing. These are now four separate snapshots residing in your details drawing sheet.

Note: You could have also used Paste as Block option of the right-click shortcut menu to insert the objects as a Block into a separate drawing using the Multiple Design Environment. See Chapter 19 for creating Blocks.

Named Views are saved with the drawing. This means that you can save and close the drawing, come back to it later and display the desired views. To display any of the named views created, open the drawing and access the View dialog box. Inside the Current View: list box, select the desired view and click on the Set Current button. This will place a small triangle in front of the selected view, and its name will appear in the Current View: area. Click on the OK button to display the view. You are now ready to edit the current view. The Details button in the View dialog box will display view properties as shown in Figure 11–31.

You can delete, rename, set current, and view details by selecting any of these options from the right-click shortcut menu. In the View dialog box, highlight a view and right-click. Select any of the options from the shortcut menu shown in Figure 11–32.

FIGURE 11–30 When four views are created, the View dialog box will display all four views.

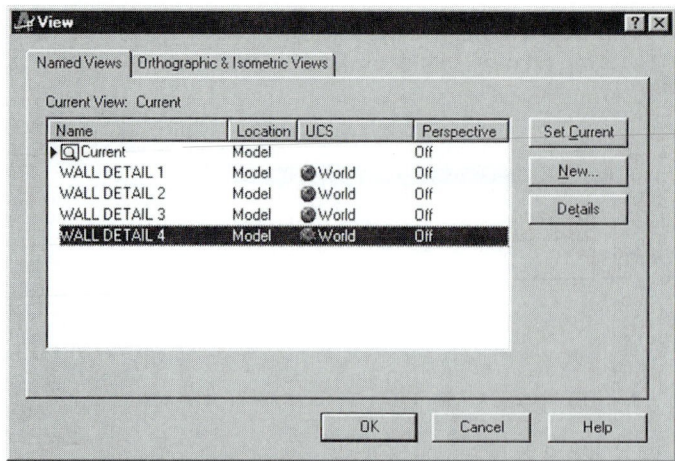

FIGURE 11–31 The View Details dialog box.

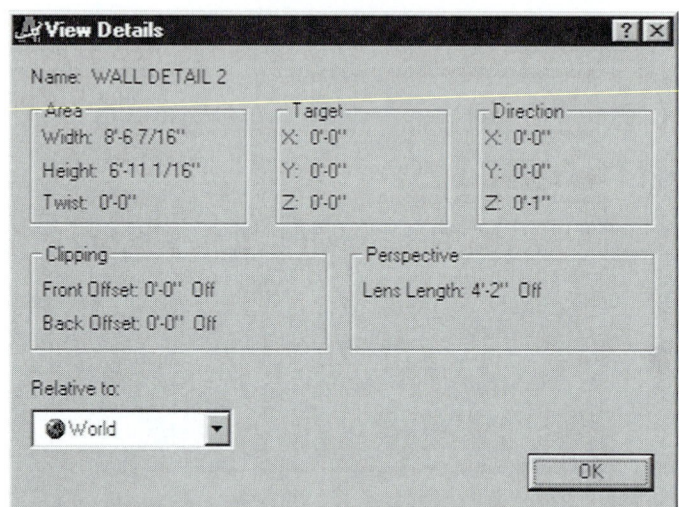

FIGURE 11–32 The right-click shortcut menu will allow you to delete, rename, set current, and view details of the selected view.

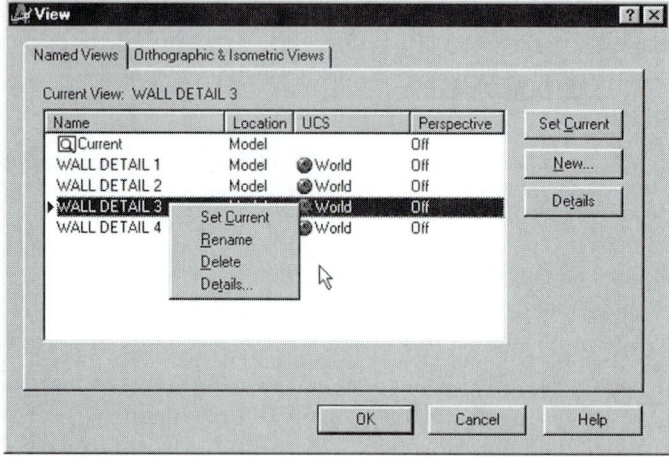

11.9 USING THE –VIEW COMMAND

You can also create and set views by entering –V or –VIEW at the command line. The command line procedure for the –VIEW command is as follows:

```
Command: -VIEW ~EnterKey~
Enter an option [?/Orthographic/Delete/Restore/Save/Ucs/Window]: (enter
an option)
```

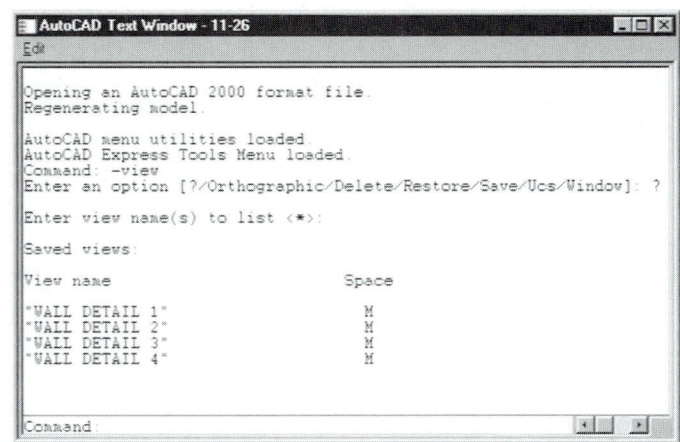

FIGURE 11–33 The –View command allows you to manage views. When you enter * after the ?, AutoCAD will display the AutoCAD Text Window and list all the views created for that drawing. Notice the M under Space for Model Space.

?: Entering ? will allow you to enter a view name or list all the defined views. The command line option is as follows:
Enter view name(s) to list < * > : *(enter a view name or press the ~EnterKey~)*
If you press the ~EnterKey~ , AutoCAD will display the AutoCAD Text Window for the current drawing and list all the defined views in that drawing. Figure 11-33 shows the four views created for Exercise 4.

ORTHOGRAPHIC: Entering O as an option changes the view to one of the orthographic views you select.

DELETE: This option allows you to delete a view. Enter D and enter the name of the view you wish to delete.

RESTORE: This option allows you to display a view. Enter R and enter the name of the view you wish to be displayed.

SAVE: This option allows you to create a new view. Enter S and enter the view name you wish to create.

UCS: This option allows you to save the UCS with the new view created. Enter U to activate this option.

WINDOW: This option allows you to create a new view based on the window selection. Enter W and enter a view name to save. AutoCAD will then allow you to create a window selection (first and second corners).

Tips: You can create separate views in Model and Paper Space Layout. When you list the views with AutoCAD Text Window, all views created in Layouts (Paper Space) will be designated as P under the Space column. M stands for Model and P stands for Paper Space in a Layout. Views can overlap and will be displayed. But objects outside the window area created with the Window option will not be plotted. This is convenient if you do not want to plot overlapping objects from other views. Layouts and Paper Space are discussed in Chapter 22.

11.10 USING THE AERIAL VIEW WINDOW

You can view different areas of a large drawing in a separate window called Aerial View. You can zoom in to locate details or features of your drawing while viewing the entire drawing in the Aerial View or you can zoom in to areas of your drawing using the Aerial View while viewing the entire drawing in the current drawing view. To access the Aerial View window, select Aerial View from the View pull-down menu or enter AV at the command line. You can resize and float the Aerial View window as shown in Figure 11–34. The entire drawing will be displayed inside the Aerial View window, and the window itself can be moved around the screen. This feature provides a view inside a view to better navigate through large drawing files.

To activate the aerial view, click on its blue title bar. This will make the current drawing inactive. To make the drawing active, click anywhere in the drawing. The thick black rectangle

FIGURE 11–34 The
Aerial View window
with its own pull-down
and zoom features.

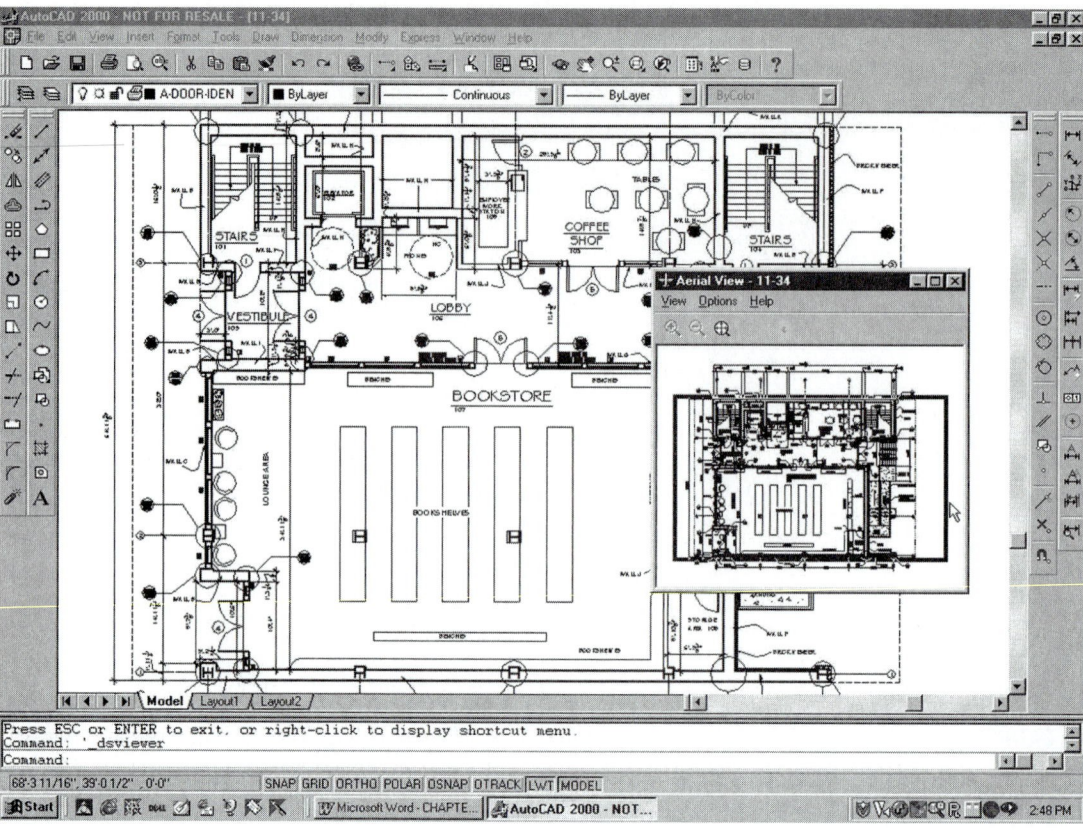

inside the aerial view represents the current drawing display. As you zoom or pan with real-time inside the current drawing, the rectangle moves to show the area you are currently working with. In Figure 11–35, the Zoom Realtime option is used to zoom in to the upper left corner of the drawing to display the stair, vestibule, elevator, HVAC/mechanical shafts, and part of the lobby areas. The Aerial View window shows the current display represented by the rectangle.

When you left-click inside the Aerial View window, the Zoom Dynamic option is activated. This is evident with the display of the X when you left-click with the display of the arrow. Use this Zoom Dynamic feature to zoom in to a portion of the drawing. To navigate through the drawing without zooming into a specific area, left-click anywhere in the drawing inside the Aerial View window, but do not select a point yet. As you move the view box around the entire drawing, you will see the pan realtime effect in the current drawing. When you reach a part of the drawing you wish to zoom in, left-click to activate the arrow in the Zoom Dynamic view box. At this point you can move the cursor to increase or decrease the magnification of the selected area. Right-click when you reach a desired magnification. This will deactivate the Zoom Dynamic operation and display the area currently zoomed in. When you increase the size of the Zoom Dynamic view box, the current drawing view updates and shows the zoomed-in location. In Figure 11–36, the Zoom Dynamic operation shown with the arrow on the edge of the view box navigates through the drawing to zoom into the exterior stairs near the handicapped ramp. The current drawing displays the zoomed-in location. This is very useful and convenient when you lose sight of where a specific feature of the drawing might be relative to the entire drawing. With the Aerial View window you see the entire drawing and navigate through out the drawing to display a required area in the active drawing as you zoom in and zoom out.

The Aerial View window bar contains three pull-down menus and three zoom buttons. The View pull-down menu contains the Zoom In, Zoom Out, and Global options. If the Zoom Out option is inactive, it can be activated by clicking on the Zoom In button. If the Zoom In option is inactive, it can be activated by clicking on the Zoom Out button. The View pull-down menu is

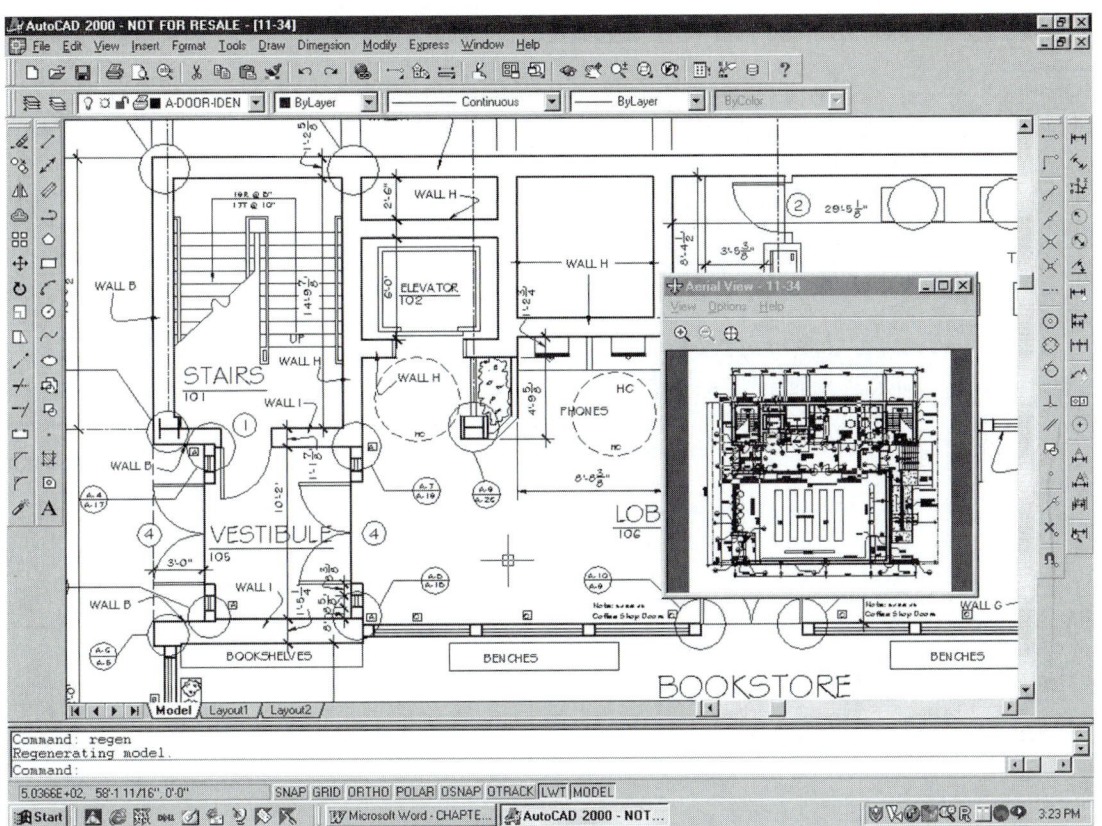

FIGURE 11–35 As you zoom in to a particular feature of the drawing, the Aerial View window shows the current display with a thick borderline.

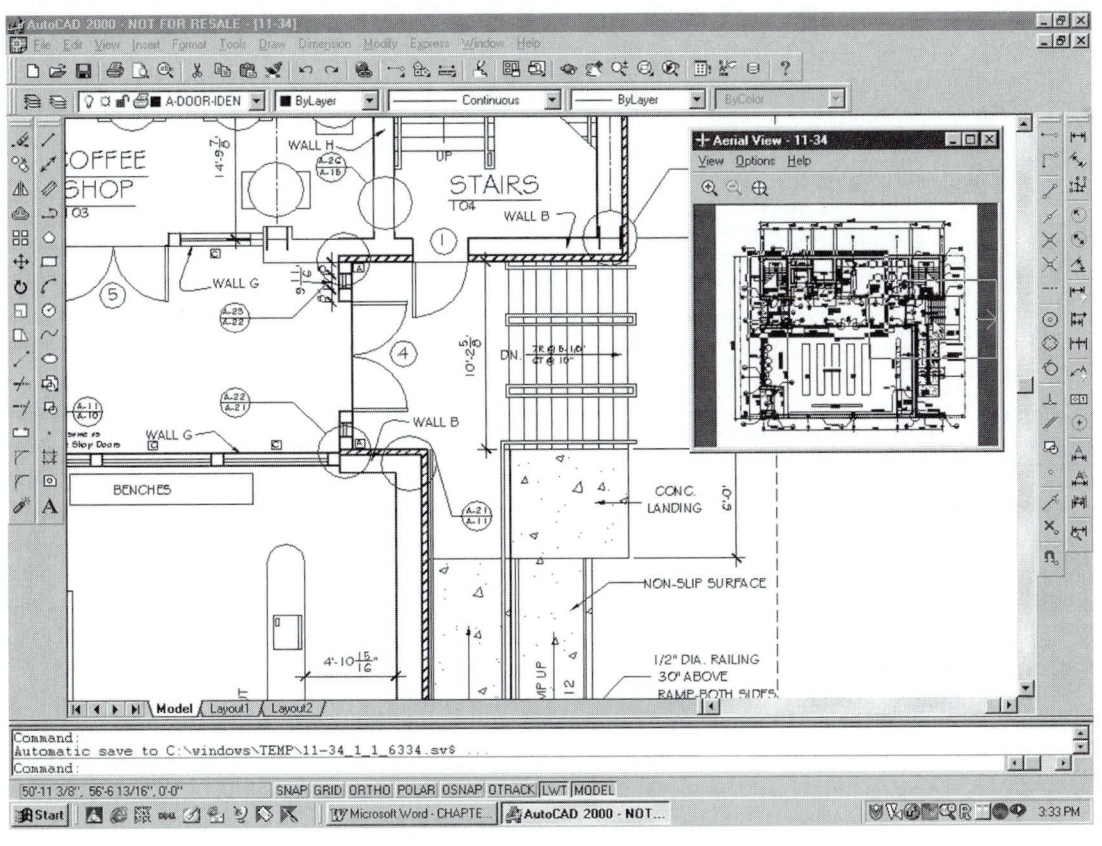

FIGURE 11–36 The Zoom Dynamic option is automatically activated when you left-click inside the Aerial View window. The exterior stair entrance near the handicapped ramp is currently zoomed-in. Notice the arrow inside the edge of the view box.

FIGURE 11–37 The View pull-down menu options.

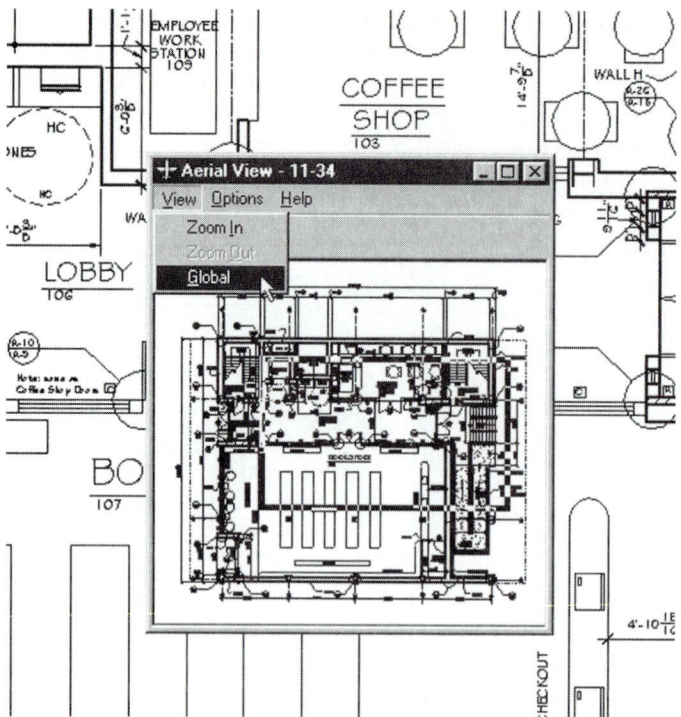

FIGURE 11–38 The Options pull-down menu.

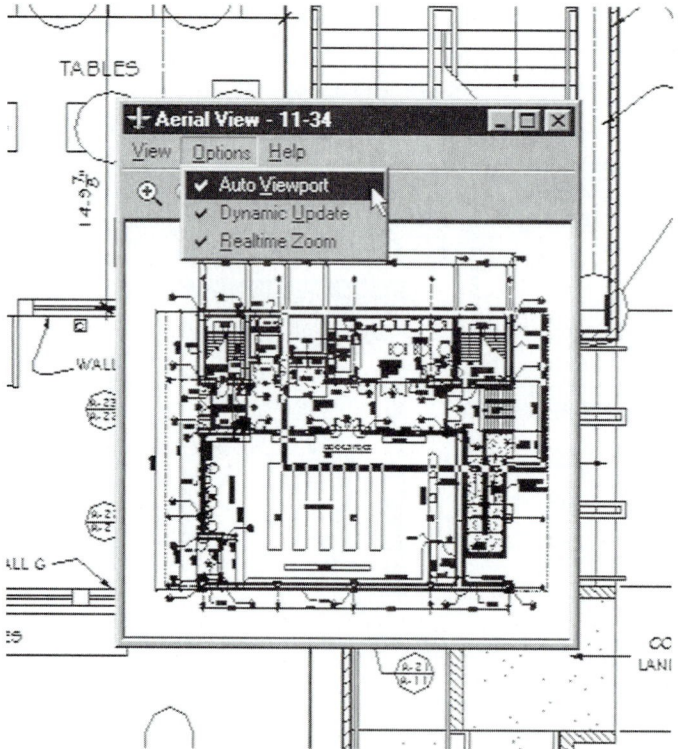

shown in Figure 11–37. The Zoom In option increases the magnification of the drawing in the Aerial View window. The Zoom Out option decreases the magnification of the drawing in the Aerial View window. The Global option will zoom to the extents of the drawing.

The Options pull-down menu shown in Figure 11–38 includes Auto Viewport, Dynamic Update, and Realtime Zoom. The Auto Viewport has no effect if you do not have any tiled viewports. Viewports are discussed in Chapter 22. When a checkmark is displayed in front of the Auto

Viewport, switching from one tiled viewport to another will automatically cause the new tiled viewport to be displayed in the Aerial View window. The Dynamic Update option allows for automatic updates in the Aerial View window display after each magnification change. The Real-time Zoom option allows you to use the ZOOM command in realtime mode inside the Aerial View window. The checkmark in front of the option indicates that the option is on. To turn the option off, select it from the list. The help pull-down menu allows you to open the Aerial View help in AutoCAD.

Tips: Use the right-click shortcut menu inside the Aerial View window to access all the button and pull-down menu options. You can also use the zoom and pan options transparently.

REVIEW QUESTIONS

1. The Zoom toolbar has eight zoom options. Name four of these options.
2. How many different ways can you access the Window option of the ZOOM command?
3. Explain the concept behind Zoom Dynamic.
4. What does "relative to full display" mean when using Zoom Scale?
5. Which Zoom option allows you to zoom to the limits of your drawing?
6. Which Zoom option allows you to place a rectangle around the objects?
7. Describe the advantages behind using the zoom and pan in realtime mode.
8. What does using ZOOM command options transparently mean?
9. Describe view resolution as it relates to view display accuracy.
10. Describe the options available to correct and adjust view display accuracy.
11. Why is it important to create views of your drawings?
12. How many different ways can you access the View dialog box?
13. Describe briefly the process behind creating a view of your drawing.
14. How do you access the Aerial View window?
15. What happens when you left-click inside the Aerial View window and move your cursor around?
16. What is the function of the Global option in the View pull-down menu of the Aerial View window?

PROBLEMS

1. Open the *EXE11-4.dwg* file. Zoom in to the lower-left corner and create a view and name it DIRECTORS AREA. Save the changes.
2. Using the same drawing above, zoom in to the upper-right corner and create a view of the stairs and name it STAIRS AREA. Save the changes.
3. Open the *EXE10-6.dwg* file. Create a view of the bathroom, kitchen, and the sun room by zooming in to each area. Save the changes.
4. Open the *EXE11-6.dwg* file. Use the Zoom Dynamic option to zoom in to the upper-left corner. Do not save the changes.
5. Open the *EXE11-2.dwg* file. Access the Aerial View window and zoom to the area where wall and roof intersect. Next, zoom to the bottom of the footing using the Realtime Zoom option of the Aerial View window. Do not save the changes.
6. Open the *EXE11-4.dwg* file. Using the Zoom and Pan Realtime options, zoom in and pan into each room and create a list of all fixtures and/or furniture in each room. Do not save the changes.
7. Open the *EXE11-5.dwg* file. Using the Zoom and Pan Realtime options, zoom in and pan into the Toilet Accessories Table and locate each item in the elevation. Do not save the changes.

Basic Editing and Modifying

CHAPTER

12

After successful completion of this chapter you should be able to:

▲ Identify the guidelines to follow when drawing and modifying.

▲ Identify, understand, and create six object selection set methods.

▲ Add and remove objects to and from the selection set.

▲ Use the ERASE command.

▲ Edit stacked objects.

▲ Use the TRIM and EXTRIM commands.

▲ Use the EXTEND and LENGTHEN commands.

▲ Use the STRETCH and MSTRETCH (Multiple Stretch) commands.

▲ Use the SCALE command.

▲ Use the MOVE and COPY commands.

▲ Use the ROTATE command.

▲ Use the MOCORO (Move Copy Rotate) command.

▲ Use the MIRROR and ALIGN commands.

▲ Use the ARRAY command.

▲ Use the CHANGE command.

▲ Use the SELECT command.

▲ Use the BREAK command.

▲ Use the GROUP command.

▲ Create a selection set based on object type and properties using the Quick Select dialog box.

▲ Edit polylines.

12.1 INTRODUCTION TO MODIFYING

All projects go through some kind of modification. It is a major part of the design, drawing, and production cycle. Drawing modifications happen due to mistakes, changes in the drawing, change orders, revisions, client requirements, and code implications, among other reasons. AutoCAD provides a wide array of commands and procedures that will help you modify objects as fast and as effectively as possible. This is where AutoCAD shines and this is where you begin to hate manual drawing and erasing with eraser in one hand and eraser shield in the other. When modifying AutoCAD drawings you should follow some of the guidelines below:

1. Before drawing from sketches, preliminaries, or mark-ups, check dimensions, notes, and references. Ask the person in charge of the project about what to draw and what is expected from you for that project.

2. Although it is possible to draw objects over existing objects, try not to make this a habit. Drawing over existing objects takes time, is redundant, and it may plot with a double thickness, which may be unacceptable.

3. Do not cut corners thinking that you will fix it next time around. You may not be the only person working on the same drawing.

4. Always understand and follow the AutoCAD standards where you work. Create everything according to those standards.

5. Study the drawing you are about to modify.

6. Understand scale factors that will affect drawing precision at modifications.

7. Remember that drawings need to be precise and at the correct scale when plotted.

8. Do not assume anything when drawing. Simply ask someone. It is better to spend 15 minutes searching and consulting than one hour of erasing.

12.2 CREATING A SELECTION SET FOR EDITING

When deleting and modifying objects, you can either select each entity one at a time using the pickbox or select the entire object as a whole with an enclosure. This enclosure to select objects is called creating a *selection set* in AutoCAD. All editing commands will eventually prompt you to create a selection set by displaying *Select objects:* prompt after accessing the editing command. When selecting more than one object, it is better to create a window around the objects so that the time to select objects for modification is kept to a minimum. A window around the object is not just for erasing or modification, it can be created for assigning or selecting specific object properties or for inserting purposes. But a window around the objects can be any shape, size, or form. The simplest window selection form is the box. The box can be a rectangle or a square. Objects can be removed from or added to the selection set. There are six different object selection methods as follows:

1. Pickbox selection.
2. Window selection.
3. Crossing selection.
4. Window Polygon (WP) selection.
5. Crossing Polygon (CP) selection.
6. Fence selection.

These selection options require you to select an object with the pickbox or create an enclosure around the objects after you select or enter an editing command. They are in no way limited to just one command. All of the editing commands that require you to *select objects* will work with any of the object selection methods. Most of the editing commands allow you to perform different selection options. For example, you can select everything on the screen by entering *All* at the Select objects: prompt, you can enter *P* to select a previously edited object, you can enter *R* to remove a selected object, or you can enter *A* to add objects to the selection set. Or you can use the *Multiple* option of the COPY command to copy the selected object into more than one location. Starting with the ERASE command, you will learn the six major object selection methods and the options associated with each command.

12.3 ERASING OBJECTS

The ERASE command allows you to delete objects. You can access the ERASE command by selecting the Erase button in the Modify toolbar, selecting Erase from the Modify pull-down menu, or by entering E or ERASE at the command line. When the Select objects: prompt appears, the crosshairs disappear and the pickbox remains. The command line procedure is as follows:

```
Command: ERASE ~EnterKey~
Select objects: (use one of the following object selection methods)
```

12.3.1 Pickbox Selection

The pickbox is used to select the objects one at a time or to create any of the above selection methods. The size of the pickbox is important in reference to the size of the objects being selected. In order for the individual objects to be selected, a portion of the object must be inside the pickbox to be selected. If the pickbox does not pick, select, or touch an object, then there is no selection. Any objects that are included in the pickbox selection set will be subject to modification. A very large pickbox can include objects that are not desired in the selection set, and a very small pickbox may make it difficult to manage object selection. You can adjust the size of the pickbox from the Options dialog box or at the command line. From the Options dialog box, click on the Selection tab and adjust the slide bar in the Pickbox Size area shown in Figure 12–1. Move the slider left to make the pickbox smaller and move it right to make it larger. When done, click on the Apply button then click on the OK button. You can also use the PICKBOX system variable at the command line and enter a size for the pickbox. Enter a numeric value from 0 to 50 that will set the object selection pickbox size in pixels. The default pickbox size is 3.

There are two different ways you can use the pickbox:

1. ***Selecting one object with the pickbox:*** Enter the editing command and left-click on the object to select it. The selected object will be highlighted and is included in the selection set. Right-click or press the ~EnterKey~ to execute the editing command.

2. ***Selecting more than one object with the pickbox:*** Enter the editing command and left-click on each object. All selected objects will be highlighted. After selecting the objects right-click or press the ~EnterKey~ to execute the editing command.

■ **EXERCISE 12–1:** *The following step-by-step exercise will help you use the ERASE command to erase a group of objects using the pickbox. Figure 12–2 shows seven tables in the coffee shop. Each table is composed of seven individual objects, six lines and one circle. Using the*

FIGURE 12–1 The Options dialog box can be used to change the size of the pickbox.

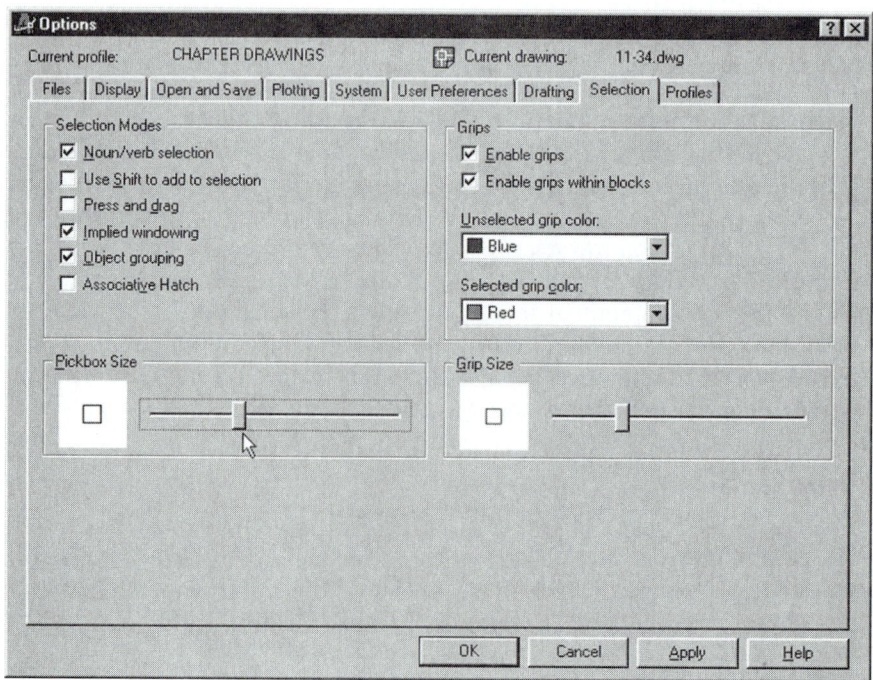

ERASE command and the Pickbox selection method 2, you will erase one of the tables. All objects that are part of the table will be selected one after another. AutoCAD will display the number of objects selected and include it in the total found area.

Step #1: Open the EXE12-1.dwg file.

Step #2: Using one of the zoom methods, zoom in to the coffee shop area.

Step #3: Use the ERASE command to erase one of the tables as follows:

Command: **E** *~EnterKey~ (or click on the Erase button in the Modify toolbar)*

Select objects: *(Select one of the lines. The line will be highlighted)*

Select objects: 1 found

Select objects: *(Select another line. The line will be highlighted)*

Select objects: 1 found, 2 total

Select objects: *(Select another line. The line will be highlighted)*

Select objects: 1 found, 3 total

Select objects: *(Select another line. The line will be highlighted)*

Select objects: 1 found, 4 total

Select objects: *(Select another line. The line will be highlighted)*

Select objects: 1 found, 5 total

Select objects: *(Select another line. The line will be highlighted)*

Select objects: 1 found, 6 total

Select objects: *(Select the circle. The circle will be highlighted)*

Select objects: 1 found, 7 total

Select objects: *~EnterKey~ (or right-click)*

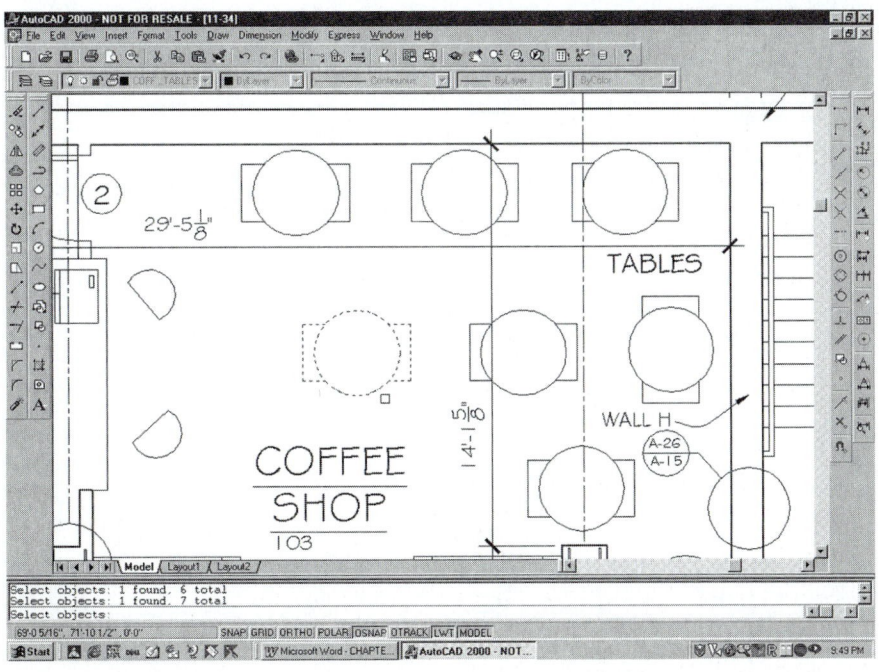

FIGURE 12–2 Using the Pickbox Selection method with the ERASE command.

The table will be erased. Notice that the selection set included seven objects to be erased. Do not save the changes.

Congratulations! You have successfully erased a table composed of seven objects.

Note: To adjust the size of the crosshairs, enter the CURSORSIZE system variable at the command line. The default value of 5 represents the size of the crosshairs as the percentage of the screen.

Tips: Pickbox is not the same as Aperture box. All Object Snap modes use a target box called Aperture, which is measured in pixels. It is controlled by the APERTURE system variable. Default size is 10 with 1 as minimum and 50 as maximum size for the Aperture box.

12.3.2   Window Selection

Rather than selecting objects one at a time, you can select a group of objects by placing a window around the objects. All objects entirely within the window will be selected. If portions of objects extend beyond the box, they will not be selected. For this to work, you must create the window by selecting the upper-left or lower-left corner of the box and dragging the cursor diagonally to select the opposite corner. This method will create a solid window box as shown in Figure 12–3.

■   **EXERCISE 12–2:**   *The following step-by-step exercise will help you erase the table shown in Figure 12–4 using the Window selection method.*

Step #1:   Open the EXE12-1.dwg file.

Step #2:   Using one of the zoom methods, zoom-in to the coffee shop area.

Step #3:   Use the ERASE command and create a window selection as follows:

Command: **E** ~EnterKey~

Select objects: *(select the first corner for the window and drag the mouse to the second corner as shown in Figure 12–4)*

FIGURE 12–3 Creating a window selection set.

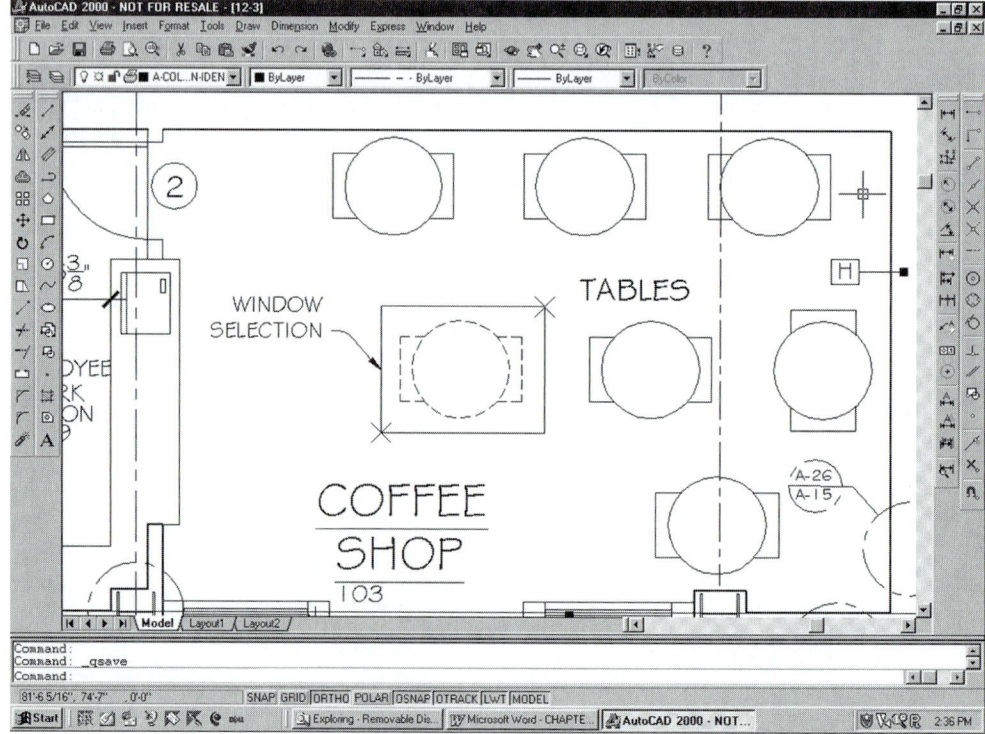

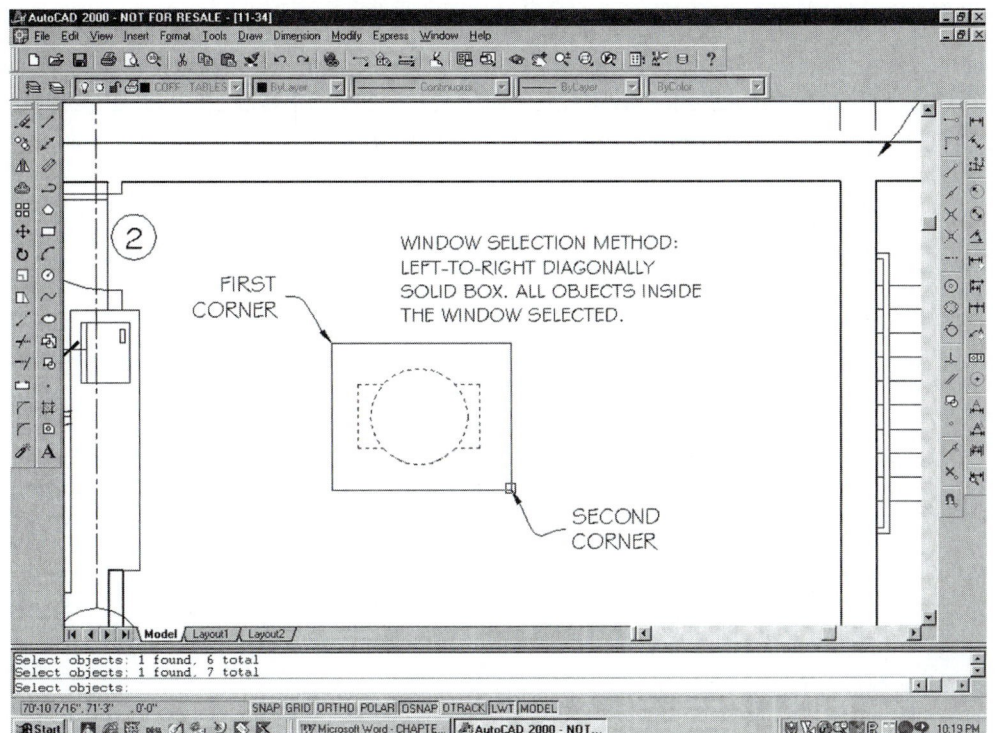

FIGURE 12–4
Selecting the first corner and then dragging the cursor to the opposite corner to select the second corner will create a solid window. All objects inside the window will be selected and subject to modification.

Specify opposite corner: *(select the second corner for the window)*

Specify opposite corner: 7 found

Select objects: ~EnterKey~

The table will be erased. Notice that the selection set included seven objects to be erased. Do not save the changes.

Congratulations! You have successfully erased the table by creating a window selection set.

You can alter the selection set by selecting more objects or by creating more window selections at the Select objects: prompt. Objects will not be erased until you press the ~EnterKey~ or use right-click. If objects do not completely fit inside the window box, they will not be selected as shown in Figure 12–5.

12.3.3 Crossing Selection

The Crossing selection method is similar to the Window selection method, except the box is created from the lower-right or upper-right corner and dragged diagonally to the opposite corner. This method will create a dashed box to distinguish it from the solid box of the Window selection method. All objects completely inside the crossing box and any objects touching the crossing box will be selected.

■ **EXERCISE 12–3:** *The following step-by-step exercise will help you erase the two circles and six lines shown in Figure 12–6 using the Crossing selection method.*

Step #1: Open the EXE12-2.dwg file.

Step #2: Use the ERASE command and create a crossing selection as follows:

Command: **E** ~EnterKey~

Select objects: *(select the first corner of the crossing and drag the mouse to the second corner as shown in Figure 12–6)*

FIGURE 12–5 Objects touching the window box will not be included in the selection set because they are not completely included inside the window box. These objects will not be subject to modification.

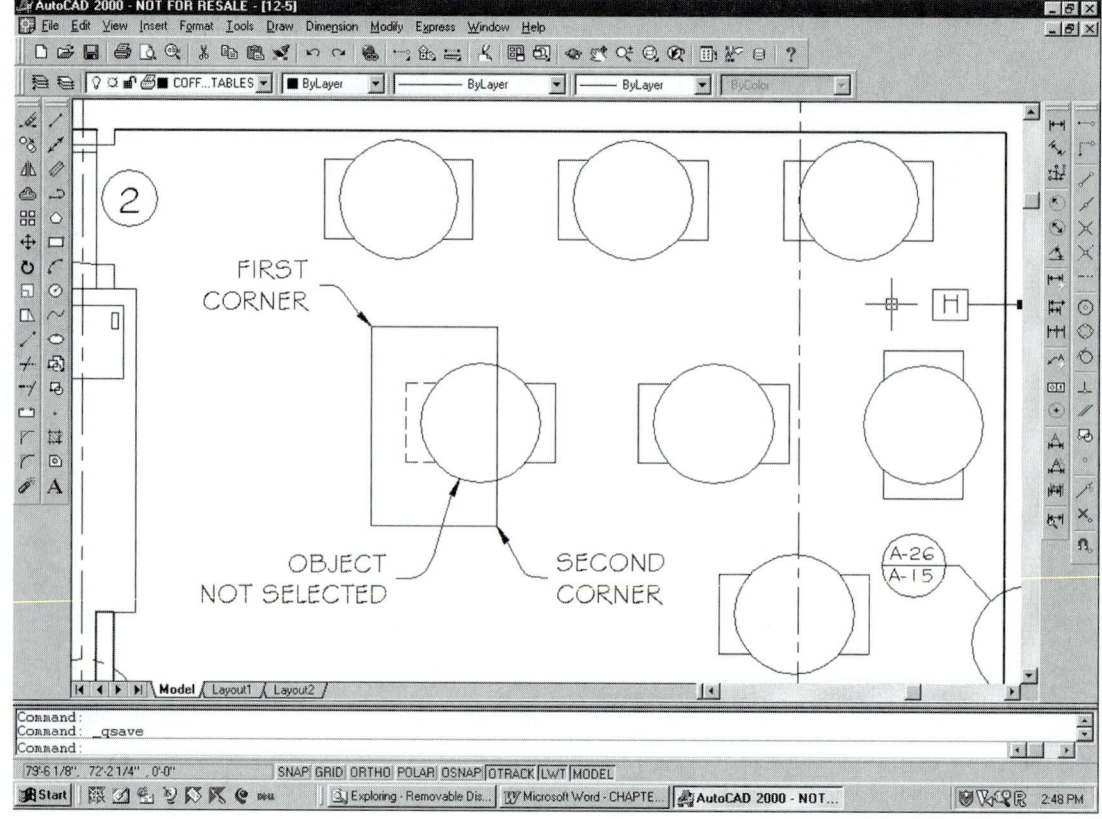

Specify opposite corner: *(select the second corner)*

Specify opposite corner: 8 found *(only the two circles and six lines will be selected)*

Select objects: ~EnterKey~

Congratulations! You have successfully erased the objects by creating a crossing selection. Do not save the changes.

> *Note: Remember, when the selection box is created from left to right it is a Window selection with a solid line; when the selection box is created from right to left it is a Crossing selection with a dashed line. All objects must be completely inside the Window box to be selected, and all objects inside and crossing the Crossing box will be selected.*

12.3.4   Window Polygon (WP) Selection

When creating a Window or Crossing selection, you are limited to selecting only two points. The Polygon option allows you to create additional points by moving around objects so as to avoid selecting other objects that would otherwise be selected with the Window selection box. To create a window as a polygon (closed object with more than one side) at any shape and in any direction, enter WP at the Select objects: prompt. This way you can create a window selection set by creating more than two points around the objects.

■   **EXERCISE 12–4:**   *The following step-by-step exercise will help you erase the objects shown with "X" in Figure 12–7 without erasing the other objects by creating a window polygon.*

Step #1:   Open the EXE12-3.dwg file.

Step #2:   Use the ERASE command and create a window polygon as follows:

Command: **ERASE** ~EnterKey~

Select objects: **WP** ~EnterKey~

First polygon point: *(turn Ortho and Osnap off and select the starting point as shown in Figure 12–8)*

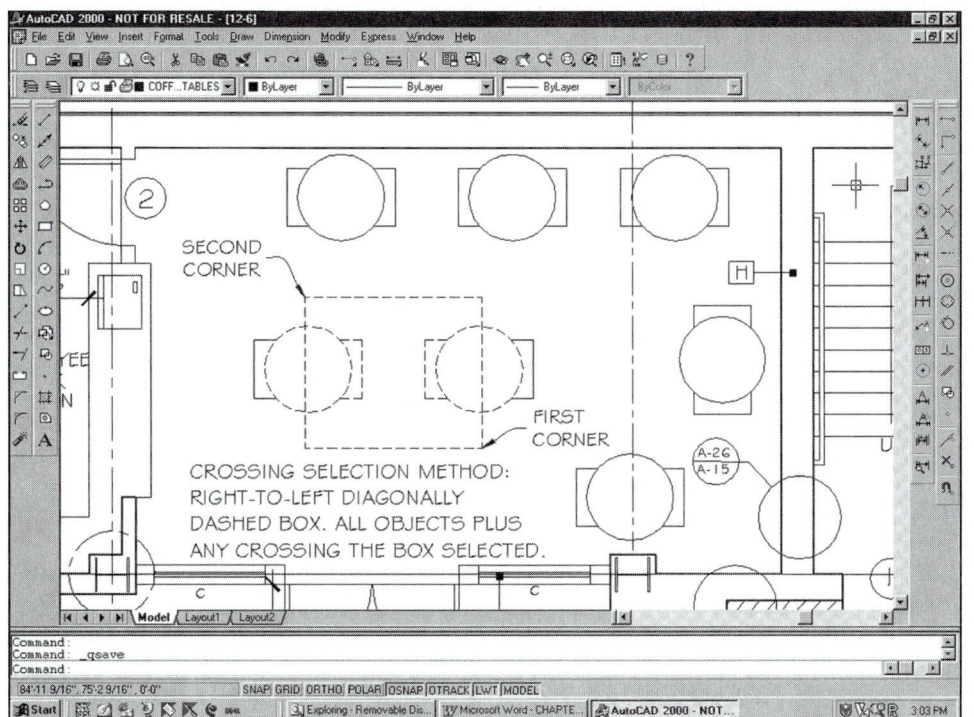

FIGURE 12–6 Using the Crossing selection method to select objects to erase.

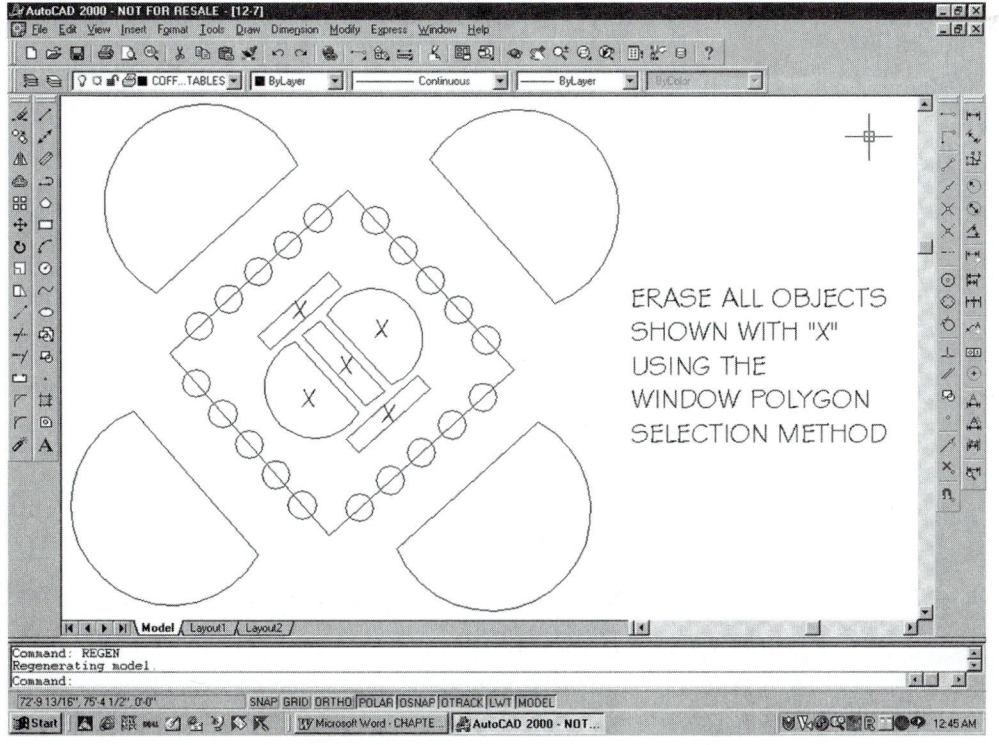

FIGURE 12–7 All objects shown with X can be erased using the Window Polygon (WP) selection method.

Specify endpoint of line or [Undo]: *(select second point)*

Specify endpoint of line or [Undo]: *(select third point)*

Specify endpoint of line or [Undo]: *(select fourth point)*

Specify endpoint of line or [Undo]: *(select ending point)*

Specify endpoint of line or [Undo]: ~EnterKey~

Congratulations! You have successfully erased the objects shown as X by creating a window polygon.

All required objects are included in the selection set as shown in Figure 12–8. Do not save the changes.

Tips: If you select a point that you did not want to select, enter U to undo the last point. The last point and the first point do not have to intersect to create the polygon. You could have selected the objects individually with the pickbox but that would have required 16 picks.

12.3.5   Crossing Polygon (CP) Selection

This is similar to the Window Polygon option, except the objects touching the crossing polygon will be included in the selection set. For example, to erase the six circles with lines going through the centers that are adjacent to the small rectangles including the five objects in the center, enter *CP* at the Select objects: prompt and specify the points as shown in Figure 12–9. Everything inside the crossing polygon and everything crossing it will be included in the selection set and will be erased as shown in Figure 12–10.

■ **EXERCISE 12–5:**   *The following step-by-step exercise will help you to create a crossing polygon and erase the objects as shown in Figure 12–9.*

Step #1:   Open the EXE12-4.dwg file.

Step #2:   Use the ERASE command and create a crossing polygon as follows:

FIGURE 12–8   The points selected for the Window Polygon depend on the objects to be included in the selection set. This task required only five picks.

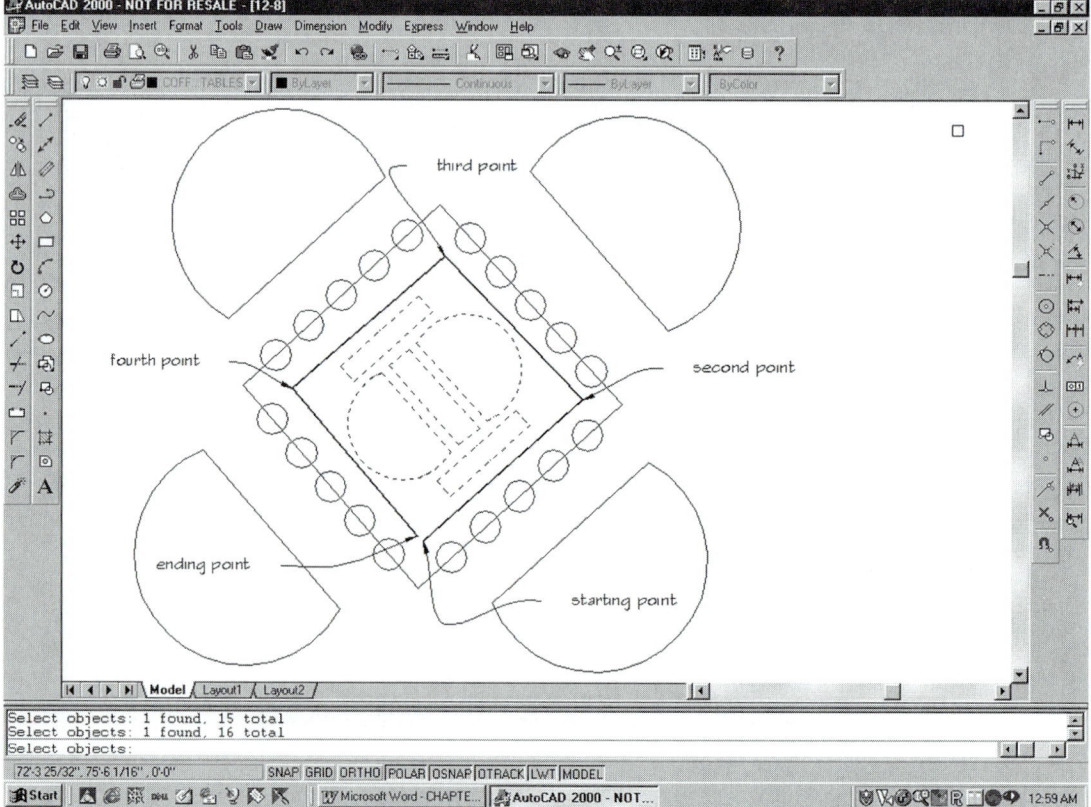

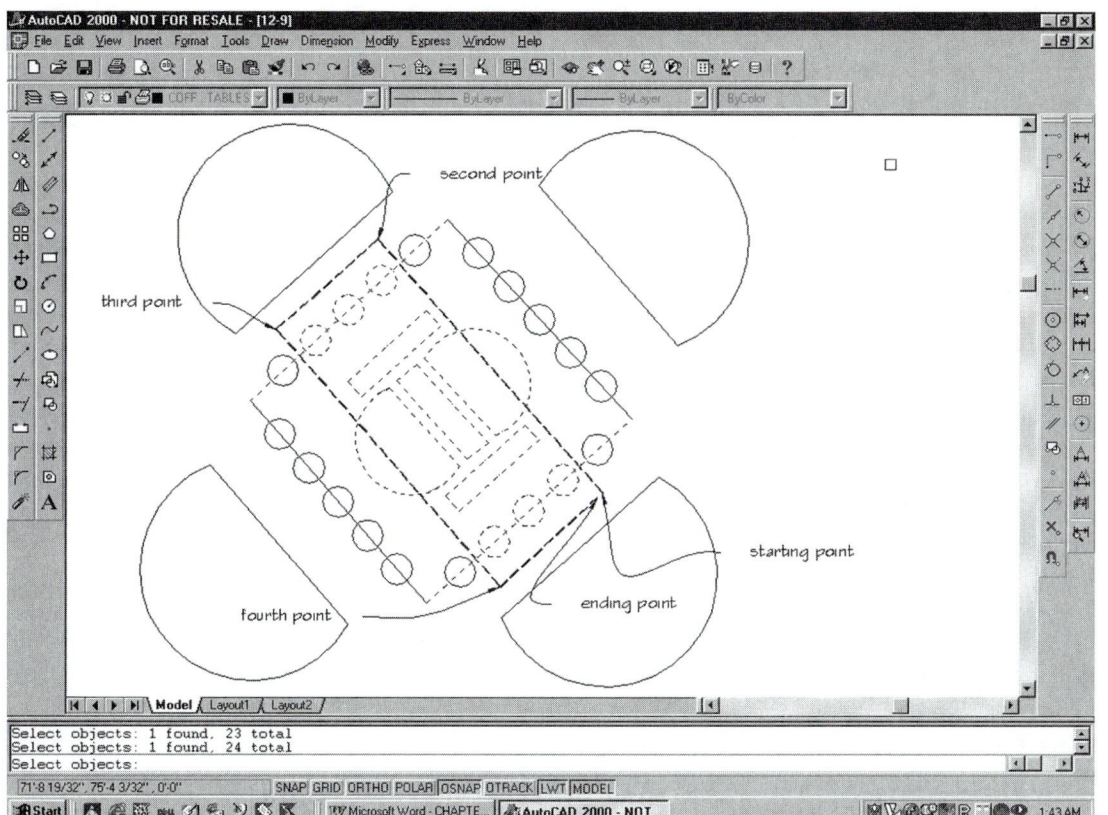

FIGURE 12–9 The Crossing Polygon (CP) selection method is similar to the Window Polygon (WP) selection method except the crossing feature is used. All objects inside the CP and all objects crossing the CP are included in the selection set.

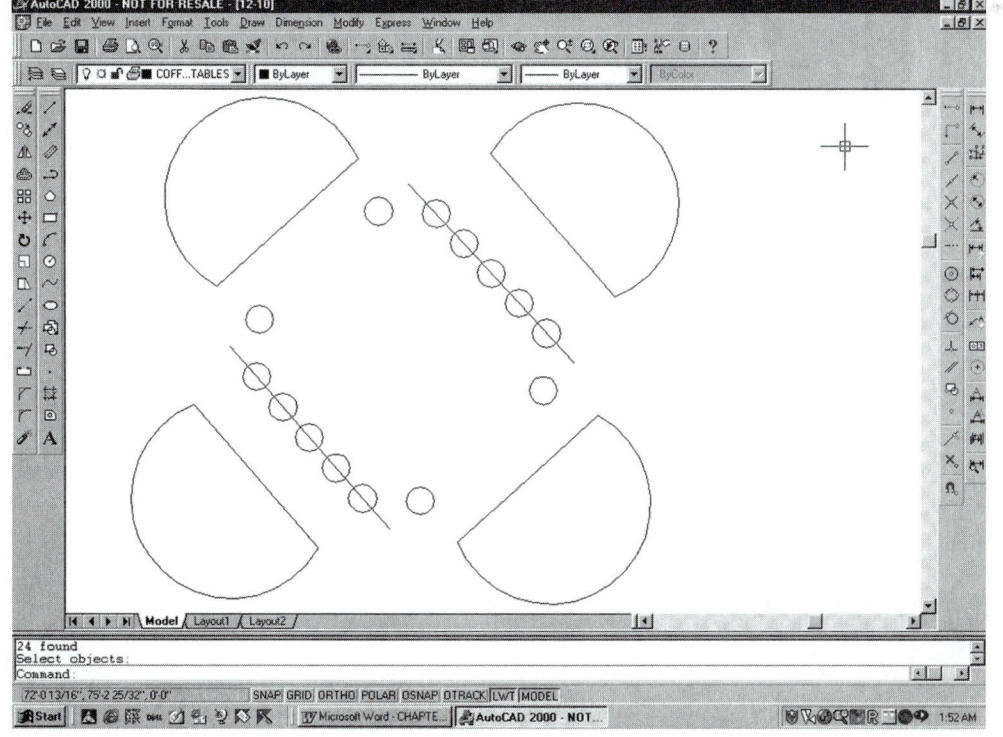

FIGURE 12–10 The end result of the Crossing Polygon (CP) selection option.

Command: **ERASE** ~EnterKey~

Select objects: **CP** ~EnterKey~

First polygon point: *(turn Ortho and Osnap off and select the starting point as shown in Figure 12–9)*

Specify endpoint of line or [Undo]: *(select second point)*

Specify endpoint of line or [Undo]: *(select third point)*

Specify endpoint of line or [Undo]: *(select fourth point)*

Specify endpoint of line or [Undo]: *(select ending point)*

Specify endpoint of line or [Undo]: ~EnterKey~

Congratulations! You have successfully erased the objects as shown in Figure 12–10 by creating a crossing polygon.

All required objects are included in the selection set as shown in Figure 12–9. Do not save the changes.

12.3.6 Fence Selection

The Fence option allows you to select several objects at the same time, without the constraints of window and crossing. You simply create a fence (displayed as dashed line) going through the objects. Any object touching or crossing the fence will be included in the selection set. For example, to erase the two large circles, two medium-size circles and the eight small circles shown in Figure 12–11, enter *F* at the Select objects: prompt. Create the fence and press the ~EnterKey~ or right-click when done. All objects crossing the fence will be erased as shown in Figure 12–12.

■ **EXERCISE 12–6:** *The following step-by-step exercise will help you to create a fence and erase the objects as shown in Figure 12–11.*

Step #1: Open the EXE12-21.dwg file.

FIGURE 12–11 The Fence selection method allows you to *fence* through the objects. All objects crossing the fence will be selected.

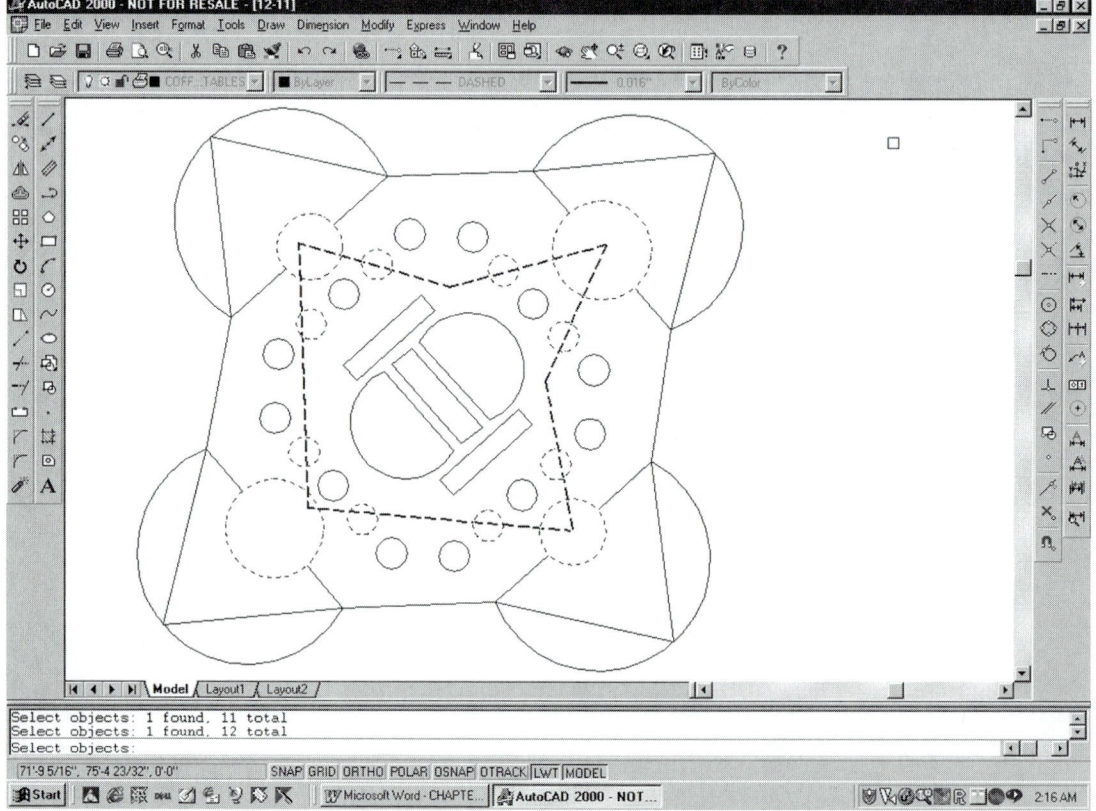

Step #2: Use the ERASE command and create a fence as follows:

Command: **ERASE** ~EnterKey~

Select objects: **F** ~EnterKey~

First fence point: *(turn Ortho and Osnap off and select a starting point)*

Specify endpoint of line or [Undo]: *(select second fence point)*

Specify endpoint of line or [Undo]: *(select third fence point)*

Specify endpoint of line or [Undo]: *(select fourth fence point)*

Specify endpoint of line or [Undo]: *(select fifth fence point)*

Specify endpoint of line or [Undo]: *(select sixth fence point)*

Specify endpoint of line or [Undo]: *(select ending point)*

Specify endpoint of line or [Undo]: ~EnterKey~

Congratulations! You have successfully erased the objects as shown in Figure 12–11 by creating a crossing polygon. All required objects are included in the selection set as shown in Figure 12–12. Do not save the changes.

Tips: The Window Polygon and the Crossing Polygon selection methods will allow the first and the last points to be crossed. However, these two points do not have to touch. Left-click when getting close to the starting point or overlap (cross) the first point.

Tips: You can also left-click on objects when no command is running and press the ~Delete~key to erase the selected objects.

Tips: You can also left-click on objects when no command is running and select Cut from the Edit pull-down menu.

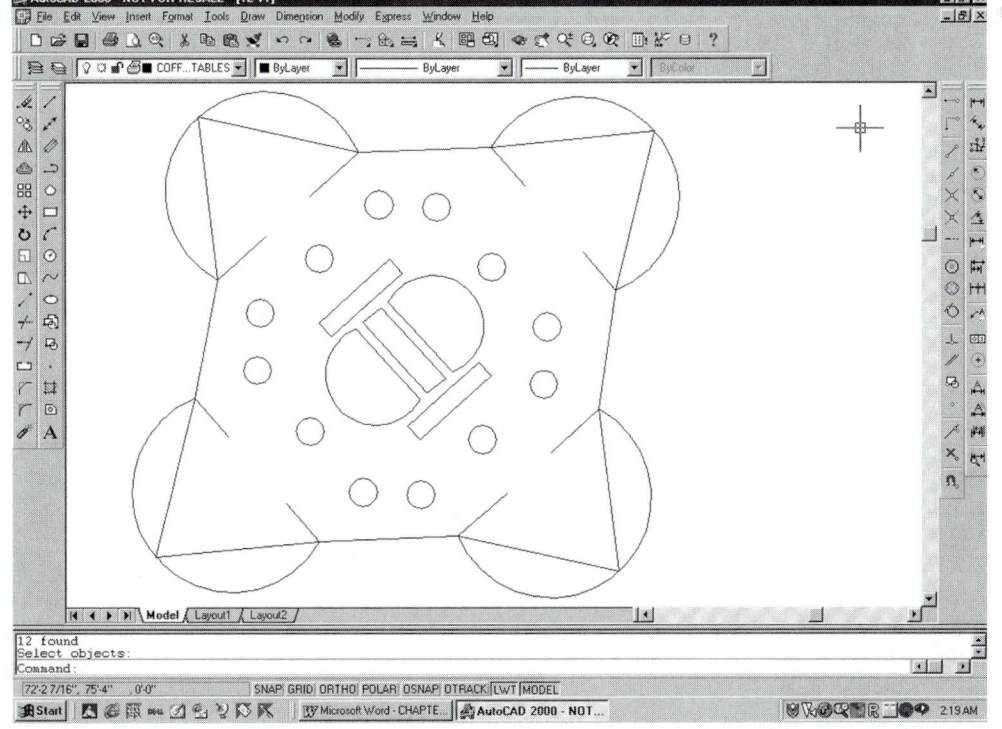

FIGURE 12–12 The end result of the Fence selection method.

12.4 REMOVING OBJECTS FROM THE SELECTION SET

When using any of the editing commands, you select objects as described previously. Each object that you select will be highlighted and will be included in the selection set. When you are selecting many objects it is possible to accidentally include an object to the selection set. Instead of starting the selection process all over again, you can remove the objects selected by mistake from the selection set by using two different methods as follows:

- **PRESS AND HOLD THE ~SHIFTKEY~ AT THE SELECT OBJECTS**   prompt and select the objects to remove them from the selection set. Objects that are removed from the selection set will be displayed as solid.

- **ENTER**   *R* (Remove) at the Select objects: prompt and select the objects to be removed from the selection set. Objects that are removed from the selection set will be displayed as solid. The command line procedure to remove objects from the selection set for the ERASE command is as follows:

```
Command: ERASE
Select objects: (select the objects to be erased. Now, suppose you
selected a line and a circle that you did not want to erase)
Select objects: R ~EnterKey~
Remove objects: (select the line you want removed from the selection set)
Remove objects: 1 found, 1 removed, 4 total
Remove objects: (select the circle you want removed from the selection set)
Remove objects: 1 found, 1 removed, 3 total
Remove objects: ~EnterKey~
```

12.5 ADDING OBJECTS TO THE SELECTION SET AFTER REMOVING OBJECTS FROM THE SELECTION SET

You can keep selecting objects at the Remove objects: prompt until all objects are removed from the selection set. To add objects to the selection set after removing objects from the selection set, enter **A** (Add) at the Remove objects: prompt and select the objects to add to the selection set. This process will restore the Select objects: prompt as follows:

```
Remove objects: A ~EnterKey~
Select objects: (keep selecting objects to include in the selection set)
```

12.6 USING THE OOPS COMMAND

When you use the ERASE command to delete one or more objects they will be removed from the drawing. If you want those erased objects to appear back in the same drawing session you can recall them by entering OOPS at the command line. Only the most recently erased objects will be brought back. You can use the OOPS command also to bring back a symbol after turning it into a block with the BLOCK or WBLOCK commands. Blocks are discussed in Chapter 19.

12.7 THE PICKAUTO SYSTEM VARIABLE

When you create a selection set by creating a window or a crossing around objects, AutoCAD by default allows you to select the first corner; you then drag the cursor to the second corner. This automatic windowing is controlled by the PICKAUTO system variable. By default, the PICKAUTO system variable is set to 1 (on). When the PICKAUTO system variable is set to 0 (off), automatic windowing is not possible, but you can still select individual objects using the pickbox to include them to the selection set. You can control the setting for the PICKAUTO system variable using the Options dialog box. Access the Options dialog box and select the Selection tab as shown in Figure 12–13. Under Selection Modes category, place a checkmark inside the Implied windowing check box to turn PICKAUTO on. Remove the checkmark to turn PICKAUTO off. Remember to click on the Apply button before clicking on the OK button.

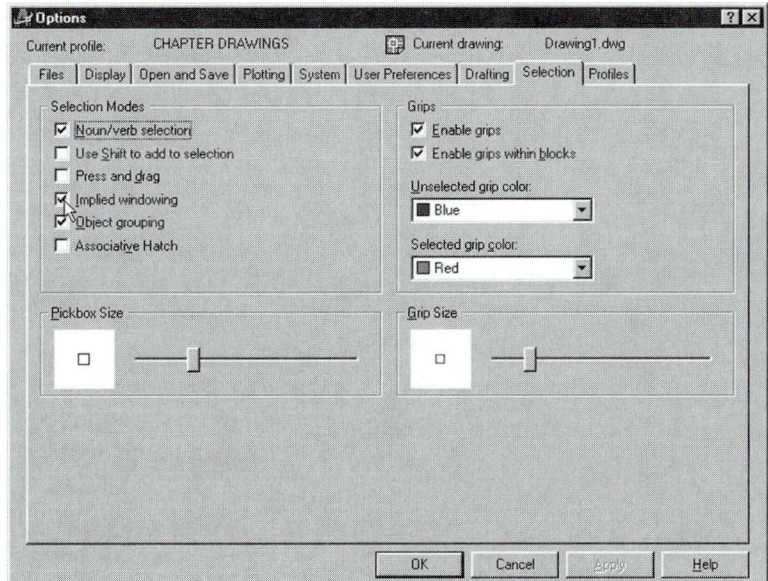

FIGURE 12–13 You can control automatic windowing from the Options dialog box.

Tips: You can still use the Window and Crossing selection methods even when the PICKAUTO system variable is set to 0 (off). Enter W (Window), C (Crossing), or BOX at the Select objects: prompt and create a window, crossing, or a box around the objects you want to select. If you use the W option when PICKAUTO is off, the window will be created solid whether you go from left to right or from right to left. If you use the C option when PICKAUTO is off, the crossing created will be dashed whether you go from left to right or from right to left. The Box option will create a Window when you go from left to right and will create a crossing when you go from right to left.

12.8 ADDING ALL OBJECTS TO THE SELECTION SET

When you use any of the editing commands, AutoCAD displays the Select objects: prompt. You can include all objects in the selection set in the current drawing by entering *A* (All) at the Select objects: prompt. For example, to erase all objects on the screen, access the ERASE command, enter *A*, and then press the ~EnterKey~.

Tips: The All option is useful when selecting many objects but leaving some objects out. For example, if you need to erase 25 objects out of 35 total objects and you can't see all the objects on the screen, select All objects and then use the Remove option to remove the 10 from the selection set.

12.9 RESELECTING A PREVIOUS SELECTION SET

If you decide to perform the same editing operation by reselecting the previously selected objects, enter *P* (Previous) at the Select objects: prompt. For example, after copying an object to a specific location, you decide to copy the same object to another location. Instead of selecting the objects again, enter the COPY command and enter *P* at the Select objects: prompt. This will highlight the previously copied object and add it to the selection set.

Tips: For a more advanced selection set use the QSELECT command to create a filtering criteria based on object type and properties. QSELECT command is discussed in Chapter 13.

12.10 EDITING STACKED OBJECTS

Sometimes an object is drawn over another object intentionally or by mistake. When both objects overlap each other exactly at the same length, they are referred to as stacked objects. It is easy to edit the top object since the object on top will be highlighted when selected. If you want to edit the object that is in the bottom, you need to send the top object to back.

■ **EXERCISE 12–7:**　*The following step-by-step exercise will allow you to bring up a rectangle object that is in the bottom of another rectangle object for editing purposes.*

Step #1:　Using the RECTANG command, draw a rectangle on the screen.

Step #2:　From the Color Control box, change the color to Red so that you can draw the second rectangle with a different color to distinguish the two rectangles.

Step #3:　Using the RECTANG command and the object snap modes, draw the second rectangle exactly on top of the first rectangle. The red rectangle will be on top.

Step #4:　From the Tools pull-down menu and from the Display Order cascading menu, select Send to Back as shown in Figure 12–14 and place the top rectangle to the bottom as follows:

Select objects: *(click on the red rectangle)*

Select objects: ~EnterKey~

The red rectangle will be moved to the bottom and the first rectangle will be moved to the top. Use the ERASE command to erase the rectangle. The red rectangle will remain.

Congratulations! You have edited a stacked rectangle object. Do not save this drawing.

The *Bring to Front* option will move a selected object on top. For this to work, the object in the bottom must extend beyond the top object so that it can be selected. At the Select objects: prompt, click on the object you want to move top and press the ~EnterKey~. AutoCAD will force the selected object to be on top of the other object. If the object you want to bring to front is not visible because it is shorter than the top object, use the *Send to Back* option. The *Bring Above Object* option will force the selected object to be displayed above the referenced object. The referenced object in this case is the object inserted into the drawing as a block or as an xref. See chapter 19 for blocks and chapter 24 for xrefs. AutoCAD will ask you to select the object first, then ask you to select the reference object. The *Send Under Object* option will perform the opposite function of the Bring Above Object option.

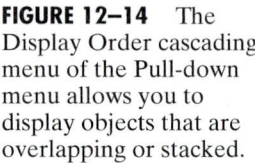

Tips: Use the selection cycling option to gain more control over which object you select with the pickbox if objects are close together. At the select objects: prompt, press and hold the ~Ctrl~ key while selecting the object. Release the ~Ctrl~ key and then repeatedly left-click to highlight different objects

FIGURE 12–14　The Display Order cascading menu of the Pull-down menu allows you to display objects that are overlapping or stacked.

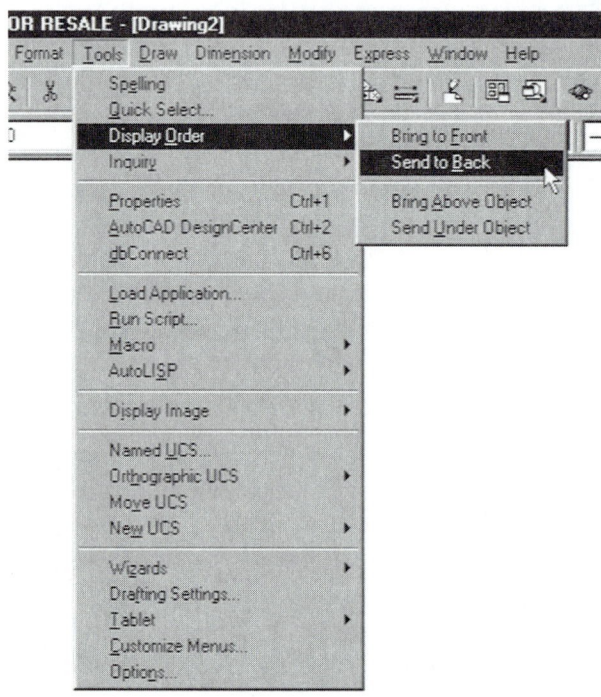

that are in the pickbox selection. After the desired object is highlighted, press the <Enter< key or right-click in the drawing area to select that object.

12.11 USING EXPRESS SELECTION TOOLS

AutoCAD allows you to exclude a selection set so that the selection methods described earlier can be reversed. For example, the normal crossing selection method includes every object inside the crossing plus any object crossing over. The *exclusionary* selection method reverses this method by selecting every object outside the crossing and not selecting any object crossing over. These exclusionary selection methods can be accessed by selecting the Selection Tools from the Express pull-down menu. You can also access the exclusionary selection methods by entering *'EX* before the object selection method. For example, to access the Exclude Window Polygon selection method, enter *'EXWP* after the editing command.

You can use the Get Selection Set option from the Selection tools to create a selection set based on layer and/or object type of selected objects as follows:

- Select Get Selection Set from the Select tools cascading menu in the Express pull-down menu.
- Select an object or objects on the desired layer. You can press the ~EnterKey~ to select objects on all layers.
- Select an object of the desired type.

AutoCAD will build a selection set that matches the selected object in relation to layer, object type, or both criteria. AutoCAD will not highlight these objects but will display the number of objects matching the criteria. After creating a selection set you can use any of the AutoCAD edit commands (e.g. MOVE). At the Select objects: prompt enter P to use the Previous selection set registered with Get Selection Set. For example, suppose you want to move all 8 circles to a new location on the layer called *Site.* Use the above procedure to select Get Selection Set and use the following command line procedure:

```
Select an object on the Source layer <*>: (select an object on the Site
layer)
Select an object of the Type you want <*>: (select a circle)
Collecting all CIRCLE objects on layer SITE...
8 objects have been placed in the active selection set
Command: MOVE~EnterKey~
Select objects: P~EnterKey~
8 found
Select objects: ~EnterKey~
Specify base point or displacement: (select the center of one of the circles)
Specify second point of displacement: (select the second point on the screen)
```

Tips: Instead of entering ALL at the Select objects: prompt to select everything on the screen and entering R to remove objects, use exclusionary selection methods to select the object you want to remove from the selection set and edit everything else around it.

12.12 USING THE TRIM COMMAND

The TRIM command will allow you to cut and remove unwanted lines, circles, arcs, ellipses, splines, construction lines, and rays that extend beyond a point of intersection. To use the TRIM command, click on the Trim button in the Modify toolbar, select Trim from the Modify pull-down menu, or enter TR or TRIM at the command line. The Modify toolbar is shown in Figure 12–15. When you access the TRIM command, AutoCAD will ask you to select cutting edges. A cutting edge is defined as *object that crosses over another object.* The cross over is the portion of the object that can be trimmed. More than one object can be selected as the cutting edges as long as these objects intersect and create the cross over. For example, you can trim the objects that cross

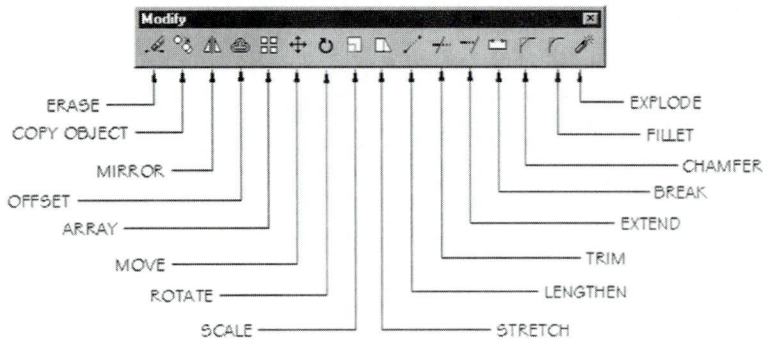

FIGURE 12–15 The Modify toolbar is used to access all of the basic editing commands.

over the four intersecting lines created with the LINE and OFFSET commands (to represent a wall) as shown in Figure 12–16A as follows:

```
Command: TRIM ~EnterKey~
Current settings: Projection=UCS,
Edge=None
Select cutting edges...
Select objects: (select all four lines
indicated as cutting edges. All four
lines will be highlighted)
Select objects: ~EnterKey~
Select object to trim or
[Project/Edge/Undo]: (select the four
crossing lines)
```

The intersecting lines will be trimmed as shown in Figure 12–16B. To trim the lines inside the walls, continue selecting the lines as shown in Figure 12–16B as follows:

```
Select object to trim or [Project/Edge/Undo]: (select the two lines
inside the walls)
Select object to trim or [Project/Edge/Undo]: ~EnterKey~
```

The unwanted lines will be trimmed as shown in Figure 12–16C.

Tips: The TRIM command has a convenient Quick Mode in which you can save time by pressing the ~EnterKey~ at the Select objects: prompt instead of selecting cutting edges. This mode will use all objects as cutting edges without highlighting them allowing you to skip a step and go straight to selecting the objects to trim.

Tips: if there are objects left over from the trim process that must be removed, use the ERASE command to erase them.

FIGURE 12–16 Using the TRIM command. **A:** four lines will be trimmed first. **B:** two lines left inside the wall will be trimmed next without leaving the TRIM command. **C:** all unwanted lines are trimmed as the wall corner is cleaned-up.

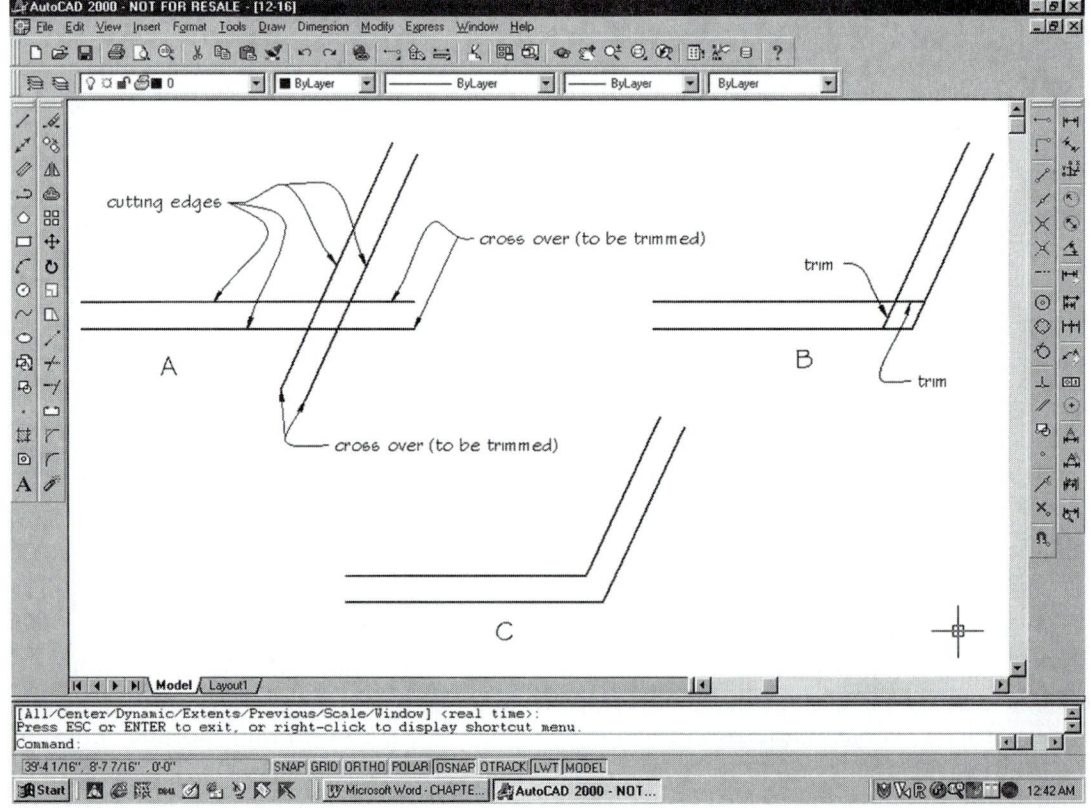

12.12.1 Using the Edge Option of the TRIM Command

The Edge option of the TRIM command is used to trim an object to its implied intersection with the Edge Extension mode. When the first TRIM command line prompt shows Edge=None, the cutting edges must cross objects to trim them. When the command line prompt shows Edge=Extend, the cutting objects can imply extended edges. Figure 12–17A shows a wall at an angle not intersecting the horizontal wall. If the angled wall was to be extended, it will intersect the horizontal wall at an implied intersection as shown with dash lines. The Edge and the Extend options of the TRIM command will trim the horizontal wall at that implied intersection. The command line procedure to trim the angled wall to the left side of the implied intersection shown in Figure 12–17A is as follows:

```
Command: TRIM ~EnterKey~
Current settings: Projection=UCS, Edge=None
Select cutting edges...
Select objects: (select the two cutting edges as shown in Figure 12-17A)
Select objects: ~EnterKey~
Select object to trim or [Project/Edge/Undo]: E ~EnterKey~
Enter an implied edge extension mode [Extend/No Extend]: E ~EnterKey~
Select object to trim or [Project/Edge/Undo]: (select the two horizontal lines)
Select object to trim or [Project/Edge/Undo]: ~EnterKey~
```

The selected wall will be trimmed to the implied edge extension as shown in Figure 12–17B.

Note: If the No Extend option is selected, the implied intersection extension will not work. Use the EDGEMODE system variable to toggle the edge mode between Extend the Cutting Edges (1) and No Extension (0). The Projection mode can be set to View for three-dimensional drawings. For two-dimensional drawings, the Projection mode is set to UCS.

Caution: Because the EDGEMODE system variable is stored in the system registry, the setting will affect all drawing sessions on your computer until you change it again.

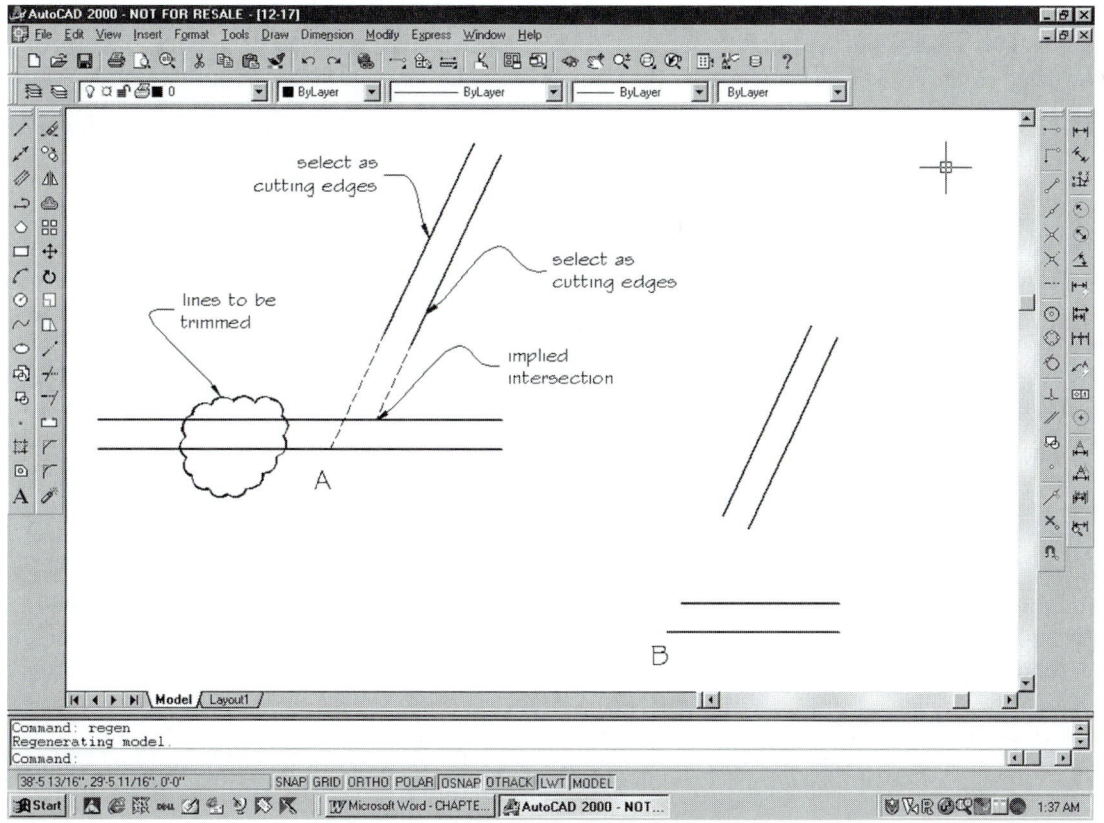

FIGURE 12–17 Using the Edge Extension mode option of the TRIM command.

FIGURE 12–18 Using the EXTRIM command. **A:** Selecting the parallel lines and the side to trim. **B:** After the extended trim operation.

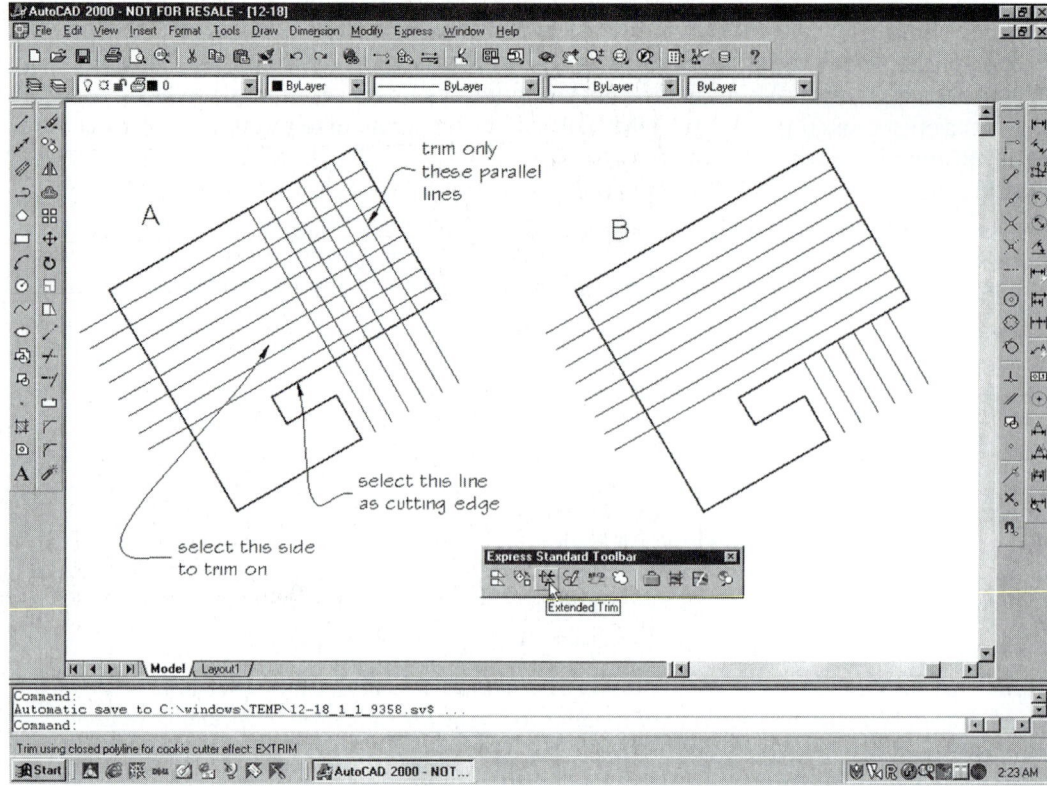

12.12.2 Using the Extended Trim Option of the TRIM Command

The Extended Trim option allows you to trim all objects that overlap a cutting edge you select. You can access this command by selecting Cookie Cutter Trim from the Modify cascading menu of the Express pull-down menu, clicking on the Extended Trim button in the Express Standard Toolbar, or entering EXTRIM at the command line. The cutting edges can be a polyline, circle, arc, line, ellipse, image, or a text. You can select only one cutting edge but you can recall the command to select another cutting edge.

■ **EXERCISE 12–8:** *The following step-by-step exercise will allow you to trim all of the parallel lines going in one direction inside the object as shown in Figure 12–18A using the EXTRIM command.*

Step #1: Open the EXE12-5.dwg file.

Step #2: Use the EXTRIM command and select the objects as follows:

Command: **EXTRIM** ~EnterKey~

Pick a polyline, line, circle, arc, ellipse, image or text for cutting edge...

Select objects: *(select the line shown as cutting edge in Figure 12–18A)*

Select objects: 1 found

Command:

Specify the side to trim on: *(select the side as shown in Fig 12–18A)*

Congratulations! You have successfully used the EXTRIM command to trim objects overlapping the cutting edge. The lines will be trimmed as shown in Figure 12–18B. Do not save the changes. You could have also selected the outside lines and selected the opposite side to trim the extended objects.

Note: When using the EXTRIM command and after specifying the side to trim, AutoCAD will zoom in to the area as it works on the objects. It will return to the previous display when trimming is completed.

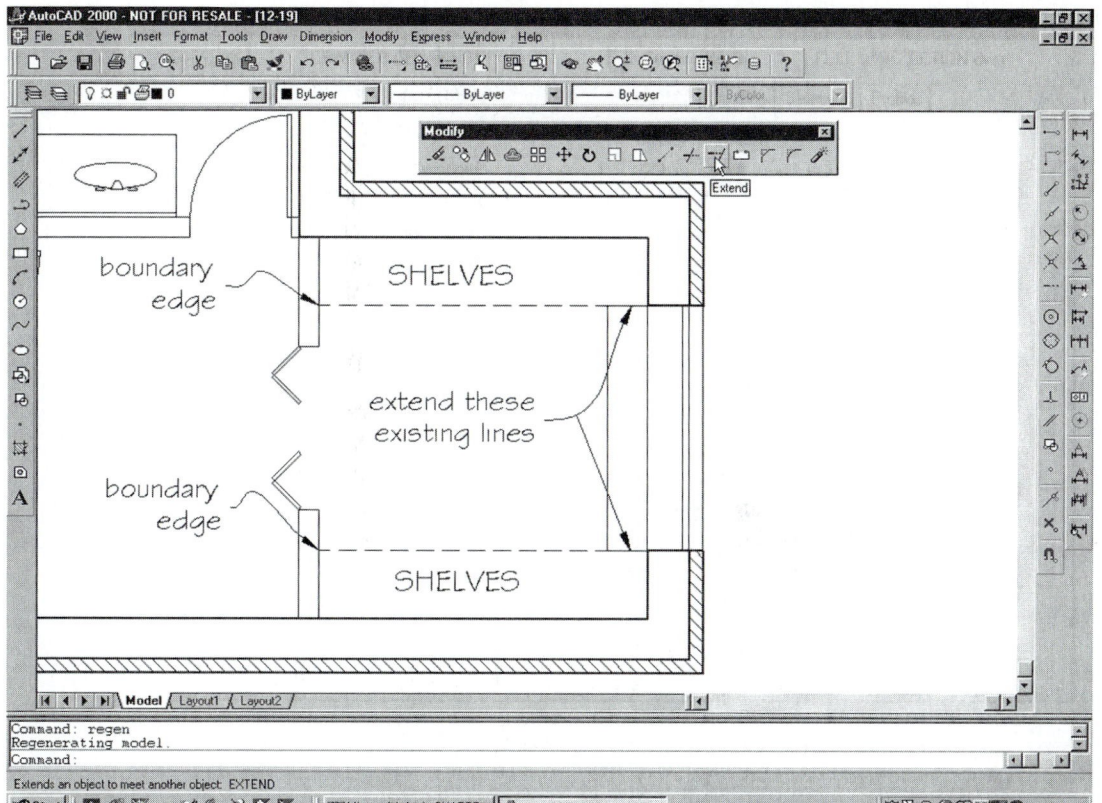

12.13 USING THE EXTEND COMMAND

The EXTEND command allows you to extend an object into another object. AutoCAD does this by lengthening the object to a boundary edge. Similar to the TRIM command, you are asked to select the boundary edges first. The boundary edge is the object that is used as the edge or the point for the extension. After selecting the boundary edge, you are asked to select the object to be extended to that edge. The boundary edges can be lines, arcs, circles, or polylines. You can extend more than one object to a common edge. To access the EXTEND command, select the Extend button in the Modify toolbar, select Extend from the Modify pull-down menu, or enter EX or EXTEND at the command line.

■ **EXERCISE 12–9:** *The following step-by-step exercise will allow you to extend the two existing lines in the Floor Plan to create the shelves as shown in Figure 12–19.*

Step #1: Open the EXE12–6.dwg file.

Step #2: Use the EXTEND command to extend the existing lines to create the shelves as follows:

Command: **EXTEND** ~EnterKey~

Current settings: Projection = UCS, Edge = None

Select boundary edges...

Select objects: *(select the first boundary edge as shown in Figure 12–19)*

Select objects: 1 found

Select objects: *(select the second boundary edge)*

Select objects: 1 found, 2 total

Select objects: ~EnterKey~

Select object to extend or [Project/Edge/Undo]: *(select the first existing line)*

FIGURE 12–20 The two existing lines are extended to the inside of the wall surface.

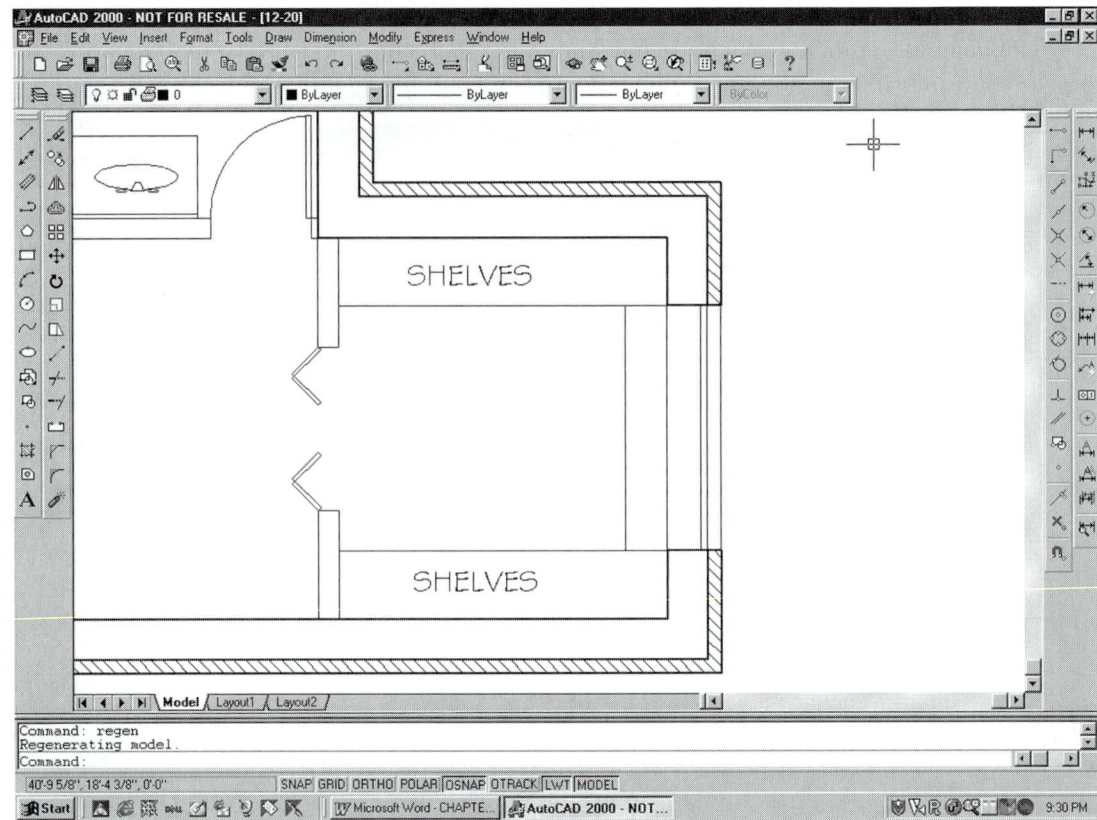

Select object to extend or [Project/Edge/Undo]: *(select the second existing line)*

Select object to extend or [Project/Edge/Undo]: ~EnterKey~

Congratulations! You have successfully used the EXTEND command to create lines from existing lines. The two existing lines will be extended into the wall as shown in Figure 12–20. Do not save the changes.

> ***AutoCAD 2000i Update:*** *By holding down the ~ShiftKey~, the TRIM command can be used as the EXTEND command and the EXTEND command can be used as the TRIM command. On the Modify toolbar select the Extend button and press the ~EnterKey~. Then select the object you want to extend. Press and hold the ~ShiftKey~, then select the object to trim. Press the ~EnterKey~ to exit the command. Use the same procedure to use the TRIM command as the EXTEND command.*

12.13.1 Using the Edge Option of the EXTEND Command

Similar to the trimming to an implied intersection, you can also extend to an implied boundary. The Edge option of the EXTEND command is used to extend objects to their implied intersection with the Edge Extension mode. Figure 12–21A shows a wall at an angle not intersecting the horizontal wall. If the angled wall was to be extended, it would intersect the horizontal wall at an implied intersection as shown with dashed lines. The Edge and the Extend options of the EXTEND command will extend the angled wall at that implied intersection. The command line procedure to extend the angled wall to the implied intersection shown in Figure 12–21A is as follows:

```
Command: EXTEND ~EnterKey~
Current settings: Projection = UCS, Edge = None
Select boundary edges...
Select objects: (select the two horizontal lines as shown in Figure 12-21A)
Select objects: ~EnterKey~
Select object to extend or [Project/Edge/Undo]: E ~EnterKey~
```

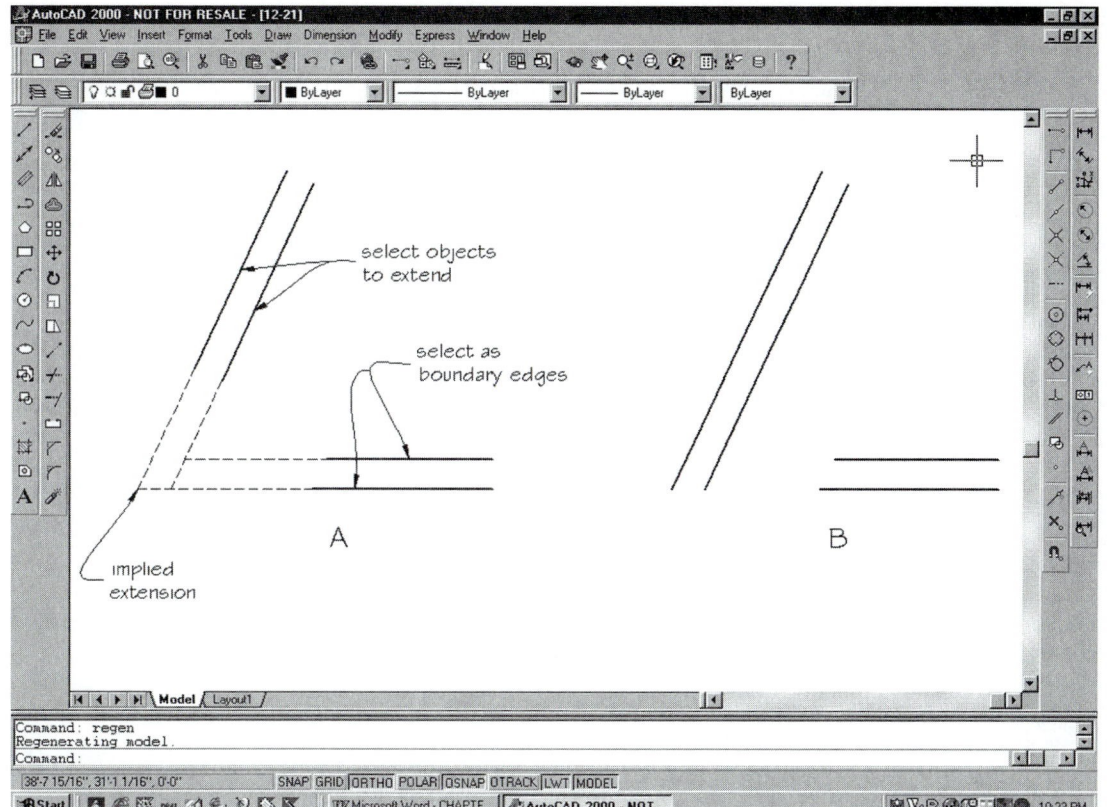

FIGURE 12–21
Extending to an implied intersection.

```
Enter implied edge extension mode [Extend/No Extend]: E ~EnterKey~
Select object to extend or [Project/Edge/Undo]: (select both objects to
extend at the endpoints closest to the implied intersection)
Select object to extend or [Project/Edge/Undo]: ~EnterKey~
```

The selected wall will be extended to the implied edge extension as shown in Figure 12–21B.

Note: Selecting which objects as boundary edges and which objects as objects to extend depends on what result you want at the end of each extend operation. Look at the big picture and determine the appropriate procedure required based on the final outcome of the project.

Tips: If you use a wide polyline as a boundary edge, the selected objects will be extended to the centerline of the polyline. If you extend a tapered polyline, it will be extended proportionally.

Tips: Most of the editing commands have an Undo option. If the command line procedure produces unwanted results, enter U at the Select objects [options]: prompt. This will undo the last item from the procedure.

Tips: Use the Fence selection option to trim and extend multiply lines in one operation.

12.14 USING THE LENGTHEN COMMAND

You can lengthen or shorten an object and change the included angle of an arc using the LENGTHEN command. Unlike the TRIM and EXTEND commands, only one object can be lengthened or shortened at a time. You can access the LENGTHEN command by clicking on the Lengthen button in the Modify toolbar, select Lengthen from the Modify pull-down menu, or enter LEN or LENGTHEN at the command line. When you first select an object, AutoCAD gives you the current length of a linear segment, the perimeter of a closed object (rectangle, polygon), included angle of an arc, and the circumference of a circle. There are four different ways to use the LENGTHEN command as follows:

```
Command: LENGTHEN ~EnterKey~
Select an object or [DElta/Percent/Total/DYnamic]: (select an object)
```

FIGURE 12–22 Using the DElta option of the LENGTHEN command. **A:** Selecting the existing line. **B:** The end result of the operation.

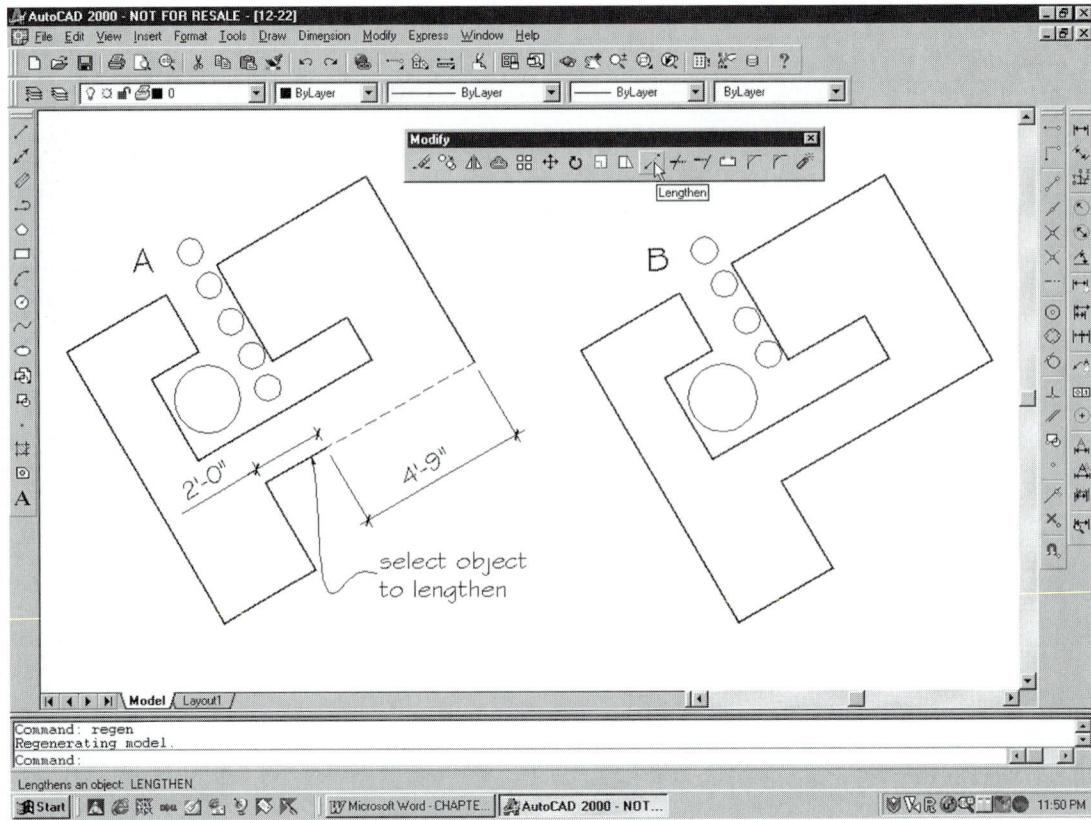

Current length: *(displays the current length of the selected object)*
Select an object or [DElta/Percent/Total/DYnamic]:

- **Delta:** This option allows you to add or subtract a desired length to or from the existing object. A positive length will lengthen and a negative length will shorten the selected object.

■ **EXERCISE 12–10:** *The following step-by-step exercise will allow you to add a length of 4'-9" to the existing line shown in Figure 12–22A to close the object.*

Step #1: Open the EXE12-7.dwg file.

Step #2: Use the Delta option of the LENGTHEN command to add an additional length of 4'-9" to the exisitng line as follows:

Command: **LEN** ~EnterKey~

Select an object or [DElta/Percent/Total/DYnamic]: *(select the line shown in Figure 12–22A)*

Current length: 2'-0"

Select an object or [DElta/Percent/Total/DYnamic]: **DE** ~EnterKey~

Enter delta length of [Angle] <0'-0">: **4'9** ~EnterKey~

Select an object to change or [Undo]: *(select the object again)*

Select an object to change or [Undo]: ~EnterKey~

Congratulations! You have successfully added a length to an existing object using the Delta option of the LENGTHEN command. The line will be lengthened an additional 4'-9" as shown in Figure 12–22B. Do not save the changes.

The Angle suboption allows you to change the included angle of a selected arc by specifying a desired angle.

- **Percent:** This option allows you to change the length of an object or the angle of an arc by a percentage. AutoCAD considers the current length of the selected object as 100

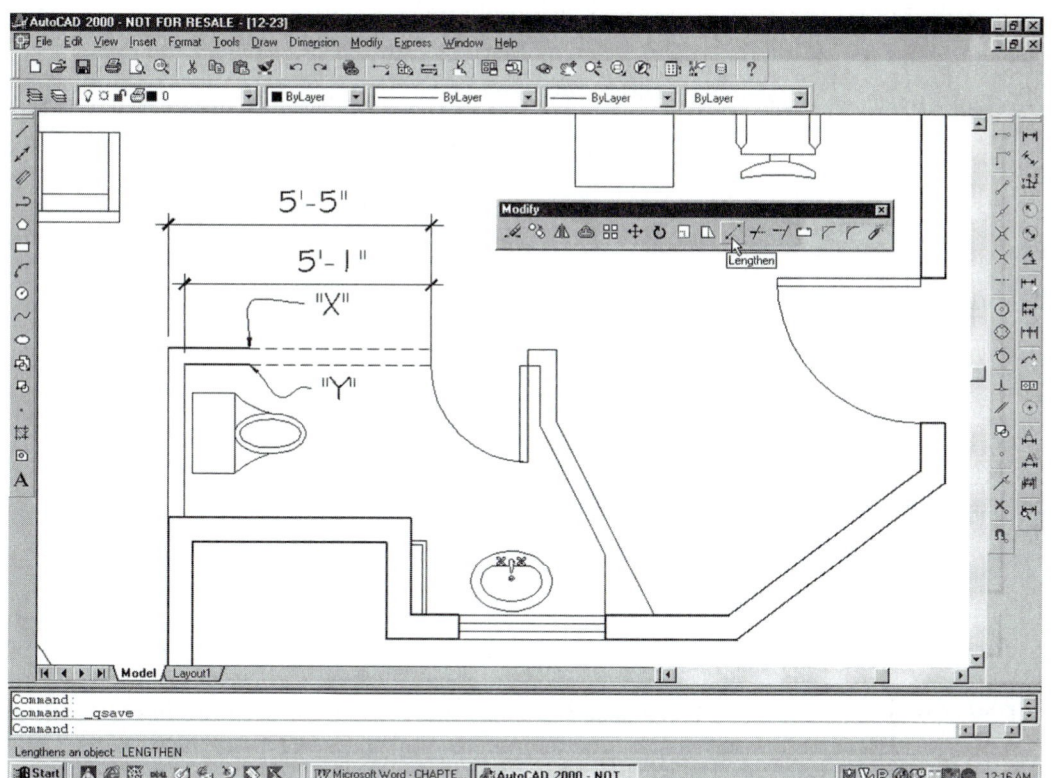

FIGURE 12–23 The Total option of the LENGTHEN comand can be used to assign a total new length to selected objects.

percent. To make the object shorter, enter less than 100 percent, to make the object longer, enter more than 100 percent. The command line procedure is as follows:

```
Command: LEN ~EnterKey~
Select an object or [DElta/Percent/Total/DYnamic]: P ~EnterKey~
Enter percent length <100.00>: (enter a desired percentage)
Select an object to change or [Undo]: (select the object you want to change)
Select an object to change or [Undo]: ~EnterKey~
```

- **Total:** This option allows you to specify a total length for the object or a total angle for the arc.

■ **EXERCISE 12–11:** *The following step-by-step exercise will allow you to create a new length for the walls X and Y to extend to the door swing as shown in Figure 12–23 with a total length of 5'-5" and 5'-1", respectively.*

Step #1: Open the EXE12-8.dwg file.

Step #2: Use the Total option of the LENGTHEN command to create a new length for the walls as follows:

Command: **LEN** ~EnterKey~

Select an object or [DElta/Percent/Total/DYnamic]: **T** ~EnterKey~

Specify total length or [Angle] <0'-1">: **5'5** ~EnterKey~

Select an object to change or [Undo]: *(select line X as shown in Figure 12–23)*

Select an object to change or [Undo]: ~EnterKey~

Command: ~EnterKey~

Select an object or [DElta/Percent/Total/DYnamic]: **T** ~EnterKey~

Specify total length or [Angle] <5'5">: **5'1** ~EnterKey~

Select an object to change or [Undo]: *(select line Y as shown in Figure 12–23)*

Select an object to change or [Undo]: ~EnterKey~

FIGURE 12–24 The result of the Total option of the LENGTHEN command.

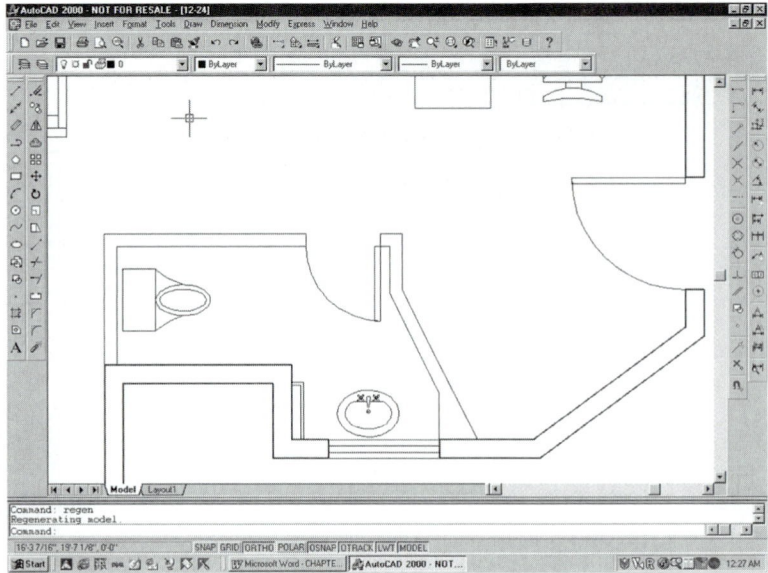

Congratulations! You have successfully created a new length for the walls using the Total option of the LENGTHEN command. The lines will now be connected to the door swing as shown in Figure 12–24. Do not save the changes.

- **DYnamic:** This option allows you to drag the endpoint of the selected object or the arc to the required length. This is called dynamically lengthening an object. At the command prompt enter DY and select the endpoint of the object to be dynamically changed. Only lines and arcs can be dynamically lengthened.

Tips: Use the LENGTHEN command to quickly find the current length of an object. Access the command, move the pickbox over the object such as a line and left-click on the object. Read the command line for length information.

Tips: The EXTEND and the LENGTHEN commands create a single entity at the conclusion of the editing procedure by completely recreating the object from the start to the endpoint. This is different than using the LINE command to add another line to make an object longer. With the LINE command you create two separate lines connected together by their start and endpoints. With the EXTEND and LENGTHEN commands, you create one single object at the end of the procedure.

12.15 USING THE SCALE COMMAND

The SCALE command allows you to change the X and Y dimensions of objects proportionately. You can change the size of an object or the entire drawing by using the SCALE command. You can access the SCALE command by clicking on the Scale button in the Modify toolbar, selecting Scale from the Modify pull-down menu, or entering SC or SCALE at the command line. To scale objects, you are asked to specify a base point after selecting the objects to scale. The base point is any point either on the object or on the screen that will be used as the point from which scaling will take place. It is at the base point that the selected objects will become smaller or larger. Selection of the base point is important because selected objects will increase away from or shrink towards this point. Figure 12–25A shows a vanity sink inside a rectangle vanity counter top. The sink needs to be smaller so that it can fit the vanity according to project specifications. You can shrink the sink by 25 percent as follows:

```
Command: SCALE ~EnterKey~
Select objects: (using an appropriate selection set method, select the
sink only)
```

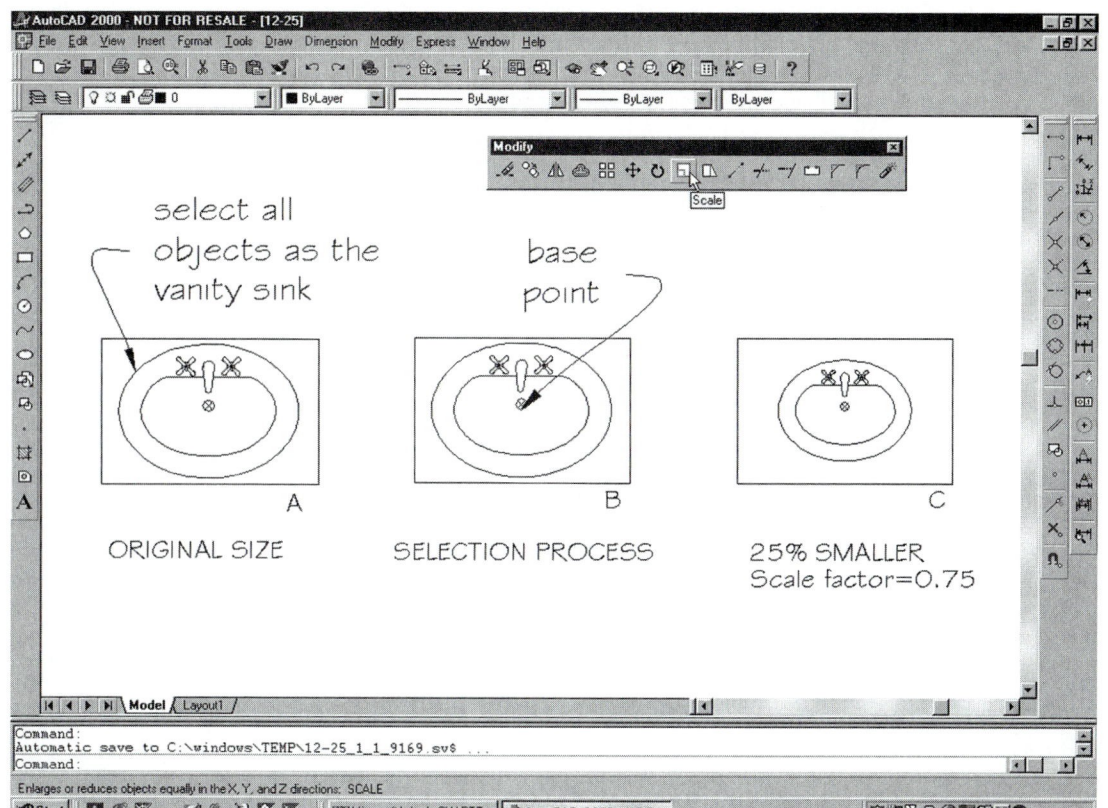

FIGURE 12–25 The SCALE command can be used to make objects smaller or larger. **A:** The sink inside the vanity counter top is selected. **B:** With the base point at the center of the drain. **C:** It is reduced by 25 percent with a 0.75 scale factor value.

```
Select objects: ~EnterKey~
Specify base point: (using object snap modes, select the center of the
drain as shown in Figure 12-25B)
Specify scale factor or [Reference]: 0.75 ~EnterKey~
```

The sink will be scaled down as shown in Figure 12–25C.

Specifying the scale factor is the default. The scale factor value you enter represents the enlargement or reduction of the object. Numbers above 1 will increase the scale, and numbers below 1 will decrease the scale. For example, a scale factor value of 3 will increase the original size of the object by three times, and a scale factor of 0.50 will shrink the original object to half size.

The Reference option allows you to scale an object in relation to an existing X or Y length. When objects are scaled in this fashion, both lengths in the X and Y direction will be scaled. For example, you can reduce the X and Y lengths of the object shown in Figure 12–26A in reference to 9'-0" (length in the X direction) as follows:

```
Command: SC ~EnterKey~
Select objects: (using an appropriate selection method, select the four
objects)
Select object: ~EnterKey~
Specify base point: (using object snap modes, select the intersection as
shown in Figure 12-26B)
Specify scale factor or [Reference]: R ~EnterKey~
Specify reference length <1>: 9' ~EnterKey~
Specify new length: 6' ~EnterKey~
The new object will be reduced to 6'-0" in the X direction and to 4'-0" in
the Y direction as shown in Figure 12-26C.
```

Note: Specifying a 0.0 or negative scale factor value is not permitted.

FIGURE 12–26 Using the Reference option of the SCALE command. Notice either X or Y lengths can be used as a reference but both will be affected by the new length.

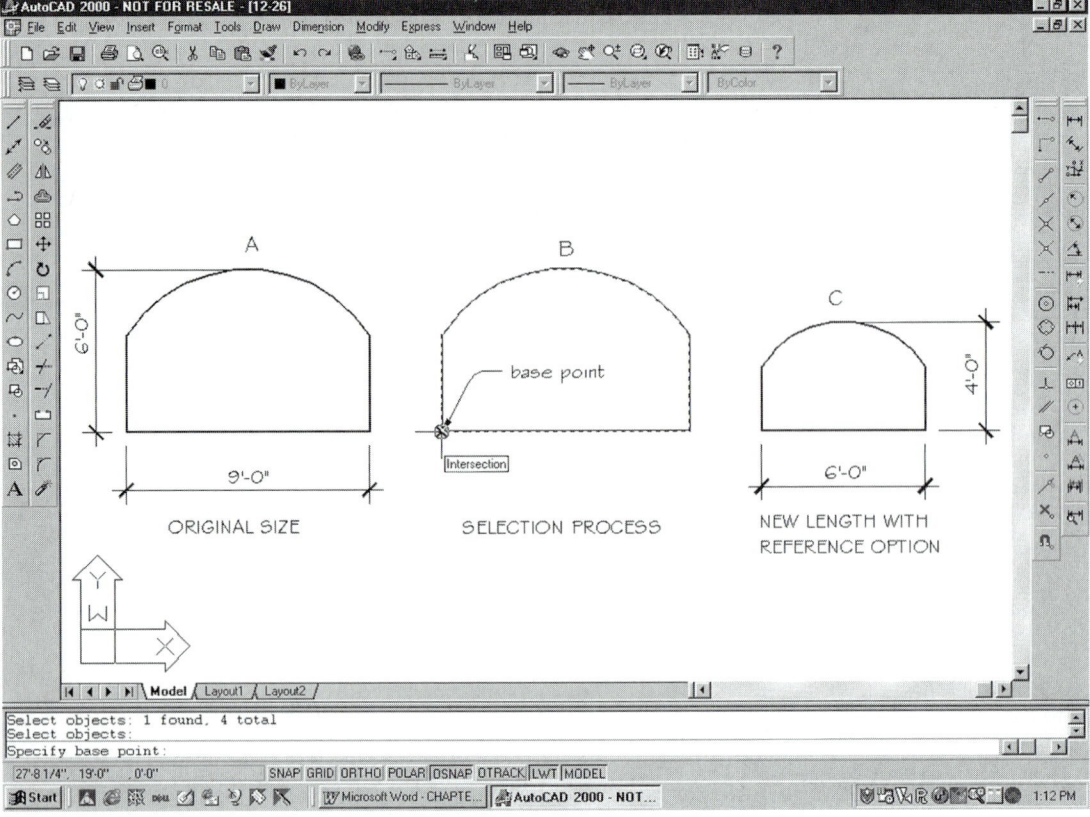

12.16 CHANGING THE SCALE OF THE ENTIRE DRAWING

You can use the SCALE command to make a drawing larger or smaller but it does not change the scale of the drawing based on the current dimensions. This method works fine if you want to increase or shrink all widths, lengths, and heights of objects associated with the drawing and if it can fit inside the existing limits. If you scale a drawing to make it larger, all dimension text, thickness and length of all walls, all regular text, all tick marks associated with architectural dimensioning, and any arrowheads for leader lines will increase in size. This method of changing the scale of an existing drawing is inappropriate because everything about this drawing is changed. The appropriate way to change the scale of an existing drawing is to change the Limits of the drawing or assign a final plot scale when plotting. Remember that when you assign new Limits to the drawing, you do so by entering the upper-right corner coordinates by using either the LIMITS or the LIMMAX commands. As you know from Chapters 2 and 3, this changes the actual scale of the drawing based on new scale factor and new paper plot size. The new Limits can be obtained from the Limits Chart shown in Chapter 2. You assign limits based on the final plot scale and final plot paper size of the drawing. For example, Figure 12–27 shows a floor plan with a final plot scale of 1/4″ =1′-0″. The Limits are based on the final plot scale and the A-size paper on which the drawing will be printed. The upper-right corner limits are 44′, 34′. When this drawing is printed on an A-size sheet, it will be at a precise scale of 1/4″ = 1′-0″. If you use the SCALE command and enter 2 as the scale factor, it will be twice as large as shown in Figure 12–28 (the base point is selected somewhere in the center of the drawing). **Although the SCALE command does change the final plot scale of the drawing from 1/4″ = 1′-0″ to 1/2″ = 1′-0″, it does not keep the original dimensions and the dimension variable values.** Hence, if keeping the dimensions and thickness of walls corresponding to the new scale is of primary concern, this method will produce incorrect dimensions and thickness but at the correct scale. For

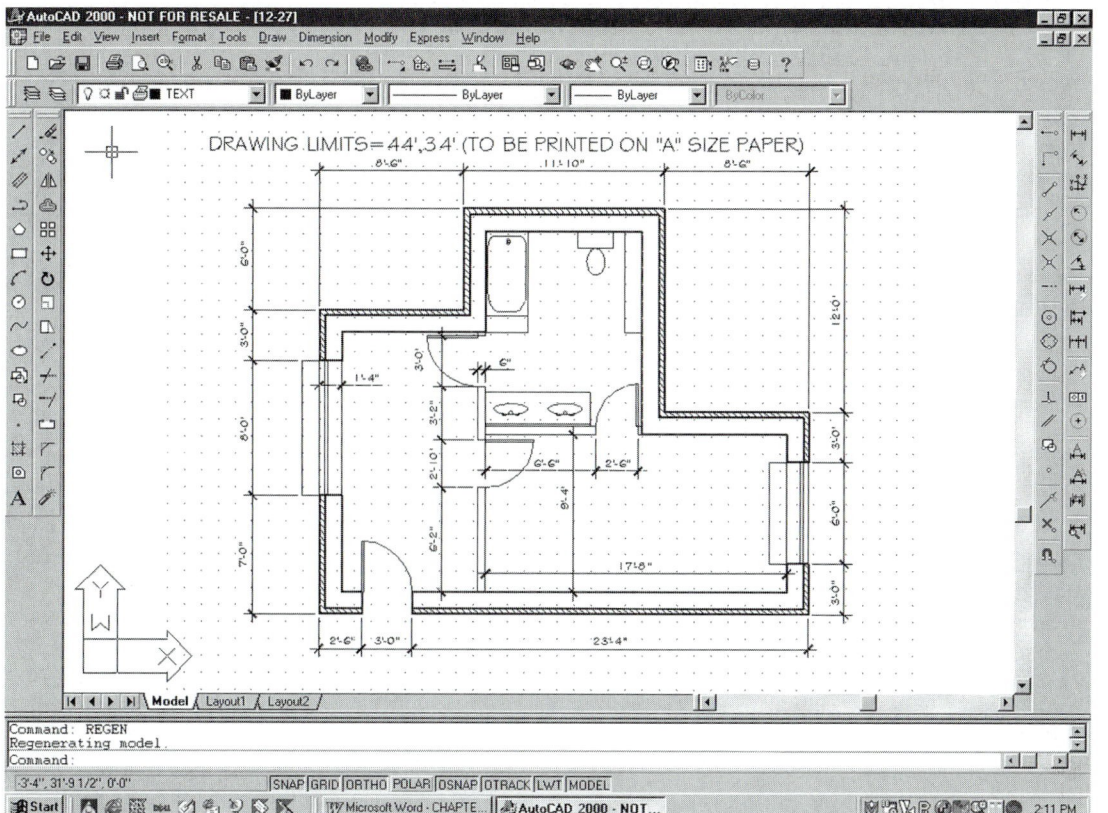

FIGURE 12–27 This floor plan is at a final plot scale of 1/4″ = 1′ = 0″ with upper-right corner limits of 44′, 34′ to be printed on A-size paper.

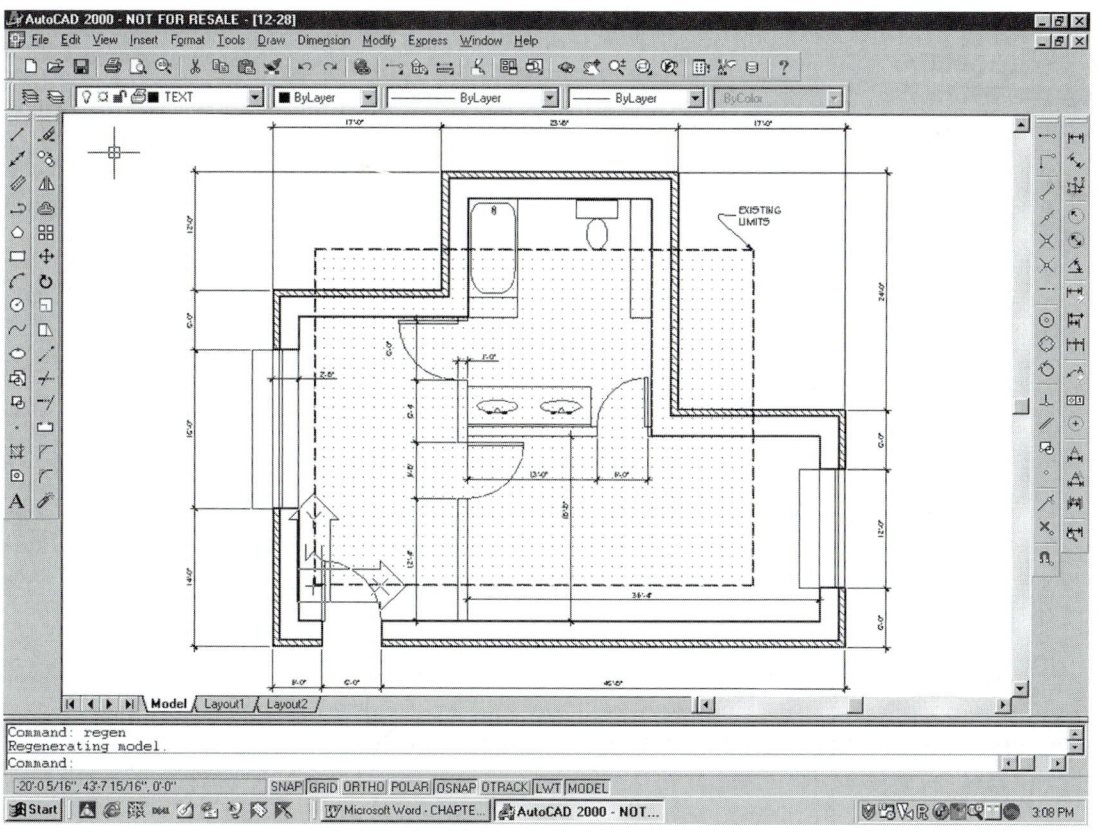

FIGURE 12–28 The same floor plan in Figure 12–27 after using the SCALE command with a scale factor of 2. Notice the dimensions and the size of the walls are displayed twice as the previous size and the drawing does not fit inside the existing limits. This is inappropriate and it does not correspond to the original dimensions and sizes of the drawing.

example, observing Figure 12–28, the door at the entrance is now 6'-0" as opposed to 3'-0", and the wall to the left of this door is now 5'-0" as opposed to 2'-6". This is fine if you want everything dimensioned and printed twice as large. This new scale also does not fit properly inside the existing Limits as shown in Figure 12–28, which are shown with bold dashed lines. When the drawing in Figure 12–28 is printed on a C (24"×18")-size paper, you can use a 1/2" scale and measure everything as it is indicated in the drawing but it will not correspond to the original dimensions and sizes of the 1/4" = 1'-0" drawing. This method of changing the scale merely makes the drawing double with dimensions and wall sizes being twice as large.

To appropriately change the scale of the drawing in Figure 12–27 from 1/4" = 1'-0" to 1/2" = 1'-0" and from A-size paper to C-size paper use the following procedure:

```
Command: LIMMAX
Enter new value for LIMMAX <44'-0",34'-0">: 48',36' ~EnterKey~
Command: (click on the Zoom All button in the Standard toolbar)
```

The drawing will now be at final plot scale of 1/2" = 1'-0" and can be plotted on C-size paper as shown in Figure 12–29. All dimensions will correspond to the original plan at the new scale. The only problem is that the dimension text height, regular text height, dimension tick marks, and extension and dimension extension lines will also be twice as large as the original size. To correspond all that to the height standards, use the Properties window or the Dimension Style Manager dialog box. Using the Properties window to change object properties is discussed in Chapter 13. Dimensioning is discussed in Chapter 18.

FIGURE 12–29   The floor plan in Figure 12–27 is now at a 1/2" = 1'-0" scale with new limits of 48', 36' and can be printed on a C-size sheet.

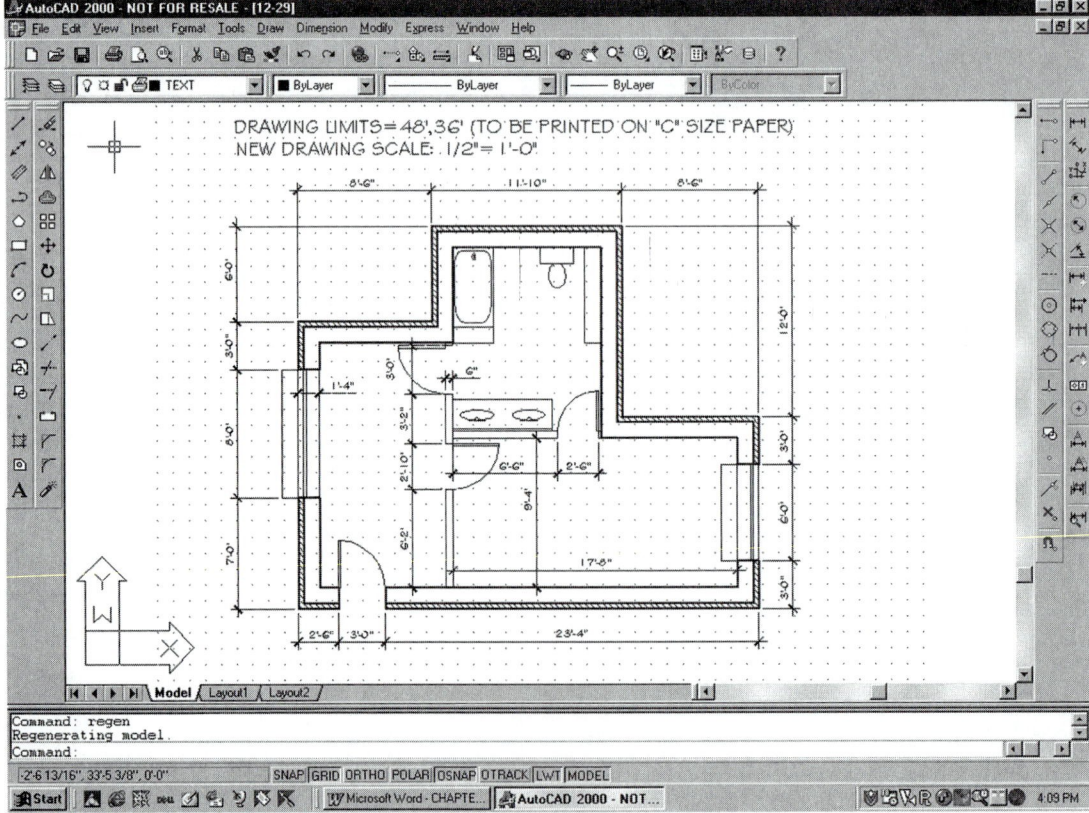

12.17 USING THE STRETCH COMMAND

While the SCALE command changes the length of objects both in the X and Y direction, the STRETCH command allows you to change objects in either one direction. To access the STRETCH command, click on the Stretch button in the Modify toolbar, select Stretch from the Modify pull-down menu, or enter S or STRETCH at the command line. When stretching objects, you must use the Crossing or the Crossing Polygon (CP) selection methods.

■ **EXERCISE 12–12:** *The following step-by-step exercise will allow you to stretch the exterior wall (hence the interior space) of the Floor Plan 5'-0" at 270 degrees shown in Figure 12–30.*

Step #1: Open the EXE12-9.dwg file.

Step #2: Use the STRETCH command to stretch the exterior wall as follows:

Command: **STRETCH** ~EnterKey~

Select objects to stretch by crossing-window or crossing-polygon...

Select objects: *(select the first corner of crossing as shown in Figure 12–30)*

Specify opposite corner: *(select the second corner of crossing)*

Select objects: ~EnterKey~

Specify base point or displacement: *(turn Ortho on and select the base point using Object Snap modes)*

Specify second point of displacement: **@5'<270** ~EnterKey~

Congratulations! You have successfully stretched the exterior wall 5'-0" at 270 degrees. The walls will be stretched as shown in Figure 12–31. Do not save the changes.

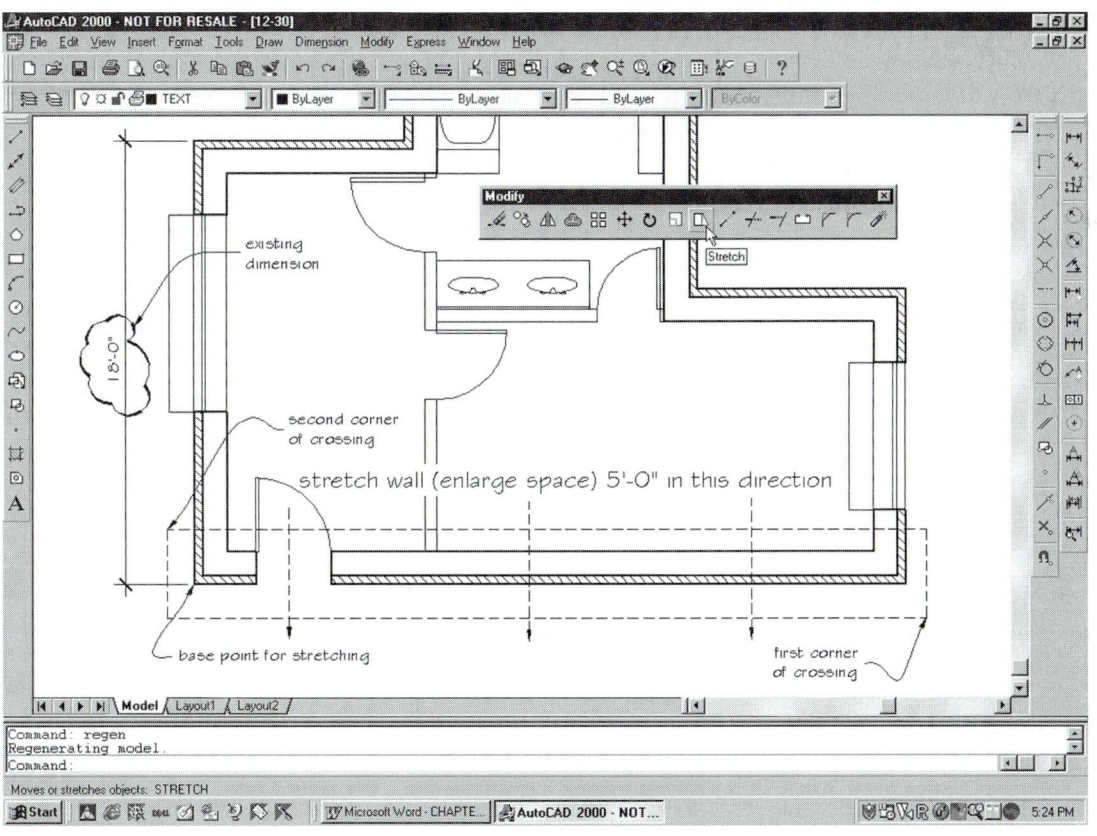

FIGURE 12–30 The STRETCH command can be used to stretch walls and other objects.

FIGURE 12–31   The walls are stretched 5'-0". Notice the updated dimension.

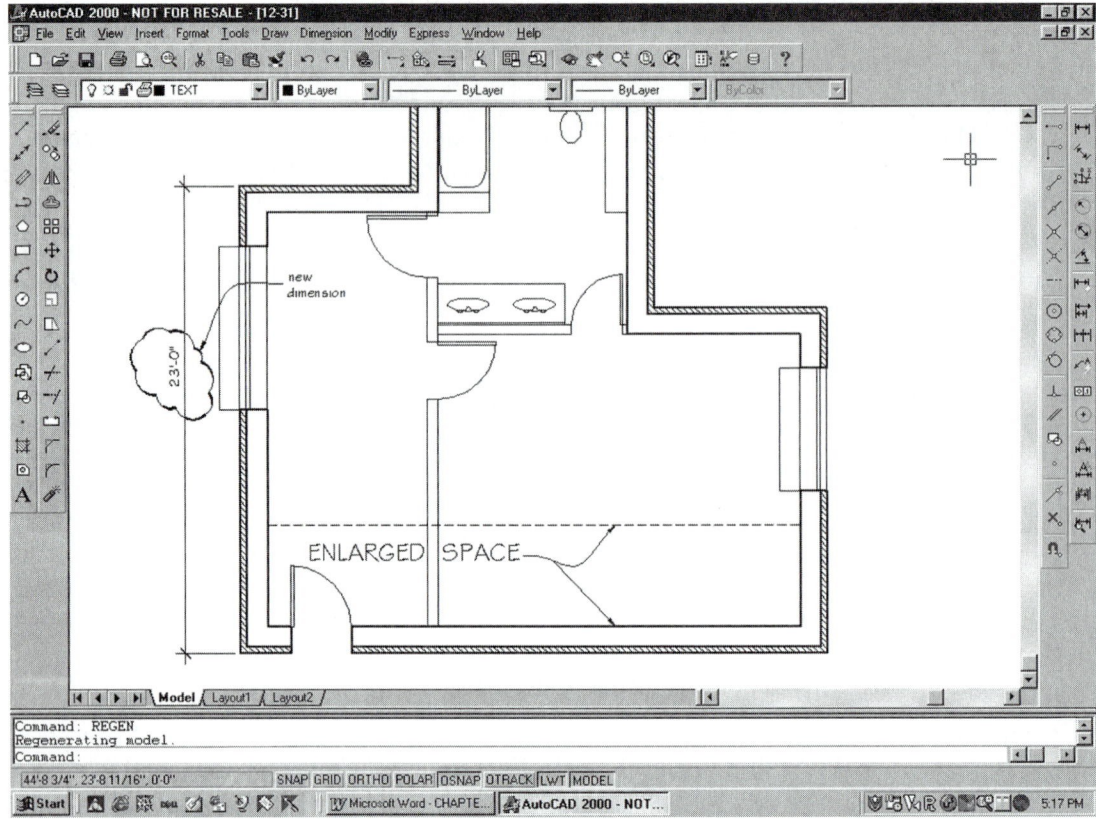

When the objects are selected with the crossing, all objects included in the selection set will be stretched. Be careful not to select objects that you do not want to include in the selection set. To stretch dimensions along with the other objects, include the dimensions in the selection set. Crossing an extension line is sufficient to include it in the selection set.

Tips: Use the Remove (R) option to remove the unwanted objects from the selection set.

Tips: Use the Crossing Polygon (CP) selection method to create a crossing around objects.

Note: To have dimensions and hatching automatically update after stretching, use associative dimensions and associative hatching. See Chapter 17 for a detailed discussion on stretching multilines and hatching inside multilines.

Tips: You must include the hatch pattern's origin to stretch a hatch pattern inside objects.

Tips: The STRETCH command is one of the most versatile and powerful editing commands in AutoCAD. When you use the STRETCH command on objects having associative dimensions and associative hatching, all dimensions and hatching will be updated along with the objects.

12.17.1   Using Multiple Entity Stretch

The Multiple Entity Stretch option allows you to select more than one crossing or crossing polygon to select objects for the STRETCH command. This tool is a part of the Express tools and is accessed from the Modify cascading option in the Express pull-down menu by clicking on the Multiple Entity Stretch button in the Express Standard Toolbar, or by entering MSTRETCH at the command line.

■   **EXERCISE 12–13:**   *The following step-by-step exercise will allow you to stretch the three areas of the drawing in Figure 12–32 at the same time.*

Step #1:   Open the EXE12-10.dwg file.

Step #2:   Use the MSTRETCH command to stretch multiple areas as follows:

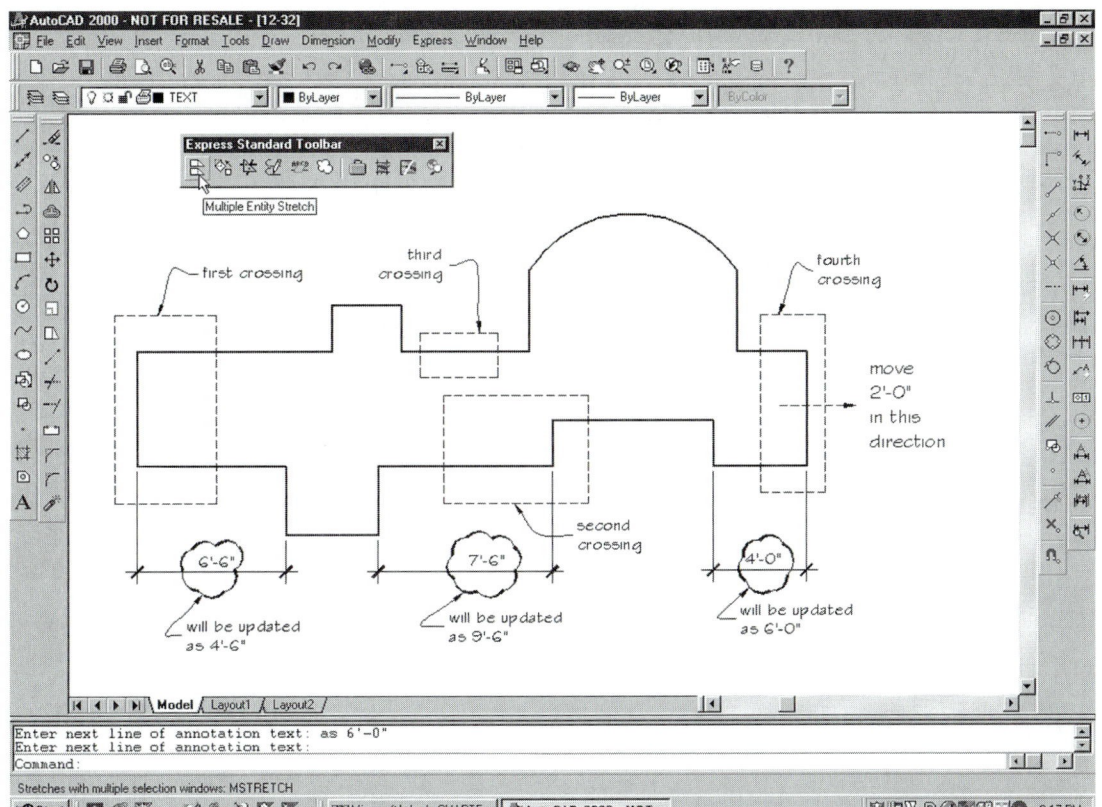

FIGURE 12–32 The MSTRETCH command can be used to stretch multiple objects at one time. Select Crossings or Crossing Polygons at the command prompt.

Command: **MSTRETCH**

Define crossing windows or crossing polygons...

Options: Crossing Polygon or Crossing First Point

Specify an option [CP/C] <Crossing first point>: *(select the lower-right corner of the first crossing as shown in Figure 12–32)*

Specify other corner: *(select the upper-left corner of the first crossing)*

Options: Crossing Polygon or Crossing First Point

Specify an option [CP/C] <Crossing first point>: *(select the lower-right corner of the second crossing)*

Specify other corner: *(select the upper-left corner of the second crossing)*

Options: Crossing Polygon or Crossing First Point

Specify an option [CP/C] <Crossing first point>: *(select the lower-right corner of the third crossing)*

Specify other corner: *(select the upper-left corner of the third crossing)*

Options: Crossing Polygon or Crossing First Point

Specify an option [CP/C] <Crossing first point>: *(select the lower-right corner of the fourth crossing)*

Specify other corner: *(select the upper-left corner of the fourth crossing)*

Options: Crossing Polygon or Crossing First Point

Specify an option [CP/C] <Crossing first point>: ~EnterKey~

 Done defining windows for stretch...

Specify an option [Remove objects] <Base point>: *(using object snap modes, select the base point)*

Second base point: *(turn ortho on)* **@2'<0** ~EnterKey~

FIGURE 12–33 The end result of the Multiple Entity Stretch operation.

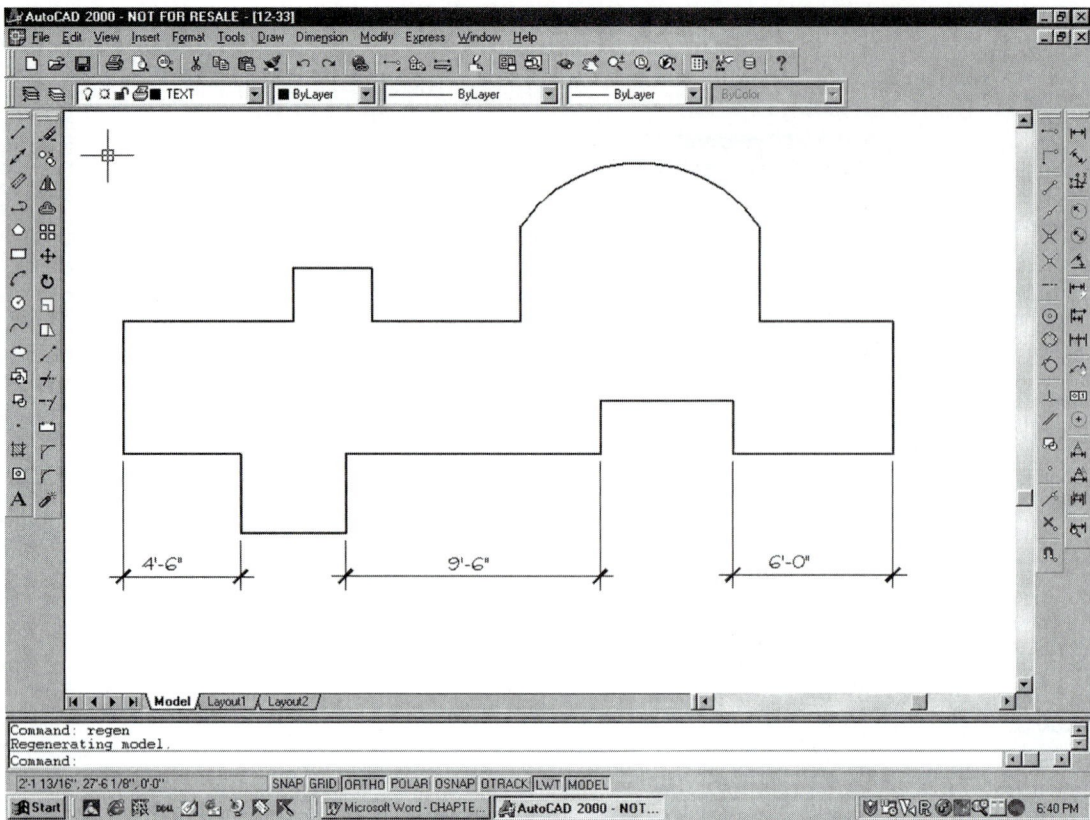

Congratulations! You have successfully stretched multiple objects using the MSTRETCH command. The objects will be stretched as shown in Figure 12–33. Use the R option to remove unwanted objects from the selection set and use the CP option to use the Crossing Polygon selection method. Do not save the changes.

12.18 USING THE MOVE COMMAND

The MOVE command allows you to move a single object or a group of objects from their existing location to a new location. The existing object moved will not remain in its original position. You can access the MOVE command by clicking on the Move button in the Modify toolbar, selecting Move from the Modify pull-down menu, or entering M or MOVE at the command line.

■ **EXERCISE 12–14:** *The following step-by-step exercise will allow you to move the two existing chairs shown in Figure 12–34 from the base point to the second point.*

Step #1: Open the EXE12-11.dwg file.

Step #2: Use the MOVE command to move the chairs as follows:

Command: **MOVE** ~EnterKey~

Select objects: *(select the first corner as shown in Figure 12–34)*

Specify opposite corner: *(select the opposite corner)*

Select objects: Specify opposite corner: 16 found

Select objects: ~EnterKey~

Specify base point or displacement: *(select the base point)*

Specify base point or displacement: Specify second point of displacement or <use first point as displacement>: *(select the second point)*

Congratulations! You have successfully moved the two chairs to a new location. The two chairs will be moved to the second point location as shown in Figure 12–35. Do not save the changes.

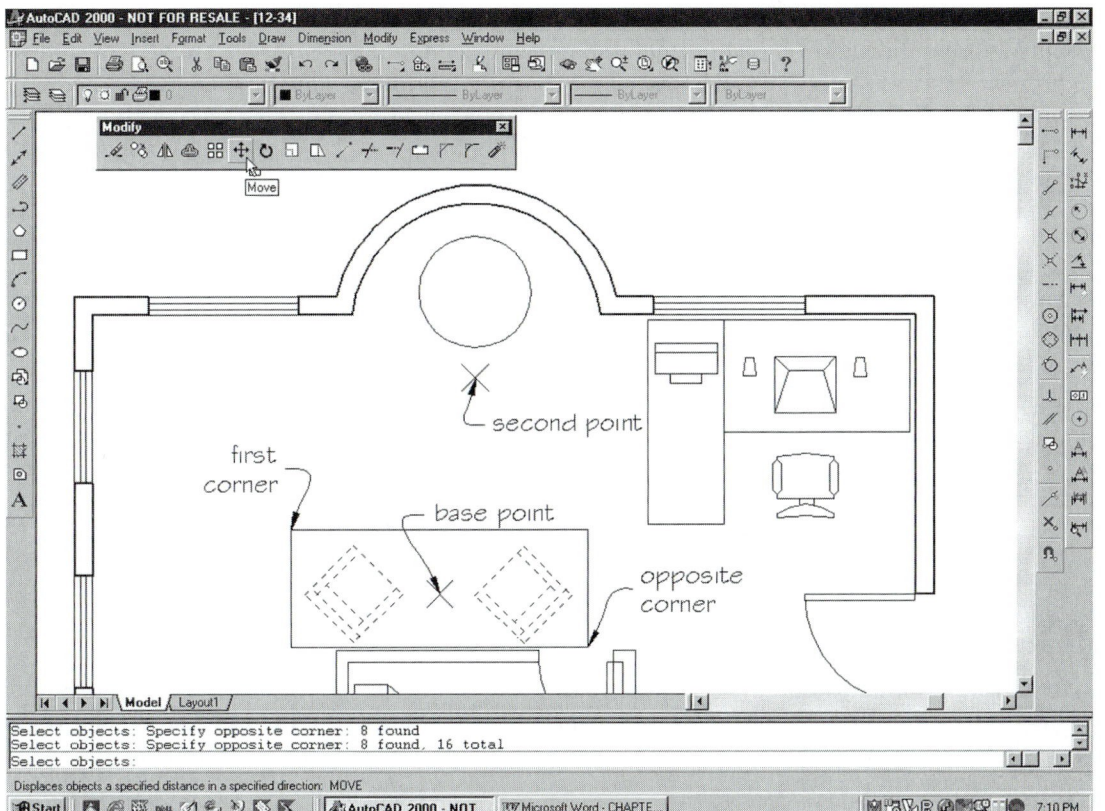

FIGURE 12–34 The MOVE command allows you to move objects from their original location to a new location. You can select objects individually or create a selection set. The two chairs are selected with a Window selection method.

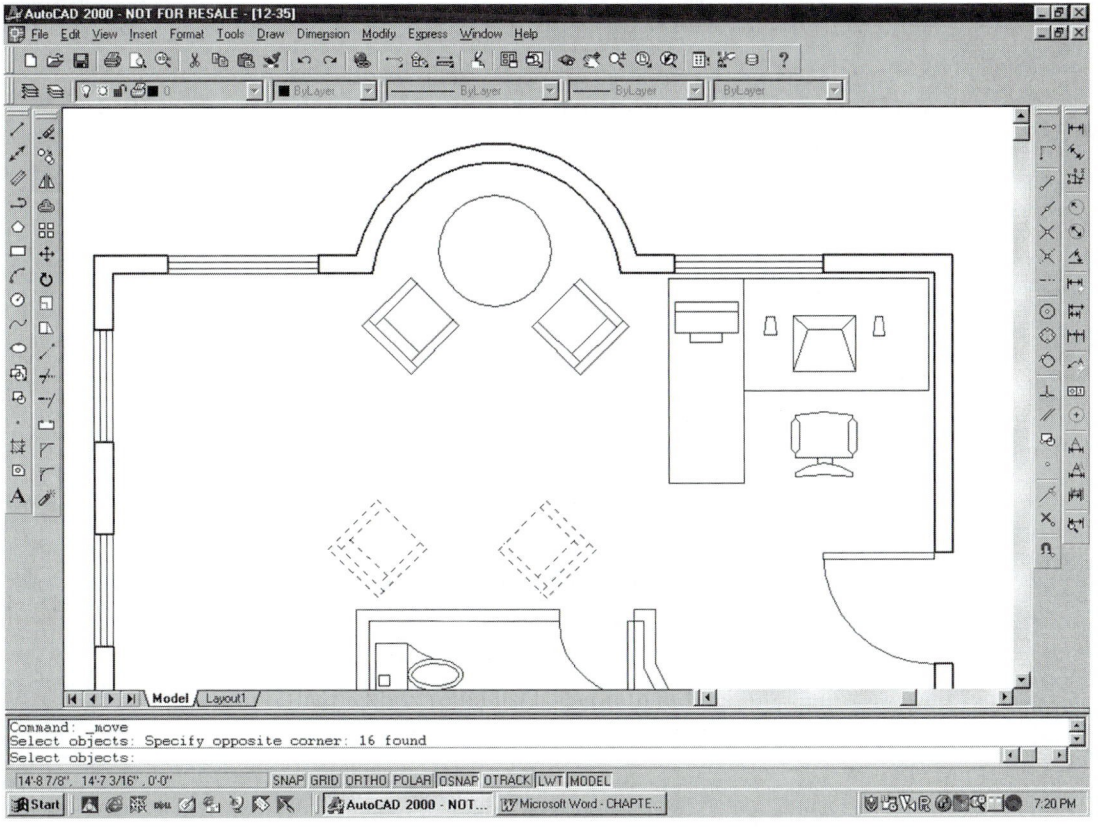

FIGURE 12–35 The two chairs will be moved to the new location.

The base point allows you to select a base point either on the object or a point near the objects. Make your decision based on the first and the second point of displacement. If you make a mistake, enter U (undo) at the Select objects: prompt. This will remove the last selected item from the selection set. Use the R (remove) option to deselect objects from the selection set. After you select the objects, you can automatically drag them to the new position. When moving at an angle, turn Ortho off.

In the above example, you selected a base point and then selected the second point for displacement. You can also move the chairs relative to the coordinates of the first point by entering base point coordinates and then entering displacement coordinates. For example, if the coordinates for the base point are 16'-9", 18'-0" and the coordinates for the second point are 17'-9", 23'-10" you can move the two chairs by coordinates as follows:

```
Specify base point or displacement: 16'9,18' ~EnterKey~
Specify second point of displacement or <use first point as
displacement>: 17'9,23'10 ~EnterKey~
```

The chairs will be moved to the same location shown in Figure 12–35.

Tips: When using editing commands, it is best to use object snap modes for precise point editing.

12.19 USING THE COPY COMMAND

The COPY command allows you to make a single copy or multiple copies of existing object or objects. To access the COPY command, click on the Copy button in the Modify toolbar, select Copy from the Modify pull-down menu, or enter CO or COPY at the command line.

■ **EXERCISE 12–15:** *The following step-by-step exercise will allow you to copy five trees to locations marked as X in Figure 12–36 by selecting one of the existing trees with the Multiple option of the COPY command.*

Step #1: Open the EXE12-12.dwg file.

Step #2: Use the COPY to copy the trees as follows:

Command: **COPY** ~EnterKey~

Select objects: *(select one tree as shown in Figure 12–36)*

Select objects: 1 found

Select objects: ~EnterKey~

Specify base point or displacement, or [Multiple]: **M** ~EnterKey~

Specify base point: *(select the center of the tree)*

Specify second point of displacement or <use first point as displacement>: *(turn Ortho off and select the first X)*

Specify second point of displacement or <use first point as displacement>: *(select the other X points)*

Specify second point of displacement or <use first point as displacement>: ~EnterKey~

Congratulations! You have successfully copied five trees to new locations. The five trees will be copied to the new locations as shown in Figure 12–37. Do not save the changes.

Tips: You can also left-click on objects when no command is running and select Copy from the Edit pull-down menu then select paste from the Edit pull-down menu to copy objects using the Clipboard. Using the Clipboard is another way to edit objects.

Tips: You can also left-click on objects when no command is running and press and hold the right mouse button to drag the selected objects to a new location and then select Move Here or Copy Here from the shortcut menu to Move and Copy objects.

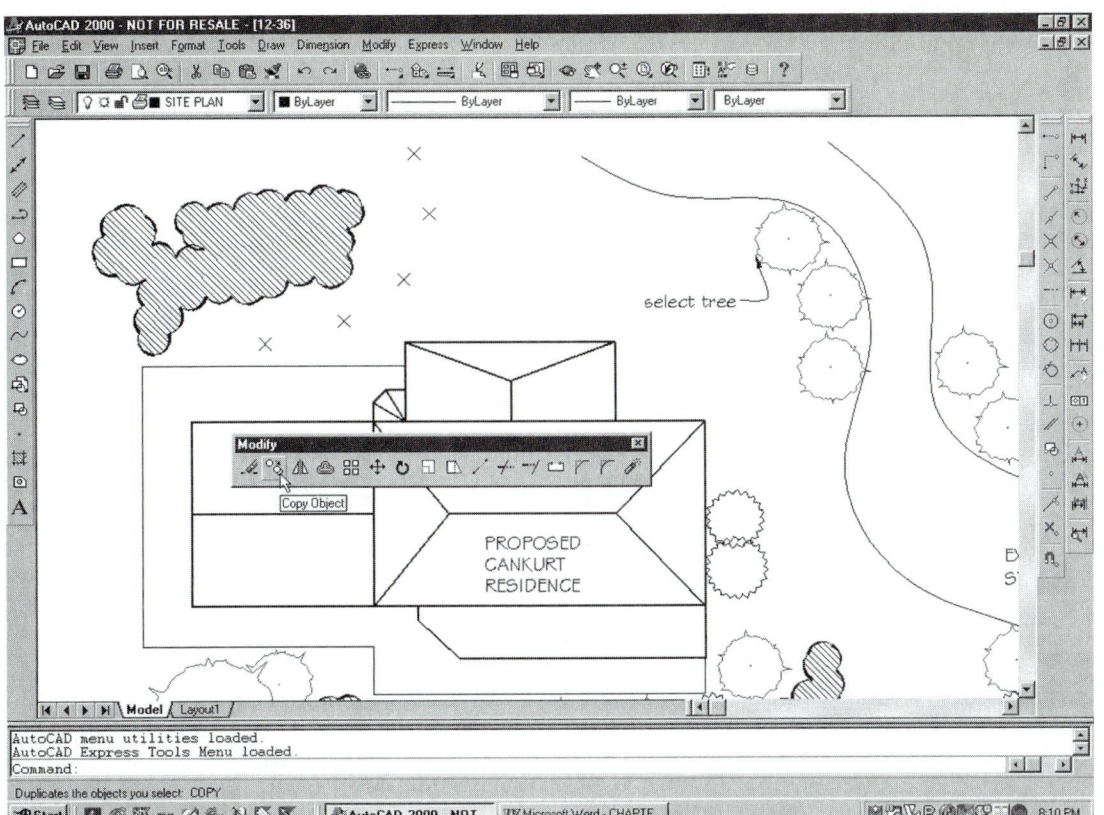

EXERCISE 12–36 The Copy command allows you to make a single copy or multiple copies of existing object or objects. In this example, an existing tree will be copied to multiple locations.

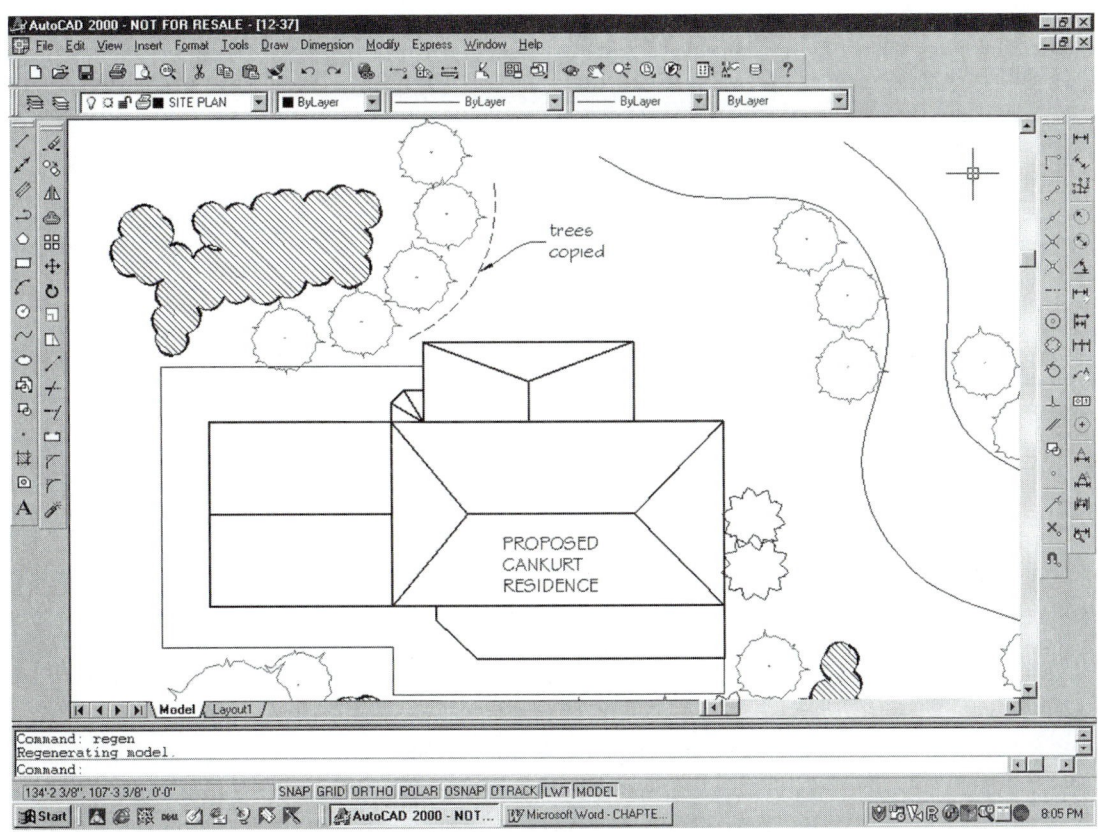

FIGURE 12–37 The end result of the Multiple option of the COPY comand.

12.20 USING THE ROTATE COMMAND

The ROTATE command allows you to rotate an existing object by a specified rotation angle. AutoCAD will rotate the selected object or objects from the base point you specify. To access the ROTATE command, click on the Rotate button in the Modify toolbar, select Rotate from the Modify pull-down menu, or enter RO or ROTATE at the command line. A plus rotation angle rotates the objects counterclockwise, and a minus rotation angle rotates the objects clockwise.

■ **EXERCISE 12–16:** *The following step-by-step exercise will allow you to rotate the floor plan in Figure 12–38 at an angle of 45 degrees from the base point.*

Step #1:   Open the EXE12-13.dwg file.

Step #2:   Use the ROTATE command as follows:

Command: **ROTATE**

Current positive angle in UCS: ANGDIR = counterclockwise ANGBASE = 0

Select objects: *(place a window around the floor plan)*

Specify base point: *(select the base point as shown in Figure 12–38)*

Specify rotation angle or [Reference]: **45** ~EnterKey~

Congratulations! You have successfully rotated an existing floor plan at 45 degrees from a specified base point. The floor plan will be rotated as shown in Figure 12–39. Do not save the changes.

To rotate objects already at an angle, use the *Reference* option to specify the reference angle (current) and the new angle (desired). For example, the furniture shown in Figure 12–40A

FIGURE 12–38 The ROTATE command will rotate objects from a selected base point clockwise or counterclockwise.

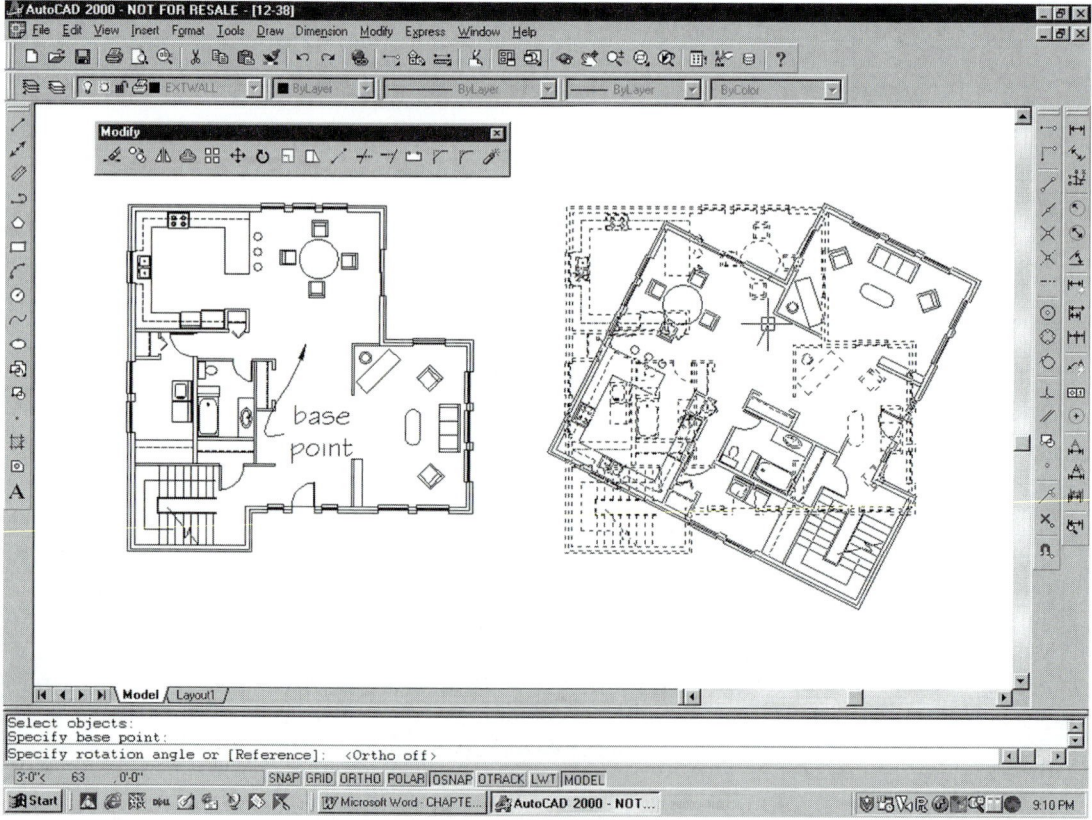

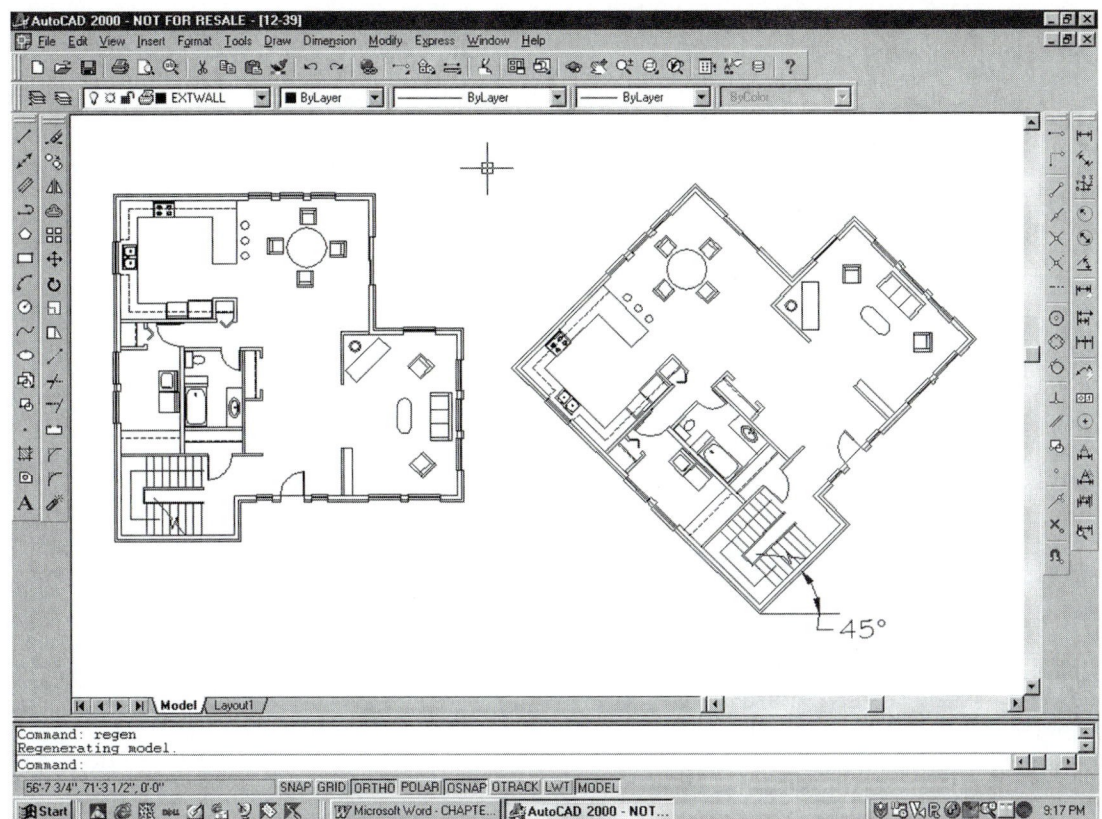

FIGURE 12–39 The floor plan is rotated 45 degrees from the base point.

is already rotated 60 degrees. To display this furniture at an angle of 30 degrees from the horizontal, use the reference (60 degrees) and the new angle (30 degrees) as follows:

```
Command: RO
Current positive angle in UCS: ANGDIR =counterclockwise ANGBASE =0
Select objects: (place a window around the furniture)
Specify base point: (select the base point)
Specify rotation angle or [Reference]: R ~EnterKey~
Specify the reference angle <0>: 60 ~EnterKey~
Specify the new angle: 30 ~EnterKey~
```

The furniture will be rotated 30 degrees as shown in Figure 12–40B.

Tips: With the Ortho mode on, you can rotate objects by moving the cursor to 0, 90, 180, and 270 degrees direction. AutoCAD will dynamically display the new rotated position as you move your cursor around the screen. You can also pick a reference line on the object or on the screen and rotate the object in relation to that reference line.

12.21 MOVE COPY ROTATE EXPRESS TOOLS

The MOCORO (Move Copy Rotate) command allows you to move, copy, rotate, and scale a selected object or objects at the same time without having to access the three separate commands. This is a very powerful command and is very convenient because you do not have to use the Previous option when you select the objects for the second, third, or fourth commands. This express tool allows you to select objects once and then perform as many of the options as needed. Even though the SCALE option is not included in the MOCORO name, it is available in the command option. The COPY option of this express command is a multiple copy, so you can use it to make multiple copies. The Move, Copy, Rotate, and Scale options can be used in any order and can be repeated as many times as needed. You can also change the base point while in the command. The MOCORO command can be accessed from the Modify cascading option of the

FIGURE 12–40   Using the Reference option of the ROTATE command.

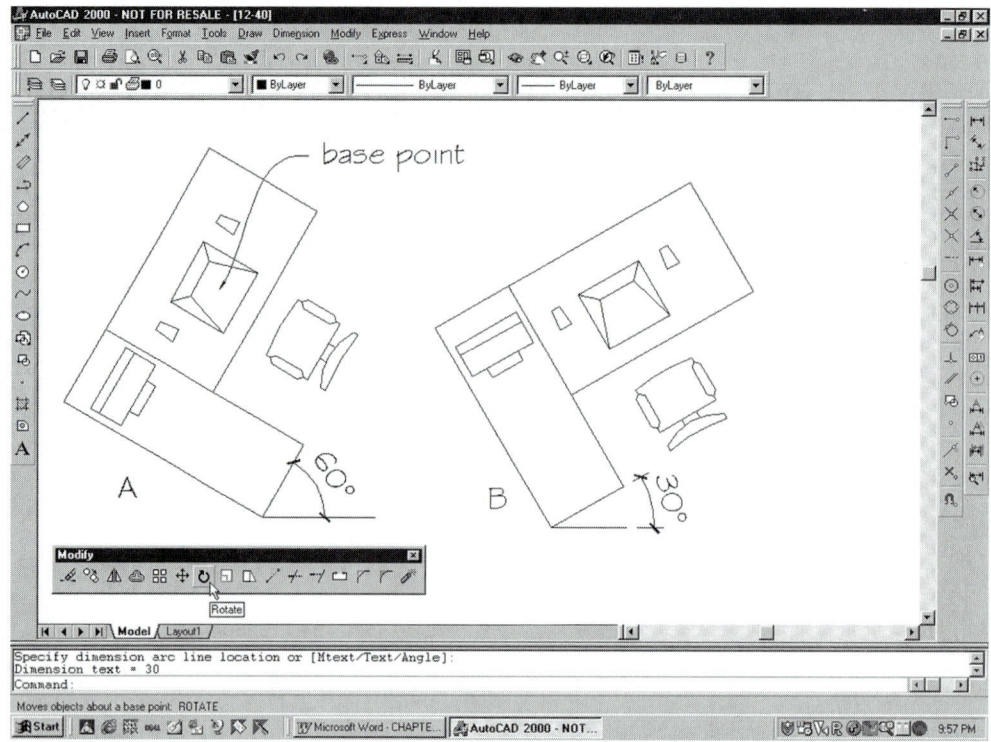

Express pull-down menu, selected from the Move Copy Rotate button in the Express Standard Toolbar, or entered at the command line.

■ **EXERCISE 12–17:**   *Figure 12–41 shows a kitchen sink that is twice as big as the current scale requires. It needs to be scaled down by half and also needs to be rotated 90 degrees and moved to the second point near the window. The following step-by-step exercise will allow you to first scale it down, then rotate, and then move it to its final location by using the MOCORO command.*

Step #1:   Open the EXE12-14.dwg file.

Step #2:   Use the MOCORO command as follows:

   Command: **MOCORO** ~EnterKey~

   Select objects: *(select the first window point and turn Ortho off)*

   Specify opposite corner: *(select the opposite corner of the window)*

   37 found

   Select objects: ~EnterKey~

   Base point: *(select the base point as the midpoint as shown in Figure 12–41)*

   [Move/Copy/Rotate/Scale/Base/Undo] <eXit>: **S** ~EnterKey~

   Second point or scale factor: **0.50** ~EnterKey~

   [Move/Copy/Rotate/Scale/Base/Undo] <eXit>: **R** ~EnterKey~

   Second point or rotation angle: **90** ~EnterKey~

   [Move/Copy/Rotate/Scale/Base/Undo] <eXit>: **M** ~EnterKey~

   Second point of displacement: *(select the second point)*

   [Move/Copy/Rotate/Scale/Base/Undo] <eXit>: ~EnterKey~

Congratulations! You have successfully used the MOCORO command. The sink will be scaled, rotated, and moved in one continuous operation as shown in Figure 12–42. Do not save the changes.

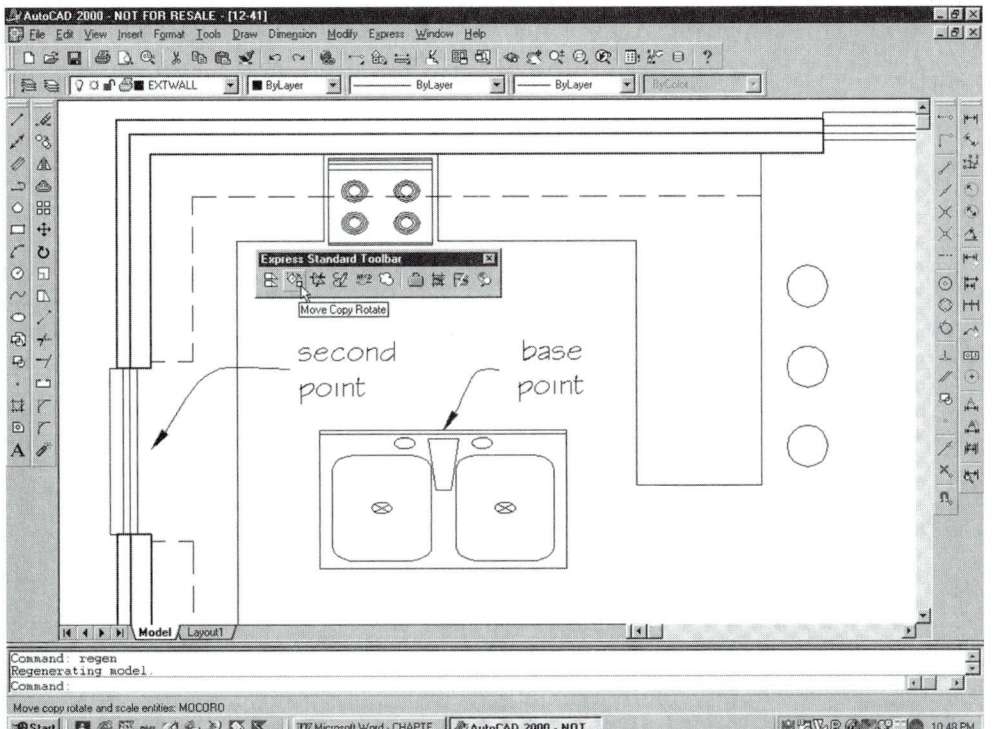

FIGURE 12–41 The MOCORO command can be used to move, copy, rotate, and scale objects in one continuous operation.

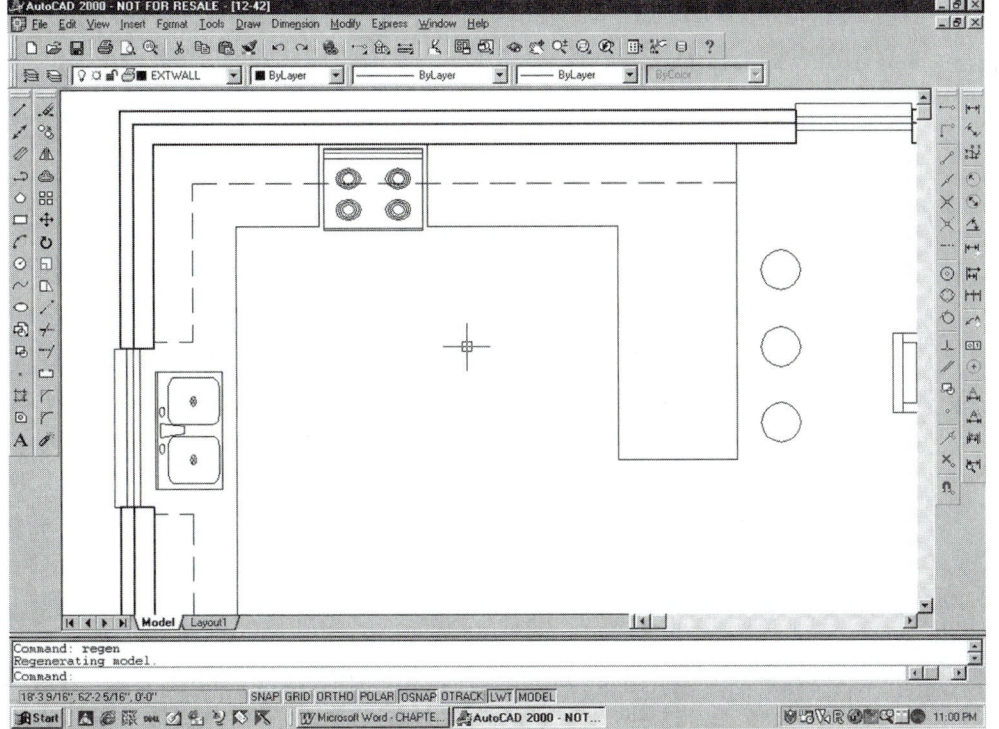

FIGURE 12–42 The final result of the MOCORO command.

12.22 USING THE MIRROR COMMAND

The MIRROR command allows you to create a mirror image of an object. This command is extremely useful when a client requires the reverse of the floor plan. You can access the MIRROR command by clicking on the Mirror button in the Modify toolbar, by selecting Mirror from the Modify pull-down menu, or by entering MI or MIRROR at the command line. Once in the MIRROR command, you are asked to select the objects, then select a mirror line. A mirror line is an imaginary hinge point about which objects are mirrored. If you select the exterior points on the object as the mirror line, the mirror image will appear attached to the initial object. If you select points outside the object as the mirror line, the mirror image will appear at the distance specified by the points. You can have the mirror line placed at any angle. At the end of the mirror operation, you have the option to delete the original objects.

■ **EXERCISE 12–18:** *The following step-by-step exercise will allow you to mirror the floor plan shown in Figure 12–43A using the imaginary mirror line.*

Step #1: Open the EXE12-15.dwg file.

Step #2: Use the MIRROR command as follows:

Command: **MIRROR** ~EnterKey~

Select objects: *(select the entire floor plan)*

Select objects: ~EnterKey~

Specify first point of mirror line: *(select the first point of mirror line as shown in Figure 12–43A)*

Specify second point of mirror line: *(select the second point of mirror line)*

Delete source objects? [Yes/No] <N>: ~EnterKey~

Congratulations! You have successfully used the MIRROR command. The floor plan will be mirrored as shown in Figure 12–43B. Do not save the changes.

FIGURE 12–43 Using the MIRROR command.

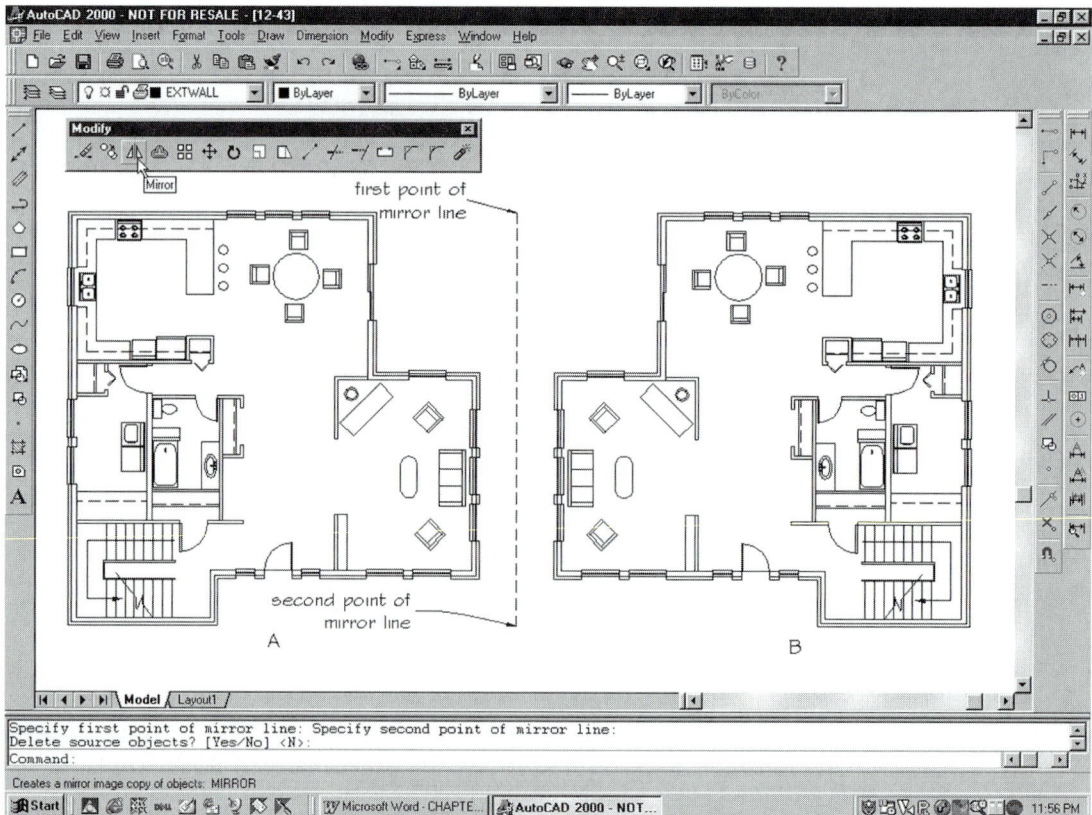

Tips: Use the MIRROR command to cut drawing time in half for symmetric objects. Create an angled reference line for mirroring objects at an angle. Turn Ortho on if mirroring horizontal or vertical.

Tips: If mirrored objects contain text, the text will be displayed backward after the mirror operation. For normal text display, turn the MIRRTEXT system variable off before using the MIRROR command.

12.23 USING THE ALIGN COMMAND

The ALIGN command allows you to move and rotate objects at the same time. Rather than specifying a rotation angle, the ALIGN command aligns several selected *source points* with the several *destination points*. The move and rotate operations take place through the alignment points. The source points define points on the source object in relation to the object's original position. The destination points define points on the destination source in relation to the object's new position. Once the points are established, AutoCAD aligns the points with an imaginary line, then moves and rotates the original position into the new position. The alignment, the movement, and the rotation are the three major components of the ALIGN command. You can access the ALIGN command by selecting Align from the 3D Operation cascading option of the Modify pull-down menu or by entering Al or ALIGN at the command line.

After selecting the objects, AutoCAD asks for three source points and three destination points. Usually it is sufficient to align two points on the object with the two points on the source object. If required, you can select the third source point and the third destination point.

■ **EXERCISE 12–19:**   *Figure 12–44 shows a kitchen cabinet plan with cabinet and appliance locations on the right side of the drawing. This design is transferred from another drawing using the Multiple Design Environment. The Floor Plan on the left represents a rectangular kitchen plan. The following step-by-step exercise will allow you to move and rotate the cabinet design plan into the kitchen plan using the ALIGN command.*

Step #1:   Open the EXE12-16.dwg file.

Step #2:   Use the ALIGN command as follows:

Command: **ALIGN** ~EnterKey~

Select objects: *(select the first window corner in the kitchen cabinet plan)*

Select objects: Specify opposite corner: *(select the opposite corner)*

Select objects: Specify opposite corner: 60 found

Select objects: ~EnterKey~

Specify first source point: *(select the first source point as shown in Figure 12–44)*

Specify first destination point: *(select the first destination point. AutoCAD will place an imaginary line between the two points)*

Specify second source point: *(select the second source point)*

Specify second destination point: *(select the second destination point. AutoCAD will place an imaginary line between the two points)*

Specify third source point or <continue>: ~EnterKey~

Scale objects based on alignment points? [Yes/No] <N>: ~EnterKey~

Congratulations! You have successfully used the ALIGN command. The kitchen cabinet plan will be moved and rotated to the new location as shown in Figure 12–45. If the distance between the source points is not equal to the distance between the destination points, enter Y at the last command: prompt. If the results are not perfect, edit the source object or the destination objects. Do not save the changes.

FIGURE 12–44 The ALIGN command uses source and destination points to move and rotate objects into a new position. The two dashed lines are actually solid lines between the alignment points.

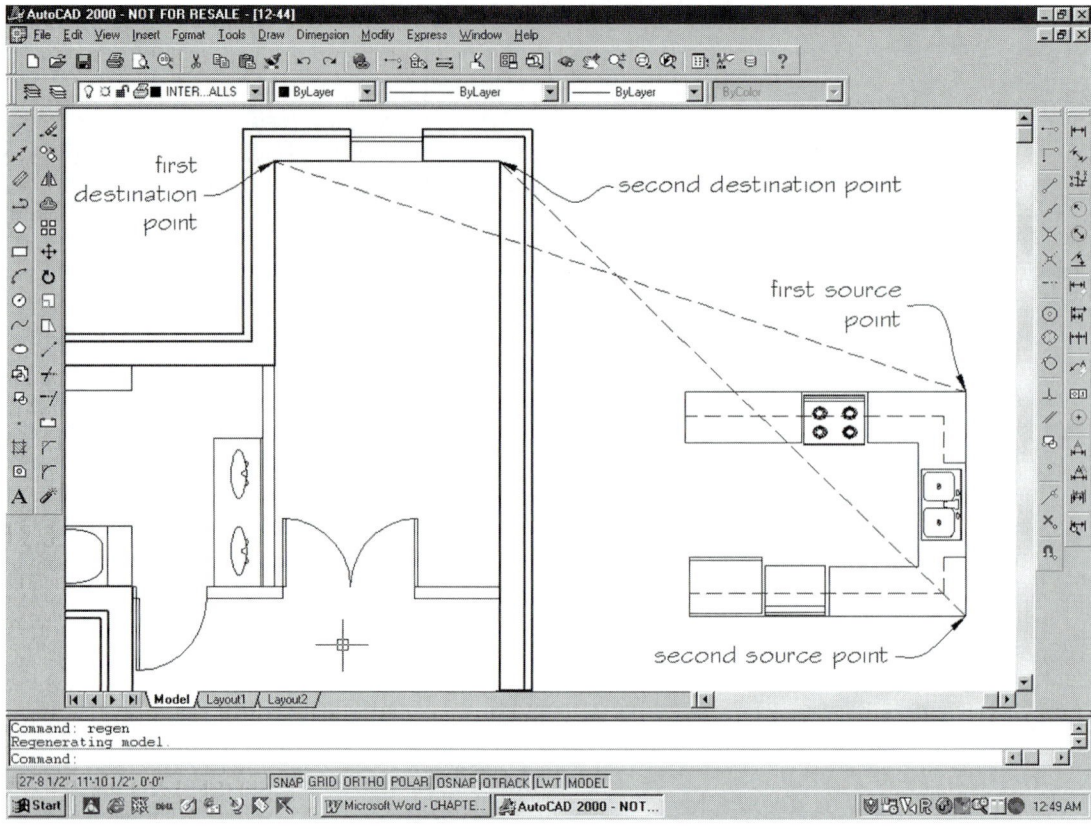

FIGURE 12–45 The kitchen cabinet plan is moved and rotated at the same time into the kitchen space of the floor plan.

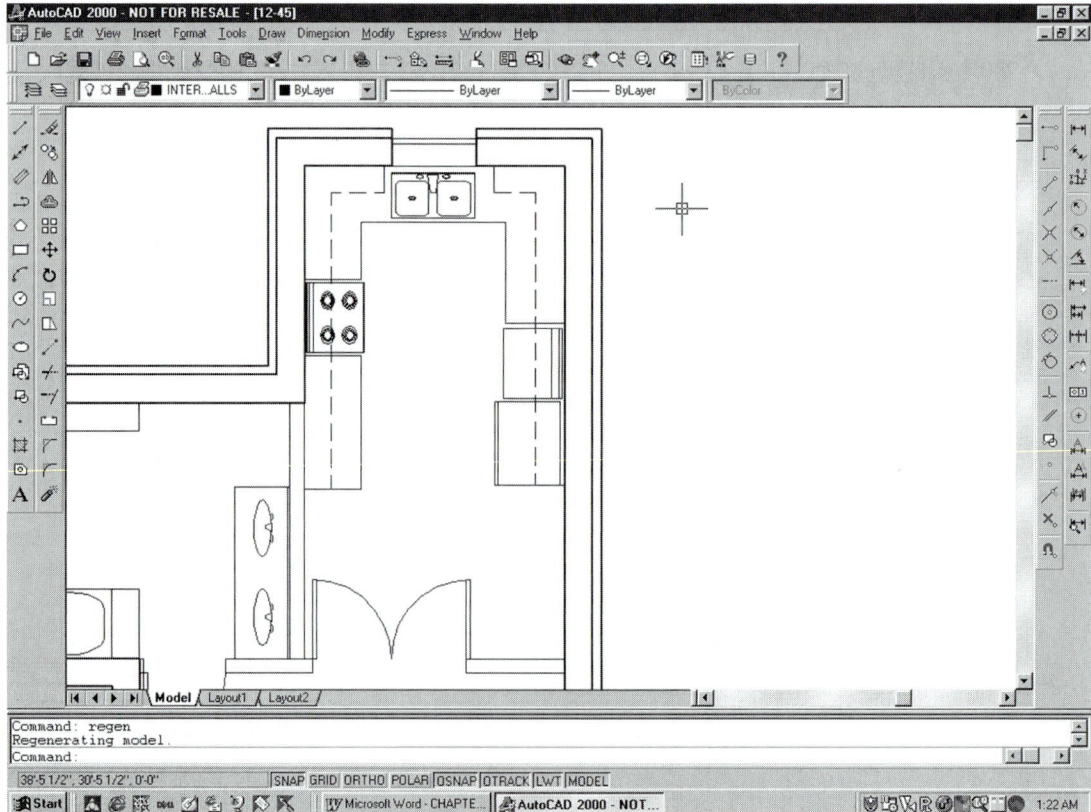

12.24 USING THE ARRAY COMMAND

The ARRAY command allows you to copy and rotate objects at the same time. You can create multiple copies of an object or group of objects reproduced in a rectangular or circular (polar) format. To access the ARRAY command, click on the Array button in the Modify toolbar, select Array from the Modify pull-down menu, or enter AR or ARRAY at the command line. When using the ARRAY command, you are asked to select the object(s) to be copied first. You are then asked to select the format of the array. There are two array formats, *Rectangular Array* and *Polar Array*.

- The **Rectangular Array** allows you to copy and rotate objects arranged in rows and columns. You are asked to specify number of rows, number of columns, distance between rows, and distance between columns. During command prompts, the rows are identified as horizontal dashed lines (- - -) and columns are identified as vertical solid lines (|||). Columns are arranged in vertical format, and rows are arranged in horizontal format. After you specify the number of columns and the number of rows for the rectangular array, you are then asked to enter the *distance between rows,* or the *distance between columns* or specify *unit cell.* The distance between rows is the total distance between objects in the Y axis direction. The distance between columns is the total distance between objects in the X axis direction. You can also enter these distances with your cursor. The points you select with your cursor that separate objects between rows and columns is the *unit cell* value. The unit cell value is the same as the distance between columns and rows.

- ■ **EXERCISE 12–20:** *Figure 12–46 shows a single structural column as Column A4. This column will be arrayed to create the drawing shown in Figure 12–48. Before arraying, however, look at Figure 12–47 and study the components of the rectangular array format, including distance between columns and rows and unit cell in relationship to other columns. The following step-by-step exercise will allow you to array the existing column as four rows and six columns.*

  Step #1: Open the EXE12-17.dwg file.

  Step #2: The following command line procedure will allow you to create a rectangular array of the 1'-0" by 1'-0" A4 column having six columns, four rows, and 2'-0" between (see Figures 12–46 and 12–47):

  Command: **ARRAY** ~EnterKey~

  Select objects: *(select column A4)*

  Select objects: ~EnterKey~

  Enter the type of array [Rectangular/Polar] <R>: ~EnterKey~

  Enter the number of rows (- - -) <1>: **4** ~EnterKey~

  Enter the number of columns (|||) <1>: **6** ~EnterKey~

  Enter the distance between rows or specify unit cell (- - -): **3'** ~EnterKey~

  Specify the distance between columns (|||): **3'** ~EnterKey~

Congratulations! You have successfully arrayed the column. The column A4 will be arrayed as shown in Figure 12–48. Do not save the changes.

You can create a rectangular array in four coordinate directions by entering either positive or negative row and column distances. For example, if you had column F1 as the original object to array, you would enter −3' as the distance between rows and −3' as the distance between columns.

- The **Polar Array** allows you to copy and rotate objects arranged around the center point of a circle. This is the center point of the polar array. After selecting the center point of array, you are asked to enter the number of items in the array. For example, if you want seven chairs arrayed around a circular table at a full 360 degrees, the number of items will be 7. You are then asked to specify the angle to fill. The angle you specify does not have to be 360 degrees—it can be any angle you require. For example, you can array the seven chairs around half the circular table by entering either 180 or −180. The plus angle will array objects counterclockwise, and the minus angle will array objects clockwise. The angle direction depends on the location of the original object and the location of the point of array. The angle direction options will be presented by + =ccw and − =cw inside the

FIGURE 12–46   The ARRAY command will be used to copy and rotate column A4 using the rectangular array format with a number of columns (six) and a number of rows (four).

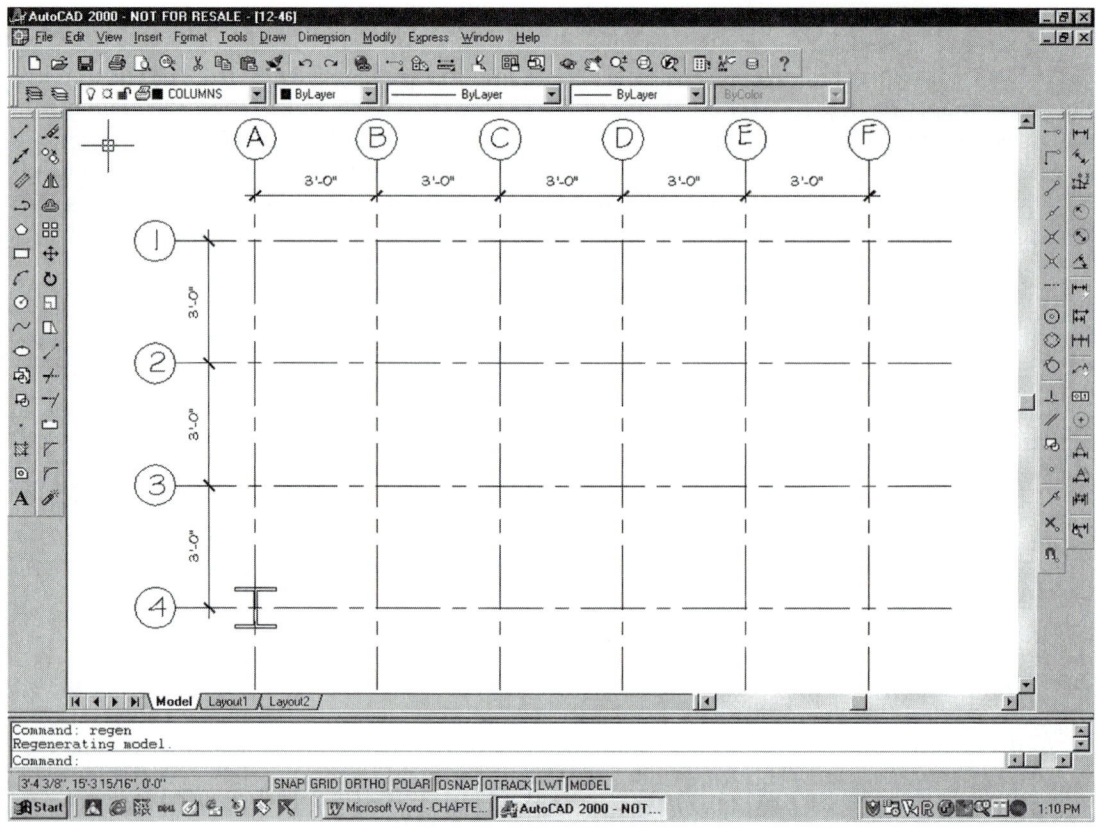

FIGURE 12–47   The distance between rows and columns must include the distance separating objects plus the width and length of the selected object.

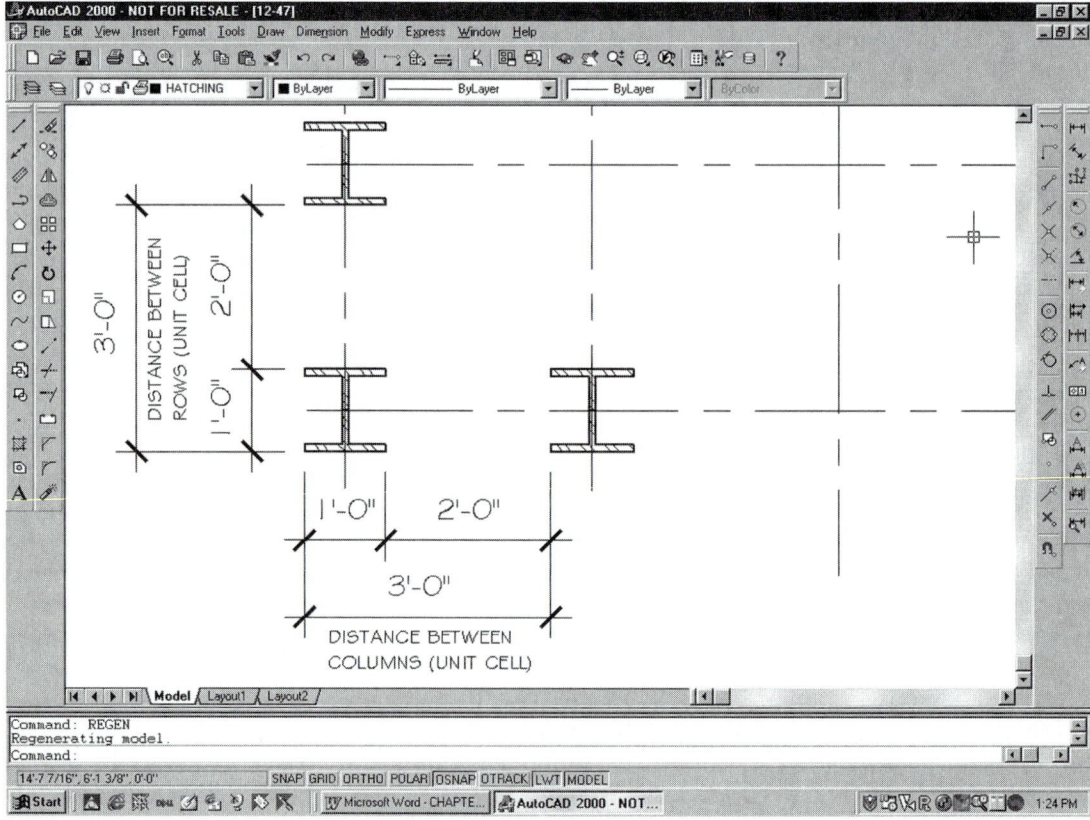

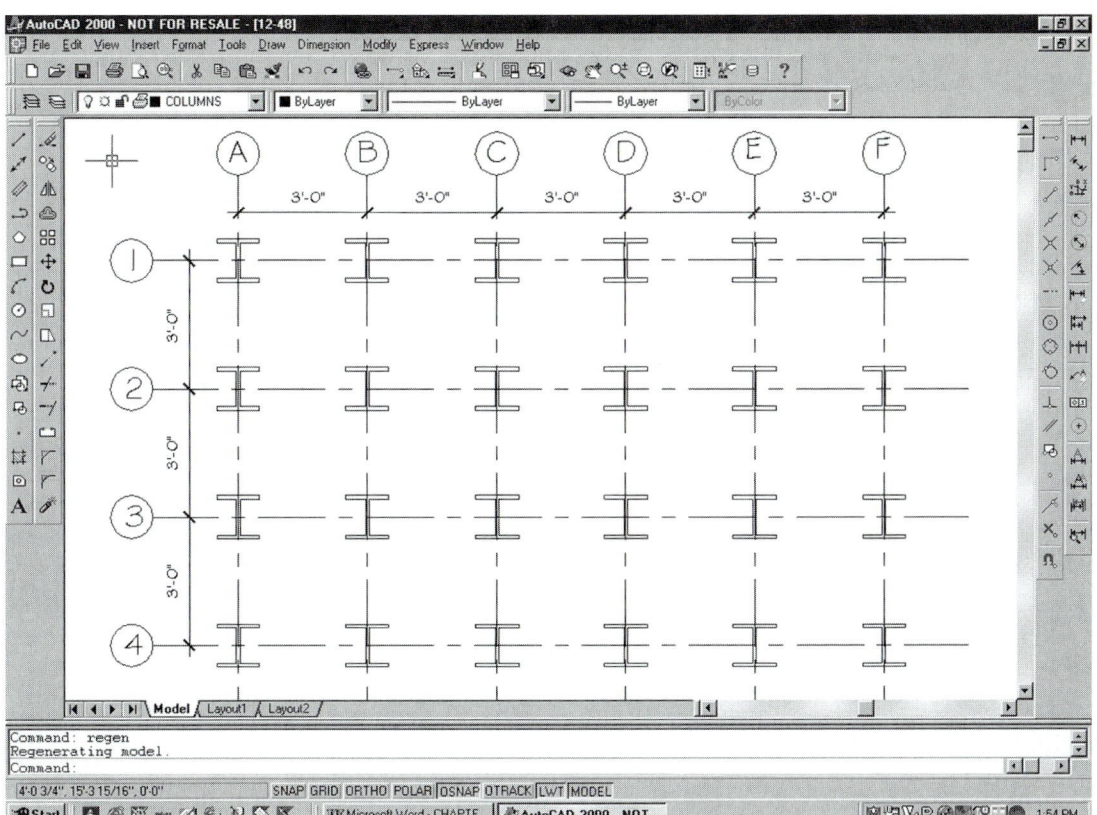

FIGURE 12–48 The final result of the Rectangular Array.

parentheses. If you want to specify a specific angle between objects, press the ~EnterKey~ and enter the number of items in the Array: prompt. You will then be asked to enter the angle between items. If you specify the number of items in the array and specify the angle to fill, AutoCAD will automatically figure out the angle between objects per given values. As the last item in the command procedure, you can have the objects rotated as they are arrayed around the center point of array or you can have the objects remain the same position and orientation as the original object. For example, if you enter Y at the Rotate arrayed objects? [Yes/No] <Y>: prompt, the original chair will be arrayed so that the face of the chair is always perpendicular to the center point of array.

■ **EXERCISE 12–21:** *The following step-by-step exercise will allow you to use Polar Array to arrange the chair shown in Figure 12–49A around the circular table so that seven chairs are displayed around 360 degrees as shown in Figure 12–49B.*

Step #1:   Open the EXE12-18.dwg file.

Step #2:   Use the ARRAY command as follows:

Command: **AR** ~EnterKey~

Select objects: *(select the chair)*

Select objects: ~EnterKey~

Enter the type of array [Rectangular/Polar] <R>: **P** ~EnterKey~

Specify center point of array: *(select the center of the circle)*

Enter the number of items in the array: **7** ~EnterKey~

Specify the angle to fill (+=ccw, −=cw) <360>: ~EnterKey~

Rotate arrayed objects? <Yes/No] <Y>: ~EnterKey~

Congratulations! You have succsessfully rotated the chair around the table. Do not save the changes.

Figure 12–50 shows the two different applications of the Polar Array.

FIGURE 12–49 The Polar Array allows you to array objects around the center point of a circle. **A:** The chair is selected for the array. **B:** Seven chairs are arrayed around 360 degrees.

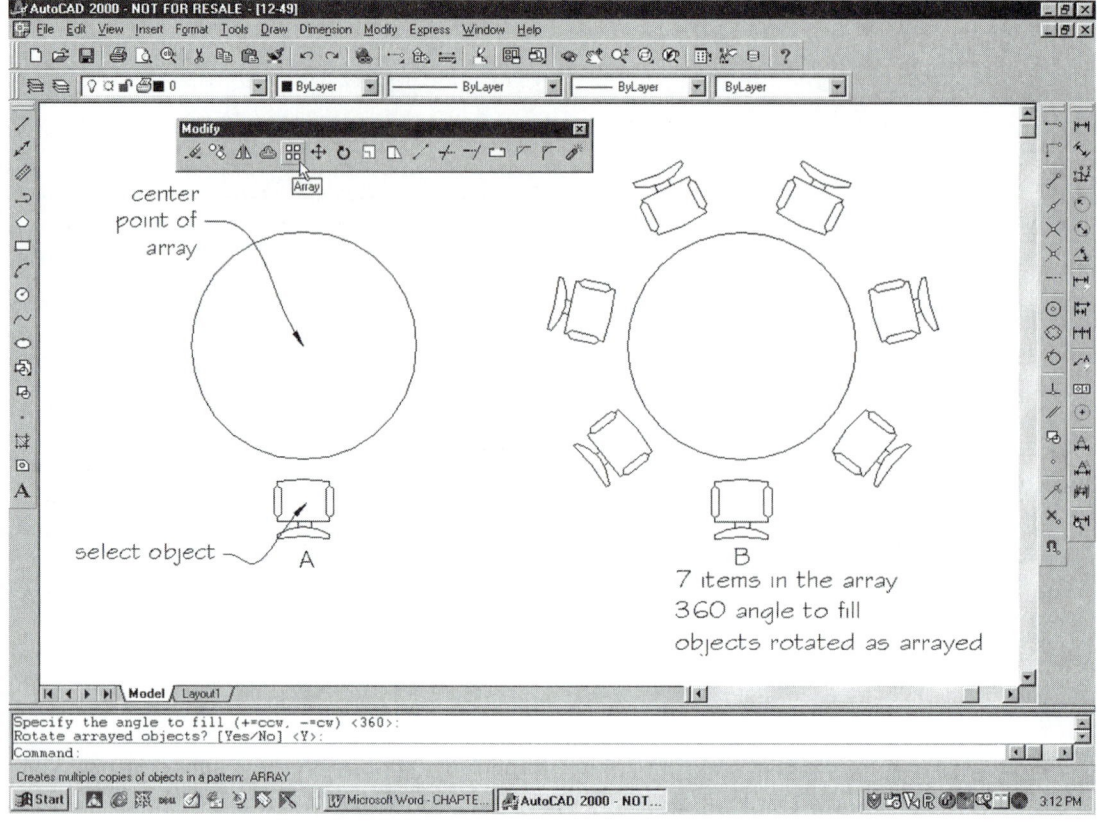

FIGURE 12–50 The original object is arrayed with 15 degrees between and at −180 degrees (left). The original object is arrayed 10 times between −270 degrees but is not rotated as arrayed.

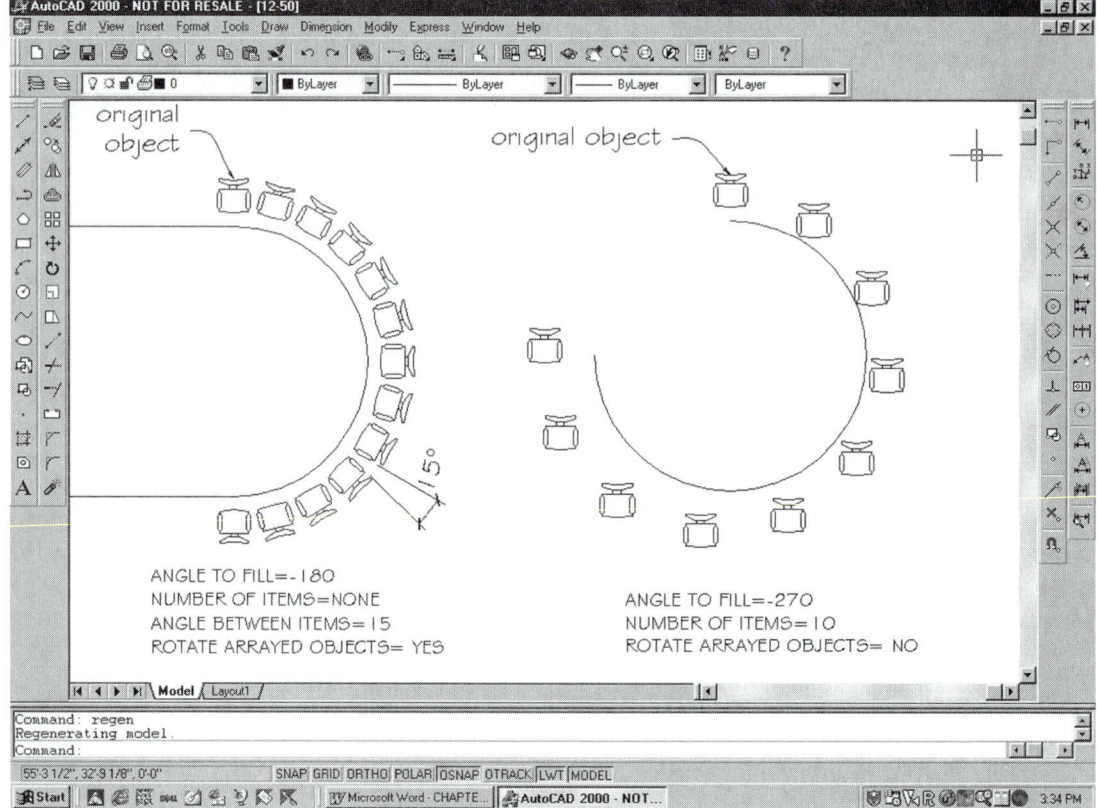

Tips: You can create a rectangular array at a specified angle by using the Rotation option of the SNAP command.

Tips: To create a linear array along a circular path (an arc or circle), use the DIVIDE or MEASURE command with a point style and size of your choice.

AutoCAD 2000i Update: *The Array dialog box allows you to array objects using a preview window. You can access the Array dialog box by selecting the Array button in the Modify toolbar or by entering ARRAY at the command line. See section 1.13.4 for more information.*

12.25 USING THE CHANGE COMMAND

The CHANGE command allows you to specify a new point location for the selected objects or to modify certain properties of selected objects. Although this command is not as powerful as the Properties window (discussed in Chapter 13), it nevertheless allows you to change the current location of objects or change object properties at the command line. To use the CHANGE command, enter CHANGE at the command line. For example, in Figure 12–51 you can change the current point location of line 1 and line 2 to a new point location as follows:

```
Command: CHANGE ~EnterKey~
Select objects: (select line 1 and line 2)
Specify change point or [Properties]: (select the change point)
```

You can also increase the size of the circle in Figure 12–51 by selecting the change point as follows:

```
Command: CHANGE ~EnterKey~
Select objects: (select the circle)
Specify change point or [Properties]: (select the change point)
```

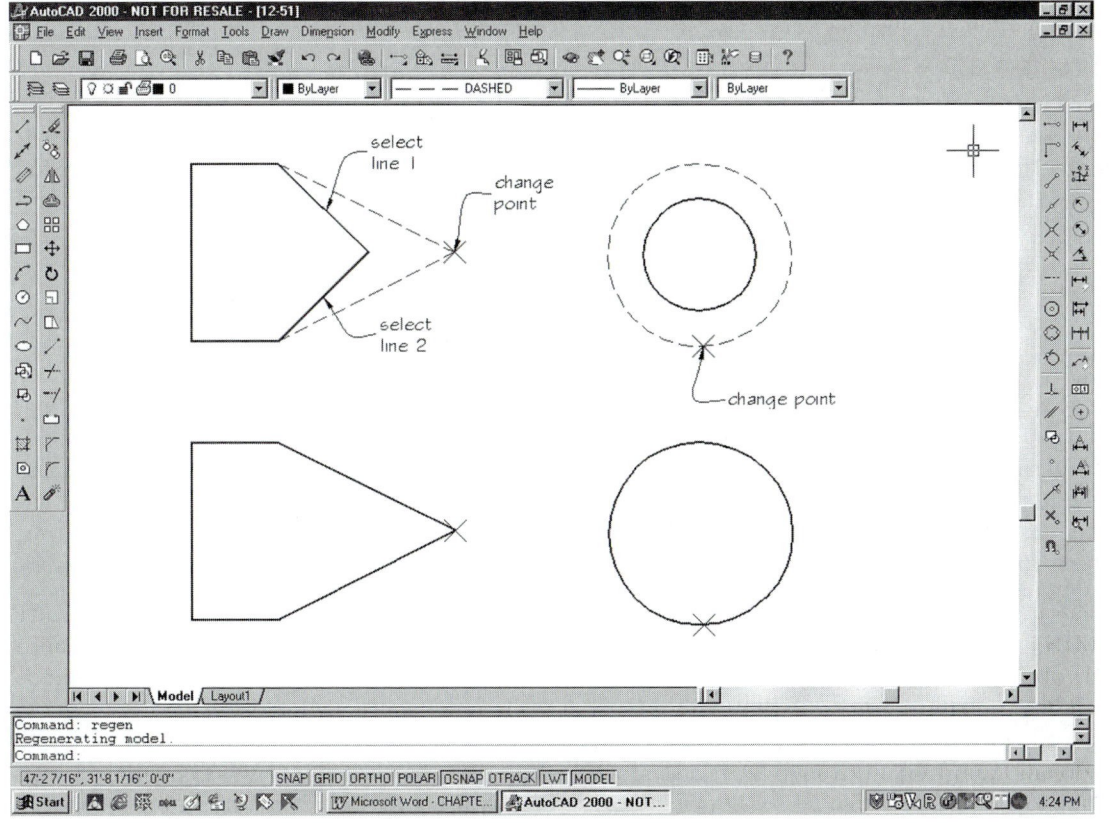

FIGURE 12–51 The CHANGE command can be used to change the current location of objects or to change the current size of a circle.

The Properties option of the CHANGE command allows you to change the following properties of objects:

COLOR:　Enter C to change the color of the selected objects. You can enter either the color name or the color number.

ELEV:　Enter E to change the elevation of the object. This is a three-dimensional option and is not used in two-dimensional drawings.

LAYER:　Enter LA to move the objects to a different layer. You must enter the name of the layer.

LTYPE:　Enter LT to change the linetype of the objects. You must enter the name of the linetype and it must be loaded into the current drawing.

LTSCALE:　Enter S to change the scale of linetypes.

LWEIGHT:　Enter LW to change the lineweight of the objects. You must enter an appropriate lineweight value.

THICKNESS:　Enter T to change the thickness of objects in 3D drawings.

PLOTSTYLE:　Enter PL to change the plotstyle of objects. This option is only available when the plot styles are on.

For example, suppose you have an object currently on layer DIMENSION. To move this object to layer HATCH use the Properties option of the CHANGE command as follows:

```
Command: CHANGE ~EnterKey~
Select objects: (select the object)
Select objects: ~EnterKey~
Specify change point or [Properties]: P ~EnterKey~
Enter property to change
[Color/Elev/LAyer/LType/ltScale/LWeight/Thickness/PLotstyle]: LA
~EnterKey~
Enter new layer name <layer DIMMENSION>:HATCH ~EnterKey~
Enter property to change
[Color/Elev/LAyer/LType/ltScale/LWeight/Thickness/PLotstyle]: ~EnterKey~
```

Tips: Instead of using the CHANGE command, you can left-click on the objects to display object properties. For example, when you left-click on any object, the Layer Control box will display the name of the layer the object is on. You can move this object to a different layer by selecting another layer from the Layer Control box located on the Object Properties toolbar. This procedure will allow you to modify object properties using the ByLayer *method. You can also assign a different color, linetype, lineweight, and plot style to selected objects by selecting a different property from the Color Control box, Linetype Control box, Lineweight Control box, and Plot Style Control box located in the Object Properties toolbar. This procedure will allow you to modify object properties using the* by object *method.*

12.26 USING THE SELECT COMMAND

The SELECT command allows you to preselect an object or group of objects for future editing. The only restriction is that you have to use the selection before using another editing command. You can still create objects. For example, suppose you have five objects you want to move from the upper-left corner of the drawing to the lower-right corner of the drawing and you are planning to work in the lower-right corner of the drawing. You can first preselect the five objects, then zoom to the lower-right corner and recall the preselection with the P (previous) option as follows:

```
Command: SELECT ~EnterKey~
Select objects: (using any of the object selection methods, select the
five objects)
Select objects: ~EnterKey~
```

This will create the selection set. Now, zoom to the lower-right corner and use the MOVE command as follows:

```
Command: MOVE ~EnterKey~
Select objects: P ~EnterKey~ (this will highlight the five objects you
have created as a selection set previously)
Select objects: ~EnterKey~
Specify base point or displacement: (select a base point)
Specify second point of displacement: (select a new location to move the
objects)
```

Caution: When you create a new selection set for future editing, the previous selection set will be deleted.

12.27 USING THE BREAK COMMAND

The BREAK command allows you to remove a portion of a line, circle, arc, or polyline. You can use the BREAK command to remove lines as openings in floor plans however; creating individual wall segments with the required openings using the LINE command is more efficient and faster. Refer to Chapter 5 section 5.9. You can access the BREAK command by selecting the Break button in the Modify toolbar, by selecting Break from the Modify pull-down menu, or by entering BR or BREAK at the command line. AutoCAD will require you to select the object first then allow you to specify the second break point or the option to specify the first break point. The command line procedure is as follows:

```
Command: BR ~EnterKey~
Select object: (select the object to break)
Specify second break point or [First point]: (select a second break point
or enter F to select first break point)
```

You have the option to select the first break point at the *Select object:* prompt as opposed to selecting the object first then selecting the first break point. If you want to select the object first then decide on the first and second break points simply select the object at the *Select object:* prompt. Then enter F to establish the first break point. Specify the first point using object snap modes or object snap tracking. Then specify second break point. After both break points are specified, the section of the object between the two points is removed. The following command line procedure will allow you to remove a portion of an existing line as follows:

Draw a line that is 15'-0" long. You will cut 4'-0" from this line starting 5'-0" from the starting point (left side). After you are finished you will have two individual line segments remaining on the screen with a 4'-0" gap between. The first line segment will measure 5'-0" and the second line segment will measure 6'-0".

```
Command: BR ~EnterKey~
Select object: (select the existing line)
Specify second break point or [First point]: F ~EnterKey~
Specify first break point: (click on the Snap From button on the Object
Snap toolbar)
_from Base point: (using the snap to endpoint click on the endpoint of
the line. This is the beginning of the line on the left side)
_endp of <Offset>: @5'<0 ~EnterKey~
Specify second break point: @4'<0 ~EnterKey~
```

If you want to specify the first break point immediately, use the following command line procedure:

```
Command: BR ~EnterKey~
Select object: (click on the Snap From button on the Object Snap toolbar)
_from Base point: (using the snap to endpoint click on the endpoint of
the line. This is the beginning of the line on the left side)
_endp of <Offset>: @5'<0 ~EnterKey~
Specify second break point or [First point]: @4'<0 ~EnterKey~
```

You can use the BREAK command also to split an object in two without removing a portion. This is accomplished by selecting the same point as both the first and second break points. The split is not actually visible on the screen until one of the objects is edited or highlighted. When using the BREAK command on circles and arcs, always work in a counterclockwise direction when selecting the first and the second break points. Otherwise, AutoCAD will remove the portion of the circle or the arc that you want to keep.

Tips: If you just want to break off the end of a line, select the line first close to the end you want to break. Then pick the second point slightly beyond the end to be cut off. When you select the second point that is not on the object, AutoCAD will select the point on the object nearest to the point you selected. This concept can be used to remove ½ of an existing line. Use Snap *to* Midpoint *object snap mode when selecting the object. Then select the second point slightly beyond and of the ends.*

12.28 CREATING AND NAMING OBJECT GROUPS

The SELECT command allows you to create a group of objects as a selection set but it does not allow you to name it or use it between multiple drawings. The GROUP command allows you to create single or multiple named selection set of objects. You can include the same object or objects in more than one group. A group can also be a part of another group. This is referred to as *nesting*. Enter G or GROUP at the command line. This will display the Object Grouping dialog box as shown in Figure 12–52.

The Object Grouping dialog box has four major areas as follows:

Group Name: This rectangular text box displays the names of groups created in the current drawing. If no groups are created, this area will be blank. The Selectable column lists whether or not the group is selectable. If a group is selectable, you can select any one of the objects belonging to that group and the entire group will be selected.

Group Identification: This area allows you to name, describe, find, and specify groups and has the following options:

- **GROUP NAME:**   This text box allows you to enter a name for the new group. No spaces are allowed.

- **DESCRIPTION:**   This text box allows you to enter a description for the group and can be up to 64 characters long.

FIGURE 12–52   The Object Grouping dialog box allows you to create a named selection set.

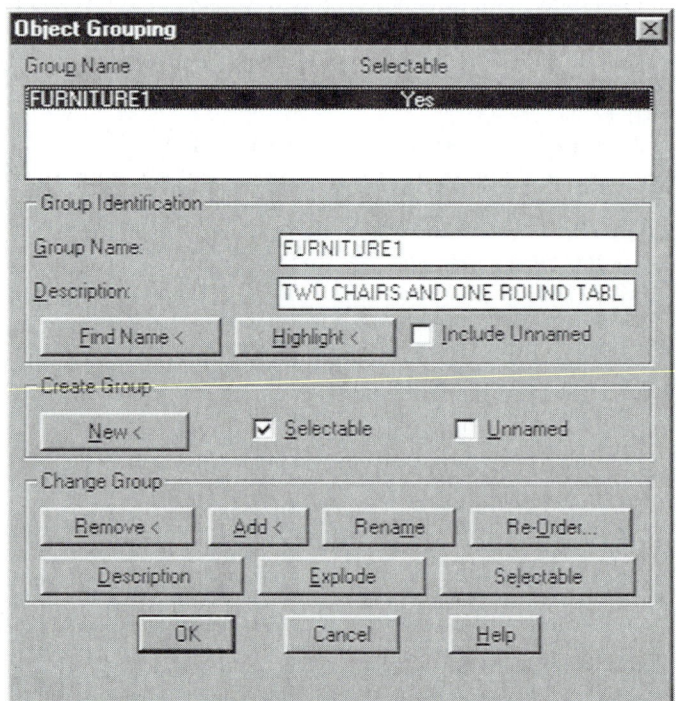

- **FIND NAME<:** Selecting this button will display the Group Member List dialog box, which will show a list of all groups to which a selected object belongs. When you select this button, the Pick a member of a group: prompt will appear. Select an object to find the group with which it is associated.

- **HIGHLIGHT<:** This button allows you to highlight the objects included in the selected or current group. This will allow you to see the areas of the drawing that identify the objects belonging to that group.

- **INCLUDE UNNAMED:** This check box lists all unnamed groups in the Object Grouping dialog box. Unnamed groups are objects inserted as a block using the AutoCAD DesignCenter or the Multiple Design Environment. See Chapter 10 for more information.

Create Group: This area allows you to create a group and has the following options:

- **NEW<:** This button will allow you to select the object or objects for the group. AutoCAD will display the Select objects for grouping: prompt after you enter a new name in the Group Name: text box.

- **SELECTABLE:** This check box allows you to either have the group selectable or not. A checkmark will make the group selectable.

- **UNNAMED:** This check box indicates whether the new group will be unnamed or named. A checkmark will allow AutoCAD to give the name *A*n*, where *n* is a number that increases with each group.

Change Group: This area allows you to edit objects inside a group and has the following options:

- **REMOVE<:** This button allows you to remove objects from a group.

- **ADD<:** This button allows you to add objects to a group.

- **RENAME:** This button allows you to change the name of the selected group.

- **RE-ORDER...:** This button allows you to change the order of objects in the group by displaying the Order Group dialog box as shown in Figure 12–53. When you create a group, objects are numbered in the order that they are selected. This dialog box allows you to reorder objects in the group.

- **DESCRIPTION:** This button allows you to change the description of the group.

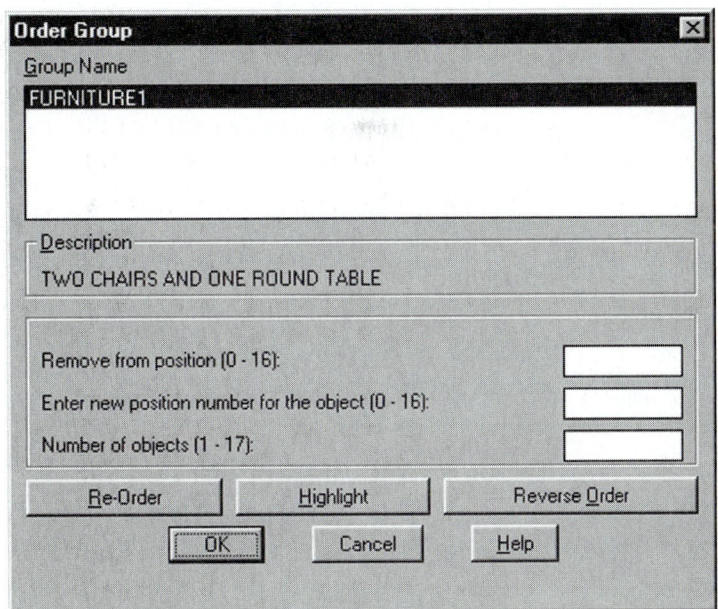

FIGURE 12–53 The Order Group dialog box allows you to change the order of objects in a group.

- **EXPLODE:**   This button allows you to delete the group description but does not delete objects in the group.

- **SELECTABLE:**   This button toggles the selectable value of groups.

The Order Group dialog box has the following areas:

- **GROUP NAME:**   This rectangular text box lists the names of groups in the current drawing.

- **DESCRIPTION:**   This area displays the description of the selected group.

- **REMOVE FROM POSITION (0-*n*):**   Selects the object to reorder where *n* is the total number of objects found in the group. Enter a desired order in the text box.

- **ENTER NEW POSITION NUMBER FOR THE OBJECT (0-*n*):**   Changes the order of objects.

- **NUMBER OF OBJECTS (1-*n*):**   Lists the number of objects to reorder.

- **RE-ORDER:**   Select this button to apply the order changes.

- **HIGHLIGHT:**   Highlights the objects in the current group.

- **REVERSE ORDER:**   Select this button to reverse the order of the groups.

12.28.1   Using the PICKSTYLE System Variable

The PICKSTYLE system variable allows you to include or exclude objects that are part of a group when editing a group and include or exclude associative hatches in the object selection methods. For example, when the PICKSTYLE is off (0), AutoCAD will not highlight all the objects belonging to a group when you enter the MOVE (or any other edit) command and select one of the objects belonging to that group and it will not include associative hatches in the selection set. See Chapter 20 for a discussion of hatching. When the PICKSTYLE is on (1), AutoCAD will highlight all the objects belonging to a group when you use an editing command and select one of the objects. When the PICKSTYLE is set to 2, AutoCAD will include associative hatches in the selection set. When the PICKSTYLE is set to 3, AutoCAD will include both in the selection set. You can also set the PICKSTYLE on or off from the Options dialog box as shown in Figure 12–54.

■ **EXERCISE 12–22:**   *Figure 12–55 shows a floor plan with two chairs and a table. The following step-by-step exercise will allow you to create and name an object group called FURNITURE1 by selecting the two chairs and the table.*

Step #1:   Open the EXE12-19.dwg file.

Step #2:   Access the Object Grouping dialog box as follows:

Command: **GROUP** ~EnterKey~

Step #3:   Inside the Object Grouping dialog box, enter FURNITURE1 inside the Group Name: text box.

Step #4:   Inside the Description: text box, enter TWO CHAIRS AND ONE ROUND TABLE.

Step #5:   Place a checkmark inside the Selectable check box and click on the New< button under the Create Group area.

Step #6:   The dialog box will disappear and the cursor will turn into a pickbox. Place a window around the two chairs and the table as shown in Figure 12–55. Press the ~EnterKey~ when done. The dialog box will reappear with the name and description of the group as shown in Figure 12–52.

Congratulations! You have successfully created and named a group. Do not save the changes.

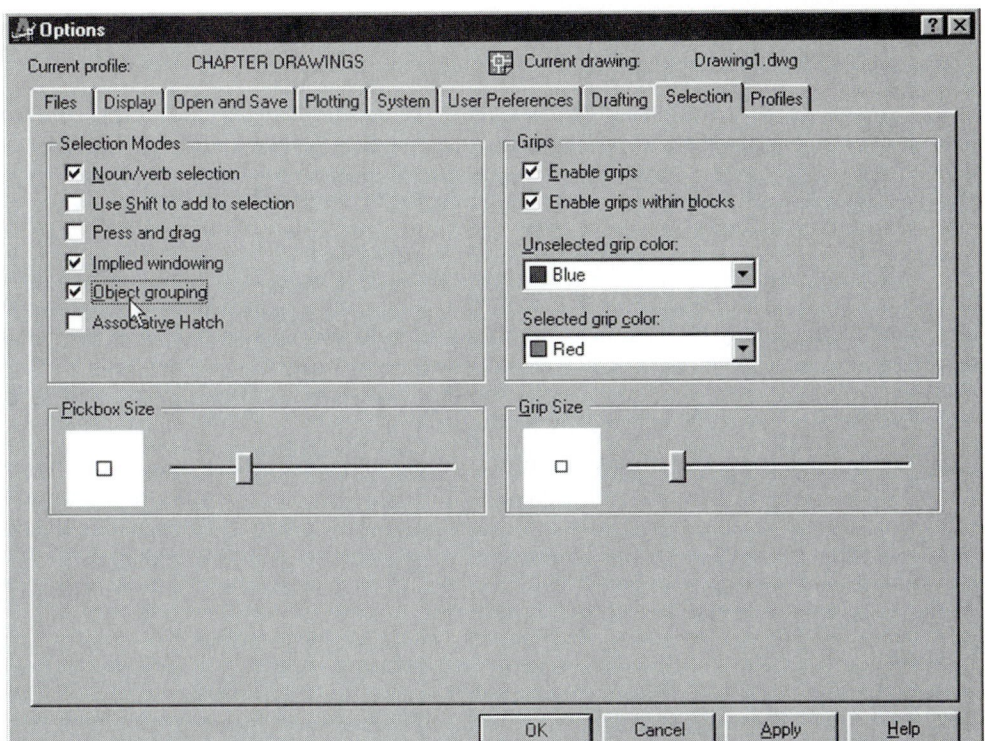

FIGURE 12–54 The Options dialog box allows you to set the PICKSTYLE system variable.

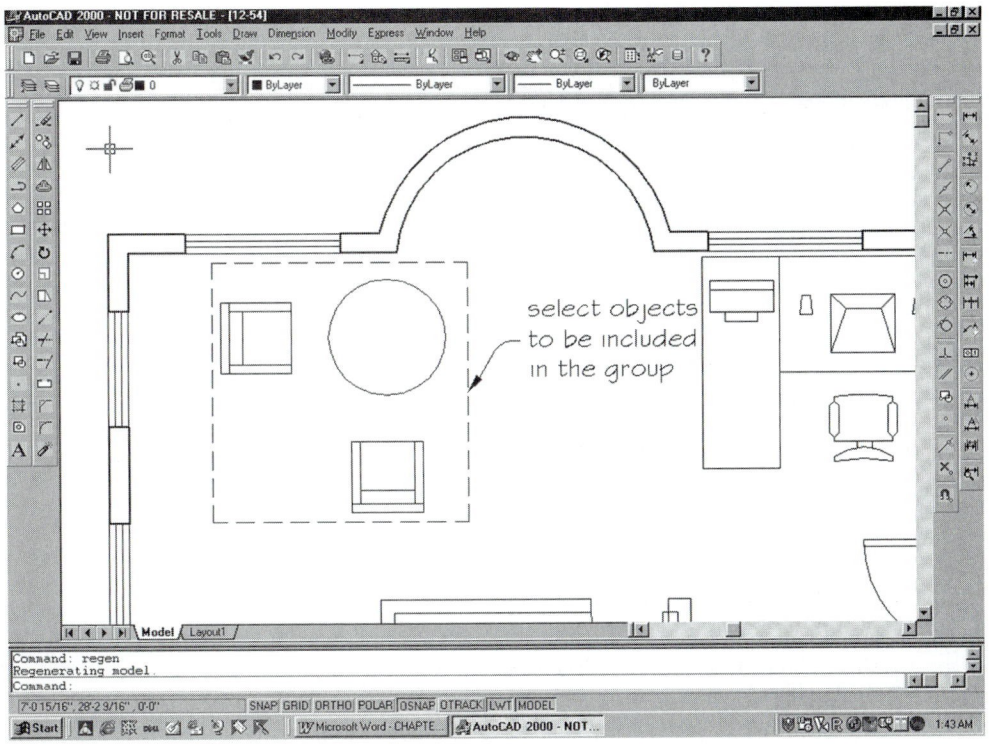

FIGURE 12–55 The two chairs and the table are selected to create a group.

12.29 CREATING A SELECTION SET BASED ON OBJECT TYPE AND PROPERTIES: USING THE QSELECT COMMAND

When you create different selection sets using the methods described in the beginning of this chapter, you select objects without any regard to their object types or properties. The QSELECT (Quick Select) command allows you to create a selection set based on object types and/or properties. For example, you can create a selection set based on a specific object's color, linetype, lineweight, layer, and starting or ending point. Using the QSELECT command, you can quickly create a selection set based on the selection criteria you specify. You can access the QSELECT command by selecting Quick Select . . . from the Tools pull-down menu as shown in Figure 12–56, by entering QSELECT at the command line, or by selecting Quick Select . . . from the right-click shortcut menu as shown in Figure 12–57. This will display the Quick Select dialog box as shown in Figure 12–58. You can also access this dialog box by selecting the Quick Select button in the Properties window or selecting the Quick Select button in the Make Block and Write Block dialog boxes. The Properties window is discussed in Chapter 13. To create a selection set for the purpose of editing or modifying objects, you must use the Quick Select dialog box to create the set before starting any of the modify commands. The Quick Select dialog box will display object types based on the types of objects in the current drawing. For example, if your drawing does not contain any circles or polylines, the Object type: drop-down list will not display the words *Circle* or *Polyline*.

FIGURE 12–56 The Quick Select dialog box can be accessed from the Tools pull-down menu.

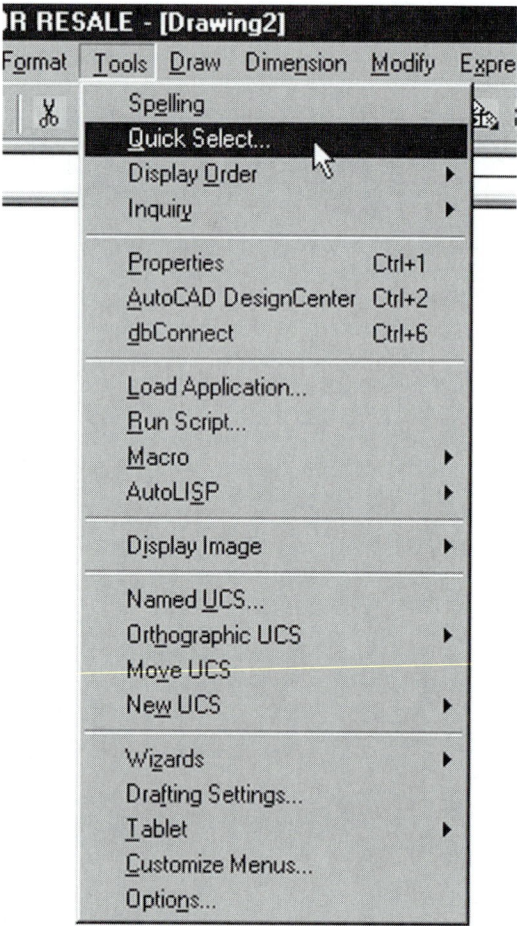

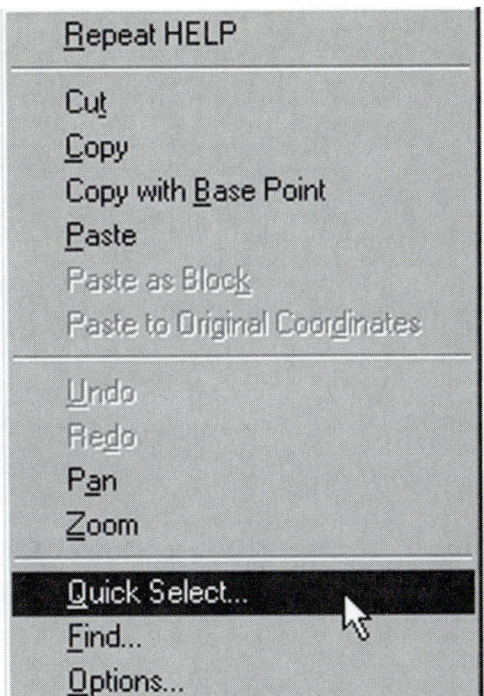

FIGURE 12–57 The Quick Select dialog box also can be accessed from the right-click shortcut menu.

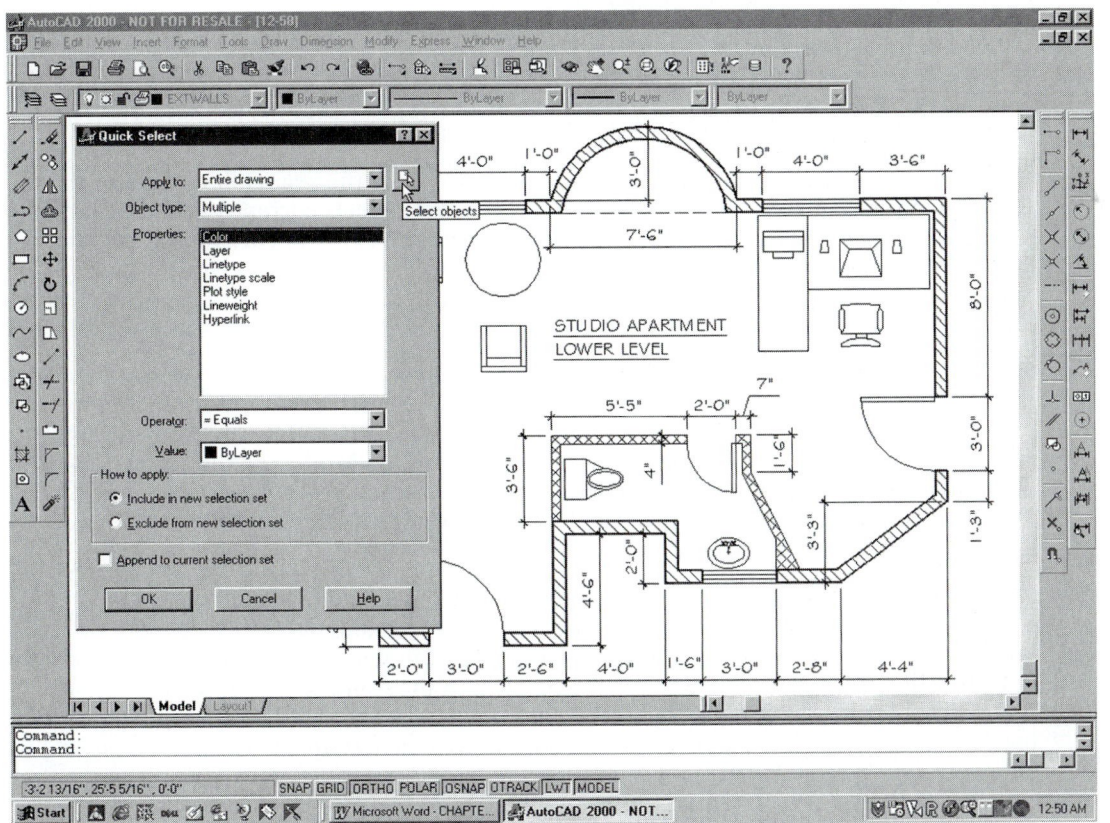

FIGURE 12–58 The Quick Select dialog box allows you to create a selection set based on the selection criteria you specify.

FIGURE 12–59 The Object type: drop-down list contains the types of objects in the current drawing.

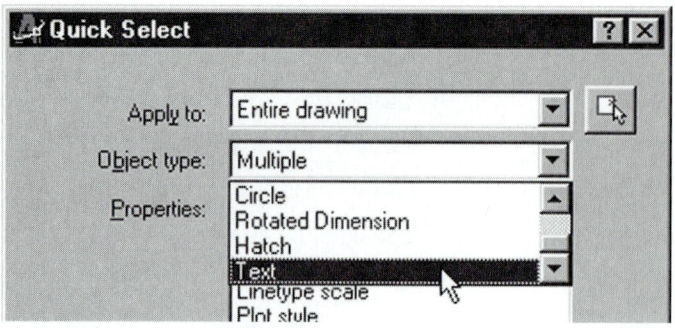

FIGURE 12–60 The Properties: drop-down list allows you to specify a specific property for the object type selected.

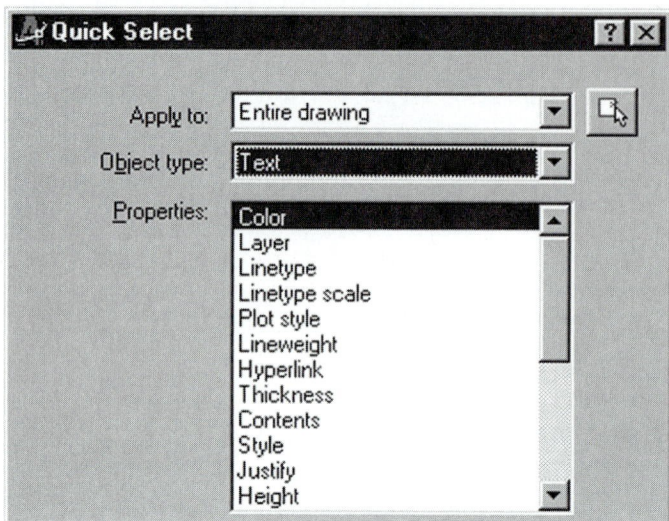

The Quick Select dialog box has the following categories:

- **APPLY TO:** (drop-down list). This area allows you to apply the selection criteria to the entire drawing or to the current selection set. If there are objects currently selected, the *Current selection* will be displayed inside this drop-down list. If no objects are selected, by default the *Entire drawing* is displayed inside this drop-down list. You can also click on the Select Objects button to select the objects on the screen to create a selection set. The Select Objects button is shown in Figure 12–58.

- **OBJECT TYPE:** (drop-down list). This area allows you to specify the type of object to search for. If you select *Multiple,* AutoCAD will search for all object types. The object type displayed depends on the type of objects you currently have in the drawing. For example, the Object type: drop-down list shown in Figure 12–59 displays Multiple, Line, Arc, Block Reference, Circle, Rotated Dimension, Hatch, and Text as the current object types belonging to the Floor Plan in the current drawing. The Multiple, Line, Arc, and Block Reference object types are not shown because of the list size.

- **PROPERTIES:** (drop-down list). This area allows you to specify the property to include in the selected object types. The Properties in the list vary, depending on the object type selected. For example, if you select Text as the object type, you can select one of the properties shown in Figure 12–60. The list will continue if you click on the down arrow. You can only specify one property to search for at a time. To create a selection set based on multiple properties, use the Quick Select dialog box repeatedly with the *Append to current selection set* check box checked.

- **OPERATOR:** (drop-down list). This area allows you to narrow your selection criteria to logical operators available for the selected property as shown in Figure 12–61. The available

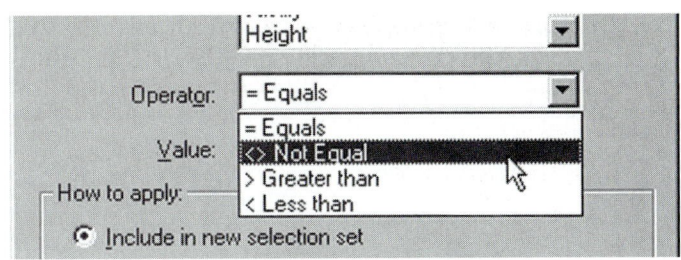

FIGURE 12–61 The Operators available will vary, depending on the type of property selected.

operators will vary, depending on the type of property selected. The operators for the Object type: Text and Properties: Color will include the following:

Operator	Meaning
= Equals	Objects will be selected if they are equal to the value of the property specified.
≠ Not Equal	Objects will be selected if they are different from the value of the property specified.
> Greater than	Objects will be selected if they are greater than the value of the property specified.
< Less than	Objects will be selected if they are less than the value of the property specified.

- **VALUE:** (drop-down list). This area allows you to specify the value you want for the property selected. Values listed will vary, depending on the type of property selected. For example, the values for the Object type: Text, Properties: Color, and Operator: =Equals will display all the colors including ByLayer and ByBlock. If the layer was selected for the Properties for the Object type: Text, then all layers will be listed in the Value: drop-down list. For numerical values such as a Radius or Diameter or Height, enter a number.

How to Apply: This category allows you to include or exclude the criteria as follows:

- **INCLUDE IN NEW SELECTION SET:** (radio button). When checked, this will include all the objects that meet the criteria as part of the selection set.

- **EXCLUDE FROM NEW SELECTION SET:** (radio button). When checked, this will select all the objects that do not meet the criteria.

- **APPEND TO CURRENT SELECTION SET:** (check box). When checked, all matching results of the criteria will be added to the current selection set as opposed to creating a new selection set.

■ **EXERCISE 12–23:** *Figure 12–62 shows a floor plan with blocks inserted into the layer 0. A new layer, called BLOCKS, has been created, and all blocks belonging to layer 0 are to be selected and placed into this new layer. The following step-by-step exercise will allow you to create a selection set based on Object type: Block Definition, Properties: Layer, Operator: =Equal and Value: 0. After the selection set is created, the selected blocks will be placed into the BLOCKS layer using the Layer Control box in the Object Properties toolbar.*

Step #1: Open the EXE12-20.dwg file.

Step #2: Access the Quick Select dialog box.

Step #3: Inside the Apply to: drop-down list, select *Entire drawing*.

Step #4: Inside the Object type: drop-down list, select *Block Reference*.

Step #5: Inside the Properties: drop-down list, select *Layer*.

Step #6: Inside the Operator: drop-down list, select =Equals.

Step #7: Inside the Value: drop-down list, select *0*.

Step #8: Inside the How to Apply: area, select *Include in new selection set*.

Step #9: Place a checkmark inside the *Append to current selection set* check box.

Step #10: Click on the OK button. This will highlight all the Block References currently on layer 0 as shown in Figure 12–63.

Step #11: From the Layer Control box, select layer BLOCKS as shown in Figure 12–64.

FIGURE 12–62 The floor plan with five blocks on layer 0.

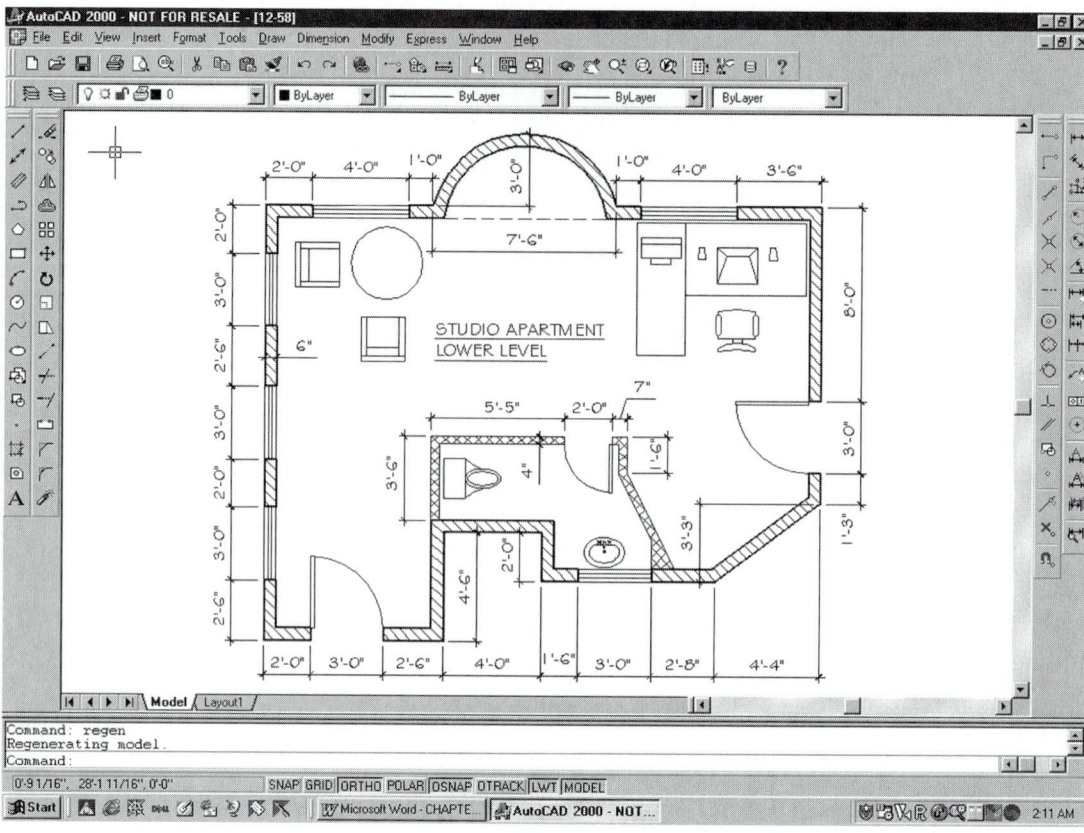

FIGURE 12–63 All five blocks are highlighted after the selection criteria.

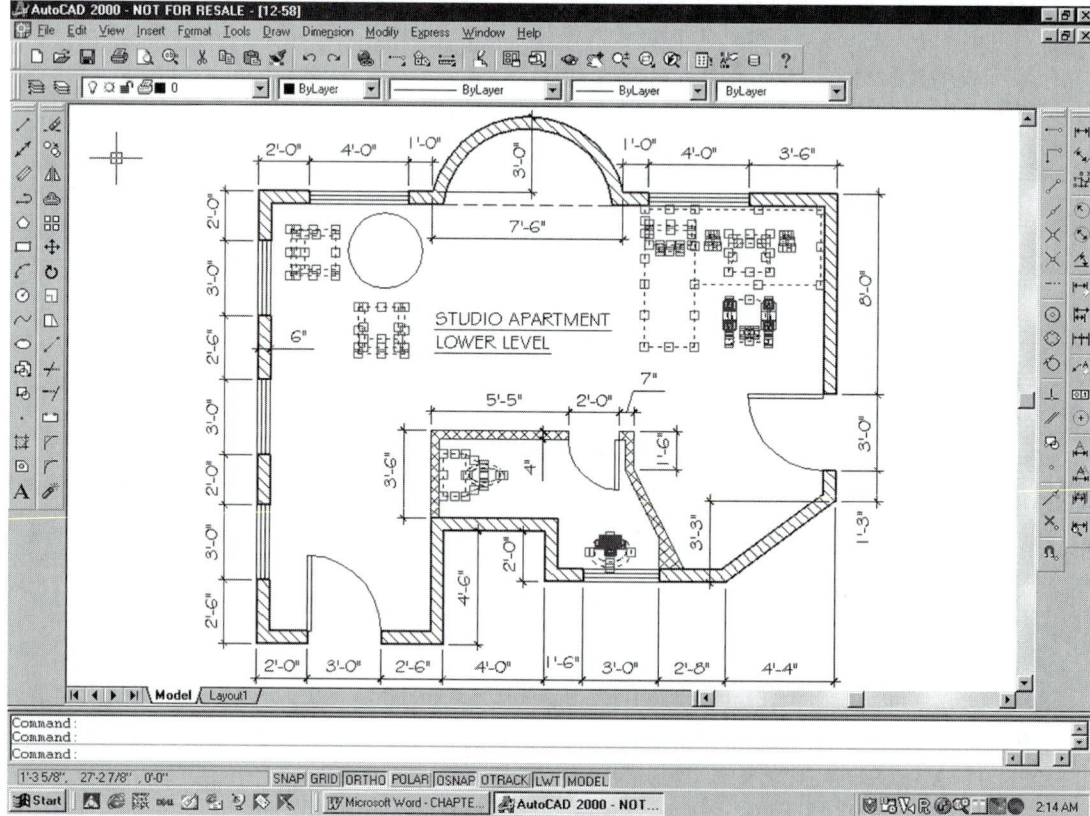

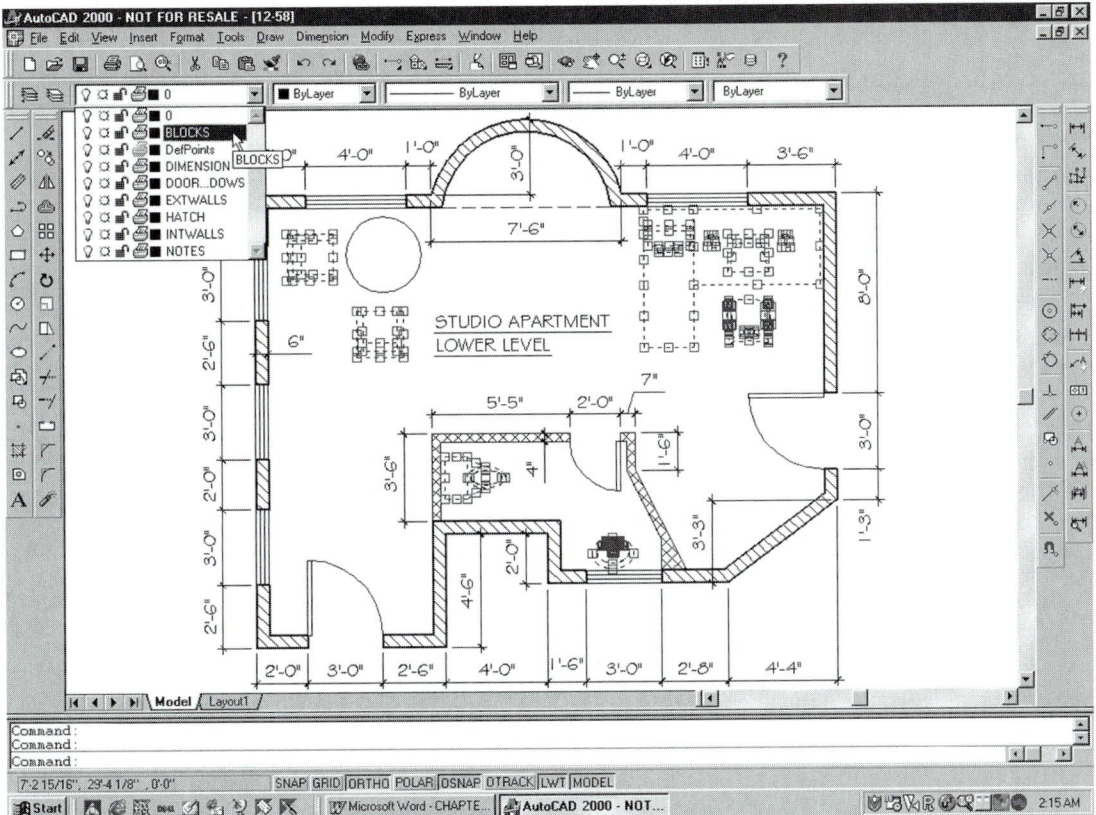

FIGURE 12–64 The selected blocks will be placed on layer BLOCKS.

Step #12: Press on the ~EscKey~ twice.

Step #13: Repeat Steps #2, #3, #4, #5, and #6. Inside the Value: drop-down list, select *BLOCKS.*

Step #14: Repeat Steps #8, and #9.

Step #15: Click on the OK button. This will highlight all the Block references currently on Layer BLOCKS. This is your assurance that the operation was successful.

Congratulations! You have successfully created a selection set based on object type and properties criteria. Do not save the changes.

Tips: For maximum editing efficiency and speed, use the Quick Select dialog box in conjunction with the Properties window.

12.30 EDITING POLYLINES

Drawing Polylines was introduced in Chapter 6. You can edit polylines using the PEDIT and the EXPLODE commands. Use the PEDIT command to edit a polyline as one object. Use the EXPLODE command to convert a *single entity* object such as a polyline into a *multi entity* object. You can also use the PEDIT command to convert a line into a polyline. To access the PEDIT command, select the Edit Polyline button from the Modify II toolbar, select Polyline from the Modify pull-down menu, or enter PE or PEDIT at the command line. You can also select an existing polyline and then right-click to display the shortcut menu and select Polyline Edit. The command sequence is as follows:

```
Command: PE ~EnterKey~
Select polyline: (select an existing polyline)
Enter an option: [Close/Join/Width/Edit vertex/Fit/Spline/Decurve/Ltype
gen/Undo]: (enter an option)
```

Because there is no default for the PEDIT command, you must enter one of the options or press the ~EnterKey~ to return to the Command: prompt. You can use any of the selection methods to select the polyline after an option. If you use the pickbox to select a wide polyline, you must place it on the edge of the polyline segment as opposed to selecting the center point. The options are explained as follows:

Close: Entering C will close an open polyline. If you select a polyline that is already closed, AutoCAD will display the Open option. Use this option to open the selected polyline. The open option is displayed only if the polyline was closed using the close option of the PLINE command.

Join: Entering J will allow you to join existing lines and arcs that are connected to create a single polyline object. In other words, this option will turn a multi entity object into a single entity object. If the object you select is a line, AutoCAD will display the following message:

```
Object selected is not a polyline.
Do you want to turn it into one? <Y>: ~EnterKey~
```

Pressing the ~EnterKey~ will allow you to select line objects. The command sequence is as follows:

```
Command: PE ~EnterKey~
Select polyline: (select one of the line segments)
Enter an option: [Close/Join/Width/Edit vertex/Fit/Spline/Decurve/Ltype
gen/Undo]: J ~EnterKey~
Select objects: (select rest of the line segments you want to turn into
polyline)
Select objects: ~EnterKey~
X segments added to polyline
Enter an option: [Close/Join/Width/Edit vertex/Fit/Spline/Decurve/Ltype
gen/Undo]: ~EnterKey~
The J option of the PEDIT command works only if the existing objects do
not cross and meet exactly.
```

AutoCAD 2000i Update: You can join objects even if they do not cross or overlap each other and multiple polylines can be edited at the same time. Select the Modify Polyline from the Modify II toolbar, then right-click in the drawing area and select Multiple from the shortcut menu. Select the polylines to be edited, then press the ~EnterKey~. Select an option and perform the editing operation. You can also enter PEDIT at the command line and enter M to access the multiple option.

Width: Entering W will allow you to change the existing width of the selected polyline(s). The width of the original polyline can be uniform, or it can vary. See section 6.3.

Edit vertex: Entering E will allow you to edit polyline vertices and points of tangency. A polyline vertex is a point where straight polyline segments meet. A point of tangency is where straight polyline segments or polyline segments or polyline arcs join. Entering this option will place an "X" marker on the first polyline vertex or point of tangency. The command sequence is as follows:

```
Command: PE ~EnterKey~
Select polyline: (select a polyline)
Enter an option: [Close/Join/Width/Edit vertex/Fit/Spline/Decurve/Ltype
gen/Undo]: E ~EnterKey~
Enter a vertex editing option
[Next/Previous/Break/Insert/Move/Regen/Straighten/Tangent/Width/eXit]
<N>: (enter an option)
```

The Edit vertex options are explained as follows:

- **NEXT:** This option will move the "X" marker to the next vertex or point of tangency.

- **PREVIOUS:** This option will move the "X" marker to the previous vertex or point of tangency.

- **BREAK:** This option will break (remove) a segment at a vertex.

- **INSERT:** This option will insert (add) a new vertex.

- **MOVE:** This option will move a vertex to a new location.

- **REGEN:** This option regenerates the screen to show the edited polylines.

- **STRAIGHTEN:** This option will draw a straight polyline segment between two vertices.

- **TANGENT:** This option will show a tangent direction to current vertex when using the Fit option of the PEDIT command.

- **WIDTH:** This option will change the current polyline width.

- **EXIT:** This option will return to the PEDIT command prompt.

Tips: Only the current "X" marker points are affected by editing functions. The Next option will move clockwise and the Previous option will move counterclockwise direction.

Fit: Entering F will fit a curve to the tangent points of each vertex.

Spline: Entering S will fit a splined curve along the polyline.

Decurve: Entering D will reverse the effects of Fit-curve or Spline-curve options.

Ltype gen: Entering L will specify a linetype generation style.

Undo: Entering U will undo the most-recent PEDIT operation.

Tips: Use the Multiple Pedit and Polyline Join tools available in the Modify cascading menu of the Express pull-down menu for more efficient polyline editing.

AutoCAD 2000i Update: *When you use the* Join *option of the PEDIT command, you can specify a* fuzz *distance to join objects with endpoints that are within this distance. You can also use the* Join Type *option to specify how objects that do not share exactly the same endpoints are joined together. There are three Join Type options: The* Extend *option will join the selected polylines by extending or trimming, the* Add *option will join the selected polylines by adding a straight segment between the nearest endpoints, and the* Both *option will join selected polylines by extending or trimming first if not will join them by adding a straight segment.*

REVIEW QUESTIONS

1. Name the six different ways to create a selection set.
2. How many different ways can you access the ERASE command?
3. What is a pickbox selection, and how can you adjust the size of the pickbox using a dialog box?
4. What is the difference between a Window selection and a Crossing selection?
5. What does CP selection mean?
6. What is the function of the PICKAUTO system variable?
7. How can you reselect a previously selected object?
8. You draw a blue line 5'-0" long and you draw a red line directly on top of the blue line 5'-0" long. Describe the process involved in erasing the blue line without erasing the red line.
9. What is the purpose of the Quick Mode of the TRIM command and how do you use it?
10. What options of the TRIM command must you use to trim an object to its implied intersection?
11. What command would you use to trim all objects that overlap a cutting edge?
12. What does the Total option of the LENGTHEN command allow you to do?
13. What command would you use to quickly find the perimeter of a rectangle?
14. What are the end results of using the SCALE command to change the scale of a drawing?
15. What is the appropriate method to change the scale of drawings?
16. Can you place a Window around the object when using the STRETCH command?
17. What command allows you to select more than one object to stretch?

18. What does the Reference option of the ROTATE command allow you to do?

19. What is the name of the command that allows you to move, copy, rotate, and scale objects one after another without using the MOVE, COPY, ROTATE, and SCALE commands individually?

20. How can you mirror a horizontal object at a 65-degree angle?

21. Describe the purpose of the source and the destination points associated with the ALIGN command.

22. Describe the difference between Rectangular and Polar Array.

23. How do you access the Object Grouping dialog box?

24. Is the group name EXISTING BUILDINGS a valid group name?

25. What is the function of the Quick Select dialog box?

26. Describe the process involved in creating a filtering criteria based on object type and properties.

PROBLEMS

1. Open the *EXE12-1.dwg* file. Zoom in to the bookstore lounge area. Erase the four chairs by creating a Window Polygon. Do not save the changes.

2. Open the *EXE12-21.dwg* file. Erase all small circles using the Fence selection method. Do not save the changes.

3. Open the *EXE12-3.dwg* file. Erase everything except the four large half circles using the All and Remove options of the ERASE command.

4. Create a new drawing. Draw a circle with blue color. Draw another circle with magenta color exactly the same size as the first circle and place it directly above the first circle. Erase the blue circle without erasing the magenta circle. Do not save the changes.

5. Using the Options dialog box, change the Object Selection Modes from Implied windowing to Press and drag. Do not save the changes.

6. Open the *EXE12-5.dwg* file. Using the Extended Trim button in the Express Standard Toolbar, trim the eight parallel lines overlapping the object at the left side. Do not save the changes.

7. Open the *EXE12-9.dwg file.* Using the STRETCH command, enlarge the bathroom space from 6'-0" to 12'-0" in the North direction. Do not save the changes.

8. Open the *EXE12-10.dwg* file. Using the MSTRETCH command, stretch the bottom three dimensions to read 6'-0", 7'-0", and 3'-6" respectively. Do not save the changes.

9. Open the *EXE12-11.dwg* file. Move the computer workstation from its current location to the upper-left corner of the space as you rotate it 90 degrees. Do not save the changes.

10. Open the *EXE12-12.dwg* file. Create one object group called TREES and include two different kinds of trees for the group. Do not save the changes.

Advanced Editing

13

After successful completion of this chapter you should be able to:

▲ Use the GRIPS command to edit objects.

▲ Use the Options dialog box to set object selection modes.

▲ Use the Properties window to edit a single object or multiple objects.

▲ Use Quick Select with the Properties window.

▲ Use Match Properties to change object properties.

13.1 AUTOMATIC EDITING

In Chapter 12, you learned to create different object selection methods and used editing commands that allowed you to perform a wide variety of editing tasks. You accomplished that by accessing the commands first then creating a selection set. This chapter takes editing to another level by allowing you to first select the objects and then automatically edit them using different editing commands. Different ways to control object selection modes will be discussed. You will also learn to modify object properties using the Properties window and have the ability to combine it with the Quick Select procedure.

13.2 EDITING OBJECTS WITH GRIPS

Each object you create has small squares, called *grips,* strategically located to identify its *grip box* locations. These grip boxes allow you to *snap,* or grab the object at its grip location point and perform a continuous set of editing operations. The grips on objects are not displayed until you select (left-click) the object before entering a command. As default, when you enter a modify command, AutoCAD will display the *Select objects:* prompt where you select the objects you want to edit. The opposite of that is possible where you select the object first and then perform the editing operation using the GRIPS system variable. When the grips on objects are displayed, you can simply move your cursor over one of the grip locations and select the grip box to grab the object at that location and perform stretch, copy, move, rotate, scale, and mirror editing operations in one continuous mode. The concept of automatically editing an object with grips is similar to the MOCORO command discussed in the previous chapter. The advantage of using the grips to edit objects is that you can select any one of the grip locations on the object as opposed to using the object snap modes to snap to a desired point on the object. You can enable or disable grips using the Options dialog box or use the GRIPS system variable at the command line. After accessing the Options dialog box, click on the Selection tab and place a checkmark inside the Enable grips check box under the Grips category to turn the grips on. The Selection tab of the Options dialog box is shown in Figure 12–54. If the checkmark is removed, the grips are not displayed when you select the objects. The Enable grips within the Blocks check box allows you to turn the grips on or off for a block in the drawing. When this check box is on and when you left click on a block, all the grips will be displayed on every object that is a part of the block. Blocks are discussed in Chapter 19.

You can also turn grips on and off by using the GRIPS system variable as follows:

```
Command: GRIPS ~EnterKey~
Enter new value for GRIPS <1>: (as default grips is on. Enter 0 to
disable grips)
```

When grips are enabled, you can left-click on objects to display its grip locations. When grips are disabled, you can left-click on objects to create a selection set and then enter the editing command to edit the selected objects. Objects such as lines, polylines, splines, and arcs will display three grip locations, one at the beginning point, one at the midpoint, and one at the endpoint of the object. A seven-sided polygon will display seven grips, and a circle will display five grips. Figure 13–1 shows some of the objects with their grip locations displayed.

The size of the grip boxes can be adjusted using the Grip Size scroll bar in the Selection tab of the Options dialog box. When the grips are displayed, they are inactive until selected. An unselected grip is a square with a blue outline. Blue is the default color but can be changed. To make a grip active, move your pickbox over one of the grip boxes and left-click. When a grip is selected, the color will turn into a solid red. Red is the default color but can be changed. To change the color of an unselected grip and the color of a selected grip use the color drop-down list in the Options dialog box. You can also use the GRIPCOLOR (unselected) and GRIPHOT (selected) system variables to change grip colors.

If you select more than one object and their grips are unselected, then all objects displaying grips will be affected by the editing operation you are planning to perform with the selected grips. You can remove highlighted objects from the selection set by holding down the ~ShiftKey~ and selecting the objects. You can remove the highlighted objects and their grips by pressing the ~EscKey~ twice (once if you are using AutoCAD 2000i). When you select a grip, AutoCAD will display the following command prompt:

```
**STRETCH**
Specify stretch point or [Base point/Copy/Undo/eXit]:
```

FIGURE 13–1 The amount and location of grips depends on the object type. Notice that the block (chair) displays many grips since it it composed of many lines.

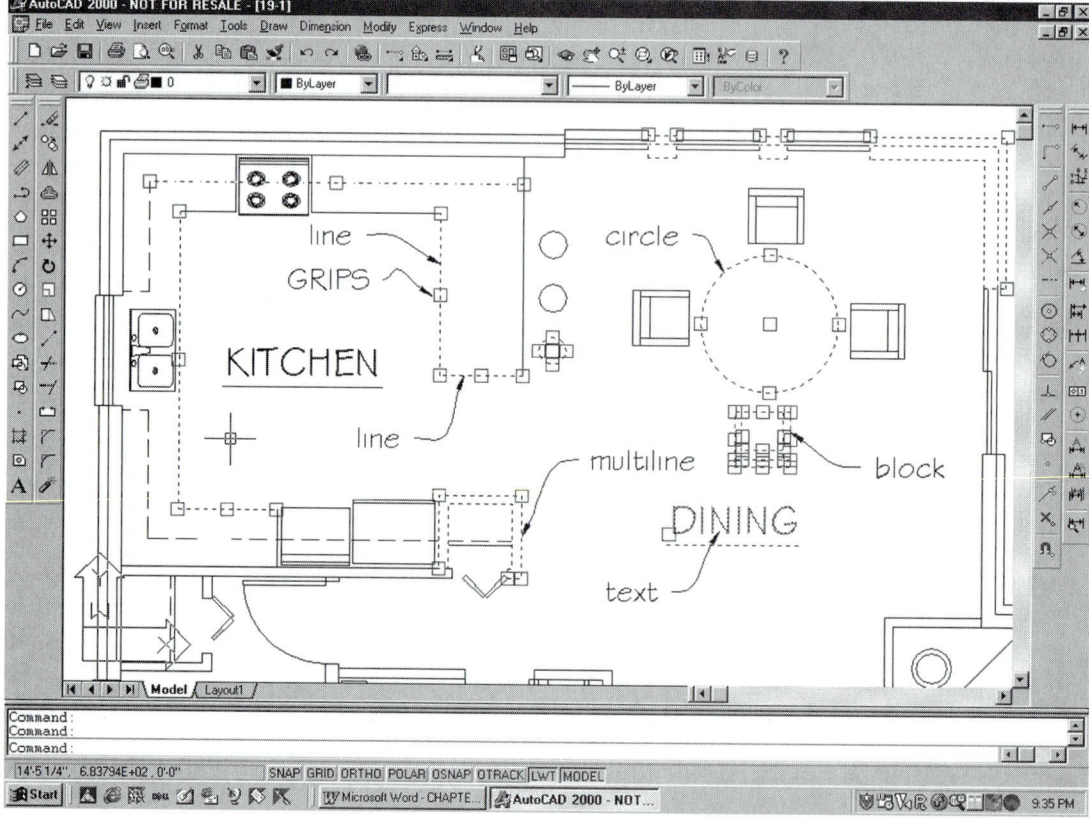

This is the first editing command option of the grips. When you move your cursor to a new location after selecting a grip, the object will be stretched using the STRETCH command. The stretch operation will take place from the selected grip to the selected point on the screen as shown in Figure 13–2. When you have seleced the stretch point, press the ~EscKey~ twice to finish the operation.

Note: Editing Multilines with grips is discussed in Chapter 17.

The *Base point* option allows you to select a new base point for the object. Enter B and press ~EnterKey~ to activate this option. You can select any point on the object or on the screen as the base point. Turn OSNAP off if you want to select a base point on the object. The *Copy* option allows you to make single or multiple copies of the selected object. Enter C and press ~EnterKey~ to copy the object to a new location. Keep selecting new points to copy the object to multiple locations. The *Undo* (U) option allows you to undo the previous operation. The *eXit* (X) option allows you to exit the command but will still display the grips on the object.

If you do not want to use the STRETCH command, you can press ~EnterKey~ to advance to the next command operation as follows:

```
**STRETCH**
Specify stretch point or [Base point/Copy/Undo/eXit]: ~EnterKey~

**MOVE**
Specify stretch point or [Base point/Copy/Undo/eXit]:
```

Move is the second editing command option of the grips. When you move your cursor to a new location, the object or objects will be moved using the MOVE command.

AutoCAD 2000i Update: You can single ~Esc~ to remove grips from objects.

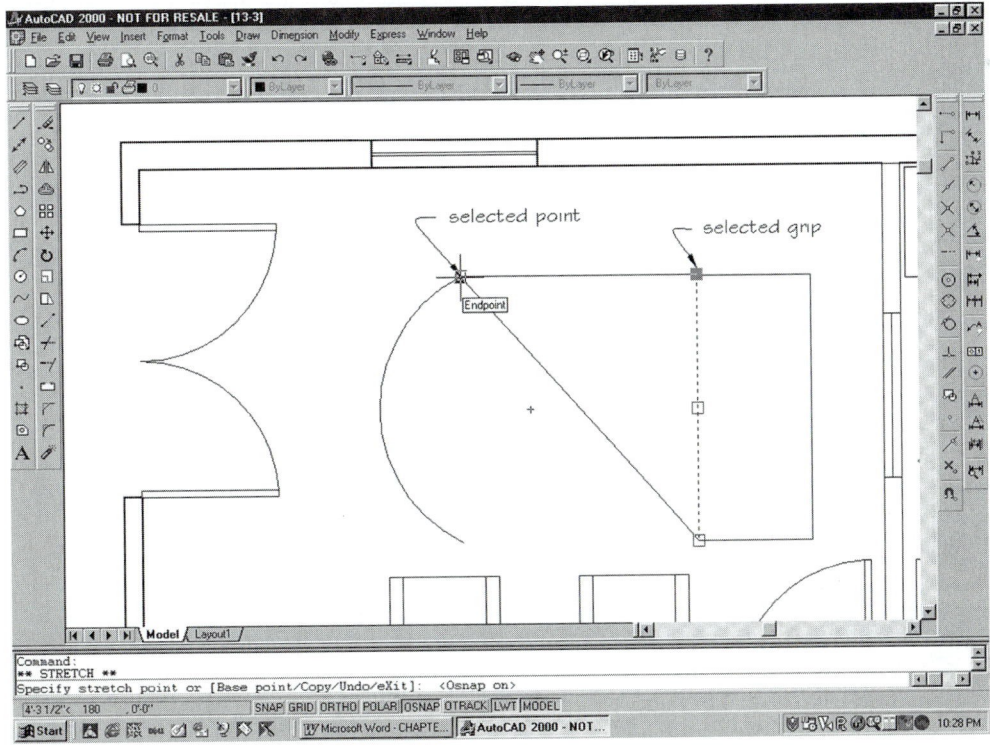

FIGURE 13–2 The Stretch command is the first editing command option of the grips. Select the grip to stretch to a desired location.

■ **EXERCISE 13–1:** *The following step-by-step exercise will help you move the two arcs shown in Figure 13–3 to the selected point at the door.*

Step #1:   Open the EXE13-1.dwg file.

Step #2:   Make sure the GRIPS system variable is on.

Step #3:   Left-click on both arcs. This will display the grips for both arcs.

Step #4:   Left-click (select) the grip as shown in Figure 13–3.

Step #5:   Press the ~EnterKey~ to advance to the MOVE command option.

Step #6:   Turn Ortho off and move the arcs to the new point location on the door as shown in Figure 13–4.

Step #7:   Press the EscKey twice to complete the operation.

Congratulations! You have successfully moved the two arcs to a new location using GRIPS. The arcs will be moved to the door as shown in Figure 13–5.

The options under the MOVE command are the same as with the STRETCH command.

When you press the ~EnterKey~ after selecting a grip, more editing options will be presented as follows:

```
**STRETCH**
Specify stretch point or [Base point/Copy/Undo/eXit]: ~EnterKey~
**MOVE**
Specify move point or [Base point/Copy/Undo/eXit]: ~EnterKey~
**ROTATE**
Specify rotation angle or [Base point/Copy/Undo/Reference/eXit]: ~EnterKey~
**SCALE**
Specify rotation angle or [Base point/Copy/Undo/Reference/eXit]: ~EnterKey~
**MIRROR**
Specify stretch point or [Base point/Copy/Undo/eXit]:
```

FIGURE 13–3   The two arcs will display five grips. The upper grip will be selected to move the arcs to the door location.

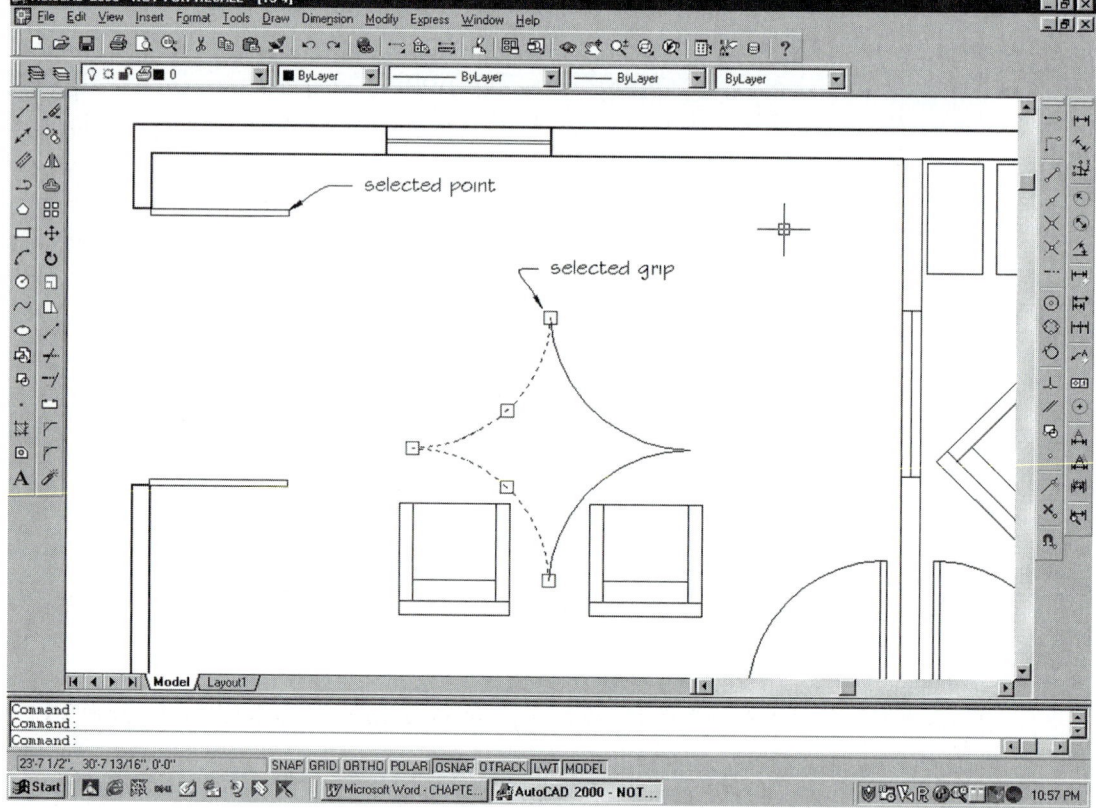

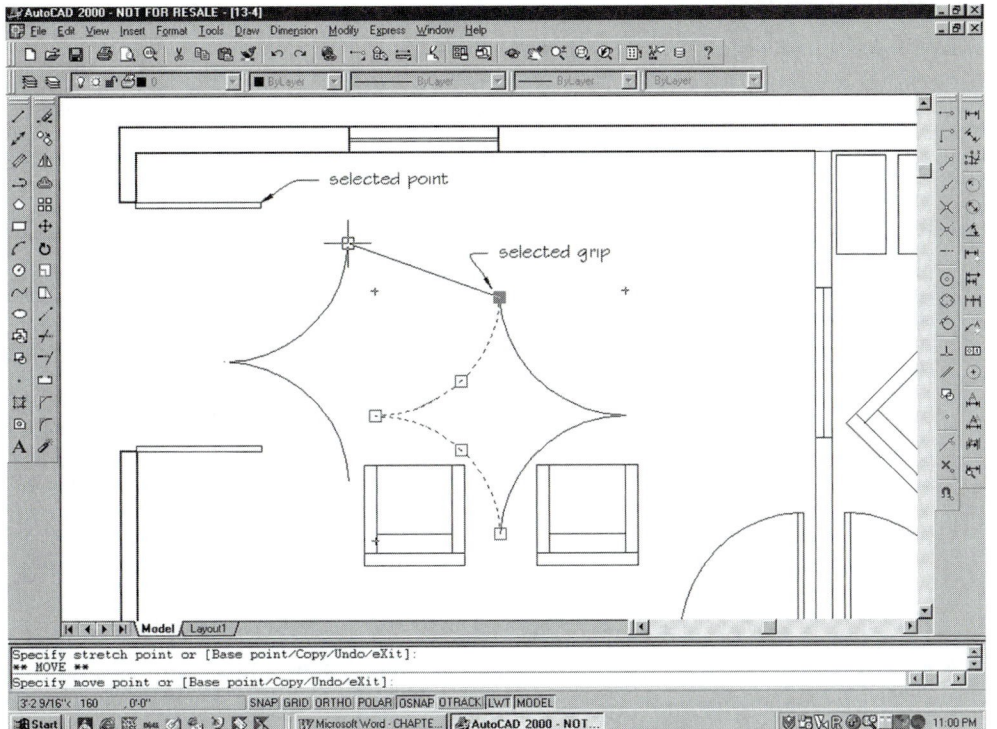

FIGURE 13–4 The selected grip is being moved to the new location. Notice both arcs moving.

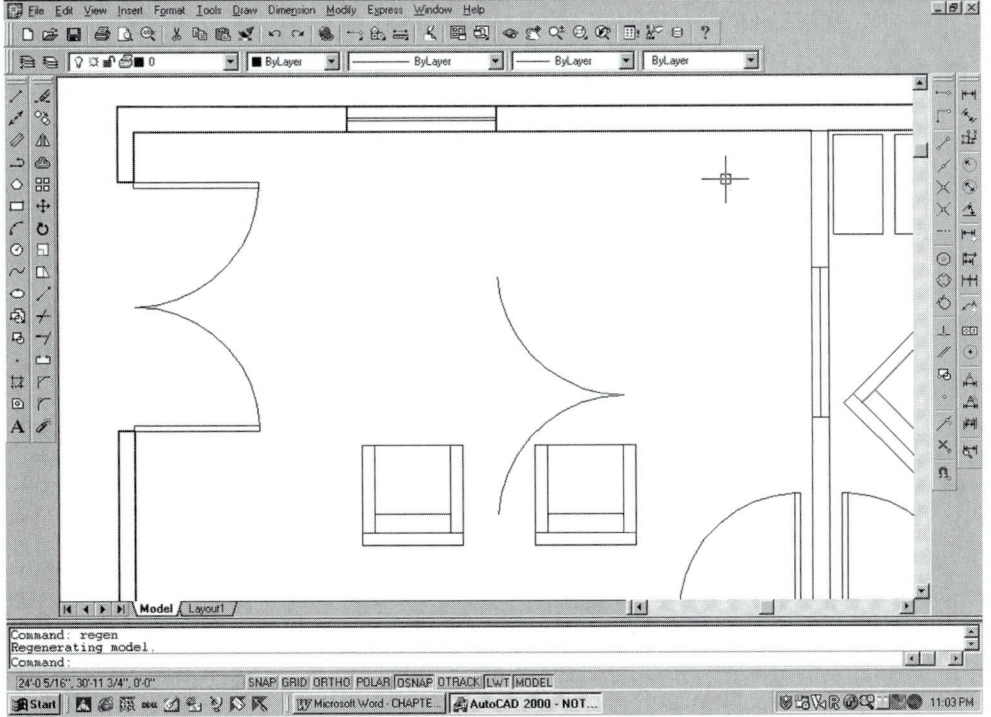

FIGURE 13–5 The final position of the two arcs moved with grips.

The ROTATE, SCALE, and MIRROR command options of grips perform the same editing operations discussed in the previous chapter.

13.3 OBJECT SELECTION MODES

You can use the Options dialog box to set system variables that will allow you to select objects first, then enter the editing command. The Selection Modes area of the Selection tab in the Options dialog box shown in Figure 12–54 allows you to set a selection mode when you select objects using the editing commands. The six options are as follows:

- **NOUN/VERB SELECTION:**   (check box). Placing a checkmark here allows you to select the object or objects before accessing an editing command. However, for this to work, grips must be disabled. If Noun/verb selection is unchecked and the grips off, then selecting the object first is not possible. If this is the case, the cursor will convert to crosshairs without the pickbox. This is your indication that selecting an object first is not possible. However, you can still enter a command and then select an object to edit. You can also use the PICKFIRST system variable to set the Noun/verb selection.

- **USE SHIFT TO ADD TO SELECTION:**   (check box). Placing a check mark here will require you to press ~ShiftKey~ to add objects to the selection set. If there is no check mark here, every object or group of objects you select is highlighted and added to the selection set. You can also use the PICKADD system variable to turn this feature on or off.

- **PRESS AND DRAG:**   (check box). Placing a checkmark here allows you to create a selection box by picking the first corner and then dragging the cursor to select the second corner. Release the left button when you are at the desired second corner location. You can also use the PICKDRAG system variable to control this feature.

- **IMPLIED WINDOWING:**   As discussed in the previous chapter, placing a checkmark here will allow you to create a window, crossing, window polygon, or crossing polygon selection set.

- **OBJECT GROUPING:**   As discussed in the previous chapter, placing a checkmark here allows AutoCAD to recognize objects belonging to a group.

- **ASSOCIATIVE HATCH:**   Placing a checkmark here allows you to select objects with the associative hatch pattern.

13.4 USING THE PROPERTIES WINDOW

The Properties window is the most comprehensive and complete editing feature in AutoCAD. Using the Properties window, you can streamline editing operations within one dialog box. When you have many objects to edit using different properties, the Properties window will provide you with the most efficient and fastest way to edit. The Properties window can be accessed by clicking on the Properties button from the Standard toolbar, selecting Properties from the Modify pull-down menu, or by entering PROPS or PROPERTIES at the command line. If you have an object or objects already selected on the screen (with or without grips), you can right-click and select Properties from the shortcut menu. The Properties window can be docked or floated or even resized to meet your editing requirements. The Properties window is shown in Figure 13–6. You can leave the Properties window docked or floating while using other commands. To close the Properties window, click on the X button in the upper right corner. The top drop-down list of the Properties window will show *No selection* if no object has been selected. You must select an object or objects to use the Properties window to modify and edit objects and their properties.

13.4.1   Changing the Properties of a Single Object

You can select a single object to modify its properties using the Properties window before or after opening the Properties window. If you select one object to modify, the object's type will be displayed on the top drop-down list of the Properties window. The selected object's properties will also be listed in the window. Object properties can be listed alphabetically or categorized. To see

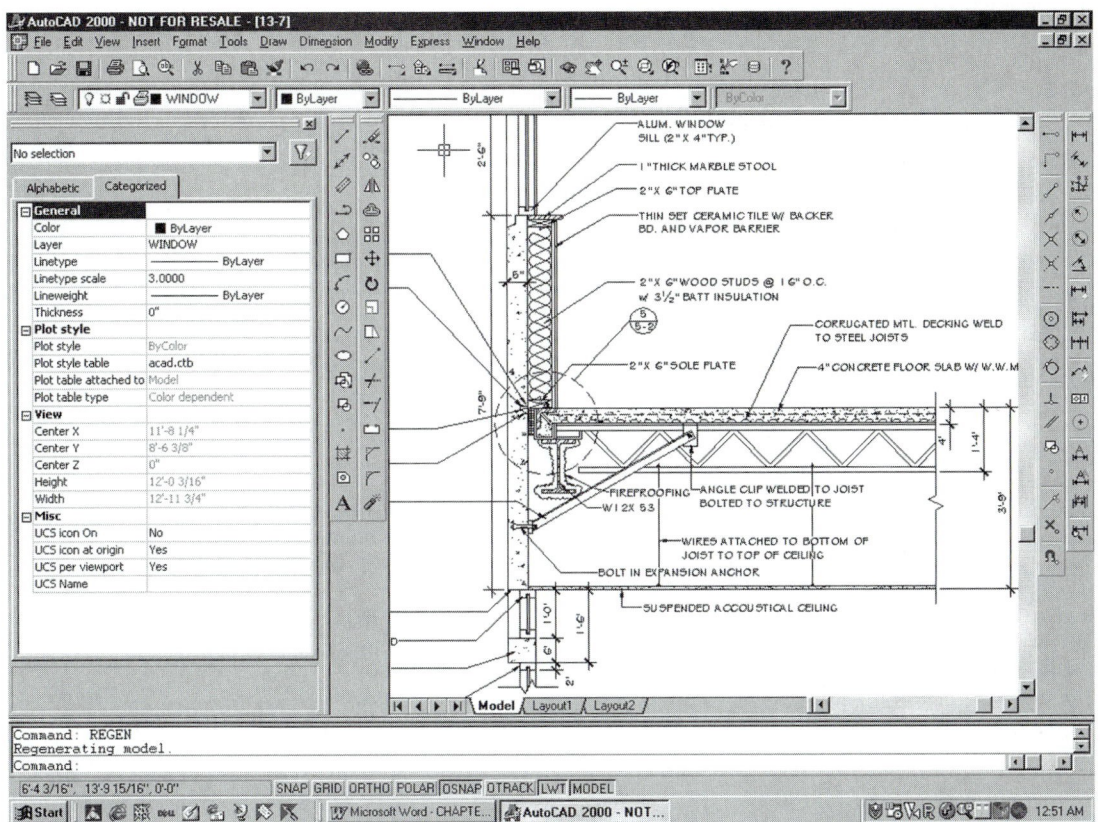

FIGURE 13–6 The Properties window allows you to edit object properties in the most streamlined fashion.

all properties associated with the selected object, select the *Alphabetic* tab. This will eliminate the need for searching a property under a specific category, but may prove more time consuming if the alphabetical list contains a long list of items. If this is the case, you will save time by searching under a specific category. To see object properties sorted by category, select the *Categorized* tab. The Alphabetic tab will list in alphabetical order the properties of the object for you to select from. For example, in Figure 13–7, the leader line is selected for editing. The top drop-down list will display *Leader* as the type of object selected. If you have the grips on, the grips of the object will be displayed. If you turn the grips off, the selected object will only be highlighted. The Alphabetic tab in Figure 13–7 contains Arrow, Arrow size, Color, Dim line color, Dim line LW, Dim scale overall, Dim style, and so on. If there are selection options within a property, a drop-down list box with a down arrow will be displayed as seen in the Arrow property of the Leader object. To change the property under a drop-down list box, click on the down arrow and select the property to change.

■ **EXERCISE 13–2:** *The following step-by-step exercise will allow you to change the leader line arrowhead shown in Figure 13–7 from Closed Filled to Dot arrow style.*

Step #1: Open the EXE13-2.dwg file.

Step #2: Open the Properties window.

Step #3: Select the leader line as shown in Figure 13–7.

Step #4: Inside the Properties window select the Alphabetic tab and click on the Arrow drop-down list down arrow. This will list all the available arrow styles as shown in Figure 13–8.

Step #5: Select the Dot arrow style. AutoCAD will immediately apply the changes to the selected leader. At this point you can see the arrowhead change from Closed filled to Dot style.

Step #6: Move your cursor in to the drawing area and press the ~EscKey~ twice. This will remove the grips and complete the editing process.

FIGURE 13–7 The Alphabetic tab of the Properties window displays all properties associated with the selected objects. The extent of the property list depends on the object or objects selected for modification. Notice there are 20 properties associated with the selected leader line.

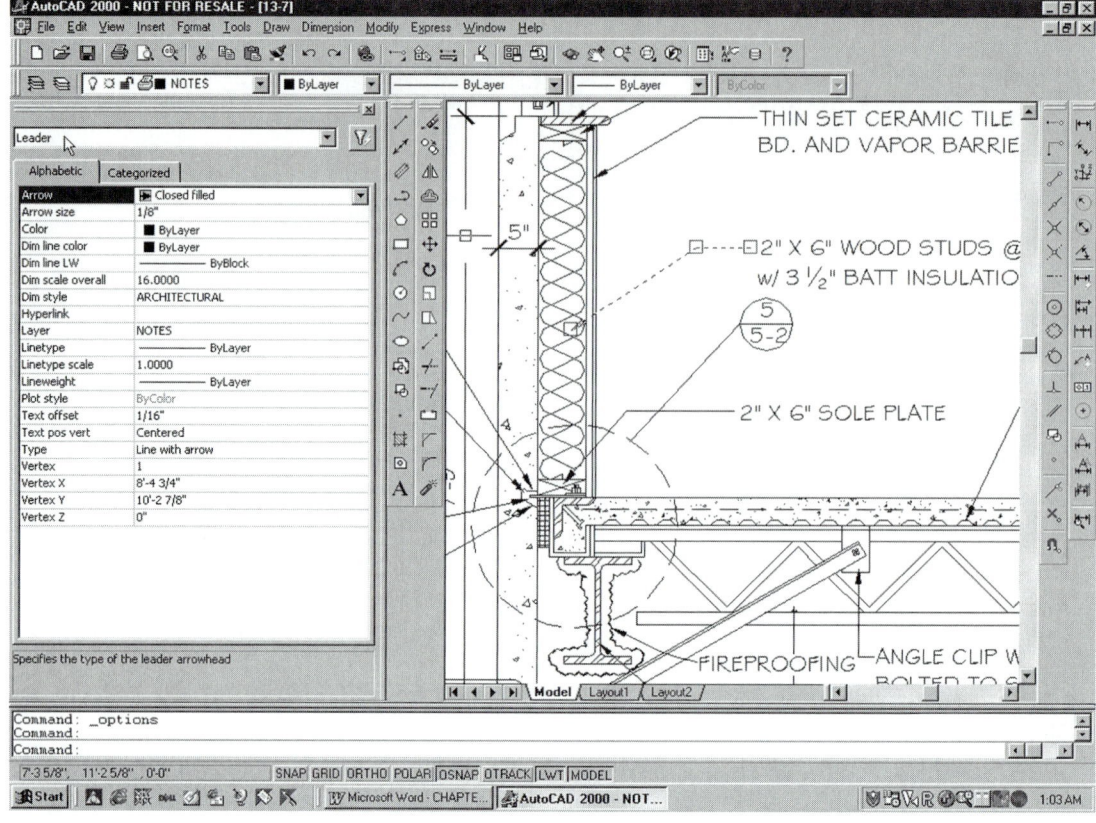

FIGURE 13–8 The Arrow property drop-down list contains all the arrowhead style. The Dot style has been selected to change the leader line arrowhead.

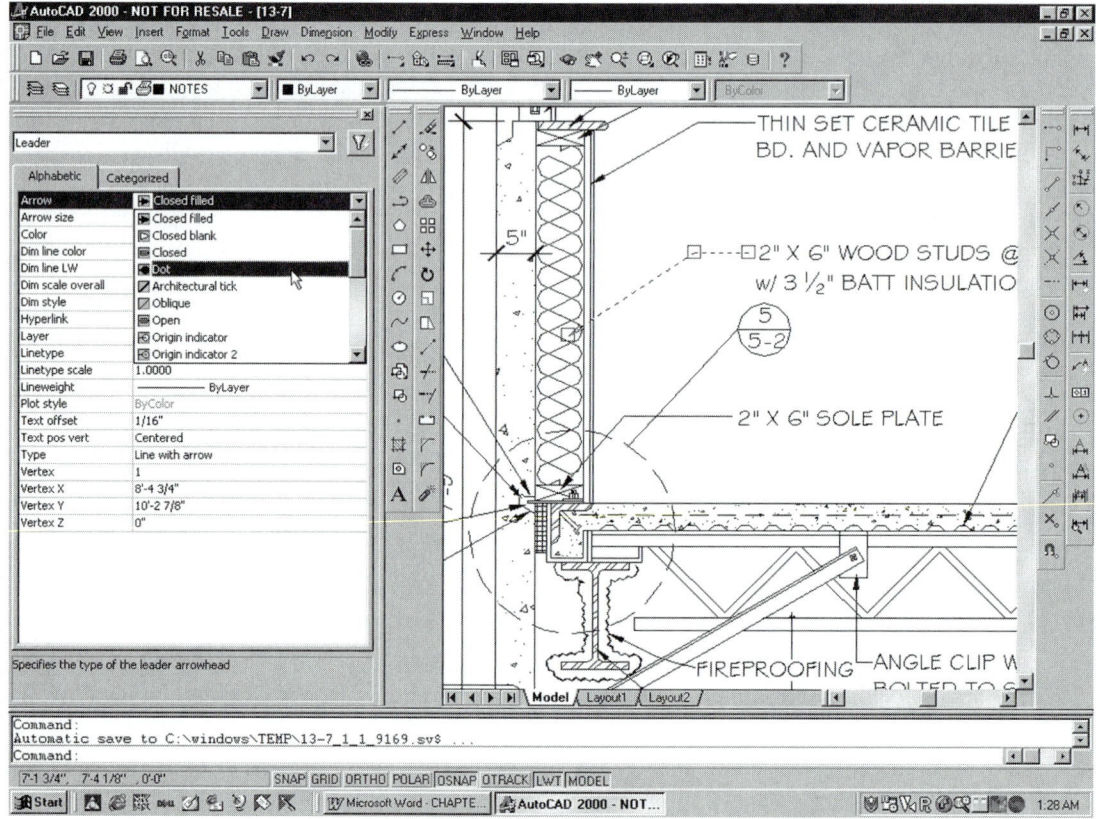

Congratulations! You have successfully used the Alphabetic tab of the Properties window to change the properties of a single object. The Dot arrow style will be displayed for the selected leader line as shown in Figure 13–9. Save the changes but do not exit the drawing.

You can select more properties of the selected object to change.

■ **EXERCISE 13-3:**   *The following step-by-step exercise will allow you to change the existing size of the Dot arrowhead style from 1/8″ to 1/16″.*

Step #1:   Continue with the EXE13-2.dwg file.

Step #2:   Select the leader line to modify. Turn grips off.

Step #3:   Inside the Properties window and under the Alphabetic tab, click on the Arrow size.

Step #4:   Highlight the current size (1/8) and enter 1/16 and then press the ~EnterKey~. This will change the size of the Dot arrowhead style as shown in Figure 13–10.

Step #5:   Move your cursor in to the drawing area and press the ~EscKey~ once.

Congratulations! You have successfully changed more properties of the same object using the Properties window. The Dot arrowhead size will now be 1/16″ as shown in Figure 13–11. Save the changes but do not exit the drawing.

You do not have to leave the Properties window and reselect the same object to modify additional properties. To modify more than one property of a selected object, click on the property list one-at-a-time and edit the current values or items. Every time you press the ~EnterKey~ the selected property will be changed. You can select as many properties as you like for change without going back to the drawing.

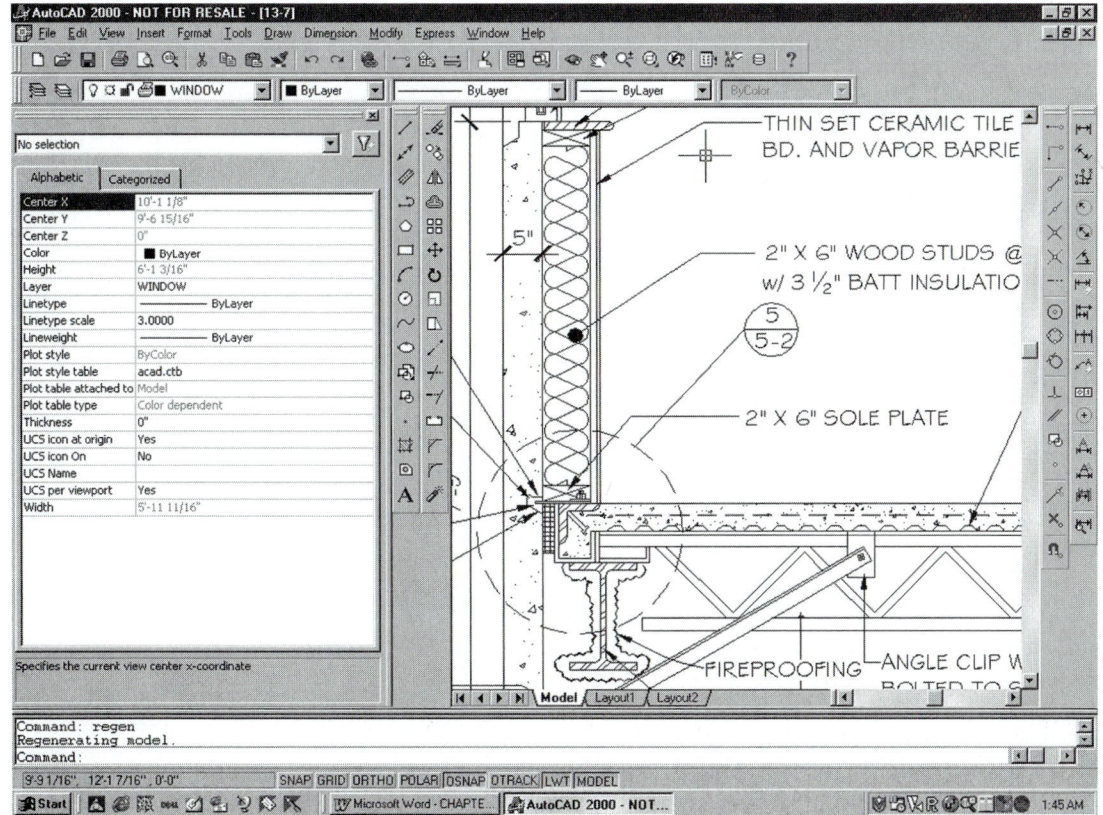

FIGURE 13–9   The selected leader line has been modified to a Dot leader line arrowhead style.

FIGURE 13–10 The
Arrow size has been
changed to 1/16″ inside
the Arrow size area of
the Alphabetic tab in
the Properties window.

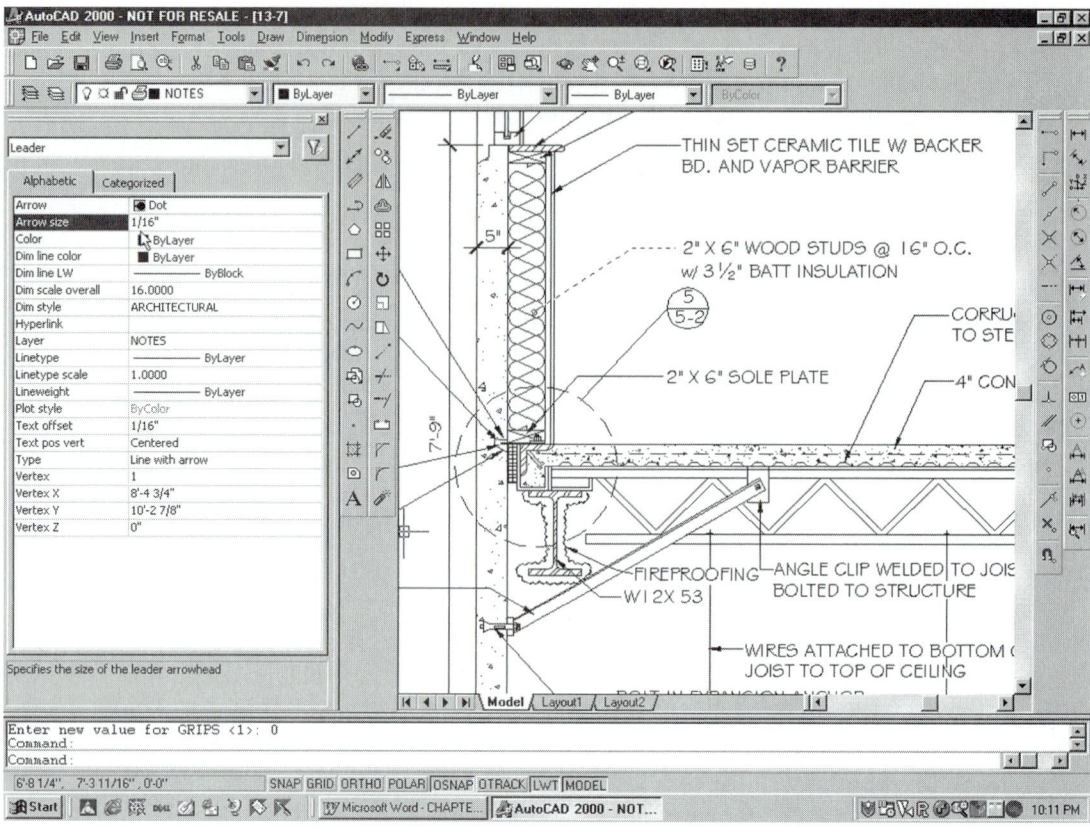

FIGURE 13–11 The
selected leader line has
been changed from 1/8″
to 1/16″ arrow size.

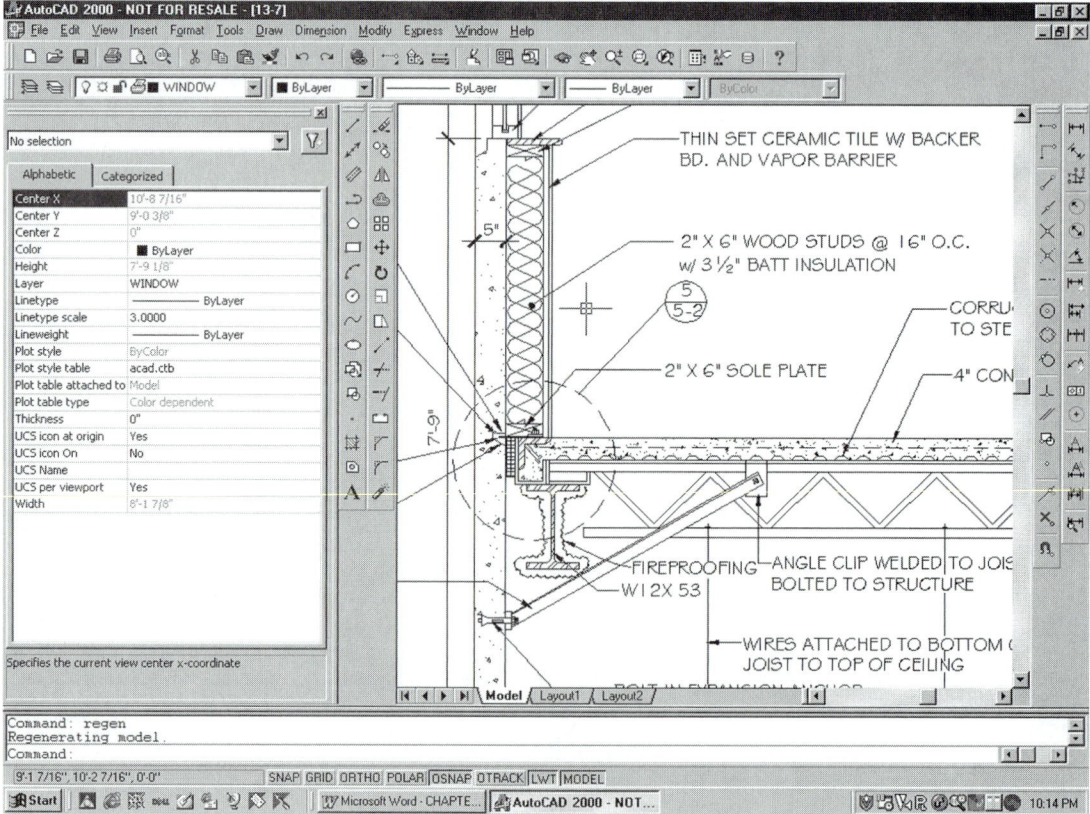

■ **EXERCISE 13–4:** *The following step-by-step exercise will allow you to change the Arrow style to Architectural tick, the Arrow size to 3/16″, the Color of the arrow to red, and the Layer of the arrow to a different layer.*

Step #1: Continue with the EXE13-2.dwg file.

Step #2: Select the leader line to modify.

Step #3: Inside the Properties window and under the Alphabetic tab, click on the arrow and then click on the Arrow drop-down list. Select Architectural tick from the list. This will change the arrow to Architectural tick.

Step #4: Select the Arrow size, highlight the current value and enter *3/16* and then press the ~EnterKey~. This will change the arrow size to *3/16″*.

Step #5: Select the color and then click on the Color drop-down list. Select Red. This will change the color of the architectural tick to red.

Step #6: Select the layer and then click on the Layer drop-down list. Select the layer you want. This will place the Architectural tick into the layer selected.

Step #7: Move your cursor in to the drawing area and press the ~EscKey~ once.

Congratulations! You have successfully changed more properties of the same object using the Alphabetic tab of the Properties window. Save the changes.

Tips: The property values that can be changed are listed as black and are visible; the property values that cannot be changed are grayed out.

You can display the properties of objects using the Categorized tab. You can expand or collapse a category by selecting the + or − signs in front of each category. With no object selection, the Categorized tab will display the following properties:

• **GENERAL:** This category allows you to change the color, layer, linetype, linetype scale, lineweight, and thickness of the selected objects as shown in Figure 13–12. Thickness is

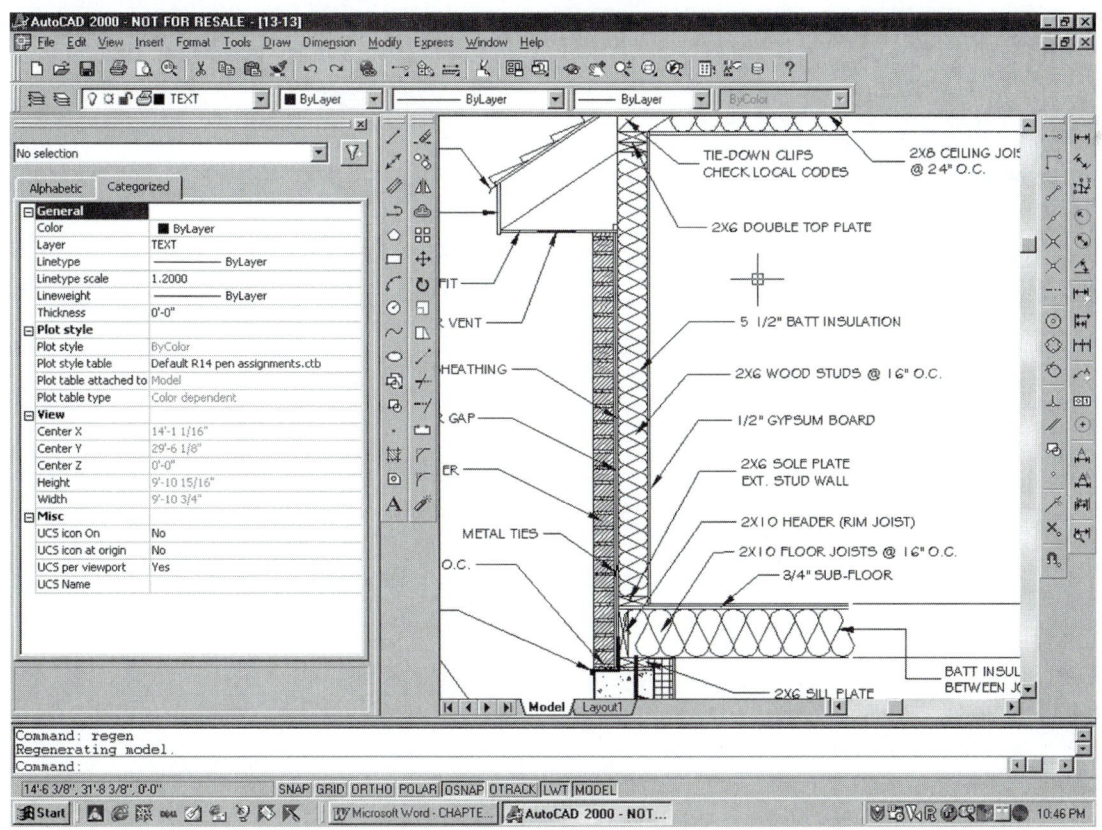

FIGURE 13–12 The Categorized tab of the Properties window without any object selection. Notice the four major categories.

associated with three-dimensional drawings and is not applicable to two-dimensional drawings. To change a value, select on the property. For numeric properties such as Linetype scale, highlight the current value and then enter a new value. For properties that require a selection from a list such as Layer, highlight the property and select a new value from the list. The object will be updated to reflect any changes you make under this category.

■ **EXERCISE 13–5:** *The following step-by-step exercise will allow you to change the lineweight of the exterior line of the brick shown in Figure 13–13 from ByLayer to 0.020".*

Step #1: Open the EXE13-3.dwg file.

Step #2: Open the Properties window.

Step #3: Turn grips off. Zoom close to the brick wall. Select the exterior line of the brick. The line will be highlighted, and the word *Line* will appear in the top drop-down list as shown in Figure 13–13.

Step #4: Inside the Properties window and under the General category, select Lineweight. From the drop-down list, select 0.020" as shown in Figure 13–14. As soon as you select 0.020", the lineweight of the selected line will change to 0.020" but will still be highlighted. While the object is still highlighted, you can change more of its properties.

Step #5: Move your cursor to the drawing area and click on the ~EscKey~ once.

Step #6: Make sure the LWT button is turned on.

Congratulations! You have successfully changed the lineweight of an object using the Categorized tab of the Properties window. The line will now be displayed solid and updated to reflect the new lineweight as shown in Figure 13–15.

FIGURE 13–13 When you select an object such as a line, the Categorized tab will display only the property categories associated with the selected object. In this case the selected line can be modified with the General category.

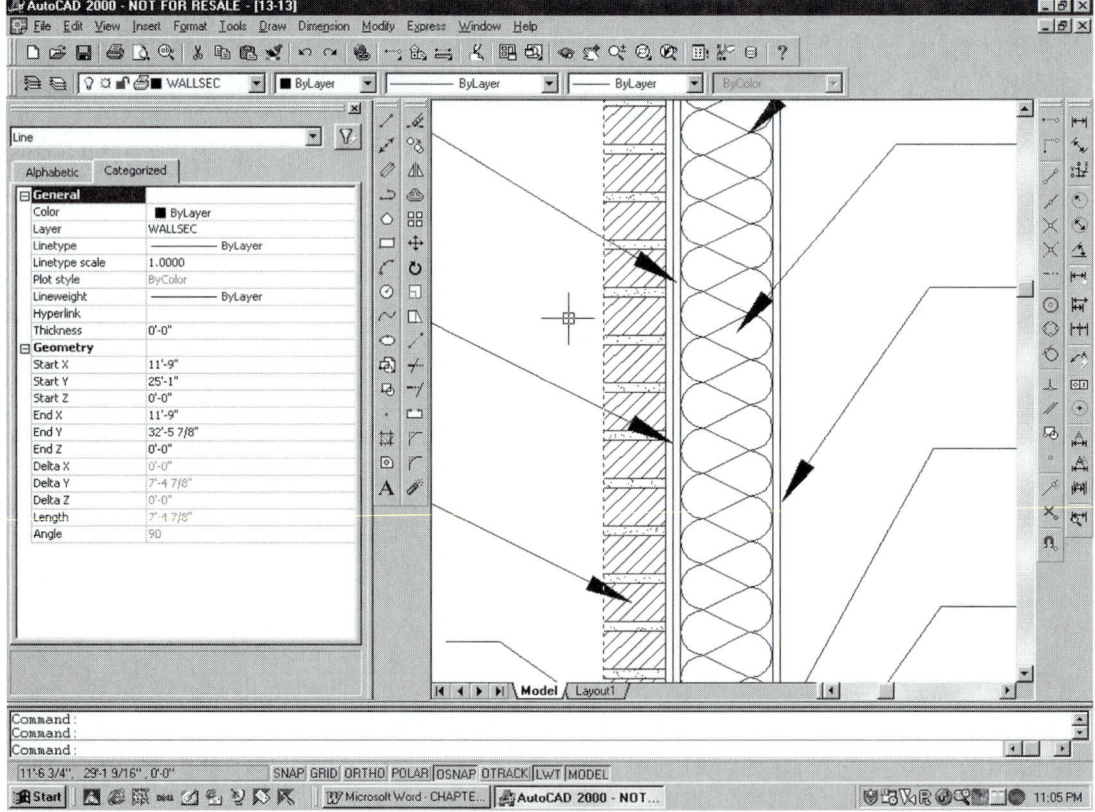

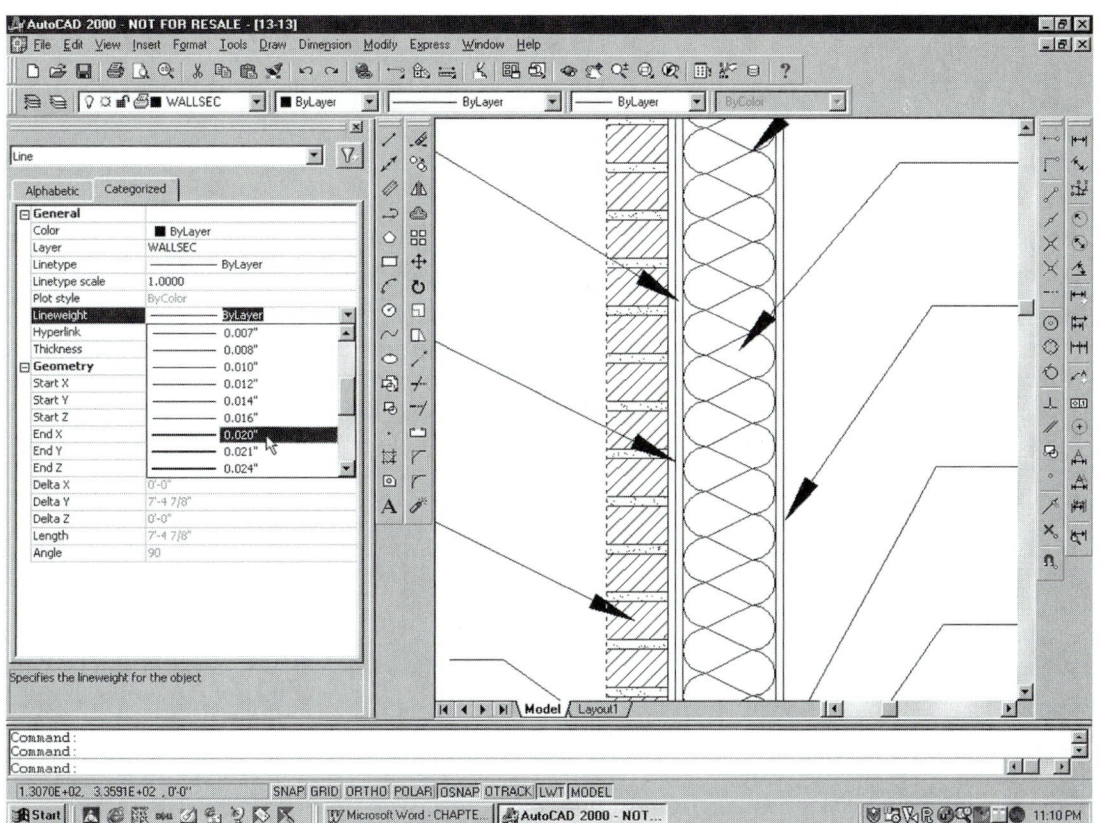

FIGURE 13–14 When you select the Lineweight category, the drop-down list will show all the available lineweights to choose from. In this example, the 0.020″ is selected for lineweight. Notice that when you select the value, AutoCAD automatically updates the line (not shown here for clarity). The line stays as dashed, allowing you to modify more properties as one continuous operation.

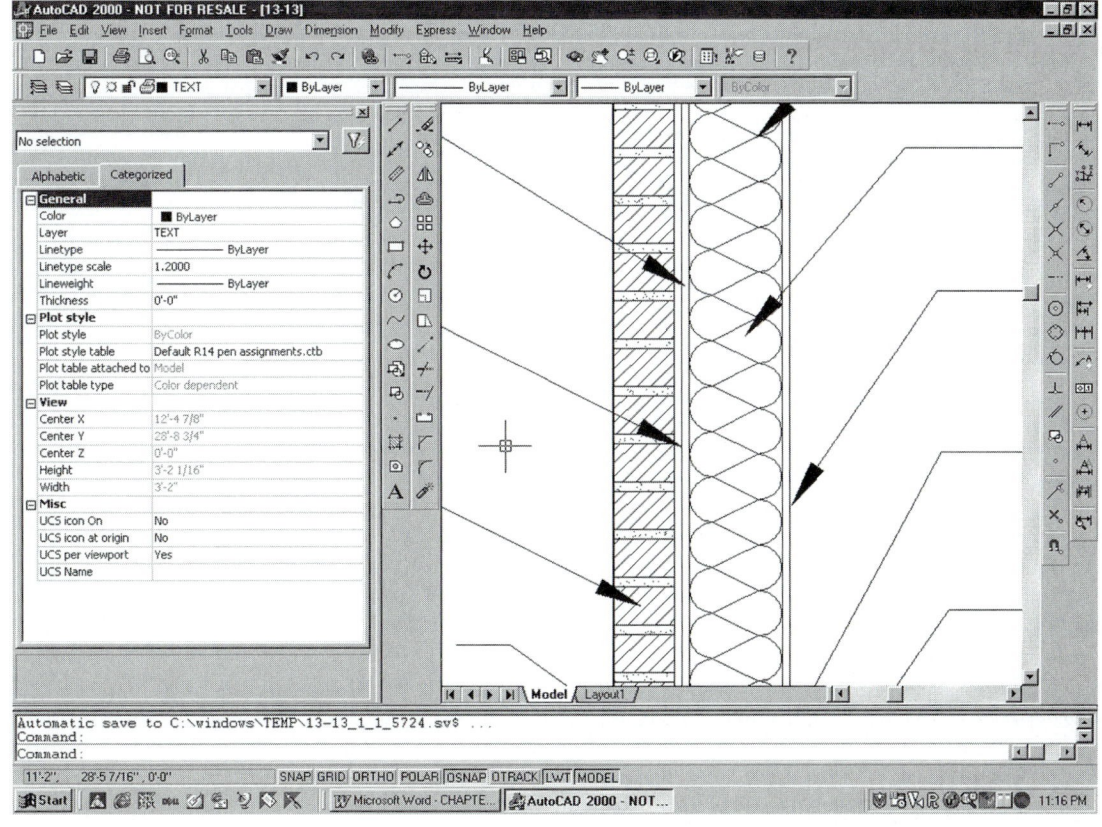

FIGURE 13–15 After pressing the ~EscKey~ once (twice if grips is on), the line will be displayed as 0.020″. Notice the Properties window is back to No selection.

- **PLOT STYLE:** This category allows you to change the plot style of the drawing. As default only the ByColor is available as the plot style. You must first create a plot style table to select it from the drop-down list. See Chapter 23 for Plotting and creating plot styles.

- **VIEW:** This category allows you to specify the current view center X, Y, Z coordinates, height, and width. You must first create views of your project. See Chapter 11 for creating views.

- **MISC:** This category allows you to modify the UCS icon. You can turn it on or off, place it at the origin, save it with the viewport, or change the coordinate system name.

Each object has unique characteristics associated with its properties. With each different object selection, the Categorized tab will display different properties unique to the selected object. With each property selection you may have more options relating to sub-properties of the selected object. Depending on the object and the category selected, AutoCAD will display selection buttons (...) that, when you click on them, will display dialog boxes associated with the property. For example, selecting a hatch pattern will display a Pattern category in addition to General and Misc (miscellaneous) categories as shown in Figure 13–16. Inside the pattern category, you can change the hatch type, hatch pattern name, hatch angle, and hatch scale of the selected hatch pattern. The options in the Pattern category are similar to the options found in the Boundary hatch dialog box. Creating hatch patterns is discussed in Chapter 20.

Once you dock the Properties window, you can change the size horizontally by selecting the vertical bar that divides the Properties window from the drawing window and moving it in either direction.

13.4.2 Changing the Properties of Multiple Objects

When you select more than one object (of the same object type), AutoCAD will display the object type followed by the number of objects selected inside the parenthesis. For example, if you select five lines, the top drop-down list will display Line (5). If you select different object types,

FIGURE 13–16
Selecting a hatch pattern will display the Pattern category and its associated properties.

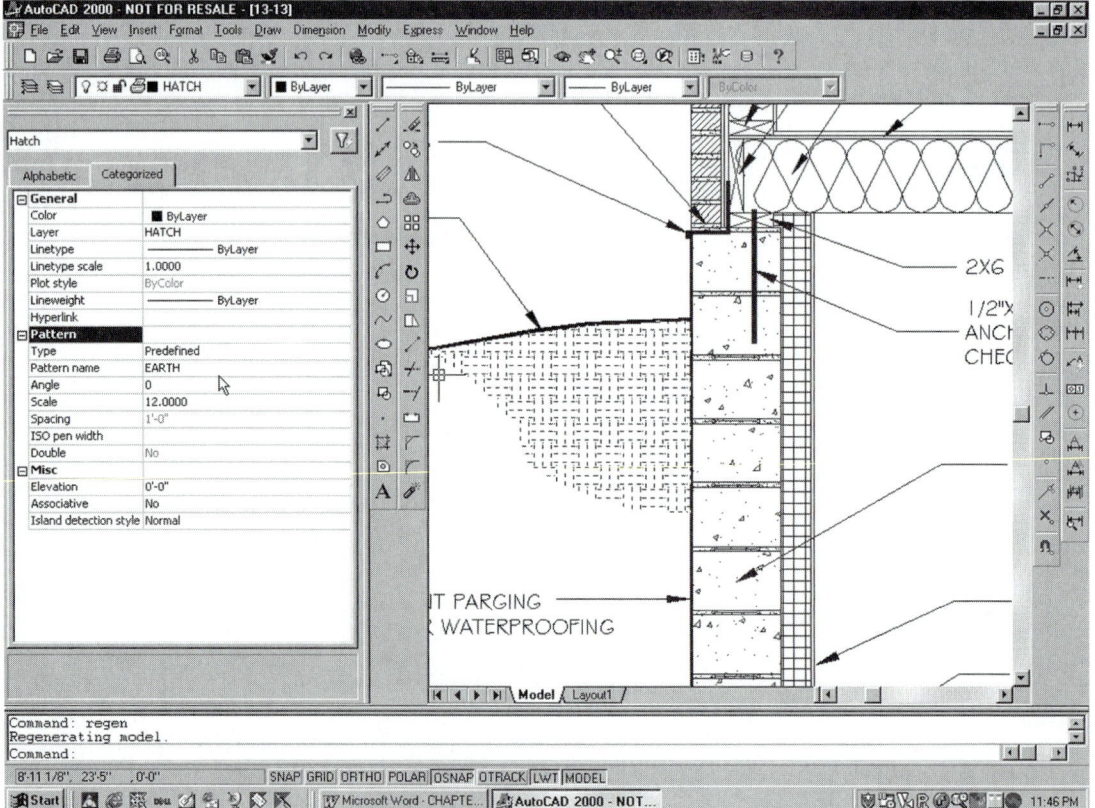

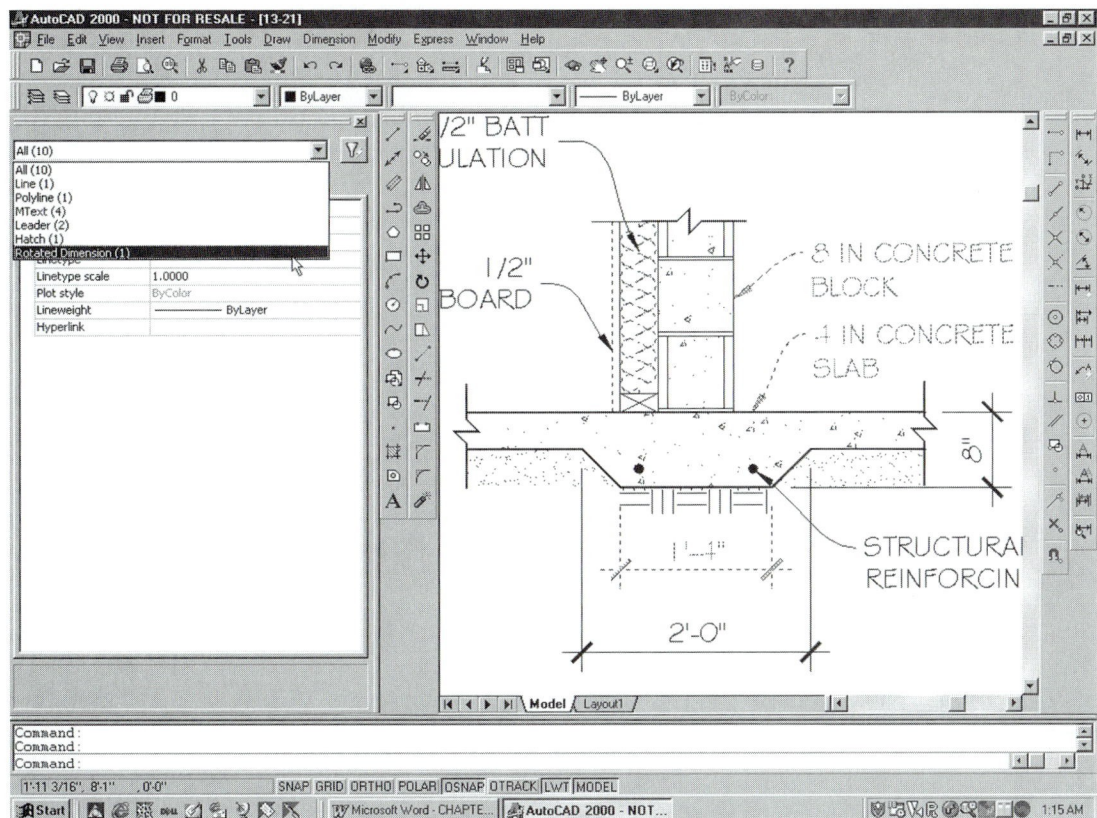

FIGURE 13–17 When you select different object types, AutoCAD will display each object type followed by the amount selected in the parenthesis. You can then select a specific object type from the list to modify.

AutoCAD will display the word "All" followed by the number of objects selected inside the parenthesis. For example, if you select two lines, one dimension, and two leader lines the top drop-down list will display All (5). Selecting different object types will only allow you to change the properties common between them. For example, you can change only the properties listed under the General category when you select different object types. But if you select more than one object (of the same object type), you can change geometrical properties along with general properties of the selected objects. You can select several circles to make them all the same radius and/or all the same color at once. When you select different object types, you can select a specific object type from the top drop-down list to display and change the properties for that object type only. In Figure 13–17 ten objects are selected. When you click on the top drop-down list arrow, each object type with the amount selected in the parenthesis will be displayed. You can select a specific object type from the list and change properties for that object type. You can continuously keep selecting the specific object types and modify. AutoCAD will keep updating them as you edit them. When you complete your editing, move your cursor to the drawing area and press the ~EscKey~ once or twice to exit.

13.5 USING QUICK SELECT WITH PROPERTIES WINDOW

You learned how to use the Quick Select in the previous chapter. You can create a powerful editing tool by combining the Quick Select and the Properties window. With the Quick Select you can create a filtered selection set based on the specific object properties. You can then use the Properties window to modify the properties of the filtered objects. This procedure will increase efficiency and decrease the amount of time it takes to modify drawings.

■ **EXERCISE 13–6** *Figure 13–18 shows a floor plan of a kitchen with a 36″ diameter table with five 12″ diameter stools. There are also four 8″ diameter stools placed on the bottom portion of the kitchen counter. The following step-by-step exercise will allow you to create a filtered selection set based on the 12″ diameter stools and change their size to 10″. Since there are*

FIGURE 13–18 The kitchen floor plan with 10 circles. A filtered selection set will be created based on the five circles around the kitchen table without affecting other circles.

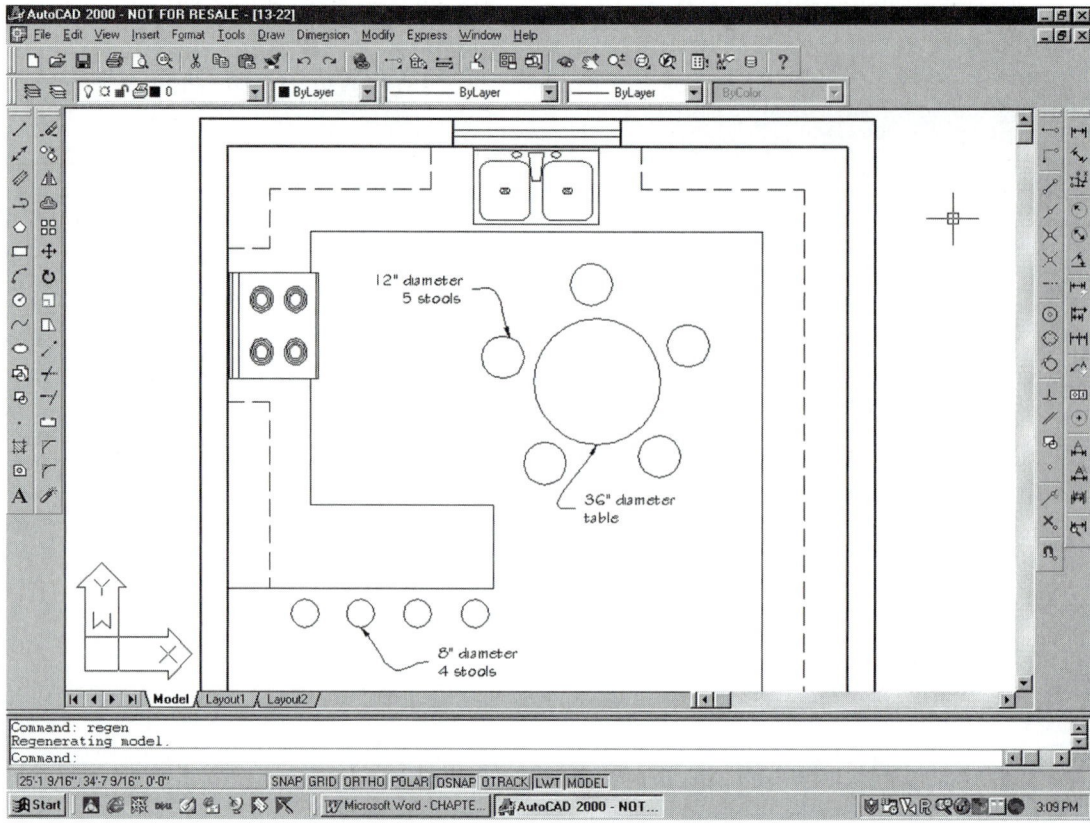

10 circles with different diameters, this procedure will only select the circles having a diameter of 12″ and will not affect other circles.

Step #1: Open the EXE13-4.dwg file.

Step #2: Access the Properties window and click on the Quick Select button.

Step #3: Inside the Quick Select dialog box, select *Entire drawing* from the Apply to: drop-down list.

Step #4: Select *Circle* from the Object type: drop down list.

Step #5: Select *Diameter* from the Properties: drop-down list.

Step #6: Select *=Equals* from the Operator: drop-down list.

Step #7: Enter *12* inside the Value text box.

Step #8: Click on the Include in new selection set radio button.

Step #9: Click on the Append to current selection set. The Quick Select dialog box should now look like in Figure 13–19.

Step #10: Click on the OK button. This procedure will select all circles having a diameter of 12″ as shown in Figure 13–20. Notice that the top drop-down list of the Properties window shows Circle (5).

Step #11: Inside the Geometry category, click on the Diameter and highlight the 1′-0″ value. Enter a value of 10 and press the ~EnterKey~. This will automatically change the diameter of the selected circles to 10″, as shown in Figure 13–20.

Step #12: Move your cursor inside the drawing and press the ~EscKey~ once (twice if the grips is on).

Congratulations! You have successfully created a filtered selection set using the Quick Select dialog box and the Properties window to edit selected objects. The edited drawing will now display five circles with 10″ diameter as shown in Figure 13–21. Do not save the changes.

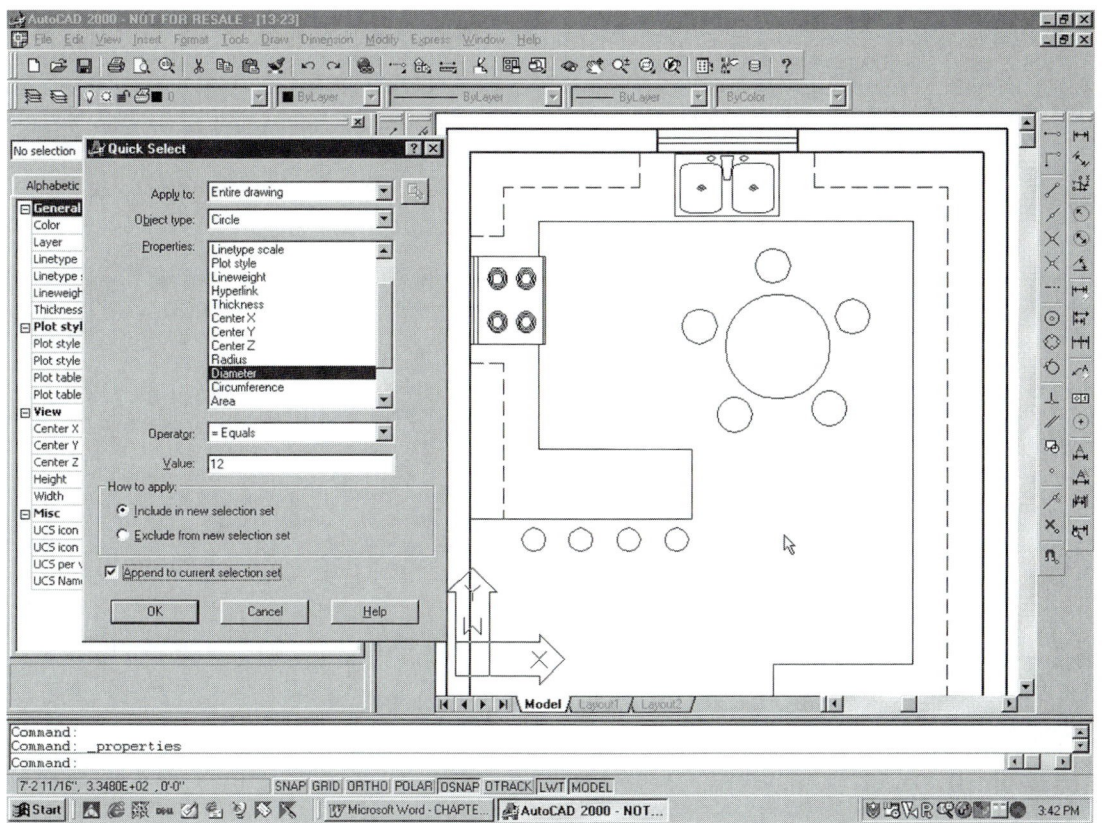

FIGURE 13–19 The Quick Select dialog box is used to create the filtered selection set. The selection set is based on the entire drawing and filters circles having a diameter of 12″.

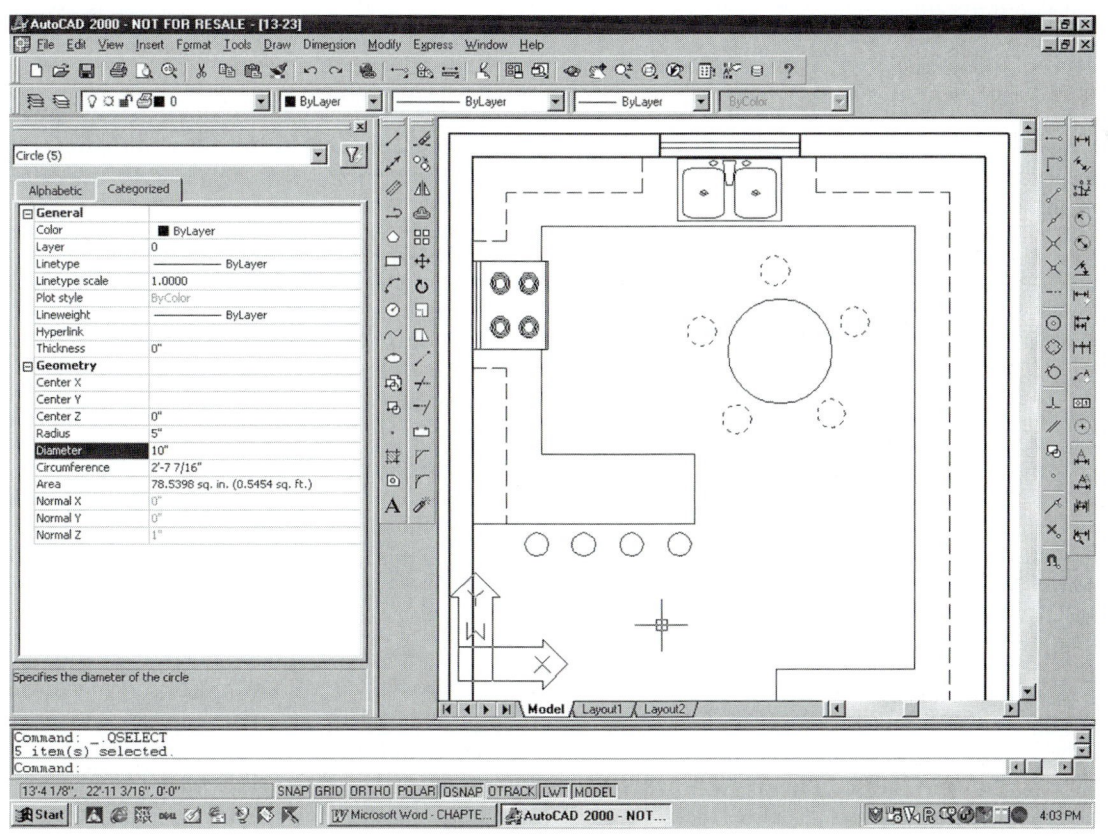

FIGURE 13–20 When the filtered selection set is created, pressing the ok button will highlight all the circles fitting to that filtered criteria. In this case only the five circles around the kitchen table are selected. Inside the properties window and under the categorized tab, the existing diameter of 1′–0″ is changed to 10″

FIGURE 13–21 Inside the drawing, the five circles are now displayed with a diameter of 10″.

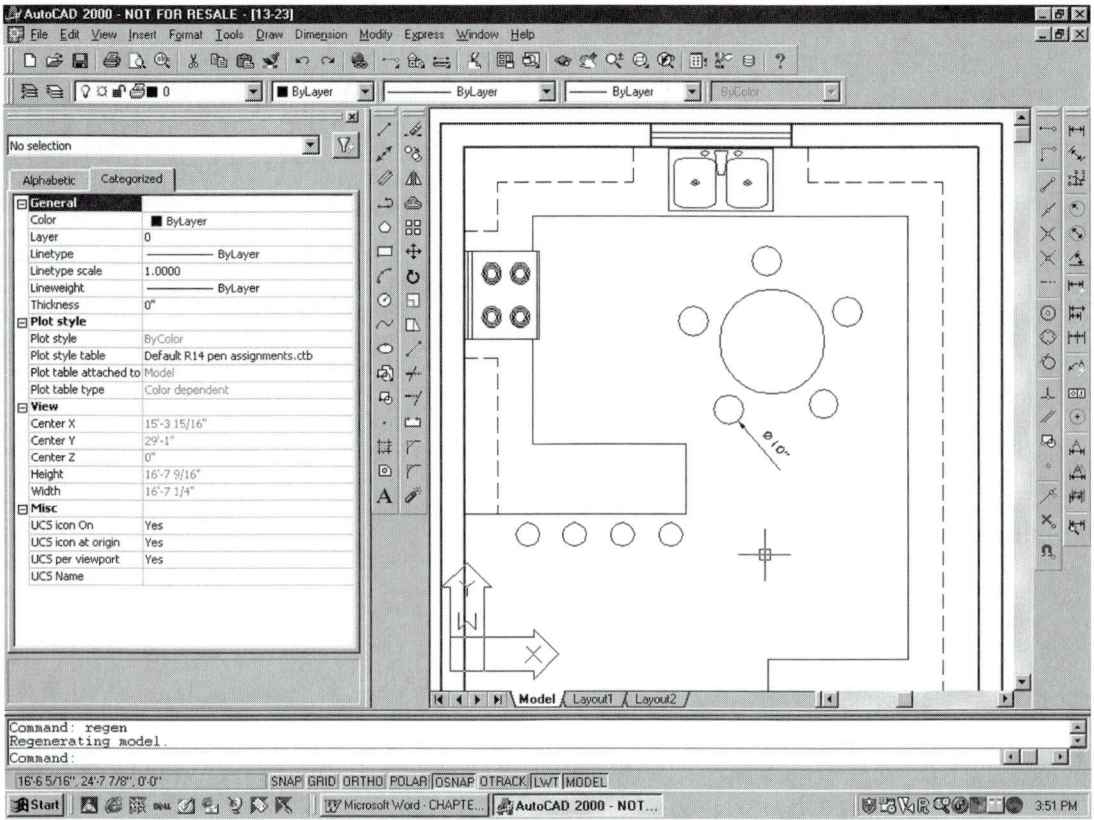

When the filtered selection set is created, pressing the OK button will highlight all the circles fitting to that filtered criteria. In this case only the five circles around the kitchen table are selected. Inside the Properties window and under the Categorized tab, the existing Diameter of 1′-0″ is changed to 10.

Tips: You can use the Properties window and the Quick Select to edit objects between multiple drawings. Use the Multiple Design Environment to open multiple drawings and edit object properties between drawings.

Note: You can access Quick Select from the right click shortcut menus.

AutoCAD 2000i Update: *You can use the Select Objects button next to the Quick Select button to select objects manually using one of the object selection methods. The PICKADD button (when set to 1) allows you to edit one group of objects within the Properties window. When you select a second group of objects, the first group will be deselected. Set the PICKADD button back to 0 (off) before closing the Properties window, otherwise the PICKADD on will carry through on all editing operations thus will not allow you to edit more than one object.*

13.6 CHANGING OBJECT PROPERTIES USING MATCH PROPERTIES

You can also change the color, layer, linetype, linetype scale, and lineweight properties of objects using the MATCHPRO command. You can copy properties from one *source object* to one or more *destination object(s)*. The source object is the object having the properties you want to copy to another object or objects. Once you select the source object, the command line will show the current active settings for the object. The cursor will turn into a pickbox with a paintbrush. Select the destination object(s) you want to have the properties of the source object. You can access the Match Properties by selecting the Match Properties button in the Standard toolbar, by selecting Match Properties from the Modify pull-down menu, or by entering MA, MATCHPROP, or PAINTER at the command line. The command line procedure is as follows:

```
Command: MATCHPROP ~EnterKey~
Select source object: (select the object
that has the properties you like to copy)
Current active settings: Color Layer Ltype
Ltscale Lineweight Thickness PlotStyle Text
Dim Hatch
Select destination object(s) or [settings]:
(select the object or objects you want the
properties painted)
```

If you want the source object properties to be painted to all objects in the current drawing, enter ALL. If you want to modify the properties to be painted, enter S for Settings. The command line procedure is as follows:

```
Select destination object(s) or [Settings]: S
~EnterKey~
```

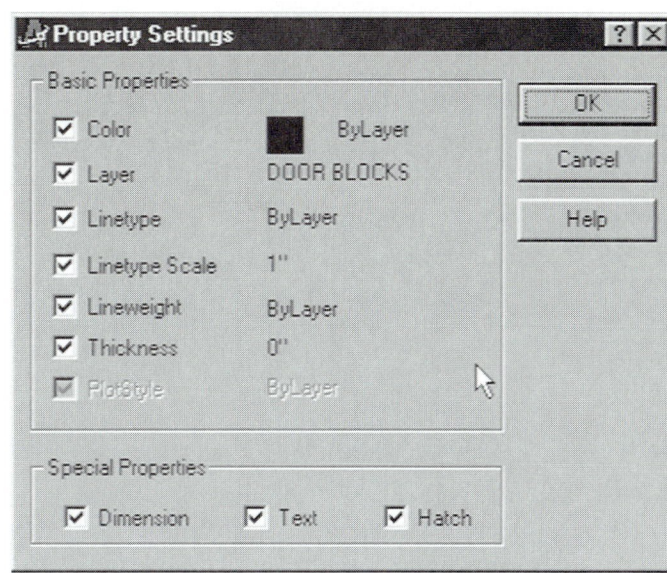

FIGURE 13–22 The Property Settings dialog box allows you to paint desired properties of one object into one or more objects.

This will display the Property Settings dialog box as shown in Figure 13–22. This dialog box shows the basic properties of the source object. The two categories are as follows:

- **BASIC PROPERTIES:** This category lists the general properties associated with the source object. The properties to be painted to destination object(s) are Color, Layer, Linetype, Linetype Scale, Lineweight, and Thickness. If you do not want a particular property painted to the destination object(s), remove the checkmark from the property check box. All properties with checkmarks will be painted to the destination object(s).

- **SPECIAL PROPERTIES:** This category allows you to select additional properties not listed in the basic properties category, such as Dimension, Text, and Hatch. If you leave the checkmarks on, these properties will also be painted to the destination object(s). For example, if you want to paint only the color, layer, and hatch style of one hatch object to another hatch object, remove all checkmarks except the Color, Layer, and Hatch.

Note: Paint is referred to as the act of copying or transferring selected properties of source object into selected destination object(s).

Tips: Use the Multiple Design Environment to paint between drawings. Select the source object from one drawing and select the destination object(s) from one or more drawings.

- **EXERCISE 13–7:** *Figure 13–23 shows a floor plan with three doors inserted as blocks. The door with dashed line is on layer DOOR BLOCKS, has a RED color, with a DASHED linetype and a 0.012″ lineweight. This door is the source object. The other three doors are on layer 0 and they do not have any of the properties of the source object. These three doors are destination objects. The following step-by-step exercise will allow you to paint the Color, Layer, Linetype, and Lineweight properties of the source object to the destination objects.*

Step #1: Open the EXE13-5.dwg file.

Step #2: From the Standard toolbar, select the Match Properties button.

Step #3: Use the following command prompt sequence:

Command: _'matchprop

Select source object: *(select the red door)*

Current active settings: Color Layer Ltype Ltscale Lineweight Thickness PlotStyle Text Dim Hatch

Select destination object(s) or [Settings]: **S** ~EnterKey~

FIGURE 13–23 The properties of the source object can be painted to other objects using the MATCHPROP command.

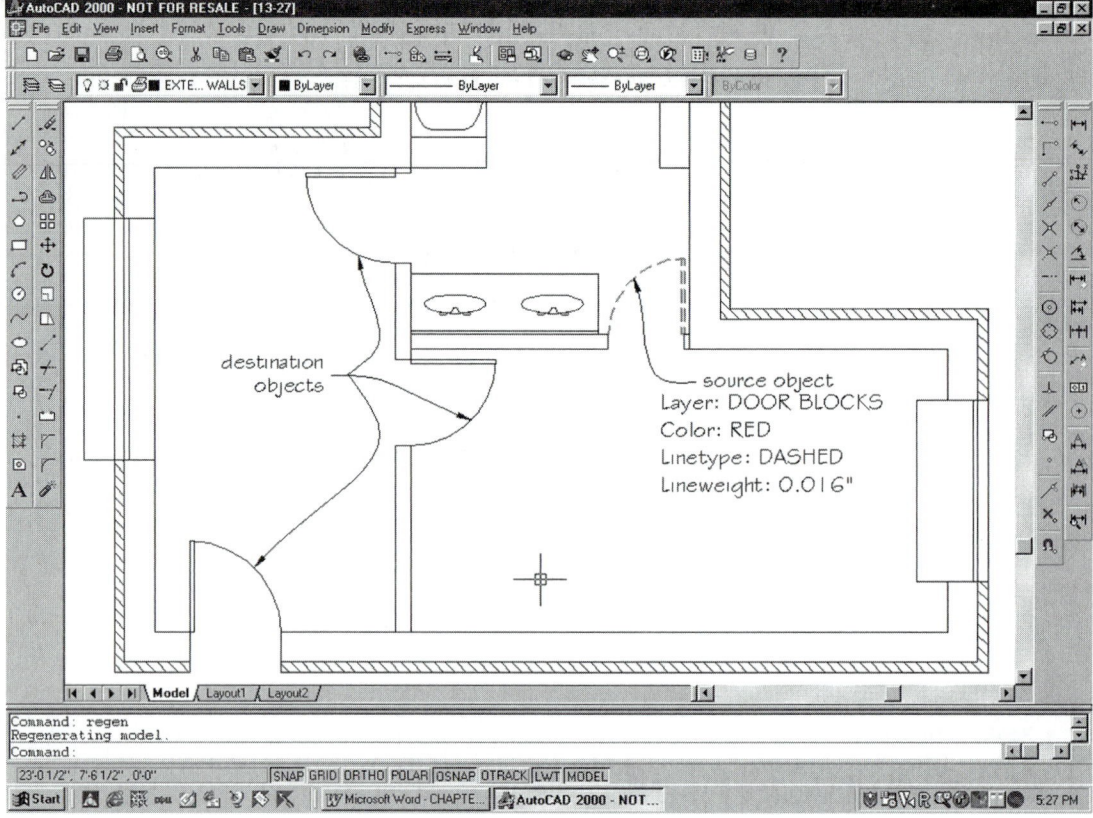

Step #4: Inside the Property Settings dialog box, remove all the checkmarks except Color, Layer, Linetype, and Lineweight and click on the OK button.

The command prompt will be as follows:

Current active settings: Color Layer Ltype Lineweight

Select destination object(s) or [Settings]: *(select the other three doors)*

Select destination object(s) or [Settings]: ~EnterKey~

Congratulations! You have successfully changed object properties using Match Properties. The selected properties of the destination objects will be changed as shown in Figure 13–24.

Tips: Use the Dimension, Text, and Hatch special properties when painting between multiple drawings. The current drawing already contains these special properties hence there is no reason to use these when painting in the current drawing.

AutoCAD 2000i Update: You can double click on an existing object to display its corresponding editing tool. When you double click on an existing text (created with the DTEXT command), the Edit Text dialog box will be displayed. When you double click on an existing hatch pattern the Edit Hatch dialog box will be displayed. When you double click on an existing line or circle the Properties window will be displayed. This feature is controlled by the DBLCLKEDIT system variable and is set to ON by default. When you set the DBLCLKEDIT system variable to OFF, you cannot double click on the objects to edit.

REVIEW QUESTIONS

1. What are grips and what function do they have in the editing process?
2. What is the difference between unselected and selected grip?

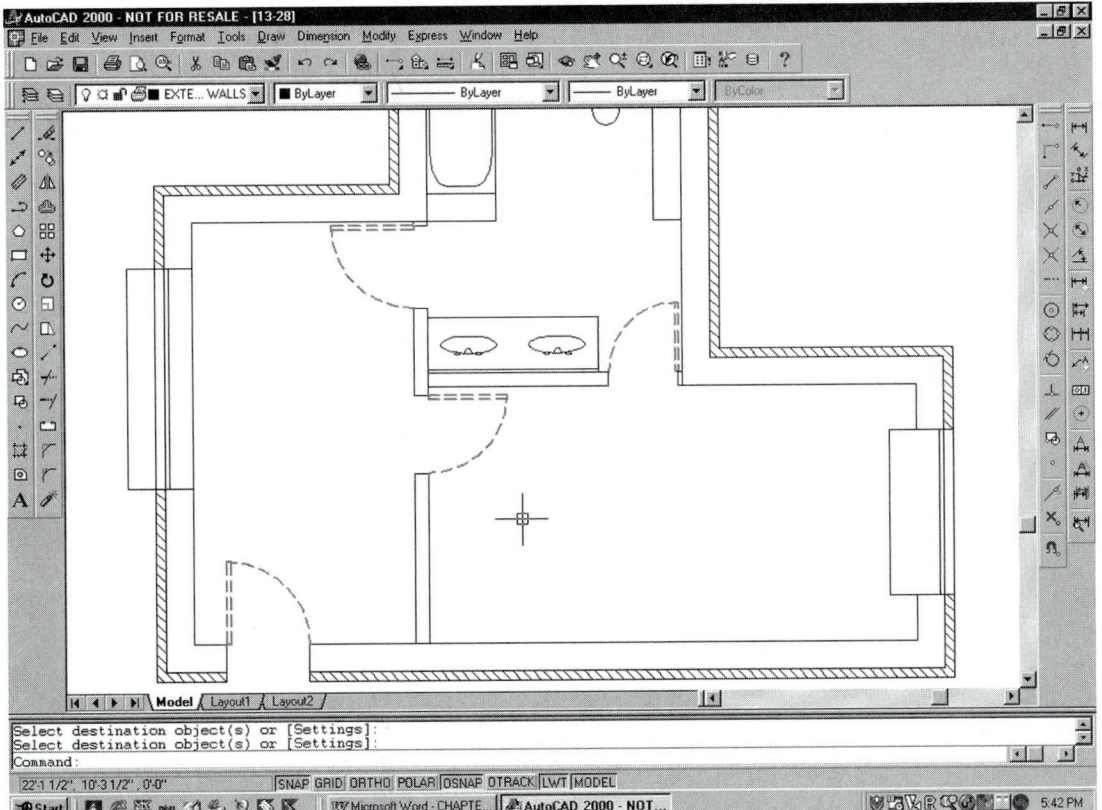

3. How can you change the color of grips?
4. Name the five commands you can use automatically with grips.
5. What does a noun/verb selection mode mean?
6. What is the function of the PICKDRAG system variable?
7. How do you access the Properties window?
8. How do you resize the Properties window?
9. What is the difference between Alphabetic and Categorized tabs of the Properties window?
10. How do you change the properties of multiple objects?
11. How do you access the Property Settings dialog box?

PROBLEMS (DO NOT SAVE ANY OF THE CHANGES)

1. Open the *EXE13-6.dwg* file. Use the Properties window to change the following:

   Change the column lines (magenta color) from default to 0.02" lineweight.
   Change all leader line arrowheads to Blue color and arrow size to 1/8".
   Change Dimension Style to STANDARD.

2. Open the *EXE13-7.dwg* file. Use the Quick Select and the Properties window to change the following:

   Change all text (excluding dimension text) size to 1 3/4".
   Change all text (including dimension text) color to RED.
   Change all leader arrowheads to Right angle.
   Change the Title of the drawing from NOTES layer to TITLE layer.

3. Open the *EXE13-5.dwg* file. Use the Properties window to change the following:

   Change all exterior walls lineweight to 0.020".
   Place the bathtub, water closet, and vanity sink blocks from layer 0 to FIXTURES layer.

4. Open the *EXE13-4.dwg* file. Use the Quick Select and the Properties window to change the following:

   Change all 8″ diameter circles to 15″ and place them from layer 0 to FURNITURE layer.
   Change the 36″ diameter table to 30″ and assign a lineweight of 0.024″.

5. Open the *EXE13-8.dwg* file. Use the Properties window to change the following:

   Change the Concrete Block hatching scale from 15 to 25.
   Change the Column lineweight from ByLayer to 0.021″.
   Change the two column designator circles from 2″ to 4″ radius. Trim the column centerlines.
   Change column letter text height to 4″. Move and adjust the letter location inside the new circle.

6. Open the *EXE10-3A.dwg* file. Use the Properties window to change the following:

   Place all objects that are on layer FURNITURE to the FIXTURES layer.
   Place all exterior walls to the EXTWALL layer.

7. Open the *EXE10-3B.dwg* file. Change the color of one of the leader-line text to green. Use the Match Properties to change the remaining text to that property.

8. Open the *EXE10-6.dwg* file. Change one of the door swings to yellow color. Use the Match Properties to change the remaining door swing colors to yellow.

9. Open the *EXE12-1.dwg* file. Zoom-in to the COFFEE SHOP area. Change the color of one of the tables to red. Use the Match Properties to change the remaining tables to red.

10. Open the *EXE12-7.dwg* file. Use the Quick Select and the Properties window to change all circles with the radius of less than 8″ to 3″.

CHAPTER 14 Creating Text Styles and Placing Text

After successful completion of this chapter you should be able to:

▲ Create architectural text styles.

▲ Use the TEXT or the DTEXT commands to create single-line text.

▲ Use the MTEXT command to create multiline text.

▲ Calculate text heights based on drawing scale factor and plotted text height.

▲ Use the Text Height Chart to find text heights for a given drawing scale and plotted text height.

▲ Create special characters using Control Codes.

▲ Use command line editing before placing text into the drawing.

▲ Use the Justify option of the DTEXT and TEXT commands to format and justify text.

▲ Use the Multiline Text Editor dialog box.

▲ Understand and use AutoStack options.

▲ Use the right-click shortcut menu to edit multiline text inside the Multiline Text Editor dialog box.

▲ Understand and use the QTEXT command.

▲ Use the DDEDIT command to edit single-line and multiline text.

▲ Use Express Text Tools to expedite text creating and editing.

14.1 CREATING TEXT STYLES

Written information in drawings is referred to as *annotation*. Annotating a drawing provides additional information in the form of general and specific notes, description of features, material identifications, text in a legend, and revision notes. AutoCAD provides a wide array of *text styles* that can be used in drawings to create annotation. The default text style is the Standard text style and uses the txt font with 0.20 height, 0 degrees rotation angle, width of 1, and 0 degrees oblique angle. A text style is a composition of fonts and characteristics that define the height, width, and slant angle of the text. You can create several text styles using the same font, but with different characteristics. The standard AutoCAD text fonts have *.shx* file extensions. Therefore the *txt.shx* font name is the Standard style name. The txt font has a rough look and is not suitable for architectural drawings. The simplex font is similar to a single-stroke lettering, whereas complex and triplex fonts represent multistroke lettering. The gothic and italic fonts are generally used where high definition of ornamental type is desired. You can start placing text on the drawing using the Standard text style, but it is usually a common procedure to create one or more text styles that have architectural characteristics and are esthetically pleasing.

FIGURE 14–1 The Text Style dialog box is used to create and format new and existing text styles. Notice the Rename . . . , Delete, and Apply buttons are inactive because a new style has not been created yet.

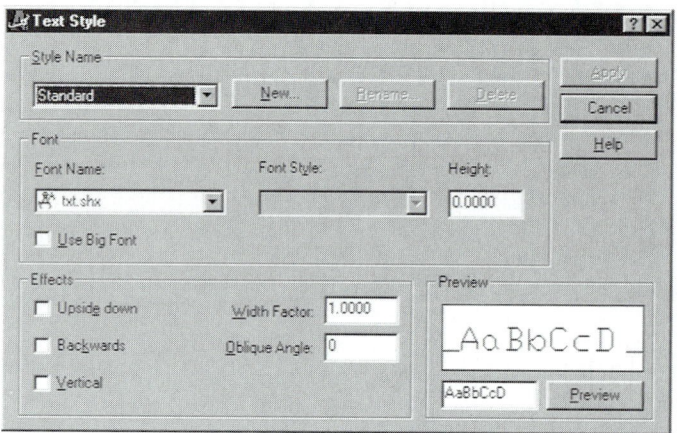

14.1.1 Using the STYLE Command

The STYLE command allows you to create text styles for your drawings. They are stored in the current drawing and can be copied to another drawing using Multiple Design Environment, AutoCAD DesignCenter, and Match Properties as you have learned in previous chapters. You can access the STYLE command by selecting Text Style . . . from the Format pull-down menu or by entering ST or STYLE at the command line. The STYLE command will display the Text Style dialog box as shown in Figure 14–1. The three major categories in the Text Style dialog box are *Style Name, Font, Effects,* and *Preview.* The following describes each category and options:

Style Name: The style name drop-down list is where you can search for any text style created previously. If there are no text styles created, the Style Name drop down list will only display the *Standard* style. The *New. . .* button allows you to create and name a new text style. The *Rename* button allows you to rename an existing text style, but you cannot rename the Standard text style. The *Delete* button allows you to delete an unused existing text style, but you cannot delete the Standard text style. That is why the Rename . . . and Delete buttons are inactive the first time you access this dialog box.

Font: This is the category where you select the font name for your new text style. The default font is txt.shx. The Font Name: drop-down list contains approximately 185 font names that you can select from. You can also use third-party font styles that are special to your projects and include it into the list. Figure 14–2 shows some of the font names available. The *Font Style:* drop down list includes special options available within the selected font. This area is inactive because the Standard text style does not contain any special font options. The *Height:* text box is used to set the current text height for all text used in the drawing. The default is 0.0000 and if not changed allows you to set a value at the command prompt when using the text commands. If you set a text height value inside the Height: text box, then the height becomes fixed for all text created and you will not be prompted for the text height when using text commands. It is common to use more than one text height during the project. Therefore it is best to leave this text box at 0.0000. The *Use Big Font* check box allows you to specify the use of a big font file. This is usually typical for Asian alphabets.

Effects: This category allows you to create and assign special effects for the new or current style. The *Upside down* check box is off by default but when it is checked, the text you create in the drawing will appear upside down. The *Backwards* check box is off by default but when it is checked, the text you create will be displayed backward. The *Vertical* check box is off by default but when it is checked, the text you create in the drawing will appear vertical starting from a top point. This option works best when the text angle is created at 270 degrees. The *Width Factor:* text box allows you to change the width of text characters relative to its height. A width factor of 1.0000 is the default. A width factor greater than 1 will expand the characters, and less than 1 will shrink the characters. The *Oblique Angle:* text box allows you to set an angle that will slant

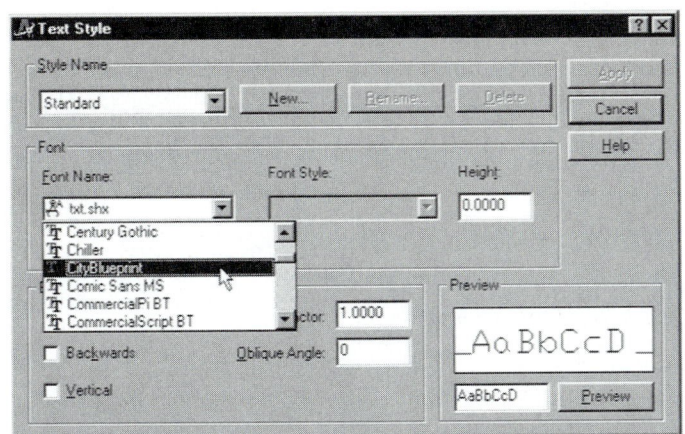

FIGURE 14–2 You can use the Font Name: drop-down list to select a font for the new text style.

the text characters forward or backward. An oblique angle of −30 degrees will slant the characters backward.

Preview: This category allows you to preview the font and the effects on the text style. This is an excellent way to see what the font will look like, including any effects selected before creating the text style. You can preview specific words using the font selected. Simply type the desired word inside the small rectangle below the Preview rectangle and then click on the Preview button.

The *Apply* button is used after establishing the name, height, and effects for the new text style. Selecting this button will apply the name and effects to the style. You must select this button for each new style created. The *Close* button will close the dialog box.

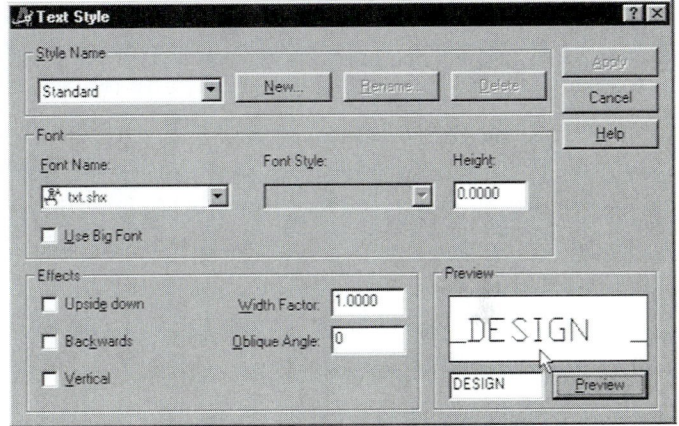

FIGURE 14–3 When the word *design* is entered and when the Preview button is selected, it will appear inside the Preview window.

Figure 14–3 shows how the word *design* will look like if the Standard text style is used. Notice that the style is not appropriate for architectural drawings.

■ **EXERCISE 14–1:** *The following step-by-step exercise will allow you to create two new text styles from CITY BLUEPRINT and STYLUS BT font names without establishing a fixed text height or any special effects.*

Step #1: Open the EXE14-1.dwg file.

Step #2: Access the Text Style dialog box.

Step #3: Click on the New . . . button. This will display the New Text Style dialog box as shown in Figure 14–4.

Step #4: Inside the New Text Style dialog box, enter CITY BLUEPRINT and click on the OK button.

Step #5: From the Font Name: drop-down list, find and select CityBlueprint.

Step #6: Click on the Apply button.

Step #7: Repeat Step #3.

Step #8: Inside the New Text Style dialog box, enter STYLUS BT and click on the OK button.

Step #9: From the Font Name: drop-down list, find and select Stylus BT and click on the OK button.

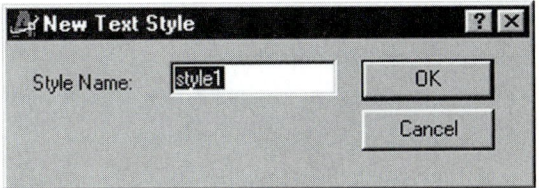

FIGURE 14–4 The New Text Style dialog box allows you to enter the name for the new text style.

Step #10: Click on the Apply and Close buttons to close the dialog box.

Congratulations! You have successfully created two new Text Styles using the Text Style dialog box. The Text Style dialog box will now display the two new text styles as shown in Figure 14–5. Save the changes.

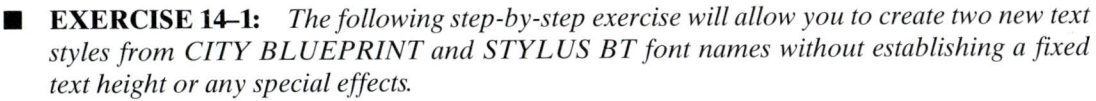

FIGURE 14–5 The Text Style dialog box after the CITY BLUEPRINT and STYLUS BT text styles are created.

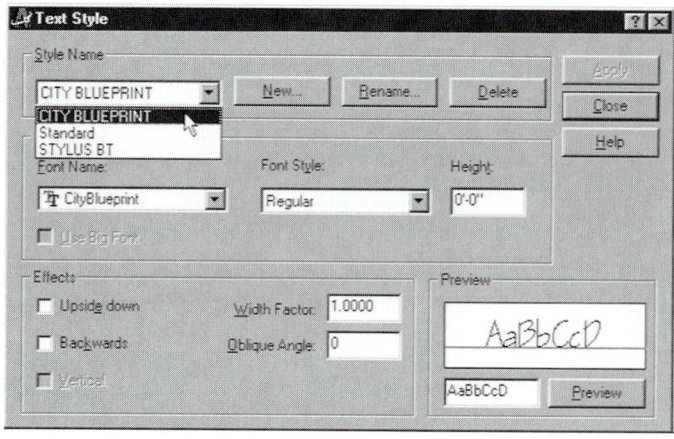

FIGURE 14–6 The AutoCAD warning dialog box.

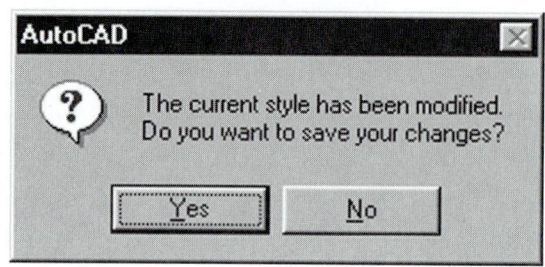

Note: Some font names have font styles. If you require a font style, select from the Font Style: drop-down list.

Caution: If you click on the Close button before clicking on the Apply button after selecting a new font name, AutoCAD will display a warning dialog box as shown in Figure 14–6. Click on the Yes button if you want to save the changes. Click on the No button if you do not want to save the changes.

Tips: Use AutoCAD DesignCenter to import and export text styles from other drawings.

*Note: You can create special text styles for isometric drawings. Create the isometric grid and snap using the Drafting Settings dialog box and create the isometric drawing. Use the Text Style dialog box and create two new text styles called **ISOP** (isometric positive 30 degree oblique angle) and **ISON** (isometric negative 30 degree oblique angle). For ISOP, enter 30 inside the Oblique Angle: text box and click on the Apply button. For ISON, enter –30 inside the Oblique Angle: text box and click on the Apply button. Click on the Close button to close the Text Style dialog box. Use the TEXT command and enter –30 as the Rotation angle (for the text) using the ISON text style. This will be used for text placed in the front view of an object. Enter 30 as the Rotation angle (for the text) using the ISON text style. This will be used for text placed in the top view of an object. Use the TEXT command and enter 30 as the Rotation angle (for the text) using the ISOP text style. This will be used for text placed in the side view of an object.*

14.2 CALCULATING TEXT HEIGHTS

Text (annotation) is created at its true size and must be adjusted for drawings using architectural scales. Adjusting the text height will provide proportionality to the text size and the drawing scale. When using the text commands, AutoCAD will ask you for a text height if you did not enter a value inside the Height: text box in the Text Style dialog box. Text heights are based on the scale of the drawings and must be calculated to correspond to the final plotted text height in drawing units and the scale factor of the drawing. For drawings having a scale of 1″=1″ there is no need to calculate a text height because the full scale of the drawing is the same as the plotted full scale of the text height. If the drawing scale is 1″=1″ and you want the text height to be plotted at 1/4″, then enter 1/4 or 0.25 at the Specify height <0.20>: prompt. The text created will be 0.25″ high. For architectural projects, the text height must be calculated as discussed in Chapter 2.

Tips: Use the Text Height Chart shown in Figure 2–8 in Chapter 2 for the text height values in reference to drawing scale. Although not a common practice, text can be placed in paper space without calculating text height.

Tips: If you leave the Height: 0.0000 inside the Text Style dialog box, you can use the TEXTSIZE system variable to change the text height for the duration of the text commands. This will allow you to set (not fix) a text height when placing text. The Specify height: prompt will still be displayed, allowing you to change your mind about a text height.

Caution: If you change the Height: 0.0000 to a different value, your text height will be fixed for the duration of the drawing. This means that AutoCAD will not display the Specify height: prompt because the text height is fixed at the Text Style dialog box and you cannot use the TEXTSIZE system variable to change the text height. If you want the flexibility to enter text heights at the command prompt, change the Height: value back to 0 in the Text Style Dialog box and click on the Apply button first then click on the Close button to close the dialog box.

Tips: Use the Properties window to quickly and efficiently change the height of existing text. Use the Quick Select method to quickly change the height of large amount of text in the drawing.

14.3 PLACING TEXT ON DRAWINGS

There are two different methods involved in creating text. The DTEXT or the TEXT commands allow you to place text one line at a time and creates single-line text objects. The MTEXT command allows you to create a multiline or paragraph text object that fits inside a boundary box defined by you.

14.4 USING THE DTEXT AND TEXT COMMANDS

The DTEXT (dynamic text) command can be used to create single-line text. It is composed of many individual single-line text segments. This means that every line of dynamic text is a single text object. To edit a dynamic text, you must select them individually or create a selection set based on the editing requirements. The DTEXT and TEXT commands perform the same functions and can be used interchangably. You can access them by selecting Single Line Text from the Text cascading menu in the Draw pull-down menu or by entering DTEXT, TEXT, or DT at the command line. AutoCAD will display the current text style name (the style you are working with last or created last) and the current text height at the command prompt. You are then asked to specify a starting point for the text or change the style or justification of the current text.

■ **EXERCISE 14–2:** *The following step-by-step exercise will allow you to create text with the STYLUS BT text style using the DTEXT command.*

Step #1: Open the EXE14-1.dwg file.

Step #2: Create the text as follows:

Command: **DTEXT** ~EnterKey~

Current text style: "STYLUS BT" Text height: 1′-0″

Specify start point of text or [Justify/Style]: *(select a starting point such as point X shown in Figure 14–7)*

Specify height <1′-0″>: **9** ~EnterKey~ *(the actual plotted text height in full scale will measure 3/16″ when the drawing scale is 1/4″ = 1′-0″. Refer to TEXT HEIGHT CHART in Chapter 2)*

Specify rotation angle of text <0>: ~EnterKey~ *(or specify any angle)*

Enter text: **THIS IS STYLUS BT FONT STYLE** ~EnterKey~

Enter text: ~EnterKey~ *(this will create a single-line text, but you may continue typing for the second line)*

FIGURE 14–7 Using the DTEXT command on a drawing having a scale of 1/4"=1'-0". The text height is entered as 9". This means that when the drawing is plotted, the text height will measure 3/16" at full-scale.

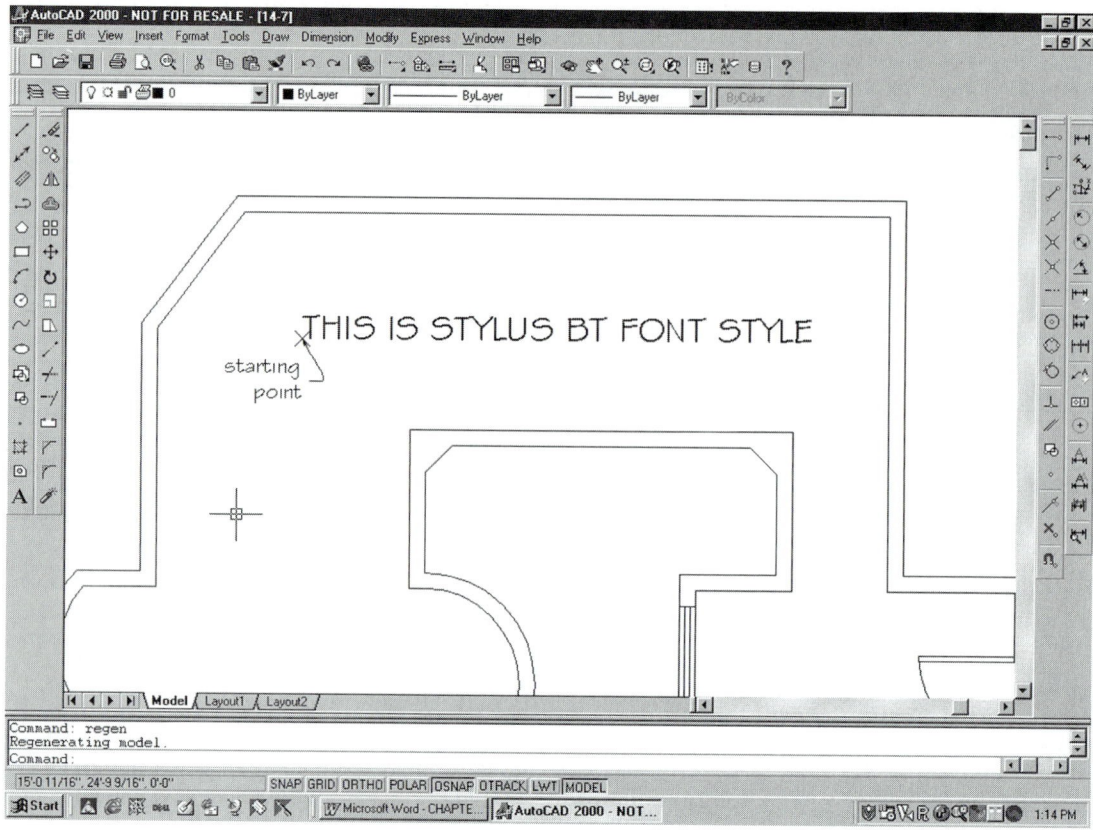

Congratulations! You have successfully created text inside a drawing using the DTEXT command. Do not save the changes.

After you specify the rotation angle for the text, the cursor leaves behind a vertical line on the screen. This vertical line is equal in size to the text height you entered at the Specify height: prompt. Each time you press the ~EnterKey~ after a text line, another text line will be created below the first text line. The Enter text: prompt is repeated for the new line of text below the previous line. To place the text you have created on the screen, press the ~EnterKey~ twice. You can also cancel the command any time by pressing the ~EscKey~. This will erase any text line not completed. You do not have to accept the next text line to be the one below the previous text line. You can continue placing text at a different location by selecting a new point anywhere on the screen by moving your mouse and selecting that point at the Enter text: prompt. Selecting a new start point will complete the line of text entered and will begin a new line of text at the point you selected. This procedure will allow you to place text continuously anywhere in the drawing and will save drafting time and increase productivity. The rotation angle of text allows you to place text at any angle on the screen. Figure 14–8 shows text created with different text height and rotation angle.

> ***AutoCAD 2000i Update:***   The DTEXT and TEXT commands are combined into a single TEXT command. On the command line, the behavior is the same as the DTEXT command and in scripts and AutoLISP applications, it is the same as the TEXT command.

14.4.1   Creating Special Characters

You can create special symbols when using the TEXT and MTEXT commands. To create special symbols you must enter its corresponding *control code*. A control code is a text symbol beginning with two (2) percent signs (%%) followed by special text and then followed by the text you want to enter. There is no space between the control code, special text, and the first letter of the text. The following list shows the most commonly used control code symbols:

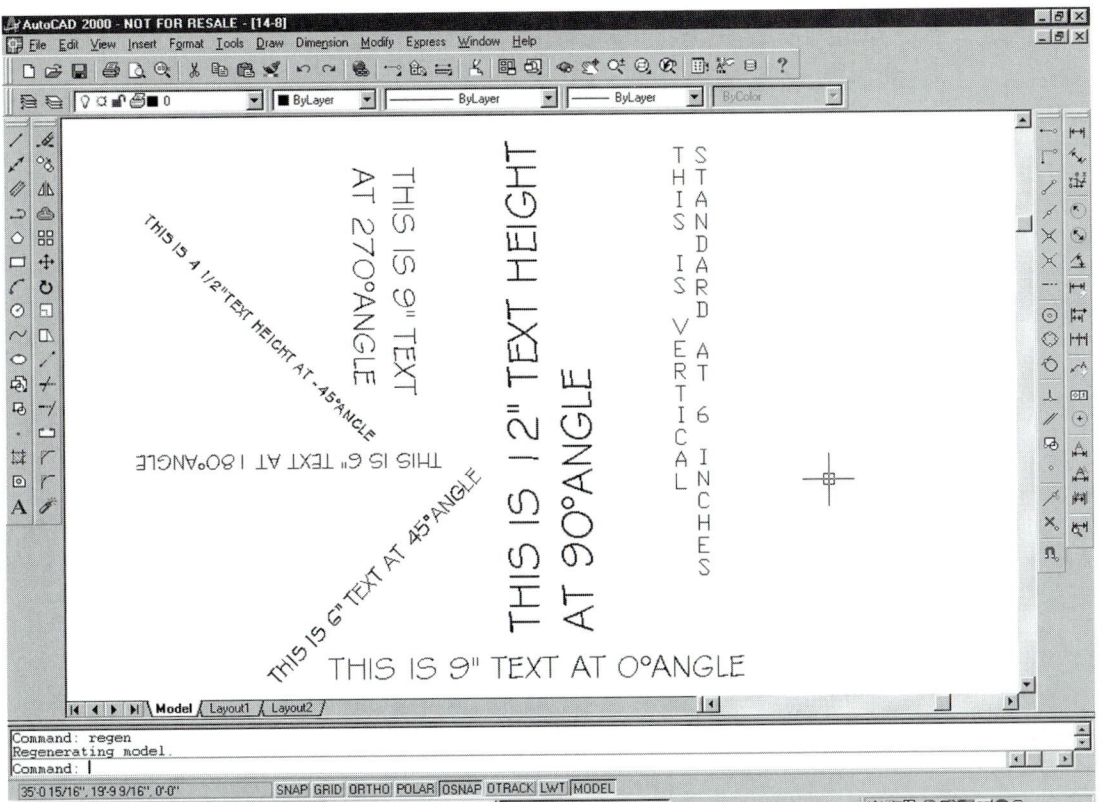

Control Code and Special Text	Symbol Created	Description
%%D	°	degree symbol
%%C	Ø	diameter symbol
%%O	—	overlining
%%U	—	underlining
%%P	±	plus and minus symbol
%%%	%	percent symbol

Note: The control code and the special character you enter will be displayed on the screen until you are finished with the text line and press the ~EnterKey~ twice.

14.4.2 Command Line Editing

When using the TEXT or the DTEXT commands, you can use the following keyboard entries to edit the text before placing it on the drawing:

- **UP ARROW KEY (↑):** Use the up arrow key to move backward through previously entered commands. Every time you press on this key, the cursor line will move up to the previous text line.

- **DOWN ARROW KEY (↓):** Use the down arrow key to move forward after using the up arrow key. This will allow you to move down from the previous commands.

- **LEFT ARROW KEY (←):** Use the left arrow key to move the cursor line left through the text lines. Position the cursor to the desired location and insert or remove letters or words that were missed or misspelled.

- **RIGHT ARROW KEY (→):** Use the right arrow key to move the cursor line back after using the left arrow key.

- **HOME:** Use the Home key to move the cursor line back to the beginning of the text line. This will move the cursor line to the left of the last text line entered.

FIGURE 14–9 The AutoCAD Text Window dialog box will display all existing text styles, including the Standard. It will show information such as font typeface, height, width factor, and obliquing angle.

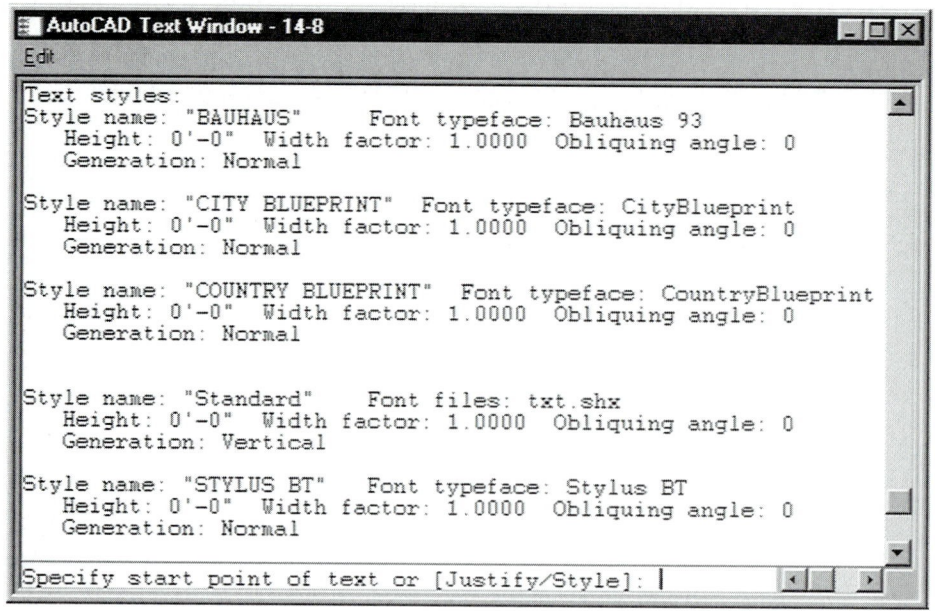

```
█ AutoCAD Text Window - 14-8                        _ □ ×
Edit

Text styles:
Style name: "BAUHAUS"       Font typeface: Bauhaus 93
    Height: 0'-0"  Width factor: 1.0000  Obliquing angle: 0
    Generation: Normal

Style name: "CITY BLUEPRINT"  Font typeface: CityBlueprint
    Height: 0'-0"  Width factor: 1.0000  Obliquing angle: 0
    Generation: Normal

Style name: "COUNTRY BLUEPRINT"  Font typeface: CountryBlueprint
    Height: 0'-0"  Width factor: 1.0000  Obliquing angle: 0
    Generation: Normal


Style name: "Standard"      Font files: txt.shx
    Height: 0'-0"  Width factor: 1.0000  Obliquing angle: 0
    Generation: Vertical

Style name: "STYLUS BT"     Font typeface: Stylus BT
    Height: 0'-0"  Width factor: 1.0000  Obliquing angle: 0
    Generation: Normal

Specify start point of text or [Justify/Style]: |
```

- **END:** Use the End key to move the cursor line to the end of the last text line entered.

- **DELETE:** Use the Delete key to delete characters or words located at the right side of the cursor line.

14.4.3 Command Line Options

The Justify and Style options can be used to set a justification or change the text style before specifying a start point for the text as follows:

Style: This option allows you to change the text style at the command line as opposed to selecting it from the Text Style dialog box. Enter **S** at the command prompt as follows:

```
Command: DTEXT ~EnterKey~
Current text style: "STYLUS BT" Text height: 6"
Specify start point of text or [Justify/Style]: S ~EnterKey~
Enter style name or [?] <STYLUS BT>: CITY BLUEPRINT (or enter the full
name of the text style you created previously)
Current text style: "CITY BLUEPRINT" Text height: 6"
Specify start point of text or [Justify/Style]: (select a starting point
for the new text style or enter an option)
```

If you want to see a listing of all the current text style in the drawing file, enter ? at the command prompt as follows:

```
Enter style name or [?] <STYLUS BT>: ? ~EnterKey~
Enter text style(s) to list <*>: ~EnterKey~
```

AutoCAD will display the AutoCAD Text Window dialog box as shown in Figure 14–9. This dialog box will display all existing text styles in the current drawing. Use the scroll bars to move up or down to see more styles. To close the dialog box press the ~F2Key~ located in the Keyboard. This dialog box can also be used to review command line history.

Justify: This option allows you to specify the text alignment based on text insertion point and the justification to other points on the screen. By default the text is left justified. This means that the starting point of the text is set to the lower left corner of the first letter. To use other justification options, enter **J** at the command prompt as follows:

```
Command: DTEXT ~EnterKey~
Current text style: "STYLUS BT" Text height: 6"
```

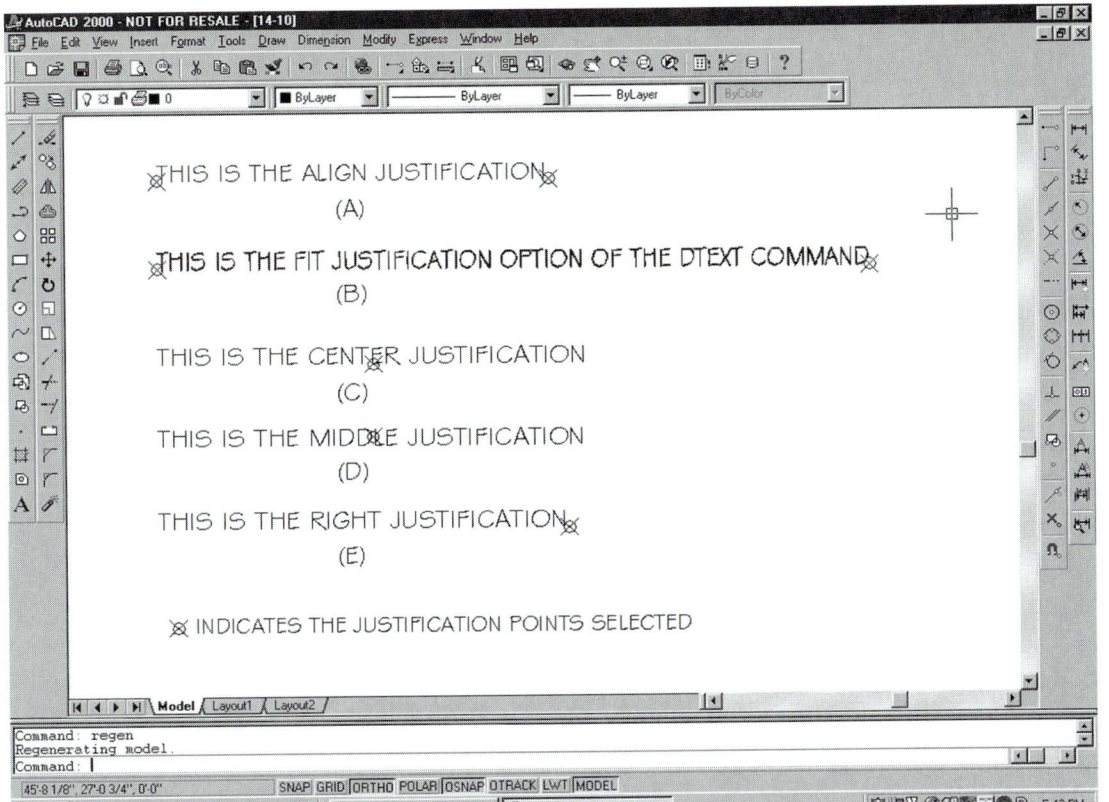

FIGURE 14–10 The first five justification options of the DTEXT and TEXT commands.

```
Specify start point of text or [Justify/Style]: J ~EnterKey~
Enter an option [Align/Fit/Center/Middle/Right/TL/TC/TR/ML/MC/MR/BL/BC/BR]:
```

ALIGN (A): This option allows you to select two points on the screen. The text height and width are adjusted as AutoCAD aligns the written text between the two points selected. See Figure 14–10A. The final text height and width depend on the distance between the two selected points and the length of the text string.

FIT (F): This option allows you to select two points on the screen. The text height you enter will be preserved along the points picked. AutoCAD fits the written text between the two points selected by adjusting the width between letters. See Figure 14–10B.

CENTER (C): This option allows you to center the text from a specified center point of text. AutoCAD will ask you to specify center point of text before allowing you to enter a text height. See Figure 14–10C.

MIDDLE (M): This option allows you to center the text both horizontally and vertically. See Figure 14–10D.

RIGHT (R): This option allows you to justify text at the lower right corner of a selected starting point. See Figure 14–10E.

There are nine more justification options that allow you to place text on the drawing in relation to top (T), middle (M), and bottom (B) with left (L), center (C), and right (R) subjustifications. For example, entering **MR** at the command prompt will allow you to justify to the Middle Bottom side of the text. Figure 14–11 shows the nine other justification options.

Tips: You can erase text characters or words by pressing the Backspace key while in the Enter text: prompt.

Tips: You can enter Justification options without entering J at the Specify start point of text or [Justify/Style]: prompt.

FIGURE 14–11 The TL, TC, TR, ML, MC, MR, BL, BC, and BR justification options. The X indicates the text insertion point.

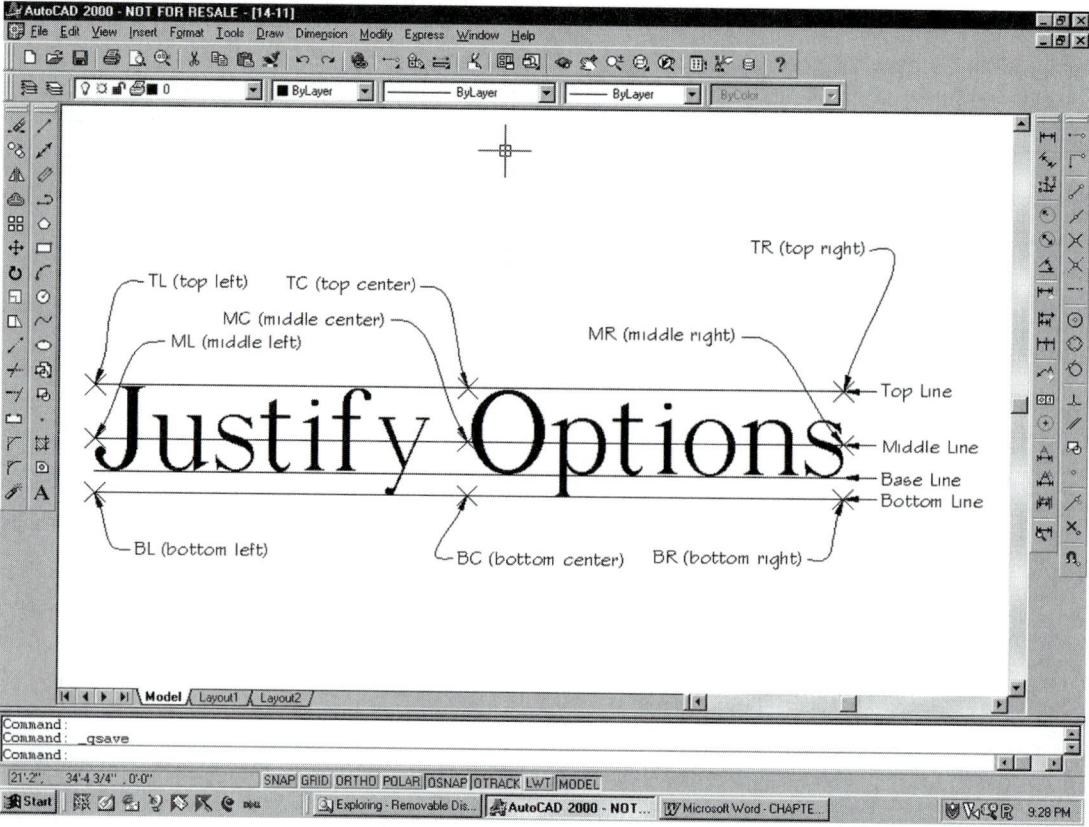

14.5 USING THE MTEXT COMMAND

The MTEXT (multiline text) command allows you to create multiline text objects that are part of a whole unit. You can access the MTEXT command by selecting the Multiline text button in the Draw toolbar, selecting Multiline Text. . . in the Text cascading menu of the Draw pull-down menu, or entering T, MT, or MTEXT at the command line. AutoCAD will ask you to specify the first and the second corners of the boundary box. The *text boundary box* is an area within which your text will be placed. The width of the text boundary box you create is the limit to the text width for each text string you create. The height of the text boundary box does not affect the text height you specify. It is automatically resized to fit the actual text height. The arrow in the bottom of the box indicates the direction of the text flow. The command line procedure is as follows:

```
Command: MTEXT ~EnterKey~
Current text style: "STYLUS BT" Text height: 6"
Specify first corner: (select the first corner)
Specify opposite corner or [Height/Justify/Line
spacing/Rotation/Style/Width]: (select the second corner)
```

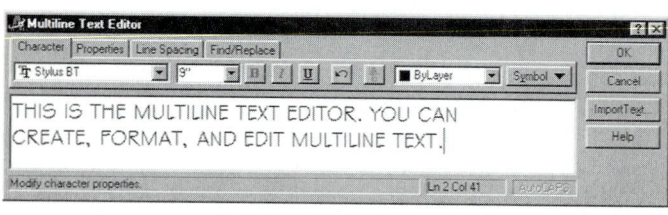

FIGURE 14–12 The Multiline Text Editor dialog box allows you to create, format, and edit multiline text.

After selecting the second corner the Multiline Text Editor dialog box will be displayed as shown in Figure 14–12.

The blinking cursor line indicates the start point of the text. A text string is created every time the cursor line moves down. The amount of text you can type before moving down automatically depends on the width of the text boundary box. You can press the ~EnterKey~ whenever you want to create a new text string. You can also use your cursor to relocate the flashing cursor line to select a new text line. When the Multiline text Editor box is filled with text, the previous text lines will be moved up so that new text line can be seen. You can use the up, down, left, and right arrows to move around the text. When you move your cursor to a section, cate-

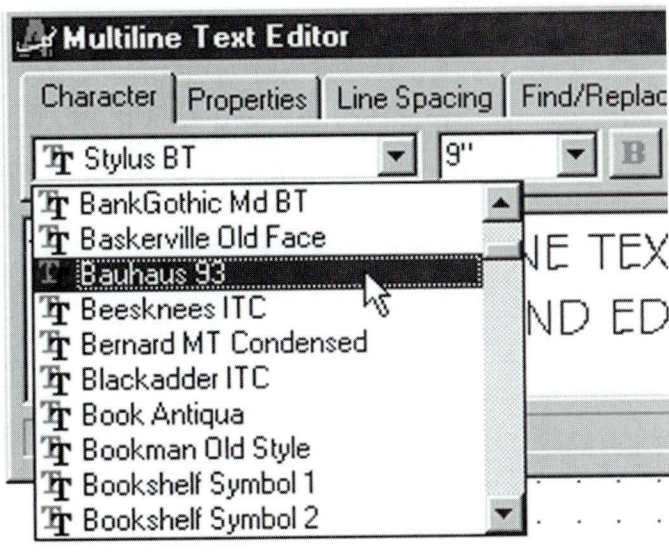

FIGURE 14–13 The Font drop-down list allows you to select a different text font to override the current text font.

gory, or button a tooltip appears showing you the description of the item. For example, move your cursor to the button that has the letter *U*, and the tooltip will show the word Underline.

There are four tabs in the Multiline Text Editor dialog box: Character, Properties, Line Spacing, Find/Replace.

Character: The Character tab has nine areas that allow you to edit and format the content and appearance of the text. The *Font* drop-down list shown in Figure 14–13 lists all available text fonts. This is similar to the Font Name: drop-down list in the Text Style dialog box (see Figure 14–5). Select a font from the list to override the font of the current text style. The *Font height* drop-down list allows you to override the current text height. Highlight the current value and enter a new text height. The *Bold* button allows you to create bold text. Not all fonts can be made bold. The *Italic* button allows you to create italic text. The .shx style fonts do not have this capability. The *Underline* button allows you to underline a text. The *Undo* button allows you to remove the previous text activity. The *Stack/Unstack* button allows you to stack a pair of characters to create a fraction. To create a horizontal fraction, enter a number followed by a forward slash (/) and another number such as 1/8 but do not press the ~EnterKey~ or the space bar. Then highlight the ⅛ with your cursor. The Stack/Unstack button will become active. Click on the Stack/Unstack button to convert the diagonal fraction with a horizontal fraction. This is called stacking. You can convert a horizontal fraction to a diagonal fraction using the same method. This is called un-stacking. You can also use the caret (^) symbol between text or numbers to remove the diagonal or horizontal fraction. This is called tolerance stacking. To create a tolerance stacking, enter a number(s) or a letter(s) followed by the caret (^) symbol and another number(s) or letter(s). Then highlight the items with your cursor and click on the Stack/Unstack button. You can also use the (#) symbol between text or numbers to create a diagonal fraction. For example, highlight an existing X#Y and click on the Stack/Unstack button to make it X/Y. The *Text color* is set to ByLayer by default. To change the color of the text string, select the desired color from the drop-down list. The *Insert symbol* button displays the symbols available to insert as shown in Figure 14–14. Select a symbol from the list to insert at the cursor line location. The Non-breaking Space joins two separate words. The *Other . . .* option displays the *Character Map* dialog box as shown in Figure 14–15. This dialog box allows you to find and insert special and unique characters into the Multiline Text Editor dialog box. To insert (copy) a character, select it from the list and click on the Select button. The selected character will be displayed inside the *Characters to copy:* text box. Click on the Copy button to copy the symbol to the Clipboard. Click on the Close button to close the dialog box. Inside the Multiline Text Editor dialog box, place the cursor line to the location you want to insert the selected character. Move your cursor on an open area inside the

FIGURE 14–14 The Insert Symbol options. Notice that you had to enter the control code and special text to create these symbols when using the DTEXT command.

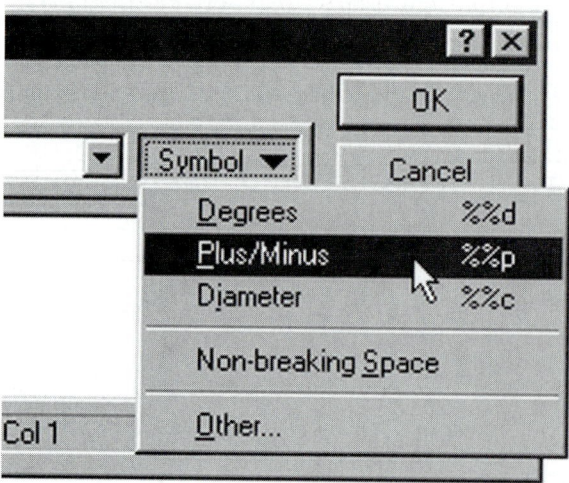

FIGURE 14–15 The Character Map dialog box allows you to copy special characters into the clipboard. You can then paste these characters into the Multiline Text Editor.

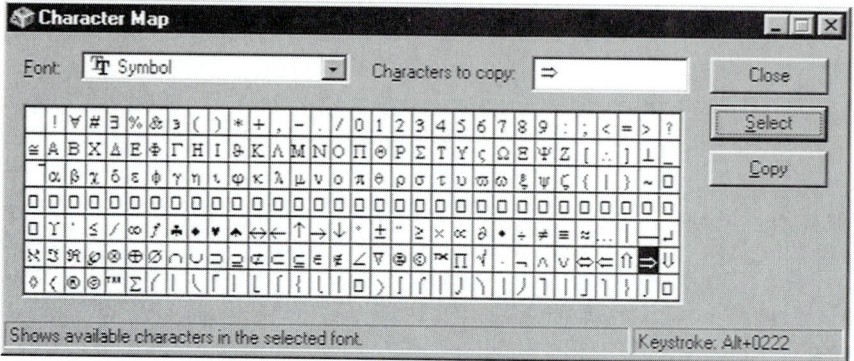

dialog box and right-click to display the *Edit text* shortcut menu. Select the *Paste* option to paste the character. Figure 14–16 shows the Σ symbol pasted between text. The *Import Text . . .* button allows you to import text from existing text files into the Multiline Text Editor.

Tips: Resize the Multiline Text Editor dialog box to see more or less of what you are typing.

Tips: You can copy text or special characters from different applications such as Microsoft Word and paste it into the Multiline Text Editor text box. The reverse of this concept is also true.

14.5.1   Assigning Different Text Heights

When using the Multiline Text Editor dialog box, you can specify a different text height for each text line or between words as follows:

1. Highlight the current text height inside the Font height list. Enter a new value such as 6. The cursor line will be flashing on the right side of 6.

2. Move your cursor and click on the location you want to create text with the new height. The cursor line will be flashing.

3. Enter desired text. The text will be created with the new text height.

4. Highlight the current text height inside the Font height list. Enter a new value such as 12. The cursor line will be flashing on the right side of 12.

5. Repeat the procedure described in step 2.

6. Enter the desired text. The text will be created with the new text height.

7. To display what you have written as text inside the drawing area, click on the OK button.

Figure 14–17 shows four different text heights (6″, 9″, 10″, and 12″) for three text lines. The fourth text line is the alphabet created by assigning 3″ for letter A, 4″ for letter B, 5″ for letter C, and

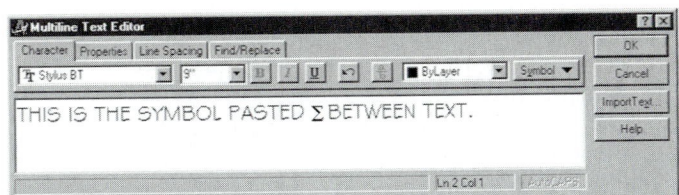

FIGURE 14–16 The Σ character is pasted between the text.

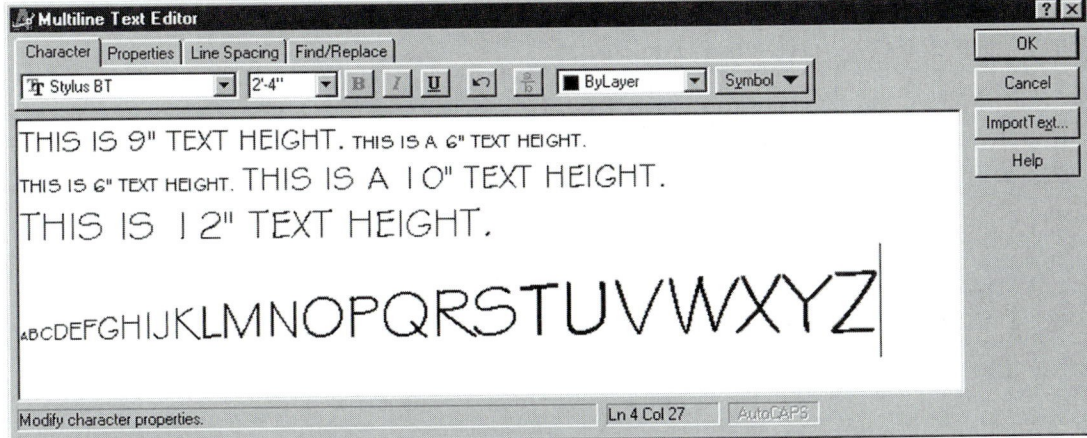

FIGURE 14–17 You can assign a different text height for each text string or even to each letter.

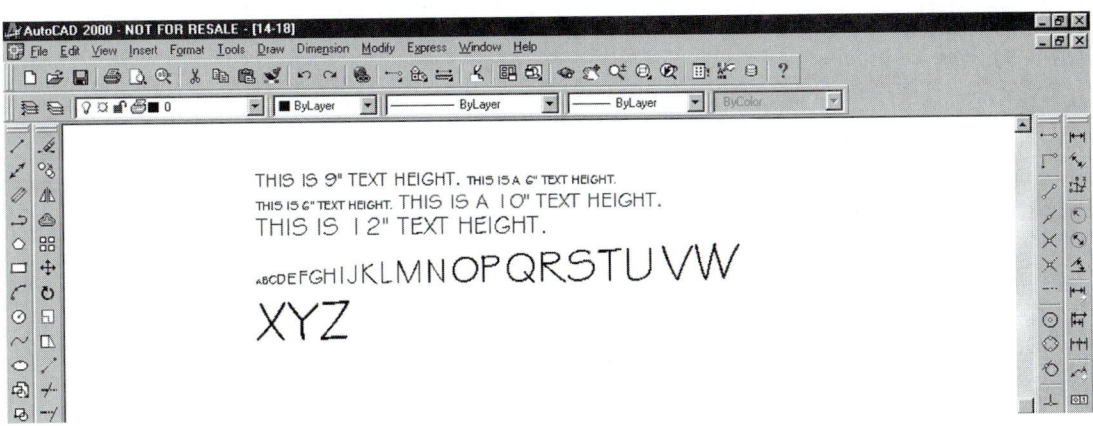

FIGURE 14–18 When you click on the OK button in the Multiline Text Editor dialog box, everything you typed will be displayed in the drawing area.

so on. Letter Z has a text height of 2′-4″ as indicated inside the Font height. Figure 14–18 shows the four text lines placed inside the drawing area.

Every time you enter a new text height, AutoCAD will save it in the Font height drop-down list. Click on the down arrow and scroll up or down the list to find the text height already entered. The partial text height list is shown in Figure 14–19.

> *Note: In addition to assigning different text heights for each text line, you can also assign a different color and use any of the available options. Just make sure that the cursor line is flashing at the new location after changing the text height.*

Properties: The Properties tab allows you to change the current text style, justification, width, and rotation. The Properties tab is shown in Figure 14–20. The *Style* drop-down list displays the current text style. To display all existing styles in the drawing file, click on the down arrow and use the scroll bars. **Selecting a different text style from the list will change all the text inside the dialog box.** To change the text style of an existing text string, select the *Character* tab and highlight the text you want to alter. From the Font drop-down list select the corresponding font style. You can select any of the font styles available in the list, but it may not correspond with the

FIGURE 14–19 The Font height drop-down list will display all text heights entered while working inside the Multiline Text Editor dialog box.

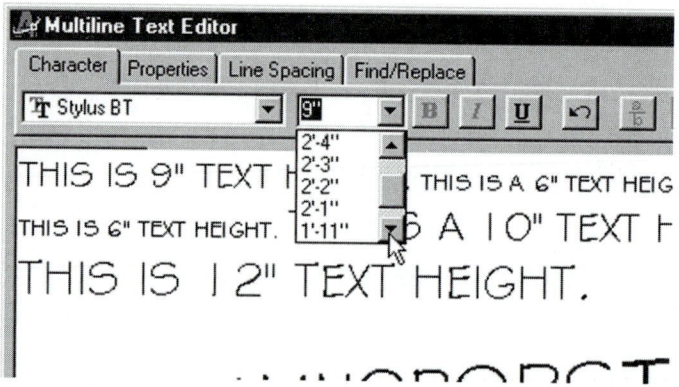

FIGURE 14–20 The Properties tab of the Multiline Text Editor.

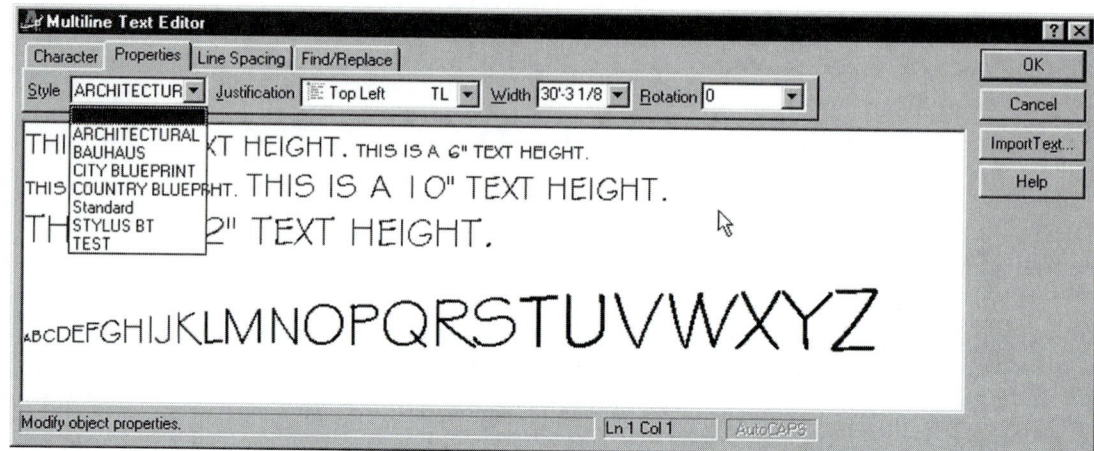

FIGURE 14–21 The Justification drop-down list.

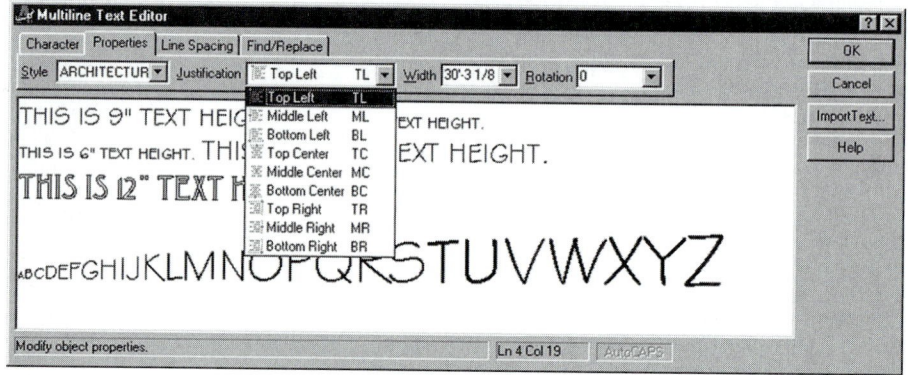

text style and font you created using the Text Style dialog box. The *Justification* drop-down list allows you to assign a new justification for the text. Figure 14–21 shows the options for the justification. In addition to the description and the two-letter abbreviation, there is an icon placed in front of the option. The justification occurs in relation to the text boundary box. The *Width* drop-down list displays the current and available text boundary box widths as shown in Figure 14–22. If you select the (*no wrap*) option, you will not be able to start a new line automatically after reaching the end of a line. The *Rotation* drop-down list allows you to select a rotation angle for the entire text in the window. See Figure 14–23. The rotation does not take effect until you select the OK button.

Line Spacing: The Line Spacing tab shown in Figure 14–24 allows you to specify the spacing between lines of text. The *At Least* line spacing option (default) adjusts the line spacing based on the largest text character. The *Exactly* line spacing option forces the line spacing to be the same

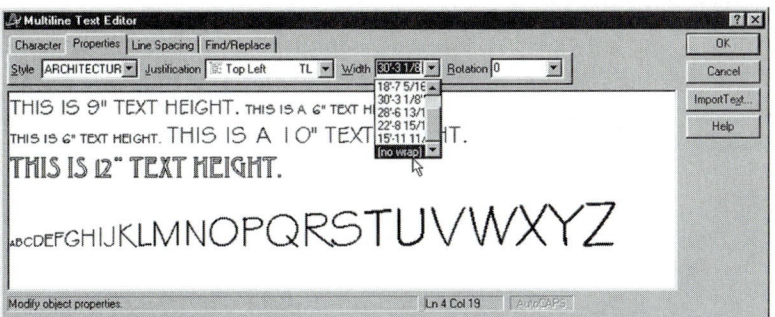

FIGURE 14–22 The Width drop-down list.

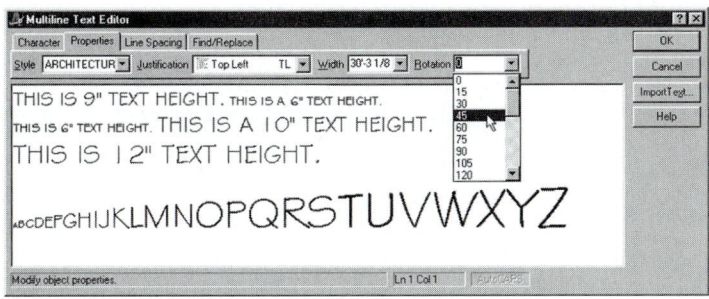

FIGURE 14–23 The Rotation drop-down list.

FIGURE 14–24 The Line Spacing drop-down list with its two options.

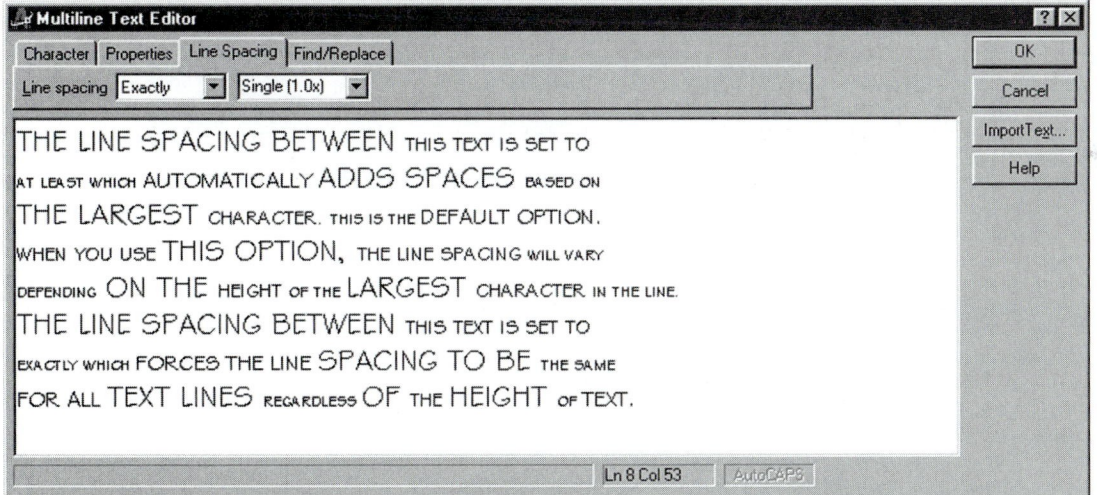

FIGURE 14–25 An example of the At Least and the Exactly Line Spacing options.

for all text lines. Figure 14–25 shows an example of the At Least and Exactly line spacing options. The *Single (1.0x)* option allows you to specify the vertical distance from the bottom of one text line to the bottom of the next text line as single spacing. The default distance is 1.66 multiplied by the height of the text characters. The *1.5 Lines (1.5x)* option provides one-and-a-half line spacing between text lines. The *Double (2.0x)* option provides double spacing between text lines. You can also type a number followed by × for a multiple of single spacing, or enter 1 for spacing to be exactly 1.0 units, regardless of the text height.

Find/Replace: This tab allows you to find and replace text using the words and characters in the current text. Enter a word inside the *Find* text box to search for. Enter a word to replace the word being searched inside the *Replace with* text box. Click on the *Find* button. AutoCAD will find and highlight the word inside the Multiline Text Editor. Click on the *Replace* button to replace the word. Click on the *Replace* button again to find and replace more of the same word. Click on the *OK* button when done. Placing a checkmark inside the *Match Case* check box matches the case of the text. For example, if you check this option when searching for the word STRUCTURAL, AutoCAD will precisely find STRUCTURAL and will skip words such as Structural and structural. Placing a checkmark inside the *Whole Word* allows AutoCAD to look for whole words as opposed to partial words. Figure 14–26 shows an example of the Find and Replace operation.

After the text is placed in the drawing, you can use the FIND command or the Find and Replace button in the Standard toolbar to search for specific text and replace it with alternative text. The Find and Replace button is shown in Figure 14–27. When you click on this button, or enter FIND at the command line, the *Find and Replace* dialog box will be displayed as shown in Figure 14–28.

FIGURE 14–26   Using the Find/Replace tab.

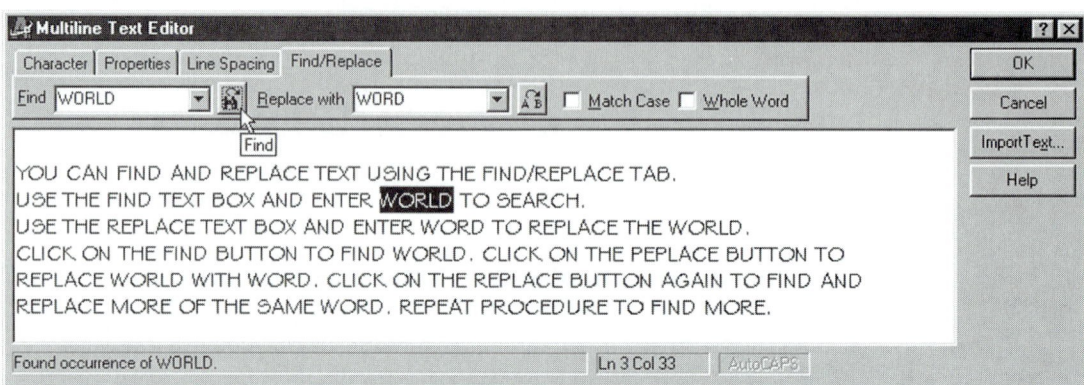

FIGURE 14–27   The Find and Replace button will display the Find and Replace dialog box.

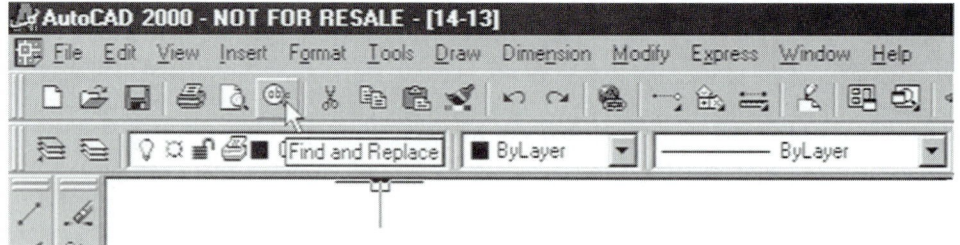

FIGURE 14–28   The Find and Replace dialog box allows you to search for specific text strings or a word and replace it with alternative text.

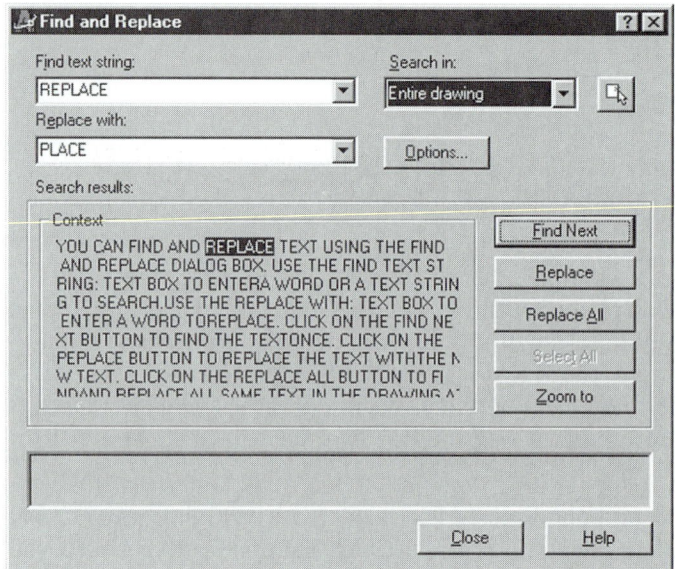

■ **EXERCISE 14–3:** *The following step-by-step procedure will give you a general idea on how to find and replace a text string.*

Step #1: Click on the *Options . . .* button to define the types of objects you want to search for. The Options . . . button will display the *Find and Replace Options* dialog box as shown in Figure 14–29. This dialog box allows you to define object types and words you want to find.

Step #2: Inside the *Find text string:* drop-down text box, enter the text you want to search for. The list also contains the six most recently used words.

Step #3: Inside the *Replace with:* drop-down text box, enter the text that will replace found text. You can also select one of the most recently used words from the list.

Step #4: Use the *Search in:* drop-down list to search the *Entire drawing* or only the Current selection. If there is no current selection, the Entire drawing will be the default. You can also click on the *Select Objects* button to select text objects in the current drawing. This will temporarily close the dialog box for you to select the text objects.

Step #5: Click on the *Find* button. The first occurrence will be displayed in the *Context* area. Notice that the Find button is replaced by the *Find Next* button.

Step #6: Click on the *Replace* button to view and replace each found text. Click on the *Replace All* to find and replace all instances that match the search format.

Step #7: When the Status field indicates that all text has been replaced, click on the *Close* button to close the dialog box.

Congratulations! You have successfully used the above steps to find and replace a text string.

Tips: You can use the Find and Replace dialog box to also find and replace dimension text, attribute text, Hypertext URL, and Hypertext name.

Tips: Double-click on the AutoCAPS button to enter text in uppercase.

14.5.2 AutoStack Options

You can automate the fractions entered in the Multiline Text Editor using the AutoStack Properties dialog box. Inside the Multiline Text Editor, enter a fraction such as 1/8 and press the space bar. The AutoStack Properties dialog box will be displayed as shown in Figure 14–30. Place a checkmark inside the *Enable AutoStacking* check box to enable AutoStacking. Placing a checkmark inside the *Remove leading blank* check box will remove the space between fraction and whole number. Placing a checkmark inside the *Convert it to a diagonal fraction* radio button will convert the fraction to a diagonal format. Placing a check mark inside the *Convert it to a horizontal fraction* radio button will convert the fraction to a horizontal format. When you enter a

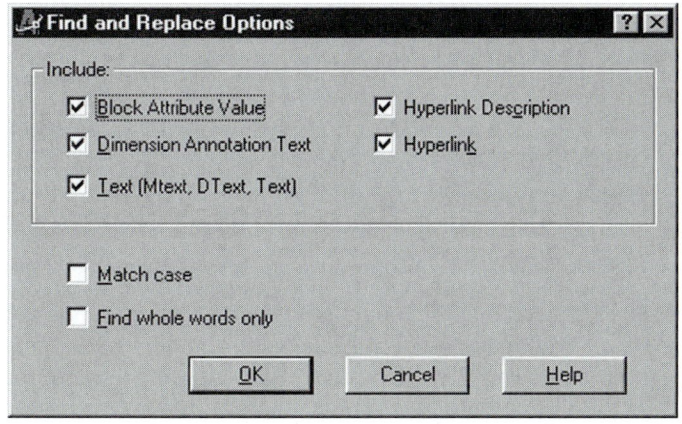

FIGURE 14–29 The Find and Replace Options dialog box.

FIGURE 14–30 The AutoStack Properties dialog box.

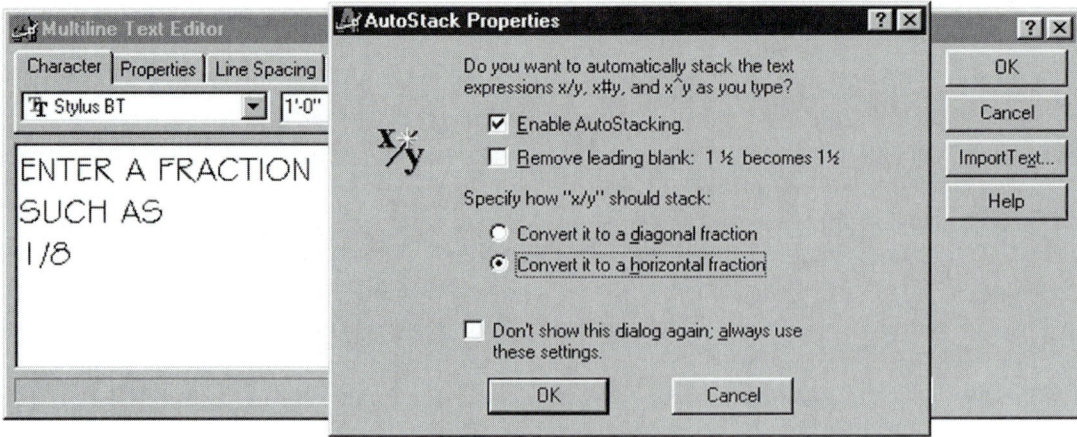

FIGURE 14–31 Examples of the AutoStacking options.

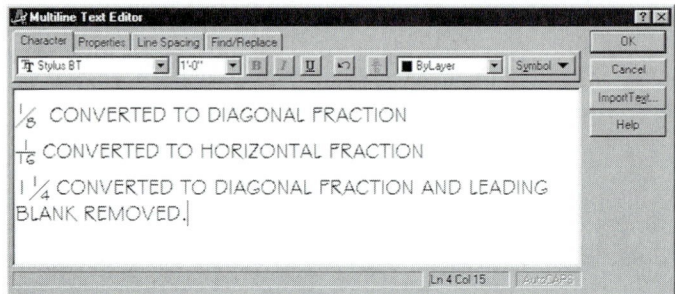

fraction followed by the space bar or a non-numeric character such as ″, the AutoStack dialog box will appear. Check the desired option and click on the OK button. The next time a fraction is entered, it will automatically be stacked in the selected format. Figure 14–31 shows examples of each option.

14.6 USING THE MTEXT SHORTCUT MENU

Inside the Multiline Text Editor dialog box, you can right-click to display a shortcut menu. When you highlight a text and right-click, a shortcut menu will be displayed as shown in Figure 14–32. The eight options are as follows:

UNDO: Selecting this option will remove the last operation. You can select Undo again to bring back the operation removed by undo.

CUT: Selecting this option will remove the selected text from the text window and place it in the Clipboard.

COPY: Selecting this option will copy the selected text to the Clipboard.

PASTE: Use this option to place text from the Clipboard into the text window. The text object(s) will be pasted at the text cursor location. Any item in the Clipboard can be pasted into the text window.

SELECT ALL: Use this option if you want to select the entire text in the text window.

CHANGE CASE: Use this option to change the selected text to all uppercase or lowercase letters.

REMOVE FORMATTING: Use this option to remove font, height, bold, italic, and underline formatting that is not part of the original text style from the selected text.

COMBINE PARAGRAPHS: Use this option to combine two paragraphs into one.

To stack an existing fraction or to unstack a stacked fraction, highlight the fraction only without the inches or feet mark and right-click. A shortcut menu will be displayed as shown in Figure 14–33. Select the Unstack option to unstack. You can stack a fraction similarly by selecting the Stack option from the shortcut menu as shown in Figure 14–34.

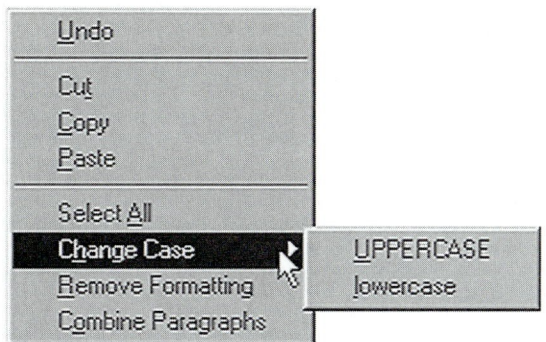

FIGURE 14–32 The right-click shortcut menu will appear after you right-click on the highlighted text.

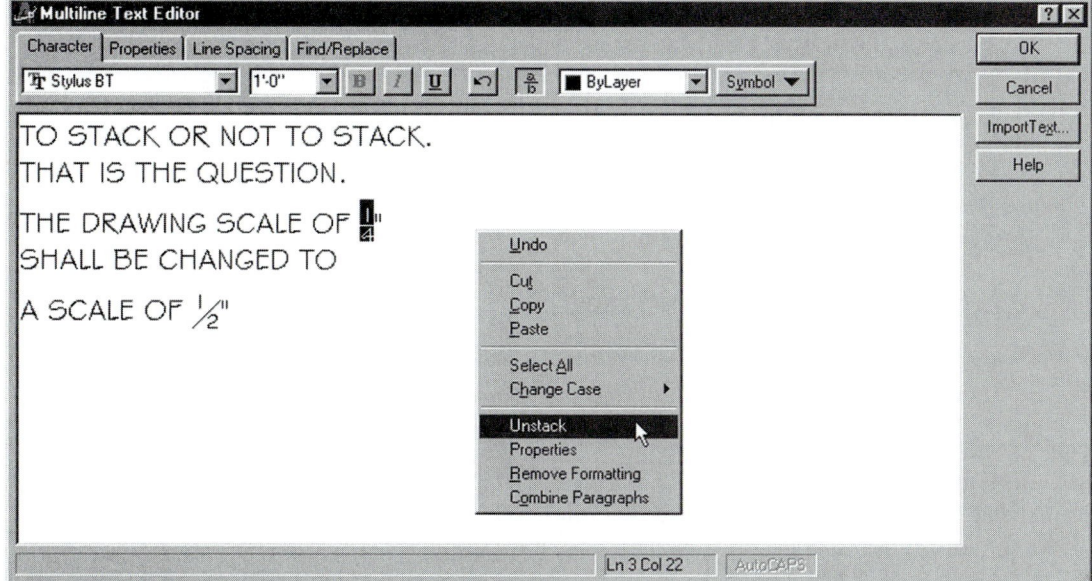

FIGURE 14–33 Using the right-click shortcut menu to unstack a fraction.

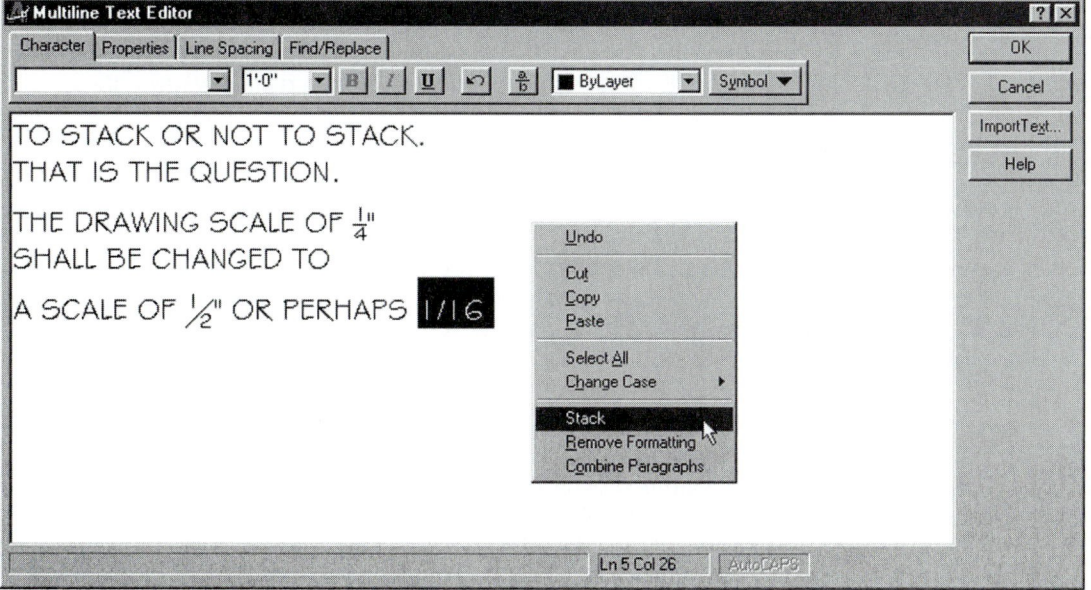

FIGURE 14–34 Using the right-click shortcut menu to stack a fraction.

FIGURE 14–35 The
Stack Properties dialog
box.

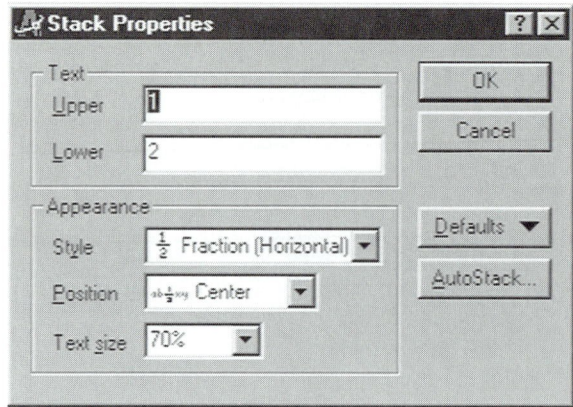

When you select the Properties option from the shortcut menu, the stack properties dialog box will be displayed as shown in Figure 14–35. Use the *Upper* and *Lower Text* boxes to edit fraction values. Use the *Style* drop-down list to select Diagonal, Horizontal, and Tolerance options. Use the *Position* drop-down list to select Top, Center, or Bottom vertical alignment position option. Use the *Text Size* drop-down list to specify percentage of text size. Clicking on the *Defaults* button will save the settings as defaults, or restore original defaults. Clicking on the *AutoStack...* button will display the AutoStack properties dialog box.

14.7 USING THE QTEXT COMMAND

Text creation is a complex process in AutoCAD. It requires more time to regenerate than line objects because each text object is composed of very small individual line segments. If your drawing contains excessive amount of text, the drawing or editing process will slow down because of text regeneration time. The QTEXT (quick text) command allows you to convert all current text on the screen to empty rectangles so that AutoCAD will skip text regeneration. The empty rectangles are created to match the text height of each text string. To activate the quick text command, enter QTEXT at the command line as follows:

```
Command: QTEXT ~EnterKey~
Enter mode [ON/OFF] <OFF>: ON ~EnterKey~
Command: REGEN ~EnterKey~
```

All text in the drawing will be displayed as empty rectangles as shown in Figure 14–36. To turn text back to normal, turn off the QTEXT and enter REGEN at the command line.

Tips: The length of QTEXT rectangles does not necessarily equal the actual length of text.

14.8 EDITING TEXT

You can edit text created with DTEXT, TEXT, and MTEXT commands using the DDEDIT command. The DDEDIT command is accessed by selecting Text ... from the Modify pull-down menu, by clicking on the Edit Text button in the Modify II toolbar, or by entering ED or DDEDIT at the command line. You can also select a text, right-click, and select Text Edit ... from the shortcut menu. The command line procedure is as follows:

```
Command: ED ~EnterKey~
DDEDIT
Select an annotation object or [Undo]: (select a single line text to edit)
```

The Edit Text dialog box will appear as shown in Figure 14–37. Use the arrow keys to navigate through the text string and use the Delete key to remove unwanted text. If you select a text created with the MTEXT command or select a dimension text or a leader text, the Multiline Text Editor dialog box will appear as shown in Figure 14–38. The blinking brackets (< >) represent the selected text. You can either use the Delete button in the keyboard to delete the contents of

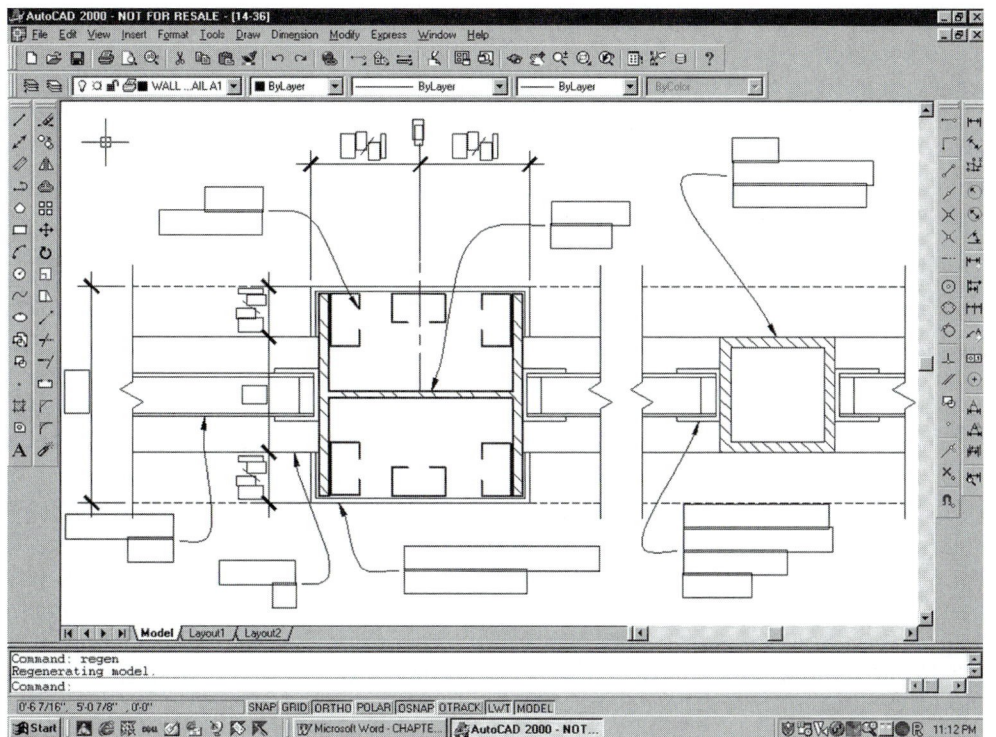

FIGURE 14–36 The QTEXT command allows you to display text into rectangles that redraw and regenerate faster than text.

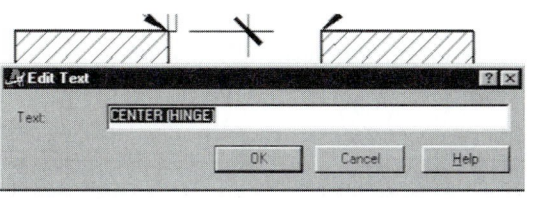

FIGURE 14–37 The Edit Text dialog box.

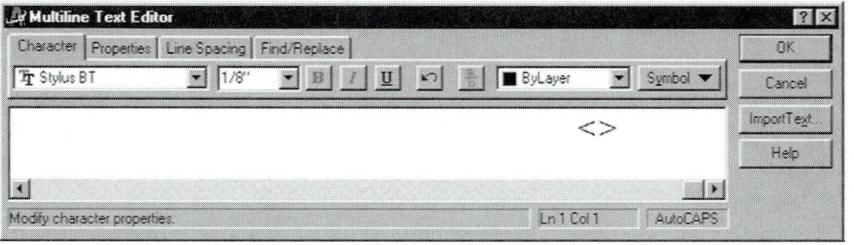

FIGURE 14–38 The Multiline Text Editor dialog box with blinking brackets (< >).

the selected text or enter new text before and/or after it. Use the arrow keys to go over the < >. When done, click on the OK button.

> *Tips: Use the Properties window to edit all text in one continuous operation. Use the Text category to change text properties. Use the Geometry category to change text insertion points. Use the Misc category to change text style effects.*

> *Tips: General Notes or text that are reused can be saved as a separate file or turned into a Wblock so that they do not have to be retyped with each use.*

14.9 EXPRESS TEXT TOOLS

The Express Text toolbar shown in Figure 14–39 has four text tool buttons that can help increase productivity when editing or modifying text. The *Text Fit* button allows you to select a text to change its length to fit inside a specific box or rectangle.

■ **EXERCISE 14–4:** *The following step-by-step exercise will allow you to fit the LIVING SPACE text inside the rectangle shown in Figure 14–39.*

Step #1: Open the EXE14-2.dwg file.

Step #2: Access the Express Text toolbar.

Step #3: Click on the Text Fit button and use the following command line procedure:

Select text to stretch or shrink: *(select the text)*

Specify end point or [Start point]: *(select a point inside the rectangle toward the lower right corner)*

Congratulations! You have successfully used the Text Fit button. The selected text will be shrunk and fit inside the rectangle as shown in Figure 14–39. If the text is small and the rectangle is large, then AutoCAD will stretch the text. This procedure only works with the single-line text. You can also enter TEXTFIT at the command line or select Text Fit from the Text cascading menu of the Express pull-down menu. Save the changes.

The *Text Mask* button allows you to mask entities from behind text. It puts a wipeout under text to remove portion of other objects underneath.

■ **EXERCISE 14–5:** *The following step-by-step exercise will allow you to wipe out portions of the joist wiring that the text crosses as shown in Figure 14–40.*

Step #1: Open the EXE14-3.dwg file.

Step #2: Access the Express Text toolbar.

FIGURE 14–39 The Text Fit express text tool allows you to stretch or shrink text.

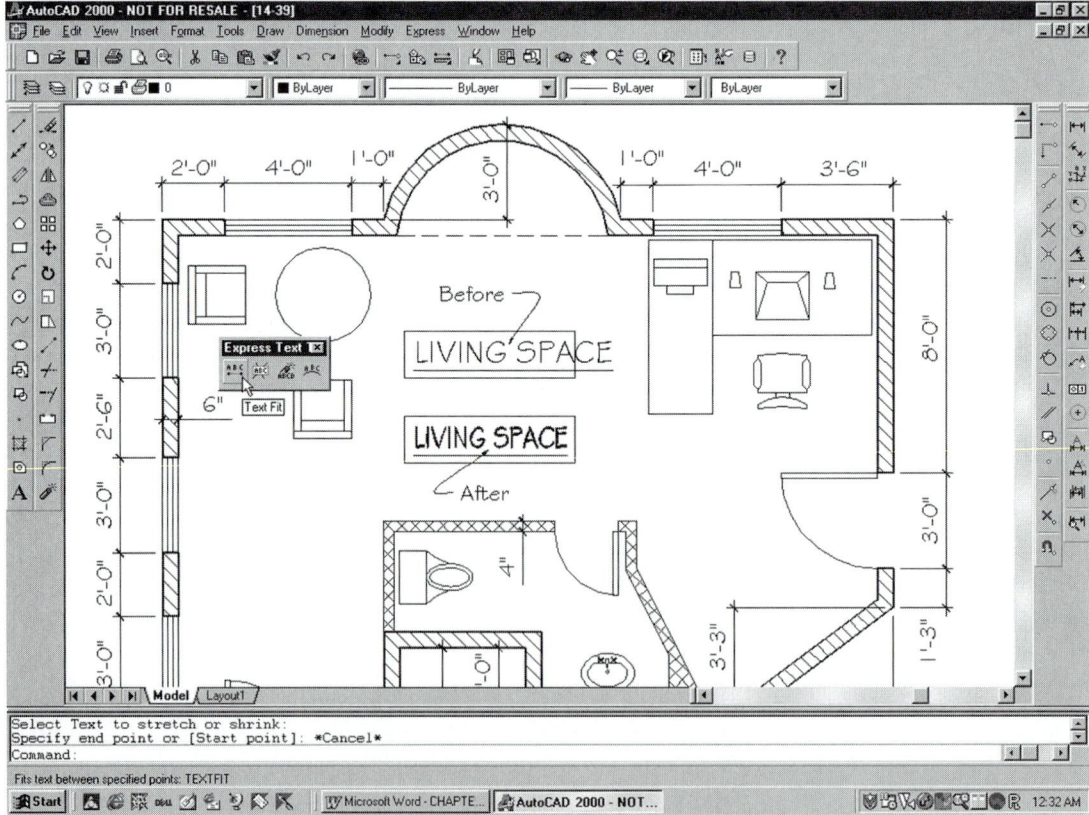

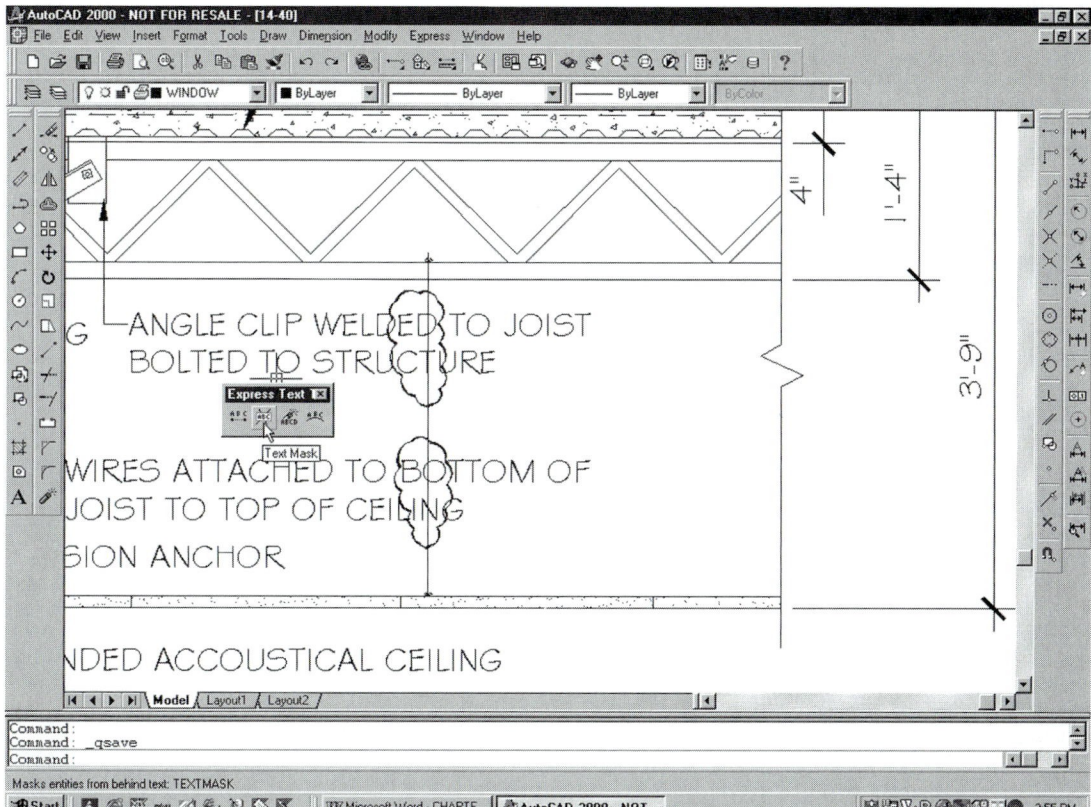

FIGURE 14–40 The Text Mask express tool allows you to mask text objects with a wipeout to block out other objects underneath.

Step #3: Click on the Text Mask button and use the following command line procedure:

Current settings: Offset factor = 0.3500, Mask type = Wipeout

Select text objects to mask or [Masktype/Offset]: *(select the text objects)*

Select text objects to mask or [Masktype/Offset]: ~EnterKey~

Wipeout created.

2 text items have been masked with a wipeout.

Congratulations! You have successfully used the Text Mask button to wipe out portions of the joist wiring. At the end of the procedure the text objects selected will be masked with a wipeout as shown in Figure 14–41. The Offset option determines how far you want the mask to extend. The Masktype option offers a choice between a wipeout, solid fill, or a three-dimensional face. The Frame option of the wipeout is automatically turned off with the Text Mask operation. You can also enter TEXTMASK at the command line or select Text Mask from the Text cascading menu of the Express pull-down menu. Do not save the changes.

Note: The Text Mask wipeout becomes an integral part of the text after it is created. This means that the text and wipeout will move together if you move the text.

The *Explode Text* button allows you to convert text objects of either single or multiple text into individual pieces. For example, you can edit individual pieces of text after exploding the text shown in Figure 14–42 as follows:

```
Click on the Explode Text button and use the following command line
procedure:
Select text to be exploded: (select the single-line or multi-line text to
be exploded)
1 text object(s) have been exploded to lines.
The line objects have been placed on layer 0.
```

FIGURE 14–41 The selected text objects after the Text Mask operation. Notice that the portions of the joist wiring have been blocked out.

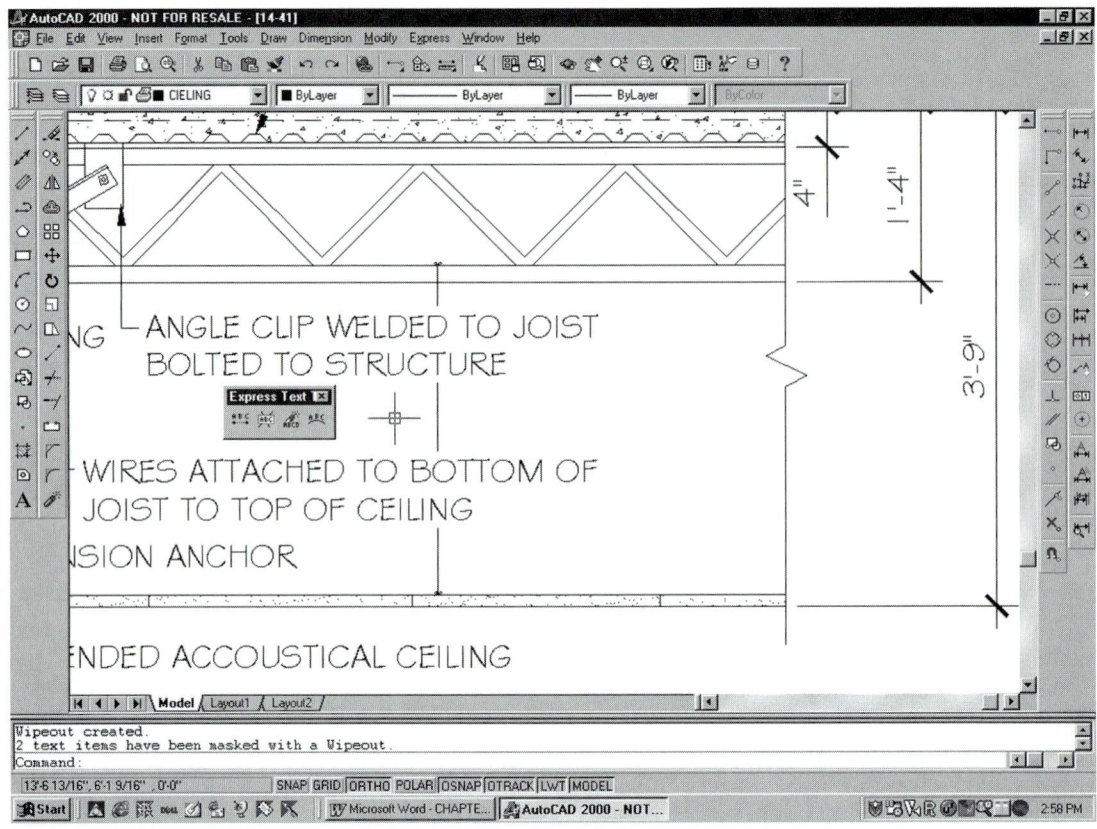

FIGURE 14–42 Using the Explode Text express tool. Notice the solid fill is removed from the individual text outlines, and each letter is turned into individual pieces. These pieces can be moved from the letter, or letters can be moved from the text.

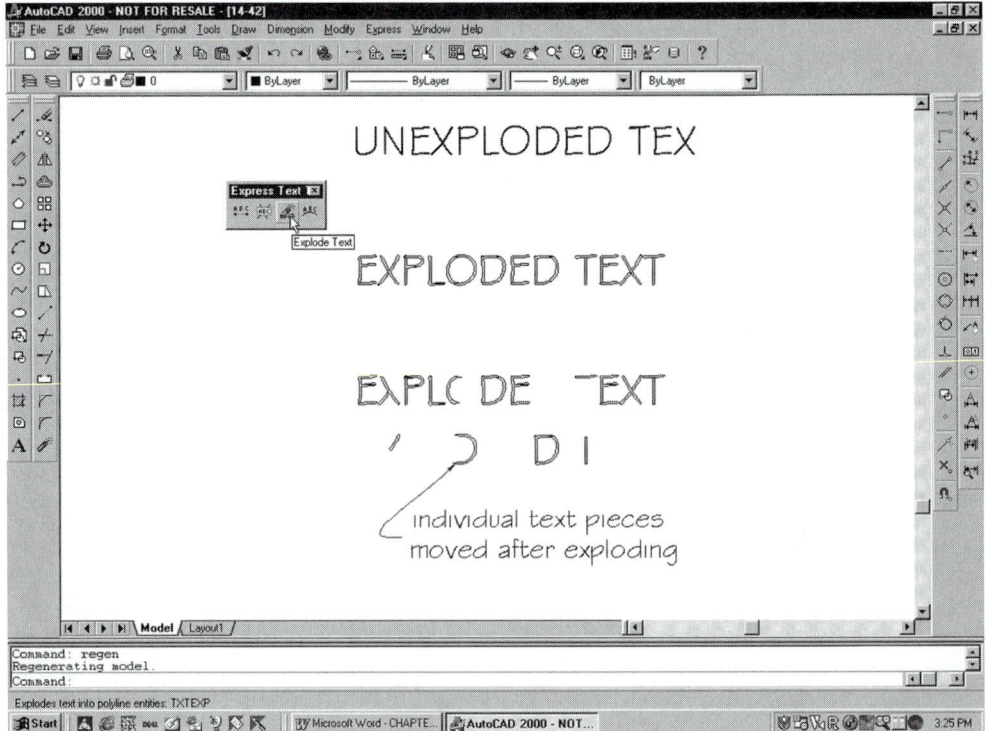

You can also enter TXTEXP at the command line or select Explode Text from the Text cascading menu of the Express pull-down menu.

Tips: You cannot use the EXPLODE command to explode text objects.

The *Arc Aligned Text* button allows you to create text around the selected arc.

■ **EXERCISE 14–6:** *The following step-by-step exercise will allow you to create text around the existing arc as shown in Figure 14–43.*

Step #1: Open the EXE14-4.dwg file.

Step #2: Access the Express Text toolbar.

Step #3: Click on the Arc Aligned Text button and use the following command line procedure:

ArcText application loaded.

Type ATEXT or ARCTEXT to start.

Select an Arc or an ArcAlignedText: *(select the existing arc)*

The ArcAlignedText Workshop – Create dialog box will be displayed as shown in Figure 14–43.

Step #4: Inside the Text: edit box, type THIS IS ARC ALIGNED TEXT 6″ HIGH.

Step #5: Under the Properties category, enter 6 as the Text height and Width factor of 1. Inside the Offset from arc: text box enter 2. This is the distance from the arc to the bottom of the text. Inside the Offset from left: text box enter 1. This is the distance from the left endpoint of the arc to the text start point. Inside the Offset from right: text box enter 1. This is the distance from the right endpoint of the arc to the text endpoint. You can assign a color to the text by selecting a color from the ByLayer drop-down list.

Step #6: Click on the OK button.

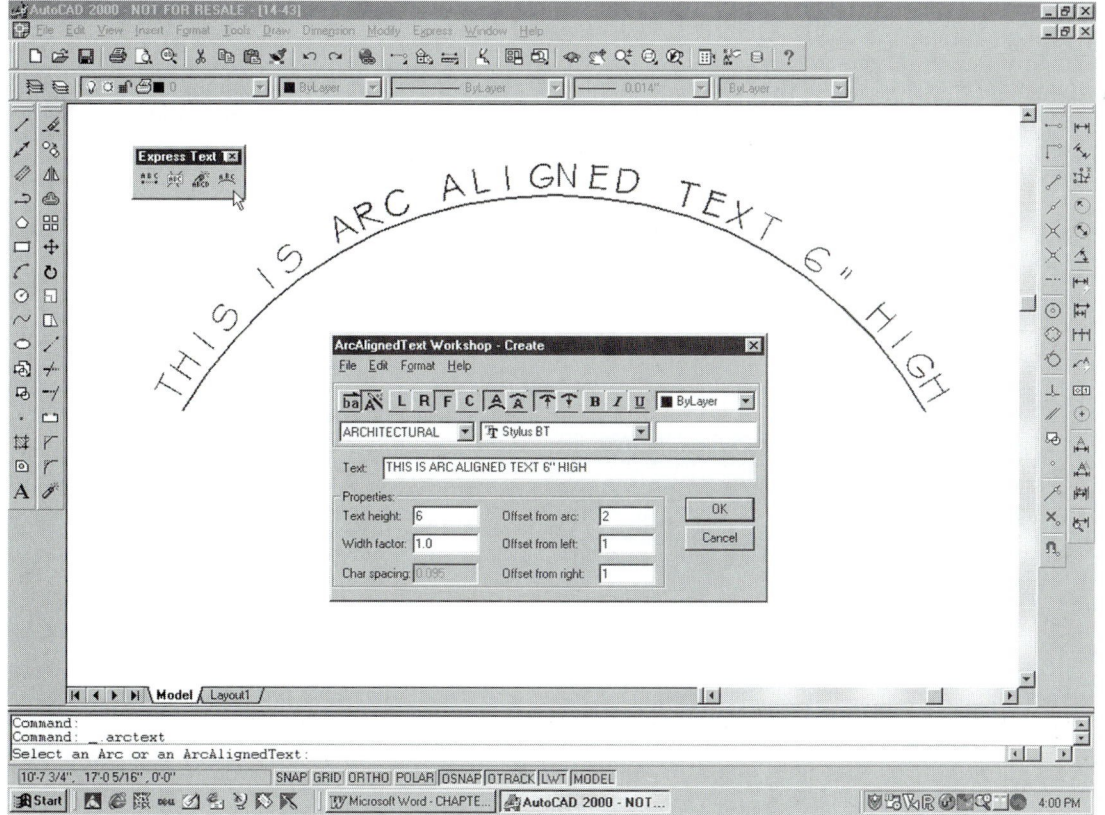

FIGURE 14–43 The Arc Aligned Text allows you to create text around an existing arc.

Congratulations! You have successfully created a text to fit around the arc. You can also enter ARCTEXT at the command line or select Arc Aligned Text from the Text cascading menu in the Express pull-down menu. This will work only if you have an arc in the drawing. Use the ARCTEXT command to edit arc-aligned text. Do not save the changes.

Caution: The ARCTEXT command does not work with a full circle.

14.9.1 Converting Single-Line Text to Multi-Line Text

You can use the TXT2MTX (Convert Text to MTEXT) command to change a single-line text to a multiline text. You can select more than one single-line text to convert them to a multiline text. If they are separated, they will be grouped together with the first single-line text object selected. This command will work on any text objects created with the TEXT or DTEXT commands. You can also access this command by selecting Convert to MTEXT from the Text cascading menu of the Express pull-down menu. The command line procedure is as follows:

```
Command: TXT2MTXT ~EnterKey~
Convert a selection set of texts into a single mtext.
Select text objects, or [Options] <Options>:
Select objects: (select one or more single-line text)
Select objects: ~EnterKey~
4 Text objects removed, 1 MText object added.
```

The four text objects will be converted to multi-line text.

If you press ~EnterKey~ at the Select objects: prompt, the Text to MText Options dialog box will be displayed as shown in Figure 14–44. The Text ordering area contains two options. Placing a checkmark inside the *Selection set order* radio button will merge the selected text objects into a single Mtext object in the order in which you select them. Placing a checkmark inside the *Sort top-down* radio button will merge the selected text objects into a single Mtext object in order of descending value. Placing a checkmark inside the *Create word-wrap MText* check box will add spaces at the end of each line to make a uniform paragraph of word-wrapped Mtext.

Tips: If you select a set of text objects created with the DTEXT command or with successive TEXT command, selecting the Sort top-down radio button and deselecting the Create word-wrap MText check box will produce the most visually similar and consistent text.

FIGURE 14–44   The Text to MText Options dialog box.

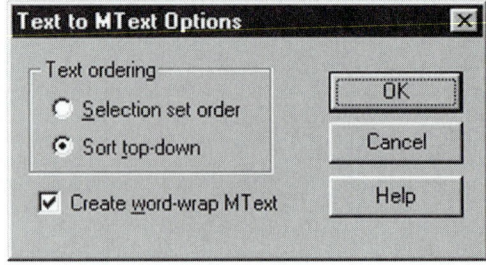

THIS SINGLE-LINE TEXT WILL BE CONVERTED TO MULTI-LINE TEXT USING THE TXT2MTXT COMMAND.

REVIEW QUESTIONS

1. What is the function of the STYLE command?
2. When using the Text Style dialog box why is it important to have the text Height set at 0.0000 units?
3. If the drawing scale is 3/8″ =1′ - 0″ and if the actual plotted text height in full scale is to be ³⁄₁₆″, what would the text height be?
4. What command is used to create single-line text?
5. What command is used to create multiline text?
6. What control code and special text is used to create the degrees symbol?
7. Which Justify option of the DTEXT command allows you to center the text both horizontally and vertically?
8. Which tab of the Multiline Text Editor dialog box allows you to change the current text style?
9. What is the function of the Find/Replace tab of the Multiline Text Editor dialog box?
10. What is the function of the AutoStack Properties dialog box?
11. What command is used to convert text into empty rectangles?
12. What does the flashing brackets (<>) represent inside the Multiline Text Editor dialog box?
13. What is the function of the Text Mask button in the Express Text toolbar?
14. What happens to a text after it has been exploded with the TXTEXP command?

PROBLEMS

1. Create a new drawing and call it *DOOR SCHEDULE*. Use Architectural Units and establish drawing Limits of 22′, 17′. Look at Figure 14–45 and use the LINE command to draw the schedule outline. Draw the rectangle 17′ by 15′. Offset the top line 12″. Offset the second line 6″ to create the 28 rows. Offset the left vertical line 36″ to create the first column. Create the second column line 60″. Create the third column line 24″. Create the fourth column line 60″. Create a new text style and call it ARCHITECTURAL. Use the Stylus BT font style. Use the new text style and the DTEXT command to create the DOOR SCHEDULE at 5″ height. Create the rest of the text at 3″ height.

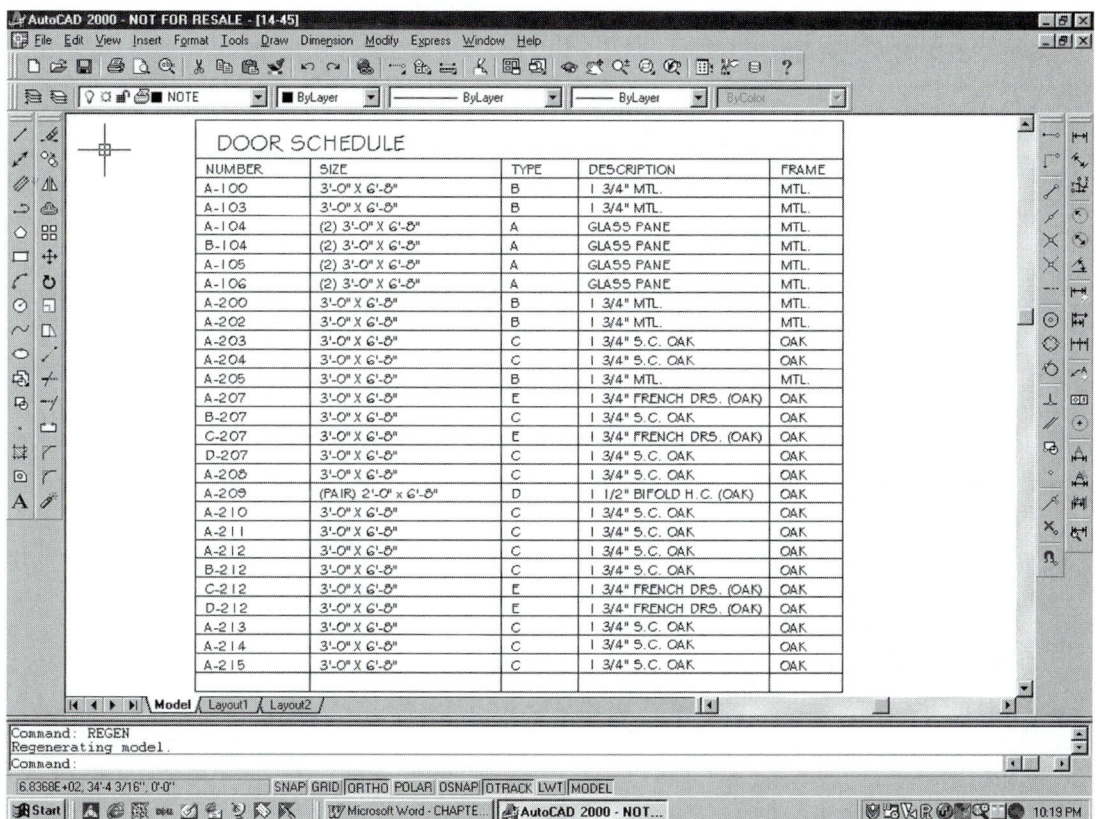

FIGURE 14–45
Problem 1.

2. Create a new drawing and call it *ROOM FINISH SCHEDULE.* Use Architectural Units and establish drawing Limits of 29′4, 22′8. Look at Figure 14–46 and use the LINE command to draw the schedule outline. Draw the rectangle 25′-7″ by 14′. Offset the top line 12″. Offset the second line 6″ to create the 26 rows. Offset the left vertical line 36″ to create the first column. Create the second column line 5′-7″. Create the third column line 24″. Create the fourth column line 4′-5″. Create the fifth column line 36″. Create the sixth column line 4′-6″. Create a new text style and call it ARCHITECTURAL. Use the Stylus BT font style. Use the new text style and the DTEXT command to create the ROOM FINISH SCHEDULE at 5″ height. Create the rest of the text at 3″ height.

3. Create a new drawing and call it *TEXT FIND AND REPLACE.* Use Architectural Units and establish drawing Limits of 44′, 34′. Create a new text style and call it MY EURO. Use the EuroRoman font style. Using a text height of 9″ create the text as shown in Figure 14–47 using the MTEXT command. Use the Find and Replace dialog box to find the words *TEXT* and replace it with the word ANNOTATION. Do not save the changes.

4. Open the *EXE14-5.dwg* file. Using the DTEXT command and the ARCHITECTURAL text style create all text as shown in Figure 14–48. Use a text height of 4″ for the title and 2″ for all other text. Place all text in NOTES layer. Save the changes.

5. Open the *EXE14-6.dwg* file. Using the DTEXT command and the ARCHITECTURAL text style create all text as shown in Figure 14–49. Use a text height of 2″ for the title and 1″ for all other text. Place all text in NOTES layer. Save the changes.

6. Open the *COM1-DOOR TYPES-SCHEDULES.dwg* file. Using the DDEDIT command change all B TYPE doors to E type. Do not save the changes.

7. Open the *COM1-DOOR TYPES-SCHEDULES.dwg* file. Using the Properties window change all room NUMBERS starting with 1 to 2. Use the Categorized tab and the Text Contents area of the Properties window. Do not save the changes.

8. Open the *COM1-DOOR TYPES-SCHEDULES.dwg* file. Use the Find and Replace dialog box to find the words *CARPET* and replace it with the word TILE. Do not save the changes.

   Hint: Place a window through the FLOOR column to select all text containing the word CARPET.

9. Open the *EXE14-7.dwg* file. Using the DTEXT command and the ARCHITECTURAL text style create all text that is missing as shown in Figure 14–50. Determine the text height from the existing text. Place all new text in the TEXT layer.

FIGURE 14–46
Problem 2.

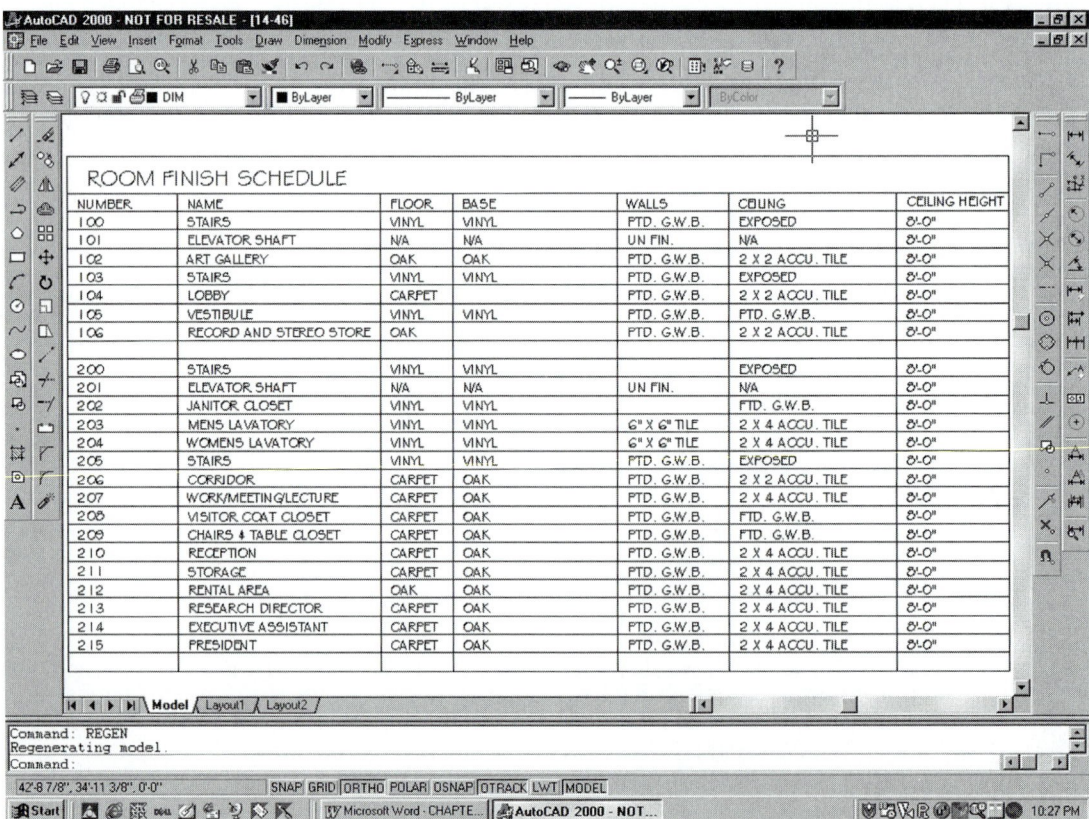

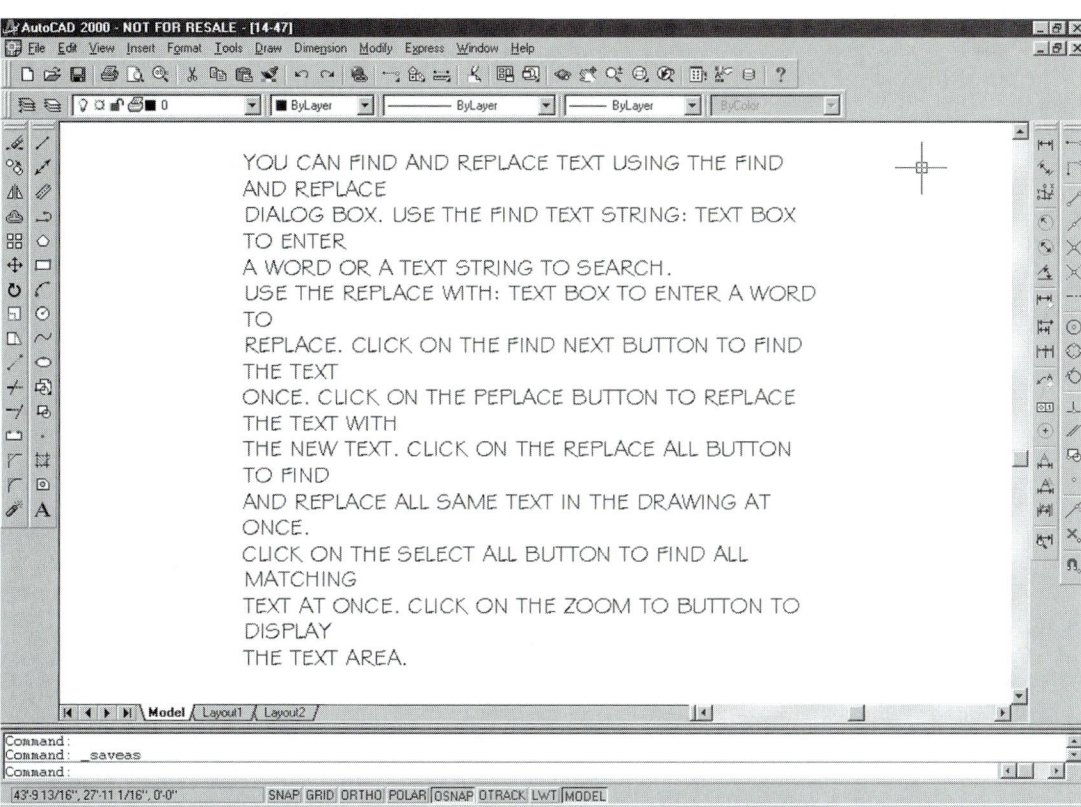

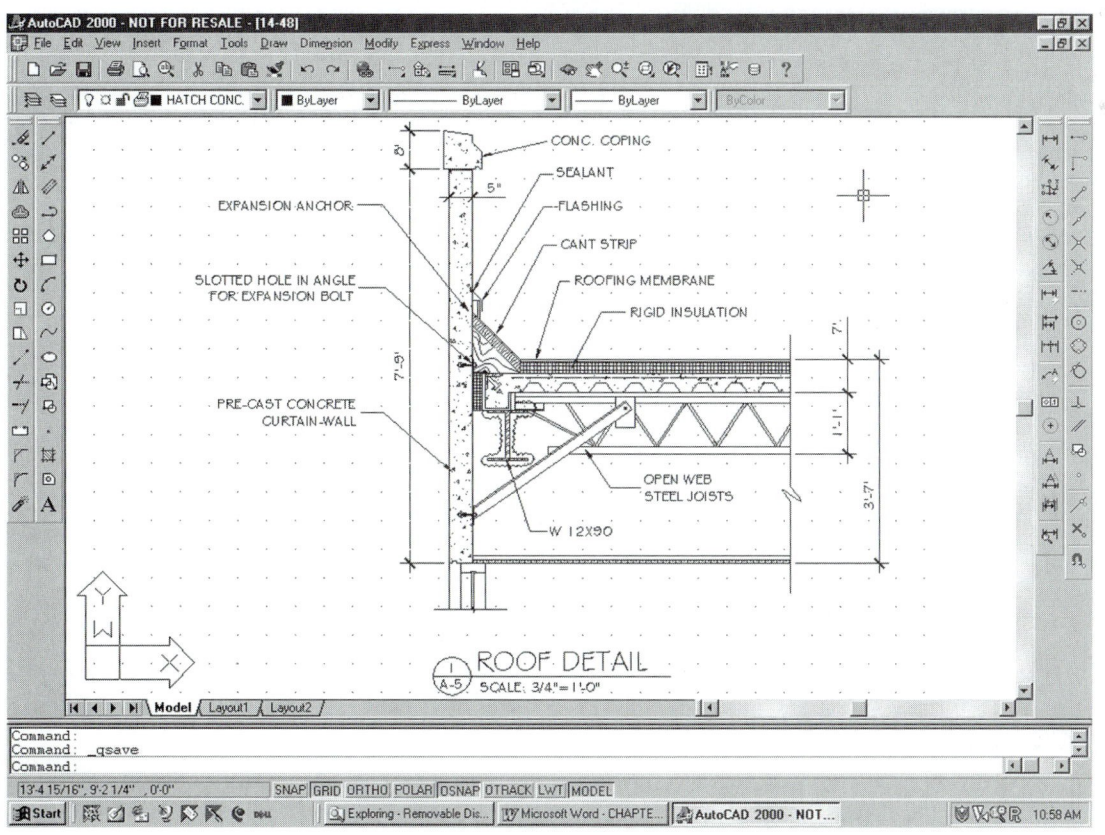

FIGURE 14–49
Problem 5.

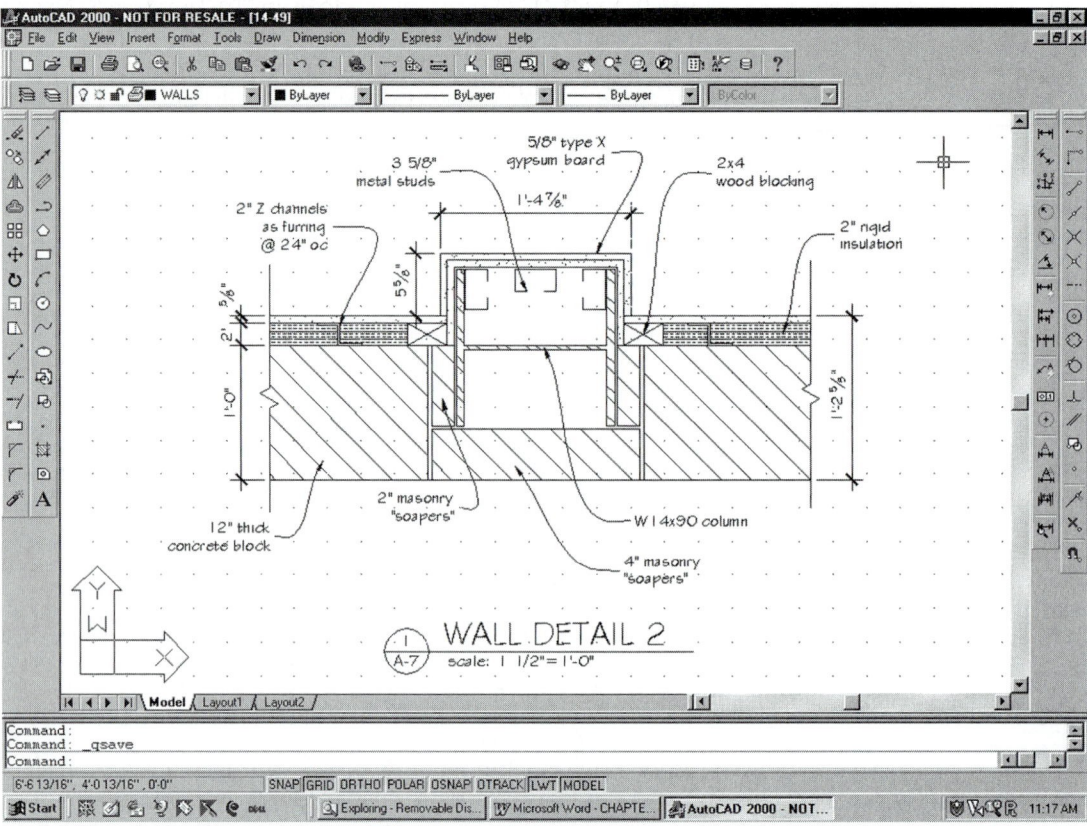

FIGURE 14–50
Problem 9.

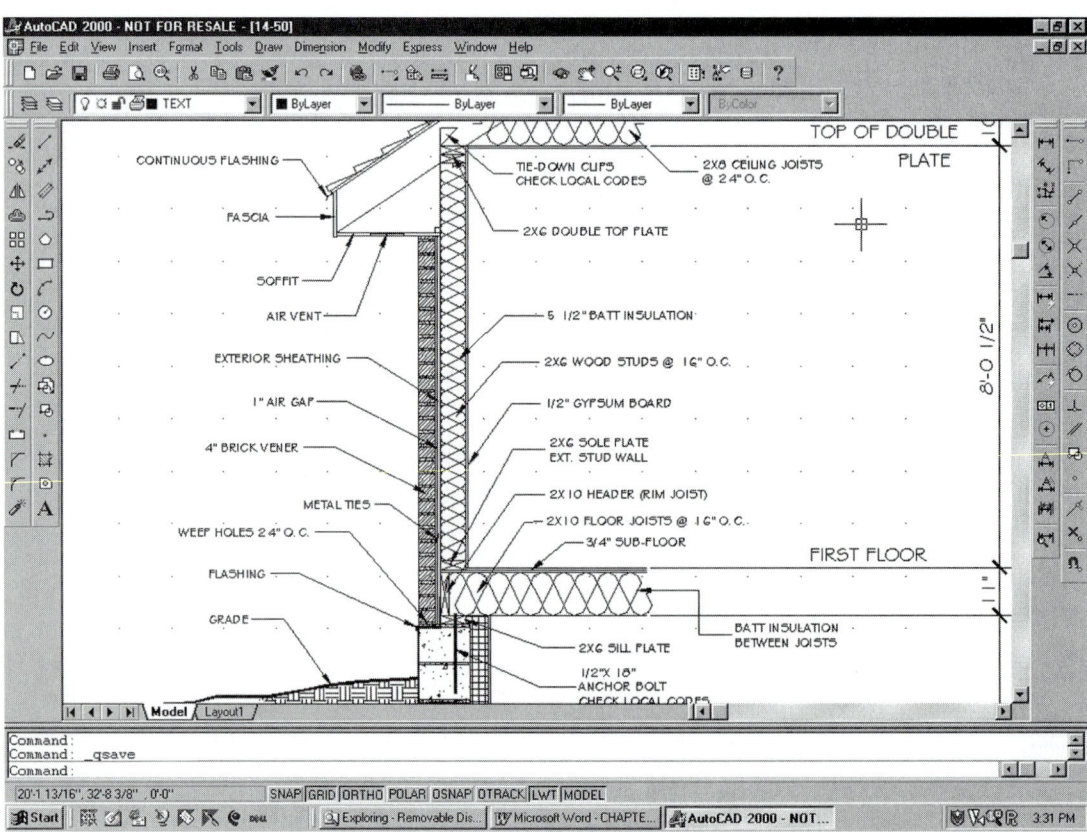

15 Managing AutoCAD Files and Establishing User Settings

After successful completion of this chapter you should be able to:

▲ Understand Microsoft's Windows® Explorer directory and file structure.

▲ Use Windows Explorer to create folders and subfolders.

▲ Use Windows Explorer to move, copy, rename, and delete folders, subfolders, and files.

▲ Format floppy diskettes and zip disks.

▲ Use the Options dialog box.

▲ Create User Profiles using different settings in the Options dialog box.

15.1 USING WINDOWS EXPLORER

Windows Explorer is a program that provides a variety of tools that allow you to manage all your drawing files. The drawings that you create and name are given a three-letter file extension of *.dwg* after you save them into the program. AutoCAD will create *Drawing1* when you create a new drawing until you save the drawing as a different file name. When naming a drawing file, you only need to enter the name without the file extension. For example, if you name a drawing OFFICE BUILDING 2000, AutoCAD will automatically add a file extension and save the drawing as OFFICE BUILDING 2000.dwg. When you search for this file to edit, you need only the name of the file. You can use Windows Explorer for the following tasks:

1. Create folders and subfolders.
2. List folders, subfolders, and files.
3. Obtain file format information.
4. Open single or multiple AutoCAD drawing files.
5. Arrange and rearrange folders, subfolders, and files.
6. Search for files.
7. Create folders, subfolders, and files.
8. Copy folders, subfolders, and files.
9. Move folders, subfolders, and files.
10. Rename folders, subfolders, and files.
11. Delete folders, subfolders, and files.
12. Format floppy and zip disks.
13. Obtain file property information.

To access the Windows Explorer, click on the Start button (located in the lower left corner of your screen) and select Windows Explorer from the Programs menu. If you created a shortcut icon on your desktop, click on the Show Desktop button on the taskbar and double-click on the

417

Windows Explorer icon. The Exploring (C:) window will be displayed as shown in Figure 15–1. The letter (C:) indicates the drive that is highlighted.

15.1.1 Directory and File Structure

The Windows Explorer is divided into two parts with a vertical *split bar*. The left part lists the contents of the computer and is called the *directory tree* (under All Folders). The right part lists the contents of the selected drive or folder you are searching for. You can move your cursor on the split bar and move it to the left or to the right to display more or less of the areas in each side of the window. In Figure 15–1 the right side shows the contents of the selected (C:) drive with all its folders. The left side shows both the contents of My Computer and the contents of the (C:) drive with all its folders. A plus (+) symbol indicates that the disk or folder contains additional folders, or subfolders. A minus (−) symbol indicates that the disk or folder has been expanded to show all its folders and subfolders. You can hide the contents of a disk or a folder by selecting the (−) symbol. For example, if you click on the (+) symbol in front of the (C:), all folders and subfolders contained in the (C:) drive will be displayed as shown in Figure 15–1. Folders that are indicated with a (+) symbol are the folders that contain subfolders. By clicking on the (+) symbol you can display its subfolders. Subfolders that are indicated with a (+) symbol contain additional folders within the subfolder. To display files (drawings) in folders or subfolders, highlight the folder or the subfolder and its contents (drawing files) are displayed in the right side of the Windows Explorer as shown in Figure 15–2. Double-clicking on the file will open the drawing. It will also launch AutoCAD if it is not already open.

All available drives in your computer are listed under My Computer. This includes all fixed drives, desktop, printers, and plotters. Each drive and folder is represented with an icon. The (C:) drive in most computers is the root directory where all programs reside. Consider the root directory as a big file cabinet where all folders and files are kept. Depending on the capacity of your (C:) drive, more programs can be loaded into the root directory and more folders can be created. In other words, more cabinet drawers can be added to the file cabinet hence more fold-

FIGURE 15–1 When you select the (C:) drive, its folders are displayed in the directory tree and the contents of the drive are displayed on the right side.

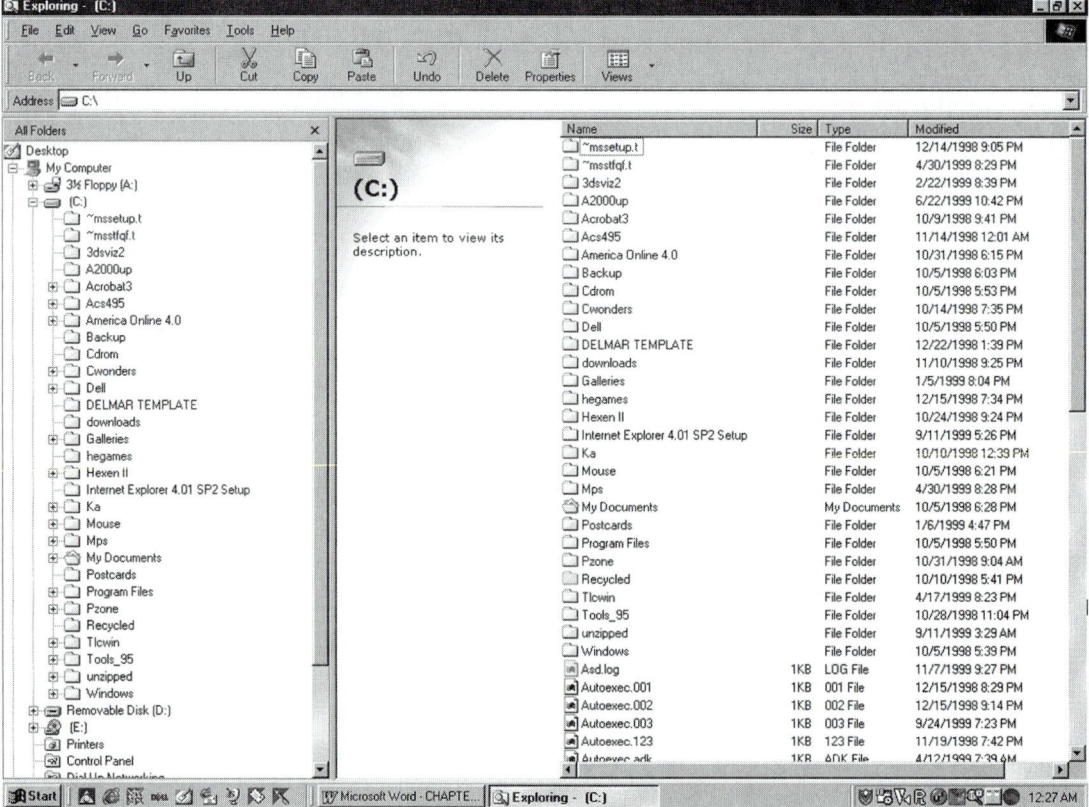

ers and files can be stored. All programs, folders, subfolders, and files reside in the root directory. The (A:) drive in most computers is the 3½ inch floppy drive and is used to insert a floppy disk to copy files from any drive to (A:) drive or vice versa. This is located directly under My Computer icon. A typical floppy disk can hold up to 1.44 megabytes (MB) of files. The (D:) drive in most computers is the removable disk drive and is indicated as Removable Disk (D:). Depending on the drive lettering hierarchy, your removable disk drive might have a different letter. A removable disk is usually a high-capacity disk such as a zip disk. To locate the removable disk drive in your computer, look for the word *zip* if your computer has a zip drive. An internal zip drive is a part of your hardware and is one of the front openings in your CPU. The most common type of zip drive is the ZIP 100 and uses the Zip100 disk. A Zip100 disk can hold 100 megabytes of information. Some removable disks come with a higher capacity zip disks, such as Zip200 or Zip250. The ZIP 250 drive can be found in new computers and use Zip 250 disks. The reason a zip disk can hold very large amounts of files (equal to 70 or more floppy disks) is that the files are compressed (condensed) using a zip utility and then copied into the zip disk or into the floppy diskette (depending on file size). A zip utility allows files to be squeezed and compressed into a very small file size. However, when these files are copied into the root directory of a computer that has no zip utility, the files cannot be decompressed and cannot be opened. A zip utility is needed to open zip files.

You can purchase zip utilities on the Internet, or one is usually included with the purchase of any System Utility software such as McAfee Office 2000 or Norton 2000. The System Utility software comes loaded with features such as diagnostic, repair, cleanup, defrag, and scandisk utilities to keep your computer in top condition and safe from viruses. With an average start/stop time of three seconds, a short format type of 10 seconds, and a capacity of up to 250 MB, a zip drive built into your computer (or external) can be an effective removable storage. Some computer manufacturers include CD-RW (CD-Recordable/Rewritable) drive as the removable disk. The (E:) drive in most computers is the CD-ROM or DVD-ROM drive. This is where the CD is placed to install software or listen to music. A DVD-ROM drive allows you to watch DVD movies and read a CD as well.

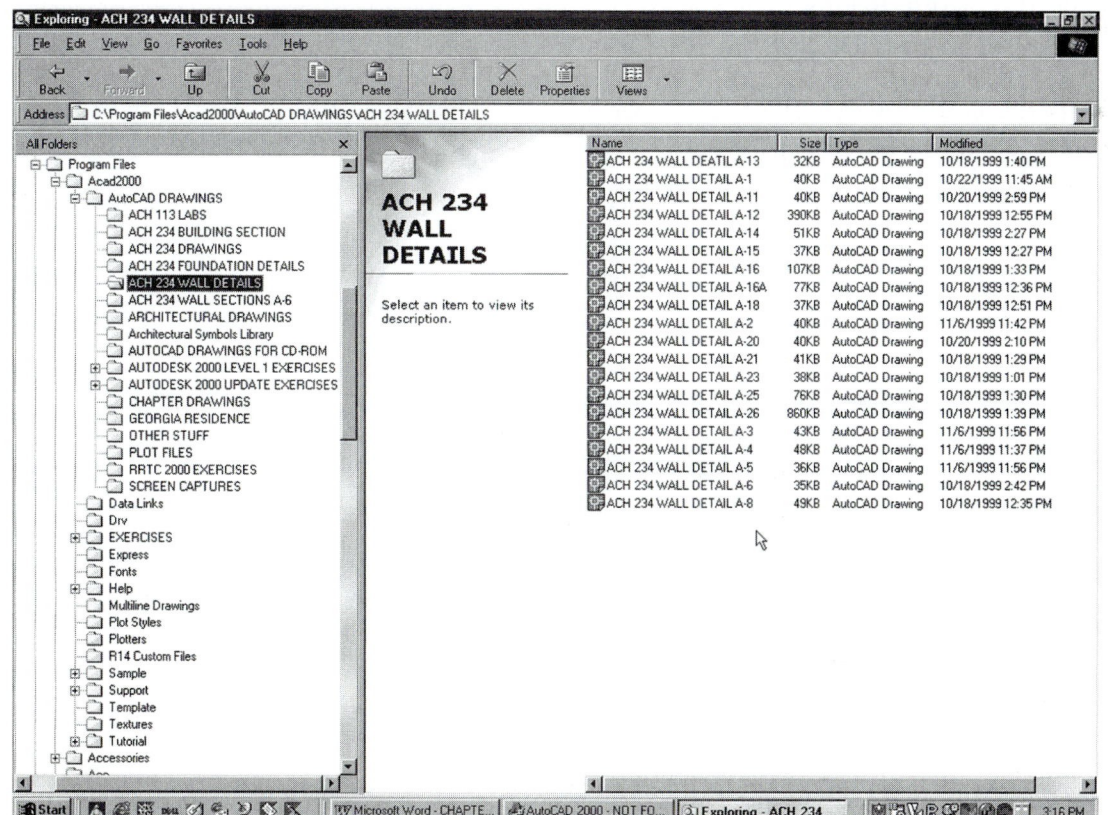

FIGURE 15–2 When you highlight (single-click) a folder in the directory tree, all its files are displayed on the right side. Think of the directory tree as a large cabinet file, the drives as the cabinet drawers, the folders as the individual file folders inside the cabinet drawers, and the drawing files as the files inside the individual file folders inside the cabinet drawers.

A typical computer CPU is designed to be laid horizontally with the monitor placed on top of it. Alternatively, the CPU can be a tower or a mini-tower type, which is placed vertically on top of the computer desk next to the monitor or on the floor. Recently a new kind of CPU has been introduced with the monitor and CPU combined as one unit, a concept similar to TVs with an integral VCR.

15.1.2 Microsoft Windows Operating Systems

A computer needs an operating system (OS) to function. The five Microsoft Windows operating systems are Windows® 95, Windows® 98, Windows® Millennium, Windows® NT, and Windows® 2000. Windows® Millennium is the successor to Windows® 98 and Windows® 95. Millenium is easier to use, more reliable, and faster with new technology integrated in its architecture. The Windows® 98 operating system incorporates FAT 32 file system technology, which allows over two gigabytes (GB) of disk space to be formatted as a single drive. Windows® 95 and 98 allow support for DVD, TV tuner, and USB peripherals that offer full-motion video and multichannel and digital surround audio. Windows® Millennium incorporates all of these features and adds new peripherals to use the latest video, sound, and graphics technology. Windows® 2000 is the successor to Windows® NT and focuses on performance, reliability, security, and manageability and is used by many businesses of all sizes. Windows® 2000 also incorporates some of the System Tools found in Windows® Millennium, such as Disk Cleanup and Defragmenter. The functions of all operating systems are very similar when it comes to file management. The Windows® Explorer in Windows® 2000 is very similar to Windows® NT, with minor differences. This chapter is based on the Windows® 98 operating system's file management. If you have a different operating system, the Exploring window may appear slightly different.

15.1.3 Creating Folders and SubFolders

Depending on your school's or company's security settings, you can create folders and subfolders in any drive. For 3½-floppy, removable disk, and CR-RW drives, you must have the appropriate disk inside the drive. For example, you can create a folder named STUDENT PROJECTS in the (C:) drive as follows:

1. Open Windows Explorer.
2. Inside the directory tree area, left-click on (C:) to highlight it.
3. From the File pull-down menu, select Folder from the New cascading menu as shown in Figure 15–3.
4. A New Folder inside a rectangle will be displayed in the right side of the Windows Explorer.
5. Type STUDENT PROJECTS and press ~EnterKey~.

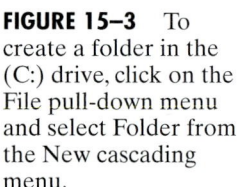
FIGURE 15–3 To create a folder in the (C:) drive, click on the File pull-down menu and select Folder from the New cascading menu.

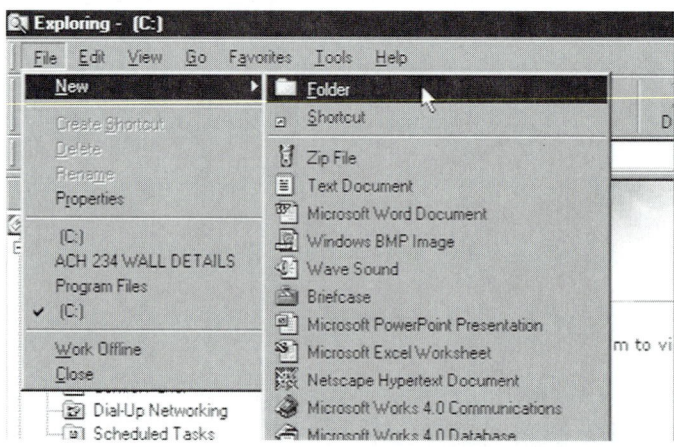

6. Move your cursor to the directory tree area and click on the (+) sign in front of the (C:).

7. The STUDENT PROJECTS folder will be listed (in alphabetical order) inside the (C:) drive as shown in Figure 15–4. Notice that this folder does not contain a (+) sign, because there are no additional subfolders created. The same folder will also be displayed in the right side of the Windows Explorer because it shows the contents of the selected drive. If you left-click on the STUDENT PROJECTS folder, the contents of the folder will be displayed in the right side. There are no files residing in this folder, so the contents of the folder will be empty. Notice that when you left-click on a folder in the directory tree, the folder icon will turn into an open folder icon.

A subfolder is a folder residing in the first folder created. You can create as many subfolders as required. Create a folder first that incorporates a general scheme and then create subfolders as you move from general to specific. For example, you can create a subfolder called LEVEL 1 DRAWINGS under the STUDENT PROJECTS folder as follows:

1. Inside the directory tree area, left-click on the STUDENT PROJECTS folder to highlight it.

2. From the File pull-down menu, select Folder from the New cascading menu.

3. A New Folder inside a rectangle will be displayed in the right side of the Windows Explorer.

4. Type LEVEL 1 DRAWINGS and press ~EnterKey~. As soon as you press the ~EnterKey~, a (+) sign will appear in front of the STUDENT PROJECTS. The LEVEL 1 DRAWINGS folder at this point is displayed in the right side of the Windows Explorer.

5. Move your cursor to the directory tree area and click on the (+) sign in front of the STUDENT PROJECTS folder. The LEVEL 1 DRAWINGS subfolder will be displayed directly under the STUDENT PROJECTS folder without the (+) sign as shown in Figure 15–5.

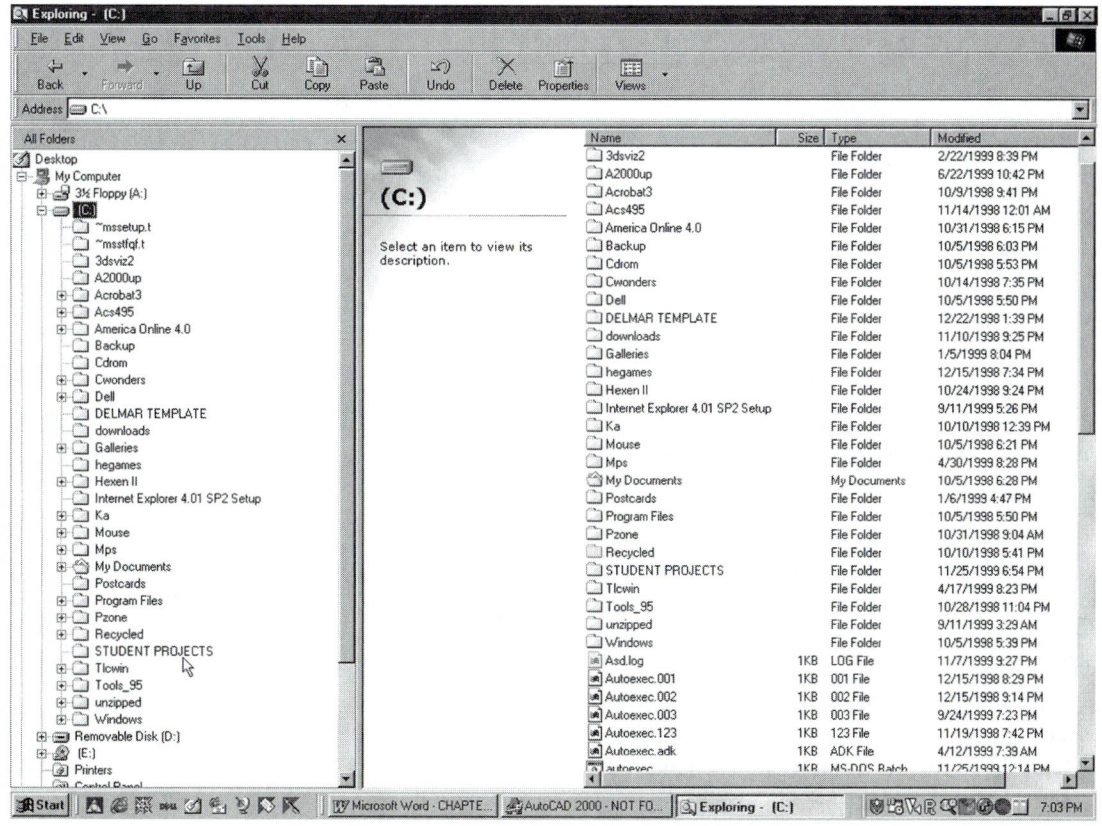

FIGURE 15–4 The STUDENT PROJECTS folder shown in directory tree and the right side of Windows® Explorer.

FIGURE 15–5 The LEVEL 1 DRAWINGS subfolder located under the STUDENT PROJECTS folder. Notice the (−) sign in front of the STUDENT PROJECTS folder. This means that all subfolders inside the STUDENT PROJECTS folder have been displayed and there is nothing more to display. Notice that there is no sign in front of the LEVEL 1 DRAWINGS subfolder. This means that this subfolder does not contain any additional subfolders or any drawing files.

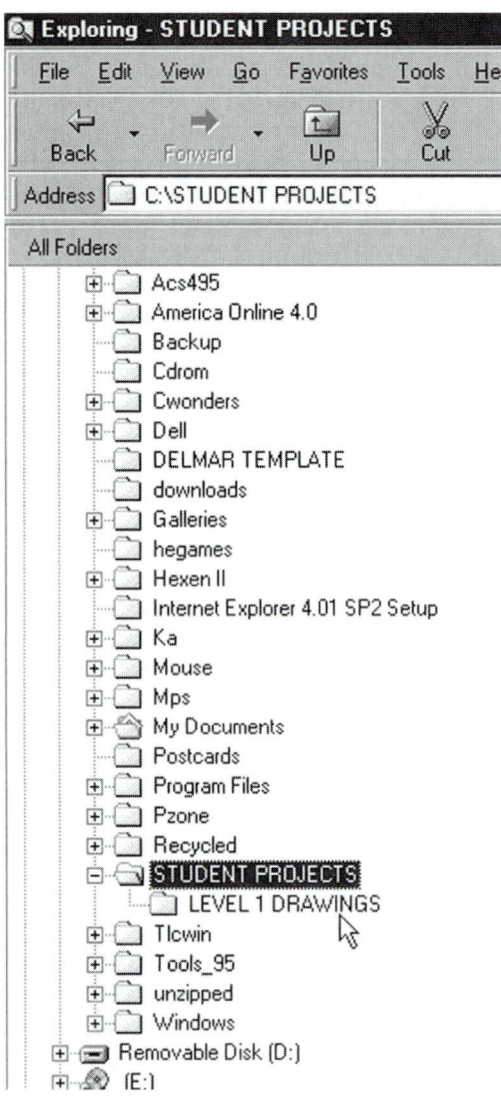

6. Inside the directory tree area, left-click on the subfolder. The Address drop-down list will display the path to the location of the selected subfolder as shown in Figure 15–6. In this case the Address is C:/STUDENT PROJECTS/LEVEL 1 DRAWINGS. This means that the LEVEL 1 DRAWINGS subfolder is located inside the STUDENT PROJECTS folder which is located inside the (C:) drive.

You can create additional subfolders inside the LEVEL 1 DRAWINGS subfolder as needed. To create folders and subfolders inside the other drives, insert the appropriate disk inside the drive. Left-click on the drive to highlight it and follow the steps described above.

Tips: Minimize the Windows Explorer by clicking on the (-) sign located in the upper right corner. This will keep the Windows Explorer open so that you can move, copy, open, rename, and delete files.

15.1.4 Formatting a Floppy Diskette or a Zip Disk

While most disks (3½ floppy or zip disk) are sold formatted, a floppy diskette purchased unformatted must be formatted. Zip disks are sold formatted for IBM compatibles or formatted for MAC-based computers. Formatting is a process that cleans a diskette or disk that prepares it for file copying. You can also format a diskette or disk to erase any existing data. You can format a floppy diskette as follows:

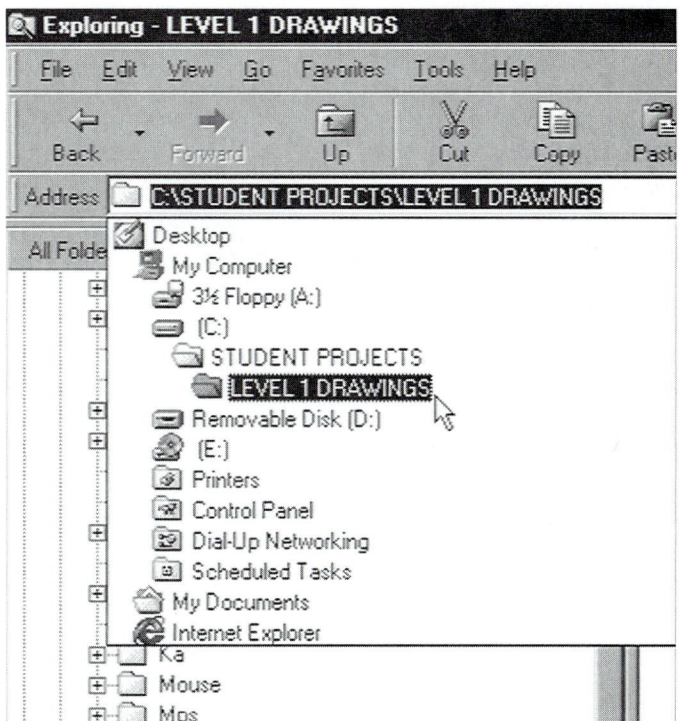

FIGURE 15–6 The Address drop-down list contains the path to the selected folder, subfolder, or drawing file.

1. Insert a 3½ floppy diskette into the (A:) drive.

2. Inside the directory tree area, click on the 3½ floppy (A:) to highlight it.

3. Right-click on the highlighted 3½ floppy (A:) and select Format … from the shortcut menu.

4. The Format – 3½ floppy (A:) dialog box will be displayed as shown in Figure 15–7. From the Capacity: drop-down list, select the diskette capacity appropriate for the diskette in the drive. Most floppy diskettes have 1.44 MB capacity, but some are with 720 KB (kilobytes), with 1K = 1000. If your floppy diskette does not say 1.44 MB, select the 720 Kb (3.5″) option.

5. Inside the Format type, click on the Quick (erase) radio button.

6. Inside the Label: text box, enter an identifying name for the diskette, such as your last name followed by the current year. This will help identify the owner of the diskette in case it is lost. Although it is not necessary to enter a label name, it is recommended for your protection.

7. Click on the Start button to begin the formatting process.

8. When formatting is complete, the Format Results – 3½ floppy (A:) dialog box will be displayed as shown in Figure 15–8. Click on the Close button to close the dialog box.

The *Quick (erase)* Format type option quickly formats and erases all information contained in the diskette. The actual disk capacity is indicated along with any bad sectors found. The *Full* Format type option performs a thorough check of the floppy diskette or zip disk and reports any bad sectors that might be found. This process takes much longer than the Quick option. The *Copy system files only* Format type creates a bootable disk without formatting. The *No label* option deletes the current label from the diskette. The *Display summary when finished* option displays the dialog box shown in Figure 15–8. The *Copy system files* option creates a bootable disk by copying system files and formats the diskette or the disk. Because system files are large files, it is recommended that you use a zip disk for this procedure.

Caution: Be careful when formatting a formatted diskette or a zip disk that contains files since all information will be erased.

FIGURE 15–7 The Format – 3½ Floppy (A:) dialog box for the Windows® 98 operating system.

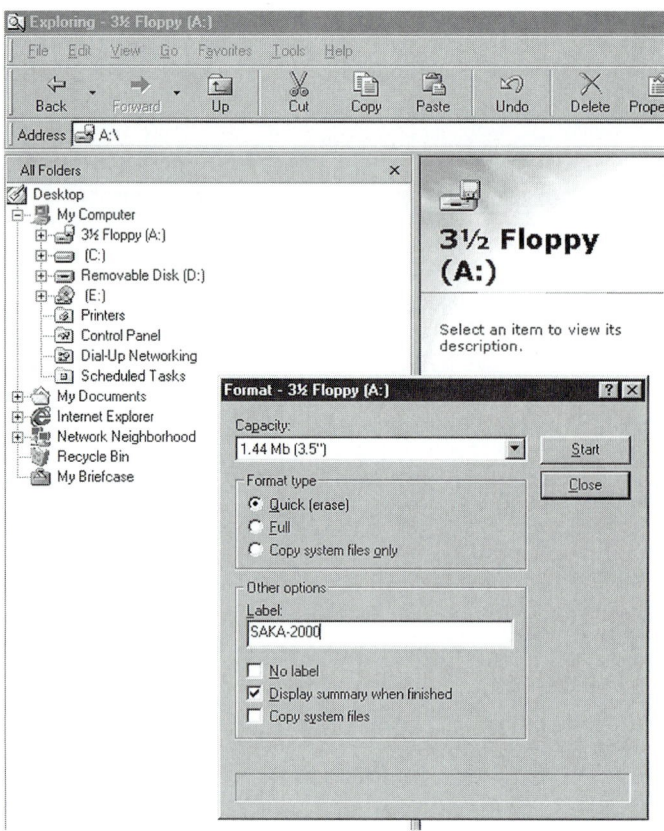

FIGURE 15–8 The Format Results – 3½ Floppy (A:) dialog box.

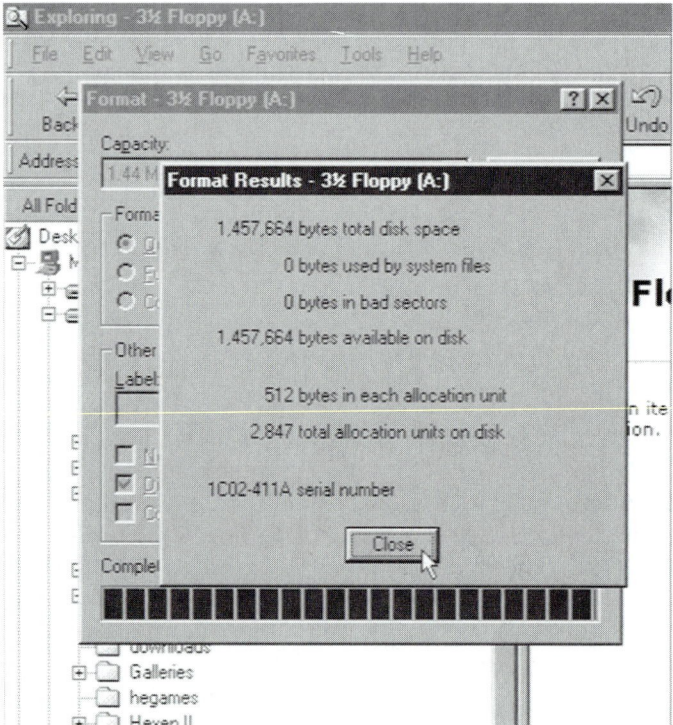

15.1.5 Copying and Moving Folders and Files

When a folder is copied from one drive to another drive that has an existing folder, all of its subfolders (if any) and files will also be copied to the new location. Folders and subfolders of the *source object* will be added onto and become a part of the *destination object*. When a file is copied to a folder, its contents are added onto the folder. You can copy a file from the (C:) drive into the (A:) drive as follows:

1. Inside the directory tree, select the folder that contains the file you wish to copy. The contents of the folder will be displayed in the right side of the Windows Explorer.

2. Place the floppy diskette into the (A:) drive.

3. Left-click on the 3½ floppy (A:) inside the directory tree and display the folder you want to copy the file to.

4. Move your cursor to the right side of the Windows Explorer and left-click on the file you want to copy.

5. While keeping your finger pressed on the left button, drag the file to the directory tree and over the folder you want to copy to. When the folder is highlighted, drop the file into this folder by releasing your finger from the left button.

6. The Copying . . . dialog box will appear as shown in Figure 15–9 to confirm the copying process.

The (+) sign attached to the cursor when dragging indicates that the file is being *copied* not *moved*. This happens automatically when copying files from one drive into another drive. When you use the same procedure within the same drive, such as copying a file from one folder in (C:) drive into another folder in the same drive, the file will actually be *moved,* not *copied*. This is because there is no (+) sign attached to the cursor while moving the cursor from one folder into another folder. To copy a file within the same drive, press the ~CtrlKey~ after you left-click on the file.

To copy or move the contents of a folder, select the source folder and drag and drop it into the destination folder. The (+) sign attached to the cursor will copy the folder. If there is no (+) sign attached to the cursor, the folder will be moved. There are more ways to copy and move folders and files. For example, you can select the file or folder and then select Copy from the Edit pull-down menu, or right-click and select Copy from the shortcut menu as shown in Figure 15–10. This procedure copies the file to the Clipboard. Select the folder or drive you want to copy to, then select Paste from the Edit pull-down menu, or right-click and select Paste from the shortcut menu. This procedure copies the file to the selected folder or drive. You can also right-click on the file to be copied, then select *Quick Copy to* . . . option from the shortcut menu. This will display the Quick Copy dialog box as shown in Figure 15–11. Inside the dialog box, enter the full path of the file (destination folder) inside the Copy to: drop-down list. Select either the Copy or Move option from the transfer Method and click on the OK button.

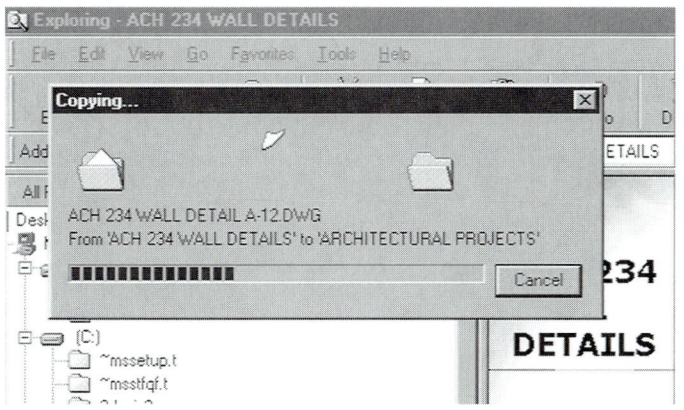

FIGURE 15–9 The Copying . . . dialog box will appear as confirmation of the copying process.

FIGURE 15–10   The right-click shortcut menu can be used to copy files or folders.

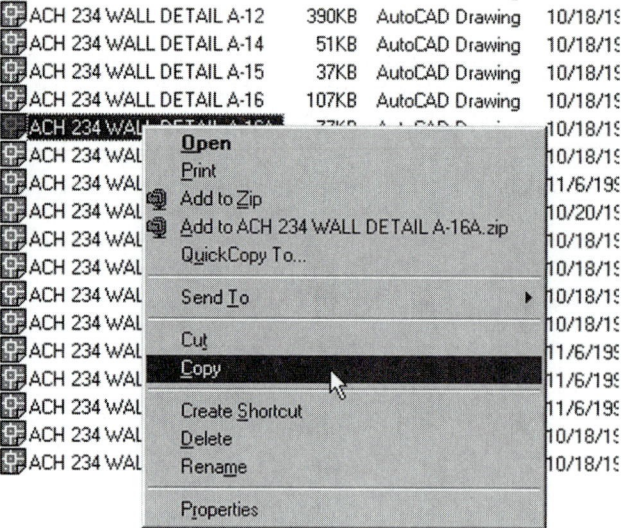

FIGURE 15–11   The Quick Copy dialog box allows you to quickly copy files and folders.

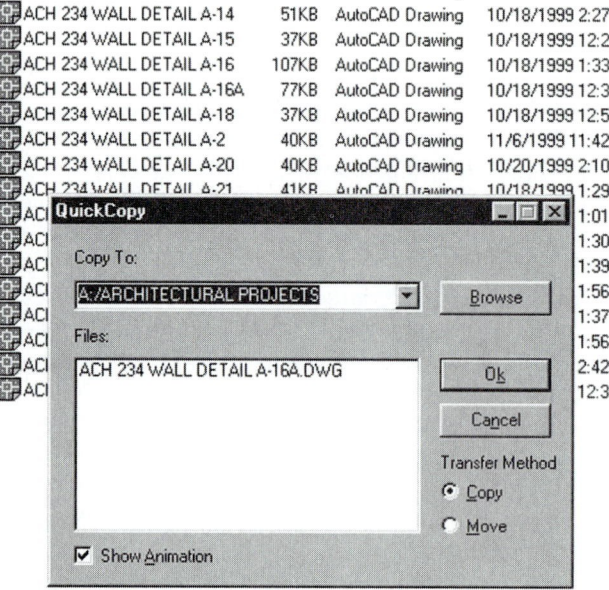

15.1.6   Renaming Folders and Files

To rename a folder or a file, left-click on the folder or the file and wait two seconds. The selected item will be highlighted and placed inside a rectangle with a flashing cursor. Enter the new name over the old name and press the ~EnterKey~. Or you can select Rename from the File pull-down menu. You can also right-click on the file or folder and select Rename from the shortcut menu. If a file is displayed with its .dwg (or any other three-letter file) extension, you must include the corresponding three-letter file extension at the end of the file name. This is especially true when renaming files inside the Select File dialog box in AutoCAD. You can avoid having to enter the file extension as follows:

1. Inside the Windows Explorer, select Folder Options . . . from the View pull-down menu.
2. Inside the Folder Options dialog box, click on the View tab.
3. Place a check mark inside the Hide file extensions for known file types check box.
4. Click on the OK button to exit.

15.1.7 Deleting Folders and Files

To delete a folder or a file, left-click on it and select Delete from the File pull-down menu, press the Delete key, or right-click and select Delete from the shortcut menu. All deleted files are sent to the Recycle Bin. To recover a deleted file, open the Recycle Bin dialog box. Select the files you want to recover and select Restore from the File pull-down menu. The selected files will be removed from the Recycle Bin and will be returned to their original location. To delete files permanently from the Recycle Bin, select Empty Recycle Bin from the File pull-down menu.

Note: This chapter is not meant to teach you everything about Windows Explorer. It is meant to teach you the basics behind simple file management operations.

15.2 SEARCH PATHS AND FILE LOCATIONS

You can specify the folders and support files in which AutoCAD searches when locating text fonts, linetypes, hatch patterns, menus, drawings to insert, and plug-ins that are not in the current folder. For example, the default file path for AutoCAD's Drawing Template File Location is C:\PROGRAM FILES\ACAD2000\template. You can create a folder in your hard drive (root directory) and have AutoCAD to always use that folder for template file storage. Use the Options dialog box to find a folder for template files as follows:

1. Right-click and select Options . . . This will display the Options dialog box.
2. Select the Files tab.
3. Click on the (+) sign in front of the Drawing Template File Location. The current location will be displayed as shown in Figure 15–12.
4. Click on the current location and then click on the Browse button.
5. Inside the Browse for Folder dialog box, find the folder you want to use for template files and click on it.
6. Click on the OK button to exit.
7. Inside the Options dialog box, click on the Apply button and then click on the OK button.

You can use any of the folders and support files inside the Search paths, file names, and file locations: list to assign and change location of files.

Other buttons in the Files tab are described as follows:

- **ADD . . . :** This button will add an item below the selected file name.

- **REMOVE:** This button will remove the selected item.

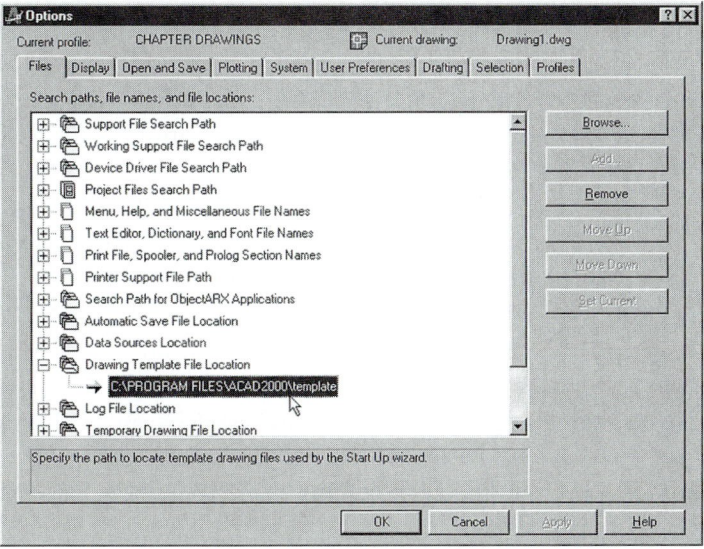

FIGURE 15–12 The Files tab of the Options dialog box.

- **MOVE UP:** This button will move the selected item above or before the preceding item and applies to search paths only.

- **MOVE DOWN:** This button will move the selected item below the following item and applies to search paths only.

- **SET CURRENT:** This button will make the selected item current and applies to spelling directories only.

15.3 CREATING USER PROFILES

A *profile* is a menu of settings and values that can be established to adjust many features of the drawing environment. These features do not affect the final plot of the drawing but affect the productivity and efficiency of each user. Creating a *user profile* allows each user of the same CAD Workstation to adjust and save drawing environment and drawing settings to meet his/her requirements. This is extremely useful if you share a computer with several other people. Each user can establish a separate user profile and save his or her choice of settings in a file. For example, if you want six text lines in the command line window and a crosshair size of 20 percent and you share your computer with someone who likes two text lines in the command line window and a crosshair size of 3 percent, creating two user profiles with different settings will allow each person to save and retrieve their own drawing settings. This process eliminates any time spent on adjusting the required features of the drawing environment each time a user starts AutoCAD. AutoCAD features such as window and layout elements, display resolution, background colors, crosshair size, file safety precautions, plot settings, right-click customization, and AutoSnap and AutoTrack settings are some of the items that can be adjusted or changed through user profiles.

A user profile is not the same as creating a Template file. Templates are created so that specific drawing aids, settings, conventions, and standards can be incorporated into the drawing that remain constant between each project and each member of the project team. A user profile deals with the performance of the user and the general appearance of the drawing screen. A user profile is established using the Options dialog box. Each AutoCAD user can establish the settings to meet individual drawing requirements.

■ **EXERCISE 15–1:** *The following step-by-step exercise will allow you to create a user profile named MY PERSONAL USER PROFILE. This profile will have AutoCAD display six text lines in the command line window and a crosshair size of 20 percent of the screen size.*

Step #1: From the Tools pull-down menu, select Options . . . (or right-click and select Options . . . from the shortcut menu).

Step #2: Inside the Options dialog box, select the Display tab.

Step #3: Inside the Display tab, change the default value from 3 to 6 in the text lines in command line window text box as shown in Figure 15–13.

Step #4: Change the crosshair size by moving the size bar from left to right until the value reads 20 as shown in Figure 15–13. At this point the required preferences have been set.

Step #5: Click on the Apply button. If you click on the Close button next, you must access the Options dialog box again to save these settings in a profile before exiting AutoCAD. Otherwise the settings will be lost when you exit AutoCAD.

Step #6: Inside the Options dialog box, select the Profiles tab.

Step #7: Click on the Add to list . . . button. The Add Profile dialog box will appear as shown in Figure 15–14.

Step #8: Inside the Add Profile dialog box, enter MY PERSONAL USER PROFILE inside the Profile name: text box and enter a profile description (optional) such as six text lines in command line window and 20 percent crosshair size inside the Description: text box as shown in Figure 15–14. Click on the Apply & Close button.

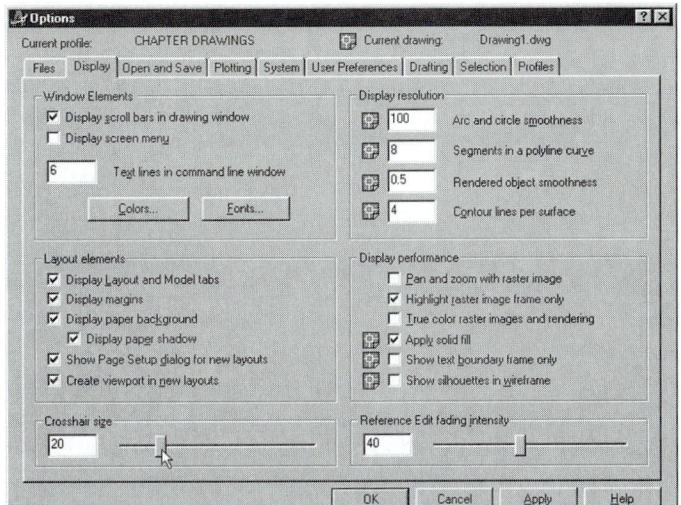

FIGURE 15–13
Changing the Text lines in command line window and the crosshair size to create a user profile.

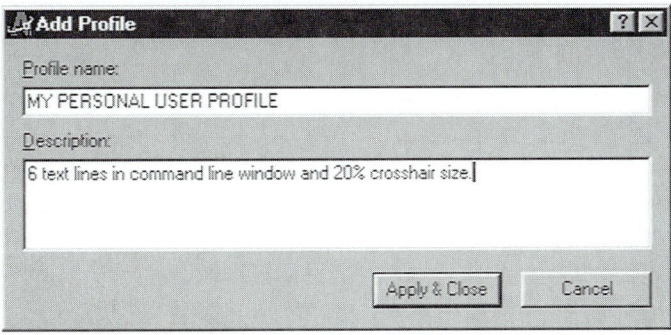

FIGURE 15–14 Using the Add Profile dialog box to enter a profile name and description.

Step #9: The new profile name will be added to the Available profiles: list inside the Options dialog box as shown in Figure 15–15.

Step #10: Click on the OK button to exit.

The established settings will become effective in the drawing screen as shown in Figure 15–16.

Congratulations! You have successfully created a user profile.

You can set an existing profile as current as follows:

1. Access the Options dialog box.
2. Select the Profile tab.
3. Select the profile you want current from the Available profiles: list.
4. Click on the Set Current button.
5. Click on the OK button.

The selected profile will be current.

When creating profiles, all settings you change are applied while you work with the Options dialog box. You can select any of the nine tabs in the Options dialog box and change settings to meet your personal drawing habits. You can set any of the existing profiles as current to see what the settings look like, but not all profile settings are visible. The buttons in the Profiles tab are described as follows:

- **SET CURRENT:** This button will set the selected profile as current.

- **ADD TO LIST . . . :** This button will display the Add Profile dialog box shown in Figure 15–14. You can enter a name and a description for the new profile.

FIGURE 15–15 The
MY PERSONAL
USER PROFILE is
added to the available
profiles list.

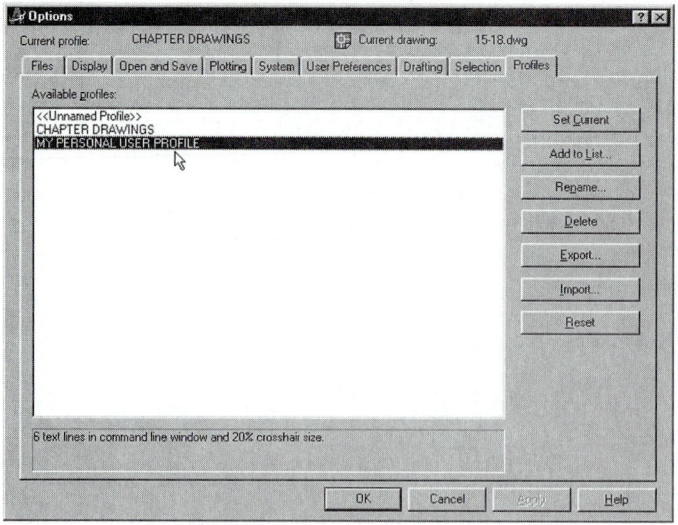

FIGURE 15–16 The
new profile settings
become effective when
you exit the Options
dialog box.

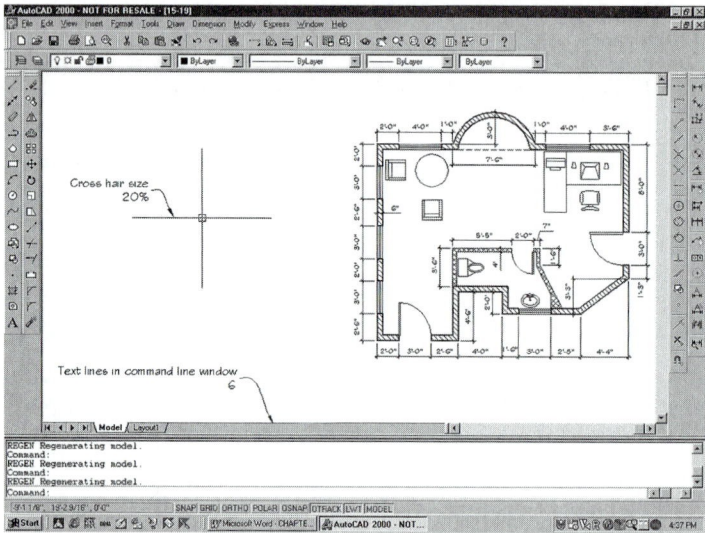

- **RENAME ...:** This button will display the Change Profile dialog box. You can change the name and the description of the selected profile.

- **DELETE:** This button will delete the selected profile. You cannot delete the current profile.

- **EXPORT...:** This button will display the Export profile dialog box. You can select a folder location to export a profile as an ARG file. This allows you to save and share profiles with different computers. Profiles of extensive nature should be saved to a floppy diskette or zip disk.

- **IMPORT...:** This button will display the Import Profile dialog box. You can import a profile that was exported.

- **RESET:** This button will reset the values of the selected profile to AutoCAD's default settings.

15.4 USING THE OPTIONS DIALOG BOX

Each of the nine tabs in the Options dialog box is introduced and discussed throughout the text at appropriate Chapters. The tab and its options specific to user profile settings are as follows:

Display Tab: The Display tab shown in Figure 15–17 has six categories: The *Layout elements* category options are discussed in Chapter 22. The *Crosshair size* category option is discussed in

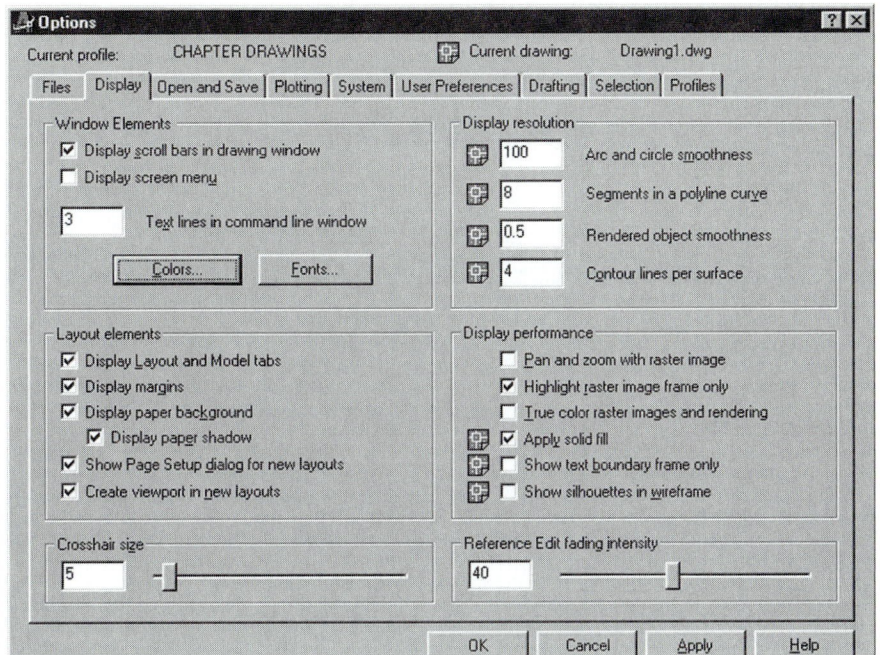

FIGURE 15–17 The Display tab of the Options dialog box.

Chapter 1. The *Display resolution* category options are discussed in Chapter 11. The *Reference Edit fading intensity* category option is discussed in Chapters 19 and 24. The remaining category options are as follows:

- **WINDOW ELEMENTS:** This category allows you to set window elements properties. The *Display scroll bars in drawing window* option toggles the display of the horizontal and vertical scroll bars on the screen. The *Display screen menu* option toggles the display of the screen menu. The *Text lines in command line window* option allows you to specify the number of lines of text shown in the command line window. The range is from 1 to 100 lines, with a default value of 3. Selecting the *Colors . . .* button will display the *Color Options* dialog box as shown in Figure 15–18. Use this dialog box to change the colors of the AutoCAD graphics and text windows. First, select an element from the *Window Element:* drop-down list, then select a color from the *Color:* drop-down list. You can also click on the pickbox/crosshairs or blank space inside the Model or Layout tabs to display the Model/Layout tab pointer and Model tab background and Layout tabs background (paper) in the Window Element: drop-down list. The *Default All* button will set all elements back to their default colors. The *Default one element* button will allow you to set colors one element at a time. After changing color settings, click on the *Apply & Close* button to exit. Selecting the *Fonts . . .* button will display the *Command Line Window Font* dialog box, as shown in Figure 15–19. Use this dialog box to change the font, font style, and font size of the command line window font. You can review the selected font settings inside the preview window under *Sample Command Line Font*. After changing the font, click on the *Apply & Close* button to exit.

User Preferences: The User Preferences tab shown in Figure 15–20 has five categories: The *AutoCAD DesignCenter* category options are discussed in Chapter 19. The *Windows Standard Behavior* category options are discussed in Chapter 1. The *Lineweight Settings . . .* option is discussed in Chapter 5. The remaining category options are as follows:

- **PRIORITY FOR COORDINATE DATA ENTRY:** This category allows you to set coordinate data entry. Placing a checkmark inside the *Running object snap* radio button allows the object snap

FIGURE 15–18 The Color Options dialog box allows you to change the colors of AutoCAD window elements.

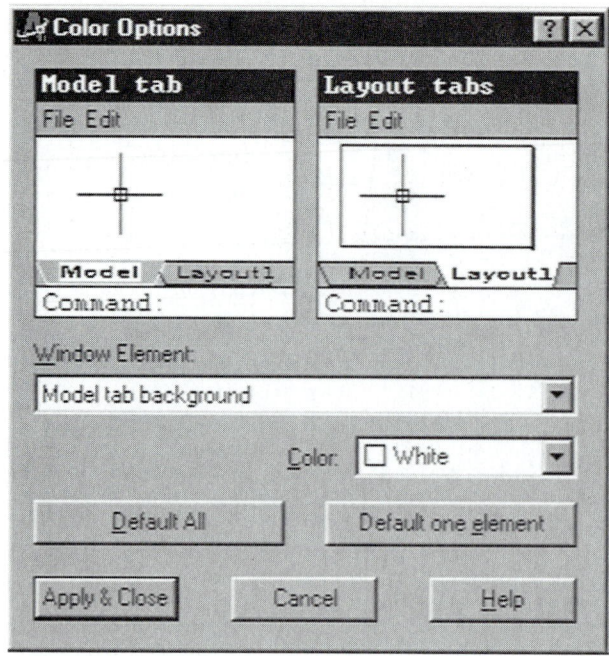

FIGURE 15–19 The Command Line Window Font dialog box allows you to change the font, font style, and font size of the command line window text.

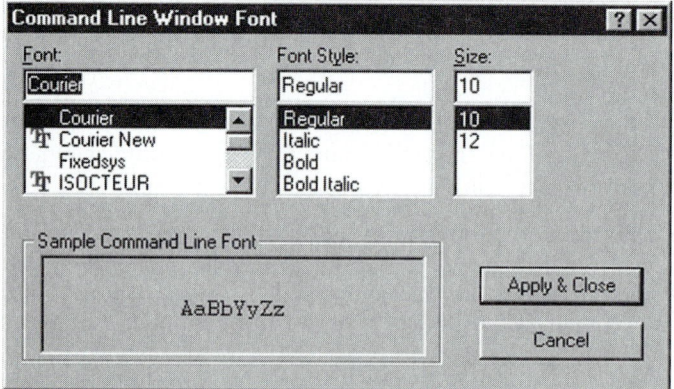

modes to override coordinates entered at the keyboard. This means that you cannot use a coordinate point entry system to establish a point on the screen, although an object snap mode can be used. Placing a checkmark inside the *Keyboard entry* radio button allows the coordinates entered at the keyboard to override object snap modes. The *Keyboard entry except scripts* option is on by default. This means that the coordinates entered at the keyboard override running object snap modes, except for coordinates provided in a script.

- **OBJECT SORTING METHODS:**   This category allows you to control the order of objects when they are displayed or plotted. The *Object selection* option will sort objects in the selection set from first to last created. The *Object snap* option will sort objects in the drawing selected with object snap modes from first to last. The *Redraws* option will sort objects that are displayed by the REDRAW command in the order they were created. The *Regens* option will sort objects that are displayed by the REGEN command in the order they were created. The *Plotting* option will sort objects in the drawing from first to last created when printing or plotting. The *PostScript output* option will sort objects in the drawing from first to last created for PostScript output.

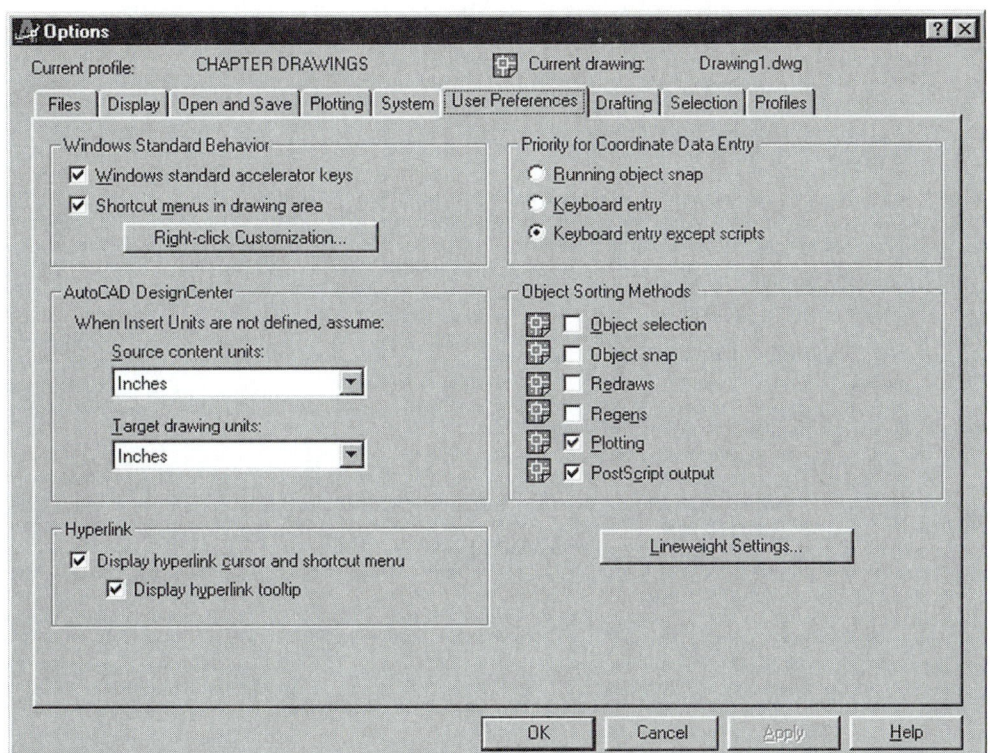

FIGURE 15–20 The User Preferences tab of the Options dialog box.

- **HYPERLINK:** AutoCAD allows you to establish file, path, and description information for a hyperlink using the Insert Hyperlink dialog box. This replaces the URL commands. The Hyperlink technology works with the application of *WHIP!*4.0, which is a free viewer provided by Autodesk. You can create hyperlinks to the Web as well as to local non-Web files. AutoCAD will display a hyperlink-sensitive cursor and a shortcut menu if the first check box is checked. AutoCAD will display a hyperlink tooltip if the second check box is checked.

Tips: Access the Options dialog box tabs by clicking on Options in various dialog boxes. For example, click on the Options . . . button in the Drafting Settings dialog box to display the Drafting tab of the Options dialog box.

REVIEW QUESTIONS

1. Name six functions you can perform with Windows Explorer.
2. What does the directory tree list in Windows Explorer?
3. What do the (+) and (−) symbols mean in front of a drive or folder?
4. What is a root directory?
5. What is the function of the (A:) drive?
6. How can you open an AutoCAD drawing in the Windows Explorer?
7. What is the difference between a floppy diskette and a zip disk?
8. How is it possible to store 100 MB of file into a zip disk?
9. What is the function of a zip utility?
10. How do you create a folder?
11. How many different ways can you copy a file using Windows Explorer?

12. What happens when you delete a file?
13. What is the purpose behind creating user profiles?
14. Which dialog box is used to create a user profile?

PROBLEMS

1. Create a user profile named YOUR LAST NAME-FAVORITES using the following settings:

   Do not display scroll bars.
   Crosshair size 10%.
   15 minutes between saves.
   Display AutoSnap aperture box.
   Grips off.
   Window background color RED.
   Model tab background color BLUE.

2. Change all color settings to default values for the profile created above and save the changes.

3. Create a user profile of the settings you use the most.

4. Create a folder in C: drive and name it MY EXE FILES. Copy all MYEXE files into this folder.

CHAPTER

16

Drawing Information at Your Fingertips

After successful completion of this chapter you should be able to:

▲ Use the Inquiry toolbar.

▲ Use the DISTANCE command.

▲ Use the DISTANCE command transparently.

▲ Use the LIST command to list object and drawing information.

▲ Use the ID command to find the coordinates of points.

▲ Use the AREA command.

▲ Use Object, Add, and Subtract options of the AREA command.

▲ Use the MASSPROP command.

16.1 USING THE INQUIRY TOOLBAR

As you progress with your AutoCAD drawings you gain a better understanding of the drawing process. You also learn more commands, options, and create complex drawings. It is very easy to be overwhelmed by the amount of information displayed in the drawing. You may find it hard to keep track of object properties and drawing settings. The Inquiry toolbar and commands help you obtain and list information about an object or about the entire drawing. It also allows you to calculate the area of an object, find the distance between two points, identify the coordinates of a point, and list the status of the drawing. The Inquiry toolbar shown in Figure 16–1 has five buttons: Distance, Area, Mass Properties, List, and Locate Point. Right-click on any toolbar and left-click on the Inquiry option to access the Inquiry toolbar. You can also access all of the commands found in the Inquiry toolbar by selecting the desired option from the Inquiry cascading menu in the Tools pull-down menu shown in Figure 16–1. This method provides three additional commands as Time, Status, and Set Variable. You can also access the Inquiry commands from the Inquiry flyout button in the Standard Toolbar as shown in Figure 16–2.

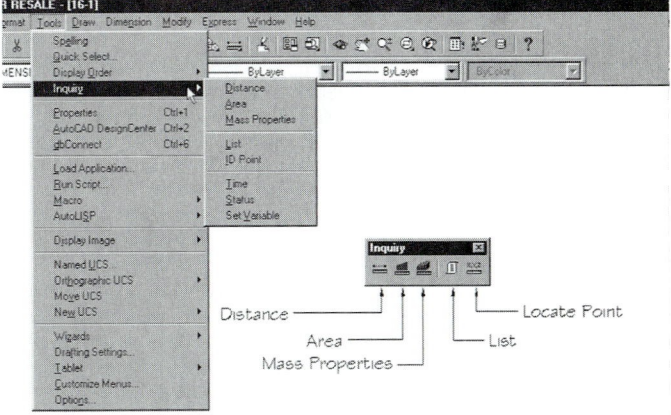

FIGURE 16–1 The Inquiry tools can be accessed from the Inquiry toolbar or from the Inquiry cascading menu in the Tools pull-down menu.

16.2 FINDING THE DISTANCE BETWEEN TWO POINTS

The Distance button in the Inquiry toolbar will allow you to measure the distance between two points. Use the object snap modes to precisely pick points. You can also enter DIST or DISTANCE at the command line to access the DISTANCE command.

435

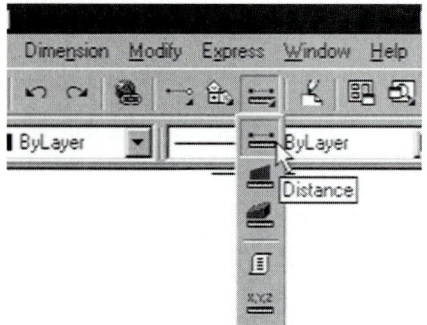

FIGURE 16–2 The Inquiry commands can also be accessed from the Inquiry flyout button in the Standard Toolbar.

■ **EXERCISE 16–1:** *The following step-by-step exercise will allow you to measure the distance between the two points as the length of the wall as shown in Figure 16–3.*

Step #1: Open the EXE12-9.dwg file.

Step #2: Access the Inquiry toolbar and use the following procedure:

Click on the Distance button in the Inquiry toolbar.

Command: '_dist Specify first point: (select the first point as shown in Figure 16–3)

Specify second point: (select the second point)

Distance = 6'-6", Angle in XY Plane = 0, Angle from XY Plane = 0

Delta X = 6'-6", Delta Y = 0'-0", Delta Z = 0'-0"

Congratulations! You have successfully obtained the length of the wall using the Distance button in the Inquiry toolbar. The distance in this case is indicated as Distance = 6'-6".

Tips: The apostrophe (') displayed before the dist *indicates that this command is a transparent command. This means that you can use the DISTANCE command while working with another command. For example, while using the LINE command to draw line objects you can place the LINE command operation* on hold *while inquiring about the distance of an existing object. The command line procedure is as follows:*

```
Command: LINE ~EnterKey~
Specify first point: (select the starting point for the line)
Specify next point or [Undo]: (select the second point for the line)
Specify next point or [Undo]: (select the third point for the line)
Specify next point or [Close/Undo]: 'DIST ~EnterKey~
>>Specify first point: (select the first point on the object that you
want to find the distance)
```

FIGURE 16–3 Finding the distance between two points of an interior partition wall.

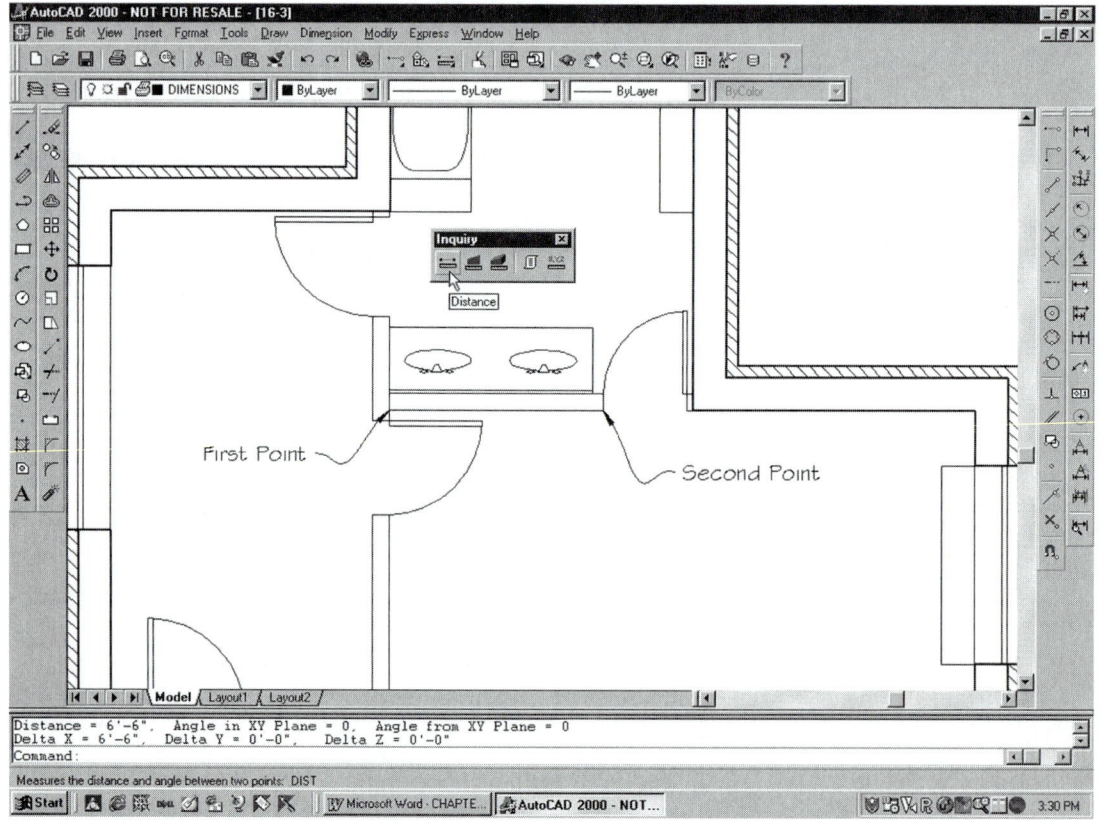

```
>>Specify second point: (select the second point on the object that you
want to find the distance)
Distance = 5'-5", Angle in XY Plane = 0, Angle from XY Plane = 0
Delta X = 5'-5", Delta Y = 0'-0", Delta Z = 0
Resuming LINE command.
Specify next point or [Close/Undo]: (continue selecting point for the line)
```

See Chapter 11 and Chapter 18 for additional information about using commands transparently.

Tips: To obtain the current length of an object use the LENGTHEN command without selecting any of its options. Simply select an object after accessing the LENGTHEN command.

16.3 LISTING OBJECT INFORMATION

Information about one or more objects in the drawing can be listed using the LIST command. You can access the LIST command by selecting the List button in the Inquiry toolbar, selecting List from the Inquiry cascading menu in the Tools pull-down menu, selecting List from the Inquiry flyout button, or by entering LI or LIST at the command line. Information about objects includes length, location, radius, width of a polyline, and object layers.

■ **EXERCISE 16–2:** *The following step-by-step exercise will allow you to list information about the three objects as shown in Figure 16–4.*

Step #1: Open the EXE16-1.dwg file.

Step #2: Use the LIST command as follows:

Command: LIST ~EnterKey~

Select objects: *(select the horizontal line as shown dashed in Figure 16–4 as LENGTH/DELTA X)*

Select objects: 1 found

Select objects: *(select the inclined line shown as dashed)*

Select objects: 1 found, 2 total

Select objects: *(select the circle shown as dashed)*

Select objects: 1 found, 3 total

Select objects: ~EnterKey~

All three objects are selected as shown in Figure 16–4. The information about the two lines and the circle are displayed in the AutoCAD Text Window dialog box as shown in Figure 16–5. If you select many objects to list their information, press the ~EnterKey~ to scroll down the list inside the AutoCAD Text Window dialog box. To exit the dialog box, press the ~F2Key~.

Congratulations! You have successfully listed object information as it relates to two wall lengths and the circle.

The data provided in the dialog box is as follows:

The *Object Type* and the *Layer* it is created on.

The AutoCAD *Space* (environment) it is created on. (See Chapter 22 for Model Space, Paper Space, and layouts.)

The X and Y coordinate points for the starting point of the two lines as *from point*.

The X and Y coordinate points for the center point of the circle as *center point*.

The *radius, circumference,* and the *area* of the circle and the X and Y coordinate points for the endpoint of the two lines as *to point*.

The *Length* represented as the horizontal distance between the two points of the horizontal line.

The Length represented as the inclined distance between the two points of the inclined line.

The *Delta X* represented as the Length of the horizontal line (Delta X = Length).

The Delta X represented as the horizontal distance between the two inclined points for the inclined line (second line).

FIGURE 16–4 The three objects are selected after accessing the LIST command.

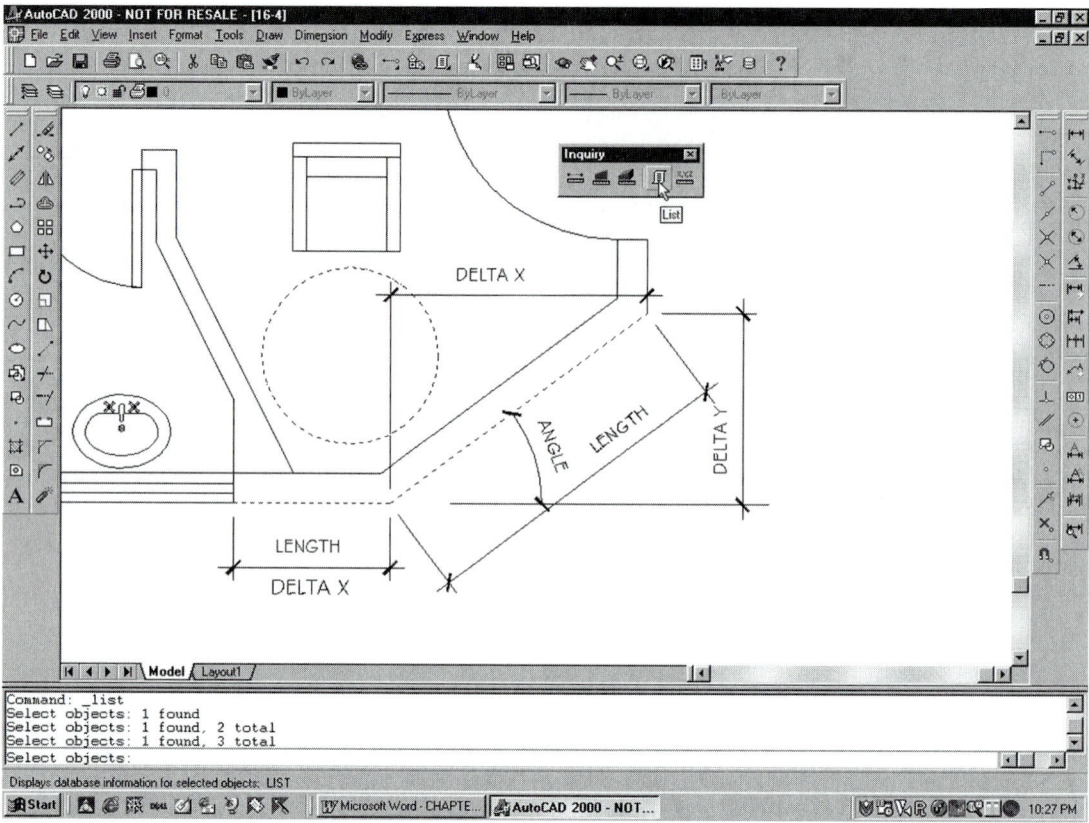

FIGURE 16–5 The AutoCAD Text Window dialog box will list data for each of the objects selected.

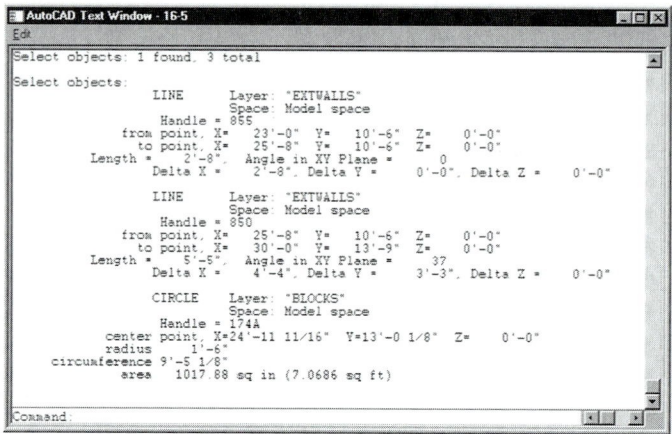

The *Angle in XY Plane* represented as the angle between the line and the horizontal plane (0 degrees for the first line and 37 degrees for the second line).

The Delta Y represented as the vertical distance between from point and the to point.

The Delta Z is used in three-dimensional drawings.

Note: The information listed in the AutoCAD Text Window dialog box depends on the type of object(s) selected. The object's type, coordinate points, layer name, and either Model Space or Paper Space are always listed. Information about object color and linetype are not listed when object color and linetype is set ByLayer.

Tips: Use the LIST command to list information about a selected single-line or multiline text. The information provided includes text style, layer location, height, contents, rotation angle, width factor, and oblique angle.

16.4 LISTING DRAWING INFORMATION

The DBLIST (Database List) command allows you to list all information for every object created in the current drawing. You do not have to select any objects. Use the DBLIST command to compare drawing information between two similar drawings. This command is also useful to find out if block references are used as opposed to creating symbols from standard AutoCAD commands. The information presented with the DBLIST command also appears inside the AutoCAD Text Window dialog box in the same order that is presented for the LIST command. The command line procedure is as follows:

```
Command: DBLIST ~EnterKey~
```

The AutoCAD Text Window dialog box will be displayed similar to the one shown in Figure 16–5. You can press the ~EnterKey~ to advance through the pages of the listing information for the entire drawing.

Tips: You can create a hard copy of the information presented by printing the contents of the Auto-CAD Text Window dialog box. Your computer must be connected to a printer.

16.5 FINDING COORDINATES FOR A POINT

You can find the X and Y coordinate locations of a point located anywhere in the drawing using the ID command. Use object snap modes for accuracy when locating points with the ID command. This command is useful when you want to find the coordinates of the start point or the endpoint of a line or the center of a circle or arc. You can access the ID command by selecting Locate Point button in the Inquiry toolbar, selecting ID Point from the Inquiry cascading menu of the Tools pull-down menu, or by entering ID at the command line. The command line procedure is as follows:

```
Command: ID ~EnterKey~
Specify point: (select the point that you want to find the coordinates)
X = 13'-6" Y = 19'-4" Z = 0'-0"
```

You can also use the ID command to identify a coordinate location on the screen. If you want AutoCAD to display blipmarks (+ signs) at the selected locations, turn the BLIPMODE system variable on. This allows you to see the coordinate locations of the selected points. The command line procedure is as follows:

```
Command: ID ~EnterKey~
Specify point: 18',21' ~EnterKey~
```

This will display a blipmark at the coordinate location X = 18' and Y = 21' measured from X = 0' and Y = 0'. You can use the @ symbol to identify a coordinate location measured from the last ID point. For example, you can identify where a point might be 2'-6" from the 18' (last known ID point on the X) and 4'-0" away from the 21' (last known ID point on the Y) as follows:

```
Command: ID ~EnterKey~
Specify point: @2'6,4' ~EnterKey~
```

16.6 FINDING AREAS OF OBJECTS AND SHAPES

The AREA command allows you to find the area and perimeter of an object. You can access the AREA command by selecting the Area button in the Inquiry toolbar, selecting Area from the Inquiry cascading menu of the Tools pull-down menu, or by entering AA or AREA at the command line. You must select at least three points on the shape to calculate the area, but the three points do not have to be connected. Shapes created as lines or polylines do not need to be closed for AutoCAD to calculate the area and perimeter values. AutoCAD will automatically connect the last point selected with the first point created. After you select the last point on the object or shape, AutoCAD automatically closes the area before calculating and displaying area calculations. The AREA command can be used to calculate the exact square footage of living space or rental space of a floor plan of a house or a commercial building. Or it can be used to determine the exact square footage sizes of structural materials such as a foundation wall and footing. You can also use the AREA command to determine wall lengths in a floor plan. You can add or subtract areas while AutoCAD displays a running total for square footage and perimeter values.

You can find the area and perimeter of any shape created with the LINE, POLYLINE, POLYGON, MULTILINE, SPLINE, RECTANGLE, or CIRCLE command or any closed or unclosed objects. If the shape is created with the LINE or the MULTILINE command, you must select intersecting points along the perimeter (or at least three points) using the *Snap to Endpoint* or *Snap to Intersection* object snap modes. If the shape is created with the POLYLINE, POLYGON, RECTANGLE, or SPLINE command, you can either select the intersecting points or use the *Object* option of the AREA command and select one of the objects that make up the shape to quickly obtain area and perimeter.

■   **EXERCISE 16–3:**   *The following step-by-step exercise will allow you to calculate the area and the perimeter of the floor plan as shown in Figure 16–6.*

Step #1:   Open the EXE16-2.dwg file.

Step #2:   Use the AREA command as follows:

Command: **AA** or **AREA** ~EnterKey~

Specify first corner point or [Object/Add/Subtract]: *(select point 1 as shown in Figure 16–6)*

Specify next corner point or press ENTER for total: *(select point 2)*

Specify next corner point or press ENTER for total: *(select point 3)*

FIGURE 16–6   The AREA command is used to calculate the area in square inches and in square feet with the perimeter of the floor plan (or any shape). In this example, nine points are selected. The floor plan is created with the LINE and the OFFSET commands.

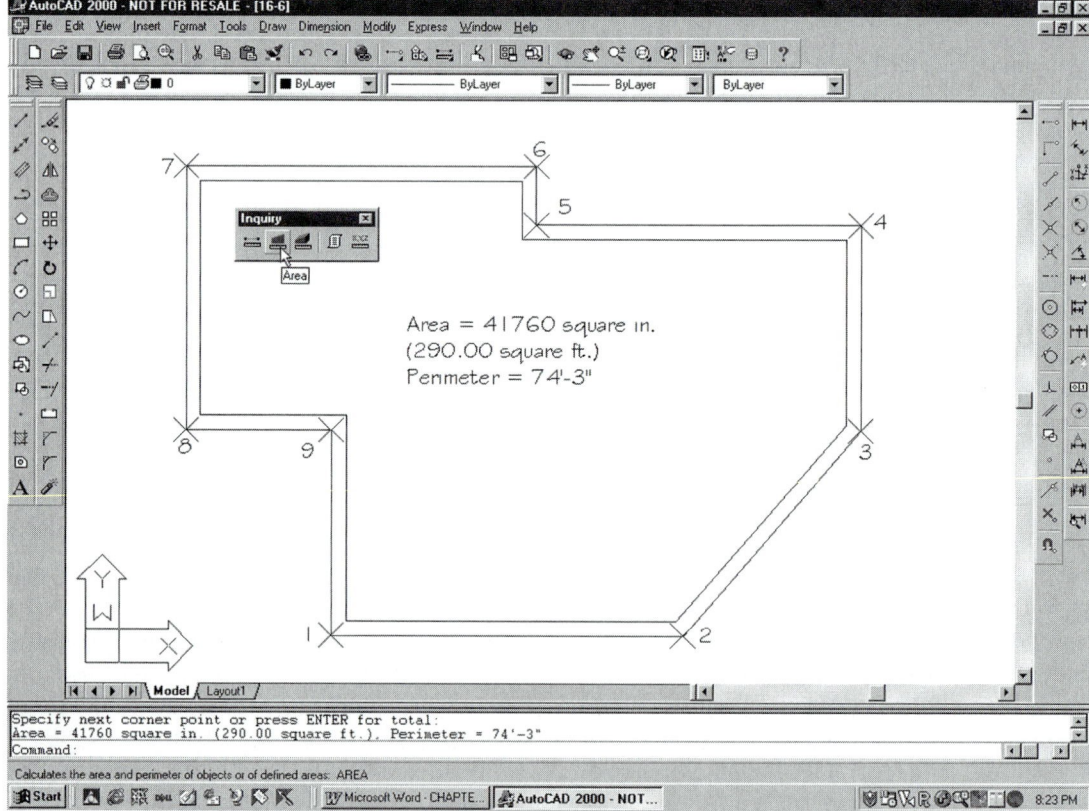

Specify next corner point or press ENTER for total: *(select point 4)*

Specify next corner point or press ENTER for total: *(select point 5)*

Specify next corner point or press ENTER for total: *(select point 6)*

Specify next corner point or press ENTER for total: *(select point 7)*

Specify next corner point or press ENTER for total: *(select point 8)*

Specify next corner point or press ENTER for total: *(select point 9)*

Specify next corner point or press ENTER for total: ~EnterKey~

Area = 41760 square in. (290.00 square ft.), Perimeter = 74'-3"

Congratulations! You have successfully calculated the area of the floor plan using the AREA command.

> *Caution: The area and perimeter values are a direct result of the* Length Precision *value assigned using the Drawing Units dialog box. You can change the precision to 0'-0" before using the AREA command to have the values displayed as feet-and-inches only.*

> *Tips: If you create floor plans using the MULTILINE command, the procedure to calculate the area would be the same as shown in EXERCISE 16–3. However, if you create floor plans using the PLINE command, you can skip selecting the corner points by simply selecting the polyline using the Object option of the AREA command.*

For the floor plan shown in Figure 16–6, you can calculate the area of the exterior walls by multiplying the wall thickness (6") by the perimeter as follows: 74'-3" × 6" = 37.125 square ft. This is useful when calculating the cubic yard of concrete in a foundation plan. Simply convert the s.f. to c.f. then to c.y.

16.6.1   Using the Object Option of the AREA Command

The Object option of the AREA command allows you to select the shape with a single click. The shape must be a circle, ellipse, spline, polygon or a polyline but does not have to be closed (except circle and ellipse). Selecting a circle with the Object option will display area and circumference.

■ **EXERCISE 16–4:**   *The following step-by-step exercise will allow you to calculate the area and the perimeter of the object created with the PLINE command with a width of 2" as shown in Figure 16–7. To calculate the area and the perimeter of this shape, use the Object option of the AREA command.*

Step #1:   Open the EXE16-3.dwg file.

Step #2:   Use the AREA command as follows:

Command: **AA** or **AREA** ~EnterKey~

Specify first corner point or [Object/Add/Subtract]: **O** ~EnterKey~

Select objects: *(select the polyline)*

Area = 14544 square in. (101.00 square ft.), Perimeter = 51'-8"

Polyline's width ignored in area calculations.

Congratulations! You have successfully calculated the area of the polyline using the AREA command.

No matter how wide the polyline is, AutoCAD will ignore the polyline's width in area calculations. The area of a wide polyline is calculated from its centerline. If the polyline is closed using the Close option of the PLINE command, AutoCAD will calculate the Perimeter value; otherwise AutoCAD will calculate the Length value. The values displayed after selecting the objects depend on the type of object selected. The following is a list of objects and values returned by AutoCAD when using the Object option:

FIGURE 16–7 The Object option of the AREA command allows you to select the shape or object. The shape must be a circle, ellipse, spline, polygon, or a polyline.

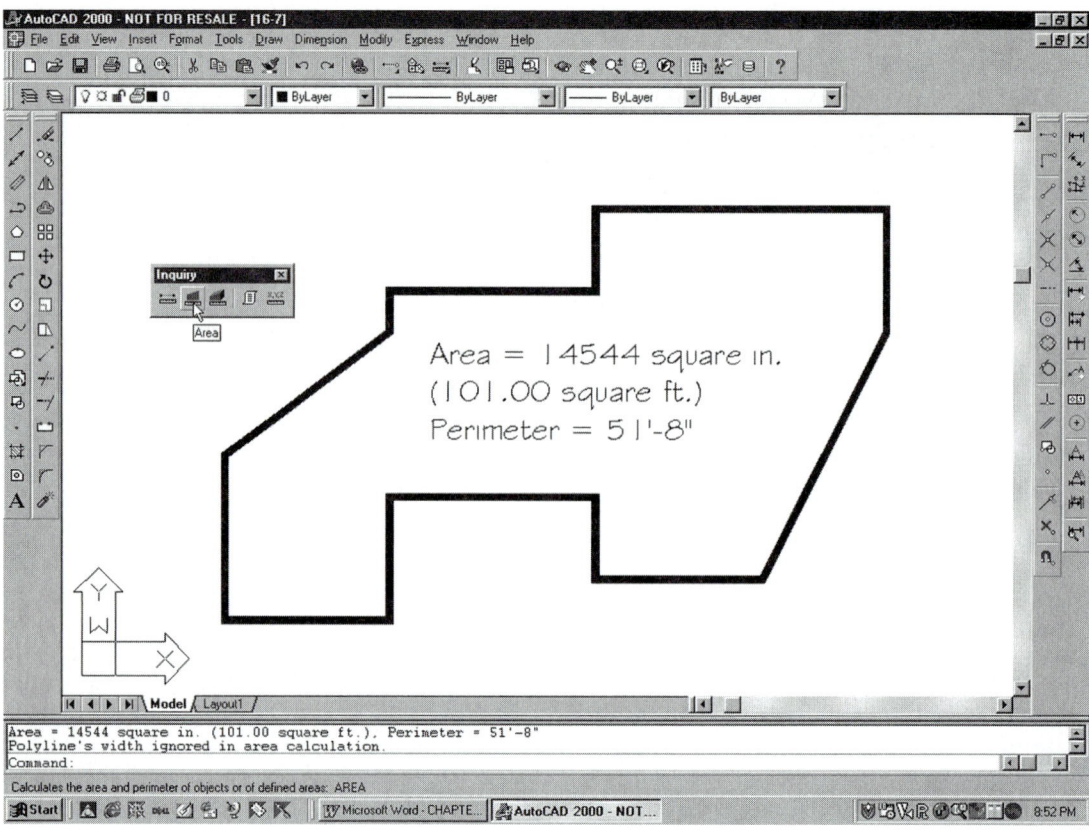

Object Selected	Numeric Value Returned (AutoCAD's Respond)
Line	Selected object does not have an area
Circle	Area and circumference
Ellipse	Area and perimeter
Polyline	Area, length, perimeter
Multiline	Selected object does not have an area
Rectangle	Area and perimeter
Polygon	Area and perimeter
Spline	Area and length
Trace	Selected object does not have an area
Sketch	Selected object does not have an area
Open Objects	Area and length
Region	Area of all objects within a region

Tips: If precise area calculations are required for projects, avoid using the PLINE command when creating objects since AutoCAD calculates area of polylines along its centerline.

16.6.2 Using the Add and Subtract Options of the AREA Command

The Add option of the AREA command allows you to automatically add the area calculations to the total area. AutoCAD will display a running total after each addition. To begin a running total, select the Add option before selecting the objects to be added to the running total. The Subtract option of the AREA command allows you to subtract areas from the running total. The Add or the Subtract option will stay in effect until the command is cancelled.

■ **EXERCISE 16–5:** *The following step-by-step exercise will allow you to calculate the total area of the object shown in Figure 16–8, including the circle and the polygon. You will add the entire shape into the running total first and then subtract the areas of the circle and the polygon from the running total.*

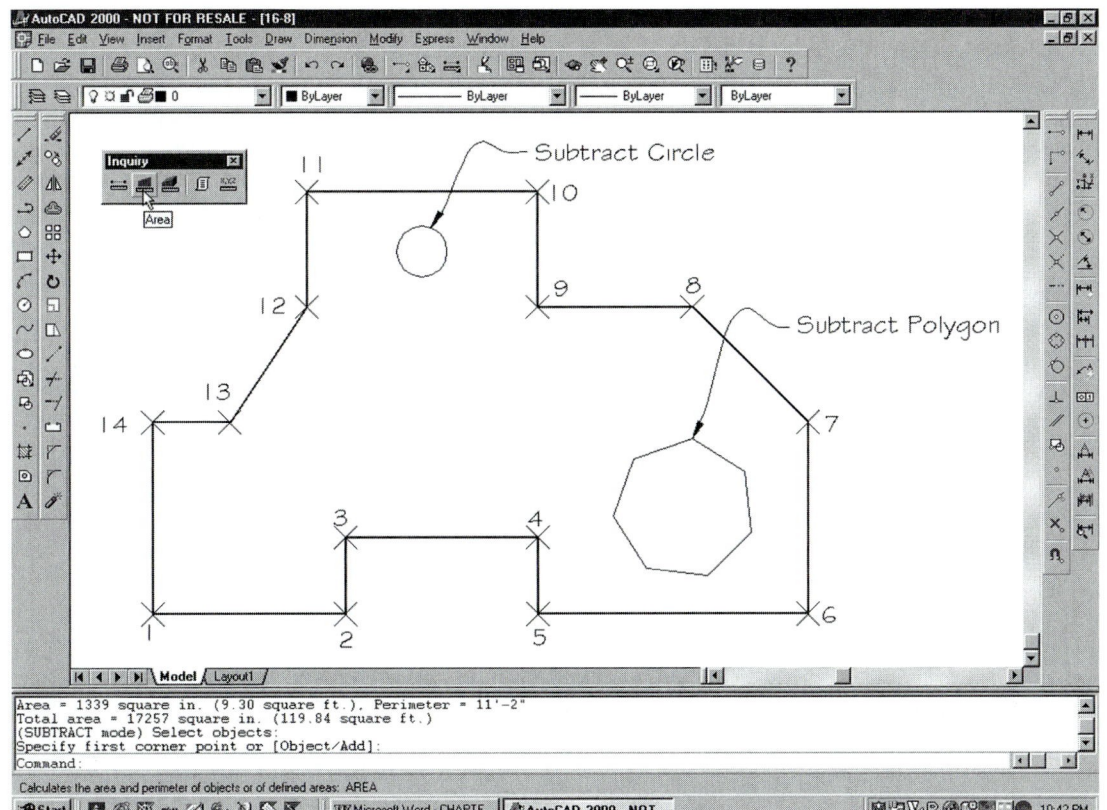

FIGURE 16–8 Using the Add and the Subtract options of the AREA command to calculate the area without the circle and polygon.

Step #1: Open the EXE16-4.dwg file.

Step #2: Click on the Area button in the Inquiry toolbar and use the following command line procedure:

Specify first corner point or [Object/Add/Subtract]: **A** ~EnterKey~

Specify first corner point or [Object/Subtract]: *(select point 1 as shown in Figure 16–8)*

Specify next corner point or press ENTER for total (ADD mode): *(select point 2)*

Specify next corner point or press ENTER for total (ADD mode): *(select point 3)*

Step #3: Select the remaining points. After selecting point 14, press ~EnterKey~ and use the following command line procedure:

Area = 18792.00 square in. (130.50 square ft.), Perimeter = 56'-10"

Total area = 18792.00 square in. (130.50 square ft.)

Specify first corner point or [Object/Subtract]: **S** ~EnterKey~

Specify first corner point or [Object/Add]: **O** ~EnterKey~

(SUBTRACT mode) Select objects: *(select the circle)*

Area = 195 square in. (1.36 square ft.), Circumference = 4'-2"

Total area = 18597 square in. (129.14 square ft.)

(SUBTRACT mode) Select objects: *(select the seven-sided polygon)*

Area = 1339 square in. (9.30 square ft.), Perimeter = 11'-2"

Total area = 17257 square in. (119.84 square ft.)

(SUBTRACT mode) Select objects: ~EnterKey~

Specify first corner point or [Object/Add]: ~EnterKey~

Congratulations! You have successfully calculated the area of the object by subtracting the circle and the polygon from the total. The area and circumference are given for the circle and area and perimeter are given for the polygon. Their areas are subtracted from the total area. You can keep selecting corner points or use the Object or the Add option to add more objects to the running total. If you are finished subtracting and want to add another object or shape to the total, enter A at the last prompt to switch to the ADD mode. Press the ~EnterKey~ when done.

16.6.3 Finding the Area of Open Objects

The object or shape does not have to be closed to find its area. If the shape is a single entity such as a polyline, select the object by using the Object option of the AREA command. If the shape is multi-entity, such as lines, select the corner points until you reach the opening.

■ **EXERCISE 16–6:** *The following step-by-step exercise will allow you to calculate the total area of the closet space as shown in Figure 16–9.*

Step #1: Open the EXE16-5.dwg file.

Step #2: Use the Area command as follows:

Command: **AREA** ~EnterKey~

Specify first corner point or [Object/Add/Subtract]: *(select point 1 as shown in Figure 16–9)*

Specify next corner point or press ENTER for total: *(select point 2)*

Specify next corner point or press ENTER for total: *(select point 3)*

Specify next corner point or press ENTER for total: *(select point 4)*

Specify next corner point or press ENTER for total: ~EnterKey~

Area = 6912 square in. (48 square ft.), perimeter = 28'-0"

FIGURE 16–9
Calculating an open area.

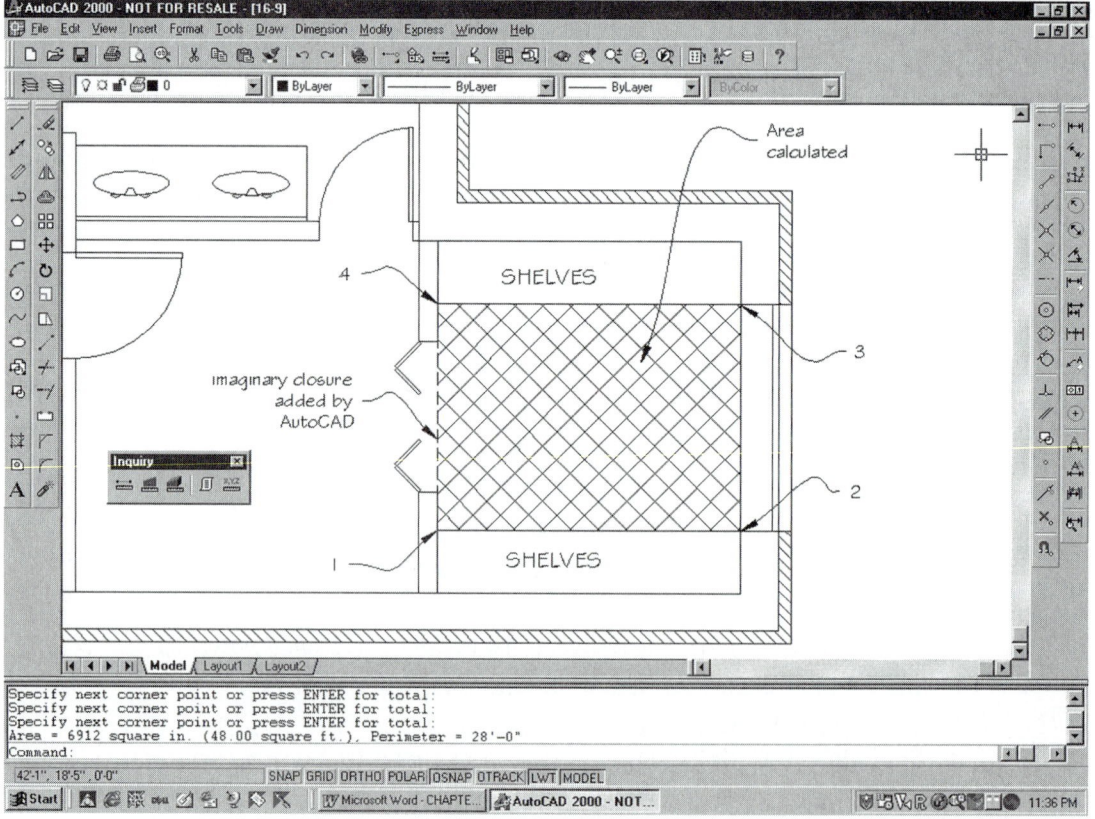

Congratulations! You have successfully calculated the area of an open object.

Tips: The LIST command is a faster alternative to using the AREA command to find lengths and areas of objects.

16.7 DISPLAYING MASS PROPERTIES OF SHAPES

The MASSPROP (Mass Properties) command allows you to calculate the area, perimeter and other properties of two-dimensional shapes and three-dimensional solid models. The MASSPROP command can be accessed by selecting Mass Properties button in the Inquiry toolbar, selecting Mass Properties from the Inquiry flyout button in the Standard Toolbar, selecting Mass Properties from the Inquiry cascading menu of the Tools pull-down menu, or by entering MASSPROP at the command line. To display the mass properties of two-dimensional objects, you must first convert the two-dimensional shape into a *region*. A region is a two-dimensional area created from closed shapes or loops. To create a region, you must use the REGION command. To access the REGION command, click on the Region button in the Draw toolbar, select Region from the Draw pull-down menu, or enter REG or REGION at the command line. You can select lines, circular arcs, elliptical arcs, circles, ellipses, closed polylines, and splines to create a region. AutoCAD will convert lines, polylines, and curves to form closed planar loops such as outside object boundaries and holes inside a region. The outside boundary is considered the *loop,* and the holes inside the region are considered the *islands.* Figure 16–10 shows two different shapes created with different commands. To convert these shapes into regions, use the RE-GION command as follows:

```
Command: REGION ~EnterKey~
Select objects: (select all objects shown in Figure 16-10A and B)
Select objects: ~EnterKey~
5 loops extracted.
5 regions created.
```

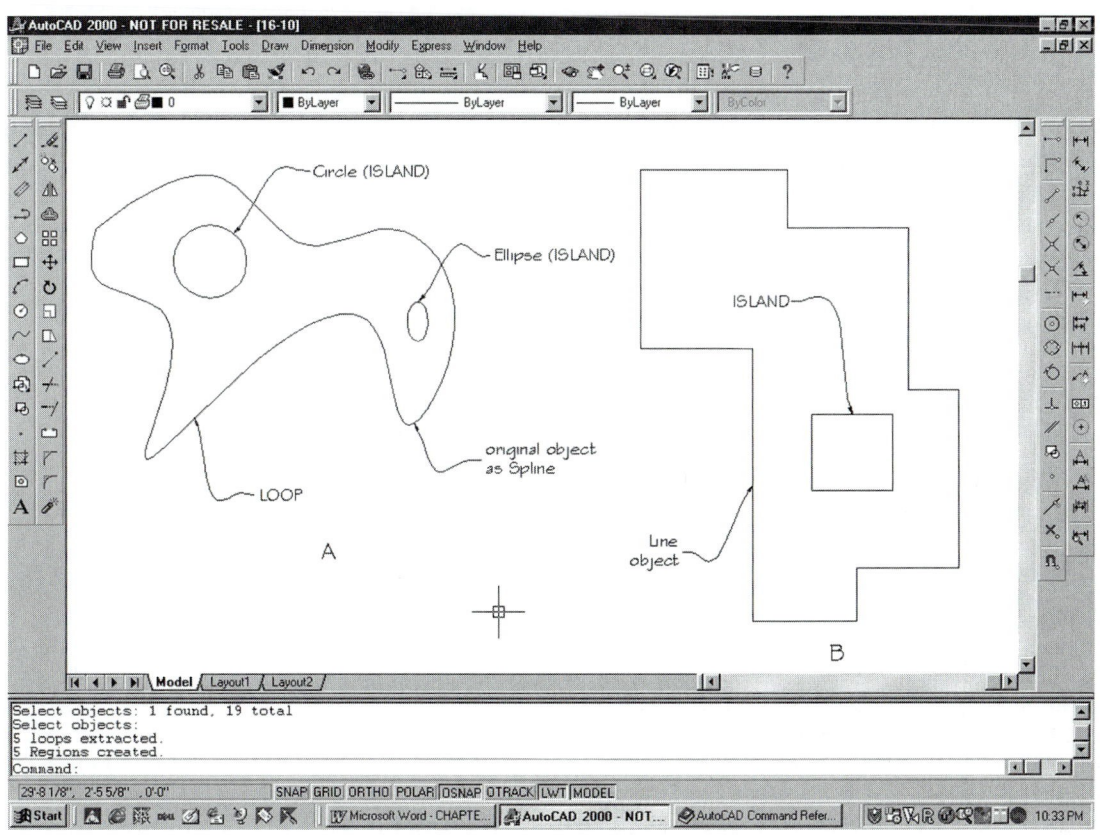

FIGURE 16–10 Before using the MASSPROP command, shapes and objects must be converted to regions using the REGION command.

```
AutoCAD Text Window - 16-11
Edit
Command: _massprop
Select objects: 1 found

Select objects: 1 found, 2 total

Select objects: 1 found, 3 total

Select objects: 1 found, 4 total

Select objects:
-----------------    REGIONS    -----------------
Area:                   81642.2937 sq in
Perimeter:              2460.2536 in
Bounding box:        X: 50.1011  --  695.5678 in
                     Y: 22.2636  --  381.4571 in
Centroid:            X: 442.0591 in
                     Y: 220.4343 in
Moments of inertia:  X: 4514757322.7834 sq in sq in
                     Y: 19305777574.2470 sq in sq in
Product of inertia:  XY: 7265923867.3412 sq in sq in
Radii of gyration:   X: 235.1579 in
                     Y: 486.2796 in
Principal moments (sq in sq in) and X-Y directions about centroid:
                     I: 387181112.8896 along [0.9740 -0.2266]
                     J: 3512017700.3137 along [0.2266 0.9740]

Write analysis to a file? [Yes/No] <N>: |
```

FIGURE 16–11 The Mass Properties information provided by the AutoCAD Text Window dialog box.

The boundary of the region consists of end-connected curves where each point shares only two edges. If you select objects that are open, intersections, and self-intersecting curves, AutoCAD will reject them. If you use the LIST command on any of the objects after a region is created, they will be listed as regions (not lines, spline, circle, or ellipse). You can now use the MASSPROP command to display mass properties of the regions as follows:

```
Command: MASSPROP ~EnterKey~
Select objects: (select all regions)
Select objects: ~EnterKey~
Write analysis to a file? [Yes/No] <N>:
~EnterKey~
```

If you wish to write a mass property report to an MPR (Mass Property Report) file, enter Y at the last command prompt. AutoCAD will display the mass properties in the text window as shown in Figure 16–11. Much of the information provided in this text window is beyond the scope of this text.

AutoCAD applies the current color, layer, linetype, and lineweight to the region. AutoCAD deletes the original objects when creating a region unless the DELOBJ (Delete Objects) system variable is set to 0. If the original object contains hatching, AutoCAD will remove the hatch associativity. To restore hatch associativity, you must erase and recreate hatching. Associative Hatching is discussed in Chapter 20.

Tips: Use the EXPLODE command to convert individual loops of regions and islands back to lines, circles, and ellipses.

REVIEW QUESTIONS

1. How do you access the Inquiry toolbar?
2. What is the function of the Inquiry toolbar?
3. Describe the purpose and procedure behind using the DISTANCE command transparently.
4. What kind of information would you receive when using the LIST command on a circle?
5. What command would you use to find the coordinates of an existing point?
6. What kind of information is returned when using the AREA command on a polygon?
7. What is the function of the Object option of the AREA command?
8. How many different ways can you access the AREA command?
9. What is the function of the MASSPROP command?

PROBLEMS

1. Open the *EXE16-6.dwg* file. Freeze the DIMENSIONS, HATCHING, and NOTES layers. Use the AREA command to calculate the area of the BASEMENT. Do not forget to go around pilasters. Hint: You should select a total of 20 corner points. The answer is 981.7420 square feet. Do not save the changes.

2. Open the *EXE16-7.dwg* file. Use the AREA command to calculate the square footage of the first floor plan. Freeze the Dimensions, Hatching, and Notes layers. Include all walls. Do not include PORCH and GARAGE areas.

3. Open the *EXE16-8.dwg* file. Use the AREA command to calculate the square footage of the second floor plan. Freeze the Dimensions, Hatching, and Notes layers. Include all walls. Do not include the Bonus Room.

4. Using the *EXE16-7.dwg* file, what is the area of the GARAGE?

5. Using the *EXE16-7.dwg* file, what is the perimeter of this house?

6. Open the *EXE16-9.dwg* file. What is the total area of this house?

7. Open the *EXE16-10.dwg* file. What is the perimeter of the PROPOSED FIVE-STORY OFFICE BUILDING?

8. Using the *EXE16-10.dwg* file. What is the area of the PROPOSED PARKING space?

9. Open the *EXE16-11.dwg* file. What is the square footage of the RENTAL AREA?

Drawing MultiLines

17

After successful completion of this chapter, you will be able to:

▲ Use the MULTILINE command to draw Multiple Lines to create architectural floor plans.

▲ Create architectural wall types and styles using the MLSTYLE command.

▲ Define the components of the MultiLine Styles Dialog Box.

▲ Utilize Polar Tracking and Polar Snap when using MultiLines.

▲ Use Blipmarks to determine MultiLine Justification reference points.

▲ Utilize the Element Properties Sub-Dialog Box of the MultiLine Styles Dialog Box.

▲ Utilize the MultiLine Properties Sub-Dialog Box of the MultiLine Styles Dialog Box.

▲ Use three different methods to calculate Offset Values when creating wall types based on project specifications.

▲ Create Shading inside the Wall Types using the BHatch command.

▲ Draw architectural floor plans, including door and window openings, using two different methods.

▲ Edit MultiLines with 12 different editing options using the MultiLine Edit Tools Dialog Box.

▲ Use the Snap From Toolbar and Object Snap Tracking to locate new MultiLines in relation to existing MultiLines.

▲ Create a door with jambs inside the wall opening.

▲ Edit and change the length of MultiLines using the STRETCH command.

▲ Edit and change the length of MultiLines using Grips.

17.1 INTRODUCTION TO MULTILINES

In the short run it is easier to use the LINE and the OFFSET commands to draw floor plans, but in the long run it is more efficient and faster to create and edit floor plans with the MLINE and MLEDIT commands. The MLINE command simply saves time and increases drawing efficiency once you understand and know its operation. Many people avoid using the MLINE command because of its complexity. But this chapter will teach you all you wanted to know about the MULTILINE command. It is especially detailed for the following reason: to put an end to the notion that MultiLines are useless and to teach the true character of this command to those who want to learn it. It will take time and patience to master this command, but when you learn it you will create floor plans faster, and editing will be much easier. You may skip this

FIGURE 17–1 A preliminary floor plan created with the *Standard* two-line *default* MultiLine Style.

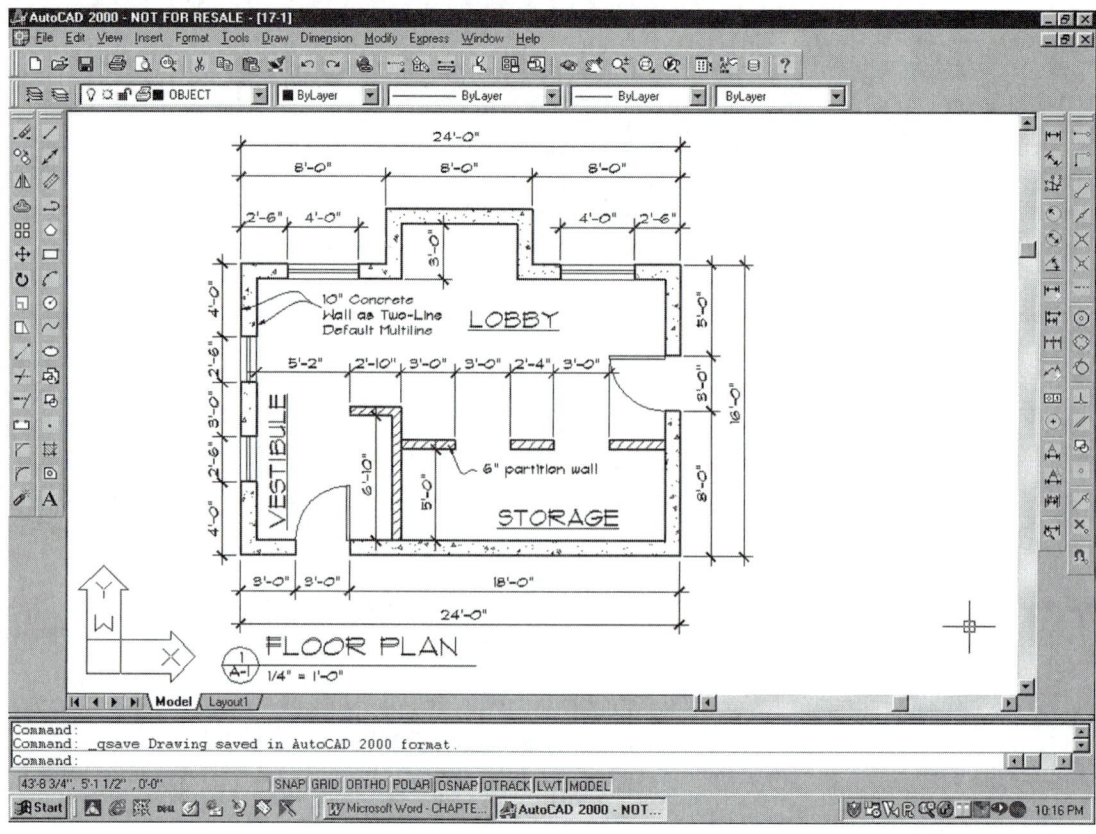

chapter if you like: just go back to Chapter 5 and get more acquainted with the LINE command. A word of caution for those who want to learn the MULTILINE command: **Do not skim through this chapter. Read every single word and perform all exercises. Read over and over again to slowly digest the complex nature of this command.**

The MLINE command allows architects and interior designers to create floor plans by drawing up to 16 parallel lines as follows:

1. When a drawing calls for the creation of *only* two parallel lines having a continuous linetype, the default Standard MultiLine Style can be used. Objects created with this method will have only two parallel lines, a continuous linetype, and open beginning and open end points. This does not require creation of a MultiLine Style other than setting the wall thickness after accessing the MLINE command. With this option a floor plan can be drawn as either a continuous operation (cutting the wall openings afterward) or as individual wall segments (establishing the wall openings as the floor plan is drawn). The desired wall and door openings are cut from the walls with the editing options of the MultiLine Edit Tools dialog box. These are all explained later in the chapter. A floor plan created with the Standard MultiLine style using the MLINE command is shown in Figure 17–1. This floor plan uses the default two-line STANDARD MultiLine style.

2. When a project calls for the creation of a floor plan with more than two parallel lines, the MLSTYLE (MultiLine Style) command is used. This method can also be used to establish some of the display options of the Standard default MultiLine Style or the display options of the new style to be created. The display options are associated with the *Joints*, *Caps*, and *Fills* categories of the MultiLine properties inside the MLSTYLE command. This method requires the creation of a new MultiLine Style and/or establishment of display option settings. Figure 17–2 shows a foundation plan with two continuous and two dashed linetypes. Notice that in Figure 17–2 there are no door or window openings, only the continuous footing and a foundation wall are created.

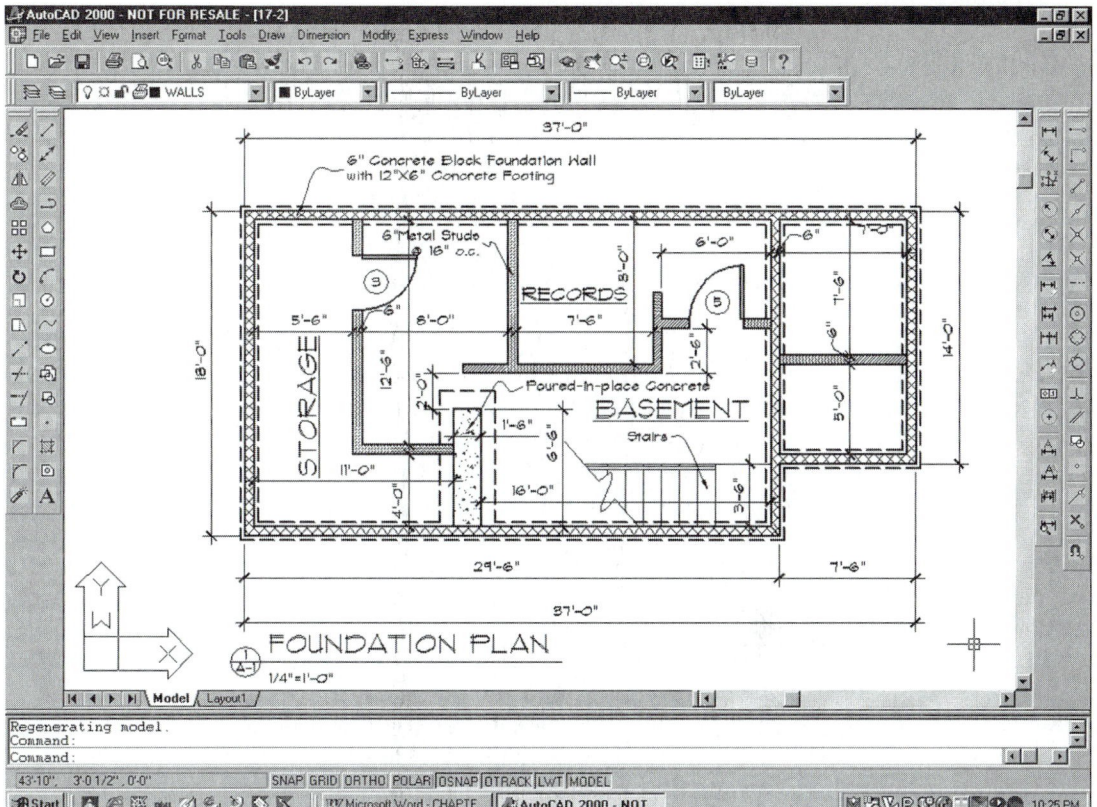

FIGURE 17–2 A Foundation Plan with two continuous and two dashed line types created with the MLSTYLE command.

17.2 ADVANTAGES OF THE MULTILINE COMMAND

The MLINE command is generally used to create floor plans in architectural drawings. Although there are many possibilities for creating and designing different wall types in floor plans, there are major advantages of using this command over the LINE or the PLINE commands as follows:

- Ease of operation and efficiency.
- Immediate use of the standard style as default two-line parallel lines without having to create a new style.
- Three different methods can be used to create new wall styles and types with or without the standard style using the MultiLine Styles dialog box. This is discussed later in the chapter. One of these methods would surely satisfy the discriminating or reluctant MultiLine user.
- The Scale option of the MLINE command allows the user to enter the wall thickness for any of the architectural drawing scales.
- More than one Justification can be used to determine point of origin for distance configuration.
- Creation of up to 16 parallel lines is possible with different color and linetype as part of the MultiLine Style to meet project-specific standards and applications.
- Provides solid coloring of the entire wall segment.
- Storing of new styles in MLN files in DXF (Data Exchange) format.
- Option to display Joints (vertices) at wall intersections to provide different Hatch (material indicator graphics) pattern applications to different wall segments with ease of editing Joints.

- Ease of editing MultiLines using the STRETCH command.
- Ease of editing MultiLines using grips.
- Ability to create openings in floor plans using a continuous MultiLine operation.
- Ability to cut openings using a single MultiLine editing operation. The LINE command would require the use of BREAK or TRIM commands with multiple operations. Cutting or Closing openings in a MultiLine is a snap. Perhaps this might get you to look closer to the MLINE command.

MultiLines are created as single objects that can serve as a single wall segment. In contrast, floor plans created with the LINE command are composed of many individual elements that make up a whole entity. Unless lines are converted to polylines, editing floor plans created with the LINE command takes more time and requires more effort to draw. In this respect it is easier to compose, dimension, hatch, and edit floor plans that are drawn with the MLINE command. Easier because wall components created with the MLINE command can be drawn, hatched, and edited with efficiency and with a minimum amount of operation steps, especially when editing a single pick usually gets the editing job done. MultiLines have characteristics of a Polyline but are not considered to be a Pline. Managing and editing MultiLines is much easier and more efficient than using the PLINE command. PLINE (Polyline) is a very complex command, and a thorough knowledge of this command is required if speed and efficiency of the MultiLine command is to be matched or exceeded. There are too many complex editing options involved with the PLINE command. It is not as straightforward as the MLEDIT (MultiLine Edit) command and it does not provide a dialog box to create a specific wall style for the creation of a floor plan.

Similarly, the TRACE command is not an efficient way to draw floor plans because it is not possible to hatch walls with this command, and establishing distances as references to the point of origin is very difficult. Even though you can establish a wall thickness, the display of the trace segment is delayed by one pick point where it might create confusion and miscalculation when drawing precise wall dimensions on floor plans. Also it is not possible to back up because the Undo option is missing and there is no option to control or edit intersections or joints of walls created with the TRACE command. The LINE command was introduced earlier and a sample floor plan was generated using the LINE and the OFFSET commands. Although this approach to creating a floor plan is simple, it requires many segments to be created and involves many operational steps when edited. Knowing the strengths and shortcomings of available commands will narrow your choices when it comes to choosing a particular command to perform a specific task such as creation of a floor plan. You must first understand the task and then study the options available to you. Knowing the inner workings of a command will help you make a viable decision.

17.3 THE MULTILINE COMMAND

The MLINE command allows you to draw multiple lines that are parallel to each other. These multiple lines are called *elements* and consist of between 1 and 16 lines. AutoCAD provides two continuous solid lines as the standard style. If more than two lines are required, a new Style must be created using the MLSTYLE command. After a style is set, it can be modified and edited using the MLEDIT command. Figure 17–3 shows a two-line MultiLine with identification of components. Notice that the default Justification is at Top and indicated as X on the drawing. The default direction is counterclockwise as indicated with arrows in the drawing. Most of the architectural applications will involve the use of two and the creation of three or more lines in AutoCAD. However, it is possible to create up to 16 parallel lines with the MLSTYLE command.

The MLINE (MultiLine) command can be accessed in three different ways:

1. From the Draw toolbar select the MultiLine button. The Draw toolbar is docked as default on the left side of the AutoCAD drawing screen next to the Modify toolbar. It is the third button from the top.
2. From the Draw pull-down menu select the MultiLine.

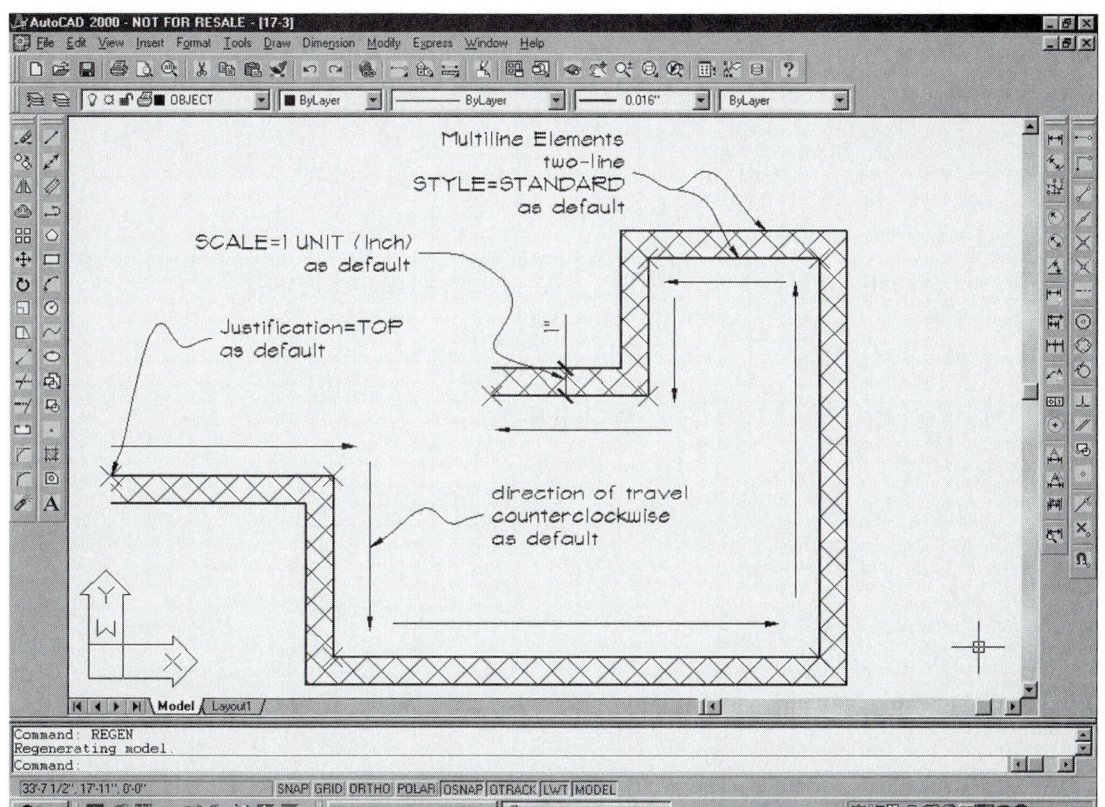

FIGURE 17–3
MultiLine Standard
two-line default values
and components. Notice
the MultiLine
Justification is at Top
indicated with "X" at
each wall intersection.
This is extremely helpful
in determining distances
on floor plans. Also
notice that the
beginning and the
ending points of this
wall are open, but can
be closed (capped)
using the MultiLine
Properties option of the
MultiLine Styles Dialog
Box.

3. Type MLINE or ML at the command line as follows:

```
Command: MLINE or Ml ~EnterKey~
Current settings: Justification = Top, Scale = 1.00, Style = STANDARD
Specify start point or [Justification/Scale/STyle]:
```

When you enter the MLine command the first time, the default values for Justification = Top, Scale = 1.00, and Style = STANDARD will appear. These default values will remain until you change it. When you change any of the options, the new values will be shown when you access the MLINE command again and will be shown as Current settings.

The MultiLine command has three options affecting its *justification* (point of origin), *scale* (the thickness of a wall, or the distance between the two lines), and *style* (the name of the style given to the MultiLine). Let's examine these three options in detail.

17.3.1   MultiLine Justification Option

This option determines how the lines originate from the definition points set by the user. AutoCAD will originate the MultiLine relative to a base point as the user defines the *From* and *To* locations. Justification is based on AutoCAD's counterclockwise direction. This means that if you draw a MultiLine in a clockwise direction, the justification will reverse itself. For example, if you set the justification to *Bottom* and start drawing clockwise, the justification will reverse itself to *Top* and vice versa. *Zero Justification* will not be affected by either direction. In a single MultiLine command, justification can be specified only once. In order to change the justification, the MLINE command must be accessed again. The three justification options are Top, Zero, and Bottom. The Top justification is the default. If you exit the drawing session with justification set to other than the default value, next time you open a file or start a new drawing the justification will appear with the default value reset.

Figure 17–4 shows a square floor plan with 12'-0" long and 1'-0" thick walls with Top Justification as the default. To draw this floor plan properly in a counterclockwise direction, a distance of 10'-0" must be entered as the dimension between starting and ending points marked with X,

FIGURE 17–4   A square floor plan created with the Top Justification option and counterclockwise direction.

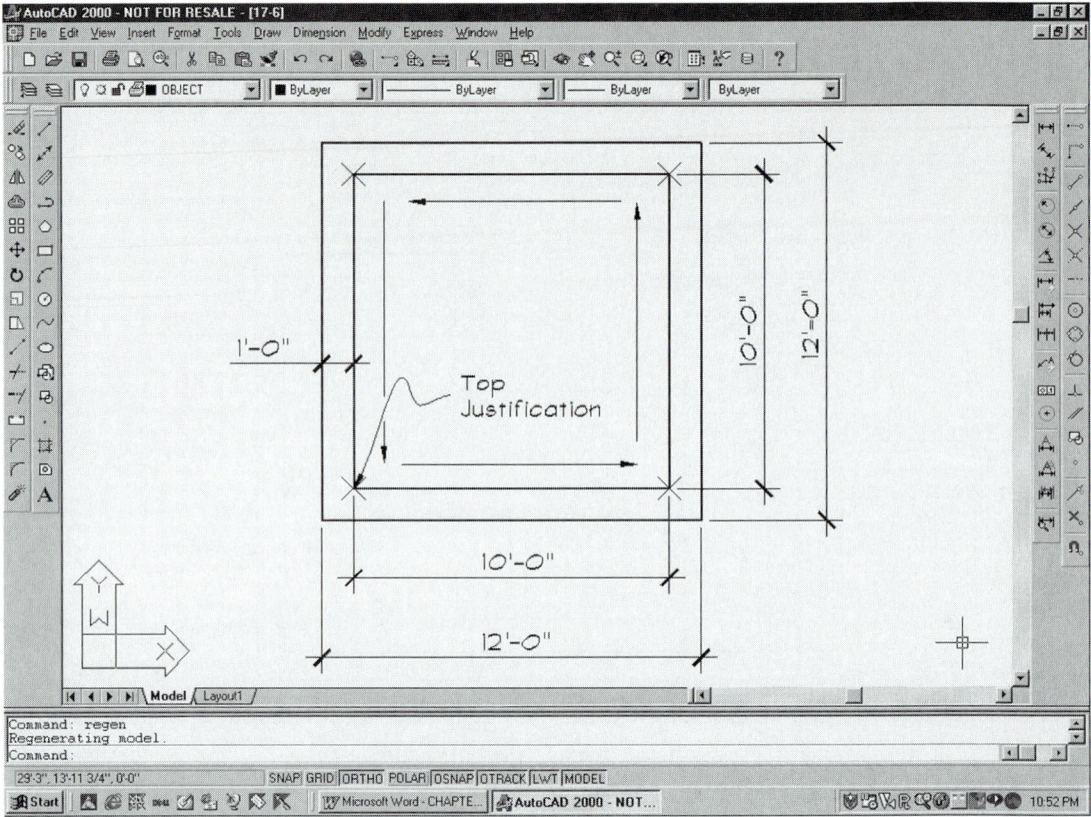

even though the overall dimension is shown as 12'-0". This is because AutoCAD starts creating the MultiLine from the top (inside corner) point of the walls. As the walls are drawn counterclockwise the inside corners of each intersection becomes the Top Justification. When the justification is set to top, inside corners of walls become the definition points.

Caution: When drawing floor plans be very careful not to inadvertently change the Justification option points during the drawing because the distance required to enter depends on the justification points.

The option to change the justification to meet personal drawing habits is another advantage of the MultiLine command. Figure 17–5 shows how changing the justification option to zero can alter the distance required to enter. With this change the distance required to enter is now 11'-0", even when the overall dimension is 12'-0". Because the walls are 12" thick, zero justification represents the center point of the wall. One half of 12" is 6" calculated on both sides and subtracted from the overall dimension of 12'-0". The 11'-0" is now the required distance to draw this floor plan using the zero justification option.

Caution: Because of this unique implication of the Justification options on the overall dimensions of the floor plans, it is extremely important that you follow very closely on screen the definition points in regards to the required distances and the application of the proper dimensions.

■   **EXERCISE 17–1:**   *The following step-by-step exercise will allow you to create the simple floor plan as shown in Figure 17–5 using the MLINE command. The justification will be set to zero.*

Step #1:   Create a new drawing and establish architectural units and limits.

Step #2:   Access the MULTILINE command and use the following command line procedure:

Command: **MLINE** ~EnterKey~ (or click on the MultiLine button in the Draw toolbar).

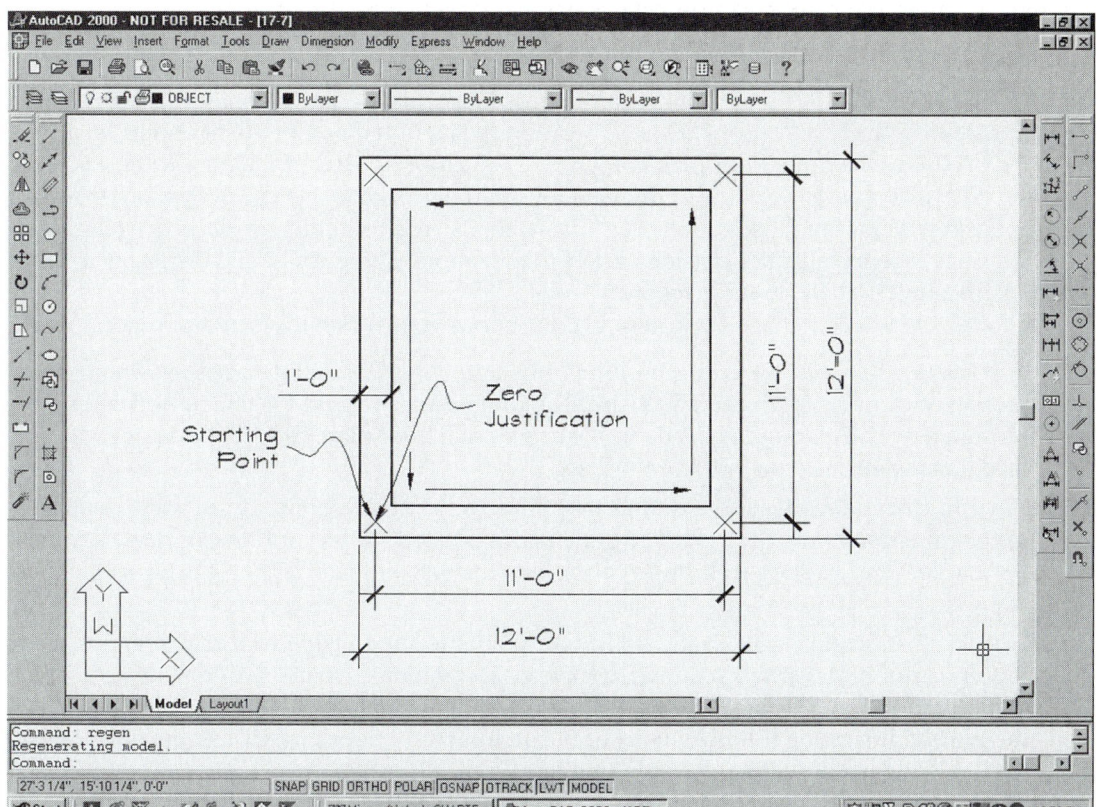

FIGURE 17–5
MultiLine Zero
Justification option
changes the dimension
needed to enter to draw
the same floor plan in
Figure 17–4.

Current settings: Justification = Top, Scale = 1.00, Style = STANDARD

Specify start point or [Justification/Scale/Style]: **J** ~EnterKey~ (this will select the justification option)

Enter justification type [Top/Zero/Bottom] <top>: **Z** ~EnterKey~ (this will set the justification option to zero)

Current settings: Justification = Zero, Scale = 1.00, Style = STANDARD

Specify start point or [Justification/Scale/STyle/]: **S** ~EnterKey~ (this will select the Scale option)

Enter mline scale <1.00>: **12** ~EnterKey~ (this will set the wall thickness as 12″)

Current settings: Justification = Zero, Scale = 12, Style = STANDARD

Specify start point or [Justification/Scale/Style]: (select the starting point as shown in Figure 17–5) ~EnterKey~

Specify next point: **@11′<0** ~EnterKey~ (this will draw the bottom horizontal portion of the wall as 11′-0″ to the East).

Specify next point or [Undo]: **@11′<90** ~EnterKey~ (this will draw the right vertical portion of the wall as 11′-0″ to the North).

Specify next point or [Close/Undo]: **@11′<180** ~EnterKey~ (this will draw the top horizontal portion of the wall as 11′-0″ to the West).

Specify next point or [Close/Undo]: **C** ~EnterKey~ (this will *close* the wall)

Congratulations! You have successfully created a 12′-0″ square using the MLINE command. Your drawing should now look like Figure 17–5. Do not save the changes.

Note: Instead of using the ~EnterKey~ to select the justification you can use the right-click shortcut menu. This method will save you from having to type the options at the command line. For the purpose of clarity and ease of recognizing commands and options

the command and its options will be used at the command prompt. The right-click will allow access to shortcut menus and is only an option.

To draw the floor plan in Figure 17–4 use the procedure shown above, but set Justification to Top, then change the Scale from 1.00 to 12 (if required) and then enter 10′ for point locations. Figure 17–6 shows the same floor plan in Figures 17–4 and 17–5 except the justification is set to Bottom. With this option the exterior intersections of the walls become the definition points for the dimensions. With the justification set to Bottom, the required dimension is the overall dimension since it represents the outside corner intersections of the walls. The distances to enter when justification is at Bottom for Figure 17–6 is 12′-0″.

The following is a list of items you should consider as you work with justification options:

1. Top Justification will set the definition points to the inside wall intersections when the direction of drawing is counterclockwise. The dimensions needed for this option can be determined by calculating the inside wall surfaces of a floor plan. Entering exterior wall surface dimensions will **not** work in this case.

2. Zero Justification will set the definition points to the center point of the walls regardless of the direction of the drawing. The dimensions needed for this option can be determined by reading the exterior wall intersection dimensions and subtracting the wall thickness from it.

3. Bottom Justification will set the definition points to the outside wall intersections when the direction of drawing is counterclockwise. The dimensions needed for this option can be determined by reading the exterior overall wall dimensions. Generally speaking this is the type of dimension found in many of the architectural floor plans. Entering interior wall surface dimensions will **not** work in this case.

4. Top Justification will reverse itself to Bottom when the direction of drawing is clockwise.

5. Bottom Justification will reverse itself to Top when the direction of drawing is clockwise.

FIGURE 17–6
MultiLine Bottom Justification option. Notice the bottom exterior intersections of the walls become the definition points for dimensions when the direction of drawing is counterclockwise.

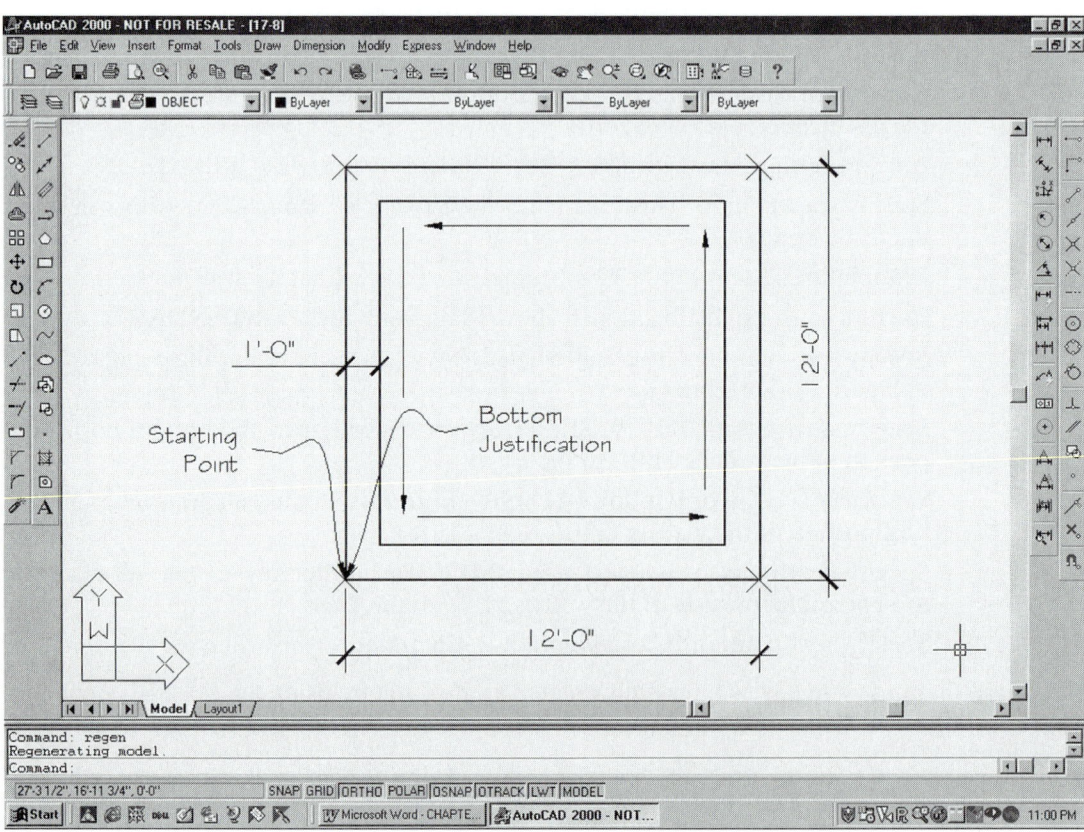

17.3.2 MultiLines and the Blip Marks

While using the MLINE command to draw walls, it is very easy to get disoriented or lose track of definition points. Sometimes it becomes extremely difficult to navigate through the drawing, hence creating walls with incorrect lengths. Unfortunately, the correct application of the MLINE command does not show itself until a distance is taken or a dimension is drawn. Drawing MultiLines with correct distances can become tricky unless you completely understand the procedures explained in this chapter and become fairly comfortable using them. It will be quite a disappointment to see the dimensions come out incorrect after spending considerable amount of time creating walls in a floor plan. This is most likely due to your misunderstanding and/or misuse of the MultiLine Justification option. The main complexity while drawing floor plans with the MULTILINE command is when the MultiLines move from counterclockwise to clockwise to counterclockwise direction and how the cursor interacts with the *visual attributes* of the MultiLines. This is inevitable because of the inherent applications of a typical floor plan configuration. To create smooth transitions between corners you must establish definition points as visual clues (points) on the screen. With the definition points visible on the screen, pointing the cursor toward the direction of drawing will give a definite clue as to the location of the MultiLine Justification.

As discussed in Chapter 5, the visible points on the screen are called *blip marks*, or *blips*. You can get a better understanding of the MultiLine Justification and the definition points created by the blip marks by performing a simple exercise on the screen as follows:

■ **EXERCISE 17–2:** *The following step-by-step exercise will help you better understand the relationship between MultiLine justification and the blip marks.*

Step #1: Draw a Standard Style (default) MultiLine starting from the bottom left corner of the screen. Make sure the BLIPMODE system variable is on. As you go up with the MultiLine, notice the cursor is "snapped" on the left line of the two-line MultiLine. This is because the default justification is Top.

Step #2: Stop near the midpoint of the screen and left-click (this will establish the first MultiLine from bottom to top direction). Move the cursor toward left and observe the location of the Justification point as a blip mark as the cursor is "snapped" to the bottom line of the MultiLine. Do not left-click here.

Step #3: Move the cursor toward right and observe the change in the location of the justification and the blip mark. As you move the cursor toward right, the cursor is "snapped" to the top line of the MultiLine. This is because the justification is now *Bottom* because the move from left to right represents an intention to move clockwise from the last known point. Establish a point here by clicking the left mouse button.

Step #4: Move the cursor up. As soon as you start moving up, the Justification becomes Top since this move is an intention to move counterclockwise from the last known point. Move up slightly and establish another point.

Step #5: Move the cursor toward right; as you guessed, the justification reverses itself and becomes Bottom. Experiment more with the justification points as you move the cursor around the screen and observe its locations.

Congratulations! You now have a better understanding of the MultiLine justification options.

Tips: Use Polar Tracking and Polar Snap to establish distances without having to type at the command line. Polar Tracking will allow MultiLines to "snap" to an increment angle established by the user. Polar Snap will allow the MultiLines to "snap" to specific distances when the cursor is moved in a specific direction, similar to Snap but without the dependence of the grid. As a result of Polar Tracking and Polar Snap, a visual display of temporary construction lines in the form of dots will appear. This is a real user performance booster since actual construction lines need never be drawn.

17.3.3 MultiLine Scale Option

The MultiLine *Scale* option determines the thickness of a wall in a floor plan or it is simply the distance between the two default lines. The Scale option has a multiplier effect on the MultiLine offset values. The value entered at the Scale option depends on the method used to create the new MultiLine Style. The method used to calculate offset values determines the value entered at the Scale option. The three different methods are discussed in detail later in the chapter.

17.3.4 MultiLine Style Option

The MultiLine *Style* option allows you to create a new wall style and access to existing styles. The MultiLine Style must be created and saved to a .mln file before it can be used. This is the MultiLine Style Definition File located in Acad2000\Common\Support. The MLSTYLE (Multi-Line Style) command is used to create a new MultiLine Style or to redefine/edit an existing style. This defines, edits, and sets the *element* (line) properties and display options of the Multi-Line. Many different wall styles can be created to meet drawing requirements. This will allow you to manipulate the current Standard style. The MLSTYLE command can be accessed in two different ways (it is not available as a toolbar):

1. From the Format pull-down menu select the MultiLine Style. The MultiLine Style dialog box will appear as shown in Figure 17–7.
2. Type MLSTYLE at the command Line as follows:

   Command: MLSTYLE ~EnterKey~

Before going into detailed explanation of the major components of the MultiLine Styles Dialog Box a brief list of steps involved in the creation of the MultiLine style needs to be identified. Each step will be explained in greater detail later in the chapter.

There are eight steps involved in the creation of a new MultiLine style as follows:

Step #1: Enter a new name inside the **Name:** (edit box).

Step #2: Enter a description inside the **Description:** (edit box).

FIGURE 17–7 The MultiLine Styles dialog box with standard default two-line style.

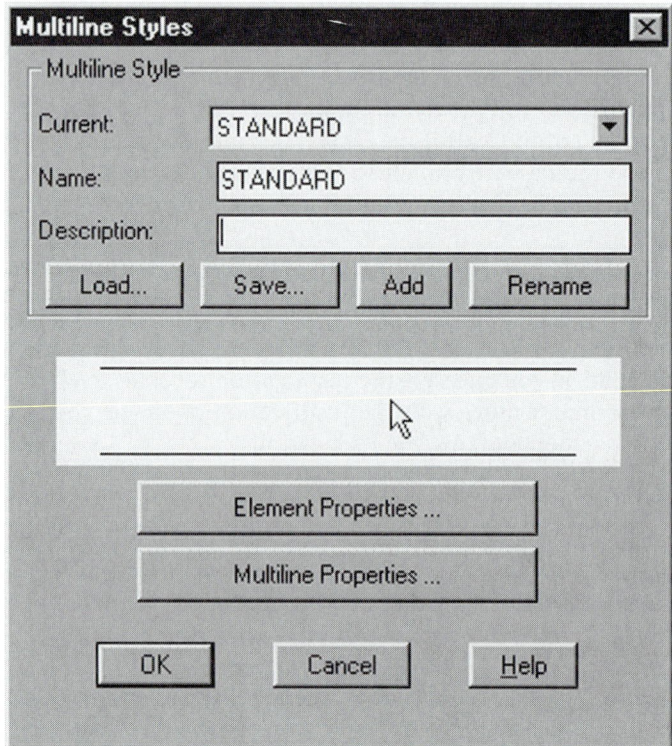

Step #3: Click on **Add:** (button).

Step #4: Click on **Element Properties:** (button). This step has three different methods to establish a new wall style and is covered later in this chapter.

Step #5: Click on **MultiLine Properties:** (button).

Step #6: Click on **Save:** (button).

Step #7: Click on **Load:** (button).
Step #8: Click on **OK:** (button).

The following are the major components of the MultiLine Styles dialog box:

- **CURRENT:** (edit text box). This area shows the current MultiLine Style. If no new wall styles have been created, the standard appears as default. This default two-line style can be seen inside the image area in the middle of the dialog box. If additional styles are present, the drop-down arrow can be used to display the existing styles and make it the current style if needed.

- **NAME:** (edit text box). This area is used to give the name of the style being created. It can be up to 31 characters without spaces. This is the **first step** in creating a new wall style, which is discussed later in this chapter. This edit text box can also be used to rename an existing style.

- **DESCRIPTION:** (edit text box). This area is used for an explicit definition of the wall style being created. AutoCAD allows up to 255 characters with spaces. The key is to be simple and concise in giving the description. This is the **second step** in creating a new wall style.

- **LOAD:** (button). This will allow you to load the style you have just created by displaying the Load MultiLine Styles Dialog Box as shown in Figure 17–8. It loads the style from the Acad.Mln MultiLine Library. This is the **seventh step** in creating a new wall style.

- **SAVE:** (button). This will allow you to save the style created or edited to an external file by displaying the Save MultiLine Style dialog box as shown in Figure 17–9. The style is saved to a .mln file. This is the **sixth step** in creating a new wall style.

- **ADD:** (button). This button will allow the MultiLine Style name to be added to the current MultiLine list file before manipulation of the standard MultiLine takes place. This is the **third step** in creating a new wall style.

- **RENAME:** (button). This will rename a current MultiLine style. The Standard style cannot be renamed because this is the origin of any new style creation. To rename an existing style, click on Rename button. The Name: (edit box) will be highlighted. Enter the new name and finally click on the Add button. The original style will be retained if the Current: (edit text box) displays the same style. Always keep track of what you do for future verification.

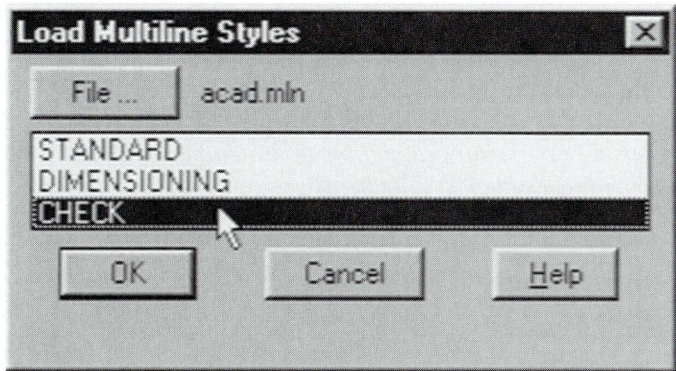

FIGURE 17–8 The Load MultiLine Styles dialog box will load the new wall style and add its name to the list of current styles. You can check this dialog box any time to verify the status of the MultiLine.

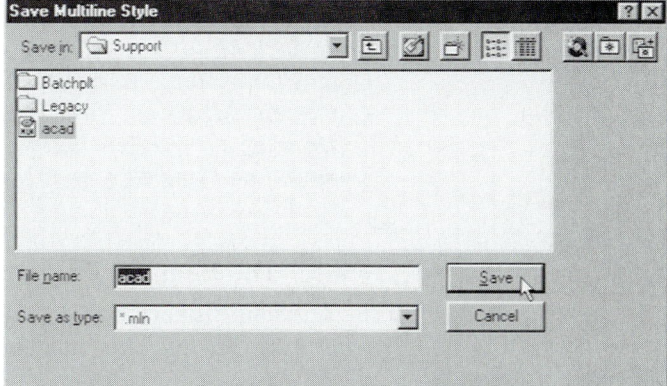

FIGURE 17–9 The Save MultiLine Style dialog box will save the new style to a .mln file.

FIGURE 17–10
Element Properties
dialog box with
standard default two-
line offset values of 0.5
and −0.5.

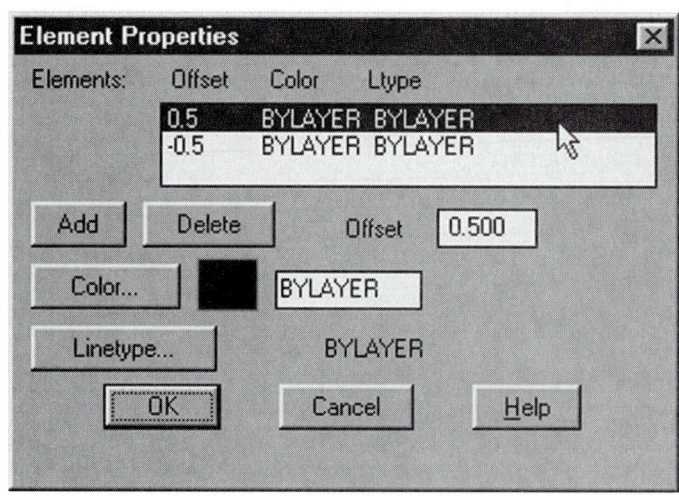

- **ELEMENT PROPERTIES:** (button). Selecting this button will display the Element Properties dialog box as shown in Figure 17–10. This will allow you to create additional lines added to the Standard two-line default MultiLine, or you can delete the default MultiLine and add your own numbers starting from scratch. This is the **fourth step** in creating a new wall style unless there is no need to have more than two lines, in which this step can be skipped. If there is a need to create more than two lines, this is the dialog box in which additional lines, called *elements,* can be added to the Standard two-line MultiLine.

- **MULTILINE PROPERTIES:** (button). Selecting this button will display the MultiLine Properties dialog box as shown in Figure 17–11. This will allow you to establish MultiLine Properties such as joints between wall intersections, end caps at start and/or end of walls set, angle of caps selected, and background fill with option to select color within the selected MultiLine style. This is the **fifth step** in creating a new wall style unless there is no need to set these options. MultiLine *joints* and/or *caps* can increase the efficiency of floor plans and are discussed later in this chapter.

Caution: There is a significant advantage to using caps on MultiLines when they are edited. The caps must be a part of the MultiLine if they are stretched using the STRETCH or the GRIP commands. Refer to the section on Stretching MultiLines.

- **OK:** (button). This is the **eighth** and **final step** in creating a new wall style.

- **CANCEL:** (button). This option will cancel the operation.

- **HELP:** (button). This option will display AutoCAD Command Reference dialog box.

Note: The progression of steps described above is intended to reflect a certain way to create a MultiLine style. It is not the only way to progress through the dialog box. You may for example, start with the Element Properties dialog box as the first step and complete the MultiLine Properties Dialog Box as the second step. You may then Name and Describe it as the third and fourth steps. The most important thing to remember is to Add, Save, Load, and click on OK (in that order) as the last four steps.

17.3.5 The Element Properties Dialog Box

The Element Properties dialog box as shown in Figure 17–10 has five major components: *Elements, Add, Delete, Color,* and *Linetype.* They are described as follows:

- **ELEMENTS**   (area). This section shows the two-line default Offset values as **decimal units.** These are the distances from the center of the standard two-line MultiLine style. Keep

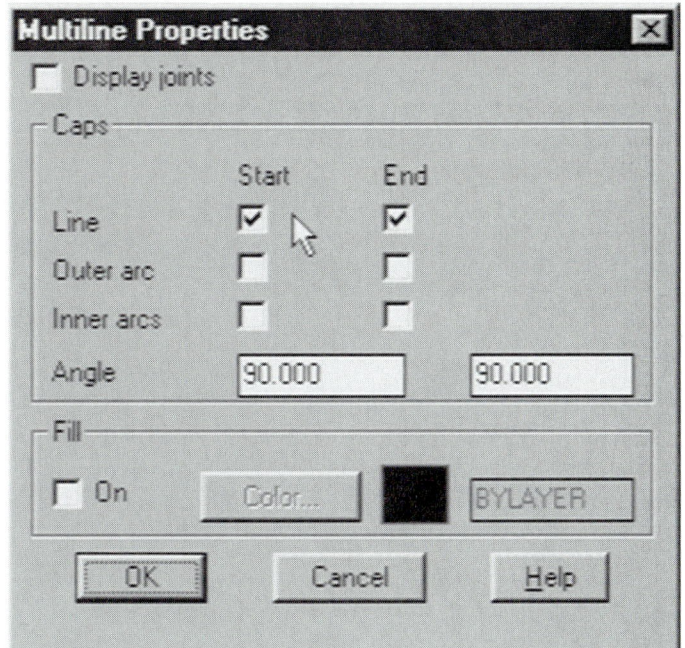

FIGURE 17–11
MultiLine Properties
dialog box.

in mind that with this area you will either be adding additional lines by referencing each additional distance to these values or deleting these lines to establish your own values from scratch. If adding additional lines, the value of **0.5** represents the upper line as being ½″ away from the zero centerline, sort of like moving in the plus (+) Y coordinate direction from the center. The value of **−0.5** represents the lower line being 1/2″ away from the zero centerline, sort of like moving in the minus (−) Y coordinate direction from the center. The logic behind the minus (−) direction is so that additional lines can be established in the lower portion of the default two-line from the reference source of zero as the center. The zero center mark is extremely important to understand to establish additional lines for the new MultiLine. The total distance from the centerline to the upper and lower line is one unit. Figure 17–12 shows the standard default two-line MultiLine style as the starting point for creating additional lines as new wall types. Notice that the centerline is imaginary at this point but can be created and made visible if needed. The total thickness for this standard wall is 1″. All additional lines are created from this centerline. Each element value can be assigned a color and a linetype if needed. The two offset values (0.5 and −0.5) are assigned a bylayer color and linetype. A new color and linetype can be assigned to any offset value. Refer to the section on the Color and Linetype button area.

- **ADD:** (button). This button will allow you to add new offset values as the new wall types are created. When you click on this button, the offset edit box will display 0.000 value. If you highlight this value and change it to a new value, you will establish the third line measured from the zero reference point in the plus direction. When you click on the Add button, the second time, the edit box will display another 0.000 for you to enter another value as the minus (−) value or any other value measured from the zero reference point.

- **DELETE:** (button). This button will delete the highlighted item from the list. You can delete the offset values entered incorrectly by highlighting the value from the Elements text area and clicking on the Delete button. You can also use this button to delete the existing standard two-line default MultiLine (0.5 and −0.5) to create your own MultiLine style from scratch by establishing a line at a 0 (zero) value and offsetting other lines from it.

FIGURE 17–12 The default Standard MultiLine style offset values determined from the center (zero) reference point.

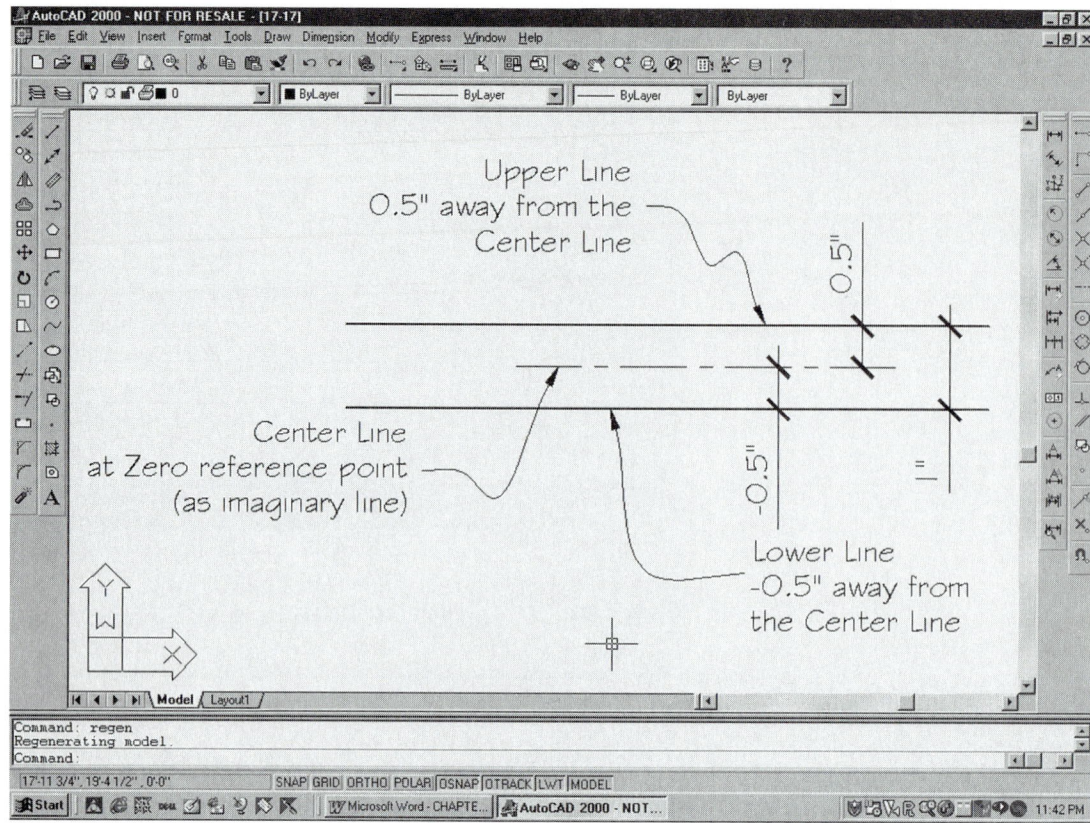

- **COLOR:** (button). This button will assign a color to the specified offset value. Selecting this box will display the Select Color dialog box. The name of the selected color will be displayed on the top of the Element Properties dialog box under Color. The selected color will also be shown in the MultiLine Styles dialog box when you return to it.

- **LINETYPE:** (button). This button will assign a new Linetype to the offset value. Selecting this button will display the Select Linetype dialog box. If a new linetype needs to be added to the list, click on *Load* to select the appropriate Linetype. Refer to Chapter 9 for creating Layers and Linetypes.

- **OK:** (button). This button will complete the creation of additional lines added to the default two-line MultiLine as offset values.

- **CANCEL:** (button). This button will cancel the operation. You must start over again if you wish to continue establishing offset values.

- **HELP:** (button). This option will display AutoCAD Command Reference Dialog Box.

17.3.6   Calculating Offset Values Using the Element Properties Dialog Box

The Element Properties dialog box is used to create the wall types required for the MultiLine style. There are three different methods to create a new MultiLine style having more than two parallel lines:

1. The equation method.
2. The alternate equation method.
3. The direct distance offset method.

17.4 USING THE EQUATION METHOD TO CALCULATE OFFSET VALUES

This method uses the existing standard default two-line offset values (0.5 and −0.5) as an existing wall and uses new offset values to add additional lines by referencing these new lines from the center point of the existing wall. New lines are calculated by establishing an *equation* by

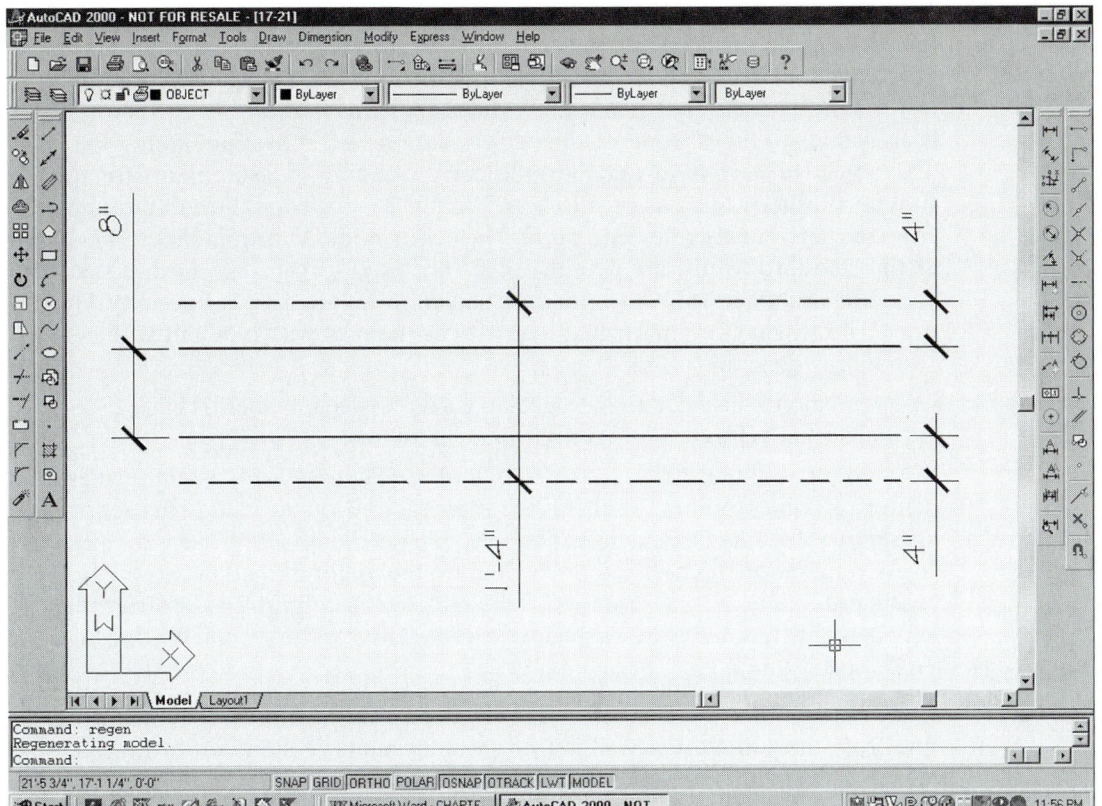

FIGURE 17–13
Architectural representation of the 8″ concrete block foundation wall with 4″ offset dashed lines as footing on both sides of the wall. Notice that the two solid lines are the standard default MultiLine style that will be used as a base to determine the two additional dashed lines as new offset values.

means of converting reference points for distances from the standard units to architectural units. The default standard MultiLine thickness value is set to one unit and can be dimensioned as one inch. If the Scale option is changed to six, the distance between the two parallel lines will then be six units or can be plotted to measure as a six-inch wall. With the Equation Method, the scale is the architectural distance between the standard default two-line MultiLine.

Furthermore, the distance between the two parallel lines must be entered as inches without the inches mark at the scale option. For example, a wall that is 24″ thick will have the Multi-Line scale option value entered as 24 without the inches mark no matter what the intended architectural scale is. If you try to enter 2′-0″ or 24″, AutoCAD will give you the following error message:

```
Requires numeric value.
```

■ **EXERCISE 17–3:** *The following step-by-step exercise will allow you to calculate the offset values needed to create a typical wall style using the Equation Method. The wall requirements are as follows:*

1. 8″ thick concrete block foundation wall with bylayer color and linetype.

2. 16″ thick footing with a red color and a dashed linetype. The dashed lines are to be placed 4″ away from the foundation wall on both sides.

3. The total wall thickness, including foundation wall and footing, is to be 1′-4″.

4. The amount of standard default lines: 2

5. The amount of new offset lines to be created: 2

6. The total amount of lines in the new wall type: 4

Step #1: Examine the architectural representation of this wall as shown in Figure 17–13. The upper dashed line representing the footing will be placed 4″ away from the upper foundation wall (solid line) and the lower dashed line representing the footing will be placed −4″ away from the bottom foundation wall (solid line).

Step #2: Refer back to the standard MultiLine offset values as shown in Figure 17–12 and determine that the values 0.5 and −0.5 represent the distance from the zero center reference point. This is important in establishing the upper and lower solid lines as the standard 1″ MultiLine. This is the 1″ MultiLine that corresponds to the 8″ concrete block foundation wall shown in Figure 17–12. The objective here is to calculate the corresponding measurements for the footing (dashed) lines as plus (+) and minus (−) offset values determined from the zero center reference point. The offset values shown in Figure 17–14 as the standard MultiLine default values are used to translate to the corresponding architectural values that are shown in Figure 17–13. In reality, Figure 17–13 is what you are trying to create as the new wall type but with corresponding decimal values.

Step #3: Set-up equation to help determine the relationship between standard (Figure 17–14) and architectural (Figure 17–13) offset values as follows:

4″ is half of 8″ (Figure 17–13). 0.5″ is half of 1″ (Figure 17–14). From the zero center reference point, 1 and −1 are the required offset values that correspond to 4″ footing dashed lines. The 1 represents the offset distance required to go from the zero center reference point to the upper dashed line as the first footing line. The −1 represents the offset distance required to go from the zero center reference point to the lower dashed line as the second footing line.

Step #4: Determine the final equation from Step #3 as follows:

If 8″ concrete block wall is to 1 unit of standard MultiLine, then 4″ of footing line from the foundation wall is to how many units of standard MultiLine? Which is to say that the equation is: $8/1 = 4/X$

Step #5: Solve for X as follows:

$8X = 4$

$X = 4/8$

$X = 0.5$

Therefore the distance from the foundation line to the footing line is 0.5 and −0.5 units. Because the offset values are determined from the zero center reference point, the final offset values would be 1 and −1.

Congratulations! You have successfully calculated the Offset values needed to create a typical wall style using the Equation Method with the wall requirements. The Elements area of the Element Properties dialog box can now be completed to look like Table 17–1.

To understand the relationship between standard MultiLine offset values shown in Figure 17–14 and the Architectural Representation as shown in Figure 17–13 of the same values look at Table 17–2.

TABLE 17–1: Contents of the Elements area for Exercise 17–3.

Offset	Color	Ltype
0.5	White	Continuous
−0.5	White	Continuous
1	Red	Dashed
−1	Red	Dashed

TABLE 17–2: Comparison of Standard and Architectural Offset Values.

Architectural Representation	Offset Values Entered
Figure 17–13	Figure 17–14
8″ Concrete foundation wall	0.5 and −0.5 as Default
4″ Footing upper dashed line	1
4″ Footing lower dashed line	−1

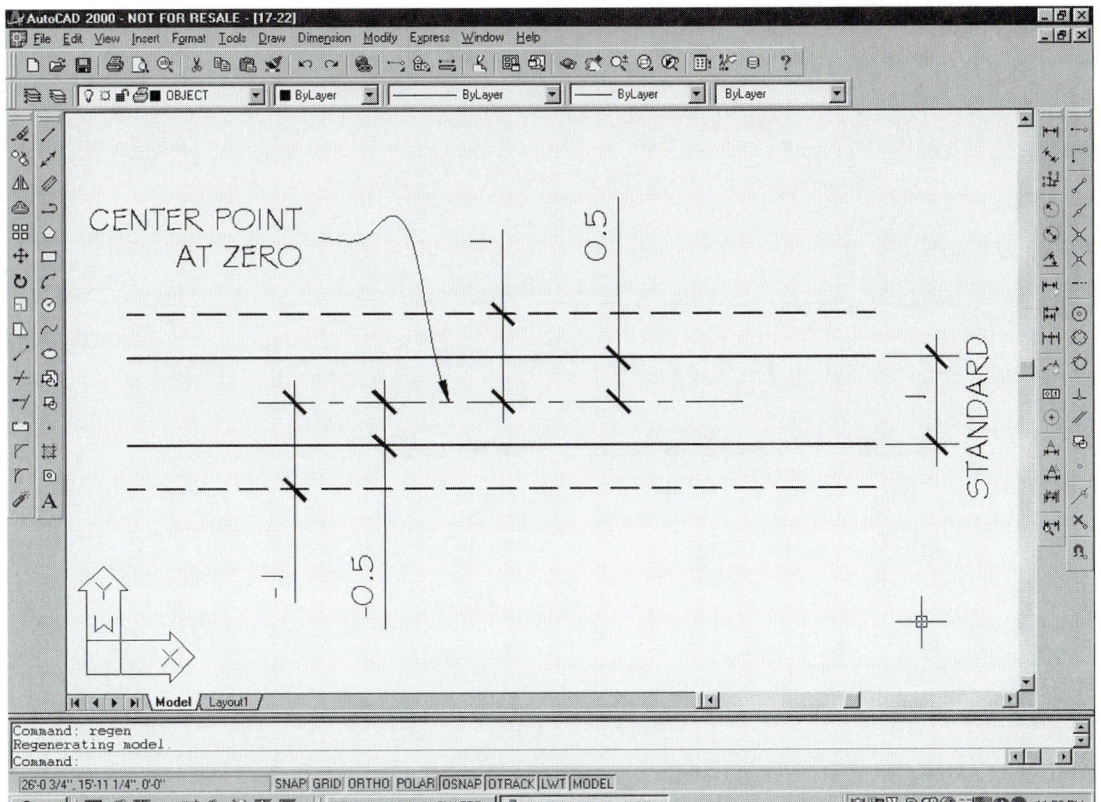

FIGURE 17–14
Corresponding Offset
values needed for the
wall type shown in
Figure 17–13.

In order to use this wall style in a floor plan it must be created using the MultiLine Styles dialog box. This procedure is explained later in the Chapter.

■ **EXERCISE 17–4:** *The following step-by-step exercise will allow you to calculate the offset values needed to create a typical wall style using the Equation Method. The wall requirements are as follows:*

1. 6″ Thick wood stud wall with a centerline (red color) at zero reference point.

2. 1/2″ Thick gypsum board on both sides of the wood stud wall with a continuous linetype and blue color.

3. Total thickness for this wall is to be 7″.

4. The amount of standard default lines: 2

5. The amount of new offset lines to be created: 3

6. The total amount of lines in the new wall type: 5

Step #1: Examine Figure 17–15 and determined that upper solid line representing the gypsum board will be placed 1/2″ away from the upper wood stud wall and the lower gypsum board line placed −1/2″ away from the lower wood stud wall. The centerline will be placed at the zero reference point.

Step #2: Examine Figure 17–16 and determine the corresponding offset values needed to create this wall style. The values of 0.5 and −0.5 represent the distance from the zero reference point for the standard default MultiLine. This is the default MultiLine that corresponds to the 6″ wood stud wall in Figure 17–15.

Step #3: Set up the equation as follows:

If 6″ (thick) wood stud wall is to 1 unit (inch) of standard default MultiLine, then 1/2″ of gypsum board is to how many units of standard MultiLine? Which is to say that the equation is $6/1 = 0.5/X$.

FIGURE 17–15
Architectural
representation of the 6"
wood stud wall with 1/2"
offset solid lines as the
gypsum board on both
sides of the wall. Notice
that the two solid inner
lines are the standard
default MultiLine style
that will be used as a
base to determine the
two additional solid
lines as new offset
values.

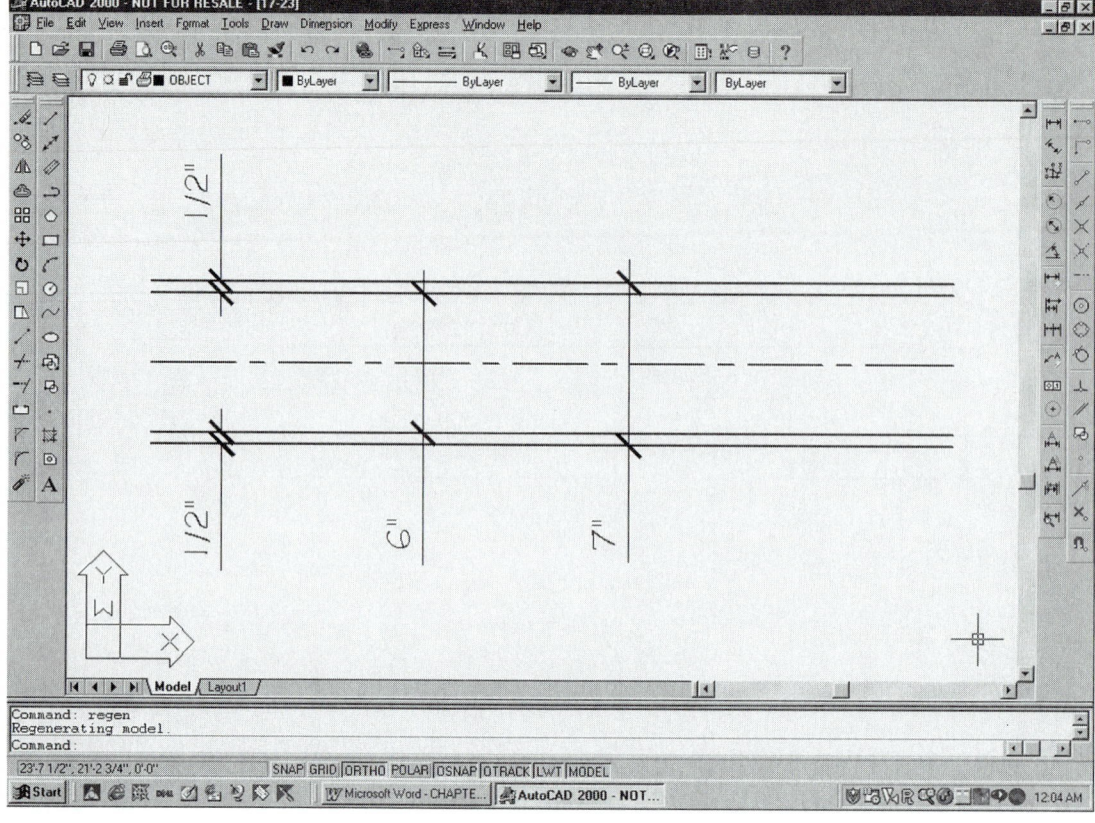

FIGURE 17–16
Corresponding offset
values needed for the
wall type shown in
Figure 17–15.

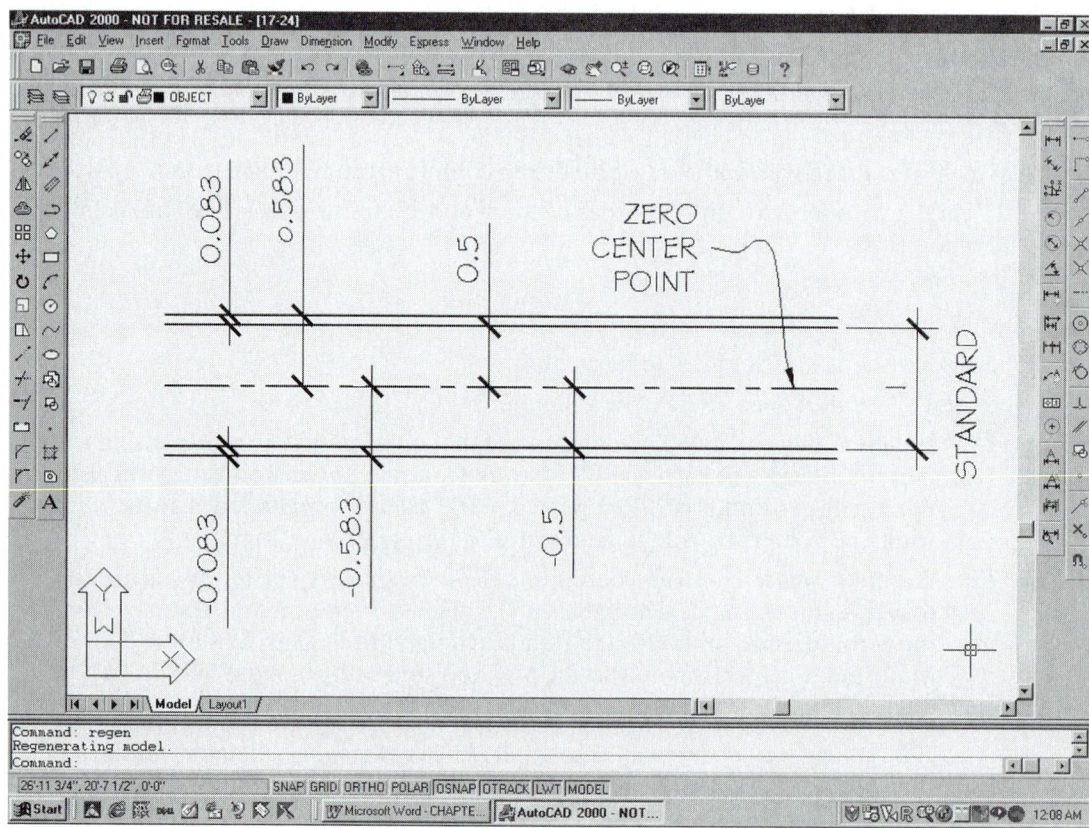

Offset	Color	Ltype
0.5	White	Continuous
−0.5	White	Continuous
0.583	Blue	Continuous
−0.583	Blue	Continuous
0	Red	Centerline

TABLE 17–3: Contents of the Elements area for Exercise 17–4.

Architectural Representation	Offset Values Entered
Figure 17–15	Figure 17–16
6″ Wood stud wall	0.5 and −0.5 (default)
Centerline of wood stud wall	0
1/2″ Gypsum board upper line	0.583
1/2″ Gypsum board lower line	−0.583

TABLE 17–4: Comparison of Standard and Architectural Offset Values.

Step #4: Solve for X as follows:

$6X = 0.5$

$X = 0.5/6$

$X = 0.083 + 0.5$ (measured from the zero reference point) $= 0.583$ and $−0.583$ respectively.

Congratulations! You have successfully calculated the offset values needed to create a typical wall style using the Equation Method with the wall requirements. The Elements area of the Element Properties dialog box can now be completed to look like Table 17–3.

To understand the relationship between the standard MultiLine offset values (Figure 17–16) and the Architectural Representation (Figure 17–15) of the same values take a look at Table 17–4.

The final *Offset* values for the gypsum board can also be calculated as follows:

```
1/2" is 1/12 of 6" where 1/12 = 0.083.
```

The 0.083 is the required offset distance from the upper wood stud wall line in the minus direction, hence −0.083 is the required offset distance from the lower wood stud wall line (Figure 17–16). Notice that the values 0.083 and −0.083 represent the 1/2″ gypsum board on both sides of the wood stud wall in Figure 17–15. The offset value for the centerline line is 0 (zero). Because the new offset values need to be determined from the zero reference point the final values are calculated as follows:

```
0.083 + 0.5 = 0.583 and −0.583 respectively.
```

The Exercise in the following pages will allow you to actually create the wall type calculated in Exercise 17–4.

Tips: When using the MLINE command to draw a wall style that was created with the Equation Method, use the style option to locate it first, use the justification option to set dimension definition points second, and use the scale option to set the thickness of the default wall last. For Exercise 17–3 the scale option should be set to 8. For Exercise 17–4 the scale option should be set to 6.

17.5 MULTIPLE USE OF THE MULTILINE SCALE OPTION

You can use the same MultiLine style on different architectural projects having different architectural scales. AutoCAD will automatically adjust the offset values needed for that scale. For example, if you need to change the foundation wall thickness from 8″ to 10″ for Exercise 17–3 you only need to change the scale option to 10 (Scale = 10). AutoCAD will adjust the footing dashed lines from 4″ to 5″ on both sides of the foundation wall. In other words, a foundation wall created as a new wall type for one drawing can also be used for other drawings regardless of its wall thickness. This is possible only because there is a proportional relationship between the thickness of the foundation wall with the thickness of the footing. This concept does not work with the stud wall and the gypsum board as in the case of Figures 17–15 and 17–16 because different offset values will make the gypsum board thickness unacceptable even though a new stud wall thickness is established. Hence, if the new offset values as architectural dimensions are acceptable then there is no need to create separate MultiLine styles for the representation of different wall thickness'. When Auto-CAD creates offset values for the new scale option it does so by recalculating each of the offset values proportionate to the scale value entered. In reality all numbers refer to the corresponding two-line default MultiLine style. The new proportionate offset values created for different scale options may not be appropriate or acceptable for a specific drawing. This scale relationship is especially true for Exercise 17–4. This is where a 1/2″ gypsum board is an acceptable dimension as a finish material for a 6″ stud wall with a scale of 6. But it is not acceptable as an 11/16″ gypsum board or any other material (unless it is specifically required) for a say 8″ concrete wall with a scale of 8. Auto-CAD recalculates the new offset value of 11/16″ for the 8″ wall as follows:

If 1/2″ is the representation of the finish material for a 6″ wall, what will be the thickness of the finish material if the wall is changed to 8″? Driving the equation from previous theories:

If 6 is to 1/2, then 8 is to what? Plug in the numbers as follows:

```
6/0.5 = 8/X (solve for X)
6X = (8) (0.5)
6X = 4
X = 4/6
X = 0.666 or 11/16″ if the precision of the drawing units is set to 0′-0 1/16″.
If the precision of the drawing units is set to 0′-0 1/8″, then it will be
5/8″, if it is set to 0′-0 1/4″ it will be 3/4″, and if it is set to 0′-0 1/2″ it
will be 1/2″. Hence for a 10″ wall the finish material would be 13/16″ and for
a 12″ wall it will be 1″ at the 0′-0 1/16″ drawing units precision. If the
precision is changed, the new values will change as well. Depending on the
values obtained and the settings of the precision for the units of a project,
a new wall style might be necessary to create.
```

Caution: The selection of a precision value affects the values obtained as dimensions and distances in AutoCAD. Set the precision value as required by the drawing to display dimension values to the nearest 1″ to 1/256″ but always remember that the Offset values in MultiLines will change as you change the precision value. Always keep track of your precision and Offset values as they will have a great impact on overall architectural dimensions.

17.6 USING THE ALTERNATE EQUATION METHOD TO CALCULATE OFFSET VALUES

The equation method shown earlier allows the user to find Offset values based on the two-line Standard default MultilLine and converting any new additional lines into architectural representations by entering the thickness assigned to the Standard default MultiLine as units. With the Alternate Equation Method the zero reference point will again serve as the beginning point. With this method the Offset values are obtained as true to their architectural characters. In Exercise 17–3, the two-line Standard default MultiLine will be taken as 8″ not 1″ and must be entered in the Offset area as 4 and −4 not 0.5 and −0.5. This will require you to *delete* 0.5 and −0.5 and *add* 4 and −4 as the new default values measured from the zero center reference point. The upper dashed footing line measured from the zero center reference point will now be 8 and the bottom dashed footing line will now be −8. The Elements area of the Element Properties dialog box would now look like Table 17–5 as follows:

TABLE 17–5: Contents of the Elements area for Exercise 17–3 using the Alternate Equation Method.

Offset	**Color**	**Ltype**
4	White	Continuous
−4	White	Continuous
8	Red	Dashed
−8	Red	Dashed

Architectural Representation	Offset Values Entered
8″ Concrete block wall	4 and −4 (taken as default)
4″ Footing for upper dashed line	8
4″ Footing for bottom dashed line	−8

TABLE 17–6: Comparison of Standard and Architectural Offset Values.

Offset	Color	Ltype
0	Red	Center
3	White	Continuous
−3	White	Continuous
3.5	Blue	Continuous
−3.5	Blue	Continuous

TABLE 17–7: Contents of the Elements area for Exercise 17–4.

For the alternate equation method to work for Exercise 17–3, the scale must be entered as 1 (Scale = 1) when using the MULTILINE command. Scale = 1 represent the 8″ foundation wall. To understand the relationship between standard MultiLine offset values and architectural representation for Exercise 17–3, take a look at Table 17–6.

As you can see from Tables 17–5 and 17–6, the alternate equation method allows the user to enter the offset values as architectural dimensions taken directly from Figure 17–13. There is no need to deal with conversions or equations for the offset values. This method may seem more architectural friendly, but be very careful because this method requires you to create a new conversion for the scale value. This is because for Exercise 17–3 the standard default two-line is now 8″ as opposed to 1″. Therefore the scale value for this wall type must be set to 1 (scale = 1) for it to plot at 8″. If the same wall is used as a 12″ wall, then the scale value must be set as 1.50 (scale = 1.50) as follows (or a new wall style must be created if scale = 1 is to be used):

If 8″ of concrete block foundation wall is to 1″ (1 unit) in Scale, THEN 12″ of new wall is equal to how many units in scale? Establish the equation as:

```
8/1 = 12/X (solve for X)
8X = 12
X = 12/8
X = 1.50 This is the number that must be entered as the scale when
drawing a wall that is 12″ thick.
```

With this set up and as with the equation method AutoCAD will automatically recalculate the footing values as 6″.

For Exercise 17–4 the Elements area of the Element Properties dialog box will look like Table 17–7.

For these offset values to work, the MultiLine Scale must be entered as 1.

The alternate equation method can be seen as the reverse of the equation method where the architectural dimensions are taken from the center reference (zero) point without establishing an equation to reference a standard decimal MultiLine. Both methods provide good performance but with different approaches to offset values and scale. The common denominator for the equation and the alternate equation methods is that they both utilize the centerline of an existing wall to calculate offset lines.

17.7 USING THE DIRECT DISTANCE OFFSET METHOD TO CALCULATE OFFSET VALUES

This method allows you to start from scratch by removing the default 0.5 and −0.5 offset values from the Elements section of the Element Properties dialog box. Once these two values are deleted a beginning point of 0 (zero) will be established. This 0 (zero) point indicates the bottom line of any new MultiLine. Additional lines will then be established as offset values taken

TABLE 17–8:
Contents of the Elements area for Exercise 17–3.

Offset	Color	Ltype
0	Red	Dashed
4	White	Continuous
12	White	Continuous
16	Red	Dashed

TABLE 17–9:
Contents of the Elements area for Example 17–4.

Offset	Color	Ltype
0	Blue	Continuous
0.5	White	Continuous
3.5	Red	Center
6.5	White	Continuous
7	Blue	Continuous

from the 0 (zero) reference point. With this method you basically have to ignore the standard default two-line MultiLine and start establishing lines from your own 0 (zero) point going up in the + (plus) direction. When you are ready to use the MultiLine command with this method, you need to set the scale option to 1 (Scale = 1). If the scale is set to 2 then all offset dimensions will double giving you twice as big a wall. If the scale is set to 0.25, then all offset dimensions will be ¼ of their original size. With this method the wall style in Exercise 17–3 would look like the wall style in Figure 17–17 where 0 (zero) is the starting point for the footing line. All other values are referenced from that point. For Exercise 17–3 the Elements area of the Element Properties dialog box will look like Table 17–8.

Notice that for these offset values to work, the scale must be entered as 1 and default offset values of 0.5 and −0.5 must be deleted.

For Exercise 17–4 the Elements area of the Element Properties dialog box will look like Table 17–9.

With this method the wall style in Exercise 17–4 would have the offset values shown in Figure 17–18.

Each method requires a different approach to MultiLine scale and corresponding architectural scale. Before selecting a method, look at its strengths and weaknesses and then use the method you feel most comfortable with. Keep track of your calculations and share relevant information with peers and co-workers. When everyone agrees on a method to use, make it a part of the office standards.

■ **EXERCISE 17–5:** *The following step-by-step exercise will allow you to create the wall type used in Exercise 17–4 using the Equation Method. By following the steps one at a time, you will learn the necessary steps involved in the use of the MultiLine Styles dialog box to create a new wall type. Before creating the wall type consider the following:*

A. Establish drawing standards in appropriate template drawings.

B. Create all wall types inside AutoCAD Template Drawings so these can be a part of the office conventions.

C. Keep name and descriptions of all wall types simple and easy to recognize and associate. Do not place any spaces inside the Name area.

Step #1: Verify and acknowledge from Figure 17–16 that the 0.5 and −0.5 represent the distance from the zero center reference point to the upper and lower standard default MultiLine. This is represented by 6″ in Figure 17–15. You are to calculate the corresponding values of the 1/2″ gypsum board on both sides of the wood stud wall to the 1 unit Standard default MultiLine as plus (+) and minus (−) offset values.

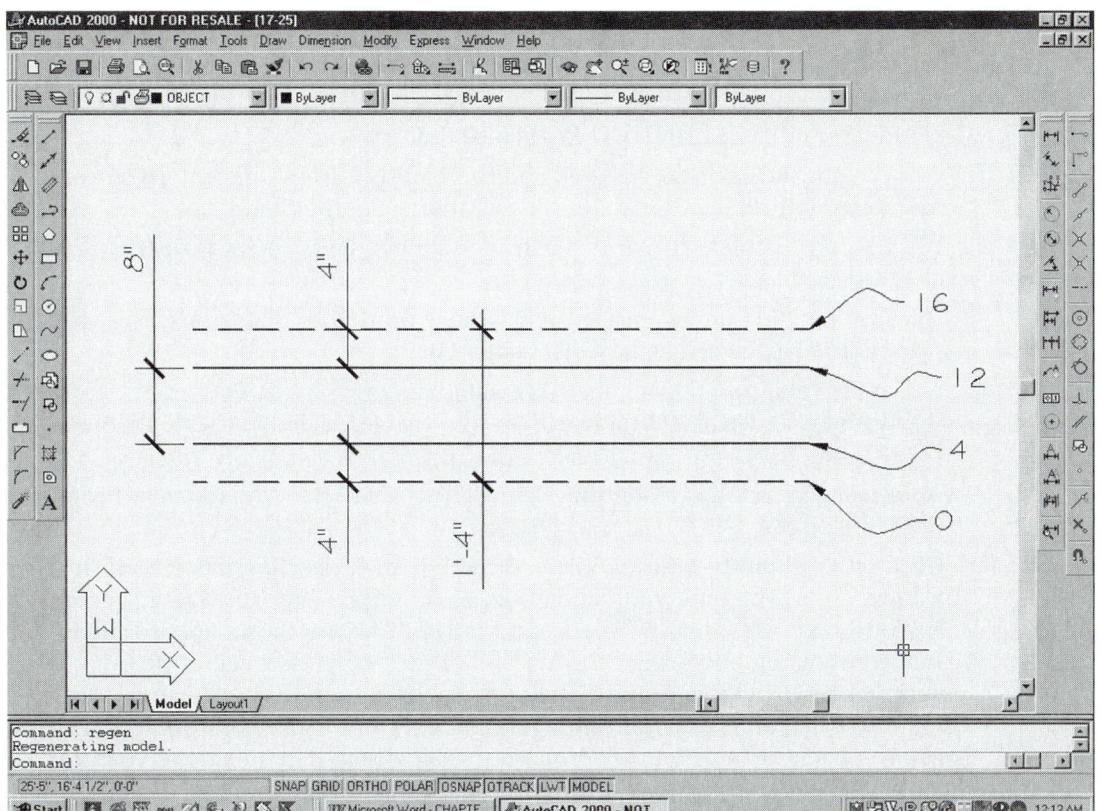

FIGURE 17–17 The offset values established from the zero reference point for Exercise 17–3 using the Direct Distance Offset method. Notice that numbers 0, 4, 12, and 16 are entered in the Elements area of the Element Properties dialog box for this option.

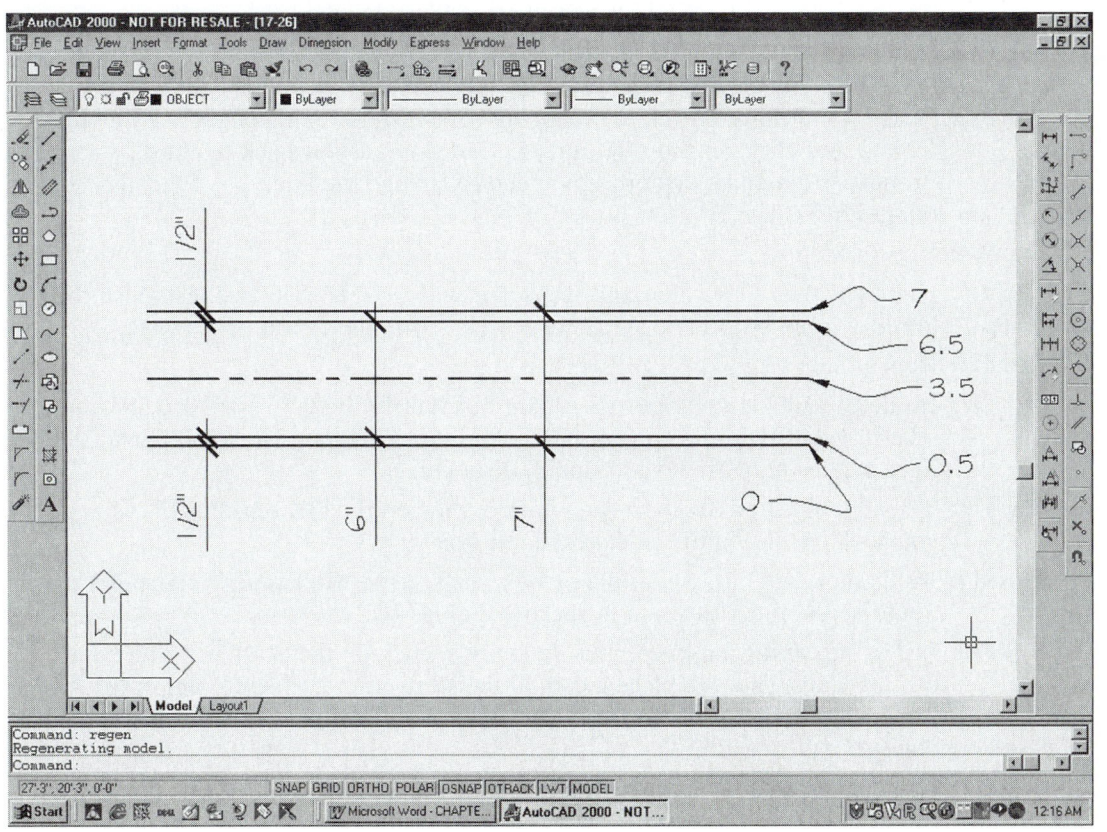

FIGURE 17–18 The corresponding values for Exercise 17–4 using the Direct Distance Offset Method.

Step #2:   Access the MultiLine Styles dialog box.

Step #3:   Inside Name: (edit text box) type INTERIORWALL.

Step #4:   Inside Description: (edit text box) type 6 INCH WOOD STUD WALL WITH 1/2 INCH GYPSUM BOARD BOTH SIDES.

Step #5:   Click on the Add button. This will add the wall style to the current list so you can perform further editing later such as adding another line.

Step #6:   Click on the Element Properties button to access the Element Properties dialog box.

Step #7:   Click on the Add button inside the Element Properties dialog box. This will place a 0.000 value inside the Offset edit box.

Step #8:   Leave the value as 0.000 because this will place a line inside the center of the wood stud wall. The 0.000 value will now be visible inside the Elements: area.

Step #9:   Click on the Color button to access the Select Color dialog box. Click on red color and click on the OK button. This will get you back to the Element Properties dialog box.

Step #10:   Click on the Linetype button inside the Element Properties dialog box. This will access Select Linetype dialog box. If centerline linetype has not been loaded previously, click on the Load button to access the Load or Reload Linetypes dialog box. Under the available Linetypes, select center (linetype) and click on the OK button. This will get you back to the Select Linetype dialog box. Click on the center (linetype) and click on the OK button. This will get you back to the Element Properties dialog box. If the linetype you are looking for has already been loaded, just click on it inside the Select Linetype dialog box.

Step #11:   Click on the Add button inside the Element Properties dialog box. This will place a 0.000 value inside the Offset edit box.

Step #12:   Highlight the 0.000 value and replace it with 0.583. This will establish the upper gypsum board line as 1/2″ or 3 1/2″ from the center of the wall.

Step #13:   Click on the Color button to access the Select Color dialog box. Click on blue (color) and click on the OK button. This will get you back to the Element Properties dialog box (there is no need to change the linetype of the gypsum board line).

Step #14:   Repeat Step 7.

Step #15:   Highlight the 0.000 value and replace it with −0.583. This will establish the lower gypsum board line as 1/2″ or −3 1/2″ from the center of the wall.

Step #16:   Repeat Step 13.

Step #17:   Inside the Element Properties dialog box, verify the 0.5, −0.5, 0, 0.583, and −0.583 values with its appropriate colors and linetypes. No scroll bar to the right means there are no additional offset values.

Step #18:   When all required numbers are verified, click on the OK button. This will get you back to the MultiLine Styles dialog box.

Step #19:   Inside the MultiLine Styles dialog box, click on the MultiLine Properties button to access the MultiLine Properties dialog box.

Step #20:   Inside the MultiLine Properties dialog box, click on the Start and End boxes of Line Caps. This will place a cap on the start-point and end-point of Multi-Lines. Click on the OK button. This will get you back to the MultiLine Styles dialog box.

Step #21:   Look at the MultiLine Style you just created. There should be five lines representing the new wall type with red as the centerline (AutoCAD does not show the linetypes as dashed but as solid for viewing purposes), blue as upper and lower lines, and black as standard default lines, which represent the 6″ wood stud wall.

Step #22: Inside the MultiLine Styles dialog box, click on the Save button. The Save MultiLine Style dialog box will appear. Inside this dialog box, verify file name as acad and Save as type as *.mln and click on the Save button. This will bring you back to the MultiLine Styles dialog box.

Step #23: Inside the MultiLine Styles dialog box, click on the Load button. This will display the Load MultiLine Styles dialog box. Inside this dialog box under File, find INTERIORWALL and highlight it then click on the OK button. This will bring you back to the MultiLine Styles dialog box.

Step #24: Take another look inside the graphics area for final verification of the new MultiLine style. If all is to your satisfaction, click on the OK button and you will be ready to draw with the new wall type using the MLINE command.

Congratulations! You have successfully created a wall type shown in Figure 17–15 by calculating offset values using the Equation method. You are now ready to use this wall type by simply accessing the MLINE command. The MultiLine justification can be set to your requirements. The MultiLine scale should be set to 6 for a 6″ wall. The MultiLine style should read INTERIORWALL.

17.8 USING THE MULTILINE PROPERTIES DIALOG BOX

The MultiLine Properties dialog box allows you to display joints and caps as well as the fill options of the new or standard MultiLines. The MultiLine Properties dialog box shown in Figure 17–11 has three major parts: display joints, caps, and fill. They are explained as follows:

Display Joints: (check box). Placing a checkmark in this box will allow the intersections of walls to be displayed as joints on the screen as you create the floor plan as shown in Figure 17–19. The

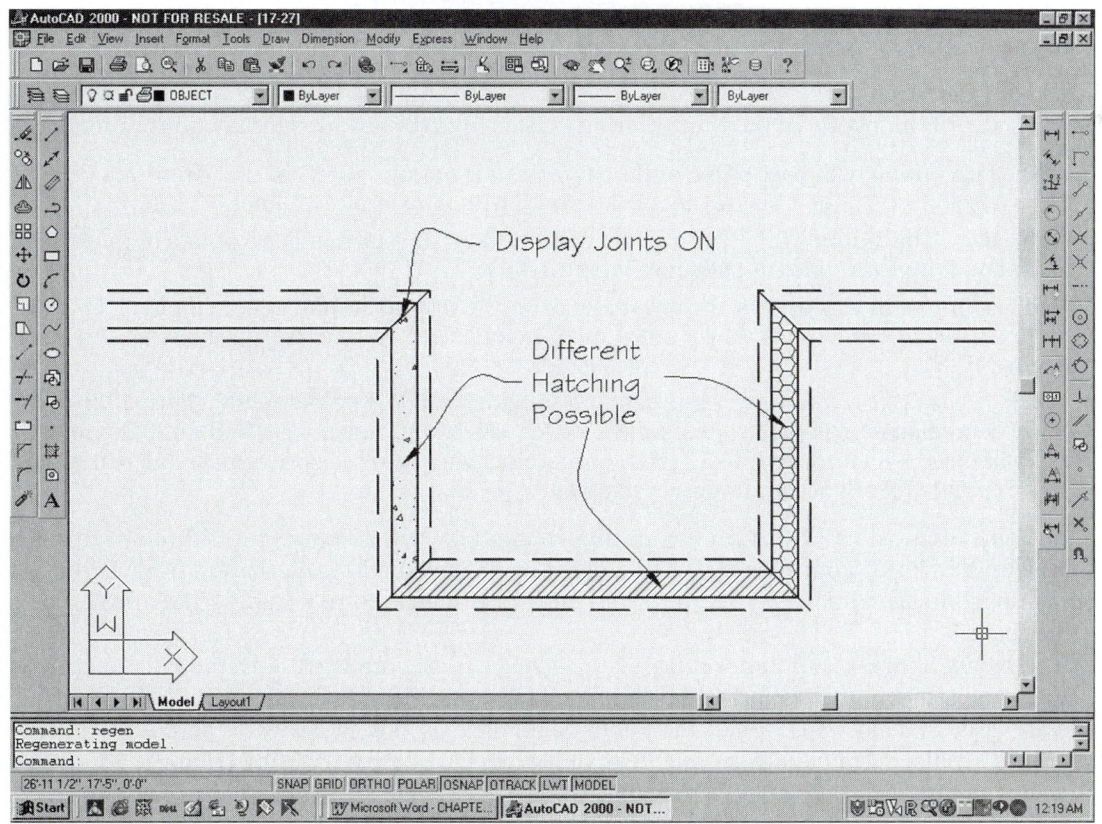

FIGURE 17–19 Display Joints ON will allow for different hatch pattern applications for different wall segments by providing a separation as miters at intersections.

FIGURE 17–20 The
wall style created in
Exercise 17–3 shown
with Line Caps ON for
Start and End. It also
shows a hatch pattern.

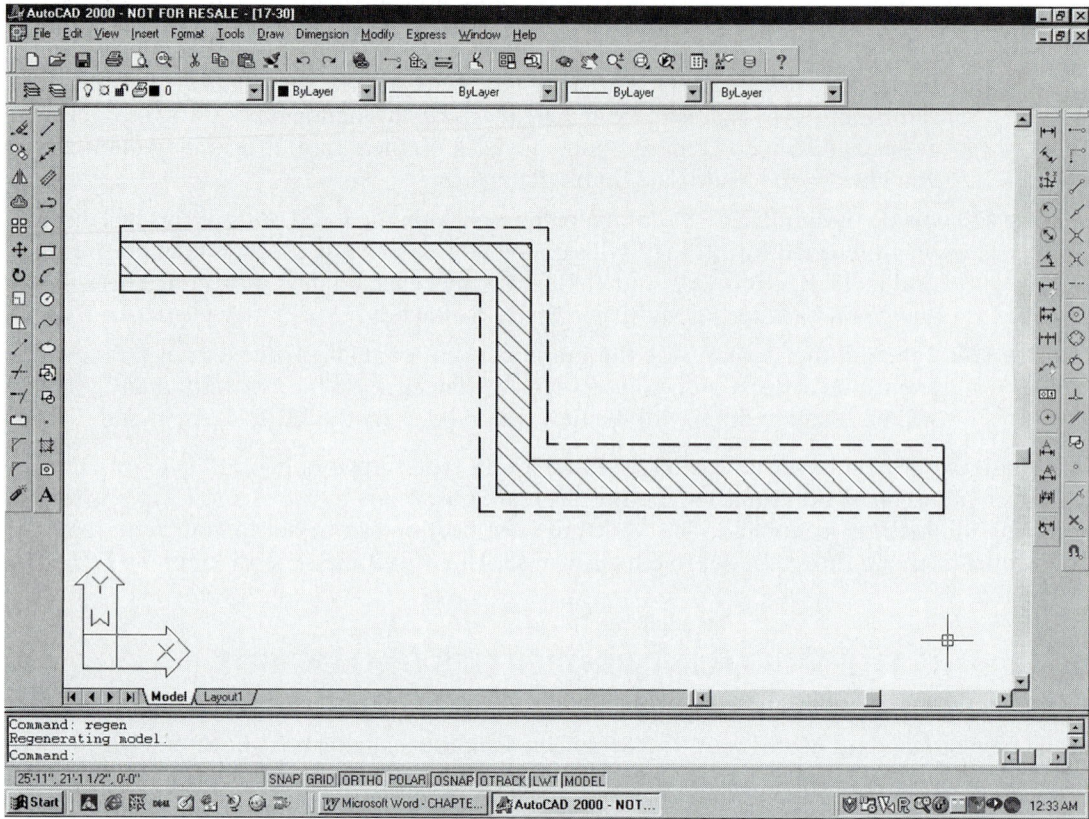

creation of joints will allow you to break walls into individual segments for applying different hatch patterns between joints. This may or may not be a desirable option, depending on the hatching specifications and the drawing requirements.

Caps area Start and End: (check boxes).   This area will allow you to place caps (close ends) on Start, End, or both points of the MultiLine style. This option has four subselections as follows:

LINE: This option will place a line at the Start or End or both points of the MultiLine style as shown in Figure 17–20. This will cover the entire MultiLine up to 16 lines.

OUTER ARC: This option will place a semicircle between the start and end points of the *uppermost* and *lowermost* lines as shown in Figure 17–21.

INNER ARCS: With this option the emphasis is on the *arcs* as in plural not singular. This option will place semicircles on all inner lines except the top and bottom lines as shown in Figure 17–22.

ANGLE: This option will draw a line cap at a specified angle. The default angle is 90 degrees. A 30 degree angle will place a line or arc 30 degrees counterclockwise, and a 120 degree angle will place a line or arc 120 degrees counterclockwise or 60 degrees clockwise. AutoCAD at this point will not accept minus (−) angles.

Fill: This area of the MultiLine Properties dialog box will allow you to fill the MultiLine solid with a color of your choice. When a checkmark is placed inside the On box, the Color button becomes available. When the Color button is checked, the Select Color dialog box will appear.

The Filling/Shading sometimes referred to as *poche* is accomplished with the Fill On option. The true architectural material symbols or graphics are achieved with the HATCH command and are discussed in Chapter 20. If the Filling/Shading is used together with the HATCH command, the results may not be desirable. To avoid too much density, try using Filling/Shading and Hatching separately.

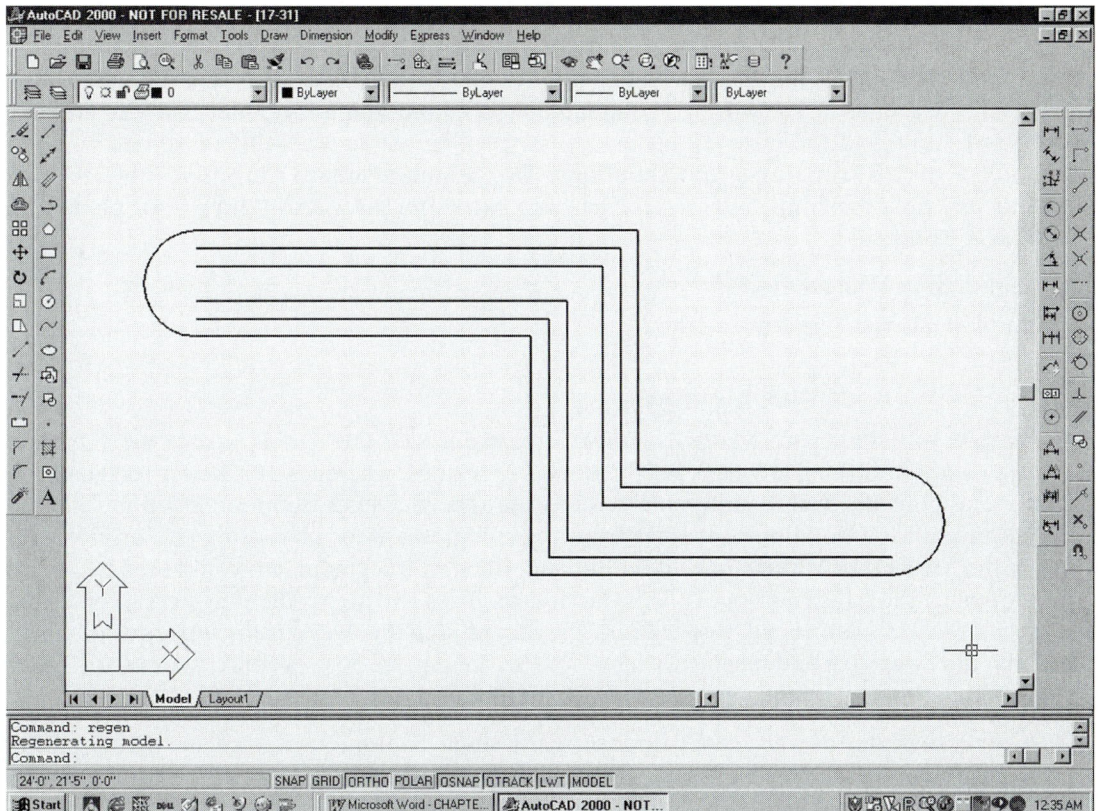

FIGURE 17–21 This wall type has 6 lines with Outer arc Caps ON for Start and End. Notice that only the upper and lower lines receive arc closure.

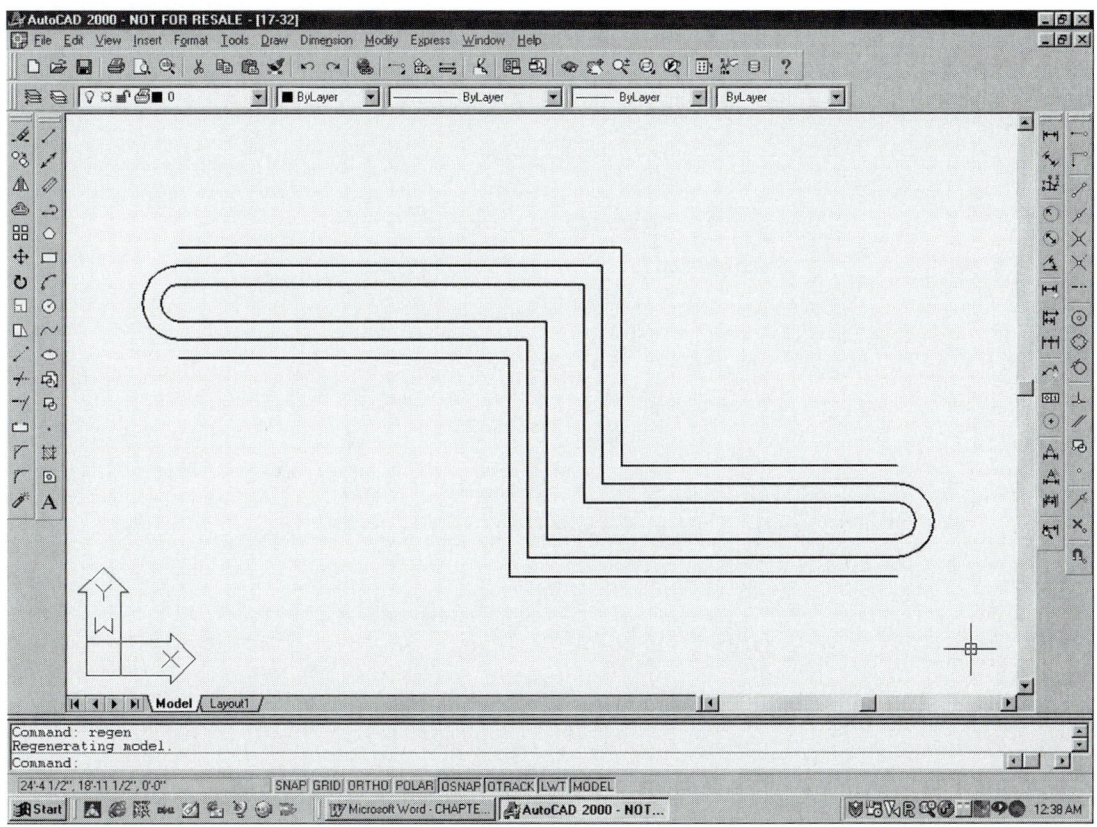

FIGURE 17–22 The six line wall type in Figure 17–21 has now drawn with Inner arcs Caps ON for Start and End.

17.9 DRAWING FLOOR PLANS WITH THE MULTILINE COMMAND

After creation of a MultiLine style using one of the three methods described earlier, the actual floor plan is drawn using the MLINE command. Please note that it is not necessary to create a new MultiLine style if the project calls for a floor plan having two parallel lines with no color and no caps. If this is the case, you should use the default standard MultiLine style without spending any time creating a new style. There are two different ways to draw floor plans with the MLINE command:

1. Continuous Wall method.
2. Individual Wall Segments method.

17.9.1   Continuous Wall Method

This method will allow you to create a *single continuous wall segment* as part of the complete floor plan without placing any gaps for the door and window openings. It is better to start from a corner and draw the walls counterclockwise to keep the wall justifications consistent. You can then cut the window and door openings from the completed floor plan using one or more options of the MLEDIT (MultiLine Edit) command. Each wall segment cut would then be closed (capped) using the LINE command. This method requires two steps. The first step involves the drawing of the walls as one single operation. The second step involves cutting the required openings from the floor plan and placing the *caps* for the openings. The procedure to draw the Floor Plan in Figure 17–23 with the Continuous Wall method is as follows:

1. Create the exterior walls of the floor plan as a single continuous wall segment as shown in Figure 17–24.
2. Create the interior walls of the floor plan as a single continuous piece referenced from a selected corner.

FIGURE 17–23 The Floor Plan as the final product for drawing walls using either the Continuous Wall or the Individual Wall Segments methods.

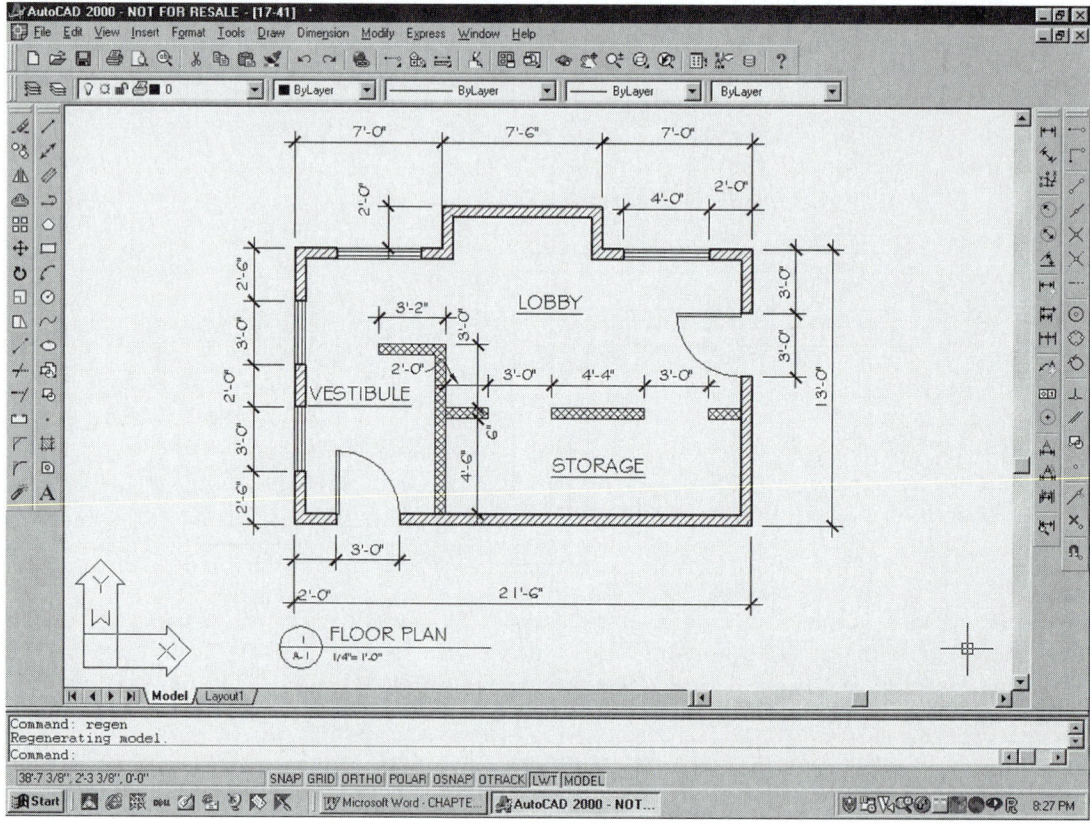

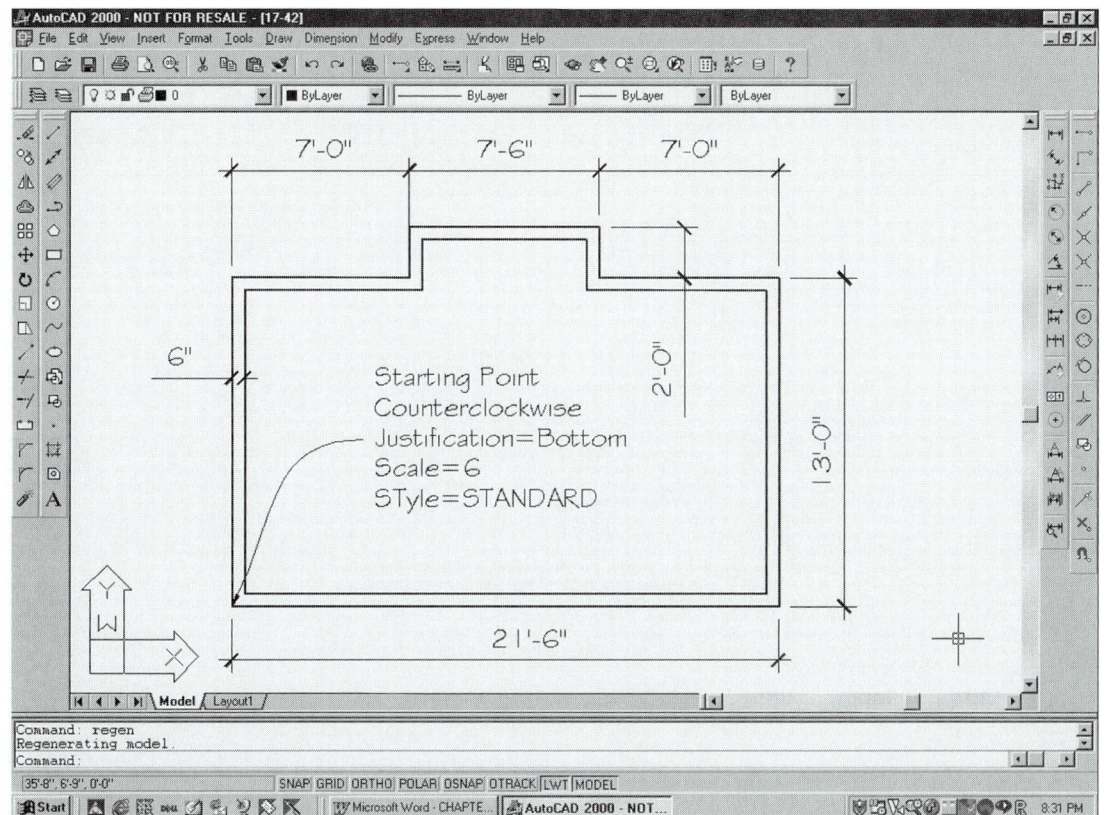

3. Use the Cut All option of the MLEDIT command to cut the required door and window openings from the exterior and interior walls. The MLEDIT command is discussed later in the chapter.

4. Use the Line command to cap the ends of the openings or use the Element Properties dialog box to automatically add caps to the walls as shown in Figure 17–25.

5. Insert doors, windows, furniture, or fixtures as blocks. Blocks are discussed in Chapter 19.

6. Create the necessary dimensions, hatching, and text as shown in Figure 17–23. Dimensioning is discussed in Chapter 18. Hatching is discussed in Chapter 20. Creating text is discussed in Chapter 14.

Caution: After an opening in a floor plan is cut, the LINE command can be used to close the sides of the openings. This operation is not the same as placing line caps on the Start and End of the Multi-Line using the MultiLine Properties dialog box of the MLSTYLE command. This procedure is discussed next as the second method of creating a floor plan. When the LINE command is used to provide the caps, the caps do not become a part of the MultiLine; instead they act as separate objects. This will create significant editing problems in the future if a wall is edited using the STRETCH command. Stretching MultiLines is discussed at the end of the chapter.

17.9.2 Individual Wall Segments Method

This method will allow you to create individual wall segments one at a time with the desired openings or gaps between the wall segments of the floor plan without ever leaving the MLINE command. With this method the MultiLine caps are placed on Start and End points of the MultiLine style, where each wall segment becomes a closed single entity. The caps placed in this fashion become a part of the total wall segment where future editing operations will select the entire wall segment, including its caps. This method will work best with the STRETCH command as an editing operation. However, this method will require you to use the MLSTYLE command

FIGURE 17–25 All openings for doors and windows are cut at required locations on exterior and interior walls. At each opening an enclosure is drawn using the LINE command so as to provide a cap at the opening locations. This wall cap can also be created using the MultiLine Properties dialog box.

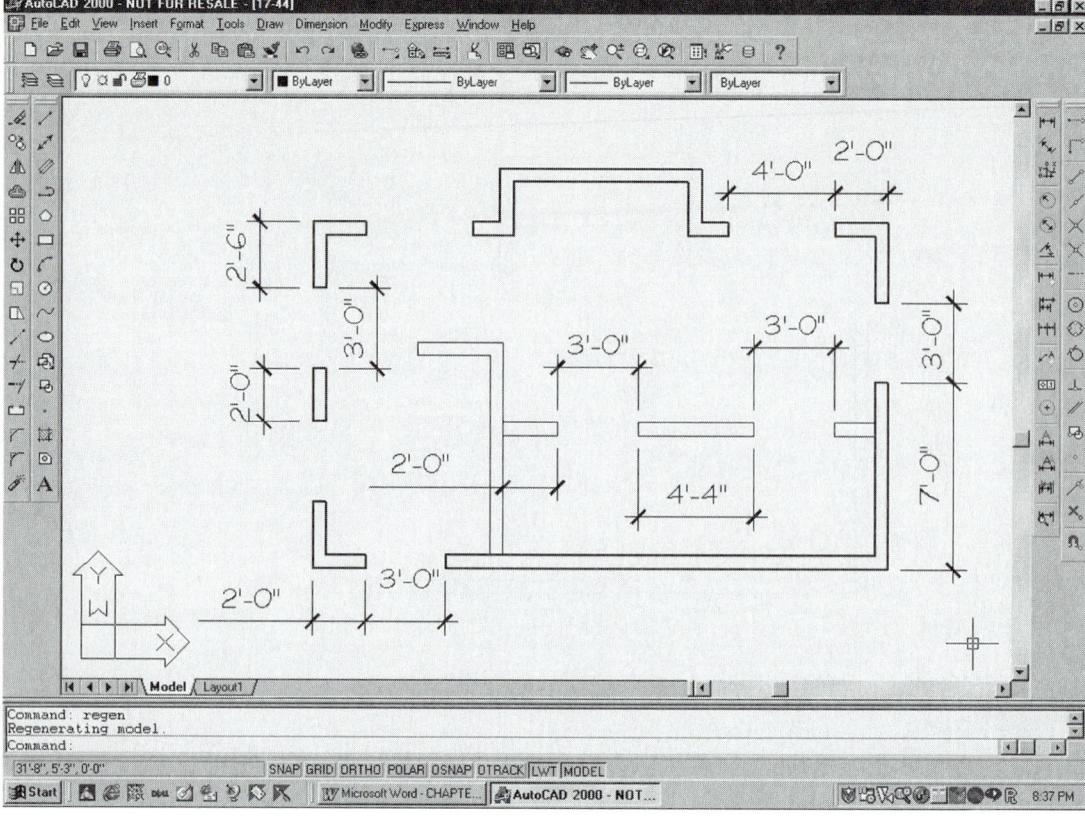

FIGURE 17–26 Exterior walls are created as individual wall segments with the desired gaps in between.

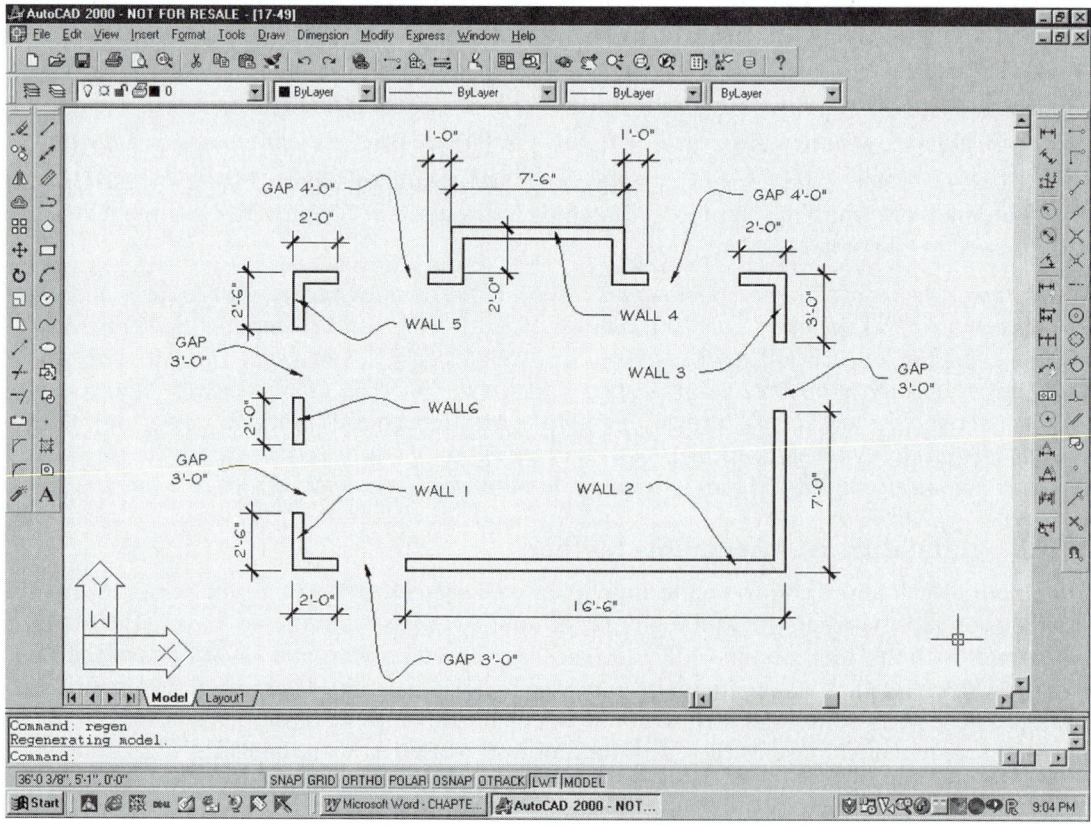

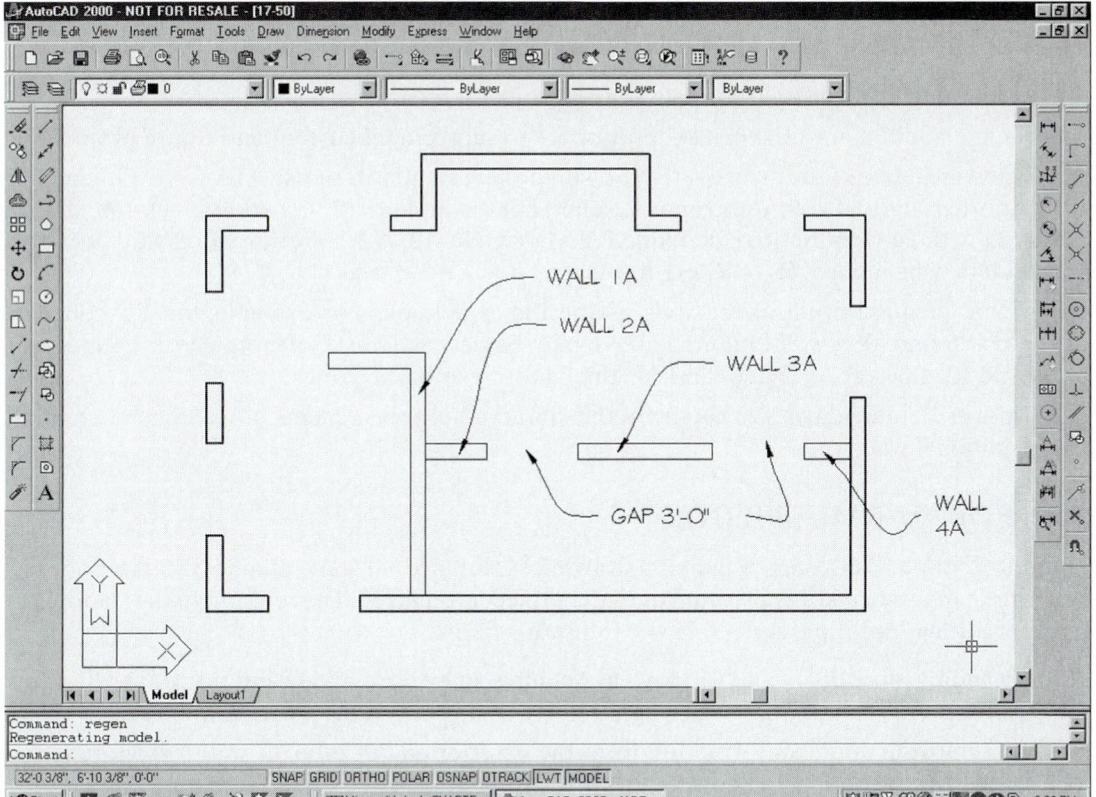

FIGURE 17–27 Interior walls are created as individual wall segments with the desired gaps in between.

to create a new MultiLine style with the caps on. With the Individual Wall Segments method, wall openings are created using the MLINE command as opposed to using the MLEDIT command to cut the walls after they are drawn. The procedure to draw the floor plan in Figure 17–23 using this method is as follows:

1. Create exterior individual wall segments 1, 2, 3, 4, 5, and 6 as shown in Figure 17–26. After drawing each wall segment, finish the MULTILINE command by pressing ~EnterKey~ at the command prompt but do not exit the command. Press the ~EnterKey~ to access the MULTILINE command again. Type the @ symbol followed by the distance and the angle (polar coordinates) of the desired opening or use Polar Angle and Polar Snap. AutoCAD will start the next MultiLine at the required distance away from the last wall segment.

2. Create interior individual wall segments 1A, 2A, 3A, and 4A as shown in Figure 17–27. Use the same method shown above to create the gaps between wall segments.

3. Use procedures 5 and 6 of the Continuous Wall method to finish the project.

The Individual Wall Segments method is the preferred method because there is no need to cut openings and the floor plan is ready for windows and doors. However, if the door and window locations on the floor plan are not readily available and if it is to be provided as the drawing evolves, then the Continuous Wall method is the *preferred* choice. Combining the two options will make the floor plan operation an ideal one.

17.10 DEVELOPING A LIBRARY OF MULTILINES

There can be many wall types involved in the creation of different floor plans. Although Auto-CAD provides only one MultiLine style, you should create as many wall styles as possible using the steps shown earlier in this chapter. The most important aspect of the creation of this library is that you pay close attention to creation and management of the wall types being created. It is best to create the wall types library as part of the architecture office standards or architectural drawing conventions. The following is a list of items to consider when creating the *library of MultiLines:*

1. Create a MultiLine style consistent with project standards.

2. Create additional wall types as appropriate to supplement current and future projects.

3. Keep the name of the style consistent with project standards or use AIA CAD Guidelines. Another method is to use common sense. For example, a 12″ concrete block foundation wall with 24″ footing may be named: FND-CONC-12. A 6″ interior wood stud partition wall may be named: INT-WDST-6.

4. Keep the description of the style as specific as possible. For example, the 12″ concrete block foundation wall in item 3 above may be described as: Concrete Block Foundation Wall 12″ thick as solid lines and 24″ thick footing as dashed lines.

5. Inform all individuals working with this library about the general procedures of creating additional wall types.

[17.11] EDITING MULTILINES

Revising floor plans is a part of the total drawing experience. At some architectural/interior design firms it may even be a daily ritual until the project is finalized. The revision of the floor plans involves editing MultiLine style(s) in the following manner:

1. By adding more doors and windows as openings in exterior and/or interior walls, which requires the actual *cutting* (removing) of parts or sections of the existing wall surfaces.

2. By removing doors and windows from the exterior and/or interior walls, which requires the *welding* (undoing the cutting) of the existing openings.

3. By changing the locations or the lengths of the walls, which requires the *moving* (removal), adding a *vertex* to show a new grip location, or *stretching* of the existing walls.

4. By cleaning up the undesired intersections of two or more different or similar wall types that form a *cross, tee,* or *joint.*

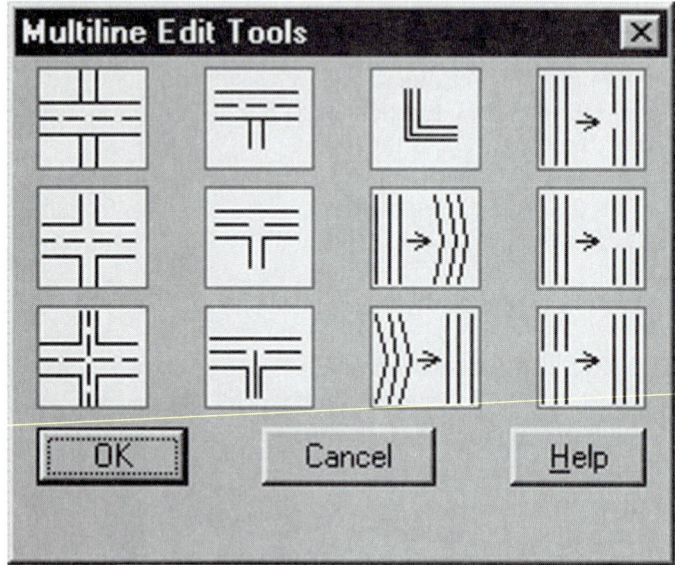

FIGURE 17–28 The MultiLine Edit Tools Dialog Box with 12 different editing option buttons.

With the exception of stretching of the MultiLines, all of the above editing operations can be performed with the editing options set inside the MultiLine Edit Tools dialog box as shown in Figure 17–28.

MultiLine editing can be a straightforward, concise, and easy process if all the 12 editing options of the Multi-Line Edit Tools are understood and put in perspective with the methods and procedures described earlier. From the start of the project, the objective of the floor plan should be to minimize the use of the multilLine editing involved. For example, caps should always be used for individual wall segments, and gaps should be established for all openings so as to eliminate the lengthy process of using the Cut All option of the MLEDIT command. If possible, the precise locations of exterior and interior wall intersections should be established without any overlapping wall intersections so as to eliminate the intersection clean-ups later in the project. But for most architects and designers revisions of the floor plan is inevitable. For that purpose the MultiLine Edit Tools dialog box provide sufficient editing arsenal.

Since MultiLines are not two-dimensional polylines (they are a special species of their own!) they cannot be edited using the BREAK, EXTEND, TRIM, LENGTHEN, OFFSET, CHAMFER, and FILLET commands unless the MultiLines are exploded. Exploding MultiLines is not

Unusable Command =	Usable Command =	MultiLine Edit Tools Option
Break	_____	Cut all
Extend	Stretch (grips)	_____
Trim	_____	Cross, tee, corner joint, and cut
Lengthen	Stretch (grips)	_____
Offset	Array	_____
Chamfer	_____	Corner joint
Fillet	_____	Corner joint

TABLE 17–10:
Corresponding Commands for MultiLine Editing Options.

recommended because it removes the associativity between line segments. AutoCAD does not recognize MultiLines as objects to be edited with editing commands. The following error messages will be given respectively at the command prompt: "object can't be broken," "cannot extend this object," "cannot trim this object," "this object has no length definition," "cannot offset that object," "chamfer requires 2 lines," and "fillet requires 2 lines, arcs, or circles." Talk about a bad project day! But, luckily, for every unusable AutoCAD command on MultiLines there is at least one usable command and one or more MultiLine Editing options available to do the same job. Table 17–10 illustrates a breakdown of such commands and MultiLine Editing Tools options that can be used in lieu of those "unfriendly to the MultiLine commands." Another option to work around this is to use the grips of the MultiLines to perform Stretch, Move, Rotate, Scale, and Mirror operations. Enabling grips on MultiLines is a very effective and powerful editing operation. In most of the editing cases the MultiLine Editing Tools can be considered as the *trim and break heaven* of the MLEDIT and the MLINE commands.

Tips: MultiLines can be EXPLODED for editing purposes. When a MultiLine is exploded, it automatically turns into individual line segments that can be edited using any of the modify commands. However, an exploded MultiLine loses its singular unity as well as its associative integrity. Because of its unique composition and the associative attributes connected with the DIMENSION and HATCH commands, it is highly recommended that the MultiLines not be exploded unless all alternative avenues are exhausted and the consequences are understood.

To edit MultiLines use the MLEDIT (MultiLine Editor) command. It can be accessed in three different ways as shown below:

1. From the Modify II toolbar select the Edit MultiLine button.
2. From the Modify pull-down menu select MultiLine....
3. Enter MLEDIT at the command prompt.

The MultiLine Edit Tools dialog box will appear as shown in Figure 17–28.

The MultiLine Editing tools help not only to control and clean up the undesired intersections but also to cut and mend a previously cut MultiLine. It will cut a portion of a wall as the openings for doors and windows along with the welding of those cuts. The MultiLine Edit Tools dialog box has four columns. Each column has four types of editing tools corresponding to intersections. The first column edits MultiLines that cross, the second column edits MultiLines that form a tee, the third column edits the joints and vertices of the MultiLines, and the fourth column performs cuts and welds. The individual graphics on the image buttons should serve as the final results that can be expected after the editing option. When you click on the individual editing button, the name will appear on the lower left corner of the dialog box. Let's take a look at each of the editing buttons.

17.11.1 Editing MultiLines that Cross

Closed Cross: This option will close the intersection of two MultiLines. The first MultiLine selected will be trimmed and will appear on the bottom (background), while the second MultiLine will remain unchanged and will appear on top (foreground). This means that whichever MultiLine

FIGURE 17–29 The results achieved by using the Closed Cross option of the MultiLine Edit Tools. Notice that the **MultiLine** selected first appears trimmed and on the bottom.

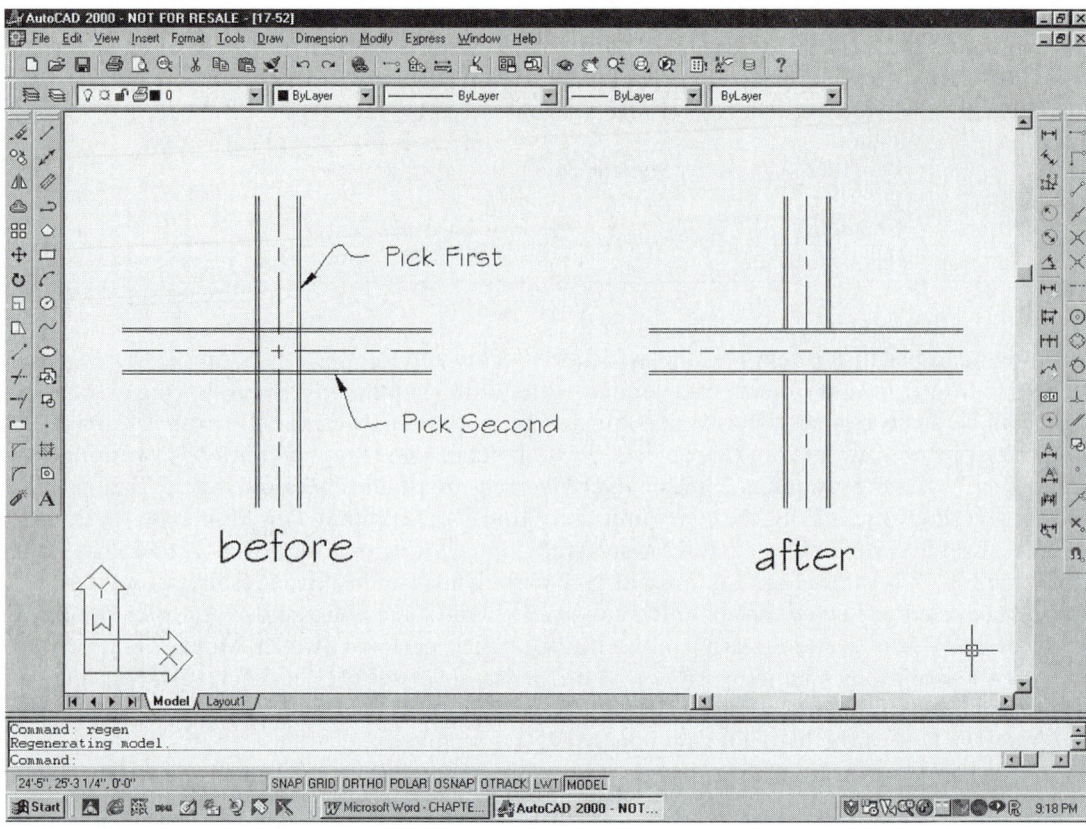

you want to appear on top as unchanged should be selected *second*. Figure 17–29 shows the intersection of the two MultiLines.

Open Cross: This option will trim *all* of the elements of the first selected MultiLine and will trim *only* the outside elements of the second MultiLine. Notice that the centerline of the first selected MultiLine is trimmed, but the centerline and the inside line of the second selected MultiLine remain. This is shown in Figure 17–30.

Merged Cross: This option will trim all the exterior lines of the first and second MultiLine but will not trim the centerlines as shown in Figure 17–31. This editing function can be useful when four interior walls intersect.

17.11.2   Editing MultiLines that Form a Tee

Closed Tee: This option will trim the first selected wall where it intersects the second wall. An example would be where the exterior wall crosses over the interior wall or vice versa. This option can be performed on four different locations where walls intersect. The end result depends on which wall on which side is picked first. Figure 17–32 shows an example of a brick and block exterior wall intersected by an interior partition wall. To trim the partition wall that extends beyond the exterior wall so that it is located on the inside of the floor plan, the partition wall is picked first on the inside part of the floor plan.

Open Tee: This option is similar to the Closed Tee option except it will trim the outside wall lines at intersections as shown in Figure 17–33. With this option the inside wall intersection will not be trimmed. To completely trim the outside and inside lines use the Merged Tee option described next. This could be applicable to the intersection of similar walls where the intersecting lines need to be trimmed without resorting to the EXPLODE command. Notice that in Figure 17–33 centerlines of both walls will not meet at an intersection but will meet if the Merged Tee option is used.

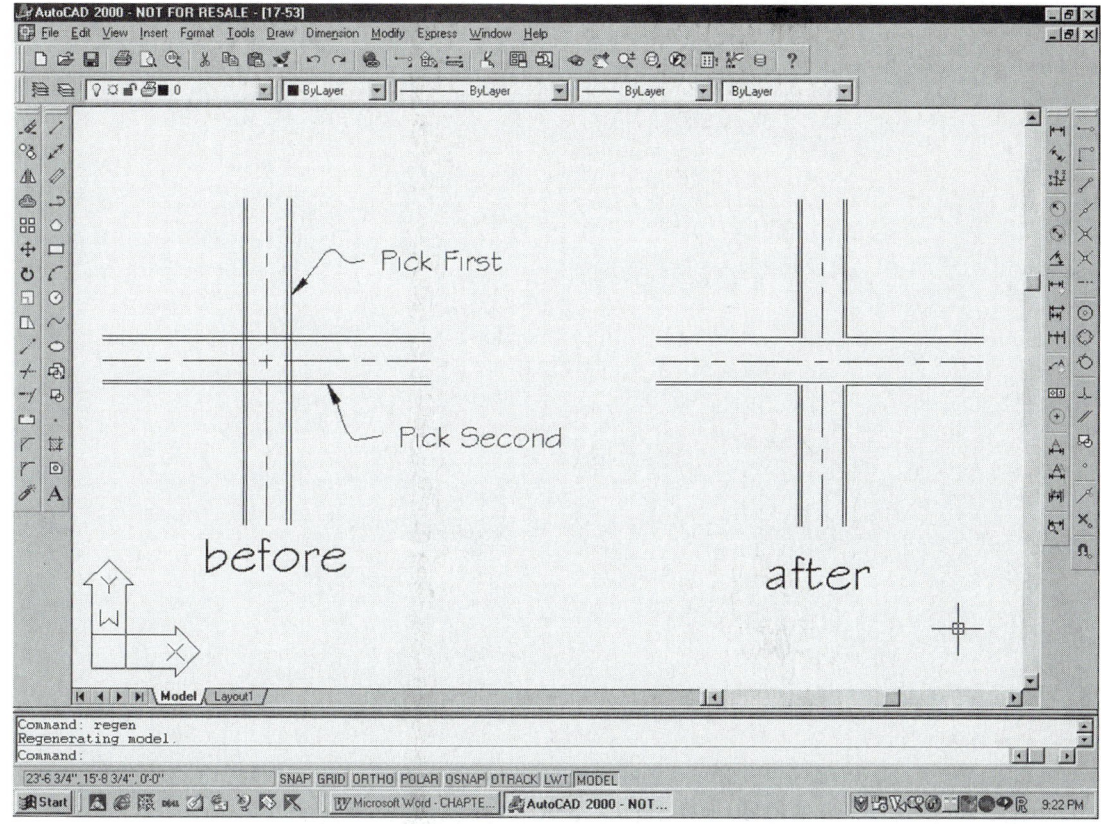

FIGURE 17–30 Using the Open Cross option.

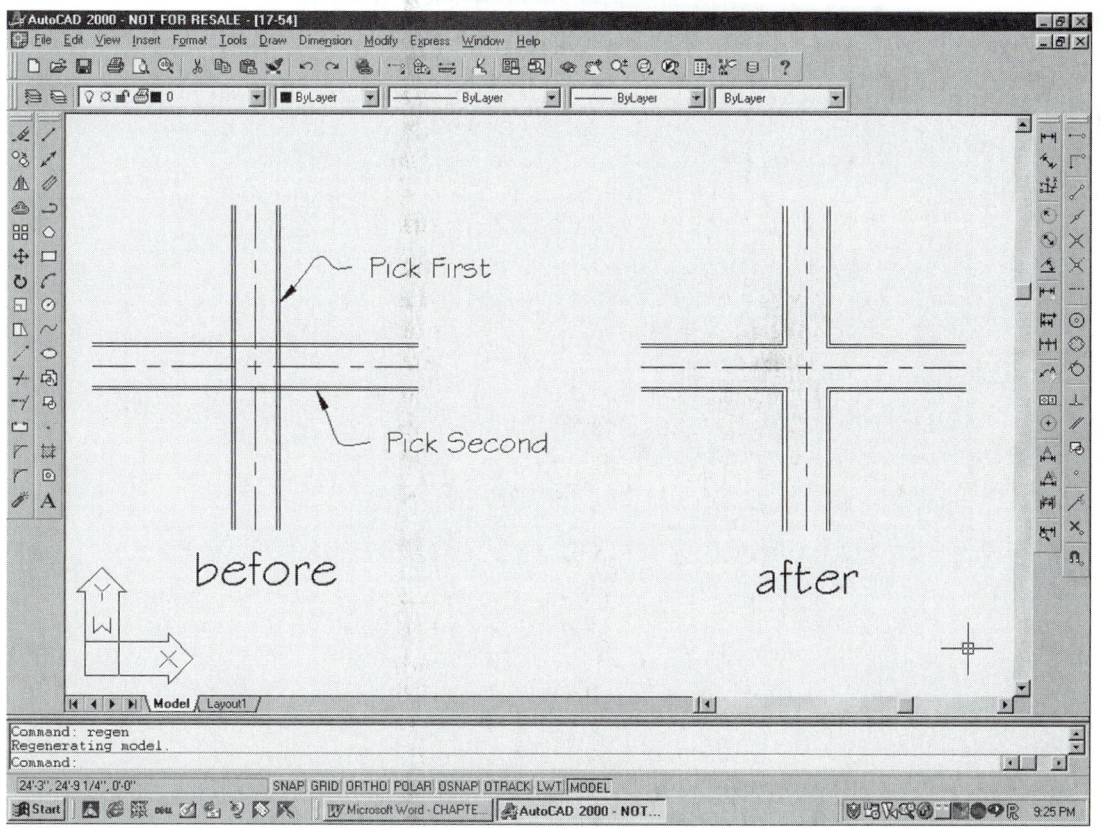

FIGURE 17–31 Using the Merged Cross option.

FIGURE 17–32 The
Closed Tee option will
clean up the
intersections of walls.
Notice that the
intersection is closed.

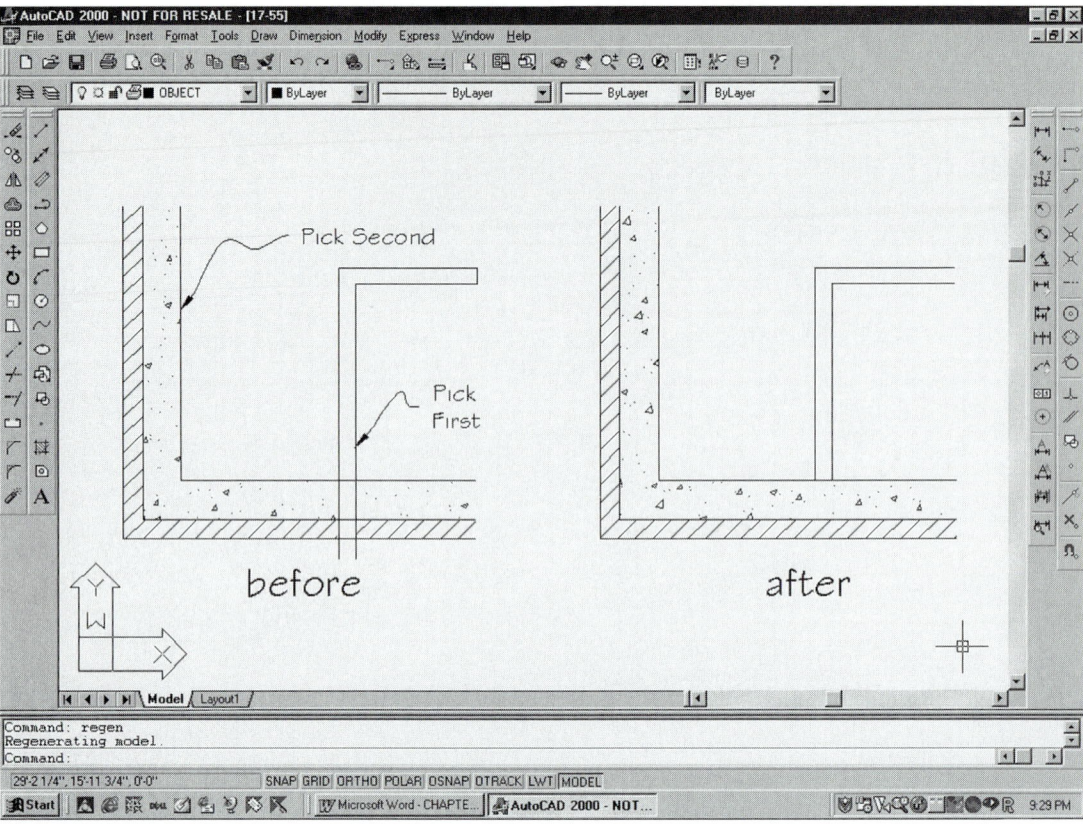

FIGURE 17–33 Using
the Open Tee editing
option.

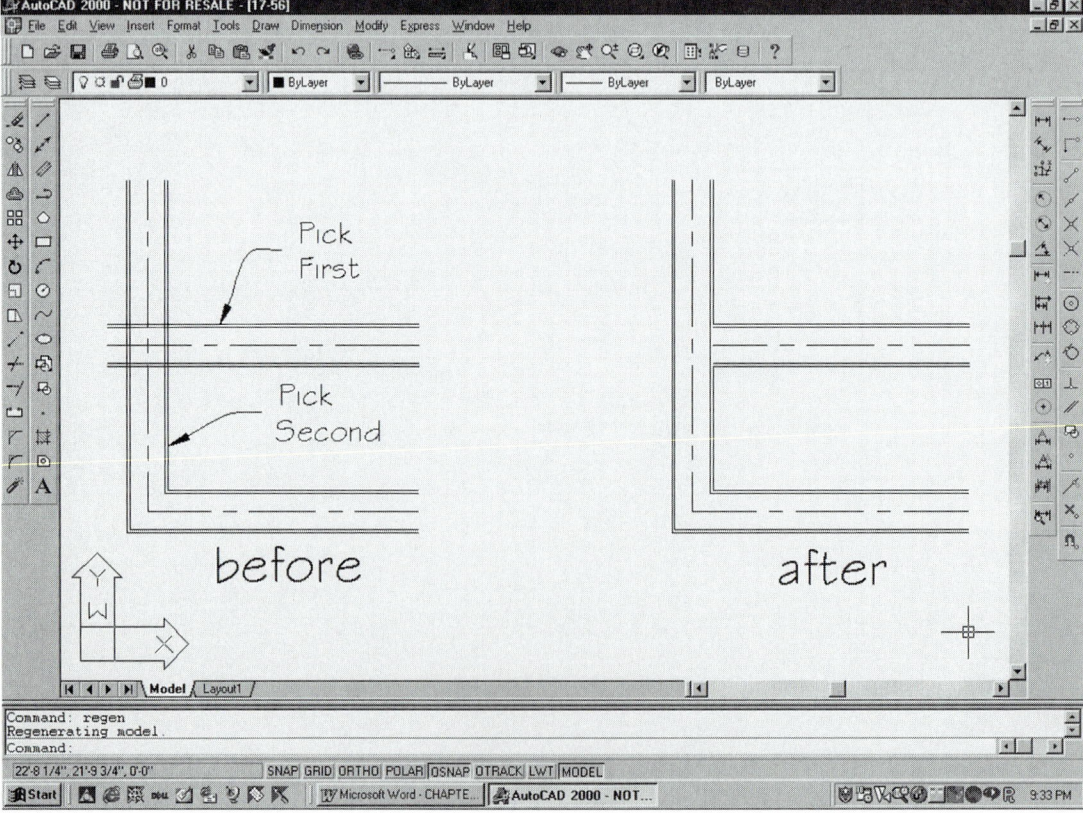

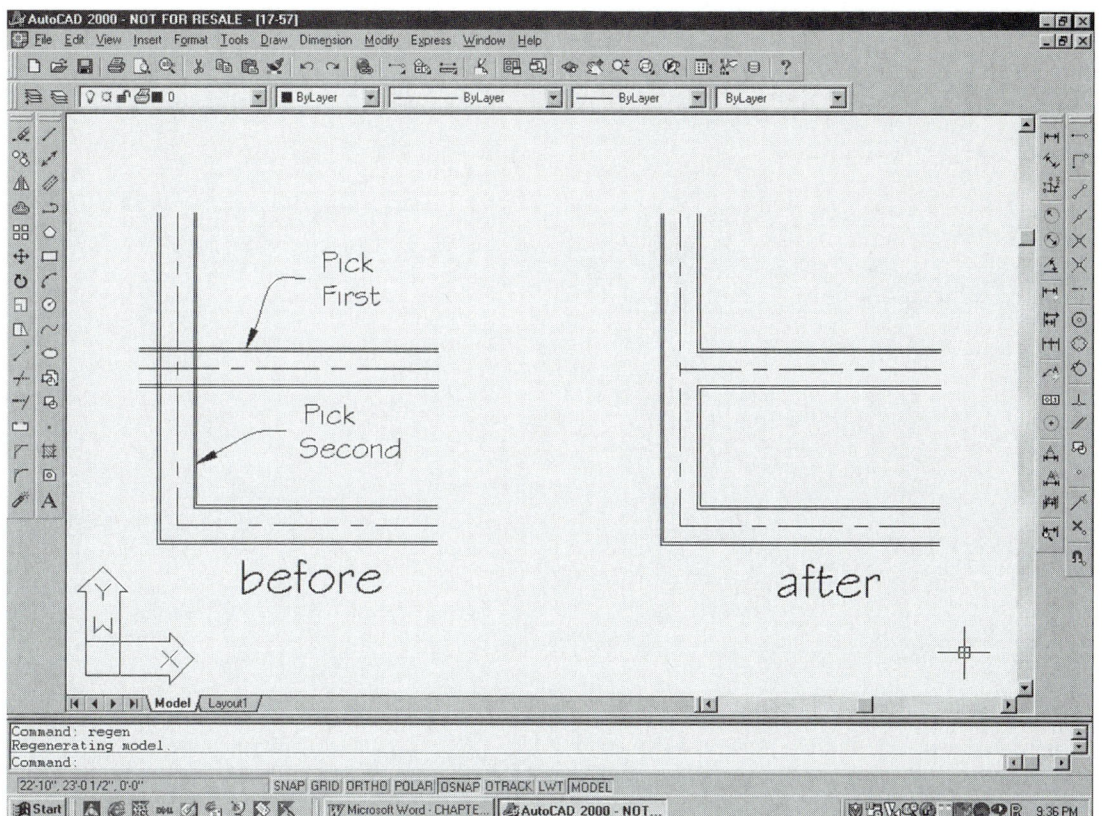

Merged Tee:　This option will do everything the Open Tee does plus it will trim the inside wall line intersections and will merge the centerlines of the walls as shown in Figure 17–34.

17.11.3 Editing Joints and Vertices of MultiLines

This area of the MultiLine Edit Tools dialog box will trim corners and vertexes of the walls that intersect as follows:

Corner Joint:　This option will *lengthen* or *shorten* each of the two MultiLines by creating a *trimmed* corner joint. The first selected wall will be trimmed or extended to its intersection with the second wall. Figure 17–35 shows an example of a brick and block exterior wall similar to Figure 17–32. When two of the same wall types intersect the corner joint editing option will trim the intersection as shown in Figure 17–35.

Add Vertex:　This option will add a vertex to an existing MultiLine at a location of your choice. This new vertex can later be used to add a new grip location to the existing MultiLine so that it can be edited using the STRETCH, MOVE, ROTATE, SCALE, and MIRROR commands automatically with grips. This is a very powerful option because a grip can be located at a specific location on a wall and can be used to alter the shape of the wall. In Figure 17–36 a simple square floor plan with brick and block is shown. The right side wall is required to be moved to a new location previously determined with both sides at a 45 degree angle as shown in Figure 17–36. By using the Add Vertex option a new vertex is added to the mid-point of the wall. This provides the additional grip point needed to select the wall at that location. By displaying the grips and by selecting the new grip the wall is stretched to the new location. This editing option can be very useful when specific points of the walls on the floor plan need to be altered or moved to a new location.

Delete Vertex:　This option will remove any vertex added by the Add Vertex option. Simply pick the vertex you want deleted from the wall surface.

FIGURE 17–35 The Corner Joint editing option will clean up the two wall intersections.

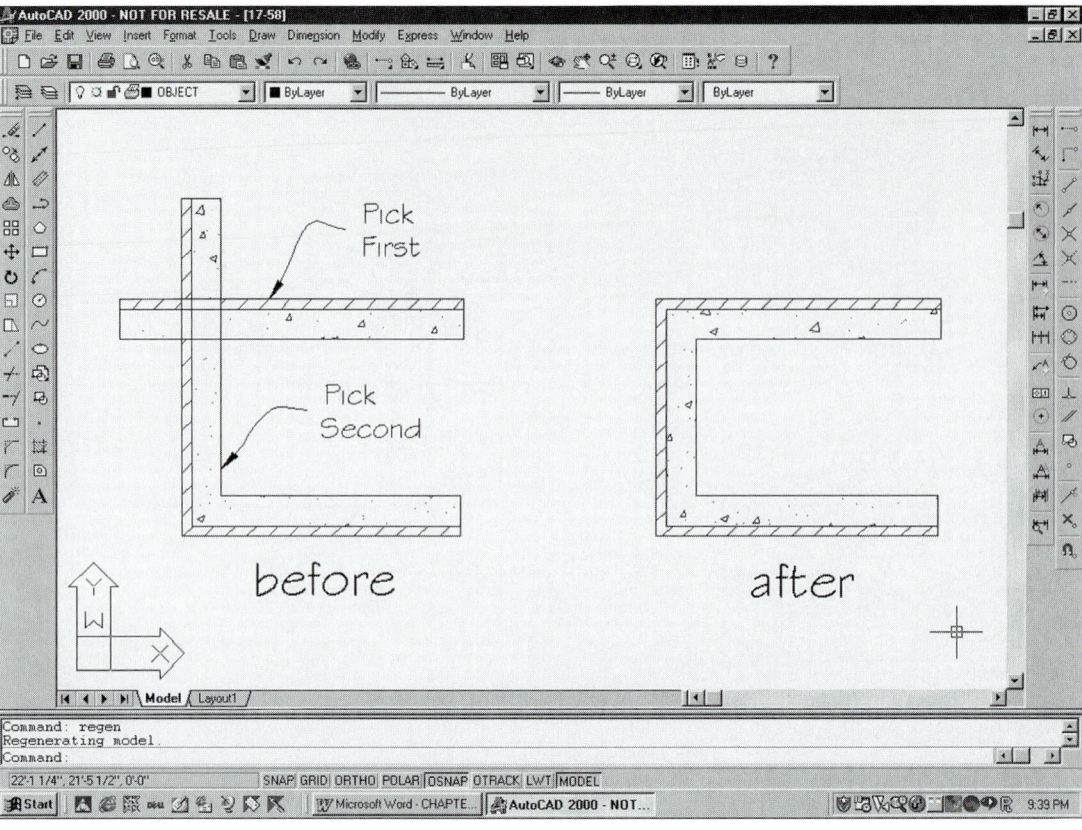

FIGURE 17–36 The Add Vertex option creates a new grip location to stretch the wall from that location to a new location. It can also be moved, rotated, scaled, and mirrored automatically as needed.

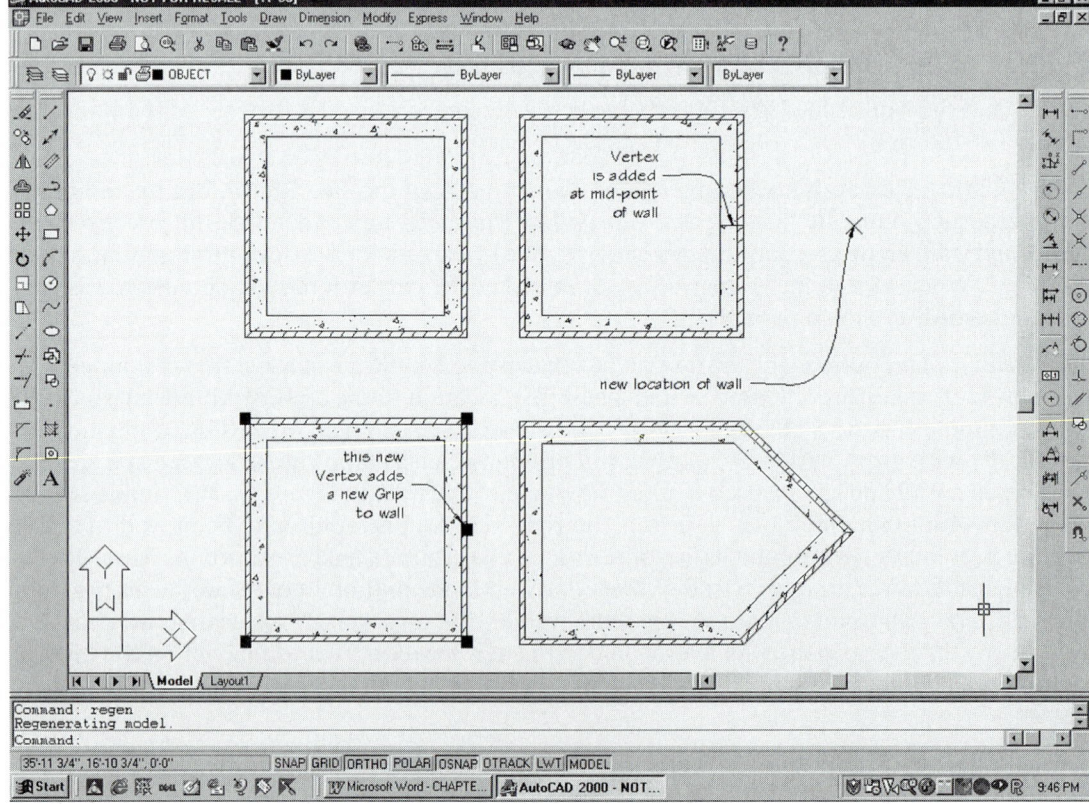

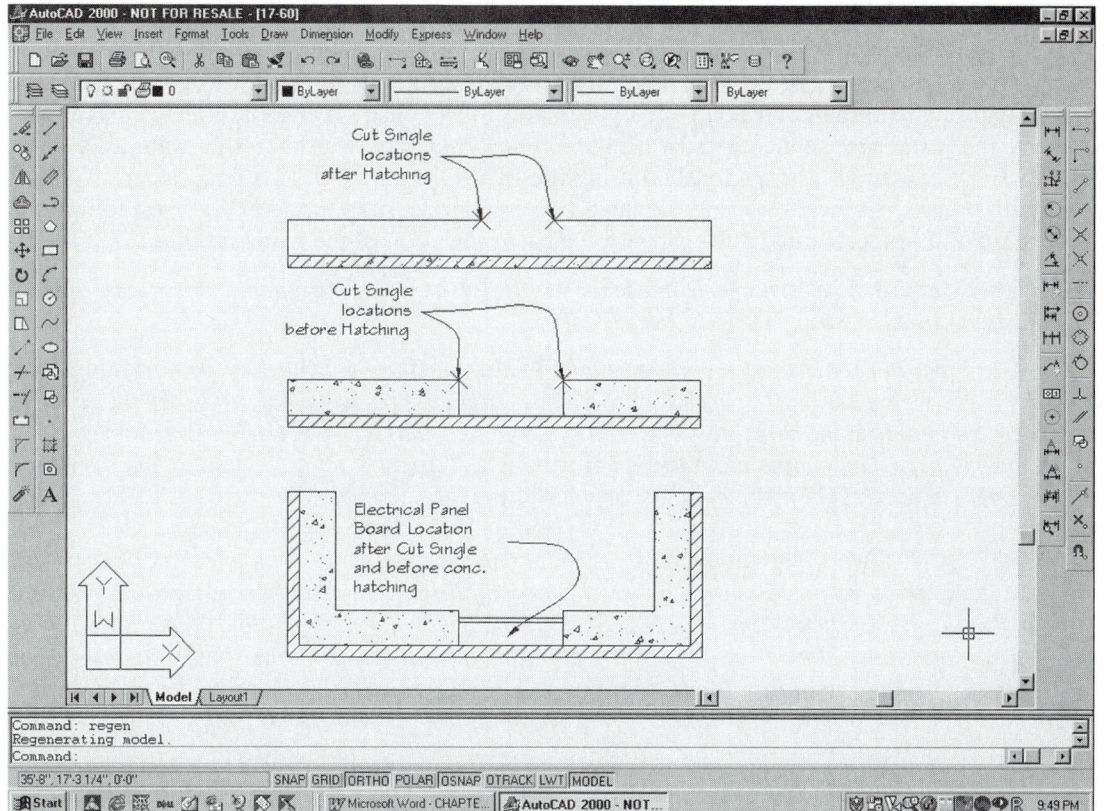

FIGURE 17–37 Using the Cut Single option.

17.11.4   Cutting and Welding MultiLines

The last column of editing tools in the MultiLine Edit Tools dialog box deal with cutting (removing a portion of the wall for doors, windows, or any other purpose) a single or the entire wall thickness at a specified location. This area of editing can also reverse the cutting process (restoring that portion of the wall that was cut previously) by simply welding the wall by connecting the gap created by cutting. If the Individual Wall Segment method is used to create the floor plan, the amount of cutting and welding is reduced to a minimum if not eliminated, thus increasing the productivity and decreasing the time needed to complete the floor plan. But as mentioned earlier, revising floor plans is a major part of the design and drafting process. I suggest you be prepared to use these editing tools. As the user of AutoCAD and the producer of floor plans you are the major decision-maker on choosing the most effective methods described in this chapter.

Cut Single: This option will cut a single element between two points. It does not break the Multi-Line. In Figure 17–37 a brick and block wall is shown. In the top example a single cut is to be performed to provide an electrical panel board location. If the wall hatching is performed before the single cut, any gap created within the boundaries of the hatch pattern will cause the hatch pattern to dissipate into other areas of the drawing and undesired results may be created. Therefore, it is strongly suggested that you perform wall hatching after all the cuts are made. In the middle example, cutting a single line for the placement of the electrical panel board within the concrete wall before hatching is recommended. After the single cut is performed, the sides of the concrete wall are closed with the LINE command to create the boundaries needed for hatch pattern applications. The final plan is presented in the bottom example, including the cut and the hatching.

Cut All: This option will cut all of the MultiLine elements between two points. This cutting operation only affects the appearance of the MultiLine. It does not break the MultiLine into two separate pieces. The MultiLine will remain as a whole unit consistent with its previous attributes, but now an additional wall segment is added to the floor plan. This option is used to provide openings for door and window insertions on floor plans. Be very careful not to place hatching before the openings and be precise with the use of the Cut All Locations option. Use the Snap From object snap mode with the Polar Snap and coordinates to establish precise cut points. You can also visually verify the precise locations by using *blipmarks* at exact coordinates. A point as X in the precise location can also be established using the POINT command. This point location can be used as a precise cut location using the Snap to Node object snap mode or by using Temporary Tracking Point mode. Figure 17–38 shows a typical application of the Cut All option.

Caution: Any hatch pattern visible inside the MultiLine will not be cut and will remain inside the MultiLine after the wall is cut single or cut all.

Tips: In order to have the hatch pattern trimmed while cutting the MultiLine you must apply the hatch pattern after the cutting operation(s) is done. Applying the hatch pattern before the openings are cut will not trim the hatching along with the wall(s). If the hatch pattern has been applied before the cut is made, you should erase the hatch pattern and apply it after everything has been done, preferably at the end of the drawing just before plotting.

■ **EXERCISE 17–6:**   *The following step-by-step exercise will allow you to cut a door opening in a predetermined location on a given portion of a floor plan as shown in Figure 17–39. The final product is shown in Figure 17–42. A hatch pattern will not be created at this time. For efficiency and quick flow of information and procedures the Snap From object snap mode will be used to locate cut points. Remember that you can also use Polar Distance Entry method to locate the same points. You should try to become familiar with Polar Snap, Polar Tracking, and Object Snap Tracking features of AutoCAD so that you may utilize them to increase efficiency and boost productivity in your drawings. AutoSnap AutoTrack modes are discussed in Chapter 7.*

Step #1:   Open the EXE17-1.dwg file.

FIGURE 17–38   Using the Cut All option.

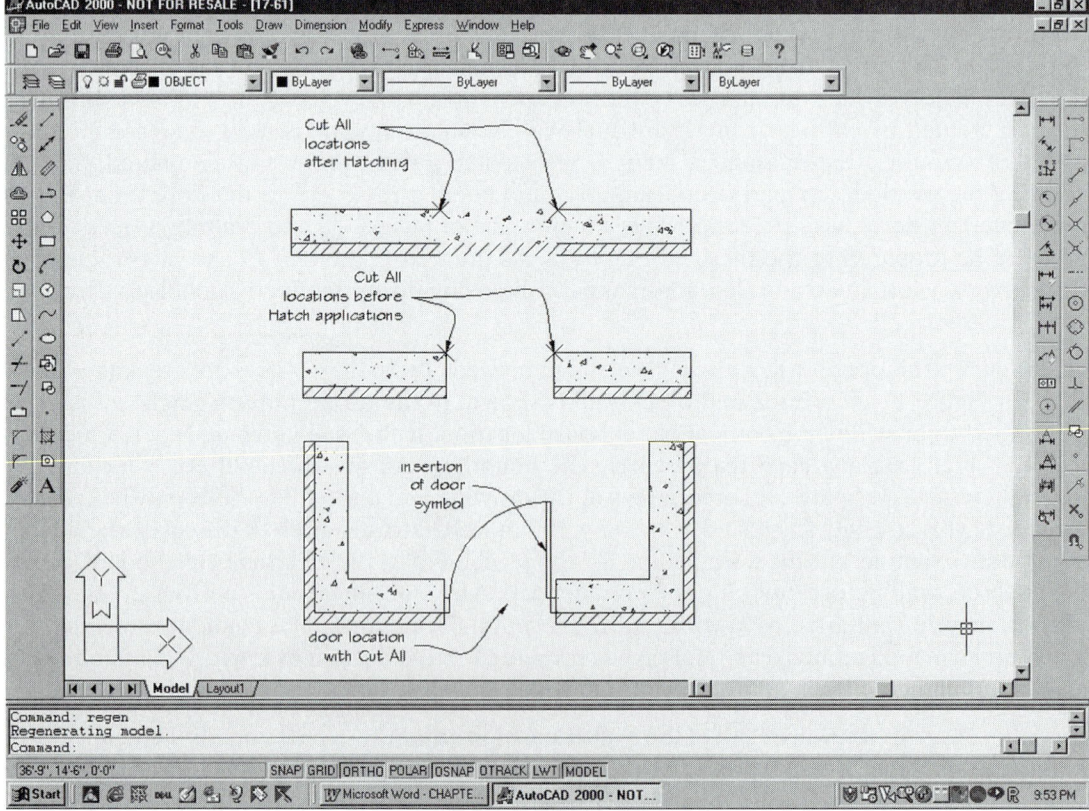

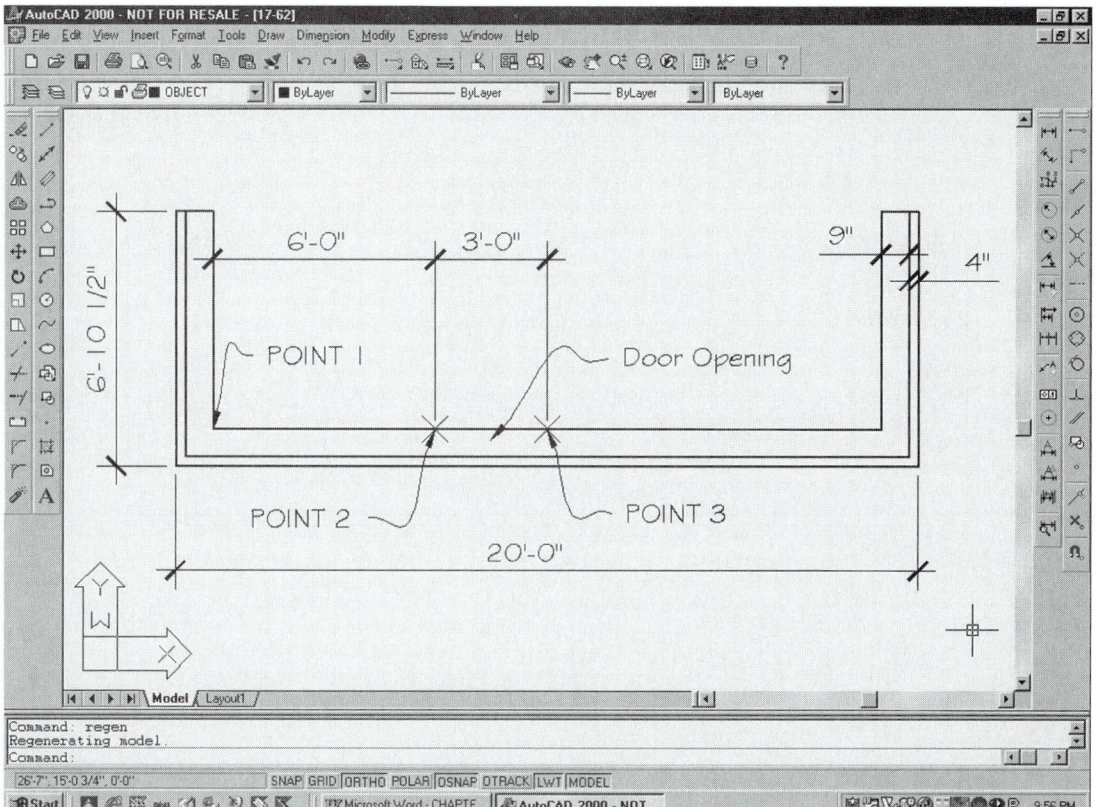

FIGURE 17–39 The Cut All option of the MLEDIT command will be used to cut the door opening.

Step #2: Using the Cut all option of the MLEDIT command, cut the door opening as follows:

Command: **MLEDIT** ~EnterKey~ (the MultiLine Edit Tools dialog box will appear. Click on the Cut All button and click on the OK button).

Select mline: (Inside the Object Snap toolbar click on the Snap From button).
Select mline: _ from Base point: (Click on the Snap to Endpoint button or use running object snap modes).
Select mline: _ from Base point: _ endp of (Click on point 1 as shown in Figure 17–39).
Select mline: _ from Base point: _ endp of <offset>: **@6'<0** ~EnterKey~ (this will establish point 2 as a + sign if you have the blipmode system variable on).
Select second point: **@3'<0** ~EnterKey~ (this will make the actual cut).
Select mline or [Undo]: ~EnterKey~ (this will finish the cut operation at that location).
Your drawing should now look like Figure 17–40, without the X's.

Tips: If you had more openings to cut, do not press the ~EnterKey~. Instead, continue with the Cut All option using the Snap From and Snap to Endpoint object snap modes. This will allow you to cut more than one opening as a continuous operation without ever leaving the Cut All option of the MLEDIT command. This is very significant because you can perform one cut after another without having to exit the command.

Step #3: After the cut is made, place the side wall lines (caps) using the LINE command and object snap modes as follows:

Command: **LINE** ~EnterKey~

_ line specify first point: (Click on Snap to Endpoint).

_ line specify first point: _ endp of (Click on point 2 as shown in Figure 17–39).
Specify next point or [Undo]: (Click on the end point of the bottom line).

FIGURE 17–40 The 3'-0"
wall opening is cut from
the wall. Notice all three
wall lines are cut.

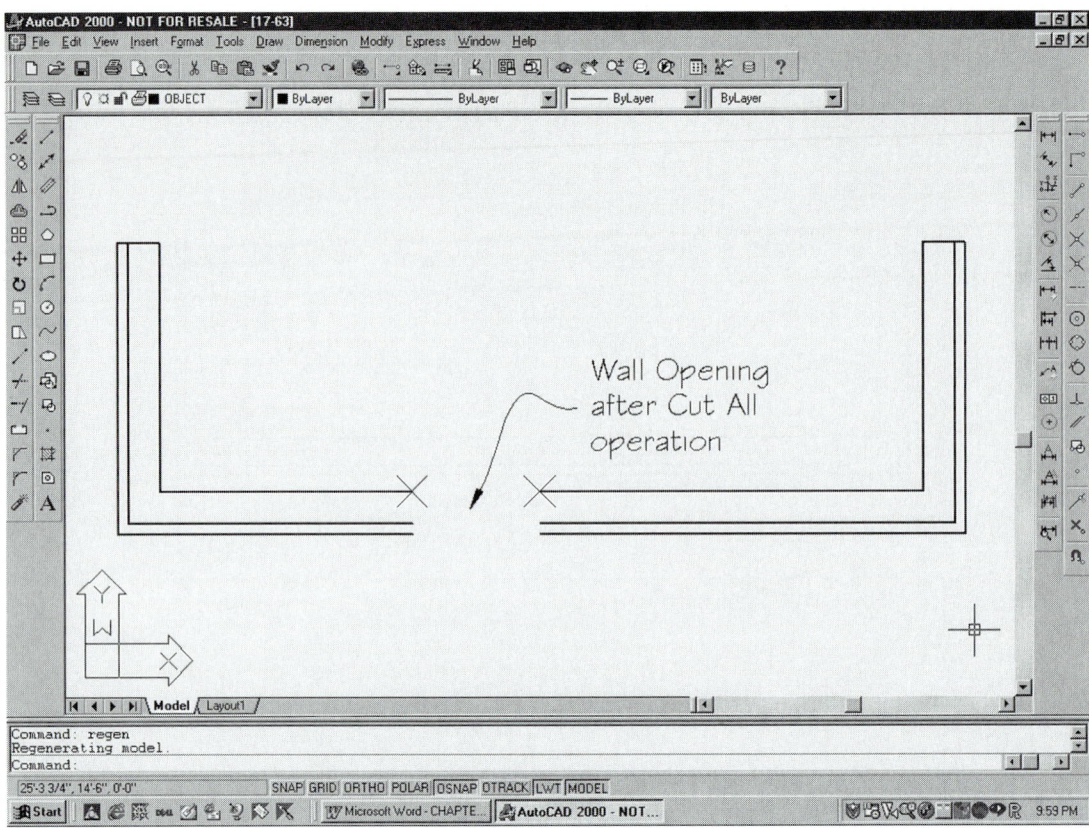

Specify next point or [Close/Undo]: ~EnterKey~
Perform the same operation for the other side of the cut.

Step #4: Draw the door as follows and by looking at Figure 17–41:

Command: **LINE** ~EnterKey~

_ line specify first point: (Click on snap to endpoint).
_ line specify first point: _ endp of (Click on point 1 as shown in Figure 17–41).
Specify next point or [Undo]: **@3'<90** ~EnterKey~
Specify next point or [Undo]: **@2<180** ~EnterKey~ (this will draw the door
as 2" thick).
Specify next point or [Close/Undo]: **@3'<270** ~EnterKey~
Specify next point or [Close/Undo]: **@2<0** ~EnterKey~ (this will finish the
door as 3' by 2" rectangle).

Step #5: Draw the door swing using the ARC command as follows:
From the Draw pull-down menu click on Draw, click on Arc, and click on Center, Start, End option.

Command: _ arc specify start point of arc or [CEnter]: _ c Specify center point
of arc: (Click on Point 1 as the center point of the arc).

Specify start point of arc: (Click on Point 2 as the start point of the arc).
Specify end point of arc [Angle/chord Length]: (Click on point 3 as the end
point of the arc).

Congratulations! You have successfully used the MLEDIT command to cut the door opening and created the door. Your drawing should now look like Figure 17–42., without hatching.

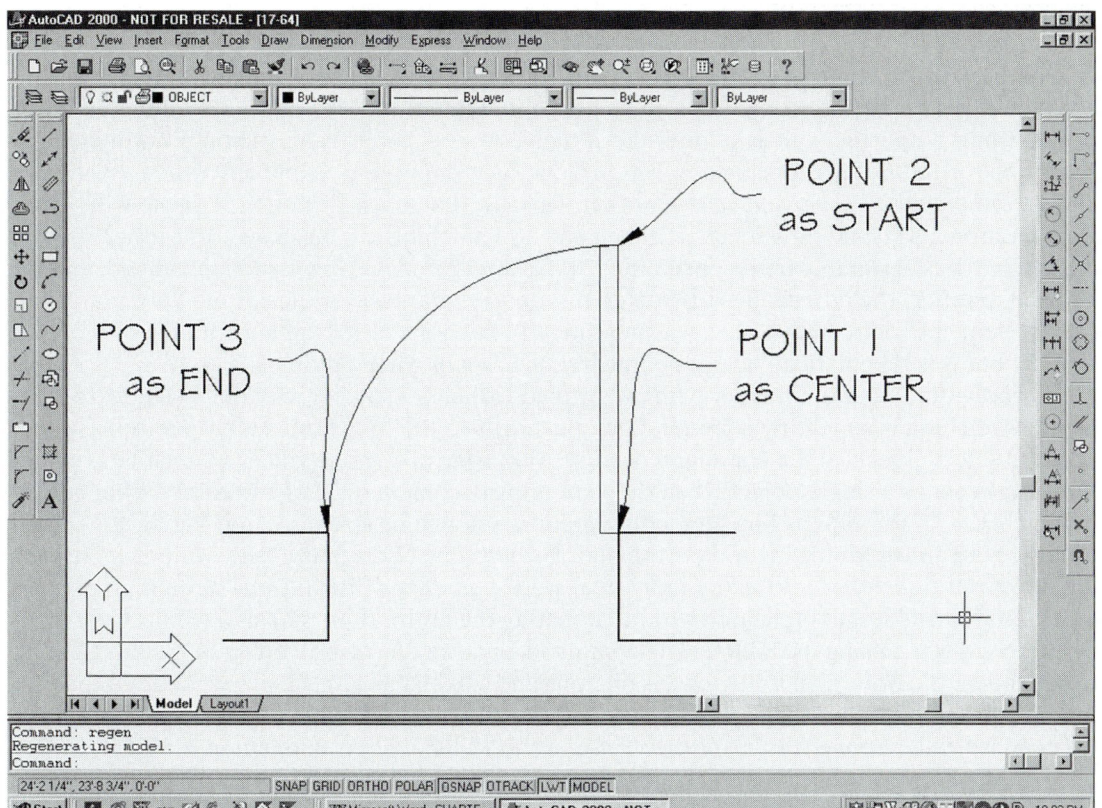

FIGURE 17–41 A close-up of the wall opening that shows the actual drawing of the door and its swing using the LINE and the Center, Start, End option of the ARC command.

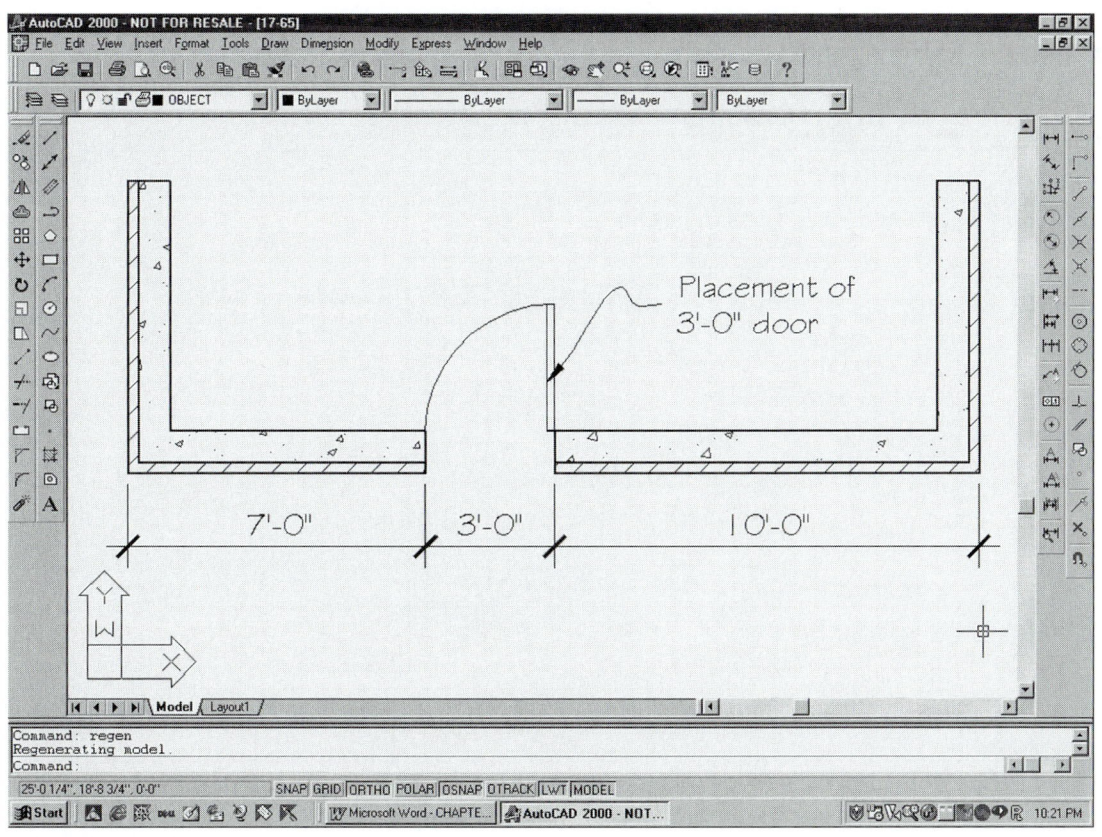

FIGURE 17–42 Exercise 17–6 showing the door opening, the door, and the door swing.

17.12 STRETCHING MULTILINES

One of the greatest challenges of the floor plan editing operations is to have the dimensions and hatch patterns as part of the wall to change as the individual wall segments are edited. In other words, when a specific wall is edited, the dimension and hatch values should automatically change to reflect the current changes. This automatic updating is possible only when *associative dimensioning* and *associative hatching* are on. This is a time-saving method because with a single operation a wall and its associated dimension and hatching can be changed together. On the other hand, it is extremely time-consuming if walls are erased, redrawn, redimensioned, and re-hatched to reflect the new changes. If you do this on a regular basis while editing floor plans, you are not being efficient and you are wasting time. It may not change the appearance of the final product but it will be noticed when too much time is spent when editing a floor plan.

The individual walls of the floor plan can be made longer or shorter with the STRETCH command. Stretching is an editing command but a true gift to the MultiLine Edit operations. When asked to select objects at the command prompt, a *crossing box* (not a window) must be created. MultiLines act as a single object when they are moved, copied, rotated, or erased. When a wall is stretched with the caps as line segments, the line itself will be stretched, not the MultiLine. In order for the entire MultiLine to be stretched, the caps must be a part of the MultiLine. Breaking down the floor plan into many individual wall segments will make the stretching process more tailored and less complicated without affecting the entire floor plan as a whole. Care must be exercised when using the STRETCH command because the desired effect of the STRETCH command on the floor plan is not always obvious and can be hard to achieve when used the first time. Be prepared to use the UNDO command to restart the stretching operation. The following exercise will demortrate the effective use of the STRETCH command on MultiLines.

■ **EXERCISE 17–7:** *The following step-by-step exercise will allow you to edit the three wall segments using the STRETCH command as shown in Figure 17–43. The three wall segments are created with the MLINE command using the Individual Wall Segment method discussed*

FIGURE 17–43 Partial Floor Plan for Exercise 17–7. Notice the walls are created with the Individual Wall Segments method. Three wall segments are created with two wall openings. From the five wall lengths given, three will be increased and two will be decreased using the STRETCH command.

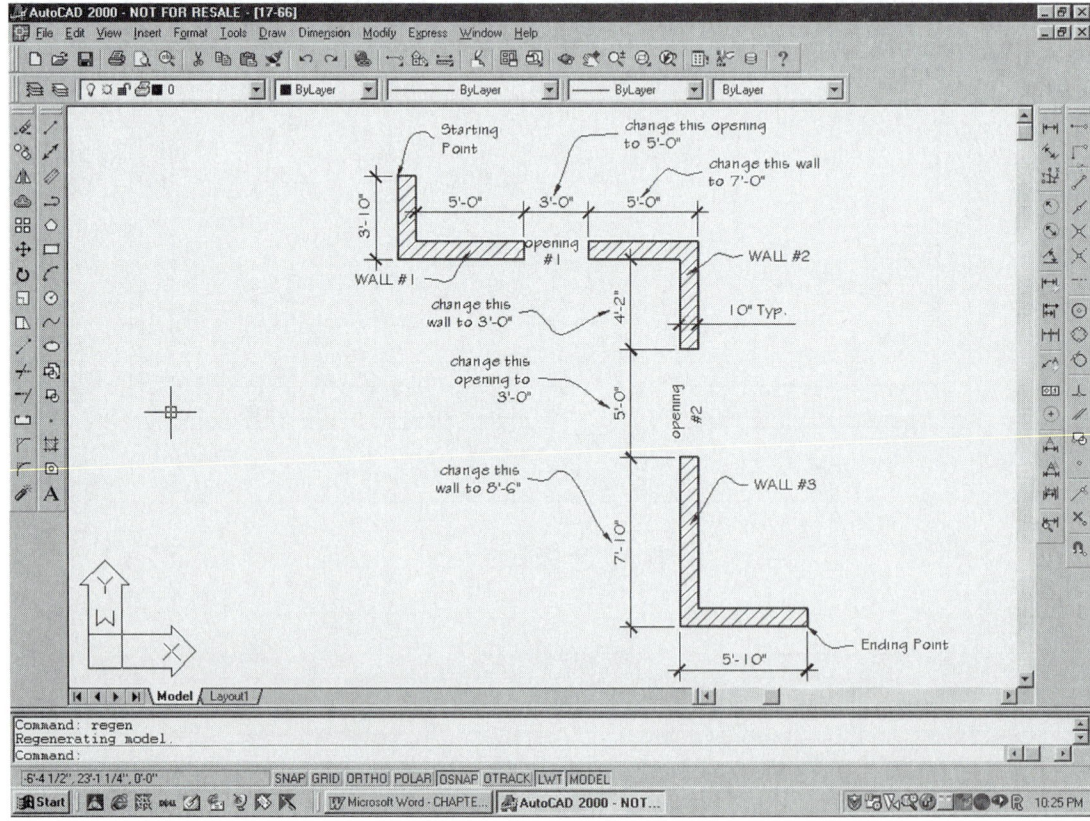

earlier. There are five wall lengths shown with notes to edit. Three wall lengths will be increased in length, and two wall lengths will be decreased (shortened) in length. Spend a few minutes looking at Figure 17–43 to become familiar with what is given and understand what needs to be done. Appropriate steps will be shown to change the individual wall lengths to achieve the end result shown in Figure 17–51.

Step #1: Open the EXE17-2.dwg file.

Step #2: Use the STRETCH command as follows:

Command: **STRETCH** ~EnterKey~

Select objects to stretch by crossing-box or crossing-polygon. . .
Select objects: (by looking at Figure 17–44, perform STRETCH operation #1 by selecting the first corner).
Select objects: specify opposite corner: (Select the second corner of the STRETCH operation #1. Make sure the 5'-0" and 4'-2" are included.)
Select objects: ~EnterKey~ (this will end the crossing-window process).
Specify base point or displacement: (select base point #1 as endpoint or intersection).
Specify second point of displacement: **@1'2<90** ~EnterKey~ (this will decrease/ shorten the wall to 3'-0" as follows: 4'-2" minus 1'-2" as entered is equal to 3'-0", and because going in the direction of 90º at 1'-2" will cause the 4'-2" to shrink to 3'-0").

Note: Notice that with the STRETCH operation #1 the opening #2 changed from 5'-0" to 6'-2". You can see this automatic change if you create associative dimensions for floor plans. Now the STRETCH operation #2 must be performed according to this new dimension. See Figure 17–45.

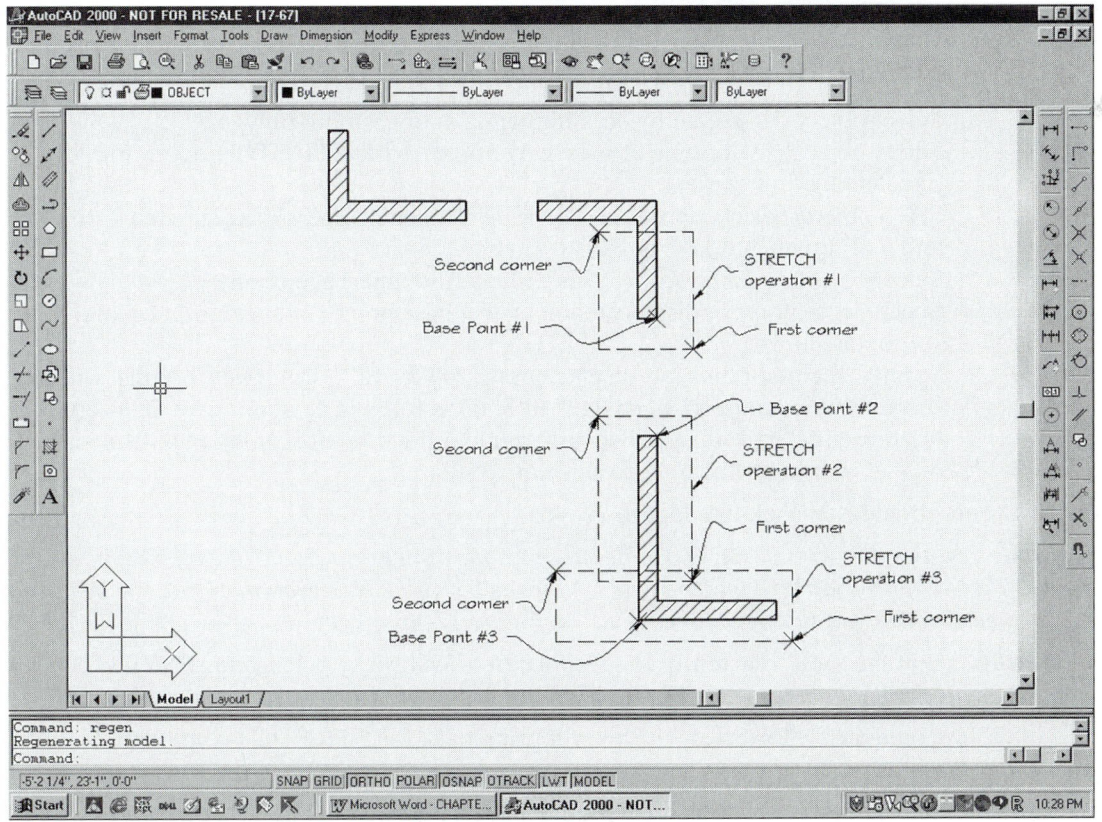

FIGURE 17–44 Editing the two wall segments using the STRETCH command. Notice the STRETCH operations #1, #2, and #3.

FIGURE 17–45 The wall segments after the STRETCH operation #1.

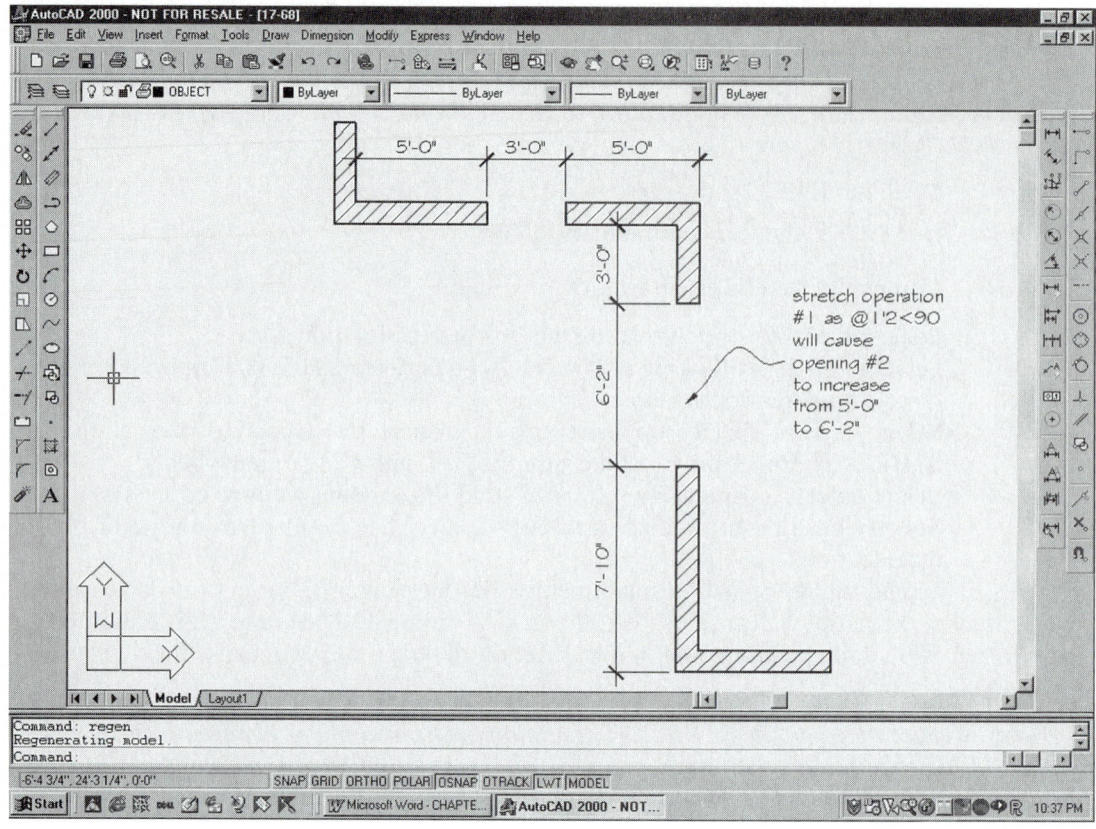

Step #3: Edit the 5'-0" opening (currently 6'-2") by performing STRETCH operation #2 as shown in Figure 17–44 as follows:

Command: ~EnterKey~ (this will bring back the STRETCH command if no other command has been used; otherwise type STRETCH or click on Stretch toolbar).

Select objects to stretch by crossing-window or crossing-polygon . . .
Select object: (by looking at Figure 17–44, perform STRETCH operation #2 by selecting first corner).
Select objects: select opposite corner: (Select second corner. Make sure the 7'-10" and 6'-2" are included).
Select objects: ~EnterKey~ (this will end the object selection).
Specify base point or displacement: (select base point #2 as endpoint or intersection as shown).
Specify second point of displacement: **@3'2<90** ~EnterKey~ (this will shorten the opening #2 from 6'-2" to 3'-0" as follows: 6'-2" minus 3'-2" as entered is equal to 3'-0", and because going in the direction of 90° at a distance of 3'-2" will cause the 6'-2" to shrink to 3'-0").

Your drawing should now look like Figure 17–46.

Note: Notice that with STRETCH operation #2, the dimension 7'-10" of wall #3 is now 11'-0" (3'-2" plus 7'-10" is equal to 11'-0"). Now the STRETCH operation #3 must be performed according to this new dimension. See Figure 17–46.

Step #4: Edit the 7'-10" (currently 11'-0") portion of Wall #3 by performing STRETCH operation #3 shown in Figure 17–44 as follows (zoom out first, if necessary):

Command: ~EnterKey~ (this will bring back the STRETCH command).

Select objects to stretch by crossing-window or crossing-polygon . . .
Select objects: (by looking at Figure 17–44, perform STRETCH operation #3 by selecting first corner).

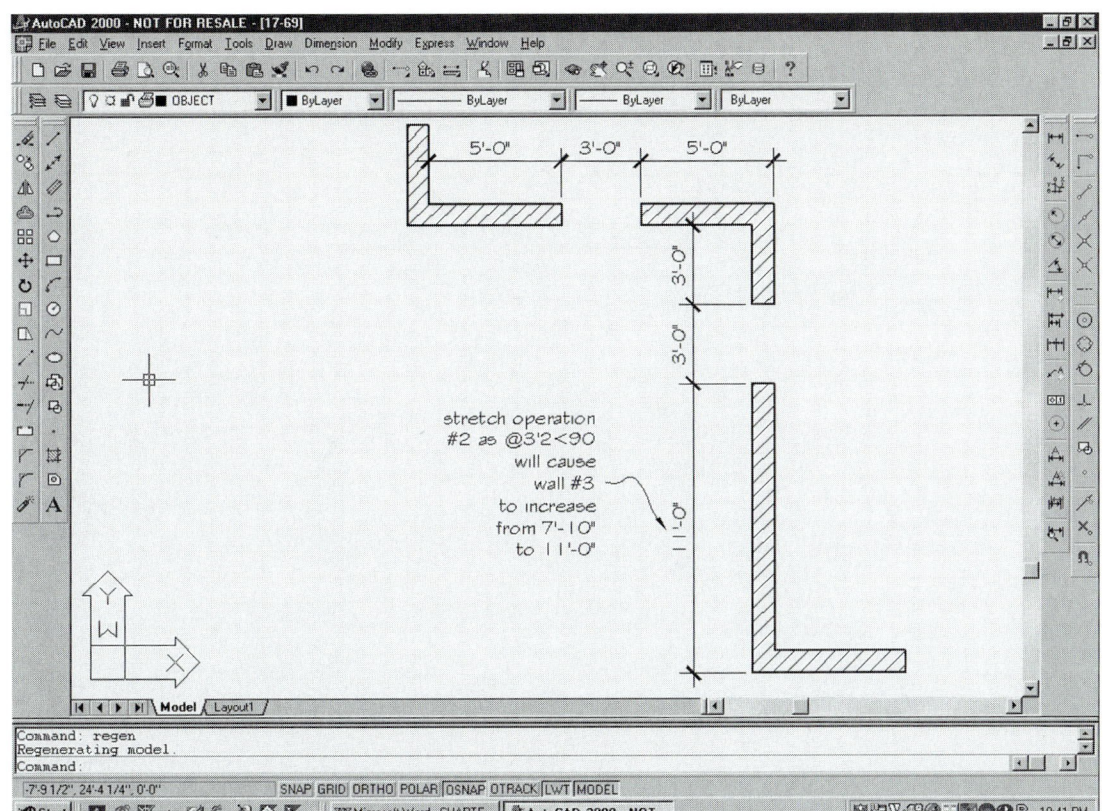

FIGURE 17–46
The wall segments
after STRETCH
operation #2.

Select objects: specify opposite corner: (Select second corner. Make sure the 11′-0″ and 5′-10″ are included).
Select objects: ~EnterKey~
Select base point or displacement: (select base point #3 as endpoint or intersection).
Select second point of displacement: **@2′6<90** ~EnterKey~ (this will shorten wall #3 from 11′-0″ to 8′-6″ as follows: 11′-0″ minus 2′-6″ as entered is equal to 8′-6″, and because going in the direction of 90 degrees at a distance of 2′-6″ will cause the 11′-0″ to shrink to 8′-6″).

Your drawing should now look like Figure 17–47.

Step #5: Edit opening #1 by performing STRETCH operation #4 shown in Figure 17–48 as follows:

Command: ~EnterKey~ (this will bring back the STRETCH command).

Select objects to stretch by crossing-window or crossing-polygon . . .
Select objects: (by looking at Figure 17–48, perform STRETCH operation #4 by selecting first corner).
Select objects: specify opposite corner: (Select second corner. Make sure the 5′-10″, 8′-6″, 3′-0″, 3′-0″, 3′-0″, and 5′-0″ are included).
Select objects: ~EnterKey~
Select base point or displacement: (select base point #4 as endpoint or intersection).
Select second point of displacement: **@2′<0** ~EnterKey~ (this will increase the opening from 3′-0″ to 5′-0″).

Your drawing should now look like Figure 17–49.

Step #6: Edit the 5′-0″ portion of wall #2 by performing STRETCH operation #5 as shown in Figure 17–50 and as follows:

Command: ~EnterKey~ (this will bring back the STRETCH command).

FIGURE 17–47   The wall segments after STRETCH operation #3.

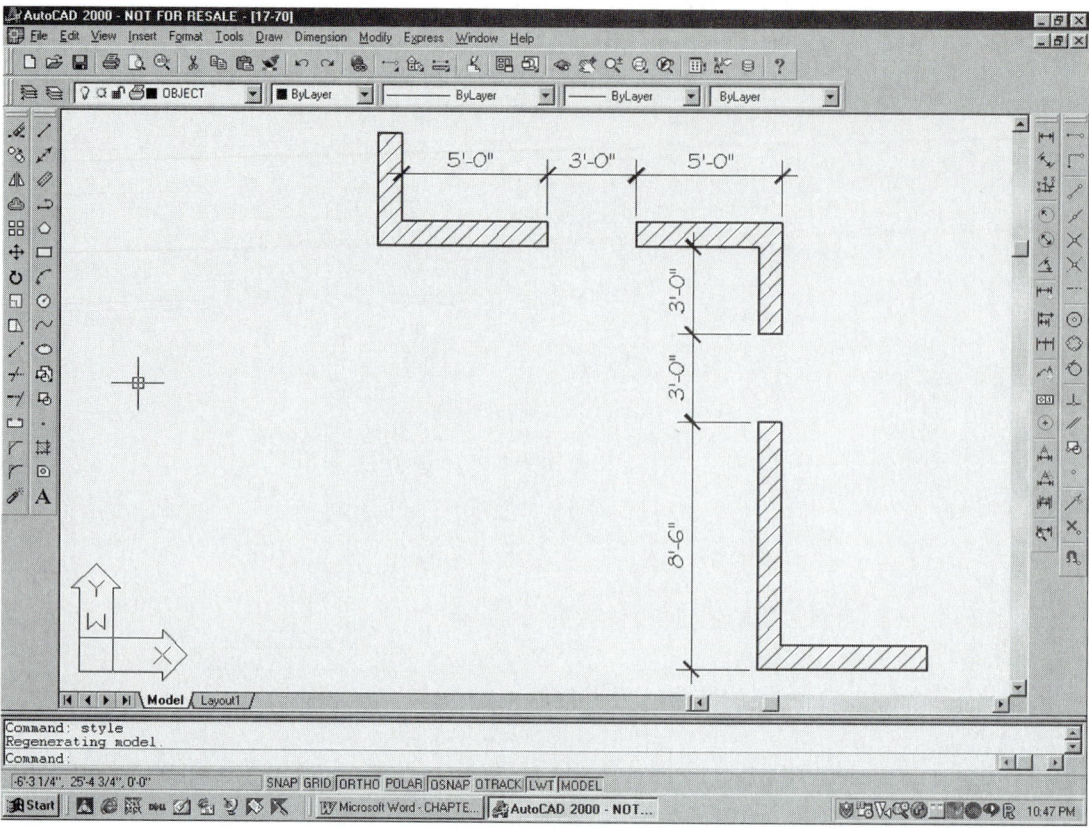

FIGURE 17–48 Performing STRETCH operation #4.

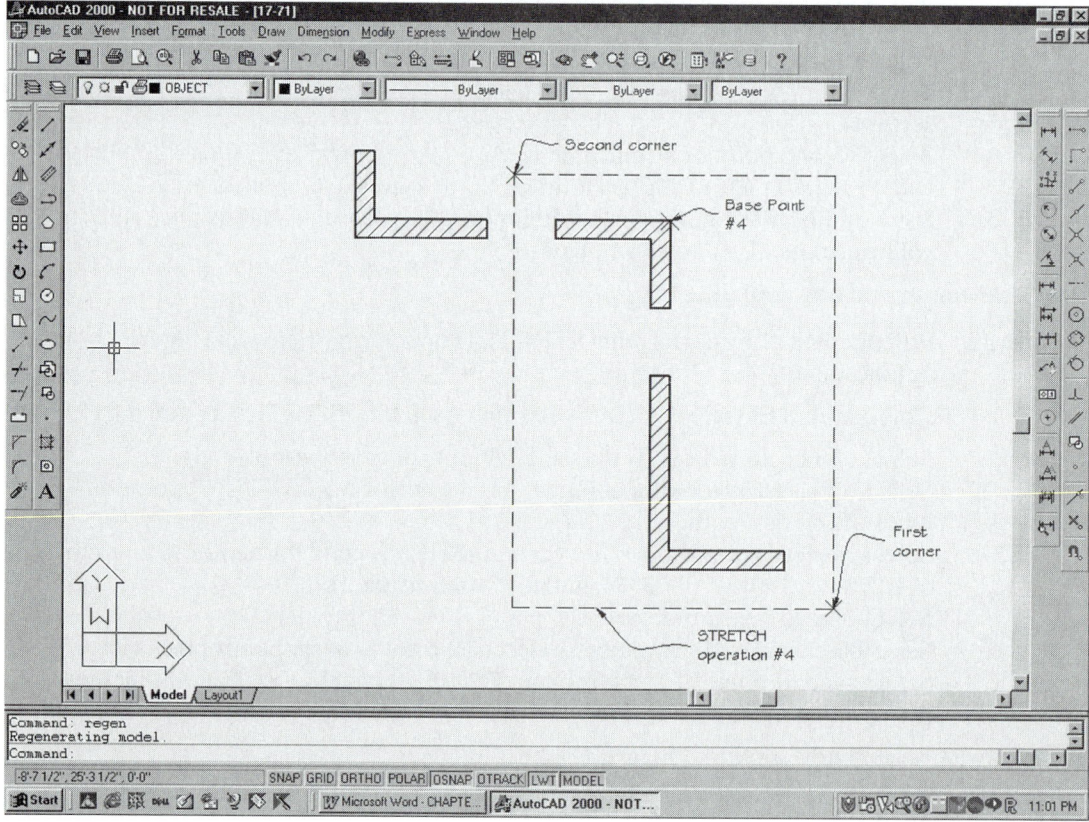

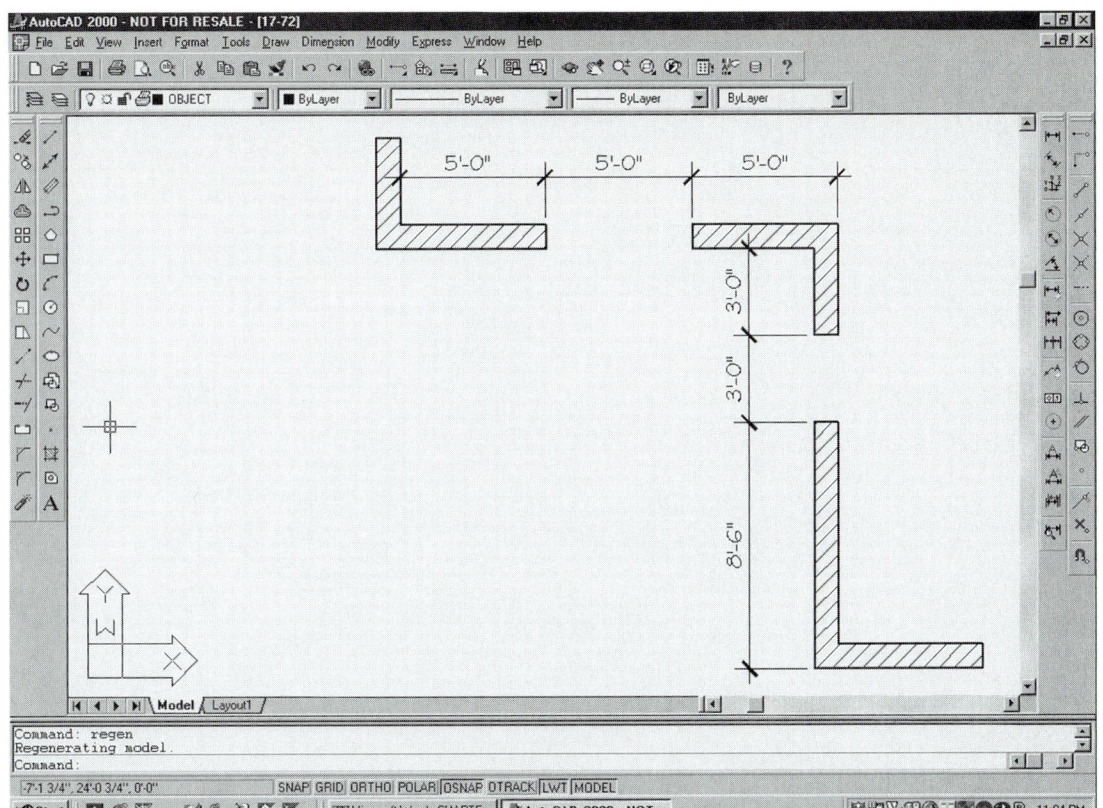

FIGURE 17–49
The wall segments
after the STRETCH
operation #4.

Select objects to stretch by crossing-window or crossing-polygon . . .
Select objects: (by looking at Figure 17–50, perform STRETCH operation #5
by selecting first corner).
Select objects: specify opposite corner: (Select second corner. Make sure the
5'-10", 8'-6", 3'-0", 3'-0", 5'-0", and 5'-0" are included).
Select objects: ~EnterKey~
Select base point or displacement: (select base point #5 as endpoint or intersection).
Select second point of displacement: **@2'<0** ~EnterKey~ (this will increase
the 5'-0" wall length to 7'-0").

Congratulations! You have successfully used the STRETCH command to edit a MultiLine
drawing. Your drawing should now look like Figure 17–51. This is the final composition of the
wall segments after editing the partial floor plan shown in Figure 17–43. Do not save the
changes.

*Tips: Notice that in the Exercise 17–7 there is no scientific reason behind the sequence of the
STRETCH operations. They are selected merely on the basis of vertical/horizontal operations or on
personal choice. You as the end user should have a game plan first and sketch out the operations in
your head to determine the sequence of events needed to get to the final product as efficiently and as
quickly as possible. The selection of sequence of stretching operations should be based on personal
and project requirements and your skill level. Keep in mind that other individuals on the project team
might be involved in working on and editing the same project you have been working on. Once
you understand the true essence of Stretch operations pertaining to the editing of floor plans with
MultiLines along with its strengths and weaknesses, you will then be at a better position to make
effective decisions to increase productivity in the long run.*

FIGURE 17–50
Performing STRETCH
operation #5.

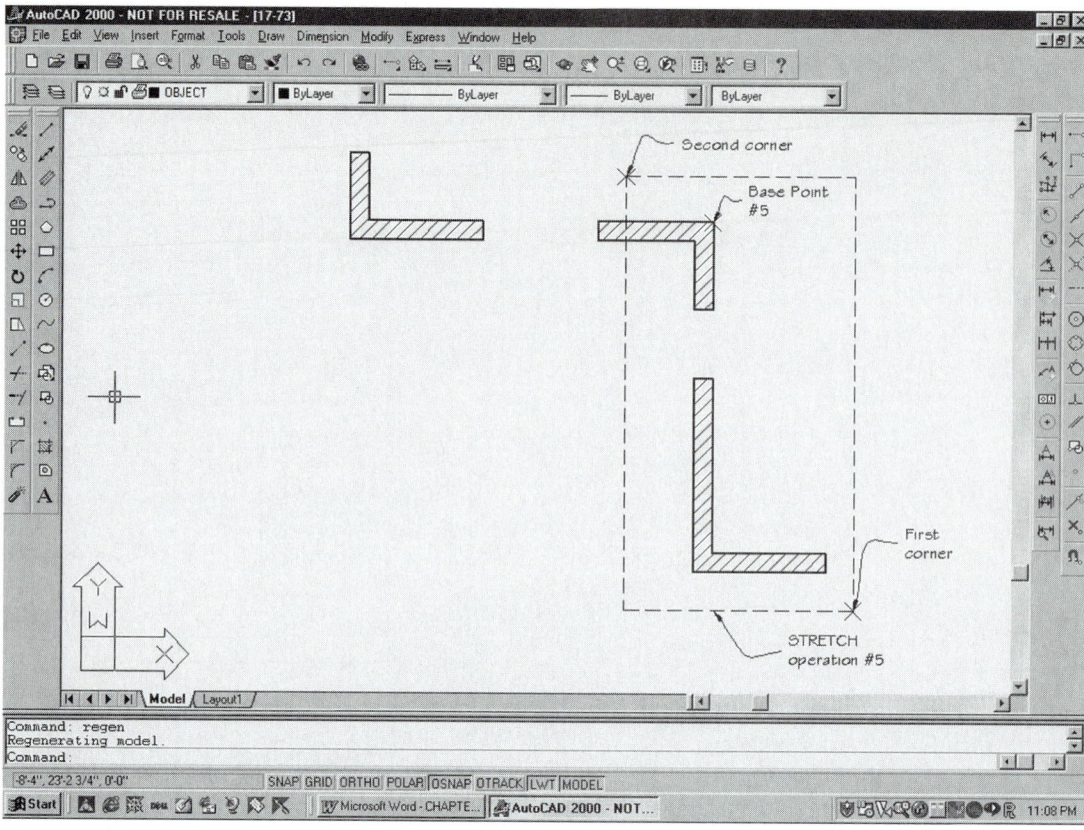

FIGURE 17–51 The
final composition of the
edited wall segments
after five Stretch
operations. Notice the
dimensions and
hatching are
automatically updated
to reflect the changes
performed. These
updates are possible
only when the
associative
dimensioning (dimaso)
and associative hatching
(through dialog box) are
turned on when initially
dimensioning and
hatching.

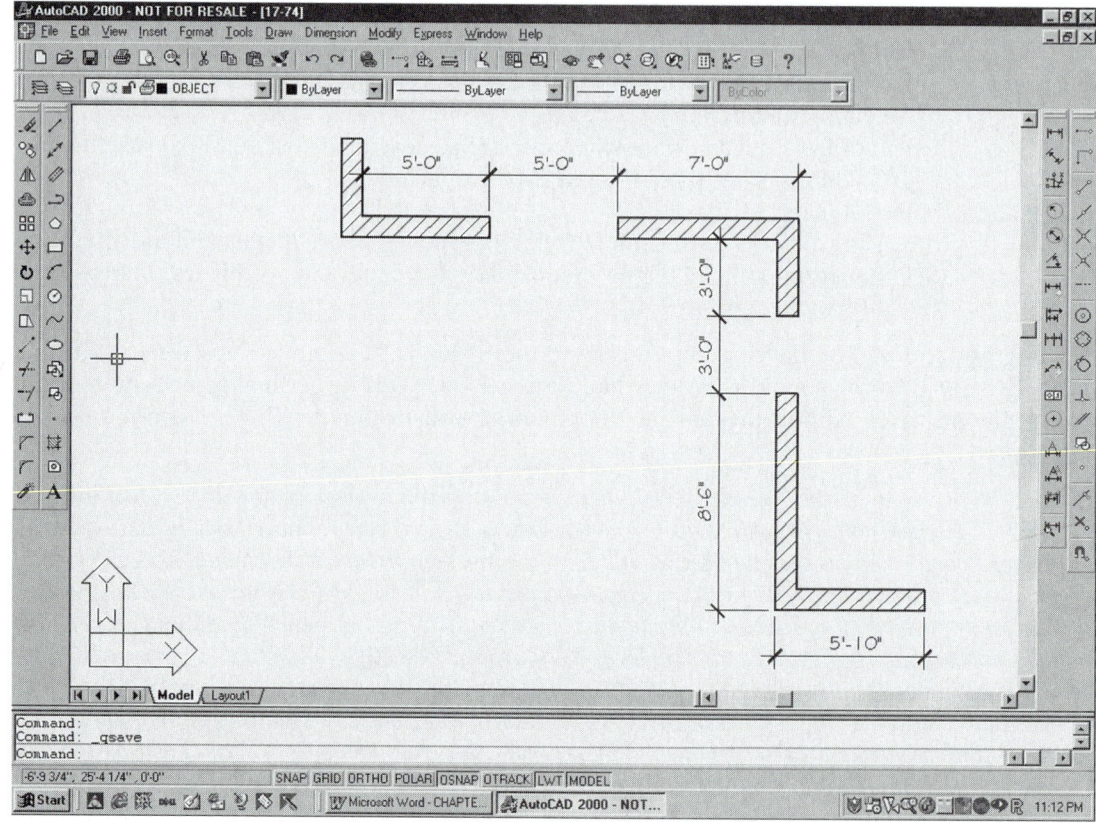

17.13 AUTOMATICALLY EDITING MULTILINES WITH GRIPS

The Stretch operation requires the selection of MultiLines by crossing box or crossing polygon. These two crossing operations give you maximum flexibility when editing MultiLines. The crossing box allows you to place a rectangle or square around the wall to be edited. Sometimes it becomes necessary to place an odd-shaped window around a wall. In this situation a closed figure with three or more sides at any angle can be placed using the crossing polygon (CP) option. The use of grips takes editing a step further by automatically editing the objects without placing a crossing box or crossing polygon around them. Once the grips are activated, selecting any of the grips on the MultiLine will allow you to perform stretch, move, rotate, scale or mirror editing operations. In order for this type of automatic editing to work, the GRIPS system variable must be on. AutoCAD places three grip locations on LINES, POLYLINES, MULTILINES, and ARCS. One grip is located at the starting point, the other at the midpoint, and the third at the endpoint. When a MultiLine is selected, any of its three grips may be used to perform the stretching operation. However, if a wall is to be increased or decreased in length, the endpoint grips should be used. If associative dimensions are to be stretched with the walls, then the grips at the dimension definition point locations must also be selected. The dimension definition point locations may not always be on the side of the walls where MultiLine justification points are located. Refer to Chapter 18 on Architectural Dimensioning and read the section on Associative Dimensioning and Editing Dimensions. Also refer to Chapter 13 for more information about grips.

■ **EXERCISE 17–8:** *The following step-by-step exercise will allow you to edit the same floor plan in Exercise 17–2 using the grips of individual wall segments. Appropriate steps will be shown to change the individual wall lengths using grips to achieve the same results of Exercise 17–7.*

Step #1: Open the EXE17-2.dwg file.

Step #2: Turn the HATCH layer off.

Step #3: Select wall #2 as shown in Figure 17–52. Three grip locations will appear as small squares.

Step #4: Click on grip #1 to select it. Once selected, the grip will become a solid color depending on the grip color selected. Turn Ortho on and use the Stretch automatic editing option (the first item on a series of editing options) of grips as follows:

STRETCH

Specify stretch point or [Base point/Copy/Undo/eXit]: <ortho on> @1'2<90 ~EnterKey~ (this will shrink the 4'-2" portion of wall #2 to 3'-0").
Command: ~EscKey~
Command: ~EscKey~ (pressing the ~EscKey~ twice will remove grip locations and end the stretch with grips operation)

Tips: Use Grip locations to verify MultiLine justification points. This procedure is similar to using the blipmarks. The grips will be displayed on the justification point. Notice that in the above example, the grip locations on wall #2 are on the top Justification. Do a List to check it out.

Caution: In order to stretch and update associative dimensions along with the walls, grips at the dimension definition point locations must be selected. The dimension definition points are the first and second extension line origins selected on the objects when dimensioning occurs. These points must also be located on the side of the walls where MultiLine justification points are located. Using the grips to automatically stretch the MultiLine along with its associative dimension is only possible if the MultiLine justification points in the wall are on the same side of the dimension definition point locations. For example, in Figure 17–52 the vertical portion of wall #2 has the MultiLine justification points on the right-hand side and the dimension definition points on the left-hand side. Because they are on the opposite side, the 4'-2" dimension will not update when wall #2 is moved 1'-2" north from grip #1 location. However, it will update the associative hatching inside wall #2. Always turn

FIGURE 17–52 Using the Grips to edit the partial floor plan for Exercise 17–8. The Hatch layer is turned off for ease of selecting objects.

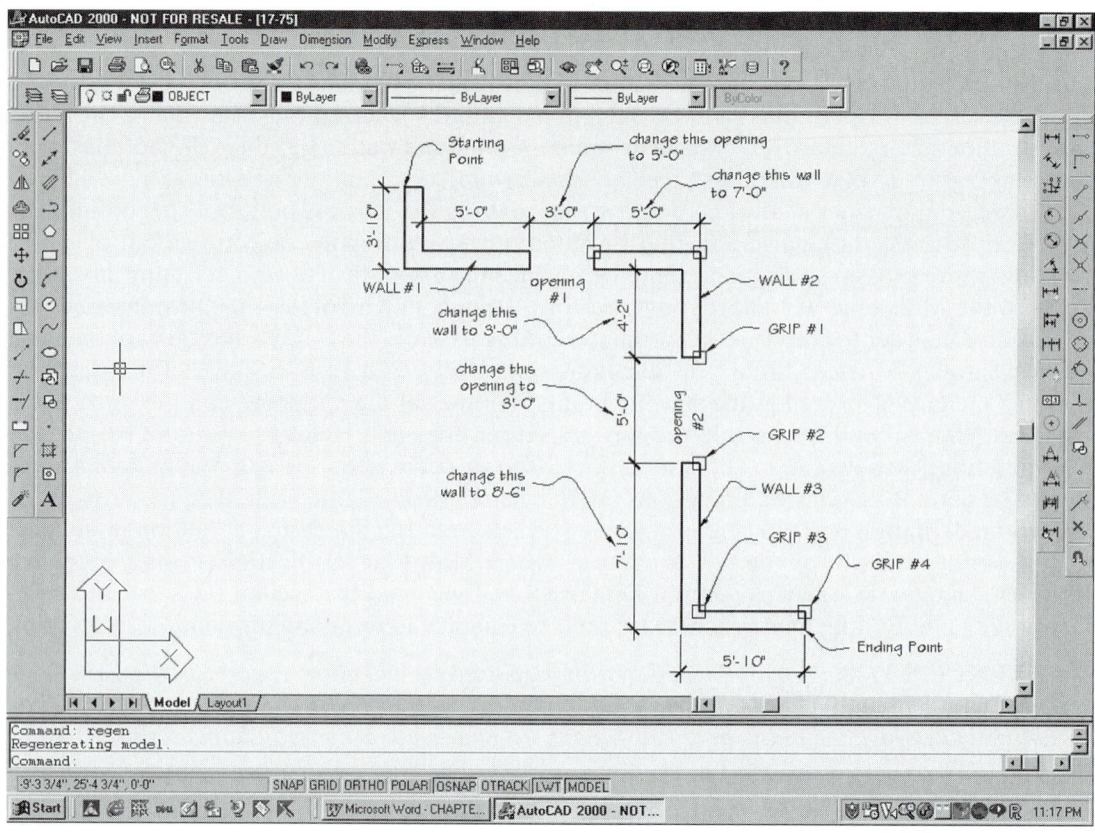

off the Hatch layer before selecting MultiLines; otherwise you will end up selecting the hatch instead. See Figure 17–53.

Because the dimension for wall #2 did not automatically update with the Grips/Stretch editing option, it is best to dimension the walls again after the editing. You might also consider placing dimensions on the MultiLine justification locations, but this is not always possible or feasible. Under normal conditions, the exterior and the overall dimensions will be created on floor plans with the bottom justification.

Step #5:   Using Figure 17–52 click on wall #3. Three grip locations will appear. Click on grip #2 to select it. Use the Grip/Stretch operation to stretch wall #3 as follows:

STRETCH

Specify stretch point or [Base point/Copy/Undo/eXit]: <ortho on> **@3'2<90** ~EnterKey~ (this will increase the 7'-10" portion of the Wall #3 to 11'-0" therefore shrinking opening #2 from 5'-0" to 3'-0").
Command: ~EscKey~
Command: ~EscKey~

Your drawing should now look like Figure 17–54, without hatching.

Step #6:   Using Figure 17–52, click on wall #3 again. Click on grip #3 to select it. Use the Grip/Stretch operation to stretch wall #3 as follows:

STRETCH

Specify stretch point or [Base point/Copy/Undo/eXit]: <ortho on> **@2'6<90** ~EnterKey~ (this will shrink that corner of the wall from 11'-0" to 8'-6"). Notice that only one corner of this wall is moved at a distance of 2'-6" in the direction of 90 degrees. The other corner of the same wall did not move simply

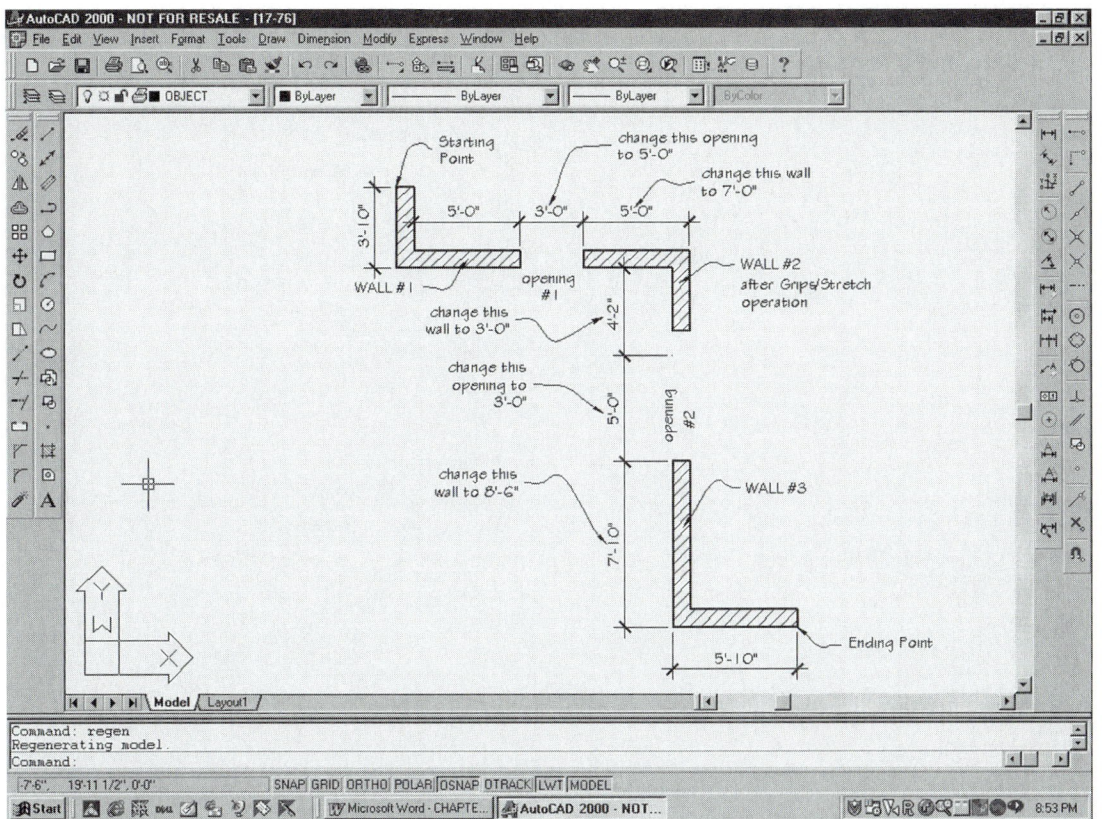

FIGURE 17–53 Notice the 4'-2" dimension did not update to 3'-0" after the Grip/Stretch operation because the associative dimension definition point locations are not at the same side as the MultiLine Justification locations.

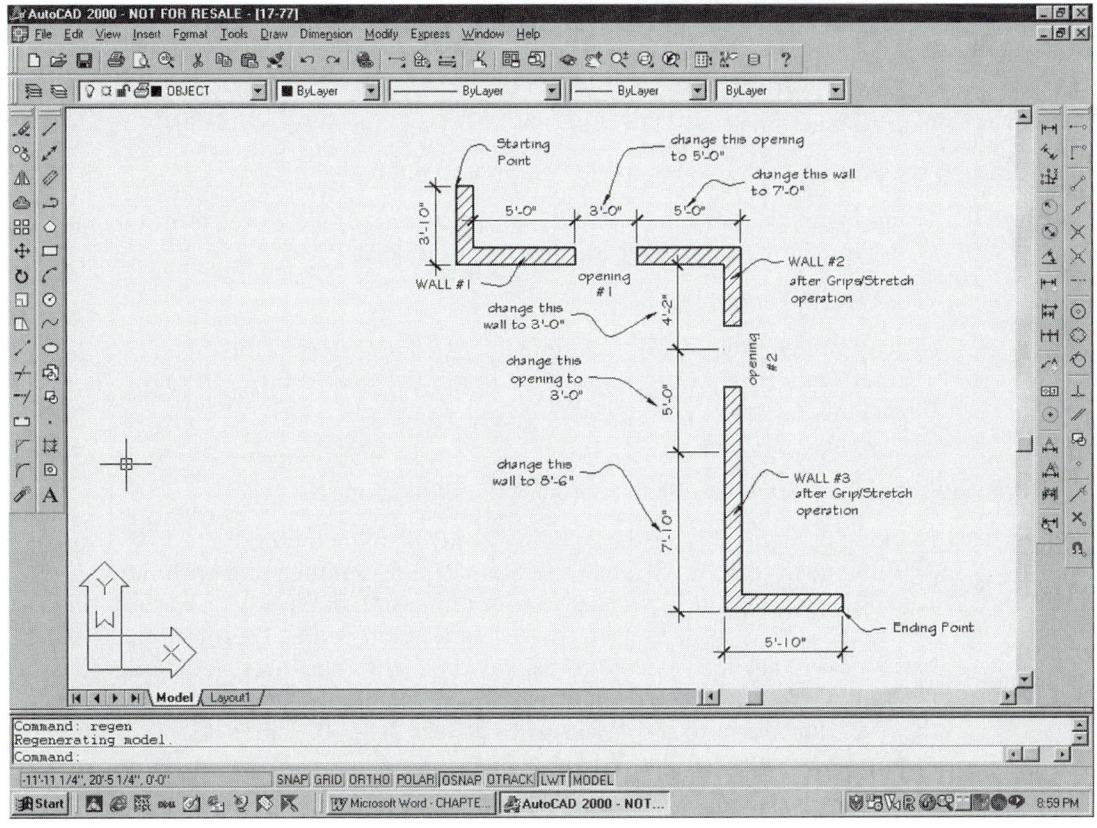

FIGURE 17–54 The wall segments after two Grips/Stretch operations. Notice the 7'-10" dimension did not automatically update.

FIGURE 17–55
Selecting grip #3, which
is located on the top
justification of the wall,
will only move the left
corner of the wall.
Notice that the right
corner needs to be
stretched also.

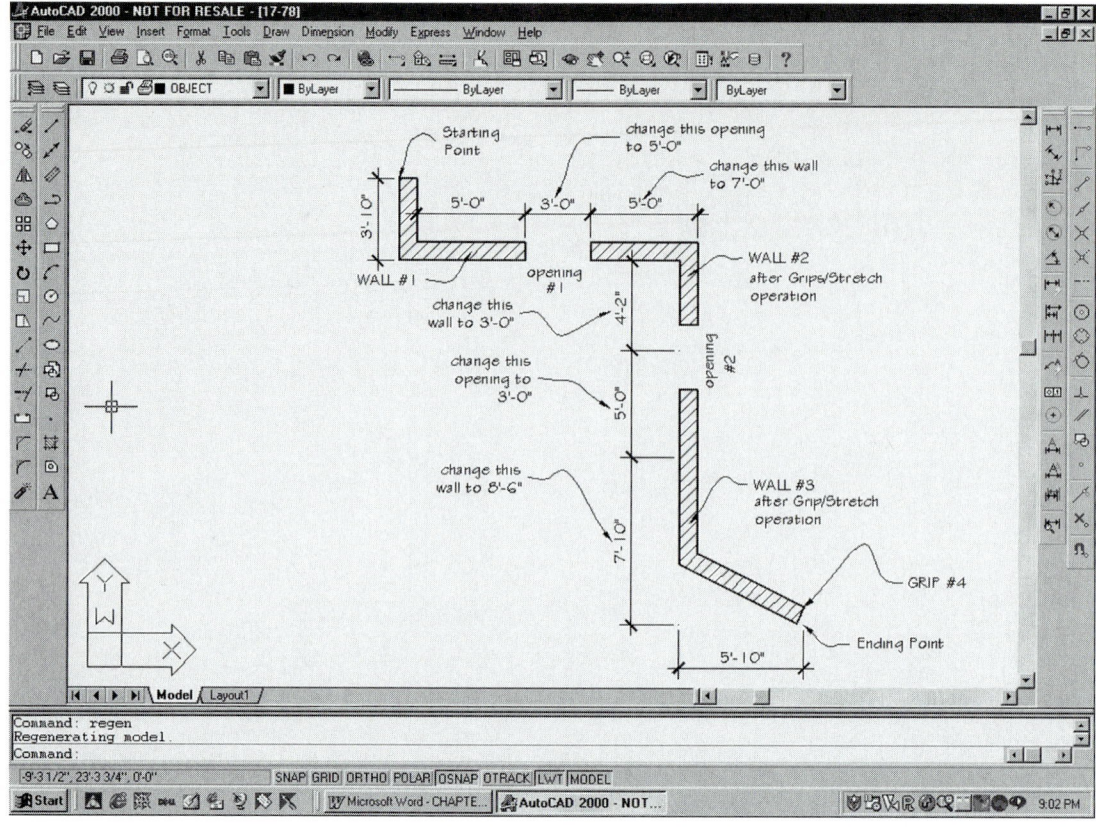

because the grips are at the top justification of the wall. If the justification had been at bottom, the entire bottom portion would have been moved. This means that you have to perform another Grip/Stretch operation to put this wall in its final location.
Command: ~EscKey~
Command: ~EscKey~

Your drawing should now look like Figure 17–55, without hatching.

Step #7:   Using Figure 17–55, select wall #3 and click on grip #4 to select it. Use the Grip/Stretch operation to stretch wall #3 as follows:

STRETCH

Specify stretch point or [Base point/Copy/Undo/eXit]: <ortho on> **@2'6<90**
~EnterKey~ (this will shrink that corner of the wall from 11'-0" to 8'-6").
Command: ~EscKey~
Command: ~EscKey~

Your drawing should now look like Figure 17–56, without hatching.

Step #8:   Looking at Figure 17–57, the opening #1 needs to be increased to 5'-0" from 3'-0" by means of Grip/Stretch operation. You will notice that with the horizontal portion of wall #2, the associative dimension definition point locations are on the same side as the MultiLine justification points. Therefore the 3'-0" and 5'-0" will also be selected to display their grips and stretched along with the wall. Select wall #2 to display its grips but **do not select grip** #5 yet. Select the 3'-0" dimension to display its grips. Select the 5'-0" dimension to display its grips. Now select grip #5 and stretch as follows:

STRETCH

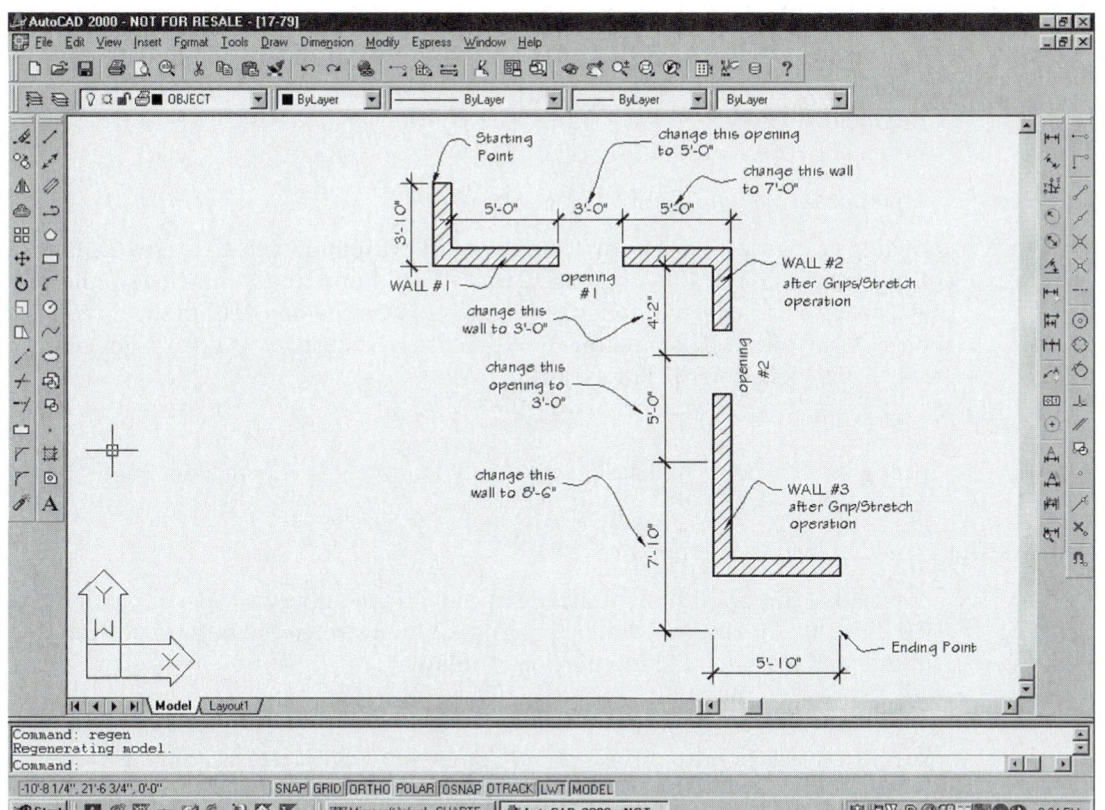

FIGURE 17–56
Selecting grip #4 will move the right corner of wall #3 to its final position. Notice the 5'-10" dimension did not move with the wall.

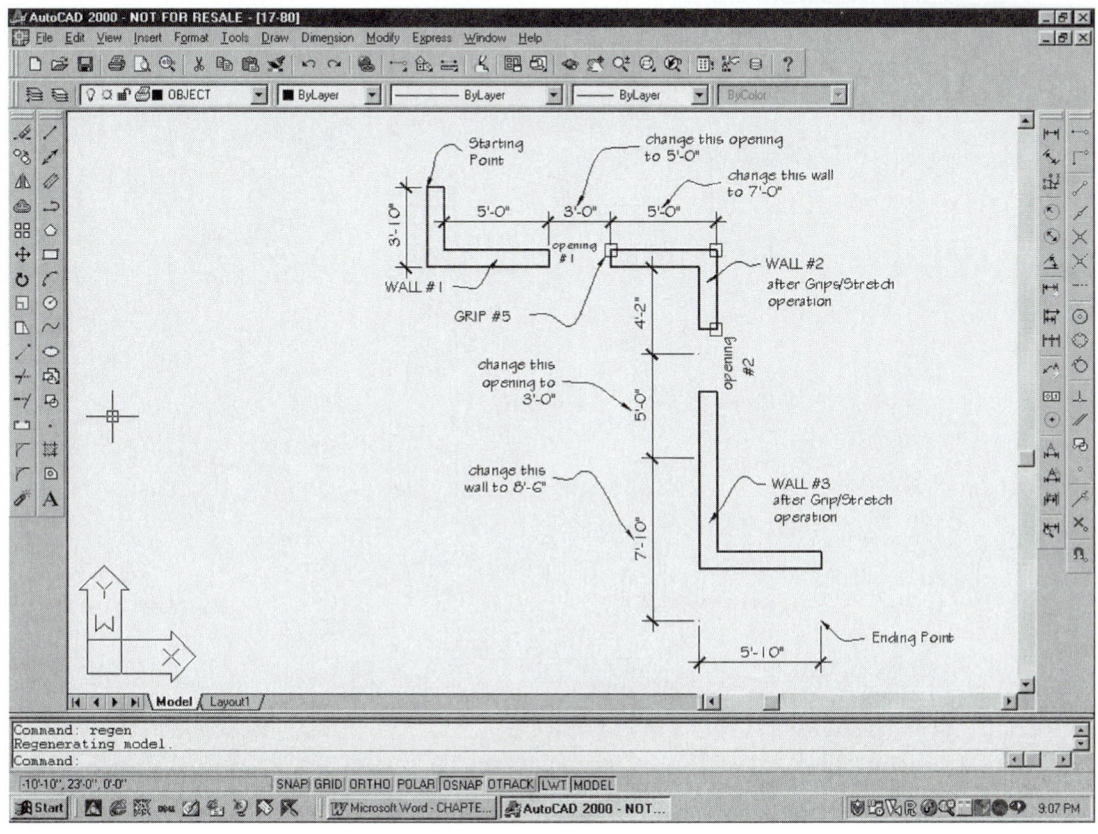

FIGURE 17–57
Selecting grip #5 will increase opening #1.

Specify stretch point or [Base point/Copy/Undo/eXit]: <ortho on>: **@2'<0**
~EnterKey~ (this will increase the 3'-0" opening #1 to 5'-0" and update the
dimension).
Command: ~EscKey~
Command: ~EscKey~

Your drawing should now look like Figure 17–58.

Step #9:   Looking at Figure 17–59, notice that the 5'-0" portion of wall #2 is now 3'-0".
In order to increase this dimension to 7'-0" and update its dimension, the
3'-0" needs to be selected, and grip #6 needs to be stretched 4'-0" in the direction of 0° as follows: Click on the 3'-0" dimension to display its grips. Click on
wall #2 and click on grip #6 to select it.

STRETCH

Specify stretch point or [Base point/Copy/Undo/eXit]: <ortho on> **@4'<0**
~EnterKey~

Your drawing should now look like Figure 17–60.

Step #10:   Notice that this operation misarranged and did not move wall #2 completely.
Continue the operation by selecting grip #7, then stretch the bottom portion
of this wall to match the top portion as follows:

STRETCH

Specify stretch point or [Base point/Copy/Undo/eXit]: <ortho on> **@4'<0**
~EnterKey~ (this will align wall #2 completely).

Command: ~EscKey~

FIGURE 17–58   The
wall segments after
Grip/Stretch operation.
Notice by selecting the
two dimensions and the
wall at grip #5, the 3'-0"
is updated to 5'-0".

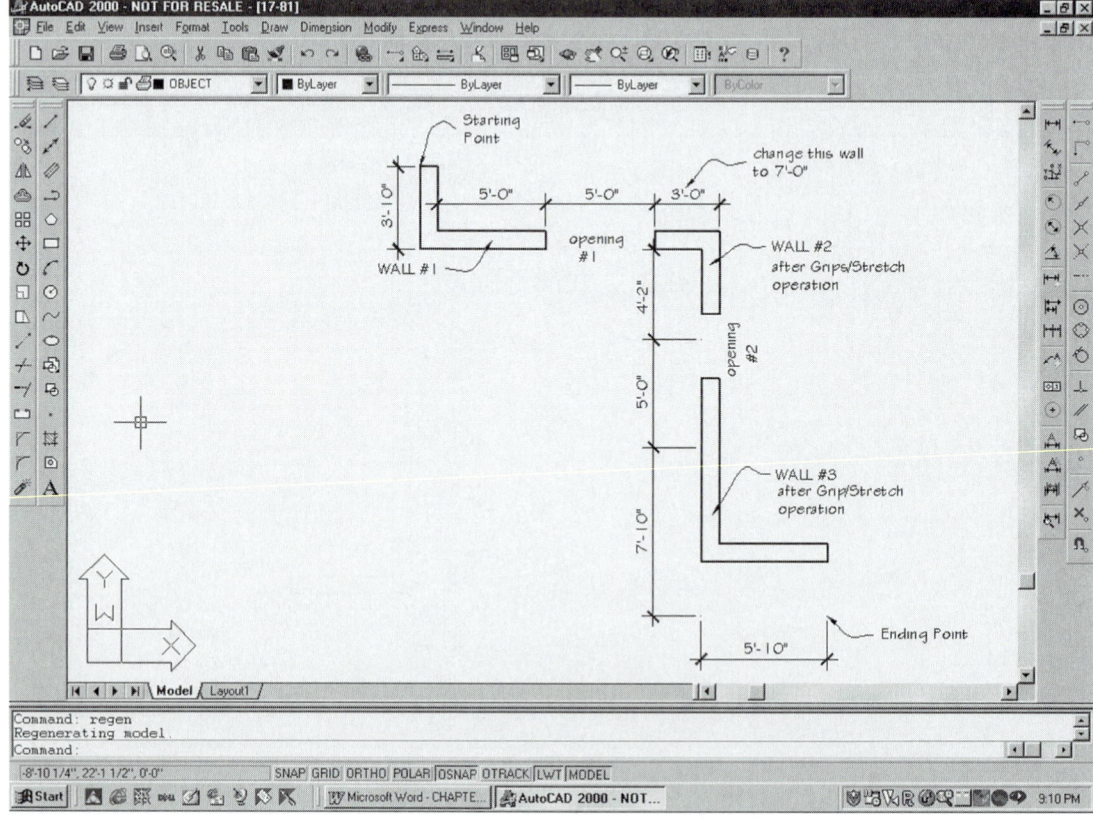

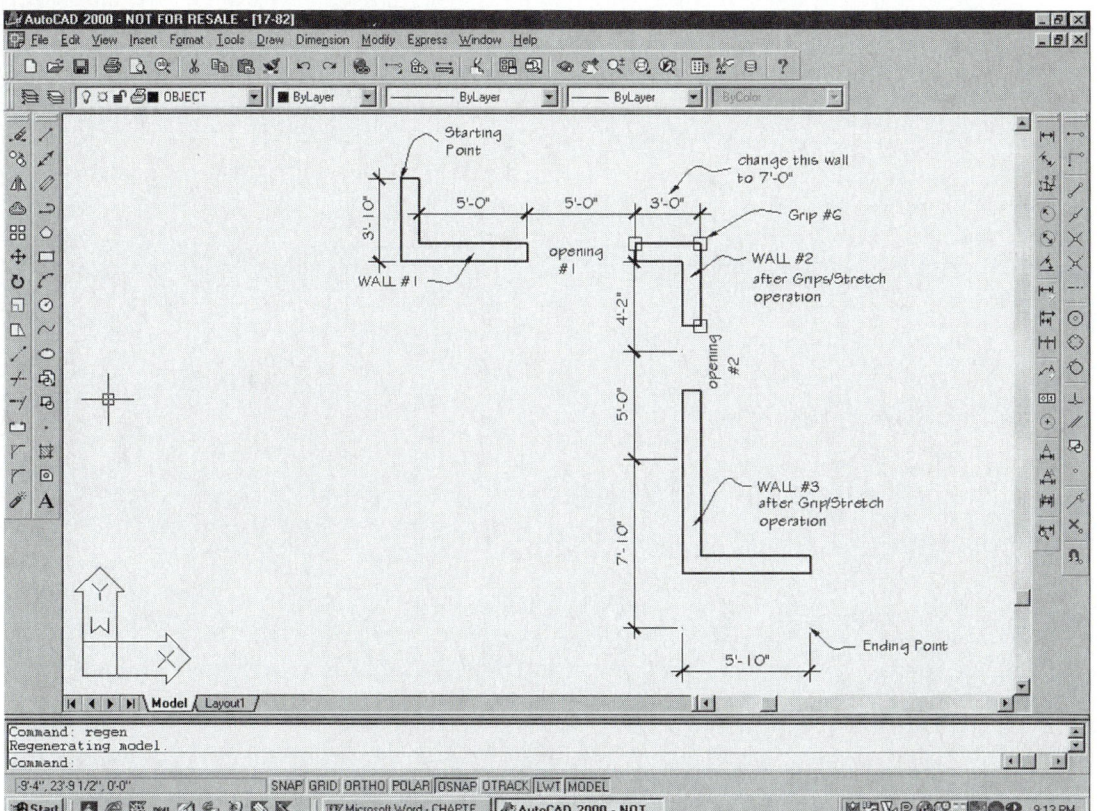

FIGURE 17–59 Before grip #6 operation.

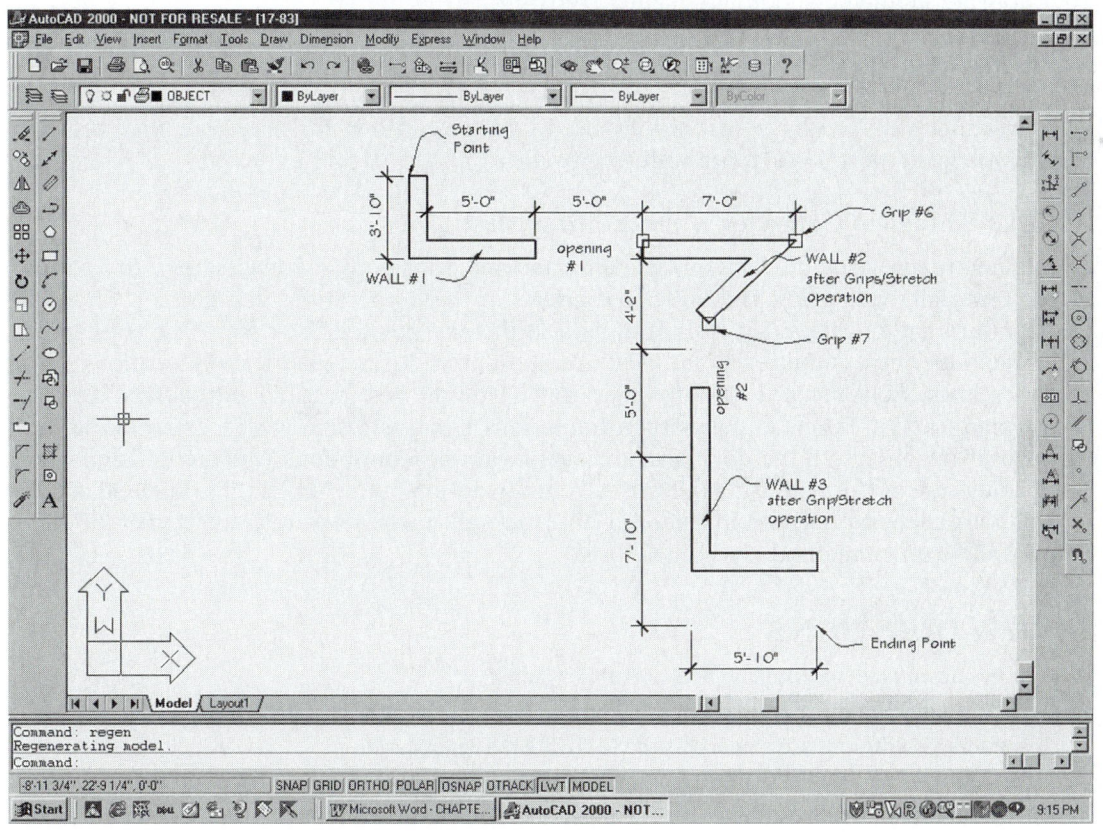

FIGURE 17–60 After grip #6 operation, wall #2 does not completely move to its correct position yet.

FIGURE 17–61 After grip #7 operation, wall #2 is aligned.

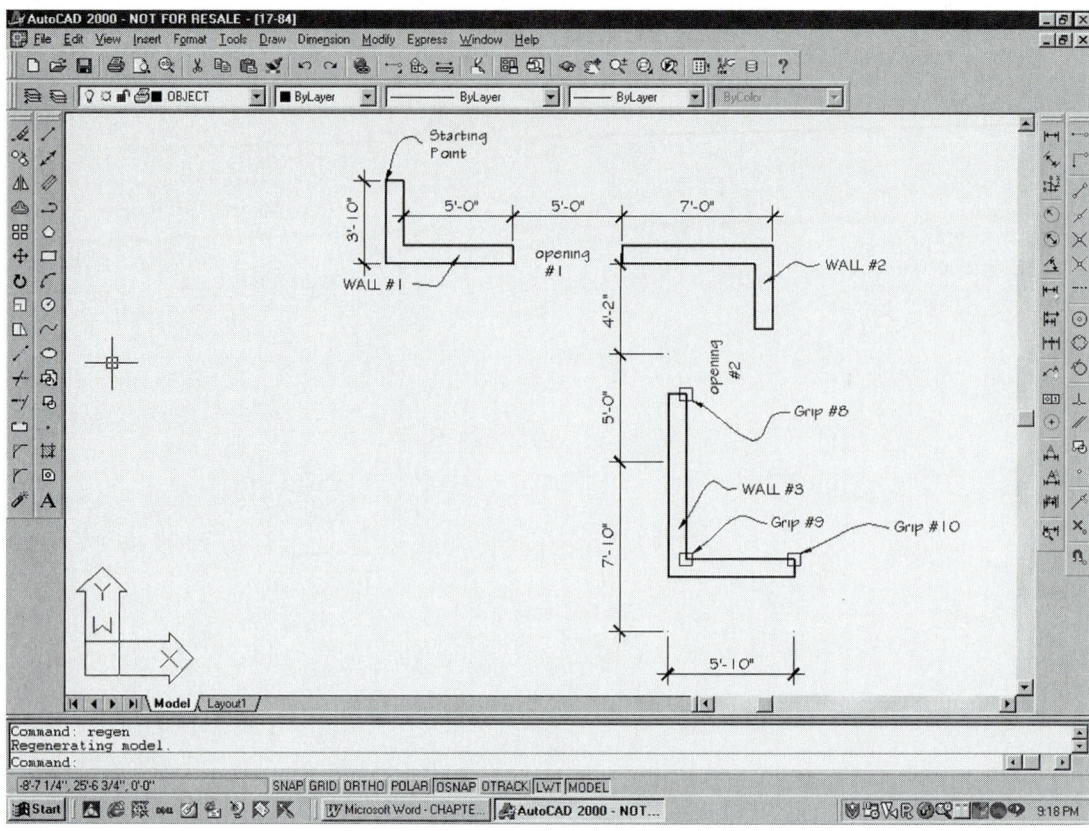

Your drawing should now look like Figure 17–61.

> **Step #11:**   Using Figure 17–61, move wall #3 a distance of 4'-0" at grip locations #8, #9, and #10.

Congratulations! You have successfully used grips to edit a MultiLine. Your final drawing should look like Figure 17–61, with wall #3 moved.

17.13.1   Things to Consider when Editing MultiLines

Editing floor plans using the STRETCH command and grips is not a flawless operation for the novice, especially with grips. The undesired effects of these operations can be seen when the hatch pattern and/or dimension do not update to the new revised floor plan. The conflict between the dimension definition point locations and the MultiLine justification locations is the primary reason. However, if the floor plan is drawn with the best possible method and if all the editing operations are done knowing their limitations, less frustration will be experienced during the drawing process. If the floor plan is created with the Continuous Wall method and when the openings are performed using the Cut All editing option of the MLEDIT command, hatching will not update. Notice that in Exercise 17–7 the wall segments were created with the Individual Wall Segment method.

REVIEW QUESTIONS

1. List five advantages of using the MULTILINE command.
2. What style of MultiLine is used when the project calls for only two parallel lines?
3. List the three different ways to access the MULTILINE command.
4. What option of the MULTILINE command determines how lines originate from a definition point?
5. Why is it important to have the blip marks appear on the wall intersections?
6. What option of the MULTILINE command determines the wall thickness?

7. Which Dialog Box must be accessed to create a new wall style?

8. Name the eight steps involved in the creation of a new MultiLine Style.

9. Which Dialog Box allows you to add additional lines to the standard MultiLine style?

10. Which Dialog Box allows you to add color to the MultiLine?

11. Describe briefly the concept behind drawing floor plans using the Continuous Wall method.

12. Describe briefly the concept behind drawing floor plans using the Individual Wall Segments method.

13. Name the Dialog Box that uses 12 different editing options for MultiLines.

14. Can a MultiLine be trimmed? If not, why?

15. What is the corresponding MultiLine Edit Tools Option for the BREAK command used on MultiLines?

16. After the MultiLine is cut using the Cut All option, the sides of the opening should be closed using the LINE command. Can this line entity be turned into a pline using the PEDIT command so as to make the MultiLine a single whole entity? If not why?

17. Which editing option should be used to trim all of the intersecting elements of the first selected Multi-Line and to trim only the outside elements of the second MultiLine?

18. Which editing option would work like a chamfer or fillet operation on MultiLines?

19. Does the Cut All option of the MultiLine editing break the MultiLine into two separate pieces?

20. Name the two editing commands where MultiLines can be edited with most efficiency and flexibility.

PROBLEMS

1. For the wall type shown in Figure 17–62, calculate the offset values using the Equation method. Enter your answers next to the question marks.

Offset	Color	Ltype
0.5	White	Continuous
−0.5	White	Continuous
?	White	Continuous
?	White	Continuous

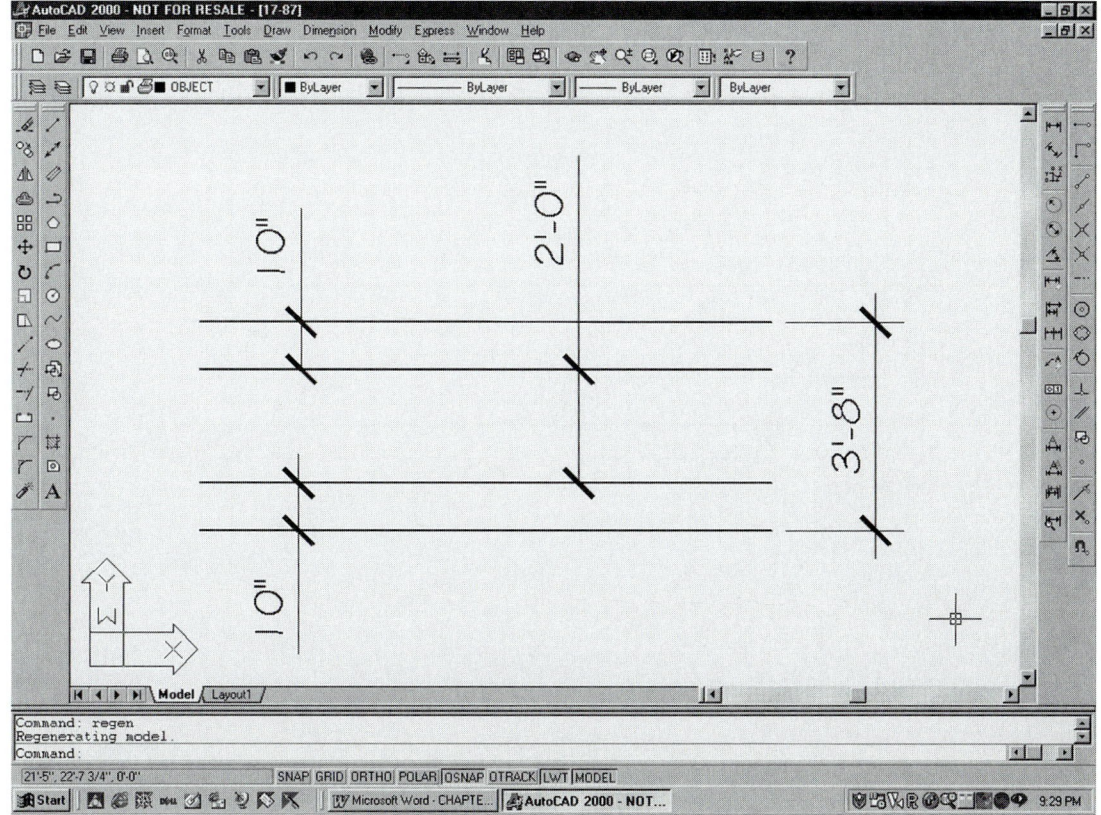

FIGURE 17–62 Wall Type for Problem 1.

2. For the wall type shown in Figure 17–63, calculate the offset values using the Direct Distance Offset method. Enter your answers next to the question marks.

Offset	Color	Ltype
?		
?		
?		
?		
?		

3. Draw the floor plan shown in Figure 17–64 using the MultiLine method of your choice.

4. Open the *EXE17-3.dwg* file. Create the 4″ thick interior partition walls as shown in Figure 17–65. Use the points as a reference. Do not save the changes.

5. Start a new drawing with a 1/4″=1′-0″ scale to be printed on A-size paper horizontally. Save the drawing as MYEXE17-5. Create appropriate layers. Create a wall style and call it STUDIO APT with caps on. Draw the floor plan as shown in Figure 17–66. The exterior walls are 6″ thick and the interior walls are 4″ thick. Use the Individual Wall Segment method to create the walls. Draw all windows and doors. Do not create dimensions or hatching.

6. Using a template drawing, create a new MultiLine style and call it BRICK AND BLOCK. Use 4″ brick, 2″ air space, and 10″ concrete block. Use the equation method.

7. Using a template drawing, create a new MultiLine style and call it CAVITY WALL. Use 12″ concrete block, 4″ air space, and 10″ concrete block. Use the Direct Distance Offset method.

8. Start a new drawing with a 1/4″=1′-0″ scale to be printed on C-size paper horizontally. Save the drawing as MYEXE17-8. Create appropriate layers. Create a wall style and call it BRICK with caps on. Draw the floor plan as shown in Figure 17–67. The wall composition from exterior to interior is as follows: 4″ brick, 2″ air space, and 10″ concrete block. Interior walls are 6″ thick. Use the Continuous Wall method and use the MLEDIT Cut All option to cut all door and window openings. Draw all windows and doors. Do not create dimensions or hatching.

9. Start a new drawing with a 1/4″=1′-0″ scale to be printed on C-size paper horizontally. Save the drawing as MYEXE17-9. Create appropriate layers. Create a wall style and call it BRICK2 with caps on.

FIGURE 17–63 Wall Type for Problem 2.

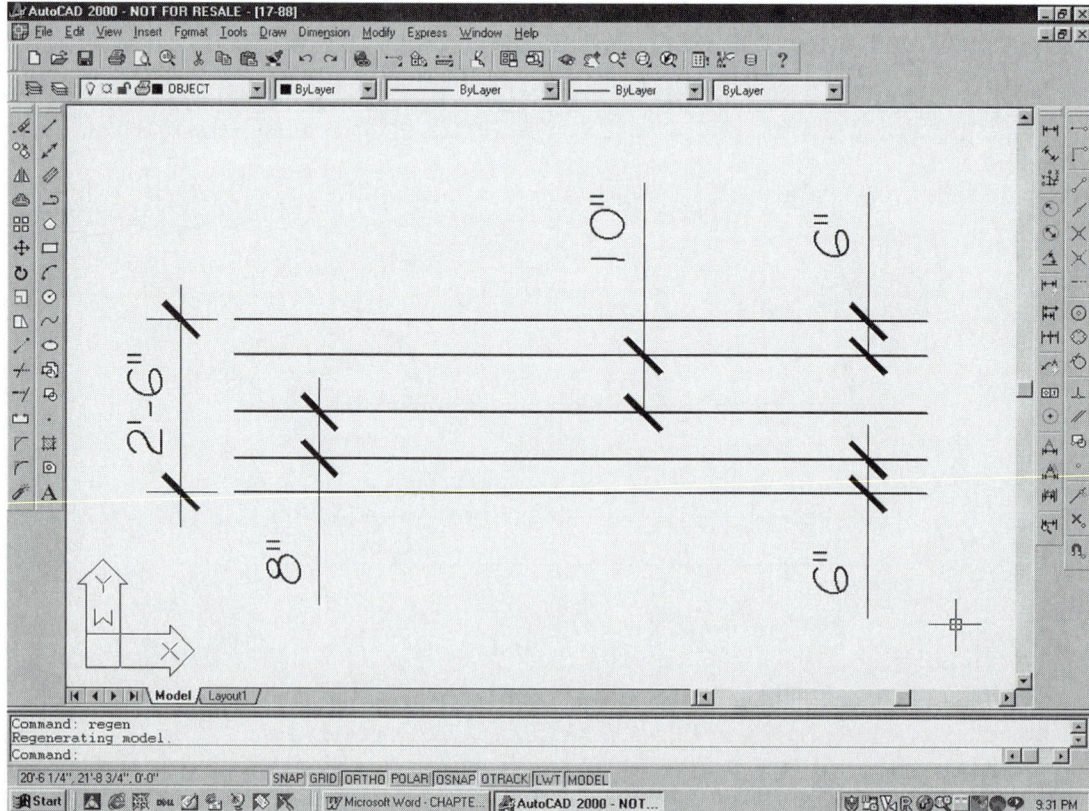

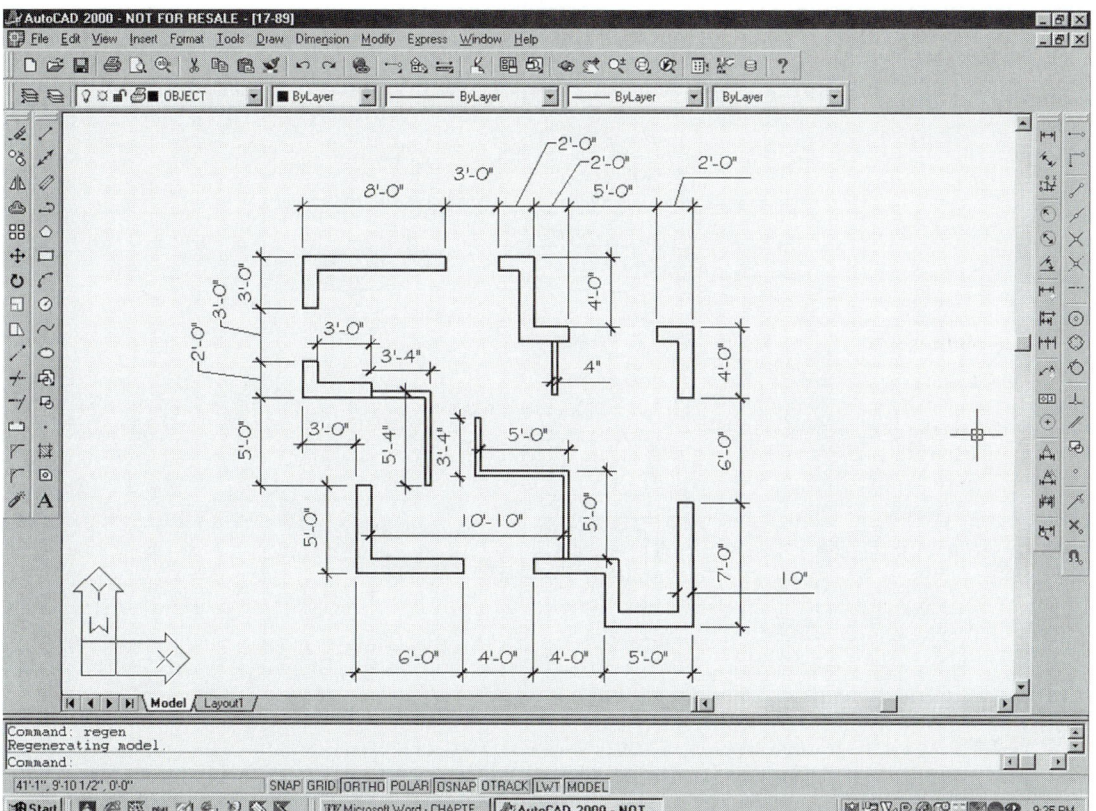

FIGURE 17–64 Floor plan for Problem 3.

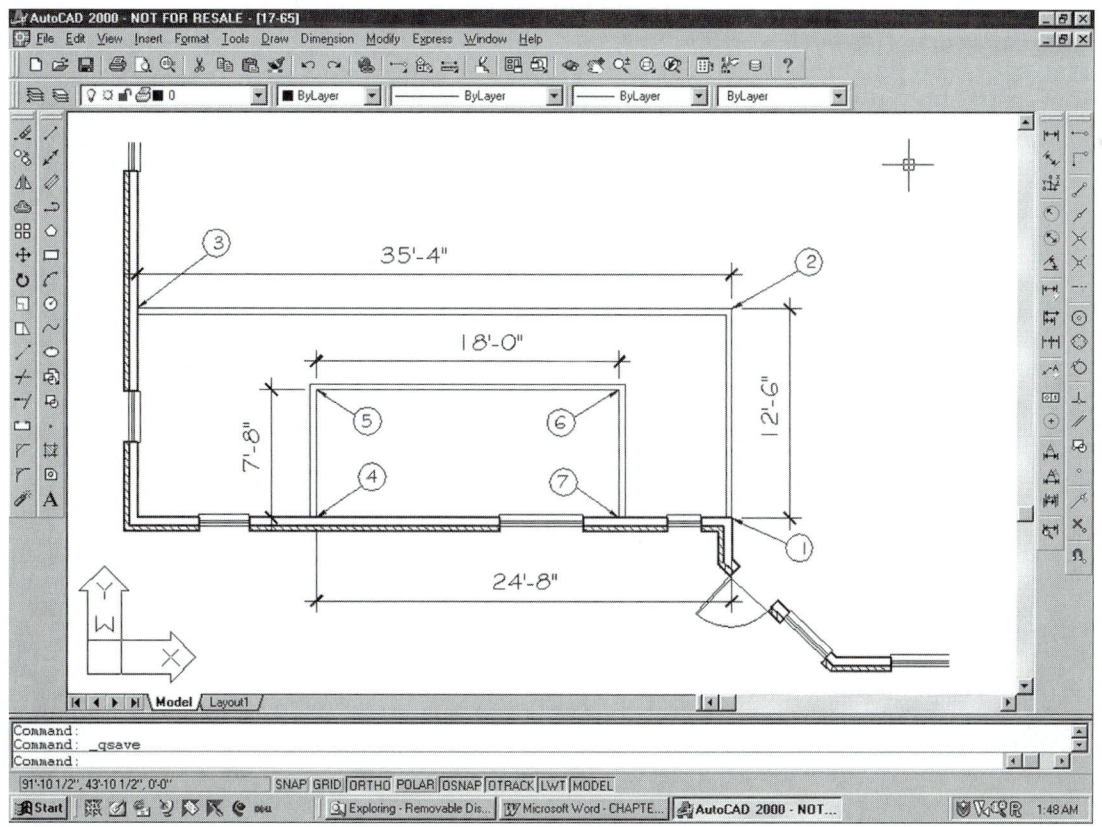

FIGURE 17–65 Partition wall for Problem 4.

FIGURE 17–66
Problem 5.

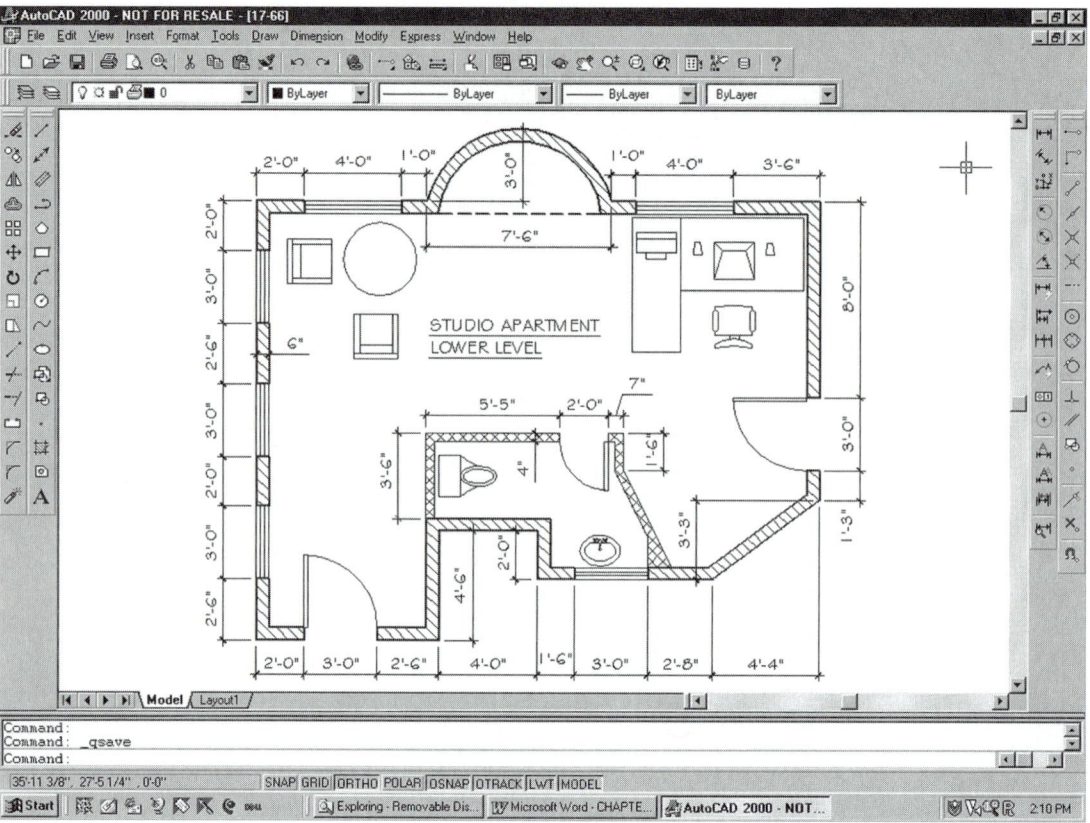

FIGURE 17–67
Problem 8.

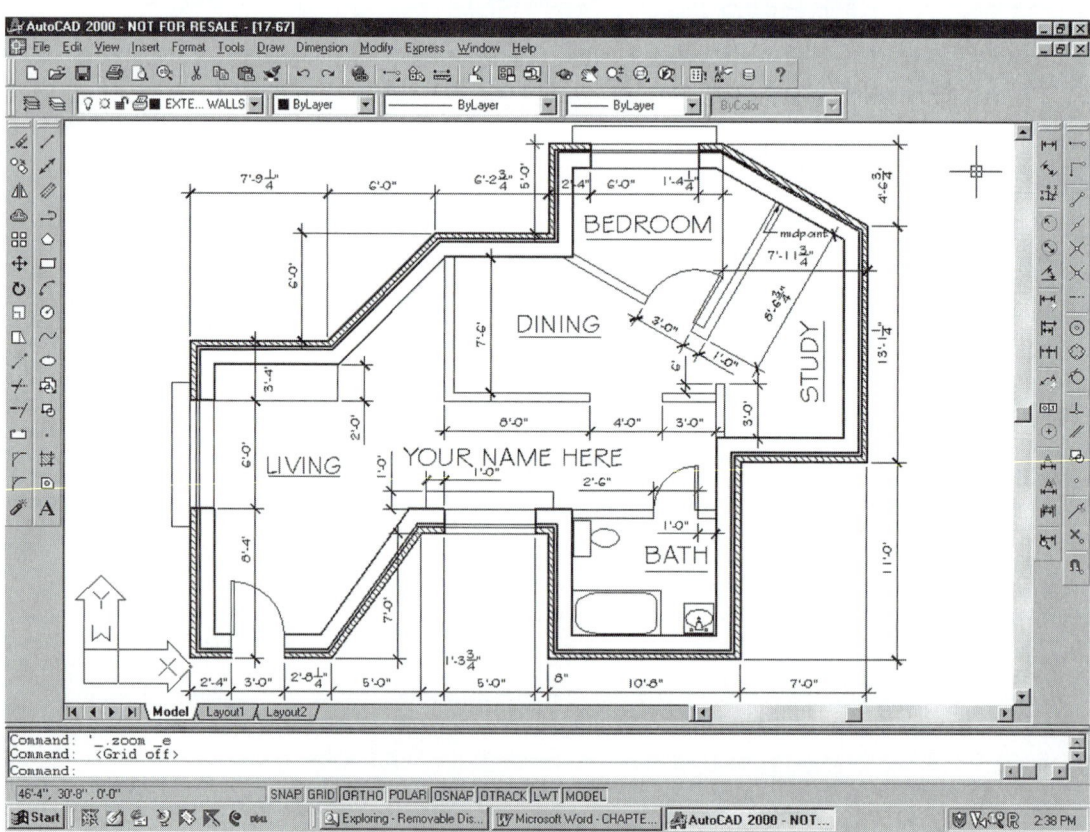

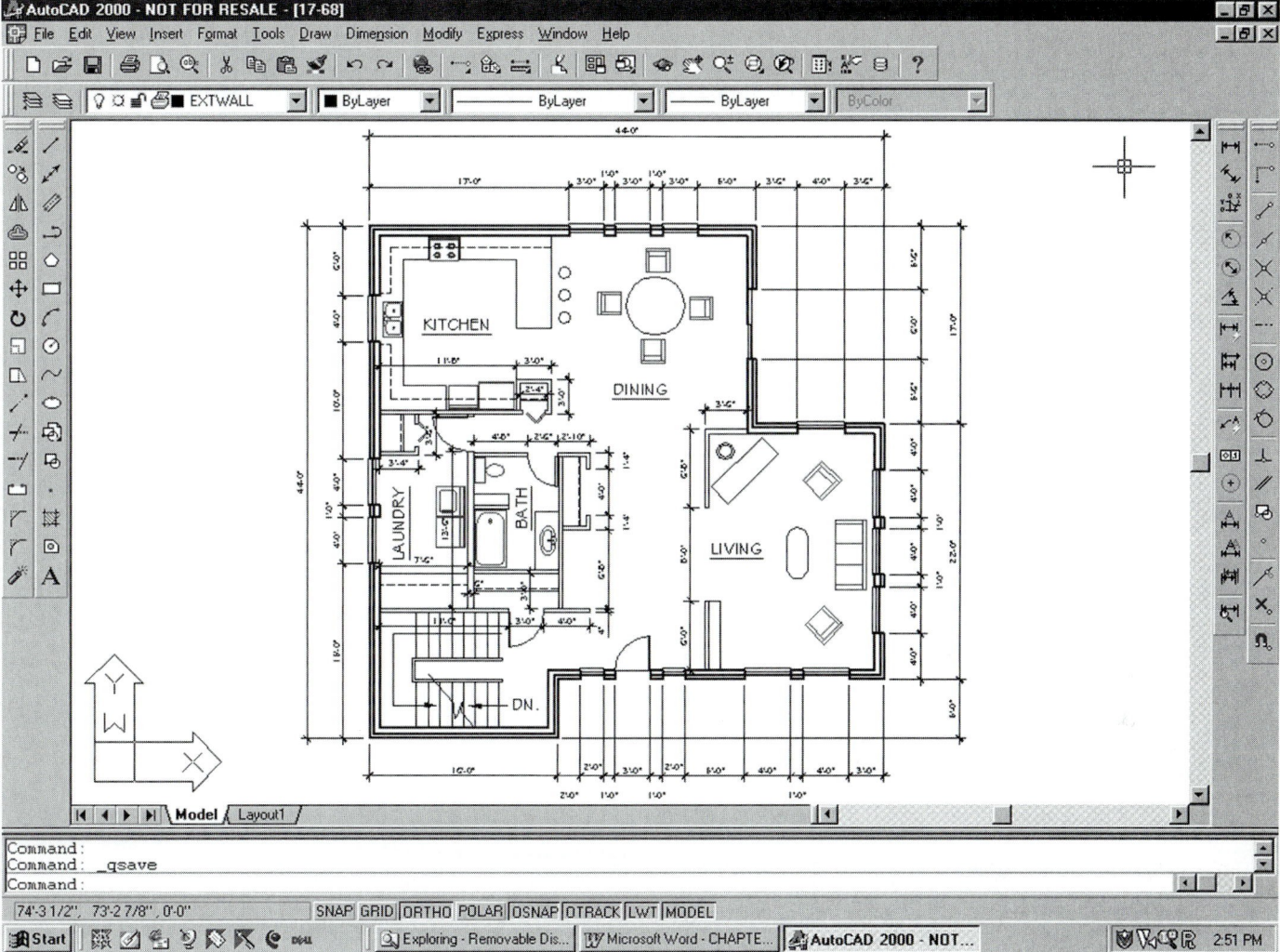

FIGURE 17–68   Problem 9.

Draw the Floor Plan as shown in Figure 17–68. The wall composition from exterior to interior is as follows: 4″ Brick and 6″ studs. Interior walls are 4″ except the wall between laundry and bath, which is 6″ thick. Use the Individual Wall Segment method to create the walls. Draw all windows and doors. Do not create dimensions or hatching.

10. Open the *MYEXE17-5.dwg* file. Using the STRETCH command, enlarge the upper portion of the floor plan 4′-6″ in the north direction. Do not change window dimensions.

11. Open the *MYEXE17-8.dwg* file. Using the STRETCH command, enlarge the living space 5′-0″ in the west direction. Do not change door size.

12. Open the *MYEXE17-9.dwg* file. Using grips, enlarge the upper portion of the kitchen 6′-0″ in the north direction.

Architectural Dimensioning

After successful completion of this chapter you should be able to:

▲ Understand architectural dimensioning principles.

▲ Understand architectural dimensioning conventions.

▲ Identify architectural dimensioning components.

▲ Understand architectural dimensioning arrangements.

▲ Understand and control dimensioning variables.

▲ Understand the effects of units and precision on dimensioning variables and size options.

▲ Create architectural dimension styles.

▲ Modify and override existing dimension styles.

▲ Use dimensioning applications effectively and efficiently.

▲ Use the quick dimension toolbar to automatically dimension drawings.

▲ Use the quick leader toolbar to automatically create notes with leader lines.

▲ Place dimensions on drawings using the dimension toolbar.

▲ Create dimension styles using the dimension style manager dialog box.

▲ Create dimension substyles.

▲ Use dimensioning variables transparently.

▲ Understand associative and non associative dimensioning.

▲ Edit and update dimensions using five different techniques.

▲ Stretch, extend, and trim dimensions.

18.1 ARCHITECTURAL DIMENSIONING PRINCIPLES

Adding specific information to a design that shows length measurements, wall thickness, distances and angles between objects, and annotation helps builders and contractors physically build the objects in the drawings by reading the construction documents through graphics and dimensions. The dimensions in the drawings help convey sufficient information about measurements, distances, lengths, thickness, width, perimeter, areas and angles. Dimensioning is the process of adding such information to a drawing. Dimensioning is an integral part of architectural drawing and requires special attention and consideration. Dimensioning can be a tedious, time-consuming, and frustrating task unless certain guidelines and standards are established. If enough time is spent on planning, understanding, and settings of the dimensioning standards, less time will be spent on editing and revising dimensions. There are six major principles governing the creation and use of architectural dimensioning on drawings:

1. Conventions.
2. Variables.
3. Components.
4. Arrangements.
5. Styles.
6. Applications.

Each dimensioning principle brings a wealth of knowledge and unlimited flexibility to the user, increasing productivity and making dimensioning less time consuming. Let's take a look at these principles.

18.1.1 Architectural Dimensioning Conventions

The AEC field would most benefit from establishing CAD dimensioning standards shared between the three user groups. The architecture field currently uses a particular dimensioning technique that is somewhat consistent throughout the profession. This brings coherency to projects when viewed by other CAD users, architects, designers, engineers, clients, interior designers, and contractors. Establishing standards in CAD dimensioning across the disciplines may not be a "pressing" issue, but each firm should establish its own standards. This can be a standard dimensioning technique called "Architectural Dimensioning Conventions." The ideal scenario would be to have all the architects, designers, engineers, and consultants working on the same project perform tasks that are shared by common standards and adhere to specific architectural dimensioning techniques.

18.1.2 Dimensioning Variables

A dimensioning variable is a setting that controls how dimensioning components are presented on the drawing. These dimensioning variables govern the size, shape, color, spacing, and attributes associated with each dimensioning element. For example, an architectural tick mark placed at the ends of dimension lines is a dimensioning variable. The size and color of the architectural tick mark can be controlled by either using a dialog box or by typing the corresponding dimensioning variable name at the command line. In both cases the tick mark size and/or color can change according to its value set by the architectural dimensioning conventions. The ability to control dimensioning variables at the command line is useful for previous release users, but the driving force behind AutoCAD 2000 is a positive movement away from keyboard dependence. Because all of the architectural dimensioning variables can be controlled through the use of the Dimension Style Manager dialog box and its affiliated dialog boxes, new users should use toolbar buttons and dialog boxes when dimensioning.

There are many applications and options available when placing dimensions on objects. For this reason some of the dimensioning variables or options do not necessarily apply to the architecture, interior design, or construction fields. Therefore some of the dimensioning variables, methods, or options will not be covered in great length and detail but will be mentioned briefly so as to give the reader an idea of its existence. The concentration in this chapter is on the most useful and necessary options for dimensioning architectural drawings using dialog boxes.

AutoCAD's Dimension Style Manager feature allows the user to turn a time-consuming task of dimensioning into a time-saving function through the use of many dialog boxes. There are more than 60 dimensioning variables that affect dimensioning in a generic sense. These dimensioning variables are listed in Appendix A. All dimensioning variables, except the ones that deal with tolerances, can be applicable to architectural dimensioning conventions.

18.1.3 Architectural Dimensioning Components

To establish architectural dimensioning conventions, the dimensioning variables that govern size, format, color, location, height, spacing, offset, justification and appearance must be individually determined and set. The components that make up the dimensioning styles and variables can be

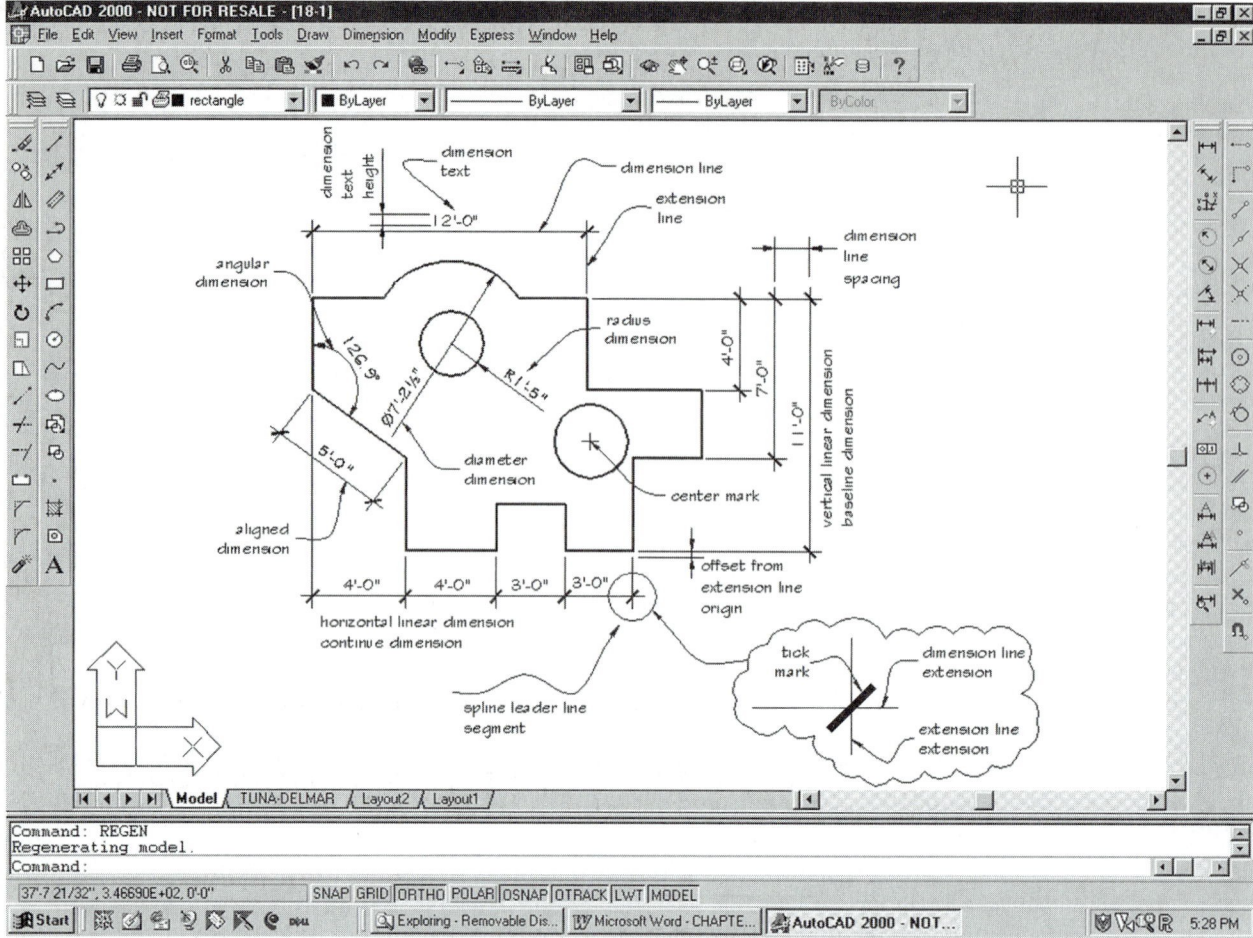

FIGURE 18–1

Architectural dimensioning components are variables that can be controlled using dialog boxes or at the command line.

established, managed, and edited individually or as a group. Different variables allow you to create a dimension style that accommodates projects with different settings. Typical architectural dimensioning features and components are shown in Figure 18–1.

18.1.4   Architectural Dimensioning Arrangements

One of the most important aspects of architectural dimensioning is its text alignment with the dimension lines. Architectural dimensions are arranged in a specific orientation called *aligned*. This is achieved by aligning the dimension line and the dimension text parallel with the object surface being dimensioned. On the other hand, Mechanical drawing dimensions are arranged in a unidirectional direction. The term *unidirectional* refers to the placement of all dimensioning text horizontally on the drawing. In a unidirectional dimensioning arrangement, arrowheads are used instead of architectural tick marks and the dimension text is usually centered inside the dimension line. Figure 18–2 shows the comparison between aligned and unidirectional dimensioning arrangements.

18.1.5   Architectural Dimension Styles

A dimension style controls dimensioning variables in the drawing. Before discussing dimensioning applications, a *dimensioning style* applicable to architectural drawings will be created. This dimension style will be called Architectural. When a dimension is created in the drawing, its format and appearance will be governed by this dimension style. For architects and designers this issue becomes especially important because even thought the default standard dimension style can be used on preliminary drawings, concerns about the drawing scale, scale factor, tick marks, and architectural format and appearance come into play. More styles can be created from the existing architectural style as specific applications become necessary. The Architectural

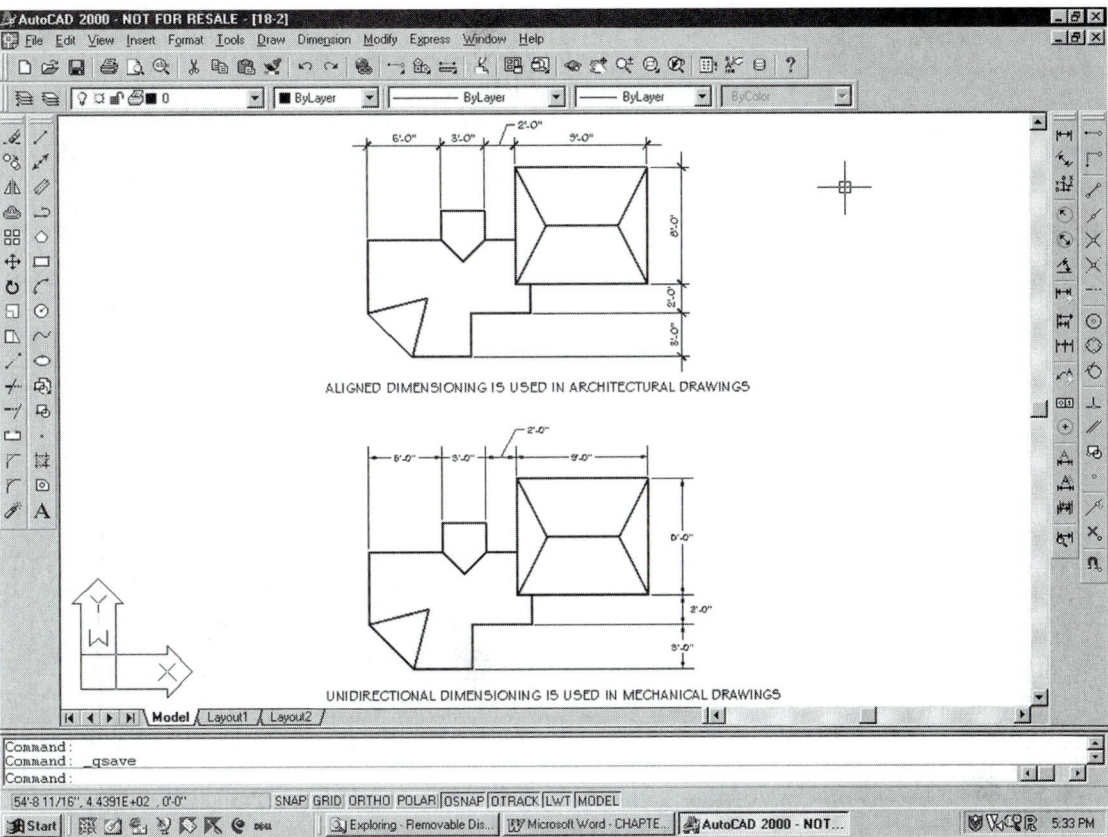

FIGURE 18–2 The aligned and unidirectional dimensioning arrangements.

dimensioning style can also serve as the *master template style* from which additional styles with slight variations can be created based on the properties of the same style. A new dimension style is created using the Dimension Style Manager dialog box, which is accessed as follows:

1. From the Dimension toolbar (this is the first vertical docked toolbar on the right side of the screen), click on the Dimension Style button (this is the last button in the Dimension toolbar).

2. Right-click on the empty area next to the Help toolbar (this is the last toolbar on the Standard toolbar), and a *shortcut menu* will appear. Move the cursor over ACAD and left-click on Dimension. If the Dimension toolbar is not docked or not floating, this will display the Dimension toolbar. Inside the Dimension toolbar, click on Dimension Style button.

3. Enter DDIM or DIMSTYLE at the command line.

4. From the Dimension pull-down menu click on Style. . . .

5. From the Format pull-down menu pick Dimension Style. . . .

The Dimension Style Manager dialog box will appear as shown in Figure 18–3. The Dimension toolbar is shown in Figure 18–4.

18.1.6 Dimensioning Applications

Once you create a dimension style that fits the project requirements, you can then start applying the new style when dimensioning. The Dimension toolbar is the primary source for creating dimensions and provides many different dimensioning applications. For example, you can create angular or linear dimensions as desired with the new dimension style in effect. You can also switch between dimension styles and update existing dimensions in the drawing as desired. We will first create a new architectural dimension style, then apply this new style to some dimensioning applications. Later we will edit and revise existing dimensions using different techniques.

FIGURE 18–3 The Dimension Style Manager dialog box with ARCHITECTURAL and default STANDARD dimension styles.

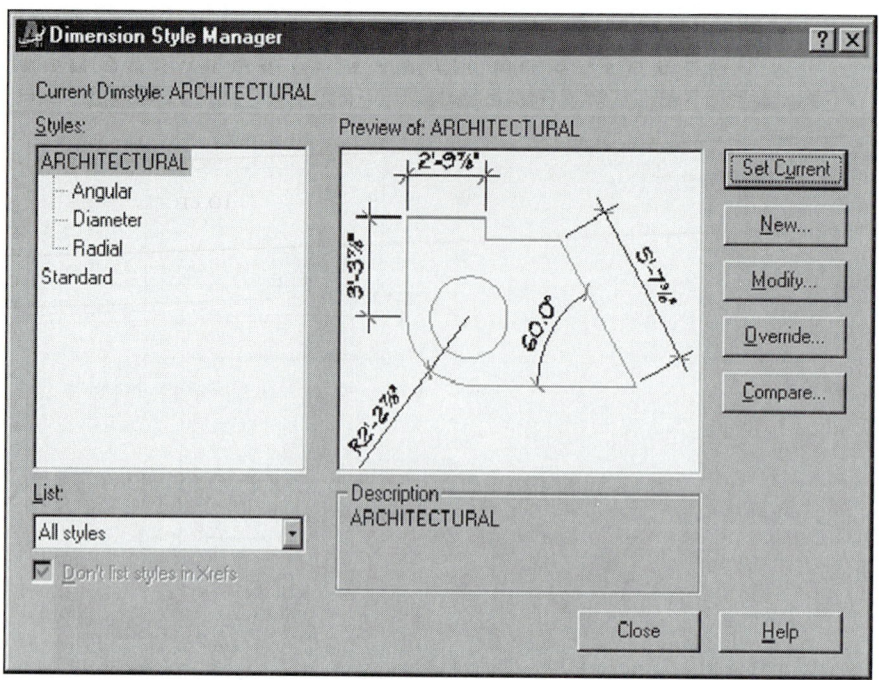

FIGURE 18–4 The Dimension toolbar is used to create dimensions and access the Dimension Style Manager dialog box.

18.2 USING THE DIMENSION STYLE MANAGER DIALOG BOX

The Dimension Style Manager dialog box shown in Figure 18–3 will allow you to perform the following dimensioning tasks:

1. Create a new dimension style.
2. Preview the current or an existing dimension style.
3. Customize dimensioning variables.
4. Modify an existing dimension style.
5. List current dimensioning variables.
6. Compare dimension styles including a list of variables.
7. Rename and delete current dimension styles.
8. Override dimensioning variables.
9. Manage all other dimensioning issues.

Each time you create a new dimension style, modify an existing dimension style, or override an existing dimension style, AutoCAD will replace the Dimension Style Manager dialog box with the task-specific dialog box. For example, when you modify the standard (default/existing) dimension style by selecting the Modify... button in the Dimension Style Manager dialog box, the Modify Dimension Style: Standard dialog box will be displayed. Don't let this dialog box intimidate you—it is not as complicated as it seems! Each specific area will be discussed in detail and each category will include a dimensioning variable that can be typed at the command line to change its value or setting. Also where applicable, a recommendation about a size or value will be included to help you establish architectural dimensioning conventions. Let's examine the areas of the Dimension Style Manager dialog box.

Current Dimstyle: (area)   This area displays the current dimension style. The standard dimension style is the default dimension style that AutoCAD provides as a base to create additional styles. When you first open this dialog box, the standard style is displayed. If a new dimension style is not created or if the current style is not changed, the standard style and its dimensioning variables will be assigned when dimensioning. For the mechanical drafting field the default standard style can be used immediately without creating a new style because most of the dimension settings and variables are in tune with that field. If you begin dimensioning an architectural drawing with standard dimension style, the default variable settings and scale will not work properly. You must create a new style or modify existing settings to correspond to architectural drawing settings.

Styles: (list box)   This area will display all the available dimension styles created previously including the default standard style. If there are no dimension styles created, the list box will display only the standard style.

List: (drop-down menu)   This area controls the dimension styles displayed in the Styles: list box. The list contains All styles and Styles in use. Selecting All styles will display all the available dimension styles, while Styles in use will display only the dimension styles that are referenced.

Don't List Styles in Xrefs: (check box)   This box controls the listing of dimension styles in externally referenced drawings. If you place a checkmark here, AutoCAD will not list dimension styles when that drawing file is externally referenced into another file. Xrefs are discussed in Chapter 24.

Preview of: (area)   This is the dimension style *image display window,* which is used as the preview pane. You can preview the dimensioning variables inside this window. The New, Modify, and Override Dimension Style dialog boxes each contain the image display window. This area will list the name of the style being used and will show a sample drawing with dimensioning variables. The sample drawing inside the image display window includes dimension lines, extension lines, dimension text style and height, radius, and angular dimension. Each time a dimensioning variable is changed, this preview window will automatically update the sample drawing to reflect the changes in dimensioning variables or settings.

Description: (text box)   This text area will list all the dimension variable settings after the dimension style has been created. This is a quick reference area where all of the dimensioning variables that are changed can be seen at a glance. Since the Description text box is a small rectangle, it will not display all of the new dimensioning variables and their settings. To read all of the variables, place the cursor at the end of the last text line and press the right arrow key on your keyboard. This will advance the text until it is finished. The style must be current to view its description.

Set Current: (button)   When a new dimension style is created or when an existing style needs to be used for dimensioning, the Set Current button is used to make it current. There are two different ways to make a dimension style current:

1. Click on the desired dimension style under the Styles: list box and then click on the Set Current button in the Dimension Style Manager dialog box.
2. Click on the desired dimension style inside the Dim Style Control drop-down menu in the Dimension toolbar.

Setting a dimension current in one way will make it current in the other way. A dimension style must be made current to take effect in the drawing. If you right-click on a highlighted style inside the Styles: list box, a shortcut menu will be displayed where you can *set current,*

FIGURE 18–5 The Create New Dimension Style dialog box is used to create a new dimension style.

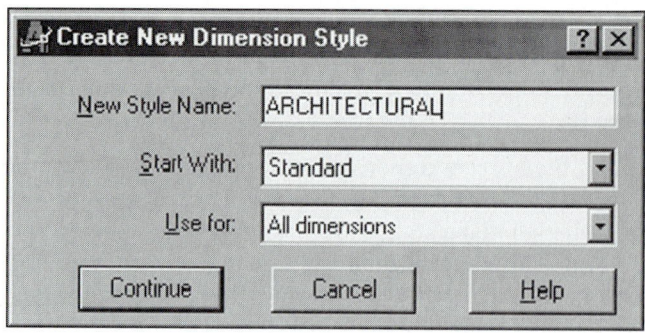

rename, or *delete* the dimension style. To delete an existing dimension style, right-click on the style to be deleted and click on Delete from the shortcut menu. When deleting an existing style make sure that it is not current and not being currently used; otherwise AutoCAD will give you the following message:

```
Dimension style ARCHITECTURAL is in use and cannot be deleted.
```

When the existing style is in use or current, the Delete option of the shortcut menu will not be available. The right-click option is not available inside the Dim Style Control drop-down menu in the Dimension toolbar. A dimension style must be made current to modify or override its settings.

New. . . : (button)   This button is used to create and define new dimension styles. It will also allow you to set an existing dimension style on which to start the new dimension style and select a dimensioning variable to which you want the new style to apply. Selecting this button will display the Create New Dimension Style dialog box as shown in Figure 18–5.

Modify . . . : (button)   Selecting this button will display the Modify Dimension Style dialog box shown in Figure 18–6. The contents of this dialog box are identical to the New Dimension Style dialog box as shown in Figure 18–9 and are used to modify and change the dimensioning variables of an existing dimension style rather than creating a new dimension style. Using the Modify. . . button to change dimensioning variables will have a global effect on dimensions. This means that during a dimensioning application, if a variable is changed using the Modify . . . button, it will change all the dimensions having the same variable. This is termed a *global effect.* For example, if the original tick mark size of ⅛″ is determined to be too small after dimensioning a large drawing, the Modify. . . button can be used to change the tick mark size variable for the entire draw-

FIGURE 18–6 The Modify Dimension Style dialog box showing the ARCHITECTURAL dimension style.

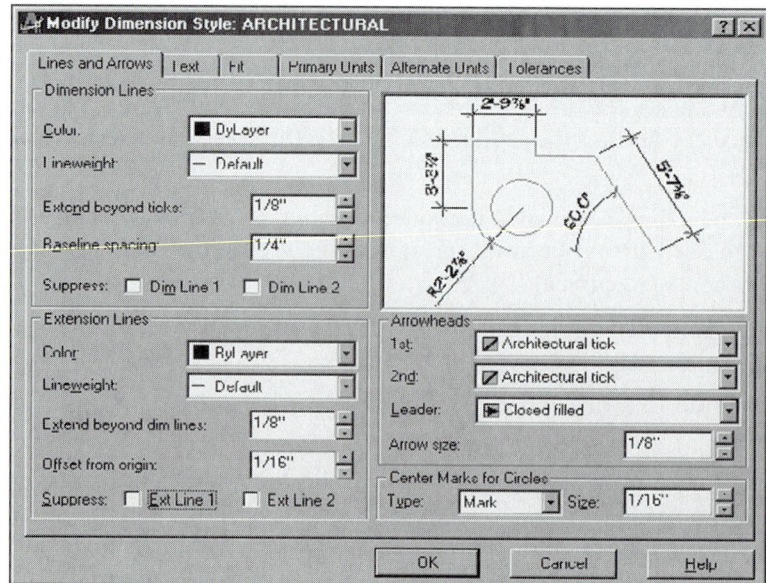

ing of the current style. On the other hand, if only a single or a few of the *new* dimensions need to have a different dimensioning variable value, the Override. . . button is used (see below). It is important to remember that the Modify. . . button is used to change a single or more dimensioning variables using the current dimension style. When using the Modify. . . button to edit dimensioning variables for the current dimensioning style, AutoCAD will automatically save all the changes to the current dimensioning style. When all the changes are saved, every existing dimension will update to reflect the new settings for each of the dimensioning variables changed. All of the new dimensions will have the new settings as objects are dimensioned on the screen.

Override. . . : (button)   Selecting this button will display the Override Current Style dialog box as shown in Figure 18–7. The contents of this dialog box are identical to the New and Modify Dimension Style dialog boxes, and this box is used to override dimensioning variables of an existing dimension style rather than creating a new dimension style. When this dialog box is used to change one or more dimensioning variables, the changes are *not* saved to the current dimension style. The existing dimensions in the drawing are not affected by these changes. Only the new dimension(s) will reflect the changes in the drawing. Although the Override option affects only the new dimensions to be performed in the drawing, it can be used in conjunction with the command line to change selected dimensions in the drawing. If all the existing dimensions are selected, it will have a global effect similar to using the Modify. . . button. In order for the changes to take effect on selected dimensions, a *dimension update* must be performed after using the Override. . . button to change one or more dimensioning variables. A dimension update can be performed using the Dimension Update button in the Dimension toolbar or at the command line as follows:

```
Command: DIM ~EnterKey~ (for dimension)
Dim: UP ~EnterKey~ (for update)
Select objects: (select the dimension or dimensions to override)
Select objects: ~EnterKey~ (this will update the dimension with an override)
Dim: ~EscKey~ (this will complete the operation)
```

This will allow you to keep the original dimensioning variable settings while also allowing you to change only one or more dimensions on the drawing. Temporary overrides can be set to dimension styles without having a global effect on the entire dimensions. AutoCAD will display

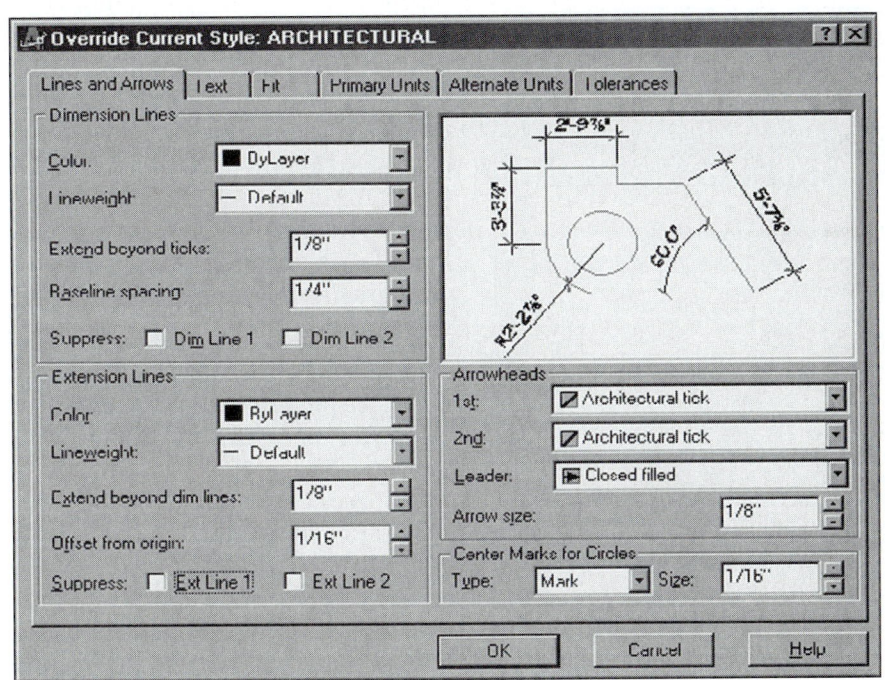

FIGURE 18–7 The Override Current Style dialog box. The current style is Architectural.

overrides as unsaved changes under the dimension style in the Styles: list box. After changing dimensioning variables to modify one or more specific dimensions on the drawing, the <style overrides> will be displayed under the current dimension style inside the Styles: list box. You can remove overrides using the Dimension Style Manager dialog box as follows:

1. Click on the <style overrides> and click on the Override. . . button.

2. Inside the Override Current Style dialog box, change the variable(s) back to its original value(s) and click on OK button.

3. Highlight the dimension style and click on the Set current button. Click on OK button inside the Alert dialog box. Now the Dimension Style Manager dialog box will no longer display the <style overrides>.

When you *undo* an Override, the existing dimensions with the new variable will not be changed back to the original settings; only the new dimensions will be performed as if no override has taken place. To change the existing dimensions with the new variable back to its original settings, a dimension update must be performed as shown earlier. To override existing dimensioning variables at the command line, you can either enter the name of the dimensioning variable at the command line or enter the name of the dimensioning variable after the DIMOVERRIDE command. This command will also allow you to *clear* overrides.

Caution: Setting another style current will discard style overrides. AutoCAD will give you an alert as to whether you would like to discard the style overrides.

Tips: It is more efficient and quicker to use the Override Current Style dialog box to change dimensioning variables rather than using the variables at the command line. In the dialog box you can pick an existing dimension style, alter the variable, and make a new style. By using a dialog box you can also look at the big picture by viewing the dimension style image display window. This will allow you to see the effects of dimensioning variables when altered in the dialog box. This is a great way to check on the appropriateness of a particular dimensioning setting. In certain projects requiring specific dimension styles not compatible with firm standards, it is better to generate a new style in order to prevent conflicts with dimension geometry.

Tips: To increase productivity and efficiency, utilize the Modify and Override buttons in the Dimension Style Manager dialog box to your advantage. Remember that when the Modify. . . button is used, all existing dimensions will be changed to the new settings. When the Override. . . button is used, only the new dimensions placed after the override will have the new settings. To change existing dimensions after the override, use the DIM (dimension) and UP (update) commands at the command line or use the Dimension Update button on the Dimension toolbar and select the dimensions to override. If a specific dimension does not update automatically after the Modify. . . button is used, try the Dimension Update button to update it manually.

Compare. . . : (button)   This button will allow you to compare the properties and variables of two dimension styles or list all the properties and variables of one dimension style by displaying the Compare Dimension Styles dialog box as shown in Figure 18–8. The Compare: drop-down menu is used to pick the first dimension style for the comparison. The With: drop-down menu is used to pick the second dimension style to compare it with the first dimension style. If With: drop-down menu is set to <none>, or if it is set to the same dimension style, all of the properties and variables for the dimension style will be displayed. When comparing two dimension styles or listing the properties of one dimension style, the comparison results are displayed automatically inside the list box. In Figure 18–8 the

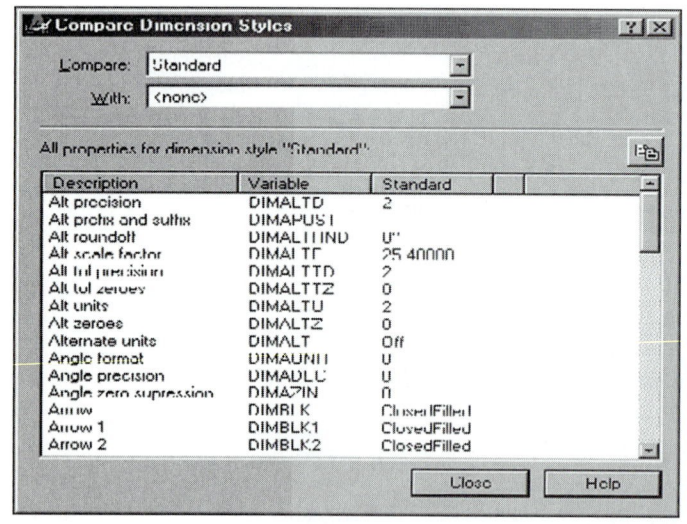

FIGURE 18–8
Compare Dimension Styles dialog box with Standard dimension style variables.

standard dimension style is compared with <none> to list all of its variables. Notice that scrolling through the list will show the 61 different dimensioning variables that can be set using the standard style. There are three columns in the Compare Dimension Styles dialog box as follows:

DESCRIPTION: This heading describes the dimension style variable. For example, if you click on the down arrow until the dimension variable DIMBLK is visible, the description will read: Arrow. This means Arrowhead block name.

VARIABLE: This heading will list the name of the dimensioning variable such as DIMBLK. This dimension variable controls the property of the Arrowheads assigned to ends of the dimension lines.

STANDARD: This heading will list all the dimensioning variables and their values that differ for the dimension style Standard. The value for DIMBLK under Standard is Closed Filled. In this case the properties and dimensioning variables will be listed under Standard.

Use this dialog box to compare different dimension styles with each other or list all of the variables in one dimension style. You can also print the contents of the comparison area by clicking on the print icon above the scroll bar.

Close: (button) This button will close the Dimension Style Manager dialog box when all the tasks are done.

Help: (button) This button will display the AutoCAD Command Reference dialog box where you can get quick reference to commands found inside Dimension Style Manager dialog box.

18.3 USING THE CREATE NEW DIMENSION STYLE DIALOG BOX

The Create New Dimension Style dialog box shown in Figure 18–5 is used to create a new dimension style and has the following major components.

New Style Name: (text box) This is where you enter the name of the new dimension style. The new dimension style name can be project specific or can be general.

Start With: (drop-down menu) If you have an existing style that you want to use as a base for the new style, this is where you highlight the existing style. Starting with an existing style will save you keystrokes because you change only the dimensioning variables in the new style that will differ from the variables you start with. If you want to start from scratch, use the standard style, where all variables will be based on the AutoCAD Standard dimension style. Some of your dimensioning applications will involve the use of substyles, in which a specific dimensioning variable will have a different value for a specific type of application. Instead of changing a dimensioning variable each time a specific application is used, a substyle is created by changing a dimensioning variable once and is used by making the substyle current for a specific dimensioning application. This method is different than using the Override. . . button inside the Dimension Style Manager dialog box. Overriding dimensioning settings is discussed later in the chapter.

Use for: (drop-down menu) AutoCAD has 12 dimensioning applications that fall into six major categories: linear, angular, radius, diameter, ordinate dimensions, and leaders and tolerances. The 12 dimensioning applications are available as buttons inside the Dimension toolbar or they can be accessed through the command line. Using the Dimension toolbar and dimensioning applications are discussed in detail later in the chapter. When you create a new dimension style you are basically creating a *dimensioning template*. By using the New Dimension Style dialog box you are determining the format and properties of *lines and arrows, text, fit, primary units, alternate units,* and *tolerances* of all the dimensioning applications. The dimensioning template that you create will take some time and patience to complete. Once it is complete and fully functional, all dimensioning variable settings will apply to all dimensioning applications. Not all drawings would use all the settings of the dimensioning template. When the project calls for variations on the type of dimensioning you are performing, the Use for: drop-down menu is used. This will create a substyle that applies only to a specific dimensioning application within the original dimension style. It will allow you to create a specific dimension style with varying dimensioning elements, depending on the type of dimension being performed. Here are some examples:

The Angular substyle is created when angular dimensions need to have a color or arrow size setting different from the Linear dimensions.

The Diameter substyle is created when diameter dimensions need to have leader lines with an arrowhead style and arrowhead size different from the Linear dimensions that use architectural tick marks.

Continue: (button) Once the New Style Name is typed and the Start With and Use for drop-down menus are selected, you are ready to establish dimensioning variables. When Continue is selected, AutoCAD will display the New Dimension Style dialog box as shown in Figure 18–9. This is where you select and define all dimensioning variables. This is the command center for all the dimensioning operations.

Tips: When creating a new dimension style the first time, use the standard inside the Start With drop-down menu and use the All dimensions inside the Use for drop-down menu. This will help you look at all standard dimension variables and establish a template for an "architectural" dimension style based on all major dimensioning applications. You can then set different settings and variables for different dimensioning applications.

Cancel: (button) This button will cancel the selections made inside the Create New Dimension Style dialog box. When this operation is cancelled AutoCAD will take you back to the Dimension Style Manager dialog box.

Help: (button) This button will display the AutoCAD command reference dialog box, where you can read a brief description of the buttons and drop-down menus associated with the Create New Dimension Style dialog box.

FIGURE 18–9 The New Dimension Style dialog box will help you establish the dimensioning variables and it starts with the Lines and Arrows tab.

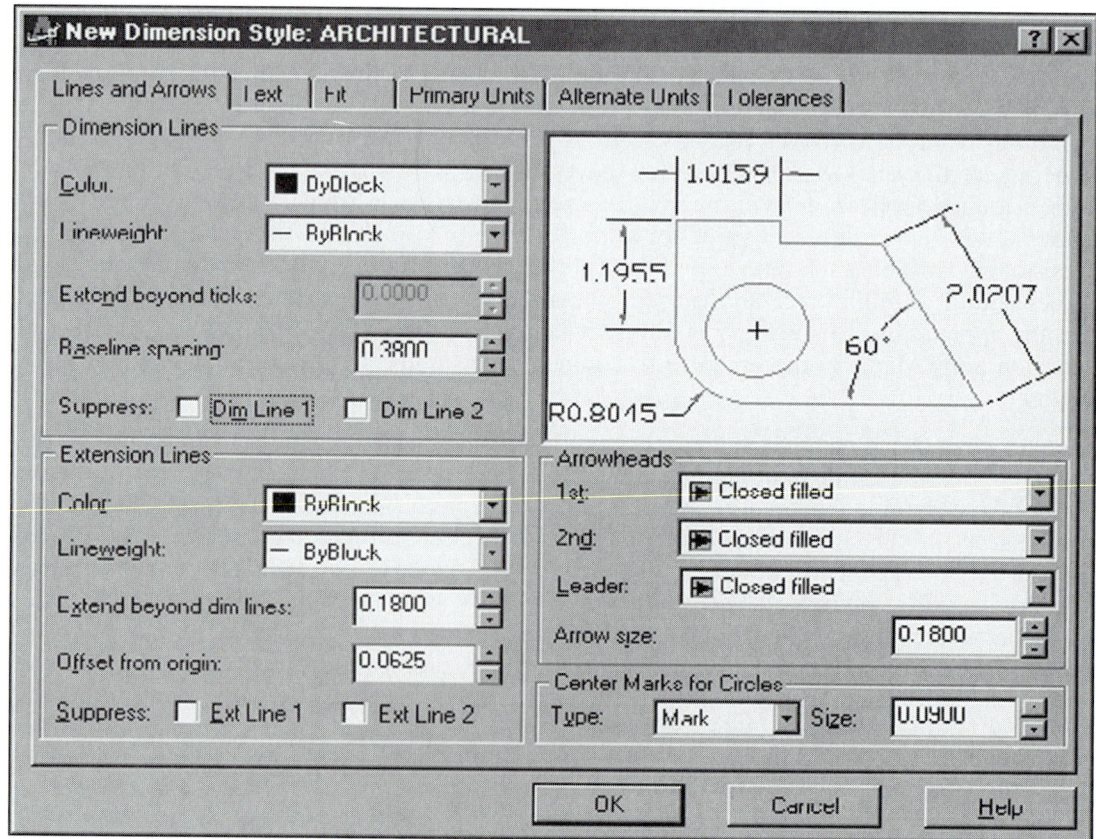

■ **EXERCISE 18–1:** *The following step-by-step exercise will allow you to create a new dimension style named Architectural based on the standard style.*

Step #1: Access the Dimension Style Manager dialog box.

Step #2: Inside the Dimension Style Manager dialog box, click on the standard style and click on the Set Current button.

Step #3: Click on the New... button.

Step #4: Inside the Create New Dimension Style dialog box, enter ARCHITECTURAL inside the New Style Name: text box.

Step #5: Inside the Start with: drop-down menu, select Standard.

Step #6: Inside the Use for: drop-down menu, select All dimensions and click on the Continue button.

This will display the New Dimension Style: Architectural dialog box. This is where you will set all the dimensioning variables. The setting of all the dimensioning variables is discussed in detail in Section 18.4, Using the New Dimension Style Dialog Box. For now, click on the OK button. This will create the Architectural dimensioning style. Congratulations! You have successfully created a new dimension style called Architectural.

Once you create the Architectural dimensioning style, it can be used as the foundation for a new substyle. In AutoCAD dimensioning terms, the copy of Architectural can be used to create the substyles that can be used for different dimensioning applications. The substyles are created within a style and use the current style as a copy. That is why you will see the Copy of STANDARD (in this case Copy of ARCHITECTURAL) inside the New Style Name: text box. A substyle is created with one of the seven options found inside the Use for: drop-down menu. When a substyle is created within a style, it will be listed under the main style in a tree-like manner.

■ **EXERCISE 18–2:** *The following step-by-step exercise will allow you to create the Diameter Substyle with a text height of 3/16″ and a text color of red to be used only when creating Diameter dimensions.*

Note: Don't worry about the use of the Text tab in the New Dimension Style: ARCHITECTURAL: Diameter dialog box at this point. This dialog box and all of its tabs will be discussed later in the chapter.

Before starting this exercise, set the drawing units to architectural and the precision to 0′-0 1/16″.

Step #1: Click on the Dimension Style button inside the Dimension toolbar.

Step #2: Inside the Dimension Style Manager dialog box, highlight the ARCHITECTURAL and click on the Set Current button and click on the New... button.

Step #3: Inside the Create New Dimension Style dialog box, click on the down arrow of the Use for: drop-down menu and select Diameter dimensions. Notice that when anything other than All dimensions is selected, the New Style Name: text box becomes unavailable because you are creating a substyle based on a specific dimensioning application and not based on all dimensioning applications.

Step #4: Inside New Style Name: text box ARCHITECTURAL: Diameter should read and be inactive. Select ARCHITECTURAL inside the Start With: drop-down menu. If Architectural style is not created or does not exist, select Standard.

Step #5: Click on the Continue button.

Notice that when you selected the Diameter dimensions category, ARCHITECTURAL: Diameter appeared inside the New Style Name: text box. This means that AutoCAD has created a substyle called Diameter within the Architectural dimensioning style.

Step #6: Inside the New Dimension Style: ARCHITECTURAL: Diameter dialog box, click on the Text tab.

Step #7: Inside the Text Appearance category and inside the Text color: drop-down menu, click on the down arrow and select color red.

Step #8: Inside the Text height: drop-down menu, click on the up arrow and select 3/16″ and click on the OK button.

Step #9: Inside the Dimension Style Manager dialog box, notice the Diameter listed under the Architectural dimensioning style as the substyle. Under Preview of: ARCHITECTURAL: Diameter image display window, you will see an example of the diameter symbol and the diameter dimension text with red color. Also notice the text inside the Description text box will read as follows:

ARCHITECTURAL + Text height = 3/16″,

Text color = 1 (red)

Step #10: Click on the Close button to close the Dimension Style Manager dialog box.

Congratulations! You have successfully created a Diameter substyle from Architectural style. Now, whenever you use the Architectural dimensioning style for diameter dimensions, the dimension text height will be 3/16″ and the diameter dimension text color will be red. For all other dimensioning applications (such as a Radius dimension), the dimension text height and the dimension text color will be default.

You can create Linear, Angular, Radius, Diameter, Ordinate dimensions, and Leaders and Tolerances substyles using the steps described above without using the New Style Name: text box that is based on a specific dimensioning style. All dimensions refer to all dimensioning applications that include all of the six dimensioning applications used for creating a brand new dimensioning style from scratch. When All dimensions is selected, the New Style Name: text box becomes active and it will show Copy of whatever style is selected from the Start With: drop-down menu. The advantage to creating a substyle is that instead of creating a dimension style for each one of the different dimensioning characteristics, you create a dimensioning style (template) once and have the application settings, such as the Diameter, to their own unique characteristics. When a different category is used, it will be listed under the original style name.

18.4 USING THE NEW DIMENSION STYLE DIALOG BOX

The New Dimension Style dialog box as shown in Figure 18–9 has six tabs that will allow you to set all of the dimensioning variable settings. These tabs are Lines and Arrows, Text, Fit, Primary Units, Alternate Units, and Tolerances. Let's take a look at each individual category: (notice that the new dimension style has been named Architectural).

Note: The values shown inside the drop-down menus for each tab are the direct result of the Drawing Units type and the Drawing Units precision values entered at the start of the drawing. If Architectural Units and a precision of 0′ −0 1/16″ are selected, then all the numerical values inside the available drop-down menus will be at 0′ −0 1/16″ increment. The values will initially show the 0′ −0 and the inches values, but when the down arrow on the drop-down menu is used to reach the value of zero inches (0″), the consecutive numbers will have only an inch value. You can see the results of the values selected for each dimensioning option inside the image display window. For example, when the Arrowheads area is changed to Architectural tick style, the default Closed filled arrowheads will turn into tick marks inside the image display window. To work with the following dimensioning option values at 1/16″ increments, set the Units to Architectural and the precision to 0′ −0 1/16″ prior to establishing styles.

Lines and Arrows: (tab)   This tab has four separate categories relating to the geometry of the dimensioning variables. It is used to establish dimensioning features and variables relating to the following categories: *dimension lines, extension lines, arrowheads,* and *center marks for circles.*

Dimension Lines: This area will help you establish dimension line properties. This is the component that describes the length of the dimension. It starts from a specific dimension extension line on one side of the object and terminates at the other dimension extension line. The dimension line itself has three parts: extension lines, dimension text, and arrowheads as shown in Figure 18–10. Usually the dimension line is solid and continuous, with the dimension text placed on top of the dimension line for architectural applications. However, it can be broken to accommodate the dimension text inside. Refer to Text tab and Text Placement section for placing text inside the dimension line. When a dimension is placed in a drawing to indicate the length of an object, the dimension line, extension lines, dimension text, and dimension line terminators will be displayed as part of the dimension. These four components make up a typical dimension that is considered to be a single entity by default. This means that all four elements act and respond together to AutoCAD commands as a whole. As far as changing the color is concerned, the dimension line with the tick marks, the two extension lines, and the dimension text can be controlled separately. For example, when the color of a dimension line is changed from default to red color, only the dimension line and the tick marks will have red color. The extension lines and the dimension text will retain their default colors. Therefore, when establishing dimension line properties, these four components can be set independently from each other to suit dimensioning requirements.

Inside the Dimension Lines category of the Lines and Arrows tab there are five variables affecting the properties of Dimension Lines:

- **COLOR:** (drop-down menu). This option will assign a color to the dimension line and to the arrowheads. The default color is ByBlock but can be set to ByLayer. ByBlock means that the four components of a typical dimension (dimension line, extension lines, arrowheads, and dimension text) will assume the current color and line type settings when the dimension is created in the drawing. All associative dimensions are considered to be *block objects* when they are created. Associative dimensioning is discussed later in this chapter. Blocks are symbols created for multiple use and are discussed in Chapter 19. If the Dimension Line Color is set to ByBlock, the dimensions will be shown as default colors in the image display window regardless of layer settings. If it is set to ByLayer, it will assume the current layer name, layer color, and layer line type. To assign a color to the dimension lines, click on

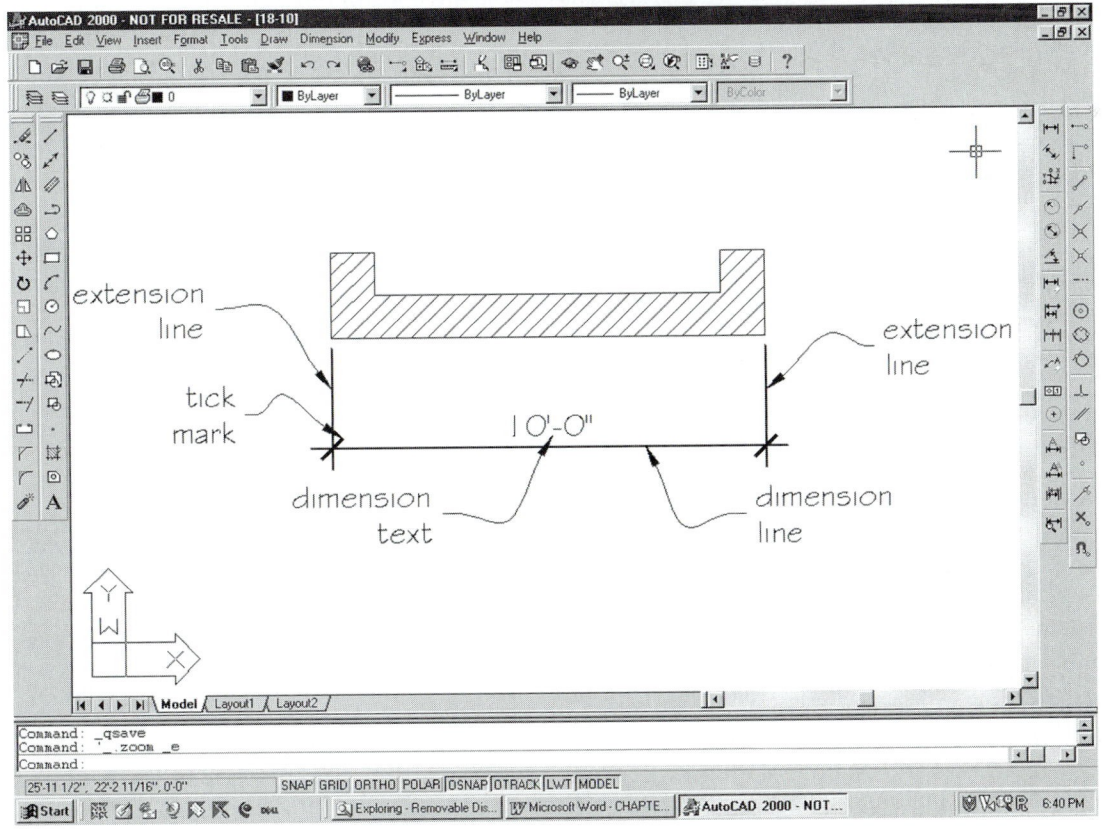

FIGURE 18–10
Dimension line, extension line, dimension text, and dimension line terminators (tick marks).

the drop-down menu arrow, locate the desired color, and click on it. If a color other than the seven major colors is desired, go to the bottom of the color list, click on Other..., and select a different color from the Select Color dialog box. AutoCAD stores the color values in the DIMCLRD (dimension line color) variable. The default is 0, which is ByBlock. The DIMCLRD variable will assign and change colors to dimension lines, arrowheads (tick marks), and dimension leader lines created with the LEADER command. The Color drop-down menu, on the other hand, will assign or change only the color of the dimension lines and arrowheads. When using the command line, you must enter the corresponding number of the color, not the color name.

- **LINEWEIGHT:** (drop-down menu). This option will assign a specific lineweight to dimension lines if you do not wish to use Plot Styles to control line thickness. Lineweights are discussed in Chapter 9, and Plot Styles are discussed in Chapter 23. AutoCAD assigns a width value to all graphical entities, including dimension lines but not to TrueType fonts and raster images. The values are standard lineweights assigned to ByLayer and ByBlock. The default line weight is ByBlock and is an integer representing 100th of a millimeter. To assign a different lineweight to the dimension line, click on the drop-down menu arrow and scroll down to see the available line weights. AutoCAD stores the lineweight values in the DIMLWD (dimension line lineweight) variable. The DIMLWD variable will change the lineweight of a dimension line at the command line.

- **EXTEND BEYOND TICKS:** (drop-down menu). This option will determine how far the dimension line extends beyond the extension lines. This is called the dimension line extension and is shown in Figure 18–1. This area is initially inactive because the distance to extend the dimension line past the extension line option is only available when Architectural tick, Oblique, Integral, or None options are used as Arrowheads. To create a dimension line extension, you must first establish architectural tick marks as Arrowheads. The desired value for the dimension line extension is directly proportional to the scale of the drawing being dimensioned. For a floor plan at a scale of $1/4'' = 1' - 0''$, a dimension line extension value of $1/8''$ is adequate. The dimension variable DIMDLE (dimension line extension) can be entered at the command line to change its value.

- **BASELINE SPACING:** (drop-down menu). This option will control the distance between two or more dimension baselines when the Baseline Dimension application is used. This application takes effect when the Baseline Dimension toolbar inside the Dimension toolbar is used. It sets the distance of the second dimension line from the baseline of the previous dimension or a selected dimension. The default value for this spacing is $3/8''$ (0.375). The Baseline Dimension application is discussed later in this chapter. For general architectural dimensioning purposes this option can be ignored because most of the architectural drawings use continue (chain) dimensioning. The dimension variable DIMDLI (dimension line increment) can be entered at the command line to change its value.

- **SUPPRESS: DIM LINE 1 AND DIM LINE 2** (check boxes). In architectural dimensioning a dimension line is intersected by two extension lines. It usually includes two tick marks at intersections as shown in Figure 18–1. The Dim Line 1 refers to the first dimension line location established by the first extension line origin. The Dim Line 2 refers to the second dimension line location established by the second extension line origin. With no suppression, a typical dimension with dimension text above the dimension line will include the dimension line, two extension lines, dimension text, and two arrowheads as shown in Figure 18–11. When the dimension text is placed above the dimension line, only the tick mark(s) and the dimension extension line(s) will be suppressed. When a checkmark is placed inside the Suppress: Dim Line 1 only, AutoCAD will suppress the first dimension line by not displaying the tick mark at the first extension line origin when the dimension text is placed above the dimension line. When a checkmark is placed inside the Suppress: Dim Line 2 only, AutoCAD will suppress the second dimension line. When both dimension lines are suppressed, AutoCAD will remove the tick marks from both extension line origins. Notice that when both Dim Line 1 and Dim Line 2 are suppressed, the Color, Lineweight, and Extend beyond ticks variables for dimension lines are no longer available to change. When the dimension text is centered inside the dimension line, the dimension line will be broken into two pieces. The Suppress option will allow you to keep either the first, second, or both dimension lines and their tick marks from being displayed if the dimension text is placed in

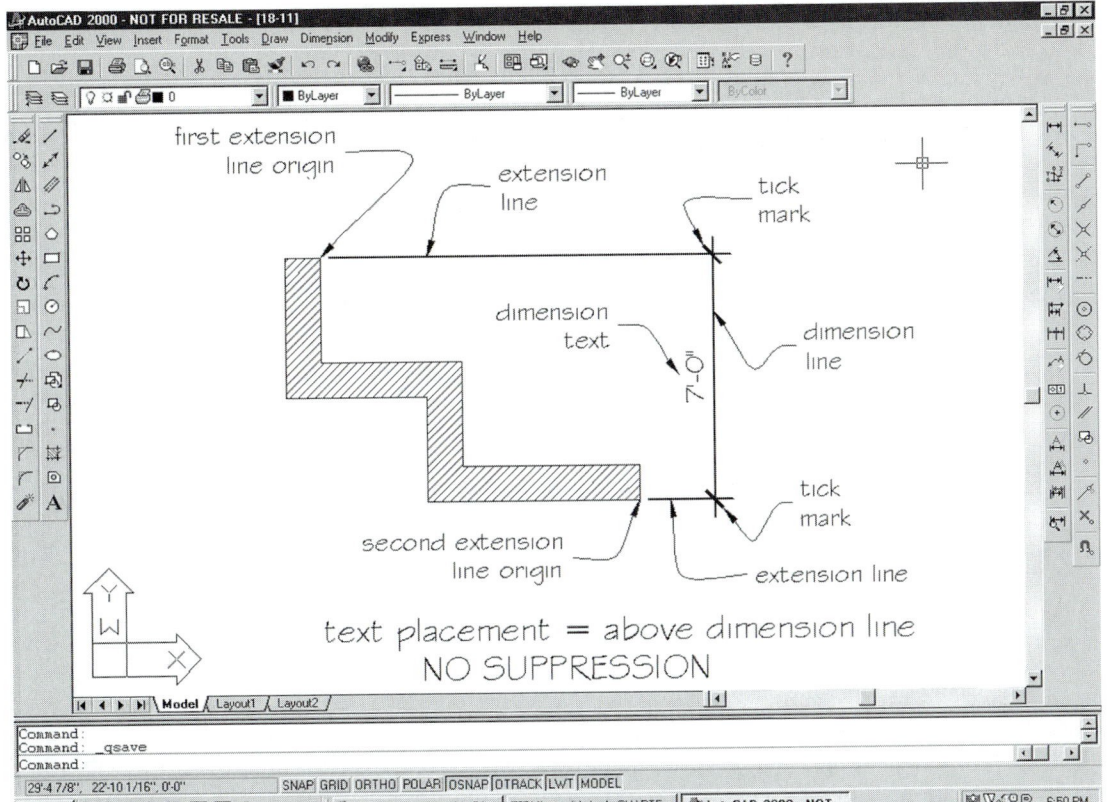

the center of the dimension line. With no suppression, a typical dimension with dimension text centered in the dimension line will include the two pieces of the dimension line, two extension lines, dimension text, and two tick marks as shown in Figure 18–12. When a check mark is placed inside the Suppress: Dim Line 1 only, AutoCAD will suppress the first dimension line by not displaying the first dimension line and the first tick mark as shown in Figure 18–12. When a check mark is placed inside the Suppress: Dim Line 2 only, AutoCAD will suppress the second extension line by not displaying the second dimension line and the second tick mark as shown in Figure 18–13. When both dimension lines are suppressed when the dimension text is centered inside the dimension line, both pieces of the dimension line will not be displayed as shown in Figure 18–13. The DIMSD1 (suppress first dimension line) and DIMSD2 (suppress second dimension line) dimensioning variables can be used at the command line to suppress dimension lines.

Tips: The check boxes and the radio buttons inside the dialog boxes are point sensitive. You don't have to precisely click on the inside of a pick box or a radio button to make it active or inactive. You can either pick the text next to the check box or radio button or click on the empty space right side of the check box or radio button text without going outside the boundaries.

Extension Lines: This area will help you establish extension line properties. This is the component that describes the beginning and ending point of the dimension by means of an extension line from an object point that is called the *extension line origin*. See Figure 18–12. When the Linear or Aligned dimension is used, AutoCAD will ask you to pick two points on the object or select the object itself. The first point picked for dimensioning is the *first extension line origin*, and the second point picked for dimensioning is the *second extension line origin*. After two points are picked on the object, extension lines are displayed by default. Extension lines have similar characteristics of dimension lines where one or both extension lines can be suppressed and both ends can be extended beyond the dimension line.

Inside the Extension Lines area there are five variables affecting the properties of Extension Lines:

FIGURE 18–12 When the dimension text is placed in the center of the dimension line, the dimension line is broken. With no suppression two pieces of the dimension line will be displayed. When the first dimension line is suppressed, the first part of the dimension line including the tick mark will not be displayed.

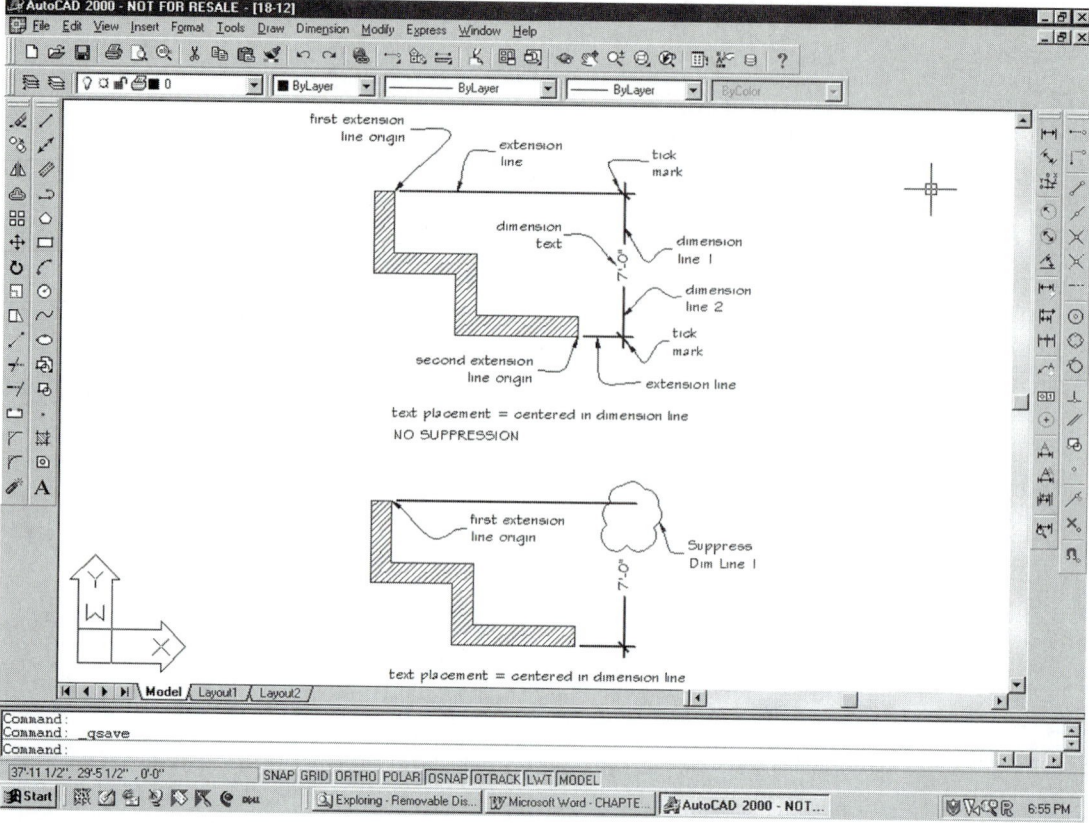

FIGURE 18–13 When the second dimension line is suppressed, the second part of the dimension line including the tick mark will not be displayed. When both dimension lines are suppressed, both dimension lines, including tick marks, will not be displayed.

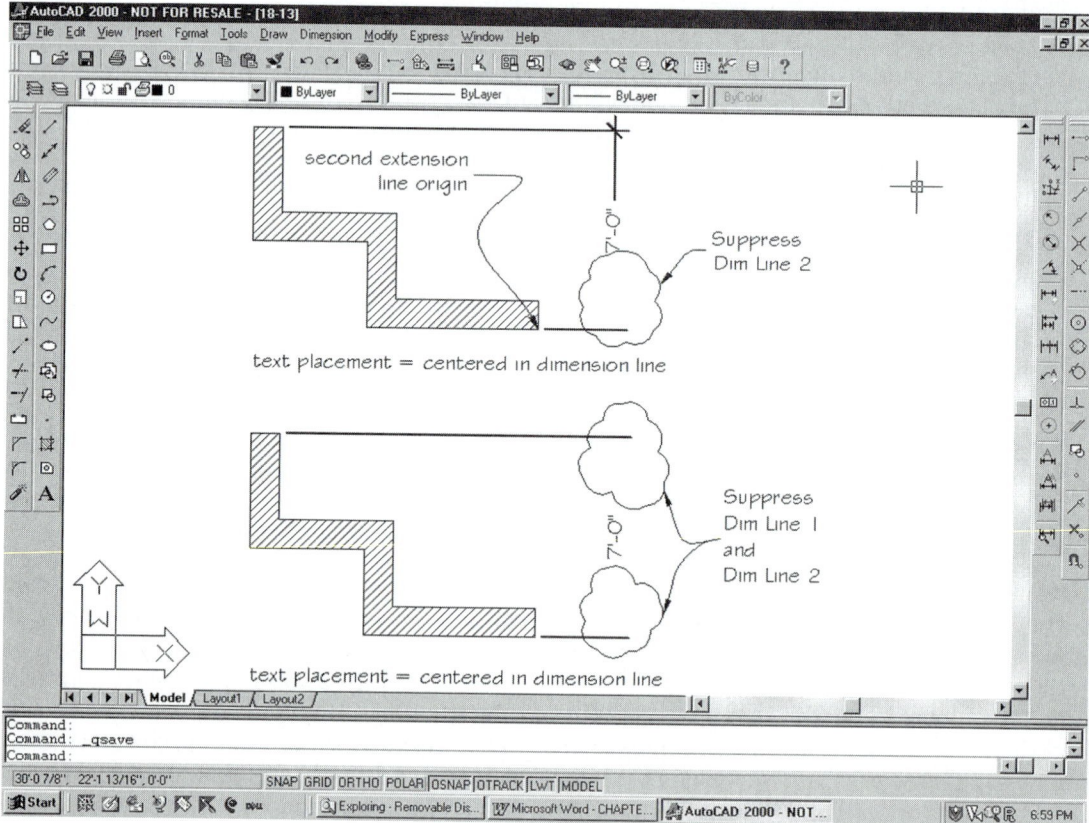

- **COLOR:** (drop-down menu). This option will assign a color to the extension lines similar to the area for Dimension Lines Color section. AutoCAD stores the color values inside the DIMCLRE (extension line color) variable, and the default value is 0, which is ByBlock. The same principles governing the DIMCLRD (dimension line color) apply to the DIMCLRE dimensioning variable.

- **LINEWEIGHT:** (drop-down menu). This option will assign a specific lineweight to the extension line. The properties of the lineweight are identical to the dimension line lineweight discussed earlier. AutoCAD stores the line weight value in the DIMLWE (extension line lineweight) dimension variable.

- **EXTEND BEYOND DIM LINES:** (drop-down menu). This option will determine how far the extension lines extend beyond the dimension line. This is called the extension line extension and is shown in Figure 18–1. Unlike the Dimension Line Extension variable, this area is active when any of the Arrowheads options is picked. The values inside this menu are similar to the values inside the Extend beyond ticks drop-down menu discussed earlier. When this value is 0″, the extension line does not extend past the dimension line. As with any variable, you can see this inside the image display window. Because the 0″ represent the beginning of no extension line extension, only the up arrow is available. The DIMEXE (extension above dimension line) dimensioning variable can be used at the command line to change this variable.

- **OFFSET FROM ORIGIN:** (drop-down menu). This option will determine the gap between the object and the first and second extension line origins. This is the gap between the object and the beginning of extension lines as shown in Figure 18–1. This is called the extension origin offset, and its value depends on the scale of the drawing. A value of 0″ is not recommended because this will place the extension lines directly on top of the object line. A value of 1/16″ or 1/8″ is adequate. The DIMEXO (extension line origin offset) dimensioning variable can be used at the command line to change the value of offset from origin.

- **SUPPRESS: EXT LINE 1 AND EXT LINE 2:** (check boxes). Extension lines are a reference source originating from an object and extended to intersect the dimension line at some distance. For most of the dimensioning applications both extension lines will be needed. When an object line or edge can be used as a reference source, the extension line at that location can be omitted by suppressing it. Extension line suppression is similar to the dimension line suppression where the same procedure is used to suppress either the first, second, or both extension lines. The Ext Line 1 refers to the first extension line origin, and the Ext Line 2 refers to the second extension line origin when the dimension is created. With no suppression, both extension lines will be displayed. When a checkmark is placed inside the Suppress: Ext Line 1 only, AutoCAD will suppress the first extension line. When a checkmark is placed inside the Suppress: Ext Line 2 only, AutoCAD will suppress the second extension line. When both boxes are checked, AutoCAD will suppress both extension lines. The DIMSE1 (suppress the first extension line) and DIMSE2 (suppress the second extension line) dimensioning variables can be used at the command line to suppress extension lines. By default DIMSE1 and DIMSE2 are turned off (0). To turn DIMSE1 or DIMSE2 on, enter ON or 1 at the command line.

Arrowheads: This area will help you establish the properties of dimension arrowheads. When the dimension line and the extension lines intersect an arrowhead style and size is specified. The arrowhead style for architectural dimensioning is the tick marks. There are two different kinds of tick marks for architectural dimensioning: architectural tick and oblique. The architectural tick arrowhead style has heavy line, whereas the oblique arrowhead style has lighter line. The architectural tick marks are preferred because of their bold properties. A different arrowhead style can also be specified for the first and second dimension line. The DIMBLK (arrowhead block name) dimensioning variable can be used at the command line if both arrowheads are to be the same.

Inside the Arrowheads area there are four variables affecting the properties of the arrowheads:

- **ARROWHEADS 1ST:** (drop-down list). This option will select the arrowhead style for the first extension line origin. When the first arrowhead style is picked from the drop-down list, the second arrowhead style will automatically change to match it. The default arrowhead style is Closed filled. There are 20 different arrowhead styles to choose from, as shown in Figure 18–14. To see the complete list of arrowhead styles, click on the down arrow and use the scroll bar. A graphical representation of the corresponding arrowhead style is shown on the left side of the arrowhead style. As an arrowhead option number 21, AutoCAD will allow you to create user defined arrowhead blocks. To set architectural tick marks as the arrowhead style, click on the drop-down list and click on the Architectural tick option. The DIMBLK1 (first arrowhead block name) can be used to change the arrowhead style at the command line.

- **ARROWHEADS 2ND:** (drop-down list). This option will select the arrowhead style for the second extension line origin. The procedure to select an arrowhead for the second extension line origin is same as for the first one. To change arrowhead styles at the command line, use DIMBLK (arrowhead block name) if both arrowheads are the same. To establish separate arrowheads for the first and second extension line origin, you must first turn the DIMSAH (separate arrowhead blocks) dimensioning variable ON. Then you can use DIMBLK1 (first arrowhead block name), and DIMBLK2 (second arrowhead block name) to assign two different arrowhead styles.

The User Arrow… option of the Arrowheads area will help you create a new arrowhead style based on your own design. In order to create a user arrow, you must first design the arrowhead style and turn it into a block. Blocks are discussed in Chapter 19. When the User Arrow… option is picked, the Select Custom Arrowhead Block dialog box will appear. Inside this dialog box select the name of your custom arrow block from the Select from Drawing Blocks: (drop-down list).

FIGURE 18–14 The 20 different arrowhead styles.

- **LEADER:** (drop-down list). This area will help you establish the arrowhead style for dimension leader lines. A leader is used to point to a specific feature of a drawing followed by a specific note as annotation. This controls the arrowhead style for the leader lines drawn using the LEADER and the QLEADER commands. The options for the leader arrowhead style are the same as dimension line arrowheads style. Leader lines are discussed in detail under Dimensioning Applications.

- **ARROW SIZE:** (drop-down menu). This area will help you establish a size for arrowheads used as dimension line terminators and for the arrowhead style for the leader lines. For closed filled arrowheads the default size is 3/16″. This is sufficient for the application of leader lines, but can be changed to 1/8″ for smaller scale drawings. The size of the architectural tick marks as dimension line terminators is also controlled by Arrow Size drop-down value menu. The size of a 45 degree angle tick mark is measured either horizontally or vertically from endpoint to endpoint. A 1/8″ tick mark is large enough for a 1/4″ = 1′−0″ scale drawings. To change the arrow size, click on the up or down arrow in the drop-down value menu. Figure 18–15 shows examples of the closed filled and architectural tick arrowhead styles. The dimensioning variable that controls the arrow size including tick marks and leader lines is DIMASZ (dimension arrow size).

Center Marks for Circles   This area will help you control the appearance of center marks or centerlines every time a circle or arc is dimensioned. Circles and Arcs are dimensioned using the Radius Dimension or Diameter Dimension toolbars in the Dimension toolbar. You can also use DIMDIAMETER and DIMRADIUS commands at the command line to dimension circles and arcs.

Inside the Center Marks for Circles area there are two variables affecting the properties of Center Marks:

Type: (drop-down menu)   This area controls the types of marks placed in circles and arcs. Inside this list are three center mark type options: Mark, Line, and None.

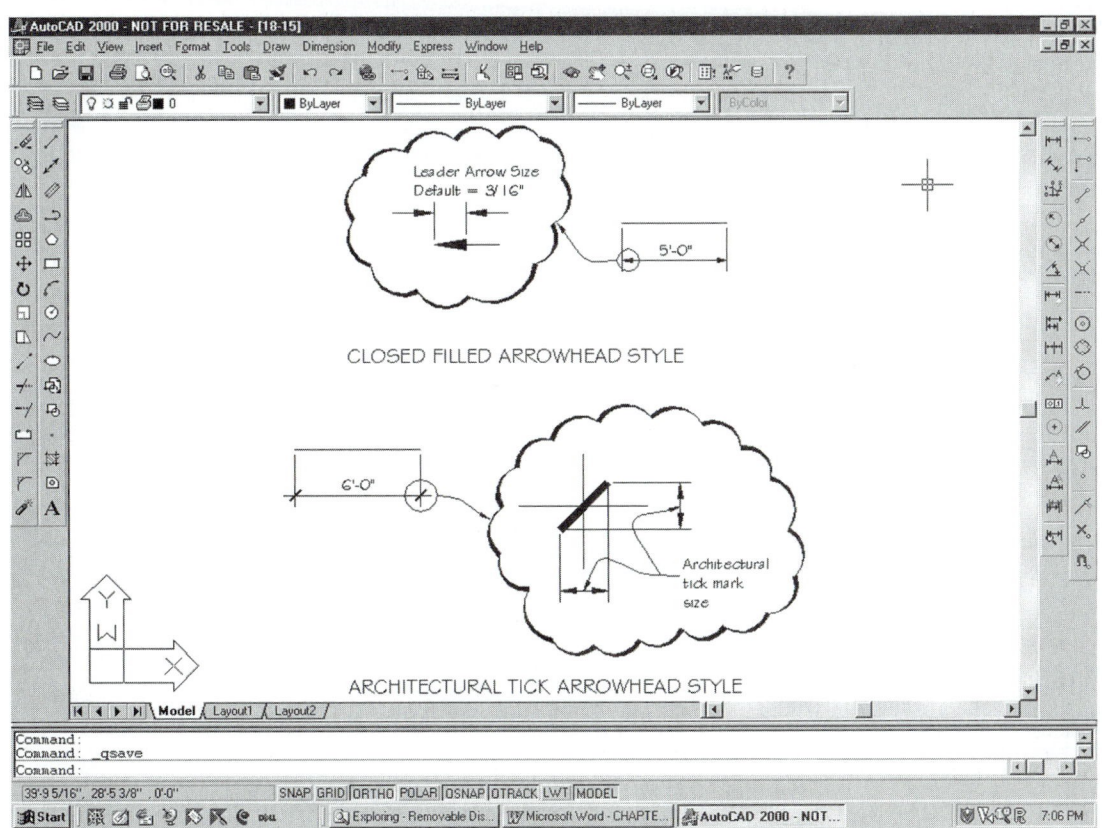

FIGURE 18–15   A typical closed filled and architectural tick arrowhead styles.

- **MARK:**   This option will place a center mark (without centerlines) when dimensioning circles and arcs. This is a vertical and a horizontal line placed in the center of the circle or arc along with the leader line and the dimension text. When a circle or arc is picked for a radius or a diameter dimension, a center mark is placed in the center of the circle or arc. If the dimension is placed inside the circle or arc, the center mark will not be displayed. If the dimension is placed outside the circle or arc, the center mark will be displayed. The default value for the center mark size is 3/32″ but will read as 0.0900 when Drawing Units is set to decimal and the precision is set to 0.0000. The size of the center mark is controlled by the Size drop-down list. This value is measured from the center point of the center mark to the end point of the center mark. The center mark size for circles and arcs can be changed at the command line with the DIMCEN (dimension center mark) dimensioning variable. If the DIMCEN value is a positive number, a center mark will be drawn. If the DIMCEN value is a negative number, a centerline will be drawn.

- **LINE:**   This option will create a centerline when dimensioning circles and arcs. When a centerline is placed, it will use a center mark and add four additional lines at each quadrant. The gap between the endpoint of the center mark to the beginning point of the centerline is same as the default center mark value of 0.0900″ (3/32″). The additional lines at four quadrants intersect the circle at a point of tangency and extend pass this intersection. The amount that the centerlines extend beyond the circle or arc is controlled by the Size option. A negative value for the DIMCEN variable will change the centerline size at the command line.

- **NONE:**   This option will not place a center mark or a centerline in a circle or arc. If the Size of the center mark or the centerline is set to zero, the None option will be default.

Size: (drop-down menu)   This area will change the size of the center mark and the centerline for the Center Marks for Circles category. For example, if a value of 1/4″ is selected, the center mark and the centerline size will measure 1/4″ when plotted as shown in Figure 18–16. If the diameter of a circle or arc is less than 0.375″, the Centerlines will not be shown. Therefore the

FIGURE 18–16   The center mark and centerline size of 1/4″.

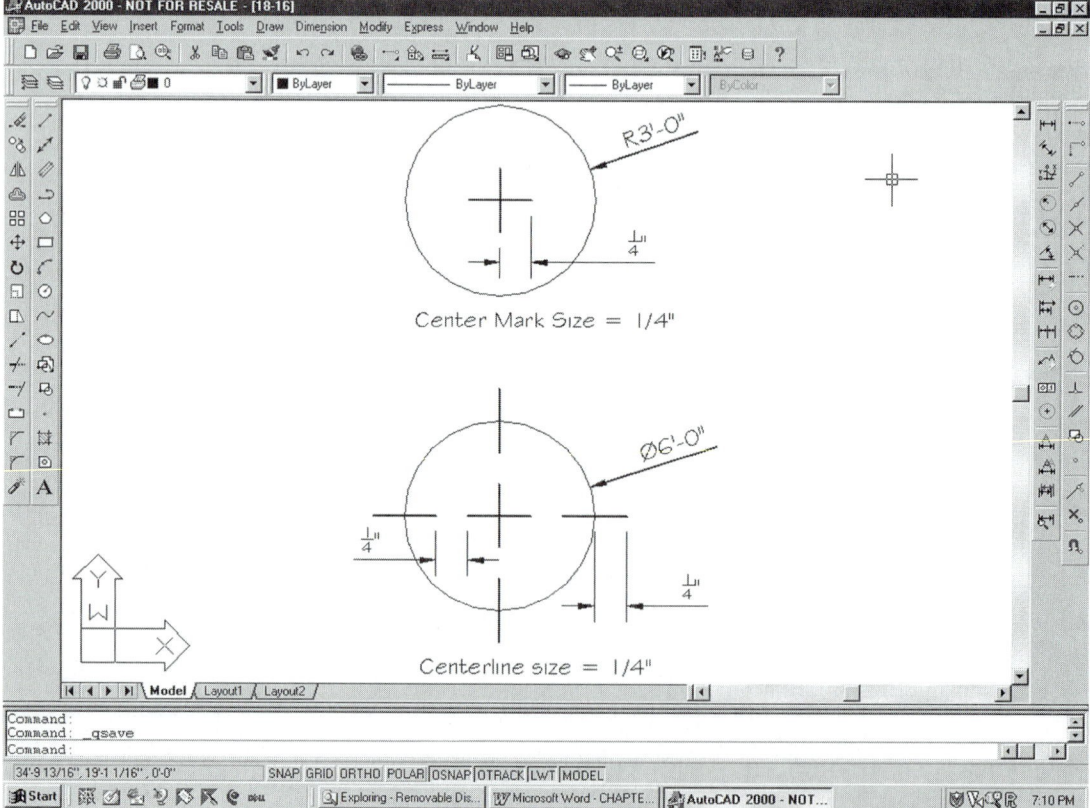

appearance of centerlines will depend on the size of the circle or arc being drawn. For example, if a circle is drawn with a 0.0900" radius, the center mark will cover the entire circle and a centerline will not be drawn.

Tips: When dimensioning circles and arcs, AutoCAD uses a leader line and text to indicate a diameter or a radius dimension. The leader line attached to a radius or a diameter dimension is controlled by the Arrowheads and Arrow size options, not by the Leader option of the arrowheads. When tick marks are used as the arrowheads style, the diameter or the radius dimensions will have tick marks at the ends of the leader lines. This may not be a desirable feature on the drawing. To have the diameter or radius dimensions use closed filled arrowheads style while the linear dimensions use tick marks under the same dimension style, create Angular and Diameter substyles. You can also click on the Override. . . button and change the arrowheads style to closed filled before dimensioning a circle or arc.

While the DIMDIAMETER and the DIMRADIUS commands allow you to draw center marks and centerlines for circles and arcs, they include the leader line and the dimension text. If no leader line and no dimension text are required, type DIMCENTER at the command line and pick the circle or the arc. When the DIMCENTER command is used in conjunction with the DIMCEN variable only the Center Marks or Centerlines will be drawn.

Note: When the DIMCENTER command is used in conjunction with the DIMCEN variable, the Center Marks and Centerlines are composed of separate entities. This means that the Center Mark in a circle has two separate lines, one vertical one horizontal. If the Center Mark is to be erased both lines must be selected. This also means that the Centerlines in a circle are composed of six individual separate lines, two for the Center Mark and four for the Centerlines.

Text: (tab)   This tab has three separate categories relating to the appearance, placement and alignment of dimension text and a dimension style image display window similar to other tabs. The categories are *Text Appearance, Text Placement,* and *Text Alignment.* The text tab is shown in Figure 18–17.

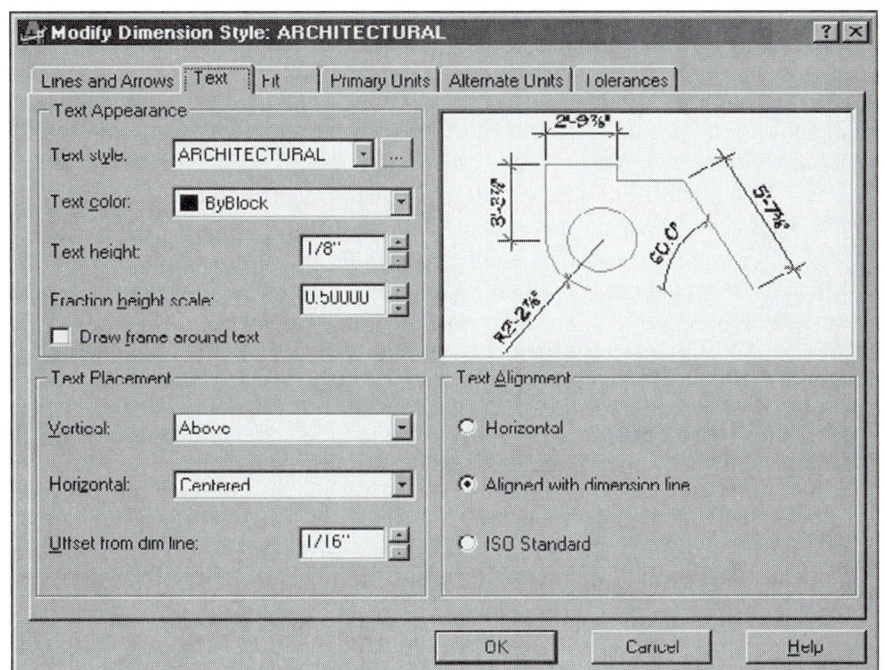

FIGURE 18–17 The Text tab of the Modify Dimension Style dialog box controls how dimension text is created, placed, and aligned.

Let's take a look at the categories and how the adjustments work with different settings:

Text Appearance: This area will help you control the dimension text format and dimension text size.

Inside the Text Appearance category of the Text tab there are five variables affecting the properties of the dimension text:

- **TEXT STYLE:**   (drop-down list). This area will display and set the current style for dimension text. If there is an existing text styles it can be selected from the list. If there are no existing styles, a new dimension text style can be created using the (…) button next to the list. When this button is picked, the Text Style dialog box will appear. The Text Style dialog box is used to create, define, and modify text styles, as discussed in Chapter 14. The text style should be architectural and can be used for dimension text as well as dimension leader text and any other text on the drawing. The names of the text styles are stored in the DIMTXSTY (dimension text style) system variable. To work with a different text style, pick the style from the Text Style drop-down list or enter DIMTXSTY at the command line and enter the name of the text style to be used.

- **TEXT COLOR:**   (drop-down menu). This area will help you assign a color to dimension text. The color options inside the drop-down menu are similar to dimension and extension line color drop-down menus. You can also enter the color number at the command line when the DIMCLRT (dimension text color) variable is used.

- **TEXT HEIGHT:**   (drop-down menu). This area will help you assign a specific height for the dimension text. A dimension text height of 1/8″ (when plotted) is recommended for typical architectural dimensioning purposes. If a fixed text height is assigned (a height greater than zero) when establishing dimension text style using the Text Style dialog box, that specific text height will override the text height set inside the Text Height drop-down menu. If you want to control the text height inside the Text Height drop-down menu on the Text tab, make sure the text height inside the Text Style dialog box is set to 0″. When you change the text height to 0″ inside the Text Height drop-down menu (not inside the Text Style dialog box), AutoCAD will set the dimension text height to the lowest denominator of the Drawing Units Precision value. For example, if the precision is 0′-0 1/16″, then the 0″ inside the Text Height drop-down value menu will be automatically set to 1/16″. This means that you can never have a text height of 0″ when you use this drop-down menu inside the New, Modify, and Override Dimension Style dialog boxes. AutoCAD stores the dimension text height values in the DIMTXT (dimension text height) dimensioning variable where you can enter the text height at the command line. When the Height value inside the Text Style dialog box is higher than 0″, the DIMTXT dimensioning variable will not have any effect on the dimension text even though it will change the values in the Text Height drop-down value menu.

Tips: To control the dimension text height and text height for all other text, set the Text height inside the Text Style dialog box to 0″. The Text Height drop-down menu also controls the text height for the leader lines drawn immediately after the Text Height value selected, but the next time the Text Height is changed it will not automatically update them, even with the DIM and UP commands. This is because the leader text is not a part of the dimension text component. The height for consecutive leader text is not controlled by the dimension text height but is controlled by the Properties window. Figure 18–18 shows three types of dimension text applications: the first is a dimension text for a square object, the second is a dimension text called annotation for a dimension leader, and the third is a dimension text for the diameter of a circle.

- **FRACTION HEIGHT SCALE:**   (drop-down menu). This area will help you establish the scale of dimension fractions relative to the dimension text. For this option to work you need to have two prerequisites: 1. You need to have AutoCAD measure dimensions that have fractions by establishing the Primary Units precision set to at least 1/2″ or higher increment in the Primary Units tab; 2. You need to have AutoCAD use a Diagonal or Horizontal Fraction format using the Fraction format drop-down list. Figure 18–19 shows three dimensions with three different fraction formats. If the Not Stacked option is selected, the Fraction height scale will not work. If a dimension has no fraction, the Fraction height scale will have no

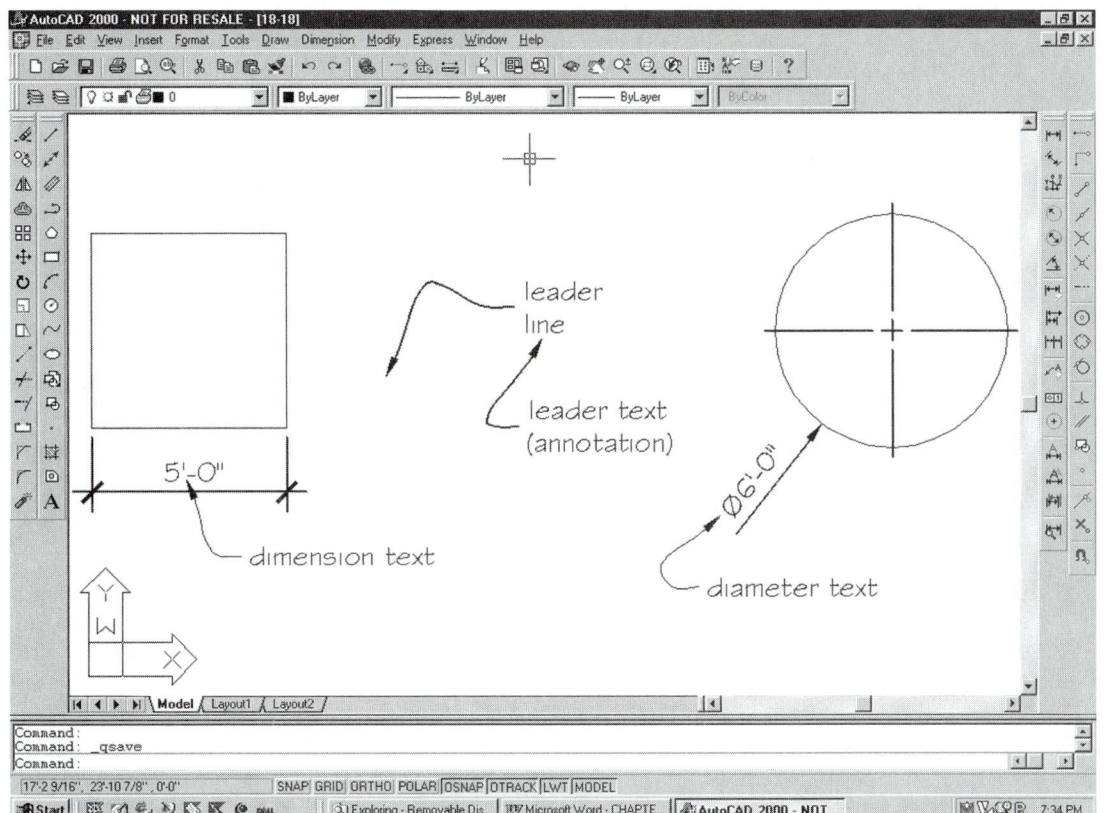

FIGURE 18–18 Three types of dimension text applications. The dimension text height is set to 1/8″ for all three applications. When the text height is changed to a different value, the leader line text height will not change.

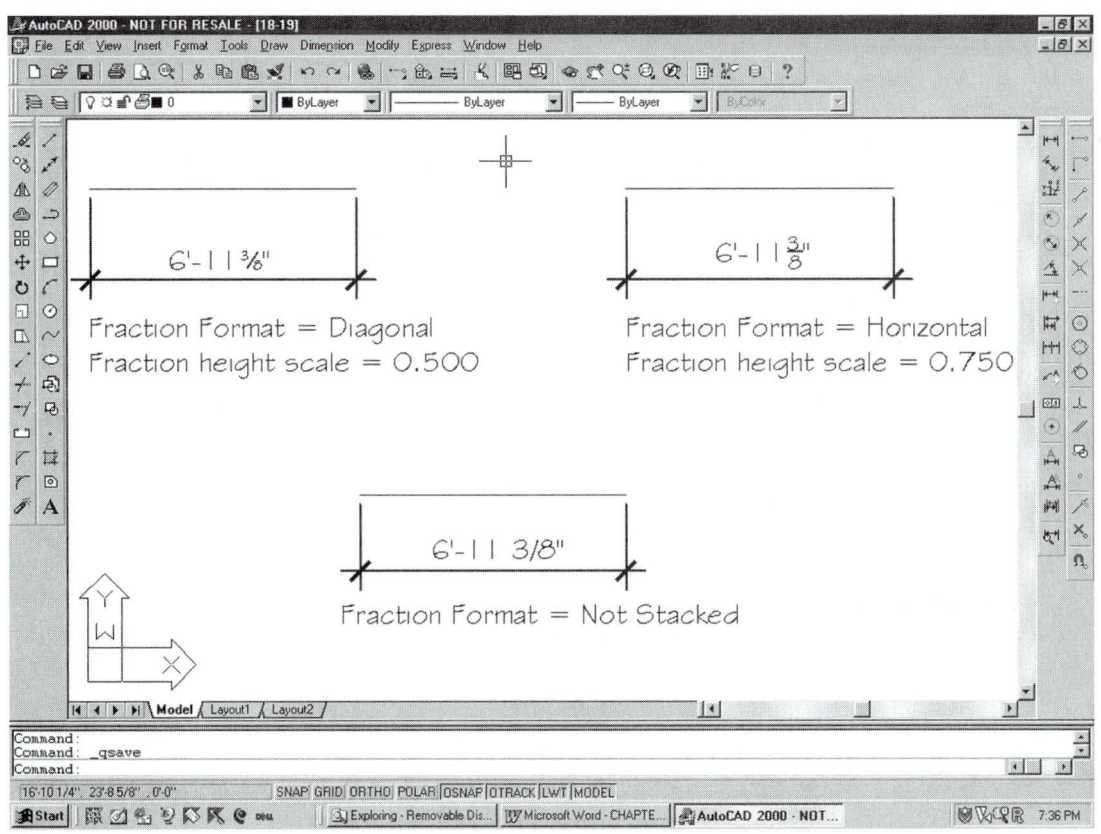

FIGURE 18–19 The Fraction height scale area controls the fraction text height in relationship to the dimension text height.

bearing on the dimension. The Fraction height scale is controlled by the DIMTFAC (fraction and tolerance text height scaling factor) dimensioning variable at the command line. The default value for DIMTFAC is 1, meaning that the fraction text height is equal to the dimension text height. For the proper scaling of the fractions in relation to the dimension text, change the value of DIMTFAC to 0.5 or 0.75 at the command line.

- **DRAW FRAME AROUND TEXT:**   (check box). This area will allow you to draw a frame around the dimension text. The frame is a rectangular object drawn around the dimension text that becomes an integral part of the dimensioning component. This means that if the frame around text is erased, the dimension text, dimension line, extension lines, and the tick marks will be erased also. The size and the distance of the frame from the dimension line and the placement of the dimension text inside the frame are controlled by three factors: 1. The value inside the Offset from dim line drop-down menu (discussed under Text Placement); 2. The value inside the Text height drop-down menu; 3. The dimension numbers that make up the dimension text. To better understand the relationship between these variables, let's identify the Offset from dim line variable factor as X, the Text height variable factor as Y, and the dimension numbers that make up the dimension text factor as Z. Figure 18–20 shows a typical dimension text with the frame around it. The text, the frame, and the dimension line have seven major distances identified by the three factors. The distances A, C, D, E, and G are equal to factor X, the distance B is equal to factor Y, and the distance F is equal to factor Z. When the dimension text is placed in the center of the dimension line, the frame simply drops down and the dimension line starts from the midpoint of the frame. When the Draw frame around text check box is checked, the offset from dim line drop-down menu will have negative values.

Text Placement: This area will help you control the placement of dimension text in relationship to the text alignment discussed in the beginning of the chapter. Let's first set AutoCAD so

FIGURE 18–20 The relationship between dimension text, dimension line, and the frame around text.

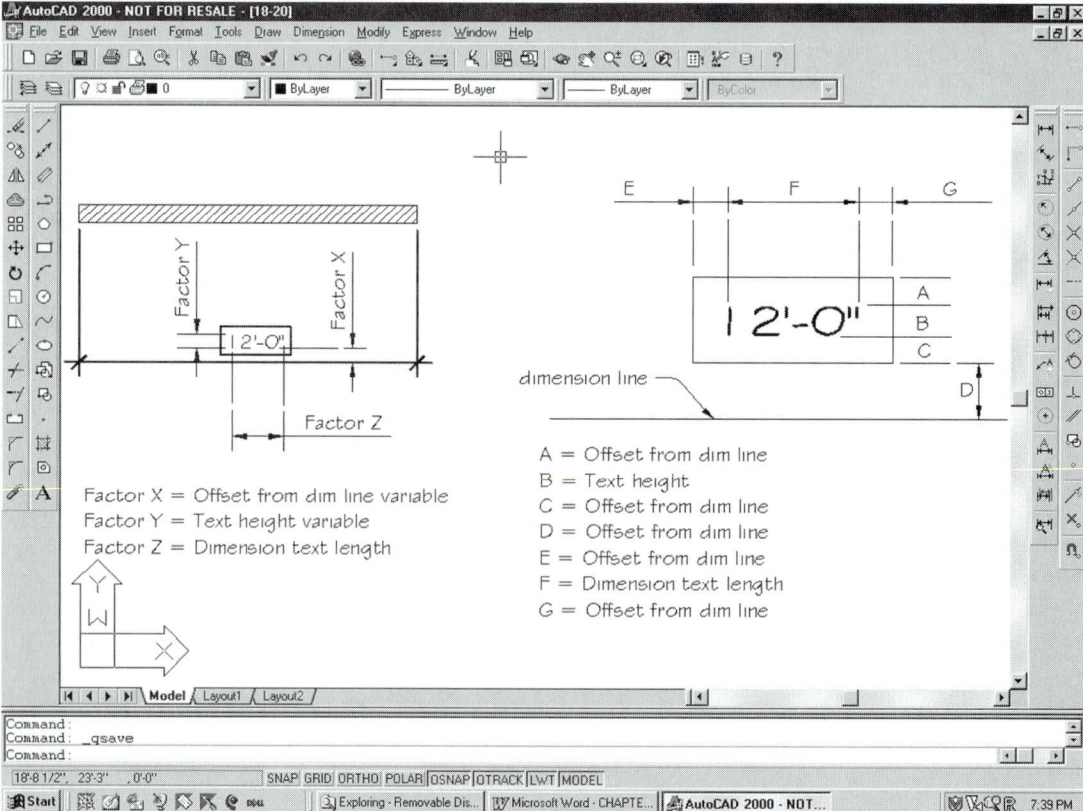

that the dimensions are arranged in a specific orientation, called *aligned,* and then discuss the effects of text placement on that text alignment. To align the text with dimension lines, go to the Text Alignment section (next to Text Placement) and click inside the Align with dimension line radio button. You will notice inside the image display window that the dimension text is aligned with the dimension lines. With this alignment, let's move on to the Text Placement options:

Inside the Text Placement category of the Text tab there are four variables affecting the placement of the dimension text:

- **VERTICAL:** (drop-down menu). This area will help you control the vertical positioning of the dimension text along the dimension line. Inside the Vertical drop-down menu, there are four different Vertical position options (when the text alignment is set to Align with dimension line) as follows:

- **CENTERED:** This option will center the dimension text between the extension lines. The dimension text is centered in a gap provided in the dimension line. When AutoCAD positions the text inside the extension lines, it calculates to see if there is enough space to fit the dimension text and at least a space equal to the Offset from dim line value on both sides. AutoCAD uses the value of the Offset from dim line on both sides plus the length of the dimension text as the minimum length required for the dimension text to be placed inside the extension lines. If there is enough space between the extension lines equal to the Offset from dim line value on both sides plus the dimension text, AutoCAD will place only the dimension text inside the extension lines by breaking the dimension line at the extension lines. AutoCAD will simply remove the dimension line, place the dimension text, and keep the tick marks and dimension line extensions. AutoCAD will automatically provide the gap so that the text can be centered between the extension lines. When the dimension text is centered in the dimension line, the gap between the dimension text and the dimension line on both sides is controlled by the Offset from dim line option, which also controls the Draw frame around text option. The DIMTAD (vertical position of dimension text) dimensioning variable controls the vertical position of dimension text in relation to the dimension line. When the DIMTAD is set to 0 (zero) at the command line, the dimension text is centered in the dimension line vertically. This will change the Vertical Text Placement from Above to Centered inside the Override Current Style dialog box. Also with DIMTAD set to 0 (zero) the <style overrides> will appear under the ARCHITECTURAL dimension style. This is AutoCAD's way to remind you that a dimension override has occurred. If you click on the Modify. . . button while the <style overrides> is highlighted and change the Vertical Text Placement back to Above setting, the <style overrides> will disappear. This is AutoCAD's way to remind you that the dimensioning variable you set at the command line is undone.

- **ABOVE:** This option will place the dimension text above the dimension line in all locations when the text placement is aligned with dimension line. This is the option used in the architectural, interior design, and building construction professions. The distance from the dimension line to the bottom of the text is controlled by the Offset from dim line drop-down menu. When the DIMTAD dimensioning variable is set to 1, the dimension text will be placed above the dimension line, except when the dimension line is not horizontal and the DIMTIH (text inside align) dimensioning variable is turned on. The DIMTIH dimensioning variable is discussed under the Text Alignment section.

- **OUTSIDE:** This option will place the dimension text on the outside of the dimension line farthest from the first and second extension line origins. In the dimensioning example shown in Figure 18–21, the Vertical area is set to Outside, the Horizontal area is set to Centered, and the Aligned with dim line selection button is picked. With these settings the dimensions labeled as "A" are placed on top of the dimension lines because this is the farthest point away from the object surface that is used to pick dimension points. On the other hand, the dimensions labeled as "B" are placed on the bottom of the dimension lines because this is the farthest point from the object surface that is used to pick dimension points. The distance between the dimension line and the baseline of the dimension text (dimension A) and the distance between the dimension line and the upper line of the dimension text (dimension B) is controlled by the Offset from dim line drop-down menu.

FIGURE 18–21 The Outside option will place the dimension text on the outside of the dimension line farthest away from the *defpoints*.

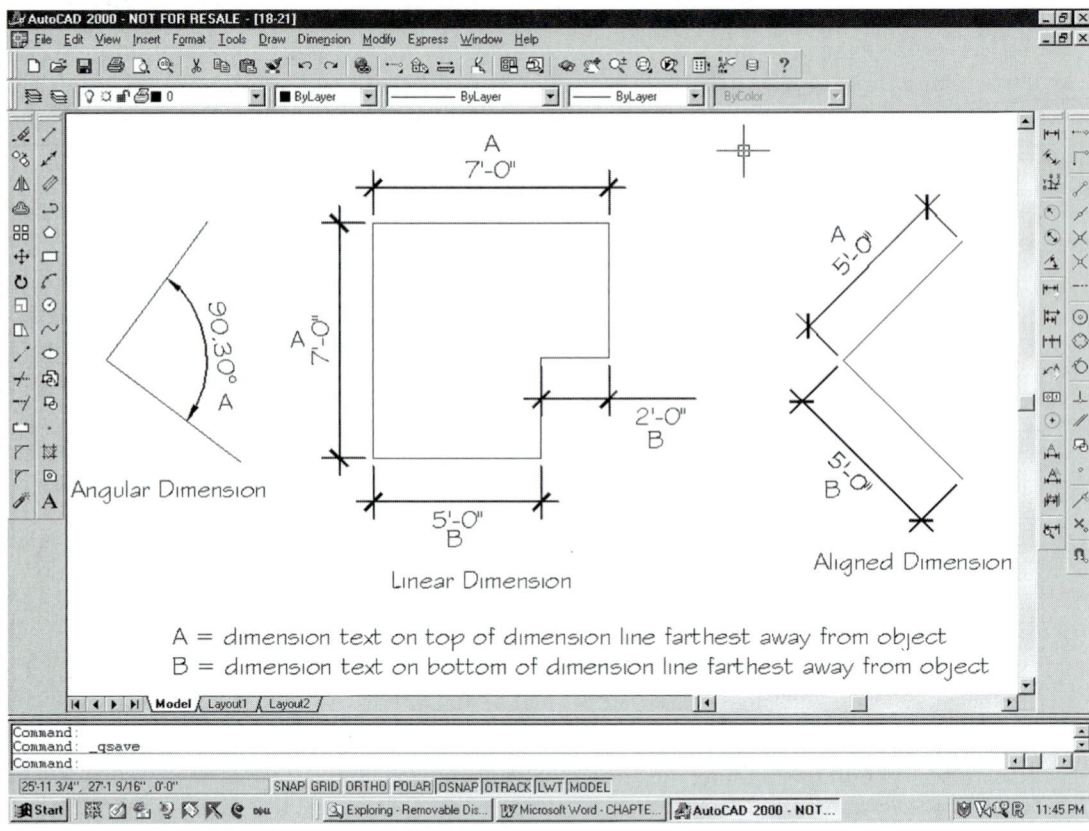

When the DIMTAD dimensioning variable is set to 2, the dimension text will be placed on the outside of the dimension line.

JIS: This option will allow you to perform dimensioning for the *Japanese Industrial Standards.* (JIS). When the DIMTAD dimensioning variable is set to 3, the dimensions will conform to JIS.

Horizontal: (drop-down menu) This area will help you control the horizontal positioning of the dimension text along the dimension line. Inside the Horizontal drop-down menu, there are five different Horizontal position options (when the Text Alignment is set to Align with dimension line) as follows:

- **CENTERED:** This option will center the dimension text horizontally along the dimension line. When the Horizontal Text Placement is set to Centered and the Vertical Text Placement is set to Above, the dimensions will conform to architectural dimensioning standards. The DIMJUST (horizontal position of dimension text) dimensioning variable controls the horizontal position of dimension text in relation to the dimension line at the command line. When the DIMJUST value is 0 (zero), the dimension text is centered in the dimension line horizontally.

- **AT EXT LINE 1:** This option will place the dimension text next to the first extension line origin as horizontally justified. When this option is picked, AutoCAD will simply move the dimension text horizontally and locate it next to the first extension line origin. Figure 18–22 shows an object dimensioned when the Horizontal Text Placement is At Ext Line 1 and the Vertical Text Placement is set to Above. Point 1 indicates the first extension line origin, and point 2 indicates the second extension line origin for the corresponding dimension. The distance between the extension line and the dimension text is equal to twice the arrowhead size plus the value inside the Offset from dim line drop-down menu. For example, if the arrowhead size (tick marks) is set to 1/8″ and the Offset from dim line is set to 1/8″, then the distance between the extension line and the dimension text is equal to 3/8″ as shown in Figure 18–23. When DIMJUST value is 1, the dimension text is placed next to first extension line.

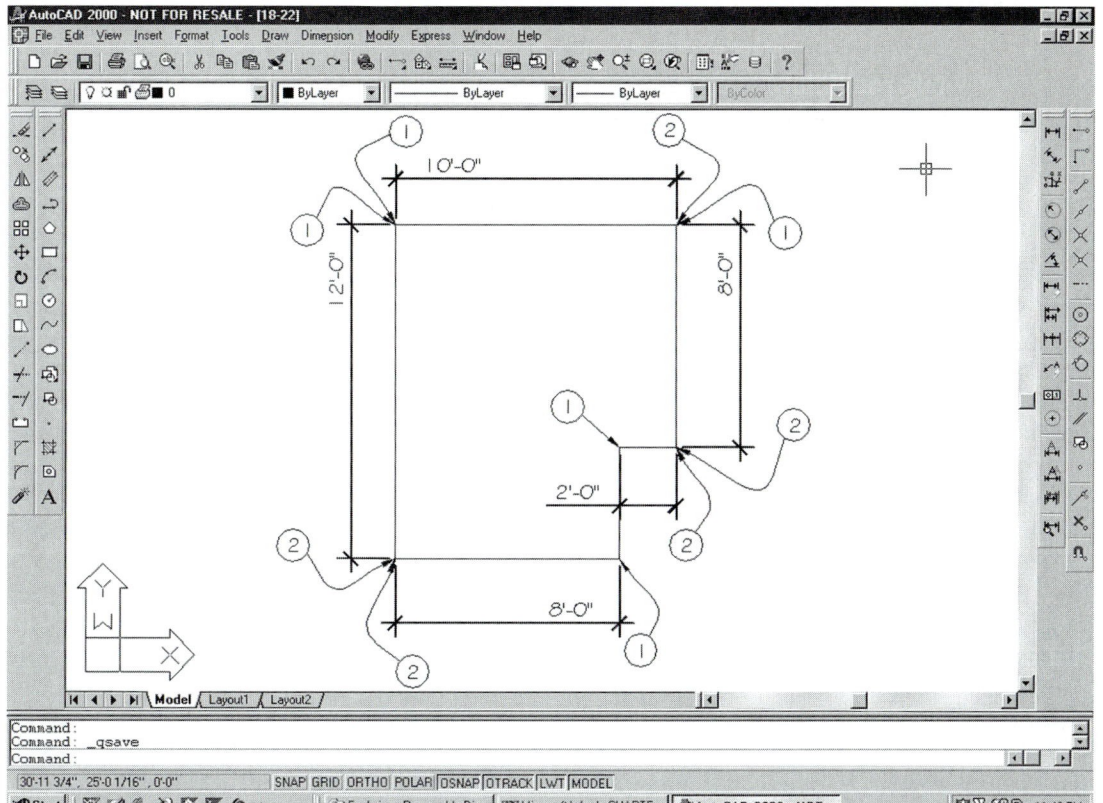

FIGURE 18–22
Example of an object dimensioned when Horizontal Text Placement is set at the first extension line and the Vertical Text Placement is set at Above.

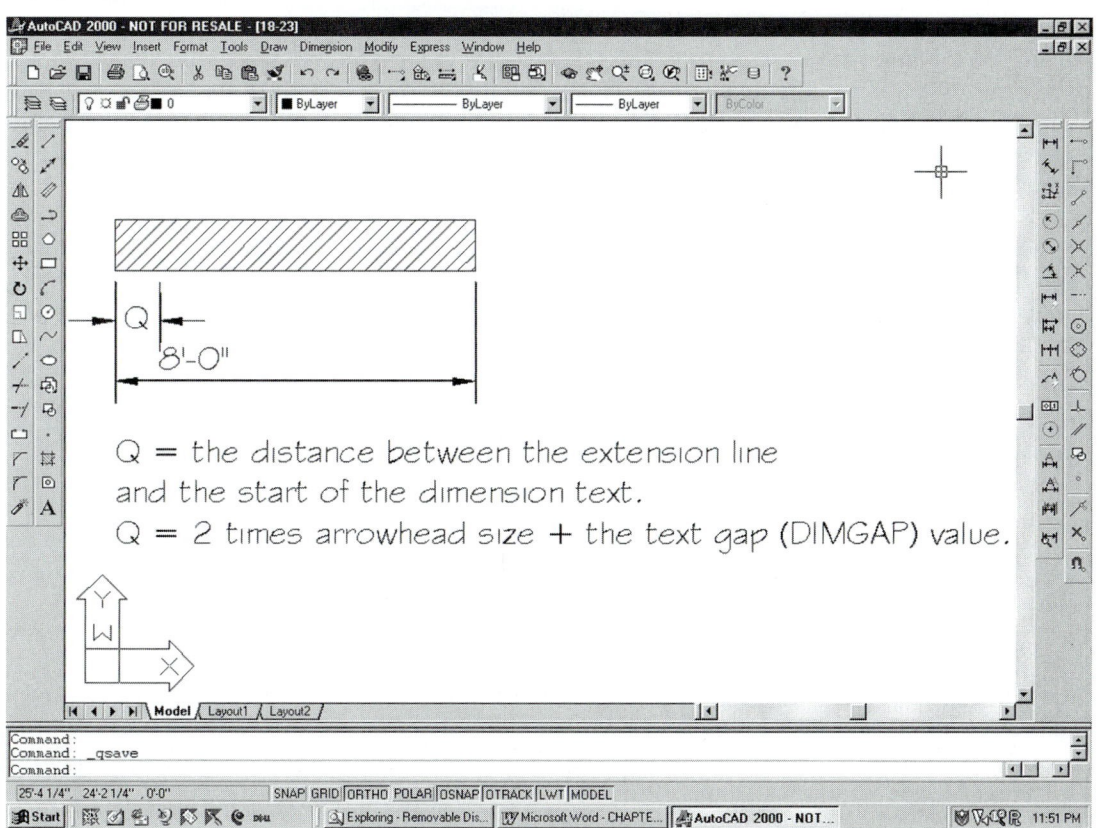

FIGURE 18–23   A close-up of a dimension with the distance between the extension line and the dimension text as "Q" when there is enough space to place the dimension text between extension lines. Q = 2 × (DIMGAP + DIMASZ). In this example DIMGAP = 1/8″, DIMASZ = 1/8″. Q = 2 × 1/8″ + 1/8″ = 3/8″. See DIMGAP dimensioning variable below.

- **AT EXT LINE 2:**   This option will place the dimension text next to the second extension line origin. When the DIMJUST value is 2, the dimension text is placed next to the second extension line origin.

- **OVER EXT LINE 1:**   This option will place the dimension text over or along the first extension line origin. When the DIMJUST value is 3, the dimension text is placed over the first extension line.

- **OVER EXT LINE 2:**   This option will place the dimension text over or along the second extension line origin. When the DIMJUST value is 4, the dimension text is placed over the second extension line.

Offset From Dim Line: (drop-down menu)   This area will help you control the size of the gap between the dimension line and the dimension text. When the Vertical Text Placement is set to above, the Offset from dim line option will control the distance between the dimension line and the baseline of the dimension text. For a floor plan with a 1/4″ = 1′-0″ drawing scale, the recommended value for Offset from dim line is 1/16″ and should not be more than 1/8″ as this will provide too much of a gap and pull the dimension text away from the dimension line. Never set this value to 0″ because this will place the dimension text directly on top of the dimension line unless it is called for. The Offset from dim line value will also set the gap between the annotation (leader line text) and the hook line created with the LEADER command or with the Quick Leader button in the Dimension toolbar. These are discussed later in the chapter. When the Offset from dim line value is increased, some of the dimensions that fit inside the extension lines will be placed outside the extension lines. When a dimension text is placed outside because there is not enough space inside, AutoCAD will extend the dimension line and place the text above and along the dimension line when the Vertical Text Placement is set to Above. When the Vertical Text Placement is set to Centered, AutoCAD will break the dimension line outside and center the dimension text on the open side of the dimension line. The DIMGAP (gap from dimension line to text) dimensioning variable will control the Offset from dim line option at the command line. The default value for DIMGAP is 3/32″. When the DIMGAP value is negative, AutoCAD will draw frame around text.

The DIMTAD dimensioning variable controls the vertical position of dimension text above the dimension line when it is set to 1. The DIMGAP dimensioning variable controls the actual gap between the dimension text and the dimension line, while the DIMTVP (text vertical position) dimensioning variable controls the vertical position of the dimension text above or below the dimension line when the DIMTAD is off. For the DIMTVP to work DIMTAD must be turned off. When DIMTAD is set to 0 at the command line, the Vertical Text Placement will show Centered inside the Override Current Style dialog box. Setting DIMTVP to 1 is equal to setting DIMTAD on. Figure 18–24 shows eight of the same dimensions with different DIMTVP settings. To place the dimension text below the dimension line, use a negative DIMTVP value. You can use a DIMTVP value higher than 1 to place the dimension text above the dimension line. DIMTVP settings will not work when DIMTAD is on (DIMTVP = 1).

> *Note: AutoCAD uses the DIMGAP value when calculating the minimum length required for the components of the dimension line as described under Vertical Text Placement except when the dimension text is located over extension lines. If the Offset from dim line value is increased, the gap between the dimension line and the dimension text also increases. If there is not enough room inside the dimension length to accommodate the new DIMGAP value with the dimension line and the dimension text, AutoCAD will place the dimension text on the side of the dimension line. The dimension text will be moved inside only if there is room for tick marks (arrowheads), dimension text, and a space between them at least as large as the DIMGAP value.*

Text Alignment: This area will help you control the horizontal or aligned orientation of the dimension text discussed previously under Architectural Dimensioning Arrangements.

Inside the Text Alignment category of the Text tab there are three variables affecting the alignment of the text with the dimension lines:

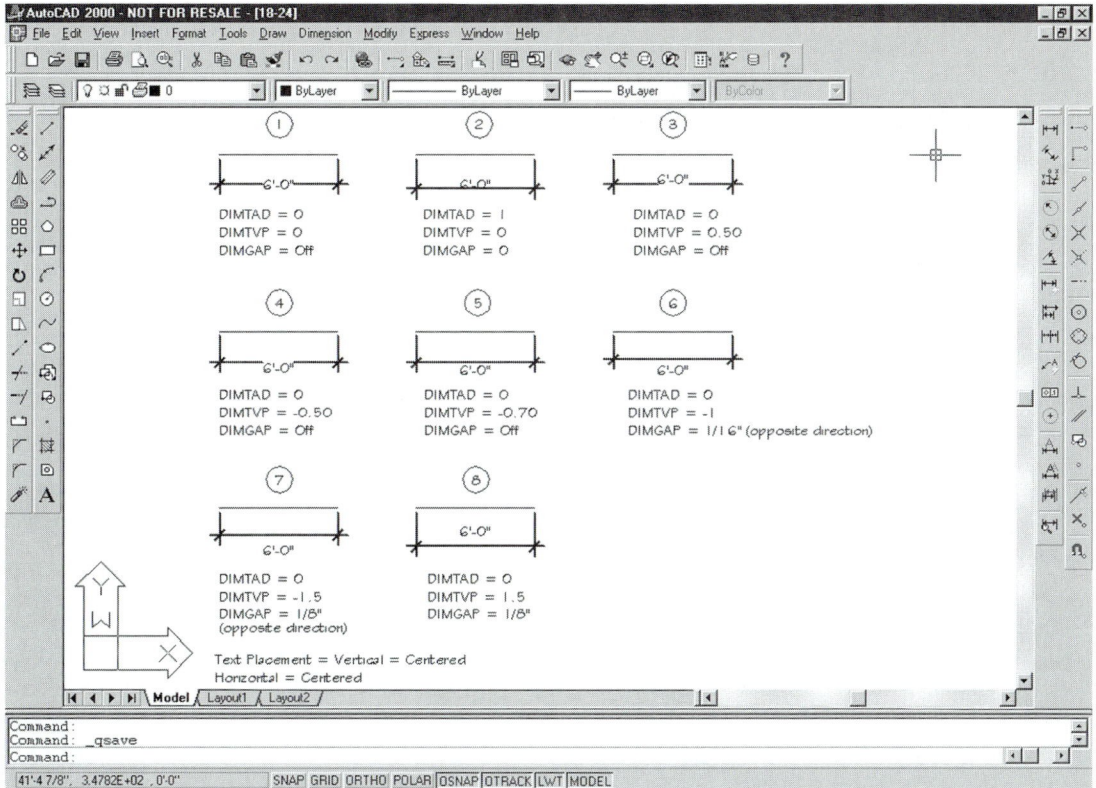

- **HORIZONTAL:** (radio button). This option will arrange dimensions in a *unidirectional* orientation where all the dimension text will be placed horizontally on the drawing. This option is used commonly on mechanical drawings.

- **ALIGNED WITH DIMENSION LINE:** (radio button). This option will align the dimension text with the dimension line. When using the Linear, Aligned, and Angular dimensioning applications, dimension text will be placed parallel to the dimensioned surface. This option is used for architectural *aligned* dimensioning. The DIMTIH (text inside align) and the DIMTOH (text outside align) dimensioning variables can be entered at the command line to control text alignment. DIMTIH controls the position of the dimension text inside the extension lines for all dimensioning applications except Ordinate dimensioning application. When DIMTIH is on (default), AutoCAD will align dimension text horizontally as in the case of mechanical drawings. When DIMTIH is off, AutoCAD will align dimension text with the dimension line. DIMTOH controls the position of the dimension text outside the extension lines. When DIMTOH is on (default), AutoCAD will place the dimension text horizontally outside the extension lines. When DIMTOH is off, AutoCAD will align the dimension text with the dimension line outside the extension lines. To have the dimension text align with the dimension lines at the command line, DIMTIH and DIMTOH must be turned off.

- **ISO STANDARD:** (radio button). ISO stands for International Standardization Organization. This organization is dedicated to establishing global standards in drafting. The ISO option will align the dimension text with the dimension line when the dimension text is inside the extension lines (similar to architectural dimensioning). But ISO will align the dimension text horizontally when the dimension text is outside the extension lines (similar to mechanical dimensioning but can be used for architectural).

Fit: (tab)   This tab has four separate categories relating to the placement of the dimension text, tick marks, arrowheads, leader lines, and the dimension lines and a dimension style image display window similar to other tabs. The categories are *Fit Options, Text Placement,*

FIGURE 18–25 The Fit tab of the Modify Dimension Style dialog box controls how dimension text, tick marks, arrowheads, leader lines, and the dimension lines are placed on the drawing.

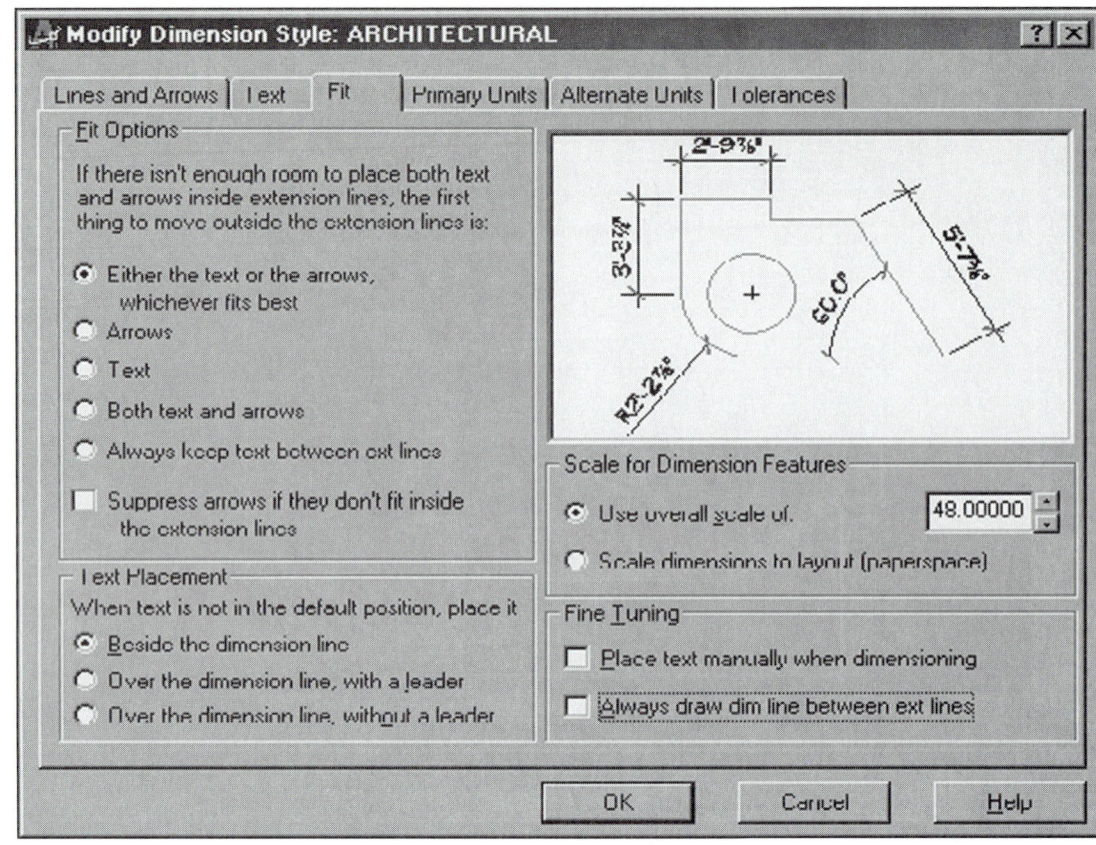

Scale for Dimension Features, and *Fine Tuning.* The Fit tab is shown in Figure 18–25. The following will explain each category and how the adjustments will work with different settings:

Fit Options: This area controls the placement of dimension text and tick marks inside or outside the extension lines, depending on the available space between the extension line origins. When there is enough space between the first and second extension line origin, AutoCAD will place dimension text and arrowheads between the extension lines unless Horizontal Text Placement is set to Over Ext Line 1 or 2. When there is not enough space, dimension text and arrowheads will be placed according to the Fit Options.

Inside the Fit Options category there are six variables affecting the placement of dimension text and tick marks and arrowheads. These six variables are used as possible choices when responding to the following statement inside the Fit Options category:

If there isn't enough room to place both text and arrows inside extension lines, the first thing to move outside the extension lines is. . .

- **EITHER THE TEXT OR THE ARROWS, WHICHEVER FITS BEST:**   (radio button). When this radio button is checked AutoCAD will place the dimension text and arrowheads as follows:

1. When there is enough space, the dimension text and the tick marks and arrowheads will be placed between the extension lines.

2. When there is enough space for tick marks and arrowheads only, it will be placed between the extension lines and the dimension text will be placed outside the extension lines. Some examples are shown in Figure 18–26.

3. When there is not enough space for the dimension text and the tick marks, both will be placed outside the extension lines.

The DIMATFIT (fit arrowheads and text) dimensioning variable will determine how dimension text and tick marks are arranged when there is not enough space to fit them both be-

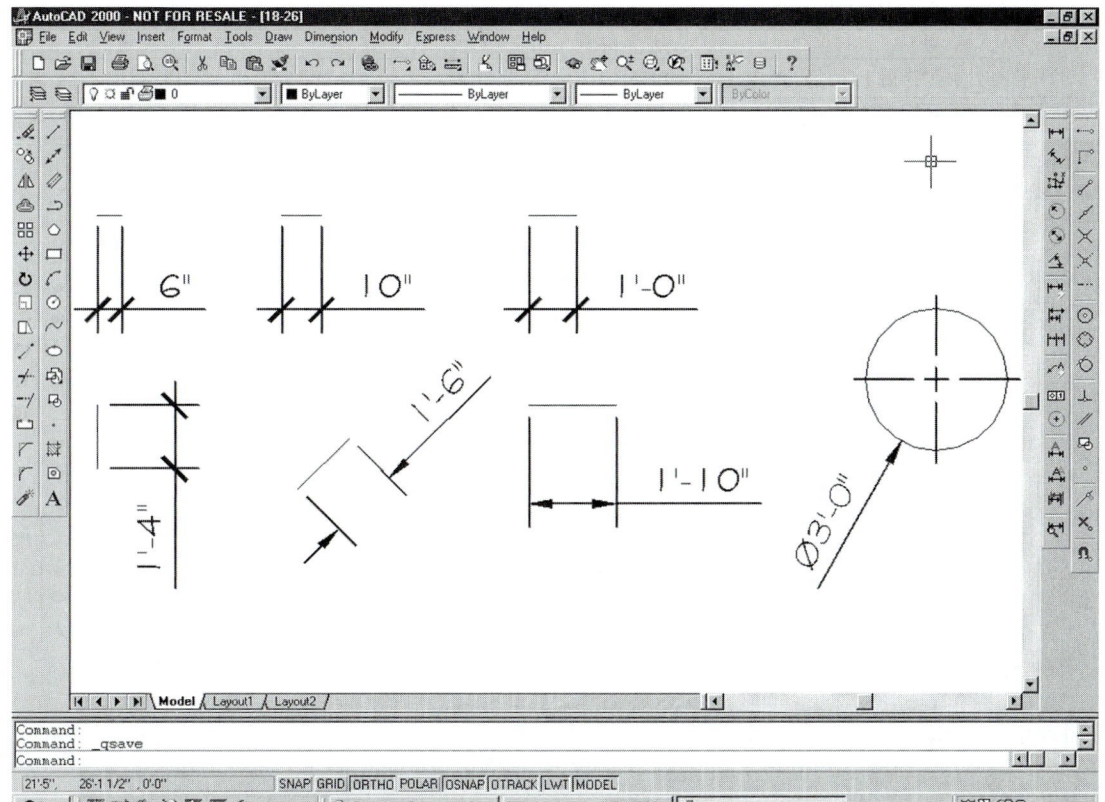

FIGURE 18–26 When there is enough space for tick marks and arrowheads only, AutoCAD will place the dimension text outside and place the tick marks and arrowheads inside the extension lines.

tween the extension lines at the command line. When DIMATFIT is set to 3, the Either the text or the arrows, whichever fits best option is used.

- **ARROWS:** (radio button). When this radio button is checked, AutoCAD will place the tick marks and arrowheads as follows:

1. When there is enough space for dimension text and tick marks and arrowheads, they will be placed between the extension lines.

2. When there is enough space for tick marks and arrowheads only, they will be placed between the extension lines, and the dimension text will be placed outside the extension lines as shown in Figure 18–26.

3. When there is not enough space for the tick marks and arrowheads, the dimension text and the tick marks and arrowheads will be placed outside the extension lines.

When DIMATFIT is set to 1 at the command line, Arrows option is used.

- **TEXT:** (radio button). When this radio button is checked, AutoCAD will place the dimension text and tick marks and arrowheads as follows:

1. When there is enough space, the dimension text and the tick marks and arrowheads will be placed between the extension lines.

2. When there is not enough space for dimension text, both text and tick marks and arrowheads will be placed outside the extension lines.

When DIMATFIT is set to 2 at the command line, Text option is used.

- **BOTH TEXT AND ARROWS:** (radio button). When this radio button is checked, AutoCAD will place the dimension text and the tick marks and arrowheads outside the extension lines when there is not enough space to place them both between the extension lines. When DIMATFIT is set to 0 at the command line, the both text and arrows option is used.

- **ALWAYS KEEP TEXT BETWEEN EXT LINES:** (radio button). When this radio button is checked, AutoCAD will force the dimension text between the extension lines. This may not always produce desirable effects but could be used for dimensioning interior partition walls. Dimension text can be moved outside the extension lines with or without a leader using editing techniques discussed later in the chapter. This option is controlled by the DIMTIX (place text inside extensions) dimensioning variable at the command line. When DIMTIX is off, the Either the text or the arrows, whichever fits best option will be used, so the dimension text will be placed inside the extension lines if there is enough room. For Radius and Diameter dimensions that do not fit inside the circle or arc, DIMTIX has no effect because AutoCAD will always place the text outside the circle or arc. When there is enough room inside a circle or arc to place the radius or diameter dimension text, turning DIMTIX off will place the dimension text inside the circle or arc. When DIMTIX is on, the dimension text will be forced between the extension lines even if AutoCAD normally will place the dimension text outside the extension lines.

- **SUPPRESS ARROWS IF THEY DON'T FIT INSIDE EXTENSION LINES:** (check box). When this box is checked, AutoCAD will suppress tick marks and arrowheads if there is not enough space between the extension lines. When the dimension text is forced inside the extension lines, the tick marks and arrowheads are placed on the outside of the extension lines. Checking this option will not display the tick marks and arrowheads. The DIMSOXD (suppress outside extension dimensions) dimensioning variable will suppress dimension lines.

Text Placement: This area will justify the dimension text when it is not in its default position.

Inside the Text Placement category of the Fit tab there are three variables affecting the placement of dimension text when it is not in the default position. These three variables are used as possible choices when responding to the following statement inside the text placement category:

When text is not in the default position, place it. . .

- **BESIDE THE DIMENSION LINE:** (radio button). When this radio button is checked, AutoCAD will place the dimension text beside the dimension line. The DIMTMOVE (dimension text movement) dimensioning variable controls the movement options under Text Placement category at the command line. When DIMTMOVE is set to 0, the dimension text will be placed beside the dimension line.

- **OVER THE DIMENSION LINE, WITH A LEADER:** (radio button). When this radio button is checked, AutoCAD will move the dimension text away from the dimension line and create a leader connecting the dimension text to the dimension line. When DIMTMOVE dimensioning variable is set to 1, a leader is added and the dimension text is moved away from the dimension line.

- **OVER THE DIMENSION LINE, WITHOUT A LEADER:** (radio button). When this radio button is checked, AutoCAD will move the dimension text away from the dimension line while keeping the dimension line in the same place. This option is useful especially in dimensioning tight places. When the DIMTMOVE dimensioning variable is set to 2, the dimension text is moved without a leader being created.

Scale for Dimension Features: This area will allow you to set the scale factor for all the dimensioning variables for the entire drawing or establish paper space scaling.

Inside the Scale for dimension features category of the Fit tab there are two variables affecting the scale for all dimensioning variables for the current dimension style and the scaling between paper space and model space:

- **USE OVERALL SCALE OF:** (radio button and menu). This area will allow you to enter the scale factor for the drawing scale. The scale factor is calculated based on the final plot scale. When a scale factor is entered, AutoCAD will set the scale for all dimensioning variables that specify distance, size, and spacing including the dimension text height and tick marks and arrowhead sizes. The scale factor for dimensioning applications is referred to as the *overall scale factor.* For a final plot scale of 1/4″ = 1′-0″ enter 48 inside this box. The DIMSCALE (overall scale factor) dimensioning variable is entered at the command line to change the scale factor for dimensions.

Tips: The Overall Scale Factor (DIMSCALE) should be set to the scale factor of the drawing first. This will display all the dimensioning variable values at their proper scale inside the image display windows of each tab of the New, Modify, and Override Dimension Style dialog boxes.

- **SCALE DIMENSIONS TO LAYOUT (PAPER SPACE):** (radio button). When you compose your drawings in Layouts (paper space), the objects and their dimensions are in Model (model space). When you draw and dimension in Model, you establish drawing units and drawing limits based on the drawing scale and the size of the final plot of your drawing. The dimensions you create in Model are based on the objects you create in Model. If the scale factor of your drawing is 48 (1/4″ = 1′-0″ drawing scale), then the overall scale of dimension features will also be 48. If the overall scale of dimension features is not the same as the scale factor of your drawing, dimensioning settings will not be plotted to scale. Generally speaking, there is no need to create dimensions in Layout (paper space). Layouts are used primarily to establish the final composition of the drawing and the set-up for plotting. Paper Space and Layouts are discussed in Chapter 22. You can create dimensions in Layouts and in Model. If you create objects in Model, you should dimension them in Model because AutoCAD places dimension definition points in the space where the object geometry is drawn. It is much easier to create, manage, and edit dimensions in the space where the objects are created. However, you can create dimension in Model for objects created in Layouts and create dimension in Layouts for objects created in Model. When you pick this radio button the DIMSCALE will read as <0′-0″> at the command line and the *Use overall scale of* radio button and drop-down menu will be disabled. If you dimension in Layouts, you need to set the scale factor inside the Measurement Scale category in the Primary Units tab to equal the value inside the Use overall scale of the Scale for Dimension Features category in the Fit tab.

Note: The Scale factor inside the Measurement Scale category in the Primary Units tab is controlled by the DIMLFAC (length scale) dimensioning variable. When a value is entered for the scale factor, AutoCAD will multiply the distances measured in Layouts for dimensioning by the value set for the scale factor. When the scale factor for the Layout (DIMLFAC) matches the scale factor (Use overall scale of) for the Model (DIMSCALE), you can create dimensions in both environments. AutoCAD will calculate the scale factor value for the Layout automatically if you use the DIMLFAC variable from the DIM command prompt and select the Viewport option. To accomplish this, you must enter DIM at the command line, then enter DIMLFAC and select the Viewport option, and then select the viewport you want to assign a scale factor in Layout. AutoCAD will automatically calculate the Scale factor value for the Layout and assign the negative of this value to DIMLFAC. The dimensions created in Layouts will not display in Model, but the dimensions created in Model and Model space viewports will be displayed in Layouts. The DIMLFAC scaling method does not work for ordinate dimensions.

Fine Tuning: This area will help you control additional settings that will fine-tune the dimensioning placement.

Inside the Fine Tuning category of the Fit tab there are two variables affecting the fine tuning:

- **PLACE TEXT MANUALLY WHEN DIMENSIONING:** (check box). Checking this option will ignore any Horizontal Text Placement settings under the Text Placement category and will allow the user to define the location of the dimension text. This option is extremely useful in hard-to-control places where maximum placement flexibility is needed. The DIMUPT (user-positioned text) dimensioning variable controls the manual placement of the dimension text and dimension line at the command line. When DIMUPT is off, the cursor controls only the dimension line location. When DIMUPT is on, the cursor controls both the text position and the dimension line location.

- **ALWAYS DRAW DIM LINE BETWEEN EXT LINES: (CHECK BOX).** Checking this option will draw dimension lines between the extension line origins even when AutoCAD will otherwise place the tick marks outside. When there is not enough space to fit the dimension line inside the extension lines, this option can be used to force the dimension line between the extension lines. The DIMTOFL (force line inside extension lines) dimensioning system variable controls this option at the command line. When DIMTOFL is off, no dimension lines will be drawn inside the extension lines when the arrowheads are placed outside. When DIMTOFL is on, dimension lines will be drawn inside the extension lines.

Primary Units: (tab)   This tab has two separate categories relating to the format and precision of how distances are measured between two points that are defined by the first and second extension line origins. The Primary Units tab is shown in Figure 18–27. The categories are *Linear Dimensions* and *Angular Dimensions*. Under the Linear Dimensions category there are two subcategories: *Measurement Scale* and *Zero Suppression*. Under the Angular dimensions category there is one subcategory, Zero Suppression.

Linear Dimensions: This area will help you control the unit measurement of straight lines such as horizontal, vertical, or angled surfaces.

Inside the Linear Dimensions category there are seven variables and two subcategories, called Measurement Scale and Zero Suppression, affecting the format and precision for linear dimensions:

- **UNIT FORMAT:** (drop-down list). This area will help you establish how you want AutoCAD to measure distances using a specific unit format. This is where the unit for measuring distances is established. Inside the Unit Format drop-down list there are six options similar to the Drawing Units options. Windows Desktop will dimension objects using the decimal format units under Control Panel Settings of the operating system of the computer. To find this setting, click on the Start button located on the lower left corner of the desktop and click on the Settings area. Click on the Control Panel and find the Regional Settings icon and double click on it. Once inside the Regional Settings Properties dialog box, click on the Number tab. The DIMLUNIT (dimension linear units) dimensioning variable is used to select the Unit Format for all dimensioning types except Angular at the command line. The default value for DIMLUNIT is 2, which is set for decimal units.

FIGURE 18–27 The Primary Units tab of the Modify Dimension Style box.

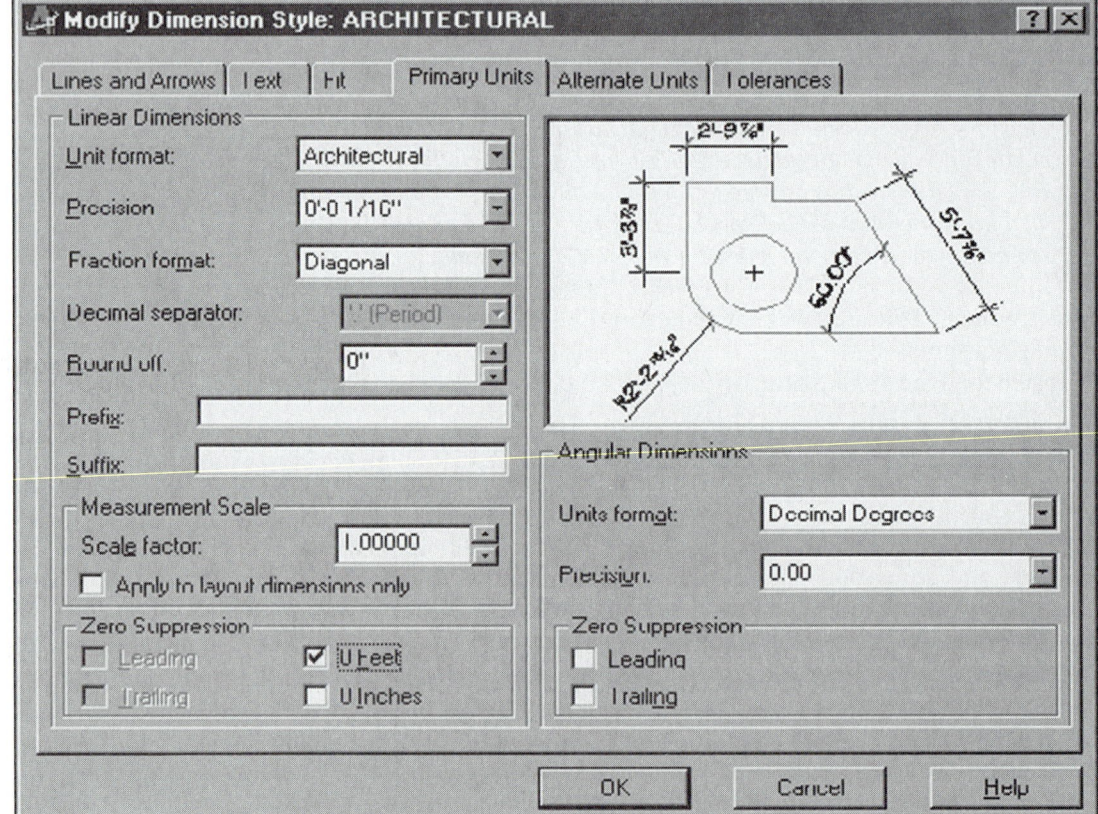

Precision	Line Drawn as 6'-2" Dim Text	Line Drawn as 9'-7 1/2" Dim Text	Line Drawn as 2'-5 5/8" Dim Text	Line Drawn as 15'-4 3/32" Dim Text
0'-0"	6'-2"	9'-8"	12'-6"	15'-4"
0'-0 1/2"	6'-2"	9'-7 1/2"	12'-5 1/2"	15'-4"
0'-0 1/4"	6'-2"	9'-7 1/2"	12'-5 3/4"	15'-4"
0'-0 1/8"	6'-2"	9'-7 1/2"	12'-5 5/8"	15'-4 1/8"
0'-0 1/16"	6'-2"	9'-7 1/2"	12'-5 5/8"	15'-4 1/8"
0'-0 1/32"	6'-2"	9'-7 1/2"	12'-5 5/8"	15'-4 3/32"
0'-0 1/64"	All Dimensions Will Be Displayed Same As Above			
0'-0 1/128"	All Dimensions Will Be Displayed Same As Above			
0'-0 1/256"	All Dimensions Will Be Displayed Same As Above			

TABLE 18–1:
Comparison of four dimension text with nine different precision settings.

- **PRECISION:** (drop-down list). This area will help you select the number of digits displayed after the decimal point when Decimal, Engineering, Scientific, and Windows Desktop units are used. The default value is 0.0000 (four digits), with a maximum of 0.00000000 (eight digits). For Architectural and Fractional units, the precision values relate to the smallest desired fractional denominator. The default value for Architectural precision is 0'-0 1/16" with a maximum precision value of 0'-0 1/256". The default value for Fractional precision is 0 1/16 with a maximum precision value of 0 1/256. For architectural dimensioning, a precision value of 0'-0" would mean no fractional values will be displayed. A precision value of 0'-0 1/16" would mean the lengths of objects are dimensioned at 1/16" fractional denominator, providing that the lengths of the objects are drawn at that precision. For example, a line drawn with a length of 15'-8 3/16" can be dimensioned and displayed as the dimension text using at least a precision of 0'-0 1/16" or higher because of the 1/16" increment. Table 18–1 shows how the dimension text will be displayed for four different line lengths when the lines are dimensioned with Architectural Unit Format and with different Precision settings under the Linear Dimensions category. The lines are drawn with the Drawing Units Type set to Architectural and the Drawing Units Precision value set to 0'-0 1/32". The same results would have been achieved even when the Drawing Units Precision is set to 0'-0".

As discussed previously, the Drawing Units Precision will affect the values inside the drop-down menus of the Dimension Style dialog boxes. It will not affect the length precision values when entered at the command line. For example, you could have the Drawing Units Precision set at 0'-0" and still draw a line with a length of 15'-4 3/32" as long as you enter the length as 15'4-3/32 at the command line. The settings under the Drawing Units Precision does not limit you to a certain precision, the only requirement is to have the Drawing Units Type correspond to Unit Format of the Linear Dimensions. The accuracy of your drawings is maintained regardless of coordinate display precision.

Tips: As long as you enter the correct precision values for the object lengths, the Drawing Units Precision does not have to be set to that precision. But you must select the corresponding Drawing Units Type for this to work. To avoid any misinterpretation or miscalculations, always match the Drawing Units Type and the Drawing Units Precision with the Unit Format and the Precision of the Linear Dimensions.

- **FRACTION FORMAT:** (drop-down list). This area will help you select a fraction format for the fractions of the dimensions by allowing the dimension fractions to be stacked horizontally, diagonally, or not stacked. Architectural drawings quite often include dimensions with fractions such as a dimension of 12'-6 5/8". The 5/8" part of the dimension text is called the fraction, with the number 5 the upper fraction and number 8 the lower fraction. The line between the upper and lower fraction numbers is called the fraction separator. Stacking will move the upper fraction slightly above the dimension text and the lower fraction slightly below the dimension text. The Fraction Format option controls the stacking of the fraction numbers and the geometry of the fraction separator. Under the Fraction Format area, there are three options. *Horizontal* will provide the stacking of the fraction numbers and a horizontal line as the fraction separator. *Diagonal* will provide the stacking of the fraction numbers and a diagonal line as the fraction separator. You may not always want the dimension fractions to be stacked. If this is the case, *Not Stacked* will leave the upper and the lower fraction numbers aligned with the dimension text. You can also control the height of the fraction numbers by using the Fraction height scale (DIMTFAC) drop-down menu under the Text tab as discussed previously. When the Fraction Format is set to *Not Stacked,* the Fraction Height Scale will have no effect. The Fraction Format option will only work when the Unit Format of the Linear Dimensions is set to Architectural or Fractional. It will not work with Scientific, Decimal, Engineering, or Windows Desktop units. The DIMFRAC (fraction format) dimensioning variable will control the Fraction Format at the command line. The default value for DIMFRAC is 0, which is the Horizontal Fraction Format. When DIMFRAC is set to 1, the Diagonal Fraction Format will be used. When DIMFRAC is set to 2, the Not Stacked Fraction Format will be used.

- **DECIMAL SEPARATOR:**   (drop-down list). This area will help you establish a single character separator for decimal format. There are three Decimal separator options: "." (period) will provide a period as a Decimal separator; "," (comma) will provide a comma as a Decimal separator; and " " (Space) will provide a space between the number and the decimal units for the dimension text. The Decimal separator will only work with dimensions using decimal format. The DIMDSEP (decimal separator) dimensioning variable will control the Decimal separator characters at the command line. The default for DIMDSEP is "." (period).

- **ROUND OFF:**   (drop-down menu). This area will help you set rounding guidelines for dimension text and is used for all dimensioning applications except Angular. The values inside the drop-down menu represent the settings for the Drawing Units Type and the Drawing Units Precision. For Decimal units, if you enter a value of 0.25, all dimension text will be rounded to the nearest 0.25 unit. For Architectural units, if you select a value of 1/16″, all dimension text will be rounded to the nearest 16th of an inch. If the round-off value is higher than zero, it will take precedence over the precision values of the Linear Dimensions. This will cause the Round-off option to be used independently from the precision and the unit Format of the Linear Dimensions. If the round-off value is 0″, the precision values will take precedence over the round-off values. The Round-off option is controlled by the DIMRND (round off) dimensioning variable. The round-off digits edited after the decimal point depend on the precision value or the precision set by DIMDEC dimensioning variable.

Prefix: (text box)   Sometimes it is necessary to place a special character or a note in front of the dimension text. This area will allow you to enter text, text control codes, or characters found on the keyboard in front of the dimension text. For example, to place a ± (plus or minus) symbol in front of the dimension text, type %%p inside the Prefix text box. This will place the ± *in* front of all the existing dimension text. If you want to place a prefix for one or more of the new dimensions, use the Override. . . button and then type %%p inside the Prefix text box. The next dimension(s) you perform will have the prefix in front of that dimension text and will not affect any existing dimension text on the screen. To have a space between the prefix and the dimension text, press the space bar after the prefix. Text control codes are discussed in Chapter 14. The prefix option is controlled by the DIMPOST (text prefix and suffix) dimensioning variable at the command line. To type the prefix at the command line, use the < > (brackets) symbol after the prefix. To place a space between the prefix and the dimension text, type the prefix first enter the space bar second and use the < > last. The < > represent the actual dimension text. You must type the prefix and the space key and the < > for the prefix to work at the command line.

Suffix: (text box)   This area will allow you to enter text, text control codes, or characters found on the keyboard at the end of the dimension text. The Suffix option is controlled by the DIMPOST (text prefix and suffix) dimensioning variable. You must type the suffix after the < > for the suffix to work at the command line.

Caution: Using Prefix and Suffix options will add characters to the dimension text string. Depending on the prefix and suffix text size, the total dimension text will be placed outside the extension lines if there is not enough room to accommodate dimension text plus the prefix and the suffix.

Caution: When you place a prefix or suffix for the dimension text, it will override any default prefixes and suffixes assigned by AutoCAD, such as the diameter or the radius symbols used with the Radius Dimension and the Diameter Dimension toolbars and the DIMDIAMETER (DDI) and the DIMRADIUS (DRA) commands. Before dimensioning a circle or an arc, make sure the Prefix and Suffix edit boxes are clear unless you want a prefix or a suffix for the diameter or the radius dimension. If you specify tolerances, AutoCAD will add the prefix and suffix to the tolerances as well as to the main dimension text.

Tips: A prefix or suffix is not used on every dimension but used as a special note or application placed in front or after the dimension text. It might be more efficient to create a special dimension style called SUFFIX AND PREFIX and use it when needed without using the Override. . . button. You can also enter a prefix or suffix when using the Linear Dimension and Angular Dimension toolbars inside the Dimension toolbar. When you select an object to dimension, AutoCAD will give you two options to edit the dimension text at the command line. The Mtext option will display the Multiline Text Editor dialog box, where the < > symbol is the dimension text. You can either type in front of it for prefix or type after it for suffix. You can also delete the < > (dimension text) and type a special note. The Text option will allow you to type a new dimension text or a special note. This is discussed later in the chapter under Dimensioning Applications.

Measurement Scale: This area will help you control the scale factor for linear dimension measurements and the application of dimensioning in Layouts (paper space).

Inside the Measurement Scale section there are two variables, Scale factor and Apply to layout dimensions, that only affect the measurement scale for linear dimensions:

- **SCALE FACTOR:**   (drop-down menu). **This is not the same scale factor discussed under the Scale for Dimension Features category.** The Scale factor for Measurement Scale is a scale value in which AutoCAD multiplies the dimension measurement by the value entered here. It is a length scale for linear dimension measurements, including radii, diameters, and coordinates. For example, if you enter 2 as the value for the Scale factor under Measurement Scale, the dimension values will be twice as much as the original measurement. The lengths of the measured objects will not increase or decrease by the scale factor values, only the dimension measurements will. Notice that the default value inside the Scale factor drop-down menu is 1. The Scale factor is controlled by the DIMLFAC (length scale) dimensioning variable at the command line. The default value for DIMLFAC is 1. When a value is entered as the Scale factor and the Apply to layout dimensions only check box is activated, the dimensions will not be affected by the scale factor value in Model.

  Note: The Scale factor for Measurement Scale does not work on angular dimensions and it does not apply to the rounding values of the linear dimensions.

- **APPLY TO LAYOUT DIMENSIONS ONLY:**   (check box). If you create dimensions in Layouts (paper space), click on this check box and enter the scale factor value of the drawing inside the Scale factor drop-down menu discussed above. You must also click on the Scale dimensions to layout (paper space) radio button under the Scale for Dimension Features category inside the Fit tab to be able to dimension in Layouts for the drawings created in Model. When this check box is activated, the value inside the Scale factor drop-down menu is used to compute a scale factor based on the scaling between the Layout and the Model space viewport. When this check box is not activated and a value is entered inside the Scale factor drop-down menu, the dimension measurements in Model are simply multiplied by that value.

Zero Suppression: This area will help you control the suppression of zeros for leading, trailing, feet, and inches of the Linear Dimensions of the Primary Units.

Inside the Zero Suppression section of the Linear Dimensions category there are four variables affecting decimal and feet and inch measurements:

- **LEADING:**   (check box). Checking this option will remove the zero from a decimal dimension value less than one. For example, a dimension of 0.5000 will have a leading zero before the decimal point. This option will remove the zero before the decimal point to read

.5000. This option will only work on Scientific, Decimal, Engineering, Fractional, and Windows Desktop Unit Formats.

- **TRAILING:** (check box). Decimal units have zeros after the decimal point based on the precision settings. Checking the Trailing option will remove all the trailing zeros in all decimal dimension units. For example, a dimension text of 74.00000 will become 74, and 15.50 will become 15.5 after this option is checked.

- **0 FEET:** (check box). This option is used to remove the feet portion of the feet and inches dimensions that are less than one foot in architectural drawings. For this to work, the length of the object must be less than one foot and the Unit Format must be set to Architectural. When floor plans are dimensioned, walls that are less than 1'-0″ should be dimensioned as inches only. For example, a partition wall 6″ thick should be dimensioned as 6″ not 0'-6″. The 0 Feet check box option will remove the 0' from the 0'-6″.

- **0 INCHES:** (check box). This option is used to remove the inch portion of a feet and inch dimension when the feet portion is any number and the inches portion is zero. For example, if this option is checked, a dimension of 12'-0″ will become 12'. Removing the 0″ after the feet value is not a common practice in architectural drawings, but removing the 0″ before the feet value is common. This option will not affect dimensions higher than 0″ with fractions of an inch after the feet value. For example, a dimension of 16'-0 5/8″ will not change whether it is entered as 16'5/8 or 16'0-5/8 at the command line.

Angular Dimensions: This area will help you control the current angle format for angular dimensions, including precision and suppression.

Inside the Angular Dimensions category there are two variables and one subcategory, Zero Suppression, similar to Linear Dimensions Zero Suppression affecting the current angle format:

- **UNITS FORMAT:** (drop-down list). This area will help you set the angular unit format for dimensioning angles. Angles are dimensioned using the Angular Dimension toolbar or by typing DIMANGULAR (DAN) at the command line. Circles, arcs, and the angle formed by two intersecting lines can be used as angle measurements. When using circles, two points must be picked on the circle. When using arcs, a single point must be picked. When two lines intersect each other a certain angle, that angle can be measured by picking the two lines. The Units Format for Angular Dimensions has four selections. The *Decimal Degrees* option is used for most of the drafting applications, including architectural. The Decimal Degrees option will use the decimal parts of the degree measurement. The *Degrees Minutes Seconds* option is used when minute and second precision are needed for the decimal degrees. It is mostly used in civil engineering and surveying applications, but architectural, mechanical, and structural applications are common also. For example, if the angle between two surfaces is 67.85 degrees when this option is used, the dimension text will read as 67° 51'0″ (67 degrees, 51 minutes, and 0 seconds). Since there are 60 minutes in one degree, 0.85 degrees will be equal to 51 minutes ($0.85 \times 60 = 51$). The Precision in this case is set to 0d00'00.0″. The *gradians* are units of angular measurement based on *gradients*. One gradient is equal to 0.9 degrees, and 1 degree is equal to 1.11 gradient because there are 400 gradients in 360 degrees. With the unit format as *gradians* (g) and a precision of 0.000 g, the 67.85 degree angle will measure 75.389 g ($67.85 \times 1.11111 = 75.389$). The *radians* (r) units are based on a complete circle (360°) being equal to 2π radians where π is equal to 3.14. A 90 degree angle will have $\pi/2$ radians. With the unit format as *radians* and a precision of 0.000r, the 67.85 degree angle will measure 1/184r. The Units Format for the Angular Dimensions is controlled by the DIMAUNIT (angular units) dimensioning variable at the command line.

- **PRECISION:** (drop-down list). This area will help you select the number of decimal places to display in angular dimensions. For decimal degrees the precision can be set to 0, which means the angular dimension will be displayed with no decimal place. If it is set to 0.00000000, the angular dimension will be displayed with eight decimal places. Gradians and radians precision are same as decimal degrees except there will be a "g" at the end of the precision for gradians and there will be an "r" at the end of the precision for radians. The precision for the angular dimensions is controlled by the DIMADEC (angle precision) dimensioning variable at the command line. The default value for DIMADEC is 0 with a maximum of 8.

Zero Suppression: This area will help you control the leading and the trailing zeros of the angular dimensions.

Inside the Zero Suppression option there are two variables affecting decimal angular measurements:

- **LEADING:** (check box). Checking this box will remove the zero from a decimal angular dimension less than one. For example, an angular dimension of 0.5000 degrees will read as .5000° when the precision is set to 0.0000.

- **TRAILING:** (check box). Checking this box will remove all the trailing zeros in all decimal angular dimensions. For example, an angular dimension of 60.5500 degrees will read as 60.55° when the precision is set to 0.0000. The Zero Suppression for angular dimensions is controlled by the DIMAZIN (angle zero suppression) dimensioning variable at the command line.

Alternate Units: (tab) This tab has three separate categories relating to the format, precision, and scale of alternate dimensioning practices. Alternate Units, or Dual Dimensioning, will help you include millimeters (mm) or any other alternate unit you need to display as part of the primary dimensioning units. The dimension style image display window is also a part of this tab. The Alternate Units tab is shown in Figure 18–28. The categories are Alternate Units, Zero Suppression, and Placement.

- **DISPLAY ALTERNATE UNITS:** (check box). This check box is off by default. If it is checked, all the options and variables inside the Alternate Units tab will become active. This check box will turn the Alternate Units on and off. This is controlled by the DIMALT (alternate units) dimensioning variable at the command line. DIMALT is off by default.

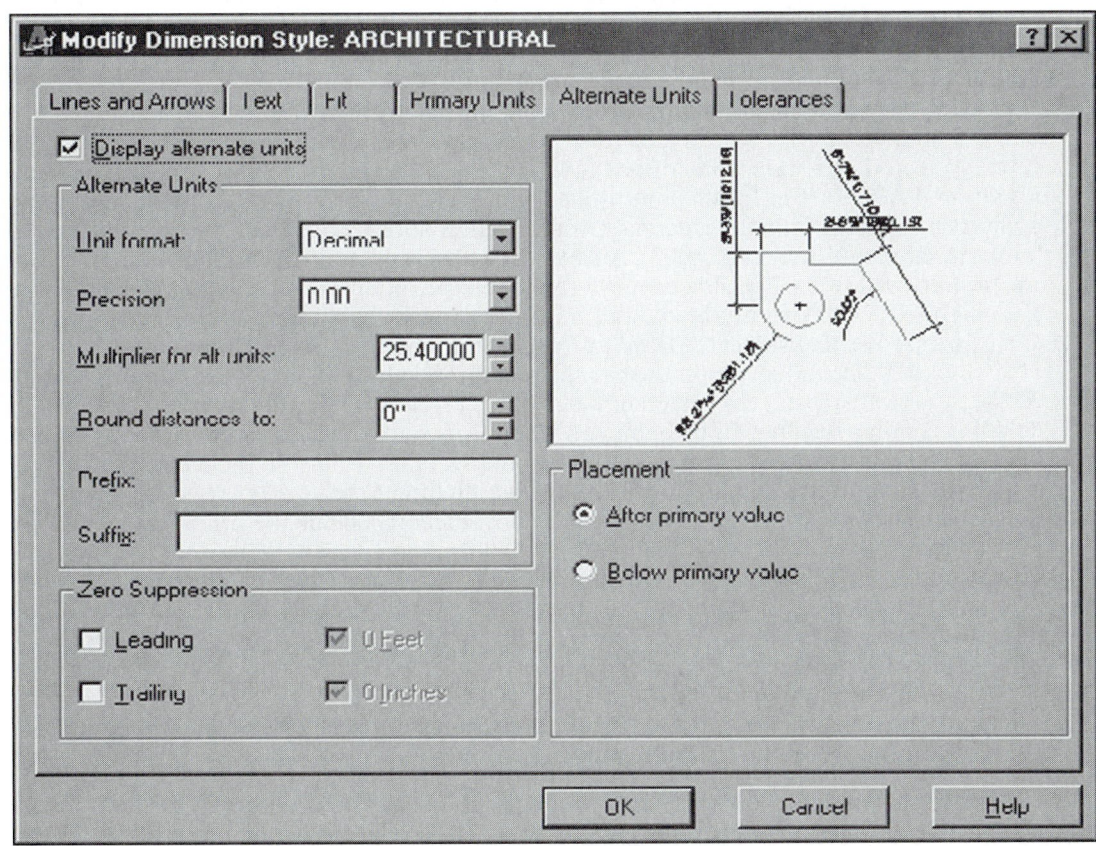

FIGURE 18–28 The Alternate Units tab can be used to include metric units as well as user defined units as part of the Primary Units applications.

Alternate Units: While the primary units represent a major source of information relating to the measurement of lengths and distances in the drawings, an alternate method for dimensions can be included with the primary units if it is required. Some drawings might require millimeters or meters displayed in brackets preceding inch measurements. This type of dimensioning is called *alternate dimensioning* where alternate units are displayed next to inch (or feet and inches) measurements inside the brackets, except for Angular dimensioning.

Inside the Alternate Units category there are six variables similar to the ones inside the Linear Dimensions category of the Primary Units tab:

- **UNIT FORMAT:**   (drop-down list). This area will help you establish how you want AutoCAD to measure distances using an alternate unit format. The options inside the drop-down list are similar to the ones inside the Unit Format drop-down list of the Linear Dimensions category. In addition to the Scientific, Decimal, Engineering, Architectural, Fractional, and Windows Desktop dimension length units, Architectural Stacked and Fractional Stacked are also included in the alternate unit format. The actual display of the alternate unit values are governed by the dimension text of the primary unit, the value entered inside the Multiplier for alt units drop-down menu, and the option selected inside the Unit Format drop-down list. **The values inside the brackets are the representation of the dimension text of the primary unit multiplied by the value of the Multiplier for alt units and converted into the alternate unit format.** AutoCAD will take the value inside the Multiplier for alt units and multiply it by dimension text of the primary unit and then convert it into the alternate unit format and then place it inside the brackets next to the dimension text. The default multiplier for alternate units is 25.4000. This is the metric equivalent of one inch. To deal with metric units, some conversions are in order: 1″ = 25.4000 (mm), 1″ = 2.5400 cm, and 1″ = 0.0254 m. With the default multiplier in place, when Decimal is selected from the Unit Format list the dimension text of the primary unit will be multiplied by 25.4000 and then converted to decimal format to be placed inside the brackets. This will produce millimeter equivalents inside the brackets for primary units. For example, draw a line measuring 5′-8″ using architectural primary units. With the default multiplier (25.4000) in place, select Decimal from the Unit Format list and set the precision to 0.00. Click on the Linear Dimension toolbar inside the Dimension toolbar and select the line to measure. The dimension text will read 5′-8″ [1727.20]. The value inside the brackets is the millimeter equivalent of 5′-8″. AutoCAD will first multiply 5′-8″ with 25.4000 (5′-8″ × 25.4000 = 143′-11 3/16″) and then convert it to the selected alternate unit format (143′-11″ = 1727 and 3/16″ = 0.1875 and 1727 + 0.1875 = 1727.20). The 25.4000 multiplier will only give millimeter equivalents for the primary units using only the Decimal Unit format. If another alternate unit format is used with the same multiplier (25.4000), AutoCAD will simply multiply the dimension text of the primary unit by 25.400 and convert it to the selected alternate unit format. For example, keeping the 25.4000 inside the default multiplier, select Architectural Stacked from the Unit Format list and select 0′-0 1/4″ for precision. The 5′-8″ line will now read as 5′-8″ [143′-11 1/4″]. The value inside the brackets is the result of 25.4000 being multiplied by 5′-8″ (143′-11 3/16″) and converted into 0′-0 1/4″ precision of Architectural Stacked (143′-11 1/4″). Similar results will be achieved when different unit formats are used. You can even have your own multiplier value. For example, enter 10 inside the Multiplier for alt units area (do not use up and down arrows just highlight the current value and type 10) and select Decimal from the Unit Format, then select 0.0000 as the precision value. The 5′-8″ dimension text will now read 5′-8″ [680.0000]. AutoCAD will multiply 5′-8″ with 10 (5′-8″ × 10 = 56′-8″) and convert it into Decimal units format with a precision of 0.0000 (56′-8″ = 680.0000 decimal units). You can enter 0.0254 inside the Multiplier for alt units area and select Decimal as Alternate Unit Format and have all your feet and inch dimensions include meter equivalents inside the brackets. With the 0.0254 as the multiplier, the 5′-8″ dimension text will now read as 5′-8″ [1.7272]. The Unit Format for Alternate Units is controlled by the DIMALTU (alternate unit format) dimensioning variable at the command line, and the default value is 2.

- **PRECISION:**   (drop-down list). This area will help you select the number of decimal places similar to the Precision for Primary Units area. The Precision for alternate units is controlled by the DIMALTD (alternate precision) dimensioning variable at the command line. The default value for DIMALTD is 2 for 0.00 precision.

- **MULTIPLIER FOR ALTERNATE UNITS:** (drop-down list). This area will help you establish the multiplier value for alternate units. AutoCAD will multiply this value with the primary dimension text value and convert it to the selected primary unit format and display it inside the brackets next to the primary dimension text as discussed under alternate unit format area. Entering 0.5 for a multiplier will have the alternate unit values displayed as half of the primary dimension text values. Entering 1 for a multiplier will have the alternate unit values displayed as the conversions of the same primary dimension text values. You must enter a value higher than 0. AutoCAD will not accept a value of 0 as a multiplier. The multiplier value has no effect on the angular dimensions and does not effect the rounded values. The multiplier is controlled by the DIMALTF (alternate scale factor). The default value for DIMALTF is 25.4000 which is the number of millimeters in an inch.

- **ROUND DISTANCES TO:** (drop-down menu). This area is similar to the Round off drop-down menu inside the Linear Dimensions category of the Primary Units tab. It works in the same manner as the primary units round off, where it will set rounding guidelines for the alternate unit dimension text. It is used for all dimensioning applications except Angular Dimensioning. The alternate rounding values are controlled by the DIMALTRND (alternate round off) dimensioning variable at the command line. The default value for DIMALTRND is 0″.

- **PREFIX:** (text box). This area will help you include a prefix for the alternate unit dimension text. The features and the application of the Alternate Units Prefix are the same as the Primary Units Prefix. The Prefix option is controlled by the DIMAPOST (alternate prefix and suffix) dimensioning variable at the command line. Place a space after the prefix if you want a space between the prefix and the alternate unit dimension text. If you use the command line to add the alternate prefix, make sure the Display Alternate Units check box is on. If it is off, your prefix will still be registered but not applied.

- **SUFFIX:** (text box). This area will help you include a suffix for the alternate unit dimension text. For example, to include millimeters after the alternate unit dimension text, including a space between the alternate dimension text and the millimeters abbreviation, click inside the Suffix text box and press the space bar and type mm. Click on the OK button and close the Dimension Style Manager dialog box. The suffix option is controlled by the DIMAPOST (alternate prefix and suffix) dimensioning variable.

Zero Suppression: This area will help you control the suppression of zeros for leading, trailing, feet, and, inches of the Alternate Unit dimensions. The Leading, Trailing, 0 Feet, and 0 Inches check boxes work in the same manner as those in the Primary Units section. The Zero Suppression for Alternate Units is controlled by the DIMALTZ (alternate zeros) dimensioning variable at the command line. The values for DIMALTZ are the same as DIMZIN.

Placement: This area will help you control the placement of Alternate Unit dimensions.

Inside the Placement section of the Alternate Units there are two variables affecting the placement of alternate unit dimensions:

- **AFTER PRIMARY VALUE:** (radio button). This option will place the alternate unit dimension text after the primary unit dimensions as shown in Figure 18–29A.

- **BELOW PRIMARY VALUE:** (radio button). This option will place the alternate unit dimension text below the primary unit dimensions as shown in Figure 18–29B. To avoid overcrowding, make sure you leave enough space between the object and the location of the dimension text.

Tolerances: (tab) Tolerances are not included in this textbook because this area does not apply to architectural dimensioning.

FIGURE 18–29   Using the Alternate Units Placement options. Notice the required space for the dimension text to fit inside the extension lines.

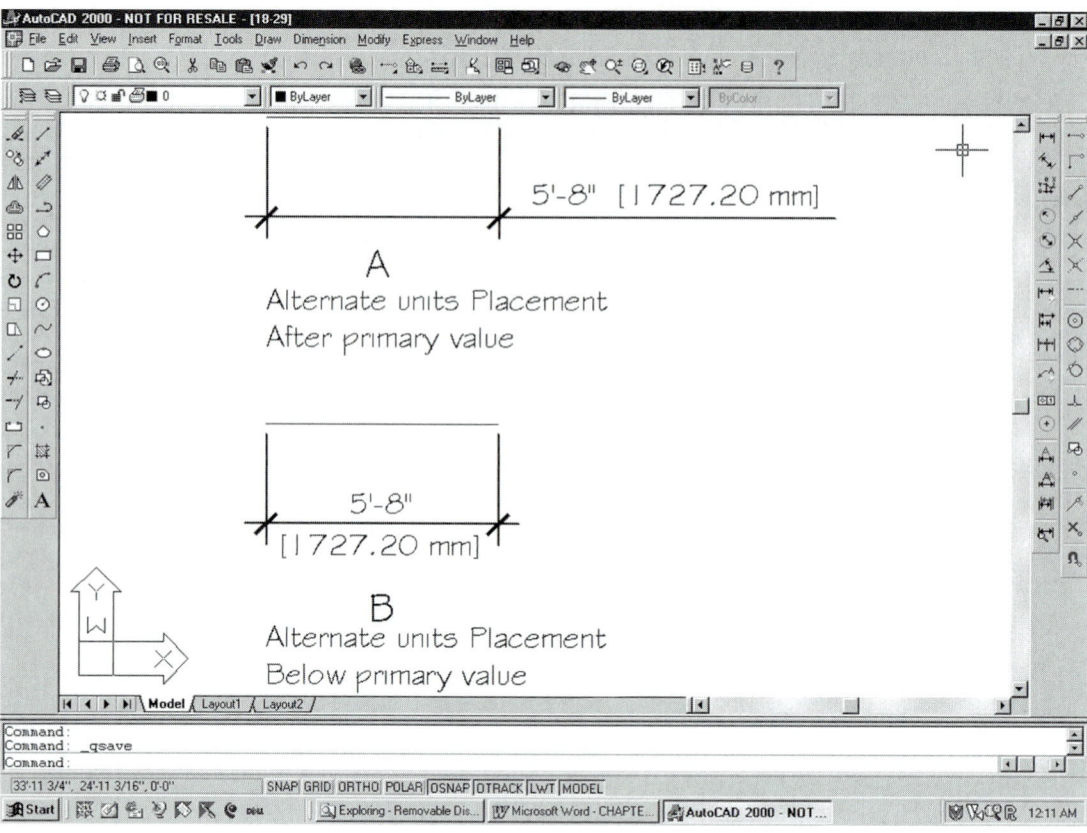

18.5 DIMENSIONING APPLICATIONS

Throughout this chapter, you learned to create, manage, override and modify dimension styles using the dialog boxes and the dimensioning variables. The New, Modify, and Override Dimension Style dialog boxes offer you the most flexibility and the most graphical user interface. With the exception of *tolerances,* the dialog boxes offer 55 dimensioning variables and settings in which only 16 have been modified to fit architectural dimensioning applications. The initial setting of 16 variables can be used for most architectural dimensioning purposes with the possibility of setting more as they become necessary. Before using these settings for dimensioning, you should compare their values with the default values of the standard dimension style to better understand their purposes. Table 18–2 shows the comparison of the 16 dimensioning variables of the Architectural dimension style with the standard dimension style. You should establish these settings before continuing with this chapter.

These are the dimensioning variables and settings that make architectural dimensioning applications possible. Remember that the DIMSCALE (overall scale factor) is one of the most important settings for the dimension style. **The Overall Scale Factor (use overall scale of drop-down menu) must be set to the scale factor of the drawing.** After establishing all of the dimensioning settings per dimensioning conventions, you are now ready to apply these settings to actual dimensioning tasks using the Dimension Toolbar, Dimension pull-down menu, and typing dimensioning commands directly at the command line. Creating several architectural dimensioning styles before hand will help you see and understand all of the dimensioning variables and settings from an architectural point of view. There are six major dimensioning applications as follows:

1. Linear dimensioning.
2. Angular dimensioning.
3. Radius dimensioning.

Dimensioning Variable	What It Changes	Architectural	Standard
DIMBLK	Arrowhead style	ArchTick	ClosedFilled
DIMASZ	Arrow size	1/8″	3/16″
DIMDLE	Dimension line extension	1/8″	0
DIMEXE	Extension line extension	1/8″	3/16″
DIMFRAC	Fraction format	1	0
DIMLUNIT	Dimension line unit	4	2
DIMSCALE	Overall scale factor	48.0000	1.0000
DIMDEC	Unit precision	3	4
DIMTXT	Text height	1/8″	3/16″
DIMTIH	Text inside align	Off	On
DIMGAP	Gap from dim line to text	1/16″	1/16″
DIMTOH	Text outside align	Off	On
DIMTAD	Vertical position of dim text	1	0
DIMTXSTY	Dim text style	Architectural	Standard
DIMZIN	Zero suppression	3	0
DIMSTYLE	Dimension style	Architectural	Standard

TABLE 18–2:
Comparison of Architectural with standard dimensioning variables.

4. Diameter dimensioning.

5. Ordinate dimensioning.

6. Leaders and tolerances.

When you create a new dimension style using the Create New Dimension Style dialog box, you have the opportunity to create a new style based on the current style, another style, or the standard style. You can start a new style and use it for all or any one of the above dimensioning application categories as mentioned in the beginning of this chapter. One of the great benefits of creating just one style and using it to establish different variables for each category is that each dimensioning application can use different settings, format, and variables and can be used on an as-needed basis. For example, suppose the diameter dimensions for your project require you to use a different color dimension line, different arrowhead style, different DIMGAP value, and a different text style than the current style. You don't have to keep using the Override... button to go back and forth to perform the tasks that can be done with just a click of a button. You can do the same for Linear, Angular, Radius, Ordinate, and Leader dimensioning. The possibilities with the Create New Dimension Style dialog box and its contents are endless, and so is the flexibility.

All of the aforementioned dimensioning applications can be accessed using the Dimension toolbar shown in Figure 18–4. The Dimension toolbar is divided into six sections. The first four sections contain three buttons, each relating to a specific dimensioning application, the fifth section relates to dimension editing. The last section contains the Dimension Style Control drop-down menu and the Dimension Style button to access the Dimension Style Manager dialog box. The first section contains the Linear, Aligned, and Ordinate Dimension buttons. The second section contains the Radius, Diameter, and Angular Dimension buttons. The third section contains the Quick, Baseline, and Continue Dimension buttons. The fourth section contains the Quick Leader, Tolerance, and Center Mark buttons. The fifth section contains the Dimension Edit, Dimension Text Edit, and Dimension Update buttons.

Tips: Dimensioning accuracy is a direct result of the drawing accuracy. When entering distances at the command line or when using the Polar Snap and Polar Tracking along with Object Tracking, be as precise as possible and turn SNAP and OTRACK on when required. Always use Object Snap modes to accurately snap to the desired locations precisely. Zoom in if you must to get a precise snap point. Always remember that there may be other points very close to the point you are snapping to and never underestimate the possibility of snapping to the end point of an extension line, leader

arrowhead, a point, or hatching. Always read the tool tips; your best source of correct snap confirmation. Never alter a dimension value by more than what appears inside the brackets unless you are asked to do so.

Let's take a look at these buttons in the Dimension toolbar as we work with dimensioning applications:

18.5.1 Linear Dimension

This is the first button in the Dimension toolbar. The majority of your dimensions will be linear, meaning straight. A horizontal, vertical, or slanted line can be dimensioned to produce a vertical or horizontal distance, a specific angle can be assigned to the dimension text, and the dimension line can be rotated to match an angled surface using the Linear Dimension button. You can also enter DIMLINEAR or DLI at the command line or select Linear from the Dimension pull-down menu.

■ **EXERCISE 18–3:** *The following step-by-step exercise will allow you to dimension a simple object, create overrides, and update the dimension.*

Step #1: Create a new drawing and establish architectural units and drawing limits of 22', 17'.

Step #2: Use the procedures described so far to create the ARCHITECTURAL dimension style and set it current.

Step #3: Using the LINE command, draw a rectangle measuring 12'-6 7/8" × 2'-4 1/2" as shown in Figure 18–30. Do not create hatching.

Step #4: To dimension the 12'-6 7/8" measurement, click on the Linear Dimension button inside the Dimension toolbar and follow the command sequence as follows: (When dimensioning, the points you pick on the object are the first and second extension line origins.)

Command: _dimlinear

Specify first extension line origin or <select object>: (using object snap modes, click on point 1. This is the first extension line origin for the first dimension).

Specify second extension line origin: (using object snap modes, click on point 2. This is the second extension line origin for the first dimension).

Specify dimension line location or [Mtext/Text/Angle/Horizontal/Vertical/Rotated]: (move the cursor up or down vertically to determine the dimension line location and left click).

Step #5: Use the DIMLINEAR command at the command line to dimension the 2'-4 1/2" measurement as follows:

Command: **DIMLINEAR** ~EnterKey~

Specify first extension line origin or <select object>: (using object snap modes, click on point 2 as shown in Figure 18–30. This is the first extension line origin for the second dimension).

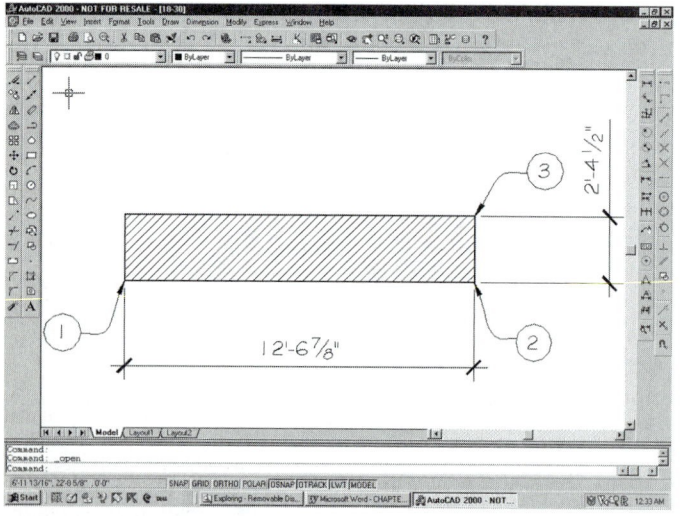

FIGURE 18–30 The rectangle object created will be dimensioned.

Specify second extension line origin: (using object snap modes, click on point 3. This is the second extension line origin for the second dimension).

Specify dimension line location or

[Mtext/Text/Angle/Horizontal/Vertical/Rotated]: (move the cursor left to right horizontally to determine the dimension line location and left click).

Notice that the dimension text 2'-4 1/2" is placed outside the extension lines and toward the top (right side) of the second extension line origin. If the first extension line origin was selected at point 3 and the second extension line origin was selected at point 2, then the dimension text would be placed toward the bottom (left side) of the second extension line origin. If there is not enough room to place the dimension text inside the extension lines, the dimension text will be located on the side of the second extension line origin when points are picked. The dimension text is displayed outside the extension lines because there is not enough room to place the dimension text between the extension lines as defined by DIMATFIT dimensioning variable.

Step #6: Place the dimension text inside the extension lines as follows:

Click on the Override. . . button inside the Dimension Style Manager dialog box and click on the Fit tab inside the Override Current Style dialog box. Place a checkmark inside the Always keep text between ext lines (DIMTIX) radio button and click on the OK button. Close the Dimension Style Manager dialog box. Update the dimension text at the command line as follows:

Command: **DIM** ~EnterKey~

Dim: **UP** ~EnterKey~

Select objects: (pick the dimension text).

Select objects: ~EnterKey~ (or right click).

Dim: ~EscKey~ (this will end the dimension update operation).

You can also click on the Dimension Update button in the Dimension toolbar.

The dimension text 2'-4 1/2" will now be placed between the extension lines but the dimension line will be broken completely as shown in Figure 18–31.

Step #7: Place the dimension line inside the extension lines as follows:

Highlight the <style overrides> inside the Dimension Style Manager dialog box and click on the Override. . . button. Select the Fit tab inside the Override Current Style dialog box and click inside the Always draw dim line between ext lines (DIMTOFL) check box under the Fine Tuning section. Click on the OK button. Notice the text inside the Description text box inside the Dimension Style Manager dialog box will read as follows:

ARCHITECTURAL + Dim Line forced = On,

Text inside = On

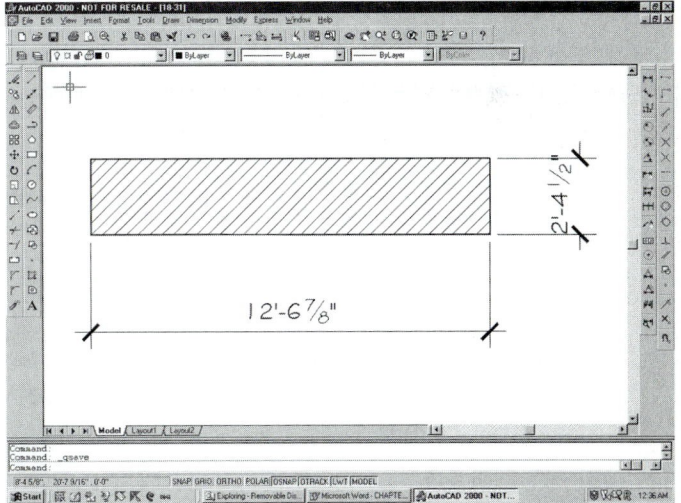

These are the current Overrides you have established so far for the current dimension style. This means that the DIMTIX and the DIMTOFL dimensioning variables are on.

Step #8: Close the Dimension Style Manager dialog box.

Step #9: Update the dimension as previously shown.

FIGURE 18–31 The 2'-4 1/2" dimension placed between inside the extension line but without the dimension line.

The dimension line will be placed inside the extension lines as shown in Figure 18–32.

Step #10:   Move the dimension text to the bottom of the dimension line so that it will not touch the tick marks as follows:

Click on the Dimension Style button in the Dimension toolbar and click on the Override. . . button inside the Dimension Style Manager dialog box. Inside the Fit tab and under the Fit Options category, select the Both text and arrows radio button. Under the Text Placement category, select the Over the dimension line, without a leader radio button. Under the Fine Tuning category, select the Place text manually when dimensioning check box and click on the OK button. Notice the text inside the Description text box inside the Dimension Style Manager dialog box will read as follows:

ARCHITECTURAL + Dim Line forced = On,

Fit: text movement = 2, (DIMUPT) = On

Fit: arrow and text = 0

Step #11:   Close the Dimension Style Manager dialog box.

Step #12:   Update the dimension as follows:

Click on the Dimension Text Edit button in the Dimension toolbar. At the Select Dimension: command prompt, select the dimension text. Move the dimension text to the bottom of the dimension line as shown in Figure 18–33.

Congratulations! You have successfully created a linear dimension and created overrides and updated the dimension to look like Figure 18–33.

Referring to the dimension text of 2′-4 1/2″, the value inside the Fraction height scale can be changed to make the fraction smaller or larger. Setting the appropriate Fraction height scale will save you from editing some of the dimensions with fractions. You can also select all the overrides at one time while you are inside the Override Current Style dialog box by going into the different tabs and changing the settings that you desire. Knowing the required variables will save you time by allowing you to set all the overrides in one continuous operation. You can then perform one dimension update and select all the dimensions one after another to have the new settings take effect. To get back to dimensioning with the current style without the overrides, right-click on the <style overrides> and select delete. The updated dimensions will re-

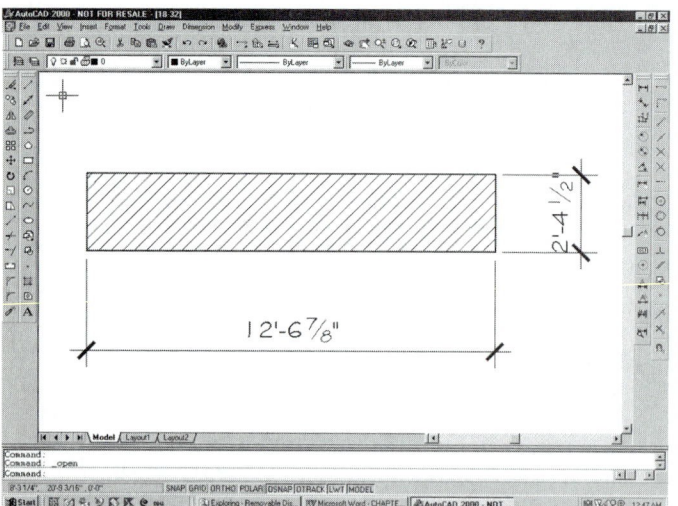

FIGURE 18–32   The dimension text placed inside the extension lines with the dimension line. Notice the dimension text is too close to the tick marks.

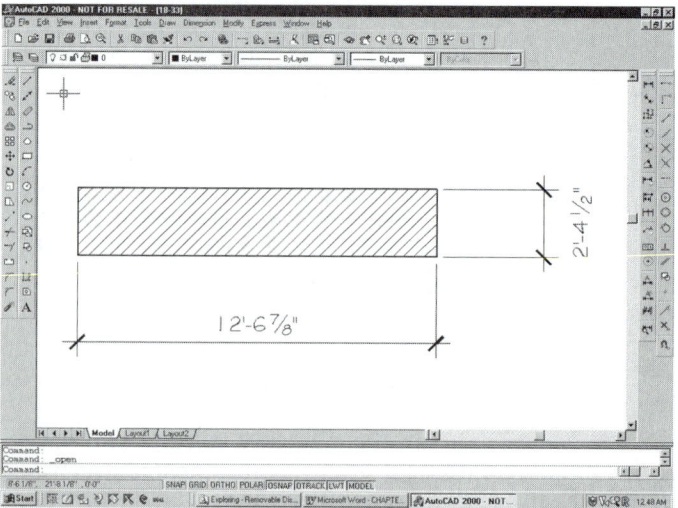

FIGURE 18–33   The final position of the dimension text as it is moved outside the extension lines.

main with their respected overrides until another dimension update is performed to change it to the current settings.

When you pick point 1 and point 2 or point 2 and pont 3 in Figure 18–30 for dimensioning, you are establishing the first and second extension line origins. However, you can just pick the object without picking extension line origins to dimension. For example, you can dimension the lower horizontal line by selecting the line as follows:

```
Command: DLI ~EnterKey~ (or click on the Linear Dimension button in the
Dimension toolbar).
Specify first extension line origin or <select object>: ~EnterKey~ (or
right click)
Select object to dimension: (select the lower horizontal line of the
object to dimension).
Specify dimension line location or
[Mtext/Text/Angle/Horizontal/Vertical/Rotated]: (move the cursor up or
down vertically to determine the dimension line location and left click).
```

Before you select the object to dimension, AutoCAD will give you six options to choose from as follows:

- **MTEXT:**   This option will allow you to change the dimension text by accessing the Multiline Text Editor dialog box. You can enter a new dimension text or a special character or use dimension control codes to replace the existing dimension text. This dialog box is discussed in Chapter 14. The brackets symbol (< >) inside the Multiline text Editor dialog box represents the existing dimension text. The blinking vertical line in front of the < > represents the cursor location. To erase the current text, press the Delete button on the keyboard twice. The Multiline Text Editor dialog box will now have only the vertical blinking line. To replace the existing dimension text with a new one, type a new dimension, new text, or special character or use dimension control codes. To move around the typed text, use the Backspace and direction arrows on your keyboard. If you want the existing dimension text to be a part of the new dimension text, type the new text inside, in front, or after the < >.

- **TEXT:**   This option will allow you to change the existing dimension text at the command line. This can be a convenient way to type the desired text rather than using the Multiline Text Editor dialog box because the Text option will retain the current text height established while creating the dimension style. This option will display the current dimension text inside the brackets. You can either accept the default dimension text by pressing ~EnterKey~ or type a new dimension value.

- **ANGLE:**   This option will allow you to change the current dimension text angle. With the Angle option, AutoCAD will simply rotate the dimension text by the specified value.

- **HORIZONTAL:**   This option will allow you to dimension horizontal distances only. When you select a horizontal surface to dimension, AutoCAD will automatically place a horizontal distance by placing the dimension line and the dimension text parallel to the horizontal surface. When you select a vertical surface to dimension, AutoCAD will automatically place a vertical distance by placing the dimension line and the dimension text parallel to the vertical surface (when text alignment is not horizontal). When a slanted surface is dimensioned, AutoCAD will automatically place a horizontal or a vertical distance by placing the dimension line and the dimension text horizontally or vertically depending on the selection of the dimension line location.

- **VERTICAL:**   This option will allow you to dimension vertical distances only. When you select the Vertical option, AutoCAD will give you only the vertical distance (delta Y).

- **ROTATED:**   This option will allow you to specify an angle for the extension lines. This is different than setting an angle for the dimension text.

■   **EXERCISE 18–4:**   *The following step-by-step exercise will allow you to create the object shown in Figure 18–34 and dimension the two circles drawn parallel to the hypotenuse of the triangle using the Rotate option as shown in Figure 18–39.*

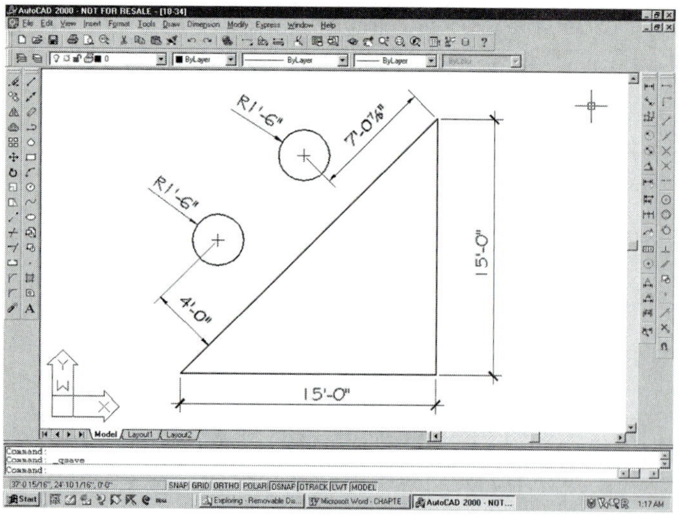

FIGURE 18–34 The triangle with 15'-0" base and height and the two circles offset 4'-0" from the hypotenuse. The dimensions to locate the two circles in two different locations are accomplished by using the Rotated option of the Dimlinear command.

Step #1: Use the drawing settings established in Exercise 18–3 and erase everything on the screen.

Step #2: Draw the horizontal and the vertical lines of the triangle shown in Figure 18–34 as 15'-0".

Step #3: Draw another line connecting the end points of the vertical and the horizontal lines as the hypotenuse of the triangle.

Step #4: Draw the two circles, 4'-0" offset from the hypotenuse with a radius of 1'-6" and locate the circles 1/3 of the hypotenuse distance and dimension the circles from the hypotenuse and from the upper corner of the triangle as follows:

Offset the hypotenuse 4'-0" using the OFFSET command as follows:

Command: **OFFSET** ~EnterKey~

Specify offset distance or [Through] <Through>: **4'** ~EnterKey~

Select object to offset or <exit>: (select the hypotenuse).

Specify point on side to offset: (pick a point on the upper side of the hypotenuse).

Select object to offset or <exit>: ~EnterKey~

Your drawing should now look like Figure 18–35.

Step #5: Divide the offset line into three equal units using the DIVIDE command and the PDMODE system variable as follows:

Command: **PDMODE** ~EnterKey~

Enter new value for PDMODE <0>: **2** ~EnterKey~ (this will place + signs on the line when using the DIVIDE command).

Command: **DIVIDE** ~EnterKey~

Select object to divide: (pick the line).

Enter the number of segments or [Block]: **3** ~EnterKey~ (this will divide the line into three equal units by placing two + signs as points on the line).

Your drawing should now look like Figure 18–36.

Step #6: Draw two circles with a radius of 1'-6" and place them at the intersections of the two + signs using the CIRCLE and the NODE object snap mode as follows:

Command: **CIRCLE** ~EnterKey~

Specify center point for circle or [3P/2P/Ttr (tan tan radius)]: (click on the *Snap to Node* button inside the Object Snap toolbar).

Specify center point for circle or [3P/2P/Ttr (tan tan radius)]: _nod of (click on the center of the first + sign).

Specify radius of circle or [Diameter]: **1'6** ~EnterKey~

Command: ~EnterKey~ (this should bring back the circle command).

CIRCLE Specify center point for circle or [3P/2P/Ttr (tan tan radius)]: (click on the *Snap to Node* button inside the Object Snap toolbar).

Specify center point for circle or [3P/2P/Ttr (tan tan radius)]: _nod of (click on the center of the second + sign).

Specify radius of circle or [Diameter] <1'-6">: ~EnterKey~

Erase the Points (+ signs) and the line using the erase command.

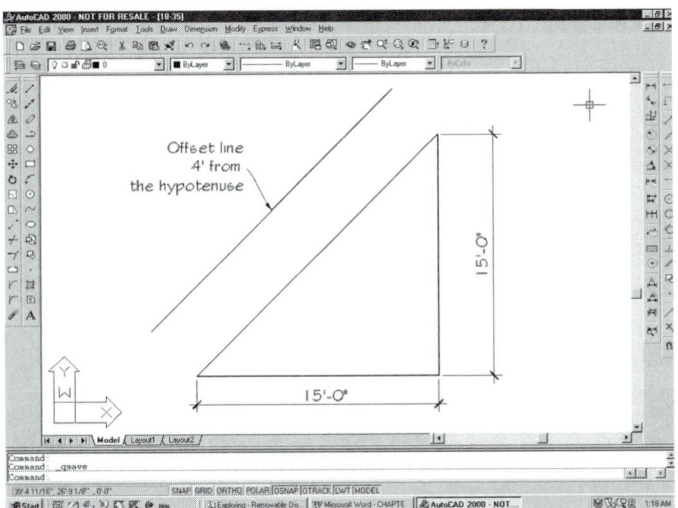

FIGURE 18–35 A line is offset 4'-0" from the hypotenuse. This line will be used to place two circles 1/3 the distance from the end points.

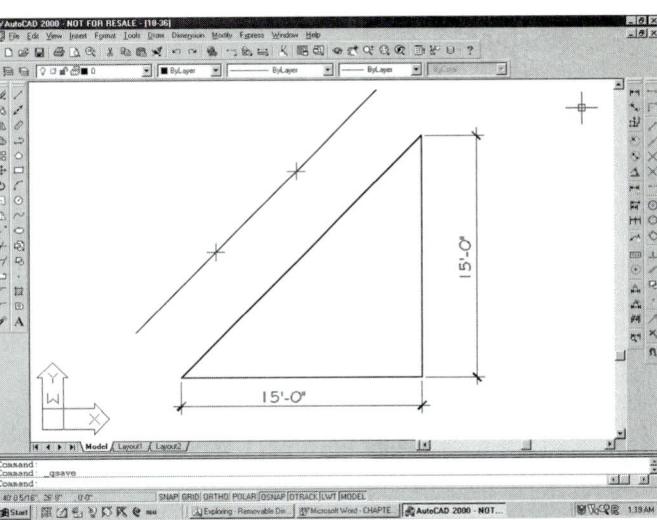

FIGURE 18–36 Using the DIVIDE command, the line is divided into three equal units with two points using the PDMODE system variable.

Your drawing should now look like Figure 18–37 without the line going through the circles.

Step #7: Dimension the upper circle from the upper corner of the triangle by using the Rotated option of the DIMLINEAR command. Notice that if you were to draw a line perpendicular to the hypotenuse of the triangle, the line will be at an angle of 135 degrees to the horizontal or 45 degrees to the vertical using the default orientation of angle measurement as counterclockwise. You can specify any of the two angles as the angle of dimension line (the rotation angle) as shown in Figure 18–38 as follows:

Command: **DIMLINEAR** ~EnterKey~

Specify first extension line origin or <select object>: (select point 1).

Specify second extension line origin: (turn ORTHO off and select point 2).

Specify dimension line location or

[Mtext/Text/Angle/Horizontal/Vertical/Rotated]: **R** ~EnterKey~

Specify angle of dimension line <0>: **135** (or 45) ~EnterKey~

Specify dimension line location or

[Mtext/Text/Angle/Horizontal/Vertical/Rotated]: (left click on the location shown).

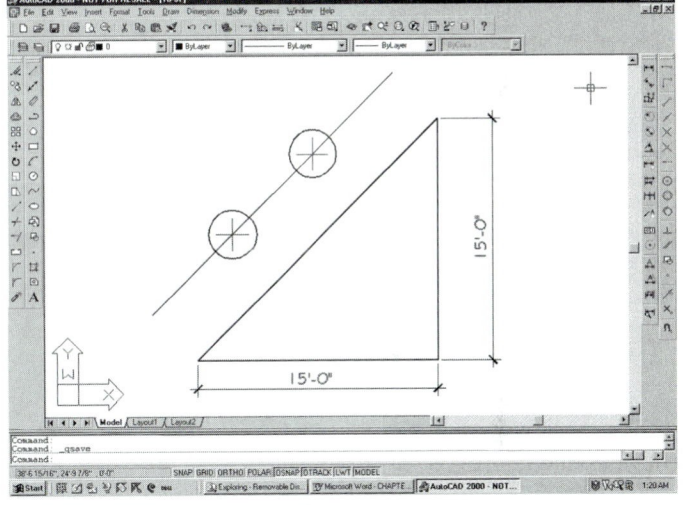

FIGURE 18–37 Using the CIRCLE command and the Snap to Node object snap mode, two circles are drawn.

Your drawing should now look like Figure 18–38. Notice that the dimension line is parallel to the hypotenuse, and the extension lines are perpendicular to the hypotenuse.

Step #8: By looking at Figure 18–39, dimension the lower circle from the lower corner of the triangle as the offset distance between the hypotenuse and the center of the circle as follows:

Command: **DLI** ~EnterKey~(or click on the Linear Dimension button in the Dimension toolbar).

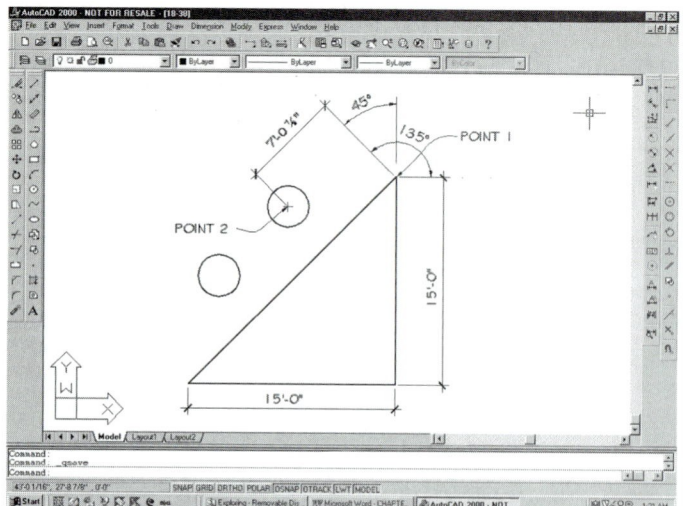

FIGURE 18–38 Using the Rotated option of the Dimlinear command, the first dimension is taken as the distance from Point 1 to Point 2 as 7'-0 7/8".

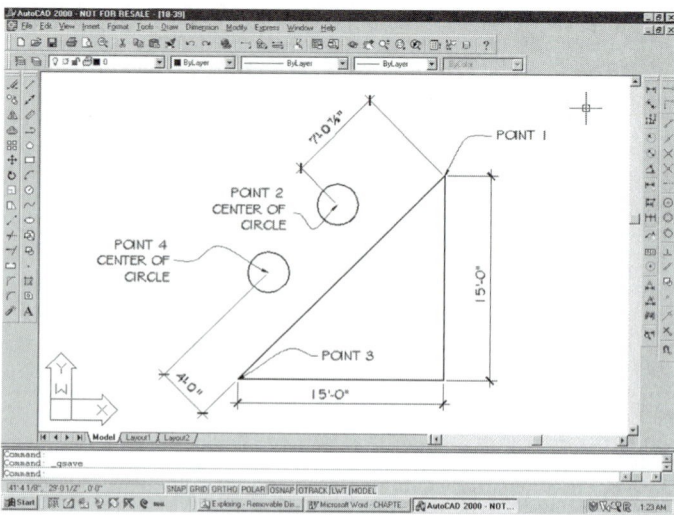

FIGURE 18–39 The second circle is dimensioned using the Rotated option of the DIMLINEAR comand from point 3 to point 4, which is the 4'-0" offset distance.

Specify first extension line origin or <select object>: (select point 3).

Specify second extension line origin: (turn ORTHO off and select point 4).

Specify dimension line location or

[Mtext/Text/Angle/Horizontal/Vertical/Rotated]: **R** ~EnterKey~

Specify angle of dimension line: **135** (or 45) ~EnterKey~

Specify dimension line location or

[Mtext/Text/Angle/Horizontal/Vertical/Rotated]: (left-click on the location shown).

Congratulations! You have successfully created the object shown in Figure 18–34 and used the Rotated option of the DIMLINEAR command to dimension the circles. Your drawing should now look like Figure 18–39.

18.5.2 Aligned Dimension

When objects are drawn at an angle, the Linear Dimension button or the DIMLINEAR command will only provide a horizontal or a vertical distance. The Aligned Dimension button in the Dimension toolbar will dimension the angled surfaces and draw the dimension line parallel to the angled surface. This is called aligning the dimension line with the inclined surface. The aligned dimensions are achieved using the DIMALIGNED or the DAL command. You can also access the DIMALIGNED command by selecting Aligned from the Dimension pull-down menu. You can select either the first and the second extension lines as origins or select the object to dimension. For example, you can dimension any of the lines of the triangle shown in Figure 18–40 as follows:

```
Click on the Aligned Dimension button inside the Dimension toolbar.
Command: _dimaligned
Specify first extension line origin or <select object>: (click on point A).
Specify second line origin: (click on point B).
Specify dimension line location or
[Mtext/Text/Angle]: (left click on the location shown).
```

Before you specify the dimension line location, you can use the Mtext, Text, or the Angle option as described previously. The lines from point B to point C and point C to point A can be

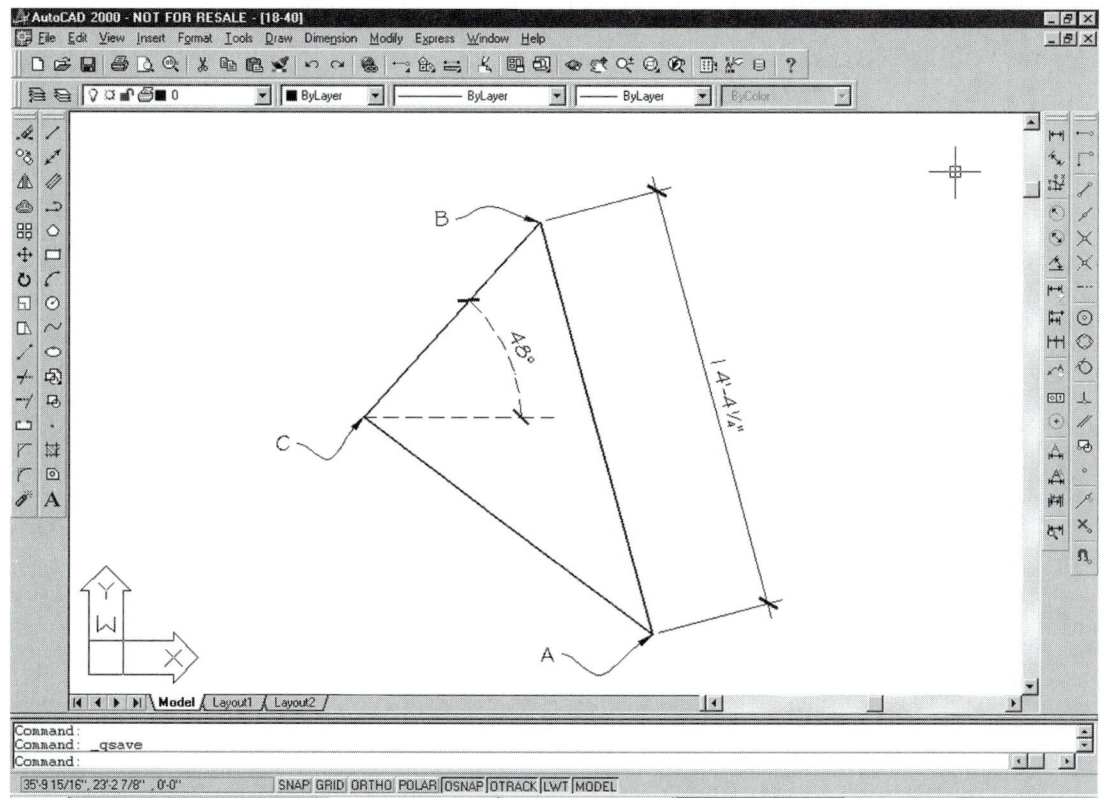

FIGURE 18–40 The Aligned Dimension is used to dimension angled surfaces.

dimensioned the same way because these lines are all inclined. To dimension the distance from point A to point B (not the same distance as the line from point B to point C) shown in Figure 18–41, will require you to use the Rotated option of the DIMLINEAR command. Because the dimension line to dimension the distance from point A to point B must be parallel to the line from point B to point C, a 48 degree rotation must be used as follows:

```
Command: DIMLINEAR ~EnterKey~
Specify first extension line origin or <select object>: (click on point A).
Specify second extension line origin: (click on point B).
Specify dimension location or
[Mtext/Text/Angle/Horizontal/Vertical/Rotated]: R ~EnterKey~
Specify angle of dimension line <0>: 48 ~EnterKey~
Specify dimension line location or
[Mtext/Text/Angle/Horizontal/Vertical/Rotated]: (left click on the
location shown).
```

The dimensioned drawing is shown in Figure 18–41.

Note: You can create isometric dimensions as follows: Select the Aligned Dimension button from the Dimension toolbar or select Aligned from the Dimension pull-down menu. Select the first and the second extension line origins or press the ~EnterKey~ to select the object. Place the dimension text at the required position. From the Dimension pull-down menu, select Oblique and select the dimension. Enter 30 at the Enter obliquing angle: prompt for dimensions placed in the front view of an object and enter −30 for dimensions placed in the side view of an object. This will convert the aligned dimension to the proper isometric oblique angle. You can also use the Dimension Edit button in the dimension toolbar, enter O for the Oblique option, select the dimension, and enter the appropriate angle. If you want the dimension text to be aligned with the dimension line, select the Aligned with dimension line radio button in the Text Alignment category of the Text tab of the Dimension Style dialog box.

FIGURE 18–41 To
dimension the inclined
surfaces that require a
parallel dimension line,
the Rotated option of
the DIMLINEAR
command must be used.

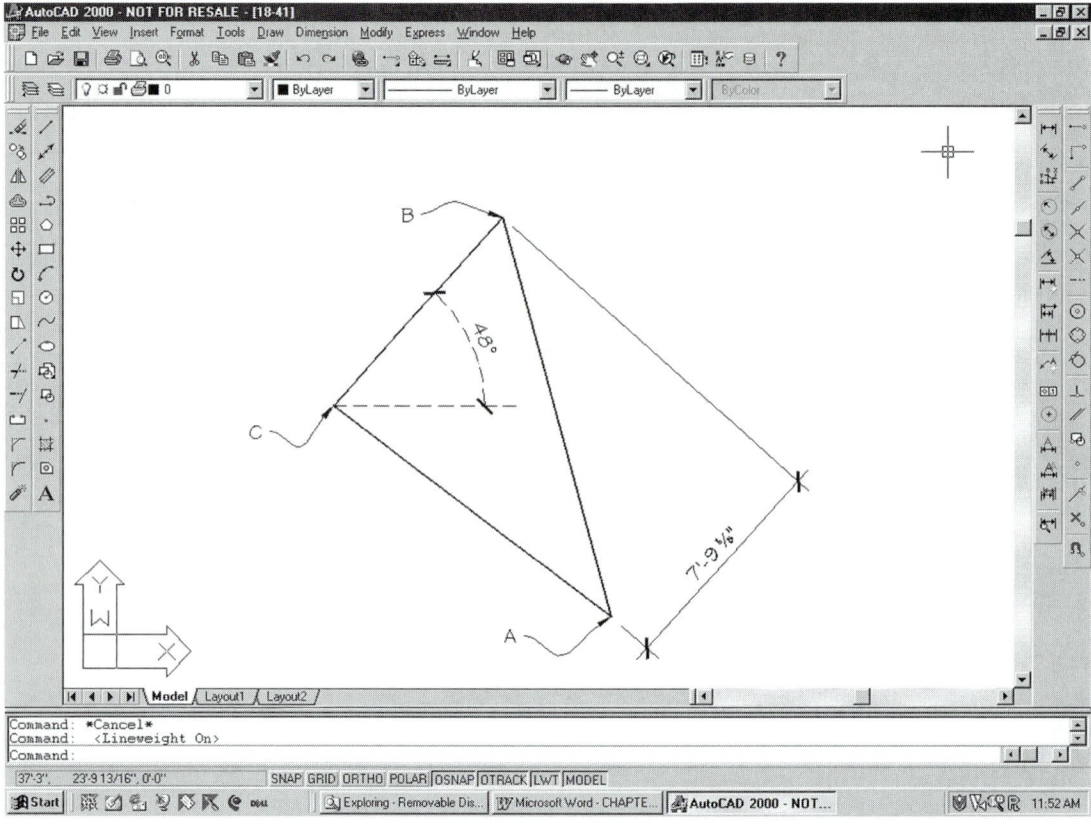

18.5.3   Ordinate Dimension

Ordinate dimensioning is referred to as arrowless dimensioning and it is mostly used in mechanical and electronics drafting. It will locate the X and Y coordinates of the points picked by providing an extension line and a value without an arrow or a tick mark. The ordinate dimensioning will work best if the Ortho is on. The ordinate dimensioning can also be performed using the DIMORDINATE or DOR commands at the command line, or by selecting Ordinate from the Dimension pull-down menu. Because all of the ordinate dimensions originate from a primary datum point, it is recommended that the UCS (User Coordinate System) be moved to the lower left corner or to the appropriate datum feature corner of the object.

18.5.4   Radius Dimension

The Radius Dimension button allows you to place a radius symbol and a radius dimension text for a circle or an arc. The DRA, DIMRAD, or DIMRADIUS commands can be typed at the command line to get a radius dimension, or you can access the DIMRADIUS command by selecting RADIUS from the Dimension pull-down menu. When using the radius dimension, a leader line, an arrowhead (tick mark), and the dimension text with the radius symbol will be placed inside or outside the circle or arc, depending on the radius size. A center mark or a centerline can be placed in the center of the circle or arc using the center marks for circles category of the Lines and Arrows tab inside the New, Modify, or Override Dimension Style dialog boxes. A radius dimension should use Closed filled arrowhead at the end of the leader line. If the Arrowhead style is set to Architectural tick for the Architectural style, the radius dimensions will have tick marks on the circles and arcs.

18.5.5   Diameter Dimension

The Diameter Dimension button allows you to place a diameter symbol and a diameter dimension text for a circle or an arc. The DDI or DIMDIAMETER command can be typed at the command line or you can select Diameter from the Dimension pull-down menu. The command sequence for the DIAMETER command is similar to the RADIUS command. You can also use

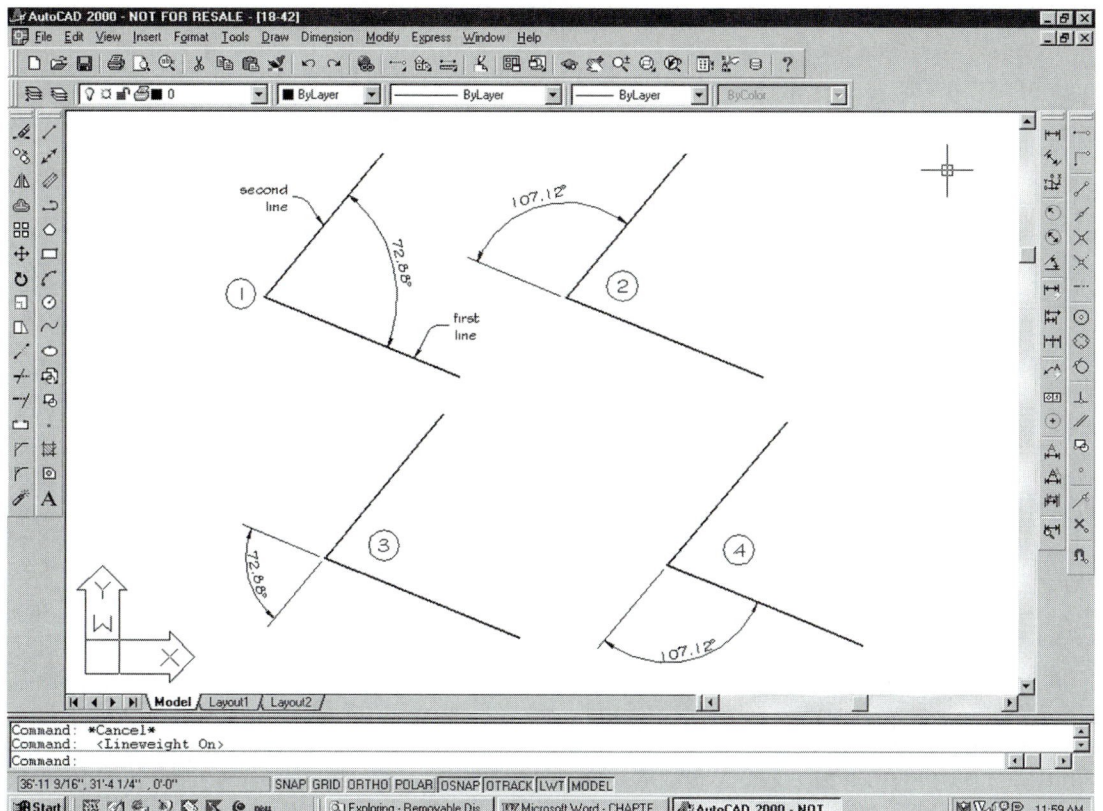

the Mtext, Text, or the Angle options to change the text value or the angle of the text. To use Closed filled arrowheads at the end of the leader lines you need to create a Diameter Sub-style similar to Radius Sub-style. Follow the procedures described at the beginning of the chapter to create the Diameter Sub-style.

18.5.6   Angular Dimension

The Angular Dimension button allows you to dimension the angle between any two nonparallel objects including lines, circles, and arcs. It will also provide an angular dimension using three points on the screen. AutoCAD will provide a dimension line and a value of the angle in degrees. This value depends on the type of angular unit selected. The DAN or the DIMANGULAR command can be typed at the command line or you can select Angular from the Dimension pulldown menu.

18.5.6.1 Angular Dimensioning Between Two Lines   By selecting the first and the second line, you can dimension the angle between the two lines shown in Figure 18–42 as follows:

```
Click on the Angular Dimension button on the Dimension toolbar.
Command: _dimangular
Select arc, circle, line, or <specify vertex>: (select the first line).
Select second line: (select the second line).
Specify dimension arc line location or [Mtext/Text/Angle]: (click on the
inside area of the lines).
```

The dimension arc line location is similar to the dimension line location of the DIMLINEAR command. With the angular dimensioning the dimension line becomes the arc line. The dimension arc location can be selected freely once the two objects are picked. The first angle in Figure 18–42 is the angle between the two lines where the dimension arc location is inside the lines. The other three angles are dimensioned by moving the cursor counterclockwise and by selecting the appropriate locations for the arc lines. Notice that the first dimension arc line uses the two lines as extension arc lines similar to extension lines of the DIMLINEAR command.

FIGURE 18–43 When placing an angular dimension on the circle, selecting the circle at a specific point will become the first angle endpoint. The second angle endpoint will determine the value of the angle.

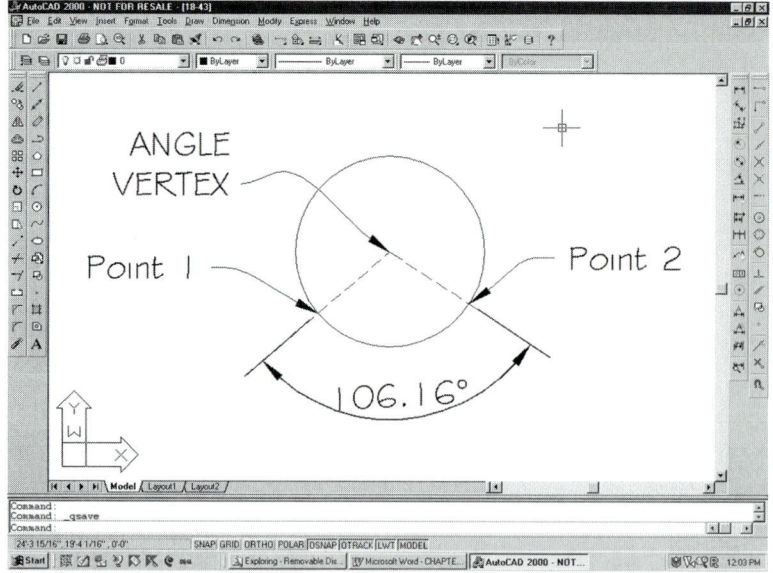

The third dimension arc line has two extension arc lines. To have arrowheads at the end of the dimension arc line locations instead of tick marks, create Angular substyle similar to the Diameter and the Radius substyles shown previously. Once you create a substyle, you can use the Modify... button to change any of the dimensioning variables applicable to the specific substyle.

18.5.6.2 Angular Dimensioning of Arcs and Circles   The Angular Dimensioning can be used to dimension the included angle of an arc or a specified portion of a circle. When a circle or arc is selected, the center point becomes the *vertex* point, which is the vertex of the angle. AutoCAD will automatically snap to the center of the circle or the arc and will ask for the second angle endpoint. The circle in Figure 18–43 is dimensioned by picking two points as the origin points for the arc extension line locations as follows:

```
Command: DIMANGULAR ~EnterKey~
Select arc, circle, line or <specify vertex>: (turn ORTHO and OSNAP off
and select point 1. This is an arbitrary location).
Specify second angle endpoint: (select point 2. This is an arbitrary
location. Notice that even with ORTHO and OSNAP off, the center of the
circle is selected as the angle vertex point).
Specify dimension arc line location or [Mtext/Text/Angle]: (move the
mouse away from the bottom of the circle and click on the location).
```

The dashed lines are not a part of the angular dimensioning; they merely represent the extensions of the first and the second angle endpoints that establish the angle vertex. You can experiment with the dimension arc line location by moving the cursor counterclockwise and clockwise and then up and down from the center of the circle. You will discover that a combination of arrangements is possible with different angle values at each location.

18.5.6.3 Angular Dimensioning Using Three Points   You do not have to have a line, arc, or circle to place an angular dimension. You can place an angular dimension through three points on the screen. These points can be existing or established on the screen while using the angular dimension. This is accomplished by using the <specify vertex> option of the DIMANGULAR command. Figure 18–44 shows three points on the screen. Point 1 is picked as the vertex point, point 2 is picked as the first angle endpoint, and point 3 is picked as the second angle endpoint as follows:

```
Right click on the command line to display a shortcut menu. This will
give you access to the last six commands. Click on DIMANGULAR.
Command: DIMANGULAR
```

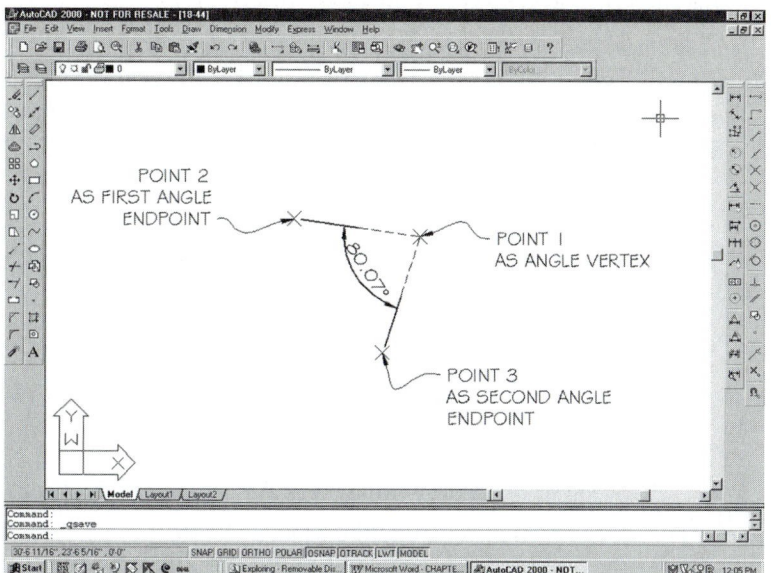

```
Select arc, circle, line, or <specify vertex>: (click on the right button).
Specify angle vertex: (click on the snap to node button on the Object
snap toolbar).
Specify angle vertex: _nod of (click on point 1).
Specify first angle endpoint: (click on the Snap to node button on the
Object snap toolbar).
Specify first angle endpoint: _nod of (click on point 2).
Specify second angle endpoint: (click on the Snap to node button on the
Object snap toolbar).
Specify second angle endpoint: _nod of (click on point 3).
Specify dimension arc line location or [Mtext/Text/Angle]: (select a
point somewhere in the middle).
Dimension text: 80.07 (this is the angular dimension text value in degrees).
```

18.5.7 Quick Dimension

The Quick Dimension button in the Dimension toolbar allows you to create a series of Continuous, Staggered, Baseline, Ordinate, Radius, Diameter, and Datum Point dimensions with a quick selection of geometry, thus reducing the number of extension line origins picked on the screen. The Baseline and Continue Dimensions will be discussed after the Quick Dimensioning. The QDIM command can be typed at the command line to create quick dimensions, or you can select QDIM from the Dimension pull-down menu. The Quick Dimension is extremely useful when creating a series of continuous dimensions in architectural drawings and can substitute for a conventional dimensioning application. The Quick Dimensioning offers many advantages that increase productivity significantly. When using the QDIM command, you can either select individual objects to be dimensioned or you can simply select the geometry to be dimensioned using any of the object selection methods. When selecting individual objects, you do not have to use object snap modes as you would with conventional dimensioning. With Quick Dimensioning, selecting the objects to be dimensioned will automatically create the required series of dimensions on the drawing. When selecting the geometry as a single selection, you can utilize the Window, Crossing, Window Polygon, Crossing Polygon, and Fence selection options among other selection methods. A good working knowledge of the object selection methods will increase the productivity of your Quick Dimensioning tasks. Selecting objects using any of the two methods described above will create a *dimension point* on the object geometry. This Dimension point is different than dimension definition points (defoints), which are discussed under Associative Dimensioning. When all of the dimensioning points are selected, AutoCAD will create quick dimensioning from the dimensioning points. The default for Quick Dimensioning is Continuous, which means chain dimensioning.

■ **EXERCISE 18–5:**   *The following step-by-step exercise will allow you to dimension the lower portion of the object shown in Figure 18–45 using the QDIM command. It requires just three mouse-clicks to chain dimension the lower portion using the QDIM command. Using a combination of Linear Dimension and Continue Dimension method would have required many picks on the object. For the QDIM to work properly for architectural dimensioning, the Architectural dimensioning style should be created and made current as previously discussed.*

Step #1:   Open the EXE18-1.dwg file.

Step #2:   Use the QDIM command as follows:

Command: **QDIM** ~EnterKey~(or click on the Quick Dimension button in the Dimension toolbar).

Select geometry to dimension: *(when the cursor turns into a pickbox, create a crossing box by clicking on point 1 as shown in Figure 18–46).*

Specify opposite corner: *(moving the mouse from right to left click on point 2).*

Your drawing should now look like Figure 18–46.

Specify other corner: 13 found *(six vertical lines, five horizontal lines, and two semicircles are selected).*

In reality, your selection method created eight dimension points as shown in Figure 18–47.

Select geometry to dimension: *(right click).*

Specify dimension line position, or

[Continuous/Staggered/Baseline/Ordinate/Radius/Diameter/datumPoint/Edit] <Continuous>: *(moving the mouse to the bottom of the drawing click on a dimension line location).*

Congratulations! You have successfully used the QDIM command. The seven chain dimensions originating from eight dimension points will now create the continuous dimensions for the building as shown in Figure 18-48.

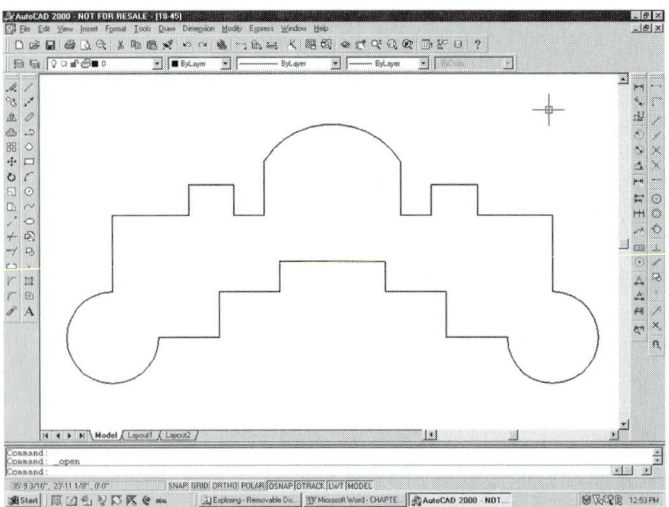

FIGURE 18–45   The footprint of this building requires only three mouse clicks to create seven dimensions as chain dimensioning using Quick Dimensioning (QDIM).

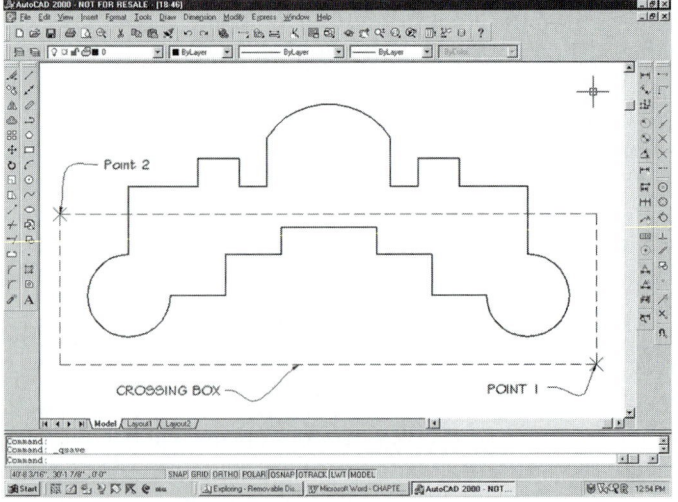

FIGURE 18–46   At Select geometry to dimension prompt, a crossing box is used to select six vertical lines.

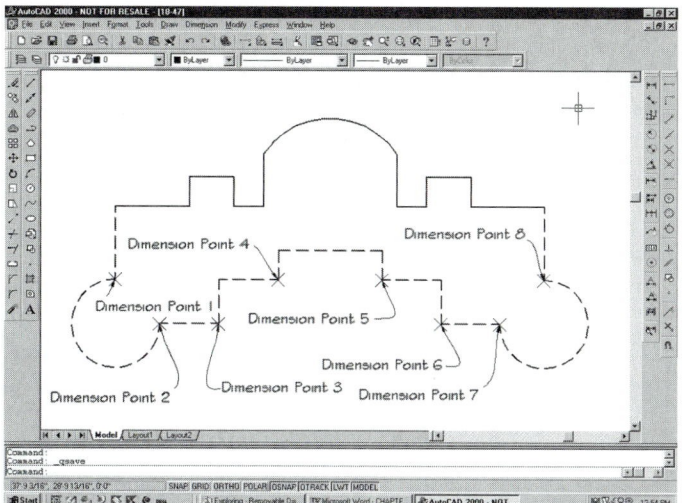

FIGURE 18–47 When the crossing box is completed, the entities inside or crossing the box will appear as dashed lines. This is where the selection will create the eight dimension points where continuous dimensions will originate.

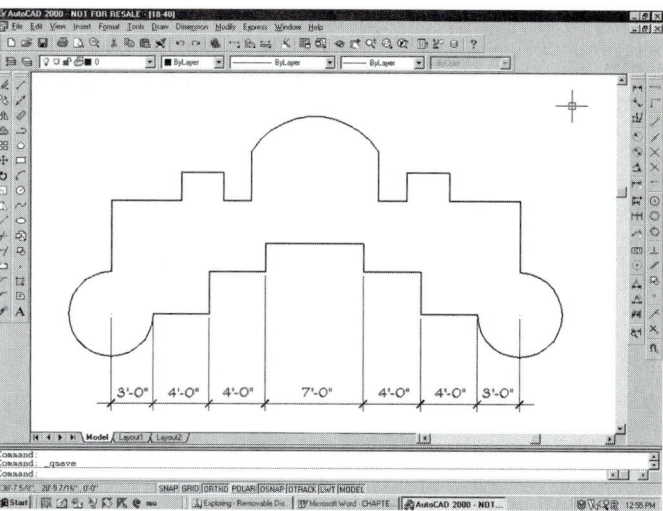

FIGURE 18–48 After the dimension line position is selected the chain dimensions are placed on the bottom portion of the building.

The crossing selection box is used to select vertical lines on the lower part of the building. Because the crossing box does not have to enclose the entire object it only needs to cross entities to select it. In this case the two vertical lines crossed the box and the other four vertical lines are inside the crossing box as well as the horizontal lines. The creation of the crossing box in relation to the objects selected determines the *dimension points* in which the continuous (chain) dimensioning originates. When the crossing box is created in a different manner the resulting continuous dimension would be different. The object selection method is an important part of Quick Dimensioning concept. A much higher degree of efficiency can be achieved by using a specific selection method and applying it properly in the drawing.

The Staggered option of the QDIM command will create a series of Staggered dimensions with staggered dimension text as shown in Figure 18–49. The procedure for creating Staggered dimensions is similar to the continuous option where the selection of objects through a crossing box determines the amount of Staggered dimensions. For example, in Figure 18–49 there are four Staggered dimensions, each starting from the opposite outside corner of the building. The first Staggered dimension is between the two opposite outside corners of the building. AutoCAD will automatically place the dimension text for each dimension line in a staggered fashion.

The Baseline option will create a series of Baseline dimensions. The Ordinate option will create a series of Ordinate dimensions. The Radius option will create a series of Radius dimensions. The Diameter option will create a series of Diameter dimensions. The Datum Point option will set a new datum point for the Baseline and Ordinate dimensions. At the Select new datum point command prompt, select a new location. The Edit option will allow you to edit a series of dimensions by adding or removing dimension points from existing dimensions. The default is Remove. After selecting the object geometry to dimension, enter E for the Edit option and select a dimension point to remove or enter A for the Add option to add a dimension point to object geometry to dimension. After removing or adding dimension points, press the ~EnterKey~ to select a dimension line position. To add a dimension point, enter A at the Indicate dimension point to remove, or [Add/eXit] <eXit>: command prompt. At the Indicate dimension point to add, or [Remove/eXit] <eXit>: command prompt, click on the dimension points to add.

Caution: The QDIM command will recognize and create dimensions for lines, arcs, circles, polylines, and points. The QDIM command does not recognize objects created with multilines. To dimension

FIGURE 18–49 The Staggered option of the QDIM command will stagger the dimension text as the dimension lines start from one outside corner to the opposite outside corner of the building.

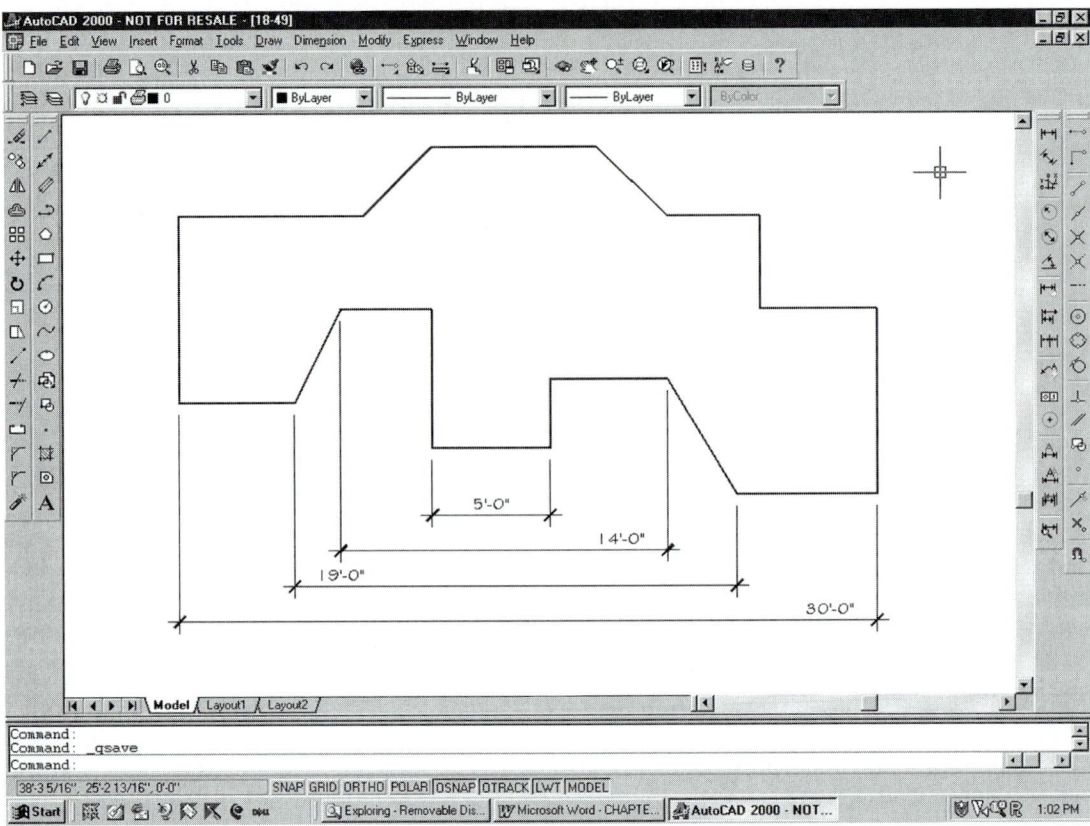

multilines using the QDIM command, turn multilines into individual segments by exploding them. Or use the LINE command and the OFFSET command to create parallel lines for floor plans. Also, when using the QDIM command to create dimensions, you will not be able to place the dimension text manually even when the DIMUPT (user positioned text) is on. To place text manually when using the QDIM command, use the Dimension Text Edit button in the Dimension toolbar after the dimension is created. Refer to Editing Dimensions for more information.

18.5.8 Baseline Dimension

The Baseline Dimension button on the Dimension toolbar will allow you to create baseline dimensions where a series of offset dimensions originate from a corner of the object. Each dimension is independent on the others because each dimension is created from the baseline of the previous dimension or a selected dimension. Each dimension is referenced from the originating point that is common for all baseline dimensions. Baseline dimensioning is commonly used in mechanical drafting. Baseline dimensions are created by entering DBA or DIMBASELINE at the command line or by selecting Baseline from the Dimension pull-down menu. Since baseline dimensions originate from a common point, a reference dimension must be created prior to using the DIMBASELINE command. This is called the fist dimension of the baseline. This first dimension is created by selecting the first and the second extension line origins on the object when using Linear Dimensions, by specifying a feature location when using the Ordinate Dimensions, and by selecting arc, circle, or line when using the Angular dimensions. After establishing the first dimension, the Baseline Dimension button in the Dimension toolbar can be used to create the next series of baseline dimensions. Figure 18–50 shows a baseline dimension.

The first dimension of the baseline that is the origination point for the other dimensions can be established on any corner of the drawing. The Undo option will deselect a second extension

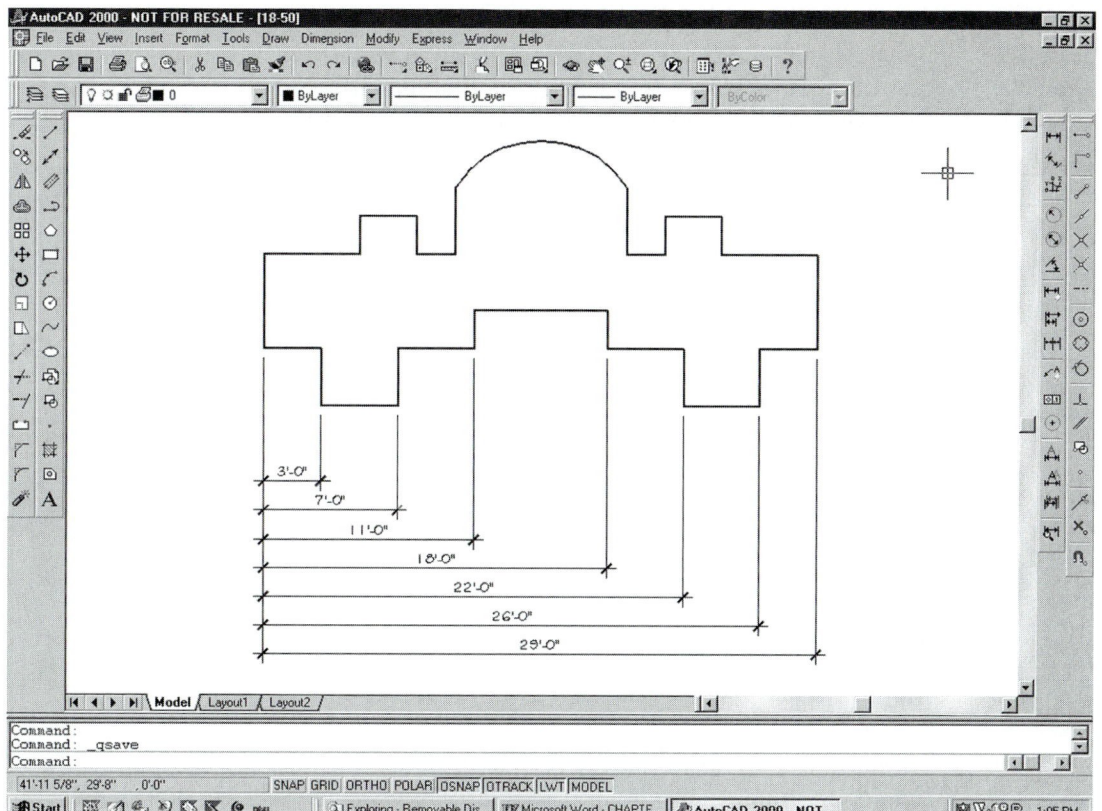

FIGURE 18–50 To create Baseline Dimensions, a dimension must exist prior to using the DIMBASELINE command. The first and second extension line origins are used to create the first dimension of the baseline. This is where all the other dimensions will originate.

line origin. If the DIMBASELINE command does not follow immediately after the Linear, Ordinate, or Angular dimensions, AutoCAD will give the following respond:

```
Select baseline dimension:
```

You can select any Linear, Ordinate, or Angular dimension to start the Baseline Dimensioning. You can also use the <Select> option by pressing ~EnterKey~ to get the Select baseline dimension: prompt.

18.5.9 Continue Dimension

The Continue Dimension button on the Dimension toolbar will allow you to create chain dimensions on the drawings, a series of shorter dimensions that add up to the overall dimension. Architectural drawings utilize continue dimensions the most. When creating Continue dimensions, each dimension is dependent on the other dimensions because it is created from the second extension line of the previous dimension or a selected dimension where each dimension is referenced from the previous point. When Linear Continue dimensions are created, AutoCAD will suppress the first extension line. Continue dimensions are created by entering DCO or DIMCONTINUE at the command line or by selecting Continue from the Dimension pull-down menu. If there are no dimensions in the current drawing and you select an object, AutoCAD will prompt you for a Linear, Ordinate, or Angular dimension to use as reference for the next dimension. If the previous dimension was a Linear, Ordinate, or Angular dimension, the origin of that dimension's second extension line is used for the origin of the next dimension's first extension line. Because continue dimensions originate from the previous dimension points along a continuous string chained together, a reference dimension must exist prior to using the DIMCONTINUE command. Similar to the Baseline Dimension concept, this is called the first dimension of the chain dimensions. The first dimension is created by selecting the first and second extension line origins on the object when using Linear Dimensions, by specifying a feature location when using the Ordinate Dimensions, and by selecting arc, circle, or line when using the Angular dimensions. After establishing the first dimension, the Continue Dimension button in the Dimension toolbar can be used to create chain dimensions.

■ **EXERCISE 18–6:**   *The following step-by-step exercise will allow you to create continue dimensions for the drawing shown in Figure 18–51. Before using the DIMCONTINUE command, the DIMLINEAR command will be used to create the first dimension as the origination point. The second extension line origin of the previous dimension will be the chain dimension.*

Step #1:   Open the EXE18-2.dwg file.

Step #2:   Create the first dimension as follows:

Command: **DIMLINEAR** ~EnterKey~

Specify first extension line origin or <select object>: *(click on the first extension line origin as shown in Figure 18–51).*

Specify second extension line origin: *(click on the second extension line origin)*

Specify dimension line location or

[Mtext/Text/Angle/Horizontal/Vertical/Rotated]: *(move the cursor down and select a dimension line location and left-click).*

The drawing will now look like Figure 18–52.

Step #3:   Create Continue Dimensions as follows:

Click on the Continue Dimension button in the Dimension toolbar.

Specify a second extension line origin or [Undo/Select] <Select>: *(using the object snap modes, click on the first point after the first linear dimension going from left to right. This is shown as the first X on the right side of the 7'-0" dimension in Figure 18–52).*

FIGURE 18–51   To create Continue Dimensions, a dimension must exist prior to using the DIMCONTINUE command. The first and second extension line origins are used to create the first linear dimension.

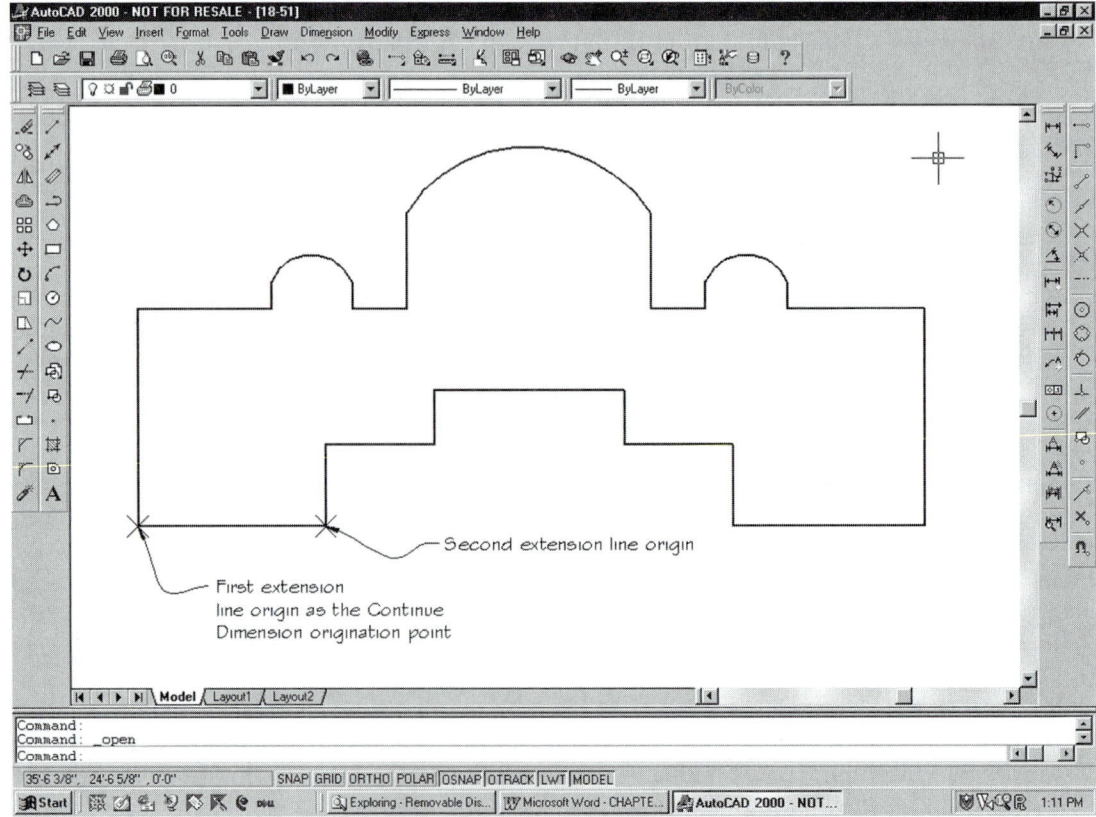

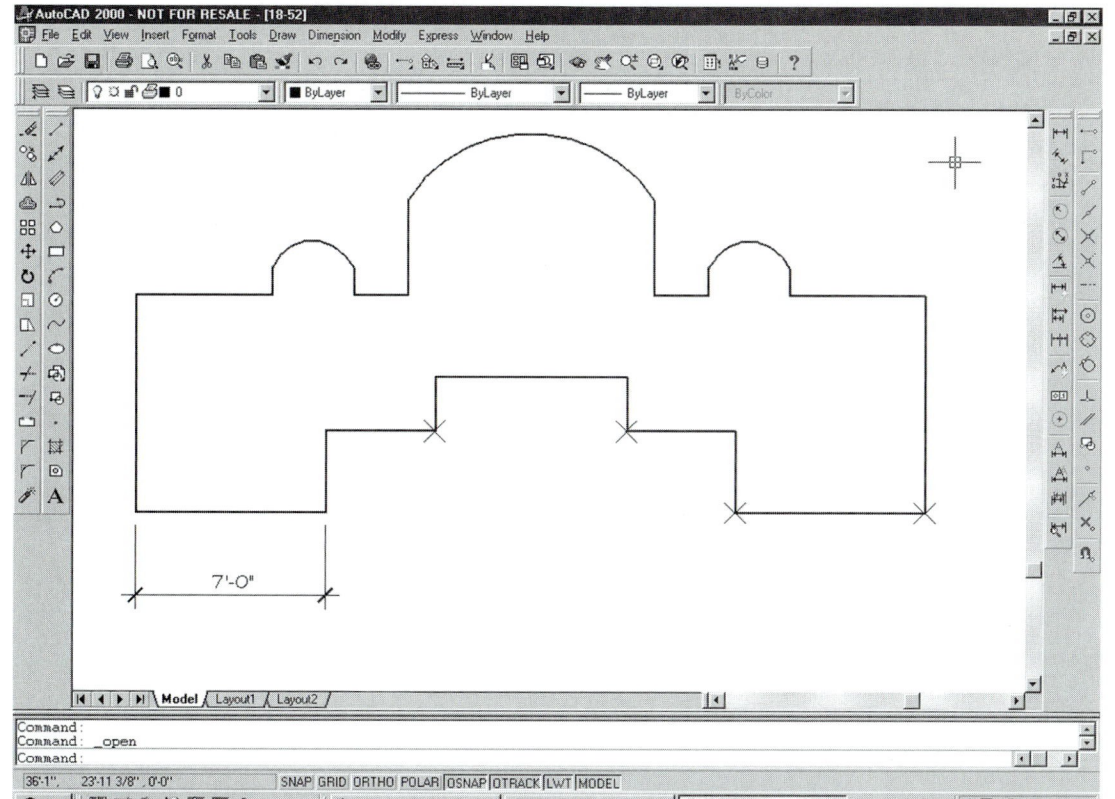

FIGURE 18–52 The first dimension is created for the chain dimensioning to follow. The Xs on the drawing indicate the second extension line origins. Each X point is referenced from the second extension line origin of the previous dimension.

Dimension text = 4'-0"

Specify a second extension line origin or [Undo/Select] <Select>: *(click on the next X point).*

Dimension text = 7'-0"

Specify a second extension line origin or [Undo/Select] <Select>: *(click on the next X point).*

Dimension text = 4'-0"

Specify a second extension line origin or [Undo/Select] <Select>: *(click on the last X point).*

Dimension text = 7'-0"

Specify a second extension line origin or [Undo/Select] <Select>:

Select continue dimension: ~EnterKey~ *(to exit the command).*

The X points on the drawing are for illustration purposes. This does not mean you should establish points at those locations using the POINT command.

Congratulations! You have successfully used the Continue Dimension. Your drawing will now look like Figure 18–53.

You can use the <Select> option by pressing ~EnterKey~ to get the Select continue dimension: prompt where you can select any of the existing Linear, Ordinate, or Angular dimensions.

18.5.10 Quick Leader

The Quick Leader button in the Dimension toolbar will allow you to quickly place leaders and their annotations without requiring several extra steps. It also gives you the option to establish leader settings through the leader Settings dialog box. A leader is a line object with a specific

FIGURE 18–53 The
Continue dimensions
originate from the
second extension line
origins of the previous
dimension.

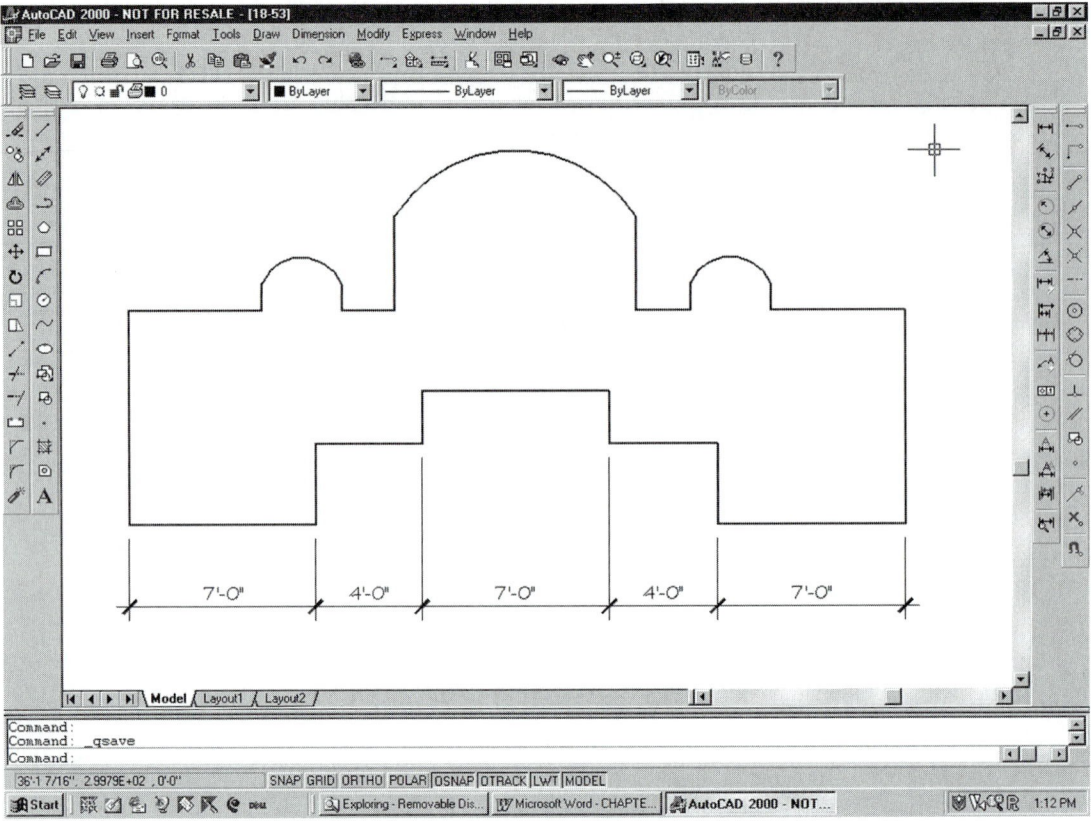

arrowhead style attached to the beginning point and an annotation attached to the ending point that is connected to a specified object on the screen. Annotation refers to the notes typed as text. A leader line does not have to include annotation; it can simply be attached to an existing text or an existing object. A block can also be attached to a leader line. You can have single or multiple lines of annotation attached to the end of the leader. Leader lines are a quick and easy way to add specific notes to drawing features and are used to identify specific components of architectural elements such as building materials on building elevations or structural components on a typical wall section. A typical leader has four major components as shown in Figure 18–54.

1. **First Leader Point:** This is the starting point of the leader line. It usually has an arrowhead style attached to it. Figure 18–54 shows a leader with a closed filled arrowhead style. The arrowhead can be set to none to suppress or another arrowhead style can be attached. The arrowhead style and size are controlled by the current dimension style settings. But you can still control the arrowhead size and customize leader line and annotation format and properties using the Leader Settings dialog box. This dialog box is explained shortly. You may recall that in the Architectural dimensioning style, the Leader: drop-down menu under the Arrowheads category inside the Lines and Arrows tab of the New, Modify, and Override dialog boxes is set to Closed filled for the arrowhead style. And the Arrow size: drop-down menu is set to 1/8″. Unless a Leader substyle is created, or leader properties are changed using the Properties window, leader lines have the same properties as dimension lines settings inside the current dimension style. Creating individual substyles was discussed earlier.

2. **First Leader Line Segment:** This is the line attached to the end of the arrowhead and can be of any length and any angle. The line between the first leader point and the second leader point is considered to be the first leader segment. Using the Leader Settings dialog box, leader lines can be set to have a Straight or a Spline (smooth curves) format, and the angle in which a leader line is drawn can be set to a variety of values. You can also set the angle of the first and the second leader line segments to meet your requirements.

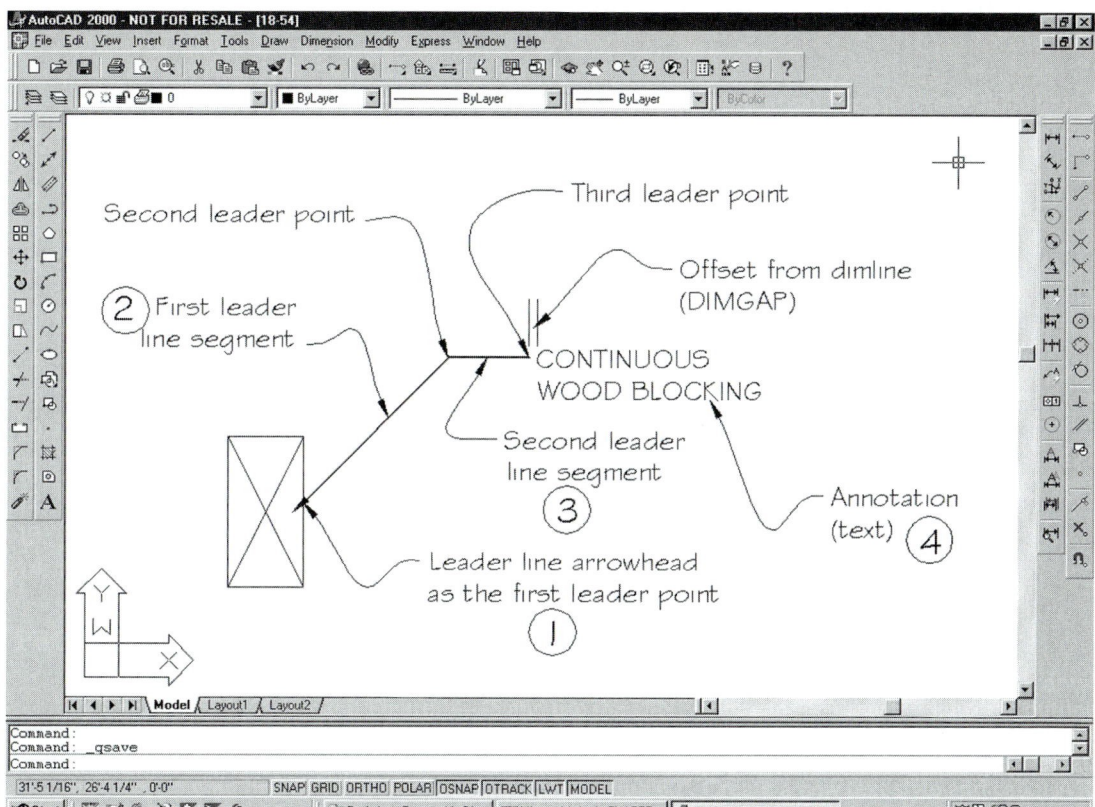

FIGURE 18–54 The four major components of a typical leader.

3. **Second Leader Line Segment:** This is the shoulder of a leader line and is the continuation of the leader line from the second leader point. The number of leader points can be set to a maximum or can be set to have no limits to suit your drawing needs. The second leader line segment can be set to be horizontal or at a different angle using the Leader Settings dialog box. You can also set the limitations on the number of leader points. The distance between the endpoint of the last leader line segment (third leader point in Figure 18–54) and the beginning of the annotation is controlled by the DIMGAP dimensioning variable. You can also control this distance using the Offset from dim line: drop-down menu under the Text Placement category of the Text tab in the New, Modify, and Override Dimension Style dialog boxes.

4. **Annotation:** This is the text part attached to the leader line. It can be a single or a multiple lines of text or it can be a Block reference.

The Quick Leader is created by selecting the Quick Leader button in the Dimension toolbar, entering QLEADER or LE at the command line, or by selecting Leader from the Dimension pull-down menu. The QLEADER command will allow you to customize annotation type and format, number of leader points allowed, leader line geometry, angle constraints for the first and second leader line segments, and annotation attachment options. **The LEADER command is different than the QLEADER command.** The LEADER command does not have the flexibility for customization and does not provide you with a dialog box to change settings. The Leader command is discussed later.

18.5.10.1 Using the Leader Settings Dialog Box   When a leader line is created, its color, lineweight, and arrowhead style and size are controlled by the current dimension style settings. When a Leader Sub-style is created, the same properties are controlled under the Sub-style settings. The Leader Settings dialog box will help you establish and control other properties of the

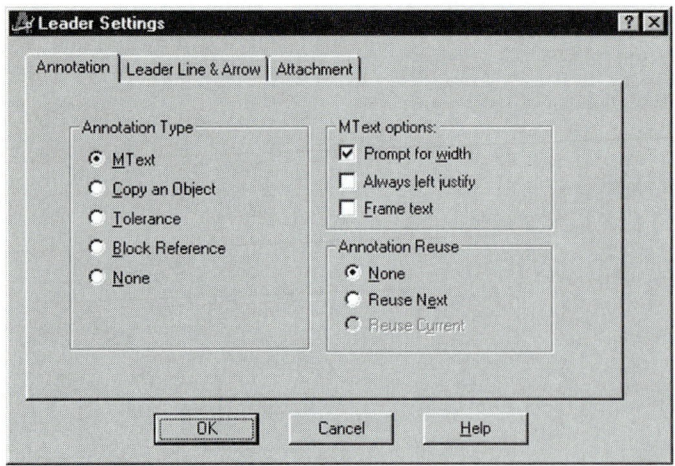

FIGURE 18–55 The Leader Settings dialog box will help you establish settings for leader lines.

leader lines including the arrowhead style. The Leader Settings dialog box shown in Figure 18–55 can be accessed as follows:

```
From the Dimension toolbar, click on the
Quick Leader button and follow the command
line procedure shown below:
Command: _qleader
Specify first leader point, or [Settings]
<Settings>: ~EnterKey~.
```

Let's examine the three tabs and their settings:

Annotation: (tab) This tab will help you define the leader annotation type that will be attached to the leader lines. There are three categories as follows:

Annotation Type: This category will help you set the leader annotation type. The type you select will change the QLEADER command's leader line annotation prompt at the command line. It has five options as described below:

- **MTEXT:** (radio button). When this button is checked, AutoCAD will prompt you to create MText (multiline text) annotation. After establishing the number of leader points on the screen, you will have two options for annotation. You can press the ~EnterKey~ to use the Multiline Text Editor dialog box or you can start typing annotation immediately.

- **COPY AN OBJECT:** (radio button). Checking this button will prompt you to copy an existing multiline text, single line text, block reference, or tolerance object to the leader line after establishing the number of leader points specified.

- **TOLERANCE:** (radio button). Checking this button will prompt you to create a feature control frame that display geometric tolerances by displaying the Geometric Tolerance dialog box after establishing the number of leader points specified.

- **BLOCK REFERENCE:** (radio button). Checking this button will prompt you to insert a block to the endpoint of the last leader line segment.

- **NONE:** (radio button). Checking this button will create a leader line without annotation. This is useful when you want to attach a leader line to an existing text without typing any annotation.

MText options: This category will help you specify multiline text options. The three options under the MText options category will be available only when the MText radio button is checked under the Annotation type. The three options are as follows:

- **PROMPT FOR WIDTH:** (check box). When this box is checked, AutoCAD will prompt you to specify a width for the MText word wrapping. When the MText and Prompt for width are selected you can create a text boundary or enter a width value. A leader line from right to left will always be right justified, and a leader line from left to right will always be left justified. When the leader line is pulled to the left, the starting point for the annotation (the vertical blinking line) will always be on the right side of the Multiline Text Editor dialog box text boundary area.

- **ALWAYS LEFT JUSTIFY:** (check box). When this box is checked, the MText annotation will be left justified. This means that when the Multiline Text Editor dialog box appears, the starting point for the annotation (the vertical blinking line) will always be on the left even when the leader line is from right to left.

- **FRAME TEXT:** (check box). When this box is checked, a box is placed around the annotation.

Annotation Reuse: This category will help you set options for reusing leader line annotation. The three options are as follows:

- **NONE:** (radio button). If this button is checked, you cannot reuse leader line annotation.

- **REUSE NEXT:** (radio button). Checking this button will allow you to reuse the previous leader line annotation. This is useful if you have a series of notes that will be used over several times. When this button is checked, AutoCAD will remember the last annotation used and will apply the same annotation each time you reissue the QLEADER command.

- **REUSE CURRENT:** (radio button). AutoCAD will automatically select this button when the annotation is reused several times after checking the Reuse Next button. When the Reuse Current button is checked, the Annotation Type category options will not be available.

■ **EXERCISE 18–7:**   *The following step-by-step exercise will allow you to create the leader line and the annotation shown in Figure 18–56 by using the Annotation tab of the Leader Settings dialog box.*

Step #1:   Open the EXE18-3.dwg file.

Step #2:   Click on the Quick Leader button in the Dimension toolbar and use the following command line procedure:

Command: _qleader

Specify first leader point, or [Settings] <Settings>: ~EnterKey~ *(this will display the Leader Settings dialog box as shown in Figure 18–55).*

Step #3:   Inside the Annotation tab click on the MText radio button and click on the OK button.

Specify first leader point, or [Settings] <Settings>: *(turn ORTHO off and click on the Snap to Nearest button in the Object Snap toolbar).*

Specify first leader point, or [Settings] <Settings>: _nea to *(select the plywood material, that is the first leader point as shown in Figure 18–56).*

Specify next point: **@36<45** ~EnterKey~ *(this will draw the first leader line segment 3'-0" long at 45 degrees. This is the second leader point).*

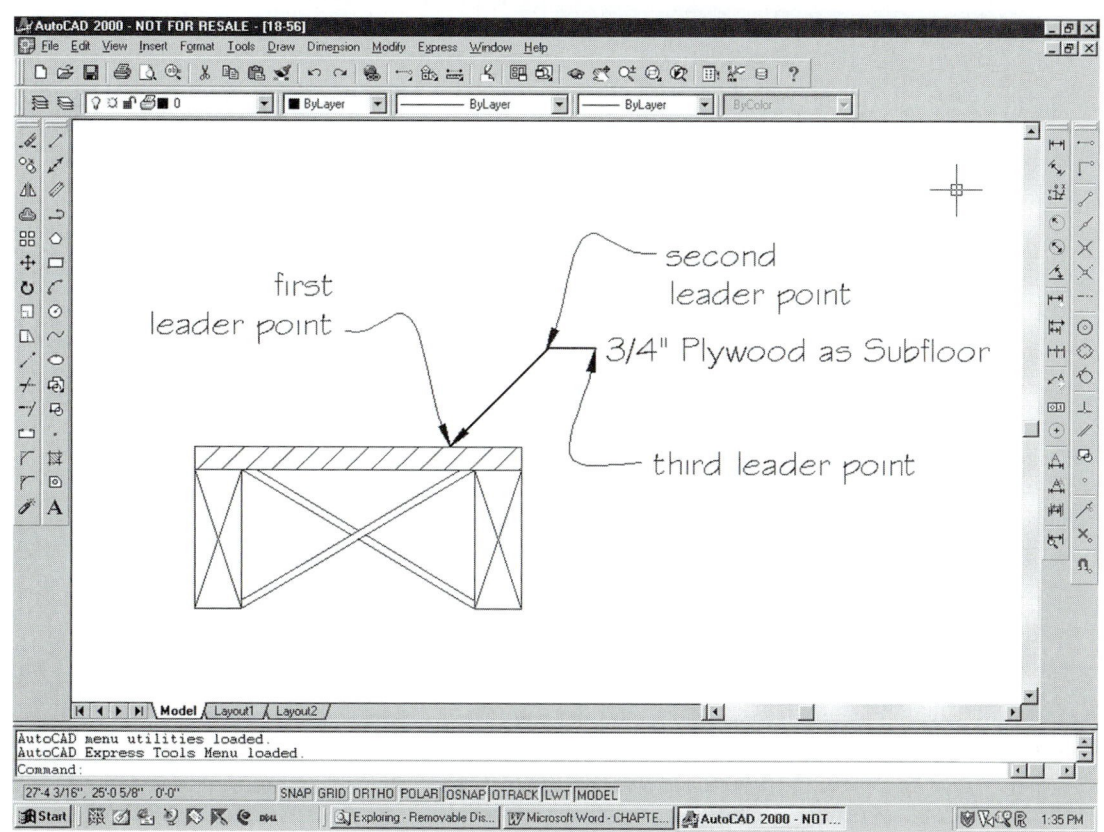

FIGURE 18–56 Using the QLEADER command to place a simple leader line with annotation. Note that you can set the angles for the first and second leader line segments using the Leader Line & Arrow tab rather than typing at the command line.

Specify next point: **@12<0** ~EnterKey~ *(this will draw the second leader line segment horizontal 1'-0" long. This is the third leader point).*

Specify text width <0">: ~EnterKey~

Enter first line of annotation text <MText>: **3/4" Plywood as Subfloor** ~EnterKey~

Enter next line of annotation text: ~EnterKey~

Congratulations! You have successfully created a leader line segment with annotation.

■ **EXERCISE 18–8:** *The following step-by-step exercise will allow you to attach an existing block named* wall detail reference *to a leader line in a partial floor plan by using the Annotation tab of the Leader Settings dialog box as shown in Figure 18–57. The block already exists in the drawing. See Chapter 19 for creating blocks.*

Step #1: Open the EXE18-4.dwg file.

Step #2: Use the QLEADER command as follows:

Command: **QLEADER** ~EnterKey~

Specify first leader point, or [Settings] <Settings>: ~EnterKey~ *(This will display the Leader Settings dialog box).*

Step #3: Inside the Annotation tab click on the Block Reference button and click on the OK button.

Specify first leader point, or [Settings] <Settings>: *(Turn Ortho off and click on the Snap to Nearest button in the Object Snap toolbar).*

Specify first leader point, or [Settings] <Settings>: _nea to *(Select the upper left section of the circle on the floor plan. This is the first leader point as shown in Figure 18–57).*

FIGURE 18–57 Using the Block Reference button inside the Annotation Type will allow you to attach a Block to the leader line.

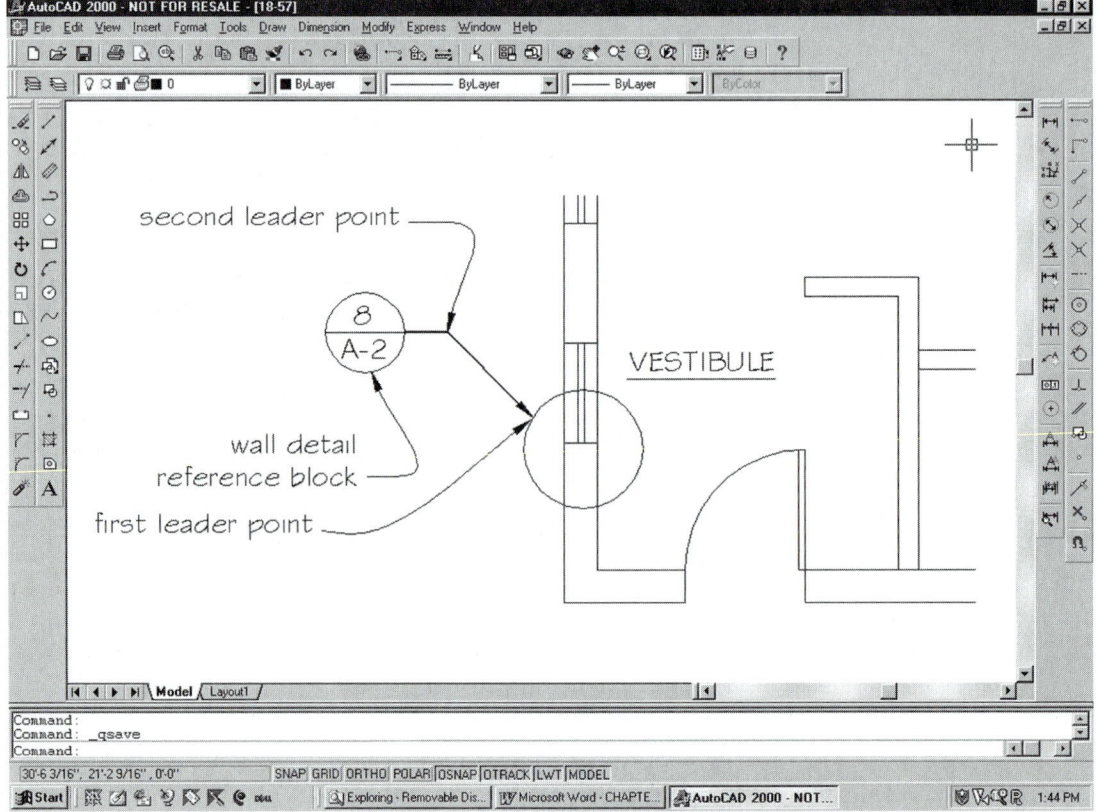

Specify next point: *(Move the cursor approximately 45 degrees and draw the first leader line segment. This is the second leader point).*

Specify next point: *(Turn Ortho on and move the cursor from right to left and draw the second leader line segment. This is the third leader point).*

Specify next point: Enter block name or [?]: **wall detail reference** ~EnterKey~

Specify insertion point or [Scale/X/Y/Z/Rotate/PScale//PX/PY//PZ/Protate]: *(click on the Snap to Endpoint and select the endpoint of the leader line).*

Enter X scale factor, specify opposite corner, or [Corner/XYZ] <1>: ~EnterKey~

Enter Y scale factor <use X scale factor>: ~EnterKey~

Specify rotation angle <0>: ~EnterKey~

Congratulations! You have successfully attached an existing block to a leader line. Do not save the changes.

Note: When Copy an Object, Tolerance, Block Reference, or None radio button is checked, the Attachment tab of the leader Settings dialog box will disappear.

Leader Line & Arrow: (tab) This tab will help you establish the leader line and arrowhead format as shown in Figure 18–58.

The four categories are as follows:

- **LEADER LINE:** This category will help you establish the format of the leader lines. The two options are as follows:

- **STRAIGHT:** (radio button). Checking this button will create leader line segments composed of straight lines for all leader line segments. If the last leader line segment is at an angle greater than 15 degrees from the horizontal, a small hook line will connect the leader to the annotation. You have been using the Straight leader line format so far.

- **SPLINE:** (radio button). Checking this button will create leader line segments composed of smooth curves called Spline for all leader line segments. This is most common in architectural drawings.

- **NUMBER OF POINTS:** This category will help you set and limit the number of leader line points AutoCAD will prompt you to specify before prompting for the leader line annotation. The two options are as follows:

- **NO LIMIT:** (check box). The No Limit check box will allow you to create unlimited leader points before using annotation. When the No Limits box is checked, the Maximum drop-down menu will not be available and the QLEADER will not prompt you for leader line points until you press ~EnterKey~ twice.

- **MAXIMIM:** (drop-down menu). When you want to limit the amount of leader line points before using annotation, place that number inside the Maximum drop-down menu. The default is 2 maximum leader line points. For example, if you click on the up arrow in the Maximum drop-down menu until 4 is displayed, the QLEADER command will automatically prompt you to specify annotation after you select three leader line points. Two leader line points are equal to one leader line segment. The first point you pick on the screen is the first leader line point; the second point you pick on the screen will create the first leader line segment; and the third point you pick on the screen will create the second leader line segment. Remember to set the number of points to one more than the number of leader line segments you want to create.

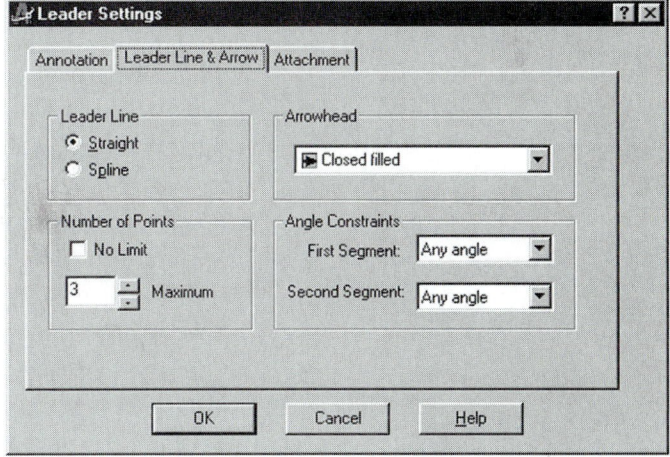

FIGURE 18–58 The Leader Line & Arrow tab of the Leader Settings dialog box will allow you to control leader line and arrowhead style format.

Arrowhead: This category will help you select the arrowhead style for the first leader point. You can select an arrowhead from the Arrowhead drop-down list. This is the same list as the ones inside the New, Modify, and Override Dimension Style dialog boxes. When you select a leader arrowhead style other than Closed filled in this dialog box, you will be creating a <style overrides> inside the Dimension Style Manager dialog box. Each time you select a different arrowhead style, the Leader: drop-down menu under the Arrowheads category inside the Lines and Arrows tab of the Modify Dimension Style dialog box will show the new arrowhead style. If you want to attach a block as a leader line arrowhead, click on User Arrow. . .This will display the Select Custom Arrow Block dialog box. If you have blocks created, a list of blocks in the drawing will be displayed. Select one of the custom blocks to use as the arrowhead. If you select None, arrowhead will be suppressed and no arrowhead will be shown.

Angle Constraints: This category will help you set angle constraints for the first and second leader lines. The two options are as follows:

- **FIRST SEGMENT:**   (drop-down list). The Any Angle setting will allow you to establish the first leader line segment (two leader points) at any angle you desire. You can set this angle to be Horizontal, 90 degrees, 45 degrees, 30 degrees, or 15 degrees.

- **SECOND SEGMENT:**   (drop-down list). This will set the angle of the second leader line segment. The angle options are the same as for the First Segment. Since Spline leader lines are created as smooth curved lines, the First and Second Segment should be set to Any Angle for a spline character.

Tips: Use Polar Tracking inside the Drafting Settings dialog box to draw the first leader line segment at 45 degrees after the first leader line point without setting Angle Constraints inside the Leader Settings dialog box.

■ **EXERCISE 18–9:**   *The following step-by-step exercise will allow you to create the Spline leader line and the annotation as shown in Figure 18–59 by using the Leader Line & Arrow tab of the Leader Settings dialog box.*

Step #1: Open the EXE18-4.dwg file and erase the wall detail circle.

Step #2: Right click inside the command line. This will display a shortcut menu. Highlight Recent Commands and pick QLEADER. If you have not used the QLEADER command during the last six commands it will not be displayed.

Command: QLEADER

Specify first leader point, or [Settings] <Settings>: ~EnterKey~ *(this will display the Leader Settings dialog box)*

Step #3: Click on the Leader Line & Arrow tab and click on the Spline radio button. Under the Number of Points category, click on the Maximum drop-down menu up arrow and set it to 5. Make sure the Angle Constraints for the First and Second Segment is set to Any Angle. Click on the OK button.

Specify first leader point, or [Settings] <Settings>: *(turn Ortho and OSNAP off and select the first leader point as shown in Figure 18-59).*

Specify next point: *(select the second leader point, this is the first leader line segment).*

Specify next point: *(select the third leader point, this is the second leader line segment).*

Specify next point: *(select the fourth leader point, this is the third leader line segment).*

Specify next point: *(select the fifth and last leader point, this is the fourth and last leader line segment allowed).*

Specify text width <0">: ~EnterKey~

Enter first line of annotation text <MText>: **Wall Composition:** ~EnterKey~

Enter next line of annotation text: **2X6** ~EnterKey~

Enter next line of annotation text: **wood studs** ~EnterKey~

Enter next line of annotation text: **@16" O.C.** ~EnterKey~

Enter next line of annotation text: ~EnterKey~

Congratulations! You have successfully created a spline leader line with annotation.

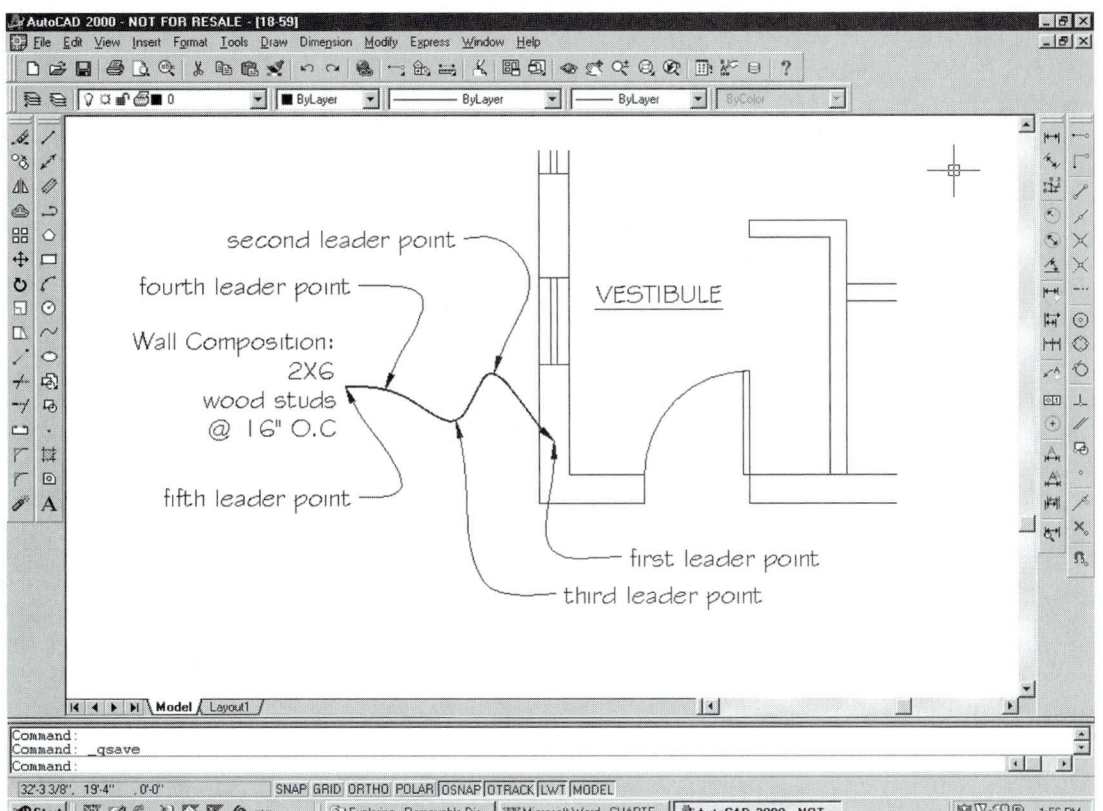

FIGURE 18–59 Using the Leader Line & Arrow tab to create the Spline Leader Line.

Attachment: (tab) This tab will help you control how the leader line is attached to the multiline text as annotation. Figure 18–60 shows the Attachment tab of the Leader Settings dialog box. Inside the Multiline Text Attachment category there are five options for the Text on left side or for the Text on right side and a check box to underline the bottom of the annotation. If the annotation is on the left side of the leader line, use the attachment options in the left column. If the annotation is on the right side of the leader line, use attachment options in the right column. Select the attachment option that best suit your needs.

The five options are as follows:

TOP OF TOP LINE: (radio button). This option will attach the leader line at the top portion of the top multiline and single-line text line.

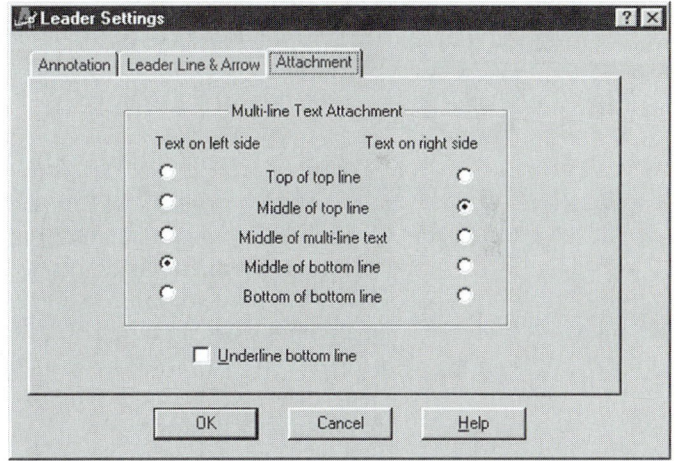

MIDDLE OF TOP LINE: (radio button). This option will attach the leader line at the middle portion of the top multi-line and single-line text line.

MIDDLE OF MULTILINE TEXT: (radio button). This option will attach the leader line at the middle portion of the multiline text.

FIGURE 18–60 The Attachment tab will control how leader lines are attached to annotation on the left and right side.

MIDDLE OF BOTTOM LINE: (radio button). This option will attach the leader line at the middle portion of the bottom multiline text line.

BOTTOM OF BOTTOM LINE: (radio button). This option will attach the leader line at the bottom portion of the bottom multiline text line.

UNDERLINE BOTTOM LINE: (check box). This option will underline the bottom of the multiline or the single-line text line. When this box is checked, the Multiline Text Attachment options will not be available to use.

Figure 18–61 shows the attachment options for the Multiline Text Attachment category.

FIGURE 18–61   The Multiline Text Attachment options will provide you with unlimited flexibility when attaching the last leader line segment to the annotation.

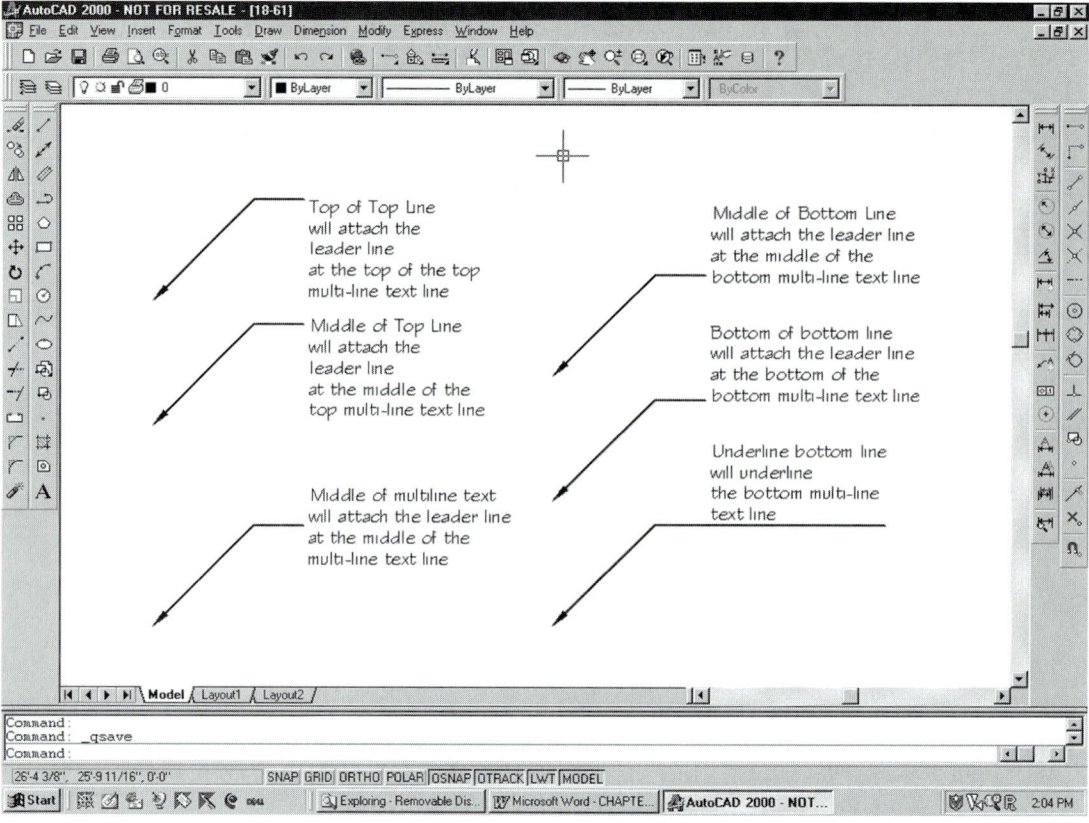

Tip: You can reconfigure leader line segments without moving the arrowhead by using the STRETCH command. Place a Crossing box around the leader line segments but do not include the arrowhead in the selection set. You can also use the Stretch option of the Grip command.

18.5.11   Using the LEADER Command

The Leader command will allow you to draw leader line segments and attach annotation. It does not have the customization features of the QLEADER command, but can be used if needed. The initial command prompts are similar to the LINE command where you can draw the leader line from point to point. With the Leader command there is no limit on the number of leader line points. You can type LEADER at the command line to access the Leader command. Other properties of the leader line associated with color, size, and style are controlled by the current dimension style settings. When you type LEADER at the command line, AutoCAD will display the following prompts:

```
Command: LEADER ~EnterKey~
Specify leader start point: (select the first leader point)
Specify next point: (turn Ortho off if you want to draw the first leader
line segment at an angle and select the second leader point)
Specify next point or [Annotation/Format/Undo] <Annotation>: (if you
want to draw the second leader line segment, select the third leader
point. Turn ORTHO on if you want this to be horizontal)
```

AutoCAD will allow you to enter as many points as you like until you enter A or press ~EnterKey~ where you can enter annotation or select options for annotation. The Annotation option is the default when you press ~EnterKey~ after specifying leader line points. You can type the required text at the next command prompt.

To get the options within the Annotation, press ~EnterKey~ before typing the annotation. The command sequence will be as follows:

```
Enter first line of annotation text or <options>: ~EnterKey~
Enter an annotation option [Tolerance/Copy/Block/None/Mtext] <Mtext>:
```

If you press ~EnterKey~ , the Multiline Text Editor dialog box will be displayed where you can type single or multiline annotation and click on the OK button when finished. AutoCAD will place the annotation on top of the horizontal leader line. The Tolerance, Copy, Block, and None options are the same as with the QLEADER command. Type T, C, B, or N to access these options.

To use the Format option of the LEADER command, enter F after the last leader line segment. The command sequence will be as follows:

```
Specify next point or [Annotation/Format/Undo] <Annotation>: F
~EnterKey~
Enter leader format option [Spline/STraight/Arrow/None] <Exit>:
```

Pressing ~EnterKey~ will get you back to where you were before you entered F. The Spline, Straight, Arrow, and None options are same as with the QLEADER command. If you previously set Format to draw Spline leader line segments, enter ST to change the leader line segments back to Straight format if you are still inside the LEADER command. When you leave the LEADER command, AutoCAD will automatically default to drawing Straight leader line segments. The Undo option will remove the last leader line segment if you happen to draw an extra leader line segment unintentionally. This option is handy because you do not have to start drawing a new leader line segment from scratch just because you have one too many.

Tips: To have multiple leader line segments, point to the same object or annotation and create the first leader line segment using the QLEADER or the LEADER command. Then create other leader line segments without annotation and attach it to the existing leader line segment using the Snap to Nearest object snap mode.

18.5.12 Tolerance

The Tolerance button in the Dimension toolbar will provide you with the tools necessary to create Geometric Dimension and Tolerance symbols. This is used in the mechanical drafting field and will not be covered in this textbook.

18.5.13 Center Mark

The Center Mark button in the Dimension toolbar will invoke the DIMCENTER command and allow you to place center marks or centerlines inside circles and arcs without placing dimension line, arrowhead, and dimension text. This is done using the Radius Dimension or the Diameter Dimension buttons inside the Dimension toolbar or using DIMDIAMETER and DIMRADIUS commands at the command line. See Figure 18–16. When dimensioning circles and arcs, the placement of center marks and centerlines are controlled by the Center Marks for Circles category inside the Lines and Arrows tab of the New, Modify, and Override Dimension Style dialog boxes. To place center marks or centerlines inside circles and arcs without the dimension line, arrowhead, and the dimension text, use the center mark button in the Dimension toolbar. The command sequence to place center marks or centerlines inside circles and arcs are as follows:

```
Command: DIMCENTER ~EnterKey~(or click on the Center Mark button in the
Dimension toolbar).
Select arc or circle: (select the arc or the circle)
```

AutoCAD will automatically place a center mark or centerline inside the arc or the circle, depending on the settings under current dimension style. If the Center Marks for circles Type is set to None, you will not be able to select the circle or the arc after entering DIMCENTER at the command line. AutoCAD will give you the following response:

```
Command: DIMCENTER ~EnterKey~
DIMCEN = 0.0, not drawing center cross. *Invalid*
```

The DIMCEN (dimension center mark) dimensioning variable controls the center mark and centerline sizes at the command line.

The center marks and centerlines placed inside arcs and circles using the DIMCENTER command are composed of individual lines. To erase a center mark two lines must be erased; to erase a centerline six individual lines must be erased. The center marks and centerlines placed inside circles and arcs using the Radius Dimension and Diameter Dimension buttons in the Dimension toolbar are composed of single entities. Selecting one of the lines in centerlines will select the other five lines, including the dimension line, arrowhead, and the dimension text.

Before discussing the Dimension Edit and Dimension Text Edit buttons in the Dimension toolbar and editing dimensions in general, *Transparency, Dimensioning Mode, Dimension Definition Points (Defpoints),* and *Associative Dimensioning* need to be explained.

18.6 CHANGING DIMENSIONING VARIABLES DURING DIMENSIONING

So far you learned to change dimensioning variables using the New, Modify, and Override buttons inside the Dimension Style Manager dialog box and using the Dimension Update button in the Dimension toolbar was briefly introduced. While these methods are effective and efficient, you can also change dimensioning variables while using dimensioning commands and applications. The ability to use one command while using another command is called Transparency. The command used is said to be Transparent and in the case of its application it is said to be entered Transparently. With dimensioning, this is referred to as using a dimensioning variable while using a dimensioning command. For some dimensioning commands, you can enter the dimensioning variable immediately after issuing the dimensioning command or after selecting the object at the Specify dimension line location: command prompt. For dimensioning commands having a command prompt that start with the word *specify,* you can enter the variable at any command line. For dimensioning commands having a command prompt that starts with the word *select,* you can enter the variable at any command line after entering *apostrophe (').* Two right angle brackets (>>) will be displayed in front of the prompts for transparent commands. The current value for the variable will be displayed inside the brackets < > for both methods.

For example, you can change the gap from dimension line to text using the DIMGAP variable from 1/16″ to 3/16″, just when you start using the DIMLINEAR command as follows:

```
Command: DIMLINEAR ~EnterKey~
Specify first extension line origin or <select object>: DIMGAP
~EnterKey~
Enter new value for dimension variable <1/16">: 3/16 ~EnterKey~
Specify first extension line origin or <select object>: (you can enter
another variable or ~EnterKey~)
Select object to dimension: (select the object to dimension)
Specify dimension line location or
[Mtext/Text/Angle/Horizontal/Vertical/Rotated]: (select the dimension
line location)
The dimension will be displayed with a DIMGAP value of 3/16".
```

You can change as many variables as you need to, providing that you enter each variable after the command line that starts with the word *specify.*

The following dimensioning commands do not require apostrophe (') before the dimensioning variable since the command prompts start with the word *specify:*

```
DIMLINEAR (linear dimension)
DIMALIGNED (aligned dimension)
DIMORDINATE (ordinate dimension)
QLEADER (quick leader)
```

The following dimensioning commands require apostrophe (') before the dimensioning variable since the command prompts start with the word *select*:

```
DIMRADIUS (radius dimension)
DIMDIAMETER (diameter dimension)
DIMANGULAR (angular dimension)
```

```
QDIM (quick dimension)
DIMBASELINE (baseline dimension)
DIMCONTINUE (continue dimension)
DIMCENTER (center mark)
```

The dimensioning variable names can also be entered without the DIM prefix for the dimensioning commands that do not require apostrophe ('). For example, to change the dimension text height using the DIMLINEAR command, enter TXT. The following command line procedure will allow you to change dimension line color to red, tick mark size to 1/4″, dimension text height to 3/16″, and place dimension text inside extension lines at different command lines while using the QDIM command:

```
Command: QDIM ~EnterKey~
Select geometry to dimension: 'DIMCLRD ~EnterKey~(notice the apostrophe
before the dimensioning variable).
>>Enter new value for DIMCLRD <0>: 1 ~EnterKey~
Resuming QDIM command.
Select geometry to dimension: (select an object)
1 found
Select geometry to dimension: 'DIMASZ ~EnterKey~
>>Enter new value for DIMASZ <0'-0 1/8″>: 0.25 ~EnterKey~
Resuming QDIM command.
Select geometry to dimension: (select an object or enter the next
variable)
1 found, 2 total
Select geometry to dimension: 'DIMTXT ~EnterKey~
>>Enter new value for DIMTXT <0'-0 1/8″>: 3/16 ~EnterKey~
Resuming QDIM command.
Select geometry to dimension: (select an object or enter the next
variable)
1 found, 3 total
Select geometry to dimension: 'DIMTIX ~EnterKey~
>>Enter new value for DIMTIX <OFF>: ON ~EnterKey~
Specify dimension line position, or
[Continuous/Staggered/Baseline/Ordinate/Radius/Diameter/datumPoint/Edit]
<Continuous>: (you can enter more variables here also or select the
dimension line position)
```

Notice that with the apostrophe (') rule, the name of the dimensioning variable is listed after the Enter new value for command prompt such as >>Enter new value for DIMTIX <OFF>, as opposed to Enter new value for dimension variable <XX>.

Each time a dimensioning variable is used Transparently, it is saved under <style overrides> that appear under the current dimension style. This does not affect the settings for substyles.

18.7 DIMENSIONING MODE

Throughout this chapter, you have learned to access dimensioning commands by entering the full command name or command aliases at the command line, selecting the command from the pull-down menu, toolbar, status bar, or shortcut menu. AutoCAD gives you even more flexibility by allowing you to enter dimensioning commands without the DIM prefix. To be able to do this, AutoCAD has to be in Dimensioning mode. Entering DIM or DIM1 at the command line will change the prompt from "Command" to "Dim", allowing you to start Dimensioning Mode. The DIM or DIM1 command prompt indicates that you are in Dimensioning mode and you can enter dimensioning commands without the DIM prefix instead of the full command name. If a command alias is known, it will take less typing strokes to enter a command, but sometimes it is difficult to recall command aliases or there is no command alias for a specific command. DIM and DIM1 are provided only for compatibility with previous release of AutoCAD.

The DIM command will allow you to enter as many dimensioning commands you require until you press ~EnterKey~ to exit the command. The DIM1 command will allow you to use only

Dimensioning Command	Command Alias	Dimensioning Mode
Command		
DIMLINEAR (Horizontal)		Horizontal
DIMLINEAR (Rotated)		Rotated
DIMLINEAR (Vertical)		Vertical
DIMALIGNED	DAL	Aligned
DIMANGULAR	DAN	Angular
DIMBASELINE	DBA	Baseline
DIMCENTER	DCE	Center
DIMCONTINUE	DCO	Continue
DIMRADIUS	DRA	Radius
DIMDIAMETER	DDI	Diameter
DIMORDINATE	DOR	Ordinate
DIMOVERRIDE	DOV	Override
LEADER	LE	Leader
DIMSTYLE (Variables)		Variables
DIMSTYLE (Restore)		Restore
DIMSTYLE (Apply)		Update
DIMSTYLE (Save)		Save
DIMSTYLE (Status)		Status
DIMTEDIT		Tedit
DIMEDIT (Home)		Hometext
DIMEDIT (Text)		Newtext
DIMEDIT (Oblique)		Oblique
DIMEDIT (Rotate)		Trotate

one dimensioning command. AutoCAD will then automatically return to the Command: prompt. While using the DIM or DIM1 commands, you can exit any time by entering E, EXIT or ~EscKey~.

The following command line procedure will allow you to access the Horizontal option of the DIMLINEAR command using Dimensioning mode:

```
Command: DIM ~EnterKey~
Dim: HORIZONTAL or HOR ~EnterKey~
Specify first extension line origin or <select object>:
```

Table 18–3 shows dimensioning commands and their dimensioning mode command equivalents including command aliases.

18.8 ASSOCIATIVE DIMENSIONING

Associative Dimensioning allows dimensions to change in length and value as the object that is attached to changes. The associative nature of dimensioning is extremely useful when drawings are revised and edited. When associative dimensioning is on, any changes made to objects will automatically update the dimension text and dimension line. The dimensioning variable that creates associative dimensioning is DIMASO (associative dimensioning). By default DIMASO is on. When the associative dimensioning is on, the dimensions associated with the object are considered to be a single unit. Editing an object will also change the dimensions associated with the object. When the associative dimensioning is off, the association between the dimension and the object is broken and so are the components of the dimension. This means that when the object is edited, the dimensions do not update to reflect the changes made to the object. This also means that the components of the dimension (dimension line, dimension text, tick marks, and extension lines) are now disassociated from each other and they are now individual objects.

AutoCAD is sensitive about this issue (who can blame it!). When you dimension an object while DIMASO is off, AutoCAD will not allow you to place the dimension at the Specify dimension line location command prompt. AutoCAD will stun you by making the dimension disappear! AutoCAD will simply place the dimension at the command line and await your response. It is only when you press ~EnterKey~ that the dimension will be placed on the drawing. This is AutoCAD's way of telling you that the associative dimensioning is not on. This is important because **you cannot turn a nonassociative dimensioning into an associative dimensioning** later during a project. You can turn an associative dimensioning into a nonassociative dimensioning by exploding it. You can use the Explode button in the Modify toolbar or enter EXPLODE at the command line to explode an associative dimensioning. You can check to see if associative dimensioning is on as follows:

```
Command: DIMASO ~EnterKey~
Enter new value for DIMASO <ON>: ~EnterKey~
This will keep associative dimensioning on until you access the DIMASO
dimensioning variable and turn it off as follows:
Command: DIMASO ~EnterKey~
Enter new value for DIMASO <ON>: OFF ~EnterKey~
```

Note: A nonassociative dimension is no longer a part of the current dimension style settings after it is created. Any changes made to the dimensioning variables will not affect an existing nonassociative dimension. It is only effective when the dimension is created. Any subsequent changes will not affect a nonassociative dimension.

The DIMLINEAR, DIMALIGNED, DIMANGULAR, DIMORDINATE, DIMDIAMETER, DIMRADIUS, DIMBASELINE, and DIMCONTINUE commands are affected by the nonassociative dimensioning. When DIMASO is off, the dimensions created by these dimensioning commands will be nonassociative.

The QDIM and QLEADER commands are not affected by the nonassociative dimensioning. The dimensions created by the QDIM command will retain their associative dimensioning character even when the DIMASO is off.

18.9 DIMENSION DEFINITION POINTS

When you create associative dimensions, every dimension includes a definition point defining the dimension location. These definition points are called *defpoints*. When you edit dimensions, the actual editing operation is based on the selection of dimension definition points that are small dots on the screen. Figure 18–62 shows dimension definition point locations for a radius, a diameter, and a linear dimension. For a radius dimension, the defpoints are located on the dimension text, at the object selection point, and at the center point. For a diameter dimension, the defpoints are located on the dimension line, at the object selection point, and on the opposite point. For a linear dimension, the defpoints are located at the first extension line origin, at the midpoint of the dimension line, at the intersection of second extension line origin and dimension line, and at the second extension line origin. Because defpoints are small dots on the screen and because their location is on the object geometry, it is difficult to see them. You can see the defpoints located on the first and second extension line origins of a linear dimension by creating the dimension and erasing the object. You can also see the defpoint located at the center of the circle by creating a radius dimension without the center mark and without the centerline. Because a Diameter dimension locates two opposite points on the circle, a defpoint is not located at the center. You will have to zoom in to see the defpoints.

When you create associative dimensions, AutoCAD will automatically create a layer called Defpoints and create dimension definition points on this layer. This layer does not plot.

FIGURE 18–62 The location of dimension definition points created by the associative dimensioning.

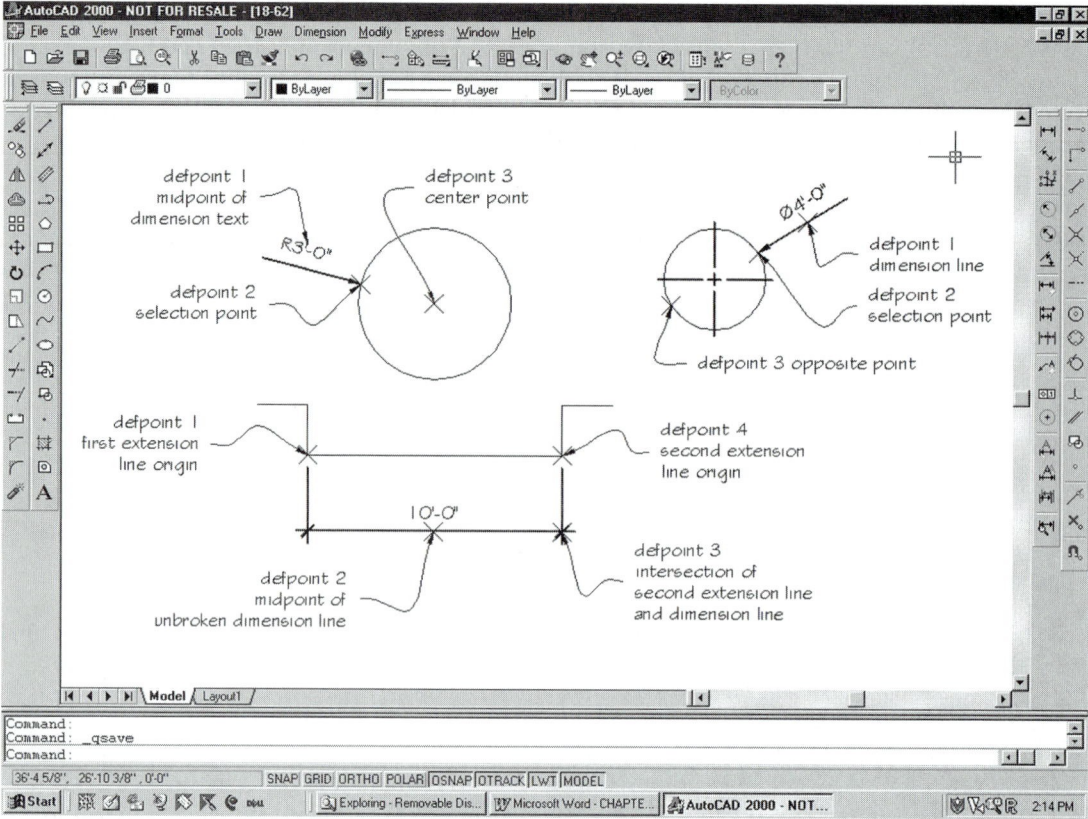

18.10 EDITING DIMENSIONS

You can edit associative dimensions using five different techniques shown below:

1. Using the DIMTEDIT and DIMEDIT commands and the Dimension Edit and the Dimension Text Edit buttons in the Dimension toolbar.

2. Using the Dimension Style Manager dialog box in conjunction with dimension editing tools at the command line. This will edit dimensioning variables that control dimension text placement and format.

3. Using AutoCAD editing commands.

4. Using the Properties window.

5. Using the right-click shortcut menu.

In addition to the five editing techniques, you can also use the Wipeout button in the Express Standard Toolbar to break one of the overlapping extension lines and retain the other. This is explained later in the chapter.

Each editing technique gives you the tools you need to modify dimensions efficiently and effectively. Try each technique and experiment with it until you become comfortable with the procedures. A good working knowledge of editing techniques can increase productivity considerably. The most important aspect of editing is that dimensions are automatically updated to reflect any changes performed by the specific editing technique. Let's take a look at the editing techniques.

18.10.1 Editing Dimension Text at the Command Line and Using the Dimension Toolbar (DIMTEDIT and DIMEDIT Commands)

You can edit dimension text by entering a new dimension text, changing the rotation angle of the dimension text, moving the dimension text to a new location, or moving it back to its original position at the command line using the DIMTEDIT and DIMEDIT commands.

The DIMTEDIT (Dimension Text Edit) command will help you control text alignment at the command line. You have to select the dimension object first to edit. You can access the DIMTEDIT command by entering it at the command line, selecting Dimension Text Edit button in the Dimension toolbar, or selecting Align Text from the Dimension pull-down menu. The DIMTEDIT command will present you with the following text alignment options:

```
Command: DIMTEDIT ~EnterKey~(or click on the Dimension Text Edit button
in the Dimension toolbar).
Select dimension:(select one dimension to edit)
Specify new location for dimension text or
[Left/Right/Center/Home/Angle]:
```

When you select a dimension, you can manually move the dimension text to a desired location. This will turn the DIMUPT (user-positioned text) dimensioning variable on. If you do not wish to manually place dimension text, you can choose one of the following options to automatically move dimension text:

LEFT: This option will position the horizontal dimension text on the left side and the vertical dimension text on the bottom side of the dimension line.

RIGHT: This option will position the horizontal dimension text on the right side and the vertical text on the up side of the dimension line.

CENTER: This option will center the dimension text on the dimension line.

HOME: This option will return the dimension text to its default position. It will not return the dimension text to its previous position. The default position is the dimension text position settings inside Text Placement category of the Text tab in the New, Modify, or Override Dimension Style dialog boxes.

ANGLE: This option will allow you to place the dimension text at the angle you specify. This is similar to the Rotate option of the DIMEDIT command. You can specify the angle by typing it or you can select two points on the screen to define the angle. AutoCAD will rotate the text around its center point. Entering an angle of 0 degrees will place the dimension text in its default orientation.

Figure 18–63 shows the five options of the DIMTEDIT command.

The DIMEDIT (Dimension Edit) command will help you move, change, and rotate dimension text. It will also allow you to convert the extension lines of linear dimensions oblique. You select the editing option first, then select one or more dimensions to edit. The dimensions selected will change according to the editing option. You can access the DIMEDIT command by entering it at the command line or by selecting Dimension Edit button in the Dimension toolbar. The DIMEDIT command will present you the following editing options:

```
Command: DIMEDIT ~EnterKey~(or click on the Dimension Edit button in the
Dimension toolbar).
Enter type of dimension editing [Home/New/Rotate/Oblique] <Home>:
```

You can choose one of the following options to edit:

HOME: This option will move dimension text back to its default position. This is the default option and is identical to the Home option of the DIMTEDIT command.

NEW: This option will allow you to edit existing text or enter new text by displaying the Multiline Text Editor dialog box.

ROTATE: This option will rotate the dimension text and is similar to the Angle option of the DIMTEDIT command. You can also access this option by entering TROTATE or TR at the Dim: prompt.

OBLIQUE: This option will change the extension lines to oblique angle. When a dimension is created, the extension lines are normally perpendicular to dimension lines. This option will change the angle of the extension lines. This might be useful when extension lines conflict with object geometry. You can also access this option by selecting Oblique from the Dimension pull-down menu.

Figure 18–64 shows the four options of the DIMEDIT command.

FIGURE 18–63 The five options of the DIMTEDIT command will control text alignment and position.

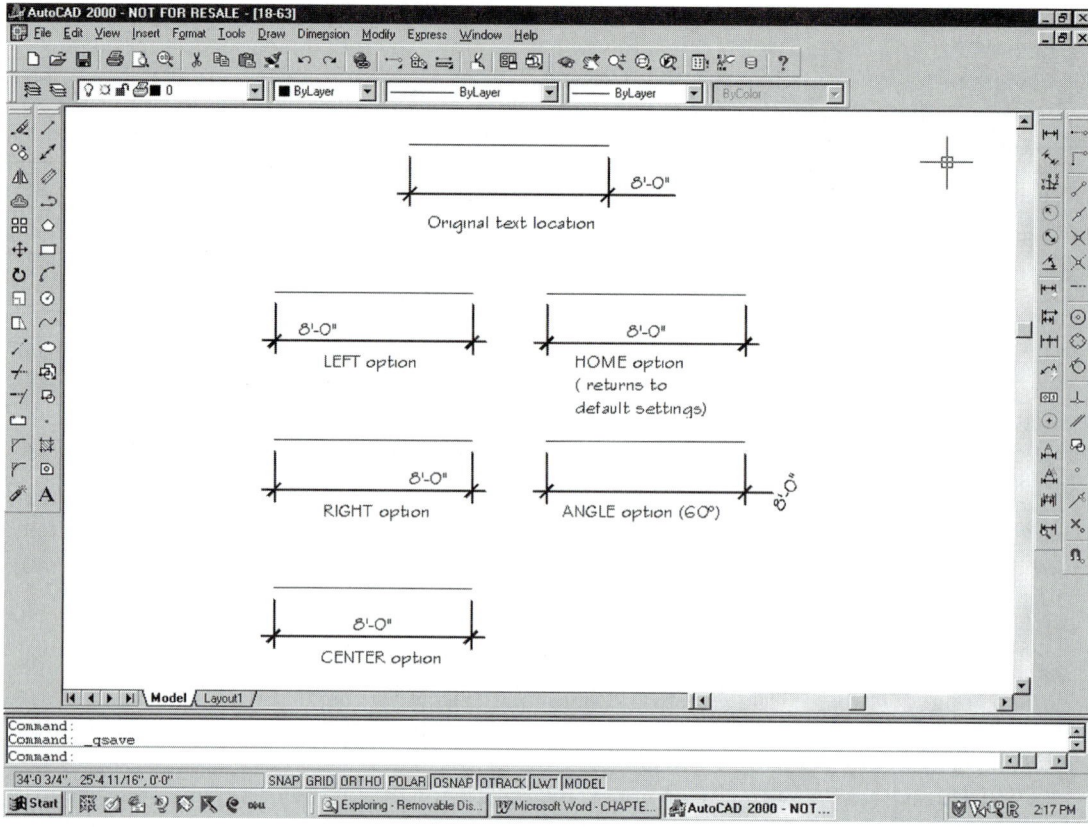

FIGURE 18–64 The four options of the DIMEDIT command will allow you to edit dimension text and format extension lines at an oblique angle.

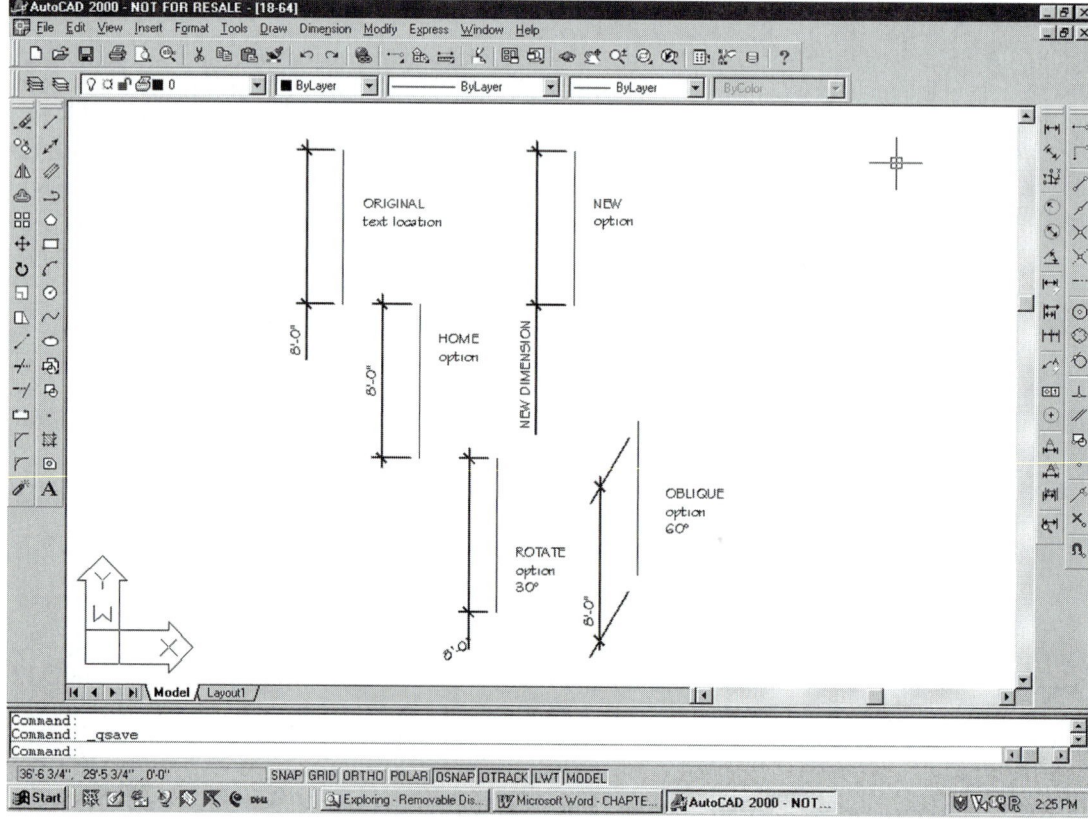

18.10.2 Editing Dimensions Using the Dimension Style Manager Dialog Box

This type of editing is performed using the dimensioning variables at the command line or at the Dimension Style Manager dialog box. The placement of dimension text in relation to the dimension line and extension lines are controlled by the Fit tab in the Dimension Style Manager dialog box. The Fit tab and its categories were covered in detail previously in this chapter. You can edit specific dimensions that do not properly display in the drawing by using the Fit tab in the Dimension Style Manager dialog box.

For example, after dimensioning the drawing shown in Figure 18–65 you discover that the dimensions for the exterior walls are not properly placed. In this case the wall thickness dimensions are placed outside the dimension lines directly on top of the other dimension because the space between the extension lines are too small to fit the wall thickness dimensions. Figure 18–66 shows the current settings of the Fit tab when the drawing was dimensioned. This represents the default settings except for the overall scale of (scale factor) 48. The drawing is created using the LINE command and offsetting the lines 1'-0". It is dimensioned using the QDIM command with a crossing box to select walls. This represents the default settings.

■ **EXERCISE 18–10:** *The following step-by-step exercise will allow you to edit the dimensions displayed improperly in Figure 18–65.*

Step #1: Open the EXE18-5.dwg file.

Step #2: Access the Dimension toolbar and click on the Dimension Style button.

Step #3: Inside the Dimension Style Manager dialog box, select the ARCHITECTURAL style and click on the Set Current button.

Step #4: Click on the Modify... button.

Step #5: Inside the Modify Dimension Style: ARCHITECTURAL dialog box, select the Fit tab.

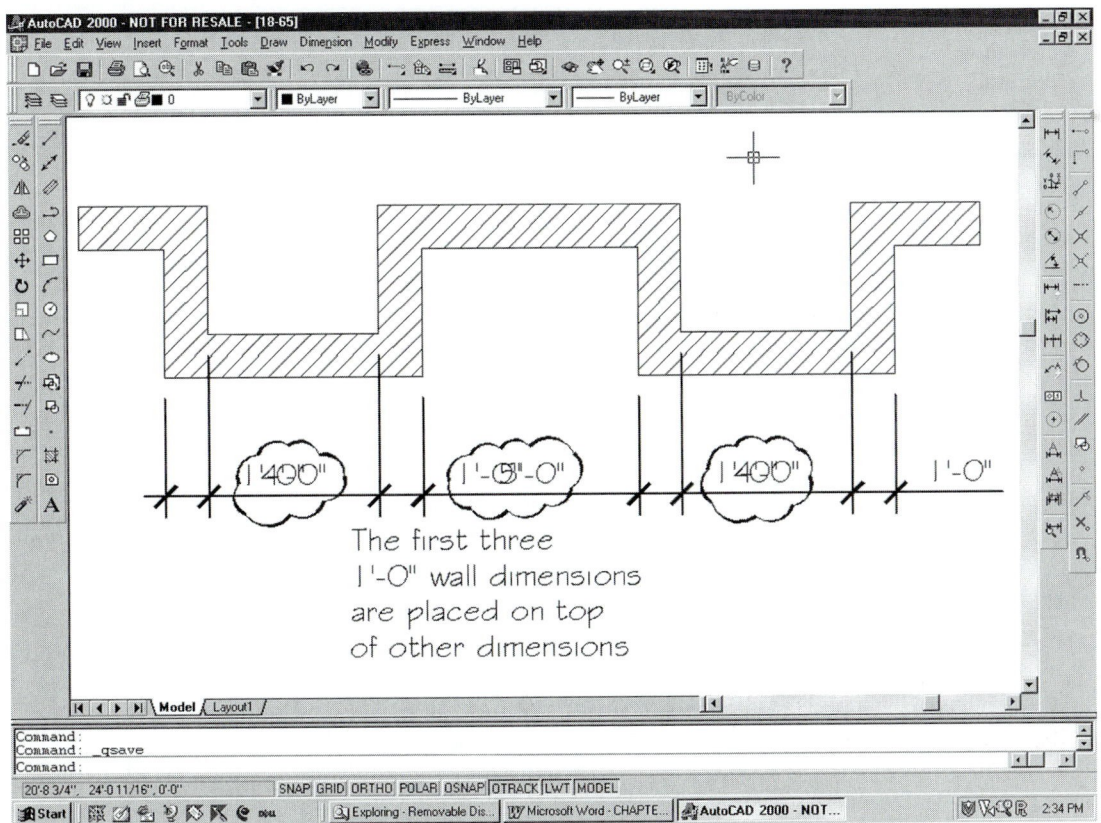

FIGURE 18–65 The drawing is dimensioned using the QDIM command. The wall thickness dimensions move to the side to cover other dimensions. You can edit these dimensions using the Dimension Style Manager dialog box.

Step #6: Under Fit Options category, click on Always keep text between ext lines radio button.

Step #7: Under Text Placement category, click on Over the dimension line, without a leader radio button.

Step #8: Under Fine Tuning category, click on Always draw dim line between ext line check box.

Step #9: Click on the OK button and close the Dimension Style Manager dialog box.

The drawing will now look like Figure 18–67. This does not edit the dimensions completely because the 1'-0" dimensions need to be moved outside the extension lines for a proper look.

Step #10: Click on the Dimension Text Edit button in the Dimension toolbar.

Step #11: At the Select dimension: command prompt, select the first 1'-0" dimension on the left. These dimensions are shown inside the revision clouds as shown in Figure 18–67.

Step #12: At the Specify new location for dimension text or [Left/Right/Center/Home/Angle]: command prompt move the dimension and place it slightly toward left.

Step #13: Perform procedure shown in Step #10, #11, and #12 on the other dimensions.

Congratulations! You have successfully modified the dimensions placed improperly. The final edited drawing will now look like Figure 18–68. You may need to update dimensions if necessary.

FIGURE 18–66 The current settings of the Fit tab inside the Dimension Style Manager dialog box. Changing the appropriate settings will allow dimensions to display properly for Figure 18–65.

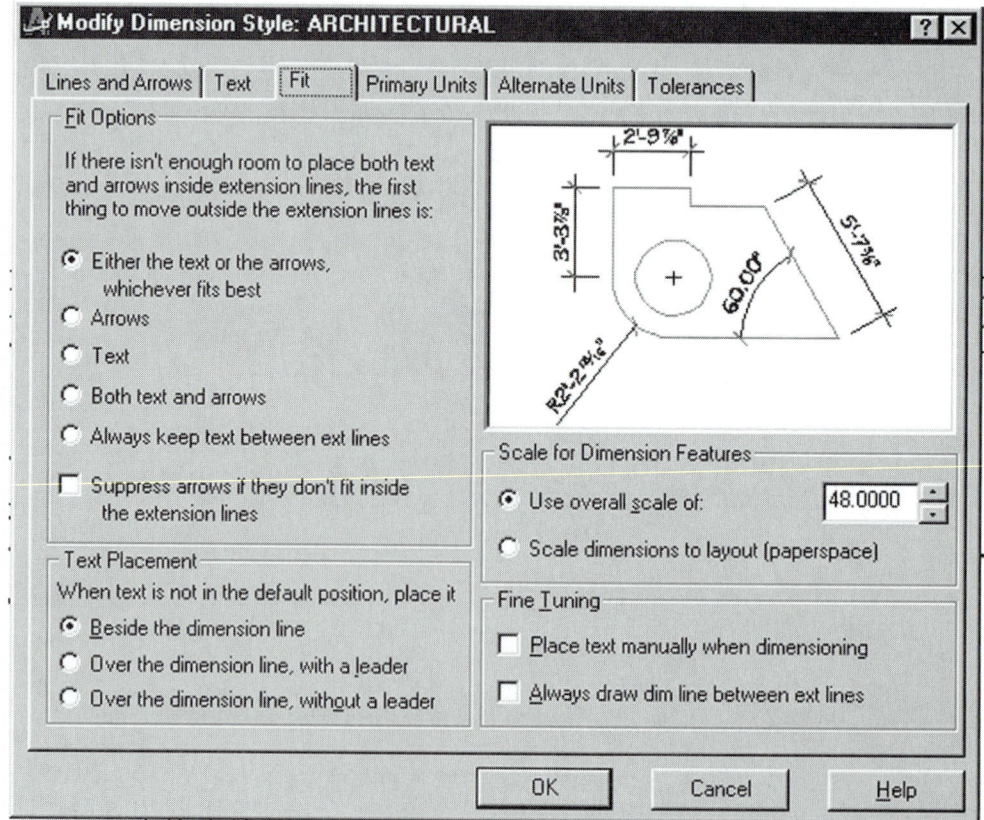

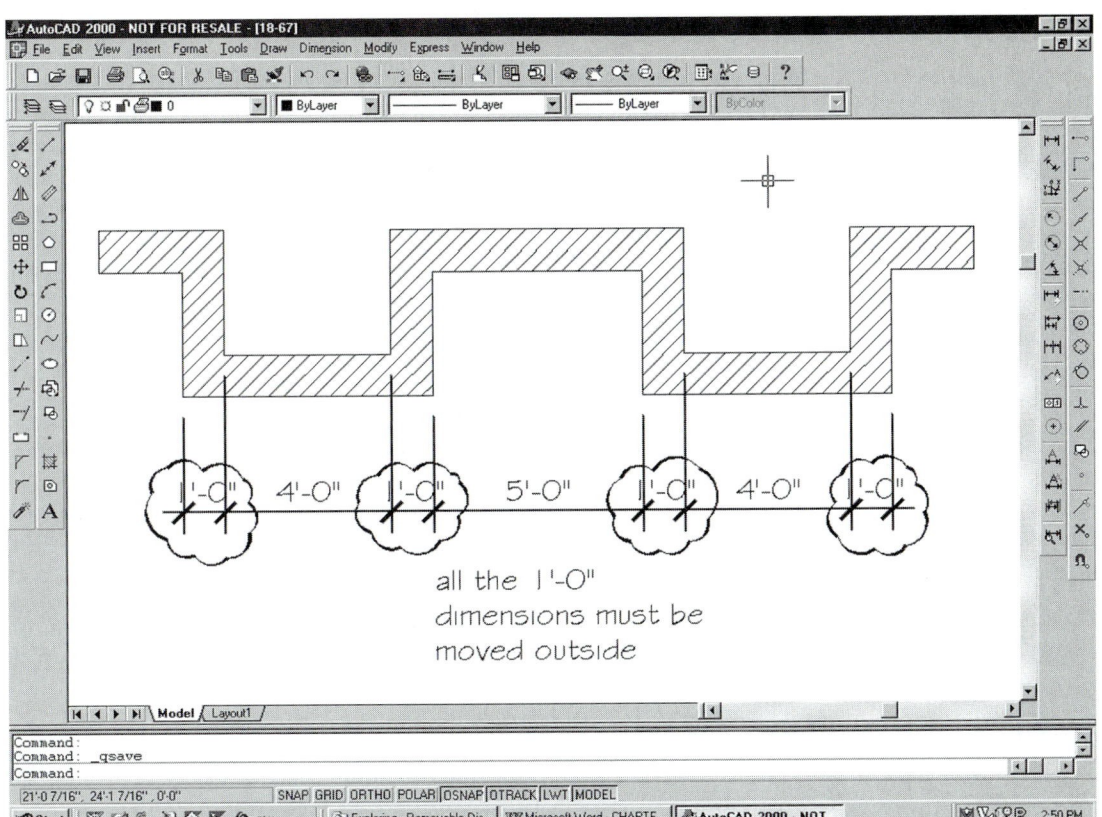

FIGURE 18–67 The 1'-0" dimensions will be placed outside the extension lines using additional editing techniques.

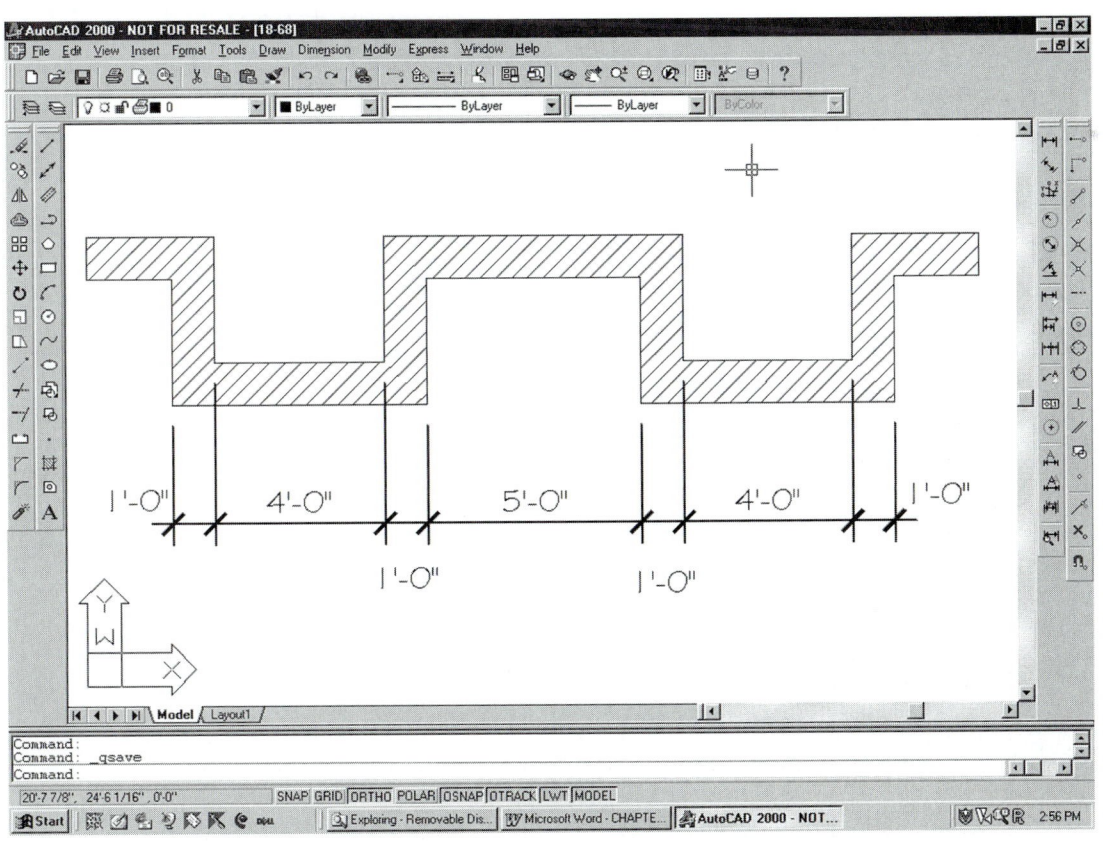

FIGURE 18–68 The dimensions on the drawing are now edited so they are displayed properly. This procedure involved changing settings inside the Fit tab and using the Dimension Text Edit button in the Dimension toolbar.

18.10.3 Editing Dimensions Using AutoCAD Commands

You can edit associative dimensions using the STRETCH, EXTEND, TRIM, MIRROR, RO-TATE, and SCALE commands and also using grips. The most efficient command in editing is the STRETCH command. The grips are effective but require more selection points than the STRETCH command. When using the above commands to edit dimensions, you must be very careful to include all the dimension definition points in the selection set. You can include defpoints more effectively by using the Snap to Node button in the Object Snap toolbar because each dimension definition point is a point object. The defpoints are not affected by changes you make to the PDMODE or PDSIZE system variables. When using commands to edit dimensions, the system variable that controls the recalculation of dimensions while dragging should be turned on. This system variable is called DIMSHO and is on by default. DIMSHO will allow you to see dimensions when they are moved, dragged, or stretched.

18.10.3.1 Using the STRETCH Command to Edit Dimensions   An object and its associative dimension can be stretched to change its length and value. If DIMASO is on before dimensioning, the dimension text will be automatically updated to reflect the changes. The dimension line will be stretched to the new length. When using the STRETCH command to edit dimensions, be sure to include the defpoints by creating the appropriate selection method.

■ **EXERCISE 18–11:**   *The following step-by-step exercise will allow you to edit the wall and its dimension shown in Figure 18–69. The wall will be increased to 8'-0" using the STRETCH command.*

Step #1:   Open the EXE18-6.dwg file.

Step #2:   Click on the STRETCH button in the Modify toolbar.

Step #3:   Create a crossing box as shown in Figure 18–70 by using the following command sequence:

Command: _stretch

FIGURE 18–69   The 4'-0" wall is to be increased to 8'-0" using the STRETCH command. The existing dimension is to be updated at the same time.

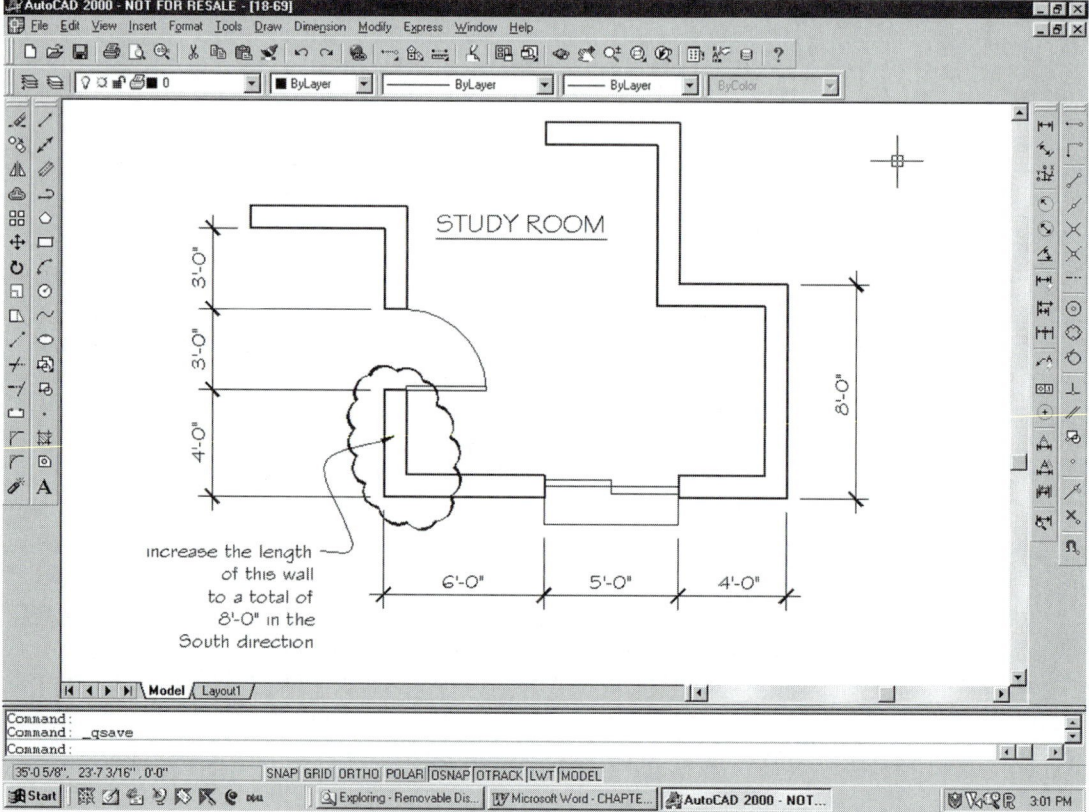

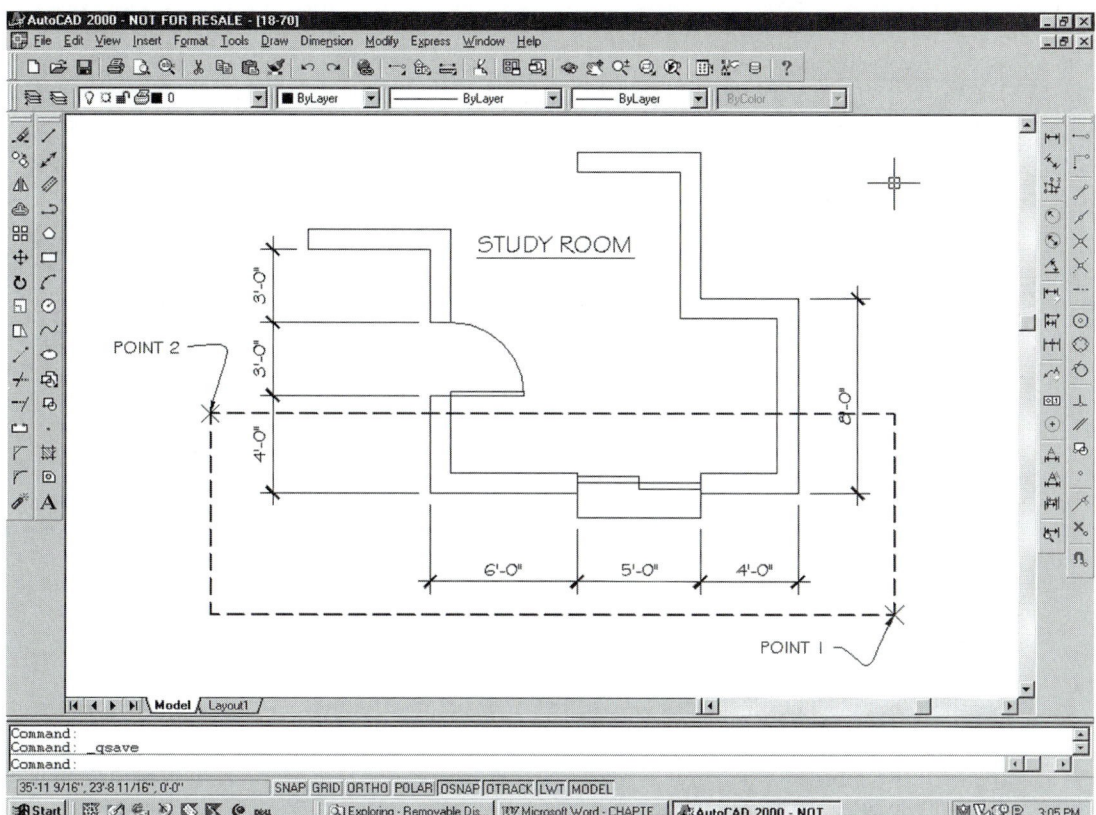

Select object to stretch by crossing-window or crossing-polygon...

Select object: *(select point 1).*

Specify opposite corner: 13 found *(select point 2).*

Select objects: ~EnterKey~

Specify base point or displacement: *(using object snap modes, select the lower left corner of the wall).*

Specify second point or displacement: *(turn Ortho on)* **@4′<270** ~EnterKey~

Congratulations! You have successfully used the STRETCH command to edit the wall and its associative dimensions. The drawing will now look like Figure 18–71. Bottom dimensions are moved along with the wall.

18.10.3.2 Editing Dimensions Using Grips   For the GRIPS to work properly on drawings created with Multilines, the dimension definition points (defpoints) must be located on the side of the objects where multiline justification points are located. This is illustrated as an exercise in Chapter 17, Drawing Multilines. Multilines are single objects even when two or more parallel lines make up the multilines. Grips are displayed on only one side of the multiline. The side on which the grips are displayed is not necessarily the side where multiline justification points are displayed. Generally speaking, if the multilines are created with the Bottom justification option, then the dimensions at the exterior side as overall dimensions will have the defpoints located at the same side as the multiline justification points.

■ **EXERCISE 18–12**   *The following step-by-step exercise will allow you to enlarge the Storage area using grips as shown in Figure 18–72. The drawing is created using the MULTILINE command. The existing space is to be converted to a new storage area. This requires the space and the 4′-0″ dimension is to be moved and updated to a new value.*

Step #1:   Open the EXE18-7.dwg file.

First you need to move the 8′-0″ vertical dimension 6′-3″ to the right using the grips.

FIGURE 18–71 The drawing after editing dimensions. Notice the dimensions moved and updated with two pick points.

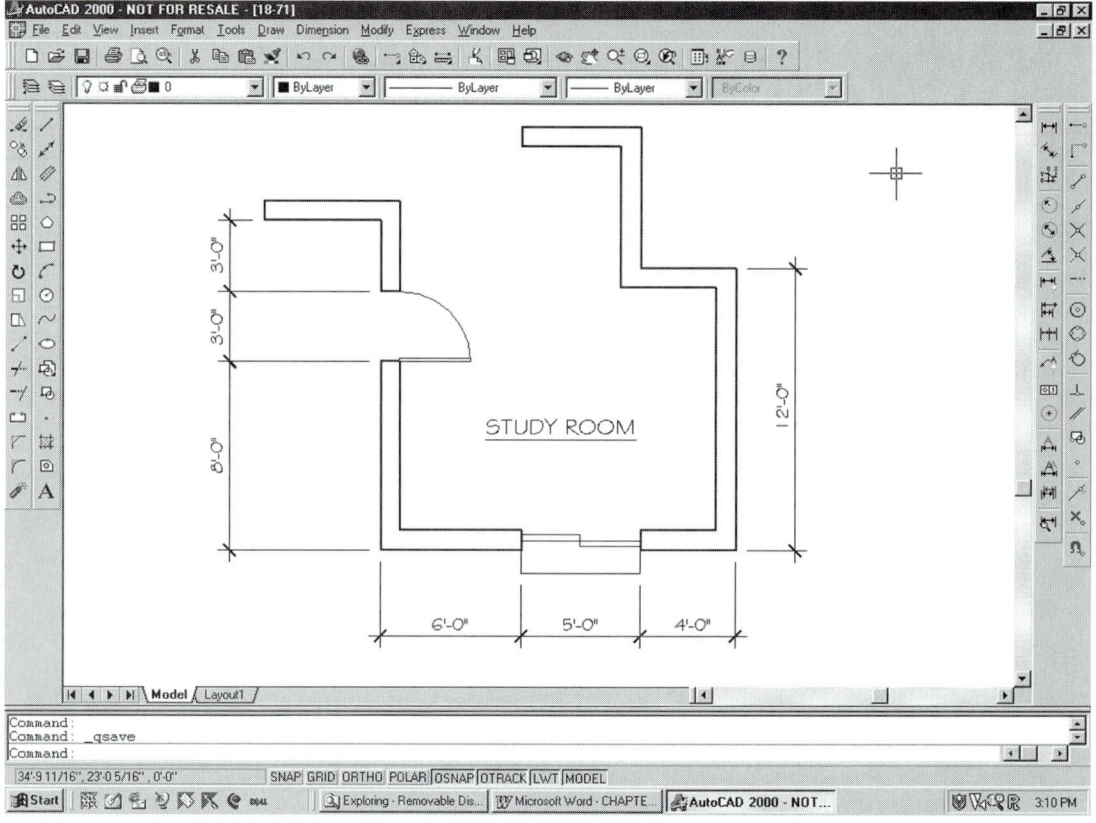

FIGURE 18–72 The proposed new storage area requires the existing space to be enlarged horizontally from left to right. This will be accomplished by using grips.

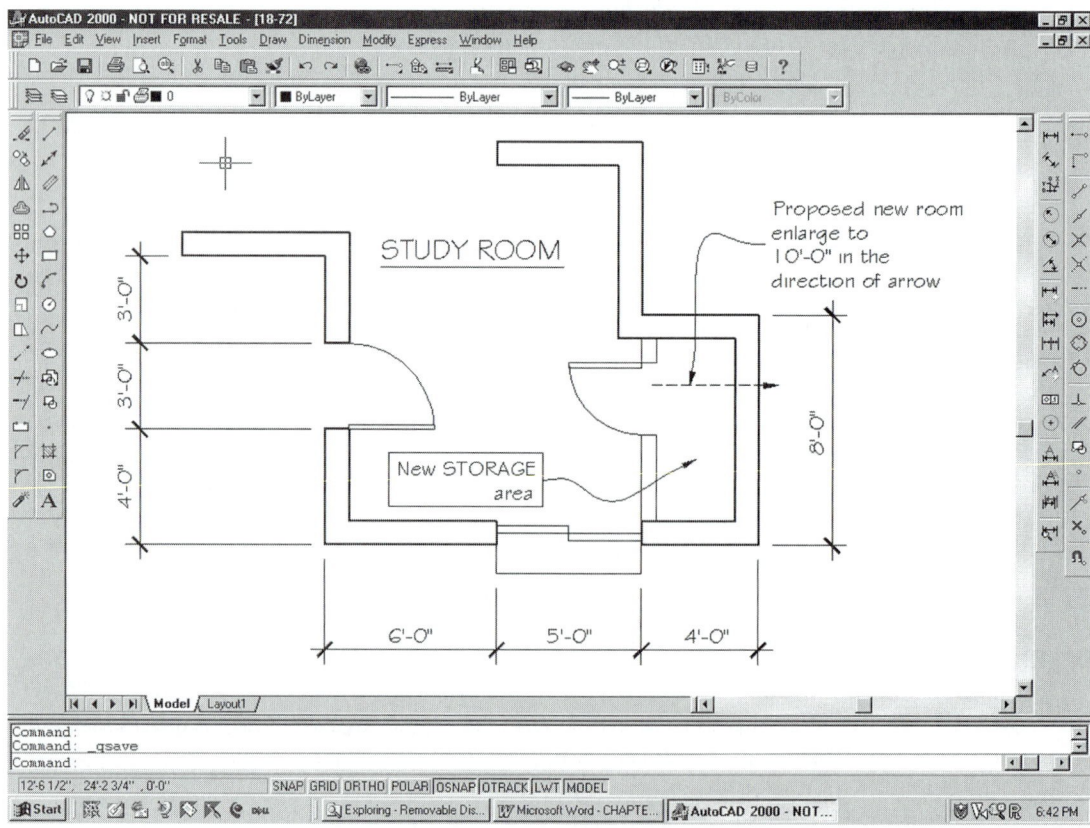

Step #2: Select the 8'-0" dimension to display its grips.

Step #3: Select the grip located at the midpoint of the dimension line.

Step #4: Press ~EnterKey~ to display Move option of grips. The command sequence is as follows:

MOVE

Specify move point or [Base point/Copy/Undo/eXit]: **@6'3<0** <**EnterKey**<

Command: ~EscKey~

Command: ~EscKey~ (*you must press this key twice to exit grips when using AutoCAD 2000*)

The drawing will now look like Figure 18–73. The dimension has been moved to make room for stretching of the wall.

Step #5: Select the wall as shown in Figure 18–73 to display its grips.

Step #6: Select the dimension shown in Figure 18–73 to display its grips.

Step #7: After the grips are displayed, select the grip that is located at the lower right corner of the wall. Turn the Ortho on. The command sequence is as follows:

STRETCH

Specify stretch point or [Base point/Copy/Undo/eXit]: **@6'<0** ~EnterKey~

Command:

Step #8: Select the grip that is located at the upper right corner of the wall. The command sequence is as follows:

STRETCH

Specify stretch point or [Base point/Copy/Undo/eXit]: **@6'<0** ~EnterKey~

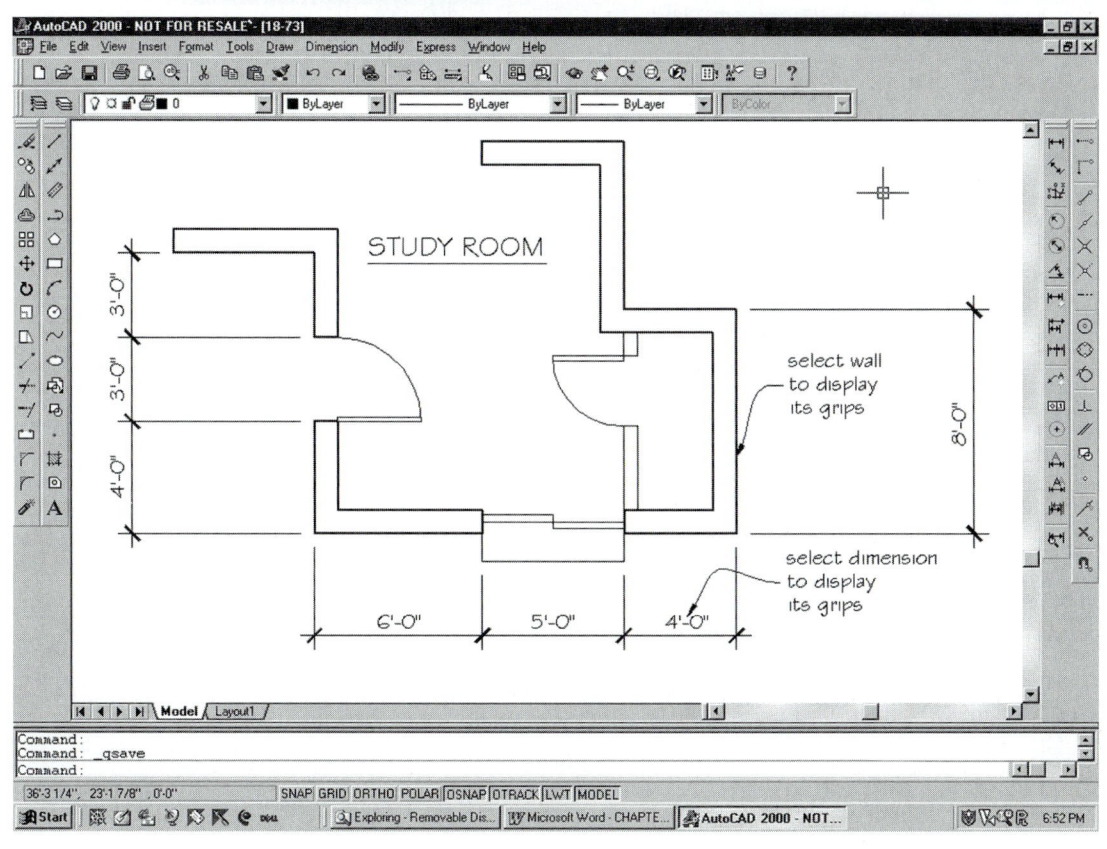

FIGURE 18–73 The 8'-0" vertical dimension is moved 6'-3" toward the right. This will provide just enough space for the dimension origin gap.

Command: ~EscKey~

Command: ~EscKey~

Step #9:   Edit the new dimension (10′-0″) using the Home option of the DIMEDIT command.

Congratulations! You have successfully used grips to enlarge a space in a floor plan and updated the dimension. The final drawing will now look like Figure 18–74.

Tips: You can use grips to change the current dimension style of selected objects to a different dimension style. To do this, left click on the dimension(s) and select a dimension style from the Dim Style Control drop-down menu then hit the ~EscKey~ twice. This will change the current dimension style of selected dimensions to another dimension style.

18.10.3.3 Using the EXTEND Command to Edit Dimensions

You can use the EXTEND command to extend linear and ordinate dimensions. To extend a linear dimension, first select the object that you want the dimension to extend to. This is called the boundary edge. Then select the dimension. The dimension selected will be automatically extended to the selected object. AutoCAD will ask you to select the second object to extend. If you have more dimensions to be extended, you may select them at this point; otherwise press the ~EnterKey~ to finish the editing operation. You can also use the Project/Edge/Undo options to meet your editing requirements. You can select the boundary edges and the dimensions consecutively. Notice that AutoCAD extends only the dimension line. To move the dimension text to the desired position on the new dimension line (without moving the dimension line), use the Dimension Edit button in the Dimension toolbar or by using the DIMEDIT command.

18.10.3.4. Using the TRIM Command to Edit Dimensions

The TRIM command can be used to break a portion of an existing dimension to display a new dimension text for the new di-

FIGURE 18–74   The final Storage room with updated dimension.

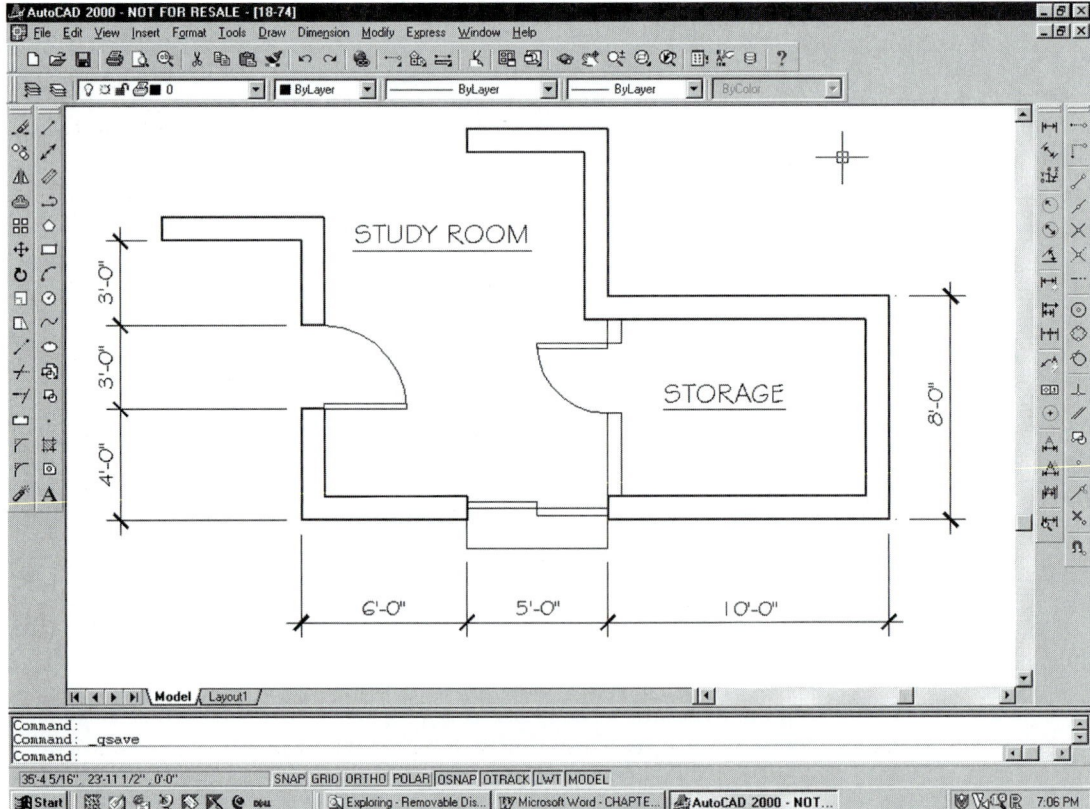

mension line. There are two points to consider. The *cutting edges* refer to the objects crossing the existing dimension line. The *objects to trim* refer to the dimension to be broken at the selected location. At the Select objects: command prompt, select the object(s) as the *cutting edge*, at the Select object to trim: command prompt, select the existing dimension as the *object to trim* and press the ~EnterKey~ to finish the editing operation. You can also use the Project/Edge/Undo options to meet your editing requirements. The new dimension can be moved between tick marks or to a new location using the Dimension Edit button in the Dimension toolbar or by using the DIMEDIT command.

18.10.3.5 Editing Dimensions Using the Object Properties Window   The Object Properties window was discussed in Chapter 13. All properties displayed in the Properties window are the settings established by the current dimension style when the dimension is created. You can edit the dimensioning variable settings of a dimension style by changing the dimension properties directly on the Object Properties window. Editing dimensioning variable settings through the Properties window does not affect the current dimension style settings. You can also use the Properties window to view and evaluate the current dimension variable settings. Editing through the Properties window can enhance productivity and can streamline dimension editing by allowing you to edit and see the results all in one drawing session. As you modify dimensions with the Properties window, the drawing will be automatically updated. When modifying objects, you can enter a new value or select a value from the list provided.

Caution: The dimension definition points (defpoints) and grips will be displayed for each selected dimension when using the Properties window. Each defpoint has a grip point, but not every grip point locates a defpoint. When using grips to edit dimensions, you do not have to know the exact location of defpoints. If you use editing commands other than grips to edit dimensions, you must include in your selection set all the defpoints of the dimensions to be edited. Use the Snap to Node object snap mode to include defpoints more easily.

Tip: To quickly access the Properties window, select one or more objects, right click in the drawing area to display the shortcut menu, and select Properties.

18.10.3.6 Editing Dimensions Using the Shortcut Menu   You can edit dimension text position, change precision of dimension text, and save the modified dimension settings to a new dimension style by selecting one or more dimensions with a left click and then right click on the screen to use the shortcut menu. When you select a dimension and then right click, a shortcut menu will be displayed as shown in Figure 18–75.

The shortcut editing options are as follows:

Dimension Text Position: This area will allow you to modify the dimension text position with six options as follows:

ABOVE DIM LINE: Selecting this option will place the dimension text above the dimension line.

CENTERED: Selecting this option will place the dimension text in the center of the dimension line.

HOME TEXT: Selecting this option will place the dimension text to its default position.

MOVE TEXT ALONE: Selecting this option will move only the dimension text to a new location.

MOVE WITH LEADER: Selecting this option will move the dimension text and attach a leader to it.

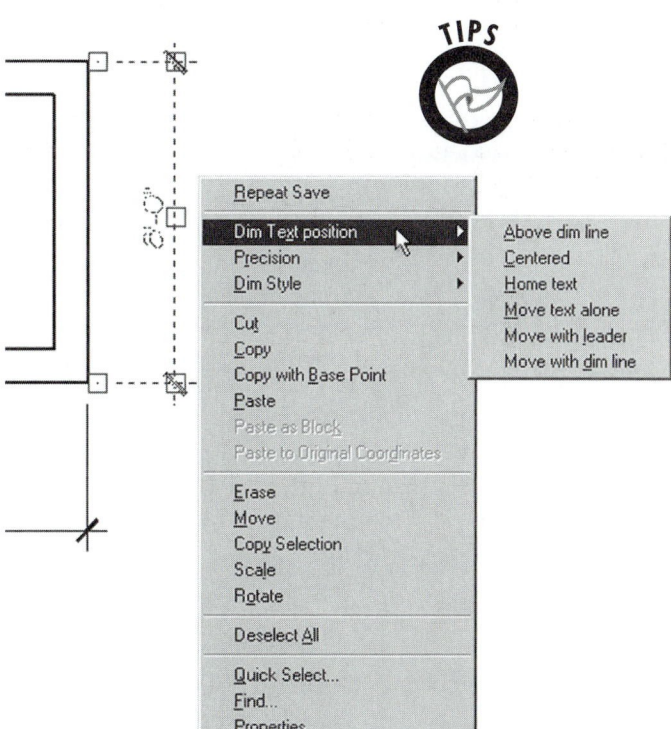

FIGURE 18–75   When you select one or more dimensions, a shortcut menu will appear. You can edit dimensions using this shortcut.

MOVE WITH DIM LINE: Selecting this option will move the dimension text along with the dimension line to a new location.

PRECISION: This area will allow you to set a new dimension unit precision to the dimension text. This will not affect the Linear Dimensions Unit format Precision setting for the current dimension style.

DIM STYLE: This area will allow you to save a modified dimension variable setting to a new or existing style. The option above the bar is called Save as New Style... and is explained as follows:

SAVE AS NEW STYLE...:   Selecting this option will save the properties of the selected dimensions as a new dimension style by displaying the Save As New Dimension Style dialog box. Entering a new style name and then clicking the OK button will create a new dimension style and add it to the Styles: list box in the Dimension Style Manager dialog box. This will be a new addition to the current dimension styles list.

The options below the Save as New Style... bar will show the current and the available dimension styles. Selecting a dimension style from the list will assign that dimension style to the selected dimensions.

18.11 USING THE WIPEOUT COMMAND TO BREAK ONE OF THE OVERLAPPING EXTENSION LINES

Projects that require extensive interior and exterior dimensions will have some of the extension lines overlap each other. This might happen when you dimension a recessed corner both horizontally and vertically as shown in Figure 18–76. In manual drafting practices you would leave a gap for one of the extension lines and keep the other so that the entire dimension has a better readable character. You can accomplish the same task by using the WIPEOUT and the DRAWORDER commands.

The WIPEOUT command will place a blank image on top of the two intersecting extension lines by masking both extension lines. This procedure will break the crossing but will keep the dimensions intact. If you use the BREAK command to achieve the same result, you would have to explode the dimension first and break the extension line where the intersection occurs. This is not a good practice because when you explode a dimension, the associative dimensioning character is lost.

You can access the WIPEOUT command from the Express pull-down menu by selecting Draw and Wipeout. Or you can use the Express Standard Toolbar and select the Wipeout button. When a wipeout is used to break a portion of two intersecting extension lines, one extension line needs to be put on the bottom of the other extension line so that the other extension line can be displayed as a continuous extension line again. This is accomplished by using the DRAWORDER command. The DRAWORDER command will move one of the broken extension lines to the bottom of the masking done with the WIPEOUT command.

■   **EXERCISE 18–13:**   *The following step-by-step exercise will allow you to use a wipeout on the intersection of the two extension lines shown in Figure 18–76 and place the vertical extension line to the bottom of the other using the DRAWORDER command:*

Step #1:   Open the EXE18-8.dwg file.

Step #2:   From the Express Standard Toolbar, click on the Wipeout button and follow the command line procedure below:

Command: _. WIPEOUT Select first point or [Frame/New from Polyline] <New>: **F** ~EnterKey~

Select an option [Off/On] <ON>: **OFF** ~EnterKey~

Regenerating model.

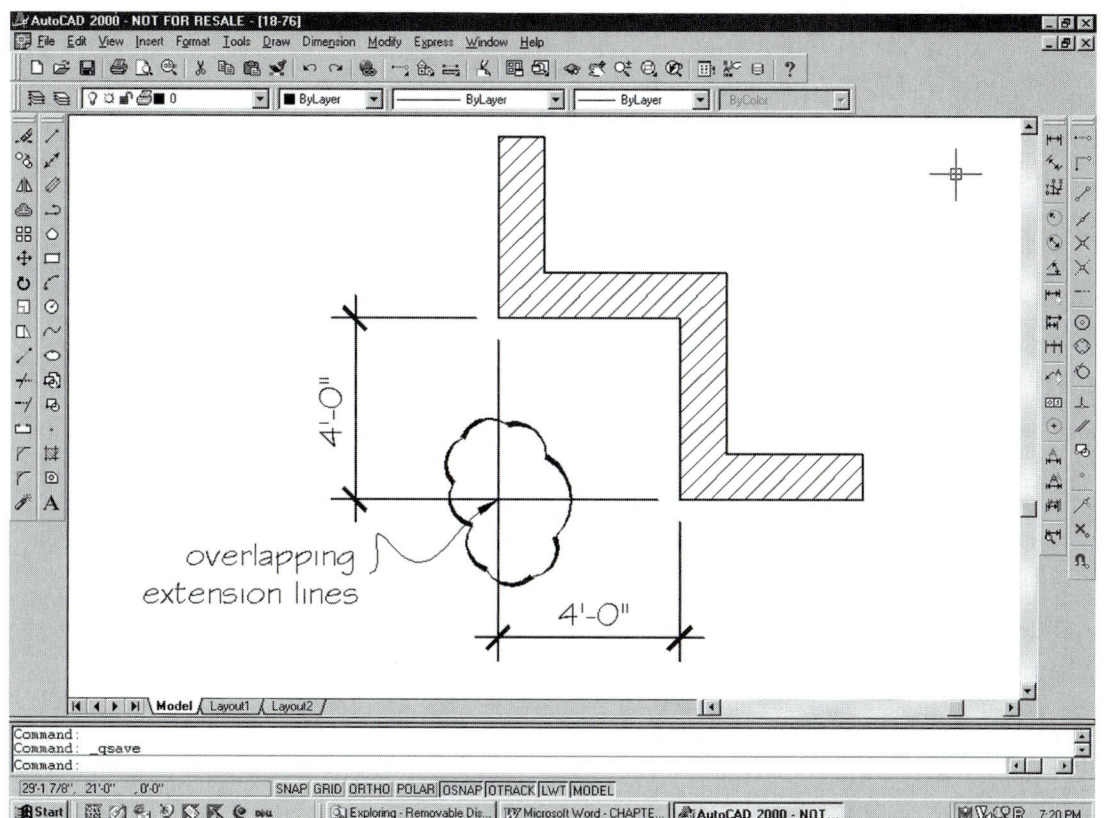

Command: ~EnterKey~

WIPEOUT select first point or [Frame/New from Polyline] <New>: *(select the first point to place a box around the two intersecting extension lines)*

Specify next point: *(select the second point)*

Specify next point or [Undo]: *(select the third point)*

Specify next point or [Undo/Close]: *(select the fourth point)*

Specify next point or [Undo/Close]: **C** ~EnterKey~

The drawing will now look like Figure 18–77.

Now place the vertical extension line to the bottom of the horizontal extension line using the DRAWORDER command with the following continued steps:

Step #3: Click on the Draworder button in the Modify II toolbar and follow the command procedure below:

Command: _draworder

Select objects: *(select the vertical extension line)*

Select objects: ~EnterKey~

Enter object ordering option [Above object/Under object/Front/Back] <Back>: **F** ~EnterKey~

Congratulations! You have successfully used a wipeout to break an extension line. The drawing will now look like Figure 18–78.

FIGURE 18–77 The *wipeout* will place a blank image by creating a box around the intersection of two overlapping extension lines. Notice both extension lines are broken.

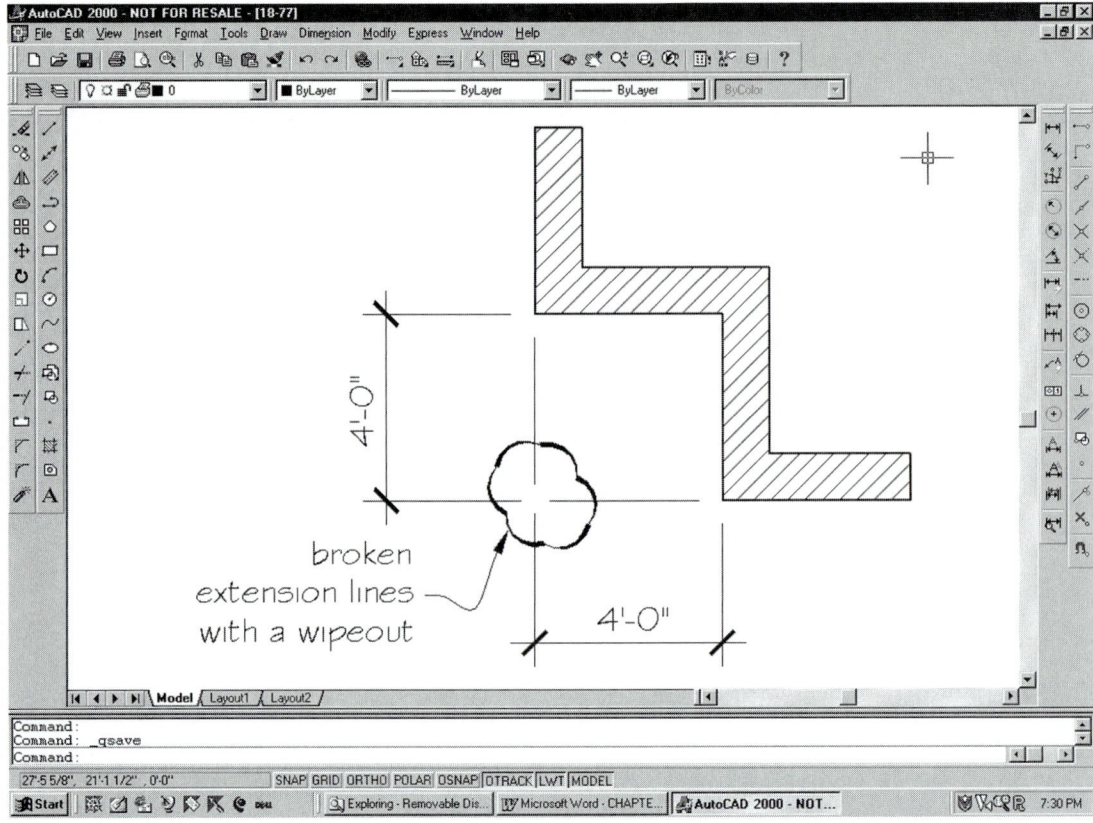

FIGURE 18–78 Using the DRAWORDER command, the vertical extension line is placed to the bottom of the horizontal extension line by bringing it to Front.

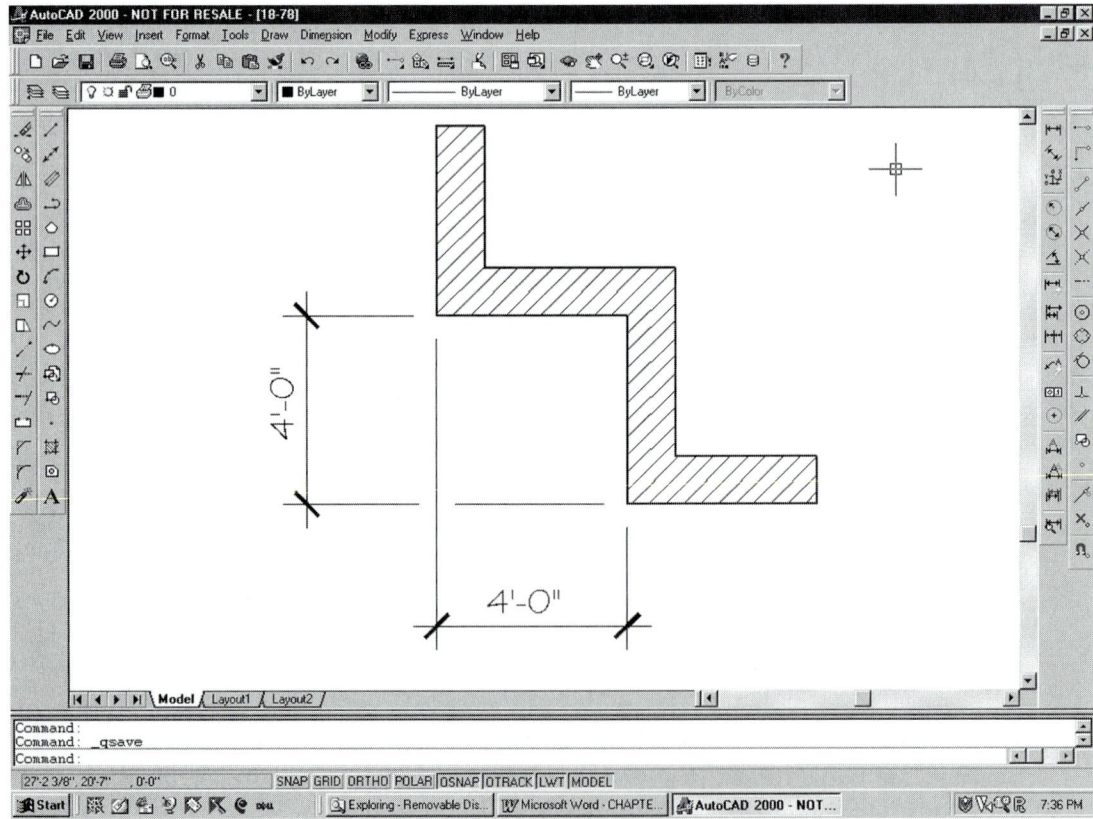

REVIEW QUESTIONS

1. Name the six major principles governing the creation and use of architectural dimensioning in projects.
2. What kind of goals should the architecture firm establish toward achieving uniformity and high efficiency in dimensioning?
3. How can you access a list of all the dimensioning variables in AutoCAD?
4. What is the function of the following dimensioning variables?

   DIMDLE:

   DIMTXT:

   DIMGAP:

   DIMLUNIT:

   DIMTIH:
5. Describe the function of the Description text box inside the Dimension Style Manager dialog box.
6. After what function does the <*style overrides*> message appear under the current dimension style inside the Dimension Style Manager dialog box?
7. What is the name of the command used to create dimension overrides?
8. What is a substyle and how can you create one?
9. In what way does the Drawing Units Type and the Drawing Units Precision settings established from the Format pull-down menu affect the dimensioning variable settings inside the dialog boxes?
10. Describe the two different ways to dimension an object when using the DIMLINEAR or DIMALIGNED commands?
11. What prerequisites are required for the Fraction height scale setting to work?
12. Which dimensioning setting forces the dimension text between extension lines?
13. Which dimensioning setting will allow you to display all dimensioning variable values at their proper scale inside the image display window?
14. How does the Crossing option of the QDIM command work?
15. What are the major components of a typical leader line?
16. What is the major difference between the QLEADER and the LEADER command?
17. Which setting inside the Leader Settings dialog box allows you to attach a block to the endpoint of the last leader line segment?
18. How do you access the Leader Settings dialog box?
19. How do you change a dimensioning variable while using dimensioning commands?
20. What is a dimensioning mode?
21. What is the name of the variable that controls associative dimensioning?
22. What are dimension defpoints?
23. How do you trim a dimension?

PROBLEMS

1. Open the *EXE18-9.dwg* file. By using the JAMB dimension style, create all the dimensions as shown in Figure 18–79. Use the QLEADER command to create all spline leader lines with annotation. Save the drawing as MYEXE18-14.
2. Open the *EXE18-10.dwg* file. Use the QLEADER command to create the missing leader lines with annotation as shown in Figure 18–80.
3. Open the *EXE18-11.dwg* file. Use the Dimension toolbar and the ARCHITECTURAL dimension style and create all exterior and interior dimensions.
4. Open the *EXE18-12.dwg* file. Extend the two dimensions using the EXTEND command as shown in Figure 18–81. Edit dimension text so that it is centered in the dimension line. Your finished drawing should look like Figure 18–82.
5. Open the *EX18-13.dwg* file. Show the new dimension for the upper portion of the new wall using the TRIM command as shown in Figure 18–83. Use the Dimension Edit button in the Dimension toolbar to move dimension text home. Your finished drawing should look like Figure 18–84.
6. Open the *EXE18-14.dwg* file. Use the right-click shortcut menu to edit the six dimensions with the six options of the Dim Text Position as shown in Figure 18–85. Your final drawing should look like Figure 18–86.

FIGURE 18-79
Problem 1.

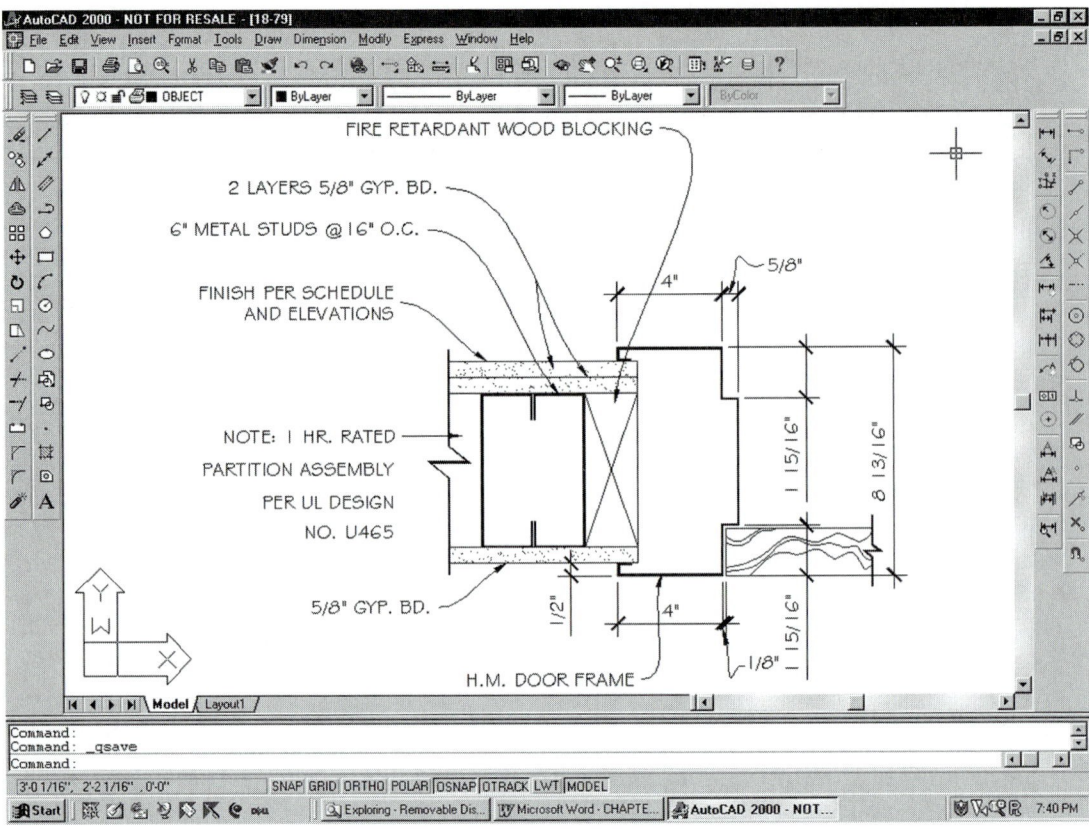

FIGURE 18-80
Problem 2.

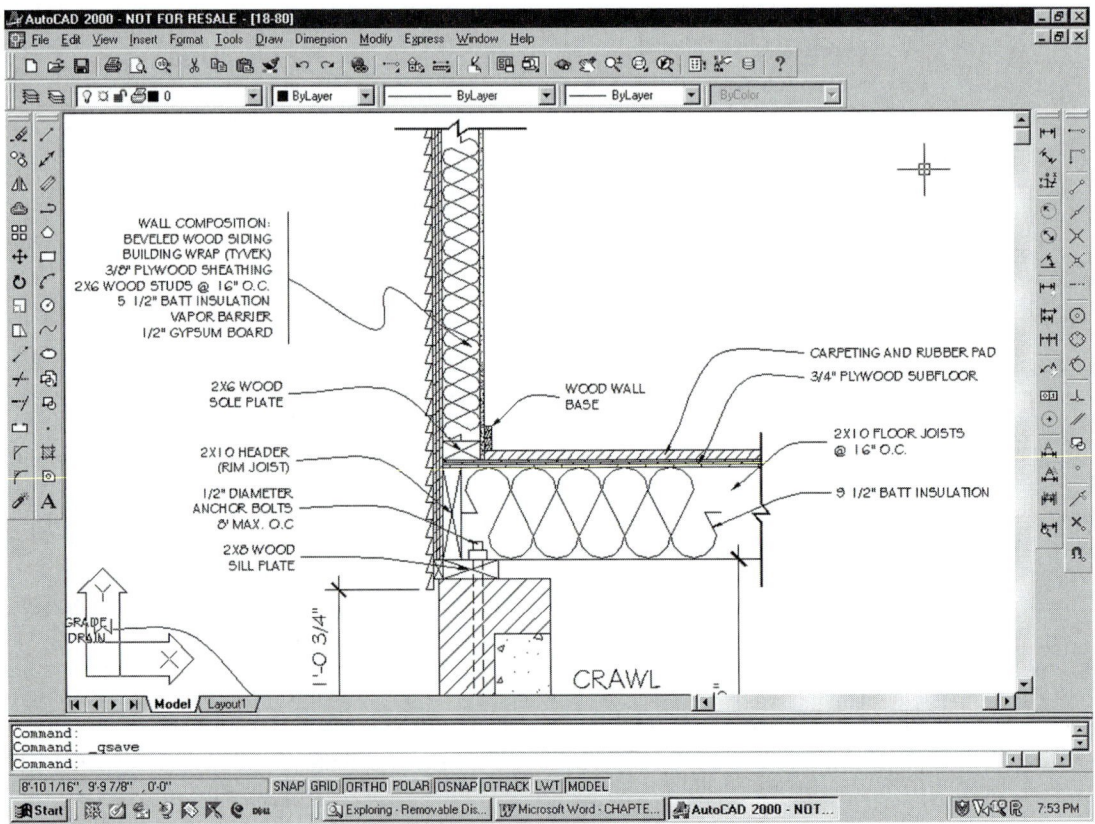

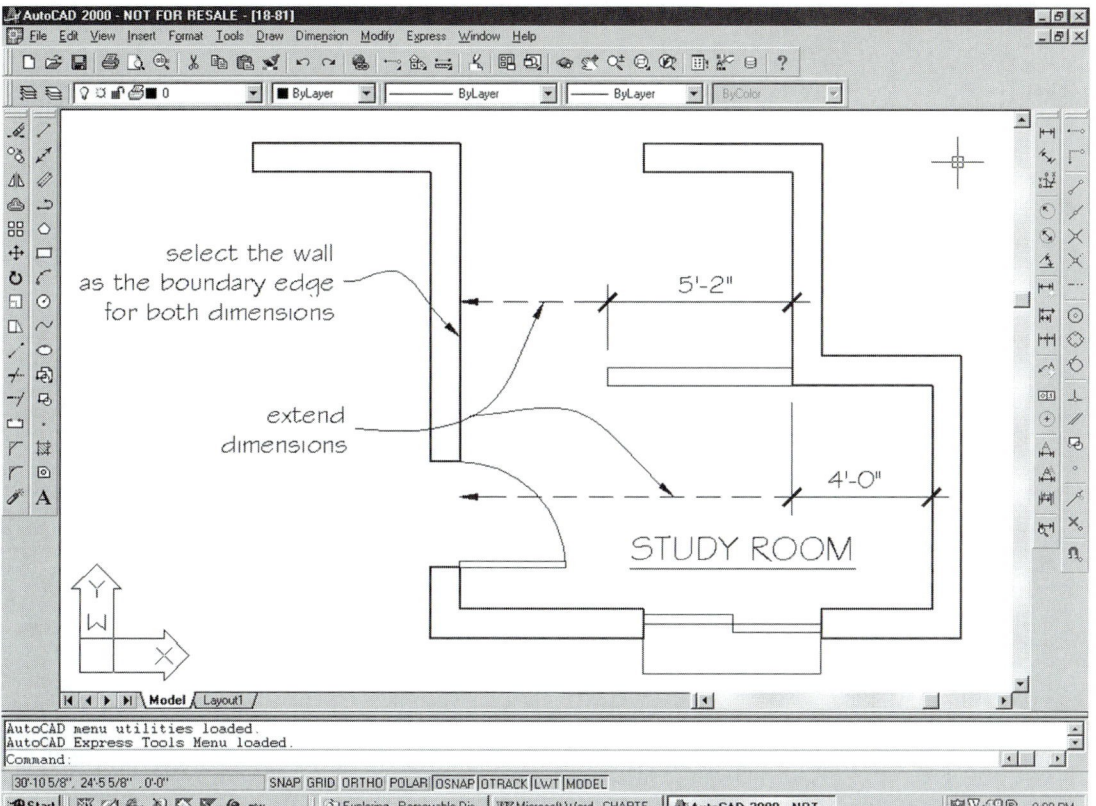

FIGURE 18–81
Problem 4.

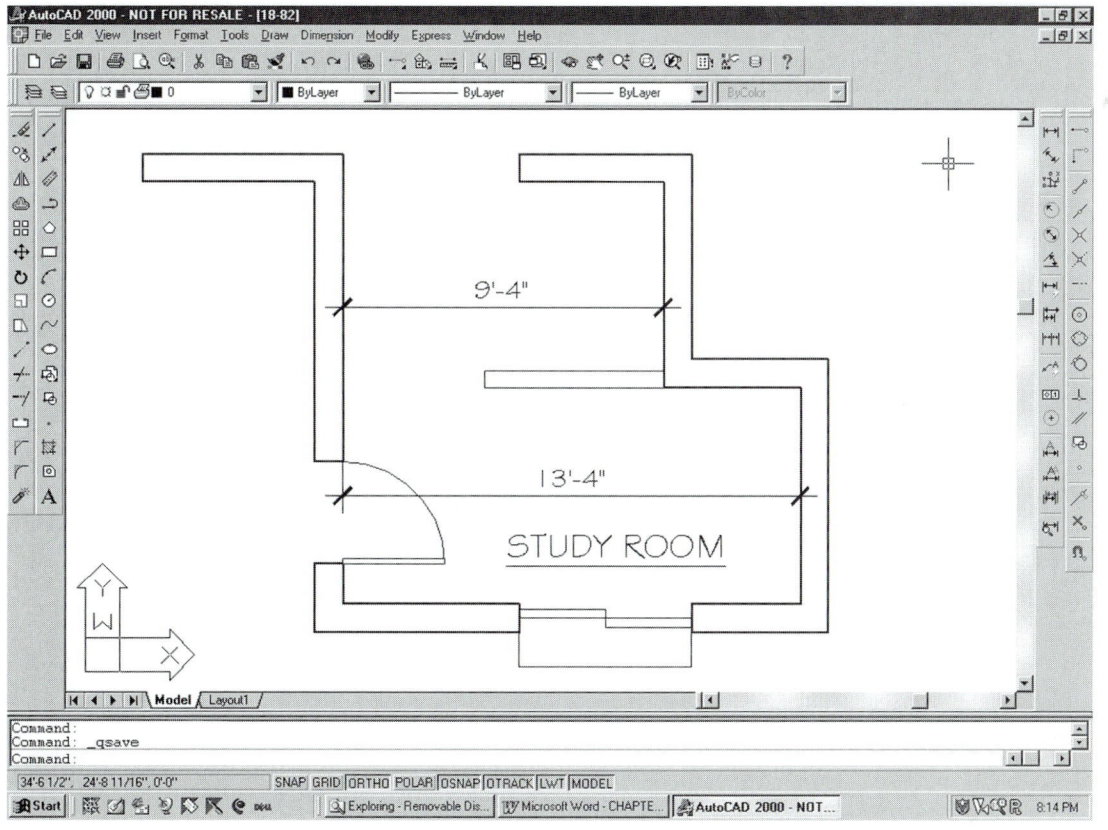

FIGURE 18–82 Final
for Problem 4.

FIGURE 18–83
Problem 5.

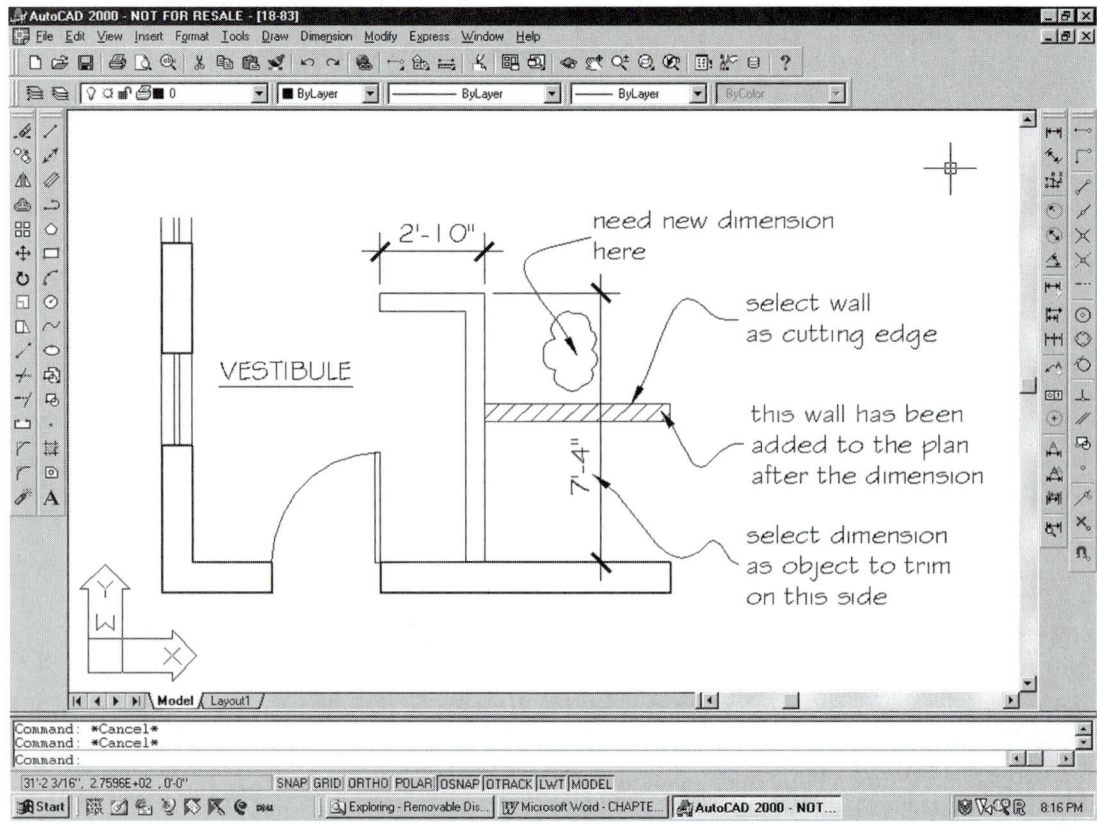

FIGURE 18–84 Final
for Problem 5.

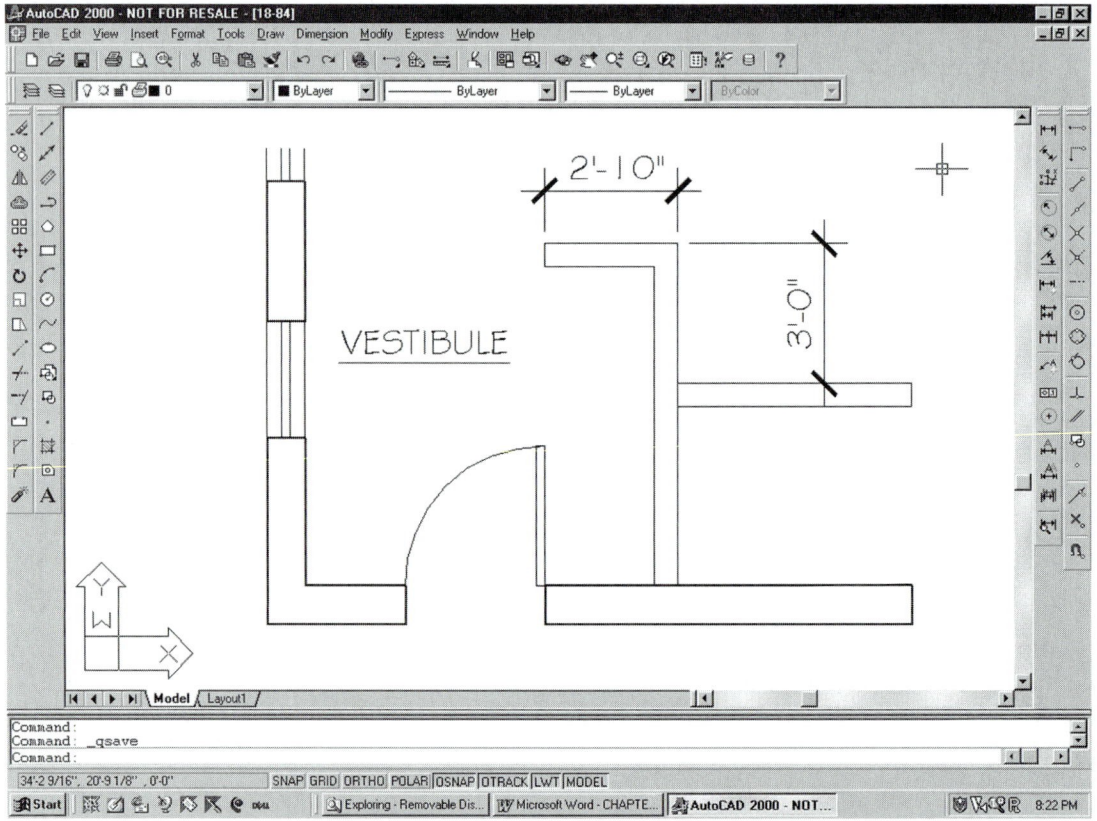

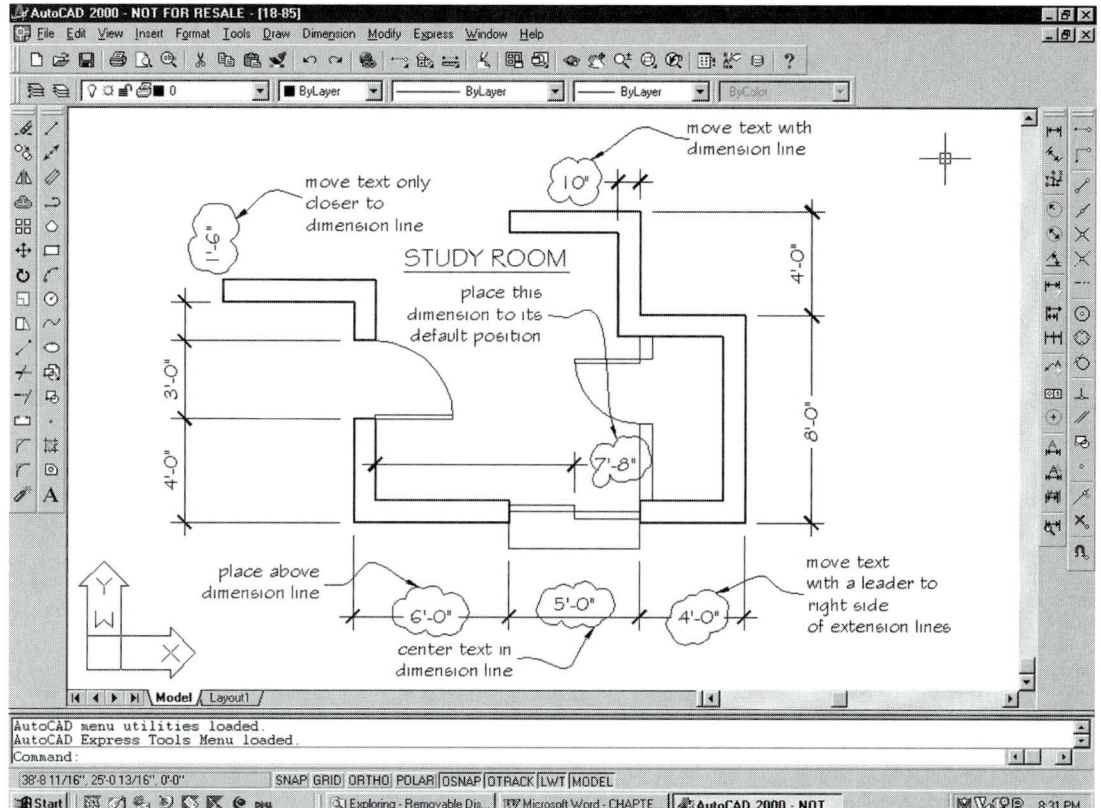

FIGURE 18–85
Problem 6.

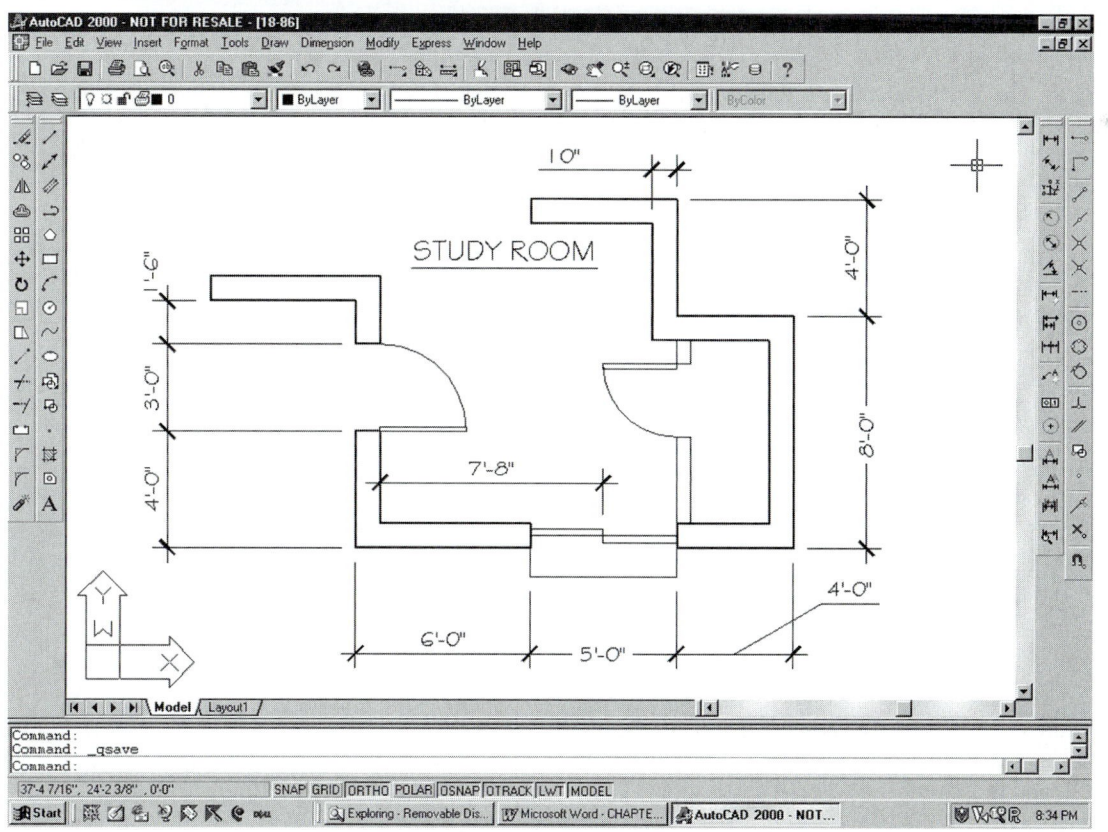

FIGURE 18–86 Final
for Problem 6.

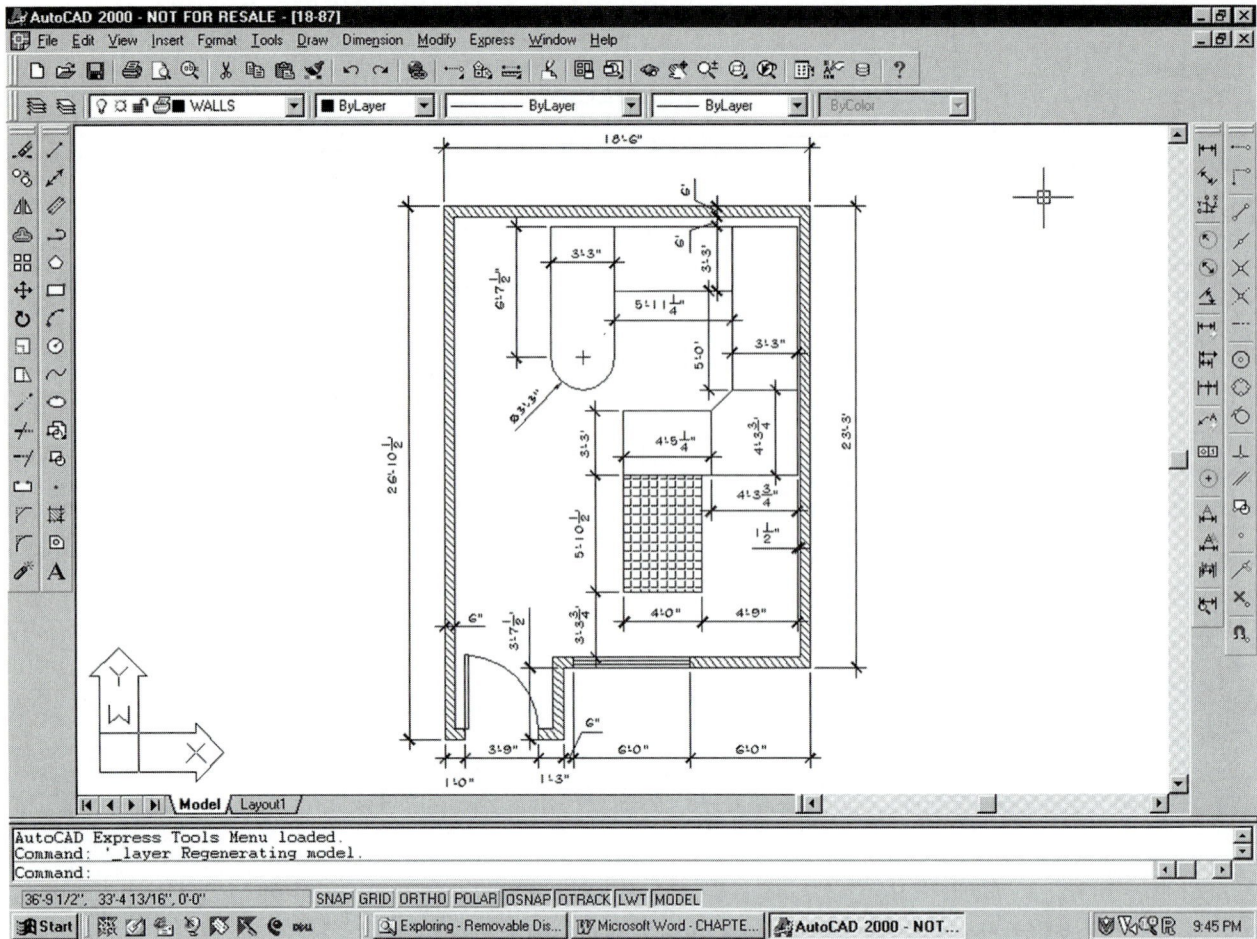

FIGURE 18–87 The Floor Plan as dimensioned for Problem 7.

7. Open the *EXE18-15.dwg* file. Dimension the drawing as shown in Figure 18–87.

8. Open the *EXE18-16.dwg* file. Create all dimensions, leader lines with annotation, and text as shown in Figure 18–88. Use the appropriate layers for each task.

9. Open the *EXE18-17.dwg* file. Dimension the drawing as shown in Figure 18–89.

10. Open the *EXE18-18.dwg* file. Edit the existing dimensions as shown in Figure 18–90.

11. Open the *EXE18-19.dwg* file. Create all dimensions and leader lines with annotation as shown in Figure 18–91. Use the appropriate layers.

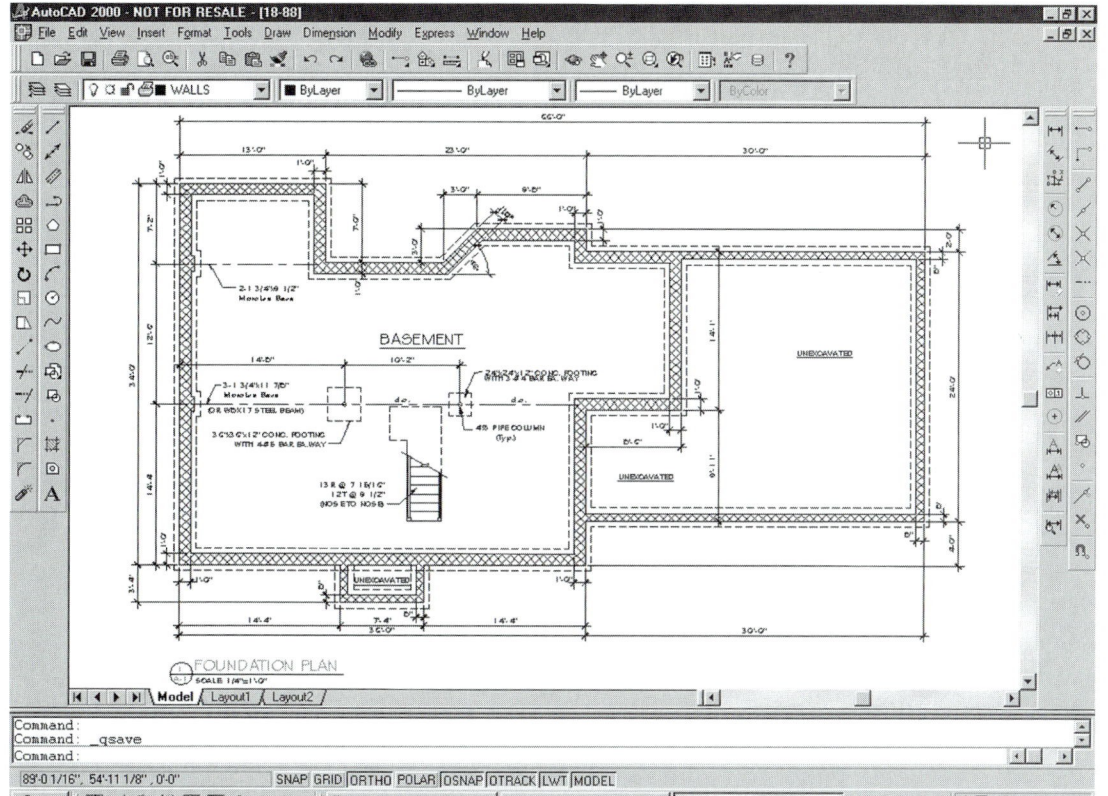

FIGURE 18–88 The Floor Plan as dimensioned for Problem 8.

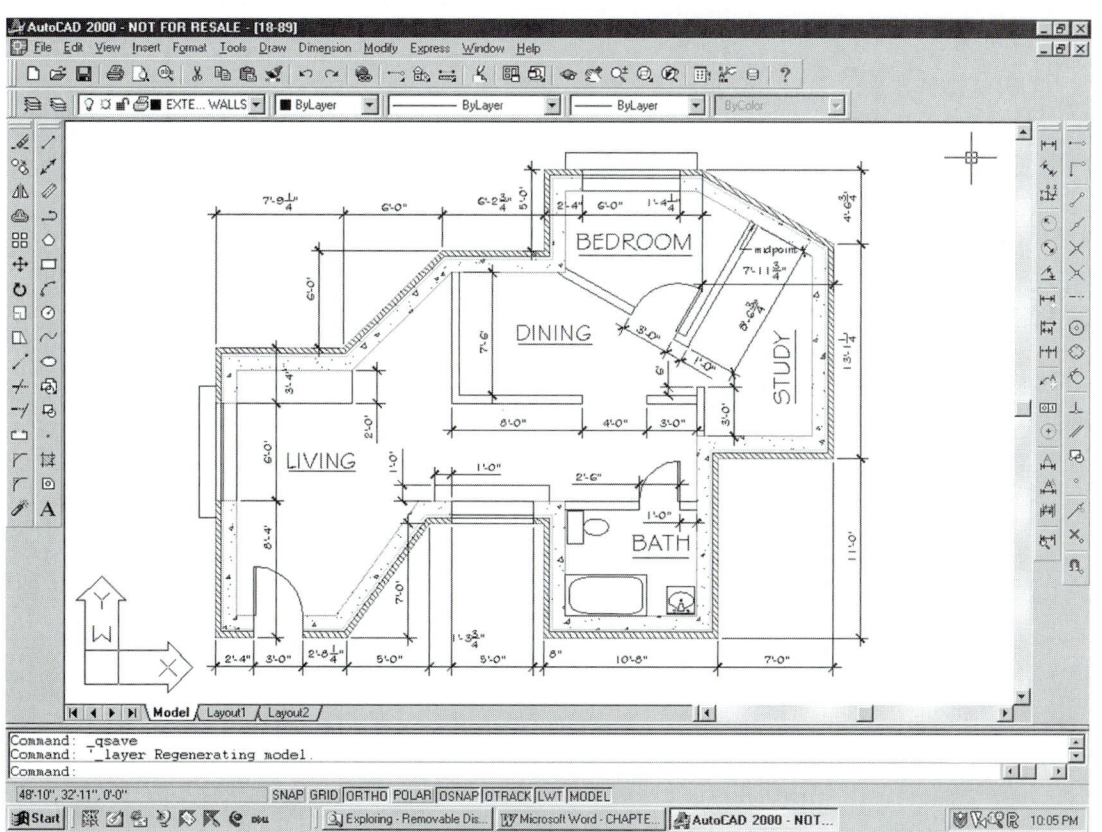

FIGURE 18–89 The Floor Plan as dimensioned for Problem 9.

FIGURE 18–90 The edited dimensions for Problem 10.

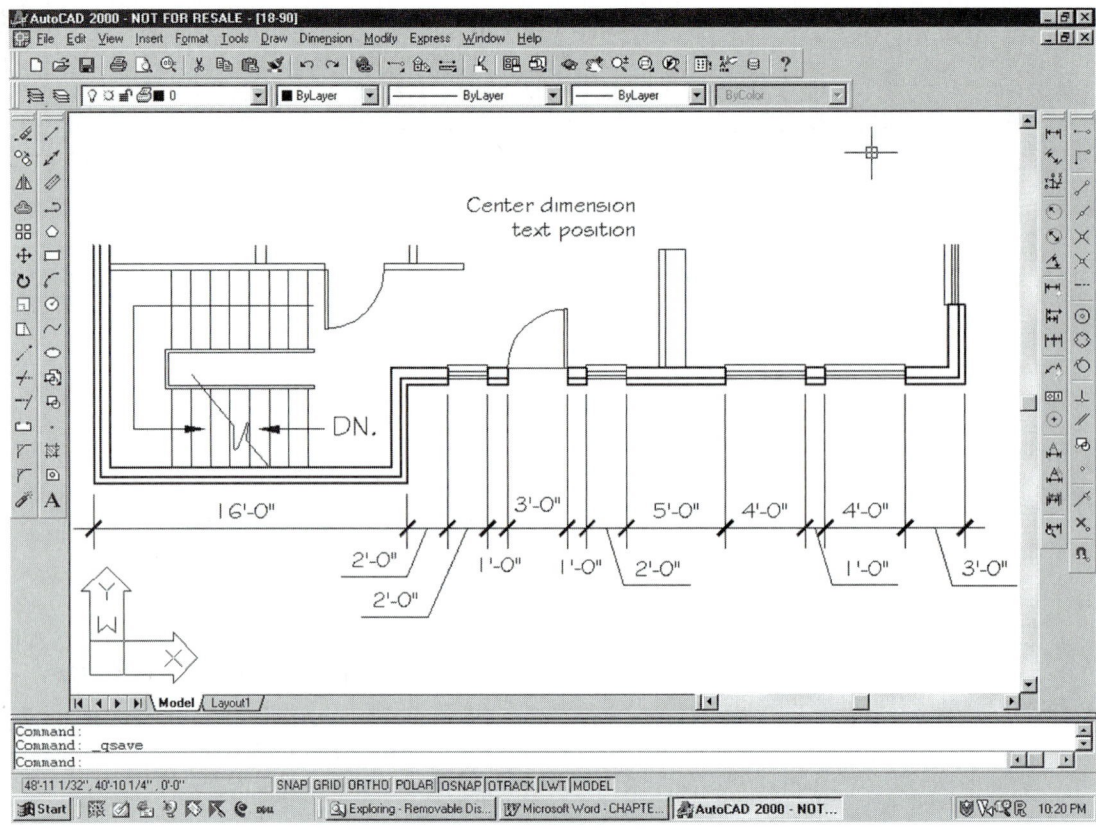

FIGURE 18–91 The detail as dimensioned for Problem 11.

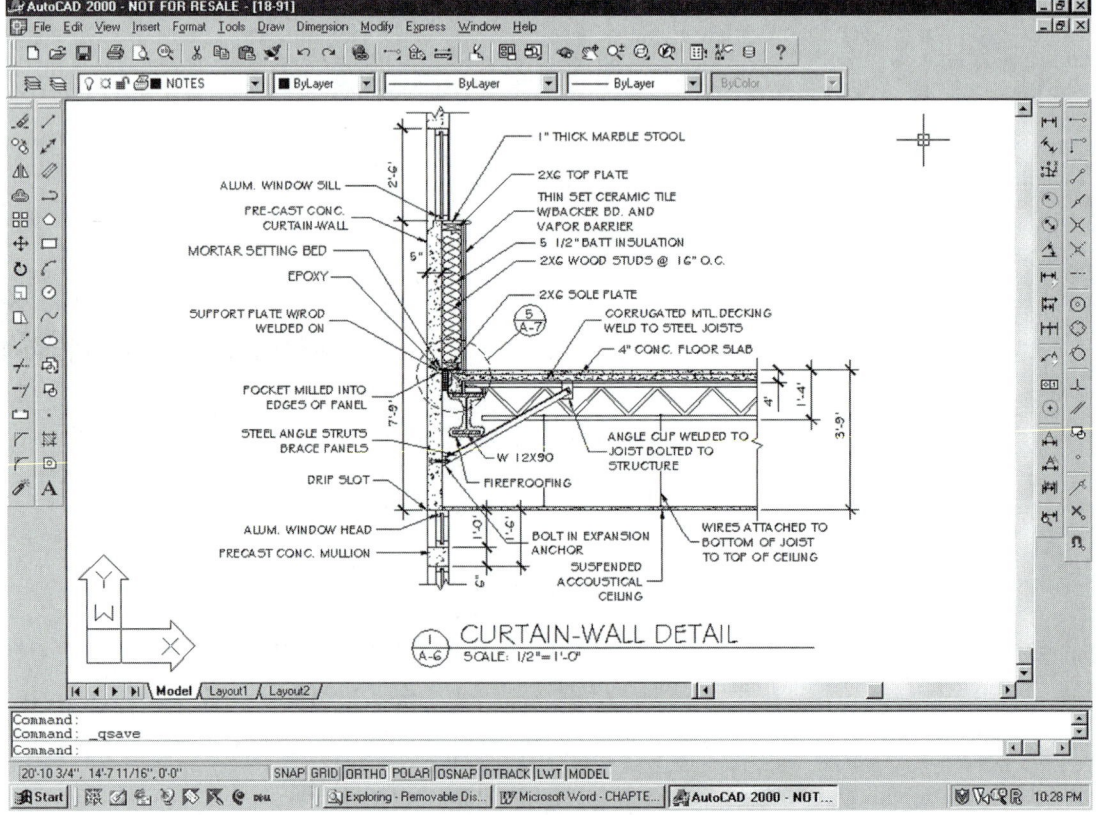

FALSE CHIMNEY

CHAPTER 19 *Creating Architectural Symbols*

After successful completion of this chapter you should be able to:

▲ Identify the role of architectural symbols in drawings.

▲ Create blocks and wblocks using three different techniques.

▲ Insert blocks and wblocks into drawings at any scale.

▲ Use Cut/Copy and Paste to copy or move symbols from one drawing into another.

▲ Use the Multiple Design Environment (MDE) to manage blocks and wblocks within several drawings in the same AutoCAD session.

▲ Use AutoCAD DesignCenter (ADC) to view, copy, and insert symbols from one drawing into another.

▲ Use the Refedit toolbar to edit and update blocks and wblocks.

▲ Create an architectural symbols library.

▲ Use Express tools to increase efficiency when using blocks.

19.1 THE ROLE OF ARCHITECTURAL SYMBOLS

Architectural drawings contain many symbols. These symbols appear as a shape, a view, or a component of an assembly on any working drawing. In a foundation plan the symbol can be a footing composed of lines or circles. In a floor plan it can be the door composed of lines and an arc to show the door swing, or a washing machine in the laundry room. In an elevation it can be the elevation mark composed of a circle and lines, one of a window on the façade of the building. In a mechanical plan it could be one of the many ceiling diffusers or the emergency exit sign near the door. To draw these symbols one at a time and copy them multiple times in a single drawing would take a considerable amount of time and surely would be a waste of time. One of the greatest tools of AutoCAD is its ability to make and insert symbols, called blocks and wblocks, into drawings at a specified scale and store them within a specific drawing file. This ability to make, insert, and store symbols is a great production booster and a real time-saving feature. Figure 19–1 shows a floor plan with blocks inserted as doors, windows, furniture, fixtures, and drawing name and number symbols.

19.2 BLOCKS

A block is a group of objects representing a specific symbol in the drawing. These entities grouped together form a single, named *block definition*. Once a block definition is created, it can be inserted, scaled, and rotated inside the current drawing or it can be inserted into another drawing file using the AutoCAD DesignCenter (ADC). AutoCAD DesignCenter is an excellent feature to copy and insert blocks from one drawing into another. A block is considered to be an internal symbol that can be locally accessed in the current drawing or it can be copied or inserted

FIGURE 19-1   A floor plan with inserted blocks as doors, windows, furnishings, fixtures, and drawing designator symbols.

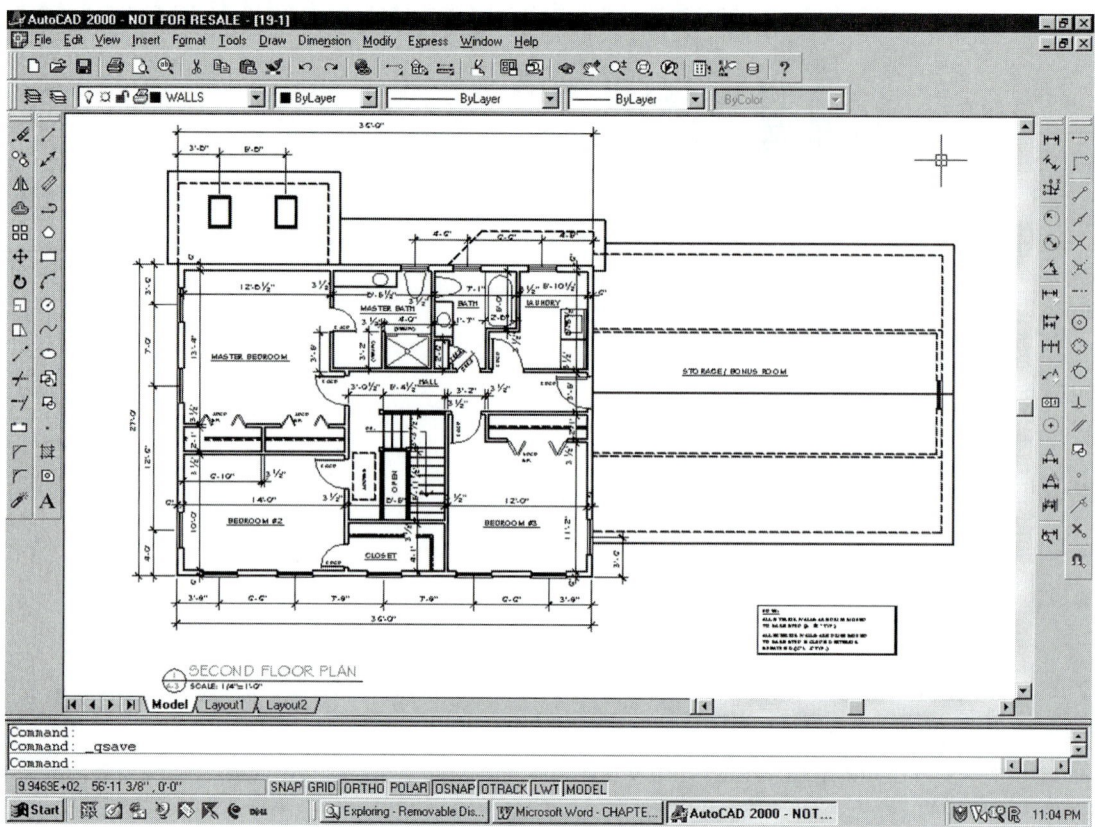

FIGURE 19-1   A floor plan with inserted blocks as doors, windows, furnishings, fixtures, and drawing designator symbols.

into another drawing using ADC. For a project that is small in size and scope, creating blocks for multiple use and inserting as needed is sufficient. For a much more coherent, uniform, and efficient block insertion procedures use the ADC to select, drag, and drop block(s) from one drawing into another drawing. For example, a symbol representing a major part of a drawing can be created as a block and inserted in the current drawing whenever it is needed, but it can also be copied into another file having the same or different drawing units using ADC.

19.3 WBLOCKS

A wblock is a group of objects representing a specific symbol in the drawing that is used to write a block definition as a separate drawing file. A wblock can be created from an object, an existing block, or an entire drawing that can be used globally and inserted into any drawing with or without ADC. Since a wblock has a .dwg file extension, it can easily be accessed and used as frequently as needed. This will greatly increase drawing efficiency and speed.

Whether you create a block or a wblock, local or global access is possible with the use of AutoCAD DesignCenter. The greatest time saving feature of a block or a wblock is that you create it once and insert it many times into any drawing. When a block or a wblock is inserted into a drawing, it will become a permanent part of the drawing, but its content is not added to the current drawing file. On very large size projects, inserting symbols in this manner will help you save file size.

19.4 SYMBOLS LIBRARY

For ongoing large projects, company- and project-specific custom blocks can be created as part of the *architectural symbols library*. The contents of this library can be determined, and each individual symbol can be created and made into a block while other firm standards are being established. After the symbols are given a block definition, the W(WriteBlock) command can be

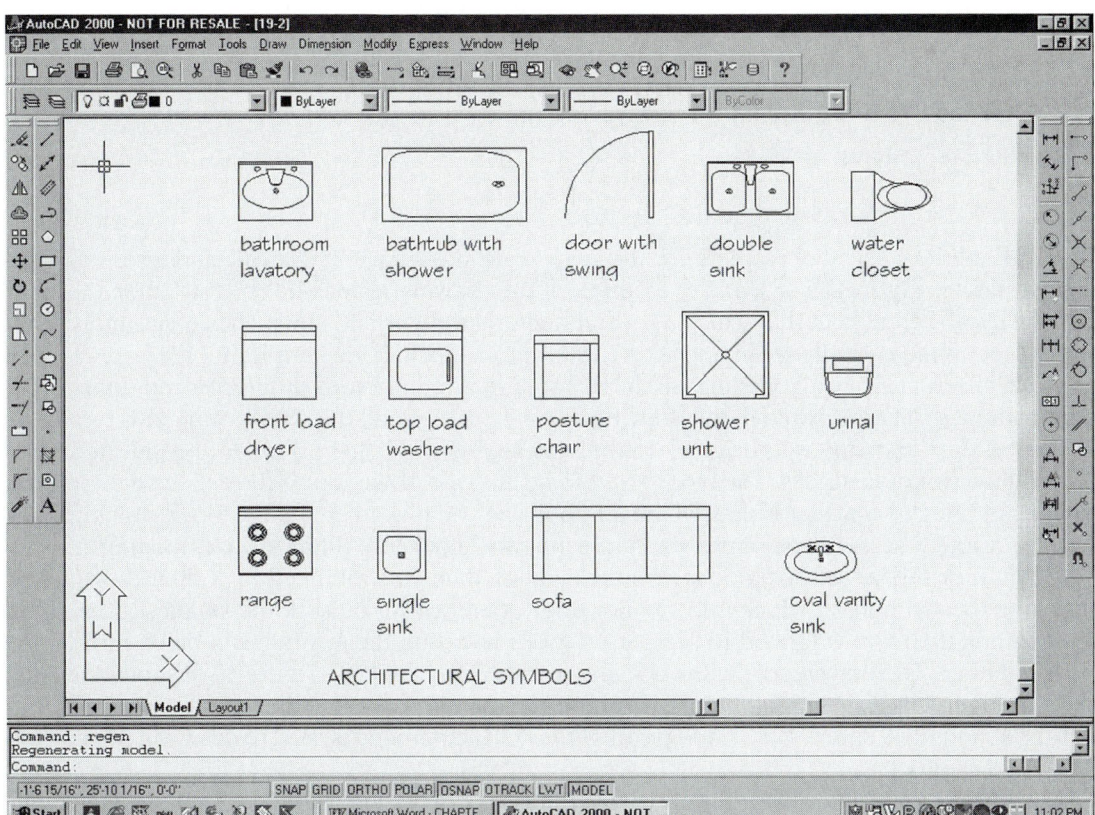

FIGURE 19–2 A sample of an architectural symbols library.

used to create a series of files that can be used to create a symbols Library. Using this file, each block can be inserted into another file using the ADC. Furthermore, many blocks can be created in one master drawing and used as a symbols library. If this process is done once, there will be no need to create the same symbol again. Only the additional symbols need to be created. Figure 19–2 shows the architectural symbols library file with 14 blocks. More symbols can be added to the library as needed. For a detailed discussion on symbols library, see Section 19.11.

19.5 SIZE AND SCALE OF BLOCKS

A block can be any symbol that you intend to use more than once in the current or in any other drawing. It is defined as one object but may contain many objects. You can draw the symbol using any AutoCAD commands. Before drawing the symbol, determine its size in terms of X and Y scale. This is important because when the symbol is made into a block and inserted into the drawing, AutoCAD will ask for the X and the Y scale factor value established either on the dialog box or on the screen. This means that if the block is to vary in size from one insertion location to another, the different scale values must be established or calculated in relation to the original X and Y values of the block. Certain blocks, such as electrical outlet symbols, appliances, and water closets have X and Y values as standard measurements. For blocks that do not vary in size with different insertion applications, the symbols can be created in the current drawing using current drawing scale and settings at their actual size and inserted at X = 1 and Y = 1 scale factor values. Other blocks, such as doors, bathtubs, windows, HVAC equipment, custom cabinets and furniture, and structural columns have varying X and Y values. For blocks that vary in size with different insertion locations, the symbols can be drawn to fit inside a one square unit and inserted at the required X and Y scale factor values. This will allow you to create a block or a wblock that varies in size when inserted. With this method you create the block once and insert it at any X and Y scale factor many times in the current drawing or use the ADC to drag and drop into another drawing.

There are three different methods to create blocks and wblocks:

1. Current drawing scale method.
2. One Inch Square Method.
3. One Foot Square Method.

19.5.1 Current Drawing Scale Method

With this method a symbol is created at the same scale as the current drawing and inserted in the current drawing as inches or feet. For example, if the drawing scale is 1/4″ = 1′-0″, then the symbol will also be created at that scale, using architectural units as feet and inches. You simply draw the object on the current screen and then turn it into a block. For example, in Figure 19–3 there are four different size wall openings in the drawing that require four different sized doors. With this method, a door is created in the drawing using the LINE and the ARC commands by selecting one of the door sizes as its original symbol size. In Figure 19–3, the 3′-0″ door is selected to be the original size of the block. The block size can be any one of the four different-sized doors. The important thing to consider is that, whatever door size you pick to create the block, you must adjust the X and Y scale factor values when inserting the block into different size openings.

If you pick the largest size door to be the symbol, then you will need to scale it down when inserting the symbol as a block into smaller door openings. If you pick the smallest door to be the symbol, then you will need to scale it up when inserting the symbol as a block into larger door openings. The drawing in Figure 19–3 has a scale of 1/4″ = 1′-0″. Figure 19–4 shows the 3′-0″ door in Figure 19–3 magnified before it is made into a block. Notice that the door has a thickness of 2″ and the Center, Start, End option of the ARC command is used to draw the door swing with 3′-0″ radius.

Because a typical door has equal X and Y values, it can be said that the ratio between X and Y is 1:1. This door will be inserted in the drawing it is created using X and Y insertion scale factor values as decimal inches. Since this door has an X and Y value of 3′-0″ (as the drawing is created), AutoCAD will register the insertion X and Y unit values as 1. In other words, when this door symbol is made into a block and inserted into an opening that has the same unit size as the block, the X and Y values are automatically equal to 1 unit (1″). This means that when the door symbol shown in Figure 19–4 is made into a block and is inserted into the 3′-0″ opening (which is the same size as the block), its X and Y scale values are automatically registered as 1 unit. When inserting this block into the 3′-0″ opening as a 3′-0″ door, you simply accept the default X and Y values (X = 1 and Y = 1) and insert the door without changing the X or Y scale values. However, when this block is inserted into an opening that has a size other than 3′-0″, the new value for the X and Y scale must be calculated based on the original 36″ door. A simple way to calculate the required X and Y scale value is to come up with an equation that would adjust the X and Y scale values of the block to the new insertion value for the selected opening. For example, if this 3′-0″ door as a block is inserted into an opening that requires a 2′-0″ door, then the adjustment would be made as follows:

```
If 36 units for the door symbol is to 1 unit for the block definition,
Then 24 units will be to X unit for the block insertion definition.
```

The X represents the block scale value for the 2′-0″ door. Putting the variables in to the equation form will give us the following:

```
36/1 = 24/X
```

Now solve for X as follows:

```
36 X = 24
X = 24/36
X = 0.6666
```

Therefore, when inserting this block into a 2′-0″ opening that requires a 2′-0″ door, use X = 0.6666 and Y = 0.6666 as the insertion scale factor values. Since X = Y, only X needs a value. The X and Y insertion scale factor values must be entered as unit inches.

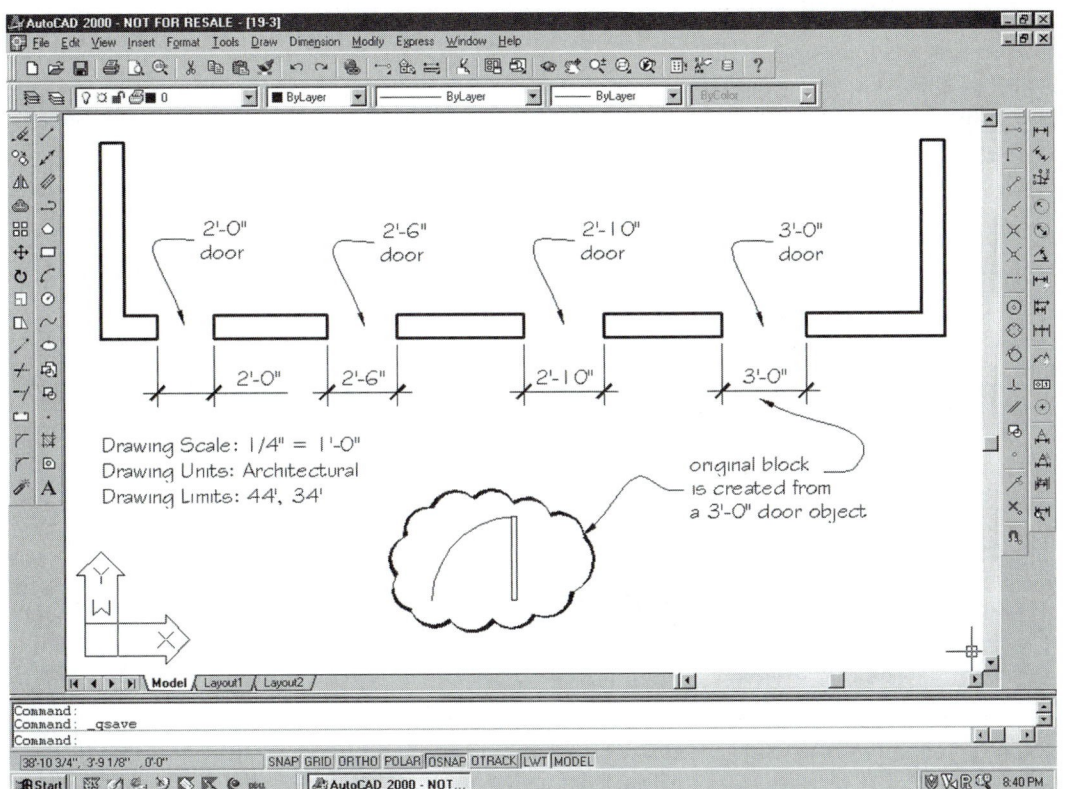

FIGURE 19–3 The drawing with four different door openings. The 3'-0" door is selected to be the symbol for the block to be inserted in all the other door openings. The door symbol will be made into a block and inserted into different openings with different X and Y scale values.

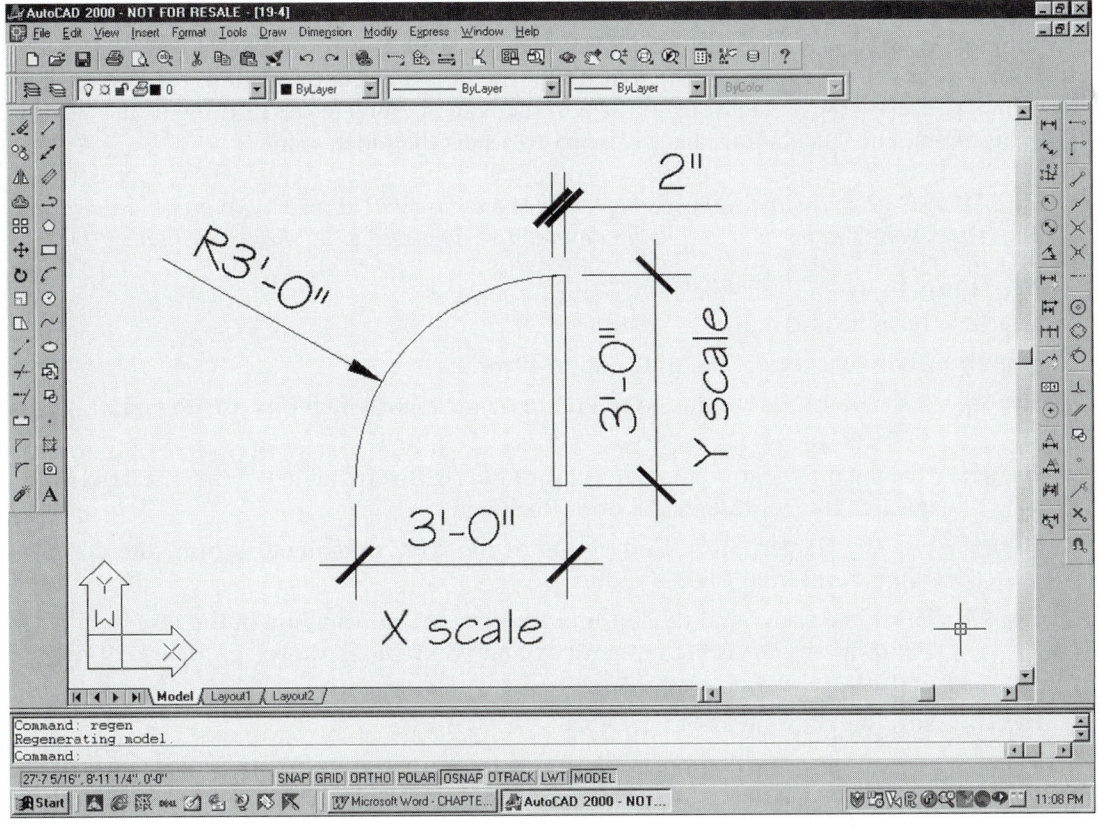

FIGURE 19–4 The 3'-0" door is drawn as a symbol. It will then be given a block definition. Notice the X and Y scale values are equal.

TABLE 19-1: Comparison
of X and Y scale factor
for different size doors
as block.

Size of Door Used as Block	X and Y Scale Factor When Inserting the Block as the Door Size			
	2'-0"	2'-6"	2'-10"	3'-0"
2'-0"	1.0000	1.2500	1.4166	1.5000
2'-6"	0.8000	1.0000	1.1333	1.2000
2'-10"	0.7058	0.8823	1.0000	1.0588
3'-0"	0.6666	0.8333	0.9444	1.0000

If the same block is to be inserted into the 2'-6" opening, the equation would be as follows:

```
36/1 = 30/X (the value of 30 representing the 2'-6" opening).
36 X = 30
X = 30/36
X = 0.8333
```

The last opening of 2'-10" would have an X and Y insertion scale value of 0.9444.

Consequently, if the 2'-6" door was selected as the original symbol and made into a block, the X and Y insertion scale value for other openings would be different and have to be calculated. Table 19–1 shows the different X and Y scale factors needed for different door size symbols.

19.5.2   One Inch Square Method

With this method the symbol is created to fit inside a one unit square box using either the default AutoCAD settings or the current drawing settings. In other words, the one square inch object can be created using decimal units and 12, 9 as drawing limits or using architectural units and corresponding drawing limits. The symbol is then fit inside this square. After the symbol is created, the X and Y unit value of the symbol will equal one inch. This means that if the block is inserted in a drawing with X and Y scale factor value of 1, then the symbol will be a one square inch object. If it is inserted in a drawing with X and Y scale factor of 36 (X= 36 and Y = 36), then the symbol will be a 36 square inch object. If the object is a door symbol, you simply enter the X and Y insertion scale factor as the size of the wall opening in the drawing as inches only. With this method no calculations are necessary to adjust the block scale.

■ **EXERCISE 19–1:**   *The following step-by-step exercise will allow you to create a door symbol inside a one square inch box using default drawing settings as shown in Figure 19–5.*

Step #1:   Start a new drawing from scratch.

Step #2:   Turn the grid on.

Step #3:   Zoom-in close to the center of the drawing.

Step #4:   Use the LINE command to create a one square inch box as shown in Figure 19–5A.

Step #5:   Use the OFFSET command to offset the right vertical line of the box 0.0416" inward. This represents the door thickness.

Step #6:   Use the Center, Start, End option of the ARC command to draw the door swing. Notice the 1.0000" radius.

Step #7:   Erase the upper and the left line and trim the bottom line of the box so that the only object visible is the door and its swing as shown in Figure 19–5B and 19–5C.

Step #8:   Save the drawing as MY DOOR SYMBOL.

Congratulations! You have successfully used the One Inch Square method to create a door symbol. You can turn this symbol into a block or a wblock. This is discussed later in the chapter.

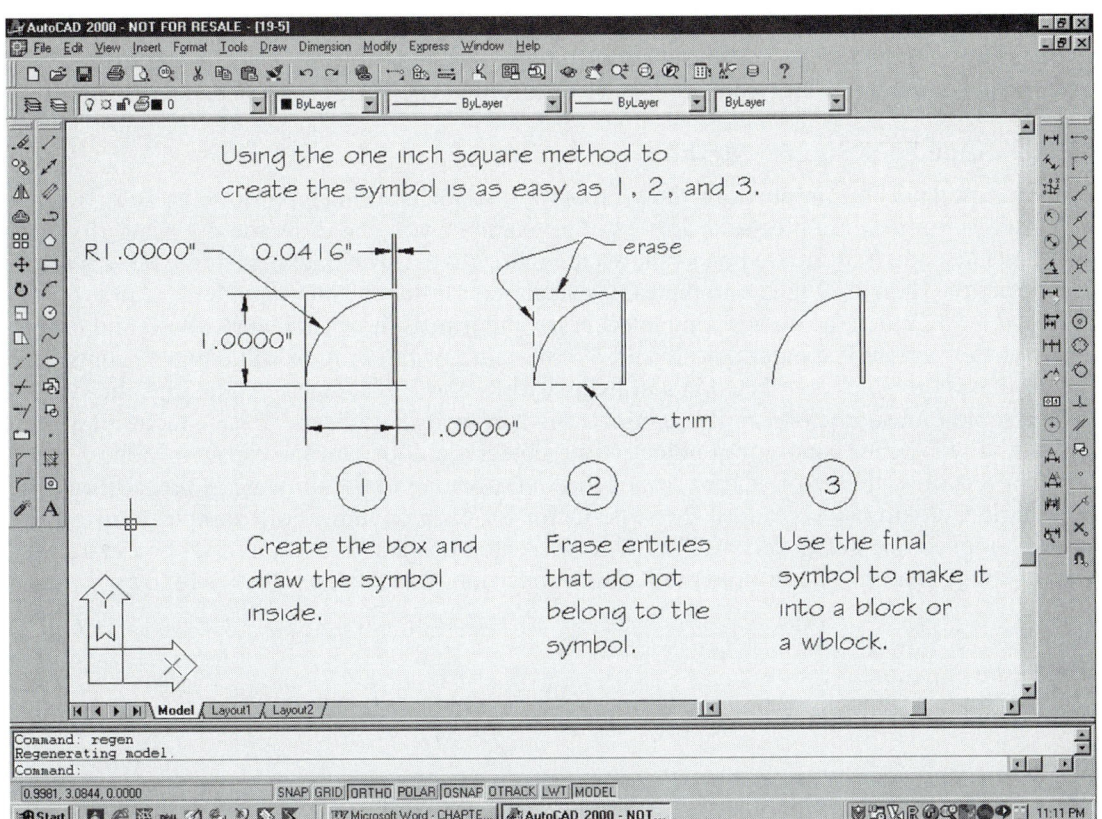

FIGURE 19–5 The door symbol is created inside the one square inch box. A, Step one creates the one inch square box and the door with the swing. B, Step two deletes the unwanted lines. C, Step three shows the final door symbol before it is made into a block.

Tips: To calculate the thickness of the door inside the one square inch box so that when inserted in any size door opening it will be 2″ thick, use the following drawing data and formula:

Drawing Units: Architectural

Drawing Scale: 1/4″ = 1′-0″

Drawing Scale Factor: 48

Now establish the equation as follows: If 2″ is the representation of a typical door thickness in a drawing that has a scale factor of 48

Then, What would be the door thickness represented inside a one square inch box at a scale factor of 1?

Write the equation as follows: 2″/48 = X/1

48X = 2″

X = 2″/48 = 0.0416

The 0.0416 is good for the drawings that have scale factors of 48, 64, 96, and 128. If the drawing you are working on has a scale factor other than what is shown above, divide the 2″ by the scale factor of the drawing. For example if you are creating a door symbol in a drawing that has a scale factor of 24 (1/2″ = 1′-0″ scale), draw the door inside a one square inch area with a door thickness of 0.0833 (2″/24 = 0.0833).

To insert the door block in any size wall opening, enter the X and Y scale factor as inches. For example, to insert the one square inch door as a block in a 2′-6″ opening, enter 30 as the X and Y insertion scale factor. To insert the same block in a 2′-10″ opening, enter 34 as the X and Y insertion scale factor. The One Inch Square method is the most efficient and effective method, since it allows you to create any symbol inside a one square inch box and insert it at the true scale without any conversions to find insertion scale factor values. This method is extremely useful for symbols that vary in X and Y scale. The wall openings shown in Figure 19–3 require uniform door values in the X direction. For symbols that vary in X and Y directions, this method becomes more effective and faster. For example, in large projects you might have equipment that vary in X and Y directions. Instead of creating one equipment for one size and then create another at a different size, you would simply create the symbol to fit inside a one square inch box once and insert it at different sizes using different X and Y insertion scale factor values.

19.5.3   One Foot Square Method

With this method, you simply draw the symbol to fit inside a one square foot box. This could be an existing or a new architectural drawing. For example, you can draw the door and the door swing inside a one foot square box as shown in Figure 19–6A. The thickness of the door is calculated from the ratio of 12 inches to the value calculated for the one inch square method as *0.0416 × 12 = 0.4992″*. When the door is completed, erase and trim as shown in Figure 19–6B and 19–6C.

After the symbol is created, the X and Y unit value of the symbol will equal 12 units. This means that if the block is inserted in a drawing with X and Y scale factor value of 1, the symbol will be a one foot square object. If it is inserted in a drawing with X and Y scale factor of 3, then the symbol will be a 3 square foot object. If the object is a door symbol, you simply enter the X and Y insertion scale factor as foot size of the wall opening in the drawing as feet without the feet mark. But you have to adjust the scale factor for each opening. For example, to insert the door symbol shown in Figure 19–6C as a block created inside a one square foot box in a 2′-10″ wall opening, you must determine the X and Y insertion scale factor values as follows:

```
If 1" is to 12". Then X is to 34" (2'-10" wall opening).
```

Create the equation as follows:

```
1/12 = X/34
```

And solve for X as follows:

```
12 X = 34
X = 34/12
X = 2.8333
```

FIGURE 19–6   The door is created inside the one square foot box. A, Step one creates the one square foot box and the door with the swing. B, Step two deletes the unwanted lines. C, Step three shows the final door symbol before it is made into a block.

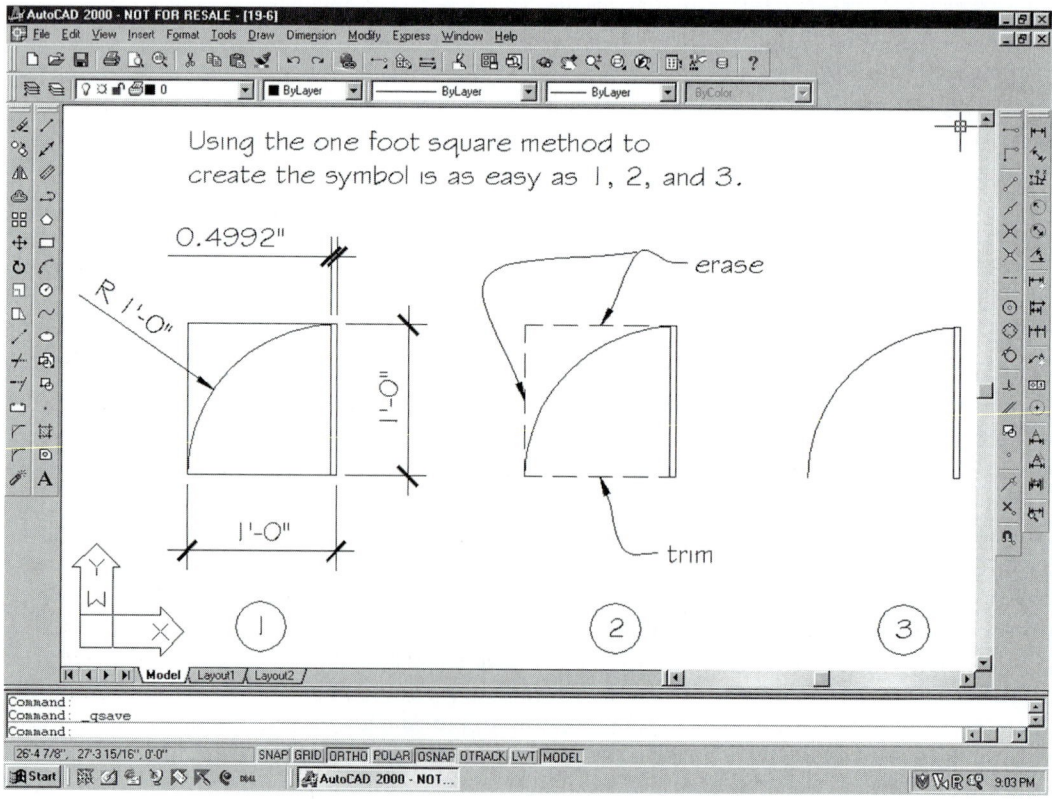

Therefore, to insert the door symbol as a block in a 2'-10" opening enter 2.8333 as the X insertion scale factor value. If the wall opening required a 2'-0" door, the X insertion scale factor value will be entered as 2. If the wall opening required a 2'-6" door, the X insertion scale factor value will be entered as 2.5. This formula and equation will work for symbols created to fit inside a one square foot box.

Tips: Try experimenting with the three different methods shown. One of the biggest advantages of creating blocks and wblocks with the One Inch Square method is that the X and Y insertion scale factor values always equal to the required X and Y values in inches in the drawing. This will help you avoid calculating conversions.

19.6 CALCULATING INSERTION SCALE FACTORS

If you create a symbol using the Current Drawing Scale method and create a block or a wblock from it and then insert it into a drawing having a different scale, you can use the methods described above to determine X and Y insertion scale values.

Example 1: Suppose you create a symbol inside a drawing having a 1/4"=1'-0" scale and create a block or a wblock then decide to insert the symbol into a drawing having a scale of 3"=1'-0". If the block is inserted at the same size that it was created, the proper insertion scale factor would be determined from the method used to create the block. If the block is inserted at a different size, the proper insertion scale factor must be calculated based on the method used to create the original block. Refer to examples in sections 19.5.1, 19.5.2, and 19.5.3. Also refer to Table 19–1.

Example 2: Suppose you create a symbol inside a drawing having a 1/4"=1'-0" scale and create a wblock then decide to insert the symbol into a Title Block (.dwt file). This block can be a drawing title symbol used for the identification of individual drawings inserted into a Template. When inserting this block in a Layout Paper Space, use the reciprocal of the scale factor of the drawing used to create the block to determine the X and Y insertion scale values. For example, for the block created inside a 1/4"=1'-0" drawing, use 0.020833 (1/48=0.020833) as the X insertion value. Since the block is inserted in paper space that has a scale factor of 1, and the original block is created inside a drawing having a scale factor of 48, the reciprocal of 48 is 0.020833. When inserting the same block inside a Model Space in a Layout, the insertion scale values are determined from the procedures explained above and depend on the method used to create the block.

19.7 COLOR AND LINETYPE OF BLOCKS AND WBLOCKS

Before you create a symbol, think about its color and linetype when you insert a block or a wblock in a drawing with layers and colors already established. Most architectural drawings have layers created just for symbols. There are two methods you can use to create symbols before they are made into a block or a wblock: the Bylayer method and the Byblock method.

Bylayer Method: If you want the block or the wblock to maintain its own specific layer, color, linetype, and lineweight regardless of the layer, color, and linetype it is to be inserted on, assign a layer, color, linetype, and lineweight before drawing the symbol. Most symbols will require only a layer and a color. Set color and linetype to BYLAYER in this case. A block created using the Bylayer method will retain the property characteristics of the layer on which it is drawn. For example, suppose that you create an exit sign block on Fire Protection layer with the color blue, DOT2 linetype, and a lineweight of 0.020". When you insert this block, it will be displayed as having a blue color with DOT2 linetype and a 0.020" lineweight regardless of the layer on which it is inserted. Whatever the color, linetype, lineweight, and layers you use to create the block, it will retain its properties when it is inserted on a different layer. For the above example, if the Fire Protection layer does not exist in the drawing it is inserted in, AutoCAD will automatically create the Fire Protection layer.

■ **EXERCISE 19–2:**   *The following step-by-step exercise will allow you to create a symbol using the Bylayer Method:*

Step #1:   Create a new drawing or use and existing drawing to draw the symbol.

Step #2:   Click on the Layers button in the Object Properties toolbar.

Step #3:   Inside the Layer Properties Manager dialog box, create a new layer and call it MY BLOCK.

Step #4:   Assign a red color to this layer.

Step #5:   Assign a DASHED linetype to this layer.

Step #6:   Assign a 0.020″ lineweight to this layer. Turn the LWT button on in the Status Bar.

Step #7:   Right-click on the MY BLOCK layer and select Make Current. Click on the OK button to close the Layer Properties Manager dialog box.

Step #8:   Draw the symbol.

Congratulations! You have successfully created a symbol using the Bylayer Method. This will set the properties (color, linetype, and lineweight) of the symbol as a function of the layer it is created on.

Byblock Method: If the block or the wblock can assume the color and linetype of the layer on which it is inserted, create the symbol on layer 0 and set color and linetype to BYBLOCK. For example, suppose that you create a water closet symbol on layer 0, turn it into a block, and insert it on the Fixtures layer. The water closet will become a part of the Fixtures layer. If you explode the water closet block, the individual objects that make up the block will revert back to layer 0. If you create the same block with objects drawn on layer 0 with color and linetype set to Bylayer, when inserted the block will have the color and linetype of the current layer.

The following guidelines will help you manage blocks and wblocks efficiently in your projects:

• If a block is created on layer 0 and assigned a color, linetype, and lineweight of Bylayer, it is placed on the current layer, all properties of the current layer will apply to the block.

• If a block is created to have color, linetype, and lineweight specified with Byblock, it will assume the current properties of the drawing it is inserted in.

If you create a symbol using Bylayer but want to change it to Byblock, use the Properties window to change the properties of the symbol to layer 0, delete any layers (other than 0), and set color and linetype to Byblock. If you create a symbol using Byblock but want to change it to Bylayer, use the Layer Properties Manager dialog box to create a layer and assign a color to the symbol. Then use the Linetype Manager dialog box if you need to assign a different linetype to the symbol.

19.8 CREATING BLOCK DEFINITION

After the symbol is drawn using one of the three different techniques shown above and at the appropriate size and scale, it is ready to be given a block definition. A symbol is not a block until it is turned into a block. To make a block from an existing symbol, select the Make Block button in the Draw toolbar, type BLOCK at the command line, or from the Draw pull-down menu select Block and then select the Make. . .option. You can also type B or BMAKE at the command line to access the Block Definition dialog box. Whichever method you select, the Block Definition dialog box will appear as shown in Figure 19–7.

When you create a block, you create a *block definition* similar to the definition points established by the dimensioning applications. A block definition is an object composed of many entities but is a single object when inserted into a drawing. There are seven major steps involved in creating a block:

Step #1:   Name the block.

Step #2:   Select the base point as the insertion point in the block.

Step #3:   Select the objects for the block.

Step #4: Determine the faith of the original symbol.

Step #5: Create a preview icon for the block.

Step #6: Select insertion units for the block.

Step #7: Describe the block.

The Block Definition dialog box has six major categories to help you with these seven steps as follows:

Name: (drop-down list box). This is where you enter the name of the block and is the **first step** in creating a block. The block name can be up to 255 characters, including letters, numbers, and spaces, and is not case sensitive. If you enter an extended block name and receive an error message, enter the EXTNAMES system variable at the command line to make sure it is On (1). When EXTNAMES is Off (0), blocks and wblocks along with layers and text styles use Release 14 symbol parameters. If you send data to other firms, clients, contractors, or builders that use software that do not support long filenames, limit the name to eight characters or less and do not use spaces. For example, to create a block from a 3'-0" door-symbol, enter DOOR-3' inside the Name: drop-down text box as shown in Figure 19–7. If the block name already exists, Auto-CAD will give you the following message:

```
DOOR-3' is already defined.
Do you want to re-define it?
```

If you select No, the existing block will not be redefined. If you select Yes, AutoCAD will save the new block and replace the old one. This message will not be displayed until Step 5 is completed and the OK button is picked. You can select an existing block definition to rename it or change its base point by selecting the down arrow on the right of the Name: drop-down text box. Figure 19–8 shows the existing blocks listed under the Name: drop-down text box.

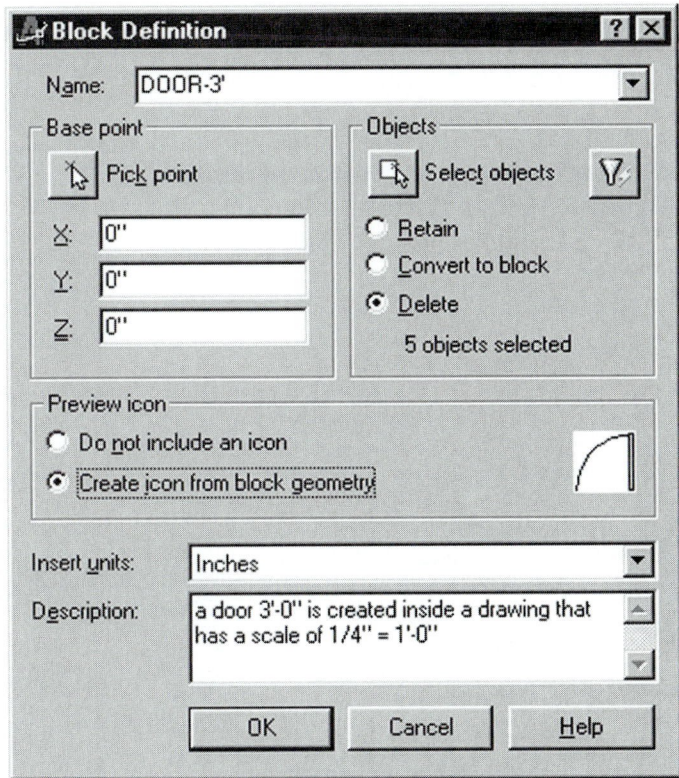

FIGURE 19–7 The Block Definition dialog box is used to create a block from an existing symbol.

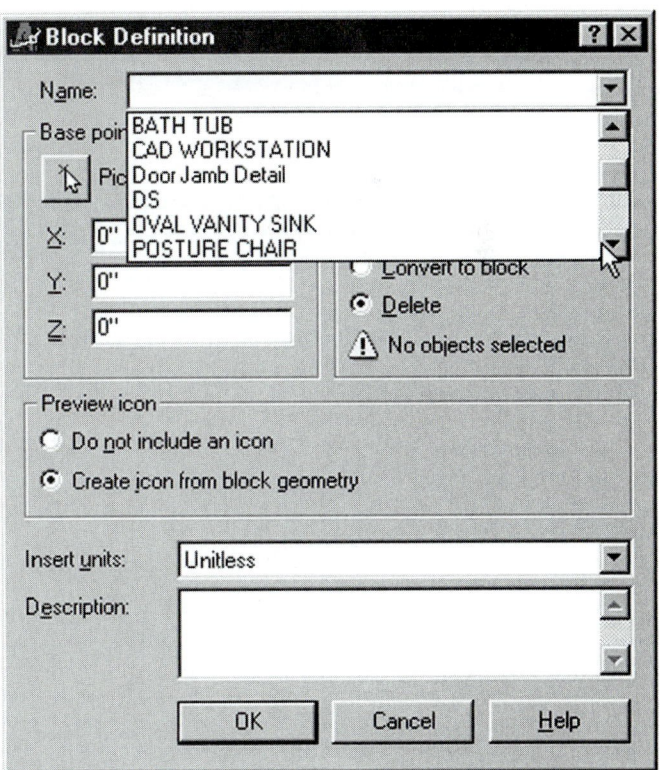

FIGURE 19–8 The down arrow next to the Name: drop-down text box can be used to list the existing blocks created in the current drawing.

Base point: (category).   The Base point is used to establish the insertion point of the block. Insertion point is where the base point of a block is placed when the block is inserted into a drawing. This is the **second step** in creating a block. When a block is inserted into a drawing, the symbol is placed with the base point on the cursor as the insertion point. AutoCAD will give you the opportunity to rotate the symbol if necessary according to the base point and the location of the insertion. Determine the best place for the insertion point. Keep in mind the overall scheme of the drawing along with the drawing requirements. For example, the ideal base point location for the door symbol shown in Figure 19–4 would be the lower right corner of the door shown in Figure 19–9. This is the best place on the door because a typical door is drawn at the intersection or corner of a wall opening.

It is very important to keep track of the base point locations on symbols because blocks may not always be inserted exactly at 0 degrees rotation angle. For example, in Figure 19–10 there are four wall openings that require four doors to be inserted at different rotation angles.

Knowing the precise base point location in the door symbol will allow you to adjust the rotation angle at each insertion point location. Figure 19–11 shows the rotation angle values for the four base point locations for the door symbol shown in Figure 19–9. After the symbol is given a block definition, it can be inserted into the drawing with the following rotation angles: base point location 1 = 0 degrees, Base point location 2=90 degrees, base point location 3=180 degrees, and base point location 4=90 degrees. Last insertion must be mirrored using the MIRROR command.

Tips: Always keep a copy of the symbols library handy with the base points shown on the symbols. If you forget the base point location, insert the block near the intended location, rotate it at the desired angle and copy it.

Figure 19–12 shows some of the symbols and their base point locations.

Pick point: (button). This button will allow you to select the base point location manually. When this button is selected, the dialog box will disappear and the drawing screen will return. Auto-CAD will give you the following command prompt:

```
Command: _block Specify insertion base point:
```

FIGURE 19–9   The ideal place for the base point location as the insertion point for the door block.

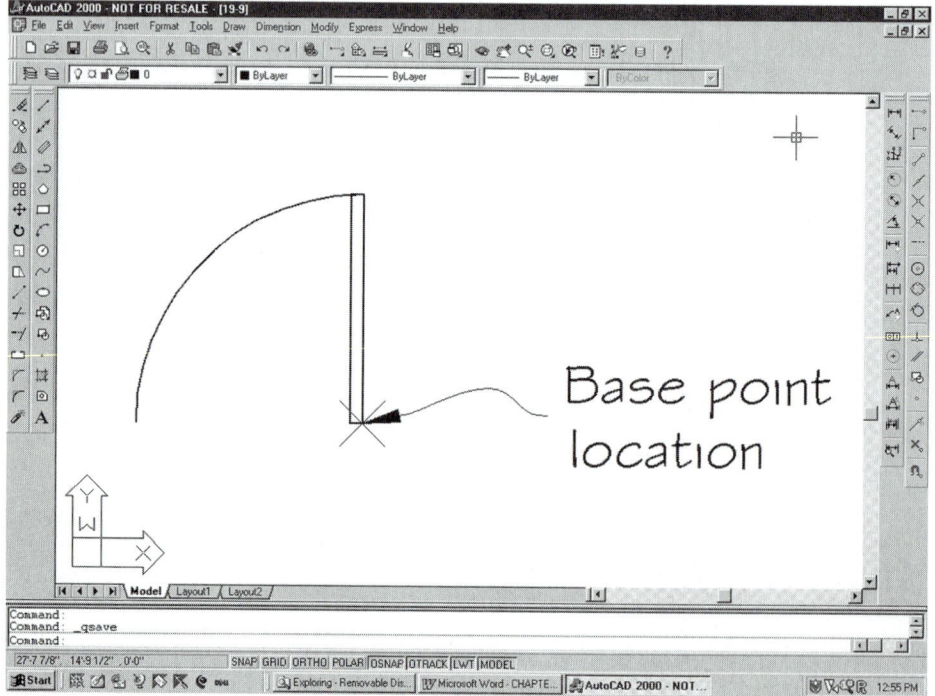

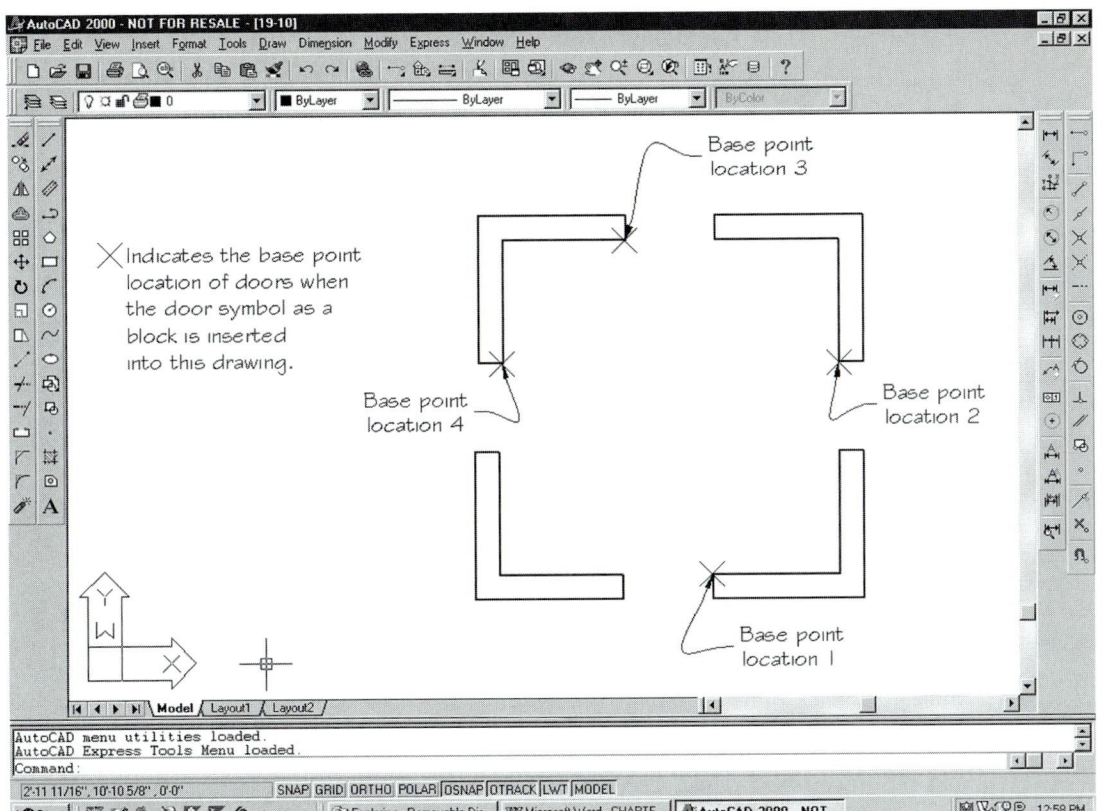

FIGURE 19–10 The four wall openings that require different insertion Rotation angle values for the door symbol in Figure 19–9.

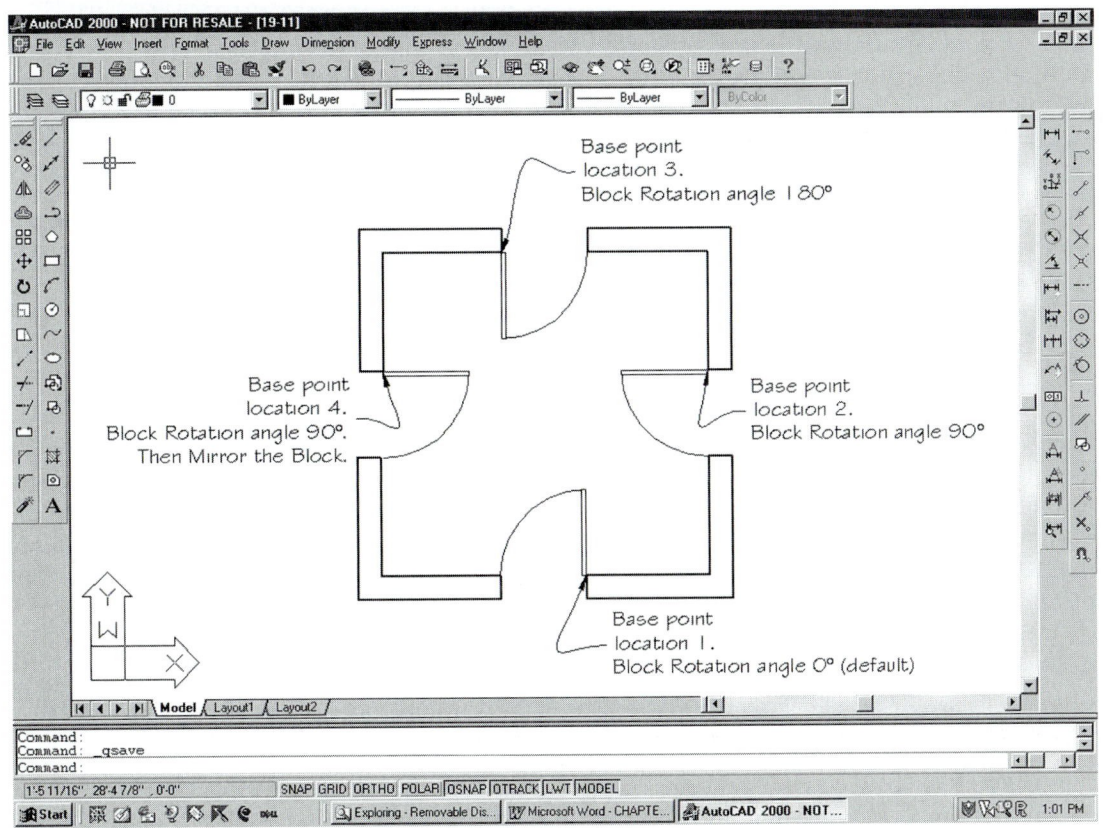

FIGURE 19–11 The Block insertion Rotation angle values for Base point location 1 through 4.

FIGURE 19–12 Some
of the symbols with
their base point
locations as insertion
points shown as Xs on
the symbol.

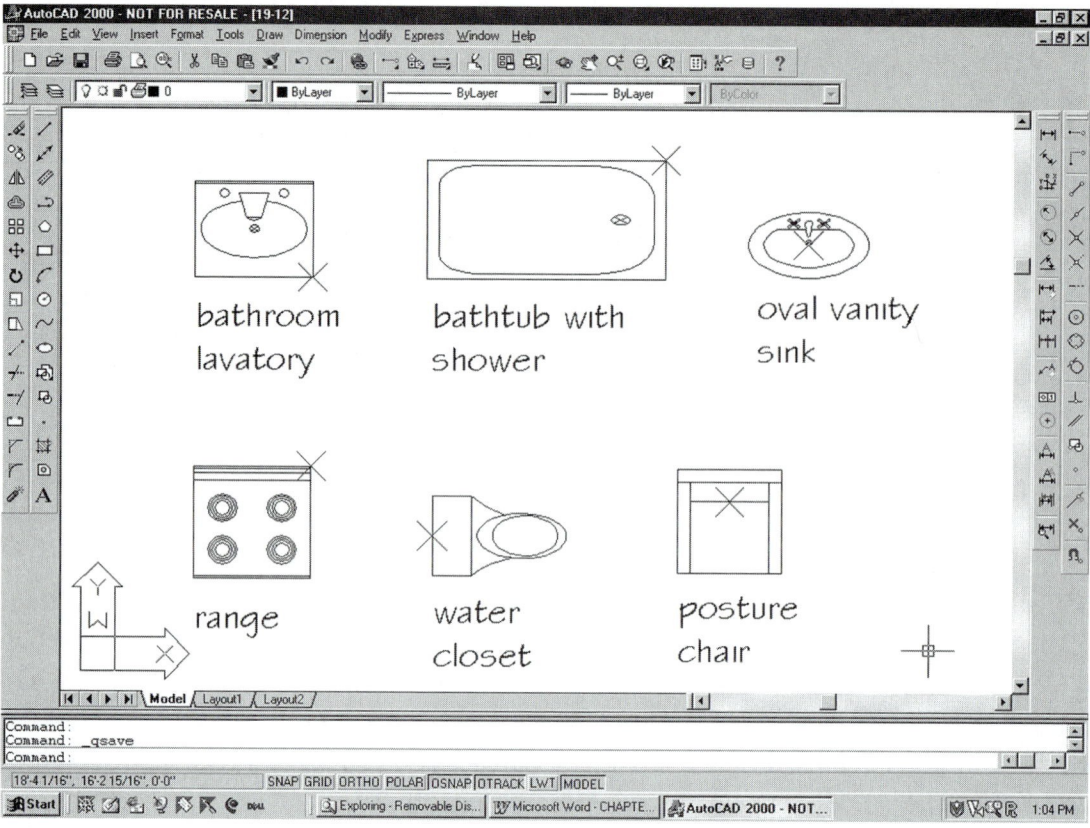

To create the door symbol shown in Figure 19–4 as a block with a name *door,* select the base
point location on the door as shown in Figure 19–9. Be sure to turn Ortho On when selecting
the base point location as the insertion point. After the base point location is selected, the Block
Definition dialog box will return. You can automatically enter the X and Y coordinate locations
for the base point in the X: and Y: text box areas. If you know the precise X and Y coordinate
locations, enter these values in the appropriate areas.

Objects: (category).   This category will help you select the objects that make up the block in the
current drawing. This selection set defines the objects that will create the block. This is the **third
step** in creating a block.

   Select objects: (button). When this button is picked, the drawing screen will return and AutoCAD will prompt you to select the objects that will create the block as follows:

```
Select objects: (select the objects that will define the block)
```

You can use any selection methods to select the entities. For example, to create the door block
in Figure 19–9, simply create a window around the objects to select the door symbol. When you
have finished selecting the objects, press the ~EnterKey~ and the Block Definition dialog box
will return. When no objects are selected, AutoCAD will display the message *No objects selected.*
You must select an object or objects to create a block definition in the current drawing. Under
the Select objects button, there are three options dealing with the status of the symbol after the
block is created. This is the **fourth step** in creating a block. The three options are as follows:

- **RETAIN:**   (radio button). Selecting this option will retain the selected objects in the current
  drawing after the block is created. Click on this radio button if you want the objects to remain
  in the current drawing as individual objects. If you draw the door symbol in the current drawing and do not intend to use it again, there is no need to retain the original symbol.

- **CONVERT TO BLOCK:**   (radio button). Selecting this option will convert the selected objects
  into a block in the current drawing after the block is created.

- **DELETE:** (radio button). Selecting this option will delete the selected objects from the drawing after the block is created.

Quick Select: (button). Quick Select will help you simplify creating blocks by allowing you to create a filtered selection set based on the objects properties on the screen. In addition to selecting objects directly on the screen, you can select objects based on their object types and object properties for block definition. When you click on the Quick Select button on the right of the Select objects button, the Quick Select Dialog box will be displayed. You can use this dialog box to specify the filtering criteria and how you want AutoCAD to define the selection set from the criteria. This technique of creating a filtered selection set is extremely powerful when the object selection for a block or a wblock is based on specific types and properties.

Note: When using Quick Select, you can only select one Property and one Value for the selected Object Type. For example, you cannot search for a CIRCLE with a BLUE color and HIDDEN linetype at the same time. You cannot search for objects that are not in the current drawing. If you use Multiple as the Object type, use Quick Select repeatedly with the Append to current selection set check box checked.

Preview Icon: (Category). This category will help you determine whether to save a preview icon after the block definition is completed. This is the **fifth step** in creating a block. There are two options as follows:

- **DO NOT INCLUDE AN ICON:** (radio button). Selecting this radio button will not display a preview icon. Select this option if you create just a few blocks and do not expect to use them in another drawing.

- **CREATE ICON FROM BLOCK GEOMETRY:** (radio button). Selecting this radio button will create a preview icon to be saved with the block definition from the geometry of the objects and will display an image of the symbol. For example, for the door symbol in Figure 19–9, selecting this radio button will create a preview icon and display the image of the door shown in Figure 19–13. When this radio button is checked, the same icon will appear in the Palette area of the ADC window as shown in Figure 19–14. This window will allow you to view and copy data from one drawing into another. Copying a block definition from one drawing into another drawing using the ADC is discussed later in the chapter.

Insert Units: (Drop-Down List). This is the **sixth step** in creating a block. When you use the ADC, you can insert blocks from one drawing into another. The Insert Units category will allow you to specify the units of the block to be scaled when dragged and dropped from one drawing into another drawing. The insert units should correspond to the current drawing units. For example, if a block having a different unit scale was to be inserted into this drawing using the ADC, the value inside the Insert units: drop-down list area will convert the block to the selected units. When using the ADC, if the drawing units containing the block do not match the units of the block being copied, AutoCAD will convert the block scale to the current drawing scale. This is called *automatic scaling.* For example, if a 1'-0" by 2'-0" filing cabinet block created using decimal inches is inserted into a drawing having a unit scale of millimeters (mm), AutoCAD will automatically convert the unit scale to millimeters. When the same cabinet is measured inside the metric drawing after it is being inserted, the dimensions will be 304.80 by 609.60 millimeters. If Unspecified-Unitless is selected, the block will not be scaled when inserted. However, you can set which units to automatically use for a block inserted into the current drawing with the INSUNITS (insertion units) system variable. The INSUNITS values are as follows:

```
0 = Unspecified (no units), 1 = inches, 2 = feet, 3 = miles, 4 =
millimeters, 5 = centimeters, 6 = meters, 7 = kilometers, 8 =
microinches, 9 = mils, 10 = yards, 11 = angstroms, 12 = nanometers,
13 = microns, 14 = decimeters, 15 = decameters, 16 = hectometers, 17 =
gigameters, 18 = astronomical units, 19 = light years, 20 = parsecs.
```

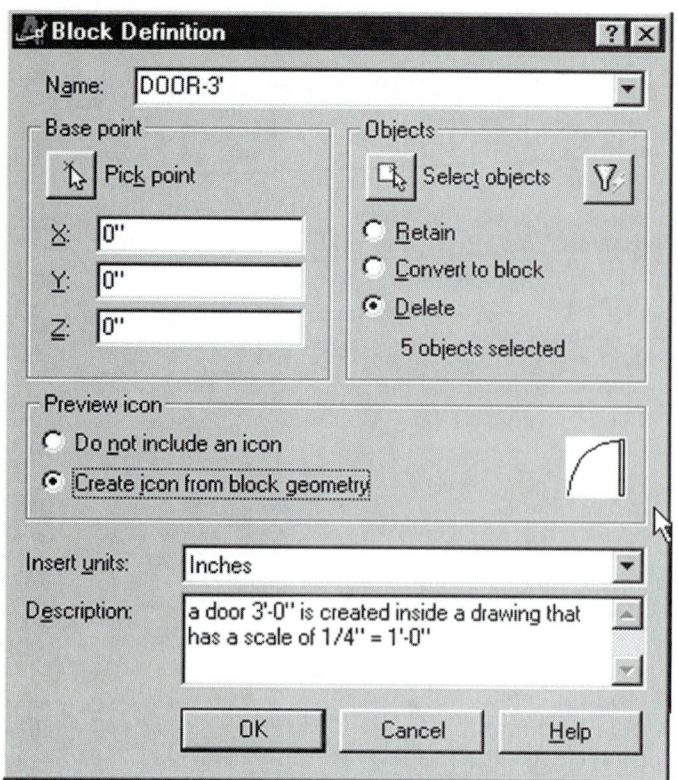

FIGURE 19–13   The Block Definition dialog box with the door preview icon.

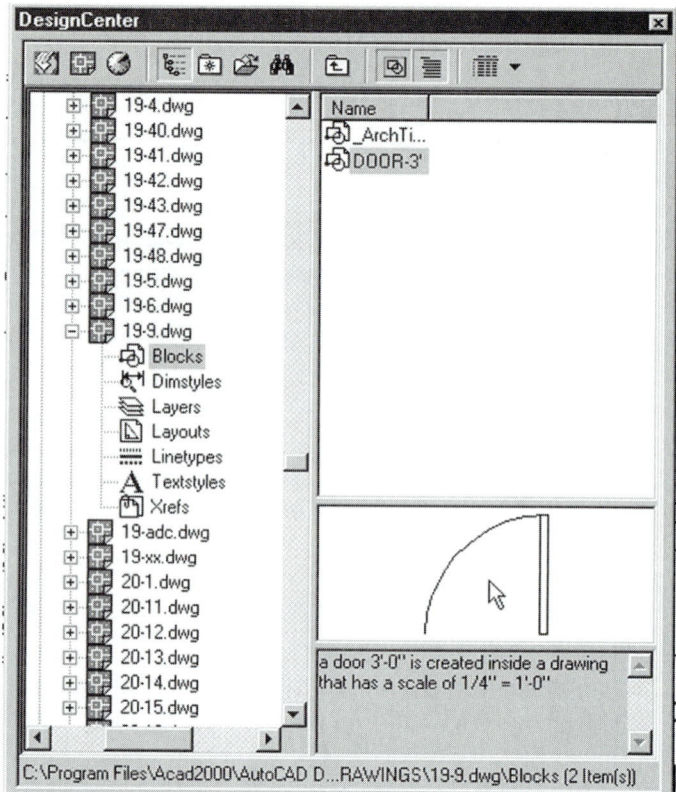

FIGURE 19–14   The door preview icon in the Palette area of the ADC window.

You can set the insertion units option to keep blocks the correct size each time it is copied into a drawing having different units when using the ADC as follows:

From the Format pull-down menu select Units . . .. Inside the Drawing Units dialog box select the appropriate unit from the *Drawing units for DesignCenter blocks* area. This will scale the blocks to the selected units that are inserted into this drawing from other drawings.

Description: (Text Box).   This area is used to enter a description of the block. This is the **seventh step** in creating a block. The description can include information such as project number, symbol specifications, created by, method of creation, and a symbols library reference number. For example, Figure 19–13 shows a description for the door block.

The **OK** button is used when everything in the Block Definition dialog box is complete. When the OK button is selected, the symbol is officially made into a block. You can use the Block Definition dialog box to verify that the block was created properly. Pick the down arrow next to the Name: drop-down list box. A list of all created blocks will be displayed. Select the block you want to view. If the Create icon from block geometry radio button was checked when creating the block, the block symbol will appear as the icon.

The **Cancel** button will cancel the entire operation of creating the block.

The **Help** button will display the AutoCAD Command Reference dialog box where you can read to obtain information about this dialog box and its contents.

19.9 CREATING WBLOCKS

Creating a wblock is referred to as creating a drawing file from three different sources: from an existing block, an existing drawing, or objects in a drawing. The procedure is similar to creating blocks. To create a wblock, enter W or WBLOCK at the command line. The Write Block dialog box will be displayed as shown in Figure 19–15. This dialog box has four categories: as *Source, Base point, Objects,* and *Destination.* The Base point and Objects categories are exactly the same as in the Block Definition dialog box.

There are four major steps involved in creating a wblock:

Step #1: Select a source for the wblock.

Step #2: Select the base point as the insertion point for the wblock.

Step #3: Select the block, drawing, or the object(s) for the wblock.

Step #4: Determine the faith of the wblock.

Step #5: Enter the destination for the file name and location.

Step #6: Select insertion units.

Source: (Category). This category will allow you to select a source for the wblock. The three options are as follows:

- **BLOCK:** (radio button). This option will create a wblock from an existing block. If you want to create a wblock from a block you have created previously select this radio button. When this option is selected, you can use the down arrow to find and select an existing block name.

- **ENTIRE DRAWING:** (radio button). This option will create a wblock from the entire drawing. All entities in the current drawing will be converted to a wblock.

- **OBJECTS:** (radio button). This option will allow you to create a wblock from existing objects.

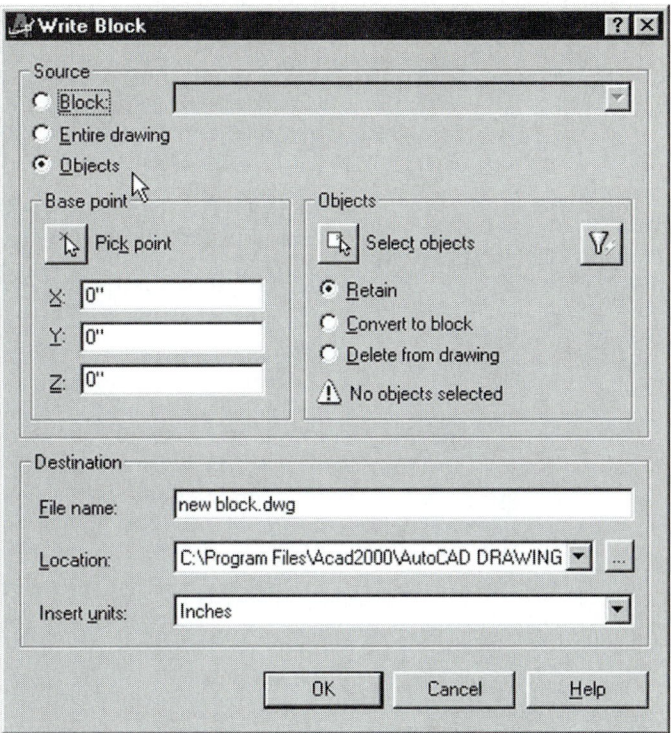

FIGURE 19–15 The Write Block dialog box is used to create a wblock.

Base Point: (Category) This is the same as the base point category in the Block Definition dialog box. If the Block radio button is picked as the source, the base point category will be grayed out because the X and Y Base point values of the block will be used as the wblock. If the Entire drawing radio button is picked as the source, the Base point category will be grayed out because the base point location will be assigned as 0,0. If the Objects radio button is picked as the source, you can either pick the base point on the drawing or enter X and Y base point locations in the dialog box.

Objects: (Category) This is the same as the Base point category in the Block Definition dialog box. If the Block radio button is picked as the source, the Objects category will be grayed out because the elements of the block will be used as the wblock. If the Entire drawing radio button is picked as the source, the Objects category will be grayed out since the entire drawing will be selected as the objects. If the Objects radio button is picked as the source, you can select the objects on the drawing as part of the wblock.

Quick Select: (Button) This is the same button found in the Block Definition dialog box. It is available only when the Objects radio button is selected as the source.

Destination: (Category) This category will allow you to select a file name, file location, and file insertion units as follows:

- **FILE NAME:** (text window). This area is where you enter the name of the wblock. The same guidelines apply as in the Block Definition dialog box. If the Block radio button is picked as the source, the selected block name will appear in the File name: text window. This means that a separate drawing file will be created as a wblock with the same name block residing inside a different file. You can enter a different file name if you like.

- **LOCATION: (DROP-DOWN LIST).**   This area will list the file location of the current drawing where the wblock will be created and saved as a .dwg file. If you want the wblock to be created and saved in a different location, you can browse by selecting the box with ellipses (…) next to it. This will display the Browse for Folder dialog box. Using the scroll bars find the location of the folder you are looking for. Select the folder and click on the OK button. AutoCAD will automatically place this folder in the Location: drop-down list.

- **INSERT UNITS:**   (drop-down list): This area will allow you to select the insertion units of the wblock when the ADC is used.

The **OK** button is used when everything in the Write Block dialog box is complete. When the OK button is selected, the Block, Entire drawing, or the Objects officially become a wblock with a .dwg file extension.

The **Cancel** button will cancel the entire Write Block operation.

Tips: If you are planning to use a block or a wblock on a previous AutoCAD release or another software that does not support long file names, use a short file name composed of eight characters or less without any spaces.

19.10 INSERTING BLOCKS AND WBLOCKS

When a block is created, it can be inserted into the current drawing using the Insert Block button in the Draw toolbar. You can also insert a block by picking the Insert pull-down menu and selecting Block. . . , or you can type I or INSERT at the command line. This will display the Insert dialog box as shown in Figure 19–16. To insert a block into another file, use the ADC. A wblock can also be inserted using the same procedure. Before inserting a block or a wblock, try to remember the insertion point that you have established and think about the X and Y insertion scale factors. Which method did you use to create the block or the wblock? What was the original size of the block or the wblock? Where is the final insertion location of the block or the wblock in the drawing? Does this location require you to insert the block or the wblock at different X and Y scales? Does the block or the wblock require rotation? Try to answer the questions and work out mentally or on paper before inserting.

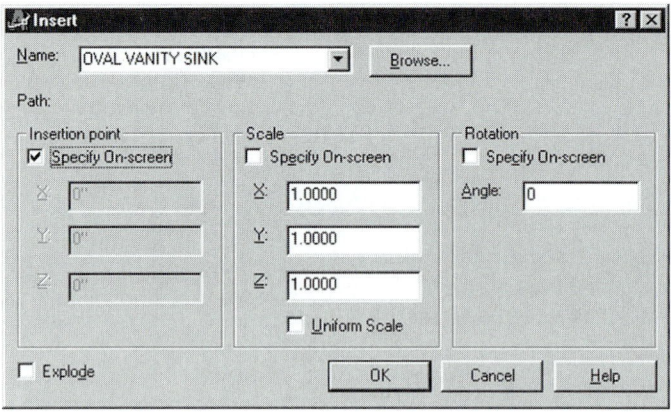

FIGURE 19–16   The Insert dialog box is used to insert blocks and wblocks into drawings.

The Insert dialog box has six major categories as follows:

Name: (Drop-Down List).   This category will allow you to select the name of the block in the current drawing file. Blocks created in other files will not be listed. To insert blocks that are not listed, use the ADC to copy the blocks from one file into another file or use the Browse . . . button to insert a wblock. The last block that you have inserted during the current drawing session will become the default block name for the subsequent use of the Insert dialog box.

Browse. . . (Button).   This button will allow you to search for the wblock with the .dwg file extension. Selecting this button will display the Select Drawing File dialog box. Using this dialog box, you can locate the folder where the drawing file was saved when the Write Block dialog box was used. When you select the file name and click on the Open button, the Insert dialog box will show the file location in the Path: text area. Because of the text length limitations the Path: text area may not show the complete path to the file.

Insertion Point: (Category).   This category will allow you to choose which insertion point settings to use when inserting the block or the wblock as follows:

- **SPECIFY ON-SCREEN:** (check box). If you place a checkmark inside this check box, you will be prompted to specify the insertion point location of the block inside the drawing using the *pickbox*. If you know the precise X and Y coordinate values of the insertion point location in the drawing, remove the check mark and enter the values inside the X : text box and the Y: text box as follows:

    Using the cursor, left-click inside the X: text box and highlight the existing value. Type the required X value and press the ~TabKey~; this will highlight the existing value inside the Y: text box. Type the required Y value.

Scale: (Category).   This category will allow you to establish the X and Y scale factor values for the block to be inserted as follows:

- **SPECIFY ON-SCREEN:** (check box): If you place a check mark inside this check box, you will be prompted to specify the X and Y scale factor values of the inserted block at the command line inside the drawing. If you know the precise X and Y scale factor values when inserting a block, remove the check mark and enter the X scale factor value inside the X: text box and the Y scale factor value inside the Y: text box.

- **UNIFORM SCALE:** (check box). If the block does not require different X and Y insertion scale factor values with different insertion locations place a check mark inside this check box. This will allow a single value for X to be entered as the uniform scale. Notice that when you place a check mark here, the Y and Z scale factor value text boxes are grayed out.

Tips: If you specify a negative X and Y scale factor value, a mirror image of the block will be inserted in the drawing. For example, in Figure 19–17 the door on the right is inserted with X and Y scale factor value of 1 and the door on the left is inserted with X and Y scale factor value of −1. The door is created using the Current Drawing Scale method as a 3'-0" door, hence X and Y is equal to 1.

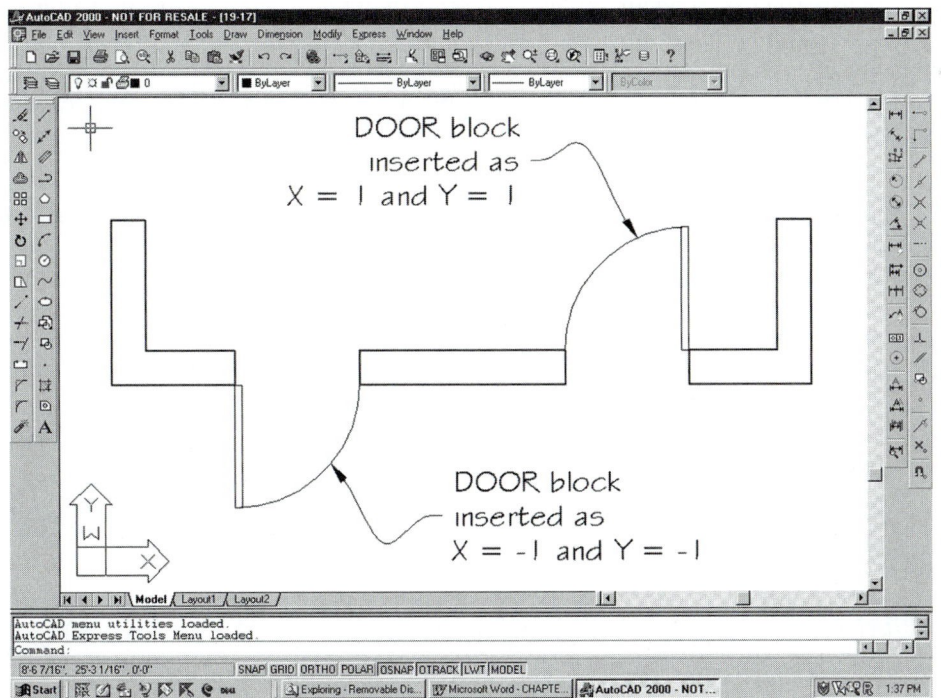

FIGURE 19–17 With a negative X and Y insertion scale factor values, the 3'-0" Door block is inserted on the left as the mirror image of the same door on the right.

Tips: When inserting blocks created with the Current Drawing Scale method, let AutoCAD do the math for you! Inside the Insert dialog box, remove the check mark inside the Specify On-screen check box in the Scale category. Highlight the existing value inside the X: text box and enter the desired number (length) with a forward slash followed by the number (length) used for the original block symbol. For example, to insert the 3'-0" door into a 2'-0" wide (requiring a 24" door size) opening as discussed in section 19.5.1, enter 24/36 inside the X" text box and click on the Uniform scale check box and then click on the OK button. If X does not equal Y, do not click on the Uniform scale check box and enter numbers for both X and Y.

Tips: When inserting blocks created with the One Foot Square method, let AutoCAD do the math for you! Inside the Insert dialog box, remove the check mark inside the Specify On-screen check box in the Scale category. Highlight the existing value inside the X: text box and enter the desired number (length) with a forward slash followed by 12 (the 12" square used for the original block symbol). For example, to insert the door into a 2'–10" wide (requiring a 34" door size) opening as discussed in section 19.5.3, enter 34/12 inside the X" text box and click on the Uniform scale check box and then click on the OK button. If X does not equal Y, do not click on the Uniform scale check box and enter numbers for both X and Y.

Rotation: (Category).   This category will allow you to specify on-screen or preset the rotation angle of the inserted block as follows:

- **SPECIFY ON-SCREEN:**   (check box). If you place a checkmark here, you will be prompted to specify the rotation angle of the inserted block at the command line inside the drawing. If you know the rotation angle, do not place a checkmark here.

- **ANGLE:**   (text box). Enter the rotation angle of the inserted block here when you remove the check mark from the Specify On-screen check box.

Explode: (Check Box).   When there is no check mark inside this check box, the block definition will include all the objects as one whole unit when the block is inserted. This concept is similar to the Polylines, Multilines, Associative Dimensioning, and Associative Hatching. If you place a check mark here, the block will be exploded as it is inserted into the drawing. When a block is exploded, it will lose its block definition character and the objects of the block will be converted to single elements. You can explode blocks if they require quick editing and if maintaining the block definition is not important. When you select Explode, you can only specify the X scale factor value.

Selecting the **OK** button will insert the block in the drawing. Selecting the **Cancel** button will cancel the insert block operation.

Note: When you create dimensions in the drawing, the arrowheads that you select for the dimension style will be inserted into the drawing as a block with the exception of Closed filled arrowhead style. For example, if you select Right angle as the arrowhead style, the right angle will be inserted as a block at the intersections of extension and dimension line every time you create a dimension. You can verify this by entering INSERT at the command line and looking into the Name: drop-down list. The name _Open 90 will appear. Similarly, if you use Architectural tick as the arrowheads style, the block name would be _ArchTick. This could be helpful because you can insert the arrowhead styles as blocks if necessary with different scales. Look at these as additional graphical symbols that you might use one day.

Tips: When you include the objects for the block definition, do not include text. Instead, assign attributes to symbols. Attributes are discussed in Chapter 21.

19.11 CREATING ARCHITECTURAL SYMBOLS LIBRARY

To manage blocks and wblocks more effectively and insert them efficiently, a symbols library containing all the symbols as blocks should be created. Creating an architectural symbols library requires some planning. It is very important to keep track of all the activities and all the symbols while creating the library. AutoCAD already gives you the option to create an icon from each symbol and an option to write the description for each symbol before it is made into a block. As you have learned so far, you can create and insert blocks using the BLOCK, WBLOCK, and INSERT commands. There are streamlined procedures that will allow you to quickly copy or move objects and insert blocks from one drawing into another drawing, tools that will provide direct access to your library and view, drag, and drop block definitions from folders to current drawing. These methods are possible with the Multiple Design Environment and the ADC. The following guidelines will help you create an effective architectural symbols library:

- Use a separate file to draw symbols. Create each symbol using one of the three methods described earlier. Use the convert to block option in the Block Definition dialog box. If you choose the Current Drawing Scale method, create a large-size drawing with architectural units and limits because each symbol is created in feet and inches at the drawing scale. Select an appropriate scale for the drawing. For example, a scale of 1/16″ = 1′–0″ is too small to create five symbols on a D-size sheet. Either change the paper size or use a larger scale, such as 1/4″ = 1′–0″. If you choose the One Inch Square method, use either the current architectural drawing or the AutoCAD default drawing settings.

- Create each symbol in the drawing one at a time using AutoCAD commands. Be creative and add as much detail as you possibly can. Identify each symbol with a name or establish a code name for each drawing. For example, WC-M1-05-99 can be the Water Closet (WC) symbol created with Method 1 (M1) as the fifth symbol (05) in the library created in 1999.

- Name the current drawing as *symbols as blocks file.*

- Use the BLOCK command to convert each symbol into a block. Use easy to understand names for the blocks. Follow the guidelines described under Creating Blocks.

- Create a folder called *architectural symbols library* in the hard drive and copy the *symbols as blocks file* drawing into this folder.

- Use the WBLOCK command to create a file from each symbol. Open the *symbols as blocks file* drawing inside the Write Block dialog box, select the objects radio button as the Source. Under Destination, enter a different file name for each symbol inside the File name: text box. For the Location select the architectural symbols library folder in the hard drive. Retain and select the object and click on the OK button. This will create a file containing the block and place it in the architectural symbols library folder. Repeat this procedure for each symbol. Each block will be located in the *architectural symbols library* folder as an individual file.

- Assign one person to create, maintain, update, and copy the architectural symbols library folder to all workstation hard drives.

- Create a back up disk and keep it in a safe place.

- Print a copy of the *symbols as blocks file* drawing and distribute to each person, showing the symbols and insertion points with a brief description of the symbol. Plot a large copy and place it in a conspicuous place.

- To add additional symbols to the library, open the symbols as blocks file drawing inside the architectural symbols library folder. Create the symbol and turn it into a block. Create a wblock from the block and keep it in the same folder.

A file is created from each block because a file containing a single block can be inserted globally using the Browse . . . button in the Insert dialog box without using the ADC. The following guidelines will help you utilize the architectural symbols library in your projects:

- When the insertion of many blocks is necessary, you can insert the file containing all the symbols in the corner of the drawing and insert the blocks in the current drawing as they are needed. Use the INSERT command and click on the Browse. . . button to find the *symbols as blocks*.dwg. This is the file located in the *architectural symbols library* folder. When you insert this file into the current drawing, all the blocks will come with the drawing. Just click on the Insert Block button in the Draw toolbar and look inside the Insert dialog box and under the *symbols as blocks file* Name: drop-down list, you will see all the blocks listed alphabetically. You can also erase the entire drawing after it is inserted. The blocks will remain in the current drawing.

- To insert blocks using the Multiple Design Environment (MDE) and the ADC, refer to the appropriate chapters and sections.

Tips: Create individual blocks for design and documentation drawings. For design drawings, create blocks or wblocks for appliances, casework, ceiling fixtures, electric equipment, furniture, plumbing fixtures, and site symbols by using one of the three methods described earlier. For documentation drawings, create blocks or wblocks for break marks, detail marks, elevation marks, section marks, and title marks by using the One Inch Square method and inserting it at the required scale in paper space or model space.

19.12 NESTING BLOCKS

When a *block reference* becomes a part of another block, it is referred to as a nesting block. For example, a floor plan containing several blocks as fixtures can be made into a block. The fixtures are nesting blocks inside a larger block. The nesting block structure can become complicated if the nested block contains objects that are on layer 0 or that have color, linetype, and lineweight created using Byblock. You cannot insert or create blocks that reference themselves. To use nesting blocks as effectively as possible without any complications, create each block, including any nesting blocks, on layer 0 with all properties set to Bylayer. This will help you control the color, linetype, and lineweight of the blocks by using the properties of the layer on which each is inserted. You can also create block objects set to Byblock and assign each its own color, linetype, and lineweight. Use the Properties window to change the layer, color, linetype, and lineweight of the objects before creating the block.

■ **EXERCISE 19–3:**   *The following step-by-step exercise will allow you to create a window symbol as a wblock using the One Inch Square method and insert into four different size wall openings. The floor plan for the window insertions is shown in Figure 19–18. There are four different size window openings and the typical window insertion for window opening 1 is shown in Figure 19–19. The components and the size of the window including dimensions are shown in Figure 19–20.*

Step #1:   Start a new drawing using the Start from scratch option.

Step #2:   Using the Drawing Units dialog box, set Length Type to architectural and Precision to 0′–0 1/16″. Under the Drawing units for DesignCenter blocks category, select Inches inside the When inserting blocks into this drawing, scale them to: drop-down menu.

Step #3:   Set Drawing Limits to 44′–0″, 34′–0″ and zoom to the limits of the drawing (perform Zoom All).

Step #4:   Use the MULTILINE command to draw the floor plan shown in Figure 19–18 with four different size window openings. Use the Individual Wall Segment method to create wall caps. The walls are 10″ thick concrete block. Save the drawing as MY BLOCKS EXERCISE and exit the drawing.

Step #5:   To create the window symbol using the One Inch Square method, the window must be fit inside a one square inch box. Examine how the window will be inserted

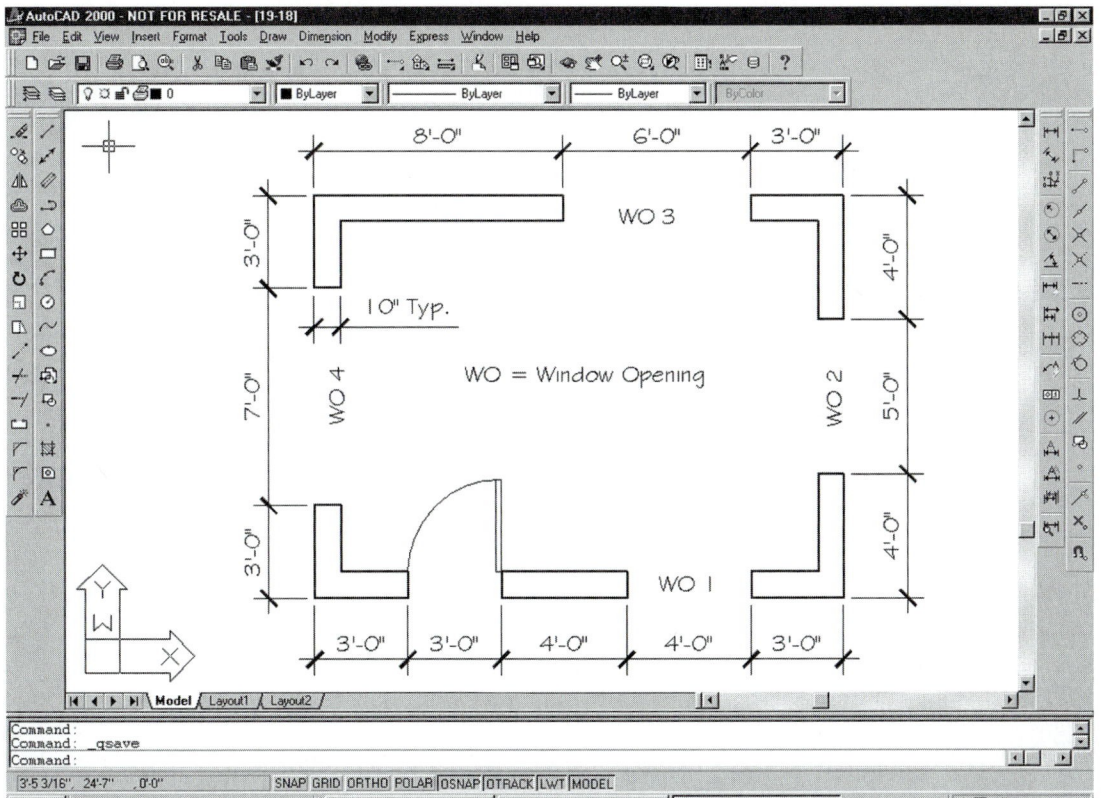

FIGURE 19–18 This floor plan requires four different size windows to be inserted as a block. The window will be drawn to fit inside a one square inch box.

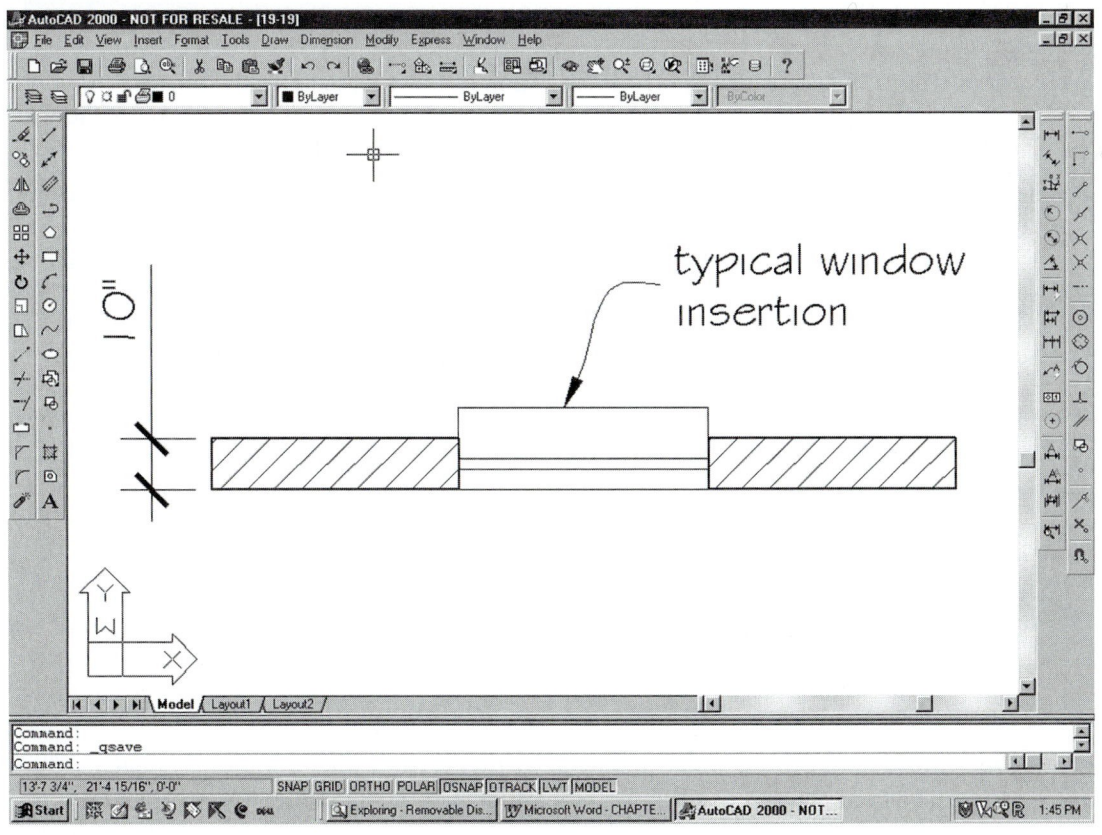

FIGURE 19–19 The typical window insertion for the floor plan. Notice that the window will require different X and Y insertion scale factor values.

FIGURE 19–20 The
window with
dimensions having a 6″
sill and a 2″ glass with 4″
separation inside the 10″
block wall.

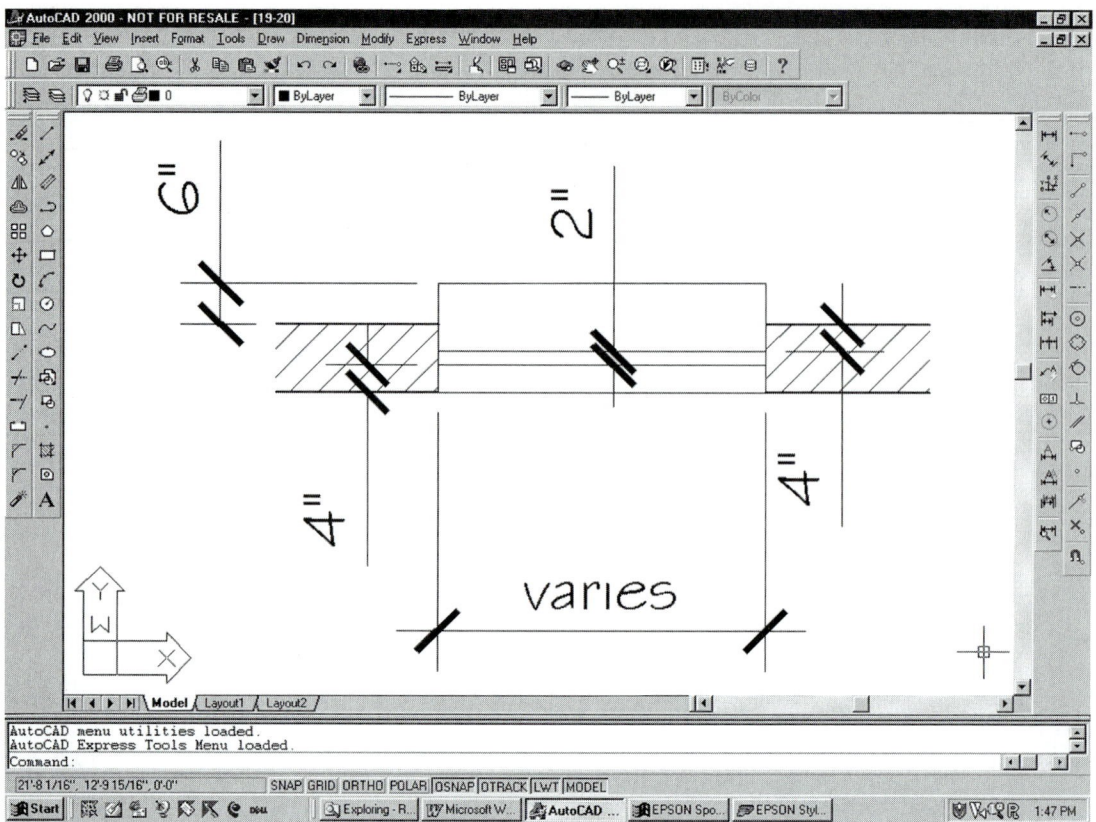

by looking at Figure 19–19. Also examine the size, scale, and components of the window by looking at Figure 19–20. Recognize that the X dimension for the window varies but the Y dimension is always 16″ (10″ wall + 6″ sill).

Step #6: Create a new drawing from scratch using default settings. Inside the drawing, zoom in and draw a one square inch box using the LINE command. Since the window must be created inside this box, the total width of the window, including the 6″ sill, must be fit inside the one square inch box. The total width of the window is 16″ in the Y direction. And the total width of the box is 1″ in the Y direction. Therefore, every inch in the Y direction for the wall is equal to 0.0625″ in the one square inch box (1″ / 16 = 0.0625″). Then the 6″ sill is equal to 0.375″ inside the box (6 × 0.0625 = 0.375). In theory the box must be divided into 16 equal units so that the sill and the glass locations can be located proportionately to the original window width. The 2″ glass is equal to 0.125″ (2 × 0.0625 = 0.125) and the 4″ wall distance on both side of the glass is equal to 0.25″ each (4 × 0.0625 = 0.25).

Step #7: Using the OFFSET command, offset the top horizontal line 0.375″ inside the box. Offset the new line 0.250″. Offset the bottom horizontal line 0.250″ and the remaining distance will be 0.125″. Figure 19–21 shows the initial symbol and a close-up of the one square inch box as the window symbol with the offset lines and distances.

Step #8: Erase the first offset line and trim the two vertical lines as shown in Figure 19–22. The final product as the window symbol is shown in Figure 19–23. This is the *one square inch* representation of the original window shown in Figure 19–20. Notice that no manipulation is required in the X direction.

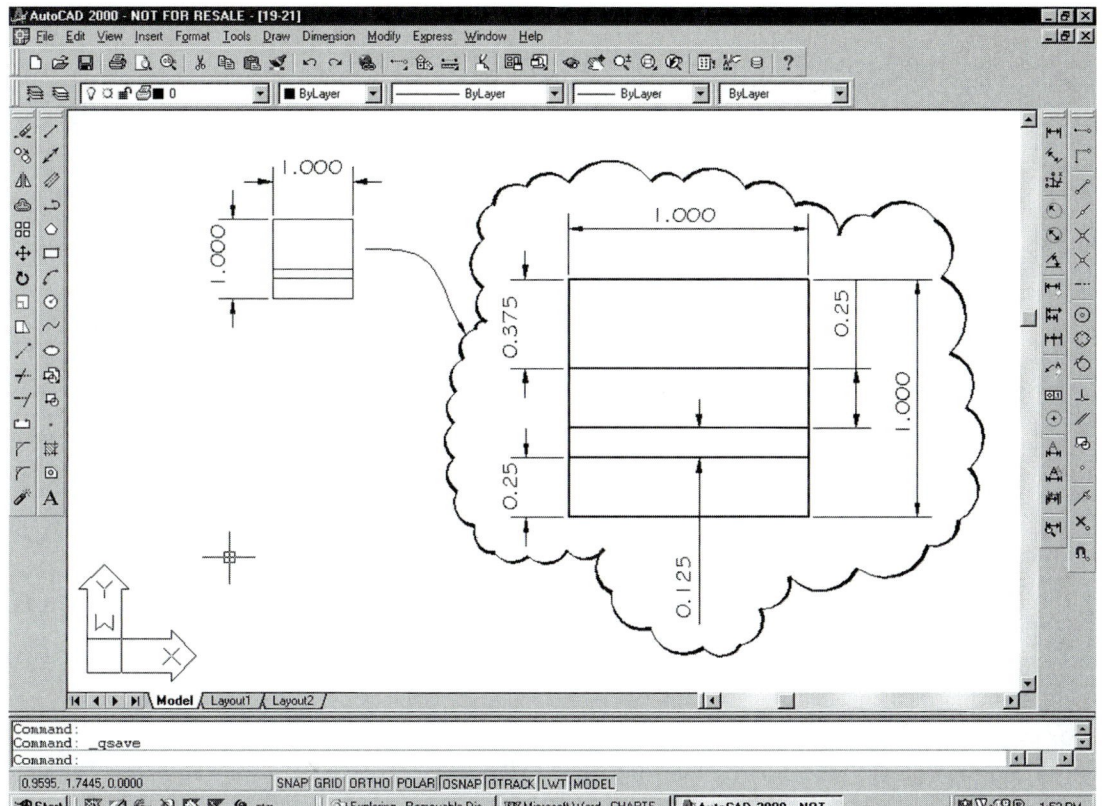

FIGURE 19–21 The one square inch box is created with the corresponding components.

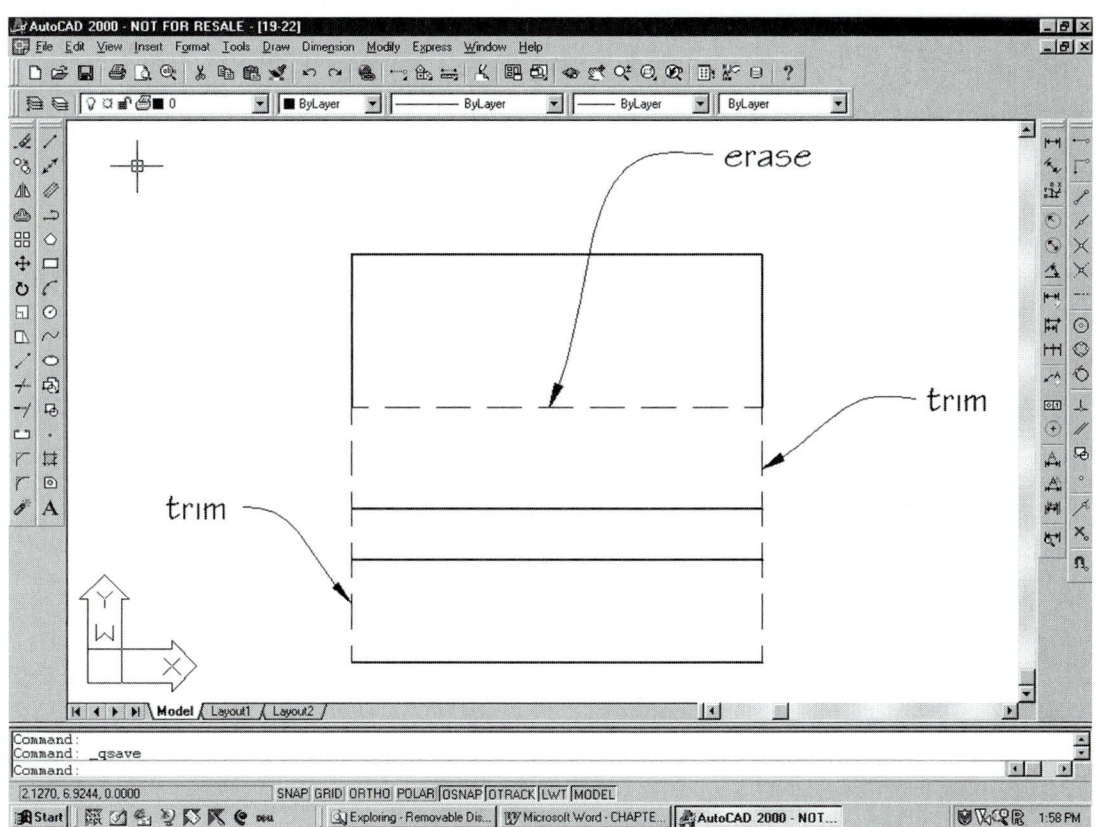

FIGURE 19–22 To give the final look for the window symbol, the first offset line is erased and the lower vertical lines are trimmed.

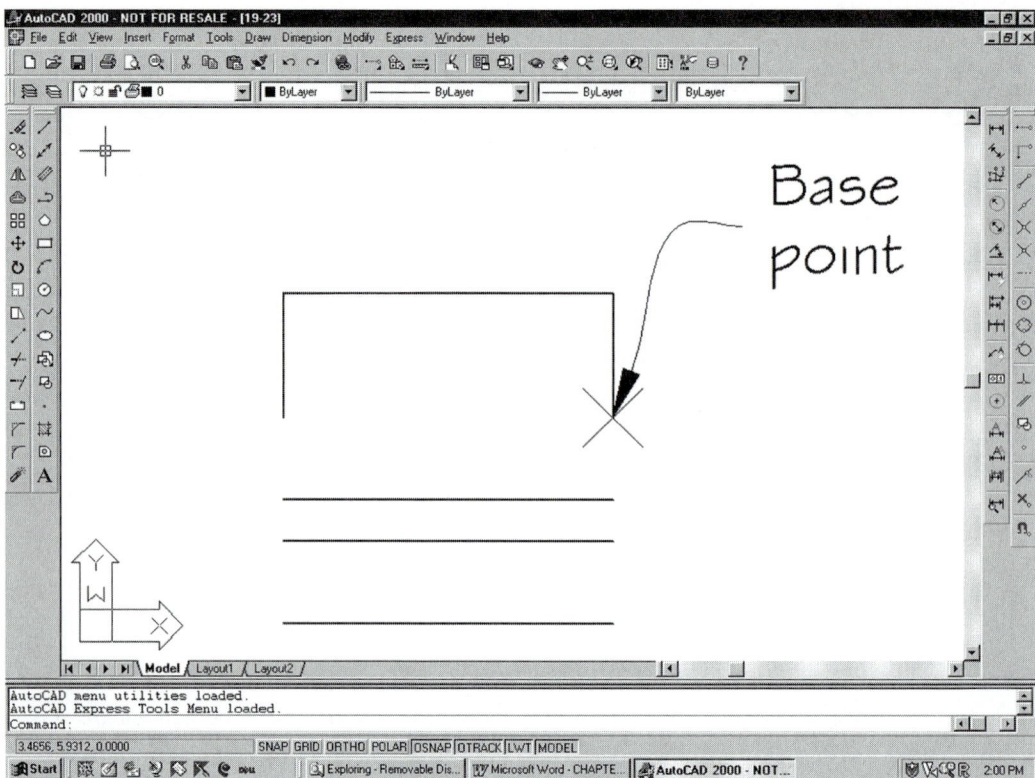

Step #9: Use the WBLOCK (W) command to access the Write Block dialog box. Select the Objects radio button as the source. Select the base point as the insertion point shown in Figure 19–23. Select the Delete from drawing radio button and click on the Select objects button.

Step #10: Select the objects on the screen. Inside the File name: text window, enter WINDOW 1INCH SQ.

Step #11: Determine the file location. Select Inches as the Insert units and click on the OK button. This will create the wblock and create the WINDOW 1INCH SQ.dwg file.

Step #12: Close the drawing without saving. Open MY BLOCKS EXERCISE.dwg file. Click on the Insert Block button in the Draw toolbar.

Step #13: Inside the Insert dialog box, select the Browse . . . button and locate the WINDOW 1 INCH SQ.dwg file. Place check marks inside the Specify On-screen check boxes for the Insertion point, Scale, and Rotation categories. Click on the OK button.

Step #14: Use the following command line procedure to insert the first window into the Window Opening (WO) 1 location shown in Figure 19–18:

Command: _insert

Specify insertion point or [Scale/X/Y/Z/Rotate/PScale/PX/PY/PZ/Protate]: *(select the insertion point for the first window as shown in Figure 19–24).*

Enter X scale factor, specify opposite corner, or [Corner/XYZ] <1>: **48** ~EnterKey~

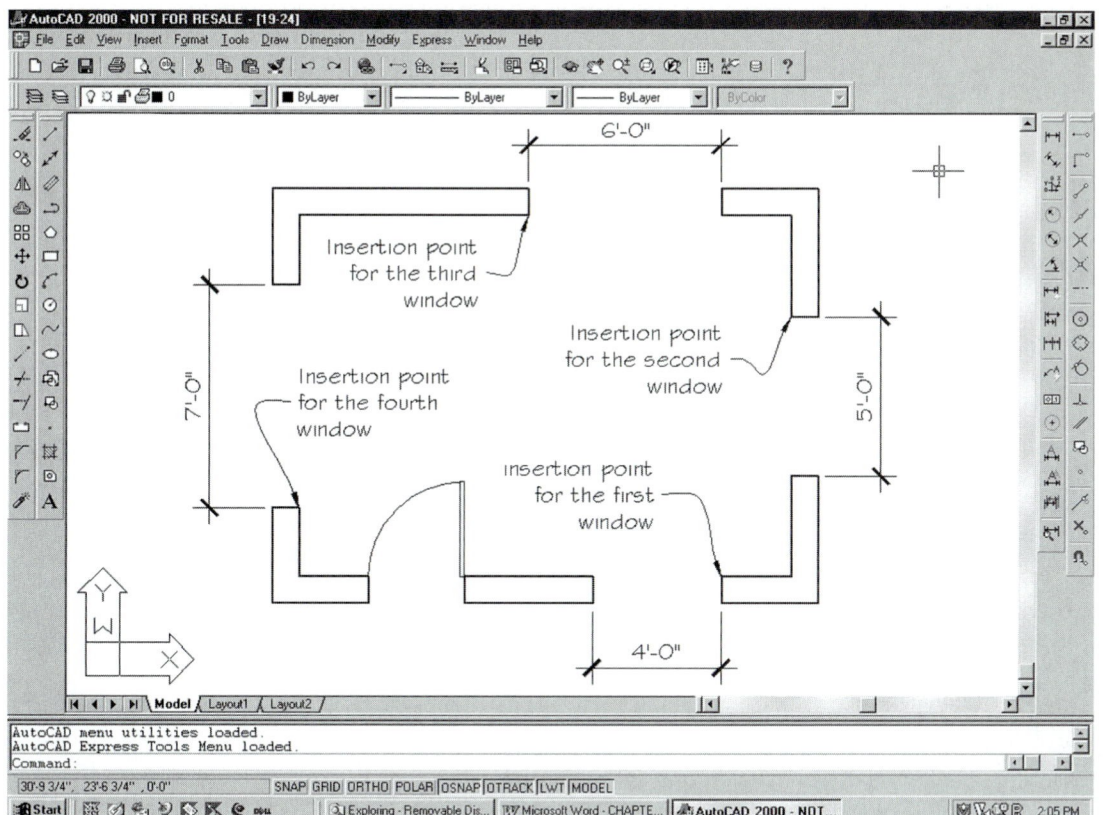

FIGURE 19–24 The insertion point locations for the four windows.

Enter Y scale factor, use X scale factor>: **16** ~EnterKey~

Specify rotation angle <0>: ~EnterKey~

The window will be inserted into the window opening 1 location as shown in Figure 19–25.

Step #15: Repeat Step #14 to insert the block into window opening 2 location with the following values (see Figure 19–24 for insertion point locations):

```
X = 60, Y = 16, and Rotation = 90°.
```

The inserted window is shown in Figure 19–26.

Step #16: Repeat Step #14 to insert the block into window opening 3 location with the following values:

```
X = −72, Y = −16, and Rotation = 0°.
```

The inserted window is shown in Figure 19–27.

Step #17: Repeat Step #14 to insert the block into window opening 4 location with the following values:

```
X = 84, Y = 16, and Rotation = 270°
```

The inserted window is shown in Figure 19–28.

Congratulations! You have successfully created a wblock from a window symbol and inserted at various locations with varying X scale factor and rotation angle values.

FIGURE 19–25 The inserted wblock in its final location in the floor plan.

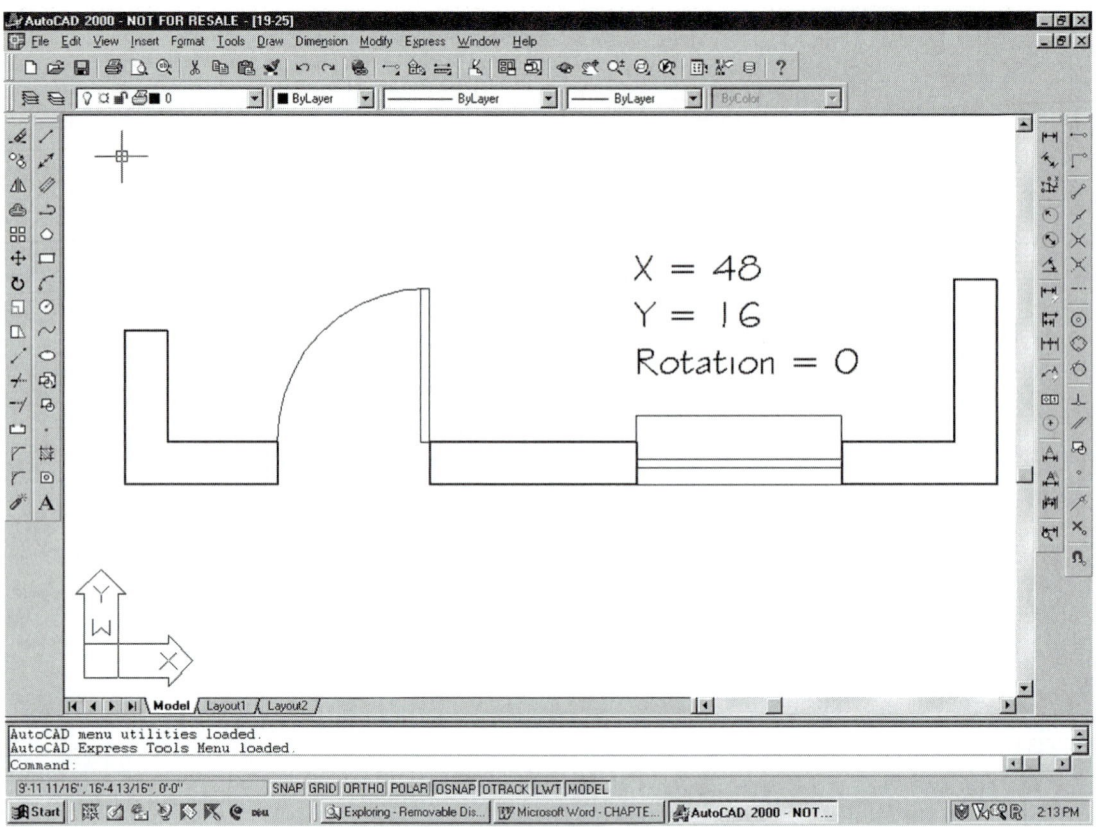

FIGURE 19–26 The wblock is inserted into window opening 2 location.

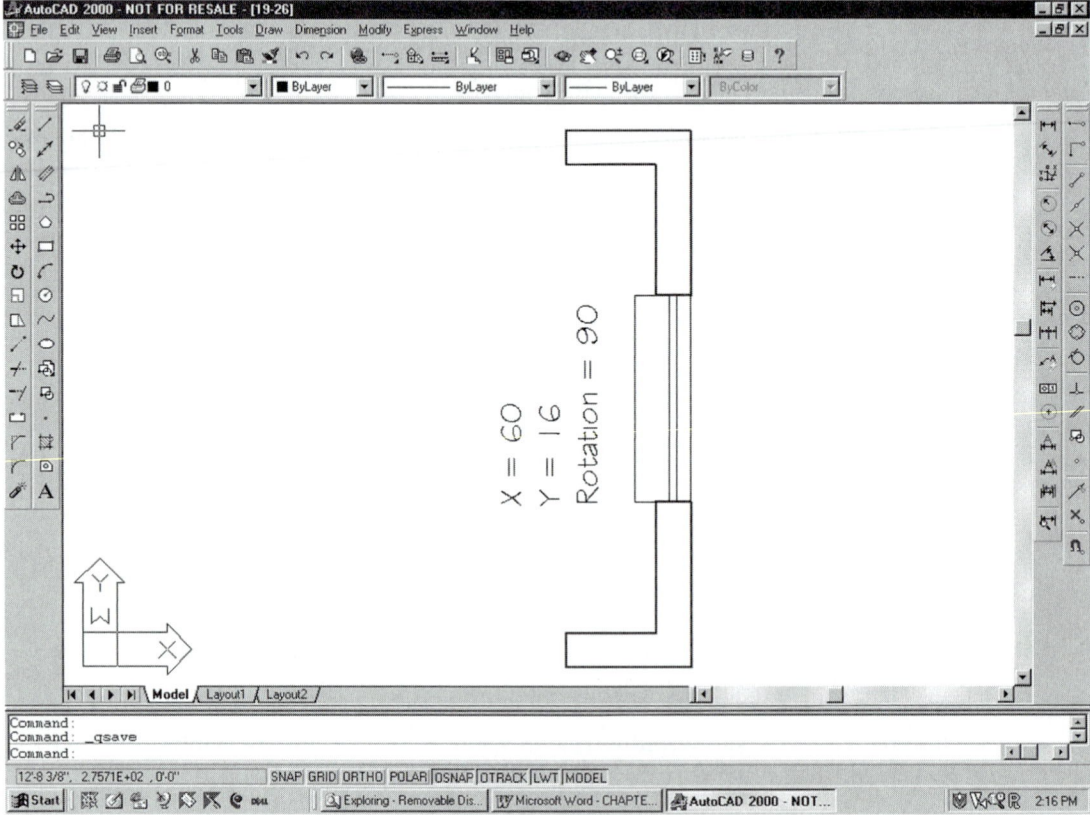

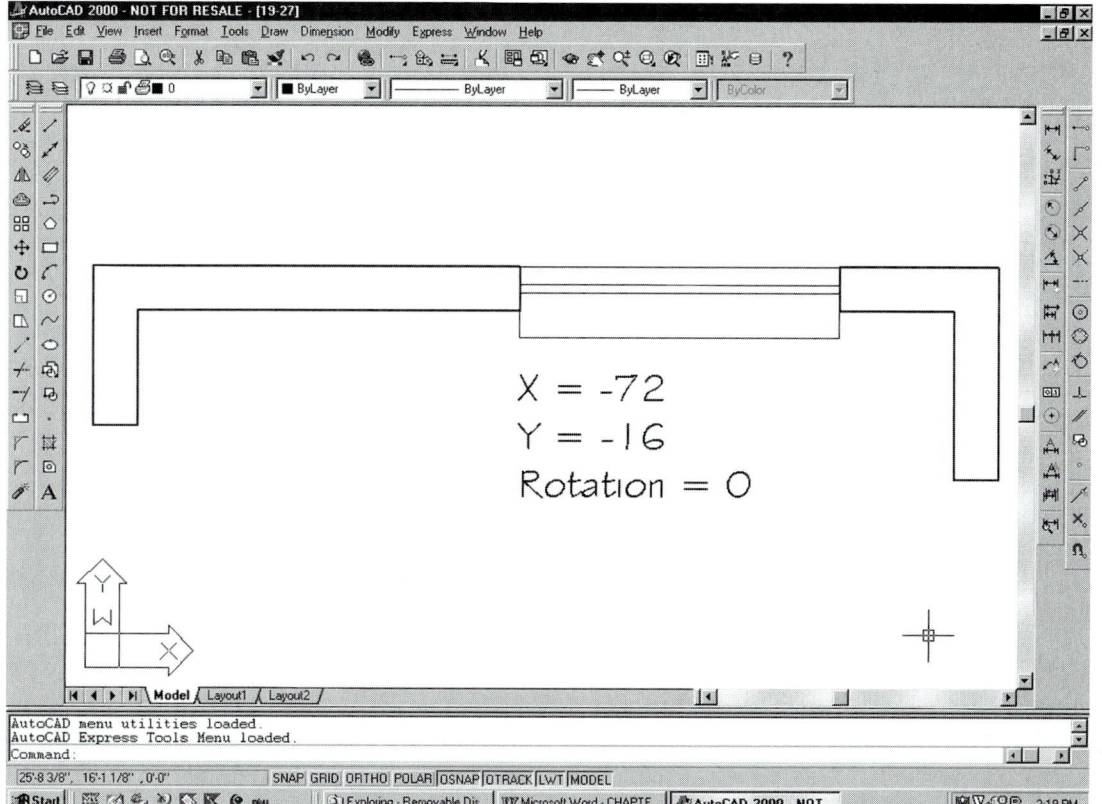

FIGURE 19–27 The wblock is inserted into window opening 3 location.

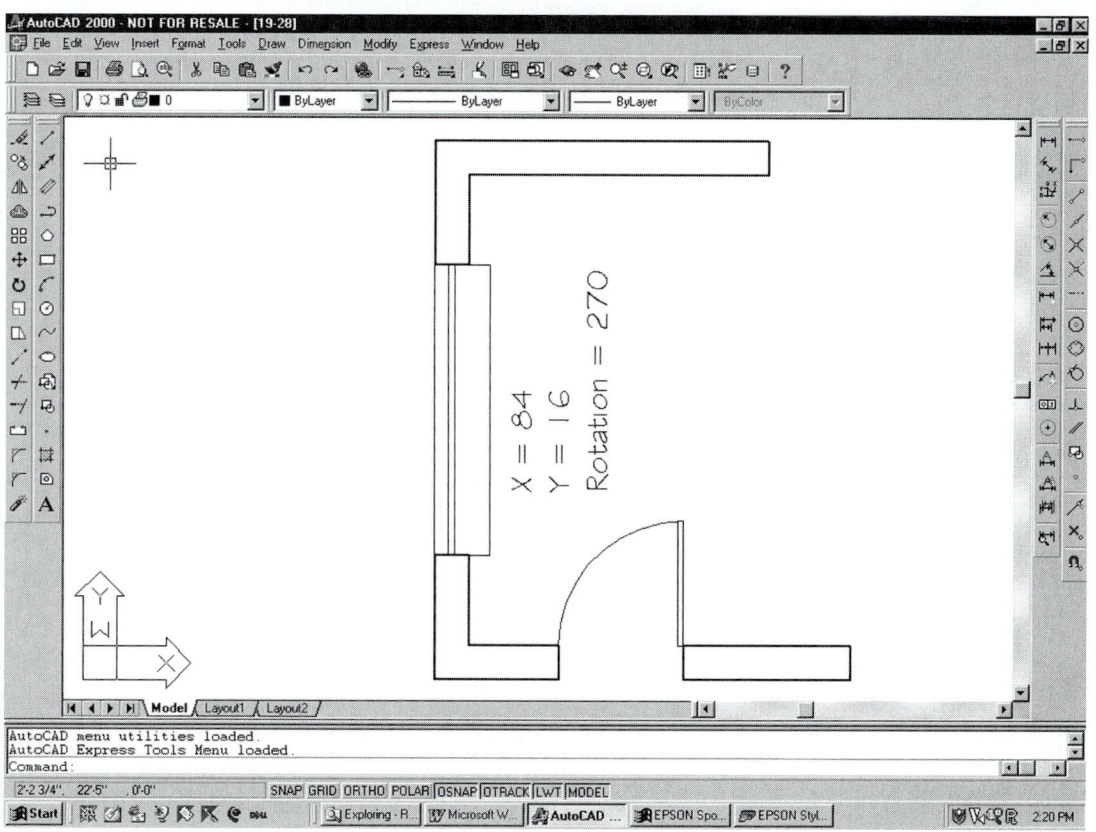

FIGURE 19–28 The last window is inserted into window opening 4 location.

19.13 MULTIPLE BLOCK INSERTIONS

You can insert multiple copies of the same block in a drawing using the MINSERT (multiple insert) command. The MINSERT command combines the ARRAY and the INSERT commands into one. The ARRAY command creates multiple copies of selected objects in a rectangular or polar format. The INSERT command inserts block and wblocks in drawings.

■ **EXERCISE 19–4:**   *The following step-by-step exercise will allow you to insert six copies of the CAD workstation block into the floor plan as shown in Figure 19–29. Before using the MINSERT command, determine the Number of rows, Number of columns, Unit of cell or distance between rows, and the Distance between columns. For the CAD workstations in Figure 19–29, the following values are determined:*

```
Number of rows = 2
Number of columns = 3
Unit of cell or distance between rows = 11'-0". This is the distance
between rows from the insertion point of one block to the other.
Distance between columns = 11'-0". This is the length of the computer
desk (5'-0") plus the distance between the desks (6'-0") as columns.
```

Notice that the insertion starts from the lower left corner of the floor plan. The Starting Point location on the floor plan is the initial insertion point location.

Step #1:   Open the EXE19-1.dwg file.

Step #2:   Use the MINSERT command as follows:

```
Command: MINSERT ~EnterKey~
```

Enter block name or [?] <xxxx>: CAD WORKSTATION ~EnterKey~

FIGURE 19–29   The floor plan with multiple insertions of the CAD workstation block.

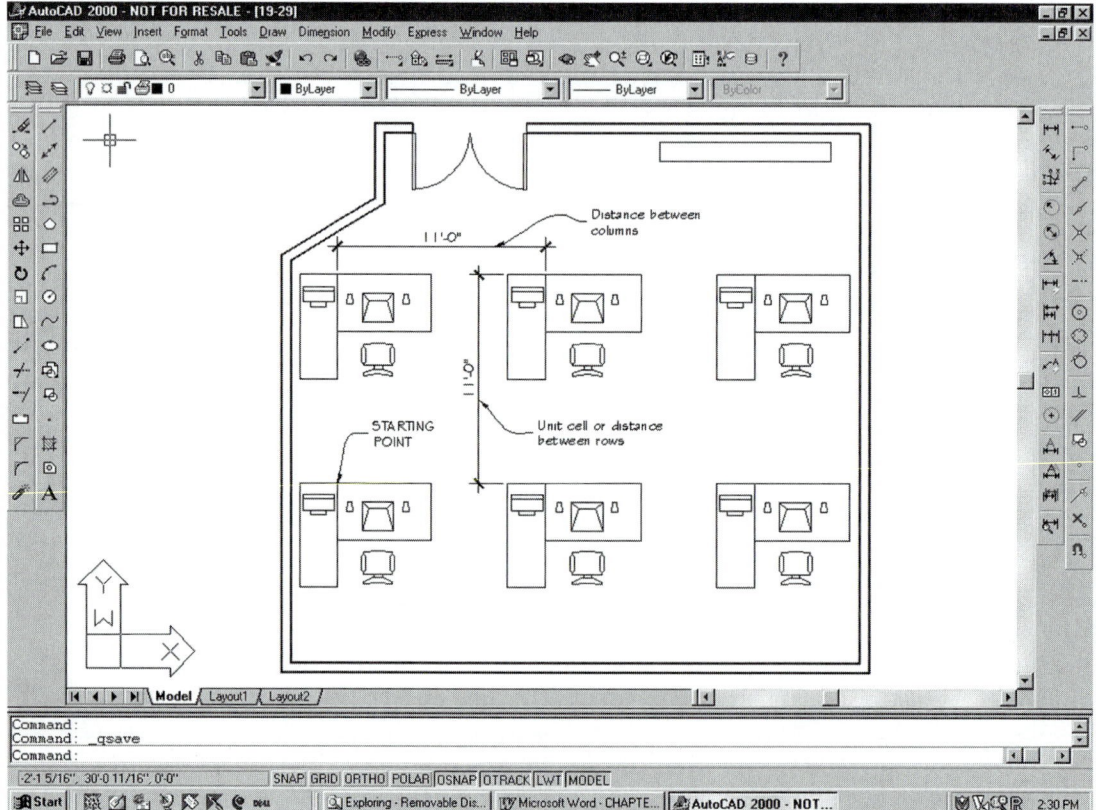

Specify insertion point or [Scale/X/Y/Z/Rotate/PScale/PX/PY/PZ/PRotate]: (select the starting point).

Enter X scale factor, specify opposite corner, or [Corner/XYZ] <1>: ~EnterKey~

Enter Y scale factor <use X scale factor>: ~EnterKey~

Specify rotation angle <0>: ~EnterKey~

Enter number of rows (---) <1>: 2 ~EnterKey~

Enter number of columns (| | |) <1>: 3 ~EnterKey~

Enter distance between rows or specify unit cell (---): 11′ ~EnterKey~

Specify distance between columns (| | |): **11′** ~EnterKey~

Congratulations! You have successfully used the MINSERT command. The block will be inserted as shown in Figure 19–29.

NUMBER OF ROWS: This is the number of times the block is inserted and displayed as rows in a horizontal fashion.

NUMBER OF COLUMNS: This is the number of times the block is inserted and displayed as columns in a vertical fashion.

To eliminate confusion, the command line prompt indicates the direction with horizontal (---) and vertical (| | |) lines inside the parentheses. When you specify the rotation angle of the individual block, AutoCAD will automatically set the angle of the other blocks for the entire array. If you specify more than one row, you will be prompted to enter the distance between rows or specify a unit cell. The distance between the insertion points on the block horizontally and vertically is the unit cell, which is the distance between rows and columns. This distance includes the length of the object plus any distance separating the objects. You can enter the unit cell with the pickbox by placing a window in the drawing. When you specify two points to define the window, the width and the height of the window represent the distance between rows and columns. Blocks inserted using the MINSERT command cannot be exploded.

Before specifying the insertion point for the block with the MINSERT command, you can preset the scale factor and the rotation angle. Presetting can increase speed when multiple block insertions are used. It will also allow you to see the scaled size and rotation angle before you pick the insertion point. When using the MINSERT command, the following command prompt will appear after the block name is entered:

```
Specify insertion point or [Scale/X/Y/Z/Rotate/PScale/PX/PY/PZ/PRotate]:
```

You can use the preset options in two different ways. The first method is the Preset Scale(s) option. If you enter the S option at the Specify insertion point: prompt, you can set the scale factor, insertion point, and rotation angle. The command line procedure is as follows:

```
Command: MINSERT ~EnterKey~
Insert block name or [?] <CAD WORKSTATION>: ~EnterKey~
Specify insertion point or [Scale/X/Y/Z/Rotate/PScale/PX/PY/PZ/PRotate]:
S ~EnterKey~
Specify scale factor for XYZ axis: (enter a scale factor)
Specify insertion point: (select the insertion point) Specify insertion
point or [Scale/X/Y/Z/Rotate/PScale/PX/PY/PZ/PRotate]: S ~EnterKey~
Specify rotation angle: (enter the rotation angle)
Enter number of rows (—) <1>: ~EnterKey~ (if inserting one block)
Enter number of columns (|||) <1>: ~EnterKey~ (if inserting one block)
```

The second method is the Temporary Preset Scale (PS) option. If you enter the PS option, you will be asked to specify the scale factor for preview display purposes only. If the scale factor you entered did not come out right, you will get another prompt to specify a new scale factor value.

This option will allow you to see the *preset* scale or rotation angle as you drag the block in place. The dragging effect is controlled by the DRAGMODE system variable. Make sure this system variable is set to Auto. After you select the insertion point, the normal command prompts will be displayed. The command line procedure is as follows:

```
Command: MINSERT ~EnterKey~
Insert block name or [?] <CAD WORKSTATION>: ~EnterKey~
Specify insertion point or [Scale/X/Y/Z/Rotate/PScale/PX/PY/PZ/PRotate]:
PS ~EnterKey~
Specify preview scale factor for XYZ axes: (enter a scale to preview for
example, 18)
Specify insertion point: (select the insertion point)
Enter X scale factor, specify opposite corner, or [Corner/XYZ] <1>:
(enter a new X scale factor or enter 18 if it is acceptable)
Enter Y scale factor <use X scale factor>: (enter Y scale factor or
~EnterKey~ to accept 18)
Specify rotation angle: (enter the rotation angle)
Enter number of rows (—) <1>: ~EnterKey~ (if inserting one block)
Enter number of columns (|||) <1>: ~EnterKey~ (if inserting one block)
```

To use Temporary Preset variables, enter P followed by the option you want to preset. For example, to temporarily preset the rotation angle enter PR.

The scale factor value entered has the same effect as the SCALE command. For example, if you enter 0.5 as the scale factor for XYZ axis, the blocks will be displayed as half the original size. You can set the scale factor on the screen by specifying the block insertion point and an opposite corner. When you enter the Corner option, you will be prompted to specify a corner point. The corner point and the insertion point determine the X and Y scale factor values.

Note: In the above example, if different desk sizes were required, you would create a single block as the desk using the One Inch Square method. You would then use the INSERT command and insert the desks individually at different X and Y scale factor values. Finally, you would create another block from the other elements that make up the CAD workstation using the Current Drawing Scale method because those items do not vary in size, and insert using the MINSERT command. A good deal of coordination is required for these situations.

19.14   INSERTING BLOCKS USING THE MULTIPLE DESIGN ENVIRONMENT

In today's high-tech office, more and more design firms are streamlining their design and production environment by increasing productivity through improved data and file accessibility. Multiple Design Environment (MDE) and AutoCAD DesignCenter (ADC) provide faster and more efficient access to design data. Both MDE and ADC were introduced in Chapter 10. Working across drawings in this fashion makes it convenient to insert and copy data and bring unmatched flexibility to productivity. This chapter discusses the application of the cut, copy, and paste procedures pertaining to blocks. For a more detailed discussion on this topic, refer to Chapter 10.

19.14.1   Select, Drag, and Drop Copying

When you have more than one drawing open, you can copy existing blocks from one drawing into another drawing by selecting the block, dragging it across, and dropping it into another. When blocks are copied with this fashion they are inserted into the new drawing. You can insert blocks from one drawing into another using the following procedure:

1. Inside the source drawing, select the block. Do not select a grip.
2. Drag the block into the target drawing and drop it inside the drawing.

19.14.2 Using the Windows Clipboard to Cut, Copy, and Paste

You can place blocks on the Windows Clipboard by copying or cutting it from a drawing. You can then paste them from the Windows Clipboard into a different drawing. Refer to Chapter 10 for additional information. The Paste as Block option in the Edit pull-down menu will insert blocks on the Clipboard from the source drawing into the target drawing as a block similar to the INSERT command. The Copy with Base Point option will allow you to select the base point of the objects after they are selected.

■ **EXERCISE 19–5:** *The following step-by-step exercise will allow you to copy a chair that is not a block from the source drawing into the target drawing as a block. Figure 19–30 shows two drawings tiled vertically. The source drawing on the right contains a chair that is not a block. The chair is part of a furniture arrangement for a CAD Workstation. The target drawing on the left is a floor plan.*

Step #1: Open the EXE19-2A.dwg file. This is the source drawing.

Step #2: Open the EXE 19-2B.dwg file. This is the target drawing.

Step #3: From the Windows pull-down menu, select Tile Vertically. The drawings will be displayed as shown in Figure 19–30 without the chairs around the table.

Step #4: Left-click inside the source drawing to make it current.

Step #5: From the Edit pull-down menu, select Copy with Base Point.

Step #6: Select the front line midpoint as the base point on the chair.

Step #7: Place a window around the chair to select it and press the ~EnterKey~

Step #8: Make the target drawing active.

Step #9: From the Edit pull-down menu, select Paste as Block.

Step #10: Insert the chair near the south quadrant of the circle (kitchen table).

Step #11: Array the chair around the table as shown in Figure 19–30.

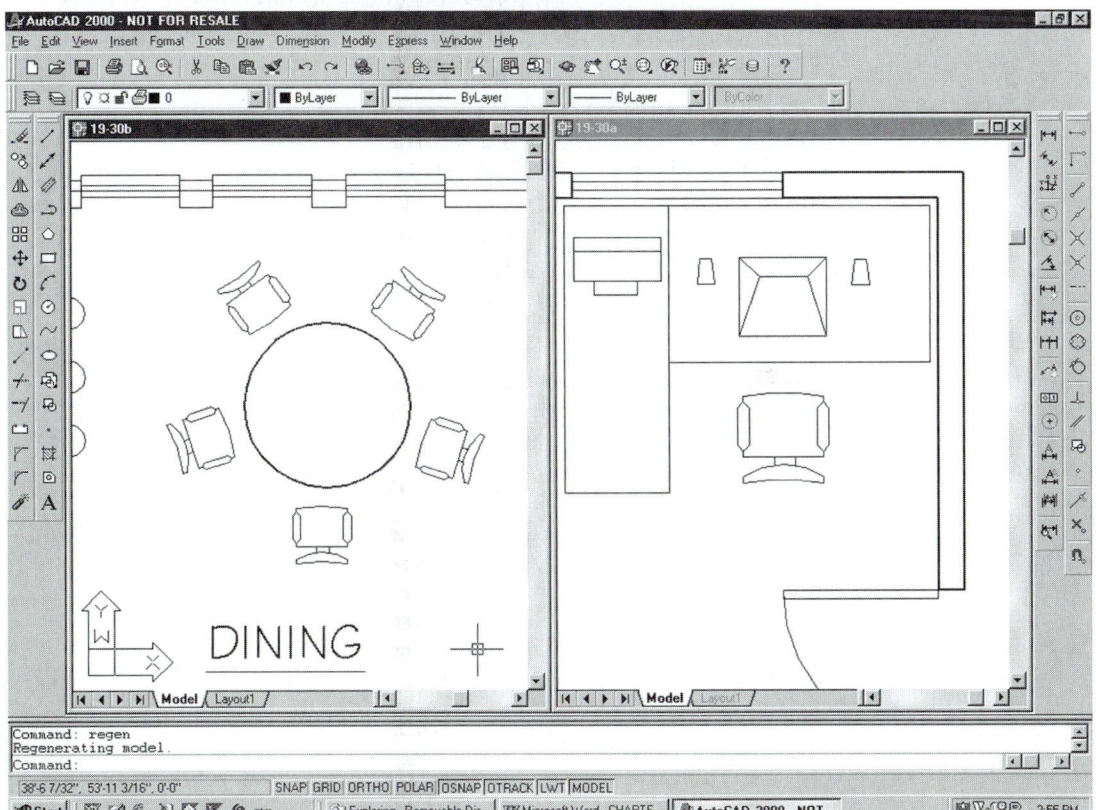

FIGURE 19–30 Using the MDE to copy the chair in the source drawing and insert it as a block into the kitchen plan in the target drawing. Notice the chair has been arrayed.

Congratulations! You have successfully copied a chair as a block from a source drawing into a target drawing. The chair will be inserted as a block definition. You can also right click in the source drawing and select Copy with Base Point from the shortcut menu to select a base point and select the objects. You can then make the target drawing current and right-click in the drawing and select Paste as Block.

AutoCAD will automatically assign a name to the inserted object, such as A$C638144D2. You can check the assigned name by entering LIST at the command line and selecting the inserted chair. You can rename the block using the RENAME command.

To use the architectural symbols library with the MDE, use the following guidelines:

- Open the symbols as blocks file drawing next to the current drawing. This file contains all the current symbols as blocks. Use any of the selection methods shown above to insert as many blocks as necessary into the current drawing.

- When selecting the blocks with left-click, the grips will be displayed on the block. Zoom-in close to the block and left-click on one of the objects on the block; do not select a grip.

19.15 INSERTING BLOCKS USING THE AUTOCAD DESIGNCENTER

AutoCAD DesignCenter (ADC) provides easy access to information on your desktop, network, or the Internet. You can copy drawing contents from one drawing into another drawing. Drawing contents include blocks, dimension styles, layers, linetypes, text styles, and xrefs. This chapter discusses the copying of blocks using the ADC. For a more detailed discussion of the ADC, refer to Chapter 10. You can look at a tree list in the tree view to locate a specific file having a specific block. You can then select the content source in the palette and copy it into the target drawing. It is the palette area that you left-or right-click on the block to copy or insert into another drawing. The following guidelines will help you find the content source you need:

- Use the Tree toggle View to locate the required file containing the block.
- Pick the plus (+) sign next to the file name to see the content of the file. This will display the available blocks, dimstyles, layers, layouts, linetypes, textstyles, and xrefs.
- Selecting blocks will display all the blocks in the palette area.
- Selecting an individual block name in the palette area will display the icon and the description of the block if the Create icon from block geometry was checked and a description was entered inside the Block Definition dialog box when the block was created.

The Insert units category in the Block Definition dialog box supports automatic scaling of blocks inserted using the ADC. If this option is used and a unit is selected while creating the block, any block inserted into a drawing whose drawing unit is different then the blocks will be automatically scaled to match the new units. If you specified the creation of icon from block geometry and entered a description for the block inside the Block Definition dialog box, the icon and the description will appear in the palette area of the ADC. To see the preview and description of the selected block, click on the Preview and Description buttons in the DesignCenter toolbar. Figure 19–31 shows the blocks residing inside the 19-adc.dwg file using the DesignCenter toolbar. The drawing on the right represents the target drawing.

The following guidelines will help you copy blocks from the ADC into another drawing more effectively and efficiently:

- You can left-click, drag, and drop a block into another drawing. If you use the left button while dragging, the block will be inserted when it is dropped into the drawing. The inserted block will maintain its block definition in the new drawing. If you left-click, drag, and drop a block into a drawing, the block is automatically scaled. The automatic scaling is controlled by the Insert units drop-down menu inside the Block Definition and the Write Block dialog boxes. When you insert a block in this fashion, you will not be able to

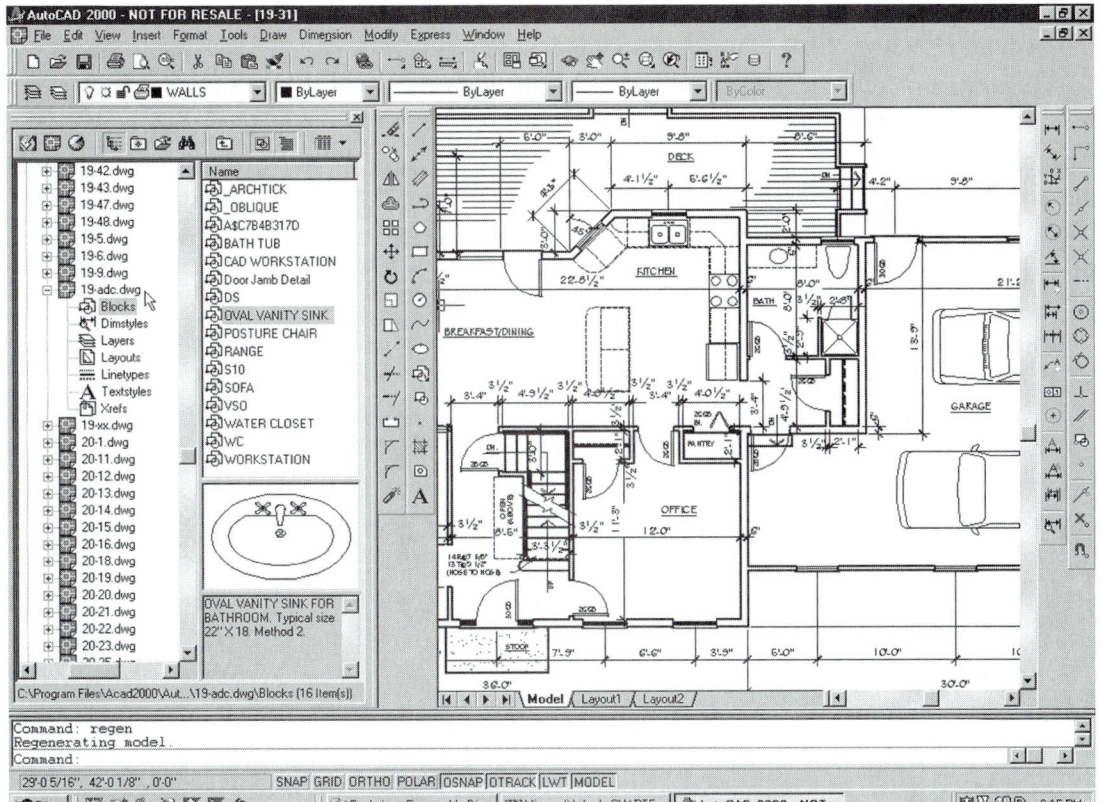

FIGURE 19-31 The DesignCenter toolbar shown floating here is used to gain access to drawing contents, desktop, network, or the Web.

adjust the X and Y scale factor values for the block. You may use the SCALE command to adjust the scale, but this would change the X and Y units of the block equally when it is inserted.

- You can right-click, drag, and drop a block into another drawing. When you right-click, drag, and drop a block, a shortcut menu will appear. You can use either the Insert Block... or the Cancel option. If you select the Insert Block option, the Insert dialog box will appear. You can use the Browse... button to search for another file or specify the insertion point, scale, and rotation angle of the block to be inserted.

- You can right-click on the block in the palette area and select either the Insert Block... or the Copy option from the shortcut menu. Choosing the Insert Block... option will insert the block and add a block definition into the drawing by displaying the Insert dialog box. Choosing the Copy option will place the block on the Clipboard. You can then use the Paste as Block option from the Edit pull-down menu to insert the block.

- You can enter the ACDCINSERTBLOCK (AutoCAD DesignCenter Insert Block) command at the command line to use the Insert dialog box to insert a block.

- You can double click on the block in the palette area. This will display the Insert dialog box.

- You can insert or copy one block at a time.

To use the architectural symbols library folder with the ADC, use the following guidelines:

- Open the ADC and dock it next to the current file.

- In the tree view area of the ADC, find the architectural symbols library folder.

- Pick the + sign in front of the folder. All the wblock files along with the *symbols as blocks file* will be listed with a .dwg extension.

- Pick the + sign in front of the symbols as blocks file.dwg and left-click on Blocks. This will place all the blocks in this file on the palette area.
- Inside the palette area, left-click on one of the blocks. The block icon and the description will be displayed on the bottom of the palette area.

When you pick the + sign in front of one of the wblock files and left click on Blocks, the specific block will not be listed in the palette area (except the _Arch Tick). This is because the file itself is a block with a .dwg file extension. The file does not contain a block. This is why you created the symbols as blocks file drawing containing all the blocks and created a wblock from it. You can have individual wblocks display their own symbol as a block as follows:

1. Open the drawing file containing the single block. Notice that the symbol is not a block but the file is a block.
2. Use the BLOCK command to create block from the symbol. Inside the Block Definition dialog box, enter a different name. Select the Retain radio button and complete the rest as shown previously.

   Note: When you use the ADC to insert blocks from the architectural symbols library, an architectural symbols library.cdc file will be created as the design center preview cache file.

There are two types of unit control settings that relate to the AutoCAD DesignCenter:

1. **Source Content Units:** When no insert units are specified (INSUNITS = 0), the INSUNITSDEFSOURCE (insertion units definition source) system variable will set a unit value to the source block. Using a number from 1 to 20 will set units to be used automatically for an object being inserted into the current drawing. The numbers correspond to the INSUNITS values.

2. **Target Drawing Units:** When no insert units are specified (INSUNITS = 0), the INSUNITSDEFTARGET (insertion units definition target) system variable will set a unit value to the target block. Using a number from 1 to 20 will set units to be used automatically in the current drawing.

You can set the Source Content Units and the Target Drawing Units inside the Options dialog box while using the AutoCAD DesignCenter as follows:

1. Open the AutoCAD DesignCenter.
2. In the drawing area, right click and select Options. . . from the shortcut menu. The Options dialog box will appear.
3. Inside the Options dialog box select the User Preferences tab.
4. Under the ADC category, select a unit inside the Source content units: drop-down list and select a unit inside the Target drawing units: drop-down list.

■ **EXERCISE 19–6:**   *The following step-by-step exercise will allow you to insert the sofa and the posture chair blocks from the symbols as blocks file drawing and the water closet, oval vanity sink, and CAD workstation blocks from the individual drawing files inside the architectural symbols library folder into the current floor plan.*

Step #1:   Copy the architectural symbols library folder (and its contents) into your hard drive. Open the EXE19-3.dwg file.

Step #2:   Open the ADC and dock it.

Step #3:   In the DesignCenter toolbar, click on the Tree Toggle View and locate the symbols as blocks file.dwg file containing the blocks. This file is inside the architectural symbols library folder. Pick the + sign next to the file name to display blocks and other contents of the drawing.

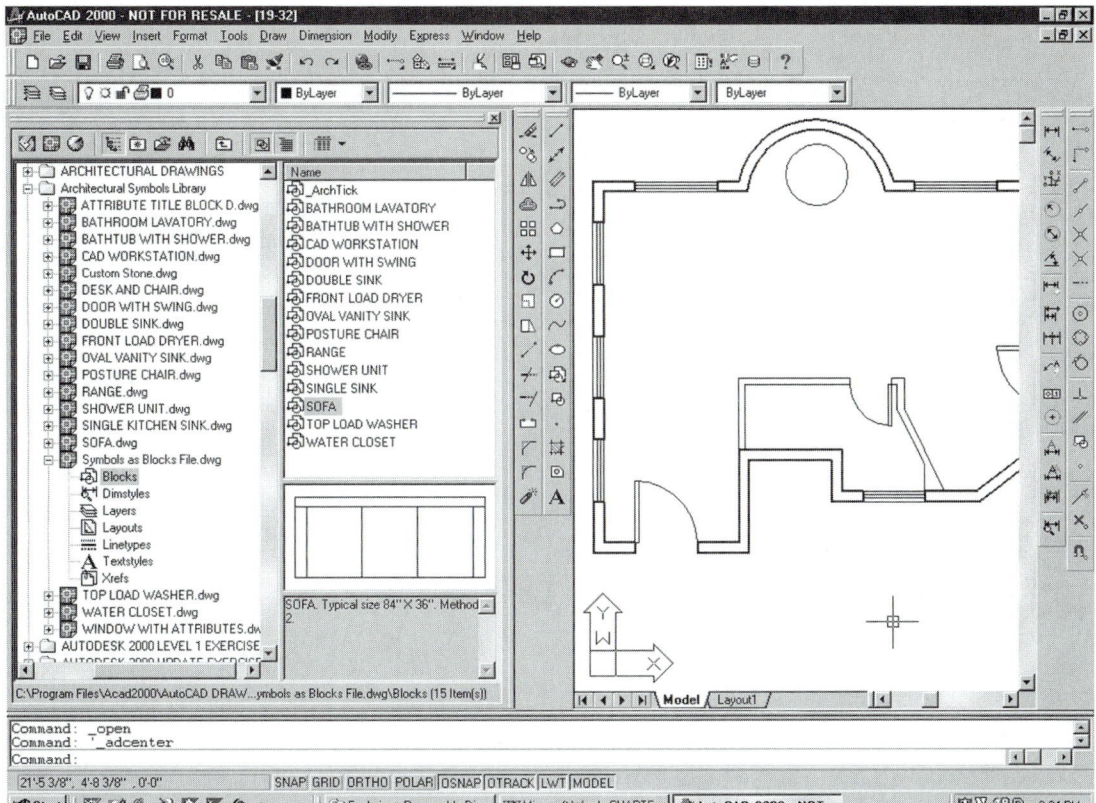

FIGURE 19–32 The AutoCAD DesignCenter tree view area showing the Tree View and the location of the SOFA and the POSTURE CHAIR blocks.

Step #4: Left-click on Blocks to display all the blocks on the palette. This file contains 15 blocks as shown in Figure 19–32.

Step #5: Inside the palette area, select the sofa block. The image and description of the block will be displayed as shown in Figure 19–32. In Figure 19–32, the sofa block is located in C:\Program Files\Acad2000\CAD DRAWINGS\Architectural Symbols Library\Symbols as Blocks File.dwg\Blocks. The icon and the description for the blocks will be shown in the bottom of the palette area. You can adjust the size of the DesignCenter toolbar by clicking on the vertical separation bar and moving it left or right.

Step #6: Turn OSNAP off inside the target drawing.

Step #7: Inside the Palette area left-click on the sofa block. While holding down the left-button, drag and drop the block into the upper-left corner of the floor plan.

Step #8: Inside the palette area, right-click on the posture chair and select Insert Block. . . from the shortcut menu. Inside the Insert dialog box, place a checkmark inside the Uniform Scale check box, and click on the OK button. Insert the block into the locations shown in Figure 19–33 (use the Rotation Angle area to specify the appropriate angles for the rotation).

Step #9: Pick the + sign next to water closet.dwg. Notice that this file is a wblock, and inside the file there are no blocks. The architectural symbols library folder has the water closet.dwg file that is a wblock. Since you cannot copy a file from the ADC (you can only copy drawing contents), you cannot use this file to

FIGURE 19–33　The floor plan with the inserted sofa and the posture chair blocks.

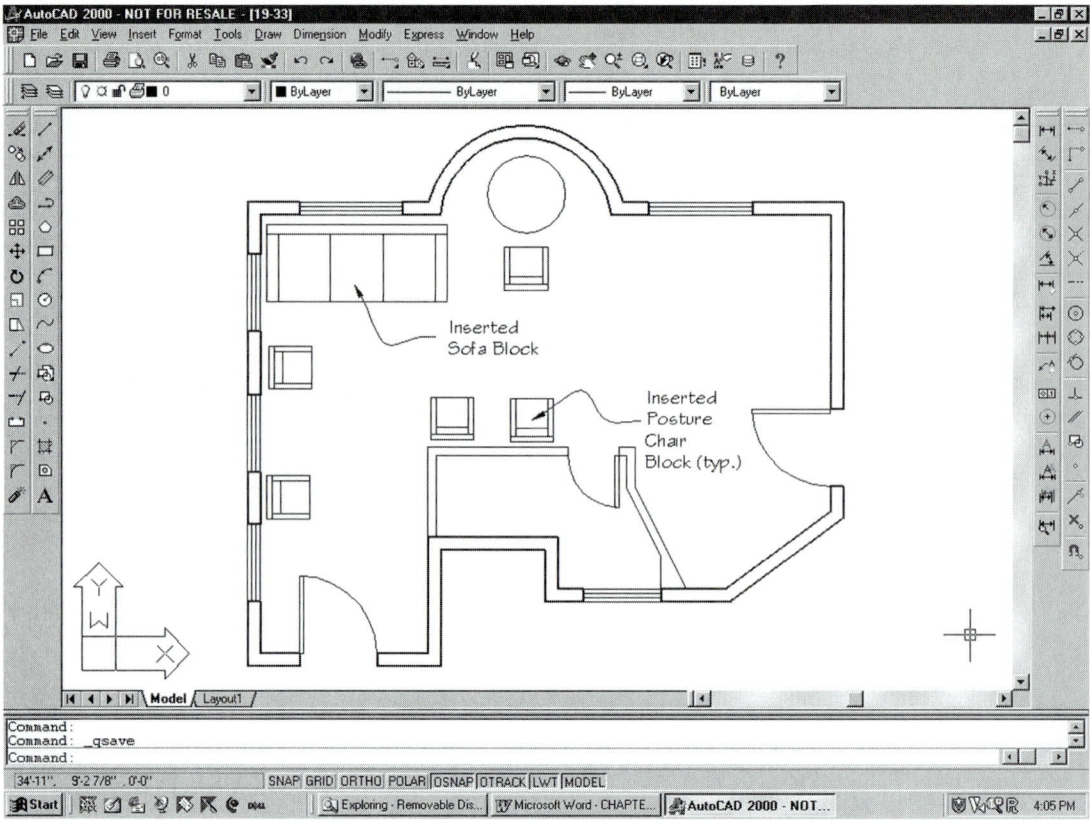

insert or copy the water closet. In this case use the INSERT command and click on the Browse. . . button to find the water closet.dwg file and insert it into the drawing.

Tips: Therefore, when using the Write Block dialog box to create a wblock it is best to have the block as the source so that you have a block and a file of the block.

Step #10:　Go back to the *symbols as blocks file*.dwg and select Blocks**.** Select the water closet block and insert it in the floor plan inside the bathroom. This wblock is created using the One Inch Square method. If it is inserted as X = 1″ and Y = 1″ it will not be inserted at the correct size. A typical water closet measures 20″ long by 28″ deep. Therefore the water closet must have insertion scale factor values of X = 28 and Y = 20 units (this depends on how the symbol was drawn and which side is X and which side is Y). Use the procedure as used in Step #8. Inside the Insert dialog box, adjust the X and Y scale factor values as required. The block will be inserted at the desired scale. This is where one advantage for the One Inch Square method comes into play. If for any reason you need to adjust the X and Y scale factor values, it is much easier to simply enter the width and length (true size) of a symbol in real units. However, you can still adjust the X and Y scale factor values for the blocks created with the other methods, you just need to calculate and interpolate from the original values.

Step #11:　Insert the oval vanity sink and the CAD workstation blocks using the procedures shown above. The final drawing with all the inserted blocks is shown in Figure 19–34.

Congratulations! You have successfully used the ADC to insert blocks into a target drawing.

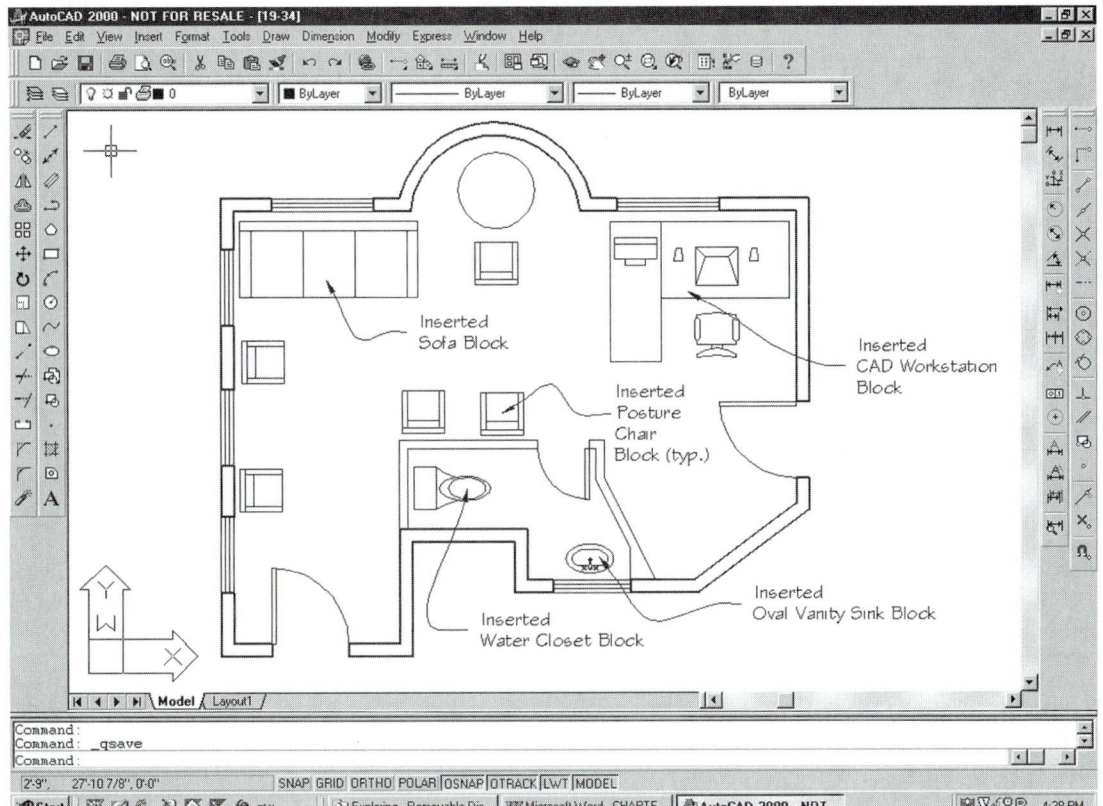

FIGURE 19–34 The floor plan with five blocks inserted from the ADC.

19.16 RENAMING BLOCKS

You can change the name of an existing block by using the RENAME command. The command line procedure to rename a block is as follows:

```
Command: RENAME ~EnterKey~
```

The Rename dialog will be displayed as shown in Figure 19–35. Use the following guidelines to rename a block:

1. Inside the Rename dialog box, select Blocks under Named Objects. All available blocks will be displayed under the Items text box on the right.

2. Select the block name you want to change. The name will appear in the Old Name: text box.

3. Enter the new name inside the text box below the Old Name: text box.

4. Click on the Rename to: button. The new name will appear in the Items text box and the old name will be deleted.

5. Click on the OK button to close the Rename dialog box.

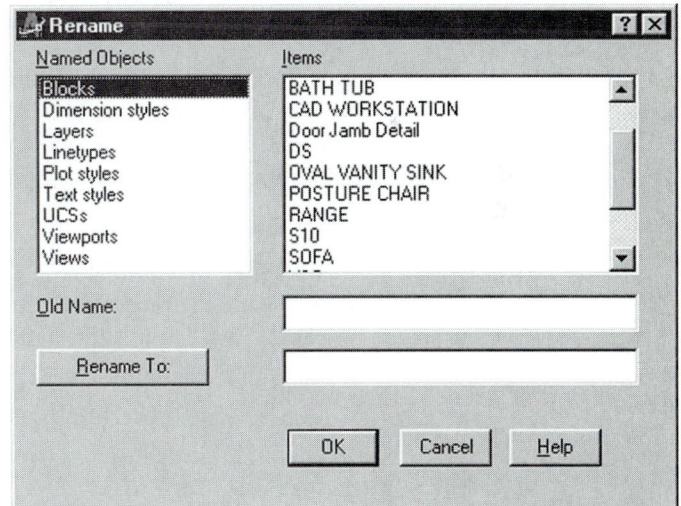

FIGURE 19–35 The Rename dialog box can be used to rename a block.

19.17 EDITING BLOCKS

You can edit blocks either by exploding the block or by using the Refedit toolbar.

19.17.1 Exploding Blocks

You can explode an existing block using the Explode button in the Modify toolbar or by entering EXPLODE at the command line. When a block is exploded, it will lose its block definition character and all the objects that make up the block will return to their original components. Two methods can be used to explode blocks. The first method is to place a checkmark inside the Explode: (check box) inside the Insert dialog box discussed earlier in the chapter. When this box is checked, the inserted block will be exploded as it is displayed on the screen. If a block created using the Bylayer method is exploded, the objects that make up the block will assume the characteristics of layer 0. The second method is to use the EXPLODE command after the block is inserted in the drawing. The EXPLODE command can also break apart any polylines, multilines, associative dimensions, and associative hatching in the drawing. The command sequence to explode a block is as follows:

```
Command: X or EXPLODE ~EnterKey~
Select objects: (select the block to explode)
```

When a block is exploded, you can edit the individual components of the block using the Auto-CAD editing commands. A block can be exploded to redefine its shape or size.

If you insert more than one block in the current drawing and want to edit just one block but do not want the changes to affect the other blocks with the same name, use the following procedure:

1. Explode the block.
2. Edit the block as required.
3. Redefine the block by recreating it. Use the Make Block button in the draw toolbar or enter BLOCK at the command line.
4. Give the block a different name.
5. Use the same insertion point or select a new insertion point.
6. Give the block a new definition.
7. Select the objects for the block.

Only the block you redefined will be edited. Other blocks in the drawing with the original block name will not be affected. This is called *single block editing*.

If you insert more than one block in the current drawing and want the editing operation to affect all the blocks with the same name, use the following procedure:

1. Explode the block.
2. Edit the block as required.
3. Redefine the block by recreating it. Use the Make Block button in the draw toolbar or enter BLOCK at the command line.
4. Give the block the same name it had before.
5. Use the same insertion point or select a new insertion point.
6. Give the block a new definition, for example, CAD workstation without the side desk and speakers.
7. Select the objects for the block.
8. AutoCAD will give you the following message:

CAD WORKSTATION is already defined.
Do you want to re-define it?

9. Select the Yes button.

All the blocks in the current drawing with the same name will be edited. This is called a *Global Block Editing*.

19.17.2 Using the Refedit Toolbar

You can edit blocks without exploding them using the REFEDIT command or the Refedit toolbar. This is called *in-place xref and block editing.* The following guidelines will help you use the Refedit toolbar effectively:

- You can only edit one block at a time.
- When you edit a block using this procedure, all other blocks having the same name will also be edited.
- You cannot use the REFEDIT command on a nonuniformly scaled block.

Enter REFEDIT at the command line or from the Modify pull-down menu select In-place Xref and Block Edit and select Edit Reference. Both options will give you the Select reference: prompt. When you select the block, the Reference Edit dialog box will be displayed as shown in Figure 19–36.

The Reference Edit dialog box has three major categories as follows:

- **REFERENCE NAME:** (text box). This category will show the block reference selected for in-place editing. If you select a block that is part of a wblock (inserted drawings with block components) or part of one or more nested block references, the nested references will also be displayed. The nested references will be displayed only if the selected block is part of a nested reference. If the selected item is xref, the AutoCAD file icon will appear in front of the xref name, and the drawing file will be displayed in the Preview: image box. The icon in front of a block is the same icon in the Make Block button in the Draw toolbar. The name of the block will be grayed out. Select the block name to highlight it.

- **PREVIEW:** (image box). This category will display the image of the selected block. You can cycle through multiple references when you select the Next button. The icon inside the

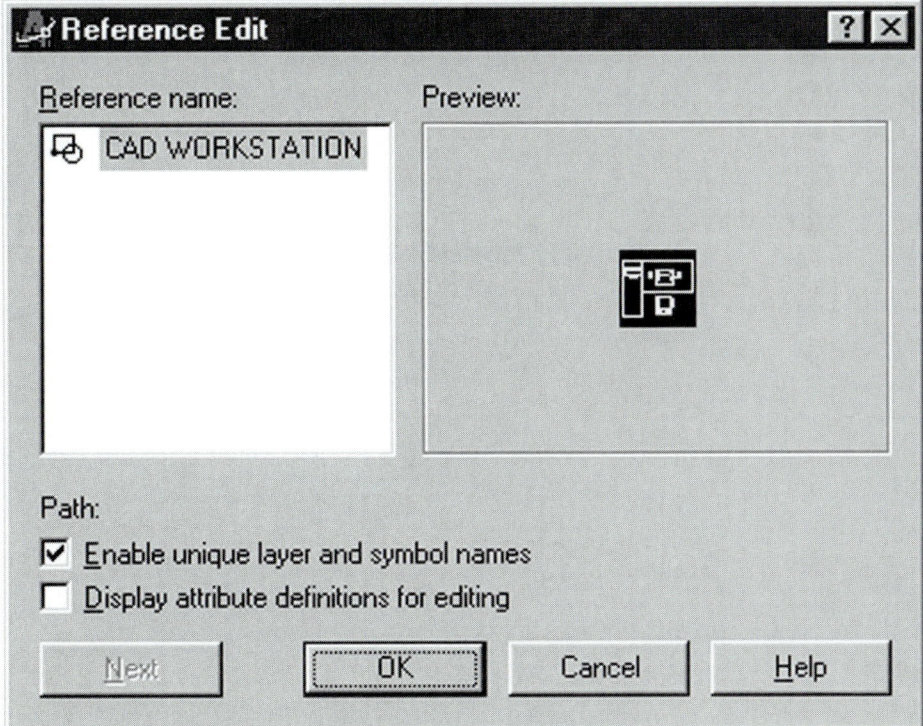

FIGURE 19–36 The Reference Edit dialog box is used to edit a block or an Xref.

Preview: image box is the last saved image in the drawing. This image box is not updated when changes are saved back to the reference.

- **PATH:** (text line). This category applies to xrefs. It will display the file location of the selected xref. If a drawing is inserted as a block inside a current drawing, no path will be displayed. A block that is a part of the current file will not have a path.

- **ENABLE UNIQUE LAYER AND SYMBOL NAMES:** (check box). This category applies to xrefs. Refer to the chapter on Using External References.

- **DISPLAY ATTRIBUTE DEFINITIONS FOR EDITING:** (check box). This category applies to blocks with attributes. Refer to the chapter on Assigning Attributes to Blocks.

- **NEXT:** (button). Selecting this button will allow you to cycle through the references available for selection.

Click on the OK button to select a block reference. AutoCAD will display the following prompt:

```
Command:_refedit
Select reference:
Select nested objects: (select the individual entities within the block
reference that you want to edit)
```

When you select the objects you want to edit within the specific block definition, AutoCAD will form a working set from the selected objects. If you have more than one of the same block and you select a specific one at the Select reference: prompt, you must select nested objects from that specific block. After you select the nested objects from the block definition click on the right button or press ~EnterKey~. The Refedit toolbar will be displayed as shown in Figure 19–37. Using the buttons in the Refedit toolbar, you can add or remove objects from the working set, and you can discard or save changes to the block reference.

The Refedit (Reference Edit) toolbar has five buttons and a reference display box.

FIGURE 19–37 The Refedit toolbar.

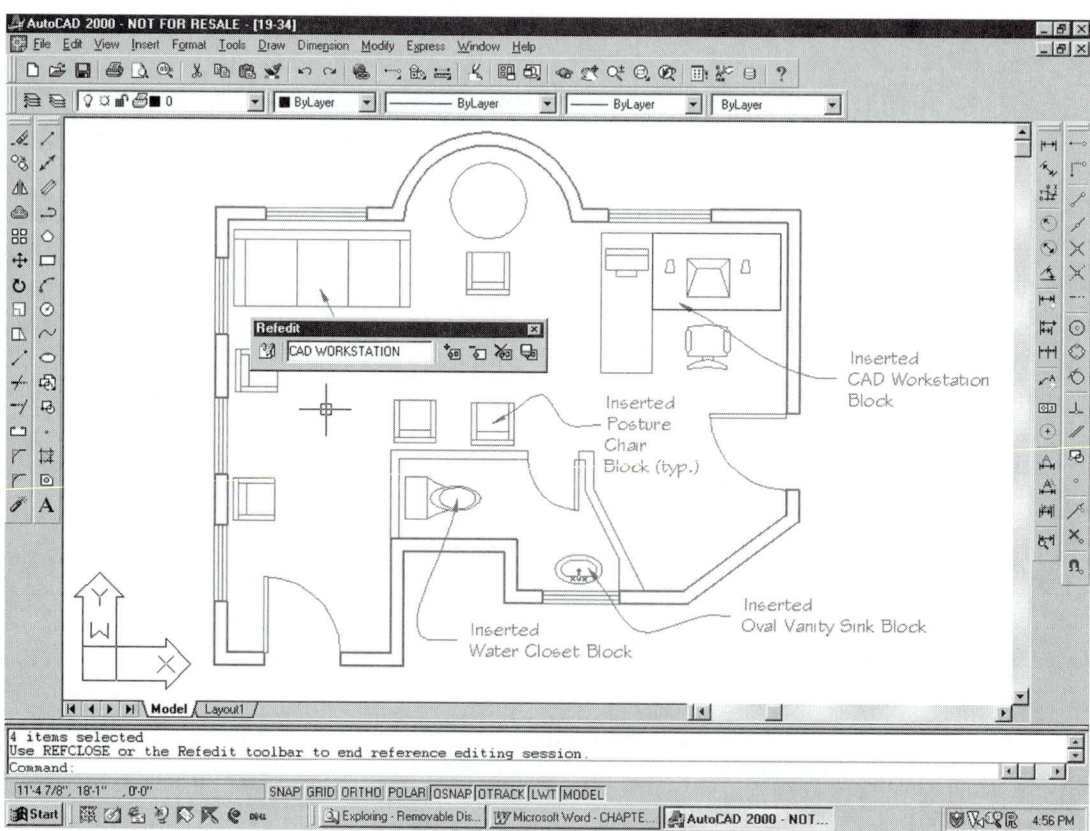

- **EDIT BLOCK OR XREF** (button). This button has the same effect as the REFEDIT command. You can access the Refedit toolbar by right clicking on any toolbar and selecting Refedit. Selecting this button is the first step in editing a block in-place that will display the Select reference: prompt.

- **REFERENCE DISPLAY BOX.** This area will show the name of the block being edited.

- **ADD OBJECTS TO WORKING SET** (button). Selecting this button will add objects to the selection set. You can also use the REFSET command and enter ADD to add objects to working set.

- **REMOVE OBJECTS FROM WORKING SET** (button). Selecting this button will remove objects from the selection set. You can also use the REFSET command and enter REM to remove objects from the working set.

- **DISCARD CHANGES TO REFERENCE** (button). Selecting this button will discard all the changes that you made to the block with the Refedit toolbar. After selecting this button, the Refedit toolbar will automatically disappear. You can also use the REFCLOSE command and enter DISC to discard changes to reference.

- **SAVE BACK CHANGES TO REFERENCE** (button). Selecting this button will save all the changes that you made to the block. All blocks with the same name will be updated in the drawing. After selecting this button, the Refedit toolbar will automatically disappear. You can also use the REFCLOSE command and enter SAV to save back changes to reference.

After you select nested objects in the block to edit (after establishing the working set), all other objects in the drawing will appear faded. This fading of the objects other than the ones in the working set will help you identify which objects belong to the working set before you perform the editing operation. This fading effect is controlled by the XFADECTL system variable. The XFADECTL system variable controls the fading intensity for references when blocks and xrefs are edited in place. The default value is 50 percent fading with a minimum of 0 percent and maximum fading value of 90 percent. For the objects outside the working set to be faded, the SHADEMODE system variable must be set to 2D Wireframe. You can control the fading intensity by also using the Reference Edit fading intensity category inside the Display tab of the Options dialog box.

Note: The XEDIT system variable controls whether or not a reference can be edited. The default value for XEDIT is 1, meaning editing a reference is allowed. When XEDIT is set to 0, editing a reference is not allowed. The REFEDITNAME system variable stores the referenced file name that indicates whether a drawing is in the in-place-reference-editing phase.

■ **EXERCISE 19–7:** *The following step-by step exercise will allow you to edit a block using the Refedit toolbar. Figure 19–38 shows a floor plan with two offices. The WORKSTATION block is inserted inside both offices. It is later discovered that the Workstations are too large to fit inside Office 1 and Office 2. The side desk including the printer is to be removed from the workstation in both offices without exploding the block.*

Using the Refedit toolbar to edit one workstation will automatically edit the other block with the same name.

Step #1: Open the EXE19-4.dwg file.

Step #2: Zoom-in on the workstation block in Office 1.

Step #3: Right-click on any toolbar and select Refedit. The Refedit toolbar will be displayed.

Step #4: Inside the Refedit toolbar, click on the Edit block or xref button and use the following command line procedure:

Command:_refedit

Select reference: *(select the workstation block)*

FIGURE 19–38   The floor plan with two WORKSTATION blocks inserted in Office 1 and Office 2. One block will be edited suing the Refedit toolbar so that the side desk and the printer is deleted from the WORKSTATION.

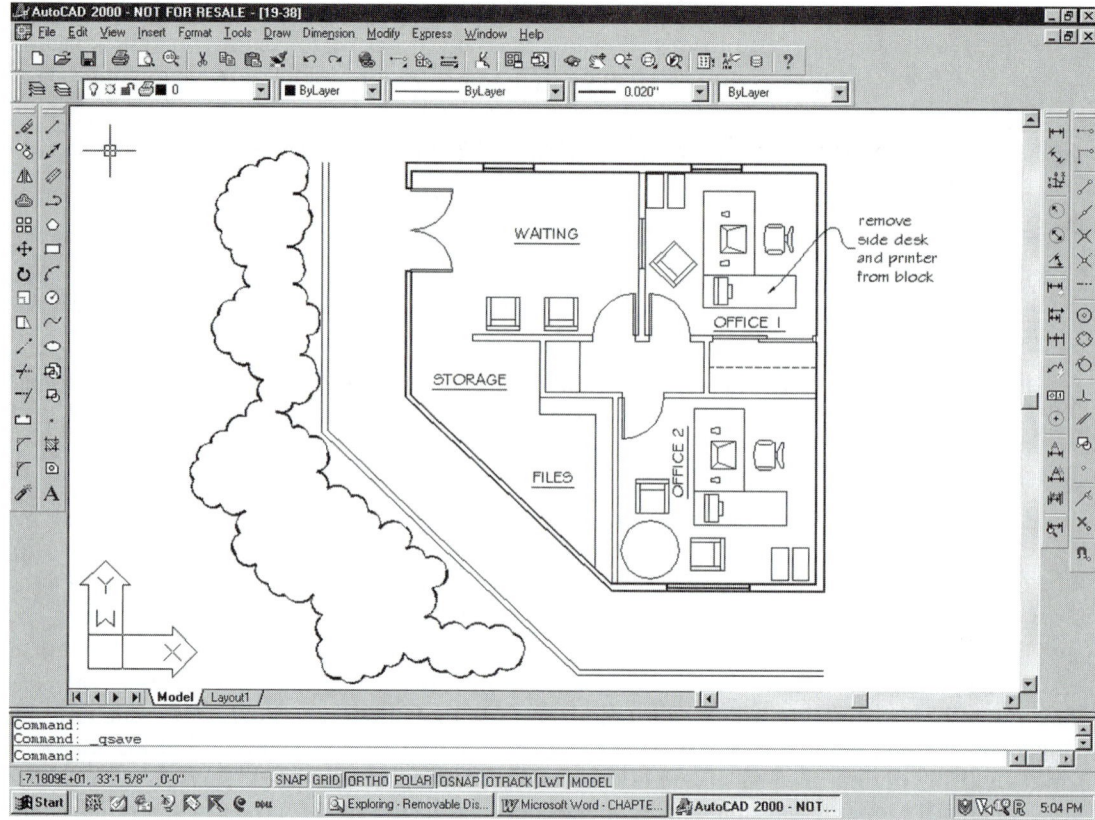

The Reference Edit dialog box will appear. Select the block reference name and click on the OK button.

Select nested objects: *(place a window around the entire block)*

59 entities added

Select nested objects: ~EnterKey~

Command: **ERASE** ~EnterKey~

Select objects: *(select the lines that make up the side desk including the printer)*

Select objects: ~EnterKey~

Step #5:   Click on the *Save back changes to reference* button in the Refedit toolbar. Click on the OK button in the AutoCAD message dialog box.

The following will appear at the command prompt:

Command: _refclose

Enter option [Save/Discard reference changes] <Save>: _sav

Regenerating model.

14 objects removed from WORKSTATION

2 block instances updated

WORKSTATION redefined.

Congratulations! You have successfully edited a block using the Refedit toolbar by removing the side desk and the printer from an existing block. The other block will be automatically edited to reflect the changes. The edited blocks are shown in Figure 19–39.

AutoCAD 2000i Update: You can trim and extend to objects within blocks. You no longer have to explode a block to trim or extend within blocks.

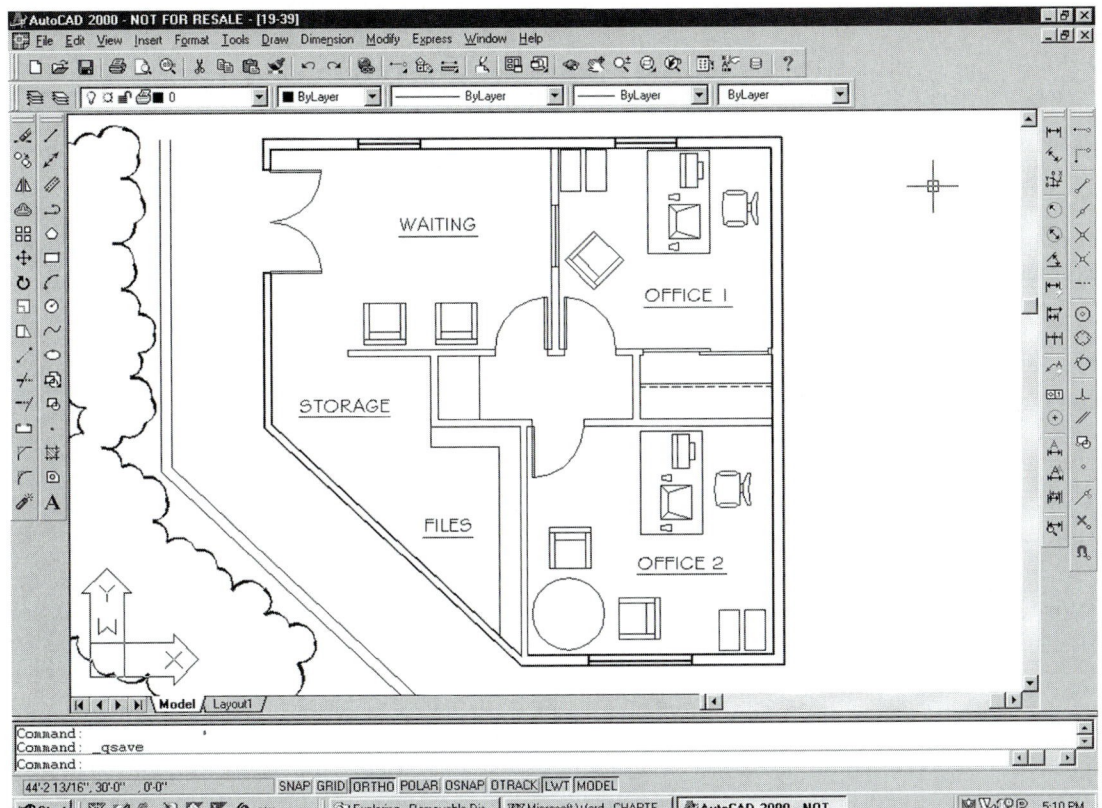

FIGURE 19–39 The workstation blocks in Office 1 and Office 2 after using the Refedit toolbar. Notice the workstations are small enough now to fit in the offices.

19.18 EXPRESS BLOCK TOOLS

There are four express tools that you can use when working with blocks. You can access these tools by clicking on the Express pull-down menu and selecting Blocks. Inside the Blocks are the first express tools explained as follows:

List Xref/Block Entities: This express tool will display the properties of objects nested in external references or blocks and is similar to the LIST command used to obtain information from a drawing. Or you can enter XLIST at the command line. Nested objects are considered to be the individual entities that make up the block definition. When you select this express tool, AutoCAD will give you the following command prompt:

```
Command: xlist
Select nested xref or block object to list: (select
the object that defines the block to list)
```

Every time you select an object, the Xref/Block Nested Object List dialog box will be displayed as shown in Figure 19–40. Inside this dialog box, the object, layer, color, and linetype settings of the object selected will be displayed.

Copy Nested Entities: This express tool will allow you to copy nested objects inside blocks and xrefs similar to the COPY command but without exploding the block. Or you can enter NCOPY at the command line. When you select this express tool, AutoCAD will give you the following command prompt:

```
Command: ncopy
Select nested objects to copy: (select the individual entities that make
up the block definition)
```

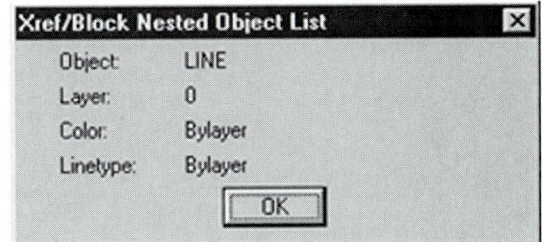

Xref/Block Nested Object List	
Object:	LINE
Layer:	0
Color:	Bylayer
Linetype:	Bylayer
	OK

FIGURE 19–40 The Xref/Block Nested Object List dialog box can be used to list objects that define the block reference.

```
Specify base point or displacement, or [Multiple]: (similar to the copy
command, specify the base point or ~EnterKey~ for multiple copy)
Specify second point of displacement or <use first point as
displacement>: (specify the second point to move)
```

Trim to Block Entities: This express tool will allow you to trim entities crossing nested objects in blocks or xrefs similar to the TRIM command but without exploding the block. Or you can enter BTRIM at the command line. For example, if a line crosses a block and needs to be trimmed, AutoCAD will not recognize the selected block as a valid cutting edge when the TRIM command is used. Instead it will display the following message:

```
1 was not a valid edge
```

You can trim the same line by using the above express tool or enter BTRIM at the command line. AutoCAD will now recognize the block as a valid cutting edge by highlighting the nested object. You can then select the object (line) to trim. The command line procedure is similar to the TRIM command.

Extend to Block Entities: This express tool will allow you to extend entities into the nested objects in block xrefs similar to the EXTEND command but without exploding the block. Or you can enter BEXTEND at the command line. For example, if a line is to be extended into a block, AutoCAD will not recognize the block as a valid edge when the EXTEND command is used. Instead it will display the following message:

```
1 was not a valid edge
```

You can extend the same line into the block by using the above express tool or enter BEXTEND at the command line. AutoCAD will now recognize the block as a valid edge by highlighting the nested object. You can then select the object (line) to extend. The command line procedure is similar to the EXTEND command.

19.19 PURGING OBJECTS FROM A DRAWING

You can use the Write Block dialog box to store an entire drawing as a wblock. To accomplish this, select the Entire drawing radio button in the Write Block dialog box and give the wblock a name. This method will allow you to save the entire drawing to a disk as if you had used the SAVE command. In this case, all unused blocks will be removed (purged) from the drawing. If your drawing contains unused blocks, this method will reduce the size of your drawing. AutoCAD stores all named objects such as blocks with the drawing. You can use the PURGE command or the new Purge dialog box (see chapter 1) to remove any unused named objects. Purging unused named objects frees disk space and simplifies drawing management. To access the PURGE command, select Purge from the Drawing Utilities cascading menu in the File pulldown menu, or enter PU or PURGE at the command line. The command sequence to purge an unused block is as follows:

```
Command: PURGE
Enter type of unused objects to purge
[Blocks/Dimstyles/LAyers/LTypes/Plotstyles/SHapes/textSTyles/Mlinestyles/
All]: B
Enter name(s) to purge <*>: (enter the name of the block or enter to see
a list of all unused blocks)
Verify each name to be purged? [Yes/No] <Y>:
Purge block "SINK"? <N>: Y
```

This method allows you to see unused blocks individually and gives you the option to answer yes or no. You can use the All option to remove all unused named objects. This is a very efficient way to clean up a drawing that is cluttered with named objects. If there are no unused named objects to purge, AutoCAD will give you the following command line response:

```
No unreferenced _ found.
```

In addition to blocks, you can also purge unused dimension styles, layers, linetypes, plot styles, shapes, text styles, and multiline styles.

Caution: You cannot purge default named objects such as layer "0", standard text style, standard dimension style, standard multiline style, and continuous linetype.

Tips: You can delete unused named objects while in their dialog boxes. For example, you can click on the Delete button in the Style dialog box to delete an unused text style. For a named object to be purged, it must be unused in the drawing. If it is used, it must be removed, erased, or deleted from the drawing or from its appropriate location.

AutoCAD 2000i Update: The Purge dialog box allows you to purge all unused objects one at a time. Refer to section 1.13.3 for more information. To display the Purge dialog box select Purge from the Drawing Utilities cascading menu from the File pull-down menu or enter PURGE at the command line.

REVIEW QUESTIONS

1. Describe the difference between a block and a wblock.
2. Describe the main procedures in creating a symbols library.
3. Why are the size and scale of blocks important?
4. Describe briefly the three different methods used to create blocks.
5. How is a block created using the Bylayer method?
6. What are the six major steps involved in creating a block.
7. What is the function of the Quick Select button inside the Block Definition dialog box?
8. What command is used to insert blocks?
9. What does nesting blocks mean?
10. What command is used to insert multiple blocks.
11. Describe the advantages of using the ADC to insert blocks.
12. Describe the two different methods to edit blocks.

PROBLEMS

1. Using the dimensions and graphics from the Architectural Graphic Standards, draw a chair, washer, and dryer. Create three separate blocks using the Current Drawing Scale method. Insert these blocks into *MYEXE7-1.dwg* file using the ADC. Save the changes.

2. Draw the oval vanity sink and the bathtub with shower symbols from the symbols library shown in Figure 19–2 and create two separate wblocks using the One Inch Square method. Obtain dimensions from Architectural Graphic Standards or manufacturer's catalogs. Insert these blocks into MYEXE 9-2.dwg file. Save the changes.

3. Draw a simple floor plan with one bathroom, kitchen, living room, and bedroom. Using the ADC, insert furniture, fixtures, and appliances from the symbols library.

4. Open the *EXE19-5.dwg* file. Create and insert a kitchen sink, stove, and refrigerator into the kitchen. Create and insert an oval vanity sink, water closet, and shower into the bathroom. Create and insert two doors that are shown missing. Use the appropriate layers for block insertions. Do not save the changes.

5. Open the *EXE19-6.dwg* file. Insert the washer and the dryer blocks you created in Problem 1 into the laundry room. Insert the water closet, oval vanity sink, and the bathtub into both bathrooms.

6. Open the *EXE19-7.dwg* file. Design a window and create a wblock using the One Inch Square method. Insert the WINDOW into six different locations.

7. Open the *EXE19-8.dwg* file. Insert the appropriate blocks into proper locations.

8. Open the *EXE19-9.dwg* file. Create a door using the One Inch Square method. Insert the door block into three different locations.

9. Open the *EXE19-10.dwg* file. Insert two CAD workstation blocks from the symbols library into the office space. Use the Refedit toolbar to edit the blocks by removing the chair and the computer.

Creating Architectural Graphic Patterns

After successful completion of this chapter you should be able to:

▲ Create hatch patterns using the Boundary Hatch dialog box.

▲ Identify components of the Boundary Hatch dialog box.

▲ Create hatch patterns in Model and Layouts.

▲ Create hatch patterns by picking points and selecting objects.

▲ Understand island detection methods and styles.

▲ Create crosshatching.

▲ Understand associative and nonassociative hatching.

▲ Use predefined hatch patterns.

▲ Create hatch boundaries as polyline and region.

▲ Turn hatch visibility on and off.

▲ Use the HATCH command to create hatch patterns.

▲ Understand direct hatching.

▲ Create batt insulation using two different techniques.

▲ Edit hatch patterns and hatch boundaries.

▲ Use the HATCHEDIT command and the HATCH EDIT dialog box.

▲ Use the Super Hatch Express Tool to create hatch objects from images, blocks, xrefs, and wipeouts.

20.1 CREATING HATCH PATTERNS

Architectural drawings use graphic patterns to indicate material type, graphic layout, and as shading on plans, elevations, sections, and other presentation techniques. These graphic patterns are called *hatch patterns* in AutoCAD. A hatch pattern is defined in the drawing as a graphical hatch object having either an associative or nonassociative character. A hatch pattern is not considered to be a part of drawing contents such as blocks, dimension styles, layers, layouts, linetypes, text styles, and Xrefs but AutoCAD 2000i offers hatch pattern files that can be dragged and dropped into any drawing using the ADC. Refer to section 1.13.2 for additional information. Figure 20–1 shows a typical wall section with hatch patterns as poured-in-place concrete, gypsum board, compacted earth, plywood, and batt insulation. Figures 20–2 and 20–3 shows elevations with hatch patterns as glass, concrete, vinyl siding, and fiberglass shingles.

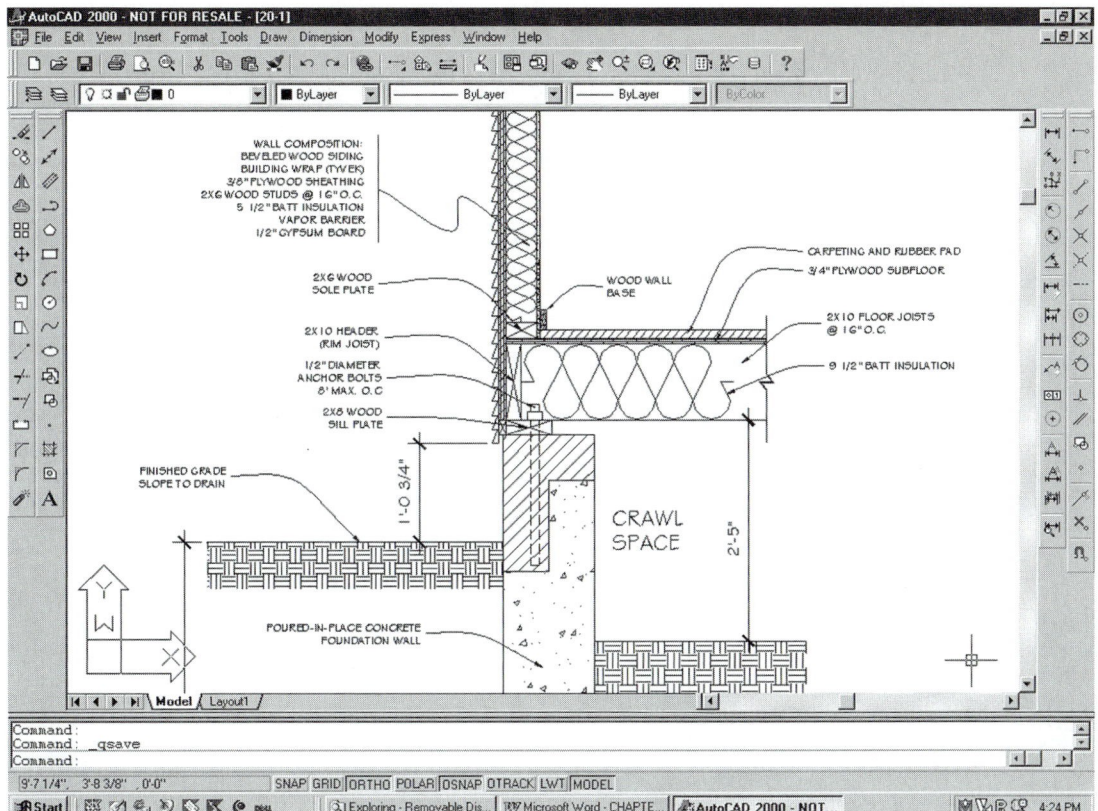

FIGURE 20–1 A typical wall section with hatch patterns.

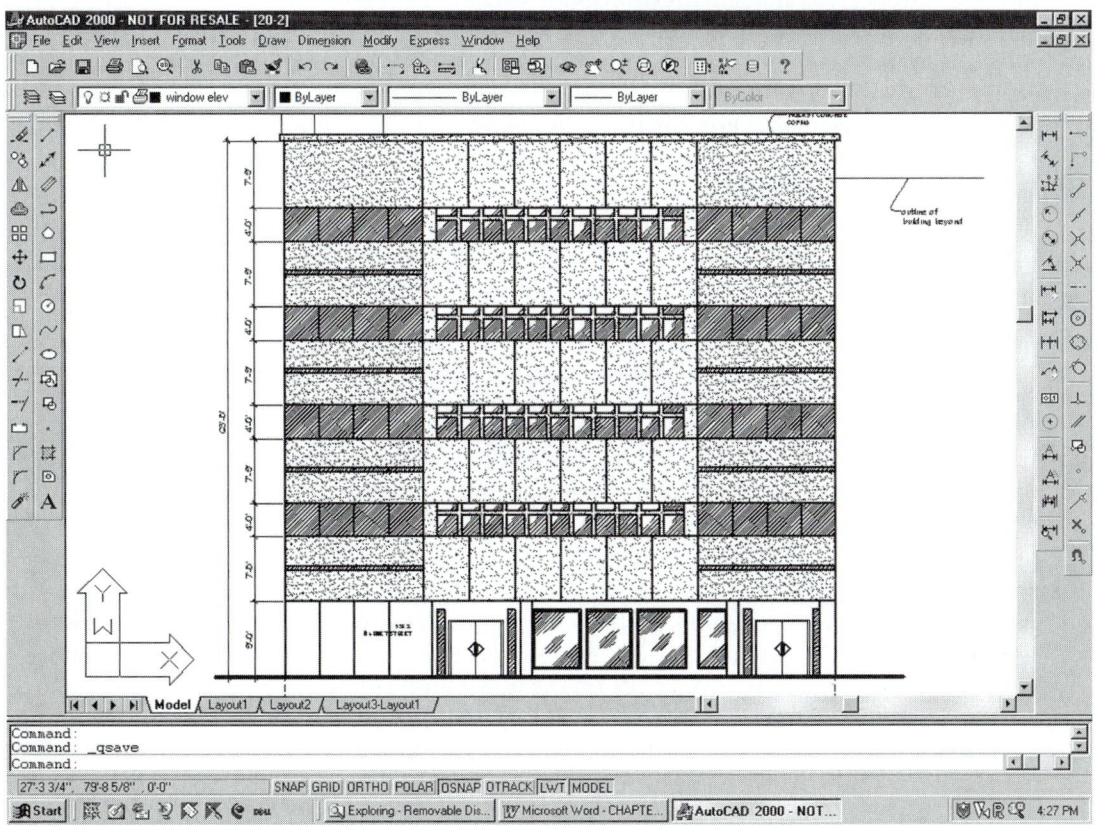

FIGURE 20–2 An office building elevation with hatch patterns.

FIGURE 20–3   A house elevation with hatch patterns.

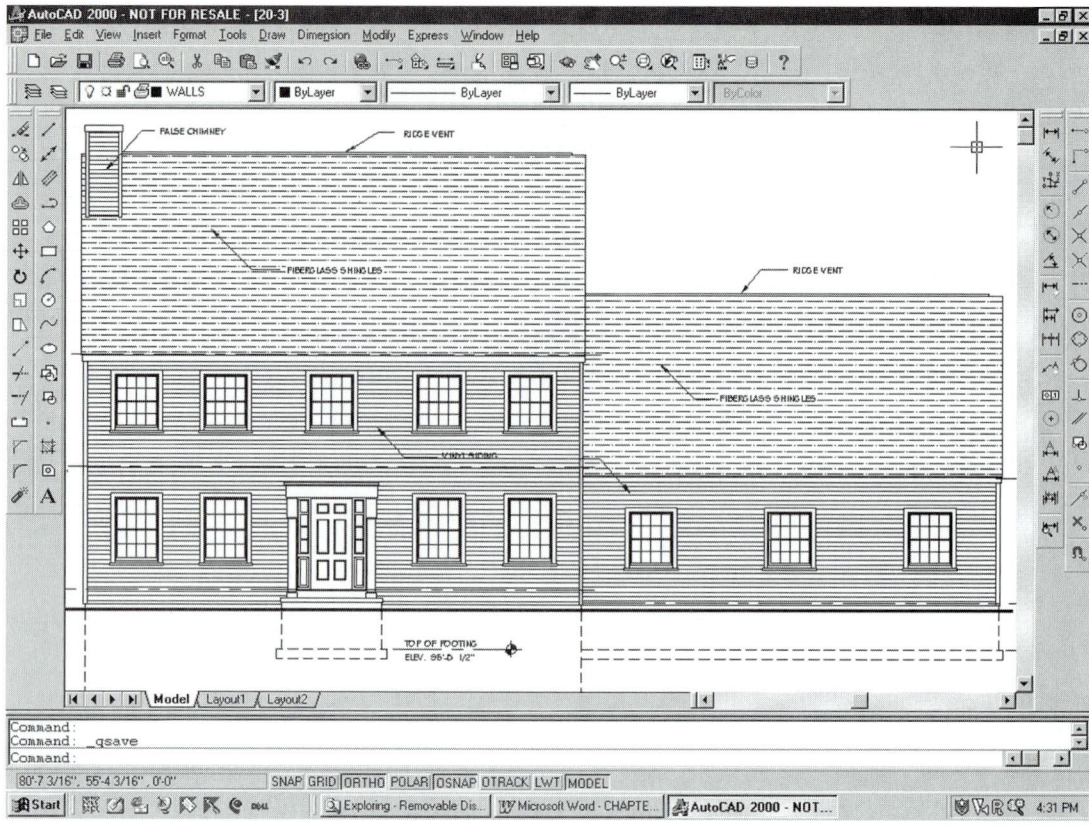

AutoCAD offers many hatch patterns to choose from. To create a hatch pattern, click on the Hatch button in the Draw toolbar, select Hatch. . . from the Draw pull-down menu, or enter H or BHATCH at the command line. The Boundary hatch dialog box will be displayed as shown in Figure 20–4.

The Boundary hatch dialog box has two tabs: *Quick* and *Advanced*.

20.1.1   Using the Quick Tab

You can simplify the hatching process by quickly creating a hatch boundary and apply a hatch pattern in any enclosed area in the drawing using the Quick tab. The Quick tab has the following areas:

- **TYPE:**   (drop-down list). This area shows the types of hatch patterns available to use. The *predefined* type includes AutoCAD's standard hatch patterns and is the default hatch pattern type. These patterns are stored in the acad.pat and acadiso.pat files. You can control the angle and scale of any predefined hatch pattern. The *user-defined* pattern will allow you to draw a pattern of lines based on the current linetype in the drawing. You can control the angle and spacing of the user defined line patterns. The *custom* pattern uses a pattern defined in a custom .pat file added to AutoCAD. You can control the angle and scale of any custom pattern.

- **PATTERN:**   (drop-down list). This area shows the predefined patterns available to use. When you use the Boundary Hatch dialog box the first time, the default hatch pattern of ANSI31 will be displayed. This hatch pattern consists of 45 degree hatch lines running counterclockwise from the X axis. If you click on the down button, a complete text list of the hatch patterns will be displayed in alphabetical order starting with ANSI31 as shown in Figure 20–5. The six most recently used predefined hatch patterns will also appear on top of the list. To select a hatch pattern from the list, simply click on the hatch pattern and the name of the selected pattern will be displayed in the Pattern: drop-down list. This Pattern: drop down list is available only when the hatch pattern type is set to Predefined. You can

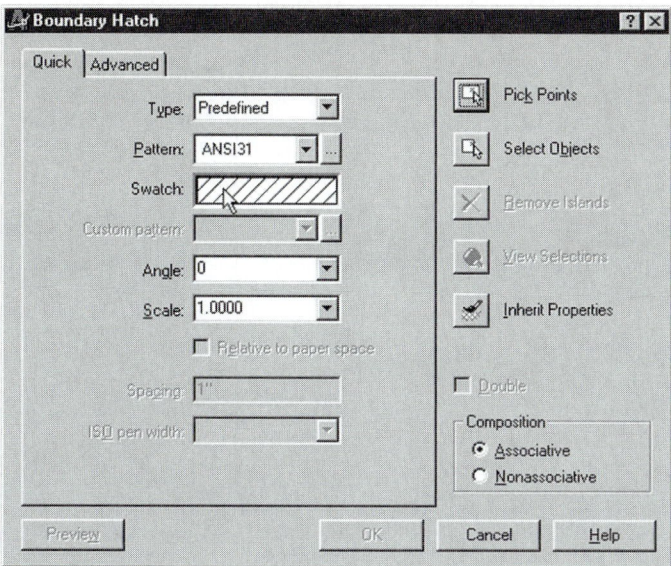

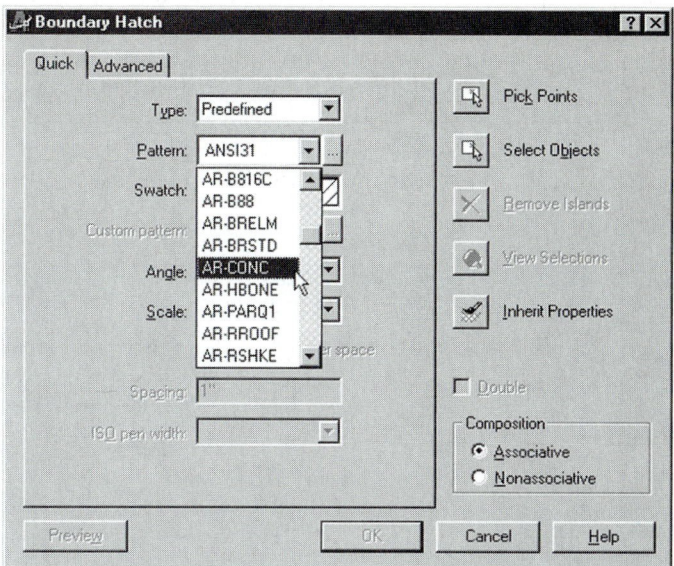

FIGURE 20–4 The Boundary Hatch dialog box is used to create hatch patterns.

FIGURE 20–5 The Pattern: drop-down list will display all the available hatch patterns. Selecting a hatch pattern will display a preview image of the hatch pattern inside the Swatch: display box.

set a hatch pattern current at the command line using the HPNAME system variable. After entering HPNAME at the command line, AutoCAD will prompt you to enter a new value for the HPNAME. The new value is the name of the hatch pattern to be set current. If a new hatch pattern is set using this method, the new name will be displayed as the current pattern the next time the Boundary Hatch dialog box is accessed. The […] button will allow you to see the preview images of all the predefined and custom patterns by displaying the Hatch Pattern Palette dialog box as shown in Figure 20–6. The four tabs inside this dialog box show hatch patterns according to ANSI, ISO, Other Predefined, and Custom types. Selecting the ANSI tab will list all ANSI patterns that are included in AutoCAD. Selecting the ISO tab will list all ISO patterns that are included in AutoCAD. Selecting the Other Predefined tab will list all patterns other than ANSI and ISO. Selecting the Custom tab will list all patterns defined in a custom .pat file added to AutoCAD. To select any of the patterns as the current hatch pattern, click on the pattern name or icon and click on the OK button.

- **SWATCH:** (display box). This area will display a preview of the selected pattern. If you click inside the Swatch display box, the Hatch Pattern Palette dialog box will be displayed.

- **CUSTOM PATTERN:** (drop-down list). This area will list the available custom hatch patterns. It is available only if a custom pattern is added to AutoCAD and when Type is set to Custom. The [. . .] button will allow you to see the preview images of all custom patterns by displaying the Hatch Pattern Palette dialog box. The HPNAME system variable can be entered at the command line to specify a different custom pattern.

- **ANGLE:** (drop-down list). This area will allow you to specify the angle for the current hatch pattern relative to the X axis of the current User Coordinate System (UCS). 0 degrees is the default angle for the hatch pattern. Clicking on the down arrow will display a list of available angles at 15-degree increments starting with 0 degrees and ending with 345 degrees. Figure 20–7 shows some of the angles displayed inside the Angle: drop-down list. To make an angle current, click on the angle from the list. If the angle you want is not listed, highlight the current angle and enter the new angle. You can set the hatch pattern angle at the command line by using the HPANG system variable. If a new angle is set using this method, it will be displayed as the current angle the next time the Boundary Hatch dialog box is accessed during the current drawing session.

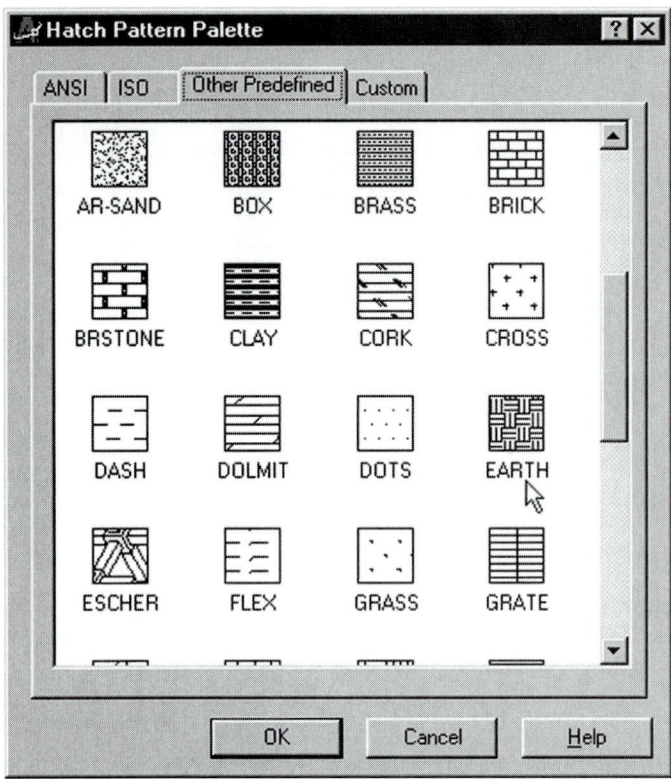

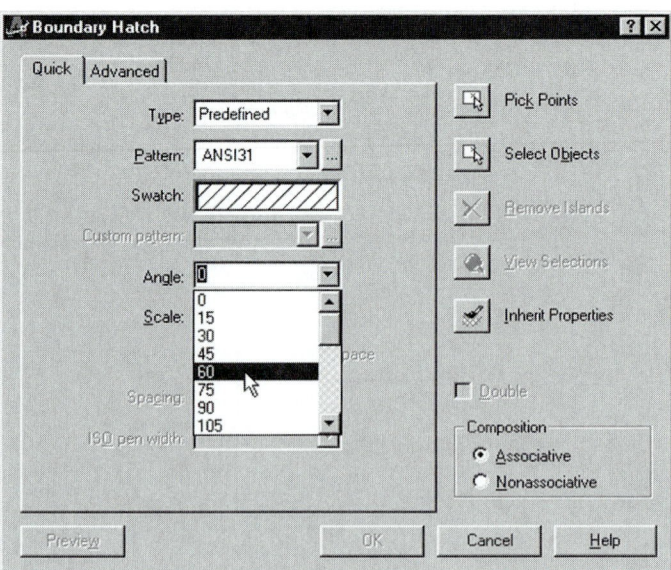

FIGURE 20–7   The Angle: drop-down list is used to select the angle for the hatch pattern, or a new angle can be entered.

FIGURE 20–6   The Hatch Pattern Palette dialog box will help you select ANSI, ISO, Other Predefined, or Custom hatch pattern type.

- **SCALE:**   (drop-down list). This area will allow you to specify a scale for the current hatch pattern. The default scale is 1.00. At full scale (1″ = 1″) and at a scale factor of 1, the ANSI31 hatch pattern will have the 45 degree lines displayed as 1 unit apart. If the scale is set to 2.00, the distance between the 45 degree lines will be two units. Figure 20–8 shows examples of ANSI31 hatch pattern with scale values of 1.00, 2.00, and 5.00. The HPSCALE system variable can be entered at the command line to specify a new scale value. Notice that the drawing in Figure 20–8 is at full scale. If you are using a different scale, adjust the scale by entering a higher or lower scale value. It might become a cumbersome procedure to find the appropriate scale for a hatch pattern using an architectural scale such as 1/4″ = 1′–0″ because the hatch pattern scale references the model space at full scale. For a drawing that is not at full scale this becomes a problem. For example, if you use ANSI31 with a scale of 1.00 to hatch a wall segment in a floor plan with a scale of 1/4″ = 1′–0″, the wall segment will be hatched solid because the drawing scale factor does not correspond to the hatch scale factor in model space. This is true for the hatch patterns listed in the ANSI tab when used in architectural settings. Figure 20–9 shows a 1/4″ = 1′–0″ scale floor plan with ANSI31 hatch pattern with a scale of 1.00 and 20.00. Notice that the 1.00 scale hatch pattern is applied solid and the 20.00 scale hatch pattern is at a more appropriate scale. You can apply the hatch pattern at the appropriate scale using two different methods:

1. Reference the hatch pattern scale to Paper Space. This is accomplished by selecting the Relative to paper space check box inside the Boundary Hatch dialog box, which is explained below. Keep in mind that a scale value less than one will result in a denser pattern, and a scale value more than one will result in a looser pattern. If no hatch pattern appears after setting a hatch scale, the message *"Hatch spacing too dense, or dash size too small"* will be displayed.

2. Set a different hatching scale value in Model. This is accomplished by adjusting the scale of a hatch pattern when applying it to drawings with architectural scale in model space (see

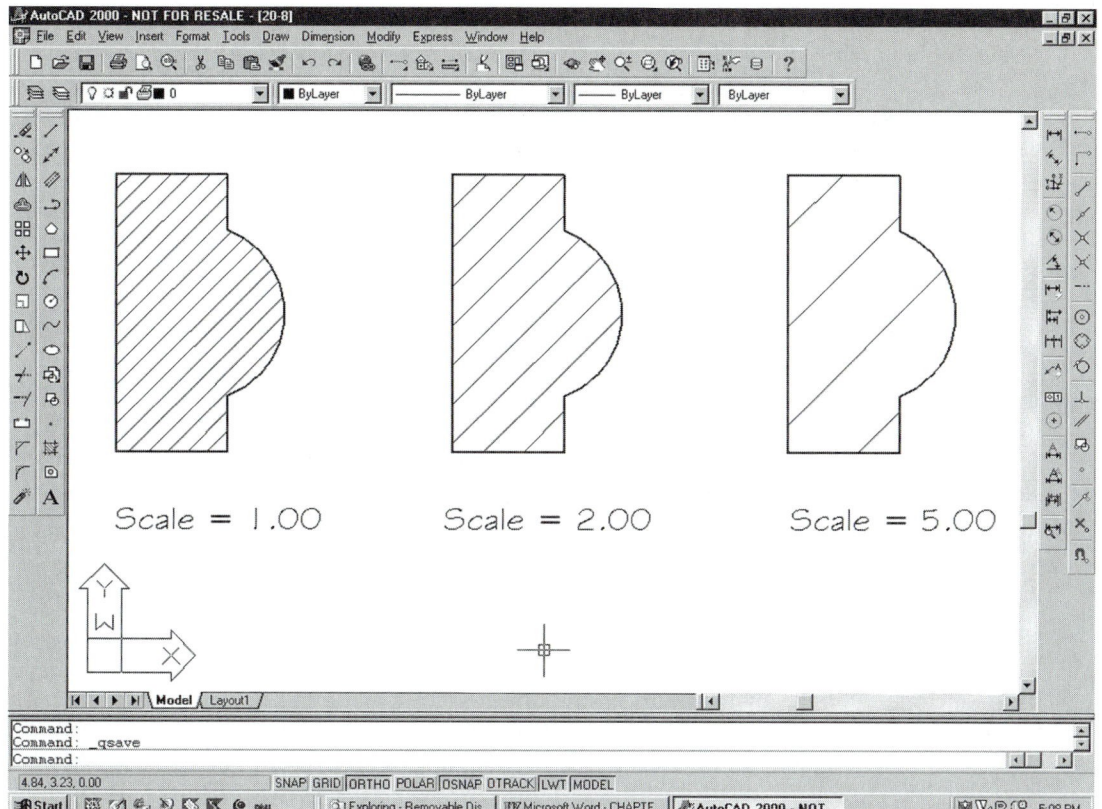

FIGURE 20–8
Examples of the
ANSI31 hatch pattern
with three different
scales. The drawing has
a 1″ = 1″ scale.

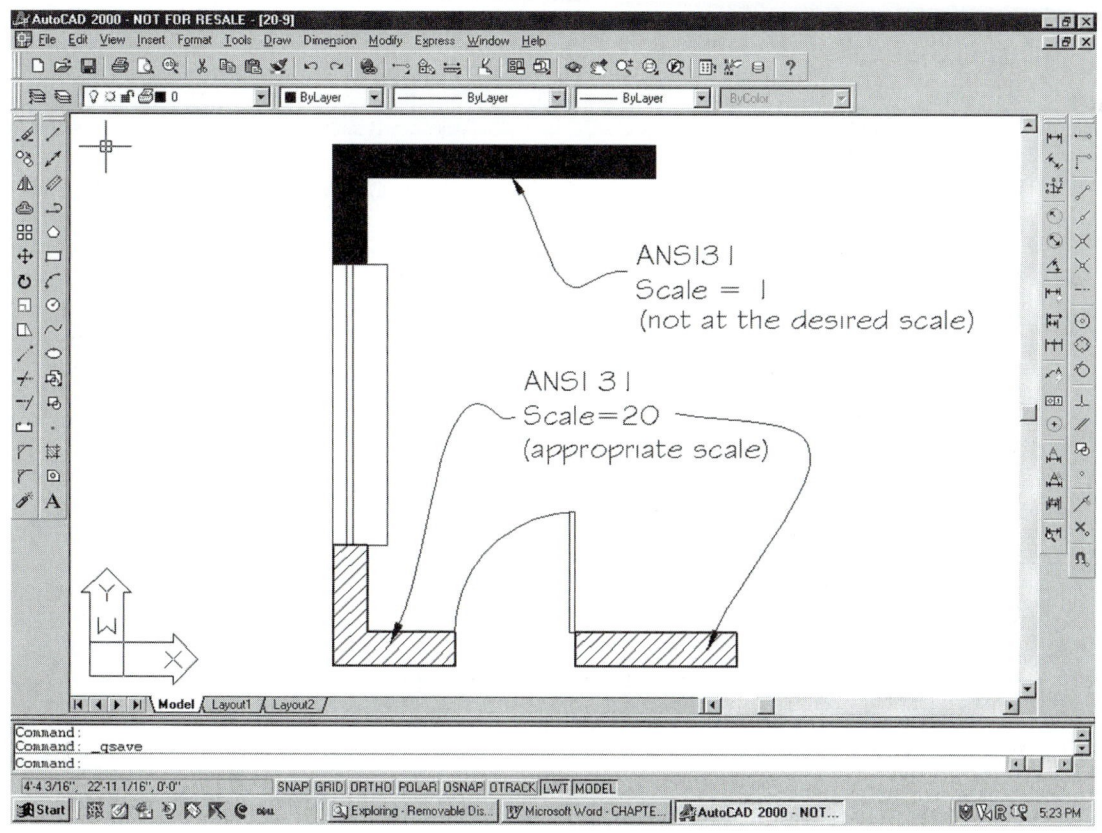

FIGURE 20–9 Example
of the ANSI31 hatch
pattern on a floor plan
with a 1/4″ = 1′–0″ scale.
Notice the 1.00 scale
hatch pattern is applied
solid.

Figure 20–9). Also, Figure 20–24 shows a wall segment having a 1/8″ = 1′–0″ architectural scale with a hatch pattern of ANSI31 using three different hatch scales in model space.

- **RELATIVE TO PAPER SPACE:** (check box). Checking this box will scale the hatch patterns inside the ANSI tab relative to paper space units. This is appropriate if plotting is done through paper space with 1″ = 1″ plot scale. In this case the selected ANSI hatch pattern with a scale of 1.00 will be scaled correctly at any architectural scale drawing. However, in order for this to work you must select a Layout tab and apply hatching in Layout. Figure 20–10 shows the same floor plan in Figure 20–9 in Layout 1 tab with ANSI31 hatch pattern with a scale of 1.00. Some of the hatch patterns in the Other Predefined tab work in the same way as the ANSI patterns. Use the Layout tab and apply hatching in Layout with a scale of 1.00 and place a checkmark inside the Relative to paper space check box.

- **SPACING:** (text box). This area will allow you to specify the spacing of lines in a user-defined hatch pattern. It is available only when the hatch Type is set to User defined. The HPSPACE system variable can be entered at the command line to specify spacing for a user-defined hatch pattern.

- **ISO PEN WIDTH:** (drop-down list). This area will allow you to scale an ISO predefined hatch pattern based on the pen width you choose. It is available only when the hatch type is set to Predefined and when the Pattern is set to one of the available ISO patterns.

- **PICK POINTS:** (button). This button controls the way you define an area to be hatched by selecting an internal point of a closed object. AutoCAD will determine an internal boundary from an existing object by highlighting the object to be hatched. This is called the boundary definition. This method of hatching depends on the Island Detection method selected from the Advanced tab. AutoCAD detects objects inside the outer boundary as islands. Islands are usually not hatched. When objects within objects are created, islands are formed and therefore detected. When an island is detected, AutoCAD includes it in the boundary definition.

FIGURE 20–10   The ANSI31 hatch pattern applied in layout 1 with a scale of 1.00 when the Relative to paper space check box is checked.

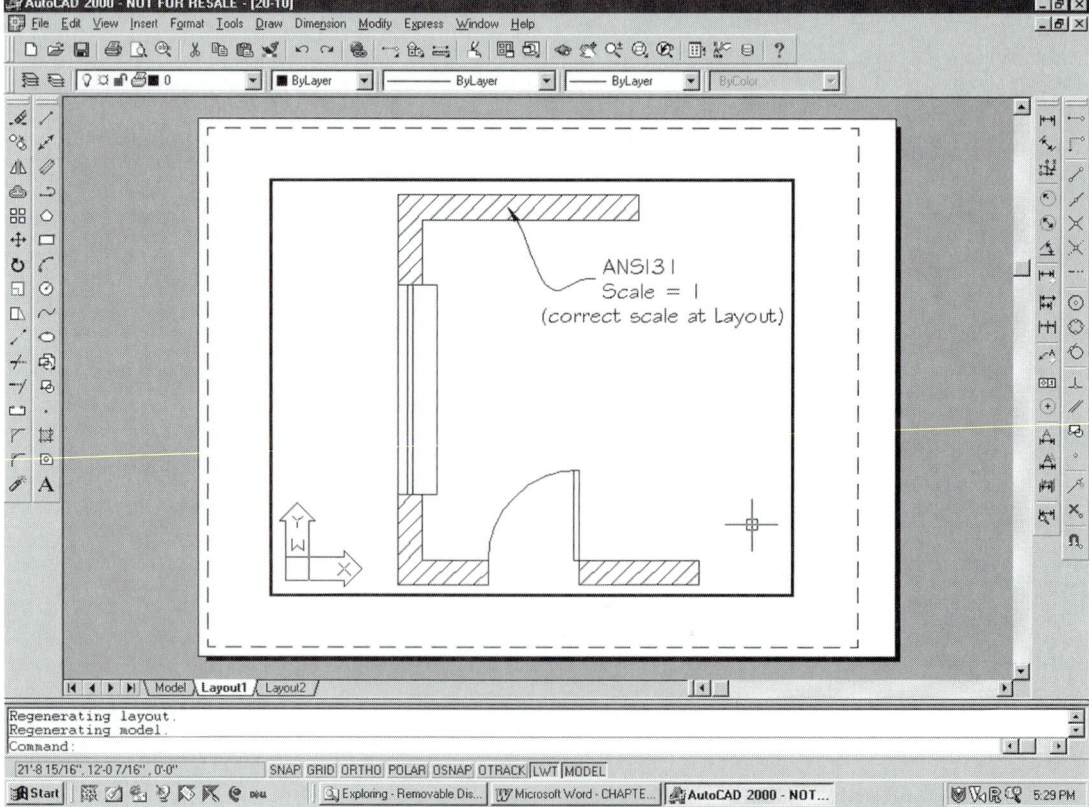

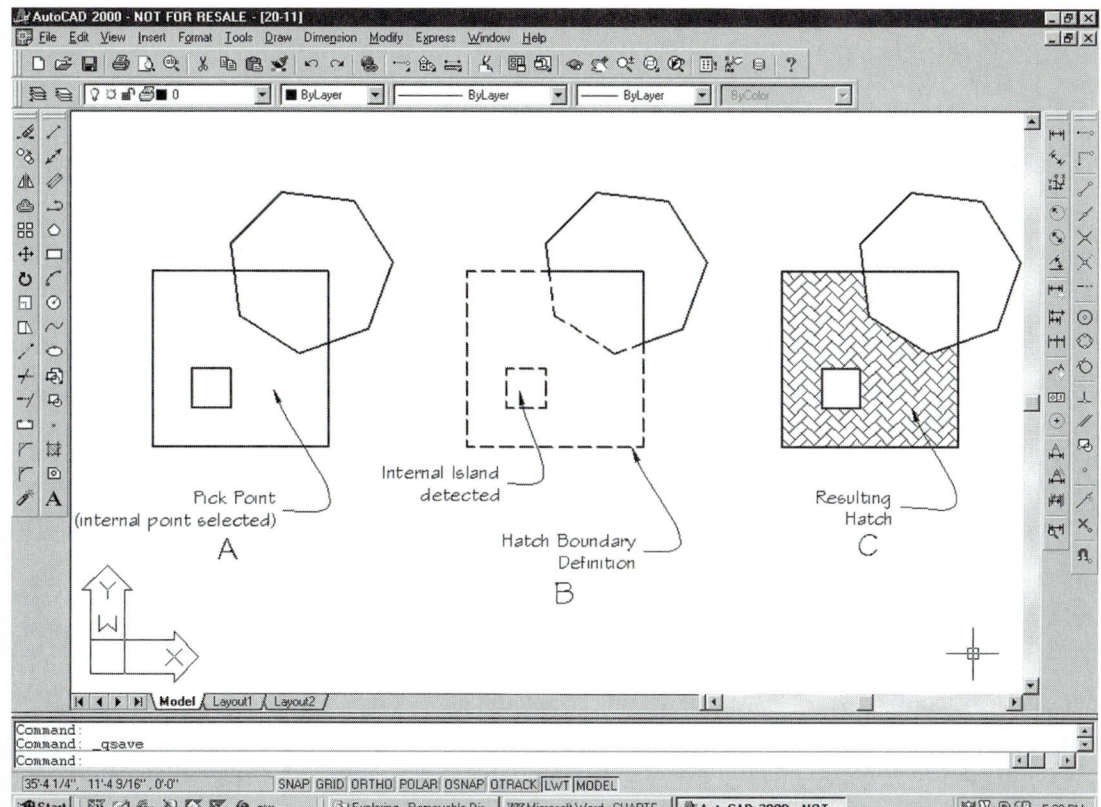

FIGURE 20–11
Selecting the Pick Points button will prompt you to select an internal point to be hatched.

Figure 20–11A shows a seven-sided polygon crossing a square and a smaller square inside the large square. When you select the Pick Points button, the Boundary Hatch dialog box temporarily disappears and AutoCAD prompts you to select an internal point within the region to be hatched. When the *Island detection method* inside the Advanced tab is set to *Flood* and when the *Island detection style* is set to *Normal,* AutoCAD automatically detects objects within the outermost boundary as islands and includes them in the definition of the boundary. Notice that the small square is detected as an internal island within the large square and therefore is not hatched. When you select the Pick Points button, the command line procedure will be as follows:

```
Command: _bhatch
Select internal point: (select a point within the area such as
the internal point of the large square as shown in Figure 20-11A)
Analyzing the selected data...
Analyzing internal islands...(both squares will be selected
automatically as shown in Figure 20-11B)
Select internal point: (right click and select Enter. This will display
the Boundary Hatch dialog box. You can also enter U or UNDO to undo the
last selection.)
```

Click on the OK button. The selected boundary will be hatched as shown in Figure 20–11C. While selecting internal point(s) you can right click in the drawing area at any time. This will display a shortcut menu as shown in Figure 20–12. From this shortcut menu, you can undo the selection, change the selection method, change the island detection style, or preview the hatch before applying.

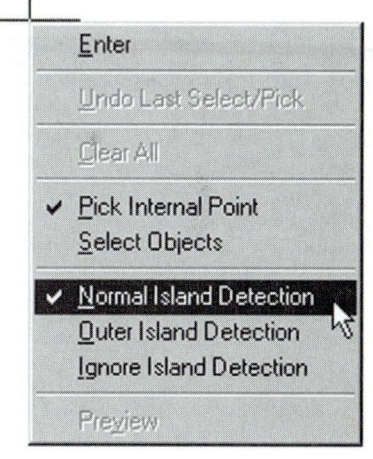

FIGURE 20–12 When you right click after selecting the internal point, a shortcut menu will be displayed with options to choose from.

- **SELECT OBJECTS:** (button). This is the second method to define an area to be hatched. With this method, you simply click on the objects to define the boundary. If the object is a closed polygon, selecting one entity will highlight the entire object. If the closed object is made out of individual entities, you must select all entities that define the object or you can use any of the selection methods to define the boundary. When you define boundaries with this method, the interior islands are not detected automatically because you are not selecting an internal point. To detect internal islands, you must select the objects within the selected boundary to be hatched. This method of hatching also depends on the Island Detection Method selected from the Advanced tab in the Boundary Hatch dialog box.

Figure 20–13 shows the same objects in Figure 20–11. When you click on the Select Objects button, the Boundary Hatch dialog box temporarily disappears and AutoCAD prompts you to select objects to define the boundary to be hatched. When the four lines that define the large square are selected, the small square and the parts of the polygon are not detected and therefore hatching will be applied to the entire area of the large square. The command line procedure for the Select Objects option is as follows:

```
Command: _bhatch
Select objects: (select the four lines of the large square as shown in
Figure 20-13A)
Select objects: 1 found, 4 total (four lines will be selected as shown in
Figure 20-13B)
Select objects: ~EnterKey~ (this will display the Boundary Hatch dialog
box)
Click on the OK button. The selected boundary will be hatched as shown in
Figure 20-13C.
```

Figure 20–14 shows the resulting hatch when four lines of the large and four lines of the small square are selected.

Figure 20–15 shows the resulting hatch when all objects are selected. Notice that the two islands are detected within the large square.

- **REMOVE ISLANDS:**   (button). Selecting this button will remove any of the internal islands (objects) from the boundary definition. For this option to work, you must use the Pick Points

FIGURE 20–13   The Select Objects button in the Boundary Hatch dialog box will allow you to select objects individually or by any object selection methods. Notice that the entire large square is hatched when the small square is not selected.

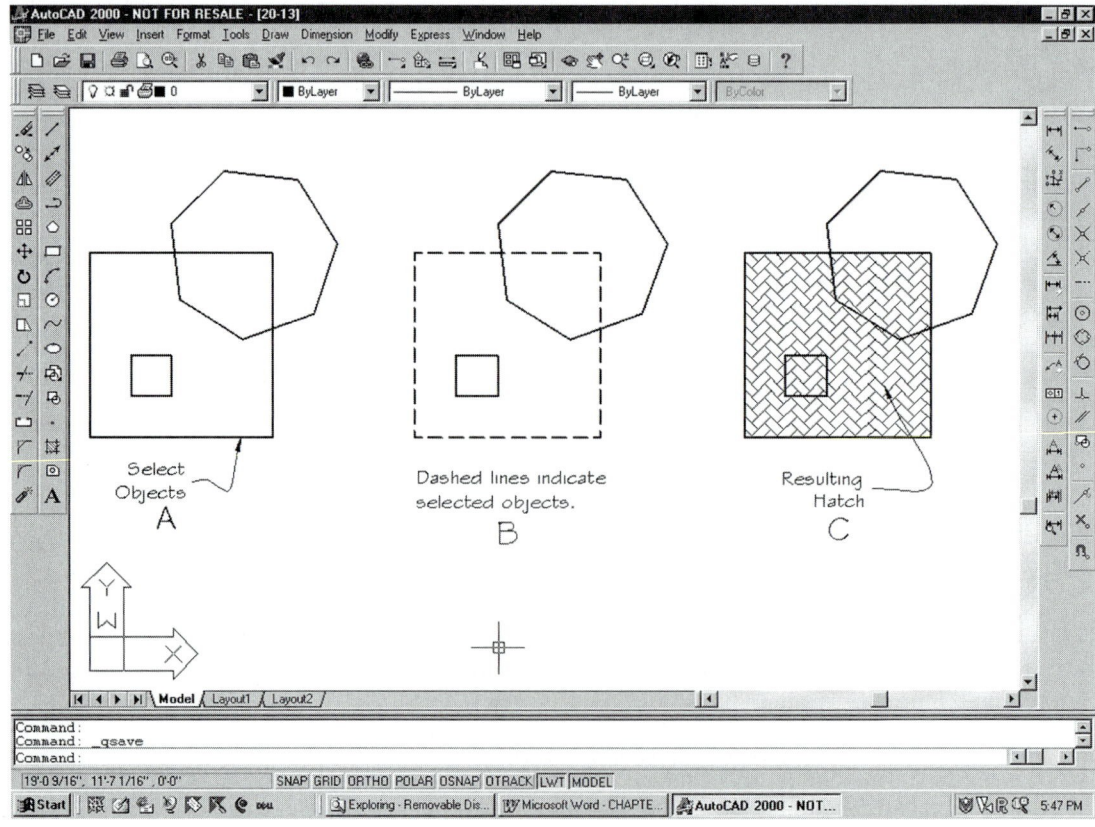

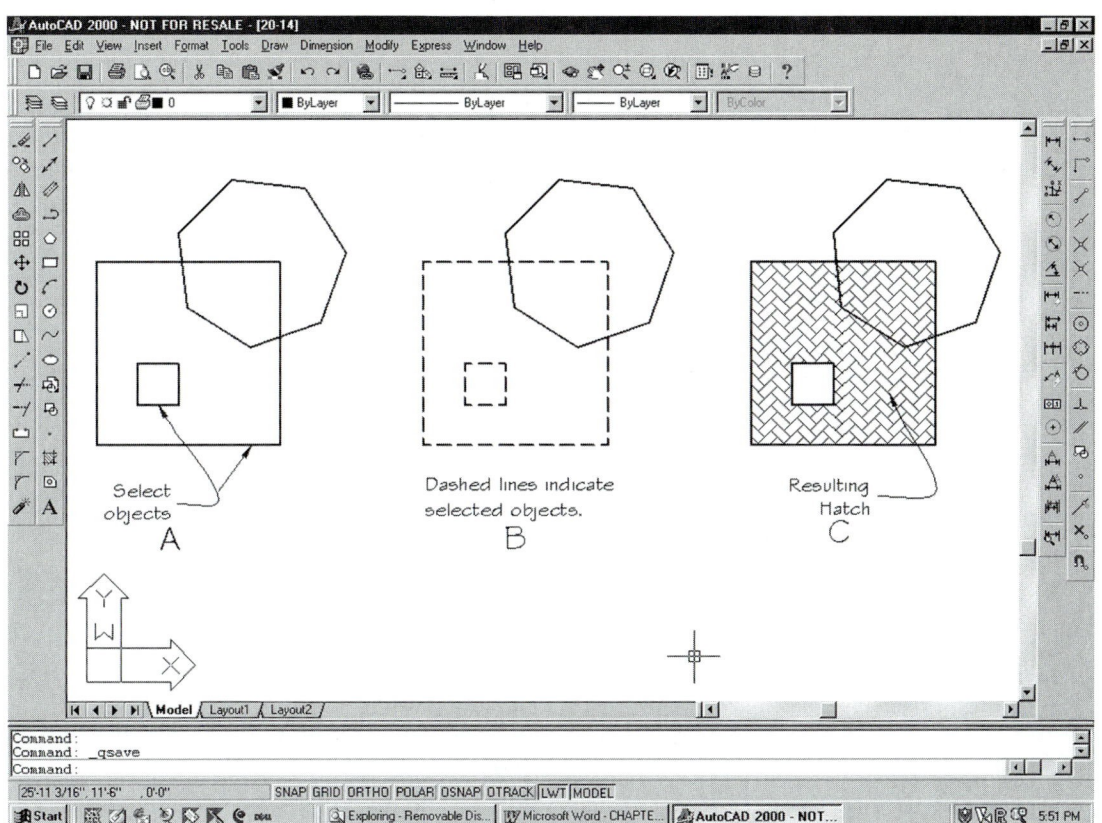

FIGURE 20–14 When the small square is selected along with the large square, the internal island is detected and the small square will not be hatched.

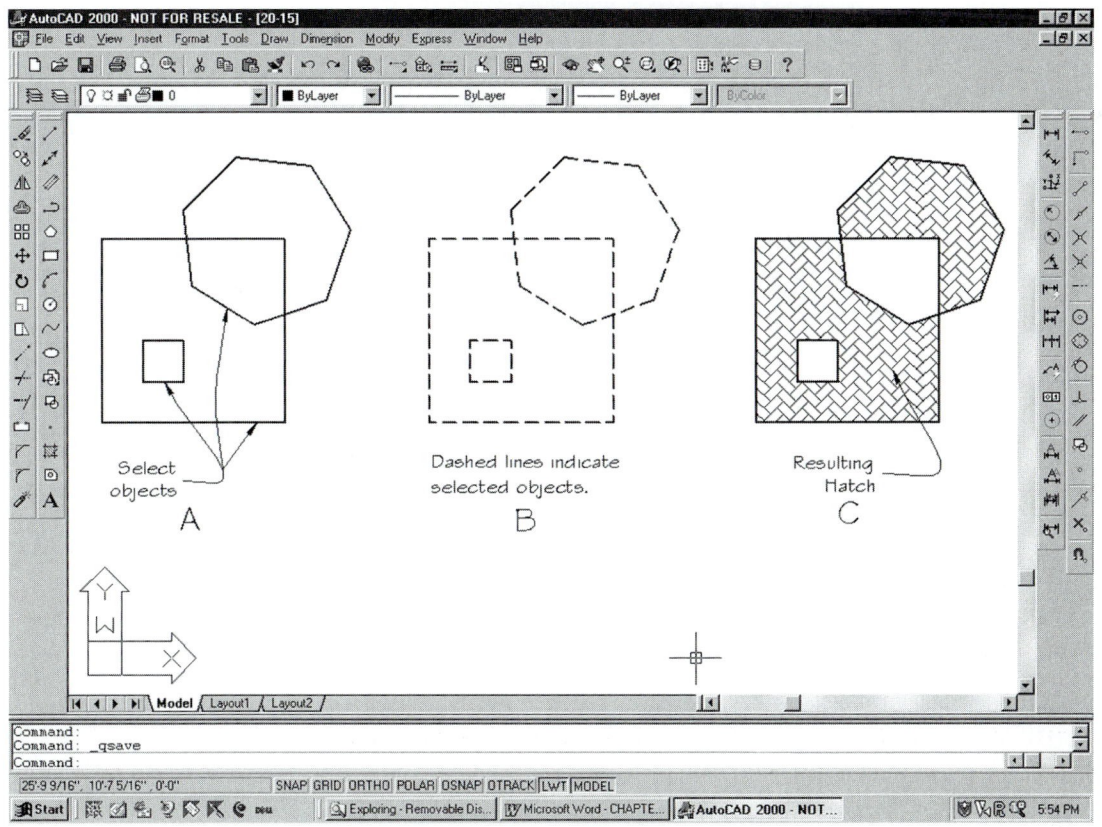

FIGURE 20–15 When all the objects are selected, all internal islands will be detected and therefore will not be hatched.

method to define the internal boundaries first, then select the Remove Islands button to select the internal islands to remove from the detection. However, you cannot remove the outer boundary.

In Figure 20–16A the Pick Points button is used to select the internal point to be hatched. After selecting the internal point, the Remove Islands button is picked from the Boundary Hatch dialog box. Finally the small square is selected as the island to be removed from the boundary selection. As a result, the small square will also be hatched. The command line procedure for the Remove Islands option is as follows:

```
Command: _bhatch
Select internal point: (select the internal point of the large square)
Analyzing the selected data...
Analyzing internal islands...(objects selected for boundary will be
selected as shown in Figure 20-16B)
Select internal point: (right click and select Enter)
Inside the Boundary hatch dialog box, click on the Remove Islands button.
Select island to remove: (select the small square)
<Select island to remove>/Undo: ~EnterKey~
```

Inside the Boundary hatch dialog box, click on the OK button. The selected boundary will be removed from island detection and will be hatched as shown in Figure 20–16C.

- **VIEW SELECTIONS:** (button). When this button is selected, the Boundary Hatch dialog box will temporarily disappear and AutoCAD will display the currently defined boundaries showing the boundary hatch settings last previewed. This option is available only when an internal point is selected or objects are selected.

- **INHERIT PROPERTIES:** (button). Selecting this button will allow you to inherit the properties of the hatch pattern of one object and apply it to another object. The existing hatch must have *associative hatch* properties.

FIGURE 20–16 The Remove Islands button will remove objects as internal islands from the boundary selection when Pick Points button is used to select internal points.

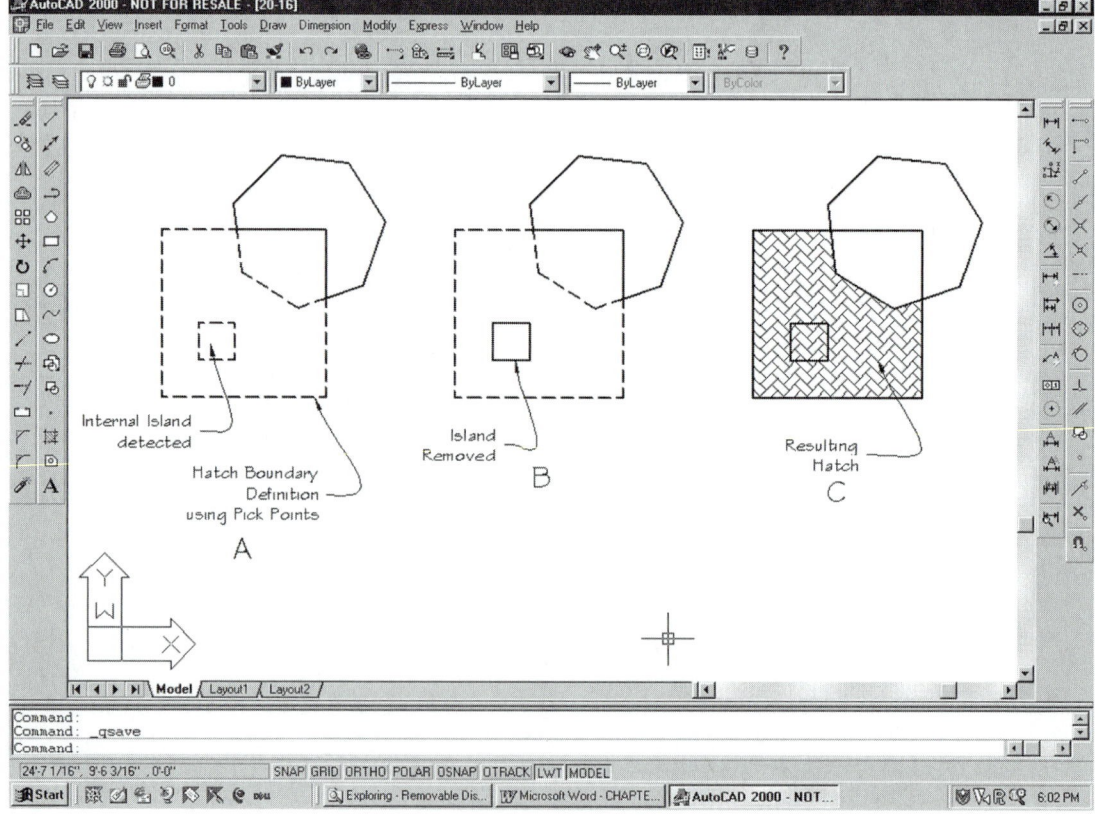

■ **EXERCISE 20–1:**   *The following step-by-step exercise will allow you to hatch the missing rigid insulation between the z-furring channels as shown in Figure 20–17 by using the Inherit Properties button in the Boundary Hatch dialog box. Notice that the rigid insulation hatch pattern on the left side of the drawing is existing and will be used to inherit its properties.*

Step #1:   Open the EXE20-1.dwg file.

Step #2:   Make the hatching layer current.

Step #3:   Click on the Hatch button in the Draw toolbar.

Step #4:   Inside the Boundary Hatch dialog box select the Inherit Properties button and use the following command line procedure:

Command: _bhatch

Select associative hatch object: *(select the existing associative hatch object as shown in Figure 20–17. This is the hatch whose properties you want to inherit)*

Inherited properties: Name <INSUL>, Scale <2.0000>, Angle <0>

Select internal point: *(select internal point 1 as shown in Figure 20–17).*

Analyzing the selected data...

Analyzing internal islands...

Select internal point: *(select internal point 2 as shown in Figure 20–17).*

Select internal point: ~EnterKey~ *(the Boundary Hatch dialog box will appear).*

Step #5:   Inside the Boundary Hatch dialog box click on the Preview button.

<Hit enter or right-click to return to the dialog>

AutoCAD will display the preview of the rigid insulation hatch pattern that you have selected.

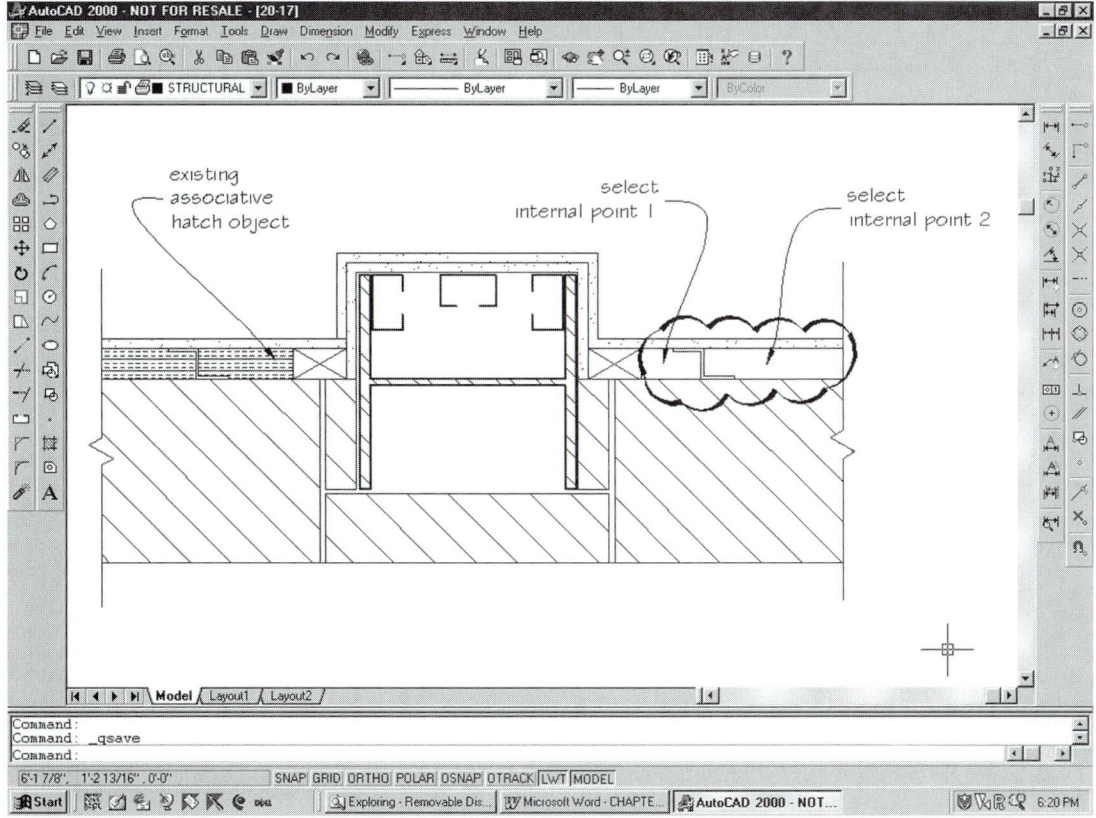

FIGURE 20–17 The Inherit Properties button will allow you to use the same hatch pattern with set properties on one or more objects.

Step #6: Press the ~EnterKey~. The Boundary Hatch dialog box will return. You can change any of the hatch options at this time if you like.

Step #7: Click on the OK button. The final hatch pattern will be applied.

Congratulations! You have successfully inherited the properties of an existing hatch pattern to apply it to a different area of the drawing.

- **DOUBLE:** (pick-box). Selecting this option will draw a second set of lines displayed at 90 degrees to the original lines. This is referred to as *crosshatching*. It is available only for the user-defined type of hatch. The HPDOUBLE system variable can be entered at the command line to create the double effect. Placing a checkmark inside the Double pick-box will set the HPDOUBLE system variable to 1 (on). You can actually use the user-defined as a hatch type that is composed of horizontal lines offset 1 unit from each other to create a floor tile pattern. Figure 20–18 shows two identical floor plans with a scale of 1/4″ = 1′–0″. Both floor plans have a 7′–6″ × 6′–6″ area hatched using two different hatch types to create a 6″ × 6″ tile pattern.

- ■ **EXERCISE 20–2:** *The following step-by-step exercise will allow you to create the hatch pattern as shown in the left side of Figure 20–18.*

Step #1: Open the EXE20-2.dwg file.

Step #2: Click on the Hatch button in the Draw toolbar. This will display the Boundary Hatch dialog box.

Step #3: Select the Quick tab and set the Type to User-defined. Set the Angle to 0 and set the Spacing to 6″.

Step #4: Place a checkmark inside the Double check box. The Swatch display box should now display crosshatching (horizontal and vertical lines crossing each other at a 90 degree angle).

FIGURE 20–18 Two identical floor plans with the same floor tile pattern created by using two different hatch type and pattern and different settings.

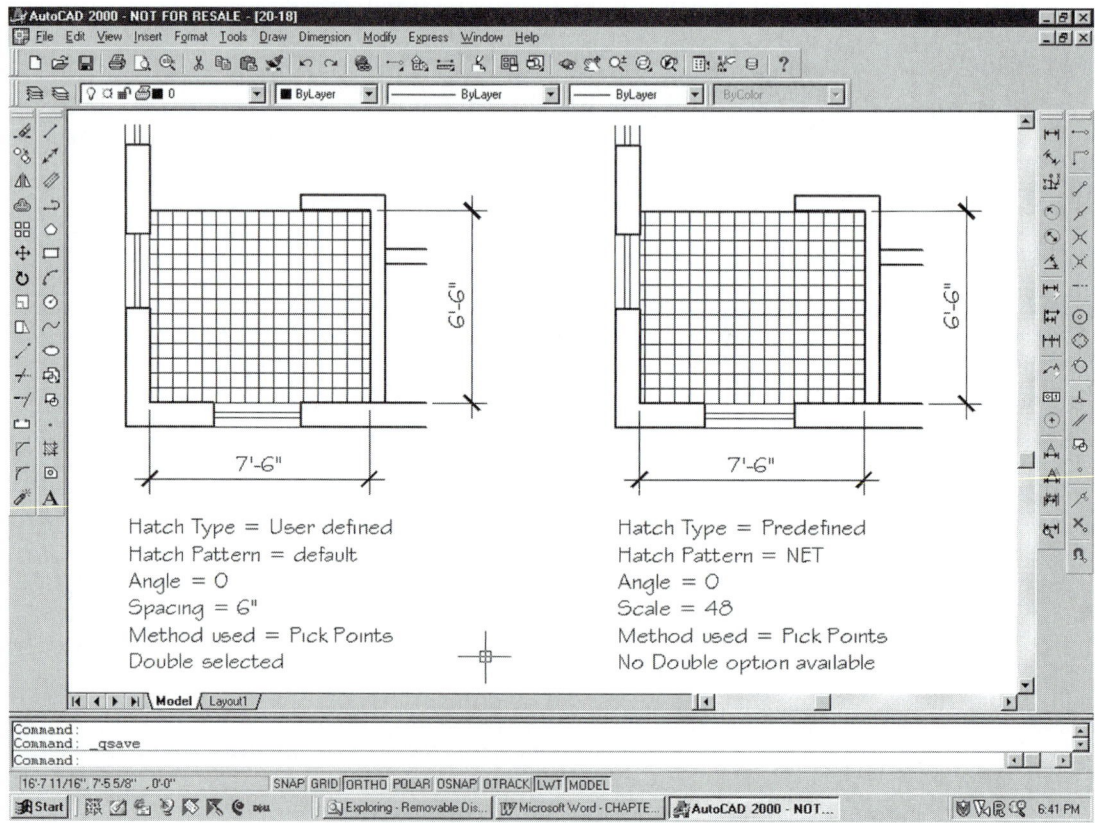

Step #5: Click on the Pick Points button and select the floor area as the internal point. The floor boundary will be displayed as dashed lines.

Step #6: Press the ~EnterKey~.

Step #7: Inside the Boundary Hatch dialog box click on the OK button.

Congratulations! You have successfully created a hatch pattern in a floor plan using the Boundary Hatch dialog box. This will create a 6″ × 6″ floor tile pattern as shown in Figure 20–18.

Composition: (category). This category will allow you to select either associative or nonassociative composition for the hatch pattern. The two options are *associative* and *nonassociative*.

- **ASSOCIATIVE:** (radio button). Selecting this option will apply the hatch pattern as associative. This means that the hatch pattern is associated with its boundaries. An associative hatch pattern is automatically updated when the boundary area is edited. For example, when you stretch an object having an associative hatch pattern, the hatch pattern will automatically update to reflect any changes. An associative hatch pattern is a whole unit similar to associative dimension. This means that if you select one hatch line segment to erase, the entire hatch pattern will be erased. You can explode an associative hatch pattern using the EXPLODE command. This will create individual hatch line segments but will remove hatch boundary associativity.

- **NONASSOCIATIVE:** (radio button). Selecting this option will create a nonassociative hatch pattern. This means that the hatch pattern is not associated with its boundaries. A nonassociative hatch pattern is not automatically updated when the boundary area is edited. A nonassociative hatch pattern is still a whole unit. For example, if you select one hatch line segment to move, the entire hatch pattern will be moved. Exploding a nonassociative hatch pattern will create individual hatch line segments.

- **PREVIEW:** (button). Selecting this option after picking points or selecting objects to be hatched will allow you to preview the hatch pattern before you apply it. After selecting this option the Boundary hatch dialog box will temporarily disappear and the currently defined boundaries with the current hatch settings will be displayed. This will give you the opportunity to see if any changes are needed before the hatch pattern is applied. If you are satisfied with the hatch pattern results, click on the OK button to apply hatching.

Tips: You can select more than one internal point or objects for hatching, but if you plan to edit the boundary or the hatch pattern later, multiple hatch patterns will be edited at the same time. This may produce undesired effects therefore you should create hatching one area at a time.

TIPS

20.1.2 Using the Advanced Tab

Under regular use and applications the Quick tab provides enough tools to create fast and efficient boundary hatching. The Advanced tab provides additional tools to create and hatch more complex areas. For large and complex areas to be hatched, AutoCAD evaluates the entire region that is visible on the screen to create the boundary and any islands that need to be detected. This tab is used to improve the hatching process and resolve some of the complex issues. The Advanced tab is shown in Figure 20–19.

The Advanced tab has four categories as follows:

Island Detection Style: (category). This category will allow you to specify the method for hatching objects within the outermost hatch boundary. If there are no internal islands and boundaries to be detected, specifying an island detection style will have no effect on the hatch pattern method. However, if there are any internal islands or boundaries within the outermost hatch boundary their application can be controlled using three island detection styles as follows:

- **NORMAL:** (radio button). This island detection style will hatch every other island starting from the outermost boundary and moving inward. When AutoCAD detects an internal island, the hatching is turned off automatically until it detects the next internal island. You

FIGURE 20–19 The Advanced tab of the Boundary Hatch dialog box is used to establish island detection styles and methods, including current viewport boundary settings.

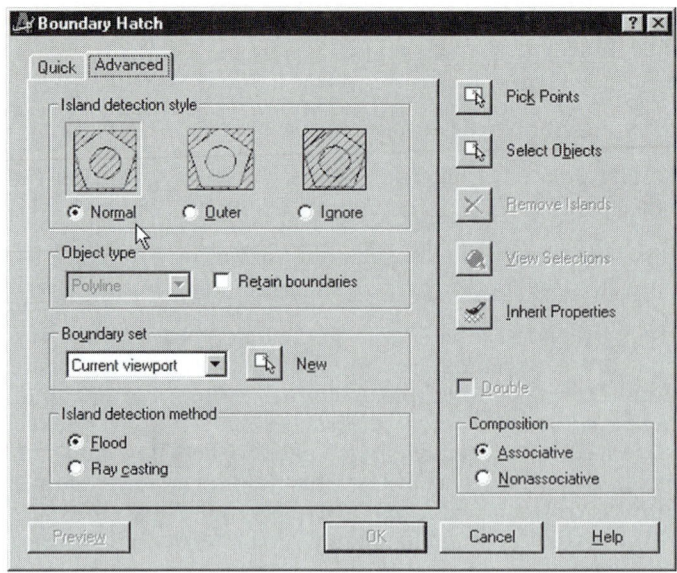

can also set the Normal style by entering **,N** after the HPNAME system variable at the command line as follows:

```
Command: HPNAME ~EnterKey~
Enter new value for HPNAME <"ANSI31">: BRASS,N ~EnterKey~
```

The Brass hatch pattern is now set current with island detection style as Normal.

Figure 20–20 shows an example of how Normal Island detection style can be used to hatch an elevation of a building.

- **OUTER:**   (radio button). This island detection style will hatch only the outermost area and will leave all internal islands blank. You can also set the Outer style by entering **,O** after the HPNAME system variable at the command line. Figure 20–21 shows the effect of the Outer style.

- **IGNORE:**   (radio button). This island detection style will ignore all internal islands and will hatch through them. You can also set the Ignore style by entering **,I** after the HPNAME system variable at the command line.

  Note: The Normal, Outer, and Ignore Island detection styles are also available from the shortcut menu when you right-click in the drawing area after you specify points or select objects for hatching.

Object Type: (category). This category will allow you to retain hatch boundaries as objects and control the type of the new boundary object. A boundary is created as a polyline or region.

- **RETAIN BOUNDARIES:**   (check box). This option will allow you to keep the boundary of a hatched area as a polyline or a region. When this option is selected, the Object type will display Polyline and Region as the boundary object type. When Polyline is selected as the Object type, AutoCAD will create a polyline boundary around the outermost edges of the selected internal point. Figure 20–22 shows a kitchen plan with the ANSI31 hatch pattern. The drawing on the left shows the original line objects used as the boundary for the hatching. The drawing on the right shows the original boundary created and converted to polyline after the hatching is applied with the Retain boundaries option checked and Polyline as the Object type. This is useful when you have a floor plan and want to apply different hatching to indicate spaces and later remove it from the floor plan as polyline boundaries. For example, a schematic rental plan of an office building with rental spaces can be created from the original office plan with this option. After the rental spaces are hatched, the hatching can be removed from the complex plan

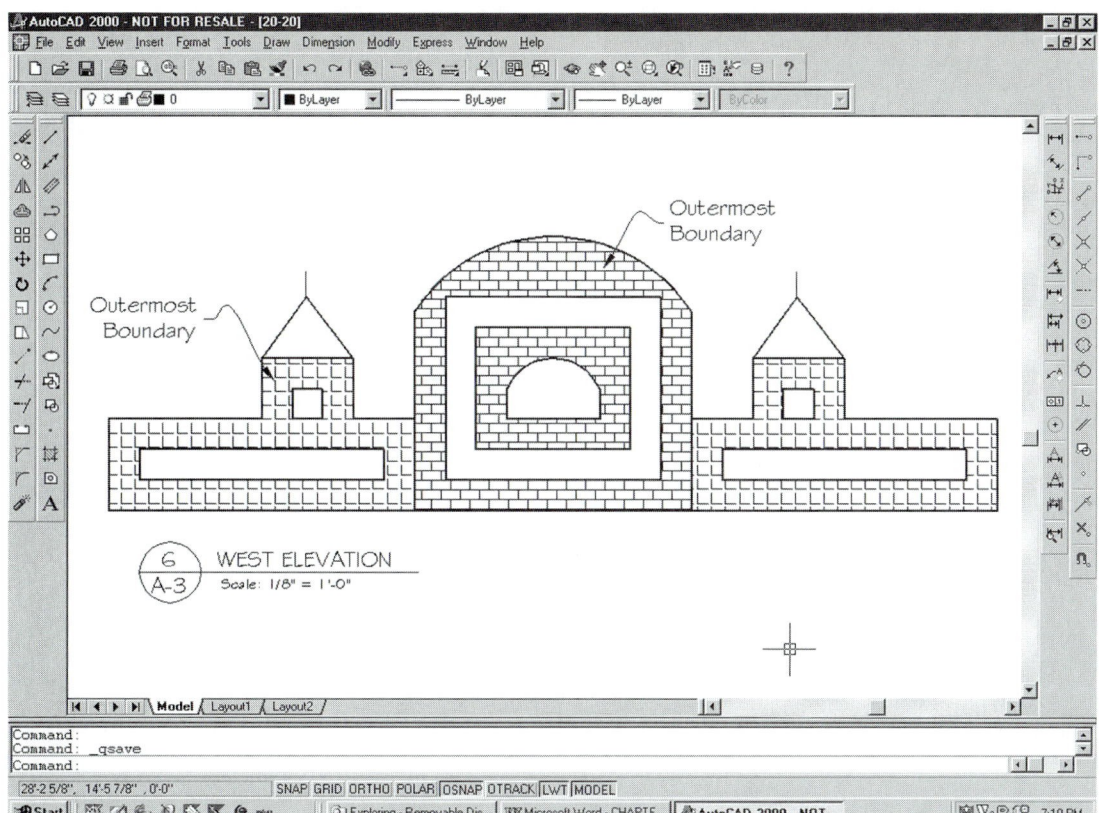

FIGURE 20–20 The Normal Island detection style will hatch every other feature on this elevation starting from the outer boundary.

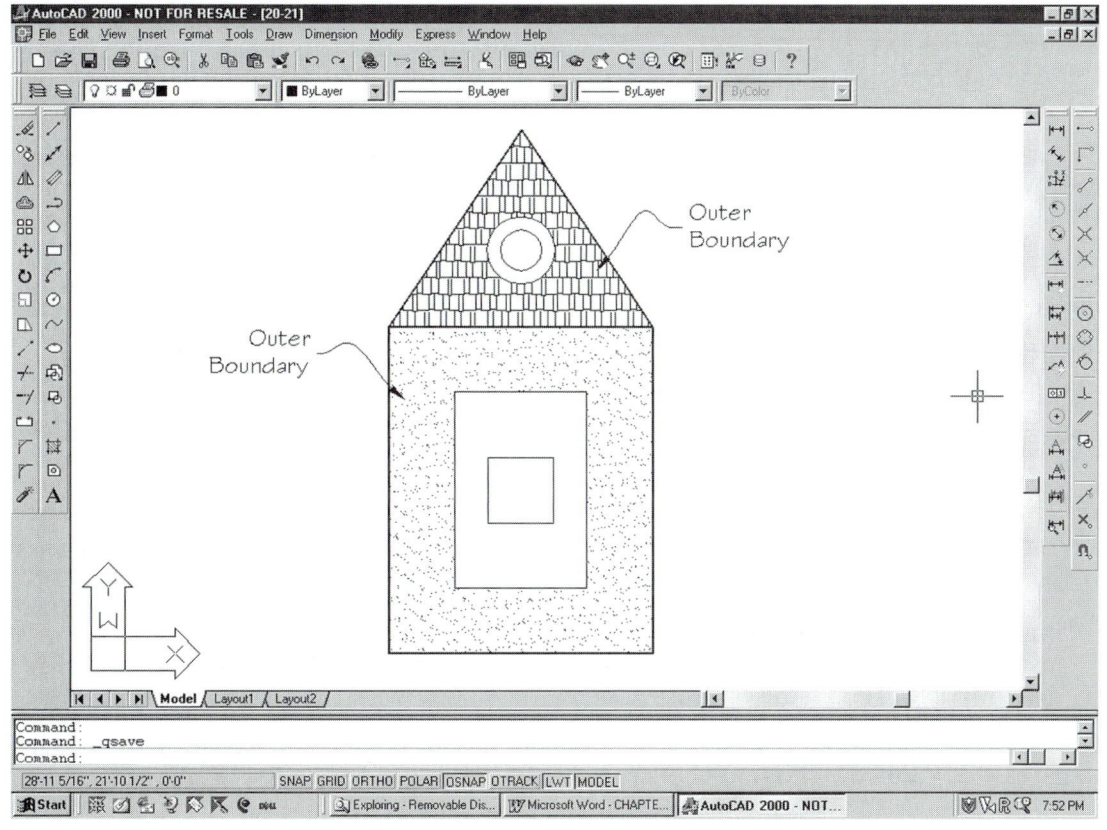

FIGURE 20–21 The Outer Island detection style will hatch only the outermost area, leaving the internal islands blank.

FIGURE 20–22 A hatch pattern and a boundary as a polyline is created from an existing line object.

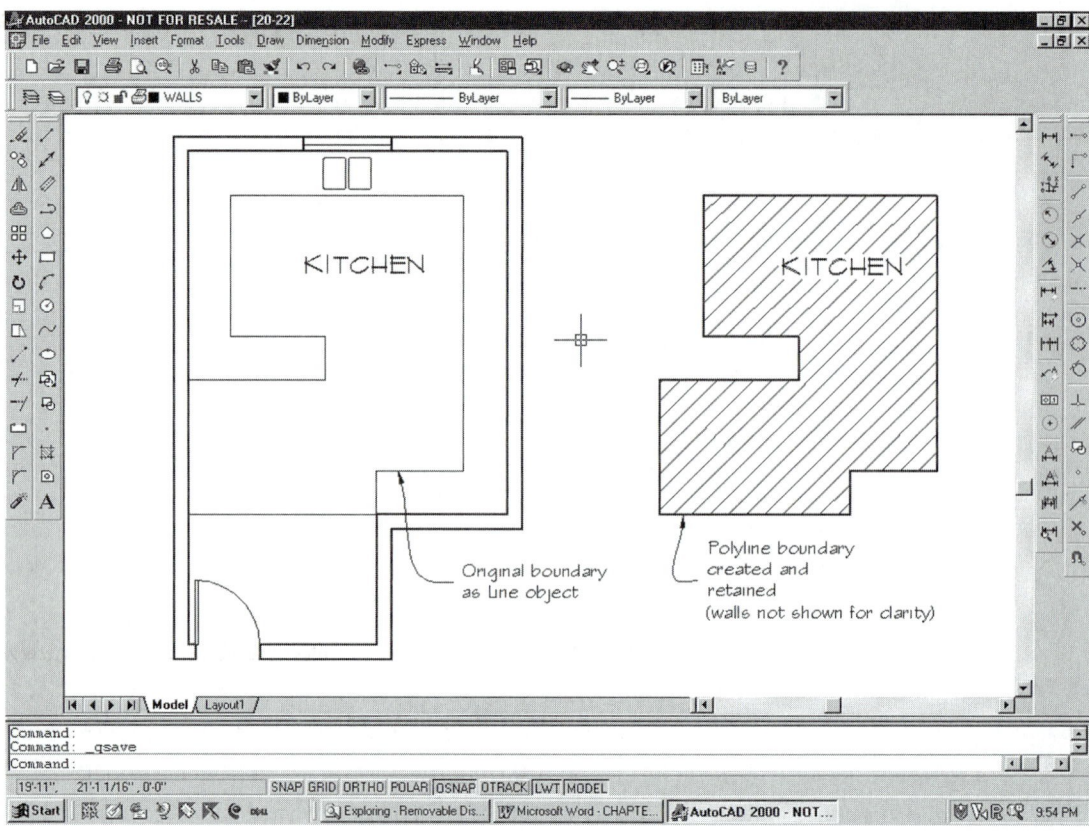

and the plan presented as a simple schematic rental plan to the client. You can also add a boundary as a region. Regions are two-dimensional closed objects. In addition to applying hatching and shading to regions, you can also analyze properties such as their area and moments of inertia.

Boundary Set: (category). This category will allow you to define objects that AutoCAD analyzes when defining a boundary when the Pick Points method is used to select an internal point. By default, when you define a boundary using the Pick Points method, AutoCAD analyzes and evaluates the entire drawing. This process can take a considerable amount of time on large projects. To speed up the process, you can redefine the boundary set and disregard certain objects without having to hide or remove those objects. With this method AutoCAD analyzes fewer objects.

- **CURRENT VIEWPORT:** The current viewport boundary set is the default where AutoCAD defines the boundary set from all objects visible in the current viewport. If there is a current boundary established, it will be discarded.

- **EXISTING SET:** This option is displayed only when you define a boundary using the New button.

- **NEW:** (button). Selecting this button will prompt you to select objects from which you want to create the new boundary set. When you select this option, the Boundary hatch dialog box will temporarily disappear and AutoCAD will prompt you to select objects. Existing boundary sets are discarded and replaced with the new boundary set. Only the objects that can be hatched are included in the new boundary set. If there are no objects to be hatched, AutoCAD will retain the current set.

Island Detection Method: (category). This category specifies whether to include or exclude internal islands within the outermost boundary.

- **FLOOD:** (radio button). Selecting this option will include internal islands as boundary objects. As a result, the detected internal islands will not be hatched.

- **RAY CASTING:** (radio button). Selecting this option will exclude internal islands as boundary objects. As a result, the entire object will be hatched.

20.2 USING ANSI HATCH PATTERNS

There are eight predefined ANSI hatch patterns in the Hatch Pattern Palette dialog box. These hatch patterns are mostly used in section views on mechanical drawings but can also be used on architectural drawings. The ANSI31 pattern is a general section line symbol used in mechanical drawings but it can be used in floor plans to indicate brick as a material. The ANSI37 hatch pattern can be used in architectural drawings to indicate concrete block as a material. Figure 20–23 shows two wall segments with the ANSI31 hatch pattern using two different hatch scales. Notice that the hatch scale of 96 represents the scale factor for the 1/8″ = 1′–0″ drawing scale. When the hatch scale is set to 96, the distance between the hatch lines will be 1′–5″. As the hatch scale is decreased, the distance between the hatch lines will also decrease. It might be less complicated to use the Relative to paper space check box to create ANSI hatch patterns in layouts as shown in Figure 20–10.

Figure 20–24 shows three wall segments with the ANSI37 hatch pattern using three different hatch scales. Notice that the drawing scale is 1/4″ = 1′–0″. The distance between hatch lines is the same as in Figure 20–23.

You might have to experiment with the hatch scales to find the appropriate hatch scale that meets your drawing requirements.

Tips: If you plan to plot through paper space at 1″ = 1″ plot scale, create hatch patterns in Layouts.

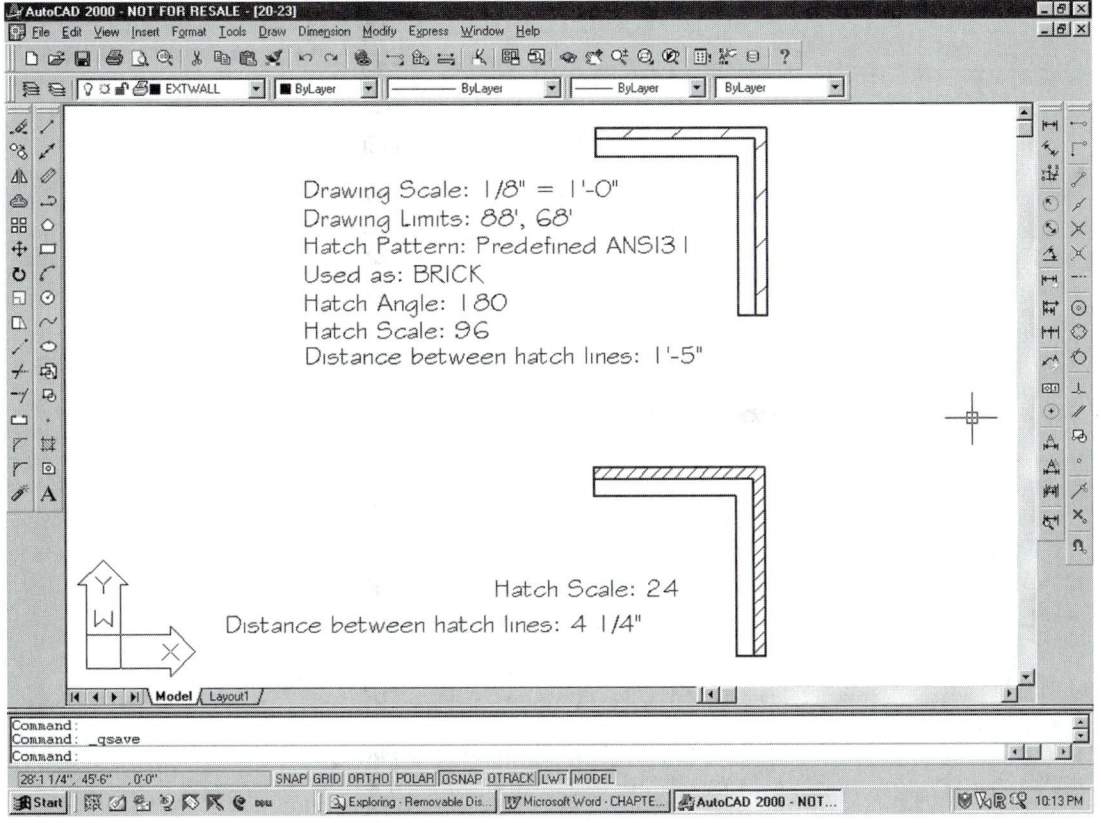

FIGURE 20–23 Three wall segments in architectural units, limits, and scale using three different hatch scales for the ANSI31 hatch pattern.

FIGURE 20–24 Three wall segments in architectural scale using three different hatch scales for the ANSI37 hatch pattern.

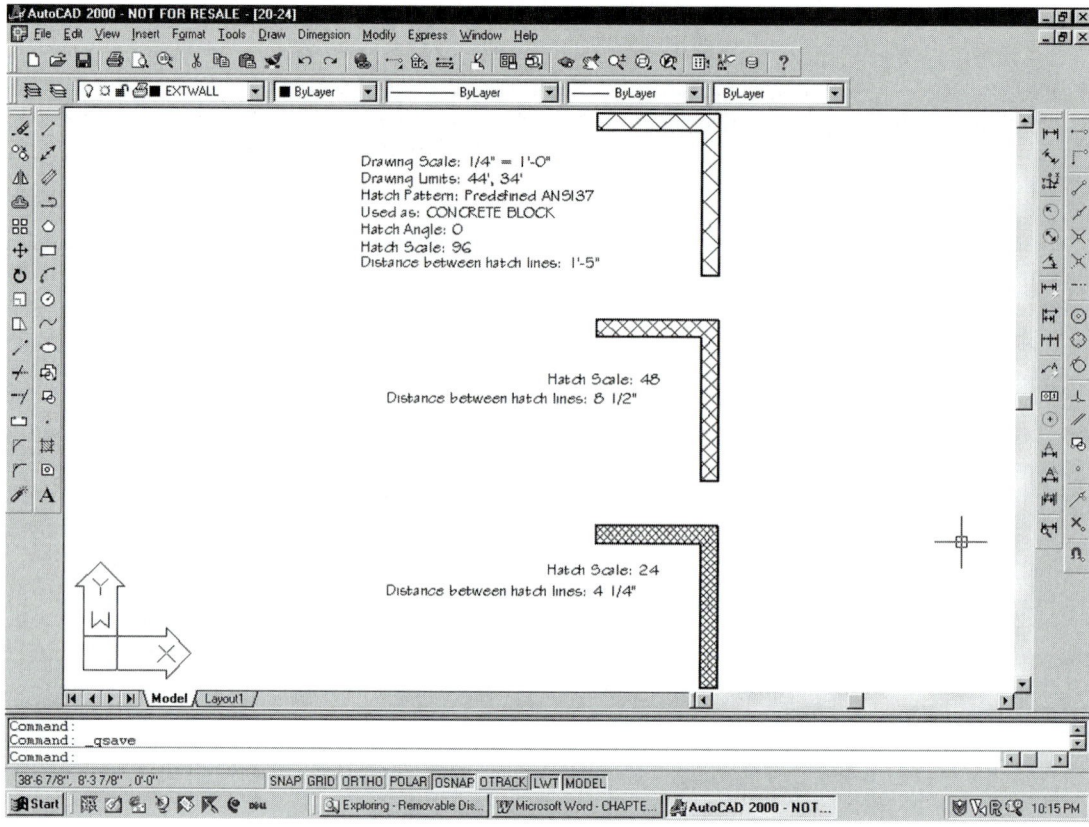

Drawing Scale: 1/4" = 1'-0"
Drawing Limits: 44', 34'
Hatch Pattern: Predefined ANSI37
Used as: CONCRETE BLOCK
Hatch Angle: 0
Hatch Scale: 96
Distance between hatch lines: 1'-5"

Hatch Scale: 48
Distance between hatch lines: 8 1/2"

Hatch Scale: 24
Distance between hatch lines: 4 1/4"

20.3 USING OTHER PREDEFINED HATCH PATTERNS

There are 46 hatch patterns in the Other Predefined tab. The first hatch pattern in the list is the SOLID hatch pattern. Selecting this hatch pattern will hatch any shape object solid. It is much simpler to use the SOLID hatch pattern as opposed to using the SOLID command to hatch objects solid because the SOLID command requires triangulation that might become very complicated for uniquely shaped objects. Some of the hatch patterns in this list are very specific to architectural applications. For example, the AR-CONC hatch pattern can be used to represent poured-in-place-concrete. The ANGLE hatch pattern can be used to represent tiled façade. The AR-BRSTD hatch pattern can be used to represent standard architectural brick. The AR-HBONE hatch pattern can be used to represent an exterior tiled walkway, and the EARTH hatch pattern can be used to represent compacted soil in a wall or building section.

Not all architecture-specific hatch patterns work with the same scale. To create visually appealing hatch patterns without knowing what scale to use, click on the Preview button to try different values or create hatching in Layouts. When a hatch scale of 1.00 is used in a layout, the corresponding scale in model space can be obtained by selecting the Model button in the Status Bar. Keep records of the hatch scales that work for future use. Some hatch patterns will give the same scale results in model and layout. For example, the partial floor plan with the AR-CONC hatch pattern shown in Figure 20–25 will display the same hatch configuration in both model space and in layout.

The following guidelines will help you save time when creating hatch patterns:

- Create a list of company standard hatch scales for all the hatch patterns used in projects. This will help everyone create hatch patterns at consistent scales.

- Try to create hatch patterns in Layouts, especially if you are planning to plot from paper space at a scale of 1″ = 1″.

- Create User defined hatch patterns for maximum flexibility.

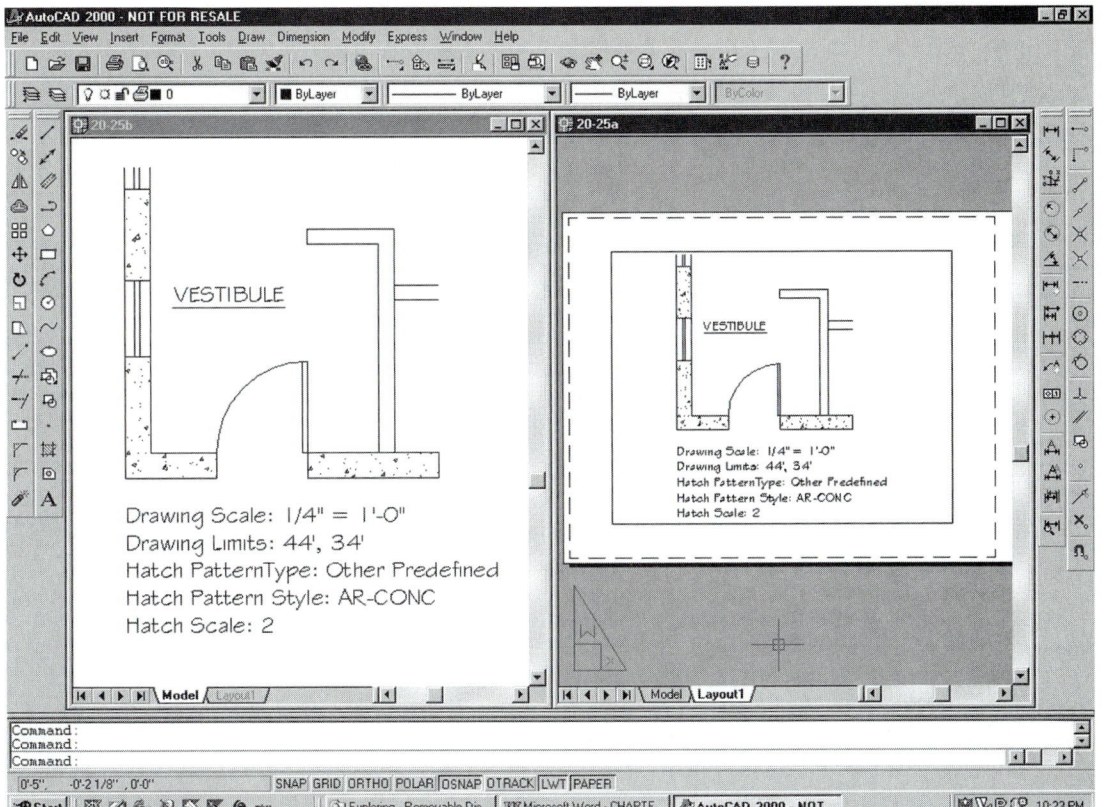

FIGURE 20–25 The AR-CONC hatch pattern will give same scale results in both Model Space and Layout.

- Create hatching one area at a time to eliminate future editing problems.
- Zoom in close to the area you are hatching. The hatching process is much faster when AutoCAD does not have to search the entire screen to find boundaries.
- Apply hatching as the last task in the drawing.
- Turn off other layers so that other objects do not interfere with selecting internal points or selecting objects to hatch.
- For complex areas, create and retain boundaries as polyline or region. This will help you pick and choose specific hatch regions for presentation purposes.
- Use the *nonassociative* composition if you are planning to custom edit individual segments of the hatch pattern.

Tips: When creating hatch patterns, make sure the object is completely closed. Even a very small gap that can be very difficult to detect will result in AutoCAD displaying the Boundary Definition Error dialog box. The same error will also be displayed when the entire object you are hatching is not visible on the screen even though you pick a point inside the boundary area. When this happens, pick the OK button and zoom out until the entire object is visible on the screen. You might have to cancel and reapply hatching if necessary.

AutoCAD 2000i Update: *AutoCAD DesignCenter (ADC) provides access to hatch patterns that can be selected from the palette, then dragged and dropped inside objects in the target drawing. The source drawing does not need to be opened. Refer to section 1.13.2 for more information. To visually see the hatch pattern being dropped at the correct scale right click on the hatch pattern and select BHATCH... from the list. Inside the Boundary Hatch dialog box, enter the appropriate scale of the hatch pattern being used in the Scale: list box and press the ~EnterKey~. Select the hatch pattern, then drag it into the drawing area. Observe the scale of the hatch pattern being dragged. Drop the hatch pattern inside*

the object in the drawing area to finish the hatch operation. Remember that these hatch patterns are not coming from an open drawing. They are the acad.pat or acadiso.pat files in the Support folder that are in the AutoCAD 2000i folder in your computer. The file path is displayed in the bottom of the DesignCenter. When you access ADC, click on the Desktop button located on top. Inside the Tree View area, navigate to the Support directory and click on acad.pat to display the available hatch patterns in the palette area.

20.4 HATCH VISIBILITY

By default, all hatch patterns created are visible on the screen. However, you can control the visibility of the hatch patterns using the FILL command or the FILLMODE system variable. The command line procedure to remove visibility with the FILL command is as follows:

```
Command: FILL ~EnterKey~
Enter mode [ON/OFF] <ON>: OFF ~EnterKey~
Command: REGEN ~EnterKey~
The actual removal of the hatch visibility is accomplished only after
regenerating the current drawing. The command line procedure to remove
visibility with the FILLMODE system variable is as follows:
Command: FILLMODE ~EnterKey~
Enter new value for FILLMODE <1>: 0 ~EnterKey~
Command: REGEN ~EnterKey~
```

To turn hatch pattern visibility back, enter ON or 1 after the command and the system variable and type REGEN.

Tips: You can also control hatch pattern visibility from the Options dialog box. Right click in the drawing area and select Options. . . from the shortcut menu. Select the display tab. In the Display performance category, place a checkmark inside the Apply solid fill check box to turn visibility on or remove the check mark to turn visibility off. Click on the Apply button and then click on the OK button. You must still enter REGEN at the command line for the setting to take effect.

20.5 USING THE HATCH COMMAND

You can create hatch patterns without using the Boundary Hatch dialog box by entering HATCH at the command line. Hatch patterns created with the HATCH command are nonassociative but they are not exploded. The Pick Points option is not available with the HATCH command, so boundary creation is accomplished by selecting objects. You can select objects individually or create a window, crossing-window, window-polygon (WP), crossing-polygon (CP), or fence (F) as a selection method. The command sequence is as follows:

```
Command: HATCH ~EnterKey~
Enter a pattern name or [?/Solid/User defined] <ANSI31>: (enter the name
of the hatch pattern)
Specify a scale for the pattern <1.00>: (enter a scale for the pattern)
Specify an angle for the pattern <0>: (enter an angle for the pattern)
Select objects to define hatch boundary or <direct hatch>,
Select objects: (select objects to define a boundary or press the
~EnterKey~ for a direct hatch option)
When you enter ? at the first command prompt, the command sequence will
be as follows:
Enter a pattern name or [?/Solid/User defined] <ANSI31>: ? ~EnterKey~
Enter pattern(s) to list <*>:
```

You can enter a pattern name or names, or press ~EnterKey~ to accept the wildcard (*), which will list all the hatch patterns by displaying the AutoCAD Text Window as shown in Figure 20–26. The list will include a brief description of each hatch pattern. The list is three pages

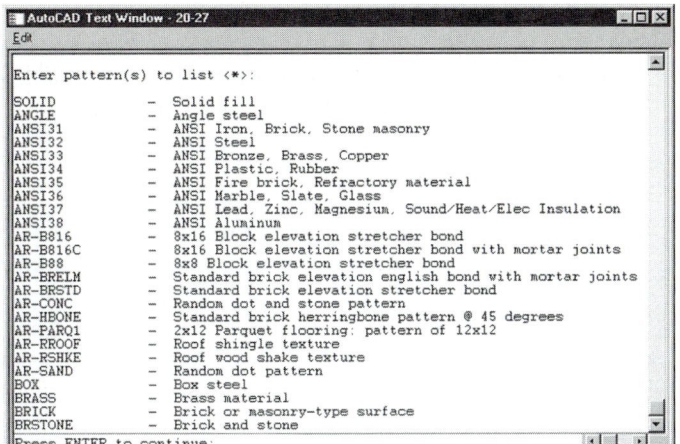

long, so use the ~EnterKey~ to scroll through the list or press ~F2Key~ to return to the AutoCAD screen.

```
When you enter SOLID at the first command prompt, the solid hatch pattern
will be used as follows:
Enter a pattern name or [?/Solid/User defined] <ANSI31>: S ~EnterKey~
Select objects: (select objects to be hatched solid)
Entering U (user defined) at the first command prompt will allow you to
set angle, spacing, and double option for the hatch pattern. The command
line procedure is as follows:
Enter a pattern name or [?/Solid/User defined] <ANSI31>: U ~EnterKey~
Specify angle for crosshatch lines <0>: (specify the angle)
Specify spacing between the lines <1.00>: (specify the spacing)
Double hatch area? [Yes/No] <N>: (if you want crosshatching enter Y if
not press ~EnterKey~)
Select objects to define hatch boundary or <direct hatch>,
Select objects: (select objects to be hatched)
```

You can set the hatch scale or the hatch line spacing to match paper space units. The hatch scale and the hatch line spacing in model space in relation to paper space is controlled by the scale factor of the current drawing. For example, if you want to plot a drawing at 3/8″ = 1′–0″ scale, then the scale factor is 32. When you enter a hatch scale or hatch line spacing value of *32XP*, AutoCAD will automatically control hatch scale and hatch line spacing created in model space to match paper space units. The command line sequence for the hatch scale and hatch line spacing are as follows:

```
Specify a scale for the pattern <1.00>: 32XP ~EnterKey~
Specify spacing between the lines <1.00>: 32XP ~EnterKey~
```

Tips: Enter a large-scale factor value when selecting large boundaries. This will save regeneration and plot time.

You can also enter the Island detection style as N (Normal), O (Outer), or I (Ignore) with a comma after the hatch pattern name at the command line as follows:

```
Command: HATCH ~EnterKey~
Enter a pattern name or [?/Solid/User defined] <ANSI31>: AR-CONC,N
~EnterKey~ (for Normal island detection style)
```

You can explode a hatch pattern by entering * before the hatch pattern name as follows:

```
Command: HATCH ~EnterKey~
Enter a pattern name or [?/Solid/User defined] <ANSI31>: *ANSI37 ~EnterKey~
```

The ANSI37 hatch pattern will be displayed as single lines.

Tips: Because the HATCH command will only allow you to select objects, select any text inside the hatch boundary in addition to the objects if you don't want hatching to be applied over the text. When you select the text, AutoCAD will place an imaginary box around the text and the hatch pattern will not be applied inside the imaginary box.

20.6 DIRECT HATCHING

Direct Hatching will allow you to create a hatch boundary without selecting any objects. With direct hatching option, you can create a polyline boundary around the object or you can delete the polyline around the object to display only the hatch pattern. Figure 20–27 shows two objects using the same hatch pattern. The object on the left is hatched with the boundary and the object on the right is hatched without the boundary. The command sequence for both is as follows:

```
Command: HATCH ~EnterKey~
Enter a pattern name or [?/Solid/User defined] <ANSI31>: ~EnterKey~
Specify a scale for the pattern <1.00>: 40 ~EnterKey~
Specify an angle for the pattern <0>: ~EnterKey~
Select objects to define hatch boundary or <direct hatch>,
Select objects: ~EnterKey~
Retain polyline boundary? [Yes/No] <N>: (enter Y for the left drawing, N
for the right drawing)
Specify start point: (select point 1)
Specify next point or [Arc/Close/Length/Undo]: (select point 2)
Specify next point or [Arc/Close/Length/Undo]: (select point 3)
Specify next point or [Arc/Close/Length/Undo]: (select point 4)
Specify next point or [Arc/Close/Length/Undo]: (select point 5)
Specify next point or [Arc/Close/Length/Undo]: (select point 6)
Specify next point or [Arc/Close/Length/Undo]: (select point 7)
Specify next point or [Arc/Close/Length/Undo]: (select point 1)
Specify start point for new boundary or <apply hatch>: ~EnterKey~
```

FIGURE 20–27 Direct hatching can be used to create hatch boundaries without selecting objects.

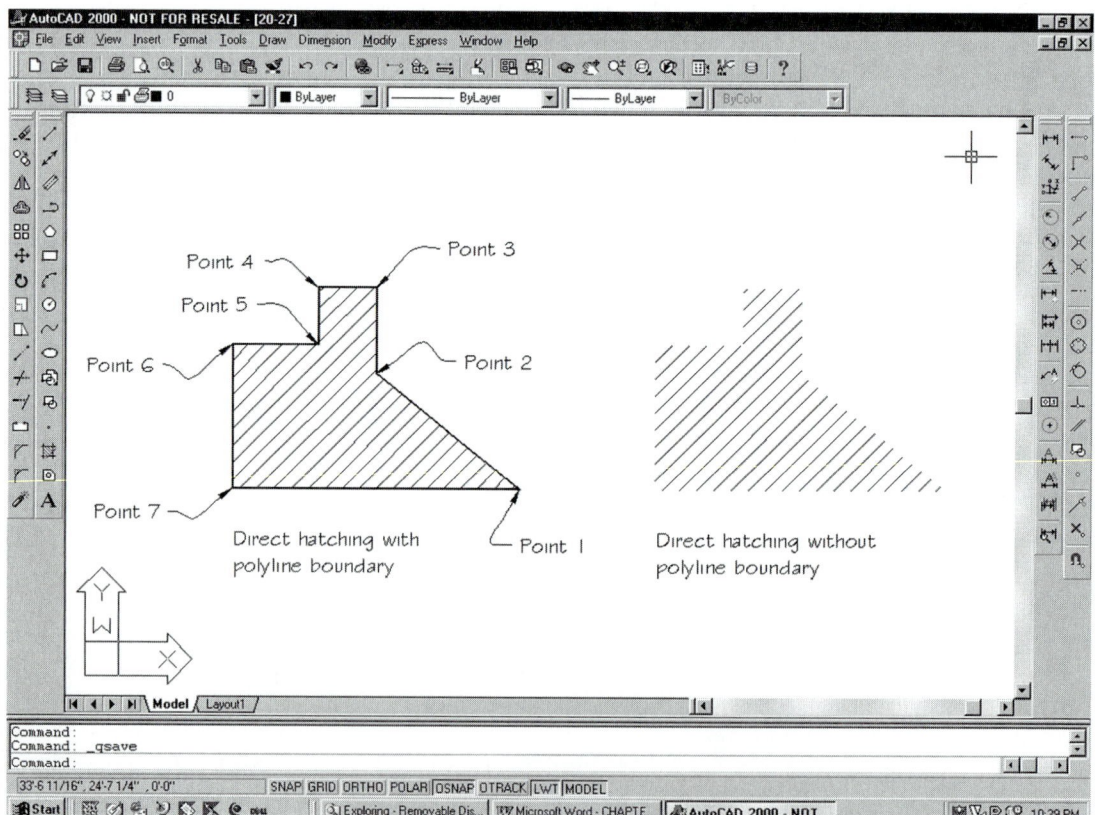

20.7 CREATING BATT INSULATION

A typical residential wall section will include batt insulation as part of graphical symbols as shown in Figures 20–1 and 20–28. For example, a 2 × 6 wood stud wall @ 16 o.c. will have 5 1/2″ batt insulation as a graphical symbol. Commercial construction also uses batt insulation usually between metal studs. There are two different ways to create batt insulation as follows:

User-Defined Hatch Method: This method uses the Boundary Hatch dialog box to create the batt insulation hatching. Figure 20–28 shows a typical wall section with 2 × 6 wood stud frame construction.

■ **EXERCISE 20–3:** *The following step-by-step exercise will allow you to create batt insulation inside the wall shown in Figure 20–28.*

Step #1: Open the EXE20-3.dwg file.

Step #2: Load the linetype called *batting* and make it the current linetype.

Step #3: Click on the Hatch button in the Draw toolbar. The Boundary Hatch dialog will be displayed.

Step #4: Select User defined as the Type and set the Angle to 90.

Step #5: Set Spacing to 6, and click on the Pick Points button and use the following command line procedure:

Command: _ bhatch

Select internal point: *(click on the inside area of the stud wall).*

Selecting everything visible. . .

Analyzing the selected data. . .

Analyzing internal islands. . .

Select internal point: ~EnterKey~

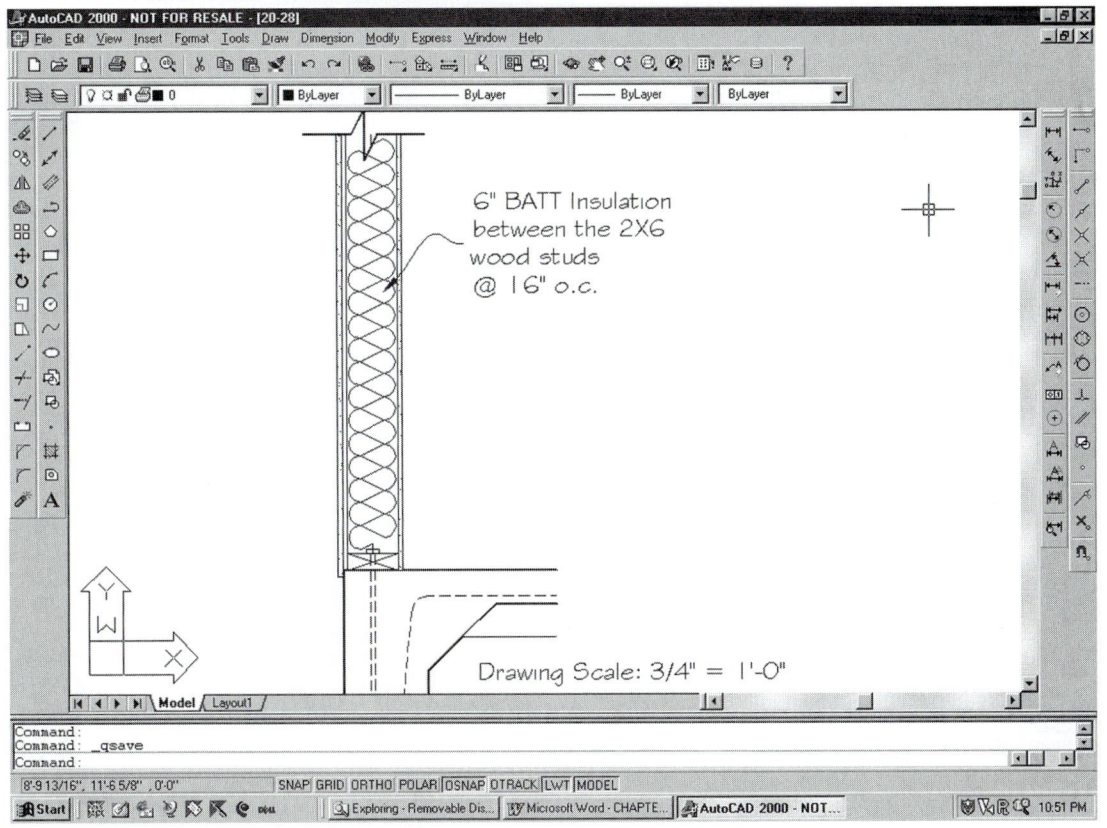

FIGURE 20–28
Creating a batt insulation using the User-Defined hatch method. Adjust hatch spacing to fit different wall composition.

Step #6: Inside the Boundary Hatch dialog box, click on the OK button.

Step #7: If the hatch pattern is not centered inside the wall move the bottom endpoint of the batt insulation to the midpoint of the anchor bolt or the midpoint of the sole plate if necessary.

Congratulations! You have successfully created batt insulation using the User-Defined hatch method. Your drawing should now look like Figure 20–28.

LINE Command Method: This method uses the LINE command with the batting linetype. Figure 20–29 shows a wall section with 2 × 10 floor joists and 9 1/2″ batt insulation.

■ **EXERCISE 20–4:** *The following step-by-step exercise will allow you to create batt insulation inside the floor joist shown in Figure 20–29.*

Step #1: Open the EXE20-4.dwg file.

Step #2: Load the BATTING Linetype and make it the current linetype.

Step #3: Click on the Line button in the Draw toolbar and use the following command line procedure:

Command: _line

Specify first point: *(click on the inside midpoint of the header line).*

Specify next point or [Undo]: *(click on the Snap to Perpendicular and select the vertical cut line).*

Specify next point or [Undo]: ~EnterKey~

Command: **LTSCALE** ~EnterKey~

Enter new linetype scale factor <1.00>: **4.9** ~EnterKey~

Congratulations! You have successfully created batt insulation using the Line Command method.

FIGURE 20–29
Creating a batt insulation using the Line Command method. Adjust the LTSCALE to fit insulation between joist lines.

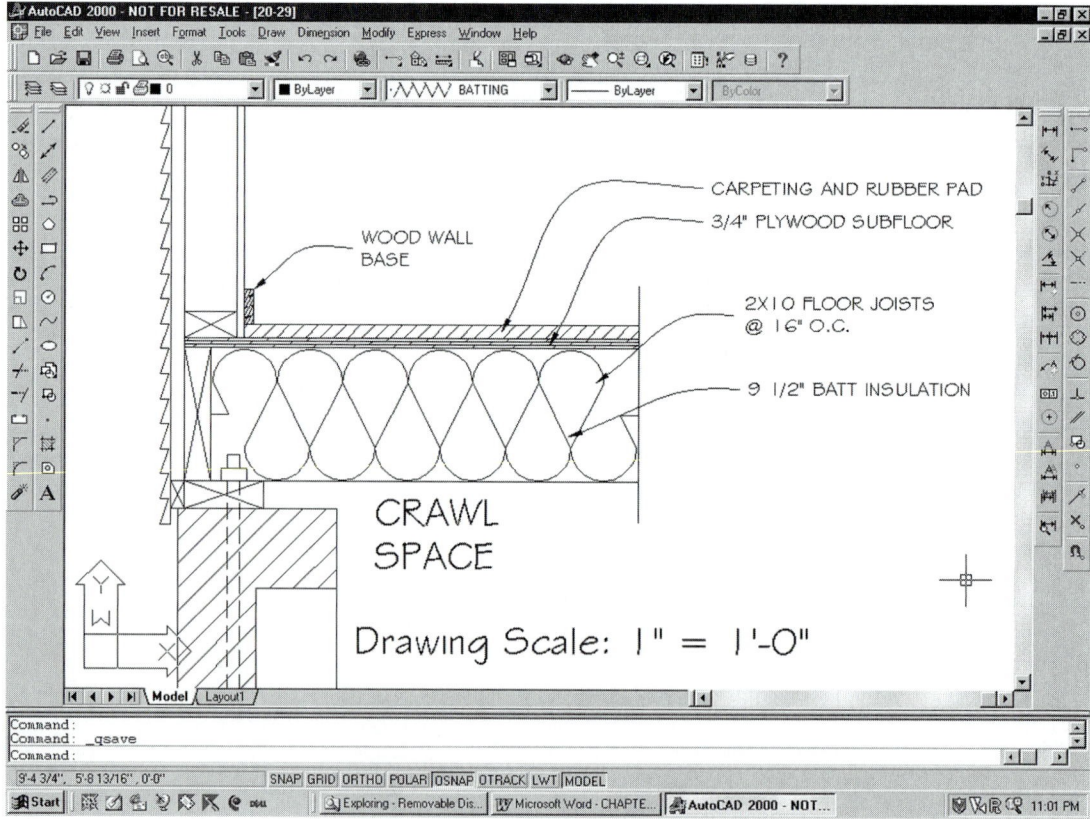

Note: There is no magic number for the line type scale value for the second method. Adjust the LTSCALE system variable value until the BATT insulation fits tight between the joist lines.

20.8 EDITING HATCH PATTERNS AND BOUNDARIES

You can edit hatch patterns and hatch boundaries of *associative hatching* without erasing the existing hatch pattern. Associative hatches are updated to match any changes made to their hatch boundaries. When the associative hatch boundary is edited, the hatch pattern will also change to reflect the editing procedure. When you select a hatch pattern itself to edit its boundary, the hatch pattern to hatch boundary associativity will be broken unless the entire boundary is selected. The hatch boundary is referred to as the objects that contain the hatch pattern. To keep the hatch pattern to hatch boundary associativity intact, select only the boundary, not the hatch pattern. For example, the upper wall of the drawing in Figure 20–30 is stretched 3′–0″. As the hatch boundary is stretched, the hatch pattern is updated automatically to match editing. Figure 20–31 shows the same drawing in Figure 20–30 stretched with a nonassociative hatching. Notice that when a nonassociative hatch pattern is edited it is not updated.

Note: When an interior island is erased inside a hatched object, the associative hatch pattern will be revised to fill the island area. When you move interior islands, the hatch will redraw to fill the gap.

You can use grips and editing commands such as ERASE, MOVE, STRETCH, COPY, ROTATE, and SCALE to edit hatch boundaries and hatch patterns. The hatch pattern to hatch boundary associativity is preserved when you copy, move, or mirror boundaries. The grip for a hatch pattern will appear at the center of the hatch pattern. When you edit hatch patterns using grips, follow the steps described below:

1. From the Tools pull-down menu, click on Options...
2. Inside the Options dialog box, click on the Selection tab.

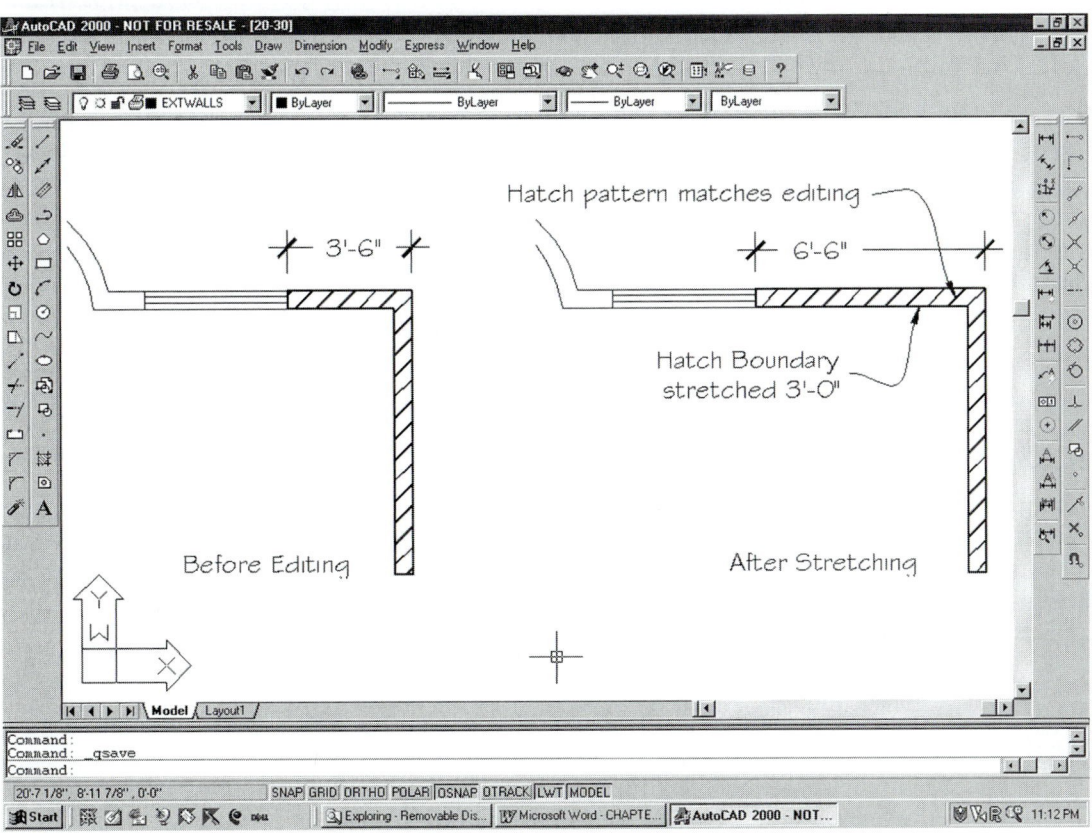

FIGURE 20–30 When an associative hatch boundary is edited, the existing hatch pattern will be updated automatically to reflect the changes.

FIGURE 20–31 When a nonassociative hatch pattern is edited, it will not be updated to reflect the changes.

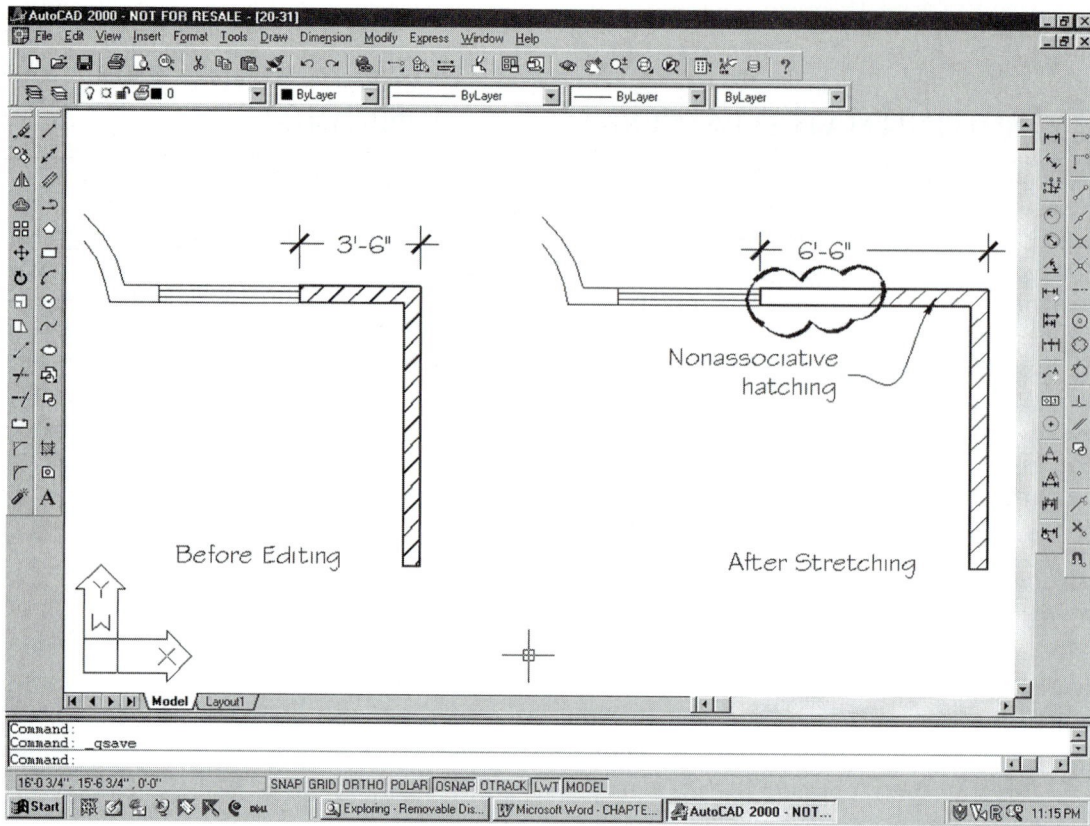

3. Under the Grips category, place a checkmark in the Enable grips and Enable grips within blocks check boxes.

4. Click on the Apply and the OK buttons to close the Options dialog box.

5. Select the hatch pattern to edit.

You can edit a hatch pattern but not the hatch boundary. Selection of hatch patterns and hatch boundaries depends on the settings of the PICKSTYLE system variable. To select a hatch pattern without selecting the hatch boundary, set PICKSTYLE to 0 or 1. To select a hatch pattern with its boundary, set PICKSTYLE to 2 or 3. For example, to erase a hatch pattern but not the hatch boundary, set the PICKSTYLE system variable to 0 or 1. To erase the hatch pattern and the hatch boundary, set the PICKSTYLE system variable to 2 or 3.

Tips: Associative hatch patterns are updated even if they are on layers that are turned off.

Tips: You can use the Properties window to change hatch pattern properties.

20.8.1   Using the HATCHEDIT Command

A more efficient way to edit a hatch pattern is by using the HATCHEDIT command. You can enter HE or HATCHEDIT at the command line, select Hatch. . . from the Modify pull-down menu, or click on the Edit Hatch button in the Modify II toolbar. The Modify II toolbar is shown in Figure 20–32.

The command sequence is as follows:

```
Command: HE or HATCHEDIT ~EnterKey~
Select associative hatch object: (select a hatch pattern, it does not
have to be associative)
```

The Hatch Edit dialog box will be displayed as shown in Figure 20–33. You can also use the shortcut menu to quickly access the Hatch Edit dialog box as follows:

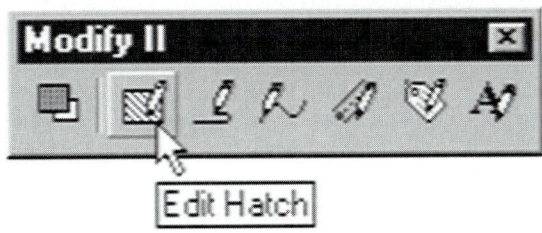

FIGURE 20–32 The Edit Hatch button in the Modify II toolbar can be used to quickly edit an existing hatch pattern.

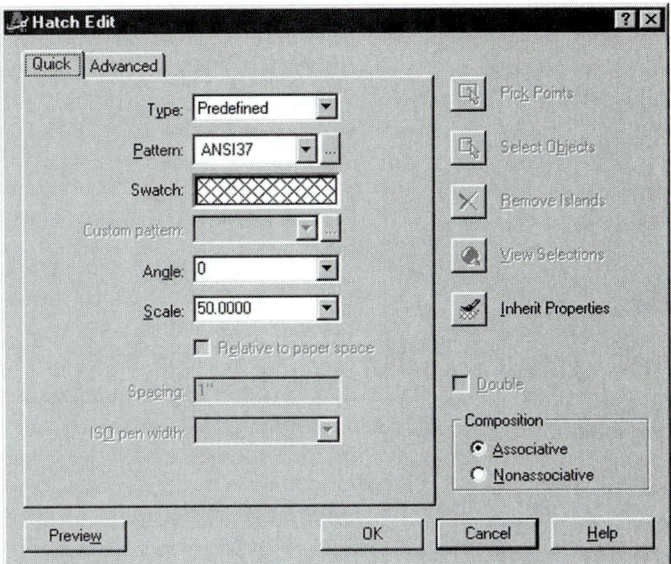

FIGURE 20–33 The Hatch Edit dialog box is used to quickly edit an existing hatch pattern.

1. Set the PICKSTYLE system variable to 0 or 1.
2. Select a hatch pattern. A single grip box will appear in the center of the hatch pattern.
3. Right click on the hatch pattern and select Hatch Edit. . . from the shortcut menu. The Hatch Edit dialog box will be displayed.

The Hatch Edit dialog box will show only the option settings related to the selected hatch pattern. The features inside this dialog box are the same as the Boundary Hatch dialog box. Use the Hatch Edit dialog box to perform the following tasks:

- Change the hatch type.
- Change the hatch pattern.
- Change the hatch angle.
- Change the hatch scale. You can also verify the hatch scale of an existing hatch pattern that you forgot by using the Hatch Edit dialog box.
- Change hatch spacing.
- Change hatch composition.
- Inherit properties.
- Change any settings inside the Advanced tab.

After you make the changes, click on the Preview button to review the new settings before you apply it to the current drawing.

Caution: *If you erase all or part of the exterior hatch boundary (leaving an existing hatch boundary open) and edit later, the hatch associativity is broken but the pattern stays the same. See Figure 20–34.*

Tips: If you copy a polyline boundary of a hatch created with the Retain boundaries category in the Boundary Hatch dialog box, the polyline boundary will be copied but the original boundary will remain. See Figure 20–22.

Tips: You can use the Multiple Design Environment to select, drag, and drop hatch patterns to copy from one drawing into another. You can also use Windows Edit options to cut, copy, and paste hatch patterns to the Windows clipboard.

FIGURE 20–34 When the associative hatch boundary is open, the hatch editing operation will result in a nonassociative hatch pattern.

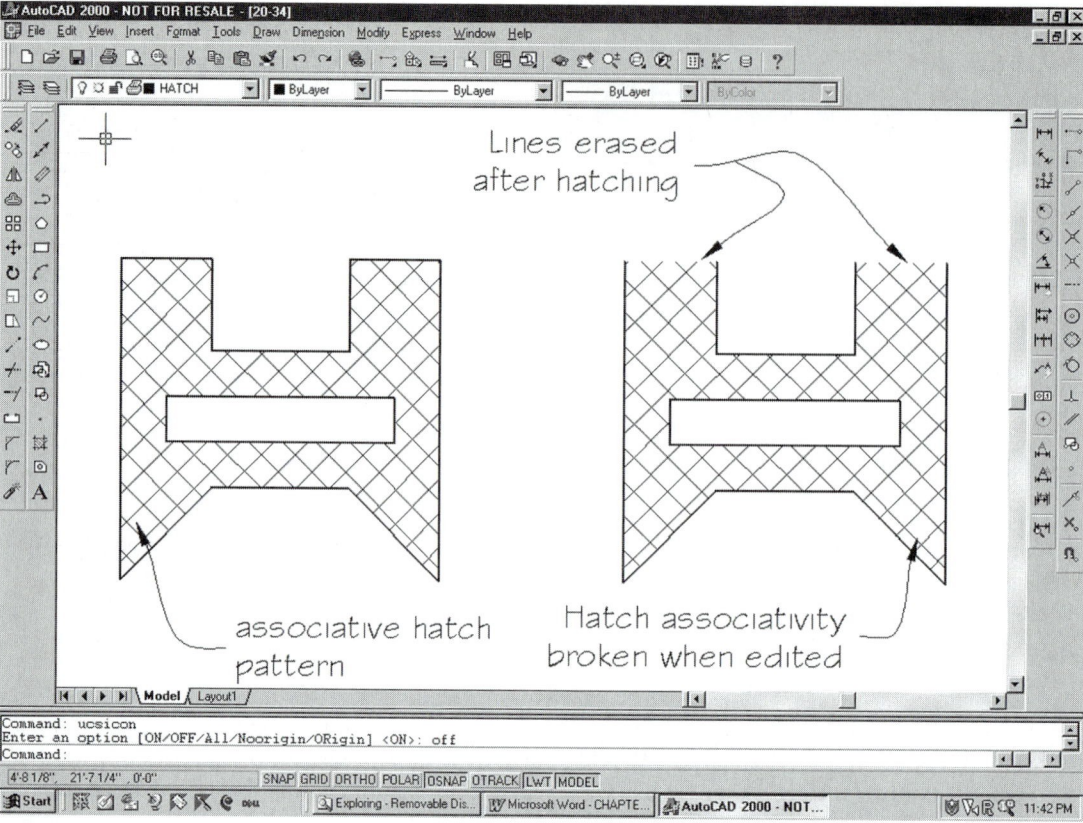

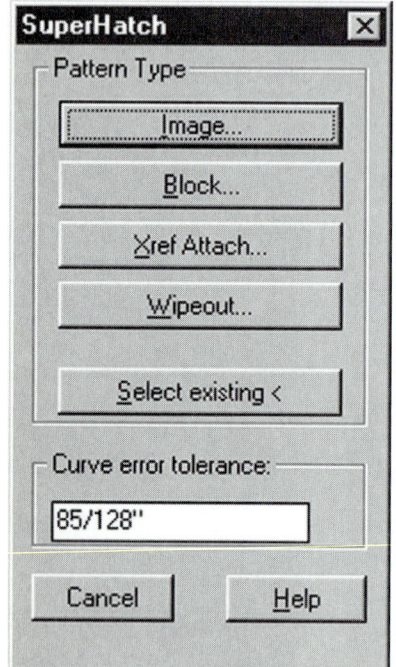

FIGURE 20–35 The SuperHatch dialog box will allow you to use an image, block, xref, or wipeout objects as a hatch pattern.

You can remove hatch associativity only without editing hatch pattern or hatch boundary as follows:

1. From the Modify pull-down menu select Hatch...
2. Select an associative hatch pattern.
3. Inside the Hatch Edit dialog box and under the Composition category place a checkmark inside the Nonassociative radio button.

20.9 USING THE SUPER HATCH EXPRESS TOOL

The Super Hatch express tool allows you to create hatch patterns using images, blocks, xrefs, and wipeouts. To access Super Hatch, pick the Express pull-down menu select Draw and select Super Hatch... You can also enter SUPERHATCH at the command line. The Super Hatch patterns are not hatch objects, therefore are not associative. When you start Super Hatch, the SuperHatch dialog box will be displayed as shown in Figure 20–35.

The SuperHatch dialog box has two categories: Pattern Type and Curve error tolerance.

Pattern Type: (category). This category will allow you to select pattern types for hatching. There are five options under this category.

• **IMAGE...:** (button). Selecting this option will display the Select Image File dialog box as shown in Figure 20–36. This is where you select an image for the hatch pattern. The image can be a photograph or a drawing saved as an image file in the hard drive. You can view and attach raster or bitmapped bitonal, eight-bit gray, eight-bit color, or 24-bit color image files to a drawing. To see all image files in your computer, select all image files from the Files of type: drop-down list. Select the image file you are looking for. The Preview image box should display the image file you have selected. If the image file is what you want to use as an

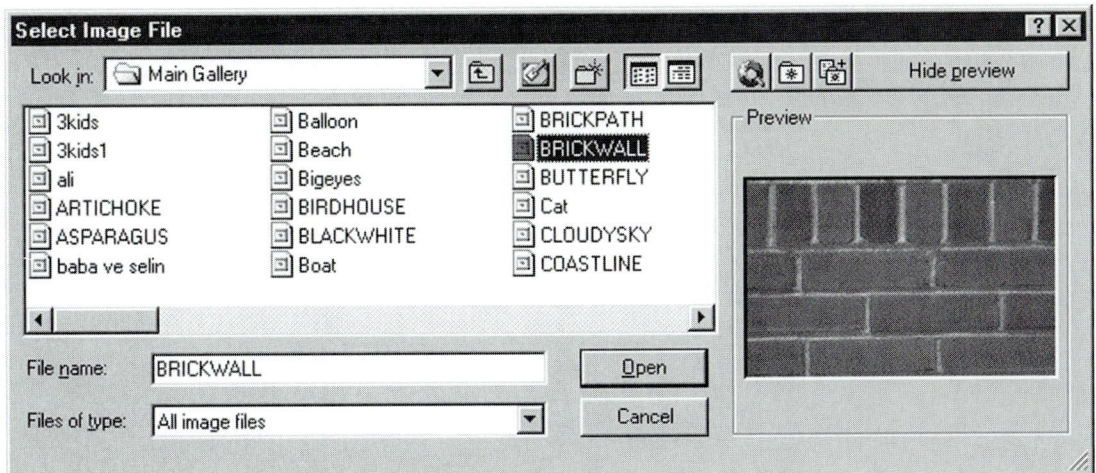

FIGURE 20–36 The Select Image File dialog box will allow you to select the image file.

image hatch pattern, click on the Open button. This will display the Image dialog box as shown in Figure 20–37. The Image dialog box is very similar to the Insert dialog box. Establish insertion point, scale, and rotation for the image to be inserted as a hatch pattern on the dialog box or select Specify on-screen. Insert the image in the current drawing. You can also enter IMAGEATTACH at the command line to access the Select Image File dialog box.

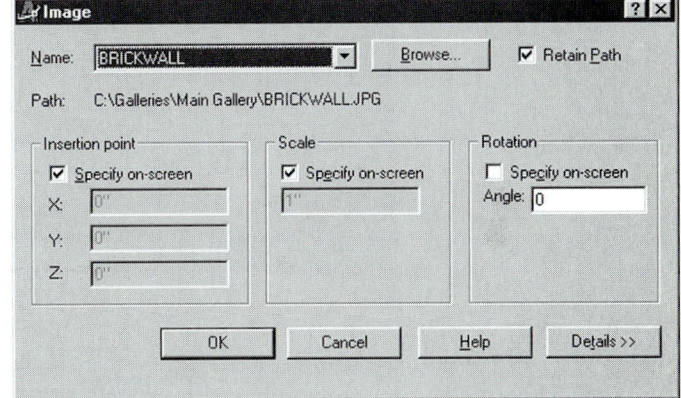

FIGURE 20–37 The Image dialog box will allow you to insert the selected image as a hatch pattern in the current drawing.

■ **EXERCISE 20–5:** *Figure 20–38 shows a simple house elevation. The following step-by-step exercise will allow you to use the SuperHatch dialog box to create hatching from a BRICK image file.*

Step #1: Open the EXE20-5.dwg file.

Step #2: Click on the Express pull-down menu. Select Draw and select Super Hatch... The SuperHatch dialog box will appear.

Step #3: Click on the Image... button. The Select Image File dialog box will appear. Select the file containing the BRICK image and click on the Open button. This will display the Image dialog box.

Step #4: From the Image dialog box, enter a scale of **40**. The scale value will help you define how close you can get to the actual brick dimension in the image. A higher scale value will increase the size of the bricks in the image. A smaller scale value will decrease the size of the bricks in the image. For Insertion point and Rotation, select Specify on-screen. Click on the OK button.

Step #5: Inside the drawing, the image will be displayed as a rectangular object attached to the cursor. This rectangular object measures 40″ in the horizontal dimension and the vertical dimension is 64 percent of the horizontal dimension. Use the following command procedure:

Insertion point <0,0>: *(select the insertion point shown in Figure 20–38).*

Specify rotation angle <0>: ~EnterKey~

Is the placement of this IMAGE acceptable? [Yes/No] <Yes>: *(If the image scale is not acceptable, type N and the Select Image File dialog box will be displayed. Click on the Open button and change the scale of the image inside the Image dialog box. Otherwise press ~EnterKey~).*

Selecting visible objects for boundary detection...Done.

FIGURE 20–38 House elevation showing internal points, closures, and attach image point.

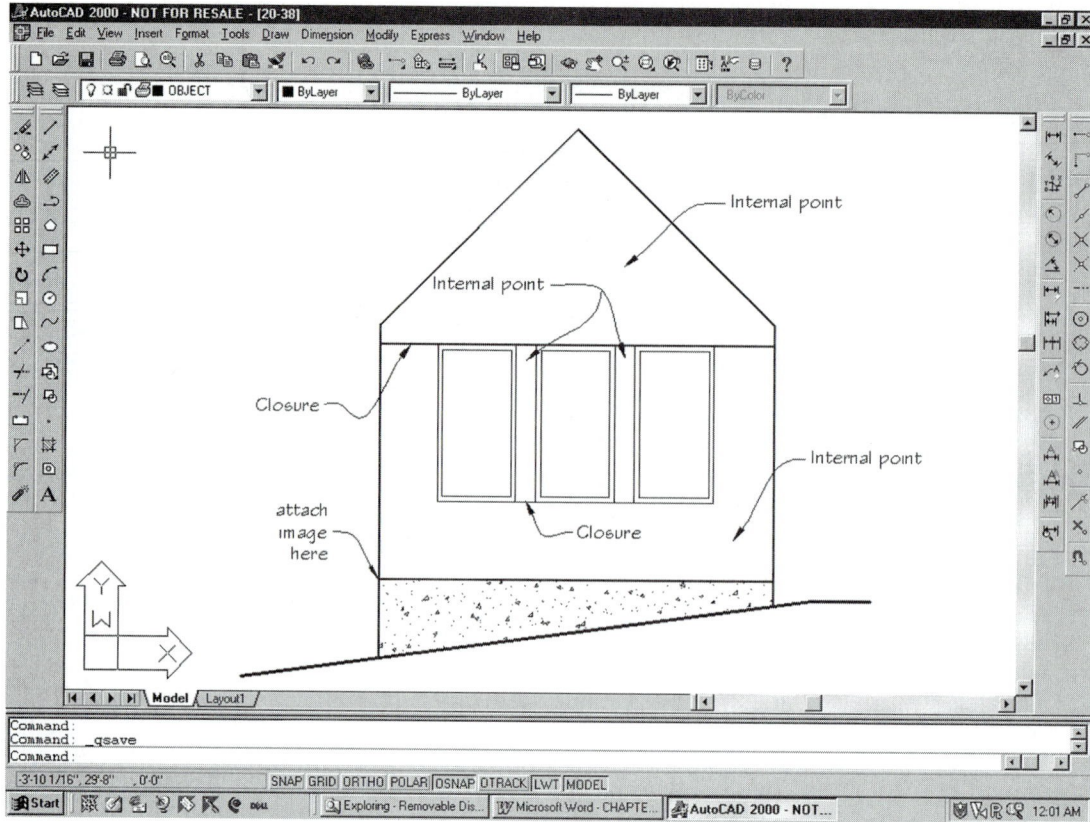

Specify an option [Advanced options] <Internal point>: *(select the internal points shown).*

Specify an option [Advanced options] <Internal point>: ~EnterKey~

Preparing hatch objects for display... Done.

Use TFRAMES to toggle object frames on and off.

Step #6: The drawing will now display many of the 40″ × 26″ boxes containing brick images that are separated by object frames. Object frames are lines around the individual brick images. From the Express Standard toolbar, click on the Toggle frames button or enter TFRAMES at the command line as follows:

```
Command: TFRAMES ~EnterKey~
IMAGE/WIPEOUT frames are toggled OFF.
```

This will remove all the frames around the boxes from the drawing.

Congratulations! You have successfully used the SuperHatch dialog box to attach an image. The completed drawing is shown in Figure 20–39. The TFRAMES are for images and wipeouts only. You might have to repeat some of the lines around window frames if necessary.

Selecting the Advanced options before selecting internal points as boundaries for hatching will allow you to create a Boundary set or turn on or off Island detection. The command line procedure is as follows:

```
Specify an option [Advanced options] <Internal point>: A ~EnterKey~
Enter an option [Boundary set/Island detection] <eXit>: B ~EnterKey~
Specify candidate set for boundary [New/Everything] <Everything>: N
~EnterKey~
Select objects: (select the objects to create new boundary)
You can also press ~EnterKey~ to select everything as the new boundary.
The Island detection option works as follows:
```

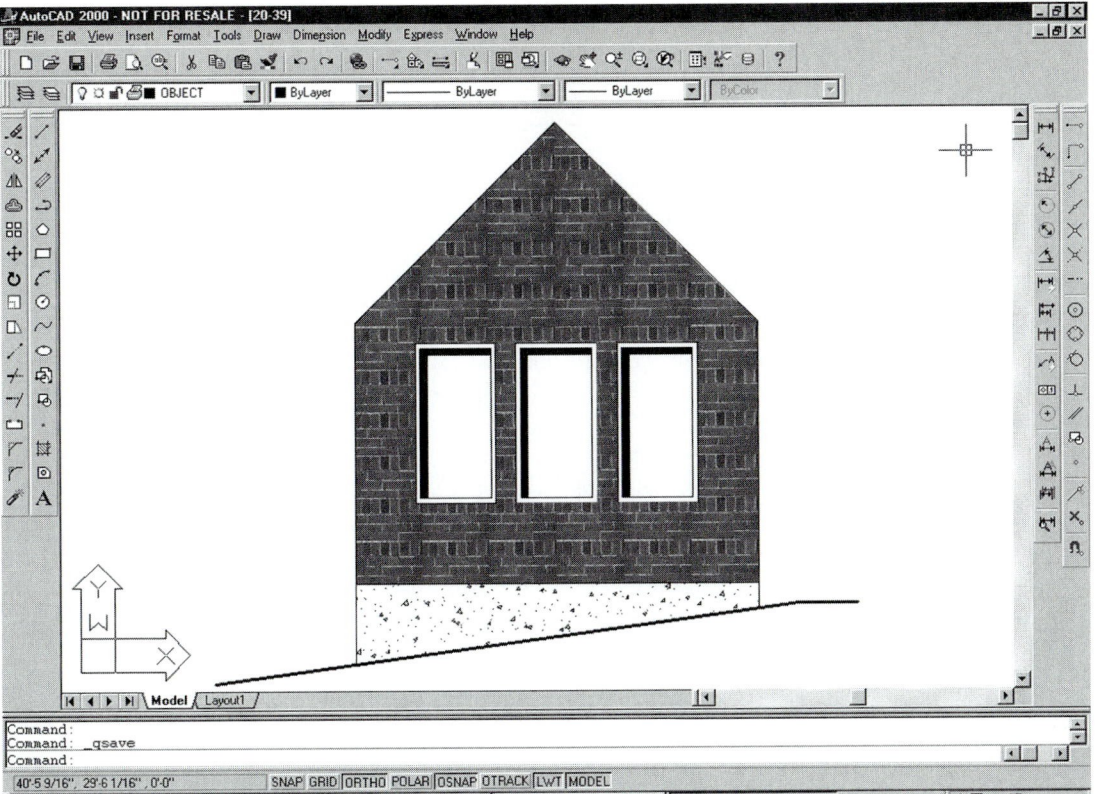

FIGURE 20–39 The completed elevation with BRICK image used as a hatch pattern. Notice heavier outline.

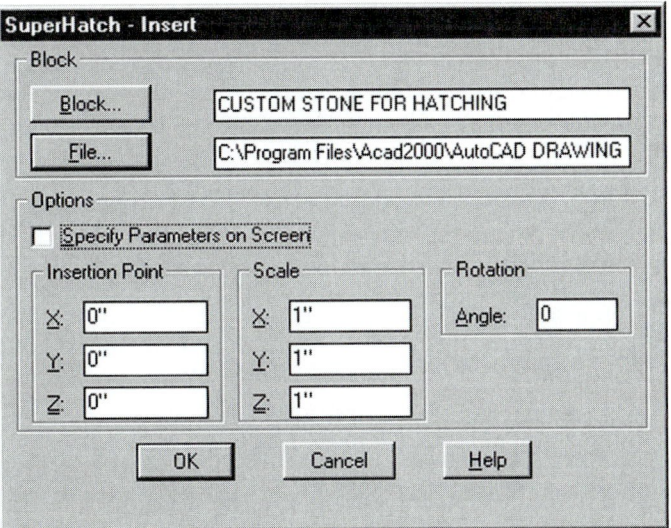

FIGURE 20–40 The SuperHatch–Insert dialog box is used to insert a block or a wblock as the hatch pattern.

```
Enter an option [Boundary set/Island detection] <eXit>: I ~EnterKey~
Do you want island detection? [Yes/No] <Yes>: ~EnterKey~
```

- **BLOCK…:** (button). You can use hatch images on object surfaces such as elevations and sections to display a rendered effect. You can use custom blocks as repeated hatch patterns such as bricks, stones, roof tiles, or any façade treatments. Selecting this option will display the SuperHatch–Insert dialog box as shown in Figure 20–40. This dialog box will allow you to specify the block or wblock for the hatch pattern. You can create a specific block or wblock to be used as a hatch pattern.

After selecting a block or a file and after placing a check mark in the Specify Parameters on Screen check box, the command line procedure will be as follows:

```
Specify insertion point or [Scale/X/Y/Z/Rotate/PScale/PX/PY/PZ/PRotate]:
(specify insertion point or select other options)
Enter X scale factor, specify opposite corner, or [Corner/XYZ] <1>:
(specify the X scale factor)
Enter Y scale factor <use X scale factor>: (specify the Y scale factor
or press ~EnterKey~)
Specify rotation angle <0>: (specify the rotation angle or press ~EnterKey~)
Is the placement of this block acceptable? [Yes/No] <Yes>: (see step #5
in Exercise 20-5 for image insertion instructions).
The block will be displayed inside the magenta color rectangle.
Specify fillet radius for rectangles <0'-0">: (enter a fillet radius or
press ~EnterKey~)
Specify line width for rectangles <0'-0">: (enter a line width or press
~EnterKey~)
Specify thickness for rectangles <0'-0">: (enter a thickness or press
~EnterKey~)
Select a window around the block to define column and row tile distances.
Current rectangle modes: Width = 0'-1"
Specify block [Extents] first corner <magenta rectang>: (you can specify
a frame for tiling block insertion or press ~EnterKey~ to accept the
magenta rectangle)
Selecting visible objects for boundary detection...Done.
Specify an option [Advanced options] <Internal point>: (select an
internal point for hatch boundary or enter A for Advanced options)
```

Use TFRAMES to toggle block object frames on and off. For large drawings the hatch pattern will take some time to be displayed. Figure 20–41 shows the same elevation in Figure 20–38 with a custom stone block as the hatch pattern.

- **XREF ATTACH. . .:** (button). This button will allow you to use an externally referenced drawing (xref) as a hatch pattern by displaying the Select Reference File dialog box. The process is similar to inserting an xref. External References are discussed in Chapter 24. The command line procedure for using an xref as hatching is similar to the block hatching procedure.

- **WIPEOUT. . .:** (button). This button will allow you to select a wipeout as a hatch pattern. A wipeout is a blank image AutoCAD places on top of the objects in an area you want to hide. A wipeout will hide selected areas of the drawing. See the WIPEOUT command for more information. You can use this option to select an internal point or Advanced options and select boundaries as wipeout and use TFRAMES to toggle object frames on or off. This will hide selected areas from hatching or from any other object. The command line procedure is similar to the Image and Block options.

- **SELECT EXISTING** <: (button). This button will allow you to select an existing image, block, xref, or wipeout for a hatch pattern.

Curve Error Tolerance: (category). This category will allow you to specify error tolerance for curves. If the drawing contains curved objects such as circles, arcs and splined polylines, the SUPERHATCH command will hatch curved boundaries by placing a series of short line segments inside the curved objects. This is called *traversing arc segments*. This category will let you control the precision of traversing arc segments. You can specify a distance between a midpoint of a typical short line segment and the arc. If you enter a large error value inside the text, box fewer segments will be created, allowing faster AutoCAD performance. The down side to this is that arcs will appear less smooth. If you enter a small error value, smooth hatching will be created along arcs but will result in slower AutoCAD performance. The concept is similar to the View Resolution effect on curved surfaces where the VIEWRES system variable controls the smoothness of curves in the drawing.

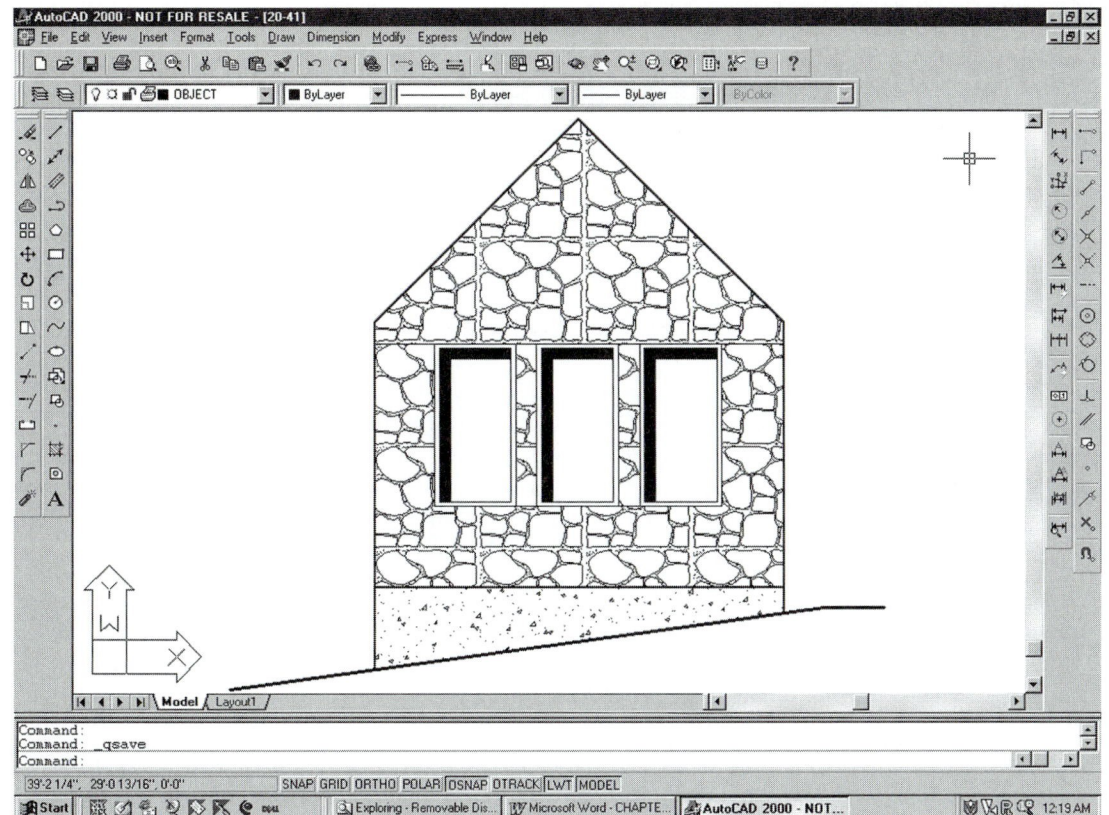

FIGURE 20–41 Using the Block... button in the SuperHatch dialog box, a custom created stone block is used as hatching.

TIPS

Tips: Splines, circles in non-uniformly scaled block insertions, ellipses inside block insertions, and Text and Mtext as block insertions are not supported by the boundary command. Therefore the SUPERHATCH command cannot create boundary edges from them.

20.10 EDITING SUPER HATCH PATTERNS

Super hatch pattern objects are created as unnamed groups. In AutoCAD, groups are created from objects using the GROUP command. You can use the GROUP command to turn off selection of the super hatch pattern object group to edit individual units containing super hatch pattern objects. To edit individual segments within super hatch patterns use the following procedure:

- Enter GROUP at the command line. This will display the Object Grouping dialog box as shown in Figure 20–42.

- Inside the dialog box, place a check mark in the Include unnamed check box under the Group Identification category. Under the Group Name, the unnamed super hatch patterns will be displayed as *A1 and *A2. More can be displayed according to the super hatch patterns used. Select the *A1 group as shown in Figure 20–42. The Description will now read *Superhatch*.

- Click on the Selectable button under the Change Group category. Make sure the word No appears under Selectable next to the Group Name.

- Repeat the same procedure for other groups.

- Click on the OK button.

You can now edit individual super hatch objects.

FIGURE 20–42 The Object Grouping dialog box is used to turn off the entire selection of super hatch objects.

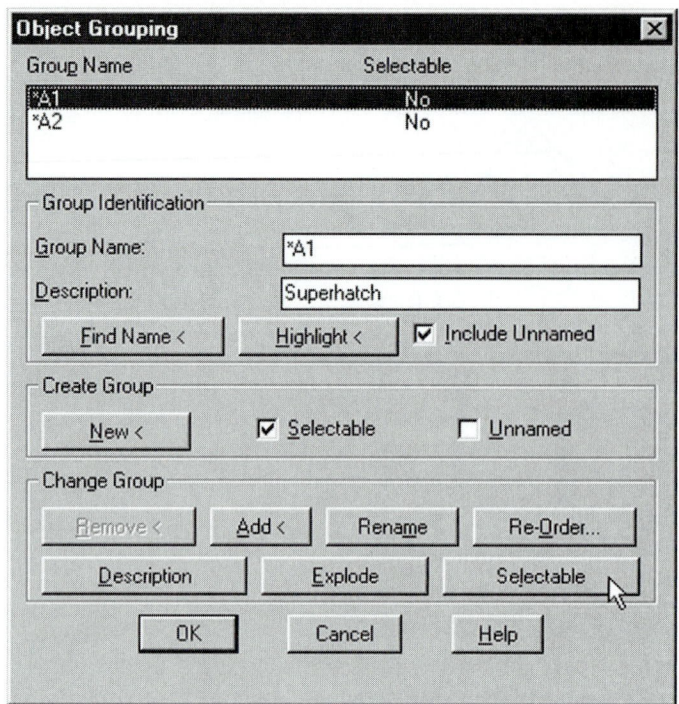

■ **EXERCISE 20–6:**   *The following step-by-step exercise will allow you to create six different hatch patterns for the building elevation shown in Figure 20–43. The boundaries for six hatch patterns are indicated as B1, B2, B3, B4, B5, and B6.*

Step #1:   Open the EXE20-6.dwg file.

Step #2:   Zoom in to the roof area. Click on the Hatch button in the Draw toolbar and set the following parameters in the Boundary Hatch dialog box for the B1 area:

Type: Predefined

Pattern: AR-RSHKE

Angle: 0

Scale: 0.50

Step #3:   Click on the Pick Points button.

Step #4:   Select the internal points shown as B1 and press ~EnterKey~.

Step #5:   Inside the Boundary Hatch dialog box, click on the OK button.

Step #6:   Right click in the drawing area and select Repeat Hatch from the shortcut menu to return to the Boundary Hatch dialog box. Establish settings for B2 boundary as follows:

Type: User defined

Angle: 0

Spacing: 2″

Step #7:   Repeat Steps #3, #4, and #5 for B2.

Your drawing will now look like Figure 20–44.

Step #8:   Repeat Step #6 and establish settings for B3 boundary area as follows:

Type: Predefined

Pattern: ANGLE

Angle: 0

Scale: 20.00

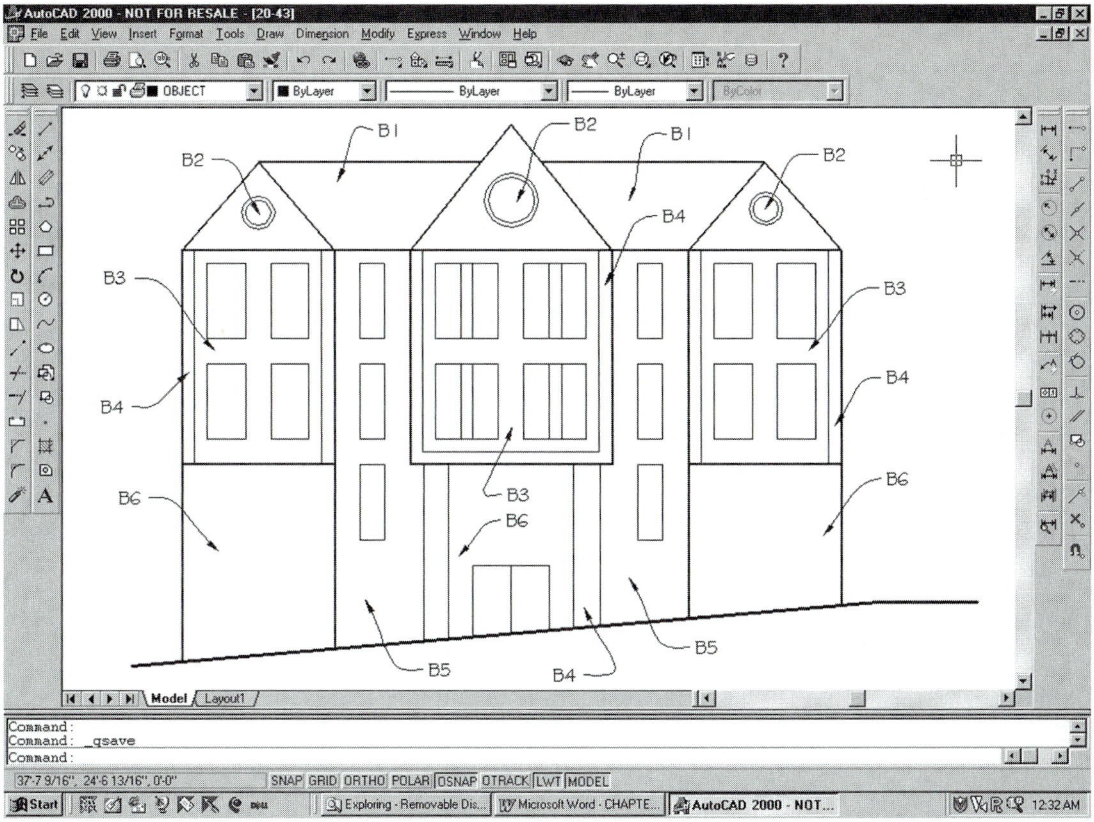

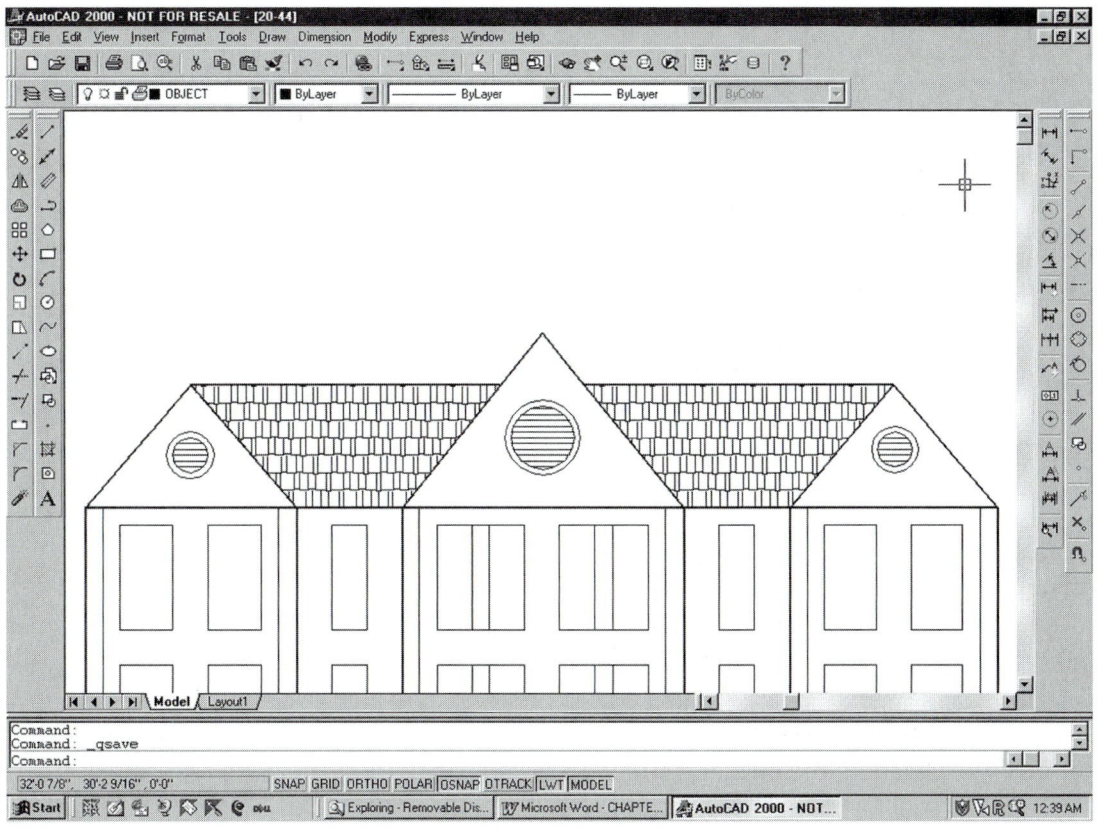

FIGURE 20–43 The building elevation with six boundary areas.

FIGURE 20–44 The hatch patterns for B1 and B2 boundaries created.

FIGURE 20–45
Building elevation with hatching completed for B1, B2, B3, and B4 boundary areas.

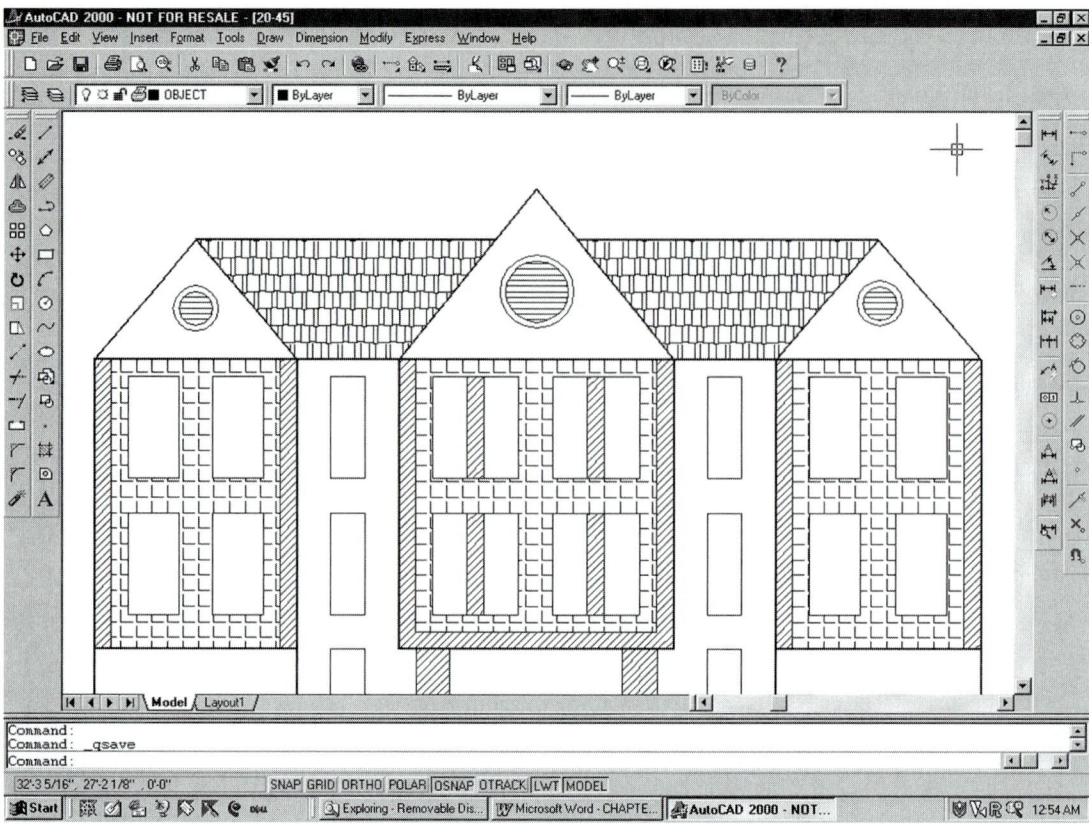

Step #9:   Repeat Steps #3, #4, and #5 for B3.

Step #10:   Repeat Step #6 and establish settings for B4 boundary area as follows:

Type: Predefined

Pattern: ANSI31

Angle: 0

Scale: 15.00

Step #11:   Repeat Steps #3, #4, and #5 for B4.

Your drawing will now look like Figure 20–45.

Step #12:   Repeat Step #6 and establish settings for B5 boundary area as follows:

Type: Predefined

Pattern: AR-SAND

Angle: 0

Scale: 7.00

Step #13:   Repeat Steps #3, #4, and #5 for B5.

Step #14:   Repeat Step #6 and establish settings for B6 boundary area as follows:

Type: Predefined

Pattern: AR-BRSTD

Angle: 0

Scale: 1.00

Step #15:   Repeat Steps #3, #4, and #5 for B6.

Congratulations! You have successfully created and applied six different hatch patterns for the building elevation. The final drawing will now look like Figure 20–46.

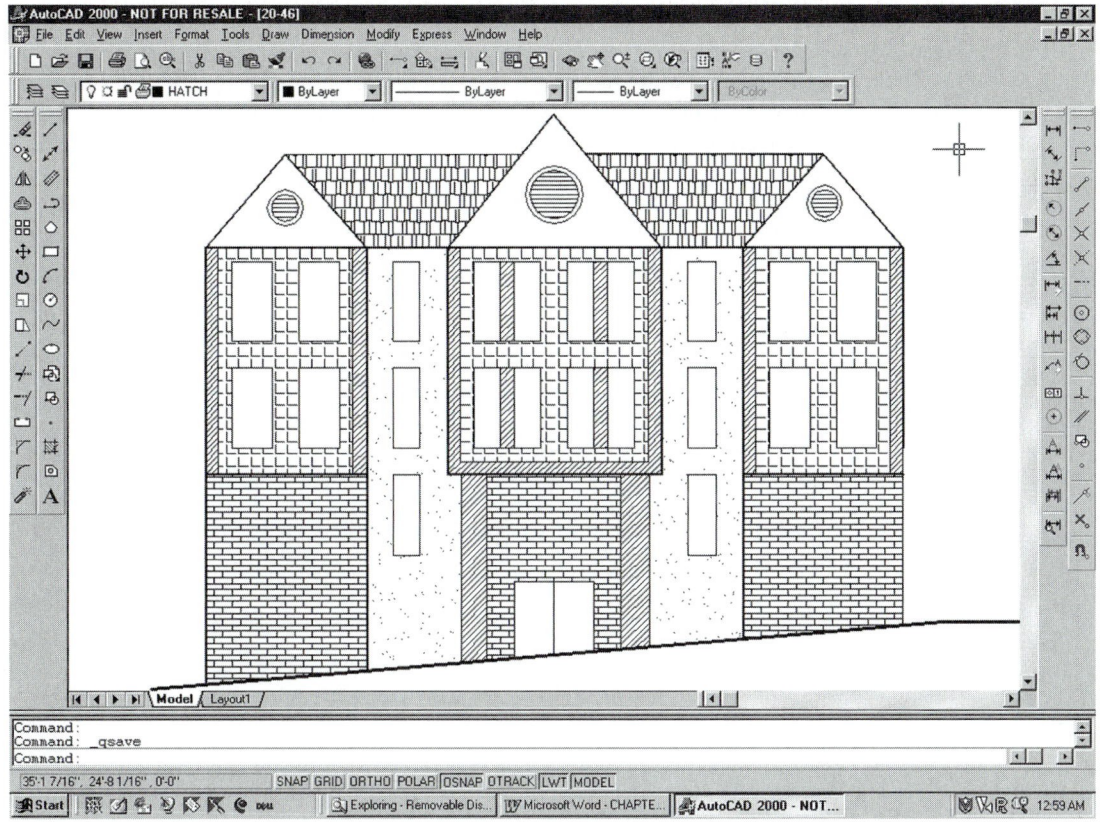

REVIEW QUESTIONS

1. Describe three different ways to access the Boundary Hatch dialog box.
2. How many different hatch types are available in the Type: drop-down list of the Boundary Hatch dialog box?
3. If the ANSI31 hatch pattern has 45-degree hatch lines at a 0 degree default angle, what angle must be entered to have the ANSI31 hatch lines appear as vertical lines?
4. How do you reference hatch scale to paper space?
5. What is the name of the system variable that controls hatch spacing?
6. What are the two different methods used when creating a hatch boundary for hatching?
7. How can you inherit the properties of one existing hatch pattern and apply it to another object?
8. What is the best way to create crosshatching?
9. What is the advantage of having an associative hatch pattern?
10. What is considered to be an island?
11. Describe the three different island detection styles.
12. Can a hatch pattern be created without any objects on the screen? If so, how?
13. What is the advantage behind using the SOLID hatch pattern to hatch objects solid as opposed to using the SOLID command?
14. What is the name of the system variable that controls the visibility of hatch patterns?
15. Can you create hatch patterns without the Boundary hatch dialog box? If so, how?
16. Where does the grip for a hatch pattern appear in the object?
17. What is the PICKSTYLE system variable used for?
18. How do you access the Hatch Edit dialog box?
19. Describe the functions of the super hatch.

PROBLEMS

1. Using the Chapter Tutorial drawing in Chapter 17, Drawing Multilines, create and apply a hatch pattern of your choice for the exterior walls and a hatch pattern for the interior walls for the floor plan.

2. Create a custom stone symbol as a block similar to the one shown in Figure 20–45 and use the Super Hatch Block option to create a stone elevation of a house.

3. Scan a photograph elevation of a building that you find interesting in an architectural magazine. Create an image file and use the Super Hatch Image option to create a hatch pattern on one of your projects.

Assigning Attributes to Symbols

After successful completion of this chapter you should be able to:

▲ Understand the function of attributes.

▲ Create and assign attributes to blocks using the Attribute Definition dialog box.

▲ Understand attribute modes.

▲ Assign attributes using the –ATTDEF command.

▲ Assign attributes to existing blocks.

▲ Understand the function of the ATTDIA system variable.

▲ Control attribute visibility.

▲ Understand the function of the ATTMODE system variable.

▲ Suppress attribute prompts.

▲ Edit attributes before creating the block with the Edit Attribute Definition dialog box.

▲ Edit attributes before creating the block with the Properties window.

▲ Edit attributes before creating the block using the CHANGE command.

▲ Edit attributes after creating and inserting the block with the Edit Attributes dialog box.

▲ Edit attributes after creating and inserting the block using the ATTE command.

▲ Edit attributes one at a time or globally.

▲ Redefine attributes.

▲ Assign attributes to title blocks.

▲ Extract attributes to create door and window schedules.

21.1 WHAT ARE ATTRIBUTES?

Attributes are text information attached to symbols that are included in the block definition. They contain valuable information about the type, manufacturer, size, material, and price of a specific piece of furniture or equipment in the drawing. You can attach specific information to describe the block in greater detail by creating more labels, called *tags*. Attributes are entered as values that are stored in a database. When written information becomes a part of the block definition, it can be made visible or it can be hidden from the block. In addition to being used as a label, the attribute information can later be extracted from the drawing and a bill of materials can be printed. Figure 21–1 shows a block inserted with attributes. The workstation desk, chair, quarter round unit, and side table are pieces of furniture with their own attributes that are part of the block. Attributes can be created, attached, and edited using dialog boxes or using specific commands at the command line.

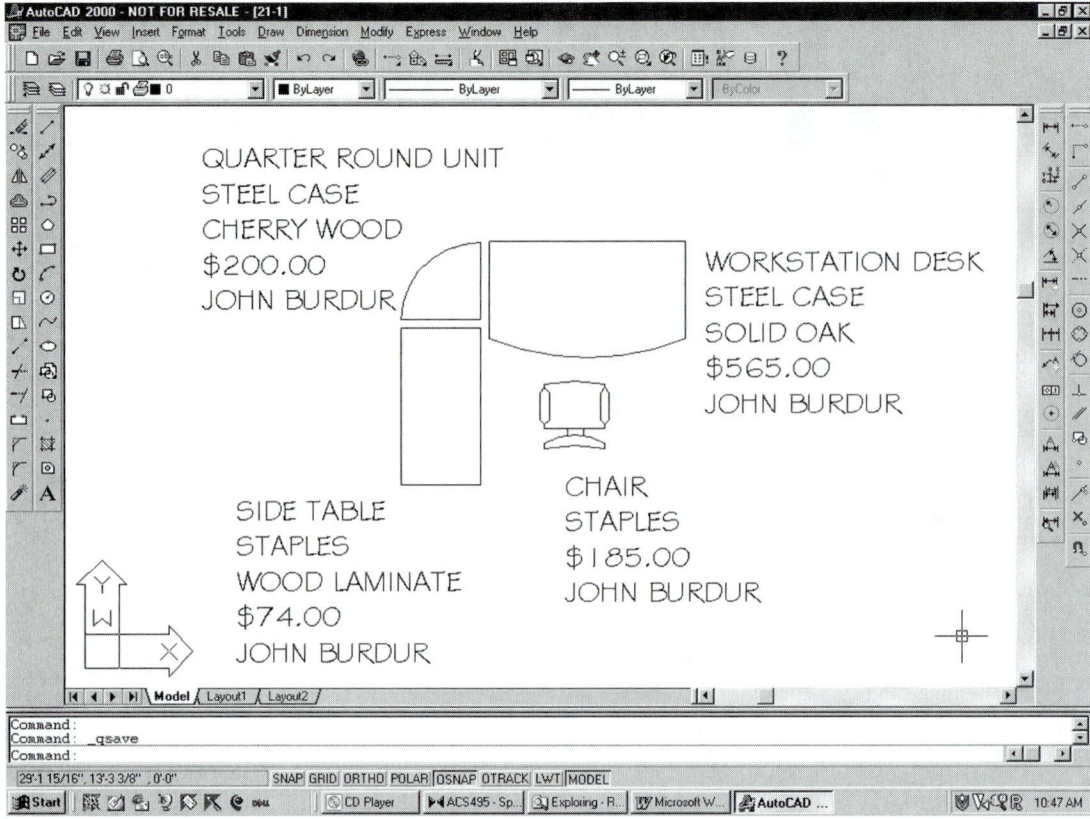

21.2 ASSIGNING ATTRIBUTE INFORMATION

There are three major steps involved in assigning attributes to blocks:

1. Create the symbol to which attributes will be assigned. For example, this could be the four furniture components of the CAD workstation symbol shown in Figure 21–1.

2. Determine what information about the block is needed and assign that information as attribute tags using a dialog box or the command line.

3. Create a block from the symbol making sure that all objects including attribute tags are selected.

When the block is inserted, all attribute tags will be displayed as assigned values as shown in Figure 21–1. Once the symbol is created, enter ATTDEF (attribute definition) at the command line or select Block, then select Define Attributes. . . from the Draw pull-down menu. The Attribute Definition dialog box will be displayed as shown in Figure 21–2. This dialog box will allow you to create, assign, and insert information as attributes relating to the specific symbol. The Attribute Definition dialog box has four major categories: Mode, Attribute, Insertion Point, and Text Options.

Mode: (Category). This category will allow you to set the visibility and the format of the attributes. The four options are as follows:

- **INVISIBLE:** (check box). This option controls the visibility of the attribute when the block is inserted in the current drawing. If you do not want the attribute to be visible, place a checkmark in the Invisible check box. You can still assign attributes to the block, but when the block is inserted the attributes will not be displayed. If you want the attribute to be displayed when the block is inserted, do not place a checkmark here. Attributes are normally not displayed during plotting unless the attribute information is needed. For the purpose of creating, assigning, and inserting attributes in this chapter, the Invisible check box will not be checked. You can control the visibility of the attributes at the command line using the ATTDISP command, which is discussed later in the chapter.

- **CONSTANT:** (check box). If the attribute value is to be the same during block insertions, place a checkmark in the Constant check box. This means that all current and future insertions of the block will produce a constant value for the attribute. If you want Auto-CAD to prompt you for a new attribute value because different values are to be used at different block insertions, do not place a checkmark here. If this option is checked, the Verify and Preset options will not be available.

- **VERIFY:** (check box). If you want AutoCAD to give you a prompt to remind you about the attribute value you entered, place a check mark in the Verify check box. Keeping this option on will allow you to check and verify the attribute value before it is assigned and before the block is inserted.

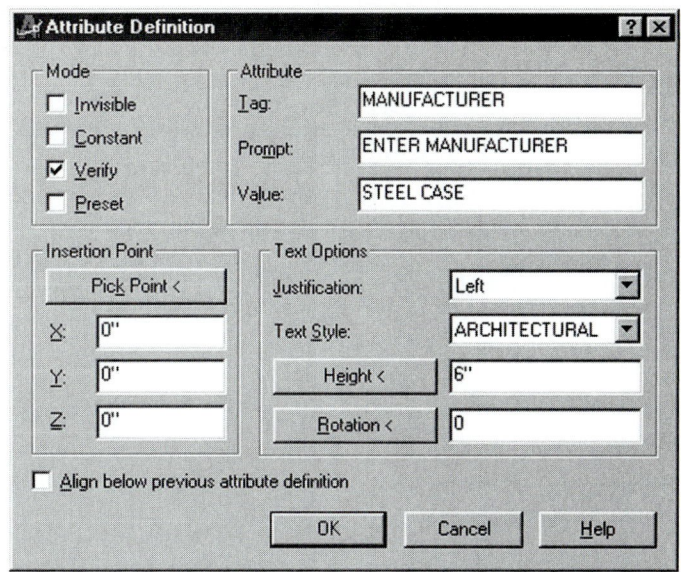

FIGURE 21–2 The Attribute Definition dialog box is used to create, assign, and insert attributes to symbols on the current drawing.

- **PRESET:** (check box). If you do not want AutoCAD to display prompts about the attribute values, place a checkmark in the Preset check box. All attributes will assume default values during insertions of the block. Because attribute values might change, not placing a check mark in this option will give you greater flexibility in controlling attribute values during block insertions.

If no checkmark is placed in any of the above options, AutoCAD will display the attributes as Normal when you use the ATTDISP (attribute display) command, which is explained later in the chapter.

Attribute: (Category).　This category will allow you to create attributes that will be attached to the symbol before it is turned into a block. The three attributes are as follows:

- **TAG:** (text area). This is where you decide what specific attribute will be attached to the block by asking what information about the block is needed in the drawing. This information is called a Tag. A tag is similar to a label, and in AutoCAD it is the name given to the attribute. A tag can be composed of letters and numbers but no spaces. For example, the following can be assigned as a Tag:

Type: This tag can be a name or number given to the block. For example, the name *workstation desk* can be the value assigned to type.

Manufacturer: This tag can be the name given to the manufacturer.

Material: This tag can be the material used to manufacture the type.

Size: This tag can be the size or dimensions assigned to the individual furniture as the type.

Price: This tag can be assigned as a dollar value to the furniture or the equipment.

Person: This tag can have the first and last name of the individual assigned to the type.

The attribute is inserted as a text and will be displayed as the tag, such as *manufacturer*. When all the attribute information is completed, a block is created from the symbol. When the block is inserted, the manufacturer attribute tag will be displayed as a value, such as *steel case*.

- **PROMPT:** (text area). This is the area where you create a statement you want AutoCAD to ask you about the value of the tag. For example, for the Manufacturer assigned as the Tag the question can be *What is the name of the Manufacturer?* Or *Enter Manufacturer.* For the Material as the Tag, the prompt can be *What is the Material of this product?* Or *Enter Material.* The second prompts are better questions to ask because they are short and to the point. A prompt can be composed of letters, numbers, and spaces. If the Constant option under Mode is checked, the Prompt text area will be inactive.

- **VALUE:** (text area). This is the text that is actually displayed in the drawing as the default attribute when the block is inserted. For example, the value for the tag assigned as material for the workstation desk can be entered as SOLID OAK or PLASTIC LAMINATE. The value for the tag assigned as manufacturer for the workstation desk can be entered as STEELCASE or ETHAN ALLEN. A value can be composed of letters, numbers, and spaces. It is not necessary to enter anything here because AutoCAD will prompt you for a Value if the Constant option is not checked. This might be a better option if furniture and equipment purchases are with multiple manufacturers. You can choose to enter a value at the insertion time. You can include a message instead of the actual value. The message might say something like, SELECT FROM THE LIST ONLY or CALL INTERIOR DESIGN DEPARTMENT.

Use the ~TabKey~ to move from tag to prompt to value text areas faster. If you entered information incorrectly, you can correct it by highlighting the text and reentering the correct information before closing the Attribute Definition dialog box. If you discover a mistake after closing the dialog box, you can still edit attributes using the Enter Attributes dialog box when you insert the block. This is discussed later in the chapter.

Text Options: (Category). This category will allow you to set the justification, style, height, and rotation of the attribute text.

- **JUSTIFICATION:** (drop-down list). This area will allow you to select the justification for the attribute text by displaying the 15 different text justification options. To see all the options, click on the down arrow next to the drop-down list and use the scroll bars on the right. By default text is left justified when inserted as attributes. This means that the attribute will be inserted with the insertion point at the lower left corner of the first letter of the text. For more information regarding text justification options, refer to Chapter 14.

- **TEXT STYLE:** (drop-down list). This area will allow you to select a text style to be used for the attribute. If no text style has been created, you can either accept the default standard text style or use the STYLE command to create a new text style. If one or more text styles exist, use the down arrow to see the available text styles and click on the one you want to use. Notice that in Figure 21–2 the text style is selected as Architectural.

- **HEIGHT <:** (button and text box). The text box area is used to enter the text height value of the attribute. For example, if you want the attribute text height to be plotted at 1/8″ when the drawing scale is set to 1/4″ = 1′-0″, enter 6 inside this text box. See the Text Height Chart in Chapter 2. You can also set the text height value at the command line by clicking on the Height button. The Attribute Definition dialog box will temporarily disappear, and the following command line will appear:

```
Command: _attdef
Height: (enter a new value for the attribute text height and press
~EnterKey~)
```

The dialog box will return, and the new text height value will be displayed in the Height text box. You can also set the text height by selecting two points on the screen. This is useful when the text height is to match the height of an existing object or text and no dimensional value is available. If this is the case, select the points on the objects using object snap modes. The new text height value will be displayed when the dialog box returns.

- **ROTATION <:** (button and text box). The text box area is used to enter the rotation value for the attribute text. It functions in the same manner as the Height < button and text box. Enter a new rotation angle value in the text box or click on the Rotation button to assign a new value at the command line. You can also assign a new rotation angle by selecting two points on the screen. The default Rotation angle is 0 degrees.

Insertion Point: (category). This category will allow you to enter the X and Y coordinate locations for the attribute insertion or select the insertion point on the screen.

- **PICK POINTS <:** (button). Selecting this button will allow you to pick the insertion point for the attribute on the current drawing. The Attribute Definition dialog box will temporarily disappear when you click on this button. Once you pick the insertion point on the screen, the dialog box will return showing the X and Y coordinates of the insertion points picked.

- **X:** (text area). This area is where you enter the X coordinate value for the attribute insertion point directly in the dialog box without picking a point on the screen. If you know the precise X coordinate value of the insertion, enter it here.

- **Y:** (text area). This area is where you enter the Y coordinate value for the attribute insertion point directly in the dialog box without picking a point on the screen. If you know the precise Y coordinate value of the insertion, enter it here.

- **Z:** (text area). The Z coordinate value is used when three-dimensional drawings are used. Enter 0 or use default 0.0000 value for two-dimensional drawings.

- **ALIGN BELOW PREVIOUS ATTRIBUTE DEFINITION:** (check box). This option is not available for the first attribute text insertion. When you create the first attribute you insert the text by using the Pick Points button or the X and Y coordinates. When you create the second attribute, this option becomes available allowing you to insert the second attribute text below the previous text with same justification. This is very useful when you want all attributes to align below previous ones.

OK: (Button). After you click on the Pick Points button and select the insertion point for the first attribute text, the Attribute Definition dialog box will return. When you are satisfied with all the categories, click on the OK button to place the attribute.

Figure 21–3 shows the first attribute tag displayed as type for the workstation desk shown in Figure 21–1. Figure 21–4 shows 19 tags created for all furniture that are part of the CAD workstation symbol. Don't be alarmed if tags of type, manufacturer, material, price, and person are displayed without their assigned values. When the symbol is assigned a block definition and when it is inserted in the drawing, all tags will be automatically converted to assigned values as shown in Figure 21–1.

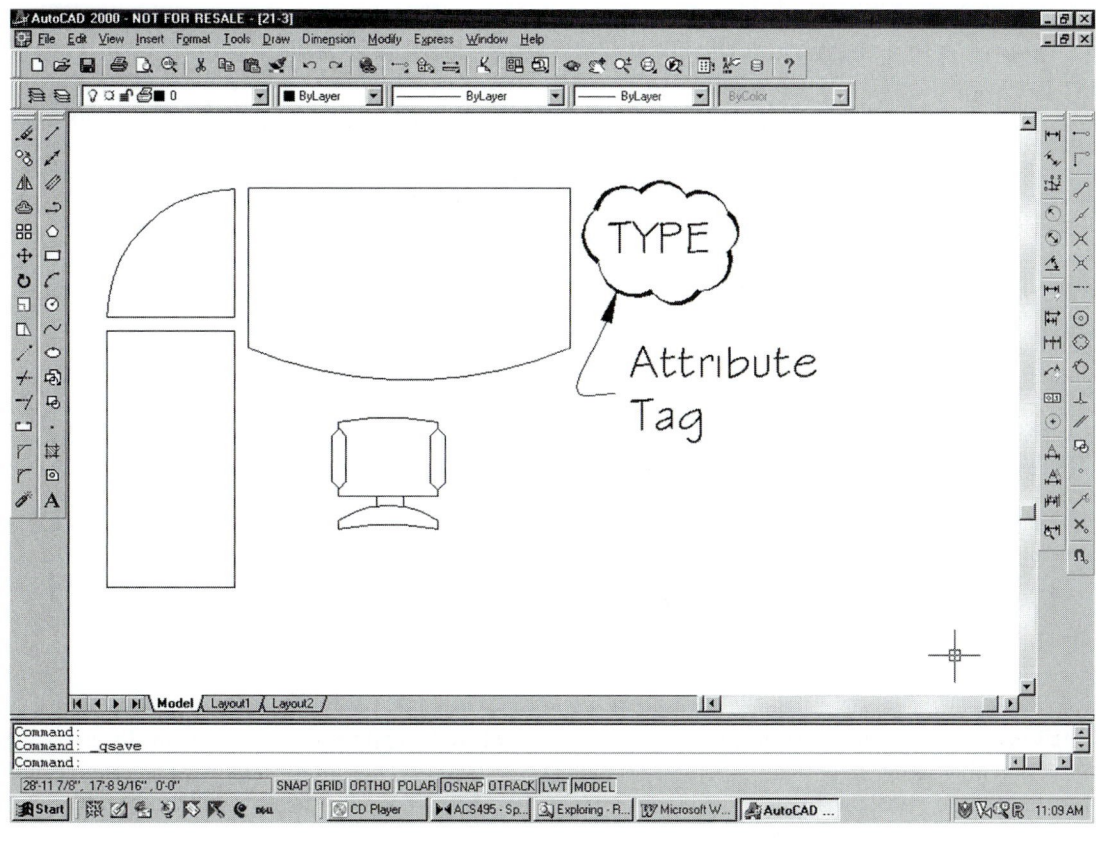

FIGURE 21–3 When the first attribute tag is displayed it will not show the assigned value. All consecutive attributes will be displaed as tags. When the symbol is created as a block or a wblock and when it is inserted in the drawing all tags will be automatically displayed as assigned values.

FIGURE 21–4 All 19 attributes that are part of the CAD workstation symbol are displayed as tags when they are first completed. This symbol is not a block yet.

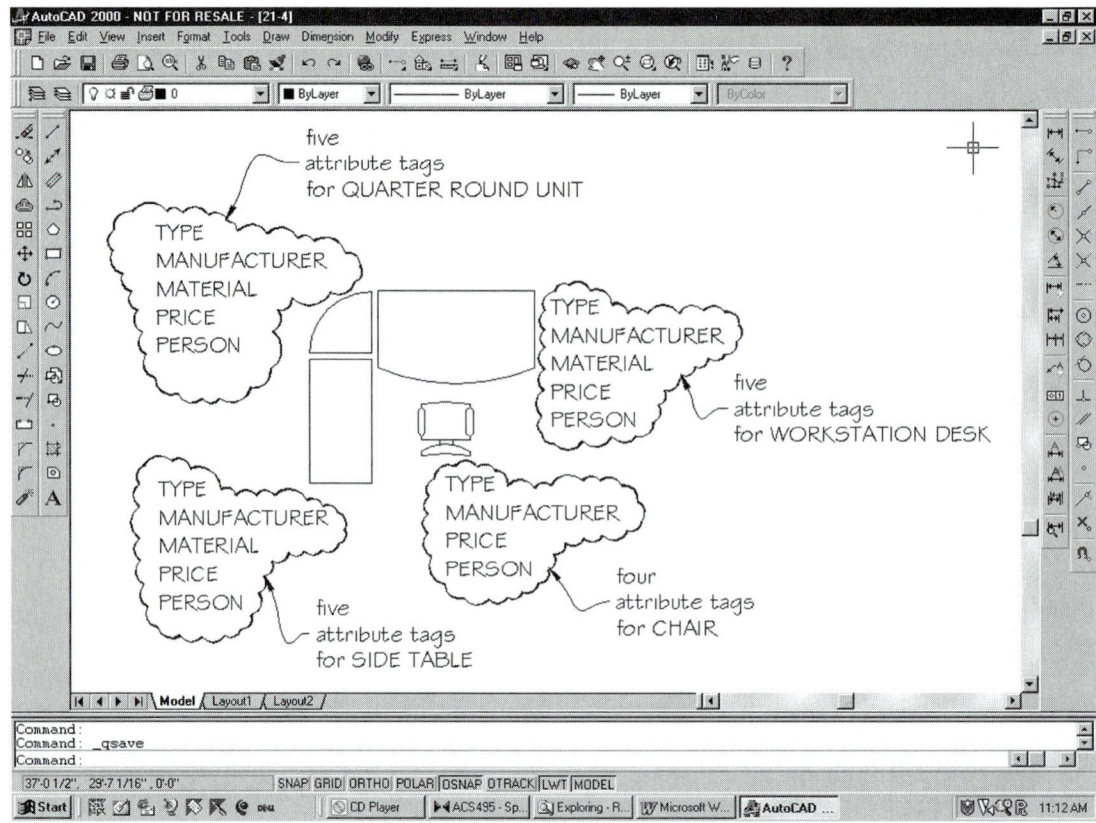

Note: The amount of attributes needed for each symbol depends on the information required by the project guidelines. More or fewer attribute tags might be required for different symbols. Product-related data can include Sweet's Catalog Numbers or Manufacturer Product Code Numbers. Establish this data earlier in the project to increase productivity when assigning attributes.

In order for the assigned attribute tags to appear as values, a block must be created from the symbol and the attributes. Use the Make Block button in the Draw toolbar or enter B, BMAKE, or BLOCK at the command line to access the Block Definition dialog box. You can also create a WBLOCK from the symbol and attributes. When creating the block or the wblock, make sure that you include the attributes with the objects. If you do not include the attributes when selecting the objects for the block, the attributes will not become a part of the block. Refer to Chapter 19 for more information about blocks and wblocks.

21.3 ASSIGNING ATTRIBUTES AT THE COMMAND LINE

You can assign attributes at the command line using the –ATTDEF (attribute definition) command. AutoCAD will present attribute modes for you to set as follows:

```
Command: -ATTDEF ~EnterKey~
Current attribute modes: Invisible=N Constant=N Verify=Y Preset=N
Enter an option to change [Invisible/Constant/Verify/Preset] <done>:
```

You can change attribute modes by entering I, C, V, or P or pressing ~EnterKey~ to finish attribute modes. When you enter an option, it will act as a toggle switch. For example, entering I for Invisible will toggle from N (no or normal) to Y (yes) and will place a checkmark inside the Invisible check box under the Mode category of the Attribute Definition dialog box. The next three prompts will allow you to assign attributes as follows:

```
Enter attribute tag name: (enter a tag name such as SIZE) ~EnterKey~
Enter attribute prompt: (enter an attribute prompt such as ENTER SIZE)
~EnterKey~
Enter default attribute value: (enter an attribute value such as 3'-0")
~EnterKey~
```

The rest of the command prompts are similar to the categories found in the Attribute Definition dialog box as follows:

```
Current text style: "ARCHITECTURAL" Text height: 0'-6"
Specify start point of text or [Justify/Style]: (select the insertion point
for the attribute text or enter J for Justification or S for text style)
When you select the insertion point for the attribute text, AutoCAD will
prompt you to specify the text height as follows:
Specify height <0'-6">: (enter the text height or press ~EnterKey~ to
accept default value)
Specify rotation angle of text <0>: (enter a rotation angle value for
the text or press ~EnterKey~ to accept default value)
This will display the attribute tag name on the screen. If you select the
Justify option before specifying start point of text, AutoCAD will prompt
you to select the text justification as follows:
Specify start point of text or [Justify/Style]: J ~EnterKey~
Enter an option
[Align/Fit/Center/Middle/Right/TL/TC/TR/ML/MC/MR/BL/BC/BR]: (enter an
option)
If you select the Style option before specifying start point of text,
AutoCAD will prompt you to enter a text style as follows:
Specify start point of text or [Justify/Style]: S ~EnterKey~
Enter style name or [?] <ARCHITECTURAL>: (enter? to see available styles,
enter the style name, or press ~EnterKey~ to accept default text style)
```

You can add additional attributes to symbols by pressing the ~EnterKey~. This will repeat the entire attribute definition sequence. Each sequence will assign a new attribute tag. When you reach the second attribute text positioning prompt, the previous attribute text will be highlighted. If you press ~EnterKey~, the new attribute text will be positioned directly below the first text or you can specify a new location. After all attribute tags are assigned, use the BLOCK or the WBLOCK command to create a block or wblock from the symbol. When the block is inserted, all the attribute tags will convert to attribute values.

21.4 ASSIGNING ATTRIBUTES TO EXISTING BLOCKS

You can assign attributes to existing blocks using the Attribute Definition dialog box or entering –ATTDEF at the command line. If you use the original block name you are basically creating the same block twice. This will cause AutoCAD to display the following message:

```
CAD WORKSTATION is already defined.
Do you want to redefine it?
```

If you press the No button, AutoCAD will not allow you to create a new block from itself using the same name. If you press the Yes button, AutoCAD will display the following message:

```
Block CAD WORKSTATION references itself.
```

To avoid seeing the error messages, always use a different name for existing blocks. Rather than re-creating the same block, add ATT as the suffix for the block name. For example, if you have an existing block named Circuit Control Panel and you wish to add attributes, use the following guidelines:

- Open or insert the Circuit Control Panel block.
- Assign attributes as discussed previously.
- Use the BLOCK or WBLOCK command to create block or the file.

- Inside the Block Definition dialog box highlight the Circuit Control Panel inside the Name: text box and rename it as Circuit Control Panel ATT. This will remind you that a second block has been created with attributes.
- Create the block or wblock as discussed in Chapter 19.
- Insert the block or the file as discussed in Chapter 19.

21.5 INSERTING BLOCKS WITH ATTRIBUTES USING THE COMMAND LINE

The ATTDIA (attribute dialog entry interface) system variable controls whether the INSERT command or the block insertion procedure uses a dialog box for entering attribute values for attribute prompts. By default the ATTDIA system variable is turned off (0). This means that the attribute values can be verified and checked for correctness using the command line. If an attribute value is to be corrected, it can be typed at the command line in response to the attribute prompt. First use the Insert Block button in the Draw toolbar or enter INSERT at the command line to insert the block with attributes. Figure 21–5 shows a WINDOW block inserted with attributes on the east elevation of a house. The attribute tags for the window are entered as SIZE, TYPE, FRAME-MATERIAL, MANUFACTURER, GLAZING, and ROUGH OPENING from top to bottom.

When inserting blocks with attributes, the insertion process is similar to inserting blocks up until the actual insertion. After inserting the block, AutoCAD will prompt you for all the attributes, and you will have the option to enter a new attribute value at the command line. Of course, this all depends on the options selected under the Mode category in the Attribute Definition dialog box or at the command line. After using the Insert dialog box to locate the block or the wblock, the block will appear attached to the pickbox ready to be inserted. The command sequence to insert the window block shown in Figure 21–5 with attributes is as follows:

FIGURE 21–5 The window block inserted on the east elevation of a house with six attributes.

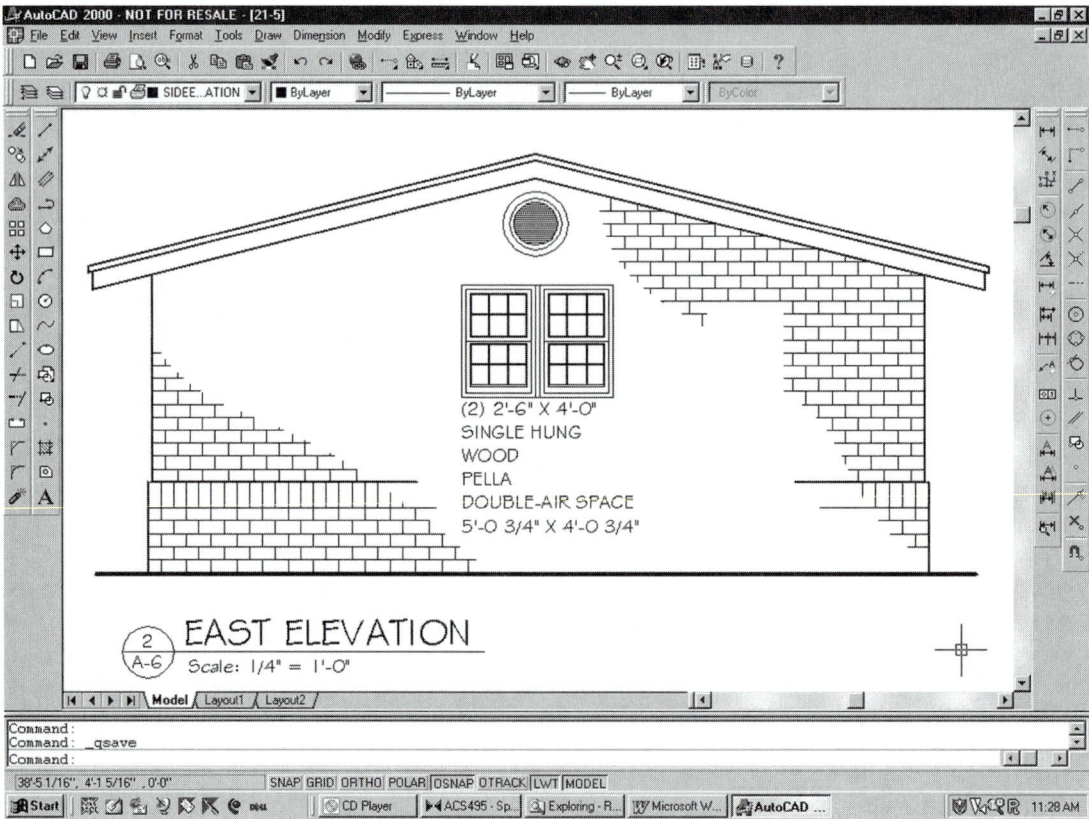

```
Command: _insert
Specify insertion point or [Scale/X/Y/Z/Rotate/PScale/PX/PY/PZ/PRotate]:
(specify the insertion point of the block with attributes or enter an
option)
Enter attribute values
ENTER ROUGH-OPENING <5'-0 3/4" X 4'-0 3/4">: (This is the attribute
prompt for the ROUGH OPENING attribute tag with the attribute value shown
inside the brackets. Enter a new value or press ~EnterKey~ to accept the
default attribute value. If the Constant Mode option is checked, you will
not be prompted for a new attribute value. If the Verify mode is not
checked, you will not be reminded about the attribute value. If the
Preset option is checked, all attribute prompts will be disabled.)
ENTER GLAZING <DOUBLE-AIR SPACE>: (This is the attribute prompt for the
GLAZING attribute tag with the attribute value shown inside the brackets.)
ENTER MANUFACTURER <PELLA>: (This is the attribute prompt for the
MANUFACTURER attribute tag with attribute value shown inside the
brackets.)
ENTER FRAME MATERIAL <WOOD>: (This is the attribute prompt for the FRAME-
MATERIAL attribute tag with attribute value shown inside the brackets.)
ENTER TYPE <SINGLE HUNG>: (This is the attribute prompt for the TYPE
attribute tag with attribute value shown inside the brackets.)
ENTER SIZE <(2) 2'-6" X 4'-0">: (This is the attribute prompt for the
SIZE attribute tag with attribute value shown inside the brackets.)
Verify attribute values
```

The entire process will repeat itself giving you a second chance to correct any mistakes before the block and its attributes are inserted.

21.6 INSERTING BLOCKS WITH ATTRIBUTES USING A DIALOG BOX

If the ATTDIA system variable is turned on (1), you can have the same process shown above using a dialog box to verify the attribute values. To use the dialog box, turn the ATTDIA system variable on as follows:

```
Command: ATTDIA ~EnterKey~
Enter new value for ATTDIA <0>: 1
~EnterKey~
```

Use the Insert Block button in the Draw toolbar, or enter I or INSERT at the command line to insert the block with attributes. After you establish the insertion point, scale, and rotation, the Enter Attributes dialog box will be displayed as shown in Figure 21–6. The Block name: area will display the name of the block with attributes. The attribute prompts are displayed on the left side, and the corresponding attribute values are displayed in the attribute value text box. If there are more than eight attribute prompts and values, they can be displayed by clicking on the Next button. To display the first eight attributes, click on the Previous button. These buttons are not available in Figure 21–6 because there are only five attribute prompts and values. Notice that in Figure 21–6 the oval vanity sink ATT is the block with five attributes: manufacturer, type, price, size, and color.

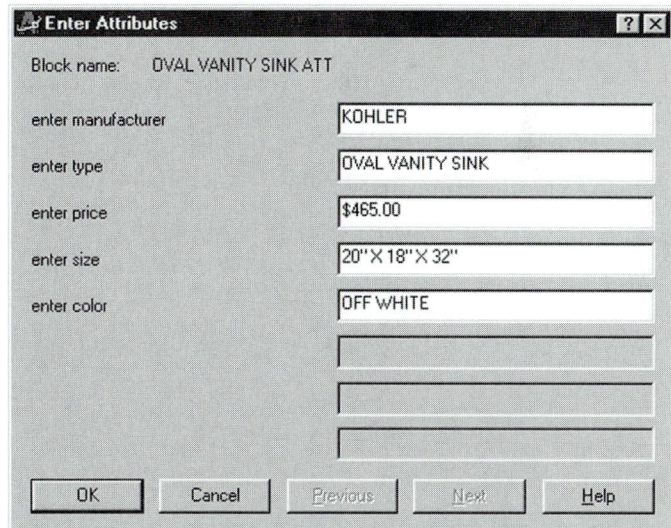

FIGURE 21–6 The Enter Attributes dialog box is used to check and verify attribute values before a block with attributes is inserted in the drawing.

To change an attribute value, highlight the desired attribute value and enter the new value. When finished, click on the OK button to close the Enter Attributes dialog box. The block with new attribute values will be inserted.

Tips: It is more efficient and effective to verify attribute tags and values that are visible, not constant, and not preset using the Enter Attributes dialog box. This will allow you to enter new attribute values and request the attribute value each time the block is inserted. Check only the Verify Mode and set the ATTDIA system variable to 1 before inserting blocks with attributes.

21.7 CONTROLLING ATTRIBUTE VISIBILITY

All blocks should include some type of information attached as an attribute. Even information considered insignificant may on occasion prove to be significant. Attributes do not have to be tags or values attached to symbols. They can convey a hidden message or a specific direction provided to the designer or the CAD manager during the design or production phase of the project. For example, all electrical outlet or electrical switch blocks might contain the following message: DO NOT INSERT MORE THAN 12'-0" APART or MAX. ELEV. 48" or IF INSERTED WITHIN 5' OF SINK OR LAVATORY USE GFCI. This information can boost production by reducing the redline cycle on working drawings. In this case the attribute tag could be entered as IMPORTANT MESSAGE and the prompt could be entered as ENTER IMPORTANT MESSAGE and the value as the message itself. Be careful not to display these messages on the drawing.

When the attribute is a tag, its visibility on the drawing can be controlled globally using the ATTDISP (attribute display) command at the command line. You can also access the ATTDISP command by selecting Display and then Attribute display from the View pull-down menu. The command prompt is as follows:

```
Command: ATTDISP ~EnterKey~
Enter attribute visibility setting [Normal/On/Off] <Normal>:
The three options are described below:
```

- **Normal:** (option). This option will display all attributes according to the settings established using the Attribute Definition dialog box or using the –ATTDEF command. This is the default attribute display option. It is important to know that if the invisible mode is checked, attributes will not be displayed.
- **On:** (option). This option will display all attributes, regardless of ATTDEF settings.
- **Off:** (option). This option will not display any attributes, regardless of ATTDEF settings.

After you change the visibility using the ATTDISP command, AutoCAD will regenerate the drawing if the REGENAUTO system variable is on. The current visibility setting is stored in the ATTMODE (attribute mode) system variable, which contains the current settings of the ATTDISP command. The command prompt is as follows:

```
Command: ATTMODE ~EnterKey~
Enter new value for ATTMODE <1>:
```

The three settings are described below:

- **0:** (Off). This will set the ATTDISP to Off.
- **1:** (Normal). This will set the ATTDISP to Normal.
- **2:** (On). This will set the ATTDISP to On.

Tips: When defining invisible attributes, use the ATTDISP command to view them. Turn off attribute display to increase display speed and minimize drawing text clutter.

21.8 SUPPRESSING ATTRIBUTE PROMPTS

When drawings use blocks with attributes that always keep their default values, the attribute prompts can be suppressed by using the ATTREQ (attribute request) system variable. This system variable determines whether the INSERT command uses default attribute settings or displays prompts at the command line or dialog box attribute values. The command prompt is as follows:

```
Command: ATTREQ ~EnterKey~
Enter new value for ATTREQ <1>:
The two options are as follows:
```

- **1:** (On). This will allow AutoCAD to display prompts for attributes at the command line. This is the default setting.
- **0:** (Off). This will suppress prompts and dialog box attribute values as specified by ATTDIA system variable.

When your drawing involves inserting many blocks with attributes, spend some time on establishing system variables to your advantage before inserting. When attribute values vary, set ATTREQ to 1 to use attribute prompts to change attribute values at the command line or in the dialog box.

21.9 EDITING ATTRIBUTES

An attribute is considered to be text information attached and made a part of a block. When the attribute is attached to the block, the block and the text become one object. However, when the attribute is created and inserted in the symbol it is only a text. The attribute does not become associated with the symbol until it is made into a block with the symbol. Therefore attributes can be edited either before they are included in the block definition or after the block is created.

21.9.1 Editing Attribute Definition Before Creating the Block

You can attach attributes to symbols using the Attribute Definition dialog box or at the command line as discussed previously. Before using the Block Definition dialog box to create the block from the attribute text and the symbol, you can change attribute tag, prompt, and default values using three different methods as follows:

1. Use the DDEDIT command or the Edit Text button in the Modify II toolbar or select Text... from the Modify pull-down menu.

When you click on the Edit Text button in the Modify II toolbar, the command prompt will be as follows:

```
Command: _ ddedit
Select an annotation object or [Undo]: (select the annotation text to be edited)
```

The Edit Attribute Definition dialog box will be displayed as shown in Figure 21–7. Use this dialog box to edit the Attribute text before creating a block definition.

2. Use the Properties window to edit text. The Properties window is discussed in Chapter 13. When you select one attribute text, a grip will be displayed and the word *Attribute* will appear in the Properties window text box. Select the Categorized tab and click on the plus sign (+) in front of Text category. This will display all editing options associated with the attribute text, including tag, prompt, value, style, justify, and height. For example, to change the attribute tag, click on the attribute tag text, enter a new value, and press the ~EnterKey~. In the drawing area press the ~EscKey~ twice, and this will automatically change the attribute tag in the drawing. You can change the attribute prompt and value using the same procedure, but these changes will not take effect until you create a block definition from the symbol and the attributes and insert in the drawing. Be careful when you select more than one attribute because any attribute editing will change all the attributes in the drawing. You can also enter MO or DDMODIFY at the command line to access the Properties window. Figure 21–8 shows the oval vanity sink symbol with two attributes. When the manufacturer tag is selected, the Properties window will display Tag, Prompt, and Value assigned to the attribute as shown in Figure 21–8.

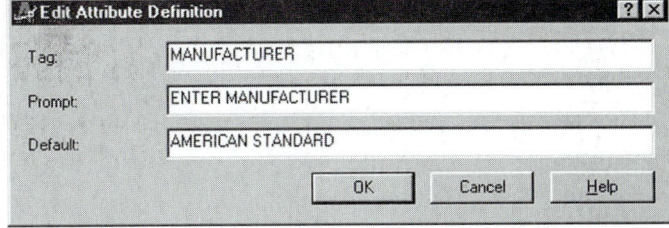

FIGURE 21–7 The Edit Attribute Definition dialog box will allow you to change attribute tag, prompt, and default (value) before you create a block definition from the symbol and the attributes.

FIGURE 21–8 The Properties window shown docked here can be used to edit properties of the attribute text. Notice that all properties associated with the attributes is found under the Text category.

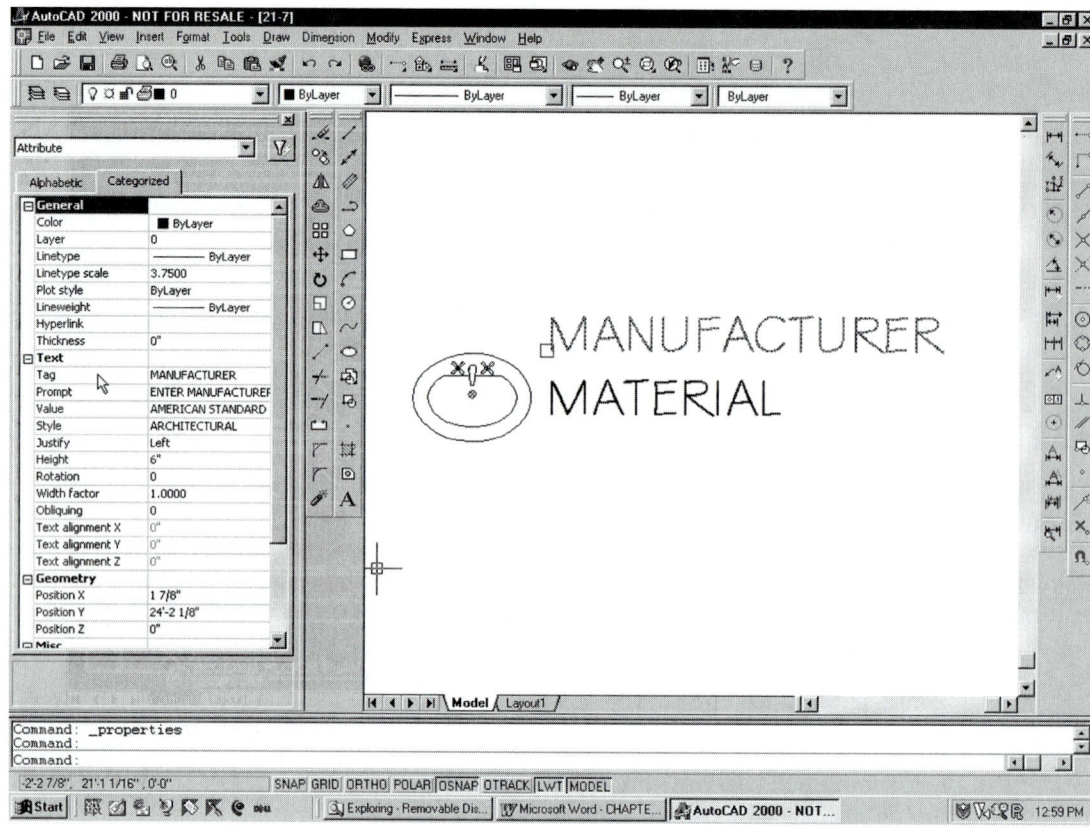

3. Use the CHANGE command to change the current position or the properties of the attribute text. The command line procedure is as follows:

```
Command: CHANGE ~EnterKey~
Select objects: (select one or more attribute text)
Specify change point or [Properties]: ~EnterKey~
Specify new text insertion point <no change>: (select a new
insertion point for the attribute text)
Enter new text style <ARCHITECTURAL>: (enter a new text style or
press ~EnterKey~ to accept default text style)
Specify new height <0'-6">: (enter a new text height or press
~EnterKey~ to accept default text height)
Specify new rotation angle <0>: (enter a new rotation angle or press
~EnterKey~ to accept default rotation angle)
Enter new tag <LOCATION>: (enter a new tag or press ~EnterKey~ to
accept default attribute tag)
Enter new prompt <ENTER LOCATION>: (enter a new prompt or press
~EnterKey~ to accept default attribute prompt)
Enter new default value <OFFICE 209>: (enter a new attribute value
or press ~EnterKey~ to accept default value)
When you press ~EnterKey~ after the last command prompt, the entire
procedure will repeat itself twice allowing you to catch any
mistakes you might have missed the first or second time around.
The Properties option will allow you to change the color, layer,
linetype, and lineweight of the attribute text. The command line
procedure is as follows:
Specify change point or [Properties]: P ~EnterKey~
Enter property to change
[Color/Elev/LAyer/LType/1tScale/LWeight/Thickness]: (enter an
option)
```

21.9.2 Editing Attribute Definition After Creating the Block

Once a block definition is created from the symbol and its attributes, you can edit attributes using a dialog box or using the command line.

21.9.3 Editing Attributes Using a Dialog Box

You can edit individual nonconstant attribute values associated with a specific block using the ATTEDIT (attribute edit) command. You can edit individual or all attribute values of one or more blocks one at a time using the ATTEDIT command. To access the ATTEDIT command, click on the Edit Attribute button in the Modify II toolbar, select Attribute and Single from the Modify pull-down menu, or enter ATE or ATTEDIT at the command line. The command line procedure is as follows:

```
Command: ATE or ATTEDIT ~EnterKey~
Select block reference: (select the inserted block or one of its
attributes)
```

The Edit Attributes dialog box will be displayed as shown in Figure 21–9. This dialog box is similar to the Enter Attribute dialog box as shown in Figure 21–6. To change any of the attributes,

highlight and enter the new text. When you click on the OK button, the attribute will be changed. You can edit attributes one at a time using this method. Figure 21–9 shows the five attribute values within the oval vanity sink ATT block. If there are more than eight attributes, use Next and the Previous buttons to navigate through the list.

To edit attribute values, highlight the individual attribute value and enter a new value. When finished click on the OK button. The block attribute will be updated on the screen.

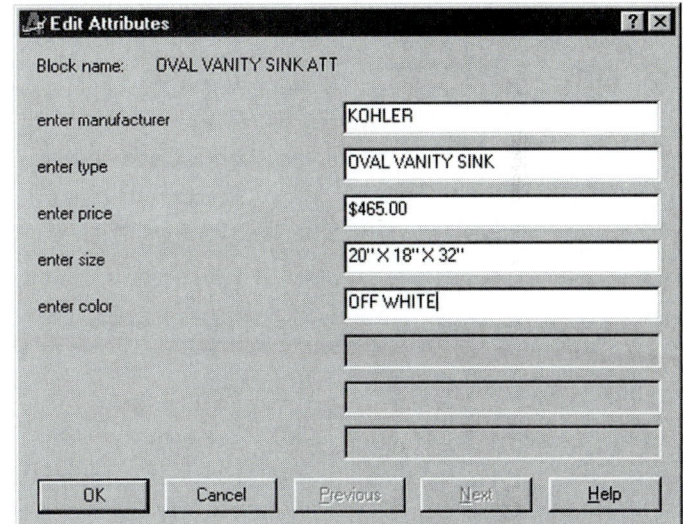

FIGURE 21–9 The Edit Attributes dialog box will allow you to edit one block at a time in the drawing.

21.9.4 Editing Attributes at the Command Line

You can edit both attribute values and attribute properties individually or globally independent of a block by entering ATTE or –ATTEDIT at the command line or selecting Attribute and Global from the Modify pull-down menu. The command line procedure is as follows:

```
Command: ATTE or -ATTEDIT ~EnterKey~
Edit attributes one at a time? [Yes/No] <Y>:
```

Responding Yes will allow you to edit the same attribute on many insertions of the same block one at a time without leaving the ATTE command. You can edit any or all of the attributes. Attributes must be visible on the screen and parallel to the current UCS. Responding No will allow you to change specific letters, numbers, and words of a single attribute but will affect all insertions of the same block on a global scale. The command prompt for the Yes option will present additional options as follows:

```
Enter block name specification <*>:
Enter attribute tag specification <*>:
Enter attribute value specification <*>:
```

Each attribute editing technique will allow you to place restrictions for determining the exact block and attribute specifications to edit. You can set restrictions so that only attributes having a specific value or name are selected. To selectively edit attributes, respond to the above prompts with a name or a value then press the ~EnterKey~. Make sure that the block name, attribute tag, and attribute value match the name, tag, and value entered for the selection set. To select individual attributes to edit, press ~EnterKey~ to the above prompts. The command prompt will continue as follows:

```
Select Attributes: (select one or more attributes to edit)
```

Figure 21–10 shows two of the same block inserted with four attributes. The attribute tags are item, catalog, price, and location and are inserted as office desk-chair, CF-6478-TR, $645.00, and room 2-107 respectively. The drawing on the left represents the original block with original attributes. The drawing on the right represents the edited catalog attribute with a different text value and a different text height. You can select one attribute or place a window around the entire attributes. When you select one attribute, AutoCAD will place an X on the left corner of the selected attribute. The X represents the attribute that is being edited.

■ **EXERCISE 21–1:** *The following step-by-step exercise will allow you to edit the attributes of the inserted block using the ATTE command.*

Step #1: Open the EXE21-1.dwg file.

Step #2: Edit the Attributes using the ATTE command as follows:

Command: **ATTE** ~EnterKey~

Edit attributes one at a time? [Yes/No] <Y>: ~EnterKey~

Enter block name specification <*>: ~EnterKey~

Enter attribute tag specification <*>: ~EnterKey~

Enter attribute value specification <*>: ~EnterKey~

Select Attributes: *(select the CF-6478-TR attribute)*

Select Attributes: 1 found

Select Attributes: ~EnterKey~

1 attribute selected. *(X is placed at the beginning of the attribute line)*

Enter an option [Value/Position/Height/Angle/Style/Layer/Color/Next] <N>: **V** ~EnterKey~

Enter type of value modification [Change/Replace] <R>: ~EnterKey~

Enter new attribute value: **CF-3905-KT** ~EnterKey~

Enter an option [Value/Position/Height/Angle/Style/Layer/Color/Next] <N>: **H** ~EnterKey~

Specify new height <0′–6″>: **4** ~EnterKey~

Enter an option [Value/Position/Height/Angle/Style/Layer/Color/Next] <N>: ~EnterKey~

Congratulations! You have successfully edited the value and height of one attribute. The attribute value and the attribute text height will be changed as shown in Figure 21–10.

After you select an attribute, there are eight editing options to select from as follows:

• **Value:** (option). This option will allow you to edit the attribute value of the selected attribute. You have two suboptions to select from: Change or Replace. Pressing ~EnterKey~ will replace the existing attribute value with a new value that you enter. You can change any part of the attribute by entering *C* as the Change option. AutoCAD will ask you to enter the string to change. A *string* is any single part or sequence of consecutive characters in the attribute. For example, in Figure 21–10 you can change only the number 7 in the room 2-107 attribute to read room 2-109 without retyping the entire value as follows:

```
Enter type of value modification [Change/Replace] <R>: C ~EnterKey~
Enter string to change: 7 ~EnterKey~
Enter new string: 9 ~EnterKey~
Enter an option [Value/Position/Height/Angle/Style/Layer/Color/Next]
<N>: ~EnterKey~
```

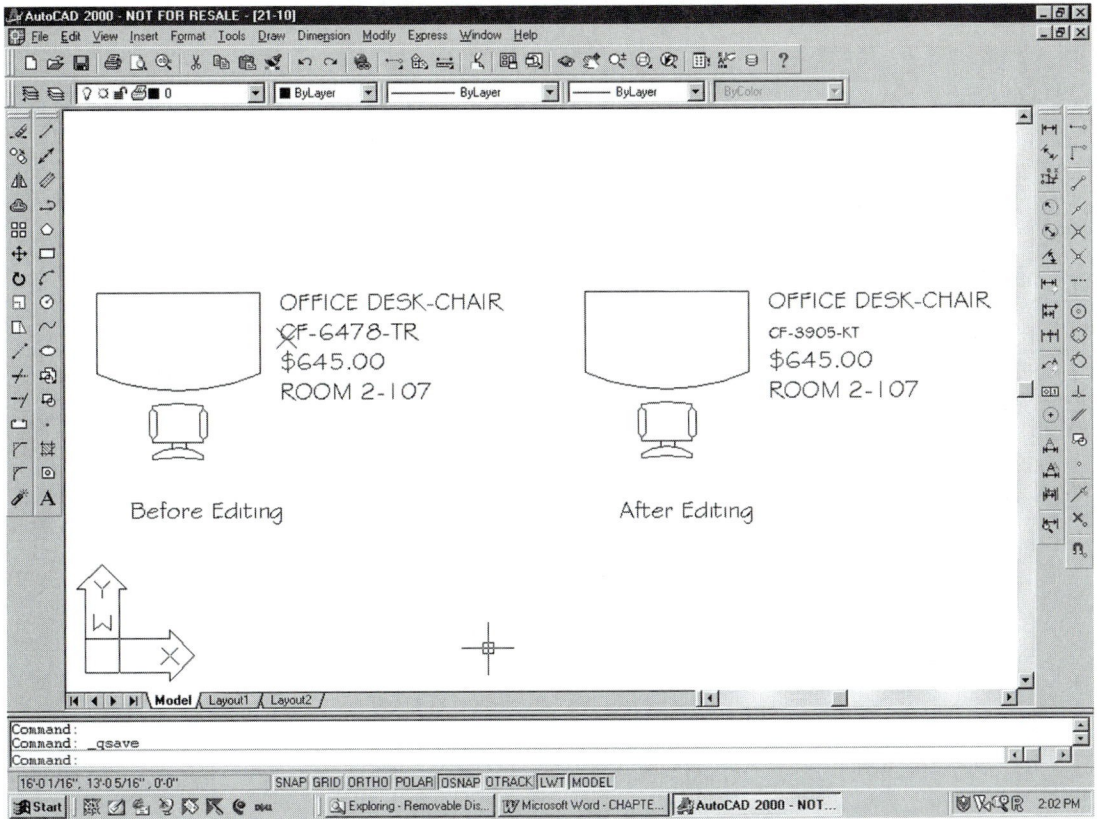

This will change the existing attribute value from ROOM 2-107 to ROOM 2-109.

- **Position:** (option). This option will allow you to select a new text insertion point. The command line procedure is as follows:

```
Enter an option [Value/Position/Height/Angle/Style/Layer/Color/Next]
<N>: P ~EnterKey~
Specify new text insertion point <no change>: (select a new text
insertion point for the attribute text)
```

This will move the attribute text to a new position. Figure 21–11 shows the office desk-chair attribute value text moved to a new location.

- **Height:** (option). This option will allow you to enter a new text height for the selected attribute.

- **Angle:** (option). This option will allow you to enter a new text angle for the selected attribute.

- **Style:** (option). This option will allow you to enter a new text style for the selected attribute.

- **Layer:** (option). This option will allow you to enter a new layer name for the selected attribute.

- **Color:** (option). This option will allow you to enter a new color name or a color number between 1 and 255 for the selected attribute. You can also enter BYLAYER or BYBLOCK.

- **Next:** (option). When you select more than one attribute or place a window around the attributes to select all, AutoCAD assumes that you will be editing one attribute after another. When you are finished editing one attribute, pressing ~EnterKey~ will cause the X to move from one attribute to the next. If there are no additional attributes to edit, the process ends. You can also enter N to move to the next attribute without editing the current.

FIGURE 21–11 The
Position option will
allow you to move the
selected attribute text to
a new location.

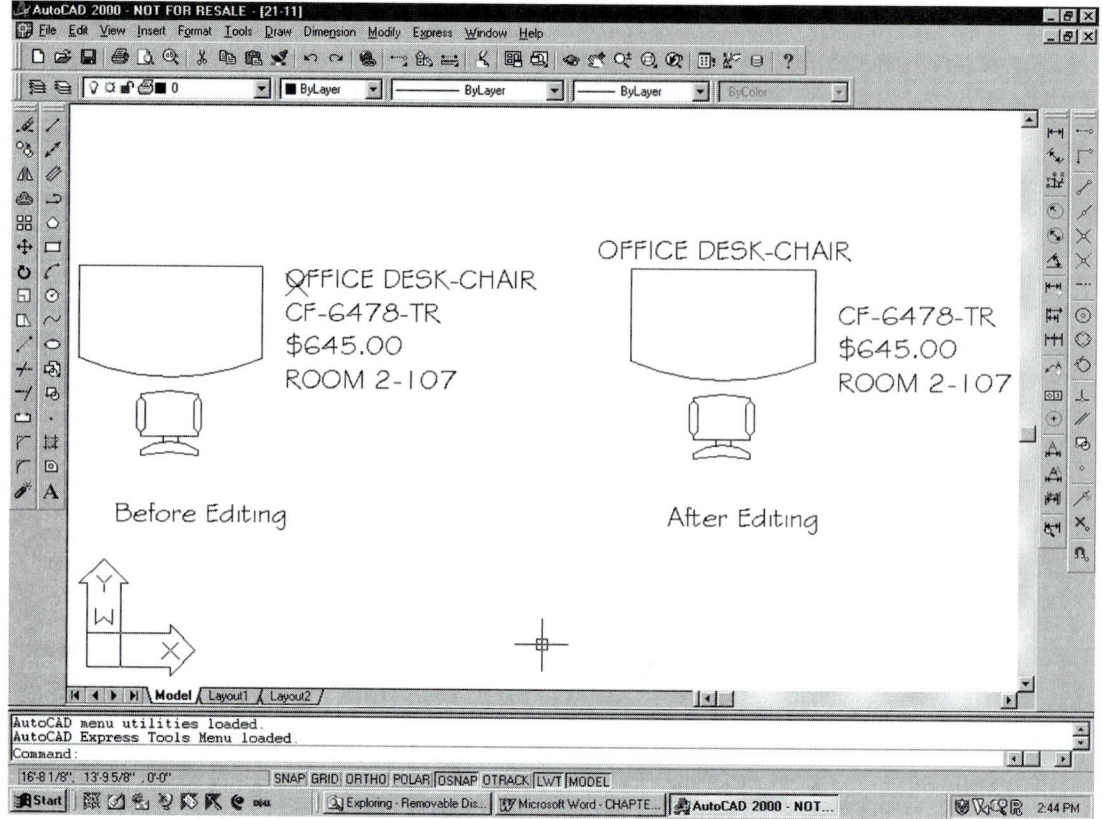

*Caution: If the original attribute is created with aligned or fit text option, the command prompt will
not include the Angle option. If the original attribute is created with aligned text option, the command prompt will not include the Height option.*

*Tips: At the Height option, you can also specify a point for the new text height. The new text height
becomes the distance between the selected point on the screen and the starting point of the text. The
same concept is applicable to the Angle option.*

You can edit attributes globally by responding *no* to the ATTE command. Figure 21–12 shows
four blocks inserted with attributes. The ATTE command will be used to edit the 8″ concrete
block attribute to 10″ on two blocks as follows:

```
Command: ATTE or -ATTEDIT ~EnterKey~
Edit attributes one at a time? [Yes/No] <Y>: N ~EnterKey~
Performing global editing of attribute values.
Edit only attributes visible on the screen? [Yes/No] <Y>: ~EnterKey~
Enter block name specification <*>: ~EnterKey~
Enter attribute tag specification <*>: ~EnterKey~
Enter attribute value specification <*>: ~EnterKey~
Select attributes: (select the 8″ concrete block attribute from two
blocks on the right)
Select Attributes: ~EnterKey~
2 attributes selected.
Enter string to change: 8 ~EnterKey~
Enter new string: 10 ~EnterKey~
```

The two attributes will be changed to 10″ concrete block as shown in Figure 21–12.

*Tips: Use any of the selection methods such as Window, Crossing, WP, CP, and Fence to your ad-
vantage.*

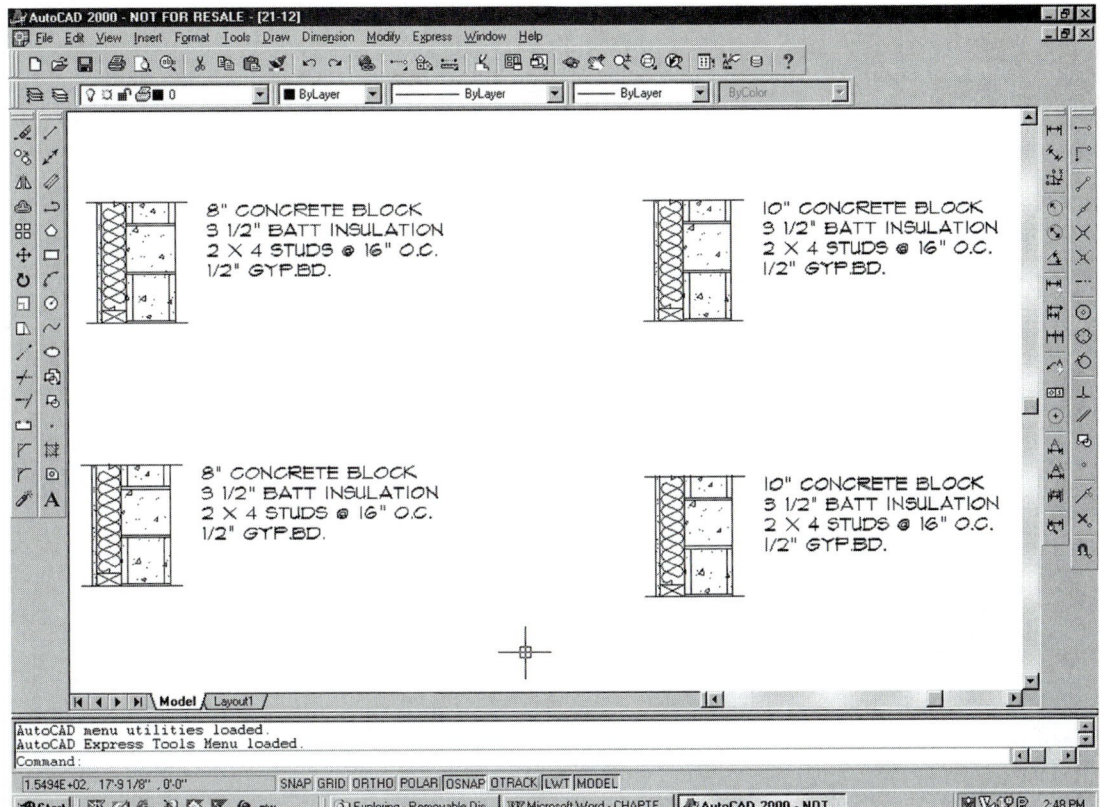

FIGURE 21–12 The global editing of attributes.

21.10 REDEFINING ATTRIBUTES

There might be a situation in which an existing block and its associated attributes need to be revised. You can redefine a block and update its attributes using the ATTREDEF command. When redefining a block and its attributes, the block must be exploded prior to redefining it. Figure 21–13 shows the same block in Figure 21–12. The following changes are to be made to the block:

```
Change 2 X 4 wood studs to 2 X 2 wood furring with 2" rigid insulation.
Remove batt insulation hatch and replace it with net hatching.
Change the 3 1/2" batt insulation attribute value to 2" rigid insulation.
To perform all these changes, the block must be redefined with its
attributes.
```

■ **EXERCISE 21–2:** *The following step-by-step exercise will allow you to perform the changes described above.*

Step #1: Open the EXE21-2.dwg file.

Step #2: Explode the block. When attributes are exploded they will return to their attribute tag text.

Step #3: Erase the batt insulation and move the gypsum board 2″ toward the concrete block.

Step #4: Create the rigid insulation by using the net hatch pattern.

Step #5: Use the Edit Attribute Definition dialog box and change the 3 1/2″ batt insulation to 2″ rigid insulation and 2 × 4 studs @ 16″ O.C. to 2 × 2 furring vertical.

Step #6: Use the Block Definition dialog box and create a new block from the new objects and attributes.

Step #7: Insert the block with new definition as shown in Figure 21–13.

FIGURE 21–13 After redefining the block and the components of the wall with 2″ rigid insulation, and 2 × 2 vertical furring.

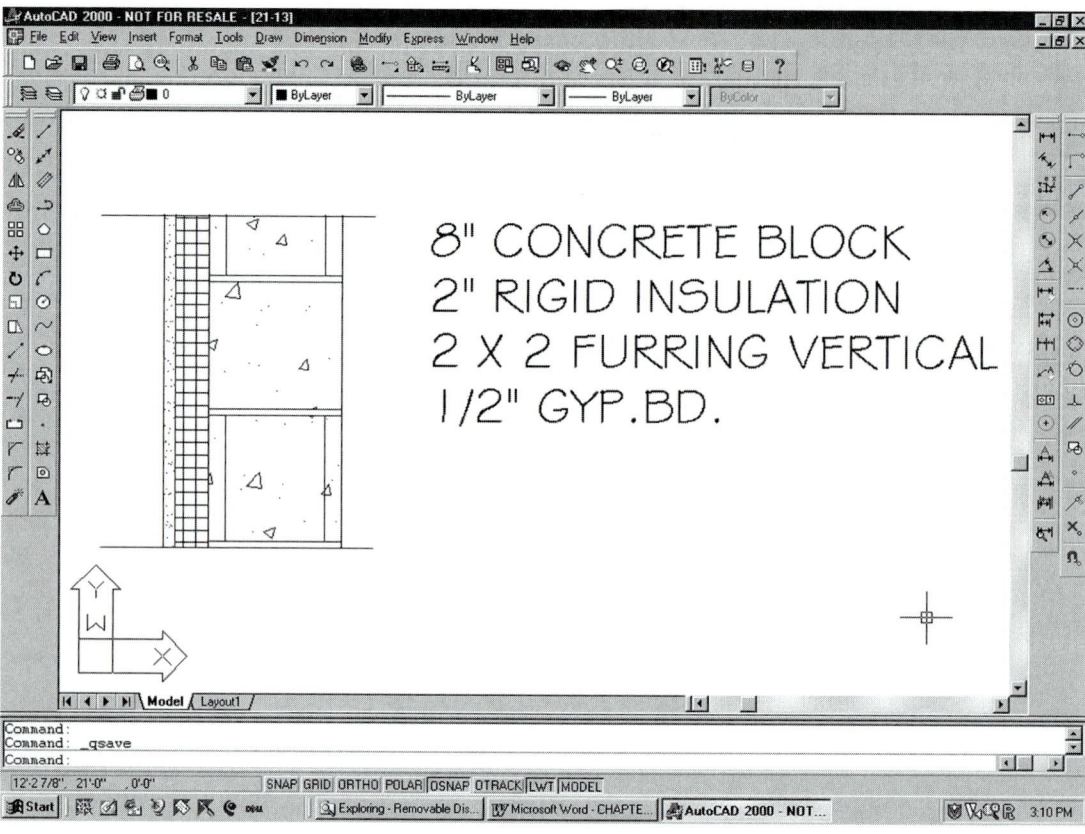

Congratulations! You have successfully redefined a block and changed its attributes.

Note: If you assign new attributes to the existing block reference, the default attribute values will be used. Previous attributes in the new block definition will retain their previous attribute values. If you do not include any previous attributes in the new block definition, AutoCAD will delete them from the definition.

21.11 ASSIGNING ATTRIBUTES TO TITLE BLOCKS

When a title block is used in a new drawing, a great deal of text must be entered to indicate the title block information. This can be a time-consuming task. Title block information is generally composed of variable data for the current drawing file. This variable data can be assigned as attributes and can be edited while inserting the title block into the new drawing. Information that is constant should be created as text and placed in the title block prior to assigning attributes. The title block may include revision data. If you leave title block information areas empty and complete them after you insert the title block into the new drawing file, you are spending too much time creating and placing text inside each area. If you create text objects with arbitrary values using templates and edit them using the Properties window or the DDEDIT command, you are also spending too much time editing each text object. Because attributes are extremely powerful text information tools, always assign attributes to automate title block documentation task. When you assign attributes to the title block areas, the attribute definition will include attribute tags as ordinary text objects. When you create a block definition (Block) or a file definition (WBlock) and when you insert the title block into another drawing, you will be prompted to enter attribute values for each attribute tag. Think of the text objects that are constant in a title block as the database and the attributes as the values stored in the database. Each time you insert the title block, the database is accessed and different values are entered. Figure 21–14 shows a title block with typical text objects without any attributes. Figure 21–15 shows the same

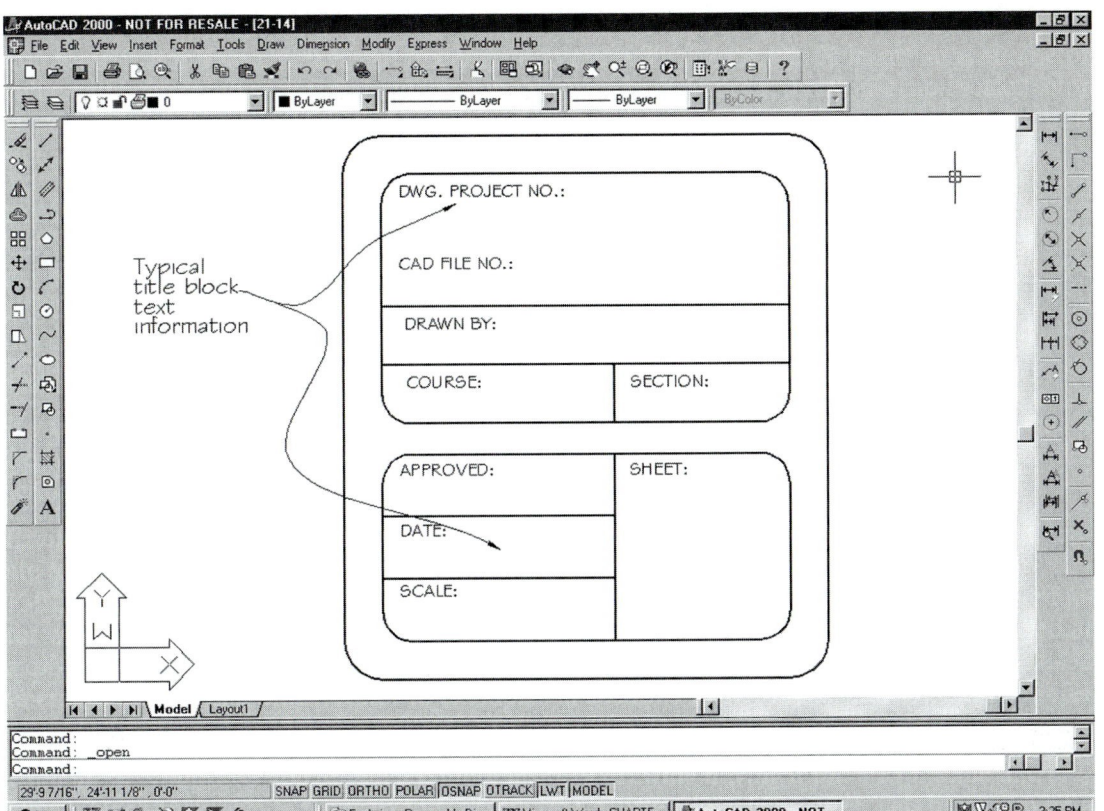

FIGURE 21–14 A title block information with blank areas.

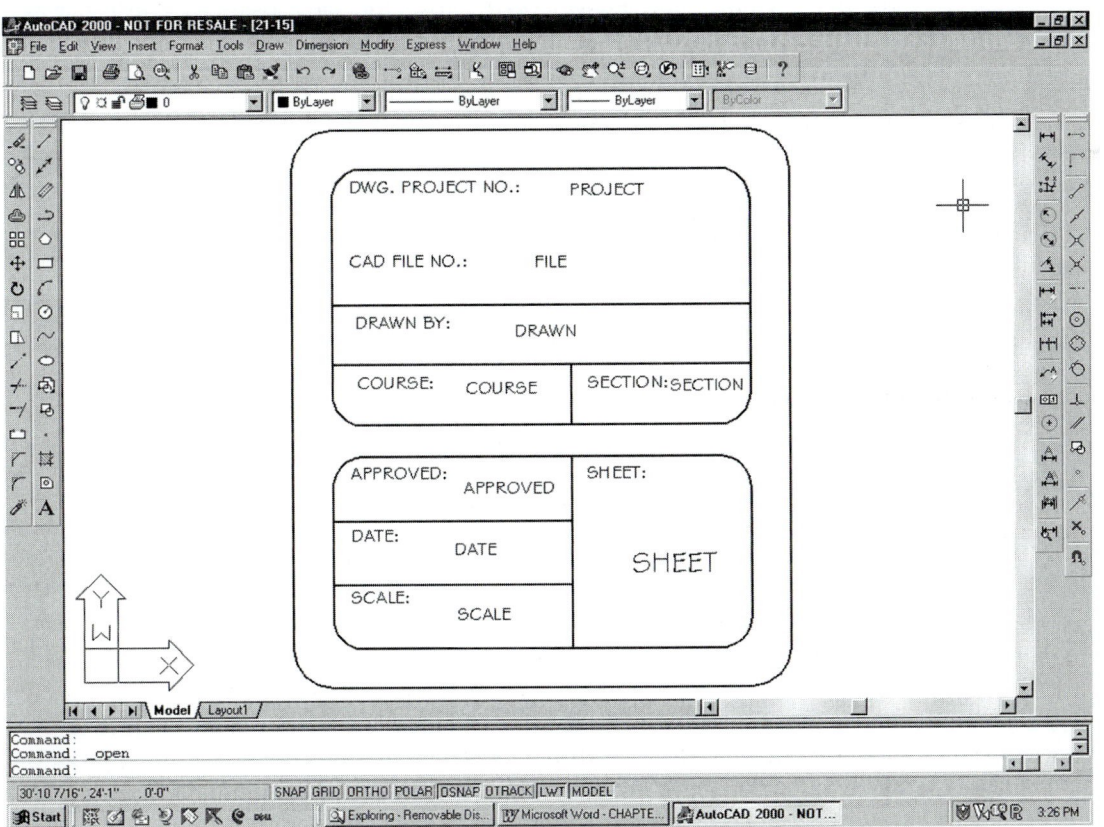

FIGURE 21–15 A title block with assigned attribute tags.

FIGURE 21–16 A title block inserted as a block with attribute values that can be changed each time it is inserted.

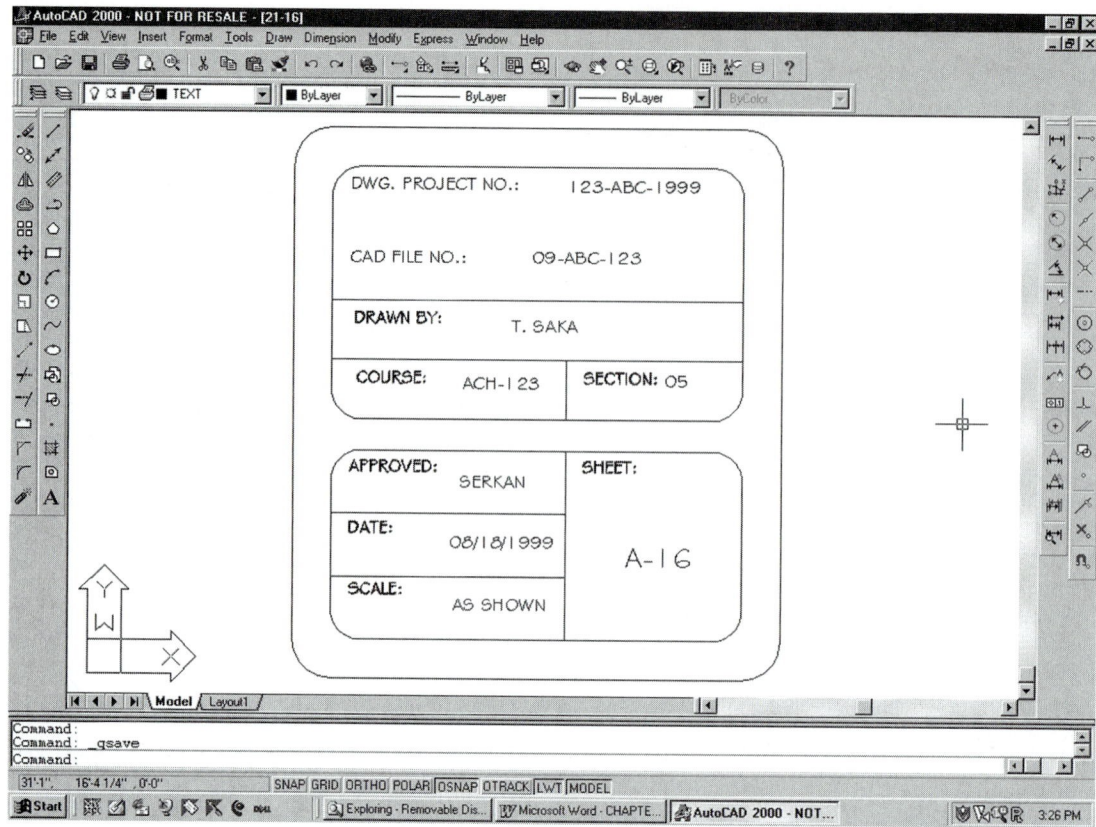

title block with assigned attribute tags. Figure 21–16 shows the same title block inserted as a block with attribute values.

The following procedure will help you assign attributes to a title block:

• Open an existing template or create a new one with title block information.

• Using the ATTDEF command, assign attribute tag, prompt, and value to each text object.

• Create a block or a wblock using the title block and attributes.

• Turn the ATTDIA system variable on to use a dialog box to enter different attribute values. Otherwise type attribute values at the command line.

• Insert the block or the file into the current drawing.

• If necessary, edit attributes as discussed previously.

This will allow you to enter title block attribute values without using the text command.

Tips: Create and place the title block attributes in a layer called title block attributes. This will allow you to freeze the layer containing attributes and reduce regeneration time. When you are ready to plot, thaw the frozen layer. Determine the exact text height for each attribute tag and place it in its precise location. Use same procedures for the revision block data. Use the WBLOCK command to create a .dwg file from the title block. Include any specific messages or reminder to the user inside the attribute prompt.

21.12 EXTRACTING ATTRIBUTES

You can extract information stored in the attributes in a drawing and create a separate written text file using a database software program such as Notepad or any other text-editing program. You can use the extracted information in a spreadsheet or database to produce schedules, parts list, and bill of materials (BOM). When attributes are extracted from the block, the current drawing geometry or information does not change. The extracted information list can be used to create a door, window, and room-finish schedule for the floor plans. Before extracting attribute information, a template file must be created. This template file will allow AutoCAD how to format the file structure containing extracted attribute information.

21.12.1 Creating an Extraction Template File

The extraction template file contains all of the attribute tag information assigned to a block and is composed of three elements: a character (C) or numeric (N) data, a maximum field name length, and a decimal allowance. For example, the manufacturer, type, size, model, and price attribute tags are a part of the extraction template file as shown in Table 21–1. The data written to a specific field must be classified as character or numeric type. Characters such as *a, b, c, d, e, #, H, <,* and *"* are always considered to be a character type, but numerical values such as 6, 2, 34, and 105 do not have to be numeric type. Numbers that represent a value such as price, length, and weight can be stored as characters or numbers. The field length is the allowance given to the character or the numerical data. Each field in the template file will extract specific information from the block. Each line in the template file information represents one field to be written in the attribute information file, including the name of the field, its character or numerical length, and numerical precision.

The following template file information format shows four possible fields:

MNFR	Cwww000	*(Character values without decimal places)*
TYPE	Cwww000	*(Character values without decimal places)*
PRICE	Nwwwddd	*(Numerical values with decimal places)*
SIZE	Nwww000	*(Numerical values without decimal places)*

The C represents character, N represents numeric value, the www represent three digits for the number of spaces that will be reserved for the attribute, and the ddd represent three digits for the number of decimal places in the numerical value. For example, a listing of C025000 represents character data with 25 spaces allocated for the attribute and no space allocated for decimal places. A listing of N008003 represents a numerical entry with eight spaces and three decimal places.

Any group of fields in any order is acceptable, but the template file must include at least one attribute tag field. The attribute tag fields determine which attributes (blocks) are included in the attribute file. If a block contains some of the attributes specified, the values for the missing attributes are registered as blanks for characters and zeros for numerical data. Each field can only appear once in the template file. Message and comment fields should not be included in the template file.

In addition to listing attribute extraction information, the template file can be created to extract block property information. You can see all information related to the block by selecting the block and examining the General, Geometry, and Misc tabs in the Properties window or entering LIST at the command line and selecting the block. The following template file shows six possible fields:

BL:NAME	Cwww000	*(Block name)*
BL:XCI	Nwwwddd	*(X coordinate for block insertion)*
BL:YCI	Nwwwddd	*(Y coordinate for block insertion)*
BL:LAYER	Cwww000	*(Block insertion layer name)*
BL:ROTA	Nwwwddd	*(Block insertion rotation angle)*
BL:LEVEL	Nwww000	*(Block nesting level)*

TABLE 21–1: Example of extraction template file information.

Attribute Tag	Character (C) or Numeric Data (N)	Maximum Field Length	Decimal Places
Manufacturer	C	050	000
Type	C	050	000
Size	N	015	003
Model	C	020	000
Price	N	006	003

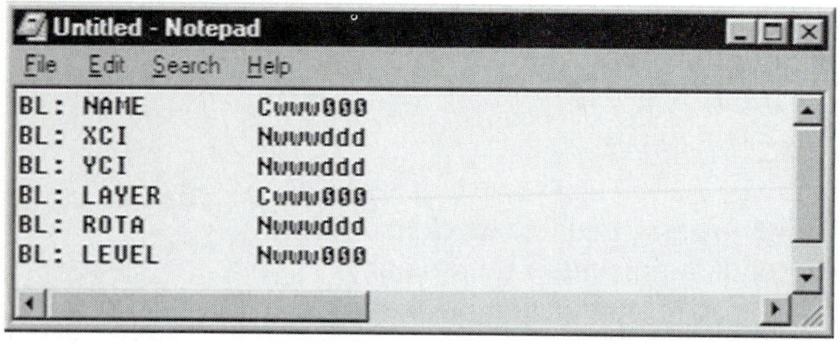

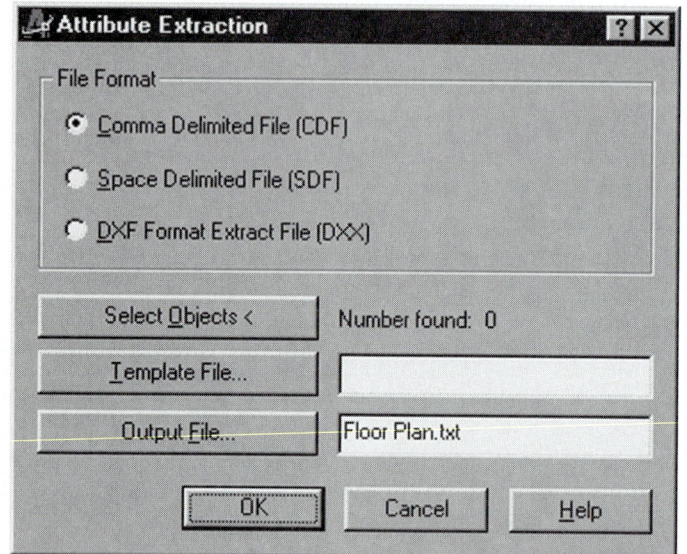

FIGURE 21-17
Creating the attribute extraction template using Notepad.

To create the actual template, use the following procedure:

- Open a drawing that contains blocks with attributes, such as a floor plan with doors and windows as blocks containing attributes.

- From the Start menu, select Programs, Accessories, and select Notepad.

- Enter the required template information in Notepad. Figure 21–17 shows a typical template entry.

- When the template is complete, save the template with a *.txt* file extension by using the SaveAs option from the File pull-down menu. For example, DRSCH.txt can be a template file for the door schedule.

- Exit Notepad and return to AutoCAD.

21.12.2 Using the Attribute Extraction Dialog Box

After the template file is created, attributes from blocks can be extracted. For example, after each door, window, and room designation is inserted into the floor plan as a block with attributes, a schedule can be created and maintained by using the DDATTEXT (dynamic dialog attribute extraction) or ATTEXT (attribute extraction) commands. Entering either of these commands at the command line will display the Attribute Extraction dialog box as shown in Figure 21–18. This dialog box will allow you to write all door, window, and finish material information to a file format. It also specifies template and output file names for the information to be extracted.

The Attribute Extraction dialog box has the following categories:

- **FILE FORMAT:** (category). This category will allow you to determine the format for the file to extract specific attribute data. There are three file formats:

Comma Delimited File (CDF): This file format will create a file containing one record for each block reference in the current drawing that has at least one matching attribute tag in the template file. A record is a specific component of a block with attributes, such as a solid core door type. Each additional listing of components to the same door is record. All of the doors that share a common record are considered to be a field. You can further divide records by size, shape, and type. A template file is a file that lists each field with an attribute tag. When creating a file, each field of each record is separated by a comma, and a single quotation mark encloses the character fields.

Space Delimited File (SDF): This file format will create a file containing one record for each block reference in the current drawing that has at least one matching attribute tag in the template file. The fields of each record have a fixed width; therefore, character separators are not allowed.

Drawing Interchange File (DXF): This will produce a file format containing only block reference, attribute, and end-of-sequence objects. This type of format requires no template. This is a subset of the AutoCAD normal DXF format and is distinguished by the *.dxx* file extension.

FIGURE 21-18 The Attribute Extraction dialog box will allow you to write text information to a file format.

- **SELECT OBJECTS** <: (button). Selecting this button will close the Attribute Extraction dialog box temporarily to allow you to select the blocks with attributes. When the dialog box returns, the number of objects selected will be registered in the Number found: area.

- **TEMPLATE FILE...:** (button). This button will allow you to specify a Template Extraction File for CDF and SDF formats. You can either enter the file name in the space provided next to the button or click on the button to search for the existing template file. When this button is selected the Output File dialog box will be displayed as shown in Figure 21–19. From the file list, the DRSCH.txt can be selected for door schedule extraction.

- **OUTPUT FILE...:** (button). This button will allow you to select an output file name. You can either enter the file name in the space provided or click on the button to search for existing files.

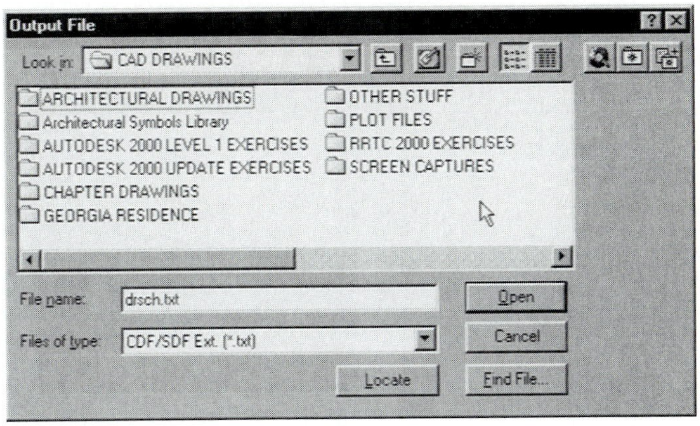

FIGURE 21–19 The Output File dialog box is similar to a standard file selection dialog box and will allow you to specify a template extraction file format. Notice that the default file extension is *.txt*. If you select DXF as the file format, the Template File option will not be available.

To extract attribute information, use the following procedure:

- Enter DDATTEXT or ATTEXT at the command line.
- Inside the Attribute Extraction dialog box, select the file format to be used for extraction.
- Click on the Select Objects < button to select a single block or multiple blocks with attributes in the drawing.
- Click on the Template File... button to specify the template file to use or enter the template file name.
- Click on the Output File... button to specify the output attribute information or enter the file name.
- Click on the OK button.

REVIEW QUESTIONS

1. List some of the benefits of assigning attributes to symbols.
2. How do you access the Attribute Definition dialog box?
3. Under what circumstances should you select the Constant attribute mode when defining attributes?
4. What does the default attribute value mean?
5. What command is used to assign attributes at the command line?
6. What does the ATTDISP system variable control?
7. What is the function of the ATTDIA system variable?
8. Describe the three different methods used to edit attributes before creating a block definition?
9. What are the steps involved in creating a template file to extract attribute information from blocks with attributes?

PROBLEMS

1. Draw the elevation of a double hung window as shown in Figure 21–20. Use architectural units, precision, and limits. Do not create dimensions. Assign the following attributes to the window:

Tag	Prompt	Value
Type	*Enter type*	*Double hung*
Manufacturer	*Enter manufacturer*	*Pella*
Catalog	*Enter catalog number*	*PDBH-490-12*
Frametype	*Enter frame type*	*Wood*
R.O.	*Enter rough opening*	*4'-0 3/4" × 5'-0 1/2"*
Glazing	*Enter glazing type*	*Double-low E*
Price	*Enter price*	*$112.00*

Do not create a block yet.

FIGURE 21–20 The Window elevation for Problem 1.

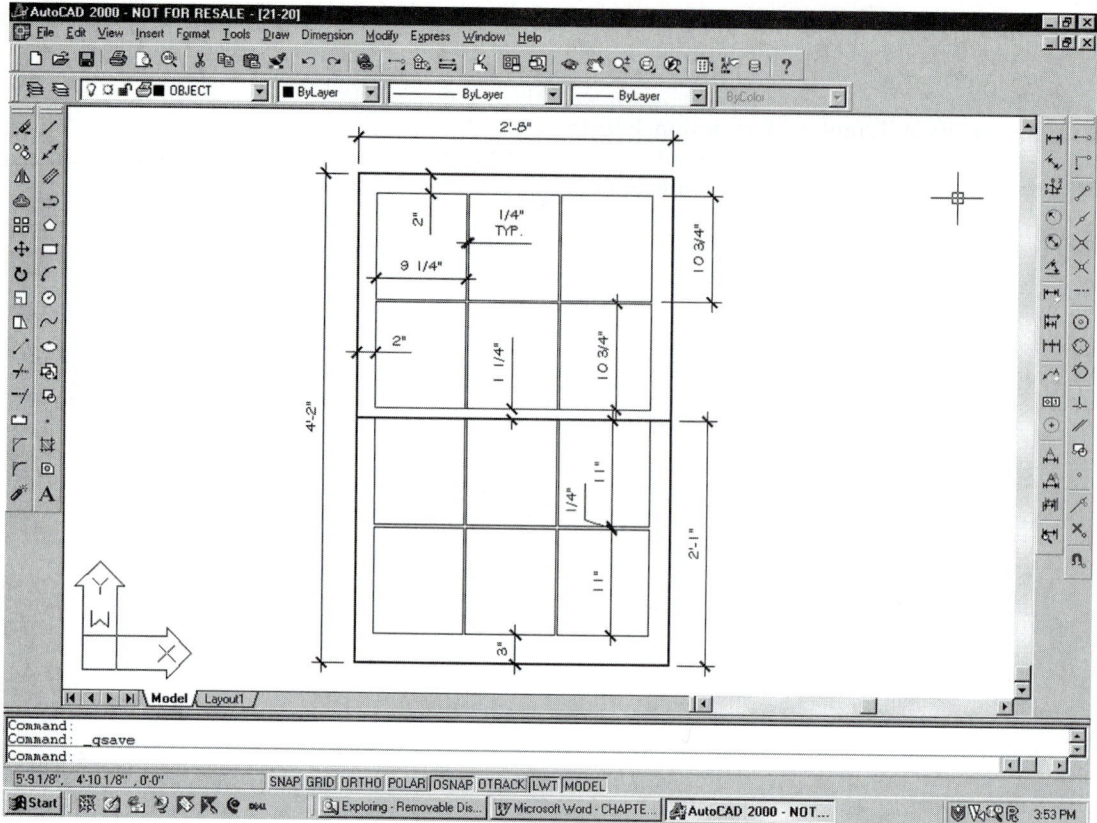

2. Before creating a block definition for the window in Exercise 1, change the manufacturer tag to peach tree, change the catalog to PQT-359-08, and change the price to $79.00. Create a Wblock with attributes and call it ATT-WDH. Save the changes. Use the upper-left corner of the window as the insertion point.

3. Open the *EXE21-3.dwg* file. Insert the ATT-WDH block into the points shown as X. Display all attributes and then turn attribute display off. Save the changes.

4. Using the same drawing above, turn attribute display on. Change the manufacturer, catalog, and price tags to their original values for only one of the windows. Do not save the changes.

5. Draw the elevation of the door as shown in Figure 21–21. Use architectural units, precision, and limits. Use the SPLINE command to create wood grains. Do not create dimensions. Assign the following attributes to the window:

Tag	Prompt	Value
Type	*Enter type*	*SC door*
Manufacturer	*Enter manufacturer*	*Pella*
Catalog	*Enter catalog number*	*PDSCDR-608-36*
Frametype	*Enter frame type*	*Wood*
SIZE	*Enter size*	*3'-0" × 6'-8"*
Price	*Enter price*	*$238.00*

Do not create a block yet.

6. Before creating a block definition for the door in Exercise 5, change the manufacturer tag to steel case, change the catalog to PKSSC-909-08, and change the price to $179.00. Create a wblock with attributes and call it ATT-SCDOOR. Save the changes. Use the upper-right corner of the door as the insertion point.

7. Open the *EXE21-4.dwg* file. Insert the ATT-SCDOOR block into the point shown as X. Display all attributes and then turn attribute display off. Save the changes.

8. Using the same drawing above, turn attribute display on. Change the manufacturer, catalog, and price tags to their original values for the door. Do not save the changes.

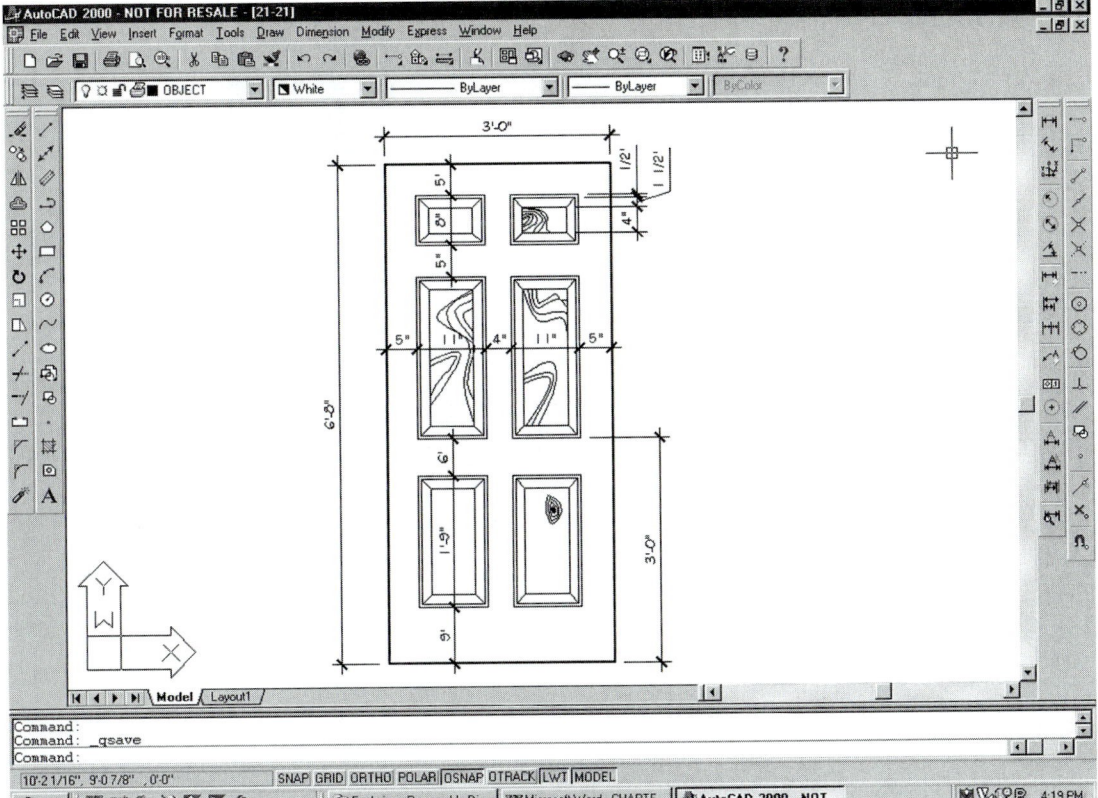

FIGURE 21–21 The
Door elevation for
Problem 5.

9. Open the *EXE21-5.dwg* file. Insert the CAD workstation attributes block into the office space. Inside the Enter Attributes dialog box, change the following attributes:

   Enter Person: Enter your name

   Enter Material: Steel

   Enter Person: Enter your name

10. After inserting the revised CAD workstation attributes block, change the other two names to your name using the Edit Attributes dialog box.

Layouts and Paper Space

CHAPTER

22

After successful completion of this chapter you should be able to:

▲ Understand model space, paper space, and layouts.

▲ Understand model space and paper space viewports.

▲ Create layouts using four different methods.

▲ Create tiled and untiled floating viewports.

▲ Copy layouts using ADC.

▲ Delete and rename layouts.

▲ Change layout display settings using the Options dialog box.

▲ Use the Page Setup dialog box.

▲ Create polygonal floating viewports in paper space.

▲ Convert paper space objects to viewports.

▲ Scale viewports.

▲ Clip viewports.

▲ Lock viewport scale.

22.1 MODEL SPACE, LAYOUTS, AND PAPER SPACE

There are two different environments that you work with in AutoCAD: *model* and *layout*. Throughout this text you have been creating drawings in the model environment with the Model tab active. The Model tab is located at the lower-left corner of the drawing screen as shown in Figure 22–1. When you start a new drawing as described in Chapter 3, you are automatically in model, working with the model of your drawing. When you are in model with the Model tab active, you are in model space. You create your drawings at full scale in model space with Model tab active. The model space can be thought of as the environment where you create object geometry including dimensions, notes, text, and hatching. The model space is where you create your drawings. There are three items that will remind you that you are working in model space:

1. The UCS icon located in the lower left corner of the drawing. This icon has two arrows pointing in the X and Y direction. The arrows of the UCS icon represent the X and Y coordinates.

2. The Model tab located below the UCS icon is highlighted when you are in model space. The Model tab represents the current model of your drawing environment.

3. The Model button in the Status bar represents the model space. When the word *Model* is displayed in this button, you are in model space.

The environment used to layout, compose, and prepare drawings for plotting is called the *layout*. A layout is a paper space environment that allows you to compose the model of your drawing on a selected sheet of paper for printing and plotting. A layout can be thought of as the environment where you setup the drawing sheet the way you want it to print or plot in paper space. The Layout tabs are at the lower left area of the drawing window next to the Model tab. When you first open a drawing, AutoCAD displays two default layouts tabs. These are the Layout1 and Layout2 tabs as shown in Figure 22–1. Layout tabs allow you to organize different views of your drawing on separate sheets called layouts. These layouts can easily be selected from the bottom of the screen to show different aspects of your drawing. When you click on one of the Layout tabs, the paper space environment is activated. Once in Paper space of your drawing layout, you can switch from Paper space to Model space by selecting the Paper or Model button in the Status Bar. Paper space in a layout represents the environment where the drawing is arranged prior to printing and plotting. There are three items that will remind you that you are in paper space:

1. The UCS icon for paper space is represented by a 90 degree triangle located at the lower left corner of the drawing as shown in Figure 22–2.

2. The Layout1 (or any other layout) tab located in the lower left corner of the drawing (next to the Model tab) is highlighted, and the paper space icon is displayed.

3. The Paper button in the Status Bar represents the paper space. When the word Paper is displayed in this button, you are in paper space.

Note: When you first select the Layout1 tab, AutoCAD will display the Page Setup – Layout1 dialog box. This is because AutoCAD thinks that you are ready to print or plot your drawing. Click on the OK button to exit this dialog box. The Page Setup dialog box allows you to specify plot parameters such as plot device, paper size, plot orientation, and plot area in each Layout. Page Setup is discussed later in the chapter. Printing and Plotting are discussed in Chapter 23.

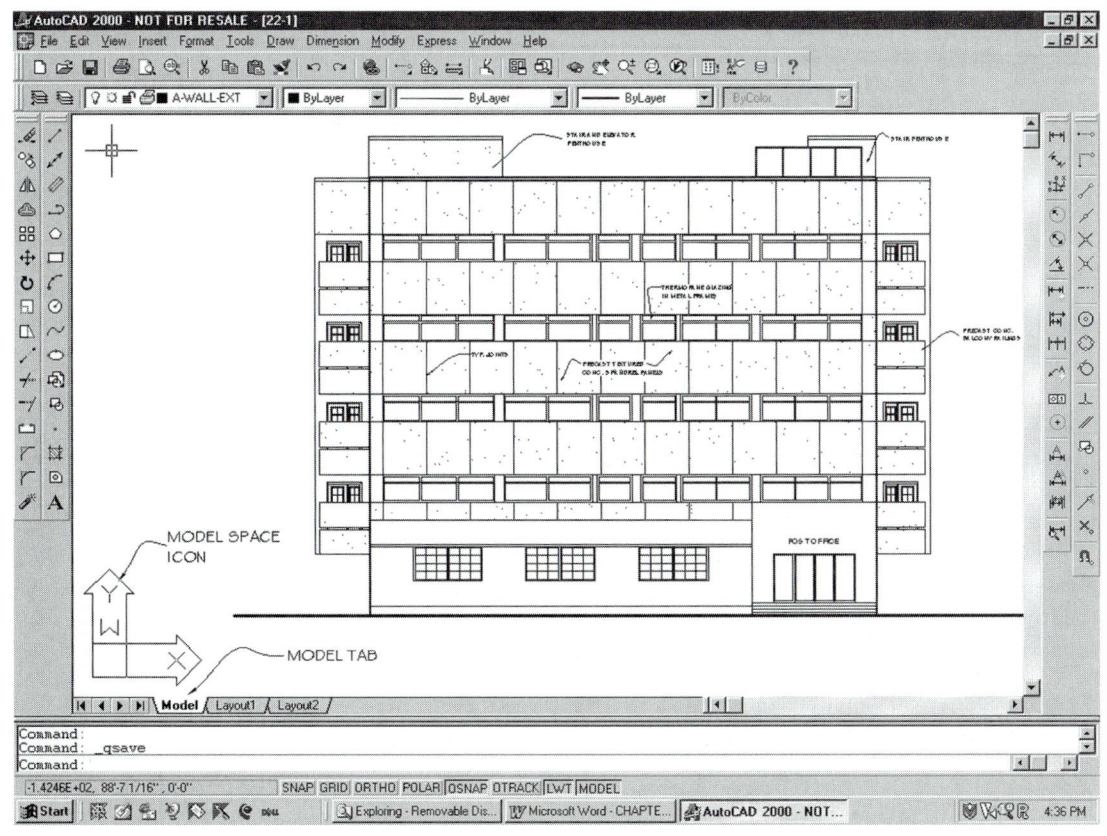

FIGURE 22–1 The model space environment is used to create the objects that are part of your drawing, including dimensions, notes, text, and hatching. The Model tab located at the lower left corner of the drawing screen is on by default every time you start a new drawing.

FIGURE 22–2 When
you select the Layout1
tab, the drawing will
appear in paper space.
Notice the Paper button
is active in the Status
bar next to the LWT
button.

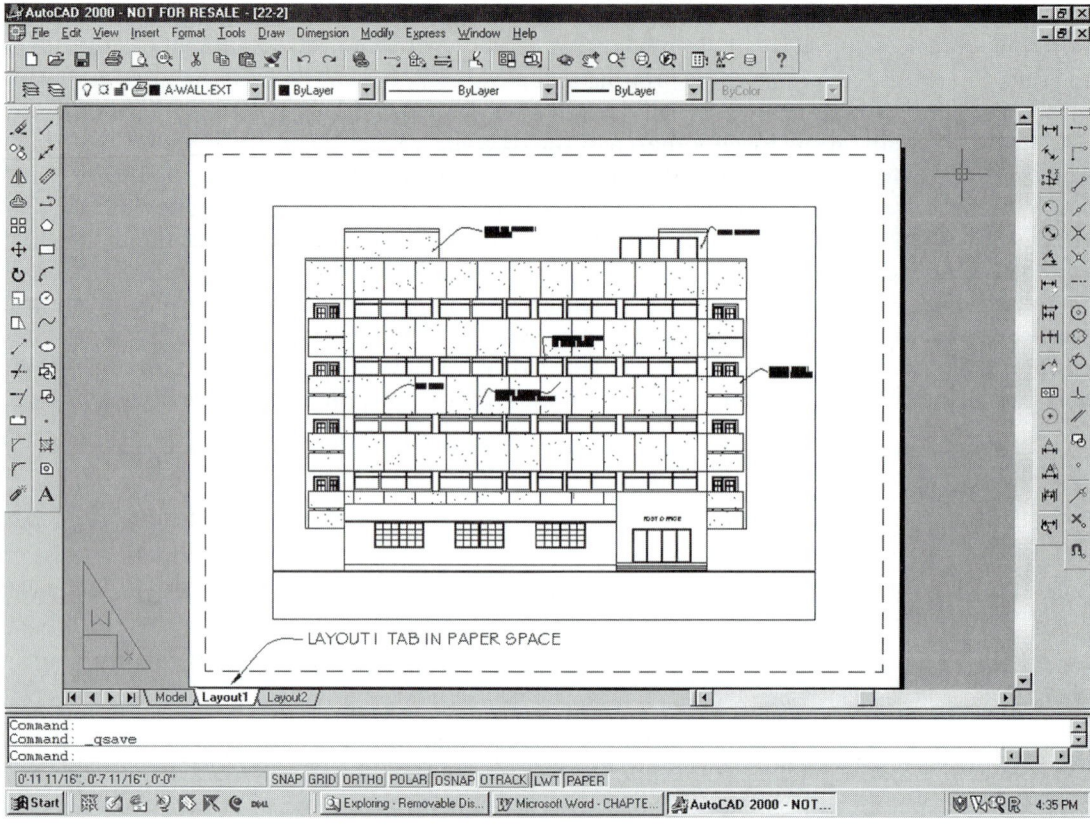

22.2 MODEL SPACE AND PAPER SPACE VIEWPORTS

Viewports allow you to divide the Model or the Layout into tiles to compose the final layout of the drawing. Viewports multiply the image of your drawing; however, you are still working with only one database. There are two types of viewport utilities:

1. Tiled viewports created in model space. This is called Model Space viewports.
2. Untiled, floating, and overlapping viewports created in paper space. This is called Paper Space viewports.

22.2.1   Tiled Viewports

Tiled viewports are preset viewports that you can create in model space of the Model tab. Tiled viewports are mostly created for orthographic drawings in mechanical drafting. Display commands such as ZOOM and PAN, and drawing tools such as Grid, Snap, and Ortho, are set independently in each viewport. With tiled viewports, you cannot freeze layers in active (current), or in new viewports. You can only freeze layers in All viewports. This creates a problem when arranging drawings in model space with different views. When you create an object in the Model Space viewport, the same object appears in all the other viewports. To control the display of objects in each viewport, you must create a layer for objects and freeze that layer in each of the active or current viewports. Model Space viewport does not allow you to freeze layers in current or new viewports. Model space viewport allows you to freeze layers in all viewports only.

22.2.2   Untiled Viewports

Untiled viewports are floating viewports that are created in paper space. These viewports are separate objects that can be moved, copied, erased, stretched, and scaled, and can overlap. You can use grips to alter the size and position of an untiled viewport. You can create multiple drawing composition of your drawing in paper space layout using untiled viewports. These viewports can be arranged on the layout as needed. You can create different views of your drawings with different scales using floating viewports of different sizes in paper space. Paper space allows you to create different views at different scales of your drawing inside a layout. The creation of the multiple-scale drawings is possible by creating untiled viewports inside the paper space. By default, there is only one viewport in the layout (paper space) area. Additional preset size viewports at different sizes and shapes can be created in paper space to accommodate different size drawings. A viewport is a hole cut in paper space to access the model of your drawing. Each viewport created in paper space cuts a hole in paper so that the model of your drawing is displayed and accessed inside each viewport. With untiled floating viewports, you can freeze layers in *active* (current), or in *new* viewports. This allows you to control the display of objects created in viewports. This chapter will explore the use of the Layout tabs and creating tiled and untiled viewports. You will learn how to create multiple viewports to arrange multiple-scale layouts of your drawing. The creation of multiple viewports allows you to display your drawing at different scales within the same layout. Once a final layout of your drawing is created, it can be plotted in paper space of your layout.

22.3 CREATING LAYOUTS

So far you have been creating drawings in model. When you are ready to plot, you can either plot in model or use the Layout1 tab to switch to paper space environment. A layout allows you to compose and arrange different views of your drawing and use title blocks in paper space for plotting. The general description of the layout(s) and paper space is as follows:

1. A layout is a complete drawing setup tool that allows you to compose your drawing inside a specified sheet the way you want it to plot.

2. You can create several different layouts in the same drawing to plot the drawing on different sheet sizes, at different scales, and with different details. For example, you can create different layouts as A-1, A-2, S-1, S-2, P-1, and so on. Or you can create different layouts as floor plan, site plan, electrical plan, framing plan, and so on.

3. You can create a new layout from an existing template.

4. You can show different views of your drawing inside the viewports that can be arranged on the layout as needed.

5. Each layout represents an individual plot output sheet, or an individual sheet with different viewports represent different parts of the drawing with different scales.

6. Tabs at the bottom of the drawing area let you switch from the model to any of the layouts you created for plotting purposes.

7. Layout(s) displays visual representation of your drawing inside paper space that is the drawing sheet.

8. When in Layout, you can switch between working in paper space to create viewports and working on the Model (inside a viewport) of the drawing. The Paper/Model button on the Status bar toggles between the Layout and the Model of the drawing.

When you create a drawing with the Use a Wizard or Start from Scratch setup options, AutoCAD will display two layout tabs as default. These are identified as the Layout1 and Layout2 tabs next to the Model tab. You can easily and quickly create layouts using four different methods:

22.3.1 Creating a New Layout from Scratch

You can create a new layout from scratch using four different methods:

1. Use the **New** option of the **LAYOUT** command as follows:

```
Command: LAYOUT ~EnterKey~
Enter layout option [Copy/Delete/New/Template/Rename/Saveas/Set/?]
<set>: N ~EnterKey~
Enter new layout name <Layout2>: FLOOR PLAN ~EnterKey~
```

FIGURE 22–3 The Floor Plan layout tab created using the New option of the LAYOUT command.

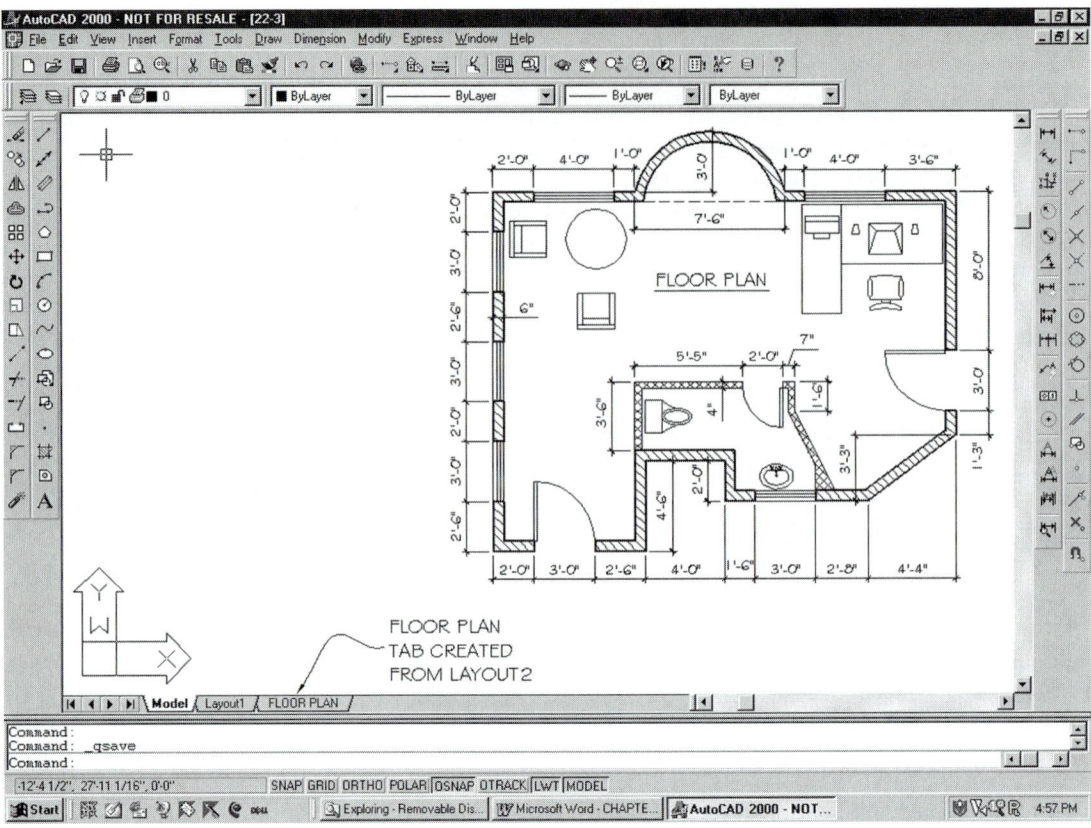

The Floor Plan tab will be created as shown in Figure 22–3. You can select this layout tab to prepare the floor plan for plotting or to create viewports to represent different views at different scales.

The other options for the LAYOUT command are as follows:

COPY: This option allows you to copy an existing layout to create a new layout.

DELETE: This option allows you to delete an existing layout. You cannot delete the Model tab.

TEMPLATE: This option displays the Select File dialog box, which allows you to select a .dwg drawing or a .dwt template file to use as a template for the new layout. If the file has existing layouts, this option will display the Insert Layout(s) dialog box.

RENAME: This option allows you to rename a layout.

SAVEAS: This option allows you to save the layout(s) in a drawing template (.dwt) file. Auto-CAD uses the last current layout as the default for the layout(s).

SET: This option makes the layout current.

?: This option lists all layouts in the drawing.

2. Select New Layout from the Layout cascading menu in the Insert pull-down menu as shown in Figure 22–4.

3. Select the New Layout button from the Layouts toolbar as shown in Figure 22–5.

4. Right-click on the Layout tab and select New layout from the shortcut menu as shown in Figure 22–6.

22.3.2 Creating A New Layout from Template

You can create a new layout from an existing template based on the title block, borderline, and drawing settings information stored in an existing drawing (.dwg) or template (.dwt) file. This option can be selected by using the Template option of the LAYOUT command, selecting Layout from Template. . . from the Layout cascading menu in the Insert pull-down menu, selecting Layout from Template button in the Layouts toolbar, or by selecting From template. . . from the

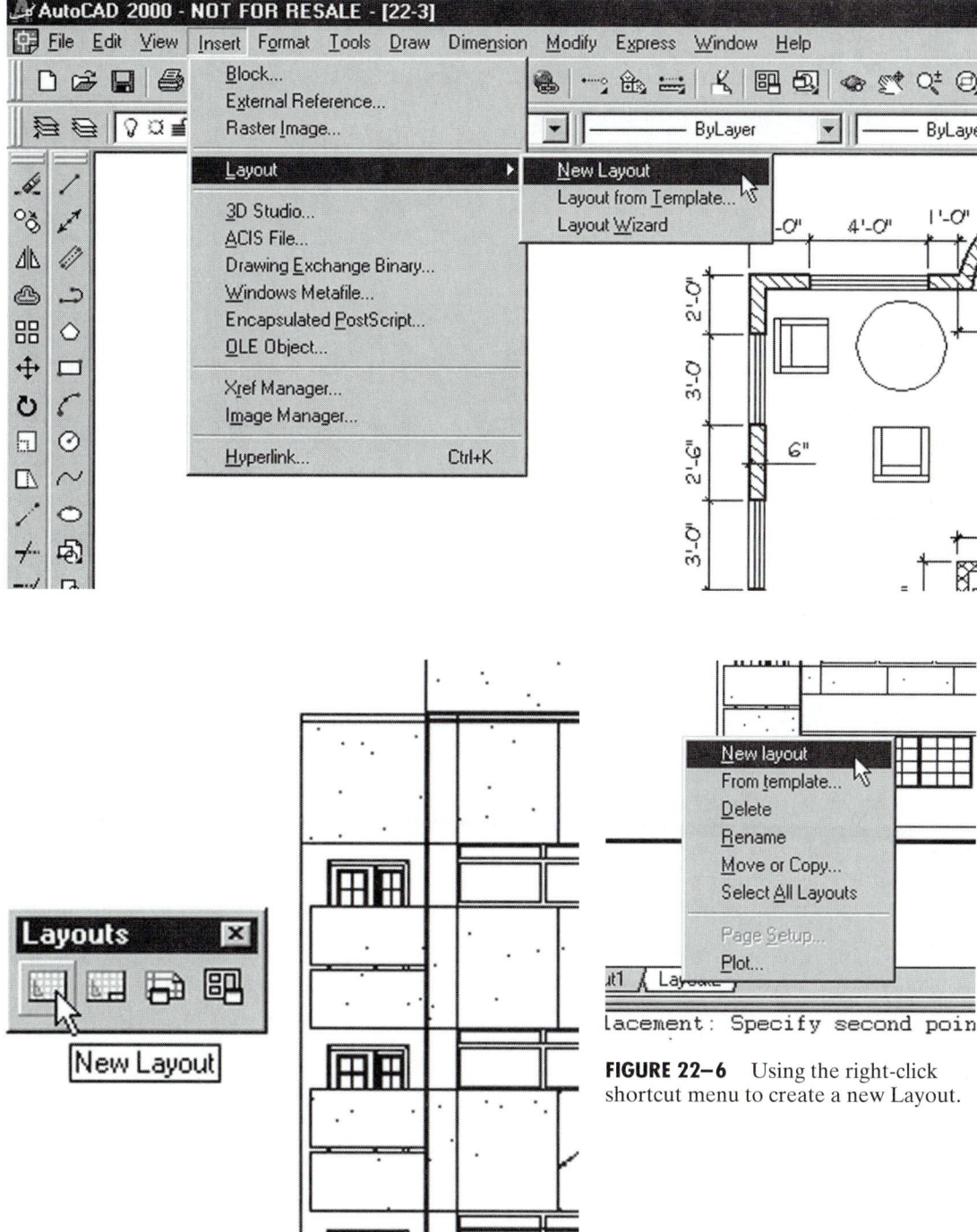

FIGURE 22–4 Using the Insert pull-down menu to create a new layout.

FIGURE 22–5 Using the Layouts toolbar to create a new layout.

FIGURE 22–6 Using the right-click shortcut menu to create a new Layout.

right-click shortcut menu. When you select this option, the Select File dialog box will be displayed as shown in Figure 22–7.

■ **EXERCISE 22–1:** *The following step-by-step exercise will allow you to create a new Layout from the existing Architectural, English units–Color Dependent Plot Styles template for the building elevation as shown in Figure 22–10.*

Step #1: Open the EXE22–1.dwg file.

Step #2: Right-click on the Layout1 tab and select From template…from the shortcut menu. See Figure 22–6. This will display the Select File dialog box as shown in Figure 22–7.

FIGURE 22–7 The Select File dialog box is used to select an existing template or a drawing for the layout.

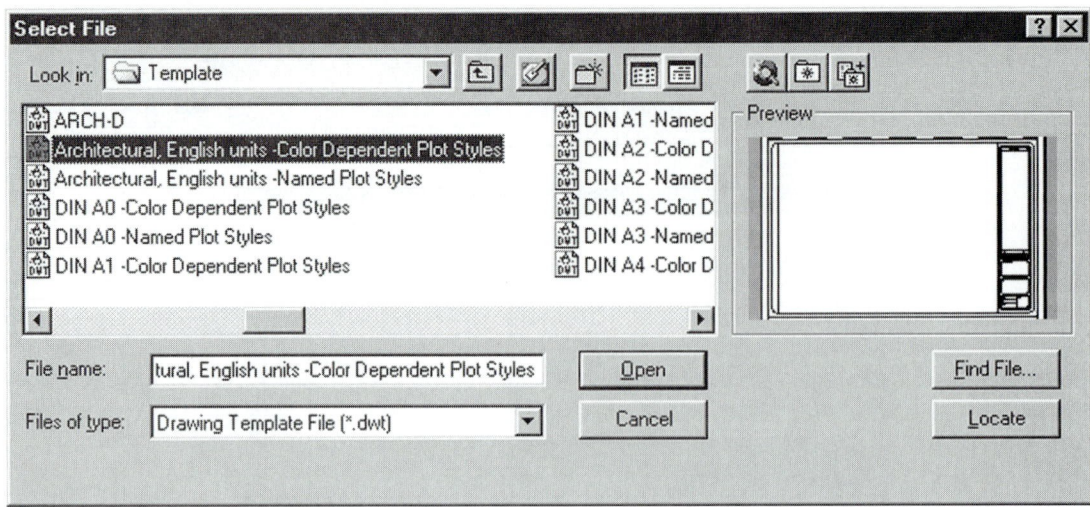

FIGURE 22–8 The Insert Layout(s) dialog box will insert the selected template or drawing into the layout.

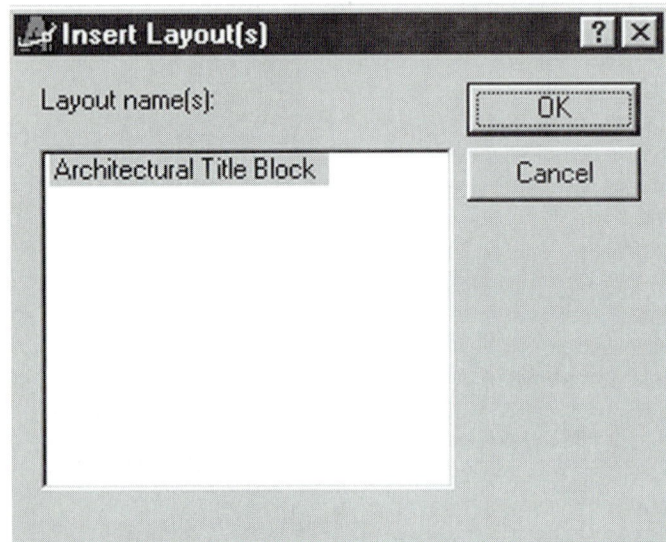

Step #3: Inside the Select File dialog box select the Architectural, English units–Color Dependent Plot Styles template.

Step #4: Click on the Open button. This will display the Insert Layout(s) dialog box as shown in Figure 22–8.

Step #5: Click on the OK button. The Architectural Title Block layout tab will be displayed as shown in Figure 22–9.

Step #6: Left-click on the Architectural Title Block tab. The title block will appear in Paper space.

Step #7: Left-click on the Paper button in the Status Bar to switch to Model. The drawing will appear in model space as shown in Figure 22–10. If the drawing does not appear, zoom to the extents of the drawing. The drawing will be active in Model space, but the title block will not be available to work on. In other words, the viewport is open and the drawing is accessed in model space.

Step #8: Left-click on the Model button in the Status bar to switch back to paper space (PAPER). The title block will be active in Paper space, but the drawing will not be available to work on. In other words, the viewport is closed, and only the title block is available to work on. However, the drawing is available for view.

Step #9: Save the changes.

Congratulations! You have successfully created a new layout called Architectural Title Block from an existing template. In Figure 22–10, the solid rectangle closest to the drawing is the default viewport. This viewport is provided by the template selected. The heavy lines outside the viewport represent the borderline in paper space, including the title block information located in the right side of the layout. The dashed lines outside the borderline represent the maximum printable area.

22.3.3   Creating a New Layout by Copying an Existing Layout

You can create a new layout from an existing layout using the *Copy* option of the LAYOUT command or by selecting Move or Copy. . . from the right-click shortcut menu. If you use the

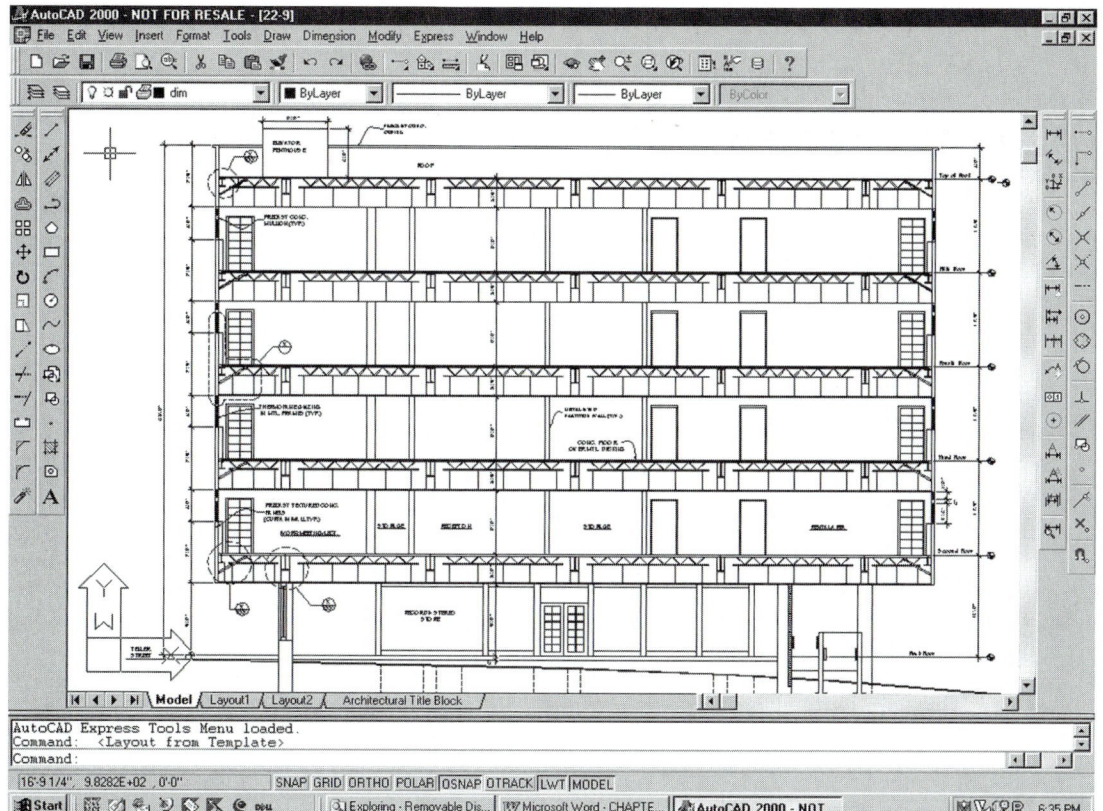

FIGURE 22–9 The Architectural Title Block is created as the new layout. Notice the existing Layout1 and Layout2 tabs.

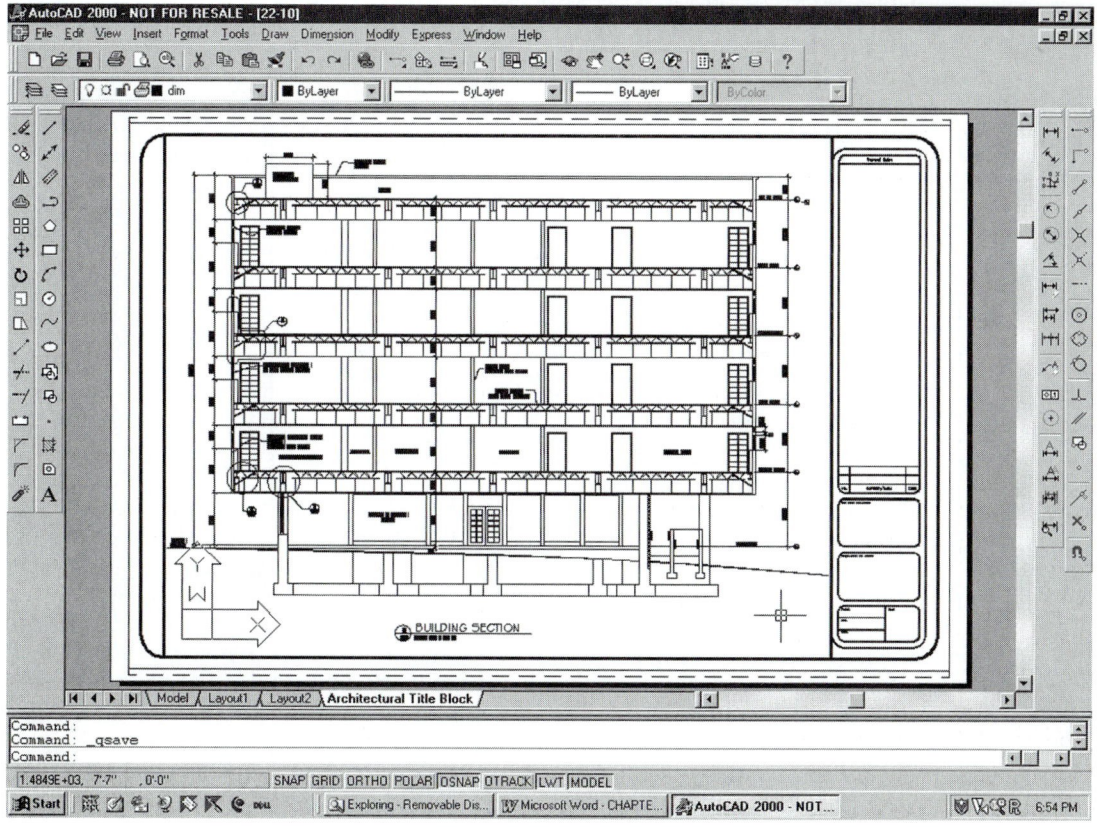

FIGURE 22–10 The existing architectural template is inserted inside the new layout.

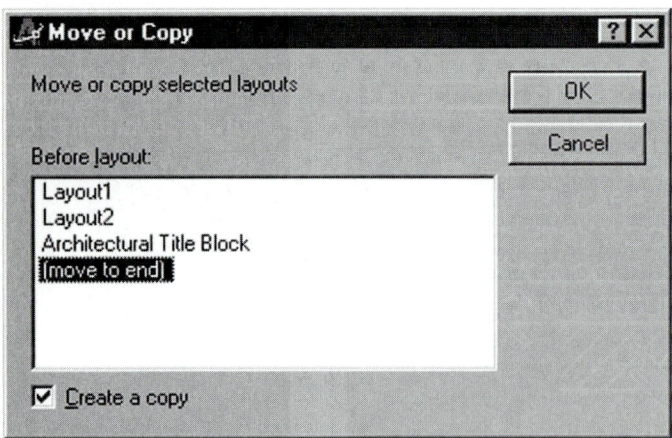

FIGURE 22–11 The Move or Copy dialog box is used to move, copy, or rearrange the layout tabs.

Copy option of the LAYOUT command, enter the name of the layout to copy and then enter the name for the new layout. The current layout is the default layout to copy. If you do not enter a new name for the layout, AutoCAD will use the current layout name followed by a number in the parentheses. The right-click shortcut menu option does not allow you to change the layout to be copied. Instead, the current layout tab is copied. When you select this option, the Move or Copy dialog box will appear as shown in Figure 22–11. Place a checkmark inside the Create a copy check box and then select the layout from the list you want the new layout tab to be. This will copy the selected layout with an additional suffix. Use the Rename option to rename the layout. For example, you can create a copy of Layout1 and place it at the end of the last layout as follows:

1. Right-click on the Layout1 tab and select Move or Copy...

2. Inside the Move or Copy dialog box, place a checkmark inside the Create a copy check box and select the (move to end) from the Before layout: text box.

3. Click on the OK button. The Layout1(2) tab will appear next to the last layout tab as shown in Figure 22–12.

Note: Copied layouts will have an additional suffix in the layout name. For example, if you copy the Site Plan layout, AutoCAD will create Site Plan (2) layout. If there is already a Site Plan (2) layout, the copied layout will be named Site Plan (3).

FIGURE 22–12 The Layout1(2) is created by copying the Layout1 tab and displaying it at the end of the Layout tabs.

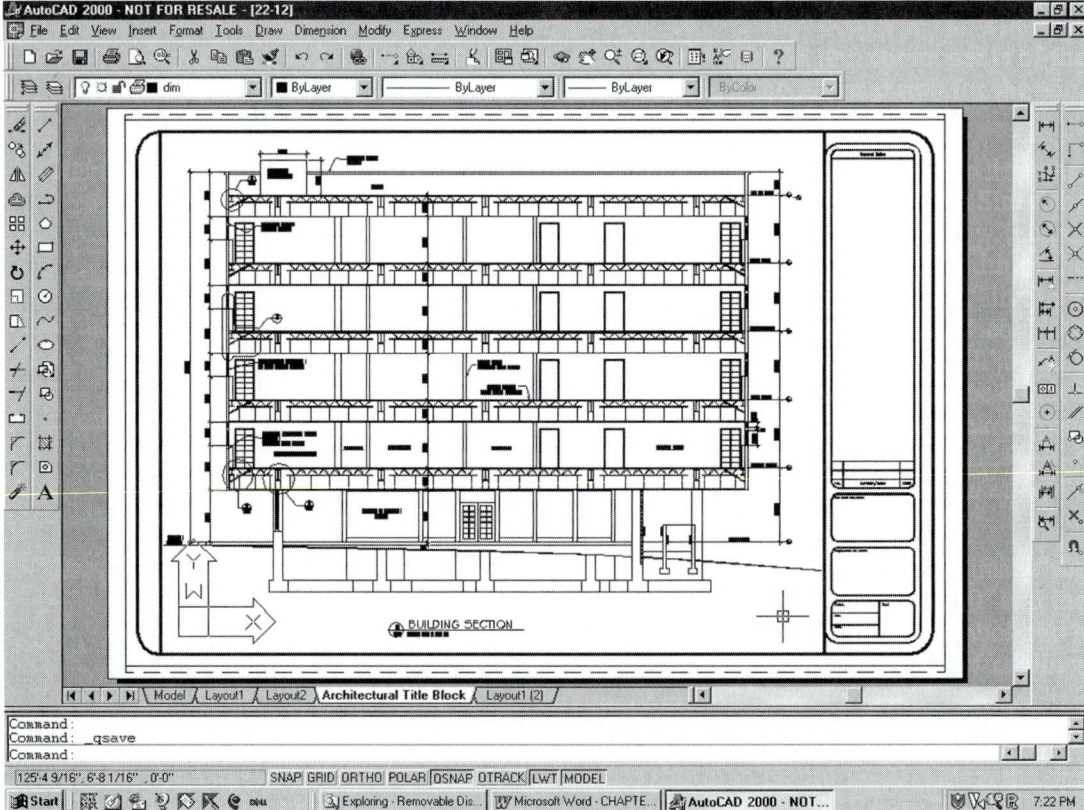

22.3.4 Creating a New Layout by Using the Layout Wizard

You can create a new layout by using the Create Layout Wizard. To use this wizard, select Create Layout. . . from the Wizards cascading menu in the Tools pull-down menu as shown in Figure 22–13. You can also select Layout Wizard from the Layout cascading menu in the Insert pull-down menu. The Layout Wizard contains a series of pages that walk you through the process of creating a new layout. It also allows you to choose a plot device, select plot settings, insert a title block (template drawing), and specify a viewport setup. After the Wizard is completed, the settings that you specify will be saved with the drawing. The first page in the Layout Wizard is the **Begin** page as shown in Figure 22–14. The left side of the page identifies the eight pages that you must complete to create layout. Enter the name of the new layout you are creating, such as Alpman Residence, as shown in Figure 22–14. Click on the Next> button to continue.

The **Printer** page shown in Figure 22–15 allows you to select a configured printer or plotter for the new layout. Select the appropriate printer or plotter from the list and click on the Next> button. If you make a mistake, click on the <Back button to go back one page or click on the Cancel button to cancel the operation.

The **Paper Size** page shown in Figure 22–16 allows you to select a size of paper supported by the printer or plotter. If you select Millimeters inside the Drawing units, the paper size is measured in metric units. If you select Inches, the paper size is measured in Imperial units. The Pixels option allows the paper size to be measured in dots per inch. Click on the Next> button to continue.

The **Orientation** page shown in Figure 22–17 allows you to select the orientation of the drawing being printed or plotted. The Portrait option plots the drawing vertically, and the Landscape option plots the drawing horizontally. Your selection should correspond to the Limits of your drawing. The paper icon in the left side of the options shows the orientation for the selected option. Click on the Next> button to continue.

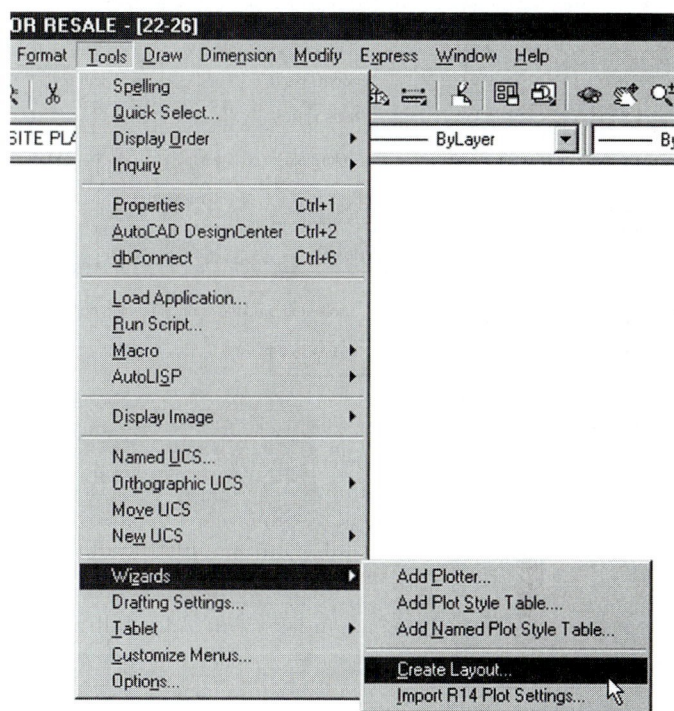

FIGURE 22–13 The Create Layout. . . is selected from the Wizards cascading menu in the Tools pull-down menu.

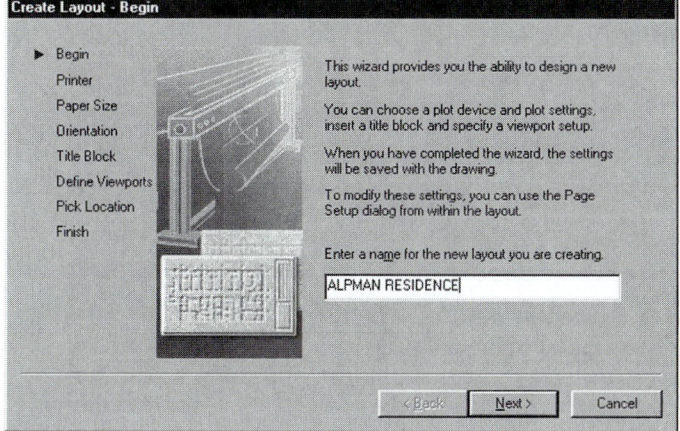

FIGURE 22–14 The Begin page of the Create Layout dialog box is used to assign a name to the layout being created.

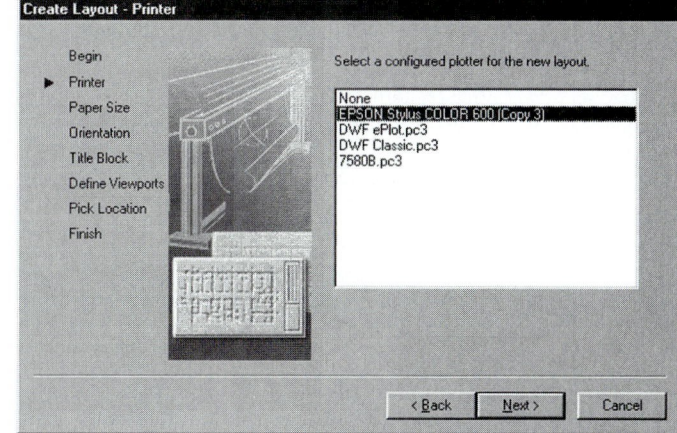

FIGURE 22–15 The Printer page of the Create Layout dialog box is used to select a printer or a plotter that is already configured.

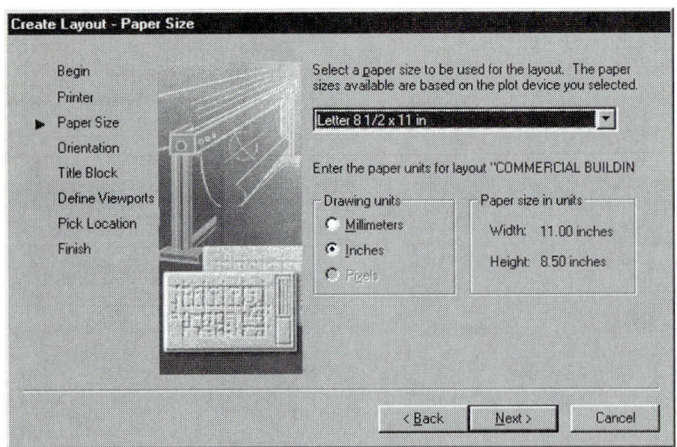

FIGURE 22–16 The Paper Size page of the Create Layout dialog box is used to select the paper size for the layout.

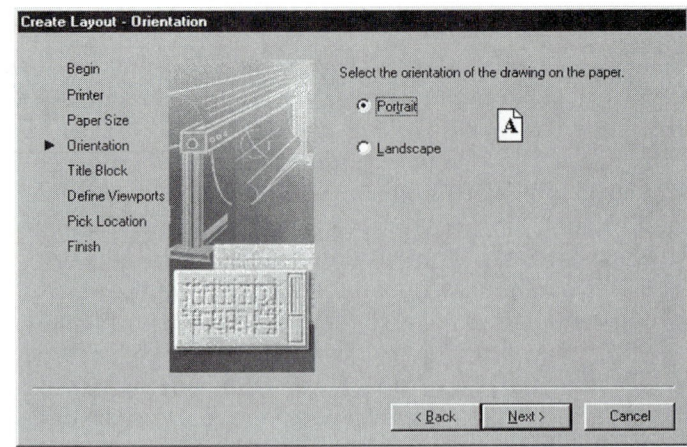

FIGURE 22–17 The Orientation page of the Create Layout dialog box is used to select the orientation of the selected paper size.

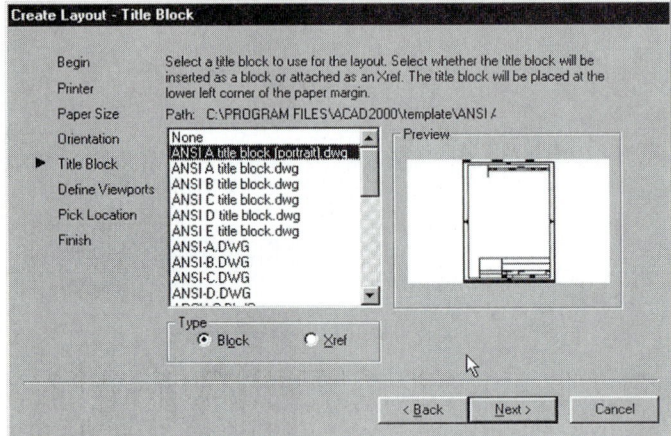

FIGURE 22–18 The Title Block page of the Create Layout dialog box is used to select a title block for the layout. Select None if no title block is required.

The **Title Block** page shown in Figure 22–18 allows you to select a title block to be used for the layout. Select a title block from the list and select whether the title block will be inserted as a Block or attached as an Externally Referenced File (xref). Xrefs are discussed in Chapter 24. Click on the Next> button to continue.

The **Define Viewports** page shown in Figure 22–19 allows you to specify the viewport size and type. You can add viewport(s) to the layout as required. The Viewport setup category allows you to select a viewport type. Selecting None will not create a paper space viewport for the layout. Selecting Single will create a single paper space viewport. Selecting Std. 3D Engineering Views will create top, front, side, and isometric views of the three-dimensional drawing. Selecting Array will create a rectangular array of viewports. The Viewport scale: dropdown list allows you to select the scale for the drawing

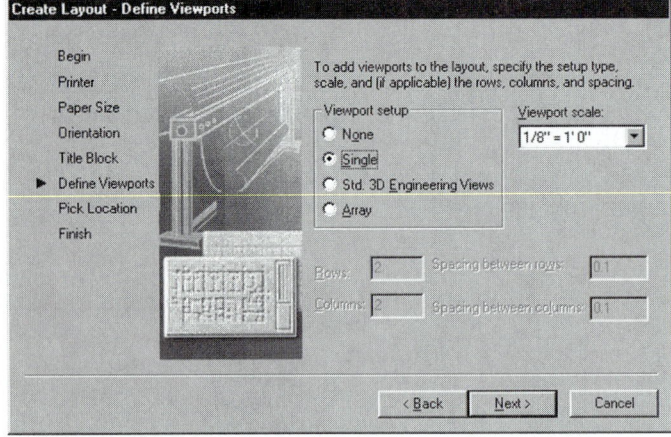

FIGURE 22–19 The Define Viewports page of the Create Layout dialog box is used to specify the viewport type and the viewport scale.

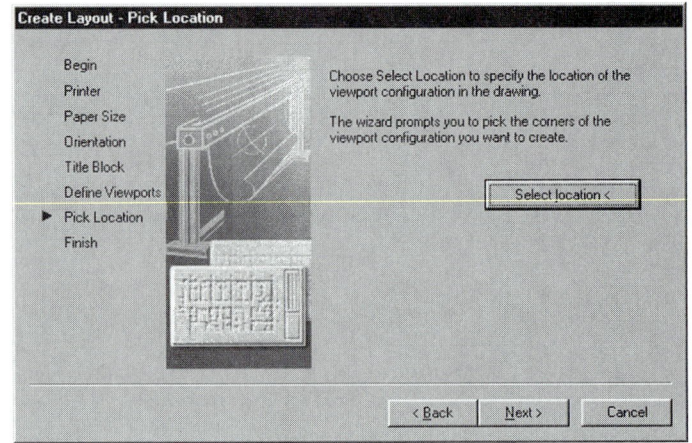

FIGURE 22–20 The Pick Location page of the Create Layout dialog box is used to create the viewport for the laypout.

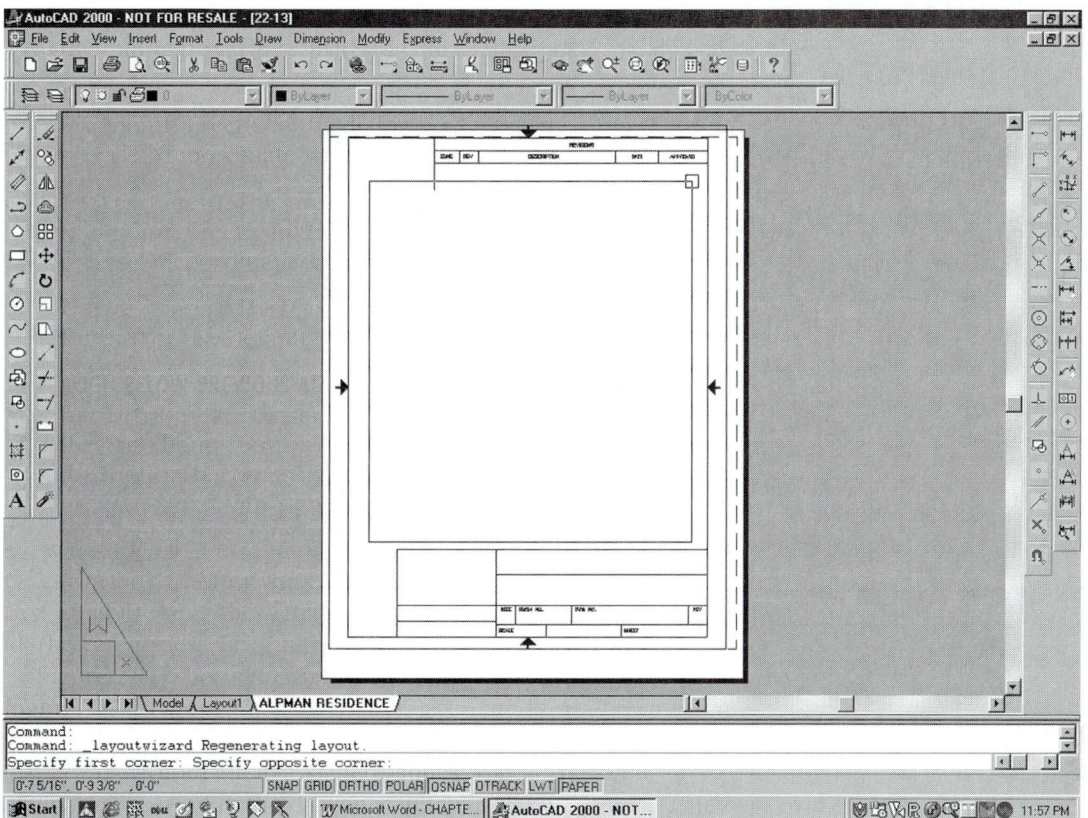

FIGURE 22-21 You create the viewport inside the selected title block.

inside the viewport. The Scaled to fit option fits the drawing inside the viewport. However, if the drawing is to be plotted at a precise scale, the corresponding scale must be selected from the list. For example, the new layout for Alpman Residence will be printed on a Letter (A size) 8½″ × 11″ paper using ANSI A title block (portrait) .dwg at a scale of 1/8″=1′–0″ inside a single viewport. The Rows: and Columns: text box options are only available when the Std. 3D Engineering Views and Array options are selected. Click on the Next> button to continue.

The **Pick Location** page shown in Figure 22–20 allows you to specify the corners of the viewport rectangle. In other words, you are ready to create the single viewport you specified in Define Viewports page. When you click on the Select location<button, AutoCAD will display the new layout in paper space as shown in Figure 22–21. At this point the cursor will turn into a pickbox. Move the cursor to the first corner of the viewport and select a point. Then move the cursor diagonally to select the other corners of the viewport as shown in Figure 22–21. After selecting the second corner, AutoCAD will display the Finish page, which is the last page of the Create Layout dialog box as shown in Figure 22–22. When you click on the Finish button to complete the operation, the drawing will be displayed inside the single viewport at the selected scale as shown in Figure 22–23.

FIGURE 22-22 The Finish page of the Create Layout dialog box is the last page and completes the creation of the new layout.

Note: There are other ways to create viewports and establish drawing scale for plotting without using Create layout Wizard. See Chapter 23.

FIGURE 22–23 The new layout tab as the Alpman Residence is created. Notice the title block in paper space with single viewport and the floor plan at 1/8″=1′–0″ scale.

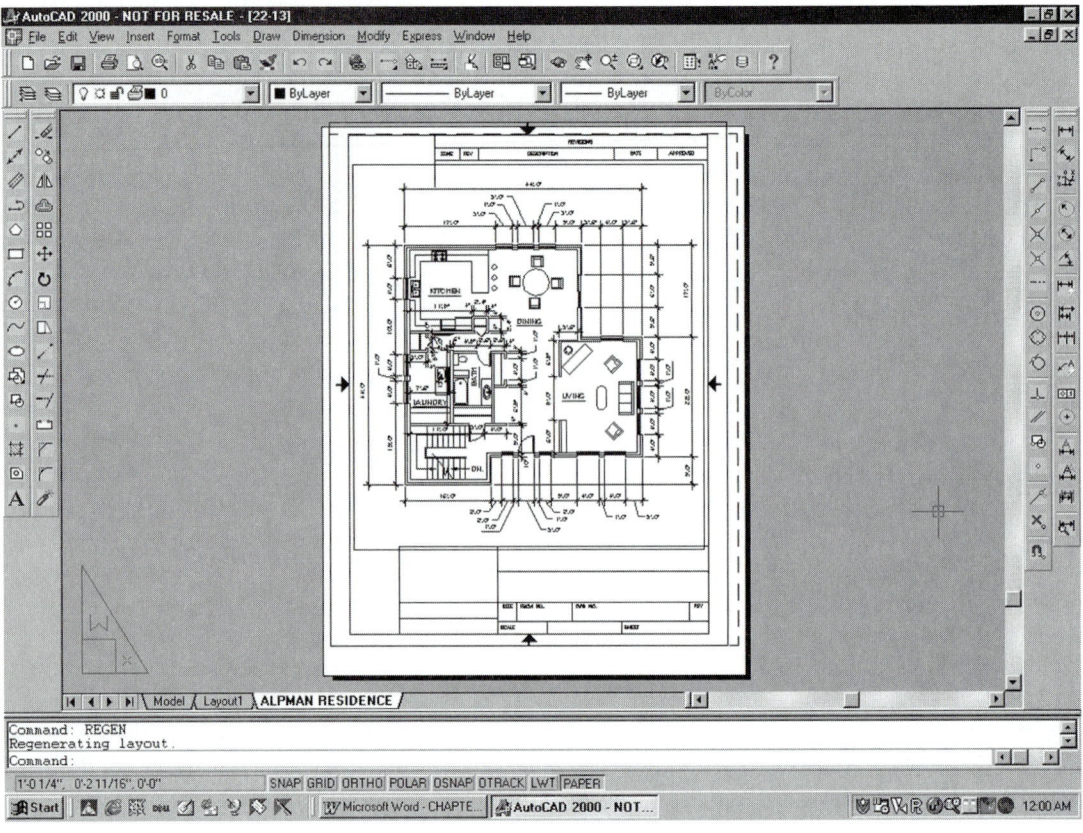

22.4 COPYING LAYOUTS USING AUTOCAD DESIGNCENTER

Layouts are included as part of drawing contents that can be viewed using the AutoCAD DesignCenter (ADC). To copy a layout from an existing drawing to the current drawing, locate the source drawing inside the tree view area. Select Layouts to display the available layouts inside the palette area. Use the options discussed in Chapter 10 to copy the selected layout(s) into the target drawing. Figure 22–24 shows the layouts displayed inside the tree view area and the layout displayed in the palette area.

22.5 DELETING LAYOUTS

You can delete one or more existing layouts using the Delete option of the LAYOUT command or by using the Delete option from the right-click shortcut menu. When you use the Delete option of the LAYOUT command, you are asked to enter the name of the layout to be deleted. When you select Delete from the right-click shortcut menu, AutoCAD will display an alert box warning you that the layout will be

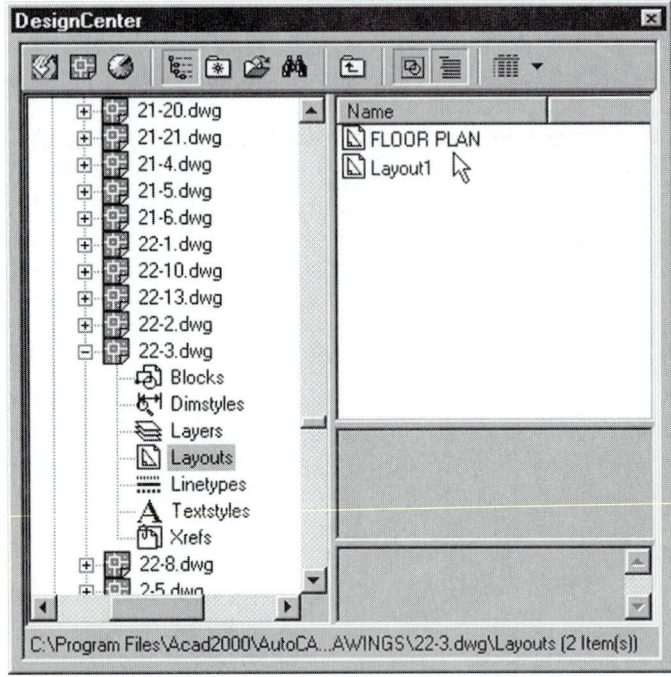

FIGURE 22–24
Layouts can be copied into another drawing using the AutoCAD DesignCenter.

permanently deleted. Click on the OK button to delete the layout. Use the ~ShiftKey~ and ~CtrlKey~ to select more than one layout tab to delete. You can also pick Select All Layouts from the right-click shortcut menu and then select Delete to delete all layouts. The Model tab cannot be deleted, and there will always be one Paper space layout.

22.6 RENAMING LAYOUTS

Layouts are better understood if they have a descriptive name. You can rename a nondescriptive layout or any layout using the Rename option of the LAYOUT command or using the Rename from the right-click shortcut menu. When you use the Rename option of the LAYOUT command, you are asked to enter the name of the layout to be renamed. The current layout is provided as the default layout to be renamed. After you rename the layout, the new name is displayed on the tab. When you select Rename from the right-click shortcut menu, the Rename Layout dialog box will be displayed. Enter a new name in the text box and select the OK button.

22.7 WORKING WITH LAYOUT ELEMENTS

A layout contains many elements, including viewports, title block, and notes. Arranging these elements in a layout allows you to see exactly what will be plotted. The preview of the layout displays a paper border that accurately indicates the plot area for the layout based on the paper size, scale factor, paper orientation, and viewport size. The layout also accurately displays the current linetypes, lineweights, color, hatch patterns, and orientation. This information is displayed in a WYSIWYG (What You See Is What You Get) fashion. With WYSIWYG layouts, the output of your project is simplified, giving you the full control of your output, saving you time and eliminating guesswork. Plotting becomes easier and more efficient because Plot Setups are stored on a per layout basis. In a layout, the rectangular outline with a shadow indicates the paper size of the currently configured plotting device as shown in Figures 22–2, 22–10, 22–12, 22–21, and 22–23. The display of the paper background in paper space and several settings that affect the display of layouts can be controlled using the Display tab of the Options dialog box as shown in Figure 22–25.

The Layout elements area has the following options:

DISPLAY LAYOUT AND MODEL TABS: This check box is on by default and toggles the display of the Model and Layout tabs. If you remove the checkmark, AutoCAD will not display the Model and Layout tabs.

DISPLAY MARGINS: This check box is on by default and toggles the display of dashed lines in layouts. The dashed lines indicate the printable area.

DISPLAY PAPER BACKGROUND: This check box is on by default and toggles the display of the page in layouts. Placing a check mark inside this check box will remove the paper and the shadow and will display only the printable area (dashed lines) and the viewport.

DISPLAY PAPER SHADOW: This check box is on by default and toggles the display of the shadow under the page in layouts.

SHOW PAGE SETUP DIALOG FOR NEW LAYOUTS: This check box is on by default and displays the Page Setup dialog box when you create a new layout.

CREATE VIEWPORT IN NEW LAYOUTS: This check box is on by default and toggles the creation of a single viewport for the layout. When this option is on, AutoCAD will automatically create a single viewport in layout Paper space.

When there are too many layout tabs to display at the same time, you can use the buttons to scroll forward and back as shown in Figure 22–26.

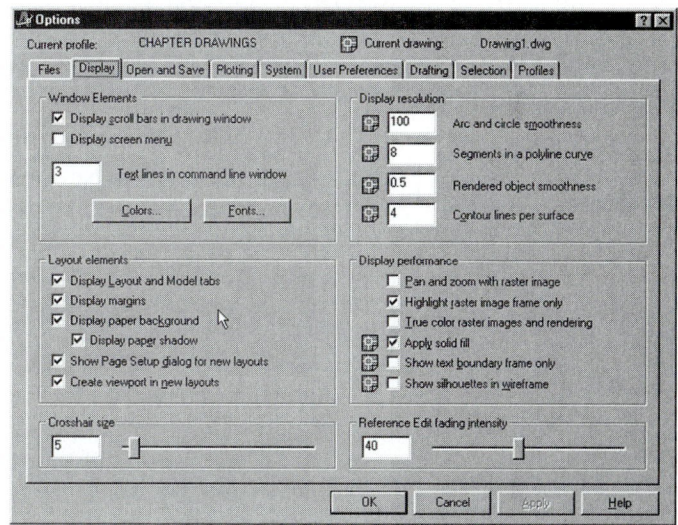

FIGURE 22–25 The Display tab of the Options dialog box allows you to change settings that affect the display of layouts.

FIGURE 22–26 The Forward and Back buttons can be used to scroll through the tabs if there are too many layouts to be displayed.

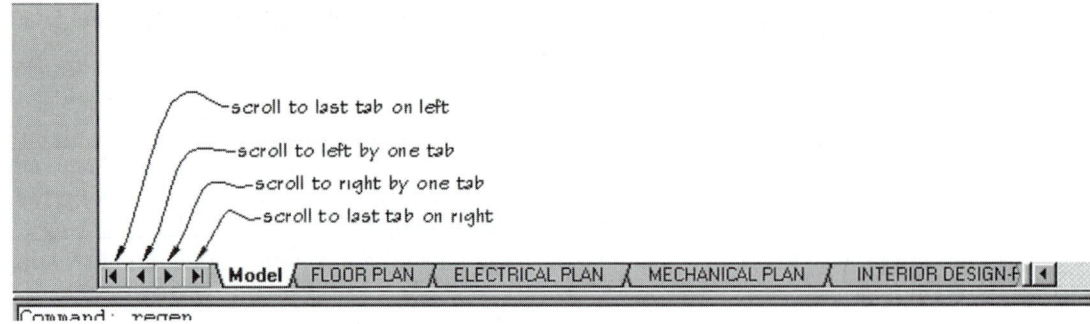

scroll to last tab on left
scroll to left by one tab
scroll to right by one tab
scroll to last tab on right

Model ⟋ FLOOR PLAN ⟋ ELECTRICAL PLAN ⟋ MECHANICAL PLAN ⟋ INTERIOR DESIGN-

Command: regen

22.8 PAGE SETUP

The layout settings that you create control the final output of your drawing. Page setup allows you to specify plot parameters and additional layout settings such as plot device, paper size, paper orientation, plot area, plot offset, and plot scale. After you configure the page setup for your layouts, you can name and save them into the drawing file for later use. This is very convenient when you want to change a layout's page setup settings from one configuration to another. You can also import named page setups from other AutoCAD 2000 drawings. Most of the parameters of how the drawing is plotted can be established using the Page Setup dialog box. When plotting drawings, the Plot dialog box can also be used to establish plot settings. The only difference between the Page Setup dialog box and the Plot dialog box is that the Page Setup dialog box does not provide a Plot Preview button. The Plot dialog box is discussed in Chapter 23. You can establish a unique page setup for each layout. The Page Setup dialog box is a productivity tool that allows you to quickly prepare a drawing for plotting. You can use the Page Setup dialog box in Model tab or in Layouts tab. When you use the Page Setup dialog box in Model, AutoCAD will display the Page Setup–Model dialog box. When you use the Page Setup dialog box in Layout, AutoCAD will display the Page Setup–Layout1 (or the name of the layout) dialog box. You can access the Page Setup dialog box by selecting Page Setup. . .from the File pull-down menu, selecting the Page Setup button in the Layouts toolbar, or by entering PAGE-SETUP at the command line. You can also right-click on the Model or the Layout tab and select Page Setup. . . from the shortcut menu. The Page Setup dialog box contains two tabs: Plot Device and Layout Settings. The Plot Device tab is discussed in Chapter 23. The Layout Settings tab is shown in Figure 22–27.

There are six categories in the Layout Settings tab of the Page Setup dialog box as follows:

PAPER SIZE AND PAPER UNITS: The paper size: drop-down list contains a list of paper sizes to choose from. Select the appropriate size for the selected plotter. The Printable area (dashed lines in paper space): displays the area of the plot in inches or millimeters.

DRAWING ORIENTATION: This category controls the orientation of the drawing on the paper. The image changes to show the effect of the different settings. Select the Portrait radio button to orient the drawing vertically on the paper. Select the Landscape button to orient the drawing horizontally on the paper. Place a check mark inside the Plot upside-down check box to plot the drawing upside-down.

PLOT AREA: The Layout option plots everything within the printable area of the selected paper size. The Display option will plot the current display of the drawing. When plotting from Model tab, the layout option is replaced by the Limits option. The Window < button allows you to select a portion of the drawing to be plotted.

PLOT SCALE: When plotting a layout in paper space, the Scale: drop-down list should be set to 1:1, since the layout is created at actual size to fit on the paper. When plotting from Model tab, you can select the appropriate scale from the list. The Custom: text box allows you to specify a custom scale by entering the appropriate numbers. Plotting at a precise scale is discussed in Chapter 23. If you place a checkmark inside the Scale lineweights check box, the lineweights are scaled in proportion to the plot scale. If not selected (default), lineweights plot at their assigned values.

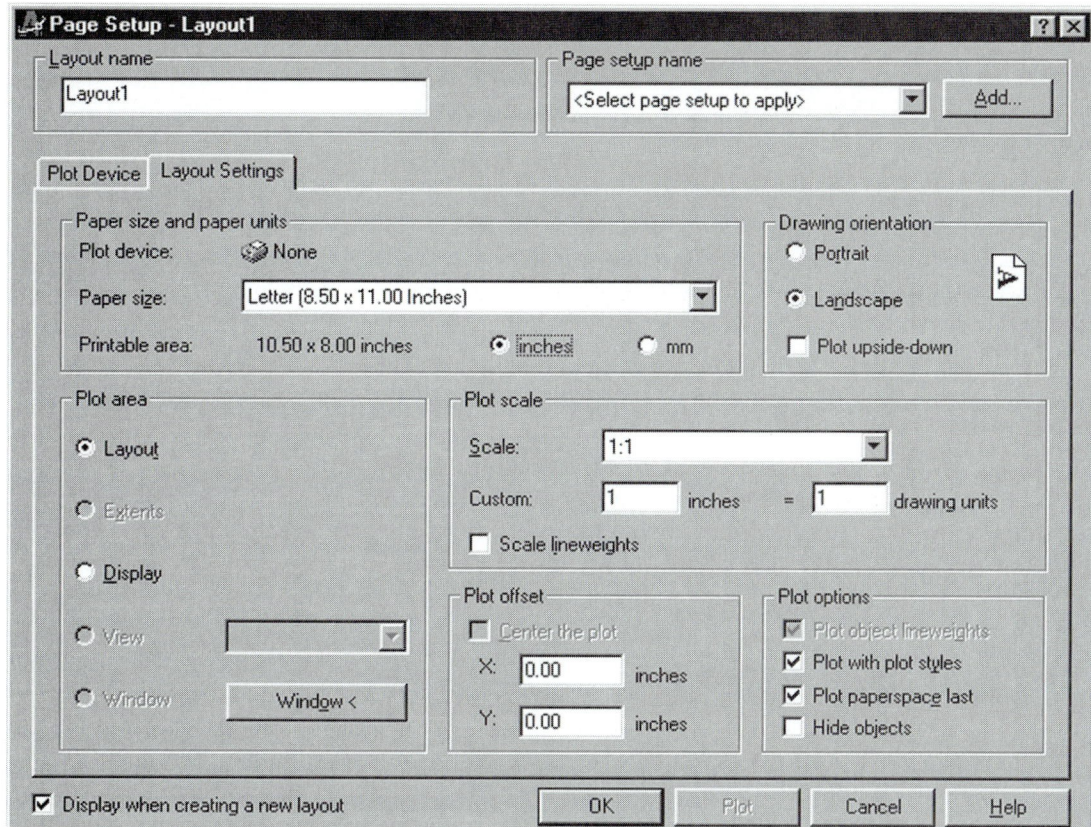

FIGURE 22–27 The Layout Settings tab in the Plot dialog box will be covered in detail in Chapter 23. The Layout Settings tab of the Page Setup dialog box allows you to set paper size, paper units, drawing orientation, plot area, and plot origin.

PLOT OFFSET: By default, the lower-left corner of the plot area starts printing at the lower-left corner of the drawing area. You can move the drawing in the X and Y direction to fit inside the page margin. The Center the plot option automatically calculates X and Y offsets so that the drawing is centered on the plot paper.

PLOT OPTIONS: The Plot with lineweights option allows you to plot the drawing with assigned lineweights. The Plot with plot styles option applies plot styles that are defined for objects or in a plot style table. See Chapter 23. The Plot paper space last option allows you to plot paper space objects after model space objects. The Hide objects option removes hidden lines for objects in the layout.

22.9 CREATING TILED VIEWPORTS

By default, the Model tab drawing area has one viewport that is the entire drawing area. You can divide the Model tab drawing area into various viewports called *tiled viewports*. Tiled viewports are created in model space and are mostly used to set up the top, front, right, and isometric viewports for mechanical and three-dimensional drawings. Each viewport can be considered as a different "tile" or view of the same drawing. Tiled viewports can be used in architectural drawings to set up several views at different magnification factors. You can create tiled viewports using the Viewports dialog box as shown in Figure 22–28. To access the Viewports dialog box, click on the Display Viewports Dialog button in the Standard, Layouts, or Viewports toolbar. The Standard toolbar is shown in Figure 22–29. The Viewports toolbar is shown in Figure 22–30. You can also select New Viewports . . . from the Viewports cascading menu in the View pull-down menu or enter VPORTS at the command line.

The Viewports dialog box has two tabs as follows:

New Viewports: This tab allows you to name and select a viewport configuration. Enter a new name inside the New name: text box to specify the name for the viewport configuration. The Standard viewports: list box displays the available viewport configurations. Selecting a viewport

FIGURE 22–28 The Viewports dialog box is used to create preset viewport configurations that are nonoverlapping and nonfloating.

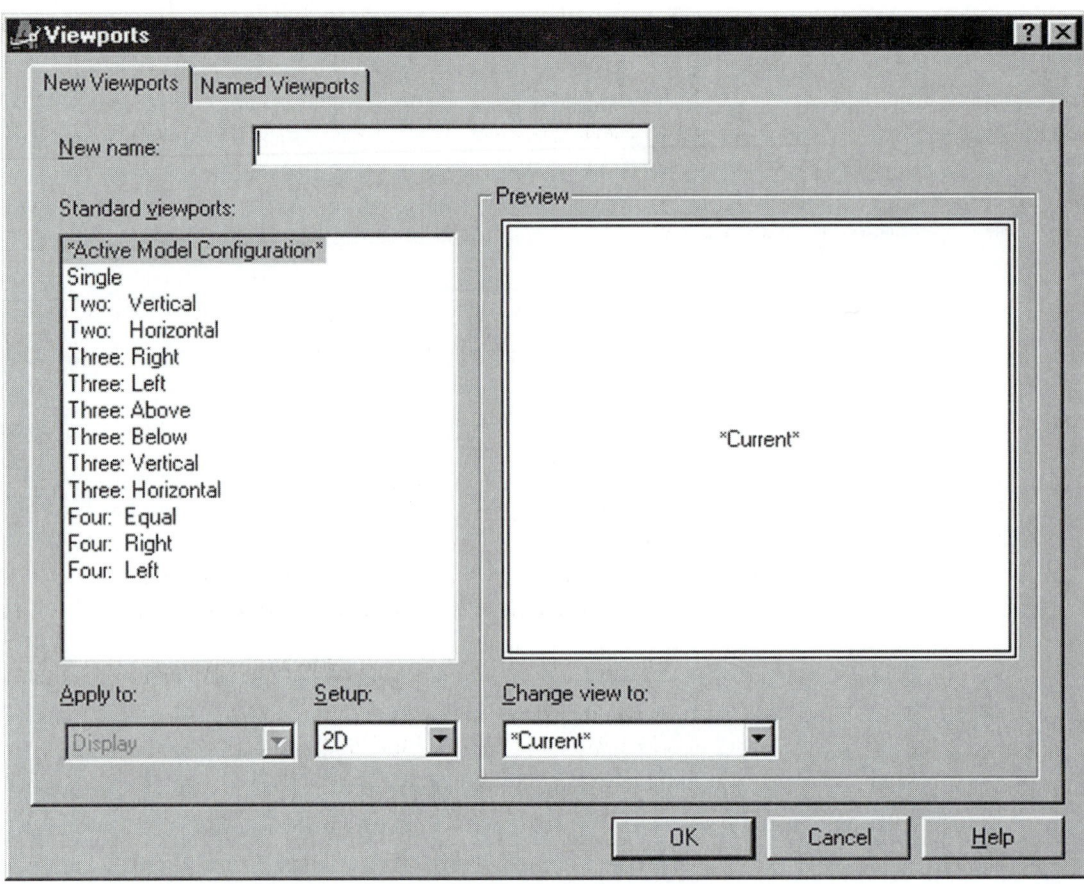

FIGURE 22–29 You can select the Display Viewports Dialog button in the Standard toolbar to display the Viewports dialog box.

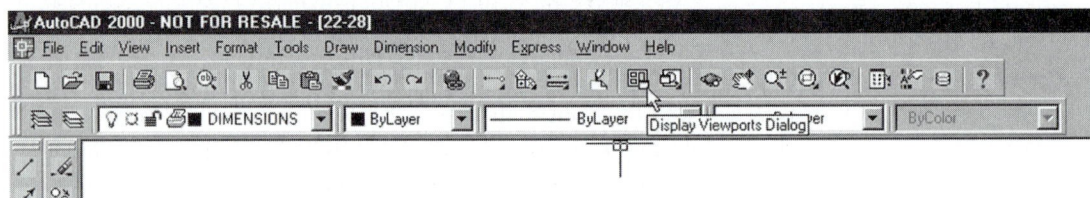

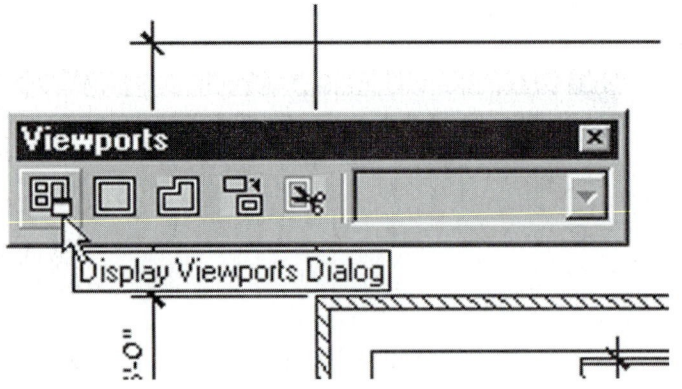

FIGURE 22–30 The Viewports toolbar.

configuration displays the arrangement and location of the largest viewport inside the Preview window area. For example, if you select the Three:Left viewport configuration, AutoCAD will display the largest viewport on the left side and the two viewports on the right side as shown in Figure 22–31. The Apply to: drop-down list allows you to specify the viewport configuration to Display or Current Viewport. Select Display if you want the viewport configuration to apply to the entire drawing area as shown in Figure 22–32. Select Current Viewport to have the new viewport configuration in the active viewport only as shown in Figure 22–33. The Setup: drop-down list allows you to select two-dimensional or three-dimensional configurations. When 2D is selected, all viewports show the same drawing with the same orientation as shown in Figure 22–32. When 3D is selected, the different viewports display various three-dimensional views of the drawing. Figure 22–34 shows isometric view in the largest viewport and top and front views on the other viewports. You can change the drawing display inside the viewport by selecting a new view from the Change view to: drop-down list. Click on the OK button to

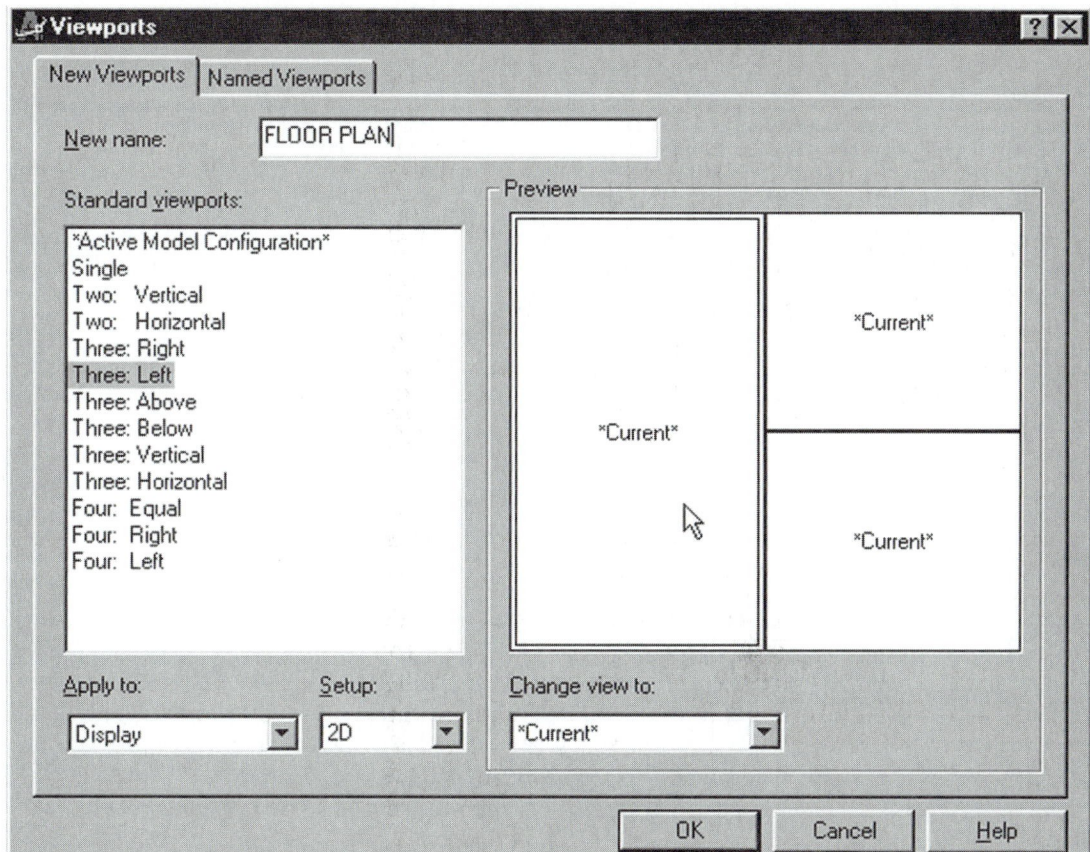

FIGURE 22-31
Selecting Three: Left viewport configuration will display two small viewports on the right and one large viewport on the left.

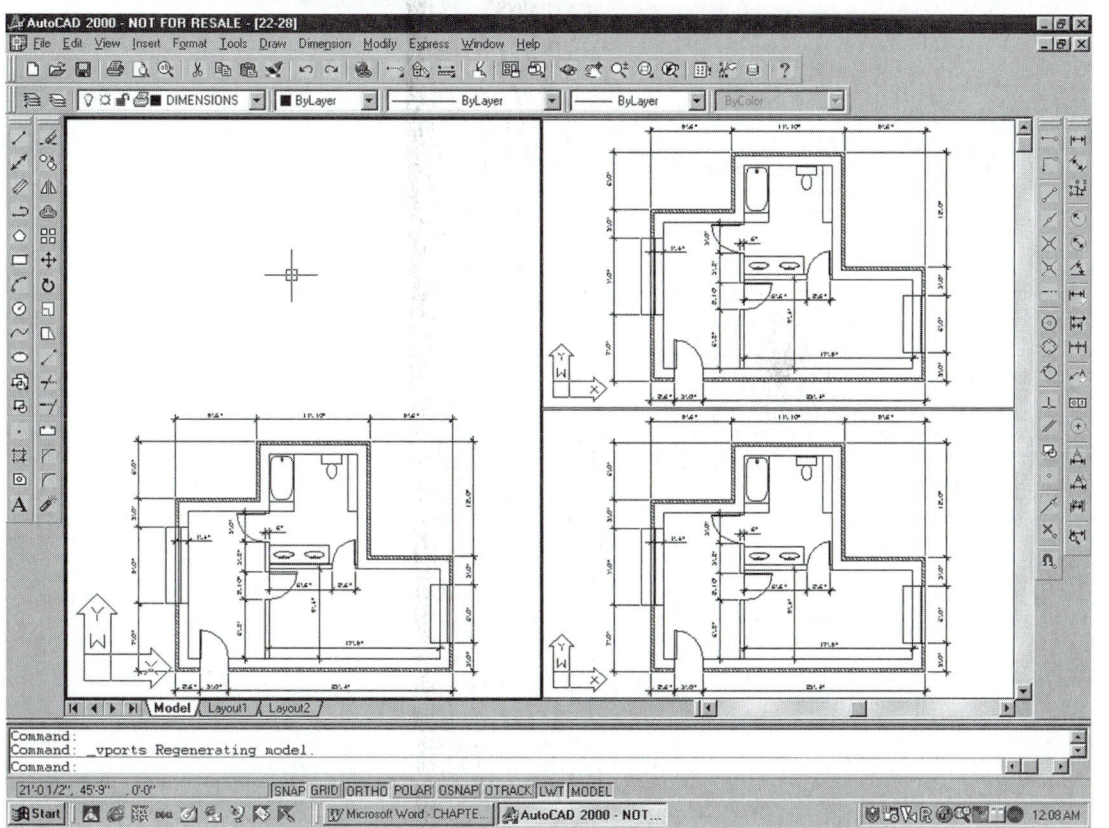

FIGURE 22-32 A viewport configuration can be applied to the entire drawing area. In this case the Three: Left viewport configuration is applied by selecting the OK button in the Viewports dialog box. This means that there are three viewports in the drawing, and the left viewport is the largest viewport. Notice that the left viewport is active.

FIGURE 22–33 A viewport configuration can be applied to the active viewport. In this case Two: Horizontal viewport configuration is selected and applied to the current (left) viewport. Therefore the left viewport now has two horizontal viewports, and the entire drawing has a total of four equal viewports.

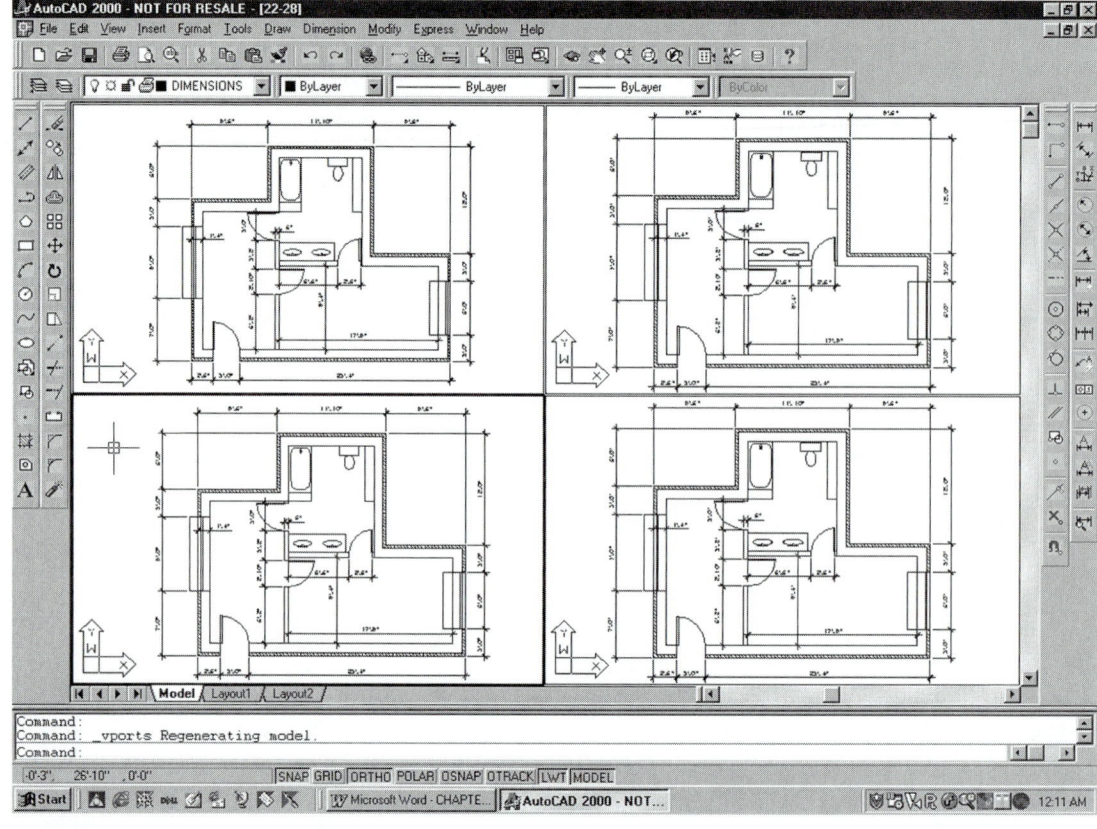

FIGURE 22–34 The 3D Setup option will display at least one isometric view and several other views of the drawing.

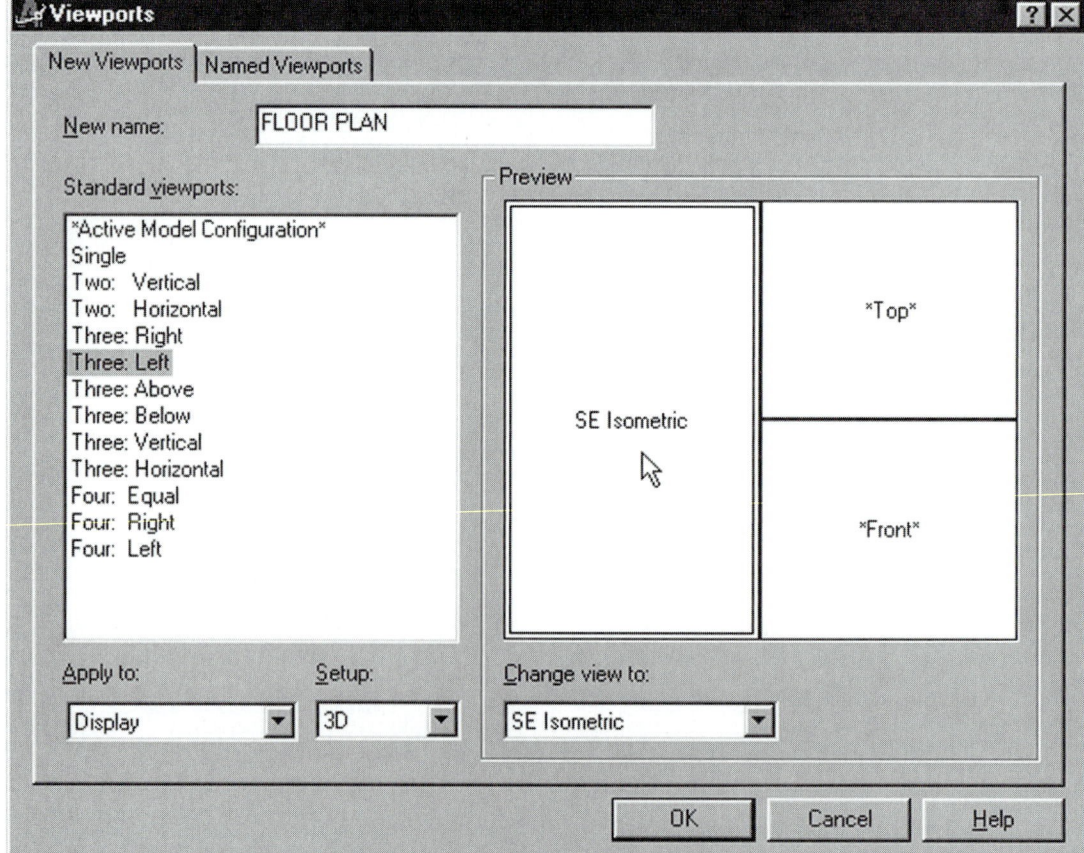

apply any changes made to the Viewports dialog box. Only one viewport can be active at any time. The active viewport has a bold outline around its edges. When you move your cursor around the drawing, you will notice that when you are inside the active viewport your cursor will turn into crosshairs and pickbox. When you are outside the current viewport, your cursor will turn into an arrow. To make a viewport active, click on the inside area of the viewport.

Named Viewports: This tab displays the names of saved viewport configurations. Select the named viewport configuration and select the OK button to apply it to the drawing area. Named viewport configurations cannot be applied to the active viewport.

> *Note: You cannot set a precise scale for the drawings inside the viewports when using tiled viewports. You can use the ZOOM/PAN Realtime or the SCALE commands to alter the magnification of each drawing in its viewport. Use Untiled/Floating viewports in paper space to assign a precise scale to each viewport created.*

> *Caution: Tiled viewports are preset. You cannot edit them.*

22.10 CREATING RECTANGULAR FLOATING VIEWPORTS IN PAPER SPACE

The paper space environment in Layout is used to create untiled viewports. Viewports created in paper space are called *floating viewports*. Floating viewports are untiled viewports and can overlap. These floating viewports are holes cut into the paper in the layout tab so that the model of your drawing can be seen. Floating viewports are separate objects and you can use most of the editing commands to edit them. For example, you can move, copy, stretch, and erase floating viewports in paper space. You can create rectangular floating viewports using five different methods.

22.10.1 Using the Viewports Dialog Box

You can create floating viewports in paper space using the Viewports dialog box (described previously) as shown in Figure 22–35. This dialog box is slightly different than the one shown in Figure 22–31. If the current environment is paper space, selecting a viewport configuration from the Viewports dialog box will display the Viewport Spacing: text box as shown in Figure 22–35. You can use this setting to specify the space around the edges of the floating viewports. Select any of the *Current* viewports inside the Preview window to specify a different viewport spacing for each viewport.

> *Note: When you select the Layout tab, your drawing will be displayed in paper space with one large viewport. You must erase this viewport if you want to use the Viewports dialog box to create a different viewport configuration. If you do not use the Viewports dialog box, you can use the editing commands to create your own viewports in paper space.*

■ **EXERCISE 22–2:** *The following step-by-step exercise will allow you to create a Three: Right viewport configuration with 1/4" space between the viewports as shown in Figure 22–39 using the Viewports dialog box in paper space.*

Step #1: Open the EXE22-2.dwg file.

Step #2: Make sure the Model tab is active as shown in Figure 22–36.

Step #3: Click on the Layout1 tab. If you are using any of the layout tabs the first time, the Page Setup–Layout1 dialog box will appear. Click on the OK button to enter paper space as shown in Figure 22–37.

Step #4: You should be in paper space now. Use the ERASE command to erase the viewport shown as the solid rectangle in Figure 22–37. The drawing will disappear as shown in Figure 22–38. In reality the drawing is covered by paper because the viewport acting as the hole cut in paper is now deleted. When you create another viewport or viewports at different sizes, the drawing will

FIGURE 22–35 The Viewports dialog box creates untitled/floating viewports in paper space layout.

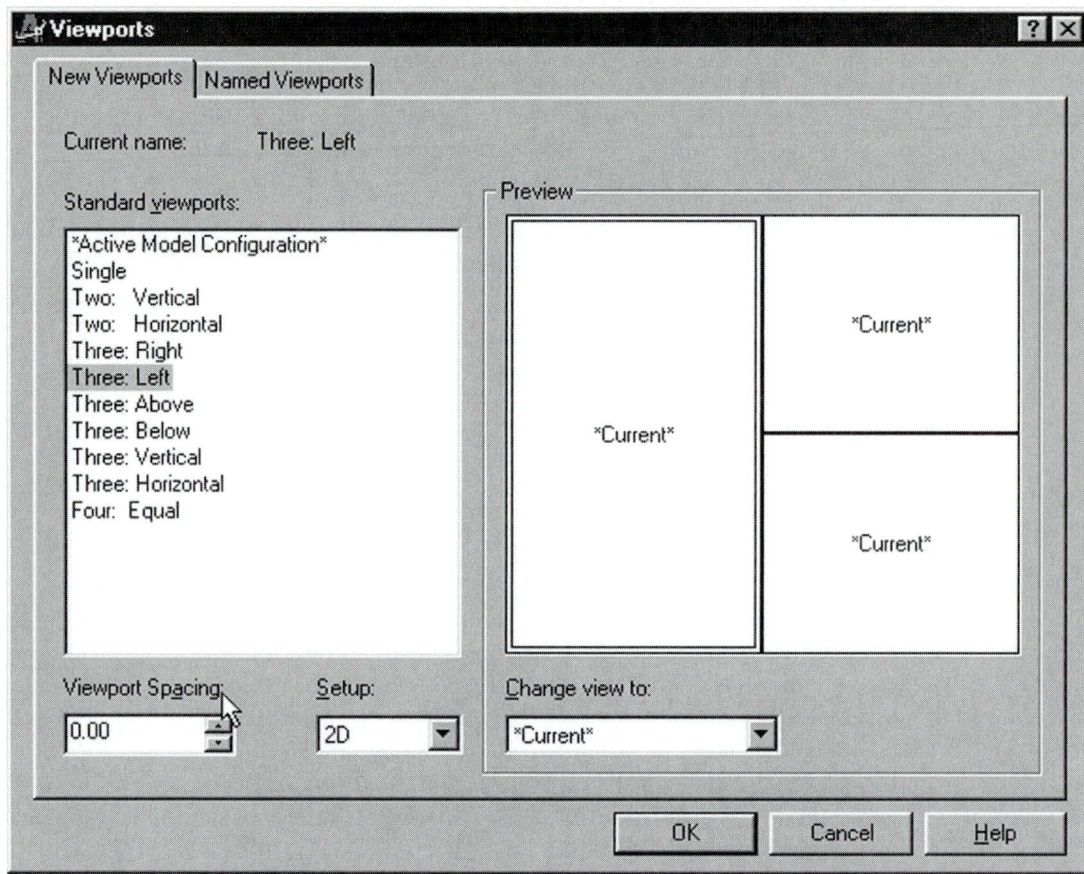

FIGURE 22–36 The drawing displayed with the Model tab on.

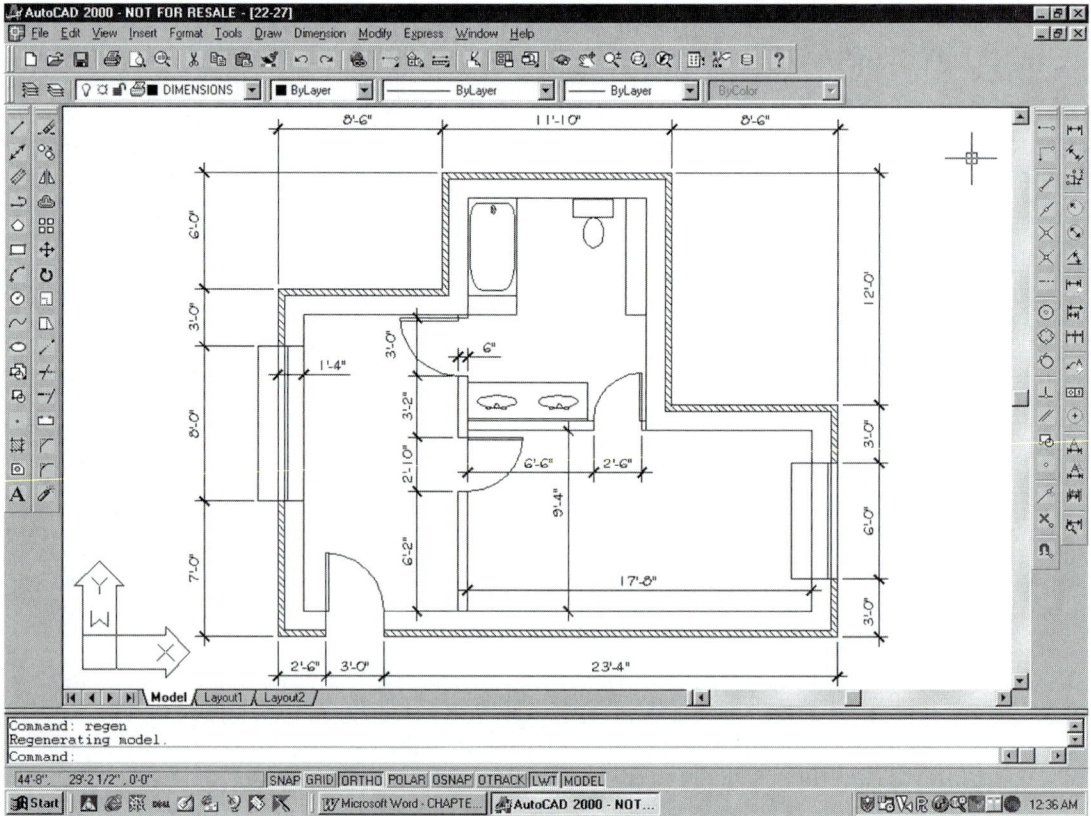

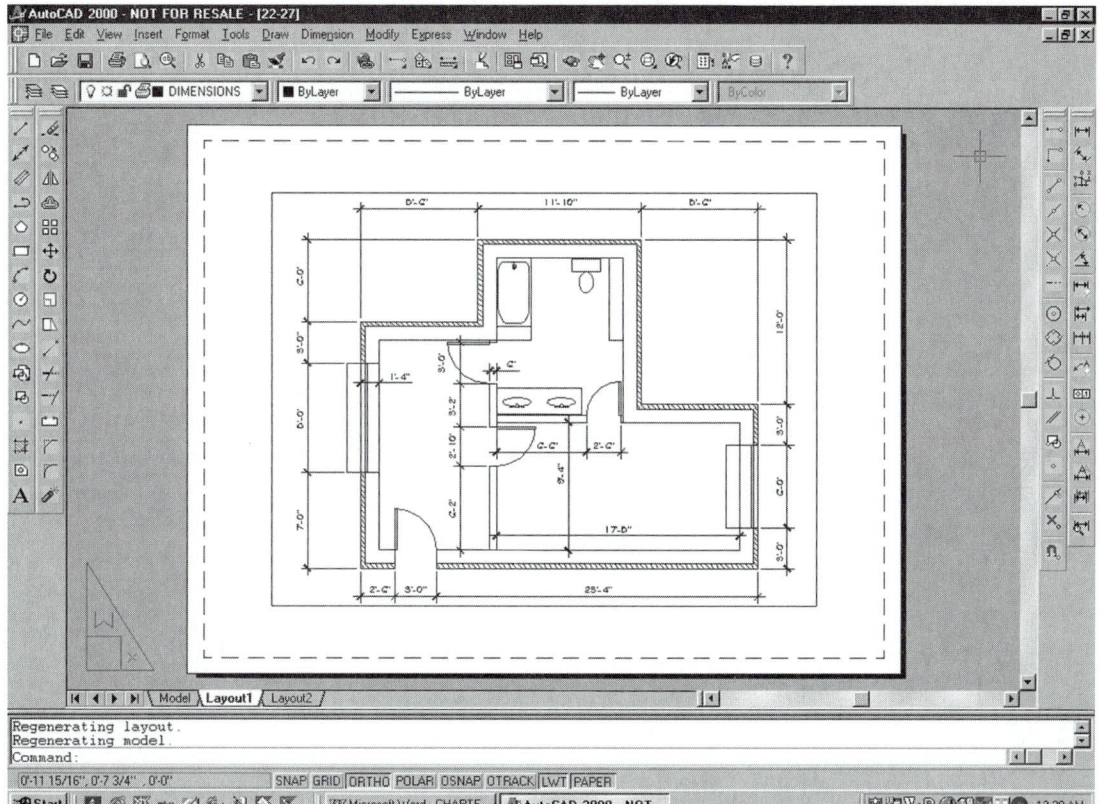

FIGURE 22–37
Selecting the Layout tab will display the same drawing in paper space. Notice the rectangular paper outline with shadow (paper size), the rectangular dashed line (printable area), and the rectangular solid line (default viewport), and the drawing inside the viewport.

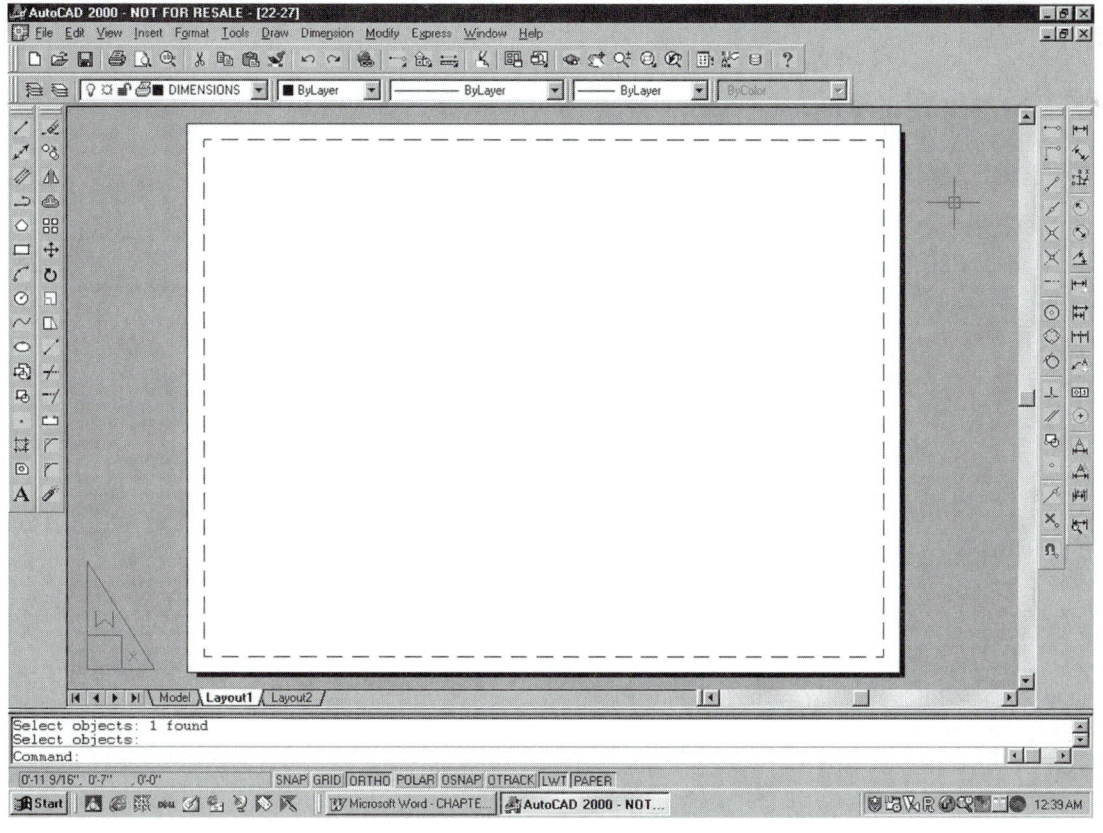

FIGURE 22–38 When the viewport is erased, the drawing is covered with paper. In other words, you do not see the drawing because there are no holes cut in paper (no viewport created) yet.

FIGURE 22–39 The drawing with three viewports in paper space.

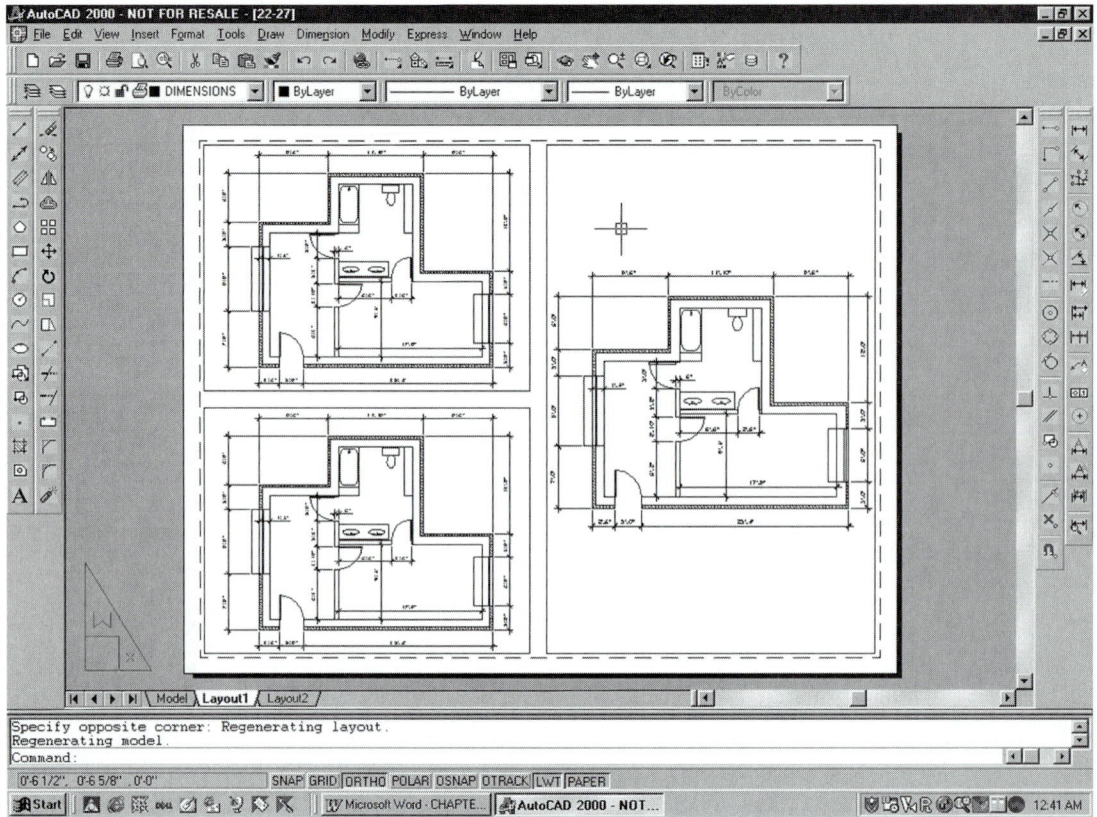

be seen again inside the viewports because you are actually cutting holes in paper.

Step #5:   Access the Viewports toolbar and click on the Display Viewports Dialog button. The Viewports dialog box will be displayed as shown in Figure 22–35.

Step #6:   Inside the dialog box, select the Three: Right option from the Standard viewports: list box and enter 0.25 inside the Viewport Spacing: list box.

Step #7:   Click on the OK button to exit the dialog box.

Step #8:   AutoCAD will ask you to create one rectangle that will display three viewports at the Command: prompt. Select the lower left corner inside the dashed lines (printable area) as the first corner of the viewport and select the upper right corner inside the dashed lines as the other corner of the viewport. As an alternative, you can press the ~EnterKey~ to fit the viewports inside the paper space. The problem with the fit option is that the viewports might go over the dashed lines. Any object inside the viewport that overlaps the dashed lines will be out of the printable area range.

Congratulations! You have successfully created three viewports using the Viewports dialog box. The drawing will be displayed in three viewports in paper space as shown in Figure 22–39. These viewports are actually three holes cut in paper, and the drawing (model) is displayed in each viewport.

22.10.2 Using the Current Viewport

You can use the current viewport to create additional different-size floating and overlapping viewports. You can use grips to resize the existing viewport and then use the editing commands to create additional viewports.

■   **EXERCISE 22–3:**   *The following step-by-step exercise will allow you to create three floating viewports from one drawing as shown in Figure 22–48 using the current viewport.*

Step #1:   Open the EXE22-3.dwg file.

Step #2: Click on the Layout1 tab. If you are using any of the layout tabs the first time, the Page Setup – Layout1 dialog box will appear. Click on the OK button to enter paper space, as shown in Figure 22–40.

Step #3: Turn Ortho off and Left-click on the viewport to display its grips as shown in Figure 22–41.

Step #4: Resize the viewport using the **STRETCH** option of grips as shown in Figure 22–42.

Step #5: Press the ~EscKey~ twice to remove grips.

Step #6: Use the COPY command to copy the viewport to the right side as shown in Figure 22–43.

Step #7: Use grips to enlarge the second viewport as shown in Figure 22–44.

Step #8: Use the COPY command to copy the last viewport to the bottom of the paper as shown in Figure 22–45.

Step #9: Use the grips to fit the third viewport inside the dashed lines as shown in Figure 22–46.

Step #10: Click on the Paper button in the Status bar to switch from paper space to model space.

Step #11: Move your cursor inside the upper-left viewport and left-click to make it active.

Step #12: Use the DISPLAY commands to magnify the corner of the elevation as shown in Figure 22–47.

Step #13: Move to the right viewport and make that viewport active. Use the zoom and pan realtime to display a portion of the elevation. Repeat the same procedure for the bottom viewport. Figure 22–48 shows three different views of the same drawing at different scales.

Step #14: Refer section 22.14 to scale drawings in Viewports.

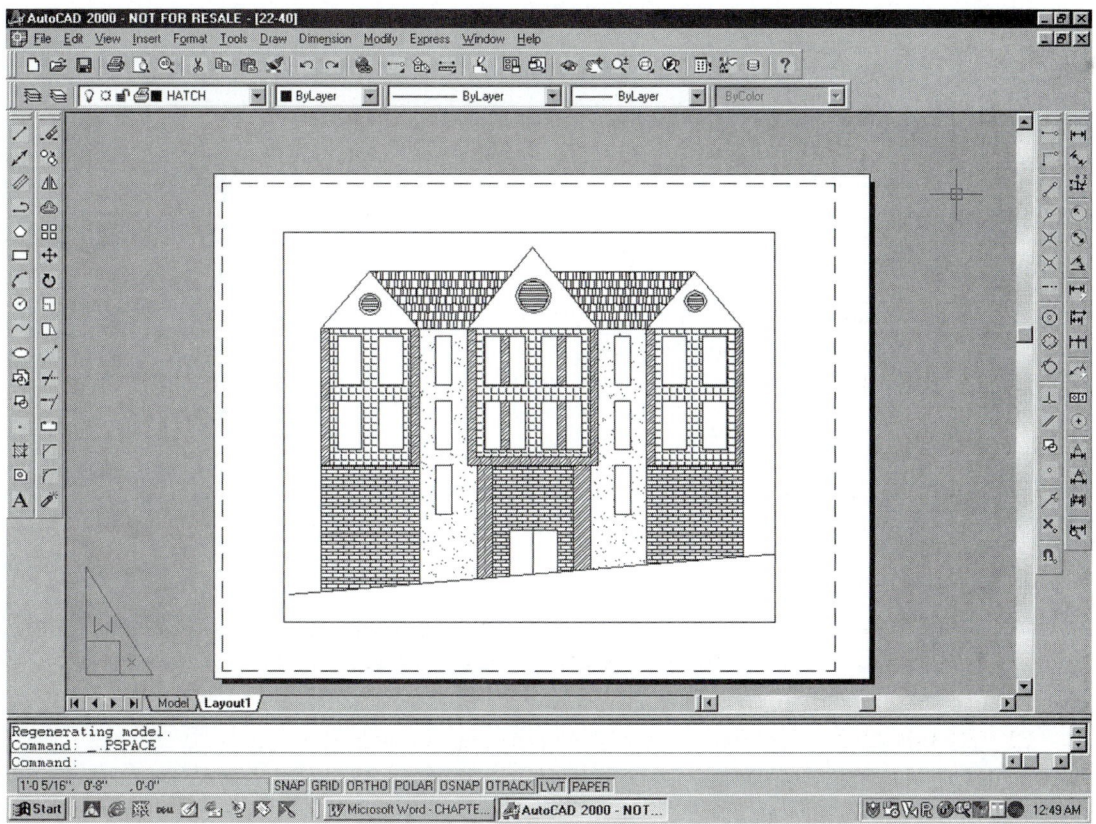

FIGURE 22–40 The elevation drawing displayed in paper space Layout1.

FIGURE 22–41
Selecting the viewport
will display its grips.
Grips will be used to
resize the viewport.

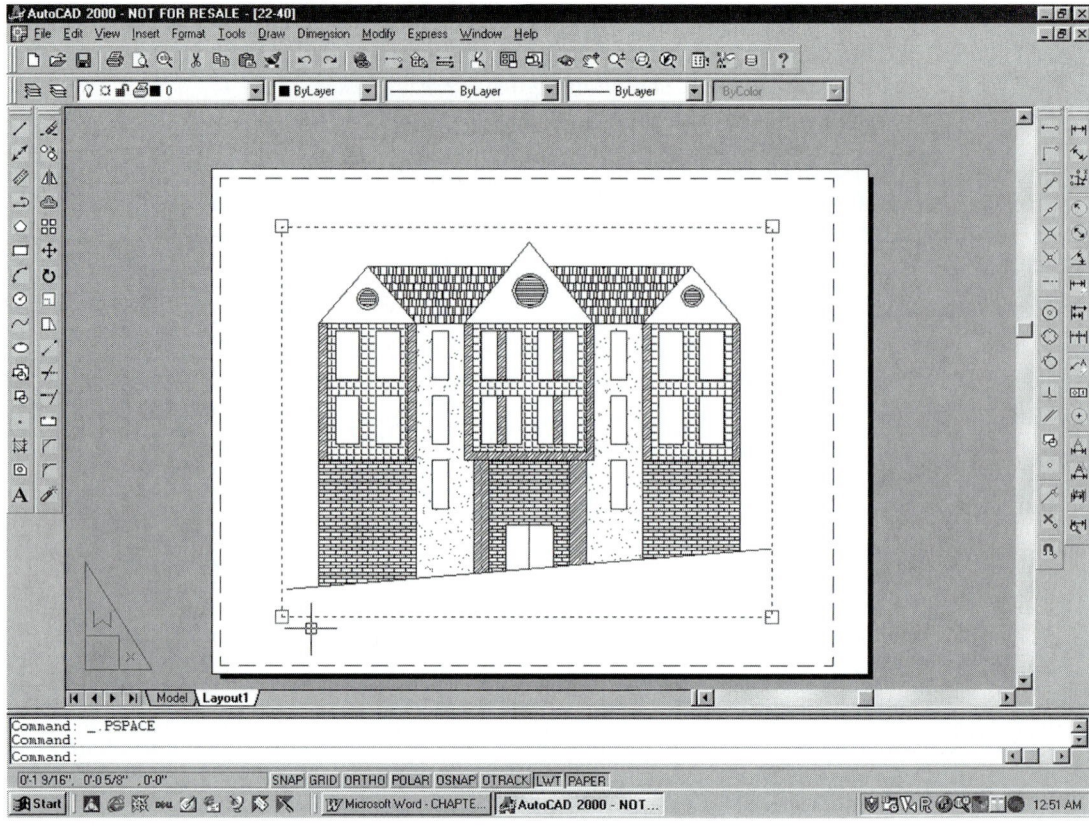

FIGURE 22–42   The
existing viewport is
resized at the upper left
corner of the paper.
Notice that only a
portion of the drawing
is visible in the
viewport.

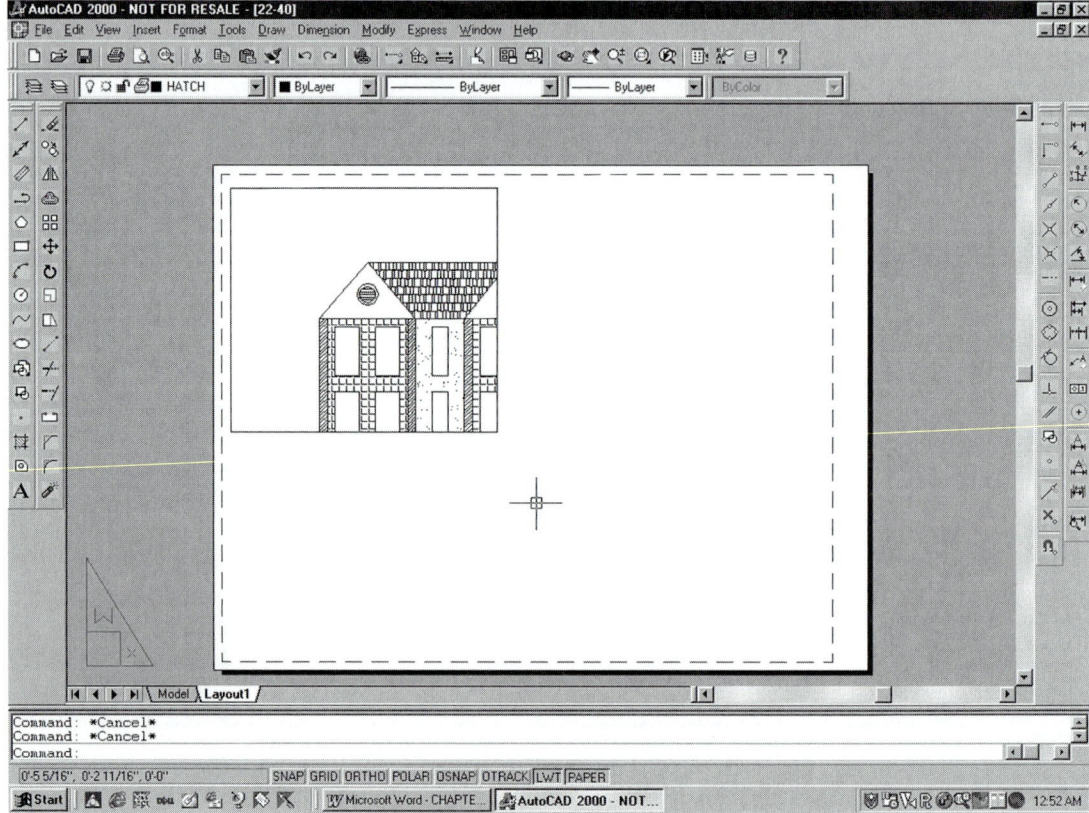

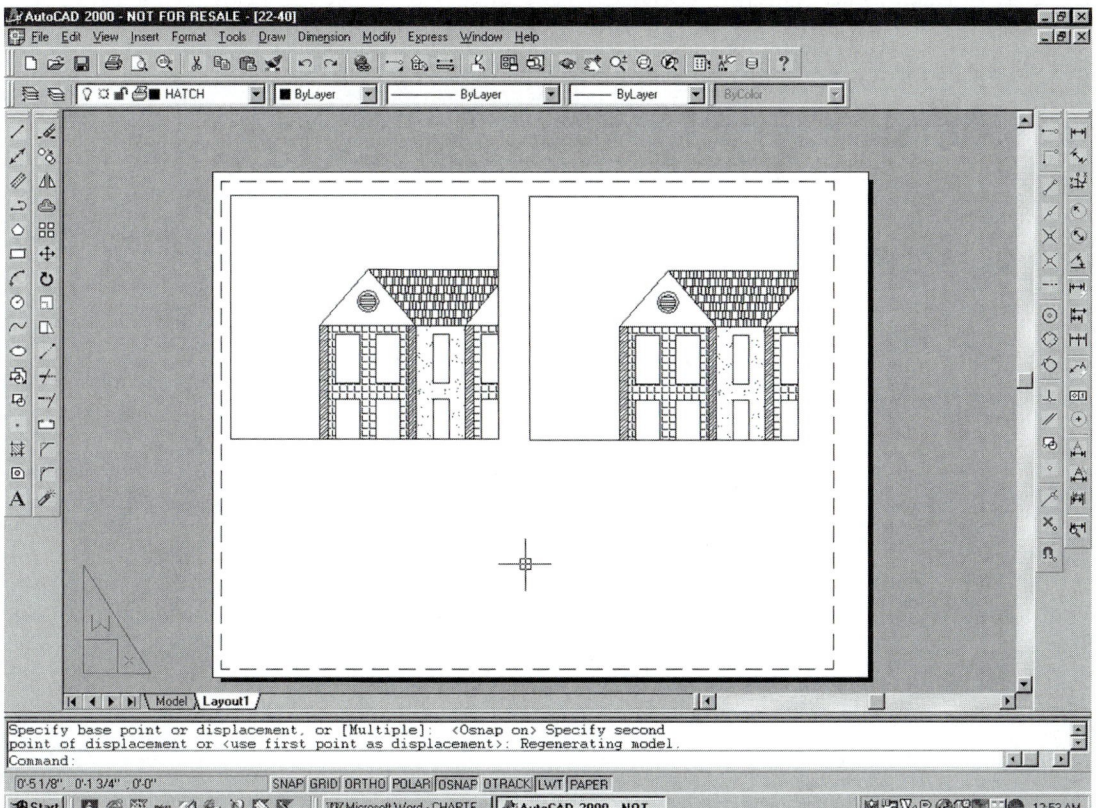

FIGURE 22–43 The viewport is copied to the right side of the paper. Notice the viewports are created inside the dashed lines (printable area).

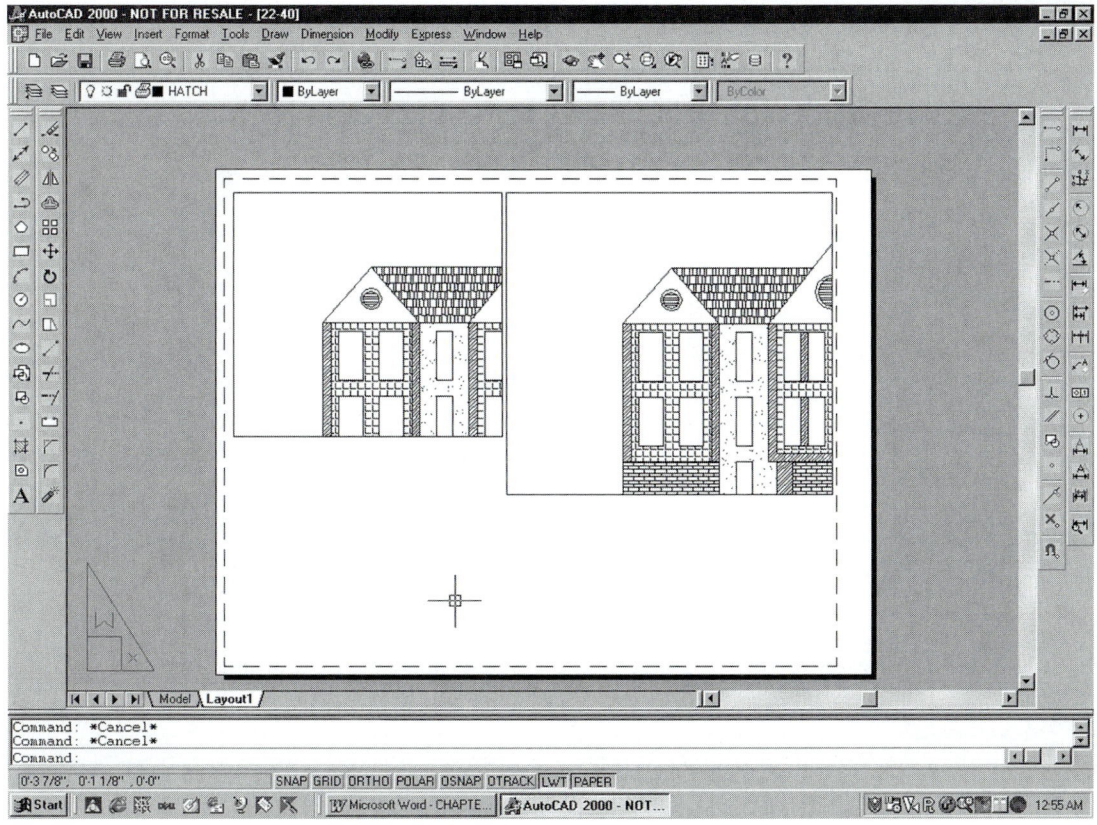

FIGURE 22–44 The viewport is enlarged to show more of the elevation.

FIGURE 22–45 The second viewport is copied to the bottom of the paper. Notice the overlapping/floating viewports.

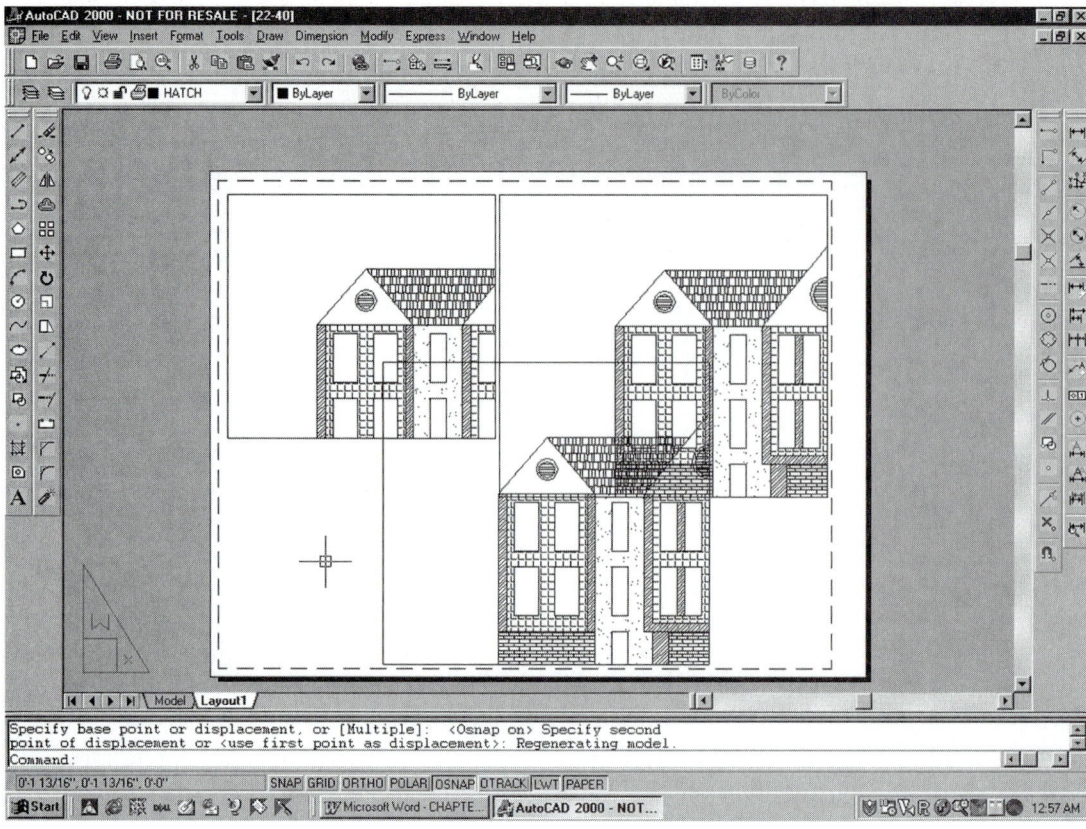

FIGURE 22–46 The third viewport is resized with grips.

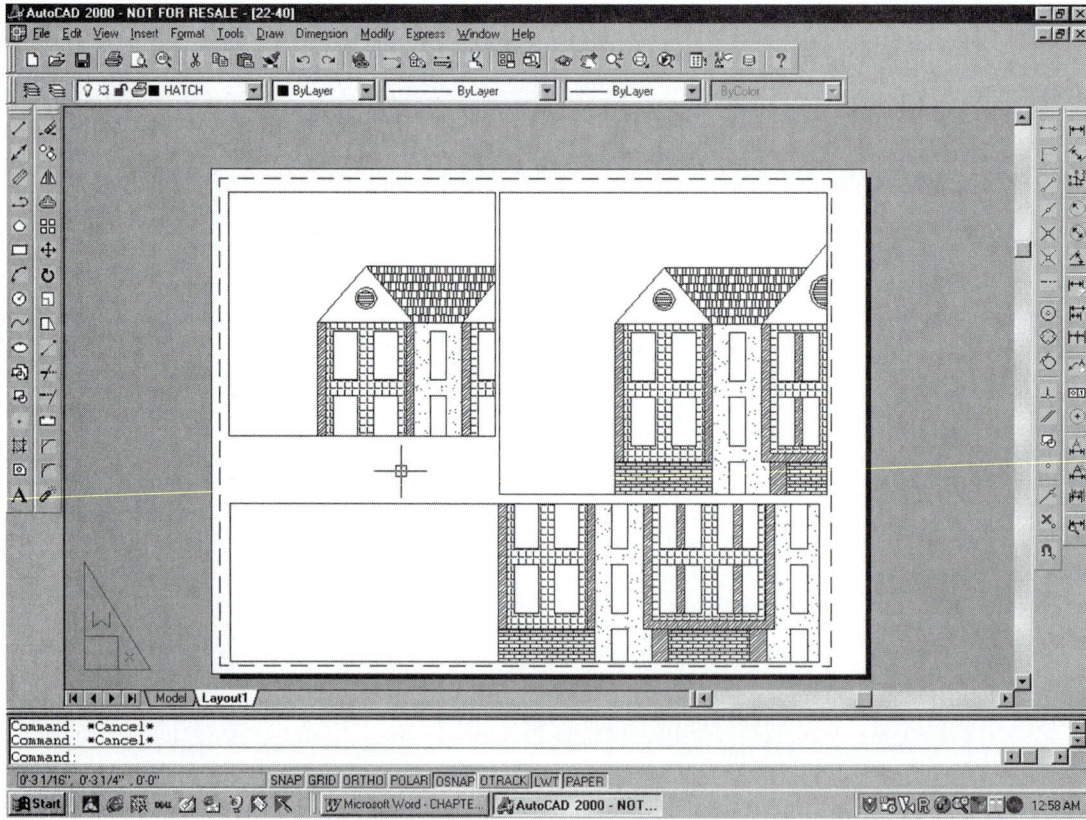

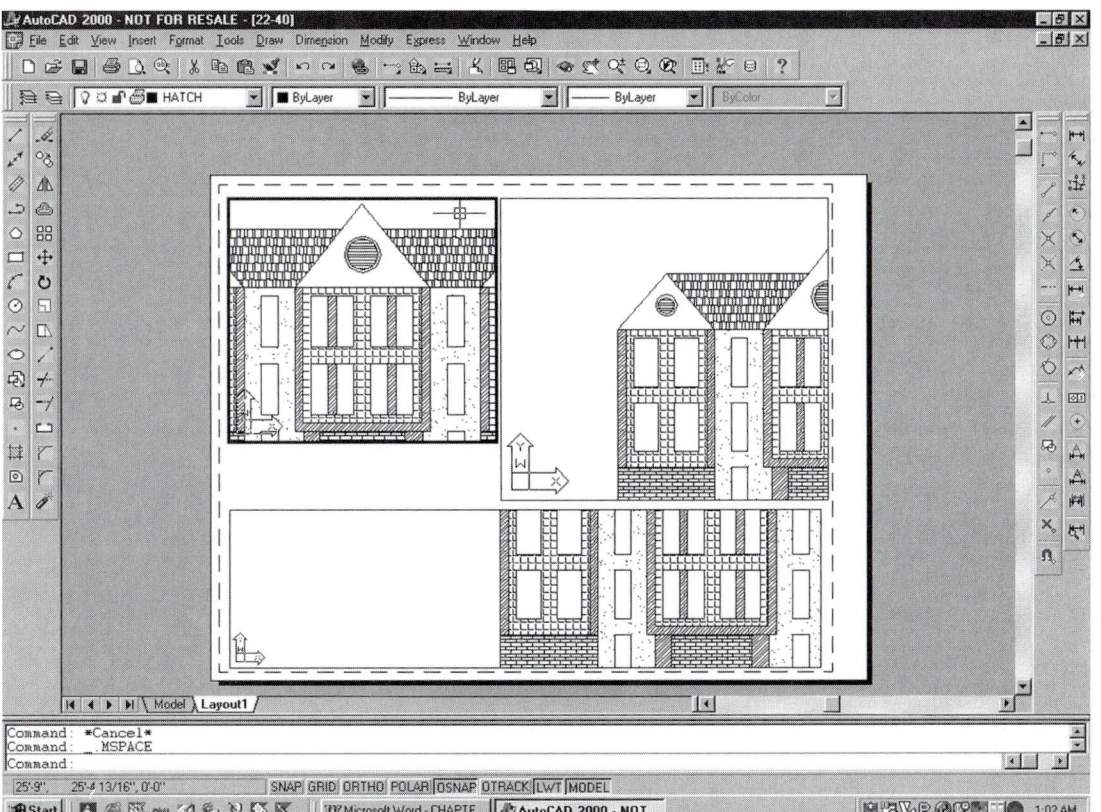

FIGURE 22—47 Pan and zoom realtime is used to display a portion of the elevation inside the first viewport in Model space. Notice that each viewport provides access to its own model space.

FIGURE 22—48 The three viewports displaying different portions of the same elevation. Each drawing in each viewport is displayed at a different magnification in its own model space.

Congratulations! You have successfully created three floating viewports from the default current viewport using the editing commands.

22.10.3   Using the Viewports Toolbar

You can create rectangular viewports using the Single Viewport button in the Viewports toolbar as shown in Figure 22–49. The procedure is the same as described above. You can delete the default viewport and use this button to create a new single viewport. AutoCAD will ask you to specify the corners of the rectangle for the viewport. Select the first and the second corner to create the viewport. Repeat this procedure if more viewports are needed.

22.10.4   Using the View Pull-Down Menu

You can create rectangular tiled viewports in Model or untiled floating rectangular viewports in paper space layout using the View pull-down menu. The Viewports cascading menu in the View pull-down menu is shown in Figure 22–50.

The first six options deal with creating rectangular viewports as follows:

NAMED VIEWPORTS. . .:   Selecting this option will display the Named Viewports tab of the Viewports dialog box. If you have named viewports, select the named viewport configuration and click on the OK button to apply it to the drawing area. Named viewport configurations cannot be applied to the active viewport.

NEW VIEWPORTS. . .:   Selecting this option will display the New Viewports tab of the Viewports dialog box. Select the required option from the Standard viewports: list and click on the OK button.

1 VIEWPORT: Selecting this option allows you to create a single viewport. If you use this option in paper space layout, you need to erase the default viewport and create a new one. If you use this option in Model tab, the current viewport will be replaced with this single viewport.

2 VIEWPORTS: When you select this option, AutoCAD asks you to select a vertical or horizontal viewport arrangement. If you use this option in paper space layout, you need to erase the

FIGURE 22–49 The Viewports toolbar can be used to create a single viewport in paper space Layout.

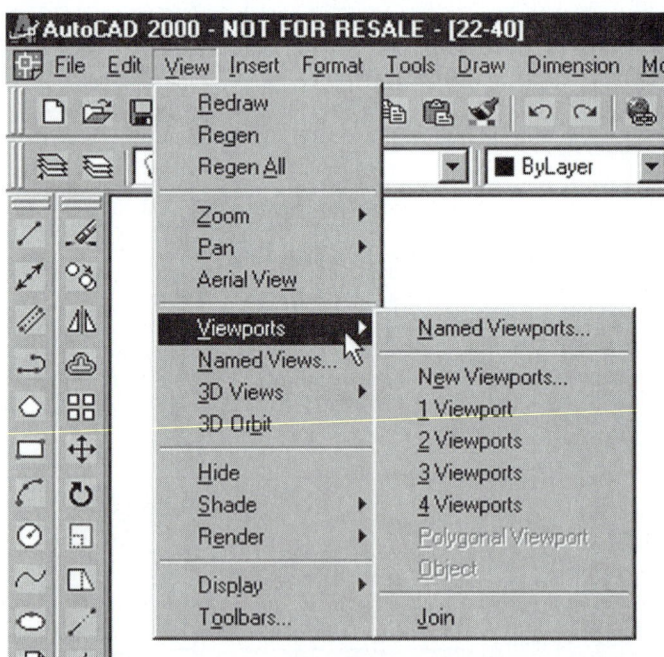

FIGURE 22–50   The Viewports cascading menu options in the View pull-down menu.

default viewport and create the new viewport arrangement. The command line procedure in paper space is as follows:

```
Enter viewport arrangement [Horizontal/Vertical] <Vertical>: (enter H
for horizontal or press ~EnterKey~ for vertical viewport arrangement)
Specify first corner or [Fit] <Fit>:
```

You can create two rectangular viewports by selecting the first and the opposite corner inside the paper space. AutoCAD will create two horizontal or two vertical viewports. The Fit option automatically fits the viewports inside the available paper. If you use this option in Model tab, two viewports will be created without specifying corners.

3 VIEWPORTS: When you select this option, AutoCAD asks you to select one of the viewport arrangement options as follows:

```
Enter viewport arrangement
[Horizontal/Vertical/Above/Below/Left/Right] <Right>: (select an option)
Specify first corner or [Fit] <Fit>: (specify first corner or use the
Fit option)
```

If you use this option in paper space, you need to erase the default viewport and create the new viewport arrangement. If you use this option in Model tab, the current viewport will be replaced by three viewports.

4 VIEWPORTS: This option allows you to create four equal viewports. If you use this option in paper space, you need to erase the default viewport and create the new viewport arrangement. If you use this option in Model tab, the current viewport will be replaced by four equal viewports.

22.10.5 Using the MV, MVIEW, or –Vports Commands

Floating viewports can also be created using the MV, MVIEW, and –VPORTS commands. These commands are identical when used in paper space. The command line procedure is as follows:

```
Command: MV, MVIEW, or -VPORTS ~EnterKey~
Specify corner of viewport or
[ON/OFF/Fit/Hideplot/Lock/Object/Polygonal/Restore/2/3/4] <Fit>:
```

The default option allows you to create a viewport by specifying the two corners of the viewport. The 2, 3, and 4 options allow you to create preset viewport configurations similar to the Viewports dialog box and the Viewports cascading menu option in the View pull-down menu. You must be in paper space to work with these commands; otherwise AutoCAD will automatically switch to paper space. The other options are as follows:

ON: This option activates the model space display inside a viewport.

OFF: This option deactivates the model space display inside a viewport. When you enter this option, AutoCAD will ask you to select objects. Select the viewport you want to turn off and press the ~EnterKey~. AutoCAD will deactivate the model space. This means that when you click on the Paper button in the Status bar, AutoCAD will give you the following message at the command line:

```
There are no active model space viewports.
```

To activate model space display, enter ON after the MV command, select the viewport, and press the ~EnterKey~. When you click on the Paper button, the model space will be activated.

FIT: This option is the default and will create a single rectangular floating viewport that covers the entire printable area.

HIDEPLOT: This option removes the hidden lines in a three-dimensional drawing when plotted.

LOCK: This option allows you to lock the magnification display of the drawing inside a viewport. When you lock a viewport, its current scale is locked and you cannot use display commands such as ZOOM and PAN in model space. However, you can still edit objects inside a locked viewport. This option is covered later in the chapter.

RESTORE: This option will convert saved viewport configurations into individual floating viewports.

OBJECT: This option allows you to convert a closed object created in paper space into a floating viewport. This option is covered later in the chapter.

POLYGONAL: This option allows you to create nonrectangular floating viewports in paper space. This option is covered next.

Note: You can create up to 64 viewports in Paper Space. The MAXACTVP (maximum active viewports) system variable can be used to control the amount of viewports displayed. The default is 64 with a minimum of two. Use the REGENALL command to regenerate all viewports after setting a new value for MAXACTVP.

Tips: Create a Viewports layer and make this layer nonplottable. This will allow only the objects inside the viewports to plot, but not the outline of the viewports. Make this layer plottable if viewports must be plotted.

22.11 CREATING POLYGONAL FLOATING VIEWPORTS IN PAPER SPACE

You can create nonrectangular floating viewports in paper space. The viewport can be any polygonal shape. You can create polygonal floating viewports by selecting the Polygonal option of the MV, MVIEW, and –VPORTS commands, by selecting the Polygonal Viewport button in the Viewports toolbar, or by selecting the Polygonal Viewport from the Viewports cascading menu in the View pull-down menu. The command line prompts for drawing the outline of the viewport are similar to those for drawing a polyline. The outline of the polygon can include straight lines and arc segments. You can create polygonal floating viewports in paper space as follows:

1. Open the drawing in Model tab.

2. Click on the Layout1 (or any other Layout) tab. If you are using any of the layout tabs for the first time, the Page Setup – Layout1 dialog box will appear. Click on the OK button to enter paper space.

3. Use the ERASE command to erase the default viewport or use grips to resize the current viewport.

4. Click on the Polygonal Viewport button in the Viewports toolbar. The command line procedure is as follows:

```
Specify start point: (select the start point of the polygon)
Specify next point or [Arc/Close/Length/Undo]: (turn ortho off and
select the next point or any of the options)
Specify next point or [Arc/Close/Length/Undo]: (select additional
points to create the desired closed polygon)
Specify next point or [Arc/Close/Length/Undo]: ~EnterKey~
```

The polygon will be created as a viewport and the drawing will be displayed inside the viewport. You can create more polygonal viewports in paper space using the procedure described above. Figure 22–51 shows four polygonal viewports (for four wall details) created in paper space. You can switch to model space and make one of the viewports active. You can then use the display commands such as ZOOM and PAN realtime to adjust the magnification of the drawing to display a specific portion of the drawing inside the polygonal viewport. Figure 22–52 shows four wall details displayed inside the polygonal viewports with different magnification factors. Notice the upper-left viewport is current (active) in model space.

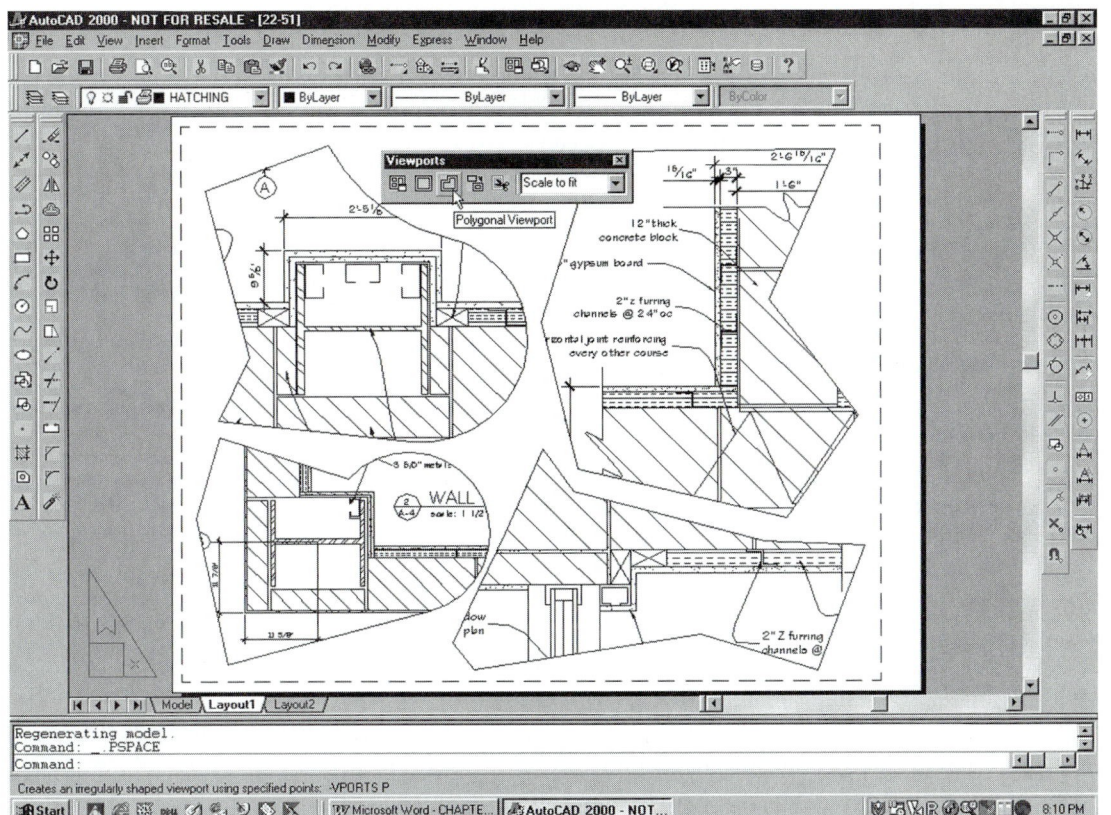

FIGURE 22–51 You can create non-rectangular (polygonal) floating viewports in paper space. Notice the arc as part of the two viewports.

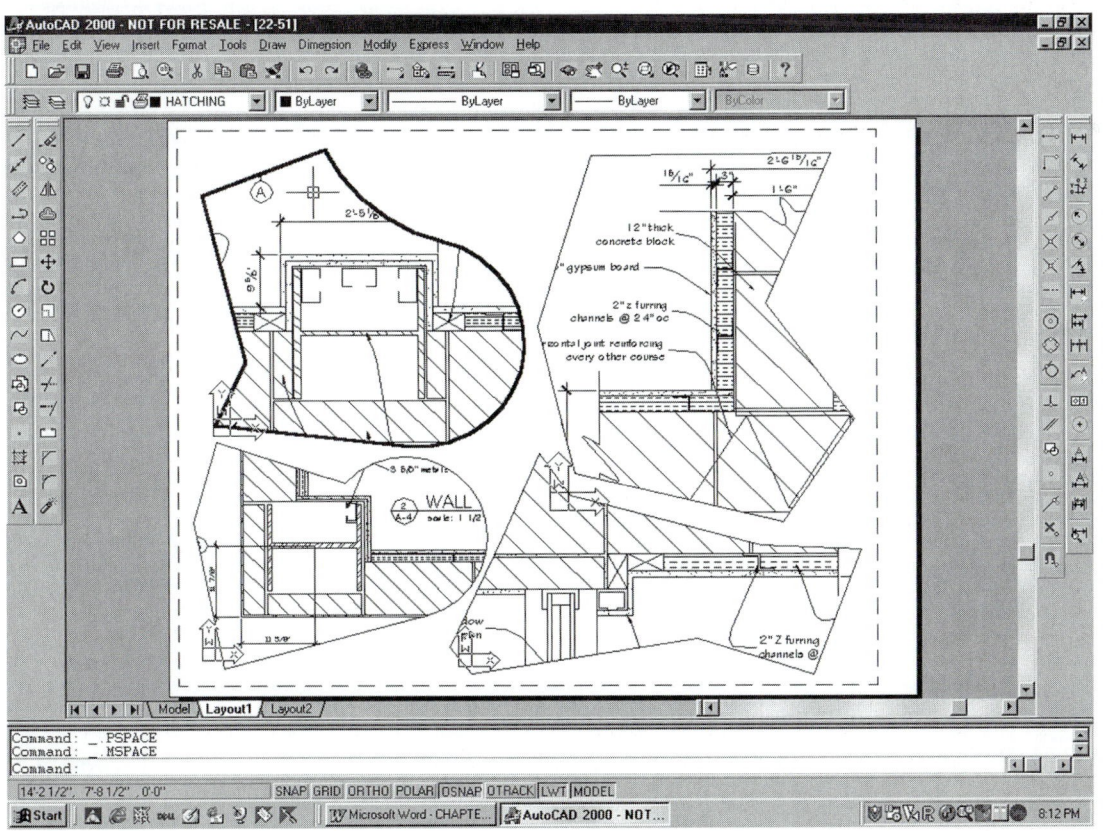

FIGURE 22–52 You can switch to Model space and use display commands to change the size of the detail of the drawing in each polygonal viewport. The viewport in the upper left corner has bold outline around its edges. This is the active viewport. You can also work and edit objects in model space of each viewport.

22.12 CONVERTING PAPER SPACE OBJECTS TO VIEWPORTS

In addition to creating polygonal viewports, you can convert existing objects created in paper space into viewports. The objects to be converted into viewports can be a closed polyline, polygons, circles, splines, ellipses, or regions. You can convert a circle, a triangle (using the POLYGON command), a rectangle (using the RECTANG command), and a seven-sided polygon (using the POLYGON command) into viewports as follows:

1. Open the drawing in Model tab.

2. Click on the Layout1 (or any other Layout) tab. If you are using any of the layout tabs the first time, the Page Setup–Layout1 dialog box will appear. Click on the OK button to enter paper space.

3. Erase the default viewport.

4. In paper space, create a circle, a triangle, a rectangle, and a seven-sided polygon as shown in Figure 22–53.

5. Click on the Convert Object to Viewport button in the Viewports toolbar. You can also use the Object option of the MV, MVIEW, and –VPORTS commands or use the Object option of the Viewports cascading menu in the View pull-down menu.

6. At the Select object to clip viewport: command prompt, select the object to convert to viewport. Repeat the same procedure for other objects.

7. Switch to Model space and use the ZOOM and PAN realtime to change the magnification of the drawing in each viewport.

Figure 22–54 shows the four objects turned into viewports. Each viewport displays different parts of the floor plan with different magnification.

Caution: Objects drawn with the LINE command cannot be converted into a viewport.

Tips: The Viewports toolbar is the fastest way to create viewports one-at-a-time. Have this toolbar open when you are creating and managing viewports in paper space.

FIGURE 22–53 The circle, rectangle, triangle, and seven-sided polygon created in paper space can be turned into separate viewports.

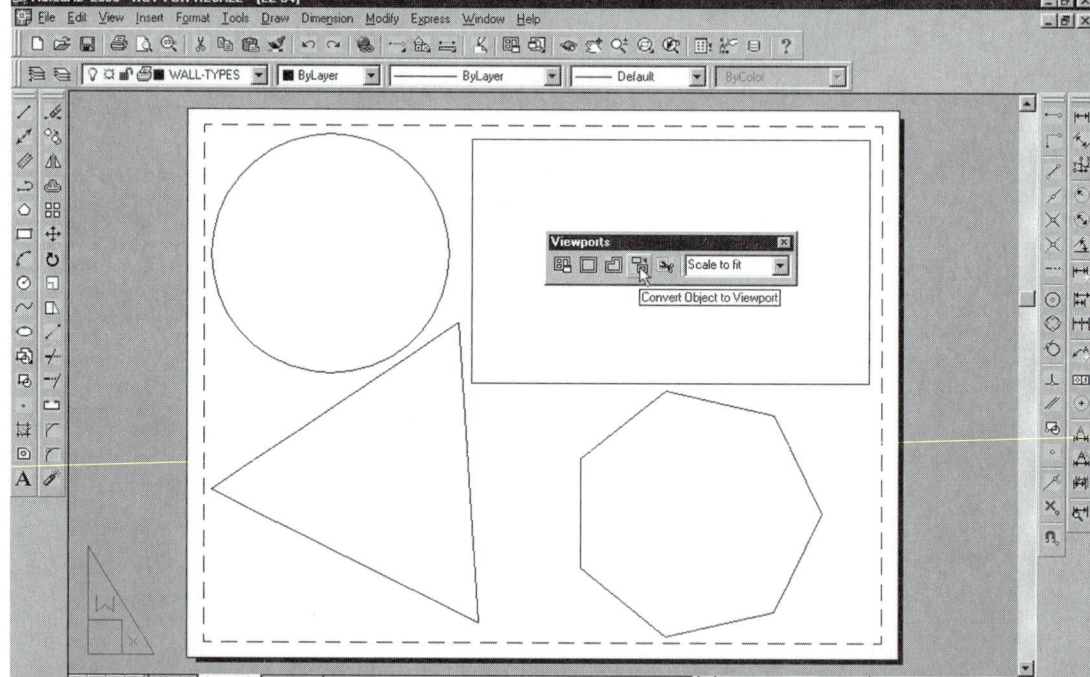

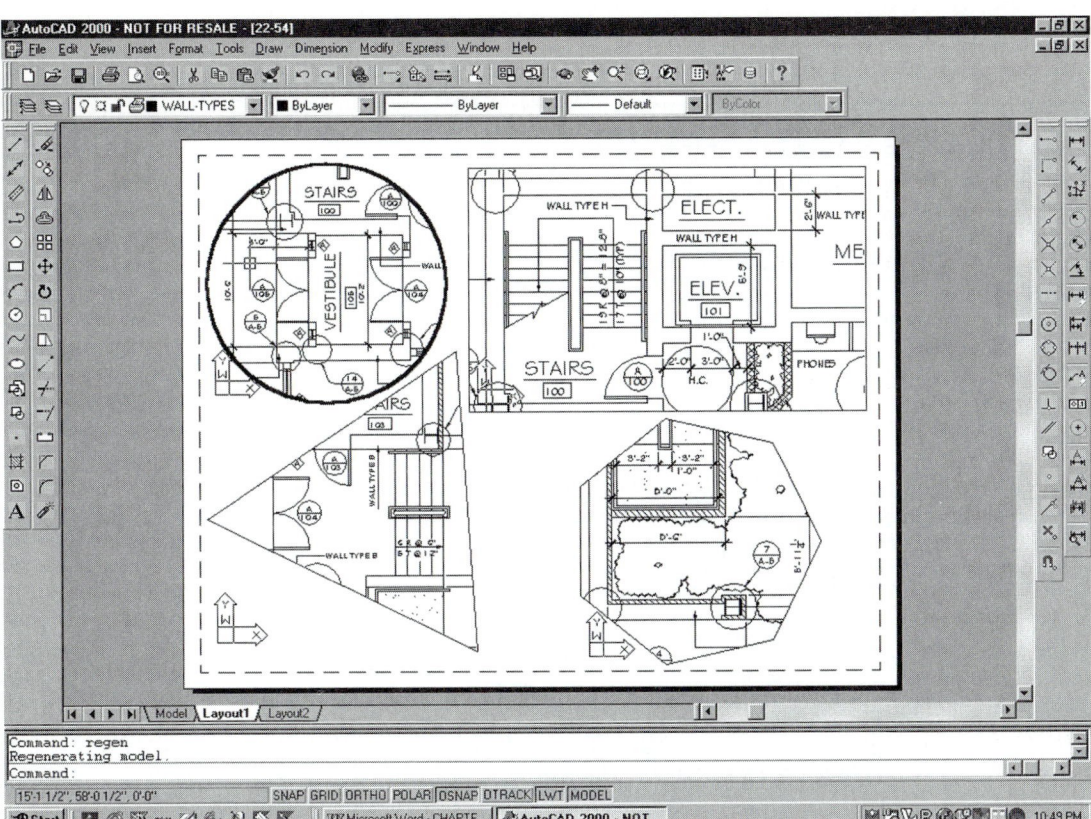

FIGURE 22–54 Four different viewports displaying four different areas of the floor plan.

22.13 SWITCHING BETWEEN MODEL SPACE AND PAPER SPACE

After you create layout(s) and create viewports in paper space, you can continue working on your drawing from the Model tab or the Layout tab. To work with the model of your project, click on the Model tab or enter MODEL at the command line. To move from Model tab to paper space, click on the Layout1 tab. While in a layout, you can work in paper space or in model space by making a viewport current. To make a viewport current (while in paper space), double-click inside the viewport. This will cut a hole in the viewport and bring you to model space. To make paper space current, double-click on any area outside a viewport. You can also switch between model space and paper space in a layout by selecting either Paper or Model from the status bar. You can also enter MSPACE or PSPACE at the command line. The last active viewport will be made current when switching to model space.

When you are in paper space, AutoCAD inserts a piece of "paper" over the drawing and cuts a hole, called a viewport, in this "paper." In paper space, display commands such as ZOOM and PAN affect the entire paper space. Objects that you draw in paper space appear only once. You can create text in paper space at full scale. In paper space, all the viewports are closed and you can draw on top of them. Editing commands in paper space edits objects drawn in paper space.

22.14 SCALING VIEWPORTS

Before plotting drawings from a layout, you should set the viewport display scale relative to paper space so that objects in viewports plot at the required drawing scale. You can set a precise scale to the drawing inside a viewport using the viewport scale drop-down list shown in Figure 22–55. The list contains architectural and mechanical drawing scales,

FIGURE 22–55 The
viewport scale drop-
down list is used to
assign a precise scale to
viewports. The list
contains predetermined
scales including most of
the architectural scales.

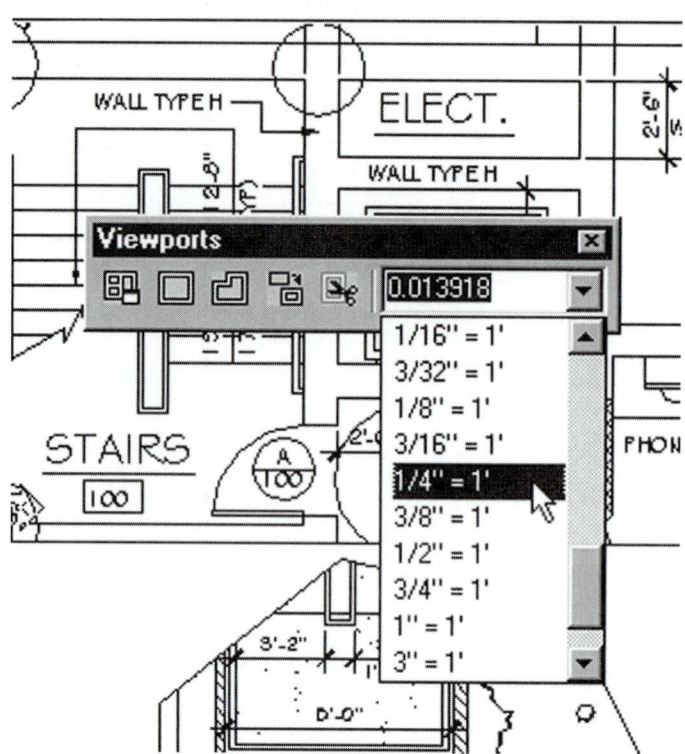

including Scale to Fit, 1:1, and other scales. You can scale the drawing inside the viewport as follows:

1. Make sure you are in model space (MODEL should be displayed in the PAPER/MODEL toggle in the Status bar).
2. Click inside the viewport you want to scale to make it active.
3. The current scale of the viewport will be displayed in the Viewports toolbar.
4. Select the required drawing scale from the drop-down list.

Recently used scales will be listed at the top of the list. If a scale is not available, you can type the scale directly in the viewport scale box. You must type the scale as a decimal number or a drawing scale factor number. For example, to set a precise scale of 1″=10′ enter **0.008333** (1 divided by 120) or enter **1:120**. The 120 is the scale factor for the scale of 1″=10′. The 1 1/2″=1′ scale is not listed under the architectural scales but in reality selecting **1:8** or entering **0.125** will set the scale to 1 1/2″=1′–0″.

Figure 22–56 shows the circle viewport set at 1/4″=1′ scale, the rectangle viewport set at 1/8″=1′ scale, the triangle viewport set at 3/16″=1′ scale, and the polygon viewport set at 1/8″=1′ scale.

Note: Using the ZOOM and PAN realtime does not affect the current scale. Using the ZOOM command options will affect the current scale.

You can also use the reciprocal of the scale factor XP to change the scale of the viewports. For example, you can set a scale of 1″=40′ to a site plan in a viewport as follows:

1. Make the viewport active in model space.
2. Use the ZOOM command as follows:

```
Command: ZOOM ~EnterKey~
Specify corner of window, enter a scale factor (nX or nXP), or
[All/Center/Dynamic/Extents/Previous/Scale/Window] <real time>:
1/480XP ~EnterKey~
The current viewport will now be at the 1"=40' scale (480 is the scale
factor).
```

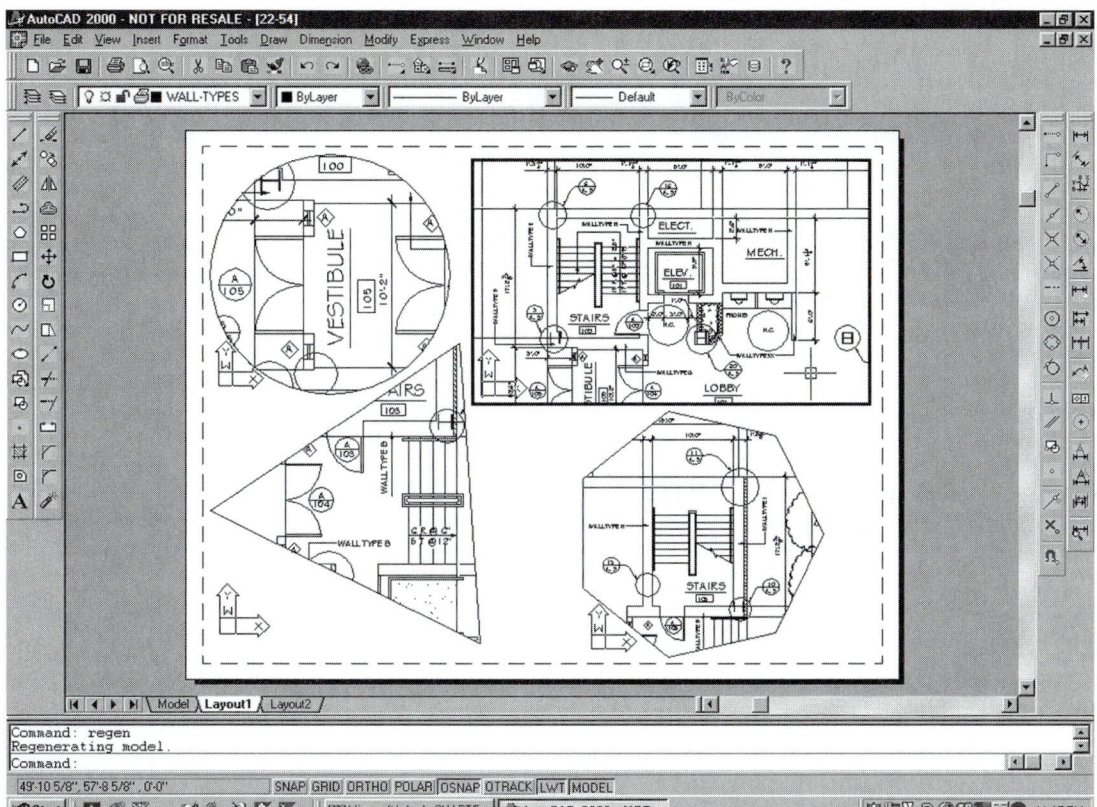

22.15 CLIPPING EXISTING VIEWPORTS

You can clip a floating viewport to a custom-drawn viewport. You can change the current rectangular shape of the default (or any other) viewport into a polygonal viewport without erasing the viewport, or you can select an existing closed object inside the viewport to clip as follows:

In paper space, click on the Clip Existing Viewport button in the Viewports toolbar and use the following command line procedure:

```
Select viewport to clip: (select the outline of the viewport to be
clipped)
Select clipping object or [Polygonal] <Polygonal>: (select an object
inside the viewport or press the ~EnterKey~ to create a polygonal clip)
```

If you select an object for clipping, AutoCAD will convert the object into a clipping boundary. This will become the new viewport. Objects that are valid for clipping are closed polylines, polygons, circles, ellipses, closed splines, and regions.

The Polygonal option allows you to create a clipping boundary. The command line procedure is as follows:

```
Specify start point: (turn ortho and osnap off and select the first point
to create the clipping boundary)
Specify next point or [Arc/Close/Length/Undo]: (select all points
required to create the clipping boundary)
```

The Arc, Close, Length, and Undo suboptions are similar to the functions of the PLINE command options.

22.16 LOCKING VIEWPORT SCALE

After you set a precise scale to a viewport, you can lock that scale so that it is not altered by accident. This is similar to layer locking. By locking the viewport scale, you are preventing the use

FIGURE 22–57 Using the right-click shortcut menu to lock a viewport scale.

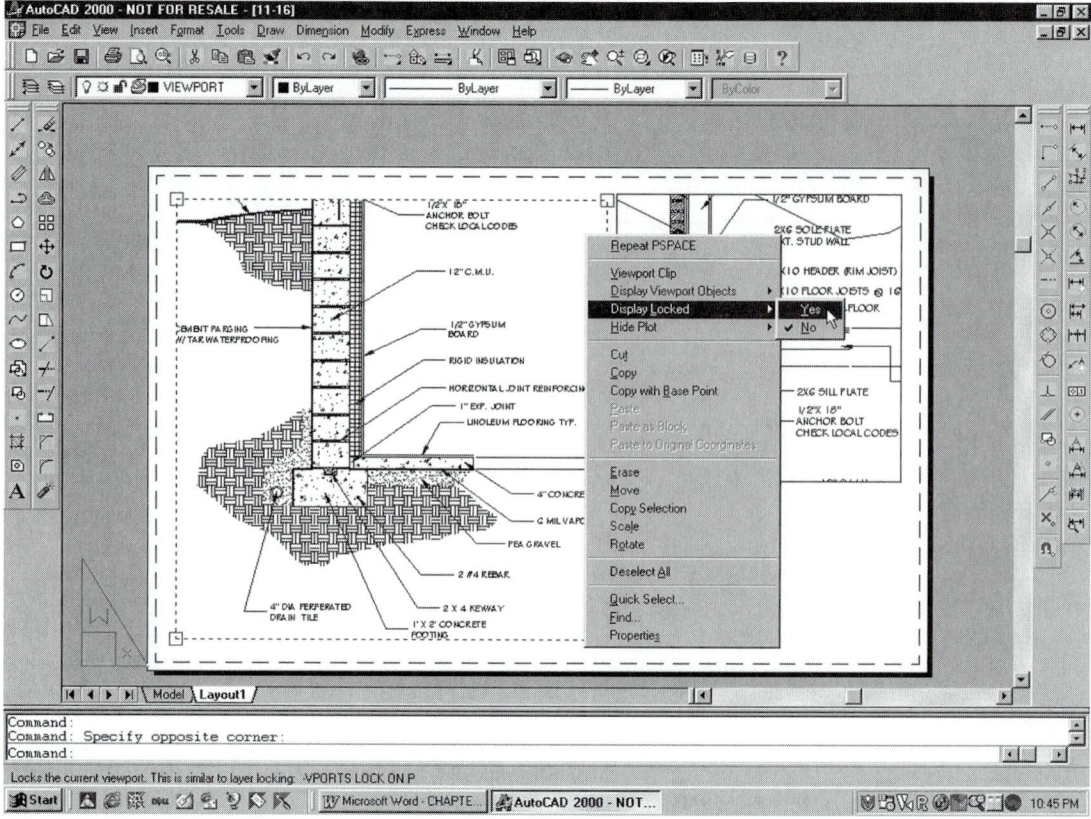

of zoom command options in Model space. After locking the viewport scale, if you are in model space and attempt to zoom, AutoCAD will display the message "Viewport is view-locked. Switching to Paper space" at the command line. All zooming is now performed in paper space. You will return automatically to model space with the viewport scale unchanged when you complete the display command. You can lock viewport scale as follows:

1. Switch to paper space.
2. Left-click on the viewport outline you want to lock scale. The grips will be displayed if you have the grips on.
3. Right-click in the drawing area and a shortcut menu will be displayed as shown in Figure 22–57.
4. Select the Display Locked menu option and select Yes. A checkmark in front of No means the viewport scale is not locked. A checkmark in front of Yes means the viewport scale is locked.

Tips: You can still use editing commands to stretch, move, and copy viewports in paper space.

You can use the right-click shortcut menu to clip a viewport. The Display Viewport Objects option allows you to turn off a viewport, making its objects invisible. Select Yes to turn off the selected viewport.

REVIEW QUESTIONS

1. What is the function of the Model and the Layout tabs?
2. What does the paper space environment allow you to do?
3. Name two items that indicate you are in paper space?
4. When you first select a Layout tab, what dialog box does AutoCAD display?

5. What does a Viewport allow you to do in paper space and in model space?

6. What is the difference between a tiled and an untiled viewport?

7. Describe two different methods to create layouts.

8. Name four items that you can setup using the Create Layout dialog box?

9. The preview of the layout displays a paper border that accurately indicates the plot area for the layout based on what settings?

10. What does WYSIWYG stand for and what does it do for AutoCAD?

11. The display of the paper background in paper space and several settings that affect the display of layouts can be controlled using which tab of what dialog box?

12. What does Page Setup allow you to do?

13. You can create rectangular floating viewports using five different methods. Describe two methods.

14. Describe the process to create polygonal floating viewports in paper space.

15. How do you convert a paper space object into a viewport?

16. How do you establish a plot scale for a viewport?

17. How do you lock viewport scale?

PROBLEMS

1. Open the *EXE22-1.dwg* file. Rename the Architectural Title Block layout to Building Section. Access the paper space and delete the default viewport. Using the Viewports dialog box, create Three:Above viewports. Use the Zoom and Pan realtime to fit the entire building section into the top viewport. Show the upper-left corner as enlarged detail in the bottom-left viewport. Show the lower-left corner as enlarged detail in the bottom-right viewport. Your drawing should now look like Figure 22–58. Do not save the changes.

2. Open the *EXE10-6.dwg* file. Create a new layout from the existing Architectural, English units – Color Dependent Plot Styles template and rename it Floor Plan. Select the Floor Plan Layout tab. Switch to model space and zoom to the extents of the drawing. Switch back to paper space. Erase the default viewport. The drawing should now disappear. Use the View pull-down menu to create four floating viewports as shown in Figure 22–59. Switch back to model space. Arrange the views of the

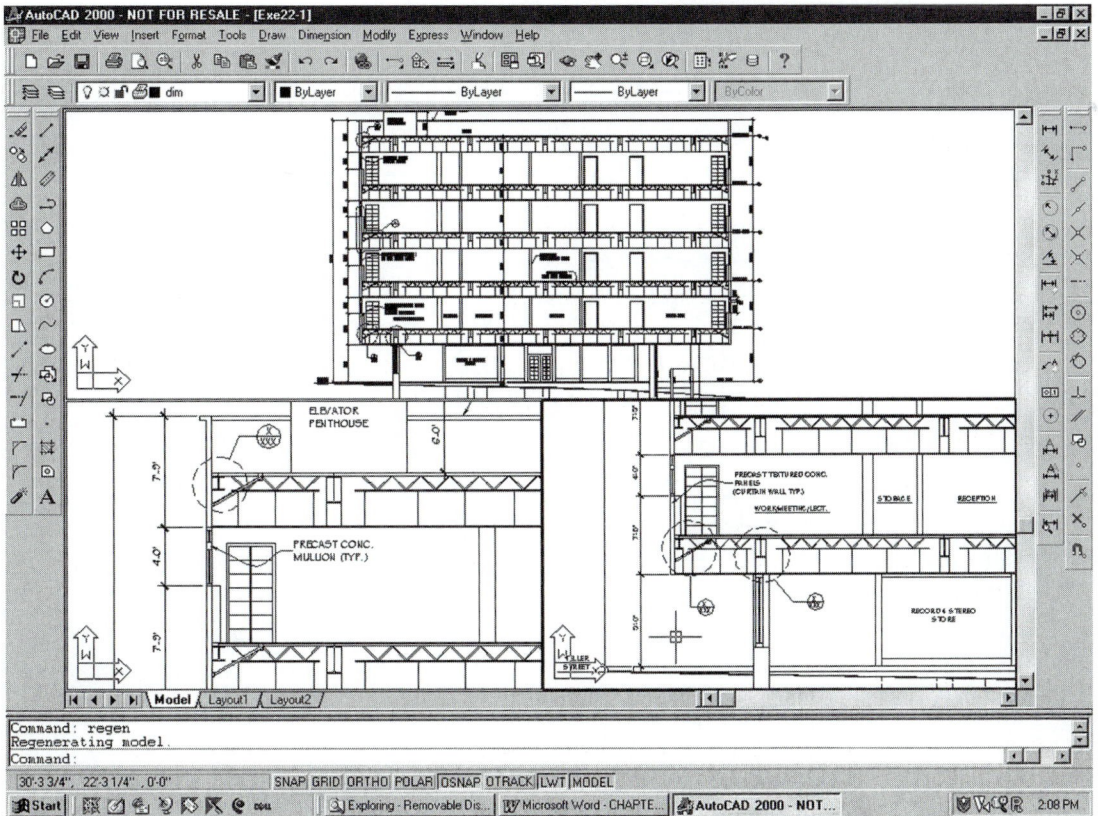

FIGURE 22–58
Problem 1.

FIGURE 22–59
Problem 2.

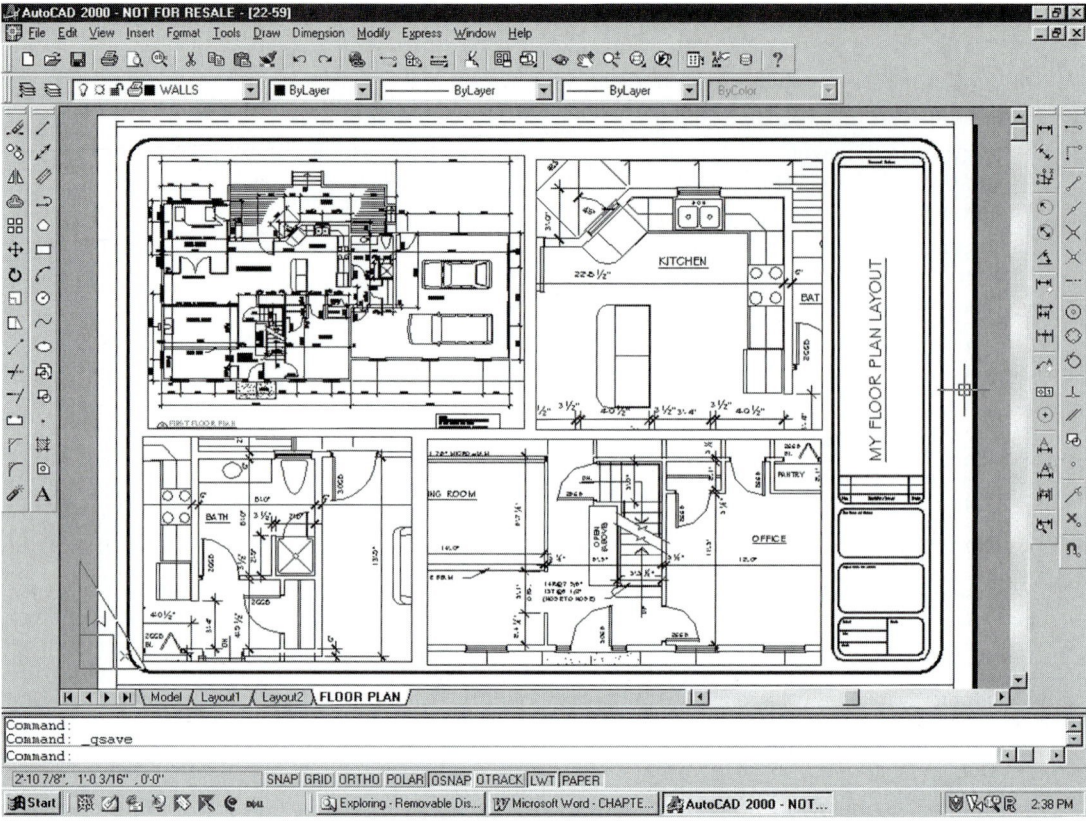

FIGURE 22–60
Problem 3.

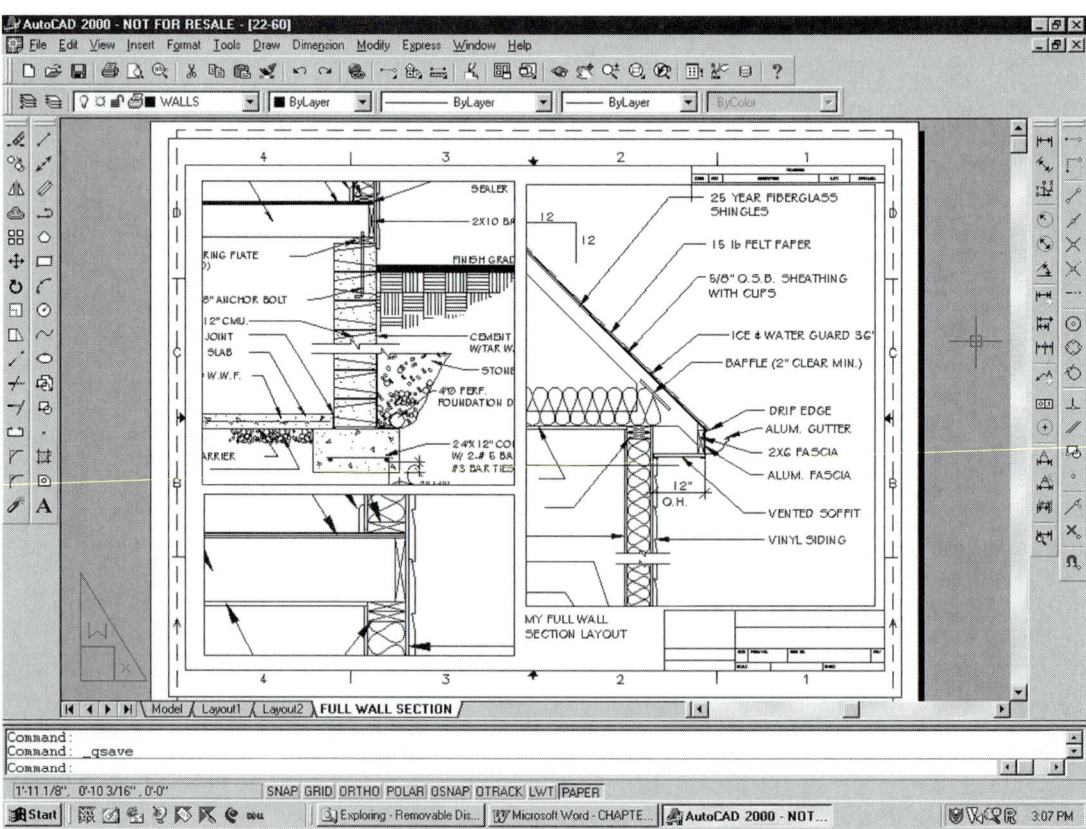

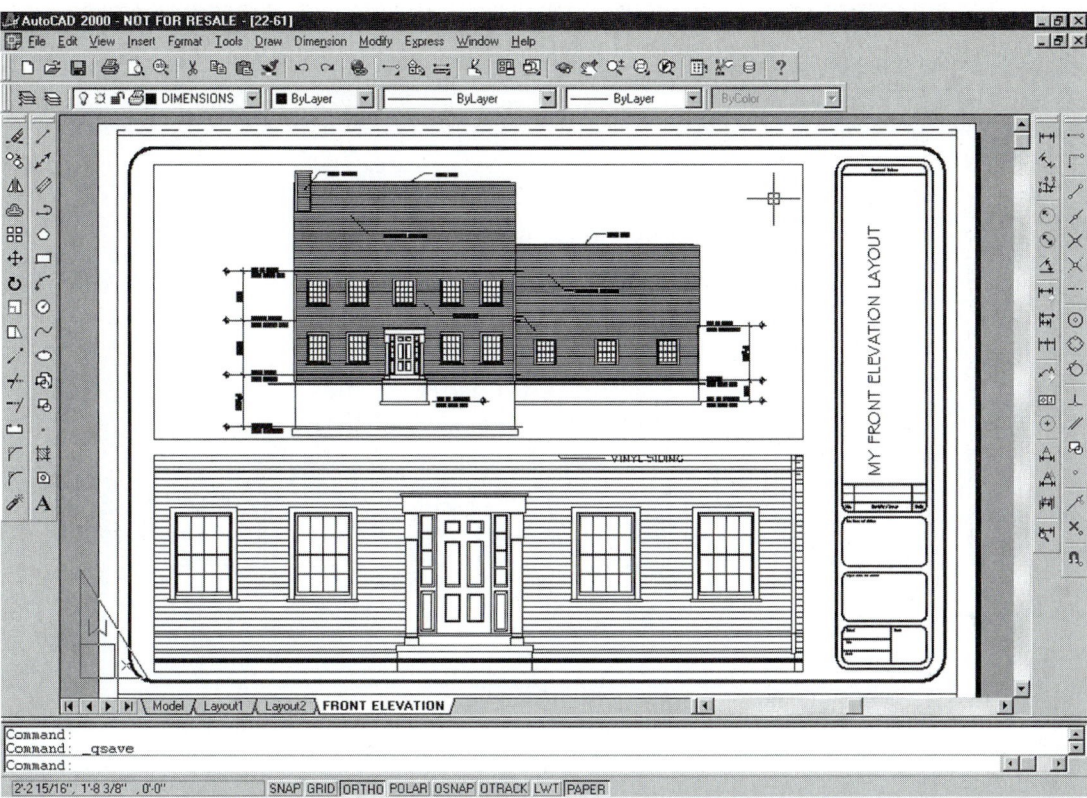

FIGURE 22–61
Problem 4.

drawing in viewports as shown in Figure 22–59. Switch back to paper space. Use the DTEXT command to type My Floor Plan Layout at 1/2″ text height inside the title block as shown in Figure 22–59. Do not save the changes.

3. Open the *EXE22-4.dwg* file. Create a new Layout from the existing ANSI C-Named Plot Styles template and rename it Full Wall Section. Select the Full Wall Section layout tab. Switch to model space and zoom to the extents of the drawing. Switch back to paper space. Erase the default viewport. The drawing should now disappear. Use the MVIEW command to create three floating viewports as shown in Figure 22-60. Switch back to model space. Arrange the views of the drawing in viewports as shown in Figure 22-60. Switch back to paper space. Use the DTEXT command to type My Full Wall Section Layout at 1/4″ text height as shown in Figure 22–60. Do not save the changes.

4. Open the *EXE22-5.dwg* file. Create a new Layout from the existing Architectural, English units — Named Plot Styles template and rename it Front Elevation. Select the Front Elevation Layout tab. Switch to model space and zoom to the limits of the drawing. Switch back to paper space. Use grips to resize the existing viewport and copy the viewport to the bottom of the drawing. Switch back to model space. Use the Viewports toolbar to set the upper viewport to 1/4″ = 1′–0″ scale. Use Pan realtime to position the drawing. Set the bottom viewport to 3/4″= 1′–0″ scale and use Pan realtime to show the front entrance as shown in Figure 22–61. Switch back to paper space. Lock both viewport scales. Use the DTEXT command to type My Front Elevation Layout at 1/2″ text height as shown in Figure 22–61. Do not save the changes.

5. Open the *EXE10-6.dwg* file. Click on the Layout1 tab. The Page Setup – Layout1 dialog box will appear. Click on the OK button to close the dialog box. Erase the default viewport. The drawing will disappear. Create two polygonal viewports as shown in Figure 22–62 using the Viewports toolbar. Switch back to model space. Set the largest viewport to 3/8″ =1′–0″ scale and adjust the view as shown in Figure 22–62. Set the other viewport to 3/16″ = 1′–0″ scale and adjust the view as shown. Lock both viewport scales. Use the DTEXT command to type My Polygonal Viewports at 3/8″ text height in paper space as shown in Figure 22–62. Do not save the changes.

6. Open the *EXE22-4.dwg* file. Click on the Layout1 tab. The Page Setup – Layout1 dialog box will appear. Click on the OK button to close the dialog box. Erase the default viewport. The drawing will disappear. Create a circle and a nine-sided polygon as shown in Figure 22–63. Convert these two objects to two viewports. Switch back to model space. Use the Zoom and Pan realtime to adjust the magnification of the drawings as shown in Figure 22–63. Switch back to paper space. Use the DTEXT command to type My Objects to Viewports at 3/8″ text height. Do not save the changes.

FIGURE 22–62
Problem 5.

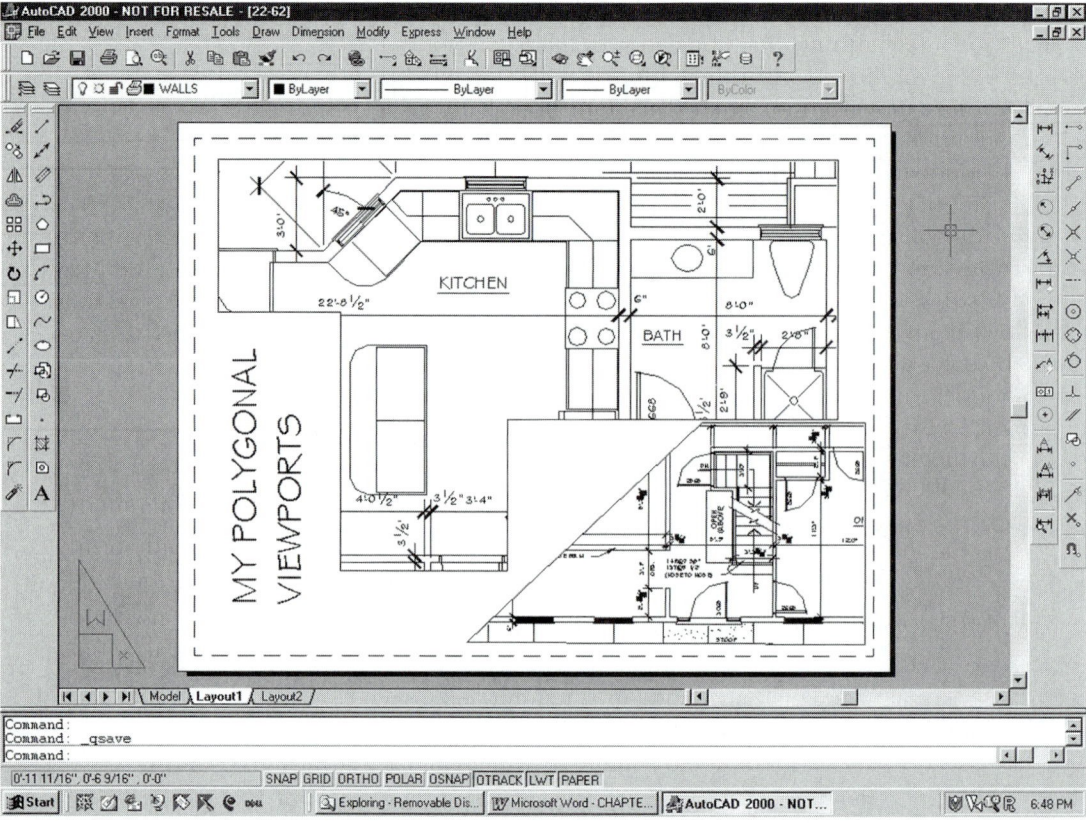

FIGURE 22–63
Problem 6.

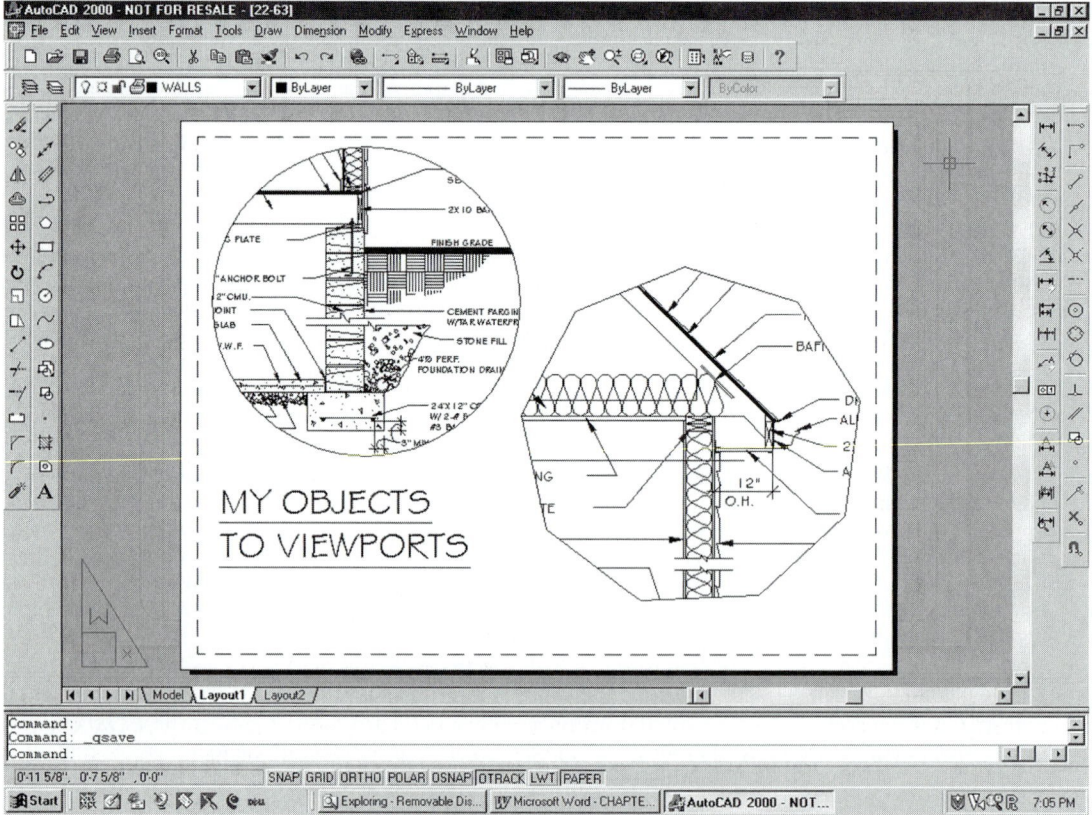

CHAPTER

23

Printing and Plotting

After successful completion of this chapter you should be able to:

▲ Understand printing and plotting procedures.

▲ Understand the concept behind plot styles.

▲ Use the Add Plot Style Table dialog box to create plot style tables.

▲ Create and modify color-dependent plot style tables.

▲ Create and modify named plot style tables.

▲ Attach plot style tables to drawings and layouts.

▲ Use the Plot dialog box to print and plot.

▲ Print and plot from the Model tab.

▲ Print and plot from paper space layouts.

▲ Edit plot style tables.

▲ Apply color-dependent and named plot styles.

23.1 INTRODUCTION TO PRINTING AND PLOTTING

Printing is the process of creating a hard copy of your drawing using a printing device such as a laser or ink-jet printer. These printers allow you to obtain the final copy of your drawing on 8 1/2″ × 11″ (A size) paper or 11″ × 17″ (B size) paper. Plotting is referred to as the process of creating a hard copy of your drawing using a plotter capable of plotting the final copy of your drawing on 18″ × 24″ (C size) paper, 24″ × 36″ (D size) paper, or 36″ × 48″ (E size) paper. After making a print or plot of your drawings, you can make a blueprint and send it to appropriate individuals. You can also send the contents of your drawing files to those who will use it by creating a plot file. These files have .plt extensions. You can send copies of your drawings electronically over the Internet to another firm, to a client, or to your consultants or you can send copies of your drawing files by floppy or zip disk. No matter how you send files, obtaining a paper copy through printing or plotting is the most dependable method. You have been introduced to layouts, paper space, viewports, and model space in Chapter 22. Each Layout tab can be configured to print or plot different view of your project using different plotting settings such as paper size, scale, and orientation. Creating layouts allows you to print and plot with maximum flexibility with varying settings. Each layout you create is a preview of how the drawing will appear prior to printing and plotting. This streamlined operation of interlacing layouts with plot settings offer you the WYSIWYG layouts. The process of plotting might seem a bit overwhelming at first, but after familiarizing yourself you will be able to plot faster, more easily, and with outmost consistency. Before plotting, you must configure a printer and/or plotter in AutoCAD 2000. This process will most likely be performed by the CAD manager, IT manager, or by the computer services department. The purpose of this chapter is to discuss the basic process behind printing and plotting your drawings at the most efficient way possible.

23.2 PLOTTING PROCEDURES

You can print and plot from the Model tab (model space) or from the Layout tab (paper space). Typically, paper space layouts provide more flexibility and functionality. When plotting from the Model tab, the plot scale is selected to reflect the scale of the drawing. When plotting from paper space layout, the plot scale is set to 1:1. The general procedures for both methods are similar. The general printing and plotting procedures are as follows:

1. Configure and install printing and/or plotting devices.
2. Create the drawing in Model tab.
3. If you are creating a layout, create untiled floating viewports in paper space.
4. If a title block and other desired items are required, create a layout from a template.
5. Use the Page Setup or the Plot dialog box to specify printing and plotting settings. The Plot dialog box is discussed later in the chapter.
6. Use plot style tables if required to do so.
7. Print or plot the drawing.

23.3 PLOT STYLES

In earlier versions of AutoCAD, *pen assignments* were used to assign a particular color with a particular pen width when printing and plotting. AutoCAD 2000 expands this ability with a new feature called *plot styles*. Plot styles allows you to plot objects with properties (color, linetype, lineweight, and so on) other than the properties shown in the drawing. For example, in one layout you can plot the walls of a floor plan using a gray scale and the electrical equipment with a heavier lineweight. This means that the walls of the floor plan will be plotted with less emphasis, and the electrical equipment in the floor plan will stand out. In another layout you can plot with opposite effect. You can use plot styles to determine how objects appear when the drawing is plotted including:

1. Color, linetype, and lineweight.
2. Line end, join, and fill styles for wide lineweights.
3. Color screening, gray scaling, and dithering.
4. Fill patterns and pen numbers.

Plot styles are device independent and are attached at plot time using the plot style table (pen assignments) list in the Plot dialog box. There are two plot styles as follows:

- **COLOR PLOT STYLES:**　A color plot style table contains 255 colors. Each color is associated with a particular set of plotting parameters. You assign plot settings to each color in the table to determine how your drawing will plot. AutoCAD automatically assigns color styles to objects and layers based on their color. Objects having the same color are plotted with the same properties. This plot style is very similar to the way R14 pen assignments work with AutoCAD 2000. You cannot delete, add, or rename the color-dependent plot styles. The color-dependent plot styles are stored in the Plot Styles folder with .ctb (for color dependent) extension. The styles in a color plot can be taught of as a set of pens. Each pen has specific characteristics, such as thickness and color. Each pen can be assigned a different color in the drawing file. For example you can assign a thick black pen to the color red. Everything red in the drawing will be plotted with a thick black line. You can assign a color plot style table using the Page Setup dialog box or the Plot dialog box. The Plot dialog box is discussed later in the chapter.

- **NAMED PLOT STYLES:**　With a named plot style you can associate each object in the drawing with a specific set of plotting parameters. You can define any combination of color, linetype, lineweight, dithering, or other property for a plot and give it a name. For example, you can assign specific properties to walls in a floor plan with a named plot style and call it "New Construction." You can assign plot styles to objects by layer or by object. With named plot styles you plot each object differently even if they are the same color. Named plot styles are stored with a .stb (for style table) extension. You can assign a named plot style for a layer using the Layer Properties Manager dialog box. Click on the plot style icon for the layer you want to set. This is the same procedure you would use to assign a color or line-type to a layer. To assign a named plot style for an object, select the object and use the Properties window to change the plot style option to the style you like to use. You can also assign a named plot style to an object by selecting the object (grips will be displayed), and select the plot style from the Object Properties toolbar. When done, press the ~EscKey~ twice to clear the grips.

You do not have to use plot styles in AutoCAD. If you wish to print or plot objects as they appear on the screen, then plot styles are not required. If no plot style is used, the objects are plotted as defined in the drawing as WYSIWYG. If you wish to change some of the object properties at plot time only, then you should use one of the plot styles described above. When you use a plot style table, the objects are plotted as defined by the plot style table. If you are using a previous version of AutoCAD, by default you will use color plot style tables. You can use AutoCAD 2000 drawing templates to create color or named plot styles. AutoCAD provides two versions of each predefined template—one that uses color plot styles and one that uses named plot styles. When you use a template to start a new drawing, the new drawing plot style type is the same as the template. You can create templates based on both plot style types.

Caution: Some laser printers produce output using only black ink or toner. These devices will not plot exactly as the plot style dictates. You can use only one plot style table per layout.

A drawing uses either color or named plot styles. The plot style type for a drawing is determined when the drawing is first created. The default plot style is selected in the Options dialog box in the Plotting tab as shown in Figure 23–1. The Default plot style behavior for new

FIGURE 23–1 The Plotting tab of the Options dialog box is used to set default plot style types and tables for the new drawing.

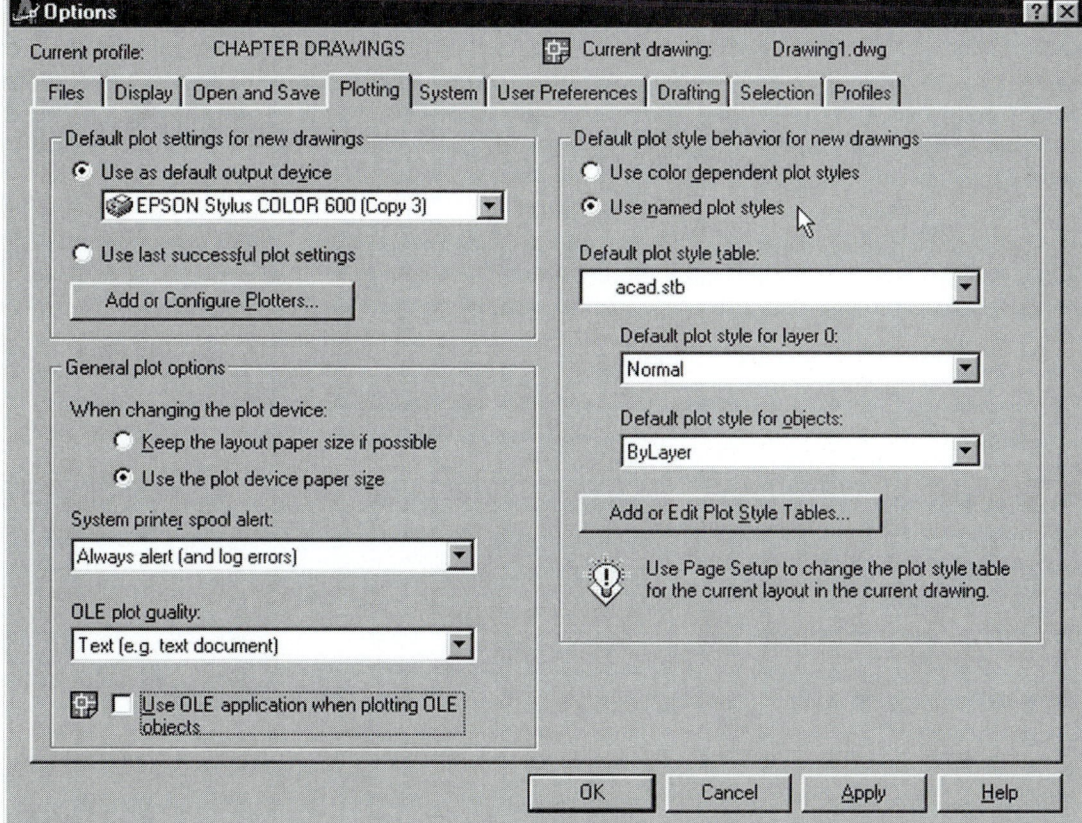

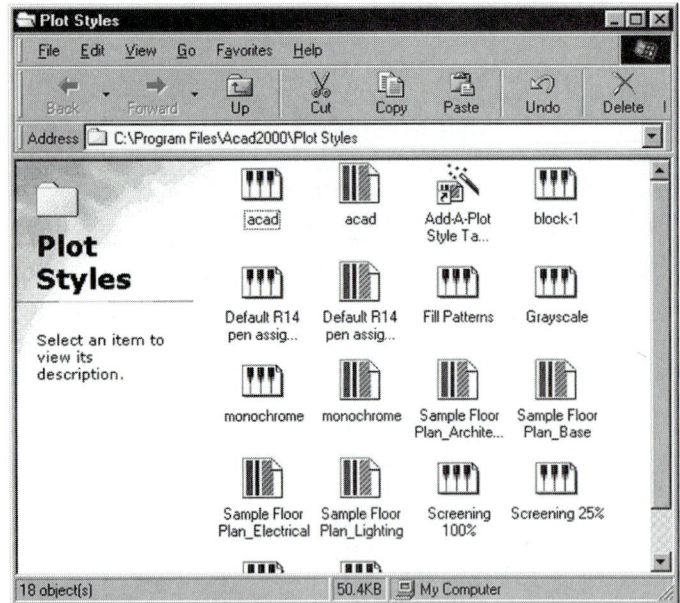

FIGURE 23–2 The Plot Style dialog box shows the available plot styles in the Plot Styles folder.

drawings category on the right side of the Plotting tab has two options. By default, the Use color dependent plot styles radio button is checked. This means that the new drawings will be assigned a set of plotting parameters based on the color of the objects. If you check the Use named plot styles radio button, the plotting parameters will be applied on a layer-by-layer or on an object-by-object basis. If you select the Use named plot styles option, the Default plot style for layer 0: drop-down list and the Default plot style for objects: drop-down list will be activated. You have the option to select the default plot style for layer 0 and for objects. The Default plot style table: drop down-list is used to set a default plot style table. When None is selected, objects in the new drawing will be plotted based on their current on screen properties. You can also change the plot style table from the Page Setup and Plot dialog boxes. The Add or Edit Plot Style Tables . . . button displays the Plot Styles dialog box as shown in Figure 23–2. This dialog box allows you to edit existing plot style tables and create new plot style tables. You can also select Plot Style Manager . . . from the File pull-down menu or enter STYLESMANAGER at the command line to access the Plot Styles dialog box. This dialog box displays icons for each of the saved and standard plot style tables. The icons ending with .ctb are the color plot styles and the icons ending with .stb are the named plot styles. If you double-click on the Add-A-Plot Style Table Wizard icon, the Plot Style Table Editor dialog box will be displayed. This dialog box is used to edit the plot style table and is discussed later in the chapter.

The default plot style type applies to all new AutoCAD 2000 and 2000i drawings and to drawings from previous releases that are opened in AutoCAD 2000. When a drawing is open, the current plot style type is set according to the type used in the drawing previously. The default plot style type is applied to the Model tab and to the Layout tabs. You can change the current plot style type at any time by using the Page Setup dialog box (before plotting) and Plot dialog box (during plotting).

Tips: When you open a drawing, the current plot style type as named or color is indicated on the Object Properties toolbar. If the name ByColor is grayed out in the Plot Style Control box (disabled), then the Color plot styles are active as shown in Figure 23–3. If the name ByLayer is active in the Plot Style control box (enabled) as shown in Figure 23–4, then the Named plot styles are in use.

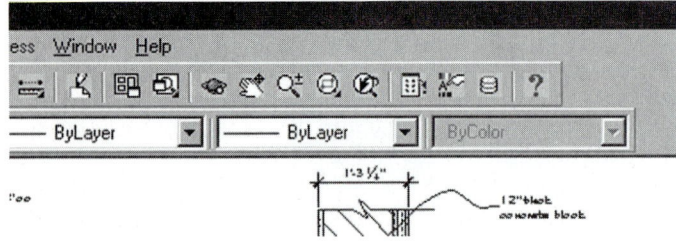

FIGURE 23–3 The Plot Style Control box will be disabled with the name *ByColor* when color plot styles are used.

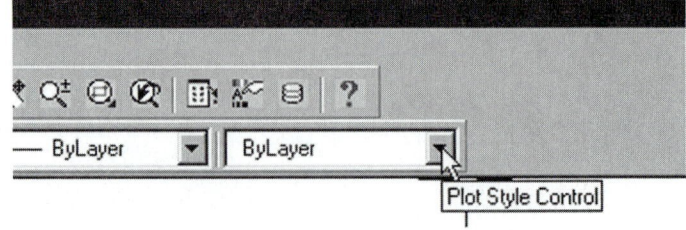

FIGURE 23–4 The Plot Style Control box will be enabled with the name *ByLayer* when named plot styles are used.

23.4 CREATING PLOT STYLE TABLES

Plot styles are organized into plot style tables. Plot style tables are created using the Add-A-Plot Style Table Wizard. To access this wizard, select Add Plot Style Table . . . from the Wizards cascading menu of the Tools pull-down menu as shown in Figure 23–5 or double-click on the Add-A-Plot Style Table Wizard icon in the Plot Styles dialog box discussed previously. You can also use the Page Setup or Plot dialog boxes to access the Add Plot Style Table dialog box. Read the introductory page and click on the Next> button.

The Add Plot Style Table dialog box will be displayed as shown in Figure 23–6. This dialog box contains five pages.

The first page is the **Begin** page and contains four options as follows:

START FROM SCRATCH: This option allows you to create a new plot style table from scratch. When this option is used, the Browse File page is skipped because the new plot style table is not based on any current settings.

USE AN EXISTING PLOT STYLE TABLE: This option allows you to copy an existing plot style table to be used as a template for a new style. When this option is selected, the Table Type page is skipped because the plot style type is determined by the file selected.

USE MY R14 PLOTTER CONFIGURATION (CFG): This option allows you to copy pen assignments from the acad14.cfg file to be used as a template for a new style.

USE A PCP OR PC2 FILE: A PCP file is a partial plot configuration file that contains single plotter device-independent settings. Previous releases (R12, 13, and 14) uses PCP files. A PC2 file is a full plot configuration file that contains both device-dependent and device-independent settings. Release 14 uses PC2 files. A PC3 file is an AutoCAD 2000 plotter configuration file. The Add-A-Plotter wizard creates PC3 files. These files are stored in the ACAD2000/Plotters folder. Select this option if you want to use PCP or PC2 files.

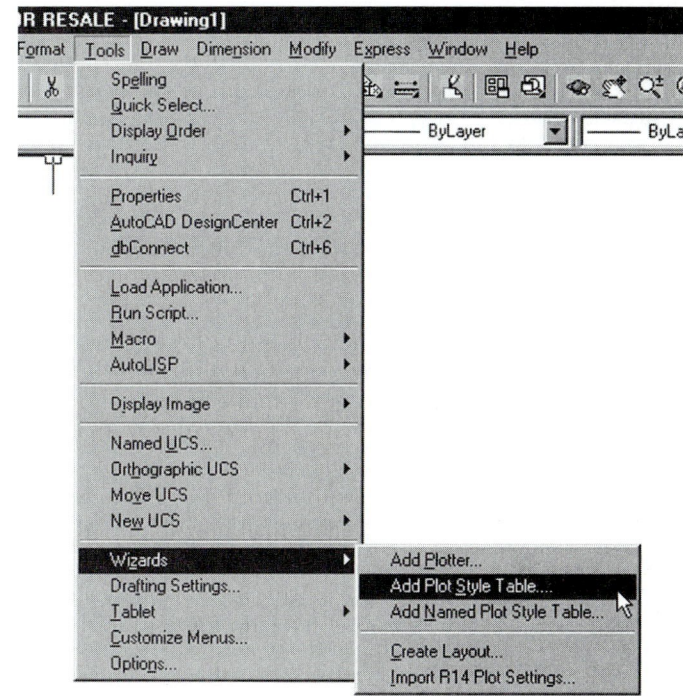

FIGURE 23–5 The Tools pull-down menu can be used to access the Add Plot Styles Table dialog box.

Click on the Next> button to go to the **Table Type** page as shown in Figure 23–7. This page will not be displayed if the Use an existing plot style table option is selected. This page shows the two plot style types. The default plot style is the color-dependent plot styles table, which creates

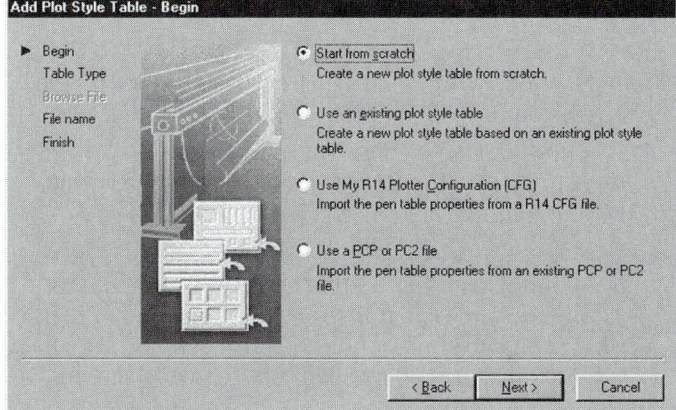

FIGURE 23–6 The Add Plot Style Table–Begin (page) dialog box with four options.

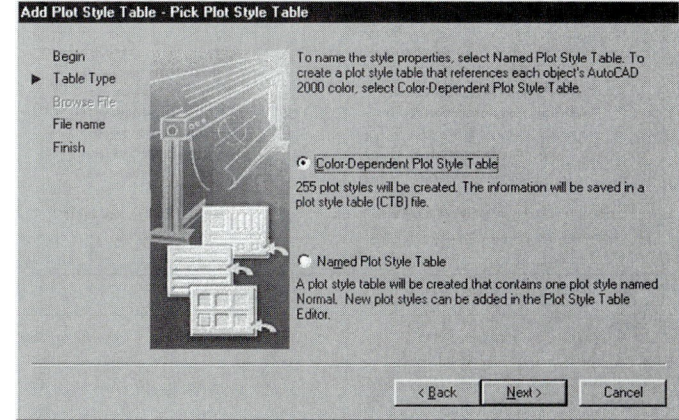

FIGURE 23–7 The Add Plot Style Table–Pick Plot Style Table page allows you to select the appropriate plot style table.

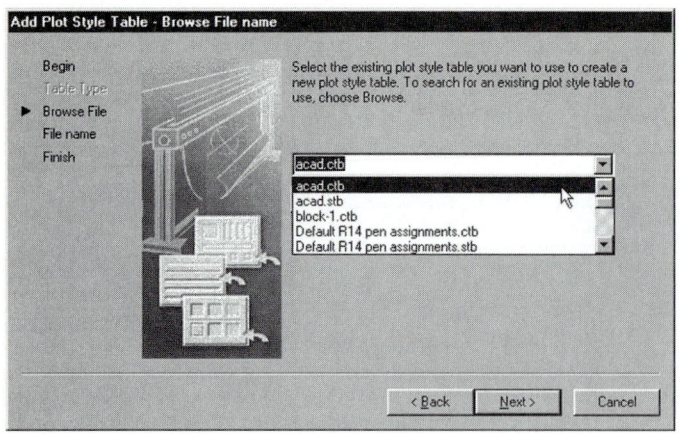

FIGURE 23–8 The Browse File name page allows you to select or find the file on which the plot style is to be based on.

255 color-dependent plot styles. The information will be saved in a plot style table with .ctb file extension. If you want each object in the drawing to be associated with a particular set of plotting parameters, select the named plot style table.

If you used any of the options other than Start from scratch in the first page, the **Browse File** page will be displayed as the next page as shown in Figure 23–8. This page allows you to select the file on which the plot style table is to be based on. You can select the plot style table from the list or click on the Browse . . . button to display the Select File dialog box.

After selecting the file, click on the Next> button to display the **File name** page as shown in Figure 23–9. If you make a mistake, click on the <Back button to go back to the previous page. The File name page allows you to enter a name for the new plot style table. A file extension of .ctb is added to color-dependent plot style tables and a file extension of .stb is added to named plot style tables. Click on the Next> button to display the **Finish** page.

The **Finish** page is shown in Figure 23–10. This final page allows you to edit the plot style table before it is used or attach it to the new drawing. Editing plot style tables are discussed later in the chapter. To attach this plot style table to all new drawings (by default), place a checkmark inside the check box at the bottom of the page. This means that the plot style table you created will be listed in the Plot style table (pen assignments) category of the Page Setup dialog box. This check box is only available if the color-dependent or named plot styles is selected from the Default plot style behavior for new drawings category of the Plotting tab in the Options dialog box as shown in Figure 23–1.

When you click on the Finish button, AutoCAD will assign the new plot style table name to the existing plot style tables list. To confirm that the plot style table is created, select Plot Style Manager from the File pull-down menu. Figure 23–11 shows the addition of ARCHITECTURAL.stb inside the Plot Styles dialog box. Figure 23–12 shows the same plot style table in the Plotting tab of the Options dialog box.

The new plot style tables are also listed in the Plot dialog box. The Plot dialog box is discussed next.

Note: The Wizards cascading menu in the Tools pull-down menu also contains the Add Named Plot Style Table . . . or the Add Color-Dependent Plot Style Table . . . options. The plot style type set for the drawing determines the option. The pages in these Wizards are similar to the Add Plot Style Table Wizard.

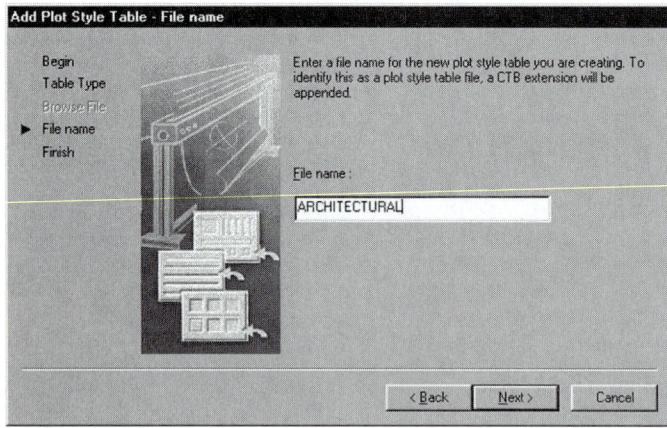

FIGURE 23–9 The File name page is used to enter a name for the new plot style table.

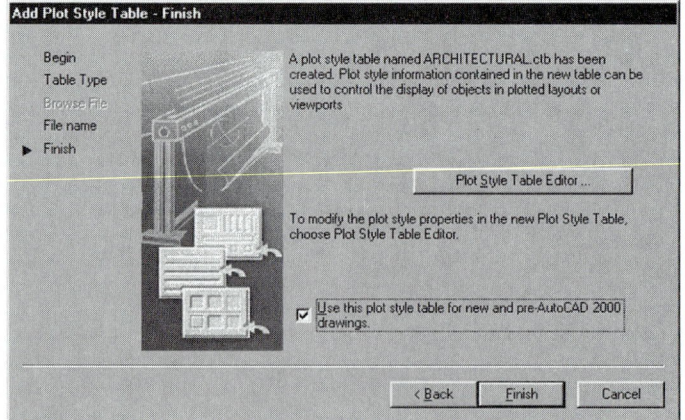

FIGURE 23–10 The Finish page allows you to attach the new plot style table to new drawings or edit before using.

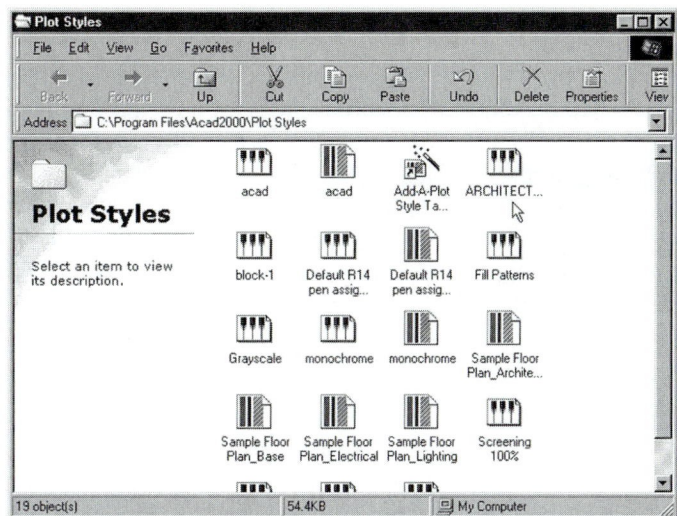

FIGURE 23–11 The new plot style created with the Add Plot Style Table Wizard will be listed in the Plot Styles dialog box.

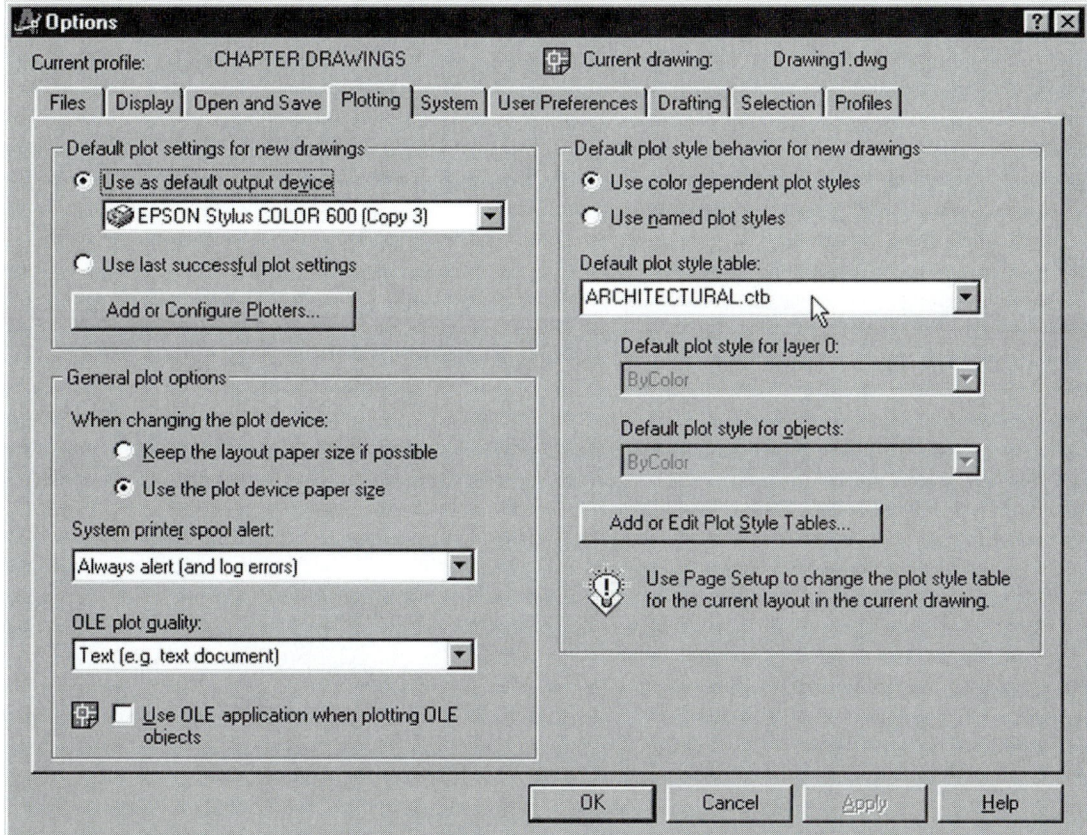

FIGURE 23–12 The new plot style created with the Add Plot Style Table Wizard will also be listed in the Plotting tab of the Options dialog box.

Tips: You must select a plot style behavior that meets your drawing requirements before you create the new drawing. Once you create a new drawing it will use either color-dependent plot styles or named plot styles.

Caution: You cannot change the plot style behavior after you create a new drawing. However, you can use a utility in the AutoCAD 2000 Migration Assistance (Ama.exe) to change plot style behavior of existing drawings.

23.5 PRINTING AND PLOTTING FROM THE MODEL TAB

You can print and plot from the Model tab using the Plot dialog box. When you are ready to plot, click on the Plot button in the Standard toolbar, enter PLOT at the command line, or select Plot . . . from the File pull-down menu. You can also right-click on the Model tab and select Plot . . . from the shortcut menu. When you access the Plot dialog box, AutoCAD will display the Fast Track to Plotting Help dialog box as shown in Figure 23–13. If you wish to view an in-depth help on plotting, click on the Yes button: otherwise click on the No button. If you do not want this dialog box displayed again, place a checkmark in front of the Do not show this dialog again check box. The Plot dialog box will be displayed as shown in Figure 23–14.

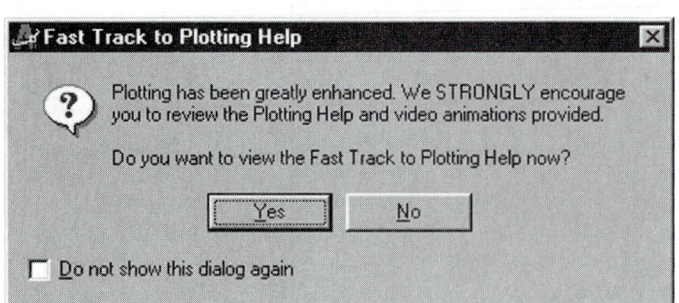

FIGURE 23–13 The Fast Track to Plotting Help dialog box allows you to see more information on the new plotting procedures.

Note: Using the Plot dialog box allows you to temporarily override Page Setup settings for printing and plotting. It also gives you more options such as What to plot, Plot to file, Full Preview, and Partial Preview options.

The Plot dialog box has two tabs: Plot Device and Plot Settings (The Plot Settings tab would be displayed as the Layout Settings tab if you were to plot a drawing using the paper space Layout tab). The Plot Device and Layout Settings tab in the Page Setup dialog box is similar to the one in the Plot dialog box. The Layout Settings tab in the Page Setup dialog box was briefly discussed in Chapter 22. The top of the dialog box has two categories: Layout name and Page setup name. When plotting from the Model tab, the Layout name will appear as Model. You can tem-

FIGURE 23–14 The Plot dialog box is used to print or plot drawings from the Model tab or from paper space in Layout tabs. Notice that Model is used as the Layout name.

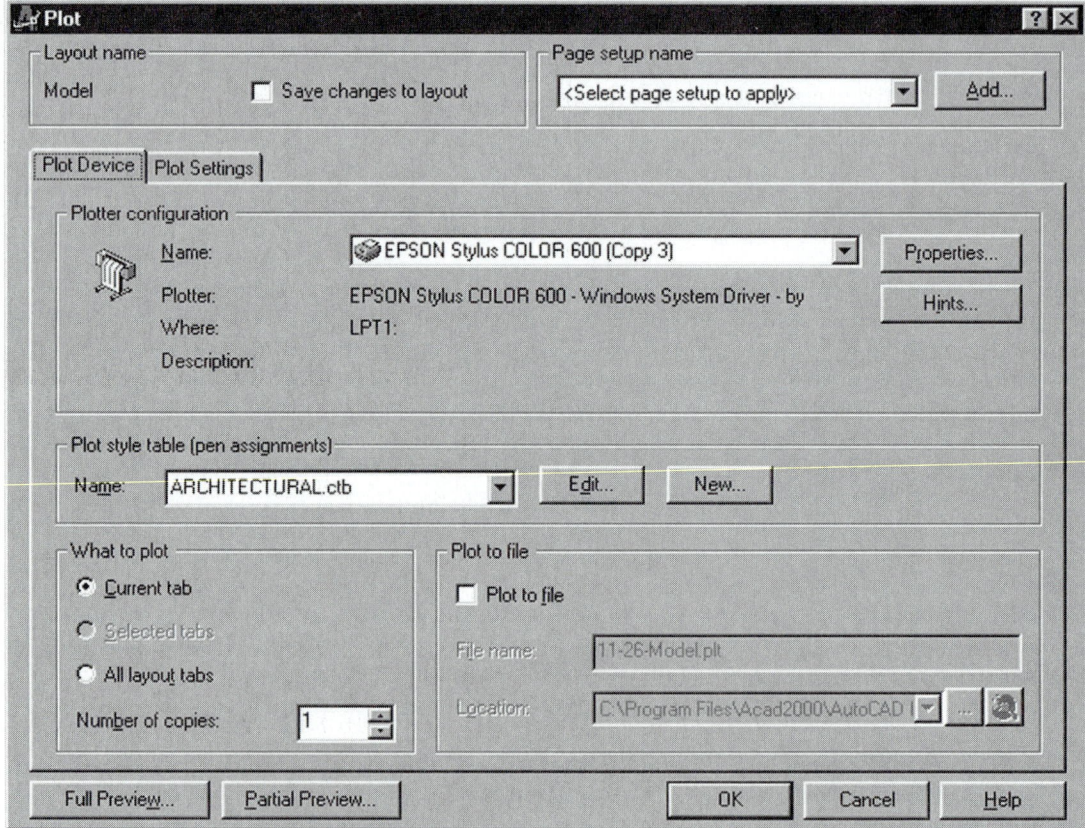

porarily override page setup settings by removing the checkmark from the Save changes to layout check box. When you plot from a layout, the plot settings default to layout settings. If you need to make changes to the layout before plotting, you can save changes back to the page setup by checking the box in the Save changes to layout check box. The Page setup name category contains the named page setups that are saved in other drawings. The two default options are <Select page setup to apply> and <Previous Plot>. The <Select page setup to apply> option allows you to select a named page setup. The <Previous Plot> option allows you to use the plot settings of the previous plot. To select a named page setup, select the named setup you wish to use from the Page setup name drop-down list. The Add . . . button allows you to add a user-defined page setup. When you click on the Add . . . button, the User Defined Page Setups dialog box will appear as shown in Figure 23–15. Inside the new page setup name: text box enter the name of the new page setup to which you wish to save the current plot settings. All named setups in the active drawing are listed in the Page setups: list box. The Location column shows named setups for model (Layout tab if paper space Layout is used). The Rename button allows you rename the selected page setup. The Delete button allows you to delete the selected page setup. The Import . . . button allows you to import named setups that are saved in another drawing file without actually opening the drawing. This button will display the Select File dialog box. Select the file you wish to import the user defined page setup and click on the Open button. The Import user defined page setup(s) dialog box will be displayed as shown in Figure 23–16. Select the page setup from the list and click on the OK button to import to the current drawing.

Plot Device: This tab is used to select the printing and plotting device, plot appearance settings, and what to plot. It also allows you to change the properties of the selected plot device. The Plot Device tab has the following categories:

PLOTTER CONFIGURATION: This category allows you to select the name of the printer or plotter configured in AutoCAD. The Name: drop-down list will show all the available printers and/or plotters connected to and configured for the computer you are working with. Windows system printers and plotters do not require any additional configuration to be used with AutoCAD. They are always available in the Plotter configuration Name: drop-down list and are distinguished from AutoCAD–based plot devices by a printer icon as shown

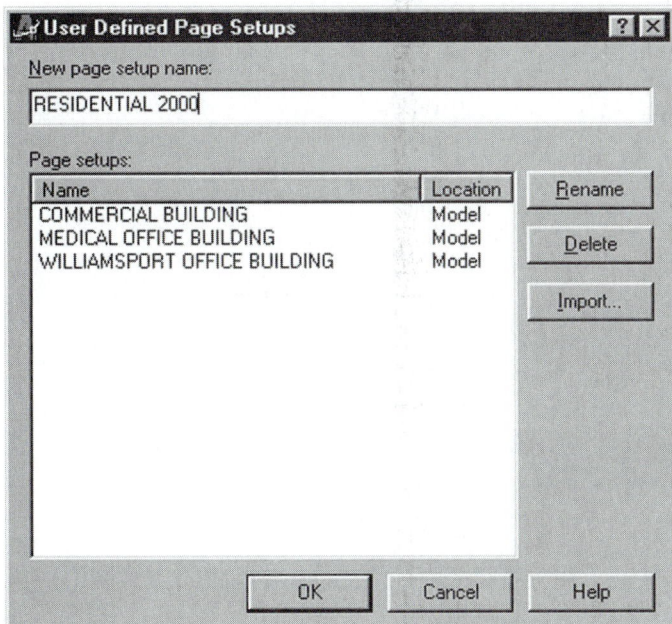

FIGURE 23–15   The User Defined Page Setups dialog box allows you to select a different named page setup to be used for the current plot.

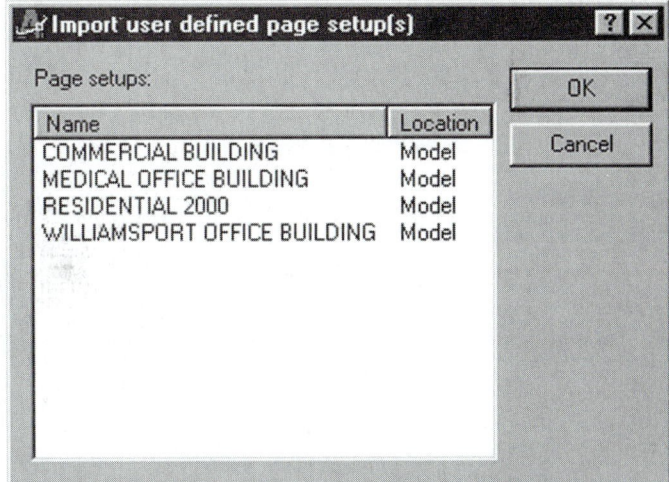

FIGURE 23–16   The Import user defined page setup(s) dialog box allows you to import a page setup from another drawing file without opening that file.

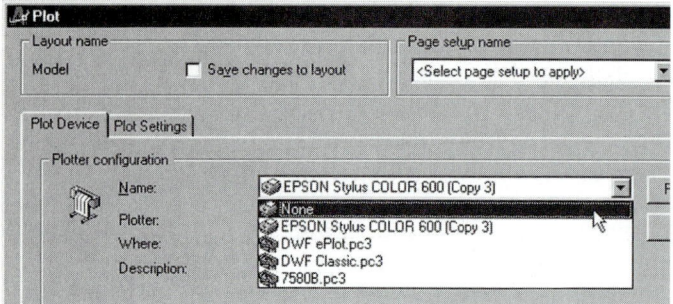

FIGURE 23–17 The Name: drop-down list will show all configured and installed printers and plotters. Note the different icons for Windows system printers and AutoCAD plot devices.

in Figure 23–17. The Plotter: area will display the name of the printer or plotter with its driver name. The Where: area will display the location of the plot. A local plot will plot the drawing to a local print or plot machine. A file plot will plot to a floppy disk, zip disk, or to the selected drive in your computer. The Description: area will display a description of the plot device if a description is given while configuring the plotter. Configuring a plotter and adding new plot devices are discussed later in the chapter.

The Properties . . . button will display the Plotter Configuration Editor dialog box for the selected printer or plotter as shown in Figure 23–18. This dialog box allows you to change device and document settings. For example, you can select a different paper size for Windows system printers or Autodesk plotter drivers as follows:

1. Select Custom Properties from the Device and Document Settings tab.
2. Click on the Custom Properties . . . button to display the custom properties dialog box for the printer or the plotter driver you have selected as shown in Figure 23–19.
3. Select a paper size from the list and click on the OK button.

The Hints . . . button will display the AutoCAD Help dialog box, where you can obtain more information on printing and plotting.

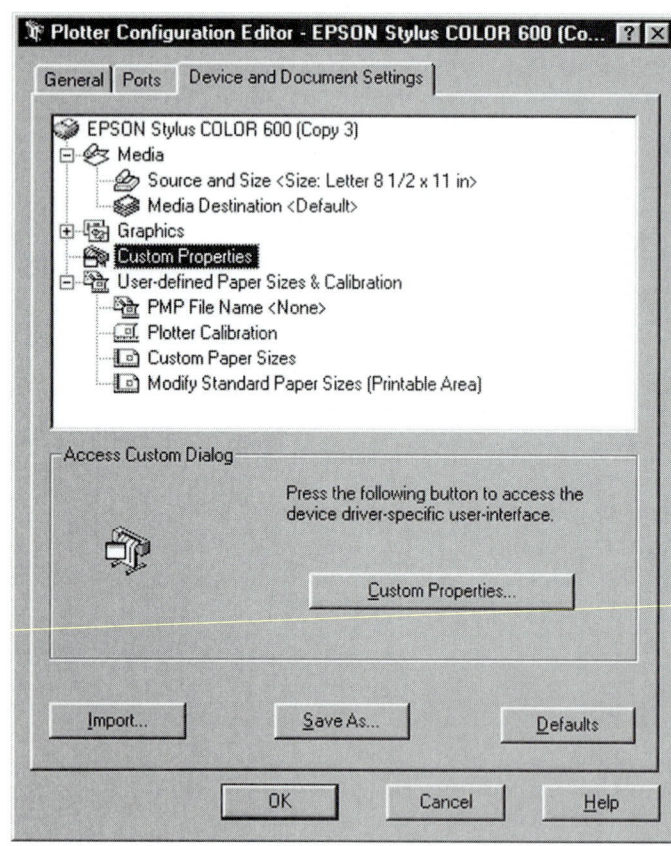

FIGURE 23–18 The Plotter Configuration Editor dialog box allows you to edit document and device settings for the selected printer or plotter.

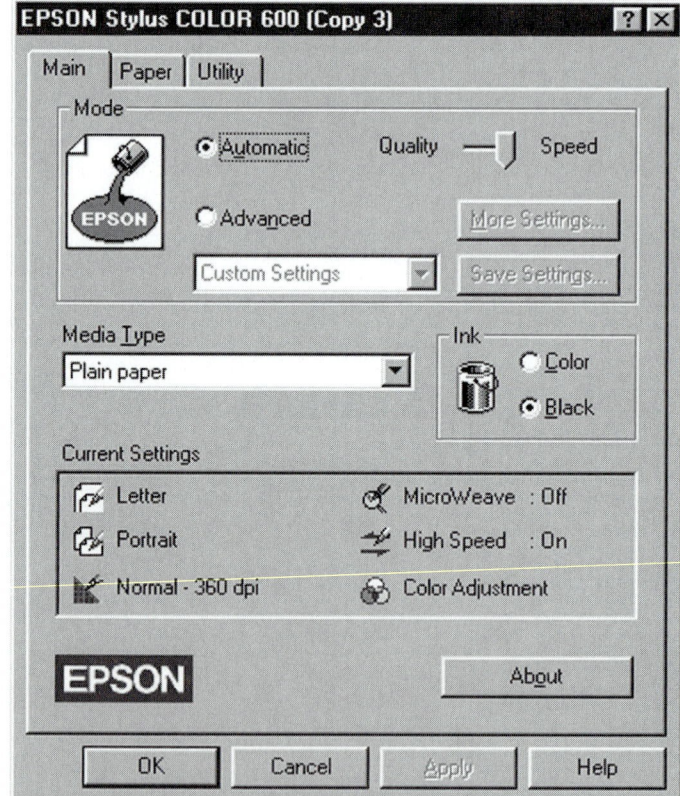

FIGURE 23–19 The custom properties for the selected printer or plot can be used to create a different paper size. The Epson Stylus Color 600 printer is shown here.

PLOT STYLE TABLE (PEN ASSIGNMENTS):   This category is used to select a plot style table. The Name: drop-down list shows the available plot style tables as shown in Figure 23–20. Select a plot style table from the list to attach to your drawing for plotting. Selecting *None* from the list will plot your drawing without using any plot style tables. Selecting the Default R14 Pen Assignments.ctb plot style table will plot your drawing with the same pen assignments as your last plotted with Release 14. This option is only available if Release 14 was installed in your computer when AutoCAD 2000 was installed. Selecting monochrome.ctb will plot all object colors in black. Use this option if you want to plot your drawing with black color even when your drawing has many colors. Selecting acad.ctb will plot objects in your drawing the way they appear on the screen using the standard color-dependent plot style

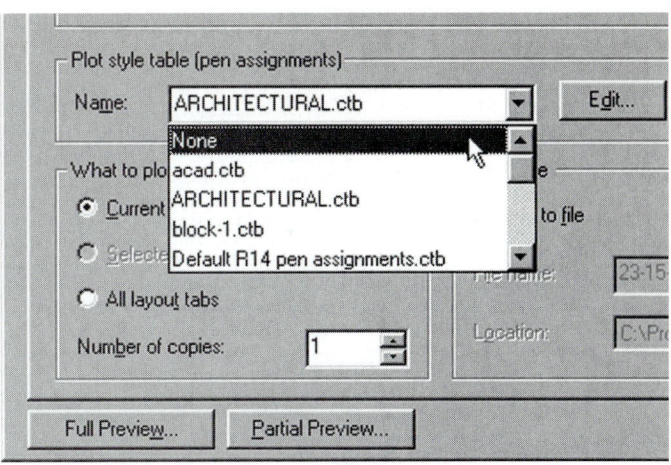

FIGURE 23–20   The Name: drop-down list in the Plot style table category lists all available plot style tables.

tables. You can also attach Fill Patterns.ctb, Greyscale,ctb, and Screening.ctb plot style tables to your drawing. The Edit . . . button will display the Plot Style Table Editor dialog box and is discussed later in the chapter. This dialog box is used to edit the current plot style table. The New . . . button will display the Add Plot Style Table dialog box. This dialog box is used to create a new plot style table and was discussed previously.

WHAT TO PLOT: This category allows you to make more than one plot of selected tabs. The Current tab is the default and will plot the current model tab. The Selected tabs will plot all selected tabs. This is not available because there is only one Model tab. If you are plotting from the Layout tab and want to select more than one tab, hold down the ~CtrlKey~ and select the desired tabs. The All layout tabs will plot all layout tabs in paper space. The Number of copies: value list allows you to make two or more prints of the current or selected tabs.

PLOT TO FILE: This category allows you to specify the file name and location for plot files. Creating plot files is useful if you need to use a plotter connected to another computer. You can copy the plot file to a floppy disk or zip disk and then transfer the file to another computer. AutoCAD creates the plot file with a .plt extension. Place a checkmark inside the Plot to file check box to create a plot file. By default, the name of the plot file will be the same as the current drawing name and will be saved in the current folder. If you want to save the plot file to a different file name, enter a file name inside the File name: text box. You can also save it to another folder by specifying the name of the folder inside the Location: text box. When you click on the . . . button next to the Location: text box, the Browse for Folder dialog box will be displayed, allowing you to select a folder from the list.

Plot Settings: This tab is used to specify paper size, drawing orientation, plot area and scale, plot offset, and plot options. The Plot Settings tab shown in Figure 23–21 has the following categories:

PAPER SIZE AND PAPER UNITS: This category allows you to select the paper size and the units to plot. Paper size: drop-down list lists the available paper sizes based on the current plot device shown in the Plot device: area. Each paper size has a predefined printable area based on the manufacturer specification. Select the appropriate paper size from the list. The Printable area: shows the actual printable area in inches or millimeters. Select the Inches radio button to show the printable area in inches. Select the mm radio button to show the printable area in millimeters.

DRAWING ORIENTATION: This category is used to select the orientation of the drawing on the paper for plotters that support landscape or portrait orientation. The plot rotation is controlled by the paper size and drawing orientation you specify. The paper icon under drawing orientation represents the paper orientation in the plot device. The letter "A" inside the icon represents the drawing orientation on the plot paper. The paper orientation represent the direction of the sheet seed in the printer/plotter. Selecting the Portrait radio button will plot your drawing with the long edge at the side of the paper. This means that the paper is vertical and the drawing can be rotated to the desired orientation on the paper. Selecting the Landscape radio button will plot your drawing with the long edge at the top of the paper. This means that the paper is horizontal and the drawing can be rotated to the desired orientation on the

FIGURE 23–21 The
Plot Settings tab of the
Plot dialog box allows
you to establish plot
settings.

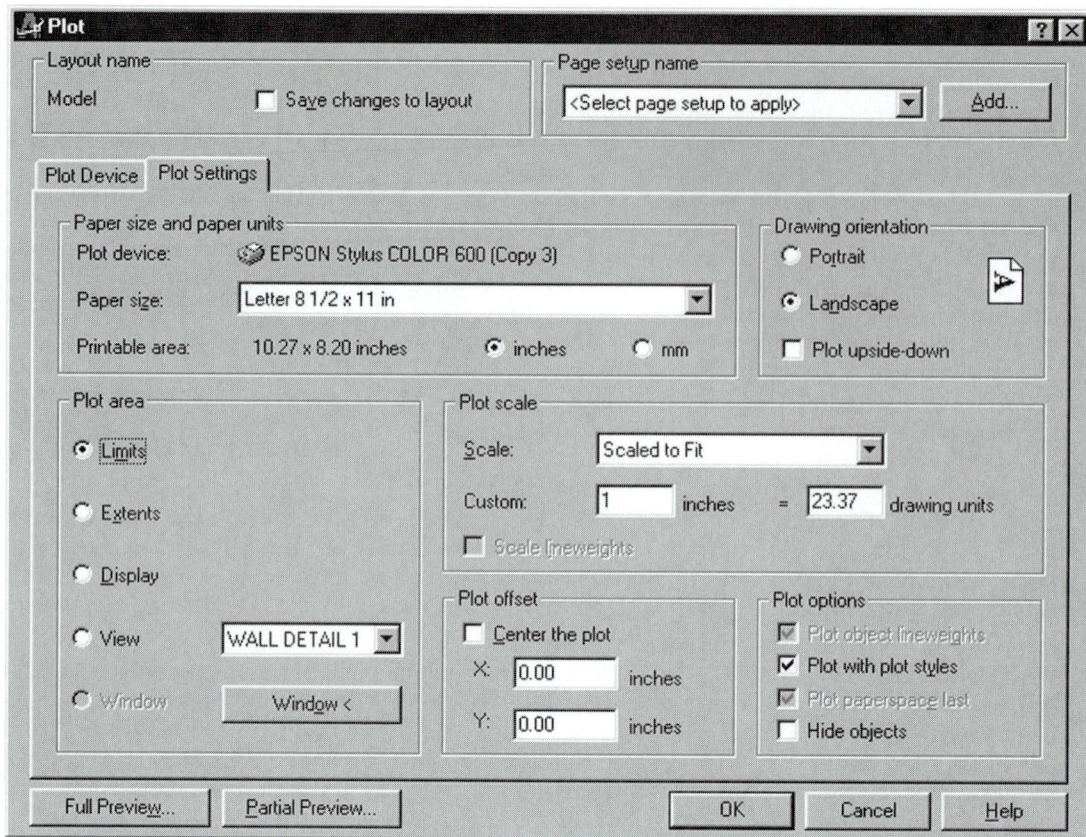

paper. When a paper size is listed twice, it has the ability to be used in either portrait or landscape orientation. For example, in Figure 23–22, the position of the paper icon is the result of selecting letter (8.5″ × 11″) paper size and a landscape drawing orientation. In this case, the 8.5″ × 11″ paper from the printer is rotated 90 degrees to view the drawing. In Figure 23–23, the position of the paper icon is the result of selecting ANSI A (11″ × 8.5″) paper size and a landscape drawing orientation. In this case, the 8.5″ × 11″ paper from the printer is not rotated to view the drawing. The Plot upside-down option will plot the drawing upside down, rotated by 180 degrees.

PLOT AREA: This category allows you to specify which area of your drawing to plot. The Limits option will plot all parts of your drawing inside the specified limits of your drawing. Zoom to the limits (all option of the zoom command) of your drawing before selecting this option. This will make the lower left corner of the limits (0,0,0) equal to the origin of the plot. Also, make sure that the drawing is inside the limits. Any parts of your drawing that is outside the limits will not be plotted. The Extents option will plot the entire drawing, including any objects drawn outside the limits. It is similar to the Extents option of the ZOOM command. Before using this option, zoom to the extents of your drawing to include all objects in the plot area. Some objects may be clipped off if they are at the very extreme edge of the screen. The Display option will plot what is currently displayed on the screen. Before using this option, make sure the view you want to plot is displayed on the screen by using the ZOOM or PAN realtime command. The View option will plot a previously saved view. If you created named views, use this option to plot a selected view. This option makes it convenient to plot pre-defined areas of your drawing. If there are no saved views in the current drawing, this option will not be available. The Window option allows you to create a window on the screen and plot the objects that are inside the window. The lower left corner of the window becomes the origin of the plot. This option appears grayed out until you select the Window . . . button. When you select this button, the Plot dialog box will temporarily disappear. Inside the drawing area, define the two opposite corners of the window to be plotted. You will be returned to the Plot dialog box.

PLOT SCALE: This category allows you to scale the drawing to fit on the selected sheet. Remember that in AutoCAD you have the option to assign a drawing scale based on paper size (Lim-

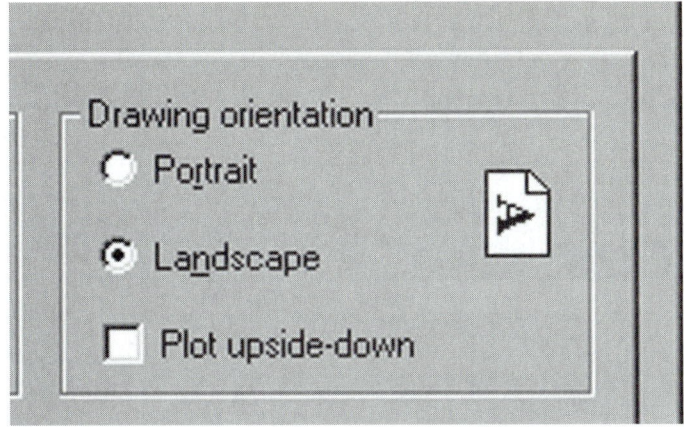

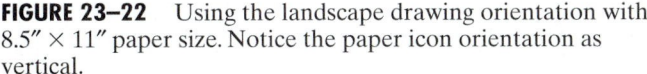

FIGURE 23-22 Using the landscape drawing orientation with 8.5″ × 11″ paper size. Notice the paper icon orientation as vertical.

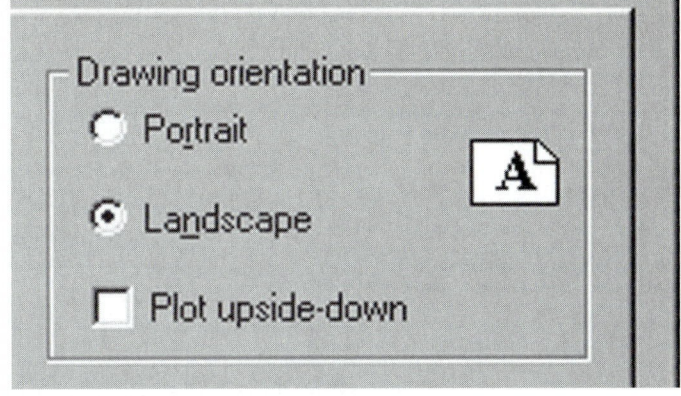

FIGURE 23-23 Using the landscape drawing orientation with 11″ × 8.5″ paper size. Notice the paper icon orientation as horizontal.

its) or scale your drawings during plotting. To set a scale to the drawing, select the appropriate scale from the Scale: drop-down list. Most of the architectural scales are represented in this list, as shown in Figure 23–24. When plotting from Model tab, drawings are assigned a plot scale from this list. When you select a scale from the list, the scale is represented as the ratio of plotted units to drawing units inside the Custom: text box and the drawing units text box, respectively. For example, if you select the 1/4″=1′0″ option from the Scale: drop-down list, the Custom text box will display 1 and the drawing units text box will display 48. The value of 1 represents the plotted units, and the value of 48 represents the drawing units. The scale itself represents the ratio of 1:48. Notice that 48 is also the scale factor for a 1/4″=1′-0″ scale drawing. The Custom option of the Scale: drop-down list is used to specify a custom plot-to-drawing ratio. When you select this option from the list, you can enter a custom plot unit-to-drawing unit ratio. For example, to have the drawing plotted at 1 1/2″=1′-0″ scale, enter 1.5 inside the Custom: text box and enter 12 inside the drawing units text box or enter 1 inside the custom: test box and enter 8 inside the drawing units text box. This is to say that the 1 1/2″=1′-0″ scale can be registered as 1.5=12 or 1=8. The Scaled to fit option will automatically adjust the drawing to fit inside the specified paper. This is similar to NTS (not to scale) drawings. Use this option to fit a large-scale drawing (intended to plot on a large paper) into a small paper size. The Scale lineweights option is only available when plotting from paper space layouts.

PLOT OFFSET: This category allows you to specify an offset distance for the drawing from the lower-left corner of the plot paper. This is useful if you preview the drawing and discover that the drawing needs to be moved either in the X or in the Y coordinates direction. You can enter positive or negative values as needed. You can center the drawing on the plot paper by placing a checkmark inside the Center the plot check box.

PLOT OPTIONS: This category allows you to specify options for the plot. The Plot object lineweights option allows you to plot lineweights that are assigned to objects. This box is checked by default. The Plot with plot styles option allows you to plot the drawing with all plot styles attached. The Plot paper space last option is not available when plotting from Model tab. The Hide objects option removes hidden lines from objects. This option affects only objects drawn in paper space and when plotted from the layout tab.

FULL PREVIEW ... button will display the drawing as it would appear on the plot paper when it is plotted. This might take some time for large drawings but is a quick way to check the plot before actually plotting. AutoCAD temporarily removes the Plot dialog box. At this time, the cursor will change into a magnifying glass with plus and minus signs. You can left-click and drag the cursor up to enlarge the preview image. If items need to be changed, right-click on the drawing and select Exit from the shortcut menu. This will take you back to the Plot dialog box. You can change settings according to your specifications and then click on the Full preview ... button one more time to preview the plot. When you are satisfied, you can right-click and select Plot from the shortcut menu. The right-click shortcut menu is shown in Figure 23–25. This will print or plot your drawing.

FIGURE 23–24 Some of the available architectural scales inside the Scale: drop-down list.

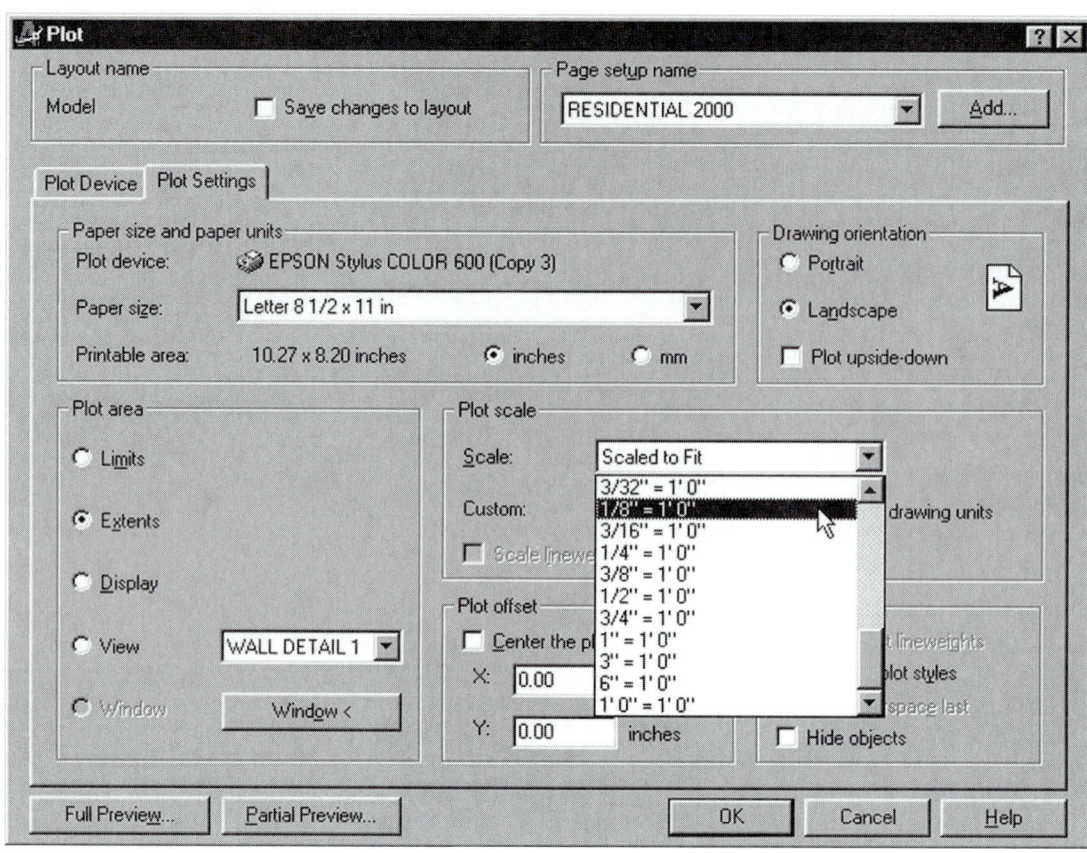

FIGURE 23–25 The shortcut menu offers Exit and Plot options and additional preview options.

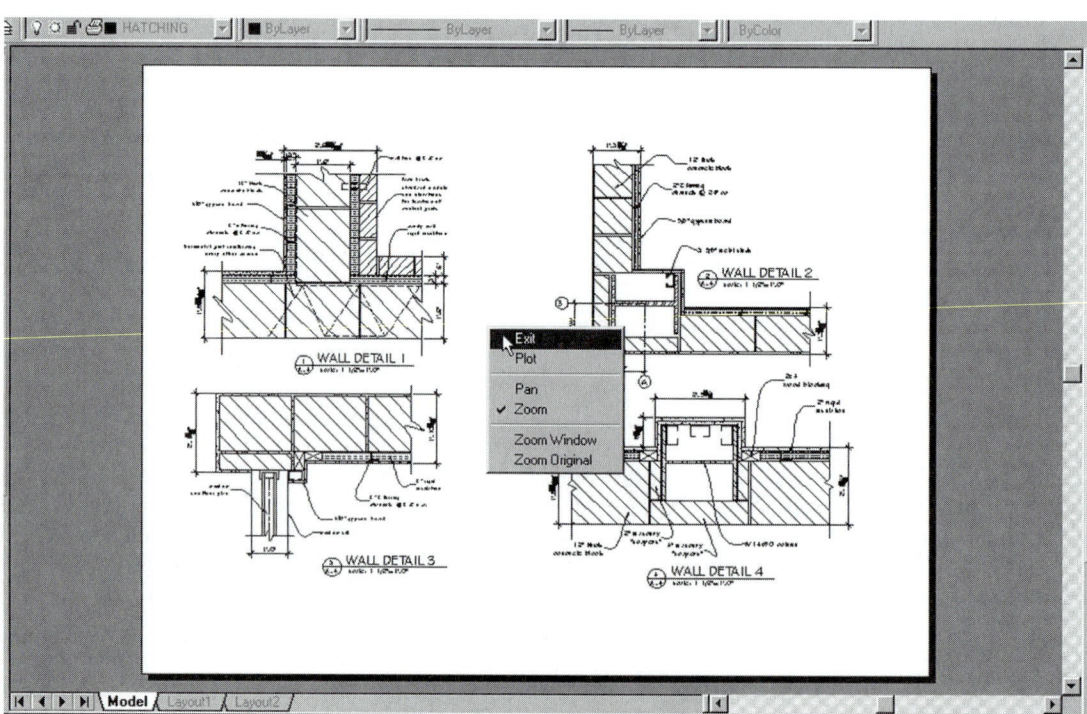

PARTIAL PREVIEW... button will quickly display a partial preview of the plot area relative to the paper size and the printable area as shown in Figure 23–26. AutoCAD provides information regarding paper size, printable area, and effective area. Partial plot previews are useful to see any advance notices of any warnings that may be encountered before plotting. Click on the OK button to get back to the Plot dialog box.

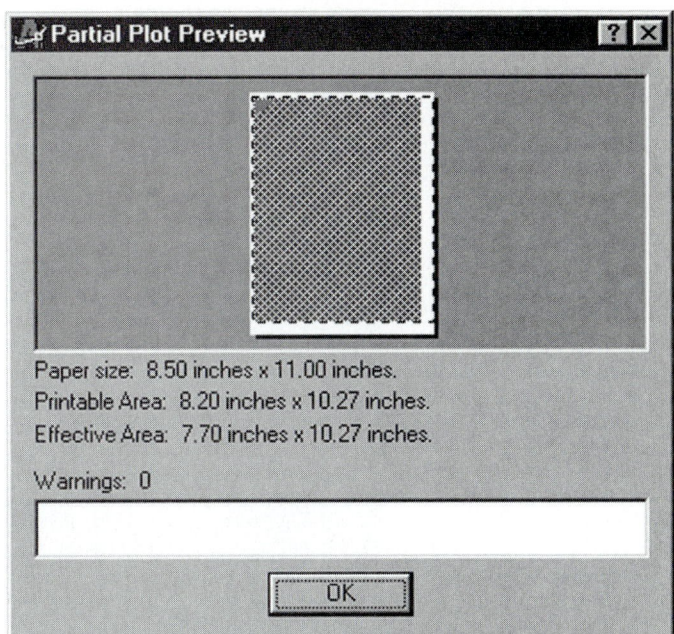

- ■ **EXERCISE 23–1:** *The following step-by-step exercise will allow you to plot a black and white hard copy of the Building Section drawing from the Model tab. This drawing is created at a scale of 1/4″=1′-0″ and is to be plotted on a "D" (36″ × 24″) size sheet. Drawing Limits are 144′, 96′. The drawing is to be plotted without a title block and borderline. Before starting this exercise make sure that the plotter has been configured and working properly. Also, make sure that the appropriate size sheet is inserted into the plotter.*

Step #1: Open the EXE22-1.dwg file. Make sure the Model tab is active.

Step #2: Zoom to the limits of the drawing (Zoom All).

Step #3: Click on the Plot button in the Standard toolbar. The Fast Track to Plotting help dialog box will be displayed. Click on the No button.

Step #4: Inside the Plot dialog box select the Plot Device tab.

Step #5: Inside the Plotter configuration category select the Name of the Printer that is configured in your computer. See Figure 23–14.

Step #6: Inside the Plot style table (pen assignments) category select monochrome.ctb from the Name: drop-down list.

Step #7: Inside the What to plot category select the Current tab radio button.

Step #8: Inside the Number of copies: drop-down list select 1.

Step #9: Select the Plot Settings tab.

Step #10: Inside the Paper size and paper units category, select 36″ × 24″ (or the corresponding size) from the Paper size: drop-down list.

Step #11: Inside the Plot area category, select the Limits radio button.

Step #12: Inside the Drawing orientation category, select the Landscape radio button.

Step #13: Inside the Plot scale category, select the 1/4″=1′-0″ from the Scale: drop-down list. The Custom: list should display 1 inches = 48 drawing units. 48 is the scale factor for the drawing scale.

Step #14: Inside the Plot offset category, place a check mark inside the Center the plot check box.

Step #15: Click on the Full Preview... button. The drawing will be displayed in the center of the 36″ × 24″ paper at a 1/4″=1′-0″ scale.

Step #16: Right-click inside the drawing and select Plot from the shortcut menu.

Congratulations! You have successfully plotted the Building Section drawing at a 1/4″=1′-0″ scale on a 36″ × 24″ D-size sheet without a title block.

FIGURE 23–26 The Partial Plot Preview dialog box will be displayed when the Partial preview... button is selected.

23.6 PRINTING AND PLOTTING FROM PAPER SPACE LAYOUTS

You can print and plot from paper space layouts using the Plot dialog box. When you are ready to plot, click on the Layout1 or any other layout created for the drawing. Your drawing will be displayed in paper space as shown in Figure 23–27. The paper image represents the paper size, the dashed line represents the printable area of the specified paper, and the

FIGURE 23-27 The drawing will be displayed in paper space with one default viewport.

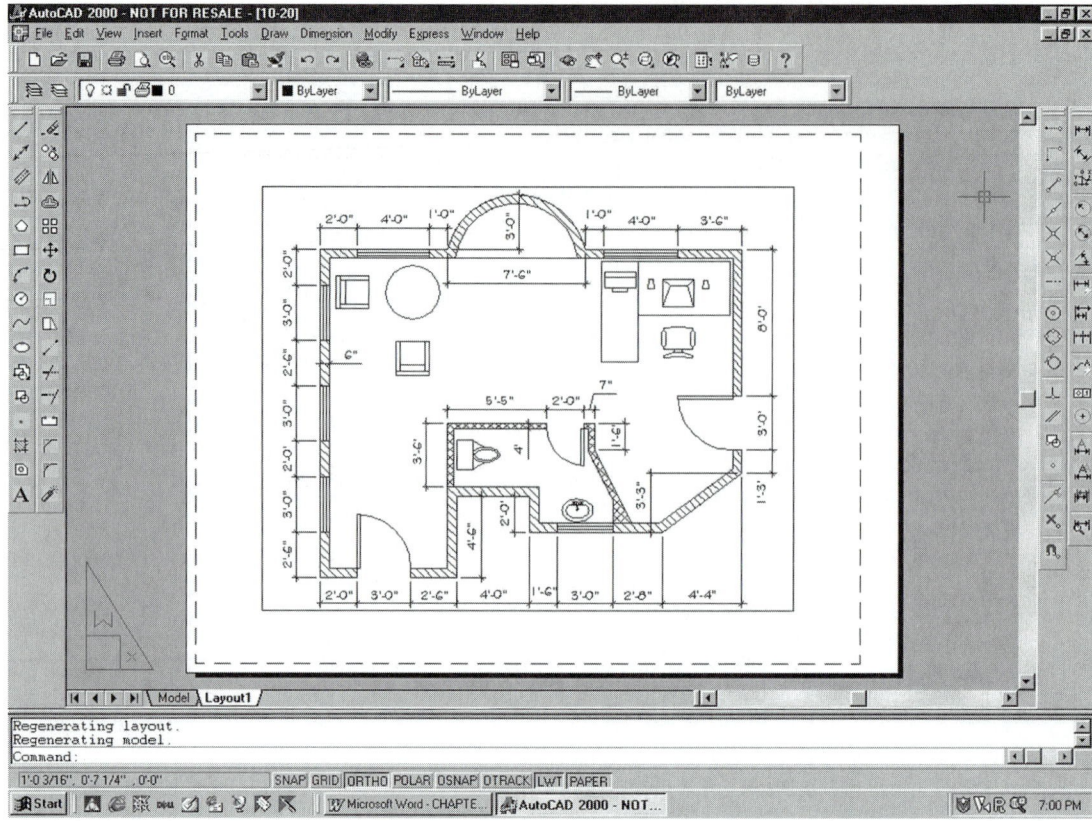

solid line represents the default viewport. You can create more floating viewports if they are required. To set a scale for the viewport, use the Viewports toolbar scale drop-down list. You must be in model space to set the scale of the viewport drawings. When you are ready to plot your drawing, switch back to paper space and click on the Plot button in the Standard toolbar, or right-click on the Layout tab and select Plot . . . from the shortcut list. The Plot dialog box will appear as shown in Figure 23–28.

The Plot dialog box in paper space layout is similar to the Plot Device tab of the Plot dialog box in Model tab, except the Layout name category shows the name of the Layout tab. In Figure 23–28 the layout name is displayed as Layout1. The Plot Device tab offers the same categories as in the Plot dialog box of the Model tab. The Plot Settings tab as shown in Figure 23–29 is also similar to the one in Figure 23–24, but the Plot area category has the Layout radio button as opposed to the Limits radio button. The default plot area is the layout in which the drawing is plotted for the selected layout. When plotting from paper space layouts, the plot scale is set to 1:1. When you create viewports in addition to the default viewport in paper space, you set the drawing scale in each viewport by selecting the appropriate scale from the Viewports toolbar in model space.

■ **EXERCISE 23–2:** *The following step-by-step exercise will allow you to plot a color hard copy of the Site Plan drawing from the Layout1 tab using a Template. This drawing is created at a scale of 1"=10' and is to be plotted on a 36" × 24" D-size sheet. Drawing limits are 360', 240'. The drawing is to be plotted with the title block and borderline. Before starting this exercise, make sure that the plotter has been configured and is working properly. Also, make sure that the appropriate-size sheet is inserted into the plotter.*

Step #1:   Open the EXE16-10.dwg file. Make sure the Model tab is active.

Step #2:   Zoom to the limits of the drawing (Zoom All).

Step #3:   Right-click on the Layout1 tab and select From template . . . from the shortcut menu.

Step #4:   Select Architectural, English units–Color Dependent Plot Styles template from the Select File dialog box and click on the Open button.

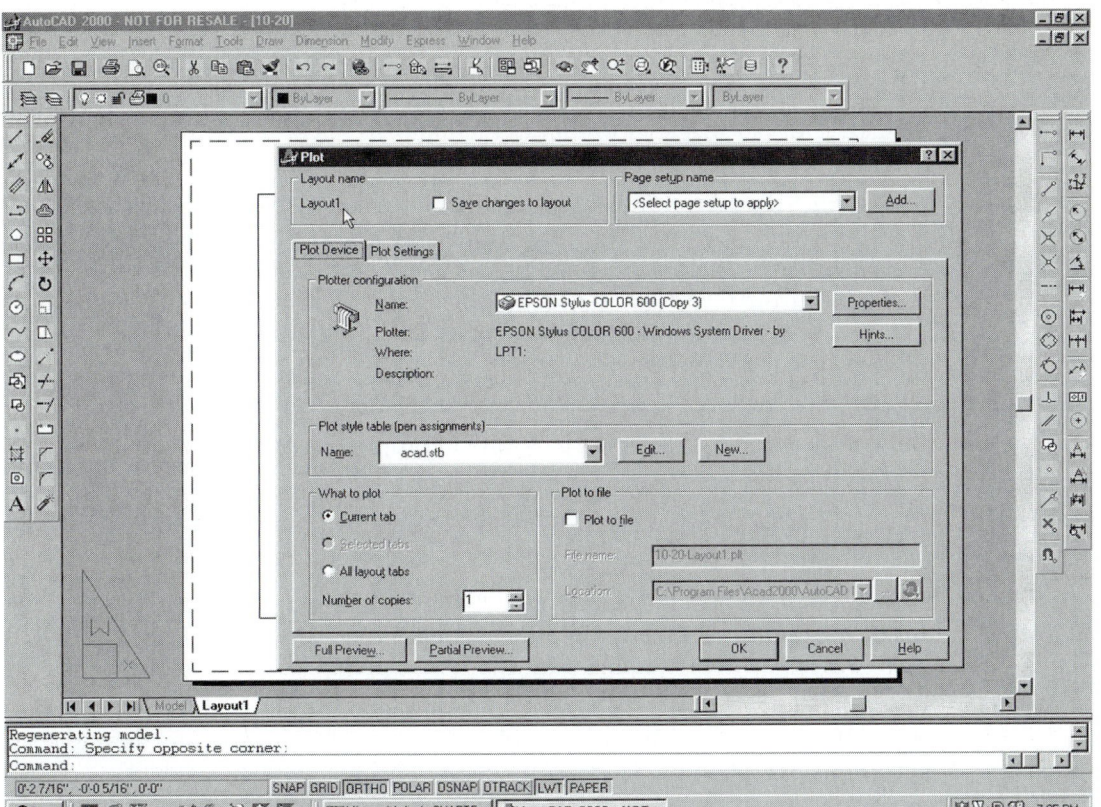

FIGURE 23–28 The Plot dialog box in Layout1 is similar to the Plot dialog box in Model tab.

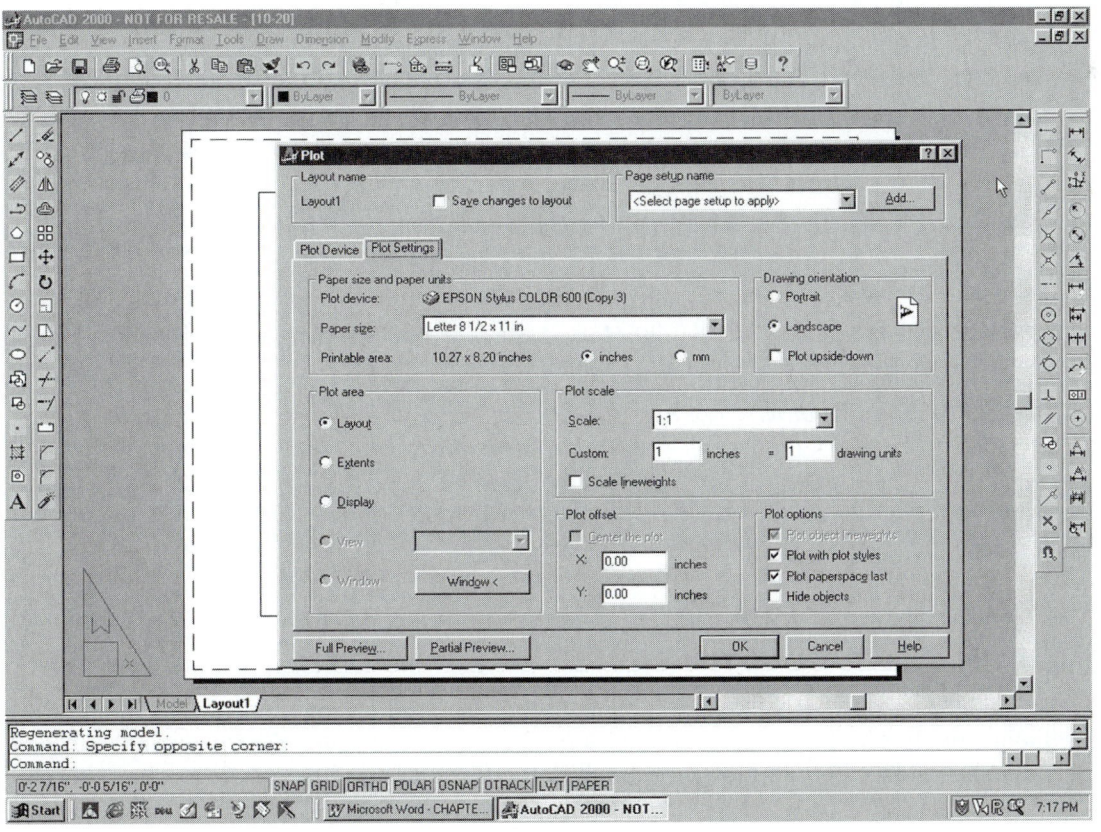

FIGURE 23–29 The Plot Settings tab of the Plot dialog box in paper space layouts.

Step #5:   Inside the Insert Layout(s) dialog box click on the OK button.

Step #6:   Left-click on the Architectural Title Block tab. The Title Block template will be displayed in paper space without the drawing.

Step #7:   Switch to Model space and zoom to the limits of the drawing. The drawing will now be displayed inside the viewport.

Step #8:   Access the Viewports toolbar and highlight the existing scale value inside the Viewport Scale Control list. Enter 0.0083333 and press the ~EnterKey~. Since there is no scale corresponding to 1″=10′ inside the list, the 0.0083333 is obtained from the reciprocal of the scale factor, which is 1/120=0.0083333. This will display the Site Plan drawing at the 1″=10′ scale inside the title block, which is 36″ × 24″.

Step #9:   Switch to paper space and lock the viewport scale.

Step #10:   In paper space, fill in the title block with appropriate text at full scale.

Step #11:   Freeze the Viewport layer.

Step #12:   Click on the Plot button in the Standard toolbar. The Fast Track to Plotting help dialog box will be displayed. Click on the No button.

Step #13:   Inside the Plot dialog box, select the Plot Device tab.

Step #14:   Inside the Plotter configuration category, select the Name of the Printer that is configured in your computer.

Step #15:   Inside the Plot style table (pen assignments) category, select acad.ctb from the Name: drop-down list. This will plot objects in your drawing the way they appear on the screen using the standard color-dependent plot style tables.

Step #16:   Inside the What to plot category, select the Current tab radio button.

Step #17:   Inside the Number of copies: drop-down list select 1.

Step #18:   Select the Plot Settings tab.

Step #19:   Inside the Paper size and paper units category, select the 36″ × 24″ size (or the corresponding size) from the Paper size: drop-down list.

Step #20:   Inside the Plot area category, select the Layout radio button.

Step #21:   Inside the Drawing orientation category, select the Landscape radio button.

Step #22:   Inside the Plot scale category, select 1:1 from the Scale: drop-down list. The Custom: list should display 1 inches = 1 drawing units. This is because you are plotting through paper space.

Step #23:   Click on the Full Preview … button. The drawing will be displayed in the center of the Title Block (36″ × 24″ paper) at a 1″=10′.

Step #24:   Right-click inside the drawing and select Plot from the shortcut menu.

Congratulations! You have successfully plotted the Site Plan drawing at a 1″=10′ scale on a 36″ × 24″ D-size sheet with Title Block template.

> ***AutoCAD 2000i Update:***   *The new plotting features include Merge control, Device filters, Paper size filters, Plot stamp, and True color in plot styles. Plot Merge Control gives you control of overlapping objects. Device and Paper Size Filters enables you to filter unwanted printers and paper sizes. Plot Stamp allows you to create data about the plot. True Color Plot Styles allows you to plot drawings with presentation quality. Refer to section 1.13.5 for more information. The Plot dialog box includes the Plot stamp area.*

23.7 EDITING PLOT STYLE TABLES

You can edit both color-dependent and named plot style tables using the Plot Style Table Editor dialog box. To access this dialog box, click on the Edit … button in the Plot style table (pen assignments) category of the Plot Device tab in the Plot or Page Setup dialog box or double-click on the icon for the desired plot style table in the Plot Styles dialog box. The Plot Style Table Editor dialog box will be displayed as shown in Figure 23–30.

The General tab contains general information about the plot style table as shown in Figure 23–30. You can enter a description inside the Description text box. The File Information category displays information such as number of styles, path of the plot style, and version. If you place a checkmark inside the Apply global scale factor to non-ISO linetypes check box, AutoCAD will scale all non-ISO linetypes and fill patterns by the value entered in the Scale factor text box. The Form View tab as shown in Figure 23–31 is used to edit color-dependent plot style tables. Choose an AutoCAD color from the Plot styles: drop-down list. Then select a value from the Properties category for that color. For example, if you select Color 1 (red) from the Plot styles: list, select Black from the Color: drop-down list under the Properties category, and then click on the Save & Close button, all objects in the drawing having red color will be plotted with black color. To select all colors from the list, select Color 1 and then scroll to the bottom of the list while holding down the ~ShiftKey~. When you select all 255 colors, and if you select Black from the Color: drop-down list, all object colors on the drawing will plot with the color black. This is same as using the Mono-chrome.ctb plot style table. You can use the Use object color from the Color: drop-down list to control which property is used at plotting for any other plot property. This is what is meant by *color-dependent plot style* behavior. When you highlight more than one AutoCAD color in the list, the Properties list displays the common values and blanks out values that are not

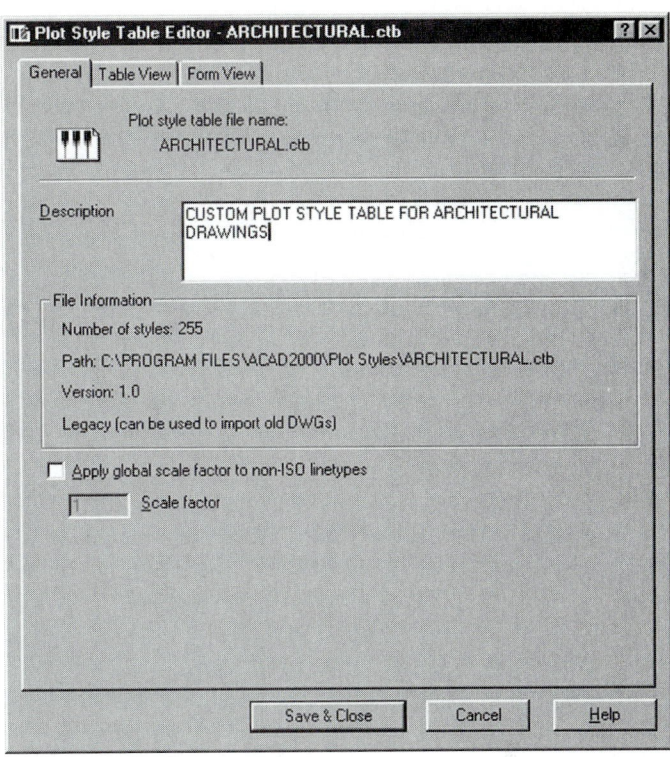

FIGURE 23–30 The Plot Style Table Editor dialog box is used to edit both color-dependent and named plot style tables.

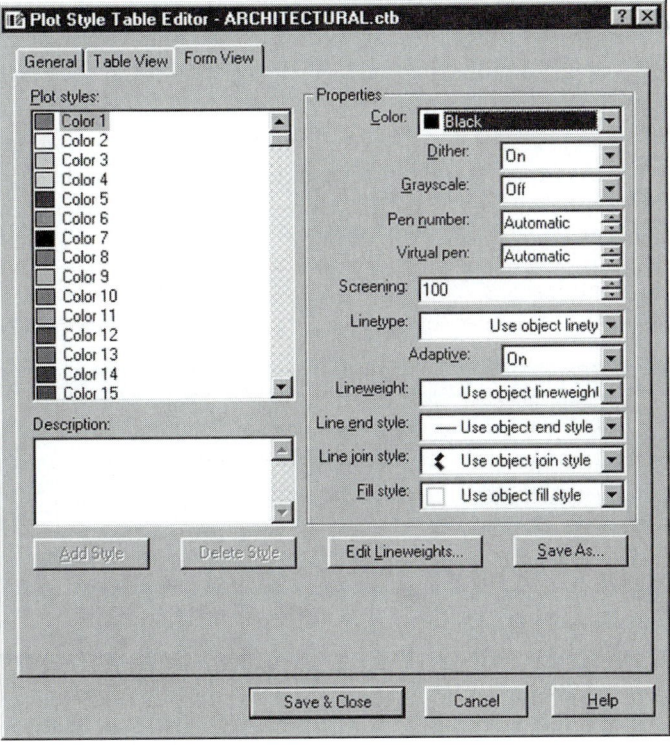

FIGURE 23–31 The Form View tab of the Plot Style Editor dialog box can be used to edit color-dependent plot style properties.

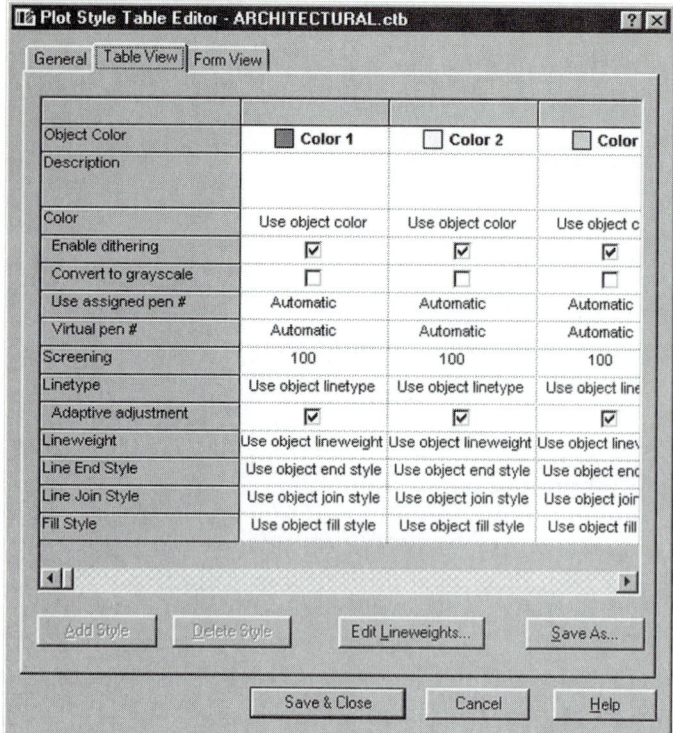

FIGURE 23–32   The Table View tab of the Plot Style Table Editor dialog box can be used to edit named plot style properties.

common. The Properties category allows you to edit properties of selected plot styles. Select the values to be changed using the drop-down list for each property. Some of the properties you can modify are lineweights, dithering, grayscale, linetypes, line end and join styles, fill patterns, and pen numbers. Click on the Save As . . . button to change the plot style table name.

The Table View tab of the Plot Style Table Editor dialog box shown in Figure 23–32 is used to edit named plot styles. To modify plot style attributes, first use the scroll bar to display the plot style (AutoCAD color) to be edited. Then select the value to be changed from the list. Click on the Save As . . . button to save the plot style table with a different name. When done, click on the Save & Close button to save the changes and exit the dialog box.

23.7.1   Applying Color-Dependent Plot Styles

To apply a color-dependent plot style, use the following procedures:

1. Make sure the Use color-dependent plot styles option is selected as the default plot style behavior in the Options dialog box. You can assign different plot style tables to the Model tab and Layout tabs.

2. Select a plot style table, such as acad.ctb, from the Plot style table (pen assignments) in the Plot or Page Setup dialog box.

23.7.2   Applying Named Plot Styles

To apply named plot styles, use the following procedures:

1. Make sure the Use named plot styles option is selected as the default plot style behavior in the Options dialog box.

2. Select a plot style table for the Model tab or the Layout tab.

You can assign plot styles to object and layers. A plot style assigned to an object will override a plot style assigned to a layer. To assign a plot style to a layer, select the current plot style listed for the layer as shown in Figure 23–33. The Select Plot Style dialog box will be displayed as shown in Figure 23–34. This dialog box lists the plot styles available in the plot style table attached to the selected tab. You can select a different plot style table from the Active plot style table: drop-down list. If you click on the Editor . . . button, the Plot Style Table Editor dialog box will be displayed.

FIGURE 23–33   You can select the current plot style listed for the layer to display the Select Plot Style dialog box.

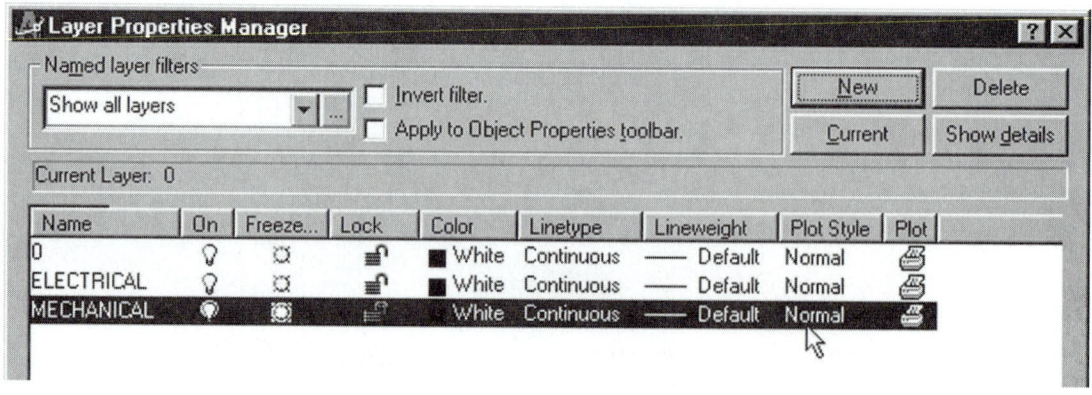

Named plot styles can be applied to objects in two different ways:

1. From the Properties window, click on the Categorized tab. Click on the Plot Style and select the plot style from the drop-down list as shown in Figure 23–35.

2. Select the plot style from the Plot Style Control drop-down list in the Object Properties toolbar as shown in Figure 23–36.

Note: If the current drawing is set to use a named plot style table, the default plot style for objects will be ByLayer. This means that the objects in the drawing will retain the properties assigned to their layer. The default plot style for a layer is Normal.

Named Plot Style Example: You have a proposed site plan and three layers named Building A, Building B, and Building C along with other layers. You have three buildings as Building A, Building B, and Building C on the site plan that will be constructed in three different phases. Each phase of construction could have a separate Layout tab and could be named as Phase 1, Phase 2, and Phase 3. Each Phase tab could have a different named plot style table file attached to the tab. Furthermore, each plot style table file could use the same plot style names but these styles could be defined differently in each table file. For example, Building A could plot BLUE in the Phase 1 tab while other layers plot gray on the same tab. Building B could plot BLUE in the Phase 2 tab while other layers plot gray on this tab. And finally Building C could plot BLUE in the Phase 3 tab while other layers plot gray on this tab.

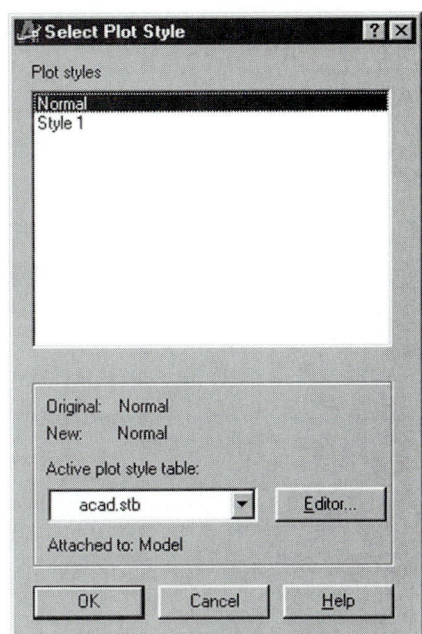

FIGURE 23–34 The Select Plot Style dialog box.

FIGURE 23–35 The Properties window can be used to assign a new named plot style to an object.

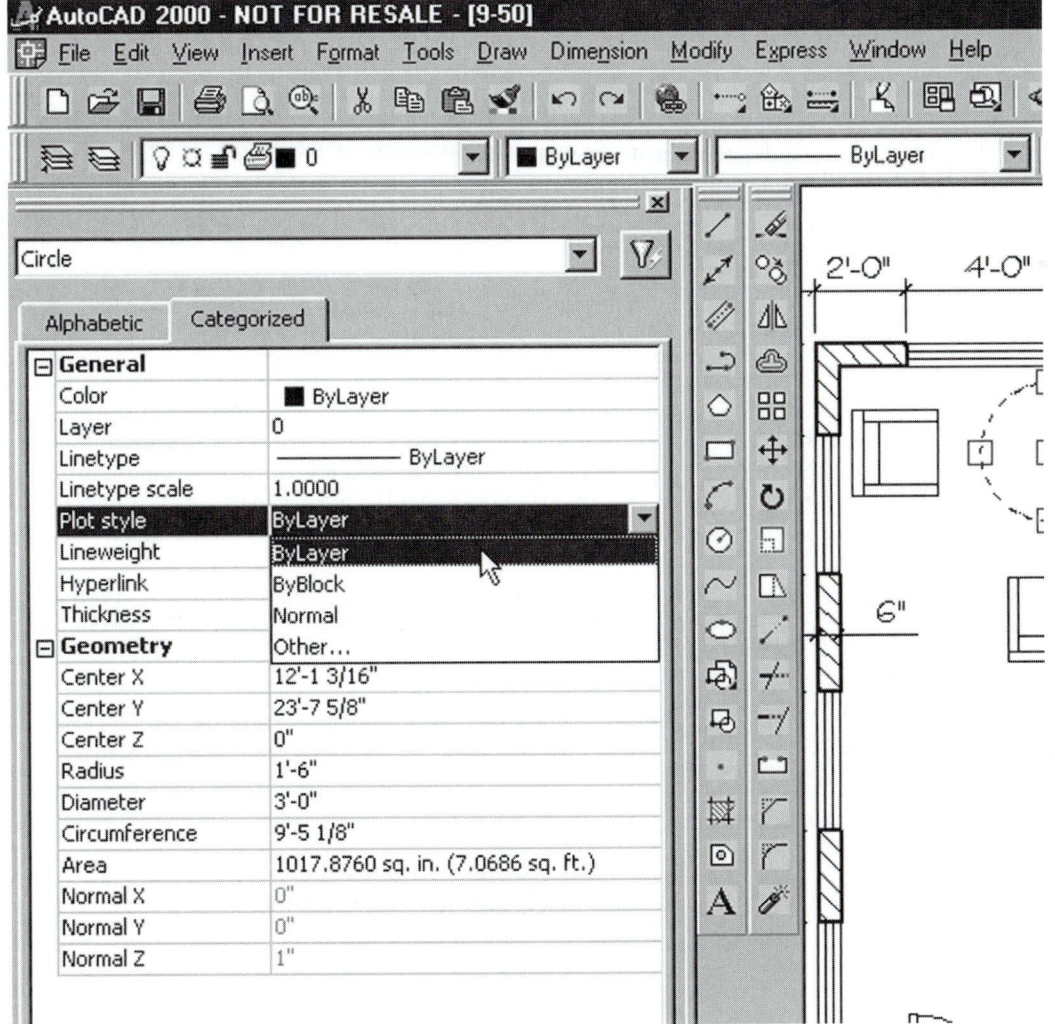

FIGURE 23–36 The Plot Style Control box drop-down list can be used to assign a new named plot style to an object.

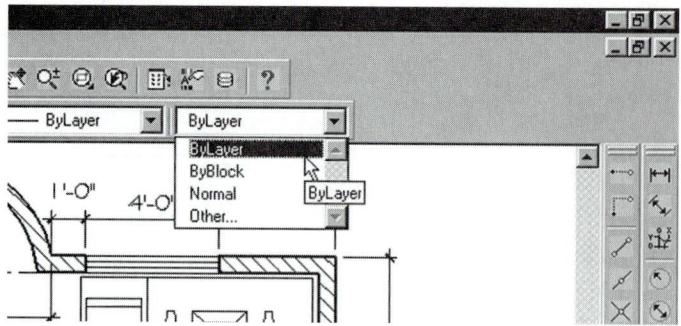

REVIEW QUESTIONS

1. What is the function of plot styles?
2. What are the names of the two different plot styles?
3. How do you access the Add Plot Style Table dialog box?
4. What does a color-dependent plot style table mean?
5. What is the function of the Page Setup dialog box?
6. What is the difference between a page setup in Model tab and page setup in Paper space layout tab?
7. What is the correlation between paper size and drawing orientation in the Plot dialog box?
8. How do you assign a custom plot scale using the Plot dialog box?
9. How do you import user-defined page setups?
10. What must you enter inside the Custom: inches = drawing units area to plot a drawing at a scale of 1 1/2″=1′-0″?

PROBLEMS

1. Open the *EXE23-1.dwg* file. Plot this drawing in Model tab without a title block using a final plot scale of 1 1/2″=1′-0″ on a 36″ × 24″ sheet. Do not plot with color.

2. Open the *EXE10-3B.dwg* file. Create a layout called *Partial Wall Section* from the ANSI C–Color Dependent Plot Styles template. Plot this drawing in this new layout and inside the new template with title block and borderline in paper space using a final plot scale of 1 1/2″=1′-0″.

3. Open the *EXE10-6.dwg* file. Create a layout called *Residential Floor Plan* from the Architectural, English units–Color Dependent Plot Styles template. Fill in the title block information. Plot this drawing in this new layout and inside the new template with title block and borderline in paper space using a final plot scale of 1/4″=1′-0″. Plot with existing colors.

4. Open the *EXE12-1.dwg* file. Create a layout called *Commercial Floor Plan* from the Architectural, English units–Color Dependent Plot Styles template. Fill in the title block information. Plot this drawing in this new layout and inside the new template with title block and borderline in paper space using a final plot scale of 1/4″=1′-0″. Plot with existing colors.

5. Open the *EXE12-20.dwg* file. Assign different colors of your choice to existing layers. Plot this drawing in Model tab using a final plot scale of 1/4″=1′-0″ on a 11″ × 8 1/2″ paper. Plot with colors.

6. Open the *EXE13-8.dwg* file. Plot this drawing in Model tab using a final plot scale of 1″=1′-0″ on a 11″ × 8 1/2″ paper. Plot with colors.

7. Open the *EXE16-7.dwg* file. Create a layout called *Kitchen Plan* from the ANSI A (portrait)–Color Dependent Plot Styles template. Plot only the kitchen area in this new layout and inside the new template with title block and borderline in paper space using a final plot scale of 1/2″=1′-0″. Plot with existing colors.

8. Open the *EXE22-2.dwg* file. Assign different colors of your choice to existing layers. Plot this drawing in Model tab using a final plot scale of 1/4″=1′-0″ on a 11″ × 8 1/2″ sheet. Plot with colors.

9. Open the *EXE22-5.dwg* file. Create a Layout called *Front Elevation* from the Architectural, English units–Color Dependent Plot Styles template. Plot this drawing in this new layout and inside the new template with title block and borderline in paper space using a final plot scale of 1/4″=1′-0″. Plot with existing colors.

CHAPTER 24

Externally Referenced Drawings

After successful completion of this chapter you should be able to:

▲ Understand the function of external references.

▲ Reference an existing drawing into the current drawing using the Reference toolbar.

▲ Bind external references and dependent objects.

▲ Use the Xref Manager dialog box.

▲ Detach, reload, and unload external references.

▲ Use the Xbind dialog box to add or remove only the portions of the xref.

▲ Clip external references.

▲ Edit external references using the Refedit toolbar.

▲ Use external references in paper space layouts.

▲ Create and compose a multiple scale drawing from a template in a multiview layout.

▲ Use the Layer Properties Manager dialog box to control layer display in viewports.

24.1 EXTERNAL REFERENCES

One of the most powerful attributes of AutoCAD is the ability of the building design and construction team to reuse and share drawing data. Most architectural projects require that all members of the design and production team have access to the current drawing database. It is important to have access to up-to-date drawing information for everyone involved in the project to ensure the quality, precision and correctness of the projects. The design and construction of buildings involve several teams of consultants to work in collaboration. In addition to the architectural and engineering firms, many projects require landscape architects, interior designers, contractors, subcontractors, and facility managers for the design, construction, and management of buildings. One way to provide consistent drawing information to clients, consultants, and contractors is to use externally referenced files, or xrefs. Externally referenced drawings allow you to reference, or "borrow," needed information pertaining to a specific drawing and to combine it with the existing data. For example, a reflected ceiling plan can be created by externally referencing only the base floor plan. Or a structural framing plan can be generated by externally referencing only the base column grid plan. With external references you can also compose a drawing sheet in paper space layouts containing multiple-scale drawings. In Chapter 22, you learned about paper space and layouts. Using the XREF command, you will learn to reference needed drawings into separate viewports with different scales to compose the final outcome of your project.

Externally referenced drawing files are not added to the contents of the current drawing file if they are only attached as a reference. Therefore, using xrefs helps keep your drawing file size to a minimum. When you insert a wblock as a drawing file, the contents of the drawing file are copied into the current drawing file, taking up a lot of disk space. An externally referenced drawing file is displayed each time the base drawing is accessed. When you update the base drawing, all drawings that are referenced (attached) will be updated. You can create a drawing that serves as the base drawing, such as a floor plan with required information. You can then externally reference this drawing into another drawing to create electrical, mechanical, plumbing, and framing plans.

24.2 THE XREF COMMAND

The XREF command allows you to reference a drawing file into the master (current) drawing using the Xref Manager dialog box. To access this dialog box, select the External Reference button in the Reference or Insert toolbar, select Xref Manager ... from the Insert pull-down menu, or enter XR or XREF at the command line. The Reference toolbar is shown in Figure 24–1, and the Insert pull-down menu is shown in Figure 24–2.

When you access the Xref Manager dialog box the first time, no reference file name will be listed and only the Attach ... button will be active. The Xref Manager dialog box is shown in Figure 24–3.

FIGURE 24–1 The Reference toolbar is used to reference drawings into current drawing.

Using a reference file is similar to inserting a drawing, with the following exceptions:

1. When you open a drawing that uses reference files, the current version of each reference file is used.

2. If changes are made to the original attached reference file (xref), the master (current) drawing will always reflect the current changes.

3. Any changes to the original referenced drawing are automatically updated in the master drawing only if it is attached.

4. You can attach and then detach a reference file without leaving behind unreferenced blocks and layers, whereas inserting a drawing (with the INSERT command) can pose problems in this respect.

5. You can reference drawings and not have to worry about duplicate block names, layer names, and so on.

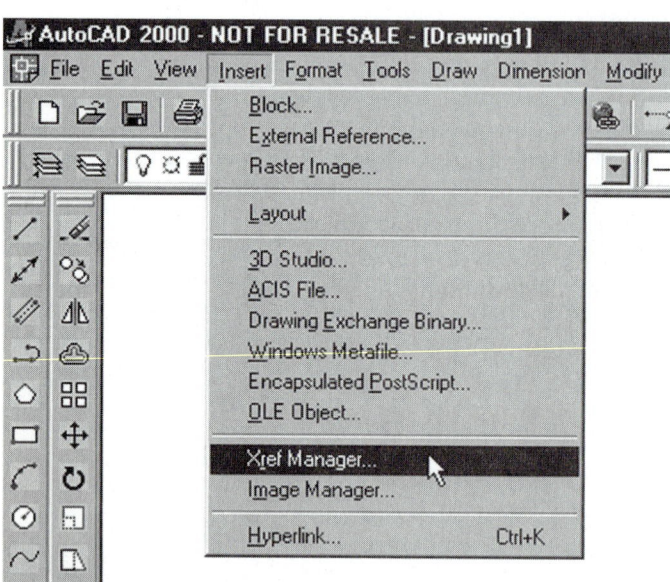

FIGURE 24–2 The Insert pull-down menu can be used to access the XREF command.

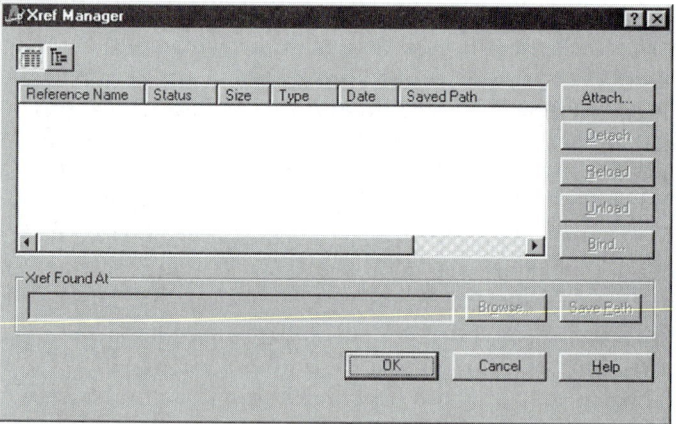

FIGURE 24–3 The Xref Manager dialog box allows you to attach a reference file when a file is first referenced. It also allows you to detach, reload, unload, and bind xrefs.

AutoCAD will reload each xref drawing whenever the master drawing is loaded. Therefore, every time a drawing is accessed, the most recently saved version of the xref will be loaded. For example, if a CAD team member is working on the elevations and the designer is working on the floor plan, every time the xref floor plan is loaded for the elevations, they will be updated. However, this is possible only if the Attach option of the Xref Manager dialog box is used and if computers are networked.

24.3 ATTACHING EXTERNAL REFERENCES

You can attach an external reference into the current file using two different methods:

1. Click on the Attach . . . button in the Xref Manager dialog box.
2. Click on the External Reference Attach button in the reference toolbar. This is the second button in the toolbar.

Either method will display the Select Reference File dialog box as shown in Figure 24–4. This is a standard file dialog box with a drawing Preview area and a Find File . . . button. Use this dialog box to locate the file to be referenced into the current drawing. Click on the Open button to display the External Reference dialog box as shown in Figure 24–5.

The name of the xref is displayed inside the Name: drop down box. The path of the selected xref is displayed in the Path: area. The Reference Type category allows you to select one of the two reference type options. The Attachment option (default) allows you to attach a drawing as an external reference. The Overlay option allows you to see what your drawing would look like with another drawing overlaid on it. The major difference between Attachment and Overlay is the way in which nested xrefs are handled in the drawing. A nested drawing is a drawing containing other referenced drawings. When a nested drawing is overlaid, any nested drawing within the drawing file will not be displayed. When a nested drawing is attached, all objects will be displayed. In other words, any nested overlay will not be carried into the master drawing that is an attached xref. The Insert point, Scale, and Rotation categories of the External Reference dialog box are similar to the Insert dialog box used to insert a block.

When you click on the OK button, AutoCAD will load the xref and present the following command prompt:

```
Specify insertion point or [Scale/X/Y/Z/Rotate/Pscale/PX/PY/PZ/PRotate]:
```

At this point, select an insertion point or enter an option. The drawing will be attached as an xref.

Tips: If the drawing is not displayed on the screen, use the Extents option of the ZOOM command. This will display the drawing to fit the extents of the drawing area.

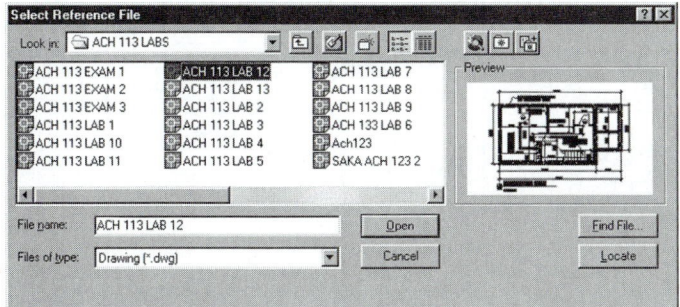

FIGURE 24–4 The Select Reference File dialog box allows you to find the file to be referenced.

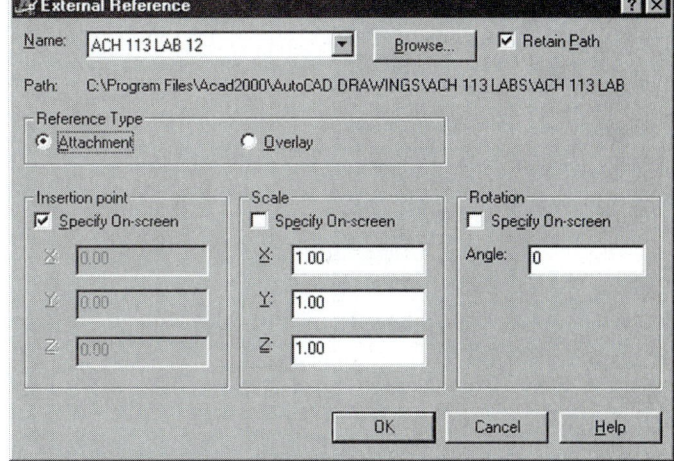

FIGURE 24–5 The External Reference dialog box allows you to specify how an external reference is placed in the current drawing.

24.4 DETACHING, RELOADING, AND UNLOADING EXTERNAL REFERENCES

Once you externally reference a drawing using the Attachment option, you can use the Xref Manager dialog box to access other reference options. The Xref Manager dialog box will display all the drawings that are attached to the current drawing. Figure 24–6 shows three drawings that are attached to the current drawing. The two elevations and the floor plan are individual drawings that are attached to the master drawing. If one of the elevations is revised, the latest version of the xref elevation will be displayed when the master drawing is opened. The master drawing is the current drawing containing xref attachments. The Xref Manager dialog box will now show the three drawings that are attached as shown in Figure 24–7.

The file names in the Reference Name column can be displayed either in List view or Tree view. These two buttons are located at the upper-left corner of the Xref Manager dialog box. The List View button is active by default and provides six columns as follows:

REFERENCE NAME: This column lists the names of the existing external reference files.

STATUS: This column describes the current status of each reference file. *Loaded* status means that the xref is attached to the drawing. *Unloaded* status means that the xref is not displayed. *Unreferenced* status means that the xref has nested xrefs that are not found and therefore not displayed. *Not Found* status means that the reference file was not found in the search paths. *Unresolved* status means that the xref file is missing or cannot be found. *Orphaned* status means that the nested xref was not found.

SIZE: This column shows the size of the reference file in KB (kilobytes).

TYPE: This column indicates whether the reference file was attached or overlaid.

DATE: This column shows the last modified date for each of the listed reference file.

SAVED PATH: This column lists the path name saved with the reference file.

The Tree View displays external references with the standard AutoCAD 2000 drawing file icon as the sheet of paper with a paper clip as shown in Figure 24–8. A plus sign (+) in front of the

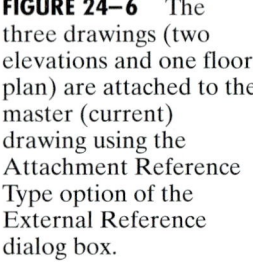

FIGURE 24–6   The three drawings (two elevations and one floor plan) are attached to the master (current) drawing using the Attachment Reference Type option of the External Reference dialog box.

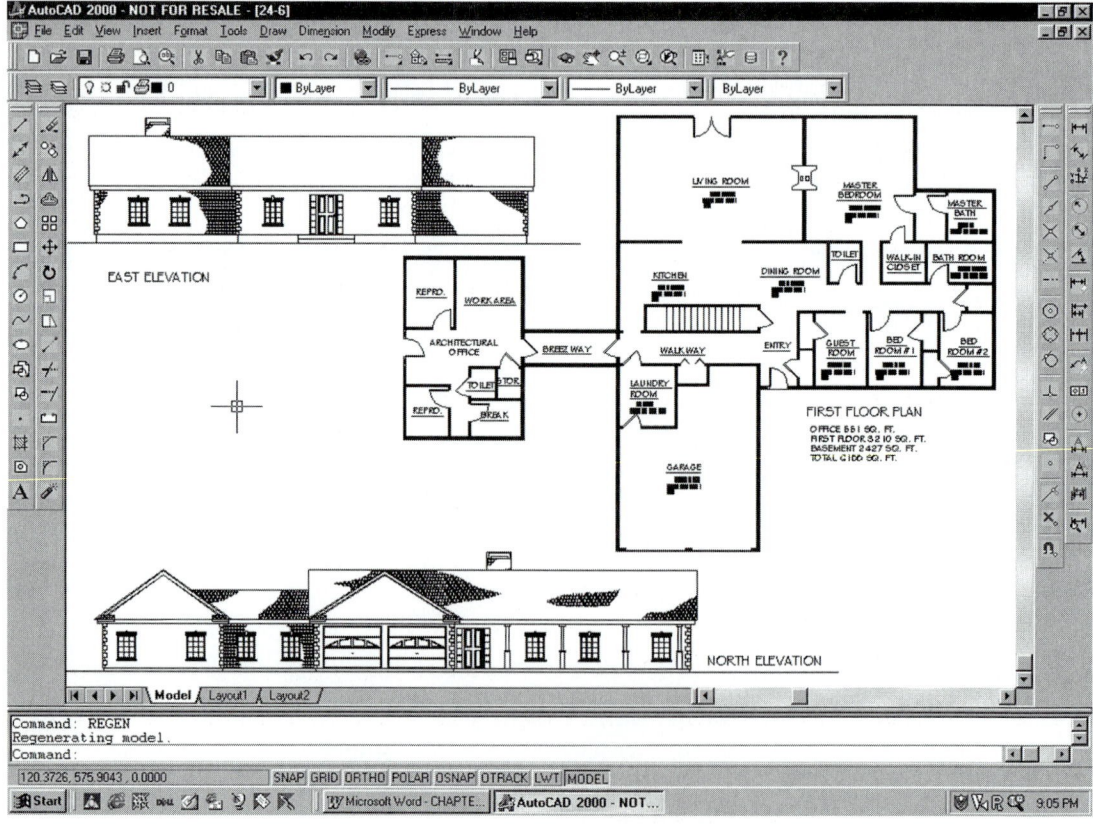

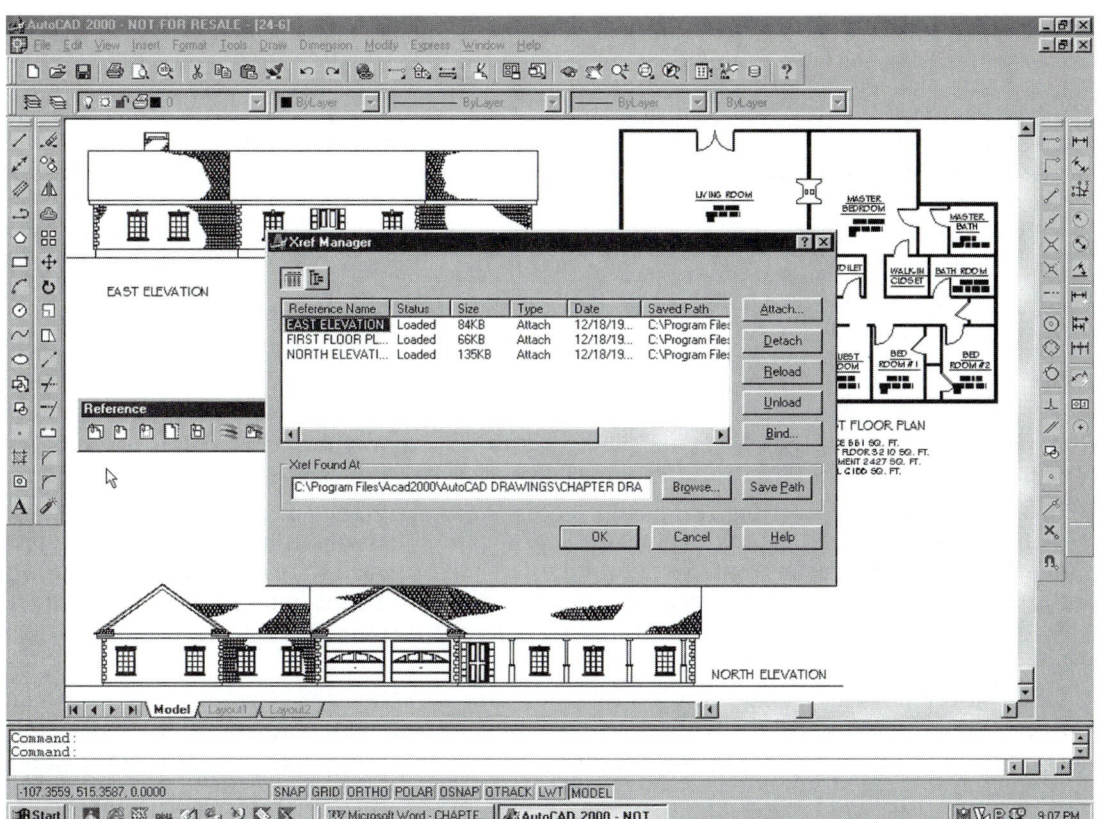

FIGURE 24–7 The Xref Manager dialog box showing the three externally referenced (attached) drawings using the List View box.

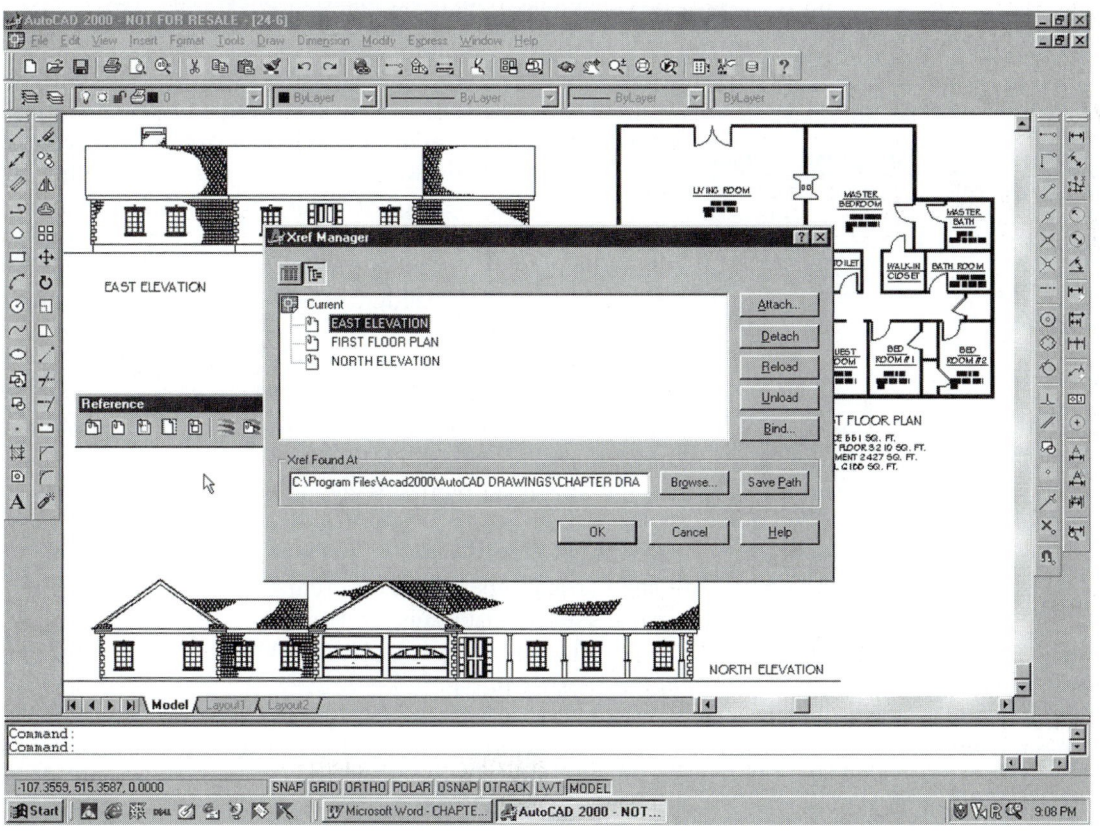

FIGURE 24–8 The Xref Manager dialog box showing the three externally referenced (attached) drawings using the Tree View box.

reference file icon indicates nested xrefs. To display the nested xrefs, click on the plus sign. If there is an xref whose status is unloaded, the icon will be grayed out. If there is a question mark in front of the xref, the file is not found. If there is an upward arrow, the xref is reloaded. If there is a downward arrow, the xref is unloaded.

Tips: In the List View display option, the column widths can be adjusted to display more or less of the information displayed. Move your cursor to the vertical line separating the columns until the cursor changes into a double arrow. Press and drag the column to the desired width.

The attachment of the xref remains permanent until you detach it. To remove or detach the attached xref, highlight the reference file in the Xref Manager dialog box and click on the Detach button. The reference file that is detached will be removed from the Reference Name list. When you detach an externally referenced file, all drawing data, including nested xrefs, are removed from the current drawing. For the actual detachment to occur, you must click on the OK button. If you accidentally select a file and click on Detach button, click on the Cancel button to prevent the detachment.

You can update an externally referenced file by highlighting the reference file name and selecting the Reload button. Selecting the Reload button will force AutoCAD to read and display the most recent version of the reference file. This is useful when referenced files are modified when the disk version of the file is different from the version currently displayed.

You can temporarily remove an externally reference file without actually detaching it by unloading it. To unload the xref, highlight the reference file and click on the Unload button. An unloaded xref is not displayed. To display the xref again, click on the Reload button.

24.5 BINDING EXTERNAL REFERENCES

The Bind . . . button of the Xref Manager dialog box allows you to make referenced files a permanent part of the current drawing. To bind an xref, you must first attach it to the current file. When this option is used, the reference files function as a Wblock rather than an xref. Think of binding as inserting a drawing using the INSET command. After the binding process you can edit the externally referenced drawing inside the current drawing as opposed to editing the externally referenced drawing in its own file. When the xref is attached to the current drawing, all drawing contents are renamed so that the xref name precedes the actual object name. The names are separated by a vertical pipe symbol (|). Drawing contents that are carried into another drawing such as blocks, dimension styles, layers, linetypes, and text styles, depend on the external file for their characteristics. For example, an externally referenced (attached) file named *East Elevation* with a layer named *Wall* will be displayed as follows:

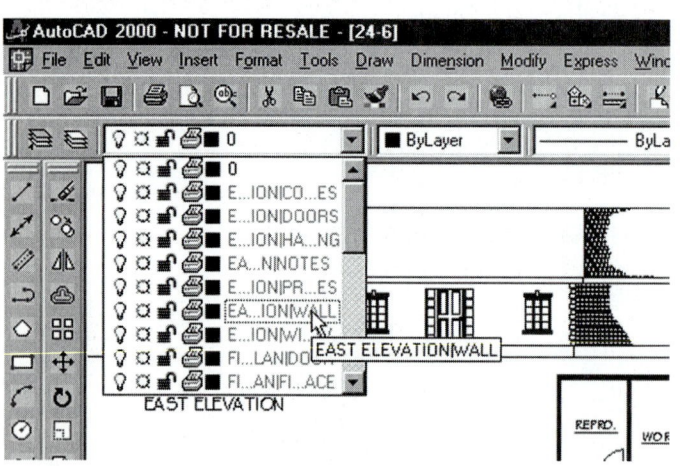

FIGURE 24–9 The layer names for the attached xref are separated by a vertical pipe symbol and are grayed out.

```
East Elevation|Wall
```

The vertical pipe symbol is created so that the xref-layer name can be distinguished from the same layer name in the master drawing. The layers for the xref (attached) drawings are not available for editing. The layers for the file named *East Elevation* are shown in Figure 24–9.

When you bind externally referenced drawings to the current drawing, the drawing contents are renamed again to reflect the permanent status of the binding. The vertical pipe symbol is replaced by $$ signs with a number in between. To bind the xref, highlight the xref to bind and click on the Bind . . . button in the Xref Manager dialog box. This will display the Bind Xrefs dialog box as shown in Figure 24–10.

FIGURE 24–10 The Bind Xrefs dialog box is used to bind the externally referenced files permanently to the current drawing.

The Bind Xrefs dialog box has two different bind types. The Bind option converts the attached xref to local block definitions. This means that all xref files are now blocks inside the current drawing. Objects inside the bound drawing can now be edited after exploding it. The xref drawing contents will be changed to reflect the binding process. For example, after binding the *East Elevation* file with a wall layer name to the current drawing, the layer will be displayed as follows:

```
East Elevation$0$Wall
```

Figure 24–11 shows the layers for the *East Elevation* file after the binding process.

The number between the dollar signs is automatically updated when a local layer with the same name exists. For example, if East Elevation0Wall already exists in the master drawing, the layer is renamed to East Elevation1Wall. This allows unique names to be created for all xref-drawing contents that are bound to the current drawing with the Bind option.

The Insert option of the Bind Xrefs dialog box binds an attached xref into the master drawing as if a file had been inserted into a drawing. The xref-drawing contents are stripped of their file names and are displayed only as names. For example, the xref file named *North Elevation* with a layer named *Wall* will be displayed as follows:

```
Wall
```

Figure 24–12 shows the layers for the *North Elevation* after the Insert option.

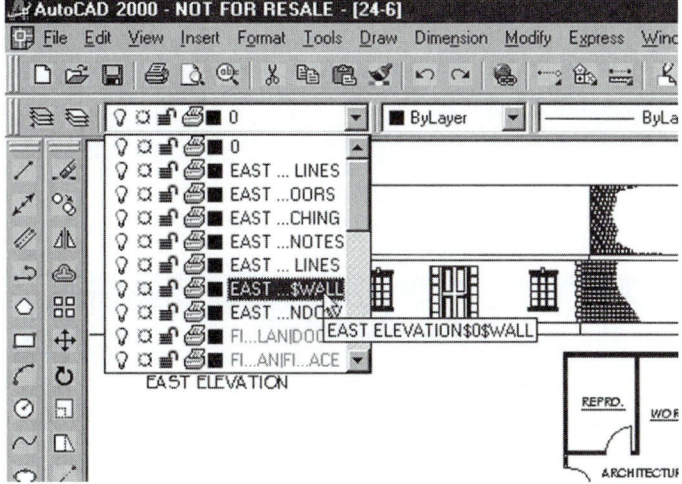

FIGURE 24–11 The layer names for the xref that is bound using the Bind option are separated by dollar signs with a number in between. Notice that the bound layers are available and objects can be added to those layers.

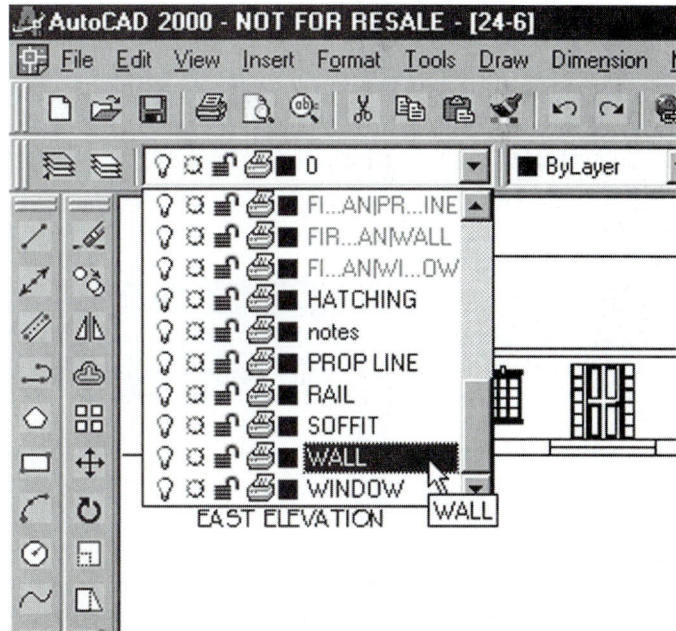

FIGURE 24–12 The layer names for the xref that is bound using the Insert option.

24.6 THE XBIND COMMAND

The Bind option allows a referenced drawing to be a permanent part of the current drawing. However, there may be cases in which you need to bind xref drawing contents individually rather than the entire xref file. The XBIND command allows you to permanently add a portion of the xref—such as a block, a layer, or a linetype—to the current drawing. To access the XBIND command, click on the External Reference Bind button from the Reference toolbar, select Object, External Reference, and Bind . . . from the Modify pull-down menu, or enter XB or XBIND at the command line. This will display the Xbind dialog box as shown in Figure 24–13. This dialog box allows you to select individual xref drawing contents for binding.

The plus sign (+) in front of the xref icon indicates that the file can be expanded. To expand the file, click on the plus sign. This will display the drawing contents for the file. In Figure 24–14, the *East Elevation* is expanded to show the contents of the drawing. A plus sign (+) in front of the icon indicates that there are specific items belonging to that drawing content. For example, in Figure 24–14 the *East Elevation* file has one or more dimension styles (Dimstyle), one or more layers (Layer), and one or more text styles (Textstyle) but no blocks or linetypes. Selecting the plus sign (+) in front of the Layer will display all the layers belonging to that file as shown in Figure 24–15.

FIGURE 24–13 The Xbind dialog box allows you to individually bind xref drawing contents to the current drawing. Three drawing files shown here indicate externally referenced (attached) drawings in the master drawing.

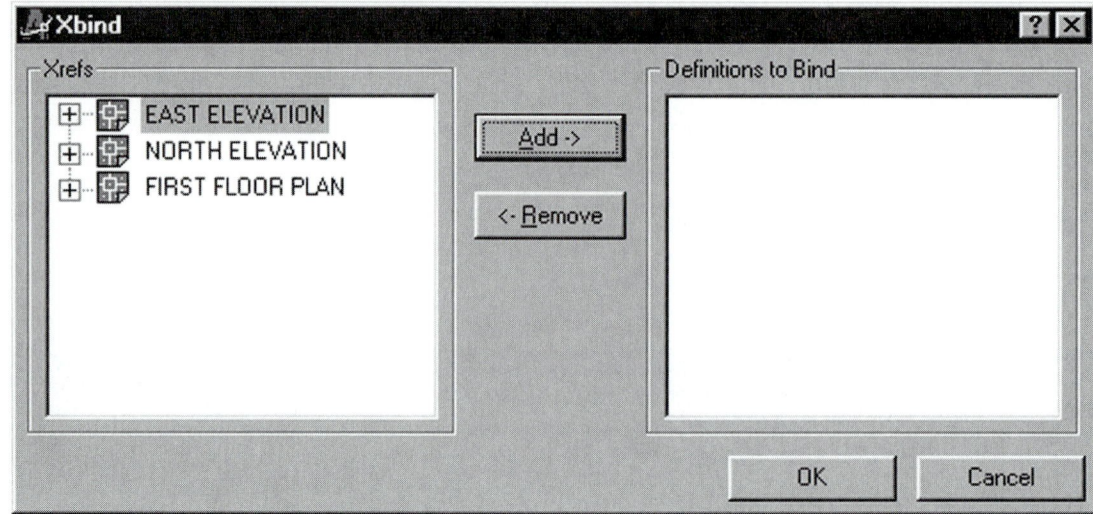

FIGURE 24–14 Selecting the plus sign in front of the drawing file will expand the file to list drawing contents.

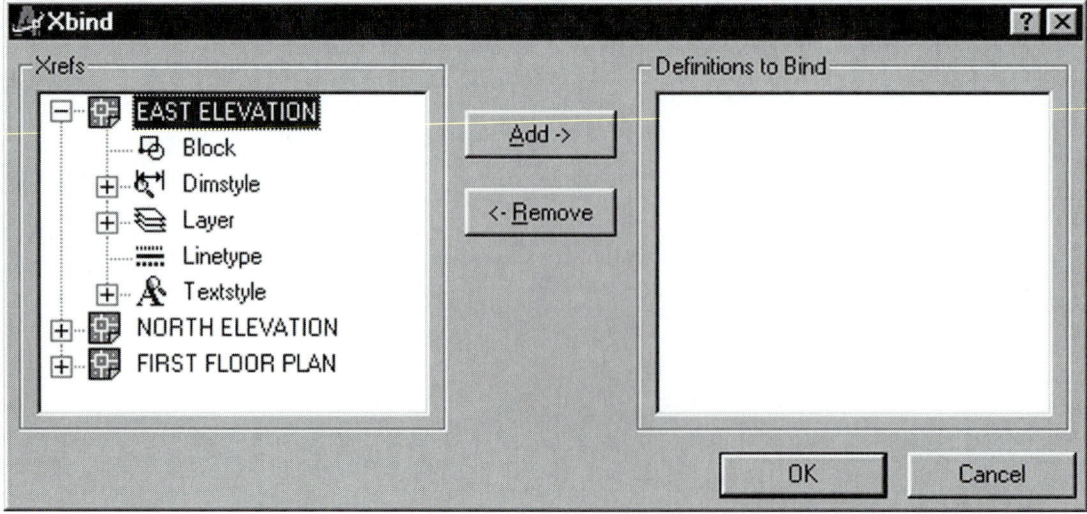

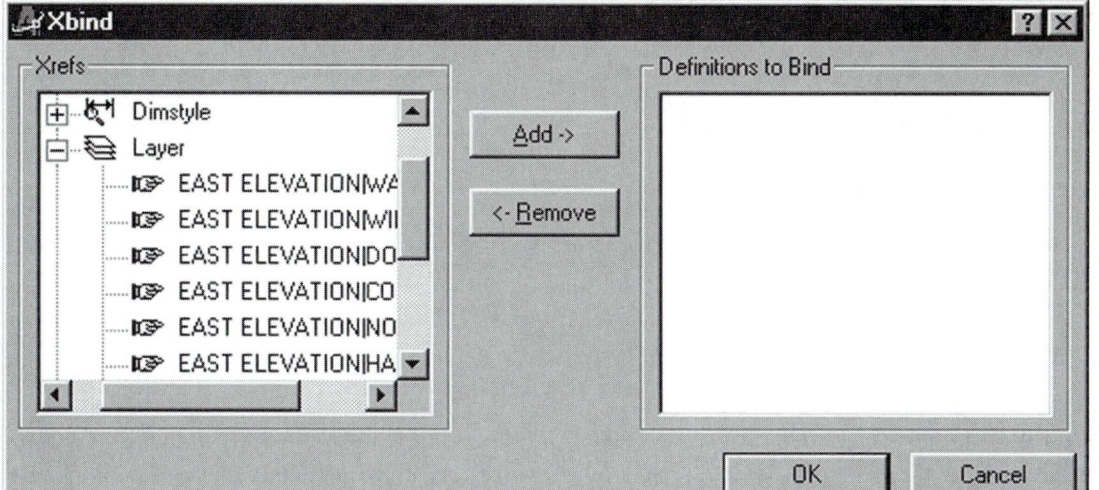

FIGURE 24–15
Selecting the plus sign in front of the layer will expand the list to show all layers.

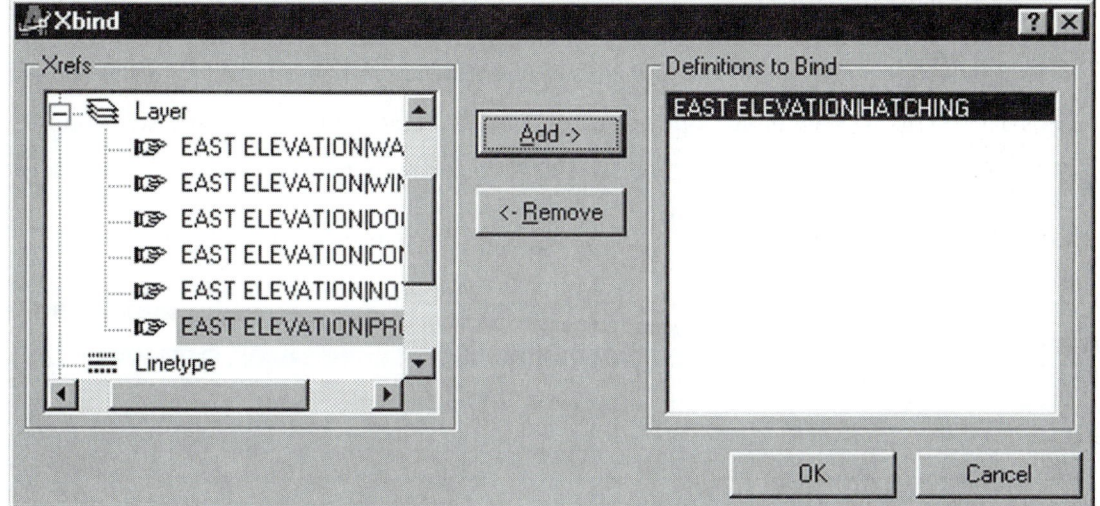

FIGURE 24–16
Selecting the item from the xrefs list and selecting the Add-> button will permanently bind the item to the master drawing.

To select an item for binding, highlight it and click on the Add button. For example, selecting East Elevation|Hatching and clicking the Add-> button will bind the layer to the current drawing. The names of all objects selected and added will be displayed inside the Definition to Bind area on the right side of the Xbind dialog box. Figure 24–16 shows the East Elevation|Hatching layer bound to the master drawing. AutoCAD will rename this layer in the same manner as items are bound using the Bind option in the Bind Xrefs dialog box. For example, the layer in Figure 24–16 will be displayed as EAST ELEVATION0HATCHING inside the Layer properties Manager dialog box.

To remove the items from the Definitions to Bind list (before exiting this dialog box), select the item and click on the <-Remove button. This will unbind the item from the current drawing and restore it to the Xrefs list. When all required layers (or items) are selected and bound to the master drawing, click on the OK button. You can then make the defined (bind) layer current and add objects to it. However, you must explode the drawing before you can edit referenced objects. New objects added after the bind or the xbind can be edited without exploding the xref.

24.7 CLIPPING EXTERNAL REFERENCES

You can display only a specific portion of a drawing by creating a boundary around the xref. All objects that are outside the boundary will be invisible. All objects that are partially inside the boundary will be trimmed. The XCLIP command allows you to create and modify clipping boundaries for the xref. To access the XCLIP command, select the External Reference Clip button from the Reference toolbar, select Xref from the Clip cascading menu in the Modify pull-down menu, or enter XC or XCLIP at the command line. The command sequence is as follows:

```
Command: XCLIP ~EnterKey~
Select objects: (select one or more xref objects)
Select objects: ~EnterKey~
Enter clipping option
[ON/OFF/Clipdepth/Delete/generate Polyline/New boundary] <New>:
~EnterKey~
Specify clipping boundary:
[Select polyline/Polygonal/Rectangular] <Rectangular>: ~EnterKey~
Specify first corner: (select the first corner for the clip)
Specify opposite corner: (select the opposite corner for the clip)
```

Figure 24–17 shows the right portion of the floor plan clipped. Options for the clipping are as follows:

ON AND OFF: You can turn on or off the clipping feature by using these options.

CLIPDEPTH: This option allows you to create a front and back clipping plane for a three-dimensional drawing.

DELETE: This option removes the clipping boundary.

GENERATE POLYLINE: This option allows you to create a polyline object for the clipping boundary.

After selecting the New boundary option, AutoCAD displays the following boundary options:

SELECT POLYLINE: This option allows you to select an existing polyline object as the boundary definition.

POLYGONAL: This option allows you to create irregular lines as the polygon boundary.

FIGURE 24–17   A portion of the floor plan clipped using the XCLIP command.

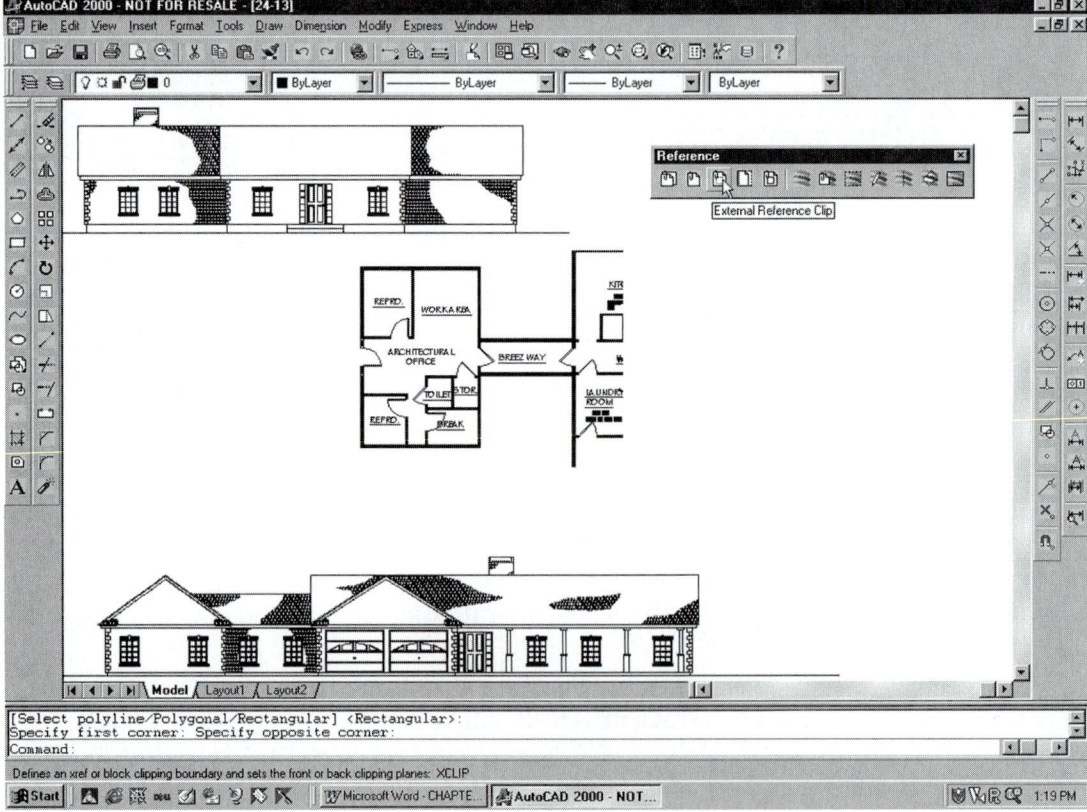

The External Reference Clip Frame button in the Reference toolbar allows you to place a frame around the clipping boundary. This is controlled by the XCLIPFRAME system variable. When this system variable is set to 1, the frame is displayed around the clipping boundary. By default, this system variable is set to 0 (off).

24.8 EDITING REFERENCED DRAWINGS

You can edit externally referenced drawings inside the current drawing without expoding it. This is called *in-place reference editing*. This allows any member of the project team to edit an externally referenced drawing inside the current drawing when it is open. Use the REFEDIT command to edit xrefs. To access this command, select the Edit block or Xref button in the Refedit toolbar, select Edit Reference from the In-place Xref and Block Edit cascading menu in the Modify pull-down menu, or enter REFEDIT at the command line. The command line procedure is as follows:

```
Command: REFEDIT
Select reference: (select the externally referenced drawing)
```

After selecting the xref, the Reference Edit dialog box will be displayed as shown in Figure 24–18. The Reference Edit dialog box has the following categories:

REFERENCE NAME: This text box displays the name of the selected reference drawing.

PREVIEW: This box displays the preview image of the selected reference drawing.

PATH: This area shows the location of the selected reference drawing.

ENABLE UNIQUE LAYER AND SYMBOL NAMES: This check box controls whether layer and symbol names of objects extracted (removed) from the referenced file will be unique or altered. This check box is on by default. In the on mode, layer names are given the prefix n, where *n* is the incremental number. If the selected reference drawing contains other references (nesting), the Reference name: box will list all nested xrefs in tree view. If there are additional nested xrefs, use the Next button to cycle through them.

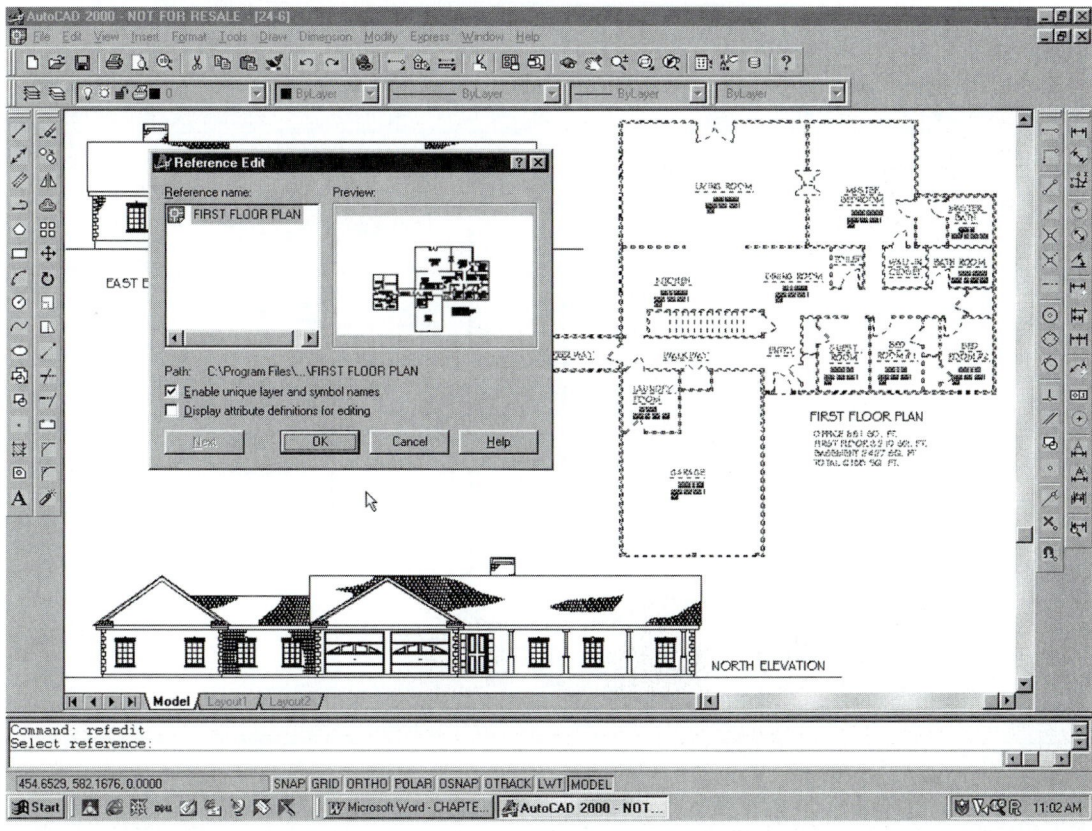

FIGURE 24–18 The Reference Edit dialog box allows you to edit externally referenced drawings in-place.

DISPLAY ATTRIBUTE DEFINITIONS FOR EDITING: This check box controls visibility of attributes in a block reference during editing. When checked, block reference attributes will be invisible but the objects and the attribute definitions will be available for editing.

Click on the **OK** button when done. AutoCAD will ask you to select nested objects in the reference drawing to edit as follows:

```
Select nested objects: (select objects to edit in the xref)
Select nested objects: ~EnterKey~
```

After you select nested objects, the Refedit toolbar will be displayed as shown in Figure 24–19. The objects you select will be a part of the *working set*. Objects that are not a part of the working set will appear grayed out during the reference editing process as shown in Figure 24–20.

Tips: Use the Refedit toolbar to edit externally referenced drawings without binding and/or exploding the entire xref. For example, you can edit objects on specific layers for an attached xref using the Refedit toolbar even though layers are not available for selec-

FIGURE 24–19 The Refedit toolbar is used to perform reference editing operations. The name of the xref drawing file is displayed in the toolbar.

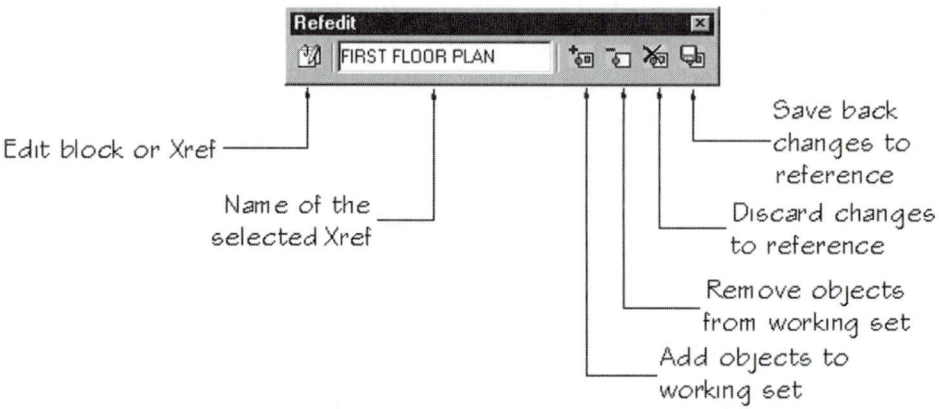

FIGURE 24–20 The objects that are not a part of the working set are grayed out during reference editing. In this case, the east elevation and north elevation are grayed out while the first floor plan is selected as part of the working set.

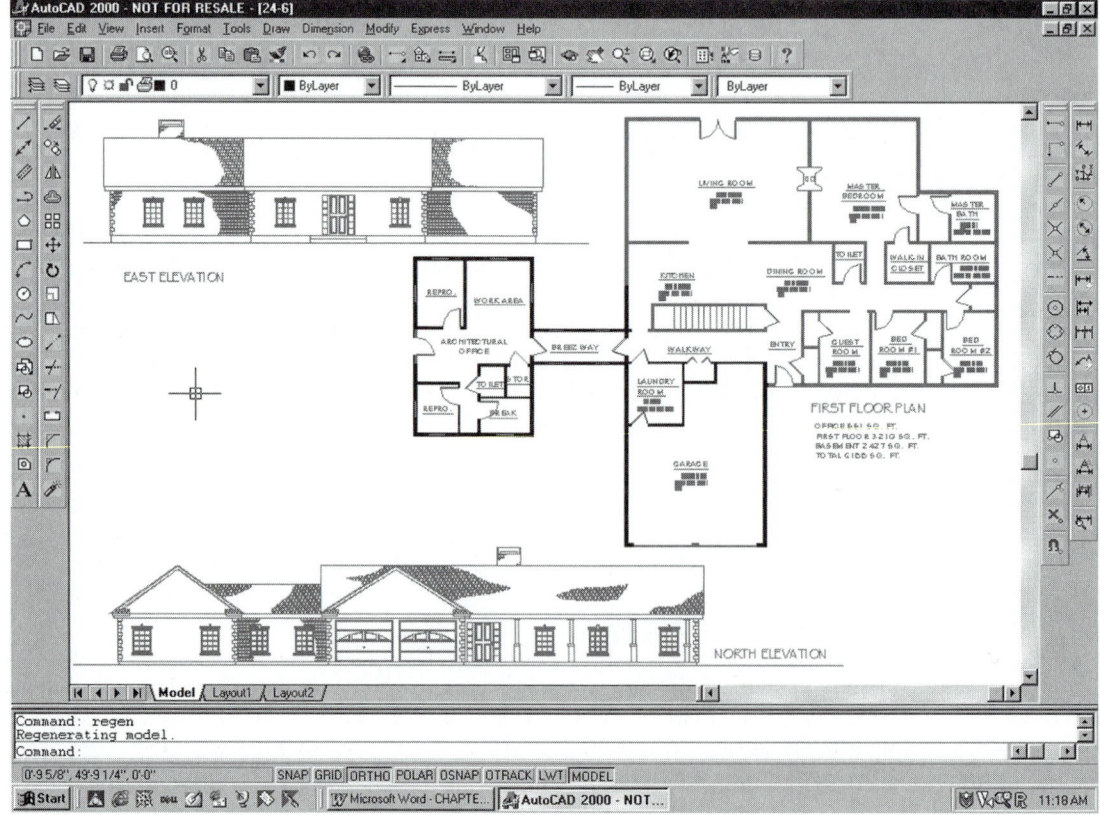

tion. This will allow you to retain the xref update feature and work with layers without binding the xref. Make sure layers are not locked. This method also allows you to update the original drawing by editing the attached xref in the current drawing.

The Refedit toolbar shown in Figure 24–19 is used to perform different reference editing functions. You can add or remove objects from the working set or you can save or discard changes to the original xref file. The Refedit toolbar buttons are described as follows:

ADD OBJECTS TO WORKING SET: This button allows you to add any objects drawn during the in-place editing to the working set. You can also add existing objects by using this button. If you add existing objects to the working set, they will be extracted from the xref. The command line procedure is as follows:

```
Transfer objects between the Refedit working set and host drawing . . .
Enter an option [Add/Remove] <Add>: A
Select objects: (select objects to be added to the working set)
```

REMOVE OBJECTS FROM WORKING SET: This button allows you to remove selected objects from the working set. If you remove a previously extracted object, it will be added back to the xref. The command line procedure is as follows:

```
Transfer objects between the Refedit working set and host drawing . . .
Enter an option [Add/Remove] <Add>: R
Select objects: (select objects to be removed from the working set)
Objects removed from the working set will appear faded.
```

DISCARD CHANGES TO REFERENCE: This button allows you to exit the in-place reference editing without saving the changes.

SAVE BACK CHANGES TO REFERENCE: This button allows you to save the editing changes and exit the in-place reference editing session. You can also use the REFCLOSE command to save or discard changes and exit the in-place reference editing session.

Note: The fading of the objects that are not a part of the working set appears as the percentage of the normal display mode. The percentage of fading is 50 percent by default and can be changed by using the Display tab in the Options dialog box. Move the slider in the Reference Edit fading intensity area or enter a new value inside the text box.

24.9 DEMAND LOADING AND ACCESS TO REFERENCED DRAWINGS

Demand loading refers to the amount of externally referenced file to be loaded while it is attached to the master drawing. When demand loading is enabled, only the required portion of the xref file necessary to regenerate the current drawing is loaded. This allows you to keep the xref file to a minimum size and improves performance. Because the entire xref file is not loaded, any objects on frozen layers and objects outside the clipping boundaries will not be displayed. Demand loading is enabled by default. You can disable this feature by using the Open and Save tab of the Options dialog box as shown in Figure 24–21.

The External References (Xrefs) category has the following options:

DEMAND LOAD XREFS: This drop-down list controls demand loading. When Enabled is selected, demand loading is turned on. When demand loading is on, others cannot edit the file. When Disabled is selected, demand loading is turned off. When Enable with copy is selected, demand loading is turned on and other users can edit the original file of the xref because the copy of the xref is used.

RETAIN CHANGES TO XREF LAYERS: This option is on by default allowing you to save all changes made to the object properties of xref dependent layers. Any changes made to layers will take precedence over the xref file layer settings. You can use the VISRETAIN system variable to control this function. By default, the VISRETAIN system variable is set to 1 (on).

ALLOW OTHER USERS TO REFEDIT CURRENT DRAWING: This option is on by default, allowing other users to edit in-place the current drawing while it is open and referenced by another drawing. This

FIGURE 24–21 The Open and Save tab of the Options dialog box allows you to control additional xref options.

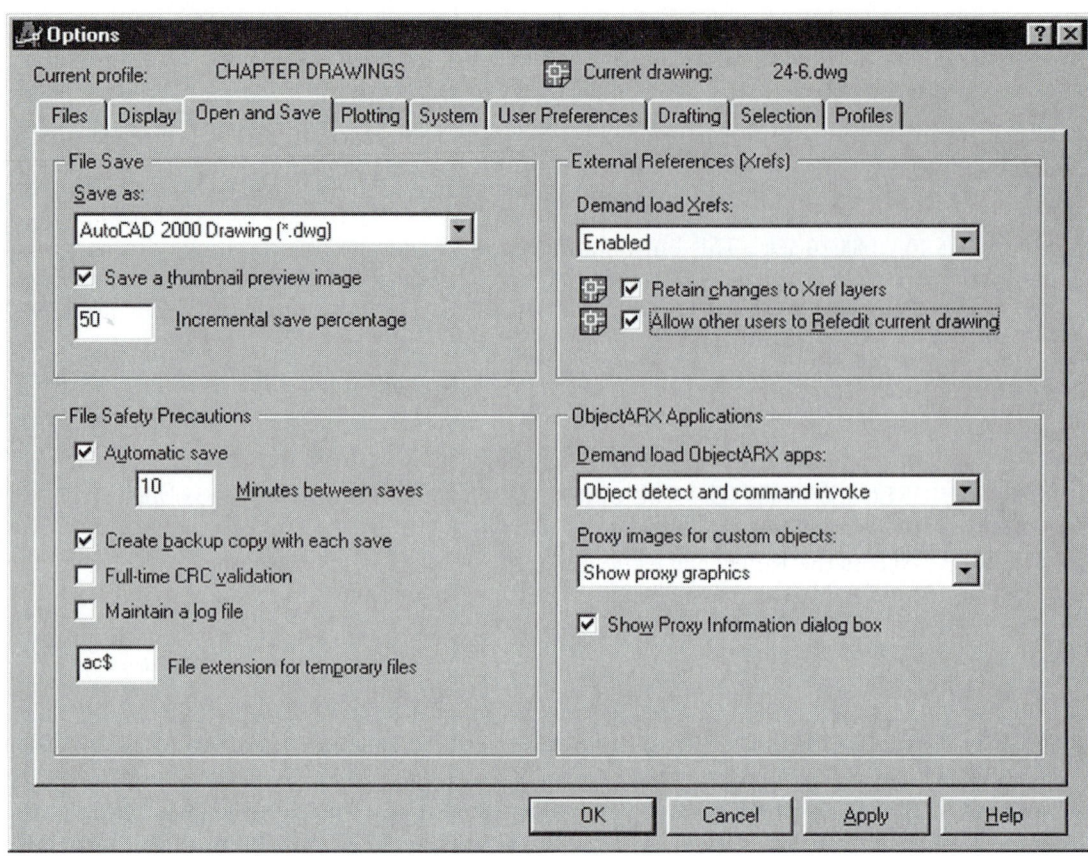

feature is also controlled by the XEDIT system variable. By default, the XEDIT system variable is on.

Tips: When demand loading is enabled (default), a write lock is placed on the original drawing when the xref is loaded. This prevents other users from changing the externally referenced drawing file. Because the file is kept open, you can change layer and clipping settings. Demand loading should be enabled because the xref file is not loaded entirely into the master drawing and cannot be opened or edited by other users on the network.

24.10 USING XREFS IN PAPER SPACE LAYOUTS

Creating multiple viewports in paper space layout allows you to compose multiple-scale drawings in one sheet. For example, you can create three viewports with different sizes in one template and externally reference three different drawings into model space of the three viewports. You can set the scale of each viewport drawing in model space and change the size of each viewport in paper space to accommodate the scale and proper viewport size of the drawing in each viewport. As you learned in Chapter 22, any drawing that is part of the viewport will be displayed in other viewports. This means that when you xref a drawing inside a viewport, the same drawing will appear in other viewports. This creates a problem because only one drawing should be displayed inside each viewport so that a precise scale can be set for that specific drawing. To control the display of drawings inside each viewport, use the Layer Properties Manager dialog box.

■ **EXERCISE 24–1:** *The following step-by-step exercise will allow you to create three viewports in paper space layout based on the architectural template and externally reference (xref) three different drawings to compose a multiple scale layout. The three drawings are a floor plan, an elevation, and a wall section. Before proceeding, copy the RES2-Floor Plan, RES2-Wall Section, and RES2-North Elevation files into your hard drive.*

Step #1: Create a new drawing by selecting the New button in the Standard toolbar.

Step #2: Inside the Create New Drawing dialog box, click on the Use a Template button.

Step #3: Inside the Select a Template: drop-down list, select the Architectural, English units—color dependent plot styles.dwt template. Click on the OK button. The Architectural Title Block layout will be highlighted and the template will be displayed in paper space as shown in Figure 24–22.

Step #4: Right-click on the Architectural Title Block layout and select Rename from the shortcut menu. Inside the Rename Layout dialog box, enter My Architectural Project. Click on the OK button. The layout name will be changed to the new name as shown in Figure 24–23.

Step #5: In paper space, click on the default viewport and resize it using grips. Make two copies of the resized default viewport and place it inside the dashed lines as shown in Figure 24–24. Each viewport will be used to externally reference a drawing file.

Step #6: Double-click on the upper-left viewport to switch to model space and to make that viewport active. You can also click on the Paper button in the Status bar to switch to model space. Figure 24–25 shows the upper-left viewport in model space as the active viewport.

Step #7: Access the Reference toolbar. Click on the External Reference Attach button. Inside the Select Reference File dialog box, find and select the RES2-Floor Plan file as shown in Figure 24–26. Click on the Open button.

Step #8: Inside the External Reference dialog box, select the Attachment option from the Reference Type category as shown in Figure 24–27. Leave everything as is and click on the OK button.

Step #9: Inside the upper-left viewport select the lower-left corner as the insertion point for the RES2-Floor Plan drawing. If the drawing does not appear, enter ZOOM and then enter E at the command line. This will perform zoom

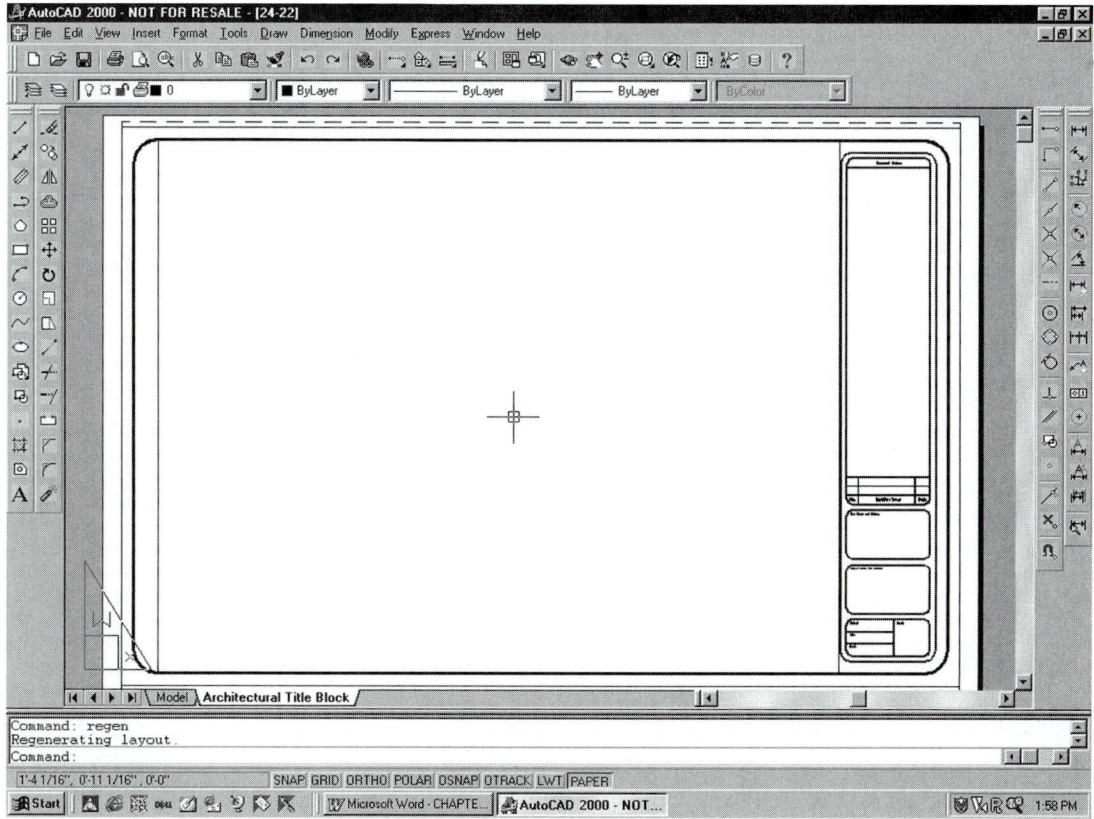

FIGURE 24–22 The Architectural D-size drawing template in paper space layout. Notice the Architectural Title Block layout name.

FIGURE 24–23 The existing layout name is renamed to My Architectural Project.

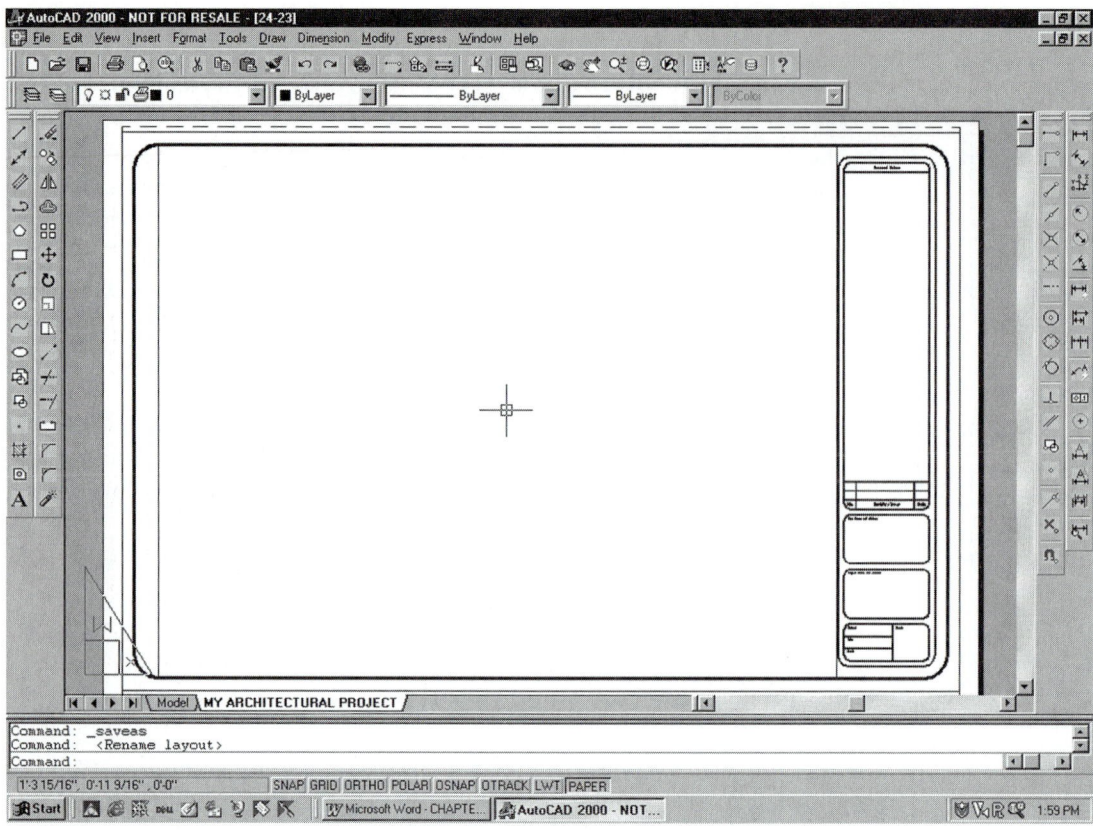

FIGURE 24–24 Three viewport are created. Each viewport will be used to externally reference a drawing file.

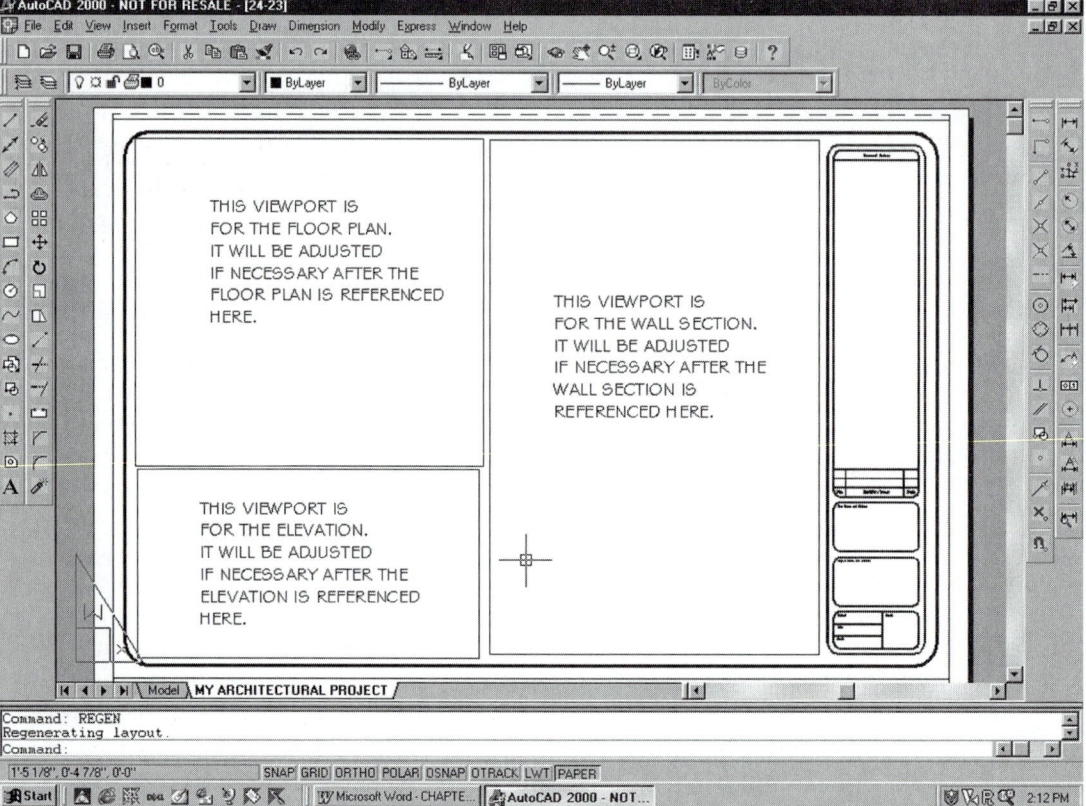

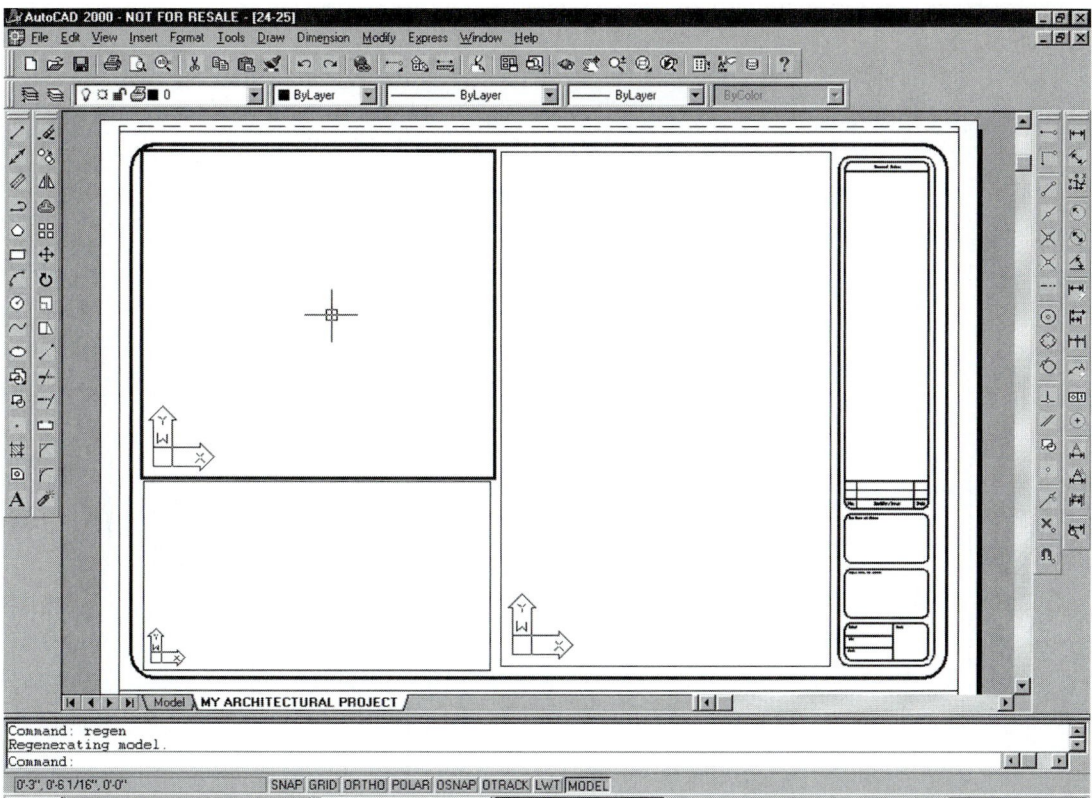

FIGURE 24–25 The upper-left viewport as the active viewport will be used to externally reference the FLOOR PLAN.

extents. The floor plan will be externally referenced inside the viewport as shown in Figure 24–28.

Step #10: Click inside the right (largest) viewport to make it active. Use the procedures described above to externally reference the RES2-Wall Section file into this viewport. Figure 24–29 shows the RES2-Wall Section externally referenced into the right viewport. Notice that both drawings are displayed inside the first and second viewports.

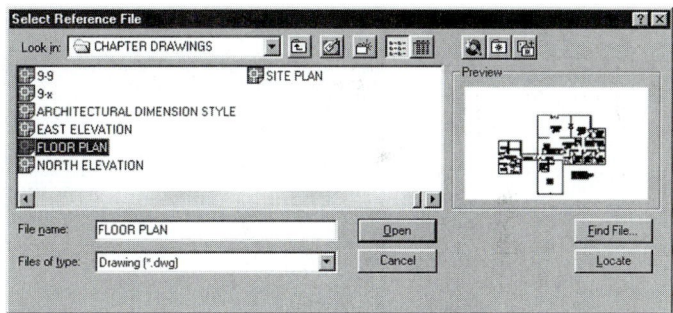

FIGURE 24–26 The RES2-Floor Plan file is selected as the reference file. The file here is shown as Floor Plan.

Step #11: While the second (right) viewport is active in model space, click on the Layers button in the Object Properties toolbar. Inside the Layer Properties Manager dialog box, select all the layers belonging to the RES2-Floor Plan file and select the Active VP Freeze icon. You are about to freeze all layers associated with the RES2-Floor Plan drawing inside the active viewport so that the RES2-Floor Plan drawing is not displayed inside this viewport. This will allow only the RES2-Wall Section to be displayed inside this active viewport. Click on the OK button when done. However, when you externally reference the RES2-North Elevation file into the third viewport, it will be displayed in all the other viewports. You have to go through this procedure of freezing all layers belonging to the drawing for each of the viewports for each of the drawings you do not wish to display. The Layer Properties Manager dialog box and the selection of all the RES2-Floor Plan layers with the Active VP Freeze icon is shown in Figure 24–30. The viewport will now display only the RES2-Wall Section. Use the ZOOM and PAN realtime commands to adjust

FIGURE 24–27 The External Reference dialog box before the file is attached to the master drawing. The file name here is shown as Floor Plan.

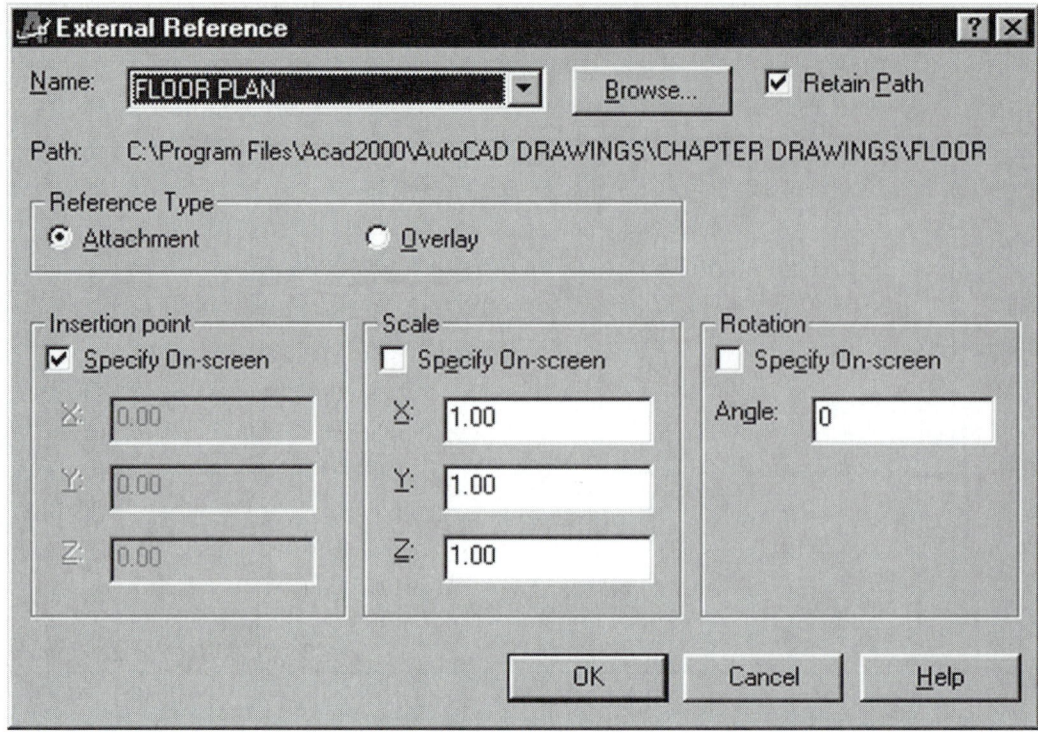

FIGURE 24–28 The RES2-Floor Plan is externally referenced (attached) into the viewport.

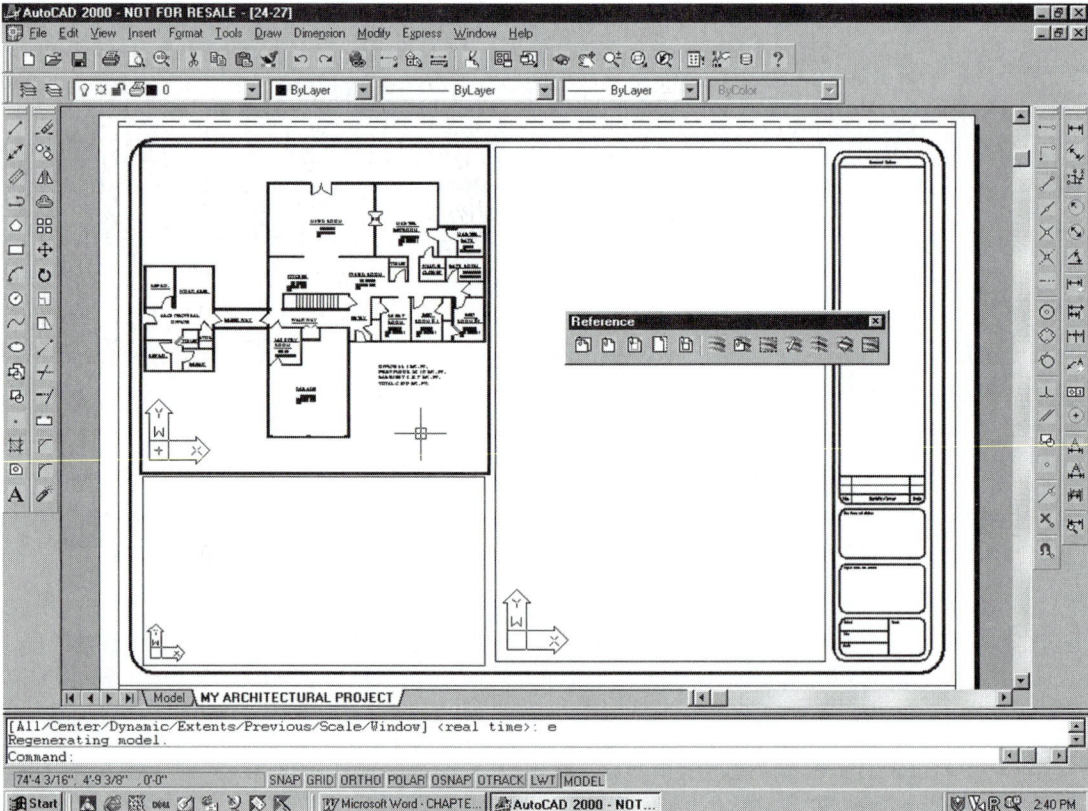

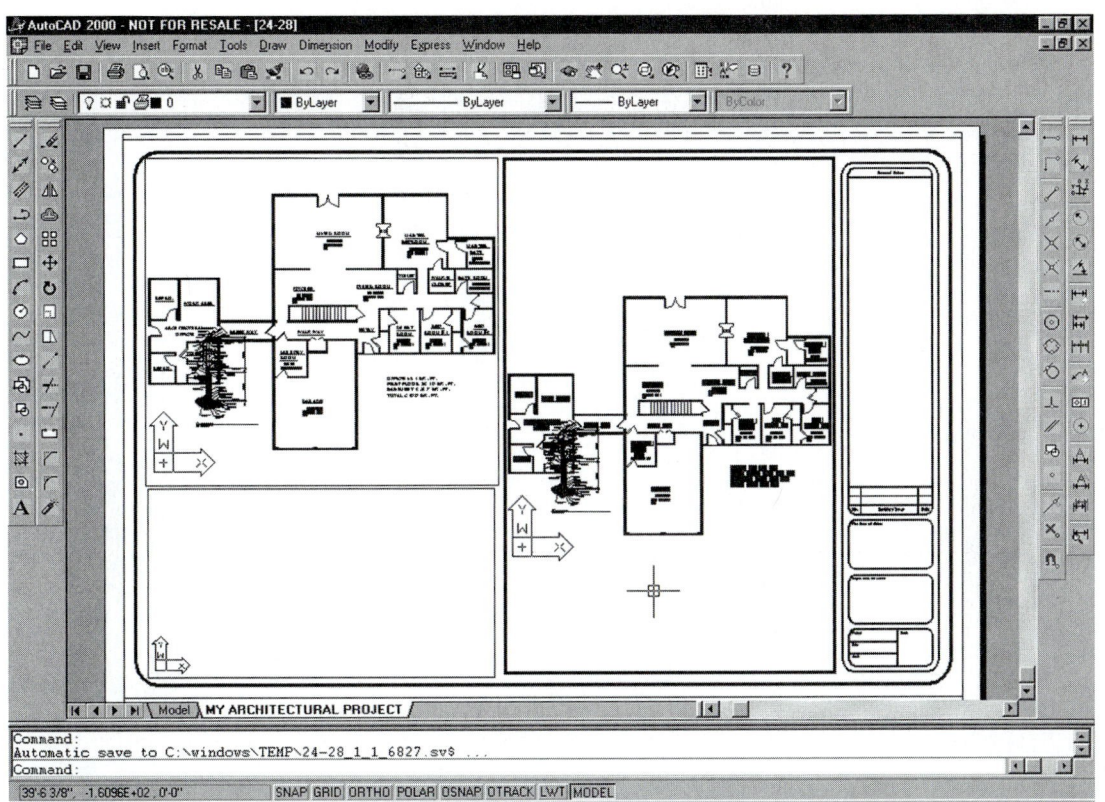

FIGURE 24–29 When externally referencing files into the viewports all drawings are displayed in each of the viewports. The RES2-Floor Plan is displayed along with the RES2-Wall Section in the second viewport. The RES2-Wall Section is displayed along with the RES2-Floor Plan in the first viewport.

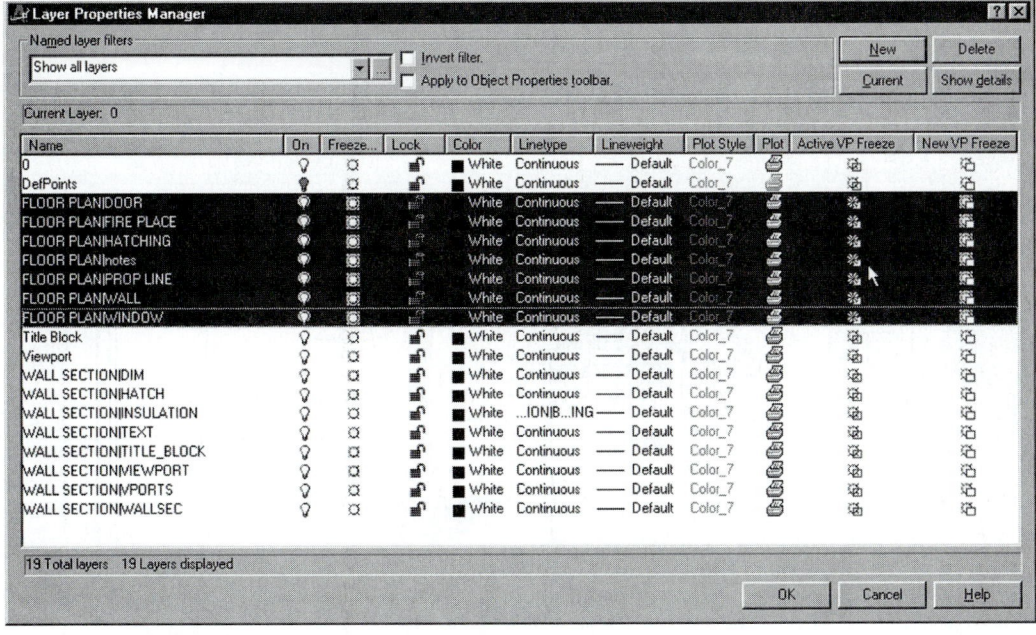

FIGURE 24–30 To control the visibility of each drawing referenced in the active viewport, select all the layers for that drawing and click on the Active VP Freeze icon. The file names here are shown as Floor Plan and Wall Section. This is possible when using a Layout to compose drawings inside a template.

the position of the drawing so that it covers most of the viewport as shown in Figure 24–31. The precise scale for each viewport will be set later.

Step #12: Make the first (upper-left) viewport active. Use the same procedure to freeze all layers belonging to the RES2-Wall Section drawing inside the active viewport. This viewport will now display only the RES2-Floor Plan drawing as shown in Figure 24–32.

FIGURE 24–31 The RES2-Wall Section is now displayed as the only drawing in the second (right) viewport.

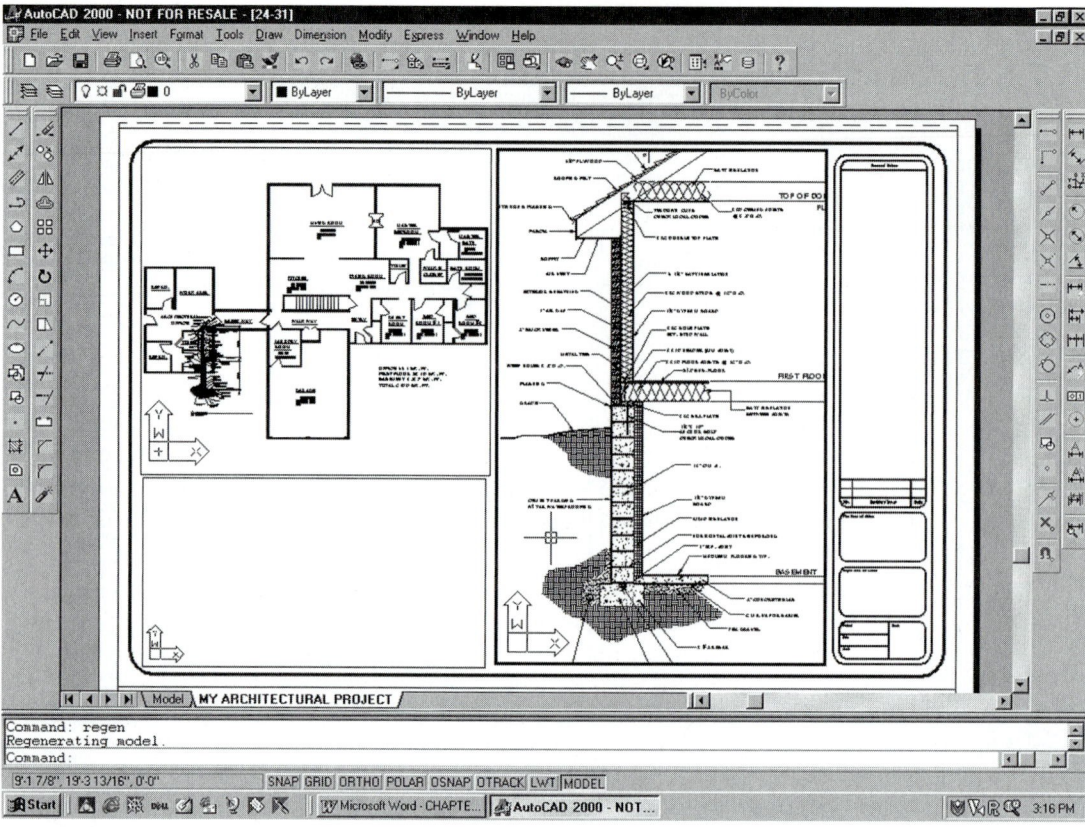

FIGURE 24–32 The first viewport after freezing all layers associated with the RES2-Wall Section drawing in active viewport.

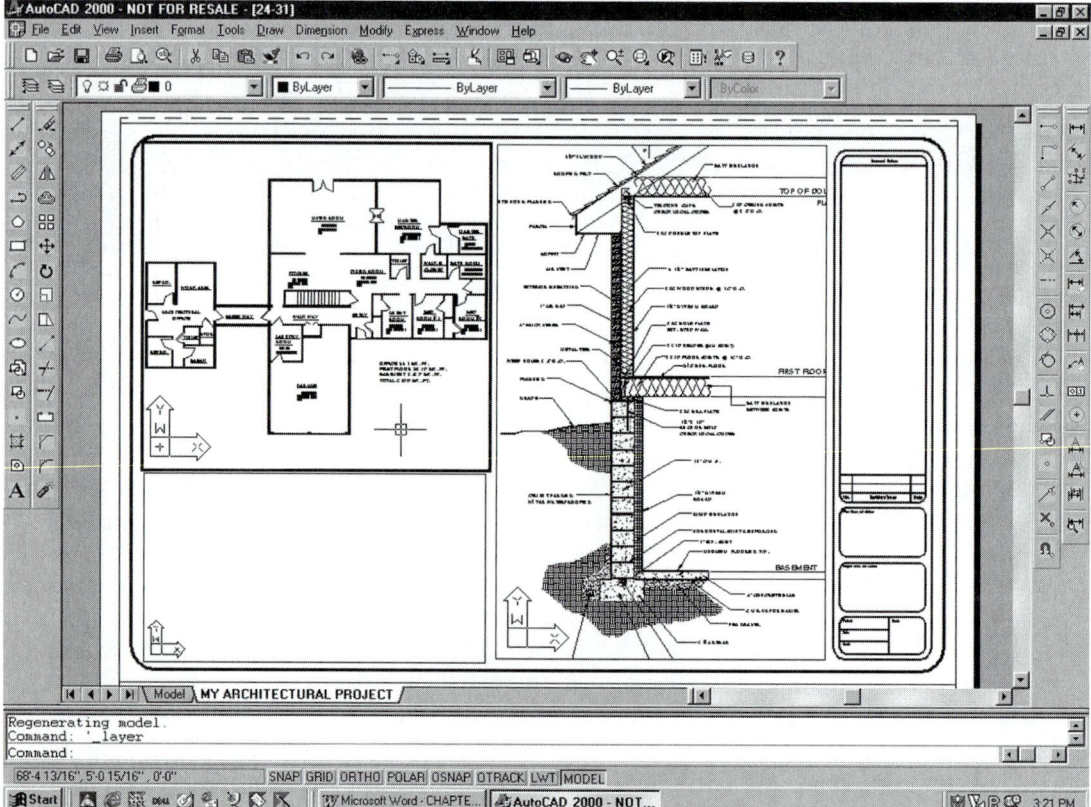

Step #13: Using the procedures described earlier, reference the RES2-North Elevation file into the third (bottom) viewport. Using the Layer Properties Manager dialog box, freeze in active viewport the RES2-Floor Plan and RES2-Wall Section file layers in this viewport.

Step #14: Make the upper left viewport active. Using the Layer Properties Manager dialog box, freeze in active viewport the RES2-North Elevation layers.

Step #15: Make the right viewport active. Using the Layer Properties Manager dialog box, freeze in active viewport the RES2-North Elevation layers. The three viewports will now display only the appropriate drawings intended for the viewports as shown in Figure 24–33. Use zoom and pan realtime to adjust magnification.

Step #16: Using the Viewports toolbar, set a precise scale for each of the viewports in model space. For the RES2-Floor Plan, set a scale of 1/8″=1′. For the RES2-Wall Section, set a scale of 3/4″=1′ scale. For the RES2-North Elevation, set a scale of 3/16″=1′. Refer to section 22.14 for scaling viewports. In paper space, adjust the size of the viewports to accommodate the scale of individual drawings. Don't worry if viewports overlap. Just make sure that the drawings don't overlap.

Step #17: In model space, adjust the display of drawings inside their viewport by using PAN realtime so that each drawing is visible inside its own viewport with its precise scale. Remember that PAN realtime does not alter the scale of your drawings set inside the viewport. Just make sure that you do not use other Zoom options. To make sure that each drawing is at the intended scale, lock the scale of each viewport in paper space.

Step #18: In paper space create a layer called My Viewports and assign the color red. Using the Properties window, place all the viewports (not the drawings) in this layer. Turn My Viewports layer off.

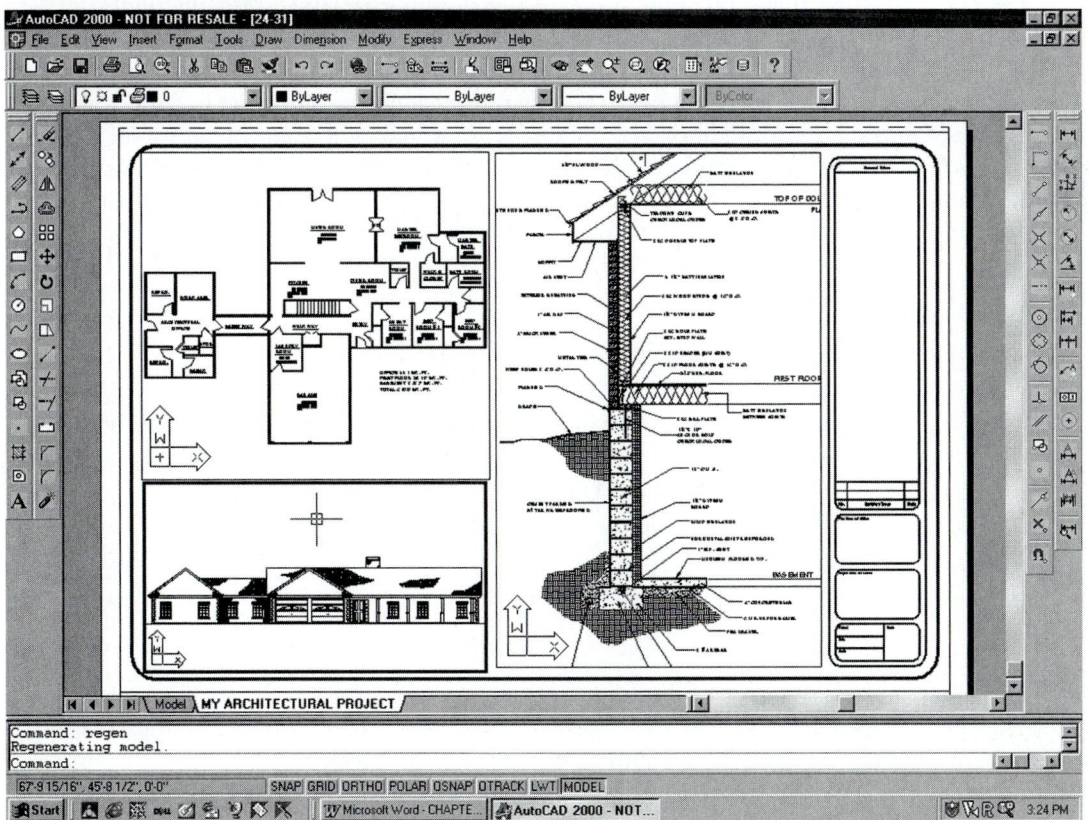

FIGURE 24–33 All viewports displaying the appropriate drawing.

FIGURE 24–34 The final composition of the three drawings at different scales inside a "D" size standard title block.

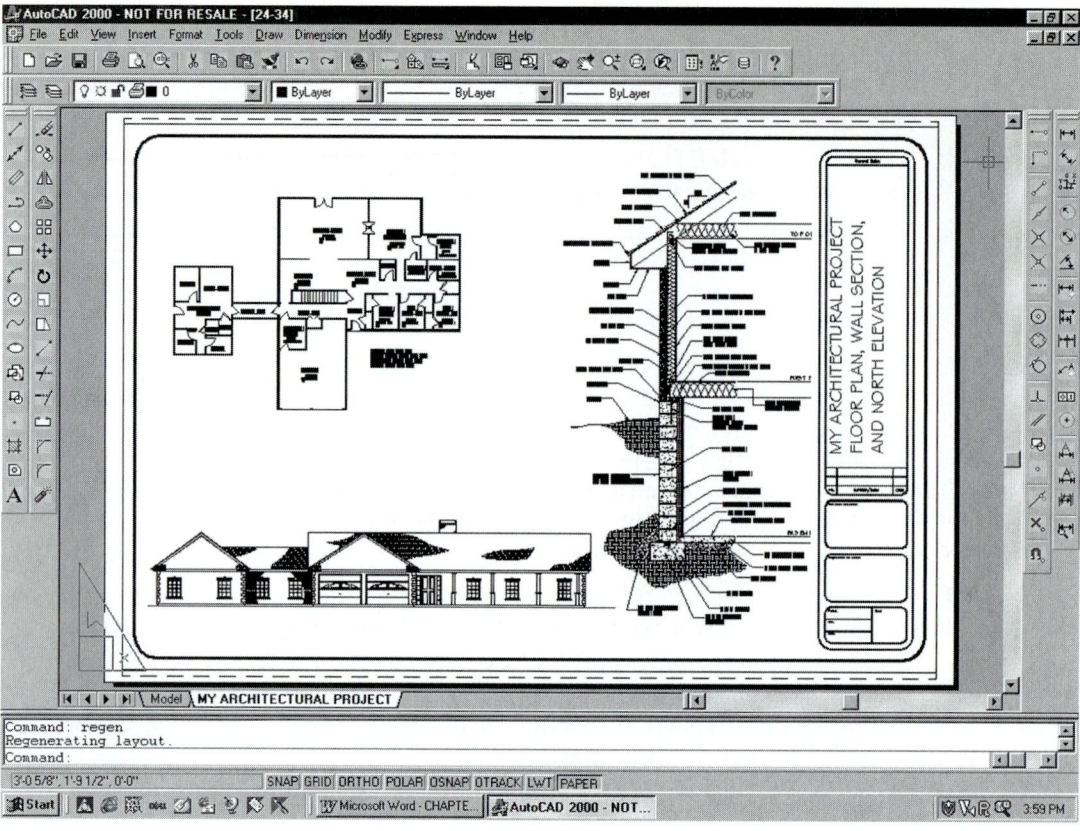

Step #19: In paper space, fill in the title block as required and as shown. The final composition of My Architectural Project layout in paper space is shown in Figure 24–34.

Congratulations! You have successfully externally referenced three drawings in paper space layout. You have also successfully controlled the display of drawings in each viewport, set a precise scale to each viewport, and composed the final look of the title block before plotting. You can now plot this drawing in paper space. You can also type the scale (as text) of each drawing in paper space using text height at full scale. Using a scale of 1:1. Refer to section 23.5.

REVIEW QUESTIONS

1. Briefly describe the general purpose behind externally referenced drawings.
2. How do you access the Xref Manager dialog box?
3. What is the difference between the Attach and Bind options in the Xref Manager dialog box?
4. What is the difference between the Attach and Overlay options in the External Reference dialog box?
5. What is the difference between Bind and Xbind?
6. What is the function of the External Reference Clip button in the Reference toolbar?
7. What is demand loading?
8. When referencing drawings into multiple viewports, how do you control the display of objects in each viewport?

PROBLEMS

1. Using Exercise 24-1 as a guide, create a new drawing from the architectural template (36″ × 24″) and name the drawing *My Xref 1*. Externally reference the following files:

   COM1-FOUNDATION PLAN file at 1/4″=1′-0″ scale.

COM1-FOUNDATION DETAIL1 file at 3/4″=1′-0″ scale.

COM1-COLUMN DETAIL 1 file at 1 1/2″=1′-0″ scale.

Create three viewports in paper space and set and lock scale for each viewport.

2. Plot *MY XREF 1.dwg* file in paper space.

3. Using Exercise 24–1 as a guide, create a new drawing from the architectural template (36″ × 24″) and name the drawing *My Xref 2*. Externally reference the following files:

COM1-WALL DETAIL 1 file at 1 1/2″=1′-0″ scale.

COM1-WALL DETAIL 2 file at 1 1/2″=1′-0″ scale.

COM1-WALL DETAIL 3 file at 1 1/2″=1′-0″ scale.

COM1-CURTAIN WALL DETAIL file at 1/2″=1′-0″ scale.

COM1-ROOF DETAIL file at 3/4″=1′-0″ scale.

Create five viewports in paper space and set and lock scale for each viewport.

4. Plot *MY XREF 2.dwg* file in paper space.

5. Using Exercise 24-1 as a guide, create a new drawing from the architectural template (36″ × 24″) and name the drawing *My Xref 3*. Externally reference the following files:

COM1-GROUND PLAN file at 1/4″=1′-0″ scale.

COM1-BATHROOM ELEVATIONS file at 1/4″=1′-0″ scale.

Create two viewports in paper space and set and lock scale for each viewport.

6. Plot *My Xref 3.dwg* file in paper space.

7. Using Exercise 24-1 as a guide, create a new drawing from the architectural template (36″ × 24″) and name the drawing *My Xref 4*. Externally reference the following files:

COM1-SOUTH ELEVATION file at 1/8″=1′-0″ scale.

COM1-WEST ELEVATION file at 1/8″=1′-0″ scale.

Create two viewports in paper space and set and lock scale for each viewport.

8. Plot *My Xref 4.dwg* file in paper space.

9. Using Exercise 24-1 as a guide, create a new drawing from the architectural template (36″ × 24″) and name the drawing *My Xref 5*. Externally reference the following files:

RES1-FIRST FLOOR PLAN file at 1/4″=1′-0″ scale.

RES1-FRONT ELEVATION file at 1/4″=1′-0″ scale.

RES1-LEFT ELEVATION file at 1/8″=1′-0″ scale.

Create three viewports in paper space and set and lock scale for each viewport.

10. Plot *My Xref 5.dwg* file in paper space.

Dimensioning Variables

You can change dimensioning variables using the dimensioning dialog boxes or at the command line. To change a dimensioning variable at the command line you must type the name of the dimensioning variable at the command line and enter a new value or turn it on. After changing a dimensioning variable value at the command line, you need to use the DIM (Dimension) and UP (Update) commands to update the existing dimensions on the drawing for the new settings to take effect. For example, suppose after selecting architectural tick as the arrowheads (dimension line terminators at extension line origins) and the arrow size (tick marks size) value of 1/16″ using a dialog box, you decide to change one dimension in the drawing to 3/16″ arrow size at the command line. The dimensioning variable that controls architectural tick size is called DIMASZ (arrow size). The following procedure will show you how to change the architectural tick arrowhead size for one existing dimension in the drawing from 1/16″ to 3/16″ at the command line:

```
Command: DIMASZ ~EnterKey~
Enter new value for DIMASZ<0'-0 1/16">:3/16 ~EnterKey~
Command: DIM ~EnterKey~
Dim: UP ~EnterKey~ (the cursor will turn into a pick box prompting you
to update a dimension)
Select objects: (select dimension)
Select objects: 1 found (this is your confirmation of the dimension to
be updated)
Select objects: ~EnterKey~ (this will update the dimension selected and
change its DIMASZ value on the screen)
Dim: ~EscKey~ (this will complete the dimension update procedure)
```

At the Select objects: command prompt you can select as many dimensioning objects as necessary, depending on how many dimensions you would like the update command to change. When a dimensioning variable is used at the command line it will have the same effect as using the Override. . . button inside the Dimension Style Manager dialog box. This operation will place <style overrides> under the current dimension style of the Styles: list box. See Using the Dimension Style Manager Dialog Box for more information on dimension overrides and dimension updates.

Instead of typing DIM (Dimension) and UP (Update) commands at the command line to update dimensions, you can click on the Dimension Update button inside the Dimension toolbar. This is a much faster way to update a dimension.

Dimensioning variables are hard to memorize and even harder to understand because they are abbreviated. However, there are some common denominators and elements found on most of the dimensioning variable names. Spending some time to look at the common elements found in all of the dimensioning variables will save you a great deal of frustration in the future, especially if you are planning on typing the dimensioning variables at the command line. All dimensioning variable names start with DIM, which stands for *dimension*. Some of the abbreviations have certain meanings and are listed below:

ASZ = arrow size

A = arrowheads as in ASZ (arrow size)

A = angle as in AUNIT (angle format)

ALT = alternate

CLR = color

D or DL = dimension line

SEP = separator or separation

D = decimal as in DSEP (decimal separator)

E = extension line

LW = line weight

S = suppress

X or EX = extension

BLK = arrowhead block

T or TX = text

STY = style

I = inside

O = outside

H = horizontal alignment

VP = vertical position

D = dimension

U = unit

UP = user position

L = linear

FRAC = fraction

RND = round off

A = angle

POS = prefix and suffix as in (POST)

Z = zeros

Establishing a relationship between letters and meanings can be like putting a jigsaw puzzle together. But when you have a good set of rules and a keen desire to learn, all complexities will start making sense. When you work and practice with the set of letters and their associations with the dimensioning variables, things will start falling into their respectful places.

The following is a list of the dimensioning variables that apply to architectural dimensioning conventions and architectural dimensioning standards:

Dimensioning Variable	What it Changes	Default Value
DIMASO	Associative dimensioning	1 (On)
DIMSTYLE	Current dimension style	Standard
DIMASZ	Arrow size	3/16″
DIMDLE	Dimension line extension	0″
DIMDLI	Dimension line increment	3/8″
DIMSD1	Suppress first dimension line	Off
DIMSD2	Suppress second dimension line	Off
DIMSE1	Suppress the first extension line	Off
DIMSE2	Suppress the second extension line	Off
DIMCLRD	Dimension line color	0 (ByBlock)
DIMCEN	Center mark size	1/16″
DIMLWD	Dimension line lineweight	-2
DIMCLRE	Extension line color	0 (ByBlock)
DIMLWE	Extension line lineweight	-2
DIMEXE	Extension line extension	3/16″

(continued)

DIMEXO	Extension line offset	1/16″
DIMBLK	Arrowhead style	Closed/Filled
DIMBLK1	First arrowhead style	Closed/Filled
DIMBLK2	Second arrowhead style	Closed/Filled
DIMLDRBLK	Leader arrow	Closed/Filled
DIMSAH	Separate arrowhead style	Off
DIMTXSTY	Dimension text style	Standard
DIMCLRT	Dimension text color	0 (ByBlock)
DIMTXT	Text height	3/16″
DIMTFAC	Fraction and tolerance text height scaling factor	1.00
DIMTAD	Vertical position of dimension text	0
DIMJUST	Horizontal text positioning	0
DIMGAP	Gap from dimension line to text	3/32″
DIMTIH	Text inside align	On
DIMTOH	Text outside align	On
DIMTVP	Text vertical position	0
DIMTIX	Place text inside extensions	Off
DIMATFIT	Fit arrowheads and text	3
DIMSOXD	Suppress outside extension dimensions	Off
DIMTMOVE	Dimension text movement	0
DIMSCALE	Overall scale factor	1
DIMUPT	User-positioned text	Off
DIMTOFL	Force line inside extension lines	0
DIMLUNIT	Dimension linear unit	2
DIMDEC	Unit precision	4
DIMFRAC	Fraction format	0
DIMDSEP	Decimal separator	.
DIMRND	Round off	0
DIMPOST	Prefix and suffix	.
DIMLFAC	Length scale	1
DIMZIN	Zero suppression	0
DIMAUNIT	Angle format	0
DIMADEC	Angle precision	0
DIMAZIN	Angle zero suppression	0
DIMALT	Alternate units	0
DIMALTZ	Alternate zeros	0
DIMALTD	Alternate precision	2
DIMALTF	Alternate scale factor	25.4000
DIMALTU	Alternate units format	2
DIMALTRND	Alternate round off	0″
DIMAPOST	Alternate prefix and suffix	—

AIA (256-Color) Layers

The following is a list of architectural layers found in the AIA CAD Layer Guidelines. The color numbers are taken from the Architectural Desktop Layer Key Style Properties dialog box.

Layer Name	Description	Descipline	Major	Minor	Color #No.
0	Default	—	—	—	0
A-Detl-Iden	Detail marks	A	Detl	Iden	111
A-Anno-Note	Notes and leaders	A	Anno	Note	211
A-Anno-Revs	Revisions	A	Anno	Revs	213
A-Sect-Iden	Section marks	A	Sect	Iden	111
A-Anno-Symb	Annotation marks	A	Anno	Symb	111
A-Flor-Appl	Appliances	A	Flor	Appl	150
A-Anno-Nplt	Cameras (Nonplotting)	A	Anno	Nplt	7
A-Flor-Case	Casework	A	Flor	Case	10
A-Flor-Case-Iden	Casework tags	A	Flor	Case	11
A-Clng-Grid	Ceiling grids	A	Clng	Grid	232
A-Clng	Ceiling objects	A	Clng	—	150
A-Cols	Columns	A	Cols	—	110
A-Comm	Communication	A	Comm	—	150
A-Ctrl-Devc	Control systems	A	Ctrl	Devc	152
A-Anno-Dims	Dimensions	A	Anno	Dims	221
A-Door	Doors	A	Door	—	150
A-Door-Iden	Door tags	A	Door	Iden	21
A-Strm	Drainage	A	Strm	—	190
A-Lite	Electric	A	Lite	—	140
A-Lite-Iden	Electrical tags	A	Lite	Iden	141
A-Flor-Evtr	Elevators	A	Flor	Evtr	232
A-Eqpm	Equipment	A	Eqpm	—	90
A-Eqpm-Iden	Equipment tags	A	Eqpm	Iden	101
A-Clng-Iden	Ceiling tags	A	Clng	Iden	11
Ap-Flor-Iden	Finish tags	A	Flor	Iden	11
A-Prot-Eqpm	Fire system equipment	A	Prot	Eqpm	90
A-Furn	Furniture	A	Furn	—	10
A-Furn-Iden	Furniture tags	A	Furn	Iden	11
A-Grid-Iden	Column grid tags	A	Grid	Iden	171
A-Grid-Layo	Layout grids	A	Grid	Layo	193
A-Lite-Clng	Ceiling lighting	A	Lite	Clng	120
A-Lite-Wall	Wall lighting	A	Lite	Wall	142
A-Elev-Symb	People elevation symbols	A	Elev	Symb	190
A-Flor-Pfix	Plumbing fixtures	A	Flor	Pfix	140
A-Plnt	Plants—outdoor	A	Plnt	—	82
A-Furn-Plnt	Plants—indoor	A	Furn	Plnt	92
A-Powr-Wall	Electrical power	A	Powr	Wall	130
A-Pkng	Parking symbols	A	Pkng	—	190
A-Wall-Open	Wall openings	A	Wall	Open	172
A-Roof	Roofs	A	Roof	—	20

(continued)

A-Area-Iden	Room tags	A	Area	Iden	131
A-Area-Bdry	Space boundaries	A	Area	Bdry	140
A-Area-Spce	Space objects	A	Area	Spce	34
A-Furn-Char-Iden	Seating tags (chairs)	A	Furn	Char	11
A-Sect	Section objects	A	Sect	—	242
A-Site	Site	A	Site	—	20
A-Flor-Strs	Stairs	A	Flor	Strs	12
A-Flor-Hral	Stair handrails	A	Flor	Hral	242
A-Lite-Swch	Electrical switches	A	Lite	Swch	140
A-Anno-Ttlb	Border and title block	A	Anno	Ttlb	111
A-Flor-Spcl	Arch. Specialties	A	Flor	Spcl	190
A-Flor-Pfix-Iden	Toilet tags	A	Flor	Pfix	151
A-Site-Util	Site utilities	A	Site	Util	190
A-Pkng-Cars	Vehicles	A	Pkng	Cars	242
A-Wall	Walls	A	Wall	—	50
A-Wall-Fire	Fire wall patterning	A	Wall	Fire	14
A-Wall-Iden	Wall tags	A	Wall	Iden	201
A-Glaz	Windows	A	Glaz	—	92
A-Glaz-Iden	Windows tags	A	Glaz	Iden	91
A-Grid	Column grids	A	Grid	—	173
A-Anno-Legn	Schedules	A	Anno	Legn	171

Note: Layers A-Grid and A-Grid-Iden use Center2 linetype. Layers A-Wall-Fire and A-Grid-Layo use Dashed2 Linetype.

Index

The American Spirit

Selected and Edited with
Introduction and Commentary by

David M. Kennedy

Stanford University

Thomas A. Bailey

The American Spirit

United States History
as Seen by Contemporaries

Thirteenth Edition

David M. Kennedy
Thomas A. Bailey

Australia • Brazil • Mexico • Singapore • United Kingdom • United States

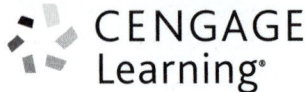

The American Spirit, United States History
as Seen by Contemporaries,
Thirteenth Edition

David M. Kennedy, Thomas A. Bailey

Product Director: Suzanne Jeans

Product Manager: Clint Attebery

Content Developer: Margaret McAndrew Beasley

Product Assistant: Andy Newton

Media Developer: Kate MacLean

IP Analyst: Alexandra Ricciardi

IP Project Manager: Brittani Morgan

Art and Cover Direction, Production
    Management, and Composition: Cenveo®
    Publisher Services

Manufacturing Planner: Sandee Milewski

Cover Image: Andrea Gingerich/Vetta/Getty
    Images

Library of Congress Control Number: 2014945090

ISBN: 978-1-305-10177-7

Cengage Learning
20 Channel Center Street
Boston, MA 02210
USA

Cengage Learning is a leading provider of customized learning solutions with
office locations around the globe, including Singapore, the United Kingdom,
Australia, Mexico, Brazil, and Japan. Locate your local office at
www.cengage.com/global.

Cengage Learning products are represented in Canada by Nelson Education, Ltd.

To learn more about Cengage Learning Solutions, visit **www.cengage.com.**

Purchase any of our products at your local college store or at our preferred
online store **www.cengagebrain.com.**

Printed in the United States of America
Print Number: 02   Print Year: 2015

About the Authors

David M. Kennedy is the Donald J. McLachlan Professor of History Emeritus at Stanford University, where he has taught for more than four decades. Born and raised in Seattle, he received his undergraduate education at Stanford and did his graduate training at Yale in American Studies, combining the fields of history, economics, and literature. His first book, *Birth Control in America: The Career of Margaret Sanger* (1970) was honored with both the Bancroft Prize and the John Gilmary Shea Prize. His study of World War I, *Over Here: The First World War and American Society* (1980) was a Pulitzer Prize finalist. In 1999 he published *Freedom from Fear: The American People in Depression and War, 1929–1945*, which won the Pulitzer Prize for

History, as well as the Francis Parkman Prize, the English-Speaking Union's Ambassador's Prize, and the Commonwealth Club of California's Gold Medal for Literature. At Stanford he has taught both undergraduate and graduate courses in American political, diplomatic, intellectual, and social history, and in American literature. He has received several teaching awards, including the Dean's Award for Distinguished Teaching. He has been a visiting professor at the University of Florence, Italy, and in 1995–1996 served as the Harmsworth Professor of American History at Oxford University. He has also served on the advisory board for the PBS television series *The American Experience* and as a consultant to several documentary films, including *The Great War*, *Cadillac Desert*, and *Woodrow Wilson*. From 1990 to 1995 he chaired the Test Development Committee for the Advanced Placement United States History examination. He is an elected Fellow of the American Academy of Arts and Sciences and of the American Philosophical Society and has served on the boards of the Pulitzer Prizes, the New York Historical Society, and the California Academy of Sciences. Married and the father of two sons and a daughter, in his leisure time he enjoys hiking, bicycling, river-rafting, sea-kayaking, flying, and fly-fishing.

Thomas A. Bailey (1903–1983) taught history for nearly forty years at Stanford University, his alma mater. Long regarded as one of the nation's leading historians of American diplomacy, he was honored by his colleagues in 1968 with election to the presidencies of both the Organization of American Historians and the Society for Historians of American Foreign Relations. He was the author, editor, or coeditor of some twenty books, but the work in which he took most pride was *The American Pageant* through which, he liked to say, he had taught American history to several million students.

Contents

17 *Manifest Destiny and Its Legacy, 1841–1848* 271

18 *Renewing the Sectional Struggle, 1848–1854* 290

19 *Drifting Toward Disunion, 1854–1861* 304

41 *The American People Face a New Century, 2001–2014*   840

Index   876

Maps

Preface

The documents collected in *The American Spirit* are meant to recapture the spirit of the American past as expressed by the men and women who lived it. Movers and shakers who tried to sculpt the contours of history share these pages with the humble folk whose lives were grooved by a course of events they sometimes only dimly understood, and not infrequently resented. In all cases, I have tried to present clear and pungent documents that combine intrinsic human interest with instructive historical perspectives. Students in American history courses will discover in these selections the satisfaction of working with primary documents—the raw human record from which meaningful historical accounts are assembled.

Taken together, the readings in the pages that follow convey a vivid sense of the wonder and the woe, the passion and the perplexity, with which Americans have confronted their lives and their times. *The American Spirit* seeks especially to stimulate reflection on the richness, variety, and complexity of American history. It also seeks to cultivate an appreciation of both the problems and the prejudices of people in the past. Accordingly, it devotes much attention to the clash of opinions and values, including the unpopular or unsuccessful side of controversial issues. It gives special emphasis to problems of social justice, including the plight of religious, ethnic, and racial minorities; the evolving status of women; the problems of the poor; the health of the American political system; environmental controversies; the responsibilities of world power; and the ongoing debate about the meaning of democracy itself.

I have revised this thirteenth edition of *The American Spirit* to make it fully compatible with its companion text, the sixteenth edition of *The American Pageant*. Every chapter in the *Pageant* has a corresponding chapter of the same title and scope in the *Spirit*. Instructors and students may use the two books together if they choose, but the chronological organization of the *Spirit* and its extensive explanatory materials make it usable with virtually any American history text. It may also be read on its own. Prologues for each chapter, headnotes for each document, explanatory inserts, and questions at the end of each headnote and at the end of every chapter will guide students in learning to appraise the documents thoughtfully and critically.

In many chapters, readers will find visual materials—cartoons, paintings, posters, charts, and tables, for example—that are treated as documents in their own right, fully equivalent in their evidentiary value and their historical interest to the more traditional verbal texts. These visual documents are here presented with the same kind of explanatory and other editorial apparatus that frames the conventional texts. It is my hope that students will thereby be encouraged to interrogate the past in new ways—not only by analyzing the written record, but by developing a critical attitude toward other kinds of historical evidence as well.

Like the sixteenth edition of *The American Pageant*, this edition of *The American Spirit* has been substantially revised to emphasize the interaction of social, economic, and cultural developments with political history. I have given special attention to identifying new documents that reflect the global context in which the American story has played out. Recent editions have incorporated much new material on Native Americans, the slave trade, indentured servants in the colonial era, disputes over governance and authority in the Revolutionary period, the environmental consequences of settlement and industrialization, the westward movement, women's history, diplomatic relations with Latin America and Asia, controversies about immigration, espionage in the Cold War era, the Reagan, Clinton, and both Bush presidencies, and the moral, religious, and political dilemmas confronting modern American society. In addition to those items, the current edition contains many new documents chosen to illustrate the ways in which Americans in past generations took sides—often bitterly opposed sides—in a variety of social, cultural, and political conflicts. In order to help students understand the American past in a global context, this edition also contains many sources that reflect international influences on American behavior, and tables comparing American economic and demographic trends with those in other countries.

In response to suggestions from users, I have made this edition considerably briefer than previous editions, consolidating it into a convenient single-volume format while still covering the full span of American history. Many lengthier documents have been eliminated, and I have compressed others so that their essential significance might be more accessible and useful to students. All this effort has been made with the help of Andy Hammann, whose grace and initiative have been indispensable.

The result of these revisions, I hope, is an up-to-date and more provocative *Spirit* whose documents will enable students to savor the taste and to feel the texture of the American past, while engaging themselves in its frequently emotional and sometimes explosive controversies and also coming to understand something of the planetary stage on which the American drama has unfolded.

D. M. K.
Stanford, California

1

New World Beginnings, 33,000 B.C.–A.D. 1769

> . . . May it not then be lawful now to attempt the possession of such lands as are void of Christian inhabitants, for Christ's sake?
>
> *William Strachey, c. 1620*

Prologue: Each ignorant of the other's existence, Native Americans and Europeans lived in isolation on their separate continents for millennia before Columbus's revolutionary voyage in 1492. For the Europeans, the Native Americans were both a wonder and a mystery, unexplained in either the Bible or the classical writings of the ancients that were being revived in the dawning age of the Renaissance. Learned European scholars earnestly debated whether the "Indians" were "true men." For their part, the Native Americans were no less baffled by the arrival of the Europeans, and they looked to their own folklore and traditions in order to understand this new race of people who had suddenly appeared among them. The Europeans, especially the Portuguese and the Spanish, had begun to penetrate and exploit Africa even before they made contact with the New World of the Americas. A fateful triangle was established as Europe drew slave labor from Africa to unlock and develop the riches of the Americas. Spain soon spread its empire over a vast American domain, exciting the jealousy of the English, who began in the late 1500s to launch their own imperial adventure in the New World.

A. The Native Americans

1. Juan Ginés de Sepúlveda Belittles the Indians (1547)[*]

Juan Ginés de Sepúlveda was an outstanding example of the "Renaissance man." A Spaniard who studied in the cradle of the Renaissance, Italy, he achieved fame as a theologian, philosopher, historian, and astronomer. When Emperor Charles V convened a debate in Valladolid, Spain, in 1550–1551 to determine the future of Spain's relationship with the American aborigines, he naturally turned to Sepúlveda as one of the most learned men in his realm. As a student of Aristotle, Sepúlveda relied heavily on the classical distinction between "civilized" Greeks and "barbarians." The selection that follows is not a transcript of the debate at Valladolid but an excerpt

---

[*]From *The Spanish Struggle for Justice in the Conquest of America*, by Lewis Hanke, pp. 122-123. Copyright © 1949 The University of Pennsylvania Press. Reprinted with permission of the University of Pennsylvania Press.

from Sepúlveda's book The Second Democrates, *published in 1547, in which he set forth his basic arguments. What differences does Sepúlveda emphasize between Europeans (especially Spaniards) and the Indians, and on what grounds does he assert the superiority of European culture?*

The Spanish have a perfect right to rule these barbarians of the New World and the adjacent islands, who in prudence, skill, virtues, and humanity are as inferior to the Spanish as children to adults, or women to men, for there exists between the two as great a difference as between savage and cruel races and the most merciful, between the most intemperate and the moderate and temperate and, I might even say, between apes and men.

You surely do not expect me to recall at length the prudence and talents of the Spanish. . . . And what can I say of the gentleness and humanity of our people, who, even in battle, after having gained the victory, put forth their greatest effort and care to save the greatest possible number of the conquered and to protect them from the cruelty of their allies?

Compare, then, these gifts of prudence, talent, magnanimity, temperance, humanity, and religion with those possessed by these half-men (*homunculi*), in whom you will barely find the vestiges of humanity, who not only do not possess any learning at all, but are not even literate or in possession of any monument to their history except for some obscure and vague reminiscences of several things put down in various paintings; nor do they have written laws, but barbarian institutions and customs. Well, then, if we are dealing with virtue, what temperance or mercy can you expect from men who are committed to all types of intemperance and base frivolity, and eat human flesh? And do not believe that before the arrival of the Christians they lived in that pacific kingdom of Saturn which the poets have invented; for, on the contrary, they waged continual and ferocious war upon one another with such fierceness that they did not consider a victory at all worthwhile unless they sated their monstrous hunger with the flesh of their enemies. . . . Furthermore these Indians were otherwise so cowardly and timid that they could barely endure the presence of our soldiers, and many times thousands upon thousands of them scattered in flight like women before Spaniards so few that they did not even number one hundred. . . . Although some of them show a certain ingenuity for various works of artisanship, this is no proof of human cleverness, for we can observe animals, birds, and spiders making certain structures which no human accomplishment can competently imitate. And as for the way of life of the inhabitants of New Spain and the province of Mexico, I have already said that these people are considered the most civilized of all, and they themselves take pride in their public institutions, because they have cities erected in a rational manner and kings who are not hereditary but elected by popular vote, and among themselves they carry on commercial activities in the manner of civilized peoples. But see how they deceive themselves, and how much I dissent from such an opinion, seeing, on the contrary, in these very institutions a proof of the crudity, the barbarity, and the natural slavery of these people; for having houses and some rational way of life and some sort of commerce is a thing which the necessities of nature itself induce, and only serves to prove that they are not bears or monkeys and are not totally lacking in reason. But on the other hand, they have established their nation in such a way that no one possesses anything individually, neither a house nor a field, which he can leave to his heirs in his will, for everything belongs to their masters whom, with improper nomenclature, they call kings, and by whose whims they live, more than by their own, ready to do the bidding and desire of these rulers and possessing no liberty. And the fulfillment of all this, not under the pressure of arms but in a voluntary and spontaneous way, is a definite sign of the servile and base soul of these barbarians. They have distributed the land in such a way that they themselves cultivate the royal and public holdings, one part belonging to the king, another to public feasts and sacrifices, with only a third reserved for their own advantage, and all this is done in such a way that they live as employees of the king, paying, thanks to him, exceedingly high taxes. . . . And if this type of servile and barbarous nation had not been to their liking and nature, it would have been easy for them, as it was not a hereditary monarchy, to take advantage of the death of a king in order to obtain a freer state and one more favorable to their interests; by not doing so, they have stated quite clearly that they have been born to slavery and not to civic and liberal life. Therefore, if you wish to reduce them, I do not say to our domination, but to a servitude a little less harsh, it will not be difficult for them to change their masters, and instead of the ones they had, who were barbarous and impious and inhuman, to accept the Christians, cultivators of human virtues and the true faith.

2. Bartolomé de Las Casas Defends the Indians (1552)*

The Dominican friar Bartolomé de Las Casas was Sepúlveda's great antagonist in the debates of 1550–1551 at Valladolid. As a young man, Las Casas had sailed with one of the first Spanish expeditions to the West Indies in 1502. A humane, sensitive priest, he was soon repelled by his countrymen's treatment of the native peoples of the New World. He eventually became bishop of Guatemala and devoted himself to reforming Spanish colonial policies, for which he was recognized as the "Protector of the Indians." His vivid and polemical account The Destruction of the Indies *did much to spread the "Black Legend" of Spain's brutal behavior in the New World—a legend not without substance, and eagerly exploited by the rival English. How are his views of the Indians different from those of Sepúlveda? What ideas did the two debaters share?*

Now if we shall have shown that among our Indians of the western and southern shores (granting that we call them barbarians and that they are barbarians) there are important kingdoms, large numbers of people who live settled lives in a society, great cities, kings, judges and laws, persons who engage in commerce, buying, selling, lending, and the other contracts of the law of nations, will it not stand proved that the Reverend Doctor Sepúlveda has spoken wrongly and viciously against peoples like these, either out of malice or ignorance of Aristotle's teaching, and, therefore, has falsely and perhaps irreparably slandered them before the entire world? From the fact that the Indians are barbarians it does not necessarily follow that they are incapable of government and have to be ruled by others, except to be taught about the Catholic faith and to be admitted to the holy sacraments. They are not ignorant, inhuman, or bestial. Rather, long before they had heard the word Spaniard they had properly organized states, wisely ordered by excellent laws, religion, and custom. They cultivated friendship and, bound together in common fellowship, lived in populous cities in which they wisely administered the affairs of both peace and war justly and equitably, truly governed by laws that at very many points surpass ours, and could have won the admiration of the sages of Athens. . . .

Now if they are to be subjugated by war because they are ignorant of polished literature, . . . I would like to hear Sepúlveda, in his cleverness, answer this question: Does he think that the war of the Romans against the Spanish was justified in order to free them from barbarism? And this question also: Did the Spanish wage an unjust war when they vigorously defended themselves against them?

Next, I call the Spaniards who plunder that unhappy people torturers. Do you think that the Romans, once they had subjugated the wild and barbaric peoples of Spain, could with secure right divide all of you among themselves, handing over so many head of both males and females as allotments to individuals? And do you then conclude that the Romans could have stripped your rulers of their authority and consigned all of you, after you had been deprived of your liberty, to wretched labors, especially in searching for gold and silver lodes and mining and refining the metals? . . . For God's sake and man's faith in him, is this the way to impose the yoke of Christ on Christian men? Is this the way to remove wild barbarism from the minds of barbarians? Is it not, rather, to act like thieves, cut-throats, and cruel plunderers and to drive the gentlest of people headlong into despair? The Indian race is not that barbaric, nor are they dull witted or stupid, but they are easy to teach and very talented in learning all the liberal arts, and very ready to accept, honor, and observe the Christian religion and correct their sins (as experience has taught) once priests have introduced them to the sacred mysteries and taught them the word of God. They have been endowed with excellent conduct, and before the coming of the Spaniards, as we have said, they had political states that were well founded on beneficial laws.

Furthermore, they are so skilled in every mechanical art that with every right they should be set ahead of all the nations of the known world on this score, so very beautiful in their skill and artistry are the things this people produces in the grace of its architecture, its painting, and its needlework. But Sepúlveda despises these mechanical arts, as if these things do not reflect inventiveness, ingenuity, industry, and right reason. For a mechanical art is an operative habit of the intellect that is usually defined as "the right way to make things, directing the acts of the reason, through which the artisan proceeds in orderly fashion, easily, and unerringly in the very act of reason." So these men are not stupid, Reverend Doctor. Their skillfully fashioned works of superior refinement awaken the admiration of all nations, because works proclaim a man's talent, for, as the poet says, the work commends the craftsman. Also, Prosper [of Aquitaine] says: "See, the maker is proclaimed by the wonderful signs of his works and the effects, too, sing of their author."

In the liberal arts that they have been taught up to now, such as grammar and logic, they are remarkably adept. With every kind of music they charm the ears of their audience with wonderful sweetness. They write skillfully and quite elegantly, so that most often we are at a loss to know whether the characters are handwritten or printed. . . .

The Indians are our brothers, and Christ has given his life for them. Why, then, do we persecute them with such inhuman savagery when they do not deserve such treatment? The past, because it cannot be undone, must be attributed to our weakness, provided that what has been taken unjustly is restored.

Finally, let all savagery and apparatus of war, which are better suited to Moslems than Christians, be done away with. Let upright heralds be sent to proclaim Jesus Christ in their way of life and to convey the attitudes of Peter and Paul. [The Indians] will embrace the teaching of the gospel, as I well know, for they are not stupid or barbarous but have a native sincerity and are simple, moderate, and meek, and, finally, such that I do not know whether there is any people readier to receive the gospel. Once they have embraced it, it is marvelous with what piety, eagerness, faith, and charity they obey Christ's precepts and venerate the sacraments. For they are docile and clever, and in their diligence and gifts of nature, they excel most peoples of the known world.

B. The Spanish in America

1. Hernán Cortés Conquers Mexico (1519–1526)[*]

In 1519 the Spanish conquistador Hernán Cortés landed in Mexico and quickly conquered the Aztecs, a powerful people who had long dominated their neighbors in the central Mexican highlands. In the passage below, Cortés, writing to his king in Spain, describes his first encounter with the Aztec ruler Moctezuma, as well as his efforts to suppress the religious practices of the Aztecs, especially those involving human sacrifice. What advantages did Cortés possess in his confrontation with the Aztecs? How did his own cultural background influence his treatment of the native people?

The Second Letter

The Second Despatch of Hernán Cortés to the Emperor: Sent from Segura de la Frontera on the 30th of October, 1520.

Very Great and Powerful, and Very Catholic Prince, Most Invincible Emperor, Our Lord . . .

We were received by that lord, Montezuma, with about two hundred chiefs, all barefooted, and dressed in a kind of livery, very rich, according to their custom, and some more so than others. They approached in two processions near the walls of the street, which is very broad, and straight, and beautiful, and very uniform from one end to the other, being about two thirds of a league long, and having, on both sides, very large houses, both dwelling places, and mosques. . . . When

---

[*]Fernando Cortes, *His Five Letters of Relation to the Emperor Charles V*, vol. 1, trans. Francis Augustus MacNutt (Cleveland, OH: The Arthur H. Clark Company, 1908), 233–236, 260–262.

I approached to speak to Montezuma, I took off a collar of pearls and glass dia-monds, that I wore, and put it on his neck, and, after we had gone through some of the streets, one of his servants came with two collars, wrapped in a cloth, which were made of coloured shells. These they esteem very much; and from each of the collars hung eight golden shrimps executed with great perfection and a span long. When he received them, he turned towards me, and put them on my neck, and again went on through the streets, as I have already indicated, until we came to a large and handsome house, which he had prepared for our reception. There he took me by the hand, and led me into a spacious room, in front of the court where we had entered, where he made me sit on a very rich platform, which had been ordered to be made for him, and told me to wait there; and then he went away.

After a little while, when all the people of my company were distributed to their quarters, he returned with many valuables of gold and silver work, and five or six thousand pieces of rich cotton stuffs, woven, and embroidered in divers ways.

Within this great mosque, there are three halls wherein stand the principal idols of marvellous grandeur in size, and much decorated with carved figures, both of stone and wood; and within these halls there are other chapels, entered by very small doors, and which have no light, and nobody but the religious are admitted to them. Within these are the images and figures of the idols, although, as I have said, there are many outside.

The principal idols in which they have the most faith and belief I overturned from their seats, and rolled down the stairs, and I had those chapels, where they kept them, cleansed, for they were full of blood from the sacrifices; and I set up images of Our Lady, and other Saints in them, which grieved Montezuma, and the natives not a little. At first they told me not to do it, for, if it became known through-out the town, the people would rise against me, as they believed that these idols gave them all their temporal goods, and, in allowing them to be ill-treated, they would be angered, and give nothing, and would take away all the fruits of the soil, and cause the people to die of want. I made them understand by the interpreters how deceived they were in putting their hope in idols, made of unclean things by their own hands, and I told them that they should know there was but one God, the Universal Lord of all, who had created the heavens, and earth, and all things else, and them, and us, who was without beginning, and immortal; that they should adore, and believe in Him, and not in any creature, or thing. I told them all I knew of these matters, so as to win them from their idolatries, and bring them to a knowl-edge of God, Our Lord; and all of them, especially Montezuma, answered that they had already told me they were not natives of this country, and that it was a long time since their forefathers had come to it, therefore they might err in some points of their belief, as it was so long since they left their native land, whilst I, who had recently arrived, should know better than they what they should believe, and hold; and if I would tell them, and explain to them, they would do what I told them, as being for the best. Montezuma and many chiefs of the city remained with me until the idols were taken away and the chapels cleansed, and the images put up, and they all wore happy faces. I forbade them to sacrifice human beings to the idols, as they were accustomed to do, for besides its being very hateful to God, Your Majesty had also prohibited it by your laws, and commanded that those who killed should be put to death. Henceforth they abolished it, and, in all the time I remained in the city, never again were they seen to sacrifice any human creature.

The figures of the idols, in which those people believe, exceed in size the body of a large man. They are made of a mass of all the seeds and vegetables which they eat, ground up and mixed with one another, and kneaded with the hearts' blood of human beings, whose breasts are opened when alive, the hearts being removed, and, with the blood which comes out, is kneaded the flour, making the quantity necessary to construct a great statue. When these are finished the priests offer them more hearts, which have likewise been sacrificed, and besmear the faces with the blood. The idols are dedicated to different things, as was the custom of the heathen who anciently honoured their gods. Thus, to obtain favours in war these people have one idol, for harvests another, and for everything in which they desire any good, they have idols whom they honour and serve.

2. Aztec Chroniclers Describe the Spanish Conquest of Mexico (1519)[*]

The Spanish Franciscan friar Bernardino de Sahagún arrived in Mexico in 1529, swiftly mastered the indigenous language Nahuatl, and proceeded to gather from his Aztec informants a history of their civilization. In the selection that follows, one of Sahagún's witnesses describes the encounter between Moctezuma and Cortés from the Aztec perspective. How does this account differ, either factually or interpretively, from Cortés's description?

The Spaniards arrived in Xoloco, near the entrance to Tenochtitlan. That was the end of the march, for they had reached their goal.

Motecuhzoma now arrayed himself in his finery, preparing to go out to meet them. The other great princes also adorned their persons, as did the nobles and their chieftains and knights. They all went out together to meet the strangers.

They brought trays heaped with the finest flowers—the flower that resembles a shield; the flower shaped like a heart; in the center, the flower with the sweetest aroma; and the fragrant yellow flower, the most precious of all. They also brought garlands of flowers, and ornaments for the breast, and necklaces of gold, necklaces hung with rich stones, necklaces fashioned in the petatillo style.

Thus Motecuhzoma went out to meet them, there in Huitzillan. He presented many gifts to the Captain and his commanders, those who had come to make war. He showered gifts upon them and hung flowers around their necks; he gave them necklaces of flowers and bands of flowers to adorn their breasts; he set garlands of flowers upon their heads. Then he hung the gold necklaces around their necks and gave them presents of every sort as gifts of welcome.

When Motecuhzoma had given necklaces to each one, Cortes asked him: "Are you Motecuhzoma? Are you the king? Is it true that you are the king Motecuhzoma?"

---

[*]From *The Broken Spears* by Miguel Leon-Portilla. © 1962, 1990 by Miguel Leon-Portilla. Expanded and Updated Edition © 1992 by Miguel Leon-Portilla.

And the king said: "Yes, I am Motecuhzoma." Then he stood up to welcome Cortes; he came forward, bowed his head low and addressed him in these words: "Our lord, you are weary. The journey has tired you, but now you have arrived on the earth. You have come to your city, Mexico. You have come here to sit on your throne, to sit under its canopy.

"The kings who have gone before, your representatives, guarded it and preserved it for your coming. The kings Itzcoatl, Motecuhzoma the Elder, Axayacatl, Tizoc and Ahuitzol ruled for you in the City of Mexico. The people were protected by their swords and sheltered by their shields.

"Do the kings know the destiny of those they left behind, their posterity? If only they are watching! If only they can see what I see!

"No, it is not a dream. I am not walking in my sleep. I am not seeing you in my dreams. . . . I have seen you at last! I have met you face to face! I was in agony for five days, for ten days, with my eyes fixed on the Region of the Mystery. And now you have come out of the clouds and mists to sit on your throne again.

"This was foretold by the kings who governed your city, and now it has taken place. You have come back to us; you have come down from the sky. Rest now, and take possession of your royal houses. Welcome to your land, my lords!"

When Motecuhzoma had finished, La Malinche translated his address into Spanish so that the Captain could understand it. Cortes replied in his strange and savage tongue, speaking first to La Malinche: "Tell Motecuhzoma that we are his friends. There is nothing to fear. We have wanted to see him for a long time, and now we have seen his face and heard his words. Tell him that we love him well and that our hearts are contented."

Then he said to Motecuhzoma: "We have come to your house in Mexico as friends. There is nothing to fear."

La Malinche translated this speech and the Spaniards grasped Motecuhzoma's hands and patted his back to show their affection for him. . . .

The Spaniards examined everything they saw. They dismounted from their horses, and mounted them again, and dismounted again, so as not to miss anything of interest. . . .

When the Spaniards entered the Royal House, they placed Motecuhzoma under guard and kept him under their vigilance. They also placed a guard over Itzcuauhtzin, but the other lords were permitted to depart.

Then the Spaniards fired one of their cannons, and this caused great confusion in the city. The people scattered in every direction; they fled without rhyme or reason; they ran off as if they were being pursued. It was as if they had eaten the mushrooms that confuse the mind, or had seen some dreadful apparition. They were all overcome by terror, as if their hearts had fainted. And when night fell, the panic spread through the city and their fears would not let them sleep.

In the morning the Spaniards told Motecuhzoma what they needed in the way of supplies: tortillas, fried chickens, hens' eggs, pure water, firewood and charcoal. Also: large, clean cooking pots, water jars, pitchers, dishes and other pottery. Motecuhzoma ordered that it be sent to them. The chiefs who received this order were angry with the king and no longer revered or respected him. But they furnished the Spaniards with all the provisions they needed—food, beverages and water, and fodder for the horses. . . .

The Aztecs begged permission of their king to hold the fiesta of Huitzilopochtli. The Spaniards wanted to see this fiesta to learn how it was celebrated. A delegation of the celebrants came to the palace where Motecuhzoma was a prisoner, and when their spokesman asked his permission, he granted it to them. . . .

On the evening before the fiesta of Toxcatl, the celebrants began to model a statue of Huitzilopochtli. They gave it such a human appearance that it seemed the body of a living man. Yet they made the statue with nothing but a paste made of the ground seeds of the chicalote, which they shaped over an armature of sticks.

When the statue was finished, they dressed it in rich feathers, and they painted crossbars over and under its eyes. They also clipped on its earrings of turquoise mosaic; these were in the shape of serpents, with gold rings hanging from them. Its nose plug, in the shape of an arrow, was made of gold and was inlaid with fine stones.

They placed the magic headdress of hummingbird feathers on its head. They also adorned it with an *anecuyotl*, which was a belt made of feathers, with a cone at the back. Then they hung around its neck an ornament of yellow parrot feathers, fringed like the locks of a young boy. Over this they put its nettle-leaf cape, which was painted black and decorated with five clusters of eagle feathers.

Next they wrapped it in its cloak, which was painted with skulls and bones, and over this they fastened its vest. The vest was painted with dismembered human parts: skulls, ears, hearts, intestines, torsos, breasts, hands and feet. They also put on its *maxtlatl*, or loincloth, which was decorated with images of dissevered limbs and fringed with amate paper. This *maxtlatl* was painted with vertical stripes of bright blue.

They fastened a red paper flag at its shoulder and placed on its head what looked like a sacrificial flint knife. This too was made of red paper; it seemed to have been steeped in blood.

The statue carried a *tehuehuelli*, a bamboo shield decorated with four clusters of fine eagle feathers. The pendant of this shield was blood-red, like the knife and the shoulder flag. The statue also carried four arrows.

Finally, they put the wristbands on its arms. These bands, made of coyote skin, were fringed with paper cut into little strips.

Early the next morning, the statue's face was uncovered by those who had been chosen for that ceremony. They gathered in front of the idol in single file and offered it gifts of food, such as round seedcakes or perhaps human flesh. But they did not carry it up to its temple on top of the pyramid.

All the young warriors were eager for the fiesta to begin. They had sworn to dance and sing with all their hearts, so that the Spaniards would marvel at the beauty of the rituals.

The procession began, and the celebrants filed into the temple patio to dance the Dance of the Serpent. When they were all together in the patio, the songs and the dance began. Those who had fasted for twenty days and those who had fasted for a year were in command of the others; they kept the dancers in file with their pine wands. (If anyone wished to urinate, he did not stop dancing, but simply opened his clothing at the hips and separated his clusters of heron feathers.)

If anyone disobeyed the leaders or was not in his proper place they struck him on the hips and shoulders. Then they drove him out of the patio, beating him and shoving him from behind. They pushed him so hard that he sprawled to the ground, and they dragged him outside by the ears. No one dared to say a word about this punishment, for those who had fasted during the year were feared and venerated; they had earned the exclusive title "Brothers of Huitzilopochtli."

The great captains, the bravest warriors, danced at the head of the files to guide the others. The youths followed at a slight distance. Some of the youths wore their hair gathered into large locks, a sign that they had never taken any captives. Others carried their headdresses on their shoulders; they had taken captives, but only with help.

Then came the recruits, who were called "the young warriors." They had each captured an enemy or two. The others called to them: "Come, comrades, show us how brave you are! Dance with all your hearts!"

At this moment in the fiesta, when the dance was loveliest and when song was linked to song, the Spaniards were seized with an urge to kill the celebrants. They all ran forward, armed as if for battle. They closed the entrances and passageways, all the gates of the patio: the Eagle Gate in the lesser palace, the Gate of the Canestalk and the Gate of the Serpent of Mirrors. They posted guards so that no one could escape, and then rushed into the Sacred Patio to slaughter the celebrants. They came on foot, carrying their swords and their wooden or metal shields.

They ran in among the dancers, forcing their way to the place where the drums were played. They attacked the man who was drumming and cut off his arms. Then they cut off his head, and it rolled across the floor.

They attacked all the celebrants, stabbing them, spearing them, striking them with their swords. They attacked some of them from behind, and these fell instantly to the ground with their entrails hanging out. Others they beheaded: they cut off their heads, or split their heads to pieces.

They struck others in the shoulders, and their arms were torn from their bodies. They wounded some in the thigh and some in the calf. They slashed others in the abdomen, and their entrails all spilled to the ground. Some attempted to run away, but their intestines dragged as they ran; they seemed to tangle their feet in their own entrails. No matter how they tried to save themselves, they could find no escape.

Some attempted to force their way out, but the Spaniards murdered them at the gates. Others climbed the walls, but they could not save themselves. Those who ran into the communal houses were safe there for a while; so were those who lay down among the victims and pretended to be dead. But if they stood up again, the Spaniards saw them and killed them.

The blood of the warriors flowed like water and gathered into pools. The pools widened, and the stench of blood and entrails filled the air. The Spaniards ran into the communal houses to kill those who were hiding. They ran everywhere and searched everywhere; they invaded every room, hunting and killing.

3. Francisco Coronado Explores the American Southwest (1541)[*]

In 1540–1542 Francisco Coronado led a Spanish expedition from Mexico into the present-day territory of Arizona and New Mexico and as far east as Kansas. Seeking fabled cities of gold, he found instead the modest villages of the Pueblo Indians, who urged him to continue eastward to a region they called Quivira. As he struggled across the vast and forbidding American wilderness, the truth gradually dawned on Coronado that Quivira held no more gold than did the land of the Pueblos. How does Coronado describe the landscape? How does his cultural background influence what he sees and how he estimates its usefulness?

While I was engaged in the conquest and pacification of the natives of this province, some Indians who were natives of other provinces beyond these had told me that in their country there were much larger villages and better houses than those of the natives of this country, and that they had lords who ruled them, who were served with dishes of gold, and other very magnificent things; and although, as I wrote Your Majesty, I did not believe it before I had set eyes on it, because it was the report of Indians and given for the most part by means of signs, yet as the report appeared to me to be very fine and that it was important that it should be investigated for Your Majesty's service, I determined to go and see it with the men I have here. I started from this province on the 23d of last April, for the place where the Indians wanted to guide me.

After nine days' march I reached some plains, so vast that I did not find their limit anywhere that I went, although I traveled over them for more than 300 leagues. And I found such a quantity of cows in these, of the kind that I wrote Your Majesty about, which they have in this country, that it is impossible to number them, for while I was journeying through these plains, until I returned to where I first found them, there was not a day that I lost sight of them. And after seventeen days' march I came to a settlement of Indians who are called Querechos, who travel around with these cows, who do not plant, and who eat the raw flesh and drink the blood of the cows they kill, and they tan the skins of the cows, with which all the people of this country dress themselves here. They have little field tents made of the hides of the cows, tanned and greased, very well made, in which they live while they travel around near the cows, moving with these. They have dogs which they load, which carry their tents and poles and belongings. These people have the best figures of any that I have seen in the Indies. They could not give me any account of the country where the guides were taking me. I traveled five days more as the guides wished to lead me, until I reached some plains, with no more landmarks than as if we had been swallowed up in the sea, where they strayed about, because there was not a stone, nor a bit of rising ground, nor a tree, nor a shrub, nor anything to go by. . . .

It was the Lord's pleasure that, after having journeyed across these deserts seventy-seven days, I arrived at the province they call Quivira, to which the guides were conducting me, and where they had described to me houses of stone, with

---

[*]George Parker Winship, trans. and ed., *The Journey of Coronado, 1540–1542* (New York: A. S. Barnes, 1904), pp. 213–220.

many stories; and not only are they not of stone, but of straw, but the people in them are as barbarous as all those whom I have seen and passed before this. . . .

The province of Quivira is 950 leagues from Mexico. Where I reached it, it is in the fortieth degree. The country itself is the best I have ever seen for producing all the products of Spain, for besides the land itself being very fat and black and being very well watered by the rivulets and springs and rivers, I found prunes like those of Spain [*or* I found everything they have in Spain] and nuts and very good sweet grapes and mulberries. I have treated the natives of this province, and all the others whom I found wherever I went, as well as was possible, agreeably to what Your Majesty had commanded, and they have received no harm in any way from me or from those who went in my company. I remained twenty-five days in this province of Quivira, so as to see and explore the country and also to find out whether there was anything beyond which could be of service to Your Majesty, because the guides who had brought me had given me an account of other provinces beyond this. And what I am sure of is that there is not any gold nor any other metal in all that country, and the other things of which they had told me are nothing but little villages, and in many of these they do not plant anything and do not have any houses except of skins and sticks, and they wander around with the cows; so that the account they gave me was false, because they wanted to persuade me to go there with the whole force, believing that as the way was through such uninhabited deserts, and from the lack of water, they would get us where we and our horses would die of hunger. And the guides confessed this, and said they had done it by the advice and orders of the natives of these provinces.

4. Don Juan de Oñate Conquers New Mexico (1599)*

Don Juan de Oñate, inspired by tales of Coronado's expedition some fifty years earlier, led a heavily armed expedition into present-day New Mexico in 1598 and proceeded to impose Spanish rule on the native Pueblo Indians. The Indians of the village of Acoma inflicted a humiliating defeat on Oñate's forces on December 4, 1599, prompting a swift and harsh reprisal from the Spanish. In the selection that follows, Oñate instructs his officers on how to deal with the Indians at Acoma (eventually they severed one foot of every adult male survivor). What motives prompted Oñate? In what ways did he try to promote the cause of Christianity among the Indians? How did he justify his action?

Instructions to you, Vicente de Zaldívar, sargento mayor [sergeant-major] of the expedition to New Mexico, my lieutenant governor and captain general for the punishment of the pueblo of Acoma for having killed Don Juan de Zaldívar Oñate, my maese de campo [second-in-command], ten other captains and soldiers, and two servants, which resulted in disrupting the general peace of the land, which is now in serious danger of revolting if the offenders are not properly punished, as their vileness would be emulated by other savages whenever they wished; in

---

*From *Don Juan de Onate: Colonizer of New Mexico, 1595-1628*, by George P. Hammond and Agapito Rey, pp. 456-459. Copyright © 1953 The University of New Mexico Press.

this situation one can see the obvious danger of slavery or death for the innocent people entrusted to my protection and care by his majesty; these innocent ones are the ministers of the holy gospel, whom the Indians would not spare any more than they did others in the past, and they would also kill the many women and children in the expedition, who would suffer without cause once the natives overcame their fear of rebelling. The greatest force we possess at present to defend our friends and ourselves is the prestige of the Spanish nation, by fear of which the Indians have been kept in check. Should they lose this fear it would inevitably follow also that the teaching of the holy gospel would be hindered, which I am under obligation to prevent, as this is the main purpose for which I came. For the gospel is the complete remedy and guide for their abominable sins, some of them nefarious and against nature. For the following just cases, such as general peace in the land, protection of the innocent, punishment of those who transgress against their king and his ministers and against their obligations to him as ruler of these Indies, to whom they voluntarily swore obedience, and furthermore to obtain redress for such serious offenses as the killing of such worthy persons, disregarding the recovery of the goods they took from us, and finally to remove such pernicious obstacles and open the way for the spreading of the holy gospel, I have determined that in the discharge of your commission to the pueblo of Acoma, you should make more use of royal clemency than of the severity that the case demands, take into serious consideration the stupidity (*brutalidad*) and incapacity of the Indians, if that is what they showed in this case rather than malice, and observe the following instructions:

First: On receiving your commission and the instructions that follow, you will acknowledge receipt of them before the secretary. With these you will have sufficient authority for what you are to do and you must bind yourself to observe and obey exactly what you are ordered, as we expect from you.

Since the good success of the undertaking depends on the pleasure of God our Lord in directing you to appropriate and effective methods, it is right that you should seek to prevent public or private offenses to Him in the expedition. You must exercise particular care in this respect, admonishing and punishing in exemplary fashion those who cause them, so that one may readily see that you take special interest in this matter.

You will proceed over the shortest route to the pueblo of Acoma, with all the soldiers and war equipment. At the places and pueblos that you pass through on the way you will treat the natives well and not allow any harm to be done them, and to this end you may issue whatever proclamations that seem desirable or necessary.

When you come to the pueblo of Acoma, you must weigh very carefully and calmly the strength of the Indians, plant at once your artillery and musketry at the places that seem most practical, and assign the captains and soldiers to their posts in battle formation, without making any noise or firing an harquebus [heavy musket].

This done, you will, in the presence of Juan Velarde, my secretary, and with the help of Don Tomás and Don Cristóbal, Indian interpreters who are expert in the language, or with the aid of any other interpreters that you may deem suitable, summon the Indians of Acoma to accept peace, once, twice, and thrice, and urge them to abandon their resistance, lay down their arms, and submit to the authority of the king our lord, since they have already rendered obedience to him as his vassals.

You will ask the people of Acoma to surrender the leaders responsible for the uprising, and the murderers, assuring them that they will be justly dealt with.

The Acomas must abandon at once the fortified place in which they live and move down into the valley, where the ministers of the holy gospel who were sent to these kingdoms and provinces by his majesty for this purpose may be able to teach them more easily the matters of our holy Catholic faith.

The Indians must deliver up the bodies of those killed, their personal belongings and weapons, and the horseshoes and other iron that they had dug up three leagues from the pueblo. You must record their answers before my secretary in the presence of as many as can conveniently be brought together to hear them. If the Indians should do all that is prescribed above and come down and submit peacefully, you will establish them in the valley at a safe place where they will not run away and disappear. You will keep them under strict guard and bring them before me in order that we may hear their pleas and administer justice.

After the Indians have been removed from the pueblo and placed under custody, you will send back to the pueblo as many soldiers as you deem necessary, burn it to the ground, and leave no stone on stone, so that the Indians may never be able again to inhabit it as an impregnable fortress.

If the Indians are entrenched and should have assembled many people and you think there is danger of losing your army in trying to storm the pueblo, you will refrain from doing so, for there would be less harm in postponing the punishment for the time being than in risking the people with you and those left here for the protection of the church of God, its ministers, and me. In this matter you must exercise the utmost care and foresight.

If the people should have deserted the pueblo, you will burn it to the ground and destroy it. You will then consult with the council of war as to whether or not it is desirable to pursue the natives, since the council must consider the matter. This must be handled with much discretion.

If God should be so merciful as to grant us victory, you will arrest all of the people, young and old, without sparing anyone. Inasmuch as we have declared war on them without quarter, you will punish all those of fighting age as you deem best, as a warning to everyone in this kingdom. All of those you execute you will expose to public view at the places you think most suitable, as a salutary example. If you should want to show lenience after they have been arrested, you should seek all possible means to make the Indians believe that you are doing so at the request of the friar with your forces. In this manner they will recognize the friars as their benefactors and protectors and come to love and esteem them, and to fear us. To execute this punishment as you may see fit, I grant you the same powers I myself hold from his majesty.

And since all matters properly discussed and thought out lead to a happy and successful end, you already know that I have named as members of the council of war of this expedition, Alonso Sánchez, contador of the royal treasury; Diego de Zubía, captain of cavalry and purveyor general; Marcos Farfán de los Godos, captain of my guard; Captain Gaspar de Villagrán, procurator general; Pablo de Aguilar Inojosa, captain of cavalry; and Gerónimo Márquez, captain of artillery. All six of them are men of much experience and well informed in all that pertains to warfare.

You will hold councils of war whenever it seems desirable to you, to them, or to the majority of them. Whatever is agreed upon by all or by the majority in council must be observed. The councils held are to be attended by my secretary who will record what may be determined. I have given these men the appropriate commissions as members of the council of war.

All of the aforesaid you will fulfill with proper diligence and care in order that God and his majesty may be served, and this offense punished.

Stamped with the seal of my office at the pueblo of San Juan Bautista on January 11, 1599. Don Juan de Oñate. By order of the governor, Juan Gutiérrez Bocanegra, secretary.

C. The African Slave Trade

1. The Conscience of a Slave Trader (1694)[*]

In September 1693, the thirty-six-gun ship Hannibal, *commanded by Thomas Phillips, set sail from England for West Africa, where Phillips bought slaves for sale on the West Indian sugar island of Barbados. What does Phillips's account reveal about the involvement of the Africans themselves in the slave trade? What was Phillips's own attitude toward the Africans? How could he reconcile such sentiments with the brutal business in which he was engaged?*

We mark'd the slaves we had bought in the breast, or shoulder, with a hot iron, having the letter of the ship's name on it, the place being before anointed with a little palm oil, which caus'd but little pain, the mark being usually well in four or five days, appearing very plain and white after.

When we had purchas'd to the number of 50 or 60 we would send them aboard, there being a cappasheir, intitled the captain of the slaves, whose care it was to secure them to the water-side, and see them all off; and if in carrying to the marine any were lost, he was bound to make them good, to us, the captain of the trunk being oblig'd to do the like, if any ran away while under his care, for after we buy them we give him charge of them till the captain of the slaves comes to carry them away: These are two officers appointed by the king for this purpose, to each of which every ship pays the value of a slave in what goods they like best for their trouble, when they have done trading; and indeed they discharg'd their duty to us very faithfully, we not having lost one slave thro' their neglect in 1300 we bought here.

There is likewise a captain of the sand, who is appointed to take care of the merchandize we have come ashore to trade with, that the negroes do not plunder them, we being often forced to leave goods a whole night on the sea shore, for want of porters to bring them up; but notwithstanding his care and authority, we often came by the loss, and could have no redress.

---

[*]Elizabeth Donnan, *Documents Illustrative of the History of the Slave Trade to America* (Washington, D.C.: The Carnegie Institution, 1930), vol 1, pp. 402-403.

When our slaves were come to the seaside, our canoes were ready to carry them off to the longboat, if the sea permitted, and she convey'd them aboard ship, where the men were all put in irons, two and two shackled together, to prevent their mutiny, or swimming ashore.

The negroes are so wilful and loth to leave their own country, that they have often leap'd out of the canoes, boat and ship, into the sea, and kept under water till they were drowned, to avoid being taken up and saved by our boats, which pursued them; they having a more dreadful apprehension of Barbadoes than we can have of hell, tho' in reality they live much better there than in their own country; but home is home, etc: we have likewise seen divers of them eaten by the sharks, of which a prodigious number kept about the ships in this place, and I have been told will follow her hence to Barbadoes, for the dead negroes that are thrown overboard in the passage. I am certain in our voyage there we did not want the sight of some every day, but that they were the same I can't affirm.

We had about 12 negroes did wilfully drown themselves, and others starv'd themselves to death; for 'tis their belief that when they die they return home to their own country and friends again.

I have been inform'd that some commanders have cut off the legs and arms of the most wilful, to terrify the rest, for they believe if they lose a member, they cannot return home again: I was advis'd by some of my officers to do the same, but I could not be perswaded to entertain the least thought of it, much less put in practice such barbarity and cruelty to poor creatures, who, excepting their want of christianity and true religion (their misfortune more than fault) are as much the works of God's hands, and no doubt as dear to him as ourselves; nor can I imagine why they should be despis'd for their colour, being what they cannot help, and the effect of the climate it has pleas'd God to appoint them. I can't think there is any intrinsick value in one colour more than another, nor that white is better than black, only we think so because we are so, and are prone to judge favourably in our own case, as well as the blacks, who in odium of the colour, say, the devil is white, and so paint him. . . .

The present king often, when ships are in a great strait for slaves, and cannot be supply'd otherwise, will sell 3 or 400 of his wives to compleat their number, but we always pay dearer for his slaves than those bought of the cappasheirs.

2. A Slave Is Taken to Barbados (c. 1750)*

Olauda Equiano was a remarkable African, born in 1745 in present-day Nigeria. After his capture as a boy by slave traders, he was taken to Barbados. He eventually bought his freedom and became a leading spokesperson for the cause of antislavery. His book The Interesting Narrative of the Life of Olaudah Equiano or Gustavus Vassa the African, *from which the following selection is taken, was a best seller in both Europe and America in the late eighteenth and early nineteenth centuries.*

---

*From *Equiano's Travels: His Autobiography, The Interesting Narrative of the Life of Olaudah Equiano or Gustavus Vassa the African.*

Although Equiano's narrative dates from nearly three centuries after the beginnings of large-scale European slave trading in Africa, it affords a unique perspective on the experience of slavery through the eyes of an African slave. Equiano's account is probably faithful, at least psychologically, to the experiences of millions of Africans in the centuries before him. How does Equiano make sense of his new surroundings, particularly the sailing vessels he sees for the first time? What differences does he see between slavery as practiced in Africa and as practiced in Barbados? What is the most difficult part of his experience as a slave?

I grew up till I was turned the age of 11, when an end was put to my happiness in the following manner. . . . One day, when all our people were gone out to their works as usual and only I and my dear sister were left to mind the house, two men and a woman got over our walls, and in a moment seized us both, and without giving us time to cry out or make resistance they stopped our mouths and ran off with us into the nearest wood. . . . The next day proved a day of greater sorrow than I had yet experienced, for my sister and I were then separated while we lay clasped in each other's arms. It was in vain that we besought them not to part us; she was torn from me and immediately carried away, while I was left in a state of distraction not to be described. I cried and grieved continually, and for several days I did not eat anything but what they forced into my mouth. At length, after many days' travelling, during which I had often changed masters, I got into the hands of a chieftain in a very pleasant country. This man had two wives and some children, and they all used me extremely well and did all they could to comfort me, particularly the first wife, who was something like my mother. Although I was a great many days' journey from my father's house, yet these people spoke exactly the same language with us. . . .

I was now carried to the left of the sun's rising, through many different countries and a number of large woods. . . .

The first object which saluted my eyes when I arrived on the coast was the sea, and a slave ship which was then riding at anchor and waiting for its cargo. These filled me with astonishment, which was soon converted into terror when I was carried on board. I was immediately handled and tossed up to see if I were sound by some of the crew, and I was now persuaded that I had gotten into a world of bad spirits and that they were going to kill me. Their complexions too differing so much from ours, their long hair and the language they spoke (which was very different from any I had ever heard) united to confirm me in this belief. Indeed such were the horrors of my views and fears at the moment that, if ten thousand worlds had been my own, I would have freely parted with them all to have exchanged my condition with that of the meanest slave in my own country. When I looked round the ship too and saw a large furnace or copper boiling and a multitude of black people of every description chained together, every one of their countenances expressing dejection and sorrow, I no longer doubted of my fate; and quite overpowered with horror and anguish, I fell motionless on the deck and fainted. When I recovered a little I found some black people about me, who I believed were some of those who had brought me on board and had been receiving their pay; they talked to me in order to cheer me, but all in vain. I asked them if we were not to be eaten by those white men with horrible looks, red faces, and loose hair. . . .

I now saw myself deprived of all chance of returning to my native country or even the least glimpse of hope of gaining the shore, which I now considered as friendly; and I even wished for my former slavery in preference to my present situation, which was filled with horrors of every kind, still heightened by my ignorance of what I was to undergo. I was not long suffered to indulge my grief; I was soon put down under the decks, and there I received such a salutation in my nostrils as I had never experienced in my life: so that with the loathsomeness of the stench and crying together, I became so sick and low that I was not able to eat, nor had I the least desire to taste anything. I now wished for the last friend, death, to relieve me; but soon, to my grief, two of the white men offered me eatables, and on my refusing to eat, one of them held me fast by the hands and laid me across I think the windlass, and tied my feet while the other flogged me severely. I had never experienced anything of this kind before, and although, not being used to the water, I naturally feared that element the first time I saw it, yet nevertheless could I have got over the nettings I would have jumped over the side. . . . While we stayed on the coast I was mostly on deck, and one day, to my great astonishment, I saw one of these vessels coming in with the sails up. As soon as the whites saw it they gave a great shout, at which we were amazed; and the more so as the vessel appeared larger by approaching nearer. At last she came to an anchor in my sight, and when the anchor was let go I and my countrymen who saw it were lost in astonishment to observe the vessel stop, and were now convinced it was done by magic. . . .

At last we came in sight of the island of Barbados, at which the whites on board gave a great shout and made many signs of joy to us. . . . Many merchants and planters now came on board, though it was in the evening. They put us in separate parcels and examined us attentively. They also made us jump, and pointed to the land, signifying we were to go there. We thought by this we should be eaten by these ugly men, as they appeared to us; and when soon after we were all put down under the deck again, there was much dread and trembling among us, and nothing but bitter cries to be heard all the night from these apprehensions, insomuch that at last the white people got some old slaves from the land to pacify us. They told us we were not to be eaten but to work, and were soon to go on land where we should see many of our country people. This report eased us much; and sure enough soon after we were landed there came to us Africans of all languages. We were conducted immediately to the merchant's yard, where we were all pent up together like so many sheep in a fold without regard to sex or age. . . . We were not many days in the merchant's custody before we were sold after their usual manner, which is this: On a signal given, (as the beat of a drum) the buyers rush at once into the yard where the slaves are confined, and make choice of that parcel they like best. The noise and clamour with which this is attended and the eagerness visible in the countenances of the buyers serve not a little to increase the apprehensions of the terrified Africans, who may well be supposed to consider them as the ministers of that destruction to which they think themselves devoted. In this manner, without scruple, are relations and friends separated, most of them never to see each other again. I remember in the vessel in which I was brought over, in the men's apartment there were several brothers who, in the sale, were sold in different lots; and it was very moving on this occasion to see and hear their cries at parting. O, ye nominal

Christians! might not an African ask you, Learned you this from your God who says unto you, Do unto all men as you would men should do unto you? Is it not enough that we are torn from our country and friends to toil for your luxury and lust of gain? Must every tender feeling be likewise sacrificed to your avarice? Are the dearest friends and relations, now rendered more dear by their separation from their kindred, still to be parted from each other and thus prevented from cheering the gloom of slavery with the small comfort of being together and mingling their sufferings and sorrows? Why are parents to lose their children, brothers their sisters, or husbands their wives? Surely this is a new refinement in cruelty which, while it has no advantage to atone for it, thus aggravates distress and adds fresh horrors even to the wretchedness of slavery.

D. New Worlds for the Taking

1. An English Landlord Describes a Troubled England (1623)[*]

England's prosperity in the early sixteenth century had been built on the backs of bleating sheep, as exports of raw wool and finished woolen cloth boomed. Beginning about 1550, however, a severe depression descended on the woolen districts. Thousands of sheepherders and weavers were pitched out of work and onto the roads of England. England suddenly seemed to be overflowing with paupers and vagabonds, as described in the following letter by a Lincolnshire landlord. What did he find most alarming?

Right honourable brother, the best news I can send you is that we are all in good health God be praised. I am now here with my son to settle some country affair, and my own private, which were never so burdensome unto me as now. For many insufficient tenants have given up their farms and sheepwalks, so as I am forced to take them into my own hands and borrow money upon use to stock them. It draweth me wholly from a contemplative life, which I most affected, and could be most willing to pass over my whole estate to the benefit of my children so as I were freed of the trouble. Our country was never in that want that now it is, and more of money than corn, for there are many thousands in these parts who have sold all they have even to their bed straw and cannot get work to earn any money. Dog's flesh is a dainty dish and found upon search in many houses, also such horse flesh as hath lain long in a deke for hounds. And the other day one stole a sheep who for mere hunger tore a leg out, and did eat it raw. All that is most certain true and yet the great time of scarcity not yet come. I shall rejoice to have a better subject to write of, and expect it with patience. In the mean time and ever

I will remain
Your honour's most loving brother to serve you
William Pelham

---

[*]*Lincolnshire Notes and Queries* (Horncatle, England: W. K. Morton, 1888), vol. 1, no. 1, pp. 15–16.

2. Hakluyt Sees England's Salvation in America (1584)*

Richard Hakluyt, a remarkable clergyman-scholar-geographer who lies buried in Westminster Abbey, deserves high rank among the indirect founding fathers of the United States. His published collections of documents relating to early English explorations must be regarded as among the "great books" of American history for their stimulation of interest in New World colonization. (Hakluyt even gambled some of his own small fortune in the company that tried to colonize Virginia.) In one of his most widely read works, Discourse Concerning the Western Planting, *published in 1584, he argued that colonizing America might provide a remedy for England's festering economic and social problems. What did he identify as the most pressing problems to be solved? In what ways did he see America providing solutions to those problems? How prophetic was he about the role the American colonies were to play in England's commerce?*

It is well worth the observation to see and consider what the like voyages of discovery and planting in the East and West Indies have wrought in the kingdoms of Portugal and Spain; both which realms, being of themselves poor and barren and hardly able to sustain their inhabitants, by their discoveries have found such occasion of employment, that these many years we have not heard scarcely of any pirate of those two nations; whereas we and the French are most infamous for our outrageous, common, and daily piracies. . . . [W]e, for all the statutes that hitherto can be devised, and the sharp execution of the same in punishing idle and lazy persons, for want of sufficient occasion of honest employment, cannot deliver our commonwealth from multitudes of loiterers and idle vagabonds.

Truth it is that through our long peace and seldom sickness . . . we are grown more populous than ever heretofore; so that now there are of every art and science so many, that they can hardly live by one another, nay, rather, they are ready to eat up one another; yes, many thousands of idle persons are within this realm, which, having no way to be set on work, be either mutinous and seek alteration in the state, or at least very burdensome to the commonwealth, and often fall to pilfering and thieving and other lewdness, whereby all the prisons of the land are daily pestered and stuffed full of them, where either they pitifully pine away, or else at length are miserably hanged. . . .

Whereas if this voyage were put in execution, these petty thieves might be condemned for certain years to the western parts, especially in Newfoundland, in sawing and felling of timber for masts of ships; . . . in burning of the firs and pine trees to make pitch, tar, rosin, and soap ashes; in beating and working of hemp for cordage; and, in the more southern parts, in setting them to work in mines of gold, silver, copper, lead, and iron; in dragging for pearls and coral; in planting of sugar cane, as the Portuguese have done in Madera; in maintenance and increasing of silk worms for silk, and in dressing the same; in gathering of cotton whereof there is plenty; in tilling of the soil for grain; in dressing of vines whereof there is great abundance for wine; olives, whereof the soil is capable, for oil; trees for

---

*Richard Hakluyt, *Discourse Concerning the Western Planting* (1584), in Charles Deane, ed., *Documentary History of the State of Maine* (Cambridge: Press of John Wilson and Son, 1877), vol. 2, pp. 36–39.

oranges, lemons, almonds, figs, and other fruits, all which are found to grow there already; . . . in fishing, salting, and drying of ling, cod, salmon, herring; in making and gathering of honey, wax, turpentine. . . .

Besides this, such as by any kind of infirmity cannot pass the seas thither, and now are chargeable to the realm at home, by this voyage shall be made profitable members, by employing them in England in making of a thousand trifling things, which will be very good merchandise for those countries where we shall have most ample vente [sales] thereof.

And seeing the savages . . . are greatly delighted with any cap or garment made of coarse woolen cloth, their country being cold and sharp in winter, it is manifest we shall find great [demand for] our clothes . . . whereby all occupations belonging to clothing and knitting shall freshly be set on work, as cappers, knitters, clothiers, woolmen, carders, spinners, weavers, fullers, shearmen, dyers, drapers, hatters, and such like, whereby many decayed towns may be repaired.

Thought Provokers

1. How might we explain the attitudes of Renaissance-era Europeans toward the newly discovered Indians? Was the concern for Christianizing the Native Americans sincere?
2. What motivated the Spanish to colonize the Americas in the sixteenth century? On balance, was the Spanish arrival good or bad for the New World? What advantages and disadvantages did the Spanish have as colonizers?
3. Why did Europeans look to Africa for labor with which to develop the riches of the New World? To what extent did Africans themselves help to promote the slave trade?
4. What were the most valid arguments used to promote English colonization in the sixteenth and seventeenth centuries? What relevance to the English did the example of Spain's colonizing venture in the New World have?

2

The Planting of English America, 1500–1733

There is under our noses the great and ample
country of Virginia; the inland whereof is found
of late to be so sweet and wholesome a climate,
so rich and abundant in silver mines, a better and
richer country than Mexico itself.

Richard Hakluyt, 1599

Prologue: The spectacular success of the Spanish conquerors excited the cupidity
and rivalry of the English and partly inspired Sir Humphrey Gilbert's ill-fated colony in
Newfoundland in 1583 and Sir Walter Raleigh's luckless venture on Roanoke Island,
off the North Carolina coast, in the 1580s. But England, though suffering from blighting
economic and social disruptions at home, was not prepared for ambitious colonial ventures until the defeat of the Spanish Armada in 1588 and the perfection of the joint-stock
company—a device that enabled "adventurers" to pool their capital. Virginia, which got
off to a shaky start in 1607, was finally saved by tobacco. In all the young colonies,
people of diverse cultures—European, Native American, and African—commingled,
and sometimes clashed.

A. England on the Eve of Empire

1. Thomas More Deplores the All-Consuming Sheep (1516)*

*Concerns over enclosure and depopulation were often expressed in strikingly moral
terms. Clergymen and pamphleteers railed against rapacious landlords who cast out
peasants from their land, unleashing hordes of drifters upon the English countryside.
In the following excerpt from his famous tract,* **Utopia,** *English humanist philosopher
Thomas More takes aim at noblemen and their voracious sheep. What images does
he invoke? What consequences does he attribute to the practice of enclosure?*

"But this is not the only problem which makes it necessary to steal. There is
another, more peculiar (so far as I know) to you Englishmen."

---

*Thomas More, *Utopia,* Clarence H. Miller, trans. (New Haven, CT: Yale University Press, 2001), pp. 22–23.

"What is that?" said the Cardinal.

"Your sheep," I said, "which are ordinarily so meek and require so little to maintain them, now begin (so they say) to be so voracious and fierce that they devour even the people themselves; they destroy and despoil fields, houses, towns. I mean that wherever in the realm finer and therefore more expensive wool is produced, noblemen, gentlemen, and even some abbots (holy men are they), not content with the annual rents and produce which their ancestors were accustomed to derive from their estates, not thinking it sufficient to live idly and comfortably, contributing nothing to the common good, unless they also undermine it, these drones leave nothing for cultivation; they enclose everything as pasture; they destroy homes, level towns, leaving only the church as a stable for the sheep; and as if too little ground among you were lost as game preserves or hunting forests, these good men turn all habitations and cultivated lands into a wilderness. And so that one glutton, a dire and insatiable plague to his native country, may join the fields together and enclose thousands of acres within one hedge, the farmers are thrown out: some are stripped of their possessions, circumvented by fraud or overcome by force; or worn out by injustices, they are forced to sell. One way or another, the poor wretches depart, men, women, husbands, wives, orphans, widows, parents with little children and a household which is numerous rather than rich, since agriculture requires many hands, they depart, I say, from hearth and home, all that was known and familiar to them, and they cannot find any place to go to. All their household furnishings, which could not be sold for much even if they could wait for a buyer, are sold for a song now that they must be removed. They soon spend that pittance in their wanderings, and then finally what else is left but to steal and to hang—justly, to be sure—or else to bum around and beg? For that matter, even as vagrants they are thrown into jail because they are wandering around idly, though no one will hire them, even when they offer their services most eagerly. For since no seed is sown, there is no farm labor, and that is all they are accustomed to. One herdsman or shepherd is sufficient to graze livestock on ground that would require many hands to cultivate and grow crops.

"And for this reason the price of grain has risen sharply in many places."

2. The Puritans Set Sail (1629)[*]

The economic turmoil that drove landless peasants into the port cities of London and Bristol, and onto the merchant ships headed for Chesapeake Bay, also helped spur a wave of devout Puritans to make their own journey across the Atlantic. What unified these future settlers of Massachusetts Bay was of course their religion, marked by a profound displeasure with the corruption and ceremonialism of the Anglican Church. But they were also deeply troubled by the overcrowding and dislocation that rocked the English economy. Prior to setting off for the New World, John Winthrop, future founder and governor of Massachusetts Bay, detailed his reasons for the Puritan migration as follows. What faults did he find with English society? What did he hope to achieve with the transatlantic migration?

---

[*]Robert C. Winthrop, *Life and Letters of John Winthrop* (Boston: Ticknor & Fields, 1864), pp. 309–310.

1. It will be a service to the Church of great consequence to carry the Gospel into those parts of the world...& to raise a Bulwark against the kingdom of Ante-Christ w[hi]ch the Jesuits labour to reare up in those parts.

2. All other churches of Europe are brought to desolation, & o[u]r sins, for w[hi]ch the Lord begins already to frown upon us & to cut us short, do threaten evil times to be coming upon us, & who knows, but that God hath provided this place to be a refuge for many whom he means to save out of the general calamity, & seeing the Church hath no place left to fly into but the wilderness, what better work can there be, then to go & provide tabernacles & food for her against she comes thither:

3. This Land grows weary of her Inhabitants, so as man, who is the most precious of all creatures, is here more vile & base then the earth we tread upon, & of less price among us than an horse or a sheep: masters are forced by authority to entertain servants, parents to maintain there [their] own children, all towns complain of the burthen of their poore, though we have taken up many unnecessary yea unlawful trades to maintain them, & we use the authority of the Law to hinder the increase of o[u]r people. . . .

4. The whole earth is the Lord[']s garden & he hath given it to the Sons of men w[i]th a gen[era]l Commission: Gen: 1:28: increase & multiply, & replenish the earth & subdue it, . . . why then should we stand striving here for places of habitation...& in the meane time suffer a whole Continent as fruitful & convenient for the use of man to lie waste w[i]thout any improvement?

5. All arts & Trades are carried in that deceitful & unrighteous course, as it is almost impossible for a good & upright man to maintain his charge & live comfortably in any of them.

6. The fountaine of Learning & Religion are so corrupted as...most children (even the best wittes & of fairest hopes) are perverted, corrupted, & utterly overthrown by the multitude of evil examples. . . .

B. *Precarious Beginnings in Virginia*

1. The Starving Time (1609)[*]

Captain John Smith—adventurer, colonizer, explorer, author, and mapmaker—also ranks among America's first historians. Writing from England some fifteen years after events that he did not personally witness, he tells a tale that had come to him at second hand. What indications of modesty or lack of it are present? What pulled the settlers through?

The day before Captain Smith returned for England with the ships [October 4, 1609], Captain Davis arrived in a small pinnace [light sailing vessel], with some sixteen proper men more. . . . For the savages [Indians] no sooner understood Smith was gone but they all revolted, and did spoil and murder all they encountered. . . .

---

[*]Edward Arber, ed., *Travels and Works of Captain John Smith* (Edinburgh: John Grant, 1910), vol. 2, pp. 497–499. (*The General History of Virginia by Captaine John Smith, sometymes Governour in those Countryes and Admirall of New England.* [London: Printed by I. D. and I. H. for Michael Sparkes, 1674]).

Now we all found the loss of Captain Smith; yea, his greatest maligners could now curse his loss. As for corn provision and contribution from the savages, we [now] had nothing but mortal wounds, with clubs and arrows. As for our hogs, hens, goats, sheep, horses, and what lived, our commanders, officers, and savages daily consumed them. Some small proportions sometimes we tasted, till all was devoured; then swords, arms, [fowling] pieces, or anything we traded with the savages, whose cruel fingers were so often imbrued in our blood that what by their cruelty, our Governor's indiscretion, and the loss of our ships, of five hundred [persons] within six months after Captain Smith's departure there remained not past sixty men, women, and children, most miserable and poor creatures. And those were preserved for the most part by roots, herbs, acorns, walnuts, berries, now and then a little fish. They that had starch [courage] in these extremities made no small use of it; yea, [they ate] even the very skins of our horses.

Nay, so great was our famine that a savage we slew and buried, the poorer sort took him up again and ate him; and so did divers one another boiled and stewed, with roots and herbs. And one amongst the rest did kill his wife, powdered [salted] her, and had eaten part of her before it was known, for which he was executed, as he well deserved. Now whether she was better roasted, boiled, or carbonadoed [broiled], I know not; but of such a dish as powdered wife I never heard of.

This was the time which still to this day [1624] we called the starving time. It were too vile to say, and scarce to be believed, what we endured. But the occasion was our own, for want of providence, industry, and government, and not the barrenness and defect of the country, as is generally supposed. For till then in three years...we had never from England provisions sufficient for six months, though it seemed by the bills of loading sufficient was sent us, such a glutton is the sea, and such good fellows the mariners. We as little tasted of the great proportion sent us, as they of our want and miseries. Yet notwithstanding they ever overswayed and ruled the business, though we endured all that is said, and chiefly lived on what this good country naturally afforded, yet had we been even in Paradise itself with these governors, it would not have been much better with us. Yet there were amongst us who, had they had the government as Captain Smith appointed but...could not maintain it, would surely have kept us from those extremities of miseries.

2. *Governor William Berkeley Reports (1671)*[*]

Sir William Berkeley, a polished Oxford graduate, courtier, and playwright, was appointed governor of Virginia in 1642, when only thirty-six years of age. Conciliatory, energetic, and courageous, he served well in his early years as both administrator and military leader. He cultivated flax, cotton, rice, and silk on his own lands, and in one year sent a gift of three hundred pounds of silk to the king. In response to specific questions from London, he prepared the able report from which the following extract is taken. From what economic and social handicaps did Virginia suffer? Which one was the most burdensome? What is significantly revealed of Berkeley's character and outlook?

[*]W. W. Hening, *The Statutes at Large...of Virginia...*(Richmond, VA: Samuel Pleasants, 1823), vol. 2, pp. 514–517.

12. What commodities are there of the production, growth, and manufacture of your plantation [colony]; and particularly, what materials are there already growing, or may be produced for shipping in the same?

Answer. Commodities of the growth of our country we never had any but tobacco, which in this yet is considerable, that it yields His Majesty a great revenue. But of late we have begun to make silk, and so many mulberry trees are planted, and planting, that if we had skillful men from Naples or Sicily to teach us the art of making it perfectly, in less than half an age [generation] we should make as much silk in an year as England did yearly expend three score years since. But now we hear it is grown to a greater excess, and more common and vulgar usage. Now, for shipping, we have admirable masts and very good oaks; but for iron ore I dare not say there is sufficient to keep one iron mill going for seven years. . . .

15. What number of planters, servants, and slaves; and how many parishes are there in your plantation?

Answer. We suppose, and I am very sure we do not much miscount, that there is in Virginia above forty thousand persons, men, women, and children, and of which there are two thousand black slaves, six thousand Christian servants [indentured] for a short time. The rest are born in the country or have come in to settle and seat, in bettering their condition in a growing country.

16. What number of English, Scots, or Irish have for these seven years last past come yearly to plant and inhabit within your government; as also what blacks or slaves have been brought in within the said time?

Answer. Yearly, we suppose there comes in, of servants, about fifteen hundred, of which most are English, few Scotch, and fewer Irish, and not above two or three ships of Negroes in seven years.

17. What number of people have yearly died, within your plantation and government, for these seven years last past, both whites and blacks?

Answer. All new plantations are, for an age or two, unhealthy, till they are thoroughly cleared of wood. But unless we had a particular register office for the denoting of all that died, I cannot give a particular answer to this query. Only this I can say, that there is not often unseasoned hands (as we term them) that die now, whereas heretofore not one of five escaped the first year. . . .

23. What course is taken about the instructing of the people, within your government, in the Christian religion; and what provision is there made for the paying of your ministry?

Answer. The same course that is taken in England out of towns: every man, according to his ability, instructing his children. We have forty-eight parishes, and our ministers are well paid, and by my consent should be better if they would pray oftener and preach less. But of all other commodities, so of this, the worst are sent us, and we had few that we could boast of, since the persecution in Cromwell's tyranny drove divers worthy men hither. But, I thank God, there are no free schools nor printing, and I hope we shall not have these hundred years. For learning has brought disobedience, and heresy, and sects into the world, and printing has divulged them, and libels against the best government. God keep us from both!

C. The Mix of Cultures in English America _____

1. The Great Indian Uprising (1622)*

From the outset, the Indians attacked the Virginia colonists with arrows, and relations between the two groups remained uneasy for many years after 1607. As if deaths from famine, exposure, improper food, and malarial fever were not enough, the colonists lost perhaps a quarter of their number in the great attack of 1622. Among other grievances, the Indians resented the clearing of their forests and the seizure of their cornfields by the whites. Edward Waterhouse, a prominent Virginia official, sent home this firsthand report. What does it reveal about how the colony subsisted, how earnest the Christianizing efforts of the colonists were, and how the disaster could be used to the advantage of the Virginians?

And such was the conceit of firm peace and amity [with the Indians] as that there was seldom or never a sword worn and a [fowling] piece seldomer, except for a deer or fowl. By which assurance of security the plantations of particular adventurers and planters were placed scatteringly and stragglingly as a choice vein of rich ground invited them, and the farther from neighbors held the better. The houses generally sat open to the savages, who were always friendly entertained at the tables of the English, and commonly lodged in their bed-chambers...[thus] seeming to open a fair gate for their conversion to Christianity.

Yea, such was the treacherous dissimulation of that people who then had contrived our destruction, that even two days before the massacre, some of our men were guided through the woods by them in safety.... Yea, they borrowed our own boats to convey themselves across the river (on the banks of both sides whereof all our plantations were) to consult of the devilish murder that ensued, and of our utter extirpation, which God of his mercy (by the means of some of themselves converted to Christianity) prevented....

On the Friday morning (the fatal day) the 22nd of March [1622], as also in the evening, as in other days before, they came unarmed into our houses, without bows or arrows, or other weapons, with deer, turkeys, fish, furs, and other provisions to sell and truck with us for glass, beads, and other trifles; yea, in some places, sat down at breakfast with our people at their tables, whom immediately with their own tools and weapons, either laid down, or standing in their houses, they basely and barbarously murdered, not sparing either age or sex, man, woman, or child; so sudden in their cruel execution that few or none discerned the weapon or blow that brought them to destruction. In which manner they also slew many of our people then at their several works and husbandries in the fields, and without [outside] their houses, some in planting corn and tobacco, some in gardening, some in making brick, building, sawing, and other kinds of husbandry—they well knowing in what places and quarters each of our men were, in regard of their daily familiarity and resort to us for trading and other negotiations, which the more willingly was by us

---

*Susan M. Kingsbury, ed., *The Records of the Virginia Company of London* (Washington, DC: Government Printing Office, 1933), vol. 3, pp. 550–551, 556–557.

continued and cherished for the desire we had of effecting that great masterpiece of works, their conversion.

And by this means, that fatal Friday morning, there fell under the bloody and barbarous hands of that perfidious and inhumane people, contrary to all laws of God and man, and nature and nations, 347 men, women, and children, most by their own weapons. And not being content with taking away life alone, they fell after again upon the dead, making, as well as they could, a fresh murder, defacing, dragging, and mangling the dead carcasses into many pieces, and carrying away some parts in derision, with base and brutish triumph. . . .

Our hands, which before were tied with gentleness and fair usage, are now set at liberty by the treacherous violence of the savages . . . so that we, who hitherto have had possession of no more ground than their waste and our purchase at a valuable consideration to their own contentment gained, may now by right of war, and law of nations, invade the country, and destroy them who sought to destroy us; whereby we shall enjoy their cultivated places. . . . Now their cleared grounds in all their villages (which are situate in the fruitfulest places of the land) shall be inhabited by us, whereas heretofore the grubbing of woods was the greatest labor.

2. A Missionary Denounces the Treatment of the Indians in South Carolina (1708)[*]

Francis Le Jau served as an Anglican missionary in South Carolina from 1706 to 1717. In his regular reports to his superiors in London, he described Indian-white relations in the southern colony and was especially critical of the Indian slave trade. What did he see as the principal harm inflicted on the Indians by whites? In what ways did the whites' treatment of the native peoples complicate his efforts to spread Christianity among them?

I perceive dayly more and more that our manner of giving Liberty to some very idle and dissolute Men to go and Trade in the Indian Settlements 600 or 800 Miles from us where they commit many Enormities & Injustices is a great Obstruction to our best designs. I have tryed to get some free Indians to live with me and wou'd Cloath them but they will not consent to it, nor part with their Children tho' they lead miserable poor lives. It is reported by some of our Inhabitants lately gone on Indian Trading that they excite them to make War amongst themselves to get Slaves which they give for our European Goods. I fear it is but too true and that the Slaves we have for necessary Service, (for our white Servants in a Months time prove good for nothing at all) are the price of great many Sins. . . .

. . . I gave you an account in my last of the desolate Condition of Renoque. it was in Octobr. or the latter End of September that the Tuscararo's Indians liveing near Cape fair Cutt off *137* of our people, most of them Palatines and some Switzers. I am not able to declare whether they were sett on by some of the partys that have

---

[*]Frank J. Klingberg, ed., *The Carolina Chronicle of Dr. Francis Le Jau, 1706–1717* (Berkeley: University of California Press, 1956), pp. 41–116. Some of the punctuation in this document has been edited to conform to modern usage.

been long at variance in that place or whether they were provoked by some great Injustice & taking their Land by force, it is so reported among us our forces are Actualy marched to Suppress those Murderers. . . . Generall Called Barnewell and 16 White men, whome 6 or 700 Indians have Joined and they are to meet the Virginians. Many wise men in this Province doubt of the Success. It is evident that our Traders have promoted Bloody Warrs this last Year to get slaves and one of them brought lately *100* of those poor Souls. It do's not belong to me to say any more upon those Melancholy Affaires I submit as to the Justice of those Proceedings to Your Wisdom. When I am asked how we are to deal with those unfortunate slaves, I content my selfe to Exhort that they be used with Xtian Charity and yt. we render their Condition as tollerable as we can. . . .

The Indian traders have always discouraged me by raising a world of Difficultyes when I proposed any thing to them relating to the Conversion of the Indians. It appears they do not care to have Clergymen so near them who doubtless would never approve those perpetual warrs they promote amongst the Indians for the onely reason of making slaves to pay for their trading goods; and what slaves! poor women and children, for the men taken prisoners are burnt most barbarously. I am Informd It was done So this Last year & the women and children were brought among us to be sold.

Thought Provokers

1. What social and economic factors contributed to the migration of Englishmen to the North American colonies?
2. Why did the early Virginia colonists experience such punishing difficulties?
3. What were the relative advantages and disadvantages of Europeans, Africans, and Indians as these three peoples commingled and clashed in seventeenth-century English America?

3

Settling the Northern Colonies, 1619–1700

To Banbury [England] came I, O profane one!
Where I saw a Puritan once
Hanging of his cat on Monday,
For killing of a mouse on Sunday.

Richard Brathwaite, 1638

Prologue: The English authorities, angered by the efforts of Puritans to de-Catholicize the established Church of England, launched persecutions that led to the founding of Plymouth in 1620 and the Massachusetts Bay Colony in 1630. The Bay Colony early fell under the leadership of Puritan (Congregational) clergymen. Although they had been victims of intolerance in old England, they in turn sought to enforce conformity in New England, sometimes with harsh measures. Partly as a result of the uncongenial atmosphere in Massachusetts Bay, other settlements sprang into existence in Connecticut and Rhode Island. These offshoot colonies, as well as the older ones, developed the pure-democracy town meeting and other significant institutions. All the colonies sometimes had troubled relationships with the Indians, notably in King Philip's War (1675–1676).

A. The Planting of Plymouth

1. Framing the Mayflower Compact (1620)*

Leaving Plymouth (England) in the overburdened Mayflower, *the plucky band of Pilgrims crossed the Atlantic. After severe storms and much seasickness, they sighted the Cape Cod coast of Massachusetts, far to the north of the site to which they had been granted patent privileges by the Virginia Company. The absence of valid rights in the Plymouth area, so William Bradford recorded, caused "some of the strangers amongst them" to utter "discontented and mutinous speeches" to the effect that when they "came ashore they would use their own liberty; for none had the power to command them, the patent they had being for Virginia, and not for New England. . . . " In an effort to hold the tiny band together, the leaders persuaded forty-one male passengers to sign a solemn pledge known as the Mayflower Compact. A constitution is "a document defining and limiting the functions of government." Was the Compact,*

_____

*B. P. Poore, ed., The Federal and State Constitutions, 2nd ed. (1878), part 1, p. 931.H1:H21.

as is often claimed, the first American constitution? In what ways did it foreshadow the development of democratic institutions?

In the name of God, amen. We whose names are underwritten, the loyal subjects of our dread sovereign lord, King James, by the grace of God, of Great Britain, France, and Ireland King, Defender of the Faith, etc., having undertaken, for the glory of God, and advancement of the Christian faith, and honor of our King and country, a voyage to plant the first colony in the northern parts of Virginia, do by these presents solemnly and mutually, in the presence of God and one another, covenant and combine ourselves together into a civil body politic, for our better ordering and preservation and furtherance of the ends aforesaid; and by virtue hereof to enact, constitute, and frame such just and equal laws, ordinances, acts, constitutions, and offices, from time to time, as shall be thought most meet and convenient for the general good of the colony, unto which we promise all due submission and obedience. In witness whereof we have hereunto subscribed our names at Cape Cod the eleventh of November, in the reign of our sovereign lord, King James, of England, France, and Ireland, the eighteenth, and of Scotland, the fifty-fourth. Anno Domini 1620.

2. Abandoning Communism at Plymouth (1623)*

Some wag has said that the Pilgrims first fell on their knees, and then on the aborigines. The truth is that a plague—probably smallpox, possibly measles—had virtually exterminated the Indians near Plymouth, and the Pilgrims got along reasonably well with the few survivors. The Native Americans taught the whites how to grow maize (corn), which helped revitalize the ragged, starving, disease-decimated newcomers. The story of the first Thanksgiving (1621) is well known, but less well known is the fact that the abundant harvest of 1623 was made possible when the Pilgrims abandoned their early scheme of quasi-communism. For seven years, there was to have been no private ownership of land, and everyone was to have been fed and clothed from the common stock. William Bradford, the historian and oft-elected governor of the colony, here tells what happened when each family was given its own parcel of land. Why did individual ownership succeed where communal enterprise had failed?

This had very good success, for it made all hands very industrious, so as much more corn was planted than otherwise would have been by any means the Governor or any other could use, and saved him a great deal of trouble, and gave far better content. The women now went willingly into the field and took their little ones with them to set corn, which before would allege weakness and inability, whom to have compelled would have been thought great tyranny and oppression.

The experience that was had in this common course and condition, tried sundry years and that amongst godly and sober men, may well evince the vanity of

---

*From *Of Plymouth Plantation 1620–1647* by William Bradford.

that conceit of Plato's and other ancients, applauded by some of later times, that the taking away of property and bringing in community [communism] into a commonwealth would make them happy and flourishing, as if they were wiser than God. For this community (so far as it was) was found to breed much confusion and discontent and retard much employment that would have been to their benefit and comfort. For the young men that were most able and fit for labor and service did repine that they should spend their time and strength to work for other men's wives and children, without any recompense. The strong, or man of parts, had no more in division of victuals and clothes than he that was weak and not able to do a quarter the other could; this was thought injustice. The aged and graver men to be ranked and equalized in labors and victuals, clothes, etc., with the meaner and younger sort, thought it some indignity and disrespect unto them. And for men's wives to be commanded to do service for other men, as dressing their meat, washing their clothes, etc., they deemed it a kind of slavery, neither could many husbands well brook it.

B. Life in Early New England

1. John Winthrop's Concept of Liberty (1645)*

Governor John Winthrop was the most distinguished lay leader in the Massachusetts Bay Colony. Cambridge educated and trained in the law, he was modest, tender, self-sacrificing, and deeply religious. After a furious quarrel broke out at Hingham over the election of a militia leader, he caused certain of the agitators to be arrested. His foes brought impeachment charges against him, but they instead were fined. After his acquittal, Winthrop delivered this famous speech to the court. It illustrates the close connection between the aristocratic lay leaders of the Bay Colony and the leading clergymen. Would the kind of liberty that Winthrop describes be regarded as liberty today?

There is a twofold liberty: natural (I mean as our nature is now corrupt) and civil or federal. The first is common to man with beasts and other creatures. By this, man, as he stands in relation to man simply, hath liberty to do what he lists. It is a liberty to evil as well as to good. This liberty is incompatible and inconsistent with authority, and cannot endure the least restraint of the most just authority. The exercise and maintaining of this liberty makes men grow more evil, and in time to be worse than brute beasts. . . .

The other kind of liberty I call civil or federal. It may also be termed moral, in reference to the covenant between God and man in the moral law, and the politic covenants and constitutions amongst men themselves. . . . Whatsoever crosseth this, is not authority, but a distemper thereof. This liberty is maintained and exercised in

---

*John Winthrop, *The History of New England from 1630 to 1649* (Boston: Little, Brown and Company, 1853), vol. 2, pp. 281–282.

a way of subjection to authority. It is of the same kind of liberty wherewith Christ hath made us free.

The woman's own choice makes such a man her husband; yet being so chosen, he is her lord, and she is to be subject to him, yet in a way of liberty, not of bondage. And a true wife accounts her subjection her honor and freedom, and would not think her condition safe and free, but in her subjection to her husband's authority.

Such is the liberty of the church under the authority of Christ, her king and husband. His yoke is so easy and sweet to her as a bride's ornaments; and if through forwardness or wantonness, etc., she shake it off at any time, she is at no rest in her spirit until she take it up again. And whether her lord smiles upon her, and embraceth her in his arms, or whether he frowns, or rebukes, or smites her, she apprehends the sweetness of his love in all, and is refreshed, supported, and instructed by every such dispensation of his authority over her. On the other side, ye know who they are that complain of this yoke and say, let us break their bands, etc., we will not have this man to rule over us.

Even so, brethren, it will be between you and your magistrates. If you stand for your natural corrupt liberties, and will do what is good in your own eyes, you will not endure the least weight of authority, but will murmur, and oppose, and be always striving to shake off that yoke. But if you will be satisfied to enjoy such civil and lawful liberties, such as Christ allows you, then will you quietly and cheerfully submit unto that authority which is set over you, in all the administrations of it, for your good. Wherein if we [magistrates] fail at any time, we hope we shall be willing (by God's assistance) to hearken to good advice from any of you, or in any other way of God. So shall your liberties be preserved, in upholding the honor and power of authority amongst you.

2. The Blue Laws of Connecticut (1672)[*]

Blue laws—statutes governing personal behavior—were to be found both in Europe and in the American colonies. They obviously could not be enforced with literal severity, and they generally fell into disuse after the Revolution. Connecticut's blue laws received unpleasant notoriety in the Reverend Samuel Peters's General History of Connecticut (1781), which fabricated such decrees as "No woman shall kiss her child on the Sabbath or fasting-day." But the valid laws of Connecticut, some of which are here reproduced with biblical chapter and verse, were harsh enough. How did the punishment fit the crime? Which offenses would still be regarded as criminal today?

1. If any man or woman, after legal conviction, shall have or worship any other God but the Lord God, he shall be put to death. (Deuteronomy 13.6. Exodus 22.20.)

2. If any person within this colony shall blaspheme the name of God, the Father, Son, or Holy Ghost, with direct, express, presumptuous, or high-handed blasphemy, or shall curse in the like manner, he shall be put to death. (Leviticus 24.15, 16.)

---

[*]George Brinley, ed., *The Laws of Connecticut* (Hartford: printed for private distribution, 1865), pp. 9–10.

3. If any man or woman be a witch, that is, has or consults with a familiar spirit, they shall be put to death. (Exodus 22.18. Leviticus 20.27. Deuteronomy 18.10, 11.)

4. If any person shall commit any willful murder, committed upon malice, hatred, or cruelty, not in a man's just and necessary defense, nor by casualty [accident] against his will, he shall be put to death. (Exodus 21.12, 13, 14. Numbers 35.30, 31.)

5. If any person shall slay another through guile, either by poisoning or other such devilish practices, he shall be put to death. (Exodus 21.14.) . . .

10. If any man steals a man or mankind and sells him, or if he be found in his hand, he shall be put to death. (Exodus 21.16.)

11. If any person rise up by false witness wittingly and of purpose to take away any man's life, he or she shall be put to death. (Deuteronomy 19.16, 18, 19.) . . .

14. If any child or children above sixteen years old, and of sufficient understanding, shall curse or smite their natural father or mother, he or they shall be put to death, unless it can be sufficiently testified that the parents have been very unchristianly negligent in the education of such children, or so provoked them by extreme and cruel correction that they have been forced thereunto to preserve themselves from death or maiming. (Exodus 21.17. Leviticus 20.9. Exodus 21.15.)

15. If any man have a stubborn or rebellious son, of sufficient understanding and years, viz. sixteen years of age, which will not obey the voice of his father, or the voice of his mother, and that when they have chastened him, he will not harken unto them; then may his father or mother, being his natural parents, lay hold on him, and bring him to the magistrates assembled in court, and testify unto them that their son is stubborn and rebellious, and will not obey their voice and chastisement, but lives in sundry notorious crimes, such a son shall be put to death. (Deuteronomy 21.20, 21.) . . .

C. Indian-White Relations in Colonial New England: Three Views of King Philip's War

1. Mary Rowlandson Is Captured by Indians (1675)[*]

Mary Rowlandson was taken prisoner in February 1675 by Indians who raided her home on the Massachusetts frontier some thirty miles west of Boston. Her account became one of the most popular "captivity narratives" that fascinated readers in England and America in the seventeenth and eighteenth centuries, providing a model for such later works as James Fenimore Cooper's The Last of the Mohicans. *What are the most harrowing aspects of Rowlandson's experience? What religious meaning did she find in the Indian attack and in her captivity?*

On the tenth of February 1675, came the Indians with great numbers upon Lancaster: their first coming was about sunrising; hearing the noise of some guns,

---

*From C. H. Lincoln, ed., *Original Narratives of Early American History: Narratives of Indian Wars, 1675–1699* (New York: Charles Scribner's Sons, 1913), pp. 118–120.

we looked out; several houses were burning, and the smoke ascending to heaven. There were five persons taken in one house; the father, and the mother and a sucking child, they knocked on the head; the other two they took and carried away alive. There were two others, who being out of their garrison upon some occasion were set upon; one was knocked on the head, the other escaped; another there was who running along was shot and wounded, and fell down; he begged of them his life, promising them money (as they told me) but they would not hearken to him but knocked him in head, and stripped him naked, and split open his bowels. . . . Thus these murderous wretches went on, burning, and destroying before them.

At length they came and beset our own house, and quickly it was the dolefulest day that ever mine eyes saw. . . . Some in our house were fighting for their lives, others wallowing in their blood, the house on fire over our heads, and the bloody heathen ready to knock us on the head, if we stirred out. Now might we hear mothers and children crying out for themselves, and one another, "Lord, what shall we do?" Then I took my children (and one of my sisters', hers) to go forth and leave the house: but as soon as we came to the door and appeared, the Indians shot so thick that the bullets rattled against the house, as if one had taken an handful of stones and threw them, so that we were fain to give back. We had six stout dogs belonging to our garrison, but none of them would stir, though another time, if any Indian had come to the door, they were ready to fly upon him and tear him down. The Lord hereby would make us the more to acknowledge His hand, and to see that our help is always in Him. But out we must go, the fire increasing, and coming along behind us, roaring, and the Indians gaping before us with their guns, spears, and hatchets to devor us. No sooner were we out of the house, but my brother-in-law (being before wounded, in defending the house, in or near the throat) fell down dead, whereat the Indians scornfully shouted, and hallowed, and were presently upon him, stripping off his clothes, the bullets flying thick, one went through my side, and the same (as would seem) through the bowels and hand of my dear child in my arms. One of my elder sisters' children, named William, had then his leg broken, which the Indians perceiving, they knocked him on [his] head. . . . [T]he Indians laid hold of us, pulling me one way, and the children another, and said, "Come go along with us"; I told them they would kill me: they answered, if I were willing to go along with them, they would not hurt me.

2. Plymouth Officials Justify the War (1675)[*]

The officials of Plymouth Colony offered the following explanation for their actions in taking up arms against the Wampanoag chief Metacom (called King Philip by the English) in 1675. What do they see as the principal offenses by the Indians? Should John Sassamon be regarded as "a faithful Indian" or as an English spy? Did the Puritan settlers go to war reluctantly or enthusiastically?

Anno Domini 1675

---

[*]David Pulsifer, ed., "Acts of the Commissioners of the United Colonies of New England," in *Plymouth Colonial Records* (1675), vol. 10, pp. 362–364.

Not to look back further than the troubles that were between the Colony of New Plymouth and Philip, sachem [chieftain] of Mount Hope, in the year 1671, it may be remembered that . . . [he] was the peccant and offending party; and that Plymouth had just cause to take up arms against him; and it was then agreed that he should pay that colony a certain sum of money, in part of their damage and charge by him occasioned; and he then not only renewed his ancient covenant of friendship with them; but made himself and his people absolute subjects to our Sovereign Lord King Charles the Second. . . .

But sometime last winter the Governor of Plymouth was informed by Sassamon, a faithful Indian, that the said Philip was undoubtedly endeavoring to raise new troubles, and was endeavoring to engage all the sachems round about in a war against us; some of the English also that lived near the said sachem, communicated their fears and jealousies concurrent with what the Indian had informed. About a week after John Sassamon had given his information, he was barbarously murdered by some Indians for his faithfulness (as we have cause to believe) to the interest of God and of the English; some time after Sassamon's death Philip, having heard that the Governor of Plymouth had received some information against him and purposed to send for or to him to appear at their next Court that they might inquire into those reports, came down of his own accord to Plymouth a little before their Court, in the beginning of March last; at which time the Council of that colony upon a large debate with him, had great reason to believe, that the information against him might be in substance true, but not having full proof thereof and hoping that the discovery of it so far would cause him to desist they dismissed him friendly; giving him only to understand that if they hear further concerning that matter they might see reason to demand his arms to be delivered up for their security; which was according to former agreement between him and them; and he engaged [pledged] on their demand they should be surrendered unto them or their order. . . .

But no sooner was our Court dissolved but we had intelligence from Lieut. John Brown of Swansea that Philip and his men continued constantly in arms, many strange Indians from several places flocked in to him & that they sent away their wives to Narragansett; and were giving our people frequent alarms by drums and guns in the night and invaded their passage towards Plymouth; and that their young Indians were earnest for a war; on the 7th of June Mr. Benjamin Church being on Rhode Island, Weetamoo and some of her chief men told him that Philip intended a war speedily with the English, some of them saying that they would help him; and that he had already given them leave to kill Englishmen's cattle and rob their houses; about the 14th and 15th of June Mr. James Brown went twice to Philip to persuade him to be quiet but at both times found his men in arms and Philip very high and not persuadable to peace; on the 14th June our Council wrote an amicable friendly letter to Philip therein showing our dislike of his practices; and advising him to dismiss his strange Indians and command his own men to fall quietly to their business that our people might also be quiet; and not to suffer himself to be abused by reports concerning us, who intended no wrong, nor hurt towards him; but Mr. Brown could not obtain an answer from him; on the 17th June Mr. Paine of Rehoboth and several others of the English going unarmed to Mount Hope to seek their horses at Philip's request, the Indians came and presented their guns at them and carried it very insolently though no way provoked by them; on the 18th or 19th Job Winslow his house was broken up and rifled by Philip's men; June the 20th being our Sabbath, the people at Swansea were alarmed by the Indians, two of our inhabitants burned out of their houses and their houses rifled; and the Indians were marching up as they judged to assault the town; and therefore entreated speedy help from us; we hereupon the 21 of June sent up some forces to relieve that town and dispatched more with speed; on Wednesday the 23 of June a dozen more of their houses at Swansea were rifled; on the 24th Thomas Layton was slain at the Fall River; on the 25th of June divers of the people at Swansea slain; and many houses burned until which time, and for several days, though we had a considerable force there both of our own and of the Massachusetts (to our grief and shame), they took no revenge on the enemy; thus slow were we and unwilling to engage ourselves and neighbors in a war; having many insolencies almost intolerable from them, of whose hands we had deserved better;

> *Josiah Winslow*
> *Thomas Hinckley*
> [Plymouth Commissioners to the United Colonies]

3. A Rhode Island Quaker Sympathizes with the Indians (1675)*

John Easton, lieutenant governor of Rhode Island and a Quaker, took a different view of the war's causes than did the officials from Plymouth, as described in the preceding selection. In what ways does he disagree with them? What does he cite as the Indians' primary grievances against the English settlers?

[The Indians] said they had been the first in doing good to the English, and the English the first in doing wrong, said when the English first came their king's father [Massasoit] was as a great man and the English as a little child, he constrained other Indians from wronging the English and gave them corn and showed them how to plant and was free to do them any good and had let them have a 100 times more land than now the king had for his own people, but their king's brother when he was king came miserably to die by being forced to court, as they judged poisoned, and another grievance was if 20 of their own Indians testified that an Englishman had done them wrong, it was as nothing, and if but one of their worst Indians testified against any Indian or their king, when it pleased the English that was sufficient.

Another grievance was when their kings sold land, the English would say it was more than they agreed to and a writing must be proof against all them, and some of their kings had done wrong to sell so much. He left his people none, and some being given to drunkenness the English made them drunk and then cheated them in bargains, but now their kings were forewarned not to part with land for nothing in comparison to the value thereof. Now whom the English had owned for king or queen they [the English] would disinherit, and make another king that would give

---

*John Easton, "A Relation of the Indian War," in Charles H. Lincoln, ed., *Narratives of the Indian Wars, 1675–1699* (New York: Charles Scribner's Sons, 1913), pp. 10–11. Some of the punctuation in this document has been edited to conform to modern usage.

or sell them their land, that now they had no hopes left to keep any land. Another grievance the English cattle and horses still increased, that when they removed 30 miles from where English had anything to do, they could not keep their corn [there] from being spoiled, they never being used to fence, and thought when the English bought land of them that they [the English] would have kept their cattle upon their own land.

Another grievance, the English were so eager to sell the Indians liquor that most of the Indians spent all in drunkenness and then ravened upon the sober Indians and, they did believe, often did hurt the English cattle, and their kings could not prevent it. We knew before [that] these were their grand complaints, but then we only endeavored to persuade that all complaints might be righted without war, but could have no other answer but that they had not heard of that way for the Governor of York and an Indian king to have the hearing of it. We had cause to think if that had been tendered it would have been accepted. We endeavored that, however, they should lay down their arms, for the English were too strong for them. They said then the English should do to them as they did when they were too strong for the English.

Thought Provokers

1. In regard to the Plymouth Pilgrims, what support does one find for this statement: "The cowards never started; the weak died on the way"? An English writer claims that the brave ones were actually those who stayed at home and fought the authorities for religious freedom instead of fleeing from them. Comment.

2. How can one justify the so-called intolerance of the Puritans, especially since they were the victims of intolerance at home? What light does this statement of Pope Leo XIII in 1885 throw on the problem: "The equal toleration of all religions . . . is the same thing as atheism"?

3. It has been said that the Puritans were misguided in following biblical law, which did not fit conditions of the seventeenth century. Comment. The blacks of South Africa have this proverb: "At first we had the land and the white man had the Bible. Now we have the Bible and the white man has the land." Comment with reference to Indian-white relations in North America.

4. In which of the colonies would you have preferred to be a settler? Explain fully why.

American Life in the Seventeenth Century, 1607–1692

Our fathers were Englishmen which came over
this great ocean, and were ready to perish in this
wilderness, but they cried unto the Lord, and he
heard their voice, and looked on their adversity.

William Bradford, Of Plymouth Plantation

Prologue: The unhealthful environment of the Chesapeake region killed off the first would-be settlers in droves. Mostly single men, the earliest Virginia and Maryland colonists struggled to put their raw colonies on a sound economic footing by cultivating tobacco. At first, indentured servants provided much of the labor supply for tobacco culture, but after discontented former servants erupted in Bacon's Rebellion in 1676, the dominant merchant-planters shifted to importing African slaves. By the end of the seventeenth century, both white and black populations in the Chesapeake were growing through natural reproduction as well as through continued immigration.

A. Indentured Servants in the Chesapeake Region

1. A Londoner Agrees to Provide a Servant (1654)*

The earliest Virginia settlers hungered for more workers so that they could plant more land in tobacco, the colony's richly profitable cash crop. Agents in England served as "brokers" who found laborers, arranged for their transportation to the New World, and drew up contracts specifying the terms of labor and the duration of the period of service. In the following contract, what sort of worker does Thomas Workman of Virginia want? What might be the implications of the contract's conspicuous failure to mention the terms of the servant's termination of service in four years' time? (Note

---

*From *The Old Dominion in the Seventeenth Century: A Documentary History of Virginia, 1606-1686,* edited by Warren M. Billings.

that inconsistency in the spelling of names, such as Garford versus Garfford, was common in the seventeenth century.)

Recorded this 20th Day of June 1654

Be it known unto all men by these presents that I Richard Garford of London Inhoulder doe Confess and acknowledge my selfe to owe and stand indebted unto Thomas Workman of the Little Creeke in the County of Lower Norffolk in Virginia, planter, his Executors Administrators or assignes the full and Just some of Tenn pounds of good and lawfull money of England to be paid uppon demand of the abovesaid Thomas Workman or his true and lawfull Atterny or Attornyes at the now dwelling house of Mr. Willyam Garford Innkeeper at the Red Lyon in fleet streete without either Equevocation fraud or delay, and to the true performance of the same well and truly to bee made and done I bind my selfe my Executors Administrators and Assignes, firmly by these presents in witnesse heereof I have hereunto sett my hand and seale this 4th day of Aprill 1653

Richard Garfford

The Condition of this obligation is such that the within bounden Richard Garford or his Assignes shall well and truly deliver or cause to be delivered unto the above mentioned Thomas Workman, his Executors Administrators or assignes here in Virginia a sound and able man servant betweene Eighteene and 25 yeres of age that shall have fower yeres to serve at the least, and that in the first second or third shipp that shall arrive in the Port of James River in Virginia from London, that then the bond above to be voyd and of noe effect or else to stand in full force and vertue

Richard Garfford

Sealed and delivered in the presence of
Thomas Ward

2. A Servant Girl Pays the Wages of Sin (1656)[*]

Single, lonely, and hard-used, indentured servants enjoyed few liberties. Those who went astray could be severely punished. In the following record from Charles City County Court, Virginia, what are the consequences of the servant girl's having borne an illegitimate child?

Whereas Ann Parke servant to Elizabeth Hatcher widdow is Complained of and proved to have Comitted Fornication and borne a Child in the time of her service: It is therefore ordered that the said Ann shall double the time of service due to be

---

[*]From *The Old Dominion in the Seventeenth Century: A Documentary History of Virginia, 1606-1686,* edited by Warren M. Billings.

performed by her to her mistress or her assigns, from the time of her departure, according to act in that Case made and provided.

3. An Unruly Servant Is Punished (1679)*

The planter-employers and masters struggled constantly to keep their hard-drinking, fractious servants in line. Sometimes matters got seriously out of hand, as in the following account from Virginia's Accomack County Court records in 1679. What were the terms of the offender's punishment? Were they justified?

The Examination of Elizabeth Bowen Widdow—saith—That on Sunday evening being the eighteenth day of May 1679 Thomas Jones her servant did come into her Roome and with a naked Rapier in his hand did tell her he would kill her and said shee had sent Will Waight to her Mothers and that shee had got a master for them, but hee would bee her Master and allso said that he would not kill her if shee would let him lye with her all night and bade her goe to bed and she answered she would not and Runn in with his Rapier and bent it, then he said he woald cutt her throat but she getting [to] the dore did run out of dores and he after her and ketched [her] in the yard and as she was standing did endeavor to cutt her throat with a knife but could not and then he threw her down and did there allso indeavour to cutt her throat but she prevented it by defending her throat with her hands and bending the knife hee took her [petti]coats and threw [them] over her head and gave her two or three blows in the face with his fist and bade her get her gun and did in this act with the Knife scurrify her throat and brest and cut her right hand with six or seven cutts very much and that she with bending the Rapier and knife cut her hands and fingers very much

Elizabeth Bowen

Whereas Elizabeth Bowin Widdow did by her examination upon oath in open Court declare that Thomas Jones her servant in a most barbarous and villanous nature sett upon and most desparately attempted to murder the said Bowin with a naked Rapier and Knife to cut her throat which had been perpatrated and committed had it not bee[n] Providentially and strongly prevented by the said Bowins resistance recieving severall wounds in her endeavours to prevent the sam[e] which was allso confessed by the said Jones: The Court takeing the same into their serious Considerations do order as a just reward for his said horrid offense and crime that the sherriff Forthwith take him into Custody and that he forthwith receive thirty nine lashes on the bare back well laid on: and to have his haire cutt off and an Iron Coller forthwith put about his neck dureing the Courts pleasure and after the time for which he was to serve his said mistriss is expired to serve his said mistriss or assignes one whole yeare according to Act for laying violent hands on his said mistriss and allso two yeares for his wounding her as aforesaid and after due punishment inflicted accordingly The Court do further order that the sherriff deliver the said Jones to the said Elizabeth Bowin or

*From *The Old Dominion in the Seventeenth Century: A Documentary History of Virginia, 1606-1686,* edited by Warren M. Billings.

order (it being by her request) and the said Bownig [sic] to Pay Court Charges the said Jones makeing satisfaction for the same after his time of service is expired—

B. Bacon's Rebellion and Its Aftermath

1. Nathaniel Bacon Proclaims His Principles (1676)[*]

Angry former indentured servants, impoverished and resentful, crowded into the untamed Virginia backcountry as the seventeenth century wore on. Governor William Berkeley's unwillingness to protect the hardscrabble planters on the frontier against Indian attacks gave rise to ugly rumors of graft and helped spark a rebellion led by the well-born planter Nathaniel Bacon. Chiefly concerned with eradicating the Indian threat along the frontier, Bacon sought from Berkeley a commission to establish a militia. Following a dramatic showdown in Jamestown, Berkeley acquiesced, granting Bacon the commission he desired. As Bacon and his men marched off toward Indian settlements, however, Berkeley rescinded his promise and once again declared Bacon to be in rebellion. In response to this latest slight, Bacon drafted his famous "Declaration of the People," printed below. What were his main grievances against Berkeley and the seaboard elite?

1. For having, upon specious pretences of public works, raised great unjust taxes upon the commonalty for the advancement of private favorites and other sinister ends, but no visible effects in any measure adequate; for not having, during this long time of his government, in any measure advanced this hopeful colony either by fortifications, towns, or trade.

2. For having abused and rendered contemptible the magistrates of justice by advancing to places of judicature scandalous and ignorant favorites.

3. For having wronged his Majesty's prerogative and interest by assuming monopoly of the beaver trade and for having in it unjust gain betrayed and sold his Majesty's country and the lives of his loyal subjects to the barbarous heathen.

4. For having protected, favored, and emboldened the Indians against his Majesty's loyal subjects, never contriving, requiring, or appointing any due or proper means of satisfaction for their many invasions, robberies, and murders committed upon us.

5. For having, when the army of English was just upon the track of those Indians, who now in all places burn, spoil, murder and when we might with ease have destroyed them who then were in open hostility, for then having expressly countermanded and sent back our army by passing his word for the peaceable demeanor of the said Indians, who immediately prosecuted their evil intentions, committing horrid murders and robberies in all places, being protected by the said engagement and word past of him the said Sir William Berkeley, having ruined and laid desolate a great part of his majesty's country, and have now drawn themselves into such obscure and remote places and are by their success so emboldened and confirmed by their confederacy so strengthened that the cries of blood are in all

---

[*]*Foundations of Colonial America: A Documentary History* by W. Keith Kavenagh, ed.

places, and the terror and consternation of the people so great, are now become not only a difficult but a very formidable enemy who might at first with ease have been destroyed.

6. And lately, when upon the loud outcries of blood, the assembly had, with all care, raised and framed an army for the preventing of further mischief and safeguard of this his Majesty's colony.

7. For having, with only the privacy of some few favorites without acquainting the people, only by the alteration of a figure, forged a commission, by we know not what hand, not only without but even against the consent of the people, for the raising and effecting civil war and destruction, which being happily and without bloodshed prevented; for having the second time attempted the same, thereby calling down our forces from the defense of the frontiers and most weakly exposed places.

8. For the prevention of civil mischief and ruin amongst ourselves while the barbarous enemy in all places did invade, murder, and spoil us, his Majesty's most faithful subjects.

Of this and the aforesaid articles we accuse Sir William Berkeley as guilty of each and every one of the same, and as one who has traitorously attempted, violated, and injured his Majesty's interest here by a loss of a great part of this his colony and many of his faithful loyal subjects by him betrayed and in a barbarous and shameful manner exposed to the incursions and murder of the heathen. And we do further declare these the ensuing persons in this list to have been his wicked and pernicious councillors, confederates, aiders, and assisters against the commonalty in these our civil commotions.

2. The Governor Upholds the Law (1676)*

The youthful Bacon, putting himself at the head of about a thousand men, chastised both the Indians and Berkeley's forces. He died mysteriously at the moment of victory, and his rebellion ended. The ferocity with which Berkeley executed Bacon's followers (more than twenty all told) shocked Charles II, who allegedly remarked, "That old fool has killed more people in that naked country than I have done for the murder of my father." Before the rebellion collapsed, Berkeley pleaded his own case with the people of Virginia as follows. What is the strongest argument in defense of his position? Comment critically on it.

But for all this, perhaps I have erred in things I know not of. If I have, I am so conscious of human frailty and my own defects that I will not only acknowledge them, but repent of and amend them, and not, like the rebel Bacon, persist in an error only because I have committed it. . . .

And now I will state the question betwixt me as a governor and Mr. Bacon, and say that if any enemies should invade England, any counselor, justice of peace, or other inferior officer might raise what forces they could to protect His Majesty's subjects. But I say again, if, after the King's knowledge of this invasion, any the greatest peer of England should raise forces against the King's prohibition, this would be now, and ever was in all ages and nations, accounted treason. . . .

Collections of the Massachusetts Historical Society, Fourth Series (Boston, 1871), vol. 9, pp. 179–181.

Now, my friends, I have lived thirty-four years amongst you, as uncorrupt and diligent as ever governor was. Bacon is a man of two years among you; his person and qualities unknown to most of you, and to all men else, by any virtuous action that ever I heard of. And that very action [against the Indians] which he boasts of was sickly and foolishly and, as I am informed, treacherously carried to the dishonor of the English nation. Yet in it he lost more men than I did in three years' war; and by the grace of God will put myself to the same dangers and troubles again when I have brought Bacon to acknowledge the laws are above him, and I doubt not but by God's assistance to have better success than Bacon hath had. The reasons of my hopes are, that I will take counsel of wiser men than myself; but Mr. Bacon hath none about him but the lowest of the people.

Yet I must further enlarge that I cannot, without your help, do anything in this but die in defense of my King, his laws and subjects, which I will cheerfully do, though alone I do it. And considering my poor fortunes, I cannot leave my poor wife and friends a better legacy than by dying for my King and you: for his sacred Majesty will easily distinguish between Mr. Bacon's actions and mine; and kings have long arms, either to reward or punish.

Now after all this, if Mr. Bacon can show one precedent or example where such acting in any nation whatever was approved of, I will mediate with the King and you for a pardon and excuse for him. But I can show him an hundred examples where brave and great men have been put to death for gaining victories against the command of their superiors.

Lastly, my most assured friends, I would have preserved those Indians that I knew were hourly at our mercy to have been our spies and intelligence, to find out our bloody enemies. But as soon as I had the least intelligence that they also were treacherous enemies, I gave out commissions to destroy them all, as the commissions themselves will speak it.

To conclude, I have done what was possible both to friend and enemy; have granted Mr. Bacon three pardons, which he hath scornfully rejected, supposing himself stronger to subvert than I and you to maintain the laws, by which only, and God's assisting grace and mercy, all men must hope for peace and safety.

3. Slavery Is Justified (1757)[*]

Following Bacon's ill-starred rebellion, tobacco culture continued to flourish. The Virginians had early learned that the path to wealth and leisure involved the use of African slaves. Even ministers of the gospel parroted the arguments in behalf of slavery, as is evident in this brutally frank letter by the Reverend Peter Fontaine, of Westover, Virginia, to his brother Moses. Is the attempt to shift the blame onto the British convincing? Was there a valid economic basis for slavery?

As to your second query, if enslaving our fellow creatures be a practice agreeable to Christianity, it is answered in a great measure in many treatises at home, to which I refer you. I shall only mention something of our present state here.

---

[*]Ann Maury, ed., *Memoirs of a Huguenot Family* (1853), pp. 351–352.

Like Adam, we are all apt to shift off the blame from ourselves and lay it upon others, how justly in our case you may judge. The Negroes are enslaved [in Africa] by the Negroes themselves before they are purchased by the masters of the ships who bring them here. It is, to be sure, at our choice whether we buy them or not; so this then is our crime, folly, or whatever you will please to call it. But our Assembly, foreseeing the ill consequences of importing such numbers amongst us, hath often attempted to lay a duty upon them which would amount to a prohibition, such as ten or twenty pounds a head. But no governor dare pass a law, having instructions to the contrary from the Board of Trade at home. By this means they are forced upon us, whether we will or will not. This plainly shows the African Company has the advantage of the colonies, and may do as it pleases with the [London] ministry.

Indeed, since we have been exhausted of our little stock of cash by the [French and Indian] war, the importation has stopped; our poverty then is our best security. There is no more picking for their [slave traders'] ravenous jaws upon bare bones, but should we begin to thrive, they will be at the same again. . . .

This is our part of the grievance, but to live in Virginia without slaves is morally impossible. Before our troubles, you could not hire a servant or slave for love or money, so that unless robust enough to cut wood, to go to mill, to work at the hoe, etc., you must starve, or board in some family where they both fleece and half starve you. There is no set price upon corn, wheat, and provisions, so they take advantage of the necessities of strangers, who are thus obliged to purchase some slaves and land. This, of course, draws us all into the original sin and the curse of the country of purchasing slaves, and this is the reason we have no merchants, traders, or artificers of any sort but what become planters in a short time.

A common laborer, white or black, if you can be so much favored as to hire one, is a shilling sterling or fifteen pence currency per day; a bungling carpenter two shillings or two shillings and sixpence per day; besides diet and lodging. That is, for a lazy fellow to get wood and water, £19.16.3 current per annum; add to this seven or eight pounds more and you have a slave for life.

C. Slavery in the Colonial Era

1. A Young African Boy Is Taken into Slavery (c. 1735)[*]

Venture Smith was the English name given to the West African author of the following account. Born in 1729, Venture was captured as a boy and brought to Rhode Island. He lived first as a slave, owned by several masters in succession, and later as a free man in Connecticut. His ancestral people, the Dukandarra of present-day Mali, were cattle and goat herders, and Venture worked with livestock as a youth in New England. He dictated this account to a scribe, Elisha Niles, in the 1790s. What must have been the most disconcerting features of Smith's forced removal from Africa to New England? What factors helped him to adjust to life in his new world?

---

[*]H. M. Selden, *A Narrative of the Life and Adventures of Venture, a Native of Africa* (Middletown, CT: J. S. Stewart, 1897; originally published 1798).

[A] message was brought...to my father, that [we were about to be] invaded by a numerous army, from a nation not far distant, furnished with musical instruments, and all kinds of arms then in use; that they were instigated by some white nation who equipped and sent them to subdue and possess the country. . . .

They then came to us in the reeds, and the very first salute I had from them was a violent blow on the head with the fore part of a gun, and at the same time a grasp around the neck. I then had a rope put about my neck, as all the women in the thicket with me, and were immediately led to my father, who was likewise pinioned and haltered for leading. In this condition we were all led to the camp. The women and myself, being submissive, had tolerable treatment from the enemy, while my father was closely interrogated respecting his money, which they knew he must have. But as he gave them no account of it, he was instantly cut and pounded on his body with great inhumanity, that he might be induced by the torture he suffered to make the discovery. All this availed not in the least to make him give up his money, but he despised all the tortures which they inflicted, until the continued exercise and increase of torment obliged him to sink and expire. He thus died without informing his enemies where his money lay. I saw him while he was thus tortured to death. The shocking scene is to this day fresh in my memory, and I have often been overcome while thinking on it. He was a man of remarkable stature. I should judge as much as six feet and six or seven inches high, two feet across the shoulders, and every way well proportioned. He was a man of remarkable strength and resolution, affable, kind and gentle, ruling with equity and moderation.

The army of the enemy was large, I should suppose consisting of about six thousand men. Their leader was called Baukurre. After destroying the old prince, they decamped and immediately marched towards the sea, lying to the west, taking with them myself and the women prisoners. . . .

. . . On a certain time, I and other prisoners were put on board a canoe, under our master, and rowed away to a vessel belonging to Rhode Island, commanded by Captain Collingwood, and the mate, Thomas Mumford. While we were going to the vessel, our master told us to appear to the best possible advantage for sale. I was bought on board by one Robertson Mumford, a steward of said vessel, for four gallons of rum and a piece of calico, and called VENTURE on account of his having purchased me with his own private venture. Thus I came by my name. All the slaves that were bought for that vessel's cargo were two hundred and sixty. . . .

The vessel then sailed for Rhode Island, and arrived there after a comfortable passage. Here my master sent me to live with one of his sisters until he could carry me to Fisher's Island, the place of his residence. I had then completed my eighth year. After staying with his sister some time, I was taken to my master's place to live. . . .

The first of the time of living at my master's own place, I was pretty much employed in the house, carding wool and other household business. In this situation I continued for some years, after which my master put me to work out of doors. After many proofs of my faithfulness and honesty, my master began to put great confidence in me. My behavior had as yet been submissive and obedient. I then began to have hard tasks imposed on me. Some of these were to pound four bushels of ears of corn every night in a barrel for the poultry, or be rigorously punished.

At other seasons of the year, I had to card wool until a very late hour. These tasks I had to perform when only about nine years old. Some time after, I had another difficulty and oppression which was greater than any I had ever experienced since I came into this country. This was to serve two masters. James Mumford, my master's son, when his father had gone from home in the morning and given me a stint to perform that day, would order me to do *this* and *that* business different from what my master had directed me. . . .

After I had lived with my master thirteen years, being then about twenty-two years old, I married Meg, a slave of his who was about my own age. . . .

[Eventually] I hired myself out at Fisher's Island, earning twenty pounds; thirteen pounds six shillings of which my master drew for the privilege and the remainder I paid for my freedom. This made fifty-one pounds two shillings which I paid him. In October following I went and wrought six months at Long Island. In that six month's time I cut and corded four hundred cords of wood, besides threshing out seventy-five bushels of grain, and received of my wages down only twenty pounds, which left remaining a larger sum. Whilst I was out that time, I took up on my wages only one pair of shoes. At night I lay on the hearth, with one coverlet over and another under me. I returned to my master and gave him what I received of my six months' labor. This left only thirteen pounds eighteen shillings to make up the full sum of my redemption. My master liberated me, saying that I might pay what was behind if I could ever make it convenient, otherwise it would be well. The amount of the money which I had paid my master towards redeeming my time, was seventy-one pounds two shillings. The reason of my master for asking such an unreasonable price, was, he said, to secure himself in case I should ever come to want. Being thirty-six years old, I left Colonel Smith once more for all. I had already been sold three different times, made considerable money with seemingly nothing to derive it from, had been cheated out of a large sum of money, lost much by misfortunes, and paid an enormous sum for my freedom.

2. The Stono River Rebellion in South Carolina (1739)[*]

Black slaves made up a majority of the population in early-eighteenth-century South Carolina. Naturally, they dreamed of freedom, and the refuge of nearby Spanish Florida held out the promise of turning their dream into reality. In 1739, a number of South Carolina slaves rose up in arms and struck out for Florida and freedom. What did their behavior suggest about the character of colonial slavery? In the following account by a white contemporary, what appear to be the greatest fears of the white slave-owning minority?

Sometime since there was a Proclamation published at Augustine, in which the King of Spain (then at Peace with Great Britain) promised Protection and Freedom to all Negroes [sic] Slaves that would resort thither. Certain Negroes belonging to Captain Davis escaped to Augustine, and were received there. They were

[*]Allen D. Candler, compiler, *The Colonial Records of the State of Georgia* (1913), vol. 22, part 2, pp. 232–236. Courtesy of Public Record Office (London)—CO 5/640ff.

demanded by General Oglethorpe who sent Lieutenant Demere to Augustine, and the Governor assured the General of his sincere Friendship, but at the same time showed his Orders from the Court of Spain, by which he was to receive all Run away Negroes. Of this other Negroes having notice, as it is believed, from the Spanish Emissaries, four or five who were Cattel-Hunters, and knew the Woods, some of whom belonged to Captain Macpherson, ran away with His Horses, wounded his Son and killed another Man. These marched f [sic] for Georgia, and were pursued, but the Rangers being then newly reduced [sic] the Countrey people could not over-take them, though they were discovered by the Saltzburghers, as they passed by Ebenezer. They reached Augustine, one only being killed and another wounded by the Indians in their flight. They were received there with great honours, one of them had a Commission given to him, and a Coat faced with Velvet. Amongst the Negroe Slaves there are a people brought from the Kingdom of Angola in Africa, many of these speak Portugueze [which Language is as near Spanish as Scotch is to English,] by reason that the Portugueze have considerable Settlement, and the Jesuits have a Mission and School in that Kingdom and many Thousands of the Negroes there pro-fess the Roman Catholic Religion. Several Spaniards upon diverse Pretences have for some time past been strolling about Carolina, two of them, who will give no account of themselves have been taken up and committed to Jayl in Georgia. The good reception of the Negroes at Augustine was spread about, Several attempted to escape to the Spaniards, & were taken, one of them was hanged at Charles Town. In the latter end of July last Don Pedr, Colonel of the Spanish Horse, went in a Launch to Charles Town under pretence of a message to General Oglethorpe and the Lieutenant Governour.

On the 9th day of September last being Sunday which is the day the Planters allow them to work for themselves, Some Angola Negroes assembled, to the number of Twenty; and one who was called Jemmy was their Captain, they suprized a Ware-house belonging to Mr. Hutchenson at a place called Stonehow [Stono]; they there killed Mr. Robert Bathurst, and Mr. Gibbs, plundered the House and took a pretty many small Arms and Powder, which were there for Sale. Next they plundered and burnt Mr. Godfrey's house, and killed him, his Daughter and Son. They then turned back and marched Southward along Pons Pons, which is the Road through Georgia to Augustine, they passed Mr. Wallace's Tavern towards day break, and said they would not hurt him, for he was a good Man and kind to his Slaves, but they broke open and plundered Mr. Lemy's House, and killed him, his wife and Child. They marched on towards Mr. Rose's resolving to kill him; but he was saved by a Negroe, who having hid him went out and pacified the others. Several Negroes joyned them, they calling out Liberty, marched on with Colours displayed and two Drums beat-ing, pursuing all the white people they met with, and killing Man Woman and Child when they could come up to them. Collonel Bull, Lieutenant Governour of South Carolina, who was then riding along the Road, discovered them, was pursued, and with much difficulty escaped & raised the Countrey. They burnt Colonel Hext's house and killed his Overseer and his Wife. They then burnt Mr. Sprye's house, then Mr. Sacheverell's, and then Mr. Nash's house, all lying upon the Pons Pons Road, and killed all the white People they found in them. Mr. Bullock got off, but they burnt his House, by this time many of them were drunk with the Rum they had taken in the Houses. They increased every minute by new Negroes coming to them, so that they were above Sixty, some say a hundred, on which they halted in a field, and set to dancing, Singing and beating Drums, to draw more Negroes to them, thinking they were now victorious over the whole Province, having marched ten miles & burnt all before them without Opposition, but the Militia being raised, the Planters with great briskness pursued them and when they came up, dismounting; charged them on foot. The Negroes were soon routed, though they behaved boldly, several being killed on the Spot, many ran back to their Plantations thinking they had not been missed, but they were there taken and Shot. Such as were taken in the field also, were, after being examined, shot on the Spot. And this is to be said to the honour of the Carolina Planters, that notwithstanding the Provocation they had received from so many Murders, they did not torture one Negroe, but only put them to an easy death. All that proved to be forced & were not concerned in the Murders & Burnings were pardoned, And this sudden Courage in the field, & the Humanity afterwards hath had so good an Effect that there hath been no farther Attempt, and the very Spirit of Revolt seems over. About 30 escaped from the fight, of which ten marched about 30 miles Southward, and being overtaken by the Planters on horseback, fought stoutly for some time and were all killed on the Spot. The rest are yet untaken. In the whole action about 40 Negroes and 20 whites were killed. The Lieutenant Governour sent an account of this to General Oglethorpe, who met the advices on his return from the Indian Nation. He immediately ordered a Troop of Rangers to be ranged, to patrole through Georgia, placed some Men in the Garrison at Palichocolas, which was before abandoned, and near which the Negroes formerly passed, being the only place where Horses can come to swim over the River Savannah for near 100 miles, ordered out the Indians in pursuit, and a Detachment of the Garrison at Port Royal to assist the Planters on any Occasion, and published a Proclamation ordering all the Constables &ca. of Georgia to pursue and seize all Negroes, with a Reward for any that should be taken. It is hoped these measures will prevent any Negroes from getting down to the Spaniards.

Thought Provokers

1. What sorts of people became indentured servants? How did the life of the servant compare with that of the slave?
2. What caused Bacon's Rebellion? Were the Baconites justified in revolting? In what ways did their rebellion foreshadow the American Revolutionary War?
3. How did slavery affect the spirit of the enslaved? of the enslavers? How did the experience of slaves in North America differ from that of slaves in the West Indies and Brazil? In which region would you rather have been a slave?

5

Colonial Society on the Eve of Revolution, 1700–1775

Driven from every other corner of the earth,
freedom of thought and the right of private
judgment in matters of conscience direct their
course to this happy country as their last asylum.

Samuel Adams, 1776

Prologue: The population of the British colonies increased amazingly, owing largely to the fertility of a pioneer people. Slaves arrived from Africa in growing numbers in the eighteenth century, and they too—like the whites—were soon increasing their ranks through their own natural fertility. Immigrants were pouring in from the British Isles and Europe, and although the English language remained predominant, the now-famed melting pot was beginning to bubble. As the population spread, the austerity of the old-time worship weakened, although it was given a temporary revival by the Great Awakening of the 1730s. The rational thought inspired by the European Enlightenment found a ready disciple in Benjamin Franklin, whose sly pokes at religion no doubt helped undermine the dominance of the clergy. Americans began dealing in international trade, straining against the commercial limitations imposed by British imperial rule. A ruling class of sorts existed in all the colonies, although the governing clique in New York received a sharp jolt in the famed Zenger libel case. The ease with which the individual colonist could rise from one social rung to another, quite in contrast with Old World rigidity, foreshadowed the emergence of a mobile, pluralistic society.

A. The Colonial Melting Pot

1. Benjamin Franklin Analyzes the Population (1751)[*]

The baby boom in the British colonies was an object of wonderment. The itinerant Swedish scientist Peter Kalm recorded that Mrs. Maria Hazard, who died in her hundredth year, left a total of five hundred children, grandchildren, great-grandchildren, and great-great-grandchildren. Benjamin Franklin, the incredibly versatile printer, businessman, philosopher, scientist, and diplomat, made the following observations in 1751. In his opinion, why were families so large, white labor so expensive, and slave labor so uneconomical?

---

[*]Jared Sparks, ed., *The Works of Benjamin Franklin* (Philadelphia: Childs & Peterson, 1840), vol. 2, pp. 313–315.

Land being thus plenty in America, and so cheap as that a laboring man that understands husbandry can, in a short time, save money enough to purchase a piece of new land sufficient for a plantation, whereon he may subsist a family, such are not afraid to marry. For, if they even look far enough forward to consider how their children, when grown up, are to be provided for, they see that more land is to be had at rates equally easy, all circumstances considered.

Hence marriages in America are more general, and more generally early, than in Europe. And if it is reckoned there that there is but one marriage per annum among one hundred persons, perhaps we may here reckon two; and if in Europe they have but four births to a marriage (many of their marriages being late), we may here reckon eight, of which, if one half grow up, and our marriages are made, reckoning one with another, at twenty years of age, our people must at least be doubled every twenty years.

But notwithstanding this increase, so vast is the territory of North America that it will require many ages to settle it fully. And till it is fully settled, labor will never be cheap here, where no man continues long a laborer for others, but gets a plantation of his own; no man continues long a journeyman to a trade, but goes among those new settlers, and sets up for himself, etc. Hence labor is no cheaper now in Pennsylvania than it was thirty years ago, though so many thousand laboring people have been imported.

The danger therefore of these colonies interfering with their mother country in trades that depend on labor, manufactures, etc., is too remote to require the attention of Great Britain. . . .

It is an ill-grounded opinion that, by the labor of slaves, America may possibly vie in cheapness of manufactures with Britain. The labor of slaves can never be so cheap here as the labor of workingmen is in Britain. Any one may compute it. Interest of money is in the colonies from 6 to 10 percent. Slaves, one with another, cost thirty pounds sterling per head. Reckon then the interest of the first purchase of a slave, the insurance or risk on his life, his clothing and diet, expenses in his sickness and loss of time, loss by his neglect of business (neglect is natural to the man who is not to be benefited by his own care or diligence), expense of a driver to keep him at work, and his pilfering from time to time, almost every slave being by nature a thief, and compare the whole amount with the wages of a manufacturer of iron or wool in England, you will see that labor is much cheaper there than it ever can be by Negroes here.

Why then will Americans purchase slaves? Because slaves may be kept as long as a man pleases, or has occasion for their labor; while hired men are continually leaving their masters (often in the midst of his business) and setting up for themselves.

2. Michel-Guillaume Jean de Crèvecoeur Discovers a New Man (c. 1770)[*]

Michel-Guillaume Jean de Crèvecoeur, a young Frenchman of noble family, served with the French army in Canada from 1758 to 1759. Upon reaching the English

---

[*]M. G. J. de Crèvecoeur, *Letters from an American Farmer* (New York: Fox, Duffield & Company, 1904; reprint), pp. 51–56.

colonies in 1759, he traveled widely, married an American woman, and settled down to an idyllic existence on his New York estate, "Pine Hill." A born farmer, he introduced into America a number of plants, including alfalfa. Probably during the decade before 1775, he wrote in English the classic series of essays known as Letters from an American Farmer (published in 1782). This glowing account was blamed for luring some five hundred French families to the wilds of the Ohio Country, where they perished. What does Crèvecoeur reveal regarding the racial composition of the colonies? What did he regard as the most important factors creating the new American man?

Whence came all these people?

They are a mixture of English, Scotch, Irish, French, Dutch, Germans, and Swedes. From this promiscuous breed, that race now called Americans have arisen. The Eastern [New England] provinces must indeed be excepted, as being the unmixed descendants of Englishmen. I have heard many wish that they had been more intermixed also. For my part, I am no wisher, and think it much better as it has happened. They exhibit a most conspicuous figure in this great and variegated picture; they too enter for a great share in the pleasing perspective displayed in these thirteen provinces. I know it is fashionable to reflect on them, but I respect them for what they have done; for the accuracy and wisdom with which they have settled their territory; for the decency of their manners; for their early love of letters; their ancient college, the first in this hemisphere;* for their industry, which to me, who am but a farmer, is the criterion of everything. There never was a people, situated as they are, who with so ungrateful a soil have done more in so short a time. . . .

In this great American asylum, the poor of Europe have by some means met together, and in consequence of various causes; to what purpose should they ask one another what countrymen they are? Alas, two-thirds of them had no country. Can a wretch who wanders about, who works and starves, whose life is a continual scene of sore affliction or pinching penury—can that man call England or any other kingdom his country? A country that had no bread for him, whose fields procured him no harvest, who met with nothing but the frowns of the rich, the severity of the laws, with jails and punishments; who owned not a single foot of the extensive surface of this planet? No! urged by a variety of motives, here they came. Everything has tended to regenerate them: new laws, a new mode of living, a new social system. Here they are become men. In Europe they were as so many useless plants, wanting vegetative mould, and refreshing showers; they withered, and were mowed down by want, hunger, and war. But now by the power of transplantation, like all other plants, they have taken root and flourished! Formerly they were not numbered in any civil lists of their country, except in those of the poor. Here they rank as citizens.

By what invisible power has this surprising metamorphosis been performed? By that of the laws and that of their industry. The laws, the indulgent laws, protect them as they arrive, stamping on them the symbol of adoption. They receive ample

---

*In fact, the Spanish universities in Mexico City and Lima, Peru, antedated Harvard by eighty-five years.

rewards for their labors; these accumulated rewards procure them lands; those lands confer on them the title of freemen, and to that title every benefit is affixed which men can possibly require. . . .

What then is the American, this new man? He is either an European, or the descendant of an European; hence that strange mixture of blood, which you will find in no other country. I could point out to you a family whose grandfather was an Englishman, whose wife was Dutch, whose son married a French woman, and whose present four sons have now four wives of different nations.

He is an American who, leaving behind him all his ancient prejudices and manners, receives new ones from the new mode of life he has embraced, the new government he obeys, and the new rank he holds. He becomes an American by being received in the broad lap of our great *alma mater*. Here individuals of all nations are melted into a new race of men whose labors and posterity will one day cause great changes in the world. Americans are the western pilgrims, who are carrying along with them the great mass of arts, sciences, vigor, and industry which began long since in the East. They will finish the great circle.

The American ought therefore to love this country much better than that wherein either he or his forefathers were born. Here the rewards of his industry follow with equal steps the progress of his labor; his labor is founded on the basis of nature, *self-interest*; can it want a stronger allurement? Wives and children, who before in vain demanded of him a morsel of bread, now, fat and frolicsome, gladly help their father to clear those fields whence exuberant crops are to arise to feed and to clothe them all; without any part being claimed, either by a despotic prince, a rich abbot, or a mighty lord. Here religion demands but little of him: a small voluntary salary to the minister, and gratitude to God. Can he refuse these?

The American is a new man, who acts upon new principles; he must therefore entertain new ideas, and form new opinions. From involuntary idleness, servile dependence, penury, and useless labor, he has passed to toils of a very different nature, rewarded by ample subsistence.

This is an American.

3. The Growth of the Colonial Population (1740–1780)*

This table shows the growth and shifting composition of the colonial population in the several decades before independence. What are the principal trends in the changing population? How might one account for regional differences in the numbers and makeup of the American people in the colonial era? Why did some areas grow faster than others? To what extent can the subsequent history of the United States be predicted from these figures?

---

*"The Thirteen Colonies: Estimated Percentages of Blacks and Whites, 1740–1780" by R. C. Simmons from *The American Colonies: From Settlement to Independence* (Copyright © R. C. Simmons 1976).

The Thirteen Colonies:
Estimated Percentages of Blacks and Whites, 1740–1780

A = Total Population   B = % of Blacks   C = % of Whites

	1740			1760			1780		
	A	B	C	A	B	C	A	B	C
Maine[a]	—	—	—	—	—	—	49,133	0.93	99.07
New Hampshire	23,256	2.15	97.85	39,093	1.53	98.47	87,802	0.62	99.38
Massachusetts	151,613	2.00	98.00	222,600	2.18	97.82	268,627	1.79	98.21
Rhode Island	25,255	9.53	90.47	45,471	7.63	92.37	52,946	5.04	94.96
Connecticut	89,580	2.90	97.10	142,470	2.65	97.35	206,701	2.85	97.15
New York	63,665	14.13	85.87	117,138	13.94	86.06	210,541	10.00	90.00
New Jersey	51,373	8.50	91.50	93,813	7.00	93.00	139,627	7.49	92.51
Pennsylvania	85,637	2.40	97.60	183,703	2.40	97.60	327,305	2.40	97.60
Delaware	19,870	5.21	94.79	33,250	5.21	94.79	45,385	6.60	93.40
Maryland	116,093	20.70	79.30	162,267	30.20	69.80	245,474	32.80	67.20
Virginia	180,440	33.25	66.75	339,726	41.38	58.62	538,004	41.00	59.00
North Carolina	51,760	21.25	78.75	110,422	30.38	69.62	270,133	33.69	66.31
South Carolina	45,000	66.67	33.33	94,074	60.94	39.06	180,000	53.89	46.11
Georgia	2,021		100.00	9,578	37.36	62.64	56,071	37.15	62.85

[a]Massachusetts, of which Maine was a part until admitted to the Union as a state in 1820, did not establish a separate administrative district for Maine until the 1770s.
Source: "The Thirteen Colonies: Estimated Percentages of Blacks and Whites, 1740-1780" by R. C. Simmons from The American Colonies: From Settlement to Independence (Copyright © R. C. Simmons 1976).

B. The Great Awakening

1. George Whitefield Fascinates Franklin (1739)[*]

The frenzied religious revival that swept the colonies in the 1730s, known as the Great Awakening, featured George Whitefield as one of the Awakeners. Although he was only twenty-five years old when Benjamin Franklin heard him in Philadelphia during the second of Whitefield's seven trips to America, he had already preached with such emotional power in England that crowds would assemble at his church door before daybreak. When orthodox clergymen denied him their pulpits, he would speak in the open air, at times to crowds of twenty thousand persons. Franklin, then thirty-six years old and a hardheaded Philadelphia businessman, was skeptical. What does

[*]John Bigelow, ed., *Autobiography of Benjamin Franklin* (Philadelphia: J. B. Lippincott & Co., 1868), pp. 251–255.

this passage from his famed autobiography, written many years later, reveal about Franklin's character and about the atmosphere of toleration in Philadelphia?

In 1739 arrived among us from Ireland the Reverend Mr. Whitefield, who had made himself remarkable there as an itinerant preacher. He was at first permitted to preach in some of our churches; but the clergy, taking a dislike to him, soon refused him their pulpits, and he was obliged to preach in the fields. The multitudes of all sects and denominations that attended his sermons were enormous, and it was a matter of speculation to me, who was one of the number, to observe the extraordinary influence of his oratory on his hearers, and how much they admired and respected him, notwithstanding his common abuse of them, by assuring them they were naturally *half beasts and half devils*. It was wonderful to see the change soon made in the manners of our inhabitants. From being thoughtless or indifferent about religion, it seemed as if all the world were growing religious, so that one could not walk through the town in an evening without hearing psalms sung in different families of every street.

And it being found inconvenient to assemble in the open air, subject to its inclemencies, the building of a house to meet in was no sooner proposed, and persons appointed to receive contributions, but sufficient sums were soon received to procure the ground and erect the building, which was one hundred feet long and seventy broad, about the size of Westminster Hall; and the work was carried on with such spirit as to be finished in a much shorter time than could have been expected. Both house and ground were vested in trustees, expressly for the use of any preacher of any religious persuasion who might desire to say something to the people at Philadelphia; the design in building not being to accommodate any particular sect, but the inhabitants in general; so that even if the Mufti of Constantinople were to send a missionary to preach Mohammedanism to us, he would find a pulpit at his service.

Mr. Whitefield, in leaving us, went preaching all the way through the colonies to Georgia. The settlement of that province had lately been begun, but, instead of being made with hardy, industrious husbandmen, accustomed to labor, the only people fit for such an enterprise, it was with families of broken shopkeepers and other insolvent debtors, many of indolent and idle habits, taken out of the jails, who, being set down in the woods, unqualified for clearing land, and unable to endure the hardships of a new settlement, perished in numbers, leaving many helpless children unprovided for. The sight of their miserable situation inspired the benevolent heart of Mr. Whitefield with the idea of building an Orphan House there, in which they might be supported and educated. Returning northward, he preached up this charity, and made large collections, for his eloquence had a wonderful power over the hearts and purses of his hearers, of which I myself was an instance.

I did not disapprove of the design, but, as Georgia was then destitute of materials and workmen, and it was proposed to send them from Philadelphia at a great expense, I thought it would have been better to have built the house there, and brought the children to it. This I advised, but he was resolute in his first project, rejected my counsel, and I therefore refused to contribute.

I happened soon after to attend one of his sermons, in the course of which I perceived he intended to finish with a collection, and I silently resolved he should get nothing from me. I had in my pocket a handful of copper money, three or four silver dollars, and five pistoles in gold. As he proceeded I began to soften, and concluded to give the coppers. Another stroke of his oratory made me ashamed of that, and determined me to give the silver; and he finished so admirably that I emptied my pocket wholly into the collector's dish, gold and all.

At this sermon there was also one of our club who, being of my sentiments respecting the building in Georgia, and suspecting a collection might be intended, had, by precaution, emptied his pockets before he came from home. Towards the conclusion of the discourse, however, he felt a strong desire to give, and applied to a [Quaker] neighbor, who stood near him, to borrow some money for the purpose. The application was unfortunately to perhaps the only man in the company who had the firmness not to be affected by the preacher. His answer was, "At any other time, Friend Hopkinson, I would lend to thee freely; but not now, for thee seems to be out of thy right senses."

2. Jonathan Edwards Paints the Horrors of Hell (1741)*

Jonathan Edwards, a New England Congregational minister, was, like George White-field, a Great Awakener. Tall, slender, and delicate, Edwards had a weak voice but a powerful mind. He still ranks as the greatest Protestant theologian ever produced in America. His command of the English language was exceptional, and his vision of hell, peopled with pre-damned infants and others, was horrifying. As he preached hellfire to his Enfield, Connecticut, congregation, there was a great moaning and crying: "What shall I do to be saved? Oh, I am going to hell!" Men and women groveled on the floor or lay inert on the benches. Would Edwards's famous sermon, "Sinners in the Hands of an Angry God," be equally effective today?

The God that holds you over the pit of hell, much as one holds a spider or some loathsome insect over the fire, abhors you, and is dreadfully provoked. His wrath towards you burns like fire; he looks upon you as worthy of nothing else but to be cast into the fire. He is of purer eyes than to bear you in his sight; you are ten thousand times as abominable in his eyes as the most hateful, venomous serpent is in ours.

You have offended him infinitely more than ever a stubborn rebel did his prince, and yet it is nothing but his hand that holds you from falling into the fire every moment. It is to be ascribed to nothing else that you did not go to hell the last night; that you were suffered to awake again in this world, after you closed your eyes to sleep. And there is no other reason to be given why you have not dropped into hell since you arose in the morning, but that God's hand has held you up. There is no other reason to be given why you have not gone to hell since you have sat here in the house of God provoking his pure eye by your sinful, wicked manner of attending his solemn worship. Yea, there is nothing else that is to be given as a reason why you do not this very moment drop down into hell.

O sinner! consider the fearful danger you are in! It is a great furnace of wrath, a wide and bottomless pit, full of the fire of wrath that you are held over in the hand of that God whose wrath is provoked and incensed as much against you as against many of the damned in hell. You hang by a slender thread, with the flames of Divine wrath flashing about it, and ready every moment to singe it and burn it asunder. . . .

---

*Jonathan Edwards, *Works* (Andover, MA: Allen, Morrill & Wardwell, 1842), vol. 2, pp. 10–11.

It would be dreadful to suffer this fierceness and wrath of Almighty God one moment; but you must suffer it to all eternity. There will be no end to this exquisite, horrible misery. When you look forward, you shall see along forever a boundless duration before you, which will swallow up your thoughts, and amaze your soul. And you will absolutely despair of ever having any deliverance, any end, any mitigation, any rest at all. You will know certainly that you must wear out long ages, millions of millions of ages in wrestling and conflicting with this Almighty, merciless vengeance. And then when you have so done, when so many ages have actually been spent by you in this manner, you will know that all is but a point [dot] to what remains. So that your punishment will indeed be infinite.

Oh! who can express what the state of a soul in such circumstances is! All that we can possibly say about it gives but a very feeble, faint representation of it. It is inexpressible and inconceivable: for "who knows the power of God's anger"!

How dreadful is the state of those that are daily and hourly in danger of this great wrath and infinite misery! But this is the dismal case of every soul in this congregation that has not been born again, however moral and strict, sober and religious, they may otherwise be. Oh! that you would consider it, whether you be young or old!

There is reason to think that there are many in this congregation, now hearing this discourse, that will actually be the subjects of this very misery to all eternity. We know not who they are, or in what seats they sit, or what thoughts they now have. It may be they are now at ease, and hear all these things without much disturbance, and are now flattering themselves that they are not the persons, promising themselves that they shall escape.

If we knew that there was one person, and but one, in the whole congregation, that was to be the subject of this misery, what an awful thing it would be to think of! If we knew who it was, what an awful sight would it be to see such a person! How might all the rest of the congregation lift up a lamentable and bitter cry over him!

But, alas! instead of one, how many is it likely will remember this discourse in hell! And it would be a wonder, if some that are now present should not be in hell in a very short time, before this year is out. And it would be no wonder if some persons that now sit here in some seats of this meeting-house, in health, and quiet and secure, should be there before tomorrow morning!

C. The Colonial Economy

I. Colonial Trade and the British Empire (1701–1770)*

Eighteenth-century British merchants established an expansive commercial network linking England's burgeoning manufacturers to the raw materials of India and the Americas, and to the lucrative markets of the European continent. The following table chronicles the Empire's growing trade. Which regions saw the greatest absolute and relative gains in trade with England? What does the table suggest about the American colonies' role in the British imperial system?

---

*From R. A. Johns, *Colonial Trade and International Exchange: The Transition from Autarky to International Trade*, p. 55. Copyright © 1988. Reproduced by kind permission of Continuum International Publishing Group.

Composition of English Trade, 1700–1770 (Annual averages of combined imports and exports)

	1701–1710		1731–1740		1761–1770	
	Annual Average (£000s)	% Total Trade	Annual Average (£000s)	% Total Trade	Annual Average (£000s)	% Total Trade
British Empire						
American continent[a]	556	5%	1,313	7%	2,843	11%
British West Indies	942	9%	1,781	9%	3,406	13%
India	582	5%	1,179	6%	2,516	10%
Ireland	579	5%	1,045	6%	2,850	11%
Europe	7,653	69%	10,555	56%	11,740	45%
Other	757	7%	3,046	16%	2,575	10%
Total	11,069	100%	18,919	100%	25,930	100%

[a]By using the monetary value of imports and exports, this table understates the importance of North American trade to the British Empire. Colonial raw materials, though cheaper than the finished goods exported to Europe, were essential to the expansion of English industry.

Source: From R. A. Johns, *Colonial Trade and International Exchange: The Transition from Autarky to International Trade*, p. 55. Copyright © 1988.

2. British Colonial Exports (1768–1772)[*]

The following table lists the principal exports of the British colonies on the eve of the Revolution. What patterns emerge from the figures below? What effect did the Navigation Acts have on the movement of goods throughout the British Empire? What do these figures suggest about the future economic development of each region?

Exports from British New World Colonies, 1768–1772 (pounds sterling)

	Great Britain	Ireland	North America	Other Europe	West Indies	Africa	Total (% Exports)
West Indies							
Sugar	3,002,750		183,700				3,186,450 (81%)
Rum	380,943		333,337				714,280 (18%)
Molasses	222		9,648				9,870 (0.3%)
Total	3,383,915		526,685				3,910,600

Continued

---

[*]Ronald Findlay and Kevin H. O'Rourke, *Power and Plenty* (Princeton, NJ: Princeton University Press, 2007).

Continued

	Great Britain	Ireland	North America	Other Europe	West Indies	Africa	Total (% Exports)
New England							
Fish/whale	40,649			57,999	115,170	440	214,258 (49%)
Livestock/meat	374			461	89,118		89,953 (20%)
Wood	5,983	167		1,352	57,769		65,271 (15%)
Potash	22,390	9					22,399 (5%)
Grains	117	23		3,998	15,764		19,902 (5%)
Rum	471	44		1,497		16,754	18,766 (4%)
Other	6,991	1,018		296	247		8,552 (2%)
Total	76,975	1,261		65,603	278,068	17,194	439,101
Middle Colonies							
Grains	15,453	9,686		175,280	178,961		379,380 (72%)
Flaxseed	771	35,185					35,956 (7%)
Wood	2,635	4,815		3,053	18,845		29,348 (6%)
Iron	24,053	695			2,921		27,669 (5%)
Livestock/meat	2,142			1,199	16,692		20,033 (4%)
Potash	12,233	39					12,272 (2%)
Other	11,082	1,310		2,227	6,191	1,077	21,887 (4%)
Total	68,369	51,730		181,759	223,610	1,077	526,545
Upper South							
Tobacco	756,128						756,128 (72%)
Grains	10,206	22,962		97,523	68,794		199,485 (19%)
Iron	28,314	416			461		29,191 (3%)
Wood	9,060	2,115		1,114	10,195		22,484 (2%)
Other	23,344	3,357		526	12,368		39,595 (4%)
Total	827,052	28,850		99,163	91,818		1,046,883
Lower South							
Rice	198,590			50,982	55,961		305,533 (55%)
Indigo	111,864						111,864 (20%)
Deerskins	37,093						37,093 (7%)
Naval Stores	31,709						31,709 (6%)
Wood	2,520	228		1,396	21,620		25,764 (5%)
Grains	302	169		1,323	11,358		13,152 (2%)
Livestock/meat	75	366		103	12,386		12,930 (2%)
Other	11,877	515		365	785	362	13,904 (3%)
Total	394,030	1,278		54,169	102,110	362	551,949

D. The Shoots of Democracy

1. The Epochal Zenger Trial (1735)*

William Cosby, a hotheadedly incompetent New York governor, peremptorily removed the chief justice of the colony and substituted a stooge, young James Delancey. New Yorkers of the "popular party" decided to strike back by supporting the New-York Weekly Journal, *edited by John Peter Zenger, a struggling printer who had earlier come from Germany as an indentured servant. Zenger's attacks on Governor Cosby brought on a famous trial for seditious libel. The outlook seemed dark after Zenger's two attorneys were summarily disbarred. But at the crucial moment, Andrew Hamilton, an aging but eminent Philadelphia lawyer, put in a surprise appearance as defense counsel. At the outset, he seemingly gave away his case when he admitted that Zenger had published the alleged libels, but he contended that because they were true, they were not libelous. The accepted law was that a libel was a libel, regardless of its truth. In the account excerpted here, Zenger describes his defense by Hamilton and the outcome of the trial. How did Hamilton's defense contribute to the development of American democracy?*

Mr. [Prosecuting] Attorney. . . . The case before the court is whether Mr. Zenger is guilty of libeling His Excellency the Governor of New York, and indeed the whole administration of the government. Mr. Hamilton has confessed the printing and publishing, and I think nothing is plainer than that the words in the information [indictment] are scandalous, and tend to sedition, and to disquiet the minds of the people of this province. And if such papers are not libels, I think it may be said there can be no such thing as a libel.

Mr. Hamilton. May it please Your Honor, I cannot agree with Mr. Attorney. For though I freely acknowledge that there are such things as libels, yet I must insist, at the same time, that what my client is charged with is not a libel. And I observed just now that Mr. Attorney, in defining a libel, made use of the words "scandalous, seditious, and tend to disquiet the people." But (whether with design or not I will not say) he omitted the word "false."

Mr. Attorney. I think I did not omit the word "false." But it has been said already that it may be a libel, notwithstanding it may be true.

Mr. Hamilton. In this I must still differ with Mr. Attorney; for I depend upon it, we are to be tried upon this information now before the court and jury, and to which we have pleaded not guilty, and by it we are charged with printing and publishing a certain false, malicious, seditious, and scandalous libel. This word "false" must have some meaning, or else how came it there? . . .

Mr. Chief Justice [Delancey]. You cannot be admitted, Mr. Hamilton, to give the truth of a libel in evidence. A libel is not to be justified; for it is nevertheless a libel that it is true [i.e., the fact that it is true makes it nonetheless a libel].

---

*J. P. Zenger, *Zenger's Own Story* (1736; reprint Columbia, MO: Press of the Crippled Turtle, 1954), pp. 20–41, passim.

Mr. Hamilton. I am sorry the court has so soon resolved upon that piece of law; I expected first to have been heard to the point. I have not in all my reading met with an authority that says we cannot be admitted to give the truth in evidence, upon an information for a libel.

Mr. Chief Justice. The law is clear, that you cannot justify a libel. . . .

Mr. Hamilton. I thank Your Honor. Then, gentlemen of the jury, it is to you we must now appeal, for witnesses, to the truth of the facts we have offered, and are denied the liberty to prove. And let it not seem strange that I apply myself to you in this manner. I am warranted so to do both by law and reason.

The law supposes you to be summoned out of the neighborhood where the fact [crime] is alleged to be committed; and the reason of your being taken out of the neighborhood is because you are supposed to have the best knowledge of the fact that is to be tried. And were you to find a verdict against my client, you must take upon you to say the papers referred to in the information, and which we acknowledge we printed and published, are false, scandalous, and seditious. But of this I can have no apprehension. You are citizens of New York; you are really what the law supposes you to be, honest and lawful men. And, according to my brief, the facts which we offer to prove were not committed in a corner; they are notoriously known to be true; and therefore in your justice lies our safety. And as we are denied the liberty of giving evidence to prove the truth of what we have published, I will beg leave to lay it down, as a standing rule in such cases, that the suppressing of evidence ought always to be taken for the strongest evidence; and I hope it will have that weight with you. . . .

I hope to be pardoned, sir, for my zeal upon this occasion. It is an old and wise caution that when our neighbor's house is on fire, we ought to take care of our own. For though, blessed be God, I live in a government [Pennsylvania] where liberty is well understood, and freely enjoyed, yet experience has shown us all (I'm sure it has to me) that a bad precedent in one government is soon set up for an authority in another. And therefore I cannot but think it mine, and every honest man's duty, that (while we pay all due obedience to men in authority) we ought at the same time to be upon our guard against power, wherever we apprehend that it may affect ourselves or our fellow subjects.

I am truly very unequal to such an undertaking on many accounts. And you see I labor under the weight of many years, and am borne down with great infirmities of body. Yet old and weak as I am, I should think it my duty, if required, to go to the utmost part of the land, where my service could be of any use, in assisting to quench the flame of prosecutions upon informations, set on foot by the government, to deprive a people of the right of remonstrating (and complaining too) of the arbitrary attempts of men in power. Men who injure and oppress the people under their administration provoke them to cry out and complain; and then make that very complaint the foundation for new oppressions and prosecutions. I wish I could say there were no instances of this kind.

But to conclude. The question before the court and you, gentlemen of the jury, is not of small nor private concern. It is not the cause of a poor printer, nor of New York alone, which you are now trying. No! It may, in its consequence, affect every freeman that lives under a British government on the main[land] of America. It is the best cause. It is the cause of liberty. And I make no doubt but your upright conduct, this day, will not only entitle you to the love and esteem of your fellow citizens; but every man who prefers freedom to a life of slavery will bless and honor you, as men who have baffled the attempt of tyranny, and, by an impartial and uncorrupt verdict, have laid a noble foundation for securing to ourselves, our posterity, and our neighbors, that to which nature and the laws of our country have given us a right—the liberty both of exposing and opposing arbitrary power (in these parts of the world, at least) by speaking and writing truth. . . .

The jury withdrew, and in a small time returned, and being asked by the clerk whether they were agreed of their verdict, and whether John Peter Zenger was guilty of printing and publishing the libels in the information mentioned, they answered by Thomas Hunt, their foreman, "Not guilty." Upon which there were three huzzas in the hall, which was crowded with people, and the next day I was discharged from my imprisonment.

[The jurors, who might have suffered fines and imprisonment, were guilty of "bad law," for at that time they had no legal alternative to finding Zenger guilty. But the trial, which was widely publicized at home and abroad, provided a setback for judicial tyranny, a partial triumph for freedom of the press, a gain for the privilege of criticizing public officials, and a boost to the ideal of liberty generally. Andrew Hamilton, in truth, was contending for the law as it should be—and as it ultimately became. Not for many years, however, did the two principles for which he argued become accepted practice in England and America: (1) the admissibility of evidence as to the truth of an alleged libel and (2) the right of the jury to judge the libelous nature of the alleged libel.]

2. Crèvecoeur Finds a Perfect Society (c. 1770)*

Crèvecoeur, the happy Frenchman dwelling on a New York farm before the Revolution (see earlier, p. 51), wrote in glowing terms of the almost classless society developing in the colonies. Can you reconcile his statements with the existence of slavery and indentured servitude, a planter aristocracy, and a tax-supported church?

He [the European traveler to America] is arrived on a new continent; a modern society offers itself to his contemplation, different from what he had hitherto seen. It is not composed, as in Europe, of great lords who possess everything, and of a herd of people who have nothing. Here are no aristocratical families, no courts, no kings, no bishops, no ecclesiastical dominion, no invisible power giving to a few a very visible one; no great manufacturers employing thousands, no great refinements of luxury. The rich and the poor are not so far removed from each other as they are in Europe.

---

*M. G. J. de Crèvecoeur, *Letters from an American Farmer* (New York: Fox, Duffield & Company, 1904; reprint), pp. 49–50.

Some few towns excepted, we are all tillers of the earth, from Nova Scotia to West Florida. We are a people of cultivators, scattered over an immense territory, communicating with each other by means of good roads and navigable rivers, united by the silken bands of mild government, all respecting the laws, without dreading their power, because they are equitable. We are all animated with the spirit of an industry which is unfettered and unrestrained, because each person works for himself.

If he [the European visitor] travels through our rural districts, he views not the hostile castle and the haughty mansion, contrasted with the clay-built hut and miserable cabin, where cattle and men help to keep each other warm, and dwell in meanness, smoke, and indigence. A pleasing uniformity of decent competence appears throughout our habitations. The meanest of our log-houses is a dry and comfortable habitation. Lawyer or merchant are the fairest titles our towns afford; that of a farmer is the only appellation of the rural inhabitants of our country. It must take some time ere he can reconcile himself to our dictionary, which is but short in words of dignity and names of honor.

There, on a Sunday, he sees a congregation of respectable farmers and their wives, all clad in neat homespun, well mounted, or riding in their own humble wagons. There is not among them an esquire, saving the unlettered magistrate. There he sees a parson as simple as his flock, a farmer who does not riot on the labor of others. We have no princes, for whom we toil, starve, and bleed: we are the most perfect society now existing in the world. Here man is free as he ought to be; nor is this pleasing equality so transitory as many others are.

Thought Provokers

---

1. Compare and contrast social conditions in the New World with those in the Old, and explain why the New World had certain advantages. In what ways did the composition of colonial society foreshadow the social structure of the modern United States?
2. Compare and contrast religion in colonial times with religion today. Did the threat of hellfire promote better morals? Reconcile the wrathful Old Testament God of Jonathan Edwards with the New Testament concept of "God is love."
3. How did imperial regulations shape the patterns of trade between Britain and her colonies? How did North American exports contribute to the economic development of the British Empire as a whole?
4. How can one reconcile the case of Zenger with the classless society described by Crèvecoeur? Can the truth be libel today?

6

The Duel for North America, 1608–1763

The most momentous and far-reaching question ever brought to issue on this continent was: Shall France remain here or shall she not?

Francis Parkman, 1884

Prologue: French exploration of North America penetrated deeply into Canada and the Mississippi Valley. At first there was elbow room for both the French and the English, but wars that were ignited in Europe spread to the New World and involved the colonists of both nations in a series of bloody clashes: King William's War (1689–1697), Queen Anne's War (1702–1713), King George's War (1744–1748), and the French and Indian War (1754–1763). Continuing rivalry between the English colonists and the French traders gradually intensified, and the showdown came in 1754 in the wilds of the Ohio Valley, where young George Washington's tiny army of Virginians was forced to surrender. The French and Indian War (called the Seven Years' War in Europe) thus began inauspiciously for the British and continued disastrously for them. In 1755 General Edward Braddock's army was almost wiped out near what is now Pittsburgh. At length, a new prime minister, William Pitt, infused life into the flagging cause. In 1759 Quebec fell to the heroic General James Wolfe, and the next year Montreal capitulated. By the Treaty of 1763, France was completely and permanently ejected from the mainland of North America. Meanwhile, the British victory both provoked fresh problems with the Indians in the Great Lakes region and caused new stirrings among the American colonists.

A. The French and Indian War

1. Benjamin Franklin Characterizes General Edward Braddock (1755)[*]

Once the French and Indian War had begun, the British aimed their main thrust of 1755 at Fort Duquesne, on the present site of Pittsburgh. Their commander was General Edward Braddock, a sixty-two-year-old veteran of European battlefields. Transportation over uncut roads from Virginia was but one of the many difficulties

---

[*]John Bigelow, ed., *Autobiography of Benjamin Franklin* (Philadelphia: J. B. Lippincott & Co., 1868), pp. 309–313.

facing the invaders, and Benjamin Franklin won laurels by rounding up 150 wag-ons. Within about ten miles of Fort Duquesne, Braddock's vanguard of some 1,200 officers and men encountered an advancing force of about 250 French and 600 Indians. Both sides were surprised, but the French, at first driven back, rallied and attacked the flanks of the crowded redcoats from nearby ravines. In Franklin's account, written some sixteen years after the event, who or what is alleged to have been responsible for the disaster?

This general [Braddock] was, I think, a brave man, and might probably have made a figure as a good officer in some European war. But he had too much self-confidence, too high an opinion of the validity of regular troops, and too mean a one of both Americans and Indians. George Croghan, our Indian interpreter, joined him on his march with one hundred of those people, who might have been of great use to his army as guides, scouts, etc., if he had treated them kindly. But he slighted and neglected them, and they gradually left them.

In conversation with him one day, he was giving me some account of his intended progress. "After taking Fort Duquesne," says he, "I am to proceed to [Fort] Niagara; and, having taken that, to [Fort] Frontenac, if the season will allow time; and I suppose it will, for Duquesne can hardly detain me above three or four days; and then I see nothing that can obstruct my march to Niagara."

Having before revolved in my mind the long line his army must make in their march by a very narrow road, to be cut for them through the woods and bushes, and also what I had read of a former defeat of 1,500 French who invaded the Iroquois country, I had conceived some doubts and some fears for the event of the campaign. But I ventured only to say, "To be sure, sir, if you arrive well before Duquesne, with these fine troops, so well provided with artillery, that place, not yet completely fortified, and as we hear with no very strong garrison, can probably make but a short resistance. The only danger I apprehend of obstruction to your march is from ambuscades of Indians, who, by constant practice, are dexterous in laying and executing them; and the slender line, near four miles long, which your army must make, may expose it to be attacked by surprise in its flanks, and to be cut like a thread into several pieces, which, from their distance, cannot come up in time to support each other."

He smiled at my ignorance, and replied, "These savages may, indeed, be a formidable enemy to your raw American militia, but upon the King's regular and disciplined troops, sir, it is impossible they should make any impression." I was conscious of an impropriety in my disputing with a military man in matters of his profession, and said no more.

The enemy, however, did not take the advantage of his army which I apprehended its long line of march exposed it to, but let it advance without interruption till within nine miles of the place; and then, when more in a body (for it had just passed a river, where the front had halted till all were come over), and in a more open part of the woods than any it had passed, attacked its advanced guard by a heavy fire from behind trees and bushes, which was the first intelligence the General had of an enemy's being near him. This guard being disordered, the General hurried the troops up to their assistance, which was done in great confusion, through wagons, baggage, and cattle; and presently the fire came upon their flank. The officers, being on horseback, were more easily distinguished, picked out as marks, and fell very fast; and the soldiers were crowded together in a huddle, having or hearing no orders, and standing to be shot at till two-thirds of them were killed; and then, being seized with a panic, the whole fled with precipitation.

The wagoners took each a horse out of his team and scampered. Their example was immediately followed by others; so that all the wagons, provisions, artillery, and stores were left to the enemy. The General, being wounded, was brought off with difficulty; his secretary, Mr. Shirley, was killed by his side; and out of 86 officers, 63 were killed or wounded, and 714 men killed out of 1,100. . . .

Captain Orme, who was one of the General's aides-de-camp, and, being grievously wounded, was brought off with him and continued with him to his death, which happened in a few days, told me that he was totally silent all the first day, and at night only said, "Who would have thought it?" That he was silent again the following day, saying only at last, "We shall better know how to deal with them another time"; and died in a few minutes after.

2. A Frenchman Reports Braddock's Defeat (1755)[*]

An anonymous Frenchman, presumably stationed at Fort Duquesne, sent the following report of the battle home to Paris. In what important respects does it differ from Franklin's account just given? Where the two versions conflict, which is to be accorded the more credence? Why? What light does this report cast on the legend that Braddock was ambushed?

M. de Contrecoeur, captain of infantry, Commandant of Fort Duquesne, on the Ohio, having been informed that the English were taking up arms in Virginia for the purpose of coming to attack him, was advised, shortly afterwards, that they were on the march. He dispatched scouts, who reported to him faithfully their progress. On the 7th instant he was advised that their army, consisting of 3,000 regulars from Old England, were within six leagues [eighteen miles] of this fort.

That officer employed the next day in making his arrangements; and on the 9th detached M. de Beaujeu, seconded by Messrs. Dumas and de Lignery, all three captains, together with 4 lieutenants, 6 ensigns, 20 cadets, 100 soldiers, 100 Canadians, and 600 Indians, with orders to lie in ambush at a favorable spot, which he had reconnoitred the previous evening. The detachment, before it could reach its place of destination, found itself in presence of the enemy within three leagues of that fort.

M. de Beaujeu, finding his ambush had failed, decided on an attack. This he made with so much vigor as to astonish the enemy, who were waiting for us in the best possible order; but their artillery, loaded with grape[shot] . . . , having opened its fire, our men gave way in turn. The Indians, also frightened by the report of the cannon, rather than by any damage it could inflict, began to yield, when M. de Beaujeu was killed.

---

[*]E. B. O'Callaghan, ed., *Documents Relative to the Colonial History of the State of New York* (Albany, NY: Weed, Parsons, Printers, 1858), vol. 10, pp. 303–304.

M. Dumas began to encourage his detachment. He ordered the officers in command of the Indians to spread themselves along the wings so as to take the enemy in flank, whilst he, M. de Lignery, and the other officers who led the French, were attacking them in front. This order was executed so promptly that the enemy, who were already shouting their "Long live the King," thought now only of defending themselves.

The fight was obstinate on both sides and success long doubtful; but the enemy at last gave way. Efforts were made, in vain, to introduce some sort of order in their retreat. The whoop of the Indians, which echoed through the forest, struck terror into the hearts of the entire enemy. The rout was complete. We remained in possession of the field with six brass twelves and sixes [cannon], four howitz-carriages of fifty, eleven small royal grenade mortars, all their ammunition, and, generally, their entire baggage.

Some deserters, who have come in since, have told us that we had been engaged with only 2000 men, the remainder of the army being four leagues further off. These same deserters have informed us that the enemy were retreating to Virginia, and some scouts, sent as far as the height of land, have confirmed this by reporting that the thousand men who were not engaged had been equally panic-stricken, and abandoned both provisions and ammunition on the way. On this intelligence, a detachment was dispatched after them, which destroyed and burnt everything that could be found.

The enemy have left more than 1000 men on the field of battle. They have lost a great portion of the artillery and ammunition, provisions, as also their general, whose name was Mr. Braddock, and almost all their officers. We have had 3 officers killed; 2 officers and 2 cadets wounded. Such a victory, so entirely unexpected, seeing the inequality of the forces, is the fruit of M. Dumas' experience, and of the activity and valor of the officers under his command.

B. Pontiac's Rebellion and Its Aftermath

I. Pontiac Rallies His Warriors (1763)*

Britain's triumph over France in 1763 proved a classic example of a Pyrrhic victory. It led first to renewed conflict with the Indians of the Great Lakes–Ohio Valley region and then to mounting problems with the seaboard colonists. Those problems eventually contributed heavily to the outbreak of the American Revolution. Almost immediately after peace was declared, the British announces that they would discontinue the French practice of supplying the Indians with arms and ammunition. Britain also made clear its intention to fortify the territory it had wrested from France. Peoples of the Five Nations, or Iroquois Confederacy, were especially embittered, as their wartime alliance with Britain had led them to expect better treatment. A coalition of Indian peoples led by the Ottawa chief, Pontiac, was ready to rise up against the

---

*From "The Pontiac Manuscript," a diary thought to be of a French priest who may have been an eyewitness to the events he describes. In Francis Parkman, *The Conspiracy of Pontiac* (New York: E. P. Dutton, 1908), vol. 2, Appendix, pp. 223–224.

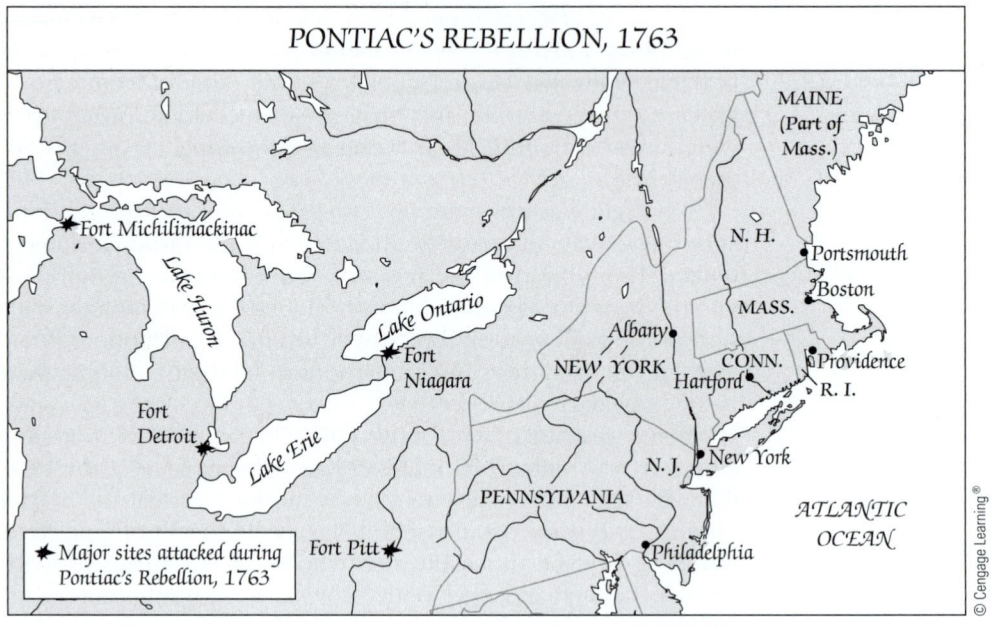

PONTIAC'S REBELLION, 1763

★ Major sites attacked during Pontiac's Rebellion, 1763

British. In April 1763 Pontiac summoned a meeting of leaders from several Indian groups at a Pottawattamie village on the banks of the Ecorse River near Detroit. There he laid out his plan to throw the British out of the land by first attacking the fort at Detroit and eventually storming all the British garrisons in the region, from Fort Pitt in the east to Michilimackinac in the west. What role does he see for France, recently expelled from the continent by British arms? How realistic was his plan?

The day fixed upon having arrived, all the Ottawas, Pondiac at their head, and the bad band of the Hurons, Takee at their head, met at the Pottawattamie village, where the pre-meditated council was to be held. Care was taken to send all the women out of the village, that they might not discover what was decided upon. Pondiac then ordered sentinels to be placed around the village, to prevent any interruption to their council. These precautions taken, each seated himself in the circle, according to his rank, and Pondiac, as great chief of the league, thus addressed them:—

"It is important, my brothers, that we should exterminate from our land this nation, whose only object is our death. You must be all sensible, as well as myself, that we can no longer supply our wants in the way we were accustomed to do with our Fathers the French. They sell us their goods at double the price that the French made us pay, and yet their merchandise is good for nothing; for no sooner have we bought a blanket or other thing to cover us than it is necessary to procure others against the time of departing for our wintering ground. Neither will they let us have them on credit, as our brothers the French used to do. When I visit the English chief, and inform him of the death of any of our comrades, instead of lamenting, as our brothers the French used to do, they make game of us. If I ask him for anything for our sick, he refuses, and tells us he does not want us, from which it is apparent he seeks our death. We must therefore, in return, destroy them without delay; there is nothing to prevent us: there are but few of them, and we shall easily overcome them,—why should we not attack them? Are we not men? Have I not shown you the belts I received from our Great Father the King of France? He tells us to strike—why should we not listen to his words? What do you fear? The time has arrived. Do you fear that our brothers the French, who are now among us, will hinder us? They are not acquainted with our designs, and if they did know them, could they prevent them? You know, as well as myself, that when the English came upon our lands, to drive from them our father Bellestre, they took from the French all the guns that they have, so that they have now no guns to defend themselves with. Therefore now is the time: let us strike. Should there be any French to take their part, let us strike them as we do the English. Remember what the Giver of Life desired our brother the Delaware to do: this regards us as much as it does them. I have sent belts and speeches to our friends the Chippeways of Saginaw, and our brothers the Ottawas of Michillimacinac, and to those of the Rivière à la Tranche, (Thames River,) inviting them to join us, and they will not delay. In the meantime, let us strike. There is no longer any time to lose, and when the English shall be defeated, we will stop the way, so that no more shall return upon our lands."

2. The Proclamation of 1763[*]

Seeking to pacify the western frontier and lay a basis for permanently orderly relations with the Indians, the British government on October 7, 1763, issued the following proclamation. What rationale does the government offer for its action? What aspects of the proclamation might have proved most unacceptable to the American colonists?

Whereas we have taken into our royal consideration the extensive and valuable acquisitions in America secured to our Crown by the late definitive treaty of peace concluded at Paris the 10th day of February last; and being desirous that all our loving subjects, as well of our kingdom as of our colonies in America, may avail themselves, with all convenient speed, of the great benefits and advantages which must accrue therefrom to their commerce, manufactures, and navigation; we have thought fit, with the advice of our Privy Council, to issue this our Royal Proclamation, hereby to publish and declare to all our loving subjects that we have, with the advice of our said Privy Council, granted our letters patent under our Great Seal of Great Britain, to erect within the countries and islands ceded and confirmed to us by the said treaty, four distinct and separate governments, styled and called by the names of Quebec, East Florida, West Florida, and Grenada, and limited and bounded as follows, . . .

[The Proclamation next outlines the territories to be embraced by these four new governments, and their general characters, and then announces the policy that so provoked the colonists.]

---

[*]Annual Register, 1763, pp. 208ff., in Henry Steele Commager, ed., *Documents in American History*, 7th ed. (New York: Appleton-Century-Crofts, 1963), pp. 47–50.

And whereas it is just and reasonable, and essential to our interest and the security of our colonies, that the several nations or tribes of Indians with whom we are connected, and who live under our protection, should not be molested or disturbed in the possession of such parts of our dominions and territories as, not having been ceded to or purchased by us, are reserved to them, or any of them, as their hunting-grounds; we do therefore, with the advice of our Privy Council, declare it to be our royal will and pleasure, that no Governor or commander in chief, in any of our colonies of Quebec, East Florida, or West Florida, do presume, upon any pretence whatever, to grant warrants of survey, or pass any patents for lands beyond the bounds of their respective governments, as described in their commissions; as also that no Governor or commander in chief of our other colonies or plantations in America do presume for the present, and until our further pleasure be known, to grant warrants of survey or pass patents for any lands beyond the heads or sources of any of the rivers which fall into the Atlantic Ocean from the west or northwest; or upon any lands whatever, which, not having been ceded to or purchased by us, as aforesaid, are reserved to the said Indians, or any of them.

And we do further declare it to be our royal will and pleasure, for the present as aforesaid, to reserve under our sovereignty, protection, and dominion, for the use of the said Indians, all the land and territories not included within the limits of our said three new governments, or within the limits of the territory granted to the Hudson's Bay Company; as also all the land and territories lying to the westward of the sources of the rivers which fall into the sea from the west and northwest as aforesaid; and we do hereby strictly forbid, on pain of our displeasure, all our loving subjects from making any purchases or settlements whatever, or taking possession of any of the lands above reserved, without our special leave and license for that purpose first obtained.

And we do further strictly enjoin and require all persons whatever, who have either wilfully or inadvertently seated themselves upon any lands within the countries above described, or upon any other lands which, not having been ceded to or purchased by us, are still reserved to the said Indians as aforesaid, forthwith to remove themselves from such settlements.

And whereas great frauds and abuses have been committed in the purchasing lands of the Indians, to the great prejudice of our interests, and to the great dissatisfaction of the said Indians; in order, therefore, to prevent such irregularities for the future, and to the end that the Indians may be convinced of our justice and determined resolution to remove all reasonable cause of discontent, we do, with the advice of our Privy Council, strictly enjoin and require, that no private person do presume to make any purchase from the said Indians of any lands reserved to the said Indians within those parts of our colonies where we have thought proper to allow settlement; but that if at any time any of the said Indians should be inclined to dispose of the said lands, the same shall be purchased only for us, in our name, at some public meeting or assembly of the said Indians, to be held for that purpose by the Governor or commander in chief of our colony respectively within which they shall lie: and in case they shall lie within the limits of any proprietary government, they shall be purchased only for the use and in the name of such proprietaries, conformable to such directions and instructions as we or they shall think proper to give for that purpose. And we do, by the advice of our Privy Council, declare and enjoin, that the trade with the said Indians shall be free and open to all our subjects whatever, provided that every person who may incline to trade with the said Indians do take out a license for carrying on such trade, from the Governor or commander in chief of any of our colonies respectively where such person shall reside, and also give security to observe such regulations as we shall at any time think fit, by ourselves or commissaries to be appointed for this purpose, to direct and appoint for the benefit of the said trade. And we do hereby authorize, enjoin, and require the Governors and commanders in chief of all our colonies respectively, as well those under our immediate government as those under the government and direction of proprietaries, to grant such licenses without fee or reward, taking especial care to insert therein a condition that such license shall be void, and the security forfeited, in case the person to whom the same is granted shall refuse or neglect to observe such regulations as we shall think proper to prescribe as aforesaid.

And we do further expressly enjoin and require all officers whatever, as well military as those employed in the management and direction of Indian affairs within the territories reserved as aforesaid, for the use of the said Indians, to seize and apprehend all persons whatever who, standing charged with treasons, misprisions of treason, murders, or other felonies or misdemeanors, shall fly from justice and take refuge in the said territory, and to send them under a proper guard to the colony where the crime was committed of which they shall stand accused, in order to take their trial for the same.

Given at our Court at St. James's, the 7th day of October 1763, in the third year of our reign.

3. Johnson Sketches a Possible Peace (1764)[*]

The British dispatched Indian commissioner Sir William Johnson to placate their Indian foes. Johnson eventually concluded a peace settlement with the Indians in 1766, ending Pontiac's Rebellion. Here, two years before the final settlement, he outlines the terms that he hopes to secure (he was largely successful). What are the key elements of his peace plan? How realistic was his expectation that the peace would hold?

Your Lordships will please to observe that for many months before the march of Colonel Bradstreet's army, several of the Western Nations had expressed a desire for peace, and had ceased to commit hostilities, that even Pontiac inclined that way, but did not choose to venture his person by coming into any of the posts. This was the state of affairs when I treated with the Indians at Niagara, in which number were fifteen hundred of the Western Nations, a number infinitely more considerable than those who were twice treated with at Detroit, many of whom are the same people, particularly the Hurons and Chippewas. In the meantime it now appears, from the very best authorities, and can be proved by the oath of several respectable persons, prisoners at the Illinois and amongst the Indians, as also from the accounts of the

---

[*]Sir William Johnson to the Board of Trade, December 26, 1764, in Francis Parkman, *The Conspiracy of Pontiac* (New York: E. P. Dutton, 1908), vol. 2, Appendix, pp. 268–270.

Indians themselves, that not only many French traders, but also French officers came amongst the Indians, as they said, fully authorized to assure them that the French King was determined to support them to the utmost, and not only invited them to the Illinois, where they were plentifully supplied with ammunition and other necessaries, but also sent several canoes at different times up the Illinois river, to the Miamis, and others, as well as up the Ohio to the Shawanese and Delawares, as by Major Smallman's account, and several others, (then prisoners,) transmitted me by Colonel Bouquet, and one of my officers who accompanied him, will appear. That in an especial manner the French promoted the interest of Pontiac, whose influence is now become so considerable, as General Gage observes in a late letter to me, that it extends even to the Mouth of the Mississippi, and has been the principal occasion of our not as yet gaining the Illinois, which the French as well as Indians are interested in preventing. This Pontiac is not included in the late Treaty at Detroit, and is at the head of a great number of Indians privately supported by the French, an officer of whom was about three months ago at the Miamis Castle, at the Scioto Plains, Muskingum, and several other places. The Western Indians, who it seems ridicule the whole expedition, will be influenced to such a pitch, by the interested French on the one side, and the influence of Pontiac on the other, that we have great reason to apprehend a renewal of hostilities, or at least that they and the Twightees (Miamis) will strenuously oppose our possessing the Illinois, which can never be accomplished without their consent. And indeed it is not to be wondered that they should be concerned at our occupying that country, when we consider that the French (be their motive what it will) loaded them with favours, and continue to do so, accompanied with all outward marks of esteem, and an address peculiarly adapted to their manners, which infallibly gains upon all Indians, who judge by extremes only, and with all their acquaintance with us upon the frontiers, have never found anything like it, but on the contrary, harsh treatment, angry words, and in short anything which can be thought of to inspire them with a dislike to our manners and a jealousy of our views. I have seen so much of these matters, and I am so well convinced of the utter aversion that our people have for them in general, and of the imprudence with which they constantly express it, that I absolutely despair of our seeing tranquility established, until your Lordships' plan is fully settled, so as I may have proper persons to reside at the Posts, whose business it shall be to remove their prejudices, and whose interest it becomes to obtain their esteem and friendship.

The importance of speedily possessing the Illinois, and thereby securing a considerable branch of trade, as well as cutting off the channel by which our enemies have been and will always be supplied, is a matter I have very much at heart, and what I think may be effected this winter by land by Mr. Croghan, in case matters can be so far settled with the Twightees, Shawanoes, and Pontiac, as to engage the latter, with some chiefs of the before-mentioned nations, to accompany him with a garrison. The expense attending this will be large, but the end to be obtained is too considerable to be neglected. I have accordingly recommended it to the consideration of General Gage, and shall, on the arrival of the Shawanoes, Delawares, &c., here, do all in my power to pave the way for effecting it. I shall also make such a peace with them, as will be most for the credit and advantage of the crown, and the security of the trade and frontiers, and tie them down to such conditions as Indians will most probably observe.

C. A New Restlessness

1. William Burke Makes a Fateful Prediction (1760)[*]

With victory against France in North America all but assured by the fall of 1759, a lively debate broke out in the English press over how best to dispose of the French colonies that had fallen into British hands. The debate centered on the relative merits of keeping either Canada or the sugar-rich islands of the Caribbean, as most observers recognized that Britain could not hope to hold onto both. William Burke, secretary of the newly acquired island of Guadalupe, had a personal stake in seeing that island retained. But in the following excerpt from his unsigned pamphlet, he lays out a broader argument for returning Canada to France. Why did he think it necessary to let France keep a foothold in North America? Did subsequent events confirm his predictions?

To view the Continent of *America* in a Commercial Light, the Produce of all the Northern Colonies is the same as that of *England*, Corn and Cattle: and therefore, except for a very few naval Stores, there is but little Trade from thence directly to *England*. Their own Commodities bear a very low Price, Goods carried from *Europe* bear a very high Price; and thus they are of Necessity driven to set up Manufactures similar to those of *England*, in which they are favoured by Cheapness of Provisions. In fact, there are Manufactures of many Kinds in these Northern Colonies, that promise in a short Time to supply their Home Consumption. From *New England* they begin even to export some things manufactured, particularly Hats, in some Quantity. In these Provinces they have Colleges and Academies for the Education of their Youth; and as they increase daily in People and in Industry, the Necessity of a Connection with *England*, with which they have no natural Intercourse by a Reciprocation of Wants, will continually diminish. But as they recede from the Sea, all these Causes will operate more strongly; they will have nothing to expect from Commerce, they must live wholly on their own Labour, and in process of Time will know little, enquire little, and care little about the Mother Country.

If, Sir, the People of our Colonies find no Check from *Canada*, they will extend themselves, almost, without bounds into the Inland Parts. They are invited to it by the Pleasantness, the Fertility, and the Plenty of that Country; and they will increase infinitely from all these Causes. What the Consequence will be, to have a numerous, hardy, independent People, possessed of a strong Country, communicating little, or not at all with *England*, I leave to your own Reflections. I hope we have not gone to these immense Expences, without any Idea of securing the Fruits of them to Posterity. If we have, I am sure we have acted with little Frugality or Foresight. This is

---

[*]William Burke, *Remarks on the Letter Address'd to Two Great Men*, 3rd ed., corr. (London: R. & J. Dodsley, 1760).

indeed a Point that must be the constant Object of the Minister's Attention, but is not a fit Subject for a publick Discussion. I will therefore expatiate no farther on this Topic; I shall only observe, that by eagerly grasping at extensive Territory, we may run the risque, and that perhaps in no very distant Period, of losing what we now possess. The Possession of *Canada*, far from being necessary to our Safety, may in its Consequence be even dangerous. A Neighbour that keeps us in some Awe, is not always the worst of Neighbours. So that far from sacrificing *Guadaloupe* to *Canada*, perhaps if we might have *Canada* without any Sacrifice at all, we ought not to desire it. . . .

2. Benjamin Franklin Dismisses Burke's Fears (1760)*

Benjamin Franklin spent most of the Seven Years' War in London as Pennsylvania's agent to the British government. Convinced that Britain should retain possession of Canada, Franklin published a lengthy rebuttal to Burke's main premise—that the French presence in North America served as a valuable buffer against American independence. Why did Franklin discount the prospects of colonial revolt? What future developments did he fail to foresee?

In short, according to this writer, our present colonies are large enough and numerous enough, and the French ought to be left in North America to prevent their increase, lest they become not only *useless* but *dangerous* to Britain.

I agree with the gentleman, that with Canada in our possession, our people in America will increase amazingly. I know, that their common rate of increase, where they are not molested by the enemy, is doubling their numbers every twenty five years by natural generation only, exclusive of the accession of foreigners.† I think this increase continuing, would probably in a century more, make the number of British subjects on that side the water more numerous than they now are on this; but I am far from entertaining on that account, any fears of their becoming either *useless* or *dangerous* to us; and I look on those fears, to be merely imaginary and without any probable foundation. . . .

The remarker thinks that our people in America, "finding no check from Canada would extend themselves almost without bounds into the inland parts, and increase infinitely from all causes." The very reason he assigns for their so extending, and which is indeed the true one, their being "invited to it by the pleasantness, fertility and plenty of the country," may satisfy us, that this extension will continue to proceed as long as there remains any pleasant fertile country within their reach. And if

---

*Leonard W. Labaree, ed., *The Papers of Benjamin Franklin*, vol. 9 (New Haven, CT: Yale University Press, 1966), pp. 77–94.

†The reason of this greater increase in America than in Europe, is, that in old settled countries, all trades, farms, offices, and employments are full, and many people refrain marrying till they see an opening, in which they can settle themselves, with a reasonable prospect of maintaining a family: but in America, it being easy to obtain land which with moderate labour will afford subsistence and something to spare, people marry more readily and earlier in life, whence arises a numerous offspring and the swift population of those countries. 'Tis a common error that we cannot fill our provinces or increase the number of them, without draining this nation of its people. The increment alone of our present colonies is sufficient for both those purposes. [Franklin's footnote]

we even suppose them confin'd by the waters of the Mississippi westward, and by those of St. Laurence and the lakes to the northward, yet still we shall leave them room enough to increase even in the *sparse* manner of settling now practis'd there, till they amount to perhaps a hundred millions of souls. This must take some centuries to fulfil, and in the mean time, this nation must necessarily supply them with the manufactures they consume, because the new settlers will be employ'd in agriculture, and the new settlements will so continually draw off the spare hands from the old, that our present colonies will not, during the period we have mention'd find themselves in a condition to manufacture even for their own inhabitants, to any considerable degree, much less for those who are settling behind them. Thus our *trade* must, till that country becomes as fully peopled as England, that is for centuries to come, be continually increasing, and with it our naval power; because the ocean is between us and them, and our ships and seamen must increase as that trade increases. . . .

[S]o difficult is it to overturn an established government, that it was not without the assistance of France and England, that the United Provinces supported themselves: which teaches us, that if the visionary danger of independence in our colonies is to be feared, nothing is more likely to render it substantial than the neighbourhood of foreigners at enmity with the sovereign government, capable of giving either aid or an asylum, as the event shall require. . . .

But what is the prudent policy inculcated by the *remarker*, to obtain this end, security of dominion over our colonies: It is, to leave the French in Canada, to "*check*" their growth, for otherwise our people may "increase infinitely from all causes." We have already seen in what manner the French and their Indians *check the growth* of our colonies. 'Tis a modest word, this, *check*, for massacring men, women and children. . . . But if Canada is restored on this principle, will not Britain be guilty of all the blood to be shed, all the murders to be committed in order to check this dreaded growth of our own people? Will not this be telling the French in plain terms, that the horrid barbarities they perpetrate with their Indians on our colonists, are agreeable to us; and that they need not apprehend the resentment of a government with whose views they so happily concur? Will not the colonies view it in this light? Will they have reason to consider themselves any longer as subjects and children, when they find their cruel enemies halloo'd upon them by the country from whence they sprung, the government that owes them protection as it requires their obedience? Is not this the most likely means of driving them into the arms of the French, who can invite them by an offer of that security their own government chuses not to afford them?

3. Andrew Burnaby Scoffs at Colonial Unity (1760)[*]

Andrew Burnaby, the broad-minded Church of England clergyman who traveled extensively in the colonies during the closing months of the French and Indian War, recorded many penetrating observations. But he scoffed at the idea that the

---

[*]Andrew Burnaby, *Travels Through the Middle Settlements in North-America in the Years 1759 and 1760* (London: J. Payne, 1775; reprinted Ithaca, NY: Great Seal Books, 1960), pp. 110–114.

Americans would one day form a mighty nation or even come together in a voluntary union. Which of his arguments were borne out when the colonies did attempt to form one nation?

An idea, strange as it is visionary, has entered into the minds of the generality of mankind, that empire is traveling westward; and everyone is looking forward with eager and impatient expectation to that destined moment when America is to give law to the rest of the world. But if ever an idea was illusory and fallacious, I will venture to predict that this will be so.

America is formed for happiness, but not for empire. In a course of 1,200 miles I did not see a single object that solicited charity. But I saw insuperable causes of weakness, which will necessarily prevent its being a potent state. . . .

The Southern colonies have so many inherent causes of weakness that they never can possess any real strength. The climate operates very powerfully upon them, and renders them indolent, inactive, and unenterprising; this is visible in every line of their character. I myself have been a spectator—and it is not an uncommon sight—of a man in the vigor of life, lying upon a couch, and a female slave standing over him, wafting off the flies, and fanning him, while he took his repose. . . .

The mode of cultivation by slavery is another insurmountable cause of weakness. The number of Negroes in the Southern colonies is upon the whole nearly equal, if not superior, to that of the white men; and they propagate and increase even faster. Their condition is truly pitiable: their labor excessively hard, their diet poor and scanty, their treatment cruel and oppressive; they cannot therefore but be a subject of terror to those who so unhumanly tyrannize over them.

The Indians near the frontiers are a still farther formidable cause of subjection. The southern Indians are numerous, and are governed by a sounder policy than formerly; experience has taught them wisdom. They never make war with the colonists without carrying terror and devastation along with them. They sometimes break up entire counties together. Such is the state of the Southern colonies.

The Northern colonies are of stronger stamina, but they have other difficulties and disadvantages to struggle with, not less arduous, or more easy to be surmounted, than what have been already mentioned. . . . They are composed of people of different nations, different manners, different religions, and different languages. They have a mutual jealousy of each other, fomented by considerations of interest, power, and ascendancy. Religious zeal, too, like a smothered fire, is secretly burning in the hearts of the different sectaries that inhabit them, and were it not restrained by laws and superior authority, would soon burst out into a flame of universal persecution. Even the peaceable Quakers struggle hard for pre-eminence, and evince in a very striking manner that the passions of mankind are much stronger than any principles of religion. . . .

Indeed, it appears to me a very doubtful point, even supposing all the colonies of America to be united under one head, whether it would be possible to keep in due order and government so wide and extended an empire, the difficulties of communication, of intercourse, of correspondence, and all other circumstances considered.

A voluntary association or coalition, at least a permanent one, is almost as difficult to be supposed: for fire and water are not more heterogeneous than the different colonies in North America. Nothing can exceed the jealousy and emulation which they possess in regard to each other. The inhabitants of Pennsylvania and New York have an inexhaustible source of animosity in their jealousy for the trade of the Jerseys. Massachusetts Bay and Rhode Island are not less interested in that of Connecticut. The West Indies are a common subject of emulation to them all. Even the limits and boundaries of each colony are a constant source of litigation.

In short, such is the difference of character, of manners, of religion, of interest, of the different colonies, that I think, if I am not wholly ignorant of the human mind, were they left to themselves there would soon be a civil war from one end of the continent to the other, while the Indians and Negroes would, with better reason, impatiently watch the opportunity of exterminating them all together.

4. A Lawyer Denounces Search Warrants (1761)*

During the French and Indian War, the American merchant-smugglers kept up a lucrative illicit trade with the French and Spanish West Indies. They argued that they could not pay wartime taxes if they could not make profits out of their friends, the enemy. Angered by such disloyalty, the royal authorities in Massachusetts undertook to revive the hated writs of assistance. Ordinary search warrants describe the specific premises to be searched; writs of assistance were general search warrants that authorized indiscriminate search of ships and dwellings for illicit goods. Colonial participation in the recent war against the French had inspired a spirit of resistance, and John Adams, later president of the United States, remembered in his old age the following dramatic episode. Why were the colonists so alarmed? Were their fears exaggerated?

When the British ministry received from General Amherst his despatches announcing his conquest of Montreal, and the consequent annihilation of the French government in America, in 1759 [actually 1760], they immediately conceived the design and took the resolution of conquering the English colonies, and subjecting them to the unlimited authority of Parliament. With this view and intention, they sent orders and instructions to the collector of the customs in Boston, Mr. Charles Paxton, to apply to the civil authority for writs of assistance, to enable the custom-house officers, tidewaiters, landwaiters, and all, to command all sheriffs and constables, etc., to attend and aid them in breaking open houses, stores, shops, cellars, ships, bales, trunks, chests, casks, packages of all sorts, to search for goods, wares, and merchandises which had been imported against the prohibitions or without paying the taxes imposed by certain acts of Parliament, called "The Acts of Trade." . . .

An alarm was spread far and wide. Merchants of Salem and Boston applied to [lawyers] Mr. Pratt, who refused, and to Mr. Otis and Mr. Thacher, who accepted, to defend them against this terrible menacing monster, the writ of assistance. Great fees were offered, but Otis, and I believe Thacher, would accept of none. "In such a cause," said Otis, "I despise all fees."

---

*C. F. Adams, ed., *The Works of John Adams* (1856), vol. 10, pp. 246–248.

I have given you a sketch of the stage and the scenery, and the brief of the cause; or, if you like the phrase better, the tragedy, comedy, or farce.

Now for the actors and performers. Mr. Gridley argued [for the government] with his characteristic learning, ingenuity, and dignity, and said everything that could be said in favor of Cockle's [deputy collector at Salem] petition, all depending, however, on the "If the Parliament of Great Britain is the sovereign legislature of all the British empire."

Mr. Thacher followed him on the other side, and argued with the softness of manners, the ingenuity, and the cool reasoning which were remarkable in his amiable character.

But Otis was a flame of fire! With a promptitude of classical allusions, a depth of research, a rapid summary of historical events and dates, a profusion of legal authorities, a prophetic glance of his eye into futurity, and a torrent of impetuous eloquence he hurried away everything before him. American independence was then and there born; the seeds of patriots and heroes were then and there sown. . . .

Every man of a crowded audience appeared to me to go away, as I did, ready to take arms against writs of assistance. Then and there was the first scene of the first act of opposition to the arbitrary claims of Great Britain. Then and there the child Independence was born. In fifteen years, namely in 1776, he grew up to manhood and declared himself free. . . .

Mr. Otis' popularity was without bounds. In May, 1761, he was elected into the House of Representatives by an almost unanimous vote. On the week of his election, I happened to be at Worcester attending a Court of Common Pleas, of which Brigadier Ruggles was Chief Justice, when the News arrived from Boston of Mr. Otis' election. You can have no idea of the consternation among the government people. Chief Justice Ruggles, at dinner at Colonel Chandler's on that day, said, "Out of this election will arise a d—d faction, which will shake this province to its foundation."

Thought Provokers

1. Did the British err in depriving France of Canada in 1763? How would the history of the English colonies have been changed in the eighteenth and nineteenth centuries if the French had been allowed to remain?

2. Compare and contrast the advantages and disadvantages of the French and the English in their intercolonial wars in America. Assess the effects of these wars on colonial attitudes.

3. The seeds of American nationalism were sown during the colonial period. In parallel columns, list those forces and factors that made for a spirit of unity or nationality and those that militated against it. Then form conclusions as to which forces predominated and what they foreshadowed.

7

The Road to Revolution, 1763–1775

We cannot be happy without being free; we cannot be free without being secure in our property; we cannot be secure in our property if, without our consent, others may, as by right, take it away; taxes imposed on us by Parliament do thus take it away.

John Dickinson, 1767

Prologue: After the Seven Years' War had saddled Britain with a staggering debt, the British government decided to tax the colonies for a portion of the cost of their continuing defense. The result was the Stamp Act of 1765, which stirred up such a furor that Parliament was forced to repeal it the next year. A renewed attempt at taxation in 1773 goaded the colonists into destroying a number of tea cargoes, notably at Boston. Parliament retaliated by passing legislation directed at Massachusetts, which, among other restrictions, closed the port of Boston. The other colonies rallied to the defense of Massachusetts, tensions increased, and the first overt fighting erupted at Lexington in 1775.

A. The Tempest over Taxation

1. Benjamin Franklin Testifies Against the Stamp Act (1766)[*]

In 1765 the British Parliament undertook to levy a direct (internal) stamp tax on the American colonies to defray one-third of the expenses of keeping a military force there. The colonists had long paid taxes voted by their own assemblies, as well as customs duties (external taxes) passed by Parliament primarily to regulate trade. But they objected heatedly to paying direct or internal taxes voted by a Parliament in which they were not specifically represented. Benjamin Franklin, then in London as a prominent colonial agent, testified as follows before a committee of the House of Commons. He made a brilliant showing with his incisive answers, especially since he had "planted" a number of questions in advance among his friends on the committee.

---

[*]*The Parliamentary History of England . . .* (1813), vol. 16, pp. 138–159, passim.

Were the Americans financially able to bear additional taxes? What defenses did they have available against the odious stamp tax?

Q. What is your name, and place of abode?

A. Franklin, of Philadelphia.

Q. Do the Americans pay any considerable taxes among themselves?

A. Certainly many, and very heavy taxes.

Q. What are the present taxes in Pennsylvania, laid by the laws of the colony?

A. There are taxes on all estates, real and personal; a poll tax; a tax on all offices, professions, trades, and businesses, according to their profits; an excise on all wine, rum, and other spirit; and a duty of ten pounds per head on all Negroes imported, with some other duties.

Q. For what purposes are those taxes laid?

A. For the support of the civil and military establishments of the country, and to discharge the heavy debt contracted in the last [Seven Years'] war. . . .

Q. Are not all the people very able to pay those taxes?

A. No. The frontier counties, all along the continent, having been frequently ravaged by the enemy and greatly impoverished, are able to pay very little tax. . . .

Q. Are not the colonies, from their circumstances, very able to pay the stamp duty?

A. In my opinion there is not gold and silver enough in the colonies to pay the stamp duty for one year.

Q. Don't you know that the money arising from the stamps was all to be laid out in America?

A. I know it is appropriated by the act to the American service; but it will be spent in the conquered colonies, where the soldiers are, not in the colonies that pay it. . . .

Q. Do you think it right that America should be protected by this country and pay no part of the expense?

A. That is not the case. The colonies raised, clothed, and paid, during the last war, near 25,000 men, and spent many millions.

Q. Were you not reimbursed by Parliament?

A. We were only reimbursed what, in your opinion, we had advanced beyond our proposition, or beyond what might reasonably be expected from us; and it was a very small part of what we spent. Pennsylvania, in particular, disbursed about 500,000 pounds, and the reimbursements, in the whole, did not exceed 60,000 pounds. . . .

Q. Do not you think the people of America would submit to pay the stamp duty, if it was moderated?

A. No, never, unless compelled by force of arms. . . .

Q. What was the temper of America towards Great Britain before the year 1763?

A. The best in the world. They submitted willingly to the government of the Crown, and paid, in all their courts, obedience to acts of Parliament. . . .

Q. What is your opinion of a future tax, imposed on the same principle with that of the Stamp Act? How would the Americans receive it?

A. Just as they do this. They would not pay it.

Q. Have not you heard of the resolutions of this House, and of the House of Lords, asserting the right of Parliament relating to America, including a power to tax the people there?

A. Yes, I have heard of such resolutions.

Q. What will be the opinion of the Americans on those resolutions?

A. They will think them unconstitutional and unjust.

Q. Was it an opinion in America before 1763 that the Parliament had no right to lay taxes and duties there?

A. I never heard any objection to the right of laying duties to regulate commerce; but a right to lay internal taxes was never supposed to be in Parliament, as we are not represented there. . . .

Q. Did the Americans ever dispute the controlling power of Parliament to regulate the commerce?

A. No.

Q. Can anything less than a military force carry the Stamp Act into execution?

A. I do not see how a military force can be applied to that purpose.

Q. Why may it not?

A. Suppose a military force sent into America; they will find nobody in arms; what are they then to do? They cannot force a man to take stamps who chooses to do without them. They will not find a rebellion; they may indeed make one.

Q. If the act is not repealed, what do you think will be the consequences?

A. A total loss of the respect and affection the people of America bear to this country, and of all the commerce that depends on that respect and affection.

Q. How can the commerce be affected?

A. You will find that, if the act is not repealed, they will take very little of your manufactures in a short time.

Q. Is it in their power to do without them?

A. I think they may very well do without them.

Q. Is it their interest not to take them?

A. The goods they take from Britain are either necessaries, mere conveniences, or superfluities. The first, as cloth, etc., with a little industry they can make at home; the second they can do without till they are able to provide them among themselves; and the last, which are much the greatest part, they will strike off immediately. They are mere articles of fashion, purchased and consumed because the fashion in a respected country; but will now be detested and rejected. The people have already struck off, by general agreement, the use of all goods fashionable in mournings. . . .

Q. If the Stamp Act should be repealed, would it induce the assemblies of America to acknowledge the right of Parliament to tax them, and would they erase their resolutions [against the Stamp Act]?

A. No, never.

Q. Is there no means of obliging them to erase those resolutions?

A. None that I know of; they will never do it, unless compelled by force of arms.

Q. Is there a power on earth that can force them to erase them?

A. No power, how great soever, can force men to change their opinions. . . .

Q. What used to be the pride of the Americans?

A. To indulge in the fashions and manufactures of Great Britain.

Q. What is now their pride?

A. To wear their old clothes over again, till they can make new ones.

2. Philadelphia Threatens Tea Men (1773)*

Parliament, faced with rebellion and a crippling commercial boycott, repealed the Stamp Act in 1766. The next year the ministry devised a light indirect tax on tea, which, being external, presumably met the colonial objections to a direct tax. Opposition to the new levy was fading when, in 1773, the London officials granted a monopoly of the tea business in America to the powerful and hated British East India Company. These arrangements would make the tea, even with the three-penny tax included, cheaper than ever. The colonists, resenting this transparent attempt to trick them into paying the tax, staged several famous tea parties. Those at Boston and New York involved throwing the tea overboard; the affair at Annapolis resulted in the burning of both vessel and cargo. At Portsmouth and Philadelphia, the tea ships were turned away. Of the reasons here given by the Philadelphians for action, which was the strongest? Was it strong enough to warrant the measures threatened?

TO CAPT. AYRES

Of the Ship *Polly*, on a Voyage

from London to Philadelphia

Sir: We are informed that you have imprudently taken charge of a quantity of tea which has been sent out by the [East] India Company, under the auspices of the Ministry, as a trial of American virtue and resolution.

Now, as your cargo, on your arrival here, will most assuredly bring you into hot water, and as you are perhaps a stranger to these parts, we have concluded to advise you of the present situation of affairs in Philadelphia, that, taking time by the forelock, you may stop short in your dangerous errand, secure your ship against the rafts of combustible matter which may be set on fire and turned loose against her; and more than all this, that you may preserve your own person from the pitch and feathers that are prepared for you.

In the first place, we must tell you that the Pennsylvanians are, to a man, passionately fond of freedom, the birthright of Americans, and at all events are determined to enjoy it.

That they sincerely believe no power on the face of the earth has a right to tax them without their consent.

That, in their opinion, the tea in your custody is designed by the Ministry to enforce such a tax, which they will undoubtedly oppose, and in so doing, give you every possible obstruction.

Pennsylvania Magazine of History and Biography, vol. 15 (Philadelphia: Pennsylvania Historical Society, 1891), p. 391.

We are nominated to a very disagreeable, but necessary, service: to our care are committed all offenders against the rights of America; and hapless is he whose evil destiny has doomed him to suffer at our hands.

You are sent out on a diabolical service; and if you are so foolish and obstinate as to complete your voyage by bringing your ship to anchor in this port, you may run such a gauntlet as will induce you in your last moments most heartily to curse those who have made you the dupe of their avarice and ambition.

What think you, Captain, of a halter around your neck—ten gallons of liquid tar decanted on your pate—with the feathers of a dozen wild geese laid over that to enliven your appearance?

Only think seriously of this—and fly to the place from whence you came—fly without hesitation—without the formality of a protest—and above all, Captain Ayres, let us advise you to fly without the wild geese feathers.

Your friends to serve,
THE COMMITTEE OF TARRING AND FEATHERING

3. Connecticut Decries the Boston Port Act (1774)*

The Boston Tea Party, which involved the destruction of three cargoes of tea by colonists thinly disguised as Indians, provoked an angry response in Parliament. Even as good a friend of America as Colonel Barré so far forgot his grammar as to burst out, "Boston ought to be punished; she is your eldest son!" Parliament speedily passed a series of punitive measures ("Intolerable Acts"), notably the act closing the port of Boston until the tea was paid for. The other colonies, deeply resentful, responded with assurances of support. Virginia raised food and money; Philadelphia contributed one thousand barrels of flour. Various groups, including the citizens of Farmington, Connecticut, passed resolutions of protest. To what extent did their resolution reflect a desire for independence?

Early in the morning was found the following handbill, posted up in various parts of the town, viz.:

To pass through the fire at six o'clock this evening, in honor to the immortal goddess of Liberty, the late infamous Act of the British Parliament for farther distressing the American Colonies. The place of execution will be the public parade, where all Sons of Liberty are desired to attend.

Accordingly, a very numerous and respectable body were assembled of near one thousand people, when a huge pole, just forty-five feet high, was erected, and consecrated to the shrine of liberty; after which the Act of Parliament for blocking up the Boston harbor was read aloud, sentenced to the flames, and executed by the hands of the common hangman. Then the following resolves were passed, *nem. con.* [unanimously]:

*Peter Force, ed., *American Archives*, Fourth Series (Washington, DC: prepared and published under authority of an act of Congress, 1837), vol. 1, p. 336.

1st. That it is the greatest dignity, interest, and happiness of every American to be united with our parent state while our liberties are duly secured, maintained, and supported by our rightful sovereign, whose person we greatly revere; whose government, while duly administered, we are ready with our lives and properties to support.

2nd. That the present Ministry, being instigated by the Devil, and led on by their wicked and corrupt hearts, have a design to take away our liberties and properties, and to enslave us forever.

3rd. That the late Act, which their malice hath caused to be passed in Parliament, for blocking up the port of Boston, is unjust, illegal, and oppressive; and that we, and every American, are sharers in the insults offered to the town of Boston.

4th. That those pimps and parasites who dared to advise their master [George III] to such detestable measures be held in utter abhorrence by us and every American, and their names loaded with the curses of all succeeding generations.

5th. That we scorn the chains of slavery; we despise every attempt to rivet them upon us; we are the sons of freedom, and resolved that, till time shall be no more, that godlike virtue shall blazon our hemisphere.

B. Britain at the Crossroads

1. Edmund Burke Urges Conciliation (1775)[*]

As a new crisis over taxation once again embroiled Britain and her colonies, Parliament split over how best to address this latest bout of American insubordination. Whig politicians, themselves on guard against arbitrary rule, were typically more sympathetic to the American cause: few more so than the Irish-born statesman and orator, Edmund Burke. In a rousing address in March of 1775, Burke proposed that Parliament revoke the tax acts that had so inflamed colonial opposition and instead secure revenues by voluntary grants from colonial assemblies. He defended his conciliatory approach by emphasizing the value of American commerce and by stressing the futility of force against "a people so numerous, so active, so growing," and so fiercely protective of their freedoms. How does Burke account for Americans' characteristic devotion to liberty? What does he see as the role of religion in shaping American attitudes?

In this Character of the Americans, a love of Freedom is the predominating feature, which marks and distinguishes the whole: and as an ardent is always a jealous affection, your Colonies become suspicious, restive, and untractable, whenever they see the least attempt to wrest from them by force, or shuffle from them by chicane, what they think the only advantage worth living for. This fierce spirit of Liberty is

---

[*]W. M. Elofson and John A. Woods, ed., *The Writings and Speeches of Edmund Burke*, vol. 3 (Oxford: Clarendon Press, 1996), pp. 121–125.

stronger in the English Colonies probably than in any other people of the earth; and this from a great variety of powerful causes; which, to understand the true temper of their minds, and the direction which this spirit takes, it will not be amiss to lay open somewhat more largely.

First, the people of the Colonies are descendents of Englishmen. England, Sir, is a nation, which still I hope respects, and formerly adored, her freedom. The Colonists emigrated from you, when this part of your character was most predominant; and they took this biass and direction the moment they parted from your hands. They are therefore not only devoted to Liberty, but to Liberty according to English ideas, and on English principles. . . .

Their governments are popular in an high degree; some are merely popular; in all, the popular representative is the most weighty; and this share of the people in their ordinary government never fails to inspire them with lofty sentiments, and with a strong aversion from whatever tends to deprive them of their chief importance.

If any thing were wanting to this necessary operation of the form of government, Religion would have given it a complete effect. Religion, always a principle of energy in this new people, is no way worn out or impaired; and their mode of professing it is also one main cause of this free spirit. The people are protestants; and of that kind, which is the most adverse to all implicit submission of mind and opinion. This is a persuasion not only favourable to liberty, but built upon it. . . .

All protestantism, even the most cold and passive, is a sort of dissent. But the religion most prevalent in our Northern Colonies* is a refinement on the principle of resistance; it is the dissidence of dissent; and the protestantism of the protestant religion. This religion, under a variety of denominations, agreeing in nothing but in the communion of the spirit of liberty, is predominant in most of the Northern provinces; where the Church of England, notwithstanding its legal rights, is in reality no more than a sort of private sect, not composing most probably the tenth of the people. The Colonists left England when this spirit was high; and in the emigrants was the highest of all: and even that stream of foreigners, which has been constantly flowing into these Colonies, has, for the greatest part, been composed of dissenters from the establishments of their several countries, and have brought with them a temper and character far from alien to that of the people with whom they mixed.

Sir, I can perceive by their manner, that some Gentlemen object to the latitude of this description; because in the Southern Colonies the Church of England forms a large body, and has a regular establishment. It is certainly true. There is however a circumstance attending these Colonies, which in my opinion, fully counterbalances this difference, and makes the spirit of liberty still more high and haughty

---

*In 1761 a study had estimated the numbers in the major New England Faiths as follows: Episcopalians 12,600, Society of Friends 16,000, Baptists 22,000, Congregationalists 440,000; see E. Stiles, *A Discourse on the Christian Union*, Boston, 1761, cited in C. Bridenbaugh, *Mitre and Sceptre, Transatlantic Faiths, Ideas, Personalities and Politics, 1689–1775*, New York, 1962, p. 12.

than in those to the Northward. It is that in Virginia and the Carolinas, they have a vast multitude of slaves. Where this is the case in any part of the world, those who are free, are by far the most proud and jealous of their freedom. Freedom is to them not only an enjoyment, but a kind of rank and privilege. Not seeing there, that freedom, as in countries where it is a common blessing, and as broad and general as the air,* may be united with much abject toil, with great misery, with all the exterior of servitude, Liberty looks amongst them, like something that is more noble and liberal. I do not mean, Sir, to commend the superior morality of this sentiment, which has at least as much pride as virtue in it; but I cannot alter the nature of man. The fact is so; and these people of the Southern Colonies are much more strongly, and with an higher and more stubborn spirit, attached to liberty than those to the Northward. Such were all the ancient commonwealths; such were our Gothick ancestors; such in our days were the Poles; and such will be all masters of slaves, who are not slaves themselves. In such a people the haughtiness of domination combines with the spirit of freedom, fortifies it, and renders it invincible.† . . .

The last cause of this disobedient spirit in the Colonies is hardly less powerful than the rest, as it is not merely moral, but laid deep in the natural constitution of things. Three thousand miles of ocean lie between you and them. No contrivance can prevent the effect of this distance, in weakening Government. Seas roll, and months pass, between the order and the execution; and the want of a speedy explanation of a single point is enough to defeat an whole system. You have, indeed, winged ministers of vengeance, who carry your bolts in their pounces to the remotest verge of the sea. But there a power steps in, that limits the arrogance of raging passions and furious elements, and says, "So far shalt thou go, and no farther." Who are you, that should fret and rage, and bite the chains of Nature?—Nothing worse happens to you, than does to all Nations, who have extensive Empire; and it happens in all the forms into which Empire can be thrown.

2. Samuel Johnson Urges the Iron Fist (1775)‡

The conservative Samuel Johnson, famed for his English dictionary, was no friend of Americans, who, he wrote, "multiplied with the fecundity of their own rattlesnakes." In 1762 he accepted a pension of £300 annually from the crown; in 1775 he repaid his royal master by publishing a pamphlet, Taxation No Tyranny, in which he proved himself to be a political babe in the woods. He privately admitted that his manuscript

---

Macbeth, III. iv. 21.

†Burke's analysis of the effects of slavery is famous and has been generally accepted. He may well have taken it from Andrew Burnaby, *Travels through the Middle Settlements in North America in the Years 1759 and 1760. With Observations upon the State of the Colonies.* This had been published in February 1775. Speaking of the Virginians, Burnaby wrote: 'Their authority over their slaves renders them vain and imperious . . . they are haughty and jealous of their liberties, impatient of restraint, and can scarcely bear the thought of being controlled by any superior power. Many of them consider the Colonies as independent states, unconnected with Great Britain, otherwise than by having the same common king, and being bound to her with natural affection' (pp. 18–20).

‡*The Works of Samuel Johnson* (Oxford: Talboys and Wheeler, 1825), vol. 6, pp. 259–262.

was revised and shortened by the royal officials. Which of his proposals would be most likely to arouse the American frontier? Which the South? Which would be most likely to stir up renewed rebellion generally? Which proposals have real merit, and which are the most fantastic?

The Dean of Gloucester has proposed, and seems to propose it seriously, that we should, at once, release our claims, declare them [the Americans] masters of themselves, and whistle them down the wind. His opinion is that our gain from them will be the same, and our expense less. What they can have most cheaply from Britain, they will still buy; what they can sell to us at the highest price, they will still sell.

It is, however, a little hard that, having so lately fought and conquered for their safety, we should govern them no longer. By letting them loose before the [Seven Years'] war, how many millions might have been saved? One wild proposal is best answered by another. Let us restore to the French what we have taken from them. We shall see our colonists at our feet, when they have an enemy so near them [Canada]. Let us give the Indians arms, and teach them discipline, and encourage them, now and then, to plunder a plantation. Security and leisure are the parents of sedition.

While these different opinions are agitated, it seems to be determined by the legislature that force shall be tried. Men of the pen have seldom any great skill in conquering kingdoms, but they have strong inclination to give advice. I cannot forbear to wish that this commotion may end without bloodshed, and that the rebels may be subdued by terror rather than by violence; and, therefore, recommend such a force as may take away not only the power but the hope of resistance, and, by conquering without a battle, save many from the sword.

If their obstinacy continues, without actual hostilities, it may, perhaps, be mollified by turning out the soldiers to free quarters, forbidding any personal cruelty or hurt. It has been proposed that the slaves should be set free, an act which, surely, the [American] lovers of liberty cannot but commend. If they are furnished with firearms for defense, and utensils for husbandry, and settled in some simple form of government within the country, they may be more grateful and honest than their masters. . . .

Since the Americans have made it necessary to subdue them, may they be subdued with the least injury possible to their persons and their possessions! When they are reduced to obedience, may that obedience be secured by stricter laws and stronger obligations!

Nothing can be more noxious to society than that erroneous clemency which, when a rebellion is suppressed, exacts no forfeiture and establishes no securities, but leaves the rebels in their former state. Who would not try the experiment which promises advantage without expense? If rebels once obtain a victory, their wishes are accomplished. If they are defeated, they suffer little, perhaps less than their conquerors. However often they play the game, the chance is always in their favor. In the meantime they are growing rich by victualing the troops we have sent against them, and, perhaps, gain more by the residence of the army than they lose by the obstruction of their post [Boston].

Their charters, being now, I suppose, legally forfeited, may be modeled as shall appear most commodious to the Mother Country. Thus the privileges [of self-government] which are found, by experience, liable to misuse will be taken away, and those who now bellow as patriots, bluster as soldiers, and domineer as legislators will sink into sober merchants and silent planters, peaceably diligent and securely rich. . . .

We are told that the subjection of Americans may tend to the diminution of our own liberties—an event which none but very perspicacious politicians are able to foresee. If slavery be thus fatally contagious, how is it that we hear the loudest yelps for liberty among the [American] drivers of Negroes?

3. Two Views of the British Empire (1767, 1775)

Benjamin Franklin played many roles in colonial America. In 1767, he commissioned the cartoon shown below, "Britannia: Her Colonies," to illustrate the importance of the North American colonies to the British Empire. Was his purpose to encourage independence or reconciliation? To whom is his cartoon principally addressed? The second cartoon, "The Wise Men of Gotham and Their Goose," is from a London magazine in 1775, after the Revolutionary War had broken out. To what audience is it addressed? What are the cartoonist's sympathies in the conflict between Britain and its American colonies? To what extent does the British cartoon of 1775 express sentiments similar to Franklin's image of 1767?

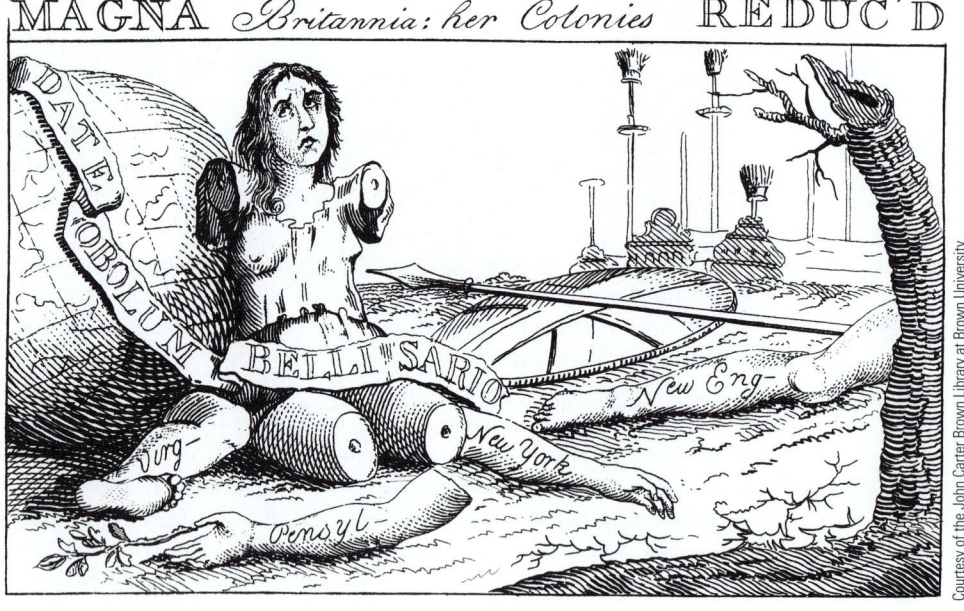

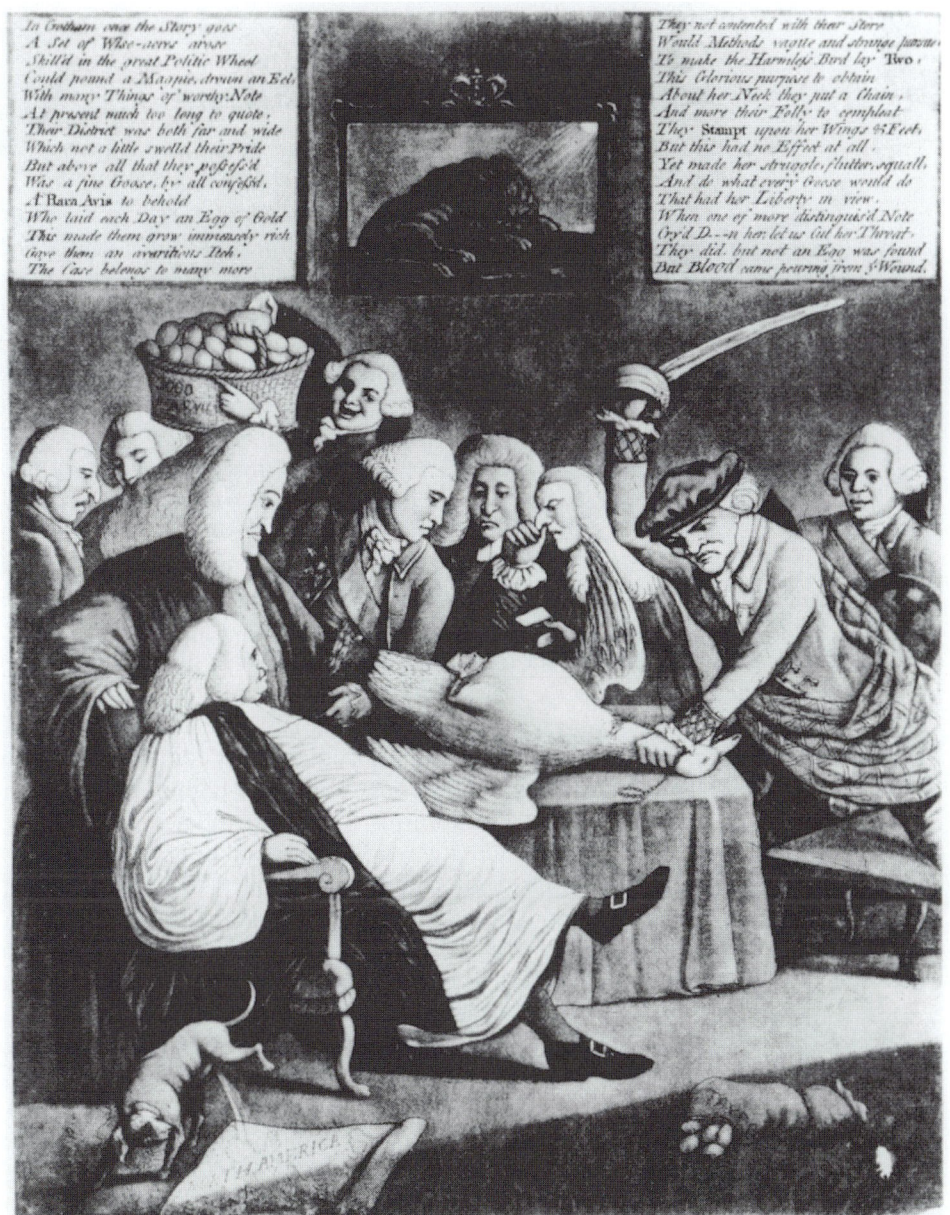

C. Loyalists Versus Patriots

1. Daniel Leonard Deplores Rebellion (1775)*

Daniel Leonard, of an aristocratic Massachusetts family, was the cleverest Tory pamphleteer in America. His writings, declared his pen adversary John Adams, "shone like the moon among the lesser stars." Forced to flee from Boston when the British troops withdrew in 1776, he subsequently became chief justice of Bermuda and dean of the English bar. He is best known in America for a series of seventeen newspaper articles, published in 1774–1775 over the signature "Massachusettensis." He warned his readers that rebellion was "the most atrocious offense" and that it would open the doors to anarchy. Legal punishment for the rebel was that he be dragged to the gallows; "that he be hanged by the neck, and then cut down alive; that his entrails be taken out and burned while he is yet alive; that his head be cut off; that his body be divided into four parts; that his head and quarters be at the king's disposal." As the clash neared between the American Patriots (Whigs) and the British troops in Massachusetts, Leonard issued this final appeal to his countrymen two weeks before the bloodshed at Lexington. What were his most convincing and least convincing arguments in support of the view that the colonists could not win?

Do you expect to conquer in war? War is no longer a simple, but an intricate science, not to be learned from books or two or three campaigns, but from long experience. You need not be told that His Majesty's generals, Gage and Haldimand, are possessed of every talent requisite to great commanders, matured by long experience in many parts of the world, and stand high in military fame; that many of the officers have been bred to arms from their infancy, and a large proportion of the army now here have already reaped immortal honors in the iron harvest of the field.

Alas! My friends, you have nothing to oppose to this force but a militia unused to service, impatient of command, and destitute of resources. Can your officers depend upon the privates, or the privates upon the officers? Your war can be but little more than mere tumultuary rage. And besides, there is an awful disparity between troops that fight the battles of their sovereign and those that follow the standard of rebellion.

These reflections may arrest you in an hour that you think not of, and come too late to serve you. Nothing short of a miracle could gain you one battle; but could you destroy all the British troops that are now here, and burn the men-of-war that command our coast, it would be but the beginning of sorrow. And yet without a decisive battle, one campaign would ruin you. This province [Massachusetts] does not produce its necessary provision when the husbandman can pursue his calling without molestation. What then must be your condition when the demand shall be increased and the resource in a manner cut off? Figure to yourselves what must be your distress should your wives and children be driven from such places as the King's troops shall occupy, into the interior parts of the province, and they, as well as you, be destitute of support.

I take no pleasure in painting these scenes of distress. The Whigs [rebels] affect to divert you from them by ridicule; but should war commence, you can expect nothing

---

*Daniel Leonard, *Massachusettensis* (London: J. Mathews, 1776; reprinted Boston, 1810), pp. 187–188.

but its severities. Might I hazard an opinion, but few of your leaders ever intended to engage in hostilities, but they may have rendered inevitable what they intended for intimidation. Those that unsheathe the sword of rebellion may throw away the scabbard; they cannot be treated with while in arms; and if they lay them down, they are in no other predicament than conquered rebels. The conquered in other wars do not forfeit the rights of men, nor all the rights of citizens. Even their bravery is rewarded by a generous victor. Far different is the case of a routed rebel host.

My dear countrymen, you have before you, at your election, peace or war, happiness or misery. May the God of our forefathers direct you in the way that leads to peace and happiness, before your feet stumble on the dark mountains, before the evil days come, wherein you shall say, we have no pleasure in them.

2. Patrick Henry Demands Boldness (1775)*

Daniel Leonard's well-justified lack of confidence in the ill-trained colonial militia was more than shared by the earl of Sandwich. In the House of Lords he scorned the colonists as "raw, undisciplined, cowardly men" and hoped that they would assemble 200,000 "brave fellows" rather than 50,000, for they would thus starve themselves out and then run at the first "sound of cannon." But the great William Pitt (now Lord Chatham), also speaking in Parliament, warned against "an impious war with a people contending in the great cause of public liberty. . . . All attempts to enforce servitude upon such men must be vain, must be futile." A few weeks later Patrick Henry, the flaming young lawyer-orator, urging warlike preparations before the Virginia Assembly, spelled out the reasons for action in his famous speech ending with the immortal words, "Give me liberty or give me death!" Which of his several arguments is the strongest?

They tell us, sir, that we are weak; unable to cope with so formidable an adversary. But when shall we be stronger? Will it be the next week, or the next year? Will it be when we are totally disarmed, and when a British guard shall be stationed in every house? Shall we gather strength by irresolution and inaction? Shall we acquire the means of effectual resistance by lying supinely on our backs and hugging the delusive phantom of hope, until our enemies shall have bound us hand and foot?

Sir, we are not weak if we make a proper use of those means which the God of nature hath placed in our power. Three millions of people armed in the holy cause of liberty, and in such a country as that which we possess, are invincible by any force which our enemy can send against us. Besides, sir, we shall not fight our battles alone. There is a just God who presides over the destinies of nations and who will raise up friends to fight our battles for us. The battle, sir, is not to the strong alone; it is to the vigilant, the active, the brave.

Besides, sir, we have no election. If we were base enough to desire it, it is now too late to retire from the contest. There is no retreat but in submission and slavery! Our chains are forged! Their clanking may be heard on the plains of Boston! The war is inevitable—and let it come! I repeat, sir, let it come!

---

*C. M. Depew, ed., *The Library of Oratory* (New York: The Globe Publishing Company, 1902), vol. 3, pp. 30–31.

It is vain, sir, to extenuate the matter. The gentlemen may cry, Peace, peace! but there is no peace. The war has actually begun! The next gale that sweeps from the north will bring to our ears the clash of resounding arms! Our brethren are already in the field! Why stand we here idle? What is it that the gentlemen wish? What would they have? Is life so dear or peace so sweet as to be purchased at the price of chains and slavery? Forbid it, almighty God. I know not what course others may take, but as for me, give me liberty or give me death!

D. The Clash of Arms

1. Conflicting Versions of the Outbreak (1775)*

British troops from Boston, seeking secret military stores and presumably rebel leaders, clashed with the colonists at Lexington and then at Concord, on April 19, 1775, in the first bloodshed of the American Revolution. Among the numerous conflicting accounts that exist, these two excerpts, representing an American version and an official British version, are noteworthy. To this day scholars have not proved who fired the first shot. What undisputed and what probable facts emerge from these accounts? How can historians extract truth from conflicting contemporary testimony?

American Version	British Version
At Lexington . . . a company of militia . . . mustered near the meeting house. The [British] troops came in sight of them just before sunrise; and running within a few rods of them, the Commanding Officer [Pitcairn] accosted the militia in words to this effect: "Disperse, you rebels—damn you, throw down your arms and disperse"; upon which the troops huzzaed, and immediately one or two officers discharged their pistols, which were instantaneously followed by the firing of four or five of the soldiers, and then there seemed to be a general discharge from the whole body. Eight of our men were killed and nine wounded. . . .	Six companies of [British] light infantry . . . at Lexington found a body of the country people under arms, on a green close to the road. And upon the King's troops marching up to them, in order to inquire the reason of their being so assembled, they went off in great confusion. And several guns were fired upon the King's troops from behind a stone wall, and also from the meetinghouse and other houses, by which one man was wounded, and Major Pitcairn's horse shot in two places. In consequence of this attack by the rebels, the troops returned the fire and killed several of them. . . .
In Lexington [the British] . . . also set fire to several other houses. . . . They pillaged almost every house they	On the return of the troops from Concord, they [the rebels] . . . began to fire upon them from behind stone walls

---

*The American version is from the *Salem* (Massachusetts) *Gazette* of April 25, 1775; the British, from the *London Gazette* of June 10, 1775. Reprinted in Peter Force, ed., *American Archives, Fourth Series* (1839), vol. 2, pp. 391–392, 945–946. For numerous other versions, see A. C. McLaughlin et al., *Source Problems in United States History* (1918), pp. 3–53.

passed. . . . But the savage barbarity exercised upon the bodies of our unfortunate brethren who fell is almost incredible. Not contented with shooting down the unarmed, aged, and infirm, they disregarded the cries of the wounded, killing them without mercy, and mangling their bodies in the most shocking manner.

and houses, and kept up in that manner a scattering fire during the whole of their march of fifteen miles, by which means several were killed and wounded. And such was the cruelty and barbarity of the rebels that they scalped and cut off the ears of some of the wounded men who fell into their hands.

2. Why an Old Soldier Fought (1898)*

Many years after the bloodshed at Lexington, Mellen Chamberlain, a prominent Massachusetts lawyer-politician-historian-librarian, published the following account of an interview with a veteran participant, Levi Preston. Why did Preston fight? What did his reasons have to do with traditional historical accounts?

When the action at Lexington, on the morning of the 19th [of April], was known at Danvers, the minute men there, under the lead of Captain Gideon Foster, made that memorable march—or run, rather—of sixteen miles in four hours, and struck Percy's flying column at West Cambridge. Brave but incautious in flanking the Redcoats, they were flanked themselves and badly pinched, leaving seven dead, two wounded, and one missing. Among those who escaped was Levi Preston, afterwards known as Captain Levi Preston.

When I was about twenty-one and Captain Preston about ninety-one, I "interviewed" him as to what he did and thought sixty-seven years before, on

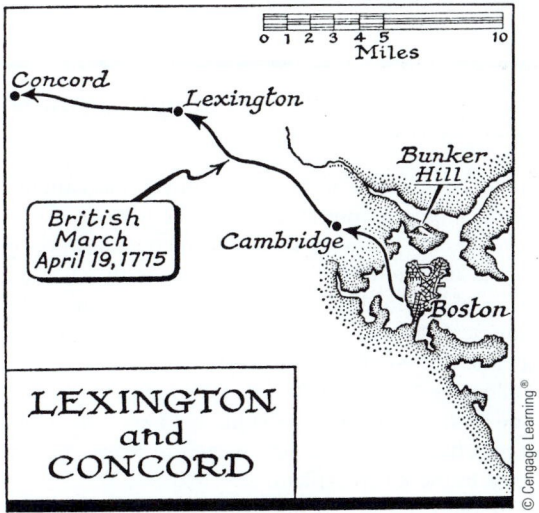

LEXINGTON
and
CONCORD

British March April 19, 1775

© Cengage Learning®

---

*Mellen Chamberlain, *John Adams, the Statesman of the American Revolution* (Boston and New York: Houghton, Mifflin and Company, 1898), pp. 248–249.

April 19, 1775. And now, fifty-two years later, I make my report—a little belated perhaps, but not too late, I trust, for the morning papers!

At that time, of course, I knew all about the American Revolution—far more than I do now! And if I now know anything truly, it is chiefly owing to what I have since forgotten of the histories of that event then popular.

With an assurance passing even that of the modern interviewer—if that were possible—I began: "Captain Preston, why did you go to the Concord fight, the 19th of April, 1775?"

The old man, bowed beneath the weight of years, raised himself upright, and turning to me said: "Why did I go?"

"Yes," I replied; "my histories tell me that you men of the Revolution took up arms against 'intolerable oppressions.' What were they?"

"Oppressions? I didn't feel them."

"What, were you not oppressed by the Stamp Act?"

"I never saw one of those stamps, and always understood that Governor Bernard [of Massachusetts] put them all in Castle William [Boston]. I am certain I never paid a penny for one of them."

"Well, what then about the tea-tax?"

"Tea-tax! I never drank a drop of the stuff; the boys threw it all overboard."

"Then I suppose you had been reading Harrington or Sidney and Locke about the eternal principles of liberty."

"Never heard of 'em. We read only the Bible, the Catechism, Watts' Psalms and Hymns, and the Almanack."

"Well, then, what was the matter? and what did you mean in going to the fight?"

"Young man, what we meant in going for those Redcoats was this: we always had governed ourselves, and we always meant to. They didn't mean we should."

Thought Provokers

1. It has been said that the American colonists attempted to reverse the maxim and have it read, "Mother countries exist for the benefit of their colonies." Comment on the reasonableness of such a position. Has mercantilism disappeared as an economic philosophy?
2. Is it justifiable for the people to take mob action against lawful measures that they deem harmful or illegal? Comment critically on the following propositions in the light of the American Revolution: (a) He who strikes a king must strike to kill. (b) Rebellion is a great crime—unless it succeeds.
3. Following the Boston Tea Party, what possible courses were open to Britain, and which one would have been most likely to keep the colonies in the empire?
4. If you had been a wealthy citizen in Massachusetts in 1776, would you have remained loyal to the king? Explain.
5. Why did each side blame the other for the first shot at Lexington? Are the people who fight in a war the best judges of its causes and significance?

8

America Secedes from the Empire, 1775–1783

And if ever there was a just war since the
world began, it is this in which America is now
engaged. . . . We fight not to enslave, but to set a
country free, and to make room upon the earth for
honest men to live in.

Thomas Paine, The Crisis, 1776

Prologue: Following the bloodshed at Lexington, the colonists raised a nondescript army and put George Washington in command. The undisciplined and unreliable amateur soldiers exasperated their leader, and not until later in the war was a nucleus of several thousand trained veterans whipped into line. Meanwhile the colonists, goaded by harsh British acts, finally declared their independence in 1776. Colonists of all creeds and colors rallied to the Patriot cause, though the situation of enslaved Africans remained especially precarious (and paradoxical). The colonists kept their flickering cause alive with secret French aid until 1778, when France formed an alliance with them following the decisive American victory over General John Burgoyne at Saratoga in 1777. Spain and Holland ultimately entered the general conflict against the British. With much of the rest of Europe unfriendly, Britain found that the war had become too big to handle. Following a crushing defeat by a joint Franco-American force at Yorktown in 1781, the British decided to cut their losses and come to terms with their rebellious subjects. The final treaty was signed in 1783. Meanwhile, the emerging republic struggled to define the guiding principles of its foreign policy.

A. The Formal Break with Britain

1. Thomas Paine Talks Common Sense (1776)[*]

Despite the shooting at Lexington, Concord, and Bunker Hill; despite the British burning of Falmouth (Maine) and Norfolk (Virginia); despite the king's hiring of German (Hessian) mercenaries, the American colonists professed to be fighting merely for reconciliation. But killing redcoats with one hand and waving the olive branch with the other seemed ridiculous to Thomas Paine, a thirty-nine-year-old agitator from

---

[*]Thomas Paine, *Common Sense* (New York: G. P. Putnam's Sons, 1894), pp. 84–101, passim.

England who had arrived in Philadelphia about a year earlier. Of humble birth, impoverished, largely self-educated, and early apprenticed to a corset maker, he was a born rebel who had failed at various undertakings. But he rocketed to fame with a forty-seven-page pamphlet published in January 1776 under the title Common Sense. *Selling the incredible total of 120,000 copies in three months, it sharply accelerated the drift toward independence. Paine urged an immediate break, not only to secure foreign assistance but also to fulfill America's moral mandate from the world. Were his views on mercantilism, isolationism, and reconciliation reasonable? Did his arguments appeal more to passion or to logic?*

In the following pages I offer nothing more than simple facts, plain arguments, and common sense: . . .

I have heard it asserted by some that, as America has flourished under her former connection with Great Britain, the same connection is necessary towards her future happiness, and will always have the same effect. Nothing can be more fallacious than this kind of argument. We may as well assert that, because a child has thrived upon milk, it is never to have meat, or that the first twenty years of our lives is to become a precedent for the next twenty. But even this is admitting more than is true. For I answer roundly that America would have flourished as much, and probably much more, had no European power taken any notice of her. The commerce by which she hath enriched herself are the necessaries of life, and will always have a market while eating is the custom of Europe.

But she [England] has protected us, say some. That she hath engrossed [monopolized] us is true, and defended the continent at our expense, as well as her own, is admitted; and she would have defended Turkey from the same motive, viz. for the sake of trade and dominion. . . .

But Britain is the parent country, say some. Then the more shame upon her conduct. Even brutes do not devour their young, nor savages make war upon their families; wherefore the assertion, if true, turns to her reproach. But it happens not to be true, or only partly so. . . . Europe, and not England, is the parent country of America. This new world hath been the asylum for the persecuted lovers of civil and religious liberty from every part of Europe. Hither have they fled, not from the tender embraces of the mother, but from the cruelty of the monster; and it is so far true of England that the same tyranny which drove the first emigrants from home pursues their descendants still. . . .

. . . Any submission to, or dependence on, Great Britain tends directly to involve this continent in European wars and quarrels, and set us at variance with nations who would otherwise seek our friendship, and against whom we have neither anger nor complaint. As Europe is our market for trade, we ought to form no partial [preferential] connection with any part of it. It is the true interest of America to steer clear of European contentions, which she never can do while, by her dependence on Britain, she is made the makeweight in the scale of British politics. . . .

Everything that is right or reasonable pleads for separation. The blood of the slain, the weeping voice of nature, cries, 'tis time to part. Even the distance at which the Almighty hath placed England and America is a strong and natural proof that the authority of the one over the other was never the design of Heaven. . . .

But if you say, you can still pass the violations over, then I ask, Hath your house been burnt? Hath your property been destroyed before your face? Are your wife and children destitute of a bed to lie on, or bread to live on? Have you lost a parent or a child by their hands, and yourself the ruined and wretched survivor? If you have not, then are you not a judge of those who have. But if you have, and can still shake hands with the murderers, then are you unworthy the name of husband, father, friend, or lover; and whatever may be your rank or title in life, you have the heart of a coward, and the spirit of a sycophant. . . .

Every quiet method for peace hath been ineffectual. Our prayers have been rejected with disdain. . . . Wherefore, since nothing but blows will do, for God's sake let us come to a final separation. . . .

Small islands, not capable of protecting themselves, are the proper objects for government to take under their care. But there is something absurd in supposing a continent to be perpetually governed by an island. In no instance hath nature made the satellite larger than its primary planet; and as England and America, with respect to each other, reverse the common order of nature, it is evident that they belong to different systems. England to Europe: America to itself. . . .

No man was a warmer wisher for a reconciliation than myself before the fatal nineteenth of April, 1775 [Lexington]. But the moment the event of that day was made known, I rejected the hardened, sullen-tempered Pharaoh of England [George III] for ever; and disdain the wretch that, with the pretended title of Father of his People, can unfeelingly hear of their slaughter, and composedly sleep with their blood upon his soul. . . .

And in order to show that reconciliation now is a dangerous doctrine, I affirm that it would be policy in the King at this time to repeal the acts, for the sake of reinstating himself in the government of the provinces; in order that *he may accomplish by craft and subtlety in the long run what he cannot do by force and violence in the short one.* Reconciliation and ruin are nearly related. . . .

You that tell us of harmony and reconciliation, can you restore to us the time that is past? Can you give to prostitution its former innocence? Neither can you reconcile Britain and America. . . . There are injuries which nature cannot forgive; she would cease to be nature if she did. As well can the lover forgive the ravisher of his mistress as the continent forgive the murders of Britain. The Almighty hath implanted in us these unextinguishable feelings for good and wise purposes. . . . They distinguish us from the herd of common animals. . . .

O! you that love mankind! You that dare oppose not only the tyranny but the tyrant, stand forth! Every spot of the old world is overrun with oppression. Freedom hath been hunted round the globe. Asia and Africa have long expelled her. Europe regards her like a stranger, and England hath given her warning to depart. O! receive the fugitive, and prepare in time an asylum for mankind.

2. Thomas Jefferson's Declaration of Independence (1776)*

Independence could hardly be undertaken without a convincing explanation, partly in the hope of eliciting foreign sympathy and military aid. The Continental Congress

---

*W. C. Ford, ed., *Journals of the Continental Congress* (1906), vol. 5, pp. 510–515.

had appointed a committee to prepare such an appeal, and the tall, sandy-haired Thomas Jefferson, then only thirty-three years old, was named chief draftsman. The Declaration (Explanation) of Independence, formally adopted on July 4, 1776, contained little new. It embodied the doctrine of natural rights and John Locke's ancient "compact theory" of government, as well as a formidable and partisan list of grievances, as though from a prosecuting attorney. But the language of the Declaration was so incisive and eloquent that this subversive document—designed primarily to subvert British rule—was magnificently successful. What persons or groups of persons are blamed, and which one is blamed the most? Does Jefferson offer any hint that the colonists themselves were partly at fault?

[I]

When, in the course of human events, it becomes necessary for one people to dissolve the political bands which have connected them with another, and to assume, among the powers of the earth, the separate and equal station to which the laws of nature and of nature's God entitle them, a decent respect to the opinions of mankind requires that they should declare the causes which impel them to the separation.

We hold these truths to be self-evident: that all men are created equal; that they are endowed by their Creator with certain unalienable rights; that among these are life, liberty, and the pursuit of happiness. That to secure these rights, governments are instituted among men, deriving their just powers from the consent of the governed. That, whenever any form of government becomes destructive of these ends, it is the right of the people to alter or to abolish it, and to institute new government, laying its foundation on such principles, and organizing its powers in such form, as to them shall seem most likely to effect their safety and happiness.

Prudence, indeed, will dictate that governments long established should not be changed for light and transient causes; and accordingly all experience hath shown that mankind are more disposed to suffer, while evils are sufferable, than to right themselves by abolishing the forms to which they are accustomed. But when a long train of abuses and usurpations, pursuing invariably the same object, evinces a design to reduce them under absolute despotism, it is their right, it is their duty, to throw off such government, and to provide new guards for their future security. Such has been the patient sufferance of these colonies; and such is now the necessity which constrains them to alter their former systems of government.

[II]

The history of the present King of Great Britain is a history of repeated injuries and usurpations, all having in direct object the establishment of an absolute tyranny over these states. To prove this, let facts be submitted to a candid world.

He has refused his assent to laws the most wholesome and necessary for the public good.

He has forbidden his governors to pass laws of immediate and pressing importance, unless suspended in their operation till his assent should be obtained, and when so suspended, he has utterly neglected to attend to them.

He has refused to pass other laws for the accommodation of large districts of people, unless those people would relinquish the right of representation in the legislature, a right inestimable to them and formidable to tyrants only.

He has called together legislative bodies at places unusual, uncomfortable, and distant from the depository of their public records, for the sole purpose of fatiguing them into compliance with his measures.

He has dissolved representative houses repeatedly for opposing, with manly firmness, his invasions on the rights of the people.

He has refused for a long time, after such dissolutions, to cause others to be elected; whereby the legislative powers, incapable of annihilation, have returned to the people at large for their exercise; the state remaining in the mean time, exposed to all the dangers of invasion from without and convulsions within.

He has endeavored to prevent the population [populating] of these states; for that purpose obstructing the laws for naturalization of foreigners, refusing to pass others to encourage their migration hither, and raising the conditions of new appropriations of lands.

He has obstructed the administration of justice by refusing his assent to laws for establishing judiciary powers.

He has made judges dependent on his will alone for the tenure of their offices and the amount and payment of their salaries.

He has erected a multitude of new offices, and sent hither swarms of officers to harass our people and eat out their substance.

He has kept among us, in time of peace, standing armies without the consent of our legislatures.

He has affected to render the military independent of and superior to the civil power.

[III]

He has combined with others to subject us to a jurisdiction [by Parliament] foreign to our constitution, and unacknowledged by our laws; giving his assent to their acts of pretended legislation:

For quartering large bodies of armed troops among us;

For protecting them, by a mock trial, from punishment for any murders which they should commit on the inhabitants of these states;

For cutting off our trade with all parts of the world;

For imposing taxes on us without our consent;

For depriving us, in many cases, of the benefits of trial by jury;

For transporting us beyond seas to be tried for pretended offenses;

For abolishing the free system of English laws in a neighboring province [Quebec], establishing therein an arbitrary government, and enlarging its boundaries so as to render it at once an example and fit instrument for introducing the same absolute rule into these colonies [a reference to the Quebec Act of 1774];

For taking away our charters, abolishing our most valuable laws, and altering fundamentally the forms of our governments;

For suspending our own legislatures and declaring themselves invested with power to legislate for us in all cases whatsoever.

[IV]

He has abdicated government here by declaring us out of his protection and waging war against us.

He has plundered our seas, ravaged our coasts, burnt our towns, and destroyed the lives of our people.

He is at this time transporting large armies of foreign mercenaries to complete the works of death, desolation, and tyranny already begun with circumstances of cruelty and perfidy scarcely paralleled in the most barbarous ages, and totally unworthy the head of a civilized nation.

He has constrained our fellow citizens, taken captive on the high seas, to bear arms against their country, to become the executioners of their friends and brethren, or to fall themselves by their hands.

He has excited domestic insurrections amongst us, and has endeavored to bring on the inhabitants of our frontiers the merciless Indian savages, whose known rule of warfare is an undistinguished destruction of all ages, sexes, and conditions.

In every stage of these oppressions we have petitioned for redress in the most humble terms; our repeated petitions have been answered only by repeated injury. A prince whose character is thus marked by every act which may define a tyrant is unfit to be the ruler of a free people.

[V]

Nor have we been wanting in attention to our British brethren. We have warned them from time to time of attempts by their legislature to extend an unwarrantable jurisdiction over us. We have reminded them of the circumstances of our emigration and settlement here. We have appealed to their native justice and magnanimity, and we have conjured them, by the ties of our common kindred, to disavow these usurpations, which would inevitably interrupt our connections and correspondence. They too have been deaf to the voice of justice and consanguinity. We must, therefore, acquiesce in the necessity which denounces [announces] our separation, and hold them, as we hold the rest of mankind, enemies in war, in peace friends.

[VI]

We, therefore, the representatives of the United States of America, in General Congress assembled, appealing to the Supreme Judge of the world for the rectitude of our intentions, do in the name and by the authority of the good people of these colonies, solemnly publish and declare, That these United Colonies are, and of right ought to be, *free and independent states*; that they are absolved from all allegiance to the British Crown, and that all political connection between them and the state of Great Britain is, and ought to be, totally dissolved; and that as free and independent states they have full power to levy war, conclude peace, contract alliances, establish commerce, and to do all other acts and things which independent states may of right do. And for the support of this Declaration, with a firm reliance on the protection of Divine Providence, we mutually pledge to each other our lives, our fortunes, and our sacred honor.

3. The Abortive Slave Trade Indictment (1776)*

Farsighted colonists had repeatedly attempted in their local assemblies to restrict or stop the odious African slave trade. But the London government, responding to the anguished cries of British (and New England) slave traders, had killed all such laws with the royal veto—five times in the case of Virginia alone. Jefferson added this grievance to the original indictment, but Congress threw it out, largely because of opposition from those parts of the South heavily dependent on the slave trade. Would this clause have added to the effectiveness of the Declaration of Independence? How, if at all, might its inclusion have changed the subsequent course of human history?

He [George III] has waged cruel war against human nature itself, violating its most sacred rights of life and liberty in the persons of a distant people who never offended him, captivating and carrying them into slavery in another hemisphere, or to incur miserable death in their transportation thither. This piratical warfare, the opprobrium of infidel powers, is the warfare of the Christian King of Great Britain. Determined to keep open a market where *men* should be bought and sold, he has prostituted his negative [royal veto] for suppressing every legislative attempt to prohibit or to restrain this execrable commerce. And that this assemblage of horrors might want no fact of distinguished dye [might lack no flagrant crime], he is now exciting those very people to rise in arms among us, and to purchase that liberty of which he has deprived them by murdering the people upon whom he also obtruded them: thus paying off former crimes committed against the liberties of one people with crimes which he urges them to commit against the lives of another.

B. Waging War for Independence

1. The Unreliable Militia (1776)†

General George Washington's makeshift army, after finally forcing the British out of Boston in March 1776, was badly defeated later in the year while defending New York City. On one occasion Washington tried to beat the fleeing militia into line with the flat of his sword. From the discouraging letter that he wrote several weeks later to the president of Congress, determine why he regarded the militiamen as poor fighters, poor soldiers, and prone to desertion.

To place any dependence upon militia is assuredly resting upon a broken staff. Men just dragged from the tender scenes of domestic life, unaccustomed to the din of arms, totally unacquainted with every kind of military skill, which (being followed by want of confidence in themselves when opposed to troops regularly trained, disciplined, and appointed, superior in knowledge and superior in arms) makes them timid and ready to fly from their own shadows.

---

*J. H. Hazelton, *The Declaration of Independence* (New York: Dodd, Mead and Company, 1906), p. 144.
†J. C. Fitzpatrick, ed., *The Writings of George Washington* (1931), vol. 6, pp. 110–112 (September 24, 1776).

Besides, the sudden change in their manner of living (particularly in the lodging) brings on sickness in many, impatience in all, and such an unconquerable desire of returning to their respective homes that it not only produces shameful and scandalous desertions among themselves, but infuses the like spirit in others.

Again, men accustomed to unbounded freedom and no control cannot brook the restraint which is indispensably necessary to the good order and government of an army, without which licentiousness and every kind of disorder triumphantly reign. . . .

The jealousies [suspicions] of a standing army, and the evils to be apprehended from one, are remote, and, in my judgment, situated and circumstanced as we are, not at all to be dreaded. But the consequence of wanting [lacking] one, according to my ideas formed from the present view of things, is certain and inevitable ruin. For, if I was called upon to declare upon oath whether the militia have been most serviceable or hurtful upon the whole, I should subscribe to the latter.

2. William Barton Describes Frontier Warfare (1779)*

Along the frontier, the warring parties and their Indian allies squared off with striking ferocity. All but two of the nations of the Iroquois Confederacy sided with the British, and throughout 1777 and 1778, warriors terrorized the frontier settlements of Pennsylvania and New York, allegedly encouraged in their brutality by British scalp buyers. When American forces counterattacked in 1779, they deployed these same harsh tactics against the Indians, as described in the wartime journal of Lieutenant William Barton, a member of the New Jersey militia who participated in the offensive. What does his account suggest about the nature of frontier warfare?

Sunday 29th. Proceeded very slowly two miles, occasioned by the roughness of the way, which we had to clear for the artillery, baggage, &c., to pass. Here we halted for one hour and a half, until the artillery, &c., should raise a difficult height, at which time an advanced party of our riflemen discovered the enemy throwing up some works on the other side of a morass, and a difficult place through which we had to pass. It appears this was intended for an ambuscade, it being on a small height, where some logs, etc. were laid up, covered with green bushes, which extended half a mile. On the right was a small town which they had destroyed themselves, making use of the timber, etc. in the above works. Moved one mile and a quarter, after all was in readiness, and within a quarter of the works, when some small parties of riflemen were sent to divert them by firing at long shot on their works. After the ground was well reconnoitered, the artillery was advanced on their left. At the same time Gen'l Poor with his brigade was endeavoring to gain their rear around their left; Gen'l Hand's brigade was following in rear of Poor. Our brigade was kept as a reserve, as was also Gen. Clinton's, until their rear should be gained; but they having a party posted on a very considerable height, over which our right flanks had to pass, we were discovered by them. Previous to this, some shells and round shot were thrown among them in their works, which caused them to give several yells, and doubtless intimidated them much. But at this discovery

---

they gave a most hideous yell and quit their works, endeavoring to prevent Gen'l Poor's ascending the height, by a loose scattering fire; but our troops pressing forward with much vigor, made them give way, leaving their dead behind, (amounting to eleven or twelve) which were scalped immediately. . . .

Monday, 30th. At the request of Maj. Piatt, sent out a small party to look for some of the dead Indians—returned without finding them. Toward morning they found them and skinned two of them from their hips down, for boot legs; one pair for the Major the other for myself. On the other side this mountain was a town said to be of the best buildings we had passed. It was destroyed by Gen. Poor the evening of the engagement. . . .

Monday, 13th. At half past 4, morning, proceeded one mile and a half; came to a considerable town, Canesaah, consisting of from sixteen to twenty huts and halted for the troops to get some refreshment and to build a bridge cross a creek; meantime a party of twenty-six men, commanded by Lt. Boyd, was sent out to a town about six miles for discovery, at which place he arrived without molestation. Here an Indian was killed and scalped by his party. He then despatched two men to inform us what had happened; after they had gone two miles they saw five Indians. They immediately run back and told the Lieutenant what they had seen, who marched on to the place with all speed, when he discovered some few of them who retreated; he pursued and killed one of them. The men then went to scalp him, which caused some dispute who should have it; at the same instant the enemy rose up from their ambuscade, when the action commenced, but they being much superior in numbers, caused him and one or two others to surrender, though not until the rest were all killed and got off. About the same time, Capt. Lodge, surveyor of the road, with a small party was discovered about one mile beyond, where the party was building a bridge. They were fired on by the Indians and one of his men wounded. The rest ran off and were pursued so closely that one of them drew out his tomahawk and was close on the heels of one of our men, when a sentinel from the party at the bridge fired at the Indian, which caused them all to run off. . . .

Tuesday, 14th. Early in the morning was ordered to destroy the corn, which we did by throwing the ears into the creek . . . At two P.M. marched and crossed the creek, and forded the main branch of Canisee and proceeded four miles down to the Chenisee castle, where we arrived about four P.M. At this place was Lieut. Boyd and one soldier found, with their heads cut off. The Lieutenant's head lay near his body; the scalp was entirely cut off; his body appeared to have been whipped and pierced in many different places. The other's head was not found. A great part of his body was skinned, leaving his ribs bare.

3. Cornwallis Surrenders (1781)[*]

After failing to secure the Carolinas, British General Charles Cornwallis retreated to the Chesapeake, entrenching his force at Yorktown. Seizing the initiative, French and American forces converged on the British encampment. George Washington's

---

[*]Charles Ross, ed., *Correspondence of Charles, First Marquis Cornwallis*, vol. 1 (London: Murray, 1859, 2nd ed.), pp. 127–131.

army encircled Yorktown by land, while the French fleet under Admiral de Grasse cut off British reinforcements by sea. Under heavy barrage from American artillery and with no hope of escape, Cornwallis capitulated on October 19, 1781. The next day, he wrote the following explanation to General Henry Clinton, Commander in Chief of the British colonial troops. How does Cornwallis account for his defeat?

I have the mortification to inform your Excellency that I have been forced to give up the posts of York and Gloucester, and to surrender the troops under my command, by capitulation, on the 19th instant, as prisoners of war to the combined forces of America and France.

I never saw this post in a very favourable light, but when I found I was to be attacked in it in so unprepared a state, by so powerful an army and artillery, nothing but the hopes of relief would have induced me to attempt its defence, for I would either have endeavoured to escape to New York by rapid marches from the Gloucester side, immediately on the arrival of General Washington's troops at Williamsburg, or I would, notwithstanding the disparity of numbers, have attacked them in the open field, where it might have been just possible that fortune would have favoured the gallantry of the handful of troops under my command, but being assured by your Excellency's letters that every possible means would be tried by the navy and army to relieve us, I could not think myself at liberty to venture upon either of those desperate attempts; therefore, after remaining for two days in a strong position in front of this place in hopes of being attacked, upon observing that the enemy were taking measures which could not fail of turning my left flank in a short time, and receiving on the second evening your letter of the 24th of September, informing me that the relief would sail about the 5th of October, I withdrew within the works on the night of the 29th of September, hoping by the labour and firmness of the soldiers to protract the defence until you could arrive. . . .

. . . [T]heir batteries opened on the evening of the 9th against our left, and other batteries fired at the same time against a redoubt advanced over the creek upon our right, and defended by about 120 men of the 23rd Regiment and marines, who maintained that post with uncommon gallantry. The fire continued incessant from heavy cannon, and from mortars and howitzers throwing shells from 8 to 16 inches, until all our guns on the left were silenced, our work much damaged, and our loss of men considerable. On the night of the 11th they began their second parallel, about 300 yards nearer to us. The troops being much weakened by sickness, as well as by the fire of the besiegers, and observing that the enemy had not only secured their flanks, but proceeded in every respect with the utmost regularity and caution, I could not venture so large sorties as to hope from them any considerable effect, but otherwise, I did everything in my power to interrupt this work by opening new embrasures for guns and keeping up a constant fire from all the howitzers and small mortars that we could man. . . . At this time we knew that there was no part of the whole front attacked on which we could show a single gun, and our shells were nearly expended. I, therefore, had only to choose between preparing to surrender next day, or endeavouring to get off with the greatest part of the troops, and I determined to attempt the latter, reflecting that, though it should prove unsuccessful in its immediate object, it might at least delay the enemy in the prosecution of further enterprises. Sixteen large boats were prepared, and upon other pretexts were ordered to be in readiness to receive troops precisely at 10 o'clock. With these I hoped to pass the infantry during the night, abandoning our baggage, and leaving a detachment to capitulate for the townspeople, and the sick and wounded, on which subject a letter was ready to be delivered to General Washington. After making my arrangements with the utmost secrecy, the light infantry, greatest part of the Guards, and part of the 23rd Regiment, landed at Gloucester; but at this critical moment the weather, from being moderate and calm, changed to a most violent storm of wind and rain, and drove all the boats, some of which had troops on board, down the river. It was soon evident that the intended passage was impracticable, and the absence of the boats rendered it equally impossible to bring back the troops that had passed, which I had ordered about two in the morning. . . . Our numbers had been diminished by the enemy's fire, but particularly by sickness, and the strength and spirits of those in the works were much exhausted, by the fatigue of constant watching and unremitting duty. Under all these circumstances, I thought it would have been wanton and inhuman to the last degree to sacrifice the lives of this small body of gallant soldiers, who had ever behaved with so much fidelity and courage, by exposing them to an assault which, from the numbers and precautions of the enemy, could not fail to succeed. I therefore proposed to capitulate; and I have the honour to enclose to your Excellency the copy of the correspondence between General Washington and me on that subject, and the terms of capitulation agreed upon. I sincerely lament that better could not be obtained, but I have neglected nothing in my power to alleviate the misfortune and distress of both officers and soldiers. . . .

Although the event has been so unfortunate, the patience of the soldiers in bearing the greatest fatigues, and their firmness and intrepidity under a persevering fire of shot and shells that, I believe, has not often been exceeded, deserved the highest admiration and praise. A successful defence, however, in our situation was, perhaps, impossible, for the place could only be reckoned an intrenched camp, subject in most places to enfilade, and the ground in general so disadvantageous that nothing but the necessity of fortifying it as a post to protect the navy, could have induced any person to erect works upon it. Our force diminished daily by sickness and other losses, and was reduced, when we offered to capitulate, on this side to little more than 3200 rank and file fit for duty, including officers, servants, and artificers; and at Gloucester about 600, including cavalry. The enemy's army consisted of upwards of 8000 French, nearly as many continentals, and 5000 militia. They brought an immense train of heavy artillery, most amply furnished with ammunition, and perfectly well manned. . . .

C. African Americans in the Revolutionary War

1. Dunmore Promises to Free the Slaves (1775)[*]

With war against Britain on the horizon, rumors swirled throughout the South that British agents would use the nearly half a million slaves who toiled on Southern

---
[*]*Virginia Gazette* (Dixon and Hunter), November 25, 1775.

plantations as instruments of war. Planters' worst fears were confirmed in November of 1775, when Lord Dunmore, the governor of Virginia, proclaimed free all slaves who joined the royal army in restoring order to the colony. How does Dunmore justify his actions?

Lord Dunmore's Proclamation

As I have ever entertained hopes that an accommodation might have taken place between *Great Britain* and this colony, without being compelled, by my duty, to this most disagreeable, but now absolutely necessary step, rendered so by a body of armed men, unlawfully assembled, firing on his Majesty's tenders, and the formation of an army, and that army now on their march to attack his Majesty's troops, and destroy the well disposed subjects of this colony: To defeat such treasonable purposes, and that all such traitors, and their abettors may be brought to justice, and that the peace and good order of this colony may be again restored, which the ordinary course of the civil law is unable to effect, I have thought fit to issue this my proclamation, hereby declaring, that until the aforesaid good purposes can be obtained, I do, in virtue of the power and authority to me given, by his Majesty, determine to execute martial law, and cause the same to be executed throughout this colony; and to the end that peace and good order may the sooner be restored, I do require every person capable of bearing arms to resort to his Majesty's STANDARD, or be looked upon as traitors to his Majesty's crown and government, and thereby become liable to the penalty the law inflicts upon such offenses, such as forfeiture of life, confiscation of lands, &c. &c. And I do hereby further declare all indented servants, Negroes, or others (appertaining to rebels) free, that are able and willing to bear arms, they joining his Majesty's troops, as soon as may be, for the more speedily reducing this colony to a proper sense of their duty to his Majesty's crown and dignity. I do further order, and require, all his Majesty's liege subjects to retain their quitrents, or any other taxes due, or that may become due, in their own custody, till such time as peace may be again restored to this at present most unhappy country, or demanded of them for their former salutary purposes, by officers properly authorized to receive the same.

2. John Page Appeals to Slaves (1775)*

In the wake of Dunmore's proclamation, planters scrambled to ward off a mass exodus of slaves to British lines. They locked slaves up for the night, withdrew boats from the shore, moved slaves inland, and established nightly patrols. Planters also appealed for their slaves' loyalty. John Page, a wealthy planter and vice president of Virginia's Committee of Safety, delivered the following plea, published in newspapers throughout the state. How convincing are the arguments he employs?

Long have the Americans, moved by compassion, and actuated by sound policy, endeavored to stop the progress of slavery. Our Assemblies have repeatedly passed

---

Virginia Gazette (Dixon and Hunter), November 25, 1775.

acts laying heavy duties upon imported Negroes, by which they meant altogether to prevent the horrid traffic; but their humane intentions have been as often frustrated by the cruelty and covetousness of a set of English merchants, who prevailed upon the king to repeal our kind and merciful acts, little indeed to the credit of his humanity. Can it then be supposed that the Negroes will be better used by the English, who have always encouraged and upheld this slavery, than by their present masters, who pity their condition, who wish, in general, to make it as easy and comfortable as possible, and who would willingly, were it in their power, or were they permitted, not only prevent any more Negroes from losing their freedom, but restore it to such as have already unhappily lost it. No, the ends of Lord Dunmore and his party being answered, they will either give up the offending Negroes to the *rigour* of the laws they have broken, or sell them in the West Indies, where every year they sell many thousands of their miserable brethren, to perish, either by the inclemency of the weather, or the cruelty of barbarous masters. Be not then, ye Negroes tempted by this proclamation to ruin yourselves. I have given you a faithful view of what you are to expect; and I declare, before GOD, in doing it I have considered your welfare, as well as that of the country. Whether you will profit by my advice I cannot tell; but this I know that whether we suffer or not, if you desert us, you most certainly will.

3. Boston King Recalls His Service (1798)*

As British ships withdrew from colonial ports at war's end, they carried away tens of thousands of African Americans. The vast majority were Loyalist property, destined for the slave plantations of the British West Indies. But a considerable number—perhaps as many as fourteen thousand—found their way to freedom in Nova Scotia and the British Isles. One of the lucky émigrés was Boston King, a runaway slave from Charleston who secured passage to Nova Scotia and published a narrative of his wartime odyssey. What do the following excerpts from his memoir reveal about the precarious situation of blacks during the war?

I determined to go to Charles-Town, and throw myself into the hands of the English. They received me readily, and I began to feel the happiness of liberty, of which I knew nothing before, altho' I was much grieved at first, to be obliged to leave my friends, and reside among strangers. In this situation I was seized with the small-pox, and suffered great hardships; for all the Blacks affected with that disease, were ordered to be carried a mile from the camp, lest the soldiers should be infected, and disabled from marching. This was a grievous circumstance to me and many others. We lay sometimes a whole day without any thing to eat or drink; but Providence sent a man, who belonged to the York volunteers whom I was acquainted with, to my relief. He brought me such things as I stood in need of; and by the blessing of the Lord I began to recover. . . .

---

*Vincent Carretta, ed., *Unchained Voices: An Anthology of Black Authors in the English-Speaking World of the Eighteenth Century* (Lexington: University Press of Kentucky, 1996), pp. 353–357.

Being recovered, I marched with the army to Chamblem. When we came to the head-quarters, our regiment was 35 miles off. I stayed at the head-quarters three weeks, during which time our regiment had an engagement with the Americans, and the man who relieved me when I was ill of the small-pox, was wounded in the battle, and brought to the hospital. As soon as I heard of his misfortune, I went to see him, and tarried with him in the hospital six weeks, till he recovered; rejoicing that it was in my power to return him the kindness he had shewed me. . . .

Soon after I went to Charles-Town, and entered on board a man of war. As we were going to Chesepeak-bay, we were at the taking of a rich prize. We stayed in the bay two days, and then sailed for New-York, where I went on shore. Here I endeavoured to follow my trade, but for want of tools was obliged to relinquish it, and enter into service. But the wages were so low that I was not able to keep myself in clothes, so that I was under the necessity of leaving my master and going to another. I stayed with him four months, but he never paid me, and I was obliged to leave him also, and work about the town until I was married. . . .

[In 1783] the horrors and devastation of war happily terminated, and peace was restored between America and Great Britain, which diffused universal joy among all parties, except us, who had escaped from slavery, and taken refuge in the English army; for a report prevailed at New-York, that all the slaves, in number 2000, were to be delivered up to their masters, altho' some of them had been three or four years among the English. This dreadful rumour filled us all with inexpressible anguish and terror, especially when we saw our old masters coming from Virginia, North-Carolina, and other parts, and seizing upon their slaves in the streets of New-York, or even dragging them out of their beds. Many of the slaves had very cruel masters, so that the thoughts of returning home with them embittered life to us. For some days we lost our appetite for food, and sleep departed from our eyes. The English had compassion upon us in the day of distress, and issued out a Proclamation, importing, That all slaves should be free, who had taken refuge in the British lines, and claimed the sanction and privileges of the Proclamations respecting the security and protection of Negroes. In consequence of this, each of us received a certificate from the commanding officer at New-York, which dispelled all our fears, and filled us with joy and gratitude. Soon after, ships were fitted out, and furnished with every necessary for conveying us to Nova Scotia.

4. Jehu Grant Petitions for a Pension (1836)[*]

In the North, slaves and free blacks sided most often with the Patriots, fighting bravely in the major battles of the Revolution. In 1777 Jehu Grant ran away from his Tory master to serve in the Connecticut militia, but his term of service was cut short when his master discovered him and dragged him back into bondage. Decades later, after Congress established pensions for Revolutionary veterans, the now free and ailing Grant filed the following petition to get his due. What reasons does he give for joining the Patriot cause?

---

[*]John C. Dann, ed., *The Revolution Remembered: Eyewitness Accounts of the War for Independence* (Chicago: University of Chicago Press, 1980), pp. 27–28.

I was then grown to manhood, in the full vigor and strength of life, and heard much about the cruel and arbitrary things done by the British. Their ships lay within a few miles of my master's house, which stood near the shore, and I was confident that my master traded with them, and I suffered much from fear that I should be sent aboard a ship of war. This I disliked. But when I saw liberty poles and the people all engaged for the support of freedom, I could not but like and be pleased with such thing (God forgive me if I sinned in so feeling). And living on the borders of Rhode Island, where whole companies of colored people enlisted, it added to my fears and dread of being sold to the British. These considerations induced me to enlist into the American army, where I served faithful about ten months, when my master found and took me home. Had I been taught to read or understand the precepts of the Gospel, "Servants obey your masters," I might have done otherwise, notwithstanding the songs of liberty that saluted my ear, thrilled through my heart. But feeling conscious that I have since compensated my master for the injury he sustained by my enlisting, and that God has forgiven me for so doing, and that I served my country faithfully, and that they having enjoyed the benefits of my service to an equal degree for the length [of] time I served with those generally who are receiving the liberalities of the government, I cannot but feel it becoming me to pray Your Honor to review my declaration on file and the papers herewith amended.

A few years after the war, Joshua Swan, Esq., of Stonington purchased me of my master and agreed that after I had served him a length of time named faithfully, I should be free. I served to his satisfaction and so obtained my freedom. He moved into the town of Milton, where I now reside, about forty-eight years ago. After my time expired with Esq. Swan, I married a wife. We have raised six children. Five are still living. I must be upward of eighty years of age and have been blind for many years, and, notwithstanding the aid I received from the honest industry of my children, we are still very needy and in part are supported from the benevolence of our friends. With these statements and the testimony of my character herewith presented, I humbly set my claim upon the well-known liberality of government.

D. Revolutionary Diplomacy

1. John Adams Contemplates a Model Treaty (1776)[*]

Even before the Continental Congress had declared independence, it recognized that friendship with France would be vital to any hope for American success in the conflict with Britain. Yet a close relationship with such a powerful imperial state came with its own dangers. It fell principally to John Adams to figure out how the colonies could maintain a beneficial connection to great nations without drowning in the treacherous swamp of European power politics. Adams jotted down his thoughts on the issue in the spare notes reprinted here and would shortly develop them more fully in what came to be known as "The Model Treaty." How might such a treaty as Adams

---

[*]John Adams, *The Works of John Adams* (1856; reprint New York: AMS Press, 1971), vol. 2, pp. 488–489.

proposed be seen as a reflection both of a new diplomatic idealism and of the diplomatic realities faced by the fledgling American government?

Is any assistance attainable from France?

What connection may we safely form with her?

1. No political connection. Submit to none of her authority; receive no governors or officers from her. 2. No military connection. Receive no troops from her. 3. Only a commercial connection; that is, make a treaty to receive her ships into our ports; let her engage to receive our ships into her ports; furnish us with arms, cannon, saltpetre, powder, duck, steel.

2. Silas Deane Works to Convince France (1776)*

While John Adams theorized about treaties, Congress dispatched Silas Deane to Paris to begin the practical process of winning French support. Eventually the work of Deane and fellow diplomats led to a wartime alliance that proved instrumental to the colonists' victory. In this selection, Deane tries to convince his French hosts of the advantages to be gained from a relationship with the American states. Why, according to Deane, should France care about the success of the Revolution? What role does "commerce" play in Deane's argument?

With whatever European States the Trade of the United Colonies may be carried on, it must of Necessity prove highly beneficial & advantageous to them, as this Commerce will consist principally of an exchange of the most Valuable raw or unmanufactured Commodities, for those which are already manufactured. The Colonies, therefore, in offering their Commerce to France, do really offer her that from which the Wealth of Great Brittain has been principally derived, and which will afford every benefit that could result even from the Sovereignty of those Colonies, without any of the Burthens necessarily attending Sovereignty. No power in Europe can have ought to apprehend from the independancy of the Colonies. In Conjunction with Great Brittain they would enable her to conquer the possessions of other States in America, but separated from her, both interest and Inclination will lead them to observe a just and peaceable conduct toward the rest of the World for many, very many ages to come; happy in having been able to secure and enjoy their own Rights, they will not think of invading those of other People, and from their Local situation, the Circumstances by which they are surrounded, their habits, Interests, & Dispositions, & above all from the immense extent of uncultivated Territory which they possess, their attention must for a Multitude of Years necessarily be fixed upon Agriculture, the most natural, beneficial and inoffensive of all human Employments. By this they will constantly produce abundant Quantities of those productions & Materials which are suited for European Consumption and European Manufactures. And to obtain suitable markets for these articles, as well as suitable supplies of European Manufactures & Commodities for their own Wants, it

---

*Silas Deane, *The Deane Papers, Collections of the New York Historical Society* (New York, 1887), vol. 19, pp. 436–437.

must ever be their Interest to pursue an inviolable Peace with the States of Europe, more especially with France; they can therefore never resolve, even were they to become sufficiently powerful, to embroil themselves with those European States who have possessions in America, by attempting the Conquest of such possessions.

3. Ségur Recalls the Arrival of Franklin and the Departure of Lafayette (1824)*

Louis-Philippe Ségur was a young and rising officer within the French military when he heard of the American colonies' decision to declare independence. Though a member of the French aristocracy, he deeply sympathized with the colonists' historic struggle to throw off their monarchical burden. In the following passage from his memoirs, Ségur recalls the effect the arrival of American diplomats had on him and other young nobles. Among Ségur's close friends was the famed Marquis de Lafayette, who would let nothing stand in the way of his participation in the colonists' cause. How might we account for the astonishing resolve of men like Lafayette to risk everything to help the Americans? Why did the physical appearance and diplomatic practices of the American representatives seem so important to Ségur and his colleagues?

Soon we witnessed the arrival in Paris of the American deputies, Sileas Deane and Arthur Lee. Shortly after, they were joined by the celebrated American, Benjamin Franklin. Words fail to describe with what eagerness and favour these envoys of a people in rebellion against its monarch were received in France in the bosom of an ancient monarchy.

Nothing was more surprising than the contrast between the luxury of our capital, the elegance of our fashions, the magnificence of Versailles, all the living traces of the monarchical pride of Louis XIV, the polished but proud haughtiness of our grand persons . . . and the Americans' almost rustic dress, simple but proud bearing, free and candid language, unadorned, powderless hair and their general antique appearance, which seemed to transport of a sudden within our walls, in the midst of the flabby, servile civilisation of the eighteenth century, some of the wise contemporaries of Plato or the republicans of Cato and Fabius.

Young French officers eager for war flocked to visit the American commissioners, questioning them on the state of their affairs, the forces at the disposal of Congress, their means of defence, and on the various scraps of news which were incessantly arriving from America, where they saw liberty fighting so bravely against British tyranny.

Our admiration was increased by the good faith and simplicity with which these envoys told us of the frequent defeats sustained by their inexperienced forces, for at that time the number of tactics of the English gave them several passing triumphs over the brave American planters, who were novices in warfare. Sileas Deane and Arthur Lee did not conceal from us that the help of some trained officers would be as agreeable to them as it would be useful. . . . [T]hree first Frenchmen of rank

---

*From *The Memoirs and Anecdotes of the Count de Ségur*, translated by Gerard Shelley, pp. 50–55. Copyright © 1928 by Scribner's.

to offer the help of their swords to the Americans were the Marquis de La Fayette, Vicomte de Noailles and myself. . . .

We all three swore secrecy concerning our arrangements with the American commissioners in order that we might have time to fathom the dispositions of our Court and to get together the necessary means for the execution of our projects. Unfortunately there was no conformity between our hopes, desires and opinions and our fortunes. Vicomte de Noailles and I depended on our parents, and had no more than the allowance they gave us. La Fayette, on the other hand, though younger and less advanced in rank than ourselves, was at the age of nineteen master of his property and person and the owner of an income of one hundred thousand pounds.

Our eagerness was too great to be discreet for long. We confided our plan to some young men we hoped to get to join our enterprise. The Court got to hear of it and the ministry ordered us to abandon it, fearing that the departure of volunteers of rank for America, which would be considered impossible without its authorisation, might open the eyes of the English to the designs it still wished to conceal from them.

Our parents, who had known nothing till then, grew alarmed and reproached us for our adventurous levity. I was struck by the surprise shown by the family of La Fayette. It pleased me all the more because it showed how badly his grandparents had known and judged his character till then. . . .

The prohibition to set out on this great adventure naturally affected us in different ways. Vicomte de Noailles and myself were bewildered, as it deprived us of all freedom and means of action. It irritated La Fayette, who decided to go his own way, being assured of all the necessary means for the success of his design.

Nevertheless he made a pretence of obeying at first. Two months later he rushed all of a sudden into my room, closed the door tightly, and sat down near my bed.

"I'm off to America," he said. "Nobody knows about it. But I love you too much to go away without telling you my secret."

"What have you done to make sure of your sailing?" I asked.

He told me that he had made a journey abroad on some plausible pretext and had bought a vessel, which was to wait for him in a Spanish port. He had fitted it out, got a good crew and filled it not only with arms and ammunition but also with a good number of officers who had agreed to share his lot. . . .

. . . His departure caused much affliction to his family, who could hardly bear to see him run so many dangers and, furthermore, sacrifice a great part of his fortune for the sake of a country so far away. . . .

Informed immediately of his disobedience, the Court gave orders for his arrest, which were carried out. So after all these sacrifices my unfortunate friend was deprived of his liberty at the very moment he was setting out to defend that of another hemisphere.

Happily he managed to deceive his warders and escaped a few days later. He crossed the Pyrenees and found his vessel on the Spanish coast together with his comrades in arms, who had almost given up hope of seeing him again. He set sail, arrived without mishap in America and was received in a manner befitting his noble and generous audacity.

Thought Provokers

1. Why were many Patriot soldiers who had volunteered to defend their liberties so untrustworthy and even cowardly?

2. Paine's *Common Sense* and the Declaration of Independence have both been referred to as the most potent propaganda documents in American history. Comment. Prepare a British rejoinder to the Declaration of Independence. The Declaration was designed primarily to achieve American independence, but it was much more than that. Assess its worldwide, long-range significance.

3. What factors helped determine whether African Americans sided with Loyalists or Patriots? How did the experience of black soldiers differ from that of whites? If you were a slave in the South, would you have tried to join the British army?

4. In what ways did America's earliest diplomatic efforts foreshadow the later course of American foreign policy?

9

The Confederation and the Constitution, 1776–1790

Should the states reject this excellent Constitution,
the probability is that an opportunity will never
again offer to make another in peace—the next will
be drawn in blood.

George Washington, on signing the Constitution, 1787

Prologue: The nation's first written constitution—the Articles of Confederation (in force 1781–1789)—provided a toothless central government. Disorders inevitably erupted, notably in Massachusetts, though they were exaggerated by those who hoped to substitute a potent federal government. Such pressures eventually bore fruit in the new Constitution framed in Philadelphia during the humid summer of 1787. A century and a quarter later, Charles A. Beard advanced the sensational thesis that propertied men had foisted the Constitution upon the less privileged classes. He underscored the fact that many of the fifty-five framers owned depreciated government securities that would rise in value with the establishment of a powerful central regime. But subsequent scholarship has concluded that Beard overemphasized economic motivation. The crucial struggle was between the big states, which had reluctantly accepted an equal vote in the Senate, and the small states, which rather promptly approved the Constitution. Several of the stronger and more self-sufficient commonwealths, notably Virginia and New York, were among the last to ratify. At almost the same moment, another popular revolution erupted in France, but with consequences quite different from those in America.

A. The Shock of Shays's Rebellion

I. Daniel Gray Explains the Shaysites' Grievances (1786)*

When debt-ridden farmers in Massachusetts failed in 1786 to persuade the state legislature to issue cheap paper money and take measures to halt farm foreclosures, violence erupted. One of the Shaysites, Daniel Gray, issued the following statement of the farmers' grievances. What was their principal complaint? Were they justified in taking up arms?

---

*George Richards Minot, ed., *History of the Insurrection in Massachusetts in 1786 and of the Rebellion Consequent Thereon* (Worcester, MA: Isaiah Thomas, 1788), as reprinted by Da Capo Press, 1971, pp. 83–84.

An *Address* to the People of the several towns in the county of *Hampshire*, now at arms.

GENTLEMEN,

We have thought proper to inform you of some of the principal causes of the late risings of the people, and also of their present movement, viz.

1st. The present expensive mode of collecting debts, which, by reason of the great scarcity of cash, will of necessity fill our gaols with unhappy debtors, and thereby a reputable body of people rendered incapable of being serviceable either to themselves or the community.

2d. The monies raised by impost and excise being appropriated to discharge the interest of governmental securities, and not the foreign debt, when these securities are not subject to taxation.

3d. A suspension of the writ of *Habeas corpus*, by which those persons who have stepped forth to assert and maintain the rights of the people, are liable to be taken and conveyed even to the most distant part of the Commonwealth, and thereby subjected to an unjust punishment.

4th. The unlimited power granted to Justices of the Peace and Sheriffs, Deputy Sheriffs, and Constables, by the Riot Act, indemnifying them to the prosecution thereof; when perhaps, wholly actuated from a principle of revenge, hatred and envy.

Furthermore, Be assured, that this body, now at arms, despise the idea of being instigated by British emissaries, which is so strenuously propagated by the enemies of our liberties: And also wish the most proper and speedy measures may be taken, to discharge both our foreign and domestic debt.

Per Order,
Daniel Gray, *Chairman of the Committee, for the above purpose.*

2. George Washington Expresses Alarm (1786)*

The retired war hero Washington, struggling to repair his damaged fortunes at Mount Vernon, was alarmed by the inability of the Congress under the Articles of Confederation to collect taxes and regulate interstate commerce. The states, racked by the depression of 1784–1788, seemed to be going their thirteen separate ways. The worthy farmers of western Massachusetts were especially hard hit, burdened as they were with inequitable and delinquent taxes, mortgage foreclosures, and the prospect of imprisonment for debt. Hundreds of them, under the Revolutionary captain Daniel Shays, formed armed mobs in an effort to close the courts and to force the issuance of paper money. "Good God!" burst out Washington on hearing of these disorders; "who, besides a Tory, could have foreseen, or a Briton have predicted them?" He wrote despairingly as follows to John Jay, the prominent New York statesman and diplomat. What single fear seems to disturb Washington most, and why?

---

*J. C. Fitzpatrick, ed., *Writings of George Washington* (Washington, DC: U.S. Government Printing Office, 1938), vol. 28, pp. 502–503 (August 1, 1786).

Your sentiments, that our affairs are drawing rapidly to a crisis, accord with my own. What the event will be is also beyond the reach of my foresight. We have errors to correct; we have probably had too good an opinion of human nature in forming our Confederation. Experience has taught us that men will not adopt, and carry into execution, measures the best calculated for their own good, without the intervention of coercive power. I do not conceive we can exist long as a nation without lodging, somewhere, a power which will pervade the whole Union in as energetic a manner as the authority of the state governments extends over the several states.

To be fearful of investing Congress, constituted as that body is, with ample authorities for national purposes, appears to me the very climax of popular absurdity and madness. Could Congress exert them for the detriment of the people without injuring themselves in an equal or greater proportion? Are not their interests inseparably connected with those of their constituents? By the rotation of appointments [annual elections], must they not mingle frequently with the mass of citizens? . . .

What then is to be done? Things cannot go on in the same train forever. It is much to be feared, as you observe, that the better kind of people, being disgusted with these circumstances, will have their minds prepared for any revolution whatever. We are apt to run from one extreme to another. To anticipate and prevent disastrous contingencies would be the part of wisdom and patriotism.

What astonishing changes a few years are capable of producing! I am told that even respectable characters speak of a monarchical form of government without horror. From thinking proceeds speaking; thence to acting is often but a single step. But how irrevocable and tremendous! What a triumph for our enemies to verify their predictions! What a triumph for the advocates of despotism to find that we are incapable of governing ourselves, and that systems founded on the basis of equal liberty are merely ideal and fallacious. Would to God that wise measures may be taken in time to avert the consequences we have but too much reason to apprehend.

3. Thomas Jefferson Favors Rebellion (1787)[*]

Thomas Jefferson was the successor to Benjamin Franklin as American minister to France, 1785 to 1789. ("I do not replace him, sir; I am only his successor," he remarked with both wit and modesty.) As an ultraliberal and a specialist in revolution, this author of the Declaration of Independence wrote as follows about Shays's Rebellion to his Virginia neighbor, James Madison. The complete crushing of the uprising had not yet occurred. What did Jefferson regard as the most important cause of the disturbance, and what was most extreme about his judgment?

I am impatient to learn your sentiments on the late troubles in the Eastern [New England] states. So far as I have yet seen, they do not appear to threaten serious consequences. Those states have suffered by the stoppage of the channels of their commerce, which have not yet found other issues. This must render money scarce, and make the people uneasy. This uneasiness has produced acts

---

[*]P. L. Ford, ed., *Writings of Thomas Jefferson* (New York: G. P. Putnam's Sons, 1894), vol. 4, pp. 361–363.

absolutely unjustifiable; but I hope they will provoke no severities from their governments. A consciousness of those in power that their administration of the public affairs has been honest may perhaps produce too great a degree of indignation; and those characters wherein fear predominates over hope may apprehend too much from these instances of irregularity. They may conclude too hastily that nature has formed man insusceptible of any other government but that of force, a conclusion not founded in truth, nor experience. . . .

Even this evil is productive of good. It prevents the degeneracy of government, and nourishes a general attention to the public affairs. I hold it that a little rebellion now and then is a good thing, and as necessary in the political world as storms in the physical. Unsuccessful rebellions indeed generally establish the encroachments on the rights of the people which have produced them. An observation of this truth should render honest republican governors so mild in their punishment of rebellions as not to discourage them too much. It is a medicine necessary for the sound health of government.

B. Clashes in the Philadelphia Convention

1. The Debate on Representation in Congress (1787)*

After Shays's Rebellion collapsed, pressures for a stronger central government mounted. Finally, in the summer of 1787, delegates from twelve states met in Philadelphia to strengthen the Articles of Confederation—actually to frame a new constitution. The most complete record of the debates was kept by James Madison of Virginia, the youthful "Father of the Constitution." A portion of his notes follows. The reader must be warned that two of the speakers, Elbridge Gerry of Massachusetts and George Mason of Virginia, not only refused to sign the Constitution but fought against its adoption. Do these debates show the Framing Fathers to be truly democratic? What were the most impressive arguments for and against popular election of representatives? Which side was right?

Resolution 4, first clause: "that the members of the first branch [House of Representatives] of the national legislature ought to be elected by the people of the several states" (being taken up),

Mr. Sherman [of Connecticut] opposed the election by the people, insisting that it ought to be by the state legislatures. The people, he said, immediately should have as little to do as may be about the government. They want [lack] information and are constantly liable to be misled.

Mr. Gerry [of Massachusetts]. The evils we experience flow from the excess of democracy. The people do not want virtue, but are the dupes of pretended patriots. In Massachusetts, it has been fully confirmed by experience that they are daily misled into the most baneful measures and opinions by the false reports circulated by designing men, and which no one on the spot can refute. . . . He had, he said, been

---

*Max Farrand, ed., *The Records of the Federal Convention of 1787* (New Haven, CT: Yale University Press, 1911), vol. 1, pp. 48–50 (May 31, 1787).

too republican heretofore: he was still, however, republican, but had been taught by experience the danger of the leveling spirit.

Mr. Mason [of Virginia] argued strongly for an election of the larger branch by the people. It was to be the grand depository of the democratic principle of the government. It was, so to speak, to be our House of Commons. It ought to know and sympathize with every part of the community, and ought therefore to be taken not only from different parts of the whole republic, but also from different districts of the larger members of it, which had in several instances, particularly in Virginia, different interests and views arising from difference of produce, of habits, etc., etc.

He admitted that we had been too democratic but was afraid we should incautiously run into the opposite extreme. We ought to attend to the rights of every class of the people. . . .

Mr. Wilson [of Pennsylvania] contended strenuously for drawing the most numerous branch of the legislature immediately from the people. He was for raising the federal pyramid to a considerable altitude, and for that reason wished to give it as broad a basis as possible. No government could long subsist without the confidence of the people. In a republican government this confidence was peculiarly essential. He also thought it wrong to increase the weight of the state legislatures by making them the electors of the national legislature. All interference between the general and local governments should be obviated as much as possible. On examination it would be found that the opposition of states to federal measures had proceeded much more from the officers of the states than from the people at large.

Mr. Madison [of Virginia] considered the popular election of one branch of the national legislature as essential to every plan of free government. . . . He thought, too, that the great fabric to be raised would be more stable and durable if it should rest on the solid foundation of the people themselves than if it should stand merely on the pillars of the legislatures. . . .

On the question for an election of the first branch of the national legislature by the people: Massachusetts, aye; Connecticut, divided; New York, aye; New Jersey, no; Pennsylvania, aye; Delaware, divided; Virginia, aye; North Carolina, aye; South Carolina, no; Georgia, aye. (Ayes—6; noes—2; divided—2.)

2. The Argument over Slave Importations (1787)[*]

The issue of slavery provoked spirited debate at Philadelphia. Should the black slave count as a whole person or as no person at all in apportioning representation in Congress? The compromise: a slave would count as three-fifths of a person. Should the further importation of slaves be shut off or allowed to continue forever? The compromise: Congress could not touch slave importation for twenty years (a concession to the South), but Congress by a simple majority rather than by a two-thirds vote could pass laws to control shipping (a concession to the commercial North). As this portion of the debate opens, according to James Madison, delegate Luther Martin of Maryland, a man of well-known liberal tendencies, is endeavoring to amend a draft article stipulating

---

[*]Max Farrand, ed., *The Records of the Federal Convention of 1787* (New Haven, CT: Yale University Press, 1911), vol. 2, pp. 364–365, 369–372.

that slave importation was not to be prohibited or taxed. What were the arguments for nonimportation and those for continued importation? What might have happened if the convention had voted to stop all slave importations at once?

[August 21.] *Mr. L. Martin* [of Maryland] proposed to vary article 7, sect. 4 so as to allow a prohibition or tax on the importation of slaves. First, as five slaves are to be counted as three freemen in the apportionment of representatives, such a clause would leave an encouragement to this traffic. Second, slaves [through danger of insurrection] weakened one part of the Union, which the other parts were bound to protect; the privilege of importing them was therefore unreasonable. Third, it was inconsistent with the principles of the Revolution, and dishonorable to the American character, to have such a feature in the Constitution.

Mr. Rutledge [of South Carolina] did not see how the importation of slaves could be encouraged by this section [as now phrased]. He was not apprehensive of insurrections, and would readily exempt the other states from the obligation to protect the Southern against them. Religion and humanity had nothing to do with this question. Interest alone is the governing principle with nations. The true question at present is whether the Southern states shall or shall not be parties to the Union. If the Northern states consult their interest, they will not oppose the increase of slaves, which will increase the commodities of which they will become the carriers.

Mr. Ellsworth [of Connecticut] was for leaving the clause as it stands. Let every state import what it pleases. The morality or wisdom of slavery are considerations belonging to the states themselves. What enriches a part enriches the whole, and the states are the best judges of their particular interest. The old Confederation had not meddled with this point; and he did not see any greater necessity for bringing it within the policy of the new one.

Mr. [Charles] Pinckney [of South Carolina]. South Carolina can never receive the plan if it prohibits the slave trade. In every proposed extension of the powers of Congress, that state has expressly and watchfully excepted that of meddling with the importation of Negroes. If the states be all left at liberty on this subject, South Carolina may perhaps, by degrees, do of herself what is wished, as Virginia and Maryland already have done. . . .

Mr. Sherman [of Connecticut] was for leaving the clause as it stands. He disapproved of the slave trade; yet, as the states were now possessed of the right to import slaves, as the public good did not require it to be taken from them, and as it was expedient to have as few objections as possible to the proposed scheme of government, he thought it best to leave the matter as we find it. He observed that the abolition of slavery seemed to be going on in the United States, and that the good sense of the several states would probably by degrees complete it. . . .

Col. Mason [of Virginia]. This infernal traffic originated in the avarice of British merchants. The British government constantly checked the attempts of Virginia to put a stop to it. The present question concerns not the importing states alone, but the whole Union. . . . Maryland and Virginia, he said, had already prohibited the importation of slaves expressly. North Carolina had done the same in substance. All this would be in vain if South Carolina and Georgia be at liberty to import. The Western people are already calling out for slaves for their new lands, and will fill that country with slaves, if they can be got through South Carolina and Georgia. Slavery discourages arts and manufactures. The poor despise labor when performed by slaves. They prevent the immigration of whites, who really enrich and strengthen a country. They produce the most pernicious effect on manners. Every master of slaves is born a petty tyrant. They bring the judgment of Heaven on a country. As nations cannot be rewarded or punished in the next world, they must be in this. By an inevitable chain of causes and effects, Providence punishes national sins by national calamities. He lamented that some of our Eastern [New England] brethren had, from a lust of gain, embarked in this nefarious traffic. . . . He held it essential, in every point of view, that the general government should have power to prevent the increase of slavery.

Mr. Ellsworth [of Connecticut], as he had never owned a slave, could not judge of the effects of slavery on character. He said, however, that if it was to be considered in a moral light, we ought to go further, and free those already in the country. As slaves also multiply so fast in Virginia and Maryland that it is cheaper to raise than import them, whilst in the sickly rice swamps foreign supplies are necessary, if we go no further than is urged, we shall be unjust towards South Carolina and Georgia. Let us not intermeddle. As population increases, poor laborers will be so plenty as to render slaves useless. Slavery, in time, will not be a speck in our country. . . .

Gen. [Charles C.] Pinckney [of South Carolina] declared it to be his firm opinion that if himself and all his colleagues were to sign the Constitution, and use their personal influence, it would be of no avail towards obtaining the assent of their constituents [to a slave trade prohibition]. South Carolina and Georgia cannot do without slaves. As to Virginia, she will gain by stopping the importations. Her slaves will rise in value, and she has more than she wants. It would be unequal to require South Carolina and Georgia to confederate on such unequal terms. . . . He contended that the importation of slaves would be for the interest of the whole Union. The more slaves, the more produce to employ the carrying trade; the more consumption also; and the more of this, the more of revenue for the common treasury. He admitted it to be reasonable that slaves should be dutied like other imports; but should consider a rejection of the clause as an exclusion of South Carolina from the Union.

[The final compromise, as written into the Constitution, permitted Congress to levy a maximum duty of ten dollars a head on each slave imported. In 1808, the earliest date permitted by the framers, Congress ended all legal importation of slaves.]

C. Debating the New Constitution _____

1. Alexander Hamilton Scans the Future (1787)[*]

Alexander Hamilton of New York, though only thirty-two, was probably the most brilliant and eloquent member of the Philadelphia assemblage. But his great contribution was in engineering the call for the convention and in campaigning for the Constitution.

---

[*]H. C. Lodge, ed., *The Works of Alexander Hamilton* (Boston and New York: Houghton, Mifflin and Company, 1904), vol. 1, pp. 420–423.

At Philadelphia, he was outvoted by his two antifederalist colleagues from New York, and his own federalist and centralist views were too extreme for the other delegates. His superlative five-hour oratorical effort championed a plan that, among other things, would have had the president and the senators holding office during good behavior, and the state governors appointed by the federal government. The scheme received one vote—his own. Hamilton evidently prepared the following memorandum shortly after the Constitution was drafted. Why would the rich be favorable to the new instrument? Why would the poor and the states' righters be unfavorable?

The new Constitution has in favor of its success these circumstances: A very great weight of influence of the persons who framed it, particularly in the universal popularity of General Washington. The good will of the commercial interest throughout the states, which will give all its efforts to the establishment of a government capable of regulating, protecting, and extending the commerce of the Union. The good will of most men of property in the several states, who wish a government of the Union able to protect them against domestic violence and the depredations which the democratic spirit is apt to make on property, and who are besides anxious for the respectability of the nation. The hopes of the creditors of the United States, that a general government, possessing the means of doing it, will pay the debt of the Union. A strong belief in the people at large of the insufficiency of the present Confederation to preserve the existence of the Union, and of the necessity of the Union to their safety and prosperity. Of course, a strong desire of a change, and a predisposition to receive well the propositions of the convention.

Against its success is to be put: The dissent of two or three important men in the convention, who will think their characters pledged to defeat the plan. The influence of many *inconsiderable* men in possession of considerable offices under the state governments, who will fear a diminution of their consequence, power, and emolument by the establishment of the general government, and who can hope for nothing there. The influence of some *considerable* men in office, possessed of talents and popularity, who, partly from the same motives, and partly from a desire of *playing a part* in a convulsion for their own aggrandizement, will oppose the quiet adoption of the new government. (Some considerable men out of office, from motives of ambition, may be disposed to act the same part.)

Add to these causes: The disinclination of the people to taxes, and of course to a strong government. The opposition of all men much in debt, who will not wish to see a government established, one object of which is to restrain the means of cheating creditors. The democratical jealousy of the people, which may be alarmed at the appearance of institutions that may seem calculated to place the power of the community in few hands, and to raise a few individuals to stations of great preeminence. And the influence of some foreign powers, who, from different motives, will not wish to see an energetic government established throughout the states.

In this view of the subject, it is difficult to form any judgment whether the plan will be adopted or rejected. It must be essentially matter of conjecture. The present appearances and all other circumstances considered, the probability seems to be on the side of its adoption. But the causes operating against its adoption are powerful, and there will be nothing astonishing in the contrary.

If it do not finally obtain, it is probable the discussion of the question will beget such struggles, animosities, and heats in the community that this circumstance, conspiring with the real necessity of an essential change in our present situation, will produce civil war. . . .

A reunion with Great Britain, from universal disgust at a state of commotion, is not impossible, though not much to be feared. The most plausible shape of such a business would be the establishment of a son of the present monarch [George III] in the supreme government of this country, with a family compact.

If the government be adopted, it is probable General Washington will be the President of the United States. This will ensure a wise choice of men to administer the government, and a good administration. A good administration will conciliate the confidence and affection of the people, and perhaps enable the government to acquire more consistency than the proposed Constitution seems to promise for so great a country.

2. George Mason Is Critical (1787)*

George Mason, a wealthy Virginia planter who owned five thousand acres, had played a leading role in the Revolutionary movement. A self-taught constitutional lawyer of high repute, a dedicated advocate of states' rights, and an undying foe of slavery, he was one of the five most frequent speakers at the Philadelphia convention. Shocked by the whittling down of states' rights, he finally refused to sign the Constitution and fought it bitterly in Virginia. His chief grievance was the compromise by which the South conceded a simple majority vote in Congress on navigation laws in return for twenty more years of African slave trade, of which he disapproved anyhow. He set forth his objections in the following influential pamphlet. Which of his criticisms relate to states' rights? Which to the rights of the South? Which seem overdrawn in the light of subsequent events?

There is no Declaration [Bill] of Rights, and the laws of the general government being paramount to the laws and constitution of the several states, the declarations of rights in the separate states are no security. . . .

The Judiciary of the United States is so constructed and extended as to absorb and destroy the judiciaries of the several states; thereby rendering law as tedious, intricate, and expensive, and justice as unattainable, by a great part of the community, as in England, and enabling the rich to oppress and ruin the poor.

The President of the United States has no Constitutional Council, a thing unknown in any safe and regular government. He will therefore be unsupported by proper information and advice, and will generally be directed by minions and favorites; or he will become a tool to the Senate—or a council of state will grow out of the principal officers of the great departments; the worst and most dangerous of all ingredients for such a council in a free country. From this fatal defect has arisen the improper power of the Senate in the appointment of public officers, and the alarming dependence and connection between that branch of the legislature and the Supreme Executive.

---

*Kate M. Rowland, *The Life of George Mason* (New York and London: G. P. Putnam's Sons, 1892), vol. 2, pp. 387–390.

Hence also sprung that unnecessary officer, the Vice-President, who, for want of other employment, is made president of the Senate, thereby dangerously blending the executive and legislative powers, besides always giving to some one of the states an unnecessary and unjust pre-eminence over the others. . . .

By declaring all treaties supreme laws of the land, the Executive and the Senate have, in many cases, an exclusive power of legislation; which might have been avoided by proper distinctions with respect to treaties, and requiring the assent of the House of Representatives, where it could be done with safety.

By requiring only a majority [of Congress] to make all commercial and navigation laws, the five Southern states, whose produce and circumstances are totally different from that of the eight Northern and Eastern states, may be ruined. For such rigid and premature regulations may be made as will enable the merchants of the Northern and Eastern states not only to demand an exorbitant freight, but to monopolize the purchase of the commodities at their own price, for many years, to the great injury of the landed interest and impoverishment of the people. And the danger is the greater as the gain on one side will be in proportion to the loss on the other. Whereas requiring two-thirds of the members present in both Houses would have produced mutual moderation, promoted the general interest, and removed an insuperable objection to the adoption of this government.

Under their own construction of the general clause [Article I, Section VIII, para. 18], at the end of the enumerated powers, the Congress may grant monopolies in trade and commerce, constitute new crimes, inflict unusual and severe punishments, and extend their powers as far as they shall think proper; so that the state legislatures have no security for the powers now presumed to remain to them, or the people for their rights.

There is no declaration of any kind for preserving the liberty of the press, or the trial by jury in civil causes [cases]; nor against the danger of standing armies in time of peace. . . .

This government will set out a moderate aristocracy; it is at present impossible to foresee whether it will, in its operation, produce a monarchy or a corrupt, tyrannical aristocracy. It will most probably vibrate some years between the two, and then terminate in the one or the other.

3. Jefferson Is Unenthusiastic (1787)*

Thomas Jefferson, the American minister in Paris, learned of the Philadelphia convention with some misgivings. While recognizing the need for a stronger central government, especially in foreign affairs, he regarded the Confederation as a "wonderfully perfect instrument," considering the times. A comparison of the United States government with the governments of continental Europe, he declared, "is like a comparison of heaven and hell. England, like the earth, may be allowed to take the intermediate station." He evidently believed that some judicious patchwork would provide the needed bolstering. Upon receiving a copy of the new Constitution, he was

---

*P. L. Ford, ed., *The Writings of Thomas Jefferson* (New York: G. P. Putnam's Sons, 1894), vol. 4, pp. 466–467 (November 13, 1787).

troubled by some of its features, particularly by the absence of a Bill of Rights. Why, in the following letter to the prominent New York jurist William Smith, did he belittle reports of anarchy? Why did he condone periodic rebellions?

I do not know whether it is to yourself or Mr. [John] Adams I am to give my thanks for the copy of the new Constitution. . . . There are very good articles in it; and very bad. I do not know which preponderate. What we have lately read in the history of Holland . . . would have sufficed to set me against a chief magistrate eligible for a long duration, if I had ever been disposed towards one. And what we have always read of the elections of Polish kings should have forever excluded the idea of one continuable for life.

Wonderful is the effect of impudent and persevering lying. The British ministry have so long hired their gazetteers to repeat, and model into every form, lies about our being in anarchy, that the world has at length believed them, the English nation has believed them, the ministers themselves have come to believe them, and what is more wonderful, we have believed them ourselves.

Yet where does this anarchy exist? Where did it ever exist, except in the single instance of [Shays's Rebellion in] Massachusetts? And can history produce an instance of rebellion so honorably conducted? I say nothing of its motives. They were founded in ignorance, not wickedness.

God forbid we should ever be twenty years without such a rebellion. The people cannot be all, and always, well informed. The part which is wrong will be discontented, in proportion to the importance of the facts they misconceive. If they remain quiet under such misconceptions, it is a lethargy, the forerunner of death to the public liberty.

We have had thirteen states independent for eleven years. There has been one rebellion. That comes to one rebellion in a century and a half for each state. What country before ever existed a century and a half without a rebellion? And what country can preserve its liberties if its rulers are not warned from time to time that their people preserve the spirit of resistance? Let them take arms. The remedy is to set them right as to facts, pardon, and pacify them.

What signify a few lives lost in a century or two? The tree of liberty must be refreshed from time to time with the blood of patriots and tyrants. It is its natural manure. Our convention has been too much impressed by the insurrection of Massachusetts; and on the spur of the moment they are setting up a kite [hawk] to keep the henyard in order.

I hope in God this article [perpetual reeligibility of the president] will be rectified before the Constitution is accepted.

4. A Storekeeper Blasts Standing Armies (1788)*

Samuel Nasson, a saddler and later a storekeeper, expressed a common fear in the Massachusetts ratifying convention. Why was this unmoneyed Massachusetts man so deeply concerned about an army?

The Debates . . . on the Adoption of the Federal Constitution (Philadelphia: J. B. Lippincott, 1836), vol. 2, pp. 136–137.

shall comprehend both the nature of the cure and the efficacy which it must derive from the Union.

The two great points of difference between a democracy and a republic are: first, the delegation of the government, in the latter, to a small number of citizens elected by the rest; secondly, the greater number of citizens and greater sphere of country over which the latter may be extended.

The effect of the first difference is, on the one hand, to refine and enlarge the public views by passing them through the medium of a chosen body of citizens, whose wisdom may best discern the true interest of their country and whose patriotism and love of justice will be least likely to sacrifice it to temporary or partial considerations. Under such a regulation it may well happen that the public voice, pronounced by the representatives of the people, will be more consonant to the public good than if pronounced by the people themselves, convened for the purpose. . . .

The other point of difference is the greater number of citizens and extent of territory which may be brought within the compass of republican than of democratic government; and it is this circumstance principally which renders factious combinations less to be dreaded in the former than in the latter. The smaller the society, the fewer probably will be the distinct parties and interests composing it; the fewer the distinct parties and interests, the more frequently will a majority be found of the same party; and the smaller the number of individuals composing a majority, and the smaller the compass within which they are placed, the more easily will they concert and execute their plans of oppression. Extend the sphere and you take in a greater variety of parties and interests; you make it less probable that a majority of the whole will have a common motive to invade the rights of other citizens; or if such a common motive exists, it will be more difficult for all who feel it to discover their own strength and to act in unison with each other. Besides other impediments, it may be remarked that, where there is a consciousness of unjust or dishonorable purposes, communication is always checked by distrust in proportion to the number whose concurrence is necessary.

Hence, it clearly appears that the same advantage which a republic has over a democracy in controlling the effects of faction is enjoyed by a large over a small republic—is enjoyed by the Union over the States composing it. Does this advantage consist in the substitution of representatives whose enlightened views and virtuous sentiments render them superior to local prejudices and to schemes of injustice? It will not be denied that the representation of the Union will be most likely to possess these requisite endowments. Does it consist in the greater security afforded by a greater variety of parties, against the event of any one party being able to outnumber and oppress the rest? In an equal degree does the increased variety of parties comprised within the Union increase this security? Does it, in fine, consist in the greater obstacles opposed to the concert and accomplishment of the secret wishes of an unjust and interested majority? Here again the extent of the Union gives it the most palpable advantage.

The influence of factious leaders may kindle a flame within their particular States but will be unable to spread a general conflagration through the other States. A religious sect may degenerate into a political faction in a part of the Confederacy; but the variety of sects dispersed over the entire face of it must secure the national councils against any danger from that source. A rage for paper money, for an abolition of debts, for an equal division of property, or for any other improper or wicked project, will be less apt to pervade the whole body of the Union than a particular member of it, in the same proportion as such a malady is more likely to taint a particular county or district than an entire State.

In the extent and proper structure of the Union, therefore, we behold a republican remedy for the diseases most incident to republican government. And according to the degree of pleasure and pride we feel in being republicans ought to be our zeal in cherishing the spirit and supporting the character of federalists.

Publius

D. Two Revolutions

1. The French Declare the Rights of Man (1789)*

By calling the Estates General, the King of France had unwittingly set in motion the makings of political revolution. Unable to resolve the issue of representation, the Estates General collapsed, and a more democratic National Assembly emerged in its place. Meanwhile, peasants rioted throughout the countryside against their many obligations to crown and church. Parisians stormed the Bastille, the city's towering symbol of despotic rule. Swept up by the popular fervor, the National Assembly dismantled a centuries-old feudal order and, like the Americans before them, announced the dawn of a new regime with a bold statement of principles, the "Declaration of the Rights of Man and Citizen." What are the parallels between the French declaration below and American Declaration of Independence (p. 97)? What accounts for the differences between the two documents?

The representatives of the French people, constituted as a National Assembly, and considering that ignorance, neglect, or contempt of the rights of man are the sole causes of public misfortunes and governmental corruption, have resolved to set forth in a solemn declaration the natural, inalienable, and sacred rights of man: so that by being constantly present to all the members of the social body this declaration may always remind them of their rights and duties; so that by being liable at every moment to comparison with the aim of any and all political institutions the acts of the legislative and executive powers may be the more fully respected; and so that by being founded henceforward on simple and incontestable principles the demands of the citizens may always tend toward maintaining the constitution and the general welfare.

In consequence, the National Assembly recognizes and declares, in the presence and under the auspices of the Supreme Being, the following rights of man and the citizen:

1. Men are born and remain free and equal in rights. Social distinctions may be based only on common utility.

---

*From Lynn Hunt, ed., *The French Revolution and Human Rights, A Brief Documentary History,* 1996, pp. 77–79, published by Bedford Books/St. Martin's Press.

2. The purpose of all political association is the preservation of the natural and imprescriptible rights of man. These rights are liberty, property, security, and resistance to oppression.

3. The principle of all sovereignty rests essentially in the nation. No body and no individual may exercise authority which does not emanate expressly from the nation.

4. Liberty consists in the ability to do whatever does not harm another; hence the exercise of the natural rights of each man has no other limits than those which assure to other members of society the enjoyment of the same rights. These limits can only be determined by the law.

5. The law only has the right to prohibit those actions which are injurious to society. No hindrance should be put in the way of anything not prohibited by the law, nor may any one be forced to do what the law does not require.

6. The law is the expression of the general will. All citizens have the right to take part, in person or by their representatives, in its formation. It must be the same for everyone whether it protects or penalizes. All citizens being equal in its eyes are equally admissible to all public dignities, offices, and employments, according to their ability, and with no other distinction than that of their virtues and talents.

7. No man may be indicted, arrested, or detained except in cases determined by the law and according to the forms which it has prescribed. Those who seek, expedite, execute, or cause to be executed arbitrary orders should be punished; but citizens summoned or seized by virtue of the law should obey instantly, and not render themselves guilty by resistance.

8. Only strictly and obviously necessary punishments may be established by the law, and no one may be punished except by virtue of a law established and promulgated before the time of the offense, and legally applied.

9. Every man being presumed innocent until judged guilty, if it is deemed indispensable to arrest him, all rigor unnecessary to securing his person should be severely repressed by the law.

10. No one should be disturbed for his opinions, even in religion, provided that their manifestation does not trouble public order as established by law.

11. The free communication of thoughts and opinions is one of the most precious of the rights of man. Every citizen may therefore speak, write, and print freely, if he accepts his own responsibility for any abuse of this liberty in the cases set by the law.

12. The safeguard of the rights of man and the citizen requires public powers. These powers are therefore instituted for the advantage of all, and not for the private benefit of those to whom they are entrusted.

13. For maintenance of public authority and for expenses of administration, common taxation is indispensable. It should be apportioned equally among all the citizens according to their capacity to pay.

14. All citizens have the right, by themselves or through their representatives, to have demonstrated to them the necessity of public taxes, to consent to them freely, to follow the use made of the proceeds, and to determine the means of apportionment, assessment, and collection, and the duration of them.

15. Society has the right to hold accountable every public agent of the administration.

16. Any society in which the guarantee of rights is not assured or the separation of powers not settled has no constitution.

17. Property being an inviolable and sacred right, no one may be deprived of it except when public necessity, certified by law, obviously requires it, and on the condition of a just compensation in advance.

2. Lafayette Writes to Washington (1790)*

A declaration of rights did not rid France of centuries-old suspicions between the different orders of society. The following year was one of mounting unrest as the National Assembly, which had replaced the defunct Estates General, debated the new distribution of power among the social classes. In the midst of this uncertainty, Lafayette, the French general who had served under George Washington in the American Revolution, wrote the following letter to his friend and mentor. How does Lafayette account for the tensions in France? What gives him cause for optimism?

Our Revolution is Getting on as Well as it Can With a Nation that Has Swalled up liberty all at once, and is still liable to Mistake licentiousness for freedom—the Assembly Have More Hatred to the Ancient System than Experience on the proper Organisation of a New, and Constitutional Governement—the Ministers are lamenting the loss of power, and Affraid to use that which they Have—and As Every thing has been destroied and Not much New Building is Yet Above Ground, there is Much Room for Critics and Calomnies.

[T]o this May be Added that We still are Pestered By two parties, the Aristocratic that is panting for a Counter Revolution, and the factious Which Aims at the division of the Empire, and destruction of all Authority and perhaps of the lifes of the Reigning Branch, Both of which parties are fomenting troubles.

And after I Have Confessed all that, My dear General, I will tell you With the Same Candour that We Have Made an Admirable, and Almost incredible destruction of all abuses, prejudices, &c. &c. that Every thing Not directly Useful to, or Coming from the people Has been levelled—that in the topographical, Moral, political Situation of France We Have Made More changes in ten Month than the Most Sanguine patriot could Have imagined—that our internal troubles and Anarchy are Much Exagerated—and that upon the Whole this Revolution, in which Nothing will be wanting But Energy of Governement just as it was in America, Will propagate implant liberty and Make it flourish throughout the world, while We must wait for a Convension in a few years to Mend Some defects which are not Now perceived By Men just Escaped from Aristocracy and despotism. . . .

Give me leave, My dear General, to present you With a picture of the Bastille just as it looked a few days after I Had ordered its demolition, with the Main Kea of that fortress of despotism—it is a tribute Which I owe as A Son to My Adoptive father, as an aid de Camp to My General, as a Missionary of liberty to its patriarch.

---

*Dorothy Twohig, ed., *The Papers of George Washington, Presidential Series*, vol. 5 (Charlottesville: University Press of Virginia, 1996), pp. 241–242.

3. Jefferson Reflects on the Path of Revolutions (1823)*

Years of turmoil and bloodshed sapped the idealism that had flourished in the early years of Revolution. An exhausted French public welcomed the stability offered by the victorious young general, Napoleon Bonaparte, who seized power in 1799 and declared himself Emperor in 1804. Across the Atlantic in Latin America, the revolutions that expelled European powers were of a more lasting nature, but they too were plagued by violence, corruption, and the persistent threat of foreign intervention. In a letter to John Adams, Thomas Jefferson reflects on the nature of revolution. What conclusions does he draw? Has subsequent history confirmed his predictions?

Your letter of Aug. 15. was received in due time, and with the welcome of every thing which comes from you. With it's opinions on the difficulties of revolutions, from despotism to freedom, I very much concur. The generation which commences a revolution can rarely compleat it. Habituated from their infancy to passive submission of body and mind to their kings and priests, they are not qualified, when called on, to think and provide for themselves and their inexperience, their ignorance and bigotry make them instruments often, in the hands of the Bonapartes and Iturbides to defeat their own rights and purposes. This is the present situation of Europe and Spanish America. But it is not desperate. The light which has been shed on mankind by the art of printing has eminently changed the condition of the world. As yet that light has dawned on the midling classes only of the men of Europe. The kings and the rabble of equal ignorance, have not yet received it's rays; but it continues to spread. And, while printing is preserved, it can no more recede than the sun return on his course. A first attempt to recover the right of self-government may fail; so may a 2d. a 3d. etc., but as a younger, and more instructed race comes on, the sentiment becomes more and more intuitive, and a 4th. a 5th. or some subsequent one of the ever renewed attempts will ultimately succeed. In France the 1st. effort was defeated by Robespierre, the 2d. by Bonaparte, the 3d. by Louis XVIII. and his holy allies; another is yet to come, and all Europe, Russia excepted, has caught the spirit, and all will attain representative government, more or less perfect. This is now well understood to be a necessary check on kings, whom they will probably think it more prudent to chain and tame, than to exterminate. To attain all this however rivers of blood must yet flow, and years of desolation pass over. Yet the object is worth rivers of blood, and years of desolation for what inheritance so valuable can man leave to his posterity?

4. The French Revolution: Conflicting Views (1790s)†

Hamilton and Jefferson, disagreeing as they did on many issues, naturally took opposite sides on the French Revolution. The philosophical Virginian, ever dedicated

---

*Lester J. Cappon, ed., *The Adams-Jefferson Letters: The Complete Correspondence Between Thomas Jefferson and Abigail and John Adams* (Chapel Hill: University of North Carolina Press, 1988), pp. 596–597.
†Convenient compilations of quotations from Hamilton and Jefferson are found in S. K. Padover, ed., *The Mind of Alexander Hamilton* (New York: Harper & Row, 1958) and *Thomas Jefferson on Democracy* (New York and London: D. Appleton-Century Company, 1939).

to liberty, rejoiced over the liberation of oppressed humanity. The practical-minded New Yorker, concerned about property, was profoundly shocked by the bloody excesses. Why did Hamilton reject the parallel to the American Revolution? Why was Jefferson so deeply concerned?

Hamilton

In France, he [Jefferson] saw government only on the side of its abuses. He drank freely of the French philosophy, in religion, in science, in politics. He came from France in the moment of a fermentation which he had a share in exciting, and in the passions and feelings of which he shared, both from temperament and situation. . . . He came electrified with attachment to France, and with the project of knitting together the two countries in the closest political bands. (1792)

The cause of France is compared with that of America during its late revolution. Would to heaven that the comparison were just. Would to heaven we could discern in the mirror of French affairs the same humanity, the same decorum, the same gravity, the same order, the same dignity, the same solemnity, which distinguished the cause of the American Revolution. Clouds and darkness would not then rest upon the issue as they now do. I own I do not like the comparison. (1793?)

There was a time when all men in this country entertained the same favorable view of the French Revolution. At the present time, they all still unite in the wish that the troubles of France may terminate in the establishment of a free and good government; and dispassionate, well-informed men must equally unite in the doubt whether this be likely to take place under the auspices of those who now govern . . . that country. But agreeing

Jefferson

But it is a fact, in spite of the mildness of their governors, the [French] people are ground to powder by the vices of the form of government. Of twenty millions of people supposed to be in France, I am of opinion there are nineteen millions more wretched, more accursed in every circumstance of human existence than the most conspicuously wretched individual of the whole United States. (1785)

You will have heard, before this reaches you, of the peril into which the French Revolution is brought by the flight of their King. Such are the fruits of that form of government which heaps importance on idiots, and of which the Tories of the present day are trying to preach into our favor. I still hope the French Revolution will issue happily. I feel that the permanence of our own leans in some degree on that; and that a failure there would be a powerful argument to prove there must be a failure here. (1791)

In the struggle which was necessary, many guilty persons fell without the forms of trial, and with them some innocent. These I deplore as much as anybody, and shall deplore some of them to the day of my death. But I deplore them as I should have done had they fallen in battle. . . . But time and truth will rescue and embalm their very liberty for which they would never have hesitated to offer up their lives. The liberty of the whole earth was depending on the issue of the in these two points, there is a great and serious diversity of opinion as to the real merits and probable issue of the French Revolution. (1794)

None can deny that the cause of France has been stained by excesses and extravagances for which it is not easy, if possible, to find a parallel in the history of human affairs, and from which reason and humanity recoil. (1794)

contest, and was ever such a prize won with so little innocent blood? (1793)

My own affections have been deeply wounded by some of the martyrs to this cause, but rather than it should have failed I would have seen half the earth desolated; were there but an Adam and an Eve left in every country, and left free, it would be better than it now is. (1793)

Thought Provokers

1. Considering the conflicting testimony regarding conditions of anarchy under the Articles of Confederation, what conclusions may be safely drawn about the true state of affairs? To what extent may Daniel Shays be regarded as one of the indirect Founding Fathers? Was his "rebellion" justified? Would Jefferson today be permitted to express publicly his views on rebellion?

2. In what sense was the Constitution a democratic document, and in what sense a conservative one? What did democracy mean to the Founding Fathers?

3. What groups seem to have been the strongest supporters of the Constitution? The strongest foes? Why? What probably would have happened in the short run and in the long run if the Constitution had failed of ratification?

4. What is meant by "enlightened self-interest" in public affairs? Were the Founding Fathers motivated by it rather than by "pocketbook patriotism"?

5. Was *The Federalist* really propaganda in the same sense as the Declaration of Independence and Paine's *Common Sense*?

6. Why did the course of revolution in France differ so markedly from that in the United States? Were there conditions in the United States that could have prompted a more violent upheaval?

Launching the New Ship of State, 1789–1800

Hamilton was honest as a man, but, as a politician, believed in the necessity of either force or corruption to govern men.

Thomas Jefferson, 1811

[Jefferson is] a man of profound ambition and violent passions.

Alexander Hamilton, 1792

Prologue: When Washington took the presidential oath at New York, the temporary capital, he was determined to get the ship of state off on an even keel. He therefore "packed" the new offices with federalists, as the supporters of the Constitution were called. The one conspicuous exception was the secretary of state, Thomas Jefferson. As a vigilant champion of states' rights, he was an antifederalist, or a foe of a powerful central government. One result was an inevitable clash between him and Secretary of the Treasury Alexander Hamilton, a staunch federalist, over foreign affairs and fiscal policy. From these heated differences there emerged, about 1793, two political parties: the Hamiltonian Federalists and the Jeffersonian Democratic-Republicans. Jefferson naturally opposed the Hamiltonian plans for assuming the state debts, establishing the Bank of the United States, and levying an excise tax on whiskey. In his eyes, all these schemes would increase the power of the federal octopus, encroach on states' rights, promote corruption, and enrich the ruling class at the expense of the common folk.

A. Conflict in the Infant Republic: Hamilton Versus Jefferson

1. Alexander Hamilton Versus Thomas Jefferson on Popular Rule (1780s–1820s)[*]

Secretary of the Treasury Hamilton, though born in humble circumstances, had developed a profound distrust of common people. In contrast, Jefferson, a Virginia

---

[*]Excerpts found for the most part in S. K. Padover, ed., *The Mind of Alexander Hamilton* (New York: Harper & Row, 1958); R. B. Morris, ed., *The Basic Ideas of Alexander Hamilton* (1957); S. K. Padover, ed., *Thomas Jefferson on Democracy* (New York and London: D. Appleton-Century Company, 1939).

planter-aristocrat, championed the common folk. Faith in the informed masses became the cornerstone of Jefferson's Democratic-Republican party; distrust of the masses and the cultivation of special interests became the cornerstone of Hamilton's Federalist party. Following are the conflicting opinions of the two great leaders over a period of years. The initial quotations from Hamilton formed a part of his five-hour speech before the Constitutional Convention in Philadelphia (see p. 120). To what extent were Hamilton and Jefferson both right in the light of subsequent history? Who, on balance, was the more sound? Note that Jefferson in particular was prone to exaggerate, and that some of these observations were written privately and in the heat of bitter partisan struggles.

Hamilton

All communities divide themselves into the few and the many. The first are the rich and well born; the other, the mass of the people. The voice of the people has been said to be the voice of God; and however generally this maxim has been quoted and believed, it is not true in fact. The people are turbulent and changing; they seldom judge or determine right. Give therefore to the first class a distinct, permanent share in the government. They will check the unsteadiness of the second; and as they cannot receive any advantage by a change, they therefore will ever maintain good government.

Can a democratic assembly, who annually [through annual elections] revolve in the mass of the people, be supposed steadily to pursue the public good? Nothing but a permanent body can check the imprudence of democracy. Their turbulent and uncontrolling disposition requires checks. (1787)

Take mankind in general, they are vicious—their passions may be operated upon. . . . Take mankind as they are, and what are they governed by? Their passions. There may be in every government a few choice spirits, who may act from more worthy motives.

Jefferson

Those who labor in the earth are the chosen people of God, if ever he had a chosen people, whose breasts he has made his peculiar deposit for substantial and genuine virtue. (1784)

Men . . . are naturally divided into two parties. Those who fear and distrust the people. . . . Those who identify themselves with the people, have confidence in them, cherish and consider them as the most honest and safe . . . depository of the public interest. (1824)

The mass of mankind has not been born with saddles on their backs, nor a favored few booted and spurred, ready to ride them legitimately, by the grace of God. (1826)

Every government degenerates when trusted to the rulers . . . alone. The people themselves are its only safe depositories. (1787)

I have such reliance on the good sense of the body of the people and the honesty of their leaders that I am not afraid of their letting things go wrong to any length in any cause. (1788)

One great error is that we suppose mankind more honest than they are. Our prevailing passions are ambition and interest; and it will be the duty of a wise government to avail itself of those passions, in order to make them subservient to the public good. (1787)

Your people, sir, is a great beast. (According to legend, c. 1792)

I have an indifferent [low] opinion of the honesty of this country, and ill forebodings as to its future system. (1783)

I said that I was affectionately attached to the republican theory. . . . I add that I have strong hopes of the success of that theory; but, in candor, I ought also to add that I am far from being without doubts. I consider its success as yet a problem. (1792)

Whenever the people are well-informed, they can be trusted with their own government; whenever things get so far wrong as to attract their notice, they may be relied on to set them to rights. (1789)

I am not among those who fear the people. They, and not the rich, are our dependence for continued freedom. (1816)

I have great confidence in the common sense of mankind in general. (1800)

My most earnest wish is to see the republican element of popular control pushed to the maximum of its practicable exercise. I shall then believe that our government may be pure and perpetual. (1816)

2. The Clash over States' Rights (1780s–1820s)*

Hamilton, distrusting and fearing the states, strove to build up a powerful central government at their expense. Jefferson, distrusting and fearing a potent central government, strove to safeguard states' rights at its expense. Which of the two men was closer to the truth in the light of subsequent history, particularly in the matter of grassroots supervision of government?

Hamilton

A firm Union will be of the utmost moment to the peace and liberty of the states, as a barrier against domestic faction and insurrection. (1787)

A state government will ever be the rival power of the general government. (1787)

As to the destruction of state governments, the great and real anxiety

Jefferson

I am not a friend to a very energetic government. It is always oppressive. It places the governors indeed more at their ease, at the expense of the people. (1787)

If ever this vast country is brought under a single government, it will be one of the most extensive corruption. (1822)

Our country is too large to have all its affairs directed by a single government.

---

*See the works of Padover and Morris previously cited (p. 134).

is to be able to preserve the national [government] from the too potent and counteracting influence of those governments.... As to the state governments, the prevailing bias of my judgment is that if they can be circumscribed within bounds consistent with the preservation of the national government, they will prove useful and salutary.

If the states were all of the size of Connecticut, Maryland, or New Jersey, I should decidedly regard the local governments as both safe and useful. As the thing now is, however, I acknowledge the most serious apprehensions that the government of the United States will not be able to maintain itself against their influence. I see that influence already penetrating into the national councils and preventing their direction.

Hence, a disposition on my part towards a liberal construction of the powers of the national government, and to erect every fence to guard it from depredations which is, in my opinion, consistent with constitutional propriety. As to any combination to prostrate the state governments, I disavow and deny it. (1792)

Public servants, at such a distance and from under the eye of their constituents, must, from the circumstance of distance, be unable to administer and overlook all the details necessary for the good government of the citizens; and the same circumstance, by rendering detection impossible to their constituents, will invite the public agents to corruption, plunder, and waste. . . .

What an augmentation of the field for jobbing, speculating, plundering, office-building, and office-hunting would be produced by an assumption of all the state powers into the hands of the general government. The true theory of our Constitution [strict construction] is surely the wisest and best—that the states are independent as to everything within themselves, and united as to everything respecting foreign nations. Let the general government be reduced to foreign concerns only, and let our affairs be disentangled from those of all other nations, except as to commerce, which the merchants will manage the better, the more they are left free to manage themselves. And our general government may be reduced to a very simple organization and a very unexpensive one: a few plain duties to be performed by a few servants. (1800)

3. The Spectrum of Disagreement (1780s–1820s)*

At the rear entrance of Jefferson's imposing Virginia home, Monticello, busts of Hamilton and Jefferson stood opposite each other. The guide used to tell tourists that Jefferson placed them there because the two men had opposed each other in life, and they might as well stand opposite each other in death. In the following quotations, what do they agree on, what are their most fundamental disagreements, and how fair are they in assessing each other?

---

*See the works of Padover and Morris previously cited (p. 134).

Hamilton

A national debt, if it is not excessive, will be to us a national blessing. (1781)

If all the public creditors receive their dues from one source . . . their interest will be the same. And having the same interests, they will unite in support of the fiscal arrangements of the government. (*c.* 1791)

Real liberty is neither found in despotism or the extremes of democracy, but in moderate governments. (1787)

Beware, my dear sir, of magnifying a riot into an insurrection, by employing in the first instance an inadequate force. 'Tis better far to err on the other side. Whenever the government appears in arms, it ought to appear like a Hercules, and inspire respect by the display of strength. (1799)

I believe the British government forms the best model the world ever produced, and such has been its progress in the minds of the many that this truth gradually gains ground. (1787)

It must be by this time evident to all men of reflection . . . that it [Articles of Confederation] is a system so radically vicious and unsound as to admit not of amendment but by an entire change in its leading features and characters. (1787)

Let me observe that an Executive is less dangerous to the liberties of the people when in office during life than for seven years. (1787)

Standing armies are dangerous to liberty. (1787)

Jefferson

No man is more ardently intent to see the public debt soon and sacredly paid off than I am. This exactly marks the difference between Colonel Hamilton's views and mine, that I would wish the debt paid tomorrow; he wishes it never to be paid, but always to be a thing wherewith to corrupt and manage the legislature [Congress]. (1792)

Were it left to me to decide whether we should have a government without newspapers, or newspapers without a government, I should not hesitate a moment to prefer the latter. (1787)

A little rebellion now and then is a good thing, and as necessary in the political world as storms in the physical. . . . It is a medicine necessary for the sound health of government. (1787)

It is her [England's] government which is so corrupt, and which has destroyed the nation—it was certainly the most corrupt and unprincipled government on earth. (1810)

But with all the imperfections of our present government [Articles of Confederation], it is without comparison the best existing or that ever did exist. . . . Indeed, I think all the good of this new Constitution might have been couched in three or four new articles, to be added to the good, old, and venerable fabric. . . . (1787)

I disapproved, also, the perpetual re-eligibility of the President. (1789)

A naval force can never endanger our liberties, nor occasion bloodshed; a land force would do both. (1786)

[Jefferson is] an atheist in religion and a fanatic in politics. (1800)

I am a Christian, in the only sense in which he [Jesus] wished anyone to be: sincerely attached to his doctrines, in preference to all others. (1803)

It was not long before I discovered he [Washington] was neither remarkable for delicacy nor good temper. . . .

The General [Washington] is a very honest man. His competitors have slender abilities, and less integrity. His popularity has often been essential to the safety of America. . . . These considerations have influenced my past conduct respecting him and will influence my future. (1781)

His [Washington's] integrity was most pure, his justice the most inflexible I have ever known.... He was, indeed, in every sense of the words, a wise, a good, and a great man. His temper was naturally irritable and high toned; but reflection and resolution had obtained a firm and habitual ascendancy over it. If ever, however, it broke its bonds, he was most tremendous in his wrath. (1814)

That gentleman [Jefferson] whom I once *very much esteemed*, but who does not permit me to retain that sentiment for him, is certainly a man of sublimated and paradoxical imagination, entertaining and propagating opinions inconsistent with dignified and orderly government. (1792)

Hamilton was indeed a singular character. Of acute understanding, disinterested, honest, and honorable in all private transactions, amiable in society, and duly valuing virtue in private life, yet so bewitched and perverted by the British example as to be under thorough conviction that corruption was essential to the government of a nation. (1818)

4. Jefferson Versus Hamilton on the Idea of a National Bank (1791)[*]

There were only three banks in the entire country when Hamilton, in 1790, proposed the Bank of the United States as the keystone of his financial edifice. Modeled on the Bank of England and located in Philadelphia, it would be capitalized at $10 million, one-fifth of which might be held by the federal government. As a private concern under strict government supervision, it would be useful to the Treasury in issuing notes, safeguarding surplus tax money, and facilitating numerous public financial transactions. Before signing such a bank bill, Washington solicited the views of his cabinet members. The opinions of Jefferson, given below, elicited a rebuttal from Hamilton, also given below. Note that Jefferson, the strict constructionist of the Constitution, based his case on the Tenth Amendment in the Bill of Rights, about to be ratified. Hamilton, the loose constructionist of the Constitution, based his views on the implied powers in Article I, Section VIII, paragraph 18, which stipulates that Congress is empowered "to make all laws which shall be necessary and proper for carrying into execution the foregoing powers." Which of the two men seems to be on sounder ground in interpreting "necessary"?

[*]H. C. Lodge, ed., *The Works of Alexander Hamilton* (1904), vol. 3, pp. 458, 452, 455, 485–486; P. L. Ford, ed., *The Writings of Thomas Jefferson* (New York: G. P. Putnam's Sons, 1895), vol. 5, pp. 285, 287.

Jefferson
February 15, 1791

I consider the foundation of the Constitution as laid on this ground—that all powers not delegated to the United States by the Constitution, nor prohibited by it to the states, are reserved to the states, or to the people (12th [10th] amend.). To take a single step beyond the boundaries thus specifically drawn around the powers of Congress is to take possession of a boundless field of power, no longer susceptible of any definition.

The incorporation of a bank, and the powers assumed by this bill, have not, in my opinion, been delegated to the United States by the Constitution.

The second general phrase is "to make all laws *necessary* and proper for carrying into execution the enumerated powers." But they can all be carried into execution without a bank. A bank therefore is not *necessary*, and consequently not authorized by this phrase.

It has been much urged that a bank will give great facility or convenience in the collection of taxes. Suppose this were true; yet the Constitution allows only the means which are "necessary," not those which are merely "convenient," for effecting the enumerated powers. If such a latitude of construction be allowed to this phrase as to give any non-enumerated power, it [the latitude] will go to every one; for there is not one [power] which ingenuity may not torture into a convenience, in some instance or other, to some one of so long a list of enumerated powers. It would swallow up all the delegated powers [of the states], and reduce the whole to one power.

Hamilton
February 23, 1791

If the *end* be clearly comprehended within any of the specified powers, and if the measure have an obvious relation to that *end*, and is not forbidden by any particular provision of the Constitution, it may safely be deemed to come within the compass of the national authority.

There is also this further criterion, which may materially assist the decision: Does the proposed measure abridge a pre-existing right of any state or of any individual? If it does not, there is a strong presumption in favor of its constitutionality. . . .

. . . "Necessary" often means no more than needful, requisite, incidental, useful, or conducive to. . . . [A] restrictive interpretation of the word "necessary" is also contrary to this sound maxim of construction: namely, that the powers contained in a constitution . . . ought to be construed liberally in advancement of the public good.

A hope is entertained that it has, by this time, been made to appear to the satisfaction of the President, that a bank has a natural relation to the power of collecting taxes—to that of regulating trade—to that of providing for the common defense—and that, as the bill under consideration contemplates the government in the light of a joint proprietor of the stock of the bank, it brings the case within the provision of the clause of the Constitution which immediately respects [relates to] the property of the United States. [Evidently Art. IV, Sec. III, para. 2: "The Congress shall have power to . . . make all needful rules and regulations respecting the territory or other property belonging to the United States. . . ."]

B. Overawing the Whiskey Boys

1. Hamilton Upholds Law Enforcement (1794)*

Secretary Hamilton's excise tax on whiskey hit the impoverished Pennsylvania fron-tiersmen especially hard. Their roads were so poor that they could profitably transport their corn and rye to market only in liquid concentrate form. If sued by the govern-ment, they were forced to incur the heavy expense of traveling three hundred miles and undergoing trial before strange judges and jurors. Numerous other grievances caused the Whiskey Boys to form armed mobs that intimidated would-be taxpayers or roughly handled the federal tax collectors. Some agents were tarred, feathered, and beaten; the home of one was burned. An outraged Hamilton, prejudiced against those who "babble republicanism," set forth these views in the press over the pen name "Tully." What are the strengths and weaknesses of his argument?

Let us see then what is this question. It is plainly this: Shall the majority govern or be governed? Shall the nation rule or be ruled? Shall the general will prevail, or the will of a faction? Shall there be government or no government? It is impossible to deny that this is the true and the whole question. No art, no sophistry can involve it in the least obscurity.

The Constitution *you* have ordained for yourselves and your posterity contains this express clause: "The Congress shall have power to lay and collect taxes, duties, imposts, and excises, to pay the debts, and provide for the common defense and general welfare of the United States." You have, then, by a solemn and deliberate act, the most important and sacred that a nation can perform, pronounced and decreed that your representatives in Congress shall have power to lay excises. You have done nothing since to reverse or impair that decree.

Your representatives in Congress, pursuant to the commission derived from you, and with a full knowledge of the public exigencies, have laid an excise. At three succeeding sessions they have revised that act, and have as often, with a degree of unanimity not common, and after the best opportunities of knowing your sense, renewed their sanction to it. You have acquiesced in it; it has gone into general operation; and *you* have actually paid more than a million of dollars on account of it.

But the four western counties of Pennsylvania undertake to rejudge and reverse your decrees. You have said, "The Congress shall have power to lay excises." They say, "The Congress shall not have this power," or—what is equivalent—"they shall not exercise it": for a power that may not be exercised is a nullity. Your representatives have said, and four times repeated it, "An excise on distilled spirits shall be collected." They say, "It shall not be collected. We will punish, expel, and banish the officers who shall attempt the collection. We will do the same by every other person who shall dare to comply with your decree expressed in the constitutional charter, and with that of your representatives expressed in the laws. The sovereignty shall not reside with you, but with us. If you presume to dispute the point by force, we are ready to measure swords with you, and if unequal ourselves to the contest, we will call in the aid of a foreign nation [Britain]. We will league ourselves with a foreign power."

---

*H. C. Lodge, ed., *The Works of Alexander Hamilton* (1904), vol. 6, pp. 414–416 (August 26, 1794).

2. Jefferson Deplores Undue Force (1794)*

Hamilton was accused of deliberately aggravating the Whiskey Rebellion so that he might strengthen the prestige of the new government with an overpowering show of might. At all events, he marched out to the disaffected region with an army of some thirteen thousand militiamen. Resistance evaporated before such a force. Jefferson was appalled that these extravagant measures should have been taken against "occasional riots," and charged that Hamilton was merely pursuing his "favorite purpose of strengthening government and increasing public debt," all under "the sanction of a name [Washington] which has done too much good not to be sufficient to cover harm also." From his luxurious home, Monticello, Jefferson wrote indignantly as follows to James Madison, his friend and neighbor. Six years later these same backcountry rebels, who had incurred Hamilton's upper-class scorn, helped elect Jefferson president. Hamilton's show of sledgehammer force no doubt helped the prestige of the national government, but in the light of Jefferson's letter, how did the government probably hurt itself?

The excise law is an infernal one. The first error was to admit it by the Constitution; the second, to act on that admission; the third and last will be to make it the instrument of dismembering the Union, and setting us all afloat to choose which part of it we will adhere to.

The information of our militia, returned from the westward, is uniform, that though the people there let them pass quietly, they were objects of their laughter, not of their fear; that a thousand men could have cut off their whole force in a thousand places of the Allegheny; that their detestation of the excise law is universal, and has now associated to it a detestation of the government; and that separation, which perhaps was a very distant and problematical event, is now near, and certain, and determined in the mind of every man.

I expected to have seen justification of arming one part of the society against another; of declaring a civil war the moment before the meeting of that body [Congress] which has the sole right of declaring war; of being so patient of the kicks and scoffs of our [British] enemies,† and rising at a feather against our friends; of adding a million to the public debts and deriding us with recommendations to pay it if we can, etc., etc.

C. The Controversial Jay Treaty _____

1. Virginians Oppose John Jay's Appointment (1794)‡

After British cruisers suddenly seized scores of American food ships bound for the French West Indies, a crisis developed. President Washington, desperately seeking to avoid hostilities, decided to send to London a pro-British Federalist, John Jay, in a last-gasp effort to preserve peace. Pro-French Jeffersonians reacted angrily, notably in

---

*P. L. Ford, *The Writings of Thomas Jefferson* (New York: G. P. Putnam's Sons, 1895), vol. 6, pp. 518–519 (December 28, 1794).
†A reference to British seizures of American ships prior to Jay's Treaty.
‡*Independent Chronicle* (Boston), August 11, 1794.

this "Address to the People of the United States" from the Democratic Society in Wythe County, Virginia. Were these Jeffersonians pro-French, pro-British, or merely partisan?

While with anxious expectation we contemplate the affairs of Europe, it will be criminal to forget our own country. A session of Congress having just passed, the first in which the people were equally represented, it is a fit time to take a retrospective view of the proceedings of government. We have watched each motion of those in power, but are sorry we cannot exclaim, "Well done, thou good and faithful servant." We have seen the nation insulted, our rights violated, our commerce ruined—and what has been the conduct of government? Under the corrupt influence of the [Hamiltonian] paper system, it has uniformly crouched to Britain; while on the contrary our allies, the French, to whom we owe our political existence, have been treated unfriendly; denied any advantages from their treaties with us; their minister abused; and those individuals among us who desired to aid their arms, prosecuted as traitors—blush, Americans, for the conduct of your government.

Citizens! Shall we Americans who have kindled the spark of liberty stand aloof and see it extinguished when burning a bright flame in France, which hath caught it from us? Do you not see, if despots prevail, you must have a despot like the rest of the nations? If all tyrants unite against free people, should not all free people unite against tyrants? Yes! Let us unite with France and stand or fall together.

We lament that a man who hath so long possessed the public confidence as the head of the Executive Department [Washington] hath possessed it, should put it to so severe a trial as he hath by a late appointment [of Jay]. The Constitution hath been trampled on, and your rights have no security. . . .

Fellow citizens!

We hope the misconduct of the Executive may have proceeded from bad advice; but we can only look to the immediate cause of the mischief. To us it seems a radical change of measures is necessary. How shall this be effected? Citizens! It is to be effected by a change of men. Deny the continuance of your confidence to such members of the legislative body as have an interest distinct from that of the people.

2. Hamilton Attacks Jay's Attackers (1795)[*]

The Federalist diplomat John Jay, who held few high cards, finally signed a treaty in London in 1794 that was keenly disappointing. Although the British belatedly agreed to evacuate the half-dozen frontier trading posts on American soil and grant certain trade concessions, they gave no satisfaction regarding the impressment of American seamen, the future seizure of ships, and the alleged inciting of the Indians of the Northwest. But to a financially shaky America, a humiliating treaty was still better than a devastating war, and Federalists defended the pact with vigor. After he was bloodily stoned from a New York platform, Alexander Hamilton contributed a series of articles to the press, from which the following excerpt is taken. How did the democratic process operate then, as compared with now?

---

[*]H. C. Lodge, ed., *The Works of Alexander Hamilton* (1904), vol. 5, pp. 195–197.

Before the treaty was known, attempts were made to prepossess the public mind against it. It was absurdly asserted that it was not expected by the people that Mr. Jay was to make any treaty; as if he had been sent, not to accommodate differences by negotiation and agreement, but to dictate to Great Britain the terms of an unconditional submission.

Before it was published at large, a sketch, calculated to produce false impressions, was handed out to the public, through a medium noted for hostility to the administration of the government. Emissaries flew through the country, spreading alarm and discontent; the leaders of [Jeffersonian] clubs were everywhere active to seize the passions of the people, and preoccupy their judgments against the treaty.

At Boston it was published one day, and the next a town-meeting was convened to condemn it; without ever being read, without any serious discussion, sentence was pronounced against it.

Will any man seriously believe that in so short a time an instrument of this nature could have been tolerably understood by the greater part of those who were thus induced to a condemnation of it? Can the result be considered as anything more than a sudden ebullition of popular passion, excited by the artifices of a party which had adroitly seized a favorable moment to furorize the public opinion? This spirit of precipitation, and the intemperance which accompanied it, prevented the body of the merchants and the greater part of the most considerate citizens from attending the meeting, and left those who met, wholly under the guidance of a set of men who, with two or three exceptions, have been the uniform opposers of the government.

The intelligence of this event had no sooner reached New York than the leaders of the clubs were seen haranguing in every corner of the city, to stir up our citizens into an imitation of the example of the meeting at Boston. An invitation to meet at the city hall quickly followed, not to consider or discuss the merits of the treaty, but to unite with the meeting at Boston to address the President against its ratification.

This was immediately succeeded by a hand-bill, full of invectives against the treaty, as absurd as they were inflammatory, and manifestly designed to induce the citizens to surrender their reason to the empire of their passions.

In vain did a respectable meeting of the merchants endeavor, by their advice, to moderate the violence of these views, and to promote a spirit favorable to a fair discussion of the treaty; in vain did a respectable majority of the citizens of every description attend for that purpose. The leaders of the clubs resisted all discussion, and their followers, by their clamors and vociferations, rendered it impracticable, notwithstanding the wish of a manifest majority of the citizens convened upon the occasion.

Can we believe that the leaders were really sincere in the objections they made to a discussion, or that the great and mixed mass of citizens then assembled had so thoroughly mastered the merits of the treaty as that they might not have been enlightened by such a discussion?

It cannot be doubted that the real motive to the opposition was the fear of a discussion; the desire of excluding light; the adherence to a plan of surprise and deception. Nor need we desire any fuller proof of the spirit of party which has stimulated the opposition to the treaty than is to be found in the circumstances of that opposition.

D. Washington Retires

1. A President Bids Farewell (1796)*

Weary of body and outraged by political abuse, Washington announced his decision to retire in his Farewell Address, which he simply gave as a gratuitous "scoop" to a Philadelphia newspaper. At first a nonpartisan but now a Federalist, he had leaned heavily on Hamilton's collaboration in its composition. The bulk of the address deals with domestic difficulties, but the part relating to foreign affairs is best known. The document was clearly partisan. It served as the opening gun in the forthcoming presidential campaign of 1796 by indirectly defending Jay's Treaty and by directly alerting the public to flagrant French intrigue in the nation's capital. Many Jeffersonian Democratic-Republicans, recognizing the attack on them, condemned the document. Why was it to the advantage of America to remain aloof? Did Washington reject all alliances in all circumstances?

Observe good faith and justice toward all nations. Cultivate peace and harmony with all. Religion and morality enjoin this conduct. And can it be that good policy does not equally enjoin it? It will be worthy of a free, enlightened, and, at no distant period, a great nation to give to mankind the magnanimous and too novel example of a people always guided by an exalted justice and benevolence. . . .

In the execution of such a plan nothing is more essential than that permanent, inveterate antipathies against particular nations and passionate attachments for others should be excluded, and that, in place of them, just and amicable feelings toward all should be cultivated. The nation which indulges toward another an habitual hatred or an habitual fondness is in some degree a slave. It is a slave to its animosity or to its affection, either of which is sufficient to lead it astray from its duty and its interest. . . .

The nation prompted by ill will and resentment sometimes impels to war the government, contrary to the best calculations of policy. The government sometimes participates in the national propensity, and adopts through passion what reason would reject. . . .

So, likewise, a passionate attachment of one nation for another produces a variety of evils. Sympathy for the favorite nation, facilitating the illusion of an imaginary common interest in cases where no real common interest exists, and infusing into one the enmities of the other, betrays the former into a participation in the quarrels and wars of the latter without adequate inducement or justification. . . .

As avenues to foreign influence in innumerable ways, such attachments are particularly alarming to the truly enlightened and independent patriot. How many opportunities do they afford to tamper with domestic factions, to practice the arts of seduction, to mislead public opinion, to influence or awe the public councils! Such an attachment of a small or weak toward a great and powerful nation dooms the former to be the satellite of the latter.

---

*J. D. Richardson, ed., *Messages and Papers of the Presidents* (1896), vol. 1, pp. 221–223.

Against the insidious wiles of foreign influence (I conjure you to believe me, fellow citizens) the jealousy of a free people ought to be *constantly* awake, since history and experience prove that foreign influence is one of the most baneful foes of republican government. . . .

The great rule of conduct for us in regard to foreign nations is, in extending our commercial relations, to have with them as little *political* connection as possible. So far as we have already formed engagements [French treaty], let them be fulfilled with perfect good faith. Here let us stop.

Europe has a set of primary interests which to us have none, or a very remote, relation. Hence she must be engaged in frequent controversies, the causes of which are essentially foreign to our concerns. Hence, therefore, it must be unwise in us to implicate ourselves by artificial ties in the ordinary vicissitudes of her politics, or the ordinary combinations and collisions of her friendships or enmities.

Our detached and distant situation invites and enables us to pursue a different course. If we remain one people, under an efficient government, the period is not far off when we may defy material injury from external annoyance; when we may take such an attitude as will cause the neutrality we may at any time resolve upon to be scrupulously respected; when belligerent nations, under the impossibility of making acquisitions upon us, will not lightly hazard the giving us provocation; when we may choose peace or war, as our interest, guided by justice, shall counsel.

Why forgo the advantages of so peculiar a situation? Why quit our own to stand upon foreign ground? Why, by interweaving our destiny with that of any part of Europe, entangle our peace and prosperity in the toils of European ambition, rivalship, interest, humor, or caprice?

It is our true policy to steer clear of permanent alliances with any portion of the foreign world, so far, I mean, as we are now at liberty to do it. For let me not be understood as capable of patronizing infidelity to existing engagements. I hold the maxim no less applicable to public than to private affairs that honesty is always the best policy. I repeat, therefore, let those engagements be observed in their genuine sense. But in my opinion it is unnecessary and would be unwise to extend them.

Taking care always to keep ourselves by suitable establishments on a respectable defensive posture, we may safely trust to temporary alliances for extraordinary emergencies.

Harmony, liberal intercourse with all nations, are recommended by policy, humanity, and interest. But even our commercial policy should hold an equal and impartial hand, neither seeking nor granting exclusive favors or preference; . . . constantly keeping in view that it is folly in one nation to look for disinterested favors from another; that it must pay with a portion of its independence for whatever it may accept under that character; that by such acceptance it may place itself in the condition of having given equivalents for nominal favors, and yet of being reproached with ingratitude for not giving more. There can be no greater error than to expect or calculate upon real favors from nation to nation. It is an illusion which experience must cure, which a just pride ought to discard.

2. Editor Benjamin Franklin Bache Berates Washington (1797)*

Benjamin Franklin Bache, grandson of "Old Ben," was a newspaper editor notorious for his malicious attacks on the Federalists in general and on Washington in particular.† He published the following tirade when the president retired, but fortunately his sentiments were not shared by the vast majority of Washington's appreciative countrymen. In retaliation, Federalist rowdies wrecked the office of the Philadelphia Aurora and manhandled editor Bache. How much of this incendiary editorial is anti-Federalist partisanship, and how much is pure libel?

"Lord, now lettest thou thy servant depart in peace, for mine eyes have seen thy salvation," was the pious ejaculation of a man who beheld a flood of happiness rushing upon mankind [Simeon, who had just seen Jesus]. If ever there was a time that would license the reiteration of the exclamation, that time is now arrived. For the man who is the source of all the misfortunes of our country is this day reduced to a level with his fellow citizens, and is no longer possessed of power to multiply evils upon the United States.

If ever there was a period for rejoicing, this is the moment. Every heart in unison with the freedom and happiness of the people ought to beat high with exultation that the name of Washington, from this day, ceases to give a currency to political iniquity and to legalize corruption. A new era is opening upon us—a new era which promises much to the people. For public measures must now stand upon their own merits, and nefarious projects can no longer be supported by a name.

When a retrospect is taken of the Washington administration for eight years, it is a subject of the greatest astonishment that a single individual should have canceled the principles of republicanism in an enlightened people, and should have carried his designs against the public liberty so far as to have put in jeopardy its very existence. Such, however, are the facts, and with these staring us in the face, this day ought to be a jubilee in the United States.

E. The Alien and Sedition Hysteria _____

1. Timothy Pickering Upholds the Repressive Laws (1798)‡

Angered by Jay's pro-British treaty, the French seized scores of American ships, thereby paving the way for the undeclared naval war of 1798–1800, during the presidency of John Adams. The pro-British Federalists, riding the wave of anti-French hysteria, undertook to curb and gag the pro-French Jeffersonians by passing the Alien and Sedition Acts of 1798. The Alien Act empowered the president to deport undesirable aliens (largely Irish and French refugees); the Sedition Act

---

Philadelphia Aurora, March 6, 1797, in Allan Nevins, ed., *American Press Opinion* (Boston and New York: D. C. Heath and Company, 1928), pp. 21–22.
†Benjamin Franklin Bache was nicknamed "Lightning Rod, Junior," an obvious reference to his inventive grandfather and to his own high-voltage journalism.
‡C. W. Upham, *Life of Timothy Pickering* (1873), vol. 3, pp. 475–476.

prescribed fines and imprisonment for false maligning of federal officials. Timothy Pickering, secretary of state under President Adams, offered the following spirited defense of the Alien and Sedition Acts. What were his views regarding (a) inferior rights of aliens and (b) the similarity between abusing free speech and committing murder?

The Alien Law has been bitterly inveighed against as a direct attack upon our liberties, when in fact it affects only foreigners who are conspiring against us, and has no relation whatever to an American citizen. It gives authority to the First Magistrate [President] of the Union to order all such aliens as he shall judge dangerous to the peace and safety of the United States, or shall have reasonable grounds to suspect are concerned in any treasonable or secret machinations against the government thereof, to depart out of our territory.

It is only necessary to ask whether, without such a power vested in some department, any government ever did, or ever can, long protect itself. The objects of this act are strangers merely, persons not adopted and naturalized—a description of men who have no lot nor interest with us, and who even manifest a disposition the most hostile to this country, while it affords them an asylum and protection. It is absurd to say that, in providing by law for their removal, the Constitution is violated. For he must be ignorant indeed who does not know that the Constitution was established for the protection and security of American citizens, and not of intriguing foreigners.

The Sedition Act has likewise been shamefully misrepresented as an attack upon the freedom of speech and of the press. But we find, on the contrary, that it prescribes a punishment only for those pests of society and disturbers of order and tranquillity "who write, print, utter, or publish any false, scandalous, and malicious writings against the government of the United States, or either house of the Congress of the United States, or the President, with intent to defame, or bring them into contempt or disrepute, or to excite against them the hatred of the good people of the United States; or to stir up sedition, or to abet the hostile designs of any foreign nation."

What honest man can justly be alarmed at such a law, or can wish unlimited permission to be given for the publication of malicious falsehoods, and with intentions the most base? They who complain of legal provisions for punishing intentional defamation and lies as bridling the liberty of speech and of the press, may, with equal propriety, complain against laws made for punishing assault and murder, as restraints upon the freedom of men's actions. Because we have the right to speak and publish our opinions, it does not necessarily follow that we may exercise it in uttering false and malicious slanders against our neighbor or our government, any more than we may under cover of freedom of action knock down the first man we meet, and exempt ourselves from punishment by pleading that we are free agents. We may indeed use our tongues, employ our pens, and carry our cudgels or our muskets whenever we please. But, at the same time, we must be accountable and punishable for making such "improper use of either as to injure others in their characters, their persons, or their property."

2. The Virginia Legislature Protests (1798)*

The Federalist Sedition Act was plainly a violation of the free speech and free press guarantees of the Constitution (First Amendment, Bill of Rights). But the Federalist Supreme Court was not yet declaring acts of Congress unconstitutional. When Jeffersonians branded the Sedition Act the "gag law," one Federalist editor replied: "Nothing can so completely gag a Jeffersonian Democrat as to restrain him from lying. If you forbid his lying, you forbid his speaking." A score or so of Jeffersonian editors were arrested, including the unbridled Benjamin Franklin Bache (see p. 147), who died before his trial. Vice President Jefferson and James Madison (who was then in private life) both feared that the Sedition Act would terrorize the Jeffersonian Democratic-Republican party into silence and destroy it. Madison, working secretly with Jefferson, drafted the following resolutions, which were approved by the Virginia legislature. Note especially the views on the "compact theory," the First Amendment, and the proposed method of voiding the Alien and Sedition Acts. Do they seem unreasonable?

[Resolved,] That this Assembly most solemnly declares a warm attachment to the union of the states, to maintain which it pledges its powers; and that, for this end, it is their duty to watch over and oppose every infraction of those principles which constitute the only basis of that union, because a faithful observance of them can alone secure its existence and the public happiness.

That this Assembly does explicitly and peremptorily declare that it views the powers of the federal government as resulting from the compact to which the states are parties, as limited by the plain sense and intention of the instrument [Constitution] constituting that compact, as no further valid than they are authorized by the grants enumerated in that compact; and that, in case of a deliberate, palpable, and dangerous exercise of other powers not granted by the said compact, the states who are parties thereto have the right, and are in duty bound, to interpose for arresting the progress of the evil, and for maintaining, within their respective limits, the authorities, rights, and liberties appertaining to them. . . .

That the General Assembly does also express its deep regret that a spirit has, in sundry instances, been manifested by the federal government to enlarge its powers by forced constructions of the constitutional charter which defines them, . . . so as to consolidate the states, by degrees, into one sovereignty, the obvious tendency and inevitable result of which would be to transform the present republican system of the United States into an absolute, or, at best, a mixed monarchy.

That the General Assembly does particularly protest against the palpable and alarming infractions of the Constitution in the two late cases of the "Alien and Sedition Acts," passed at the last session of Congress; the first of which exercises a power nowhere delegated to the federal government, and which, by uniting legislative and judicial powers to those of executive, subverts the general principles of free

---

*Jonathan Elliot, *The Debates . . . on the Adoption of the Federal Constitution* (Philadelphia: J. B. Lippincott, 1836), vol. 4, pp. 528–529.

government, as well as the particular organization and positive provisions of the federal Constitution; and the other of which acts exercises, in like manner, a power not delegated by the Constitution, but, on the contrary, expressly and positively forbidden by one of the amendments thereto—a power which, more than any other, ought to produce universal alarm, because it is leveled against the right of freely examining public characters and measures, and of free communication among the people thereon, which has ever been justly deemed the only effectual guardian of every other right.

That this state having, by its convention [of 1788] which ratified the federal Constitution, expressly declared that, among other essential rights, "the liberty of conscience and the press cannot be canceled, abridged, restrained, or modified by any authority of the United States," and, from its extreme anxiety to guard these rights from every possible attack of sophistry and ambition, having, with other states, recommended an amendment for that purpose, which amendment [the First] was, in due time, annexed to the Constitution, it would mark a reproachful inconsistency and criminal degeneracy if an indifference were now shown to the most palpable violation of one of the rights thus declared and secured, and to the establishment of a precedent which may be fatal to the other.

That the good people of the commonwealth having ever felt, and continuing to feel, the most sincere affection for their brethren of the other states, the truest anxiety for establishing and perpetuating the union of all, and the most scrupulous fidelity to that Constitution, which is the pledge of mutual friendship, and the instrument of mutual happiness, the General Assembly does solemnly appeal to the like dispositions in the other states, in confidence that they will concur with this commonwealth in declaring, as it does hereby declare, that the acts aforesaid are unconstitutional, and that the necessary and proper measures will be taken by each for cooperating with this state in maintaining unimpaired the authorities, rights, and liberties reserved to the states respectively, or to the people.

Thought Provokers

1. Which principles of Jefferson, the founder of the Democratic-Republican party, are upheld by Democrats today, and which are not? Which principles of Hamilton, the godfather of the present Republican party, are upheld by Republicans today, and which are not? Explain.
2. In 1783 Hamilton wrote, "The rights of government are as essential to be defended as the rights of individuals. The security of the one is inseparable from that of the other." Given Hamilton's handling of the Whiskey Rebellion of 1794, comment on this statement.
3. Has the federal government become more or less Hamiltonian during the past two centuries?
4. Massachusetts senator Henry Cabot Lodge once remarked that politics should stop at the water's edge. Comment with reference to foreign affairs in the 1790s.

5. Was Washington's Farewell Address necessary? What have been its most misunderstood parts, and why? Was it designed as a prescription for all future years? Which parts are still valid, and which are not?

6. Can the Alien and Sedition Acts be justified, especially in view of the excesses of editors such as Bache? If free speech ought to be curbed, who should do the curbing? Why is free speech necessary for the workings of a free government? It has been said that many a minority has become a majority because its foes were unwise enough to persecute it. Comment with reference to the Jeffersonian Democratic-Republicans of 1798.

The Triumphs and Travails of the Jeffersonian Republic, 1800–1812

We have a perfect horror at everything like
connecting ourselves with the politics of Europe.

Thomas Jefferson, 1801

Prologue: Following Jefferson's controversial election to the presidency in 1800, Jeffersonians and Federalists alike contributed to the process of nation building. Jefferson's Federalist cousin, Supreme Court Justice John Marshall, handed down a series of Court decisions that significantly strengthened the powers of the federal government at the expense of the individual states. Jefferson himself swallowed some of his constitutional scruples to accomplish the boldest achievement of his presidency—the Louisiana Purchase—which at a stroke doubled the size of the United States and guaranteed American control of the Mississippi River and its crucial ocean port at New Orleans. Jefferson proved less successful in his increasingly desperate efforts to keep the United States out of the war then raging in Europe. Though sorely provoked by British impressment of American sailors, Jefferson consistently tried to avoid fighting. He resorted finally to a self-denying trade embargo as the price he was willing to pay for peace.

A. John Marshall Asserts the Supremacy of the Constitution

Marshall Asserts the Supremacy of the Constitution (1803)*

No principle is more important to the system of constitutional democracy than the notion that the Constitution represents a higher level of law than that routinely enacted by legislatures. And no American jurist has been more instrumental in asserting that principle than the great Federalist justice John Marshall. Marshall also helped mightily to resolve the question—unclear in the early days of the republic—of where final authority to interpret the Constitution lay. In the following excerpt from his famous decision in the case of Marbury v. Madison, how does he trace the linkages between the Constitution and the concept of limited government?

---

*William Cranch, *Reports of Cases Argued and Adjudged in the Supreme Court of the United States, 1801–1815* (Newark, N.Y.: The Lawyers' Co-operative Publishing Company, 1804), vol. 1, p. 137.

The question, whether an act, repugnant to the constitution, can become the law of the land, is a question deeply interesting to the United States; but, happily, not of an intricacy proportioned to its interest. It seems only necessary to recognize certain principles, supposed to have been long and well established, to decide it.

That the people have an original right to establish, for their future government, such principles, as, in their opinion, shall most conduce to their own happiness is the basis on which the whole American fabric has been erected. The exercise of this original right is a very great exertion; nor can it, nor ought it, to be frequently repeated. The principles, therefore, so established, are deemed fundamental. And as the authority from which they proceed is supreme, and can seldom act, they are designed to be permanent.

This original and supreme will organizes the government, and assigns to different departments their respective powers. It may either stop here, or establish certain limits not to be transcended by those departments.

The government of the United States is of the latter description. The powers of the legislature are defined and limited; and that those limits may not be mistaken, or forgotten, the constitution is written. To what purpose are powers limited, and to what purpose is that limitation committed to writing, if these limits may, at any time, be passed by those intended to be restrained? The distinction between a government with limited and unlimited powers is abolished, if those limits do not confine the persons on whom they are imposed, and if acts prohibited and acts allowed, are of equal obligation. It is a proposition too plain to be contested, that the constitution controls any legislative act repugnant to it; or, that the legislature may alter the constitution by an ordinary act.

Between these alternatives there is no middle ground. The constitution is either a superior paramount law, unchangeable by ordinary means, or it is on a level with ordinary legislative acts, and, like other acts, is alterable when the legislature shall please to alter it.

If the former part of the alternative be true, then a legislative act contrary to the constitution is not law: if the latter part be true, then written constitutions are absurd attempts, on the part of the people, to limit a power in its own nature illimitable.

Certainly all those who have framed written constitutions contemplate them as forming the fundamental and paramount law of the nation, and, consequently, the theory of every such government must be, that an act of the legislature, repugnant to the constitution, is void.

This theory is essentially attached to a written constitution, and, is consequently, to be considered, by this court, as one of the fundamental principles of our society. It is not therefore to be lost sight of in the further consideration of this subject. . . .

So if a law be in opposition to the constitution; if both the law and the constitution apply to a particular case, so that the court must either decide that case conformably to the law, disregarding the constitution; or conformably to the constitution, disregarding the law; the court must determine which of these conflicting rules governs the case. This is of the very essence of judicial duty.

If, then, the courts are to regard the constitution, and the constitution is superior to any ordinary act of the legislature, the constitution, and not such ordinary act, must govern the case to which they both apply.

Those, then, who controvert the principle that the constitution is to be considered, in court, as a paramount law, are reduced to the necessity of maintaining that courts must close their eyes on the constitution, and see only the law.

This doctrine would subvert the very foundation of all written constitutions. It would declare that an act which, according to the principles and theory of our government, is entirely void, is yet, in practice, completely obligatory. It would declare that if the legislature shall do what is expressly forbidden, such act, notwithstanding the express prohibition, is in reality effectual. It would be giving to the legislature a practical and real omnipotence, with the same breath which professes to restrict their powers within narrow limits. It is prescribing limits, and declaring that those limits may be passed at pleasure.

That it thus reduces to nothing what we have deemed the greatest improvements on political institutions, a written constitution, would of itself be sufficient, in America, where written constitutions have been viewed with so much reverence, for rejecting the construction. . . .

Thus, the particular phraseology of the constitution of the United States confirms and strengthens the principle, supposed to be essential to all written constitutions, that a law repugnant to the constitution is void; and that courts, as well as other departments, are bound by that instrument.

B. The Louisiana Purchase

1. Napoleon Decides to Dispose of Louisiana (1803)*

Much of early American history was shaped by the endless rivalry between Britain and France, and the Louisiana Purchase was no exception. Having failed in his bid to establish a French empire in the Western Hemisphere, Napoleon Bonaparte resolved to use France's American holdings as a means to fund his ongoing battle with the British. In these statements, recorded by one of Napoleon's closest advisers, the strong-willed emperor detailed his reasons for selling Louisiana—a region France had only recently reacquired from Spain. How did Napoleon feel about the probability that the acquisition of such a vast tract of territory would greatly strengthen the young United States?

I know the full value of Louisiana, and I have been desirous of repairing the fault of the French negotiator who abandoned it in 1763. A few lines of a treaty have restored it to me, and I have scarcely recovered it when I must expect to lose it. But if it escapes from me, it shall one day cost dearer to those who oblige me to strip myself of it than to those to whom I wish to deliver it. The English have successively taken from France, Canada, Cape Breton, Newfoundland, Nova Scotia, and the richest portions of Asia. They are engaged in exciting troubles in St. Domingo [Haiti]. They shall not have the Mississippi which they covet. Louisiana is nothing in comparison with their conquests in all parts of the globe, and yet the jealousy they feel at the

---

The History of Louisiana, Particularly of the Cession of That Colony to the United States of America, by Barbe Marbois. Translated from the French by an American Citizen (1830).

restoration of this colony to the sovereignty of France, acquaints me with their wish to take possession of it, and it is thus that they will begin the war. They have twenty ships of war in the gulf of Mexico, they sail over those seas as sovereigns, whilst our affairs in St. Domingo have been growing worse every day since the death of Leclerc. [Charles Leclerc, Napoleon's brother-in-law, violently suppressed a Haitian rebellion led by Toussaint L'Ouverture, then died of yellow fever in 1802.] The conquest of Louisiana would be easy, if they only took the trouble to make a descent there. I have not a moment to lose in putting it out of their reach. I know not whether they are not already there. It is their usual course, and if I had been in their place, I would not have waited. I wish, if there is still time, to take from them any idea that they may have of ever possessing that colony. I think of ceding it to the United States. I can scarcely say that I cede it to them, for it is not yet in our possession. If, however, I leave the least time to our enemies, I shall only transmit an empty title to those republicans whose friendship I seek. They only ask of me one town in Louisiana, but I already consider the colony as entirely lost, and it appears to me that in the hands of this growing power, it will be more useful to the policy and even to the commerce of France, than if I should attempt to keep it. . . .

Perhaps it will also be objected to me, that the Americans may be found too powerful for Europe in two or three centuries: but my foresight does not embrace such remote fears. Besides, we may hereafter expect rivalries among the members of the Union. The confederations, that are called perpetual, only last till one of the contracting parties finds it to its interest to break them, and it is to prevent the danger, to which the colossal power of England exposes us, that I would provide a remedy. . . .

This accession of territory . . . strengthens for ever the power of the United States; and I have just given to England a maritime rival, that will sooner or later humble her pride.

2. Thomas Jefferson Alerts Robert Livingston (1802)[*]

Rumors of the secret treaty of 1800, under which Spain agreed to cede Louisiana to France, filled President Jefferson with apprehension. The extent of his concern is betrayed in this remarkable letter, addressed to the American minister in Paris, Robert R. Livingston. A distinguished lawyer and diplomat, Livingston was also famous as the financial backer of Robert Fulton's successful steamboat in 1807. Why did Jefferson feel that French occupancy of Louisiana would force the United States to reverse its "political relations"?

The cession of Louisiana . . . by Spain to France works most sorely on the United States. On the subject the Secretary of State has written to you fully. Yet I cannot forbear recurring to it personally, so deep is the impression it makes in my mind. It completely reverses all the political relations of the United States and will form a new epoch in our political course.

---

[*]P. L. Ford, *The Writings of Thomas Jefferson* (New York: G. P. Putnam's Sons, 1897), vol. 8, pp. 144–146 (April 18, 1802).

Of all nations of any consideration, France is the one which hitherto has offered the fewest points on which we could have any conflict of right, and the most points of a communion of interests. From these causes we have ever looked at her as our natural friend, as one with which we never could have an occasion of difference.* Her growth therefore we viewed as our own, her misfortunes ours.

There is on the globe one single spot, the possessor of which is our natural and habitual enemy. It is New Orleans, through which the produce of three-eighths of our territory must pass to market, and from its fertility it will ere long yield more than half of our whole produce and contain more than half our inhabitants. France, placing herself in that door, assumes to us the attitude of defiance.

Spain might have retained it quietly for years. Her pacific dispositions, her feeble state, would induce her to increase our facilities there, so that her possession of the place would be hardly felt by us. And it would not perhaps be very long before some circumstances might arise which might make the cession of it to us the price of something of more worth to her.

Not so can it ever be in the hands of France. The impetuosity of her temper, the energy and restlessness of her character . . . render it impossible that France and the United States can continue long friends when they meet in so irritable a position. They, as well as we, must be blind if they do not see this; and we must be very improvident if we do not begin to make arrangements on that hypothesis.

The day that France takes possession of New Orleans fixes the sentence which is to restrain her forever within her low-water mark. It seals the union of two nations who in conjunction can maintain exclusive possession of the ocean. From that moment we must marry ourselves to the British fleet and nation. We must turn all our attentions to a maritime force, for which our resources place us on very high grounds; and having formed and cemented together a power which may render reinforcement of her settlements here impossible to France, make the first cannon which shall be fired in Europe the signal for tearing up any settlement she may have made, and for holding the two continents of America in sequestration for the common purposes of the united British and American nations.

This is not a state of things we seek or desire. It is one which this measure, if adopted by France, forces on us, as necessarily as any other cause, by the laws of nature, brings on its necessary effect. It is not from a fear of France that we deprecate this measure proposed by her. For however greater her force is than ours compared in the abstract, it is nothing in comparison of ours when to be exerted on our soil. But it is from a sincere love of peace, and a firm persuasion that, bound to France by the interests and the strong sympathies still existing in the minds of our citizens, and holding relative positions which ensure their continuance, we are secure of a long course of peace. Whereas the change of friends, which will be rendered necessary if France changes that position, embarks us necessarily as a belligerent power in the first war of Europe. In that case, France will have held possession of New Orleans during the interval of a peace, long or short, at the end of which it will be wrested from her. . . .

---

*Jefferson conveniently overlooked the undeclared naval war of 1798–1800.

She may say she needs Louisiana for the supply of her West Indies. She does not need it in time of peace. And in war she could not depend on them because they would be so easily intercepted [by the British navy]. . . .

If France considers Louisiana, however, as indispensable for her views, she might perhaps be willing to look about for arrangements which might reconcile it to our interests. If anything could do this, it would be the ceding to us the Island of New Orleans and the Floridas. This would certainly in a great degree remove the causes of jarring and irritation between us, and perhaps for such a length of time as might produce other means of making the measure permanently conciliatory to our interests and friendships.

3. Jefferson Stretches the Constitution to Buy Louisiana (1803)*

In early 1803, Jefferson dispatched James Monroe to Paris to consummate the purchase of Louisiana for the United States. Monroe was instructed to pay up to $10 million for New Orleans and as much land to the east as he could obtain. To the surprise of Americans, Napoleon offered to sell all of Louisiana, including the vast territory to the west and north of New Orleans. The Americans readily agreed, though Jefferson worried that he was exceeding his constitutional mandate. When he had earlier opposed Hamilton's bank (see p. 139), Jefferson had argued that powers not conferred on the central government were reserved to the states. The Constitution did not specifically empower the president— or the Congress, for that matter—to annex foreign territory, especially territory as large as the nation itself. But the bargain acquisition of Louisiana seemed too breathtaking an opportunity to pass up. In the following letter to Senate leader John Breckinridge, Jefferson defends his action. Is his "guardian" analogy sound?

This treaty must, of course, be laid before both Houses, because both have important functions to exercise respecting it. They, I presume, will see their duty to their country in ratifying and paying for it, so as to secure a good which would otherwise probably be never again in their power. But I suppose they must then appeal to the nation for an additional article [amendment] to the Constitution, approving and confirming an act which the nation had not previously authorized.

The Constitution has made no provision for our holding foreign territory, still less for incorporating foreign nations into our Union. The Executive, in seizing the fugitive occurrence which so much advances the good of their country, have done an act beyond the Constitution. The Legislature, in casting behind them metaphysical subtleties, and risking themselves like faithful servants, must ratify and pay for it, and throw themselves on their country for doing for them, unauthorized, what we know they would have done for themselves had they been in a situation to do it.

It is the case of a guardian, investing the money of his ward in purchasing an important adjacent territory; and saying to him when of age, "I did this for your good. I pretend to no right to bind you: you may disavow me, and I must get out of the scrape as I can. I thought it my duty to risk myself for you."

But we shall not be disavowed by the nation, and their act of indemnity will confirm and not weaken the Constitution, by more strongly marking out its lines.

---

*A. A. Lipscomb, ed., *Writings of Thomas Jefferson* (Washington, DC: Thomas Jefferson Memorial Association, 1904), vol. 10, pp. 410–411 (August 12, 1803).

4. Lewis and Clark Meet a Grizzly (1805)*

Diplomacy done, the vast and uncharted wilderness that was the Louisiana territory remained to be explored. President Jefferson commissioned Meriwether Lewis and William Clark for the job, which took two years. The Lewis and Clark party of thirty-four soldiers and ten civilians moved up the Missouri River from St. Louis in the autumn of 1804, wintered with the Mandan Indians in present-day North Dakota, and struck out for the Pacific Ocean again in the spring of 1805. They sighted the Pacific in November 1805 and eventually returned to St. Louis nearly a year later. Along the way they collected botanical and geological specimens and made preliminary maps of the country. They also had numerous adventures, such as this one, recounted in Lewis's diary, which took place in present-day eastern Montana. What does it suggest about the task of taming the nearly trackless territory Jefferson had acquired?

Tuesday May 14th 1805.

Some fog on the river this morning, which is a very rare occurrence; the country much as it was yesterday with this difference that the bottoms are somewhat wider; passed some high black bluffs. Saw immence herds of buffaloe today also Elk deer wolves and Antelopes. Passed three large creeks one on the Starboard and two others on the Larboard side, neither of which had any runing water. Capt Clark walked on shore and killed a very fine buffaloe cow. I felt an inclination to eat some veal and walked on shore and killed a very fine buffaloe calf and a large woolf, much the whitest I had seen, it was quite as white as the wool of the common sheep. One of the party wounded a brown bear very badly, but being alone did not think proper to pursue him. In the evening the men in two of the rear canoes discovered a large brown bear lying in the open grounds about 300 paces from the river, and six of them went out to attack him, all good hunters; they took the advantage of a small eminence which concealed them and got within 40 paces of him unperceived. Two of them reserved their fires as had been previously conscerted, the four others fired nearly at the same time and put each his bullet through him. Two of the balls passed through the bulk of both lobes of his lungs. In an instant this monster ran at them with open mouth. The two who had reserved their fir[e]s discharged their pieces at him as he came towards them. Boath of them struck him, one only slightly and the other fortunately broke his shoulder, this however only retarded his motion for a moment only. The men unable to reload their guns took to flight, the bear pursued and had very nearly overtaken them before they reached the river; two of the party betook themselves to a canoe and the others seperated an[d] concealed themselves among the willows, reloaded their pieces, each discharged his piece at him as they had an opportunity. They struck him several times again but the guns served only to direct the bear to them. In this manner he pursued two of them seperately so close that they were obliged to throw aside their guns and pouches and throw themselves into the river altho' the bank was nearly twenty feet perpendicular; so enraged was this anamal that he plunged into the river only a few feet behind the

---

*Reuben Gold Thwaites, ed., *Original Journals of the Lewis and Clark Expedition, 1804–1806* (Washington, DC: Government Printing Office, 1904), vol. 2, pp. 33–34.

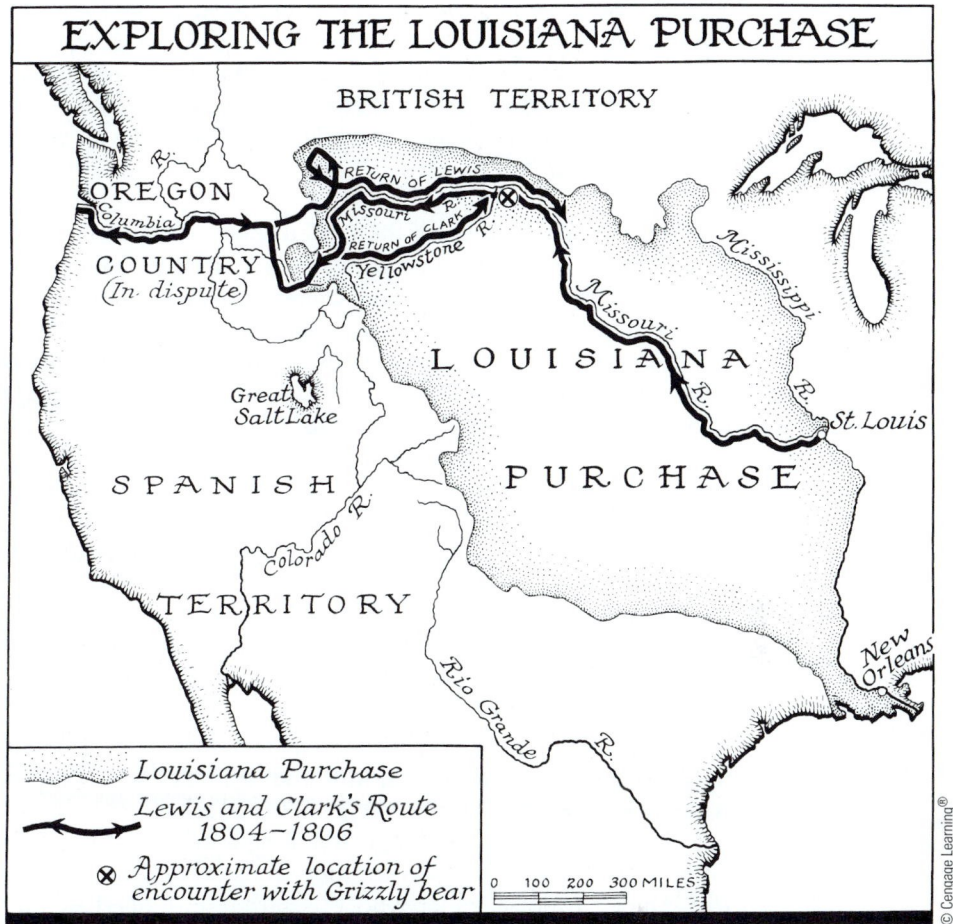

EXPLORING THE LOUISIANA PURCHASE

Louisiana Purchase
Lewis and Clark's Route 1804–1806
⊗ *Approximate location of encounter with Grizzly bear*

0   100   200   300 MILES

© Cengage Learning®

second man he had compelled [to] take refuge in the water, when one of those who still remained on shore shot him through the head and finally killed him; they then took him on shore and butch[er]ed him when they found eight balls had passed through him in different directions; the bear being old the flesh was indifferent, they therefore only took the skin and fleece, the latter made us several gallons of oil; . . .

5. A Spanish Official Warns of American Expansion (1804)*

In a secret message to Congress, Jefferson proposed the Lewis and Clark expedition as a commercial venture to establish ties with Indian tribes and extend America's influence over the region. To foreign governments, he presented the voyage as "a literary pursuit"—an endeavor they "would not be disposed to view . . . with jealousy."

---

*Donald Jackson, ed., *Letters of the Lewis and Clark Expedition, with Related Documents, 1783–1854*, vol. 1, 2nd ed. (Urbana: University of Illinois Press, 1978), pp. 184–186.

The Spanish, then involved in a bitter dispute with the United States over the precise boundaries of the Louisiana territory, were rightly skeptical of Jefferson's stated aims. In a letter to Spain's foreign minister, the Spanish governor of Louisiana, Marqués de Casa Calvo, expressed his fears about the consequences of American expansion. What do his concerns suggest about European attitudes toward North America as the nineteenth century opened?

This step on the part of the United States at the same time that it took possession of the province of Louisiana; its haste to instruct itself and to explore the course of the Missouri whose origin they claim belongs to them, extending their designs as far as the South Sea, forces us necessarily to become active and to hasten our steps in order to cut off the gigantic steps of our neighbors if we wish, as it is our duty, to preserve undamaged [intact] the dominions of the King and to prevent ruin and destruction of the *Provincias Internas* and of the Kingdom of New Spain.

The only means which presents itself is to arrest Captain Merry Weather and his party, which cannot help but pass through the nations neighboring New Mexico, its presidios or *rancherías*.

A decisive and vigorous blow will prevent immense expenditures and even countless disagreeable replies which must originate between the respective governments, and immediately we are impelled to act out of the necessity of the moment. The public claims which they manifest concerning the extensions of the province of Louisiana which the French Republic has sold to them dictate it. No less do they claim as their western limits than the mouth of the Rio Bravo up to 30 degrees north latitude, and from there the line of demarcation penetrates [undetermined] far to the north west as well as to the north, until it loses itself in the immense forests and wilderness, even though they are not [as yet] inhabited by Europeans.

What other end can the repeated designs and incursions of the Americans have, designs seen even earlier in the unfortunate one, for them, of Philip Nolan. [An Irish-American horse trader who was seized and killed by the Spanish authorities after illegally entering Texas in 1801. He is not to be confused with the fictional Philip Nolan of Edward Everett Hale's acclaimed short story of 1863, "The Man without a Country," though Hale's tale was very loosely based on legends about Nolan's exploits.]

We must not lose time, and the slightest omission can be of great consequence for the orders and confidential instruction with which I find myself. The greatest responsibility would fall upon us if we should not take, without losing a moment, steps to put a stop to these dispositions and give time for measures to be taken so that the limits of Louisiana may be arranged without compromising the interest of Spain or endangering its vast and rich possessions.

In view of what has been said above I do not doubt that Your Excellency will give orders that the most efficacious steps be taken to arrest the referred to Captain Merry and his followers, who, according to notices, number twenty-five men, and to seize their papers and instruments that may be found on them. This action may be based upon the fact that without permission of the Spanish government they have entered its territory. Since the line of demarcation has not been determined as yet, they cannot infer that it already belongs to the United States.

C. The Resort to Economic Coercion

1. A Federalist (Philip Barton Key) Attacks the Embargo (1808)*

With the nation militarily weak, Jefferson decided to force respect for the nation's rights by an economic boycott. In 1807 Congress passed his embargo, which prohibited shipments from leaving American shores for foreign ports, including the West Indies. Paralysis gradually gripped American shipping and agriculture, except for illicit trade. Representative Philip Barton Key, uncle of Francis Scott Key and a former Maryland Loyalist who had fought under George III, here assails the embargo. Why, in his view, did it play into Britain's hands? Why did he regard his proposed alternative as more effective?

But, Mr. Chairman, let us review this [embargo] law and its effects. In a commercial point of view, it has annihilated our trade. In an agricultural point of view, it has paralyzed industry.... Our most fertile lands are reduced to sterility, so far as it respects our surplus product. As a measure of political economics, it will drive (if continued) our seamen into foreign employ, and our fishermen to foreign sandbanks. In a financial point of view, it has dried up our revenue, and if continued will close the sales of Western lands, and the payment of installments of past sales. For unless produce can be sold, payments cannot be made. As a war measure, the embargo has not been advocated.

It remains then to consider its effects as a peace measure—a measure inducing peace. I grant, sir, that if the friends of the embargo had rightly calculated its effects—if it had brought the belligerents of Europe to a sense of justice and respect for our rights, through the weakness and dependence of their West India possessions—it would have been infinitely wise and desirable.... But, sir, the experience of near four months has not produced that effect....

If that be the case, if such should be the result, then will the embargo, of all measures, be the most acceptable to Britain. By occluding [closing] our ports, you give to her ships the exclusive use of the ocean; and you give to her despairing West India planter the monopoly of sugar and rum and coffee to the European world....

But, sir, who are we? What are we? A peaceable agricultural people, of simple and, I trust, virtuous habits, of stout hearts and willing minds, and a brave, powerful, and badly disciplined militia, unarmed, and without troops. And whom are we to come in conflict with? The master of continental Europe [Napoleon] in the full career of universal domination, and the mistress of the ocean [Britain] contending for self-preservation; nations who feel power and forget right.

What man can be weak enough to suppose that a sense of justice can repress or regulate the conduct of Bonaparte? We need not resort to other nations for examples. Has he not in a manner as flagrant as flagitious, directly, openly, publicly violated and broken a solemn treaty [of 1800] entered into with us? Did he not stipulate that our property should pass free even to enemy ports, and has he not burnt our ships at sea under the most causeless pretexts?

---

*Annals of Congress, 10th Congress, 1st Sess. (1808), pp. 2122–2123.

Look to England; see her conduct to us. Do we want any further evidence of what she will do in the hour of impending peril than the attack on Copenhagen?* That she prostrates all rights that come in collision with her self-preservation?

No, sir; let us pursue the steady line of rigid impartiality. Let us hold the scales of impartial neutrality with a high and steady hand, and export our products to, and bring back supplies from, all who will trade with us. Much of the world is yet open to us, and let us profit of the occasion.

At present we exercise no neutral rights. We have quit the ocean; we have abandoned our rights; we have retired to our shell. Sooner than thus continue, our merchantmen should arm to protect legitimate trade. Sir, I believe war itself, as we could carry it on, would produce more benefit and less cost than the millions lost by the continuance of the embargo.

2. A Jeffersonian (W. B. Giles) Upholds the Embargo (1808)†

Stung by Federalist criticisms of the embargo, Senator W. B. Giles of Virginia sprang to its defense. A prickly personage but a brilliant debater, he had assailed or was to assail virtually every figure prominent in public life. Bitterly anti-Hamilton and anti-British, he was more Jeffersonian than Jefferson himself. Is his argument for the coercive role of the embargo as convincing as that for the precautionary role?

Sir, I have always understood that there were two subjects contemplated by the embargo laws. The first, precautionary, operating upon ourselves. The second, coercive, operating upon the aggressing belligerents. Precautionary, in saving our seamen, our ships, and our merchandise from the plunder of our enemies, and avoiding the calamities of war. Coercive, by addressing strong appeals to the interests of both the belligerents.

The first object has been answered beyond my most sanguine expectations. To make a fair and just estimate of this measure, reference should be had to our situation at the time of its adoption. At that time, the aggressions of both the belligerents were such as to leave the United States but a painful alternative in the choice of one of three measures, to wit, the embargo, war, or submission. . . .

It was found that merchandise to the value of one hundred millions of dollars was actually afloat, in vessels amounting in value to twenty millions more; that an amount of merchandise and vessels equal to fifty millions of dollars more was expected to be shortly put afloat; and that it would require fifty thousand seamen to be employed in the navigation of this enormous amount of property. The administration was informed of the hostile edicts of France previously issued, and then in a state of execution; and of an intention on the part of Great Britain to issue her orders [in Council], the character and object of which were also known. The object was to sweep this valuable commerce from the ocean. The situation of this commerce was as well known to Great Britain as to ourselves, and her inordinate cupidity could not withstand the temptation

---

*The British, seeking to forestall Napoleon, had bombarded and captured the neutral Danish capital in 1807.
†*Annals of Congress*, 10th Congress, 2d Sess. (1808), pp. 96–106, passim.

of the rich booty she vainly thought within her power. This was the state of information at the time this measure was recommended.

The President of the United States, ever watchful and anxious for the preservation of the persons and property of all our fellow citizens, but particularly of the merchants, whose property is most exposed to danger, and of the seamen, whose persons are also most exposed, recommended the embargo for the protection of both. And it has saved and protected both. . . . It is admitted by all that the embargo laws have saved this enormous amount of property and this number of seamen, which, without them, would have forcibly gone into the hands of our enemies, to pamper their arrogance, stimulate their injustice, and increase their means of annoyance. . . .

The first effect of the embargo upon the aggressing belligerents was to lessen their inducements to war, by keeping out of their way the rich spoils of our commerce, which had invited their cupidity, and which was saved by those laws. . . .

The second effect which the embargo laws have had on the aggressing belligerents is to enhance the prices of all American produce, especially articles of the first necessity to them, to a considerable degree; and, if it be a little longer persisted in, will either banish our produce (which I believe indispensable to them) from their markets altogether, or increase the prices to an enormous amount; and, of course, we may hope will furnish irresistible inducements for a relaxation of their hostile orders and edicts.

[The effects of the embargo ultimately proved disastrous. Confronted with anarchy and bankruptcy, Jefferson engineered its repeal in 1809 and the substitution of a more limited Non-Intercourse Act.]

Thought Provokers

1. In what ways has the doctrine of "judicial supremacy" that John Marshall laid out in *Marbury v. Madison* been controversial?
2. To what extent did the Louisiana Purchase strengthen or weaken the no-alliance tradition? Did good diplomacy or good luck bring about the purchase?
3. Did it take more courage on Jefferson's part to accept Louisiana than to reject it? What becomes of the Constitution if the executive may resort to what he believes to be unconstitutional acts for the common good? What probably would have happened if, as the Federalists argued, the thirteen original states had kept all the new territory in a permanently colonial status?
4. How effective was Jefferson's embargo as an instrument of diplomacy? Does the modern history of economic sanctions as diplomatic tools—for example, against South Africa, North Korea, and Iran—prompt any reconsideration of Jefferson's adoption of such policies?
5. President Woodrow Wilson said in 1916, "The immortality of Jefferson does not lie in any one of his achievements, but in his attitude toward mankind." Comment.

12

The Second War for Independence and the Upsurge of Nationalism, 1812–1824

The war [of 1812] has renewed and reinstated the national feelings and character which the Revolution had given, and which were daily lessened.

Albert Gallatin, 1816

Prologue: The western war hawks in Congress, bitter about maritime grievances against Britain and the British-backed Indian raids on the frontier, engineered a declaration of war on Britain in 1812. But the pro-British Federalists of New England vehemently opposed "Mr. Madison's War" as a scheme of the Jeffersonian Democratic-Republicans to ruin them economically and politically. With the nation thus dangerously divided, the war went badly for the Americans, and ended with the Treaty of Ghent (1814), which essentially restored the status quo. Yet partly as a result of Andrew Jackson's stirring victory over the British at the Battle of New Orleans, an outburst of nationalism followed the otherwise frustrating War of 1812. As time went on, the chief setback to nationalism was the ominous sectional quarrel over slavery in Missouri. The volatile issue of slavery was eventually contained for a period of years by the Missouri Compromise of 1820, but it smoldered on until it finally exploded in the Civil War in 1861. In foreign affairs, meanwhile, nationalism manifested itself in the Monroe Doctrine (1823), which warned the European powers to keep their hands off the two American continents.

A. The Cauldron of War

1. Tecumseh Challenges William Henry Harrison (1810)*

The American frontiersmen blamed the British for egging the Native Americans on to attack them, but actually American greed was good enough. William Henry

---

*C. M. Depew, ed., *The Library of Oratory* (New York: The Globe Publishing Company, 1902), vol. 4, pp. 363–364.

Harrison, the aggressive governor of Indiana Territory, had negotiated a series of land-grabbing agreements with the Indians, culminating in the Treaty of Fort Wayne (1809). Two Indian tribes, ignoring the rights of all others, sold three million acres of their ancestral lands for a pittance. The gifted Shawnee chief Tecumseh, together with his visionary brother the Prophet, was then organizing the Indians against white encroachments. Absent when the Treaty of Fort Wayne was negotiated, Tecumseh journeyed angrily to Vincennes (Indiana), where, in a stormy scene, he confronted Governor Harrison and threatened to resist white occupancy of the ceded lands. How valid was his main grievance?

I would not then come to Governor Harrison to ask him to tear the treaty and to obliterate the landmark. But I would say to him: Sir, you have liberty to return to your own country.

The Being within, communing with past ages, tells me that . . . until lately there was no white man on this continent; that it then all belonged to red men, children of the same parents, placed on it by the Great Spirit that made them, to keep it, to traverse it, to enjoy its productions, and to fill it with the same race—once a happy race, since made miserable by the white people, who are never contented, but always encroaching. The way—and the only way—to check and to stop this evil is for all the red men to unite in claiming a common equal right in the land, as it was at first, and should be yet. For it never was divided, but belongs to all for the use of each. That no part has a right to sell, even to each other, much less to strangers; those who want all, and will not do with less.

The white people have no right to take the land from the Indians, because they had it first. It is theirs. They may sell, but all must join. Any sale not made by all is not valid. The late sale is bad. It was made by a part only. Part do not know how to sell. It requires all to make a bargain for all. All red men have equal rights to the unoccupied land. The right of occupancy is as good in one place as in another. There cannot be two occupations in the same place. The first excludes all others. It is not so in hunting or traveling; for there the same ground will serve many, as they may follow each other all day. But the camp is stationary, and that is occupancy. It belongs to the first who sits down on his blanket or skins which he has thrown upon the ground; and till he leaves it no other has a right.

2. Representative Felix Grundy Demands War (1811)*

Following Tecumseh's speech and the subsequent Indian raids on the frontier, Governor Harrison led an army provocatively toward the headquarters of the Indians. On the night of November 7, 1811, at Tippecanoe near the Wabash River (Indiana), he succeeded in beating back an Indian attack. This hollow but costly victory further inflamed the West, from which came Henry Clay and other leaders of the war hawks to Congress in 1811. Among them was Felix Grundy of Tennessee, three of whose brothers had been killed by the Indians. As the most famous criminal lawyer in the Southwest, he had often cheated the gallows by reducing the

---

*Annals of Congress, 12th Congress, 1st Sess., pp. 424–426 (December 9, 1811).

jury to tears. In this eloquent speech in Congress, which grievances were peculiarly western, and which ones were nationwide? What interest did westerners have in freedom of the seas?

I will now state the reasons which influenced the Committee [on Foreign Affairs] in recommending the [war] measures now before us. . . .

The true question in controversy . . . involves the interest of the whole nation. It is the right of exporting the productions of our own soil and industry to foreign markets. Sir, our vessels are now captured when destined to the ports of France, and condemned by the British Courts of Admiralty, without even the pretext of having on board contraband of war, enemies' property, or having in any other respect violated the laws of nations.

These depredations on our lawful commerce, under whatever ostensible pretense committed, are not to be traced to any maxims or rules of public law, but to the maritime supremacy and pride of the British nation. This hostile and unjust policy of that country towards us is not to be wondered at, when we recollect that the United States are already the second commercial nation in the world. The rapid growth of our commercial importance has not only awakened the jealousy of the commercial interests of Great Britain, but her statesmen, no doubt, anticipate with deep concern the maritime greatness of this republic. . . .

What, Mr. Speaker, are we now called on to decide? It is whether we will resist by force the attempt, made by the [British] government, to subject our maritime rights to the arbitrary and capricious rule of her will. For my part I am not prepared to say that this country shall submit to have her commerce interdicted, or regulated, by any foreign nation. Sir, I prefer war to submission.

Over and above these unjust pretensions of the British government, for many years past they have been in the practice of impressing our seamen from merchant vessels. This unjust and lawless invasion of personal liberty calls loudly for the interposition of this government. To those better acquainted with the facts in relation to it, I leave it to fill up the picture.

My mind is irresistibly drawn to the West. Although others may not strongly feel the bearing which the late transactions in that quarter [Tippecanoe] have on this subject, upon my mind they have great influence. It cannot be believed, by any man who will reflect, that the savage tribes, uninfluenced by other powers, would think of making war on the United States. They understand too well their own weakness and our strength. They have already felt the weight of our arms; they know they hold the very soil on which they live as tenants in sufferance. How, then, sir, are we to account for their late conduct? In one way only: some powerful nation must have intrigued with them, and turned their peaceful dispositions towards us into hostilities. Great Britain alone has intercourse with those Northern tribes. I therefore infer that if British gold has not been employed, their baubles and trinkets, and the promise of support and a place of refuge, if necessary, have had their effect.

If I am right in this conjecture, war is not to commerce by sea or land. It is already begun; and some of the richest blood of our country has already been

shed. . . . The whole Western country is ready to march; they only wait for our permission. And, sir, war once declared, I pledge myself for my people—they will avenge the death of their brethren. . . .

This war, if carried on successfully, will have its advantages. We shall drive the British from our continent. They will no longer have an opportunity of intriguing with our Indian neighbors and setting on the ruthless savage to tomahawk our women and children. That nation will lose her Canadian trade, and, by having no resting place in this country, her means of annoying us will be diminished.

3. Causes of the War (1812, 1813)

The "Second War for American Independence" was prompted by events on the frontier as well as on the high seas. The first print, entitled A Scene on the Frontiers as Practiced by the Humane British and Their Worthy Allies, *may have been inspired by the August 1812 "Massacre of Chicago," in which it was reported that British officers had purchased American scalps from Indians. The second scene,* The Tory Editor and His Apes Giving Their Pitiful Advice to the American Sailors, *presumably takes place in an Atlantic seaport, where American sailors are rejecting the counsel being offered. Why were the British depicted so differently in these two prints? What view of themselves would Americans get from these images? What do these views suggest about the relative importance of the various causes of the War of 1812?*

4. President James Madison's Fateful War Message (1812)*

Scholars once believed that Madison—mild-mannered and highly intellectual—was prodded into war by the purposeful war hawks from the West. The truth is that the president, unable to wring concessions from the British, worked hand in glove with the war hawks. In his following War Message, does he seem more concerned with purely western grievances than with national grievances? Which of his numerous charges against England carries the least conviction?

British cruisers have been in the continued practice of violating the American flag on the great highway of nations, and of seizing and carrying off persons sailing under it, not in the exercise of a belligerent right founded on the law of nations against an enemy, but of a municipal [internal] prerogative over British subjects. British jurisdiction is thus extended to neutral vessels. . . .

The practice . . . is so far from affecting British subjects alone that, under the pretext of searching for these, thousands of American citizens, under the safeguard of public law and of their national flag, have been torn from their country and from everything dear to them; have been dragged on board ships of war of a foreign nation and exposed, under the severities of their discipline, to be exiled to the most distant and deadly climes, to risk their lives in the battles of their oppressors, and to be the melancholy instruments of taking away those of their own brethren.

Against this crying enormity, which Great Britain would be so prompt to avenge if committed against herself, the United States have in vain exhausted remonstrances and expostulations. And that no proof might be wanting of their conciliatory dispositions, and no pretext left for a continuance of the practice, the British government was formally assured of the readiness of the United States to enter into arrangements such as could not be rejected if the recovery of British subjects were the real and the sole object. The communication passed without effect.

British cruisers have been in the practice also of violating the rights and the peace of our coasts. They hover over and harass our entering and departing commerce. To the most insulting pretensions they have added the most lawless proceedings in our very harbors, and have wantonly spilt American blood within the sanctuary of our territorial jurisdiction. . . .

Under pretended blockades, without the presence of an adequate force and sometimes without the practicability of applying one, our commerce has been plundered in every sea, the great staples of our country have been cut off from their legitimate markets, and a destructive blow aimed at our agricultural and maritime interests. . . .

Not content with these occasional expedients for laying waste our neutral trade, the Cabinet of Britain resorted at length to the sweeping system of blockages, under the name of Orders in Council, which has been molded and managed as might best suit its political views, its commercial jealousies, or the avidity of British cruisers. . . .

It has become, indeed, sufficiently certain that the commerce of the United States is to be sacrificed, not as interfering with the belligerent rights of Great Britain; not as supplying the wants of her enemies, which she herself supplies; but as interfering with the monopoly which she covets for her own commerce and navigation. . . .

---

*J. D. Richardson, ed., *Messages and Papers of the Presidents* (1896), vol. 1, pp. 500–504.

In reviewing the conduct of Great Britain toward the United States, our attention is necessarily drawn to the warfare just renewed by the savages on one of our extensive frontiers—a warfare which is known to spare neither age nor sex and to be distinguished by features peculiarly shocking to humanity. It is difficult to account for the activity and combinations which have for some time been developing themselves among tribes in constant intercourse with British traders and garrisons, without connecting their hostility with that influence, and without recollecting the authenticated examples of such interpositions heretofore furnished by the officers and agents of that government.

5. Federalist Congressmen Protest (1812)[*]

A group of thirty-four antiwar Federalists, outvoted in the House, prepared the following remonstrance, which was widely circulated. One of its leading authors was the unbridled Josiah Quincy, who, the year before, had declared that if the territory of Louisiana was admitted as a state, the Union was "virtually dissolved," and that like-minded men must "prepare definitely for a separation—amicably, if they can; violently, if they must." The protest of the thirty-four congressmen was in effect a reply to Madison's War Message. After minimizing or partially justifying Britain's provocative maritime practices and Indian policy, the statement continued as follows. How plausibly does it make its points regarding the futility of the war and the folly of becoming a virtual ally of France? To what extent does it describe the war as immoral?

If our ills were of a nature that war would remedy, if war would compensate any of our losses or remove any of our complaints, there might be some alleviation of the suffering in the charm of the prospect. But how will war upon the land protect commerce upon the ocean? What balm has Canada for wounded honor? How are our mariners benefited by a war which exposes those who are free, without promising release to those who are impressed?

But it is said that war is demanded by honor. Is national honor a principle which thirsts after vengeance, and is appeased only by blood? . . . If honor demands a war with England, what opiate lulls that honor to sleep over the wrongs done us by France? On land, robberies, seizures, imprisonments, by French authority; at sea, pillage, sinkings, burnings, under French orders. These are notorious. Are they unfelt because they are French? . . . With full knowledge of the wrongs inflicted by the French, ought the government of this country to aid the French cause by engaging in war against the enemy of France? . . .

It would be some relief to our anxiety if amends were likely to be made for the weakness and wildness of the project by the prudence of the preparation. But in no aspect of this anomalous affair can we trace the great and distinctive properties of wisdom. There is seen a headlong rushing into difficulties, with little calculation about the means, and little concern about the consequences. With a navy comparatively nominal, we are about to enter into the lists against the greatest marine [sea power] on the globe. With a commerce unprotected and spread over every ocean, we propose to make a profit by privateering, and for this endanger the wealth of which

---

[*]*Annals of Congress*, 12th Congress, 1st Sess., pp. 2219–2221.

we are honest proprietors. An invasion is threatened of the colonies of a power which, without putting a new ship into commission, or taking another soldier into pay, can spread alarm or desolation along the extensive range of our seaboard. . . .

The undersigned cannot refrain from asking, what are the United States to gain by this war? Will the gratification of some privateersmen compensate the nation for that sweep of our legitimate commerce by the extended marine of our enemy which this desperate act invites? Will Canada compensate the Middle states for New York; or the Western states for New Orleans?

Let us not be deceived. A war of invasion may invite a retort of invasion. When we visit the peaceable, and as to us innocent, colonies of Great Britain with the horrors of war, can we be assured that our own coast will not be visited with like horrors? At a crisis of the world such as the present, and under impressions such as these, the undersigned could not consider the war, in which the United States have in secret been precipitated, as necessary, or required by any moral duty, or any political expediency.

6. The London Times Bemoans Peace (1814)*

The British had expected to topple the United States by invading northern New York in 1814, but the redcoats were turned back at Plattsburgh by Thomas Macdonough's spectacular victory on Lake Champlain. The hard-pressed Americans, meanwhile, had completely abandoned their demands on impressment and other issues, and gladly accepted the stalemate Treaty of Ghent. The grim reality was that the British had begun the war with more than eight hundred ships in their navy, the Americans with sixteen. When the war ended, the British still dominated the seas, whereas the Americans, although they had won a dozen or so single-ship duels, were down to two or three warships. But one would hardly have thought so from the following anguished outburst in the London Times, *which irresponsibly urged nonratification of the treaty. Why was this influential journal so unhappy? Did it present a false picture of British operations?*

[The European powers] will reflect that we have attempted to force our principles on America, and have failed. Nay, that we have retired from the combat with the stripes yet bleeding on our backs—with the recent defeats at Plattsburg and on Lake Champlain unavenged. To make peace at such a moment, they will think, betrays a deadness to the feelings of honour, and shows a timidity of disposition, inviting further insult.

. . . "Two or three of our ships have struck to a force vastly superior!"—No, not two or three, but many on the ocean, and whole squadrons [to Perry and Macdonough] on the Lakes. And their numbers are to be viewed with relation to the comparative magnitude of the two navies. Scarcely is there one American ship of war which has not to boast a victory over the British flag; scarcely one British ship in thirty or forty that has beaten an American.

Our seamen, it is urged, have on all occasions fought bravely. Who denies it? Our complaint is that with the bravest seamen and the most powerful navy in the world, we retire from the contest when the balance of defeat is so heavily against us. Be it accident or be it misconduct, we enquire not now into the cause. The certain,

*London Times, December 30, 1814.

the inevitable consequences are what we look to, and these may be summed up in a few words—the speedy growth of an American navy—and the recurrence of a new and much more formidable American war. . . .

The [American] people—naturally vain, boastful, and insolent—have been filled with an absolute contempt of our maritime power, and a furious eagerness to beat down our maritime pretensions. Those passions, which have been inflamed by success, could only have been cooled by what in vulgar and emphatic language has been termed "a sound flogging." But, unfortunately, our Christian meekness has induced us rather to kiss the rod than to retaliate its exercise. Such false and feeble humanity is not calculated for the guidance of nations.

War is, indeed, a tremendous engine of justice. But when justice wields the sword, she must be inflexible. Looking neither to the right nor to the left, she must pursue her blow until the evil is clean rooted out. This is not blind rage, or blinder revenge; but it is a discriminating, a calm, and even a tender calculation of consequences. Better is it that we should grapple with the young lion when he is first fleshed with the taste of our flocks than wait until, in the maturity of his strength, he bears away at once both sheep and shepherd.

B. Disloyalty in New England

1. A Boston Paper Obstructs the War (1813)[*]

The antiwar bitterness of the New England Federalists found vigorous voice in Major Benjamin Russell's Columbian Centinel *(Boston). The editor, earlier fined twenty shillings for spitting in the face of a journalistic adversary, believed that a French-loving cabal of Virginia planter lordlings had provoked unnecessary hostilities. He charged that this Jeffersonian Democratic-Republican group, headed by President Madison, was determined to ruin the Federalists by destroying their commerce and by carving new states out of Canada—states that would outvote the New England bloc. Considering that the United States had already been at war for six months, was this editorial treasonable? What was the validity of its charges? How far did it go toward secession?*

The sentiment is hourly extending, and in these Northern states will soon be universal, that we are in a condition no better in relation to the South than that of a conquered people. We have been compelled, without the least necessity or occasion, to renounce our habits, occupations, means of happiness, and subsistence. We are plunged into a war without a sense of enmity, or a perception of sufficient provocation; and obliged to fight the battles of a cabal which, under the sickening affectation of republican equality, aims at trampling into the dust the weight, influence, and power of commerce and her dependencies.

We, whose soil was the hotbed and whose ships were the nursery of sailors, are insulted with the hypocrisy of a devotedness to sailors' rights, and the arrogance of

---

[*]*Columbian Centinel* (Boston), January 13, 1813.

pretended skill in maritime jurisprudence, by those whose country furnishes no navigation beyond the size of a ferry boat or an Indian canoe. We have no more interest in waging this sort of war, at this period and under these circumstances, at the command of Virginia, than Holland in accelerating her ruin by uniting her destiny to France. . . .

We resemble Holland in another particular. The officer [offices] and power of government are engrossed [monopolized] by executive minions, who are selected on account of their known infidelity to the interest of their fellow citizens, to foment divisions and to deceive and distract the people whom they cannot intimidate. . . .

The consequence of this state of things must then be either that the Southern states must drag the Northern states farther into the war, or we must drag them out of it; or the chain will break. This will be the "imposing attitude" of the next year. We must no longer be deafened by senseless clamors about a separation of the states. It is an event we do not desire, not because we have derived advantages from the compact, but because we cannot foresee or limit the dangers or effects of revolution. But the states are separated in fact, when one section assumes an imposing attitude, and with a high hand perseveres in measures fatal to the interests and repugnant to the opinions of another section, by dint of a geographical majority.

2. The Hartford Convention Fulminates (1814)[*]

As the war dragged on, the British extended their suffocating blockade to the coasts of New England. The New Englanders, forced to resort to costly defensive measures, complained bitterly that their federal tax payments were being used to fight the war elsewhere. Late in 1814, with Massachusetts and Connecticut as ringleaders, twenty-six delegates assembled secretly in a protest convention at Hartford, Connecticut. Although some of the Federalist extremists spoke brazenly of immediate secession, conservatives like the venerable George Cabot sat on the lid, saying, "We are going to keep you young hotheads from getting into mischief." The final resolutions, less treasonable than commonly supposed, were a manifesto of states' rights and sectionalism designed to revive New England's slipping national power, avert Jeffersonian embargoes, and keep new western states from outvoting the charter members. Which of these proposed amendments were most clearly sectional, and which one probably had the best chance of adoption at the time?

Resolved, That the following amendments of the Constitution of the United States be recommended to the states. . . .

First. Representatives and direct taxes shall be apportioned among the several states which may be included within this Union, according to their respective numbers of free persons, including those bound to serve for a term of years, and excluding Indians not taxed, and all other persons. [Aimed at reducing southern representation based on slaves.]

Second. No new state shall be admitted into the Union by Congress, in virtue of the power granted by the Constitution, without the concurrence of two-thirds of both Houses.

---

[*]Timothy Dwight, *History of the Hartford Convention* (1833), pp. 377–378.

Third. Congress shall not have power to lay any embargo on the ships or vessels of the citizens of the United States, in the ports or harbors thereof, for more than sixty days.

Fourth. Congress shall not have power, without the concurrence of two-thirds of both Houses, to interdict the commercial intercourse between the United States and any foreign nation, or the dependencies thereof.

Fifth. Congress shall not make or declare war, or authorize acts of hostility against any foreign nation, without the concurrence of two-thirds of both Houses, except such acts of hostility be in defense of the territories of the United States when actually invaded.

Sixth. No person who shall hereafter be naturalized shall be eligible as a member of the Senate or House of Representatives of the United States, nor capable of holding any civil office under the authority of the United States. [Aimed at men like Jefferson's Swiss-born secretary of the treasury, Albert Gallatin.]

Seventh. The same person shall not be elected President of the United States a second time; nor shall the President be elected from the same state two terms in succession. [Prompted by the successive two-term tenures of Jefferson and Madison, both from Virginia.]

Resolved, That if the application of these states to the government of the United States, recommended in a foregoing resolution, should be unsuccessful, and peace should not be concluded, and the defense of these states should be neglected, as it has been since the commencement of the war, it will, in the opinion of this convention, be expedient for the legislatures of the several states to appoint delegates to another convention, to meet at Boston . . . with such powers and instruction as the exigency of a crisis so momentous may require.

[The legislatures of Massachusetts and Connecticut enthusiastically approved the Hartford Resolutions. Three emissaries from Massachusetts departed for Washington with their demands, confidently expecting to hear at any moment of a smashing British victory at New Orleans, the collapse of the peace negotiations at Ghent, and the dissolution of the Union. Instead came news of the smashing British defeat at New Orleans and the signing of the peace treaty at Ghent. The Hartfordites were booted off the stage of history, amid charges of treason that cling to this day.]

3. John Quincy Adams Reproaches the Hartfordites (1815)[*]

Independent-minded John Quincy Adams, son of the second president and destined to be the sixth president, rose above the sectional prejudices of his native New England. Elected to the Senate by Massachusetts, he reluctantly voted for the Louisiana Purchase appropriation and subsequently supported Jefferson's unpopular embargo as preferable to war. The Federalists of New England now regarded him as a traitor. After serving as one of the five American negotiators of the Treaty of Ghent, he wrote

---

[*]Henry Adams, ed., *Documents Relating to New England Federalism, 1800–1815* (Boston: 1877), pp. 283–284, 321–322.

the following spirited attack on the Hartford Convention. What, in his view, was the ultimate aim of the Hartfordites?

The [Hartford] Convention represented the extreme portion of the Federalism of New England—the party spirit of the school of Alexander Hamilton combined with the sectional Yankee spirit. . . .

This coalition of Hamiltonian Federalism with the Yankee spirit had produced as incongruous and absurd a system of politics as ever was exhibited in the vagaries of the human mind. It was compounded of the following prejudices:—

1. An utter detestation of the French Revolution and of France, and a corresponding excess of attachment to Great Britain, as the only barrier against the universal, dreaded empire of France.

2. A strong aversion to republics and republican government, with a profound impression that our experiment of a confederated republic had failed for want of virtue in the people.

3. A deep jealousy of the Southern and Western states, and a strong disgust at the effect of the slave representation in the Constitution of the United States.

4. A belief that Mr. Jefferson and Mr. Madison were servilely devoted to France, and under French influence.

Every one of these sentiments weakened the attachments of those who held them to the Union, and consequently their patriotism. . . .

It will be no longer necessary to search for the objects of the Hartford Convention. They are apparent from the whole tenor of their report and resolutions, compared with the journal of their proceedings. They are admitted in the first and last paragraphs of the report, and they were:

To wait for the issue of the negotiation at Ghent.

In the event of the continuance of the war, to take one more chance of getting into their own hands the administration of the general government.

On the failure of that, a secession from the Union and a New England confederacy.

To these ends, and not to the defense of this part of the country against the foreign enemy, all the measures of the Hartford Convention were adapted.

C. The Missouri Statehood Controversy

1. Representative John Taylor Reviles Slavery (1819)[*]

The slaveholding territory of Missouri applied to Congress for admission as a state in 1819. Representative James Tallmadge of New York touched off the fireworks when he proposed an amendment to the Missouri statehood bill (a) prohibiting any further introduction of slaves and (b) freeing at age twenty-five all children born to slave parents after the admission of the state. During the ensuing debates, a leading role was played by Representative John W. Taylor, a prominent antislavery leader from New York who was to serve for twenty consecutive years in the House. The South

---

[*]*Annals of Congress*, 15th Congress, 2d Sess., pp. 1174–1176.

never forgave him, and later engineered his defeat for election as Speaker. In his speech for the Tallmadge amendment, what were the apparent contradictions in the attitude of the South toward blacks?

Having proved . . . our right to legislate in the manner proposed, I proceed to illustrate the propriety of exercising it. And here I might rest satisfied with reminding my [southern] opponents of their own declarations on the subject of slavery. How often, and how eloquently, have they deplored its existence among them! What willingness, nay, what solicitude have they not manifested to be relieved from this burden! How have they wept over the unfortunate policy that first introduced slaves into this country! How have they disclaimed the guilt and shame of that original sin, and thrown it back upon their ancestors!

I have with pleasure heard these avowals of regret and confided in their sincerity. I have hoped to see its effects in the advancement of the cause of humanity. Gentlemen now have an opportunity of putting their principles into practice. If they have tried slavery and found it a curse, if they desire to dissipate the gloom with which it covers their land, I call upon them to exclude it from the Territory in question. Plant not its seeds in this uncorrupt soil. Let not our children, looking back to the proceedings of this day, say of them, as they have been constrained to speak of their fathers, "We wish their decision had been different. We regret the existence of this unfortunate population among us. But we found them here; we know not what to do with them. It is our misfortune; we must bear it with patience."

History will record the decision of this day as exerting its influence for centuries to come over the population of half our continent. If we reject the amendment and suffer this evil, now easily eradicated, to strike its roots so deep in the soil that it can never be removed, shall we not furnish some apology for doubting our sincerity when we deplore its existence? . . .

THE MISSOURI COMPROMISE

Mr. Chairman, one of the gentlemen from Kentucky (Mr. Clay) has pressed into his service the cause of humanity. He has pathetically urged us to withdraw our amendment and suffer this unfortunate population to be dispersed over the country. He says they will be better fed, clothed, and sheltered, and their whole condition will be greatly improved. . . .

Sir, my heart responds to the call of humanity. I will zealously unite in any practicable means of bettering the condition of this oppressed people. I am ready to appropriate a territory to their use, and to aid them in settling it—but I am not willing, I never will consent, to declare the whole country west of the Mississippi a market overt for human flesh. . . .

To the objection that this amendment will, if adopted, diminish the value of a species of property in one portion of the Union, and thereby operate unequally, I reply that if, by depriving slaveholders of the Missouri market, the business of raising slaves should become less profitable, it would be an effect incidentally produced, but is not the object of the measure. The law prohibiting the importation of foreign slaves was not passed for the purpose of enhancing the value of those then in the country, but that effect has been incidentally produced in a very great degree. . . .

It is further objected that the amendment is calculated to disfranchise our brethren of the South by discouraging their emigration to the country west of the Mississippi. . . . The description of emigrants may be affected, in some measure, by the amendment in question. If slavery shall be tolerated, the country will be settled by rich planters, with their slaves. If it shall be rejected, the emigrants will chiefly consist of the poorer and more laborious classes of society. If it be true that the prosperity and happiness of a country ought to constitute the grand object of its legislators, I cannot hesitate for a moment which species of population deserves most to be encouraged by the laws we may pass.

2. Representative Charles Pinckney Upholds Slavery (1820)[*]

Angered Southerners spoke so freely of secession and "seas of blood" during the Missouri debate that the aging Thomas Jefferson likened the issue to "a fire bell in the night." The argument inevitably involved the general problem of slavery, and the view of the South was eloquently presented, in a justly famous speech, by Representative Charles Pinckney of South Carolina. Vain, demagogic, and of questionable morals, he was nevertheless touched with genius. As one of the few surviving members of the Philadelphia convention that had framed the Constitution in 1787, and as South Carolina's former governor and U.S. senator, Pinckney was in a position to command attention. What is the most alarming aspect of his speech?

A great deal has been said on the subject of slavery: that it is an infamous stain and blot on the states that hold them, not only degrading the slave, but the master, and making him unfit for republican government; that it is contrary to religion and the law of God; and that Congress ought to do everything in their power to prevent its extension among the new states.

---

[*]*Annals of Congress*, 16th Congress, 1st Sess., 1323–1328, passim.

Now, sir, . . . is there a single line in the Old or New Testament either censuring or forbidding it [slavery]? I answer without hesitation, no. But there are hundreds speaking of and recognizing it. . . . Hagar, from whom millions sprang, was an African slave, brought out of Egypt by Abraham, the father of the faithful and the beloved servant of the Most High; and he had, besides, three hundred and eighteen male slaves. The Jews, in the time of the theocracy, and the Greeks and Romans, had all slaves; at that time there was no nation without them.

If we are to believe that this world was formed by a great and omnipotent Being, that nothing is permitted to exist here but by his will, and then throw our eyes throughout the whole of it, we should form an opinion very different indeed from that asserted, that slavery was against the law of God. . . .

It will not be a matter of surprise to anyone that so much anxiety should be shown by the slaveholding states, when it is known that the alarm, given by this attempt to legislate on slavery, has led to the opinion that the very foundations of that kind of property are shaken; that the establishment of the precedent is a measure of the most alarming nature. . . . For, should succeeding Congresses continue to push it, there is no knowing to what length it may be carried.

Have the Northern states any idea of the value of our slaves? At least, sir, six hundred millions of dollars. If we lose them, the value of the lands they cultivate will be diminished in all cases one half, and in many they will become wholly useless. And an annual income of at least forty millions of dollars will be lost to your citizens, the loss of which will not alone be felt by the non-slaveholding states, but by the whole Union. For to whom, at present, do the Eastern states, most particularly, and the Eastern and Northern, generally, look for the employment of their shipping, in transporting our bulky and valuable products [cotton], and bringing us the manufactures and merchandises of Europe?

Another thing, in case of these losses being brought on us, and our being forced into a division of the Union, what becomes of your public debt? Who are to pay this, and how will it be paid? In a pecuniary view of this subject, therefore, it must ever be the policy of the Eastern and Northern states to continue connected with us.

But, sir, there is an infinitely greater call upon them, and this is the call of justice, of affection, and humanity. Reposing at a great distance, in safety, in the full enjoyment of all their federal and state rights, unattacked in either, or in their individual rights, can they, with indifference, or ought they, to risk, in the remotest degree, the consequences which this measure may produce? These may be the division of this Union and a civil war. Knowing that whatever is said here must get into the public prints, I am unwilling, for obvious reasons, to go into the description of the horrors which such a war must produce, and ardently pray that none of us may ever live to witness such an event.

[Other Southerners, so reported Representative William Plumer, Jr., of New Hampshire, "throw out many threats, and talk loudly of separation." Even "Mr. [Henry] Clay declares that he will go home and raise troops, if necessary, to defend the people of Missouri." But the Tallmadge amendment was rejected, and the famed Missouri Compromise was finally hammered out in 1820. The delicate sectional balance subsisting between the eleven free states and eleven slave states was cleverly preserved:

Maine (then a part of Massachusetts) was to come in as a free state and Missouri as a slave state. But henceforth slavery was forbidden elsewhere in the Louisiana Purchase territory north of the line of 36° 30'—the southern border of Missouri. John Quincy Adams wrote prophetically: "I take it for granted that the present question is a mere preamble—a title page to a great tragic volume."]

D. Launching the Monroe Doctrine

1. John Quincy Adams Rejects a Joint Declaration (1823)*

John Quincy Adams, President James Monroe's stiff-backed and lone-wolf secretary of state, strongly suspected the motives of British foreign secretary George Canning in approaching the American minister in London, Richard Rush, to propose a joint warning against foreign intervention in the newly independent republics of Spanish America. Adams cleverly calculated that the potent British navy would not permit these newly opened markets to be closed, and he therefore concluded that the European monarchs were powerless to intervene, no matter what the United States did. He did not share secretary of war John Calhoun's fear of the French army, which, acting as the avenging sword of the reactionary powers, was then crushing a republican uprising in Spain. Adams here records in his diary the relevant Cabinet discussion. Of the arguments he advanced against cooperation with Canning, which was strongest? Why?

Washington, November 7th.—Cabinet meeting at the President's from half-past one till four. Mr. Calhoun, Secretary of War, and Mr. Southard, Secretary of the Navy, present. The subject for consideration was the confidential proposals of the British Secretary of State, George Canning, to Richard Rush, and the correspondence between them relating to the projects of the Holy Alliance upon South America. There was much conversation without coming to any definite point. The object of Canning appears to have been to obtain some public pledge from the government of the United States, ostensibly against the forcible interference of the Holy Alliance between Spain and South America, but really or especially against the acquisition to the United States themselves of any part of the Spanish-American possessions.

Mr. Calhoun inclined to giving a discretionary power to Mr. Rush to join in a declaration against the interference of the Holy Allies, if necessary, even if it should pledge us not to take Cuba or the province of Texas; because the power of Great Britain being greater than ours to seize upon them, we should get the advantage of obtaining from her the same declaration we should make ourselves.

I thought the cases not parallel. We have no intentions of seizing either Texas or Cuba. But the inhabitants of either or both may exercise their primitive rights, and solicit a union with us. They will certainly do no such thing to Great Britain. By joining with her, therefore, in her proposed declaration, we give her a substantial and perhaps inconvenient pledge against ourselves, and really obtain nothing in return.

---

*C. F. Adams, ed., *Memoirs of John Quincy Adams* (Philadelphia: J. B. Lippincott & Co., 1875), vol. 6, pp. 177–179.

Without entering now into the enquiry of the expediency of our annexing Texas or Cuba to our Union, we should at least keep ourselves free to act as emergencies may arise, and not tie ourselves down to any principle which might immediately afterwards be brought to bear against ourselves. . . .

I remarked that the communications recently received from the Russian minister, Baron Tuyl, afforded, as I thought, a very suitable and convenient opportunity for us to take our stand against the Holy Alliance, and at the same time to decline the overture of Great Britain. It would be more candid, as well as more dignified, to avow our principles explicitly to Russia and France than to come in as a cockboat in the wake of the British man-of-war.

2. James Monroe Warns the European Powers (1823)*

Secretary Adams's cogent arguments helped turn President Monroe toward a go-it-alone policy. The president's annual message to Congress, surprisingly, contained several emphatic warnings. The Russians, who had caused some alarm by their push toward California, had privately shown a willingness to retreat to the southern bounds of present-day Alaska. But Monroe warned them and the other powers that there was now a closed season on colonizing in the Americas. At the same time, the heroic struggle of the Greeks for independence from the Turks was creating some agitation in America for intervention, and Monroe made his "you stay out" warning seem fairer by volunteering a "we'll stay out" pledge. Did he aim his main warning at noncolonization on the northwest coast or at the nonextension of monarchical systems to Spanish America? To what extent did he tie America's hands regarding the acquisition of Cuba or intervention in Greece? Did he actually threaten the European powers?

In the discussions to which this interest [Russia's on the northwest coast] has given rise, the occasion has been judged proper for asserting, as a principle in which the rights and interests of the United States are involved, that the American continents, by the free and independent condition which they have assumed and maintain, are henceforth not to be considered as subjects for the future colonization by any European powers. . . .

The political system of the Allied Powers [Holy Alliance] is essentially different . . . from that of America. This difference proceeds from that which exists in their respective [monarchical] governments; and to the defense of our own . . . this whole nation is devoted. We owe it, therefore, to candor and to the amicable relations existing between the United States and those powers to declare that we should consider any attempt on their part to extend their system to any portion of this hemisphere as dangerous to our peace and safety.

With the existing colonies or dependencies of any European power, we have not interfered and shall not interfere. But with the governments [of Spanish America] who have declared their independence and maintained it, and whose independence we have, on great consideration and on just principles, acknowledged, we could

---

*J. D. Richardson, ed., *Messages and Papers of the Presidents* (New York: Bureau of National Literature, 1896), vol. 2, pp. 209, 218–219.

not view any interposition for the purpose of oppressing them, or controlling in any other manner their destiny, by any European power in any other light than as the manifestation of an unfriendly disposition toward the United States. . . .

Our policy in regard to Europe, which was adopted at an early stage of the wars which have so long agitated that quarter of the globe, nevertheless remains the same, which is, not to interfere in the internal concerns of any of its powers; to consider the government *de facto* as the legitimate government for us; to cultivate friendly relations with it, and to preserve those relations by a frank, firm, and manly policy, meeting in all instances the just claims of every power, submitting to injuries from none.

But in regard to those [American] continents, circumstances are eminently and conspicuously different. It is impossible that the Allied Powers should extend their political system to any portion of either continent without endangering our peace and happiness. Nor can anyone believe that our southern brethren, if left to themselves, would adopt it of their own accord. It is equally impossible, therefore, that we should behold such interposition in any form with indifference.

3. A Colombian Newspaper Applauds Monroe's Doctrine (1824)*

Across South America, officials celebrated Monroe's rebuke of European intervention in the Western Hemisphere. Shortly after Monroe delivered his pronouncement, the following article, possibly written by Colombia's vice president, appeared in one of that nation's leading newspapers. Which American practices and institutions most impress the author? What does he see as the ultimate consequences of Monroe's declaration?

The United States has now begun to play among the civilized nations of the world that powerful and majestic role which befits the oldest and most powerful nation of our hemisphere. We deeply regret our inability to publish all of the message of the president to congress of December 2, for it is one of the most interesting documents which has emanated from the American government up to this time. It abounds in those suggestions and details which every free government ought to furnish its citizens in order that they may judge in regard to the interests of the nation with the proper exactness and discernment. How different is this frank and loyal mode of procedure from that horrid system which finds its stability in the secrets of the cabinet and in ministerial maneuvres. The enemies of liberty may take pleasure in the triumphs of that system on the European side of the Atlantic where its favorite principle of legitimacy has numerous partisans. In this favored continent there are no classes interested in perpetuating the ignorance of the people so that they may thrive upon prejudice and stupidity. In America man is only the slave of the law, while in a large part of the Old World people still believe and obstinately maintain that kings are an emanation of divinity. . . .

---

*Alejandro Alvarez, ed., *The Monroe Doctrine: Its Importance in the International Life of the States of the New World* (New York: Oxford University Press, 1924), pp. 120–121.

America is separated from those less fortunate regions by a vast ocean in which there will be drowned forever the hopes of those who imagine that we have not yet emerged from the darkness of the fifteenth century.

The perusal of the message which we have before us has consequently furnished us much pleasure, for the president of the United States has profited by the opportunity afforded by the differences pending with Russia to assert that the American continent is now so free and independent that henceforth it cannot be made the theater of colonization by any European power. Indeed the Americans of the North and of the South of this continent shall not again behold in their lands those hordes of foreigners, who, with the cross in one hand and a dagger in the other, would disturb the happiness and the peace which they today enjoy.

Thought Provokers

1. Why did the United States go to war with Britain in 1812? Was there any single cause whose removal would have averted hostilities?
2. Why were the Federalists so bitterly opposed to the war? Were their grievances legitimate? Were they victims of the "tyranny of the majority" or simply poor losers?
3. If the peace of Ghent was so unpopular in Britain and so popular in America, what conclusions might be drawn as to which side won the war? How is "victory" to be measured in a military contest?
4. If many leaders of the South acknowledged that slavery was a wicked institution, why did they fight its proposed abolition in Missouri?
5. Would the United States have been better off in the long run if Monroe had joined hands with Britain to keep the other European powers out of the Americas?
6. How did Latin American nations respond to the Monroe Doctrine? Were their expectations of American intervention on the continent realistic?

13

The Rise
of a Mass Democracy,
1824–1840

> I consider, then, the power to annul a law of the
> United States, assumed by one state, incompatible
> with the existence of the Union, contradicted
> expressly by the letter of the Constitution,
> unauthorized by its spirit, inconsistent with every
> principle on which it was founded, and destructive
> of the great object for which it was formed.
>
> *Andrew Jackson's South Carolina Nullification*
> *Proclamation, 1832*

Prologue: The explosive growth of the West, with its oceans of available land, weakened the old property qualifications for voting and stimulated the New Democracy of the "unwashed masses." General Andrew Jackson, idol and champion of the common people, swept into the presidency in 1828, after having lost a bitterly disputed election to John Quincy Adams four years earlier. Jackson, a frontier ruffian elevated to the White House, typified the freewheeling, entrepreneurial spirit of the age. Meanwhile, Southern anger over steadily rising tariffs led to a crisis when South Carolina tried to "nullify" the "Tariff of Abominations" passed in 1828. The classic Webster-Hayne debate of 1830 reflected the clashing sentiments of the opposing sides, and Webster's eloquent defense of the ideal of the Union touched a deep chord of nationalistic pride. Jackson himself faced down the South Carolina nullifiers and then defied the monopolistic Bank of the United States, leading to his overwhelming reelection victory over his Whig opponent, Henry Clay, in 1832. Jackson also engineered the brutal uprooting of the southeastern Indian tribes to the western plains. The surging spirit of democracy, stimulated further by the political controversies of Jackson's presidency, led to the emergence of mass-based, organized political parties (Democrats and Whigs)—something new in the American experience and, indeed, new in the experience of all the modern world. The financial crisis that erupted in 1837 helped the Whigs to elect their first president, William Henry Harrison, in 1840.

A. Background of the New Democracy _____

1. A Disgusting Spirit of Equality (1807)[*]

Freedom of opportunity in America weakened class barriers and caused the "lower orders" to be freer and easier with their "betters." Such behavior was highly offensive to English visitors from a class-ridden society, especially to those who came in the 1830s and 1840s. C. W. Janson emigrated to America from England to make his fortune, lost his money, and vented his spleen in an ill-natured book that contained numerous unpleasant truths. What specific American traits did he find annoying, and which one the most annoying? Do universal manhood suffrage and bad manners necessarily go together?

Arrived at your [New England] inn, let me suppose, like myself, you had fallen in with a landlord who at the moment would condescend to take the trouble to procure you refreshment after the family hour. . . . He will sit by your side and enter in the most familiar manner into conversation; which is prefaced, of course, with a demand of your business, and so forth. He will then start a political question (for here every individual is a politician), force your answer, contradict, deny, and, finally, be ripe for a quarrel, should you not acquiesce in all his opinions.

When the homely meal is served up, he will often place himself opposite to you at the table at the same time declaring that "though he thought he had eaten a hearty dinner, yet he will pick a bit with you."

Thus he will sit, drinking out of your glass, and of the liquor you are to pay for, belching in your face, and committing other excesses still more indelicate and disgusting. Perfectly inattentive to your accommodation, and regardless of your appetite, he will dart his fork into the best of the dish, and leave you to take the next cut.

If you arrive at the dinner hour, you are seated with "mine hostess" and her dirty children, with whom you have often to scramble for a plate, and even the servants of the inn. For liberty and equality level all ranks upon the road, from the host to the hostler.

The children, imitative of their free and polite papa, will also seize your drink, slobber in it, and often snatch a dainty bit from your plate. This is esteemed wit, and consequently provokes a laugh, at the expense of those who are paying for the board. . . .

The arrogance of domestics [servants] in this land of republican liberty and equality is particularly calculated to excite the astonishment of strangers. To call persons of this description servants, or to speak of their master or mistress, is a grievous affront.

Having called one day at the house of a gentleman of my acquaintance, on knocking at the door, it was opened by a servant-maid, whom I had never before seen, as she had not been long in his family. The following is the dialogue, word for word, which took place on this occasion:

"Is your master at home?"

"I have no master."

_____

[*]C. W. Janson, *The Stranger in America, 1793–1806* (London: J. Cundee, 1807), pp. 85–88.

"Don't you live here?"

"I stay here."

"And who are you then?"

"Why, I am Mr. —'s help. I'd have you to know, man, that I am no sarvant. None but negers are sarvants."

2. A Plea for Nonproperty Suffrage (1841)*

Until the days of Jacksonian democracy, property qualifications were generally demanded of all voters. In Virginia, where such restrictions discouraged immigration and encouraged emigration, a memorable convention met at Richmond in 1829–1830 to revise the state constitution. The result was a widening of the suffrage, in accord with the New Democracy, but a retention of certain property qualifications. One of the strongest arguments against change—an argument repeated in other conservative states—was that possession of property provided the surest guarantee of a permanent stake in the community. Grave dangers would presumably be courted if political power were put into the hands of the irresponsible, propertyless "bipeds of the forest." A popular author, George S. Camp, took sharp issue with the advocates of property qualifications in a long-lived book on democracy. In the light of his argument, is it true that the propertyless have as much of a stake in the community as the propertied?

All should have an equal voice in the public deliberations of the state, however unequal in point of circumstances, since human rights, by virtue of which alone we are entitled to vote at all, are the attributes of the man, not of his circumstances.

Should the right to vote, the characteristic and the highest prerogative of a freeman, be at the mercy of a casualty? I am rich today, worth my hundred thousands. But my wealth consists in stock and merchandise; it may be in storehouses, it may be upon the ocean. I have been unable to effect an insurance, or there is some concealed legal defect in my policy. The fire or the storms devour my wealth in an hour: am I the less competent to vote? Have I less of the capacity of a moral and intelligent being? Am I the less a good citizen? Is it not enough that I have been deprived of my fortune—must I be disfranchised by community?

My having a greater or less amount of property does not alter my rights. Property is merely the subject on which rights are exercised; its amount does not alter rights themselves. If it were otherwise, every one of us would be in some degree subject to some wealthier neighbor. And, if the representation of property were consistently carried out, the affairs of every community, instead of being governed by the majority of rational and intelligent beings, would be governed by a preponderance of houses, lands, stocks, plate, jewelry, merchandise, and money!

It is not true that one man has more at stake in the commonwealth than another. We all have our rights, and no man has anything more. If we look at the subject philosophically, and consider how much superior man is by nature to what he is by external condition, how much superior his real attributes are to what he

---

*George S. Camp, *Democracy* (New York: Harper and Brothers, 1841), pp. 145–146.

acquires from the accidents of fortune, we shall then view the distinctions of rank and wealth in their true comparative insignificance, and make as little difference on these accounts with the political as with the moral man.

3. Davy Crockett Advises Politicians (1836)*

David (Davy) Crockett—notorious Tennessee frontiersman, Indian scout, rifleman, bear hunter, and braggart—was a homespun product of the New Democracy. His scanty six months of schooling led him to scorn both grammar and "book larnin'," although he became a justice of the peace, an elected militia colonel, and a member of the state legislature. When a joking remark prompted him to campaign for Congress, he overwhelmed his two opponents with a barrage of ridicule and humorous stories. Reelected for two additional terms, he attracted wide attention in Washington with his backwoods dress, racy language, homely wit, shrewd common sense, and presumed naïveté regarding the aristocratic East. Ruggedly independent, he delighted eastern conservatives by refusing to follow President Jackson on all issues. His advice to aspiring politicians, though offered in a jocular vein, reveals the debased tone of the new manhood-suffrage democracy. Which of his recommended devices are still employed by politicians today?

"Attend all public meetings," says I, "and get some friend to move that you take the chair. If you fail in this attempt, make a push to be appointed secretary. The proceedings of course will be published, and your name is introduced to the public. But should you fail in both undertakings, get two or three acquaintances, over a bottle of whisky, to pass some resolutions, no matter on what subject. Publish them, even if you pay the printer. It will answer the purpose of breaking the ice, which is the main point in these matters.

"Intrigue until you are elected an officer of the militia. This is the second step toward promotion, and can be accomplished with ease, as I know an instance of an election being advertised, and no one attending, the innkeeper at whose house it was to be held, having a military turn, elected himself colonel of his regiment." Says I, "You may not accomplish your ends with as little difficulty, but do not be discouraged—Rome wasn't built in a day.

"If your ambition or circumstances compel you to serve your country, and earn three dollars a day, by becoming a member of the legislature, you must first publicly avow that the constitution of the state is a shackle upon free and liberal legislation, and is, therefore, of as little use in the present enlightened age as an old almanac of the year in which the instrument was framed. There is policy in this measure, for by making the constitution a mere dead letter, your headlong proceedings will be attributed to a bold and unshackled mind; whereas, it might otherwise be thought they arose from sheer mulish ignorance. 'The Government' has set the example in his [Jackson's] attack upon the Constitution of the United States, and who should fear to follow where 'the Government' leads?

---

*David Crockett, *Exploits and Adventures in Texas* . . . (1836), pp. 56–59 (a pseudo-autobiography generally ascribed to Richard Penn Smith).

"When the day of election approaches, visit your constituents far and wide. Treat liberally, and drink freely, in order to rise in their estimation, though you fall in your own. True, you may be called a drunken dog by some of the clean-shirt and silk-stocking gentry, but the real roughnecks will style you a jovial fellow. Their votes are certain, and frequently count double.

"Do all you can to appear to advantage in the eyes of the women. That's easily done. You have but to kiss and slabber [slobber over] their children, wipe their noses, and pat them on the head. This cannot fail to please their mothers, and you may rely on your business being done in that quarter.

"Promise all that is asked," said I, "and more if you can think of anything. Offer to build a bridge or a church, to divide a county, create a batch of new offices, make a turnpike, or anything they like. Promises cost nothing; therefore, deny nobody who has a vote or sufficient influence to obtain one.

"Get up on all occasions, and sometimes on no occasion at all, and make long-winded speeches, though composed of nothing else than wind. Talk of your devotion to your country, your modesty and disinterestedness, or on any such fanciful subject. Rail against taxes of all kinds, officeholders, and bad harvest weather; and wind up with a flourish about the heroes who fought and bled for our liberties in the times that tried men's souls. To be sure, you run the risk of being considered a bladder of wind, or an empty barrel. But never mind that; you will find enough of the same fraternity to keep you in countenance.

"If any charity be going forward, be at the top of it, provided it is to be advertised publicly. If not, it isn't worth your while. None but a fool would place his candle under a bushel on such an occasion.

"These few directions," said I, "if properly attended to, will do your business. And when once elected—why, a fig for the dirty children, the promises, the bridges, the churches, the taxes, the offices, and the subscriptions. For it is absolutely necessary to forget all these before you can become a thoroughgoing politician, and a patriot of the first water."

Andrew Jackson

B. The Nullification Crisis

1. Senator Robert Hayne Advocates Nullification (1830)*

The restrictive "Tariff of Abominations" of 1828 had angered the South, especially the South Carolinians, who protested vehemently against an "unconstitutional" tax levied indirectly on them to support "greedy" Yankee manufacturers. An eruption finally occurred in the Senate when Senator Robert Y. Hayne of South Carolina—fluent, skillful, and personally attractive—attacked New England's inconsistency, greed, and selfishness, notably during the War of 1812. The only way to resist usurpations by the federal government, Hayne insisted, was for the states to nullify unauthorized acts of

---

Register of Debates in Congress (1829–1830), vol. 6, part 1 (January 25, 1830) p. 58.

Congress, as foreshadowed by Jefferson in the Kentucky resolutions of 1798–1799. In this peroration of his impressive speech, is Hayne a disunionist? Was he willing to let the Supreme Court rule on the unconstitutionality of acts of Congress?

Thus it will be seen, Mr. President, that the South Carolina doctrine [of nullification] is the [Jeffersonian] Republican doctrine of 1798; that it was first promulgated by the Fathers of the Faith; that it was maintained by Virginia and Kentucky in the worst of times; that it constituted the very pivot on which the political revolution of that day turned; that it embraces the very principles the triumph of which at that time saved the Constitution at its last gasp, and which New England statesmen were not unwilling to adopt [at Hartford in 1814] when they believed themselves to be the victims of unconstitutional legislation.

Sir, as to the doctrine that the federal government is the exclusive judge of the extent as well as the limitations of its powers, it seems to me to be utterly subversive of the sovereignty and independence of the states. It makes but little difference in my estimation whether Congress or the Supreme Court are invested with this power. If the federal government in all or any of its departments is to prescribe the limits of its own authority, and the states are bound to submit to the decision and are not allowed to examine and decide for themselves when the barriers of the Constitution shall be overleaped, this is practically "a government without limitation of powers." The states are at once reduced to mere petty corporations and the people are entirely at your mercy.

I have but one word more to add. In all the efforts that have been made by South Carolina to resist the unconstitutional [tariff] laws which Congress has extended over them, she has kept steadily in view the preservation of the Union by the only means by which she believes it can be long preserved—a firm, manly, and steady resistance against usurpation.

The [tariff] measures of the federal government have, it is true, prostrated her interests, and will soon involve the whole South in irretrievable ruin. But even this evil, great as it is, is not the chief ground of our complaints. It is the principle involved in the contest—a principle which, substituting the discretion of Congress for the limitations of the Constitution, brings the states and the people to the feet of the federal government and leaves them nothing they can call their own.

Sir, if the measures of the federal government were less oppressive, we should still strive against this usurpation. The South is acting on a principle she has always held sacred—resistance to unauthorized taxation.

These, sir, are the principles which induced the immortal [John] Hampden to resist the payment [in 1637] of a tax of twenty shillings [to the English government]. Would twenty shillings have ruined his fortune? No! but the payment of half twenty shillings on the principle on which it was demanded would have made him a slave.

Sir, if in acting on these high motives, if animated by that ardent love of liberty which has always been the most prominent trait in the Southern character, we should be hurried beyond the bounds of a cold and calculating prudence, who is there with one noble and generous sentiment in his bosom that would not be disposed, in the language of [Edmund] Burke, to exclaim, "You must pardon something to the spirit of liberty!"

2. Daniel Webster Pleads for the Union (1830)*

Daniel Webster, native son of New Hampshire and adopted son of Massachusetts, sprang to the defense of New England and the Union in a running debate with Hayne that lasted two weeks and ranged over many subjects. The crowded Senate galleries thrilled to the eloquence of the two parliamentary gladiators, as the states' rightism of the South clashed head-on with the buoyant nationalism of the North. Webster's main points were that the people and not the states had formed the Constitution of 1787 (here he was historically shaky); that although the people were sovereign, the national government was supreme in its sphere and the state governments were supreme in their spheres; that if each of the twenty-four states could defy the laws of Congress at will, there would be no Union but only "a rope of sand"; and that there was a better solution than nullification if the people disapproved of their fundamental law. What was it? In Webster's magnificent peroration, memorized by countless nineteenth-century schoolchildren, are liberty and Union mutually incompatible? What objective did Webster and Hayne have in common?

If anything be found in the national Constitution, either by original provision or subsequent interpretation, which ought not to be in it, the people know how to get rid of it. If any construction be established, unacceptable to them, so as to become, practically, a part of the Constitution, they will amend it, at their sovereign pleasure. But while the people choose to maintain it as it is—while they are satisfied with it, and refuse to change it—who has given, or who can give, to the state legislatures a right to alter it, either by interference, construction, or otherwise? . . .

I profess, sir, in my career, hitherto, to have kept steadily in view the prosperity and honor of the whole country, and the preservation of our Federal Union. It is to that Union we owe our safety at home and our consideration and dignity abroad. It is to that Union that we are chiefly indebted for whatever makes us most proud of our country.

That Union we reached only by the discipline of our virtues in the severe school of adversity. It had its origin in the necessities of disordered finance, prostrate commerce, and ruined credit. Under its benign influence, these great interests immediately awoke us from the dead and sprang forth with newness of life. Every year of its duration has teemed with fresh proofs of its utility and its blessings; and although our territory has stretched out wider and wider, and our population spread farther and farther, they have not outrun its protection or its benefits. It has been to us all a copious fountain of national, social, and personal happiness.

I have not allowed myself, sir, to look beyond the Union to see what might lie hidden in the dark recess behind. I have not coolly weighed the chances of preserving liberty when the bonds that unite us together shall be broken asunder. I have not accustomed myself to hang over the precipice of disunion to see whether, with my short sight, I can fathom the depth of the abyss below. Nor could I regard him as a safe counselor in the affairs of this government whose thoughts should be mainly bent on considering not how the Union should be best preserved, but how tolerable might be the condition of the people when it shall be broken up and destroyed.

The Works of Daniel Webster, 20th ed. (Boston: Little, Brown and Company, 1890), vol. 3 (January 26, 1830), pp. 340–342.

While the Union lasts we have high, exciting, gratifying prospects spread out before us—for us and our children. Beyond that, I seek not to penetrate the veil. God grant that in my day, at least, that curtain may not rise! God grant that, on my vision, never may be opened what lies behind!

When my eyes shall be turned to behold, for the last time, the sun in heaven, may I not see him shining on the broken and dishonored fragments of a once glorious Union; on states dissevered, discordant, belligerent; on a land rent with civil feuds, or drenched, it may be, in fraternal blood! Let their last feeble and lingering glance rather behold the gorgeous ensign of the Republic, now known and honored throughout the earth, still full high advanced, its arms and trophies streaming in their original luster, not a stripe erased or polluted, not a single star obscured, bearing for its motto no such miserable interrogatory as "What is all this worth?" nor those other words of delusion and folly, "Liberty first and Union afterward"; but everywhere, spread all over in characters of living light, blazing on all its ample folds, as they float over the sea and over the land, and in every wind under the whole heavens, that other sentiment, dear to every true American heart—Liberty *and* Union, now and forever, one and inseparable!

3. South Carolina Threatens Secession (1832)[*]

As if detonated by a delayed-action fuse, the tariff issue exploded during the Jackson versus Clay campaign for the presidency in 1832. The recent tariff act of 1832, though watering down the "abominable" Tariff of 1828, aroused the South Carolinians by its reassertion of the protective principle. Excitedly summoning a special convention in Columbia, they formally declared that the two tariff acts "are unauthorized by the Constitution of the United States, and violate the true meaning and intent thereof, and are null, void, and no law, nor binding upon this State, its officers or citizens." The convention specifically forbade enforcement of the federal tariff within the borders of the state and bluntly threatened secession if the federal government employed force. Before adjourning, the delegates issued the following public appeal to the American people. Comment critically on the assumption that the other Southern states would have to follow South Carolina in dissolving the Union and that the tariff law was unconstitutional. Were the South Carolinians acting in earnest?

If South Carolina should be driven out of the Union, all the other planting states, and some of the Western states, would follow by an almost absolute necessity. Can it be believed that Georgia, Mississippi, Tennessee, and even Kentucky, would continue to pay a tribute of 50 percent upon their consumption to the Northern states, for the privilege of being united to them, when they could receive all their supplies through the ports of South Carolina without paying a single cent for tribute?

The separation of South Carolina would inevitably produce a general dissolution of the Union, and, as a necessary consequence, the protecting system, with all its pecuniary bounties to the Northern states, and its pecuniary burdens upon the Southern states, would be utterly overthrown and demolished, involving the ruin of thousands and hundreds of thousands in the manufacturing states. . . .

---

[*]*Daily National Intelligencer* (Washington, DC), December 7, 1832.

With them, it is a question merely of pecuniary interest, connected with no shadow of right, and involving no principle of liberty. With us, it is a question involving our most sacred rights—those very rights which our common ancestors left to us as a common inheritance, purchased by their common toils, and consecrated by their blood. It is a question of liberty on the one hand, and slavery on the other.

If we submit to this system of unconstitutional oppression, we shall voluntarily sink into slavery, and transmit that ignominious inheritance to our children. We will not, we cannot, we dare not submit to this degradation; and our resolve is fixed and unalterable that a protecting tariff shall be no longer enforced within the limits of South Carolina. We stand upon the principles of everlasting justice, and no human power shall drive us from our position.

We have not the slightest apprehension that the General Government will attempt to force this system upon us by military power. We have warned our brethren of the consequences of such an attempt. But if, notwithstanding, such a course of madness should be pursued, we here solemnly declare that this system of oppression shall never prevail in South Carolina, until none but slaves are left to submit to it. We would infinitely prefer that the territory of the state should be the cemetery of freemen than the habitation of slaves. Actuated by these principles, and animated by these sentiments, we will cling to the pillars of the temple of our liberties, and, if it must fall, we will perish amidst the ruins.

4. Andrew Jackson Denounces Nullification (1832)*

South Carolina's defiance of the federal government, combined with its feverish military preparations, angered its most famous native son, commander-in-chief General Andrew Jackson. Privately he issued orders to strengthen federal forces in Charleston harbor. Five days after his resounding reelection over Clay, he issued the following proclamation (ghostwritten by Secretary of State Edward Livingston) appealing to the Carolinians to forsake the treacherous paths of nullification and disunion. Is his appeal to practicalities more convincing than that to patriotism? Was he prepared to negotiate with the South Carolinians?

For what would you exchange your share in the advantages and honor of the Union? For the dream of a separate independence—a dream interrupted by bloody conflicts with your neighbors and a vile dependence on a foreign power.

If your leaders could succeed in establishing a separation, what would be your situation? Are you united at home? Are you free from the apprehension of civil discord, with all its fearful consequences? Do our neighboring [Latin American] republics, every day suffering some new revolution or contending with some new insurrection, do they excite your envy?

But the dictates of a high duty oblige me solemnly to announce that you cannot succeed. The laws of the United States must be executed. I have no discretionary power on the subject; my duty is emphatically pronounced in the Constitution.

---

*J. D. Richardson, ed., *Messages and Papers of the Presidents* (New York: Bureau of National Literature, 1896), vol. 2, pp. 654–655.

Those who told you that you might peaceably prevent their execution deceived you; they could not have been deceived themselves. They know that a forcible opposition could alone prevent the execution of the laws, and they know that such opposition must be repelled. Their object is disunion.

But be not deceived by names. Disunion by armed force is treason. Are you really ready to incur its guilt? If you are, on the heads of the instigators of the act be the dreadful consequences; on their heads be the dishonor, but on yours may fall the punishment. On your unhappy state will inevitably fall all the evils of the conflict you force upon the government of your country. . . . The consequence must be fearful for you, distressing to your fellow citizens here and to the friends of good government throughout the world.

Its enemies have beheld our prosperity with a vexation they could not conceal. It was a standing refutation of their slavish doctrines, and they will point to our discord with the triumph of malignant joy. It is yet in your power to disappoint them. There is yet time to show that the descendants of the Pinckneys, the Sumters, the Rutledges, and of the thousand other names which adorn the pages of your Revolutionary history will not abandon that Union to support which so many of them fought and bled and died.

I adjure you, as you honor their memory, as you love the cause of freedom, to which they dedicated their lives, as you prize the peace of your country, the lives of its best citizens, and your own fair fame, to retrace your steps. Snatch from the archives of your state the disorganizing edict of its convention; bid its members to reassemble and promulgate the decided expressions of your will to remain in the path which alone can conduct you to safety, prosperity, and honor.

5. Jackson Fumes in Private (1832)[*]

The Unionists of South Carolina, constituting perhaps two-fifths of the adult whites, were branded "submissionists, cowards, and Tories" by the nullifiers. But the Union men, undaunted, hanged John C. Calhoun and Governor James Hamilton, Jr., in effigy, held their own convention, and gathered weapons for their defense. One of their leaders in organizing the militia, Joel R. Poinsett, wrote of his activities to Jackson, even though the post office was infiltrated with nullifiers. The doughty general replied as follows in a letter whose original spelling, punctuation, and capitalization are here preserved as revealing of Jackson and his era. Article III, Section III, para. 1 of the Constitution states: "Treason against the United States shall consist only in levying war against them, or in adhering to their enemies, giving them aid and comfort." Was Jackson correct in branding the actions of the Carolinians treasonous? Was he more bellicose in this private letter than in his recently published proclamation?

Washington, December 9, 1832.

My D'r Sir, Your letters were this moment recd, from the hands of Col. Drayton, read and duly considered, and in haste I reply. The true spirit of patriotism that they breath fills me with pleasure. If the Union party unite with you, heart and hand in

---

[*]J. S. Bassett, ed., *Correspondence of Andrew Jackson* (Washington D.C.: The Carnegie Institution, 1929), vol. 4, p. 39 (May 30, 1829).

the text you have laid down, you will not only preserve the union, but save our native state, from that ruin and disgrace into which her treasonable leaders have attempted to plunge her. All the means in my power, I will employ to enable her own citizens, those faithful patriots, who cling to the Union to put it down.

The proclamation I have this day Issued, and which I inclose you, will give you my views, of the treasonable conduct of the convention and the Governors recommendation to the assembly—it is not merely rebellion, but the act of raising troops, positive treason, and I am assured by all the members of congress with whom I have conversed that I will be sustained by congress. If so, I will meet it at the threshold, and have the leaders arrested and arraigned for treason—I am only waiting to be furnished with the acts of your Legislature, to make a communication to Congress, ask the means necessary to carry my proclamation into compleat affect, and by an exemplary punishment of those leaders for treason so unprovoked, put down this rebellion, and strengthen our happy government both at home and abroad.

My former letter and the communication from the Dept. of War, will have informed you of the arms and equipments having been laid in Deposit subject to your requisition, to aid the civil authority in the due execution of the law, *whenever called on as the posse comitatus,* etc. etc.

The vain threats of resistance by those who have raised the standard of rebellion shew their madness and folly. You may assure those patriots who cling to their country, and this union, which alone secures our liberty prosperity and happiness, that in forty days, I can have within the limits of So. Carolina fifty thousand men, and in forty days more another fifty thousand—However potant the threat of resistance with only a population of 250,000 whites and nearly that double in blacks with our ships in the port to aid in the execution of our laws?—The wickedness, madness and folly of the leaders and the delusion of their followers in the attempt to destroy themselves and our union has not its paralel in the history of the world. The Union will be preserved. The safety of the republic, the supreme law, which will be promptly obeyed by me.

I will be happy to hear from you often, thro' Col. Mason or his son, if you think the postoffice unsafe I am with sincere respect

yr mo. obdt. servt.

[Jackson's stern words, both public and private, no doubt shook the South Carolinians. Supported by no other state and riven by a Unionist minority, they finally accepted the lower schedules of the compromise Tariff of 1833.]

C. The War on the Bank

1. Jackson Vetoes the Bank Recharter (1832)*

The charter of the Second Bank of the United States was due to expire in 1836. Senator Henry Clay, seeking a surefire issue in the presidential campaign of 1832

---

*J. D. Richardson, ed., *Messages and Papers of the Presidents* (New York: Bureau of National Literature, 1896), vol. 2, pp. 589–590 (July 10, 1832).

against Jackson, arranged in Congress for a premature recharter. The assumption was that if the president vetoed the bill, he would incur the wrath of the voters. But Jackson, his ire aroused, wielded the veto pen. He denounced the bank as monopolistic, as the tool of a favored few stockholders, as a gold mine for certain foreign investors, as a citadel of special privilege, as a menace to basic liberties, and as unconstitutional to boot (although John Marshall's Supreme Court had decreed otherwise). Jackson also complained that an incomplete investigation by a House committee had recently uncovered questionable practices that needed further probing. Is Jackson, in this veto message, resorting to electioneering demagoguery? To what extent was he Jeffersonian in his views toward states' rights and the rich?

As the [Bank] charter had yet four years to run, and as a renewal now was not necessary to the successful prosecution of its business, it was to have been expected that the Bank itself, conscious of its purity and proud of its character, would have withdrawn its application for the present, and demanded the severest scrutiny into all its transactions. . . .

The Bank is professedly established as an agent of the Executive Branch of the government, and its constitutionality is maintained on that ground. Neither upon the propriety of present action nor upon the provisions of this act was the Executive consulted. It has had no opportunity to say that it neither needs nor wants an agent clothed with such powers and favored by such exemptions. There is nothing in its legitimate functions which makes it necessary or proper. Whatever interest or influence, whether public or private, has given birth to this act, it cannot be found either in the wishes or necessities of the Executive Department, by which present action is deemed premature, and the powers conferred upon its agent not only unnecessary but dangerous to the government and country.

It is to be regretted that the rich and powerful too often bend the acts of government to their selfish purposes. Distinctions in society will always exist under every just government. Equality of talents, of education, or of wealth cannot be produced by human institutions. In the full enjoyment of the gifts of heaven and the fruits of superior industry, economy, and virtue, every man is equally entitled to protection by law.

But when the laws undertake to add to these natural and just advantages artificial distinctions, to grant titles, gratuities, and exclusive privileges, to make the rich richer and the potent more powerful, the humble members of society—the farmers, mechanics, and laborers—who have neither the time nor the means of securing like favors to themselves, have a right to complain of the injustice of their government.

There are no necessary evils in government. Its evils exist only in its abuses. If it would confine itself to equal protection, and, as heaven does its rains, shower its favors alike on the high and the low, the rich and the poor, it would be an unqualified blessing. In the act before me there seems to be a wide and unnecessary departure from these just principles.

Nor is our government to be maintained or our Union preserved by invasions of the rights and powers of the several states. In thus attempting to make our General Government strong, we make it weak. Its true strength consists of leaving individuals and states as much as possible to themselves—in making itself felt, not in its power, but in its beneficence; not in its control, but in its protection; not in binding the states more closely to the center, but leaving each to move unobstructed in its proper orbit.

Experience should teach us wisdom. Most of the difficulties our government now encounters, and most of the dangers which impend over our Union, have sprung from an abandonment of the legitimate objects of government by our national legislation, and the adoption of such principles as are embodied in this act. Many of our rich men have not been content with equal protection and equal benefits, but have besought us to make them richer by act of Congress. By attempting to gratify their desires we have in the results of our legislation arrayed section against section, interest against interest, and man against man, in a fearful commotion which threatens to shake the foundations of our Union.

2. A Boston Journal Attacks Jackson (1832)*

The Bank of the United States, as Jackson charged, had undoubtedly wielded its vast power ruthlessly, arrogantly, and at times unscrupulously. Its numerous "loans" to public men had often resembled bribes. The pro-Jackson men hated it as a despotism of wealth. The pro-bank men suspected, especially after the veto message, that Jackson was trying to establish a despotism of the masses, with himself as chief despot. Senator Daniel Webster, a paid counsel for the bank, shared these fears. The Boston Daily Atlas, *a pro-Webster journal that was rapidly becoming the most influential Whig newspaper in New England, reacted with the following counterblast against Jackson's veto message. Which charge in this editorial would be most likely to arouse the anti-Jackson Whigs in the campaign then being fought between the Democrat Jackson and the Whig Clay?*

The Bank veto . . . is the most wholly radical and basely Jesuitical document that ever emanated from any administration, in any country.

It violates all our established notions and feelings. It arraigns Congress for not asking permission of the Executive before daring to legislate on the matter, and fairly intimates a design to save the two Houses in future from all such trouble.

It impudently asserts that Congress have acted prematurely, blindly, and without sufficient examination.

It falsely and wickedly alleges that the rich and powerful throughout the country are waging a war of oppression against the poor and the weak; and attempts to justify the President on the ground of its being his duty thus to protect the humble when so assailed.

Finally, it unblushingly denies that the Supreme Court is the proper tribunal to decide upon the constitutionality of the laws!!

The whole paper is a most thoroughgoing electioneering missile, intended to secure the madcaps of the South, and as such deserves the execration of all who love their country or its welfare.

This veto seems to be the production of the whole Kitchen Cabinet [an informal group of advisors to Jackson]—of hypocrisy and arrogance; of imbecility and talent;

---

*Boston Daily Atlas, quoted in the *Daily National Intelligencer* (Washington, DC), August 9, 1832.

of cunning, falsehood, and corruption—a very firebrand, intended to destroy their opponents, but which now, thanks to Him who can bring good out of evil, bids fair to light up a flame that shall consume its vile authors.

If the doctrines avowed in this document do not arouse the nation, we shall despair that anything will, until the iron hand of despotism has swept our fair land, and this glorious Republic, if not wholly annihilated, shall have been fiercely shaken to its very foundations.

3. Cartooning the Banking Crisis (1833, 1837)

Andrew Jackson believed that the Bank of the United States was a corrupt pillar of privilege that must be destroyed. Yet when a national depression occurred shortly after the charter of the bank was revoked, many observers blamed Jackson's bank policy. In the image below, Nicholas Biddle, ex-president of the Bank of the United States and president of the Bank of Pennsylvania, is shown holding the head of a violently ill "Mother Bank," while supporters of the bank—Clay, Calhoun, and Webster—consult in the sickroom, and Jackson peers in through the window. Where are the cartoonist's sympathies? The image on p. 197, "The Times," was created during the height of the financial panic of 1837. What does it portray as the worst effects of the panic? What views of the causes and consequences of Jackson's bank policies do these images provide?

Library of Congress Prints and Photographs Division [LC-USZ62-13207]

THE TIMES.

D. Transplanting the Tribes

1. Jackson Endorses the Indian Removal (1829)[*]

By the 1820s, the once "inexhaustible" land east of the Mississippi was filling up with white people and the luckless Native Americans were being elbowed aside. In response to pressure to transplant the native tribes to a "permanent" home beyond the Mississippi River, Congress took under consideration the Indian Removal Bill. President Jackson threw his powerful weight behind the movement in the following section of his first annual message to Congress. What attitude toward Indians does Jackson's speech reveal?

The condition and ulterior destiny of the Indian tribes within the limits of some of our states have become objects of much interest and importance. It has long been the policy of government to introduce among them the arts of civilization,

[*]J. D. Richardson, ed., *Messages and Papers of the Presidents* (New York: Bureau of National Literature, 1896), vol. 2, pp. 456–459 (December 8, 1829).

in the hope of gradually reclaiming them from a wandering life. This policy has, however, been coupled with another wholly incompatible with its success. Professing a desire to civilize and settle them, we have at the same time lost no opportunity to purchase their lands and thrust them farther into the wilderness. By this means they have not only been kept in a wandering state, but been led to look upon us as unjust and indifferent to their fate. . . .

Our conduct toward these people is deeply interesting to our national character. Their present condition, contrasted with what they once were, makes a most powerful appeal to our sympathies. Our ancestors found them the uncontrolled possessors of these vast regions. By persuasion and force they have been made to retire from river to river and from mountain to mountain, until some of the tribes have become extinct and others have left but remnants to preserve for awhile their once terrible names. Surrounded by the whites with their arts of civilization, which, by destroying the resources of the savage, doom him to weakness and decay, the fate of the Mohegan, the Narragansett, and the Delaware is fast overtaking the Choctaw, the Cherokee, and the Creek. That this fate surely awaits them if they remain within the limits of the states does not admit of a doubt. Humanity and national honor demand that every effort should be made to avert so great a calamity. . . .

As a means of effecting this end, I suggest for your consideration the propriety of setting apart an ample district west of the Mississippi, and without [outside] the limits of any state or territory now formed, to be guaranteed to the Indian tribes as long as they shall occupy it, each tribe having a distinct control over the portion designated for its use. There they may be secured in the enjoyment of governments of their own choice, subject to no other control from the United States than such as may be necessary to preserve peace on the frontier and between the several tribes. There the benevolent may endeavor to teach them the arts of civilization, and, by promoting union and harmony among them, to raise up an interesting commonwealth, destined to perpetuate the race and to attest the humanity and justice of this government.

This emigration should be voluntary, for it would be as cruel as unjust to compel the aborigines to abandon the graves of their fathers and seek a home in a distant land. But they should be distinctly informed that if they remain within the limits of the states they must be subject to their laws.

2. John Ross Protests Removal (1836)*

Harassed by land-hungry settlers, many of the Indian nations reluctantly ceded their tribal lands and moved west. The Cherokee, who had already made great efforts at accommodation—adopting settled agriculture, welcoming Christian missionaries and drafting a written constitution—fiercely opposed resettlement. In 1835, a small Cherokee faction signed a removal treaty with the U.S. government. Chief John Ross, a wealthy planter who was one-eighth Cherokee by blood, fought relentlessly against the fraudulent treaty until 1838, when federal troops arrived to usher him and some

---

*Gary E. Moulton, ed., *The Papers of Chief John Ross* (Norman: University of Oklahoma Press, 1985), vol. 1, pp. 459–460.

15,000 fellow Cherokees across the Mississippi. In the following appeal to Congress, how does Ross make his case against removal?

[We] are despoiled of our private possessions, the indefeasible property of individuals. We are stripped of every attribute of freedom and eligibility for legal self-defence. Our property may be plundered before our eyes; violence may be committed on our persons; even our lives may be taken away, and there is none to regard our complaints. We are denationalized; we are disfranchised. We are deprived of membership in the human family! We have neither land nor home, nor resting place that can be called our own. And this is effected by the provisions of a compact which assumes the venerated, the sacred appellation of treaty.

We are overwhelmed! Our hearts are sickened, our utterance is paralized, when we reflect on the condition in which we are placed, by the audacious practices of unprincipled men, who have managed their stratagems with so much dexterity as to impose on the Government of the United States, in the face of our earnest, solemn, and reiterated protestations. . . .

In truth, our cause is your own; it is the cause of liberty and of justice; it is based upon your own principles, which we have learned from yourselves; for we have gloried to count your [George] Washington and your [Thomas] Jefferson our great teachers; we have read their communications to us with veneration; we have practised their precepts with success. And the result is manifest. The wildness of the forest has given place to comfortable dwellings and cultivated fields, stocked with the various domestic animals. Mental culture, industrious habits, and domestic enjoyments, have succeeded the rudeness of the savage state.

We have learned your religion also. We have read your Sacred books. Hundreds of our people have embraced their doctrines, practised the virtues they teach, cherished the hopes they awaken, and rejoiced in the consolations which they afford. To the spirit of your institutions, and your religion, which has been imbibed by our community, is mainly to be ascribed that patient endurance which has characterized the conduct of our people, under the laceration of their keenest woes. For assuredly, we are not ignorant of our condition; we are not insensible to our sufferings. We feel them! we groan under their pressure! And anticipation crowds our breasts with sorrows yet to come. We are, indeed, an afflicted people! Our spirits are subdued! Despair has well nigh seized upon our energies! But we speak to the representatives of a christian country; the friends of justice; the patrons of the oppressed. And our hopes revive, and our prospects brighten, as we indulge the thought. On your sentence, our fate is suspended; prosperity or desolation depends on your word. To you, therefore, we look! Before your august assembly we present ourselves, in the attitude of deprecation, and of entreaty. On your kindness, on your humanity, on your compassion, on your benevolence, we rest our hopes. To you we address our reiterated prayers. Spare our people! Spare the wreck of our prosperity! Let not our deserted homes become the monuments of our desolation! But we forbear! We suppress the agonies which wring our hearts, when we look at our wives, our children, and our venerable sires! We restrain the forebodings of anguish and distress, of misery and devastation and death, which must be the attendants on the execution of this ruinous compact.

E. The Emergence of Mass Political Parties

1. James Fenimore Cooper Castigates Parties (1838)*

The Jacksonian Democrats, heirs of the manhood-suffrage New Democracy, had hurrahed Jackson and Martin Van Buren into the presidential chair with frothy, slogan-filled campaigns. The more aristocratic Whigs, finally stealing the thunder of the Jacksonites, hurrahed Van Buren out of the presidential chair and William Henry Harrison into it in the frothy hard-cider campaign of 1840. The political boss had now come into his own, and the national nominating conventions had become his to manipulate. The famed author of the Leatherstocking Tales, James Fenimore Cooper, after an extended sojourn abroad, returned to the United States and was shocked by what he found. The following blast, which he published in 1838, two years before the hard-cider campaign, illustrates the bitterness that involved him in protracted public controversy, including numerous libel suits. How much of his indictment seems sound? How much of it is true today?

Party is known to encourage prejudice, and to lead men astray in the judgment of character. Thus it is we see one half the nation extolling those that the other half condemns, and condemning those that the other half extols. Both cannot be right, and as passions, interests, and prejudices are all enlisted on such occasions, it would be nearer the truth to say that both are wrong.

Party is an instrument of error, by pledging men to support its policy instead of supporting the policy of the state. Thus we see party-measures almost always in extremes, the resistance of opponents inducing the leaders to ask for more than is necessary.

Party leads to vicious, corrupt, and unprofitable legislation, for the sole purpose of defeating party. Thus have we seen those territorial divisions and regulations which ought to be permanent, as well as other useful laws, altered [gerrymandered], for no other end than to influence an election. . . .

The discipline and organization of party are expedients to defeat the intention of the institutions, by putting managers in the place of the people; it being of little avail that a majority elect, when the nomination rests in the hands of a few. . . .

Party pledges the representative to the support of the Executive, right or wrong, when the institutions intend that he shall be pledged only to justice, expediency, and the right, under the restrictions of the Constitution.

When party rules, the people do not rule, but merely such a portion of the people as can manage to get the control of party. The only method by which the people can completely control the country is by electing representatives known to prize and understand the institutions; and who, so far from being pledged to support an administration, are pledged to support nothing but the right, and whose characters are guarantees that this pledge will be respected.

The effect of party is always to supplant established power. In a monarchy it checks the king; in a democracy it controls the people.

---

*James F. Cooper, *The American Democrat* (Cooperstown, NY: H. & E. Phinney, 1838), pp. 180–181.

Party, by feeding the passions and exciting personal interests, overshadows truth, justice, patriotism, and every other public virtue, completely reversing the order of a democracy by putting unworthy motives in the place of reason.

It is a very different thing to be a democrat, and to be a member of what is called a Democratic Party; for the first insists on his independence and an entire freedom of opinion, while the last is incompatible with either.

The great body of the nation has no real interest in party. Every local election should be absolutely independent of great party divisions, and until this be done, the intentions of the American institutions will never be carried out, in their excellence. . . .

No freeman who really loves liberty and who has a just perception of its dignity, character, action, and objects will ever become a mere party man. He may have his preferences as to measures and men, may act in concert with those who think with himself, on occasions that require concert. But it will be his earnest endeavor to hold himself a free agent, and most of all to keep his mind untrammeled by the prejudices, frauds, and tyranny of factions.

2. Alexis de Tocqueville Defends Parties (1830s)*

Permanently organized political parties were a novelty in the early-nineteenth-century Western world. This was especially true of the mass-based parties based on universal manhood suffrage that emerged in the United States. Cooper was not alone in regarding parties as dangerously disruptive of the consensus and harmony presumably essential to an orderly society. But Alexis de Tocqueville (1805–1859), among the shrewdest of all students of American democracy, appraised parties differently—especially in the American context of the 1830s. What did he identify as the beneficial effects of parties? What factors in the American setting did he portray as mitigating the possibly harmful effects of parties?

It must be admitted that unlimited freedom of association in the political sphere has not yet produced in America the fatal results that one might anticipate from it elsewhere. The right of association is of English origin and always existed in America. Use of this right is now an accepted part of customs and of mores.

In our own day freedom of association has become a necessary guarantee against the tyranny of the majority. In the United States, once a party has become predominant, all public power passes into its hands; its close supporters occupy all offices and have control of all organized forces. The most distinguished men of the opposite party, unable to cross the barrier keeping them from power, must be able to establish themselves outside it; the minority must use the whole of its moral authority to oppose the physical power oppressing it. Thus the one danger has to be balanced against a more formidable one.

---

*Pages 192–194 from *Democracy in America* by Alexis de Tocqueville. Edited by J. P. Mayer and Max Lerner. Translated by George Lawrence. English translation copyright © 1965 by Harper & Row, Publishers, Inc.

The omnipotence of the majority seems to me such a danger to the American republics that the dangerous expedient used to curb it is actually something good.

Here I would repeat something which I have put in other words when speaking of municipal freedom: no countries need associations more—to prevent either despotism of parties or the arbitrary rule of a prince—than those with a democratic social state. In aristocratic nations secondary bodies form natural associations which hold abuses of power in check. In countries where such associations do not exist, if private people did not artificially and temporarily create something like them, I see no other dike to hold back tyranny of whatever sort, and a great nation might with impunity be oppressed by some tiny faction or by a single man.

The meeting of a great political convention (for conventions are of all kinds), though it may often be a necessary measure, is always, even in America, a serious event and one that good patriots cannot envisage without alarm.

That came out clearly during the convention of 1831, when all the men of distinction taking part therein tried to moderate its language and limit its objective. Probably the convention of 1831 did greatly influence the attitude of the malcontents and prepared them for the open revolt of 1832 against the commercial laws of the Union.

One must not shut one's eyes to the fact that unlimited freedom of association for political ends is, of all forms of liberty, the last that a nation can sustain. While it may not actually lead it into anarchy, it does constantly bring it to the verge thereof. But this form of freedom, howsoever dangerous, does provide guarantees in one direction; in countries where associations are free, secret societies are unknown. There are factions in America, but no conspirators. . . .

The most natural right of man, after that of acting on his own, is that of combining his efforts with those of his fellows and acting together. Therefore the right of association seems to me by nature almost as inalienable as individual liberty. Short of attacking society itself, no lawgiver can wish to abolish it. However, though for some nations freedom to unite is purely beneficial and a source of prosperity, there are other nations who pervert it by their excesses and turn a fount of life into a cause of destruction. So I think it will be thoroughly useful both for governments and for political parties if I make a comparison between the different ways in which associations are used in those nations that understand what freedom is and in those where this freedom turns into license.

Most Europeans still regard association as a weapon of war to be hastily improvised and used at once on the field of battle.

An association may be formed for the purpose of discussion, but everybody's mind is preoccupied by the thought of impending action. An association is an army; talk is needed to count numbers and build up courage, but after that they march against the enemy. Its members regard legal measures as possible means, but they are never the only possible means of success.

The right of association is not understood like that in the United States. In America the citizens who form the minority associate in the first place to show their numbers and to lessen the moral authority of the majority, and secondly, by stimulating competition, to discover the arguments most likely to make an impression on the majority, for they always hope to draw the majority over to their side and then to exercise power in its name.

Political associations in the United States are therefore peaceful in their objects and legal in the means used; and when they say that they only wish to prevail legally, in general they are telling the truth.

There are several reasons for this difference between the Americans and ourselves. In Europe there are parties differing so much from the majority that they can never hope to win its support, and yet these parties believe themselves strong enough to struggle against it on their own. When such a party forms an association it intends not to convince but to fight. In America those whose opinions make a wide gap between them and the majority can do nothing to oppose its power; all others hope to win it over.

So the exercise of the right of association becomes dangerous when great parties see no possibility of becoming the majority. In a country like the United States, where differences of view are only matters of nuance, the right of association can remain, so to say, without limits.

It is our inexperience of liberty in action which still leads us to regard freedom of association as no more than a right to make war on the government. The first idea which comes into a party's mind, as into that of an individual, when it gains some strength is that of violence; the thought of persuasion only comes later, for it is born of experience. . . .

But perhaps universal suffrage is the most powerful of all the elements tending to moderate the violence of political associations in the United States. In a country with universal suffrage the majority is never in doubt, because no party can reasonably claim to represent those who have not voted at all. Therefore associations know, and everyone knows, that they do not represent the majority. The very fact of their existence proves this, for if they did represent the majority, they themselves would change the law instead of demanding reforms.

Thereby the moral strength of the government they attack is greatly increased and their own correspondingly weakened.

Thought Provokers

1. Is it true that the coming of universal manhood suffrage made for better government? Comment. Macaulay said, "The only way in which to fit a people for self-government is to entrust them with self-government." Comment. Metternich said, "Ten million ignorances do not constitute one knowledge." Comment.
2. Southern nullification did not succeed in the 1830s, yet it has been noted that informal nullification of unpopular federal laws, amendments, and court decisions has been going on for generations. Illustrate. What better or other safeguards have a minority of the states instituted against the "tyranny of the majority"? Should Jackson have taken a stronger position in public against South Carolina?
3. Why did Jackson's veto of the bank recharter appeal so strongly to the masses? Was Jackson right? Should foreigners have been allowed to hold stock in the bank? Is it better

to have aristocratically controlled financial institutions that are sound than democratically controlled financial institutions that are less sound?

4. Explain why the Indians and the whites appeared unable to live peacefully side by side. What are the moral implications of the argument that the Indians were not putting their land to good use?

5. Are political parties necessary in a democracy? How did the Republic get along without them from approximately 1815 until the 1830s? Why did they emerge when they did?

14

Forging the National Economy, 1790–1860

Take not from the mouth of labor the bread it has earned.

Thomas Jefferson, 1801

Prologue: The Industrial Revolution spawned the factory, and in turn the factory-magnet drew from the hallowed home countless men, women, and even tiny children. Alexander Hamilton himself had stressed the spiritual value of training "the little innocents" in honest habits of industry. But the exploitation of little innocents, as well as their elders, resulted in grave abuses. For more than a century, labor fought an uphill fight against employers for a gradual improvement of its lot. Meanwhile, the spread of the factory was spurred by the canal network, the river steamboat, and then the railroad. The fast-growing states of the Ohio Valley and the Upper Mississippi Valley became less dependent on the mouth of the Mississippi as the outlet for their produce, because the new arteries of transportation carried their exports cheaply and swiftly to the cities of the eastern seaboard. The ties of the Union, conspicuously in an east-west direction, were thus greatly strengthened. Meanwhile, America's foreign trade kept pace with the rate of internal economic development.

A. The Spread of the Factory

1. Wage Slavery in New England (1832)[*]

Seth Luther, a poorly educated carpenter who helped construct New England textile factories, ranks as one of the most forceful of the early labor reformers. In numerous speeches and pamphlets, he condemned such abuses as paternalistic control, "blacklists" of troublemakers, low wages, and overlong hours. He especially deplored the exploitation of children, who were sometimes dragged to "whipping rooms." His deadly earnestness and biting sarcasm were partly responsible for the United States' first law to control child labor, enacted by Massachusetts in 1842. It prohibited children under age twelve from working more than ten hours a day. What were the most serious abuses that Luther here discusses? In what specific ways were they harmful?

A [western] member of the United States Senate seems to be extremely pleased with cotton mills. He says in the Senate, "Who has not been delighted with the

---

[*]Seth Luther, *An Address to the Working Men of New England . . .* , 2nd ed. (New York: George H. Evans, 1833), pp. 17–21.

clockwork movements of a large cotton manufactory?" He had visited them often, and always with increased delight. He says the women work in large airy apartments, well warmed. They are neatly dressed, with ruddy complexions, and happy countenances. They mend the broken threads and replace the exhausted balls or broaches, and at stated periods they go to and return from their meals with light and cheerful step. (While on a visit to that pink of perfection, Waltham [Massachusetts], I remarked that the females moved with a very light step, and well they might, for the bell rang for them to return to the mill from their homes in nineteen minutes after it had rung for them to go to breakfast. Some of these females boarded the largest part of a half a mile from the mill.)

And the grand climax [says the western senator] is that at the end of the week, after working like slaves for thirteen or fourteen hours every day, "they enter the temples of God on the Sabbath, and thank him for all his benefits. . . ." We remark that whatever girls or others may do west of the Allegheny Mountains, we do not believe there can be a single person found east of those mountains who ever thanked God for permission to work in a cotton mill. . . .

We would respectfully advise the honorable Senator to travel incognito when he visits cotton mills. If he wishes to come at the truth, he must not be known. Let him put on a short jacket and trousers, and join the "lower orders" for a short time. . . . In that case we could show him, in some of the prisons in New England called cotton mills, instead of rosy cheeks, the pale, sickly, haggard countenance of the ragged child—haggard from the worse than slavish confinement in the cotton mill. He might see that child driven up to the "clockwork" by the cowskin [whip], in some cases. He might see, in some instances, the child taken from his bed at four in the morning, and plunged into cold water to drive away his slumbers and prepare him for the labors of the mill. After all this he might see that child robbed, yes, robbed of a part of his time allowed for meals by moving the hands of the clock backwards, or forwards, as would best accomplish that purpose. . . . He might see in some, and not infrequent, instances, the child, and the female child too, driven up to the "clockwork" with the cowhide, or well-seasoned strap of American manufacture.

We could show him many females who have had corporeal punishment inflicted upon them; one girl eleven years of age who had her leg broken with a billet of wood; another who had a board split over her head by a heartless monster in the shape of an overseer of a cotton mill "paradise."

We shall for want of time . . . omit entering more largely into detail for the present respecting the cruelties practiced in some of the American mills. Our wish is to show that education is neglected, . . . because if thirteen hours' actual labor is required each day, it is impossible to attend to education among children, or to improvement among adults.

2. A Factory Girl Describes Her Treatment (1844)*

Life in the mills was harsh, but for many young women, already accustomed to toiling long hours on their family farms, mill work at least offered a modicum of

---

*Harriet Farley, ed., *The Lowell Offering* (Lowell, MA: Misses Curtis and Farley, 1844), pp. 169–171, 237.

independence. Even under the paternalistic gaze of Lowell operators, girls could accumulate personal savings, acquire new friends, and socialize with members of the opposite sex. In a series of letters, a Lowell weaver reflected on the lures and liabilities of mill work. What did she find most challenging about her job? What does she see as the redeeming qualities of her new vocation?

[April] I went into the mill to work a few days after I wrote to you. It looked very pleasant at first, the rooms were so light, spacious, and clean, the girls so pretty and neatly dressed, and the machinery so brightly polished or nicely painted. The plants in the windows, or on the overseer's bench or desk, gave a pleasant aspect to things. You will wish to know what work I am doing. I will tell you of the different kinds of work.

There is, first, the carding-room, where the cotton flies most, and the girls get the dirtiest. But this is easy, and the females are allowed time to go out at night before the bell rings—on Saturday night at least, if not on all other nights. Then there is the spinning-room, which is very neat and pretty. In this room are the spinners and doffers. The spinners watch the frames; keep them clean, and the threads mended if they break. The doffers take off the full bobbins, and put on the empty ones. They have nothing to do in the long intervals when the frames are in motion, and can go out to their boarding-houses, or do any thing else that they like. In some of the factories the spinners do their own doffing, and when this is the case they work no harder than the weavers. These last have the hardest time of all—or can have, if they choose to take charge of three or four looms, instead of the one pair which is the allotment. And they are the most constantly confined. The spinners and dressers have but the weavers to keep supplied, and then their work can stop. The dressers never work before breakfast, and they stay out a great deal in the afternoons. The drawers-in, or girls who draw the threads through the harnesses, also work in the dressing-room, and they all have very good wages—better than the weavers who have but the usual work. The dressing-rooms are very neat, and the frames move with a gentle undulating motion which is really graceful. But these rooms are kept very warm, and are disagreeably scented with the "sizing," or starch, which stiffens the "beams," or unwoven webs. There are many plants in these rooms, and it is really a good green-house for them. The dressers are generally quite tall girls, and must have pretty tall minds too, as their work requires much care and attention. . . .

At first the hours seemed very long, but I was so interested in learning that I endured it very well; and when I went out at night the sound of the mill was in my ears, as of crickets, frogs, and jewsharps, all mingled together in strange discord. After that it seemed as though cotton-wool was in my ears, but now I do not mind it at all. You know that people learn to sleep with the thunder of Niagara in their ears, and a cotton mill is no worse, though you wonder that we do not have to hold our breath in such a noise.

It makes my feet ache and swell to stand so much, but I suppose I shall get accustomed to that too. The girls generally wear old shoes about their work, and you know nothing is easier; but they almost all say that when they have worked here a year or two they have to procure shoes a size or two larger than before they came.

The right hand, which is the one used in stopping and starting the loom, becomes larger than the left; but in other respects the factory is not detrimental to a young girl's appearance. Here they look delicate, but not sickly; they laugh at those who are much exposed, and get pretty brown; but I, for one, had rather be brown than pure white. I never saw so many pretty looking girls as there are here. Though the number of men is small in proportion there are many marriages here, and a great deal of courting. I will tell you of this last sometime. . . .

You ask if the girls are contented here: I ask you, if you know of *any one* who is perfectly contented. Do you remember the old story of the philosopher, who offered a field to the person who was contented with his lot; and, when one claimed it, he asked him why, if he was so perfectly satisfied, he wanted his field. The girls here are not contented; and there is no disadvantage in their situation which they do not perceive as quickly, and lament as loudly, as the sternest opponents of the factory system do. They would scorn to say they were contented, if asked the question; for it would compromise their Yankee spirit—their pride, penetration, independence, and love of "freedom and equality" to say that they were *contented* with such a life as this. Yet, withal, they are cheerful. I never saw a happier set of beings. . . .

You ask if the work is not disagreeable. Not when one is accustomed to it. It tried my patience sadly at first, and does now when it does not run well; but, in general, I like it very much. It is easy to do, and does not require very violent exertion, as much of our farm work does. . . .

[July] You complain that I do not keep my promise of being a good correspondent, but if you could know how sultry it is here, and how fatigued I am by my work this warm weather, you would not blame me. It is now that I begin to dislike these hot brick pavements, and glaring buildings. I want to be at home—to go down to the brook over which the wild grapes have made a natural arbor, and to sit by the cool spring around which the fresh soft brakes cluster so lovingly. I think of the time when, with my little bare feet, I used to follow in aunt Nabby's footsteps through the fields of corn—stepping high and long till we came to the bleaching ground; and I remember—but I must stop, for I know you wish me to write of what I am now doing, as you already know of what I have done.

3. Disaster in a Massachusetts Mill (1860)*

The lot of women factory workers in New England seemed less idyllic after an appalling accident in the five-story Pemberton textile mill, described next. George T. Strong, a prominent New York lawyer and public-spirited citizen, poured his indignation into his diary. Who was at fault? Why might the South have taken some secret satisfaction in the tragedy?

January 11 [1860]. News today of a fearful tragedy at Lawrence, Massachusetts, one of the wholesale murders commonly known in newspaper literature as accident

---

*From *The Diary of George Templeton Strong*.

or catastrophe. A huge factory, long notoriously insecure and ill-built, requiring to be patched and bandaged up with iron plates and braces to stand the introduction of its machinery, suddenly collapsed into a heap of ruins yesterday afternoon without the smallest provocation. Some five or six hundred operatives went down with it—young girls and women mostly. An hour or two later, while people were working frantically to dig out some two hundred still under the ruins, many of them alive and calling for help, some quite unhurt, fire caught in the great pile of debris, and these prisoners were roasted. It is too atrocious and horrible to think of.

Of course, nobody will be hanged. Somebody has murdered about two hundred people, many of them with hideous torture, in order to save money, but society has no avenging gibbet for the respectable millionaire and homicide. Of course not. He did not want to or mean to do this massacre; on the whole, he would have preferred to let these people live. His intent was not homicidal. He merely thought a great deal about making a large profit and very little about the security of human life. He did not compel these poor girls and children to enter his accursed mantrap. They could judge and decide for themselves whether they would be employed there. It was a matter of contract between capital and labor; they were to receive cash payment for their services.

No doubt the legal representatives of those who have perished will be duly paid the fractional part of their week's wages up to the date when they became incapacitated by crushing or combustion, as the case may be, from rendering further service. Very probably the wealthy and liberal proprietor will add (in deserving cases) a gratuity to defray funeral charges. It becomes us to prate about the horrors of slavery! What Southern capitalist trifles with the lives of his operatives as do our philanthropes of the North?

B. The Flocking of the Immigrants

1. The Burning of a Convent School (1834)[*]

The swelling tide of Irish Catholic immigrants in the Boston area intensified a long-festering prejudice against the Catholic Church. A half-dozen riots occurred before public indignation vented itself against an Ursuline convent school in Charlestown, outside Boston. Responding to ill-founded tales of abuse suffered by incarcerated nuns, a well-organized mob of about fifty men sacked and burned the four-story brick building on August 11, 1834. (Ironically, more than half of the fifty-seven pupils were Protestant girls.) Neither the authorities nor the hundreds of approving spectators made any attempt to restrain the mob. In retaliation, angry Irish laborers began to mobilize, but were restrained by Bishop Fenwick. The following editorial from the Boston Atlas expresses the widespread condemnation voiced in the press and among responsible citizens. What did this journal find most disturbing about the outrage?

[*]Quoted in *Niles' Weekly Register* 46 (August 23, 1834): 437.

From all we can learn, the violence was utterly without cause. The institution was in its very nature unpopular, and a strong feeling existed against it. But there was nothing in the vague rumors that have been idly circulating to authorize or account for any the least act of violence. We should state, perhaps, that during the violent scenes that were taking place before the convent—while the mob were breaking the windows and staving in the doors of the institution—and while the fire was blazing upon the hill as a signal to the mob—one or two muskets were discharged from the windows of the nunnery, or some of the buildings in the vicinity.

What a scene must this midnight conflagration have exhibited—lighting up the inflamed countenances of an infuriated mob of demons—*attacking a convent of women, a seminary for the instruction of young females*; and turning them out of their beds half naked in the hurry of their flight, and half dead with confusion and terror. And this drama, too, to be enacted on the very soil that afforded one of the earliest places of refuge to the Puritans of New England—themselves flying from religious persecution in the Old World—that their descendants might wax strong and mighty, and in their turn be guilty of the same persecution in the New!

We remember no parallel to this outrage in the whole course of history. Turn to the bloodiest incidents of the French Revolution . . . and point us to its equal in unprovoked violence, in brutal outrage, in unthwarted iniquity. It is in vain that we search for it. In times of civil commotion and general excitement . . . there was some palliation for violence and outrage—in the tremendously excited state of the public mind. But here there was no such palliation. The courts of justice were open to receive complaints of any improper confinement, or unauthorized coercion. The civil magistrates were, or ought to be, on the alert to detect any illegal restraint, and bring its authors to the punishment they deserve. But nothing of the kind was detected. The whole matter was a cool, deliberate, systematized piece of brutality—unprovoked—under the most provoking circumstances totally unjustifiable—and visiting the citizens of the town, and most particularly its magistrates and civil officers, with indelible disgrace.

[Local sentiment undoubtedly supported the mobsters. The subsequent trial of the ringleaders was a farce: insults were showered on the prosecution, the nuns, and the Catholic Church. Only one culprit was convicted, and he was pardoned following a petition by forgiving Catholics. The Massachusetts legislature, bowing to intimidation, dropped all efforts to provide financial recompense. Catholic churches in the area were forced to post armed guards, and for a time insurance companies refused to insure Catholic buildings built of flammable materials. The Ursuline sisters of Charlestown finally moved to Canada, and for thirty-five years the blackened brick ruins of the school remained a monument to religious bigotry.]

2. A Southerner Defends the Catholics (1854)[*]

The great flood of Irish Catholics, uprooted by the potato famine of the mid-1840s, further aroused many "native Americans." The newcomers not only worsened already

---

[*]*Congressional Globe*, 33rd Congress, 2d session, Appendix, pp. 58–59.

stinking slums but became willing voting tools of the corrupt political machines. "Nativist" resentment found vent in the powerful Know-Nothing (American) party, which undertook to elect only "natives" to office; to raise the residence requirement for naturalization from five to twenty-one years; and to exclude Roman Catholics from office, on the popular assumption that orders from the pope took precedence over their oath to support the Constitution. Yet Know-Nothingism found little support in the South. Relatively few Catholic immigrants went there, and the Catholic Church did not cry out against slavery, as did the leading Protestant denominations of the North. Representative William T. S. Barry of Mississippi, a Presbyterian with Episco-palian leanings and one of the South's great orators, here defends the Catholics in a justly famous speech. In the light of his remarks, assess the following statements: persecution strengthens the persecuted; proscriptionists become the proscribed; intolerance has no logical halfway stopping point.

The last purpose to be achieved by the Know-Nothings is the exclusion of all Catholics from office. . . . How dare we talk of freedom of conscience, when more than a million of our citizens are to be excluded from office for conscience sake!

Yesterday, to have argued in favor of religious toleration in this country would have been absurd, for none could have been found to deny or question it. But today there is a sect [Know-Nothings] boasting that it can control the country, avowing the old Papist and monarchical doctrine of political exclusion for religious opinions' sake. The arguments by which they sustain themselves are those by which the Inquisition justified their probing the consciences and burning the bodies of men five hundred years ago, and against which Protestantism has struggled since the days of Luther.

You, sir, and I, and all of us, owe our own right to worship God according to our consciences to that very doctrine which this new [Know-Nothing] order abjures; and if the right of the Catholic is first assailed and destroyed, you, sir, or another member who believes according to a different Protestant creed, may be excluded from this House, and from other preferment, because of your religious faith.

The security of all citizens rests upon the same broad basis of universal right. Confederates who disfranchise one class of citizens soon turn upon each other. The strong argument of general right is destroyed by their united action, and the proscriptionist of yesterday is the proscribed of tomorrow. Human judgment has recognized the inexorable justice of the sentence which consigned Robespierre and his accomplices [of the French Revolution] to the same guillotine to which they had condemned so many thousand better men.

No nation can content itself with a single act of persecution; either public intelligence will reject that as unworthy of itself, or public prejudice will add others to it. If the Catholic be untrustworthy as a citizen, and the public liberty is unsafe in his keeping, it is but a natural logical consequence that he shall not be permitted to disseminate a faith which is adjudged hostile to national independence; that he shall not be allowed to set the evil example of the practice of his religion before the public; that it shall not be preached from the pulpit; that it shall not be taught in the schools; and that, by all the energy of the law, it shall be utterly exterminated.

If this [Catholic] faith be incompatible with good citizenship, and you set about to discourage it—destroy it utterly, uproot it from the land. Petty persecution will but irritate a sect which the Know-Nothings denounce as so powerful and so dangerous. This was the course which England pursued when she entertained the same fears of the Catholics three hundred years ago, and which she has lived to see the absurdity of, and has removed almost, if not quite, every disability imposed. Perhaps, however, this new [Know-Nothing] sect will not startle the public mind by proposing too much at once, and holds that it will be time enough to propose further and more minute persecution when the national sentiment is debauched enough to entertain favorably this first great departure from the unbounded toleration of our fathers.

It is the experience of this country that persecution strengthens a new creed. . . . Perhaps it is true of all times and countries. . . . In my judgment, this attempt at proscription will do more to spread Catholicism here than all the treasures of Rome, or all the Jesuitism of the Cardinals.

C. Mounting Labor Unrest

1. A One-Sided Labor Contract (c. 1832)*

The plight of the factory worker in the 1830s was such as to justify the term "wage slavery." Work contracts—often a precondition of employment—gave the employer blank-check power. The following contract was used by a textile company in Dover, New Hampshire. What feature of it would be most offensive to an active trade unionist today?

We, the subscribers [the undersigned], do hereby agree to enter the service of the Cocheco Manufacturing Company, and conform, in all respects, to the regulations which are now, or may hereafter be adopted, for the good government of the institution.

We further agree to work for such wages per week, and prices by the job, as the Company may see fit to pay, and be subject to the fines as well as entitled to the premiums paid by the Company.

We further agree to allow two cents each week to be deducted from our wages for the benefit of the sick fund.

We also agree not to leave the service of the Company without giving two weeks' notice of our intention, without permission of an agent. And if we do, we agree to forfeit to the use of the Company two weeks' pay.

We also agree not to be engaged in any combination [union] whereby the work may be impeded or the Company's interest in any work injured. If we do, we agree to forfeit to the use of the Company the amount of wages that may be due to us at the time.

We also agree that in case we are discharged from the service of the Company for any fault, we will not consider ourselves entitled to be settled with in less than two weeks from the time of such discharge.

Payments for labor performed are to be made monthly.

---

*Seth Luther, *An Address to the Working Men of New England* . . . (New York: George H. Evans, 1833), p. 36.

2. Agitation for the Ten-Hour Day (1835)*

A reduction of daily working hours from thirteen or more was a primary goal of labor in the 1830s. During a third unsuccessful strike for the ten-hour day, the Boston artisans issued the following circular. It led to the successful general strike in Philadelphia on the coal wharves. What was the employers' main objection to the ten-hour day, and how did the workers try to meet it?

In the name of the Carpenters, Masons, and Stone Cutters [we] do respectfully represent—

That we are now engaged in a cause which is not only of vital importance to ourselves, our families, and our children, but is equally interesting and equally important to every mechanic in the United States and the whole world. We are contending for the recognition of the natural right to dispose of our own time in such quantities as we deem and believe to be most conducive to our own happiness and the welfare of all those engaged in manual labor.

The work in which we are now engaged is neither more nor less than a contest between money and labor. Capital, which can only be made productive by labor, is endeavoring to crush labor, the only source of all wealth.

We have been too long subjected to the odious, cruel, unjust, and tyrannical system which compels the operative mechanic to exhaust his physical and mental powers by excessive toil, until he has no desire to eat and sleep, and in many cases he has no power to do either from extreme debility. . . .

It is for the rights of humanity we contend. Our cause is the cause of philanthropy. Our opposers resort to the most degrading obloquy to injure us—not degrading to us, but to the authors of such unmerited opprobrium which they attempt to cast upon us. They tell us, "We shall spend all our hours of leisure in drunkenness and debauchery if the hours of labor are reduced." We hurl from us the base, ungenerous, ungrateful, detestable, cruel, malicious slander, with scorn and indignation. . . .

To show the utter fallacy of their idiotic reasoning, if reasoning it may be called, we have only to say they employ us about eight months in the year during the longest and the hottest days, and in short days hundreds of us remain idle for want of work for three or four months, when our expenses must of course be the heaviest during winter. When the long days again appear, our guardians set us to work, as they say, "to keep us from getting drunk." No fear has ever been expressed by these benevolent employers respecting our morals while we are idle in short days, through their avarice. . . . Further, they threaten to starve us into submission to their will. Starve us to prevent us from getting drunk!! Wonderful wisdom!! Refined benevolence!! Exalted philanthropy!!

3. Chattel Slavery Versus Wage Slavery (1840)†

Orestes A. Brownson, a self-taught Vermonter, made his mark as a preacher, magazine editor, lecturer, reformer, socialist, transcendentalist, and writer (twenty volumes).

---

*Quoted in Irving Mark and E. I. Schwaab, *The Faith of Our Fathers* (New York: Knopf, 1952), pp. 342–343.
†*Boston Quarterly Review* 3 (1840): 368–370.

Fearless and uncompromising, he began as a Presbyterian minister and wound up as a convert to Catholicism. While preaching to groups of workers, he had become deeply interested in labor reform, and his blast, given here, was music to the ears of Southern slave owners. What are his most obvious exaggerations? Was the slave owner or the mill owner the greater hypocrite?

In regard to labor, two systems obtain: one that of slave labor, the other that of free labor. Of the two, the first is, in our judgment, except so far as the feelings are concerned, decidedly the least oppressive. If the slave has never been a free man, we think, as a general rule, his sufferings are less than those of the free laborer at wages. As to actual freedom, one has just about as much as the other. The laborer at wages has all the disadvantages of freedom and none of its blessings, while the slave, if denied the blessings, is freed from the disadvantages.

We are no advocates of slavery. We are as heartily opposed to it as any modern abolitionist can be. But we say frankly that, if there must always be a laboring population distinct from proprietors and employers, we regard the slave system as decidedly preferable to the system at wages.

It is no pleasant thing to go days without food; to lie idle for weeks, seeking work and finding none; to rise in the morning with a wife and children you love, and know not where to procure them a breakfast; and to see constantly before you no brighter prospect than the almshouse.

Yet these are no infrequent incidents in the lives of our laboring population. Even in seasons of general prosperity, when there was only the ordinary cry of "hard times," we have seen hundreds of people in a not very populous village, in a wealthy portion of our common country, suffering for the want of the necessaries of life, willing to work and yet finding no work to do. Many and many is the application of a poor man for work, merely for his food, we have seen rejected. These things are little thought of, for the applicants are poor; they fill no conspicuous place in society, and they have no biographers. But their wrongs are chronicled in heaven.

It is said there is no want in this country. There may be less in some other countries. But death by actual starvation in this country is, we apprehend, no uncommon occurrence. The sufferings of a quiet, unassuming but useful class of females in our cities, in general seamstresses, too proud to beg or to apply to the almshouse, are not easily told. They are industrious; they do all that they can find to do. But yet the little there is for them to do, and the miserable pittance they receive for it, is hardly sufficient to keep soul and body together.

And yet there is a man who employs them to make shirts, trousers, etc., and grows rich on their labors. He is one of our respectable citizens, perhaps is praised in the newspapers for his liberal donations to some charitable institution. He passes among us as a pattern of morality and is honored as a worthy Christian. And why should he not be, since our Christian community is made up of such as he, and since our clergy would not dare question his piety lest they should incur the reproach of infidelity and lose their standing and their salaries? . . .

The average life—working life, we mean—of the girls that come to Lowell, for instance, from Maine, New Hampshire, and Vermont, we have been assured, is only about three years. What becomes of them then? Few of them ever marry; fewer still

trust themselves in such conveyances but preferred making their long and weary pilgrimage on foot.

2. The Impact of the Erie Canal (1853)[*]

The Erie Canal, completed in 1825, wrote epochal new chapters in the history of American transportation and industry. Projected by western-minded New Yorkers, it was bitterly opposed by New York City, which shortsightedly clung to its seaboard orientation. When the issue was debated in the state legislature and the question arose of filling the canal with water, one eastern member exclaimed, "Give yourself no trouble—the tears of our constituents will fill it!" The most immediate result of the canal was to reduce sharply the cost of moving bulk shipments. Further results were analyzed as follows in a graphic report by the secretary of the Treasury in 1853. Why did other cities lose out in competition with New York? Which section of the United States gained the most from the canal?

Although the rates of transportation over the Erie Canal, at its opening, were nearly double the present charges . . . it immediately became the convenient and favorite route for a large portion of the produce of the Northwestern states, and secured to the City of New York the position which she now holds as the emporium of the Confederacy [Union].

Previous to the opening of the Canal, the trade of the West was chiefly carried on through the cities of Baltimore and Philadelphia, particularly the latter, which was at that time the first city of the United States in population and wealth, and in the amount of its internal commerce.

As soon as the [Great] Lakes were reached, the line of navigable water was extended through them nearly one thousand miles farther into the interior. The Western states immediately commenced the construction of similar works, for the purpose of opening a communication, from the more remote portions of their territories, with this great water-line. All these works took their direction and character from the Erie Canal, which in this manner became the outlet for almost the greater part of the West.

It is difficult to estimate the influence which this Canal has exerted upon the commerce, growth, and prosperity of the whole country, for it is impossible to imagine what would have been the state of things without it.

But for this work, the West would have held out few inducements to the settler, who would have been without a market for his most important products, and consequently without the means of supplying many of his most essential wants. That portion of the country would have remained comparatively unsettled up to the present time; and, where now exist rich and populous communities, we should find an uncultivated wilderness.

The East would have been equally without the elements of growth. The Canal has supplied it with cheap food, and has opened an outlet and created a market for the products of its manufactures and commerce.

---

[*]*Senate Executive Documents*, 32d Congress, 1st session, no. 112, pp. 278–279.

The increase of commerce, and the growth of the country, have been very accurately measured by the growth of the business of the Canal. It has been one great bond of strength, infusing life and vigor into the whole. Commercially and politically, it has secured and maintained to the United States the characteristics of a homogeneous people.

E. America in the World Economy

1. United States Balance of Trade (1820–1860)*

Throughout the first half of the nineteenth century, the United States remained a minor economic power on the world stage. Though Southern planters produced more than 80% of the world's cotton, Americans continued to import most of their manufactured goods from Europe. The following table presents the magnitude and balance of U.S. trade in the antebellum era. What patterns emerge from the figures below?

	Exports (Millions $)[a]	Imports (Millions $)	Balance of Trade (Millions $)
1821–1830	69	73	−4
1831–1840	104	120	−16
1841–1850	120	118	2
1851–1860	249	284	−35

[a]All figures are annual averages.

2. Composition of U.S. Exports (1820–1850)[†]

The table below lists American exports by broad commodity categories. What products made up the bulk of U.S. exports? Which goods grew in importance as the century progressed?

	Raw Materials	Foods		Semi-Manufactures	Finished Manufactures
		Crude	Processed		
1820	60%	4%	19%	10%	6%
1830	63%	5%	17%	7%	9%
1840	68%	5%	14%	5%	10%
1850	62%	6%	15%	4%	13%

*From Susan B. Carter, et al., eds., *Historical Statistics of the United States*, Millennial ed., vol. 5, 2006, p. 499.

[†]From Stanley L. Engerman and Robert E. Gallman, eds., *Cambridge Economic History of the United States*, vol. 2, 2000, p. 702.

3. Destination of U.S. Exports (1819–1858)*

The following table shows the primary destinations for American goods. Which regions and nations received the greatest share of U.S. exports? How had trade patterns evolved by the middle of the century?

	Europe		Americas	
	Total Europe	UK	Total Americas	Canada
1819–1828	64%	34%	34%	3%
1829–1838	71%	43%	27%	3%
1839–1848	73%	47%	24%	5%
1849–1858	73%	48%	23%	8%

4. Origin of U.S. Imports (1821–1858)†

This table lists the main sources of imports to the United States. What countries served as leading suppliers of goods shipped to America? How does the distribution of U.S. imports compare with the distribution of exports in the table above?

	Europe			Americas				Asia
	Total Europe	UK	France	Total Americas	Canada	Cuba	Brazil	Total
1821–1828	63%	40%	10%	26%	<1%	9%	2%	11%
1829–1838	64%	37%	15%	22%	1%	8%	4%	8%
1839–1848	67%	38%	19%	25%	1%	8%	5%	8%
1849–1858	66%	42%	14%	26%	4%	8%	6%	7%

Thought Provokers

1. What were the principal effects of industrialization on women and the family?
2. Compare the ways in which anti-foreignism manifests itself in the United States today with those of the 1850s and 1860s. Has the nation grown more tolerant?
3. Were the rich of the 1830s really exploiting the workers, or were they providing them with job opportunities? Would you rather have been a black slave in the South or a wage

---

*From Stanley L. Engerman and Robert E. Gallman, eds., *Cambridge Economic History of the United States*, vol. 2, 2000, p. 713.

†From Stanley L. Engerman and Robert E. Gallman, eds., *Cambridge Economic History of the United States*, vol. 2, 2000, p. 714.

slave in a New England factory? Argue both sides. In what noteworthy respects is labor better off today than it was in the 1830s, and why?

4. Why can it be asserted with plausibility that the Erie Canal won the Civil War for the North? Would there have been a Civil War if there had been no Erie Canal? Do contrasting economies tend to divide sections or to unite them because of their dependence on one another?

5. How did the role of the United States in the global economy evolve in the first half of the nineteenth century? What distinguished American manufacturers from their European counterparts?

15

The Ferment of Reform and Culture, 1790–1860

I could readily see in Emerson, notwithstanding his merit, a gaping flaw. It was the insinuation that, had he lived in those days when the world was made, he might have offered some valuable suggestions.

Herman Melville, 1849

Prologue: The War of Independence, the War of 1812, and the astonishing physical mobility of westward-pushing Americans disrupted the traditional churches and undermined cultural conventions of all sorts. Beginning in the early nineteenth century, a wave of religious revivals swept across the country, checking backsliding and summoning the people back to the hellfire religion of colonial days. The revivals of this "Second Great Awakening" inspired a host of humanitarian crusades—including campaigns for prison reform, temperance, women's rights, and, eventually, the abolition of slavery. The combined effects of industrialism and democracy initiated far-reaching changes in the character of the family and in the roles of women. Meanwhile, an impressive group of writers, based mainly in New England, laid the foundations of a distinctively American literary tradition, which contained (perhaps paradoxically) healthy doses of social utopianism and unbridled individualism.

A. Religious Ferment

1. An Englishwoman Attends a Revival (1832)[*]

Determined to expose the crude realities of American democracy to the British public, Frances Trollope could not pass up an opportunity to experience one of the frontier's celebrated camp meetings, which attracted a diverse mix of attendees, from devout evangelicals to curious spectators. Women and African Americans, both slave and free, were well represented at the gatherings, which promised salvation irrespective of race, gender, or social standing. To the uninitiated, like Trollope, the shrieks and howls that drifted from the revival tents seemed a perversion of the decorous services found in more traditional churches. What elements does Trollope find most distasteful? What do her reactions reveal about her own worldview?

[*]Frances Trollope, *Domestic Manners of the Americans* (Oxford: Oxford University Press, 1984), pp. 140–143.

We made the circuit of the tents, pausing where attention was particularly excited by sounds more vehement than ordinary. We contrived to look into many; all were strewed with straw, and the distorted figures that we saw kneeling, sitting, and lying amongst it, joined to the woful and convulsive cries, gave to each the air of a cell in Bedlam.

One tent was occupied exclusively by negroes. They were all full-dressed, and looked exactly as if they were performing a scene on the stage. One woman wore a dress of pink gauze trimmed with silver lace; another was dressed in pale yellow silk; one or two had splendid turbans; and all wore a profusion of ornaments. The men were in snow white pantaloons, with gay coloured linen jackets. One of these, a youth of coal-black comeliness, was preaching with the most violent gesticulations, frequently springing high from the ground, and clapping his hands over his head. Could our missionary societies have heard the trash he uttered, by way of an address to the Deity, they might perhaps have doubted whether his conversion had much enlightened his mind.

At midnight a horn sounded through the camp, which, we were told, was to call the people from private to public worship; and we presently saw them flocking from all sides to the front of the preachers' stand. . . . There were about two thousand persons assembled. . . .

[A]bove a hundred persons, nearly all females, came forward, uttering howlings and groans so terrible that I shall never cease to shudder when I recall them. They appeared to drag each other forward, and, on the word being given "Let us pray", they all fell on their knees; but this posture was soon changed for others that permitted greater scope for the convulsive movements of their limbs; and they were soon all lying on the ground in an indescribable confusion of heads and legs. They threw about their limbs with such incessant and violent motion, that I was every instant expecting some serious accident to occur. . . .

I saw the insidious lips approach the cheeks of the unhappy girls; I heard the murmured confessions of the poor victims, and I watched their tormentors, breathing into their ears consolations that tinged the pale cheek with red. Had I been a man, I am sure I should have been guilty of some rash act of interference; nor do I believe that such a scene could have been acted in the presence of Englishmen without instant punishment being inflicted; not to mention the salutary discipline of the treadmill, which, beyond all question, would, in England, have been applied to check so turbulent and so vicious a scene.

2. Joseph Smith Has a Vision (1820)*

Joseph Smith, prophet and first president of the Church of Jesus Christ of Latter-Day Saints (Mormons), was born in Vermont and moved as a young boy with his family to the town of Manchester, in western New York. The region was at that time pulsating with religious fervor and denominational rivalry. Pious but confused, the fourteen-year-old Smith prayed for guidance. The result, he later wrote, was a vision that led him to shun the contending existing churches and move toward the establishment of

_____

*From Joseph Smith, *The Pearl of Great Price* (Salt Lake City: Deseret Book Co., 1920), chap. 1, verses 5, 7–24, 26.

the Mormon religion. In his account of the episode, which follows, what is revealed about the religious temper of the age?

Some time in the second year after our removal to Manchester, there was in the place where we lived an unusual excitement on the subject of religion. It commenced with the Methodists, but soon became general among all the sects in that region of country. Indeed, the whole district of country seemed affected by it, and great multitudes united themselves to the different religious parties, which created no small stir and division amongst the people. . . .

I was at this time in my fifteenth year. My father's family was proselyted to the Presbyterian faith, and four of them joined that church. . . . In process of time my mind became somewhat partial to the Methodist sect, and I felt some desire to be united with them; but so great were the confusion and strife among the different denominations, that it was impossible for a person young as I was, and so unacquainted with men and things, to come to any certain conclusion who was right and who was wrong. My mind at times was greatly excited, the cry and tumult were so great and incessant. The Presbyterians were most decided against the Baptists and Methodists, and used all the powers of both reason and sophistry to prove their errors, or, at least, to make the people think they were in error. On the other hand, the Baptists and Methodists in their turn were equally zealous in endeavoring to establish their own tenets and disprove all others.

In the midst of this war of words and tumult of opinions, I often said to myself, what is to be done? Who of all these parties are right; or, are they all wrong together? If any one of them be right, which is it, and how shall I know it? While I was laboring under the extreme difficulties caused by the contests of these parties of religionists, I was one day reading the Epistle of James, first chapter and fifth verse, which reads: "If any of you lack wisdom, let him ask of God, that giveth to all men liberally, and upbraideth not; and it shall be given him."

Never did any passage of Scripture come with more power to the heart of man than this did at this time to mine. . . . I at length came to the determination to "ask of God," concluding that if He gave wisdom to them that lacked wisdom, and would give liberally, and not upbraid, I might venture. So, in accordance with this, my determination to ask God, I returned to the woods to make the attempt. It was on the morning of a beautiful, clear day, early in the spring of eighteen hundred and twenty. It was the first time in my life I had made such an attempt, for amidst all my anxieties I had never as yet made the attempt to pray vocally.

After I had retired to the place where I had previously designed to go, having looked around me, and finding myself alone, I kneeled down and began to offer up the desires of my heart to God. I had scarcely done so, when immediately I was seized upon by some power which entirely overcame me, and had such an astonishing influence over me as to bind my tongue so that I could not speak . . . and at the very moment when I was ready to sink into despair and abandon myself to destruction—not to an imaginary ruin, but to the power of some actual being from the unseen world, who had such marvelous power as I had never before felt in any being—just at this moment of great alarm, I saw a pillar of light exactly over my head, above the brightness of the sun, which descended gradually until it fell upon me.

It no sooner appeared than I found myself delivered from the enemy which held me bound. When the light rested upon me I saw two personages, whose brightness and glory defy all description, standing above me in the air. One of them spake unto me, calling me by name, and said—pointing to the other—"This is my beloved Son. Hear Him."

My object in going to inquire of the Lord was to know which of all the sects was right, that I might know which to join. No sooner, therefore, did I get possession of myself, so as to be able to speak, than I asked the personages who stood above me in the light, which of all the sects was right—and which I should join. I was answered that I must join none of them, for they were all wrong, and the personage who addressed me said that all their creeds were an abomination in His sight: that those professors were all corrupt. . . . When I came to myself again, I found myself lying on my back, looking up into heaven. When the light had departed, I had no strength; but soon recovering in some degree, I went home. And as I leaned up to the fireplace, mother inquired what the matter was. I replied, "Never mind, all is well—I am well enough off." I then said to my mother, "I have learned for myself that Presbyterianism is not true."

It seems as though the adversary was aware, at a very early period of my life, that I was destined to prove a disturber and an annoyer of his kingdom; else why should the powers of darkness combine against me? Why the opposition and persecution that arose against me, almost in my infancy . . . ? I soon found, however, that my telling the story had excited a great deal of prejudice against me among professors of religion, and was the cause of great persecution, which continued to increase; and though I was an obscure boy, only between fourteen and fifteen years of age, and my circumstances in life such as to make a boy of no consequence in the world, yet men of high standing would take notice sufficient to excite the public mind against me, and create a bitter persecution; and this was common among all the sects—all united to persecute me.

It caused me serious reflection then, and often has since, how very strange it was that an obscure boy, of a little over fourteen years of age, and one, too, who was doomed to the necessity of obtaining a scanty maintenance by his daily labor, should be thought a character of sufficient importance to attract the attention of the great ones of the most popular sects of the day, and in a manner to create in them a spirit of the most bitter persecution and reviling. But strange or not, so it was, and it was often the cause of great sorrow to myself. However, it was nevertheless a fact that I had beheld a vision.

B. Social and Humanitarian Reformers

1. William Ellery Channing Preaches Reformism (c. 1831)[*]

The famed Boston minister William Ellery Channing (1780–1842) was a leading light in the Unitarian movement, which criticized Calvinistic Puritanism for its

---

[*]William Ellery Channing, *Channing's Works* (Boston: American Unitarian Association, 1895), pp. 1001–1005.

emphasis on human depravity. Channing, in contrast, preached a gospel of human goodness, dignity, and even perfectibility. Such doctrines gave powerful impetus to the reform crusades of the early nineteenth century. In the following sermon, entitled "The Perfect Life: The Essence of the Christian Religion," how does Channing support his arguments for perfectionism? How does he portray the relationship of religious belief to worldly actions?

I believe that Christianity has one great principle, which is central, around which all its truths gather, and which constitutes it the glorious gospel of the blessed God. I believe that no truth is so worthy of acceptance and so quickening as this. In proportion as we penetrate into it, and are penetrated by it, we comprehend our religion, and attain to a living faith. This great principle can be briefly expressed. It is the doctrine that "God purposes, in his unbounded fatherly love, to perfect the human soul; to purify it from all sin; to create it after his own image; to fill it with his own spirit; to unfold it for ever; to raise it to life and immortality in heaven—that is, to communicate to it from himself a life of celestial power, virtue, and joy." The elevation of men above the imperfections, temptations, sins, sufferings, of the present state, to a diviner being,—this is the great purpose of God, revealed and accomplished by Jesus Christ; this it is that constitutes the religion of Jesus Christ,—glad tidings to all people: for it is a religion suited to fulfill the wants of every human being.

When I look into man's nature, I see that moral perfection is his only true and enduring good; and consequently the promise of this must be the highest truth which any religion can contain. The loftiest endowment of our nature is the moral power,—the power of perceiving and practising virtue, of discerning and seeking goodness. . . .

At this period, we see a mighty movement of the civilized world. Thrones are tottering, and the firmest establishments of former ages seem about to be swept away by the torrent of revolution. In this movement I rejoice, though not without trembling joy. But I rejoice, only because I look at it in the light of the great truth which I have this day aimed to enforce; because I see, as I think, in the revolutionary spirit of our times, the promise of a freer and higher action of the human mind,—the pledge of a state of society more fit to perfect human beings. I regard the present state of the world in this moral light altogether. The despotisms, which are to be prostrated, seem to be evils, chiefly as they have enslaved men's faculties, as they have bowed and weighed down the soul. The liberty, after which men aspire, is to prove a good only so far as it shall give force and enlargement to the mind; only so far as it shall conspire with Christianity in advancing human nature. Men will gain little by escaping outward despotism, if the soul continues enthralled. Men must be subjected to some law; and unless the law in their own breast, the law of God, of duty, of perfection, be adopted by their free choice as the supreme rule, they will fall under the tyranny of selfish passion, which will bow their necks for an outward yoke.

I have hope in the present struggle of the world, because it seems to me more spiritual, more moral, in its origin and tendencies, than any which have preceded it. It differs much from the revolts of former times, when an oppressed populace or peasantry broke forth into frantic opposition to government, under the goading pressure of famine and misery. Men are now moved, not merely by physical wants and sufferings, but by ideas, by principles, by the conception of a better state of society, under which the rights of human nature will be recognized, and greater justice be done to the mind in all classes of the community. There is then an element— spiritual, moral, and tending towards perfection—in the present movement; and this is my great hope.

2. Dorothea Dix Succors the Insane (1843)*

In 1840 there were only eight insane asylums in the twenty-six states. The overflow, regarded as perverse, were imprisoned or chained in poorhouses, jails, and houses of correction. Schoolteacher Dorothea Dix—a frail, soft-spoken spinster from New England who lived to be eighty-five despite incipient tuberculosis—almost single- handedly wrought a revolution. Filled with infinite compassion for these outcasts, she journeyed thousands of wearisome miles to investigate conditions and to appeal to state legislatures. Despite the powerful prejudice against women who were outspo- ken in public, she succeeded in securing modern facilities with trained attendants. Her horrifying report to the Massachusetts legislature is a classic. In the following excerpt, where does she lay the blame for the existing conditions?

I must confine myself to few examples, but am ready to furnish other and more complete details, if required. If my pictures are displeasing, coarse, and severe, my subjects, it must be recollected, offer no tranquil, refined, or composing features. The condition of human beings, reduced to the extremest states of degradation and misery, cannot be exhibited in softened language, or adorn a polished page.

I proceed, gentlemen, briefly to call your attention to the present state of insane persons confined within this Commonwealth, in cages, closets, cellars, stalls, pens! Chained, naked, beaten with rods, and lashed into obedience!

As I state cold, severe facts, I feel obliged to refer to persons, and definitely to indicate localities. But it is upon my subject, not upon localities or individuals, I desire to fix attention. And I would speak as kindly as possible of all wardens, keepers, and other responsible officers, believing that most of these have erred not through hardness of heart and willful cruelty so much as want of skill and knowl- edge, and want of consideration.

Familiarity with suffering, it is said, blunts the sensibilities, and where neglect once finds a footing, other injuries are multiplied. This is not all, for it may justly and strongly be added that, from the deficiency of adequate means to meet the wants of these cases, it has been an absolute impossibility to do justice to this mat- ter. Prisons are not constructed in view of being converted into county hospitals, and almshouses are not founded as receptacles for the insane. And yet, in the face of justice and common sense, wardens are by law compelled to receive, and the masters of almshouses not to refuse, insane and idiotic subjects in all stages of men- tal disease and privation.

Old South Leaflets (Boston: Old South Meeting House, 1904), vol. 6, pp. 490–491, 493–494, 513, 518–519.

It is the Commonwealth, not its integral parts, that is accountable for most of the abuses which have lately [existed] and do still exist. I repeat it, it is defective legislation which perpetuates and multiplies these abuses. . . .

Danvers. November. Visited the almshouse. A large building, much out of repair. Understand a new one is in contemplation. Here are fifty-six to sixty inmates, one idiotic, three insane, one of the latter in close confinement at all times.

Long before reaching the house, wild shouts, snatches of rude songs, imprecations and obscene language, fell upon the ear, proceeding from the occupant of a low building, rather remote from the principal building to which my course was directed. Found the mistress, and was conducted to the place which was called "the home" of the forlorn maniac, a young woman, exhibiting a condition of neglect and misery blotting out the faintest idea of comfort, and outraging every sentiment of decency. She had been, I learned, "a respectable person, industrious and worthy. Disappointments and trials shook her mind, and, finally, laid prostrate reason and self-control. She became a maniac for life. She had been at Worcester Hospital for a considerable time, and had been returned as incurable." The mistress told me she understood that, "while there, she was comfortable and decent."

Alas, what a change was here exhibited! She had passed from one degree of violence to another, in swift progress. There she stood, clinging to or beating upon the bars of her caged apartment, the contracted size of which afforded space only for increasing accumulations of filth, a foul spectacle. There she stood with naked arms and disheveled hair, the unwashed frame invested with fragments of unclean garments, the air so extremely offensive though ventilation was afforded on all sides save one, that it was not possible to remain beyond a few moments without retreating for recovery to the outward air. Irritation of body, produced by utter filth and exposure, incited her to the horrid process of tearing off her skin by inches. Her face, neck, and person were thus disfigured to hideousness. She held up a fragment just rent off. To my exclamation of horror, the mistress replied: "Oh, we can't help it. Half the skin is off sometimes. We can do nothing with her; and it makes no difference what she eats, for she consumes her own filth as readily as the food which is brought her." . . .

The conviction is continually deepened that hospitals are the only places where insane persons can be at once humanely and properly controlled. Poorhouses converted into madhouses cease to effect the purposes for which they were established, and instead of being asylums for the aged, the homeless, and the friendless, and places of refuge for orphaned or neglected childhood, are transformed into perpetual bedlams. . . .

Injustice is also done to the convicts. It is certainly very wrong that they should be doomed day after day and night after night to listen to the ravings of madmen and madwomen. This is a kind of punishment that is not recognized by our statutes, and is what the criminal ought not to be called upon to undergo. The confinement of the criminal and of the insane in the same building is subversive of the good order and discipline which should be observed in every well-regulated prison. . . .

Gentlemen, I commit to you this sacred cause. Your action upon this subject will affect the present and future condition of hundreds and of thousands.

3. T. S. Arthur's Ten Nights in a Barroom (1854)[*]

T. S. Arthur, an ill-educated New Yorker, became the moralistic author of seventy books and countless articles. His lurid Ten Nights in a Barroom *was the* Uncle Tom's Cabin *of the temperance crusade, and second only to* Uncle Tom's Cabin *as the best seller of the 1850s. Endorsed by the clergy, it was put on the stage for an incredible run. Although the author was a foe of saloons, he was not a teetotaler, and he consistently advocated temperance by education rather than prohibition by legislation. In his famous novel, Simon Slade's tavern (the Sickle and Sheaf) is portrayed as the ruination of quiet Cedarville. After numerous heart-tugging tragedies, the climax comes when the drunken tavern owner is murdered with a brandy bottle by his drunken son. Earlier in the book, the following conversation takes place. Enumerate and assess the arguments on both sides, and evaluate this interchange as propaganda in the battle against the bottle.*

The man, who had until now been sitting quietly in a chair, started up, exclaiming as he did so—

"Merciful heavens! I never dreamed of this! Whose sons are safe?"

"No man's," was the answer of the gentleman in whose office we were sitting; "no man's—while there are such open doors to ruin as you may find at the 'Sickle and Sheaf.' Did not you vote the anti-temperance ticket at the last election?"

"I did," was the answer, "and from principle."

"On what were your principles based?" was inquired.

"On the broad foundations of civil liberty."

"The liberty to do good or evil, just as the individual may choose?"

"I would not like to say that. There are certain evils against which there can be no legislation that would not do harm. No civil power in this country has the right to say what a citizen shall eat or drink."

"But may not the people, in any community, pass laws, through their delegated lawmakers, restraining evil-minded persons from injuring the common good?"

"Oh, certainly—certainly."

"And are you prepared to affirm that a drinking shop, where young men are corrupted—ay, destroyed, body and soul—does not work an injury to the common good?"

"Ah! but there must be houses of public entertainment."

"No one denies this. But can that be a really Christian community which provides for the moral debasement of strangers, at the same time that it entertains them? Is it necessary that, in giving rest and entertainment to the traveler, we also lead him into temptation?"

"Yes—but—but—it is going too far to legislate on what we are to eat and drink. It is opening too wide a door for fanatical oppression. We must inculcate temperance as a right principle. We must teach our children the evils of intemperance, and send them out into the world as practical teachers of order, virtue, and sobriety. If we do this, the reform becomes radical, and in a few years there will be no barrooms, for none will crave the fiery poison."

---

[*]T. S. Arthur, "Night the Sixth," *Ten Nights in a Barroom* (Boston: L. P. Crown, 1854).

"Of little value, my friend, will be, in far too many cases, your precepts, if temptation invites our sons at almost every step of their way through life. Thousands have fallen, and thousands are now tottering, soon to fall. Your sons are not safe, nor are mine. We cannot tell the day nor the hour when they may weakly yield to the solicitation of some companion, and enter the wide-open door of ruin. . . . Sir! while you hold back from the work of staying the flood that is desolating our fairest homes, the black waters are approaching your own doors."

There was a startling emphasis in the tones with which this last sentence was uttered, and I did not wonder at the look of anxious alarm that it called to the face of him whose fears it was meant to excite.

"What do you mean, sir?" was inquired.

"Simply, that your sons are in equal danger with others."

"And is that all?"

"They have been seen of late in the barroom of the 'Sickle and Sheaf.' "

"Who says so?"

"Twice within a week I have seen them going in there," was answered.

"Good heavens! No!"

"It is true, my friend. But who is safe? If we dig pits and conceal them from view, what marvel if our own children fall therein?"

"My sons going to a tavern!" The man seemed utterly confounded. "How can I believe it? You must be in error, sir."

"No. What I tell you is the simple truth."

C. The Changing Role of Women

1. The Seneca Falls Manifesto (1848)[*]

Lucretia C. Mott, a militant antislavery Quaker, received her first harsh lesson in feminism when, as a teacher, she was paid half a man's salary. Elizabeth C. Stanton, also a temperance and antislavery reformer, insisted on leaving the word "obey" out of her marriage ceremony. Both were aroused when, attending the World Anti-Slavery Convention in London in 1840, they were denied seats because of their sex. These two women sparked the memorable convention at Seneca Falls, New York, that formally launched the modern women's rights movement. The embattled women issued a flaming pronouncement in the manner of the Declaration of Independence ("all men and women are created equal"). They not only proclaimed their grievances but also passed eleven resolutions designed to improve their lot. Which of the grievances listed here remain unresolved today?

Declaration of Sentiments

When, in the course of human events, it becomes necessary for one portion of the family of man to assume among the people of the earth a position different from

---

[*]Elizabeth Cady Stanton, Susan B. Anthony, and Matilda Joslyn Gage, eds., *History of Woman Suffrage* (New York: Fowler & Wells, 1881), vol. 1, pp. 70–71.

that which they have hitherto occupied, but one to which the laws of nature and of nature's God entitle them, a decent respect to the opinions of mankind requires that they should declare the causes that impel them to such a course.

We hold these truths to be self-evident: that all men and women are created equal; that they are endowed by their Creator with certain inalienable rights; that among these are life, liberty, and the pursuit of happiness; that to secure these rights governments are instituted, deriving their just powers from the consent of the governed. Whenever any form of government becomes destructive of these ends, it is the right of those who suffer from it to refuse allegiance to it, and to insist upon the institution of a new government, laying its foundation on such principles, and organizing its powers in such form, as to them shall seem most likely to effect their safety and happiness. Prudence, indeed, will dictate that governments long established should not be changed for light and transient causes; and accordingly all experience hath shown that mankind are more disposed to suffer, while evils are sufferable, than to right themselves by abolishing the forms to which they were accustomed. But when a long train of abuses and usurpations, pursuing invariably the same object, evinces a design to reduce them under absolute despotism, it is their duty to throw off such government, and to provide new guards for their future security. Such has been the patient sufferance of the women under this government, and such is now the necessity which constrains them to demand the equal station to which they are entitled.

The history of mankind is a history of repeated injuries and usurpations on the part of man toward woman, having in direct object the establishment of an absolute tyranny over her. To prove this, let facts be submitted to a candid world.

He has never permitted her to exercise her inalienable right to the elective franchise.

He has compelled her to submit to laws, in the formation of which she had no voice.

He has withheld from her rights which are given to the most ignorant and degraded men—both natives and foreigners.

Having deprived her of this first right of a citizen, the elective franchise, thereby leaving her without representation in the halls of legislation, he has oppressed her on all sides.

He has made her, if married, in the eye of the law, civilly dead.

He has taken from her all right in property, even to the wages she earns.

He has made her, morally, an irresponsible being, as she can commit many crimes with impunity, provided they be done in the presence of her husband. In the covenant of marriage, she is compelled to promise obedience to her husband, he becoming, to all intents and purposes, her master—the law giving him power to deprive her of her liberty, and to administer chastisement.

He has so framed the laws of divorce, as to what shall be the proper causes, and in case of separation, to whom the guardianship of the children shall be given, as to be wholly regardless of the happiness of women—the law, in all cases, going upon the false supposition of the supremacy of man, and giving all power into his hands.

After depriving her of all rights as a married woman, if single, and the owner of property, he has taxed her to support a government which recognizes her only when her property can be made profitable to it.

He has monopolized nearly all the profitable employments, and from those she is permitted to follow, she receives but a scanty remuneration. He closes against her all the avenues to wealth and distinction which he considers most honorable to himself. As a teacher of theology, medicine, or law, she is not known.

He has denied her the facilities for obtaining a thorough education, all colleges being closed against her.

He allows her in Church, as well as State, but a subordinate position, claiming Apostolic authority for her exclusion from the ministry, and, with some exceptions, from any public participation in the affairs of the Church.

He has created a false public sentiment by giving to the world a different code of morals for men and women, by which moral delinquencies which exclude women from society, are not only tolerated, but deemed of little account in man.

He has usurped the prerogative of Jehovah himself, claiming it as his right to assign for her a sphere of action, when that belongs to her conscience and to her God.

He has endeavored, in every way that he could, to destroy her confidence in her own powers, to lessen her self-respect, and to make her willing to lead a dependent and abject life.

Now, in view of this entire disfranchisement of one-half the people of this country, their social and religious degradation—in view of the unjust laws above mentioned, and because women do feel themselves aggrieved, oppressed, and fraudulently deprived of their most sacred rights, we insist that they have immediate admission to all the rights and privileges which belong to them as citizens of the United States.

In entering upon the great work before us, we anticipate no small amount of misconception, misrepresentation, and ridicule; but we shall use every instrumentality within our power to effect our object. We shall employ agents, circulate tracts, petition the State and National legislatures, and endeavor to enlist the pulpit and the press in our behalf. We hope this Convention will be followed by a series of Conventions embracing every part of the country.

Resolutions

WHEREAS, The great precept of nature is conceded to be, that "man shall pursue his own true and substantial happiness." Blackstone in his Commentaries remarks, that this law of Nature being coeval with mankind, and dictated by God himself, is of course superior in obligation to any other. It is binding over all the globe, in all countries and at all times; no human laws are of any validity if contrary to this, and such of them as are valid, derive all their force, and all their validity, and all their authority, mediately and immediately, from this original; therefore,

Resolved, That such laws as conflict, in any way, with the true and substantial happiness of woman, are contrary to the great precept of nature and of no validity, for this is "superior in obligation to any other."

Resolved, That all laws which prevent woman from occupying such a station in society as her conscience shall dictate, or which place her in a position inferior to that of man, are contrary to the great precept of nature, and therefore of no force or authority.

Resolved, That woman is man's equal—was intended to be so by the Creator, and the highest good of the race demands that she should be recognized as such.

Resolved, That the women of this country ought to be enlightened in regard to the laws under which they live, that they may no longer publish their degradation by declaring themselves satisfied with their present position, nor their ignorance, by asserting that they have all the rights they want.

Resolved, That inasmuch as man, while claiming for himself intellectual superiority, does accord to woman moral superiority, it is pre-eminently his duty to encourage her to speak and teach, as she has an opportunity, in all religious assemblies.

Resolved, That the same amount of virtue, delicacy, and refinement of behavior that is required of woman in the social state, should also be required of man, and the same transgressions should be visited with equal severity on both man and woman.

Resolved, That the objection of indelicacy and impropriety, which is so often brought against woman when she addresses a public audience, comes with a very ill-grace from those who encourage, by their attendance, her appearance on the stage, in the concert, or in feats of the circus.

Resolved, That woman has too long rested satisfied in the circumscribed limits which corrupt customs and a perverted application of the Scriptures have marked out for her, and that it is time she should move in the enlarged sphere which her great Creator has assigned her.

Resolved, That it is the duty of the women of this country to secure to themselves their sacred right to the elective franchise.

Resolved, That the equality of human rights results necessarily from the fact of the identity of the race in capabilities and responsibilities.

Resolved, therefore, That, being invested by the Creator with the same capabilities, and the same consciousness of responsibility for their exercise, it is demonstrably the right and duty of woman, equally with man, to promote every righteous cause by every righteous means; and especially in regard to the great subjects of morals and religion, it is self-evidently her right to participate with her brother in teaching them, both in private and in public, by writing and by speaking, by any instrumentalities proper to be used, and in any assemblies proper to be held; and this being a self-evident truth growing out of the divinely implanted principles of human nature, any custom or authority adverse to it, whether modern or wearing the hoary sanction of antiquity, is to be regarded as a self-evident falsehood, and at war with mankind.

Resolved, That the speedy success of our cause depends upon the zealous and untiring efforts of both men and women, for the overthrow of the monopoly of the pulpit, and for the securing to woman an equal participation with men in the various trades, professions, and commerce.

2. New Yorkers Ridicule Feminists (1856)[*]

Male opponents of feminism claimed that the female crusaders were frustrated old maids (many, in fact, were married); that women would become coarsened and defeminized by entering the cutthroat arena of politics; that their husbands (if they were lucky enough to have husbands) would look after their rights; and that women,

---

[*]Elizabeth Cady Stanton et al., eds., *History of Woman Suffrage* (1881), vol. 1, pp. 629–630.

like black slaves, were divinely ordained to be inferior and would be happier in that status. An editorial in the New York Herald wondered what would happen if pregnant sea captains, generals, members of Congress, physicians, and lawyers were suddenly seized with birth pangs in critical situations. The following official report reveals the joking condescension with which the New York legislature approached the problem. How might feminists have answered these jibes?

Mr. Foote, from the Judiciary Committee, made a report on Women's Rights that set the whole House in roars of laughter:

"The Committee is composed of married and single gentlemen. The bachelors on the Committee, with becoming diffidence, have left the subject pretty much to the married gentlemen. They have considered it with the aid of the light they have before them and the experience married life has given them. Thus aided, they are enabled to state that the ladies always have the best place and choicest tidbit at the table. They have the best seat in the cars, carriages, and sleighs; the warmest place in the winter, and the coolest place in the summer. They have their choice on which side of the bed they will lie, front or back. A lady's dress costs three times as much as that of a gentleman; and, at the present time, with the prevailing fashion, one lady occupies three times as much space in the world as a gentleman.

"It has thus appeared to the married gentlemen of your Committee, being a majority (the bachelors being silent for the reason mentioned, and also probably for the further reason that they are still suitors for the favors of the gentler sex), that, if there is any inequality or oppression in the case, the gentlemen are the sufferers. They, however, have presented no petitions for redress; having, doubtless, made up their minds to yield to an inevitable destiny.

"On the whole, the Committee have concluded to recommend no measure, except that as they have observed several instances in which husband and wife have both signed the same petition. In such case, they would recommend the parties to apply for a law authorizing them to change dresses, so that the husband may wear petticoats, and the wife the breeches, and thus indicate to their neighbors and the public the true relation in which they stand to each other."

3. Lucy Stone Protests Traditional Marriage (1855)*

Lucy Stone graduated from Oberlin College (America's first coeducational institution of higher learning) in 1847 and launched herself on a lifelong career as a reformer. She was an outspoken abolitionist and advocate of women's rights. Traditionalists were so irritated with her that they rudely repeated a poem published by a Boston newspaper promising "fame's loud trumpet shall be blown" for the man who "with a wedding kiss shuts up the mouth of Lucy Stone." When she did marry Henry B. Blackwell in 1855, she hardly fell silent. Instead, with her new husband, she used the occasion to dramatize the plight of women. In her wedding declaration, which follows, what aspects of women's condition are most condemned? In what ways does this document suggest the relationship between the abolitionist and feminist crusades?

---

*Elizabeth Cady Stanton et al., eds., *History of Woman Suffrage* (1881), vol. 1, pp. 260–261.

Protest

While acknowledging our mutual affection by publicly assuming the relationship of husband and wife, yet in justice to ourselves and a great principle, we deem it a duty to declare that this act on our part implies no sanction of, nor promise of voluntary obedience to such of the present laws of marriage, as refuse to recognize the wife as an independent, rational being, while they confer upon the husband an injurious and unnatural superiority, investing him with legal powers which no honorable man would exercise, and which no man should possess. We protest especially against the laws which give to the husband:

1. The custody of the wife's person.
2. The exclusive control and guardianship of their children.
3. The sole ownership of her personal, and use of her real estate, unless previously settled upon her, or placed in the hands of trustees, as in the case of minors, lunatics, and idiots.
4. The absolute right to the product of her industry.
5. Also against laws which give to the widower so much larger and more permanent an interest in the property of his deceased wife, than they give to the widow in that of the deceased husband.
6. Finally, against the whole system by which "the legal existence of the wife is suspended during marriage," so that in most States, she neither has a legal part in the choice of her residence, nor can she make a will, nor sue or be sued in her own name, nor inherit property.

We believe that personal independence and equal human rights can never be forfeited, except for crime; that marriage should be an equal and permanent partnership, and so recognized by law; that until it is so recognized, married partners should provide against the radical injustice of present laws, by every means in their power.

We believe that where domestic difficulties arise, no appeal should be made to legal tribunals under existing laws, but that all difficulties should be submitted to the equitable adjustment of arbitrators mutually chosen.

Thus reverencing law, we enter our protest against rules and customs which are unworthy of the name, since they violate justice, the essence of law.

(Signed) *Henry B. Blackwell,*
Lucy Stone.

D. Transcendentalism and Earthly Utopias

1. Ralph Waldo Emerson Chides the Reformers (1844)[*]

Dissatisfied Europeans let off steam in the 1840s in a series of armed revolts; dissatisfied Americans let off steam in various reformist protests. Every brain was seemingly gnawed by a "private maggot." Ralph Waldo Emerson—poet, essayist, transcendentalist, and

---

[*]R. W. Emerson, *Complete Works* (Boston: Houghton, Mifflin and Company, 1884), vol. 3, pp. 240–243.

ever-popular lyceum lecturer—delivered this famous discourse on the New England reformers in 1844. A nonconformist himself, he had resigned his Unitarian pastorate in Boston after disagreeing with his congregation over the sacrament of the Lord's Supper. What might have linked the phenomena that Emerson describes and the Southern spirit of political nullification? Did Emerson oppose all reform?

What a fertility of projects for the salvation of the world!

One apostle thought all men should go to farming, and another that no man should buy or sell, that the use of money was the cardinal evil; another that the mischief was in our diet, that we eat and drink damnation. These made unleavened bread and were foes to the death to fermentation.

It was in vain urged by the housewife that God made yeast as well as dough, and loves fermentation just as dearly as he loves vegetation; that fermentation develops the saccharine element in the grain, and makes it more palatable and more digestible. No; they wish the pure wheat, and will die but it shall not ferment. Stop, dear nature, these incessant advances of thine; let us scotch these ever-rolling wheels!

Others attacked the system of agriculture, the use of animal manures in farming, and the tyranny of man over brute nature [animals]. These abuses polluted his food. The ox must be taken from the plow, and the horse from the cart; the hundred acres of the farm must be spaded. And the man must walk, wherever boats and locomotives will not carry him.

Even the insect world was to be defended—that had been too long neglected, and a society for the protection of ground-worms, slugs, and mosquitoes was to be incorporated without delay.

With these, appeared the adepts of homoeopathy, of hydropathy, of mesmerism, of phrenology, and their wonderful theories of the Christian miracles! Others assailed particular vocations, as that of the lawyer, that of the merchant, of the manufacturer, of the clergyman, of the scholar. Others attacked the institution of marriage as the fountain of social evils. Others devoted themselves to the worrying of churches and meetings for public worship, and the fertile forms of antinomianism* among the elder Puritans seemed to have their match in the plenty of the new harvest of reform.

With this din of opinion and debate, there was a keener scrutiny of institutions and domestic life than any we had known. There was sincere protesting against existing evils, and there were changes of employment dictated by conscience. . . .

In politics, for example, it is easy to see the progress of dissent. The country is full of rebellion; the country is full of kings. Hands off! Let there be no control and no interference in the administration of the affairs of this kingdom of me. Hence the growth of the doctrine and of the party of Free Trade, and the willingness to try that experiment in the face of what appear incontestable facts.

I confess the motto of the *Globe* newspaper is so attractive to me that I can seldom find much appetite to read what is below it in its columns: "The world is governed too much." So the country is frequently affording solitary examples

---

*The belief that Christian faith alone, not obedience to moral law, ensures salvation.

of resistance to the government, solitary nullifiers who throw themselves on their reserved rights; nay, who have reserved all their rights; who reply to the [tax] assessor and to the clerk of the court that they do not know the state, and embarrass the courts of law by nonjuring [refusing to take an oath] and the commander-in-chief of the militia by nonresistance.

2. Henry David Thoreau Praises Spiritual Wealth (1854)*

Henry David Thoreau, a leading transcendentalist, had worn a green coat to the Harvard chapel because the rules required black. He tried his hand at teaching, but when the authorities criticized his use of moral suasion, he whipped a dozen surprised pupils, just to show the absurdity of flogging, and forthwith resigned. While some transcendentalists sought stimulation through an experiment in communal living known as Brook Farm, Thoreau sought it in solitude. Building a hut on the shore of Walden Pond, near Concord, Massachusetts, he spent more than two years in philosophical introspection and in communion with the wildlife, including fish and moles. His experiences unfold in his classic Walden, *which was socialistic enough to become a textbook of the British Labour party. James Russell Lowell accused Thoreau of trying to make a virtue out of his indolence and other defects of character. Which of Thoreau's observations in* Walden *have been weakened or strengthened by the passage of more than a hundred years? Which ones would we regard as absurd today?*

For more than five years I maintained myself thus solely by the labor of my hands, and I found that by working about six weeks in a year, I could meet all the expenses of living. The whole of my winters, as well as most of my summers, I had free and clear for study.

I have thoroughly tried schoolkeeping, and found that my expenses were in proportion, or rather out of proportion, to my income, for I was obliged to dress and train, not to say think and believe, accordingly, and I lost my time into the bargain. As I did not teach for the good of my fellow-men, but simply for a livelihood, this was a failure.

I have tried trade. But I found that it would take ten years to get under way in that, and that then I should probably be on my way to the devil. I was actually afraid that I might by that time be doing what is called a good business.

When formerly I was looking about to see what I could do for a living, . . . I thought often and seriously of picking huckleberries. That surely I could do, and its small profits might suffice—for my greatest skill has been to want but little—so little capital it required, so little distraction from my wonted moods, I foolishly thought. While my acquaintances went unhesitantly into trade or the professions, I contemplated this occupation as most like theirs; ranging the hills all summer to pick the berries which came in my way, and thereafter carelessly dispose of them. . . . But I have since learned that trade curses everything it handles; and though you trade in messages from heaven, the whole curse of trade attaches to the business. . . .

---

*H. D. Thoreau, *Walden* (Boston: Houghton, Mifflin and Company, 1893), pp. 110–111, 112, 498, 505–506, 510.

For myself, I found that the occupation of a day-laborer was the most independent of any, especially as it required only thirty or forty days in a year to support one. The laborer's day ends with the going down of the sun, and he is then free to devote himself to his chosen pursuit, independent of his labor. But his employer, who speculates from month to month, has no respite from one end of the year to the other. . . .

I left the woods for as good a reason as I went there. Perhaps it seemed to me that I had several more lives to live, and could not spare any more time for that one. It is remarkable how easily and insensibly we fall into a particular route, and make a beaten track for ourselves. I had not lived there a week before my feet wore a path from my door to the pond-side; and though it is five or six years since I trod it, it is still quite distinct. It is true, I fear, that others may have fallen into it, and so helped to keep it open.

The surface of the earth is soft and impressible by the feet of men; and so with the paths which the mind travels. How worn and dusty, then, must be the highways of the world, how deep the ruts of tradition and conformity! I did not wish to take a cabin passage, but rather to go before the mast and on the deck of the world, for there I could best see the moonlight amid the mountains. I do not wish to go below now. . . .

However mean your life is, meet it and live it; do not shun it and call it hard names. It is not so bad as you are. It looks poorest when you are richest. The fault-finder will find faults even in Paradise. Love your life, poor as it is. You may perhaps have some pleasant, thrilling, glorious hours even in a poorhouse. The setting sun is reflected from the windows of the almshouse as brightly as from the rich man's abode; the snow melts before its door as early in the spring. I do not see but a quiet mind may live as contentedly there, and have as cheering thoughts, as in a palace.

The town's poor seem to me often to live the most independent lives of any. Maybe they are simply great enough to receive without misgiving. Most think that they are above being supported by the town; but it oftener happens that they are not above supporting themselves by dishonest means, which should be more disreputable.

Cultivate poverty like a garden herb, like sage. Do not trouble yourself much to get new things, whether clothes or friends. Turn the old; return to them. Things do not change; we change. Sell your clothes and keep your thoughts. God will see that you do not want society. If I were confined to a corner of a garret all my days, like a spider, the world would be just as large to me while I had my thoughts about me. . . .

Rather than love, than money, than fame, give me truth.

3. Emersonisms and Thoreauisms

The following pithy sayings are culled from the writings of Emerson and Thoreau, who were close transcendentalist friends and nonconformists. In what areas does there seem to be a close similarity in thinking? How many of these observations have been borne out by personalities or experiences in American history?

Government

The less government we have, the better—fewer laws, and the less confided power. *(Emerson)*

I heartily accept the motto "That government is best which governs least." Carried out, it finally amounts to this, which I also believe: "That government is best which governs not at all"; and when men are prepared for it, that will be the kind of government which they will have. *(Thoreau)*

Under a government which imprisons any unjustly, the true place for a just man is also a prison.* *(Thoreau)*

Of all debts men are least willing to pay the taxes. What a satire this [is] on government! *(Emerson)*

Reform

We are reformers in spring and summer; in autumn and winter we stand by the old; reformers in the morning, conservers at night. Reform is affirmative, conservatism negative; conservatism goes for comfort, reform for truth. *(Emerson)*

Every reform was once a private opinion. *(Emerson)*

Beware when the Great God lets loose a thinker on this planet. *(Emerson)*

There is no strong performance without a little fanaticism in the performer. *(Emerson)*

Every burned book enlightens the world. *(Emerson)*

Every reform is only a mask under cover of which a more terrible reform, which dares not yet name itself, advances. *(Emerson)*

If anything ail a man so that he does not perform his functions, if he have a pain in his bowels . . . he forthwith sets about reforming—the world. *(Thoreau)*

Wealth

The greatest man in history [Jesus] was the poorest. *(Emerson)*

If a man own land, the land owns him. *(Emerson)*

Poverty consists in feeling poor. *(Emerson)*

I would rather sit on a pumpkin, and have it all to myself, than to be crowded on a velvet cushion. *(Thoreau)*

They take their pride in making their dinner cost much; I take my pride in making my dinner cost little. *(Thoreau)*

Men have become the tools of their tools. *(Thoreau)*

To inherit property is not to be born—it is to be stillborn, rather. *(Thoreau)*

That man is the richest whose pleasures are the cheapest. *(Thoreau)*

Great Men

To be great is to be misunderstood. *(Emerson)*

Shallow men believe in luck. *(Emerson)*

Every hero becomes a bore at last. *(Emerson)*

If the single man plant himself indomitably on his instincts, and there abide, the huge world will come around to him. *(Emerson)*

Great men are they who see that spiritual is stronger than any material force; that thoughts rule the world. *(Emerson)*

---

*In 1845 Thoreau was jailed for one night for refusing to pay his poll tax to a state (Massachusetts) that supported slavery. The tax, much to his disgust, was paid by an aunt. Legend has it that Emerson visited him in jail, saying, "Why are you here?" Thoreau allegedly replied, "Why are you not here?"

The true test of civilization is, not the census, nor the size of cities, nor the crops—no, but the kind of man the country turns out. *(Emerson)*

An institution is the lengthened shadow of one man. *(Emerson)*

There are men too superior to be seen except by a few, as there are notes too high for the scale of most ears. *(Emerson)*

If a man does not keep pace with his companions, perhaps it is because he hears a different drummer. Let him step to the music he hears, however measured or far away. *(Thoreau)*

Living

Nothing can bring you peace but yourself. *(Emerson)*

The only gift is a portion of thyself. *(Emerson)*

Hitch your wagon to a star. *(Emerson)*

Nothing is so much to be feared as fear.* *(Thoreau)*

We do not quite forgive a giver. *(Emerson)*

Do not be too moral. You may cheat yourself out of much life so. Aim above morality. Be not simply good; be good for something. *(Thoreau)*

I never found the companion that was so companionable as solitude. *(Thoreau)*

The mass of men lead lives of quiet desperation. *(Thoreau)*

E. Three Views of the Indians

1. Alexis de Tocqueville Predicts the Indians' Future (1835)†

Alexis de Tocqueville, the remarkable French commentator whose observations of American life in the 1830s inspired his classic Democracy in America *(1835), speculated in that book on "the present and probable future condition of the Indian tribes." Near present-day Memphis, he actually witnessed the westward migration of some Choctaw Indians in the year immediately following the Indian Removal Act of 1830, as described in the selection that follows. What feature of white civilization did Tocqueville find most injurious to the traditional ways of Indian life? How accurate were his predictions about the Native Americans' future?*

At the end of the year 1831, while I was on the left bank of the Mississippi, at a place named by Europeans Memphis, there arrived a numerous band of Choctaws (or Chactas, as they are called by the French in Louisiana). These savages had left their country and were endeavoring to gain the right bank of the Mississippi, where they hoped to find an asylum that had been promised them by the American government. It was then the middle of winter, and the cold was unusually severe; the snow had frozen hard upon the ground, and the river was drifting huge masses of ice.

---

*Perhaps Franklin D. Roosevelt's most famous saying, uttered in his inaugural address in 1933, was "The only thing we have to fear is fear itself."

†Pages 321–339 from *Democracy in America* by Alexis de Tocqueville. Edited by J. P. Mayer and Max Lemer. Translated by George Lawrence. English translation copyright © 1965 by Harper & Row, Publishers, Inc.

The Indians had their families with them, and they brought in their train the wounded and the sick, with children newly born and old men upon the verge of death. They possessed neither tents nor wagons, but only their arms and some provisions. I saw them embark to pass the mighty river, and never will that solemn spectacle fade from my remembrance. No cry, so sob, was heard among the assembled crowd; all were silent. Their calamities were of ancient date, and they knew them to be irremediable. The Indians had all stepped into the bark that was to carry them across, but their dogs remained upon the bank. As soon as these animals perceived that their masters were finally leaving the shore, they set up a dismal howl and, plunging all together into the icy waters of the Mississippi, swam after the boat.

The expulsion of the Indians often takes place at the present day in a regular and, as it were, a legal manner. When the European population begins to approach the limit of the desert inhabited by a savage tribe, the government of the United States usually sends forward envoys who assemble the Indians in a large plain and, having first eaten and drunk with them, address them thus: "What have you to do in the land of your fathers? Before long, you must dig up their bones in order to live. . . . Beyond those mountains which you see at the horizon, beyond the lake which bounds your territory on the west, there lie vast countries where beasts of chase are yet found in great abundance; sell us your lands, then, and go to live happily in those solitudes." After holding this language, they spread before the eyes of the Indians firearms, woolen garments, kegs of brandy, glass necklaces, bracelets of tinsel, ear-rings, and looking-glasses. If, when they have beheld all these riches, they still hesitate, it is insinuated that they cannot refuse the required consent and that the government itself will not long have the power of protecting them in their rights. What are they to do? Half convinced and half compelled, they go to inhabit new deserts, where the importunate whites will not let them remain ten years in peace. In this manner do the Americans obtain, at a very low price, whole provinces, which the richest sovereigns of Europe could not purchase.

These are great evils; and it must be added that they appear to me to be irremediable. I believe that the Indian nations of North America are doomed to perish, and that whenever the Europeans shall be established on the shores of the Pacific Ocean, that race of men will have ceased to exist. The Indians had only the alternative of war or civilization; in other words, they must either destroy the Europeans or become their equals. . . .

The Spaniards pursued the Indians with bloodhounds, like wild beasts; . . . [the Americans] kindly take them by the hand and transport them to a grave far from the land of their fathers.

The Spaniards were unable to exterminate the Indian race by those unparalleled atrocities which brand them with indelible shame, nor did they succeed even in wholly depriving it of its rights; but the Americans of the United States have accomplished this twofold purpose with singular felicity, tranquilly, legally, philanthropically, without shedding blood, and without violating a single great principle of morality in the eyes of the world. It is impossible to destroy men with more respect for the laws of humanity.

2. George Catlin Dreams of a National Park to Preserve the Indian Way of Life (1832)*

George Catlin (1796–1872), a Pennsylvanian who gave up the practice of law to study art, joined an American Fur Company expedition to the upper Missouri River in 1832. He made detailed observations of the landscape and of the Indian way of life. His descriptions and paintings of Native American culture and individual Indians are among the richest sources for understanding the antebellum West, though Catlin has been criticized for inaccuracies, especially for romanticizing Indian ways. While camped in present-day South Dakota in 1832, Catlin witnessed the slaughter of hundreds of buffalo (bison) by Native Americans who sold the animals' tongues to white traders for liquor. Disgusted by this spectacle, Catlin proposed a vast national refuge for both buffalo and Native Americans—an idea that eventually blossomed into the distinctive American system of national parks, including Yellowstone National Park. How does Catlin assess the buffalo's importance to Indian life? How realistic—or romantic—was his proposal for a "nation's Park"? To what extent did the eventual national park system realize Catlin's dream?

Letter—No. 31
Mouth of Teton River, Upper Missouri

Reader! listen to the following calculations, and forget them not. The buffaloes (the quadrupeds from whose backs your beautiful robes were taken, and whose myriads were once spread over the whole country, from the Rocky Mountains to the Atlantic Ocean) have recently fled before the appalling appearance of civilized man, and taken up their abode and pasturage amid the almost boundless prairies of the West. An instinctive dread of their deadly foes, who made an easy prey of them whilst grazing in the forest, has led them to seek the midst of the vast and treeless plains of grass, as the spot where they would be least exposed to the assaults of their enemies; and it is exclusively in those desolate fields of silence (yet of beauty) that they are to be found—and over these vast steppes, or prairies, have they fled, like the Indian, towards the "setting sun"; until their bands have been crowded together, and their limits confined to a narrow strip of country on this side of the Rocky Mountains.

It is a melancholy contemplation for one who has travelled as I have, through these realms, and seen this noble animal in all its pride and glory, to contemplate it so rapidly wasting from the world, drawing the irresistible conclusion too, which one must do, that its species is soon to be extinguished, and with it the peace and happiness (if not the actual existence) of the tribes of Indians who are joint tenants with them, in the occupancy of these vast and idle plains.

And what a splendid contemplation too, when one (who has travelled these realms, and can duly appreciate them) imagines them as they *might* in future be seen, (by some great protecting policy of government) preserved in their pristine beauty and wildness, in a *magnificent park*, where the world could see for ages to come, the native Indian in his classic attire, galloping his wild horse, with sinewy

---

*George Catlin, *Letters and Notes on the Manners, Customs, and Conditions of the North American Indians* (New York, 1841), pp. 260–264.

bow, and shield and lance, amid the fleeting herds of elks and buffaloes. What a beautiful and thrilling specimen for America to preserve and hold up to the view of her refined citizens and the world, in future ages! A *nation's Park*, containing man and beast, in all the wild and freshness of their nature's beauty!

I would ask no other monument to my memory, nor any other enrolment of my name amongst the famous dead, than the reputation of having been the founder of such an institution.

Such scenes might easily have been preserved, and still could be cherished on the great plains of the West, without detriment to the country or its borders; for the tracts of country on which the buffaloes have assembled, are uniformly sterile, and of no available use to cultivating man.

There are, by a fair calculation, more than 300,000 Indians, who are now subsisted on the flesh of the buffaloes, and by those animals supplied with all the luxuries of life which they desire, as they know of none others. The great variety of uses to which they convert the body and other parts of that animal, are almost incredible to the person who has not actually dwelt amongst these people, and closely studied their modes and customs. Every part of their flesh is converted into food, in one shape or another, and on it they entirely subsist. The robes of the animals are worn by the Indians instead of blankets—their skins when tanned, are used as coverings for their lodges, and for their beds; undressed, they are used for constructing canoes—for saddles, for bridles—l'arrêts, lasos, and thongs. The horns are shaped into ladles and spoons—the brains are used for dressing the skins—their bones are used for saddle trees—for war clubs, and scrapers for graining the robes—and others are broken up for the marrow-fat which is contained in them. Their sinews are used for strings and backs to their bows—for thread to string their beads and sew their dresses. The feet of the animals are boiled, with their hoofs, for the glue they contain, for fastening their arrow points, and many other uses. The hair from the head and shoulders, which is long, is twisted and braided into halters, and the tail is used for a fly brush. In this wise do these people convert and use the various parts of this useful animal, and with all these luxuries of life about them, and their numerous games, they are happy (God bless them) in the ignorance of the disastrous fate that awaits them.

Yet this interesting community, with its sports, its wildness, its languages, and all its manners and customs, could be perpetuated, and also the buffaloes, whose numbers would increase and supply them with food for ages and centuries to come, if a system of non-intercourse could be established and preserved. But such is not to be the case—the buffalo's doom is sealed, and with their extinction must assuredly sink into real despair and starvation, the inhabitants of these vast plains, which afford for the Indians, no other possible means of subsistence; and they must at last fall a prey to wolves and buzzards, who will have no other bones to pick.

It seems hard and cruel, (does it not?) that we civilized people with all the luxuries and comforts of the world about us, should be drawing from the backs of these useful animals the skins for our luxury, leaving their carcasses to be devoured by the wolves—that we should draw from that country, some 150 or 200,000 of their robes annually, the greater part of which are taken from animals that are killed expressly for the robe, at a season when the meat is not cured and preserved, and for each of which skins the Indian has received but a pint of whiskey!

3. John James Audubon Is Pessimistic About the Indians' Fate (1843)*

The great naturalist and ornithologist John James Audubon (1785–1851) followed Catlin's route on the upper Missouri a decade later, on a hunting trip. How does his assessment of the Native Americans differ from Catlin's? What factors might account for their differing appraisals?

June 7, Wednesday [1843]. . . We reached Fort Clark and the Mandan Villages at half-past seven this morning. . . . The Mandan mud huts are very far from looking poetical, although Mr. Catlin has tried to render them so by placing them in regular rows, and all of the same size and form, which is by no means the case. But different travellers have different eyes! We saw more Indians than at any previous time since leaving St. Louis; and it is possible that there are a hundred huts, made of mud, all looking like so many potato winter-houses in the Eastern States. As soon as we were near the shore, every article that could conveniently be carried off was placed under lock and key, and our division door was made fast, as well as those of our own rooms. Even the axes and poles were put by. Our captain told us that last year they stole his cap and his shot-pouch and horn, and that it was through the interference of the first chief that he recovered his cap and horn; but that a squaw had his leather belt, and would not give it up. The appearance of these poor, miserable devils, as we approached the shore, was wretched enough. There they stood in the pelting rain and keen wind, covered with Buffalo robes, red blankets, and the like, some partially and most curiously besmeared with mud; and as they came on board, and we shook hands with each of them, I felt a clamminess that rendered the ceremony most repulsive. Their legs and naked feet were covered with mud. They looked at me with apparent curiosity, perhaps on account of my beard, which produced the same effect at Fort Pierre. They all looked very poor; and our captain says they are the *ne plus ultra* of thieves. It is said there are nearly three thousand men, women, and children that, during winter, cram themselves into these miserable hovels. . . .

After dinner we went up the muddy bank again to look at the corn-fields, as the small patches that are meanly cultivated are called. We found poor, sickly looking corn about two inches high, that had been represented to us this morning as full six inches high. We followed the prairie, a very extensive one, to the hills, and there found a deep ravine, sufficiently impregnated with saline matter to answer the purpose of salt water for the Indians to boil their corn and pemmican, clear and clean; but they, as well as the whites at the fort, resort to the muddy Missouri for their drinking water, the only fresh water at hand. Not a drop of spirituous liquor has been brought to this place for the last two years; and there can be no doubt that on

---

*Maria Audubon, *Audubon and His Journals* (New York: Charles Scribner's Sons, 1897), vol. 1, pp. 496–497; vol. 2, pp. 10–107.

this account the Indians have become more peaceable than heretofore, though now and then a white man is murdered, and many horses are stolen. As we walked over the plain, we saw heaps of earth thrown up to cover the poor Mandans who died of the small-pox. These mounds in many instances appear to contain the remains of several bodies and, perched on the top, lies, pretty generally, the rotting skull of a Buffalo. Indeed, the skulls of the Buffaloes seem as if a kind of relation to these most absurdly superstitious and ignorant beings. . . .

June 11, Sunday. . . . We have seen much remarkably handsome scenery, but nothing at all comparing with Catlin's descriptions; his book must, after all, be altogether a humbug. Poor devil! I pity him from the bottom of my soul; . . .

July 21, Friday. . . . What a terrible destruction of life, as it were for nothing, or next to it, as the tongues [of the Buffaloes] only were brought in, and the flesh of these fine animals was left to beasts and birds of prey, or to rot on the spots where they fell. The prairies are literally covered with the skulls of the victims, and the roads the Buffalo make in crossing the prairies have all the appearance of heavy wagon tracks.

Thought Provokers

1. How might a skeptical secular critic explain the religious revivalism of the early nineteenth century?

2. Article VIII of the Bill of Rights of the Constitution requires that "cruel and unusual punishments" shall not be "inflicted." In what respects did Dorothea Dix find the Constitution being widely violated? Why do reformers invariably encounter difficulties?

3. In what ways was it a man's world in the nineteenth century? How much has changed today? In what ways did the changes in women's role in the early nineteenth century represent an improvement or a deterioration from earlier conditions?

4. Is there less reformism in America today than there was in the 1840s? Assess the soundness of Emerson's remark: "Men are conservative when they are least vigorous, or when they are most luxurious. They are conservatives after dinner." It has been said that the wise man reduces his wants; the fool increases his income. Comment in the light of Thoreau's philosophy. What would happen to our economic and social structure if large numbers of people literally followed Thoreau's teachings?

5. By what means did the arrival of white pioneers transform the environment and the Native American cultures of the trans-Appalachian West?

16

The South and the Slavery Controversy, 1793–1860

Whenever I hear anyone arguing for slavery, I feel
a strong impulse to see it tried on him personally.

Abraham Lincoln, 1865

Prologue: In slavery, the Southerners had a bear by the tail: to hang on was embarrassing; to let go would be costly and seemingly dangerous. So situated, they put the best face they could on their "peculiar institution" and freely quoted the Bible to defend an archaic practice that both God and Jesus had tolerated, if not sanctioned. The abolitionists, especially the Garrisonians, harped on the evils of slavery; the white Southerners stressed its benefits. The truth lay somewhere between. Certainly most slave owners were not sadists. Self-interest, if not humanity, was a strong though not infallible deterrent to mayhem. Yet slavery was a grave moral offense, especially in a "free" society, even if the slaves did sometimes preserve their dignity and if some masters were kind. The slaves were seldom beaten to death, and as a rule, families were not needlessly separated. Slaves were discouraged from learning to read and encouraged to embrace the Christian religion, which is often the solace of the oppressed. Despite the manifest immorality of slavery, countless Northerners, with a financial stake in slave-grown cotton, deplored the boat-rocking tactics of the abolitionists.

A. The Face of Slavery

1. A Slave Boy Learns a Lesson (c. 1827)*

The amazing Frederick Douglass, sired by an unknown white father, was born in Maryland to a slave woman. He learned to read and write; after suffering much cruel usage, he escaped to the North, where, despite mobbings and beatings, he became a leading abolitionist orator and journalist. A commanding figure of a man, he raised black regiments during the Civil War, and in 1889 became U.S. minister to the republic of Haiti. He showed impartiality in his two marriages: his first wife, he quipped, was the color of his mother and his second (despite a storm of criticism) was that of his father. From the following passage in his autobiography, ascertain why slaveholders were willing to have their slaves know the Bible but not read it.

---

*Frederick Douglass et al., *Life and Times of Frederick Douglass* (Hartford, CT: Park, 1882), pp. 94–97.

The frequent hearing of my mistress reading the Bible aloud—for she often read aloud when her husband was absent—awakened my curiosity in respect to this mystery of reading, and roused in me the desire to learn. Up to this time I had known nothing whatever of this wonderful art, and my ignorance and inexperience of what it could do for me, as well as my confidence in my mistress, emboldened me to ask her to teach me to read.

With an unconsciousness and inexperience equal to my own, she readily consented, and in an incredibly short time, by her kind assistance, I had mastered the alphabet and could spell words of three or four letters. My mistress seemed almost as proud of my progress as if I had been her own child, and supposing that her husband would be as well pleased, she made no secret of what she was doing for me. Indeed, she exultingly told him of the aptness of her pupil, and of her intention to persevere in teaching me, as she felt her duty to do, at least to read the Bible. . . .

Master Hugh was astounded beyond measure, and probably for the first time proceeded to unfold to his wife the true philosophy of the slave system, and the peculiar rules necessary in the nature of the case to be observed in the management of human chattels. Of course, he forbade her to give me any further instruction, telling her in the first place that to do so was unlawful, as it was also unsafe. "For," said he, "if you give a nigger an inch, he will take an ell. Learning will spoil the best nigger in the world. If he learns to read the Bible, it will forever unfit him to be a slave. He should know nothing but the will of his master, and learn to obey it. As to himself, learning will do him no good, but a great deal of harm, making him disconsolate and unhappy. If you teach him how to read, he'll want to know how to write, and this accomplished, he'll be running away with himself."

2. A Former Slave Exposes Slavery (1850)[*]

Flogged without effect by his master, Douglass was hired out for one year to a notorious "slave breaker," who also professed to be a devout Methodist. Worked almost to death in all kinds of weather, allowed five minutes or less for meals, and brutally whipped about once a week, Douglass admitted that "Mr. Covey succeeded in breaking me—in body, soul, and spirit. My natural elasticity was crushed; my intellect languished, the disposition to read departed, the cheerful spark that lingered about my eye died out; the dark night of slavery closed in upon me; and behold a man transformed to a brute!" In this abolitionist speech in Rochester, New York, Douglass spoke from bitter experience. In what respects were the nonphysical abuses of slaves worse than the physical ones? Where was the system most unjust?

More than twenty years of my life were consumed in a state of slavery. My childhood was environed by the baneful peculiarities of the slave system. I grew up to manhood in the presence of this hydra-headed monster—not as a master—not as an idle spectator—not as the guest of the slaveholder; but as A SLAVE, eating the bread and drinking the cup of slavery with the most degraded of my brother bondmen, and sharing with them all the painful conditions of their wretched lot. In consideration of these facts, I feel that I have a right to speak, and to speak strongly. Yet, my friends, I feel bound to speak truly. . . .

---

[*]Quoted in Irving Mark and E. L. Schwaab, eds., *The Faith of Our Fathers* (New York: Alfred A. Knopf, Inc., 1952), pp. 157–159.

First of all, I will state, as well as I can, the legal and social relation of master and slave. A master is one (to speak in the vocabulary of the Southern states) who claims and exercises a right of property in the person of a fellow man. This he does with the force of the law and the sanction of Southern religion.

The law gives the master absolute power over the slave. He may work him, flog him, hire him out, sell him, and in certain contingencies kill him with perfect impunity.

The slave is a human being, divested of all rights—reduced to the level of a brute—a mere "chattel" in the eye of the law—placed beyond the circle of human brotherhood—cut off from his kind. His name, which the "recording angel" may have enrolled in heaven among the blest, is impiously inserted in a master's ledger with horses, sheep, and swine.

In law a slave has no wife, no children, no country, and no home. He can own nothing, possess nothing, acquire nothing, but what must belong to another. To eat the fruit of his own toil, to clothe his person with the work of his own hands, is considered stealing.

He toils, that another may reap the fruit. He is industrious, that another may live in idleness. He eats unbolted meal, that another may eat the bread of fine flour. He labors in chains at home, under a burning sun and biting lash, that another may ride in ease and splendor abroad. He lives in ignorance, that another may be educated. He is abused, that another may be exalted. He rests his toil-worn limbs on the cold, damp ground, that another may repose on the softest pillow. He is clad in coarse and tattered raiment, that another may be arrayed in purple and fine linen. He is sheltered only by the wretched hovel, that a master may dwell in a magnificent mansion. And to this condition he is bound down by an arm of iron.

From this monstrous relation there springs an unceasing stream of most revolting cruelties. The very accompaniments of the slave system stamp it as the offspring of hell itself. To ensure good behavior, the slaveholder relies on the whip. To induce proper humility, he relies on the whip. To rebuke what he is pleased to term insolence, he relies on the whip. To supply the place of wages, as an incentive to toil, he relies on the whip. To bind down the spirit of the slave, to imbrute and destroy his manhood, he relies on the whip, the chain, the gag, the thumb-screw, the pillory, the bowie knife, the pistol, and the bloodhound. . . .

There is a still deeper shade to be given to this picture. The physical cruelties are indeed sufficiently harassing and revolting; but they are as a few grains of sand on the sea shore, or a few drops of water in the great ocean, compared with the stupendous wrongs which it inflicts upon the mental, moral, and religious nature of its hapless victims. It is only when we contemplate the slave as a moral and intellectual being that we can adequately comprehend the unparalleled enormity of slavery, and the intense criminality of the slaveholder.

3. Human Cattle for Sale (c. 1850)*

Slave auctions, ugly affairs at best, received top billing in abolitionist propaganda. Here is an account, less sensational than many, by Solomon Northup, a free black citizen of New York State. Kidnapped in Washington, DC, and enslaved on a Louisiana plantation, he eventually managed to regain his freedom. His narrative, edited

---

*Solomon Northup, *Twelve Years a Slave* (New York: Miller, Orton & Mulligan, 1853), pp. 79–82.

and perhaps ghostwritten by a New York lawyer, bears the earmarks of credibility. What aspect of this New Orleans slave auction, held by a Mr. Freeman, would be most likely to wound Northern sensibilities?

Next day many customers called to examine Freeman's "new lot" [of slaves]. The latter gentleman was very loquacious, dwelling at much length upon our several good points and qualities. He would make us hold up our heads, walk briskly back and forth, while customers would feel of our hands and arms and bodies, turn us about, ask us what we could do, make us open our mouths and show our teeth, precisely as a jockey examines a horse which he is about to barter for or purchase.

Sometimes a man or woman was taken back to the small house in the yard, stripped, and inspected more minutely. Scars upon a slave's back were considered evidence of a rebellious or unruly spirit, and hurt his sale.

One old gentleman, who said he wanted a coachman, appeared to take a fancy to me. From his conversation with Freeman, I learned he was a resident of the city [New Orleans]. I very much desired that he would buy me, because I conceived it would not be difficult to make my escape from New Orleans on some Northern vessel. Freeman asked him $1,500 for me. The old gentleman insisted it was too much, as times were very hard. Freeman, however, declared that I was sound and healthy, of a good constitution, and intelligent. He made it a point to enlarge upon my musical attainments. The old gentleman argued quite adroitly that there was nothing extraordinary about the nigger, and finally, to my regret, went out, saying he would call again.

During the day, however, a number of sales were made. David and Caroline were purchased together by a Natchez planter. They left us, grinning broadly, and in the most happy state of mind, caused by the fact of their not being separated. Lethe was sold to a planter of Baton Rouge, her eyes flashing with anger as she was led away.

The same man also purchased Randall. The little fellow was made to jump, and run across the floor, and perform many other feats, exhibiting his activity and condition. All the time the trade was going on, Eliza [the mother] was crying aloud, and wringing her hands. She besought the man not to buy him unless he also bought herself and Emily. She promised, in that case, to be the most faithful slave that ever lived. The man answered that he could not afford it, and then Eliza burst into a paroxysm of grief, weeping plaintively.

Freeman turned round to her, savagely, with his whip in his uplifted hand, ordering her to stop her noise, or he would flog her. He would not have such work—such sniveling; and unless she ceased that minute, he would take her to the yard and give her a hundred lashes. Yes, he would take the nonsense out of her pretty quick—if he didn't, might he be d———d.

Eliza shrunk before him, and tried to wipe away her tears, but it was all in vain. She wanted to be with her children, she said, the little time she had to live. All the frowns and threats of Freeman could not wholly silence the afflicted mother. She kept on begging and beseeching them, most piteously, not to separate the three. Over and over again she told them how she loved her boy. A great many times she repeated her former promises—how very faithful and obedient she would be; how hard she would labor day and night, to the last moment of her life, if he would only buy them all together.

But it was of no avail; the man could not afford it. The bargain was agreed upon, and Randall must go alone. Then Eliza ran to him; embraced him passionately;

kissed him again and again; told him to remember her—all the while her tears falling in the boy's face like rain.

4. Cohabitation in the Cabins (c. 1834)*

As the once fertile lands of Maryland and Virginia petered out, the producing of slaves often proved more profitable than the producing of tobacco. Blacks were bred for export to the newly opened cotton lands of the booming Southwest. Frederick Douglass, in his reminiscences, here recounts how his Maryland slave breaker, Mr. Covey, laid the foundations of riches. What does Douglass find most objectionable?

In pursuit of this object [wealth], pious as Mr. Covey was, he proved himself as unscrupulous and base as the worst of his neighbors. In the beginning he was only able—as he said—"to buy one slave"; and scandalous and shocking as is the fact, he boasted that he bought her simply "as a breeder." But the worst of this is not told in this naked statement. This young woman (Caroline was her name) was virtually compelled by Covey to abandon herself to the object for which he had purchased her; and the result was the birth of twins at the end of the year. At this addition to his human stock Covey and his wife were ecstatic with joy. No one dreamed of reproaching the woman or finding fault with the hired man, Bill Smith, the father of the children, for Mr. Covey himself had locked the two up together every night, thus inviting the result.

But I will pursue this revolting subject no farther. No better illustration of the unchaste, demoralizing, and debasing character of slavery can be found than is furnished in the fact that this professedly Christian slaveholder, amidst all his prayers and hymns, was shamelessly and boastfully encouraging and actually compelling, in his own house, undisguised and unmitigated fornication, as a means of increasing his stock. It was the system of slavery which made this allowable, and which condemned the slaveholder for buying a slave woman and devoting her to this life no more than for buying a cow and raising stock from her; and the same rules were observed, with a view to increasing the number and quality of the one as of the other.

5. From Slavery to Freedom (1835)†

African-born James L. Bradley was one of many slaves who purchased their freedom out of their own hard-gained, meager earnings. Bradley eventually made his way to the Lane Seminary in Cincinnati, a hotbed of abolitionist sentiment presided over by Lyman Beecher, father of the novelist Harriet Beecher Stowe. There he wrote the following short account of his life. What did he see as the worst aspects of slavery? What did his ability to purchase his freedom imply about the character of the slave system? What was his attitude toward Christianity?

I will try to write a short account of my life, as nearly as I can remember; though it makes me sorrowful to think of my past days; for they have been very

---

*Frederick Douglass et al., *Life and Times of Frederick Douglass* (Hartford, CT: Park, 1882), pp. 150–151.
†Fourth Annual Report of the Trustees of the Cincinnati Lane Seminary (Cincinnati, OH: Lane Seminary, 1834), p. 27.

dark and full of tears. I always longed and prayed for liberty, and had at times hopes that I should obtain it. I would pray, and try to study out some way to earn money enough to buy myself, by working in the night-time. But then something would happen to disappoint my hopes, and it seemed as though I must live and die a slave, with none to pity me.

I will begin as far back as I can remember. I think I was between two and three years old when the soul-destroyers tore me from my mother's arms, somewhere in Africa, far back from the sea. They carried me a long distance to a ship; all the way I looked back, and cried. The ship was full of men and women loaded with chains; but I was so small, they let me run about on deck.

After many long days, they brought us into Charleston, South Carolina. A slave-holder bought me, and took me up into Pendleton County. I suppose that I staid with him about six months. He sold me to a Mr. Bradley, by whose name I have ever since been called. This man was considered a wonderfully kind master; and it is true that I was treated better than most of the slaves I knew. I never suffered for food, and never was flogged with the whip; but oh, my soul! I was tormented with kicks and knocks more than I can tell. My master often knocked me down, when I was young. Once, when I was a boy, about nine years old, he struck me so hard that I fell down and lost my senses. I remained thus some time, and when I came to myself, he told me he thought he had killed me. At another time, he struck me with a currycomb, and sunk the knob into my head. I have said that I had food enough; I wish I could say as much concerning my clothing. But I let that subject alone, because I cannot think of any suitable words to use in telling you.

I used to work very hard. I was always obliged to be in the field by sunrise, and I labored till dark, stopping only at noon long enough to eat dinner. When I was about fifteen years old, I took what was called the cold plague, in consequence of being over-worked, and I was sick a long time. My master came to me one day, and hearing me groan with pain, he said, "This fellow will never be of any more use to me—I would as soon knock him in the head, as if he were an opossum." His children sometimes came in, and shook axes and knives at me, as if they were about to knock me on the head. But I have said enough of this. The Lord at length raised me up from the bed of sickness, but I entirely lost the use of one of my ankles. Not long after this, my master moved to Arkansas Territory, and died. Then the family let me out; but after [line illegible] the plantation, saying she could not do with me. My master had kept me ignorant of everything he could. I was never told anything about God, or my own soul. Yet from the time I was fourteen years old, I used to think a great deal about freedom. It was my heart's desire; I could not keep it out of my mind. Many a sleepless night I have spent in tears, because I was a slave. I looked back on all I had suffered—and when I looked ahead, all was dark and hopeless bondage. My heart ached to feel within me the life of liberty. After the death of my master, I began to contrive how I might buy myself. After toiling all day for my mistress, I used to sleep three or four hours, and then get up and work for myself the remainder of the night. I made collars for horses, out of plaited husks. I could weave one in about eight hours; and I generally took time enough from my sleep to make two collars in the course of a week. I sold them for fifty cents each. One summer, I tried to take two or three hours from my sleep every night; but I found that I grew weak, and I was obliged to sleep more. With my first money

I bought a pig. The next year I earned for myself about thirteen dollars; and the next about thirty. There was a good deal of wild land in the neighborhood that belonged to Congress. I used to go out with my hoe, and dig up little patches, which I planted with corn, and got up in the night to tend it. My hogs were fattened with this corn, and I used to sell a number every day. Besides this, I used to raise small patches of tobacco, and sell it to buy more corn for my pigs. In this way I worked for five years, at the end of which time, after taking out my losses, I found that I had earned one hundred and sixty dollars. With this money I hired my own time for two years. During this period, I worked almost all the time night and day. The hope of liberty strung my nerves, and braced up my soul so much, that I could do with very little sleep or rest. I could do a great deal more work than I was ever able to do before. At the end of the two years, I had earned three hundred dollars, besides feeding and clothing myself. I now bought my time for eighteen months longer, and went two hundred and fifty miles west, nearly into Texas, where I could make more money. Here I earned enough to buy myself; which I did in 1833, about one year ago. I paid for myself, including what I gave for my time, about seven hundred dollars. . . .

I will now mention a few things, that I could not conveniently bring in, as I was going along with my story.

In the year 1828, I saw some Christians, who talked with me concerning my soul, and the sinfulness of my nature. They told me I must repent, and live to do good. This led me to the cross of Christ;—and then, oh, how I longed to be able to read the Bible! I made out to get an old spelling-book, which I carried in my hat for many months, until I could spell pretty well, and read easy words. When I got up in the night to work, I used to read a few minutes, if I could manage to get a light. Indeed, every chance I could find, I worked away at my spelling-book. After I had learned to read a little, I wanted very much to learn to write; and I persuaded one of my young masters to teach me. But the second night, my mistress came in, bustled about, scolded her son, and called him out. I overheard her say to him, "You fool! what are you doing? If you teach him to write, he will write himself a pass and run away." That was the end of my instruction in writing; but I persevered, and made marks of all sorts and shapes I could think of. By turning every way, I was, after a long time, able to write tolerably plain.

I have said a good deal about my desire for freedom. How strange it is that anybody should believe any human being *could* be a slave, and yet be contented! I do not believe there ever was a slave, who did not long for liberty. I know very well that slave-owners take a great deal of pains to make the people in the free States believe that the slaves are happy; but I know, likewise, that I was never acquainted with a slave, however well he was treated, who did not long to be free. There is one thing about this, that people in the free States do not understand. When they ask slaves whether they wish for their liberty, they answer, "No;" and very likely they will go so far as to say they would not leave their masters for the world. But at the same time, they desire liberty more than anything else, and have, perhaps, all along been laying plans to get free. The truth is, if a slave shows any discontent, he is sure to be treated worse, and worked the harder for it; and every slave knows this. This is why they are careful not to show any uneasiness when white men ask them about freedom. When they are alone by themselves, all their talk is about liberty—liberty! It is the great thought and feeling that fills the mind full all the time.

6. The Sexual Complexities of Slavery[*]

Harriet Jacobs was born into slavery in North Carolina in 1813. Both her maternal and paternal grandfathers were white, but as the daughter of an enslaved woman, Harriet became her owners' property. Her original owners treated her kindly and taught her to read and write. But at about the age of puberty, Harriet passed into the hands of another slave-owning family whose patriarch soon began subjecting her to constant sexual harassment. She repeatedly refused his advances, though at the age of sixteen, she had the first of two children with a local white lawyer, Samuel Tredwell Sawyer (later a member of Congress). Those children, too, became the property of her master. In 1835 she ran away, hid for seven years in the attic of her free black grandmother's home, eventually made her way to the North, where she befriended abolitionists like Harriet Beecher Stowe and Lydia Maria Child, and still later secured the freedom of her two children. In 1861, under the pseudonym Linda Brent, she published Incidents in the Life of a Slave Girl, *which caused a sensation with its candid descriptions of the seamy sexual side of slavery. Lydia Maria Child, who wrote a preface for the book, almost apologetically acknowledged that Jacobs' experiences were what "some will call delicate subjects and others indelicate. . . . I am well aware that many will accuse me of indecorum for presenting these pages to the public." What does the young Harriet's story reveal about the implications of slavery in otherwise "respectable" white slave-owning households? And what does it suggest about gender roles and authority patterns in those households?*

During the first years of my service in Dr. Flint's family, I was accustomed to share some indulgences with the children of my mistress. Though this seemed to me no more than right, I was grateful for it, and tried to merit the kindness by the faithful discharge of my duties. But I now entered on my fifteenth year—a sad epoch in the life of a slave girl. My master began to whisper foul words in my ear. Young as I was, I could not remain ignorant of their import. . . . He told me I was his property; that I must be subject to his will in all things. My soul revolted against the mean tyranny. But where could I turn for protection? No matter whether the slave girl be as black as ebony or as fair as her mistress. In either case, there is no shadow of law to protect her from insult, from violence, or even from death; all these are inflicted by fiends who bear the shape of men. The mistress, who ought to protect the helpless victim, has no other feelings towards her but those of jealousy and rage. The degradation, the wrongs, the vices, that grow out of slavery, are more than I can describe. . . .

Even the little child, who is accustomed to wait on her mistress and her children, will learn, before she is twelve years old, why it is that her mistress hates such and such a one among the slaves. Perhaps the child's own mother is among those hated ones. She listens to violent outbreaks of jealous passion, and cannot help understanding what is the cause. She will become prematurely knowing in evil things. Soon she will learn to tremble when she hears her master's footfall. She will be compelled to realize that she is no longer a child. If God has bestowed beauty

---

[*]Harriet Jacobs (pseud. Linda Brent), *Incidents in the Life of a Slave Girl*, ed. Lydia Maria Child (Boston, 1861), 44–51.

upon her, it will prove her greatest curse. That which commands admiration in the white woman only hastens the degradation of the female slave. . . .

I longed for some one to confide in. I would have given the world to have laid my head on my grandmother's faithful bosom, and told her all my troubles. But Dr. Flint swore he would kill me, if I was not as silent as the grave. Then, although my grandmother was all in all to me, I feared her as well as loved her. I had been accustomed to look up to her with a respect bordering upon awe. I was very young, and felt shamefaced about telling her such impure things, especially as I knew her to be very strict on such subjects. . . . But though I did not confide in my grandmother, and even evaded her vigilant watchfulness and inquiry, her presence in the neighborhood was some protection to me. Though she had been a slave, Dr. Flint was afraid of her. He dreaded her scorching rebukes. . . .

I would ten thousand times rather that my children should be the half-starved paupers of Ireland than to be the most pampered among the slaves of America. I would rather drudge out my life on a cotton plantation, till the grave opened to give me rest, than to live with an unprincipled master and a jealous mistress. The felon's home in a penitentiary is preferable. He may repent, and turn from the error of his ways, and so find peace; but it is not so with a favorite slave. She is not allowed to have any pride of character. It is deemed a crime in her to wish to be virtuous. . . .

I had entered my sixteenth year, and every day it became more apparent that my presence was intolerable to Mrs. Flint. Angry words frequently passed between her and her husband. He had never punished me himself, and he would not allow any body else to punish me. In that respect, she was never satisfied; but, in her angry moods, no terms were too vile for her to bestow upon me. Yet I, whom she detested so bitterly, had far more pity for her than he had, whose duty it was to make her life happy. I never wronged her, or wished to wrong her; and one word of kindness from her would have brought me to her feet.

7. The Sundering of Families (1874)*

The brutality of whip and branding iron was monstrous, but slavery's greatest psychological horror was the cruel separation of family members. In the following account, Lorenzo Ivy, the son of a slave cobbler on a Virginia plantation, describes his family's efforts, not always successful, to stay together. How did the spread of the cotton economy (what Ivy refers to as the "cotton fever") increase the suffering of the slaves?

Times have changed so fast in the last ten years, that I often ask myself who am I, and why am I not on my master's plantation, working under an overseer, instead of being here in this institution [Hampton Institute, in Virginia, founded as a school for freed slaves after the Civil War], under the instruction of a school-teacher. I was born in 1849. My master was very good to his slaves, and they thought a great deal of him. But all of our happy days were over when he went South and caught the cotton fever. He was never satisfied till he moved out there. He sold the house

---

*Mrs. M. F. Armstrong and Helen W. Ludlow, *Hampton and Its Students* (New York: G. P. Putnam, 1874), pp. 78–80.

before any of the black people knew anything about it, and that was the beginning of our sorrow. My father belonged to another man, and we knew not how soon we would be carried off from him. Two of my aunts were married, and one of them had ten children, and both of their husbands belonged to another man. Father and my uncles went to their masters and asked them to buy their families. They tried to, but our master wouldn't sell, and told [them] how many hundred dollars' worth of cotton he could make off us every year, and that we little chaps were just the right size to climb cotton-stalks and pick cotton. But our master and father's master had once agreed that if either one of them ever moved away, he would sell out to the other. So father's master sent for the other gentlemen who heard the conversation, and they said it was true. After a day or two's consideration, he agreed to let him have mother and the seven children for $12,000. That released us from sorrow. But it was not so with my aunts; they had lost all hope of being with their husbands any longer; the time was set for them to start; it was three weeks from the time we were sold. Those three weeks did not seem as long as three days to us who had to shake hands for the last time with those bound together with the bands of love.

Father said he could never do enough for his master for buying us. They treated us very well for the first three or four years—as the saying was with the black people, they fed us on soft corn at first and then choked us with the husk. When I was large enough to use a hoe, I was put under the overseer to make tobacco-hills. I worked under six overseers, and they all gave me a good name to my master. I only got about three whippings from each of them. The first one was the best; we did not know how good he was till he went away to the war. Then times commenced getting worse with us. I worked many a day without any thing to eat but a tin cup of buttermilk and a little piece of corn-bread, and then walk two miles every night or so to carry the overseer his dogs; if we failed to bring them, he would give us a nice flogging.

When the war closed, our master told all the people, if they would stay and get in the crop, he would give them part of it. Most of them left; they said they knew him too well. Father made us all stay, so we all worked on the remainder of the year, just as if Lee hadn't surrendered. I never worked harder in my life, for I thought the more we made, the more we would get. We worked from April till one month to Christmas. We raised a large crop of corn and wheat and tobacco, shucked all the corn and put it in the barn, stripped all the tobacco, and finished one month before Christmas. Then we went to our master for our part he had promised us, but he said he wasn't going to give us any thing, and he stopped giving us any thing to eat, and said we couldn't live any longer on his land. Father went to an officer of the Freedmen's Bureau, but the officer was like Isaac said to Esau: "The voice is like Jacob's voice, but the hands are the hands of Esau." So that was the way with the officer—he had on Uncle Sam's clothes, but he had Uncle Jeff's [Jefferson Davis's] heart. He said our master said we wasn't worth any thing, and he couldn't get any thing for us, so father said no more about it.

We made out to live that winter—I don't know how. In April, 1866, father moved to town where he could work at his trade. He hired all of us boys that were large enough to work in a brick-yard for from three to six dollars a month. That was the first time I had tasted the sweet cup of freedom.

B. The White Southern View of Slavery

1. The "Blessings" of the Slave (1849)*

Connecticut-born and Puritan-descended Solon Robinson became a Yankee ped-dler at eighteen. After he moved to Indiana, he attained prominence as a trader and agriculturist. During the course of his extensive travels through practically every state, he wrote a series of discerning sketches for the foremost agricultural maga-zines. The following contribution to a leading Southern trade journal is hardly what one would expect from a Connecticut Yankee. In what respects did Robinson appear to be too soft on slavery, and in what respects did he disagree with the abolitionists?

A greater punishment could not be devised or inflicted upon the Southern slave at this day than to give him that liberty which God in his wisdom and mercy deprived him of. . . .

Free them from control, and how soon does poverty and wretchedness over-take them! . . . I boldly and truly assert that you may travel Europe over—yea, you may visit the boasted freemen of America—aye, you may search the world over—before you find a laboring peasantry who are more happy, more contented, as a class of people, or who are better clothed and fed and better provided for in sick-ness, infirmity, and old age, or who enjoy more of the essential comforts of life, than these so-called miserable, oppressed, abused, starved slaves. . . .

I doubt whether one single instance can be found among the slaves of the South where one has injured himself at long and excessive labor. Instead of a cruel and avaricious master being able to extort more than a very reasonable amount of labor from him, his efforts will certainly produce the contrary effect. This is a well-known fact, so much so indeed that an overseer of this character cannot get employment among masters, who know that over-driving a Negro, as well as a mule, is the poorest way to get work out of either of them. These facts are well understood by all observant masters and overseers: that neither mule nor Negro can be made to do more than a certain amount of work; and that amount so small in comparison to the amount done by white laborers at the North that it is a universal observation at the South. Northern men are always the hardest masters, in the vain attempt they make to force the Negro to do even half as much as a hireling in New England is compelled to do, or lose his place and wages. . . .

It is true that some men abuse and harshly treat their slaves. So do some men abuse their wives and children and apprentices and horses and cattle. . . .

The fact is notorious that slaves are better treated now than formerly, and that the improvement in their condition is progressing; partly from their masters becom-ing more temperate and better men, but mainly from the greatest of all moving causes in human actions—self-interest. For masters have discovered in the best of all schools—experience—that their true interest is inseparably bound up with the humane treatment, comfort, and happiness of their slaves.

De Bow's Review, vol. 7 (n.s., vol. 1, 1849), pp. 217–221, 383–384.

And many masters have discovered, too, that their slaves are more temperate, more industrious, more kind to one another, more cheerful, more faithful, and more obedient under the ameliorating influences of religion than under all the driving and whipping of all the tyrannical taskmasters that have existed since the day when the children of Israel were driven to the task of making Egyptian brick without straw.

And I do most fearlessly assert, and defy contradiction, that in no part of this Union, even in Puritan New England, is the Sabbath better kept by master and slave, by employer and hireling, or by all classes, high and low, rich and poor, than in the state of Mississippi, where I have often been told that that thing so accursed of God [slavery] existed in all its most disgusting deformity, wretchedness, and sinful horror. From the small plantations, the slaves go more regularly, and better dressed and behaved, to church, often a distance of five or six miles, than any other class of laborers that I have ever been acquainted with. Upon many of the large plantations, divine service is performed more regularly, and to larger and more orderly audiences, than in some county towns. . . .

In all my tour during the past winter, I did not see or hear of but two cases of flogging: one of which was for stealing, and the other for running away from as good a master as ever a servant need to have, which is proved by the appearance and general good conduct of his Negroes. And that they are well fed I know from many days' personal observation; and I have seen some of them with better broadcloth suits on than I often wear myself; and more spare money than their master, as he will freely acknowledge. . . .

But I do seriously say that I did not see or hear of one place where the Negroes were not well fed; and I did not see a ragged gang of Negroes in the South. And I could only hear of one plantation where the Negroes were overworked or unjustly flogged, and on that plantation the master was a drunken, abusive wretch, as heartily despised by his neighbors as he was hated by his Negroes. And were it not for the consequences to themselves if they should rise upon and pull him limb from limb, his brother planters would rejoice that he had met the fate that cruelty to slaves, they are free to say, justly merits.

The two things that are most despised and hated in the South are masters that abuse and starve and ill-treat their slaves, and abolitionists, who seize upon every isolated case of the kind, and trumpet it through the land as evidence of the manner that all slaves are treated, and then call upon the people of the free states to aid the Negroes to free themselves from such inhuman bondage, peaceably if they can, forcibly if they must, no matter whose or how much blood shall flow.

2. Comparing Slave Labor and Wage Labor (1850)

In response to abolitionist attacks in the 1840s, supporters of slavery became more aggressive. Instead of simply defending the "peculiar institution," they began to argue that slavery benefited slave owners and slaves alike. Proslavery propagandists frequently compared Northern and Southern institutions in the light of this argument. The cartoon on p. 257, published in Boston, is an example of such a comparison. Why would an attack on conditions in England be an effective way to respond to criticism of slavery in America? Were there advantages to slave labor, and if so, to whom did they accrue? In what sense was wage labor really "free"?

3. George Fitzhugh Attacks Wage Slavery (1857)*

By levying charges of "wage slavery" against Northern industrialists, Southern planters sought to deflect criticism of their own coercive labor arrangements. But few went as far as writer George Fitzhugh, who argued that white workers would actually be better off in bondage. In a searing indictment of capitalist society, Fitzhugh lauded the virtues of Southern paternalism and predicted that eventually all society would be composed of masters and slaves. While Southerners generally applauded his effort to put slavery on a higher moral plane, Northerners reacted to Fitzhugh's treatise with near-universal disdain. Prominent abolitionist William Lloyd Garrison called the author "crack-brained" and "demonical," taking ample space in his weekly newspaper, The Liberator, to refute Fitzhugh's vitriolic pronouncements. What might Northerners have found most objectionable in the following excerpt? Does Fitzhugh offer an accurate portrait of Southern slavery? Are his criticisms of wage labor valid?

Until the lands of America are appropriated by a few, population becomes dense, competition among laborers active, employment uncertain, and wages low, the personal liberty of all the whites will continue to be a blessing. We have vast unsettled territories; population may cease to increase slowly, as in most countries, and many centuries may elapse before the question will be practically suggested, whether slavery to capital be preferable to slavery to human masters. But the negro has neither energy nor enterprise, and, even in our sparser population, finds, with his improvident habits, that his liberty is a curse to himself, and a greater curse to the society around him. These considerations, and others equally obvious, have induced the South to attempt to defend negro slavery as an exceptional institution, admitting, nay asserting, that slavery, in the general or in the abstract, is morally wrong, and against common right. With singular inconsistency, after making this admission, which admits away the authority of the Bible, of profane history, and of the almost universal practice of mankind—they turn round and attempt to bolster up the cause of negro slavery by these very exploded authorities. If we mean not to repudiate all divine, and almost all human authority in favor of slavery, we must vindicate that institution in the abstract.

To insist that a status of society, which has been almost universal, and which is expressly and continually justified by Holy Writ, is its natural, normal, and necessary status, under the ordinary circumstances, is on its face a plausible and probable proposition. To insist on less, is to yield our cause, and to give up our religion; for if white slavery be morally wrong, be a violation of natural rights, the Bible cannot be true. . . .

---

*George Fitzhugh, *Cannibals All! or Slaves Without Masters*, C. Vann Woodward, ed. (Cambridge, MA: Belknap Press, 1973), pp. 199–201.

The world at large looks on negro slavery as much the worst form of slavery; because it is only acquainted with West India slavery. Abolition never arose till negro slavery was instituted; and now abolition is only directed against negro slavery. There is no philanthropic crusade attempting to set free the white slaves of Eastern Europe and of Asia. The world, then, is prepared for the defence of slavery in the abstract—it is prejudiced only against negro slavery. These prejudices were in their origin well founded. The Slave Trade, the horrors of the Middle Passage, and West India slavery were enough to rouse the most torpid philanthropy.

But our Southern slavery has become a benign and protective institution, and our negroes are confessedly better off than any free laboring population in the world.

How can we contend that white slavery is wrong, whilst all the great body of free laborers are starving; and slaves, white or black, throughout the world, are enjoying comfort?

We write in the cause of Truth and Humanity, and will not play the advocate for master or for slave.

The aversion to negroes, the antipathy of race, is much greater at the North than at the South; and it is very probable that this antipathy to the person of the negro, is confounded with or generates hatred of the institution with which he is usually connected. Hatred to slavery is very generally little more than hatred of negroes.

There is one strong argument in favor of negro slavery over all other slavery: that he, being unfitted for the mechanic arts, for trade, and all skillful pursuits, leaves those pursuits to be carried on by the whites; and does not bring all industry into disrepute, as in Greece and Rome, where the slaves were not only the artists and mechanics, but also the merchants.

C. The Abolitionist Crusade

1. William Lloyd Garrison Launches The Liberator (1831)*

Mild-appearing William Lloyd Garrison, the most impassioned of the abolitionists, began publication of his incendiary weekly newspaper, The Liberator, with the following trumpet blast. Despite a subscription list of not more than three thousand and embarrassing annual deficits, he continued the journal for thirty-five years—until slavery was legally ended. The rude woodcut at the top of the front page showing a slave auction near the Capitol infuriated the South; the state of Georgia offered $5,000 for Garrison's arrest and conviction. Jailed in Baltimore for libel, mobbed in Boston, and jeered at while on the lecture platform, he not only outraged the South

---

The Liberator (Boston), January 1, 1831.

*but also angered Northern conservatives and even moderate abolitionists. What spe-
cific measures did he advocate? Did he address his appeal exclusively to the South?
Has posterity vindicated him, as he claimed it would?*

During my recent tour for the purpose of exciting the minds of the people
by a series of discourses on the subject of slavery, every place that I visited
gave fresh evidence of the fact that a greater revolution in public sentiment
was to be effected in the free states—*and particularly in New England*—than
at the South. I found contempt more bitter, opposition more active, detraction
more relentless, prejudice more stubborn, and apathy more frozen, than among
slaveowners themselves. Of course, there were individual exceptions to the
contrary.

This state of things afflicted but did not dishearten me. I determined, at
every hazard, to lift up the standard of emancipation in the eyes of the nation,
within sight of Bunker Hill and in the birthplace of liberty. That standard is now
unfurled; and long may it float, unhurt by the spoliations of time or the missiles of a desperate foe—yea, till every chain be broken, and every bondman
set free! Let Southern oppressors tremble—let their secret abettors tremble—let
their Northern apologists tremble—let all the enemies of the persecuted blacks
tremble. . . .

Assenting to the "self-evident truth" maintained in the American Declaration of
Independence "that all men are created equal, and endowed by their Creator with
certain inalienable rights—among which are life, liberty, and the pursuit of happiness," I shall strenuously contend for the immediate enfranchisement of our slave
population. . . . In Park Street Church [in Boston], on the Fourth of July, 1829, in
an address on slavery, I unreflectingly assented to the popular but pernicious doctrine of *gradual* abolition. I seize this opportunity to make a full and unequivocal
recantation, and thus publicly to ask pardon of my God, of my country, and of my
brethren the poor slaves, for having uttered a sentiment so full of timidity, injustice,
and absurdity. . . .

I am aware that many object to the severity of my language; but is there not
cause for severity? I *will be* as harsh as truth, and as uncompromising as justice. On
this subject I do not wish to think, or speak, or write, with moderation. No! No!
Tell a man whose house is on fire to give a moderate alarm; tell him to moderately
rescue his wife from the hands of the ravisher; tell the mother to gradually extricate her babe from the fire into which it has fallen—but urge me not to use moderation in a cause like the present. I am in earnest—I will not equivocate—I will
not excuse—I will not retreat a single inch—AND I WILL BE HEARD. The apathy of the
people is enough to make every statue leap from its pedestal, and to hasten the
resurrection of the dead.

It is pretended that I am retarding the cause of emancipation by the coarseness of my invective and the precipitancy of my measures. *The charge is not
true.* On this question my influence—humble as it is—is felt at this moment to a
considerable extent, and shall be felt in coming years—not perniciously, but ben-
eficially—not as a curse, but as a blessing. And posterity will bear testimony that
I was right.

2. Manifesto of the Anti-Slavery Society (1833)*

About fifty abolitionist idealists, meeting in Philadelphia, launched the American Anti-Slavery Society with the following declaration. Garrison, who would be its president twenty-two times, was chief architect of this manifesto. Later becoming more insistent and impatient, he denounced the churches as "cages of unclean birds" (because they tolerated slavery), denied the full inspiration of the Bible (because it sanctioned slavery), publicly burned a copy of the Constitution (because it upheld slavery), and as early as 1841 advocated the disruption of the Union (because it legalized slavery). The following is an edict by the American Anti-Slavery Society. Why does it demand immediate and uncompensated emancipation? What concessions does it make at this early date to the South? Which of its proposals were most (and least) politically feasible?

We further maintain that no man has a right to enslave or imbrute his brother—to hold or acknowledge him, for one moment, as a piece of merchandise—to keep back his hire by fraud—or to brutalize his mind by denying him the means of intellectual, social, and moral improvement.

The right to enjoy liberty is inalienable. To invade it is to usurp the prerogative of Jehovah. Every man has a right to his own body—to the products of his own labor—to the protection of law—and to the common advantages of society. It is piracy to buy or steal a native African and subject him to servitude. Surely, the sin is as great to enslave an American as an African.

Therefore we believe and affirm that there is no difference, in principle, between the African slave trade and American slavery;

That every American citizen who retains a human being in involuntary bondage as his property is, according to Scripture (Exodus 21:16), a mansteaker;

That the slaves ought instantly to be set free and brought under the protection of law; . . .

That all those laws which are now in force admitting the right of slavery are therefore, before God, utterly null and void. . . .

We further believe and affirm that all persons of color who possess the qualifications which are demanded of others ought to be admitted forthwith to the enjoyment of the same privileges, and the exercise of the same prerogatives, as others; and that the paths of preferment, of wealth, and of intelligence should be opened as widely to them as to persons of a white complexion.

We maintain that no compensation should be given to the planters emancipating their slaves:

Because it would be a surrender of the great fundamental principle that man cannot hold property in man;

Because slavery is a crime, and therefore [the slave] is not an article to be sold;

Because the holders of slaves are not the just proprietors of what they claim; freeing the slave is not depriving them of property, but restoring it to its rightful

---

*W. P. Garrison and F. J. Garrison, *William Lloyd Garrison, 1805–1879* (New York: The Century Co., 1885), vol. 1, pp. 410–411.

owner; it is not wrong the master, but righting the slave—restoring him to himself;

Because immediate and general emancipation would only destroy nominal, not real, property; it would not amputate a limb or break a bone of the slaves, but, by infusing motives into their breasts, would make them doubly valuable to the masters as free laborers; and

Because, if compensation is to be given at all, it should be given to the outraged and guiltless slaves, and not to those who have plundered and abused them.

We regard as delusive, cruel, and dangerous any scheme of expatriation [to Liberia] which pretends to aid, either directly or indirectly, in the emancipation of the slaves, or to be a substitute for the immediate and total abolition of slavery.

We fully and unanimously recognize the sovereignty of each state to legislate exclusively on the subject of the slavery which is tolerated within its limits; we concede that Congress, under the present national compact, has no right to interfere with any of the slave states in relation to this momentous subject;

But we maintain that Congress has a right, and is solemnly bound, to suppress the domestic trade between the several states, and to abolish slavery in those portions of our territory which the Constitution has placed under its exclusive jurisdiction [District of Columbia].

3. Theodore Dwight Weld Pillories Slavery (1839)*

Theodore Dwight Weld assumed leadership of the New York abolitionist group, which objected to the anticonstitutional tactics of Garrison's New England following. He was one of the most influential of the abolitionists, and certainly one of the great men of his era. Preacher, lecturer (until he ruined his voice), pamphleteer, organizer, and inspirational genius, he founded numerous local abolitionist societies and won countless converts to abolition, including congressmen and other public figures. His documented compilation of horror tales, published in 1839 in American Slavery As It Is, *not only became the bible of the cause but greatly influenced the writing of* Uncle Tom's Cabin. *The following statements in his Introduction have been criticized as grossly overdrawn. How exaggerated or accurate are they?*

We will prove that the slaves in the United States are treated with barbarous inhumanity; that they are overworked, underfed, wretchedly clad and lodged, and have insufficient sleep; that they are often made to wear round their necks iron collars armed with prongs, to drag heavy chains and weights at their feet while working in the field, and to wear yokes, and bells, and iron horns; that they are often kept confined in the stocks day and night for weeks together, made to wear gags in their mouths for hours or days, have some of their front teeth torn out or broken off, that they may be easily detected when they run away; that they are frequently flogged with terrible severity, have red pepper rubbed into their lacerated flesh, and hot brine, spirits of turpentine, etc., poured over the gashes to increase the torture;

---

*T. D. Weld, *American Slavery As It Is* (New York: American Anti-Slavery Society, 1839), p. 9.

that they are often stripped naked, their backs and limbs cut with knives, bruised and mangled by scores and hundreds of blows with the paddle, and terribly torn by the claws of cats, drawn over them by their tormentors; that they are often hunted with bloodhounds and shot down like beasts, or torn in pieces by dogs; that they are often suspended by the arms and whipped and beaten till they faint, and when revived by restoratives beaten again till they faint, and sometimes till they die; that their ears are often cut off, their eyes knocked out, their bones broken, their flesh branded with red-hot irons; that they are maimed, mutilated, and burned to death over slow fires.

All these things, and more, and worse, we shall prove. . . . We shall show, not merely that such deeds are committed, but that they are frequent; not done in corners, but before the sun; not in one of the slave states, but in all of them; not perpetrated by brutal overseers and drivers merely, but by magistrates, by legislators, by professors of religion, by preachers of the Gospel, by governors of states, by "gentlemen of property and standing," and by delicate females moving in the "highest circles of society."

We know, full well, the outcry that will be made by multitudes at these declarations; the multiform cavils, the flat denials, the charges of "exaggeration" and "falsehood" so often bandied; the sneers of affected contempt at the credulity that can believe such things; and the rage and imprecations against those who give them currency.

We know, too, the threadbare sophistries by which slaveholders and their apologists seek to evade such testimony. If they admit that such deeds are committed, they tell us that they are exceedingly rare, and therefore furnish no grounds for judging of the general treatment of slaves; that occasionally a brutal wretch in the free states barbarously butchers his wife, but that no one thinks of inferring from that the general treatment of wives at the North and West.

They tell us, also, that the slaveholders of the South are proverbially hospitable, kind, and generous, and it is incredible that they can perpetrate such enormities upon human beings; further, that it is absurd to suppose that they would thus injure their own property, that self-interest would prompt them to treat their slaves with kindness, as none but fools and madmen wantonly destroy their own property; further, that Northern visitors at the South come back testifying to the kind treatment of the slaves, and that the slaves themselves corroborate such representations. . . . We are not to be turned from our purpose by such vapid babblings.

4. Slavery and the Family (1840)

The following illustration depicts what was probably the abolitionists' most telling argument against slavery: the violence it wrought upon the integrity of family life. Harriet Beecher Stowe would later make that argument the central motif of her epochal antislavery novel, Uncle Tom's Cabin. *Why was this argument so powerful? Did it appeal differently to men and women? How did the illustrator here make special appeal to women's sentiments?*

D. Judgments on the Abolitionists

1. Daniel Webster Is Critical (1850)[*]

The thunderously eloquent Daniel Webster was no abolitionist, though the abolitionists liked to think of him as in their camp. He sadly disillusioned them in his famous Seventh of March speech about the Compromise of 1850 (see later, p. 271). Pleading passionately for North-South harmony, he turned upon the antislaveryites. Their pained outcry rent the heavens. At a public meeting in Faneuil Hall in Boston, the Reverend Theodore Parker declared, "I know of no deed in American history done by a son of New England to which I can compare this but the act of Benedict Arnold." In this portion of Webster's speech, is he convincing about the harm done by the abolitionists?

---

[*]*Congressional Globe*, 31st Congress, 1st session, Appendix, vol. 22, part 1, p. 275.

Then, sir, there are those abolition societies, of which I am unwilling to speak, but in regard to which I have very clear notions and opinions. I do not think them useful. I think their operations for the last twenty years have produced nothing good or valuable.

At the same time, I know thousands of them are honest and good men; perfectly well-meaning men. They have excited feelings; they think they must do something for the cause of liberty. And in their sphere of action, they do not see what else they can do than to contribute to an abolition press, or an abolition society, or to pay an abolition lecturer.

I do not mean to impute gross motives even to the leaders of these societies, but I am not blind to the consequences. I cannot but see what mischiefs their interference with the South has produced.

And is it not plain to every man? Let any gentleman who doubts of that recur to the debates in the Virginia House of Delegates in 1832, and he will see with what freedom a proposition made by Mr. Randolph for the gradual abolition of slavery was discussed in that body. Everyone spoke of slavery as he thought; very ignominious and disparaging names and epithets were applied to it.

The debates in the House of Delegates on that occasion, I believe, were all published. They were read by every colored man who could read, and if there were any who could not read, those debates were read to them by others. At that time Virginia was not unwilling nor afraid to discuss this question, and to let that part of her population know as much of it as they could learn.

That was in 1832. . . . These abolition societies commenced their course of action in 1835. It is said—I do not know how true it may be—that they sent incendiary publications into the slave states. At any event, they attempted to arouse, and did arouse, a very strong feeling. In other words, they created great agitation in the North against Southern slavery.

Well, what was the result? The bonds of the slaves were bound more firmly than before; their rivets were more strongly fastened. Public opinion, which in Virginia had begun to be exhibited against slavery, and was opening out for the discussion of the question, drew back and shut itself up in its castle.

I wish to know whether anybody in Virginia can, now, talk openly as Mr. Randolph, Gov. McDowell, and others talked there, openly, and sent their remarks to the press, in 1832.

We all know the fact, and we all know the cause. And everything that this agitating people have done, has been, not to enlarge, but to restrain, not to set free, but to bind faster, the slave population of the South. That is my judgment.

2. Abraham Lincoln Appraises Abolitionism (1854)*

Abolitionism and crackpotism were, for a time, closely associated in the public mind, and the taint of abolitionism was almost fatal to a man aspiring to public office. Southerners commonly regarded Abraham Lincoln as an abolitionist, even though

---

*R. P. Basler, ed., *The Collected Works of Abraham Lincoln* (New Brunswick, NJ: Rutgers University Press, 1953), vol. 2, pp. 255–256.

his wife's family in Kentucky were slaveholders. Lincoln set forth his views at some length in this memorable speech at Peoria, Illinois, in 1854. On the basis of these remarks, did he deserve to be called an abolitionist? In what respects might the South have resented his position?

Before proceeding, let me say that I have no prejudice against the Southern people. They are just what we would be in their situation. If slavery did not now exist among them, they would not introduce it. If it did now exist amongst us, we should not instantly give it up. This I believe of the masses North and South.

Doubtless there are individuals, on both sides, who would not hold slaves under any circumstances, and others who would gladly introduce slavery anew, if it were out of existence. We know that some Southern men do free their slaves, go North, and become tiptop abolitionists; while some Northern ones go South and become most cruel slave-masters.

When Southern people tell us they are no more responsible for the origin of slavery than we, I acknowledge the fact. When it is said that the institution exists, and that it is very difficult to get rid of it in any satisfactory way, I can understand and appreciate the saying. I surely will not blame them for not doing what I should not know how to do myself.

If all earthly power were given me, I should not know what to do as to the existing institution. My first impulse would be to free all the slaves and send them to Liberia—to their native land. But a moment's reflection would convince me that whatever of high hope (as I think there is) there may be in this in the long run, its sudden execution is impossible. If they all landed there in a day, they would all perish in the next ten days; and there are not surplus shipping and surplus money enough to carry them there in many times ten days.

What then? Free them all and keep them among us as underlings? Is it quite certain that this betters their condition? I think I would not hold one in slavery at any rate; yet the point is not clear enough for me to denounce people upon.

What next? Free them, and make them politically and socially our equals? My own feelings will not admit of this; and if mine would, we well know that those of the great mass of white people would not. Whether this feeling accords with justice and sound judgment is not the sole question, if indeed it is any part of it. A universal feeling, whether well or ill founded, cannot be safely disregarded. We cannot then make them equals.

It does seem to me that systems of gradual emancipation might be adopted; but for their tardiness in this I will not undertake to judge our brethren of the South.

When they remind us of their constitutional rights, I acknowledge them, not grudgingly but fully and fairly. And I would give them any legislation for the reclaiming of their fugitives which should not, in its stringency, be more likely to carry a free man into slavery than our ordinary criminal laws are to hang an innocent one.

E. The Rising White Southern Temper

1. Hinton Helper's Banned Book (1857)*

Hinton R. Helper, an impoverished North Carolinian who hated blacks, published a sensational book in 1857 in which he statistically contrasted the rapid economic growth of the North with the slower progress of the South. Concluding that the slaveless whites were the chief victims of the slave system, he urged upon them various means, some incendiary, to overthrow both slavery and the grip of the white oligarchy. Unable to find a publisher in the South, he aired his views in the North under the title The Impending Crisis of the South. *The Southern aristocracy reacted violently, banning the book and roughly handling a few daring souls who had obtained smuggled copies. Tens of thousands of copies in one form or another were distributed. Why was it to the advantage of the slave owners to treat the poor whites as Helper alleged they did?*

Notwithstanding the fact that the white non-slaveholders of the South are in the majority as five to one, they have never yet had any part or lot in framing the laws under which they live. There is no legislation except for the benefit of slavery and slaveholders.

As a general rule, poor white persons are regarded with less esteem and attention than Negroes, and though the condition of the latter is wretched beyond description, vast numbers of the former are infinitely worse off. A cunningly devised mockery of freedom is guaranteed to them, and that is all. To all intents and purposes, they are disfranchised and outlawed, and the only privilege extended to them is a shallow and circumscribed participation in the political movements that usher slaveholders into office.

We have not breathed away seven and twenty years in the South without becoming acquainted with the demagogical maneuverings of the oligarchy. . . . To the illiterate poor whites—made poor and ignorant by the system of slavery—they hold out the idea that slavery is the very bulwark of our liberties, and the foundation of American independence! . . .

The lords of the lash are not only absolute masters of the blacks, who are bought and sold, and driven about like so many cattle, but they are also the oracles and arbiters of all non-slaveholding whites, whose freedom is merely nominal, and whose unparalleled illiteracy and degradation is purposely and fiendishly perpetuated. How little the "poor white trash"—the great majority of the Southern people—know of the real condition of the country is, indeed, sadly astonishing.

The truth is they know nothing of public measures, and little of private affairs, except what their imperious masters, the slave-drivers, condescend to tell—and that is but precious little. And even that little, always garbled and one-sided, is never told except in public harangues. For the haughty cavaliers of shackles and handcuffs will not degrade themselves by holding private converse with those who have neither dimes nor hereditary rights in human flesh.

---

*H. R. Helper, *The Impending Crisis of the South* (New York: A. C. Bundick, 1860), pp. 42–45.

Whenever it pleases . . . a slaveholder to become communicative, poor whites may hear with fear and trembling, but not speak.

Non-slaveholders are not only kept in ignorance of what is transpiring at the North, but they are continually misinformed of what is going on even in the South. Never were the poorer classes of a people, and those classes so largely in the majority, and all inhabiting the same country, so basely duped, so adroitly swindled, or so damnably outraged.

It is expected that the stupid and sequacious [servile] masses, the white victims of slavery, will believe—and, as a general thing, they do believe—whatever the slaveholders tell them. And thus it is that they are cajoled into the notion that they are the freest, happiest, and most intelligent people in the world, and are taught to look with prejudice and disapprobation upon every new principle or progressive movement. Thus it is that the South, woefully inert and inventionless, has lagged behind the North, and is now weltering in the cesspool of ignorance and degradation.

2. The South Condemns Helperites (1859)*

Helper's appeal to the poor whites of the South fell on barren ground; most of them were illiterate or apathetic, while others could not get the book. But the free-soil Republicans of the North seized upon it for political purposes, and sixty-eight members of the House of Representatives signed an appeal for funds to distribute free 100,000 copies of a paperback abridgment. Following John Brown's fear-inspiring raid into Virginia in 1859, the Southerners were determined to keep from the speakership of the House any endorser of Helper's book. For two months they filibustered successfully against Republican John Sherman, who had ill-advisedly signed the appeal, while the flames of sectional conflict roared higher and higher. What does the following speech by Representative James Bullock Clark of Missouri (later a member of the Confederate Congress) presage about the preservation of the Union?

These [Helperite] gentlemen come in and say that the riches of the South are neglected by the bad management of the South; that the accursed plague of slavery does it; and that, therefore, non-slaveholders at the South should rise in their majesty—peaceably if they can, forcibly if they must—take their arms, subdue the slaveholders, drive out the plague of slavery, take possession of the country, and dedicate it to free labor.

That is the sentiment in the book which these gentlemen recommend to have circulated gratuitously all over the South. Are such men fit to preside over the destinies of our common country? Can the South expect from such men the maintenance of the integrity of the Constitution? Our slave property is as much our property under the Constitution, and under the guarantees of this government, as any property held at the North. Whether it is sinful to hold slaves, whether slavery is a plague and a loss, and whether it will affect our future destiny, is our own business. We suffer for that, and not they.

Congressional Globe, 36th Congress, 1st session (December 8, 1859), p. 17.

We ask none of their prayers. We need none of them. If we were in need of them, and if the only way to escape future punishment and misery were to receive benefit from the prayers of those [sixty-eight] who signed that recommendation, I should expect, after death, to sink into the nethermost Hell. [Laughter.]

Do gentlemen expect that they can distribute incendiary books, give incendiary advice, advise rebellion, advise non-intercourse in all the relations of life, spread such works broadcast over the country, and not be taken to task for it? I presume that the South has sufficient self-respect; that it understands the effect of its institutions well enough; that it has its rights, and dares to maintain them.

3. James Hammond Proclaims Cotton King (1858)*

As the resentment of the South rose, so did its confidence in its ability to stand alone as a Confederacy, if need be. It rode through the panic of 1857 with flying colors; its enormous exports of "King Cotton" overshadowed all others from America. But the North might well have responded with the cry "Grass is King!" For, as Helper pointed out in his banned book, the value of the North's hay crop, though consumed at home, was greater than that of the South's cotton crop. Yet Senator Hammond of South Carolina, a bombastic owner of some three hundred slaves, voiced the cry "Cotton is King!" in this famous Senate speech. He referred to the dangerous dependence of the enormous English textile industry on the huge imports from the South. What were the problems with his argument?

Why, sir, the South has never yet had a just cause of war. Every time she has seized her sword it has been on the point of honor, and that point of honor has been mainly loyalty to her sister colonies and sister states, who have ever since plundered and calumniated her.

But if there were no other reason why we should never have a war, would any sane nation make war on cotton? Without firing a gun, without drawing a sword, when they make war on us we can bring the whole world to our feet.

The South is perfectly competent to go on, one, two, or three years, without planting a seed of cotton. I believe that if she was to plant but half her cotton, it would be an immediate advantage to her. I am not so sure but that after three years' cessation she would come out stronger than ever she was before and better prepared to enter afresh upon her great career of enterprise.

What would happen if no cotton was furnished for three years? I will not stop to depict what everyone can imagine, but this is certain: old England would topple headlong and carry the whole civilized world with her. No, sir, you dare not make war on cotton. No power on earth dares make war upon it. Cotton is King!

[It is not surprising that cotton should have deluded the South when the British themselves conceded their fatal dependence. A writer in Blackwood's Edinburgh Magazine (February 1851, p. 216) confessed: "We rest almost entirely on the supplies obtained from a single state [nation]. No one need be told that five-sixths, often nine-tenths, of the

---

Congressional Globe, 35th Congress, 1st session (March 3, 1858), p. 961.

supply of cotton consumed in our manufactures come from America, and that seven or eight thousand persons are directly or indirectly employed in the operations which take place upon it. Suppose America wishes to bully us, to make us abandon Canada or Jamaica for example, she has no need to go to war. She has only to stop the export of cotton for six months, and the whole of our manufacturing counties are starving or in rebellion; while a temporary cessation of profit is the only inconvenience they experience on the other side of the Atlantic. Can we call ourselves independent in such circumstances?"]

Thought Provokers

1. A favorite argument of the South was that the black slave was better off than the wage slave of the North or England. (See also earlier, p. 213.) In what respects was this true? False? John Quincy Adams said, "Misery is not slavery." Comment.
2. Why could persons who had witnessed slavery in the South offer such radically differing accounts? What would have been the future of slavery if it had been left alone?
3. It has been said that the Garrison abolitionists were right in principle but wrong in method. Comment. Garrison advocated disunion as a means of ending slavery. Explain the logic or illogic of his position. Explain how you would have dealt with slavery if given "all earthly power."
4. Why did so many people in the North deplore the boat-rocking tactics of the abolitionists and often despise them? Did the abolitionists do more harm or good?
5. In what respects did Hinton R. Helper help to cause the Civil War? In what respects did the "Cotton is King" complex cause the Civil War? It has been said that cotton was a king who enslaved his subjects. Comment.

17

Manifest Destiny and Its Legacy, 1841–1848

> If you will take all the theft, all the assaults, all
> the cases of arson, ever committed in time of
> peace in the United States since the settlement of
> Jamestown in 1608 [1607], and add to them all the
> cases of violence offered to woman, with all the
> murders, they will not amount to half the wrongs
> committed in this war for the plunder of Mexico.
>
> *Theodore Parker, abolitionist clergyman, 1848*

Prologue: Hereditary British-American antipathy came to a head in 1846 over extreme American demands for the boundary line of 54° 40′ in the Oregon Country. The dispute was settled later that year by a compromise on the line of 49°. Meanwhile, the overconfident Mexicans, not unwilling to fight and encouraged by the prospect of an Anglo-American conflict over Oregon, were threatening the United States with war over the annexation of the revolted province of Texas. President James K. Polk, unable to buy coveted California from the Mexicans or to adjust other disputes with them, forced a showdown in 1846 by moving U.S. troops provocatively close to the Mexican border. In the ensuing war, the Americans were everywhere victorious—General Zachary Taylor in northern Mexico at Monterrey and Buena Vista, General Winfield Scott at Cerro Gordo and elsewhere in his spectacular drive toward Mexico City. By the terms of peace, Polk finally secured California—and an aggravated slavery problem to boot.

A. The Debate over Oregon

1. Senator Edward Hannegan Demands 54° 40' (1846)[*]

The Democratic party, when nominating Polk for the presidency at Baltimore in 1844, had demanded the annexation of the republic of Texas and the acquisition of Oregon all the way to 54° 40' Texas entered the Union as a slave state in 1845. A year later, Congress, before acquiescing in the Oregon compromise line of 49°, was debating resolutions proclaiming U.S. ownership of all the territory to the line of 54° 40'. Senator Hannegan, an intemperate orator (and drinker) from Indiana, was the most bellicose

---

[*]*Congressional Globe*, 29th Congress, 1st session, vol. 15, part 1, pp. 109–110.

spokesman for the free-soil Northwest. How does his Senate speech—reported in the third person—help to explain the existing upsurge of nationalism?

Now, if the adoption of the [Oregon] resolutions, which contained the immutable principles of truth, should bring war on us, let war come! What American was there who, through fear of war, would hesitate to declare the truth in this Chamber? He [Hannegan] also was for peace. He shrunk back from the thought of war as much as could the Senator from South Carolina [John Calhoun]. He loved peace; but if it were only to be maintained on degrading and dishonorable terms, war, even of extermination, would be far preferable. . . .

There had been a singular course pursued on this Oregon question, and with reference to which he must detain the Senate a moment. It contrasted so strangely, so wonderfully, with a precisely similar question—the annexation of Texas. Texas and Oregon were born the same instant, nursed and cradled in the same cradle—the Baltimore Convention—and they were at the same instant adopted by the Democracy throughout the land. There was not a moment's hesitation, until Texas was admitted. But the moment she was admitted, the peculiar friends of Texas turned, and were doing all they could to strangle Oregon!

But the country were not blind or deaf. The people see, they comprehend, and he trusted they would speak. It was a most singular state of things. We were told that we must be careful not to involve ourselves in a war with England on

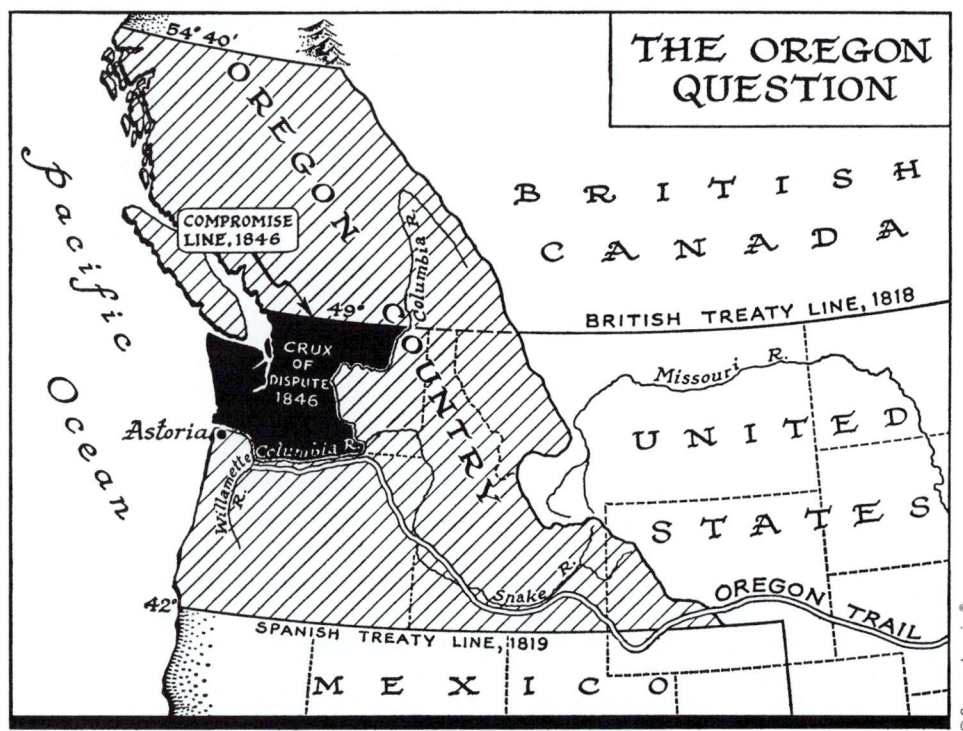

a question of disputed boundary. There was a question of disputed boundary between us and Mexico. But did we hear, from the same quarter, any warning against a collision with Mexico when we were about to consummate the annexation of Texas? We were told by those who knew something of these matters that the Nueces [River] was the proper boundary of Texas! And how did they find the friends of Texas moving on that occasion? Did we, for a single instant, halt on the banks of the Nueces? No; at a single bound we crossed the Nueces, and the blasts of our trumpets, and the prancing of our war-horses, were heard on the banks of the Rio del Norte [Rio Grande], one hundred miles beyond. Nearly one hundred miles of disputed territory gives no cause for a moment's hesitation!

There was no negotiation then, so far as Mexico was concerned: we took all. But when Oregon is brought into question, we are called on, as an act proper and right, to give away a whole empire on the Pacific, if England desire it. He never would consent to a surrender of any portion of the country north of 49°, nor one foot, by treaty or otherwise, under 54° 40'.

2. Two Pioneers Describe Oregon (1847)*

While statesmen debated, settlers continued to pour into the Oregon Country. They did not all have the same reaction to the virgin wilderness they encountered. In these two descriptions of the new territory, what observations are made by both writers? On what do they disagree? How might their different perceptions be explained?

Hezekiah Packingham to his Brother, Willamette Valley, March 1, 1847

I arrived in the Wallamette Valley on the 30th of September, and my calculations are all defeated about Oregon. I found it a mean, dried up, and drowned country. The Yam Hill is a small valley, destitute of timber. I soon got sick of this place, and then went to the mouth of the Columbia river. I can give Oregon credit for only one or two things, and these are, good health and plenty of salmon, and Indians; as for the farming country there is none here—wheat grows about the same as in Illinois; corn, potatoes, and garden vegetables cannot grow here without watering. The nights are too cold here in summer. The soil is not as good as in Illinois—the face of the country is hilly, and high mountains covered with snow all summer, and small valleys—the mountains and hills are covered with the heaviest timber that I ever saw. We have had a very hard winter here, snow fell two feet deep, and lay three weeks, by reason of which hundreds of cattle have died of starvation. The thermometer fell to three degrees above zero.—Prairie grass here is the same as in Illinois. There is no timothy nor clover. Mechanics are very numerous here. Of the ships that sailed from New York last April, but one arrived, and she was ice bound for 50 days, in latitude 50 1–2. It is supposed the other has gone to her long home. A United States man-of-war [*Shark*] was recently wrecked at the mouth of the Columbia. Money is very scarce here—and

---

*From Dale Morgan, ed., *Overland in 1846: Diaries and Letters of the California-Oregon Trail* (1963), vol. II, pp. 685–686, 691–692.

they have a kind of currency here (orders on stores and scrip)—they value property very high, but if they would put things at cash prices, they would be about the same as they are in the States. Oregon is rapidly filling up with young men, (but no girls,) of whom two-thirds are dissatisfied and many would return to the States if they were able, but the road is long and tedious, and it is hard for families to get back; my trip was pleasant until I got to the South Pass—after that the country was rugged, and bad roads. Tell young men if they intend coming to Oregon, to drive no teams unless it is their own. We were uninjured by the Indians, though they were very saucy—they have no manners; they worship idols [totem poles?], and I saw one of their gods at the mouth of the river. There is no society here except the Camelites [Campbellites—a liberal Protestant group first organized in Pennsylvania in 1810]. I shall return to the States next spring. Don't believe all that is said about Oregon, as many falsehoods are uttered respecting the country.

Hezekiah Packingham

Richard R. Howard to a Friend in Illinois, "Oregon Territory," April 6, 1847

We arrived safe in Oregon City on the 12th of September last. We reached Fort Laramie in 42 days from Independence; Fort Hall in 33 days more; the Dalles in 37 days more; and Oregon City in 16 days more—making in all 128 days. Our journey was two weeks longer than necessary had we lost no time. We met with no serious obstructions on our journey. We had to raise the front of our wagon beds two or three inches in crossing the Larimie Fork to keep the water out; sometimes we had long drives to find a good place for camping, with water and grass. [The writer gives a long detail of the necessary outfit for the journey and cautions to be used on the road— which we omit. *Illinois Journal*] No single man should come to this country. One third of the men in Oregon at this time are without wives. Nothing but men of families are wanted here to till the soil, to make this one of the greatest countries in the world. This country does not get so muddy as Illinois. There is no dust in summer here. The good land in this country is more extensive than I expected to find it. The hills are not so high as represented. From the Cascade mountains to the Pacific, the whole country can be cultivated. The natural soil of the country, especially in the bottoms, is a black loam, mixed with gravel and clay. We have good timber; but there appears to be a scarcity of good building rock. The small streams furnish us with trout the year round.

My wife to the old lady—Greeting; says she was never more satisfied with a move in her life before; that she is fast recovering her health; and she hopes you will come to Oregon, where you can enjoy what little time you have remaining in health.

The roads to Oregon are not as bad as represented. Hastings in his history* speaks of the Falls of Columbia being 50 feet and roaring loud, making the earth tremble, &c. The falls are about like that of a mill-dam. Every thing in this country now is high, except molasses, sugar and salt; but when we raise our wheat crop to trade on, we will make them pay for their high charges. I think no place where a living is to be made out of the earth can be preferable to Oregon for that purpose—and let people say what they may—all agree that it is healthy. It is certainly the healthiest

---

*The reference is to L. W. Hastings, *Emigrants' Guide to Oregon and California* (1845), a standard guidebook for travelers on the Oregon and California Trails.

country in the world, disease is scarcely known here, except among the late emigrants, ninety-nine out of a hundred of them get well the first season. I have heard of only two deaths since I have been in Oregon; one of them was a man who came here diseased and in one year died; the other was a woman who it is said was near dead ten years before she came here.

Richard R. Howard

3. A British View of the Oregon Controversy (1846)

Many Britons were bemused that the upstart Yankees were in such a bellicose mood over Oregon. This cartoon from the British magazine Punch, entitled "What? You Young Yankee-Noodle, Strike Your Own Father!" pokes fun at the Americans. What did the cartoonist find most amusing about the American position? Why is the American figure rendered as a Southerner, with a slave driver's whip in his pocket?

"WHAT? YOU YOUNG YANKEE-NOODLE, STRIKE
YOUR OWN FATHER!"

Punch (London), 1846

B. Warring over the War with Mexico

1. Charles Sumner Assails the Texas Grab (1847)[*]

Boston-bred and Harvard-polished Charles Sumner, soon to be a U.S. senator, was one of the most impressive orators of his day. Six feet four inches in height and

---

[*]*Old South Leaflets* (Boston: Old South Meeting House, 1904), vol. 6, no. 132, pp. 2–4.

blessed with a powerful voice, he could sway vast audiences. An earnest foe of war, he preached arbitration; an impassioned enemy of slavery, he demanded abolition; a devoted champion of race equality, he fought the Massachusetts law forbidding marriages between whites and blacks. In 1847, in the midst of the war with Mexico, the Massachusetts legislature adopted this document, which Sumner had prepared, blasting the annexation of Texas. Although he overplayed the slave conspiracy accusation, he made a number of telling points. Assuming that his facts are correct, how many genuine grievances did Mexico have against the United States?

The history of the annexation of Texas cannot be fully understood without reverting to the early settlement of that province by citizens of the United States.

Mexico, on achieving her independence of the Spanish Crown, by a general ordinance worthy of imitation by all Christian nations, had decreed the abolition of human slavery within her dominions, embracing the province of Texas. . . .

At this period, citizens of the United States had already begun to remove into Texas, hardly separated, as it was, by the River Sabine from the slaveholding state of Louisiana. The idea was early promulgated that this extensive province ought to become a part of the United States. Its annexation was distinctly agitated in the Southern and Western states in 1829; and it was urged on the ground of the strength and extension it would give to the "Slave Power," and the fresh market it would open for the sale of slaves.

The suggestion of this idea had an important effect. A current of emigration soon followed from the United States. Slaveholders crossed the Sabine with their slaves, in defiance of the Mexican ordinance of freedom. Restless spirits, discontented at home, or feeling the restraint of the narrow confines of our country, joined them; while their number was swollen by the rude and lawless of all parts of the land, who carried to Texas the love of license which had rendered a region of justice no longer a pleasant home to them. To such spirits, rebellion was natural.

It soon broke forth. At this period the whole [Texan] population, including women and children, did not amount to twenty thousand; and, among these, most of the older and wealthier inhabitants still favored peace. A Declaration of Independence, a farcical imitation of that of our fathers, was put forth, not by persons acting in a Congress or in a representative character, but by about ninety individuals— all, except two, from the United States—acting for themselves, and recommending a similar course to their fellow citizens. In a just cause the spectacle of this handful of adventurers, boldly challenging the power of Mexico, would excite our sympathy, perhaps our admiration. But successful rapacity, which seized broad and fertile lands while it opened new markets for slaves, excites no sentiment but that of abhorrence.

The work of rebellion sped. Citizens of the United States joined its fortunes, not singly, but in numbers, even in armed squadrons. Our newspapers excited the lust of territorial robbery in the public mind. Expeditions were openly equipped within our own borders. Advertisements for volunteers summoned the adventurous, as to patriotic labors. Military companies, with officers and standards, directed their steps to the revolted province.

During all this period the United States were at peace with Mexico. A proclamation from our government, forbidding these hostile preparations within our borders, is undeniable evidence of their existence, while truth compels us to record its impotence in upholding the sacred duties of neutrality between Mexico and the insurgents. . . .

The Texan flag waved over an army of American citizens. Of the six or eight hundred who won the [decisive] battle of San Jacinto, scattering the Mexican forces and capturing their general [Santa Anna], not more than fifty were citizens of Texas having grievances of their own to redress on that field.

The victory was followed by the recognition of the independence of Texas by the United States; while the new state took its place among the nations of the earth. . . .

Certainly our sister republic [Mexico] might feel aggrieved by this conduct. It might justly charge our citizens with disgraceful robbery, while, in seeking extension of slavery, they repudiated the great truths of American freedom.

Meanwhile Texas slept on her arms, constantly expecting new efforts from Mexico to regain her former power. The two combatants regarded each other as enemies. Mexico still asserted her right to the territory wrested from her, and refused to acknowledge its independence.

Texas turned for favor and succor to England. The government of the United States, fearing it might pass under the influence of this power, made overtures for its annexation to our country. This was finally accomplished by joint resolutions of Congress, in defiance of the Constitution, and in gross insensibility to the sacred obligations of amity with Mexico, imposed alike by treaty and by justice, "both strong against the deed." The Mexican minister regarded it as an act offensive to his country, and, demanding his passport, returned home.

2. President James Polk Justifies the Texas Coup (1845)*

The United States had tried to wrest Texas from Spain under the vague terms of the Louisiana Purchase, but had at last abandoned such claims in the swap that netted the Floridas in 1819. The Texan Americans finally staged a successful revolt against Mexico in 1835–1836, but for nine years thereafter lived in constant apprehension of a renewed Mexican invasion. Three days before President Polk took office on March 4, 1845, President John Tyler had signed a joint resolution of Congress offering the republic of Texas annexation to the United States. All that remained was for the Texans to accept the terms, and they formally did so on June 23, 1845. The tension was heightened by the keen interest of Britain and France in making Texas a satellite, with the consequent dangers of involving the United States in war. Polk, a purposeful and persistent expansionist, justified the annexation as follows in his inaugural address. Which of his arguments was the most convincing from the standpoint of the United States? Which was the least convincing from the standpoint of Mexico? Did he handle the slavery issue persuasively?

The Republic of Texas has made known her desire to come into our Union, to form a part of our Confederacy and enjoy with us the blessings of liberty secured

---

*J. D. Richardson, ed., *Messages and Papers of the Presidents* (New York: Bureau of National Literature, 1897), vol. 4, pp. 379–381.

and guaranteed by our Constitution. Texas was once a part of our country—was unwisely ceded away to a foreign power [in 1819]—is now independent, and possesses an undoubted right to dispose of a part or the whole of her territory, and to merge her sovereignty as a separate and independent state in ours. . . .

I regard the question of annexation as belonging exclusively to the United States and Texas. They are independent powers, competent to contract; and foreign nations have no right to interfere with them or to take exception to their reunion. . . . Foreign powers should therefore look on the annexation of Texas to the United States, not as the conquest of a nation seeking to extend her dominions by arms and violence, but as the peaceful acquisition of a territory once her own, by adding another member to our Confederation, with the consent of that member, thereby diminishing the chances of war and opening to them new and ever-increasing markets for their products.

To Texas, the reunion is important because the strong protecting arm of our government would be extended over her, and the vast resources of her fertile soil and genial climate would be speedily developed, while the safety of New Orleans and of our whole southwestern frontier against hostile aggression, as well as the interests of the whole Union, would be promoted by it. . . .

None can fail to see the danger to our safety and future peace if Texas remains an independent state, or becomes an ally or dependency of some foreign nation more powerful than herself. Is there one among our citizens who would not prefer perpetual peace with Texas to occasional wars, which so often occur between bordering independent nations? Is there one who would not prefer free intercourse with her, to high duties on all our products and manufactures which enter her ports or cross her frontiers? Is there one who would not prefer an unrestricted communication with her citizens, to the frontier obstructions which must occur if she remains out of the Union?

Whatever is good or evil in the local [slave] institutions of Texas will remain her own, whether annexed to the United States or not. None of the present states will be responsible for them any more than they are for the local institutions of each other. They have confederated together for certain specific objects. Upon the same principle that they would refuse to form a perpetual union with Texas because of her local institutions, our forefathers would have been prevented from forming our present Union.

3. The Cabinet Debates War (1846)*

The expansionist Polk, fearing that so-called British land-grabbers would forestall him, was eager to purchase California from Mexico. But the proud Mexicans, though bankrupt, refused to sell. They also threatened war over the annexation of Texas and defaulted on their payment of claims to Americans for damages during their recent revolutionary disturbances. Polk made a last-hope effort to buy California and adjust other disputes when he sent John Slidell to Mexico as a special envoy late in 1845, but the Mexicans refused to negotiate with Slidell. Polk then ordered General Taylor to

---

*M. M. Quaife, ed., *The Diary of James K. Polk* (Chicago: A. C. McClurg, 1910), vol. 1, pp. 384–386.

move his small army from Corpus Christi on the Nueces River (the traditional south-west border of Texas) to the Rio Grande del Norte (which the Texans extravagantly claimed as their new boundary). Still the Mexicans did not attack the provocative Yankee invader. Polk thereupon recommended to his cabinet a declaration of war, presumably on the basis of unpaid damage claims and Slidell's rejection. Both were rather flimsy pretexts. From this passage in his diary, was the president really trying to avoid a fight? Were his grounds for war valid, even after sixteen American soldiers were killed or wounded?

Saturday, 9th May, 1846.—The Cabinet held a regular meeting today; all the members present.

I brought up the Mexican question, and the question of what was the duty of the administration in the present state of our relations with that country. The subject was very fully discussed.

All agreed that if the Mexican forces at Matamoros committed any act of hostility on Gen'l Taylor's forces, I should immediately send a message to Congress recommending an immediate declaration of war.

I stated to the Cabinet that up to this time, as they knew, we had heard of no open act of aggression by the Mexican army, but that the danger was imminent that such acts would be committed. I said that in my opinion we had ample cause of war, and that it was impossible that we could stand *in statu quo*, or that I could remain silent much longer; that I thought it was my duty to send a message to Congress very soon and recommend definitive measures. I told them that I thought I ought to make such a message by Tuesday next; that the country was excited and impatient on the subject; and if I failed to do so, I would not be doing my duty.

I then propounded the distinct question to the Cabinet, and took their opinions individually, whether I should make a message to Congress on Tuesday, and whether in that message I should recommend a declaration of war against Mexico.

All except the Secretary of the Navy [George Bancroft] gave their advice in the affirmative. Mr. Bancroft dissented, but said if any act of hostility should be committed by the Mexican forces, he was then in favor of immediate war. Mr. Buchanan [Secretary of State] said he would feel better satisfied in his course if the Mexican forces had or should commit any act of hostility, but that as matters stood we had ample cause of war against Mexico, and he gave his assent to the measure.

It was agreed that the message should be prepared and submitted to the Cabinet in their meeting on Tuesday. . . .

About 6 o'clock P.M. Gen'l R. Jones, the Adjutant General of the Army, called and handed to me despatches received from Gen'l Taylor by the Southern mail which had just arrived, giving information that a part of [the] Mexican army had crossed . . . the [Rio Grande] Del Norte, and attacked and killed and captured two companies of dragoons of Gen'l Taylor's army, consisting of 63 officers and men. . . .

I immediately summoned the Cabinet to meet at 7 1/2 o'clock this evening. The Cabinet accordingly assembled at that hour; all the members present. The subject of the despatch received this evening from Gen'l Taylor, as well as the state of our relations with Mexico, were fully considered. The Cabinet were unanimously of opinion, and it was so agreed, that a message should be sent to Congress on

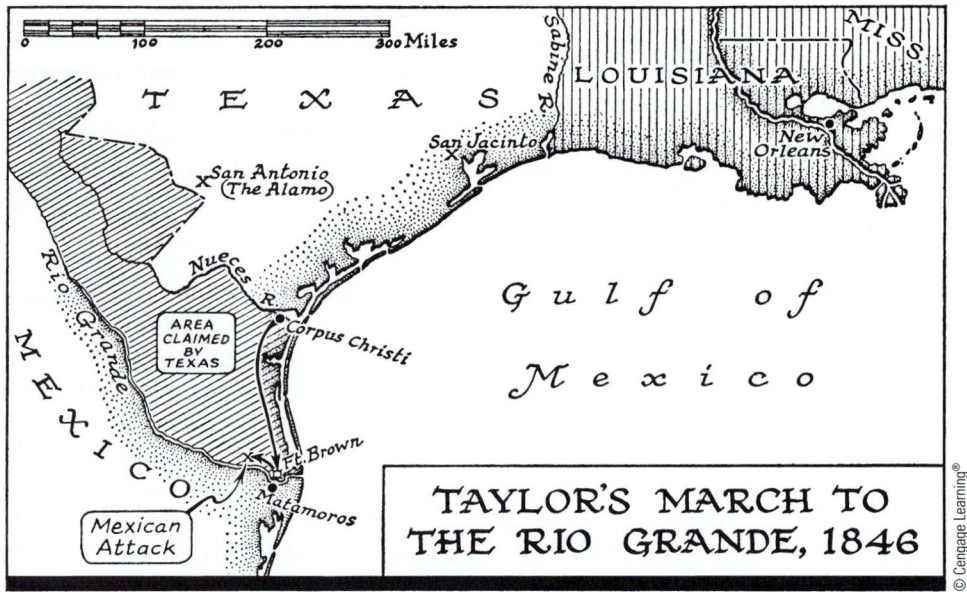

Monday laying all the information in my possession before them, and recommending vigorous and prompt measure[s] to enable the Executive to prosecute the war.

4. A Mexican Diplomat Blames America for War (1846)*

As Taylor's troops assembled along the Rio Grande, the Mexican foreign minister dispatched a fiery condemnation of American provocations. Still fuming over the annexation of Texas, he dismissed claims of Mexican aggression and absolved his country of any responsibility for the impending war. What are his chief grievances against the United States? Are his arguments convincing?

The vehement desire of the government of the United States, to extend its already immense territory at the expense of that of Mexico, has been manifest for many years; and it is beyond all doubt that in regard to Texas at least this has been their firm and constant determination: for it has been so declared categorically and officially by an authorized representative of the Union, whose assertion, strange and injurious as was its frankness, has nevertheless not been belied by the United States. . . .

[T]his incorporation of a territory which had constituted an integral part of that of Mexico during the long period of the Spanish dominion (and after her emancipation for so long a term without any interruption whatever, and which moreover had been recognized and sanctioned by the treaty of limits between the Mexican republic and the United States of America) was effected by the reprobated means of violence and fraud.

---

*Ward McAfee and J. Cordell Robinson, eds., *Origins of the Mexican War: A Documentary Source Book*, vol. 2 (Salisbury, NC: Documentary Publications, 1982), pp. 76–81.

Civilized nations have beheld with amazement, in this enlightened and refined epoch, a powerful and well consolidated state availing itself of the internal dissensions of a neighboring nation, putting its vigilance to sleep by protestations of friendship, setting in action all manner of springs and artifices, alternately plying intrigue and violence, and seizing a moment to despoil her of a precious part of her territory, regardless of the incontrovertible rights of the most unquestionable ownership and the most uninterrupted possession.

Here, then, is the true position of the Mexican republic: despoiled, outraged, condemned, it is now attempted to subject her to a humiliating degradation. The sentiment of her own dignity will now allow her to consent to such ignominy. . . .

[T]he resolve of the Mexican government is immutable. And since, in the extreme case, it is the rights of the Mexican nation which will have to be affirmed, for it is her honor which has been outraged and which will have to be avenged, her government will, if this necessity arise, call upon all her citizens to fulfill the sacred duty of defending their country.

A lover of peace, she would wish to ward off this sad contingency; and without fearing war, she would desire to avoid so great a calamity for both countries. For this she has offered herself, and will continue to offer herself, open to all honorable means of conciliation, and she anxiously desires that the present controversy may terminate in a reasonable manner.

In the actual state of things, to say that Mexico maintains a position of quasi-hostility with respect to the United States is to add a new offence to her previous injuries. Her attitude is one of defense, because she sees herself unjustly attacked, because a portion of her territory is occupied by the forces of a nation, intent, without any right whatever, to possess itself of it; her ports are threatened by the squadrons of the same power. Under such circumstances, is she to remain inactive, without taking measures suited to so rigorous an emergency?

It is then, not upon Mexico . . . that it devolves to decide if the issue shall be a friendly negotiation or an open rupture. . . . It follows, that if war should finally become inevitable, and if in consequence of this war the peace of the civilized world should be disturbed, the responsibility will not fall upon Mexico. It will all rest upon the United States; to them will the whole of it belong. . . .

The Mexican government, preparing for war, should circumstances require it, will keep alive its flattering hope that peace will not be disturbed on the new continent; and in making this declaration in the face of the world, it emphatically disclaims all responsibility for the evils which may attend a struggle which it has not provoked and which it has made every effort to avoid.

5. The President Blames Mexico (1846)*

The hundred-mile-wide expanse between the Nueces River and the Rio Grande, virtually uninhabited except for tens of thousands of wild horses, was clearly in dispute between the United States and Mexico, although the Mexicans still claimed all of

---

*J. D. Richardson, ed., *Messages and Papers of the Presidents* (New York: Bureau of National Literature, 1897), vol. 4, pp. 441–442.

revolted Texas. The blunt truth is that the Mexican title to the disputed area was then the stronger. The Whigs and other antislavery foes of the Democratic Polk, regarding him as a willing tool of the expansionist Southern "slavocracy," condemned him as a liar ("Polk the Mendacious") for his allegations that Mexico, rather than the United States, had provoked the war. In the president's war message to Congress, given here with italics we have added, what grounds are there to support this accusation? Did the United States have just grounds for war?

The grievous wrongs perpetrated by Mexico upon our citizens throughout a long period of years remain unredressed, and solemn treaties pledging her public faith for this redress have been disregarded. A government either unable or unwilling to enforce the execution of such treaties fails to perform one of its plainest duties.

Our commerce with Mexico has been almost annihilated. It was formerly highly beneficial to both nations, but our merchants have been deterred from prosecuting it by the system of outrage and extortion which the Mexican authorities have pursued against them, while their appeals through their own government for indemnity have been made in vain. Our forbearance has gone to such an extreme as to be mistaken in its character. Had we acted with vigor in repelling the insults and redressing the injuries inflicted by Mexico at the commencement, we should doubtless have escaped all the difficulties in which we are now involved.

Instead of this, however, we have been exerting our best efforts to propitiate her good will. Upon the pretext that Texas, a nation as independent as herself, thought proper to unite its destinies with our own, she has affected to believe that we have severed her rightful territory, and in official proclamations and manifestoes has repeatedly threatened to make war upon us for the purpose of reconquering Texas. In the meantime, we have tried every effort at reconciliation.

The cup of forbearance had been exhausted even before the recent information from the frontier of the [Rio Grande] Del Norte. But now, after reiterated menaces, Mexico has passed the boundary of the United States, has *invaded our territory*, and *shed American blood upon the American soil*. She has proclaimed that hostilities have commenced, and that the two nations are now at war.

As war exists, and, *notwithstanding all our efforts* to avoid it, exists by the act of Mexico herself, we are called upon by every consideration of duty and patriotism to vindicate with decision the honor, the rights, and the interests of our country.

6. Massachusetts Voices Condemnation (1847)*

The killing or wounding of sixteen American soldiers on American soil precipitated war with Mexico. But the abolitionists and the free-soil Whigs of the North, resenting an alleged grab for more slave territory, gradually increased their clamor for peace. The following mid-war resolution, drafted by the orator Charles Sumner and passed by the Massachusetts legislature in 1847, betrayed an ugly frame of mind. In what respects is this statement sound in describing the outbreak of war? In what respects is it unsound? In what respects does it verge on treason?

Old South Leaflets (Boston: Old South Meeting House, 1904), vol. 6, no. 132, pp. 10–11, 30–31.

This was the state of things when . . . General Taylor was directed, by the President of the United States, to occupy the east bank of the Rio Grande, being the extreme western part of the territory claimed by Texas, the boundaries of which had been designated as an "open question," to be determined by "negotiation." General Taylor broke up his quarters at Corpus Christi on the 11th March, and, proceeding across this disputed territory, established his post, and erected a battery, directly opposite the Mexican city of Matamoros, and, under his directions, the mouth of the Rio Grande was blockaded, so as to cut off supplies from the Mexican army at Matamoros. . . .

These were acts of war, accomplished without bloodshed. But they were nevertheless acts of unquestioned hostility against Mexico. Blockade! and military occupation of a disputed territory! These were the arbiters of the "open question" of boundary. These were the substitutes for "negotiation."

It is not to be supposed that the Mexican army should quietly endure these aggressive measures, and regard with indifference cannon pointed at their position. . . . On the 26th of April a small body of American troops, under the command of Captain Thornton, encountered Mexican troops at a place twenty miles north of General Taylor's camp. Here was the first collision of arms. The report of this was hurried to Washington. Rumor, with a hundred tongues, exaggerated the danger of the American army under General Taylor, and produced an insensibility to the aggressive character of the movement. . . .

It was under the influence of this feeling that the untoward act of May 13th was pressed through Congress, by which it was declared that "war exists by the act of Mexico." . . . The passage of this act placed the whole country in hostile array against Mexico, and impressed upon every citizen of the United States the relation of enemy of every citizen of Mexico. This disastrous condition still continues. War is still waged; and our armies, after repeated victories achieved on Mexican soil, are still pursuing the path of conquest. . . .

Resolves. Concerning the Mexican War, and the Institution of Slavery.

Resolved, That the present war with Mexico has its primary origin in the unconstitutional annexation to the United States of the foreign state of Texas while the same was still at war with Mexico; that it was unconstitutionally commenced by the order of the President, to General Taylor, to take military possession of territory in dispute between the United States and Mexico, and in the occupation of Mexico; and that it is now waged ingloriously—by a powerful nation against a weak neighbor—unnecessarily and without just cause, at immense cost of treasure and life, for the dismemberment of Mexico, and for the conquest of a portion of her territory, from which slavery has already been excluded, with the triple object of extending slavery, of strengthening the "Slave Power," and of obtaining the control of the Free States, under the Constitution of the United States.

Resolved, That such a war of conquest, so hateful in its objects, so wanton, unjust, and unconstitutional in its origin and character, must be regarded as a war against freedom, against humanity, against justice, against the Union, against the Constitution, and against the Free States; and that a regard for the true interests and the highest honor of the country, not less than the impulses of Christian duty, should arouse all good citizens to join in efforts to arrest this gigantic crime, by withholding supplies, or other voluntary contributions, for its further prosecution; by calling for the withdrawal of our army within the established limits of the United States; and in every just way aiding the country to retreat from the disgraceful position of aggression which it now occupies towards a weak, distracted neighbor and sister republic.

Resolved, That our attention is directed anew to the wrong and "enormity" of slavery, and to the tyranny and usurpation of the "Slave Power," as displayed in the history of our country, particularly in the annexation of Texas and the present war with Mexico.

C. Peace with Mexico

1. Polk Submits the Trist Treaty (1848)[*]

Hoping to win California with a minimum of bloodshed, President Polk sent special envoy Nicholas Trist to Mexico. There he was to join General Scott's army driving toward Mexico City. Trist bungled an attempt to bribe Santa Anna, the slippery Mexican dictator, and Polk recalled his negotiator in disgust. But Trist, who now saw a temporary opening, concluded a treaty anyhow. Polk, though furious at such defiance, finally decided to submit Trist's Treaty of Guadalupe-Hidalgo to the Senate. By its terms, Mexico formally yielded Texas, California, and the intervening territory; the United States bound itself to pay $18,250,000, including $3,250,000 in the damage claims owing to U.S. citizens. In Polk's diary account, what argument for the treaty seems strongest? Which one seems to carry the most weight with him?

Monday, 21st February, 1848.—I saw no company this morning. At 12 o'clock the Cabinet met; all the members present. I made known my decision upon the Mexican Treaty, which was that under all the circumstances of the case, I would submit it [to] the Senate for ratification. . . .

I assigned my reasons for my decision. They were, briefly, that the treaty conformed on the main question of limits and boundary to the instructions given to Mr. Trist in April last; and that though, if the treaty was now to be made, I should demand more territory, perhaps to make the Sierra Madre[†] the line, yet it was doubtful whether this could be ever obtained by the consent of Mexico.

I looked, too, to the consequences of its rejection. A [Whig] majority of one branch of Congress [the House] is opposed to my administration; they have falsely charged that the war was brought on and is continued by me with a view to the conquest of Mexico. And if I were now to reject a treaty made upon my own terms, as authorized in April last, with the unanimous approbation of the Cabinet, the probability is that Congress would not grant either men or money to prosecute the war. Should this be the result, the army now in Mexico would be constantly wasting and diminishing in numbers, and I might at last be compelled to withdraw them,

---

[*]M. M. Quaife, ed., *The Diary of James K. Polk* (Chicago: A. C. McClurg, 1910), vol. 3, pp. 347–348.
[†]A mountain range bordering the central plateau of Mexico.

and thus lose the two provinces of New Mexico and Upper California, which were ceded to the United States by this treaty.

Should the opponents of my administration succeed in carrying the next presidential election, the great probability is that the country would lose all the advantages secured by this treaty. I adverted to the immense value of Upper California and concluded by saying that if I were now to reject my own terms, as offered in April last, I did not see how it was possible for my administration to be sustained.

2. A Whig Journal Accepts the Pact (1848)*

The Daily National Intelligencer, *an opposition Whig newspaper, wry-facedly supported the Trist draft as an unsatisfactory way out of a bad mess. One reason for a speedy acceptance was the mounting popular clamor for all of Mexico rather than the one-half actually taken. What were the main objections to annexing still more Mexican territory?*

We regard with distrust and apprehension the proposed vast acquisition of territory by the United States. So far from paying twenty millions of dollars for it, we have not the smallest doubt that the acquisition of it will entail mischiefs upon this country which no supposed advantages to be derived from it will compensate, now or ever. Were these territories to be whelmed in the Pacific Ocean, instead of being incorporated in our Union, far better, in our opinion, would it be for the welfare and prosperity of the present population of the United States. . . .

That the annexation of *the whole* of Mexico to the United States would be fatal to this government, whoever may doubt it, we are well convinced. Add to our Senate the representation of some fifteen or twenty Mexican states, and the conservative character of that body will be destroyed. The increased representation in the other branch of the national legislature might, at first, be less injurious; but its evils cannot now be computed. Would our commercial, manufacturing, and agricultural states be content to be governed by Mexican generals, who are ignorant of civil government, and who could not understand the principles of our Constitution? *Pronunciamentos* at the head of a military array constitute the basis of their political knowledge. The Union of these states has withstood the shocks of war and of internal excitement, but it would be dissolved by the annexation of Mexico.

We would take the treaty, then, as it is, to avoid a greater national evil. We cannot reject it and continue our opposition to the war. Payment of the debts which Mexico owed our citizens at the commencement of the war is now hopeless; her means are exhausted. Her territory with its population will entail upon us increased expenditures, and evils moral and political. But it is all that Mexico can give. There can be no indemnity for the war expenses. We had better, then, as we have said, stop where we are; for if we go further, we shall only increase the evil.

The crisis should be met with firmness. By the continued prosecution of the war, we should in three months expend a larger sum than the treaty requires us to pay to our own citizens and to the Mexican government. And where is the

---

*Daily National Intelligencer (Washington, DC), February 28, 1848.

individual so lost to a sense of justice and to the common sympathies of our nature who would not rather pay the money than to expend even that much (more likely ten times as much) in prosecuting the war to the annihilation of the Mexican government and name?

3. Democrats Hail a Glorious Achievement (1848)*

A staunch pro-Polk newspaper, the Democratic Washington Daily Union, *took sharp issue with its rival, the Whig* Daily National Intelligencer. *It hailed the outcome of the war as a magnificent triumph. What does it seem to regard as the greatest intangible gain? The greatest tangible gain? How would the treaty benefit both the security and the commerce of the United States?*

It is true that the war has cost us millions of money, and, what is far more precious, the lives of some of our noblest citizens. But what great advantages has it not obtained for us? It has covered us with glory. It has extended our fame to the remotest corners of the earth. If the treaty be ratified, it will extend the area of freedom to the Southern Pacific.

The *National Intelligencer*, indeed, denies that it has "accomplished any one of the ostensible objects of the war." Yet surely nothing but the blindest party spirit could have made this extravagant assertion.

Have we not driven back the insolent enemy, who invaded Texas and shed the blood of our citizens upon our own soil? Have we not pursued him into the heart of his own country, seized all his strongholds upon the coast, and occupied his capital? Have we not subdued that vainglorious and arrogant spirit which has been productive of so many insults and so many aggressions? What has become of all those idle threats to drive us from Texas—of the silly boast of Santa Anna that he would gather his laurels upon the banks of the Sabine [River]!†

The London *Times*, in 1845, flattered the national vanity of the Mexicans with the hope that we should not be able to send men enough to encounter their troops. They were under the impression that our army dared not enter Mexico, or, if we made the attempt, that we should be driven back like chaff before the whirlwind. Their vanity deceived them; but their government flattered their arrogance and increased their infatuation.

Now they are tamed. Now they have consented to negotiate for peace, without requiring our ships to leave their coast and our troops to desert their territory. These changes in the popular sentiment have been produced by the brilliant achievements of Buena Vista and of Cerro Gordo, the capture of their castle and of their capital. Does anyone now believe that their spirit is not humbled, and that the sense of their own inferiority will not induce them to refrain from a repetition of the insults and aggressions which they had so repeatedly perpetrated upon us?

They will be stripped, too, of a large portion of their territory. They may be stripped of more, if they should wantonly insult us again. Will not the lessons they

---

Washington Daily Union, March 16, 1848.
†The southwestern border of Louisiana.

have learned operate as a "security for the future"? Will not the moral force we have gained, and the military genius we have exhibited, go beyond Mexico, and produce their impression upon the other nations of the earth?

With ample "indemnity for the past," then, and with such "security for the future"—with achievements in arms which any nation might envy—with an extension of territory to the Pacific, which gives us some of the finest harbors in the world (for one of which alone—the bay of San Francisco—Gen. Jackson was willing to give five millions of dollars)—with an immense commerce opening upon us with the richest nations of Asia—with every facility secured for our whalers in the Pacific, and with the other advantages which we will have secured—with all these, we can truly say that we have every reason to be proud of the war, and proud of the peace which it has obtained us.

4. A Mexican Official Decries the Treaty (1848)*

Overwhelmed on the battlefield and plagued by civil strife, Mexico grudgingly accepted the terms offered in the Treaty of Guadalupe-Hidalgo, ceding more than half of its territory to the United States. The end to military hostilities brought little relief to the beleaguered nation. Already weakened by wartime instability, the Mexican government found itself on the defensive against charges that it leapt too swiftly at an offer of peace. Longtime diplomat Manuel Crescencio Rejón urged the Mexican Congress to reject the treaty and reignite the conflict in the hopes of securing a more just settlement. What dangers does Rejón see in the proposed treaty? Did subsequent events confirm his predictions?

Nevertheless, insensible to everything, our national government has entered into those negotiations which are so humiliating to us, thus committing us to grave imputations of perfidy if we should reject the treaty, which we should surely do. . . .

With the borders of our conquerors brought closer to the heart of our nation, with the whole line of the frontier occupied by them from sea to sea, with their highly developed merchant marine, and with them so versed in the system of colonization by which they attract great numbers of the laboring classes from the old world, what can we, who are so backward in everything, do to arrest them in their rapid conquests, their latest invasions? Thousands of men will come daily to establish themselves under American auspices in the new territories with which we will have obliged them. There they will develop their commerce and stockpile large quantities of merchandise brought from the upper states. They will inundate us with all this, and our own modicum of wealth, already so miserable and depleted, will in the future sink to insignificance and nothingness. . . .

And what defense would be sufficient, given the fact that we do not have enough troops to guard such an extensive frontier, to prevent fraudulent crossings? Imagine what contentions will arise with the other side, what quarrels and disputes

---

*Cecil Robinson, trans. and ed., *The View from Chapultepec: Mexican Writers on the Mexican-American War* (Tucson: University of Arizona Press, 1989), pp. 96–98.

with the brazen smugglers of that republic, what continual claims and demands for indemnity, which will finally amount to such immense sums that they will provide a pretext for the threat of another war, and we will end by yielding, without resistance, the rest of our territory! . . . . Gentlemen, what is proposed to us in this fatal treaty amounts to a sentence of death, and I wonder that there could have been Mexicans who would have negotiated it and subscribed to it, thinking all the while that it would be a boon to our unfortunate country. This circumstance alone dismays me and makes me despair of the life of the republic.

5. Mexico Remembers the Despoilers (1935)*

Patriotic Mexicans can never forget the catastrophe that cost them about half of their country. Their resistance was weakened by internal political turmoil, amounting almost to civil war. The teenage boys of the military academy of Chapultepec, near Mexico City, perished heroically; legend has several throwing themselves suicidally from the battlements. In 1935, after some of the bitterness had subsided, the Ministry of Foreign Affairs in Mexico City published an elementary survey of Mexican history in which there appears the following account of the war and the treaty—with a before-and-after map. What is revealed of the weakness of Mexican resistance and the grievances against the United States? Which one seems to rankle most deeply?

In the war with the United States, and in the military operations incidental thereto, we are unable to find a single outstanding figure to represent the defense of Mexico, in the form of a hero or military leader. Invasion first of all took place from the north, and the American troops defeated our armies, not beneath them in courage, but due to interior organization, armaments, and high command. The classes that controlled material resources, and the groups at the head of the political situation, failed to rise to the occasion in that desperate situation.

A chronicle of the march of invasion makes painful reading. Our soldiers were defeated at Matamoros, at Resaca de Guerrero, and Monterrey, in spite of the sacrifices of the troops. . . .

When one follows, event by event, the military operations and the political happenings of this period, one's feelings are harrowed by the details.

In this swift historical sketch, we shall be content to mention, if no great captain representative of defense, the youthful heroes who saved the honor of Mexico: the cadets of the Military College [at Chapultepec], who fell on September 13, 1847, when the school was stormed by the invading troops, then on the point of occupying the capital of the Republic. The glorious deaths of Francisco Marquez, Agustin Melgar, Juan Escutia, Fernando Montes de Oca, Vicente Suarez, and Juan de la Barrera, in an unequal contest, without hope, crushed by an overwhelming force, are as it were a symbol and image of this unrighteous war.

---

*Alfonso Teja Zabre, *Guide to the History of Mexico* (Mexico: Ministry of Foreign Affairs, 1935), pp. 299–304, passim.

To Mexico, the American invasion contains a terrible lesson. In this war we saw that right and justice count but little in contests between one people and another, when material force, and organization, are wanting.

A great portion of Mexico's territory was lost because she had been able to administer and settle those regions, and handed them over to alien colonization [Texas].

There is no principle nor law that can sanction spoliation. Only by force was it carried out, and only by force or adroit negotiation could it have been avoided. That which Spain had been unable to colonize, and the [Mexican] Republic to settle, was occupied by the stream of Anglo-American expansion.

The war of 1847 is not, so far as Mexico is concerned, offset by anything but the courage of her soldiers. At Matamoros, at Resaca de Guerrero, at La Angostura [Buena Vista], at Vera Cruz, at Cerro Gordo, at Padierna, at Churubusco, and at Chapultepec, victory was won by a well-organized and instructed General Staff; by longer-range rifles and cannon, better-fed soldiers, abundance of money and ammunition, and of horses and wagons. . . .

The American invasion cost Mexico the total loss of Texas, whose boundaries were, without the slightest right, brought down to the Rio Grande; the Province of New Mexico and Upper California; and an outpouring of blood, energy, and wealth, offset only by material compensation in the amount of fifteen million pesos, by way of indemnity.

Thought Provokers

1. Why should Britain and America have been on friendly terms in the 1830s and 1840s, and why were they not?
2. In what ways did the U.S.–British confrontation over the Oregon country, which was resolved peacefully, affect the U.S.–Mexican confrontation that eventually led to war?
3. Polk claimed that no other power similarly situated would have refused the annexation of Texas. Do you agree or disagree? Explain how each side, at the outbreak of the Mexican War, could claim that the other was the aggressor. Were the annexation of Texas and the sending of General Taylor to the Rio Grande unconstitutional, as the abolitionists claimed? If England had held Mexico, as it did Canada, how would matters have been worked out differently?
4. Should a democratic government permit the kind of criticism that was indulged in by the Whigs and the abolitionists during the Mexican War? Compare the attitude of Massachusetts toward the War of 1812 with its attitude toward the Mexican War.
5. Did the advantages to the United States from the Mexican War outweigh the ultimate disadvantages? Emerson remarked that victory would be a dose of arsenic. Comment. Mexicans claim they would now be a rich nation if they had not been robbed of the oil and other riches of California and Texas. Comment.

18

Renewing the Sectional Struggle, 1848–1854

There is a higher law than the Constitution.

William H. Seward, in the Senate, 1850

Prologue: The electrifying discovery of gold in California in 1848 brought a frantic inrush of population, a demand for statehood, and a showdown in Congress over the future of slavery in the territories. The fruit of these debates was the great Compromise of 1850, which purchased an uneasy truce between North and South. It left the Southerners unhappy over the gains of free soil and the Northerners unhappy over being drafted as slave-catchers under the new Fugitive Slave Act of 1850. The short-lived truce was ruptured by the Kansas-Nebraska Act of 1854, which threw open the free soil of Kansas to possible slavery. To many Northerners, this repeal of the time-sanctified Missouri Compromise line of 1820 seemed like bad faith on the part of the South; to many Southerners, the open flouting of the Fugitive Slave Act, especially after 1854, seemed like bad faith on the part of the North. With distrust rapidly mounting on both sides, the days of the Union seemed numbered, even as the United States increasingly asserted its influence abroad.

A. The Wilmot Proviso Issue

1. David Wilmot Appeals for Free Soil (1847)[*]

While the Mexican War was still being fought, President Polk, his eye on California, asked Congress for $2 million with which to negotiate a peace. Representative David Wilmot of Pennsylvania proposed adding to the appropriation bill an amendment or proviso designed to bar slavery forever from any territory to be wrested from Mexico. Angry Southerners sprang to their feet; and the so-called Wilmot Proviso, though twice passing the House, was blocked in the Senate. But it became the cradle of the yet unborn Republican party, and it precipitated a debate that continued until silenced by the guns of civil war. In the following speech in Congress by Wilmot, what does he conceive the moral issue to be? How effectively does he meet the argument regarding "joint blood and treasure"? Could he properly be regarded as an abolitionist?

But, sir, the issue now presented is not whether slavery shall exist unmolested where it now is, but whether it shall be carried to new and distant regions, now free,

---

[*]*Congressional Globe*, 29th Congress, 2d session (February 8, 1847), Appendix, p. 315.

where the footprint of a slave cannot be found. This, sir, is the issue. Upon it I take my stand, and from it I cannot be frightened or driven by idle charges of abolitionism.

I ask not that slavery be abolished. I demand that this government preserve the integrity of free territory against the aggressions of slavery—against its wrongful usurpations.

Sir, I was in favor of the annexation of Texas. . . . The Democracy [Democratic party] of the North, almost to a man, went for annexation. Yes, sir, here was an empire larger than France given up to slavery. Shall further concessions be made by the North? Shall we give up free territory, the inheritance of free labor? Must we yield this also? Never, sir, never, until we ourselves are fit to be slaves. . . .

But, sir, we are told that the joint blood and treasure of the whole country [are] being expended in this acquisition, therefore it should be divided, and slavery allowed to take its share. Sir, the South has her share already; the instalment for slavery was paid in advance. We are fighting this war for Texas and for the South. I affirm it—every intelligent man knows it—Texas is the primary cause of this war. For this, sir, Northern treasure is being exhausted, and Northern blood poured upon the plains of Mexico. We are fighting this war cheerfully, not reluctantly—cheerfully fighting this war for Texas; and yet we seek not to change the character of her institutions. Slavery is there; there let it remain. . . .

Now, sir, we are told that California is ours, that New Mexico is ours—won by the valor of our arms. They are free. Shall they remain free? Shall these fair provinces be the inheritance and homes of the white labor of freemen or the black labor of slaves? This, sir, is the issue—this the question. The North has the right, and her representatives here have the power. . . .

But the South contend that, in their emigration to this free territory, they have the right to take and hold slaves, the same as other property. Unless the amendment I have offered be adopted, or other early legislation is had upon this subject, they will do so. Indeed, they unitedly, as one man, have declared their right and purpose so to do, and the work has already begun.

Slavery follows in the rear of our armies. Shall the war power of our government be exerted to produce such a result? Shall this government depart from its neutrality on this question, and lend its power and influence to plant slavery in these territories?

There is no question of abolition here, sir. Shall the South be permitted, by aggression, by invasion of the right, by subduing free territory and planting slavery upon it, to wrest these provinces from Northern freemen, and turn them to the accomplishment of their own sectional purposes and schemes?

This is the question. Men of the North, answer. Shall it be so? Shall we of the North submit to it? If we do, we are coward slaves, and deserve to have the manacles fastened upon our own limbs.

2. Southerners Threaten Secession (1849)*

After the Mexican War officially brought rich territorial plums, the northern antislaveryites became more persistent. They introduced measures in Congress for abolishing

---

Congressional Globe, 31st Congress, 1st session, part 1, pp. 26, 28, 29.

slavery in the District of Columbia and for organizing California and New Mexico as territories without slavery—that is, on the basis of the unpassed Wilmot Proviso. Outraged Southerners responded with cries of disunion. The following incendiary outbursts all occurred on the floor of the House on December 13, 1849. The most famous speaker was hale and hearty Robert Toombs of Georgia, a brilliant orator and one of the more moderate Southern planters. (He later became secretary of state for the Confederacy.) Why was the South so bitterly aroused over the question of slavery in the territories?

Mr. Meade [of Virginia]—But, sir, if the organization of this House is to be followed by the passage of these bills—if these outrages are to be committed upon my people—I trust in God, sir, that my eyes have rested upon the last Speaker of the House of Representatives. . . .

Mr. Toombs [of Georgia]—I do not, then, hesitate to avow before this House and the country, and in the presence of the living God, that if by your legislation you [Northerners] seek to drive us from the territories of California and New Mexico, purchased by the common blood and treasure of the whole people, and to abolish slavery in this District [of Columbia], thereby attempting to fix a national degradation upon half the states of this Confederacy, *I am for disunion*. And if my physical courage be equal to the maintenance of my convictions of right and duty, I will devote all I am and all I have on earth to its consummation.

From 1787 to this hour, the people of the South have asked nothing but justice—nothing but the maintenance of the principles and the spirit which controlled our fathers in the formation of the Constitution. Unless we are unworthy of our ancestors, we will never accept less as a condition of union. . . .

The Territories are the common property of the people of the United States, purchased by their common blood and treasure. You [the Congress] are their common agents. It is your duty, while they are in a territorial state, to remove all impediments to their free enjoyment by all sections and people of the Union, the slaveholder and the non-slaveholder. . . .

Mr. Colcock [of South Carolina]— . . . I here pledge myself that if any bill should be passed at this Congress abolishing slavery in the District of Columbia, or incorporating the Wilmot Proviso in any form, I will introduce a resolution in this House declaring, in terms, *that this Union ought to be dissolved*.

B. The Compromise Debates of 1850

1. John Calhoun Demands Southern Rights (1850)[*]

Two burning questions brought the sectional controversy to a furious boil in 1850. The first was the failure of Northerners loyally to uphold both the Constitution and the Fugitive Slave Law of 1793 regarding runaway slaves. The second was the effort of California to win admission as a free state, thus establishing a precedent for the

---

[*]*Congressional Globe*, 31st Congress, 1st session (March 4, 1850), pp. 453, 455.

rest of the Mexican Cession territory. The subsequent debate over the compromise measures of 1850 featured a galaxy of forensic giants: Henry Clay, John C. Calhoun, Daniel Webster, Thomas H. Benton, William H. Seward, Stephen A. Douglas, Jefferson Davis, and many others. Highly revealing was the following swan-song speech of Senator Calhoun. On the verge of death from tuberculosis, he authorized a colleague to read it for him. What were his views on the Constitution, the Union, and secession? How successfully did he place the onus of insincerity and aggression on the North? How practicable were his remedies for preserving the Union?

How can the Union be saved? To this I answer, there is but one way by which it can be, and that is by adopting such measures as will satisfy the states belonging to the Southern section that they can remain in the Union consistently with their honor and their safety. There is, again, only one way by which this can be effected, and that is by removing the causes by which this belief [that the South cannot honorably and safely remain in the Union] has been produced. Do that and discontent will cease, harmony and kind feelings between the sections be restored, and every apprehension of danger to the Union removed. The question, then, is, By what can this be done? But, before I undertake to answer this question, I propose to show by what the Union cannot be saved.

It cannot, then, be saved by eulogies on the Union, however splendid or numerous. The cry of "Union, Union, the glorious Union!" can no more prevent disunion than the cry of "Health, health, glorious health!" on the part of the physician can save a patient lying dangerously ill. So long as the Union, instead of being regarded as a protector, is regarded in the opposite character by not much less than a majority of the states, it will be in vain to attempt to conciliate them by pronouncing eulogies on it.

Besides, this cry of Union comes commonly from those whom we cannot believe to be sincere. It usually comes from our assailants. But we cannot believe them to be sincere; for, if they loved the Union, they would necessarily be devoted to the Constitution. It made the Union, and to destroy the Constitution would be to destroy the Union. But the only reliable and certain evidence of devotion to the Constitution is to abstain, on the one hand, from violating it, and to repel, on the other, all attempts to violate it. It is only by faithfully performing these high duties that the Constitution can be preserved, and with it the Union. . . .

Having now shown what cannot save the Union, I return to the question with which I commenced, How can the Union be saved? There is but one way by which it can, with any certainty; and that is by a full and final settlement, on the principle of justice, of all the questions at issue between the two sections.

The South asks for justice, simple justice, and less she ought not to take. She has no compromise to offer but the Constitution; and no concession or surrender to make. She has already surrendered so much that she has little left to surrender. Such a settlement would go to the root of the evil, and remove all cause of discontent by satisfying the South she could remain honorably and safely in the Union, and thereby restore the harmony and fraternal feelings between the sections which existed anterior to the Missouri [Compromise] agitation [1820]. Nothing else can, with any certainty, finally and forever settle the questions at issue, terminate agitation, and save the Union.

But can this be done? Yes, easily; not by the weaker party [the South], for it can of itself do nothing—not even protect itself—but by the stronger. The North has only to will it to accomplish it—to do justice by conceding to the South an equal right in the acquired territory, and to do her duty by causing the stipulations relative to fugitive slaves to be faithfully fulfilled—to cease the agitation of the slave question, and to provide for the insertion of a provision in the Constitution, by an amendment, which will restore to the South, in substance, the power she possessed of protecting herself, before the equilibrium between the sections was destroyed by the action of this government. There will be no difficulty in devising such a provision*—one that will protect the South, and which, at the same time, will improve and strengthen the government instead of impairing and weakening it.

But will the North agree to this? It is for her to answer the question. But, I will say, she cannot refuse if she has half the love of the Union which she professes to have, or without justly exposing herself to the charge that her love of power and aggrandizement is far greater than her love of the Union.

At all events, the responsibility of saving the Union rests on the North, and not the South. The South cannot save it by any act of hers, and the North may save it without any sacrifice whatever, unless to do justice, and to perform her duties under the Constitution, should be regarded by her as a sacrifice. . . .

If you, who represent the stronger portion, cannot agree to settle . . . [the question at issue] on the broad principle of justice and duty, say so; and let the states we both represent agree to separate and part in peace. If you are unwilling we should part in peace, tell us so; and we shall know what to do, when you reduce the question to submission or resistance.

If you remain silent, you will compel us to infer by your acts what you intend. In that case, California will become the test question. If you admit her, under all the difficulties that oppose her admission, you compel us to infer that you intend to exclude us from the whole of the acquired territories, with the intention of destroying, irretrievably, the equilibrium between the two sections. We would be blind not to perceive, in that case, that your real objects are power and aggrandizement, and infatuated not to act accordingly.

2. Daniel Webster Urges Concessions (1850)†

On the anvil of congressional debate was forged the great Compromise of 1850. California was admitted as a free state; the fate of slavery in the rest of the Mexican Cession territory was left to the inhabitants. The major sop to the South was the enactment of a more stringent Fugitive Slave Law. As a concession to the North, the slave trade was abolished in the District of Columbia; as a concession to the South, slavery in the District was retained. Texas received $10 million for yielding a disputed chunk of its territory to New Mexico.

---

*Calhoun evidently had in mind two presidents: one Northern, one Southern, each with crippling veto power.
†*Congressional Globe*, 31st Congress, 1st session (March 7, 1850), pp. 276, 482–483.

Senator Daniel Webster's Seventh of March speech during these congressional debates emphasized concession, compromise, moderation, and Union. He attacked the abolitionists (see earlier, p. 264) and deplored the agitation over the extension of slavery to the territories. A slave economy was geographically impossible there, he believed, and no legislative body should reenact the law of God. Finally, he took sharp issue with Calhoun's threat of secession. How good a prophet was Webster? Which of his arguments on the impracticability of peaceful secession probably carried the most weight in the North?

Mr. President, I wish to speak today, not as a Massachusetts man, nor as a Northern man, but as an American, and a member of the Senate of the United States. . . . I speak today for the preservation of the Union. "Hear me for my cause." . . .

Mr. President, I should much prefer to have heard, from every member on this floor, declarations of opinion that this Union should never be dissolved, than the declaration of opinion that in any case, under the pressure of circumstances, such a dissolution was possible. I hear with pain, and anguish, and distress, the word *secession*, especially when it falls from the lips of those who are eminently patriotic, and known to the country, and known all over the world, for their political services.

Secession! Peaceable secession! Sir, your eyes and mine are never destined to see that miracle. The dismemberment of this vast country without convulsion! The breaking up of the fountains of the great deep without ruffling the surface! Who is so foolish—I beg everybody's pardon—as to expect to see any such thing? . . .

There can be no such thing as a peaceable secession. Peaceable secession is an utter impossibility. Is the great Constitution under which we live here—covering this whole country—is it to be thawed and melted away by secession, as the snows on the mountain melt under the influence of a vernal sun—disappear almost unobserved, and die off? No, sir! No, sir! No, sir! I will not state what might produce the disruption of the states; but, sir, I see it as plainly as I see the sun in heaven—I see that disruption must produce such a war as I will not describe, in its twofold characters.

Peaceable secession! Peaceable secession! The concurrent agreement of all the members of this great Republic to separate! A voluntary separation, with alimony on one side and on the other! Why, what would be the result? Where is the line to be drawn? What states are to secede?—What is to remain American? What am I to be?—an American no longer? Where is the flag of the Republic to remain? Where is the eagle still to tower? or is he to cower, and shrink, and fall to the ground? . . .

What is to become of the army? What is to become of the navy? What is to become of the public lands? How is each of the thirty states to defend itself? I know, although the idea has not been stated distinctly, there is to be a Southern Confederacy. I do not mean, when I allude to this statement, that anyone seriously contemplates such a state of things. I do not mean to say that it is true, but I have heard it suggested elsewhere, that that idea has originated in a design to separate. I am sorry, sir, that it has ever been thought of, talked of, or dreamed of, in the wildest flights of human imagination. But the idea must be of a separation, including the slave states upon one side and the free states on the other.

Sir, there is not—I may express myself too strongly perhaps—but some things, some moral things, are almost as impossible as other natural or physical things. And

I hold the idea of a separation of these states—those that are free to form one government, and those that are slaveholding to form another—as a moral impossibility.

We could not separate the states by any such line, if we were to draw it. We could not sit down here today and draw a line of separation that would satisfy any five men in the country. There are natural causes that would keep and tie us together, and there are social and domestic relations which we could not break if we would, and which we should not if we could. . . .

And now, Mr. President, instead of speaking of the possibility or utility of secession . . . let our comprehension be as broad as the country for which we act, our aspirations as high as its certain destiny. Let us not be pigmies in a case that calls for men.

Never did there devolve on any generation of men higher trusts than now devolve upon us for the preservation of this Constitution and the harmony and peace of all who are destined to live under it. Let us make our generation one of the strongest and brightest links in that golden chain which is destined, I fully believe, to grapple the people of all the states to this Constitution for ages to come.

3. Free-Soilers Denounce Webster (1850)*

The new and more merciless Fugitive Slave Act of 1850 was the keystone of the Compromise of 1850, and Senator Webster's eloquent support of it scandalized the abolitionists. "The fame of Webster ends in this nasty law," wrote Ralph Waldo Emerson. But conservative-minded Northerners were well aware, as Emerson himself had recorded, that "cotton thread holds the Union together." Bankers, shippers, and manufacturers—holding Southern mortgages, transporting cotton, or using it in their factories—praised Webster's course as statesmanlike. Indeed, the abolitionists cried, the "Lords of the Loom" were joining hands with the "Lords of the Lash." A New Hampshire newspaper editor here assails the New England "cotton lords." Judging from this criticism, what were the political reactions to Webster's stand?

Some eight hundred of the "cotton lords" of State Street [Boston], with a few . . . Doctors of Divinity . . . of the Andover Theological Seminary, have signed a letter of thanks to Daniel Webster for his recent apostasy to freedom.

This was to be expected. There are, and always have been, men at the North whose habits, associations, and interests all lead them to love whatever degrades labor, and the man who lives by labor. Wherever Mammon is the great god, there flourishes the spirit of slavery. Wealth and luxury are ever the handmaids of oppression. The fastnesses of liberty have always been in the homes of the untitled masses. And hence the antagonism between capital and labor, which marks so strongly modern civilization.

In thanking Mr. Webster for his efforts in behalf of slavery, the "cotton" men of Boston are but signing a certificate of his servility to themselves. No such certificate, however, will commend him to the people of New England, nor of Massachusetts. Instead, it will have the very opposite effect. It is already doing a work far different from that intended.

Independent Democrat (Concord, NH), in *The Liberator* (Boston), April 19, 1850.

The honest anti-slavery masses, upon whom Webster has heretofore relied, see at once that it cannot be for any good thing done for freedom and humanity that such men praise him. To the representative of freemen, the "well done" of the enemies of freedom is the breath of infamy. That "well done" Daniel Webster has received, not only from the "cotton lords" of Massachusetts, but from the prince of cotton lords [Calhoun?] of South Carolina. He is doomed, withered, blasted; and the "thanks" of all the worshipers of Mammon and Wrong in the universe cannot save him.

[Southerners, as indicated, were generally pleased by the unexpected show of support from the Yankee Webster, but their praise was a political kiss of death to the senator. The Richmond Enquirer *remarked that the Massachusetts abolitionists—"the miserable peddlers for notoriety"—would "defame and abuse him." It further stated that his "selfish and penurious constituency"—"the moneyed men and manufacturers of New England"—were finally "aroused to the dangers that threaten the Union and their interests" (quoted in* The Liberator, *April 5, 1850).]*

C. Reactions to the Fugitive Slave Law

1. Joshua Giddings Rejects Slave-Catching (1850)*

If the South had a grievance against Northern abettors of runaway slaves, the North had a grievance against the harsh Fugitive Slave Act of 1850. No single irritant of the 1850s proved to be more persistently galling. Among the numerous features of the law, federal officers could summon bystanders to form a posse to chase the fugitive. Citizens who prevented an arrest or aided the escapee were liable to six months' imprisonment and a fine of $1,000. Few were more deeply outraged by these stipulations than fiery Joshua R. Giddings, who served for twenty years as an uncompromising antislavery congressman from Ohio. In his speech in Congress against the Fugitive Slave Act, what parts were most offensive to the South? Does the accessory-to-murder analogy hold water? What were the sources of Giddings's outrage?

Sir, what protection does this law lend to the poor, weak, oppressed, degraded slave, whose flesh has often quivered under the lash of his inhuman owner? whose youth has been spent in labor for another? whose intellect has been nearly blotted out? When he seeks an asylum in a land of freedom, this worse than barbarous law sends the officers of government to chase him down. The people are constrained to become his pursuers. Famishing, fainting, and benumbed with the cold, he drags his weary limbs forward, while the whole power of the government under the President's command, the army and navy, and all the freemen of the land, organized into a constabulary force, are on his track to drag him back to bondage, under this law. . . .

Sir, there is not a man in this body—there is not an intelligent man in the free states—but knows, if he delivers a fugitive into the custody of his pursuers, that he will be carried to the South and sold to the sugar and cotton plantations. And his life

---

*Congressional Globe, 31st Congress, 2d session (December 9, 1850), p. 15.

will be sacrificed in five years if employed on the sugar plantations, and in seven years on the cotton plantations. The men of the North, who look upon this as murder, would as soon turn out and cut the throats of the defenseless Negro as to send him back to a land of chains and whips. As soon would they do this as comply with a law which violates every principle of common justice and humanity.

The [common] law, sir, holds him who aids in a murder as guilty as he who strikes the knife to the heart of the victim. Under our law, a man is hanged if he fails to prevent a murder when it is plainly in his power to do so. Such man is held guilty of the act, and he is hanged accordingly. The man who should assist in the capture of a fugitive would be regarded by us as guilty as he under whose lash the victim expires.

I have compared this capture of a fugitive to a common murder. In doing that, I do injustice to the common murderer. To capture a slave and send him to the South, to die under a torture of five years, is far more criminal than ordinary murder.

Sir, we will not commit this crime. Let me say to the President, no power of government can compel us to involve ourselves in such guilt. No! The freemen of Ohio will never turn out to chase the panting fugitive—they will never be metamorphosed into bloodhounds, to track him to his hiding-place, and seize and drag him out, and deliver him to his tormentors. Rely upon it, they will die first. They may be shot down, the cannon and bayonet and sword may do their work upon them; they may drown the fugitives in their blood, but never will they stoop to such degradation.

Let no man tell me there is no higher law than this fugitive bill. We feel there is a law of right, of justice, of freedom, implanted in the breast of every intelligent human being, that bids him look with scorn upon this libel upon all that is called law.

2. The South Threatens Retaliation (1855)*

The Fugitive Slave Act of 1850 prompted a number of Northern states to strengthen their old "personal liberty laws" or enact new ones. Ostensibly these statutes were designed to protect the bona fide free black from the ever present danger of being kidnapped and reenslaved. Actually they operated to hamper or nullify the Fugitive Slave Act. Slaveholders who entered free states risked being sued for false arrest, jailed for kidnapping, or mobbed. Some states denied their jails to slave-catchers. Numerous attempts by Northern mobs to rescue black fugitives from the authorities led to riots and some loss of life. In 1854 angry abolitionists in Boston stormed the courthouse and shot Deputy Marshal Batchelder in a vain attempt to rescue the escaped slave Anthony Burns. In the following New Orleans editorial, what merit is there in the arguments that the North had consistently violated the Constitution, that retaliation in kind would be justified, and that one section of the nation had already seceded?

Under the Massachusetts "personal liberty law," no open action as yet has taken place. . . . Our people are scattered for the summer, hundreds spending their

---

New Orleans Bulletin, July 1855, in Allan Nevins, ed., *American Press Opinion* (Boston and New York: D. C. Heath and Company, 1928), pp. 205–206.

money in pleasure excursions or purchases in Massachusetts. No, my good friends of Bunker Hill and Lexington (and long may I be permitted to address you as such), there has been as yet no open action. Some of our [social] bees and butterflies have fluttered off among you, but we who are toiling here at home consult together about your "liberty law," and other movements, and I have leave to tell you some things which are more than hinted at, if such laws are to be enforced.

First.—Excluding your ships.

Second.—Excluding your manufactures.

Third.—Ceasing our visits to your borders, already unsafe and more or less unpleasant.

Fourth.—Requiring your citizens trading here at least to take out licenses, perhaps to furnish bond for good behavior.

How will such laws suit you? Of course not at all. They trench on that provision of the Constitution [Art. IV, sec. II] which declares that the citizens of each state shall be entitled to all the privileges and immunities of citizens in the several states. They certainly do, my conscientious friends, and such laws operate against all other rights the people of the several states have in other states under the Federal Constitution. . . . We know it! But we also know that this is precisely our objection to this "liberty law," which has made all the trouble, and that its unconstitutionality has been pronounced by our highest tribunals.

All your reasoning would have done very well, so long as you held to your bargain—so long as you yourselves submitted to the paramount law, and recognized our rights under its guarantees—so long as Massachusetts held to her obligations and place in the great American family. But now you have repudiated a right of vital importance to us, and passed a law to fine and imprison as felons our citizens who may claim their rights under that Constitution.

Why wait for a formal rupture and separation from you? You have not done so. Our compact is broken by you. There is little obligation on us to respect the rights of your citizens or their property, when you openly trample on ours. There is as little to restrain a [New Orleans] mob from taking possession of one or more of your ships as there was to restrain your [Boston] mob in the case of the Negro Burns from their assaults on the court and its officers, and from murdering the marshal Batchelder.

D. The Debate over the Kansas-Nebraska Bill

1. Stephen Douglas's Popular-Sovereignty Plea (1854)*

The Kansas-Nebraska Act of 1854 shattered the uneasy sectional truce. Senator Stephen Arnold Douglas of Illinois—a bouncy, stumpy real estate booster and transcontinental railroad enthusiast—undertook to organize Nebraska into a territory. Hoping to enlist Southern support, he held out the bait of making Kansas a slave state by means of "squatter" or "popular" sovereignty. In short, he would let the people of

---

Congressional Globe, 33d Congress, 1st session (March 3, 1854), Appendix, p. 338.

the territories themselves democratically decide whether they wanted slaves or no slaves. This meant an outright repeal, by means of the Kansas-Nebraska Act, of the time-hallowed Compromise of 1820—the compromise that had banned slavery in the Louisiana Purchase territory north of 36° 30' (see earlier, p. 178). Whatever his motives, Douglas infuriated Northern abolitionists and free-soilers by driving the Kansas-Nebraska Bill through the Senate with relentless energy. In this portion of his Senate speech, how does he define the merits of "popular sovereignty"?

When the people of the North shall all be rallied under one banner, and the whole South marshaled under another banner, and each section excited to frenzy and madness by hostility to the institutions of the other, then the patriot may well tremble for the perpetuity of the Union. Withdraw the slavery question from the political arena, and remove it to the states and territories, each to decide for itself, such a catastrophe can never happen. Then you will never be able to tell, by any Senator's vote for or against any measure, from what state or section of the Union he comes.

Why, then, can we not withdraw this vexed question from politics? Why can we not adopt the [popular sovereignty] principle of this [Kansas-Nebraska] bill as a rule of action in all new territorial organizations? Why can we not deprive these agitators of their vocation, and render it impossible for Senators to come here upon bargains on the slavery question? I believe that the peace, the harmony, and perpetuity of the Union require us to go back to the doctrines of the Revolution, to the principles of the Constitution, to the principles of the Compromise of 1850, and leave the people, under the Constitution, to do as they may see proper in respect to their own internal affairs.

Mr. President, I have not brought this question forward as a Northern man or as a Southern man. I am unwilling to recognize such divisions and distinctions. I have brought it forward as an American Senator, representing a state which is true to this principle, and which has approved of my action in respect to the Nebraska bill. I have brought it forward not as an act of justice to the South more than to the North. I have presented it especially as an act of justice to the people of those territories, and of the states to be formed therefrom, now and in all time to come.

I have nothing to say about Northern rights or Southern rights. I know of no such divisions or distinctions under the Constitution. The bill does equal and exact justice to the whole Union, and every part of it; it violates the rights of no state or territory, but places each on a perfect equality, and leaves the people thereof to the free enjoyment of all their rights under the Constitution. . . .

I say frankly that, in my opinion, this measure will be as popular at the North as at the South, when its provisions and principles shall have been fully developed and become well understood.

2. Salmon Chase Upholds Free Soil (1854)[*]

Senator Salmon P. Chase of Ohio—later Lincoln's secretary of the treasury, and still later chief justice of the Supreme Court—was an ardent free-soiler. So active

---

[*]*Congressional Globe*, 33d Congress, 1st session (February 3, 1854), Appendix, pp. 134, 140.

was he in defense of runaway slaves that he was dubbed "attorney general for the fugitive slaves." Pathologically ambitious for the presidency, he was so hand-some as to be "a sculptor's ideal of a president." He vehemently opposed both the Compromise of 1850 and the Kansas-Nebraska Act of 1854. These two measures, particularly the second, aroused so much ill feeling between the sections as to make future compromise improbable and led to the spontaneous formation of the Repub-lican party. In the light of Chase's remarks, was he justified in considering the slave power the aggressor? Was all future compromise now impossible? Was he a better prophet than Douglas?

Now, sir, who is responsible for this renewal of strife and controversy? Not we [free-soilers], for we have introduced no question of territorial slavery into Congress—not we who are denounced as agitators and factionists. No, sir; the quietists and the finalists have become agitators; they who told us that all agitation was quieted, and that the resolutions of the political conventions put a final period to the discussion of slavery.

This will not escape the observation of the country. It is slavery that renews the strife. It is slavery that again wants room. It is slavery, with its insatiate demands for more slave territory and more slave states.

And what does slavery ask for now? Why, sir, it demands that a time-honored and sacred compact [Missouri Compromise] shall be rescinded—a compact which has endured through a whole generation—a compact which has been universally regarded as inviolable, North and South—a compact the constitutionality of which few have doubted, and by which all have consented to abide. . . .

You may pass it here. You may send it to the other House. It may become law. But its effect will be to satisfy all thinking men that no compromises with slavery will endure, except so long as they serve the interests of slavery; and that there is no safe and honorable ground for non-slaveholders to stand upon, except that of restricting slavery within state limits, and excluding it absolutely from the whole sphere of federal jurisdiction.

The old questions between political parties are at rest. No great question so thoroughly possesses the public mind as this of slavery. This discussion will hasten the inevitable reorganization of parties upon the new issues which our circum-stances suggest. It will light up a fire in the country which may, perhaps, consume those who kindle it.

I cannot believe that the people of this country have so far lost sight of the maxims and principles of the Revolution, or are so insensible to the obligations which those maxims and principles impose, as to acquiesce in the violation of this compact. Sir, the Senator from Illinois [Douglas] tells us that he proposes a final settlement of all territorial questions in respect to slavery, by the application of the principle of popular sovereignty. What kind of popular sovereignty is that which allows one portion of the people to enslave another portion? Is that the doctrine of equal rights? Is that exact justice? Is that the teaching of enlightened, liberal, pro-gressive democracy?

No, sir; no! There can be no real democracy which does not fully maintain the rights of man, as man.

3. The South Is Lukewarm (1854)*

The antislavery North, as might have been expected, reacted violently against the gain for slavery (on paper) under the Kansas-Nebraska Act. Ominously, most of the opposition came not from already committed abolitionists but from citizens who had reluctantly accepted the Compromise of 1850 but had now lost all confidence in the good faith of the South. "The day of compromise is over," warned the Hartford (Connecticut) Courant. *Horace Greeley, editor of the potent* New York Tribune, *declared that Douglas and his coconspirators had "made more abolitionists than Garrison and Phillips could have made in half a century." Even the South, though on the whole mildly favorable, had its misgivings. The Columbia* South Carolinian *conceded that "practically" the Kansas-Nebraska Act would "scarcely ever benefit the South," but it would "render justice to the South" and serve as a "triumph" over abolitionism. A more realistic view was taken by an editorial in the slaveholding state of Kentucky. Why did the editor, with uncanny insight, regard the Kansas-Nebraska Act as a thing of unmitigated evil?*

The Nebraska Bill is advocated and denounced upon grounds the most opposite and for reasons the most diverse. There is the greatest contrariety of opinion as to what effect its passage will have upon the question of slavery. Southern men, of course, support it upon the ground that it will give slavery a chance to get into the territory from which it has hitherto been excluded; whilst others, with quite as much show of reason, take the ground occupied by the President, that the effect will be to prevent the admission of slave states into the Union forever.

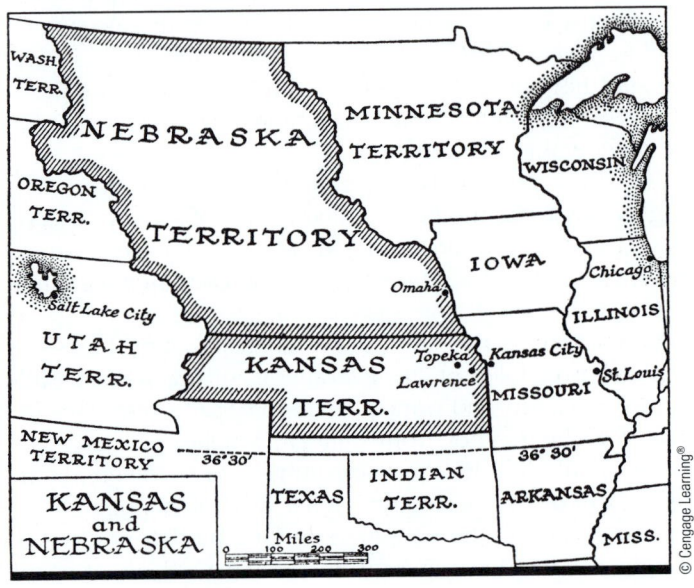

Western Citizen (Kentucky), April 21, 1854, in *Daily National Intelligencer* (Washington, DC), April 24, 1854.

A measure whose effects, in matters of so much consequence, are so uncertain; which proposes to violate and disannul a compact [Missouri Compromise] regarded by one section of our common country as sacred, and acquiesced in for a third of a century by the other—a compact the advantages of which the South has fully received on her part—should at least promise some decided practical good as the result of its passage, and should be chargeable with the production of as few evils as possible.

We believe that the adoption of the measure will be productive of evil, and only evil, continually. Even supposing that the Missouri Compromise is not a bargain that we of the slave states are bound to respect and stand to, and that we may declare it void without a breach of faith, what do we gain by its repeal? What but a revival, in a wilder and intenser and more dangerous form, of that agitation of the slavery question which was but yesterday allayed by the all but superhuman efforts of our noblest statesmen [in the Compromise of 1850]? The North regards the Missouri Compromise as a sacred compact, to the preservation of which the honor and faith of the South was pledged. If we now violate that pledge, what right have we to expect the North to respect any compromise that has been or may be made for our advantage? . . .

And what should we gain? A mere right to carry slaves into Nebraska, which we can never exercise; the mere gratification of having an old law [Missouri Compromise] repealed which the South now chooses to consider unjust to her, but which her wisest statesmen at the time of its passage regarded as highly advantageous to her—a law carried by Southern votes, and heretofore looked upon as one of the noblest achievements of Southern statesmanship.

Thought Provokers

1. If the Wilmot Proviso issue had not come up during the Mexican War, was it probable that the question of slavery in the territories would have been raised in an acute form?
2. It has been said that by the 1850s each side distrusted the other so greatly that disunion was inevitable: the North because of Southern grasping for more slave territory; the South because of Northern nullification of the Constitution and federal laws. Comment critically. Webster in 1850 was condemned as an appeaser or compromiser and hence not a statesman. Is compromise essential to statecraft?
3. Are a people ever justified in openly violating laws (like the Fugitive Slave Act) that they disapprove of and think immoral? What has been the fate of such laws in U.S. history? Should the majority always rule?
4. Was it immoral, as abolitionists alleged, for Congress to repeal the Missouri Compromise line of 1820? Why was further compromise between North and South impossible after 1854? Was the North or the South the aggressor in the 1850s with regard to the slavery issue? Which side was constitutionally right?

19

Drifting Toward Disunion, 1854–1861

It is an irrepressible conflict between opposing and enduring forces.

William H. Seward, 1858

Prologue: Popular sovereignty in Kansas degenerated into unpopular savagery. Embattled free-soilers fought embittered proslaveryites as the complaisant pro-Southern administrations of Presidents Franklin Pierce and James Buchanan continued to drift. Irate Northerners, resenting the Kansas-Nebraska grab, increasingly turned the Fugitive Slave Act into a dead letter. At the same time, the newly born Republican party, sired by the same Kansas-Nebraska Act, gathered such amazing momentum in the North as to give the Democrats a real scare in the presidential election of 1856. The sectional tension was heightened by a series of inflammatory incidents, including Representative Preston Brooks's brutal beating of Senator Charles Sumner, the proslavery *Dred Scott* decision, and John Brown's fantastic raid at Harpers Ferry. Southerners also reacted angrily against the overwhelming approval in the North of such antislavery propaganda as *Uncle Tom's Cabin* and Helper's *Impending Crisis of the South* (see p. 267). The imminent election of the Republican Lincoln in 1860 foreshadowed both secession and shooting.

A. The Impact of Uncle Tom's Cabin _____

1. Tom Defies Simon Legree (1852)[*]

Harriet Beecher Stowe, a busy mother and housewife then living in Maine, was aroused by the recent gains of slavery to write—partly on old wrapping paper—her heart-tugging novel Uncle Tom's Cabin. *Reared in New England, the daughter of famed preacher Lyman Beecher, and having lived for seventeen years in Ohio on the route of the Underground Railroad, she had developed an abhorrence of the "peculiar institution." Oddly enough, her firsthand observations of slavery were limited to a brief visit to Kentucky. In her best-selling book, she sought to mollify the South to some extent by representing the saintly slave Uncle Tom as having two kind masters; by featuring the whimsical Topsy and the angelic little Eva (who died); and by portraying the monster Simon Legree, who finally ordered Uncle Tom beaten to death,*

[*]Harriet B. Stowe, *Uncle Tom's Cabin* (Boston: J. P. Jewett, 1852), chap. 33.

as a Yankee from Vermont. In the following scene, the cotton-picking slaves have just returned from the fields, and Legree orders Tom to flog one of the sickly women for not having picked enough. What details of this episode would most offend the anti-slavery North? The proslavery South?

"And now," said Legree, "come here, you Tom. You see, I told ye I didn't buy ye jest for the common work. I mean to promote ye, and make a driver of ye; and tonight ye may jest as well begin to get yer hand in. Now, ye jest take this yer gal and flog her; ye've seen enough on't [of it] to know how."

"I beg Mas'r's pardon," said Tom; "hopes Mas'r won't set me at that. It's what I an't used to—never did—and can't do, no way possible."

"Ye'll larn a pretty smart chance of things ye never did know, before I've done with ye!" said Legree, taking up a cowhide and striking Tom a heavy blow across the cheek, and following up the infliction by a shower of blows.

"There!" he said, as he stopped to rest; "now, will ye tell me ye can't do it?"

"Yes, Mas'r," said Tom, putting up his hand, to wipe the blood that trickled down his face. "I'm willin' to work, night and day, and work while there's life and breath in me. But this yer thing I can't feel it right to do; and, Mas'r, I never shall do it—*never!*"

Tom had a remarkably smooth, soft voice, and a habitually respectful manner that had given Legree an idea that he would be cowardly and easily subdued. When he spoke these last words, a thrill of amazement went through everyone. The poor woman clasped her hands and said, "O Lord!" and everyone involuntarily looked at each other and drew in their breath, as if to prepare for the storm that was about to burst.

Legree looked stupefied and confounded; but at last burst forth:

"What! ye blasted black beast! tell *me* ye don't think it *right* to do what I tell ye! What have any of you cussed cattle to do with thinking what's right? I'll put a stop to it! Why, what do ye think ye are? May be ye think ye're a gentleman, master Tom, to be a telling your master what's right, and what an't! So you pretend it's wrong to flog the gal!"

"I think so, Mas'r," said Tom; "the poor crittur's sick and feeble; 'twould be downright cruel, and it's what I never will do, nor begin to. Mas'r, if you mean to kill me, kill me; but, as to my raising my hand agin any one here, I never shall—I'll die first!"

Tom spoke in a mild voice, but with a decision that could not be mistaken. Legree shook with anger; his greenish eyes glared fiercely, and his very whiskers seemed to curl with passion. But, like some ferocious beast, that plays with its victim before he devours it, he kept back his strong impulse to proceed to immediate violence, and broke out into bitter raillery.

"Well, here's a pious dog, at least, let down among us sinners!—a saint, a gentleman, and no less, to talk to us sinners about our sins! Powerful holy crittur, he must be! Here, you rascal, you make believe to be so pious—didn't you never hear, out of yer Bible, 'Servants, obey yer masters'? An't I yer master? Didn't I pay down twelve hundred dollars, cash, for all there is inside yer old cussed black shell? An't yer mine, now, body and soul?" he said, giving Tom a violent kick with his heavy boot; "tell me!"

In the very depth of physical suffering, bowed by brutal oppression, this question shot a gleam of joy and triumph through Tom's soul. He suddenly stretched himself up, and, looking earnestly to heaven, while the tears and blood that flowed down his face mingled, he exclaimed,

"No! no! no! my soul an't yours, Mas'r! You haven't bought it—ye can't buy it! It's been bought and paid for by One that is able to keep it. No matter, no matter, you can't harm me!"

"I can't!" said Legree, with a sneer; "we'll see—we'll see! Here, Sambo, Quimbo, give this dog such a breakin' in as he won't get over this month!"

The two gigantic Negroes that now laid hold of Tom, with fiendish exultation in their faces, might have formed no unapt personification of powers and darkness. The poor woman screamed with apprehension, and all rose, as by a general impulse, while they dragged him unresisting from the place.

2. The South Scorns Mrs. Stowe (1852)*

Northern abolitionists naturally applauded Mrs. Stowe's powerful tale; the poet John Greenleaf Whittier now thanked God for the Fugitive Slave Act, which had inspired the book. The few Northern journals that voiced criticism were drowned out by the clatter of the printing presses running off tens of thousands of new copies. Southern critics cried that this "wild and unreal picture" would merely arouse the "fanaticism" of the North while exciting the "indignation" of the South. They insisted that the slave beatings were libelously overemphasized; that the worst slave drivers were imported Northerners (like Legree); that the Southern black slave was better off than the Northern wage slave; and that relatively few families were broken up—fewer, in fact, than among soldiers on duty, Irish immigrants coming to America, sailors going to sea, or pioneers venturing West. Why did the Southern Literary Messenger *of Richmond find it important to refute Mrs. Stowe's "slanders" as follows?*

There are some who will think we have taken upon ourselves an unnecessary trouble in exposing the inconsistencies and false assertions of *Uncle Tom's Cabin*. It is urged by such persons that in devoting so much attention to abolition attacks we give them an importance to which they are not entitled. This may be true in general. But let it be borne in mind that this slanderous work has found its way to every section of our country, and has crossed the water to Great Britain, filling the minds of all who know nothing of slavery with hatred for that institution and those who uphold it. Justice to ourselves would seem to demand that it should not be suffered to circulate longer without the brand of falsehood upon it.

Let it be recollected, too, that the importance Mrs. Stowe will derive from Southern criticism will be one of infamy. Indeed she is only entitled to criticism at all as the mouthpiece of a large and dangerous faction which, if we do not put down with the pen, we may be compelled one day (God grant that day may never come!) to repel with the bayonet.

Southern Literary Messenger 18 (1852): 638, 731.

There are questions that underlie the story of *Uncle Tom's Cabin* of far deeper significance than any mere false coloring of Southern society. . . . We beg to make a single suggestion to Mrs. Stowe—that, as she is fond of referring to the Bible, she will turn over, before writing her next work of fiction, to the twentieth chapter of Exodus and there read these words—"Thou shalt not bear false witness against thy neighbor." . . .

We have not had the heart to speak of an erring woman as she deserved, though her misconduct admitted of no excuse and provoked the keenest and most just reprobation. We have little inclination—and, if we had much, we have not the time—to proceed with our disgusting labor, to anatomize minutely volumes as full of poisonous vermin as of putrescence, and to speak in such language as the occasion would justify, though it might be forbidden by decorum and self-respect.

We dismiss *Uncle Tom's Cabin* with the conviction and declaration that every holier purpose of our nature is misguided, every charitable sympathy betrayed, every loftier sentiment polluted, every moral purpose wrenched to wrong, and every patriotic feeling outraged, by its criminal prostitution of the high functions of the imagination to the pernicious intrigues of sectional animosity, and to the petty calumnies of willful slander.

B. Bleeding Kansas and "Bully" Brooks

1. Charles Sumner Assails the Slavocracy (1856)[*]

The erasing of the Missouri Compromise line in 1854 touched off a frantic tug-of-war between South and North to make Kansas either a slave or a free state. "Border ruffians," pouring into Kansas from slaveholding Missouri by the hundreds, set up a fraudulent but legal government. Resolute pioneers from the North, some of them assisted by the New England Emigrant Aid Company, countered by founding Lawrence, setting up an extralegal free-soil government, and seeking admission as a free state. Aroused by the resulting civil war, Senator Charles Sumner of Massachusetts—a handsome, egotistical, and flamingly outspoken abolitionist—assailed the slavery men in a savage two-day speech ("The Crime Against Kansas"). He singled out the slaveholding state of South Carolina and, in particular, her well-liked Senator Andrew P. Butler, who, declared Sumner, had taken as his "mistress" "the harlot, slavery." What aspects of the speech would be most offensive to a South Carolina "gentleman"?

If the slave states cannot enjoy what, in mockery of the great Fathers of the Republic, he [Butler] misnames equality under the Constitution—in other words, the full power in the national territories to compel fellow men to unpaid toil, to separate husband and wife, and to sell little children at the auction block—then, sir, the chivalric Senator will conduct the state of South Carolina out of the Union! Heroic knight! Exalted Senator! A second Moses come for a second exodus!

---

[*]*Congressional Globe*, 34th Congress, 1st session (May 19–20, 1856), Appendix, pp. 530, 543.

But not content with this poor menace . . . the Senator, in the unrestrained chivalry of his nature, has undertaken to apply opprobrious words to those who differ from him on this floor. He calls them "sectional and fanatical"; and opposition to the usurpation in Kansas he denounces as "an uncalculating fanaticism." To be sure, these charges lack all grace of originality, and all sentiment of truth; but the adventurous Senator does not hesitate. He is the uncompromising, unblushing representative on this floor of a flagrant sectionalism, which now domineers over the Republic. . . .

With regret, I come again upon the Senator from South Carolina [Butler], who, omnipresent in this debate, overflowed with rage at the simple suggestion that Kansas had applied for admission as a state; and, with incoherent phrases, discharged the loose expectoration of his speech,* now upon her representative, and then upon her people. There was no extravagance of the ancient parliamentary debate which he did not repeat. Nor was there any possible deviation from truth which he did not make, with so much of passion, I am glad to add, as to save him from the suspicion of intentional aberration.

But the Senator touches nothing which he does not disfigure—with error, sometimes of principle, sometimes of fact. He shows an incapacity of accuracy, whether in stating the Constitution or in stating the law, whether in the details of statistics or the diversions of scholarship. He cannot ope his mouth but out there flies a blunder.

[Sumner next attacks South Carolina, with its "shameful imbecility" of slavery, for presuming to sit in judgment over free-soil Kansas and block the latter's admission as a free state.]

South Carolina is old; Kansas is young. South Carolina counts by centuries; where Kansas counts by years. But a beneficent example may be born in a day; and I venture to say that against the two centuries of the older state may be already set the two years of trial, evolving corresponding virtue, in the younger community. In the one is the long wail of Slavery; in the other, the hymns of Freedom. And if we glance at special achievements, it will be difficult to find anything in the history of South Carolina which presents so much of heroic spirit in an heroic cause as appears in that repulse of the Missouri invaders by the beleaguered town of Lawrence, where even the women gave their efforts to Freedom. . . .

Were the whole history of South Carolina blotted out of existence, from its very beginning down to the day of the last election of the Senator to his present seat on this floor, civilization might lose—I do not say how little; but surely less than it has already gained by the example of Kansas, in its valiant struggle against oppression, and in the development of a new science of emigration. Already in Lawrence alone there are newspapers and schools, including a high school, and throughout this infant territory there is more mature scholarship far, in proportion to its inhabitants, than in all South Carolina. Ah, sir, I tell the Senator that Kansas, welcomed as a free state, will be a "ministering angel" to the Republic when South Carolina, in the cloak of darkness which she hugs, "lies howling."

---

*Butler suffered from a slight paralysis of the mouth.

2. The South Justifies Yankee-Beaters (1856)*

Southern fire-eaters had already used abusive language in Congress, but Sumner's epithets infuriated Congressman Brooks of South Carolina. Resenting the insults to his state and to his cousin (Senator Butler), he entered the Senate chamber and broke his cane over the head of Sumner, then sitting at his desk. The senator fell bleeding to the floor, while several other members of Congress, perhaps thinking that he was getting his just deserts, made no effort to rescue him. His nervous system shattered, Sumner was incapacitated for about three years; Brooks resigned his seat and was unanimously reelected. A resolution passed by the citizens of his district applauded his exhibition of "the true spirit of Southern chivalry and patriotism" in "chastising, coolly and deliberately, the vile and lawless Sumner." The same group sent him a new cane inscribed, "Use knock-down arguments." What does the following editorial in an Alabama newspaper suggest about the general attitude of the white South and what it portended for the Union?

There are but two papers in the state that we have seen that denounce the chastisement of Sumner by Mr. Brooks as a shameful outrage. One of them is the *Mobile Tribune*, one of the editors of which is a Yankee, and the other is a sheet, the name of which we shall not mention.

With the exception of the papers alluded to, the press of the entire state have fully approved of the course Mr. Brooks pursued, under the circumstances, and recommended that other Southern members of Congress adopt the same method of silencing the foul-mouthed abolition emissaries of the North. Indeed, it is quite apparent, from recent developments, that the shillalah [club] is the best argument to be applied to such low-bred mongrels.

More than six years ago, the abolitionists were told that if they intended to carry out their principles, they must fight. When the Emigrant Aid Societies began to send their [Yankee] tools to Kansas, they were told that if their object was to establish a colony of thieves under the name of "Free State Men," on the border of Missouri, for the purpose of keeping out Southerners and destroying slavery, they must fight. And let them understand that if they intend to carry their abolitionism into Congress, and pour forth their disgusting obscenity and abuse of the South in the Senate Chamber, and force their doctrines down the throats of Southerners, they must fight.

Let [editor Horace] Greeley be severely cowhided, and he will cease to publish his blackguardism about Southern men. Let [Senators] Wilson and Sumner and Seward, and the whole host of abolition agitators in Congress, be chastised to their heart's content, and, our word for it, they will cease to heap abuse upon our citizens.

We repeat, let our Representative in Congress use the cowhide and hickory stick (and, if need be, the bowie knife and revolver) more frequently, and we'll bet our old hat that it will soon come to pass that Southern institutions and Southern men will be respected.

Autauga (Alabama) *Citizen*, in *The Liberator* (Boston), July 4, 1856.

3. The Delicate Balance (1856)

The chart below was prepared for the 1856 presidential election. In what ways does it reflect growing tension over the slavery controversy?

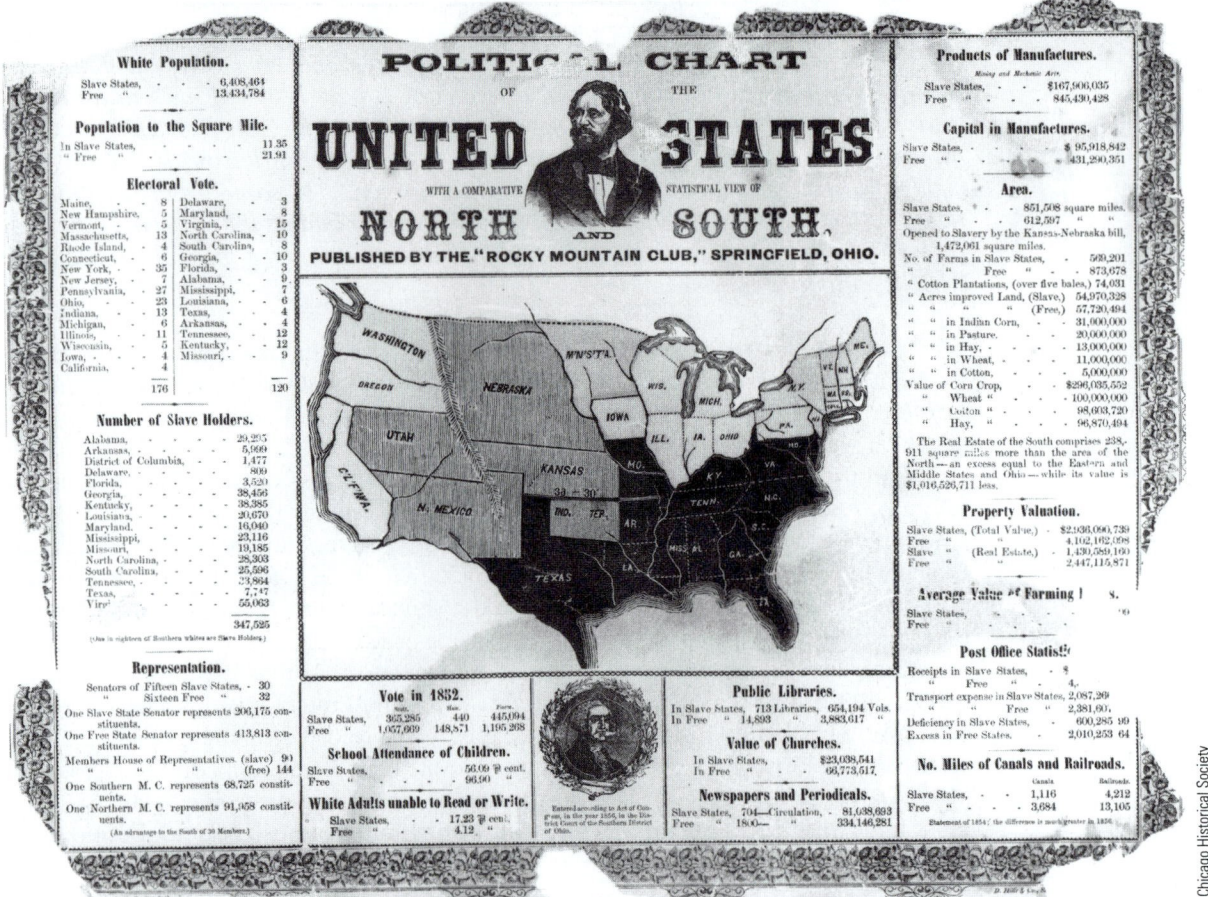

Chicago Historical Society

C. The Dred Scott Decision

1. The Pro-Southern Court Speaks (1857)*

Dred Scott, an illiterate Missouri slave, was taken by his master for several years (1834–1838) to the free state of Illinois and then to a portion of Wisconsin Territory now located in the state of Minnesota. The Minnesota area was then free territory, since it lay north of the line of 36° 30' established by the Missouri Compromise of

---

*B. C. Howard, *Reports of Cases Argued and Adjusted in the Supreme Court of the United States* (Newark, NY: The Lawyers Co-operative Publishing Company, 1857).

1820 (subsequently repealed in 1854). Scott, taken in hand by interested abolitionists, sued for his freedom on the grounds of residence on free soil. The case was appealed from the circuit court to the Supreme Court, which grappled with several basic questions: Was a slave a citizen under the Constitution? (If not, he was not entitled to sue in the federal courts.) Was Dred Scott rendered free by residence in Wisconsin Territory, under the terms of the Missouri Compromise? The Court, headed by the pro-Southern Chief Justice Roger Taney of the slaveholding state of Maryland, ruled as follows. How were the basic questions answered? What were their implications for the future?

Now . . . the right of property in a slave is distinctly and expressly affirmed in the Constitution. The right to traffic in it, like an ordinary article of merchandise and property, was guaranteed to the citizens of the United States, in every state that might desire it, for twenty years. And the government in express terms is pledged to protect it in all future time, if the slave escapes from his owner. This is done in plain words—too plain to be misunderstood. And no word can be found in the Constitution which gives Congress a greater power over slave property, or which entitles property of that kind to less protection, than property of any other description. The only power conferred is the power coupled with the duty of guarding and protecting the owner in his rights.

Upon these considerations, it is the opinion of the Court that the Act of Congress [Missouri Compromise] which prohibited a citizen from holding and owning property of this kind in the territory of the United States north of the line [of 36° 30'] therein mentioned is not warranted by the Constitution, and is therefore void; and that neither Dred Scott himself, nor any of his family, were made free by being carried into this territory; even if they had been carried there by the owner with the intention of becoming a permanent resident. . . .

Upon the whole, therefore, it is the judgment of this Court that it appears by the record before us that the plaintiff in error [Dred Scott] is not a citizen of Missouri, in the sense in which that word is used in the Constitution; and that the Circuit Court of the United States for that reason had no jurisdiction in the case, and could give no judgment in it.

2. A Virginia Newspaper Gloats (1857)*

The South was overjoyed at the Dred Scott *decision. The sanctity of slave property was ringingly reaffirmed. A slave could be taken with impunity into the territories and perhaps also into the free states. Even if the territory of Kansas should vote slavery down under popular sovereignty, slave owners could still keep their slaves. Also pleasing to the South was Chief Justice Taney's observation that in 1776 the blacks were "so far inferior that they had no rights which the white man was bound to respect." This dictum, torn out of context and applied to the present, enraged the abolitionists. What did the following editorial in a Virginia newspaper portend for an amicable solution of the slave-race problem?*

---

*Southside (Virginia) *Democrat,* in *The Liberator* (Boston), April 3, 1857.

The highest judicial tribunal in the land has decided that the blackamoors, called by the extreme of public courtesy the colored population, are not citizens of the United States. This decision must be followed by other decisions and regulations in the individual states themselves. Negro suffrage must, of course, be abolished everywhere.

Negro nuisances, in the shape of occupying promiscuous seats in our rail-cars and churches with those who are citizens, must be abated. Negro insolence and domineering arrogance must be rebuked; the whole tribe must be taught to fall back into their legitimate position in human society—the position that Divine Providence intended they should occupy. Not being citizens, they can claim none of the rights or privileges belonging to a citizen. They can neither vote, hold office, nor occupy any other position in society than an inferior and subordinate one—the only one for which they are fitted, the only one for which they have the natural qualifications which entitle them to enjoy or possess.

3. The North Breathes Defiance (1857)[*]

The antislavery North was shocked by the Dred Scott *decision. If slavery could not be barred from the territories, then the constitutional basis of popular sovereignty was in doubt, and the already unpopular Kansas-Nebraska Act of 1854 was a gigantic hoax. Especially galling was the presence of several slaveholders on the Supreme Court. Various Northern spokesmen denounced the decision as no more binding than that of a Southern debating society. Horace Greeley, editor of the influential* New York Tribune, *insisted that the Court's findings had no more "moral weight" than the judgment of "a Washington barroom." The rising politician Abraham Lincoln, referring to the "apparent partisan bias" and the numerous dissenting opinions of the Court, branded the decision "erroneous." Judging from the following reaction in a Boston religious journal, was the South justified in feeling that the North was determined to break up the Union?*

Shall this decision be submitted to? It need not be. A most righteous decision of the Supreme Court (as we believe), regarding the rights of the Cherokee nation, was made of none effect by the state of Georgia, with the connivance of President Jackson.

The people are mightier than courts or Presidents. The acts of Congress, though declared void, are not repealed. The acts of the free states, though pronounced invalid, still exist. If the people will, they can be maintained and enforced.

Is it said that this is revolutionary counsel? We answer, it is the Southern judges of the Supreme Court who are the authors of revolution. They have enacted a principle contrary to the most plain and obvious sense of the Constitution they pretend to interpret. . . . The most explicit allusion to slaves, in that instrument, describes them as held to service in the states "under the laws thereof," plainly deriving the rights of the master from local, not from common law.

The decision is also opposed to the unanimous judgment of the statesmen and jurists by whom the Constitution was formed, and to the amplest recorded

---

[*]*Christian Watchman and Reflector* (Boston), in *The Liberator* (Boston), March 27, 1857.

testimony as to their intentions. It is a doctrine not twenty years old, which those judges, conspiring with the most desperate school of Southern politicians, the men who have been for the space of a generation plotting against the Union, have dared to foist upon the Constitution. It is a sacrilege, against which the blood of our fathers cries from the ground. No man who has in his veins a drop kindred to the blood that bought our liberties can actively submit to their decree.

But if the free states will sit down in the dust, without an effort to vindicate their sovereign rights, if the majority of the people are so fallen away from the spirit of their fathers as to yield their birthright without a struggle, then it becomes the solemn duty of every conscientious freeman to regard the Union of these states as stripped henceforth of all title to his willing allegiance. If the Constitution is a charter to protect slavery, everywhere, then it is a sin against God and man to swear allegiance to it. Every man will be forced to choose between disunion and the guilt of an accomplice in the crime of slavery. May God avert such an alternative!

D. The Lincoln-Douglas Debates

I. Stephen Douglas Opposes Black Citizenship (1858)*

With the Illinois senatorship at stake, "Honest Abe" Lincoln boldly challenged Senator Douglas—the "Little Giant"—to a series of joint debates, presumably on current issues. He lost the ensuing election but placed his feet squarely on the path to the White House. The first forensic encounter occurred at Ottawa, Illinois, where the gladiators exchanged the following verbal blows before some twelve thousand partisans. How did Douglas's remarks on this occasion both please and offend the South?

We are told by Lincoln that he is utterly opposed to the Dred Scott decision, and will not submit to it, for the reason that he says it deprives the Negro of the rights and privileges of citizenship. (Laughter and applause.) That is the first and main reason which he assigns for his warfare on the Supreme Court of the United States and its decision.

I ask you, are you in favor of conferring upon the Negro the rights and privileges of citizenship? ("No, no.") Do you desire to strike out of our state constitution that clause which keeps slaves and free Negroes out of the state, and allow the free Negroes to flow in ("Never.") and cover your prairies with black settlements? Do you desire to turn this beautiful state into a free Negro colony ("No, no.") in order that when Missouri abolishes slavery she can send one hundred thousand emancipated slaves into Illinois, to become citizens and voters, on an equality with yourselves? ("Never," "No.")

If you desire Negro citizenship, if you desire to allow them to come into the state and settle with the white man, if you desire them to vote on an equality with yourselves, and to make them eligible to office, to serve on juries, and to adjudge

---

*R. P. Basler, ed., *The Collected Works of Abraham Lincoln* (New Brunswick, NJ: Rutgers University Press, 1953), vol. 3, pp. 9–11.

your rights, then support Mr. Lincoln and the Black [pro-Negro] Republican Party, who are in favor of the citizenship of the Negro. ("Never, never.")

For one, I am opposed to Negro citizenship in any and every form. (Cheers.) I believe this government was made on the white basis. ("Good.") I believe it was made by white men for the benefit of white men and their posterity for ever, and I am in favor of confining citizenship to white men, men of European birth and descent, instead of conferring it upon Negroes, Indians, and other inferior races. ("Good for you," "Douglas forever.")

Mr. Lincoln, following the example and lead of all the little abolition orators who go around and lecture in the basements of schools and churches, reads from the Declaration of Independence that all men were created equal, and then asks how can you deprive a Negro of that equality which God and the Declaration of Independence awards to him. He and they maintain that Negro equality is guaranteed by the laws of God, and that it is asserted in the Declaration of Independence. If they think so, of course they have a right to say so, and so vote. I do not question Mr. Lincoln's conscientious belief that the Negro was made his equal, and hence is his brother (Laughter.), but for my own part, I do not regard the Negro as my equal, and positively deny that he is my brother or any kin to me whatever. ("Never," "Hit him again," and cheers.) . . .

Now, I do not believe that the Almighty ever intended the Negro to be the equal of the white man. ("Never, never.") If he did, he has been a long time demonstrating the fact. (Cheers.) . . . He belongs to an inferior race, and must always occupy an inferior position. ("Good," "That's so," etc.)

I do not hold that because the Negro is our inferior that therefore he ought to be a slave. By no means can such a conclusion be drawn from what I have said. On the contrary, I hold that humanity and Christianity both require that the Negro shall have and enjoy every right, every privilege, and every immunity consistent with the safety of the society in which he lives. ("That's so.") On that point, I presume, there can be no diversity of opinion. . . . This is a question which each state and each territory must decide for itself—Illinois has decided it for herself. . . .

Now, I hold that Illinois had a right to abolish and prohibit slavery as she did, and I hold that Kentucky has the same right to continue and protect slavery that Illinois had to abolish it. I hold that New York had as much right to abolish slavery as Virginia has to continue it, and that each and every state of this Union is a sovereign power, with the right to do as it pleases upon this question of slavery, and upon all its domestic institutions.

2. Abraham Lincoln Denies Black Equality (1858)[*]

Lincoln, in his high-pitched voice, parried Douglas's charges, to the delight of his noisy Ottawa supporters, who outnumbered the Douglasites about two to one. When this particular debate ended, the Republicans bore their awkward hero in triumph from the platform—with his drawn-up trousers, said one observer, revealing the edges of his

---

[*]R. P. Basler, ed., *The Collected Works of Abraham Lincoln* (New Brunswick, NJ: Rutgers University Press, 1953), vol. 3, pp. 13, 16.

long underwear. Douglas later claimed that his opponent, beaten and exhausted, was unable to leave under his own power—a charge that angered Lincoln. In the following portion of Lincoln's contribution to the interchange at Ottawa, what portion of his stand was most offensive to Northern abolitionists? To the white South?

My Fellow Citizens: When a man hears himself somewhat misrepresented, it provokes him—at least, I find it so with myself. But when the misrepresentation becomes very gross and palpable, it is more apt to amuse him. (Laughter.) . . .

. . . Anything that argues me into his [Douglas's] idea of perfect social and political equality with the Negro is but a specious and fantastic arrangement of words, by which a man can prove a horse chestnut to be a chestnut horse. (Laughter.)

I will say here, while upon this subject, that I have no purpose directly or indirectly to interfere with the institution of slavery in the states where it exists. I believe I have no lawful right to do so, and I have no inclination to do so. I have no purpose to introduce political and social equality between the white and the black races. There is a physical difference between the two, which in my judgment will probably forever forbid their living together upon the footing of perfect equality, and inasmuch as it becomes a necessity that there must be a difference, I, as well as Judge Douglas, am in favor of the race to which I belong having the superior position.

I have never said anything to the contrary, but I hold that, notwithstanding all this, there is no reason in the world why the Negro is not entitled to all the natural rights enumerated in the Declaration of Independence, the right to life, liberty, and the pursuit of happiness. (Loud cheers.) I hold that he is as much entitled to these as the white man. I agree with Judge Douglas he is not my equal in many respects—certainly not in color, perhaps not in moral or intellectual endowment. But in the right to eat the bread, without leave of anybody else, which his own hand earns, *he is my equal and the equal of Judge Douglas, and the equal of every living man.* (Great applause.)

E. John Brown at Harpers Ferry

1. The Richmond Enquirer *Is Outraged* (1859)[*]

The fanatical abolitionist John Brown plotted a large slave insurrection at Harpers Ferry in western Virginia. Purchasing arms with about $3,000 provided by sympathetic Northern abolitionists, he launched his abortive enterprise with a score of men, including two of his own sons. After the loss of several innocent lives, most of Brown's coconspirators were captured or killed. Brown himself was wounded and thrown in jail to await trial. Most of the abolitionists who had financed his enterprise ran for cover, although many of them had evidently not known of his desperate plan to attack a federal arsenal and bring down on himself the Washington government. Southerners were angered by the widespread expressions of sympathy for Brown in

---

[*]*Richmond Enquirer*, October 25, 1859, in Edward Stone, ed., *Incident at Harpers Ferry* (Englewood Cliffs, NJ: Prentice-Hall, 1956), p. 177.

the North. A week after the raid, the influential Richmond Enquirer *wrote as follows. What is the most alarming aspect of the editorial?*

The Harper's Ferry invasion has advanced the cause of Disunion more than any other event . . . since the formation of the government; it has rallied to that standard men who formerly looked upon it with horror; it has revived, with tenfold strength, the desire of a Southern Confederacy. The heretofore most determined friends of the Union may now be heard saying, "If under the form of a Confederacy [Union] our peace is disturbed, our state invaded, its peaceful citizens cruelly murdered . . . by those who should be our warmest friends, . . . and the people of the North sustain the outrage, then let disunion come."

2. John Brown Delivers His Final Address (1859)*

Charged with three capital offenses—conspiracy with slaves, murder, and treason— Brown was given every opportunity to pose as a martyr during his trial. Before his death sentence was handed down, Brown delivered the following address to the court. While reaffirming his desire to free the slaves, Brown continued to disavow any aim on his part to incite rebellion or bring war upon the South. But in a revealing statement passed to a guard on the morning of his execution, the unrepentant Brown warned that "the crimes of this guilty land will never be purged away but with blood." How does his courtroom speech square with this statement and the events at Harpers Ferry? How does Brown justify his actions?

I have, may it please the Court, a few words to say.

In the first place, I deny everything but what I have all along admitted,—the design on my part to free the slaves. I intended certainly to have made a clean thing of that matter, as I did last winter, when I went into Missouri and there took slaves without the snapping of a gun on either side, moved them through the country, and finally left them in Canada. I designed to have done the same thing again, on a larger scale. That was all I intended. I never did intend murder, or treason, or the destruction of property, or to excite or incite slaves to rebellion, or to make insurrection.

I have another objection: and that is, it is unjust that I should suffer such a penalty. Had I interfered in the manner which I admit, and which I admit has been fairly proved (for I admire the truthfulness and candor of the greater portion of the witnesses who have testified in this case),—had I so interfered in behalf of the rich, the powerful, the intelligent, the so-called great, or in behalf of any of their friends,—either father, mother, brother, sister, wife, or children, or any of that class,—and suffered and sacrificed what I have in this interference, it would have been all right; and every man in this court would have deemed it an act worthy of reward rather than punishment.

This court acknowledges, as I suppose, the validity of the law of God. I see a book kissed here which I suppose to be the Bible, or at least the New Testament. That teaches me that all things whatsoever I would that men should do to me,

---

*F. B. Sanborn, ed., *The Life and Letters of John Brown, Liberator of Kansas, and Martyr of Virginia* (Boston: Roberts Brothers, 1891), pp. 584–585.

I should do even so to them. It teaches me, further, to "remember them that are in bonds, as bound with them." I endeavored to act up to that instruction. I say, I am yet too young to understand that God is any respecter of persons. I believe that to have interfered as I have done—as I have always freely admitted I have done—in behalf of His despised poor, was not wrong, but right. Now, if it is deemed necessary that I should forfeit my life for the furtherance of the ends of justice, and mingle my blood further with the blood of my children and with the blood of millions in this slave country whose rights are disregarded by wicked, cruel, and unjust enactments,—I submit; so let it be done!

Let me say one word further.

I feel entirely satisfied with the treatment I have received on my trial. Considering all the circumstances, it has been more generous than I expected. But I feel no consciousness of guilt. I have stated from the first what was my intention, and what was not. I never had any design against the life of any person, nor any disposition to commit treason, or excite slaves to rebel, or make any general insurrection. I never encouraged any man to do so, but always discouraged any idea of that kind.

Let me say, also, a word in regard to the statements made by some of those connected with me. I hear it has been stated by some of them that I have induced them to join me. But the contrary is true. I do not say this to injure them, but as regretting their weakness. There is not one of them but joined me of his own accord, and the greater part of them at their own expense. A number of them I never saw, and never had a word of conversation with, till the day they came to me; and that was for the purpose I have stated.

Now I have done.

3. Horace Greeley Hails a Martyr (1859)[*]

Reactions in the North to Brown's incredible raid ranged from execration to adulation. The most devoted abolitionists, who believed that slavery was so black a crime as to justify violence, defended Brown. The orator Wendell Phillips cried (amid cheers), "John Brown has twice as much right to hang Governor Wise as Governor Wise has to hang him." Ralph Waldo Emerson and Henry David Thoreau publicly likened the execution to the crucifixion of Jesus. Eccentric Horace Greeley, the influential antislavery editor of the New York Tribune, was denounced by Southerners for having given editorial aid and comfort to John Brown. Greeley replied as follows in an editorial that no doubt reflected the views of countless moderate antislavery people, who deplored the method while applauding the goal. How effectively did Greeley make the point that Brown's crime was no ordinary felony, and to what extent was he anti-Brown?

John Brown knew no limitations in his warfare on slavery—why should slavery be lenient to John Brown, defeated and a captive?

War has its necessities, and they are sometimes terrible. We have not seen how slavery could spare the life of John Brown without virtually confessing the iniquity of its own existence. We believe Brown himself has uniformly taken this view of the

---

[*]*New York Tribune*, December 3, 1859.

matter, and discountenanced all appeals in his behalf for pardon or commutation, as well as everything savoring of irritation or menace. There are eras in which death is not merely heroic but beneficent and fruitful. Who shall say that this was not John Brown's fit time to die?

We are not those who say, "If slavery is wrong, then John Brown was wholly right." There are fit and unfit modes of combating a great evil; we think Brown at Harper's Ferry pursued the latter. . . . And, while we heartily wish every slave in the world would run away from his master tomorrow and never be retaken, we should not feel justified in entering a slave state to incite them to do so, even if we were sure to succeed in the enterprise. Of course, we regard Brown's raid as utterly mistaken and, in its direct consequences, pernicious.

But his are the errors of a fanatic, not the crimes of a felon. It were absurd to apply to him opprobrious epithets or wholesale denunciations. The essence of crime is the pursuit of selfish gratification in disregard of others' good; and that is the precise opposite of Old Brown's impulse and deed. He periled and sacrificed not merely his own life—that were, perhaps, a moderate stake—but the lives of his beloved sons, the earthly happiness of his family and theirs, to benefit a despised and downtrodden race—to deliver from bitter bondage and degradation those whom he had never seen.

Unwise, the world will pronounce him. Reckless of artificial yet palpable obligations he certainly was, but his very errors were heroic—the faults of a brave, impulsive, truthful nature, impatient of wrong, and only too conscious that "resistance to tyrants is obedience to God." Let whoever would first cast a stone ask himself whether his own noblest act was equal in grandeur and nobility to that for which John Brown pays the penalty of a death on the gallows.

And that death will serve to purge his memory of any stain which his errors might otherwise have cast upon it. Mankind are proverbially generous to those who have suffered all that can here be inflicted—who have passed beyond the portals of the life to come. John Brown dead will live in millions of hearts—will be discussed around the homely hearth of toil and dreamed of on the couch of poverty and trial. . . .

Admit that Brown took a wrong way to rid his country of the curse, his countrymen of the chains of bondage, what is the right way? And are we pursuing that way as grandly, unselfishly, as he pursued the wrong one? If not, is it not high time we were? Before censuring severely his errors, should we not abandon our own?

4. Lincoln Disowns Brown (1860)*

The South quickly seized upon the John Brown raid as a club with which to belabor the fast-growing Republican party, which allegedly had connived with the conspirators. Rough-hewn Abraham Lincoln, Republican presidential aspirant, came east from Illinois for his make-or-break speech before a sophisticated eastern audience at Cooper Union in New York City. During the course of his address, which was a smashing success, he dealt with the Brown raid. How convincingly did he meet the accusation of Republican complicity, and to what extent was he both pro-Brown and anti-Brown?

---

*J. G. Nicolay and John Hay, eds., *Complete Works of Abraham Lincoln* (New York: The Century Co., 1894), vol. 5, pp. 314–319, passim.

You [Southerners] charge that we [Republicans] stir up insurrections among your slaves. We deny it; and what is your proof? Harper's Ferry! John Brown!!

John Brown was no Republican; and you have failed to implicate a single Republican in his Harper's Ferry enterprise. If any member of our party is guilty in that matter, you know it, or you do not know it. If you do know it, you are inexcusable for not designating the man and proving the fact. If you do not know it, you are inexcusable for asserting it, and especially for persisting in the assertion after you have tried and failed to make the proof. You need not be told that persisting in a charge which one does not know to be true is simply malicious slander.

Some of you admit that no Republican designedly aided or encouraged the Harper's Ferry affair, but still insist that our doctrines and declarations necessarily lead to such results. We do not believe it. . . .

Slave insurrections are no more common now than they were before the Republican Party was organized. What induced the Southampton [Nat Turner's] insurrection, twenty-eight years ago, in which at least three times as many lives were lost as at Harper's Ferry? You can scarcely stretch your very elastic fancy to the conclusion that Southampton was "got up by Black Republicanism." In the present state of things in the United States, I do not think a general, or even a very extensive, slave insurrection is possible. . . .

John Brown's effort was peculiar. It was not a slave insurrection. It was an attempt by white men to get up a revolt among slaves, in which the slaves refused to participate. In fact, it was so absurd that the slaves, with all their ignorance, saw plainly enough it could not succeed. That affair, in its philosophy, corresponds with the many attempts, related in history, at the assassination of kings and emperors. An enthusiast broods over the oppression of a people till he fancies himself commissioned by Heaven to liberate them. He ventures the attempt, which ends in little else than his own execution.

F. The Presidential Campaign of 1860

I. Fire-Eaters Urge Secession (1860)*

The surprise nomination of Abraham Lincoln for president on the Republican ticket in 1860 precipitated a crisis. Many Southern spokesmen served notice that the election of this backwoods "ape," whose opposition to slavery was grossly exaggerated, would prove that the North no longer wanted the South in the Union. The vitriolic Charleston Mercury, which had championed nullification as early as 1832, was perhaps the foremost newspaper advocating secession. What grievances does the following editorial cite? Did they justify secession?

The leaders and oracles of the most powerful party in the United States [Republican] have denounced us as tyrants and unprincipled heathens, through the civilized world. They have preached it from their pulpits. They have declared it in the halls of Congress and in their newspapers. In their schoolhouses they have taught their children (who are to rule this government in the next generation) to

---

*Charleston (South Carolina) Mercury, September 18, 1860.

look upon the slaveholder as the special disciple of the devil himself. They have published books and pamphlets in which the institution of slavery is held up to the world as a blot and a stain upon the escutcheon of America's honor as a nation.

They have established abolition societies among them for the purpose of raising funds—first to send troops to Kansas to cut the throats of all the slaveholders there, and now to send emissaries among us to incite our slaves to rebellion against the authority of their masters, and thereby endanger the lives of our people and the destruction of our property.

They have brought forth an open and avowed enemy to the most cherished and important institution of the South, as candidate for election to the Chief Magistracy of this government—the very basis of whose political principles is an uncompromising hostility to the institution of slavery under all circumstances.

They have virtually repealed the Fugitive Slave Law, and declare their determination not to abide by the decision of the Supreme Court guaranteeing to us the right to claim our property wherever found in the United States.

And, in every conceivable way, the whole Northern people, as a mass, have shown a most implacable hostility to us and our most sacred rights; and this, too, without the slightest provocation on the part of the South. . . .

Has a man's own brother, born of the same parents, a right to invade the sacred precincts of his fireside, to wage war upon him and his family, and deprive him of his property? And if he should do so, the aggrieved brother has not only a right, but it is his duty, sanctioned by every principle of right, to cut off all communication with that unnatural brother, to drive him from the sanctuary of his threshold, and treat him as an enemy and a stranger. Then why should we any longer submit to the galling yoke of our tyrant brother—the usurping, domineering, abolition North!

The political policy of the South demands that we should not hesitate, but rise up with a single voice and proclaim to the world that we will be subservient to the North no longer, but that we will be a free and an independent people. . . .

All admit that an ultimate dissolution of the Union is inevitable, and we believe the crisis is not far off. Then let it come now; the better for the South that it should be today; she cannot afford to wait.

2. The North Resents Threats (1860)*

Outstanding among Northern newspapers was the Springfield *(Massachusetts)* Republican. *Edited by the high-strung Samuel Bowles, who was known at times to drive himself forty-eight hours without sleep, it featured straightforward reporting and concise writing. Can you determine, from the following editorial, the extent to which the issue of majority rule was legitimately involved in the North-South dispute?*

The South, through the mouth of many of its leading politicians and journals, defies the North to elect Abraham Lincoln to the Presidency. It threatens secession in case he shall be elected. It arrogantly declares that he shall never take his seat. It passes resolutions of the most outrageous and insolent character, insulting every

---

*Springfield (Massachusetts) *Republican*, August 25, 1860.

man who dares to vote for what they call a "Black Republican." To make a long matter very short and plain, they claim the privilege of conducting the government in all the future, as they have in all the past, for their own benefit and their own way, with the alternative of dissolving the Union of the States.

Now, if the non-slaveholding people have any spirit at all, they will settle this question at once and forever. Look at the history of the last two administrations, in which the slave interest has had undisputed sway. This sway, the most disgraceful and shameless of anything in the history of the government, we are told must not be thrown off, else the Union will be dissolved. Let's try it! Are we forever to be governed by a slaveholding minority? Will the passage of four years more of misrule make it any easier for the majority to assume its legitimate functions?

There are many reasons why we desire to see this experiment tried this fall. If the majority cannot rule the country without the secession of the minority, it is time the country knew it. If the country can only exist under the rule of an oligarchy [of slave owners], let the fact be demonstrated at once, and let us change our institutions. We desire to see the experiment tried, because we wish to have the Southern people, who have been blinded and cheated by the politicians, learn that a "Black Republican" respects the requirements of the Constitution and will protect their interests. Harmony between the two sections of this country can never be secured until the South has learned that the North is not its enemy, but its best friend.

[The "Black Republican" Lincoln was elected president on November 6, 1860. Three days later a New Orleans newspaper declared, "The Northern people, in electing Mr. Lincoln, have perpetrated a deliberate, cold-blooded insult and outrage upon the people of the slaveholding states." On December 20, a special convention in South Carolina led the secessionist parade by voting 169 to 0 to leave the Union.]

Thought Provokers

1. Why did the fictional *Uncle Tom's Cabin* have more success, as propaganda, than the countless factual accounts published by abolitionists?
2. Compare the reaction of the North to the *Dred Scott* decision of 1857 with that of the South to the Supreme Court decision of 1954 ordering desegregation. To what extent is it true, as Republicans insisted in 1857, that the people are the court of last resort in this country?
3. Were both Douglas and Lincoln segregationists? Was Douglas more pro–popular sovereignty than he was proslavery? Was Lincoln, as often charged, an abolitionist?
4. In what ways may John Brown's raid be regarded as one of the causes of the Civil War? Since John Brown in Kansas had murdered proslavery men and run off their horses and slaves, how could he be rationally compared to Jesus? Was slavery such a grievous crime, as extreme abolitionists charged, as to justify theft and murder in fighting it?
5. Was Lincoln's election an excuse or a reason for secession? Did the white Southerners have solid grounds for fearing a Republican administration?

20

Girding for War: The North and the South, 1861–1865

It has long been a grave question whether any
government not too strong for the liberties of
its people can be strong enough to maintain its
existence in great emergencies.

Abraham Lincoln, 1864

Prologue: The seven seceding states formed a provisional government about a month before the firing on Fort Sumter forced the remaining four laggard sisters into their camp. In the ensuing conflict, the civilian front, both at home and abroad, was no less important than the fighting front. Northern diplomats strove to keep the European powers out; Southern diplomats strove to drag them in. Britain, the key nation, remained officially neutral because of self-interest. Meanwhile, in America, with dollars pouring into the maw of the war machine, conscienceless grafters and profiteers on each side grew fat. The Washington and Richmond regimes were both forced to override constitutional guarantees and deal harshly with critics.

A. Lincoln and the Secession Crisis

1. Fort Sumter Inflames the North (1861)*

Fort Sumter, in Charleston harbor, still flew the Stars and Stripes when Lincoln took office in March 1861. Unwilling either to goad the South into war or to see the garrison starved out, he compromised by announcing that he would send provisions but not reinforcements. The Southerners, who regarded provisioning as aggression, opened fire. The North rose in instant resentment. Especially important was the reaction of New York City, where the merchants and bankers involved in the cotton trade were plotting treacherous courses. What do the following recollections of a contemporary Episcopal clergyman suggest about the patriotism of the financial world and about the importance of retaining New York's loyalty?

On Sunday, April 14 [1861], the fact became known that Fort Sumter had surrendered. The excitement created by the bombardment of that fortress and its magnifi-

---

*Morgan Dix, *Memoirs of John Adams Dix* (New York: Harper and Brothers, 1883), vol. 2, p. 9.

cent defense by Anderson* was prodigious. The outrage on the government of the United States thus perpetrated by the authorities of South Carolina sealed the fate of the new-born Confederacy and the institution of slavery.

Intelligent Southerners at the North were well aware of the consequences which must follow. In the city of New York a number of prominent gentlemen devoted to the interests of the South, and desirous to obtain a bloodless dissolution of the Union, were seated together in anxious conference, studying with intense solicitude the means of preserving the peace. A messenger entered the room in breathless haste with the news: "General Beauregard has opened fire on Fort Sumter!" The persons whom he thus addressed remained a while in dead silence, looking into each other's pale faces; then one of them, with uplifted hands, cried, in a voice of anguish, "My God, we are ruined!"

The North rose as one man. The question had been asked by those who were watching events, "How will New York go?" There were sinister hopes in certain quarters of a strong sympathy with the secession movements; dreams that New York might decide on cutting off from the rest of the country and becoming a free city. These hopes and dreams vanished in a day. The reply to the question how New York would go was given with an energy worthy of herself.

2. Fort Sumter Inspirits the South (1861)†

If the Southern attack on Fort Sumter angered the North, it had an exhilarating effect on the South. Gala crowds in Charleston harbor cheered their cannonading heroes. "The Star-Spangled Banner" was rewritten to read:

> *The Star-Spangled Banner in disgrace shall wave*
> *O'er the land of the tyrant, and the home of the knave.*

The Virginia "Submissionists," who had resisted secession, were overwhelmed by the popular clamor. What does the following account from the Daily Richmond Examiner *reveal about the mood of the people? What does it portend for the secession of Virginia and the prolongation of the war?*

The news of the capture of Fort Sumter was greeted with unbounded enthusiasm in this city. Everybody we met seemed to be perfectly happy. Indeed, until the occasion we did not know how happy men could be. Everybody abuses war, and yet it has ever been the favorite and most honored pursuit of men; and the women and children admire and love war ten times as much as the men. The boys pulled down the stars and stripes from the top of the Capitol (some of the boys were sixty years old), and very properly run [sic] up the flag of the Southern Confederacy in its place. What the women did we don't precisely know, but learned from rumor that they praised South Carolina to the skies, abused Virginia, put it to the Submissionists hot and heavy with their two-edged swords, and wound up the evening's

---

*Major Robert Anderson, commander of U.S. troops in Charleston harbor.
†*Daily Richmond Examiner*, April 15, 1861, in W. J. Kimball, *Richmond in Time of War* (Boston: Houghton Mifflin, 1960), p. 4.

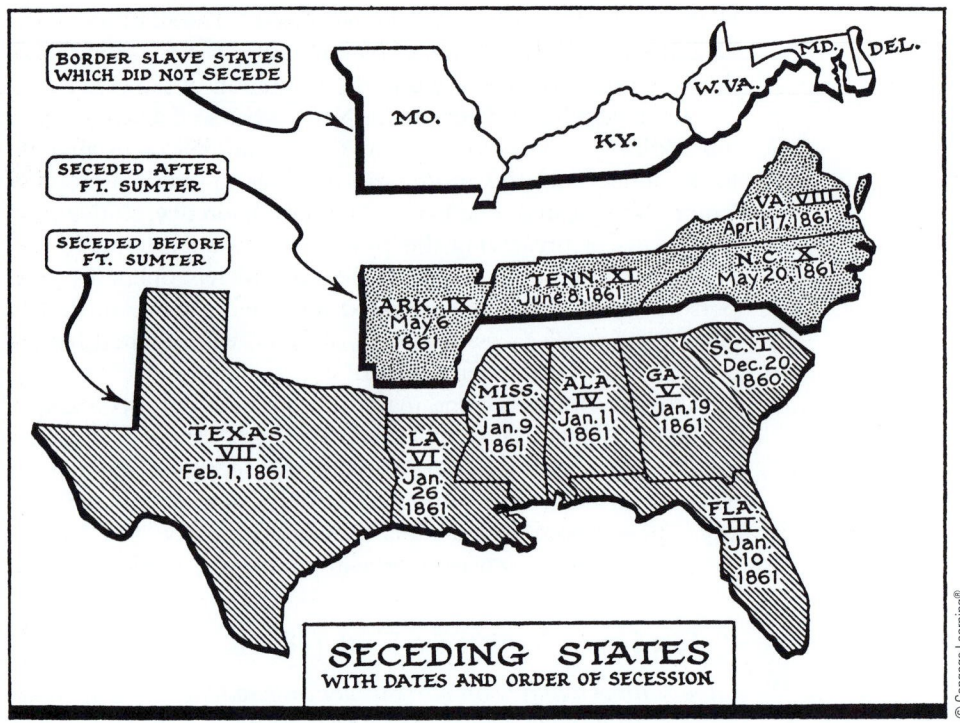

BORDER SLAVE STATES
WHICH DID NOT SECEDE

SECEDED AFTER
FT. SUMTER

SECEDED BEFORE
FT. SUMTER

MO.

KY.

W. VA.

MD.

DEL.

VA. VIII
April 17, 1861

ARK. IX
May 6
1861

TENN. XI
June 8, 1861

N.C. X
May 20, 1861

MISS.
II
Jan. 9
1861

ALA.
IV
Jan. 11
1861

GA.
V
Jan. 19
1861

S.C. I
Dec. 20
1860

TEXAS
VII
Feb. 1, 1861

LA.
VI
Jan.
26
1861

FLA.
III
Jan.
10
1861

SECEDING STATES
WITH DATES AND ORDER OF SECESSION

© Cengage Learning®

ceremonies by playing and singing secession songs until fifteen minutes after twelve on Saturday night.—The boys exploded an infinite number of crackers; the price of tar has risen 25 percent, and sky-rockets and Roman candles can be had at no price, the whole stock in trade having been used up Saturday night. We had great firing of cannon, all sorts of processions, an infinite number of grandiloquent, hifaluting speeches, and some drinking of healths, which has not improved healths; for one half the people we have met since are hoarse from long and loud talking, and the other half have a slight headache, it may be, from long and patriotic libations.

3. Alexander Hamilton Stephens's Cornerstone Speech (1861)[*]

The same convention that met at Montgomery, Alabama, in February 1861 to frame the Confederate Constitution chose Jefferson Davis as president and Alexander Hamilton Stephens of Georgia, an ex-congressman, as vice president. Stephens was a sallow-complexioned, emaciated figure (seldom weighing more than one hundred pounds) with a piping voice and a fighting spirit. Although opposing secession, he loyally (or disloyally) went along with his state. In this famous speech at Savannah,

---

[*]Henry Cleveland, *Alexander H. Stephens* (Philadelphia and Chicago: National Publishing Company, 1866), p. 721 (March 21, 1861).

three weeks before the blowup at Fort Sumter, he spelled out the philosophical basis of the Confederate Constitution. What do his remarks reveal about the white Southern attitude toward the future of slavery?

The new Constitution has put at rest forever all the agitating questions relating to our peculiar institution, African slavery, as it exists amongst us—the proper status of the Negro in our form of civilization. This was the immediate cause of the late rupture and present revolution. Jefferson, in his forecast, had anticipated this as the "rock upon which the old Union would split." He was right. What was conjecture with him is now a realized fact. But whether he fully comprehended the great truth upon which that rock stood and stands may be doubted. The prevailing ideas entertained by him and most of the leading statesmen at the time of the formation of the old Constitution were that the enslavement of the African was in violation of the laws of nature; that it was wrong in principle, socially, morally, and politically.

It was an evil they knew not well how to deal with, but the general opinion of the men of that day was that, somehow or other, in the order of Providence, the institution would be evanescent and pass away. This idea, though not incorporated in the Constitution, was the prevailing idea at the time. . . . .

Our new government is founded upon exactly the opposite idea; its foundations are laid, as its cornerstone rests, upon the great truth that the Negro is not equal to the white man; that slavery—subordination to the superior race—is his natural and normal condition. [Applause.]

This, our new government, is the first, in the history of the world, based upon this great physical, philosophical, and moral truth.

B. British Involvement

1. Southern Resentment Against England (1862)[*]

"Cotton is King!" the Southern fire-eaters had exulted before secession. England was so heavily dependent on the Southern fiber for its vast textile industry that in the event of a North-South clash, the British would presumably be forced to intervene on the side of the Confederacy. To the annoyance of Britishers, the Confederates even tried to hasten that day by burning cotton. Late in the second year of the Civil War, England was in the grip of a cotton famine; but much to the disappointment of the South, the London regime refused even to extend recognition to the Confederates. President Davis openly condemned British partiality toward the North. Why, in the view of the Southern journal quoted here, did Britain want the Union to break up but nevertheless refuse to intervene? Which of the arguments seems most farfetched?

The Confederate States are the only new power she [England] has refused to recognize, and yet they have manifested a degree of strength greater than all those we have enumerated [e.g., Belgium] put together. We have, under these circumstances, we think, some right to be indignant. We have not the smallest right to be astonished.

---

[*]*Southern Illustrated News*, October 4, 1862.

Great Britain has been trying to bring about the very state of things now existing here ever since the United States became a recognized power of the earth. She never could find it in her heart to forgive the successful revolt of the colonies. . . . . In latter days England has been jealous of the growing power of the United States to an inordinate degree. She has clearly foreseen that, if they continue united, they must become, before the close of this century, the first nation of the world, with an invincible army, a navy that must assume the empire of the seas, and a commerce that must swallow up all the commerce of the Old World.

Thus, in addition to the old grudge, she has been stimulated by the fear of losing her position among the powers of the earth. Cost what it might, she has felt that for her the greatest of all objects has been to destroy the Union. She has succeeded at last, and it is not wonderful that she should desire to see the war carried on as long as both parties may have the strength to maintain themselves. She feels that intervention would follow recognition, and this she is by no means disposed to undertake, because it might have the effect of shortening the war.

The war in question, besides removing a powerful rival from her path, is useful to her in another respect. If it should last long enough, it may be the means of getting her cotton from India into demand, and it may stimulate the production in Australia. When we consider that cotton constitutes the very basis upon which her enormous power is built, we shall see at once the importance of having it all under her own control. This she hopes to accomplish by destroying the culture in this country, which can only be done by destroying the labor which produces it. The abolition of slavery in her West India possessions was but the preliminary step to the abolition of slavery in this country. . . . .

In addition to these causes, it may be that the British Government feels itself in no condition to intervene, because of the present condition in Europe. Affairs are far from satisfactory in Italy, and any moment may witness the outbreak of a general war. As we have already observed, recognition might bring on intervention as a necessary consequence, and intervention would be sure to bring on war. This the British Government will avoid if it can. It already has a most exaggerated opinion of the strength of the Yankee Government, and is evidently very unwilling—we might almost say afraid—to come into collision with it. A late debate in Parliament plainly revealed an extraordinary degree of alarm on the subject of Canada. . . . .

These, we think, are the reasons why Great Britain—meaning the British Government—is averse to recognize us. That the majority of the people sympathize with us, while they detest the Yankees, we do not doubt.

2. A Northerner Lambastes Britain (1863)*

The South was disillusioned because England did not seem sympathetic enough; the North was angered because England seemed too sympathetic to the South. Several diplomatic crises between London and Washington were narrowly surmounted—the

---

*From *The Diary of George Templeton Strong*.

Trent *affair, the building of the cruiser Alabama, the* Laird *rams threat—but the construction of destructive Confederate commerce raiders in England rankled most deeply. Despite the serious shortage of cotton, the British prospered from an enormously expanded two-way trade with the North. George T. Strong, a prominent New York lawyer, here expresses a common view. Was his assessment of England's alleged unneutrality fair? Why was he more bitter toward England than his Southern counterpart in the preceding article?*

April 14 [1863]. We drift fast toward war with England, but I think we shall not reach that point. The shopkeepers who own England want to do us all the harm they can and to give all possible aid and comfort to our slave-breeding and woman-flogging adversary, for England has degenerated into a trader, manufacturer, and banker, and has lost all the instincts and sympathies that her name still suggests. She would declare war against us fast enough if she dared follow her sordid impulses, but there are dirty, selfish considerations on the other side.

She cannot ally herself with slavery, as she inclines to do, without closing a profitable market, exposing her commerce to [Yankee] privateers, and diminishing the supply of [Northern] breadstuffs on which her operatives depend for life. On the other side, however, is the consideration that by allowing piratical *Alabama*s to be built, armed, and manned in her ports to prey on our commerce, she is making a great deal of money.

It's fearful to think that the sympathies of England—the England of Shakespeare and Hooker, Cowper, Milton, Somers, Erskine, and others—with North or South, freedom or slavery, in this great continental battle of her children, are guided by mere considerations of profit and loss. Anglo-maniac [pro-English] Americans, like myself, are thoroughly "disillusioned."

C. Civil Liberties North and South

1. Clement Vallandigham Flays Despotism (1863)[*]

To preserve the Constitution, Lincoln was forced to take liberties with it. His arbitrary acts included a suspension of the writ of habeas corpus, and a consequent imprisonment without trial of scores of Southern sympathizers. Many Democrats in the North—dubbed Copperheads—condemned such high-handed action. The most notorious of these was Clement L. Vallandigham, an eloquent and outspoken critic of this "wicked and cruel" war. He regarded it as a diabolical attempt to end slavery and inaugurate a Republican despotism. Convicted by a military tribunal in Cincinnati of treasonable utterances, he was banished by Lincoln to the Confederacy. After a short stay, he made his way by ship to Canada. From there he ran for the governorship of Ohio in 1863 and, though defeated, polled a heavy vote. Some two months before his arrest in 1863, he delivered this flaming speech in New York to a

---

[*]C. L. Vallandigham, *Speeches, Arguments, Addresses, and Letters* (New York: J. Walter and Co., 1864), pp. 486–489.

Democratic group, assailing the recent act of Congress that authorized the president to suspend habeas corpus during the war. Is this speech treasonable? Should habeas corpus have been suspended?

[The Habeas Corpus Act] authorizes the President whom the people made, whom the people had chosen by the ballot box under the Constitution and laws, to suspend the writ of *habeas corpus* all over the United States; to say that because there is a rebellion in South Carolina, a man shall not have freedom of speech, freedom of the press, or any of his rights untrammeled in the state of New York, or a thousand miles distant. That was the very question upon which the people passed judgment in the recent [congressional] elections, more, perhaps, than any other question. . . . .

The Constitution gives the power to Congress, and to Congress alone, to suspend the writ of *habeas corpus*, but it can only be done in case of invasion or rebellion, and then only when the public safety requires it. And in the opinion of the best jurists of the land, and indeed of every one previous to these times, Congress could only suspend this writ in places actually in rebellion or actually invaded. That is the Constitution. [Cheers.] And whenever this question shall be tried before a court in the state of New York, or Ohio, or Wisconsin, or anywhere else, before honest and fearless judges worthy of the place they occupy, the decision will be that it is unconstitutional.* [Loud applause.] . . . .

Was it this which you were promised in 1860, in that grand [Lincoln] "Wide Awake" campaign, when banners were borne through your streets inscribed "Free speech, free press, and free men"? And all this has been accomplished, so far as the forms of the law go, by the Congress which has just expired. Now, I repeat again that if there is anything wanting to make up a complete and absolute despotism, as iron and inexorable in its character as the worst despotisms of the old world, or the most detestable of modern times, ... I am unable to comprehend what it is.

All this, gentlemen, infamous and execrable as it is, is enough to make the blood of the coldest man who has one single appreciation in his heart of freedom, to boil with indignation. [Loud applause.] Still, so long as they leave to us free assemblages, free discussion, and a free ballot, I do not want to see, and will not encourage or countenance, any other mode of ridding ourselves of it. ["That's it," and cheers.] We are ready to try these questions in that way. But . . . . when the attempt is made to take away those other rights, and the only instrumentalities peaceably of reforming and correcting abuses—free assemblages, free speech, free ballot, and free elections—THEN THE HOUR WILL HAVE ARRIVED WHEN IT WILL BE THE DUTY OF FREE MEN TO FIND SOME OTHER AND EFFICIENT MODE OF DEFENDING THEIR LIBERTIES. [Loud and protracted cheering, the whole audience rising to their feet.]

Our fathers did not inaugurate the Revolution of 1776, they did not endure the sufferings and privations of a seven years' war to escape from the mild and moderate control of a constitutional monarchy like that of England, to be at last, in the third generation, subjected to a tyranny equal to that of any upon the face of the globe. [Loud applause.]

---

*The Supreme Court did not hold the Habeas Corpus Act unconstitutional.

2. William Brownlow Scolds the Secessionists (1861)*

If President Lincoln had his pro-Confederate Copperheads, President Davis had his pro-Union "Tories," chiefly among the mountain whites. If Lincoln had his Vallandigham, Davis had his William G. ("Parson") Brownlow, the fiery and fearless Methodist preacher with a foghorn voice who had become editor of the Knoxville Whig. *This journal was the most influential paper in East Tennessee, and the last Union paper in the South. Though not antislavery, Brownlow was antisecession. His newspaper was suppressed late in 1861, his press was destroyed, and he was imprisoned for treason. The Confederates banished him to the Union lines—a Vallandigham case in reverse—but he returned to be elected Reconstruction governor of Tennessee in 1865. His defiant flying of a United States flag over his home led him to publish the following statement in his paper on May 25, 1861, two weeks before Tennessee seceded by a popular vote of 104,913 to 47,238. Considering the time of the incident, who acted treasonably, Brownlow or those who displayed the Confederate flag? What does this episode reveal of the strength of Unionism in Tennessee during those anxious weeks?*

It is known to this community and to the people of this county that I have had the Stars and Stripes, in the character of a small flag, floating over my dwelling, in East Knoxville, since February. This flag has become very offensive to certain leaders of the Secession party in this town, and to certain would-be leaders, and the more so as it is about the only one of the kind floating in the city. Squads of troops, from three to twenty, have come over to my house within the last several days, cursing the flag in front of my house, and threatening to take it down, greatly to the annoyance of my wife and children. No attack has been made upon it, and consequently we have had no difficulty.

It is due to the Tennessee troops to say that they have never made any such demonstrations. Other troops from the Southern states, passing on to Virginia, have been induced to do so by certain cowardly, sneaking, white-livered scoundrels residing here, who have not the melt [guts] to undertake what they urge strangers to do. One of the Louisiana squads proclaimed in front of my house, on Thursday, that they were told to take it down by citizens of Knoxville.

Now, I wish to say a few things to the public in connection with this subject. This flag is private property, upon a private dwelling, in a state that has never voted herself out of the Union or into the Southern Confederacy, and it is therefore lawfully and constitutionally under these same Stars and Stripes I have floating over my house. Until the state, by her citizens, through the ballot box, changes her federal relations, her citizens have a right to fling this banner to the breeze. Those who are in rebellion against the government represented by the Stars and Stripes have up the Rebel flag, and it is a high piece of work to deny loyal citizens of the Union the privilege of displaying their colors! . . . .

If these God-forsaken scoundrels and hell-deserving assassins want satisfaction [a duel] out of me for what I have said about them—and it has been no little—they

*W. G. Brownlow, *Sketches of the Rise, Progress, and Decline of Secession* (Philadelphia: G. W. Childs; Cincinnati: Applegate & Co., 1862), pp. 55–58, passim.

can find me on these streets every day of my life but Sunday. I am at all times prepared to give them satisfaction. I take back nothing I have ever said against the corrupt and unprincipled villains, but reiterate all, cast it in their dastardly faces, and hurl down their lying throats their own infamous calumnies.

Finally, the destroying of my small flag or of my town property is a small matter. The carving out of the state upon the mad wave of secession is also a small matter, compared with the great principle involved. Sink or swim, live or die, survive or perish, I am a Union man, and owe my allegiance to the Stars and Stripes of my country. Nor can I, in any possible contingency, have any respect for the government of the Confederate States, originating as it did with, and being controlled by, the worst men in the South. And any man saying—whether of high or low degree—that I am an abolitionist or a Black Republican, is a liar and scoundrel.

3. A North Carolinian Is Defiant (1863)*

States' rights proved about as harmful to the South as Yankee bayonets. Many Southerners, with their strong tradition of localism, resented or resisted the arbitrary central government in Richmond. William W. Holden, who attacked conscription and other harsh measures, was the recklessly outspoken editor of the Raleigh North Carolina Standard. *Probably the most influential paper in the state, it allegedly inspired wholesale desertions. In 1863, when a Georgia regiment destroyed Holden's office, he and his associates retaliated by wrecking the headquarters of a rival secessionist organ. (Scores of similar mob demonstrations occurred in the North against Copperhead journals.) What is ironic and fantastic about the extreme remedy that Holden here proposes, and what extraordinary conditions was he overlooking?*

We were told, when the government was broken up by the states south of us, that the contest was to be for liberty; that the civil power was to prevail over the military; that the common government was to be the agent of the states, and not their master; and that free institutions, not an imperial despotism, were to constitute the great object of our toils and sufferings. But the official paper [the Richmond *Enquirer*] has declared otherwise. That paper is opposed to a nobility to be established by law, but it favors a military despotism like that of France. . . . .

We know that a military despotism is making rapid strides in these [Confederate] states. We know that no people ever lost their liberties at once, but step by step, as some deadly disease steals upon the system and gradually but surely saps the fountain of life. . . . . The argument now is, we hate Lincoln so bitterly that in order to resist him successfully we must make slaves of ourselves. The answer of our people is, we will be slaves neither to Lincoln, nor Davis, nor France, nor England.

North Carolina is a state, not a province, and she has eighty thousand of as brave troops as ever trod the earth. When she calls them they will come. If the worst should happen that can happen, she will be able to take care of herself as an independent power. She will not submit, in any event, to a law of [the Confederate] Congress, passed in deliberate violation of the Constitution, investing Mr. Davis with

---

*North Carolina Standard (Raleigh), May 6, 1863.

dictatorial powers; but will resist such a law by withdrawing, if necessary, from the Confederation, and she will fight her way out against all comers. . . . . For one, we are determined not to exchange one despotism for another.

D. Abraham Lincoln Defines the Purposes of the War

1. The War to Preserve the Union (1863)*

In his 1863 Gettysburg Address, President Lincoln defined the war's purpose with unmatched eloquence. What were his principal arguments?

Four score and seven years ago our fathers brought forth on this continent, a new nation, conceived in Liberty, and dedicated to the proposition that all men are created equal.

Now we are engaged in a great civil war, testing whether that nation, or any nation so conceived and so dedicated, can long endure. We are met on a great battlefield of that war. We have come to dedicate a portion of that field, as a final resting place for those who here gave their lives that that nation might live. It is altogether fitting and proper that we should do this.

But, in a larger sense, we can not dedicate—we can not consecrate—we can not hallow—this ground. The brave men, living and dead, who struggled here, have consecrated it, far above our poor power to add or detract. The world will little note, nor long remember what we say here, but it can never forget what they did here. It is for us the living, rather, to be dedicated here to the unfinished work which they who fought here have thus far so nobly advanced. It is rather for us to be here dedicated to the great task remaining before us—that from these honored dead we take increased devotion to that cause for which they gave the last full measure of devotion—that we here highly resolve that these dead shall not have died in vain—that this nation, under God, shall have a new birth of freedom—and that government of the people, by the people, for the people, shall not perish from the earth.

2. The War to End Slavery (1865)†

Near the war's end, in his second inaugural address, Lincoln again returned to the theme of the war's purpose, but on this occasion he offered a different explanation of the war's goals and meaning than he had two years earlier at Gettysburg. What are the major differences? Which considerations do you think weighed most heavily in Lincoln's mind as the war progressed? Did his war aims change over time?

Fellow-Countrymen: At this second appearing to take the oath of the Presidential office there is less occasion for an extended address than there was at the first. Then

---

*Roy P. Basler, ed., *The Collected Works of Abraham Lincoln* (New Brunswick, NJ: Rutgers University Press, 1953), vol. 7, p. 23.

†James D. Richardson, *A Compilation of the Messages and Papers of the Presidents* (Washington, DC: Bureau of National Literature, 1911), vol. 5, pp. 3477–3478.

a statement somewhat in detail of a course to be pursued seemed fitting and proper. Now, at the expiration of four years, during which public declarations have been constantly called forth on every point and phase of the great contest which still absorbs the attention and engrosses the energies of the nation, little that is new could be presented. The progress of our arms, upon which all else chiefly depends, is as well known to the public as to myself, and it is, I trust, reasonably satisfactory and encouraging to all. With high hope for the future, no prediction in regard to it is ventured.

On the occasion corresponding to this four years ago all thoughts were anxiously directed to an impending civil war. All dreaded it, all sought to avert it. While the inaugural address was being delivered from this place, devoted altogether to *saving* the Union without war, insurgent agents were in the city seeking to *destroy* it without war—seeking to dissolve the Union and divide effects by negotiation. Both parties deprecated war, but one of them would *make* war rather than let the nation survive, and the other would *accept* war rather than let it perish, and the war came.

One-eighth of the whole population were colored slaves, not distributed generally over the Union, but localized in the southern part of it. These slaves constituted a peculiar and powerful interest. All knew that this interest was somehow the cause of the war. To strengthen, perpetuate, and extend this interest was the object for which the insurgents would rend the Union even by war, while the Government claimed no right to do more than to restrict the territorial enlargement of it. Neither party expected for the war the magnitude or the duration which it has already attained. Neither anticipated that the *cause* of the conflict might cease with or even before the conflict itself should cease. Each looked for an easier triumph, and a result less fundamental and astounding. Both read the same Bible and pray to the same God, and each invokes His aid against the other. It may seem strange that any men should dare to ask a just God's assistance in wringing their bread from the sweat of other men's faces, but let us judge not, that we be not judged. The prayers of both could not be answered. That of neither has been answered fully. The Almighty has His own purposes. "Woe unto the world because of offenses; for it must needs be that offenses come, but woe to that man by whom the offense cometh." If we shall suppose that American slavery is one of those offenses which, in the providence of God, must needs come, but which, having continued through His appointed time, He now wills to remove, and that He gives to both North and South this terrible war as the woe due to those by whom the offense came, shall we discern therein any departure from those divine attributes which the believers in a living God always ascribe to Him? Fondly do we hope, fervently do we pray, that this mighty scourge of war may speedily pass away. Yet, if God wills that it continue until all the wealth piled by the bondsman's two hundred and fifty years of unrequited toil shall be sunk, and until every drop of blood drawn with the lash shall be paid by another drawn with the sword, as was said three thousand years ago, so still it must be said "the judgments of the Lord are true and righteous altogether."

With malice toward none, with charity for all, with firmness in the right as God gives us to see the right, let us strive on to finish the work we are in, to bind up the nation's wounds, to care for him who shall have borne the battle and for his widow and his orphan, to do all which may achieve and cherish a just and lasting peace among ourselves and with all nations.

Thought Provokers

---

1. Why did the South secede? Would the North have acquiesced in peaceful coexistence if the South had not fired on Fort Sumter? Which side was the aggressor in starting the war?

2. What were the most distinctive principles of the new Confederate government? Could a government founded on such principles long endure?

3. Why did both North and South regard Britain as unduly partial to the other side? What would probably have happened if the British had intervened? To what extent was democracy an issue in the Civil War?

4. Explain why, in all of the United States' major wars, constitutional guarantees of freedom have suffered infringement. What conditions during the Civil War caused them to be more endangered than during other wars?

5. Lincoln's two speeches—the Gettysburg Address and his second inaugural address—are inscribed on facing walls of the Lincoln Memorial in Washington, DC. In what ways do they constitute a fitting summation of Lincoln's views on the war?

21

The Furnace of Civil War,
1861–1865

Among freemen there can be no successful appeal
from the ballot to the bullet, and . . . they who take
such appeal are sure to lose their case and pay the
cost.

Abraham Lincoln, 1863

Prologue: At first Lincoln's sole proclaimed war aim was to preserve the Union—to squelch secession without necessarily ending slavery. But the failure to end the war quickly by capturing Richmond in the Peninsula Campaign in the summer of 1862 turned Lincoln toward total war against the South's political, economic, and social order—including slavery. The narrow Union victory at the Battle of Antietam in September 1862 enabled Lincoln to issue the Emancipation Proclamation on January 1, 1863. The Proclamation changed the character of the war into a struggle for the preservation of the Union *and* the abolition of slavery. Many white people in the North greeted this new war aim with indignation, but the cause of antislavery added luster to the North's moral image abroad. Meanwhile, the North proceeded to drag the South back into the Union by brute force. The process was slow and frustrating, until Lincoln finally found in Ulysses S. Grant a general "who fights." General William Sherman campaigned relentlessly in Georgia and the Carolinas by warring on civilian morale as well as on uniformed armies. Lincoln, who had still not achieved military victory, was in grave danger of being unhorsed in the presidential election of 1864 by dissatisfied Democrats, but his ultimate triumph ensured a bitter-end prosecution of the war. The Confederates, finally forced to their knees by Grant's sledgehammer blows in Virginia, surrendered in the spring of 1865. Lincoln's assassination just days later brought deification in the North and grave forebodings in the South.

A. Northern War Aims

1. Congress Voices Its Views (1861)[*]

John J. Crittenden of Kentucky—at various times a cabinet member, a senator, and a congressman—achieved renown in 1860 by his efforts to work out a last-ditch compromise over slavery in the territories. After war broke out, one of his sons became a general in the Union army, another (to his father's sorrow) a general in the Confeder-

[*]*House Journal,* 37th Congress, 1st session (July 22, 1861), p. 123.

ate army. The older Crittenden, determined not to force slaveholding Kentucky and the other border states out of the Union by a crusade against slavery, shepherded the following new resolution through the House of Representatives in 1861. How was this statement designed to quiet the fears of Confederates, Southern Unionists, and border staters?

Resolved by the House of Representatives of the Congress of the United States, That the present deplorable civil war has been forced upon the country by the disunionists of the Southern states, now in arms against the constitutional government, and in arms around the capital; that in this national emergency, Congress, banishing all feelings of mere passion or resentment, will recollect only its duty to the whole country; that this war is not waged on their part in any spirit of oppression, or for any purpose of conquest or subjugation, or purpose of overthrowing or interfering with the rights or established institutions of those states, but to defend and maintain the supremacy of the Constitution, and to preserve the Union with all the dignity, equality, and rights of the several states unimpaired; and that as soon as these objects are accomplished the war ought to cease.

2. Abolitionists View the War (1863)

Lincoln at first described the Civil War as a struggle to preserve the Union, but many abolitionists had additional war aims; they saw the outbreak of the war as a divine opportunity to extinguish the evil of slavery once and for all. (Before the war began, some antislaveryites had even demanded that the North secede from the Union, to be rid of the slaveholding South.) The illustration on p. 336, "The House That Jeff Built," first published in Massachusetts, depicts the war aims of the abolitionists. How does the illustrator treat the issue of Union? If Lincoln at the start of the conflict had accepted the views advocated in this illustration, would the war have been fought differently? (The text that accompanies the illustration follows in more readable form.)

This is the House that Jeff Built.

This is the cotton, by rebels called king,
(Tho' call'd by loyalists no such thing)
That lay in the house that Jeff built.

These are the field chattels that made cotton king,
(Tho' call'd by loyalists no such thing)
That lay in the house that Jeff built.

These are the chattels, babes, mothers, and men,
To be sold by the head, in the slave pen:
A part of the house that Jeff built.

This is the thing by some call'd a man,
Whose trade is to sell all the chattels he can,
From yearlings to adults of life's longest span:
In and out of the house that Jeff built.

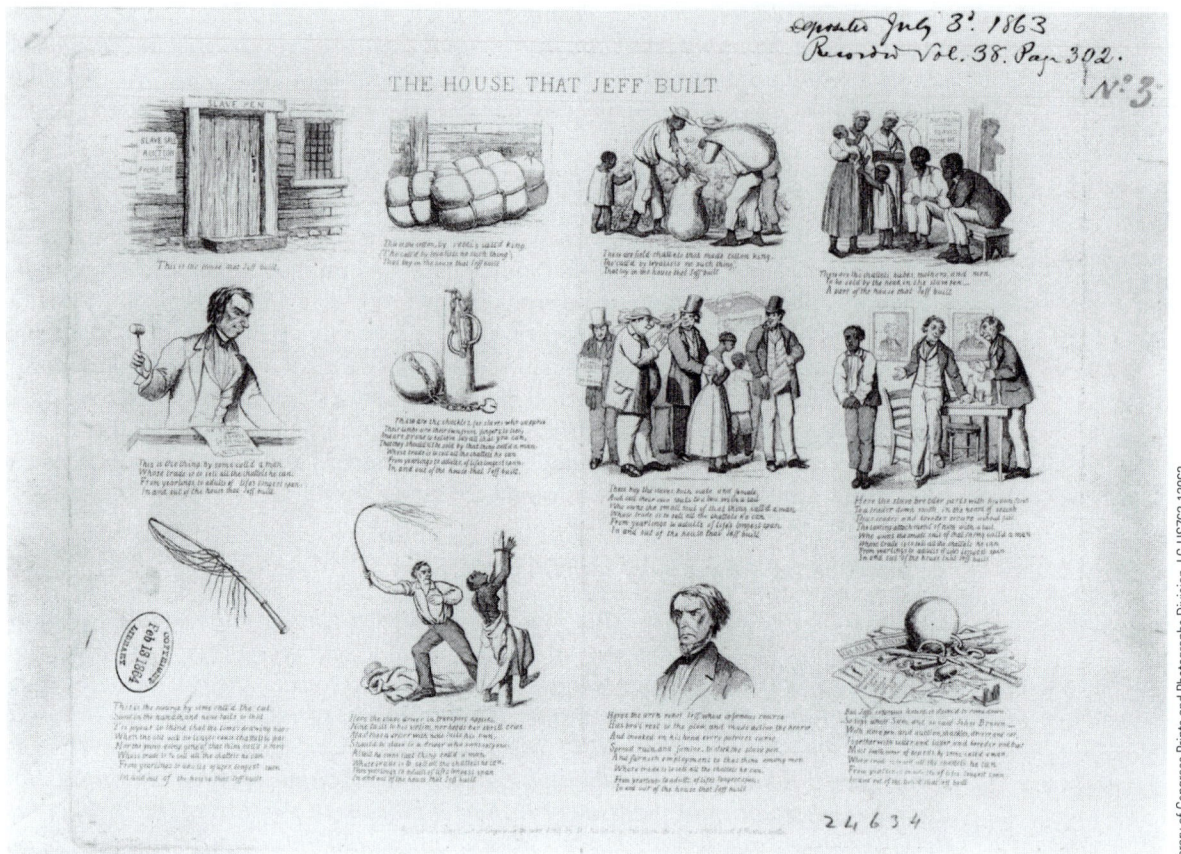

These are the shackles, for slaves who suppose
Their limbs are their own, from fingers to toes;
And are prone to believe say all that you can,
That they shouldn't be sold by that thing call'd a man:
Whose trade is to sell all the chattels he can,
From yearlings to adults of life's longest span:
In and out of the house that Jeff built.

These buy the slaves, both male and female,
And sell their own souls to a boss with a tail
Who owns the small soul of that thing called a man:
Whose trade is to sell all the chattels he can,
From yearlings to adults of life's longest span:
In and out of the house that Jeff built.

Here the slave breeder parts with his own flesh
To a trader down south in the heart of secesh
Thus trader and breeder secure without fail
The lasting attachment of him with a tail
Who owns the small soul of that thing called a man
Whose trade is to sell all the chattels he can,
From yearlings to adults of life's longest span:
In and out of the house that Jeff built.

This is the scourge that some call's the cat
Stout in the handle and nine tails to that
Tis joyous to think that the time's drawing near
When the cat will no longer cause chattels fear
Nor the going, going, gone of that thing call'd a man
Whose trade is to sell all the chattels he can,
From yearlings to adults of life's longest span:
In and out of the house that Jeff built.

Here the slave driver in transport applies
Nine tails to his victim nor heeds her shrill cries
Alas! that a driver with nine tails of his own,
Should be slave to a driver who owns only one:
Albeit he owns that thing call'd a man,
Whose trade is to sell all the chattels he can,
From yearlings to adults of life's longest span:
In and out of the house that Jeff built.

Here's the arch rebel Jeff whose infamous course
Has bro't rest in the plow, and made active the hearse,
And invoked on his head every patriot's curse.
Spread ruin and famine to stock the slave pen,
And furnish employment to that thing among men,
Whose trade is to sell all the chattels he can,
From yearlings to adults of life's longest span:
In and out of the house that Jeff built.

But Jeff's infamous house is doom'd to come down
So says uncle Sam and so said John Brown
With slave pen and auction, shackles, driver, and cat,
Together the seller and buyer and breeder and that
Most loathsome of bipeds by some call'd a man,
Whose trade is to sell all the chattels he can,
From yearlings to adults of life's longest span:
In and out of the house that Jeff built.

3. Abraham Lincoln Answers Horace Greeley's Prayer (1862)*

Bespectacled little Horace Greeley, editor of the widely read New York Tribune, *reached the heights of arrogance when he published an open letter to President Lincoln entitled "The Prayer of Twenty Millions." Professing to speak for virtually the entire population of the North, he thundered against the administration for hampering the war effort by not coming out bluntly for the emancipation of slaves. Lincoln replied as follows in a public letter. Analyze the qualities of his character that shine through this remarkable statement. Was Lincoln putting expediency above morality? What would he have done if the South had been willing to surrender, subject only to the retention of its slaves?*

Dear Sir: I have just read yours of the 19th, addressed to myself through the New York *Tribune.* If there be in it any statements, or assumptions of fact, which I may know to be erroneous, I do not, now and here, controvert them. If there be in it any inferences which I may believe to be falsely drawn, I do not now and here argue against them. If there be perceptible in it an impatient and dictatorial tone, I waive it in deference to an old friend, whose heart I have always supposed to be right.

As to the policy I "seem to be pursuing," as you say, I have not meant to leave anyone in doubt.

I would save the Union. I would save it the shortest way under the Constitution. The sooner the National authority can be restored, the nearer the Union will be "the Union as it was."

If there be those who would not save the Union unless they could at the same time save Slavery, I do not agree with them. If there be those who would not save the Union unless they could at the same time destroy Slavery, I do not agree with them. My paramount object in this struggle is to save the Union, and is not either to save or destroy Slavery.

If I could save the Union without freeing any slave, I would do it; and if I could save it by freeing all the slaves, I would do it; and if I could do it by freeing some and leaving others alone, I would also do that. What I do about Slavery and the colored race, I do because I believe it helps to save this Union; and what I forbear, I forbear because I do not believe it would help to save the Union.

I shall do less whenever I shall believe what I am doing hurts the cause, and I shall do more whenever I shall believe doing more will help the cause. I shall try to correct errors when shown to be errors; and I shall adopt new views so fast as they shall appear to be true views.

I have here stated my purpose according to my view of official duty; and I intend no modification of my oft-expressed personal wish that all men, everywhere, could be free.

---

*R. P. Basler, ed., *The Collected Works of Abraham Lincoln* (New Brunswick, NJ: Rutgers University Press, 1953), vol. 5, pp. 388–389 (August 22, 1862).

4. "A Colored Man" Reflects on the War (1863)[*]

For African Americans, the Civil War would have little meaning unless it entailed the destruction of slavery. To the extent that the North was reluctant to make emancipation and racial equality explicit goals of the war effort, African Americans proved hesitant to identify themselves fully with the Union cause. In the following document, an unidentified "colored man" expresses his ambivalence about the war. It should be noted that he was writing in New Orleans, which was under Union control and therefore, ironically, an area in which the Emancipation Proclamation was not applicable. In the course of his argument, the author repeatedly invokes the U.S. Constitution. How might the Constitution have served as symbolic common ground for those fighting for a "more perfect union" and those fighting for their "rights and liberty"?

[New Orleans, La., September? 1863]

. . . .

it is retten that a man can not Serve two master But it Seems that the Collored population has got two a rebel master and a union master the both want our Servises one wants us to make Cotton and Sugar And the Sell it and keep the money the union masters wants us to fight the battles under white officers and the injoy both money and the union black Soldiers And white officers will not play togeathe much longer the Constitution is if any man rebells against those united States his property Shall be confescated and Slaves declared and henceforth Set free forever when theire is a insurection or rebllion against these united States the Constitution gives the president of the united States full power to arm as many soldiers of African decent as he deems nescesisary to Surpress the Rebellion and officers Should be black or white According to their abillitys the Collored man Should guard Stations Garison forts and mand vessels according to his Compasitys

A well regulated militia being necessary to the cecurity of a free State the right of the people to keep and Bear arms Shall not be infringed

we are to Support the Constitution but no religious test Shall ever be required as a qualification to Any office or public trust under the united States the excitement of the wars is mostly keep up from the Churches the Say god is fighting the battle but it is the people But the will find that god fought our battle once the way to have peace is to distroy the enemy As long as theire is a Slave their will be rebles Against the Government of the united States So we must look out our white officers may be union men but Slave holders at heart the Are allways on hand when theire is money but Look out for them in the battle feild liberty is what we want and nothing Shorter

our Southern friend tells that the are fighting for negros and will have them our union friends Says the are not fighting to free the negroes we are fighting for the union and free navigation of the Mississippi river very well let the white fight for what the want and we negroes fight for what we want there are three things to fight for and two races of people divided into three Classes one wants negro Slaves the other the union the other Liberty So liberty must take the day nothing Shorter we

[*]Ira Berlin, Joseph P. Reidy, and Leslie S. Rowland, eds., *Freedom's Soldiers: The Black Military Experience in the Civil War* (New York: Cambridge University Press, 1998), pp. 109–111.

are the Blackest and the bravest race the president Says there is a wide Difference Between the black Race and the white race But we Say that white corn and yellow will mix by the taussels but the black and white Race must mix by the roots as the are so well mixed and has no tausels—freedom and liberty is the word with the Collered people

. . . .

Sure the Southern men Says the are not fighting for money the are fighting for negros the northern men Say the did not com South to free the negroes but to Save the union very well for that much what is the colored men fighting for if the makes us free we are happy to hear it And when we are free men and a people we will fight for our rights and liberty we care nothing about the union we heave been in it Slaves over two hundred And fifty years we have made the contry and So far Saved the union and if we heave to fight for our rights let us fight under Colored officers for we are the men that will kill the Enemies of the Government

. . . .

now is the united States government and constitution free or a local Government if it is free let us colored population muster in to ams and garison forts guard Station and mand vessels and then we will know wheather we are free people or not then we will know wheather you want to make brest works of us or not or make us fools ornot I heard one of most Ables and distingush lawiers Say that the Colored population was all free and Had as much liberty in the union as he had in four or five days after I went to him to get him to atend Some buiness for me he Said to me Are you free or Slave Sir Said i am free By your own speeches was you born free no Sir Said i we have been made fools of from the time Butlers fleet landed hear but I have remained At my old Stand and will untill i See what i am dowing I know very well that the white union men cannot put down the rebeles for them that was not rebles Soon will be i am Sory that I am not able to write good may the union forever Stand with peace and liberty to All good people

A Colored man

B. The Proclaiming of Emancipation

1. Lincoln Expresses Misgivings (1862)*

Preserving the Union was the officially announced war aim of the North. But to many Northern abolitionists and free-soilers, the unshackling of the slave was more important. An edict of emancipation would presumably quiet their clamor while strengthening the nation's moral position abroad. Yet such a stroke would antagonize the slaveholding but still loyal border states, as well as countless Northern Democrats who were fighting for the Union and not for "a passel of slaves." The issuance of an

---

*J. G. Nicolay and John Hay, eds., *Complete Works of Abraham Lincoln* (New York: The Century Co., 1894), vol. 8, pp. 30–33, and (1907), vol. 2, pp. 287–288.

emancipation proclamation after the current series of Northern defeats would, more-over, seem like a last-chance act of desperation. On September 13, 1862, four days before the crucial Battle of Antietam and nine days before he issued his preliminary Emancipation Proclamation, Lincoln explained his position to a visiting delegation of Northern Christians from Chicago. What arguments did he give for and against an emancipation proclamation? Was Lincoln concerned with moral considerations primarily? What were his misgivings regarding the constitutionality of emancipa-tion, and to what extent did he regard slavery as the cause of the war?

What good would a proclamation of emancipation from me do, especially as we are now situated? I do not want to issue a document that the whole world will see must necessarily be inoperative, like the Pope's bull against the comet.* Would my word free the slaves, when I cannot even enforce the Constitution in the rebel states? Is there a single court, or magistrate, or individual that would be influenced by it there? And what reason is there to think it would have any greater effect upon the slaves than the late law of Congress, which I approved, and which offers protec-tion and freedom to the slaves of rebel masters who come within our lines? Yet I cannot learn that that law has caused a single slave to come over to us.

And suppose they could be induced by a proclamation of freedom from me to throw themselves upon us, what should we do with them? How can we feed and care for such a multitude? General Butler [in New Orleans] wrote me a few days since that he was issuing more rations to the slaves who have rushed to him than to all the white troops under his command. They eat, and that is all; though it is true General Butler is feeding the whites also by the thousand, for it nearly amounts to a famine there.

If, now, the pressure of the war should call off our forces from New Orleans to defend some other point, what is to prevent the masters from reducing the blacks to slavery again? For I am told that whenever the rebels take any black prisoners, free or slave, they immediately auction them off. They did so with those they took from a boat that was aground in the Tennessee River a few days ago. And then I am very ungenerously attacked for it! For instance, when, after the late battles at and near Bull Run, an expedition went out from Washington under a flag of truce to bury the dead and bring in the wounded, and rebels seized the blacks who went along to help, and sent them into slavery, Horace Greeley said in his paper [*New York Tribune*] that the government would probably do nothing about it. What could I do?

Now, then, tell me, if you please, what possible result of good would follow the issuing of such a proclamation as you desire? Understand, I raise no objections against it on legal or constitutional grounds; for, as commander-in-chief of the army and navy, in time of war I suppose I have a right to take any measure which may best subdue the enemy. Nor do I urge objections of a moral nature, in view of pos-sible consequences of insurrection and massacre at the South.

I view this matter as a practical war measure, to be decided on according to the advantages or disadvantages it may offer to the suppression of the rebellion.

---

*The tale that a terrified Pope Calixtus III excommunicated Halley's comet by a papal bull in 1456 is base-less, but he did decree "several days of prayer for averting the wrath of God" (A. D. White, *A History of the Warfare of Science with Theology* [New York: D. Appleton & Company, 1896], p. 177).

I admit that slavery is the root of the rebellion, or at least its *sine qua non* [the factor without which it could not exist]. The ambition of politicians may have instigated them to act, but they would have been impotent without slavery as their instrument. I will also concede that emancipation would help us in Europe, and convince them that we are incited by something more than ambition. I grant, further, that it would help somewhat at the North, though not so much, I fear, as you and those you represent imagine. Still some additional strength would be added in that way to the war, and then, unquestionably, it would weaken the rebels by drawing off their laborers, which is of great importance; but I am not so sure we could do much with the blacks. If we were to arm them, I fear that in a few weeks the arms would be in the hands of the rebels; and, indeed, thus far we have not had arms enough to equip our white troops.

I will mention another thing, though it meet only your scorn and contempt. There are fifty thousand bayonets in the Union armies from the border slave states. It would be a serious matter if, in consequence of a proclamation such as you desire, they go over to the rebels. I do not think they all would—not so many, indeed, as a year ago, or six months ago—not so many today as yesterday. Every day increases their Union feeling. They are also getting their pride enlisted, and want to beat the rebels.

Let me say one thing more: I think you should admit that we already have an important principle to rally and unite the people, in the fact that constitutional government [Union] is at stake. This is a fundamental idea going down about as deep as anything.

[Lincoln made his preliminary proclamation official on January 1, 1863, when he declared "all persons held as slaves within any State, or designated part of a State, the people whereof shall then be in rebellion against the United States, shall be then, thenceforward, and forever free. . . . And I hereby enjoin upon the people so declared to be free to abstain from all violence, unless in necessary self-defense; and I recommend to them that, in all cases when allowed, they labor faithfully for reasonable wages. And I further declare and make known, that such persons of suitable condition will be received into the armed service of the United States to garrison forts, positions, stations, and other places, and to man vessels of all sorts in said service. And upon this act, sincerely believed to be an act of justice, warranted by the Constitution upon military necessity, I invoke the considerate judgment of mankind and the gracious favor of Almighty God."]

2. Jefferson Davis Deplores Emancipation (1863)[*]

Seeking to improve the military and moral position of the North, and taking advantage of the recent (limited) Union success at Antietam, Lincoln finally issued his preliminary Emancipation Proclamation on September 22, 1862, nine days after giving such excellent reasons for not doing so. Declaring anew that the preservation of the Union was still his primary goal, he announced that as of January 1, 1863, the slaves would be

---

[*]J. D. Richardson, comp., *Messages and Papers of the Confederacy* (1904), vol. 1, pp. 290–293, passim (January 12, 1863).

"forever free" in all areas still in rebellion—areas, in fact, where Lincoln was then powerless to free anybody. He further proclaimed that the Washington government would "do no act or acts to repress" the slaves "in any efforts they may make for their actual freedom." To Southerners, this seemed like an invitation to wholesale insurrection. They upbraided Lincoln "the Fiend," while seriously discussing the advisability of shooting all Yankee prisoners of war, wounded or able-bodied. President Jefferson Davis reacted bitterly as follows in his message to the Confederate congress. How did his views compare with those of Lincoln, expressed in the preceding section?

We may well leave it to the instincts of that common humanity which a beneficent Creator has implanted in the breasts of our fellow men of all countries to pass judgment on a measure by which several millions of human beings of an inferior race, peaceful and contented laborers in their sphere, are doomed to extermination, while at the same time they are encouraged to a general assassination of their masters by the insidious recommendation "to abstain from violence unless in necessary self-defense." Our own detestation of those who have attempted the most execrable measure recorded in the history of guilty man is tempered by profound contempt for the impotent rage which it discloses. . . .

In its political aspect this measure possesses great significance, and to it in this light I invite your attention. It affords to our whole people the complete and crowning proof of the true nature of the designs of the party which elevated to power the present occupant of the presidential chair at Washington, and which sought to conceal its purpose by every variety of artful device and by the perfidious use of the most solemn and repeated pledges on every possible occasion. I extract in this connection as a single example the following declaration, made by President Lincoln under the solemnity of his oath of Chief Magistrate of the United States, on the 4th of March, 1861: . . .

"I declare that I have no purpose, directly or indirectly, to interfere with the institution of slavery in the states where it exists. I believe I have no lawful right to do so; and I have no inclination to do so. . . . "

Nor was this declaration of the want of power or disposition to interfere with our social system confined to a state of peace. Both before and after the actual commencement of hostilities the President of the United States repeated in formal official communication to the Cabinets of Great Britain and France that he was utterly without constitutional power to do the act which he has just committed. . . .

This proclamation is also an authentic statement by the Government of the United States of its ability to subjugate the South by force of arms, and as such must be accepted by neutral nations, which can no longer find any justification in withholding our just claims to formal recognition.

3. Border Staters Are Alarmed (1862)*

Lincoln did not dare issue his Emancipation Proclamation until he was reasonably sure that the crucial border states would not be driven into the welcoming arms of the Confederacy. Even so, he was careful to exempt from his edict the slaves held in

---

*Quoted in the *Daily National Intelligencer* (Washington, DC), October 8, 1862.

these states, and to hold out to their owners the hope of compensated emancipation. But the border states were quick to perceive that the days of their own slave property were numbered. The fearless editor of the Louisville Journal, *George D. Prentice, a South-adopted Connecticut Yankee who had two sons in the Confederate army, had labored mightily to keep Kentucky in the Union, but even he voiced strong dissent. In his editorial, is he fair in his appraisal of the proclamation, especially its moral implications? Why did he not advocate joining the Confederacy?*

It [the Proclamation] is evidently an arbitrary act of the President as Commander-in-Chief of the army and navy of the Union. In short, it is a naked stroke of military necessity.

We shall not stop now to discuss the character and tendency of this measure. Both are manifest. The one is as unwarrantable as the other is mischievous. The measure is wholly unauthorized and wholly pernicious. Though it cannot be executed in fact, and though its execution probably will never be seriously attempted, its moral influence will be decided, and purely hurtful. So far as its own purpose is concerned, it is a mere *brutum fulmen* [futile display of force], but it will prove only too effectual for the purposes of the enemy [the South]. It is a gigantic usurpation, unrelieved by the promise of a solitary advantage, however minute and faint, but on the contrary aggravated by the menace of great and unmixed evil.

Kentucky cannot and will not acquiesce in this measure. Never! As little will she allow it to chill her devotion to the cause thus cruelly imperiled anew. The government our fathers framed is one thing, and a thing above price; Abraham Lincoln, the temporary occupant of the Executive chair, is another thing, and a thing of comparatively little worth. The one is an individual, the sands of whose official existence are running fast, and who, when his official existence shall end, will be no more or less than any other individual. The other is a grand political structure, in which is contained the treasures and the energies of civilization, and upon whose lofty and shining dome, seen from the shores of all climes, center the eager hopes of mankind.

What Abraham Lincoln, as President, does or fails to do may exalt or lower our estimate of himself, but not of the great and beneficent government of which he is but the temporary servant. The temple is not the less sacred and precious because the priest lays an unlawful sacrifice upon the altar. The loyalty of Kentucky is not to be shaken by any mad act of the President. If necessary, she will resist the act, and aid in holding the actor to a just and lawful accountability, but she will never lift her own hand against the glorious fabric because he has blindly or criminally smitten it. She cannot be so false to herself as this. She is incapable of such guilt and folly.

4. Racist Anxieties (1864)

Jefferson Davis focused on the "political aspects" of emancipation. But Lincoln's liberating manifesto stirred other fears as well. Prior to the Civil War, many critics of slavery, including Thomas Jefferson, had worried about how eventual emancipation might affect social and even sexual relations between the races. The Emancipation Proclamation compelled all Americans to confront this question, and even opponents of slavery expressed anxiety on this score. The anti-Republican illustration below, "The Miscegenation Ball," purported to depict a social event that followed a meeting of the Lincoln Central Campaign Club in New York City in September 1864. Why might readers have found this scene disturbing? How is the typical interracial couple here portrayed?

POLITICAL CARICATURE. Nº 4.

THE MISCEGENATION BALL

5. Lincoln Defends His Decision (1863)*

Despite a summer punctuated by dramatic Union victories at Vicksburg and Gettysburg, in August 1863 Lincoln was still subject to intense criticism from dissatisfied Northerners. The most prominent target for his detractors was the controversial Emancipation Proclamation. After a series of efforts to avoid the divisive step of immediate emancipation, including a plan to pay the South to release its slaves,

---

*Abraham Lincoln to James C. Conkling, reprinted in Henry J. Raymond, *History of the Administration of President Lincoln* (New York: J. C. Derby and N. C. Miller, 1864), pp. 411–413 (August 26, 1863).

Lincoln had put the historic Proclamation into effect in January. In this passage, Lincoln defends his decision against a hypothetical critic. Are idealistic or practical considerations more important to his argument?

But, to be plain. You are dissatisfied with me about the negro. Quite likely there is a difference of opinion between you and myself upon that subject. I certainly wish that all men could be free, while you, I suppose, do not. Yet, I have neither adopted nor proposed any measure which is not consistent with even your view, provided that you are for the Union. I suggested compensated emancipation; to which you replied you wished not be taxed to buy negroes. But I had not asked you to be taxed to buy negroes, except in such way as to save you from greater taxation to save the Union exclusively by other means.

You dislike the Emancipation Proclamation, and perhaps would have it retracted. You say it is unconstitutional. I think differently. I think the Constitution invests its Commander-in-Chief with the law of war in time of war. The most that can be said, if so much, is, that slaves are property. Is there, has there ever been, any question that by the law of war, property, both of enemies and friends, may be taken when needed? And is it not needed whenever it helps us and hurts the enemy? Armies, the world over, destroy enemies' property when they cannot use it; and even destroy their own to keep it from the enemy. Civilized belligerents do all in their power to help themselves or hurt the enemy, except a few things regarded as barbarous or cruel. Among the exceptions are the massacre of vanquished foes and non-combatants, male and female.

But the Proclamation, as law, either is valid or is not valid. If it is not valid it needs no retraction. If it is valid it cannot be retracted, any more than the dead can be brought to life. Some of you profess to think its retraction would operate favorably for the Union. Why better *after* the retraction than *before* the issue? There was more than a year and a half of trial to suppress the Rebellion before the Proclamation was issued, the last one hundred days of which passed under an explicit notice that it was coming, unless averted by those in revolt returning to their allegiance. The war has certainly progressed as favorably for us since the issue of the Proclamation as before.

I know as fully as one can know the opinions of others that some of the commanders of our armies in the field, who have given us our most important victories, believe the Emancipation policy and the use of colored troops constitute the heaviest blows yet dealt to the Rebellion, and that at least one of those important successes could not have been achieved when it was but for the aid of black soldiers.

Among the commanders who hold these views are some who have never had any affinity with what is called "Abolitionism," or with "Republican party politics," but who hold them purely as military opinions. I submit their opinions as entitled to some weight against the objections often urged that emancipation and arming the blacks are unwise as military measures, and were not adopted as such in good faith.

You say that you will not fight to free negroes. Some of them seem willing to fight for you; but no matter. Fight you, then, exclusively, to save the Union. I issued the Proclamation on purpose to aid you in saving the Union. Whenever you shall have conquered all resistance to the Union, if I shall urge you to continue fighting, it will be an apt time then for you to declare you will not fight to free negroes. I thought that in your struggle for the Union, to whatever extent the negroes should cease helping the enemy, to that extent it weakened the enemy in his resistance to you. Do you think differently? I thought that whatever negroes can be got to do as soldiers, leaves just so much less for white soldiers to do in saving the Union. Does it appear otherwise to you? But negroes, like other people, act upon motives. Why should they do any thing for us if we will do nothing for them? If they stake their lives for us they must be prompted by the strongest motive, even the promise of freedom. And the promise, being made, must be kept.

C. The Uncivil War

1. A Report from Antietam (1862)*

"War is at best barbarism," General William T. Sherman reportedly told a group of military academy graduates. "Its glory is all moonshine. It is only those who have neither fired a shot nor heard the shrieks and groans of the wounded who cry aloud for blood, more vengeance, more desolation. War is hell." What were the most diabolical aspects of the Battle of Antietam, as described by a sixteen-year-old Union soldier in the following account?

The next morning we had our Second battle—it was rather Strange music to hear the balls Scream within an inch of my head. I had a bullett strike me on the top of the head just as I was going to fire and a piece of Shell struck my foot—a ball hit my finger and another hit my thumb. I concluded they ment me. The rebels played the mischief with us by raising a U.S. flag. We were ordered not to fire and as soon as we went forward they opened an awful fire from their batteries on us we were ordered to fall back about ½ miles, I staid behind when our regiment retreated and a line of Skirmishers came up—I joined them and had a chance of firing about 10 times more— . . . Our Generals say they (the rebels) had as strong a position as could *possibly* be and we had to pick into them through an old chopping all grown up with bushes so thick that we couldent hardly get through—but we were so excited that the "old scratch" [the devil] himself couldent have stopt us. We rushed onto them every man for himself—all loading & firing as fast as he could see a rebel to Shoot at—at last the rebels began to get over the wall to the rear and run for the woods. The firing encreased tenfold, then it sounded like the rolls of thunder—and all the time evry man shouting as loud as he could—I got rather more excited than I wish to again. I dident *think* of getting hit but it was almost a miricle that I wasent. The rebels that we took prisoners said that they never before encountered a regiment that fought so like "Devils" (so they termed it) as we did—every one praised our regiment—one man in our company was Shot through the head no more than 4 feet from me; he was killed instantly. After the Sunday battle I took care of the

---

*Bell Irvin Wiley, *The Life of Billy Yank* (Indianapolis: Bobbs-Merrill, 1952), pp. 84–85.

wounded until 11 P.M. I saw some of the horidest sights I ever saw—one man had both eyes shot out—and they were wounded in all the different ways you could think of—the most I could do was to give them water—they were all very thirsty— . . . Our Colonel (Withington) was formerly a captain of the Mich 1st—he is just as cool as can be, he walked around amongst us at the battle the bullets flying all around him—he kept shouting to us to fire low and give it to them—

2. A Union Nurse Cares for the Gettysburg Wounded (1863)[*]

The Union victory at Gettysburg, which halted Robert E. Lee's daring assault on the North and doomed the Southern cause, came at a staggering cost. All told, some 51,000 men were killed or wounded in three agonizing days of battle. As Lee's army bitterly retreated back across the Potomac, Union nurses converged on Gettysburg to care for the mangled soldiers scattered across the battlefield. Cornelia Hancock, whose vivid letters chronicled her wartime service, described the following scene to her cousin. What circumstances complicated her task of caring for the wounded?

There are no words in the English language to express the sufferings I witnessed today. The men lie on the ground; their clothes have been cut off them to dress their wounds; they are half naked, have nothing but hard-tack to eat only as Sanitary Commissions, Christian Associations, and so forth give them. I was the first woman who reached the 2nd Corps after the three days fight at Gettysburg. I was in that Corps all day, not another woman within a half mile. Mrs. Harris was in first division of 2nd Corps. I was introduced to the surgeon of the post, went anywhere through the Corps, and received nothing but the greatest politeness from even the lowest private. . . . To give you some idea of the extent and numbers of the wounds, four surgeons, none of whom were idle fifteen minutes at a time, were busy all day amputating legs and arms. I gave to every man that had a leg or arm off a gill of wine, to every wounded in Third Division, one glass of lemonade, some bread and preserves and tobacco—as much as I am opposed to the latter, for they need it very much, they are so exhausted.

I feel very thankful that this was a successful battle; the spirit of the men is so high that many of the poor fellows said today, "What is an arm or leg to whipping Lee out of Penn." I would get on first rate if they would not ask me to write to their wives; *that* I cannot do without crying, which is not pleasant to either party. I do not mind the sight of blood, have seen limbs taken off and was not sick at all.

It is a very beautiful, rolling country here; under favorable circumstances I should think healthy, but now for five miles around, there is an awful smell of putrefaction. Women are needed here very badly, anyone who is willing to go to field hospitals . . .

---

[*]Henrietta Stratton Jaquette, *Letters of a Civil War Nurse: Cornelia Hancock, 1863–1865* (Lincoln: University of Nebraska Press, 1998), pp. 7–8.

3. The Hell of Andersonville Prison (1864)*

Andersonville was the biggest and most infamous of the Confederate stockades for Union prisoners of war. It was hastily erected in Georgia in early 1864, at a time when the South was reeling and desperately short of food, clothing, and medicine. The compound held up to thirty-two thousand prisoners in twenty-six fetid, disease-breeding acres. As many as half of them died. Union military authorities later tried the camp commander, German-born Confederate Captain Henry Wirz, and executed him for murder. Charles Ferren Hopkins was a twenty-year-old soldier with the First New Jersey Volunteers when he was captured at the Battle of the Wilderness in May 1864. Then began his ordeal at Andersonville. What were the worst conditions he had to tolerate? How did he find the will to survive? Was Wirz justly convicted of murder?

The prison was a parallelogram of about two to one as to its length and breadth, about eighteen acres at this time—it was enlarged July 1st to about twenty-seven acres—and one-third of this not habitable, being a swamp of liquid filth. This was enclosed by wooden walls of hewn pine logs, from eight to ten inches square, four feet buried in the ground, eighteen feet above, braced on the outside, cross-barred to make one log sustain the other, and a small platform making comfortable standing room for the guards, every one hundred feet, with above waist-high space below the top of stockade, reached by a ladder. A sloping roof to protect the guards from the sun and rain had been placed over them. . . . The Florida Artillery had cannon stationed at each corner of the stockade, thus commanding a range from any direction; four guns were so placed near the south gate and over the depressed section of stockade at which point the little stream entered the enclosure.

The "dead line" so much talked of and feared was a line of pine, four-inch boards on posts about three feet high. This line was seventeen feet from the stockade walls, thus leaving the distance all around the enclosure an open space, and incidentally reducing the acreage inside and giving the guards a clear view all about the stockade or "bull pen," the name given it by its inventor—the infamous General Winder. . . . To intrude inside this dead line was instant death, or wounds that would cause death, by the rifle of a watchful, ready, willing, murderous guard.

Inside the camp death stalked on every hand. Death at the hand of the guards, though murder in cold blood, was merciful beside the systematic, absolute murder inside, by slow death, inch by inch! As before stated, one-third of the original enclosure was swampy—a mud of liquid filth, voidings from the thousands, seething with maggots in full activity. This daily increased by the necessities of the inmates, being the only place accessible for the purpose. Through this mass of pollution passed the only water that found its way through the Bull Pen. . . . The air was loaded with unbearable, fever-laden stench from that poison sink of putrid mud and water, continually in motion by the activity of the germs of death. We could not get away from the stink—we ate it, drank it and slept in it (when exhaustion compelled sleep).

What wonder that men died, or were so miserable as to prefer instant death to that which they had seen hourly taking place, and so preferring, deliberately

---

*From Charles F. Hopkins, "Hell and the Survivor," in *American Heritage* (October–November 1982): 78–93.

stepping within the dead line and looking their willing murderer in the eye, while a shot was sent crashing into a brain that was yet clear.

The month of June gave us twenty-seven days of rain—not consecutively, but so frequently that no one was dry in all that time. Everything was soaked—even the sandy soil. Still, this watery month was a blessing in disguise as it gave water, plenty of which was pure to drink. The boast of Winder was that the selection of this spot for his Bull Pen was the place where disease and death would come more quickly by "natural causes," when a removal of two hundred feet east would have placed us upon a living, pure, deep and clear stream of water, properly named "Sweetwater Creek," which had we been allowed to utilize would have saved thousands of lives—but no, that was not the intent of its inventor. To kill by "natural causes" was made more possible by this location.

The average deaths per day for seven and half months were 85. But during the months of July, August, September, and October the average was 100 per day. One day in August, following the great freshet, I counted 235 corpses laying at the south gate and about. Many of those had been smothered in their "burrows" made in the side hill in which they crawled to shield themselves from sun and storm; the soil, being sandy, became rain soaked and settled down upon the occupant and became his grave instead of a protection. Others, who had no shelter, in whom life was barely existing, were rain-soaked, chilling blood and marrow, and life flitted easily away, and left but little to return to clay. These holes or burrows in both the flats and up the north slope were counted by thousands; no doubt there were some that never gave up their dead, the men buried in their self-made sepulcher. No effort was made to search unless the man was missed by a friend.

Such were Winder's "natural causes"!! These were murders committed by most "unnatural causes" and methods—systematic causes! . . .

The famous Providence Spring, so much read of, was made possible by the great storm and freshet of August 9, 1864. It broke in the stockade near the south gate, inside the dead line, and swept to the lower side and broke through there also. Near the north gate, some fifty to sixty feet south on the slope, the heavy downpour of rain rushed down the slope inside the dead line and under the strata of sand, found a clay bottom, and struck a small thread of pure water, and food-famished prisoners feasted their eyes on it for days. It grew a little larger and promised hope to those who might be able to drink of its purity. Being out of reach, all sorts of devices were invented to get some of it. The coy little life-giving stream persistently wriggled its way inside the dead line, though we were glad to welcome it to our side of death's border. Small it was but to that camp would have been like drinking diamonds—so precious were its drops to the minds of those that knew not pure water for months.

Wirz, the helpmate of the devil, concluded that even those precious drops of nature's nectar, so hardly and dangerously earned, were entirely too good for the "damned Yankees," and would in a measure defeat his "natural causes" system of death, and right here is where Providence Spring comes to our rescue. Wirz sent a force of Negroes into camp to stop the flow of water of this Providence Spring. Their efforts were in vain—fruitless, but ho! how fruitful to us poor wretches as the stream of life resented the brutal interference of Wirz, and in its wrath burst forth a torrent compared to its original flow. All the curses and demoniacal ravings of Wirz availed him nothing—he could not stop it or turn it away, being located so that it reached us eventually. We now could get water from near the dead line—pure as crystal. Wirz went so far as to lead it out of reach, yet its flow of pure water into the former reekings and seepings of the Rebel sinks was still a vast improvement, for it purified the stream and increased the flow.

4. A Southern Woman Describes the Hardship of War (1862)*

War likewise took its toll on civilians who found themselves in the path of advancing armies. After securing key victories at Forts Henry and Donelson along the Kentucky-Tennessee border, Northern troops raided nearby communities to supplement their meager supplies. In a letter to her brother, Laura Williams describes her terror-stricken town on the eve of the Union raid. What were her greatest fears? How did she prepare for the troops' impending arrival?

I am still spared to write to you once more though I must acknowledge that yesterday I thought that happy privilege would never again be permitted me. Such a day I never spent and I trust that I may never see such another in Gallatin. The men all looked like their last moments had come. Women and children were flying in every direction. Some left their homes and everything else to fly to some place of safety. Many of the families have left town to go around in the country thinking they would there be more safe. We heard the Lincolnites were about 40 miles from here and yesterday everybody was huddled around the streets looking every minute for them to come to Gallatin. They had a meeting in town and emptied and buried together every drop of whiskey in town. After our defeat at Fort Donelson everybody seems deranged. We did not expect yesterday [that] the Lincolnites would have possession of Gallatin and Nashville by this time. We heard that our forces were going to surrender Nashville without a fight, and we knew if they took that place we were gone too, but we heard that Davis had sent word for them to hold it at any hazards and he would send them as many troops as they wanted, so I am every day expecting to hear of your being at Nashville. . . . the cars have stopped on the Nashville and Louisville railroad so we have no way to send you a letter only by hand and as Rufus sent us word this morning that he was going to leave tomorrow for Bate's Regiment so I thought it the best opportunity of sending you a letter that I would have. I just wish you could be here just to see how scared the people are. I do believe the men are worse scared than the women. Some of the men (*Be it said to their shame*) did raise several white flags in town but somebody tore them down this morning. I wish you all had of been here to of shot it down. We commenced packing and hiding our clothes. I was determined they should never have my clothes. Tell Bob me and Ma put his and your clothes in a trunk and packed them away in a safe place. Your absence caused our greatest distress. If we could

Women's Letters: America from the Revolutionary War to the Present, edited by Lisa Grunwald and Stephen J. Adler (New York: Dial Press, 2008).

still get letters to you but all the communications will be cut off if we are whipped at Nashville. Everybody is in *Sack Cloth and Ashes*. I cannot half describe it to you. I wish you could be here to see and know for yourself. . . . They say Nashville presented the most awful appearance yesterday that was ever seen, that the Lincolnites were there last night and the women and children were running and screaming all over the place. Again this morning we hear no Lincolnites there so we never know when to believe anything we hear. . . .

When you come home, I reckon the Lincolnites will have all your chickens eat[en] up if they ever get here which I hope they may never do. We heard just now that Johnston was throwing shells into Washington City today. Is it so or not? Do write if you can when you get this. Be a good boy, don't rush into danger.

5. *General William T. Sherman Dooms Atlanta (1864)*[*]

General William T. Sherman, a tall, red-bearded West Pointer from Ohio, understood and liked the South better than most other Northerners did. He was in fact teaching at a military academy in Louisiana when war erupted. Yet he became one of the earliest practitioners of "total war"—that is, breaking the morale of the civilians in order to break the backbone of the military. Before leaving captured Atlanta on his spectacular march to the sea, he ordered the inhabitants to evacuate the city, pending its destruction as a military measure. In response to an appeal from the city fathers that he would work a cruel hardship on pregnant women, invalids, widows, orphans, and others in an area already overflowing with refugees, he sent the following reply. Was his position ethical?

Gentlemen: I have your letter of the 11th, in the nature of a petition to revoke my orders removing all the inhabitants from Atlanta. I have read it carefully, and give full credit to your statements of the distress that will be occasioned, and yet shall not revoke my orders, because they were not designed to meet the humanities of the case, but to prepare for the future struggles in which millions of good people outside of Atlanta have a deep interest.

We must have peace, not only at Atlanta, but in all America. To secure this, we must stop the war that now desolates our once happy and favored country. To stop war, we must defeat the rebel armies which are arrayed against the laws and Constitution that all must respect and obey. To defeat those armies, we must prepare the way to reach them in their recesses, provided with the arms and instruments which enable us to accomplish our purpose.

Now, I know the vindictive nature of our enemy, that we may have many years of military operations from this quarter; and, therefore, deem it wise and prudent to prepare in time. The use of Atlanta for warlike purposes is inconsistent with its character as a home for families. There will be no manufactures, commerce, or agriculture here for the maintenance of families, and sooner or later want will compel the inhabitants to go. Why not go now, when all the arrangements are completed

---

[*]*Memoirs of General William T. Sherman* (New York: D. Appleton and Company, 1887), vol. 2, pp. 125–127 (letter of September 12, 1864).

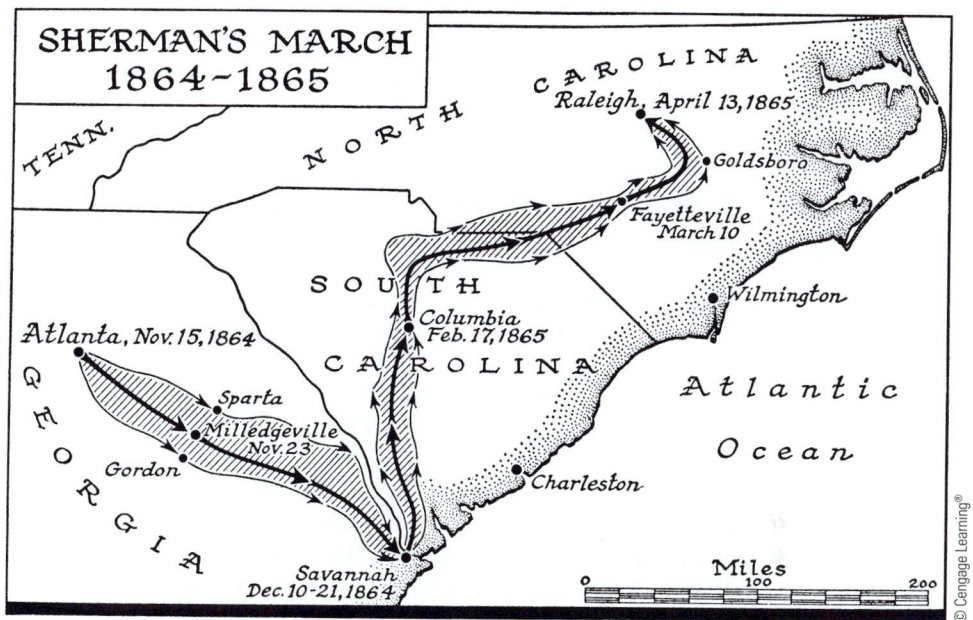

SHERMAN'S MARCH
1864-1865

for the transfer, instead of waiting till the plunging shot of contending armies will renew the scenes of the past month? Of course, I do not apprehend any such thing at this moment, but you do not suppose this army will be here until the war is over. I cannot discuss this subject with you fairly, because I cannot impart to you what we propose to do, but I assert that our military plans make it necessary for the inhabitants to go away, and I can only renew my offer of services to make their exodus in any direction as easy and comfortable as possible.

You cannot qualify war in harsher terms than I will. War is cruelty, and you cannot refine it; and those who brought war into our country deserve all the curses and maledictions a people can pour out. I know I had no hand in making this war, and I know I will make more sacrifices today than any of you to secure peace. But you cannot have peace and a division of our country. If the United States submits to a division now, it will not stop, but will go on until we reap the fate of Mexico, which is eternal war.

The United States does and must assert its authority, wherever it once had power; for, if it relaxes one bit to pressure, it is gone, and I believe that such is the national feeling. This feeling assumes various shapes, but always comes back to that of Union. Once admit the Union, once more acknowledge the authority of the national Government, and, instead of devoting your houses and streets and roads to the dread uses of war, I and this army become at once your promoters and supporters, shielding you from danger, let it come from what quarter it may. I know that a few individuals cannot resist a torrent of error and passion, such as swept the South into rebellion, but you can point out, so that we may know those who desire a government, and those who insist on war and its desolation.

You might as well appeal against the thunderstorm as against these terrible hardships of war. They are inevitable, and the only way the people of Atlanta can hope once more to live in peace and quiet at home, is to stop the war, which can only be done by admitting that it began in error and is perpetuated in pride.

We don't want your Negroes, or your horses, or your houses, or your lands, or anything you have, but we do want and will have a just obedience to the laws of the United States. That we will have, and, if it involves the destruction of your improvements, we cannot help it.

You have heretofore read public sentiment in your newspapers, that live by falsehood and excitement; and the quicker you seek for truth in other quarters, the better. I repeat then that, by the original compact of government, the United States had certain rights in Georgia, which have never been relinquished and never will be; that the South began war by seizing forts, arsenals, mints, custom-houses, etc., etc., long before Mr. Lincoln was installed, and before the South had one jot or tittle of provocation.

I myself have seen in Missouri, Kentucky, Tennessee, and Mississippi, hundreds of thousands of women and children fleeing from your armies and desperadoes, hungry and with bleeding feet. In Memphis, Vicksburg, and Mississippi, we fed thousands upon thousands of the families of rebel soldiers left on our hands, and whom we could not see starve.

Now that war comes home to you, you feel very different. You deprecate its horrors, but did not feel them when you sent carloads of soldiers and ammunition, and molded shells and shot, to carry war into Kentucky and Tennessee, to desolate the homes of hundreds and thousands of good people who only asked to live in peace at their old homes, and under the government of their inheritance.

But these comparisons are idle. I want peace, and believe it can only be reached through union and war, and I will ever conduct war with a view to perfect and early success.

But, my dear sirs, when peace does come, you may call on me for anything. Then will I share with you the last cracker, and watch with you to shield your homes and families against danger from every quarter.

Now you must go, and take with you the old and feeble, feed and nurse them, and build for them, in more quiet places, proper habitations to shield them against the weather until the mad passions of men cool down, and allow the Union and peace once more to settle over your old homes at Atlanta. Yours in haste,

W. T. Sherman, Major-General commanding

6. Georgia Damns the Yankees (1864)*

After burning much of Atlanta, General Sherman daringly cut loose from his base of supplies and headed for the sea. With the troops forced to live off the country, he detailed soldiers (loosely called "bummers") to round up poultry, livestock, and

---

*Eliza F. Andrews, *The War-Time Journal of a Georgia Girl* (New York: D. Appleton and Company, 1908), pp. 32–33.

other provisions. This type of foraging degenerated at times into pillaging, which was aggravated by bands of lawless civilians from both North and South. What light does this passage from the diary of a returning Georgia woman cast on the effectiveness of Sherman's methods, the state of Southern morale, and the prospect of North-South harmony after the war?

December 24, 1864.—About three miles from Sparta [Georgia] we struck the "Burnt Country," as it is well named by the natives, and then I could better understand the wrath and desperation of these poor people. I almost felt as if I should like to hang a Yankee myself. There was hardly a fence left standing all the way from Sparta to Gordon. The fields were trampled down and the road was lined with carcasses of horses, hogs, and cattle that the invaders, unable either to consume or to carry away with them, had wantonly shot down, to starve out the people and prevent them from making their crops. The stench in some places was unbearable; every few hundred yards we had to hold our noses or stop them with the cologne Mrs. Elzey had given us, and it proved a great boon.

The dwellings that were standing all showed signs of pillage, and on every plantation we saw the charred remains of the gin-house and packing-screw, while here and there lone chimney-stacks, "Sherman's sentinels," told of homes laid in ashes. The infamous wretches! I couldn't wonder now that these poor people should want to put a rope round the neck of every red-handed "devil of them" they could lay their hands on.

Hay ricks and fodder stacks were demolished, corn-cribs were empty, and every bale of cotton that could be found was burnt by the savages. I saw no grain of any sort, except little patches they had spilled when feeding their horses and which there was not even a chicken left in the country to eat. A bag of oats might have lain anywhere along the road without danger from the beasts of the fields, though I cannot say it would have been safe from the assaults of hungry man.

Crowds of [Confederate] soldiers were tramping over the road in both directions; it was like traveling through the streets of a populous town all day. They were mostly on foot, and I saw numbers seated on the roadside greedily eating raw turnips, meat skins, parched corn—anything they could find, even picking up the loose grains that Sherman's horses had left. I felt tempted to stop and empty the contents of our provision baskets into their laps, but the dreadful accounts that were given of the state of the country before us made prudence get the better of our generosity.

Before crossing the Oconee [River] at Milledgeville we ascended an immense hill, from which there was a fine view of the town, with Governor Brown's fortifications in the foreground and the river rolling at our feet. The Yankees had burnt the bridge; so we had to cross on a ferry. There was a long train of vehicles ahead of us, and it was nearly an hour before our turn came; so we had ample time to look about us. On our left was a field where thirty thousand Yankees had camped hardly three weeks before. It was strewn with the debris they had left behind, and the poor people of the neighborhood were wandering over it, seeking anything they could find to eat, even picking up grains of corn that were scattered around where the Yankees had fed their horses. We were told that a great many valuables were found there at first, plunder that the invaders had left behind, but the place had been picked over so often by this time that little now remained except tufts of loose cotton, piles of half-rotted grain, and the carcasses of slaughtered animals, which raised a horrible stench. Some men were plowing in one part of the field, making ready for next year's crop.

7. General Ulysses S. Grant Displays Generosity (1865)*

While Sherman was ravaging Georgia and the Carolinas, General Grant was slowly grinding his way into Virginia. Superior Union forces finally drove General Lee into a corner, and at Appomattox the sloppily dressed General Grant met with the handsomely attired General Lee to discuss terms of surrender. The following version is taken from Grant's Memoirs, which he completed on his deathbed in 1885 while suffering agony from cancer of the throat. (Although he did not live to see the two volumes published, they netted his indebted widow more than $400,000 in royalties.) At the time of the surrender negotiations, there were still several Confederate armies in the field, and there was a real possibility that the Civil War would degenerate into a protracted guerrilla war. In the light of these circumstances, comment on Grant's generosity, described in his Memoirs as follows.

Then, after a little further conversation, General Lee remarked to me again that their army was organized a little differently from the army of the United States (still maintaining by implication that we were two countries); that in their army the cavalrymen and artillerists owned their own horses; and he asked if he was to understand that the men who so owned their horses were to be permitted to retain them. I told him that as the terms were written they would not; that only the officers were permitted to take their private property. He then, after reading over the terms a second time, remarked that that was clear.

I then said to him that I thought this would be about the last battle of the war—I sincerely hoped so; and I said further I took it that most of the men in the ranks were small farmers. The whole country had been so raided by the two armies that it was doubtful whether they would be able to put in a crop to carry themselves and their families through the next winter without the aid of the horses they were then riding. The United States did not want them and I would, therefore, instruct the officers I left behind to receive the paroles of his troops to let every man of the Confederate army who claimed to own a horse or mule take the animal to his home. Lee remarked again that this would have a happy effect.

[On the day that Lee asked Grant for surrender terms (April 7, 1865), the Richmond Evening Whig published the following obituary notice:

DIED: CONFEDERACY, SOUTHERN.—At the late residence of his father, J. Davis, Richmond, Virginia, Southern Confederacy, aged 4 years. Death caused by strangulation. No funeral.*]*

---

*Personal Memoirs of U. S. Grant (New York: C. L. Webster and Co., 1886), vol. 2, pp. 492–493.

D. African Americans in the Civil War

1. An Abolitionist Officer Commands Black Troops (1869)*

In late 1861 Union forces seized Port Royal, a heavily slave-populated sea island off the South Carolina coastal town of Beaufort. For the remainder of the war, Port Royal served as a kind of laboratory for abolitionist experiments in how to deal with freed slaves. Among the most striking developments at Port Royal was the raising of the first black regiment mustered into the Union forces. Thomas Wentworth Higginson (1823–1911), a Harvard-educated Unitarian minister and outspoken abolitionist, sailed south in 1862 to take up his new command as a colonel in the black First South Carolina Volunteers. After the war, he published a remarkable book about his experiences, from which the following excerpt is taken. What did Higginson find most gratifying about the character and behavior of his troops? Is he ever condescending about them? What do his reflections suggest about the abolitionist temperament? About the freed slaves' aspirations?

Thanksgiving-Day; . . .

Already I am growing used to the experience, at first so novel, of living among five hundred men, and scarce a white face to be seen,—of seeing them go through all their daily processes, eating, frolicking, talking, just as if they were white. . . .

It needs but a few days to show the absurdity of distrusting the military availability of these people. They have quite as much average comprehension as whites of the need of the thing, as much courage (I doubt not), as much previous knowledge of the gun, and, above all, a readiness of ear and of imitation, which, for purposes of drill, counterbalances any defect of mental training. To learn the drill, one does not want a set of college professors; one wants a squad of eager, active, pliant school-boys; and the more childlike these pupils are the better. There is no trouble about the drill; they will surpass whites in that. As to camp-life, they have little to sacrifice; they are better fed, housed, and clothed than ever in their lives before, and they appear to have few inconvenient vices. They are simple, docile, and affectionate almost to the point of absurdity. The same men who stood fire in open field with perfect coolness, on the late expedition, have come to me blubbering in the most irresistibly ludicrous manner on being transferred from one company in the regiment to another. . . .

[After describing his life with the First South Carolina Volunteers, Higginson in his concluding chapters tells some of the life stories of his individual troops and reflects on the meaning of their life in slavery and under arms.]

There was another family of brothers in the regiment named Miller. Their grandmother, a fine-looking old woman, nearly seventy, I should think, but erect as a pine-tree, used sometimes to come and visit them. She and her husband had

---

*Thomas Wentworth Higginson, *Army Life in a Black Regiment* (Boston: Lee and Shepard, 1882), pp. 8–10, 247–258.

once tried to escape from a plantation near Savannah. They had failed, and had been brought back; the husband had received five hundred lashes, and while the white men on the plantation were viewing the punishment, she was collecting her children and grandchildren, to the number of twenty-two, in a neighboring marsh, preparatory to another attempt that night. They found a flat-boat which had been rejected as unseaworthy, got on board,—still under the old woman's orders,—and drifted forty miles down the river to our lines. Trowbridge happened to be on board the gunboat which picked them up, and he said that when the "flat" touched the side of the vessel, the grandmother rose to her full height, with her youngest grandchild in her arms, and said only, "My God! are we free?" By one of those co-incidences of which life is full, her husband escaped also, after his punishment, and was taken up by the same gunboat.

I hardly need point out that my young lieutenants did not have to teach the principles of courage to this woman's grandchildren.

I often asked myself why it was that, with this capacity of daring and endurance, they had not kept the land in a perpetual flame of insurrection; why, especially since the opening of the war, they had kept so still. The answer was to be found in the peculiar temperament of the races, in their religious faith, and in the habit of patience that centuries had fortified. The shrewder men all said substantially the same thing. What was the use of insurrection, where everything was against them? They had no knowledge, no money, no arms, no drill, no organization,—above all, no mutual confidence. It was the tradition among them that all insurrections were always betrayed by somebody. . . .

It always seemed to me that, had I been a slave, my life would have been one long scheme of insurrection. But I learned to respect the patient self-control of those who had waited till the course of events should open a better way. When it came they accepted it. Insurrection on their part would at once have divided the Northern sentiment; and a large part of our army would have joined with the Southern army to hunt them down. By their waiting till we needed them, their freedom was secured.

Two things chiefly surprised me in their feeling toward their former masters,—the absence of affection and the absence of revenge. I expected to find a good deal of the patriarchal feeling . . . but certainly they had not a particle. I never could cajole one of them, in his most discontented moment, into regretting "ole mas'r time" for a single instant. I never heard one speak of the masters except as natural enemies. Yet they were perfectly discriminating as to individuals; many of them claimed to have had kind owners, and some expressed great gratitude to them for particular favors received. It was not the individuals, but the ownership, of which they complained. That they saw to be a wrong which no special kindnesses could right. On this, as on all points connected with slavery, they understood the matter as clearly as Garrison or Phillips; the wisest philosophy could teach them nothing as to that, nor could any false philosophy befog them. After all, personal experience is the best logician. . . .

No doubt there were reasons why this particular war was an especially favorable test of the colored soldiers. They had more to fight for than the whites. Besides the flag and the Union, they had home and wife and child. They fought with ropes round their necks, and when orders were issued that the officers of colored troops should be put to death on capture, they took a grim satisfaction. It helped their *esprit de corps* immensely. With us, at least, there was to be no play-soldier. Though they had begun with a slight feeling of inferiority to the white troops, this compliment substituted a peculiar sense of self-respect. And even when the new colored regiments began to arrive from the North my men still pointed out this difference,— that in case of ultimate defeat, the Northern troops, black or white, would go home, while the First South Carolina must fight it out or be re-enslaved.

2. The Fifty-Fourth Massachusetts Regiment Marches South (1863)[*]

The early achievements of black regiments in the South paved the way for mass mobilization of African American troops. As the war dragged on and white enlistments dropped off, lawmakers let go of their initial misgivings about enlisting free blacks. Lincoln's Emancipation Proclamation explicitly provided for drafting freed slaves into service, and shortly thereafter, New England states formed their first black regiments, including the celebrated Fifty-Fourth Massachusetts. Composed of free blacks from nineteen states, carefully chosen to serve in the model regiment, the Fifty-Fourth distinguished itself in battle, most notably with its daring but ill-fated charge on Fort Wagner, South Carolina. What does the following account by a soldier in the regiment reveal about the Fifty-Fourth's reception in the South?

The 54th has already won the reputation here of being a first class regiment, both in drill, discipline and physical condition. When the 54th marched through the streets of this town, the citizens and soldiers lined the walks, to get a look at the first black regiment from the North. The contrabands did not believe we were coming; one of them said, "I nebber bleeve black Yankee comee here help culer men." They think now the kingdom is coming sure enough. The yarns the copperhead press have so studiously spun, that the slaves were better satisfied in their old condition than under the present order of things, is all bosh. So far as I have seen, they appear to understand the causes of the war better than a great many Northern editors. South Carolina was the pioneer in the war, and she had a double reason for it. According to one of the slaves showing, there had been a conspiracy hatching among the slaves, as far back as 1856, the year Fremont was up for the Presidency.[†] The negroes had heard through their masters that Fremont was a "damned abolitionist," they then began to lay plans to escape, or if necessary to fight. In December, 1856, after the defeat of the Republicans, one Prince Rivers went to Charleston, in the name of an organized committee, praying the Governor of the State to recommend the legislature to so modify some certain statutes that the negroes could live a

---

[*]Corporal James Henry Gooding, *On the Altar of Freedom: A Black Soldier's Civil War Letters from the Front*, Virginia Matzke Adams, ed. (Amherst: University of Massachusetts Press, 1999), pp. 26–27.
[†]John Charles Fremont, explorer of the American West and one of California's first senators (1850–1851), was nominated by the new Republican party in 1856 and ran unsuccessfully against James Buchanan. During the Civil War he was put in charge of the Western Department until his radical policy of freeing the slaves and confiscating slave owners' property led to his removal in late summer 1861.

little more like civilized people. The Governor sent him home to his master, telling him the State could not interfere with the relations existing between master and slave. Soon after that, every gun, pistol or other weapon was taken from the slaves; but the chivalry took fine care to say nothing about it in the papers. The people of the North knew nothing of these things.[*]

3. Cornelia Hancock Describes a Contraband Hospital (1863)[†]

Once the war began, thousands of former slaves fled for safety behind Union lines. Enterprising Union generals deemed these runaways "contrabands of war" and refused to turn them over to their former owners, a policy made official with the 1861 Confiscation Act. As the army pushed deeper into the South, the masses of black refugees overwhelmed the limited resources allotted for their care. Conditions were especially dreadful in camp hospitals, as described by Cornelia Hancock, a distinguished Union nurse. What were the most difficult aspects of the freedmen's experiences?

Here are gathered the sick from the contraband camps in the northern part of Washington. If I were to describe this hospital it would not be believed. North of Washington, in an open, muddy mire, are gathered all the colored people who have been made free by the progress of our Army. Sickness is inevitable, and to meet it these rude hospitals, only rough wooden barracks, are in use—a place where there is so much to be done you need not remain idle. We average here one birth per day, and have no baby clothes except as we wrap them up in an old piece of muslin, *that* even being scarce. Now the Army is advancing it is not uncommon to see from 40 to 50 arrivals [refugee slaves] in one day. They go at first to the Camp but many of them being *sick* from exhaustion soon come to us. They have nothing that any one in the North would call clothing. I always see them as soon as they arrive, as they come here to be vaccinated; about 25 a day are vaccinated. This hospital is the reservoir for all cripples, diseased, aged, wounded, infirm, from whatsoever cause; all accidents happening to colored people in all employs around Washington are brought here. It is not uncommon for a colored driver to be pounded nearly to death by some of the white soldiers. We had a dreadful case of Hernia brought in today. A woman was brought here with three children by her side; said she had been on the road for some time; a more forlorn, wornout looking creature I never beheld. Her four eldest children are still in Slavery, her husband is dead. When I first saw her she laid on the floor, leaning against a bed, her children crying around her. One child died almost immediately, the other two are still sick. She seemed to need most, food and rest, and those two comforts we gave her, but clothes she still wants. I think the women are more trouble than the men. One of the white guards called to me today and asked me if I got any pay. I told him no. He said he

---

[*]A Prince Rivers was later a color sergeant in Col. Thomas W. Higginson's 1st South Carolina Regiment (Cornish, *Sable Arm*, 91, 134).

[†]Henrietta Stratton Jaquette, ed., *Letters of a Civil War Nurse: Cornelia Hancock, 1863–1865* (Lincoln: University of Nebraska Press, 1998), pp. 31–32.

was going to be paid soon and he would give me 5 dollars. I do not know what was running through his mind as he made no other remark. I ask for clothing for women and children, both boys and girls. Two little boys, one 3 years old, had his leg amputated above the knee the cause being his mother not being allowed to ride inside, became dizzy and dropped him. The other had his leg broken from the same cause. This hospital consists of all the lame, halt, and blind escaped from slavery. We have a man & woman here without any feet theirs being frozen so they had to be amputated. Almost all have scars of some description and many have very weak eyes. There were two very fine looking slaves arrived here from Louisiana, one of them had his master's name branded on his forehead, and with him he brought all the instruments of torture that he wore at different times during 39 years of very hard slavery. I will try to send you a Photograph of him he wore an iron collar with 3 prongs standing up so he could not lay down his head; then a contrivance to render one leg entirely stiff and a chain clanking behind him with a bar weighing 50 lbs. This he wore and worked all the time hard. At night they hung a little bell upon the prongs above his head so that if he hid in any bushes it would tinkle and tell his whereabouts. The baton that was used to whip them he also had. It is so constructed that a little child could whip them till the blood streamed down their backs. This system of proceeding has been stopped in New Orleans and may God grant that it may cease all over this boasted free land, but you may readily imagine what development such a system of treatment would bring them to. With *this* class of beings, those who wish to do good to the contrabands must labor. Their standard of morality is very low.

4. A Black Corporal Demands Equal Pay (1864)[*]

Despite their accomplishments, black soldiers chafed against the discriminatory practices of the Union army. Serving in segregated units under an all-white officer corps, black troops were paid barely half the salary of white recruits, putting undue hardship on the soldiers and their families. As the war wore on, African American soldiers pressed for their sacrifices to be recognized with fairer treatment and equal pay. The Fifty-Fourth and Fifty-Fifth Massachusetts regiments, by far the most vehement in their protests, refused to collect their salaries until their grievances were addressed. In a poignant letter, Corporal John H. B. Payne justifies his stance. How does he frame his demands? What reasons does he give for joining the Union cause?

I am not willing to fight for anything less than the white man fights for. If the white man cannot support his family on seven dollars per month, I cannot support mine on the same amount.

And I am not willing to fight for this Government for money alone. Give me my rights, the rights that this Government owes me, the same rights that the white man

[*]Edwin S. Redkey, ed., *A Grand Army of Black Men: Letters from African-American Soldiers in the Union Army, 1861–1865* (New York: Cambridge University Press, 1992), pp. 208–210.

has. I would be willing to fight three years for this Government without one cent of the mighty dollar. Then I would have something to fight for. Now I am fighting for the rights of white men. White men have never given me the rights that they are bound to respect. God has not made one man better than another; therefore, one man's rights are no better than another's. They assert that because a large proportion of our race is in bondage we have a right to help free them. I want to know if it was not the white man that put them in bondage? How can they hold us responsible for their evils? And how can they expect that we should do more to blot it out than they are willing to do themselves? If every slave in the United States were emancipated at once, they would not be free yet. If the white man is not willing to respect my rights, I am not willing to respect his wrongs. Our rights have always been limited in the United States. It is true that in some places a colored man, if he can prove himself to be half-white, can vote. Vote for whom? The white man. What good do such rights ever do us—to be compelled always to be voting for the white man and never to be voted for?

Now, the white man declares that this is not our country, and that we have no right to it. They say that Africa is our country. I claim this as my native country—the country that gave me birth. I wish to know one thing, and that is this: Who is the most entitled to his rights in a country—a native of the country or the foreigner? This question can be very easily answered. Now there are foreigners who have flooded our shores. They bring nothing with them but antagonistic feelings to rule and order, and they are without the rudiments of education, and yet they can train their children to be law-abiding citizens. In their own country mis-rule reigns. Generally very poor, they have no leisure for the cultivation of their hearts' best feelings; for in their case, poverty degrades human nature. In this country their social influence is much greater than in their own. Here every avenue to distinction is open to them. . . .

The ignorant Irish can come to this country and have free access to all the rights. After they have gained their rights, they cannot appreciate them. They then want to bully the Government. They soon get tired of living under the laws of the country and commence to mutiny, riot, ransack cities, murder colored children, and burn down orphan asylums, as was done in New York.* Is the power to be given to such men to direct and govern the affairs of the Union, on which the weal or woe of the nation depends? This is productive of moral degradation and becomes one of the fruitful sources of evil in our land, from which we shall suffer most severely unless some plan is specially adopted to check its onward course. How can this nation ever expect to prosper? I wonder that God does not bring on them present deluge and disaster. I do not wonder at the conduct and disaster that transpired at Fort Pillow.† I wonder that we have not had more New York riots and Fort Pillow massacres.

---

*Opposition to the draft touched off a vicious riot in New York in 1863. For four days, a mostly Irish mob sacked Republican establishments and terrorized the city's black population, leaving scores dead or wounded.

†Until 1864, Southern armies refused to recognize African American troops as prisoners of war. When several dozen black soldiers were massacred upon surrendering at Fort Pillow, Tennessee, "Remember Fort Pillow" became a rallying cry for black regiments.

Thought Provokers

1. Why did Lincoln believe that the ideal of Union was more important than that of freeing the slave? Which had the greater emotional appeal, and why?
2. In what respects did the Emancipation Proclamation prove to be statesmanlike? Why was it so late in coming?
3. How did the war, often described as the first example of "total war," affect the civilian population? It has been argued that Sherman was a humane general because in the long run he reduced civilian suffering by bringing the war to a speedier end. Comment.
4. During his lifetime, Lincoln was widely regarded in the South and among many Northern Democrats as an inept, joke-telling buffoon. Account for his ranking today as perhaps our greatest president. Is he overrated?
5. What distinguished the experience of black soldiers in the war? What specific challenges did they face? What new opportunities did wartime service provide?

22

The Ordeal of Reconstruction, 1865–1877

The years of war tried our devotion to the Union;
the time of peace may test the sincerity of our faith
in democracy.

Herman Melville, c. 1866

Prologue: President Johnson, a rough-hewn Tennessean, favored reconstruction of the seceded states on a "soft" basis. But he soon ran afoul of the congressional Republicans. Though divided into hard-line ("radical") and more accommodating ("moderate") factions, Republicans agreed that the seceding states should not be readmitted until they had adopted the Fourteenth Amendment. This amendment, ratified in 1868, would guarantee civil rights to the blacks while reducing congressional representation in states where the ex-slave was denied a vote. But such terms were spurned by ten of the eleven high-spirited Southern states. The Republicans in Congress thereupon passed the drastic Reconstruction Act of 1867, under which black suffrage was forced upon the white South. The Congress also came within a hairsbreadth, in 1868, of removing the obstructive President Johnson by impeachment. Meanwhile, the partly black Southern legislatures, despite grievous excesses, passed stacks of long overdue social and economic legislation. The whites struck back through secret terrorist organizations and ultimately secured control of their state governments by fraud, fright, and force.

A. The Status of the South

1. Black Leaders Express Their Views (1865)[*]

From the early decades of the nineteenth century, African American preachers had served as important spokesmen for the hopes and frustrations of their communities. A group of twenty such preachers met in Savannah, Georgia, with U.S. Secretary of War Edwin McMasters Stanton and the incomparable Union general, William Tecumseh Sherman. The purpose of the meeting was to learn the views of the "colored

---

[*]Ira Berlin et al., eds., *Freedom: A Documentary History of Emancipation, 1861–1867* (New York: Cambridge University Press, 1990), vol. 3, pp. 332–337.

population . . . as to what should be done in their behalf by the Government." Speaking for the group of clergy was Garrison Frazier, a thirty-five-year veteran of the Baptist ministry who had purchased his own freedom, as well as that of his wife, a mere eight years previously. What do his answers suggest about the political knowledge and expectations of Southern black leaders in the Civil War era?

First: State what your understanding is in regard to the acts of Congress and President Lincoln's proclamation, touching the condition of the colored people in the Rebel States.

Answer: So far as I understand President Lincoln's proclamation to the Rebellious States, it is, that if they would lay down their arms and submit to the laws of the United States before the first of January, 1863, all should be well; but if they did not, then all the slaves in the Rebel States should be free henceforth and forever. That is what I understood.

Second: State what you understand by Slavery and the freedom that was to be given by the President's proclamation.

Answer: Slavery is, receiving by *irresistible power* the work of another man, and not by his *consent*. The freedom, as I understand it, promised by the proclamation, is taking us from under the yoke of bondage, and placing us where we could reap the fruit of our own labor, take care of ourselves and assist the Government in maintaining our freedom.

Third: State in what manner you think you can take care of yourselves, and how can you best assist the Government in maintaining your freedom.

Answer: The way we can best take care of ourselves is to have land, and turn it and till it by our own labor—that is, by the labor of the women and children and old men; and we can soon maintain ourselves and have something to spare. And to assist the Government, the young men should enlist in the service of the Government, and serve in such manner as they may be wanted. (The Rebels told us that they piled them up and made batteries of them, and sold them to Cuba; but we don't believe that.) We want to be placed on land until we are able to buy it and make it our own.

Fourth: State in what manner you would rather live—whether scattered among the whites or in colonies by yourselves.

Answer: I would prefer to live by ourselves, for there is a prejudice against us in the South that will take years to get over; but I do not know that I can answer for my brethren. [Mr. Lynch says he thinks they should not be separated, but live together. All the other persons present, being questioned one by one, answer that they agree with Brother Frazier.]

Fifth: Do you think that there is intelligence enough among the slaves of the South to maintain themselves under the Government of the United States and the equal protection of its laws, and maintain good and peaceable relations among yourselves and with your neighbors?

Answer: I think there is sufficient intelligence among us to do so.

Sixth: State what is the feeling of the black population of the South toward the Government of the United States; what is the understanding in respect to the present war— its causes and object, and their disposition to aid either side. State fully your views.

Answer: I think you will find there are thousands that are willing to make any sacrifice to assist the Government of the United States, while there are also many that are not willing to take up arms. I do not suppose there are a dozen men that are opposed to the Government. I understand, as to the war, that the South is the aggressor. President Lincoln was elected President by a majority of the United States, which guaranteed him the right of holding the office and exercising that right over the whole United States. The South, without knowing what he would do, rebelled. The war was commenced by the Rebels before he came into office. The object of the war was not at first to give the slaves their freedom, but the sole object of the war was at first to bring the rebellious States back into the Union and their loyalty to the laws of the United States. Afterward, knowing the value set on the slaves by the Rebels, the President thought that his proclamation would stimulate them to lay down their arms, reduce them to obedience, and help to bring back the Rebel States; and their not doing so has now made the freedom of the slaves a part of the war. It is my opinion that there is not a man in this city that could be started to help the Rebels one inch, for that would be suicide. There were two black men left with the Rebels because they had taken an active part for the Rebels, and thought something might befall them if they stayed behind; but there is not another man. If the prayers that have gone up for the Union army could be read out, you would not get through them these two weeks. . . .

Eleventh: State what, in your opinion, is the best way to enlist colored men for soldiers.

Answer: I think, sir, that all compulsory operations should be put a stop to. The ministers would talk to them, and the young men would enlist. It is my opinion that it would be far better for the State agents to stay at home, and the enlistments to be made for the United States under the direction of Gen. Sherman.

In the absence of Gen. Sherman, the following question was asked:

Twelfth: State what is the feeling of the colored people in regard to Gen. Sherman; and how far do they regard his sentiments and actions as friendly to their rights and interests, or otherwise?

Answer: We looked upon Gen. Sherman prior to his arrival as a man in the Providence of God specially set apart to accomplish this work, and we unanimously feel inexpressible gratitude to him, looking upon him as a man that should be honored for the faithful performance of his duty. Some of us called upon him immediately upon his arrival, and it is probable he would not meet the Secretary with more courtesy than he met us. His conduct and deportment toward us characterized him as a friend and a gentleman. We have confidence in Gen. Sherman, and think that what concerns us could not be under better hands. This is our opinion now from the short acquaintance and interest we have had. (Mr. Lynch states that with his limited acquaintance with Gen. Sherman, he is unwilling to express an opinion. All others present declare their agreement with Mr. Frazier about Gen. Sherman.)

Some conversation upon general subjects relating to Gen. Sherman's march then ensued, of which no note was taken.

War Dept. Adjt. Gen.'s Office
Washington, Feb. 1, 1865.

2. Carl Schurz Reports Southern Defiance (1865)*

President Johnson sent Carl Schurz—a lanky, bewhiskered, and bespectacled German American reformer—into the devastated South to report objectively on conditions there. But Schurz was predisposed to see continued defiance. He was on intimate terms with the radical Republican leaders who favored a severe reconstruction of the South, and he was financially obligated to the radical Charles Sumner. President Johnson, evidently hoping for evidence that would support his lenient policies, brushed aside Schurz's elaborate report with ill-concealed annoyance. Schurz partially financed his trip by selling a series of letters under an assumed name to the Boston Advertiser, *which presumably welcomed his pro-radical bias. In the following letter, which he wrote from Savannah to the newspaper, what class of people does he deem responsible for the trouble? What motivated them? Why were their outbursts not more serious?*

But there is another class of people here [in Savannah], mostly younger men, who are still in the swearing mood. You can overhear their conversations as you pass them on the streets or even sit near them on the stoop of a hotel. They are "not conquered but only overpowered." They are only smothered for a time. They want to fight the war over again, and they are sure in five years they are going to have a war bigger than any we have seen yet. They are meaning to get rid of this d——d military despotism. They will show us what stuff Southern men are made of. They will send their own men to Congress and show us that we cannot violate the Constitution with impunity.

They have a rope ready for this and that Union man when the Yankee bayonets are gone. They will show the Northern interlopers that have settled down here to live on their substance the way home. They will deal largely in tar and feathers. They have been in the country and visited this and that place where a fine business is done in the way of killing Negroes. They will let the Negro know what freedom is, only let the Yankee soldiers be withdrawn.

Such is their talk. You can hear it every day, if you have your ears open. You see their sullen, frowning faces at every street corner. Now, there may be much of the old Southern braggadocio in this, and I do not believe that such men will again resort to open insurrection. But they will practice private vengeance whenever they can do it with impunity, and I have heard sober-minded Union people express their apprehension of it. This spirit is certainly no evidence of true loyalty.

It was this spirit which was active in an occurrence which disgraced this city on the Fourth of July. Perhaps you have heard of it. The colored firemen of this city desired to parade their engine on the anniversary of our independence. If nobody else would, they felt like celebrating that day. A number will deny that it was a legitimate desire. At first the engineer of the fire department, who is a citizen of this town, refused his permission. Finally, by an interposition of an officer of the "Freedmen's Bureau,"† he was prevailed upon to give his consent, and the parade took place. In the principal street of the city the procession was attacked with clubs and stones by a mob opposed to the element above described, and by a crowd of boys all

---

*Joseph H. Mahaffrey, ed., "Carl Schurz's Letters from the South," *Georgia Historical Quarterly* 35 (September 1951): 244–247.
†A federal agency designed to help the ex-slaves adjust to freedom.

swearing at the d——d niggers. The colored firemen were knocked down, some of them severely injured, their engine was taken away from them, and the peaceable procession dispersed. Down with the d——d niggers. A northern gentleman who loudly expressed his indignation at the proceedings was in danger of being mobbed, and had to seek safety in a house. . . .

To return to the "unconquered" in Savannah—the occurrence of the Fourth of July shows what they are capable of doing even while the Yankee bayonets are still here. If from this we infer what they will be capable of doing when the Yankee bayonets are withdrawn, the prospect is not altogether pleasant, and Union people, white and black, in this city and neighborhood may well entertain serious apprehensions. . . .

Unfortunately, this spirit receives much encouragement from the fair sex. We have heard so much of the bitter resentment of the Southern ladies that the tale becomes stale by frequent repetition, but when inquiring into the feelings of the people, this element must not be omitted. There are certainly a good many sensible women in the South who have arrived at a just appreciation of the circumstances with which they are surrounded. But there is a large number of Southern women who are as vindictive and defiant as ever, and whose temper does not permit them to lay their tongues under any restraint. You can see them in every hotel, and they will treat you to the most ridiculous exhibitions, whenever an occasion offers.

A day or two ago a Union officer, yielding to an impulse of politeness, handed a dish of pickles to a Southern Lady at the dinner-table of a hotel in this city. A look of unspeakable scorn and indignation met him. "So you think," said the lady, "a Southern woman will take a dish of pickles from a hand that is dripping with the blood of her countrymen?"

It is remarkable upon what trifling material this female wrath is feeding and growing fat. In a certain district in South Carolina, the ladies were some time ago, and perhaps are now, dreadfully exercised about the veil question. You may ask me what the veil question is. Formerly, under the old order of things, Negro women were not permitted to wear veils. Now, under the new order of things, a great many are wearing veils. This is an outrage which cannot be submitted to; the white ladies of the neighborhood agree in being indignant beyond measure. Some of them declare that whenever they meet a colored woman wearing a veil they will tear the veil from her face. Others, mindful of the consequences which such an act of violence might draw after it, under this same new order of things, declare their resolve never to wear veils themselves as long as colored women wear veils. This is the veil question, and this is the way it stands at present.

Such things may seem trifling and ridiculous. But it is a well-known fact that a silly woman is sometimes able to exercise a powerful influence over a man not half as silly, and the class of "unconquered" above described is undoubtedly in a great measure composed of individuals that are apt to be influenced by silly women. It has frequently been said that had it not been for the spirit of the Southern women, the rebellion would have broken down long ago, and there is, no doubt, a grain of truth in it.

3. General Ulysses S. Grant Is Optimistic (1865)*

President Johnson, hoping to capitalize on Grant's enormous prestige, also sent the general on a fact-finding trip to the South. Grant spent less than a week hurriedly

---

*Senate Executive Documents, 39th Cong., 1st sess., I, no. 2, pp. 106–107.

visiting leading cities in four states. Schurz had ranged far more widely over a longer period, from July to September 1865. But just as Schurz was predisposed to see defiance, Grant was predisposed to see compliance. Bear in mind also that Schurz was an idealist, strongly pro-black, and a leading Republican politician in close touch with the radicals. Grant was none of these. Which of their reports is more credible?

I am satisfied that the mass of thinking men of the South accept the present situation of affairs in good faith. The questions which have heretofore divided the sentiment of the people of the two sections—slavery and state rights, or the right of a state to secede from the Union—they regard as having been settled forever by the highest tribunal—arms—that man can resort to. I was pleased to learn from the leading men whom I met that they not only accepted the decision arrived at as final, but, now that the smoke of battle has cleared away and time has been given for reflection, that this decision has been a fortunate one for the whole country, they receiving like benefits from it with those who opposed them in the field and in council.

Four years of war, during which law was executed only at the point of the bayonet throughout the states in rebellion, have left the people possibly in a condition not to yield that ready obedience to civil authority the American people have generally been in the habit of yielding. This would render the presence of small garrisons throughout those states necessary until such time as labor returns to its proper channel, and civil authority is fully established. I did not meet anyone, either those holding places under the government or citizens of the Southern states, who think it practicable to withdraw the military from the South at present. The white and the black mutually require the protection of the general government.

There is such universal acquiescence in the authority of the general government throughout the portions of country visited by me that the mere presence of a military force, without regard to numbers, is sufficient to maintain order. . . .

My observations lead me to the conclusion that the citizens of the Southern states are anxious to return to self-government, within the Union, as soon as possible; that whilst reconstructing they want and require protection from the government; that they are in earnest in wishing to do what they think is required by the government, not humiliating to them as citizens, and that if such a course were pointed out they would pursue it in good faith.

4. Emancipation Violence in Texas (c. 1865)[*]

In the following recollection by a former slave in Texas, what is revealed about the response of some slave owners to emancipation? What implications did such responses have for the future of the freed slaves? For federal policy during Reconstruction?

I heard about freedom in September and they were picking cotton and a white man rode up to master's house on a big, white horse and the houseboy told master a man wanted to see him and he hollered, "Light, stranger." It was a government man and he had the big book and a bunch of papers and said why hadn't master turned

[*]George P. Rawick, ed., *The American Slave: A Composite Autobiography* (Westport, CT: Greenwood Publishing Company, 1972), vol. 5, Texas Narratives, part 3, p. 78.

the niggers loose. Master said he was trying to get the crop out and he told master to have the slaves in. Uncle Steven blew the cow horn that they used to call to eat and all the niggers came running, because that horn meant, "Come to the big house, quick." The man read the paper telling us we were free, but master made us work several months after that. He said we would get 20 acres of land and a mule but we didn't get it.

Lots of niggers were killed after freedom, because the slaves in Harrison County were turned loose right at freedom and those in Rusk County weren't. But they heard about it and ran away to freedom in Harrison County and their owners had them bush-whacked, then shot down. You could see lots of niggers hanging from trees in Sabine bottom right after freedom, because they caught them swimming across Sabine River and shot them. There sure are going to be lots of souls crying against them in judgment!

5. Alfred Richardson Confronts the Ku Klux Klan in Reconstruction Era Georgia (1871)*

In 1871, a special congressional committee took testimony, in hearings conducted in both Washington and the South, about the mounting violence that was being visited upon the newly freed blacks, especially by the Ku Klux Klan. The extensive record of the committee's investigation provides grisly evidence of the dangerous situation in which black men and women found themselves in the post–Civil War South. The testimony excerpted below was given by Alfred Richardson, born a slave in Georgia in about 1837. He supported his wife and three children after emancipation by working as a carpenter. He was also politically active in the Republican party, an affiliation that brought down upon him the savage wrath of his white neighbors, virtually all of them Democrats. What does his testimony suggest about the political situation in the Reconstruction Era South? About the situation of black women? By what means did whites assert political and economic control over blacks? In the light of this testimony, how should the success or failure of Reconstruction policy be judged?

Washington, D.C., July 7, 1871

Alfred Richardson (colored) sworn and examined.

Question. Since you became a freeman have you voted?
Answer. Yes, sir.
Question. With what party have you voted?
Answer. The republican party.
Question. State to the committee whether you have been attacked in any way by anybody; if so, when and how. Tell us the whole story about it.
Answer. Yes, sir; I was attacked twice. The first time was just before last Christmas; I cannot recollect exactly what day.
Question. Tell us all the particulars.
Answer. There was a set of men came down to about a quarter of a mile of where I live. They were all disguised. They had taken out an old man by the name of

---

*Alfred Richardson, in *Testimony Taken by the Joint Select Committee to Inquire into the Condition of Affairs in the Late Insurrectionary States; Georgia, Volume I*, pp. 1–2, 12–13. *Report* No. 41, Part 6, 42d Cong., 2d sess. Senate (Washington, DC: Government Printing Office, 1872).

Charles Watson. They commenced beating him. His wife and children all ran out, and screamed and hallooed for help to stop the men from beating him to death. We, who were in town, came out to see what was the matter.

Question. You heard the outcry?

Answer. Yes, sir, and came out to see what was the matter. . . . It was the Ku-Klux, who had this old man down in the corner of the fence, knocking him and telling him he had to tell where Alfred Richardson was, and had to go with them to his house and show how he was fixed up. . . .

Question. They wanted him to tell where you were?

Answer. Yes, sir; they wanted him to tell where I was, and how I was fixed up; they said he had to go and get me out. In the mean time, while they were telling him this, a crowd of boys came on behind me, and we all ran up, after we heard what they were up to. They all broke and ran, and carried this old man with them. We followed them to the forks of the road. . . . I could not see anybody for a long time; a cloud had got over the moon. After a while I saw one fellow slipping alongside the fence. He had a pistol in his hand, as if to shoot me. When I saw him doing that, I took my pistol, and shot at him. When I shot at him there were three or four men who shot me from through the fence. I did not see them. They shot about twenty shots into my leg and hip. I went off home, and went to the doctor's office. The doctor examined me, and fixed my wounds up. In three or four days I got so that I could travel very well. Things went on till after Christmas. On the 18th of January a man by the name of John O. Thrasher came to me———

Question. Was he a white man?

Answer. Yes, sir; . . . This man told me, "There are some men about here that have something against you; and they intend to kill you or break you up. They say you are making too much money; that they do not allow any nigger to rise that way; that you can control all the colored votes; and they intend to break you up, and then they can rule the balance of the niggers when they get you off." He said, "They said they wanted me to join their party, but I told them I did not want to do it; I never knew you to do anything wrong, and these are a parcel of low-down men, and I don't want to join any such business; but I tell you, you had better keep your eyes open, for they are after you." . . . I talked to the ordinary, and the clerk of the court, and several other citizens. They said they didn't see why anybody wanted to interrupt me; that I had always kept the peace between the colored and the white people; that when there was a fuss I was the only man that could break it up and make the colored people behave themselves; that they hated to let me go away. . . . The same night this man was telling me that, I went to bed about 9 o'clock. Between 12 and 1 o'clock these men came; there were about twenty or twenty-five of them, I reckon. . . . [T]hey broke in the lower door and came up-stairs firing in every direction. I could not stand in the stairway to shoot at them. I had some small arms back in the garret. There was a door up there about large enough for one man to creep in. I thought I had better go in there, and maybe they would not find me—probably they would miss me, and I could make my escape. They all came up-stairs. My wife opened the window to call out for help, and a fellow shot at her some twelve or fifteen times through that window while she was hallooing. A whole crowd came up, and when they saw that window open, they said, "He has jumped out of the window," and they hallooed to the fellows on the ground to shoot on top of the house. Thinking I had gone out of the window, they all went down-stairs except one man. He went and looked in the cuddy-hole where I was, and saw me there. He hallooed to the rest of the fellows that he had found me; but they had got down-stairs, and some of them were on the piazza. Then he commenced firing, and shot me three times. He lodged two balls in my side, and one in the right arm. That weakened me pretty smartly. After he had shot his loads all out, he said to the rest of them, "Come back up here; I have got him; and I have shot him, but he is not quite dead; let us go up and finish him." I crept from the door of the little room where I was to the stairway; they came up-stairs with their pistols in their hands, and a man behind with a light. I shot one of them as he got on the top step. They gathered him up by the legs; and then they all ran and left me. I never saw any more of them that night; and I have not seen them since. . . .

Question. Do these bands of men ever whip women?

Answer. Yes, sir.

Question. Why do they whip women? They do not vote.

Answer. Many times, you know, a white lady has a colored lady for cook or waiting in the house, or something of that sort. They have some quarrel, and sometimes probably the colored woman gives the lady a little jaw. In a night or two a crowd will come in and take her out and whip her.

Question. For talking saucily to her mistress?

Answer. Yes, sir.

Question. Does that state of things control colored labor down there? Do these bands make the negroes work for whomever they please?

Answer. Do you mean the Ku-Klux?

Question. Yes, sir.

Answer. Well, they go sometimes so far as this: When a man is hired, if he and his employer have any dispute about the price, and there are hard words between them about the amount of money to be paid, they whip the colored man for disputing the white man's word, or having any words with him.

Question. They whip the colored man for having any dispute with his employer about what shall be paid him?

Answer. Yes, sir.

Question. Is that common?

Answer. Yes, sir; that has been done several times. Sometimes colored people are working for a part of the crop. They work on till the crop is nearly completed and ready for gathering. Then a fuss arises between them and the employer, and they are whipped off—whipped off by these men in disguise. . . . Some of the colored people swear that they do not intend to farm any more, excepting they can have peace to gather what they plant. Now, they work a part of the year and then get run off and make nothing. So they conclude it is best to go to some city and work by the day for what they can get. Every town in our State where there is any protection is overrun with colored people. Many of the farm hands are there; and there is a great mass of loafers who stand round town because they have got no work to do. Yet people's fields around in the country are running away with grass. Some men go to town and try to get hands. The colored men will ask, "In what part of the country do you live?" The man will mention such and such a place. They will say, "We can't go down there; the Ku-Klux is down there. If it wasn't for the Ku-Klux we would go down and work for you."

B. The Debate on Reconstruction Policy

1. Southern Blacks Ask for Help (1865)*

As the smoke of war cleared, blacks throughout the South gathered in Conventions of Freedmen to determine the best strategies for protecting their fragile freedom. Several of these conventions formally petitioned the Congress for help. In the following petition from a convention meeting in Alexandria, Virginia, in August 1865, what forms of support are deemed most essential? What is the freedmen's greatest fear?

We, the undersigned members of a Convention of colored citizens of the State of Virginia, would respectfully represent that, although we have been held as slaves, and denied all recognition as a constituent of your nationality for almost the entire period of the duration of your Government, and that by *your permission* we have been denied either home or country, and deprived of the dearest rights of human nature; yet when you and our immediate oppressors met in deadly conflict upon the field of battle—the one to destroy and the other to save your Government and nationality, *we*, with scarce an exception, in our inmost souls espoused your cause, and watched, and prayed, and waited, and labored for your success. . . .

When the contest waxed long, and the result hung doubtfully, you appealed to us for help, and how well we answered is written in the rosters of the two hundred thousand colored troops now enrolled in your service; and as to our undying devotion to your cause, let the uniform acclamation of escaped prisoners, "whenever we saw a black face we felt sure of a friend," answer.

Well, the war is over, the rebellion is "put down," and we are *declared* free! Four fifths of our enemies are paroled or amnestied, and the other fifth are being pardoned, and the President has, in his efforts at the reconstruction of the civil government of the States, late in rebellion, left us entirely at the mercy of these subjugated but unconverted rebels, in *everything* save the privilege of bringing us, our wives and little ones, to the auction block. . . . We *know* these men—know them *well*—and we assure you that, with the majority of them, loyalty is only "lip deep," and that their professions of loyalty are used as a cover to the cherished design of getting restored to their former relations with the Federal Government, and then, by all sorts of "unfriendly legislation," to render the freedom you have given us more intolerable than the slavery they intended for us.

We warn you in time that our only safety is in keeping them under Governors of the *military persuasion* until you have so amended the Federal Constitution that it will prohibit the States from making any distinction between citizens on account of race or color. In one word, the only salvation for us besides the power of the

---

*"Proceedings of the Convention of the Colored People of Virginia, Held in the City of Alexandria, August 2, 3, 4, 5, 1865" (Alexandria, VA, 1865), in W. L. Fleming, ed., *Documentary History of Reconstruction* (Cleveland, OH: The Arthur C. Clark Company, 1906), vol. 1, pp. 195–196.

Government, is in the *possession of the ballot*. Give us this, and we will protect ourselves. . . . But, 'tis said we are ignorant. Admit it. Yet who denies we *know* a traitor from a loyal man, a gentleman from a rowdy, a friend from an enemy? . . . All we ask is an *equal chance* with the white *traitors* varnished and japanned with the oath of amnesty. Can you deny us this and still keep faith with us? . . .

We are "sheep in the midst of wolves," and nothing but the military arm of the Government prevents us and all the *truly* loyal white men from being driven from the land of our birth. Do not then, we beseech you, give to one of these "wayward sisters" the rights they abandoned and forfeited when they rebelled until you have secured *our* rights by the aforementioned amendment to the Constitution.

2. The White South Asks for Unconditional Reintegration into the Union (1866)*

The Joint Committee on Reconstruction, composed of nine congressional representatives and six senators, held extensive hearings in the spring of 1866 about the condition of the South and various proposals for reintegrating the Southern states into the Union. One leading proposal was the legislation that eventually became the Fourteenth Amendment to the Constitution. It was designed to reduce the representation in Congress of any state that denied the freedmen the right to vote. Congressional Republicans wanted to make any state's restoration to the Union conditional on its ratification of the amendment. In the following testimony, former Confederate Vice President Alexander Stephens comments on the congressional plan. What are his main objections to it? What alternatives does he propose? Does his statement confirm or cast doubt on the concerns of blacks presented in the preceding selection?

I think the people of the State would be unwilling to do more than they have done for restoration. Restricted or limited suffrage would not be so objectionable as general or universal. But it is a matter that belongs to the State to regulate. The question of suffrage, whether universal or restricted, is one of State policy exclusively, as they believe. Individually I should not be opposed to a proper system of restricted or limited suffrage to this class of our population. . . . The only view in their opinion that could possibly justify the war that was carried on by the federal government against them was the idea of the indissolubleness of the Union; that those who held the administration for the time were bound to enforce the execution of the laws and the maintenance of the integrity of the country under the Constitution. . . . They expected as soon as the confederate cause was abandoned that immediately the States would be brought back into their practical relations with the government as previously constituted. That is what they looked to. They expected that the States would immediately have their representatives in the Senate and in the House; and they expected in good faith, as loyal men, as the term is frequently used—loyal to law, order, and the Constitution—to support the government under the Constitution. . . . Towards the Constitution of the United States the great mass of our people were always as much devoted in their feelings as any people ever were towards any laws or people . . . they resorted to secession with a view of more securely maintaining these principles. And when they found they were not successful in their object

---

Report of the Joint Committee on Reconstruction (Washington, DC, 1866), Part III, pp. 163ff.

in perfect good faith, as far as I can judge from meeting with them and conversing with them, looking to the future development of their country . . . their earnest desire and expectation was to allow the past struggle . . . to pass by and to co-operate with . . . those of all sections who earnestly desire the preservation of constitutional liberty and the perpetuation of the government in its purity. They have been . . . disappointed in this, and are . . . patiently waiting, however, and believing that when the passions of the hour have passed away this delay in representation will cease. . . .

My own opinion is, that these terms ought not to be offered as conditions precedent. . . . It would be best for the peace, harmony, and prosperity of the whole country that there should be an immediate restoration, an immediate bringing back of the States into their original practical relations; and let all these questions then be discussed in common council. Then the representatives from the south could be heard, and you and all could judge much better of the tone and temper of the people than you could from the opinions given by any individuals. . . . My judgment, therefore, is very decided, that it would have been better as soon as the lamentable conflict was over, when the people of the south abandoned their cause and agreed to accept the issue, desiring as they do to resume their places for the future in the Union, and to look to the arena of reason and justice for the protection of their rights in the Union— it would have been better to have allowed that result to take place, to follow under the policy adopted by the administration, than to delay or hinder it by propositions to amend the Constitution in respect to suffrage. . . . I think the people of all the southern States would in the halls of Congress discuss these questions calmly and deliberately, and if they did not show that the views they entertained were just and proper, such as to control the judgment of the people of the other sections and States, they would quietly . . . yield to whatever should be constitutionally determined in common council. But I think they feel very sensitively the offer to them of propositions to accept while they are denied all voice . . . in the discussion of these propositions. I think they feel very sensitively that they are denied the right to be heard.

3. The Radical Republicans Take a Hard Line (1866)*

After weeks of testimony, the Joint Committee on Reconstruction made its report. With only three Democrats among its fifteen members, and dominated by the imperious Thaddeus Stevens, the committee reflected radical Republican views on Reconstruction policy. What were its principal conclusions? In the light of the evidence provided in the previous two selections, were the committee's views justified?

A claim for the immediate admission of senators and representatives from the so-called Confederate States has been urged, which seems to your committee not to be founded either in reason or in law, and which cannot be passed without comment. Stated in a few words, it amounts to this: That inasmuch as the lately insurgent States had no legal right to separate themselves from the Union, they still retain their position as States, and consequently the people thereof have a right to immediate representation in Congress without the interposition of any conditions whatever. . . . It has even been contended that until such admission all legislation affecting their interests is, if not unconstitutional, at least unjustifiable and oppressive.

---

*Report of the Joint Committee on Reconstruction (Washington, DC, 1866), pp. 4ff.

It is believed by your Committee that these propositions are not only wholly untenable, but, if admitted, would tend to the destruction of the government. . . . It cannot, we think, be denied that the war thus waged was a civil war of the greatest magnitude. The people waging it were necessarily subject to all the rules which, by the law of nations, control a contest of that character, and to all the legitimate consequences following it. One of these consequences was that, within the limits prescribed by humanity, the conquered rebels were at the mercy of the conquerors. . . .

It is moreover contended . . . that from the peculiar nature and character of our government . . . from the moment rebellion lays down its arms and actual hostilities cease all political rights of rebellious communities are at once restored; that because the people of a state of the Union were once an organized community within the Union, they necessarily so remain, and their right to be represented in Congress at any and all times, and to participate in the government of the country under all circumstances, admits of neither question nor dispute. If this is indeed true, then is the government of the United States powerless for its own protection, and flagrant rebellion, carried to the extreme of civil war, is a pastime which any state may play at, not only certain that it can lose nothing in any event, but may even be the gainer by defeat?

It is the opinion of your committee—

I. That the States lately in rebellion were, at the close of the war, disorganized communities, without civil government, and without constitutions or other forms, by virtue of which political relation could legally exist between them and the federal government.

II. That Congress cannot be expected to recognize as valid the election of representatives from disorganized communities, which, from the very nature of the case, were unable to present their claim to representation under those established and recognized rules, the observance of which has been hitherto required.

III. That Congress would not be justified in admitting such communities to a participation in the government of the country without first providing such constitutional or other guarantees as will tend to secure the civil rights of all citizens of the republic; a just equality of representation; protection against claims founded in rebellion and crime; a temporary restoration of the right of suffrage to those who have not actively participated in the efforts to destroy the Union and overthrow the government, and the exclusion from position of public trust of, at least, a portion of those whose crimes have proved them to be enemies of the Union, and unworthy of public confidence. . . .

The necessity of providing adequate safeguards for the future, before restoring the insurrectionary States to a participation in the direction of public affairs, is apparent from the bitter hostility to the government and people of the United States yet existing throughout the conquered territory. . . .

The conclusion of your committee therefore is, that the so-called Confederate States are not, at present, entitled to representation in the Congress of the United States.

4. President Andrew Johnson Tries to Restrain Congress (1867)[*]

Alarmed by the outbreak of race riots in several Southern cities, and frustrated by the South's rejection of the Fourteenth Amendment, Congress passed the Reconstruction Act

---

[*]J. D. Richardson, ed., *A Compilation of the Messages and Papers of the Presidents* (New York: Bureau of National Literature, 1911), vol. 5, pp. 3690–3696.

on March 2, 1867. The act divided the South into military districts subject to martial law. It also stipulated that the seceding states could be restored to the Union only when they had called constitutional conventions, on the basis of universal manhood suffrage, which must guarantee black voting rights and ratify the Fourteenth Amendment. President Johnson promptly vetoed the bill, which just as promptly was passed over his veto. In his veto message, which follows, what reasons does he offer for his action? Are his arguments sound? Why might they have especially provoked the Republicans in Congress?

Washington, March 2, 1867

To the House of Representatives:

I have examined the bill "to provide for the more efficient government of the rebel States" with the care and anxiety which its transcendent importance is calculated to awaken. I am unable to give it my assent, for reasons so grave that I hope a statement of them may have some influence on the minds of the patriotic and enlightened men with whom the decision must ultimately rest.

The bill places all the people of the ten States therein named under the absolute domination of military rulers; and the preamble undertakes to give the reason upon which the measure is based and the ground upon which it is justified. It declares that there exists in those States no legal governments and no adequate protection for life or property, and asserts the necessity of enforcing peace and good order within their limits. Is this true as matter of fact? . . .

Have we the power to establish and carry into execution a measure like this? I answer, Certainly not, if we derive our authority from the Constitution and if we are bound by the limitations which it imposes.

This proposition is perfectly clear, that no branch of the Federal Government—executive, legislative, or judicial—can have any just powers except those which it derives through and exercises under the organic law of the Union. Outside of the Constitution we have no legal authority more than private citizens, and within it we have only so much as that instrument gives us. This broad principle limits all our functions and applies to all subjects. It protects not only the citizens of States which are within the Union, but it shields every human being who comes or is brought under our jurisdiction. We have no right to do in one place more than in another that which the Constitution says we shall not do at all. If, therefore, the Southern States were in truth out of the Union, we could not treat their people in a way which the fundamental law forbids.

Some persons assume that the success of our arms in crushing the opposition which was made in some of the States to the execution of the Federal laws reduced those States and all their people—the innocent as well as the guilty—to the condition of vassalage and gave us a power over them which the Constitution does not bestow or define or limit. No fallacy can be more transparent than this. Our victories subjected the insurgents to legal obedience, not to the yoke of an arbitrary despotism. . . .

Invasion, insurrection, rebellion, and domestic violence were anticipated when the Government was framed, and the means of repelling and suppressing them were wisely provided for in the Constitution; but it was not thought necessary to declare that the States in which they might occur should be expelled from the Union. Rebellions, which were invariably suppressed, occurred prior to that out of which these questions grow; but the States continued to exist and the Union remained unbroken. In Massachusetts, in

Pennsylvania, in Rhode Island, and in New York, at different periods in our history, violent and armed opposition to the United States was carried on; but the relations of those States with the Federal Government were not supposed to be interrupted or changed thereby after the rebellious portions of their population were defeated and put down. It is true that in these earlier cases there was no formal expression of a determination to withdraw from the Union, but it is also true that in the Southern States the ordinances of secession were treated by all the friends of the Union as mere nullities and are now acknowledged to be so by the States themselves. If we admit that they had any force or validity or that they did in fact take the States in which they were passed out of the Union, we sweep from under our feet all the grounds upon which we stand in justifying the use of Federal force to maintain the integrity of the Government. . . .

The United States are bound to guarantee to each State a republican form of government. Can it be pretended that this obligation is not probably broken if we carry out a measure like this, which wipes away every vestige of republican government in ten States and puts the life, property, liberty, and honor of all the people in each of them under the domination of a single person clothed with unlimited authority?

The purpose and object of the bill—the general intent which pervades it from beginning to end—is to change the entire structure and character of the State governments and to compel them by force to the adoption of organic laws and regulations which they are unwilling to accept if left to themselves. The negroes have not asked for the privilege of voting; the vast majority of them have no idea what it means. This bill not only thrusts it into their hands, but compels them, as well as the whites, to use it in a particular way. If they do not form a constitution with prescribed articles in it and afterwards elect a legislature which will act upon certain measures in a prescribed way, neither blacks nor whites can be relieved from the slavery which the bill imposes upon them. Without pausing here to consider the policy or impolicy of Africanizing the southern part of our territory, I would simply ask the attention of Congress to that manifest, well-known, and universally acknowledged rule of constitutional law which declares that the Federal Government has no jurisdiction, authority, or power to regulate such subjects for any State. To force the right of suffrage out of the hands of the white people and into the hands of the negroes is an arbitrary violation of this principle. . . .

The bill also denies the legality of the governments of ten of the States which participated in the ratification of the amendment to the Federal Constitution abolishing slavery forever within the jurisdiction of the United States [the Thirteenth Amendment] and practically excludes them from the Union. If this assumption of the bill be correct, their concurrence can not be considered as having been legally given, and the important fact is made to appear that the consent of three-fourths of the States—the requisite number—has not been constitutionally obtained to the ratification of that amendment, thus leaving the question of slavery where it stood before the amendment was officially declared to have become a part of the Constitution.

That the measure proposed by this bill does violate the Constitution in the particulars mentioned and in many other ways which I forbear to enumerate is too clear to admit of the least doubt. . . .

It is part of our public history which can never be forgotten that both Houses of Congress, in July, 1861, declared in the form of a solemn resolution that the war was and should be carried on for no purpose of subjugation, but solely to enforce the

Constitution and laws, and that when this was yielded by the parties in rebellion the contest should cease, with the constitutional rights of the States and of individuals unimpaired. This resolution was adopted and sent forth to the world unanimously by the Senate and with only two dissenting voices in the House. It was accepted by the friends of the Union in the South as well as in the North as expressing honestly and truly the object of the war. On the faith of it many thousands of persons in both sections gave their lives and their fortunes to the cause. To repudiate it now by refusing to the States and to the individuals within them the rights which the Constitution and laws of the Union would secure to them is a breach of our plighted honor for which I can imagine no excuse and to which I can not voluntarily become a party.

5. The Controversy over the Fifteenth Amendment (1866, 1870)

The Fifteenth Amendment guaranteed all adult males, regardless of race, the right to vote, and the campaign to have it ratified produced bitter arguments between the radical Republicans and their opponents. The first illustration below, titled "The Constitutional Amendment," was first published during a heated election campaign in Pennsylvania in 1866. Supporters of the Democratic candidate for governor circulated this image in an attempt to defeat the Republican gubernatorial nominee. What are its most pointed arguments?

THE FIFTEENTH AMENDMENT AND ITS RESULTS.

Respectfully dedicated to the colored Citizens of the U S of America A.D.1870 by Schneider & Fuchs 184 N. Eutaw St.
Baltimore M?

The second image, "The Fifteenth Amendment and Its Results," above, appeared in Baltimore in 1870 to celebrate the enactment of the Fifteenth Amendment. What does it find most praiseworthy about the new law? How are blacks depicted in the two prints? Were there any principled arguments against the Fifteenth Amendment?

C. Impeaching the President

1. Johnson's Cleveland Speech (1866)*

A tactless and stubborn President Johnson clashed openly with the Republicans in Congress, including the embittered Thaddeus Stevens, when he vetoed a series of

---

*Edward McPherson, *The Political History of the United States of America During the Period of Reconstruction*, 3rd ed. (Washington, DC: Philip and Salomons, 1871), pp. 134–136.

Reconstruction bills. Two of the measures designed to help the former slaves—the Civil Rights Bill and the New Freedmen's Bureau Bill—were speedily repassed over his veto. Undaunted, Johnson embarked on a speech-making tour to urge the election of congressmen favorable to his policies. But the public was in an ugly mood. Former President Jefferson Davis, though still in prison, was untried and unhanged, as were other former Confederates. A recent antiblack riot in New Orleans had resulted in some two hundred casualties. Johnson had earlier distinguished himself as a rough-and-ready stump speaker in Tennessee, but, as Secretary Seward remarked, the president of the United States should not be a stump speaker. Johnson's undignified harangue in Cleveland contained passages (here italicized) that formed the basis of some of the impeachment charges later brought by the House. What criticisms can be legitimately leveled against this speech? Which one is the most serious?

Notwithstanding the subsidized gang of hirelings and traducers [in Congress?], I have discharged all my duties and fulfilled all my pledges, and I say here tonight that if my predecessor had lived, the vials of wrath would have been poured out upon him. [Cries of "Never!" "Three cheers for the Congress of the United States!"]

. . . Where is the man or woman who can place his finger upon one single act of mine deviating from any pledge of mine or in violation of the Constitution of the country? [Cheers.] . . . Who can come and place his finger on one pledge I ever violated, or one principle I ever proved false to? [A voice, "How about New Orleans?" Another voice, "Hang Jeff Davis."] Hang Jeff Davis, he says. [Cries of "No," and "Down with him!"] . . . Hang Jeff Davis. Why don't you hang him? [Cries of "Give us the opportunity."] Have not you got the court? Have not you got the Attorney General? . . .

I will tell you what I did do. I called upon your Congress that is trying to break up the government. [Emphasis added.] [Cries, "You be d——d!" and cheers mingled with hisses. Great confusion. "Don't get mad, Andy!"] Well, I will tell you who is mad. "Whom the gods wish to destroy, they first make mad." Did your Congress order any of them to be tried? ["Three cheers for Congress."] . . .

You pretend now to have great respect and sympathy for the poor brave fellow who has left an arm on the battlefield. [Cries, "Is this dignified?"] I understand you. . . . I care not for dignity. . . . [A voice, "Traitor!"] I wish I could see that man. I would bet you now that if the light fell on your face, cowardice and treachery would be seen in it. Show yourself. Come out here where I can see you. [Shouts of laughter.] If you ever shoot a man you will do it in the dark, and pull the trigger when no one is by to see you. [Cheers.]

I understand traitors. I have been fighting them at the south end of the line, and we are now fighting them in the other direction. [Laughter and cheers.] I come here neither to criminate or recriminate, but when attacked, my plan is to defend myself. [Cheers.] . . . As Chief Magistrate, I felt so after taking the oath to support the Constitution, and when I saw encroachments upon your Constitution and rights, as an honest man I dared to sound the tocsin of alarm. ["Three cheers for Andrew Johnson."] . . .

I love my country. Every public act of my life testifies that is so. Where is the man that can put his finger upon any one act of mine that goes to prove the contrary? And what is my offending? [A voice, "Because you are not a Radical," and cry of "Veto."] Somebody says veto. Veto of what? What is called the Freedmen's

Bureau bill? . . . I might refer to the Civil Rights Bill, the results of which are very similar. I tell you, my countrymen, that though the powers of hell and Thad Stevens and his gang were by, they could not turn me from my purpose. . . .

In conclusion, beside that, Congress had taken such pains to poison their constituents against him.* But what had Congress done? Had they done anything to restore the Union of these states? No; on the contrary, they had done everything to prevent it; and because he stood now where he did when the rebellion commenced, he had been denounced as a traitor. Who had run greater risks or made greater sacrifices than himself? But Congress, factious and domineering, had [under]taken to poison the minds of the American people. [Emphasis added.]

2. Senator Lyman Trumbull Defends Johnson (1868)[†]

Johnson's unrestrained oratory backfired, and at the polls in November the Republicans won control of a two-thirds majority in both houses of Congress. They proceeded to pass the Tenure of Office Act, which was designed to entrap Johnson. Doubting its constitutionality (by indirection it was later judged unconstitutional) and seeking to bring a test case, he deliberately challenged it by removing Secretary William Stanton. The House thereupon impeached Johnson for "high crimes and misdemeanors." Most of its indictment related to Johnson's alleged violation of the Tenure of Office Act; other charges related to his "scandalous harangues." Particularly objectionable was a speech at the White House in which the president had declared that acts of Congress were not binding upon him because the South did not enjoy proper representation in it. One of the ablest of those who spoke for Johnson was Senator Lyman Trumbull of Illinois, a brilliant constitutional lawyer and a former associate of Lincoln. As one who followed principle rather than partisanship, he changed parties three times during his career. In the following speech, what is his main reason for thinking that Johnson's removal would be unfortunate?

In coming to the conclusion that the President is not guilty of any of the high crimes and misdemeanors with which he stands charged, I have endeavored to be governed by the case made, without reference to other acts of his not contained in the record, and without giving the least heed to the clamor of intemperate zealots who demand the conviction of Andrew Johnson as a test of party faith, or seek to identify with and make responsible for his acts those who from convictions of duty feel compelled, on the case made, to vote for his acquittal.

His speeches and the general course of his administration have been as distasteful to me as to anyone, and I should consider it the great calamity of the age if the disloyal element, so often encouraged by his measures, should gain political ascendancy. If the question was, Is Andrew Johnson a fit person for President? I should answer, no; but it is not a party question, nor upon Andrew Johnson's deeds and acts, except so far as they are made to appear in the record, that I am to decide.

---

*The reporter now lapses into the third person.
[†]*Congressional Globe*, 40th Cong., 2d sess. (May 7, 1868), Supplement, p. 420.

Painful as it is to disagree with so many political associates and friends whose conscientious convictions have led them to a different result, I must, nevertheless, in the discharge of the high responsibility under which I act, be governed by what my reason and judgment tell me is the truth, and the justice and law of this case. . . .

Once set the example of impeaching a President for what, when the excitement of the hour shall have subsided, will be regarded as insufficient causes, as several of those now alleged against the President were decided to be by the House of Representatives only a few months since, and no future President will be safe who happens to differ with a majority of the House and two-thirds of the Senate on any measure deemed by them important, particularly if of a political character. Blinded by partisan zeal, with such an example before them, they will not scruple to remove out of the way any obstacle to the accomplishment of their purposes, and what then becomes of the checks and balances of the Constitution, so carefully devised and so vital to its perpetuity? They are all gone.

In view of the consequences likely to flow from this day's proceedings, should they result in conviction on what my judgment tells me are insufficient charges and profits, I tremble for the future of my country. I cannot be an instrument or produce such a result; and at the hazard of the ties even of friendship and affection, till calmer times shall do justice to my motives, no alternative is left me but the inflexible discharge of duty.

[President Johnson escaped removal by the margin of a single vote, and only because seven conscientious Republican senators, including Trumbull, risked political suicide by refusing to go along with the majority.]

D. "Black Reconstruction"

1. Thaddeus Stevens Demands Black Suffrage (1867)*

The most influential radical Republican in the House, crippled and vindictive Thaddeus Stevens of Pennsylvania, loathed slavery, slaveholders, and slave breeders. He felt a deep compassion for blacks and, in fact, arranged to be buried in a black cemetery. But in his demands for black suffrage he was motivated, like many other Republicans, by a mixture of idealism and opportunism. Of the arguments for black voting that he set forth in the following speech in the House, which ones were the most selfish? The most idealistic?

There are several good reasons for the passage of this bill [for reconstructing the South].

In the first place, it is just. I am now confining my argument to Negro suffrage in the rebel states. Have not loyal blacks quite as good a right to choose rulers and make laws as rebel whites?

In the second place, it is a necessity in order to protect the loyal white men in the seceded states. The white Union men are in a great minority in each of those

---

*Congressional Globe, 39th Cong., 2d sess. (January 3, 1867), p. 252.

states. With them the blacks would act in a body; and it is believed that in each of said states, except one, the two united would form a majority, control the states, and protect themselves. Now they are the victims of daily murder. They must suffer constant persecution, or be exiled. . . .

Another good reason is, it would insure the ascendancy of the Union [Republican] Party. "Do you avow the party purpose?" exclaims some horror-stricken demagogue. I do. For I believe, on my conscience, that on the continued ascendancy of that party depends the safety of this great nation.

If impartial suffrage is excluded in the rebel states, then every one of them is sure to send a solid rebel representative delegation to Congress, and cast a solid rebel electoral vote. They, with their kindred Copperheads of the North, would always elect the President and control Congress. While Slavery sat upon her defiant throne, and insulted and intimidated the trembling North, the South frequently divided on questions of policy between Whigs and Democrats, and gave victory alternately to the sections. Now, you must divide them between loyalists, without regard to color, and disloyalists, or you will be the perpetual vassals of the free-trade, irritated, revengeful South.

For these, among other reasons, I am for Negro suffrage in every rebel state. If it be just, it should not be denied; if it be necessary, it should be adopted; if it be a punishment to traitors, they deserve it.

2. Black and White Legislatures (c. 1876)[*]

Black suffrage was finally forced on the Southern whites by their new state constitutions and by the Fifteenth Amendment to the federal Constitution (1870). Tension grew worse as designing Northern "carpetbaggers" and Unionist Southern whites ("scalawags") moved in to exploit the inexperienced former slaves. J. W. Leigh, an English clergyman turned Georgia rice planter, recorded the following observations in a personal letter. What conditions were most galling to the former Confederates?

The fact is, the poor Negro has since the war been placed in an entirely false position, and is therefore not to be blamed for many of the absurdities he has committed, seeing that he has been urged on by Northern "carpetbaggers" and Southern "scalawags," who have used him as a tool to further their own nefarious ends.

The great mistake committed by the North was giving the Negroes the franchise so soon after their emancipation, when they were not the least prepared for it. In 1865 slavery was abolished, and no one even among the Southerners, I venture to say, would wish it back. In 1868 they [Negroes] were declared citizens of the United States, and in 1870 they had the right of voting given them, and at the same time persons concerned in the rebellion were excluded from public trusts by what was called the "iron-clad" oath. And as if this was not enough, last year [1875] the Civil Rights Bill was passed, by which Negroes were to be placed on a perfect equality with whites, who were to be compelled to travel in the same cars with them, and to send their children to the same schools.

The consequence of all this is that where there is a majority of Negroes, as is the case in the states of Louisiana, Mississippi, and South Carolina, these states

---

[*]Frances B. Leigh, *Ten Years on a Georgia Plantation Since the War* (London: R. Bentley and Sons, 1883), pp. 268–292 (Appendix).

are placed completely under Negro rule, and scenes occur in the state legislatures which baffle description.

I recollect at the beginning of 1870 being at Montgomery, the capital of Alabama, and paying a visit to the State House there, when a discussion was going on with respect to a large grant which was to be made for the building of the Alabama and Chattanooga Railway, the real object of which was to put money into the pockets of certain carpetbaggers, who, in order to gain their object, had bribed all the Negroes to vote for the passing of the bill.

The scene was an exciting one. Several Negro members were present, with their legs stuck up on the desks in front of them, and spitting all about them in free and independent fashion. One gentleman having spoken for some time against the bill, and having reiterated his condemnation of it as a fraudulent speculation, a stout Negro member from Mobile sprung up and said, "Mister Speaker, when yesterday I spoke, I was not allowed to go on because you said I spoke twice on the same subject. Now what is sauce for the goose is sauce for the gander. Dis Member is saying over and over again de same thing; why don't you tell him to sit down? for what is sauce for," etc. To which the Speaker said, "Sit down yourself, sir." Another member (a carpetbagger) jumped up and shook his fist in the speaking member's face, and told him he was a liar, and if he would come outside he would give him satisfaction.

This is nothing, however, to what has been going on in South Carolina this last session. Poor South Carolina, formerly the proudest state in America, boasting of her ancient families, remarkable for her wealth, culture, and refinement, now prostrate in the dust, ruled over by her former slaves, an old aristocratic society replaced by the most ignorant democracy that mankind ever saw invested with the functions of government. Of the 124 representatives, there are but 23 representatives of her old civilization, and these few can only look on at the squabbling crowd amongst whom they sit as silent enforced auditors. Of the 101 remaining, 94 are colored, and 7 their white allies. The few honest amongst them see plundering and corruption going on on all sides, and can do nothing. . . .

The Negroes have it all their own way, and rob and plunder as they please. The Governor of South Carolina lives in luxury, and treats his soldiers to champagne, while the miserable planters have to pay taxes amounting to half their income, and if they fail to pay, their property is confiscated.

Louisiana and Mississippi are not much better off. The former has a Negro barber for its Lieutenant-governor, and the latter has just selected a Negro steamboat porter as its United States Senator, filling the place once occupied by Jefferson Davis.

3. W. E. B. Du Bois Justifies Black Legislators (1910)*

W. E. B. Du Bois, a Massachusetts-born black of French Huguenot extraction, received his Ph.D. from Harvard University in 1895. Distinguished as a teacher, lecturer, historian, economist, sociologist, novelist, poet, and propagandist, he became a militant advocate of equal rights. A founder of the National Association for the Advancement of Colored People (NAACP), he served for twenty-four years as editor of

---

*American Historical Review 15 (1910): 791–799, passim.

its chief organ. Du Bois, who was born the day before the House impeached Johnson, here writes as a scholar. In what important respects does he argue that Reconstruction legislatures have been unfairly represented? In what ways were these bodies responsible for significant achievements?

Undoubtedly there were many ridiculous things connected with Reconstruction governments: the placing of ignorant field-hands who could neither read nor write in the legislature, the gold spittoons of South Carolina, the enormous public printing bill of Mississippi—all these were extravagant and funny; and yet somehow, to one who sees, beneath all that is bizarre, the real human tragedy of the upward striving of downtrodden men, the groping for light among people born in darkness, there is less tendency to laugh and jibe than among shallower minds and easier consciences. All that is funny is not bad.

Then, too, a careful examination of the alleged stealing in the South reveals much. First, there is repeated exaggeration. For instance, it is said that the taxation in Mississippi was fourteen times as great in 1874 as in 1869. This sounds staggering until we learn that the state taxation in 1869 was only ten cents on one hundred dollars, and that the expenses of government in 1874 were only twice as great as in 1860, and that too with a depreciated currency. . . .

The character of the real thieving shows that white men must have been the chief beneficiaries. . . . The frauds through the manipulation of state and railway bonds and of banknotes must have inured chiefly to the benefit of experienced white men, and this must have been largely the case in the furnishing and printing frauds. . . .

That the Negroes, led by astute thieves, became tools and received a small share of the spoils is true. But . . . much of the legislation which resulted in fraud was represented to the Negroes as good legislation, and thus their votes were secured by deliberate misrepresentation. . . .

Granted, then, that the Negroes were to some extent venal but to a much larger extent ignorant and deceived, the question is: Did they show any signs of a disposition to learn better things? The theory of democratic governments is not that the will of the people is always right, but rather that normal human beings of average intelligence will, if given a chance, learn the right and best course by bitter experience. This is precisely what Negro voters showed indubitable signs of doing. First, they strove for schools to abolish ignorance, and, second, a large and growing number of them revolted against the carnival of extravagance and stealing that marred the beginning of Reconstruction, and joined with the best elements to institute reform. . . .

We may recognize three things which Negro rule gave to the South:
1. Democratic government.
2. Free public schools.
3. New social legislation. . . .

In South Carolina there was before the war a property qualification for office-holders, and, in part, for voters. The [Reconstruction] constitution of 1868, on the other hand, was a modern democratic document . . . preceded by a broad Declaration of Rights which did away with property qualifications and based representation directly on population instead of property. It especially took up new subjects of social legislation, declaring navigable rivers free public highways, instituting homestead exemptions, establishing boards of county commissioners, providing for a new penal code of laws, establishing universal manhood suffrage "without distinction of race or color," devoting six sections to charitable and penal institutions and six to corporations, providing separate property for married women, etc. Above all, eleven sections of the Tenth Article were devoted to the establishment of a complete public-school system.

So satisfactory was the constitution thus adopted by Negro suffrage and by a convention composed of a majority of blacks that the state lived twenty-seven years under it without essential change. And when the constitution was revised in 1895, the revision was practically nothing more than an amplification of the constitution of 1868. No essential advance step of the former document was changed except the suffrage article. . . .

There is no doubt but that the thirst of the black man for knowledge—a thirst which has been too persistent and durable to be mere curiosity or whim—gave birth to the public free-school system of the South. It was the question upon which black voters and legislators insisted more than anything else, and while it is possible to find some vestiges of free schools in some of the Southern states before the war, yet a universal, well-established system dates from the day that the black man got political power. . . .

Finally, in legislation covering property, the wider functions of the state, the punishment of crime, and the like, it is sufficient to say that the laws on these points established by Reconstruction legislatures were not only different from and even revolutionary to the laws in the older South, but they were so wise and so well suited to the needs of the new South that in spite of a retrogressive movement following the overthrow of Negro governments, the mass of this legislation, with elaboration and development, still stands on the statute books of the South.

E. The Legacy of Reconstruction _____

1. Editor E. L. Godkin Grieves (1871)*

Irish-born E. L. Godkin, a fearless liberal, founded the distinguished and long-lived New York Nation *in 1865. So biting were his criticisms that the magazine was dubbed "the weekly day of judgment." His views on the blunders of Reconstruction were aired with incisiveness. He argued that there were two ways of dealing with the postwar South: (1) reorganize the section "from top to bottom" or (2) treat the whole community as made up of "unfortunate Americans, equally entitled to care and protection, demoralized by an accursed institution for which the whole Union was responsible, and which the whole Union had connived at, and, down to 1860, had profited by." But the North, wrote Godkin, followed neither course. Which aspects of Reconstruction does he regard as the most regrettable?*

---

*The Nation (New York) 13 (December 7, 1871): 364.

The condition of the Negro after emancipation . . . attracted the carpetbagger as naturally as a dead ox attracts the buzzard. The lower class of demagogue scents an unenlightened constituency at an almost incredible distance, and travels towards it over mountain, valley, and river with the certainty of the mariner's compass.

But then we hastened his coming by our legislation. We deliberately, and for an indefinite period, excluded all the leading Southern men from active participation in the management of their local affairs, by a discrimination not unlike that which would be worked in this city [New York], but very much worse, if every man who had not at some time belonged to the Tammany Society were declared incapable of holding office.

It was before the war the time-honored custom of the Southern states, and a very good custom too, to put their ablest men, and men of the highest social standing and character, in office. The consequence was that it was these men who figured most prominently in the steps which led to the rebellion, and in the rebellion itself. When the war was over, we singled these men out, and not unnaturally, for punishment by the 14th Amendment and other legislation.

But we forgot that, as the President points out, they were no worse, so far as disloyalty went, than the rest of the community. They broke their oaths of allegiance to the United States, but the other white men of the South would have done the same thing if they had got the chance of doing it by being elevated to office, either under the United States or under the Confederacy. We forgot, too, that when putting a mutinous crew in irons, the most justly indignant captain leaves at liberty enough able-bodied seamen to work the ship. . . .

The results . . . have been positively infernal. In the idea that we were befriending the Negroes, we gave them possession of the government, and deprived them of the aid of all the local capacity and experience in the management of it, thus offering the states as a prey to Northern adventurers, and thus inflicting on the freedmen the very worst calamity which could befall a race newly emerged from barbarism— that is, familiarity, in the very first movements of enfranchisement, with the process of a corrupt administration, carried on by gangs of depraved vagabonds, in which the public money was stolen, the public faith made an article of traffic, the legislature openly corrupted, and all that the community contained of talent, probity, and social respectability put under a legal ban as something worthless and disreputable.

We do not hesitate to say that a better mode of debauching the freedmen, and making them permanently unfit for civil government, could hardly have been hit on had the North had such an object deliberately in view. Instead of establishing equal rights for all, we set up the government of a class, and this class the least competent, the most ignorant and inexperienced, and a class, too, whose history and antecedents made its rule peculiarly obnoxious to the rest of the community.

Out of this state of things Ku-Kluxing has grown . . . naturally. . . . We cannot gainsay anything anybody says of the atrocity of riding about the country at night with one's face blackened, murdering and whipping people. But we confess we condemn Ku-Kluxing very much as we condemn the cholera. . . . There is no more use in getting in a rage with Ku-Kluxery, and sending cavalry and artillery after it, than of legislating against pestilence, as long as nothing is done to remove the causes.

2. Frederick Douglass Complains (1882)*

The incredible former slave Frederick Douglass (see p. 245) raised two famous black regiments in Massachusetts during the Civil War. Among the first recruits were his own sons. Continuing his campaign for civil rights and suffrage for the freedmen, he wrote the following bitter commentary in his autobiography. One of his keenest regrets was that the federal government, despite the urgings of Thaddeus Stevens and others, failed to provide land for the freed slaves. In the light of his observations, how would free land have alleviated the conditions he describes? Why did the former slave owners make life extremely difficult for the former slaves?

Though slavery was abolished, the wrongs of my people were not ended. Though they were not slaves, they were not yet quite free. No man can be truly free whose liberty is dependent upon the thought, feeling, and action of others, and who has himself no means in his own hands for guarding, protecting, defending, and maintaining that liberty. Yet the Negro after his emancipation was precisely in this state of destitution.

The law on the side of freedom is of great advantage only where there is power to make that law respected. I know no class of my fellow men, however just, enlightened, and humane, which can be wisely and safely trusted absolutely with the liberties of any other class. Protestants are excellent people, but it would not be wise for Catholics to depend entirely upon them to look after their rights and interests. Catholics are a pretty good sort of people (though there is a soul-shuddering history behind them); yet no enlightened Protestants would commit their liberty to their care and keeping.

And yet the government had left the freedmen in a worse condition than either of these. It felt that it had done enough for him. It had made him free, and henceforth he must make his own way in the world, or, as the slang phrase has it, "root, pig, or die." Yet he had none of the conditions for self-preservation or self-protection.

He was free from the individual master, but the slave of society. He had neither money, property, nor friends. He was free from the old plantation, but he had nothing but the dusty road under his feet. He was free from the old quarter that once gave him shelter, but a slave to the rains of summer and the frosts of winter. He was, in a word, literally turned loose, naked, hungry, and destitute, to the open sky.

The first feeling toward him by the old master classes was full of bitterness and wrath. They resented his emancipation as an act of hostility toward them, and, since they could not punish the emancipator, they felt like punishing the object which that act had emancipated. Hence they drove him off the old plantation, and told him he was no longer wanted there. They not only hated him because he had been freed as a punishment to them, but because they felt that they had been robbed of his labor.

An element of greater bitterness still came into their hearts: the freedman had been the friend of the government, and many of his class had borne arms against

---

Life and Times of Frederick Douglass (Hartford, CT: Park Publishing Company, 1881), pp. 458–459.

them during the war. The thought of paying cash for labor that they could formerly extort by the lash did not in any wise improve their disposition to the emancipated slave, or improve his own condition.

Now, since poverty has, and can have, no chance against wealth, the landless against the landowner, the ignorant against the intelligent, the freedman was powerless. He had nothing left him but a slavery-distorted and diseased body, and lame and twisted limbs, with which to fight the battle of life.

Thought Provokers

1. Was the white South ever really defeated in spirit? Would the results have been more satisfactory from its point of view if it had accepted the rule of the conqueror with better grace?
2. What were the major differences between presidential and congressional Reconstruction plans? What accounts for those different approaches? Who had the better constitutional arguments? Who advocated the soundest policies?
3. It has been said that Johnson was his own worst enemy and that the white Southerners were damaged by his determination to befriend them with a "soft" policy. Comment critically.
4. Present the cases for and against *immediate* and *gradual* black suffrage. Form conclusions. Why have the excesses of the black-white legislatures been overplayed and their achievements downgraded?
5. Why did organizations like the Ku Klux Klan flourish in the Reconstruction South? In what ways did the KKK resemble a modern "terrorist" group?
6. Identify the most serious long-run mistake or lost opportunity made during Reconstruction. What have been its effects?

23

Political Paralysis in the Gilded Age, 1869–1896

> The lessons of paternalism ought to be unlearned and the better lesson taught that while the people should patriotically and cheerfully support their government, its functions do not include the support of the people.
>
> *Grover Cleveland*, Inaugural Address, *1893*

Prologue: War hero Ulysses S. Grant came to the White House in 1869, when corruption abounded at many levels of government. A great general, the politically infantile Grant proved to be a great disappointment as president. Disaffected Republicans, unable to stomach Grant for a second term, organized the Liberal Republican party in 1872 and, together with the Democrats, chose the outspoken—and outrageous—Horace Greeley as their presidential standard-bearer. Greeley went down to inglorious defeat. Politics at the national level turned into a petty and highly partisan stalemate, as the delicately balanced major parties hesitated to upset the shaky electoral standoff by emphasizing controversial issues. Rutherford B. Hayes narrowly triumphed over Democrat Samuel Tilden in 1877. As part of the arrangements that eventually secured his election, Hayes effectively ended Reconstruction in the South. With the withdrawal of federal troops from the South following Hayes's election, a regime of strict segregation relegated African Americans to second-class status. Meanwhile, mounting economic distress nurtured a rising protest movement in the agricultural regions of the South and the Midwest. In the gutter-low presidential contest of 1884, Grover Cleveland emerged triumphant. Cleveland, the first Democratic president since 1861, displayed a fierce commitment to fiscal orthodoxy and to lowering sky-high Republican-passed tariffs. Meanwhile, thanks in part to inflowing foreign investment, the American economy was maturing into an industrial behemoth whose products entered increasingly into the stream of global commerce.

A. Race Divides the South

1. A Southern Senator Defends Jim Crow (1900)[*]

Following Rutherford B. Hayes's election, the last federal troops were withdrawn from the South, and Reconstruction effectively ended. The white South proceeded rapidly

---

[*]*Congressional Record*, March 29, 1900, February 24, 1903.

to roll back the political, economic, and social gains that the freedmen had achieved with federal help in the Reconstruction Era. In the following speech, a notorious racist, South Carolina senator "Pitchfork Ben" Tillman, unabashedly defends the disfranchisement of African Americans and mocks the philanthropic educational work of Northern whites in the South. On what premises about Africans and African Americans does his defense rest? What is his attitude toward the institution of slavery itself?

The slaves of the South were a superior set of men and women to freedmen of today, and…the poison in their minds—the race hatred of the whites—is the result of the teachings of Northern fanatics. Ravishing a woman, white or black, was never known to occur in the South till after the Reconstruction era. So much for that phase of the subject....

As white men we are not sorry…for anything we have done....We took the government away from [the carpetbag Negro government] in 1876. We did take it. If no other Senator has come here previous to this time who would acknowledge it, more is the pity. We have had no fraud in our elections in South Carolina since 1884. There has been no organized Republican party in the State.

We did not disfranchise the Negroes until 1895. Then we had a constitutional convention convened which took the matter up calmly, deliberately, and avowedly with the purpose of disfranchising as many of them as we could under the Fourteenth and Fifteenth Amendments. We adopted the educational qualification as the only means left to us, and the Negro is as contented and as prosperous and as well protected in South Carolina to-day as in any State of the Union south of the Potomac. He is not meddling with politics, for he found that the more he meddled with them the worse off he got. As to his "rights"—I will not discuss them now. We of the South have never recognized the right of the Negro to govern white men, and we never will. We have never believed him to be equal to the white man, and we will not submit to his gratifying his lust on our wives and daughters without lynching him. I would to God the last one of them was in Africa, and that none of them had ever been brought to our shores....

Some people have been ready to believe and to contend that the Negro is a white man with a black skin. All history disproves that. Go to Africa. What do you find there? From one hundred and fifty million to two hundred million savages.

I happened in my boyhood, when I was about 12 years old, to see some real Africans fresh from their native jungles. The last cargo of slaves imported into this country were brought here in 1858 on the yacht *Wanderer*, landed on an island below Savannah, and sneaked by the United States marshal up the Savannah River and landed a little distance below Augusta, and my family bought some thirty of them.

Therefore I had a chance to see just what kind of people these were, and to compare the African as he is to-day in Africa with the African who, after two centuries of slavery, was brought side by side to be judged. The difference was as "Hyperion to a satyr." Those poor wretches, half starved as they had been on their voyage across the Atlantic, shut down and battened under the hatches and fed a little rice, several hundred of them, were the most miserable lot of human beings—the nearest to the missing link with the monkey—I have ever put my eyes on....

Then if God in His providence ordained slavery and had these people transported over here for the purpose of civilizing enough of them to form a nucleus and to become missionaries back to their native heath, that is a question.... But the thing I want to call your attention to is that slavery was not an unmitigated evil for the Negro, because whatever of progress the colored race has shown itself capable of achieving has come from slavery; and whether among those four million there were not more good men and women than could be found among the nine million now is to my mind a question. I would not like to assert it; but I am strongly of that belief from the facts I know in regard to the demoralization that has come to those people down there by having liberty thrust upon them in the way it was, and then having the ballot and the burdens of government, and being subjected to the strain of being tempted and misled and duped and used as tools by designing white men who went there among them....

All of the millions that are being sent there by Northern philanthropy has been but to create an antagonism between the poorer classes of our citizens and these people upon whose level they are in the labor market. There has been no contribution to elevate the white people in the South, to aid and assist the Anglo-Saxon Americans, the men who are descended from the people who fought with Marion and Sumter.* They are followed to struggle in poverty and in ignorance, and to do everything they can to get along, and they see Northern people pouring in thousands and thousands to help build up an African domination.

2. A Spokesman for the "New South" Describes Race Relations in the 1880s (1889)[†]

Henry W. Grady, editor of the Atlanta Constitution, *championed the cause of the "New South"—a South that would emulate its Northern neighbors by industrializing and modernizing its economy. Grady and other New South advocates knew that they needed the goodwill, the markets, and the capital of the North if they were to succeed. Overshadowing Northern attitudes toward the region was the question of race relations in the decades after slavery's end. In the following speech delivered in Boston in 1889, how does Grady describe the condition of the recently emancipated African Americans? Why did the North generally prove willing to believe him and to acquiesce in discrimination against blacks?*

I thank God as heartily as you do that human slavery is gone forever from the American soil.

But the freedman remains. With him a problem without precedent or parallel. Note its appalling conditions. Two utterly dissimilar races on the same soil; with equal political and civil rights, almost equal in numbers but terribly unequal in intelligence and responsibility; each pledged against fusion, one for a century in servitude to the other and freed at last by a desolating war; the experiment sought by

---

*Francis Marion and Thomas Sumter were American military heroes in the South during the American War of Independence.
†Edwin DuBois Shurter, ed., *The Complete Orations of Henry W. Grady* (New York: 1910), pp. 192–220.

neither, but approached by both with doubt—these are the conditions. Under these, adverse at every point, we are required to carry these two races in peace and honor to the end. Never, sir, has such a task been given to mortal stewardship. Never before in this republic has the white race divided on the rights of an alien race. The red man was cut down as a weed because he hindered the way of the American citizen. The yellow man was shut out of this republic because he is an alien and inferior. The red man was owner of the land, the yellow man highly civilized and assimilable—but they hindered both sections and are gone!

But the black man, affecting but one section, is clothed with every privilege of government and pinned to the soil, and my people commanded to make good at any hazard and at any cost, his full and equal heirship of American privilege and prosperity....It matters not that no two races, however similar, have lived any-where, at any time, on the same soil with equal rights in peace. In spite of these things we are commanded to make good this change of American policy which has not perhaps changed American prejudice; to make certain here what has elsewhere been impossible between whites and blacks; and to reverse, under the very worst conditions, the universal verdict of racial history. And driven, sir, to this superhuman task with an impatience that brooks no delay, a rigor that accepts no excuse, and a suspicion that discourages frankness and sincerity....

We give to the world this year a crop of 7,500,000 bales of cotton, worth $45 million, and its cash equivalent in grain, grasses, and fruit. This enormous crop could not have come from the hands of sullen and discontented labor. It comes from peaceful fields, in which laughter and gossip rise above the hum of industry and contentment runs with the singing plow....

For every Afro-American agitator, stirring the strife in which alone he prospers, I can show you a thousand Negroes, happy in their cabin homes, tilling their own land by day, and at night taking from the lips of their children the helpful message their state sends them from the schoolhouse door.

And the schoolhouse itself bears testimony. In Georgia we added last year $250,000 to the school fund, making a total of more than $1 million—and this in the face of prejudice not yet conquered—of the fact that the whites are assessed for $368 million, the blacks for $10 million, and yet 49 percent of their beneficiaries are black children...

What is the testimony of the courts? In penal legislation we have steadily reduced felonies to misdemeanors, and have led the world in mitigating punishment for crime that we might save, as far as possible, this dependent race from its own weakness....In the North, one Negro in every 466 is in jail; in the South only one in 1,865....If prejudice wrongs him in Southern courts, the record shows it to be deeper in Northern courts....

Now, Mr. President, can it be seriously maintained that we are terrorizing the people from whose willing hands come every year $1 billion of farm crops? Or have robbed a people, who twenty-five years from unrewarded slavery have amassed in one state $20 million of property?

Or that we intend to oppress the people we are arming every day? Or deceive them when we are educating them to the utmost limit of our ability? Or outlaw them when we work side by side with them? Or reenslave them under legal forms when for their benefit we have imprudently narrowed the limit of felonies and mitigated the severity of law?...

When will the black cast a free ballot? When ignorance anywhere is not dominated by the will of the intelligent; when the laborer anywhere casts a vote unhindered by his boss; when the vote of the poor anywhere is not influenced by the power of the rich; when the strong and the steadfast do not everywhere control the suffrage of the weak and shiftless—then and not till then will the ballot of the Negro be free....

Here is this vast ignorant and purchasable vote—clannish, credulous, impulsive, and passionate—tempting every art of the demagogue, but insensible to the appeal of the statesman....It must remain a faction, strong enough in every community to control on the slightest division of the whites. Under that division it becomes the prey of the cunning and unscrupulous of both parties....

It is against such campaigns as this—the folly and the bitterness and the danger of which every Southern community has drunk deeply—that the white people of the South are banded together. Just as you in Massachusetts would be banded if 300,000 black men—not one in a hundred able to read his ballot—banded in a race instinct, holding against you the memory of a century of slavery, taught by your late conquerors to distrust and oppose you, had already travestied legislation from your statehouse, and in every species of folly or villainy had wasted your substance and exhausted your credit.

3. An African American Minister Answers Henry Grady (1890)*

The Reverend Joshua A. Brockett, pastor of St. Paul's African Methodist Episcopal Church in Cambridge, Massachusetts, was deeply offended by Grady's description of life in the South and made this reply in January 1890. To which of Grady's arguments is his response most vigorous? Why do those particular issues bother him? What are his most telling rebuttals?

Henry W. Grady, of Atlanta, Ga., delivered an address before the Boston Merchants' Association at their annual banquet, on Thursday evening, December 13, 1889....In that address, beneath the glamor of eloquence, the old rebel spirit, and the old South is seen throughout. In every expression of every line in which the Negro is mentioned the old spirit of Negro hatred is manifest....

The gentleman asks the question when will the black cast a free ballot? His reply is, when ignorance anywhere is not dominated by the will of the intelligent; when the laborer casts his vote unhindered by his boss; when the strong and steadfast do not everywhere control the suffrage of the weak and shiftless. Then and not till then will the Negro be free. He also says that the Negro vote can never again control in the South. He asks of the North, "Can we solve this question?" and answers, "God knows."

Consistency, thou art a jewel! It is declared that the Negro is peaceful and industrious on the one hand, weak and shiftless on the other. If he is peaceful

---

Philadelphia Christian Recorder, January 16, 1890.

surely the South has small need to fear an uprising. Politics, then, is the only source whence danger can come to the whites. If the black vote is never to control again, why should Mr. Grady state that the condition of the people is fraught with danger from the presence of a shiftless people? Whence the need of that wail for sympathy, if, as Mr. Grady says, the colored man must down, and the white partisan might as well understand it? If the colored man is never to rise, why waste so much eloquence upon a useless subject? The problem is already solved.

Mr. Grady asserts that nearly one-half of the school fund is used to educate the Negro. If the South is leagued together to maintain itself against this beleaguering black host, why educate it?

Has Mr. Grady to learn that education and power are inseparable? I will give Mr. Grady fair warning if they continue to give one-half or thereabouts to the school fund to educate a black man, then he will rise against the greatest odds that the South can oppose; not God alone, but even I know when the black man will be free.

Mr. Grady says that the Negro has not a basis upon which to rest his political conviction, and that of 300,000 voters, not 1 in 100 can read his ballot. That is a splendid compliment to the educational system which costs the South so dear. Either the South is amazingly stupid to pay so dearly for such meager results, or the Negro is incapable of learning, or the money is not paid.

Mr. Grady states that the Negro, by every species of villainy and folly, has wasted his substance and exhausted his credit. By the side of that statement I will place another of Mr. Grady's statements, namely, that from the Negroes' willing hands comes $1 billion of farm crops. If the latter statement is true, then the character of the Negro in the former statement has been falsified. Does Mr. Grady desire to make a strong case against this villainous race at the expense of the truth? And if the former statement is true, that the Negro is villainously wasteful, the $1 billion crops are but a creation of fancy, and the Northern sons with their modest patrimony would do well to remain standing in their doors, or turn their gaze in any direction but southward.

Again, with childlike innocence, Mr. Grady asks, can it be seriously maintained that we are terrorizing the people from whose willing hands comes every year $1 billion in crops? Or that we have robbed a people who, twenty-five years from unrewarded slavery, have amassed in one state $20 million worth of property?

In Georgia, Mr. Grady's own state, the Negro's real wealth accumulated since the war, is $20 million. Its population of Negroes is 725,132. Twenty millions of dollars divided among that number will give to each person $27.58. Upon the same basis of calculation the total wealth of the Negro in the 15 Southern states, including the District of Columbia, is $146,189,834. The colored population of these states is 5,305,149. It seems an enormous sum. In those 15 states the Negro has, by the exceedingly friendly aid of their best friends, amassed a fortune of $1 a year.

Should they not, because of this rapid accumulation of wealth, balance their little account, clutch to the mule, jog down the furrow, and let the world wag on?

Look now for a moment at those billion-dollar yearly crops accumulating for 27 years, giving us the almost inconceivable sum of $27 billion, which, divided between a number of whites equal to that of blacks, each one would from this $27 billion, receive $5,089.39. Thus the blacks receive for their willing toil through

27 years $27.58, while the whites receive $5,089.39. These are both sides of the Grady picture of Negro wealth which was intended to deceive the North. Gaze upon it.

4. Booker T. Washington Accommodates to Segregation (1895)*

Noted black leader Booker T. Washington saw little hope for progress in the bitter debate over suffrage and racial equality. In a landmark address before a predominantly white Atlanta audience, Washington urged Southerners of both races to set aside their deep-seated resentments and forge ties across the color line through economic cooperation. Appealing to the sentiments of Southern whites while upholding the dignity of his race was a daunting task, one he approached "as a man... on his way to the gallows." What elements of Washington's message would white Southerners have found most attractive? How might African Americans have reacted to his advice?

[Atlanta, Ga., Sept. 18, 1895]

Mr. President and Gentlemen of the Board of Directors and Citizens: One-third of the population of the South is of the Negro race. No enterprise seeking the material, civil, or moral welfare of this section can disregard this element of our population and reach the highest success....

A ship lost at sea for many days suddenly sighted a friendly vessel. From the mast of the unfortunate vessel was seen a signal, "Water, water; we die of thirst!" The answer from the friendly vessel at once came back, "Cast down your bucket where you are." A second time the signal, "Water, water; send us water!" ran up from the distressed vessel, and was answered, "Cast down your bucket where you are." And a third and fourth signal for water was answered, "Cast down your bucket where you are." The captain of the distressed vessel, at last heeding the injunction, cast down his bucket, and it came up full of fresh, sparkling water from the mouth of the Amazon River. To those of my race who depend on bettering their condition in a foreign land or who underestimate the importance of cultivating friendly relations with the Southern white man, who is their next-door neighbour, I would say: "Cast down your bucket where you are"—cast it down in making friends in every manly way of the people of all races by whom we are surrounded.

Cast it down in agriculture, mechanics, in commerce, in domestic service, and in the professions. And in this connection it is well to bear in mind that whatever other sins the South may be called to bear, when it comes to business, pure and simple, it is in the South that the Negro is given a man's chance in the commercial world, and in nothing is this Exposition more eloquent than in emphasizing this chance. Our greatest danger is that in the great leap from slavery to freedom we may overlook the fact that the masses of us are to live by the productions of our hands, and fail to keep in mind that we shall prosper in proportion as we learn to dignify and glorify common labour, and put brains and skill into the common

*Louis R. Harlan, ed., *The Booker T. Washington Papers* (Urbana: University of Illinois Press, 1975), vol. 3, pp. 583–587.

occupations of life; shall prosper in proportion as we learn to draw the line between the superficial and the substantial, the ornamental gewgaws of life and the useful. No race can prosper till it learns that there is as much dignity in tilling a field as in writing a poem. It is at the bottom of life we must begin, and not at the top. Nor should we permit our grievances to overshadow our opportunities.

To those of the white race who look to the incoming of those of foreign birth and strange tongue and habits for the prosperity of the South, were I permitted I would repeat what I say to my own race, "Cast down your bucket where you are." Cast it down among the eight millions of Negroes whose habits you know, whose fidelity and love you have tested in days when to have proved treacherous meant the ruin of your firesides. Cast down your bucket among these people who have, without strikes and labour wars, tilled your fields, cleared your forests, builded your railroads and cities, and brought forth treasures from the bowels of the earth, and helped make possible this magnificent representation of the progress of the South. Casting down your bucket among my people, helping and encouraging them as you are doing on these grounds, and to education of head, hand, and heart, you will find that they will buy your surplus land, make blossom the waste places in your fields, and run your factories. While doing this, you can be sure in the future, as in the past, that you and your families will be surrounded by the most patient, faithful, law-abiding, and unresentful people that the world has seen. As we have proved our loyalty to you in the past, in nursing your children, watching by the sick-bed of your mothers and fathers, and often following them with tear-dimmed eyes to their graves, so in the future, in our humble way, we shall stand by you with a devotion that no foreigner can approach, ready to lay down our lives, if need be, in defense of yours, interlacing our industrial, commercial, civil, and religious life with yours in a way that shall make the interests of both races one. In all things that are purely social we can be as separate as the fingers, yet one as the hand in all things essential to mutual progress....

We shall constitute one-third and more of the ignorance and crime of the South, or one-third its intelligence and progress; we shall contribute one-third to the business and industrial prosperity of the South, or we shall prove a veritable body of death, stagnating, depressing, retarding every effort to advance the body politic....

The wisest among my race understand that the agitation of questions of social equality is the extremest folly, and that progress in the enjoyment of all the privileges that will come to us must be the result of severe and constant struggle rather than of artificial forcing. No race that has anything to contribute to the markets of the world is long in any degree ostracized. It is important and right that all privileges of the law be ours, but it is vastly more important that we be prepared for the exercise of these privileges. The opportunity to earn a dollar in a factory just now is worth infinitely more than the opportunity to spend a dollar in an opera-house....

...I pledge that in your effort to work out the great and intricate problem which God has laid at the doors of the South, you shall have at all times the patient, sympathetic help of my race; only let this be constantly in mind, that, while from representations in these buildings of the product of field, of forest, of mine, of factory, letters, and art, much good will come, yet far above and beyond material benefits will be that higher good, that, let us pray God, will come, in a blotting out of sectional differences and racial animosities and suspicions, in a determination to administer absolute justice, in a willing obedience among all classes to the mandates of law. This, coupled with our material prosperity, will bring into our beloved South a new heaven and a new earth.

5. A Southern Black Woman Reflects on the Jim Crow System (1902)*

Political disfranchisement and economic impoverishment were not the only penalties endured by Southern blacks after Reconstruction ended. Blacks felt the stigma of discrimination and restriction in all aspects of social life. How did "Jim Crow" affect the life of this Southern black woman? How—or why—did she put up with the conditions she describes?

I am a colored woman, wife and mother. I have lived all my life in the South, and have often thought what a peculiar fact it is that the more ignorant the Southern whites are of us the more vehement they are in their denunciation of us. They boast that they have little intercourse with us, never see us in our homes, churches or places of amusement, but still they know us thoroughly.

They also admit that they know us in no capacity except as servants, yet they say we are at our best in that single capacity. What philosophers they are! The Southerners say we Negroes are a happy, laughing set of people, with no thought of tomorrow. How mistaken they are! The educated, thinking Negro is just the opposite. There is a feeling of unrest, insecurity, almost panic among the best class of Negroes in the South. In our homes, in our churches, wherever two or three are gathered together, there is a discussion of what is best to do. Must we remain in the South or go elsewhere? Where can we go to feel that security which other people feel? Is it best to go in great numbers or only in several families? These and many other things are discussed over and over....

I know of houses occupied by poor Negroes in which a respectable farmer would not keep his cattle. It is impossible for them to rent elsewhere. All Southern real estate agents have "white property" and "colored property." In one of the largest Southern cities there is a colored minister, a graduate of Harvard, whose wife is an educated, Christian woman, who lived for weeks in a tumble-down rookery because he could neither rent nor buy in a respectable locality.

Many colored women who wash, iron, scrub, cook or sew all the week to help pay the rent for these miserable hovels and help fill the many small mouths, would deny themselves some of the necessaries of life if they could take their little children and teething babies on the cars to the parks of a Sunday afternoon and sit under trees, enjoy the cool breezes and breathe God's pure air for only two or three hours; but this is denied them. Some of the parks have signs, "No Negroes allowed on these grounds except as servants." Pitiful, pitiful customs and laws that make war on women and babes! There is no wonder that we die; the wonder is that we persist in living.

Fourteen years ago I had just married. My husband had saved sufficient money to buy a small home. On account of our limited means we went to the suburbs, on

---

*"The Negro Problem: How It Appears to a Southern Colored Woman," *The Independent* 54 (September 18, 1902).

unpaved streets, to look for a home, only asking for a high, healthy locality. Some real estate agents were "sorry, but had nothing to suit," some had "just the thing," but we discovered on investigation that they had "just the thing" for an unhealthy pigsty. Others had no "colored property." One agent said that he had what we wanted, but we should have to go to see the lot after dark, or walk by and give the place a casual look; for, he said, "all the white people in the neighborhood would be down on me." Finally, we bought this lot. When the house was being built we went to see it. Consternation reigned. We had ruined his neighborhood of poor people; poor as we, poorer in manners at least. The people who lived next door received the sympathy of their friends. When we walked on the street (there were no sidewalks) we were embarrassed by the stare of many unfriendly eyes.

Two years passed before a single woman spoke to me, and only then because I helped one of them when a little sudden trouble came to her. Such was the reception, I a happy young woman, just married, received from people among whom I wanted to make a home. Fourteen years have now passed, four children have been born to us, and one has died in this same home, among these same neighbors. Although the neighbors speak to us, and occasionally one will send a child to borrow the morning's paper or ask the loan of a pattern, not one woman has ever been inside of my house, not even at the times when a woman would doubly appreciate the slightest attention of a neighbor. . . .

A colored woman, however respectable, is lower than the white prostitute. The Southern white woman will declare that no Negro women are virtuous, yet she placed her innocent children in their care. . . .

White agents and other chance visitors who come into our homes ask questions that we must not dare ask their wives. They express surprise that our children have clean faces and that their hair is combed. . . .

We were delighted to know that some of our Spanish-American heroes were coming where we could get a glimpse of them. Had not black men helped in a small way to give them their honors? In the cities of the South, where these heroes went, the white school children were assembled, flags waved, flowers strewn, speeches made, and "My Country, 'tis of Thee, Sweet Land of Liberty," was sung. Our children who need to be taught so much, were not assembled, their hands waved no flags, they threw no flowers, heard no thrilling speech, sang no song of their country. And this is the South's idea of justice. Is it surprising that feeling grows more bitter, when the white mother teaches her boy to hate my boy, not because he is mean, but because his skin is dark? I have seen very small white children hang their black dolls. It is not the child's fault, he is simply an apt pupil.

B. The Populist Crusade in the South

1. Tom Watson Supports a Black-White Political Alliance (1892)*

Populism in the South seemed to offer the prospect of a political alliance of poor farmers, black as well as white, that would be strong enough to overthrow the conservative

---

*Thomas Watson, "The Negro Question in the South," *The Arena* 6 (October 1892): 540–550.

"Bourbon" regimes holding power in the Southern states. Some forward-looking Populist leaders, among them Georgia's Tom Watson, tried to overcome the racial differences that, they argued, irrationally overshadowed the common economic interests of black and white agrarians and that kept the Bourbons in control. On one occasion in 1892, Watson summoned dozens of armed white farmers to his home to protect a black colleague who had taken refuge from a lynch mob. Only a few years later, when the Populist dream of an interracial political alliance had died, Watson reversed his views and emerged as one of the South's premier racists. In the selection below, whom does Watson blame for the racial tensions of the postbellum South? What are the limits of his program for interracial cooperation?

The Negro Question in the South has been for nearly thirty years a source of danger, discord, and bloodshed. It is an ever-present irritant and menace.

Several millions of slaves were told that they were the prime cause of the civil war; that their emancipation was the result of the triumph of the North over the South; that the ballot was placed in their hands as a weapon of defence against their former masters; that the war-won political equality of the black man with the white must be asserted promptly and aggressively, under the leadership of adventurers who had swooped down upon the conquered section in the wake of the Union armies.

No one, who wishes to be fair, can fail to see that, in such a condition of things, strife between the freedman and his former owner was inevitable....

Quick to take advantage of this deplorable situation, the politicians have based the fortunes of the old parties upon it. Northern leaders have felt that at the cry of "Southern outrage" they could not only "fire the Northern heart," but also win a unanimous vote from the colored people. Southern politicians have felt that at the cry of "Negro domination" they could drive into solid phalanx every white man in all the Southern states.

Both the old parties have done this thing....You might beseech a Southern white tenant to listen to you upon questions of finance, taxation, and transportation; you might demonstrate with mathematical precision that herein lay his way out of poverty into comfort; you might have him "almost persuaded" to the truth, but if the merchant who furnished his farm supplies (at tremendous usury) or the town politician (who never spoke to him excepting at election times) came along and cried, "Negro rule!" the entire fabric of reason and common sense which you had patiently constructed would fall, and the poor tenant would joyously hug the chains of an actual wretchedness rather than do any experimenting on a question of mere sentiment.

...Let the South ask relief from Wall Street; let it plead for equal and just laws on finance; let it beg for mercy against crushing taxation, and Northern [Democrats]... would hint "Negro rule!" and the white farmer and laborer of the South had to choke down his grievance....

Reverse the statement, and we have the method by which the black man was managed by the Republicans.

Reminded constantly that the North had emancipated him; that the North had given him the ballot; that the North had upheld him in his citizenship; that the South was his enemy, and meant to deprive him of his suffrage and put him "back into slavery," it is no wonder he has played as nicely into the hands of the Republicans as his former owner has played into the hands of the Northern Democrats.

Now consider: here were two distinct races dwelling together, with political equality established between them by law. They lived in the same section; won their livelihood by the same pursuits; cultivated adjoining fields on the same terms; enjoyed together the bounties of a generous climate; suffered together the rigors of cruelly unjust laws; spoke the same language; bought and sold in the same markets; classified themselves into churches under the same denominational teachings; neither race antagonizing the other in any branch of industry; each absolutely dependent on the other in all the avenues of labor and employment; and yet, instead of being allies, as every dictate of reason and prudence and self-interest and justice said they should be, they were kept apart, in dangerous hostility, that the sordid aims of partisan politics might be served!...

That such a condition is most ominous to both sections and both races, is apparent to all.

If we were dealing with a few tribes of red men or a few sporadic Chinese, the question would be easily disposed of. The Anglo-Saxon would probably do just as he pleased, whether right or wrong, and the weaker man would go under.

But the Negroes number 8,000,000. They are interwoven with our business, political, and labor systems. They assimilate with our customs, our religion, our civilization. They meet us at every turn,—in the fields, the shops, the mines. They are a part of our system, and they are here to stay....

The People's Party will settle the race question. First, by enacting the Australian ballot system [the "secret" ballot, which protects the confidentiality of the voter's choice—so-called because it originated in Australia]. Second, by offering to white and black a rallying point which is free from the odium of former discords and strifes. Third, by presenting a platform immensely beneficial to both races and injurious to neither. Fourth, by making it to the *interest* of both races to act together for the success of the platform. Fifth, by making it to the *interest* of the colored man to have the same patriotic zeal for the welfare of the South that the whites possess....

The white tenant lives adjoining the colored tenant. Their houses are almost equally destitute of comforts. Their living is confined to bare necessities. They are equally burdened with heavy taxes. They pay the same high rent for gullied and impoverished land....

Now the People's Party says to these two men, "You are kept apart that you may be separately fleeced of your earnings. You are made to hate each other because upon that hatred is rested the keystone of the arch of financial despotism which enslaves you both. You are deceived and blinded that you may not see how this race antagonism perpetuates a monetary system which beggars both."

This is so obviously true it is no wonder both these unhappy laborers stop to listen. No wonder they begin to realize that no change of law can benefit the white tenant which does not benefit the black one likewise; that no system which now does injustice to one of them can fail to injure both. Their every material interest is identical. The moment this becomes a conviction, mere selfishness, the mere desire to better their conditions, escape onerous taxes, avoid usurious charges, lighten their rents, or change their precarious tenements into smiling, happy homes, will drive these two men together, just as their mutually inflamed prejudices now drive them apart....

The question of social equality does not enter into the calculation at all....

...They will become political allies, and neither can injure the other without weakening both. It will be to the interest of both that each should have justice. And on these broad lines of mutual interest, mutual forbearance, and mutual support the present will be made the stepping-stone to future peace and prosperity.

2. The Wilmington Massacre (1898)[*]

In 1894 white Populists and black Republicans in North Carolina formed a success-ful anti-Bourbon coalition and gained control of the state government. Four years later, conservative Bourbon Democrats overturned the Populist-Republican "fusion" government in a campaign marked by flagrant fraud and intimidation. The cli-max came in Wilmington, North Carolina, on November 11, 1898, when a mob murdered several African Americans and deposed by force the elected city admin-istration. The following eyewitness account describes the uprising in detail. In what ways does this account shed light on the death of the Populist dream of interracial political action? How does the speaker draw on the contemporary developments in the Spanish-American War to drive home his point?

Nine Negroes massacred outright; a score wounded and hunted like partridges on the mountain; one man, brave enough to fight against such odds would be hailed as a hero anywhere else, was given the privilege of running the gauntlet up a broad street, where he sank ankle deep in the sand, while crowds of men lined the sidewalks and riddled him with a pint of bullets as he ran bleeding past their doors; another Negro shot twenty times in the back as he scrambled empty handed over a fence; thousands of women and children fleeing in terror from their humble homes in the darkness of the night, out under a gray and angry sky, from which falls a cold and bone-chilling rain, out to the dark and tangled ooze of the swamp amid the crawling things of night, fearing to light a fire, startled at every footstep, cower-ing, shivering, shuddering, trembling, praying in gloom and terror: half-clad and barefooted mothers, with their babies wrapped only in a shawl, whimpering with cold and hunger at their icy breasts, crouched in terror from the vengeance of those who, in the name of civilization, and with the benediction of the ministers of the Prince of Peace, inaugurated the reformation of the city of Wilmington the day after the election by driving out one set of white office holders and filling their places with another set of white office holders—the one being Republican and the other Democrat....All this happened, not in Turkey, nor in Russia, nor in Spain, not in the gardens of Nero, nor in the dungeons of Torquemada, but within three hundred miles of the White House, in the best State in the South, within a year of the twen-tieth century, while the nation was on its knees thanking God for having enabled

---

[*]Charles S. Morris, speech to the Interdenominational Association of Colored Clergymen, Boston, January 1899. From the papers of Charles H. Williams, Wisconsin State Historical Society, Madison, Wisconsin.

it to break the Spanish yoke from the neck of Cuba. This is our civilization. This is Cuba's kindergarten of ethics and good government. This is Protestant religion in the United States, that is planning a wholesale missionary crusade against Catholic Cuba. This is the golden rule as interpreted by the white pulpit of Wilmington.

Over this drunken and blood-thirsty mob they stretch their hands and invoke the blessings of a just God. We have waited two hundred and fifty years for liberty, and this is what it is when it comes. O Liberty, what crimes are committed in thy name! A rent and bloody mantle of citizenship that has covered as with a garment of fire, wrapped in which as in a shroud, forty thousand of my people have fallen around Southern ballot boxes....A score of intelligent colored men, able to pass even a South Carolina election officer, shot down at Phoenix, South Carolina, for no reason whatever, except as the Charleston *News and Courier* said, because the baser elements of the community loved to kill and destroy. The pitiful privilege of dying like cattle in the red gutters of Wilmington, or crouching waist deep in the icy waters of neighboring swamps, where terrified women gave birth to a dozen infants, most of whom died of exposure and cold. This is Negro citizenship! This is what the nation fought for from Bull Run to Appomattox!

What caused all this bitterness, strife, arson, murder, revolution and anarchy at Wilmington? We hear the answer on all sides—"Negro domination." I deny the charge. It is utterly false, and no one knows it better than the men who use it to justify crimes that threaten the very foundation of republican government; crimes that make the South red with blood, white with bones and gray with ashes; crimes no other civilized government would tolerate for a single day. The colored people comprise one-third of the population of the State of North Carolina; in the Legislature there are one hundred and twenty representatives, seven of whom are colored. There are fifty senators, two of whom are colored—nine in all out of one hundred and seventy. Can nine Negroes dominate one hundred and sixty white men? That would be a fair sample of the tail wagging the dog. Not a colored man holds a state office in North Carolina; the whole race has less than five per cent of all the offices in the state. In the city of Wilmington the Mayor was white, six out of ten members of the board of aldermen, and sixteen out of twenty-six members of the police force were white; the city attorney was white, the city clerk was white, the city treasurer was white, the superintendent of streets was white, the superintendent of garbage was white, the superintendent of health was white, and all the nurses in the white wards were white; the superintendent of the public schools was white, the chief and assistant chief of the fire department, and three out of five fire companies were white; the school committee has always been composed of two white men and one colored; the board of audit and finance is composed of five members, four of whom were white, and the one Negro was reported to be worth more than any of his white associates. The tax rate under this miscalled Negro regime was less than under its predecessors; this is Negro domination in Wilmington. This is a fair sample of that Southern scarecrow—conjured by these masters of the black art everywhere....

The Good Samaritan did not leave his own eldest son robbed and bleeding at his own threshold, while he went way off down the road between Jerusalem and Jericho to hunt for a man that had fallen among thieves. Nor can America afford to go eight thousand miles from home to set up a republican government in the

Philippines while the blood of citizens whose ancestors came here before the May-flower, is crying out to God against her from the gutters of Wilmington.

C. The Spread of Segregation

1. The Supreme Court Declares That Separate Is Equal (1896)*

In the closing years of the nineteenth century, most Southern states passed Jim Crow laws mandating segregated public facilities for whites and blacks. Louisiana passed a statute in 1890 that provided for "equal but separate accommodations for the white and colored races" on railroads in the state and prohibited persons from occupying a railcar or waiting room other than one reserved for their race. Black Louisianans brought suit against this law as a way of challenging the spreading practice of segregation. Interestingly, the plaintiffs had some support from the railroads, which objected to the added costs entailed in providing separate cars. By a seven-to-one majority, however, the U.S. Supreme Court upheld the Louisiana statute in the case of Plessy v. Ferguson, *thus helping to cement the system of segregation into place until it was dismantled by the civil rights movement in the post–World War II period. (The lone dissenter was Justice John Harlan, a former slave owner whose views had changed dramatically after emancipation and the passage of the Thirteenth, Fourteenth, and Fifteenth Amendments to the Constitution. He wrote, "in the eye of the law, there is in this country no superior, dominant, ruling class of citizens. . . . Our Constitution is color-blind. . . . The law regards man as man, and takes no account of his surroundings or of his color when his civil rights as guaranteed by the supreme law of the land are involved.") In the following excerpt from the majority's opinion, what are the principal rationales offered for the Court's conclusions? In what ways did the opinion ultimately prove vulnerable? (It was reversed in 1954 in the case of* Brown v. Board of Education, *which held that separate educational facilities are inherently unequal.)*

By the Fourteenth Amendment, all persons born or naturalized in the United States, and subject to the jurisdiction thereof, are made citizens of the United States and of the State wherein they reside; and the States are forbidden from making or enforcing any law which shall abridge the privileges or immunities of citizens of the United States, or shall deprive any person of life, liberty or property without due process of law, or deny to any person within their jurisdiction the equal protection of the laws.

The proper construction of this amendment was first called to the attention of this court in the *Slaughter-house cases* [1873], which involved, however, not a question of race, but one of exclusive privileges. The case did not call for any expression of opinion as to the exact rights it was intended to secure to the colored race, but it was said generally that its main purpose was to establish the citizenship of the negro; to give definitions of citizenship of the United States and of the States, and

---

United States Reports (1896), vol. 163, p. 537.

to protect from the hostile legislation of the States the privileges and immunities of citizens of the United States, as distinguished from those of citizens of the States.

The object of the amendment was undoubtedly to enforce the absolute equality of the two races before the law, but in the nature of things it could not have been intended to abolish distinctions based upon color, or to enforce social, as distinguished from political equality, or a commingling of the two races upon terms unsatisfactory to either. Laws permitting, and even requiring, their separation in places where they are liable to be brought into contact do not necessarily imply the inferiority of either race to the other, and have been generally, if not universally, recognized as within the competency of the state legislatures in the exercise of their police power. The most common instance of this is connected with the establishment of separate schools for white and colored children, which has been held to be a valid exercise of the legislative power even by courts of States where the political rights of the colored race have been longest and most earnestly enforced....

So far, then, as a conflict with the Fourteenth Amendment is concerned, the case reduces itself to the question whether the statute of Louisiana is a reasonable regulation, and with respect to this there must necessarily be a large discretion on the part of the legislature. In determining the question of reasonableness it is at liberty to act with reference to the established usages, customs and traditions of the people, and with a view to the promotion of their comfort, and the preservation of the public peace and good order. Gauged by this standard, we cannot say that a law which authorizes or even requires the separation of the two races in public conveyances is unreasonable, or more obnoxious to the Fourteenth Amendment than the acts of Congress requiring separate schools for colored children in the District of Columbia, the constitutionality of which does not seem to have been questioned, or the corresponding acts of state legislatures.

We consider the underlying fallacy of the plaintiff's argument to consist in the assumption that the enforced separation of the two races stamps the colored race with a badge of inferiority. If this be so, it is not by reason of anything found in the act, but solely because the colored race chooses to put that construction upon it. The argument necessarily assumes that if, as has been more than once the case, and is not unlikely to be so again, the colored race should become the dominant power in the state legislature, and should enact a law in precisely similar terms, it would thereby relegate the white race to an inferior position. We imagine that the white race, at least, would not acquiesce in this assumption. The argument also assumes that social prejudices may be overcome by legislation, and that equal rights cannot be secured to the negro except by an enforced commingling of the two races. We cannot accept this proposition. If the two races are to meet upon terms of social equality, it must be the result of natural affinities, a mutual appreciation of each other's merits and a voluntary consent of individuals. As was said by the Court of Appeals of New York in *People* v. *Gallagher*, "this end can neither be accomplished nor promoted by laws which conflict with the general sentiment of the community upon whom they are designed to operate. When the government, therefore, has secured to each of its citizens equal rights before the law and equal opportunities for improvement and progress, it has accomplished the end for which it was organized and performed all of the functions respecting social advantages with which it is endowed." Legislation is powerless to eradicate racial instincts or to abolish distinctions based upon physical differences, and the attempt to do so can only result in accentuating the difficulties of the present situation. If the civil and political rights of both races be equal one cannot be inferior to the other civilly or politically. If one race be inferior to the other socially, the Constitution of the United States cannot put them upon the same plane.

2. A Justice of the Peace Denies Justice (1939)*

The Jim Crow system that emerged in the South at the end of the nineteenth century denied black Southerners the right to vote. For more than half a century, various tactics were employed to ensure that blacks could not exercise political power at the ballot box. In the selection that follows, a justice of the peace in North Carolina describes how he foiled black attempts to register to vote. What were his principal methods? How does he justify his actions?

In 1900 I was a Red Shirt;† that was what they called us, though we didn't actually wear red shirts as they did in some sections. But the legislature had fixed it so we could disfranchise the nigger, and we aimed to tote our part in gettin' it done. Judge Farmer organized the county; they was about thirty-five of us around here that called ourselves Red Shirts. Up to 1900 the niggers had rushed in to register whether or no, and with control of the vote they had put in nigger officeholders all over the county. They wa'n't but one white family in the county that could get a office under the nigger rule of the time, and that was Dr. Hughes's. Dr. Hughes was so good to all the pore folks, goin' when they sent for him and not chargin' 'em a cent, that they'd give him anything he asked for. When the registration book was opened in 1900, the Red Shirts was ordered to get their rifles and shotguns and protect the registration from the niggers. When the word come to me, I remember I was in the field plowin'. I got my gun and hurried out to where the rest of the Red Shirts was assembled with shotguns.

Word come that the federal authorities was comin' to protect the nigger vote; if they had, it would o' meant war. We wa'n't totin' shotguns just for show. Well, the upshot was not a nigger come nigh the registration book that day, from sunrise to sunset. Nigger rule was over!

Two years after, when I first took hold o' registerin' voters, a right smart o' niggers come to register at first, claimin' they could meet the requirements. Some wrote the Constitution, I reckon, as good as a lot o' white men, but I'd find somethin' unsatisfactory, maybe an *i* not dotted or a *t* not crossed, enough for me to disqualify 'em. The law said "satisfactory to the registrar." A few could get by the grandfather clause,‡ for they was some free niggers before the Civil War, but they couldn't get by an undotted *i* or a uncrossed *t*. They wa'n't no Republicans in the

---

*From *Such As Us: Southern Voices of the Thirties* edited by Tom E. Terrill and Jerrold Hirsch. Copyright © 1978 by the University of North Carolina Press.
†A vigilante group that intimidated blacks.
‡If a man's father or grandfather could have voted on January 1, 1867, he did not have to meet other voting requirements.

South before the Civil War; the free niggers always voted like their old masters told 'em to—and 'twa'n't Republican! That's what the war was fought over, politics; they didn't care so much about freein' the slaves as they did the Republican party....

Politics is the rottenest thing in the world. I ought to know, for I've been in it thirty years and over. Not meanin' to brag, I can say I've been honest and my hands is clean. I wouldn't twist a principle for no man. That's how come I got the influence I have in the county. The candidates come to me for advice and want me to get out and work for 'em, because they know I know practically everybody in the county—they ain't a man over forty I don't know—and can't nobody bring nothin' against my integrity. Not meanin' to brag now, my life counts much as my word; folks'll listen to a honest man. My methods ain't like some; I don't get out in the final heat of the campaign and hurrah and shout. By that time my work's all done. It's durin' the off season like this, when nobody's thinkin' politics much, that I do my workin', in a quiet homely way. I get votes pledged to my candidate— a man that won't stand by his pledge ain't worth his salt—and when the campaign gets hot I stay out'n the fight, knowin' the precincts is already lined up for my man.

D. The United States Emerges as an Industrial Giant

1. United States Balance of Trade and Share of World Exports (1870–1910)*

Fueled by rapid innovation, government incentives, and a seemingly endless supply of cheap labor, American industry flourished in the decades after the Civil War. By the 1890s, the United States had surpassed Great Britain in total industrial output. Though America's booming population hungrily consumed the vast majority of goods produced by the nation's farms and factories, increased exports and a shrinking demand for foreign manufactures tilted the U.S. balance of trade. The following table shows the development of U.S. trade between 1870 and 1910. What patterns emerge from the figures below?

	Total Exports (Millions $)	Total Imports (Millions $)	Balance of Trade (Millions $)	Exports as % GNP	U.S. as % of World Exports
1870	393	436	−43	4.7%	7.9%
1880	836	668	168	7.6%	13.2%
1890	858	789	69	6.4%	—
1900	1,394	850	544	7.5%	15.0%
1910	1,745	1,557	188	5.6%	12.3%

*From Stanley L. Engerman and Robert E. Gallman, eds., *Cambridge Economic History of the United States*, vol. 2, 2000, p. 688.

2. Composition of United States Exports (1869–1908)*

Though manufacturing accounted for a growing share of labor and GDP, the United States remained a leading agricultural exporter well into the twentieth century. The table that follows presents the composition of American exports in the decades after the Civil War. What categories of goods grew in importance as the century progressed?

	Raw Materials	Foods		Semi-Manufactures	Finished Manufactures
		Crude	Processed		
1869–1878	44%	15%	20%	5%	16%
1879–1888	34%	21%	25%	5%	15%
1889–1898	33%	17%	26%	7%	17%
1899–1908	29%	13%	22%	12%	25%

3. Destination of United States Exports (1869–1908)†

The following table lists the primary destinations of exports from the United States. Which regions imported the largest volume of American goods? How did the relative importance of European and Latin American markets shift in the late nineteenth and early twentieth centuries?

	Europe		Americas	
	Total Europe	UK	Total Americas	Canada
1869–1878	81%	54%	17%	6%
1879–1888	81%	52%	14%	5%
1889–1898	79%	48%	16%	6%
1899–1908	72%	36%	19%	8%

4. Distribution of Long-Term Foreign Investments in the United States (1803–1880)‡

Though foreign investment never accounted for more than 15 percent of the total stock of U.S. capital in the nineteenth century, key economic sectors benefited greatly from the infusion of funds from abroad. In particular, foreign investment in government-guaranteed bonds helped fuel state construction of canals and

---

*From Stanley L. Engerman and Robert E. Gallman, eds., *Cambridge Economic History of the United States,* vol. 2, 2000, p. 702.
†From Stanley L. Engerman and Robert E. Gallman, eds., *Cambridge Economic History of the United States,* vol. 2, 2000, p. 713.
‡From Stanley L. Engerman and Robert E. Gallman, eds., *Cambridge Economic History of the United States,* vol. 2, 2000, p. 742.

turnpikes during the midcentury transportation revolution. The following table shows the distribution of foreign capital by sector. What historical developments account for the trends in the figures below?

Years	Federal Government	State and Local Government	1st and 2nd U.S. and Other Banks	Turnpikes and Canals	Railroads
1803	72.1 %	0.0 %	22.5 %	0.3 %	0.0 %
1838[a]	0.0 %	3.0 %	41.2 %	25.5 %	15.2 %
1853	12.2 %	59.7 %	3.0 %	1.1 %	23.5 %
1856	6.2 %	55.0 %	2.8 %	1.0 %	34.4 %
1869	71.9 %	7.7 %	0.0 %	0.4 %	17.5 %
1880	19.9 %	7.8 %	0.0 %	0.0 %	72.0 %

[a]Government loans distributed on the basis of their announced purposes.

Thought Provokers

1. How might one explain the fact that Grant was a success as a general but an embarrassment as a president?
2. What might have been the consequences for whites and blacks in the South if the election of 1876 had gone to Tilden?
3. In the light of the conditions in the South in the late nineteenth century, could Reconstruction be considered a success or a failure? Why has this period been called the darkest hour in the history of African Americans?
4. What were the strengths and weaknesses of populism in the South? Did the Populist crusade advance or hinder the struggle of black Southerners for social justice?
5. How and why did legally sanctioned segregation emerge in the South? Why did the segregationist regime endure for so long?
6. How did American participation in the global economy evolve over the course of the nineteenth century? How do these patterns reflect shifts in the domestic economic structure of the United States?

24

Industry Comes of Age, 1865–1900

> That is the most perfect government in which an injury to one is the concern of all.
>
> *Motto of the Knights of Labor*

Prologue: Some railroad companies after 1865 had more employees than many state governments—and more power to inflict harm. When cutthroat competition failed to eliminate abuses, Congress finally passed the precedent-shattering Interstate Commerce Act of 1887. But this pioneer measure fell far short of providing adequate safeguards. Competing industries had meanwhile been merging as monopolistic trusts, notably Rockefeller's Standard Oil Company. Congress belatedly tried to restrain these monsters with the rather toothless Sherman Anti-Trust Act of 1890. The emerging "Titans of Industry"—notably Andrew Carnegie—also developed an articulate social and economic philosophy to justify the new social order they were helping to create. The new industrial regime transformed the lives of working Americans and stimulated the trade union movement. The Knights of Labor, who in the 1870s and 1880s made the most successful attempt until then to organize the nation's army of toilers, amassed considerable numerical strength. But they overreached themselves in the 1880s, and the wage-conscious American Federation of Labor, with its component skilled unions, forged to the front. Advancing industrialization, meanwhile, inflicted incalculable damage on the environment—and on the humans who inhabited it.

A. The Problem of the Railroads

1. Railroad President Sidney Dillon Supports Stock Watering (1891)*

Critics of the railroads especially condemned "stock watering"—the practice of issuing stocks and bonds grossly in excess of the value of the property. The more the stock was watered, the higher the freight and passenger rates would have to be to ensure a normal return on the investment. Sidney Dillon, a later president of the Union Pacific Railroad, stoutly defended stock watering. Beginning his career at the age of seven as a water boy—appropriately enough—on a New York railway, he ultimately amassed a fortune by building railroads, including the Union Pacific. Present at the "wedding of the rails" in Utah in 1869, marking completion of the transcontinental

---

*Sidney Dillon, "The West and the Railroads," *North American Review* 152 (April 1891): 445–448, passim.

railroad, he retained one of the final silver spikes until his death. Here he attacks regulatory legislation in an article for a popular magazine. What is his social philosophy? Why does he place his faith in competition and the courts?

Statutory enactments interfere with the business of the railway, even to the minutest details, and always to its detriment. This sort of legislation proceeds on the theory that the railroad is a public enemy; that it has its origin in the selfish desire of a company of men to make money out of the public; that it will destroy the public unless it is kept within bounds; and that it is impossible to enact too many laws tending to restrain the monster. The advocates of these statutes may not state their theory in these exact words. But these words certainly embody their theory, if they have any theory at all beyond such prejudices as are born of the marriage between ignorance and demagogism.

Many of the grievances that are urged against railways are too puerile to be seriously noticed, but the reader will pardon a few words as to "overcapitalization."...

Now, it is impossible to estimate in advance the productive power of this useful and untiring servant. Sometimes a railway is capitalized too largely, and then it pays smaller dividends; sometimes not largely enough, and then the dividends are much in excess of the usual interest of money. In the former case stockholders are willing to reduce the face of their shares, or wait until increase of population increases revenue; in the latter they accept an enlarged issue. But, as a matter of reason and principle, the question of capitalization concerns the stockholders, and the stockholders only. A citizen, simply as a citizen, commits an impertinence when he questions the right of any corporation to capitalize its properties at any sum whatever....

Then as to prices, these will always be taken care of by the great law of competition, which obtains wherever any human service is to be performed for a pecuniary consideration. That any railway, anywhere in a republic, should be a monopoly is not a supposable case. If between two points, A and B, a railway is constructed, and its charges for fares and freight are burdensome to the public and unduly profitable to itself, it will not be a long time before another railway will be laid between these points, and then competition may be safely trusted to reduce prices. We may state it as an axiom that no common carrier can ever maintain burdensome and oppressive rates of service permanently or for a long period....

Given a company of men pursuing a lawful and useful occupation,—why interfere with them? Why empower a body of other men, fortuitously assembled, not possessing superior knowledge, and accessible often to unworthy influences, to dictate to these citizens how they shall manage their private affairs? Wherever such management conflicts with public policy or private rights, there are district attorneys and competent lawyers and upright courts to take care that the commonwealth or the citizen shall receive no detriment.

2. General James B. Weaver Deplores Stock Watering (1892)*

General James B. Weaver, a walrus-mustached veteran of the Civil War, had early experienced extortion when he had to borrow $100 at 33 1/3 percent interest to finish law school. Fiery orator and relentless foe of the railroads and other "predatory"

*J. B. Weaver, *A Call to Action* (Des Moines: Iowa Printing Company, 1892), pp. 412–413.

corporations, he won the presidential nomination of the People's party (Populists) in 1892 (see p. 485). His book A Call to Action, *published during the campaign, condemned stock waterers. To what extent does the following excerpt cast doubts on the testimony of railroad president Dillon, whose article, presented in the previous selection, he sharply attacks? What is Weaver's view of the citizens' "impertinence"?*

In their delirium of greed the managers of our transportation systems disregard both private right and the public welfare. Today they will combine and bankrupt their weak rivals, and by the expenditure of a trifling sum possess themselves of properties which cost the outlay of millions. Tomorrow they will capitalize their booty for five times the cost, issue their bonds, and proceed to levy tariffs upon the people to pay dividends upon the fraud.

Take for example the Kansas Midland. It cost $10,200 per mile. It is capitalized at $53,024 per mile. How are the plain plodding people to defend themselves against such flagrant injustice?

Mr. Sidney Dillon, president of the Union Pacific,...is many times a millionaire, and the road over which he presides was built wholly by public funds and by appropriations of the public domain. The road never cost Mr. Dillon nor his associates a single penny. It is now capitalized at $106,000 per mile! This company owes the government $50,000,000 with accruing interest which is destined to accumulate for many years. The public lien exceeds the entire cost of the road, and yet this government, which Mr. Dillon defies, meekly holds a second mortgage to secure its claim....

It is pretty clear that it would not be safe for the public to take the advice of either Mr. Dillon or Mr. Gould [a railroad promoter] as to the best method of dealing with the transportation problem.

[Responding to a mounting public outcry, in 1887 Congress passed the Interstate Commerce Act, the first regulatory legislation of its kind in U.S. history. Among various reforms, it forbade unreasonable or unjust rates, discriminatory rates or practices, the payment of rebates, the pooling of profits among competing lines, and a higher charge for a short haul than for a long haul. In practice, however, the law proved to be riddled with loopholes, and subsequent legislation was required to provide adequate safeguards.]

B. The Trust and Monopoly

1. John D. Rockefeller Justifies Rebates (1909)*

John D. Rockefeller, who amassed a fortune of nearly $1 billion dollars, lived to give away more than half of his "oil-gotten gains" in philanthropy. A prominent lay Baptist, he yearly donated one-tenth of his income to charities and, in 1859, helped

*J. D. Rockefeller, *Random Reminiscences of Men and Events* (1909), pp. 107–109, 111–112. Copyright 1909, Doubleday & Company, Inc.

a Cincinnati black man to buy his slave wife. As a founding father of the mighty Standard Oil Company, he here puts the best possible face on railroad rebates, which were finally banned by the Interstate Commerce Act. He tactfully neglects to add that at one time his company also extorted secret payments ("drawbacks") from the railways on shipments by his competitors. What were the advantages to the railroads of the rebate system? To what extent did they, rather than Standard Oil, profit from these under-the-counter deals?

Of all the subjects that seem to have attracted the attention of the public to the affairs of the Standard Oil Company, the matter of rebates from railroads has perhaps been uppermost. The Standard Oil Company of Ohio, of which I was president, did receive rebates from the railroads prior to 1880, but received no advantages for which it did not give full compensation.

The reason for rebates was that such was the railroads' method of business. A public rate was made and collected by the railroad companies, but, so far as my knowledge extends, was seldom retained in full; a portion of it was repaid to the shippers as a rebate.

By this method the real rate of freight which any shipper paid was not known by his competitors nor by other railroad companies, the amount being a matter of bargain with the carrying company. Each shipper made the best bargain that he could, but whether he was doing better than his competitor was only a matter of conjecture. Much depended upon whether the shipper had the advantage of competition of carriers.

The Standard Oil Company of Ohio, being situated at Cleveland, had the advantage of different carrying lines, as well as of water transportation in the summer. Taking advantage of those facilities, it made the best bargains possible for its freights. Other companies sought to do the same.

The Standard gave advantages to the railroads for the purpose of reducing the cost of transportation of freight. It offered freights in large quantity, carloads and trainloads. It furnished loading facilities and discharging facilities at great cost. It provided regular traffic, so that a railroad could conduct its transportation to the best advantage and use its equipment to the full extent of its hauling capacity without waiting for the refiner's convenience. It exempted railroads from liability for fire and carried its own insurance. It provided at its own expense terminal facilities which permitted economies in handling. For these services it obtained contracts for special allowances on freights. But notwithstanding these special allowances, this traffic from the Standard Oil Company was far more profitable to the railroad companies than the smaller and irregular traffic, which might have paid a higher rate.

To understand the situation which affected the giving and taking of rebates, it must be remembered that the railroads were all eager to enlarge their freight traffic. They were competing with the facilities and rates offered by the boats on lake and canal and by the pipe lines. All these means of transporting oil cut into the business of the railroads, and they were desperately anxious to successfully meet this competition....

The profits of the Standard Oil Company did not come from advantages given by railroads. The railroads, rather, were the ones who profited by the traffic of the

Standard Oil Company, and whatever advantage it received in its constant efforts to reduce rates of freight was only one of the many elements of lessening cost to the consumer which enabled us to increase our volume of business the world over because we could reduce the selling price.

How general was the complicated bargaining for rates can hardly be imagined; everyone got the best rate that he could. After the passage of the Interstate Commerce Act, it was learned that many small companies which shipped limited quantities had received lower rates than we had been able to secure, notwithstanding the fact that we had made large investments to provide for terminal facilities, regular shipments, and other economies.

I well remember a bright man from Boston who had much to say about rebates and drawbacks. He was an old and experienced merchant, and looked after his affairs with a cautious and watchful eye. He feared that some of his competitors were doing better than he in bargaining for rates, and he delivered himself of this conviction:

"I am opposed on principle to the whole system of rebates and drawbacks—unless I am in it."

2. An Oil Man Goes Bankrupt (1899)*

Rockefeller's great passion was not so much a love of power or money as a dislike of waste and inefficiency. Having begun as a $3.50-a-week employee, he ultimately moved into the chaotically competitive oil business with a vision that enabled him to see far ahead and then "around the corner." Overlooking no detail, he insisted that every drop of solder used on his oil cans be counted. By acquiring or controlling warehouses, pipelines, tankers, railroads, oil fields, and refineries, he helped forge the United States' first great trust in 1882. He produced a superior product at a lower price but, in line with existing ethics, resorted to such "refined robbery" as ruthless price-cutting, dictation to dealers, deception, espionage, and rebates. George Rice, one of his ill-starred competitors, here complains to the U.S. Industrial Commission. What are his principal grievances?

I am a citizen of the United States, born in the state of Vermont. Producer of petroleum for more than thirty years, and a refiner of same for twenty years. But my refinery has been shut down during the past three years, owing to the powerful and all-prevailing machinations of the Standard Oil Trust, in criminal collusion and conspiracy with the railroads to destroy my business of twenty years of patient industry, toil, and money in building up, wholly by and through unlawful freight discriminations.

I have been driven from pillar to post, from one railway line to another, for twenty years, in the absolutely vain endeavor to get equal and just freight rates with the Standard Oil Trust, so as to be able to run my refinery at anything approaching a

---

Report of the U.S. Industrial Commission (Washington, DC: Government Printing Office, 1899), vol. 1, pp. 687, 704.

profit, but which I have been utterly unable to do. I have had to consequently shut down, with my business absolutely ruined and my refinery idle.

This has been a very sad, bitter, and ruinous experience for me to endure, but I have endeavored to the best of my circumstances and ability to combat it the utmost I could for many a long waiting year, expecting relief through the honest and proper execution of our laws, which have [has] as yet, however, never come. But I am still living in hopes, though I may die in despair....

Outside of rebates or freight discriminations, I had no show with the Standard Oil Trust, because of their unlawfully acquired monopoly, by which they could temporarily cut only my customers' prices, and below cost, leaving the balance of the town, nine-tenths, uncut. This they can easily do without any appreciable harm to their general trade, and thus effectually wipe out all competition, as fully set forth. Standard Oil prices generally were so high that I could sell my goods 2 to 3 cents a gallon below their prices and make a nice profit, but these savage attacks and [price] cuts upon my customers' goods...plainly showed...their power for evil, and the uselessness to contend against such odds.

C. The New Philosophy of Materialism

1. Andrew Carnegie's Gospel of Wealth (1889)*

Andrew Carnegie, the ambitious Scottish steel magnate, spent the first part of his life in the United States making a half-billion or so dollars and the rest of it giving his fortune away. Not a gambler or speculator at heart, he gambled everything on the future prosperity of the United States. His social conscience led him to preach "the gospel of wealth," notably in the following magazine article. Why does he believe that the millionaire is a trustee for the poor and that direct charity is an evil?

This, then, is held to be the duty of the man of wealth: first, to set an example of modest, unostentatious living, shunning display or extravagance; to provide moderately for the legitimate wants of those dependent upon him; and after doing so to consider all surplus revenues which come to him simply as trust funds, which he is called upon to administer, and strictly bound as a matter of duty to administer in the manner which, in his judgment, is best calculated to produce the most beneficial results for the community—the man of wealth thus becoming the mere agent and trustee for his poorer brethren, bringing to their service his superior wisdom, experience, and ability to administer, doing for them better than they would or could do for themselves....

Those who would administer wisely must, indeed, be wise, for one of the serious obstacles to the improvement of our race is indiscriminate charity. It were better for mankind that the millions of the rich were thrown into the sea than so spent as

---

*Andrew Carnegie, "Wealth," *North American Review* 148 (June 1889): 661–664.

to encourage the slothful, the drunken, the unworthy. Of every thousand dollars spent in so-called charity today, it is probable that $950 is unwisely spent; so spent, indeed, as to produce the very evils which it proposes to mitigate or cure.

A well-known writer of philosophic books admitted the other day that he had given a quarter of a dollar to a man who approached him as he was coming to visit the house of his friend. He knew nothing of the habits of this beggar; knew not the use that would be made of this money, although he had every reason to suspect that it would be spent improperly. This man professed to be a disciple of [conservative English social theorist] Herbert Spencer; yet the quarter-dollar given that night will probably work more injury than all the money which its thoughtless donor will ever be able to give in true charity will do good. He only gratified his own feelings, saved himself from annoyance—and this was probably one of the most selfish and very worst actions of his life, for in all respects he is most worthy.

In bestowing charity, the main consideration should be to help those who will help themselves; to provide part of the means by which those who desire to improve may do so; to give those who desire to rise the aids by which they may rise; to assist, but rarely or never to do all. Neither the individual nor the race is improved by almsgiving. Those worthy of assistance, except in rare cases, seldom require assistance. The really valuable men of the race never do, except in cases of accident or sudden change. Everyone has, of course, cases of individuals brought to his own knowledge where temporary assistance can do genuine good, and these he will not overlook.

But the amount which can be wisely given by the individual for individuals is necessarily limited by his lack of knowledge of the circumstances connected with each. He is the only true reformer who is as careful and as anxious not to aid the unworthy as he is to aid the worthy, and, perhaps, even more so, for in almsgiving more injury is probably done by rewarding vice than by relieving virtue.

The rich man is thus almost restricted to following the examples of Peter Cooper, Enoch Pratt of Baltimore, Mr. Pratt of Brooklyn, Senator Stanford,* and others, who know that the best means of benefiting the community is to place within its reach the ladders upon which the aspiring can rise—parks, and means of recreation, by which men are helped in body and mind; works of art, certain to give pleasure and improve the public taste; and public institutions of various kinds, which will improve the general condition of the people;—in this manner returning their surplus wealth to the mass of their fellows in the forms best calculated to do them lasting good. . . .

The man who dies leaving behind him millions of available wealth, which was his to administer during life, will pass away "unwept, unhonored, and unsung," no matter to what uses he leaves the dross which he cannot take with him. Of such as these the public verdict will then be: "The man who dies thus rich dies disgraced."

---

*Cooper founded an institute in New York City for educating the working classes; Enoch Pratt established a free library in Baltimore; Charles Pratt created an institute in Brooklyn for training skilled workers; and Leland Stanford endowed Stanford University.

Such, in my opinion, is the true Gospel concerning Wealth, obedience to which is destined some day to solve the problem of the Rich and the Poor, and to bring "Peace on earth, among men good will."

2. Russell Conwell Deifies the Dollar (c. 1900)*

The Reverend Russell H. Conwell was a remarkable Baptist preacher from Philadelphia who founded Temple University and had a large hand in establishing three hospitals. He delivered his famous lecture, "Acres of Diamonds," more than six thousand times. The proceeds went toward the education of some ten thousand young men. His basic theme was that in seeking riches, people were likely to overlook the opportunities (the "acres of diamonds") in their own backyards. Critics charged that Conwell was merely throwing the cloak of religion about the materialistic ideals of his time, especially since he combined philanthropy with dollar chasing. In the following excerpt from his famous lecture, what is his attitude toward the poor? How might one reconcile this brand of Christianity with the teachings of Christ, who said to the young man, "Go and sell that thou hast, and give to the poor" (Matthew 19:21)?

You have no right to be poor. It is your duty to be rich.

Oh, I know well that there are some things higher, sublimer than money! Ah, yes, there are some things sweeter, holier than gold! Yet I also know that there is not one of those things but is greatly enhanced by the use of money.

"Oh," you will say, "Mr. Conwell, can you, as a Christian teacher, tell the young people to spend their lives making money?"

Yes, I do. Three times I say, I do, I do, I do. You ought to make money. Money is power. Think how much good you could do if you had money now. Money is power, and it ought to be in the hands of good men. It would be in the hands of good men if we comply with the Scripture teachings, where God promises prosperity to the righteous man. That means more than being a goody-good—it means the all-round righteous man. You should be a righteous man. If you were, you would be rich.

I need to guard myself right here. Because one of my theological students came to me once to labor with me, for heresy, inasmuch as I had said that money was power.

He said: "Mr. Conwell, I feel it my duty to tell you that the Scriptures say that money 'is the root of all evil.'"...

So he read: "The *love* of money is the root of all evil." Indeed it is. The *love* of money is the root of all evil. The love of money, rather than the *love* of the good it secures, is a dangerous evil in the community. The desire to get hold of money, and to hold on to it, "hugging the dollar until the eagle squeals," is the root of all evil. But it is a grand ambition for men to have the desire to gain money, that they may use it for the benefit of their fellow men.

Young man! you may never have the opportunity to charge at the head of your nation's troops on some Santiago's heights.† Young woman! you may never be

---

*R. H. Conwell, "Acres of Diamonds" in Thomas B. Reed, ed., *Modern Eloquence* (Philadelphia: John D. Morris & Co., 1900), vol. 4, pp. 314–320.
†Santiago de Cuba was the site of a decisive U.S. victory over Spanish forces in the Spanish-American War of 1898.

called on to go out in the seas like Grace Darling to save suffering humanity.* But every one of you can earn money honestly, and with that money you can fight the battles of peace; and the victories of peace are always grander than those of war. I say then to you that you ought to be rich....

No man has a right to go into business and not make money. It is a crime to go into business and lose money, because it is a curse to the rest of the community. No man has a moral right to transact business unless he makes something out of it. He has also no right to transact business unless the man he deals with has an opportunity also to make something. Unless he lives and lets live, he is not an honest man in business. There are no exceptions to this great rule....

It is cruel to slander the rich because they have been successful. It is a shame to "look down" upon the rich the way we do. They are not scoundrels because they have gotten money. They have blessed the world. They have gone into great enterprises that have enriched the nation and the nation has enriched them. It is all wrong for us to accuse a rich man of dishonesty simply because he secured money. Go through this city and your very best people are among your richest people. Owners of property are always the best citizens. It is all wrong to say they are not good.

D. The Rise of the New South

1. Henry Grady Issues a Challenge (1889)†

The industrialized South—the New South—was slow to rise from the ashes of civil conflict. A kind of inferiority complex settled over the area. Henry W. Grady, eloquent editor of the Atlanta Constitution, *did more than anyone else to break the spell. With Irish wit, he preached the need for diversified crops, a readjustment of the freed slaves, the encouragement of manufacturing, and the development of local resources. In demand as a speaker, he broadcast his message widely and with demonstrable effect. The South of the 1880s was experiencing a marvelous economic boom, and new industries were spreading like its own honeysuckle. Following is a selection from a speech in Boston in which Grady contrasted the broken-down South of Reconstruction days with the new industrialized South. What major lesson must this passage have impressed upon his Northern listeners?*

I attended a funeral once in Pickens county in my state [Georgia]. A funeral is not usually a cheerful object to me unless I could select the subject. I think I could, perhaps, without going a hundred miles from here, find the material for one or two cheerful funerals. Still, this funeral was peculiarly sad. It was a poor "one-gallus" fellow, whose breeches struck him under the armpits and hit him at the other end about the knee—he didn't believe in décolleté clothes.

---

*Grace Darling was the daughter of a British lighthouse keeper who heroically helped her father rescue passengers from a shipwreck in 1838.
†Joel C. Harris, *Life of Henry W. Grady* (New York: Cassell and Company, Ltd., 1890), pp. 204–205. Shortly after delivering this speech, Grady contracted pneumonia and died.

They buried him in the midst of a marble quarry—they cut through solid marble to make his grave—and yet a little tombstone they put above him was from Vermont. They buried him in the heart of a pine forest, and yet the pine coffin was imported from Cincinnati. They buried him within the touch of an iron mine, and yet the nails in his coffin and the iron in the shovel that dug his grave were imported from Pittsburgh. They buried him by the side of the best sheep-grazing country on earth, and yet the wool in the coffin bands and the coffin bands themselves were brought from the North. The South didn't furnish a thing on earth for that funeral but the corpse and the hole in the ground.

There they put him away and the clods rattled down on his coffin, and they buried him in a New York coat and a Boston pair of shoes and a pair of breeches from Chicago and a shirt from Cincinnati, leaving him nothing to carry into the next world with him to remind him of the country in which he lived, and for which he fought for four years, but the chill of blood in his veins and the marrow in his bones.

Now we have improved on that. We have got the biggest marble-cutting establishment on earth within a hundred yards of that grave. We have got a half-dozen woolen mills right around it, and iron mines, and iron furnaces, and iron factories. We are coming to meet you. We are going to take a noble revenge, as my friend Mr. Carnegie said last night, by invading every inch of your territory with iron, as you invaded ours [in the Civil War] twenty-nine years ago.

2. Life in a Southern Mill (1910)*

From Charles Dickens's England to the modern-day Third World, the onset of industrialization has repeatedly wrenched people out of traditional habits of life and forced harsh accommodation to the discipline of the factory floor. The rapidly industrializing late-nineteenth-century South was no exception, as the following excerpt from a congressional investigation illustrates. What were the hardest conditions of life in the Southern textile mills? Were there any distinctively Southern aspects to these mill workers' plight?

In many mill villages the mill whistles blow at 4.30 or 5 A.M. to awaken the inhabitants, and in winter employees begin work in the mills before daybreak and they work until after nightfall.

When a mill is operated longer than its nominal working schedule, the machinery is started before the announced time of beginning work in the morning and at noon, and, in some cases, continues to run later than the announced time of stopping work at noon and in the evening. Mill managers, when questioned as to this practice, said that employees are not required to work before or after the announced scheduled time. In reality, however, employees are required to be at their machines whenever the machines are running. Otherwise the work gets in bad condition, and in the case of weavers dockage is made for imperfections, which are liable to occur when the weaver is not attending the looms.

Report on Condition of Woman and Child Wage-Earners in the United States, U.S. Congress, 61st Cong., 2d sess., Senate Document No. 645 (Washington, DC: Government Printing Office, 1910), pp. 280–291.

The practice of requiring employees to begin before the announced beginning time and to work after the announced stopping time is called by them "stealing time."...

Taking the 28 North Carolina mills which employed women or children at night, all together, the children working by day in all these mills were 25.32 per cent of all the day employees there, and the 437 children working by night in all these mills were 26.29 per cent of all the night workers....

In only 2 establishments investigated did the night force work more than 5 nights a week. In each of these mills, both of which were in North Carolina, an additional half day's work on Saturday was demanded, and this demand caused much dissatisfaction. In 1 of these 2 establishments the night shift worked 11 hours and 15 minutes nightly from Monday to Friday, inclusive, and on Saturday resumed at noon and worked until 6.15 in the evening, making a total of 62 hours and 30 minutes a week. In the other mill the night shift worked 11 hours and 30 minutes nightly, from Monday to Friday, inclusive, and on Saturday resumed at 3 P.M. and worked until 10 P.M., making a total of 64 hours and 30 minutes....

In cases where both the mother and father worked at night, the mother nearly always did her housework, including her washing and ironing. This means that on one day at least the mother went from 18 to 24 hours without sleeping. One woman, who gave as her reason for working at night that she could take care of her home, garden, cow, and boy during the day, was found at 11 in the morning hanging up her clothes. She had had no sleep during the preceding 24 hours....

In one of these mills the day shift worked 66 hours per week and the night shift 60 hours. Owing to a scarcity of help, day workers were frequently requested to return to the mill immediately after supper and work until midnight, and frequently some one was sent to the homes of employees early in the evening or at midnight to request day workers to come and work half of the night. Some employees usually declined to do overtime work. Others worked alternate nights as a regular custom.

Ordinarily this overtime work was paid for at the time it was performed and there was no record to show its extent. In the case of one family, however, the names of workers were entered on both the day roll and the night roll and this record showed that 4 children, 2 boys, doffers, one 10 and one 15 years old, and 2 girls, spinners, one 11 and one 13, and also a youth 17 years old, all members of the same family, had been paid for 78 to 84 hours of work per week. They had worked this number of hours, less a little time for supper and breakfast, on days when extra work was done. It was found that during a considerable part of the eight months that this family had been at this mill these children had worked two or three half nights each week, in addition to day work. After working from 6 A.M. to 6 P.M., with 35 minutes for dinner, they had returned to the mill, usually every other night, immediately after supper and worked until midnight, when they went home for four or five hours of sleep before beginning the next day's work...

The father of this family was apparently an active, hard-working man. He expressed the opinion that night work in addition to day work was rather hard on the children, but said that he was trying to get money to buy a home.... No member of this family could read or write.

E. Labor in Industrial America _____

1. In Praise of Mechanization (1897)*

As capitalists competed for markets and profits, they pushed their workers ever harder. Factory laborers came to dread the "speedup"—the order to produce more goods in less time. The already screeching din of the shop floor then whined to an even higher pitch as machines were made to run faster—and more dangerously. Some observers claimed that the peculiarly profit-hungry and competitive U.S. business environment rendered the conditions of labor in the United States particularly intolerable. Yet new workers by the millions fled the farms of both America and Europe to seek work tending the rattling industrial machines. In the following comments by a French economist who visited the United States near the end of the nineteenth century, how does he appraise the overall impact of mechanization? Is he convincing? What differences does he see between work conditions in Europe and those in the United States? What does he identify as the principal complaints of U.S. workers? Does he consider them justified?

"The pay here is good, but the labor is hard," said an Alsatian blacksmith employed in a large factory. I could verify nearly everywhere the truth of this remark, for I have seen such activity both in the small industry, where the tailors in the sweating-shops in New York worked with feverish rapidity, and in the great industry, where the butchers of the Armour packing house prepared 5800 hogs a day, where the cotton weavers tended as many as eight looms, or where the rolling-mill in Chicago turned out 1000 tons of rails in a day. Everywhere the machine goes very rapidly, and it commands; the workman has to follow....

In the Senate inquiry of 1883, upon education and labor, a weaver of Fall River, who had been a member of the Massachusetts Legislature, and who was then secretary of the Weavers' Union, said that he had worked seventeen years in England, and that conditions were much better than in America. The manufacturers there were not so desirous as they are here of working their men like horses or slaves; they do not work with the extraordinary rapidity which is customary at Fall River. In England, one man manages a pair of looms with two assistants; one between the looms and the other behind. In America, the manufacturer, with one or two exceptions, will not hear of that, and whatever the number of spindles they do not wish that a man shall have more than one assistant. The spindle is turned more rapidly; the laborers have more to do and for each loom Fall River produces more....

The manufacturers judge that the movement [to mechanize] has been advantageous to workmen, as sellers of labor, because the level of salaries has been raised, as consumers of products, because they purchase more with the same sum, and as laborers, because their task has become less onerous, the machine doing nearly everything which requires great strength; the workman, instead of bringing his muscles into play, has become an inspector, using his intelligence. He is told that his specialized labor is degrading because monotonous. Is it more monotonous to overlook with the eye

---

*E. Levasseur, "The Concentration of Industry, and Machinery in the United States," *Annals of the American Academy of Political and Social Science* 9, no. 2 (March 1897): 12–14, 18–19, 21–24.

for ten hours several automatic looms, and to attach, from time to time, one thread to another with the finger, than to push for fourteen hours against the breast the arm of a hand-loom, pressing at the same time the pedals with the feet?

In proportion as the machines require more room, the ceilings become higher, the workshops larger, the hygienic conditions better. From a sanitary standpoint, there is no comparison between the large factory to-day and the hut of the peasant, or the tenement of the sweating system. The improvement of machinery and the growing power of industrial establishments, have diminished the price of a great number of goods, and this is one of the most laudable forward movements of industry whose object is to satisfy, as well as possible, the needs of man.

The laboring classes do not share this optimism. They reproach the machine with exhausting the physical powers of the laborer; but this can only apply to a very small number of cases, to those where the workman is at the same time the motive power, as in certain sewing-machines. They reproach it with demanding such continued attention that it enervates, and of leaving no respite to the laborer, through the continuity of its movement. This second complaint may be applicable in a much larger number of cases, particularly in the spinning industries and in weaving, where the workman manages more than four looms. They reproach the machine with degrading man by transforming him into a machine, which knows how to make but one movement, and that always the same. They reproach it with diminishing the number of skilled laborers, permitting in many cases the substitution of unskilled workers and lowering the average level of wages. They reproach it with depriving, momentarily at least, every time that an invention modifies the work of the factory, a certain number of workmen of their means of subsistence, thus rendering the condition of all uncertain. They reproach it, finally, with reducing absolutely and permanently the number of persons employed for wages, and thus being indirectly injurious to all wage-earners who make among themselves a more disastrous competition, the more the opportunities for labor are restricted....

The chief of the Labor Bureau of New York has made a suggestive comparison: the United States and Great Britain, he says, are the countries which own and use the most machines. Compare the general condition of laborers in those countries with that of any country whatever in the world, where machines are unknown, except in the most primitive forms. Where is the superiority? It is almost a paradox, and yet it is a truth that machines bring about a much larger employment and improvement, not only because they increase production, but because they multiply the chances of employment, and incidentally the consumption of products. In fact, the census of the United States shows that the proportion of laborers to the total number of inhabitants has increased in the same period that the machine has taken most complete possession of manufactures. From 1860 to 1890, while the population of the United States doubled, the number of persons employed in industry increased nearly threefold (increase of 172 per cent), and at the same time the mechanical power, measured by horse-power, increased fourfold. Inventions have created new industries, such as photography, electricity, telegraphy, electrotyping, railroading, manufacture of bicycles, etc., and have thus given to labor much more employment than they have withdrawn from it. Thus, even in old industries, transformed by machinery, the progress of consumption has generally maintained a demand for hands.

There is no social evolution which does not produce friction. That which urges industry toward machinery and large factories appears to me to-day irresistible, because it leads to cheapness, which the consumer seeks first of all, and which is one of the objects of economic civilization. It is Utopia to believe that the world could come back by some modification of the social order, or of mechanical motive powers to the system of the little family workshop. Such a workshop is far from being an ideal, as the sweating system proves.

2. A Tailor Testifies (1883)*

In 1883 a Senate investigating committee heard the testimony of several workers about the conditions of labor in the United States' burgeoning industries. The witness who gave the following account had been a tailor for some thirty years. What changes in work conditions had he seen in his lifetime? Were they for good or ill? What did they imply for his family life?

Senator Pugh. Please give us any information that you may have as to the relation existing between the employers and the employees in the tailoring business in this city, as to wages, as to treatment of the one by the other class, as to the feeling that exists between the employers and the employed generally, and all that you know in regard to the subject that we are authorized to inquire into?

A. During the time I have been here the tailoring business is altered in three different ways. Before we had sewing machines we worked piecework with our wives, and very often our children. We had no trouble then with our neighbors, nor with the landlord, because it was a very still business, very quiet; but in 1854 or 1855, and later, the sewing machine was invented and introduced, and it stitched very nicely, nicer than the tailor could do; and the bosses said: "We want you to use the sewing machine; you have to buy one." Many of the tailors had a few dollars in the bank, and they took the money and bought machines. Many others had no money, but must help themselves; so they brought their stitching, the coat or vest, to the other tailors who had sewing machines, and paid them a few cents for the stitching. Later, when the money was given out for the work, we found out that we could earn no more than we could without the machine; but the money for the machine was gone now, and we found that the machine was only for the profit of the bosses; that they got their work quicker, and it was done nicer....The machine makes too much noise in the place, and the neighbors want to sleep, and we have to stop sewing earlier; so we have to work faster. We work now in excitement—in a hurry. It is hunting; it is not work at all; it is a hunt.

Q. You turn out two or three times as much work per day now as you did in prior times before the war?

A. Yes, sir; two or three times as much; and we have to do it, because the wages are two-thirds lower than they were five or ten years back....

---

*U.S. Congress, Senate Committee on Education and Labor, *Report of the Committee of the Senate upon the Relations Between Labor and Capital* (Washington, DC: Government Printing Office, 1885), vol. 1, pp. 413–421.

Senator Blair. What proportion of them are women and what proportion men, according to your best judgment?

A. I guess there are many more women than men.

Q. The pay of the women is the same as the pay of the men for the same quantity of work, I suppose?

A. Yes; in cases where a manufacturer—that is, a middleman—gets work from the shop and brings it into his store and employs hands to make it, women get paid by the piece also. If the manufacturer gets $.25 for a piece, he pays for the machine work on that piece so many cents to the machine-worker, he pays so many cents to the presser, so many cents to the finisher, and so many to the button-sewer—so much to each one—and what remains is to pay his rent and to pay for the machinery.

Q. What is your knowledge as to the amount that workers of that class are able to save from their wages?

A. I don't know any one that does save except those manufacturers.

Q. As a class, then, the workers save nothing?

A. No.

Q. What sort of house-room do they have? What is the character, in general, of the food and clothing which they are able to purchase with what they can make by their labor?

A. They live in tenement houses four or five stories high, and have two or three rooms.

Q. What is the character of their clothing?

A. They buy the clothing that they make—the cheapest of it.

Q. What about the character of food that they are able to provide for themselves?

A. Food? They have no time to eat dinner. They have a sandwich in the middle of the day, and in the evening when they go away from work it is the same, and they drink lager or anything they can get.

Q. They are kept busy all the time and have but little opportunity for rest?

A. Yes.

Q. What is the state of feeling between the employers and their employees in that business? How do you workingmen feel towards the people who employ you and pay you?

A. Well, I must say the workingmen are discouraged. If I speak with them they go back and don't like to speak much about the business and the pay. They fear that if they say how it is they will get sent out of the shop. They hate the bosses and the foremen more than the bosses, and that feeling is deep.

3. The Life of a Sweatshop Girl (1902)[*]

Sadie Frowne was approximately sixteen years old when she dictated the following account of her life to a reporter from The Independent magazine in 1902. What are the greatest differences between her life in Poland and her life in the United States?

---

[*]"The Story of a Sweatshop Girl," *The Independent* 54, no. 2808 (September 25, 1902): 2279–2282.

What are the best and worst parts of her job in a garment factory? What is her attitude toward her job? Toward her labor union?

[Our] grocer's shop [in Poland] was only one story high, and had one window, with very small panes of glass. We had two rooms behind it, and were happy while my father lived, altho[ugh] we had to work very hard. By the time I was six years of age I was able to wash dishes and scrub floors, and by the time I was eight I attended to the shop while my mother was away driving her wagon or working in the fields with my father. She was strong and could work like a man.

When I was a little more than ten years of age my father died....

We struggled along till I was nearly thirteen years of age and quite handy at housework and shop keeping, so far as I could learn them there. But we fell behind in the rent and mother kept thinking more and more that we should have to leave Poland and go across the sea to America where we heard it was much easier to make money. Mother wrote to Aunt Fanny, who lived in New York, and told her how hard it was to live in Poland, and Aunt Fanny advised her to come and bring me.... She said we should come at once, and she went around among our relatives in New York and took up a subscription for our passage.

We came by steerage on a steamship in a very dark place that smelt dreadfully. There were hundreds of other people packed in with us, men, women and children, and almost all of them were sick. It took us twelve days to cross the sea, and we thought we should die, but at last the voyage was over, and we came up and saw the beautiful bay and the big woman with the spikes on her head and the lamp that is lighted at night in her hand [Statue of Liberty]....

So I went to work in Allen street (Manhattan) in what they call a sweatshop, making skirts by machine. I was new at the work and the foreman scolded me a great deal.

"Now, then," he would say, "this place is not for you to be looking around in. Attend to your work. That is what you have to do."

I did not know at first that you must not look around and talk, and I made many mistakes with the sewing, so that I was often called a "stupid animal." But I made $4 a week by working six days in the week. For there are two Sabbaths here—our own Sabbath, that comes on a Saturday, and the Christian Sabbath that comes on a Sunday. It is against our law to work on our own Sabbath, so we work on their Sabbath.

In Poland I and my father and mother used to go to the synagogue on the Sabbath, but here the women don't go to the synagogue much, tho[ugh] the men do. They are shut up working hard all the week long and when the Sabbath comes they like to sleep long in bed and afterward they must go out where they can breathe the air. The rabbis are strict here, but not so strict as in the old country....

I get up at half-past five o'clock every morning and make myself a cup of coffee on the oil stove. I eat a bit of bread and perhaps some fruit and then go to work. Often I get there soon after six o'clock so as to be in good time, tho[ugh] the factory does not open till seven. I have heard that there is a sort of clock that calls you at the very time you want to get up, but I can't believe that because I don't see how the clock would know.

At seven o'clock we all sit down to our machines and the boss brings to each one the pile of work that he or she is to finish during the day, what they call in English their "stint." This pile is put down beside the machine and as soon as a skirt is done it is laid on the other side of the machine. Sometimes the work is not all finished by six o'clock and then the one who is behind must work overtime. Sometimes one is finished ahead of time and gets away at four or five o'clock, but generally we are not done till six o'clock.

The machines go like mad all day, because the faster you work the more money you get. Sometimes in my haste I get my finger caught and the needle goes right through it. It goes so quick, tho[ugh], that it does not hurt much. I bind the finger up with a piece of cotton and go on working. We all have accidents like that. Where the needle goes through the nail it makes a sore finger, or where it splinters a bone it does much harm. Sometimes a finger has to come off. Generally, tho[ugh], one can be cured by a salve.

All the time we are working the boss walks about examining the finished garments and making us do them over again if they are not just right. So we have to be careful as well as swift. But I am getting so good at the work that within a year I will be making $7 a week, and then I can save at least $3.50 a week. I have over $200 saved now.

The machines are all run by foot power, and at the end of the day one feels so weak that there is a great temptation to lie right down and sleep. But you must go out and get air, and have some pleasure. So instead of lying down I go out, generally with Henry [her coworker]. Sometimes we go to Coney Island, where there are good dancing places, and sometimes we go to Ulmer Park to picnics....

For the last two winters I have been going to night school at Public School 84 on Glenmore avenue. I have learned reading, writing and arithmetic. I can read quite well in English now and I look at the newspapers every day. I read English books, too, sometimes....

I am going back to night school again this winter. Plenty of my friends go there. Some of the women in my class are more than forty years of age. Like me, they did not have a chance to learn anything in the old country. It is good to have an education; it makes you feel higher. Ignorant people are all low. People say now that I am clever and fine in conversation.

We have just finished a strike in our business. It spread all over and the United Brotherhood of Garment Workers was in it. That takes in the cloakmakers, coatmakers, and all the others. We struck for shorter hours, and after being out four weeks won the fight. We only have to work nine and a half hours a day and we get the same pay as before. So the union does good after all in spite of what some people say against it—that it just takes our money and does nothing.

I pay 25 cents a month to the union, but I do not begrudge that because it is for our benefit. The next strike is going to be for a raise of wages, which we all ought to have. But tho[ugh] I belong to the Union I am not a Socialist or an Anarchist. I don't know exactly what those things mean. There is a little expense for charity, too. If any worker is injured or sick we all give money to help....

I have many friends and we often have jolly parties. Many of the young men like to talk to me, but I don't go out with any except Henry.

Lately he has been urging me more and more to get married—but I think I'll wait.

4. The Knights of Labor Champion Reform (1887)*

The blue-eyed, ruddy-complexioned Terence V. Powderly, a nimble-witted son of Irish immigrants, became a machinist and joined the secret order of the all-embracing Knights of Labor. He ultimately rose to be its influential head as Grand Master Workman and saw the organization attain a maximum strength of some 700,000 members—skilled and unskilled, white and black. But lawyers, bankers, gamblers, and liquor dealers were barred. The Knights strove primarily for social and economic reform on a broad front, rather than the piecemeal raising of wages that was the chief concern of the skilled crafts unions. Powderly favored the substitution of arbitration for strikes, the regulation of trusts and monopolies, and the replacement of the wage system with producers' cooperatives. Shot at from the front by conservatives, who accused him of communism, he was sniped at from the rear by some of his own following. In the following selection, Powderly defends the Knights against charges in 1887 that they were "breaking up." What does he identify as the Knights' most important goals? Which of these goals would be approved by the modern-day labor movement? How relevant were they to the problems of workers in late-nineteenth-century America?

It is true, the Knights are breaking up. We are at last forced to acknowledge the truth so long, so stubbornly, resisted. We are breaking up—breaking up as the plowman breaks up the soil for the sowing of new seed. We are breaking up old traditions. We are breaking up hereditary rights, and planting everywhere the seed of universal rights. We are breaking up the idea that money makes the man and not moral worth. We are breaking up the idea that might makes right. We are breaking up the idea that legislation is alone for the rich. We are breaking up the idea that the Congress of the United States must be run by millionaires for the benefit of millionaires. We are breaking up the idea that a few men may hold millions of acres of untilled land while other men starve for the want of one acre. We are breaking up the practice of putting the labor of criminals [convict labor] into competition with honest, industrious labor and starving it to death. We are breaking up the practice of importing [European] ignorance, bred of monarchies and dynamite, in order to depreciate intelligent, skilled labor at home. We are breaking up the practice of employing little children in factories, thus breeding a race deformed, ignorant, and profligate. We are breaking up the idea that a man who works with his hands has need neither of education nor of civilized refinements. We are breaking up the idea that the accident of sex puts one-half of the human race beyond the pale of constitutional rights. We are breaking up the practice of paying woman one-third the wages paid man simply because she is a woman. We are breaking up the idea that a man may debauch an infant [minor] girl and shield himself from the penalty behind

---

a law he himself has made. We are breaking up ignorance and intemperance, crime and oppression, of whatever character and wherever found.

Yes, the Knights of Labor are breaking up, and they will continue their appointed work of breaking up until universal rights shall prevail; and while they may not bring in the millennium, they will do their part in the evolution of moral forces that are working for the emancipation of the race.

[With Samuel Gompers at the helm, the skilled crafts American Federation of Labor emerged in 1886. By 1890 it had overshadowed the fast-fading Knights of Labor. Skilled carpenters, striking for their own narrow objectives, could not easily be replaced by strikebreakers; unskilled workers could be. The skilled crafts became weary of sacrificing themselves on the altar of large social objectives. This, in brief, was the epitaph of the Knights of Labor.]

5. Samuel Gompers Condemns the Knights (c. 1886)[*]

Samuel Gompers, a stocky Jewish cigar maker born in a London tenement, emerged as the potent leader of the skilled crafts American Federation of Labor. Once asked what organized labor wanted, he is said to have replied, "More"—by which he meant more wages, more power, more liberty, more leisure, more benefits. He and his skilled crafts workers battled the unskilled laborers of the Knights of Labor to defeat revolutionary schemes for remaking U.S. society. What are the principal weaknesses of the Knights of Labor from the skilled union point of view? Which one is the most serious in the eyes of Gompers?

In 1886 a definite order went out from D.A. [District Assembly No.] 49 [of the Knights of Labor] to make war on the International Cigarmakers' Unions. It was the culmination of years of friction developing over Knights of Labor encroachments on trade union functions.

The two movements were inherently different. Trade unions endeavored to organize for collective responsibility persons with common trade problems. They sought economic betterment in order to place in the hands of wage-earners the means to wider opportunities.

The Knights of Labor was a social or fraternal organization. It was based upon a principle of cooperation, and its purpose was reform. The Knights of Labor prided itself upon being something higher and grander than a trade union or political party. Unfortunately, its purposes were not always exemplified through the declarations and the acts of its members.

The order admitted to membership any person, excluding only lawyers and saloonkeepers. This policy included employers among those eligible. Larger employers gradually withdrew from the order, but the small employers and small businessmen and politicians remained.

---

[*]From Samuel Gompers, *Seventy Years of Life and Labor* (New York: E. P. Dutton & Company, 1925), pp. 176, 244–245, 284.

The order was a hodgepodge with no basis for solidarity, with the exception of a comparatively few trade assemblies. The aggressive policy inaugurated in 1886 [against the Cigarmakers' Unions] was not due to any change of heart or program, but solely to the great increase in the membership of the Knights of Labor that made it seem safe to put declarations into effect.

When the order began to encroach upon the economic field, trouble was inevitable, for such invasion was equivalent to setting up a dual organization to perform a task for which they were entirely unfitted. It was particularly unfortunate when it endeavored to conduct strikes. The Knights of Labor was a highly centralized organization, and this often placed decision upon essential trade policies in the hands of officers outside the trade concerned. Strikes are essentially an expression of collective purpose of workers who perform related services and who have the spirit of union growing out of joint employment....

Talk of harmony with the Knights of Labor is bosh. They are just as great enemies of trade unions as any employer can be, only more vindictive. I tell you they will give us no quarter, and I would give them their own medicine. It is no use trying to placate them or even to be friendly. They will not cooperate with a mere trades union, as they call our organization. The time will come, however, when the workingmen of the country will see and distinguish between a natural and an artificial organization.

6. Capital Versus Labor (1871)

The contest between labor and capital in nineteenth-century America was often bitter and always complicated. Workers were generally praised for their industriousness, but they were also frequently blamed for strikes and for the unrest that sometimes violently rocked the nation. Capitalists were admired for their ingenuity and entrepreneurial energy, but they were also criticized for their alleged greed and their supposed insensitivity to the circumstances of their employees. In the cartoon on page 431, the famous illustrator Thomas Nast portrays both sides of this complex relationship between labor and capital. Why does Nast choose to depict the laborer with his family and the capitalist alone at the office? In what ways was organized labor oppressive? Who had more at risk: the laborer or the capitalist? Which side does Nast favor? Why?

F. The Environmental Impact of Industrialization

1. Upton Sinclair Describes the Chicago Stockyards (1906)*

In The Jungle, *one of the most provocative novels ever written about social conditions in the United States, the muckraking writer Upton Sinclair penned a devastating description of Chicago's meatpacking industry at the opening of the twentieth century. In the passage below, the novel's protagonist, Lithuanian immigrant Jurgis Rudkus, first encounters Chicago. The city's landscape and its very atmosphere have been transformed by the huge slaughterhouse complex around the city's sprawling, fetid stockyards. What were the most noxious environmental effects of the meatpacking industry? Why did the city of Chicago tolerate them? How did the particular technologies of the era contribute to this environmental catastrophe?*

A full hour before the party [Rudkus and his traveling companions] reached the city they had begun to note the perplexing changes in the atmosphere. It grew darker all the time, and upon the earth the grass seemed to grow less green. Every minute, as the train sped on, the colours of things became dingier; the fields were grown parched and yellow, the landscape hideous and bare. And along with the thickening smoke they began to notice another circumstance, a strange, pungent odour. They were not sure that it was unpleasant, this odour; some might have called it sickening, but their taste in odours was not developed, and they were only sure that it was curious. Now, sitting in the trolley car, they realized that they were on their way to the home of it—that they had travelled all the way from Lithuania to it. It was now no longer something far off and faint, that you caught in whiffs; you could literally taste it, as well as smell it—you could take hold of it, almost, and examine it at your leisure. They were divided in their opinions about it. It was an elemental odour, raw and crude; it was rich, almost rancid, sensual and strong. There were some who drank it in as if it were an intoxicant; there were others who put their handkerchiefs to their faces. The new emigrants were still tasting it, lost in wonder, when suddenly the car came to a halt, and the door was flung open, and a voice shouted—"Stockyards!"

They were left standing upon the corner, staring; down a side street there were two rows of brick houses, and between them a vista: half a dozen chimneys, tall as the tallest of buildings, touching the very sky, and leaping from them half a dozen columns of smoke, thick, oily, and black as night. It might have come from the centre of the world, this smoke, where the fires of the ages still smoulder. It came as if self-imperilled, driving all before it, a perpetual explosion. It was inexhaustible; one stared, waiting to see it stop, but still the great streams rolled out. They spread in vast clouds overhead, writhing, curling; then, uniting in one giant river, they streamed away down the sky, stretching a black pall as far as the eye could reach.

Then the party became aware of another strange thing. This, too, like the odour, was a thing elemental; it was a sound—a sound made up of ten thousand little sounds.

---

*From Upton Sinclair, *The Jungle* (New York: Doubleday, Page & Company, 1906), pp. 31–33, 42.

You scarcely noticed it at first—it sunk into your consciousness, a vague disturbance, a trouble. It was like the murmuring of the bees in the spring, the whispering of the forest; it suggested endless activity, the rumblings of a world in motion. It was only by an effort that one could realize that it was made by animals, that it was the distant lowing of ten thousand cattle, the distant grunting of ten thousand swine....

There were two hundred and fifty miles of track within the yards, their guide went on to tell them. They brought about ten thousand head of cattle every day, and as many hogs, and half as many sheep—which meant some eight or ten million live creatures turned into food every year. One stood and watched, and little by little caught the drift of the tide, as it set in the direction of the packing houses. There were groups of cattle being driven to the chutes, which were roadways about fifteen feet wide, raised high above the pens. In these chutes the stream of animals was continuous; it was quite uncanny to watch them, pressing on to their fate, all unsuspicious—a very river of death.

2. An Engineer Describes Smoke Pollution (1911)*

Herbert Wilson, chief engineer for the U.S. Geological Survey, undertook a comprehensive survey of air quality in major American cities in the first years of the twentieth century. In the following report, he describes the effects of smoke pollution, mostly from coal-burning furnaces. What are the worst kinds of damage inflicted by burning coal? What would it have been like to live in a city perpetually enshrouded by coal smoke and dust? What problems associated with burning fossil fuels persist today?

The smoke nuisance is one of the greatest dangers of modern times, insidiously attacking the health of the individual, lowering his vitality, increasing the death rate, and causing untold loss and injury to property. The damage which this evil inflicts can hardly be estimated in money; it is equally impossible to estimate the amount of suffering, disease and death and the general effect of lowered vitality caused by this nuisance....

The Smoke Committee of Cleveland, discussing the losses occasioned by smoke, reported:

> There are approximately 400 retail dry goods stores in Cleveland doing business of from $10,000 to $3,000,000 or $4,000,000 a year. The owners of some of these stores estimate, and the same estimate is given in other cities, that on all white goods a clear loss of 10 per cent must be figured. Taking the single items of underwear, shirt waists, linens and white dress goods for the eleven department stores, the proprietors conservatively estimate their combined loss at $25,000....
>
> But a greater cost than all of these must be considered in the loss to the 100,000 homes in Cleveland. The constant need of cleaning walls, ceilings, windows, carpets, rugs and draperies, for redecorating and renewing, can be realized only by the house owner or housekeeper. To this should be added the increased laundry bills for household linen, the dry cleaning for clothing, and the great additional wear resulting from this constant renovation, necessitating frequent renewal. Consider also the permanent injury to books, pictures and similar articles. Though impossible of computation, it will be seen that the total of these items aggregates millions of dollars.

---

*Herbert M. Wilson, *The American City* 4 (May 1911): 210–212.

The City Forester of St. Louis declared that more than 4 per cent of the city trees are killed every year by smoke. In that city it has been found impossible to grow evergreen conifers, except the dwarf juniper and the Austrian pine. Only the hardiest of roses grow in that city. The trees which suffer the greatest injury are the oaks, hickories and conifers, and these are especially ideal park trees and far more valuable for beauty and permanence than the softer wooded varieties....

Turning now to the losses in fuel combustion: our present method of burning coal with smoke is costing the people of this country, unnecessarily, $90,000,000. It is estimated that 8 per cent of the coal used in the production of power, light and heat, or in all about 20,000,000 tons of coal, are going up the chimneys each year in smoke.

The prime source of the pollution of the atmosphere is smoke. The death rate is higher in the city than in the country, and the larger the city the higher the death rate....

It must be understood that smoke, aside from the looks and tangible shapes in which it presents itself, is one of the most poisonous gases polluting the very air we breathe. So apparent is this fact that physicians in our larger cities state their ability to tell at a moment's glance at the lungs in a post-mortem examination whether the man has lived more than thirty days in such a city or not. In the former case their examination proves that the blood, instead of showing red, is black as soot can make it.

Medical men the world over are unanimous in the declaration that the breathing of coal smoke predisposes the lungs to tuberculosis and even more violent lung trouble, such as pneumonia, as well as to many other acute diseases. We know that lung diseases are more prevalent in smoky cities; that the death rate of children due to diseases of the respiratory organs is especially great in coal and iron districts; that tuberculosis is more rapidly fatal in smoky regions.

In addition to all the above, there is the psychological effect of smoke. The city enveloped in a sooty fog is a gloomy city and the children reared therein are in danger of growing up with too much toleration for dirt and too little of that full enthusiasm for the beautiful and clean things of life which sunlight and God's blue sky encourage about as well as anything else in this world.

Thought Provokers

---

1. Which of the so-called railroad abuses of the post–Civil War period are the easiest to justify? The hardest? In view of the fact that railway rates were becoming progressively lower when the Interstate Commerce Act was passed in 1887, why should the public have complained?

2. Comment critically on the advantages and disadvantages of the monopolistic trust from the standpoint of the consumer. Was the attempted distinction between "good" and "bad" trusts a valid one?

3. To what extent was Carnegie selfish in his gospel of wealth? Is it better to have large private benefactions or to have the government tax wealth and engage in benefactions itself? Why is it difficult to give away large sums of money intelligently?

4. Why was the South, which has many natural resources and is being rapidly industrialized today, so slow to industrialize after the Civil War?

5. What features of working-class life must have been most troubling to laborers in the late nineteenth century? How is industrial labor different today?

6. The United States has long had an organized labor movement, but why has the United States never had a labor party of the sort that emerged in Britain, Germany, and other industrializing countries?

7. Why did nineteenth-century Americans tolerate the environmental ravages of rampant industrialization?

25

America Moves
to the City,
1865–1900

Th' worst thing we can do f'r anny man is to do
him good.

*F. P. Dunne ("Mr. Dooley"), paraphrasing
Andrew Carnegie, 1906*

Prologue: The robust growth of cities transformed the face of the United States in the decades following the Civil War. The inpouring of the New Immigration from southern and eastern Europe, beginning conspicuously in the 1880s, raised vexing social questions. It aggravated already festering slum conditions, stimulated agitation to halt cheap foreign labor, and revived anti-Catholic outcries. Protestant denominations, already theologically challenged by Charles Darwin's theory of evolution, were further discomforted by the arrival of hundreds of thousands of new Roman Catholic immigrants. Meanwhile, northern white reformers now largely left the recently freed blacks in the South to their own devices. The temperance crusade intensified, as did the still frustrated campaign for woman suffrage. Meanwhile, new work patterns in the booming cities provided new opportunities and challenges for women, which in turn sparked fresh debate on women's role, marital relations, and sexual morality.

A. The Lures and Liabilities of City Life

1. Sister Carrie Is Bedazzled by Chicago (1900)[*]

In his novel Sister Carrie, *Theodore Dreiser painted a classic portrait of a young woman from the countryside who seeks her fate in the big city—in this case, Chicago. Among the features of urban life that the novel's heroine, Carrie Meeber, finds most alluring are the huge department stores. Dreiser considered department stores such a distinctive innovation that he paused in his narrative to describe them at length. What effect do they have on Carrie Meeber? In what ways do they symbolize the new cultural realities of urban life?*

[*]Theodore Dreiser, *Sister Carrie* (New York: New American Library, 1961; first published 1900), pp. 25–27.

At that time the department store was in its earliest form of successful operation, and there were not many. The first three in the United States, established about 1884, were in Chicago. Carrie was familiar with the names of several through the advertisements in the *Daily News*, and now proceeded to seek them. The words of Mr. McManus [a store manager who had interviewed Carrie for a job] had somehow managed to restore her courage, which had fallen low, and she dared to hope that this new line would offer her something. Some time she spent in wandering up and down, thinking to encounter the buildings by chance, so readily is the mind, bent upon prosecuting a hard but needful errand, eased by that self-deception which the semblance of search, without the reality, gives. At last she inquired of a police officer, and was directed to proceed "two blocks up," where she would find The Fair.

The nature of these vast retail combinations, should they ever permanently disappear, will form an interesting chapter in the commercial history of our nation. Such a flowering out of a modest trade principle the world had never witnessed up to that time. They were along the line of the most effective retail organization, with hundreds of stores co-ordinated into one and laid out upon the most imposing and economic basis. They were handsome, bustling, successful affairs, with a host of clerks and a swarm of patrons. Carrie passed along the busy aisles, much affected by the remarkable displays of trinkets, dress goods, stationery, and jewelry. Each separate counter was a showplace of dazzling interest and attraction. She could not help feeling the claim of each trinket and valuable upon her personally, and yet she did not stop. There was nothing there which she could not have used—nothing which she did not long to own. The dainty slippers and stockings, the delicately frilled skirts and petticoats, the laces, ribbons, haircombs, purses, all touched her with individual desire, and she felt keenly the fact that not any of these things were in the range of her purchase. She was a work seeker, an outcast without employment, one whom the average employee could tell at a glance was poor and in need of a situation.

It must not be thought that anyone could have mistaken her for a nervous, sensitive, high-strung nature, cast unduly upon a cold, calculating, and unpoetic world. Such certainly she was not. But women are peculiarly sensitive to their adornment.

Not only did Carrie feel the drag of desire for all which was new and pleasing in apparel for women, but she noticed too, with a touch at the heart, the fine ladies who elbowed and ignored her, brushing past in utter disregard of her presence, themselves eagerly enlisted in the materials which the store contained. Carrie was not familiar with the appearance of her more fortunate sisters of the city. Neither had she before known the nature and appearance of the shopgirls with whom she now compared poorly. They were pretty in the main, some even handsome, with an air of independence and indifference which added, in the case of the more favored, a certain piquancy. Their clothes were neat, in many instances fine, and wherever she encountered the eye of one it was only to recognize in it a keen analysis of her own position—her individual shortcomings of dress and that shadow of manner which she thought must hang about her and make clear to all who and what she was. A flame of envy lighted in her heart. She realized in a dim way how much the city held—wealth, fashion, ease—every adornment for women, and she longed for dress and beauty with a whole heart.

2. Cleaning Up New York (1897)*

The cities grew so fast that municipal governments were hard-pressed to provide ade-
quate sanitation facilities and other essential urban services. New York City commis-
sioner George E. Waring, Jr., here describes the situation in late-nineteenth-century
New York before a concerted effort was made to clean up the city. What features of
urban life were the worst contributors to unsanitary conditions? Which city dwellers
suffered the most from those conditions?

Before 1895 the streets were almost universally in a filthy state. In wet weather
they were covered with slime, and in dry weather their air was filled with dust.
Artificial sprinkling in summer converted the dust into mud, and the drying winds
changed the mud to powder. Rubbish of all kinds, garbage, and ashes lay neglected
in the streets, and in the hot weather the city stank with the emanations of putrefy-
ing organic matter. It was not always possible to see the pavement, because of the
dirt that covered it. One expert, a former contractor of street-cleaning, told me that
West Broadway could not be cleaned, because it was so coated with grease from
wagon-axles; it was really coated with slimy mud. The sewer inlets were clogged
with refuse. Dirty paper was prevalent everywhere, and black rottenness was seen
and smelled on every hand.

The practice of standing unharnessed trucks and wagons in the public streets
was well-nigh universal in all except the main thoroughfares and the better
residence districts. The Board of Health made an enumeration of vehicles so standing on Sunday, counting twenty-five thousand on a portion of one side of the
city; they reached the conclusion that there were in all more than sixty thousand.
These trucks not only restricted traffic and made complete street-cleaning practically impossible, but they were harbors of vice and crime. Thieves and highway-
men made them their dens, toughs caroused in them, both sexes resorted to them,
and they were used for the vilest purposes, until they became, both figuratively
and literally, a stench in the nostrils of the people. In the crowded districts they
were a veritable nocturnal hell. Against all this the poor people were powerless to
get relief. The highest city officials, after feeble attempts at removal, declared that
New York was so peculiarly constructed (having no alleys through which the rear
of the lots could be reached) that its commerce could not be carried on unless this
privilege were given to its truckmen; in short, the removal of the trucks was "an
impossibility...."

The condition of the streets, of the force, and of the stock was the fault of
no man and of no set of men. It was the fault of the system. The department was
throttled by partizan control—so throttled it could neither do good work, command
its own respect and that of the public, nor maintain its material in good order. It was
run as an adjunct of a political organization. In that capacity it was a marked success. It paid fat tribute; it fed thousands of voters, and it gave power and influence
to hundreds of political leaders. It had this appointed function, and it performed it
well....

---

*George E. Waring, Jr., *Street-Cleaning* (New York: Doubleday and McClure, 1897), pp. 13–21.

New York is now thoroughly clean in every part, the empty vehicles are gone.... "Clean streets" means much more than the casual observer is apt to think. It has justly been said that "cleanliness is catching," and clean streets are leading to clean hallways, and staircases and cleaner living-rooms. A recent writer says:

> It is not merely justification of a theory to say that the improvement noticed in the past two and a half years in the streets of New York has led to an improvement in the interior of its tenement-houses. A sense of personal pride has been awakened in the women and children, the results of which have been noticeable to every one engaged in philanthropic work among the tenement dwellers. When, early in the present administration, a woman in the Five Points district was heard to say to another, "Well, I don't care; my street is cleaner than yours is, anyhow," it was felt that the battle was won.

Few realize the many minor ways in which the work of the department has benefited the people at large. For example, there is far less injury from dust to clothing, to furniture, and to goods in shops; mud is not tracked from the streets on to the sidewalks, and thence into the houses; boots require far less cleaning; the wearing of overshoes has been largely abandoned; wet feet and bedraggled skirts are mainly things of the past; and children now make free use as a playground of streets which were formerly impossible to them. "Scratches," a skin disease of horses due to mud and slush, used to entail very serious cost on truckmen and liverymen. It is now almost unknown. Horses used to "pick up a nail" with alarming frequency, and this caused great loss of service, and, like scratches, made the bill of the veterinary surgeon a serious matter. There are practically no nails now to be found in the streets.

The great, the almost inestimable, beneficial effect of the work of the department is shown in the large reduction of the death-rate and in the less keenly realized but still more important reduction in the sick-rate. As compared with the average death-rate of 26.78 of 1882–94, that of 1895 was 23.10, that of 1896 was 21.52, and that of the first half of 1897 was 19.63. If this latter figure is maintained throughout the year, there will have been fifteen thousand fewer deaths than there would have been had the average rate of the thirteen previous years prevailed. The report of the Board of Health for 1896, basing its calculations on diarrheal diseases in July, August, and September, in the filthiest wards, in the most crowded wards, and in the remainder of the city, shows a very marked reduction in all, and the largest reduction in the first two classes.

3. Jacob Riis Photographs the New York Tenements (1890)

Police reporter Jacob A. Riis, a Danish-born immigrant who had known rat-infested slums in Denmark, aimed his talented pen at the squalid tenements of late-nineteenth-century New York. He was shocked by the absence of privacy, sanitation, and playgrounds, and by the presence of dirt, stench, and vermin. The advent of flash photography allowed Riis to pair his searing exposés with evocative images from the windowless rooms that housed New York's immigrant poor. Eventually published in a book-length investigation, Riis's photos offered well-to-do Americans a glimpse into the lives of the "other half." What emotions are the following images meant to evoke? What might Riis's audiences have found most appalling about the conditions captured in the photos below?

Bettmann/Corbis

4. Jacob Riis Documents the Tenement Problem (1890)[*]

In the appendix to his best-selling report, Riis presented a vast array of statistics that brought the conditions of New York's tenements into sharp relief. Despite the opposition of heartless landlords who worked hand in glove with corrupt politicians, Riis's investigations helped to eliminate some of these foul firetraps, especially the dark "rear tenements." What do the following figures reveal about the problems facing New York slum dwellers?

POPULATION STATISTICS

Population of:

New York City, 1880.	1,206,299
London, 1881	3,816,483
Philadelphia, 1880	846,980

Population density to the square mile in:

New York City, 1880.	30,976
Tenth Ward, 1880	276,672
New York City, 1890.	38,451
Tenth Ward, 1890	334,080

Death-rate per 1,000 of population in:

New York City, 1889.	25.2
London, 1889	17.4
Philadelphia, 1889	19.7

---

[*]Jacob A. Riis, *How the Other Half Lives: Studies Among the Tenements of New York* (New York: Charles Scribner's Sons, 1890), pp. 299–303.

POLICE STATISTICS

	Males	Females
Arrests made by the police in 1889 62,274		19,926
Number of arrests for:		
Drunkenness and disorderly conduct 20,253		8,981
Disorderly conduct 10,953		7,477
Assault and battery 4,534		497
Theft 4,399		721
Robbery. 247		10
Vagrancy 1,686		947
Prisoners unable to read or write 2,399		1,281

Number of:	
Lost children found in the streets, 1889 2,968
Sick and destitute cared for, 1889. 2,753
Sick found in the streets 1,211
Pawnshops in the city, 1889 110
Cheap lodging-houses, 1889 270
Saloons, 1889 7,884

TENEMENTS

Number of Tenements in New York, December 1, 1888	32,390
Number built from June 1, 1888, to August 1, 1890	3,733
Rear tenements in existence, August 1, 1890.	2,630
Total number of tenements, August 1, 1890	37,316
Estimated population of tenements, August 1, 1890	1,250,000
Estimated number of children under five years in tenements, 1890 . . .	163,712

B. The New Immigration

1. Mary Antin Praises America (1894)*

The bomb assassination of Czar Alexander II in 1881 touched off an outburst of anti-Semitism in Russia that resulted in countless riots, burnings, pillagings, rapes, and murders. Tens of thousands of Jewish refugees fled to America then and later. Mary Antin, a thirteen-year-old Polish Jew, joined her father in Boston in 1894. She later distinguished herself as an author and a welfare worker. In her autobiographical account, excerpted here, what did these Jewish immigrants find most gratifying in America?

In our flat we did not think of such a thing as storing the coal in the bathtub. There was no bathtub. So in the evening of the first day my father conducted us to the public baths. As we moved along in a little procession, I was delighted with the illumination of the streets. So many lamps, and they burned until morning, my father said, and so people did not need to carry lanterns.

---

*From *The Promised Land* by Mary Antin. Copyright 1912 by Houghton Mifflin Company.

In America, then, everything was free, as we had heard in Russia; the streets were as bright as a synagogue on a holy day. Music was free; we had been serenaded, to our gaping delight, by a brass band of many pieces, soon after our installation on Union Place.

Education was free. That subject my father had written about repeatedly, as comprising his chief hope for us children, the essence of American opportunity, the treasure that no thief could touch, nor even misfortune or poverty. It was the one thing that he was able to promise us when he sent for us; surer, safer, than bread or shelter.

On our second day I was thrilled with the realization of what this freedom of education meant. A little girl from across the alley came and offered to conduct us to school. My father was out, but we five between us had a few words of English by this time. We knew the word *school*. We understood. This child, who had never seen us till yesterday, who could not pronounce our names, who was not much better dressed than we, was able to offer us the freedom of the schools of Boston! No application made, no questions asked, no examinations, rulings, exclusions; no machinations, no fees. The doors stood open for every one of us. The smallest child could show us the way.

The incident impressed me more than anything I had heard in advance of the freedom of education in America. It was a concrete proof—almost the thing itself. One had to experience it to understand it.

[Distressingly common was the experience of Anzia Yezierska, whose impoverished family came from Russia to New York City in 1901. Buoyed up by the hope of finding green fields and open places, she found herself in a smelly, crowded slum. God's blue sky was not visible; the landscape was the brick wall of the next building; and there was no place for the pasty-faced children to play. One of her despairing companions said, "In Russia, you could hope to run away from your troubles in America. But from America where can you go?"]

2. The American Protective Association Hates Catholics (1893)[*]

The flood of cheap southern European labor in the 1880s, predominantly Roman Catholic, rearoused nativist bigots. The most powerful group, the secretive American Protective Association (APA), claimed a million members by 1896. Among its various activities, it circulated forged documents revealing alleged papal orders to "exterminate" non-Catholics. In Toledo, Ohio, the local branch gathered Winchester rifles for defense. The APA was especially alarmed by the Irish Catholic political machines, which in cities like New York and Chicago had secured a semimonopoly of public offices, including the fire department and the police department. In the following secret oath of the APA, are the economic or the political prohibitions more damaging?

---

[*]From *Documents of American Catholic History*, edited by J. Tracy Ellis. Copyright © 1951.

I do most solemnly promise and swear that I will always, to the utmost of my ability, labor, plead, and wage a continuous warfare against ignorance and fanaticism; that I will use my utmost power to strike the shackles and chains of blind obedience to the Roman Catholic Church from the hampered and bound consciences of a priest-ridden and church-oppressed people; that I will never allow anyone, a member of the Roman Catholic Church, to become a member of this order, I knowing him to be such; and I will use my influence to promote the interest of all Protestants everywhere in the world that I may be; that I will not employ a Roman Catholic in any capacity, if I can procure the services of a Protestant.

I furthermore promise and swear that I will not aid in building or maintaining, by my resources, any Roman Catholic church or institution of their sect or creed whatsoever, but will do all in my power to retard and break down the power of the Pope, in this country or any other; that I will not enter into any controversy with a Roman Catholic upon the subject of this order, nor will I enter into any agreement with a Roman Catholic to strike or create a disturbance whereby the Catholic employees may undermine and substitute their Protestant co-workers; that in all grievances I will seek only Protestants, and counsel with them to the exclusion of all Roman Catholics, and will not make known to them anything of any nature matured at such conferences.

I furthermore promise and swear that I will not countenance the nomination, in any caucus or convention, of a Roman Catholic for any office in the gift of the American people, and that I will not vote for, or counsel others to vote for, any Roman Catholic, but will vote only for a Protestant, so far as may lie in my power (should there be two Roman Catholics in opposite tickets, I will erase the name on the ticket I vote); that I will at all times endeavor to place the political positions of this government in the hands of Protestants, to the entire exclusion of the Roman Catholic Church, of the members thereof, and the mandate of the Pope.

To all of which I do most solemnly promise and swear, so help me God. Amen.

3. President Cleveland Vetoes a Literacy Test (1897)[*]

In 1897 Congress passed a bill excluding all prospective immigrants who could not read or write twenty-five words of the Constitution of the United States in some language. One of the several goals of the exclusionists was to bar anarchists and other radical labor agitators. Cleveland, ever ruggedly independent, vetoed the bill. What is his most effective argument against it?

It is not claimed, I believe, that the time has come for the further restriction of immigration on the ground that an excess of population overcrowds our land.

It is said, however, that the quality of recent immigration is undesirable. The time is quite within recent memory when the same thing was said of immigrants who, with their descendants, are now numbered among our best citizens.

[*]J. D. Richardson, ed., *Messages and Papers of the Presidents* (New York: Bureau of National Literature, 1897), vol. 9, pp. 758–759.

It is said that too many immigrants settle in our cities, thus dangerously increasing their idle and vicious population. This is certainly a disadvantage. It cannot be shown, however, that it affects all our cities, nor that it is permanent; nor does it appear that this condition, where it exists, demands as its remedy the reversal of our present immigration policy.

The claim is also made that the influx of foreign laborers deprives of the opportunity to work those who are better entitled than they to the privilege of earning their livelihood by daily toil. An unfortunate condition is certainly presented when any who are willing to labor are unemployed, but so far as this condition now exists among our people, it must be conceded to be a result of phenomenal business depression and the stagnation of all enterprises in which labor is a factor. With the advent of settled and wholesome financial and economic governmental policies, and consequent encouragement to the activity of capital, the misfortunes of unemployed labor should, to a great extent at least, be remedied. If it continues, its natural consequences must be to check the further immigration to our cities of foreign laborers and to deplete the ranks of those already there. In the meantime those most willing and best entitled ought to be able to secure the advantages of such work as there is to do....

The best reason that could be given for this radical restriction of immigration is the necessity of protecting our population against degeneration and saving our national peace and quiet from imported turbulence and disorder.

I cannot believe that we would be protected against these evils by limiting immigration to those who can read and write in any language twenty-five words of our Constitution. In my opinion, it is infinitely more safe to admit a hundred thousand immigrants who, though unable to read and write, seek among us only a home and opportunity to work than to admit one of those unruly agitators and enemies of governmental control who can not only read and write, but delight in arousing by inflammatory speech the illiterate and peacefully inclined to discontent and tumult.

Violence and disorder do not originate with illiterate laborers. They are, rather, the victims of the educated agitator. The ability to read and write, as required in this bill, in and of itself affords, in my opinion, a misleading test of contented industry and supplies unsatisfactory evidence of desirable citizenship or a proper apprehension of the benefits of our institutions.

If any particular element of our illiterate immigration is to be feared for other causes than illiteracy, these causes should be dealt with directly, instead of making illiteracy the pretext for exclusion, to the detriment of other illiterate immigrants against whom the real cause of complaint cannot be alleged.

[President Taft, following Cleveland's example in 1897, successfully vetoed a literacy test in 1913, as did President Wilson in 1915. Finally, in 1917, such a restriction was passed over Wilson's veto. Wilson had declared that the prohibition was "not a test of character, of quality, or of personal fitness." In fact, a literacy test denied further opportunity to those who had already been denied opportunity.]

4. Four Views of the Statue of Liberty (1881, 1885, 1886)

The Statue of Liberty was a gift from the French people to the American people, intended to symbolize the friendship between the two republics. Even before the dedication ceremonies in 1886, the statue had become a symbol of America itself. What particular aspects of America did the statue symbolize? At the dedication ceremonies, President Grover Cleveland and other speakers explained that the statue represented the beneficent effect of American ideals, and they emphasized the theme of international friendship and peace. Later, Lady Liberty came to signify a warm welcome to foreign immigrants. The following prints provide four images of the statue and four images of America. What interpretations of the meaning of America are being expressed in these images? What different groups or perspectives are represented in these prints? Are there any similarities among the four images?

The Warning Light, 1881

Bartenders' Statue of License Lightening New York, 1885

Erecting the New York Political Statue, 1886

Our Statue of Liberty—She Can Stand It, 1886

5. Jane Addams Observes the New Immigrants (1910)*

A tireless advocate on behalf of the poor, Jane Addams established Hull House, Chicago's world-famous settlement house, just as a new wave of immigrants poured onto American shores. As the old stock of Irish and German Americans worked their way out of the cramped tenements and dusty factories of Chicago's West Side, new-comers from southern and eastern Europe filed in to take their place. In a memoir published twenty years after she first opened the doors of Hull House to the immi-grant poor, Jane Addams reflected on the character and influence of this new crop of foreign-born. How does she portray the new immigrant pool? What differences does she observe between immigrants and their native-born children?

Halsted Street has grown so familiar during twenty years of residence, that it is difficult to recall its gradual changes,—the withdrawal of the more prosperous Irish and Germans, and the slow substitution of Russian Jews, Italians, and Greeks. . . .

This substitution of the older inhabitants is accomplished industrially also, in the south and east quarters of the ward. The Jews and Italians do the finishing for the great clothing manufacturers, formerly done by Americans, Irish and Germans, who refused to submit to the extremely low prices to which the sweating system has reduced their successors. As the design of the sweating system is the elimina-tion of rent from the manufacture of clothing, the "outside work" is begun after the clothing leaves the cutter. An unscrupulous contractor regards no basement as too dark, no stable loft too foul, no rear shanty too provisional, no tenement room too small for his work-room, as these conditions imply low rental. Hence these shops abound in the worst of the foreign districts where the sweater easily finds his cheap basement and his home finishers. . . .

We learned to know many families in which the working children contributed to the support of their parents, not only because they spoke English better than the older immigrants and were willing to take lower wages, but because their parents gradually found it easy to live upon their earnings. A South Italian peasant who has picked olives and packed oranges from his toddling babyhood, cannot see at once the difference between the outdoor healthy work which he has performed in the varying seasons, and the long hours of monotonous factory life which his child encounters when he goes to work in Chicago. An Italian father came to us in great grief over the death of his eldest child, a little girl of twelve, who had brought the largest wages into the family fund. In the midst of his genuine sorrow he said: "She was the oldest kid I had. Now I shall have to go back to work again until the next one is able to take care of me." The man was only thirty-three and had hoped to retire from work at least during the winters. No foreman cared to have him in a factory, untrained and unintelligent as he was. It was much easier for his bright, English-speaking little girl to get a chance to paste labels on a box than for him to secure an opportunity to carry pig iron. The effect on the child was what no one concerned thought about, in the abnormal effort she made thus prematurely to bear the weight of life. Another little girl of thirteen, a Russian-Jewish child employed in

---

*Jane Addams, *Twenty Years at Hull-House* (New York: Macmillan Company, 1910), pp. 97–233.

a laundry at a heavy task beyond her strength, committed suicide, because she had borrowed three dollars from a companion which she could not repay unless she confided the story to her parents and gave up an entire week's wages—but what could the family live upon that week in case she did!...

From our very first months at Hull-House we found it much easier to deal with the first generation of crowded city life than with the second or third, because it is more natural and cast in a simpler mold. The Italian and Bohemian peasants who live in Chicago, still put on their bright holiday clothes on a Sunday and go to visit their cousins. They tramp along with at least a suggestion of having once walked over plowed fields and breathed country air. The second generation of city poor too often have no holiday clothes and consider their relations a "bad lot."...

Possibly the South Italians more than any other immigrants represent the pathetic stupidity of agricultural people crowded into city tenements, and we were much gratified when thirty peasant families were induced to move upon the land which they knew so well how to cultivate. The starting of this colony, however, was a very expensive affair in spite of the fact that the colonists purchased the land at two dollars an acre; they needed much more than raw land, and although it was possible to collect the small sums necessary to sustain them during the hard time of the first two years, we were fully convinced that undertakings of this sort could be conducted properly only by colonization societies such as England has established, or, better still, by enlarging the functions of the Federal Department of Immigration.

An evening similar in purpose to the one devoted to the Italians was organized for the Germans, in our first year. Owing to the superior education of our Teutonic guests and the clever leading of a cultivated German woman, these evenings reflected something of that cozy social intercourse which is found in its perfection in the fatherland. Our guests sang a great deal in the tender minor of the German folksong or in the rousing spirit of the Rhine, and they slowly but persistently pursued a course in German history and literature, recovering something of that poetry and romance which they had long since resigned with other good things. We found strong family affection between them and their English-speaking children, but their pleasures were not in common, and they seldom went out together.

6. Global Migrations (1870–2001)*

Uprooted by the industrial revolution, millions of Old World residents departed in search of economic opportunity—some leaving the countryside for nearby factories, others piling onto crowded ships to cross the Atlantic. As an emerging industrial giant with thousands of employers clamoring for cheap labor, the United States attracted nearly half of all international migrants. The following table shows the percentage of foreign-born in parts of Europe and the Americas. Which countries took in the largest share of immigrants? In what ways did immigration patterns established in the nineteenth century persist into the twentieth?

---

*Timothy J. Hatton and Jeffrey G. Williamson, *Global Migration and the World Economy: Two Centuries of Policy and Performance.* Table 2.2 and excerpt from page 16, © 2005 Massachusetts Institute of Technology, by permission of The MIT Press.

Percentages of Foreign-Born in European and New World Populations, 1870–1910 and 2000

	1870–1871	1890–1891	1910–1911	2000–2001
Europe				
Germany	0.5	0.9	1.9	8.9[b]
France	2.0	3.0	3.0	10.0
United Kingdom	0.5	0.7	0.9	4.3
Denmark	3.0	3.3	3.1	5.8
Norway	1.6	2.4	2.3	6.3
Sweden	0.3	0.5	0.9	11.3
New World				
Australia	46.5	31.8	17.1	23.6
New Zealand	63.5	41.5	30.3	19.5
Canada	16.5	13.3	22.0	17.4
United States	14.4	14.7	14.7	11.1
Argentina	12.1	25.5	29.9	5.0
Brazil	3.9	2.5	7.3[a]	

[a]1900.

[b]Foreign nationals.

Sources: For 1870–1910 figures, Germany: Ferenczi and Willcox 1929 (223); United Kingdom: Carrier and Jeffrey 1953 (15); France, Denmark, Norway, and Sweden: Foreign-born from Ferenczi and Willcox 1929 (308, 381), population from Mitchell 1983 (3–7); Australia (excludes aborigines): Price 1987 (9); New Zealand (excludes Maoris): New Zealand Bureau of Statistics 1883 (107), 1897 (62), and 1918 (76), and Dominion Bureau of Statistics 1942 (1:44); United States: U.S. Bureau of the Census 1926 (4); Argentina (1869, 1895, and 1914): Solberg 1978 (150); Brazil: Conselo Nacional do Estatistica 1958 (28). Figures for 2000–2001 are from OECD 2003.

C. The Anti-Saloon Crusade

1. Frances Willard Prays in a Saloon (1874)[*]

An independent girl, Frances E. Willard defied her novel-hating father by openly reading Scott's Ivanhoe *on her eighteenth birthday. At first an educator of females, she gained fame as an advocate of temperance and woman suffrage. She was one of the founders of the Woman's Christian Temperance Union (WCTU), which grew out of the praying-in-saloons crusade of 1873–1874. Willard stressed not so much the social and economic evils of drinking as the need for protecting the home and the Christian way of life. The saloon, often in league with gambling and prostitution, was riding high from 1870 to 1900. Some towns had one for every two hundred inhabitants, and the swinging doors, the heavy brass rails, and the nude Venus over the huge gilded mirror were familiar sights. Willard here describes her experiences in Pittsburgh. How effective is this approach, and how would it be received today?*

[*]Frances E. Willard, *Glimpses of Fifty Years* (Woman's Temperance Publication Association, 1892), pp. 340–341.

We paused in front of the saloon that I have mentioned. The ladies ranged themselves along the curbstone, for they had been forbidden in any wise to incommode the passers-by, being dealt with much more strictly than a drunken man or a heap of dry-goods boxes would be.

At a signal from our gray-haired leader, a sweet-voiced woman began to sing, "Jesus the water of life will give," all our voices soon blending in that sweet song. I think it was the most novel spectacle that I recall. There stood women of undoubted religious devotion and the highest character, most of them crowned with the glory of gray hairs. Along the stony pavement of that stoniest of cities rumbled the heavy wagons, many of them carriers of beer; between us and the saloon in front of which we were drawn up in line, passed the motley throng, almost every man lifting his hat and even the little newsboys doing the same. It was American manhood's tribute to Christianity and to womanhood, and it was significant and full of pathos.

The leader had already asked the saloonkeeper if we might enter, and he had declined, else the prayer meeting would have occurred inside his door. A sorrowful old lady, whose only son had gone to ruin through that very death-trap, knelt on the cold, moist pavement and offered a broken-hearted prayer, while all our heads were bowed.

At a signal we moved on and the next saloonkeeper permitted us to enter. I had no more idea of the inward appearance of a saloon than if there had been no such place on earth. I knew nothing of its high, heavily corniced bar, its barrels with the ends all pointed toward the looker-on, each barrel being furnished with a faucet, its shelves glittering with decanters and cut glass, its floors thickly strewn with sawdust, and here and there a round table with chairs—nor of its abundant fumes, sickening to healthful nostrils.

The tall, stately lady who led us placed her Bible on the bar and read a psalm, whether hortatory or imprecatory I do not remember, but the spirit of these crusaders was so gentle, I think it must have been the former.

Then we sang "Rock of Ages" as I thought I had never heard it sung before, with a tender confidence to the height of which one does not rise in the easy-going, regulation prayer meeting, and then one of the older women whispered to me softly that the leader wished to know if I would pray. It was strange, perhaps, but I felt not the least reluctance, and kneeling on the sawdust floor, with a group of earnest hearts around me, and behind them, filling every corner and extending out into the street, a crowd of unwashed, unkempt, hard-looking drinking men, I was conscious that perhaps never in my life, save beside my sister Mary's dying bed, had I prayed as truly as I did then. This was my Crusade baptism. The next day I went on to the West and within a week had been made president of the Chicago W.C.T.U.

2. Samuel Gompers Defends the Saloon (c. 1886)[*]

The Knights of Labor, joining the foes of the saloon, refused to admit liquor sellers to their membership. Their leader, Terence V. Powderly, even accused certain employers

---

[*]From Samuel Gompers, *Seventy Years of Life and Labor* (New York: E. P. Dutton & Company, 1925), pp. 176, 244–245, 284.

of encouraging drink so that the employees would become more content with their underpaid lot. (This argument assumes that docility is preferable to efficiency.) But Samuel Gompers of the American Federation of Labor had a good word to say for the attractively lighted "poor man's club," even though it drained away the family's grocery money. Did the advantages offset the disadvantages?

The saloon was the only club the workingmen had then. For a few cents we could buy a glass of beer and hours of congenial society. Talk in these meeting places had a peculiar freedom from formality that engendered good-fellowship and exchange of genuine intimacies.

The saloon rendered a variety of industrial services. Frequently, wages were paid there—in checks which the saloonkeeper cashed. Of course, it was embarrassing to accept that service without spending money with him.

All too frequently the saloonkeeper also served as an employment agent. But on the other hand the saloonkeeper was often a friend in time of strikes and the free lunch [salty foods to stimulate thirst] he served was a boon to many a hungry striker.

Nearly every saloon had a room or a hall back of it or over it that could be rented for a nominal sum. Of course, the saloon was counting on increased receipts due to gatherings held in the hall. These rooms were practically the only meeting places available to unions, which were poor and small in numbers.

[The continued callousness of "booze barons" resulted in the launching of the Anti-Saloon League in 1893. It supplemented the efforts of the Prohibition party, organized in 1869, and the Woman's Christian Temperance Union, organized in 1874. With mounting zeal, the reformers harped on the following arguments: (1) Alcohol was a debauching force in U.S. politics. (2) The rapid mechanization of industry required sobriety for safety and efficiency. (3) The liquor sellers were saddling the taxpayers with the occupants of prisons and poorhouses. But prohibition in the localities and the states was slow in coming. By 1905 only four states had entered the "dry" column: Kansas, Maine, Nebraska, and North Dakota. Success was slowest in the large urban areas, where huge colonies of immigrants had brought with them Old World drinking habits.]

D. The Changing Role of Women

1. The Life of a Working Girl (1905)*

Dorothy Richardson, a fairly well educated, obviously middle-class young woman, was compelled by necessity to seek employment in a New York sweatshop around the turn of the century. She recorded her experiences in a remarkable book, The Long Day, excerpted here. What is her attitude toward the immigrant working-class girls

---

*From Dorothy Richardson, *The Long Day: The Story of the New York Working Girl as Told by Herself* (New York: The Century Co., 1905), as it appears in William L. O'Neill, *Women at Work* (Chicago: Quadrangle Books, 1972), pp. 203–214.

who became her companions and workmates? Why did these young women work? How were their working conditions different from those of today? Elsewhere in her book, Richardson quoted one of her fellow workers who spoke of "long ago, when they used to treat the girls so bad. Things is ever so much better now." How might the conditions here described have been worse in an earlier day?

Bessie met Eunice and me at the lower right-hand corner of Broadway and Grand Street, and together we applied for work in the R——— Underwear Company, which had advertised that morning for twenty operators.

"Ever run a power Singer?" queried the foreman.

"No, but we can learn. We're all quick," answered Bessie, who had volunteered to act as spokesman.

"Yes, I guess you can learn all right, but you won't make very much at first. All come together?...So! Well, then, I guess you'll want to work in the same room," and with that he ushered us into a very inferno of sound, a great, yawning chaos of terrific noise. The girls, who sat in long rows up and down the length of the great room, did not raise their eyes to the newcomers, as is the rule in less strenuous workrooms. Every pair of eyes seemed to be held in fascination upon the flying and endless strip of white that raced through a pair of hands to feed itself into the insatiable maw of the electric sewing-machine. Every face, tense and stony, bespoke a superb effort to concentrate mind and body, and soul itself, literally upon the point of a needle. Every form was crouched in the effort to guide the seam through the presser-foot. And piled between the opposing phalanxes of set faces were billows upon billows of foamy white muslin and lace—the finished garments wrought by the so-many dozen per hour, for the so-many cents per day,—and wrought, too, in this terrific, nerve-racking noise.

The foreman led us into the middle of the room, which was lighted by gas-jets that hung directly over the girls' heads, although the ends of the shop had bright sunshine from the windows. He seemed a good-natured, respectable sort of man, of about forty, and was a Jew. Bessie and me he placed at machines side by side, and Eunice a little farther down the line. Then my first lesson began. He showed me how to thread bobbin and needle, how to operate ruffler and tucker, and also how to turn off and on the electric current which operated the machinery. My first attempt to do the latter was productive of a shock to the nerves that could not have been greater if, instead of pressing the harmless little lever under the machine with my knee, I had accidently exploded a bomb. The foreman laughed good-naturedly at my fright.

"You'll get used to it by and by," he shouted above the noise; "but like as not for a while you won't sleep very good nights—kind of nervous; but you'll get over that in a week or so," and he ducked his head under the machine to adjust the belt....

I leaned over the machine and practised at running a straight seam. Ah, the skill of these women and girls, and of the strange creature opposite, who can make a living at this torturing labor! How many different, how infinitely harder it is, as compared with running an ordinary sewing-machine. The goods that my nervous fingers tried to guide ran every wrong way. I had no control whatever over the fearful velocity with which the needle danced along the seam. In utter discouragement, I stopped trying for a moment, and watched the girl at my right. She was a swarthy, thick-lipped Jewess, of the type most common in such places, but I looked at her with awe and admiration. In Rachel Goldberg's case the making of muslin, lace-trimmed corset-covers was an art rather than a craft. She was a remarkable operator even among scores of experts at the R————. Under her stubby, ill-kept hands ruffles and tucks and insertion bands and lace frills were wrought with a beauty and softness of finish, and a speed and precision of workmanship, that made her the wonder and envy of the shop....

Result of my first hour's work: I had spoiled a dozen garments. Try as I would, I invariably lost all control of my materials, and the needle plunged right and left—everywhere, in fact, except along the straight and narrow way laid out for it....

As I spoiled each garment I thrust it into the bottom of a green pasteboard box under the table, which held my allotment of work, and from the top of the box grabbed up a fresh piece. I glanced over my shoulder and saw that Bessie was doing the same thing, although what we were going to do with them, or how account for such wholesale devastation of goods, we were too perturbed to consider. At last, however, after repeated trials, and by guiding the seam with laborious care, I succeeded in completing one garment without disaster; and I had just started another, when—crash!—flying shuttles and spinning bobbins and swirling wheels came to a standstill. My sewing-machine was silent, as were all the others in the great workroom. Something had happened to the dynamo.

There was a howl of disappointment....

Rachel Goldberg had finished four dozen of extrafine garments, which meant seventy-five cents, and it was not yet eleven o'clock. She would make at least one dollar and sixty cents before the day was over, provided we did not have any serious breakdowns. She watched the clock impatiently—every minute she was idle meant a certain fraction of a penny lost,—and crouched sullenly over her machine for the signal.

2. An Italian Immigrant Woman Faces Life Alone in the Big City (c. 1896)*

Rosa Cavalleri came from her native Lombardy, in Italy, to Chicago in 1884. Although she never knew her exact birth date, she was probably about eighteen years old when she arrived in the United States. In later years she recounted her life story to Marie Hall Ets, who was a social worker at the Chicago Commons, a settlement house founded in 1894 by Dr. Graham Taylor, an associate of the pioneering urban reformer Jane Addams. What were the most important concerns in Cavalleri's life? Who helped her? What evidence does this account provide of the existence of an immigrant "community"? What was the role of the municipal government in Rosa Cavalleri's life?

---

*From Marie Hall Ets, *Rosa: The Life of an Italian Immigrant* (Minneapolis: University of Minnesota Press, 1970), pp. 228–231. Copyright © 1970 by the University of Minnesota.

The year my Leo was born I was home alone and struggled along with my children. My husband went away because he was sick—he went by a doctor in St. Louis to get cured. The doctor said he must stay away from his home one year and gave him a job to do all the janitor work around his house for five dollars a month and his board. So me, I used to go all around to find the clothes to wash and the scrubbing. The city hall was helping me again in that time—they gave me a little coal and sometimes the basket of food. Bob, the sign painter downstairs, he helped me the most. He was such a good young man. He used to bring a big chunk of coal and chop it up right in my kitchen and fix the stove.

I was to the end of my nine months, but the baby never came. So I went by one woman, Mis' Thomas, and I got part of the clothes washed. Then I said, "Oh Mis' Thomas, I've got to go. I've got the terrible pains!"

She said, "You can go when you finish. You've got to finish first."

"No, I go. Otherwise I'll have to stay in your bed." When I said that she got scared I would have the baby there, so she let me go.

I went by the midwife, Mis' Marino, and told her to come; then I went home. When I saw it was my time, I told Domenico something and sent him with all the children to the wife of Tomaso. I told those people before, when they see the children come they must keep them all night—it's my time. It was really, really my time, and I had such a scare that I would be alone a second time. So when I heard a lady come in the building—she lived downstairs—I called to her. She said, "I have no time." And she didn't come up.

I was on my bed all alone by myself and then I prayed Sant' Antoni with all my heart. I don't know why I prayed Sant' Antoni—the Madonna put it in my mind. And then, just when the baby was born, I saw Sant' Antoni right there! He appeared in the room by me! I don't think it was really Sant' Antoni there, but in my imagination I saw him—all light like the sun. I saw Sant' Antoni there by my bed, and right then the door opened and the midwife came in to take care of the baby! It was February seventh and six below zero. There I had him born all alone, but Mis' Marino came when I prayed Sant' Antoni. She washed the baby and put him by me, but then she ran away. She didn't light the fire or nothing.

Oh, that night it was *so* cold! And me in my little wooden house in the alley with the walls all frosting—thick white frosting. I was crying and praying, "How am I going to live?" I said. "Oh, Sant' Antoni, I'll never live till tomorrow morning! I'll never live till the morning!"

And just as I prayed my door opened and a lady came in. She had a black shawl twice around her neck and head and that shawl came down to her nose. All I could see was half the nose and the mouth. She came in and lighted both the stoves. Then she came and looked at me, but I couldn't see her face. I said, "God bless you!"

She just nodded her head up and down and all the time said not one word, only "Sh, sh."

Then she went down in the basement herself, nobody telling her nothing, and she got the coal and fixed the fire. Pretty soon she found that little package of camomile tea I had there on the dresser and she made a little tea with the hot water. And that woman stayed by me almost till daylight. But all the time she put her finger to her mouth to tell me to keep still when I tried to thank her. And I never knew where that lady came from! I don't know yet! Maybe she was the spirit of that kind girl, Annina, in Canaletto? I don't know. I really don't know! I was *so* sick and I didn't hear her voice or see her face. All the time she put her finger on her mouth and said, "Sh, sh." And when the daylight came she was gone.

About seven o'clock morning my children came home. And Mis' Marino, that midwife, she came at eight o'clock and said, "It's so cold I thought I'd find you dead!"

Then here came the city hall, or somebody, with a wagon. They wanted to take me and my new baby to the hospital. But how could I leave all my children? I started to cry—I didn't want to go. And my children cried too—they didn't want me to leave them. So then they didn't make me. They pulled my bed away from the frosting on the wall and put it in the front room by the stove. And my baby, I had him wrapped up in a pad I made from the underskirt like we do in *Italia*. But that baby froze when he was born; he couldn't cry like other babies—he was crying weak, weak.

My Visella was bringing up the wood and the coal and trying to make that room warm. But she was only a little girl, she didn't know, and she filled that stove so full that all the pipes on the ceiling caught fire. I had to jump up from the bed and throw the pails of water so the house wouldn't burn down. Then God sent me help again. He sent that Miss Mildred from the settlement house. She didn't know about me and my Leo born; she was looking for some other lady and she came to my door and saw me. She said, "Oh, I have the wrong place."

I said, "No, lady, you find the right place."

So she came in and found out all. Then she ran away and brought back all those little things the babies in America have. She felt sorry to see my baby banded up like I had him. She didn't know then, Miss Mildred, that the women in *Italia* always band their babies that way. And she brought me something to eat too—for me and for my children. That night another young lady from the Commons, Miss May, she came and slept in my house to take care of the fire. She was afraid for the children—maybe they would burn themselves and the house. Oh, that Miss Mildred and Miss May, they were angels to come and help me like that! Four nights Miss May stayed there and kept the fire going. They were high-up educated girls—they were used to sleeping in the warm house with the plumbing—and there they came and slept in my wooden house in the alley, and for a toilet they had to go down to that shed under the sidewalk. They were really, really friends! That time I had my Leo nobody knew I was going to have the baby—I looked kind of fat, that's all. These women in the settlement house were so surprised. They said, "Why you didn't tell us before, Mis' Cavalleri, so we can help you?"

You know that Mis' Thomas—I was washing her clothes when the baby started to come—she wanted a boy and she got a baby girl right after my baby was born. When I went there the next week to do the washing I had to carry my baby with me. When she saw him she said, "Well better I have a girl than I have a boy that looks like your baby! He looks for sure like a monkey!"

In the first beginning he did look like a monkey, but in a few weeks he got pretty. He got so pretty all the people from the settlement house came to see him. After two or three months there was no baby in Chicago prettier than that baby.

When the year was over for him, my husband came home from St. Louis. He didn't send me the money when he was there—just two times the five dollars—so he brought twenty-five dollars when he came back. Oh, he was so happy when he saw that baby with exactly, exactly his face and everything—the same dark gold hair and everything—and so beautiful. But he saw that baby was so thin and pale and couldn't cry like the other babies. "Better I go by a good doctor and see," he said. "I've got twenty-five dollars—I'm going to get a good doctor." So he did.

But the doctor said, "That baby can't live. He was touched in the lungs with the cold. Both lungs got froze when he was born."

And sure enough he was all the time sick and when it was nine months he died. My first Leo and my second Leo I lose them both. Oh, I was brokenhearted to lose such a beautiful baby!

Thought Provokers

1. What was most novel about city life? How are cities different today?
2. If the New Immigrants were disillusioned by America, why didn't more of them return to the Old Country? Why did they congregate in slums?
3. How has America's role in the pattern of global migration changed in the last century and a half? Why?
4. Critics have charged that one reason that the saloon prospered was that the churches and the community failed to provide wholesome alternatives. Discuss.
5. What was new about the "new woman" at the end of the nineteenth century? Why did women in growing numbers work for wages? Did female workers deserve special protection?

26

The Great West and the Agricultural Revolution, 1865–1896

Many, if not most, of our Indian wars have
had their origin in broken promises and acts of
injustice upon our part.

President Hayes, 1877

Prologue: The fence-erecting white men inevitably clashed with the wide-roaming Indians of the plains. As land greed undermined ethical standards, many settlers acted as though the Indians had no more rights than the buffalo, which were also ruthlessly slaughtered. The seemingly endless frontier wars ended finally when the Native Americans, cooped up on reservations, were forced to adopt in part the economic life of their conquerors. The honest farmer and the fraudulent speculator were now free to open the Far West under the Homestead Act of 1862. Much of the settlement occurred in areas with only scanty rainfall, and when crops failed, or when overproduction came, the farmer was trapped. Agitation for relief vented itself most spectacularly in 1892, when the Populist party waged a colorful campaign for the presidency under General James B. Weaver. Although he carried six western states, he ran well behind the second-place Republicans as the Democrats again swept Grover Cleveland to victory.

A. The Plight of the Indian

1. Harper's Weekly Decries the Battle of the Little Bighorn (1876)*

As the white men closed in, the western Indians were forced to make numerous treaties with Washington that confined them to reservations and guaranteed needed supplies. But rascally government contractors cheated them with moldy flour, rotten beef, and moth-eaten blankets. In 1875 the discovery of gold on the Sioux reservation in the Dakotas brought stampeding thousands of miners, who brutally ignored treaty guarantees. The Indians fled the reservation (many had never agreed to live there in the first place), and the U.S. Army was sent to bring them back. The dashing Colonel

*Harper's Weekly 20 (August 5, 1876): 630–631.

George Armstrong Custer, with only 264 men, rashly attacked a hostile force that turned out to number several thousand. In 1876 Custer and his entire command were wiped out near the Little Bighorn River (Montana) in what the white men called a "massacre" and the Indians a "battle" and legend has long described as "Custer's last stand." What does this account in the reformist Harper's Weekly *see as the principal mistake in dealing with Native Americans? Who was basically responsible for the situation that had developed?*

The fate of the brave and gallant Custer had deeply touched the public heart, which sees only a fearless soldier leading a charge against an ambushed [lurking] foe, and falling at the head of his men and in the thick of the fray. A monument is proposed, and subscriptions have been made. But a truer monument, more enduring than brass or marble, would be an Indian policy intelligent, moral, and efficient. Custer would not have fallen in vain if such a policy should be the result of his death.

It is a permanent accusation of our humanity and ability that over the Canadian line the relations between Indians and whites are so tranquil, while upon our side they are summed up in perpetual treachery, waste, and war. When he was a young lieutenant on the frontier, General Grant saw this, and watching attentively, he came to the conclusion that the reason of the difference was that the English respected the rights of the Indians and kept faith with them, while we make solemn treaties with them as if they were civilized and powerful nations, and then practically regard them as vermin to be exterminated.

The folly of making treaties with the Indian tribes may be as great as treating with a herd of buffaloes. But the infamy of violating treaties when we have made them is undeniable, and we are guilty both of the folly and the infamy.

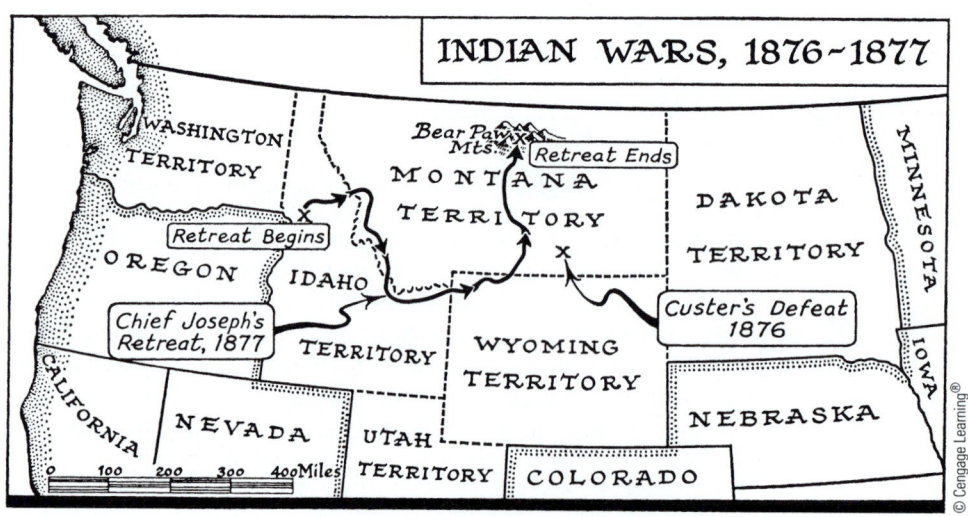

We make treaties—that is, we pledge our faith—and then leave swindlers and knaves of all kinds to execute them. We maintain and breed pauper colonies. The savages, who know us, and who will neither be pauperized nor trust our word, we pursue, and slay if we can, at an incredible expense. The flower of our young officers is lost in inglorious forays, and one of the intelligent students of the whole subject rises in Congress and says, "The fact is that these Indians, with whom we have made a solemn treaty that their territory should not be invaded, and that they should receive supplies upon their reservations, have seen from one thousand to fifteen hundred [gold] miners during the present season entering and occupying their territory, while the Indians, owing to the failure of this and the last Congress to make adequate appropriations for their subsistence, instead of being fattened, as the gentleman says, by the support of this government, have simply been starved."...

It is plain that so long as we undertake to support the Indians as paupers, and then fail to supply the food; to respect their rights to reservations, and then permit the reservations to be overrun; to give them the best weapons and ammunition, and then furnish the pretense of their using them against us; to treat with them as men, and then hunt them like skunks—so long we shall have the most costly and bloody Indian wars, and the most tragical ambuscades, slaughters, and assassinations.

The Indian is undoubtedly a savage, and a savage greatly spoiled by the kind of contact with civilization which he gets at the West. There is no romance, there is generally no interest whatever, in him or his fate. But there should be some interest in our own good faith and humanity, in the lives of our soldiers and frontier settlers, and in the taxation to support our Indian policy. All this should certainly be enough to arouse a public demand for a thorough consideration of the subject, and the adoption of a system which should neither be puerile nor disgraceful, and which would tend to spare us the constant repetition of such sorrowful events as the slaughter of Custer and his brave men.

2. She Walks with Her Shawl Remembers the Battle of the Little Bighorn (1876)[*]

The Indian encampment that Custer attacked on June 25, 1876, was one of the largest gatherings of Indians ever to assemble on the Great Plains—including Hunkpapas, Oglalas, Minneconjous, Brulés, Blackfeet, Two Kettles, Sans Arcs, and Northern Cheyennes, among others. She Walks with Her Shawl was a young Hunkpapa woman who witnessed the Battle of the Little Bighorn and gave the following account to an interviewer fifty-five years later, in 1931. In what ways might the Indians' account of the battle have differed from the whites' account? How reliable is testimony that has been filtered through more than a half-century of memory?

I was born seventy-seven winters ago, near Grand River, [in present] South Dakota. My father, Slohan, was the bravest man among our people. Fifty-five years

---

[*]*Lakota and Cheyenne: Indian Views of the Great Sioux War, 1876–1877*, edited by Greene, Jerome A. Reproduced with permission of University of Oklahoma Press in the format republish in a book via Copyright Clearance Center.

ago we packed our tents and went with other Indians to Peji-sla-wakpa (Greasy Grass). We were then living on the Standing Rock Indian reservation [Great Sioux Reservation, Standing Rock Agency]. I belonged to Sitting Bull's band. They were great fighters. We called ourselves Hunkpapa. This means confederated bands. When I was still a young girl (about seventeen) I accompanied a Sioux war party which made war against the Crow Indians in Montana. My father went to war 70 times. He was wounded nearly a dozen times.

But I am going to tell you of the greatest battle. This was a fight against Pehin-hanska (Colonel Custer). I was several miles from the Hunkpapa camp when I saw a cloud of dust rise beyond a ridge of bluffs in the east. The morning was hot and sultry. Several of us Indian girls were digging wild turnips. I was then 23 years old. We girls looked towards the camp and saw a warrior ride swiftly, shouting that the soldiers were only a few miles away and that the women and children including old men should run for the hills in an opposite direction.

I dropped the pointed ash stick which I had used in digging turnips and ran towards my tipi. I saw my father running towards the horses. When I got to my tent, mother told me that news was brought to her that my brother had been killed by the soldiers. My brother had gone early that morning in search for a horse that strayed from our herd. In a few moments we saw soldiers on horseback on a bluff just across the Greasy Grass (Little Big Horn) river. I knew that there would be a battle because I saw warriors getting their horses and tomahawks.

I heard Hawkman shout, Ho-ka-he! Ho-ka-he! (Charge.) The soldiers began firing into our camp. Then they ceased firing. I saw my father preparing to go to battle. I sang a death song for my brother who had been killed.

My heart was bad. Revenge! Revenge! For my brother's death. I thought of the death of my young brother, One Hawk. Brown Eagle, my brother's companion on that morning had escaped and gave the alarm to the camp that the soldiers were coming. I ran to a nearby thicket and got my black horse. I painted my face with crimson and unbraided my black hair. I was mourning. I was a woman, but I was not afraid.

By this time the soldiers (Reno's men) were forming a battle line in the bottom about a half mile away. In another moment I heard a terrific volley of carbines. The bullets shattered the tipi poles. Women and children were running away from the gunfire. In the tumult I heard old men and women singing death songs for their warriors who were now ready to attack the soldiers. The chanting of death songs made me brave, although I was a woman. I saw a warrior adjusting his quiver and grasping his tomahawk. He started running towards his horse when he suddenly recoiled and dropped dead. He was killed near his tipi.

Warriors were given orders by Hawkman to mount their horses and follow the fringe of a forest and wait until commands were given to charge. The soldiers kept on firing. Some women were also killed. Horses and dogs too! The camp was in great commotion.

Father led my black horse up to me and I mounted. We galloped towards the soldiers. Other warriors joined in with us. When we were nearing the fringe of the woods an order was given by Hawkman to charge. Ho-ka-he! Ho-ka-he! Charge! Charge! The warriors were now near the soldiers. The troopers were all on foot. They shot straight, because I saw our leader killed as he rode with his warriors.

The charge was so stubborn that the soldiers ran to their horses and, mounting them, rode swiftly towards the river. The Greasy Grass river was very deep. Their horses had to swim to get across. Some of the warriors rode into the water and tomahawked the soldiers. In the charge the Indians rode among the troopers and with tomahawks unhorsed several of them. The soldiers were very excited. Some of them shot into the air. The Indians chased the soldiers across the river and up over a bluff.

Then the warriors returned to the bottom where the first battle took place. We heard a commotion far down the valley. The warriors rode in a column of fives. They sang a victory song. Someone said that another body of soldiers were attacking the lower end of the village. I heard afterwards that the soldiers were under the command of Long Hair (Custer). With my father and other youthful warriors I rode in that direction.

We crossed the Greasy Grass below a beaver dam (the water is not so deep there) and came upon many horses. One soldier was holding the reins of eight or ten horses. An Indian waved his blanket and scared all the horses. They got away from the men (troopers). On the ridge just north of us I saw blue-clad men running up a ravine, firing as they ran.

The dust created from the stampeding horses and powder smoke made everything dark and black. Flashes from carbines could be seen. The valley was dense with powder smoke. I never heard such whooping and shouting. "There was never a better day to die," shouted Red Horse. In the battle I heard cries from troopers, but could not understand what they were saying. I do not speak English.

Long Hair's troopers were trapped in an enclosure. There were Indians everywhere. The Cheyennes attacked the soldiers from the north and Crow King from the South. The Sioux Indians encircled the troopers. Not one got away! The Sioux used tomahawks. It was not a massacre, but [a] hotly contested battle between two armed forces. Very few soldiers were mutilated, as oft has been said by the whites. Not a single soldier was burned at the stake. Sioux Indians do not torture their victims.

After the battle the Indians took all the equipment and horses belonging to the soldiers. The brave men who came to punish us that morning were defeated; but in the end, the Indians lost. We saw the body of Long Hair. Of course, we did not know who the soldiers were until an interpreter told us that the men came from Fort Lincoln, then [in] Dakota Territory. On the saddle blankets were the cross saber insignia and the letter seven.

The victorious warriors returned to the camp, as did the women and children who could see the battle from where they took refuge. Over sixty Indians were killed and they were also brought back to the camp for scaffold-burial.* The Indians did not stage a victory dance that night. They were mourning for their own dead.

3. Chief Joseph's Lament (1879)†

Chief Joseph, a noble-featured and humane Nez Percé, resisted being removed from his ancestral lands in Oregon and penned up on a reservation in Idaho. After an

---

*Native Americans often buried their dead not in the ground but by laying them out on aerial scaffolding.
†*North American Review* 128 (April 1879): 431–432.

amazing flight of about a thousand miles, he was finally captured in 1877 near the Canadian border. The miserable remnants of his band were deported to Indian Territory (now Oklahoma), where many died of malaria and other afflictions. Chief Joseph appealed personally to the president, and subsequently the Nez Percés were returned to the Pacific Northwest. In the following narrative, what formula does he offer for ending white-Indian wars?

At last I was granted permission to come to Washington and bring my friend Yellow Bull and our interpreter with me. I am glad I came. I have shaken hands with a good many friends, but there are some things I want to know which no one seems able to explain. I cannot understand how the government sends a man out to fight us, as it did General Miles, and then breaks his word. Such a government has something wrong about it. . . .

I have heard talk and talk, but nothing is done. Good words do not last long unless they amount to something. Words do not pay for my dead people. They do not pay for my country, now overrun by white men. They do not protect my father's grave. They do not pay for my horses and cattle.

Good words do not give me back my children. Good words will not make good the promise of your war chief, General Miles. Good words will not give my people good health and stop them from dying. Good words will not get my people a home where they can live in peace and take care of themselves.

I am tired of talk that comes to nothing. It makes my heart sick when I remember all the good words and all the broken promises. There has been too much talking by men who had no right to talk. Too many misinterpretations have been made; too many misunderstandings have come up between the white men and the Indians.

If the white man wants to live in peace with the Indian, he can live in peace. There need be no trouble. Treat all men alike. Give them the same laws. Give them all an even chance to live and grow.

All men are made by the same Great Spirit Chief. They are all brothers. The earth is the mother of all people, and all people should have equal rights upon it. You might as well expect all rivers to run backward as that any man who was born a free man should be contented penned up and denied liberty to go where he pleases. If you tie a horse to a stake, do you expect he will grow fat? If you pen an Indian up on a small spot of earth and compel him to stay there, he will not be contented nor will he grow and prosper.

I have asked some of the Great White Chiefs where they get their authority to say to the Indian that he shall stay in one place, while he sees white men going where they please. They cannot tell me.

I only ask of the government to be treated as all other men are treated. If I cannot go to my own home, let me have a home in a country where my people will not die so fast. I would like to go to Bitter Root Valley [western Montana]. There my people would be healthy; where they are now, they are dying. Three have died since I left my camp to come to Washington. When I think of our condition, my heart is heavy. I see men of my own race treated as outlaws and driven from country to country, or shot down like animals.

I know that my race must change. We cannot hold our own with the white men as we are. We only ask an even chance to live as other men live. We ask to be recognized as men. We ask that the same law shall work alike on all men. If an Indian breaks the law, punish him by the law. If a white man breaks the law, punish him also.

Let me be a free man—free to travel, free to stop, free to work, free to trade where I choose, free to choose my own teachers, free to follow the religion of my fathers, free to think and talk and act for myself—and I will obey every law or submit to the penalty.

Whenever the white man treats the Indian as they treat each other, then we shall have no more wars. We shall all be alike—brothers of one father and mother, with one sky above us and one country around us and one government for all. Then the Great Spirit Chief who rules above will smile upon this land and send rain to wash out the bloody spots made by brothers' hands upon the face of the earth. For this time the Indian race are waiting and praying. I hope no more groans of wounded men and women will ever go to the ear of the Great Spirit Chief above, and that all people may be one people.

4. Theodore Roosevelt Downgrades the Indians (1885)[*]

Sickly and bespectacled young Theodore Roosevelt, the future president, invested more than $50,000 of his patrimony in ranch lands in Dakota Territory. He lost most of his investment but gained robust health and valuable experience. With little sympathy for Native Americans, he felt that the government had "erred quite as often on the side of too much leniency as on the side of too much severity." The following account, based in part on firsthand observations, appears in one of his earliest books. What light do his observations cast on the allegation that whites robbed Native Americans of their lands? What is his proposed solution to the problem?

There are now no Indians left in my immediate neighborhood, though a small party of harmless Grosventres occasionally passes through. Yet it is but six years since the Sioux surprised and killed five men in a log station just south of me, where the Fort Keogh trail crosses the river; and, two years ago, when I went down on the prairies toward the Black Hills, there was still danger from Indians. That summer the buffalo hunters had killed a couple of Crows, and while we were on the prairie a long-range skirmish occurred near us between some Cheyennes and a number of cowboys. In fact, we ourselves were one day scared by what we thought to be a party of Sioux; but on riding toward them they proved to be half-breed Crees, who were more afraid of us than we were of them.

During the past century a good deal of sentimental nonsense has been talked about our taking the Indians' land. Now, I do not mean to say for a moment that gross wrong has not been done the Indians, both by government and individuals, again and again. The government makes promises impossible to perform, and then fails to do even what it might toward their fulfilment; and where brutal and reckless

---

[*]Theodore Roosevelt, *Hunting Trips of a Ranchman* (New York: G. P. Putnam's Sons, 1885), pp. 17–19.

frontiersmen are brought into contact with a set of treacherous, revengeful, and fiendishly cruel savages a long series of outrages by both sides is sure to follow.

But as regards taking the land, at least from the Western Indians, the simple truth is that the latter never had any real ownership in it at all. Where the game was plenty, there they hunted; they followed it when it moved away to new hunting-grounds, unless they were prevented by stronger rivals; and to most of the land on which we found them they had no stronger claim than that of having a few years previously butchered the original occupants.

When my cattle came to the Little Missouri the region was only inhabited by a score or so of white hunters; their title to it was quite as good as that of most Indian tribes to the lands they claim; yet nobody dreamed of saying that these hunters owned the country. Each could eventually have kept his own claim of 160 acres, and no more.

The Indians should be treated in just the same way that we treat the white settlers. Give each his little claim; if, as would generally happen, he declined this, why then let him share the fate of the thousands of white hunters and trappers who have lived on the game that the settlement of the country has exterminated, and let him, like these whites, who will not work, perish from the face of the earth which he cumbers.[*]

The doctrine seems merciless, and so it is; but it is just and rational for all that. It does not do to be merciful to a few, at the cost of justice to the many. The cattle-men at least keep herds and build houses on the land; yet I would not for a moment debar settlers from the right of entry to the cattle country, though their coming in means in the end the destruction of us and our industry.

5. Carl Schurz Proposes to "Civilize" the Indians (1881)[†]

Carl Schurz, a notable "Forty-Eighter," or liberal refugee from the failed German revolution of 1848, had a prominent military career on the Union side in the Civil War and in 1877 became secretary of the interior. A lifelong reformer, he fought against slavery and political corruption and considered himself a friend to the Indians. What is his preferred solution to the "Indian problem"? Is he condescending to Native Americans or simply realistic? In what ways do his comments reveal attitudes about gender roles in nineteenth-century America?

I am profoundly convinced that a stubborn maintenance of the system of large Indian reservations must eventually result in the destruction of the red men, however faithfully the Government may endeavor to protect their rights. It is only a question of time.... What we can and should do is, in general terms, to fit the Indians, as much as possible, for the habits and occupations of civilized life, by work and education; to individualize them in the possession and appreciation of property, by allotting to them lands in severalty, giving them a fee simple title individually to the parcels of land they cultivate, inalienable for a certain period, and to obtain their consent to a

---

[*]In the Dawes Act of 1887, Congress made provision for granting the Indians individual allotments, as Roosevelt here suggests.
[†]Carl Schurz, "Present Aspects of the Indian Problem," *North American Review* 133 (July 1881): 6–10, 12–14, 16–18, 20–24.

disposition of that part of their lands which they cannot use, for a fair compensation, in such a manner that they no longer stand in the way of the development of the country as an obstacle, but form part of it and are benefited by it.

The circumstances surrounding them place before the Indians this stern alternative: extermination or civilization. The thought of exterminating a race, once the only occupant of the soil upon which so many millions of our own people have grown prosperous and happy, must be revolting to every American who is not devoid of all sentiments of justice and humanity. To civilize them, which was once only a benevolent fancy, has now become an absolute necessity, if we mean to save them.

Can Indians be civilized? This question is answered in the negative only by those who do not want to civilize them. My experience in the management of Indian affairs, which enabled me to witness the progress made even among the wildest tribes, confirms me in the belief that it is not only possible but easy to introduce civilized habits and occupations among Indians, if only the proper means are employed. We are frequently told that Indians will not work. True, it is difficult to make them work as long as they can live upon hunting. But they will work when their living depends upon it, or when sufficient inducements are offered to them. Of this there is an abundance of proof. To be sure, as to Indian civilization, we must not expect too rapid progress or the attainment of too lofty a standard. We can certainly not transform them at once into great statesmen, or philosophers, or manufacturers, or merchants; but we can make them small farmers and herders. Some of them show even remarkable aptitude for mercantile pursuits on a small scale. I see no reason why the degree of civilization attained by the Indians in the States of New York, Indiana, Michigan, and some tribes in the Indian Territory, should not be attained in the course of time by all. I have no doubt that they can be sufficiently civilized to support themselves, to maintain relations of good neighborship with the people surrounding them, and altogether to cease being a disturbing element in society. The accomplishment of this end, however, will require much considerate care and wise guidance. That care and guidance is necessarily the task of the Government which, as to the Indians at least, must exercise paternal functions until they are sufficiently advanced to take care of themselves....

...The failure of Sitting Bull's attempt to maintain himself and a large number of followers on our northern frontier in the old wild ways of Indian life will undoubtedly strengthen the tendency among the wild Indians of the North-west to recognize the situation and to act accordingly. The general state of feeling among the red men is therefore now exceedingly favorable to the civilizing process....

The Indian, in order to be civilized, must not only learn how to read and write, but how to live....Such considerations led the Government, under the last administration, largely to increase the number of Indian pupils at the Normal School at Hampton, Va., and to establish an institution for the education of Indian children at Carlisle, in Pennsylvania, where the young Indians would no longer be under the influence of the Indian camp or village, but in immediate contact with the towns, farms, and factories of civilized people, living and working in the atmosphere of civilization. In these institutions, the Indian children, among whom a large number of tribes are represented, receive the ordinary English education, while there are various shops and a farm for the instruction of the boys, and the girls are kept busy in the kitchen, dining-room, sewing-room, and with other domestic work. In the summer, as many as possible of the boys are placed in the care of intelligent and philanthropic farmers and their families, mostly in Pennsylvania and New England, where they find instructive employment in the field and barn-yard. The pupils are, under proper regulations, permitted to see as much as possible of the country and its inhabitants in the vicinity of the schools....

Especial attention is given in the Indian schools to the education of Indian girls, and at Hampton a new building is being erected for that purpose. This is of peculiar importance. The Indian woman has so far been only a beast of burden. The girl, when arrived at maturity, was disposed of like an article of trade. The Indian wife was treated by her husband alternately with animal fondness, and with the cruel brutality of the slave-driver. Nothing will be more apt to raise the Indians in the scale of civilization than to stimulate their attachment to permanent homes, and it is woman that must make the atmosphere and form the attraction of the home. She must be recognized, with affection and respect, as the center of domestic life. If we want the Indians to respect their women, we must lift up the Indian women to respect themselves. This is the purpose and work of education. If we educate the girls of to-day, we educate the mothers of to-morrow, and in educating those mothers we prepare the ground for the education of generations to come. Every effort made in that direction is, therefore, entitled to especial sympathy and encouragement....

As the third thing necessary for the absorption of the Indians in the great body of American citizenship, I mentioned their individualization in the possession of property by their settlement in severalty upon small farm tracts with a fee simple title. When the Indians are so settled, and have become individual property-owners, holding their farms by the same title under the law by which white men hold theirs, they will feel more readily inclined to part with such of their lands as they cannot themselves cultivate, and from which they can derive profit only if they sell them, either in lots or in bulk, for a fair equivalent in money or in annuities. This done, the Indians will occupy no more ground than so many white people; the large reservations will gradually be opened to general settlement and enterprise, and the Indians, with their possessions, will cease to stand in the way of the "development of the country." The difficulty which has provoked so many encroachments and conflicts will then no longer exist. When the Indians are individual owners of real property, and as individuals enjoy the protection of the laws, their tribal cohesion will necessarily relax, and gradually disappear. They will have advanced an immense step in the direction of the "white man's way."

6. A Native American Tries to Walk the White Man's Road (1890s)[*]

From 1883 to 1890, Sun Elk, a Taos Indian, attended the Carlisle Indian School in Pennsylvania, where he learned typesetting. In the following passage, he describes

---

[*]From Edwin R. Embree, *Indians of the Americas.* Copyright © 1939 by Houghton Mifflin Company.

his return to his pueblo in New Mexico. Did his Carlisle education prove beneficial to him? In what ways does his experience suggest the limitations of the reformers' efforts to "civilize" Native Americans?

When I was about thirteen years old I went down to St. Michael's Catholic School. Other boys were joining the societies and spending their time in the kivas [sacred ceremonial chambers] being purified and learning the secrets. But I wanted to learn the white man's secrets. I thought he had better magic than the Indian. . . . So I drifted a little away from the pueblo life. My father was sad but he was not angry. He wanted me to be a good Indian like all the other boys, but he was willing for me to go to school. He thought I would soon stop. There was plenty of time to go into the kiva.

Then at the first snow one winter . . . a white man—what you call an Indian Agent—came and took all of us who were in that school far off on a train to a new kind of village called Carlisle Indian School, and I stayed there seven years. . . .

Seven years I was there. I set little letters together in the printing shop and we printed papers. For the rest we had lessons. There were games, but I was too slight for foot and hand plays, and there were no horses to ride. I learned to talk English and to read. There was much arithmetic. It was lessons: how to add and take away, and much strange business like you have crossword puzzles only with numbers. The teachers were very solemn and made a great fuss if we did not get the puzzles right.

There was something called Greatest Common Denominator. I remember the name but I never knew it—what it meant. When the teachers asked me I would guess, but I always guessed wrong. We studied little things—fractions. I remember that word too. It is like one half of an apple. And there were immoral fractions. . . .

They told us that Indian ways were bad. They said we must get civilized. I remember that word too. It means "be like the white man." I am willing to be like the white man, but I did not believe Indian ways were wrong. But they kept teaching us for seven years. And the books told how bad the Indians had been to the white men—burning their towns and killing their women and children. But I had seen white men do that to Indians. We all wore white man's clothes and ate white man's food and went to white man's churches and spoke white man's talk. And so after a while we also began to say Indians were bad. We laughed at our own people and their blankets and cooking pots and sacred societies and dances. I tried to learn the lessons—and after seven years I came home. . . .

It was a warm summer evening when I got off the train at Taos station. The first Indian I met, I asked him to run out to the pueblo and tell my family I was home. The Indian couldn't speak English, and I had forgotten all my Pueblo language. But after a while he learned what I meant and started running to tell my father "Tulto is back. . . ."

I went home with my family. And next morning the governor of the pueblo and the two war chiefs and many of the priest chiefs came into my father's house. They did not talk to me; they did not even look at me. When they were all assembled they talked to my father.

The chiefs said to my father, "Your son who calls himself Rafael has lived with the white men. He has been far away from the pueblo. He has not lived in the kiva nor learned the things that Indian boys should learn. He has no hair. He has no blankets. He cannot even speak our language and he has a strange smell. He is not one of us."

The chiefs got up and walked out. My father was very sad. I wanted him to be angry, but he was only sad. So I would not be sad and was very angry instead.

And I walked out of my father's house and out of the pueblo. I did not speak. My mother was in the other room cooking. She stayed in the other room but she made much noise rattling her pots. Some children were on the plaza and they stared at me, keeping very still as I walked away.

I walked until I came to the white man's town, Fernandez de Taos. I found work setting type in a printing shop there. Later I went to Durango and other towns in Wyoming and Colorado, printing and making a good living. But this indoor work was bad for me. It made me slight of health. So then I went outside to the fields. I worked in some blacksmith shops and on farms.

All this time I was a white man. I wore white man's clothes and kept my hair cut. I was not very happy. I made money and I kept a little of it and after many years I came back to Taos.

My father gave me some land from the pueblo fields. He could do this because now the land did not belong to all the people, as it did in the old days; the white man had cut it up and given it in little pieces to each family, so my father gave me a part of his, and I took my money and bought some more land and some cattle. I built a house just outside the pueblo. I would not live in the pueblo so I built outside a house bigger than the pueblo houses all for myself.

My father brought me a girl to marry. Her name was Roberta. Her Indian name was P'ah-tah-zhuli (little deer bean). She was about fifteen years old and she had no father. But she was a good girl and she came to live with me in my new house outside the pueblo.

When we were married I became an Indian again. I let my hair grow, I put on blankets, and I cut the seat out of my pants.

B. Life on the Frontier

1. Westward the Course of Empire Takes Its Way (1868)

Images of the western American frontier flooded popular magazines and newspapers in the East (and in Europe) in the mid-nineteenth century. The 1868 print on page 473, "Across the Continent" by Francis F. Palmer, presents a typical figurative rendering of the frontier, an allegorical scene in which "civilization" meets the wilderness. How does the artist portray the contrast between the East and the West? Which visual elements signify "civilization," and which signify "wilderness"? What role do the Indians play in this image? What awaits settlers in the West? What are they bringing with them?

ACROSS THE CONTINENT.
"WESTWARD THE COURSE OF EMPIRE TAKES ITS WAY."

2. A Pioneer Woman Describes the Overland Trail (1862)*

Thousands of men, women, and children trekked into the trans-Mississippi West in the nineteenth century. In this description of the overland crossing to California in 1862, what appear to be the greatest hardships the pioneers faced? What is the writer's attitude toward Indians? What might have motivated the Indians to act as they did? Was white settlement compatible with Indian life? Was there a missed opportunity for a different kind of relationship between white settlers and Native Americans?

Monday, July 28   …Came past a camp of thirty six wagons who have been camped for some time here in the mountains. They have had their cattle stampeded four or five times. There was a woman died in this train yesterday. She left

---

*From *The Diary of Jane Gould Torillott (Journey from Mitchel Co., Iowa to California by Land)*, in Lillian Schlissel, ed., *Women's Diaries of the Westward Journey* (New York: Schocken Books, 1982), pp. 222–225.

six children, one of them only two days old. Poor little thing, it had better have died with its mother. They made a good picket fence around the grave....

Sunday, August 3 ...We passed by the train I have just spoken of. They had just buried the babe of the woman who died days ago, and were just digging a grave for another woman that was run over by the cattle and wagons when they stampeded yesterday. She lived twenty-four hours, she gave birth to a child a short time before she died. The child was buried with her. She leaves a little two year old girl and a husband. They say he is nearly crazy with sorrow....

Tuesday, August 5 ...Did not start very early. Waited for a train to pass. It seems today as if I *must* go to home to fathers to see them all. I can't wait another minute. If I could only *hear* from them it would do some good, but I suppose I shall have to wait whether I am patient or not....

Sunday, August 10 Traveled five or six miles when we came to Snake River. We stayed till two o'clock then traveled till about four or five, when *we* from the back end of the train saw those on ahead all get out their guns. In a short time the word came back that a train six miles on had been attacked by the Indians, and some killed and that was cause enough for the arming. In a short time were met by two men. They wanted us to go a short distance from the road and bring two dead men to their camp, five miles ahead.

Albert unloaded his little wagon and sent Gus back with them and about forty armed men from both trains, to get them. We learned that a train of eleven wagons had been plundered of all that was in them and the teams taken and the men killed. One was Mr. Bullwinkle who left us the 25th of last month, at the crossing of Green River. He went on with this Adams train. Was intending to wait for us but we had not overtaken him yet. He was shot eight times. His dog was shot four times before he would let them get to the wagon. They took all that he had in his wagon, except his trunks and books and papers. They broke open his trunks and took all that they contained. (He had six.) It is supposed that they took six thousand dollars from him, tore the cover from his wagon, it was oilcloth. He had four choice horses. They ran away when he was shot, the harnesses were found on the trail where it was cut from them when they went. It was a nice silver one. The Captain had a daughter shot and wounded severely. This happened yesterday. This morning a part of their train and a part of the Kennedy train went in pursuit of the stock. They were surrounded by Indians on ponies, two killed, several wounded and two supposed to be killed. They were never found. One of those killed was Capt. Adams' son, the other was a young man in the Kennedy train. Those that we carried to camp were those killed this morning. Mr. Bullwinkle and two others were buried before we got to the camp. There were one hundred and fifty wagons there and thirty four of ours. Capt. Kennedy was severely wounded. Capt. Hunter of Iowa City train was killed likewise by an Indian. We camped near Snake River. We could not get George to ride after the news, he *would* walk and carry his loaded pistol to help.

Monday, August 11 ...The two men we brought up were buried early this morning with the other three, so they laid five men side by side in this vast wilderness, killed by guns and arrows of the red demons. The chief appeared yesterday in a suit of Mr. Bullwinkle's on the battlefield....

Tuesday, August 12   Capt. Adams' daughter died this morning from the effects of her wound. Was buried in a box made of a wagon box. Poor father and mother lost one son and one daughter, all of his teams, clothing and four thousand dollars. Is left dependent on the bounty of strangers....In the evening we took in Mrs. Ellen Ives, one of the ladies of the plundered train. Her husband goes in the wagon just ahead of us. She was married the morning she started for California. Not a very pleasant wedding tour....

Thursday, August 13 [sic]   ...After going up the canyon about four miles, we came to a wagon that had been stopped. There was a new harness, or parts of one, some collars and close by we saw the bodies of three dead men, top of the ground. They had been dead two or three weeks. Some one had been along and thrown a little earth over them, but they were mostly uncovered again. One had his head and face out, another his legs, a third, his hands and arms. Oh! it is a horrid thing. I wish all of the Indians in Christendom were exterminated....

Friday, August 15   We were aroused this morning at one o'clock by the firing of guns and yelling of Indians, answered by our men. The Capt. calling, "come on you red devils." It did not take us long to dress, for once. I hurried for the children and had them dress and get into our wagon, put up a mattress and some beds and quilts on the exposed side of the wagon to protect us. The firing was from the willows and from the mouth of the corrall. There were two other trains with us. There are one hundred and eleven wagons of all and two hundred or more men. The firing did not continue long nor do any harm. Our men shot a good many balls into the willows but I presume they were not effectual. We sat and watched and waited till morning. Yoked the cattle and turned them out with a heavy guard and several scouts to clear the bushes. Cooked our breakfast and started. There were ball holes through two or three wagon covers....We nooned in a little valley but kept our eyes open to all that might be hidden in the bushes and behind the rocks.

3. Taming the Canadian Frontier (1877)*

In managing their own western territories, Canadians sought to avoid the lawlessness and fierce Indian warfare that accompanied frontier settlement in the United States. Canada's more punishing climate and terrain delayed the peopling of its frontier until the 1870s, when plans were adopted to build a transcontinental railroad linking east and west. Before construction could begin in earnest, the Canadian government dispatched the newly established North West Mounted Police (known colloquially as the "Mounties") to negotiate with Indian tribes and pave the way for orderly settlement. The following article from a Canadian newspaper reflects on the success of the Mounties in the first years of operation. What lessons did Canadians draw from the American model of frontier settlement? How does the author account for the orderly settlement of Canada's western provinces?

*William M. Baker, ed., Winnipeg *Daily Free Press*, July 5, 1877, cited in William M. Baker, ed., *The Mounted Police and Prairie Society* (Regina, Saskatchewan: Canadian Plains Research Center, 1998), p. 33.

The different results of the very different kinds of policy adopted towards the aborigines of the United States and Canada respectively afford a convincing proof of the superior wisdom of the system of justice and humanity not only professed but carried out by the Canadian Government. The Americans are never wholly without an Indian war on their hands, and probably the contest between the races will intermittently continue until the red man is finally driven off every inch of territory covered by the star-spangled banner. In British North America, on the contrary, the Indians are permitted to enjoy their existence under the protection of the laws, and, if they do not prove very industrious or productive members of the commonwealth, they are at any rate law-abiding and peaceful citizens, whose loyal and not unimportant aid might be reckoned on with confidence should the Dominion ever be threatened with hostile invasion. The basis of this happy state of the relations between the white and red population of Canada is undoubtedly the treatment in good faith of the weaker race.

4. Opening Montana (1867)[*]

Elizabeth Chester Fisk, born in 1846 in Connecticut, was among the first white women to settle in Montana, and in her letters to her New England family, she chronicled its early growth with a sharp but sympathetic eye. What did she find to be the most appealing aspects of life in the rugged frontier town of Helena? What did she miss most about her native Connecticut? What were the raw new community's greatest problems?

Helena, Montana, July [21], 1867

My dear Mother:

Our steamer reached Fort Benton on the afternoon of Sunday last. We came into port amid the firing of cannon and shouts of the people assembled on shore. We had been long and anxiously expected and many fears entertained concerning our safety. Our passengers were more delighted than words can express to know that their long "Misery" was at an end....

Fort Benton was a pleasanter town than I expected to see and wore an air of life and animation. The ox and mule teams awaited their loads of freight were drawn up on the river banks, while further back, on the broad plain on which the town is built, were hundreds of cattle and mules feeding on the rich grass.... Our route lay over the most beautiful prairie, a level natural highway. At evening we came to Sun River where we were delayed four hours waiting for the coach from Helena.... While our coach stopped to change horses, I stretched myself out on the seat and took a little nap, awoke thoroughly chilled and entering the little cabin warmed myself by the fire and drank a cup of hot tea. Soon we came to the

---

[*]© Rex C. Myers, Editor, *Lizzie: The Letters of Elizabeth Chester Fisk, 1864–1893* (Missoula, MT: Mountain Press Publishing Company, 1989), pp. 25–48.

crossing of the Dearborn, and forded the stream and rushed on our way as before. The rain was falling fast and at every steep hill our gentleman passengers (I was the only lady) were obliged to unload and walk up the mountain side. They were wet to the skin and a more dismal looking party could not have been found. . . .

I am much pleased with this country, and can already think of it as home. We passed through Prickly Pear Canyon on our way from Benton. Here is some of the most beautiful scenery in the world. The loftiest mountains, their peaks covered with snow, towered above our heads, while in the valley were the most lovely wild flowers in bloom—roses...blue bells, and many other of whose names I cannot tell. The mountains rise all about our home, their sides sometimes covered with pine and cedar and again only with the green grass. The snow still lingers on the tallest peaks and the wind is cold and wintery which sweeps down from their sides. . . .

Helena, Sept. 2nd/67

My dear Fannie:

[F]or two weeks I have been enjoying your most troublesome complaint, diarrhea....[M]edicine seemed to have no effect unless I entirely abstained from food....But I am well again now, which is to be chiefly attributed to the exercise I have taken, both out and in doors, not less than to food better adapted to an invalid. . . .

I made bread on Saturday and would like to send you a piece; it is very nice. Fabricated some pie, too, after my most approved style and sent some to the office hoping to get [an editorial] puff, but it doth not appear. Can you credit my words when I tell you that, in this country where milk well watered is one dollar per gallon, and eggs one dollar and a half per dozen, I made cream pies. And today, I have been guilty of the further extravagance of cooking for supper a spring chicken for which I paid only $1.25 in [gold] dust. Such is the fact, and not a bone is left to tell the tail [sic], but we had visitors at tea, Stuart and Jackey, and we don't have chickens every day.

Today has been election, the day so long [and] anxiously awaited and on which events so much depends. We can as yet have no idea of the result, but can only hope that our territory will have no such delegate in Congress as James M. Cavanaugh.

The day has been one of much interest yet in this city it passed off very quietly. Had it not been for an event which occurred late in the day we might have been proud of the manner in which our citizens conducted themselves. The negroes of course voted and this raised some disaffection among the rebels. Late in the afternoon an Irishman shot a negro without the slightest provocation and for no reason at all, unless it were the color of his skin. The colored man cannot live it is thought, and the son of Erin will without doubt be hung, with little delay and not much of a trial. The Vigilantes keep things in order here, and I truly believe there is less of crime in this city than in any town east, of the same number of inhabitants. This I consider high praise, remembering the elements of which society is in a great measure composed. . . .

What would you think of a town with no grass, no trees, no flowers, only dust and stone in the streets and yards. Such is our town.... Nothing grows here without irrigation. This however might easily be accomplished since ditches run through all the principal streets. I intended making a garden another year. Send along the seeds please, both flower and vegetable, as soon as you gather them and they will be in season....

Your sister
Lizzie

Helena, May 24th, 1868

My dear Mother:

...I sent you a long letter by Tuesday's mail, but as news has just come to us that the eastward-bound coach was robbed yesterday, near Pleasant Valley [Idaho], I deem it possible that this letter of mine may have been one of those torn up by the desperadoes, and cast to the winds. We seem to be living over again in the early days in the history of our territory when murders, robberies, depredations and lawlessness were on every side and the Vigilantes were engaged in their terrible, awe-inspiring works. These Vigilantes must again organize in every part of our domain and bring miscreants to swift punishment. Mild measures will never do for reckless savages or still more daring white men....

I have not much faith in mankind. The world is selfish, supremely selfish, and no part of it more so than...Montana. People coming here, leave behind all the grace and goodness they ever possessed, and live only for money getting. They are true to no principle of right or justice, make friends only to advance their own interests.... The temptation is often great to make my home, when I shall gain it, my world, to seek no companionship outside its little circle.

Could I only decide the question—Shall I, too, selfishly address myself to money getting and ignore the claims of society upon me, or shall my influence be used to bring about a better state of things and beget a little public spirit. I should then with all my heart and soul address myself to the one or the other.

Love untold for all.
L. C. Fisk

5. Sodbusters in Kansas (1877)[*]

Migrants to the treeless prairies had to invent new ways of living—including new kinds of houses—at least until they could import more traditional building materials from the East. The following diary entries were written by a Kansas homesteader in Snyder's Kill Creek, Kansas. What is most novel and what is most traditional about the physical and social setting described in the diary?

---

[*]From John Ise, ed., *Sod-House Days: Letters from a Kansas Homesteader, 1877–78*. Copyright © 1937 Columbia University Press.

Wednesday, March 28, 1877   Noah staked two of the corners of my claim this morning, before he went out to herd the cattle and Jim and I followed him, looking for a place to make our dugout. We found a spot about 3/4 mile from Snyder's house where a patch of wild sunflowers had killed the grass. Here we began to dig, and by noon had made some progress. We laid off the ground 10×14 feet, and we'll have to dig it about 6 feet deep. Just before dinner I wished myself back home, and would have started for Osborne, but Jim persuaded me to stay. After dinner we went back to the hole and in about two hours had dug about half of it to the depth of two feet. And then we were stopped by a shower coming up, which bid fair to keep on till night, but did not, though the clouds hung very low. We went back to the house, and Snyder fixed the handle to our ax. My dugout is at the head of the prettiest draw on my claim, and if the clouds clear off we will have it finished by the middle of next week. This afternoon Bevvy Neuschwanger rode up to see Mrs. Snyder and while they were talking we made off and put in a little more work on the claim. Talk about hard work will you? Just try digging in the ground out here two feet from the surface—oh, I should have written 6 inches from the surface. The ground is packed just as hard as could be, and it is no fun to pick and shovel it. It is damp as far as we have gone down (some 27 inches) and sticky as putty. Sometimes we can throw out lumps as big as your head. About 3 o'clock we had a little shower and then we quit work and went back to the house. We wanted a little instruction about putting the handle into the axe, and Snyder offered to do it for us, for which we were glad enough and by the time it was dark, the axe was fixed. Now our possessions consist of an axe, shovel and tincup, besides our clothing.

The prairie chickens are about as pretty a bird as you will come across. They are about as big as a half-grown barnyard fowl, and are not much shyer. The folks say they become more numerous as the land is broken up. The law forbids a man shooting them on any claim but his own, but if a poor fellow shoots a couple on somebody else's claim for food, no one thinks of having him up for it. The folks here all talk German more than English, but they can all get along, even if they cannot use the latter tongue very fluently. I talk English altogether and they may talk what they please. . . .

Wednesday, April 4, 1877   About 8 o'clock I got to shoveling the dirt away from the cellar door and got through about 10, when I went digging a place in the hill to put a hen house. Here the cattle and fowls are all put into half-dugouts—that is, part dugout and part log, sod, or stone, with straw roofs. That was mean digging, with the busted pick and in gravelly ground. The gravel is as firmly packed as though it had been rammed down. Finished that about 4 o'clock and then started digging for a well where old man Gsell said there was water. He found it out by the use of a forked branch of a peach tree. That was the first time I ever saw forks used for finding water, but I have heard it said that the black shale will draw the switch as well as water. And when you strike shale before you get to water it is no use to go any deeper, but if you strike the water first, go ahead and make your reservoir in the shale and you will always have a supply. These two days' work were the hardest I have done in 6 months. I got $1 a day and board, so there is $1.50 earned. L. & J. were at work at the house—dugout—while I was away. I got back to Snyder's about

7 o'clock. Had bean soup for supper. It was hot today, and I worked without coat or vest.

Thursday, April 5, 1877   This was another hot day, and we had heavy work too, laying up sod. Snyder broke a lot for us this a.m. and we began laying up the wall. It is 20 inches thick. These "Kansas brick" are from 2 to 4 inches thick, 12 wide and 20 long and the joints between them we fill with ground. Just before sunset we got the ridgepole into position on the crotches, so that the room will be about 7 feet high. We expect to get the roof in and have the place in condition to live in by the end of the week. The sod is heavy and when you take 3 or 4 bricks on a litter or hand barrow, and carry it 50 to 150 feet, I tell you it is no easy work. We quit just before sunset. Had supper about 7:30. I could hardly walk today—the result of that bareback ride. It was awfully hot right after dinner, and Levin fetched water from Snyder's in a jug. That water tasted good.

6. John Wesley Powell Reports on the "Arid Region" (1879)*

In 1869, the one-armed explorer John Wesley Powell (1834–1902) led the first party to float down the mighty Colorado River through the Grand Canyon. He later led many scientific expeditions throughout the American West, and he served from 1881 to 1894 as the head of the United States Geological Survey. In 1879 he filed his "Report on the Lands of the Arid Region of the United States," a comprehensive analysis of the topography and climate of the Great Basin, including Utah. (The Great Basin lies between the Sierra Nevada and Rocky Mountain ranges.) In the excerpt from Powell's famous "Report" that follows, what did he identify as the distinguishing geological and meteorological characteristics of the region? What features of this region did Powell find most different from the eastern part of North America? What were the eventual social and environmental effects of his recommended method for making the region suitable for large-scale settlement?

In order to set forth the characteristics of these lands and the conditions under which they can be most profitably utilized, it is deemed best to discuss first a somewhat limited region in detail as a fair type of the whole....It is proposed to take up for this discussion only the area embraced in Utah Territory....

Having determined from the operations of irrigation that one cubic foot per second of water will irrigate from 80 to 100 acres of land when the greatest economy is used, and having determined the volume of water or number of cubic feet per second flowing in the several streams of Utah by the most thorough methods available under the circumstances, it appears that within the territory, excluding a small portion in the southeastern corner where the survey has not yet been completed, the amount of land which it is possible to redeem by this method is about 2,262 square miles, or 1,447,920 acres. Of course this amount does not lie in a continuous body, but is scattered in small tracts along the water courses....That is, 2.8 per cent of the

---

*J. W. Powell, *Report on the Lands of the Arid Region of the United States* (Washington, DC: Government Printing Office, 1879), pp. 6, 7–10, 23–24.

lands under consideration can be cultivated by utilizing all the available streams during the irrigating season....

This statement of the facts relating to the irrigable lands of Utah will serve to give a clearer conception of the extent and condition of the irrigable lands throughout the Arid Region. Such as can be redeemed are scattered along the water courses, and are in general the lowest lands of the several districts to which they belong....

The Arid Region is somewhat more than four-tenths of the total area of the United States, and as the agricultural interests of so great an area are dependent upon irrigation it will be interesting to consider certain questions relating to the economy and practicability of distributing the waters over the lands to be redeemed.

There are two considerations that make irrigation attractive to the agriculturist. Crops thus cultivated are not subject to the vicissitudes of rainfall; the farmer fears no droughts; his labors are seldom interrupted and his crops rarely injured by storms. This immunity from drought and storm renders agricultural operations much more certain than in regions of greater humidity. Again, the water comes down from the mountains and plateaus freighted with fertilizing materials derived from the decaying vegetation and soils of the upper regions, which are spread by the flowing water over the cultivated lands. It is probable that the benefits derived from this source alone will be full compensation for the cost of the process.

C. The Farmers' Protest Movement

1. The Evolving Wheat Economy (1852–1914)[*]

In the second half of the nineteenth century, settlers across Europe and the Americas poured onto their respective frontiers, bringing vast tracts of land under cultivation. Linked to commercial centers by rapidly expanding transportation networks, farmers from Russia's distant steppes to Argentina's fertile pampas flooded global markets with new supplies of cotton and grain. The following tables trace the evolution of the global wheat economy. What do these figures suggest is the relationship between production volume, transportation cost, and prices? How might the falling price of wheat have affected the lives of American farmers?

---

[*]Wilfred Malenbaum, *The World Wheat Economy, 1885–1939* (Cambridge, MA: Harvard University Press, 1953), pp. 238–239; C. Knick Harley, "Transportation, the World Wheat Trade, and the Kuznets Cycle, 1850–1913," *Explorations in Economic History* 17 (1980): 220–223.

Wheat Production, 1885–1914 (5-year averages, millions of bushels)

	1885–1889[a]	1889–1894	1894–1899	1899–1904	1904–1909	1909–1914
Argentina	19.9	47.3	59.6	93.3	158.1	147.1
Australia	25.9	31.3	27.3	42.7	59.3	90.5
British Isles	75.6	69.6	59.4	58.2	55.6	60.8
Canada	38.3	40.9	51.8	76.6	104.0	197.1
France	302.9	287.8	326.2	338.6	332.2	317.6
Indian Peninsula	265.8	247.2	240.6	249.0	301.7	351.8
Russia[b]	357.5	360.4	452.2	545.1	620.3	791.7
United States	515.6	628.3	686.5	713.8	671.8	694.4

[a]Four-year average.
[b]Including the countries of the former Soviet Union.

Freight Rates from Producing Areas, 1868–1913 (cents per bushel)

	1868–1872	1880–1884	1896–1899	1910–1913
Chicago–New York				
Lake+Canal	21.9	8.6	4.8	5.4
Lake+Rail	25.8	11.7	6.6	6.2
All Rail	35.0	15.7	11.8	9.6
To Liverpool from:				
New York	14.2	8.6	5.7	4.9
Odessa	18.6	10.4	6.2	6.6
Calcutta	32.4	26.7	12.5	15.6
Argentina	—	—	12.6	9.6

Wheat Prices, Various Locations, 1852–1913 (gold dollars per bushel)

	1852–1856	1868–1872	1880–1884	1895–1899	1910–1913
Liverpool	$1.70	$1.52	$1.31	$0.88	$1.07
New York	$1.71	$1.39	$1.20	$0.83	$1.05
Odessa	$0.97	$1.15	$1.12	$0.72	—

2. An Iowan Assesses Discontent (1893)*

Farm distress increased during the 1890s, to a large extent in the South but more spectacularly on the western plains. The four "d's"—drought, debt, deflation, and depression—played their dismal role, but the basic trouble was overproduction of grain. Farmers simply could not control prices that were determined by the world supply, and they vented their spleen on scapegoats nearer at hand, notably the railroads. Freight rates had fallen substantially since the Civil War, but no rates seemed fair to farmers whose grain prices were so low that they could not make a profit. And inequities persisted, despite the Interstate Commerce Act of 1887. A prominent Iowa journalist here analyzes some of the grievances that caused these hardy children of the soil to beat their Farmers' Alliances into a political plowshare. In the following essay, what are the farmers' most pressing complaints?

Nothing has done more to injure the [western] region than these freight rates. The railroads have retarded its growth as much as they first hastened it. The rates are often four times as large as Eastern rates....The extortionate character of the freight rates has been recognized by all parties, and all have pledged themselves to lower them, but no state west of the Missouri has been able to do so.

In the early days, people were so anxious to secure railways that they would grant any sort of concession which the companies asked. There were counties in Iowa and other Western states struggling under heavy loads of bond-taxes, levied twenty-five years ago, to aid railways of which not one foot has been built. Perhaps a little grading would be done, and then the project would be abandoned, the bonds transferred, and the county called upon by the "innocent purchaser" to pay the debt incurred by blind credulity. I have known men to sacrifice fortunes, brains, and lives in fighting vainly this iniquitous bond-swindle.

Railways have often acquired mines and other properties by placing such high freight rates upon their products that the owner was compelled to sell at the railroad company's own terms. These freight rates have been especially burdensome to the farmers, who are far from their selling and buying markets, thus robbing them in both directions.

Another fact which has incited the farmer against corporations is the bold and unblushing participation of the railways in politics. At every political convention their emissaries are present with blandishments and passes and other practical arguments to secure the nomination of their friends. The sessions of these legislatures are disgusting scenes of bribery and debauchery. There is not an attorney of prominence in Western towns who does not carry a pass or has not had the opportunity to do so. The passes, of course, compass the end sought. By these means, the railroads have secured an iron grip upon legislatures and officers, while no redress has been given to the farmer.

The land question, also, is a source of righteous complaint. Much of the land of the West, instead of being held for actual settlers, has been bought up by speculators and Eastern syndicates in large tracts. They have done nothing to improve the land and

---

*F. B. Tracy, "Why the Farmers Revolted," *Forum* 16 (October 1893): 242–243.

have simply waited for the inevitable settler who bought cheaply a small "patch" and proceeded to cultivate it. When he had prospered so that he needed more land, he found that his own labor had increased tremendously the value of the adjacent land....

Closely connected with the land abuse are the money grievances. As his pecuniary condition grew more serious, the farmer could not make payments on his land. Or he found that, with the ruling prices, he could not sell his produce at a profit. In either case he needed money, to make the payment or maintain himself until prices should rise. When he went to the moneylenders, these men, often dishonest usurers, told him that money was very scarce, that the rate of interest was rapidly rising, etc., so that in the end the farmer paid as much interest a month as the moneylender was paying a year for the same money. In this transaction, the farmer obtained his first glimpse of the idea of "the contraction of the currency at the hands of Eastern money sharks."

Disaster always follows the exaction of such exorbitant rates of interest, and want or eviction quickly came. Consequently, when demagogues went among the farmers to utter their calamitous cries, the scales seemed to drop from the farmers' eyes, and he saw gold bugs, Shylocks, conspiracies, and criminal legislation *ad infinitum*. Like a lightning flash, the idea of political action ran through the Alliances. A few farmers' victories in county campaigns the previous year became a promise of broader conquest, and with one bound the Farmers' Alliance went into politics all over the West.

3. Mrs. Mary Lease Raises More Hell (c. 1890)*

As the plains seethed with protest, the Populist party emerged from the Farmers' Alliance. Kansas spawned the most picturesque and vocal group of orators. A flaming speaker in great demand was the Irish-born Mrs. Mary E. Lease, a tall, magnetic lawyer known as "Patrick Henry in petticoats." Noting that corn was so cheap that it was being burned as fuel, she demanded the raising of less corn and "more hell." Noting also the disparity between the wealthy families and the people allegedly living out of garbage cans, she insisted on drastic measures. In the following selection, which are substantial grievances and which are demagogic outpourings? Which of her complaints seem to be the most serious?

This is a nation of inconsistencies. The Puritans fleeing from oppression became oppressors. We fought England for our liberty and put chains on four million of blacks. We wiped out slavery and by our tariff laws and national banks began a system of white wage slavery worse than the first.

Wall Street owns the country. It is no longer a government of the people, by the people, and for the people, but a government of Wall Street, by Wall Street, and for Wall Street.

The great common people of this country are slaves, and monopoly is the master. The West and South are bound and prostrate before the manufacturing East.

---

*Elizabeth N. Barr, "The Populist Uprising," in W. E. Connelley, ed., *History of Kansas, State and People* (New York: The American Historical Society, 1928), vol. 2, p. 1167.

Money rules, and our Vice-President is a London banker. Our laws are the output of a system which clothes rascals in robes and honesty in rags.

The parties lie to us and the political speakers mislead us. We were told two years ago to go to work and raise a big crop, that was all we needed. We went to work and plowed and planted; the rains fell, the sun shone, nature smiled, and we raised the big crop that they told us to; and what came of it? Eight-cent corn, ten-cent oats, two-cent beef, and no price at all for butter and eggs—that's what came of it.

Then the politicians said we suffered from overproduction. Overproduction, when 10,000 little children, so statistics tell us, starve to death every year in the United States, and over 10,000 shopgirls in New York are forced to sell their virtue for the bread their niggardly wages deny them.

Tariff is not the paramount question. The main question is the money question.... Kansas suffers from two great robbers, the Santa Fe Railroad and the loan companies. The common people are robbed to enrich their masters....

We want money, land, and transportation. We want the abolition of the national banks, and we want the power to make loans direct from the government. We want the accursed foreclosure system wiped out. Land equal to a tract thirty miles wide and ninety miles long has been foreclosed and bought in by loan companies of Kansas in a year.

We will stand by our homes and stay by our fireside by force if necessary, and we will not pay our debts to the loan-shark companies until the government pays its debts to us. The people are at bay; let the bloodhounds of money who have dogged us thus far beware.

4. William Allen White Attacks the Populists (1896)[*]

The embittered farmers and laborites, organized into the People's (Populist) party, met in a frenzied convention in Omaha, Nebraska, in July 1892. They nominated General James B. Weaver for president and adopted a scorching platform. In addition to other grievances, they pilloried corruption among politicians and judges, the subsidized and "muzzled" press, the impoverishment of labor, the shooting of strikers, and the hypocrisy of the two major parties. More specifically, the platform demanded distribution of monopolized land to actual settlers; government ownership of the telegraphs, telephones, and railroads ("The railroad corporations will either own the people or the people must own the railroads"); reduction of bloated fortunes by a graduated income tax; and inflation of the currency by issuing more paper money and coining all silver produced.

Four years later, the Populists nominated William Jennings Bryan and temporarily fused with the Democratic party, which also nominated Bryan, in a bid for national power. In Emporia, Kansas, newspaperman William Allen White had long been critical of the Populists and now wrote a famous editorial denouncing them: "What's the Matter with Kansas?" White's piece was reprinted and widely distributed by Republicans backing William McKinley for president against Bryan. The editorial vaulted White to national prominence, and he later became a friend and adviser to presidents from Theodore Roosevelt to Franklin D. Roosevelt. As White saw

---

[*]*Emporia Gazette*, August 15, 1896.

matters in 1896, Kansas desperately needed new investment capital from the North-
east, and the Populist agitation was scaring it away. How valid is his argument?
Were the Populists not simply the victims of agricultural distress, but in some way
also contributors to it?

In five years ten million people have been added to the national population, yet instead of gaining a share of this—say, half a million—Kansas has apparently been a plague spot and, in the very garden of the world, has lost population by ten thousands every year.

Not only has she lost population, but she has lost money. Every moneyed man in the state who could get out without loss has gone. Every month in every community sees someone who has a little money pack up and leave the state. This has been going on for eight years. Money has been drained out all the time. In towns where ten years ago there were three or four or half a dozen money-lending concerns, stimulating industry by furnishing capital, there is now none, or one or two that are looking after the interests and principal already outstanding.

No one brings any money into Kansas any more. What community knows over one or two men who have moved in with more than $5,000 in the past three years? And what community cannot count half a score of men in that time who have left, taking all the money they could scrape together?

Yet the nation has grown rich; other states have increased in population and wealth—other neighboring states. Missouri has gained over two million, while Kansas has been losing half a million. Nebraska has gained in wealth and population while Kansas has gone downhill. Colorado has gained every way, while Kansas has lost every way since 1888.

What's the matter with Kansas?...

Go east and you hear them laugh at Kansas; go west and they sneer at her; go south and they "cuss" her; go north and they have forgotten her. Go into any crowd of intelligent people gathered anywhere on the globe, and you will find the Kansas man on the defensive. The newspaper columns and magazines once devoted to praise of her, to boastful facts and startling figures concerning her resources, are now filled with cartoons [and] jibes....

What's the matter with Kansas?

We all know; yet here we are at it again. We have an old mossback Jacksonian who snorts and howls because there is a bathtub in the State House; we are running that old jay for Governor. We have another shabby, wild-eyed, rattle-brained fanatic who has said openly in a dozen speeches that "the rights of the user are paramount to the rights of the owner"; we are running him for Chief Justice, so that capital will come tumbling over itself to get into the state....Then, for fear some hint that the state had become respectable might percolate through the civilized portions of the nation, we have decided to send three or four harpies out lecturing, telling the people that Kansas is raising hell and letting the corn go to weed.

Oh, this is a state to be proud of! We are a people who can hold up our heads! What we need is not more money, but less capital, fewer white shirts and brains, fewer men with business judgment, and more of those fellows who boast that they are "just ordinary clodhoppers"...who hate prosperity, and who think, because a man believes in national honor, he is a tool of Wall Street. We have had a few of them—some hundred fifty thousand—but we need more.

We need several thousand gibbering idiots to scream about the "Great Red Dragon" of Lombard Street. We don't need population, we don't need wealth, we don't need well-dressed men on the streets, we don't need cities on the fertile prairies; you bet we don't! What we are after is the money power. Because we have become poorer and ornerier and meaner than a spavined, distempered mule, we, the people of Kansas, propose to kick; we don't care to build up, we wish to tear down.

"There are two ideas of government," said our noble [William Jennings] Bryan at Chicago. "There are those who believe that if you legislate to make the well-to-do prosperous, this prosperity will leak through on those below. The Democratic idea has been that if you legislate to make the masses prosperous their prosperity will find its way up and through every class and rest upon them."

That's the stuff! Give the prosperous man the dickens! Legislate the thriftless man into ease, whack the stuffing out of the creditors and tell the debtors who borrowed the money five years ago when money "per capita" was greater than it is now, that the contraction of currency gives him a right to repudiate.

Whoop it up for the ragged trousers; put the lazy, greasy fizzle, who can't pay his debts, on the altar, and bow down and worship him. Let the state ideal be high. What we need is not the respect of our fellow men, but the chance to get something for nothing.

Oh, yes, Kansas is a great state. Here are people fleeing from it by the score every day, capital going out of the state by the hundreds of dollars; and every industry but farming paralyzed, and that crippled, because its products have to go across the ocean before they can find a laboring man at work who can afford to buy them. Let's don't stop this year. Let's drive all the decent, self-respecting men out of the state. Let's keep the old clodhoppers who know it all....not mill hands to eat our meat, nor factory hands to eat our wheat, nor cities to oppress the farmer by consuming his butter and eggs and chickens and produce....

What's the matter with Kansas?

Nothing under the shining sun. She is losing her wealth, population and standing. She has got her statesmen, and the money power is afraid of her....[S]he seems to have an overproduction. But that doesn't matter. Kansas never did believe in diversified crops. Kansas is all right. There is absolutely nothing wrong with Kansas. "Every prospect pleases and only man is vile."

D. The Pullman Strike

I. A Populist Condemns George Pullman (1894)*

George M. Pullman, who invented the popular upper-and-lower-berth Pullman Palace Car, made a fortune in manufacturing and controlling his brainchild. A generous philanthropist with his millions, he built for his employees the model town of Pullman (now

---

*Congressional Record, 53d Cong., 2d sess. (July 10, 1894), p. 7231.

in Chicago). But when the depression came and the company slashed wages about 25 percent, the workers struck. They were joined by Eugene V. Debs's powerful American Railway Union. According to Debs, the management had said, "There is nothing to arbitrate." Senator William A. Peffer, a Populist from Kansas who combed his long whiskers with his fingers while delivering even longer speeches, here presents his views. What are the two main grievances of the Pullman workers? How legitimate are they?

Without going into all the details, I will state by way of preface that the Pullman Company established what most people in this world believed to be an ideal community, in which all the citizens should have equal rights, in which none should have special privileges. The object was to build a community where the best modern scientific principles of hygiene, drainage, sewerage, grading, lighting, watering, and every other convenience should abound.

But while the company was doing that, while the world was looking on applauding, the company, like every other corporation of which I have ever known anything, held all of the power, all of the reins within its own grasp. That is to say, while there was sewerage, while there was light, while there was water, while there were parks, and all those desirable things, at the end of every month or of every week, as the case might be, when pay day came around, the charges that were set up against the residents of the town of Pullman for their lots and for their conveniences were deducted from their pay (just as the clothing of a soldier or extra rations or a lost gun were deducted from his pay) and the balance found to be due was paid to these people. Among these charges were rents and stated dues for the purchase of property.

After a while hard times began to pinch the company as it did everybody else, and it began to reduce the pay of the men. The men submitted patiently. Another reduction came and the men again submitted, only asking, however, that their rent charges should be reduced, that their taxes should be reduced, to correspond to the amount of reduction in their wages.

Then it was found that these poor people were absolutely defenseless, absolutely powerless in the hands of a corporation that had no soul. They asked to have a reduction of their rent charges and of other charges; they asked for a little time to turn around.

All these things were denied them. Finally, the Pullman citizens came to the conclusion that they might as well starve in defense of their rights as to starve while the proprietors of the town, the organizers and controllers of the corporation, were feasting on the fat things that these men had made for them. Now the trouble is on hand, and the leader of this great corporation [George M. Pullman] is off at the seashore, or on a lake, or on an island, or somewhere, refusing to entertain even a newspaper man, except to say, "I have nothing to say; the company at Chicago will look after the company's interest there"—heartless, soulless, conscienceless, Mr. President, this tyrant of tyrants.

2. Pullman Defends His Company (1894)*

The bloody disorders attending the Pullman strike led to an investigation by the U.S. Strike Commission. George M. Pullman took the stand and testified that his

---

*Senate Executive Documents, 53d Cong., 3d sess., 1894, vol. 2, no. 7, pp. 555–556.

company had undertaken to manufacture cars at a loss so as to keep his men employed. But he conceded that it was better to operate at a slight loss than to incur the larger losses resulting from idle factories. He also testified that the salaries of management (including his own) had not been cut; that the Pullman Company still had about $25 million in undivided profits; and that the dividends paid to stockholders had ranged from 12 percent to the current 8 percent. Commissioner Worthington extracted the following information from Pullman. How sound is Pullman's position on arbitration? How does his general business philosophy square with that prevalent in the United States today?

Commissioner Worthington. Now, let me ask you right there, Mr. Pullman, what do you see that is objectionable, in a business point of view, under the existing state of affairs, . . . in submitting to disinterested persons the question as to whether under all the circumstances wages might not be increased somewhat of your employees?

Mr. Pullman. I think I have made that as plain in this [written] statement as I can make it if I should repeat it a thousand times.

Commissioner Worthington. Is that the only reason you can give?

Mr. Pullman. What do you mean by that, "The only reason"?

Commissioner Worthington. The reason you give here (in the statement), "It must be clear to every businessman and to every thinking workman that no prudent employer could submit to arbitration the question whether he should commit such a piece of business folly." Is that the only answer to it?

Mr. Pullman. Well now, I have a little memorandum here which is practically the same thing on the question of arbitration. Of course there are matters which are proper subjects of arbitration—matters of opinion.

Commissioner Worthington. What are those matters that are proper subjects for arbitration?

Mr. Pullman. A matter of opinion would be a proper subject of arbitration, as, for instance, a question of title, or a disagreement on a matter of opinion. . . . But as to whether a fact that I know to be true is true or not, I could not agree to submit to arbitration. Take the case in hand: the question as to whether the shops at Pullman shall be continuously operated at a loss or not is one which it was impossible for the company, as a matter of principle, to submit to the opinion of any third party; and as to whether they were running at a loss on contract work in general, as explained to the committee of the men in my interview with them—that was a simple fact that I knew to be true, and which could not be made otherwise by the opinion of any third party.

Commissioner Worthington. You use the expression, "Impossible to be submitted." Why is it impossible?

Mr. Pullman. Because it would violate a principle.

Commissioner Worthington. What principle?

Mr. Pullman. The principle that a man should have the right to manage his own property.

Commissioner Worthington. The decision of arbitrators would not be compulsory, would it?

Mr. Pullman. I still think, having managed the property of the Pullman Company for twenty-seven years, that I am perhaps as well calculated to manage it for the interests of its stockholders and for the interests of the public—for the general interest—as some man who is not interested, who comes in to arbitrate certain points.

3. Starvation at Pullman (1894)[*]

The Pullman strike was finally broken by federal bayonets, and the company allegedly imported more docile workers to replace those who had struck. A group signing themselves "The Starving Citizens of Pullman" appealed to Governor John Altgeld of Illinois for relief. After examining conditions personally, the governor wrote the following letter to George M. Pullman. Does the evidence here given support the charge of discrimination?

Sir: I examined the conditions at Pullman yesterday, visited even the kitchens and bedrooms of many of the people. Two representatives of your company were with me and we found the distress as great as it was represented. The men are hungry and the women and children are actually suffering. They have been living on charity for a number of months and it is exhausted. Men who had worked for your company for more than ten years had to apply to the relief society in two weeks after the work stopped.

I learn from your manager that last spring there were 3,260 people on the payroll; yesterday there were 2,220 at work, but over 600 of these are new men, so that only about 1,600 of the old employees have been taken back, thus leaving over 1,600 of the old employees who have not been taken back. A few hundred have left, the remainder have nearly all applied for work, but were told that they were not needed. These are utterly destitute. The relief committee on last Saturday gave out two pounds of oatmeal and two pounds of cornmeal to each family. But even the relief committee has exhausted its resources.

Something must be done and at once. The case differs from instances of destitution found elsewhere, for generally there is somebody in the neighborhood able to give relief; this is not the case at Pullman. Even those who have gone to work are so exhausted that they cannot help their neighbors if they would. I repeat now that it seems to me your company cannot afford to have me appeal to the charity and humanity of the state to save the lives of your old employees. Four-fifths of those people are women and children. No matter what caused this distress, it must be met.

[Mr. Pullman turned a deaf ear to appeals for relief, and humane citizens were forced to help the destitute. "Mr. Dooley" (F. P. Dunne) referred to the time "whin God quarried his heart." Reconcile Pullman's attitude in this instance with his large private philanthropies, including a bequest of $1.2 million for a free manual training school in Pullman.]

---

[*]John P. Altgeld, *Live Questions* (Chicago: Geo. S. Bowen & Son, 1899), pp. 422–423 (August 21, 1894).

E. William Jennings Bryan's Cross of Gold (1896)*

At the Democratic party's presidential nominating convention in Chicago in 1896, William Jennings Bryan of Nebraska made an eloquent and impassioned speech denouncing the gold standard and advocating inflation. Although a well-known ex-congressman and free-silver orator, Bryan was not then regarded as one of the front-runners for the presidential nomination. Tall, lean, smooth-shaven, hawk-nosed, and wide-mouthed, "the Boy Orator of the Platte" hushed the vast assemblage of some fifteen thousand with his masterful presence. The "cross of gold" analogy to the Crucifixion of Christ was one he had already used a number of times, but never before so effectively. Projecting his organlike voice to the outer reaches of the vast hall, he had the frenzied crowd cheering his every sentence as he neared the end. The climax swept the delegates off their feet and won Bryan the presidential nomination the next day. How do you account for the success of his memorable speech? To what different kinds of prejudice does Bryan appeal?

I would be presumptuous, indeed, to present myself against the distinguished gentlemen to whom you have listened if this were a mere measuring of abilities. But this is not a contest between persons. The humblest citizen in all the land, when clad in the armor of a righteous cause, is stronger than all the hosts of error. I come to speak to you in defense of a cause as holy as the cause of liberty—the cause of humanity....

We [silverites] do not come as aggressors. Our war is not a war of conquest. We are fighting in the defense of our homes, our families, and posterity. We have petitioned, and our petitions have been scorned. We have entreated, and our entreaties have been disregarded. We have begged, and they have mocked when our calamity came. We beg no longer; we entreat no more; we petition no more. We defy them!...

The gentleman from New York [Senator David Hill]...says he wants this country to try to secure an international agreement. Why does he not tell us what he is going to do if he fails to secure an international agreement?...Our opponents have tried for twenty years to secure an international agreement, and those are waiting for it most patiently who do not want it at all....

We go forth confident that we shall win. Why? Because upon the paramount issue of this campaign there is not a spot of ground upon which the enemy will dare to challenge battle. If they [the Republicans] tell us that the gold standard is a good thing, we shall point to their platform and tell them that their platform pledges the party to get rid of the gold standard and substitute bimetallism. If the gold standard is a good thing, why try to get rid of it?...

Mr. Carlisle† said in 1878 that this was a struggle between "the idle holders of idle capital" and "the struggling masses, who produce the wealth and pay the taxes of the country"; and, my friends, the question we are to decide is: upon which side

---

*C. M. Depew, ed., *The Library of Oratory* (New York: The Globe Publishing Company, 1902), vol. 14, pp. 415, 418, 420–425, passim.
†John G. Carlisle of Kentucky, formerly a distinguished member of Congress, was President Cleveland's secretary of the treasury in 1896.

will the Democratic Party fight—upon the side of "the idle holders of idle capital" or upon the side of "the struggling masses"? That is the question which the party must answer first, and then it must be answered by each individual hereafter. The sympathies of the Democratic Party, as shown by the platform, are on the side of the struggling masses who have ever been the foundation of the Democratic Party.

There are two ideas of government. There are those who believe that, if you will only legislate to make the well-to-do prosperous, their prosperity will leak through on those below. The Democratic idea, however, has been that if you legislate to make the masses prosperous, their prosperity will find its way up through every class which rests upon them.

You come to us and tell us that the great cities are in favor of the gold standard. We reply that the great cities rest upon our broad and fertile prairies. Burn down your cities and leave our farms, and your cities will spring up again as if by magic. But destroy our farms, and the grass will grow in the streets of every city in the country.

My friends, we declare that this nation is able to legislate for its own people on every question, without waiting for the aid or consent of any other nation on earth; and upon that issue we expect to carry every state in the Union. I shall not slander the inhabitants of the fair state of Massachusetts nor the inhabitants of the state of New York by saying that, when they are confronted with the proposition, they will declare that this nation is not able to attend to its own business. It is the issue of 1776 over again. Our ancestors, when but three millions in number, had the courage to declare their political independence of every other nation. Shall we, their descendants, when we have grown to seventy millions, declare that we are less independent than our forefathers?

No, my friends, that will never be the verdict of our people. Therefore, we care not upon what lines the battle is fought. If they say bimetallism is good but that we cannot have it until other nations help us, we reply that, instead of having a gold standard because England has, we will restore bimetallism, and then let England have bimetallism because the United States has it. If they dare to come out in the open field and defend the gold standard as a good thing, we will fight them to the uttermost.

Having behind us the producing masses of this nation and the world, supported by the commercial interests, the laboring interests, and the toilers everywhere, we will answer their demand for a gold standard by saying to them: You shall not press down upon the brow of labor this crown of thorns; you shall not crucify mankind upon a cross of gold.

[The Cleveland Democrats, with their devotion to the gold standard, were appalled by the nomination of Bryan. "What a burlesque on a Democratic convention," wrote Postmaster General William Wilson in his diary. "May God help the country!" He stressed the youth, ambition, and Populist leanings of the candidate, while noting that Bryan's "utter ignorance of the great diplomatic, financial, and other questions a President has constantly to dispose of, will be lost sight of in the fanaticism of the one idea he represents." (F. P. Summers, The Cabinet Diary of William L. Wilson, 1896–1897 *[Chapel Hill: University of North Carolina Press, 1957], p. 116.) Conservatives, then and later, generally agreed that Bryan was strong on sound but weak on substance.]*

Thought Provokers

1. It has been said that there was no Indian problem but a white problem; no black problem but a white problem. Comment critically. Why were Indian-white relations different in Canada? Did George Armstrong Custer bring on his own death?
2. What were the best and worst things about life on the frontier? How was the frontier experience for men different from that for women?
3. Farmers, to be successful, had to be good businesspeople, and many failed because they were not. It was charged that they illogically put the blame for their failures on other factors. Comment. Other critics accused them of not doing well because they had fallen into habits of indolence. Would greater energy and larger harvests have cured the basic ills?
4. Is a company like Pullman's justified in cutting wages when it has a large surplus of money? Does management have a higher obligation to the investor than to the laborer? Is the businessperson the best interpreter of the public interest? Is a large-scale business a purely private matter?
5. Why was William Jennings Bryan's famous "Cross of Gold" speech so moving yet ultimately so ineffective?

27

Empire and Expansion, 1890–1909

It has been a splendid little war [with Spain];
begun with the highest motives, carried on with
magnificent intelligence and spirit, favored by that
fortune which loves the brave.

John Hay, 1898

Prologue: As the nineteenth century neared its sunset, as the frontier closed and factories and farms poured out exportable surpluses, Americans increasingly looked outward. Spain, struggling to crush a rebellion in Cuba, became the focus of American wrath and ambition. Goaded by the new "yellow journalism," the pro-business administration of William McKinley forced a showdown with Spain over Cuba and soon found itself at war in both the Caribbean and the far Pacific, where Spain's Philippine colony was ripe for plucking. Although Cuba was freed from Spanish domination, the United States long compromised Cuba's full independence under the terms of the controversial Platt Amendment. The liberated Filipinos also chafed under American rule, mounting a bloody insurrection that dragged on for seven years. Imperialists and anti-imperialists hotly debated the wisdom and morality of America's new international role. Meanwhile, mounting immigration from Asia spurred an energetic nativist backlash against Chinese and Japanese newcomers alike. Theodore Roosevelt, assuming the presidency after McKinley's assassination in 1901, pursued an especially assertive foreign policy. He secured the Panama Canal Zone for the United States and proceeded to build an isthmian canal. With the "Roosevelt Corollary" to the Monroe Doctrine, he asserted the right of the United States to intervene throughout the Caribbean and Central America. By mediating a settlement at the end of the Russo-Japanese War in 1905, he won the Nobel Peace Prize. And by interceding in the quarrel between California and Japan over Japanese immigration, he hammered out the "Gentlemen's Agreement" to stem the flow of Japanese immigrants.

A. Yellow Journalism in Flower

1. Joseph Pulitzer Demands Intervention (1897)[*]

The oppressed Cubans revolted in 1895, and the Spanish commander, General Valeriano ("Butcher") Weyler, tried to crush them by herding them into pesthole concentration

---

[*]*New York World*, February 13, 1897.

camps. *Atrocities on both sides were inevitable, but the United States heard little of Cuban misdeeds. The American yellow press, with Joseph Pulitzer's* New York World *and William Randolph Hearst's* New York Journal *competing in sensationalism, headlined lurid horror tales. The basic principle of the so-called new journalism seemed to be "Anything to Sell a Paper," regardless of the truth. A* World *reporter wrote from Cuba that slaughtered rebels were fed to dogs and that children of high-ranking Spanish families clamored for Cuban ears as playthings. The following editorial in Pulitzer's* World *demanded action. What point or points probably made the heaviest impact on the American public?*

How long are the Spaniards to drench Cuba with the blood and tears of her people?

How long is the peasantry of Spain to be drafted away to Cuba to die miserably in a hopeless war, that Spanish nobles and Spanish officers may get medals and honors?

How long shall old [Cuban] men and women and children be murdered by the score, the innocent victims of Spanish rage against the patriot armies they cannot conquer?

How long shall the sound of rifles in Castle Morro [in Cuba] at sunrise proclaim that bound and helpless prisoners of war have been murdered in cold blood?

How long shall Cuban women be the victims of Spanish outrages and lie sobbing and bruised in loathsome prisons?

How long shall women passengers on vessels flying the American flag be unlawfully seized and stripped and searched by brutal, jeering Spanish officers, in violation of the laws of nations and of the honor of the United States?*

How long shall American citizens, arbitrarily arrested while on peaceful and legitimate errands, be immured in foul Spanish prisons without trial?†

How long shall the navy of the United States be used as the sea police of barbarous Spain?

How long shall the United States sit idle and indifferent within sound and hearing of rapine and murder?

How long?

2. William Randolph Hearst Stages a Rescue (1897)‡

William Randolph Hearst, the irresponsible California playboy who had inherited some $20 million from his father, was even more ingenious than his archrival Joseph Pulitzer. He is said to have boasted (with undue credit to himself) that it cost him $3 million to bring on the Spanish-American War. He outdid himself in the case of Evangelina Cisneros, a "tenderly nurtured" Cuban girl of eighteen who was imprisoned in Havana on charges of rebellion and reportedly faced a twenty-year incarceration with depraved fellow inmates. The yellow press pictured her as a beautiful young woman whose only crime had been to preserve her virtue against the lustful advances of a "lecherous" Spanish officer. Hearst's New York Journal *whipped up a*

---

*The most highly publicized case actually involved an examination by a police matron.
†By 1897 there were few, if any, U.S. citizens in Cuban prisons, even naturalized Americans of Cuban birth.
‡*New York Journal*, October 10, 1897.

storm of sympathy for the girl and inspired appeals to the Spanish queen and to the pope. All else failing, a Journal *reporter rented a house next to the prison, drugged the inmates, sawed through the cell bars, and—using a forged visa—escaped with Señorita Cisneros disguised as a boy. What does this account in the* Journal *reveal about the character and the techniques of the new yellow journalism?*

EVANGELINA CISNEROS RESCUED BY THE JOURNAL

**AN AMERICAN NEWSPAPER ACCOMPLISHES AT A SINGLE
STROKE WHAT THE RED TAPE OF DIPLOMACY
FAILED UTTERLY TO BRING ABOUT IN
MANY MONTHS**

By Charles Duval
(Copyright, 1897, by W. R. Hearst)

Havana, Oct. 7, via Key West, Fla., Oct. 9.—Evangelina Cosio y Cisneros is at liberty, and the *Journal* can place to its credit the greatest journalist coup of this age. It is an illustration of the methods of new journalism and it will find an endorsement in the heart of every woman who has read of the horrible sufferings of the poor girl who has been confined for fifteen long months in Recojidas Prison.

The *Journal*, finding that all other methods were unavailing, decided to secure her liberation through force, and this, as the specially selected commissioner of the *Journal*, I have succeeded in doing.

I have broken the bars of Recojidas and have set free the beautiful captive of monster Weyler, restoring her to her friends and relatives, and doing by strength, skill, and strategy what could not be accomplished by petition and urgent request of the Pope.

Weyler could blind the Queen to [the] real character of Evangelina, but he could not build a jail that would hold against *Journal* enterprise when properly set to work.

Tonight all Havana rings with the story. It is the one topic of conversation; everything else pales into insignificance.

B. The Declaration of War

1. President McKinley Submits a War Message (1898)*

Despite Spain's belated concessions, McKinley sent his war message to Congress on April 11, 1898. His nerves were giving way under the constant clamor for war; his heart went out to the mistreated Cubans. (He had anonymously contributed $5,000 for their relief.) He realized that Spain's offer of an armistice, at the discretion of its commander, did not guarantee peace. The rebels had to agree on terms, and Spain had shown a talent for breaking promises and protracting negotiations. Further delay would only worsen the terrible conditions. Among the reasons that McKinley

---

*James D. Richardson, ed., *Messages and Papers of the Presidents* (New York: Bureau of National Literature, 1899), vol. 10, pp. 147, 150, passim.

here gives Congress for intervention, which are the soundest and which the weakest? Was there danger in intervening for humanitarian reasons?

The grounds for such intervention may be briefly summarized as follows:

First. In the cause of humanity and to put an end to the barbarities, bloodshed, starvation, and horrible miseries now existing there, and which the parties to the conflict are either unable or unwilling to stop or mitigate. It is no answer to say this is all in another country, belonging to another nation, and is therefore none of our business. It is specially our duty, for it is right at our door.

Second. We owe it to our citizens in Cuba to afford them that protection and indemnity for life and property which no government there can or will afford, and to that end to terminate the conditions that deprive them of legal protection.

Third. The right to intervene may be justified by the very serious injury to the commerce, trade, and business of our people and by the wanton destruction of property and devastation of the island.

Fourth, and which is of the utmost importance. The present condition of affairs in Cuba is a constant menace to our peace, and entails upon this government an enormous expense. With such a conflict waged for years in an island so near us and with which our people have such trade and business relations; when the lives and liberty of our citizens are in constant danger and their property destroyed and themselves ruined; where our trading vessels are liable to seizure and are seized at our very door by warships of a foreign nation; the expeditions of filibustering [free-booting] that we are powerless to prevent altogether, and the irritating questions and entanglements thus arising—all these and others that I need not mention, with the resulting strained relations, are a constant menace to our peace and compel us to keep on a semi-war footing with a nation with which we are at peace.

These elements of danger and disorder already pointed out have been strikingly illustrated by a tragic event which has deeply and justly moved the American people. I have already transmitted to Congress the report of the Naval Court of Inquiry on the destruction of the battleship *Maine* in the harbor of Havana during the night of the 15th of February. The destruction of that noble vessel has filled the national heart with inexpressible horror. Two hundred and fifty-eight brave sailors and marines and two officers of our Navy, reposing in the fancied security of a friendly harbor, have been hurled to death, [and] grief and want brought to their homes and sorrow to the nation.

The Naval Court of Inquiry, which, it is needless to say, commands the unqualified confidence of the government, was unanimous in its conclusion that the destruction of the *Maine* was caused by an exterior explosion—that of a submarine mine.* It did not assume to place the responsibility. That remains to be fixed.

In any event, the destruction of the *Maine*, by whatever exterior cause, is a patent and impressive proof of a state of things in Cuba that is intolerable. That condition is thus shown to be such that the Spanish government cannot assure safety and security to a vessel of the American Navy in the harbor of Havana on a mission of peace, and rightfully there....

---

*Assuming that the outside explosion theory is correct—and it has been seriously challenged—the *Maine* might have been blown up by Cuban insurgents seeking to involve the United States in the war.

[McKinley here refers to the offer by the Spanish minister to arbitrate the Maine and simply adds, "To this I have made no reply."]

The long trial has proved that the object for which Spain has waged the war cannot be attained. The fire of insurrection may flame or may smolder with varying seasons, but it has not been, and it is plain that it cannot be, extinguished by present methods. The only hope of relief and repose from a condition which can no longer be endured is the enforced pacification of Cuba. In the name of humanity, in the name of civilization, in behalf of endangered American interests which give us the right and the duty to speak and to act, the war in Cuba must stop. . . .

The issue is now with the Congress. It is a solemn responsibility. I have exhausted every effort to relieve the intolerable condition of affairs which is at our doors. Prepared to execute every obligation imposed upon me by the Constitution and the law, I await your action.

Yesterday, and since the preparation of the foregoing message, official information was received by me that the latest decree of the Queen Regent of Spain directs General Blanco, in order to prepare and facilitate peace, to proclaim a suspension of hostilities, the duration and details of which have not yet been communicated to me.

This fact, with every other pertinent consideration, will, I am sure, have your just and careful attention in the solemn deliberations upon which you are about to enter. If this measure attains a successful result, then our aspirations as a Christian, peace-loving people will be realized. If it fails, it will be only another justification for our contemplated action.

[The president had prepared the foregoing war message a week or so before he submitted it; the delay was primarily to permit U.S. citizens to flee Cuba. A few hours before McKinley finally moved, cablegrams from Minister Stewart Woodford in Madrid brought the news that Spain, having already revoked reconcentration (the policy of herding Cuban rebels into concentration camps), had met the rest of the president's demands by authorizing an armistice. So, at the end of a message that urged war, McKinley casually tacked on the two foregoing paragraphs hinting that hostilities might be avoided. Eight days later a bellicose Congress overwhelmingly passed what was in effect a declaration of war. Several years after the event, General Woodford told the journalist and reformer O. G. Villard, "When I sent that last cable to McKinley, I thought I should wake up the next morning to find myself acclaimed all over the United States for having achieved the greatest diplomatic victory in our history." Instead, he learned of the war message. (O. G. Villard, Fighting Years *[New York: Harcourt, Brace and Co., 1939], p. 136.)]*

2. Professor Charles Eliot Norton's Patriotic Protest (1898)*

Lovable and immensely popular, Charles Eliot Norton served for many years at Harvard as professor of the history of the fine arts. After war broke out, he shocked public opinion with a speech in Cambridge urging young men not to enlist. The press

---

Public Opinion 24 (June 23, 1898): 775–776.

denounced him as one of the "intellectual Copperheads" (a reference to the northern Democrats who opposed the Civil War). McKinley had recommended war in the interest of civilization; Norton here urges an opposite course. Who had the sounder arguments? Was it more patriotic to protest than to acquiesce?

And now of a sudden, without cool deliberation, without prudent preparation, the nation is hurried into war, and America, she who more than any other land was pledged to peace and good will on earth, unsheathes her sword, compels a weak and unwilling nation to a fight, rejecting without due consideration her [Spain's] earnest and repeated offers to meet every legitimate demand of the United States. It is a bitter disappointment to the lover of his country; it is a turning back from the path of civilization to that of barbarism.

"There never was a good war," said [Benjamin] Franklin. There have indeed been many wars in which a good man must take part....But if a war be undertaken for the most righteous end, before the resources of peace have been tried and proved vain to secure it, that war has no defense. It is a national crime. The plea that the better government of Cuba, and the relief of the *reconcentrados*, could only be secured by war is the plea either of ignorance or of hypocrisy.

But the war is declared; and on all hands we hear the cry that he is no patriot who fails to shout for it, and to urge the youth of the country to enlist, and to rejoice that they are called to the service of their native land. The sober counsels that were appropriate before the war was entered upon must give way to blind enthusiasm, and the voice of condemnation must be silenced by the thunders of the guns and the hurrahs of the crowd.

Stop! A declaration of war does not change the moral law. "The Ten Commandments will not budge" at a joint resolve of Congress....No! the voice of protest, of warning, of appeal is never more needed than when the clamor of fife and drum, echoed by the press and too often by the pulpit, is bidding all men fall in and keep step and obey in silence the tyrannous word of command. Then, more than ever, it is the duty of the good citizen not to be silent, and spite of obliquity, misrepresentation, and abuse, to insist on being heard, and with sober counsel to maintain the everlasting validity of the principles of the moral law.

C. The Debate over Imperialism

1. Albert Beveridge Trumpets Imperialism (1898)[*]

Albert J. Beveridge delivered this famous speech, "The March of the Flag," at Indianapolis on September 16, 1898, before McKinley had decided to keep the Philippines. Born to an impoverished family, Beveridge had spent his youth at hard manual labor but ultimately secured a college education with prizes won in oratorical contests. The cadences of his spellbinding oratory were such that "Mr. Dooley" (F. P. Dunne) said you could waltz to

---

[*]C. M. Depew, ed., *The Library of Oratory* (New York: The Globe Publishing Company, 1902), vol. 14, pp. 438–440.

them. The year after making this address, Beveridge was elected to the U.S. Senate from Indiana at the remarkably youthful age of thirty-six. How convincing is his reply to the anti-imperialists' warnings against the annexation of noncontiguous territory and to their argument that no more land was needed? What were his powers as a prophet?

Distance and oceans are no arguments. The fact that all the territory our fathers bought and seized is contiguous is no argument. In 1819 Florida was further from New York than Porto Rico is from Chicago today; Texas, further from Washington in 1845 than Hawaii is from Boston in 1898; California, more inaccessible in 1847 than the Philippines are now.... The ocean does not separate us from lands of our duty and desire—the oceans join us, a river never to be dredged, a canal never to be repaired.

Steam joins us; electricity joins us—the very elements are in league with our destiny. Cuba not contiguous! Porto Rico not contiguous! Hawaii and the Philippines not contiguous! Our navy will make them contiguous. [Admirals] Dewey and Sampson and Schley have made them contiguous, and American speed, American guns, American heart and brain and nerve will keep them contiguous forever.

But the Opposition is right—there is a difference. We did not need the western Mississippi Valley when we acquired it, nor Florida, nor Texas, nor California, nor the royal provinces of the far Northwest. We had no emigrants to people this imperial wilderness, no money to develop it, even no highways to cover it. No trade awaited us in its savage fastnesses. Our productions were not greater than our trade. There was not one reason for the land-lust of our statesmen from Jefferson to Grant, other than the prophet and the Saxon within them.

But today we are raising more than we can consume. Today we are making more than we can use. Today our industrial society is congested; there are more workers than there is work; there is more capital than there is investment. We do not need more money—we need more circulation, more employment. Therefore we must find new markets for our produce, new occupation for our capital, new work for our labor. And so, while we did not need the territory taken during the past century at the time it was acquired, we do need what we have taken in 1898, and we need it now.

Think of the thousands of Americans who will pour into Hawaii and Porto Rico when the republic's laws cover those islands with justice and safety! Think of the tens of thousands of Americans who will invade mine and field and forest in the Philippines when a liberal government, protected and controlled by this republic, if not the government of the republic itself, shall establish order and equity there! Think of the hundreds of thousands of Americans who will build a soap-and-water, common-school civilization of energy and industry in Cuba, when a government of law replaces the double reign of anarchy and tyranny!—think of the prosperous millions that Empress of Islands will support when, obedient to the law of political gravitation, her people ask for the highest honor liberty can bestow, the sacred Order of the Stars and Stripes, the citizenship of the Great Republic!

What does all this mean for every one of us? It means opportunity for all the glorious young manhood of the republic—the most virile, ambitious, impatient, militant manhood the world has ever seen. It means that the resources and the commerce of these immensely rich dominions will be increased as much as American energy is greater than Spanish sloth; for Americans henceforth will monopolize those resources and that commerce.

[The Treaty of Paris, by which the United States acquired the Philippines, received Senate approval by a close vote on February 6, 1899. The imperialists had little to add to the materialistic-humanitarian arguments presented by McKinley and Beveridge. The anti-imperialists stressed the folly of annexing noncontiguous areas in the tropics thickly populated by alien peoples. They also harped on the folly of departing from the principles of freedom and nonintervention as set forth in the Declaration of Independence, Washington's Farewell Address, the Monroe Doctrine, and the Emancipation Proclamation. Senator George F. Hoar of Massachusetts assailed the imperialists with these words: "If you ask them what they want, you are answered with a shout: 'Three cheers for the flag! Who will dare to haul it down? Hold on to everything you can get. The United States is strong enough to do what it likes. The Declaration of Independence and the counsel of Washington and the Constitution of the United States have grown rusty and musty. They are for little countries and not for great ones. There is no moral law for strong nations. America has outgrown Americanism.'" (Congressional Record, 55th Cong., 3d sess., 1899, p. 495.)]

2. Mark Twain Denounces Imperialism (c. 1900)*

To the most fervent opponents of empire, more hung in the balance than simply the fate of the Philippines—their struggle was to protect the very essence of the American republic. Harvard philosophy professor William James fumed that temptation for empire had caused America "to puke up its ancient soul," while industrialist Andrew Carnegie questioned whether the United States would "remain as we are, solid… republican, American," or wantonly grasp at "the phantom of Imperialism." Noted satirist Mark Twain, who served as vice president of the American Anti-Imperialist Society, captured these sentiments when he revised a popular Civil War era anthem into a searing critique of America's imperial venture. His updated "Battle Hymn of the Republic" was never published but was found in his papers after his death. What does it reveal about the tenor of the imperialist debate? What are his chief objections to acquiring the Philippines?

Battle Hymn of the Republic
(Brought Down to Date)

Mine eyes have seen the orgy of the launching of the Sword;
He is searching out the hoardings where the stranger's wealth is
    stored;
He hath loosed his fateful lightnings, and with woe and death
    has scored;
      His lust is marching on.

---

*Frederick Anderson, ed., *A Pen Warmed Up in Hell: Mark Twain in Protest* (New York: Harper & Row, 1972), p. 4.

I have seen him in the watch-fires of a hundred circling camps,
They have builded him an altar in the Eastern dews and damps;
I have read his doomful mission by the dim and flaring lamps—
     His night is marching on.

I have read his bandit gospel writ in burnished rows of steel:
"As ye deal with my pretensions, so with you my wrath shall
    deal;
Let the faithless son of Freedom crush the patriot with his heel;
     Lo, Greed is marching on!"

We have legalized the strumpet and are guarding her retreat;[*]
Greed is seeking out commercial souls before his judgment seat;
O, be swift, ye clods, to answer him! be jubilant my feet!
     Our god is marching on!

In a sordid slime harmonious, Greed was born in yonder ditch,
With a longing in his bosom—and for others' goods an itch—
As Christ died to make men holy, let men die to make us rich—
     Our god is marching on.

3. The Nation Denounces Atrocities (1902)[†]

Many of the Filipino tribes were simple peoples who knew little of so-called civilized warfare. Some of them would horribly mutilate and torture American captives, sometimes fastening them down to be eaten alive by insects. The infuriated white soldiers retaliated by shooting a few prisoners and by administering the "water cure"—forcing buckets of dirty water into Filipinos, deflating them with rifle butts, and repeating the painful process. In certain areas the Americans herded the populace into reconcentration camps, somewhat after the manner of "Butcher" Weyler in Cuba. General Jacob ("Hell Roaring Jake") Smith was "admonished" by the War Department for an order (not carried out) to kill all males over ten years of age on the island of Samar. How sound is the parallel that the New York Nation *here draws between Spanish behavior in Cuba and U.S. behavior in the Philippines?*

Even if the condemnation of barbarous warfare in the Philippines by the imperialist press is somewhat belated, we welcome it, as we welcome everything that compels Americans to give attention to a subject to which too many of them have become increasingly indifferent. Silence, we know, is consistent with shame, and may be one of the signs of its existence; and the fact that only a few of the more unblushing or foolish newspapers have defended Gen. Smith's policy of extermination shows what the general sentiment is.

---

[*]In Manila the Government has placed a certain industry under the protection of our flag. (M.T.)
[†]*Nation* (New York) 74 (May 8, 1902): 357.

To allege the provocation which our soldiers had is to set up a defense which President Roosevelt brushed aside in advance. To fall back on the miserable sophistry that "war is hell" is only another way of making out those who engage in that kind of war to be fiends. It is, besides, to offer an excuse for ourselves which we did not tolerate for an instant in the case of Spanish atrocities. That is our present moral humiliation in the eyes of the world.

We made war on Spain four years ago for doing the very things of which we are now guilty ourselves. As the Chicago *News* pointedly observes, we are giving Spain as good reason to interfere with us on the ground of humanity as we had to interfere with her. Doubtless she would interfere if she were strong enough and thought she could acquire some islands in the virtuous act.

4. Cartoonists Tackle the Philippines Question (c. 1900)

Proponents of empire portrayed their cause as a noble civilizing mission, the moral obligation of the "white man's burden," which British poet Rudyard Kipling urged the United States to shoulder. Critics retorted that such appeals rang hollow in the face of a mounting insurrection and the brutal slaughter of Philippine natives. The following cartoons dramatize both sides of the imperialist debate. How do these cartoons portray the Filipino population? What do the images reveal about the logic of each side's argument?

"Speaking from Experience." Judge, *no date available.*

"School Begins." Puck, January 25, 1899.

D. The Monroe Doctrine in the Caribbean

1. Roosevelt Launches a Corollary (1904)[*]

The corrupt and bankrupt "banana republics" of the Caribbean were inclined to over-borrow, and Roosevelt believed they could properly be "spanked" by European creditors. But the British-German spanking of Venezuela in 1902 resulted in the sinking of two Venezuelan gunboats and the bombardment of a fort and village. Such interventions foreshadowed a possibly permanent foothold and a consequent violation of the Monroe Doctrine. Sensing this danger, Roosevelt, in his annual message to Congress of 1904, sketched out his famous corollary to the Monroe Doctrine. Monroe had in effect warned the European powers in 1823, "Hands off." Roosevelt was now saying that since the United States would not permit the powers to lay their hands on, he had an obligation to do so himself. In short, he would intervene to keep them from intervening. In the statement embodied in his annual message, how does he justify this newly announced U.S. role, and what assurances does he give to the Latin American countries?

[*]*A Compilation of the Messages and Papers of the Presidents* (New York: Bureau of National Literature, 1906), vol. 16 (December 6, 1904), pp. 7053–7054.

It is not true that the United States feels any land hunger or entertains any projects as regards the other nations of the Western Hemisphere, save such as are for their welfare. All that this country desires is to see the neighboring countries stable, orderly, and prosperous. Any country whose people conduct themselves well can count upon our hearty friendship. If a nation shows that it knows how to act with reasonable efficiency and decency in social and political matters, if it keeps order and pays its obligations, it need fear no interference from the United States.

Chronic wrongdoing, or an impotence which results in a general loosening of the ties of civilized society, may in America, as elsewhere, ultimately require intervention by some civilized nation, and in the Western Hemisphere the adherence of the United States to the Monroe Doctrine may force the United States, however reluctantly, in flagrant cases of such wrongdoing or impotence, to the exercise of an international police power. If every country washed by the Caribbean Sea would show the progress in stable and just civilization which, with the aid of the Platt amendment, Cuba has shown since our troops left the island, and which so many of the republics in both Americas are constantly and brilliantly showing, all question of interference by this Nation with their affairs would be at an end.

Our interests and those of our southern neighbors are in reality identical. They have great natural riches, and if within their borders the reign of law and justice obtains, prosperity is sure to come to them. While they thus obey the primary laws of civilized society, they may rest assured that they will be treated by us in a spirit of cordial and helpful sympathy. We would interfere with them only in the last resort, and then only if it became evident that their inability or unwillingness to do justice at home and abroad had violated the rights of the United States or had invited foreign aggression to the detriment of the entire body of American nations. It is a mere truism to say that every nation, whether in America or anywhere else, which desires to maintain its freedom, its independence, must ultimately realize that the right of such independence cannot be separated from the responsibility of making good use of it.

2. A Latin American Protests (1943)*

Following up his new corollary to the Monroe Doctrine, Roosevelt arranged with the local authorities to take over and administer the customhouses of the bankrupt Santo Domingo. The European creditors then had no real excuse for interfering, for they received their regular payments. In his annual message of 1905, Roosevelt added a refinement to his corollary to the Monroe Doctrine: to prevent European creditors from taking over customhouses (and perhaps staying), the United States had an obligation to take over the customhouses. In subsequent years, and pursuant to the Roosevelt Corollary to the Monroe Doctrine, the marines landed and acted as international policemen, notably in Haiti, Santo Domingo, and Nicaragua. The Latin Americans, cherishing their sovereign right to revolution and disorder, bitterly resented this bayonet-enforced twisting of Monroe's protective dictum. Below, an outspoken Mexican diplomat, with a Ph.D. from Johns Hopkins University, expresses his wrath. It has been said that

---

*Luis Quintanilla, *A Latin American Speaks* (New York: The Macmillan Company, 1943), pp. 125–126.

the Roosevelt Corollary was so radically different from the original Monroe Doctrine (see p. 180) that the two should never have been associated. Was Roosevelt's corollary a logical extension or a radical revision of the Monroe Doctrine?

No document has proved more harmful to the prestige of the United States in the Western Hemisphere [than the Roosevelt Corollary]. No White House policy could be more distasteful to Latin Americans—not even, perhaps, outspoken imperialism. Latin Americans are usually inclined to admire strength, force, a nation *muy hombre* [very manly]. This was imperialism without military glamour....Moreover, it was a total distortion of the original Message. Monroe's Doctrine was defensive and negative: defensive, in that it was essentially an opposition to eventual aggression from Europe; negative, in that it simply told Europe what it should not do—not what the United States should do.

The Monroe Doctrine of later corollaries became aggressive and positive; aggressive, because, even without actual European attack, it urged United States "protection" of Latin America—and that was outright intervention; positive, because instead of telling Europe what not to do, it told the United States what it should do in the Western Hemisphere. From a case of America vs. Europe, the corollaries made of the Doctrine a case of the United States vs. America.

President Monroe had merely shaken his head, brandished his finger, and said to Europe, "Now, now, gentlemen, if you meddle with us, we will not love you any more," while Teddy Roosevelt, brandishing a big stick, had shouted, "Listen, you guys, don't muscle in—this territory is ours."

In still another corollary, enunciated to justify United States intervention [in Santo Domingo], the same Roosevelt said: "It is far better that this country should put through such an arrangement [enforcing fulfillment of financial obligations contracted by Latin American states] rather than to allow any foreign country to undertake it." To intervene in order to protect: to intervene in order to prevent others from so doing. It is the "Invasion for Protection" corollary, so much in the limelight recently, in other parts of the world.

[Latin American bitterness against this perversion of the Monroe Doctrine festered for nearly three decades. A sharp turn for the better came in 1933, when President Franklin D. Roosevelt, implementing a policy initiated by President Herbert Hoover, formally renounced the doctrine of intervention in Latin America. Thus what the first Roosevelt gave, the second Roosevelt took away.]

E. Tensions with Asia

1. Californians Petition for Chinese Exclusion (1877)[*]

Uprooted by the tumultuous disintegration of the Chinese Empire and drawn to the promise of economic prosperity, some three hundred thousand Chinese immigrants

---

[*]Cheng-Tsu Wu, ed., *"Chink!": A Documentary History of Anti-Chinese Prejudice in America* (New York: World Publishing, 1972), pp. 113–120.

made their way to the United States in the second half of the nineteenth century. While employers eagerly recruited the Chinese to dig mines and lay down miles of track across the booming West, white workers resented the influx of cheap, alien competition. During the depression of the 1870s, labor leaders unleashed a torrent of abuse against the Chinese, casting them as stooges of industry and blaming them for undercutting white wages. In 1877, the California State legislature submitted the following petition to Congress advocating the exclusion of all immigrants from China. How does the petition justify restricting Chinese immigration? What parallels does it draw between the Chinese in California and African Americans in the East?

A perfect equality of political rights, and a universal cooperation of the entire people, or at least its moral capability of cooperating in the making and administering the laws, being the cornerstone of the permanence of every republic...we should not invite a national element into our midst whose social character and moral relations are so repulsive to those fundamental principles upon which our society, and indeed every civilized society, is founded, that we can neither socially amalgamate with it, nor entrust it with the prerogatives and duties of participation in the administration of our Government....

In appealing to Congress for protection against the contingency of an overwhelming immigration of Mongolians, the Legislature of California is solely actuated by the love and care for the safety and maintenance of our institutions, and the consciousness that a condition of slavery in our midst must unavoidably be the result of an unrestrained immigration of Mongolians. The Representatives of the people of California deem it a solemn duty to manifest to the National Congress the conviction that, if this immigration be not discouraged, the time is not far when degraded labor will have become as identified with the pecuniary interests of a portion of the people of this State, and as inimical to the fundamental principles of a democratic government, as Negro labor in the now rebellious States.

Even the position of the small number of free Negroes in the free States teaches us that no republican government ought to suffer the presence of a race which must, socially and politically, be always separate and distinct, and the antipathy to which is stronger in regulating its position and disabilities in society than the laws of the land.... [I]t is not alone a legalized state of slavery, which undermines the foundation of a republic, but that social relation which is the necessary consequence of the settlement in *one* community of two entirely uncongenial races, and which tends to produce, though the inferior race may be nominally free, the respective positions of a governing and a servile class, is just as dangerous to the permanence of republican institutions and ought to be as much guarded against as slavery itself....

The free States in the East could only then fully appreciate the evils and complications which threaten the social system of California, if they were as much exposed to the danger of becoming colonies of free Negroes as California to the immigration of millions of Mongolians. Though the free Negro speaks our language, though he grows up among us, worships the same God as ourselves, and is accustomed to our institutions, yet the free states find the presence of a comparatively small population of this race exceedingly annoying, and fraught with dangers not only to the peace of their own community, but to the harmony between their laws and the constitutional policy of the National Legislature. What may be the difficulties and dangers which California will have to encounter, if she is not to be protected from the unlimited influx of a race which already comprises the eighth part of her entire population, which is utterly a stranger to our language, to the fundamental principles of enlightened religion, to our consciousness of moral obligations, and, with a few individual exceptions, even to a sense of the most common properties of life....

The Mongolian is not only by degrees diminishing the means of subsistence of our white workingmen, but he is a serious impediment in the way of the immigration of the poor and humble classes of our own race from the Eastern States and Europe. As labor is undignified and despised in the slave States, because it is performed by a race which is inferior in nature and in social standing, the unrestrained immigration of Mongolians to this State, and their intrusion into every mechanical profession, will have the same humiliating and demoralizing influence upon the working classes of our citizens. No American or European workman, even if he could work for the wages of the Mongolian, will work with him at the same workbench, in the same workshop, or, in those branches which the Chinaman does succeed in monopolizing, even in the same profession. The Chinese will infinitely more degrade labor than the Negro in the slave States has done.

2. The New York Times *Satirizes the California Exclusionists (1880)*[*]

A key leader of California's Anti-Chinese movement was pro-labor firebrand Dennis Kearney, a recent immigrant from Ireland whose venomous tirades against the Chinese appealed to San Francisco's disgruntled working class. In 1877, bands of Kearney's mostly Irish followers launched vicious raids against the Chinese, lopping off men's pigtails and lynching several unfortunate victims. Responding to rumors of renewed violence, the New York Times *published a mock-serious editorial cynically proposing the expulsion of all Chinese from the American mainland as a solution to the problem. What parallels does the article draw between the treatment of American Indians and the treatment of Chinese immigrants? Do you think this kind of satire was effective—or was it likely to be misread?*

There is every reason to believe that within a few days a San Francisco mob will make an attack on the Chinamen. The preparations for this attack are in open progress, and Mr. Denis Kearney, the eminent California statesman whom Mr. Hayes once honored with a long interview at the White House, is now appealing to his followers to furnish money for erecting a neat and serviceable gallows on the Sand Lots whereon to hang the wretches who are guilty of the crime of being Chinamen. As the Mayor of the city is the ally and tool of Kearney, no protection will be given by him to the Chinese, and the fate of these unhappy heathen, in case the anticipated riot takes place, can easily be imagined.

---

[*]"The Chinese Must Go," *New York Times,* February 26, 1880, p. 4.

There are a few weak sentimentalists in the Eastern States who would look upon a massacre of the Chinese in San Francisco as a shameful crime....Such people, however, have nothing to do with real politics, and their opinions are of very little consequence.

Practical men are growing tired of the foolish sentimentality which is talked in Eastern cities concerning the Chinese. We are told that because the United States has made a treaty with China guaranteeing protection to Chinese residing in this country, it is a disgraceful breach of faith to permit the San Francisco Chinamen to be persecuted and massacred. Suppose it is. What of it? Can China compel us to keep a treaty, and if not, can we be expected to keep it? The United States has made numerous treaties with our Indian tribes, and violated them whenever the Northwestern voter has desired to seize the land of the Indians. It is one of the fundamental principles of our Government that we are under no obligation to keep treaties made with Indians, since the latter are weak and powerless. We keep treaties made with nations like England and France, who are able to resent bad faith and dishonesty on our part, but the Indians can be cheated with impunity. We can apply the same reasoning to the treaty which exists between the United States and China. We can violate it with impunity, since China cannot possibly invade our coasts with a powerful fleet and batter down our towns. As for pretending that we must keep a treaty because it would be dishonorable to do otherwise, that is mere sentimental nonsense. To tell a Government that has recognized no law of honesty at home in its dealings with weak copper-colored people, that it must be honorable when dealing with weak yellow people, is a waste of breath.

Of course, it would be possible to put an end to lawless persecution of the Chinese, provided it were popular to do so, but it so happens that it would be unpopular. Which great political party is foolish enough to risk losing the votes of the Pacific States by undertaking to do justice to the Chinese? What if it is morally right to do justice even to yellow heathen? Politicians do not make a practice of doing right because it is right. They are practical men, and their rule of conduct is to do what will secure votes. It would not pay for any politician or any party to take up the cause of the Chinamen. Votes are not to be obtained in that way....

What, then, is the use of the sentimental talk concerning the poor Chinamen, and the duty of keeping our treaty with China, which we hear from visionary people who know nothing of politics? Denis Kearney and his followers intend to drive out the Chinamen, and there is no more reason for protecting the Chinese against him than there has been for protecting the Indians against white men who wanted their lands. The question of the right and wrong of the matter is of no consequence, since the motive which governs in our public affairs is a desire to secure votes, not a sentimental desire to do right for the right's sake. The sooner the Chinamen are exterminated the sooner San Francisco will be at peace. If any one calls this a brutal and shameful doctrine, it may be retorted that such a criticism comes rather late in the day. We have systematically treated the Indians with the same technical injustice with which the Chinese are now threatened, and so long as our people accept quietly the profits of such a policy, it behooves them to remain quiet concerning the persecution of the Chinese and the violation of our treaty obligations with China.

3. A Christian Chinese Protests Restrictions on Civil Liberties (1892)*

In 1882 Congress passed the Chinese Exclusion Act, the only immigration statute in American history to specifically target a single national group. The 1892 Geary Act extended exclusion for another decade and required Chinese Americans to carry certificates of residence or risk deportation. Empowered by the new provision, police officers across the West raided Chinese neighborhoods and arrested those who could not provide proper documentation. In court, the burden of proving one's legal status fell upon the accused Chinese, revoking the presumption of innocence central to American jurisprudence. Jee Gam, a baptized Christian and leader in the Chinese community, published the following critique of the Geary Act. What are Gam's principal objections to the measure? Who is his target audience, and how does he craft his essay to appeal to their sentiments?

I am a Chinaman and a Christian. I am not any less Chinese for being a follower of Christ. My love to Jesus has intensified rather than belittled my love for my native country. I am proud of China, for it is a great country. I admire her, for she has a wonderful future. What a glorious nation she will be when she embraces Christianity! I praise her authentic history, for it goes back 4,800 years.

I honor all things that are honorable in my country. I blush for whatever has marred her record. I pray for her daily, that she may speedily become a Christian nation.

I am in some sense also an American, for I have lived in America almost twice as long as in China. I love this country. I teach my children who are native-born Americans to sing the National hymns. And just as I rejoice in whatever is honorable to America, and commend her example to my countrymen, so I am pained when unjust and oppressive laws are permitted to be placed upon her statute books. Such a law as the Geary Act seems to me to be one which dishonors America, as well as injures my countrymen and native land....

[The] Geary Act is an oppression of the weak. China is a great and powerful nation, but not just now in condition to fight a power like America. At any rate, America thinks so, and it looks to us cowardly for her to take undue advantage of a weaker nation. We all despise a man who stabs another in the back; how much more despicable when the person so attacked is weaker than he!

See how this law injures China.

1. It discriminates against her subjects. It says all Chinese laborers must register or be deported, but says this of no others. If America is fair in her dealing, she ought never for a moment to allow discrimination to exist within her borders. Her laws ought to be applicable to all people, regardless of nationality. To single out the despised Chinese, the only people who hold no votes, shows cowardliness. Would America venture to enact a similar law against any of the European powers?

And now, what harm is in the registration law? Why do the Chinese object? Every American has to register. These have been the questions and assertions of many friends. My answer to these is as follows: An American if he fails to register

*Judy Yung et al., ed., *Chinese American Voices: From the Gold Rush to the Present* (Berkeley: University of California Press, 2006), pp. 86–90.

forfeits only the right of voting at that particular election. For that no harm can come to him. But there is a vast difference in the Geary registration, for it means that the Chinese must register, or be forcibly removed from this country. So one registration is voluntary, while the other is compelled. In other words, the former law makes a person a free man, the other law makes one a slave, a criminal, or even a dog. For the only class that are required to give photographs are the criminals, and the only animal that must wear a tag is a dog. The Chinese decline to be counted in with either of these classes, so they refuse to register, and I do not blame them;

2. A registration paper will add trouble to its owner instead of protection. A laborer will have to carry the paper with him wherever he goes. Suppose he is in a strange town, and some hoodlums should play the part of officers, and should demand the showing of his paper, and, when he complies, suppose they should immediately tear it to pieces. Now, how can this man prove his loss? He has no witness but himself, and the Court will not believe him unless he has some white witness to corroborate his testimony. Consequently, his request for a renewal will be denied....

3. This Act withdraws some sacred rights such as in the Declaration of Independence are declared to be inalienable. The right to a free, untrammelled pursuit of happiness, the right of habeas corpus, the right to be adjudged innocent until proven guilty. The Geary Act says, when a Chinese is arrested under the provision of this Act, he shall be adjudged to be unlawfully within the United States, *unless* he shall establish by *affirmative proof,* to the satisfaction of such Justice, Judge or Commissioner, his lawful right to remain here. Now if that law which says every person arrested and charged with a crime is presumed to be innocent until he is proven guilty will hold good for a white man, *why not for a Chinaman also?* In other words, the people must make out a case against the accused before he can be convicted of the crime charged. If he choose to be silent, the law says that is his privilege, and judgment must not be entered against him for doing so. This also should apply to the Chinese as well as other people, but the Geary Act says No, and therefore it is un-American, barbarous and inhuman. It is unchristian, for it is contrary to the teaching of Christ....

If the United States should enforce this disgraceful Geary law, China will most assuredly retaliate. The lives of missionaries and the properties of missions will be in danger. The leading commercial interest, which is now held by America in China, will be given to the nations of Europe. If America can afford to lose that, I am sure China can also. But is that the best policy? Not conflict, but peace and harmony. Let not this infamous act mar the progress of Christianity in China, as the English opium has done: for while the gospel sent to China by the people of England is saving one soul, her opium, that she so wrongfully and selfishly forced into China, is destroying a thousand.

I never can forget the remark made by the Chinese mandarin to a British minister: "Sir, I wish you would take back with you the opium your country sent us." What a blush went over the face of the British representative! What a great stumbling block to Christianity! Let America regain her good name by repealing the Geary law.

Our sincere thanks are due to all our Christian friends. Their sympathy and prayers have greatly comforted us; and may God overrule all injustice and wrong to His glory, and the final triumph of the right!

4. President Roosevelt Anticipates Trouble (1905)*

Secretary of State John Hay, attempting to halt European land-grabbing in China, had induced the reluctant powers to accept his famed Open Door policy in 1899–1900. But Russia's continued encroachments on China's Manchuria led to the exhausting Russo-Japanese War of 1904–1905, during which the underdog Japanese soundly thrashed the Russian army and navy. President Roosevelt, who was finally drafted as peace mediator, wrote the following letter to his close friend Senator Henry Cabot Lodge. Drunk with victory, Japan was becoming understandably cocky, while the race-conscious California legislature was preparing to erect barriers against Japanese immigrants. Why did Roosevelt regard the attitude of Californians as bigoted, foolish, and dangerous?

That Japan will have her head turned to some extent I do not in the least doubt, and I see clear symptoms of it in many ways. We should certainly as a nation have ours turned if we had performed such feats as the Japanese have in the past sixteen months; and the same is true of any European nation. Moreover, I have no doubt that some Japanese, and perhaps a great many of them, will behave badly to foreigners. They cannot behave worse than the State of California, through its Legislature, is now behaving toward the Japanese.

The feeling on the Pacific slope, taking it from several different standpoints, is as foolish as if conceived by the mind of a Hottentot. These Pacific Coast people wish grossly to insult the Japanese and to keep out the Japanese immigrants on the ground that they are an immoral, degraded, and worthless race; and at the same time that they desire to do this for the Japanese, and are already doing it for the Chinese, they expect to be given advantages in Oriental markets; and with besotted folly are indifferent to building up the navy while provoking this formidable new power—a power jealous, sensitive, and warlike, and which if irritated could at once take both the Philippines and Hawaii from us if she obtained the upper hand on the seas.

Most certainly the Japanese soldiers and sailors have shown themselves to be terrible foes. There can be none more dangerous in all the world. But our own navy, ship for ship, is I believe at least as efficient as theirs, although I am not certain that our torpedo boats would be handled as well as theirs. At present we are superior to them in number of ships, and this superiority will last for some time. It will of course come to an end if Hale[†] has his way, but not otherwise.

I hope that we can persuade our people on the one hand to act in a spirit of generous justice and genuine courtesy toward Japan, and on the other hand to keep the navy respectable in numbers and more than respectable in the efficiency

---

*From E. E. Morrison, ed., *The Letters of Theodore Roosevelt.* Copyright © 1951 by the President and Fellows of Harvard College.
[†]Maine Senator Eugene Hale, chairman of the Senate Naval Affairs Committee.

of its units. If we act thus we need not fear the Japanese. But if, as Brooks Adams [a prominent historian, whose work *The Law of Civilization and Decay* (1895) deeply influenced Roosevelt] says, we show ourselves "opulent, aggressive, and unarmed," the Japanese may sometime work us an injury.

5. Japan Resents Discrimination (1906)[*]

The San Francisco Board of Education precipitated a crisis in 1906 by ordering all Asian students to attend a specially segregated school. The sensitive Japanese rose in instant resentment against what they regarded as a deliberate and insulting act of discrimination. The Tokyo Mainichi Shimbun, *a reputable journal, reacted as follows. Where was Japanese national pride most deeply wounded?*

The whole world knows that the poorly equipped army and navy of the United States are no match for our efficient army and navy. It will be an easy work to awake the United States from her dream of obstinacy when one of our great admirals appears on the other side of the Pacific.... The present situation is such that the Japanese nation cannot rest easy by relying only upon the wisdom and statesmanship of President Roosevelt. The Japanese nation must have a firm determination to chastise at any time the obstinate Americans.

Stand up, Japanese nation! Our countrymen have been HUMILIATED on the other side of the Pacific. Our poor boys and girls have been expelled from the public schools by the rascals of the United States, cruel and merciless like demons.

At this time we should be ready to give a blow to the United States. Yes, we should be ready to strike the Devil's head with an iron hammer for the sake of the world's civilization.... Why do we not insist on sending [war]ships?

6. The Gentlemen's Agreement (1908)[†]

The San Francisco school incident revealed anew that a municipality or a state could take legal action that might involve the entire nation in war. Roosevelt soothed the Japanese, but not the Californians, by adopting the Asians' side of the dispute. He publicly branded the action of the school board as a "wicked absurdity," and he brought that entire body to Washington, where he persuaded the members to come to terms. The San Franciscans agreed to readmit Japanese children to the public schools on the condition that Roosevelt would arrange to shut off the influx of Japanese immigrants. This he did in the famous Gentlemen's Agreement, which consisted of an understanding growing out of an extensive exchange of diplomatic notes. These were officially summarized as follows in the annual report of the U.S. commissioner-general of immigration. In what ways did these agreements leave the fundamental issues unresolved?

---

[*]T. A. Bailey, *Theodore Roosevelt and the Japanese-American Crises* (Stanford University Press, 1934), p. 50, October 22, 1906.
[†]*Annual Report of the Secretary of Commerce and Labor, 1908* (1908), pp. 221–222.

In order that the best results might follow from an enforcement of the regulations, an understanding was reached with Japan that the existing policy of discouraging the emigration of its subjects of the laboring classes to continental United States should be continued and should, by cooperation of the governments, be made as effective as possible.

This understanding contemplates that the Japanese Government shall issue passports to continental United States only to such of its subjects as are non-laborers or are laborers who, in coming to the continent, seek to resume a formerly acquired domicile, to join a parent, wife, or children residing there, or to assume active control of an already possessed interest in a farming enterprise in this country; so that the three classes of laborers entitled to receive passports have come to be designated "former residents," "parents, wives, or children of residents," and "settled agriculturists."

With respect to Hawaii, the Japanese Government stated that, experimentally at least, the issuance of passports to members of the laboring classes proceeding thence would be limited to "former residents" and "parents, wives, or children of residents." The said government has also been exercising a careful supervision over the subject of the emigration of its laboring class to foreign contiguous territory [Mexico, Canada].

[The honor system Gentlemen's Agreement worked reasonably well until 1924, when Congress in a fit of pique slammed the door completely in the faces of the Japanese. The resulting harvest of ill will had much to do with the tragic events that eventually led to Pearl Harbor and World War II.]

Thought Provokers

1. Does the press in a democracy have an ethical responsibility to pursue sober policies, even if such tactics hurt circulation? Has the press shown more responsibility in recent years than in 1898?
2. Were patriotic Spaniards justified in resenting American attitudes and accusations in 1897–1898? Should the United States have accepted arbitration of the *Maine* dispute?
3. To what extent were anti-imperialists idealists? Was there anything morally objectionable in their attitude? How did each side of the imperialist debate view the native population in the Philippines?
4. With reference to the Roosevelt Corollary to the Monroe Doctrine, are nations entitled to complete sovereignty if they fail to exercise it properly? When certain states of the United States defaulted on their debts to British creditors in the 1830s, Britain did not attempt to take over American customhouses. Why? Are there different rules of international behavior for small nations and large nations?
5. Why did California residents feel threatened by the Chinese? Why were East Coast audiences not more sympathetic to the plight of Chinese immigrants? Why did Japan especially resent California's discrimination in 1906? Was the Gentlemen's Agreement with Japan better than exclusion by act of Congress?

28

Progressivism and the Republican Roosevelt, 1901–1912

Men with the muckrake are often indispensable
to the well-being of society, but only if they know
when to stop raking the muck.

Theodore Roosevelt, 1906

Prologue: A wave of political reform, known as the Progressive movement, washed over the United States as the new century opened. Progressivism was inspired by muckraking journalists who exposed corruption, the adulteration of food and drugs, and the exploitation of labor; by socialists who called attention to the growing class divisions in the industrial United States; by ministers of the gospel alarmed at the grinding poverty in which many Americans lived; and by feminists who clamored for fair treatment for families, women, and children. Theodore Roosevelt embraced many of the tenets of Progressivism when he became president in 1901. He fought to tame the big corporations and to protect consumers from dangerous products. Among his major achievements as a reformer was the invigoration of the campaign to conserve the nation's fast-disappearing natural resources, especially the forests. Other Progressives championed the cause of woman suffrage, still a subject of hot controversy. The presidential election of 1912 was unusual in U.S. history. It featured three plausible candidates—William Howard Taft, Theodore Roosevelt, and Woodrow Wilson—and amounted to a referendum on which of the competing philosophies of Progressivism would prevail.

A. The Heyday of Muckraking

1. Exposing the Meatpackers (1906)[*]

In 1906 Upton Sinclair, the youthful and prolific socialist writer, published his novel The Jungle, *a damning exposure of conditions in the Chicago meatpacking plants. Seeking to turn people to socialism, he succeeded in turning their stomachs. The uproar that followed publication of his novel caused President Roosevelt to initiate an official investigation, and the following sober report was hardly less*

---

[*]*Congressional Record*, 59th Cong., 1st sess. (June 4, 1906), p. 7801.

shocking than The Jungle. *It confirmed the essential truth of Sinclair's exposé, except for such lurid scenes as men falling into vats and emerging as lard. Which aspects of this official investigation revealed conditions most detrimental to the public health?*

Meat scraps were also found being shoveled into receptacles from dirty floors, where they were left to lie until again shoveled into barrels or into machines for chopping. These floors, it must be noted, were in most cases damp and soggy, in dark, ill-ventilated rooms, and the employees in utter ignorance of cleanliness or danger to health expectorated at will upon them. In a word, we saw meat shoveled from filthy wooden floors, piled on tables rarely washed, pushed from room to room in rotten box carts, in all of which processes it was in the way of gathering dirt, splinters, floor filth, and the expectoration of tuberculous and other diseased workers.

Where comment was made to floor superintendents about these matters, it was always the reply that this meat would afterwards be cooked, and that this sterilization would prevent any danger from its use. Even this, it may be pointed out in passing, is not wholly true. A very considerable portion of the meat so handled is sent out as smoked products and in the form of sausages, which are prepared to be eaten without being cooked. . . .

As an extreme example of the entire disregard on the part of employees of any notion of cleanliness in handling dressed meat, we saw a hog that had just been killed, cleaned, washed, and started on its way to the cooling room fall from the sliding rail to a dirty wooden floor and slide part way into a filthy men's privy. It was picked up by two employees, placed upon a truck, carried into the cooling room and hung up with other carcasses, no effort being made to clean it. . . .

In one well-known establishment we came upon fresh meat being shoveled into barrels, and a regular proportion being added of stale scraps that had lain on a dirty floor in the corner of a room for some days previous. In another establishment, equally well known, a long table was noted covered with several hundred pounds of cooked scraps of beef and other meats. Some of these meat scraps were dry, leathery, and unfit to be eaten; and in the heap were found pieces of pigskin, and even some bits of rope strands and other rubbish. Inquiry evoked the frank admission from the man in charge that this was to be ground up and used in making "potted ham."

All of these canned products bear labels, of which the following is a sample:

ABATTOIR No.—
THE CONTENTS OF THIS PACKAGE HAVE BEEN
INSPECTED ACCORDING TO THE ACT OF
CONGRESS OF MARCH 3, 1891.

[The agitation and investigation inspired by Sinclair's The Jungle *had much to do with bringing about the passage by Congress of the Meat Inspection Act and the Pure Food and Drug Act of 1906.]*

2. Theodore Roosevelt Roasts Muckrakers (1906)*

President Roosevelt, though recognizing some unpalatable truths in Upton Sinclair's The Jungle, *was critical. He wrote the author bluntly that Sinclair had said things that should not have been written unless backed up "with testimony that would satisfy an honest man of reasonable intelligence." Privately he declared that Sinclair had reflected unfairly on both honest and dishonest capitalism in Chicago. Finally, nauseated by excessive sensationalism, Roosevelt made the following famous attack (which gave rise to the term* muckraker*) in a Washington speech. What are the strengths and weaknesses of his argument that hysterical and indiscriminate muckraking was doing more harm than good?*

In Bunyan's *Pilgrim's Progress* you may recall the description of the Man with the Muck-rake [manure rake], the man who could look no way but downward, with the muck-rake in his hand; who was offered a celestial crown for his muck-rake, but who would neither look up nor regard the crown he was offered, but continued to rake himself the filth of the floor.

In *Pilgrim's Progress* the Man with the Muck-rake is set forth as the example of him whose vision is fixed on carnal instead of on spiritual things. Yet he also typifies the man who in this life consistently refuses to see aught that is lofty, and fixes his eyes with solemn intentness only on that which is vile and debasing.

Now it is very necessary that we should not flinch from seeing what is vile and debasing. There is filth on the floor, and it must be scraped up with the muck-rake: and there are times and places where this service is the most needed of all the services that can be performed. But the man who never does anything else, who never thinks or speaks or writes save of his feats with the muck-rake, speedily becomes, not a help to society, not an incitement to good, but one of the most potent forces for evil.

There are—in the body politic, economic, and social—many and grave evils, and there is urgent necessity for the sternest war upon them. There should be relentless exposure of and attack upon every evil man, whether politician or businessman; every evil practice, whether in politics, in business, or in social life. I hail as a benefactor every writer or speaker, every man who, on the platform, or in book, magazine, or newspaper, with merciless severity makes such attack, provided always that he in his turn remembers that the attack is of use only if it is absolutely truthful. The liar is no whit better than the thief, and if his mendacity takes the form of slander, he may be worse than most thieves. It puts a premium upon knavery untruthfully to attack an honest man, or even with hysterical exaggeration to assail a bad man with untruth. An epidemic of indiscriminate assault upon character does no good, but very great harm. The soul of every scoundrel is gladdened whenever an honest man is assailed, or even when a scoundrel is untruthfully assailed.

Now, it is easy to twist out of shape what I have just said....Some persons are sincerely incapable of understanding that to denounce mudslinging does not mean the endorsement of whitewashing, and both the interested individuals who need

---

*Theodore Roosevelt, "The Man with the Muck-Rake," *Putnam's Monthly and the Critic* 1 (October 1906): 42–43.

whitewashing and those others who practice mudslinging like to encourage such confusion of ideas. One of the chief counts against those who make indiscriminate assault upon men in business or men in public life is that they invite a reaction which is sure to tell powerfully in favor of the unscrupulous scoundrel who really ought to be attacked, who ought to be exposed, who ought, if possible, to be put in the penitentiary. If Aristides is praised overmuch as just, people get tired of hearing it;* and overcensure of the unjust finally and from similar reasons results in their favor.

Any excess is almost sure to invite a reaction; and, unfortunately, the reaction, instead of taking the form of punishment of those guilty of the excess, is very apt to take the form either of punishment of the unoffending or of giving immunity, and even strength, to offenders. The effort to make financial or political profit out of the destruction of character can only result in public calamity. Gross and reckless assaults on character, whether on the stump or in newspaper, magazine, or book, create a morbid and vicious public sentiment, and at the same time act as a profound deterrent to able men of normal sensitiveness and tend to prevent them from entering the public service at any price.

[Roosevelt thus threw muck at the muckrakers. They resented his attack, claiming that even if they exaggerated, they were exposing evil conditions and promoting desirable legislation. (At the same time, they made money selling their magazine articles and books.) But Roosevelt was unconvinced. In 1911 he went so far as to write privately: "I think the muckrakers stand on a level of infamy with the corruptionists in politics. After all, there is no great difference between violation of the eighth [no stealing] and the ninth [no lying] commandments; and to sell one's vote for money is morally, I believe, hardly as reprehensible as to practice slanderous mendacity for hire" (Roosevelt Letters, vol. 7, p. 447). The truth is that he continued with intemperate muckraking himself, attacking "malefactors of great wealth," "nature fakers," and others. "You're the chief muckraker," Speaker Joseph G. Cannon told him flatly in 1906.]

B. The Plight of Labor

1. From the Depths (1906)

Many observers in the Progressive era saw poverty as proof of the moral weakness of the poor. For others, poverty and the glaring inequalities of wealth in America were evidence of the immorality of a society based on capitalism. What perspective does the famous image by William Balfour Ker titled "From the Depths," shown on page 519, convey? Why are the poor positioned under the floor and in the dark? Are their hands supporting the scene above or seeking to disrupt it?

---

*An allusion to Plutarch's story of the Athenian who voted for the banishment of Aristides (called "the Just") because he was tired of hearing everyone call him just.

2. Child Labor in the Coal Mines (1906)*

Another significant contribution to the muckraking movement was John Spargo's book The Bitter Cry of the Children. *An English-born socialist, Spargo had come to America in 1901 at the age of twenty-five. He was especially stirred by the rickety children of the New York tenement districts. Their mothers had no time to prepare proper meals; needlework labor in the sweatshops ran from twelve to twenty hours a day, at a wage ranging from ten cents to a cent and a half an hour. In Spargo's description of work in the coal mines, what were the various kinds of hazards involved?*

Work in the coal breakers is exceedingly hard and dangerous. Crouched over the chutes, the boys sit hour after hour, picking out the pieces of slate and other refuse from the coal as it rushes past to the washers. From the cramped position they have to assume, most of them become more or less deformed and bent-backed like old men. When a boy has been working for some time and begins to get round-shouldered, his fellows say that "He's got his boy to carry round whenever he goes."

The coal is hard, and accidents to the hands, such as cut, broken, or crushed fingers, are common among the boys. Sometimes there is a worse accident: a terrified shriek is heard, and a boy is mangled and torn in the machinery, or disappears in the chute to be picked out later smothered and dead. Clouds of dust fill the breakers and are inhaled by the boys, laying the foundations for asthma and miners' consumption.

I once stood in a breaker for half an hour and tried to do the work a twelve-year-old boy was doing day after day, for ten hours at a stretch, for sixty cents a day. The gloom of the breaker appalled me. Outside the sun shone brightly, the air was pellucid, and the birds sang in chorus with the trees and the rivers. Within the breaker there was blackness, clouds of deadly dust enfolded everything, the harsh, grinding roar of the machinery and the ceaseless rushing of coal through the chutes filled the ears. I tried to pick out the pieces of slate from the hurrying stream of coal, often missing them; my hands were bruised and cut in a few minutes; I was covered from head to foot with coal dust, and for many hours afterwards I was expectorating some of the small particles of anthracite I had swallowed.

I could not do that work and live, but there were boys of ten and twelve years of age doing it for fifty and sixty cents a day. Some of them had never been inside of a school; few of them could read a child's primer. True, some of them attended the night schools, but after working ten hours in the breaker the educational results from attending school were practically nil. "We goes fer a good time, an' we keeps de guys wot's dere hoppin' all de time," said little Owen Jones, whose work I had been trying to do....

As I stood in that breaker I thought of the reply of the small boy to Robert Owen [British social reformer]. Visiting an English coal mine one day, Owen asked a twelve-year-old lad if he knew God. The boy stared vacantly at his questioner: "God?" he said, "God? No, I don't. He must work in some other mine." It was hard to realize amid the danger and din and blackness of that Pennsylvania breaker that such a thing as belief in a great All-good God existed.

---

*John Spargo, *The Bitter Cry of the Children* (New York: Macmillan, 1906), pp. 163–165.

From the breakers the boys graduate to the mine depths, where they become door tenders, switch boys, or mule drivers. Here, far below the surface, work is still more dangerous. At fourteen or fifteen the boys assume the same risks as the men, and are surrounded by the same perils. Nor is it in Pennsylvania only that these conditions exist. In the bituminous mines of West Virginia, boys of nine or ten are frequently employed. I met one little fellow ten years old in Mt. Carbon, W. Va., last year, who was employed as a "trap boy." Think of what it means to be a trap boy at ten years of age. It means to sit alone in a dark mine passage hour after hour, with no human soul near; to see no living creature except the mules as they pass with their loads, or a rat or two seeking to share one's meal; to stand in water or mud that covers the ankles, chilled to the marrow by the cold draughts that rush in when you open the trap door for the mules to pass through; to work for fourteen hours—waiting—opening and shutting a door—then waiting again—for sixty cents; to reach the surface when all is wrapped in the mantle of night, and to fall to the earth exhausted and have to be carried away to the nearest "shack" to be revived before it is possible to walk to the farther shack called "home."

Boys twelve years of age may be *legally* employed in the mines of West Virginia, by day or by night, and for as many hours as the employers care to make them toil or their bodies will stand the strain. Where the disregard of child life is such that this may be done openly and with legal sanction, it is easy to believe what miners have again and again told me—that there are hundreds of little boys of nine and ten years of age employed in the coal mines of this state.

3. Sweatshop Hours for Bakers (1905)*

The abuse of labor in dangerous or unhealthful occupations prompted an increasing number of state legislatures, exercising so-called police powers, to pass regulatory laws. In 1898 the Supreme Court upheld a Utah statute prohibiting miners from working more than eight hours a day, except in emergencies. In 1905, however, the Court, by a five-to-four decision in the case of Lochner v. New York, *overthrew a state law forbidding bakers to work more than ten hours a day. The majority held that the right of both employers and employees to make labor contracts was protected by the Fourteenth Amendment. How might one describe the social conscience of the majority of the Supreme Court in the light of this memorable decision written by Justice Rufus W. Peckham?*

The question whether this act is valid as a labor law, pure and simple, may be dismissed in a few words. There is no reasonable ground for interfering with the liberty of person or the right of free contract, by determining the hours of labor, in the occupation of a baker. There is no contention that bakers as a class are not equal in intelligence and capacity to men in other trades or manual occupations, or that they are not able to assert their rights and care for themselves without the protecting arm of the state interfering with their independence of judgment and of action. They are in no sense wards of the state.

---

*Lochner v. New York, 198 U.S. 45 (1905), 57, 59, 61.

Viewed in the light of a purely labor law, with no reference whatever to the question of health, we think that a law like the one before us involves neither the safety, the morals, nor the welfare of the public, and that the interest of the public is not in the slightest degree affected by such an act. The law must be upheld, if at all, as a law pertaining to the health of the individual engaged in the occupation of a baker. It does not affect any other portion of the public than those who are engaged in that occupation. Clean and wholesome bread does not depend upon whether the baker works but ten hours per day or only sixty hours a week. The limitation of the hours of labor does not come within the police power on that ground....

We think that there can be no fair doubt that the trade of a baker, in and of itself, is not an unhealthy one to that degree which would authorize the legislature to interfere with the right to labor, and with the right of free contract on the part of the individual, either as employer or employee.

In looking through statistics regarding all trades and occupations, it may be true that the trade of baker does not appear to be as healthy as some other trades, and is also vastly more healthy than still others. To the common understanding the trade of a baker has never been regarded as an unhealthy one. Very likely physicians would not recommend the exercise of that or of any other trade as a remedy for ill health. Some occupations are more healthy than others, but we think there are none which might not come under the power of the legislature to supervise and control the hours of working therein, if the mere fact that the occupation is not absolutely and perfectly healthy is to confer that right upon the legislative department of the government....

...We do not believe in the soundness of the views which uphold this law. On the contrary, we think that such a law as this, although passed in the assumed exercise of the police power, and as relating to the public health, or the health of the employees named, is not within that power, and is invalid. The act is not, within any fair meaning of the term, a health law, but is an illegal interference with the rights of individuals, both employers and employees, to make contracts regarding labor upon such terms as they may think best, or which they may agree upon with the other parties to such contracts.

Statutes of the nature of that under review, limiting the hours in which grown and intelligent men may labor to earn their living, are mere meddlesome interferences with the rights of the individual, and they are not saved from condemnation by the claim that they are passed in the exercise of the police power and upon the subject of the health of the individual whose rights are interfered with, unless there be some fair ground, reasonable in and of itself, to say that there is material danger to the public health, or to the health of the employees, if the hours of labor are not curtailed.

[Justice Oliver Wendell Holmes, the great dissenter, filed a famous protest in the bakers' case. He argued that a majority of the people of New York State evidently wanted the law and that the Court ought not to impose its own social philosophy. "The Fourteenth Amendment," he solemnly declared, referring to a famous work by an archconservative British social theorist, "does not enact Mr. Herbert Spencer's Social Statics." As for the right to work more than ten hours, the mayor of New York remarked, "There were no journeymen bakers that I know of clamoring for any such liberty." Possibly chastened by Holmes's vigorous views, the Court relented and

in 1908 unanimously approved an Oregon statute prohibiting the employment of women in factories and other establishments more than ten hours in one day. In 1917 the Court upheld an Oregon ten-hour law for both men and women.]

4. The Triangle Shirtwaist Company Fire Claims 146 Lives (1911)*

One of the most grisly catastrophes ever to befall American workers occurred at the Triangle Shirtwaist Company's New York City garment factory on March 25, 1911. Trapped in a burning building in which many exit doors had been locked to discourage workers from taking unauthorized breaks, 146 laborers, mostly young women, perished. The resulting outrage encouraged the enactment of more stringent building codes and fed the growing movement for laws regulating working conditions, especially for women. (For more on women's labor laws, see the documents in Chapter 31, section D.) In the account of the fire that follows, what conditions seemed most responsible for the high loss of life? How might they have been remedied? How much of the public outrage about the fire was owed to the fact that so many of the dead were young women?

At 4:35 o'clock yesterday afternoon fire springing from a source that may never be positively identified was discovered in the rear of the eighth floor of the ten-story building at the northwest corner of Washington Place and Greene Street, the first of three floors occupied as a factory of the Triangle Shirtwaist Company.

At 11:30 o'clock Chief Croker made this statement:

"Everybody has been removed. The number taken out, which includes those who jumped from windows, is 141..."

At 2 o'clock this morning Chief Croker estimated the total dead as one hundred and fifty-four. He said further, "I expect something of this kind to happen in these so-called fire-proof buildings, which are without adequate protection as far as fire-escapes are concerned."

More than a third of those who lost their lives did so in jumping from windows. The firemen who answered the first of the four alarms turned in found 30 bodies on the pavements of Washington Place and Greene Street. Almost all of these were girls, as were the great majority of them all....

Inspection by Acting Superintendent of Buildings Ludwig will be made the basis for charges of criminal negligence on the ground that the fire-proof doors leading to one of the inclosed tower stairways were locked....

It was the most appalling horror since the Slocum disaster and the Iroquois Theater fire in Chicago. Every available ambulance in Manhattan was called upon to cart the dead to the morgue—bodies charred to unrecognizable blackness or reddened to a sickly hue—as was to be seen by shoulders or limbs protruding through flame-eaten clothing. Men and women, boys and girls were of the dead that littered the street; that is actually the condition—the streets were littered.

The fire began in the eighth story. The flames licked and shot their way up through the other two stories. All three floors were occupied by the Triangle Waist Company.

---

*New York World, March 26, 1911.

The estimate of the number of employees at work is made by Chief Croker at about 1,000. The proprietors of the company say 700 men and girls were in their place....

Before smoke or flame gave signs from the windows, the loss of life was fully under way. The first signs that persons in the street knew that these three top stories had turned into red furnaces in which human creatures were being caught and incinerated was when screaming men and women and boys and girls crowded out on the many window ledges and threw themselves into the streets far below.

They jumped with their clothing ablaze. The hair of some of the girls streamed up aflame as they leaped. Thud after thud sounded on the pavements. It is a ghastly fact that on both the Greene Street and Washington Place sides of the building there grew mounds of the dead and dying.

And the worst horror of all was that in this heap of the dead now and then there stirred a limb or sounded a moan.

Within the three flaming floors it was as frightful. There flames enveloped many so that they died instantly. When Fire Chief Croker could make his way into these three floors, he found sights that utterly staggered him, that sent him, a man used to viewing horrors, back and down into the street with quivering lips.

The floors were black with smoke. And then he saw as the smoke drifted away bodies burned to bare bones. There were skeletons bending over sewing machines.

The elevator boys saved hundreds. They each made twenty trips from the time of the alarm until twenty minutes later when they could do no more. Fire was streaming into the shaft, flames biting at the cables. They fled for their own lives.

Some, about seventy, chose a successful avenue of escape. They clambered up a ladder to the roof. A few remembered the fire escape. Many may have thought of it but only as they uttered cries of dismay.

Wretchedly inadequate was this fire escape—a lone ladder running down to a rear narrow court, which was smoke filled as the fire raged, one narrow door giving access to the ladder. By the score they fought and struggled and breathed fire and died trying to make that needle-eye road to self-preservation....

Shivering at the chasm below them, scorched by the fire behind, there were some that still held positions on the window sills when the first squad of firemen arrived.

The nets were spread below with all promptness. Citizens were commandeered into service, as the firemen necessarily gave their attention to the one engine and hose of the force that first arrived.

The catapult force that the bodies gathered in the long plunges made the nets utterly without avail. Screaming girls and men, as they fell, tore the nets from the grasp of the holders, and the bodies struck the sidewalks and lay just as they fell. Some of the bodies ripped big holes through the life-nets....

Concentrated, the fire burned within. The flames caught all the flimsy lace stuff and linens that go into the making of spring and summer shirtwaists and fed eagerly upon the rolls of silk.

The cutting room was laden with the stuff on long tables. The employees were toiling over such material at the rows and rows of machines. Sinisterly the spring day gave aid to the fire. Many of the window panes facing south and east were drawn down. Draughts had full play.

The experts say that the three floors must each have become a whirlpool of fire. Whichever way the entrapped creatures fled they met a curving sweep of flame.

Many swooned and died. Others fought their way to the windows or the elevator or fell fighting for a chance at the fire escape, the single fire escape leading into the blind court that was to be reached from the upper floors by clambering over a window sill!

On all of the three floors, at a narrow window, a crowd met death trying to get out to that one slender fire escape ladder.

It was a fireproof building in which this enormous tragedy occurred. Save for the three stories of blackened windows at the top, you would scarcely have been able to tell where the fire had happened. The walls stood firmly. A thin tongue of flame now and then licked around a window sash.

C. Battling over Conservation

1. Roosevelt Defends the Forests (1903)[*]

Greedy or shortsighted Americans had long plundered the nation's forests with heedless rapacity. President Roosevelt, a onetime Dakota cattle rancher and an accomplished naturalist, provided the lagging conservation movement with dynamic leadership. Using the Forest Reserve Act of 1891, he set aside some 150 million acres of government-owned timberland as national forest reserves—more than three times as much as his three immediate predecessors had preserved. The large timber companies complained bitterly, though in fact the worst predators on the forests were the small-fry lumbermen who had neither the incentive nor the resources to adopt long-term, sustained-yield logging practices. In this speech at Stanford University, Roosevelt explained the basis of his forest policy. His argument clearly demonstrates that he was not a preservationist, pure and simple. What are the implications of the distinction he draws between "beauty" and "use"? What does he mean when he says that "the whole object of forest protection" is "the making and maintaining of prosperous homes"?

I want today, here in California, to make a special appeal to all of you, and to California as a whole, for work along a certain line—the line of preserving your great natural advantages alike from the standpoint of use and from the standpoint of beauty. If the students of this institution have not by the mere fact of their surroundings learned to appreciate beauty, then the fault is in you and not in the surroundings. Here in California you have some of the great wonders of the world. You have a singularly beautiful landscape, singularly beautiful and singularly majestic scenery, and it should certainly be your aim to try to preserve for those who are to come after you that beauty, to try to keep unmarred that majesty.

Closely entwined with keeping unmarred the beauty of your scenery, your great natural attractions, is the question of making use of, not for the moment merely, but for future time, of your great natural products. Yesterday I saw for the first time a grove of your great trees, a grove which it has taken the ages several thousands of years to build up; and I feel most emphatically that we should not turn

---

[*]From Theodore Roosevelt at Leland Stanford Junior University, Palo Alto, California, May 12, 1903, in *Theodore Roosevelt, Presidential Addresses and State Papers of Theodore Roosevelt* (New York: P. F. Collier, 1905), vol. 1, pp. 383–390.

into shingles a tree which was old when the first Egyptian conqueror penetrated to the valley of the Euphrates, which it has taken so many thousands of years to build up, and which can be put to better use.

That, you may say, is not looking at the matter from the practical standpoint. There is nothing more practical in the end than the preservation of beauty, than the preservation of anything that appeals to the higher emotions in mankind. But, furthermore, I appeal to you from the standpoint of use. A few big trees, of unusual size and beauty, should be preserved for their own sake; but the forests as a whole should be used for business purposes, only they should be used in a way that will preserve them as permanent sources of national wealth. In many parts of California the whole future welfare of the state depends upon the way in which you are able to use your water supply; and the preservation of the forests and the preservation of the use of the water are inseparably connected.

I believe we are past the stage of national existence when we could look on complacently at the individual who skinned the land and was content, for the sake of three years' profit for himself, to leave a desert for the children of those who were to inherit the soil. I think we have passed that stage. We should handle, and I think we now do handle, all problems such as those of forestry and of the preservation and use of our waters from the standpoint of the permanent interests of the home maker in any region—the man who comes in not to take what he can out of the soil and leave, having exploited the country, but who comes to dwell therein, to bring up his children, and to leave them a heritage in the country not merely unimpaired, but if possible even improved. That is the sensible view of civic obligation, and the policy of the state and of the nation should be shaped in that direction. It should be shaped in the interest of the home maker, the actual resident, the man who is not only to be benefited himself, but whose children and children's children are to be benefited by what he has done....

I appeal to you, as I say, to protect these mighty trees, these wonderful monuments of beauty. I appeal to you to protect them for the sake of their beauty, but I also make the appeal just as strongly on economic grounds; as I am well aware that in dealing with such questions a farsighted economic policy must be that to which alone in the long run one can safely appeal. The interests of California in forests depend directly of course upon the handling of her wood and water supplies and the supply of material from the lumber woods and the production of agricultural products on irrigated farms. The great valleys which stretch through the state between the Sierra Nevada and coast ranges must owe their future development as they owe their present prosperity to irrigation. Whatever tends to destroy the water supply of the Sacramento, the San Gabriel, and the other valleys strikes vitally at the welfare of California. The welfare of California depends in no small measure upon the preservation of water for the purposes of irrigation in those beautiful and fertile valleys which cannot grow crops by rainfall alone. The forest cover upon the drainage basins of streams used for irrigation purposes is of prime importance to the interests of the entire state.

Now keep in mind that the whole object of forest protection is, as I have said again and again, the making and maintaining of prosperous homes. I am not advocating forest protection from the aesthetic standpoint only. I do advocate the keeping of big trees, the great monarchs of the woods, for the sake of their beauty, but

I advocate the preservation and wise use of the forests because I feel it essential to the interests of the actual settlers. I am asking that the forests be used wisely for the sake of the successors of the pioneers, for the sake of the settlers who dwell on the land and by doing so extend the borders of our civilization. I ask it for the sake of the man who makes his farm in the woods or lower down along the sides of the streams which have their rise in the mountains.

2. The West Protests Conservation (1907)*

The new forest reserve policies often worked a hardship on honest western settlers, who sometimes had to get permission from a federal official before they could lawfully cut a stick of firewood. The government, they charged, was more concerned with preserving trees than people. The governor of Colorado, disturbed by the large-scale withdrawals of western timber and coal lands by Washington, summoned a Public Lands Convention to meet in Denver in 1907. The deliberations of this body inspired the following editorial in a San Francisco newspaper. Did the West really oppose conservation? Was the East unfair in its demands?

The convention which has just adjourned at Denver is the first body of importance that has dealt with the subject of the disposal of the public lands of the United States. Considering the fact that the country has been in the real estate business for more than a century, and that during that period it has, by hook and crook, chiefly by crook, disposed of the major part of its holdings, it seems like a case of locking the stable door after nearly all of the horses have been stolen. The only question left to determine is whether the people who have permitted the theft of the horses, and who lent a hand in the stealing, shall be allowed to enjoy the most of the benefits which may accrue from taking good care of the steeds which still remain in the stalls.

The Far West, in which all the lands—coal-bearing, forest, pasture, and agricultural—still remaining in the possession of the government are to be found, has formally gone on record in this matter, and demands that the new states be treated with the same consideration as those commonwealths which have already divided their patrimony among their individual citizens. The Denver Convention in its resolutions recognizes the wisdom of treating the lands of the nation as a public trust, but it insisted that this trust should be administered for the benefit of the states wherein the lands still remaining are situated and not for the benefit of the people of the older states of the Union, who have no lands, forests, mines, or pastures that are not in the possession of private individuals.

Congress will be unable to resist the justice of this contention. As a rule, that body is not overswift to recognize the rights of those sections of the Union with a small representation in the Lower House, but the American people, when they understand the matter thoroughly, may be depended upon to prevent an injustice. Just now the popular impression at the East is that the Far West is opposed to the conservation of its forests, and that it supports the efforts of unscrupulous grabbers to steal the public domain. But the campaign of education inaugurated by the Pub-

---

*San Francisco Chronicle, June 22, 1907.

lic Lands Convention will soon convince it that all that is asked for is even justice for the new states, and that demands that the profits arising from the eleventh-hour reform shall not be absorbed by the states that have eaten their cake and now wish to share with those who have scarcely had a chance to nibble theirs.

3. Gifford Pinchot Advocates Damming the Hetch Hetchy Valley (1913)[*]

The city of San Francisco's proposal to dam the Tuolumne River, creating a reservoir in the Hetch Hetchy Valley within the boundaries of Yosemite National Park, stirred passionate debate in the early twentieth century. The controversy vividly demonstrated the division of "conservationists" into utilitarians and preservationists. The issue came to a dramatic climax in 1913, when Congress passed the Raker Act, authorizing construction of the dam. In his testimony before the House Committee on the Public Lands, famed conservationist Gifford Pinchot (1865–1946), chief forester of the United States in the Theodore Roosevelt administrations, offered the following rationale for construction of the Hetch Hetchy dam. What is Pinchot's chief justification for building the dam? In what ways does he deserve his title as one of the founding fathers of the modern conservation movement?

Mr. Pinchot. So we come now face to face with the perfectly clean question of what is the best use to which this water that flows out of the Sierras can be put. As we all know, there is no use of water that is higher than the domestic use. Then, if there is, as the engineers tell us, no other source of supply that is anything like so reasonably available as this one; if this is the best, and, within reasonable limits of cost, the only means of supplying San Francisco with water, we come straight to the question of whether the advantage of leaving this valley in a state of nature is greater than the advantage of using it for the benefit of the city of San Francisco.

Now, the fundamental principle of the whole conservation policy is that of use, to take every part of the land and its resources and put it to that use in which it will best serve the most people, and I think there can be no question at all but that in this case we have an instance in which all weighty considerations demand the passage of the bill....

...I believe if we had nothing else to consider than the delight of the few men and women who would yearly go into the Hetch Hetchy Valley, then it should be left in its natural condition. But the considerations on the other side of the question to my mind are simply overwhelming, and so much so that I have never been able to see that there was any reasonable argument against the use of this water supply by the city of San Francisco....

Mr. Raker.[†] Taking the scenic beauty of the park as it now stands, and the fact that the valley is sometimes swamped along in June and July, is it not a fact that if a beautiful dam is put there, as is contemplated, and as the picture is given by the engineers, with the roads contemplated around the reservoir and with other trails, it will be more beautiful than it is now, and give more opportunity for the use of the park?

---

[*]U.S. Congress, House of Representatives, Committee on the Public Lands, Hearings, *Hetch Hetchy Dam Site*, 63d Cong., 1st sess. (June 25–28, July 7, 1913), p. 25ff.
[†]John E. Raker, representative from California.

Mr. Pinchot. Whether it will be more beautiful, I doubt, but the use of the park will be enormously increased. I think there is no doubt about that.

Mr. Raker. In other words, to put it a different way, there will be more beauty accessible than there is now?

Mr. Pinchot. Much more beauty will be accessible than now.

Mr. Raker. And by putting in roads and trails the Government, as well as the citizens of the Government, will get more pleasure out of it than at the present time?

Mr. Pinchot. You might say from the standpoint of enjoyment of beauty and the greatest good to the greatest number, they will be conserved by the passage of this bill, and there will be a great deal more use of the beauty of the park than there is now.

Mr. Raker. Have you seen Mr. John Muir's[*] criticism of the bill? You know him?

Mr. Pinchot. Yes, sir; I know him very well. He is an old and a very good friend of mine. I have never been able to agree with him in his attitude toward the Sierras for the reason that my point of view has never appealed to him at all. When I became Forester and denied the right to exclude sheep and cows from the Sierras, Mr. Muir thought I had made a great mistake, because I allowed the use by an acquired right of a large number of people to interfere with what would have been the utmost beauty of the forest. In this case I think he has unduly given away to beauty as against use.

4. John Muir Damns the Hetch Hetchy Dam (1912)[†]

John Muir (1838–1914), born in Scotland and raised in Wisconsin, arrived in California in 1868 and established himself as an eminent naturalist and passionate crusader for wilderness preservation. On what grounds does he disagree with Gifford Pinchot's position on the Hetch Hetchy dam? In what ways do their two arguments continue to resonate in debates today about the environment?

Yosemite is so wonderful that we are apt to regard it as an exceptional creation, the only valley of its kind in the world; but Nature is not so poor as to have only one of anything. Several other yosemites have been discovered in the Sierra that occupy the same relative positions on the range and were formed by the same forces in the same kind of granite. One of these, the Hetch Hetchy Valley, is in the Yosemite National Park about twenty miles from Yosemite....

...[As] the Merced River flows through Yosemite, so does the Tuolumne through Hetch Hetchy. The walls of both are of gray granite, rise abruptly from the floor, are sculptured in the same style and in both every rock is a glacier monument....

...Hetch Hetchy Valley, far from being a plain, common, rock-bound meadow, as many who have not seen it seem to suppose, is a grand landscape garden, one of Nature's rarest and most precious mountain temples. As in Yosemite, the sublime rocks of its walls seem to glow with life, whether leaning back in repose or

---

[*]John Muir (1838–1914), a Scottish-born American naturalist, was a leading critic of the Hetch Hetchy dam proposal. See the next selection.

[†]John Muir, *The Yosemite* (Garden City, NY: Doubleday and Co., 1962; originally published 1912), pp. 192–202.

standing erect in thoughtful attitudes, giving welcome to storms and calms alike, their brows in the sky, their feet set in the groves and gay flowery meadows, while birds, bees, and butterflies help the river and waterfalls to stir all the air into music—things frail and fleeting and types of permanence meeting here and blending, just as they do in Yosemite, to draw her lovers into close and confiding communion with her.

Sad to say, this most precious and sublime feature of the Yosemite National Park, one of the greatest of all our natural resources for the uplifting joy and peace and health of the people, is in danger of being dammed and made into a reservoir to help supply San Francisco with water and light, thus flooding it from wall to wall and burying its gardens and groves one or two hundred feet deep. This grossly destructive commercial scheme has long been planned and urged (though water as pure and abundant can be got from sources outside of the people's park, in a dozen different places), because of the comparative cheapness of the dam and of the territory which it is sought to divert from the great uses to which it was dedicated in the Act of 1890 establishing the Yosemite National Park.

The making of gardens and parks goes on with civilization all over the world, and they increase both in size and number as their value is recognized. Everybody needs beauty as well as bread, places to play in and pray in, where Nature may heal and cheer and give strength to body and soul alike. This natural beauty-hunger is made manifest in the little window-sill gardens of the poor, though perhaps only a geranium slip in a broken cup, as well as in the carefully tended rose and lily gardens of the rich, the thousands of spacious city parks and botanical gardens, and in our magnificent National Parks—the Yellowstone, Yosemite, Sequoia, etc.—Nature's sublime wonderlands, the admiration and joy of the world. Nevertheless, like anything else worth while, from the very beginning, however well guarded, they have always been subject to attack by despoiling gain-seekers and mischief-makers of every degree from Satan to Senators, eagerly trying to make everything immediately and selfishly commercial, with schemes disguised in smug-smiling philanthropy, industriously, shampiously crying, "Conservation, conservation, panutilization," that man and beast may be fed and the dear Nation made great. Thus long ago a few enterprising merchants utilized the Jerusalem temple as a place of business instead of a place of prayer, changing money, buying and selling cattle and sheep and doves....

That anyone would try to destroy such a place seems incredible; but sad experience shows that there are people good enough and bad enough for anything. The proponents of the dam scheme bring forward a lot of bad arguments to prove that the only righteous thing to do with the people's parks is to destroy them bit by bit as they are able. Their arguments are curiously like those of the devil, devised for the destruction of the first garden—so much of the very best Eden fruit going to waste; so much of the best Tuolumne water and Tuolumne scenery going to waste....

These temple destroyers, devotees of ravaging commercialism, seem to have a perfect contempt for Nature, and, instead of lifting their eyes to the God of the mountains, lift them to the Almighty Dollar.

Dam Hetch Hetchy! As well dam for water-tanks the people's cathedrals and churches, for no holier temple has ever been consecrated by the heart of man.

5. "Beauty as Against Use" (1920s)

When Gifford Pinchot used the phrase "beauty as against use" in his testimony before the House Committee on Public Lands in 1913, he succinctly summarized the terms of the debate about natural resources in the opening years of the century (see p. 528). Conservationists like Pinchot, who advocated that national resources be utilized efficiently, faced two enemies: on the one hand, commercial interests that exploited natural resources, and on the other hand, preservationists like John Muir who celebrated the beauty of nature and wanted to preserve it unspoiled for all time. The following images by Herbert Johnson, titled "National Park as the People Inherited It" and "The Logical Finish If We Let Down the Bars," illustrate the starkly contrasting ways in which conservation issues were often posed. Why did conservationists and preservationists alike find it so difficult to combine beauty and use? If the artist had drawn a third, middle panel in this scene, what would it have looked like? If forced to choose, which of these images would Theodore Roosevelt have endorsed? Why?

D. The Crusade for Woman Suffrage

1. Senator Robert Owen Supports Women (1910)*

Wedded to the tried and true, President William Howard Taft was no enthusiast for woman suffrage. He believed the issue was one that should be handled by the individual states. As late as 1912 he wrote privately, "I cannot change my view...just to suit the exigencies of the campaign, and if it is going to hurt me, I think it will have to hurt me." But the embattled women now had an increasingly strong argument. Rapid industrialization after the Civil War had lured millions of women from the home into the office and the factory, where they were competing with men. By 1910 four states—Wyoming, Colorado, Utah, and Idaho—had granted unrestricted suffrage to women, and the Progressive upheaval of the era added great impetus to the reform. Senator Robert L. Owen of Oklahoma, who had earlier demanded citizenship for Native Americans, here makes a speech to a learned society favoring woman suffrage. What ideas about the nature of womanhood underlie his argument? What changes in society does he think woman suffrage will entail?

Women compose one-half of the human race. In the last forty years, women in gradually increasing numbers have been compelled to leave the home and enter the factory and workshop. Over seven million women are so employed, and the remainder of the sex are employed largely in domestic services. A full half of the work of the world is done by women. A careful study of the matter has demonstrated the vital fact that these working women receive a smaller wage for equal work than men do, and that the smaller wage and harder conditions imposed on the woman worker are due to the lack of the ballot.

Many women have a very hard time, and if the ballot would help them, even a little, I should like to see them have it....Equal pay for equal work is the first great reason justifying this change of governmental policy.

There are other reasons which are persuasive: First, women, take it all in all, are the equals of men in intelligence, and no man has the hardihood to assert the contrary....

The man is usually better informed with regard to state government, but women are better informed about house government, and she can learn state government with as much facility as he can learn how to instruct children, properly feed and clothe the household, care for the sick, play on the piano, or make a house beautiful....

The woman ballot will not revolutionize the world. Its results in Colorado, for example, might have been anticipated. First, it did give women better wages for equal work; second, it led immediately to a number of laws the women wanted, and the first laws they demanded were laws for the protection of the children of the state, making it a misdemeanor to contribute to the delinquency of a child; laws for the improved care of defective children; also, the Juvenile Court for the

---

Annals of the American Academy of Political and Social Science 35, Supplement (May 1910): 6–9, passim.

conservation of wayward boys and girls; the better care of the insane, the deaf, the dumb, the blind; the curfew bell to keep children off the streets at night; raising the age of consent for girls; improving the reformatories and prisons of the state; improving the hospital services of the state; improving the sanitary laws affecting the health of the homes of the state. Their [women's] interest in the public health is a matter of great importance. Above all, there resulted laws for improving the school system.

Several important results followed. Both political parties were induced to put up cleaner, better men, for the women would not stand a notoriously corrupt or unclean candidate. The headquarters of political parties became more decent, and the polling places became respectable. The bad women, enslaved by mercenary vice, do not vote, and good women do vote in as great proportion as men. Every evil prophecy against granting the suffrage has failed. The public men of Colorado, Wyoming, Utah, and Idaho give it a cordial support.

The testimony is universal:

First, it has not made women mannish; they still love their homes and children just the same as ever, and are better able to protect themselves and their children because of the ballot.

Second, they have not become office-seekers, nor pothouse politicians. They have not become swaggerers and insolent on the streets. They still teach good manners to men, as they always have done. It [suffrage] has made women broader and greatly increased the understanding of the community at large of the problems of good government; of proper sanitation, of pure food, or clean water, and all such matters in which intelligent women would naturally take an interest.

It has not absolutely regenerated society, but it has improved it. It has raised the educational qualification of the suffrage, and has elevated the moral standard of the suffrage, because there are more criminal men than criminal women. . . .

The great doctrine of the American Republic that "all governments derive their just powers from the consent of the governed" justifies the plea of one-half of the people, the women, to exercise the suffrage. The doctrine of the American Revolutionary War that taxation without representation is unendurable justifies women in exercising the suffrage.

2. Jane Addams Demands the Vote for Women (1910)[*]

Jane Addams (1860–1935) was a multitalented reformer who battled for women's rights, urban reform, and international peace (she was awarded the Nobel Peace Prize in 1931). In 1889 she helped to found Chicago's Hull House, one of the earliest settlement houses that worked to improve living conditions in the slums. A keen observer of the conditions that shaped people's lives in the new environment of the cities, she soon found in the movement toward urbanization a powerful set of arguments on behalf of granting the vote to women. In the following selection, what points are most effective in her demand for the suffrage? Does she view the

---

[*]Jane Addams, "Why Women Should Vote," *Ladies' Home Journal* 27 (January 1910): 21–22.

suffrage as an extension of women's traditional role or as a means for transform-
ing that role?

This paper is an attempt to show that many women today are failing to discharge their duties to their own households properly simply because they do
not perceive that as society grows more complicated it is necessary that woman
shall extend her sense of responsibility to many things outside of her own home
if she would continue to preserve the home in its entirety. One could illustrate
in many ways. A woman's simplest duty, one would say, is to keep her house
clean and wholesome and to feed her children properly. Yet if she lives in a
tenement house, as so many of my neighbors do, she cannot fulfill these simple
obligations by her own efforts because she is utterly dependent upon the city
administration for the conditions which render decent living possible. Her basement will not be dry, her stairways will not be fireproof, her house will not be
provided with sufficient windows to give light and air, nor will it be equipped
with sanitary plumbing, unless the Public Works Department sends inspectors
who constantly insist that these elementary decencies be provided. Women who
live in the country sweep their own dooryards and may either feed the refuse of
the table to a flock of chickens or allow it innocently to decay in the open air
and sunshine. In a crowded city quarter, however, if the street is not cleaned by
the city authorities no amount of private sweeping will keep the tenement free
from grime; if the garbage is not properly collected and destroyed a tenement-
house mother may see her children sicken and die of diseases from which she
alone is powerless to shield them, although her tenderness and devotion are
unbounded. She cannot even secure untainted meat for her household, she cannot provide fresh fruit, unless the meat has been inspected by city officials and
[unless] the decayed fruit, which is so often placed upon sale in the tenement
districts, has been destroyed in the interests of public health. In short, if woman
would keep on with her old business of caring for her house and rearing her
children she will have to have some conscience in regard to public affairs lying
quite outside of her immediate household. The individual conscience and devotion are no longer effective....

...[There] are certain primary duties which belong to even the most conservative women....The first of these...is woman's responsibility for the members of
her own household that they may be properly fed and clothed and surrounded by
hygienic conditions. The second is a responsibility for the education of children:
(a) that they may be provided with good schools; (b) that they may be kept free
from vicious influences on the street; (c) that when working they may be protected
by adequate child-labor legislation.

(a) The duty of a woman toward the schools which her children attend is
so obvious that it is not necessary to dwell upon it. But even this simple obligation cannot be effectively carried out without some form of social organization
as the mothers' school clubs and mothers' congresses testify, and to which the
most conservative women belong because they feel the need for wider reading
and discussion concerning the many problems of childhood. It is, therefore,
perhaps natural that the public should have been more willing to accord a vote

to women in school matters than in any other, and yet women have never been members of a Board of Education in sufficient numbers to influence largely actual school curriculi. If they had been kindergartens, domestic science courses and school playgrounds would be far more numerous than they are. More than one woman has been convinced of the need of the ballot by the futility of her efforts in persuading a business man that young children need nurture in something besides the three r's. Perhaps, too, only women realize the influence which the school might exert upon the home if a proper adaptation to actual needs were considered. An Italian girl who has had lessons in cooking at the public school will help her mother to connect the entire family with American food and household habits....

(b) But women are also beginning to realize that children need attention outside of school hours; that much of the petty vice in cities is merely the love of pleasure gone wrong, the overrestrained boy or girl seeking improper recreation and excitement. It is obvious that a little study of the needs of children, a sympathetic understanding of the conditions under which they go astray, might save hundreds of them. Women traditionally have had an opportunity to observe the plays of children and the needs of youth, and yet in Chicago, at least they had done singularly little in this vexed problem of juvenile delinquency until they helped to inaugurate the Juvenile Court movement a dozen years ago....

(c) As the education of her children has been more and more transferred to the school, so that even children four years old go to the kindergarten, the woman has been left in a household of constantly-narrowing interests, not only because the children are away, but also because one industry after another is slipping from the household into the factory. Ever since steam power has been applied to the process of weaving and spinning woman's traditional work has been carried on largely outside of the home. The clothing and household linen are not only spun and woven, but also usually sewed, by machinery; the preparation of many foods has also passed into the factory and necessarily a certain number of women have been obliged to follow their work there, although it is doubtful, in spite of the large number of factory girls, whether women now are doing as large a portion of the world's work as they used to do. Because many thousands of those working in factories and shops are girls between the ages of fourteen and twenty-two there is a necessity that older women should be interested in the conditions of industry. The very fact that these girls are not going to remain in industry permanently makes it more important that some one should see to it that they shall not be incapacitated for their future family life because they work for exhausting hours and under unsanitary conditions.

If woman's sense of obligation had enlarged as the industrial conditions changed she might naturally and almost imperceptibly have inaugurated the movements for social amelioration in the line of factory legislation and shop sanitation. That she has not done so is doubtless due to the fact that her conscience is slow to recognize any obligation outside of her own family circle, and because she was so absorbed in her own household that she failed to see what the conditions outside actually were. It would be interesting to know how far the consciousness that she had no vote and could not change matters operated in this direction. After all, we see only those things to which our attention has been drawn, we feel responsibility for those things which are brought to us as matters of responsibility. If conscientious women were convinced that it was a civic duty to be informed in regard to these grave industrial affairs, and then to express the conclusions which they had reached by depositing a piece of paper in a ballot-box, one cannot imagine that they would shirk simply because the action ran counter to old traditions....

In a complex community like the modern city all points of view need to be represented; the resultants of diverse experiences need to be pooled if the community would make for sane and balanced progress. If it would meet fairly each problem as it arises, whether it be connected with a freight tunnel having to do largely with business men, or with the increasing death rate among children under five years of age, a problem in which women are vitally concerned, or with the question of more adequate street-car transfers, in which both men and women might be said to be equally interested, it must not ignore the judgments of its entire adult population.

To turn the administration of our civic affairs wholly over to men may mean that the American city will continue to push forward in its commercial and industrial development, and continue to lag behind in those things which make a city healthful and beautiful. After all, woman's traditional function has been to make her dwelling-place both clean and fair. Is that dreariness in city life, that lack of domesticity which the humblest farm dwelling presents, due to a withdrawal of one of the naturally cooperating forces? If women have in any sense been responsible for the gentler side of life which softens and blurs some of its harsher conditions, may they not have a duty to perform in our American cities?

In closing, may I recapitulate that if woman would fulfill her traditional responsibility to her own children; if she would educate and protect from danger factory children who must find their recreation on the street; if she would bring the cultural forces to bear upon our materialistic civilization; and if she would do it all with the dignity and directness fitting one who carries on her immemorial duties, then she must bring herself to the use of the ballot—that latest implement for self-government. May we not fairly say that American women need this implement in order to preserve the home?

3. A Woman Assails Woman Suffrage (1910)[*]

As late as 1910 many women plainly did not want to shoulder the heavy civic responsibilities that would come with the ballot. One argument was that each sex was superior in its own sphere—women in the home, men in the outside world—and that a separation was best for all concerned. Agitators for woman suffrage feared that if their cause were submitted to a vote by all women, it would be defeated. The suffragists argued that the women who wanted the vote ought to have it. Mrs. Gilbert

───────────

[*]*Annals of the American Academy of Political and Social Science* 35, Supplement (May 1910): 16–21, passim.

E. Jones, an opponent of votes for women, here pleads her case before a scholarly group. How do her views differ from those of Senator Owen, just given? Which of them esteemed women more highly? How do Jones's views compare with those of Jane Addams (see p. 533)?

The anti-suffragists are not organizing or rushing into committees, societies, or associations, and their doings are not being cried out from the house-tops. Yet they show by undeniable facts, easily verified, that woman suffrage bills and proposals have been defeated and turned down at the rate of once in every twenty-seven days in the state legislatures for the last twelve years....

A great many states have granted to women school suffrage, but only a partisan or sectarian issue will bring out the woman's vote. In Massachusetts women have voted on school boards, and after thirty years' training, only 2 or 3 percent of the women register to vote. This hardly can be pronounced "success," or worth while....

Taxation without representation is tyranny, but we must be very careful to define what we mean by the phrase. If we adopt the suffrage attitude, "I pay taxes, therefore I should vote," the natural conclusion is that everybody who pays taxes should vote, or we have a tyrannical form of government. Remember that this argument is used in an unqualified way. We have a "tyranny" here, we are told, because some women pay taxes, yet do not vote. If this is true without any qualification, it must be true not only of women, but of everybody. Accordingly, this government is tyrannical if corporations pay taxes, but do not vote; if aliens pay taxes, but do not vote; if minors pay taxes, but do not vote; if anybody pays taxes, but does not vote. The only correct conclusion is, not that women should vote because some of them pay taxes, but that every taxpayer should be given the privilege of the ballot....

A very conscientious investigation by this League* cannot find that the ballot will help the wage-earning woman. Women must resort to organization, association, and trade unions, and then they can command and maintain a standard wage. Supply and demand will do the rest. Women are not well trained and often very deficient and unskilled in most of their occupations. They are generally only supplementary workers and drop their work when they marry. When married, and home and children are to be cared for, they are handicapped way beyond their strength. Married women should be kept out of industry, rather than urged into it, as scientists, physicians, and sociologists all state that as women enter into competitive industrial life with men, just so does the death rate of little children increase and the birth rate decrease.

Anti-suffragists deplore the fact that women are found in unsuitable occupations. But the suffragists glory in the fact that there are women blacksmiths, baggage masters, brakemen, undertakers, and women political "bosses" in Colorado.

The suffragists call this progress, independence, and emancipation of women. "Anti's" ask for more discrimination and better selection of industrial occupations for wage-earning women. Knowing that the average woman has

---

*The National League for the Civic Education of Women, an anti-suffrage group.

half of the physical strength of the average man, and the price she must pay when in competition with him is too great for her ultimate health and her hope of motherhood, the "Anti's" ask for caution and extreme consideration before new activities are entered upon. . . .

The suffrage leaders say that a woman without the vote has no self-respect. We must then look to the suffrage states to find the fulfillment of the woman's true position, complete—worthy, exalted, and respected. But what do we find when we look at Utah! Women have voted there for forty years. Mormonism and woman suffrage were coincident. By the very nature of its teachings, as indicated by Brigham Young, the basis of the Mormon Church is woman—and the Mormon Church is the greatest political machine in the four suffrage States. . . .

The question of woman suffrage should be summed up in this way: Has granting the ballot to women in the two suffrage states where they have had it for forty years brought about any great reforms or great results? No—Wyoming has many more men than women, so the results cannot be measured. The Mormon women of Utah are not free American citizens. They are under the Elder's supreme power, and vote accordingly, and polygamy has been maintained by the woman's vote, and is still to be found, although forbidden, because women have political power.

Have the saloons been abolished in any of the suffrage states? No.

Do men still drink and gamble? Yes, without a doubt.

Have the slums been done away with? Indeed no.

Are the streets better cleaned in the states where women vote? No, they are quite as bad as in New York City and elsewhere.

Have the red-light districts been cleared away? Decidedly not, and they can be reckoned upon as a political factor, when they are really needed.

Have women purified politics? No, not in the least.

Have women voted voluntarily? Some do; but thousands are carried to the polls in autos and carriages; otherwise they would not vote.

Has pure food and pure milk been established by the woman's vote? Not at all.

Have women's wages been increased because women vote? No, indeed.

Have women equal pay for equal work? Not any more than in New York City.

Are there laws on the statute books that would give women equal pay for equal work? No, and never will be.

Are women treated with more respect in the four suffrage states than elsewhere? Not at all—certainly not in Utah.

[The "anti's" also argued that women were adequately represented by their menfolk; that women already exercised a strong influence indirectly ("harem government"); that suffrage would end chivalry; that women were already overburdened in the home; that family quarrels over partisan issues would increase the divorce rate; that females were too emotional; and that women, if allowed to vote, would soon be serving on juries and forced to hear "indecent testimony." Despite such objections, some of them frivolous, nationwide woman suffrage finally triumphed with the passage of the Nineteenth Amendment in 1920.]

4. Images of the Suffrage Campaign (1900–1915)

Opponents of woman suffrage long argued that a woman's place was in the home, not in the public world of politics. But in the first years of the twentieth century, suffragists like Carrie Chapman Catt and Jane Addams began to turn that argument on its head. They stressed the roles that women already played outside the home, and argued further that modern women needed the vote precisely in order to fulfill their traditional duties as homemakers and mothers. What views of women's nature and social role are expressed in the following pro-suffrage cartoons? What arguments for woman suffrage do these images represent? Which do you think proved most persuasive?

Lou Rogers, New York Call, May 1912, courtesy of The Wisconsin Historical Society

But when the hounds of Starvation Wages, Broken Laws, Intolerable Hours, Cold, Hunger and Discouragement pursue her, where is her place and what is her protection?   1912

Place Is at Home.   1915

51,010 Teachers — **72,261 Saleswomen and Clerks** — **50,000 Stenographers** — **7,362 Telephone Operators N.Y. City** — **12,877 Trained Nurses** — **371 College Presidents and Professors**

16,000 Waitresses — **152,771 General Servants** — **6,509 Charwomen** — **22,309 Clothing Trades Workers** — **33,000 Book Keepers** — **100,000 Sewing Machine Workers**

Woman's Place Is in the Home. We're Going Home. 1915

E. The Election of 1912

1. Theodore Roosevelt Proposes Government Regulation (1912)*

Provoked by the failure of his successor, William Howard Taft, to pursue Progressive policies, Theodore Roosevelt attempted to wrest the Republican presidential nomination from Taft in 1912. Having failed in that effort, Roosevelt became the candidate of one of the most vigorous third parties in U.S. history, the Progressive, or "Bull Moose," party. In the ensuing election campaign, Roosevelt strenuously attacked the Democratic platform's call for strengthening the antitrust laws, and defended his own proposal for more extensive government regulation of the economy. In discussing the trust issue, however, Roosevelt went beyond the narrow technicalities of economic policy and raised fundamental questions of political philosophy. In the remarks excerpted here, what are Roosevelt's most telling arguments against antitrust laws? What was his underlying philosophy of government? Was that philosophy new in the context of the U.S. political tradition?

As construed by the Democratic platform, the Anti-Trust Law would, if it could be enforced, abolish all business of any size or any efficiency. The promise thus to apply and construe the law would undoubtedly be broken, but the mere fitful effort thus to apply it would do no good whatever, would accomplish widespread harm, and would bring all trust legislation into contempt....

What is needed is...a National industrial commission...which should have complete power to regulate and control all the great industrial concerns engaged in inter-State business—which practically means all of them in this country. This commission should exercise over these industrial concerns like powers to those exercised over the railways by the Inter-State Commerce Commission....

Our proposal is to help honest business activity, however extensive, and to see that it is rewarded with fair returns so that there may be no oppression either of business men or of the common people. We propose to make it worth while for our business men to develop the most efficient business agencies for use in international trade; for it is to the interest of our whole people that we should do well in international business....

We favor co-operation in business, and ask only that it be carried on in a spirit of honesty and fairness. We are against crooked business, big or little. We are in favor of honest business, big or little. We propose to penalize conduct and not size. But all very big business, even though honestly conducted, is fraught with such potentiality of menace that there should be thoroughgoing Governmental control over it, so that its efficiency in promoting prosperity at home and increasing the power of the Nation in international commerce may be maintained, and at the same time fair play insured to the wage-workers, the small business competitors, the investors, and the general public. Wherever it is practicable we propose to

---

*Theodore Roosevelt, *Progressive Principles: Selections from Addresses Made During the Presidential Campaign of 1912*, ed. Elmer H. Youngman (New York: Progressive National Service, 1913), pp. 141–152, 216–217.

preserve competition; but where under modern conditions competition has been eliminated and cannot be successfully restored, then the Government must step in and itself supply the needed control on behalf of the people as a whole....

The people of the United States have but one instrument which they can efficiently use against the colossal combinations of business—and that instrument is the Government of the United States (and of course in the several States the governments of the States where they can be utilized). Mr. Wilson's proposal* is that the people of the United States shall throw away this, the one great instrument, the one great weapon they have with which to secure themselves against wrong. He proposes to limit the governmental action of the people and therefore to leave unlimited and unchecked the action of the great corporations whose enormous power constitutes so serious a problem in modern industrial life. Remember that it is absolutely impossible to limit the power of these great corporations whose enormous power constitutes so serious a problem in modern industrial life except by extending the power of the Government. All that these great corporations ask is that the power of the Government shall be limited. No wonder they are supporting Mr. Wilson, for he is advocating for them what they hardly dare venture to advocate for themselves. These great corporations rarely want anything from the Government except to be let alone and to be permitted to work their will unchecked by the Government. All that they really want is that governmental action shall be limited. In every great corporation suit the corporation lawyer will be found protesting against extension of governmental power. Every court decision favoring a corporation takes the form of declaring unconstitutional some extension of governmental power. Every corporation magnate in the country who is not dealing honestly and fairly by his fellows asks nothing better than that Mr. Wilson's programme be carried out and that there be stringent limitations of governmental power.

There once was a time in history when the limitation of governmental power meant increasing liberty for the people. In the present day the limitation of governmental power, of governmental action, means the enslavement of the people by the great corporations who can only be held in check through the extension of governmental power.

2. Woodrow Wilson Asks for "a Free Field and No Favor" (1912)[†]

Two "progressive" candidates—Theodore Roosevelt and Woodrow Wilson—faced off in the crucial election of 1912. (William Howard Taft, the Republican candidate, finished a distant third.) The election amounted, in effect, to a referendum on which variant of Progressivism would prevail. In Woodrow Wilson's remarks that follow, what are his principal differences from Theodore Roosevelt? What is the meaning of his distinction between "benevolence" and "justice"? Which of the two candidates' philosophies was more forward looking, and which more backward looking?

---

[*]Roosevelt refers here to the "New Freedom" platform of presidential candidate Woodrow Wilson. See the next selection.
[†]Woodrow Wilson, *The New Freedom: A Call for the Emancipation of the Generous Energies of a People*, ed. William Bayard Hale (Garden City, NY: Doubleday, Page, 1913), pp. 191–222.

Mr. Roosevelt attached to his platform some very splendid suggestions as to noble enterprises which we ought to undertake for the uplift of the human race; but when I hear an ambitious platform put forth, I am very much more interested in the dynamics of it than in the rhetoric of it....You know that Mr. Roosevelt long ago classified trusts for us as good and bad, and he said that he was afraid only of the bad ones. Now he does not desire that there should be any more bad ones, but proposes that they should all be made good by discipline, directly applied by a commission of executive appointment. All he explicitly complains of is lack of publicity and lack of fairness; not the exercise of power, for throughout that plank the power of the great corporations is accepted as the inevitable consequence of the modern organization of industry. All that it is proposed to do is to take them under control and regulation....

If the government is to tell big business men how to run their business, then don't you see that big business men have to get closer to the government even than they are now? Don't you see that they must capture the government, in order not to be restrained too much by it?...

I don't care how benevolent the master is going to be, I will not live under a master. That is not what America was created for. America was created in order that every man should have the same chance as every other man to exercise mastery over his own fortunes....If you will but hold off the adversaries, if you will but see to it that the weak are protected, I will venture a wager with you that there are some men in the United States, now weak, economically weak, who have brains enough to compete with these gentlemen and who will presently come into the market and put these gentlemen on their mettle....

I agree that as a nation we are now about to undertake what may be regarded as the most difficult part of our governmental enterprises. We have gone along so far without very much assistance from our government. We have felt, and felt more and more in recent months, that the American people were at a certain disadvantage as compared with the people of other countries, because of what the governments of other countries were doing for them and our government omitting to do for us.

It is perfectly clear to every man who has any vision of the immediate future, who can forecast any part of it from the indications of the present, that we are just upon the threshold of a time when the systematic life of this country will be sustained, or at least supplemented, at every point by governmental activity. And we have now to determine what kind of governmental activity it shall be; whether, in the first place, it shall be direct from the government itself, or whether it shall be indirect, through instrumentalities which have already constituted themselves and which stand ready to supersede the government.

I believe that the time has come when the governments of this country, both state and national, have to set the stage, and set it very minutely and carefully, for the doing of justice to men in every relationship of life. It has been free and easy with us so far; it has been go as you please; it has been every man look out for himself; and we have continued to assume, up to this year when every man is dealing, not with another man, in most cases, but with a body of men whom he has not seen, that the relationships of property are the same that they always were. We have great tasks before us, and we must enter on them as befits men charged with the responsibility of shaping a new era.

We have a great program of governmental assistance ahead of us in the cooperative life of the nation; but we dare not enter upon that program until we have freed the government. That is the point. Benevolence never developed a man or a nation. We do not want a benevolent government. We want a free and a just government. Every one of the great schemes of social uplift which are now so much debated by noble people amongst us is based, when rightly conceived, upon justice, not upon benevolence. It is based upon the right of men to breathe pure air, to live; upon the right of women to bear children, and not to be overburdened so that disease and breakdown will come upon them; upon the right of children to thrive and grow up and be strong; upon all these fundamental things which appeal, indeed, to our hearts, but which our minds perceive to be part of the fundamental justice of life.

Politics differs from philanthropy in this: that in philanthropy we sometimes do things through pity merely, while in politics we act always, if we are righteous men, on grounds of justice and large expediency for men in the mass. Sometimes in our pitiful sympathy with our fellow-men we must do things that are more than just. We must forgive men. We must help men who have gone wrong. We must sometimes help men who have gone criminally wrong. But the law does not forgive. It is its duty to equalize conditions, to make the path of right the path of safety and advantage, to see that every man has a fair chance to live and to serve himself, to see that injustice and wrong are not wrought upon any....

The reason that America was set up was that she might be different from all the nations of the world in this: that the strong could not put the weak to the wall, that the strong could not prevent the weak from entering the race. America stands for opportunity. America stands for a free field and no favor.

Thought Provokers

1. In what ways did the muckrakers represent both the best and the worst features of a free press in the United States?
2. Was government protection necessary to improve the lot of the laborer in the industrializing United States? How justifiable were special laws to guard women and youthful workers?
3. What motives inspired Roosevelt's crusade for conservation? How different or similar is the attitude of the West today toward efforts at government control of the environment?
4. Were women powerless without the ballot? How has the suffrage changed the position of women? How has the nation's political agenda changed as a result of woman suffrage?
5. What elements of conservatism can be found in Roosevelt's and Wilson's "progressive" philosophies? In what ways did their proposals foreshadow later U.S. political developments?

29

Wilsonian Progressivism in Peace and War, 1913–1920

We dare not turn from the principle that morality
and not expediency is the thing that must guide us.

Woodrow Wilson, 1913

Prologue: Victorious in the election of 1912, Woodrow Wilson energetically set out to achieve landmark reforms in tariff policy, banking, and antitrust legislation. Triumphant at home, Wilson was soon embroiled in explosive diplomatic troubles abroad, beginning with Mexico in 1914. In that same year, war broke out in Europe, straining the United States' historic commitment to neutrality and testing all of Wilson's considerable political skills. The United States maintained a shaky neutrality for more than two years after war engulfed Europe in the summer of 1914. In practice, however, U.S. policies favored the Allies (chiefly Britain and France) against Germany and Austria-Hungary (the Central Powers). Facing ultimate starvation, the Germans finally proclaimed a desperate all-out campaign of submarine warfare in January 1917. As U.S. merchant ships were torpedoed on the high seas, Wilson reluctantly asked for a declaration of war. With a substantial minority dissenting, Congress agreed. War mobilization proceeded in the United States with unprecedented emotional fervor, deliberately cultivated by the government. Civil liberties were endangered, and "pacifists" were harassed. Wilson eventually rallied public opinion with his fourteen-point peace proposal, and U.S. troops made a significant military contribution in the final days of fighting. But Wilson proved incapable of securing congressional approval of the peace treaty he had helped to negotiate. The treaty's flaws soon became apparent, helping to fuel a second world war just two decades later.

A. Campaigning for Monetary Reform

1. Louis Brandeis Indicts Interlocking Directorates (1914)[*]

Populists, muckrakers, Progressives, and Wilsonian Democrats alike had condemned the monopolistic "money trust." In 1912 the Democratic House of Representatives appointed the famed Pujo Committee, which launched a searching investigation. The next year it released a sensational report stating that 341 directorships in 112 corporations controlled resources amounting to $22.245 billion. Many of these directorships,

---

[*]L. D. Brandeis, *Other People's Money* (New York: Stokes, 1914), pp. 51–53.

including the Wall Street House of Morgan, were interlocking. Louis D. Brandeis, a brilliant young liberal destined to be a Supreme Court justice, develops this aspect in the following partial summary of the Pujo Committee's findings. What was the most objectionable feature of interlocking directorates from the standpoint of the public?

The practice of interlocking directorates is the root of many evils. It offends laws human and divine. Applied to rival corporations, it tends to the suppression of competition and to violation of the Sherman [antitrust] law. Applied to corporations which deal with each other, it tends to disloyalty and to violation of the fundamental law that no man can serve two masters. In either event it tends to inefficiency; for it removes incentive and destroys soundness of judgment. It is undemocratic, for it rejects the platform: "A fair field and no favors," substituting the pull of privilege for the push of manhood. It is the most potent instrument of the Money Trust. Break the control so exercised by the investment bankers over railroads, public-service and industrial corporations, over banks, life-insurance and trust companies, and a long step will have been taken toward attainment of the New Freedom.

The term "interlocking directorates" is here used in a broad sense as including all intertwined conflicting interests, whatever the form, and by whatever device effected. The objection extends alike to contracts of a corporation, whether with one of its directors individually, or with a firm of which he is a member, or with another corporation in which he is interested as an officer or director or stockholder. The objection extends likewise to men holding the inconsistent position of director in two potentially competing corporations, even if those corporations do not actually deal with each other.

A single example will illustrate the vicious circle of control—the endless chain—through which our financial oligarchy now operates:

J. P. Morgan (or a partner), a director of the New York, New Haven & Hartford Railroad, causes that company to sell to J. P. Morgan & Co. an issue of bonds. J. P. Morgan & Co. borrow the money with which to pay for the bonds from the Guaranty Trust Company, of which Mr. Morgan (or a partner) is a director. J. P. Morgan & Co. sell the bonds to the Penn Mutual Life Insurance Company, of which Mr. Morgan (or a partner) is a director. The New Haven spends the proceeds of the bonds in purchasing steel rails from the United States Steel Corporation, of which Mr. Morgan (or a partner) is a director. The United States Steel Corporation spends the proceeds of the rails in purchasing electrical supplies from the General Electric Company, of which Mr. Morgan (or a partner) is a director. The General Electric Company sells supplies to the Western Union Telegraph Company, a subsidiary of the American Telephone and Telegraph Company; and in both Mr. Morgan (or a partner) is a director.

2. J. P. Morgan Denies a Money Trust (1913)*

J. Pierpont Morgan, bulbous-nosed but august, appeared before the Pujo Committee with eight attorneys. (Their estimated fees for two days were $45,000.) He denied not only the existence of a money trust but even the possibility of its existence.

---

*Letter from Messrs. J. P. Morgan & Co.... (privately printed, February 25, 1913), pp. 8–9, 12, 17–18.

Less convincing was his claim that he neither possessed nor desired great financial power. A subsequent letter from the House of Morgan to the Pujo Committee summarized the influential financier's point of view. To what extent does this statement refute the charges against the bankers?

There have been spread before your Committee elaborate tables of so-called interlocking directorates, from which exceedingly mistaken inferences have been publicly drawn. In these tables it is shown that 180 bankers and bank directors serve upon the boards of corporations having resources aggregating $25,000,000,000, and it is implied that this vast aggregate of the country's wealth is at the disposal of these 180 men.

But such an implication rests solely upon the untenable theory that these men, living in different parts of the country, in many cases personally unacquainted with each other, and in most cases associated only in occasional transactions, vote always for the same policies and control with united purpose the directorates of the 132 corporations on which they serve.

The testimony failed to establish any concerted policy or harmony of action binding these 180 men together, and, as a matter of fact, no such policy exists. The absurdity of the assumption of such control becomes more apparent when one considers that, on the average, these directors represent only one quarter of the memberships of their boards. It is preposterous to suppose that every "interlocking" director has full control in every organization with which he is connected, and that the majority of directors who are not "interlocking" are mere figureheads, subject to the will of a small minority of their boards.

Perhaps the greatest harm in the presentation referred to lay in the further unwarranted inference, to which has been given wide publicity, that the vast sum of $25,000,000,000 was in cash or liquid form, subject to the selfish use or abuse of individuals. Such an idea excites the public mind to demand the correction of a fancied situation which does not and, in our belief, never can exist....

Such growth in the size of banks in New York and Chicago has frequently been erroneously designated before your Committee as "concentration," whereas we have hitherto pointed out [that] the growth of banking resources in New York City has been less rapid than that of the rest of the country. But increase of capital, and merger of two or more banks into one institution (with the same resources as the aggregate of the banks merging into it), has been frequent, especially since January 1, 1908.

These mergers, however, are a development due simply to the demand for larger banking facilities to care for the growth of the country's business. As our cities double and treble in size and importance, as railroads extend and industrial plants expand, not only is it natural, but it is necessary, that our banking institutions should grow in order to care for the increased demands put upon them. Perhaps it is not known as well as it should be that in New York City the largest banks are far inferior in size to banks in the commercial capitals of other and much smaller countries....

For a private banker to sit upon...a directorate is in most instances a duty, not a privilege. Inquiry will readily develop the fact that the members of the leading banking houses in this country—and it was the leading houses only against which animad-versions were directed—are besought continually to act as directors in various corporations, whose securities they may handle, and that in general they enter only those boards which the opinion of the investing public requires them to enter, as an evidence of good faith that they are willing to have their names publicly associated with the management.

Yet, before your Committee, this natural and eminently desirable relationship was made to appear almost sinister, and no testimony whatever was adduced to show the actual working of such relationships.

3. William McAdoo Exposes the Bankers (c. 1913)*

President Wilson, the foe of special privilege, was determined to break the so-called money monopoly. The need for a more flexible currency had been brought home to the nation by the disastrous "bankers' panic" of 1907. Wilson therefore threw the weight of his dynamic personality behind the Federal Reserve Bill introduced in Congress in 1913. The big bankers, most of them conservative Republicans, fought it passionately. They favored a huge new central bank with themselves in control; they were forced, however, to accept a twelve-district Federal Reserve System, with a government-appointed Federal Reserve Board in control. Lanky, black-haired William G. McAdoo, Wilson's secretary of the treasury (and son-in-law), here describes the initial opposition of the bankers. In what respect were they most seriously wrong?

As time went by, we observed that the public generally—I mean the ordinary, average citizen—was in favor of the Federal Reserve Bill. The bankers in the larger money centers were almost to a man bitterly opposed to it, and many businessmen shared their views. Sentiment among the smaller banks was divided—those against the bill being largely in the majority.

At the national convention of the American Bankers' Association, held in Boston, October, 1913, only two delegates attempted to speak in favor of the legislation; each was howled down until the chairman managed to make himself heard, and begged the convention to give them the courtesy of attention.

Dr. Joseph French Johnson, professor of political economy at New York University, said at a dinner of the Academy of Political Science that the bill, if passed, would bring on a dangerous credit expansion and that it would cause "a collapse of the banking system." He added that "blacksmiths could not be expected to produce a Swiss watch." The blacksmiths were, in this case, I suppose, the Democrats, and the Federal Reserve Bill was the Swiss watch. So I infer, and I fancy that another meaning, to the effect that Professor Johnson himself was an excellent watchmaker, lurked in the background.

And from Chicago came reports of a speech of Senator Lawrence Y. Sherman, Republican member of the Senate from Illinois. In addressing the Illinois Bankers'

---

*From *Crowded Years* by William Gibbs McAdoo.

Association he said: "I would support a law to wind a watch with a crowbar as cheerfully as I will support any such bill."

But James B. Forgan, banking magnate of Chicago, was more direct in his expression of opinion. He said nothing about crowbars and blacksmiths and Swiss watches. He declared that the bill was "unworkable, impractical, and fundamentally bad." It would bring about, he said, "the most damnable contraction of currency ever seen in any country."

Forgan's idea that the currency would be damnably contracted was not shared by all the opponents of the Glass-Owen [Federal Reserve] Bill. Many bankers and economists proved, to their own satisfaction by figures and diagrams, that the Federal Reserve System would produce an extraordinary inflation. These vast and irreconcilable differences of opinion between the various groups of our adversaries had the effect of lessening my respect for so-called banking experts. I found that they could take the same set of facts and reach two diametrically opposite conclusions.

For example, Forgan estimated that the currency would be contracted to the extent of $1,800,000,000, while Senator Elihu Root, using the same data, predicted an inflation of at least $1,800,000,000.

President Arthur T. Hadley, of Yale, who had a high reputation as an economist, believed that the bill, if passed, would lead to inflation on an unparalleled scale, with a consequent depreciation. He was so deeply moved that he wrote a personal letter to President Wilson on July 1, 1913, for the purpose of pointing out to the President that the Act would "involve the country in grave financial danger." Practically all of our gold would leave for Europe, he thought. He was greatly mistaken. There is now in the United States about 45 percent of all the gold in the world.

Frank A. Vanderlip, president of the National City Bank of New York, declared that the notes of the Federal Reserve Banks would be "fiat money," and James J. Hill, the famous railroad builder and financier, said the plan was "socialistic." James R. Mann, Republican leader of the House, condemned the bill as all wrong, badly conceived, and impossible as a practical measure. However, he added bitterly, it did not matter; the national banks would not go into the system, anyway. Most of them would become state banks, and the Federal Reserve would just lie down and die for lack of support. Saying this, he washed his hands of the whole affair.

[The Federal Reserve System, approved by Congress late in 1913, not only carried the nation triumphantly through World War I but remains the bulwark of the nation's financial structure. The sneers of the bankers gave way to cheers. Currency expansion to meet growing needs was abundantly provided by the issuance of Federal Reserve notes, backed in part by promissory notes and other assets held by the member banks. The national banks, authorized during the Civil War, were required to join the Federal Reserve System. Wall Street's grip on money and credit was thus weakened, and interlocking directorates were curbed the next year (1914) by the Clayton Anti-Trust Act.]

B. War with Germany

1. President Wilson Breaks Diplomatic Relations (1917)*

After stern warnings from President Wilson, Germany generally avoided sinking unresisting passenger ships without warning. But in March 1916 a German submarine torpedoed a French liner, the Sussex, and caused some eighty casualties, including injuries to several Americans. Wilson indignantly presented an ultimatum to Berlin threatening a severance of diplomatic relations—an almost certain prelude to war—unless Germany discontinued these inhumane tactics. The Germans reluctantly acquiesced. Finally, however, driven to the wall by the British blockade, they dramatically announced, on January 31, 1917, the opening of unrestricted submarine warfare on virtually all ships plying the war zone, including U.S. vessels. Wilson, whose hand had now been called, went sorrowfully before Congress to deliver this speech. Was he naive or idealistic? Was he hasty in accepting the German U-boat challenge?

I think that you will agree with me that, in view of this [submarine] declaration...this Government has no alternative, consistent with the dignity and honor of the United States, but to take the course which...it announced that it would take....

I have, therefore, directed the Secretary of State to announce to His Excellency the German Ambassador that all diplomatic relations between the United States and the German Empire are severed....

Notwithstanding this unexpected action of the German Government, this sudden and deeply deplorable renunciation of its assurances, given this Government at one of the most critical moments of tension in the relations of the two governments, I refuse to believe that it is the intention of the German authorities to do in fact what they have warned us they will feel at liberty to do. I cannot bring myself to believe that they will indeed pay no regard to the ancient friendship between their people and our own, or to the solemn obligations which have been exchanged between them, and destroy American ships and take the lives of American citizens in the willful prosecution of the ruthless naval program they have announced their intention to adopt. Only actual overt acts on their part can make me believe it even now.

If this inveterate confidence on my part in the sobriety and prudent foresight of their purpose should unhappily prove unfounded—if American ships and American lives should in fact be sacrificed by their naval commanders in heedless contravention of the just and reasonable understandings of international law and the obvious dictates of humanity—I shall take the liberty of coming again before the Congress, to ask that authority be given me to use any means that may be necessary for the protection of our seamen and our people in the prosecution of their peaceful and legitimate errands on the high seas. I can do nothing less. I take it for granted that all neutral governments will take the same course.

---

*Congressional Record, 64th Cong., 2d sess. (February 3, 1917), pp. 2578–2579.

We do not desire any hostile conflict with the Imperial German Government. We are the sincere friends of the German people, and earnestly desire to remain at peace with the Government which speaks for them. We shall not believe that they are hostile to us unless and until we are obliged to believe it; and we purpose nothing more than the reasonable defense of the undoubted rights of our people.

We wish to serve no selfish ends. We seek merely to stand true alike in thought and in action to the immemorial principles of our people which I sought to express in my address to the Senate only two weeks ago—seek merely to vindicate our right to liberty and justice and an unmolested life. These are the bases of peace, not war. God grant we may not be challenged to defend them by acts of willful injustice on the part of the Government of Germany!

[Wilson first undertook to arm U.S. merchantmen against the submarines ("armed neutrality"). When this tactic failed and German U-boats began to sink U.S. vessels, he again went before Congress, on April 2, 1917. Referring principally to these sinkings, he asked for a formal resolution acknowledging the fact that Germany had "thrust" war on the United States. "We have no quarrel with the German people," he declared—only with their government. With militaristic forces rampant, "there can be no assured security for the democratic governments of the world." Hence, "The world must be made safe for democracy." War is "terrible." "But the right is more precious than peace, and we shall fight for the things which we have always carried nearest our hearts—for democracy, for the right of those who submit to authority to have a voice in their own governments, for the rights and liberties of small nations, for a universal dominion of right by such a concert of free peoples as shall bring peace and safety to all nations and make the world itself at last free."]

2. Representative Claude Kitchin Assails the War Resolution (1917)[*]

Congress responded promptly to Wilson's request for a war resolution. But the lop-sided vote was far from unanimous—82 to 6 in the Senate, 373 to 50 in the House—revealing a widespread opposition to hostilities, especially in the German American areas. A flaming antiwar speech came from the lips of Claude Kitchin of North Carolina, an eloquent and beloved string-tie congressman, whose outburst produced a deluge of unflattering letters and telegrams. "Go to Germany," demanded one detractor. "They need fertilizer!" Ascertain what truth there was in Kitchin's allegation that Wilson's inconsistent and unneutral policies were taking the nation into war. Did Kitchin deserve to be called pro-German?

Great Britain every day, every hour, for two years has violated American rights on the seas. We have persistently protested. She has denied us not only entrance into the ports of the Central Powers but has closed to us by force the ports of

---

[*]*Congressional Record*, 65th Cong., 1st sess. (April 5, 1917), pp. 332–333.

neutrals. She has unlawfully seized our ships and our cargoes. She has rifled our mails. She has declared a war zone sufficiently large to cover all the ports of her enemy. She made the entire North Sea a military area—strewed it with hidden mines and told the neutral nations of the world to stay out or be blown up. We protested.* No American ship was sunk, no American life was destroyed, because we submitted and did not go in. We kept out of war. We sacrificed no honor. We surrendered permanently no essential rights. We knew that these acts of Great Britain, though in plain violation of international law and of our rights on the seas, were not aimed at us. They were directed at her enemy. They were inspired by military necessity. Rather than plunge this country into war, we were willing to forgo for the time our rights. I approved that course then; I approve it now.

Germany declares a war zone sufficiently large to cover the ports of her enemy. She infests it with submarines and warns the neutral world to stay out, though in plain violation of our rights and of international law. We know that these acts are aimed not directly at us but intended to injure and cripple her enemy, with which she is in a death struggle.

We refuse to yield; we refuse to forgo our rights for the time. We insist upon going in.

In my judgment, we could keep out of the war with Germany as we kept out of the war with Great Britain, by keeping our ships and our citizens out of the war zone of Germany as we did out of the war zone of Great Britain. And we would sacrifice no more honor, surrender no more rights, in the one case than in the other. Or we could resort to armed neutrality, which the President recently urged and for which I voted on March 1.

But we are told that Germany has destroyed American lives while Great Britain destroyed only property. Great Britain destroyed no American lives because this nation kept her ships and her citizens out of her war zone which she sowed with hidden mines.

But are we quite sure that the real reason for war with Germany is the destruction of lives as distinguished from property, that to avenge the killing of innocent Americans and to protect American lives war becomes a duty?

Mexican bandits raided American towns, shot to death sleeping men, women, and children in their own homes. We did not go to war to avenge these deaths. . . .

We were willing to forgo our rights rather than plunge this country into war while half the world was in conflagration. I approved that course then; I approve it now.

Why can we not, why should we not, forgo for the time being the violation of our rights by Germany, and do as we did with Great Britain, do as we did with Mexico, and thus save the universe from being wrapped in the flames of war?

I have hoped and prayed that God would forbid our country going into war with another for doing that which perhaps under the same circumstances we ourselves would do.

---

*Kitchin was mistaken. The United States did not formally protest against the British mined zone; more than two years later, it merely reserved its rights.

C. The War for the American Mind _____

1. Abusing the Pro-Germans (1918)*

The several million enemy aliens in the United States were under suspicion, especially those who did not buy Liberty Bonds. One of them was Robert Paul Prager, a young German residing in Illinois. He had tried to enlist in the navy but was rejected because he had lost an eye. After he had spoken out for socialism, he was seized by a drunken mob in 1918, stripped of his clothes, wrapped in an American flag, and hanged. A patriotic jury acquitted the ringleaders. This was the worst outrage of its kind, but another almost occurred, as Secretary of War N. D. Baker relates in the following letter. What does it reveal of the American state of mind at this time? Why was such an incident much less likely to occur in World War II?

The spirit of the country seems unusually good, but there is a growing frenzy of suspicion and hostility toward disloyalty. I am afraid we are going to have a good many instances of people roughly treated on very slight evidence of disloyalty. Already a number of men and some women have been "tarred and feathered," and a portion of the press is urging with great vehemence more strenuous efforts at detection and punishment. This usually takes the form of advocating "drum-head courts-martial"† and "being stood up against a wall and shot," which are perhaps none too bad for real traitors, but are very suggestive of summary discipline to arouse mob spirit, which unhappily does not take time to weigh evidence.

In Cleveland a few days ago a foreign-looking man got into a street car and, taking a seat, noticed pasted in the window next to him a Liberty Loan poster, which he immediately tore down, tore into small bits, and stamped under his feet. The people in the car surged around him with the demand that he be lynched, when a Secret Service man showed his badge and placed him under arrest, taking him in a car to the police station, where he was searched and found to have two Liberty Bonds in his pocket and to be a non-English Pole. When an interpreter was procured, it was discovered that the circular which he had destroyed had had on it a picture of the German Emperor, which had so infuriated the fellow that he destroyed the circular to show his vehement hatred of the common enemy. As he was unable to speak a single word of English, he would undoubtedly have been hanged but for the intervention and entirely accidental presence of the Secret Service agent.

I am afraid the grave danger in this sort of thing, apart from its injustice, is that the German Government will adopt retaliatory measures. While the government of the United States is not only not responsible for these things, but very zealously trying to prevent them, the German Government draws no fine distinctions.

_____
*Frederick Palmer, *Newton D. Baker* (New York: Dodd, Mead, 1931), vol. 2, pp. 162–163.
†Originally a hasty court-martial in the field, around a drum as a table.

2. Robert La Follette Demands His Rights (1917)*

Senator Robert M. La Follette of Wisconsin—undersized, pompadoured, and fiery—was one of the most eloquent reformers of his generation. Representing a state with a heavy concentration of German Americans, he had spoken out vehemently against war with Germany and had voted against it. He and his five dissenting colleagues were pilloried in the press as traitors for voting their consciences. On October 6, 1917, La Follette rose and quoted (from the press) a charge to a federal grand jury in Texas by a district judge. The jurist reportedly had said that these six senators ought to be convicted of treason and shot. "I wish I could pay for the ammunition," he continued. "I would like to attend the execution, and if I were in the firing squad I would not want to be the marksman who had the blank shell." La Follette then went on to present this classic defense of free speech. Why was free speech so severely threatened in this particular war?

But, sir, it is not alone Members of Congress that the war party in this country has sought to intimidate. The mandate seems to have gone forth to the sovereign people of this country that they must be silent while those things are being done by their Government which most vitally concern their well-being, their happiness, and their lives.

Today—for weeks past—honest and law-abiding citizens of this country are being terrorized and outraged in their rights by those sworn to uphold the laws and protect the rights of the people. I have in my possession numerous affidavits establishing the fact that people are being unlawfully arrested, thrown into jail, held incommunicado for days, only to be eventually discharged without ever having been taken into court, because they have committed no crime. Private residences are being invaded, loyal citizens of undoubted integrity and probity arrested, cross-examined, and the most sacred constitutional rights guaranteed to every American citizen are being violated.

It appears to be the purpose of those conducting this campaign to throw the country into a state of terror, to coerce public opinion, to stifle criticism, and suppress discussion of the great issues involved in this war.

I think all men recognize that in time of war the citizen must surrender some rights for the common good which he is entitled to enjoy in time of peace. But, *sir, the right to control their own Government, according to constitutional forms, is not one of the rights that the citizens of this country are called upon to surrender in time of war.*

Rather, in time of war, the citizen must be more alert to the preservation of his right to control his Government. He must be most watchful of the encroachment of the military upon the civil power. He must beware of those precedents in support of arbitrary action by administrative officials which, excused on the plea of necessity in wartime, become the fixed rule when the necessity has passed and normal conditions have been restored.

Congressional Record, 65th Cong., 1st sess. (October 6, 1917), pp. 7878–7879.

More than all, the citizen and his representative in Congress in time of war must maintain his right of free speech. More than in times of peace, it is necessary that the channels for free public discussion of governmental policies shall be open and unclogged.

I believe, Mr. President, that I am now touching upon the most important question in this country today—and that is the right of the citizens of this country and their representatives in Congress to discuss in an orderly way, frankly and publicly and without fear, from the platform and through the press, every important phase of this war; its causes, the manner in which it should be conducted, and the terms upon which peace should be made....

I am contending for this right, because the exercise of it is necessary to the welfare, to the existence, of this Government, to the successful conduct of this war, and to a peace which shall be enduring and for the best interest of this country....

Mr. President, our Government, above all others, is founded on the right of the people freely to discuss all matters pertaining to their Government, in war not less than in peace....How can that popular will express itself between elections except by meetings, by speeches, by publications, by petitions, and by addresses to the representatives of the people?

Any man who seeks to set a limit upon those rights, whether in war or peace, aims a blow at the most vital part of our Government. And then as the time for election approaches, and the official is called to account for his stewardship—not a day, not a week, not a month, before the election, but a year or more before it, if the people choose—they must have the right to the freest possible discussion of every question upon which their representative has acted, of the merits of every measure he has supported or opposed, of every vote he has cast and every speech that he has made. And before this great fundamental right every other must, if necessary, give way, for in no other manner can representative government be preserved.

3. The Supreme Court Throttles Free Speech (1919)*

The 1917 Espionage Act gave the federal government broad powers to curtail anti-war activism by banning all efforts to interfere with the draft or with the conduct of war. Arrested and tried for distributing leaflets urging conscripts to resist the draft, Socialist party leader Charles Schenck appealed his conviction to the Supreme Court. In a unanimous decision delivered by Chief Justice Oliver Wendell Holmes, Jr., the Court upheld the Espionage Act, holding that the right to free speech must be balanced against the countervailing interests of the state to protect itself in times of war. The case also established the "clear and present danger" test for limiting speech. How does Holmes justify the Court's decision to uphold the conviction? Does his reasoning leave room for political dissent in times of war?

---

*Schenck v. United States, 249 U.S. 47 (1919), p. 52.

We admit that in many places and in ordinary times the defendants in saying all that was said in the circular would have been within their constitutional rights. But the character of every act depends upon the circumstances in which it is done.... The most stringent protection of free speech would not protect a man in falsely shouting fire in a theatre and causing a panic. It does not even protect a man from an injunction against uttering words that may have all the effect of force.... The question in every case is whether the words used are used in such circumstances and are of such a nature as to create a clear and present danger that they will bring about the substantive evils that Congress has a right to prevent. It is a question of proximity and degree. When a nation is at war many things that might be said in time of peace are such a hindrance to its effort that their utterance will not be endured so long as men fight and that no Court could regard them as protected by any constitutional right. It seems to be admitted that if an actual obstruction of the recruiting service were proved, liability for words that produced that effect might be enforced.... If the act, (speaking, or circulating a paper,) its tendency and the intent with which it is done are the same, we perceive no ground for saying that success alone warrants making the act a crime.

D. Woodrow Wilson Versus Theodore Roosevelt on the Fourteen Points (1918)*

President Wilson's war aims speeches were lofty and eloquent but rather vague and long-winded. An American journalist in Russia suggested that he compress his views into crisp, placardlike paragraphs. This he did in his famed Fourteen Points, address to Congress on January 8, 1918. By promising independence (self-determination) to minority groups under enemy rule and by raising up hopes everywhere for a better tomorrow, the Fourteen Points undermined the foe's will to resist while simultaneously inspiring the Allies. George Creel's propaganda machine broadcast the points in leaflet form throughout the world, while Allied rockets and shells showered them over enemy lines. German desertions multiplied. Form some judgment as to whether Wilson's aims were completely clear and consistent. Determine which ones would be most likely to weaken the resistance of Germany and Austria-Hungary. The frustrated Colonel Roosevelt fulminated against the Fourteen Points in the Kansas City Star. Given that before 1917 he had been anti-Wilson, pro-tariff, anti-German, pro-Ally, and internationalist-minded, what are the most important inconsistencies in his position?

---

*Congressional Record, 65th Cong., 2d sess. (January 8, 1918), p. 691, and Kansas City Star, October 30, 1918. The full text can also be found in Ralph Stout, ed., Roosevelt in the Kansas City "Star" (1921), pp. 241–242, 243–246.

Wilson's Points

I. Open covenants of peace, openly arrived at, after which there shall be no private international understandings of any kind, but diplomacy shall proceed always frankly and in the public view.

[Wilson finally meant secret negotiations but public commitments. He had earlier laid himself open to criticism by landing the marines in Haiti and Santo Domingo in 1915 and 1916 to restore order.]

II. Absolute freedom of navigation upon the seas, outside territorial waters, alike in peace and in war, except as the seas may be closed in whole or in part by international action [of the League of Nations] for the enforcement of international covenants.

[Big-navy Britain, fearing to blunt its blockade weapon, refused to accept this point.]

III. The removal, so far as possible, of all economic barriers, and the establishment of an equality of trade conditions among all the nations consenting to the peace, and associating themselves [in the League of Nations] for its maintenance.

[This meant, although not too clearly put, that the United States could still maintain tariffs but could not discriminate among fellow members of the League of Nations. Any commercial favors granted to one fellow member would automatically be extended to all.]

IV. Adequate guarantees given and taken that national armaments will be reduced to the lowest point consistent with domestic safety.

[This meant a force no larger than necessary to control domestic disorders and prevent foreign invasion.]

Roosevelt's Complaints

The President has recently waged war on Haiti and San Domingo, and rendered democracy within these two small former republics not merely unsafe, but non-existent. He has kept all that he has done in the matter absolutely secret. If he means what he says, he will at once announce what open covenant of peace he has openly arrived at with these two little republics, which he has deprived of their right of self-determination.

It makes no distinction between freeing the seas from murder, like that continually practiced by Germany, and freeing them from blockade of contraband merchandise, which is the practice of a right universally enjoyed by belligerents, and at this moment practiced by the United States. Either this proposal is meaningless, or it is a mischievous concession to Germany.

The third point promises free trade among all the nations, unless the words are designedly used to conceal President Wilson's true meaning. This would deny to our country the right to make a tariff to protect its citizens, and especially its workingmen, against Germany or China or any other country. Apparently this is desired on the ground that the incidental domestic disaster to this country will prevent other countries from feeling hostile to us. The supposition is foolish. England practiced free trade and yet Germany hated England particularly....

Either this is language deliberately used to deceive, or else it means that we are to scrap our army and navy, and prevent riot by means of a national constabulary, like the state constabulary of New York or Pennsylvania.

Wilson's Points

V. A free, open-minded, and absolutely impartial adjustment of all [wartime] colonial claims, based upon a strict observance of the principle that, in determining all such questions of sovereignty, the interests of the populations concerned must have equal weight with the equitable claims of the Government whose title is to be determined.

[German colonies captured by Britain and Japan might be returned, if this course seemed "equitable."]

VI. The evacuation of all Russian territory [inhabited by Russians], and such a settlement of all questions affecting Russia as will secure the best and freest cooperation of the other nations of the world in obtaining for her an unhampered and unembarrassed opportunity for the independent determination of her own political development and national policy, and assure her of a sincere welcome into the society of free nations, under institutions of her own choosing; and, more than a welcome, assistance also of every kind....

[Wilson had in mind having the German invader evacuate Russian territory, and helping the Russian Poles and other non-Russian nationalities to achieve self-determination. He would also lend a helping hand to the new Bolshevik government.]

VII. Belgium, the whole world will agree, must be evacuated and restored, without any attempt to limit the sovereignty which she enjoys in common with all other free nations. No other single act will serve as this will serve to restore confidence among the nations in the laws which they have

Roosevelt's Complaints

Unless the language is deliberately used to deceive, this means that we are to restore to our brutal enemy the colonies taken by our allies while they were defending us from this enemy. The proposition is probably meaningless. If it is not, it is monstrous.

Point VI deals with Russia. It probably means nothing, but if it means anything, it provides that America shall share on equal terms with other nations, including Germany, Austria, and Turkey [the Central Powers], in giving Russia assistance. The whole proposition would not be particularly out of place in a college sophomore's exercise in rhetoric.

Point VII deals with Belgium and is entirely proper and commonplace.

Wilson's Points	Roosevelt's Complaints

Wilson's Points

themselves set and determined for the government of their relations with one another. Without this healing act the whole structure and validity of international law is forever impaired.

[Germany, disregarding a neutrality treaty of 1839, had struck through Belgium at France in 1914. The war-minded Roosevelt at first approved this act as one of military necessity, but he soon changed his views. The word "restored" in Point VII implied that the Germans would be assessed an indemnity for the damage they had done.]

VIII. All French territory should be freed and the invaded portions restored, and the wrong done to France by Prussia in 1871 in the matter of Alsace-Lorraine, which has unsettled the peace of the world for nearly fifty years, should be righted, in order that peace may once more be made secure in the interest of all.

[Wilson intended that Alsace-Lorraine, seized by Prussia (Germany) in 1871, should be returned to France.]

IX. A readjustment of the frontiers of Italy should be effected along clearly recognizable lines of nationality.

[Wilson would extend "self-determination" to nearby Italian peoples not under the Italian flag.]

X. The peoples of Austria-Hungary, whose place among the nations we wish to see safeguarded and assured, should be accorded the freest opportunity of autonomous development.

[This point raised difficulties because of the quarreling minorities of the "succession states" that rose from the ruins of Austria-Hungary.]

Roosevelt's Complaints

Point VIII deals with Alsace-Lorraine and is couched in language which betrays Mr. Wilson's besetting sin—his inability to speak in a straightforward manner. He may mean that Alsace and Lorraine must be restored to France, in which case he is right. He may mean that a plebiscite must be held, in which case he is playing Germany's evil game.

Point IX deals with Italy, and is right.

Point X deals with the Austro-Hungarian Empire, and is so foolish that even President Wilson has abandoned it.

[Wilson later stressed independence rather than local autonomy.]

Wilson's Points

XI. Rumania, Serbia, and Montenegro should be evacuated; occupied territories restored; Serbia accorded free and secure access to the sea; and the relations of the several Balkan states to one another determined by friendly counsel along historically established lines of allegiance and nationality; and international guarantees of the political and economic independence and territorial integrity of the several Balkan states should be entered into.

[This point was also invalidated by the "succession states," including Yugoslavia, which embraced Serbia.]

XII. The Turkish portions of the present Ottoman Empire should be assured a secure sovereignty, but the other nationalities which are now under Turkish rule should be assured an undoubted security of life and an absolutely unmolested opportunity of autonomous development, and the Dardanelles should be permanently opened as a free passage to the ships and commerce of all nations under international guarantees.

[Wilson's ideal was self-determination for the Greeks, Armenians, Arabs, and other non-Turks in the Turkish empire, much of whose land became mandates of France and Britain under the League of Nations.]

XIII. An independent Polish state should be erected which should include the territories inhabited by indisputably Polish populations, which should be assured a free and secure access to the sea, and whose political and economic independence and territorial integrity should be guaranteed by international covenant.

[Poland was to be restored from the territory of Germany, Russia, and Austria-Hungary, despite injustices to German and other minorities.]

Roosevelt's Complaints

Point XI proposes that we, together with other nations, including apparently Germany, Austria, and Hungary, shall guarantee justice in the Balkan Peninsula. As this would also guarantee our being from time to time engaged in war over matters in which we had no interest whatever, it is worth while inquiring whether President Wilson proposes that we wage these wars with the national constabulary to which he desired to reduce our armed forces.

Point XII proposes to perpetuate the infamy of Turkish rule in Europe, and as a sop to the conscience of humanity proposes to give the subject races autonomy, a slippery word which in a case like this is useful only for rhetorical purposes.

Point XIII proposes an independent Poland, which is right; and then proposes that we guarantee its integrity in the event of future war, which is preposterous unless we intend to become a military nation more fit for overseas warfare than Germany is at present.

Wilson's Points

XIV. A general association [League] of nations must be formed under specific covenants for the purpose of affording mutual guarantees of political independence and territorial integrity to great and small states alike.

In regard to these essential rectifications of wrong and assertions of right, we feel ourselves to be intimate partners of all the governments and peoples associated together against the Imperialists. We cannot be separated in interest or divided in purpose. We stand together until the end.

Roosevelt's Complaints

In its essence Mr. Wilson's proposition for a League of Nations seems to be akin to the Holy Alliance of the nations of Europe a century ago, which worked such mischief that the Monroe Doctrine was called into being especially to combat it. If it is designed to do away with nationalism, it will work nothing but mischief. If it is devised in sane fashion as an addition to nationalism and as an addition to preparing our own strength for our own defense, it may do a small amount of good. But it will certainly accomplish nothing if more than a moderate amount is attempted, and probably the best first step would be to make the existing league of the Allies a going concern.

E. The Face of War

1. General John Pershing Defines American Fighting Tactics (1917–1918)*

Generals, it has often been said, have a habit of fighting the previous war—a maxim to which jut-jawed General John J. Pershing, commander of the American Expeditionary Force, was no exception. Pershing had studied Civil War tactics at West Point in the late nineteenth century and saw no reason why they should not be applied in France in the twentieth century. He expressed criticism bordering on contempt for the French and British fascination with fixed, entrenched warfare. Pershing insisted, therefore, that U.S. troops be trained in battle techniques different from those offered to European troops. This approach contributed to appallingly high U.S. casualty rates when the American soldiers, or "doughboys," eventually entered combat. How does Pershing here defend his tactical preferences? What factors might have motivated him to adopt them?

It was my opinion that the victory could not be won by the costly process of attrition, but it must be won by driving the enemy out into the open and engaging him in a war of movement. Instruction in this kind of warfare was based upon individual and group initiative, resourcefulness and tactical judgment, which were also of great advantage in trench warfare. Therefore, we took decided issue with the

---

*John J. Pershing, *My Experiences in the World War* (New York: Frederick A. Stokes Company, 1931), vol. 1, pp. 150–154; vol. 2, p. 358.

Allies and, without neglecting thorough preparation for trench fighting, undertook to train mainly for open combat, with the object from the start of vigorously forcing the offensive....

For the purpose of impressing our own doctrine upon officers, a training program was issued which laid great stress on open warfare methods and offensive action. The following is a pertinent extract from my instructions on this point:

> The above methods to be employed must remain and become distinctly our own. All instruction must contemplate the assumption of a vigorous offensive. This purpose will be emphasized in every phase of training until it becomes a settled habit of thought.

Intimately connected with the question of training for open warfare was the matter of rifle practice. The earliest of my cablegrams on this subject was in August, in which it was urged that thorough instruction in rifle practice should be carried on at home because of the difficulty of giving it in France:

> Study here shows value and desirability of retaining our existing small arms target practice course. In view of great difficulty in securing ranges in France due to density of the population and cultivation. Recommend as far as practicable the complete course be given in the United States before troops embark. Special emphasis should be placed on rapid fire.

The armies on the Western Front in the recent battles that I had witnessed had all but given up the use of the rifle. Machine guns, grenades, Stokes mortars, and one-pounders had become the main reliance of the average Allied soldier. These were all valuable weapons for specific purposes but they could not replace the combination of an efficient soldier and his rifle. Numerous instances were reported in the Allied armies of men chasing an individual enemy throwing grenades at him instead of using the rifle. Such was the effect of association that continuous effort was necessary to counteract this tendency among our own officers and men and inspire them with confidence in the efficacy of rifle fire.

[On September 5, 1918, Pershing issued the following instructions to his army, then preparing for its first major battle at St. Mihiel.]

Combat Instructions

> From a tactical point of view, the method of combat in trench warfare presents a marked contrast to that employed in open warfare, and the attempt by assaulting infantry to use trench warfare methods in an open warfare combat will be successful only at great cost. Trench warfare is marked by uniform formations, the regulation of space and time by higher commands down to the smallest details...fixed distances and intervals between units and individuals...little initiative....Open warfare is marked by...irregularity of formations, comparatively little regulation of space and time by higher commanders, the greatest possible use of the infantry's own fire power to enable it to get forward, variable distances and intervals between units and individuals...brief orders and the greatest possible use of individual initiative by all troops engaged in the action....The infantry commander must oppose machine guns by fire from his rifles, his automatics and his rifle grenades and must close with their crews under cover of this fire and of ground beyond their flanks....The success of every unit from the platoon to the division must be exploited to the fullest extent. Where strong resistance is encountered,

reënforcements must not be thrown in to make a frontal attack at this point, but must be pushed through gaps created by successful units, to attack these strong points in the flank or rear.

2. A "Doughboy" Describes the Fighting Front (1918)*

Of the two million young American men who served in the American Expeditionary Force, about half saw combat. Many of these troops had been raised on heroic stories about grandfathers and uncles who had fought in the Civil War, and they expected the war in France to provide the same kind of opportunities for glory that their fore- bears had found at Antietam and Shiloh, Bull Run and Fredericksburg. For the most part, they were bitterly disappointed when they discovered that modern warfare was a decidedly unheroic, dirty, impersonal, and bloody business. The following pas- sages, taken from the battlefield diary of a thirty-one-year-old draftee from upstate New York who was assigned to an engineering company, vividly convey one soldier's reactions to his baptism of fire. What aspects of combat did he find most remarkable? How does his description of warfare fit with General Pershing's expectations about the role of the individual rifleman and the tactics of mobility and "open warfare"?

Thursday, September 12, 1918. Hiked through dark woods. No lights allowed, guided by holding on the pack of the man ahead. Stumbled through underbrush for about half mile into an open field where we waited in soaking rain until about 10:00 P.M. We then started on our hike to the St. Mihiel [France] front, arriving on the crest of a hill at 1:00 A.M. I saw a sight which I shall never forget. It was the zero hour and in one instant the entire front as far as the eye could reach in either direction was a sheet of flame, while the heavy artillery made the earth quake. The barrage was so intense that for a time we could not make out whether the Americans or Germans were putting it over. After timing the interval between flash and report we knew that the heaviest artillery was less than a mile away and consequently it was ours. We waded through pools and mud across open lots into a woods on a hill and had to pitch tents in mud. Blankets all wet and we are soaked to the skin. Have carried full pack from 10:00 P.M. to 2:00 A.M., without a rest.... Despite the cannonading I slept until 8:00 A.M. and awoke to find every discharge of 14-inch artillery shaking our tent like a leaf. Remarkable how we could sleep. No breakfast.... The doughboys had gone over the top at 5:00 A.M. and the French were shelling the back areas toward Metz.... Firing is incessant, so is rain. See an air battle just before turning in.

Friday, September 13, 1918. Called at 3:00 a.m. Struck tents and started to hike at 5:00 a.m. with full packs and a pick. Put on gas mask at alert position and hiked about five miles to St. Jean, where we unslung full packs and went on about four miles further with short packs and picks. Passed several batteries and saw many dead horses who gave out at start of push. Our doughboys are still shoving and "Jerry" [the Germans] is dropping so many shells on road into no man's land that we

---

*From the diary of Eugene Kennedy. Courtesy of Eugene Kennedy Collection, Hoover Institution on War, Revolution, and Peace, Stanford University.

stayed back in field and made no effort to repair shell-torn road. Plenty of German prisoners being brought back....Guns booming all the time.

Saturday, September 14, 1918. Hiked up to same road again with rifle, belt, helmet, gas-mask, and pick....First time under shell fire. Major Judge's horse killed. Gibbs has a finger knocked off each hand [by a sniper's bullet] while burying some of our men killed in opening drive. Clothing, bandages, equipment of all sorts, dead horses and every kind of debris strewn all over....

Tuesday, September 17, 1918. Rolled packs and hiked with them up to road. Worked near town that is reduced to heap of stone. Trenches are 20 feet deep and in some places 15 feet across. The wire entanglement is beyond description. Several traps left by Germans. Man in our division had his arm blown off picking up a crucifix.

[Along with thousands of other doughboys, Kennedy was soon shifted from the St. Mihiel engagement to the major American battleground a few miles to the north, in the Argonne forest between the Meuse and Aire Rivers. Here he describes his role in this, the largest U.S. action of the war.]

Thursday, October 17, 1918. Struck tents at 8:00 A.M. and moved about four miles to Chatel. Pitched tents on a side hill so steep that we had to cut steps to ascend. Worked like hell to shovel out a spot to pitch tent on. Just across the valley in front of us about two hundred yards distant, there had occurred an explosion due to a mine planted by the "Bosche" [Germans] and set with a time fuse. It had blown two men (French), two horses, and the wagon into fragments....Arriving on the scene we found Quinn ransacking the wagon. It was full of grub. We each loaded a burlap bag with cans of condensed milk, peas, lobster, salmon, and bread. I started back...when suddenly another mine exploded, the biggest I ever saw. Rocks and dirt flew sky high. Quinn was hit in the knee and had to go to hospital....At 6:00 P.M. each of our four platoons left camp in units to go up front and throw three foot and one artillery bridge across the Aire River. On way to river we were heavily shelled and gassed....We put a bridge across 75-foot span....Third platoon men had to get into water and swim or stand in water to their necks. The toughest job we had so far.

Friday, October 18, 1918. Bright but cool. Men of third platoon who swam river are drying their clothes....Waiting for night to work under cover of darkness. Started up front at 6:00 P.M....Worked one half hour when "Jerry" shelled us so strong that we had to leave job. We could hear snipers' bullets sing past us and had to make our way back carefully along railroad track bank dodging shells every few steps. Gas so thick that masks had to be kept on, adding to the burden of carrying a rifle, pick, shovel, and hand saw. Had to run from one dug-out to another until it let up somewhat, when we made a break for road and hiked to camp about 3 kilometers, gas masks on most of the way, shells bursting both sides of road.

Monday, October 21, 1918. Fragment from shell struck mess-kit on my back....Equipment, both American and German, thrown everywhere, especially Hun helmets and belts of machine gunners....Went scouting...for narrow-gauge rails to replace the ones "Jerry" spoiled before evacuating. Negro engineers working on railroad same as at St. Mihiel, that's all they are good for....

Friday, November 1, 1918. Started out at 4:00 A.M. The drive is on. Fritz is coming back at us. Machine guns cracking, flares and Verry lights, artillery from both sides. A real war and we are walking right into the zone, ducking shells all the way. The artillery is nerve racking and we don't know from which angle "Jerry" will fire next. Halted behind shelter of railroad track just outside of Grand Pre after being forced back off main road by shell fire. Trees splintered like toothpicks. Machine gunners on top of railroad bank....."Jerry" drove Ewell and me into a two-by-four shell hole, snipers' bullets close.

Sunday, November 3, 1918. Many dead Germans along the road. One heap on a manure pile....Devastation everywhere. Our barrage has rooted up the entire territory like a ploughed field. Dead horses galore, many of them have a hind quarter cut off— the Huns need food. Dead men here and there. The sight I enjoy better than a dead German is to see heaps of them. Rain again. Couldn't keep rain out of our faces and it was pouring hard. Got up at midnight and drove stakes to secure shelter-half over us, pulled our wet blankets out of mud and made the bed all over again. Slept like a log with all my equipment in the open. One hundred forty-two planes sighted in evening.

Sunday, November 10, 1918. First day off in over two months....Took a bath and we were issued new underwear but the cooties [lice] got there first....The papers show a picture of the Kaiser entitled "William the Lost," and stating that he had abdicated. Had a good dinner. Rumor at night that armistice was signed. Some fellows discharged their arms in the courtyard, but most of us were too well pleased with dry bunk to get up.

F. The Struggle over the Peace Treaty

1. The Text of Article X (1919)*

Wilson regarded the League of Nations as the backbone of the Treaty of Versailles, and Article X of the League Covenant, which he had partly authored, as the heart of the League. He envisaged the members of the League constituting a kind of police force to prevent aggression. What weaknesses are contained in the wording of this article?

[The Members of the League undertake to respect and preserve, as against external aggression, the territorial integrity and existing political independence of all Members of the League. In case of any such aggression, or in case of any threat or danger of such aggression, the Council shall advise upon the means by which the obligation shall be fulfilled.

[All member nations were represented in the Assembly of the League of Nations; only the great powers (originally Britain, France, Italy, and Japan) were represented in the Council. The same general scheme was adopted by the United Nations in 1945.]

---

*Senate Executive Documents, 67th Cong., 4th sess. (1923), vol. 8, no. 348, p. 3339.

2. Wilson Testifies for Article X (1919)*

The already ominous mood of the Senate grew uglier when Wilson conspicuously snubbed that body in framing the peace. The Republican majority was led by the aristocratic Senator Henry Cabot Lodge of Massachusetts, who was also chairman of the potent Committee on Foreign Relations. He was determined to Republicanize and Americanize the pact by adding reservations that would adequately safeguard U.S. interests. To avert such a watering down, Wilson met with the entire Foreign Relations Committee at the White House on August 19, 1919, and underwent about three and a half hours of grilling. Much of the discussion revolved about Article X. How persuasive is Wilson's defense?

[*The President.*] Article X is in no respect of doubtful meaning, when read in the light of the Covenant as a whole. The Council of the League can only "advise upon" the means by which the obligations of that great article are to be given effect to. Unless the United States is a party to the policy or action in question, her own affirmative vote in the Council is necessary before any advice can be given, for a unanimous vote of the Council is required. If she is a party, the trouble is hers anyhow. And the unanimous vote of the Council is only advice in any case. Each Government is free to reject it if it pleases.

Nothing could have been made more clear to the [Paris] conference than the right of our Congress under our Constitution to exercise its independent judgment in all matters of peace and war. No attempt was made to question or limit that right.

The United States will, indeed, undertake under Article X to "respect and preserve as against external aggression the territorial integrity and existing political independence of all members of the League," and that engagement constitutes a very grave and solemn moral obligation. But it is a moral, not a legal, obligation, and leaves our Congress absolutely free to put its own interpretation upon it in all cases that call for action. It is binding in conscience only, not in law.

Article X seems to me to constitute the very backbone of the whole Covenant. Without it the League would be hardly more than an influential debating society. . . .

Senator [*Warren G.*] *Harding.* Right there, Mr. President, if there is nothing more than a moral obligation on the part of any member of the League, what avail Articles X and XI?

The President. Why, Senator, it is surprising that the question should be asked. If we undertake an obligation we are bound in the most solemn way to carry it out. . . . There is a national good conscience in such a matter. . . .

When I speak of a legal obligation, I mean one that specifically binds you to do a particular thing under certain sanctions. That is a legal obligation. Now a moral obligation is of course superior to a legal obligation, and, if I may say so, has a greater binding force.

Senate Documents, no. 76, 66th Cong., 1st sess. (August 19, 1919), vol. 13, pp. 6, 19.

[Never too respectful of the "bungalow-minded" members of the Senate, Wilson remarked several days later that Senator Harding, destined to be his successor, "had a disturbingly dull mind, and that it seemed impossible to get any explanation to lodge in it."]

3. The Lodge-Hitchcock Reservations (1919)[*]

Wilson finally agreed to accept mildly interpretative Senate reservations that the other powers would not have to approve. He balked, however, at the more restrictive terms of the fourteen Lodge reservations. These were made a part of the resolution of ratification and would require the assent of three of the four other major powers (Britain, France, Italy, Japan). To Wilson, such a course was unmanly and humiliating; besides, he detested Senator Lodge. He insisted that the Republican Lodge reservations, notably the one on Article X, devitalized the entire treaty. In the following, on the left appears the Lodge reservation to Article X, which Wilson resentfully rejected, and on the right appears the Democratic interpretative reservation, which Senator Hitchcock (the Senate minority leader) drafted after consulting Wilson.[†] This version Wilson was willing to accept. What are the main differences between the two versions? Are those differences substantial enough to justify Wilson's refusal to accept the Lodge reservation?

Lodge Reservation to Article X (November 1919)

The United States assumes no obligation to preserve the territorial integrity or political independence of any other country or to interfere in controversies between nations—whether members of the League or not—under the provisions of Article X, or to employ the military or naval forces of the United States under any article of the treaty for any purpose, unless in any particular case the Congress, which, under the Constitution, has the sole power to declare war or authorize the employment of the military or naval forces of the United States, shall by act or joint resolution so provide.

Hitchcock Reservation to Article X (November 1919)

That the advice mentioned in Article X of the covenant of the League which the Council may give to the member nations as to the employment of their naval and military forces is merely advice which each member nation is free to accept or reject according to the conscience and judgment of its then existing Government, and in the United States this advice can only be accepted by action of the Congress at the time in being, Congress alone under the Constitution of the United States having the power to declare war.

---

[*]From *Woodrow Wilson and the Great Betrayal* by Thomas A. Bailey. Copyright © 1945 by Thomas A. Bailey. Copyright renewed © 1973 by Thomas A. Bailey.
[†]The Hitchcock reservation follows almost verbatim a reservation that Wilson had himself secretly drafted in September 1919, on which Hitchcock based his. Ibid., p. 393.

4. Wilson Defeats Henry Cabot Lodge's Reservations (1919)*

The debate in the Senate ended in November 1919, and Lodge was ready for a vote on the Treaty of Versailles with his Fourteen Reservations attached. In general, these reaffirmed the United States' traditional or constitutional safeguards. But Wilson believed that if the odious Lodge reservations were voted down, the treaty would then be approved without "crippling" reservations. Yet the Democrats, now a minority, could not muster a simple majority, much less the two-thirds vote needed to approve a treaty. The naturally stubborn Wilson, shielded from disagreeable realities by his anxious wife, believed that the great body of public opinion was behind him and would prevail. He evidently had not been told, or would not believe, that public opinion was shifting around in favor of reservations. When the Democratic senator Hitchcock suggested compromise, Wilson sternly replied, "Let Lodge compromise." Mrs. Wilson tells the story. How does she describe the president's basic position?

All this time the fight for the reservations to the Covenant of the League was being pressed in the Senate. Deprived of Executive leadership because of the illness of my husband, friends of the Treaty were on the defensive. The ground gained on the Western tour had been gradually lost until things were worse than when he started. Friends, including such a valued and persuasive friend as Mr. Bernard M. Baruch, begged Mr. Wilson to accept a compromise, saying "half a loaf is better than no bread." I cannot be unsympathetic with them, for in a moment of weakness I did the same. In my anxiety for the one I loved best in the world, the long-drawn-out fight was eating into my very soul, and I felt nothing mattered but to get the Treaty ratified, even with those reservations.

On November 19th the Senate was to vote on the reservations. Senator Hitchcock came to tell me that unless the Administration forces accepted them, the Treaty would be beaten—the struggle having narrowed down to a personal fight against the President by Lodge and his supporters. In desperation I went to my husband. "For my sake," I said, "won't you accept these reservations and get this awful thing settled?"

He turned his head on the pillow and stretching out his hand to take mine answered in a voice I shall never forget: "Little girl, don't you desert me; that I cannot stand. Can't you see that I have no moral right to accept any change in a paper I have signed without giving to every other signatory, even the Germans, the right to do the same thing? It is not I that will not accept; it is the Nation's honor that is at stake."

His eyes looked luminous as he spoke, and I knew that he was right. He went on quietly: "Better a thousand times to go down fighting than to dip your colours to dishonorable compromise."

I felt like one of his betrayers to have ever doubted. Rejoining Senator Hitchcock outside, I told him that for the first time I had seen the thing clearly and I would never ask my husband again to do what would be manifestly dishonorable. When I went back to the President's room, he dictated a letter to Senator Hitchcock,

---

*Edith B. Wilson, *My Memoir* (1939), pp. 296–297. Copyright 1938, 1939 by Edith Bolling Wilson.

saying: "In my opinion the resolution in that form [embodying the reservations] does not provide for ratification but rather for nullification of the Treaty....I trust that all true friends of the Treaty will refuse to support the Lodge resolution."

That same day the Senate voted. The Administration forces, voting against ratification with the Lodge reservations, defeated it. The vote was then on the ratification of the Treaty without reservations—the Treaty as Mr. Wilson had brought it from France. The result was defeat.

When the word came from the Capitol, I felt I could not bear it and that the shock might be serious for my husband. I went to his bedside and told him the fatal news. For a few moments he was silent, and then he said: "All the more reason I must get well and try again to bring this country to a sense of its great opportunity and greater responsibility."

G. The Treaty in Global Perspective

1. Germany Protests (1919)[*]

Exhausted from four years of brutal warfare and assuaged by Wilson's calls for a just peace, the German people expelled their bellicose Kaiser and laid down their arms in November of 1918. Wilson's moral leadership, inspiring as it was to millions of war-weary Europeans, held little sway over the hard-nosed prime ministers of Britain and France, David Lloyd George and Georges Clemenceau. The final version of the treaty presented to the German delegation ignored the American president's appeals for restraint. It called on Germany to disarm, pay steep reparations, and accept full responsibility for starting the war. German representatives, who had pinned their hopes on Wilson's idealistic pronouncements, were understandably dismayed. What are the German delegation's main complaints about the treaty?

I have the honour to transmit to you herewith the observations of the German Delegation on the draft Treaty of Peace.[†] We came to Versailles in the expectation of receiving a peace proposal based on the agreed principles. We were firmly resolved to do everything in our power with a view to fulfilling the grave obligations which we had undertaken. We hoped for the peace of justice which had been promised to us. We were aghast when we read in that document the demands made upon us by the victorious violence of our enemies. The more deeply we penetrate[d] into the

---

[*]Arthur S. Link, ed. *The Papers of Woodrow Wilson* (Princeton, NJ: Princeton University Press, 1978), vol. 59, pp. 579–581.

[†]"Observations of the German Delegation on the Conditions of Peace," printed in U.S. Department of State, *Papers Relating to the Foreign Relations of the United States: The Paris Peace Conference, 1919*, vol. 6, pp. 800–901. This document begins with a lengthy preface aimed at showing the unjust and unfair nature of the peace treaty by contrasting it with numerous quotations from the speeches and other public statements of the Allied leaders, especially Wilson, both before and after the Armistice. The main body of the document sets forth in great detail the German government's comments on the treaty and its counterproposals to bring about a peace more acceptable to Germany. Brockdorff-Rantzau well summarizes the main points of the document in the above letter. For a discussion of the immediate background of the "Observations," see Klaus Schwabe, *Woodrow Wilson, Revolutionary Germany, and Peacemaking, 1918–1919* (Chapel Hill: University of North Carolina Press, 1985), pp. 356–362.

spirit of this Treaty, the more convinced we became of the impossibility of carrying it out. The exactions of this Treaty are more than the German people can bear....

Although the exaction of the cost of the war has been expressly renounced, yet Germany,...cut in pieces and weakened, must declare herself ready in principle to bear all the war expenses of her enemies, which would exceed many times over the total amount of German State and private assets. Meanwhile her enemies demand in excess of the agreed conditions reparation for damage suffered by their civil population, and in this connexion Germany must also go bail for her allies. The sum to be paid is to be fixed by our enemies unilaterally and to admit of subsequent modification and increase. No limit is fixed save the capacity of the German people for payment, determined not by their standard of life but solely by their capacity to meet the demands of their enemies by their labour. The German people would thus be condemned to perpetual slave labour.

In spite of these exorbitant demands, the reconstruction of our economic life is at the same time rendered impossible. We must surrender our merchant fleet. We are to renounce all foreign securities. We are to hand over to our enemies our property in all German enterprises abroad, even in the countries of our allies....

Even in internal affairs we are to give up the right of self-determination. The International Reparations Commission receives dictatorial powers over the whole life of our people in economic and cultural matters. Its authority extends far beyond that which the Emperor, the German Federal Council and the Reichstag combined ever possessed within the territory of the Empire. This Commission has unlimited control over the economic life of the State, of communities and of individuals. Further the entire educational and sanitary system depends on it. It can keep the whole German people in mental thralldom. In order to increase the payments due by the thrall, the Commission can hamper measures for the social protection of the German worker.

In other spheres also Germany's sovereignty is abolished. Her chief waterways are subjected to international administration; she must construct in her territory such canals and railways as her enemies wish; she must agree to treaties, the contents of which are unknown to her, to be concluded by her enemies with the new States on the east, even when they concern her own frontiers. The German people is excluded from the League of Nations to which is entrusted all work of common interest to the world.

Thus must a whole people sign the decree for its own proscription, nay, its own death sentence.

2. Jan Christiaan Smuts Predicts Disaster (1919)[*]

Some observers feared that the harsh provisions of the treaty would eventually lead to resumed hostilities on the European mainland. None was more prescient than the future prime minister of South Africa, Jan Christiaan Smuts, who predicted that "this Peace may well become an even greater disaster to the world than the war was."

---

[*]Arthur S. Link, ed., *The Papers of Woodrow Wilson* (Princeton, NJ: Princeton University Press, 1978), vol. 59, pp. 149–150.

He laid out his concerns in the following letter to Woodrow Wilson. What were his chief objections to the treaty? Did subsequent events confirm his fears?

The more I have studied the Peace Treaty as a whole, the more I dislike it. The combined effect of the territorial and reparation clauses is to make it practically impossible for Germany to carry out the provisions of the Treaty. And then the occupation clauses come in to plant the French on the Rhine indefinitely, even beyond the already far too long period of fifteen years, under an undefined regime of martial law. East and West blocks of Germans are put under their historic enemies. Under this Treaty Europe will know no peace; and the undertaking to defend France against aggression may at any time bring the United States also into the fire.

I am grieved beyond words that such should be the result of our statesmanship. I admit it was hard to appear to fight for the German case with our other Allies, especially with devastated France. But now that the Germans can state their own case, I pray you will use your unrivalled power and influence to make the final Treaty a more moderate and reasonable document. I fear there may be a temptation to waive aside objections which will be urged by the Germans, but which will be supported by the good sense and conscience of most moderate people. I hope this temptation will be resisted and that drastic revision will be possible even at the eleventh hour.

Democracy is looking to you who have killed Prussianism—the silent masses who have suffered mutely appeal to you to save them from the fate to which Europe seems now to be lapsing.

Forgive my importunity; but I feel the dreadful burden resting on you, and write from motives of pure sympathy.

3. Ho Chi Minh Petitions for Rights (1919)[*]

Wilson's Fourteen Points—particularly his eloquent appeal for self-determination—drew applause from Europe's colonies, many of which sent delegates to Paris to make their case for independence. One such hopeful was a young Vietnamese nationalist who called himself "Nguyen the Patriot," known to later generations of Americans as the Vietcong leader Ho Chi Minh. Decades before he led Vietnamese communists in a protracted war against France and the United States, Ho drafted a measured appeal for reform in French Indochina. Seeking swift economic recovery after years of warfare, France had no intention of relaxing its grip on the resource-rich colony; preoccupied with more pressing matters in the negotiations, neither Britain nor the United States saw fit to acknowledge Vietnamese claims. What did Ho Chi Minh hope to achieve by submitting the petition? How might subsequent events have turned out differently had France honored these requests?

With the victory of the Allies, all subject peoples are trembling with hope as they consider the prospect of the era of justice and law which is to begin for them

---

[*]Robert Joseph Gowen, "Ho Chi Minh in the Paris Peace Conference of 1919: A Documentary Footnote," *International Studies,* vol. 12, no. 1 (January 1973), pp. 134–135.

by virtue of the solemn and precise commitments which the Allied Powers have made before the whole world in the struggle of Civilization against Barbarism.

In the expectation that the principle of nationality will cease to be an ideal and become a reality by an effective recognition of the sacred duty of all nations to determine their own futures, the people of the ancient Empire of Annam, now known as French Indo-China, present to the noble Governments of the *Entente* in general, and to the honourable French Government in particular, the following humble demands:

(1) A general amnesty for all native political prisoners;
(2) Reform of Indo-Chinese justice by granting to the native population the same judicial guarantees as those possessed by the Europeans and the complete and definitive elimination of Courts "of exception," which are instruments of terror and oppression against the most decent and respectable segment of the Annamite people;
(3) Freedom of the Press and of opinion;
(4) Freedom of association and assembly;
(5) Freedom to emigrate and to travel abroad;
(6) Academic and creative freedom for the technical and professional schools for the native population in all the Provinces;
(7) Replacement of rule by decree by the rule of law;
(8) Permanent representation in the French Parliament by elected natives in order to keep it informed of native aspirations.

The Annamite people, in presenting the demands enumerated above, rely on the sense of world justice of all the Powers and commend themselves in particular to the benevolence of the noble French nation, which holds their destiny in its hands and which, being a Republic, is deemed to have taken them under its protection. In demanding the protection of the French people, the Annamite people do not think that they have abased themselves. On the contrary they make the demand with pride, for they know that the French nation represents liberty and justice and will never renounce its sublime ideal of universal brotherhood. Accordingly, hearing the voice of the oppressed, the French nation will do its duty regarding France and humanity.

Thought Provokers

1. What were the good and bad features of interlocking directorates? Should private bankers have been permitted to write the Federal Reserve Act? To what extent did Wilson's tariff and banking legislation conform to the political philosophy defined in his campaign of 1912 (see pp. 543–545)?
2. Was the United States, before it became a belligerent in 1917, truly neutral with respect to the Great War that broke out in Europe in 1914?
3. To what extent were Wilson's own policies to blame for the United States' entry into the war? Could—or should—the confrontation with Germany have been avoided?

4. Why was there more anti-enemy hysteria in the United States in 1917–1918 than during World War II, when the nation was in graver danger? Why did conscientious objectors fare so badly? Why did the government mount such a vigorous propaganda effort?

5. Were the doughboys well prepared for the war they found in France? What was most surprising about the conditions they encountered?

6. What were Wilson's purposes in announcing the Fourteen Points? Why did the announcement come so late in the war (in January 1918, nine months after U.S. entry)?

7. Would the world have been different if the United States had accepted Article X and signed the Treaty of Versailles? In the last analysis, who was more responsible for keeping the United States out of the League of Nations, Wilson or Lodge?

8. Why did some international leaders criticize the Treaty of Versailles? Why did these objections carry so little weight in 1919? What were the treaty's consequences?

30

American Life in the "Roaring Twenties," 1920–1929

You are all a lost generation.

*Attributed by Ernest Hemingway
to Gertrude Stein, 1926*

Prologue: Disappointed at the results of their intervention in the European war, Americans turned inward in the postwar decade. They repudiated all things allegedly "foreign," including radical political ideas and, especially, immigrants. A revived Ku Klux Klan vented its hatred on Catholic and Jewish newcomers, as well as on blacks. Three centuries of virtually unrestricted immigration to the United States came to a halt with the passage of the restrictive Immigration Act of 1924. The prohibition "experiment" divided "wets" from "drys." In religion, fundamentalists warred against modernists, most famously in the Scopes "monkey trial" in Tennessee. "Flappers" flamboyantly flaunted the new freedom of young women, one of whose champions was Margaret Sanger, pioneer of the birth control movement. Meanwhile, a mass consumption economy began to flower fully, typified by the booming automobile industry and the emergence of advertising and the huge entertainment industries of radio and the movies. A literary renaissance blossomed, led by F. Scott Fitzgerald, William Faulkner, Sherwood Anderson, Eugene O'Neill, Sinclair Lewis, and Ernest Hemingway. Many of these writers sharply criticized the materialist culture of the decade, symbolized by rampant speculation on the stock market, which crashed in 1929. Religious conservatives and liberals argued ever more bitterly about biblical inerrancy as fundamentalists gathered strength.

A. The Great Immigration Debate

1. Theodore Roosevelt Preaches "Americanism" (1915)[*]

In the early years of the twentieth century, Americans again confronted the challenge that had been emblazoned on their national seal since 1776: E Pluribus Unum— Out of Many, One. Between 1901 and 1920, some 14.5 million immigrants poured

---

[*]Theodore Roosevelt, "Americanism," an address delivered before the Knights of Columbus, Carnegie Hall, New York, October 12, 1915; printed in Philip Davis, ed., *Immigration and Americanization: Selected Readings* (Boston: Ginn and Company, 1920), pp. 648–649.

into the United States. The vast majority of these predominantly Catholic and Jewish newcomers came from southern and eastern Europe. Many old-stock Americans feared that these so-called "new" immigrants would not fully assimilate into American life. Former president Theodore Roosevelt addressed this topic in a widely circulated statement against "hyphenated Americans." Is he perceptive or paranoid when he speaks of hyphenated Americans as possibly "bringing this nation to ruin"?

There is no room in this country for hyphenated Americanism. When I refer to hyphenated Americans, I do not refer to naturalized Americans. Some of the very best Americans I have ever known were naturalized Americans, Americans born abroad. But a hyphenated American is not an American at all. This is just as true of the man who puts "native" before the hyphen as of the man who puts German or Irish or English or French before the hyphen. Americanism is a matter of the spirit and of the soul. Our allegiance must be purely to the United States. We must unsparingly condemn any man who holds any other allegiance. But if he is heartily and singly loyal to this Republic, then no matter where he was born, he is just as good an American as any one else.

The one absolutely certain way of bringing this nation to ruin, of preventing all possibility of its continuing to be a nation at all, would be to permit it to become a tangle of squabbling nationalities, an intricate knot of German-Americans, Irish-Americans, English-Americans, French-Americans, Scandinavian-Americans or Italian-Americans, each preserving its separate nationality, each at heart feeling more sympathy with Europeans of that nationality, than with the other citizens of the American Republic. The men who do not become Americans and nothing else are hyphenated Americans; and there ought to be no room for them in this country. The man who calls himself an American citizen and who yet shows by his actions that he is primarily the citizen of a foreign land, plays a thoroughly mischievous part in the life of our body politic. He has no place here; and the sooner he returns to the land to which he feels his real heart-allegiance, the better it will be for every good American. There is no such thing as a hyphenated American who is a good American. The only man who is a good American is the man who is an American and nothing else.

2. Randolph Bourne Defends Cultural Pluralism (1916)*

Even as influential figures such as Theodore Roosevelt demanded cultural unity, others such as the radical social critic Randolph Bourne celebrated diversity. Rejecting the metaphor of the "melting pot"—which supposedly blended all the various cultural ingredients that immigrants brought with them into a single, uniform national identity—Bourne thought of America as a symphony, where each instrument contributed its distinctive part to the harmony and beauty of the whole. How realistic is Bourne's vision that ethnic differences are compatible with national cohesion?

---

*Randolph S. Bourne, "Trans-National America," *Atlantic Monthly* 118 (July 1916): 87, 90, 91, 93.

We have needed the new peoples—the order of the German and Scandinavian, the turbulence of the Slav and Hun—to save us from our own stagnation....The foreign cultures have not been melted down or run together, made into some homogeneous Americanism, but have remained distinct but coöperating to the greater glory and benefit, not only of themselves but of all the native "Americanism" around them.

What we emphatically do not want is that these distinctive qualities should be washed out into a tasteless, colorless fluid of uniformity. Already we have far too much of this insipidity,—masses of people who are cultural half-breeds, neither assimilated Anglo-Saxons nor nationals of another culture....

...[A] truer cultural sense would have told us that it is not the self-conscious cultural nuclei that sap at our American life, but these fringes. It is not the Jew who sticks proudly to the faith of his fathers and boasts of that venerable culture of his who is dangerous to America, but the Jew who has lost the Jewish fire and become a mere elementary, grasping animal. It is not the Bohemian who supports the Bohemian schools in Chicago whose influence is sinister, but the Bohemian who has made money and has got into ward politics. Just so surely as we tend to disintegrate these nuclei of nationalistic culture do we tend to create hordes of men and women without a spiritual country, cultural outlaws, without taste, without standards but those of the mob. We sentence them to live on the most rudimentary planes of American life....This is the cultural wreckage of our time, and it is from the fringes of the Anglo-Saxon as well as the other stocks that it falls. America has as yet no impelling integrating force. It makes too easily for this detritus of cultures. In our loose, free country, no constraining national purpose, no tenacious folk-tradition and folk-style hold the people to a line....

America is a unique sociological fabric, and it bespeaks poverty of imagination not to be thrilled at the incalculable potentialities of so novel a union of men. To seek no other goal than the weary old nationalism,—belligerent, exclusive, inbreeding, the poison of which we are witnessing now in Europe,—is to make patriotism a hollow sham, and to declare that, in spite of our boastings, America must ever be a follower and not a leader of nations....

The failure of the melting-pot, far from closing the great American democratic experiment, means that is has only just begun. Whatever American nationalism turns out to be, we see already that it will have a color richer and more exciting than our ideal has hitherto encompassed. In a world which has dreamed of internationalism, we find that we have all unawares been building up the first international nation. The voices which have cried for a tight and jealous nationalism of the European pattern are failing. From that ideal, however valiantly and disinterestedly it has been set for us, time and tendency have moved us further and further away. What we have achieved has been rather a cosmopolitan federation of national colonies, of foreign cultures, from whom the sting of devastating competition has been removed. America is already the world-federation in miniature, the continent where for the first time in history has been achieved that miracle of hope, the peaceful living side by side, with character substantially preserved, of the most heterogeneous peoples under the sun. Nowhere else has such contiguity been anything but the breeder of misery. Here, notwithstanding our tragic failures of adjustment, the outlines are already too clear not to give us a new vision and a new orientation of the American mind in the world.

3. Samuel Gompers Favors Restriction (1924)*

Samuel Gompers, the nation's most prominent spokesman for organized labor, long favored immigration restrictions. Along with many other labor activists, he insisted that unrestricted immigration harmed the American worker by providing a steady flow of cheap foreign labor, thus depressing wage rates and standards of living for workers already in the country. Until 1924 Gompers avoided linking the cause of labor with the ethnocentric arguments of the nativists. Here, however, he conspicuously combines the two—borrowing extensively from Gino Speranza, one of the most outspoken advocates of ethnic quotas. Why might Gompers have decided to take advantage of the ethnic issue?

The United States enacts immigration legislation for certain definite reasons, some of which are: First, protection of American standards of living against attack by low-wage workers coming in masses from countries where the conditions of labor are vastly inferior to the conditions of labor in the United States; second, prevention of an influx of persons who, because of physical, mental or moral conditions, are undesirable either as residents or citizens; third, safeguarding American citizenship and American social and political institutions against the undermining influence of immigrant masses either hostile to those institutions or unable to understand them. All of these reasons are worthy and valid.... Every effort to enact immigration legislation must expect to meet a number of hostile forces, and, in particular, two hostile forces of considerable strength. One of these is composed of corporation employers who desire to employ physical strength ("broad backs") at the lowest possible wage and who prefer a rapidly revolving labor supply at low wages to a regular supply of American wage earners at fair wages. The other is composed of racial groups in the United States who oppose all restrictive legislation because they want the doors left open for an influx of their countrymen regardless of the menace to the people of their adopted country....

On this always delicate but none the less important phase of the question there has been an interesting contribution by Mr. Gino Speranza, who has written a series of articles. Mr. Speranza's remarks are so appropriate and so concise that a somewhat generous quotation seems advisable:

> That a democracy such as ours should want a preponderance of citizens as nearly resembling in character, history, political and social antecedents as those of the historic dominant stock which founded and gave life to the nation, is neither unfairly discriminatory, nor intolerant, nor narrowminded.... The greater the homogeneity of its citizenship the better knit and spiritually united will be this or any other democracy. On the other hand, large admixtures of aliens far removed in their history, antecedents and ideals from those of the original dominant stock unavoidably place too great a strain not only on the assimilative powers of any nation but on the political, social and spiritual life of any democracy....
>
> Personally I believe that the danger point in too large an admixture of too historically and culturally differing elements from the historic American stock has already been reached in this country. While such evidence is too voluminous to be summarized here, I may dwell on one aspect of it which has received practically no attention in our study of the alien masses in our midst: The PERSISTENCE of RACIAL CHARACTERISTICS....

---

*From Samuel Gompers, "America Must Not Be Overwhelmed," *American Federationist* 31, April 1924, pp. 313–317.

...That *physical* racial characteristics persist, most of us, I think, are ready to recognize even without the confirmation of biology and ethnology. But that mental and *moral* racial characteristics persist with equal tenacity most of us have yet to learn.

By mental and moral racial characteristics I mean those qualities, good and bad, those particular traits and mental and moral points of view which differentiate, and naturally divide off humanity into large groupings or nations or peoples who think and feel very much alike within the group. They are the result, partly of environmental forces operating for long periods, and largely of heredity, habits and special historical experience. It is such mental and moral "bent" which profoundly affects and differentiates political thought, moral and religious outlook, and the social and spiritual ideals of the various racial or national groupings. In other words, it is the mental and moral outlook which very largely shapes the various forms of government, the various social systems and the various religious beliefs. Stated in the simplest form: It is mind and will which make history....

For a good many reasons, industrial, constitutional and political, the viewpoint set forth by Mr. Speranza is worthy of consideration and should be pondered by every American who has a desire for the perpetuation of American institutions....

...However much Americans may wish well for peoples in other lands and however much they may be and are willing to contribute to assist downtrodden and despoiled peoples in other lands, they are unwilling that the United States should be made a dumping ground for the despairing hordes of ruined and bankrupt countries throughout the world. It is better far that if necessity forces matters to such an undesirable climax that there be at least one country in the world where decent standards prevail than that there be no such country....

There is no reason in the world why the United States should not, if it desires, exercise a controlling and determining voice in regard to immigrants. There is no reason why there should not be a selection as to nationality, if the United States wished to make such a selection, nor would such a selection, if made, imply any unfriendly discrimination against those nationalities not invited. It would imply that the United States wished to maintain certain characteristics and that in the event of certain racial mixtures those characteristics could not be maintained.

What the United States desires in the present instance is a carefully selected immigration of small numbers of persons most likely to become citizens and most likely to join intelligently and willingly in the effort to maintain standards of working conditions, standards of life and living and standards of citizenship, which have been built up through decades of hard and persistent effort. The labor movement would, if it could, prevent all immigration for five years. This it can not do, but it does support with all of its strength the effort to restrict as much as possible the immigration of the immediate future.

4. Two Views of Immigration Restriction (1921, 1924)

The following cartoons capture the conflicting perspectives that fueled the historical debate over immigration—and that continue to color the national conversation today. Those who favored restriction considered the United States perfectly justified in refusing to become the bottomless sink into which other countries might cast off their least productive inhabitants. Those who criticized restriction saw profound irony, if not outright hypocrisy, in a nation of immigrants that closed its doors to those who simply sought a better life in the New World. To what extent are these cartoons, and the sentiments they represent, guilty of oversimplifying a complex problem?

That immigration problem again!

Pease in Newark News

You can't come in. The quota for 1620 is full.

B. The Reconstituted Ku Klux Klan

1. Tar-Bucket Terror in Texas (1921)*

The swelling anti-immigrant sentiment of the war era was also partly responsible for the revival of the Ku Klux Klan in the 1920s. The bedsheets, hoods, and lashes were old, but the principles, aside from hatred of blacks, were new. The revamped Klan was anti-foreign, anti-Catholic, anti-Jewish, and anticommunist. It professed to uphold Christianity, the Bible, prohibition, clean movies, the law, the Constitution, public schools, the home, and marriage vows. It undertook to persuade unchaste people, especially women, to mend their ways by giving them a dose of the lash and a coat of tar and feathers. The press reported in 1921 that an African American bellboy had been branded on the forehead with the letters KKK; that in Florida an Episcopal archdeacon had been whipped, tarred, and feathered; and that there had been forty-three tar-bucket parties in Texas in six months. The Houston Chronicle *here addresses a protest to the Klan members. Does it register any sympathy for the Klan? What does it see as the Klan's greatest outrages?*

Boys, you'd better disband. You'd better take your sheets, your banners, your masks, your regalia, and make one fine bonfire.

Without pausing to argue over the objects you have in mind, it is sufficient to say that your methods are hopelessly wrong. Every tradition of social progress is against them. They are opposed to every principle on which this Government is founded. They are out of keeping with civilized life.

You seem to forget that the chief advantage of democracy is to let in the daylight, to prevent secret punishment, to insure a fair hearing for every person, to make impossible that kind of tyranny which can only flourish in the dark.

The newspapers of last Sunday were disgraced with the account of four illegal, unnecessary, and wholly ineffectual outrages. Without assuming that your organization was directly responsible for any or all of them, it was, in large measure, indirectly responsible. Your organization has made the thought of secretly organized violence fashionable.

It matters not who can get into your organization or who is kept out; any group of men can ape your disguise, your methods, and your practices. If outrages occur for which you are not accountable—and they will—you have no way of clearing yourselves, except by throwing off your disguise and invoking that publicity you have sought to deny. Your role of masked violence, of purification by stealth, of reform by terrorism is an impossible one. Your position is such that you must accept responsibility for every offense which smacks of disguised tyranny....

Who was responsible for the Tenaha case, where a woman was stripped naked and then covered with tar and feathers? Has there ever been any crime committed in this state so horrible or one that brought such shame on Texas? Is there any member of the Ku Klux Klan in Texas so pure and holy that he can condemn even the

---

*Houston Chronicle, quoted in Literary Digest 70 (August 27, 1921): 12.

vilest woman to such disgrace and torture? Masked men did it, and the world was told in press dispatches that they were the hooded Klansmen of Texas.

If that outrage was done by Ku Klux Klansmen, then every decent man who was inveigled into the order should resign immediately. If it was not the work of the real order, its members should disband because of this one act, if for no other reason.

The Ku Klux Klan, as recently rejuvenated, serves no useful purpose. On the other hand, it makes room for innumerable abuses. The community—meaning the whole nation—is against it, and the community will grow more resolutely against it as time goes on. Those who brought it into being, no matter what their intentions, would better bring about its dissolution before the storm breaks.

2. A Methodist Editor Clears the Klan (1923)*

The brutal excesses of the Ku Klux Klan (or its imitators) brought it into disrepute, and by the mid-1920s it was rapidly disintegrating. For several years, however, with its hundreds of thousands of members, it remained a potent political force. The Reverend Bob Shuler (Methodist), editor of Shuler's Magazine *and the fundamentalist pastor of a large Los Angeles church, published the following advertisement in the Eugene (Oregon) Register. What biases formed the basis of his pro-Klan views? Is vigilantism ever justified? How valid is the author's comparison of the Klan with the Knights of Columbus, an American Roman Catholic society for men, founded in 1882?*

This editor has repeatedly affirmed privately and publicly that he is not a member of the Ku Klux or any other secret organization. But when it comes to secret societies, he sees no difference absolutely between the Ku Klux and many others, the Knights of Columbus, for instance. The Knights of Columbus has an oath, just as binding, or more so, than the Ku Klux oath. Moreover, the Knights of Columbus' oath is not one-half so American as the Ku Klux. If you charge that the Ku Klux has put over mobs, I answer that the Knights of Columbus has put over two mobs to where any other secret organization on earth has ever put over one.

This editor has been favored recently by being permitted to look over documentary evidence as to the tenets, principles, and aims of the Ku Klux Klan. He finds that this organization stands with positive emphasis for Americanism as opposed to foreign idealism; for the principles of the Christian religion as opposed to Roman Catholicism and infidelity; for the American public schools and for the placing of the Holy Bible in the schoolrooms of this nation; for the enforcement of the laws upon the statute books and for a wholesome respect for the Constitution of the United States; for the maintenance of virtue among American women, sobriety and honor among American men, and for the eradication of all agencies and influences that would threaten the character of our children. So the principles of the Klan are not so damnable as pictured, it would seem.

This organization is opposing the most cunning, deceitful, and persistent enemy that Americanism and Protestant Christianity have ever had—the Jesuits. Speaking

---

*Eugene Register, *quoted in* Literary Digest *76 (January 20, 1923): 18–19.

of "invisible empires," of forces that creep through the night and do their dirty work under cover, influences that are set going in the secret places of darkness, the Jesuits are the finished product. They have burned, killed, defamed, blackmailed, and ruined their enemies by the hundreds. History reeks with it. Though I disagree with the logic of the Klan, the members of that organization declare that they can only fight such a foe by using his own fire.

As to the charge that the Ku Klux Klan has functioned in mob violence in their efforts to correct conditions, I have this to say: I am convinced that most of the mobs reported have not been ordered and directed by the Klan as an organization. I am moreover convinced that many of them have been put over by forces opposed to the Klan and for the purpose of seeking to place the guilt for mob rule upon the Klan. The most of these mobs have been, according to investigation, not Ku Klux mobs at all, but gatherings of indignant citizens, bent on correcting conditions that the officers of the law refused to correct. The way to cause the Ku Klux to retire from the field is for the officers of the law to take that field and occupy it.

The Ku Klux has the same right to exist so long as it obeys the law that any other organization has. We have not heard of any investigation of the Knights of Columbus, although their un-American oaths are historic and their mob activities have been repeatedly published and heralded from platforms far and near.

C. The Wets Versus the Drys

1. A German Observes Bootlegging (1928)*

Before the end of World War I, most of the states had decreed the prohibition of alcoholic beverages. Nationwide prohibition, authorized by the Eighteenth Amendment in 1919, resulted largely from the spirit of self-sacrifice aroused by the war. A militant majority was thus able to force its will upon a large and vocal minority, especially in the big cities, where the foreign-born population was accustomed to the regular consumption of alcohol. The "Sea Devil," Felix von Luckner, a German naval hero who had destroyed some $25 million worth of Allied commerce with his raider the Seeadler (Sea Eagle) during World War I, visited the United States as a lecturer and recorded his curious experiences with alcohol. What did he see as the good and bad features of prohibition? What conditions made enforcement peculiarly difficult?

My first experience with the ways of prohibition came while we were being entertained by friends in New York. It was bitterly cold. My wife and I rode in the rumble seat of the car, while the American and his wife, bundled in furs, sat in front. Having wrapped my companion in pillows and blankets so thoroughly that only her nose showed, I came across another cushion that seemed to hang uselessly on the side. "Well," I thought, "this is a fine pillow; since everyone else is so warm and cozy, I might as well do something for my own comfort. This certainly does no one

*From *This Was America,* ed. Oscar Handlin (Cambridge, MA: Harvard University Press, 1949), pp. 495–496.

any good hanging on the wall." Sitting on it, I gradually noticed a dampness in the neighborhood that soon mounted to a veritable flood. The odor of fine brandy told me I had burst my host's peculiar liquor flask.

In time, I learned that not everything in America was what it seemed to be. I discovered, for instance, that a spare tire could be filled with substances other than air, that one must not look deeply into certain binoculars, and that the Teddy Bears that suddenly acquired tremendous popularity among the ladies very often had hollow metal stomachs.

"But," it might be asked, "where do all these people get the liquor?" Very simple. Prohibition has created a new, a universally respected, a well-beloved, and a very profitable occupation, that of the bootlegger who takes care of the importation of the forbidden liquor. Everyone knows this, even the powers of government. But this profession is beloved because it is essential, and it is respected because its pursuit is clothed with an element of danger and with a sporting risk....

Yet it is undeniable that prohibition has in some respects been signally successful. The filthy saloons, the gin mills which formerly flourished on every corner and in which the laborer once drank off half his wages, have disappeared. Now he can instead buy his own car, and ride off for a weekend or a few days with his wife and children in the country or at the sea. But, on the other hand, a great deal of poison and methyl alcohol has taken the place of the good old pure whiskey. The number of crimes and misdemeanors that originated in drunkenness has declined. But by contrast, a large part of the population has become accustomed to disregard and to violate the law without thinking. The worst is that, precisely as a consequence of the law, the taste for alcohol has spread ever more widely among the youth. The sporting attraction of the forbidden and the dangerous leads to violations. My observations have convinced me that many fewer would drink were it not illegal.

2. Fiorello La Guardia Pillories Prohibition (1926)*

Wholesale violations of the prohibition law became so notorious that in 1926 a Senate judiciary subcommittee held extended hearings. It uncovered shocking conditions. Stocky, turbulent, fiery Fiorello ("the Little Flower") La Guardia, then a congressman from New York and later the controversial reform mayor of New York City, expressed characteristically vigorous views. Which of his statistics seem least susceptible to proof? Which of his arguments would probably carry the most weight with the average taxpayer?

It is impossible to tell whether prohibition is a good thing or a bad thing. It has never been enforced in this country.

There may not be as much liquor in quantity consumed to-day as there was before prohibition, but there is just as much alcohol.

At least 1,000,000 quarts of liquor is consumed each day in the United States. In my opinion such an enormous traffic in liquor could not be carried on without the

---

*Hearings Before the Subcommittee of the Committee on the Judiciary, U.S. Senate, Sixty-ninth Congress, First Session (April 5–24, 1926), on . . . Bills to Amend the National Prohibition Act, vol. 1, pp. 649–651.

knowledge, if not the connivance, of the officials entrusted with the enforcement of the law.

I am for temperance; that is why I am for modification.

I believe that the percentage of whisky drinkers in the United States now is greater than in any other country of the world. Prohibition is responsible for that....

At least $1,000,000,000 a year is lost to the National Government and the several states and counties in excise taxes. The liquor traffic is going on just the same. This amount goes into the pockets of bootleggers and into the pockets of the public officials in the shape of graft....

I will concede that the saloon was odious, but now we have delicatessen stores, pool rooms, drug stores, millinery shops, private parlors, and 57 other varieties of speakeasies selling liquor and flourishing.

I have heard of $2,000 a year prohibition agents who run their own cars with liveried chauffeurs.

It is common talk in my part of the country that from $7.50 to $12 a case is paid in graft from the time the liquor leaves the 12-mile limit until it reaches the ultimate consumer. There seems to be a varying market price for this service created by the degree of vigilance or the degree of greed of the public officials in charge.

It is my calculation that at least $1,000,000 a day is paid in graft and corruption to Federal, state, and local officers. Such a condition is not only intolerable, but it is demoralizing and dangerous to organized government....

The Prohibition Enforcement Unit has entirely broken down. It is discredited; it has become a joke. Liquor is sold in every large city....

Only a few days ago I charged on the floor of the House that 350 cases of liquor of a seizure of 1,500 made by Federal officials and stored in the Federal building at Indianapolis, Ind., had been removed. The Department of Justice, under date of April 9, 1926, confirmed my charge. The Attorney General admits that since this liquor was in the possession of the Federal authorities in the Federal building at Indianapolis, 330 cases are missing. If bootleggers can enter Federal buildings to get liquor, the rest can be easily imagined....

I have been in public office for a great many years. I have had the opportunity to observe first the making of the present prohibition laws as a member of Congress, and later as president of the Board of Aldermen of the largest city in this country its attempted enforcement. In order to enforce prohibition in New York City I estimated at the time would require a police force of 250,000 men and a force of 200,000 men to police the police.

3. The WCTU Upholds Prohibition (1926)*

Mrs. Ella A. Boole, president of the Woman's Christian Temperance Union (WCTU), appeared before the same Senate judiciary subcommittee. Hailing from the same metropolitan area as La Guardia, Boole was a member of the Daughters of the American Revolution (DAR), held a Ph.D. from the University of Wooster, and was a

Hearings Before the Subcommittee of the Committee on the Judiciary, U.S. Senate, Sixty-ninth Congress, First Session (April 5–24, 1926), *on ... Bills to Amend the National Prohibition Act,* vol. 1, pp. 1068–1071.

Presbyterian. She had run unsuccessfully for the U.S. Senate on the Prohibition ticket in 1920. What values underlay her insistence on enforcing unpopular laws, despite widespread flouting?

You have listened to testimony of shocking conditions due to corruption of officials, and lack of enforcement, some of which suggested no remedy except a surrender to those who violate the law, while the propaganda of all these organizations is encouraging continued violation. Permit me to show another side of the picture, and propose that instead of lowering our standards we urge that the law be strengthened, and in that way notice be served on law violators that America expects her laws to be enforced and to be obeyed....

Enforcement has never had a fair trial. Political patronage, leakage through the permit system, connivance at the violation of law, and spread of the propaganda that it is not obligatory to obey a law unless you believe in it, and to the effect that the responsibility for the enforcement of law rested with the officers alone, when it should be shared by the individual citizen, have materially hindered the work of enforcement—all this with the result that the United States has not derived from prohibition what it would have derived had all the people observed the law and had there been hearty cooperation of the press and the people....

It is not easy to get at the facts about the effect of prohibition on health, morals, and economic [life] because they are interwoven with other causes, and partial statistics may be misleading. But the elimination of a preventable cause of poverty, crime, tuberculosis, the diseases of middle life, unhappy homes, and financial depression brings results insofar as the law is observed and enforced....

The closing of the open saloon with its doors swinging both ways, an ever-present invitation for all to drink—men, women, and boys—is an outstanding fact, and no one wants it to return. It has resulted in better national health, children are born under better conditions, homes are better, and the mother is delivered from the fear of a drunken husband. There is better food. Savings-banks deposits have increased, and many a man has a bank account to-day who had none in the days of the saloon.

The increase in home owning is another evidence that money wasted in drink is now used for the benefit of the family. Improved living conditions are noticeable in our former slum districts. The Bowery and Hell's Kitchen* are transformed.

Safety-first campaigns on railroads and in the presence of the increasing number of automobiles are greatly strengthened by prohibition.

The prohibition law is not the only law that is violated. Traffic laws, anti-smuggling laws, as well as the Volstead [prohibition] Act, are held in contempt. It is the spirit of the age.

Life-insurance companies have long known that drinkers were poor risks, but they recognize the fact that prohibition has removed a preventable cause of great financial loss to them.

---

*The Bowery and Hell's Kitchen were two notorious immigrant ghettos in turn-of-the-century New York.

The wonderful advances in mechanics in the application of electricity and in transportation demand brains free from the fumes of alcohol, hence law enforcement and law observance contribute to this progress....

Your attention has been called to the failures. We claim these have been the result of lax enforcement. The machinery of enforcement should be strengthened.

[The federal enforcement machinery finally broke down, and the Eighteenth Amendment was repealed in 1933. Prohibition had done much good but at a staggering cost. In addition to the evils already noted, gangsterism was flourishing, and the courts and jails were clogged. With repeal, the control of liquor went back to state and local governments.]

D. New Goals for Women

1. Margaret Sanger Campaigns for Birth Control (1920)[*]

Few feminists could rival Margaret Sanger in energy, daring, and genius for organization and publicity. Prosecuted in 1914 for publishing a radical journal, The Woman Rebel, *she fled to England, where she made the acquaintance of the noted sexual theorist Havelock Ellis. She returned to the United States in 1915 and launched herself on a lifelong crusade for birth control. Despite being arrested several more times in subsequent years, she persevered in founding the American Birth Control League (later Planned Parenthood) in 1921. For the next decade and more, Sanger tirelessly championed her cause. What arguments does she emphasize here in favor of contraception? What was her view of women? Of men? Of the relation between the sexes? Critics sometimes accused her of drinking too deeply from the well of racism and nativism that seemed to overflow in the 1920s. Do the remarks that follow offer any evidence in support of such a charge?*

What effect will the practice of birth control have upon woman's moral development?...It will break her bonds. It will free her to understand the cravings and soul needs of herself and other women. It will enable her to develop her love nature separate from and independent of her maternal nature.

It goes without saying that the woman whose children are desired and are of such number that she can not only give them adequate care but keep herself mentally and spiritually alive, as well as physically fit, can discharge her duties to her children much better than the overworked, broken and querulous mother of a large, unwanted family....

To achieve this she must have a knowledge of birth control. She must also assert and maintain her right to refuse the marital embrace except when urged by her inner nature....

---

[*]Margaret Sanger, *Woman and the New Race* (New York: Brentano's, 1920), passim.

What can we expect of offspring that are the result of "accidents"—who are brought into being undesired and in fear? What can we hope for from a morality that surrounds each physical union, for the woman, with an atmosphere of submission and shame? What can we say for a morality that leaves the husband at liberty to communicate to his wife a venereal disease?

Subversion of the sex urge to ulterior purposes has dragged it to the level of the gutter. Recognition of its true nature and purpose must lift the race to spiritual freedom. Out of our growing knowledge we are evolving new and saner ideas of life in general. Out of our increasing sex knowledge we shall evolve new ideals of sex. These ideals will spring from the innermost needs of women. They will serve these needs and express them. They will be the foundation of a moral code that will tend to make fruitful the impulse which is the source, the soul and the crowning glory of our sexual natures.

When mothers have raised the standards of sex ideals and purged the human mind of its unclean conception of sex, the fountain of the race will have been cleansed. Mothers will bring forth, in purity and in joy, a race that is morally and spiritually free....

Birth control itself, often denounced as a violation of natural law, is nothing more or less than the facilitation of the process of weeding out the unfit, of preventing the birth of defectives or of those who will become defectives. So, in compliance with nature's working plan, we must permit womanhood its full development before we can expect of it efficient motherhood. If we are to make racial progress, this development of womanhood must precede motherhood in every individual woman. Then and then only can the mother cease to be an incubator and be a mother indeed. Then only can she transmit to her sons and daughters the qualities which make strong individuals and, collectively, a strong race.

2. The Supreme Court Declares That Women Are Different from Men (1908)*

When a Portland, Oregon, laundry violated an Oregon statute limiting the number of hours that women could work in a day, the laundry owner was convicted and fined ten dollars. The owner, Curt Muller, appealed his conviction all the way to the U.S. Supreme Court, which affirmed his guilt in the case of Muller v. Oregon in 1908. On what grounds did the Court rest its decision? Could feminists in the early twentieth century support the Court's reasoning in this case?

On February 19, 1903, the legislature of the State of Oregon passed an act (Session Laws, 1903, p. 148), the first section of which is in these words:

"Sec. 1. That no female (shall) be employed in any mechanical establishment, or factory, or laundry in this State more than ten hours during any one day. The hours of work may be so arranged as to permit the employment of females at any time so that they shall not work more than ten hours during the twenty-four hours of any one day."

*Muller v. Oregon (208 U.S. 412), pp. 416–423.

Section 3 made a violation of the provisions of the prior sections a misdemeanor, subject to a fine of not less than $10 nor more than $25. On September 18, 1905, an information was filed in the Circuit Court of the State for the county of Multnomah, charging that the defendant "on the 4th day of September, a.d. 1905, in the county of Multnomah and State of Oregon, then and there being the owner of a laundry, known as the Grand Laundry, in the city of Portland, and the employer of females therein, did then and there unlawfully permit and suffer one Joe Haselbock, he, the said Joe Haselbock, then and there being an overseer, superintendent and agent of said Curt Muller, in the said Grand Laundry, to require a female, to wit, one Mrs. E. Gotcher, to work more than ten hours in said laundry on said 4th day of September, A.D. 1905, contrary to the statutes in such cases made and provided, and against the peace and dignity of the State of Oregon."

A trial resulted in a verdict against the defendant, who was sentenced to pay a fine of $10. The Supreme Court of the State affirmed the conviction, *State* v. Muller, 48 Oregon, 252, whereupon the case was brought here on writ of error.

The single question is the constitutionality of the statute under which the defendant was convicted so far as it affects the work of a female in a laundry. . . .

That woman's physical structure and the performance of maternal functions place her at a disadvantage in the struggle for subsistence is obvious. This is especially true when the burdens of motherhood are upon her. Even when they are not, by abundant testimony of the medical fraternity continuance for a long time on her feet at work, repeating this from day to day, tends to injurious effects upon the body, and as healthy mothers are essential to vigorous offspring, the physical well-being of woman becomes an object of public interest and care in order to preserve the strength and vigor of the race.

Still again, history discloses the fact that woman has always been dependent upon man. He established his control at the outset by superior physical strength, and this control in various forms, with diminishing intensity, has continued to the present. As minors, though not to the same extent, she has been looked upon in the courts as needing especial care that her rights may be preserved. Education was long denied her, and while now the doors of the school room are opened and her opportunities for acquiring knowledge are great, yet even with that and the consequent increase of capacity for business affairs it is still true that in the struggle for subsistence she is not an equal competitor with her brother. Though limitations upon personal and contractual rights may be removed by legislation, there is that in her disposition and habits of life which will operate against a full assertion of those rights. She will still be where some legislation to protect her seems necessary to secure a real equality of right. Doubtless there are individual exceptions, and there are many respects in which she has an advantage over him; but looking at it from the viewpoint of the effort to maintain an independent position in life, she is not upon an equality. Differentiated by these matters from the other sex, she is properly placed in a class by herself, and legislation designed for her protection may be sustained, even when like legislation is not necessary for men and could not be sustained. It is impossible to close one's eyes to the fact that she still looks to her brother and depends upon him. Even though all restrictions on political, personal and contractual rights were taken away, and she stood, so far as statutes are concerned, upon an absolutely equal plane with him, it would still be true that she is so constituted that she will rest upon and look to him for protection; that her physical structure and a proper discharge of her maternal functions—having in view not merely her own health, but the well-being of the race—justify legislation to protect her from the greed as well as the passion of man. The limitations which this statute places upon her contractual powers, upon her right to agree with her employer as to the time she shall labor, are not imposed solely for her benefit, but also largely for the benefit of all. Many words cannot make this plainer. The two sexes differ in structure of body, in the functions to be performed by each, in the amount of physical strength, in the capacity for long-continued labor, particularly when done standing, the influence of vigorous health upon the future well-being of the race, the self-reliance which enables one to assert full rights, and in the capacity to maintain the struggle for subsistence. This difference justifies a difference in legislation and upholds that which is designed to compensate for some of the burdens which rest upon her....

For these reasons,...we are of the opinion that it cannot be adjudged that the act in question is in conflict with the Federal Constitution, so far as it respects the work of a female in a laundry, and the judgment of the Supreme Court of Oregon is Affirmed.

3. The Supreme Court Declares That Men and Women Are Equal (1923)[*]

Fifteen years after the Muller *case—and three years after passage of the Nineteenth Amendment, which enfranchised women—the Supreme Court reversed its ruling in Muller and declared in the case of Adkins v.* Children's Hospital *that sexual inequalities were rapidly disappearing. The case involved a federal statute regulating women's wages in Washington, D.C. Justice George Sutherland, speaking for the Court majority, invalidated the regulation in the following decision. How does his reasoning differ from that of the Court majority in the* Muller *case? Justice Oliver Wendell Holmes, Jr., dissented from Sutherland's opinion, declaring that it would take more than the Nineteenth Amendment to convince him that there were no differences between men and women. Does Sutherland's or Holmes's position provide the superior foundation for legislation regarding women? Why might feminists have disagreed over the Adkins case?*

The question presented for determination by these appeals is the constitutionality of the Act of September 19, 1918, providing for the fixing of minimum wages for women and children in the District of Columbia....

In the *Muller* case the validity of an Oregon statute, forbidding the employment of any female in certain industries more than ten hours during any one day was upheld. The decision proceeded upon the theory that the difference between the sexes may justify a different rule respecting hours of labor in the case of women than in the case of men. It is pointed out that these consist in differences of physical

---

[*]*Adkins v. Children's Hospital* (261 U.S. 525), pp. 539–562.

structure, especially in respect of the maternal functions, and also in the fact that historically woman has always been dependent upon man, who has established his control by superior physical strength. . . . But the ancient inequality of the sexes, otherwise than physical, as suggested in the *Muller* case has continued "with diminishing intensity." In view of the great—not to say revolutionary—changes which have taken place since that utterance, in the contractual, political and civil status of women, culminating in the Nineteenth Amendment, it is not unreasonable to say that these differences have now come almost, if not quite, to the vanishing point. In this aspect of the matter, while the physical differences must be recognized in appropriate cases, and legislation fixing hours or conditions of work may properly take them into account, we cannot accept the doctrine that women of mature age, *sui juris*, require or may be subjected to restrictions upon their liberty of contract which could not lawfully be imposed in the case of men under similar circumstances. To do so would be to ignore all the implications to be drawn from the present day trend of legislation, as well as that of common thought and usage, by which woman is accorded emancipation from the old doctrine that she must be given special protection or be subjected to special restraint in her contractual and civil relationships. In passing, it may be noted that the instant statute applies in the case of a woman employer contracting with a woman employee as it does when the former is a man.

E. Cultural Upheaval in the Roaring Twenties _____

1. An African American Reflects on Jazz (1925)*

Drawing on a mix of influences from its native city of New Orleans, jazz was more than just the sum of its parts—more improvisational than ragtime, more upbeat than the melancholy blues, and more soulful than the music of brass marching bands. Brought north by African Americans with the Great Migration of World War I, jazz exploded in popularity in the 1920s, giving expression to the dynamism and rebelliousness of the age. Though adopted—often clumsily—by white ensembles, it remained the province of black virtuosos like Duke Ellington and Louis Armstrong for much of the decade. In the following essay, Jamaican-born journalist and historian J. A. Rogers portrays jazz as emblematic of the times. Is Rogers entirely sympathetic to the new musical form? What does he see as the role of jazz in American culture?

Jazz is a marvel of paradox: too fundamentally human, at least as modern humanity goes, to be typically racial, too international to be characteristically national, too much abroad in the world to have a special home. And yet jazz in spite of it all is one part American and three parts American Negro, and was originally the nobody's child of the levee and the city slum. Transplanted exotic—a rather hardy one, we admit—of the mundane world capitals, sport of the sophisticated,

---

*J. A. Rogers, "Jazz at Home," *Survey Graphic,* vol. 6, no. 6 (March, 1925), pp. 665–712.

it is really at home in its humble native soil wherever the modern unsophisticated Negro feels happy and sings and dances to his mood. It follows that jazz is more at home in Harlem than in Paris, though from the look and sound of certain quarters of Paris one would hardly think so. It is just the epidemic contagiousness of jazz that makes it, like the measles, sweep the block. But somebody had to have it first: that was the Negro.

What after all is this taking new thing, that, condemned in certain quarters, enthusiastically welcomed in others, has nonchalantly gone on until it ranks with the movie and the dollar as the foremost exponent of modern Americanism? Jazz isn't music merely, it is a spirit that can express itself in almost anything. The true spirit of jazz is a joyous revolt from convention, custom, authority, boredom, even sorrow—from everything that would confine the soul of man and hinder its riding free on the air. The Negroes who invented it called their songs the "Blues," and they weren't capable of satire or deception. Jazz was their explosive attempt to cast off the blues and be happy, carefree happy even in the midst of sordidness and sorrow. And that is why it has been such a balm for modern ennui, and has become a safety valve for modern machine-ridden and convention-bound society. It is the revolt of the emotions against repression. . . .

In its elementals, jazz has always existed. It is in the Indian war-dance, the Highland fling, the Irish jig, the Cossack dance, the Spanish fandango, the Brazilian *maxixe*, the dance of the whirling dervish, the hula hula of the South Seas, the danse du *ventre* of the Orient, the carmagnole of the French Revolution, the strains of Gypsy music, and the ragtime of the Negro. Jazz proper, however, is something more than all these. It is a release of all the suppressed emotions at once, a blowing off of the lid, as it were. It is hilarity expressing itself through pandemonium; musical fireworks.

The direct predecessor of jazz is ragtime. That both are atavistically African there is little doubt, but to what extent it is difficult to determine. In its barbaric rhythm and exuberance there is something of the bamboula, a wild, abandoned dance of the West African and the Haytian Negro . . . With its cowbells, auto horns, calliopes, rattles, dinner gongs, kitchen utensils, cymbals, screams, crashes, clankings and monotonous rhythm it bears all the marks of a nerve-strung, strident, mechanized civilization. It is a thing of the jungles—modern man-made jungles. . . .

This makes it difficult to say whether jazz is more characteristic of the Negro or of contemporary America. As was shown, it is of Negro origin plus the influence of the American environment. It is Negro-American. Jazz proper however is in idiom—rhythmic, musical and pantomimic—thoroughly American Negro; it is his spiritual picture on that lighter comedy side, just as the spirituals are the picture on the tragedy side. The two are poles apart, but the former is by no means to be despised and it is just as characteristically the product of the peculiar and unique experience of the Negro in this country. The African Negro hasn't it, and the Caucasian never could have invented it. Once achieved, it is common property, and jazz has absorbed the national spirit, that tremendous spirit of go, the nervousness, lack of conventionality and boisterous good-nature characteristic of the American, white or black, as compared with the more rigid formal natures of the Englishman or German. . . .

Jazz reached the height of its vogue at a time when minds were reacting from the horrors and strain of war. Humanity welcomed it because in its fresh joyousness men found a temporary forgetfulness, infinitely less harmful than drugs or alcohol. It is partly for some such reasons that it dominates the amusement life of America today. No one can sensibly condone its excesses or minimize its social danger if uncontrolled; all culture is built upon inhibitions and control. But it is doubtful whether the "jazz-hounds" of high and low estate would use their time to better advantage. In all probability their tastes would find some equally morbid, mischievous vent. Jazz, it is needless to say, will remain a recreation for the industrious and a dissipator of energy for the frivolous, a tonic for the strong and a poison for the weak....

For the Negro himself, jazz is both more and less dangerous than for the white—less in that, he is nervously more in tune with it; more, in that at his average level of economic development his amusement life is more open to the forces of social vice. The cabaret of better type provides a certain Bohemianism for the Negro intellectual, the artist and the well-to-do. But the average thing is too much the substitute for the saloon and the wayside inn. The tired longshoreman, the porter, the housemaid and the poor elevator boy in search of recreation, seeking in jazz the tonic for weary nerves and muscles, are only too apt to find the bootlegger, the gambler and the demi-monde who have come there for victims and to escape the eyes of the police.

Yet in spite of its present vices and vulgarizations, its sex informalities, its morally anarchic spirit, jazz has a popular mission to perform. Joy, after all, has a physical basis. Those who laugh and dance and sing are better off even in their vices than those who do not. Moreover jazz with its mocking disregard for formality is a leveler and makes for democracy....At all events jazz is rejuvenation, a recharging of the batteries of civilization with primitive new vigor. It has come to stay, and they are wise, who instead of protesting against it, try to lift and divert it into nobler channels.

2. Advertising Targets Women as Consumers (1924, 1929)

As firms began to produce a growing array of standardized consumer goods, they turned to advertisers to help develop brand loyalty and bolster demand. In 1920, businesses spent nearly three billion dollars on advertising—a fifteen-fold increase from forty years prior. Since women were typically responsible for household purchases, professional advertisers appealed directly to their sentiments and tastes. As a reflection of the times, print ads from the "Roaring Twenties" demonstrate both the popularization of the flapper and the persistence of more traditional gender norms. Who are the target audiences for each of the following advertisements? What do the ads reveal about the lives of American women during this period?

Her habit of measuring time in terms of dollars gives the woman in business keen insight into the true value of a Ford closed car for her personal use.

This car enables her to conserve minutes, to expedite her affairs, to widen the scope of her activities. Its low first cost, long life and inexpensive operation and upkeep convince her that it is a sound investment value.

And it is such a pleasant car to drive that it transforms the business call which might be an interruption into an enjoyable episode of her busy day.

TUDOR SEDAN, $590   FORDOR SEDAN, $685   COUPE, $525   (All prices f. o. b. Detroit)

CLOSED CARS

May 1924 Good Housekeeping

Your Children ___
___ is their food safe ?

YOU, as a conscientious mother, buy the best food for your children, prepare it with scrupulous care and cook it correctly. Yet, in spite of all, you may be giving your children food which is not wholesome—possibly dangerous!

For even the best food becomes unsafe to eat unless it is *kept* at the proper degree of cold, which medical authorities agree should be 50 degrees or less—always. Above that temperature, bacteria multiply, food is contaminated—becomes a menace to health.

There is only one way to be sure that your children's food is fresh and healthful—correct refrigeration. There is one refrigerator that assures you of scientifically perfect refrigeration at all times—the General Electric. Faithfully, quietly, day and night, it maintains a temperature safely below the danger point—50 degrees.

The General Electric is ideal for the home. Its simple mechanism, which you never need to oil, is mounted on top of

The price of this new all-steel refrigerator—the small-family model—is now
$215 AT THE FACTORY

the cabinet and hermetically sealed in a steel casing. It has a simple accessible temperature control, makes a generous supply of ice cubes, creates no radio interference. It has the only *all-steel*, warpproof cabinet—easily-cleaned, sanitary.

Your dealer will be glad to explain the spaced payment plan, which makes it so easy to own this faithful watchman of the family health. If there is not a dealer near you, write Electric Refrigeration Dept., General Electric Co., Hanna Building, Cleveland, Ohio, for booklet S-9.

An unmatched record

There are now more than 300,000 homes enjoying the comfort and protection of General Electric Refrigerators—and not one of the owners has ever had to pay a single dollar for repairs or service.

GENERAL ⓖⓔ ELECTRIC
ALL-STEEL REFRIGERATOR

Thought Provokers

1. How is it that the proponents of cultural pluralism and the champions of immigration restriction both pointed to immigrants' resistance to assimilation to justify their positions? Could the United States have continued indefinitely to allow unlimited immigration?
2. What was the relation of the revived Ku Klux Klan in the 1920s to the original Klan of Reconstruction days? Why does the United States periodically spawn violent vigilante-style movements?
3. Was prohibition a typically American "experiment"? Under what circumstances does the government have a right to regulate personal behavior, such as drinking alcoholic beverages or using narcotic drugs?
4. In what ways was the urbanized economic order of the 1920s a new frontier for women? How did the spreading practice of birth control reflect changes in the values and styles of family life? Does an emphasis on gender difference or on gender equality form a better basis for public policy?

31

The Politics
of Boom and Bust,
1920–1932

The country is in the midst of an era of prosperity
more extensive and of peace more permanent than
it has ever before experienced.

President Calvin Coolidge, 1928

Prologue: In 1920 Warren G. Harding, campaigning on a promise to return to
"normalcy" in the nation's war-strained affairs, won the presidency by a landslide vote.
As president, Harding soon turned his back on the United States' recent comrades-in-
arms and made a separate peace with recent enemies. Harding was spared the worst
embarrassments of his scandal-ridden administration by his death in 1923. Puritanical
and tight-lipped Calvin Coolidge succeeded him. Onetime Progressive Herbert Hoover
defeated earthy New York Democrat Al Smith for the presidency in 1928, but his
administration was almost immediately engulfed by the steepest and deepest economic
downturn in U.S. history—known ever after as the Great Depression—which set the
stage for Franklin D. Roosevelt's election in 1932.

A. The Depression Descends

1. The Plague of Plenty (1932)*

*In his acceptance speech of 1928, delivered in the Stanford University football
stadium, Hoover optimistically envisioned the day when poverty would be banished
from the United States. A popular Republican slogan was "a chicken in every pot,
a car in every garage." The next year the stock market collapsed and depression
descended. Hoover, a "rugged individualist" who had pulled himself up by his own
bootstraps, was unwilling to turn Washington into a gigantic soup kitchen for the
unemployed. He struggled desperately to halt the depression, but in general his
efforts were too little and too late. To boost morale, he issued a number of cheery
statements to the effect that prosperity was just around the corner. The following*

---

*Unemployment in the United States. Hearings Before a Subcommittee of the Committee on Labor, House of
Representatives, Seventy-second Congress, First Session, on H.R. 206…(1932), pp. 98–99.

testimony of a newspaper editor, Oscar Ameringer of Oklahoma City, was given in 1932 before a House committee. What is particularly paradoxical about the situation he describes?

During the last three months I have visited, as I have said, some twenty states of this wonderfully rich and beautiful country. Here are some of the things I heard and saw:

In the state of Washington I was told that the forest fires raging in that region all summer and fall were caused by unemployed timber workers and bankrupt farmers in an endeavor to earn a few honest dollars as firefighters. The last thing I saw on the night I left Seattle was numbers of women searching for scraps of food in the refuse piles of the principal market of that city. A number of Montana citizens told me of thousands of bushels of wheat left in the fields uncut on account of its low price that hardly paid for the harvesting. In Oregon I saw thousands of bushels of apples rotting in the orchards. Only absolute[ly] flawless apples were still salable, at from 40 to 50 cents a box containing 200 apples. At the same time, there are millions of children who, on account of the poverty of their parents, will not eat one apple this winter.

While I was in Oregon the Portland *Oregonian* bemoaned the fact that thousands of ewes were killed by the sheep raisers because they did not bring enough in the market to pay the freight on them. And while Oregon sheep raisers fed mutton to the buzzards, I saw men picking for meat scraps in the garbage cans in the cities of New York and Chicago. I talked to one man in a restaurant in Chicago. He told me of his experience in raising sheep. He said that he had killed 3,000 sheep this fall and thrown them down the canyon, because it cost $1.10 to ship a sheep, and then he would get less than a dollar for it. He said he could not afford to feed the sheep, and he would not let them starve, so he just cut their throats and threw them down the canyon.

The roads of the West and Southwest teem with hungry hitchhikers. The camp fires of the homeless are seen along every railroad track. I saw men, women, and children walking over the hard roads. Most of them were tenant farmers who had lost their all in the late slump in wheat and cotton. Between Clarksville and Russellville, Ark., I picked up a family. The woman was hugging a dead chicken under a ragged coat. When I asked her where she had procured the fowl, first she told me she had found it dead in the road, and then added in grim humor, "They promised me a chicken in the pot, and now I got mine."

In Oklahoma, Texas, Arkansas, and Louisiana I saw untold bales of cotton rotting in the fields because the cotton pickers could not keep body and soul together on 35 cents paid for picking 100 pounds....

As a result of this appalling overproduction on the one side and the staggering underconsumption on the other side, 70 per cent of the farmers of Oklahoma were unable to pay the interests on their mortgages. Last week one of the largest and oldest mortgage companies in that state went into the hands of the receiver. In that and other states we have now the interesting spectacle of farmers losing their farms by foreclosure and mortgage companies losing their recouped holdings by tax sales.

The farmers are being pauperized by the poverty of industrial populations, and the industrial populations are being pauperized by the poverty of the farmers. Neither has the money to buy the product of the other, hence we have overproduction and underconsumption at the same time and in the same country.

I have not come here to stir you in a recital of the necessity for relief for our suffering fellow citizens. However, unless something is done for them and done soon, you will have a revolution on hand. And when that revolution comes it will not come from Moscow, it will not be made by the poor Communists whom our police are heading up regularly and efficiently. When the revolution comes it will bear the label "Laid in the U.S.A." and its chief promoters will be the people of American stock.

2. Rumbles of Revolution (1932)*

Franklin Roosevelt was later acclaimed as the messiah whose New Deal saved the United States for capitalism by averting armed revolution. He was quoted as saying that if he failed, he would be not the worst but the last president of the United States. Certainly in 1932 the signs were ominous. Hundreds of midwestern farmers were picketing the highways to keep their underpriced produce from reaching market, overturning milk trucks, overpowering armed deputies, and releasing prisoners from jail. With increasing millions of desperate people out of work and with thousands defying the police, the worst might have happened. The testimony in the following selection of Oscar Ameringer, the Oklahoma newspaperman, is impressive. Does it confirm that the talk of revolution was to be taken seriously?

Some time ago a cowman came into my office in Oklahoma City. He was one of these double-fisted gentlemen, with the gallon hat and all. He said, "You do not know me from Adam's ox."

I said: "No; I do not believe I know you."...

He said, "I came to this country without a cent, but, knowing my onions, and by tending strictly to business, I finally accumulated two sections of land and a fine herd of white-faced Hereford cattle. I was independent."

I remarked that anybody could do that if he worked hard and did not gamble and used good management.

He said, "After the war, cattle began to drop, and I was feeding them corn, and by the time I got them to Chicago the price of cattle, considering the price of corn I had fed them, was not enough to even pay my expenses. I could not pay anything."

Continuing, he said, "I mortgaged my two sections of land, and to-day I am cleaned out; by God, I am not going to stand for it."

I asked him what he was going to do about it, and he said, "We have got to have a revolution here like they had in Russia and clean them up."

I finally asked him, "Who is going to make the revolution?"

---

*Unemployment in the United States, Hearings Before a Subcommittee of the Committee on Labor, House of Representatives, Seventy-second Congress, First Session, on H.R. 206…(1932), pp. 100–101.

He said, "I just want to tell you I am going to be one of them, and I am going to do my share in it."

I asked what his share was and he said, "I will capture a certain fort. I know I can get in with twenty of my boys," meaning his cowboys, "because I know the inside and outside of it, and I [will] capture that with my men."

I rejoined, "Then what?"

He said, "We will have 400 machine guns, so many batteries of artillery, tractors, and munitions and rifles, and everything else needed to supply a pretty good army."

Then I asked, "What then?"

He said, "If there are enough fellows with guts in this country to do like us, we will march eastward and we will cut the East off. We will cut the East off from the West. We have got the granaries; we have the hogs, the cattle, the corn; the East has nothing but mortgages on our places. We will show them what we can do."

That man may be very foolish, and I think he is, but he is in dead earnest; he is a hard-shelled Baptist and a hard-shelled Democrat, not a Socialist or a Communist, but just a plain American cattleman whose ancestors went from Carolina to Tennessee, then to Arkansas, and then to Oklahoma. I have heard much of this talk from serious-minded prosperous men of other days.

As you know, talk is always a mental preparation for action. Nothing is done until people talk and talk and talk it, and they finally get the notion that they will do it.

I do not say we are going to have a revolution on hand within the next year or two, perhaps never. I hope we may not have such; but the danger is here. That is the feeling of our people—as reflected in the letters I have read. I have met these people virtually every day all over the country. There is a feeling among the masses generally that something is radically wrong. They are despairing of political action. They say the only thing you do in Washington is to take money from the pockets of the poor and put it into the pockets of the rich. They say that this Government is a conspiracy against the common people to enrich the already rich. I hear such remarks every day.

I never pass a hitchhiker without inviting him in and talking to him. Bankers even are talking about that. They are talking in irrational tones. You have more Bolshevism among the bankers to-day than the hod carriers, I think. It is a terrible situation, and I think something should be done and done immediately.

B. Herbert Hoover Clashes with Franklin Roosevelt

1. On Public Versus Private Power (1932)

a. Hoover Upholds Free Enterprise[*]

President Hoover, the wealthy conservative, instinctively shied away from anything suggesting socialism. In 1931 he emphatically vetoed the Muscle Shoals Bill, which would have put the federal government in the electric power business on the Tennessee River. (An expanded version later created the Tennessee Valley Authority

---

[*]*New York Times*, November 1, 1932 (speech at Madison Square Garden, New York, October 31, 1932).

[TVA] under President Roosevelt.) Hoover ringingly reaffirmed his basic position in a speech during the Hoover-Roosevelt presidential campaign of 1932. Why was he so strongly opposed to federally owned electric power? Why would he have found local community ownership more acceptable?

I have stated unceasingly that I am opposed to the Federal Government going into the power business. I have insisted upon rigid regulation. The Democratic candidate has declared that under the same conditions which may make local action of this character desirable, he is prepared to put the Federal Government into the power business. He is being actively supported by a score of Senators in this campaign, many of whose expenses are being paid by the Democratic National Committee, who are pledged to Federal Government development and operation of electrical power.

I find in the instructions to campaign speakers issued by the Democratic National Committee that they are instructed to criticize my action in the veto of the bill which would have put the Government permanently into the operation of power at Muscle Shoals, with a capital from the Federal Treasury of over $100,000,000. In fact thirty-one Democratic Senators, being all except three, voted to override that veto.

In that bill was the flat issue of the Federal Government permanently in competitive business. I vetoed it because of principle and not because it especially applied to power business. In that veto, I stated that I was firmly opposed to the Federal Government entering into any business, the major purpose of which is competition with our citizens....

From their utterances in this campaign and elsewhere it appears to me that we are justified in the conclusion that our opponents propose to put the Federal Government in the power business.

b. Roosevelt Pushes Public Power[*]

Franklin Roosevelt, who as governor of New York had shown much concern for the Niagara–St. Lawrence River power resources, had already locked horns with the private utility magnates. As president, he later had a large hand in launching the TVA project, which also involved fertilizer, flood control, and improved navigation. He presented his views on public power as follows during the campaign of 1932. Are his arguments more convincing than Hoover's?

I therefore lay down the following principle: That where a community—a city or county or a district—is not satisfied with the service rendered or the rates charged by the private utility, it has the undeniable basic right, as one of its functions of government, one of its functions of home rule, to set up, after a fair referendum to its voters has been had, its own governmentally owned and operated service....

My distinguished opponent is against giving the Federal Government, in any case, the right to operate its own power business. I favor giving the people this right where and when it is essential to protect them against inefficient service or exorbitant charges.

---

[*]*Roosevelt's Public Papers*, vol. 1, pp. 738, 741–742 (speech at Portland, Oregon, September 21, 1932).

As an important part of this policy, the natural hydro-electric power resources belonging to the people of the United States, or the several States, shall remain forever in their possession.

To the people of this country I have but one answer on this subject. Judge me by the enemies I have made. Judge me by the selfish purposes of these utility leaders who have talked of radicalism while they were selling watered stock to the people, and using our schools to deceive the coming generation.

My friends, my policy is as radical as American liberty. My policy is as radical as the Constitution of the United States.

I promise you this: Never shall the Federal Government part with its sovereignty or with its control over its power resources, while I am President of the United States.

2. On Government in Business (1932)

a. Hoover Assails Federal Intervention*

Hoover's conservative nature recoiled from the prospect of government in business, especially on the scale envisaged by the TVA. Annoyed by Democratic charges that he was a complete reactionary, he struck back in a major campaign speech at Madison Square Garden. Laboriously written by himself (he was the last president to scorn ghostwriters), it was perhaps the best conceived of his campaign. "Every time the Federal Government extends its arm," he declared, "531 Senators and Congressmen become actual boards of directors of that business." What truth is there in his charge that government in business invites a species of servitude?

There is one thing I can say without any question of doubt—that is, that the spirit of liberalism is to create free men. It is not the regimentation of men. It is not the extension of bureaucracy. I have said in this city [New York] before now that you cannot extend the mastery of government over the daily life of a people without somewhere making it master of people's souls and thoughts.

Expansion of government in business means that the Government, in order to protect itself from the political consequences of its errors, is driven irresistibly, without peace, to greater and greater control of the Nation's press and platform. Free speech does not live many hours after free industry and free commerce die.

It is a false liberalism that interprets itself into Government operation of business. Every step in that direction poisons the very roots of liberalism. It poisons political equality, free speech, free press, and equality of opportunity. It is the road not to liberty but to less liberty. True liberalism is found not in striving to spread bureaucracy, but in striving to set bounds to it....

Even if the Government conduct of business could give us the maximum of efficiency instead of least efficiency, it would be purchased at the cost of freedom. It would increase rather than decrease abuse and corruption, stifle initiative and invention, undermine development of leadership, cripple mental and spiritual

---

New York Times, November 1, 1932 (speech at Madison Square Garden, New York, October 31, 1932).

energies of our people, extinguish equality of opportunity, and dry up the spirit of liberty and progress.

Men who are going about this country announcing that they are liberals because of their promises to extend the Government in business are not liberals; they are reactionaries of the United States.

b. Roosevelt Attacks Business in Government*

The Reconstruction Finance Corporation (RFC), established late in the Hoover administration, was designed primarily to bail out hard-pressed banks and other big businesses—"a bread line for bankers." Charles G. Dawes, former vice president of the United States, hastily resigned as the head of the RFC so that his Chicago bank might secure an emergency loan of $80 million to stave off bankruptcy. The Democrats, who argued that loans to ordinary citizens were no less imperative, attacked this presumed favoritism. How well does Roosevelt, in the following campaign speech, refute the Republican philosophy of separating government and business?

Some of my friends tell me that they do not want the Government in business. With this I agree, but I wonder whether they realize the implications of the past. For while it has been American doctrine that the Government must not go into business in competition with private enterprises, still it has been traditional, particularly in Republican administrations, for business urgently to ask the Government to put at private disposal all kinds of Government assistance.

The same man who tells you that he does not want to see the Government interfere in business—and he means it, and has plenty of good reasons for saying so—is the first to go to Washington and ask the Government for a prohibitory tariff on his product. When things get just bad enough, as they did two years ago, he will go with equal speed to the United States Government and ask for a loan; and the Reconstruction Finance Corporation is the outcome of it.

Each group has sought protection from the government for its own special interests, without realizing that the function of Government must be to favor no small group at the expense of its duty to protect the rights of personal freedom and of private property of all its citizens.

3. On Balancing the Budget (1932)

a. Hoover Stresses Economy†

Hoover, the Iowa orphan, was dedicated to strict economy, a sound dollar, and the balanced budget. He was alarmed by proposals in the Democratic House to unbalance the budget further by voting huge sums to provide jobs for the unemployed. One proposed public works scheme called for the construction of twenty-three hundred new post offices. The upkeep and interest charges on these would cost $14 million a year, whereas, he noted, "the upkeep and rent of buildings at present in use amounts

---

Roosevelt's Public Papers, vol. 1, p. 748 (Commonwealth Club speech, San Francisco, September 23, 1932).
†*New York Times*, May 28, 1932 (Washington press conference of May 27, 1932).

*to less than $3,000,000." Hoover unburdened himself as follows at a press confer-
ence. In the light of subsequent developments, did he overemphasize the effects of
an unbalanced budget in relation to uneconomical public works? (Since 1932 the
federal Treasury has more often than not shown an annual deficit.)*

The urgent question today is the prompt balancing of the Budget. When that
is accomplished, I propose to support adequate measures for relief of distress and
unemployment.

In the meantime, it is essential that there should be an understanding of the
character of the draft bill made public yesterday in the House of Representatives for
this purpose. That draft bill supports some proposals we have already made in aid
to unemployment, through the use of the Reconstruction Finance Corporation, to
make loans for projects which have been in abeyance and which proposal makes
no drain on the taxpayer. But in addition it proposes to expend about $900,000,000
for Federal public works.

I believe the American people will grasp the economic fact that such action
would require appropriations to be made to the Federal Departments, thus creating
a deficit in the Budget that could only be met with more taxes and more Federal
bond issues. That makes balancing of the Budget hopeless.

The country also understands that an unbalanced budget means the loss of
confidence of our own people and of other nations in the credit and stability of the
Government, and that the consequences are national demoralization and the loss
of ten times as many jobs as would be created by this program, even if it could be
physically put into action....

This is not unemployment relief. It is the most gigantic pork barrel ever proposed
to the American Congress. It is an unexampled raid on the public Treasury.

b. Roosevelt Stresses Humanity[*]

*The Democratic platform of 1932, which assailed Republican extravagance and
deficits, had come out squarely for a balanced budget. A favorite slogan of the
Democrats was, "Throw the spenders out." When Roosevelt died thirteen years later,
the national debt (including war costs) had risen some $19 billion to $258 billion.
During the campaign of 1932, Roosevelt expressed his views on a balanced budget
as follows. In the light of these views, did his later record constitute a breach of faith
with the voters?*

Let us have the courage to stop borrowing to meet continuing deficits. Stop the
deficits! Let us have equal courage to reverse the policy of the Republican leaders
and insist on a sound currency....

This dilemma can be met by saving in one place what we would spend in
others, or by acquiring the necessary revenue through taxation. Revenues must
cover expenditures by one means or another. Any Government, like any family, can

---

[*]*Roosevelt's Public Papers*, vol. 1, pp. 662, 663, 810. (The first two paragraphs are taken from a radio
address from Albany, July 30, 1932; the last paragraph is taken from a speech at Pittsburgh, October 19,
1932.)

for a year spend a little more than it earns. But you and I know that a continuation of that habit means the poorhouse....

The above two categorical statements are aimed at a definite balancing of the budget. At the same time, let me repeat from now to election day so that every man, woman, and child in the United States will know what I mean: If starvation and dire need on the part of any of our citizens make necessary the appropriation of additional funds which would keep the budget out of balance, I shall not hesitate to tell the American people the full truth and ask them to authorize the expenditure of that additional amount.

4. On Restricted Opportunity (1932)

a. Roosevelt Urges Welfare Statism*

"Why change?" cried Republicans in the campaign of 1932. "Things could be worse." A slight business upturn did occur in the summer, but a sag soon followed—resulting, claimed Hoover, from fear of a Rooseveltian revolution. Roosevelt himself jeered that the "no change" argument was like saying, "Do not swap toboggans while you are sliding downhill." He set forth his own concept of change in his memorable Commonwealth Club speech in San Francisco. Was his argument regarding the overbuilding of the United States' industrial plant sound in the light of subsequent history?

A glance at the situation today only too clearly indicates that equality of opportunity, as we have known it, no longer exists. Our industrial plant is built; the problem just now is whether under existing conditions it is not overbuilt.

Our last frontier has long since been reached, and there is practically no more free land. More than half of our people do not live on the farms or on lands, and cannot derive a living by cultivating their own property. There is no safety valve in the form of a Western prairie, to which those thrown out of work by the Eastern economic machines can go for a new start. We are not able to invite the immigration from Europe to share our endless plenty. We are now providing a drab living for our own people....

Recently a careful study was made of the concentration of business in the United States. It showed that our economic life was dominated by some six hundred odd corporations, who controlled two-thirds of American industry. Ten million small business men divided the other third. More striking still, it appeared that if the process of concentration goes on at the same rate, at the end of another century we shall have all American industry controlled by a dozen corporations, and run by perhaps a hundred men. Put plainly, we are steering a steady course toward economic oligarchy, if we are not there already.

Clearly, all this calls for a re-appraisal of values. A mere builder of more industrial plants, a creator of more railroad systems, an organizer of more corporations, is as likely to be a danger as a help. The day of the great promoter or the financial Titan, to whom we granted anything if only he would build, or develop, is over.

Roosevelt's Public Papers, vol. 1, pp. 750–753 (speech of September 23, 1932).

Our task now is not discovery or exploitation of natural resources, or necessarily producing more goods. It is the soberer, less dramatic business of administering resources and plants already in hand, of seeking to re-establish foreign markets for our surplus production, of meeting the problem of underconsumption, of adjusting production to consumption, of distributing wealth and products more equitably, of adapting existing economic organizations to the service of the people. The day of enlightened administration has come.

b. Hoover Calls for New Frontiers*

Roosevelt's annoying vagueness prompted Hoover to refer to "a chameleon on plaid." Smarting from the New Dealish overtones of the Commonwealth Club speech, Hoover struck back in his Madison Square Garden speech. Did he interpret the United States' past and future with greater accuracy than Roosevelt did?

But I do challenge the whole idea that we have ended the advance of America, that this country has reached the zenith of its power, the height of its development. That is the counsel of despair for the future of America. That is not the spirit by which we shall emerge from this depression. That is not the spirit that made this country. If it is true, every American must abandon the road of countless progress and unlimited opportunity. I deny that the promise of American life has been fulfilled, for that means we have begun the decline and fall. No nation can cease to move forward without degeneration of spirit.

I could quote from gentlemen who have emitted this same note of pessimism in economic depressions going back for a hundred years. What Governor Roosevelt has overlooked is the fact that we are yet but on the frontiers of development of science, and of invention. I have only to remind you that discoveries in electricity, the internal combustion engine, the radio—all of which have sprung into being since our land was settled—have in themselves represented the greatest advances in America.

The philosophy upon which the Governor of New York proposes to conduct the Presidency of the United States is the philosophy of stagnation, of despair. It is the end of hope. The destinies of this country should not be dominated by that spirit in action. It would be the end of the American system.

C. Appraising Hoover _____

1. Hoover Defends His Record (1932)†

Hoover smarted under charges that he had not fought the "Hoover depression" with every ounce of energy for the benefit of all the people. Such accusations, he asserted, were "deliberate, intolerable falsehoods." At times he put in an eighteen-hour day, remarking that his office was a "compound hell." When he spoke wearily at St. Paul during the last stages of the 1932 campaign, a man was stationed behind him ready

---

*New York Times, November 1, 1932 (speech at Madison Square Garden, New York, October 31, 1932).
†New York Times, October 5, 1932 (speech of October 4, 1932).

to thrust forward an empty chair if he collapsed. In a major speech at Des Moines, he thus refuted charges that he was a "see-nothing, do-nothing president." What is the least convincing part of this recital?

We have fought an unending war against the effect of these calamities upon our people. This is no time to recount the battles on a thousand fronts. We have fought the good fight to protect our people in a thousand cities from hunger and cold.

We have carried on an unceasing campaign to protect the Nation from that unhealing class bitterness which arises from strikes and lockouts and industrial conflict. We have accomplished this through the willing agreement of employer and labor, which placed humanity before money through the sacrifice of profits and dividends before wages.

We have defended millions from the tragic result of droughts.

We have mobilized a vast expansion of public construction to make work for the unemployed.

We [have] fought the battle to balance the Budget.

We have defended the country from being forced off the gold standard, with its crushing effect upon all who are in debt.

We have battled to provide a supply of credits to merchants and farmers and industries.

We have fought to retard falling prices.

We have struggled to save homes and farms from foreclosure of mortgages; battled to save millions of depositors and borrowers from the ruin caused by the failure of banks; fought to assure the safety of millions of policyholders from failure of their insurance companies; and fought to save commerce and employment from the failure of railways.

We have fought to secure disarmament and maintain the peace of the world; fought for stability of other countries whose failure would inevitably injure us. And, above all, we have fought to preserve the safety, the principles, and ideals of American life. We have builded the foundations of recovery. . . .

Thousands of our people in their bitter distress and losses today are saying that "things could not be worse." No person who has any remote understanding of the forces which confronted this country during these last eighteen months ever utters that remark. Had it not been for the immediate and unprecedented actions of our government, things would be infinitely worse today.

2. Roosevelt Indicts Hoover (1932)[*]

Roosevelt did not use kid gloves in his ghostwritten campaign speeches. (The one at Topeka, Kansas, represented his own efforts and those of some twenty-five assistants.) Though crediting Hoover with "unremitting efforts," he assailed him for having claimed credit for prosperity while disclaiming responsibility for the depression; for having placed the blame for the depression on wicked foreigners instead of on shortsighted Republican economic policies; for having marked time and issued

---

[*]*Roosevelt's Public Papers*, vol. 1, p. 677 (speech of August 20, 1932).

airily optimistic statements when he should have grasped the bull by the horns. At Pittsburgh, Roosevelt cried, "I do indict this Administration for wrong action, for delayed action, for lack of frankness and for lack of courage." At Columbus, Ohio, he presented the following bill of particulars. What part of his indictment is most unfair?

Finally, when facts could no longer be ignored and excuses had to be found, Washington discovered that the depression came from abroad. In October of last year, the official policy came to us as follows: "The depression has been deepened by events from abroad which are beyond the control either of our citizens or our Government"—an excuse, note well, my friends, which the President still maintained in his acceptance speech last week.

Not for partisan purposes, but in order to set forth history aright, that excuse ought to be quietly considered. The records of the civilized Nations of the world prove two facts: first, that the economic structure of other Nations was affected by our own tide of speculation, and the curtailment of our lending helped to bring on their distress; second, that the bubble burst in the land of its origin—the United States.

The major collapse in other countries followed. It was not simultaneous with ours. Moreover, further curtailment of our loans, plus the continual stagnation in trade caused by the Grundy [Hawley-Smoot] tariff, has continued the depression throughout international affairs.

So I sum up the history of the present Administration in four sentences:

First, it encouraged speculation and overproduction, through its false economic policies.

Second, it attempted to minimize the [1929 stock market] crash and misled the people as to its gravity.

Third, it erroneously charged the cause to other Nations of the world.

And finally, it refused to recognize and correct the evils at home which had brought it forth; it delayed relief; it forgot reform.

Thought Provokers

1. What puzzled people most about the impact of the Great Depression? Who was hardest hit? Why was there not more radicalism in the Depression-era United States?
2. Hoover was a former associate of Woodrow Wilson, as was Franklin Roosevelt. In what ways might they both be considered "Wilsonians"? What were the sharpest differences between them?
3. No other man in the United States had a higher reputation than Hoover in the 1920s, and none rated lower in public esteem in the early 1930s. Was this reversal of public opinion justified? Should Hoover be admired for the constancy of his beliefs, even under severe criticism?

32

The Great Depression and the New Deal, 1933–1939

> I pledge you, I pledge myself, to a new deal for the
> American people.
>
> *Franklin D. Roosevelt, Accepting Nomination of*
> *Democratic National Convention, 1932*

Prologue: The Great Depression lay heavily upon the land as Roosevelt boldly set up numerous New Deal agencies designed to provide relief, recovery, and reform. He presided over one of the most active periods of political innovation in the Republic's history. His programs forever changed the structure of U.S. social and economic life, although they never did fully defeat the devastating depression. Roosevelt ignored campaign pledges to reduce government expenses, balance the budget, prune the bureaucracy, maintain a sound currency, and eliminate the improper use of money in politics. But he honored other promises, directly or indirectly, in the reciprocal tariff program, the repeal of prohibition, the insurance of bank deposits, and the encouragement of labor unions. Roosevelt, a knowledgeable naturalist, also initiated several environmental programs, including enormous construction projects aimed at taming the great rivers of the Tennessee, Missouri, Columbia, and Colorado. On the left, critics complained that the New Deal was not radical enough. Yet conservative critics of the New Deal cried that Roosevelt promoted class hatred by setting the poor against the rich. New Dealers retorted that they were merely putting need above greed. The voters endorsed Roosevelt so resoundingly at the polls in 1934 and 1936 that he was emboldened to unveil his scheme for "packing" the Supreme Court in 1937. Though soundly rebuffed, he won an unprecedented third-term election in 1940, with a strong assist from the crisis in Europe and a new war-born prosperity.

A. A World in Depression

1. Jan Christiaan Smuts Blames the Versailles Treaty (1933)[*]

Hoping to bring stability to collapsing world markets, representatives from more than sixty nations assembled in London in June 1933 to stabilize international currencies and revive world trade. South Africa's Jan Christiaan Smuts, who fourteen

---

[*]From "Speeches at the Conference," The Times/NI Syndication Limited, June 14, 1933, p. 9. Reprinted by permission.

years earlier had predicted the calamitous consequences of the Treaty of Versailles (see p. 571), took the conference as an opportunity to chide world leaders for prior failures and encourage more prudent action to address the crisis at hand. What new dangers did he foresee in the event of continued economic chaos? What does he present as the chief impediments to the success of the London conference?

It may appear presumption on my part to speak thus early in this debate, but I may claim a special privilege. I am one of the very few members of this Conference—I believe there are only three of us—who were also members of the Peace Conference 14 years ago. When I had to sign the Versailles Treaty I gave expression to the fears for the future which oppressed my mind. Those fears were generally scouted at the time. Unfortunately they have come true; not only have they come true, but much worse has happened. The Great War has in effect been followed, not by a peace, but by an economic war almost as devastating in its consequences. Once more I am filled with fear for the future; I am filled with fear for the future if this Conference fails, only now my fear is shared by all serious people, and it goes much deeper, as it is a fear for the future of our European system and of civilization itself.

You will forgive me if I speak my mind quite frankly. I could scarcely use stronger language than was used by the Preparatory Commission of Experts who drafted the agenda for this Conference. This body, not of idealists, but of sober and cautious financiers and economists, say quite plainly that failure to arrest the present downward tendencies would shake the whole system of international finance to its foundations, standards of living would be lowered, and the social system as we know it could hardly survive. That is the situation we are up against. That is the problem set us to solve. The problem is to raise world prices, to re-establish stable currencies, and to set going once more international trade, which has declined to a third of what it was three years ago. The problem is not only all-important, but most urgent. We have always been too late for the march of events, and we may once more be too late—with fatal results. . . .

If we meet, not for action, but for leisurely debates, if there is much more delay at this Conference, nobody knows what the irresistible march of events may not produce. Everywhere the moving finger is writing on the wall. The position from one end of the world to the other is worsening, not only financially, but also politically, and the way out is becoming steadily more difficult. Hence the anxiety to see this Conference become not a mere debating body but a council of action, of swift and effective action and assistance to our European civilization in its deep distress. . . .

The world calls for courageous leadership and thinks it does not always get it from the politicians. Where, as here, the whole European order is threatened, we should ignore all merely national or sectional points of view, and concentrate our forces. The forces of economic and social decay are threatening our fair civilization. They can only be met successfully on a united front and with courageous leadership by this Conference. Only in that way can we turn this Conference into a decisive battlefield and win the fight for economic and social recovery and regain eventual prosperity.

2. John Maynard Keynes Praises Roosevelt (1933)[*]

In a nod to powerful inflationist interests in Congress, Franklin D. Roosevelt took the United States off the gold standard in April 1933, promising to revisit the issue in London that summer. Then, in a stunning departure from his previous assurances to European powers, Roosevelt cabled his famous "bombshell message" to the conference, withdrawing his support for currency negotiations. Dismissing stabilization efforts as the "old fetishes of so-called international bankers," Roosevelt declared that the United States would pursue an independent monetary agenda. His cavalier pronouncement effectively killed negotiations in London and drew a torrent of criticism from European leaders. Almost alone in his praise of Roosevelt was British economist John Maynard Keynes, who applauded the inflationary logic of the president's recovery efforts. What does he present as the choice facing the European powers? Why does he take such a dim view of Europe's economic policies?

It is a long time since a statesman has cut through the cob-webs as boldly as the President of the United States cut through them yesterday.

He has told us where he stands, and he invites the Conference to proceed to substantial business. But he is prepared to act alone if necessary; and he is strong enough to do so, provided that he is well served by the experts to whom he entrusts the technique of his policy....

[T]he President's message has an importance which transcends its origins. It is, in substance a challenge to us to decide whether we propose to tread the old, unfortunate ways, or to explore new paths; paths new to statesmen and to bankers, but not new to thought. For they lead to the managed currency of the future, the examination of which has been the prime topic of post-war economics.

Since the days of the Peace Conference every constructive proposal which might have saved us from our repeated errors has fallen to the ground. The Treasury and the Bank of England have depended on their sense of smell alone. Eyes have been blind and ears have been deaf. But a man should be able to see much farther ahead than he can smell. As one reads President Roosevelt's words on the future of monetary policy it seems possible that at last that noble organ the nose is yielding place to eyes and ears....

[O]n the broad political issue—on the things which it should be the business of Presidents and Prime Ministers to understand—he is magnificently right in forcing a decision between two widely divergent policies. The Economic Conference will be a farce unless it brings this divergence to a head. If the opposed parties are not inclined to join issue in public on the fundamental choice which America has presented to the world in unambiguous form, it is much better that the Conference should adjourn.

On the one side we have a group of European countries of great political and military importance, but increasingly segregated from the currents of world trade. They disbelieve in official expansionist policies as a means of restoring economic life.

---

[*]Source: *The Collected Works of John Maynard Keynes, Volume 21. Activities 1931–1939: World Crises and Policies in Britain and America*, Eds., Elizabeth Johnson and Donald Moggridge. Copyright © 2012 The Royal Economic Society. Reprinted with the permission of Cambridge University Press.

They cling fanatically to their gold perches, though most of them are poised there precariously. They see no virtue in a rising price level, putting their faith in a 'revival of confidence', which is to come somehow by itself through business men gradually deciding that the world is safe for them.

On the other side, the United States of America invites us to see whether without uprooting the order of society which we have inherited we cannot, by the employment of common sense in alliance with scientific thought, achieve something better than the miserable confusion and unutterable waste of opportunity in which an obstinate adherence to ancient rules of thumb has engulfed us. Nor is the prescription alarming. We are to put men to work by all the means at our disposal until prices have risen to a level appropriate to the existing debts and other obligations fixed in terms of money; and thereafter we are to see to it that the purchasing power of our money shall be kept stable. We are offered, indeed, the only possible means by which the structure of contract can be preserved and confidence in a monetary economy restored.

The Dominions and India, unanimous and unhesitating, beckon us towards this side. South America must necessarily follow in the North American orbit. How can we hesitate? To suppose that the Europeans are children of ancient wisdom holding up to us a restraining finger to protect us from dangerous innovation would be a ludicrous mistake.

B. The Face of the Great Depression

1. César Chávez Gets Tractored off the Land (1936)[*]

César Chávez, born in Arizona in 1927, became famous in the 1960s as the president of the United Farm Workers of America, a labor union organized to protect migratory farmworkers, mostly Mexicans and Mexican Americans, who harvested many of the crops in the American West. Here he tells of his eviction from his boyhood home near Yuma, Arizona, in the depths of the Great Depression. How did he assess the Depression's impact on his father and the rest of his family? In what ways might the experience of the Depression have contributed to his later commitment to organizing the farmworkers?

Oh, I remember having to move out of our house. My father had brought in a team of horses and wagon. We had always lived in that house, and we couldn't understand why we were moving out. When we got to the other house, it was a worse house, a poor house. That must have been around 1934. I was about six years old.

It's known as the North Gila Valley, about fifty miles north of Yuma. My dad was being turned out of his small plot of land. He had inherited this from his father, who had homesteaded it. I saw my two, three other uncles also moving out. And for the same reason. The bank had foreclosed on the loan.

---

[*]From Studs Terkel, *Hard Times.* Copyright © 1970, Studs Terkel.

If the local bank approved, the Government would guarantee the loan and small farmers like my father would continue in business. It so happened the president of the bank was the guy who most wanted our land. We were surrounded by him: he owned all the land around us. Of course, he wouldn't pass the loan.

One morning a giant tractor came in, like we had never seen before. My daddy used to do all his work with horses. So this huge tractor came in and began to knock down this corral, this small corral where my father kept his horses. We didn't understand why. In the matter of a week, the whole face of the land was changed. Ditches were dug, and it was different. I didn't like it as much.

We all of us climbed into an old Chevy that my dad had. And then we were in California, and migratory workers. There were five kids—a small family by those standards. It must have been around '36. I was about eight. Well, it was a strange life. We had been poor, but we knew every night there was a bed *there*, and that *this* was our room. There was a kitchen. It was sort of a settled life, and we had chickens and hogs, eggs and all those things. But that all of a sudden changed. When you're small you can't figure these things out. You know something's not right and you don't like it, but you don't question it and you don't let that get you down. You sort of just continue to move.

But this had quite an impact on my father. He had been used to owning the land and all of a sudden there was no more land. What I heard . . . what I made out of conversations between my mother and my father—things like, we'll work this season and then we'll get enough money and we'll go and buy a piece of land in Arizona. Things like that. Became like a habit. He never gave up hope that some day he would come back and get a little piece of land.

I can understand very, very well this feeling. These conversations were sort of melancholy. I guess my brothers and my sisters could also see this very sad look on my father's face.

2. A Salesman Goes on Relief (1930s)*

Ben Isaacs was a door-to-door clothing salesman when the Depression hit. His weekly income suddenly plummeted from $400 to $10, and then to nothing. Eventually he had to go on relief. What was the most difficult part of his experience? What does he think about the surge of post–World War II prosperity?

I was in business for myself, selling clothing on credit, house to house. And collecting by the week. Up to that time, people were buying very good and paying very good. But they start to speculate, and I felt it. My business was dropping from the beginning of 1928. They were mostly middle-class people. They weren't too rich, and they weren't too poor.

All of a sudden, in the afternoon, October, 1929 . . . I was going on my business and I heard the newspaper boys calling, running all around the streets and giving news and news: stock market crashed, stock market crashed. It came out just like lightning. . . .

We lost everything. It was the time I would collect four, five hundred dollars a week. After that, I couldn't collect fifteen, ten dollars a week. I was going around trying to collect enough money to keep my family going. It was impossible. Very few people could pay you. Maybe a dollar if they would feel sorry for you or what.

We tried to struggle along living day by day. Then I couldn't pay the rent. I had a little car, but I couldn't pay no license for it. I left it parked against the court. I sold it for $15 in order to buy some food for the family. I had three little children. It was a time when I didn't even have money to buy a pack of cigarettes, and I was a smoker. I didn't have a nickel in my pocket.

Finally people started to talk me into going into the relief. They had open soup kitchens. Al Capone,* he had open soup kitchens somewhere downtown, where people were standing in line. And you had to go two blocks, stand there, around the corner, to get a bowl of soup.

Lotta people committed suicide, pushed themselves out of buildings and killed themselves, 'cause they couldn't face the disgrace. Finally, the same thing with me.

I was so downcasted that I couldn't think of anything. Where can I go? What to face? Age that I can't get no job. I have no trade, except selling is my trade, that's all. I went around trying to find a job as a salesman. They wouldn't hire me on account of my age. I was just like dried up. Every door was closed on me, every avenue. Even when I was putting my hand on gold, it would turn into dust. It looked like bad luck had set its hand on my shoulder. Whatever I tried, I would fail. Even my money.

I had two hundred dollar in my pocket. I was going to buy a taxi. You had to have your own car to drive a taxi, those days. The man said: You have to buy your car from us. Checker Cab Company. So I took the two hundred dollar to the office, to make a down payment on the taxi. I took the money out—he said the kind of car we haven't got, maybe next week. So I left the office, I don't know what happened. The two hundred dollar went away, just like that. I called back: Did you find any money on the table? He said no, no money.

Things were going so bad with me, I couldn't think straight. Ordinarily, I won't lose any money. But that time, I was worrying about my family, about this and that. I was walking the street just like the easy person, but I didn't know whether I was coming or going.

I didn't want to go on relief. Believe me, when I was forced to go to the office of the relief, the tears were running out of my eyes. I couldn't bear myself to take money from anybody for nothing. If it wasn't for those kids—I tell you the truth—many a time it came to my mind to go commit suicide. Than go ask for relief. But somebody has to take care of those kids....

I went to the relief and they, after a lotta red tape and investigation, they gave me $45 a month. Out of that $45 we had to pay rent, we had to buy food and clothing for the children. So how long can that $45 go? I was paying $30 on the rent. I went and find another a cheaper flat, stove heat, for $15 a month. I'm telling you, today a dog wouldn't live in that type of a place. Such a dirty, filthy, dark place.

---

*Al Capone was a notorious Chicago gangster.

I couldn't buy maybe once a week a couple of pounds of meat that was for Saturday. The rest of the days, we had to live on a half a pound of baloney. I would spend a quarter for half a pound of baloney. It was too cold for the kids, too unhealthy. I found a six-room apartment for $25 a month. It was supposed to be steam heat and hot water. Right after we move in there, they couldn't find no hot water. It wasn't warm enough for anybody to take a bath. We had to heat water on the stove. Maybe the landlord was having trouble with the boiler. But it was nothing like that. The landlord had abandoned the building. About two months later, all of a sudden—no water. The city closed it for the non-payment of the water bill.

My wife used to carry two pails of water from the next-door neighbors and bring it up for us to wash the kids and to flush the toilet with it, and then wash our hands and face with it, or make tea or something, with that two pails of water. We lived without water for almost two months.

Wherever I went to get a job, I couldn't get no job. I went around selling razor blades and shoe laces. There was a day I would go over all the streets and come home with fifty cents, making a sale. That kept going until 1940, practically. 1939 the war started. Things start to get a little better. My wife found a job in a restaurant for $20 a week. Right away, I sent a letter to the relief people: I don't think I would need their help any more. I was disgusted with relief, so ashamed. I couldn't face it any more.

My next-door neighbor found me a job in the factory where he was working. That time I was around fifty. The man said, "We can't use you." They wouldn't hire nobody over forty-five. Two weeks later, this same man said, "Go tell Bill (the name of the foreman) I sent you. He'll hire you." They hire me. They give me sixty cents an hour. Twenty-year-old boys, they were paying seventy, seventy-five cents an hour. They were shortage of hand, that's why they hire me....

But in those days, we were all on relief and they were going around selling razor blades and shoe laces.

We were going to each other's. That was the only way we could drown our sorrow. We were all living within a block of each other. We'd come to each other's house and sit and talk and josh around and try to make a little cheerfulness.

Today we live far away from the rest of our friends. Depression days, that time, we were all poor. After things got better and people became richer and everyone had their own property at different neighborhoods, we fall apart from each other.

3. A Boy in Chicago Writes to President Roosevelt (1936)[*]

In an unprecedented outpouring, tens of thousands of Americans in the depression wrote directly to the president about their plight. Their letters, often written in rough English, nevertheless provide eloquent testimony about the personal bond that many people felt with the president and with his wife, Eleanor, and they offer vivid glimpses of the predicaments in which millions of Americans found themselves. The following

---

[*]From *Down and Out in the Great Depression: Letters from the Forgotten Man*, by Robert S. McElvaine. Copyright © 1983 by the University of North Carolina Press. Foreword © 2008 by the University of North Carolina Press.

letter was written by a twelve-year-old boy in Chicago in February 1936. What does he think is the Depression's worst impact on his family?

Mr. and Mrs. Roosevelt.
Wash. D.C.
Dear Mr. President:

    I'm a boy of 12 years. I want to tell you about my family. My father hasn't worked for 5 months. He went plenty times to relief, he filled out application. They won't give us anything. I don't know why. Please you do something. We haven't paid 4 months rent, Everyday the landlord rings the door bell, we don't open the door for him. We are afraid that will be put out, been put out before, and don't want to happen again. We haven't paid the gas bill, and the electric bill, haven't paid grocery bill for 3 months. My brother goes to Lane Tech. High School. he's eighteen years old, hasn't gone to school for 2 weeks because he got no carfare. I have a sister she's twenty years, she can't find work. My father he staying home. All the time he's crying because he can't find work. I told him why are you crying daddy, and daddy said why shouldn't I cry when there is nothing in the house. I feel sorry for him. That night I couldn't sleep. The next morning I wrote this letter to you. in my room. Were American citizens and were born in Chicago, Ill. and I don't know why they don't help us Please answer right away because we need it. will starve Thank you.
    God bless you.

[Anonymous]
Chicago, Ill.

4. Hard Times in a North Carolina Cotton Mill (1938–1939)*

Sam T. Vassar was a black North Carolinian who worked in a cotton mill. The cotton textile industry was among the economic sectors hardest hit by the Great Depression, and Vassar, along with thousands of other mill workers, lost his job. How did he survive? What is his attitude toward welfare?

    "At present I belong to the ranks of the unemployed. I have regular employment only four months of the annum, and sometimes that is just part-time." Sam T. Mayhew throws away the end of a fat cigar and settles back comfortably to be interviewed. The black expanse of face above hefty shoulders is interrupted by an impressive black mustache, which presents itself before the discontent in the big black eyes registers.
    "The past year it was just part-time. We worked at the gin [cotton mill] a few days the first of September and then were laid off till the middle, when the gin

*From *Such as Us: Southern Voices of the Thirties*, edited by Tom E. Terrill and Jerrold Hirsch. Copyright © 1978 by the University of North Carolina Press.

started running again. The gin shut down for the year on December 24, which gave me around 78 working days, 26 days to the month, for the year. I am paid $2 a day at the gin. So my income this year was 2 times 78—$156, I believe it is. I've got it all figured out and set down here in this little book. Now, to get an estimate of how much my family of seven has to live on, divide $156 by 12. I've figured it out; it's less than 50 cents a week, 7 and a fraction cents a day apiece for us, with everything we eat and wear coming out of the store. It's [wrong]...to say folks can't live that cheap; they can and do when they have to, such living as it is.

"Since February, I've been getting a little relief help from the government. Everything they've give since my first trip to Jackson I've set down in this little book; it starts out with 24 pounds of flour, 5 pounds of butter, 3 pounds of prunes and beans and ends up with 17 grapefruits and 3 pounds of butter, which is all they give me last week. I've figured up what the government has give me since February—counting flour at 75 cents, butter at 30 and so forth—and it comes to exactly $14.60. I've estimated that is just one-fourth of what we ought to have to live on, to eat. Several times I've asked for clothes the women make at the sewing room, but each time those have been denied.

"There's three grown folks and four children at my house, but what these children really ought to eat is more expensive than what we could manage on. I read considerably about the diet children ought to have—milk, butter, eggs, cereals, and fruits—but I can't stretch my income to provide it. I'm particular concerned into diets and meals, because at my house I have to do practically all the cooking since my wife has been physically and mentally incapacitated. My mother always taught her boys as well as girls to do every kind of work that came to hand, from cooking to washing, and it's well she did. The way I start the day is this: first, I make a fire in the stove, heat some lard in my frying pan, cut up an onion in the hot grease, then sift some flour and pepper and salt in the pan, and when the mixture is brown add a little water. This is the main dish for breakfast. Sometimes I stir up some egg bread with a spoon to serve with this onion gravy, sometimes biscuits.

"After breakfast the children get off to school and are gone till three-thirty in the afternoon. By time they get home, I try to have them a hot dish of dried peas or beans and some prunes or canned fruit if we have any. When there's meat, I season the beans with a little slice which I cut up into six pieces—I can't eat hog meat myself on account of high blood pressure—but when meat's out, I put a spoonful of lard in the pot for seasoning. Lunch? We don't have any lunch; two meals a day is all we have winter and summer. The children don't get very hungry, because they're used to it; sometimes when they see other children at school with candy and cakes, it's right hard on them. But they know I don't have so much as a nickel extra to give them to buy an apple or orange, and they don't complain.

"Sam Junior is in the eighth grade at school. He is the *Virginian-Pilot* paper boy and makes eighty cents a week, which only about takes care of his school supplies and book rentals. I don't know what Sam Junior wants to be yet; sometimes I think I ought to talk to him and help him decide. Then I'm afraid I won't be able to help him reach his achievement, which would make him more disappointed than if he had never planned anything. So, I'm just waiting, not saying yet what I'd like to see him do....

"No, I never thought about settling up North. There's no such hard distinction about color there, though. Four or five years ago, when I was trying without success to get the welfare to buy me a new artificial limb, I wrote to President Roosevelt asking him to interfere in my behalf, stating my circumstances and needs. In a short while here came a letter from the president, assuring me that the matter would be attended to through the proper agencies at once. I know it wasn't long before the welfare office at Jackson ordered me a new limb! My typewriter* already had more than paid for itself—the limb was around $125—in what it has done for me personally and toward the advancement of education among our race, not to mention the pleasure it is to conduct business matters in a businesslike way."

C. Voices of Protest

1. Senator Huey P. Long Wants Every Man to Be a King (1934)[†]

Senator Huey P. Long of Louisiana (1893–1935) helped Franklin Roosevelt win the Democratic party's nomination for the presidency in 1932. But Long quickly made himself a thorn in Roosevelt's flesh, especially with his demands for radical redistribution of the nation's income. Roosevelt worried that Long might emerge as a rival for leadership of the Democratic party and might even be elected president in 1940, but Long's career was cut short by an assassin's bullet in 1935. Long was a flamboyant personality and a sulfurous speaker. His radio audiences included millions of spellbound and supposedly sympathetic listeners. In the excerpt from his radio address of February 23, 1934, given here, what appear to be the main sources of his popular appeal? How responsible were his proposals? In what ways did he represent an alternative to Roosevelt's New Deal?

Now, we have organized a society, and we call it share-our-wealth society, a society with the motto "Every man a king."

Every man a king, so there would be no such thing as a man or woman who did not have the necessities of life, who would not be dependent upon the whims and caprices and ipse dixit of the financial martyrs for a living. What do we propose by this society? We propose to limit the wealth of big men in the country. There is an average of $15,000 in wealth to every family in America. That is right here today.

We do not propose to divide it up equally. We do not propose a division of wealth, but we propose to limit poverty that we will allow to be inflicted upon any man's family. We will not say we are going to try to guarantee any equality, or $15,000 to families. No; but we do say that one third of the average is low enough for any one family to hold, that there should be a guaranty of a family wealth of around $5,000; enough for a home, an automobile, a radio, and the ordinary conveniences, and the opportunity to educate their children; a fair share of the income of this land thereafter to that family so there will be no such thing as merely the

---

*The typewriter had been purchased earlier out of Vassar's meager savings.
[†]Senator Huey P. Long, "Every Man a King," *Congressional Record*, March 1, 1934.

select to have those things, and so there will be no such thing as a family living in poverty and distress.

We have to limit fortunes. Our present plan is that we will allow no one man to own more than $50 million. We think that with that limit we will be able to carry out the balance of the program. It may be necessary that we limit it to less than $50 million. It may be necessary, in working out of the plans, that no man's fortune would be more than $10 million or $15 million. But be that as it may, it will still be more than any one man, or any one man and his children and their children, will be able to spend in their lifetimes; and it is not necessary or reasonable to have wealth piled up beyond that point where we cannot prevent poverty among the masses.

Another thing we propose is [an] old-age pension of $30 a month for anyone that is 60 years old. Now, we do not give this pension to a man making $1,000 a year, and we do not give it to him if he has $10,000 in property, but outside of that we do.

We will limit hours of work. There is not any necessity of having overproduction. I think all you have got to do, ladies and gentlemen, is just limit the hours of work to such an extent as people will work only so long as is necessary to produce enough for all of the people to have what they need. Why, ladies and gentlemen, let us say that all of these labor-saving devices reduce hours down to where you do not have to work but four hours a day; that is enough for these people, and then praise be the name of the Lord, if it gets that good. Let it be good and not a curse, and then we will have 5 hours a day and five days a week, or even less than that, and we might give a man a whole month off during a year, or give him two months; and we might do what other countries have seen fit to do, and what I did in Louisiana, by having schools by which adults could go back and learn the things that have been discovered since they went to school.

We will not have any trouble taking care of the agricultural situation. All you have to do is balance your production with your consumption. You simply have to abandon a particular crop that you have too much of, and all you have to do is store the surplus for the next year, and the Government will take it over. When you have good crops in the area in which the crops that have been planted are sufficient for another year, put in your public works in the particular year when you do not need to raise any more, and by that means you get everybody employed. When the Government has enough of any particular crop to take care of all of the people, that will be all that is necessary; and in order to do all of this, our taxation is going to be to take the billion-dollar fortunes and strip them down to frying size, not to exceed $50 million and if it is necessary to come to $10 million, we will come to $10 million. We have worked the proposition out to guarantee a limit upon property (and no man will own less than one third the average), and guarantee a reduction of fortunes and a reduction of hours to spread wealth throughout this country. We would care for the old people above 60 and take them away from this thriving industry and give them a chance to enjoy the necessities and live in ease, and thereby lift from the market the labor which would probably create a surplus of commodities.

Those are the things we propose to do. "Every man a king." Every man to eat when there is something to eat; all to wear something when there is something to wear. That makes us all a sovereign.

You cannot solve these things through these various and sundry alphabetical codes. You can have the NRA and PWA and CWA and the UUG and GIN and any other kind of "dadgummed" lettered code. You can wait until doomsday and see twenty-five more alphabets, but that is not going to solve this proposition. Why hide? Why quibble? You know what the trouble is. The man that says he does not know what the trouble is is just hiding his face to keep from seeing the sunlight.

God told you what the trouble was. The philosophers told you what the trouble was; and when you have a country where one man owns more than 100,000 people, or a million people, and when you have a country where there are four men, as in America, that have got more control over things than all the 130 million people together, you know what the trouble is.

We had these great incomes in this country; but the farmer, who plowed from sunup to sundown, who labored here from sunup to sundown for six days a week, wound up at the end of the time with practically nothing....

Get together in your community tonight or tomorrow and organize one of our share-our-wealth societies. If you do not understand it, write me and let me send you the platform; let me give you the proof of it.

This is Huey P. Long talking, United States Senator, Washington, D.C. Write me and let me send you the data on this proposition. Enroll with us. Let us make known to the people what we are going to do. I will send you a button, if I have got enough of them left. We have got a little button that some of our friends designed, with our message around the rim of the button, and in the center "Every man a king." Many thousands of them are meeting through the United States, and every day we are getting hundreds and hundreds of letters. Share-our-wealth societies are now being organized, and people have it within their power to relieve themselves from this terrible situation.

2. Father Coughlin Demands "Social Justice" (1934, 1935)*

Father Charles E. Coughlin (1891–1979), a Canadian-born Roman Catholic priest, was a master of the new medium of the radio, rivaled perhaps only by Franklin Roosevelt. Speaking from the pulpit of his parish church in the modest working-class community of Royal Oak, Michigan, he commanded audiences of millions of listeners for his weekly broadcasts in the 1930s. It was said that a stroller could walk through certain neighborhoods on a summer Sunday afternoon and not miss a word of Father Coughlin's sermon as his voice wafted from radios through parlor windows into the streets. At first, Coughlin supported the New Deal, but he grew more critical and more viciously anti-Semitic, as well as passionately isolationist, as time went on. In the portions of his radio addresses reprinted here, to what social groups does he seem primarily to be speaking? What does he mean by "social justice"? How much of an alternative to the New Deal did he represent?

*The Rev. Chas. E. Coughlin, *A Series of Lectures on Social Justice* (Royal Oak, MI: Radio League of the Little Flower, 1935), pp. 16–19, 232–236.

Permit me to refer to the attitude of the National Union* towards public and private property. In diagnosing the economic ills of America we are convinced that there is a growing tendency to diminish the ownership of private property. In one sense, there is too little of private ownership. This is caused, first, by an economic system which persistently tends to concentrate wealth in the hands of a few, and, second, by an obnoxious system of taxation which discourages private ownership.

On the other hand, there are some things which, by their nature, should be owned nationally or publicly. Among these things there are listed the Central Bank which will have the sole right of issuing, coining and regulating the value of money be it currency or credit. In no sense does the National Union propose to nationalize any other bank. The local banking system must be kept intact. Its functions of safeguarding depositors' money and of extending local loans upon a reasonable basis must not be destroyed. It is regrettable that more than $773-million, or 23 per cent of the capital stock of these banks is now owned by the government. It would be a benediction, however, if the government nationalized the Federal Reserve Bank, whose capital stock is valued at approximately $140-million.

Then there are the natural resources scattered throughout the nation. The ownership and development of Niagara Falls, of the St. Lawrence Waterway, which is capable of generating one million two hundred thousand horsepower, of Boulder Dam, of the Tennessee Valley project, of the Grand Coulee on the Colorado—these and other natural resources should be owned and developed by the nation. In no sense should they be farmed out for private exploitation. The National Union further subscribes in its principles to a permanent public works program of reforestation, of land reclamation, of slum clearance, of national highway building and of other public activities whereat the idle factory workers may be employed during slack industrial seasons.

Relative to the many public utilities, the National Union regards the great majority of their holding companies as economic maladies. In many cases these holding companies were born in iniquity. By their nature they deceived the investing public. By their desire for greedy gain, oftentimes they marked up their values three, four and five times the tangible value of their physical properties. On this false basis they sold their securities to an unsuspecting public.

However, the National Union is not convinced that the ownership and the operation of public utilities should be nationalized. We prescribe that these should be kept in private hands subject to governmental supervision. At all times we must avoid the communistic tendency to sovietize industry or public service enterprises. Two extremes confront us: The one is advocating the national ownership of those things which should be retained in private hands; the other is advocating and supporting the private ownership of those things which should be owned in public.

Thus, while we cling to this twofold principle of ownership—one public, the other, private—let it also be noted that even private ownership must be subject to public regulation for the public good.

---

*Coughlin helped to found the National Union for Social Justice in 1934. It condemned communism and Roosevelt's New Deal alike, advocating for nationalization of basic industries and the banking system. It all but disappeared after failing to influence the 1936 presidential election, which FDR won in a massive landslide.

Relying upon that principle, the theory is sustained that, for the public welfare, the government may enact salutary laws to regulate not only personal liberties but also property and industrial liberties. Private ownership must be protected against corporate ownership. Small business must be safeguarded reasonably against monopolistic business. Were we to permit private ownership and small business gradually to be assimilated by corporate and monopolistic creations, then we are only preparing the way either for state capitalism or for communism.

3. Norman Thomas Proposes Socialism (1934)*

Norman Thomas (1884–1968), a Princeton University graduate and ordained Presbyterian minister, succeeded Eugene Debs as head of the Socialist party and was several times the party's presidential candidate, but he always polled fewer than one million popular votes, and he never won a single electoral vote. Here he lays out the Socialist program for coping with the depression. What are his main criticisms of the New Deal? Why did socialism not establish more of a foothold in Depression America?

All that I have said implies an importance in America of an immediate program of social insurance, unemployment relief, agricultural aid, and the guarantee of civil liberty, including the right of all workers to organize. It certainly implies that immediate concern for peace and an immediate program for preserving it, such as we have already discussed. But the essential feature of any immediate program for Socialism which is of value, and the one thing which will make an immediate program a sound beginning of the transitional period, is a redistribution of the national income on a basis that will give to workers collectively the fruits of their labor. Without this there is no cure for unemployment, bitter poverty, recurring crises and ultimate collapse. Now a kind of patchwork job of limited redistribution of income can be done, as everybody knows, by a program of high taxation on the rich and various social benefits for the poor. But this can never reach to the heart of our problem. Redistribution of the national income should not be a process of intervention by government to restore to the robbed a small portion of what has been taken from them. It should be a process of ending exploitation and establishing a scheme of things in which production is naturally and logically for use rather than for the private profit of an owning class. There is no such scheme of things which does not require social ownership. It follows that the immediate and essential objective of any desirable program must be the socialization and proper management of key industries. Socialization is not identical with nationalization. Increasingly it must be on an international scale. Immediately it may include ownership and operation by bona fide consumers' coöperatives. But practically the next steps toward socialization will require a process by which the national government will take over ownership. Such nationalization will fall short of socialization if, for instance, railroads

---

should be taken over for military purposes, or banks in order to make a state capitalism more efficient. True socialization can never lose sight of the great purpose of shared abundance. . . .

. . . On March 4, 1933, a Socialist administration ought to have begun with the socialization of banking. In rapid succession it would have taken over railroads, coal mines, and the power and oil industries. Then, as I have already indicated, it would have turned its attention to other monopolies. Any worthwhile agricultural program will compel the government to set up socialized marketing agencies and to take over and run as a public non-profit-making organization the dairy trust and probably the packing houses. In some cases it might not be necessary or desirable for the government to acquire all the existing property of, let us say, the power corporations or the dairy trust. It might condemn those facilities necessary for building up a great and economical system in conjunction with resources and facilities already in possession of governmental agencies, federal, state, and local.

This brief discussion of the necessity for capturing political power brings us face to face with the most challenging of all our American failures. That is, our failure to organize any strong party which consciously represents the great masses of workers who look toward the coöperative commonwealth. The debates on philosophy and tactics carried on with so much bitterness by our working-class parties and sects leave the masses almost untouched. Neither their discontent nor their rising hopes have yet found expression in a mighty and militant party.

4. Dr. Francis E. Townsend Promotes Old-Age Pensions (1933)*

Dr. Francis E. Townsend (1867–1960) was an obscure sixty-six-year-old physician in 1933 when he penned a letter to his local newspaper in Long Beach, California, that set off a tidal wave of enthusiasm for his old-age pension plan. Within weeks, "Townsend Clubs" sprouted up all over the country to promote Dr. Townsend's proposal, and by the following year the clubs claimed to have more than two million members. What were the main features of Townsend's idea? How practical was it? To what extent was the Social Security Act of 1935 a response to pressure from the Townsendites?

It is estimated that the population of the age of 60 and above in the United States is somewhere between nine and twelve millions. I suggest that the national government retire all who reach that age on a monthly pension of $200 a month or more, on condition that they spend the money as they get it. This will insure an even distribution throughout the nation of two or three billions of fresh money each month. Thereby assuring a healthy and brisk state of business, comparable to that we enjoyed during war times.

Where is the money to come from? More taxes? Certainly. We have nothing in this world we do not pay taxes to enjoy. But do not overlook the fact that we are already paying a large proportion of the amount required for these pensions in the form of life insurance policies, poor farms, aid societies, insane asylums and

---

*Dr. Francis E. Townsend, *New Horizons (An Autobiography)* (New York: J. L. Stewart, 1943), pp. 137–140.

prisons. The inmates of the last two mentioned institutions would undoubtedly be greatly lessened when it once became assured that old age meant security from want and care. A sales tax sufficiently high to insure the pensions at a figure adequate to maintain the business of the country in a healthy condition would be the easiest tax in the world to collect, for all would realize that the tax was a provision for their own future, as well as the assurance of good business now.

Would not a sales tax of sufficient size to maintain a pension system of such magnitude exhaust our taxability from our sources?, I am asked. By no means— income and inheritance taxes would still remain to us, and would prove far more fertile sources of Government income than they are today. Property taxes could be greatly reduced and would not constitute a penalty upon industry and enterprise.

Our attitude toward Government is wrong. We look upon Government as something entirely foreign to ourselves; as something over which we have no control, and which we cannot expect to do us a great deal of good. We do not realize that it can do us infinite harm, except when we pay our taxes. But the fact is, we must learn to expect and demand that the central Government assume the duty of regulating business activity. When business begins to slow down and capital shows signs of timidity, stimulus must be provided by the National Government in the form of additional capital. When times are good and begin to show signs of a speculative debauch such as we saw in 1929, the brakes must be applied through a reduction of the circulation medium. This function of the Government could be easily established and maintained through the pension system for the aged.

D. The Struggle to Organize Labor

1. Tom Girdler Girds for Battle (1937)*

The New Dealers, with their strong appeal to the low-wage voter, encouraged the unionization of labor, notably through the Wagner Act of 1935. "Big steel" (including the U.S. Steel Corporation) reluctantly accepted unionization by the CIO (Committee for Industrial Organization). "Little steel," led by the tough-fisted but mild-appearing Tom Girdler, who became a hero to conservatives, struck back. At his Republic Steel Company's plant in Chicago on Memorial Day 1937, the police fired upon and killed ten strikers, while wounding many others. Several additional lives were lost in Ohio cities. Girdler, appearing before a Senate committee, here justifies his opposition. Are the tactics of the CIO defensible (if accurately reported)? Are the accusations regarding communism convincing?

First of all let me make it clear that the fundamental issue in this strike is not one involving wages, hours, or working conditions in Republic [Steel Company] plants. This is not a strike in the sense that a large body of our employees quit work because of grievances against the company. What has happened is that an

---

*"Delivery or Non-Delivery of Mail in Industrial Strife Areas," Senate Committee on Post Offices, *Hearings*, 75th Cong., 1st sess. (1937), pp. 207–210.

invading army descended upon our plants and forced many of our employees from their jobs.

Fully 23,000 of our employees have remained at work throughout the strike despite threats and violence, and many additional thousands have been kept from work against their will.

The basic issue of this strike is the right of American citizens to work, free from molestation, violence, coercion, and intimidation by a labor organization whose apparent policy is either to rule or to ruin American industry....

The difficulties in the present dispute arise from the fact that the company will not enter into a contract, oral or written, with an irresponsible party; and the C.I.O., as presently constituted, is wholly irresponsible....

The irresponsibility of the C.I.O. is well established by the fact that 200 strikes and walk-outs have taken place in the plants of the General Motors Corporation since that corporation signed an agreement with the C.I.O. which called for an end of strikes during the period of the agreement....

Further evidence of the irresponsible character of the C.I.O. is to be seen in the lawless and terroristic conduct of its members since the beginning of the present strike. Republic plants have been surrounded by armed crowds who call themselves pickets and who, by force and violence, have imprisoned in the plants thousands of employees who refused to heed the strike call and remained at work. These men have been prevented from returning to their families when their work is done, and other employees who want to work have been prevented from getting into the plants.

Airplanes delivering food to workers besieged in the plants have been fired upon by armed mobs about the gates. The delivery of the United States mails has been interfered with. Railroad tracks have been dynamited. Families of men who are at work in the plants in certain communities have been threatened, coerced, and stoned. Defiance of law and order has been so flagrant that in some communities law enforcement has completely collapsed.

These illegal practices have not been peculiar to the Republic strike. They have characterized C.I.O. methods since the beginning of its organization drive in many industries. They have more than confirmed the conclusion reached by this company before the present strike ever started that the C.I.O. was and is an irresponsible and dangerous force in America....

We believe that the C.I.O. with its terroristic methods and Communistic technique of picketing constitutes the most dangerous threat to the preservation of democracy in the United States....

Now, let me state a few fundamental conclusions which I have reached about the C.I.O.

First. The C.I.O. has denied to free American citizens who refuse to pay tribute to it the right to work.

Second. The C.I.O. encourages and promotes violence and disregard of law. If this is done under instructions and approval of its leaders, it amounts to a confession on their part that they are deliberately adopting the methods of force and terrorism which have proved so successful for the dictators of Europe. If this is done without their approval and occurs because they cannot control their own men, it is a confession that the C.I.O. is an irresponsible party and that a contract with it would not be worth the paper upon which it is written.

Third. The C.I.O. is associated with Communism. Many of its leaders and organizers are avowed Communists. The *Daily Worker*, the official newspaper of the Communist Party of the United States, gives the C.I.O. its full support. Can any organization which welcomes the support of the International Communist Party still claim that it adheres to the principles of democracy?

2. John Lewis Lambastes Girdler (1937)*

John L. Lewis—gruff, domineering, shaggy-browed—had risen from the depths of the coal mines to the head of the potent United Mine Workers of America. Seeking new worlds to conquer, he undertook to unionize mass production industries through his Committee for Industrial Organization (CIO). The clash between him and Tom Girdler—both strong-minded men—became so noisy that FDR himself burst out, "A plague on both your houses." Four years later, in 1941, Girdler's "little steel" was forced to accept unionization. In this impassioned speech over a radio hookup, Lewis betrayed his anger. What was his loudest complaint? Why did he regard people like Girdler as more dangerous than communists?

Five of the corporations in the steel industry elected to resist collective bargaining and undertook to destroy the steel-workers' union. These companies filled their plants with industrial spies, assembled depots of guns and gas bombs, established barricades, controlled their communities with armed thugs, leased the police power of cities, and mobilized the military power of a state to guard them against the intrusion of collective bargaining within their plants.

During this strike eighteen steel workers were either shot to death or had their brains clubbed out by police, or armed thugs in the pay of the steel companies....

The steel workers have now buried their dead, while the widows weep and watch their orphaned children become objects of public charity. The murder of these unarmed men has never been publicly rebuked by any authoritative officer of the state or federal government. Some of them, in extenuation, plead lack of jurisdiction, but murder as a crime against the moral code can always be rebuked without regard to the niceties of legalistic jurisdiction by those who profess to be the keepers of the public conscience.

[Tom] Girdler, of Republic Steel, in the quiet of his bedchamber, doubtless shrills his psychopathic cackles as he files notches on his corporate gun and views in retrospect the ruthless work of his mercenary killers....

The United States Chamber of Commerce, the National Association of Manufacturers, and similar groups representing industry and financial interests are rendering a disservice to the American people in their attempts to frustrate the organization of labor and in their refusal to accept collective bargaining as one of our economic institutions.

Vital Speeches 3 (September 15, 1937): 731 (speech of September 3, 1937).

These groups are encouraging a systematic organization of vigilante groups to fight unionization under the sham pretext of local interests. They equip these vigilantes with tin hats, wooden clubs, gas masks, and lethal weapons, and train them in the arts of brutality and oppression. They bring in snoops, finks [strikebreakers], hatchet gangs, and Chowderhead Cohens to infest their plants and disturb the communities.

Fascist organizations have been launched and financed under the shabby pretext that the C.I.O. movement is Communistic. The real breeders of discontent and alien doctrines of government and philosophies subversive of good citizenship are such as these who take the law into their own hands. No tin-hat brigade of goose-stepping vigilantes or bibble-babbling mob of blackguarding and corporation-paid scoundrels will prevent the onward march of labor, or divert its purpose to play its natural and rational part in the development of the economic, political, and social life of our nation. . . .

Do those who have hatched this foolish cry of Communism in the C.I.O. fear the increased influence of labor in our democracy? Do they fear its influence will be cast on the side of shorter hours, a better system of distributed employment, better homes for the underprivileged, social security for the aged, a fairer distribution of the national income?

Certainly the workers that are being organized want a voice in the determination of these objectives of social justice.

E. Conservation in the New Deal

1. Backcountry Poets Reflect on the Civilian Conservation Corps (1934, 1935)[*]

The Civilian Conservation Corps (CCC) was one of the most popular New Deal programs. From its inception in 1933 to its demise in 1942, more than three million young men served in the CCC, for periods ranging from six months to two years. Each received bed and board and a monthly salary of $30, of which he was required to send $25 home to his family. The CCC built trails in the national parks and forests, fought wildfires, helped to erect dams and bridges, and planted millions of trees in the nation's denuded forestlands. The CCC provided more than much-needed income to depression-pinched young men and their families. It also acquainted millions of city dwellers with the outdoors, many for the first time in their lives, and helped to spread the ideals of conservation. In these two specimens of barracks poetry from CCC enlistees, published in the CCC national newspaper, Happy Days, *what do they identify as the most positive and the most negative aspects of their service? How might the attitudes shaped by CCC service have carried over into the World War II and postwar eras?*

---

[*]From Edwin G. Hill, *In the Shadow of the Mountain: The Spirit of the CCC*, p. 175. Copyright © 1990.

What Might Have Been
(To Mr. Roosevelt)
By Raymond Kraus
Co. 1232, Olympia, Wash.

A pauper's life we might have led,
And died revolting for our bread;
We might have shed each other's blood,
And died face down within the mud.
But all because we have this man,
Whose only words are there: "I can!"
Our nation shall evolve on high,
And we shall see a brighter sky.
He gave to us the chance to say,
I've earned my bread and keep today,
The chance to smile, to toil, to sweat,
This damn depression thus forget.

The Wail of a Spike Camper
By R. F. McMahon, Co. 1744
Avery, Idaho

I joined a brand new outfit
They called it the CCC
They issued me my clothing
And put three shots in me.
They sent me out to a spike camp
Put a cot beneath my frame
They gave me a thousand-pound hammer
And a pick to go with same.
They fed me mush and eggs and bacon
I never got to town
It looks to me like I'm a sucker
Until my time runs down.

2. A Daughter of the Plains Struggles with Dust Storms (1934)*

Mother Nature and carelessly exploitative farming practices combined in the 1930s to lay waste much of the Great Plains from the Dakotas to Texas. The "Dust Bowl," a region around the Texas and Oklahoma panhandles, was so cruelly blighted by enormous dust storms during the Depression years that it came to stand as a symbol of the accumulated devastation of centuries of unbridled development. The great dust storms helped to spur a renewed conservation effort in the New Deal era. Ann

---

*Reprinted from *Dust Bowl Diary* by Ann Marie Low. Copyright © 1984 by the University of Nebraska Press.

*Marie Low, who lived in North Dakota, recorded in her diary some of the storms'
worst ravages. What were the major hardships that she had to endure?*

[*April 25, 1934, Wednesday*] Last weekend was the worst dust storm we ever had.
We've been having quite a bit of blowing dirt every year since the drouth started, not
only here, but all over the Great Plains. Many days this spring the air is just full of
dirt coming, literally, for hundreds of miles. It sifts into everything. After we wash the
dishes and put them away, so much dust sifts into the cupboards we must wash them
again before the next meal. Clothes in the closets are covered with dust.

Last weekend no one was taking an automobile out for fear of ruining the
motor. I rode Roany to Frank's place to return a gear. To find my way I had to ride
right beside the fence, scarcely able to see from one fence post to the next.

Newspapers say the deaths of many babies and old people are attributed to
breathing in so much dirt.

[*May 7, 1934, Monday*] The dirt is still blowing. Last weekend Bud [her brother]
and I helped with the cattle and had fun gathering weeds. Weeds give us greens
for salad long before anything in the garden is ready. We use dandelions, lamb's
quarter, and sheep sorrel. I like sheep sorrel best. Also, the leaves of sheep sorrel,
pounded and boiled down to a paste, make a good salve.

Still no job. I'm trying to persuade Dad I should apply for rural school #3 out
here where we went to school. I don't see a chance of getting a job in a high school
when so many experienced teachers are out of work.

He argues that the pay is only $60.00 a month out here, while even in a grade
school in town I might get $75.00. Extra expenses in town would probably eat up
that extra $15.00. Miss Eston, the practice teaching supervisor, told me her salary
has been cut to $75.00 after all the years she has been teaching in Jamestown. She
wants to get married. School boards will not hire married women teachers in these
hard times because they have husbands to support them. Her fiancé is the sole
support of his widowed mother and can't support a wife, too. So she is just stuck
in her job, hoping she won't get another salary cut because she can scarcely live on
what she makes and dress the way she is expected to.

Dad argues the patrons always stir up so much trouble for a teacher at #3 some
teachers have quit in mid-term. The teacher is also the janitor, so the hours are long.

I figure I can handle the work, kids, and patrons. My argument is that by
teaching here I can work for my room and board at home, would not need new
clothes, and so could send most of my pay to Ethel [her sister] and Bud.

In April, Ethel had quit college, saying she did not feel well.

[*May 21, 1934, Monday*] Ethel has been having stomach trouble. Dad has been
taking her to doctors though suspecting her trouble is the fact that she often goes
on a diet that may affect her health. The local doctor said he thought it might be
chronic appendicitis, so Mama took Ethel by train to Valley City last week to have a
surgeon there remove her appendix.

Saturday Dad, Bud, and I planted an acre of potatoes. There was so much dirt
in the air I couldn't see Bud only a few feet in front of me. Even the air in the house
was just a haze. In the evening the wind died down, and Cap came to take me to
the movie. We joked about how hard it is to get cleaned up enough to go anywhere.

The newspapers report that on May 10 there was such a strong wind the experts in Chicago estimated 12,000,000 tons of Plains soil was dumped on that city. By the next day the sun was obscured in Washington, D.C., and ships 300 miles out at sea reported dust settling on their decks.

Sunday the dust wasn't so bad. Dad and I drove cattle to the Big Pasture. Then I churned butter and baked a ham, bread, and cookies for the men, as no telling when Mama will be back.

[*May 30, 1934, Wednesday*] Ethel got along fine, so Mama left her at the hospital and came to Jamestown by train Friday. Dad took us both home.

The mess was incredible! Dirt had blown into the house all week and lay inches deep on everything. Every towel and curtain was just black. There wasn't a clean dish or cooking utensil. There was no food. Oh, there were eggs and milk and one loaf left of the bread I baked the weekend before. I looked in the cooler box down the well (our refrigerator) and found a little ham and butter. It was late, so Mama and I cooked some ham and eggs for the men's supper because that was all we could fix in a hurry. It turned out they had been living on ham and eggs for two days.

Mama was very tired. After she had fixed starter for bread, I insisted she go to bed and I'd do all the dishes.

It took until 10 o'clock to wash all the dirty dishes. That's not wiping them—just washing them. The cupboards had to be washed out to have a clean place to put them.

3. Franklin Roosevelt Creates the Tennessee Valley Authority (1933)*

During the famed "Hundred Days" that marked the beginning of his first administration in 1933, Franklin Roosevelt took one especially bold initiative with huge environmental implications: the creation of the Tennessee Valley Authority (TVA), designed as a comprehensive program for the planned development of the Tennessee River watershed. Beginning at Muscle Shoals, Alabama, a dam site that the government had controlled since World War I but had never utilized, the TVA built dams to control flooding and to generate electrical power, and it encouraged modern, scientific farming practices in the upper South region it served. It also displaced thousands of people whose land was destined to be drowned by the huge reservoirs that built up behind the dams, and it provoked the bitter opposition of privately owned power companies. In the following message to Congress calling for the creation of the TVA, how does Roosevelt justify this extraordinary undertaking? Roosevelt later proposed similar programs for other major river systems, but almost none came to fruition. Why did the TVA approach prove so limited in its application elsewhere?

[The White House] *April 10, 1933*

---

*From Edgar B. Nixon, ed., *Franklin D. Roosevelt and Conservation, 1911–1945*, pp. 151–152, 341–344, 489–491. Copyright © 1957 by the U.S. Government Printing Office.

To the Congress: The continued idleness of a great national investment in the Tennessee Valley leads me to ask the Congress for legislation necessary to enlist this project in the service of the people.

It is clear that the Muscle Shoals development is but a small part of the potential public usefulness of the entire Tennessee River. Such use, if envisioned in its entirety, transcends mere power development: it enters the wide fields of flood control, soil erosion, afforestation, elimination from agricultural use of marginal lands, and distribution and diversification of industry. In short, this power development of war days leads logically to national planning for a complete river watershed involving many States and the future lives and welfare of millions. It touches and gives life to all forms of human concerns.

I, therefore, suggest to the Congress legislation to create a Tennessee Valley Authority—a corporation clothed with the power of government but possessed of the flexibility and initiative of a private enterprise. It should be charged with the broadest duty of planning for the proper use, conservation and development of the natural resources of the Tennessee River drainage basin and its adjoining territory for the general social and economic welfare of the nation. This Authority should also be clothed with the necessary power to carry these plans into effect. Its duty should be the rehabilitation of the Muscle Shoals development and the coordination of it with the wider plan.

Many hard lessons have taught us the human waste that results from lack of planning. Here and there a few wise cities and counties have looked ahead and planned. But our nation has "just grown." It is time to extend planning to a wider field, in this instance comprehending in one great project many States directly concerned with the basin of one of our greatest rivers.

This in a true sense is a return to the spirit and vision of the pioneer. If we are successful here we can march on, step by step, in a like development of other great natural territorial units within our borders.

4. Roosevelt Promotes Natural Resources Planning (1935)[*]

At his ancestral estate in Hyde Park, New York, Roosevelt had long taken a special interest in studying and adopting techniques of sound ecological management, and he became a quite knowledgeable arborist. In 1935 he advocated a national program of comprehensive resource planning and environmental management. He explained his objectives in the message to Congress that follows. What are his principal concerns? How do his ideas about natural resources management compare with those of his distant cousin, Theodore Roosevelt (see p. 525)? Did the two Roosevelts share a common understanding of "Nature"?

Jan. 24, 1935

To the Congress: During the three or four centuries of white man on the American Continent, we find a continuous striving of civilization against Nature. It is

---

[*]From Edgar B. Nixon, ed., *Franklin D. Roosevelt and Conservation, 1911–1945*, pp. 341–344. Copyright © 1957 by the U.S. Government Printing Office.

only in recent years that we have learned how greatly by these processes we have harmed Nature and Nature in turn has harmed us.

We should not too largely blame our ancestors, for they found such teeming riches in woods and soil and water—such abundance above the earth and beneath it—such freedom in the taking, that they gave small heed to the results that would follow the filling of their own immediate needs. Most of them, it is true, had come from many peopled lands where necessity had invoked the preserving of the bounties of Nature. But they had come here for the obtaining of a greater freedom, and it was natural that freedom of conscience and freedom of government should extend itself in their minds to the unrestricted enjoyment of the free use of land and water.

Furthermore, it is only within our own generation that the development of science, leaping forward, has taught us where and how we violated nature's immutable laws and where and how we can commence to repair such havoc as man has wrought.

In recent years little groups of earnest men and women have told us of this havoc; of the cutting of our last stands of virgin timber; of the increasing floods, of the washing away of millions of acres of our top soils, of the lowering of our watertables, of the dangers of one crop farming, of the depletion of our minerals—in short the evils that we have brought upon ourselves today and the even greater evils that will attend our children unless we act.

Such is the condition that attends the exploitation of our natural resources if we continue our planless course....

If the misuse of natural resources alone were concerned, we should consider our problem only in terms of land and water. It is because misuse extends to what men and women are doing with their occupations and to their many mistakes in herding themselves together that I have chosen, in addressing the Congress, to use the broader term "National Resources."

For the first time in our national history we have made an inventory of our national assets and the problems relating to them. For the first time we have drawn together the foresight of the various planning agencies of the Federal Government and suggested a method and a policy for the future.

I am sending you herewith the report of the National Resources Board, appointed by me on June 30, 1934 to prepare the comprehensive survey which so many of us have sought so long. I transmit also the report made by the Mississippi Valley Committee of the Public Works Administration, which Committee has also acted as the Water Planning Committee in the larger report....

In this inventory of our national wealth we follow the custom of prudent people toward their own private property. We as a Nation take stock of what we as a Nation own. We consider the uses to which it can be put. We plan these uses in the light of what we want to be, and what we want to accomplish as a people. We think of our land and water and human resources not as static and sterile possessions but as life-giving assets to be directed by wise provision for future days. We seek to use our natural resources not as a thing apart but as something that is interwoven with industry, labor, finance, taxation, agriculture, homes, recreation, good citizenship. The result of this interweaving will have a greater influence on the future American standard of living than all the rest of our economics put together.

F. The Supreme Court Fight and After

1. Harold Ickes Defends His Chief (1937)[*]

The ultraconservative Supreme Court had repeatedly overthrown crucial New Deal measures for economic and social reform. Roosevelt, intoxicated by his heady majorities of 1932, 1934, and 1936, concluded that in a true democracy the "horse-and-buggy" Court ought to catch up with the will of the people. Two weeks after his second inauguration, he sprang his clever Supreme Court scheme on a surprised Congress and nation. Among other changes, he proposed increasing the membership of the Court from nine to fifteen by appointing additional (New Deal) justices to offset those aged seventy or more who were unwilling to retire. Critics cried that this was "packing" the Court; supporters replied that this was "unpacking" the Court by offsetting reactionaries. "Honest Harold" Ickes, the acid-tongued secretary of the interior, here tells how he defended Roosevelt before an audience of Texans. Given that the Court scheme had not received mention in the Democratic platform or in Roosevelt's speeches during the recent campaign of 1936, how persuasive is Ickes's argument regarding a popular mandate?

Then I switched to a discussion of the constitutional situation, with special reference to the recent proposal of the President to change the judiciary system. I could hear a gasp go up as I disclosed my purpose to discuss this issue. A week or ten days ago the Texas State Senate, with only three or four votes opposing, had gone on record as being against the President's proposal. The House decided neither to approve nor disapprove.

I waded right into the constitutional issue with both feet. In my first sentence I asked where had the Supreme Court gotten its supposed power to pass upon the constitutionality of acts of Congress. I read the Tenth Amendment and then I said that this power had been usurped.[†]

I then went on to discuss the supposed checks and balances in our tripartite Federal system, pointing out that while there were ample checks and balances with respect to the legislative and executive branches, there wasn't a single check on the judiciary except that of impeachment, which was slow and cumbersome and of doubtful efficacy when it came to a court of nine men. I remarked in passing that one could not be impeached for being too old, that that was not a crime but merely a misfortune.

I argued that the people had given the President a mandate at the last election to provide them with such social and economic legislation as is implicit in the term "New Deal." I said that he would be recreant to his trust if he didn't do all within his power to give the people what he had promised them and what they had shown so unmistakably that they wanted.

[†]The Tenth Amendment reserved undelegated powers to the states, but the function of judicial review, "usurped" by the Supreme Court, is generally regarded as implicit in the views of the Founding Fathers and in the Constitution.

I expressed the opinion that the people wanted the benefits of the New Deal now. I pointed out that while those who are opposing the President pretend to do it on the basis that a constitutional amendment is the proper procedure, it would take all of twenty years to get such an amendment through.

With respect to an act or acts of Congress limiting the powers of the Supreme Court so as to provide, for instance, that no law could be held to be unconstitutional except on a two-thirds or three-quarters majority, I ventured to predict that any such law would be declared unconstitutional by the Supreme Court and therefore would be ineffective.

2. Republicans Roast Roosevelt (1940)[*]

The Roosevelt-Willkie presidential campaign of 1940 generated new bitterness. Roosevelt's challenge to the two-term tradition, combined with his unsuccessful attempt to pack the Supreme Court and purge certain members of Congress hostile to him, accentuated fears of dictatorship. The Democrats argued that Roosevelt had saved capitalism by averting, whatever the monetary cost and confusion, a revolutionary uprising. The Republican platform, invoking the Preamble to the Constitution, found the New Deal wanting on many counts. In the light of subsequent developments, which is the more valid accusation?

Instead of leading us into More Perfect Union the Administration has deliberately fanned the flames of class hatred.

Instead of the Establishment of Justice the Administration has sought the subjection of the Judiciary to Executive discipline and domination.

Instead of insuring Domestic Tranquility the Administration has made impossible the normal friendly relation between employers and employees and has even succeeded in alienating both the great divisions of Organized Labor.

Instead of Providing for the Common Defense the Administration, notwithstanding the expenditure of billions of our dollars, has left the Nation unprepared to resist foreign attack.

Instead of promoting the General Welfare the Administration has Domesticated the Deficit, Doubled the Debt, Imposed Taxes where they do the greatest economic harm, and used public money for partisan political advantage.

Instead of the Blessings of Liberty the Administration has imposed upon us a Regime of Regimentation which has deprived the individual of his freedom and has made of America a shackled giant.

Wholly ignoring these great objectives, as solemnly declared by the people of the United States [in the Constitution], the New Deal Administration has for seven long years whirled in a turmoil of shifting, contradictory, and overlapping administrations and policies. Confusion has reigned supreme. The only steady undeviating characteristic has been the relentless expansion of the power of the Federal government over the everyday life of the farmer, the industrial worker, and the businessman. The emergency demands organization—not confusion. It demands free and intelligent cooperation—not incompetent domination. It demands a change.

---

[*]K. H. Porter and D. B. Johnson, eds., *National Party Platforms, 1840–1956* (Urbana: University of Illinois Press, 1961).

The New Deal Administration has failed America.

It has failed by seducing our people to become continuously dependent upon government, thus weakening their morale and quenching the traditional American spirit.

3. Assessing the New Deal (1935, 1936)

That most newspaper publishers in the 1930s were critical of the New Deal may help explain why many newspaper cartoonists took a dim view of Roosevelt and his reform program. The print below, by Herbert Johnson of the Saturday Evening *Post, is a typical example of traditional conservative criticism of the New Deal. It is worth noting that C. D. Batchelor, the cartoonist who produced the image below, refused to support the anti–New Deal views of his publisher at the* New York Daily News. *Would the "forgotten man" in the second print be likely to see himself as the "taxpayer" in the first image? Why or why not? Which image had a greater political appeal in the 1930s? How did Franklin Roosevelt work to counter the opposition of the press lords of his day?*

"Yes, You Remembered Me"

Thought Provokers

1. In what respects was the Great Depression a global phenomenon? Why did it prove so difficult to find a global solution to the crisis?

2. What might have happened if the federal government had refused to provide relief for the millions of unemployed, as well as for the impoverished farmers? Was planned scarcity immoral?

3. What were the greatest hardships Americans suffered during the Great Depression? Why was there not more radical protest against "hard times"?

4. To what extent did Roosevelt's critics offer realistic alternatives to the New Deal? How did Roosevelt outmaneuver his opponents?

5. Is the right to work without first joining a union a basic right? Why did the CIO call management fascist, and why did management call the CIO communist?

6. Were the New Deal's natural resource and conservation policies on balance helpful or harmful to the environment? How should environmental concerns be balanced with other human needs?

7. Why did Roosevelt's Supreme Court proposal stir up such a hornet's nest? Was Roosevelt justified in breaking his platform promises regarding economy and a balanced budget? Did the New Deal change the basic character of the American people? Of the federal government?

33

Franklin D. Roosevelt and the Shadow of War, 1933–1941

The epidemic of world lawlessness is spreading....
There must be positive endeavors to preserve peace.

Franklin D. Roosevelt, 1937

Prologue: The same depression that generated the New Deal at home accelerated the rise of power-hungry dictators abroad: Hitler, Mussolini, and the Japanese warlords. Congress tried to insulate the nation from the imminent world war by arms embargoes and other presumed safeguards. But when Hitler attacked Poland in 1939, the American people found themselves torn between two desires: they wanted to avoid involvement, but they feared for their future security if they failed to support the democracies. Under Roosevelt's prodding, Congress repealed the arms embargo in 1939, and the administration gradually took a series of steps that removed any pretense of neutrality. Most Americans—except the diehard isolationists—were willing to risk hostilities in an effort to help the democracies and halt the aggressors. Roosevelt took the gamble but lost when a shooting war developed with Germany in the Atlantic and when Japan attacked the U.S. naval base at Pearl Harbor, Hawaii, on December 7, 1941.

A. The Struggle Against Isolationism

1. Two Views of Isolationism (1936, 1938)

As Europe and Asia moved toward a new world war in the 1930s, Americans remembered with great bitterness and regret their country's involvement in World War I. Revisionist histories and congressional investigations of the World War I–era munitions industry reinforced the idea that America's involvement in the Great War of 1914–1918 had been a terrible mistake. Many Americans, especially in the arch-isolationist Midwest, resolved never again to allow their country to be drawn into a foreign war. Yet other Americans, particularly in the great cities of the eastern seaboard, argued that the United States could not safely ignore the threat posed by Nazi Germany and militaristic Japan. These internationally minded Americans accused their isolationist countrymen of being hopelessly naive about the dangers their country faced. The cartoon below, by C. D. Batchelor of the New York Daily News, *makes the pro-isolationist case; the one on page 641, by Albert Hirschfeld of the* New Masses, *makes the pro-internationalist case. Which is more persuasive as propaganda? Were the two images aimed at the same sectors of the American public?*

The isolationist

Al Hirschfeld. Reproduced by arrangement with Hirschfeld's exclusive representative, the Margo Feiden Galleries Ltd., New York, www.alhirschfeld.com.

2. Roosevelt Pleads for Repeal of the Arms Embargo (1939)*

The arms-embargoing Neutrality Acts of 1935 and 1937 made no distinction between aggressor and victim. When Hitler wantonly launched World War II in September 1939, the United States could not legally sell munitions to the unprepared democracies, although U.S. sentiment and self-interest both cried aloud for aid to Britain and France. A worried Roosevelt summoned Congress into special session and made the following dramatic appeal. He was wrong on two counts. First, the arms embargo, as purely domestic legislation, was not a departure from long-established international law. Second, the Jeffersonian Embargo and Non-Intercourse Acts did not cause the War of 1812; they came within a few days of averting it. What does this excerpt suggest about Roosevelt's technique as a politician? What did he see as the most dangerous loophole in the existing legislation?

Congressional Record, 76th Cong., 2d sess. (September 21, 1939), pp. 10–11.

Beginning with the foundation of our constitutional Government in the year 1789, the American policy in respect to belligerent nations, with one notable exception, has been based on international law....

The single exception was the policy adopted by this nation during the Napoleonic Wars, when, seeking to avoid involvement, we acted for some years under the so-called Embargo and Non-Intercourse Acts. That policy turned out to be a disastrous failure—first, because it brought our own nation close to ruin, and, second, because it was the major cause of bringing us into active participation in European wars in our own War of 1812. It is merely reciting history to recall to you that one of the results of the policy of embargo and non-intercourse was the burning in 1814 of part of this Capitol in which we are assembled.

Our next deviation by statute from the sound principles of neutrality, and peace through international law, did not come for 130 years. It was the so-called Neutrality Act of 1935—only 4 years ago—an Act continued in force by the Joint Resolution of May 1, 1937, despite grave doubts expressed as to its wisdom by many Senators and Representatives and by officials charged with the conduct of our foreign relations, including myself.

I regret that the Congress passed that Act. I regret equally that I signed that Act.

On July 14th of this year, I asked the Congress, in the cause of peace and in the interest of real American neutrality and security, to take action to change that Act.

I now ask again that such action be taken in respect to that part of the Act which is wholly inconsistent with ancient precepts of the law of nations—the [arms] embargo provisions. I ask it because they are, in my opinion, most vitally dangerous to American neutrality, American security, and American peace.

These embargo provisions, as they exist today, prevent the sale to a belligerent by an American factory of any completed implements of war, but they allow the sale of many types of uncompleted implements of war, as well as all kinds of general material and supplies. They, furthermore, allow such products of industry [e.g., copper] and agriculture [e.g., cotton] to be taken in American-flag ships to belligerent nations. There in itself—under the present law—lies definite danger to our neutrality and our peace.

3. Senator Arthur Vandenberg Fights Repeal (1939)*

Senator Arthur H. Vandenberg of Michigan—voluble orator, longtime newspaper reporter, and author of books on Alexander Hamilton—was a leader of the Republican isolationists and a serious contender for the presidential nomination in 1940. Later, in 1945, he underwent a spectacular conversion to internationalism and rose to heights of statesmanship in supporting the Marshall Plan for the rehabilitation of postwar Europe. While fighting against the repeal of the arms embargo in 1939, he wrote in his diary that he deplored Roosevelt's "treacherous" and "cowardly" idea that the United States could be "half in and half out of this war." Hating Hitlerism, he felt that the honorable course would be to go in or to stay out—and he much preferred to stay out. In this speech in the Senate against the repeal of the arms embargo, what does he regard as both unneutral and unethical?

---

*Congressional Record, 76th Cong., 2d sess. (October 4, 1939), p. 95.

Mr. President, I believe this debate symbolically involves the most momentous decision, in the eyes of America and of the World, that the United States Senate has confronted in a generation.

In the midst of foreign war and the alarms of other wars, we are asked to depart basically from the neutrality which the American Congress has twice told the world, since 1935, would be our rule of conduct in such an event. We are particularly asked to depart from it through the repeal of existing neutrality law establishing an embargo on arms, ammunition, and implements of war. We are asked to depart from it in violation of our own officially asserted doctrine, during the [first] World War, that the rules of a neutral cannot be prejudicially altered in the midst of a war.

We are asked to depart from international law itself, as we ourselves have officially declared it to exist. Consciously or otherwise, but mostly consciously, we are asked to depart from it in behalf of one belligerent whom our personal sympathies largely favor, and against another belligerent whom our personal feelings largely condemn. In my opinion, this is the road that may lead us to war, and I will not voluntarily take it....

The proponents of the change vehemently insist that their steadfast purpose, like ours, is to keep America out of the war, and their sincere assurances are presented to our people. But the motive is obvious, and the inevitable interpretation of the change, inevitably invited by the circumstances, will be that we have officially taken sides.

Somebody will be fooled—either the America which is assured that the change is wholly pacific, or the foreigners who believe it is the casting of our die. Either of these disillusionments would be intolerable. Each is ominous. Yet someone will be fooled—either those at home who expect too much, or those abroad who will get too little.

There is no such hazard, at least to our own America, in preserving neutrality in the existing law precisely as we almost unanimously notified the world was our intention as recently as 1935 and 1937. There is no such jeopardy, at least to our own America, in maintaining the arms embargo as it is. No menace, no jeopardy, to us can thus be persuasively conjured.

Therefore millions of Americans and many members of the Congress can see no reason for the change, but infinite reason to the contrary, if neutral detachment is our sole objective. I am one who deeply holds this view. If I err, I want to err on America's side.

[Despite such pleas, the arms embargo was repealed early in November 1939. The vote was 55 to 24 in the Senate, 243 to 172 in the House.]

4. Charles Lindbergh Argues for Isolation (1941)[*]

After France fell to Hitler in 1940, the embattled British stood alone. U.S. interventionists called for a helping hand to Britain; the isolationists called for hands off. The isolationist America First group proclaimed, "We have nothing to fear from a Nazi-European victory." Boyish-faced, curly-haired Colonel Charles A. Lindbergh, who had narrowed the Atlantic with his historic solo flight in 1927, stressed the width of the ocean in his new role as a leading isolationist orator. After inspecting

---

[*]Source: http://www.charleslindbergh.com/americanfirst/speech2.asp.

Germany's aircraft facilities in 1938, he stoutly maintained that Hitler (who decorated him) could never be conquered in the air. If Lindbergh proved so wrong in an area in which he was a specialist, form some judgment about the assessment of the U.S. strategic position that he made in this speech before a New York mass meeting in April 1941. To what extent is interventionism undemocratic, assuming that Lindbergh's figures were correct? Is his analysis of public opinion trustworthy?

We have weakened ourselves for many months, and still worse, we have divided our own people, by this dabbling in Europe's wars. While we should have been concentrating on American defense, we have been forced to argue over foreign quarrels. We must turn our eyes and our faith back to our own country before it is too late. And when we do this, a different vista opens before us.

Practically every difficulty we would face in invading Europe becomes an asset to us in defending America. Our enemy, and not we, would then have the problem of transporting millions of troops across the ocean and landing them on a hostile shore. They, and not we, would have to furnish the convoys to transport guns and trucks and munitions and fuel across three thousand miles of water. Our battleships and our submarines would then be fighting close to their home bases. We would then do the bombing from the air and the torpedoing at sea. And if any part of an enemy convoy should ever pass our navy and our air force, they would still be faced with the guns of our coast artillery, and behind them the divisions of our Army.

The United States is better situated from a military standpoint than any other nation in the world. Even in our present condition of unpreparedness no foreign power is in a position to invade us today. If we concentrate on our own defenses and build the strength that this nation should maintain, no foreign army will ever attempt to land on American shores.

War is not inevitable for this country. Such a claim is defeatism in the true sense. No one can make us fight abroad unless we ourselves are willing to do so. No one will attempt to fight us here if we arm ourselves as a great nation should be armed. Over a hundred million people in this nation are opposed to entering the war. If the principles of democracy mean anything at all, that is reason enough for us to stay out. If we are forced into a war against the wishes of an overwhelming majority of our people, we will have proved democracy such a failure at home that there will be little use fighting for it abroad.

The time has come when those of us who believe in an independent American destiny must band together and organize for strength. We have been led toward war by a minority of our people. This minority has power. It has influence. It has a loud voice. But it does not represent the American people. During the last several years I have traveled over this country from one end to the other. I have talked to many hundreds of men and women, and I have letters from tens of thousands more, who feel the same way as you and I.

[Public opinion polls during these months showed contradictory desires. A strong majority of the American people wanted to stay out of war, but a strong majority favored helping Britain even at the risk of war. The Lend-Lease Act of 1941 received about two-to-one support in the public opinion polls and more than that in congressional voting.]

5. The New York Times *Rejects Isolationism (1941)**

The New York Times *challenged Lindbergh's views in a lengthy and well-reasoned editorial that brilliantly set forth the case for intervention. What are its principal points?*

Those who tell us now that the sea is still our certain bulwark, and that the tremendous forces sweeping the Old World threaten no danger to the New, give the lie to their own words in the precautions they would have us take.

To a man they favor an enormous strengthening of our defenses. Why? Against what danger would they have us arm if none exists? To what purpose would they have us spend these almost incredible billions upon billions for ships and planes, for tanks and guns, if there is no immediate threat to the security of the United States? Why are we training the youth of the country to bear arms? Under pressure of what fear are we racing against time to double and quadruple our industrial production?

No man in his senses will say that we are arming against Canada or our Latin-American neighbors to the south, against Britain or the captive states of Europe. We are arming solely for one reason. We are arming against Hitler's Germany—a great predatory Power in alliance with Japan.

It has been said, times without number, that if Hitler cannot cross the English Channel he cannot cross three thousand miles of sea. But there is only one reason why he has not crossed the English Channel. That is because forty-five million determined Britons, in a heroic resistance, have converted their island into an armed base, from which proceeds a steady stream of sea and air power. As Secretary [of State Cordell] Hull has said: "It is not the water that bars the way. It is the resolute determination of British arms. Were the control of the seas by Britain lost, the Atlantic would no longer be an obstacle—rather, it would become a broad highway for a conqueror moving westward."

That conqueror does not need to attempt at once an invasion of continental United States in order to place this country in deadly danger. We shall be in deadly danger the moment British sea power fails; the moment the eastern gates of the Atlantic are open to the aggressor; the moment we are compelled to divide our one-ocean Navy between two oceans simultaneously.

The combined Axis fleets [German, Italian, Japanese] outmatch our own: they are superior in numbers to our fleet in every category of vessel, from warships and aircraft-carriers to destroyers and submarines.[†] The combined Axis air strength will be much greater than our own if Hitler strikes in time—and when has he failed to strike in time? The master of Europe will have at his command shipways that can outbuild us, the resources of twenty conquered nations to furnish his materials, the oil of the Middle East to stoke his engines, the slave labor of a continent—bound by no union rules, and not working on a forty-hour week—to turn out his production.

---

†Three foreign fleets are not necessarily equal to the sum of all their parts. There are different languages and signals, different caliber guns and ammunition, different types of maneuvers, and so forth.

Grant Hitler the gigantic prestige of a victory over Britain, and who can doubt that the first result, on our side of the ocean, would be the prompt appearance of imitation Nazi regimes in a half-dozen Latin-American nations, forced to be on the winning side, begging favors, clamoring for admission to the Axis? What shall we do then? Make war upon these neighbors, send armies to fight in the jungles of Central or South America; run the risk of outraging native sentiment and turning the whole continent against us? Or shall we sit tight while the area of Nazi influence draws ever closer to the Panama Canal, and a spreading checkerboard of Nazi airfields provides ports of call for German planes that may choose to bomb our cities?

But even if Hitler gave us time, what kind of "time" would we have at our disposal?

There are moral and spiritual dangers for this country as well as physical dangers in a Hitler victory. There are dangers to the mind and heart as well as to the body and the land.

Victorious in Europe, dominating Africa and Asia through his Axis partners, Hitler could not afford to permit the United States to live an untroubled and successful life, even if he wished to. We are the arch-enemy of all he stands for: the very citadel of that "pluto-democracy" which he hates and scorns. As long as liberty and freedom prevailed in the United States there would be constant risk for Hitler that our ideas and our example might infect the conquered countries which he was bending to his will. In his own interest he would be forced to harry us at every turn.

Who can doubt that our lives would be poisoned every day by challenges and insults from Nazi politicians; that Nazi agents would stir up anti-American feeling in every country they controlled; that Nazi spies would overrun us here; that Hitler would produce a continual series of lightning diplomatic strokes—alliances and "non-aggression pacts" to break our will; in short, that a continuous war of nerves, if nothing worse, would be waged against us?

And who can doubt that, in response, we should have to turn our own nation into an armed camp, with all our traditional values of culture, education, social reform, democracy and liberty subordinated to the single, all-embracing aim of self-preservation? In this case we should indeed experience "regimentation." Every item of foreign trade, every transaction in domestic commerce, every present prerogative of labor, every civil liberty we cherish, would necessarily be regulated in the interest of defense.

B. The Lend-Lease Controversy

1. FDR Drops the Dollar Sign (1940)*

A serious student of history, Roosevelt was determined to avoid the blunders of World War I. The postwar quarrel with the Allies over debts lingered in his memory as he groped for some means of bolstering the hard-pressed British without getting involved in a repayment wrangle. Keeping his new brainstorm under his hat until his triumphant reelection over Wendell Willkie—he might have lost if he had revealed

---

The Public Papers and Addresses of Franklin D. Roosevelt, 1940 Volume (New York: MacMillan, 1941), pp. 606–608.

it before then—he outlined his scheme at one of his breezy, off-the-cuff press confer-ences. How did he propose to eliminate the root of the debt difficulty?

It is possible—I will put it that way—for the United States to take over British [war] orders, and, because they are essentially the same kind of munitions that we use ourselves, turn them into American orders. We have got enough money to do it. And thereupon, as to such portion of them as the military events of the future deter-mine to be right and proper for us to allow to go to the other side, either lease or sell the materials, subject to mortgage, to the people on the other side. That would be on the general theory that it may still prove true that the best defense of Great Britain is the best defense of the United States, and therefore that these materials would be more useful to the defense of the United States if they were used in Great Britain than if they were kept in storage here.

Now, what I am trying to do is to eliminate the dollar sign. That is something brand new in the thoughts of practically everybody in this room, I think—get rid of the silly, foolish old dollar sign.

Well, let me give you an illustration: Suppose my neighbor's home catches fire, and I have a length of garden hose four or five hundred feet away. If he can take my garden hose and connect it up with his hydrant, I may help him to put out his fire. Now, what do I do? I don't say to him before that operation, "Neighbor, my garden hose cost me $15; you have got to pay me $15 for it." What is the transaction that goes on? I don't want $15—I want my garden hose back after the fire is over. All right. If it goes through the fire all right, intact, without any damage to it, he gives it back to me and thanks me very much for the use of it. But suppose it gets smashed up—holes in it—during the fire; we don't have to have too much formality about it, but I say to him, "I was glad to lend you that hose; I see I can't use it any more, it's all smashed up." He says, "How many feet of it were there?" I tell him, "There were 150 feet of it." He says, "All right, I will replace it." Now, if I get a nice garden hose back, I am in pretty good shape.

In other words, if you lend certain munitions and get the munitions back at the end of the war, if they are intact—haven't been hurt—you are all right. If they have been damaged or have deteriorated or have been lost completely, it seems to me you come out pretty well if you have them replaced by the fellow to whom you have lent them.

[After the United States entered the war, supplies provided by foreign countries to U.S. forces were credited to their account as reverse lend-lease. The total value of U.S. lend-lease was over $50 billion, less some $7 billion in reverse lend-lease. Some cash was involved in the final settlement of accounts.]

2. Senator Burton Wheeler Assails Lend-Lease (1941)[*]

Like the interventionists, Roosevelt believed that the salvation of Britain through large-scale military aid was crucial for the defense of the United States. But so strong was isolationist opposition that the proposed Lend-Lease Act could not be entitled

---

[*]Reprinted in *Congressional Record*, 77th Cong., 1st sess. (speech of January 12, 1941), Appendix, pp. 178–179.

"An Act to Intervene in World War II for the Defense of Britain." The official title was "An Act Further to Promote the Defense of the United States." As finally passed, the new law virtually pledged the United States to the full extent of its economic resources to provide military supplies for those who were fighting aggression. Fiery Senator Burton K. Wheeler of Montana, "a born prosecutor" who had run for vice president on the left-wing La Follette Progressive ticket of 1924, was one of the most vehement isolationists. In the following radio speech, how prophetic is he?

The lend-lease policy, translated into legislative form, stunned a Congress and a nation wholly sympathetic to the cause of Great Britain.... It warranted my worst fears for the future of America, and it definitely stamps the President as war-minded.

The lend-lease-give program is the New Deal's Triple-A foreign policy; it will plow under every fourth American boy.

Never before have the American people been asked or compelled to give so bounteously and so completely of their tax dollars to any foreign nation. Never before has the Congress of the United States been asked by any President to violate international law. Never before has this Nation resorted to duplicity in the conduct of its foreign affairs. Never before has the United States given to one man the power to strip this Nation of its defenses. Never before has a Congress coldly and flatly been asked to abdicate.

If the American people want a dictatorship—if they want a totalitarian form of government and if they want war—this bill should be steamrollered through Congress, as is the wont of President Roosevelt.

Approval of this legislation means war, open and complete warfare. I, therefore, ask the American people before they supinely accept it, Was the last World War worth while?

If it were, then we should lend and lease war materials. If it were, then we should lend and lease American boys. President Roosevelt has said we would be repaid by England. We will be. We will be repaid, just as England repaid her war debts of the first World War—repaid those dollars wrung from the sweat of labor and the toil of farmers with cries of "Uncle Shylock." Our boys will be returned—returned in caskets, maybe; returned with bodies maimed; returned with minds warped and twisted by sights of horrors and the scream and shriek of high-powered shells.

Considered on its merits and stripped of its emotional appeal to our sympathies, the lend-lease-give bill is both ruinous and ridiculous....

It gives to one man—responsible to no one—the power to denude our shores of every warship. It gives to one individual the dictatorial power to strip the American Army of our every tank, cannon, rifle, or anti-aircraft gun. No one would deny that the lend-lease-give bill contains provisions that would enable one man to render the United States defenseless, but they will tell you, "The President would never do it." To this I say, "Why does he ask the power if he does not intend to use it?" Why not, I say, place some check on American donations to a foreign nation?...

I say in the kind of language used by the President—shame on those who ask the powers—and shame on those who would grant them.

[Talk of "plowing under every fourth American boy" spurred Roosevelt into declaring at his press conference of January 14, 1941, that this was "the most untruthful, the most dastardly, unpatriotic thing that has ever been said. Quote me on that. That really is the rottenest thing that has been said in public life in my generation." What measure of truth was there in Wheeler's charge?]

C. War in the Atlantic

1. Framing the Atlantic Charter (1941)*

Roosevelt finally met with Prime Minister Winston Churchill in deepest secrecy off the coast of Newfoundland in August 1941. Major items of discussion were lend-lease shipments, common defense, and the halting of Japanese aggression. Churchill later wrote that for Roosevelt—the head of a technically neutral state—to meet in this way with the prime minister of a belligerent state was "astonishing" and amounted to "warlike action." The most spectacular offspring of the conference was the unofficial Atlantic Charter, which in 1942 became the cornerstone of Allied war aims. An admixture of the old Wilson Fourteen Points (see p. 557) and the New Deal, it held out seductive hope to the victims of the dictators. What aspects of the Atlantic Charter come closest to "warlike action"?

The President of the United States of America and the Prime Minister, Mr. Churchill, representing His Majesty's Government in the United Kingdom, being met together, deem it right to make known certain common principles in the national policies of their respective countries on which they base their hopes for a better future for the world.

First, their countries seek no aggrandizement, territorial or other;

Second, they desire to see no territorial changes that do not accord with the freely expressed wishes of the peoples concerned [self-determination, one of Wilson's Fourteen Points; in part Points V and XII of the fourteen];

Third, they respect the right of all peoples to choose the form of government under which they will live; and they wish to see sovereign rights and self-government restored to those who have been forcibly deprived of them [territorial restoration, Points VI, VII, VIII, XI of the fourteen];

Fourth, they will endeavor, with due respect for their existing obligations, to further the enjoyment by all states, great or small, victor or vanquished, of access, on equal terms, to the trade and to the raw materials of the world which are needed for their economic prosperity [Point III of the fourteen];

Fifth, they desire to bring about the fullest collaboration between all nations in the economic field with the object of securing, for all, improved labor standards, economic advancement, and social security [a combination of the objectives of the League of Nations and the New Deal];

Department of State Bulletin 5 (August 14, 1941): 125–126.

Sixth, after the final destruction of the Nazi tyranny, they hope to see established a peace which will afford to all nations the means of dwelling in safety within their own boundaries, and which will afford assurance that all the men in all the lands may live out their lives in freedom from fear and want;

Seventh, such a peace should enable all men to traverse the high seas and oceans without hindrance [freedom of the seas, Point II of the fourteen];

Eighth, they believe that all of the nations of the world, for realistic as well as spiritual reasons, must come to the abandonment of the use of force. Since no future peace can be maintained if land, sea, or air armaments continue to be employed by nations which threaten, or may threaten, aggression outside of their frontiers, they believe, pending the establishment of a wider and permanent system of general security [the United Nations, replacing the League of Nations], that the disarmament of such nations is essential. They will likewise aid and encourage all other practicable measures which will lighten for peace-loving peoples the crushing burden of armaments [Point IV of the fourteen].

2. The Chicago Tribune *Is Outraged (1941)*[*]

A highly influential mouthpiece of midwestern isolationism was the Chicago Tribune, *self-elected "The World's Greatest Newspaper." Violently anti-Roosevelt and anti-intervention, it resorted to extreme measures, including the publication of Washington's secret war plans three days before Pearl Harbor. To what extent does the* Tribune's *editorial on the Atlantic Conference confirm Churchill's later observation that the deliberations amounted to "warlike action"?*

Mr. Roosevelt's dangerous ambition always to do what no other President ever did, and to be the man who shakes the world, led him to meet Mr. Churchill, as is now disclosed, at sea. There, he, the head of a nation which is not at war, and the head of the British empire, which is at war, signed their names to an eight-point war and peace program, as if both countries not only were fighting side by side but saw their way to victory....

For Mr. Churchill the event would be, he could hope, that last step which would bring him what he has awaited as his salvation—the final delivery on Mr. Roosevelt's commitments, the delivery of the United States with all its man power into the war at all points. Mr. Churchill would appreciate that Mr. Roosevelt in the eyes of the world became his full ally....

Mr. Roosevelt himself had that end in view. As head of a nation at peace he had no right to discuss war aims with the ruler of a country at war. He had no right to take a chair at such a conference. He had no regard for his constitutional duties or his oath of office when he did so. He not only likes to shatter traditions, he likes to shatter the checks and restraints which were put on his office. He is thoro[ugh]ly unAmerican. His ancestry is constantly emerging. He is the true descendant of that

---

[*]Editorial against Atlantic Charter (August 15, 1941) as quoted in *A Century of Tribune Editorials* (1947), pp. 129–130.

James Roosevelt, his great-grandfather, who was a Tory in New York during the Revolution and took the oath of allegiance to the British king.*...

He comes of a stock that has never fought for the country and he now betrays it, altho[ugh] it has repudiated his program and him with it....

The American people can rest assured that Mr. Churchill was paying little attention to the rehash of the Wilsonian futilities, to the freedom of the seas and the freedom of peoples such as the [British-ruled] people of India, for instance. What he wanted to know of Mr. Roosevelt was: When are you coming across? And it is the answer to that question that concerns the American people, who have voted 4 to 1 that they are not going across at all unless their government drags them in against their will.

One phrase in the statement would have Mr. Churchill's complete approval—"after final destruction of the Nazi tyranny." To that he committed the President of the United States in circumstances as spectacular and theatrical as could be arranged. Mr. Roosevelt pledged himself to the destruction of Hitler and the Nazis. In the circumstances in which this was done Mr. Churchill would insist that it was the pledge of a government, binding upon the country.

The country repudiates it. Mr. Roosevelt had no authority and can find none for making such a pledge. He was more than outside the country. He was outside his office. The spectacle was one of two autocratic rulers, one of them determining the destiny of his country in the matter of war or peace absolutely in his own will, as if his subjects were without voice.

The country rejects that idea of its government.

3. FDR Proclaims Shoot-on-Sight (1941)†

Lend-Lease carried an implied commitment that the United States would guarantee delivery of arms, although the law specifically forbade "convoying vessels by naval vessels of the United States." Roosevelt got around this restriction by setting up a system of patrols by U.S. warships working in collaboration with the British. On September 4, 1941, the U.S. destroyer Greer in Icelandic waters trailed a German submarine for three and one-half hours while radioing its position to nearby British aircraft. The U-boat finally fired two torpedoes (which missed), whereupon the Greer retaliated with depth bombs (which also missed). Seven days later, after presumably taking time to verify the facts, Roosevelt went on the radio with this sensational shoot-on-sight speech. What liberties did he take with the truth? Did the crisis justify his doing so?

The Navy Department of the United States has reported to me that, on the morning of September fourth, the United States destroyer *Greer*, proceeding in full daylight toward Iceland, had reached a point southeast of Greenland. She was

---

*James Roosevelt, only fifteen years old when the fighting began, was a student at Princeton from 1776 to 1780. His father, a staunch patriot, was forced to flee New York City. There is no evidence that young James took the alleged oath; the probabilities are strong that he did not. (Information provided by Elizabeth B. Drewry, director of the Franklin D. Roosevelt Library.)

†*Department of State Bulletin* 5 (September 13, 1941): 193, 195, 197.

carrying American mail to Iceland. She was flying the American flag. Her identity as an American ship was unmistakable.

She was then and there attacked by a submarine. Germany admits that it was a German submarine. The submarine deliberately fired a torpedo at the *Greer*, followed later by another torpedo attack. In spite of what Hitler's propaganda bureau has invented, and in spite of what any American obstructionist organization may prefer to believe, I tell you the blunt fact that the German submarine fired first upon this American destroyer without warning, and with deliberate design to sink her.

Our destroyer, at the time, was in waters which the Government of the United States has declared to be waters of self-defense—surrounding outposts of American protection in the Atlantic.

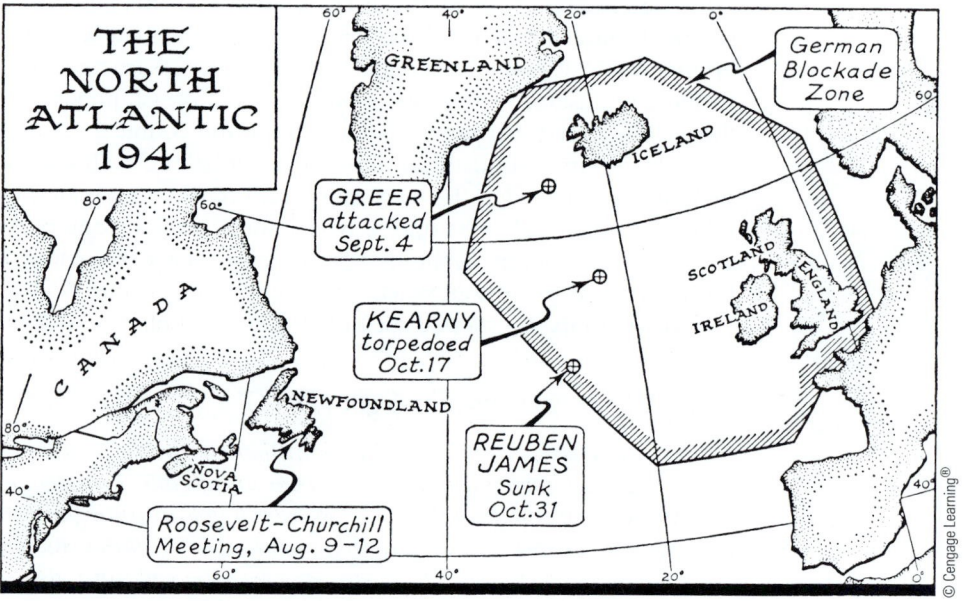

In the north, outposts have been established by us in Iceland, Greenland, Labrador, and Newfoundland. Through these waters there pass many ships of many flags. They bear food and other supplies to civilians; and they bear [lend-lease] matériel of war, for which the people of the United States are spending billions of dollars, and which, by Congressional action, they have declared to be essential for the defense of our own land.

The United States destroyer, when attacked, was proceeding on a legitimate mission. . . .

Generation after generation, America has battled for the general policy of the freedom of the seas.[*] That policy is a very simple one—but a basic, fundamental one. It means that no nation has the right to make the broad oceans of the world,

---

[*]The traditional American concept of freedom of the seas did not include the armed convoying of gift Lend-Lease munitions through German-proclaimed war zones to the enemies of Germany.

at great distances from the actual theater of land war, unsafe for the commerce of others....

It is no act of war on our part when we decide to protect the seas which are vital to American defense. The aggression is not ours. Ours is solely defense.

But let this warning be clear. From now on, if German or Italian vessels of war enter the waters, the protection of which is necessary for American defense, they do so at their own peril.

[Patrolling led to convoying by presidential edict, despite the express terms of the Lend-Lease Act, and convoying led to shooting. In October 1941 the U.S. destroyer Kearny *suffered torpedo damage and a loss of eleven lives in a battle with German submarines southwest of Iceland. Later that month the U.S. destroyer* Reuben James *was torpedoed and sunk while on convoy duty. An undeclared shooting war with Hitler was now being waged in the Atlantic.]*

D. Blowup in the Pacific

1. Harold Ickes Prepares to "Raise Hell" (1941)*

New Japanese aggression in south Indochina, despite warnings from Washington, finally prompted Roosevelt to clamp down a complete embargo on shipments going to Japan when he froze all Japanese assets in the United States on July 25, 1941. Faced with the loss of critical oil supplies, the Tokyo warlords were confronted with agonizing alternatives: yielding some of the fruits of their aggression in the Far East or fighting the United States and its allies. The United States was by no means ready for war in the vast Pacific, and the administration seriously considered a three-month truce; Roosevelt favored six months. But this proposal was never formally presented to Japan. The outspoken secretary of the interior, Harold Ickes, recorded in his secret diary the story as he heard it. What does this account (written on November 30) reveal of the inner workings of the federal government? Why did the truce scheme fail?

Our State Department has been negotiating for several days with Saburo Kurusu, the special envoy sent over from Japan, and with Ambassador Kichisaburo Nomura. I have had a suspicion for a long time that the State Department would resume a policy of appeasement toward Japan, if it could get away with it.

Our State Department, according to a story that I have heard, had actually proposed what it called a "truce" for three months with Japan. We were to resume shipments of cotton and other commodities, but the most important item on the list was gasoline for "civilian" purposes. Now anyone who knows anything about Japan and about the situation there knows that there is very little, if any, civilian use of gasoline.... Then a strong protest came in from General Chiang Kai-shek

*From *The Secret Diary of Harold L. Ickes, Vol. III:* The Lowering Clouds, 1939–1941 by Harold L. Ickes. Copyright © 1954 by Simon & Schuster, Inc. Copyright renewed © 1982 by Simon & Schuster, Inc.

[Jiang Jieshi] to the effect that to do this would destroy the morale of the Chinese. It was the intention of the State Department to crowd the thing through without even giving Halifax [British ambassador] a chance to refer it to Churchill. However, the British fought for and obtained a sufficient delay to consult Churchill, and he was strongly opposed.

The strong opposition of China and Britain caused the appeasers of the State Department to pause. They went to the White House, and in the end the President refused to go through with the deal.

If it had not been for the strenuous intervention of Churchill and Chiang Kai-shek, the appeasers in the State Department, with the support of the President, would have resumed at least a partial commercial relationship with Japan, as the result of which we would have sent Japan cotton and gasoline and other commodities....

If this negotiation with Japan had been consummated, I would have promptly resigned from the Cabinet with a ringing statement attacking the arrangement and raising hell generally with the State Department and its policy of appeasement. I have no doubt that the country would have reacted violently. As a matter of fact, some of the newspapers indicated that they were uneasy and printed editorials deprecating any attempt at even a partial resumption of relationship with Japan. I believe that the President would have lost the country on this issue and that hell would have been to pay generally.

Now matters are very tense indeed so far as Japan is concerned. The morning papers carry headlines announcing that Japan has solemnly declared her determination "to purge American and British influence from East Asia for the honor and pride of mankind." So it may be, after all, that there will be a clash in the Pacific.

2. Tōgō Blames the United States (1952)*

Instead of appeasement, Secretary of State Hull presented stern terms to the two Japanese envoys in his note of November 26, 1941. Japan would have to withdraw its armed forces from China, after four years of aggression, and from Indochina as well. In return, the United States would unfreeze Japanese assets and make some other secondary concessions. Such loss of face was so abhorrent to the Japanese warlords that Hull had little hope that the terms would be accepted. The next day he told Secretary of War Stimson, "I have washed my hands of it, and it is now in the hands of you and [Secretary of the Navy] Knox—the Army and Navy." Here, the reaction of Japan is described by the foreign minister, Shigenori Tōgō, who later died in prison while serving a twenty-year sentence as a war criminal. Where did he lay the blame for the breakdown of negotiations?

Ambassador Grew, then in Tokyo, later said that when the note of 26 November was sent, the button which set off the war had been pushed.

On the 26th and 27th Secretary Hull held special press conferences at which he gave a full account of the Japanese-American negotiations; the American press

---

responded by reporting almost unanimously that it was Japan's choice whether to accept the Hull Note or go to war. Later—in wartime—an American chronicler wrote that even a Monaco or a Luxemburg would have taken up arms against the United States if it had been handed such a memorandum as that which the State Department presented to the Japanese government....

It is therefore no longer arguable at this time of day that the American authorities, having made all necessary preparations in the expectation that the negotiations would break down and a war ensue, delivered the Hull Note anticipating that Japan would reject it, thus compelling her to elect between total surrender and war. Indeed, remembering that the question of how to insure that Japan should fire the first shot had been in the forefront in the War Cabinet's discussions in Washington, it seems not unwarrantable to construe the note as going beyond the forcing of a choice—it is not too much to say that it was the throwing down of a challenge to Japan, or at the least constituted an ultimatum without time limit.

This we knew in Tokyo—though we could not then know of the words and acts of the high American officials which confirmed our deduction—from the drastic terms of the note and the inclusion among them of conditions never theretofore suggested. Our interpretation was confirmed by the reaction to Hull's disclosures by the American press—which played up, as if at the urging of the governmental authorities, the choice between the terms of the Hull Note and war—and by the plainly visible tightening of the encirclement of Japan.

So far as concerns my own state of mind upon receipt of the Hull Note, I can never forget the despair which overpowered me. I had fought and worked unflaggingly until that moment; but I could feel no enthusiasm for the fight thereafter. I tried as it were to close my eyes and swallow the Hull Note whole, as the alternative to war, but it stuck in the craw. In contrast to my dejection, many of the military men were elated at the uncompromising attitude of the United States, as if to say, "Didn't we tell you so?"—they were by no means easy to be patient with.

[The Japanese later argued that they were forced to break out of the economic encirclement resulting from Roosevelt's embargo-freezing order of July 25, 1941. This view found surprising support in 1944 from one U.S. ally, Captain Oliver Lyttleton, British minister of production. In a London speech he declared, "Japan was provoked into attacking the Americans at Pearl Harbor. It is a travesty on history ever to say that America was forced into the war....It is incorrect to say that America was ever truly neutral." The subsequent uproar in the United States forced Lyttleton hastily to soften his remarks. (New York Times, June 21, 22, 1944.)]

3. Cordell Hull Justifies His Stand (1948)[*]

Isolationist Senator Vandenberg, writing in his diary just after Pearl Harbor, felt that the United States would have had to yield "relatively little" to pacify Japan, and feared that "we may have driven her needlessly into hostilities through our dogmatic

---

[*]From Cordell Hull, *Memoirs of Cordell Hull, Vol. II.* Copyright © 1948.

diplomatic attitudes." "We 'asked for it,'" he added, "and we 'got it.'" Secretary of State Hull, the soft-spoken Tennessean, here outlines three possible alternatives in his Memoirs. Assuming that the ultimate security of the United States required the halting of the Japanese, and knowing that the U.S. Navy was not ready for Japan, form conclusions regarding the wisdom of Hull's choice among the three possibilities. Were other courses open?

There were three methods to meet the danger from Japan. One was by a preventive attack. But democracies do not engage in preventive attacks except with greatest difficulty. Had I suggested to the President that he go to Congress and ask for a declaration of war against Japan at some time after the invasion of southern Indo-China, he could have made a good case concerning the dangers to us inherent in Japan's course of aggression. But, remembering the fact that on August 13, 1941, only three weeks after Japan invaded southern Indo-China, the House of Representatives sustained the Selective Service Act by a majority of just one vote, it seems most unlikely that the President could have obtained a declaration.

Nor would the military and naval authorities have been ready for a preventive attack. The fact that they pleaded for more time solely to prepare our defenses in the Pacific was proof in itself that they were not prepared to take the offensive.

A preventive attack, moreover, would have run counter to our determination to pursue the course of peace to the end, with the hope, however microscopic, that even at the last hour the Japanese might have a change of heart.

The second method to meet the danger was to agree to Japan's demands. This would have given us peace—that is, until Japan, after strengthening herself through the concessions we should have made, was ready to move again. But it would have denied all the principles of right living among nations which we had supported; it would have betrayed the countries [China, Britain] that later became our allies; and it would have given us an infamous place in history.

When we realize that Japan was ruthlessly invading peaceful countries, that the United States had pleaded with her from the beginning to cease her course of military conquest in partnership with Hitler, and that all problems in the Pacific would have practically settled themselves if Japan had adopted a policy of peace, it is evident that Japan had no right to make demands upon us. Japan negotiated as if we, too, were an aggressor, as if both countries had to balance their aggressions. Japan had no more right to make demands upon us than an individual gangster has to make demands upon his intended victim.

The third method was simply to continue discussions with Japan, to convince her that her aggressions cost her more than they were worth, to point out to her that her partnership with Hitler could be as dangerous to her as it was to the rest of the world, to lay before her proposal after proposal which in the long run would have given her in peace the prosperity her military leaders were seeking in conquest.

It was this third that we chose. Of the three, it was the only American method.

[The Tokyo warlords claimed that they had only two choices: surrender or war. Actually they had a third choice: accommodation. Considerable loss of face would have been better than loss of the war. The argument that Hull's note of November 26

provoked the Japanese into an attack is weakened by two facts. First, the naval force that attacked Pearl Harbor had left its rendezvous in Japan twenty-four hours earlier. Second, early in November the imperial conference had unanimously decided on war, provided that diplomacy had not produced a satisfactory accord by December 1.]

Thought Provokers

1. What would have been the outcome of World War II in Europe (or in Asia) if the United States had been truly neutral? Would the results have been to the nation's best interests?
2. Have events since 1945 given support to the view that a democratic United States could exist as a kind of fortified island?
3. Lend-Lease was designed to defend the United States by helping others fight the United States' potential enemies with U.S. weapons. Was there an element of immorality in this policy? Would the United States have kept out of the war if the Lend-Lease Act had not been passed?
4. Assuming that the Atlantic Charter was a warlike step, was it justified? Roosevelt believed that a Hitler victory would be ruinous for the United States, and to combat isolationist pressures he repeatedly misrepresented facts (*Greer* case) or usurped powers (convoying). Was he justified in using such methods to arouse the American people to an awareness of their danger?
5. With regard to the diplomatic breakdown preceding Pearl Harbor, it has been said that both Japan and the United States were right if one conceded their major premises. Explain fully, and form a conclusion.

34

America in World War II, 1941–1945

No matter how long it may take us to overcome
this premeditated invasion [Pearl Harbor], the
American people in their righteous might will win
through to absolute victory.

Franklin D. Roosevelt, War Message, 1941

Prologue: The nation was plunged into war by the worst military disaster in its history—the Japanese surprise attack at Pearl Harbor, Hawaii, on December 7, 1941. Caught flat-footed, the United States quickly whipped itself into fighting shape. War production revived the depression-drugged economy, stimulating the growth of numerous "boomtowns," many of them in the South and West. A panicky government interned some 110,000 Japanese Americans in so-called relocation centers, and a few race riots involving blacks and Latinos blotted the wartime record, but for the most part the United States' many racial and ethnic minorities were willing and welcome partners in the war effort. Millions of new defense-related jobs created unprecedented employment opportunities for women. As the mighty U.S. economic machine went into high gear, the tide of battle slowly began to turn. U.S. troops fought their way agonizingly up the chains of Pacific islands from New Guinea toward Japan. In Europe the hard-pressed and ever suspicious Soviet Union, eager to have the Western Allies share equally in the bloodletting, clamored ceaselessly for a second front. After frustrating postponements, the Western Allies at last invaded the northern French coast on D-Day, June 6, 1944. After Germany was hammered into inglorious defeat in May 1945, Japan was atom-bombed into submission in August 1945. World War II ended as the nuclear age dawned, ushered in by an ominous mushroom-shaped cloud. At war's end, revelations about the Nazis' genocidal persecution of Europe's Jews jarred the world's conscience and excited continuing controversy about whether the Allies might have been able to prevent or mitigate the Holocaust.

A. War and American Society

1. The War Transforms the Economy (1940–1950)*

As war orders flooded the nation's factories, the decade-old blight of depression was banished, and the face of the United States was transformed. Millions of workers pulled up stakes and moved to the bustling war production centers. Older cities were bursting with war workers, many of them desperate for housing. New towns appeared almost overnight, especially in the wide-open West. The billions of dollars of war contracts financed a virtual revolution in the U.S. economy, conferring enormous advantages on certain businesses and regions. What do the tables below suggest were the largest and most lasting impacts of the war? How might one explain the different effects of mobilization on different regions?

Table 1 Major War Supply Contracts and War Facilities, 1940–1945 (in thousands of dollars)

| State | Major War Supply Contracts, June 1940–Sept. 1945 | | Major War Facilities Projects, June 1940–June 1945 | |
	Combat Equipment	Other	Industrial	Military
Arizona	94,854	31,115	100,592	134,116
California	14,255,117	2,195,524	1,013,778	1,511,447
Colorado	244,634	116,920	170,350	174,479
Idaho	12,049	6,421	27,049	101,992
Montana	12,966	15,081	12,956	41,106
Nevada	1,521	32,402	151,542	88,050
New Mexico	11,133	9,356	13,325	101,506
North Dakota	1,582	5,938	120	1,572
Oregon	1,629,809	182,825	100,603	163,842
South Dakota	201	4,584	150	65,908
Texas	3,749,561	2,224,979	1,166,836	837,582
Utah	79,136	34,345	284,394	153,097
Washington	3,408,305	379,331	341,058	327,949
Wyoming	12,770	68,419	25,535	23,431

Table 1: U.S. Bureau of the Census, *County Data Book: A Supplement to the Statistical Abstract of the United States* (Washington, DC: U.S. Government Printing Office, 1947), 7; *Table 2*: U.S. Bureau of the Census, *Statistical Abstract of the United States* (Washington, DC: U.S. Government Printing Office, 1951), 196; *Table 3*: U.S. Bureau of the Census, *Historical Statistics of the United States: Colonial Times to 1970*, Bicentennial Ed., Part I (Washington, DC: U.S. Government Printing Office, 1975), 242–245; *Table 4*: U.S. Bureau of the Census, *Statistical Abstract of the United States* (Washington, DC: U.S. Government Printing Office, 1951), 30–31.

Table 2 Paid Civilian Employment in the Executive Branch of the Federal Government, 1938 and 1945, by State

State or Other Area	December 1938	June 1945
Continental U.S.	831,833	2,915,476
Washington, D.C., metro. area	119,874	257,808
48 states	711,959	2,657,668
Arizona	7,477	17,900
California	48,334	317,236
Colorado	8,692	28,839
Idaho	3,780	9,877
Montana	8,157	9,150
Nevada	1,819	6,753
New Mexico	7,201	16,206
North Dakota	3,820	6,047
Oregon	9,113	18,827
South Dakota	3,886	10,488
Texas	27,777	149,899
Utah	3,886	37,665
Washington	15,520	100,359
Wyoming	3,095	5,067

Source: U.S. Bureau of the Census, Statistical Abstract of the United States, (Washington, D.C.: U.S. Government Printing Office, 1951), 196.

Table 3 Personal Income: Select Western States, 1940, 1948 (in millions of dollars)

State	Total Income		Per Capita Income	
	1940	1948	1940	1948
Arizona	251	879	502	1,274
California	5,802	17,633	835	1,752
Colorado	615	1,810	544	1,433
Idaho	235	725	—	1,407
Montana	316	876	566	1,616
Nevada	101	283	890	1,814
New Mexico	198	655	373	1,084
North Dakota	218	813	340	1,401
Oklahoma	851	2,390	366	1,140
Oregon	671	2,278	648	1,621
South Dakota	231	916	360	1,497
Texas	2,762	9,142	430	1,199
Utah	266	810	482	1,241
Washington	1,140	3,608	655	1,600
Wyoming	151	429	606	1,595

Source: U.S. Bureau of the Census, Historical Statistics of the United States: Colonial Times to 1970, Bicentennial Ed., Part I (Washington, D.C.: U.S. Government Printing Office, 1975), 242–245.

Table 4 Population Growth of Western States, 1920–1950

Division and State	1920	1930	1940	1950	Percent Increase 1940 to 1950
United States	105,710,620	122,775,016	131,669,275	150,697,361	14.5
Mountain	3,336,101	2,701,789	4,150,003	5,074,998	22.3
Montana	548,889	537,606	559,456	501,024	5.6
Idaho	431,866	455,032	524,873	588,637	12.1
Wyoming	194,402	225,565	290,742	290,529	15.9
Colorado	939,629	1,035,296	1,123,296	1,325,089	18.0
New Mexico	360,350	423,317	531,818	681,157	28.1
Arizona	334,162	435,573	499,261	749,587	50.1
Nevada	77,407	91,058	110,247	160,083	45.2
Utah	449,396	507,847	550,310	688,862	25.2
Pacific	5,566,871	8,164,423	9,733,262	14,486,527	48.8
Washington	1,356,621	1,563,396	1,726,191	2,378,963	37.0
Oregon	783,389	753,786	1,089,684	1,521,311	39.6
California	3,426,861	5,677,251	6,907,387	10,586,223	53.3

2. A Black American Ponders the War's Meaning (1942)*

Blacks had bitter memories of World War I, when they had clamored in vain to play a major role in the "war to make the world safe for democracy." Despite urgent manpower needs, in 1917–1918 African Americans had been deemed unfit for combat assignments and relegated mostly to "labor battalions" in the army. At home they won only limited access to war-related jobs and were the victims of several bloody race riots at war's end. In the light of this sorry record, it was an open question whether blacks would support the Allied cause in World War II. Japanese propagandists tried to exploit the United States' vexed history of race relations by claiming brotherhood with African Americans as another "people of color" oppressed by white rule. On what grounds did the black author of the following essay decide to support the war? Was he being realistic? Might he have been disillusioned or pleased with the course of the civil rights movement after the war?

War had no heroic traditions for me. Wars were white folks'. All wars in historical memory. The last war, and the Spanish-American War before that, and the Civil War. I had been brought up in a way that admitted of no heroics. I think my parents were right. Life for them was a fierce, bitter, soul-searching war of spiritual and economic attrition; they fought it without heroics, but with stubborn heroism.

---

*J. Saunders Redding, "A Negro Looks at This War," *American Mercury* 55 (November 1942): 585–592.

Their heroism was screwed up to a pitch of idealism so intense that it found a safety valve in cynicism about the heroics of white folks' war. This cynicism went back at least as far as my paternal grandmother, whose fierce eyes used to lash the faces of her five grandchildren as she said, "An' he done som'pin big an' brave away down dere to Chickymorgy an' dey made a iron image of him 'cause he got his head blowed off an' his stomick blowed out fightin' to keep his slaves." I cannot convey the scorn and the cynicism she put into her picture of that hero-son of her slave-master, but I have never forgotten.

I was nearly ten when we entered the last war in 1917. The European fighting, and the sinking of the *Lusitania*, had seemed as remote, as distantly meaningless to us, as the Battle of Hastings. Then we went in and suddenly the city was flag-draped, slogan-plastered, and as riotously gay as on circus half-holidays. I remember one fine Sunday we came upon an immense new billboard with a new slogan: give! to make the world safe for democracy. My brother, who was the oldest of us, asked what making the world safe for democracy meant. My father frowned, but before he could answer, my mother broke in.

"It's just something to say, like..."—and then she was stuck until she hit upon one of the family's old jokes—"like 'Let's make a million dollars.'" We all laughed, but the bitter core of her meaning lay revealed, even for the youngest of us, like the stone in a halved peach....

And so, since I have reached maturity and thought a man's thoughts and had a man's—a Negro man's—experiences, I have thought that I could never believe in war again. Yet I believe in this one.

There are many things about this war that I do not like, just as there are many things about "practical" Christianity that I do not like. But I believe in Christianity, and if I accept the shoddy and unfulfilling in the conduct of this war, I do it as voluntarily and as purposefully as I accept the trash in the workings of "practical" Christianity. I do not like the odor of political pandering that arises from some groups. I do not like these "race incidents" in the camps. I do not like the world's not knowing officially that there were Negro soldiers on Bataan with General Wainwright.* I do not like the constant references to the Japs as "yellow bastards," "yellow bellies," and "yellow monkeys," as if color had something to do with treachery, as if color were the issue and the thing we are fighting rather than oppression, slavery, and a way of life hateful and nauseating. These and other things I do not like, yet I believe in the war....

This is a war to keep men free. The struggle to broaden and lengthen the road of freedom—our own private and important war to enlarge freedom here in America—will come later. That this private, intra-American war will be carried on and won is the only real reason we Negroes have to fight. We must keep the road open. Did we not believe in a victory in that intra-American war, we could not believe in nor stomach the compulsion of this. If we could not believe in the realization of democratic freedom for ourselves, certainly no one could ask us to die for the preservation of that ideal for others. But to broaden and lengthen the road

---

*Bataan was an area in the Philippines through which Jonathan Wainwright's captured American garrison was cruelly forced to march to prisoner-of-war camps in May 1942—the "Bataan Death March."

of freedom is different from preserving it. And our first duty is to keep the road of freedom open. It must be done continuously. It is the duty of the whole people to do this. Our next duty (and this, too, is the whole people's) is to broaden the road so that more people can travel it without snarling traffic. To die in these duties is to die for something....

I believe in this war, finally, because I believe in the ultimate vindication of the wisdom of the brotherhood of man. This is not foggy idealism. I think that the growing manifestations of the interdependence of all men is an argument for the wisdom of brotherhood. I think that the shrunk compass of the world is an argument. I think that the talk of united nations and of planned interdependence is an argument.

More immediately, I believe in this war because I believe in America. I believe in what America professes to stand for. Nor is this, I think, whistling in the dark. There are a great many things wrong here. There are only a few men of good will. I do not lose sight of that. I know the inequalities, the outraged hopes and faith, the inbred hate; and I know that there are people who wish merely to lay these by in the closet of the national mind until the crisis is over. But it would be equally foolish for me to lose sight of the advances that are made, the barriers that are leveled, the privileges that grow. Foolish, too, to remain blind to the distinction that exists between simple race prejudice, already growing moribund under the impact of this war, and theories of racial superiority as a basic tenet of a societal system—theories that at bottom are the avowed justification for suppression, defilement and murder.

I will take this that I have here. I will take the democratic theory. The bit of road of freedom that stretches through America is worth fighting to preserve. The very fact that I, a Negro in America, can fight against the evils in America is worth fighting for. This open fighting against the wrongs one hates is the mark and the hope of democratic freedom. I do not underestimate the struggle. I know the learning that must take place, the evils that must be broken, the depths that must be climbed. But I am free to help in doing these things. I count. I am free (though only a little as yet) to pound blows at the huge body of my American world until, like a chastened mother, she gives me nurture with the rest.

3. A Woman Remembers the War (1984)*

With millions of men in the armed forces and the nation's factories straining to keep them supplied, women were drawn by the millions into nontraditional jobs. For many of those women, the war represented not simply a bloody conflict of global proportions but also an unanticipated opportunity for economic freedom and personal growth. In the following selection, one war worker looks back on her experience in a plant in California. What does she remember most and least fondly about her wartime job? What aspects of it challenged her most? What was most fulfilling about it? What were the war's principal effects on her?

---

*From Mark Jonathan Harris, Franklin D. Mitchell, and Steven J. Schecter, *The Homefront: America During World War II*, (New York, Putnam) pp. 126–129. Copyright © 1984.

When the war started I was twenty-six, unmarried, and working as a cosmetics clerk in a drugstore in Los Angeles. I was running the whole department, handling the inventory and all that. It seemed asinine, though, to be selling lipstick when the country was at war. I felt that I was capable of doing something more than that toward the war effort.

There was also a big difference between my salary and those in defense work. I was making something like twenty-two, twenty-four dollars a week in the drugstore. You could earn a much greater amount of money for your labor in defense plants. Also it interested me. There was a certain curiosity about meeting that kind of challenge, and here was an opportunity to do that, for there were more and more openings for women.

So I went to two or three plants and took their tests. And they all told me I had absolutely no mechanical ability. I said, "I don't believe that." So I went to another plant, A.D.E.L. I was interviewed and got the job. This particular plant made the hydraulic-valve system for the B-17. And where did they put women? In the burr room. You sat at a workbench, which was essentially like a picnic table, with a bunch of other women, and you worked grinding and sanding machine parts to make them smooth. That's what you did all day long. It was very mechanical and it was very boring. There were about thirty women in the burr room, and it was like being in a beauty shop every day. I couldn't stand the inane talk. So when they asked me if I would like to work someplace else in the shop, I said I very much would.

They started training me. I went to a blueprint class and learned how to use a micrometer and how to draw tools out of the tool crib and everything else. Then one day they said, "Okay, how would you like to go into the machine shop?"

I said, "Terrific."

And they said, "Now, Adele, it's going to be a real challenge, because you'll be the only woman in the machine shop." I thought to myself, Well, that's going to be fun, all those guys and Adele in the machine shop. So the foreman took me over there. It was a big room, with a high ceiling and fluorescent lights, and it was very noisy. I walked in there, in my overalls, and suddenly all the machines stopped and every guy in the shop just turned around and looked at me. It took, I think, two weeks before anyone even talked to me. The discrimination was indescribable. They wanted to kill me.

My attitude was, "Okay, you bastards, I'm going to prove to you I can do anything you can do, and maybe better than some of you." And that's exactly the way it turned out. I used to do the rework on the pieces that the guy on the shift before me had screwed up. I finally got assigned to nothing but rework.

Later they taught me to run an automatic screwing machine. It's a big mother, and it took a lot of strength just to throw that thing into gear. They probably thought I wasn't going to be able to do it. But I was determined to succeed. As a matter of fact, I developed the most fantastic biceps from throwing that machine into gear. Even today I still have a little of that muscle left.

Anyway, eventually some of the men became very friendly, particularly the older ones, the ones in their late forties or fifties. They were journeymen tool and die makers and were so skilled that they could work anywhere at very high salaries. They were sort of fatherly, protective. They weren't threatened by me. The younger men, I think, were.

Our plant was an open shop, and the International Association of Machinists was trying to unionize the workers. I joined them and worked to try to get the union in the plant. I proselytized for the union during lunch hour, and I had a big altercation with the management over that. The employers and my lead man and foreman called me into the office and said, "We have a right to fire you."

I said, "On what basis? I work as well or better than anybody else in the shop except the journeymen."

They said, "No, not because of that. Because you're talking for the union on company property. You're not allowed to do that."

I said, "Well, that's just too bad, because I can't get off the grounds here. You won't allow us to leave the grounds during lunch hour. And you don't pay me for my lunch hour, so that time doesn't belong to you, so you can't tell me what to do." And they backed down.

I had one experience at the plant that really made me work for the union. One day while I was burring I had an accident and ripped some cartilage out of my hand. It wasn't serious, but it looked kind of messy. They had to take me over to the industrial hospital to get my hand sutured. I came back and couldn't work for a day or two because my hand was all bandaged. It wasn't serious, but it was awkward. When I got my paycheck, I saw that they had docked me for time that I was in the industrial hospital. When I saw that I was really mad.

It's ironic that when the union finally got into the plant, they had me transferred out. They were anxious to get rid of me because after we got them in I went to a few meetings and complained about it being a Jim Crow union. So they arranged for me to have a higher rating instead of a worker's rating. This allowed me to make twenty-five cents an hour more, and I got transferred to another plant. By this time I was married. When I became pregnant I worked for about three months more, then I quit.

For me defense work was the beginning of my emancipation as a woman. For the first time in my life I found out that I could do something with my hands besides bake a pie. I found out that I had manual dexterity and the mentality to read blueprints and gauges, and to be inquisitive enough about things to develop skills other than the conventional roles that women had at that time. I had the consciousness-raising experience of being the only woman in this machine shop and having the mantle of challenge laid down by the men, which stimulated my competitiveness and forced me to prove myself. This, plus working in the union, gave me a lot of self-confidence.

B. Japanese Internment

1. Yamato Ichihashi Relates His Relocation Experience (1942)[*]

After Pearl Harbor, the Pacific coast erupted in panic over rumors of Japanese invasion or possible sabotage. In early 1942, the secretary of war ordered the evacuation of Japanese Americans from Arizona, California, Oregon, and Washington.

After Midwestern governors objected to the inflow of Japanese Americans into their states, evacuation was abandoned in favor of internment. As the government scrambled to house the 120,000 detainees, many were packed into makeshift assembly centers, such as the horse stables at the Santa Anita racetrack where Japanese-born Stanford University professor Yamato Ichihashi spent the first two months of his internment. What does Ichihashi find most troubling about his new surroundings?

This is our 12th day here, and of course I have used all my spare time (very limited because of numerous visitors) in looking over the Camp as well as in obtaining as much reliable information possible. I have already learned a great many interesting things concerning the community life, including even gambling and commercial vice, which are said to have now been suppressed. One has to be even careful of his own immediate neighbors. Here goes my first story touching on matters which, I think, will interest you.

First of all, whether it was so intended or not, the Wartime Civil Control Administration under the Army's authority, has established in this Center a truly classless community (a Soviet ideal unrealized as yet in Russia). Residents (inmates more appropriately) are not recognized as individuals; we are numbered for identification and are treated exactly alike, except babies one year and younger as regards foods. We are fed, quartered and forced to do our own washing, including sheets, shirts, and what not. Washing facilities are wholly inadequate. They do not allow to have washing done by a laundry outside. Why I do not know. Criticisms relative [to] any matter are not tolerated by the management; a few days [ago] a doctor was railroaded from here because he, as a scientist, has tried to bring about improvements. It is very dangerous for any individual to try [not to go] along the line....

...At no time was the Camp prepared to receive evacuees; each arrival faced many hardships which could have been avoided; in particular their feeding was undescribably bad, and that was our experience, although we are informed by older residents that general conditions have been vastly improved in more recent days. The population is mixed: citizens and enemy aliens; they are differentiated in the Camp; it is an impossible combination. Many of the youngsters have been appointed [to administrative positions], and they act like petty bureaucrats—the word most commonly heard is *order*. More on this later.

In management of the classless community, the government has apparently adopted the lowest conceivable standard of treating human beings; thousands are still housed in stables; a stable for one animal is now occupied from five to six persons. They are still odorous and poor of ventilation. Of course, barracks are constructed exactly like our old fashioned wood-shed; each barrack is partitioned into six sections so that inmates have 4 walls, all constructed of rough pine boards nailed in a manner so that on the average [there is] 1/2 inch spaces between these wall boards; you can not only hear what goes on in the barrack, but can see, if you want, what goes on next door. There is no privacy anywhere; we have become veritable animals as far as our living is concerned. In addition, to be thrown into a community mostly composed of lowly, uncouth rustics, is in itself very painful for cultured persons. Some times these intangibles are more difficult to bear; but despite all, we are determined to be philosophic about everything; this is easy to talk about, but extremely difficult to face as realities.

A little more prosaically, meals served consist mostly of vegetables and rice, and meat or fish is very rarely served; when the latter is served it is done in very small quantities. Butter is not used with bread; nor do we get fats and oils and already our skin shows the result. Because of the coarseness of foods, digestive organs have a hard time in functioning properly. Diarrhoea is very prevalent, often causing panics in the lavatories, and this is no exaggeration.

Yet we are forced to face the shortage of medics and drugs and other necessary elements: there is one doctor to each 3,000 persons and only 3 dentists and some nurses. One need not observe more [than] the length of a line formed by those waiting in front of the hospital or the dental clinic to appreciate the inadequacy of facilities along these lines. Emergency cases are frequent. So far one death has occurred, but babies are born every day, often three to four; there are 800 potential mothers among the inmates. Physicians are [over]worked. I do not understand why the management fails to take advantage of the doctors present in the Camp; there are a number of unemployed ones.

There naturally exist a number of things which require reform or elimination in order to correct the general condition. But politics and graft prevent any efforts along these lines, according to older residents; for the time being, these must be seen as rumors; I have no means of verifying one way or other....

I must now proceed to the mess hall 1/2 hour ahead [of time] so as to join the line in order to get into the hall on time, so I had better to put an abrupt end here, since there is no real end no matter [what] you write.

2. A Japanese American Is Convicted (1943)*

Though later upheld by the Supreme Court, the constitutionality of Japanese removal was questioned at the time and has been hotly debated ever since. One young Japanese American citizen, Gordon K. Hirabayashi, refused to register for deportation and deliberately violated the 8:00 P.M. curfew imposed on Japanese Americans in his native city of Seattle. He was tried and convicted for both offenses, and the Supreme Court, in the decision excerpted here, upheld his conviction. What were Hirabayashi's principal reasons for denying the military orders? How does the Court justify the government's actions? Are the Court's arguments convincing? (In early 1985 a federal court in San Francisco overturned Hirabayashi's conviction of forty-three years earlier.)

Appellant asserted that the indictment should be dismissed because he was an American citizen who had never been a subject of and had never borne allegiance to the Empire of Japan, and also because the Act of March 21, 1942, was an unconstitutional delegation of Congressional power. On the trial to a jury it appeared that appellant was born in Seattle in 1918, of Japanese parents who had come from Japan to the United States, and who had never afterward returned to Japan; that he

---

*Hirabayashi v. United States, 320 U.S. 83 (1943).

was educated in the Washington public schools and at the time of his arrest was a senior in the University of Washington; that he had never been in Japan or had any association with Japanese residing there....

Appellant does not deny that he knowingly failed to obey the curfew order as charged in the second count of the indictment.... His contentions are only that... even if the regulation were in other respects lawfully authorized, the Fifth Amendment prohibits the discrimination made between citizens of Japanese descent and those of other ancestry....

The war power of the national government is "the power to wage war successfully." It extends to every matter and activity so related to war as substantially to affect its conduct and progress. The power is not restricted to the winning of victories in the field and the repulse of enemy forces. It embraces every phase of the national defense, including the protection of war materials and the members of the armed forces from injury and from the dangers which attend the rise, prosecution and progress of war....

[O]ur inquiry must be whether in the light of all the facts and circumstances there was any substantial basis for the conclusion, in which Congress and the military commander united, that the curfew as applied was a protective measure necessary to meet the threat of sabotage and espionage which would substantially affect the war effort and which might reasonably be expected to aid a threatened enemy invasion. The alternative which appellant insists must be accepted is for the military authorities to impose the curfew on all citizens within the military area, or on none. In a case of threatened danger requiring prompt action, it is a choice between inflicting obviously needless hardship on the many, or sitting passive and unresisting in the presence of the threat. We think that constitutional government, in time of war, is not so powerless and does not compel so hard a choice if those charged with the responsibility of our national defense have reasonable ground for believing that the threat is real....

There is support for the view that social, economic and political conditions which have prevailed since the close of the last century, when the Japanese began to come to this country in substantial numbers, have intensified their solidarity and have in large measure prevented their assimilation as an integral part of the white population....

As a result of all these conditions affecting the life of the Japanese, both aliens and citizens, in the Pacific Coast area, there has been relatively little social intercourse between them and the white population. The restrictions, both practical and legal, affecting the privileges and opportunities afforded to persons of Japanese extraction residing in the United States, have been sources of irritation and may well have tended to increase their isolation, and in many instances their attachments to Japan and its institutions....

Whatever views we may entertain regarding the loyalty to this country of the citizens of Japanese ancestry, we cannot reject as unfounded the judgment of the military authorities and of Congress that there were disloyal members of that population....[and] that in a critical hour such persons could not readily be isolated and separately dealt with, and constituted a menace to the national defense and safety, which demanded that prompt and adequate measures be taken to guard against it.

Appellant does not deny that, given the danger, a curfew was an appropriate measure against sabotage....

But appellant insists that the exercise of the power is inappropriate and unconstitutional because it discriminates against citizens of Japanese ancestry, in violation of the Fifth Amendment. The Fifth Amendment contains no equal protection clause and it restrains only such discriminatory legislation by Congress as amounts to a denial of due process....Congress may hit a particular danger where it is seen, without providing for others which are not so evident or so urgent....Distinctions between citizens solely because of their ancestry are by their very nature odious to a free people whose institutions are founded upon the doctrine of equality. For that reason, legislative classification or discrimination based on race alone has often been held to be a denial of equal protection....[Yet, b]ecause racial discriminations are in most circumstances irrelevant and therefore prohibited, it by no means follows that, in dealing with the perils of war, Congress and the Executive are wholly precluded from taking into account those facts and circumstances which are relevant to measures for our national defense and for the successful prosecution of the war, and which may in fact place citizens of one ancestry in a different category from others. "We must never forget, that it is *a constitution* we are expounding," "a constitution intended to endure for ages to come, and, consequently, to be adapted to the various *crises* of human affairs."* The adoption by Government, in the crisis of war and of threatened invasion, of measures for the public safety, based upon the recognition of facts and circumstances which indicate that a group of one national extraction may menace that safety more than others, is not wholly beyond the limits of the Constitution and is not to be condemned merely because in other and in most circumstances racial distinctions are irrelevant.

C. The Second-Front Controversy

1. Eisenhower Urges the Earliest Possible Second Front (1942)[†]

The German "blitzkrieg" invasion of the Soviet Union was six months old by the time the United States entered World War II in December 1941, and by that date the Soviets had already suffered hundreds of thousands of casualties. From the outset, the Soviet leader, Joseph Stalin, emphasized that what he most urgently needed from his British and American allies was for them to open a second front in Western Europe that would help to reduce the ferocious German pressure on the Soviets in the East. American military planners agreed, though political considerations, logistical bottlenecks, and strategic disagreements with the British combined to delay a full-scale second front for two and one-half more years, until D-Day, June 6, 1944—just eleven months before the conclusion of the war in Europe. The simmering controversy over the second front exacerbated Soviet suspicions of the West and significantly soured U.S.–Soviet relations, helping to set the stage for the Cold War that followed. In the

---

*The quotation is from John Marshall's decision in *McCulloch v. Maryland* (1819).
[†]Eisenhower, Dwight D., *The Papers of Dwight David Eisenhower: The War Years, Vol. I*, p. 151, copyright © 1970 The Johns Hopkins University Press.

*following document from February 28, 1942, Dwight D. Eisenhower, then the head
of the army's War Plans Division and soon to become supreme allied commander
in Europe (and later president of the United States), laid out the strategic case for
the earliest possible second front. What are his chief points? What are his principal
worries about the Soviet Union?*

The task of keeping Russia in the war involves, in the opinion of the War
Plans Division, immediate and definite action. It is not sufficient to urge upon the
Russians the indirect advantages that will accrue to them from Allied operations in
distant parts of the world, although these operations may be designed to free our
forces for a later offensive against Germany, or to keep Japan from immediately
attacking Siberia. Russia's problem is to sustain herself during the coming summer,
and she must not be permitted to reach such a precarious position that she will
accept a negotiated peace, no matter how unfavorable to herself, in preference to a
continuation of the fight.

There are two important ways in which this result can probably be brought
about. The first is by direct aid through lease-lend; the second is through the early
initiation of operations that will draw off from the Russian front sizable portions of
the German Army, both air and ground. Such an operation must be so conceived,
and so presented to the Russians, that they will recognize the importance of the
support rendered. Air, possibly ground, attack from England is indicated. Air operations can be initiated long before a sizable land attack could be staged.

2. Churchill Explains to Stalin That There Will Be No Second Front in 1942 (1942)[*]

*Stalin sent his foreign minister, Vaycheslav Molotov, to London and Washington in
May 1942 to secure agreement on an early second front. Winston Churchill tried
to dampen Soviet hopes, but Roosevelt assured Molotov that the Americans would
open such a front in 1942—a promise that Churchill almost immediately persuaded
Roosevelt to break. It fell to Churchill to carry that discouraging news to Stalin. The
British prime minister wrote that his mission to Moscow was "like carrying a large
lump of ice to the North Pole." Churchill later reported to Roosevelt on his meeting
with the Soviet leader in August 1942. How does he characterize Stalin's reaction?
What seem to be Churchill's underlying anxieties about the British-American-Soviet
alliance?*

[W]e all repaired to the Kremlin at eleven p.m. and were received only by
Stalin and Molotov with the interpreter. Then began a most unpleasant discussion.
Stalin handed me the enclosed document to which see also my reply. When it was
translated I said I would answer it in writing and that he must understand we have
made up our minds upon the course to be pursued and that reproaches were vain.
Thereafter we argued for about two hours, during which he said many disagreeable

---

[*]Winston Churchill.

things, especially about our being too much afraid of fighting the Germans, and if we tried it like the Russians we should find it not so bad, that we had broken our promise about Sledgehammer [a proposed Allied invasion of Nazi-occupied France, planned for 1942], that we had failed in delivering the supplies promised to Russia and only sent remnants after we had taken all we needed for ourselves. Apparently these complaints were addressed as much to the United States as to Britain.

I repulsed all his contentions squarely but without taunts of any kind. I suppose he is not used to being contradicted repeatedly but he did not become at all angry or even animated. On one occasion I said, "I pardon that remark only on account of the bravery of the Russian troops." Finally he said we could carry it no further. He must accept our decision and abruptly invited us to dinner at eight o'clock tonight.

Accepted the invitation [but] said I would leave by plane at dawn the next morning, i.e., fifteenth. Joe seemed somewhat concerned at this and asked could I not stay longer. I said certainly, if there was any good to be done, and that I would wait one more day anyhow. I then exclaimed there was no ring of comradeship in his attitude. I had travelled far to establish good working relations. We had done our utmost to help Russia and would continue to do so. We had been left entirely alone for a year against Germany and Italy. Now that the three great nations were allied, victory was certain provided we did not fall apart, and so forth. I was somewhat animated in this passage and before it could be translated he made the remark that he liked the temperament or spirit of my utterance. Thereafter the talk began again in a somewhat less tense atmosphere.

He plunged into a long discussion of two Russian trench mortar-firing rockets which he declared were devastating in their effects and which he offered to demonstrate to our experts if they could wait. He said he would let us have all information about them, but should there not be something in return. Should there not be an agreement to exchange information of inventions. I said that we would give them everything without any bargaining except only those devices which, if carried in aeroplanes over the enemy lines and shot down, would make our bombing of Germany more difficult. He accepted this. He also agreed that his military authorities should meet our generals and this was arranged for three o'clock this afternoon.... All this part of the talk was easier, but when [special American emissary to the Soviet Union Averell] Harriman asked about the plans for bringing American aircraft across Siberia, to which the Russians have only recently consented after long American pressing, he replied, curtly, "Wars are not won with plans." Harriman backed me up throughout and we neither of us yielded an inch nor spoke a bitter word....

It is my considered opinion that in his heart so far as he has one Stalin knows we are right and that six divisions on Sledgehammer would do him no good this year. Moreover I am certain that his sure-footed and quick military judgement makes him a strong supporter of Torch. I think it not impossible that he will make amends. In that hope I persevere. Anyhow I am sure it was better to have it out this way than any other. There was never at any time the slightest suggestion of their not fighting on and I think myself that Stalin has good confidence that he will win.

3. Stalin Resents the Delay of the Second Front (1943)*

At their meeting in Casablanca, Morocco, in January 1943, Roosevelt and Churchill announced their intention to invade Italy later that year, thus postponing the planned major attack across the English Channel until 1944. As the second front continued to be delayed, Stalin grew increasingly embittered. In this secret message to Churchill on June 24, 1943, he gave full vent to his anger. From the viewpoint of the Western Allies, what part of Stalin's attitude might have been most alarming?

When you now write that "it would be no help to Russia if we threw away a hundred thousand men in a disastrous cross-Channel attack," all I can do is remind you of the following.

First, your own Aide-Mémoire of June 1942, in which you declared that preparations were under way for an invasion, not by a hundred thousand, but by an Anglo-American force exceeding one million men at the very start of the operation.

Second, your February [1943] message, which mentioned extensive measures preparatory to the invasion of Western Europe in August or September 1943, which, apparently, envisaged an operation, not by a hundred thousand men, but by an adequate force.

So when you now declare: "I cannot see how a great British defeat and slaughter would aid the Soviet armies," is it not clear that a statement of this kind in relation to the Soviet Union is utterly groundless and directly contradicts your previous and responsible decisions, listed above, about extensive and vigorous measures by the British and Americans to organize the invasion this year, measures on which the complete success of the operation should hinge?

I shall not enlarge on the fact that this responsible decision, revoking your previous decisions on the invasion of Western Europe, was reached by you and the President without Soviet participation and without inviting its representatives to the Washington conference, although you cannot but be aware that the Soviet Union's role in the war against Germany and its interest in the problems of the second front are great enough.

There is no need to say that the Soviet Government cannot become reconciled to this disregard of vital Soviet interests in the war against the common enemy.

You say that you "quite understand" my disappointment. I must tell you that the point here is not just the disappointment of the Soviet Government, but the preservation of its confidence in its Allies, a confidence which is being subjected to severe stress. One should not forget that it is a question of saving millions of lives in the occupied areas of Western Europe and Russia, and of reducing the enormous sacrifices of the Soviet armies, compared with which the sacrifices of the Anglo-American armies are insignificant.

---

*Ministry of Foreign Affairs of the USSR, *Correspondence Between the Chairman of the Council of Ministers of the USSR and the Presidents of the USA and the Prime Ministers of Great Britain During the Great Patriotic War of 1941–1945* (1957), vol. 2, pp. 75–76.

4. Roosevelt and Stalin Meet Face to Face (1943)*

At the Iranian capital of Teheran, Roosevelt and Stalin met face to face at last in November 1943, for the first of just two such occasions (the other was at Yalta, in the Soviet Crimea, in early 1945). Talk of the second front dominated much of the discussion among Churchill, Roosevelt, and Stalin. In the following exchange, how does the second-front question reveal the tensions in the "Grand Alliance"? How does the second-front issue foreshadow U.S.–Soviet problems in the postwar era?

Bohlen Minutes

Secret

The President said that since there was no agenda for the conference he thought it would be a good idea to have a report from the military staffs who had met this morning, and if there was no objection they might hear from General Brooke, Marshal Voroshilov and General Marshall....

[The three generals—representing Great Britain, the Soviet Union, and the United States, respectively—addressed various issues relating to the planned Allied invasion of northern France, which they code-named "Overlord." The first stage of that operation would commence six months later on "D-Day," June 6, 1944.]

Marshal Stalin then inquired who will command Overlord.

The President replied that it had not yet been decided....

Marshall Stalin stated that the Russians do not expect to have a voice in the selection of the Commander-in-Chief; they merely want to know who he is to be and to have him appointed as soon as possible....

[Marshall Stalin] said that Overlord was the most important and nothing should be done to distract attention from that operation. He felt that a directive should be given to the military staffs, and proposed the following one:

(1). In order that Russian help might be given from the east to the execution of Overlord, a date should be set and the operation should not be postponed. (2). If possible the attack in southern France should precede Overlord by two months, but if that is impossible, then simultaneously or even a little after Overlord. An operation in southern France would be a supporting operation as contrasted with diversionary operations in Rome or in the Balkans, and would assure the success of Overlord. (3). The appointment of a Commander-in-Chief for Overlord as soon as possible. Until that is done the Overlord operation cannot be considered as really in progress. Marshall Stalin added that the appointment of the Commander-in-Chief was the business of the President and Mr. Churchill but that it would be advantageous to have the appointment made here.

The President then said he had been most interested in hearing the various angles discussed from Overlord to Turkey.... The President then said he was in

---

*Foreign Relations of the United States, 1943 (Washington, DC: Government Printing Office), pp. 533–539.

favor of adhering to the original date for Overlord set at Quebec, namely, the first part of May.

Marshal Stalin said he would like to see Overlord undertaken during the month of May; that he did not care whether it was the 1st, 15th or 20th, but that a definite date was important.

The Prime Minister said it did not appear that the points of view were as far apart as it seemed. The British Government was anxious to begin Overlord as soon as possible but did not desire to neglect the great possibilities in the Mediterranean merely for the sake of avoiding a delay of a month or two.

Marshal Stalin said that the operations in the Mediterranean have a value but they are really only diversions.

The Prime Minister said in the British view the large British forces in the Mediterranean should not stand idle but should be pressing the enemy with vigor. He added that to break off the campaign in Italy where the allied forces were holding a German army would be impossible.

Marshall Stalin said it looked as though Mr. Churchill thought that the Russians were suggesting that the British armies do nothing.

The Prime Minister said that if landing craft is [*are*] taken from the Mediterranean theater there will be no action. He added that at Moscow the conditions under which the British Government considered Overlord could be launched had been fully explained, and these were that there should not be more than 12 mobile German divisions behind the coastal troops and that German reinforcements for sixty days should not exceed 15 Divisions. He added that to fulfill these conditions it was necessary in the intervening period to press the enemy from all directions. He said that the Divisions now facing the allies in Italy had come [for] the most part [from] France, and to break off the action in Italy would only mean that they would return to France to oppose Overlord. Turning again to the question of Turkey, The Prime Minister said that all were agreed on the question of Turkey's entrance into the war. . . .

Marshal Stalin interposed to ask how many French Divisions were being trained in North Africa.

General Marshall replied that for the present there were five Divisions ready and four in training, and that one of these five was in Italy with the American Fifth Army and another was en route. He said that from the battle experience gained it would be possible to decide how best to utilize the other French Divisions.

The President then proposed that instead of three directives to the three Staffs that one directive be agreed upon here. He then proposed a joint directive as follows: (1). That the military staffs should assume that Overlord is the dominating operation. (2). That the Staffs make recommendations in regard to other operations in the Mediterranean area, having carefully in mind the possibility of causing a delay in Overlord.

Marshal Stalin said he saw no need for any military committee here, that the questions involved should be decided at the conference. He also saw no need for any political sub-committee. Marshal Stalin then said he wished to ask Mr. Churchill an indiscreet question, namely, do the British really believe in Overlord or are they only saying so to reassure the Russians.

5. Two Allies, One War? (1941–1945)*

While American forces directed their efforts at defeating Japan and lending material support to the European war effort, the Red Army poured millions of lives into defeating Hitler's well-oiled war machine. Russian civilians were likewise disproportionately affected by the war—in four years, as many as seventeen million Soviet noncombatants either died of starvation or were killed by advancing armies. What do the following tables suggest about the wartime experiences of the two countries? Do the figures shed light on the lasting legacy of the second-front controversy?

Red Army Personnel Losses, June 22, 1941–May 9, 1945

Year	Killed or Missing	Sick or Wounded	Total Casualties	Key Events
1941	2,993,803	1,314,291	4,308,094	6/22/1941: Germany Invades the U.S.S.R. 12/7/1941: Japan Attacks Pearl Harbor
1942	2,993,536	4,087,265	7,080,801	
1943	1,977,127	5,506,520	7,483,647	2/2/1943: Germans Surrender at Stalingrad 7/10/1943: Allies Begin Italian Campaign
1944	1,412,335	5,090,869	6,503,204	6/6/1944: D-Day
1945	631,633	2,191,748	2,823,381	5/7/1945: Germany Surrenders
Total U.S.S.R.	10,008,434	18,190,693	28,199,127	
Total U.S.A.	405,399	671,846	1,077,245	

Civilian Consumption in World War II, 1941–1945 (1940 = 100)

	1941	1942	1943	1944	1945
Meat					
U.S.A.	101	99	103	108	102
U.S.S.R.	80	52	48	46	45
Clothing					
U.S.A.	116	109	114	110	102
U.S.S.R.	61	10	10	11	18
Shoes					
U.S.A.	120	106	95	88	93
U.S.S.R.	65	8	7	10	15

---

*I. C. B. Dear, ed., *The Oxford Companion to World War II* (Oxford: Oxford University Press, 1995), p. 1218; David M. Glantz and Jonathan M. House, *When Titans Clashed: How the Red Army Stopped Hitler* (Lawrence: University Press of Kansas, 1995), p. 292; Geofrey T. Mills and Hugh Rockoff, eds., *The Sinews of War: Essays on the Economic History of World War II* (Ames: Iowa State University Press, 1993), p. 87; United States Department of Veterans Affairs.

D. America and the Holocaust

1. John W. Pehle Wants to Bomb Auschwitz (1944)*

As evidence of Nazi Germany's wholesale slaughter of European Jews continued to mount, perhaps the most agonizing decision facing Allied leaders was whether to bomb Auschwitz and Birkenau, two of Hitler's most notorious death camps. Initially even Jewish groups were reluctant to push for such a plan since carpet-bombing the camps had the potential of killing thousands of Jewish prisoners. Others argued that destroying the gas chambers would not prevent Hitler from pursuing his goal of extermination by other means. But in a letter to the assistant secretary of war, United States War Refugee Board Director John W. Pehle set aside these and other concerns and called for a raid on the two principal death mills. What does he see as the potential benefits of such an attack?

I send you herewith copies of two eye-witness descriptions of the notorious German concentration and extermination camps of Auschwitz and Birkenau.... No report of Nazi atrocities received by the Board has quite caught the gruesome brutality of what is taking place in these camps of horror as have these sober, factual accounts of conditions in Auschwitz and Birkenau. I earnestly hope that you will read these reports.

The destruction of large numbers of people apparently is not a simple process. The Germans have been forced to devote considerable technological ingenuity and administrative know-how in order to carry out murder on a mass production basis, as the attached reports will testify. If the elaborate murder installations at Birkenau were destroyed, it seems clear that the Germans could not reconstruct there for some time.

Until now, despite pressure from many sources, I have been hesitant to urge the destruction of these camps by direct, military action. But I am convinced that the point has now been reached where such action is justifiable if it is deemed feasible by competent military authorities. I strongly recommend that the War Department give serious consideration to the possibility of destroying the execution chambers and crematories in Birkenau through direct bombing action. It may be observed that there would be other advantages of military nature to such an attack. The Krupp and Siemens factories, where among other things cases for hand grenades are made, and a Buna plant, all within Auschwitz, would be destroyed. The destruction of the German barracks and guardhouses and the killing of German soldiers in the area would also be accomplished. The morale of underground groups might be considerably strengthened by such a dramatic exhibition of Allied air support and a number of the people confined in Auschwitz and Birkenau might be liberated in the confusion resulting from the bombing. That the effecting of a prison break by such methods is not without precedent is indicated by the description in the enclosed copy of a recent *New York Times* article of the liberation from Amiens prison of 100 French patriots by the RAF.

---

*Michael J. Neufeld and Michael Berenbaum, eds., *The Bombing of Auschwitz: Should the Allies Have Attempted It?* (Bedford/St. Martin's Press, 2000), p. 278.

Obviously, the War Refugee Board is in no position to determine whether the foregoing proposal is feasible from a military standpoint. Nevertheless in view of the urgency of the situation, we feel justified in making the suggestion. I would appreciate having the views of the War Department as soon as possible.

2. John J. McCloy Opposes Bombing Auschwitz (1944)*

The decision not to bomb Auschwitz or the connecting railways ranks among the most controversial choices made by the United States during World War II. Critics have often held up the decision as indisputable proof that American leaders were indifferent to the plight of Jews. But as others have noted, the Allies faced numerous practical and strategic considerations in choosing their course of action. Bombing connecting railways would have required considerable resources and frequent return missions, as Germany had the capacity to rebuild the railways within days of attack. Prisoners destined for Auschwitz could also be diverted elsewhere or disposed of by other means. In a letter to John W. Pehle, Assistant Secretary of War John J. McCloy listed several other objections to carrying out the raids. What were his principal considerations? Are his arguments convincing?

The Operations Staff of the War Department has given careful consideration to your suggestion that the bombing of these camps be undertaken. In consideration of this proposal the following points were brought out:

a. Positive destruction of these camps would necessitate precision bombing, employing heavy or medium bombardment, or attack by low flying or dive bombing aircraft, preferably the latter.

b. The target is beyond the maximum range of medium bombardment, dive bombers and fighter bombers located in United Kingdom, France, or Italy.

c. Use of heavy bombardment from United Kingdom bases would necessitate a hazardous round trip flight unescorted of approximately 2000 miles over enemy territory.

d. At the present critical stage of the war in Europe our strategic air forces are engaged in the destruction of industrial target systems vital to the dwindling war potential of the enemy, from which they should not be diverted. The positive solution to this problem is the earliest possible victory over Germany, to which end we should exert our entire means.

e. This case does not at all parallel the Amiens mission because of the location of the concentration and extermination camps and the resulting difficulties encountered in attempting to carry out the proposed bombing.

Based on the above, as well as the most uncertain, if not dangerous effect such a bombing would have on the object to be attained, the War Department has felt that it should not, at least for the present, undertake these operations.

---

*Michael J. Neufeld and Michael Berenbaum, eds., *The Bombing of Auschwitz: Should the Allies Have Attempted It?* (Bedford/St. Martin's Press, 2000), pp. 279–280.

I know that you have been reluctant to press this activity on the War Department. We have been pressed strongly from other quarters, however, and have taken the best military opinion on its feasibility, and we believe the above conclusion is a sound one.

3. The War Refugee Board Reports on Rescue Efforts (1945)*

Responding to charges of State Department indifference to the refugee crisis, Roosevelt created a separate War Refugee Board in January of 1944 to aid in the rescue and resettlement of Jews trapped on the periphery of Nazi-controlled Europe. With the daring assistance of individuals like Raoul Wallenberg—the Swedish banker who helped rescue thousands of Hungarian Jews—the War Refugee Board was able to save as many as 200,000 Jews from extermination. In 1945, the Board published the following report of its activities. What strategies did the Board employ in its rescue efforts? What difficulties did the Board encounter?

The operations planned and developed by the Board to pull victims out of enemy hands to the safe neutral areas contiguous to Nazi territory involved complex problems of planning, organization, coordination, negotiation and the use of unusual techniques. Full use had to be made of the resourcefulness, ingenuity and contacts of resistance groups and underground operators. Evacuation from German-controlled territory for specially marked victims was not possible on an official and open basis. Funds and supplies were sent in to trusted agents in enemy areas to hide refugees from the Nazis, maintain and safeguard them and transport them through underground channels to safety. Lesser German officials were bribed. False identification papers were supplied. Food was provided families of the resistance groups who concealed and protected the refugees. Border officials were bribed to pass refugees. Exit and entrance visas were procured and transportation by boat or by rail was provided for evacuation to safe areas. Tens of thousands were rescued from the Nazis by these clandestine means....

The Board's efforts to save the persecuted Jews in Hungary required the use of every resource and technique developed for the rescue of people in the hands of the enemy. Hungary, the last remaining refuge for Jews in Axis Europe, had an abnormal population of about one million Jews. When the German army overran Hungary in March 1944, all these Jews were in mortal danger. Reports soon came through of a wave of violent persecutions of the Jews in Hungary and the War Refugee Board geared its programs to the pressing emergency.

Direct rescue was difficult from Hungary which was surrounded by Nazi-controlled territory. Intense psychological pressures were therefore exerted on the authorities and people of Hungary. Strong warnings and condemnations were issued by the President, by the Congress, the Secretary of State, Archbishop Spellman and other prominent American Christians to the people of Hungary.

---

*United States War Refugee Board, *Final Summary Report of the Executive Director, War Refugee Board* (Washington, DC: Government Printing Office, September 15, 1945), pp. 17–26.

Appeals were made to the neutral governments to offer safe haven to Hungarian Jews and to inform the Nazis of their willingness to receive these suffering people. The governments of Sweden, Switzerland, Spain and Portugal were urged to issue protective citizenship to Jews in Hungary claiming family or business ties with those countries. Many thousands were granted such special neutral protection.

Raoul Wallenberg, a young Swedish businessman, volunteered to proceed to Hungary for the War Refugee Board to aid in the rescue and relief of the persecuted Jews. The Swedish Government granted him diplomatic status and stationed him in Budapest for the purpose of rendering protection to these people. The Board furnished Wallenberg detailed plans of action, but made it clear that he could not act in Hungary as a representative of the Board. Wallenberg, supplied with funds from the Board and the American Jewish Joint Distribution Committee, carried on a relentless campaign in Hungary in behalf of the Jews. He issued Swedish protective passports by the thousands and hired extra buildings as official Swedish quarters to house several hundred rabbis and communal leaders under the protection of the extraterritoriality which attached to such buildings. He constantly pressed the Hungarian authorities for better treatment of Jews and succeeded in having thousands brought back to Budapest from the forced labor marches. In all, approximately 20,000 Jews received the safety of Swedish protection in Hungary....

The many warnings and appeals addressed to the Hungarian authorities by the United States and other democratic peoples resulted in the Horthy puppet government sending a message in July 1944 through the medium of the International Red Cross to the Governments of the United States and Great Britain stating that Hungary was willing to permit the emigration of certain categories of Jews. This offer in effect said "we will permit Jews to leave Hungary if the United States and Great Britain will take care of them." It was publicly accepted by the United States and by the British Government, but no Jews were ever formally released by the German-controlled Horthy government.

Despite the difficulties in effecting direct rescue from Hungary, unremitting efforts were made to assist underground rescue operations by developing avenues of escape and finding havens of refuge in neutral and Allied territories. In addition, funds from America were transferred to Hungary via Switzerland and Sweden to keep Jews in hiding, to sustain them pending rescue or liberation, and to finance the rescue work of resistance groups in Rumania and Slovakia. These groups helped thousands to escape from Hungary through underground channels. Rescues were also developed through Yugoslav Partisan territory which had well established contacts with underground workers in Hungary. The flow of refugees through this channel was accelerated as the result of Board negotiations with Marshal Tito's representatives and the Allied military authorities in Italy. Relief supplies were provided for the maintenance of refugees in Yugoslavia and arrangements were made for evacuation from Yugoslavia to Italy by boat or plane. Approximately 7,000 Jews were enabled to escape from Hungary by this route.

4. The Christian Century *Grapples with the Holocaust (1945)**

Only after Allied troops entered German-occupied territories in April of 1945 did Americans come face to face with the indisputable evidence of Nazi crimes. Even General Dwight D. Eisenhower, who had received regular dispatches of German atrocities, was shocked by what he saw when he inspected one of the liberated camps, writing to his wife that he "never dreamed that such cruelty, bestiality, and savagery could really exist in the world." The photographs in particular—of piles of naked corpses and hollow-eyed survivors—forced audiences to grapple with seemingly incomprehensible evil. In a moving essay, the editors of The Christian Century *wrestled with their own past skepticism and with the implications of Nazi brutality for the human race. Why were the authors so hesitant to accept earlier reports of genocide? What conclusions do they draw about human beings' capacity for evil?*

The horrors disclosed by the capture of the nazi concentration camps at Buchenwald, Belsen, Limburg and a dozen other places constitute one of those awful facts upon which a paper such as this feels under obligation to comment, but concerning which it is almost physically impossible to write. What can be said that will not seem like tossing little words up against a giant mountain of ineradicable evil? What human emotion can measure up to such bestiality except a searing anger which calls on heaven to witness that retribution shall be swift and terrible and pitiless? How can men (and, it is alleged, women) who have been capable of such deeds be thought of or dealt with save as vicious brutes who must be exterminated both to do justice and in mercy to the future of the race?

We have found it hard to believe that the reports from the nazi concentration camps could be true. Almost desperately we have tried to think that they must be wildly exaggerated. Perhaps they were products of the fevered brains of prisoners who were out for revenge. Or perhaps they were just more atrocity-mongering, like the cadaver factory story of the last war. But such puny barricades cannot stand up against the terrible facts. The evidence is too conclusive. It will be a long, long time before our eyes will cease to see those pictures of naked corpses piled like firewood or of those mounds of carrion flesh and bones. It will be a long, long time before we can forget what scores of honorable, competent observers tell us they have seen with their own eyes. The thing is well-nigh incredible. But it happened.

What does it mean? That Germans are beyond the pale of humanity? That they are capable of a fiendish cruelty which sets them apart from all the rest of us? No, not that. For one thing, we read that a large portion of the victims in these concentration camps were Germans. We do not believe that the sort of Germans who were subjected to this torture under any conceivable circumstances would themselves have become torturers. For another thing, we have reason to know that mass cruelty in most revolting forms has not been confined to Germany. We have seen photographs that missionaries smuggled out of raped Nanking. We have

---

read the affidavits of men who escaped from the Baltic states and eastern Poland. We know what horrors writers like Dallin and William Henry Chamberlin believe would be revealed if the prison camps in the Soviet Arctic were opened to the world's inspection. We know, too, the frightful things that have happened in this country when lynching mobs ran wild—things so horrible that they can only be told in whispers.

No, the horror of the nazi concentration camps is the horror of humanity itself when it has surrendered to its capacity for evil. When we look at the pictures from Buchenwald we are looking, to be sure, at the frightful malignity of nazism, this perversion of all values which in its final extremity is actually intent, as Hitler himself has said, on reducing all European life to "ruin, rats and epidemics." But in the nazis and beyond them we are looking into the very pit of hell which men disclose yawning within themselves when they reject the authority of the moral law, when they deny the sacredness of human personality, when they turn from the worship of the one true God to the worship of their own wills, their own states, their own lust for power.

Buchenwald and the other memorials of nazi infamy reveal the depths to which humanity can sink, and has sunk, in these frightful years. They reveal the awful fate which may engulf all civilizations unless these devils of our pride and of our ruthlessness and of the cult of force are exorcised.

E. The Face of Battle

1. A Soldier at Anzio (1944)[*]

The Allies launched the Italian campaign hoping to knock the Axis power swiftly out of the war while appeasing the Soviet Union by taking action in the European theater. Hitler's subsequent decision to deploy sixteen German divisions to halt the Allied advance transformed the anticipated sideshow into a bloody stalemate that lasted almost until war's end. Decorated World War II veteran Audie Murphy describes the grueling siege on the Anzio beachhead in his best-selling 1949 memoir, To Hell and Back. *What did he find most terrifying about his experience in battle?*

As if the fire were a prearranged signal for action, all hell erupts. From a dozen points come bursts of automatic fire. Branches and leaves clipped from the trees rain amid the whizzing steel.

Two men caught in the open squirm frantically for the doubtful cover of a slight ridge. Bullets kick all about them. They twist in every direction, but the spurting lead follows. The gunner finally gets his range. The bodies writhe like stricken worms. The gun fires again. The bodies relax and are still.

"Where are our goddam tanks?" fumes Kerrigan. "They're never up when we need them."

---

[*]From *To Hell and Back* by Audie Murphy. Copyright © 1949 by Audie Murphy, © 1977 by Pamela Murphy.

Other men have the same idea. From all along our lines comes the call. "Tanks. Get the goddam tanks."

A scream rises from a wounded man, but the noise is lost in the whistle of an incoming shell. The German artillery has begun a barrage. The shells fall to our rear, forming a wall between us and reinforcements; between us and the possibility of retreat.

Now a second barrage is hurled directly upon us. Flames spurt; and the earth seems to roll weirdly.

From right and left comes the cry: "Medics! Medics! Over here. For chrisake, come up! Over here. This way."

We open up with everything we have, shooting blindly. The mass fire is supposed to still the enemy guns until we are close enough to pry out their positions. But the Germans are dug in too well. The fiery blanket woven by their guns never lifts. We may as well be hurtling naked bodies against a wall of spears. . . .

Rain falls in slanting black streaks, turning our area into a sea of mud. It pulls at our feet like quicksand. We slant the bottoms of our foxholes. Water drains to the lower ends; and we dip it out with our helmets. But when the storms really strike, we give up. For hours we crouch in ankle-deep water.

The enemy never lets up. During the day, if one sticks his head above the surface of the ground, he risks sudden slaughter. Often we must use ration cans as chamber pots, hurling them from the holes like grenades after they have served their purpose. When shells hit close, the soft walls of the dugouts crumble. Like turtles we dig ourselves out of the mud and try repairing the damage before another shell arrives or the water rises in our foxholes.

The rain is not without its blessing. As long as it keeps the ground swampy, enemy armor bogs down and cannot move against us.

Once every twenty-four hours we slip into the ruins of the house and heat our tins of rations in the embers of a small fire. This can be done only at night. We are in plain sight of enemy observers. By day, smoke would show and bring the artillery down on us.

Stomachs go lumpy and sour. The bitter odor of vomit is everywhere. And it seems that the intestines themselves will be squirted out in diarrheal discharges. . . .

Through our hearts and minds, resignation and futility crawl like worms. We cannot advance. And we cannot retreat another yard without adding further peril to the slim security of our beachhead.

Rumors slide from hole to hole. The British are pulling out, while the pulling is good, leaving us holding a gigantic and ferocious wildcat with a very small grip by a very short tail. The Germans are only waiting until our build-up is worthy of a major attack. They will then thrust through the middle of our defenses, split our forces, and drive us into the sea. We believe nothing; doubt nothing.

Our function we know. It is to hold the lines until enough men and materiel arrive to try again cracking the iron wall that lies before us. We listen to the moan of the wind, curse existence, and snarl at one another. There is no escape with honor except on the litter of the medics or in the sack of the burial squads.

2. An Airman Recounts the Regensburg Raid (1943)[*]

Throughout the war, the prospect of crippling the German economy through precision bombing raids on industrial targets captivated American war planners. An air war over Germany held the promise of minimizing military casualties while drawing on the United States' unrivaled industrial might. In 1943, the Allies established sixty high-value targets deep inside Germany, including a fighter aircraft plant at Regensburg. The August 17 raid on Regensburg proved disastrous. Of the 146 aircraft that took off that day, 24 failed to return—a staggering casualty rate that eclipsed any damage inflicted on the German plant. Pilot Harry H. Crosby describes the problems his team encountered on the ill-fated Regensburg mission in his poignant memoir. What were the most challenging facets of aerial combat?

Two squadrons of E.A. (enemy aircraft) came up behind and below us, just off to our right, twelve ME-109s and eleven FW-190s. They drew up even with us—and then careened toward us, their guns blinking. Our interphone became a static of voices and the plane shook with the chatter of our guns.

Off to port, the same thing. German fighters were crisscrossing at us.

Ahead of us, flying all alone and slightly off to our right, a single Messerschmitt kept in position with us. Was that their control officer, radioing directions about whom to hit, and how?

The Germans came up parallel, in singles or pairs, made a U-turn to their left and then a hard right and then hit us from the side. Up ahead the other groups were getting it, but not as bad. Then what seemed to be the whole German Air Force came up and began to riddle our whole task force.

Other groups began to lose planes.

Jack Kidd and Blakely tried to fit us in tighter with the groups ahead.

Now we began to have a new problem. As other planes were hit, we had to fly through their debris. I instinctively ducked as we almost hit an escape hatch from a plane ahead. When a plane blew up, we saw their parts all over the sky. We smashed into some of the pieces. One plane hit a body which tumbled out of a plane ahead.

A crewman went out the front hatch of a plane and hit the tail assembly of his own plane. No chute. His body turned over and over like a bean bag tossed into the air.

An unusual hit. In a plane ahead all four engines got smacked at once, all burst into flames, and then the whole plane exploded. "No chutes," I wrote.

Our gunners worried about their friends. No matter how violent the battle, they always looked for parachutes. In the heat of our present violence, McClelland, from the ball, came in on interphone. "Sir, I counted sixty chutes in the air at once."

We were getting some of them. At first, the E.A. had yellow noses—the Abbeville Kids, we called them. Now we saw blue, red, and black planes, other units vectoring toward us. When B-17s blew up, they tended to be black, from oil fires. When the Germans blew up, they were orange. Hits in their gas tanks.

---

[*]From Harry H. Crosby, *A Wing and a Prayer: The "Bloody 100th" Bomb Group of the U.S. Eighth Air Force in Action over Europe in World War II*, 1993, pp. 94–95, published by iUniverse.

I saw two of them go at once, as they hit us from the front and starboard, their debris shredding us. A German pilot came out of his plane, drew his legs into a ball, his head down. Papers flew out of his pockets. He did a triple somersault through our formation. No chute.

3. A Marine Assaults Peleliu (1944)*

As they fought their way across the Pacific islands, thousands of American soldiers scrambled onto unprotected beaches under a hailstorm of enemy fire. In the following passage, Marine infantryman E. B. Sledge describes the landing at Peleliu, one of the Palau islands marked as a stepping-stone in the long campaign to recapture the Philippines. Sledge was a fresh recruit. What parts of the assault most surprised him?

We waited a seeming eternity for the signal to start toward the beach. The suspense was almost more than I could bear. Waiting is a major part of war, but I never experienced any more supremely agonizing suspense than the excruciating torture of those moments before we received the signal to begin the assault on Peleliu. I broke out in a cold sweat as the tension mounted with the intensity of the bombardment. My stomach was tied in knots. I had a lump in my throat and swallowed only with great difficulty. My knees nearly buckled, so I clung weakly to the side of the tractor. I felt nauseated and feared that my bladder would surely empty itself and reveal me to be the coward I was. But the men around me looked just about the way I felt. Finally, with a sense of fatalistic relief mixed with a flash of anger at the navy officer who was our wave commander, I saw him wave his flag toward the beach. Our driver revved the engine. The treads churned up the water, and we started in—the second wave ashore.

We moved ahead, watching the frightful spectacle. Huge geysers of water rose around the amtracs ahead of us as they approached the reef. The beach was now marked along its length by a continuous sheet of flame backed by a thick wall of smoke. It seemed as though a huge volcano had erupted from the sea, and rather than heading for an island, we were being drawn into the vortex of a flaming abyss. For many it was to be oblivion.

The lieutenant braced himself and pulled out a half-pint whiskey bottle.

"This is it, boys," he yelled.

Just like they do in the movies! It seemed unreal....

Our bombardment began to lift off the beach and move inland. Our dive bombers also moved inland with their strafing and bombing. The Japanese increased the volume of their fire against the waves of amtracs. Above the din I could hear the ominous sound of shell fragments humming and growling through the air.

"Stand by," someone yelled.

---

*From *With the Old Breed: At Peleliu and Okinawa* by E. B. Sledge, copyright © 1981 by E. B. Sledge. Introduction copyright © 2007 by Presidio Press, a division of Random House, Inc.

I picked up my mortar ammo bag and slung it over my left shoulder, buckled my helmet chin strap, adjusted my carbine sling over my right shoulder, and tried to keep my balance. My heart pounded. Our amtrac came out of the water and moved a few yards up the gently sloping sand.

"Hit the beach!" yelled an NCO moments before the machine lurched to a stop.

The men piled over the sides as fast as they could. I followed Snafu, climbed up, and planted both feet firmly on the left side so as to leap as far away from it as possible. At that instant a burst of machine-gun fire with white-hot tracers snapped through the air at eye level, almost grazing my face. I pulled my head back like a turtle, lost my balance, and fell awkwardly forward down onto the sand in a tangle of ammo bag, pack, helmet, carbine, gas mask, cartridge belt, and flopping canteens. "Get off the beach! Get off the beach!" raced through my mind....

Shells crashed all around. Fragments tore and whirred, slapping on the sand and splashing into the water a few yards behind us. The Japanese were recovering from the shock of our prelanding bombardment. Their machine gun and rifle fire got thicker, snapping viciously overhead in increasing volume.

Our amtrac spun around and headed back out as I reached the edge of the beach and flattened on the deck. The world was a nightmare of flashes, violent explosions, and snapping bullets. Most of what I saw blurred. My mind was benumbed by the shock of it....

I caught a fleeting glimpse of a group of Marines leaving a smoking amtrac on the reef. Some fell as bullets and fragments splashed among them. Their buddies tried to help them as they struggled in the knee-deep water.

I shuddered and choked. A wild desperate feeling of anger, frustration, and pity gripped me. It was an emotion that always would torture my mind when I saw men trapped and was unable to do anything but watch as they were hit. My own plight forgotten momentarily, I felt sickened to the depths of my soul. I asked God, "Why, why, why?" I turned my face away and wished that I were imagining it all. I had tasted the bitterest essence of war, the sight of helpless comrades being slaughtered, and it filled me with disgust.

F. Dropping the Atomic Bomb

1. Japan's Horrified Reaction (1945)[*]

With Germany knocked out of the war, President Truman journeyed to Potsdam, near Berlin, in July 1945, to concert plans with Stalin and the British leaders. He was there informed that U.S. scientists had experimentally detonated the first atomic bomb in history. The conferees now called on the Japanese to surrender or be destroyed, although the Potsdam ultimatum made no reference, as perhaps it should have, to the existence of the fantastic new weapon. When Tokyo brushed aside the demand for surrender, Truman ordered the dropping of atomic bombs (the only two the United States then

---

[*]*Nippon Times* (Tokyo), August 10, 1945.

*bad)** on Hiroshima (August 6) and Nagasaki (August 9). The horrified reaction of the* Nippon Times *is herewith given. Determine whether there was force in the Japanese charge of hypocrisy, and whether there is any moral difference between atomic bombing and large-scale incendiary bombing of civilian centers. (The Japanese had already bombed civilian centers, beginning with Shanghai in 1932.) Did the Japanese refusal to respond to the Potsdam ultimatum justify the bombing?*

How can a human being with any claim to a sense of moral responsibility deliberately let loose an instrument of destruction which can at one stroke annihilate an appalling segment of mankind? This is not war; this is not even murder; this is pure nihilism. This is a crime against God and humanity which strikes at the very basis of moral existence. What meaning is there in any international law, in any rule of human conduct, in any concept of right and wrong, if the very foundations of morality are to be overthrown as the use of this instrument of total destruction threatens to do?

The crime of the Americans stands out in ghastly repulsiveness all the more for the ironic contradiction it affords to their lying pretensions. For in their noisy statements, they have always claimed to be the champions of fairness and humanitarianism. In the early days of the China Affair [beginning in 1937], the United States repeatedly protested against the bombing operations of the Japanese forces, notwithstanding the fact that the Japanese operations were conducted on a limited scale against strictly military objectives. But where its own actions are concerned, the United States seems to see no inconsistency in committing on an unimaginably vast scale the very same crime it had falsely accused others of committing.

This hypocritical character of the Americans had already been amply demonstrated in the previous bombings of Japanese cities. Strewing explosives and fire bombs indiscriminately over an extensive area, hitting large cities and small towns without distinction, wiping out vast districts which could not be mistaken as being anything but strictly residential in character, burning or blasting to death countless thousands of helpless women and children, and machine-gunning fleeing refugees, the American raiders had already shown how completely they violate in their actual deeds the principles of humanity which they mouth in conspicuous pretense.

But now beside the latest technique of total destruction which the Americans have adopted, their earliest crimes pale into relative insignificance. What more barbarous atrocity can there be than to wipe out at one stroke the population of a whole city without distinction[†]—men, women, and children; the aged, the weak, the infirm; those in positions of authority, and those with no power at all; all snuffed out without being given a chance of lifting even a finger in either defense or defiance!

The United States may claim, in a lame attempt to raise a pretext in justification of its latest action, that a policy of utter annihilation is necessitated by Japan's failure to heed the recent demand for unconditional surrender. But the question of surrendering or not surrendering certainly can have not the slightest relevance to the question of whether it is justifiable to use a method which under any circumstance

---

*The third bomb was not scheduled to be ready until about August 24, two weeks after the dropping of the second one.

†At Hiroshima about 150,000 people were killed and wounded out of a total population of some 350,000. The firebomb raid on Tokyo of March 10, 1945, killed an estimated 83,000 people.

is strictly condemned alike by the principles of international law and of morality. For this American outrage against the fundamental moral sense of mankind, Japan must proclaim to the world its protest against the United States, which has made itself the archenemy of humanity.

2. Why Did the United States Drop the Atomic Bombs? (1946)*

Almost immediately after the atomic bombings of Hiroshima and Nagasaki, critics began challenging both the moral and strategic rationales for the attacks. In an especially influential article published in the Saturday Review of Literature *in June 1946, the magazine's editor, Norman Cousins, and veteran diplomat (and later Secretary of the Air Force) Thomas K. Finletter raised some unsettling questions about what they called the "mountainous blunder" of nuclear warfare. They accused the Truman administration of not simply wanting to end the war with Japan, but of using atomic arms primarily to intimidate the Soviet Union and freeze it out of the postwar peace settlement in Asia. How persuasive is their view? Were "power politics" regarding the Soviets and the desire to end the Japanese war as swiftly as possible necessarily incompatible aims? Was one more morally justifiable than the other?*

Why, then, did we drop it? Or, assuming that the use of the bomb was justified, why did we not demonstrate its power in a test under the auspices of the UN, on the basis of which an ultimatum would be issued to Japan—transferring the burden of responsibility to the Japanese themselves?

In speculating upon possible answers to these questions, some facts available since the bombing may be helpful. We now know, for example, that Russia was scheduled to come into the war against Japan by August 8, 1945. Russia had agreed at Yalta to join the fight against Japan ninety days after V-E day [Victory in Europe Day, May 8, 1945, the date of Germany's official surrender]. Going after the knockout punch, we bombed Hiroshima on August 5 [U.S. time, August 6 in Japan], Nagasaki on August 7 [actually August 8 U.S. time, August 9 in Japan]. Russia came into the war on August 8, as specified. Japan asked for surrender terms the same day.

Can it be that we were more anxious to prevent Russia from establishing a claim for full participation in the occupation against Japan than we were to think through the implications of unleashing atomic warfare? Whatever the answer, one gthing seems likely: There was not enough time between July 16, when we knew at New Mexico that the bomb would work, and August 8, the Russian deadline date, for us to have set up the very complicated machinery of a test atomic bombing involving time-consuming problems of area preparations; invitations and arrangements for observers (the probability being that the transportation to the South Pacific would in itself exceed the time limit); issuance of an ultimatum and the conditions of fulfillment, even if a reply limit was set at only forty-eight hours or less—just to mention a few.

---

*Norman Cousins and Thomas K. Finletter, "A Beginning for Sanity," review of A Report on the International Control of Atomic Energy, by a Board of Consultants for the Secretary of State's Committee on Atomic Energy, *The Saturday Review of Literature,* June 15, 1946, pp. 7–8.

No; any test would have been impossible if the purpose was to knock Japan out before Russia came in—or at least before Russia could make anything other than a token of participation prior to a Japanese collapse.

It may be argued that this decision was justified, that it was a legitimate exercise of power politics in a rough-and-tumble world, that we thereby avoided a struggle for authority in Japan similar to what we have experienced in Germany and Italy, that unless we came out of the war with a decisive balance of power over Russia, we would be in no position to checkmate Russian expansion.

3. Harry Truman Justifies the Bombing (1945)*

German scientists were known to be working on an atomic bomb, and Roosevelt was persuaded to push forward with an ultrasecret competing project that ultimately cost some $2.5 billion. The charge was made—without proof—that Truman had to use the new weapon or face an investigation of squandered money. More probable was his desire to end the Far Eastern war speedily, before the bothersome Russians came in. The evidence is strong that they hurried up their six-day participation following the dropping of the first bomb. At all events, President Truman accepted full responsibility for his decision and later defended it in his Memoirs, as excerpted here. Did he make the decision by himself? Did he try to use the bomb as a lawful weapon? In the light of conditions at the time, rather than hindsight, was he justified in his action?

My own knowledge of these [atomic] developments had come about only after I became President, when Secretary [of War] Stimson had given me the full story. He had told me at that time that the project was nearing completion, and that a bomb could be expected within another four months. It was at his suggestion, too, that I had then set up a committee of top men and had asked them to study with great care the implications the new weapon might have for us. . . .

It was their recommendation that the bomb be used against the enemy as soon as it could be done. They recommended further that it should be used without specific warning, and against a target that would clearly show its devastating strength. I had realized, of course, that an atomic bomb explosion would inflict damage and casualties beyond imagination. On the other hand, the scientific advisers of the committee reported, "We can propose no technical demonstration likely to bring an end to the war; we see no acceptable alternative to direct military use." It was their conclusion that no technical demonstration they might propose, such as over a deserted island, would be likely to bring the war to an end. It had to be used against an enemy target.

The final decision of where and when to use the atomic bomb was up to me. Let there be no mistake about it. I regarded the bomb as a military weapon, and never had any doubt that it should be used. The top military advisers to the President recommended its use, and when I talked to Churchill, he unhesitatingly told me that he favored the use of the atomic bomb if it might aid to end the war.

Memoirs of Harry S. Truman: Vol. 1. Years of Decisions. Doubleday & Co., Inc. Copyright © 1955 by Time Inc., renewed 1983 by Margaret Truman Daniel.

In deciding to use this bomb I wanted to make sure that it would be used as a weapon of war in the manner prescribed by the laws of war. That meant that I wanted it dropped on a military target. I had told Stimson that the bomb should be dropped as nearly as possibly upon a war production center of prime military importance....

Four cities were finally recommended as targets: Hiroshima, Kokura, Niigata, and Nagasaki. They were listed in that order as targets for the first attack. The order of selection was in accordance with the military importance of these cities, but allowance would be given for weather conditions at the time of the bombing.

[The devastating impact of the atomic bomb, together with the Soviet Union's sudden entry into the war against Japan, undoubtedly forced the Japanese surrender sooner than would otherwise have been possible. Even so, the fanatical military men in Tokyo almost won out for a last-ditch stand.

*In 1959, during interchanges with the students of Columbia University, former president Truman vigorously justified his action. He noted that "when we asked them to surrender at Potsdam, they gave us a very snotty answer. That is what I got.... They told me to go to hell, words to that effect." Mr. Truman insisted that the dropping of the bomb was "just a military maneuver, that is all," because "we were destroying the factories that were making more munitions." He then concluded: "All this uproar about what we did and what could have been stopped—should we take these wonderful Monday morning quarterbacks, the experts who are supposed to be right? They don't know what they are talking about. I was there. I did it. I would do it again." (*Truman Speaks *[New York: Columbia University Press, 1960], pp. 73–74.)]*

Thought Provokers

---

1. It has been said that the four years of World War II did more to transform U.S. society than twelve years of the Great Depression and eight years of the New Deal. Comment.
2. How did the courts justify restricting the civil liberties of Japanese Americans during World War II? How did Japanese Americans respond to internment?
3. If the situation had been reversed, would Stalin have been more willing than the other Allies to open a second front? Explain. How did the Soviet experience in World War II shape Stalin's desire for a second front?
4. Should the Allied powers have done more to intervene against the Holocaust? What options did they have at their disposal? What practical and psychological factors shaped the actions of Allied leaders? Why were so many people reluctant to believe the stories of Nazi atrocities?
5. How did new technologies and battle tactics shape the experience of soldiers in World War II? What elements of war did soldiers find most difficult to adjust to?
6. Does the probability that the Germans or the Japanese would have used the atomic bomb against the United States, if they had developed it first, strengthen the moral position of the United States? If Truman had announced at Potsdam that the United States had the atomic bomb, would the Japanese have been likely to surrender at once? Was the United States shortsighted in establishing a precedent that might one day be used against it? Comment on Secretary of War Henry Stimson's view that the dropping of the bomb would prove war to be so horrible that there could never be another.

35

The Cold War Begins, 1945–1952

I have been asked whether I have any regrets
about any of the major decisions I had to make
as President. I have none.

Harry S. Truman, 1960

Prologue: The United States stood triumphant at the end of World War II, but the
return of peace provided only short-lived relief to an aching world, as a new "Cold
War" contest between the Soviet Union and the United States began to take shape.
President Truman in 1947 deeply shaped American Cold War policy for the next four
decades when he proclaimed the Truman Doctrine, designed in the short run to shore up
communist-threatened Greece and Turkey, but aimed in the long run at defining a global
policy of "containment" of communist expansionism.

In 1948 Truman implemented the Marshall Plan, designed to rehabilitate war-torn
Western Europe. The Marshall Plan proved conspicuously successful in attaining its
objectives. But continuing fear of the Soviet Union forced the United States, despite its
ancient antialliance tradition, to negotiate in 1949 an epochal military defense alliance
in the form of the North Atlantic Treaty Organization (NATO). The "containment" policy
suffered a severe blow in 1949, when communists emerged the victors in China's civil
war. The "fall" of China touched off bitter political warfare between Republicans and
Democrats in the United States and contributed to the rise of McCarthyism—fanatical
and often irresponsible pursuit of alleged communist "traitors" in the United States. The
outbreak of a shooting war in Korea in 1950 seemed to confirm the worst fears about
communist intentions and provided the opportunity for a massive U.S. military buildup.

Americans had been spared the worst ravages of World War II. In contrast to the
plight of other combatants, their homeland had not been scorched by fighting, they
had lost relatively few fighting men, and their economy was snapped out of depression
and whipped into robust trim as a result of the war effort. Confident of the future, Americans immediately after the war launched a baby boom that added some 50 million
persons to the nation's population over the next decade and a half. The beginnings of
vast changes in family life and especially in the role of women emerged as Americans
moved en masse to the burgeoning suburbs.

A. The Truman Doctrine _____

1. George Kennan Proposes Containment (1946)*

As the Grand Alliance crumbled in the postwar months, U.S. policymakers groped for ways to understand the Soviet Union and to respond to Soviet provocations. On February 22, 1946, the scholarly chargé d'affaires at the U.S. embassy in Moscow, George F. Kennan, sent his famous "Long Telegram" to the State Department, giving his views of the sources of Soviet conduct. A later version of this message was published anonymously in Foreign Affairs *(July 1947). Kennan's ideas proved immensely influential in defining the so-called containment doctrine that dominated U.S. strategic thinking for the next two decades or more of the Cold War.*

Kennan argued that the Soviet Union regarded itself as encircled by hostile capitalist countries. In Soviet eyes, capitalist governments hoped to avert economic conflict among themselves by seeking war against the socialist world. Kennan denied the accuracy of these Soviet perceptions but insisted that they nonetheless motivated Soviet behavior. Painting the Soviet leaders as insecure, fearful, and cynical, he wrote: "In the name of Marxism they sacrificed every single ethical value in their methods and tactics. Today they cannot dispense with it. It is fig leaf of their moral and intellectual respectability. Without it they would stand before history, at best, as only the last of that long succession of cruel and wasteful Russian rulers who have relentlessly forced their country on to ever new heights of military power in order to guarantee the external security of their internally weak regimes. That is why Soviet purposes must always be solemnly clothed in trappings of Marxism, why no one should underrate importance of dogma in Soviet affairs." Kennan then went on to analyze the practical implications of this diagnosis and to recommend U.S. countermeasures. How prophetic was he? In his memoirs many years later, Kennan pleaded that he had never meant to suggest the kind of massive U.S. military buildup that the containment doctrine was later used to justify. Was he in fact misunderstood? If so, why?

In general, all Soviet efforts on unofficial international plane will be negative and destructive in character, designed to tear down sources of strength beyond reach of Soviet control. This is only in line with basic Soviet instinct that there can be no compromise with rival power and that constructive work can start only when communist power is dominant. But behind all this will be applied insistent, unceasing pressure for penetration and command of key positions in administration and especially in police apparatus of foreign countries. The Soviet regime is a police regime par excellence, reared in the dim half world of Tsarist police intrigue, accustomed to think primarily in terms of police power. This should never be lost sight of in gauging Soviet motives.

In summary, we have here a political force committed fanatically to the belief that with US there can be no permanent modus vivendi, that it is desirable and necessary that the internal harmony of our society be disrupted, our traditional

_____

Foreign Relations of the United States, 1946, vol. 6 (Washington, DC: Government Printing Office).

way of life be destroyed, the international authority of our state be broken, if Soviet power is to be secure. This political force has complete power of disposition over energies of one of world's greatest peoples and resources of world's richest national territory, and is borne along by deep and powerful currents of Russian nationalism. In addition, it has an elaborate and far flung apparatus for exertion of its influence in other countries, an apparatus of amazing flexibility and versatility, managed by people whose experience and skill in underground methods are presumably without parallel in history. Finally, it is seemingly inaccessible to considerations of reality in its basic reactions. For it, the vast fund of objective fact about human society is not, as with us, the measure against which outlook is constantly being tested and re-formed, but a grab bag from which individual items are selected arbitrarily and tendentiously to bolster an outlook already preconceived. This is admittedly not a pleasant picture. Problem of how to cope with this force is undoubtedly greatest task our diplomacy has ever faced and probably greatest it will ever have to face. It should be point of departure from which our political general staff work at present juncture should proceed. It should be approached with same thoroughness and care as solution of major strategic problem in war, and if necessary, with no smaller outlay in planning effort. I cannot attempt to suggest all answers here. But I would like to record my conviction that problem is within our power to solve—and that without recourse to any general military conflict. And in support of this conviction there are certain observations of a more encouraging nature I should like to make:

(One) Soviet power, unlike that of Hitlerite Germany, is neither schematic nor adventuristic. It does not work by fixed plans. It does not take unnecessary risks. Impervious to logic of reason, and it is highly sensitive to logic of force. For this reason it can easily withdraw—and usually does—when strong resistance is encountered at any point. Thus, if the adversary has sufficient force and makes clear his readiness to use it, he rarely has to do so. If situations are properly handled there need be no prestige engaging showdowns.

(Two) Gauged against western world as a whole, Soviets are still by far the weaker force. Thus, their success will really depend on degree of cohesion, firmness and vigor which western world can muster. And this is factor which it is within our power to influence.

(Three) Success of Soviet system, as form of internal power, is not yet finally proven. It has yet to be demonstrated that it can survive supreme test of successive transfer of power from one individual or group to another. Lenin's death was first such transfer, and its effects wracked Soviet state for 15 years after. Stalin's death or retirement will be second. But even this will not be final test. Soviet internal system will now be subjected, by virtue of recent territorial expansions, to series of additional strains which once proved severe tax on Tsardom. We here are convinced that never since termination of civil war have mass of Russian people been emotionally farther removed from doctrines of communist party than they are today. In Russia, party has now become a great and—for the moment—highly successful apparatus of dictatorial administration, but it has ceased to be a source of emotional inspiration. Thus, internal soundness and permanence of movement need not yet be regarded as assured.

(Four) All Soviet propaganda beyond Soviet security sphere is basically negative and destructive. It should therefore be relatively easy to combat it by any intelligent and really constructive program.

For these reasons I think we may approach calmly and with good heart problem of how to deal with Russia. As to how this approach should be made, I only wish to advance, by way of conclusion, following comments:

(One) Our first step must be to apprehend, and recognize for what it is, the nature of the movement with which we are dealing. We must study it with same courage, detachment, objectivity, and same determination not to be emotionally provoked or unseated by it, with which doctor studies unruly and unreasonable individual.

(Two) We must see that our public is educated to realities of Russian situation. I cannot over-emphasize importance of this. Press cannot do this alone. It must be done mainly by government, which is necessarily more experienced and better informed on practical problems involved. In this we need not be deterred by [ugliness] of picture. I am convinced that there would be far less hysterical anti-Sovietism in our country today if realities of this situation were better understood by our people. There is nothing as dangerous or as terrifying as the unknown. It may also be argued that to reveal more information on our difficulties with Russia would reflect unfavorably on Russian American relations. I feel that if there is any real risk here involved, it is one which we should have courage to face, and sooner the better. But I cannot see what we would be risking. Our stake in this country, even coming on heels of tremendous demonstrations of our friendship for Russian people, is remarkably small. We have here no investments to guard, no actual trade to lose, virtually no citizens to protect, few cultural contacts to preserve. Our only stake lies in what we hope rather than what we have; and I am convinced we have better chance of realizing those hopes if our public is enlightened and if our dealings with Russians are placed entirely on realistic and matter of fact basis.

(Three) Much depends on health and vigor of our own society. World communism is like malignant parasite which feeds only on diseased tissue. This is point at which domestic and foreign policies meet. Every courageous and incisive measure to solve internal problems of our own society, to improve self-confidence, discipline, morale and community spirit of our own people, is a diplomatic victory over Moscow worth a thousand diplomatic notes and joint communiqués. If we cannot abandon fatalism and indifference in face of deficiencies of our own society, Moscow will profit—Moscow cannot help profiting by them in its foreign policies.

(Four) We must formulate and put forward for other nations a much more positive and constructive picture of sort of world we would like to see than we have put forward in past. It is not enough to urge people to develop political processes similar to our own. Many foreign peoples, in Europe at least, are tired and frightened by experiences of past, and are less interested in abstract freedom than in security. They are seeking guidance rather than responsibilities. We should be better able than Russians to give them this. And unless we do, Russians certainly will.

(Five) Finally we must have courage and self-confidence to cling to our own methods and conceptions of human society. After all, the greatest danger that can befall us in coping with this problem of Soviet Communism, is that we shall allow ourselves to become like those with whom we are coping.

2. Harry Truman Appeals to Congress (1947)*

A crisis developed early in 1947 when the bankrupt British served notice on Washington that they could no longer afford to support the "rightist" government of Greece against communist guerrillas. If Greece fell, Turkey and all the eastern Mediterranean countries would presumably collapse, like falling dominoes. After hurried consultations in Washington, President Truman boldly went before Congress to ask for $400 million to provide military and economic assistance to Greece and Turkey. This was a great deal of money, he conceded, but a trifling sum compared with the more than a third of a trillion dollars already expended in the recent war to guarantee freedom. On what grounds did he base his appeal? Were there any dangers in this approach?

I am fully aware of the broad implications involved if the United States extends assistance to Greece and Turkey, and I shall discuss these implications with you at this time.

One of the primary objectives of the foreign policy of the United States is the creation of conditions in which we and other nations will be able to work out a way of life free from coercion. This was a fundamental issue in the war with Germany and Japan. Our victory was won over countries which sought to impose their will, and their way of life, upon other nations.

To insure the peaceful development of nations, free from coercion, the United States has taken a leading part in establishing the United Nations. The United Nations is designed to make possible lasting freedom and independence for all its members. We shall not realize our objectives, however, unless we are willing to help free peoples to maintain their free institutions and their national integrity against aggressive movements that seek to impose upon them totalitarian regimes. [Applause.] This is no more than a frank recognition that totalitarian regimes imposed upon free peoples, by direct or indirect aggression, undermine the foundations of international peace and hence the security of the United States.

The peoples of a number of countries of the world have recently had totalitarian regimes forced upon them against their will. The Government of the United States has made frequent protests against coercion and intimidation, in violation of the Yalta Agreement, in Poland, Rumania, and Bulgaria. I must also state that in a number of other countries there have been similar developments. . . .

I believe that it must be the policy of the United States to support free peoples who are resisting attempted subjugation by armed minorities or by outside pressures.

I believe that we must assist free peoples to work out their own destiny in their own way.

I believe that our help should be primarily through economic and financial aid, which is essential to economic stability and orderly political processes.

The world is not static and the status quo is not sacred. But we cannot allow changes in the status quo in violation of the Charter of the United Nations by such methods as coercion, or by such subterfuge as political infiltration. In helping free

---

Congressional Record, 80th Cong., 1st sess. (March 12, 1947), p. 1981.

and independent nations to maintain their freedom, the United States will be giving effect to the principles of the Charter of the United Nations....

This is a serious course upon which we embark. I would not recommend it except that the alternative is much more serious. [Applause.]...

The free peoples of the world look to us for support in maintaining their freedoms.

If we falter in our leadership, we may endanger the peace of the world—and we shall surely endanger the welfare of our own Nation.

Great responsibilities have been placed upon us by the swift movement of events.

I am confident that the Congress will face these responsibilities squarely. [Applause, the members rising.]

3. The Chicago Tribune *Dissents (1947)*[*]

The nation was momentarily stunned by Truman's bombshell. Critics complained that the initial appropriation would be but a drop in the bucket (as it was), that the Soviet Union (though not mentioned by name) would be gravely offended, and that the United Nations was being rudely bypassed. (Speed was of the essence, and the administration concluded that the Soviets would paralyze action in the United Nations.) The Chicago Tribune, *a powerful isolationist newspaper, was vehemently anti-British, anti-communist, and anti-Roosevelt. Which of its arguments against the Truman Doctrine are persuasive?*

Mr. Truman made as cold a war speech yesterday against Russia as any President has ever made except on the occasion of going before Congress to ask for a declaration of war....

The outcome will inevitably be war. It probably will not come this year or next year, but the issue is already drawn. The declaration of implacable hostility between this country and Russia is one which cannot be tempered or withdrawn....

Mr. Truman's statement constituted a complete confession of the bankruptcy of American policy as formulated by Mr. Roosevelt and pursued by himself. We have just emerged from a great war which was dedicated to the extinction of the three nations [Germany, Italy, Japan] which were as vocally opposed to Russia as Mr. Truman proclaims himself to be now. If communism was the real danger all along, why did Mr. Roosevelt and Mr. Truman adopt Russia as an ally, and why, at Teheran, Yalta, and Potsdam, did they build up Russia's power by making her one concession after another?

The Truman speech also leaves the United Nations as a meaningless relic of mistaken intentions. The world league to insure a lasting peace is a fraud and a sham, so impotent that Mr. Truman proposes that the United States ignore it and seek peace by force and threat of force—the very means which the U.N. was intended to exclude in international dealings.

---

[*]Editorial against Truman Doctrine (March 13, 1947).

The one hope that is left is Congress, but even its peremptory refusal to follow Truman into his anti-communist crusade will not wholly undo the damage which the President has already done. His words cannot be unsaid, nor can their effect upon Russia be canceled out. Already, as witness Moscow's recall of the Soviet Ambassador from Washington, the nations are engaging in the usual preliminaries to war.

When the country views the terrible predicament in which it now finds itself, it cannot avoid the conclusion that wisdom at all times counseled the United States to follow Americanism only, to dedicate itself to the pursuit of its own interests, and to let Europe's wars alone. We have fought two of them without avail, and Mr. Truman is calling upon us to fight a third.

We were drawn into these wars primarily at the behest of Britain, and that nation, by dumping the Greek and Turkish problems into Mr. Truman's lap, is summoning us to the struggle again. If the United States can be induced to crush Russia, Britain again will rise to a station of security and comparative eminence, for it will be the only other surviving major nation.

For 10 years the United States has been dominated by alien interests. These interests, primarily financial, have bought up every newspaper, radio station, columnist, and commentator, and every so-called organization of public opinion that could be purchased. It has killed our sons by the hundreds of thousands and brought the nation to bankruptcy. It will use whatever tactics seem best to rush into World War III. It will coerce the timid and fool the stupid.

Congress must cease being a catspaw for this movement and think of America's interest first—even exclusively.

[The dangers involved in the Truman Doctrine were great, but the dangers of drifting seemed greater. Congress, by better than a two-to-one vote in both houses, finally approved the initial appropriation early in 1948.]

4. The World Through Soviet Eyes (1946)*

As the Cold War came to an end in the late 1980s and early 1990s, Russian and American scholars for the first time gained open access to Soviet archives. Among the documents that came to light in 1990 was the following telegram sent to the Soviet foreign ministry in Moscow by Soviet ambassador to the United States Nikolai Novikov on September 27, 1946. It is in many ways a companion piece to George Kennan's famous "Long Telegram" from Moscow in February of the same year, reprinted in part earlier in this section (see p. 691). Like Kennan, who tried to explain the sources of Soviet conduct to his superiors in Washington, Novikov attempted to identify the taproots of U.S. foreign policy and the outlines of U.S. international strategy. In what ways does his analysis confirm Kennan's appraisal of the ways in which the Soviets viewed the rest of the world? In what ways does Novikov's portrait of American policy constitute a mirror image of Kennan's rendering of Soviet policy? How accurate are Novikov's assessments?

*From *Origins of the Cold War: The Novikov, Kennan, and Roberts 'Long' Telegrams of 1946.* (Kenneth M. Jensen, editor) Washington, DC: Endowment of the United States Institute of Peace, 1993. 1200 words from the Novikov Telegram. Reprinted by permission of the United States Institute of Peace.

The foreign policy of the United States, which reflects the imperialist tendencies of American monopolistic capital, is characterized in the postwar period by a striving for world supremacy. This is the real meaning of the many statements by President Truman and other representatives of American ruling circles: that the United States has the right to lead the world. All the forces of American diplomacy—the army, the air force, the navy, industry, and science—are enlisted in the service of this foreign policy. For this purpose broad plans for expansion have been developed and are being implemented through diplomacy and the establishment of a system of naval and air bases stretching far beyond the boundaries of the United States, through the arms race, and through the creation of ever newer types of weapons....

Obvious indications of the U.S. effort to establish world dominance are...to be found in the increase in military potential in peacetime and in the establishment of a large number of naval and air bases both in the United States and beyond its borders.

In the summer of 1946, for the first time in the history of the country, Congress passed a law on the establishment of a peacetime army, not on a volunteer basis but on the basis of universal military service. The size of the army, which is supposed to amount to about one million persons as of July 1, 1947, was also increased significantly. The size of the navy at the conclusion of the war decreased quite insignificantly in comparison with wartime. At the present time, the American navy occupies first place in the world, leaving England's navy far behind, to say nothing of those of other countries.

Expenditures on the army and navy have risen colossally, amounting to 13 billion dollars according to the budget for 1946–47 (about 40 percent of the total budget of 36 billion dollars). This is more than ten times greater than corresponding expenditures in the budget for 1938, which did not amount to even one billion dollars.

Along with maintaining a large army, navy, and air force, the budget provides that these enormous amounts also will be spent on establishing a very extensive system of naval and air bases in the Atlantic and Pacific oceans. According to existing official plans, in the course of the next few years 228 bases, points of support, and radio stations are to be constructed in the Atlantic Ocean and 258 in the Pacific. A large number of these bases and points of support are located outside the boundaries of the United States. In the Atlantic Ocean bases exist or are under construction in the following foreign island territories: Newfoundland, Iceland, Cuba, Trinidad, Bermuda, the Bahamas, the Azores, and many others; in the Pacific Ocean: former Japanese mandated territories—the Marianas, Caroline and Marshall Islands, Bonin, Ryukyu, Philippines, and the Galapagos Islands (they belong to Ecuador).

The establishment of American bases on islands that are often 10,000 to 12,000 kilometers from the territory of the United States and are on the other side of the Atlantic and Pacific oceans clearly indicates the offensive nature of the strategic concepts of the commands of the U.S. army and navy. This interpretation is also confirmed by the fact that the American navy is intensively studying the naval approaches to the boundaries of Europe. For this purpose, American naval vessels in the course of 1946 visited the ports of Norway, Denmark, Sweden, Turkey, and Greece. In addition, the American navy is constantly operating in the Mediterranean Sea.

All of these facts show clearly that a decisive role in the realization of plans for world dominance by the United States is played by its armed forces....

The present policy of the American government with regard to the USSR is also directed at limiting or dislodging the influence of the Soviet Union from neighboring countries. In implementing this policy in former enemy or Allied countries adjacent to the USSR, the United States attempts, at various international conferences or directly in these countries themselves, to support reactionary forces with the purpose of creating obstacles to the process of democratization of these countries. In so doing, it also attempts to secure positions for the penetration of American capital into their economies. Such a policy is intended to weaken and overthrow the democratic governments in power there, which are friendly toward the USSR, and replace them in the future with new governments that would obediently carry out a policy dictated from the United States. In this policy, the United States receives full support from English diplomacy....

The numerous and extremely hostile statements by American government, political, and military figures with regard to the Soviet Union and its foreign policy are very characteristic of the current relationship between the ruling circles of the United States and the USSR. These statements are echoed in an even more unrestrained tone by the overwhelming majority of the American press organs. Talk about a "third war," meaning a war against the Soviet Union, and even a direct call for this war—with the threat of using the atomic bomb—such is the content of the statements on relations with the Soviet Union by reactionaries at public meetings and in the press. At the present time, preaching war against the Soviet Union is not a monopoly of the far-right, yellow American press represented by the newspaper associations of Hearst and McCormick. This anti-Soviet campaign also has been joined by the "reputable" and "respectable" organs of the conservative press, such as the *New York Times* and *New York Herald Tribune*. Indicative in this respect are the numerous articles by Walter Lippmann in which he almost undisguisedly calls on the United States to launch a strike against the Soviet Union in the most vulnerable areas of the south and southeast of the USSR.

The basic goal of this anti-Soviet campaign of American "public opinion" is to exert political pressure on the Soviet Union and compel it to make concessions. Another, no less important goal of the campaign is the attempt to create an atmosphere of war psychosis among the masses, who are weary of war, thus making it easier for the U.S. government to carry out measures for the maintenance of high military potential. It was in this very atmosphere that the law on universal military service in peacetime was passed by Congress, that the huge military budget was adopted, and that plans are being worked out for the construction of an extensive system of naval and air bases.

Of course, all of these measures for maintaining a high military potential are not goals in themselves. They are only intended to prepare the conditions for winning world supremacy in a new war, the date for which, to be sure, cannot be determined now by anyone, but which is contemplated by the most bellicose circles of American imperialism.

Careful note should be taken of the fact that the preparation by the United States for a future war is being conducted with the prospect of war against the

Soviet Union, which in the eyes of American imperialists is the main obstacle in the path of the United States to world domination. This is indicated by facts such as the tactical training of the American army for war with the Soviet Union as the future opponent, the siting of American strategic bases in regions from which it is possible to launch strikes on Soviet territory, intensified training and strengthening of Arctic regions as close approaches to the USSR, and attempts to prepare Germany and Japan to use those countries in a war against the USSR.

B. The Marshall Plan

1. Secretary George Marshall Speaks at Harvard (1947)*

By June 1947 it was painfully evident that the Truman Doctrine was merely a child on an adult's errand. The hunger and economic prostration produced by the war were providing an alarming hotbed for the propagation of communism in Europe, especially in Italy and France. A communist takeover of all Western Europe appeared to be a distinct (and depressing) possibility. At this critical juncture the secretary of state, General George C. Marshall, speaking at the Harvard University commencement exercises, made the following breathtaking proposal. To what extent is it both selfish and unselfish? What is its relation to the Truman Doctrine?

The truth of the matter is that Europe's requirements for the next three or four years of foreign food and other essential products—principally from America—are so much greater than her present ability to pay that she must have substantial additional help or face economic, social, and political deterioration of a very grave character. . . .

Aside from the demoralizing effect on the world at large and the possibilities of disturbances arising as a result of the desperation of the people concerned, the consequences to the economy of the United States should be apparent to all. It is logical that the United States should do whatever it is able to do to assist in the return of normal economic health in the world, without which there can be no political stability and no assured peace. Our policy is directed not against any country or doctrine but against hunger, poverty, desperation, and chaos. Its purpose should be the revival of a working economy in the world so as to permit the emergence of political and social conditions in which free institutions can exist.

Such assistance, I am convinced, must not be on a piecemeal basis as various crises develop. Any assistance that this Government may render in the future should provide a cure rather than a mere palliative. Any government that is willing to assist in the task of recovery will find full cooperation, I am sure, on the part of the United States Government. Any government which maneuvers to block the recovery of other countries cannot expect help from us. Furthermore, governments, political parties, or groups which seek to perpetuate human misery in order to profit therefrom politically or otherwise will encounter the opposition of the United States.

Department of State Bulletin 16 (June 15, 1947; speech of June 5, 1947): 1159–1160.

It is already evident that, before the United States Government can proceed much further in its efforts to alleviate the situation and help start the European world on its way to recovery, there must be some agreement among the countries of Europe as to the requirements of the situation and the part those countries themselves will take in order to give proper effect to whatever action might be undertaken by this Government.

It would be neither fitting nor efficacious for this Government to undertake to draw up unilaterally a program designed to place Europe on its feet economically. This is the business of the Europeans. The initiative, I think, must come from Europe. The role of this country should consist of friendly aid in the drafting of a European program and of later support of such a program so far as it may be practical for us to do so. The program should be a joint one, agreed to by a number, if not all, European nations.

2. Senator Arthur Vandenberg Is Favorable (1947, 1948)*

Tax-burdened Americans, having spent billions in World War II, were reluctant to pour more treasure down the "European rathole." Eloquent Senator Vandenberg of Michigan (see p. 642), a recent convert from isolationism to internationalism, was one of the foremost champions in Congress of the Marshall Plan. In the following excerpts from letters to his constituents, what are his arguments for the Marshall Plan? In what ways does he see the plan as serving the self-interest of the United States?

I have no illusions about this so-called "Marshall Plan." . . . Furthermore, I certainly do not take it for granted that American public opinion is ready for any such burdens as would be involved unless and until it is far more effectively demonstrated to the American people that this (1) is within the latitudes of their own available resources and (2) serves their own intelligent self-interest.

. . . I am entirely willing to admit that America herself cannot prosper in a broken world. But it is equally true that if America ever sags, the world's hopes for peace will sag with her. Meanwhile, however, there are some very realistic problems which we must face—including the basic fact that even our friends in Western Europe will soon be totally devoid of dollar exchange and therefore unable to buy commodities from us which are indispensable to their own self-rehabilitation. I must confess that this poses a tough conundrum in international economics entirely aside from considerations of "charity" or "communism." . . .

So we have no alternative but to do the best we can, in the absence of certified knowledge, and to balance one "calculated risk" against another. . . .

You are entirely right that an "international WPA"[†] can't save Europe from communism or anything else. Is somebody proposing one? I hadn't heard about it. The so-called "Marshall Plan" is the exact opposite, if it runs true to form—and it's our business to see that it does. It is a program geared to self-help. It requires

*From *The Private Papers of Senator Vandenberg* by Arthur H. Vandenberg, Jr. Copyright 1952 by Arthur Vandenberg, Jr.; copyright © renewed 1980 by Mrs. Myron Sands and Joe Alex Morris.
†Works Progress Administration—a New Deal agency designed to provide employment on public works.

beneficiary countries to proceed specifically to do the things for themselves which will put them on their own feet (and off ours) by 1951—and our aid is progressively contingent upon concurrent results.

...I respectfully submit that we do "know enough" to know what will happen if it, or something like it, doesn't work. We know that independent governments, whatever their character otherwise, will disappear from Western Europe; that aggressive communism will be spurred throughout the world; and that our concept of free men, free government, and a relatively free international economy will come up against accumulated hazards which can put our own, precious "American way of life" in the greatest, kindred hazard since Pearl Harbor....

Let's be equally frank in our "calculations" as to what happens if the iron curtain reaches the Atlantic; if peace and justice are at the mercy of expanding, hostile totalitarian aggression, and if the greatest creditor and capitalist nation on earth should find itself substantially isolated in a communist world where the competition would force us into complete regimentation of ourselves beyond anything we have ever experienced.

This question of "what the Bill will cost" is a very interesting one. Unfortunately, the critics of the Bill have nothing to say about what the failure to pass the Bill will cost. You can get some direct and specific idea on this latter point by reading the testimony before our Senate Foreign Relations Committee by Secretary of Defense Forrestal and Secretary of the Army Royall, who both assert that without legislation of this character they would find it necessary immediately to ask for heavily increased appropriations for military defense. Why? Because it is infinitely cheaper to defend ourselves by economic means.

In other words, in the final analysis, peace is cheaper than war. War has no bargains. Peace does. There is no guarantee that this European Recovery Plan will "work." But certainly there is an even chance that it can succeed. In my opinion, we cannot afford not to take that chance.

3. Moscow's Misrepresentations (c. 1947)[*]

The Marshall Plan certainly would not have received congressional approval if the American people had not been convinced that their security depended on preventing Western Europe from falling under the sway of Soviet communism. Humanitarian instincts, gratitude to former allies, the creation of prosperous customers for surplus goods—all these points were argued, but security was unquestionably paramount. U.S. critics of the Marshall Plan charged that the poor people of the United States needed help, and that Washington should not subsidize socialism (in Britain and elsewhere). The following description of the Marshall Plan was prepared by Soviet propagandists for a children's magazine. How accurate is it?

The American papers immediately raised a great noise about this [Marshall] plan. In different terms, they emphasized "the magnanimity" of America which had decided to help war-stricken Europe.

---

[*]Pages 198–200 from *My Three Years in Moscow* by Walter Bedell Smith. Copyright 1949 by Walter Bedell Smith.

However, actually, this cunning plan pursued entirely different aims. The American capitalists want to use the help of the Marshall Plan to overwhelm Europe and bring it into subjection to themselves. The government of the Soviet Union at once recognized the real meaning of the Marshall Plan, and definitely refused to take part in setting it up. So also did the governments of the other democratic lands—Poland, Czechoslovakia, Bulgaria, Yugoslavia, Rumania, Hungary, and also Finland.* But sixteen European states adopted the Marshall Plan against the wishes of their peoples.

Let us see now how the U.S.A. is preparing to carry out the Marshall Plan, and what it promises the European countries which have fallen for the American bait.

Representatives of these sixteen European states met together and calculated that they had to receive from the U.S.A. 29 billion dollars to restore their economies. The Americans answered that this sum was too high, and asked for its reduction to 20–22 billion dollars.

The Americans, moreover, attached the following condition: they themselves will dictate to each European country what branch of economy it must develop and what it must curtail. For example, they say to Britain: "You Britishers, build fewer ships for yourselves; you will buy ships from us in America." They propose to the French a reduction in the production of automobiles—American factories can make automobiles for France.

It goes without saying that this was very useful for American capitalists. In America everybody is fearfully awaiting "the economic crisis," i.e., the time when many factories and industries suddenly close and millions of people are left without work. At that time it will be difficult for the manufacturers to get rid of their output. A man out of work has nothing with which to buy them. So the American capitalists are greatly concerned how to sell profitably their output in Europe. Further, the European countries inevitably will become dependent on America: once they make a few machines, tools, and automobiles, it means that willy-nilly they must defer to the Americans.

According to the Marshall Plan, the American capitalists want to restore all the great factories of Western Germany. In other countries they are hastening to close many factories, while in Germany, on the contrary, they are opening them up. Their purpose there, too, is quite understandable: clearly, the U.S.A. considers Western Germany as its colony. By controlling the big industries there which can also make armaments, it will be easy for the Americans to frighten the European countries dependent on them.

The American capitalists counted on using the Marshall Plan to stir up trouble between the peoples of the democratic countries and the Soviet Union. The Americans proposed to these countries as follows: "We will give you dollars if only you will abandon your friendship with the Soviet Union. But if you don't, we won't give you anything." But the peoples of these countries did not fall for the American capitalists' trick. They answered the Americans: "We will not exchange our freedom and independence for dollars." . . .

---

*Soviet pressures on these satellite countries kept them from accepting the Marshall Plan.

But this isn't all. The American capitalists have still another dastardly aim. After using the Marshall Plan to reduce the European countries, they want to unite them in a military alliance for a future war against the democratic states.

The Marshall Plan is highly profitable to the United States. For the European countries it brings only poverty. Any land which wants to receive "aid" by means of this plan will be entirely dependent on America. Its economy will not be assisted: on the contrary, it will fall into greater ruin because the country will have to close many of its industries and plants, and hundreds of thousands of people will be out of work. That is why both in America itself and in all other lands progressive people are opposing the Marshall Plan with all their strength.

C. The Korean Crisis and NSC-68 _____

1. Senator Tom Connally Writes Off Korea (1950)*

Secretary of State Dean Acheson made a memorable speech to the National Press Club of Washington early in 1950. He outlined the United States' "defensive perimeter" in the Far East but conspicuously omitted from it the Republic of South Korea and the Nationalist China of Jiang Jeishi (Chiang Kai-shek) in exile on the island of Formosa (Taiwan). He stated that the areas thus excluded would have to depend on themselves for defense and on "the commitments of the entire civilized world under the Charter of the United Nations." Some three months later Senator Connally, chairman of the powerful Senate Foreign Relations Committee, gave the following interview. Critics of the Truman administration later charged that the Acheson and Connally statements were open invitations to the Soviet-backed North Korean communists to invade South Korea, as they did in June 1950. Was this accusation fair?

Question. Do you think the suggestion that we abandon South Korea is going to be seriously considered?

Answer. I am afraid it is going to be seriously considered because I'm afraid it's going to happen, whether we want it to or not. I'm for Korea. We're trying to help her—we're appropriating money now to help her. But South Korea is cut right across by this line—north of it are the Communists, with access to the mainland—and Russia is over there on the mainland. So that whenever she takes a notion, she can just overrun Korea, just like she probably will overrun Formosa when she gets ready to do it. I hope not, of course.

Question. But isn't Korea an essential part of the defense strategy?

Answer. No. Of course, any position like that is of some strategic importance. But I don't think it is very greatly important. It has been testified before us that Japan, Okinawa, and the Philippines make the chain of defense which is absolutely necessary. And, of course, any additional territory along in that area would be that much more, but it's not absolutely essential.

---

*Reprinted from *U.S. News and World Report* 28 (May 5, 1950): 30. Copyright 1950, U.S. News and World Report.

2. Truman Accepts the Korean Challenge (1950)*

President Truman was forced to make a series of agonizing decisions: the Truman Doctrine (1947), the Marshall Plan (1947), the Berlin airlift (1948), the North Atlantic Pact (1949), the Korean intervention (1950). Speaking later (1959) at Columbia University, he was asked, "Mr. President, what was the most complicated, the one single, most difficult decision you had to make?" Unhesitatingly he replied: "Korea. The reason for that was the fact that the policies of our allies and the members of the United Nations were at stake at the same time as ours." Here in his Memoirs he explains more fully the reasons for intervening with armed forces to support the South Korean republic, a special ward of the United Nations. Remembering that the League of Nations had collapsed in the 1930s because it failed to act resolutely, assess the validity of Truman's view that his intervention in Korea averted World War III.

On Saturday, June 24, 1950, I was in Independence, Missouri, to spend the weekend with my family and to attend to some personal family business.

It was a little after ten in the evening, and we were sitting in the library of our home on North Delaware Street when the telephone rang. It was the Secretary of State calling from his home in Maryland.

"Mr. President," said Dean Acheson, "I have very serious news. The North Koreans have invaded South Korea."

My first reaction was that I must get back to the capital, and I told Acheson so. . . .

The plane left the Kansas City Municipal Airport at two o'clock, and it took just a little over three hours to make the trip to Washington. I had time to think aboard the plane. In my generation, this was not the first occasion when the strong had attacked the weak. I recalled some earlier instances: [Japan in] Manchuria, [Italy in] Ethiopia, [Germany in] Austria. I remembered how each time that the democracies failed to act it had encouraged the aggressors to keep going ahead.

Communism was acting in Korea just as Hitler, Mussolini, and the Japanese had acted ten, fifteen, and twenty years earlier. I felt certain that if South Korea was allowed to fall, Communist leaders would be emboldened to override nations closer to our own shores. If the Communists were permitted to force their way into the Republic of Korea without opposition from the free world, no small nation would have the courage to resist threats and aggression by stronger Communist neighbors. If this was allowed to go unchallenged it would mean a third world war, just as similar incidents had brought on the second world war. It was also clear to me that the foundations and the principles of the United Nations were at stake unless this unprovoked attack on Korea could be stopped.

Memoirs by Harry S. Truman: Years of Trial and Hope (1956), vol. 2, pp. 331–333. Published by Doubleday and Company. Copyright © 1956 by Time, Inc.

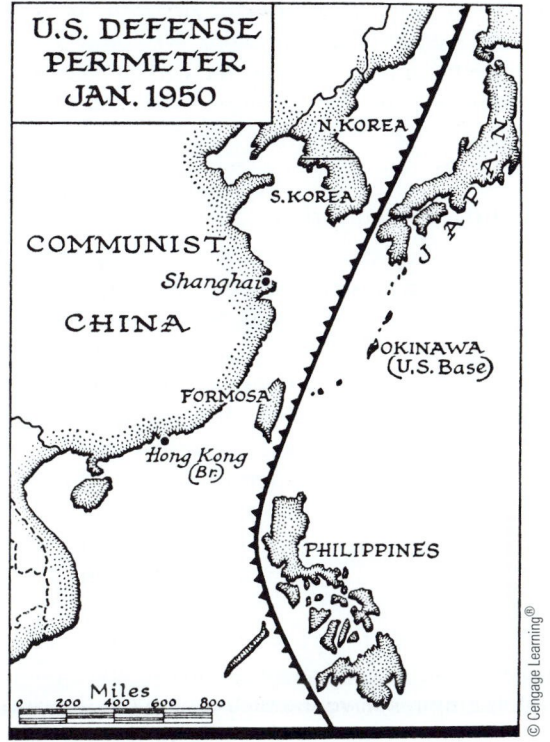

U.S. DEFENSE PERIMETER JAN. 1950

3. NSC-68 Offers a Blueprint for the Cold War (1950)*

Jolted by the communist success in China and the Soviet development of an atomic bomb, President Truman in early 1950 ordered a far-reaching reassessment of U.S. Cold War policies. The result was a lengthy secret document, declassified only a quarter of a century later, known as National Security Council Memorandum Number 68 (NSC-68). The memorandum assessed the balance of Soviet and U.S. power in the world and made sweeping recommendations for a vigorous U.S. military buildup. It laid out, in effect, a blueprint for U.S. foreign policy for the next two decades. It advised against negotiating with the Soviet Union until the United States had time "to build up strength," although it conceded that some discussions with the Soviets were probably necessary "to gain public support for the [buildup] and to minimize the immediate risks of war." NSC-68 also advocated the development of hydrogen bombs and the expansion of conventional military forces, and it frankly acknowledged that substantial tax increases would be necessary to finance this effort. On what premises about the state of the world and the character of the

*Foreign Relations of the United States, 1950 (Washington, DC: Government Printing Office), pp. 237–238, 272–286.

Soviet Union does NSC-68 build its argument? Are those premises justifiable? What policy choices does the memorandum present? Why does it choose the particular policies it recommends? What does it see as the United States' strengths and liabilities in the confrontation with the Soviet Union? What obstacles to developing those strengths does it identify?

I. Background of the Present Crisis

Within the past thirty-five years the world has experienced two global wars of tremendous violence. It has witnessed two revolutions—the Russian and the Chinese—of extreme scope and intensity. It has also seen the collapse of five empires—the Ottoman, the Austro-Hungarian, German, Italian and Japanese—and the drastic decline of two major imperial systems, the British and the French. During the span of one generation, the international distribution of power has been fundamentally altered. For several centuries it had proved impossible for any one nation to gain such preponderant strength that a coalition of other nations could not in time face it with greater strength. The international scene was marked by recurring periods of violence and war, but a system of sovereign and independent states was maintained, over which no state was able to achieve hegemony.

Two complex sets of factors have now basically altered this historical distribution of power. First, the defeat of Germany and Japan and the decline of the British and French Empires have interacted with the development of the United States and the Soviet Union in such a way that power has increasingly gravitated to these two centers. Second, the Soviet Union, unlike previous aspirants to hegemony, is animated by a new fanatic faith, antithetical to our own, and seeks to impose its absolute authority over the rest of the world. Conflict has, therefore, become endemic and is waged, on the part of the Soviet Union, by violent or nonviolent methods in accordance with the dictates of expediency. With the development of increasingly terrifying weapons of mass destruction, every individual faces the ever-present possibility of annihilation should the conflict enter the phase of total war....

The issues that face us are momentous, involving the fulfillment or destruction not only of this Republic but of civilization itself. They are issues which will not await our deliberations. With conscience and resolution this Government and the people it represents must now make new and fateful decisions....

Four possible courses of action by the United States in the present situation can be distinguished. They are:

a. Continuation of current policies, with current and currently projected programs for carrying out these policies;

b. Isolation;

c. War; and

d. A more rapid building up of the political, economic, and military strength of the free world than provided under *a*, with the purpose of reaching, if possible, a tolerable state of order among nations without war and of preparing to defend ourselves in the event that the free world is attacked....

On the basis of current programs, the United States has a large potential military capability but an actual capability which, though improving, is declining relative to the U.S.S.R., particularly in light of its probable fission bomb capability and possible thermonuclear bomb capability. The same holds true for the free world as a whole relative to the Soviet world as a whole. If war breaks out in 1950 or in the next few years, the United States and its allies, apart from a powerful atomic blow, will be compelled to conduct delaying actions, while building up their strength for a general offensive....

There are some who advocate a deliberate decision to isolate ourselves. Superficially, this has some attractiveness as a course of action, for it appears to bring our commitments and capabilities into harmony by reducing the former and by concentrating our present, or perhaps even reduced, military expenditures on the defense of the United States.

This argument overlooks the relativity of capabilities. With the United States in an isolated position, we would have to face the probability that the Soviet Union would quickly dominate most of Eurasia, probably without meeting armed resistance. It would thus acquire a potential far superior to our own, and would promptly proceed to develop this potential with the purpose of eliminating our power, which would, even in isolation, remain as a challenge to it and as an obstacle to the imposition of its kind of order in the world. There is no way to make ourselves inoffensive to the Kremlin except by complete submission to its will. Therefore isolation would in the end condemn us to capitulate or to fight alone and on the defensive, with drastically limited offensive and retaliatory capabilities in comparison with the Soviet Union. (These are the only possibilities, unless we are prepared to risk the future on the hazard that the Soviet Empire, because of over-extension or other reasons, will spontaneously destroy itself from within.)...

Some Americans favor a deliberate decision to go to war against the Soviet Union in the near future. It goes without saying that the idea of "preventive" war—in the sense of a military attack not provoked by a military attack upon us or our allies—is generally unacceptable to Americans....

The ability of the United States to launch effective offensive operations is now limited to attack with atomic weapons. A powerful blow could be delivered upon the Soviet Union, but it is estimated that these operations alone would not force or induce the Kremlin to capitulate and that the Kremlin would still be able to use the forces under its control to dominate most or all of Eurasia. This would probably mean a long and difficult struggle during which the free institutions of Western Europe and many freedom-loving people would be destroyed and the regenerative capacity of Western Europe dealt a crippling blow.

Apart from this, however, a surprise attack upon the Soviet Union, despite the provocativeness of recent Soviet behavior, would be repugnant to many Americans. Although the American people would probably rally in support of the war effort, the shock of responsibility for a surprise attack would be morally corrosive. Many would doubt that it was a "just war" and that all reasonable possibilities for a peaceful settlement had been explored in good faith. Many more, proportionately, would hold such views in other countries, particularly in Western Europe and particularly after Soviet occupation, if only because the Soviet Union would liquidate articulate opponents. It would, therefore, be difficult after such a war to create a satisfactory international order among nations. Victory in such a war would have brought us little if at all closer to victory in the fundamental ideological conflict....

A program for rapidly building up strength and improving political and economic conditions will place heavy demands on our courage and intelligence; it will be costly; it will be dangerous. But half-measures will be more costly and more dangerous, for they will be inadequate to prevent and may actually invite war. Budgetary considerations will need to be subordinated to the stark fact that our very independence as a nation may be at stake....

The United States is currently devoting about 22 percent of its gross national product ($255 billion in 1949) to military expenditures (6 percent), foreign assistance (2 percent), and investment (14 percent), little of which is in war-supporting industries....

From the point of view of the economy as a whole, the program might not result in a real decrease in the standard of living, for the economic effects of the program might be to increase the gross national product by more than the amount being absorbed for additional military and foreign assistance purposes. One of the most significant lessons of our World War II experience was that the American economy, when it operates at a level approaching full efficiency, can provide enormous resources for purposes other than civilian consumption while simultaneously providing a high standard of living. After allowing for price changes, personal consumption expenditures rose by about one-fifth between 1939 and 1944, even though the economy had in the meantime increased the amount of resources going into Government use by $60–$65 billion (in 1939 prices).

4. Secretary Acheson Defends NSC-68 (1969)*

Many government officials criticized NSC-68 as too simplistic in its view of the world and too rigid and aggressive in its definition of U.S. policies. But its leading architect, Secretary of State Dean Acheson, stoutly defended the recommendations of NSC-68. In the passage from his memoirs that follows, what are his views on the relation of public opinion to foreign policy? How should one judge his admission that he and his colleagues "made our points clearer than truth"? What were the major obstacles to acceptance of NSC-68's recommendations? How were those obstacles overcome?

The purpose of NSC-68 was to so bludgeon the mass mind of "top government" that not only could the President make a decision but that the decision could be carried out. Even so, it is doubtful whether anything like what happened in the next few years could have been done had not the Russians been stupid enough to have instigated the attack against South Korea and opened the "hate America" campaign....

The task of a public officer seeking to explain and gain support for a major policy is not that of the writer of a doctoral thesis. Qualification must give way

---

*From *Present at the Creation: My Years in the State Department* by Dean Acheson. Copyright © 1969 by Dean Acheson.

to simplicity of statement, nicety and nuance to bluntness, almost brutality, in carrying home a point. It is better to carry the hearer or reader into the quadrant of one's thought than merely to make a noise or to mislead him utterly. In the State Department we used to discuss how much time that mythical "average American citizen" put in each day listening, reading, and arguing about the world outside his own country. Assuming a man or woman with a fair education, a family, and a job in or out of the house, it seemed to us that ten minutes a day would be a high average. If this were anywhere near right, points to be understandable had to be clear. If we made our points clearer than truth, we did not differ from most other educators and could hardly do otherwise....

Such an analysis was decried by some liberals and some Kremlinologists. The real threat, they said, lay in the weakness of the Western European social, economic, and political structure. Correct that and the Russian danger would disappear. This I did not believe. The threat to Western Europe seemed to me singularly like that which Islam had posed centuries before, with its combination of ideological zeal and fighting power. Then it had taken the same combination to meet it: Germanic power in the east and Frankish in Spain, both energized by a great outburst of military power and social organization in Europe. This time it would need the added power and energy of America, for the drama was now played on a world stage.

If these were the intentions of the Kremlin, what were its capabilities for realizing and ours for frustrating them? Ours was demonstrably the potentially stronger society, but did it have the strength now, and would it have it in the future, to frustrate the Kremlin design? At the end of the war we were the most powerful nation on earth, with the greatest army, navy, and air force, a monopoly of the most destructive weapon, and all supported by the most productive industry and agriculture. But now our army had been demobilized, our navy put in mothballs, and our air force no longer had a monopoly of atomic weapons. In three or four years at the most we could be threatened with devastating damage, against which no sure protection appeared. Surely we produced far more aluminum, for instance, than the Soviet Union; but while we splashed it over the front of automobiles, in Russia more went into military aircraft than here. On the other hand, our almost minute army cost many times what theirs did. A brief comparison of the pay, care, and equipment of private soldiers showed why. Half the total effort of their rival society went into creating military power, which in a short time at present rates could top ours. What relation did these facts have to foreign policy, national security, the existence of a spacious environment for free societies? How much of our national product would we need to divert, as sensible insurance, to an arms effort we loathed? The paper recommended specific measures for a large and immediate improvement of military forces and weapons, and of the economic and morale factors which underlay our own and our allies' ability to influence the conduct of other societies....

In explaining to the nation the course it recommended, I made clear, also—in an address in Dallas on June 13, 1950—those it would not recommend. We should not pull down the blinds, I said, and sit in the parlor with a loaded shotgun, waiting. Isolation was not a realistic course of action. It did not work and it had not been cheap. Appeasement of Soviet ambitions was, in fact, only an alternative form of isolation. It would lead to a final struggle for survival with both our moral and military positions weakened. A third course, euphemistically called preventive war, adopted with disastrous results in other times by other types of people and governments than ours, would take the form of nuclear attack on the Soviet Union. It would not solve problems; it would multiply them. Then as now nothing seemed to me more depressing in the history of our own country than the speeches of the 1850s about "the irrepressible conflict." War is not inevitable. But talk of war's inevitability had, in the past, helped to make it occur.

While NSC-68 did not contain cost estimates, that did not mean we had not discussed them. To carry through the sort of rearmament and rehabilitation-of-forces program that we recommended, at the rate we thought necessary, for ourselves and with help for our allies, would require, our group estimated, a military budget of the magnitude of about fifty billion dollars per annum. This was a very rough guess, but, as the existing ceiling was thirteen and a half billion, the proposal—or rather the situation out of which it grew—required considerable readjustment of thinking. It seemed better to begin this process by facing the broad facts, trends, and probabilities before getting lost in budgetary intricacies. If that begins before an administration has decided what it *wants* to do, or made what diplomats used to call a decision "in principle"—in essence—the mice in the Budget Bureau will nibble to death the will to decide.

[The enormous cost of NSC-68's recommendations, which called for a fourfold jump in military spending to about $50 billion, or more than 13 percent of the United States' gross national product, posed a formidable barrier to its implementation. In mid-1950 the document remained, in historian Walter LaFeber's words, "a policy in search of an opportunity." The needed opportunity soon appeared in the form of the Korean War, which, Acheson later admitted, "saved us" from persisting with an insufficiently aggressive foreign policy and an underfinanced military establishment. The Defense Department budget quadrupled during the Korean War and stayed at that high level even after the conclusion of hostilities, as the United States in the 1950s pursued the biggest peacetime military buildup in its history.]

D. The New Shape of Postwar Society

1. Dr. Benjamin Spock Advises the Parents of the Baby-Boom Generation (1957)

The post–World War II baby boom exploded in a U.S. society that was fast-moving and fragmented. Parents could no longer assume, as they once had, that their children would grow up to inhabit a world much like the one the older generation had known. Moreover, the remarkable geographical mobility of Americans in the postwar era meant that many families now faced the responsibilities of child rearing without the traditional support and advice of grandparents and other relatives, who were now likely to live hundreds of miles away. Confronted with these uncertainties, Americans turned to books for guidance, especially to Dr. Benjamin Spock's The

Common Sense Book of Baby and Child Care, *first published in 1945 and possibly the most widely used advice book in U.S. history. What historical factors does Spock see as unique to the modern era? He has been accused of opposing the women's movement. What is his view of the mother's role?*

The Working Mother*

To work or not to work? Some mothers *have* to work to make a living. Usually their children turn out all right, because some reasonably good arrangement is made for their care. But others grow up neglected and maladjusted. It would save money in the end if the government paid a comfortable allowance to all mothers of young children who would otherwise be compelled to work. You can think of it this way: useful, well-adjusted citizens are the most valuable possessions a country has, and good mother care during early childhood is the surest way to produce them. It doesn't make sense to let mothers go to work making dresses in a factory or tapping typewriters in an office, and have them pay other people to do a poorer job of bringing up their children.

A few mothers, particularly those with professional training, feel that they must work because they wouldn't be happy otherwise. I wouldn't disagree if a mother felt strongly about it, provided she had an ideal arrangement for her children's care. After all, an unhappy mother can't bring up very happy children.

What about the mothers who don't absolutely have to work but would prefer to, either to supplement the family income or because they think they will be more satisfied and therefore get along better at home? That's harder to answer.

The important thing for a mother to realize is that the younger the child the more necessary it is for him to have a steady, loving person taking care of him. In most cases, the mother is the best one to give him this feeling of "belonging," safely and surely. She doesn't quit on the job, she doesn't turn against him, she isn't indifferent to him, she takes care of him always in the same familiar house. If a mother realizes clearly how vital this kind of care is to a small child, it may make it easier for her to decide that the extra money she might earn, or the satisfaction she might receive from an outside job, is not so important, after all.

What children need most from parents or substitutes. The things that are most vital in the care of a child are a little bit different at different age periods. During the first year, a baby needs a lot of motherly care. He has to be fed everything he eats, he eats often, and his food is usually different from the adults'. He makes a great deal of laundry work. In cities he usually has to be pushed in his carriage for outings. For his spirit to grow normally, he needs someone to dote on him, to think he's the most wonderful baby in the world, to make noises and baby talk at him, to hug him and smile at him, to keep him company during wakeful periods.

A day nursery or a "baby farm" is no good for an infant. There's nowhere near enough attention or affection to go around. In many cases, what care there is *is matter-of-fact or mechanical rather than warm-hearted. Besides, there's too much risk of epidemics of colds and diarrhea.*

---

*From *Baby and Child Care* by Dr. Benjamin Spock. Copyright © 1945, 1946, 1957, 1968, 1976 by Benjamin Spock, M.D.

2. A Working Mother Lauds the New "Two-Income Family" (1951)*

Dr. Spock might have advised mothers to stay at home, but even as he wrote, a quiet revolution in women's status was grinding inexorably forward as more and more women—including mothers—took up wage labor jobs. In the 1960s the women's movement would burst noisily into public consciousness, and women would storm all kinds of previously male bastions in the workplace and elsewhere; but in the 1940s and 1950s the issue of working women was still controversial. When the following article appeared in Harper's Magazine *in 1951, one reader wrote to the editor that she was "violently agitated" by it. Another wrote that he and his wife were "singing hallelujahs that the days of financial necessity which compelled for a time two-income living have passed." Still another lamented that the spectacle of women trading home and hearth for factory and office "is contrary to all standards, ethics, etc. which Western civilization has practiced and protected. . . . Woe to Western civilization and especially to the family unit as we know it—for it is the hub around which our civilization revolves, and when that is gone, everything is gone—if such thoughts as are expressed, and evidently supported, by Mrs. Mavity [author of the article] ever become universally accepted by society." In her article that follows, what does Nancy Barr Mavity see as the root cause driving women into the workplace? What role does she assign to the Great Depression and World War II?*

I am a wife, a mother, and a grandmother, and I have been a continuous job-holder since I graduated from college. Besides all that, I am a dodo.

I never used to think of myself as a dodo, but it has been brought home to me by my married daughter and her contemporaries that I most certainly am. These young people have perpetrated a revolution right under the noses of my generation. There have been no parades, no crusading arguments or lectures or legislative lobbying. They did not fight for a revolution—they simply are one.

The whole argument of marriage versus a career which burned like a roaring fire when I was my daughter's age is now as dead as wet ashes. The revolution that we were so vociferous about as a matter of principle has taken place unobtrusively as a matter of hard necessity.

My daughter and her friends and the young married women who work in my office do not call themselves career women. They do not harangue about the right to develop their individual capacities. They do not discuss the primary function of woman as a homemaker. They do not argue the propriety of muscling in on the labor market. They just plain work. . . .

Under present circumstances, a single pay envelope will not meet the needs of a white-collar-class family. It is as simple as that. . . .

Through a good many years of my life I heard men say, "I'd be ashamed to let my wife work." The standard of a man's success in America was—and to some extent still is—his earning capacity. It was a symbol of his masculine prowess and an extension of his virility. To maintain his social, his economic, and his psychological position as titular head of the family by virtue of being its source of supply, he often had to relinquish long-term goals for temporary advantages and to sacrifice his natural aptitudes to the demands of an immediate and steady job. No wonder Thoreau said that "most men lead lives of quiet desperation."

No wonder, then, that men jealously guarded their prerogatives. To be a "good provider" was one of the chief criteria—and in the eyes of many was *the* criterion—of man's achievement. Every woman of my generation who worked in what was called a "man's job" knew what it was to walk on eggs. With a diplomacy that would make Machiavelli look like a coal-heaver in a conference of foreign ministers the masculine ego had to be protected from the slightest scratch in both marital and occupational relations.

This often made the women of my generation hopping mad. What we did not realize was that the restrictions foisted on us by the masculine ego were not prompted by innate sex cussedness. They were imposed by a cultural code which men dared not flout under penalty of losing face, and which they would keep women from flouting, if they could, for the same reason. But something has happened to alter this code, something that has convinced men as well as women that the rigid demarcation of their spheres of action made them both the losers....

These young people were children during the great depression of the thirties. They learned the facts of economic life by experiencing or observing the collapse of financial security. They were married either just before or during or after the late war, and when their husbands were called into the armed forces the young wives had to learn to stand alone in a practical as well as an emotional sense.

Once the war was over and husbands returned, few of them had had a chance to accumulate any savings. The allotments they received from the government were insufficient to support their families in accordance with middle-class standards of living. Wives with or without children either had to produce income or throw themselves on the mercy of relatives who had problems of their own....

How does a two-income family cope with the problem of bringing up young children? Not so long ago a woman of proved vocational ability was adjured to divide her life into two—or, more rarely, three—periods. She might work until she produced a baby, but then she must either bury her vocation altogether, exchanging it for that of housewife-and-mother, or else lay it away for long years with the rather feeble hope of resuscitating it after the children were grown. That picture has now changed out of all recognition. Indeed, one hears wives arguing that children, instead of constituting the unanswerable argument against the two-income family, are strong arguments in its favor.

"If it weren't for the children," said one wife to me, "I'd be tempted to try to get along on one salary, even if it meant skimping. But we need two incomes to enable us to have a house with a yard that the children can play in; to live in a neighborhood where I don't have to worry about their playmates; to provide a guitar for the musical one and dancing lessons for the one who needs to improve her muscular coordination—not to mention teeth-straightening and medical insurance and the bonds we are stowing away for their education...."

The depression years, the war years, and the postwar years have cracked the old economic-social family mold. These were forces outside the control of individual women, but they have learned a lesson from circumstances. The working wives of 1951 have learned to recognize the mistakes of my generation, and are determined not to repeat them.

3. Lewis Mumford Laments the Suburban Exodus (1961)*

Americans by the millions abandoned the cities and joined the exodus to suburbia in the 1940s and 1950s. Most migrating Americans were young married couples just beginning to form families and have children. They took up residence in spanking new neighborhoods that they obviously preferred to the crowded, and expensive, turmoil of the cities. Yet countless observers found much to criticize in the new suburban way of life that was quickly becoming an American norm. What aspects of that lifestyle does the following article criticize? How persuasive is the criticism? If life in the suburbs was really as thin and conformist as the author claims, why did all those millions of people keep moving to suburbia? How was the raw, historyless character of suburban life any different from life on the thinly populated frontier?

The ultimate outcome of the suburb's alienation from the city became visible only in the twentieth century.... In the mass movement into the suburban areas a new kind of community was produced, which caricatured both the historic city and the archetypal suburban refuge: a multitude of uniform, unidentifiable houses, line up inflexibly, at uniform distances, on uniform roads, in a treeless communal waste, inhabited by people of the same class, the same income, the same age group, witnessing the same television performances, eating the same tasteless pre-fabricated foods, from the same freezers, conforming in every outward and inward respect to a common mold, manufactured in the central metropolis. Thus the ultimate effect of the suburban escape in our time is, ironically, a low-grade uniform environment from which escape is impossible....

As an attempt to recover what was missing in the city, the suburban exodus could be amply justified, for it was concerned with primary human needs. But there was another side: the temptation to retreat from unpleasant realities, to shirk public duties, and to find the whole meaning of life in the most elemental social group, the family, or even in the still more isolated and self-centered individual. What was properly a beginning was treated as an end....

[T]oo soon, in breaking away from the city, the part became a substitute for the whole, even as a single phase of life, that of childhood, became the pattern for all the seven ages of man. As leisure generally increased, play became the serious business of life; and the golf course, the country club, the swimming pool, and the cocktail party became the frivolous counterfeits of a more varied and significant life. Thus in reacting against the disadvantages of the crowded city, the suburb itself became an over-specialized community, more and more committed to relaxation and play as ends in themselves. Compulsive play fast became the acceptable alternative to compulsive work: with small gain either in freedom or vital stimulus....

---

*Lewis Mumford, *The City in History: Its Origins, Its Transformations, and Its Prospects* (New York: Harcourt, Brace & World, 1961).

On the fringe of mass Suburbia, even the advantages of the primary neighborhood group disappear. The cost of this detachment in space from other men is out of all proportion to its supposed benefits. The end product is an encapsulated life, spent more and more either in a motor car or within the cabin of darkness before a television set.... Every part of this life, indeed, will come through official channels and be under supervision. Untouched by human hand at one end: untouched by human spirit at the other. Those who accept this existence might as well be encased in a rocket hurtling through space, so narrow are their choices, so limited and deficient their permitted responses....

Does this explain in some degree the passiveness and docility that has crept into our existence?... Suburbia offers poor facilities for meeting, conversation, collective debate, and common action—it favors silent conformity, not rebellion or counterattack. So Suburbia has become the favored home of a new kind of absolutism: invisible but all-powerful.

Thought Provokers

1. Why did George Kennan's views of Soviet behavior prove so influential? What is the role of ideas in the formulation of foreign policy? Was the Truman Doctrine a balanced, proportionate response to the crisis that President Truman faced in the 1940s? To what extent did the Cold War proceed from each side's misperception of the other?
2. To what extent was the Marshall Plan an act of altruism? of self-interest?
3. NSC-68 has been called perhaps the single most important document of the Cold War. Comment. What difference might it have made if NSC-68 had been published in 1950 and publicly discussed?
4. Was Korea a necessary war for the United States? What would have happened if the Americans had stayed out?
5. Did the baby-boom generation have a unique upbringing and thus a historically unique set of values? What was distinctive about the condition of the American family in the early Cold War era? What forces worked most powerfully to change the role of women?

36

American Zenith, 1952–1963

We must guard against the acquisition of
unwarranted influence, whether sought or
unsought, by the military-industrial complex.

Dwight D. Eisenhower, 1961

Prologue: War hero Dwight D. Eisenhower ascended triumphantly to the White House in 1953. Worried about the budget-busting implications of President Harry Truman's military buildup, Eisenhower and Secretary of State John Foster Dulles tried to define a new strategic doctrine. It emphasized "massive retaliation" with nuclear weapons against the Soviets if they dared to break the peace. At the same time, Eisenhower took some hesitant steps toward promoting nuclear disarmament, although he proved unable to thaw the Cold War with Russia. After Stalin's death in 1953, the more subtle Nikita Khrushchev emerged as the undisputed Soviet leader. The Soviet Union matched the U.S. hydrogen bomb in 1953, and tensions further heightened in 1956 when the Soviets crushed an uprising in Hungary and backed President Nasser of Egypt during the Suez explosion. The Soviets jolted the Americans in 1957 by launching two satellites—Sputniks—into earth orbit. Eisenhower's administration, like Truman's, was badgered and embarrassed by the anticommunist crusade of Senator Joe McCarthy. McCarthyism cruelly wounded many individuals and left scars on the body politic that took decades to heal. The Supreme Court in 1954 ordered the desegregation of schools, notably in the South. The white South at first resisted massively, but the Court's decision imparted momentum to the rising wave of the civil rights movement, which was to crest in the 1960s as a new feminist movement gathered momentum. Americans knew unprecedented prosperity in the 1950s, but affluence had its critics. Many of them came to power when the New Frontier arrived with the election of Senator John F. Kennedy to the presidency in 1960.

A. The McCarthy Hysteria

1. Joseph McCarthy Upholds Guilt by Association (1952)[*]

Senator Joseph R. McCarthy of Wisconsin, hitherto unknown to fame, rocketed into the headlines in 1950 when he declared in a political speech that there were

---

[*]Quoted from Senator Joseph McCarthy, *McCarthyism: The Fight for America* (New York: Devin-Adair Company, 1952), pp. 7, 79–80.

scores of known communists in the State Department.* The collapse of the Nation-
alist China of Jiang Jeishi (Chiang Kai-shek) and the bloodily indecisive Korean
War gave point to his charges while accelerating the hunt for scapegoats. A few
"pinks" and communist sympathizers were exposed and driven out of government.
But persons with liberal or nonconformist ideas were indiscriminately branded as
communists, with a subsequent loss of reputation and jobs. In McCarthy's view,
birds that waddled like ducks, quacked like ducks, and associated with ducks
were presumed to be ducks. Anti-McCarthyites cited the axiom that it was better
to let ten guilty men escape than to condemn one innocent man. But though the
McCarthy-led red scare often assumed the character of a witch hunt, the fear of
communist espionage was not altogether unfounded. The Soviet Union actively
employed American citizens to collect information on the most sensitive matters of
national security—including the atomic bomb project. Many Soviet spies had ties
to the Communist party of the United States and were ideologically sympathetic to
the Soviet cause.

In a secret project dubbed "Venona," American intelligence officials intercepted
and decoded numerous messages sent between Moscow and Soviet operatives in the
United States. Those documents, finally released to the public in 1995, reveal the
extent of the espionage network and shed new light on the American concern about
communist infiltration. Among the people implicated by Venona were Julius and
Ethel Rosenberg, the only two American civilians executed for conspiracy to commit
espionage during the Cold War. Their highly publicized trial in 1951—during which
Ethel's own brother, David Greenglass, testified against them—became one of the
iconic moments in the United States' decades-long confrontation with communism.
McCarthy here defends his tactics. How convincing is he?

One of the safest and most popular sports engaged in today by every
politician and office seeker is to "agree with McCarthy's aim of getting rid of
Communists in government," but at the same time to "condemn his irresponsible
charges and shotgun technique." It is a completely safe position to take. The
Communist Party and their camp followers in press and radio do not strike back
as long as you merely condemn Communism in general terms. It is only when
one adopts an effective method of digging out and exposing the under-cover
dangerous, "sacred cow" Communists that all of the venom and smear of the
Party is loosed upon him.

I suggest to you, therefore, that when a politician mounts the speaker's rostrum
and makes the statement that he "agrees with McCarthy's aims but not his methods,"
that you ask him what methods he himself has used against Communists. I suggest
you ask him to name a single Communist or camp follower that he has forced out
of the government by his methods....

Is not a person presumed innocent until proven guilty?

Yes.

---

*The Senator's sensational accusations led to the coinage of a new word, "McCarthyism," usually defined
as a type of ad hominem political character assassination based on inflammatory and unsubstantiated
claims of subversive affiliations and intent.

Why do you condemn people like Acheson, Jessup, Lattimore, Service, Vincent,* and others who have never been convicted of any crime?

The fact that these people have not been convicted of treason or of violating some of our espionage laws is no more a valid argument that they are fit to represent this country in its fight against Communism than the argument that a person who has a reputation of consorting with criminals, hoodlums, gamblers, and kidnappers is fit to act as your baby sitter because he has never been convicted of a crime.

A government job is a privilege, not a right. There is no reason why men who chum with Communists, who refuse to turn their backs upon traitors† and who are consistently found at the time and place where disaster strikes America and success comes to international Communism, should be given positions of power in government....

I have not urged that those whom I have named be put in jail. Once they are exposed so the American people know what they are, they can do but little damage....

Strangely enough, those who scream the loudest about what they call guilt by association are the first to endorse innocence by association.

For example, those who object most strongly to my showing Jessup's affinity for Communist causes, the Communist money used to support the publication over which he had control, and his close friendship and defense of a Communist spy [Hiss], also argue Hiss' innocence by association. The argument is that Hiss was innocent because Justices Frankfurter and Reed testified they were friends of his, because Acheson chummed and walked with him each morning, because Hiss was the top planner at the United Nations conference and helped to draft the Yalta agreement.

We are not concerned with guilt by association because here we are not concerned with convicting any individual of any crime. We are concerned with the question of whether the individual who associates with those who are trying to destroy this nation, should be admitted to the high councils of those planning the policies of this nation: whether they should be given access to top secret material to which even Senators and Congressmen are not given access.

2. A Senator Speaks Up (1950)‡

The infiltration of a few communists into government was perhaps inevitable, but the embarrassed Truman administration played into the hands of the McCarthyites by its cover-up tactics. In the interests of free debate, the Constitution exempts from libel suits anything that may be said on the floor of Congress. Senator McCarthy clearly

---

*Professors Philip C. Jessup and Owen Lattimore were prominent officials or advisers who were allegedly "soft" on communism; John S. Service and John C. Vincent were foreign service officers similarly branded by McCarthy.

†After State Department official Alger Hiss was convicted of perjury in connection with Soviet espionage, his friend Secretary of State Acheson loyally but indiscreetly declared, "I do not intend to turn my back [on him]."

‡*Congressional Record*, 81st Cong., 2d sess. (June 1, 1950), pp. 7894–7895.

abused this privilege. At a time when he was riding high and many Republicans regarded him as a political asset, the tall and gray-haired Republican Margaret Chase Smith of Maine, the only female U.S. senator, courageously spoke out against his excesses. (Later McCarthy vindictively invaded Maine in an unsuccessful effort to defeat her for reelection.) Why does she believe that McCarthy's tactics, whatever his aims, are contrary to the Constitution and basically un-American?*

I think that it is high time for the United States Senate and its Members to do some real soul searching, and to weigh our consciences as to the manner in which we are performing our duty to the people of America, and the manner in which we are using or abusing our individual powers and privileges.

I think it is high time that we remembered that we have sworn to uphold and defend the Constitution. I think it is high time that we remembered that the Constitution, as amended, speaks not only of the freedom of speech but also of trial by jury instead of trial by accusation.

Whether it be a criminal prosecution in court or a character prosecution in the Senate, there is little practical distinction when the life of a person has been ruined.

Those of us who shout the loudest about Americanism in making character assassinations are all too frequently those who, by our own words and acts, ignore some of the basic principles of Americanism—

The right to criticize.

The right to hold unpopular beliefs.

The right to protest.

The right of independent thought.

The exercise of these rights should not cost one single American citizen his reputation or his right to a livelihood, nor should he be in danger of losing his reputation or livelihood merely because he happens to know someone who holds unpopular beliefs. Who of us does not? Otherwise none of us could call our souls our own. Otherwise thought control would have set in.

The American people are sick and tired of being afraid to speak their minds lest they be politically smeared as Communists or Fascists by their opponents. Freedom of speech is not what it used to be in America. It has been so abused by some that it is not exercised by others.

The American people are sick and tired of seeing innocent people smeared and guilty people whitewashed. But there have been enough proved cases, such as the Amerasia case, the Hiss case, the Coplon case, the Gold case,† to cause nation-wide distrust and strong suspicion that there may be something to the unproved, sensational accusations. . . .

Today our country is being psychologically divided by the confusion and the suspicions that are bred in the United States Senate to spread like cancerous tentacles of "know nothing, suspect everything" attitudes. . . .

---

*Senator Smith simultaneously presented "a Declaration of Conscience" signed by six fellow senators.
†*Amerasia* was a communist-tainted magazine that acquired confidential government documents. Judith Coplon, a Justice Department employee, and Harry Gold, a Philadelphia biochemist, were both convicted in 1950 of spying for the Soviet Union.

As a United States Senator, I am not proud of the way in which the Senate has been made a publicity platform for irresponsible sensationalism. I am not proud of the reckless abandon in which unproved charges have been hurled from this [Republican] side of the aisle. I am not proud of the obviously staged, undignified countercharges which have been attempted in retaliation from the other [Democratic] side of the aisle.

I do not like the way the Senate has been made a rendezvous for vilification, for selfish political gain at the sacrifice of individual reputations and national unity. I am not proud of the way we smear outsiders from the floor of the Senate and hide behind the cloak of congressional immunity, and still place ourselves beyond criticism on the floor of the Senate.

As an American, I am shocked at the way Republicans and Democrats alike are playing directly into the Communist design of "confuse, divide, and conquer." As an American, I do not want a Democratic administration whitewash or cover-up any more than I want a Republican smear or witch hunt.

As an American, I condemn a Republican Fascist just as much as I condemn a Democratic Communist. I condemn a Democratic Fascist just as much as I condemn a Republican Communist. They are equally dangerous to you and me and to our country. As an American, I want to see our Nation recapture the strength and unity it once had when we fought the enemy instead of ourselves.

3. McCarthy Inspires Fear at Harvard (1954)[*]

Senator McCarthy overplayed his hand, notably in the televised investigation of the army. To millions of viewers he exposed his vindictiveness, arrogance, and intellectual dishonesty. Apologists claimed that his anticommunist zeal, whether sincere or not, destroyed all sense of fair play. His bubble burst when the Senate "condemned" him in 1954 by a formal vote—not, curiously enough, for his abuses of U.S. citizens but for his contemptuous attitude toward the Senate itself. A petition urging the censure of McCarthy was circulated at Harvard University, and two undergraduates who refused to sign it gave their reasons in the first of the following letters to the Harvard Crimson. An English-born student named J. C. P. Richardson, who was backing the petition, took sharp issue with them in the second letter. Who had the sounder position?

To the Editors of the *Crimson*:

This afternoon my roommate and I were asked to sign a petition advocating the censure of Senator Joseph R. McCarthy. We both refused. And yet, we both hope that the censure motion is adopted.

Discussing our actions, we came to the conclusion that we did not sign because we were afraid that sometime in the future McCarthy will point to us as having signed the petition, and, as he had done to others, question our loyalty.

---

[*]Cited in *Congressional Record*, 83d Cong., 2d sess., p. A6909.

We are afraid that of the thousands of petition signers, one will be proved a Communist, and as a result, McCarthy, or someone like him, will say, because we were both co-signers and classmates of the Communist, that we, too, are Reds.

The fact that two college students and others like us will not sign a petition for fear of reprisal indicates only too clearly that our democracy is in danger. It is clear that McCarthy is suppressing free speech and free actions by thrusting fear into the hearts of innocent citizens.

Let us hope that the Senators of the United States are not victims of the same fear that has infected us.

K. W. L. '58
M. F. G. '58

To the Editors of the Crimson:

The letter sent to you by two Harvard students and published yesterday can safely be said to represent the viewpoint of about one half of those who did not sign the anti-McCarthy petition.

The position taken by the authors is common and understandable, but it is by no means justifiable. In a free society, when opinions become unpopular and dangerous, it is most important that they be expressed. To yield to the climate of fear, to become a scared liberal, is to strengthen the very forces which one opposes. Courage must complement conviction, for otherwise each man will become a rubber-stamp, content to spend the rest of his life echoing popular beliefs, never daring to dissent, never having enough courage to say what he thinks, and never living as an individual, but only as part of the crowd.

Yes, our democracy is in danger, but as long as men are not afraid to express their view in spite of the consequences, it shall flourish. Only when fear is allowed to limit dissension does democracy falter.

The blame for America's present intellectual intolerance rests as heavily on those who have bowed to it as it does on those who encourage it.

Sincerely,
J. C. Peter Richardson '56

B. The Supreme Court and the Black Revolution

I. The Court Rejects Segregation (1954)*

The Fourteenth Amendment (1868) made African Americans citizens and assured them "the equal protection of the laws." The Southern states established "separate but equal" facilities in the schools, public toilets, and transportation. In many instances, however, the facilities for blacks, though "separate," were not "equal" to those for whites. In 1892 a Louisianan by the name of Plessy, of one-eighth African descent, was jailed for insisting on sitting in a railroad car reserved for whites. The case was appealed to the Supreme Court, where Plessy lost by a seven-to-one vote (see p. 405). The Court held that separate but equal public conveyances did not violate the Fourteenth Amendment. This principle was applied to educational facilities

---

*Brown v. Board of Education of Topeka, 347 U.S. 492–495 (1954).

until May 17, 1954, when the Supreme Court, by a nine-to-zero vote, reversed its basic policy and decreed that separate educational facilities were not equal within the meaning of the Fourteenth Amendment. In the heart of the decision given here, what ground is there for the white Southern complaint that this was a sociological rather than a legal decision? Are separateness and inequality inseparable?

In approaching this problem, we cannot turn the clock back to 1868 when the [Fourteenth] Amendment was adopted, or even to 1896 when Plessy v. Ferguson was written. We must consider public education in the light of its full development and its present place in American life throughout the Nation. Only in this way can it be determined if segregation in public schools deprives the plaintiffs of the equal protection of the laws.

Today, education is perhaps the most important function of state and local governments. Compulsory school attendance laws and the great expenditures for education both demonstrate our recognition of the importance of education to our democratic society. It is required in the performance of our most basic public responsibilities, even service in the armed forces. It is the very foundation of good citizenship. Today it is a principal instrument in awakening the child to cultural values, in preparing him for later professional training, and in helping him to adjust normally to his environment. In these days, it is doubtful that any child may reasonably be expected to succeed in life if he is denied the opportunity of an education. Such an opportunity, where the state has undertaken to provide it, is a right which must be made available to all on equal terms.

We come then to the question presented: Does segregation of children in public schools solely on the basis of race, even though the physical facilities and other "tangible" factors may be equal, deprive the children of the minority group of equal educational opportunities? We believe that it does....

Such considerations apply with added force to children in grade and high schools. To separate them from others of similar age and qualifications, solely because of their race, generates a feeling of inferiority as to their status in the community that may affect their hearts and minds in a way unlikely ever to be undone. The effect of this separation on their educational opportunities was well stated by a finding in the Kansas case by a court which nevertheless felt compelled to rule against the Negro plaintiffs:

"Segregation of white and colored children in public schools has a detrimental effect upon the colored children. The impact is greater when it has the sanction of the law; for the policy of separating the races is usually interpreted as denoting the inferiority of the Negro group. A sense of inferiority affects the motivation of a child to learn. Segregation with the sanction of law, therefore, has a tendency to [retard] the educational and mental development of Negro children, and to deprive them of some of the benefits they would receive in a racial[ly] integrated school system."

Whatever may have been the extent of psychological knowledge at the time of Plessy v. Ferguson, this finding is amply supported by modern authority. Any language in Plessy v. Ferguson contrary to this finding is rejected.

We conclude that in the field of public education the doctrine of "separate but equal" has no place. Separate educational facilities are inherently unequal. Therefore, we hold that the plaintiffs and others similarly situated for whom the actions have been brought are, by reason of the segregation complained of, deprived of the equal protection of the laws guaranteed by the Fourteenth Amendment.

2. One Hundred Representatives Dissent (1956)*

Chief Justice Earl Warren, a gray-haired, open-faced California governor turned judge, had already come under some fire for his liberal views. Bitter was the outcry of white Southerners against the "Earl Warren Communist Court." Although the desegregation decision called for gradual implementation, the social upheaval that it foreshadowed was enormous. One hundred Southern members of Congress—nineteen senators and eighty-one House members—issued the following manifesto in 1956. The first part of it declared that since the Constitution does not mention education, the schools are solely the concern of the states under reserved powers (Tenth Amendment). How persuasive is the manifesto's contention that the Court's decision would worsen, rather than improve, race relations?

In the case of Plessy v. Ferguson, in 1896, the Supreme Court expressly declared that under the Fourteenth Amendment no person was denied any of his rights if the states provided separate but equal public facilities. This decision has been followed in many other cases. It is notable that the Supreme Court, speaking through Chief Justice Taft, a former President of the United States, unanimously declared in 1927 in Lum v. Rice that the "separate but equal" principle is "...within the discretion of the state in regulating its public schools and does not conflict with the Fourteenth Amendment."

This interpretation, restated time and time again, became a part of the life of the people of many of the states and confirmed their habits, customs, traditions, and way of life. It is founded on elemental humanity and common sense, for parents should not be deprived by Government of the right to direct the lives and education of their own children.

Though there has been no constitutional amendment or act of Congress changing their established legal principle almost a century old, the Supreme Court of the United States, with no legal basis for such action, undertook to exercise their naked judicial power and substituted their personal political and social ideas for the established law of the land.

This unwarranted exercise of power by the court, contrary to the Constitution, is creating chaos and confusion in the states principally affected. It is destroying the amicable relations between the white and Negro races that have been created through ninety years of patient effort by the good people of both races. It has planted hatred and suspicion where there has been heretofore friendship and understanding.

Without regard to the consent of the governed, outside agitators are threatening immediate and revolutionary changes in our public school systems. If done, this is certain to destroy the system of public education in some of the states.

---

*Congressional Record, 84th Cong., 2d sess. (March 12, 1956), pp. 4515–4516.

With the gravest concern for the explosive and dangerous conditions created by this decision and inflamed by outside meddlers:

We reaffirm our reliance on the Constitution as the fundamental law of the land.

We decry the Supreme Court's encroachments on rights reserved to the states and to the people, contrary to established law and to the Constitution.

We commend the motives of those states which have declared the intention to resist forced integration by any lawful means.

We appeal to the states and people who are not directly affected by these decisions to consider the constitutional principles involved against the time when they too, on issues vital to them, may be the victims of judicial encroachment.

Even though we constitute a minority in the present Congress, we have full faith that a majority of the American people believe in the dual system of government which has enabled us to achieve our greatness and will in time demand that the reserved rights of the states and of the people be made secure against judicial usurpation.

We pledge ourselves to use all lawful means to bring about a reversal of this decision, which is contrary to the Constitution, and to prevent the use of force in its implementation.

In this trying period, as we all seek to right this wrong, we appeal to our people not to be provoked by the agitators and troublemakers invading our states and to scrupulously refrain from disorder and lawless acts.

3. Eisenhower Sends Federal Troops (1957)[*]

Following the school desegregation decision of the "Earl Warren Court," Southern white resistance mounted. A showdown occurred in the autumn of 1957, when angry mobs in Little Rock, Arkansas, prevented nine black pupils from attending the all-white Central High School. When the governor of the state refused to provide proper protection, President Eisenhower backed up the federal court by sending in federal troops. Under their protective bayonets, the African American pupils attended the school despite disagreeable incidents. The ugly episode became a hot issue in the Cold War. Little Rock rapidly became the best-known U.S. city as communist propagandists had a field day, ignoring the fact that the federal government was trying to help the blacks. President Eisenhower addressed the American people on a nationwide radio and television hookup, explaining why he had regretfully resorted to drastic action. Was he on sound legal ground? Why was he concerned about the foreign implications of the affair?

For a few minutes this evening I want to talk to you about the serious situation that has arisen in Little Rock. To make this talk I have come to the President's office in the White House. I could have spoken from Rhode Island, where I have been staying recently, but I felt that, in speaking from the house of Lincoln, of Jackson, and of Wilson, my words would better convey both the sadness I feel in the action I was compelled today to take and the firmness with which I intend to pursue this

Vital Speeches 24 (October 15, 1957): 11–12 (address of September 24, 1957).

course until the orders of the Federal Court at Little Rock can be executed without unlawful interference.

In that city, under the leadership of demagogic extremists, disorderly mobs have deliberately prevented the carrying out of proper orders from a Federal Court. Local authorities have not eliminated that violent opposition and, under the law, I yesterday issued a Proclamation calling upon the mob to disperse.

This morning the mob again gathered in front of the Central High School of Little Rock, obviously for the purpose of again preventing the carrying out of the Court's order relating to the admission of Negro children to that school.

Whenever normal agencies prove inadequate to the task and it becomes necessary for the Executive Branch of the Federal Government to use its powers and authority to uphold Federal Courts, the President's responsibility is inescapable.

In accordance with that responsibility, I have today issued an Executive Order directing the use of troops under Federal authority to aid in the execution of Federal law at Little Rock, Arkansas. This became necessary when my Proclamation of yesterday was not observed, and the obstruction of justice still continues....

Our personal opinions about the decision have no bearing on the matter of enforcement; the responsibility and authority of the Supreme Court to interpret the Constitution are very clear....

Mob rule cannot be allowed to override the decisions of our courts.

Now, let me make it very clear that Federal troops are not being used to relieve local and state authorities of their primary duty to preserve the peace and order of the community. Nor are the troops there for the purpose of taking over the responsibility of the School Board and the other responsible local officials in running Central High School. The running of our school system and the maintenance of peace and order in each of our states are strictly local affairs, and the Federal Government does not interfere, except in very special cases and when requested by one of the several states. In the present case the troops are there, pursuant to law, solely for the purpose of preventing interference with the orders of the Court....

In the South, as elsewhere, citizens are keenly aware of the tremendous disservice that has been done to the people of Arkansas in the eyes of the nation, and that has been done to the nation in the eyes of the world.

At a time when we face grave situations abroad because of the hatred that Communism bears toward a system of government based on human rights, it would be difficult to exaggerate the harm that is being done to the prestige and influence and, indeed, to the safety of our nation and the world.

Our enemies are gloating over this incident and using it everywhere to misrepresent our whole nation. We are portrayed as a violator of those standards of conduct which the peoples of the world united to proclaim in the Charter of the United Nations. There they affirmed "faith in fundamental human rights" and "in the dignity and worth of the human person," and they did so "without distinction as to race, sex, language, or religion."

And so, with deep confidence, I call upon citizens of the State of Arkansas to assist in bringing to an immediate end all interference with the law and its processes. If resistance to the Federal Court order ceases at once, the further presence of Federal troops will be unnecessary and the city of Little Rock will return to its normal habits of peace and order—and a blot upon the fair name and high honor of our nation will be removed.

Thus will be restored the image of America and of all its parts as one nation, indivisible, with liberty and justice for all.

4. The Arkansas Democrat Protests (1958)*

Occupying federal troops—the first in the South since 1877—remained for eight months, until the nine African American pupils could attend the high school without serious molestation. Many white Southerners who were resigned to gradual integration of the schools bitterly resented President Eisenhower's armed intervention. In the light of the following article in a Little Rock newspaper, explain why. Where is the editor on the weakest ground? The strongest ground?

Little Rock's Central High School is still under military occupation. The troops are still there—on the campus, in the building.

The troops are still there, despite the fact that their presence is resented by the big majority of the students, the parents, and the people in general throughout the South.

The troops continue to stand guard during school hours, on the grounds and within the corridors and classrooms, despite the fact that there is no law or precedent—Federal or State—that permits them to do so.

There is not even an order, or so much as a sanction, from the U.S. Supreme Court that makes its own "laws" on mixing of races in the public schools.

Federal troops continue to occupy Central High—in defiance of the Constitution, law, and precedent—while the Congress of the United States sits out the sessions and does nothing.

Never before in the history of America has any area of our so-called Free Republic been so shamefully treated.

When two sections of this country were at war with each other, no troops ever patrolled the public school buildings and grounds from day to day. After the South had been beaten down, Federal forces kept the vanquished under the iron heel for the duration of the "Reconstruction" period. But not once did they molest the public schools with troop occupation.

Education, or attempted education, under the scrutiny of armed troops is un-American, un-Godly.

It is not even Communistic. Russia, in all her cruelty, has never bothered school children in occupied territory by stationing armed soldiers on the grounds and in the buildings. Germany never did it.

No other nation, however barbaric and cruel and relentless, ever—in the history of the human race—resorted to such tactics—only the United States, which sets itself up as a world example of peace, freedom, and democracy, forces the military upon a free school.

How much longer will Congress sit idly by and let such brazen violation of American principle and law continue on and on and on?

---

*"Editorial—Anti–Little Rock Intervention" by Karr Shannon in *Arkansas Democrat* (March 10, 1958).

5. Martin Luther King, Jr., Asks for the Ballot (1957)*

While the Supreme Court adjudicated, African Americans were taking the struggle for civil rights into their own hands. The first mass protest against the detested segregation laws erupted in Montgomery, Alabama. On December 1, 1955, a dignified black woman named Rosa Parks refused to move out of the "whites only" seating section of a city bus. For this, she was arrested; at that moment, "somewhere in the universe," one black leader later commented, "a gear in the machinery had shifted." Her arrest sparked a hugely successful boycott of the bus system by Montgomery's African Americans and catapulted into prominence a young black minister of the gospel, the Reverend Martin Luther King, Jr., who assumed a conspicuous leadership role in the boycott. He swiftly emerged as the nation's premier black spokesman and, until his murder in 1968, led a civil rights crusade that changed the face of American society. As early as 1957, he identified political rights as the key to improving the condition of African Americans in the South—where in some states fewer than 5 percent of eligible black voters were casting their ballots in the 1950s. In the speech reprinted here, what benefits does King think will flow from enfranchisement? What does he see as the federal government's role in securing black rights? Was his faith in the power of the ballot misplaced?

Three years ago the Supreme Court of this nation rendered in simple, eloquent and unequivocal language a decision which will long be stenciled on the mental sheets of succeeding generations. For all men of good will, this May 17 decision came as a joyous daybreak to end the long night of enforced segregation. It came as a great beacon light of hope to millions of distinguished people throughout the world who had dared only to dream of freedom. It came as a legal and sociological deathblow to the old Plessy doctrine of "separate-but-equal." It came as a reaffirmation of the good old American doctrine of freedom and equality for all people.

Unfortunately, this noble and sublime decision has not gone without opposition. This opposition has often risen to ominous proportions. Many states have risen up in open defiance. The legislative halls of the South ring loud with such words as "interposition" and "nullification." Methods of defiance range from crippling economic reprisals to the tragic reign of violence and terror. All of these forces have conjoined to make for massive resistance.

But, even more, all types of conniving methods are still being used to prevent Negroes from becoming registered voters. The denial of this sacred right is a tragic betrayal of the highest mandates of our democratic traditions and it is democracy turned upside down.

So long as I do not firmly and irrevocably possess the right to vote I do not possess myself. I cannot make up my mind—it is made up for me. I cannot live as a democratic citizen, observing the laws I have helped to enact—I can only submit to the edict of others.

So our most urgent request to the President of the United States and every member of Congress is to give us the right to vote.

Give us the ballot and we will no longer have to worry the federal government about our basic rights.

Give us the ballot and we will no longer plead to the federal government for passage of an antilynching law; we will by the power of our vote write the law on the statute books of the Southern states and bring an end to the dastardly acts of the hooded perpetrators of violence.

Give us the ballot and we will transform the salient misdeeds of bloodthirsty mobs into the calculated good deeds of orderly citizens.

Give us the ballot and we will fill our legislative halls with men of good will, and send to the sacred halls of Congress men who will not sign a Southern Manifesto,* because of their devotion to the manifesto of justice.

Give us the ballot and we will place judges on the benches of the South who will "do justly and love mercy," and we will place at the head of the Southern states governors who have felt not only the tang of the human, but the glow of the divine.

Give us the ballot and we will quietly and nonviolently, without rancor or bitterness, implement the Supreme Court's decision on May 17, 1954.

C. The Promise and Problems of a Consumer Society _____

1. John Kenneth Galbraith Criticizes the Affluent Society (1958)†

America knew fabulous prosperity in the postwar era—or did it? In an influential book first published in the late 1950s, Harvard economist John Kenneth Galbraith probingly questioned the implications of the United States' apparent affluence. His ideas contributed significantly to discussion among policymakers about the kinds of social reforms that later were enacted as the Great Society programs. What is the distinction that Galbraith draws between the private and the public realms? How convincing is his argument? What does the relationship between private and public goods suggest about the character of American values?

The final problem of the productive society is what it produces. This manifests itself in an implacable tendency to provide an opulent supply of some things and a niggardly yield of others. This disparity carries to the point where it is a cause of social discomfort and social unhealth. The line which divides our area of wealth from our area of poverty is roughly that which divides privately produced and marketed goods and services from publicly rendered services. Our wealth in the first is not only in startling contrast with the meagerness of the latter, but our wealth in privately produced goods is, to a marked degree, the cause of crisis in the supply of public services. For we have failed to see the importance, indeed the urgent need, of maintaining a balance between the two....

---

*In March 1956 more than ninety Southerners, led by Senator Walter George, presented in Congress their "Declaration of Constitutional Principles," commonly known as the "Southern Manifesto." The document condemned the Supreme Court decision on segregation in education as a usurpation of the powers of the states and encouraged the use of "every lawful means" to resist its implementation.

†From *The Affluent Society*, Fourth Edition, by John Kenneth Galbraith. Copyright © 1958, 1969, 1976, 1984 by John Kenneth Galbraith.

The contrast was and remains evident not alone to those who read. The family which takes its mauve and cerise, air-conditioned, power-steered and power-braked automobile out for a tour passes through cities that are badly paved, made hideous by litter, blighted buildings, billboards and posts for wires that should long since have been put underground. They pass on into a countryside that has been rendered largely invisible by commercial art. (The goods which the latter advertise have an absolute priority in our value system. Such aesthetic considerations as a view of the countryside accordingly come second. On such matters, we are consistent.) They picnic on exquisitely packaged food from a portable icebox by a polluted stream and go on to spend the night at a park which is a menace to public health and morals. Just before dozing off on an air mattress, beneath a nylon tent, amid the stench of decaying refuse, they may reflect vaguely on the curious unevenness of their blessings. Is this, indeed, the American genius?

2. Newton Minow Criticizes the "Vast Wasteland" of Television (1961)[*]

Newton N. Minow, chairman of the Federal Communications Commission in the John F. Kennedy administration, delivered the following address to the National Association of Broadcasters in 1961. Delivered, ironically, in what some observers regard as the "golden age" of television programming, his remarks have become a classic indictment of the cultural vapidity of television—called a medium, some have said, because so little of it is rare or well done. How fair is Minow's critique? What might explain the dismal situation that Minow describes? Has programming changed substantially in the intervening years?

It may...come as a surprise to some of you, but I want you to know that you have my admiration and respect. Yours is a most honorable profession. Anyone who is in the broadcasting business has a tough row to hoe. You earn your bread by using public property. When you work in broadcasting you volunteer for public service, public pressure, and public regulation. You must compete with other attractions and other investments, and the only way you can do it is to prove to us every three years that you should have been in business in the first place.

I can think of easier ways to make a living.

But I cannot think of more satisfying ways.

I admire your courage—but that doesn't mean I would make life any easier for you. Your license lets you use the public's airwaves as Trustees for 180,000,000 Americans. The public is your beneficiary. If you want to stay on as Trustees, you must deliver a decent return to the public—not only to your stockholders. So, as a representative of the public, your health and your product are among my chief concerns....

I have confidence in your health.

But not in your product....

[In] today's world, with chaos in Laos and the Congo aflame, with Communist tyranny on our Caribbean doorstep and relentless pressure on our Atlantic alliance,

[*]Newton N. Minow, "Program Control: The Broadcasters Are Public Trustees," *Vital Speeches* 27 (June 15, 1961): 533–535.

with social and economic problems at home of the gravest nature, yes, and with technological knowledge that makes it possible, as our President has said, not only to destroy our world but to destroy poverty around the world—in a time of peril and opportunity, the old complacent, unbalanced fare of Action-Adventure and Situation Comedies is simply not good enough.

Your industry possesses the most powerful voice in America. It has an inescapable duty to make that voice ring with intelligence and with leadership. In a few years, this exciting industry has grown from a novelty to an instrument of overwhelming impact on the American people. It should be making ready for the kind of leadership that newspapers and magazines assumed years ago, to make our people aware of their world.

Ours has been called the jet age, the atomic age, the space age. It is also, I submit, the television age. And just as history will decide whether the leaders of today's world employed the atom to destroy the world or rebuild it for mankind's benefit, so will history decide whether today's broadcasters employed their powerful voice to enrich the people or debase them. . . .

Like everybody, I wear more than one hat. I am the Chairman of the FCC. I am also a television viewer and the husband and father of other television viewers. . . . I invite you to sit down in front of your television set when your station goes on the air and stay there without a book, magazine, newspaper, profit and loss sheet or rating book to distract you—and keep your eyes glued to that set until the station signs off. I can assure you that you will observe a vast wasteland.

You will see a procession of game shows, violence, audience participation shows, formula comedies about totally unbelievable families, blood and thunder, mayhem, violence, sadism, murder, western badmen, western good men, private eyes, gangsters, more violence, and cartoons. And, endlessly, commercials—many screaming, cajoling, and offending. And most of all, boredom. True, you will see a few things you will enjoy. But they will be very, very few. And if you think I exaggerate, try it. . . .

I do not accept the idea that the present over-all programming is aimed accurately at the public taste. The ratings tell us only that some people have their television sets turned on and of that number, so many are tuned to one channel and so many to another. They don't tell us what the public might watch if they were offered half a dozen additional choices. A rating, at best, is an indication of how many people saw what you gave them. Unfortunately, it does not reveal the depth of the penetration, or the intensity of reaction, and it never reveals what the acceptance would have been if what you gave them had been better—if all the forces of art and creativity and daring and imagination had been unleashed. I believe in the people's good sense and good taste, and I am not convinced that the people's taste is as low as some of you assume. . . .

Certainly, I hope you will agree that ratings should have little influence where children are concerned. The best estimates indicate that during the hours of 5 to 6 p.m. 60% of your audience is composed of children under 12. And most young children today, believe it or not, spend as much time watching television as they do in the schoolroom. I repeat—let that sink in—most young children today spend as much time watching television as they do in the schoolroom. It used to be said that there were three great influences on a child: home, school, and church. Today, there is a fourth great influence, and you ladies and gentlemen control it.

If parents, teachers, and ministers conducted their responsibilities by following the ratings, children would have a steady diet of ice cream, school holidays, and no Sunday School. What about your responsibilities? Is there no room on television to teach, to inform, to uplift, to stretch, to enlarge the capacities of our children? Is there no room for programs deepening their understanding of children in other lands? Is there no room for a children's news show explaining something about the world to them at their level of understanding? Is there no room for reading the great literature of the past, teaching them the great traditions of freedom? There are some fine children's shows, but they are drowned out in the massive doses of cartoons, violence, and more violence. Must these be your trademarks? Search your consciences and see if you cannot offer more to your young beneficiaries whose future you guide so many hours each and every day.

3. Betty Friedan Launches the Modern Feminist Movement (1963)*

Throughout the 1950s, millions of women followed the advice of the day's leading experts—they married young, took on the responsibilities of motherhood, and maintained a stable home for their husbands and children. While some found fulfillment in the domestic sphere, many others felt isolated in their suburban ranch homes, stifled by the drudgery of housework. In 1963, writer Betty Friedan tapped into these women's silent desperation—what she described as "the problem that has no name." An instant best seller, her Feminine Mystique sparked a vigorous debate about the role of women in society and helped revitalize the feminist movement. What does Friedan see as the source of women's anxieties? What historical developments gave rise to "the problem that has no name"?

The problem lay buried, unspoken, for many years in the minds of American women. It was a strange stirring, a sense of dissatisfaction, a yearning that women suffered in the middle of the twentieth century in the United States. Each suburban wife struggled with it alone. As she made the beds, shopped for groceries, matched slipcover material, ate peanut butter sandwiches with her children, chauffeured Cub Scouts and Brownies, lay beside her husband at night—she was afraid to ask even of herself the silent question—"Is this all?"

For over fifteen years there was no word of this yearning in the millions of words written about women, for women, in all the columns, books and articles by experts telling women their role was to seek fulfillment as wives and mothers....

They learned that truly feminine women do not want careers, higher education, political rights—the independence and the opportunities that the old-fashioned feminists fought for. Some women, in their forties and fifties, still remembered painfully giving up those dreams, but most of the younger women no longer even thought about them. A thousand expert voices applauded their femininity, their adjustment, their new maturity. All they had to do was devote their lives from earliest girlhood to finding a husband and bearing children....

In the fifteen years after World War II, this mystique of feminine fulfillment became the cherished and self-perpetuating core of contemporary American culture. Millions of women lived their lives in the image of those pretty pictures of the American suburban housewife, kissing their husbands goodbye in front of the picture window, depositing their stationwagonsful of children at school, and smiling as they ran the new electric waxer over the spotless kitchen floor....

But on an April morning in 1959, I heard a mother of four, having coffee with four other mothers in a suburban development fifteen miles from New York, say in a tone of quiet desperation, "the problem." And the others knew, without words, that she was not talking about a problem with her husband, or her children, or her home. Suddenly they realized they all shared the same problem, the problem that has no name....

Gradually I came to realize that the problem that has no name was shared by countless women in America....

Just what was this problem that has no name? What were the words women used when they tried to express it? Sometimes a woman would say "I feel empty somehow...incomplete." Or she would say, "I feel as if I don't exist." Sometimes she blotted out the feeling with a tranquilizer....

Sometimes a woman would tell me that the feeling gets so strong she runs out of the house and walks through the streets. Or she stays inside her house and cries. Or her children tell her a joke, and she doesn't laugh because she doesn't hear it....

It is no longer possible to ignore that voice, to dismiss the desperation of so many American women. This is not what being a woman means, no matter what the experts say. For human suffering there is a reason; perhaps the reason has not been found because the right questions have not been asked, or pressed far enough. I do not accept the answer that there is no problem because American women have luxuries that women in other times and lands never dreamed of; part of the strange newness of the problem is that it cannot be understood in terms of the age-old material problems of man: poverty, sickness, hunger, cold. The women who suffer this problem have a hunger that food cannot fill....

If I am right, the problem that has no name stirring in the minds of so many American women today is not a matter of loss of femininity or too much education, or the demands of domesticity. It is far more important than anyone recognizes. It is the key to these other new and old problems which have been torturing women and their husbands and children, and puzzling their doctors and educators for years. It may well be the key to our future as a nation and a culture. We can no longer ignore that voice within women that says: "I want something more than my husband and my children and my home."

D. Eisenhower Says Farewell (1961)*

Dwight Eisenhower, the war hero, presided over nearly eight years of peaceful U.S. relations with the rest of the world. Yet Eisenhower also presided over the largest

*From *Public Papers of the Presidents of the United States: Dwight D. Eisenhower, 1960–1961* (Washington, DC: National Archives and Records Service, 1961), pp. 1036–1039.

peacetime buildup of armaments in U.S. history up to that time. In his final message to the American people as president, the popular ex-soldier sounded a surprising warning about the economic, political, and social consequences of the garrison state that the United States was apparently becoming. His speech is justly remembered as one of the most telling criticisms of the domestic consequences of the Cold War. What are the most worrisome aspects of the "military-industrial complex" that Eisenhower described? Why did he wait until he was on his way out of office to express his alarm?

Good evening, my fellow Americans:

First, let me express my gratitude to the radio and television networks for the opportunity to express myself to you during these past eight years and tonight.

Three days from now, after half a century in the service of our country, I shall lay down the responsibilities of office as, in traditional solemn ceremony, the authority of the President is vested in my successor.

This evening I come to you with a message of leave-taking and farewell, and to share a few final thoughts with you, my countrymen. . . .

We now stand ten years past the midpoint of a century that has witnessed four major wars among great nations. Three of these involved our own country. Despite these holocausts America is today the strongest, the most influential, and most productive nation in the world. Understandably proud of this pre-eminence, we yet realize that America's leadership and prestige depend, not merely upon our unmatched material progress, riches, and material strength, but on how we use our power in the interests of world peace and human betterment. . . .

Crises there will continue to be. In meeting them, whether foreign or domestic, great or small, there is a recurring temptation to feel that some spectacular and costly action could become the miraculous solution to all current difficulties. A huge increase in newer elements of our defense; development of unrealistic programs to cure every ill in agriculture; a dramatic expansion in basic and applied research— these and many other possibilities, each possibly promising in itself, may be suggested as the only way to the road we wish to travel.

But each proposal must be weighed in the light of a broader consideration: the need to maintain balance in and among national problems—balance between the private and the public economy, balance between cost and hoped for advantage—balance between the clearly necessary and the comfortably desirable; balance between our essential requirements as a nation and the duties imposed by the nation upon the individual; balance between actions of the moment and the national welfare of the future. Good judgment seeks balance and progress; lack of it eventually finds imbalance and frustration.

The record of many decades stands as proof that our people and their government have, in the main, understood these truths and have responded to them well, in the face of stress and threat. But threats, new in kind or degree, constantly arise. I mention two only.

A vital element in keeping the peace is our military establishment. Our arms must be mighty, ready for instant action, so that no potential aggressor may be tempted to risk his own destruction.

Our military organization today bears little relation to that known by any of my predecessors in peacetime, or indeed by the fighting men in World War II or Korea.

Until the latest of our world conflicts, the United States had no armaments industry. American makers of plowshares could, with time and as required, make swords as well. But now we can no longer risk emergency improvision of national defense; we have been compelled to create a permanent armaments industry of vast proportions. Added to this, three and a half million men and women are directly engaged in the defense establishment. We annually spend on military security more than the net income of all United States corporations.

This conjunction of an immense military establishment and a large arms industry is new in American experience. The total influence—economic, political, even spiritual—is felt in every city, every state house, every office of the federal government. We recognize the imperative need for this development. Yet we must not fail to comprehend its grave implications. Our toil, resources and livelihood are all involved; so is the very structure of our society.

In the councils of government, we must guard against the acquisition of unwarranted influence, whether sought or unsought, by the military-industrial complex. The potential for the disastrous rise of misplaced power exists and will persist.

We must never let the weight of this combination endanger our liberties or democratic processes. We should take nothing for granted. Only an alert and knowledgeable citizenry can compel the proper meshing of the huge industrial and military machinery of defense with our peaceful methods and goals, so that security and liberty may prosper together.

Akin to, and largely responsible for the sweeping changes in our industrial-military posture, has been the technological revolution during recent decades.

In this revolution, research has become central; it also becomes more formalized, complex, and costly. A steadily increasing share is conducted for, by, or at the direction of, the federal government.

Today, the solitary inventor, tinkering in his shop, has been overshadowed by task forces of scientists in laboratories and testing fields. In the same fashion, the free university, historically the fountainhead of free ideas and scientific discovery, has experienced a revolution in the conduct of research. Partly because of the huge costs involved, a government contract becomes virtually a substitute for intellectual curiosity. For every old blackboard there are now hundreds of new electronic computers.

The prospect of domination of the nation's scholars by federal employment, project allocations, and the power of money is ever present and is gravely to be regarded.

Yet, in holding scientific research and discovery in respect, as we should, we must also be alert to the equal and opposite danger that public policy could itself become the captive of a scientific-technological elite.

It is the task of statesmanship to mold, to balance, and to integrate these and other forces, new and old, within the principles of our democratic system—ever aiming toward the supreme goals of our free society.

Thought Provokers

1. Did Senator McCarthy help or hinder the cause of anticommunism? Were any of his charges justified? Is U.S. society peculiarly vulnerable to his kind of demagoguery? What finally stopped McCarthy? Did McCarthyism perish with Joseph McCarthy?

2. Progressives and liberals have historically argued that the courts should take a hands-off approach toward legislation in the economic realm, yet they applauded the Supreme Court's activist role in civil rights matters. Were they being inconsistent? What were the greatest obstacles to the success of the civil rights movement? What were its greatest assets?

3. What, if anything, was new about the sources and character of American prosperity in the 1950s? Does the Public Broadcasting Service (PBS) provide an attractive alternative to the "sins" of the commercial broadcasters as described by Newton Minow?

4. What drove the changes in women's status in the 1950s? In what ways did those changes amount to progress?

5. How prophetic was Eisenhower's warning about the "military-industrial complex"? Is that complex more or less powerful now than in Eisenhower's day? To what extent was it an inevitable product of the Cold War?

37

The Stormy Sixties, 1963–1973

And so, my fellow Americans: ask not what your country can do for you—ask what you can do for your country.

President John F. Kennedy, 1961

Prologue: Youthful President John F. Kennedy launched his administration with high hopes and great vigor. Young people seemed particularly attracted to the tough-minded yet idealistic style of Kennedy's presidency. Yet Kennedy's record in office, before his tragic assassination in 1963, was spotty. He presided over a botched invasion of Cuba in 1961 and in the same year took the first fateful steps into the Vietnam quagmire. In 1962 he displayed remarkable restraint to resolve a hair-trigger standoff with the Russians over the emplacement of Soviet missiles in Cuba. Sobered by this brush with the prospect of nuclear holocaust, Kennedy initiated a new policy of realistic accommodation with the Soviets—while the Soviets, determined never again to be so humiliated, began a massive military buildup. At home, the black revolution, led most conspicuously by Martin Luther King, Jr., exploded. Lyndon Johnson, ascending to the presidency after Kennedy's death, won election in his own right in 1964 and promptly threw his support behind the cause of civil rights. In a remarkable burst of political leadership, Johnson persuaded the Congress to pass a vast array of social welfare legislation, known collectively as the Great Society programs. But Johnson's dreams for a happier America were blasted by the mounting unpopularity of the war in Vietnam, which had drawn half a million U.S. troops by the mid-1960s. Bedeviled by the Vietnam problem, Johnson withdrew from the 1968 presidential race, paving the way for the election of Richard Nixon.

A. The Cuban Missile Crisis

1. President Kennedy and His Military Chiefs Take Stock of the Situation (1962)[*]

After the abortive Bay of Pigs invasion in 1961, the United States watched Castro's Cuba for further trouble. Officials in Washington knew that the Soviet Union was

---

[*]*The Presidential Recordings, John F. Kennedy: The Great Crises, September–October 21,* 1962, vol. II, eds. Timothy Naftali and Philip Zelikow (New York: W.W. Norton & Co., 2001), 581–588.

736

sending Castro immense quantities of weapons, which Moscow repeatedly claimed were defensive.* In mid-October 1962, high-flying U.S. spy planes returned with startling photographic evidence that Soviet technicians were installing nuclear missiles in Cuba with a striking range of about twenty-two hundred miles. President Kennedy was informed of the situation on October 16, initiating a thirteen-day round of tense consultation with his civilian and military advisers. The stakes could not have been higher, as the two nuclear-armed superpowers stood on the brink of an atomic Armageddon. Meeting with the Joint Chiefs of Staff on October 19, Kennedy offered his own assessment of the situation, which met with an openly derisive, nearly insubordinate response from some of the chiefs, notably Air Force General Curtis LeMay, who were urging a swift and massive invasion of Cuba. What are the principal strategic considerations that Kennedy emphasizes? Why were the military leaders so antagonistic? Should the president have followed their advice?

President Kennedy: Let me just say a little, first, about what the problem is, from my point of view.

First, I think we ought to think of why the Russians did this. Well, actually, it was a rather dangerous but rather useful play of theirs. If we do nothing, they have a missile base there with all the pressure that brings to bear on the United States and damage to our prestige.

If we attack Cuba, the missiles, or Cuba, in any way then it gives them a clear line to take Berlin, as they were able to do in Hungary under the Anglo war in Egypt. We will have been regarded as—they think we've got this fixation about Cuba anyway— we would be regarded as the trigger-happy Americans who lost Berlin. We would have no support among our allies. We would affect the West Germans' attitude towards us. And [people would believe] that we let Berlin go because we didn't have the guts to endure a situation in Cuba. After all, Cuba is 5[,000] or 6,000 miles from them. They don't give a damn about Cuba. And they do care about Berlin and about their own security. So they would say that we endangered their interests and security and reunification [of Germany] and all the rest, because of the preemptive action that we took in Cuba. So I think they've got...I must say I think it's a very satisfactory position from their point of view....

If you take the view, really, that what's basic to them is Berlin and there isn't any doubt [about that]. In every conversation we've had with the Russians, that's what....Even last night we [Soviet foreign minister Andrei Gromyko and I] talked about Cuba for a while, but Berlin—that's what Khrushchev's committed himself to personally. So, actually, it's a quite desirable situation from their point of view...

So I don't think we've got any satisfactory alternatives. When we balance off that our problem is not merely Cuba but it is also Berlin and when we recognize the importance of Berlin to Europe, and recognize the importance of our allies to us, that's what has made this thing be a dilemma for three days. Otherwise, our answer would be quite easy.

---

*The Soviets were correct in the sense that the so-called offensive weapons aimed at the United States were defensive in that they would deter an invasion of Cuba.

LeMay: I don't think they're going to make any reprisal if we tell them that the Berlin situation is just like it's always been. If they make a move we're going to fight. Now I don't think this changes the Berlin situation at all, except you've got to make one more statement on it.

So I see no other solution. This blockade and political action, I see leading into war. I don't see any other solution for it. It will lead right into war. This is almost as bad as the appeasement at Munich.... *[This remark was inflammatory. LeMay's not-so-subtle reference was to the notorious conference at Munich, Germany, in 1938, when British Prime Minister Neville Chamberlain capitulated to Adolf Hitler's demands, an episode that had long blighted the reputation of Kennedy's father, Joseph P. Kennedy, then the U.S. ambassador to Great Britain, who was widely—and more than a little unfairly—accused of cowardly support for Chamberlain's policies.]*

I think that a blockade and political talk would be considered by a lot of our friends and neutrals as being a pretty weak response to this. And I'm sure a lot of our own citizens would feel that way, too. In other words, you're in a pretty bad fix at the present time.

President Kennedy: What did you say?

LeMay: You're in a pretty bad fix.

President Kennedy: You're in there with me. [*Slight laughter, a bit forced.*] Personally.

2. President Kennedy Proclaims a "Quarantine" (1962)*

On October 22, after briefing key congressional leaders, Kennedy went on radio and television with a bombshell address that caught the Soviets off guard. In this excerpt, what options did he leave for himself if the initial "quarantine" should fail? What were the risks in Kennedy's strategy? Were they worth it?

Acting, therefore, in the defense of our own security and of the entire Western Hemisphere,...I have directed that the following *initial* steps be taken immediately:

First: To halt this offensive buildup, a strict quarantine on all offensive military equipment under shipment to Cuba is being initiated. All ships of any kind bound for Cuba from whatever nation or port will, if found to contain cargoes of offensive weapons, be turned back. This quarantine will be extended, if needed, to other types of cargo and carriers. We are not at this time, however, denying the necessities of life, as the Soviets attempted to do in their Berlin blockade of 1948.

Second: I have directed the continued and increased close [aerial] surveillance of Cuba and its military buildup....

Third: It shall be the policy of this Nation to regard any nuclear missile launched from Cuba against any nation in the Western Hemisphere as an attack by the Soviet Union on the United States, requiring a full retaliatory response upon the Soviet Union.

Public Papers of the Presidents of the United States: John F. Kennedy: 1962 (Washington, DC: National Archives and Records Service, 1963), pp. 807–808 (October 22, 1962).

Fourth: As a necessary military precaution, I have reinforced our base at Guantanamo [Cuba], evacuated today the dependents of our personnel there, and ordered additional military units to be on a standby alert basis.

Fifth: We are calling tonight for an immediate meeting of the Organ of Consultation under the Organization of American States, to consider this threat to hemispheric security and to invoke Articles 6 and 8 of the Rio Treaty in support of all necessary action. . . . Our other allies around the world have also been alerted.

Sixth: Under the Charter of the United Nations, we are asking tonight that an emergency meeting of the Security Council be convoked without delay to take action against this latest Soviet threat to world peace. Our resolution will call for the prompt dismantling and withdrawal of all offensive weapons in Cuba, under the supervision of U.N. observers, before the quarantine can be lifted.

Seventh and finally: I call upon Chairman Khrushchev to halt and eliminate this clandestine, reckless, and provocative threat to world peace and to stable relations between our two nations. I call upon him further to abandon this course of world domination, and to join in an historic effort to end the perilous arms race and to transform the history of man.

3. Premier Khrushchev Proposes a Swap (1962)[*]

During the tense six days after Kennedy's proclamation of a "quarantine," Soviet technicians in Cuba worked feverishly to emplace the missiles. A number of approaching Soviet merchant ships, presumably loaded with "offensive" weapons, turned back. Several, not carrying such cargoes, were allowed to reach Cuba. Premier Khrushchev, at first disposed to give some ground in a letter of October 26 to Kennedy, took a tougher stand in the following message of October 27 and proposed a swap. The U.S. missiles in Turkey were so obsolete that two months earlier President Kennedy had given orders for their withdrawal, but they were still there. He and his advisers felt that to remove them, as Khrushchev asked, on an exchange basis would weaken the morale of Turkey, the eastern anchor of the North Atlantic Treaty Organization (NATO). Was Kennedy right to risk nuclear incineration for the sake of Turkey? How much plausibility was there in Khrushchev's proposal?

Our purpose has been and is to help Cuba, and no one can challenge the humanity of our motives aimed at allowing Cuba to live peacefully and develop as its people desire. You want to relieve your country from danger and this is understandable. However, Cuba also wants this. All countries want to relieve themselves from danger.

But how can we, the Soviet Union and our government, assess your actions which, in effect, mean that you have surrounded the Soviet Union with military bases, surrounded our allies with military bases, set up military bases literally around our country, and stationed your rocket weapons at them? This is no secret. High-placed American officials demonstratively declare this. Your rockets are stationed in Britain and in Italy and pointed at us. Your rockets are stationed in Turkey.

---

[*]*Department of State Bulletin* 47 (November 12, 1962): 742.

You are worried over Cuba. You say that it worries you because it lies at a distance of 90 miles across the sea from the shores of the United States. However, Turkey lies next to us. Our sentinels are pacing up and down and watching each other. Do you believe that you have a right to demand security for your country and the removal of such weapons that you qualify as offensive, while not recognizing this right for us?...

That is why I make this proposal: We agree to remove those weapons from Cuba which you regard as offensive weapons. We agree to do this and to state this commitment in the United Nations. Your representatives will make a statement to the effect that the United States, on its part, bearing in mind the anxiety and concern of the Soviet state, will evacuate its analogous weapons from Turkey. Let us reach an understanding on what time you and we need to put this into effect.

After this, representatives of the U.N. Security Council could control on-the-spot the fulfillment of these commitments.

4. Kennedy Advances a Solution (1962)[*]

President Kennedy skillfully avoided an argument over a missile swap by ignoring his opponent's suggestion. Referring to Khrushchev's more promising letter of the previous day, he advanced the following proposals on October 27. The tension was building up, and an air strike against Cuba was scheduled for three days later, before the nuclear missiles could become fully operative. In this letter, what restrictions was Kennedy prepared to place on the United States?

Dear Mr. Chairman:

I have read your letter of October 26th with great care and welcomed the statement of your desire to seek a prompt solution to the problem. The first thing that needs to be done, however, is for work to cease on offensive missile bases in Cuba and for all weapons systems in Cuba capable of offensive use to be rendered inoperable, under effective United Nations arrangements.

Assuming this is done promptly, I have given my representatives in New York instructions that will permit them to work out this weekend—in cooperation with the Acting Secretary General and your representative—an arrangement for a permanent solution to the Cuban problem along the lines suggested in your letter of October 26th. As I read your letter, the key elements of your proposals—which seem generally acceptable as I understand them—are as follows:

1) You would agree to remove these weapons systems from Cuba under appropriate United Nations observation and supervision; and undertake, with suitable safeguards, to halt the further introduction of such weapons systems into Cuba.

2) We, on our part, would agree—upon the establishment of adequate arrangements through the United Nations to ensure the carrying out and continuation of these commitments—(a) to remove promptly the quarantine measures now in effect and (b) to give assurances against an invasion of Cuba. I am confident that other nations of the Western Hemisphere would be prepared to do likewise.

---

[*]*Department of State Bulletin* 47 (November 12, 1962): 743.

If you will give your representative similar instructions, there is no reason why we should not be able to complete these arrangements and announce them to the world within a couple of days.

[The next day, October 28, 1962, Khrushchev consented to Kennedy's terms, and a great sense of relief swept over the world. Kennedy himself had privately reckoned that the odds in favor of a nuclear blowup ran as high as fifty-fifty.]

B. President Johnson's Great Society

1. Michael Harrington Discovers Another America (1962)*

Some books shape the course of history. Michael Harrington's The Other America, *published in 1962, was such a book. It shook middle-class Americans out of their complacent assumption that the problem of poverty had been solved in their country. With reasoned yet passionate argument, Harrington forcefully documented the existence of an "invisible" America populated by hopelessly impoverished people. The book's millions of readers—many of them idealistic young people—helped form the political constituency that made possible the Johnson administration's War on Poverty in the late 1960s. Who are the poor people Harrington describes? Why are they "invisible"? What does Harrington identify as historically new about their condition? Are the problems he describes now resolved?*

There is a familiar America. It is celebrated in speeches and advertised on television and in the magazines. It has the highest mass standard of living the world has ever known.

In the 1950's this America worried about itself, yet even its anxieties were products of abundance....

While this discussion was carried on, there existed another America. In it dwelt somewhere between 40,000,000 and 50,000,000 citizens of this land. They were poor. They still are....

The millions who are poor in the United States tend to become increasingly invisible. Here is a great mass of people, yet it takes an effort of the intellect and will even to see them....

There are perennial reasons that make the other America an invisible land.

Poverty is often off the beaten track. It always has been. The ordinary tourist never left the main highway, and today he rides interstate turnpikes. He does not go into the valleys of Pennsylvania where the towns look like movie sets of Wales in the thirties. He does not see the company houses in rows, the rutted roads (the poor always have bad roads whether they live in the city, in towns, or on farms), and everything is black and dirty. And even if he were to pass through such a place by

---

accident, the tourist would not meet the unemployed men in the bar or the women coming home from a runaway sweatshop....

It is a blow to reform and the political hopes of the poor that the middle class no longer understands that poverty exists. But, perhaps more important, the poor are losing their links with the great world. If statistics and sociology can measure a feeling as delicate as loneliness..., the other America is becoming increasingly populated by those who do not belong to anybody or anything. They are no longer participants in an ethnic culture from the old country; they are less and less religious; they do not belong to unions or clubs. They are not seen, and because of that they themselves cannot see. Their horizon has become more and more restricted; they see one another, and that means they see little reason to hope....

Here is the most familiar version of social blindness: "The poor are that way because they are afraid of work. And anyway they all have big cars. If they were like me (or my father or my grandfather), they could pay their own way. But they prefer to live on the dole and cheat the taxpayers."

This theory, usually thought of as a virtuous and moral statement, is one of the means of making it impossible for the poor ever to pay their way. There are, one must assume, citizens of the other America who choose impoverishment out of fear of work (though, writing it down, I really do not believe it). But the real explanation of why the poor are where they are is that they made the mistake of being born to the wrong parents, in the wrong section of the country, in the wrong industry, or in the wrong racial or ethnic group. Once that mistake has been made, they could have been paragons of will and morality, but most of them would never even have had a chance to get out of the other America.

There are two important ways of saying this: The poor are caught in a vicious circle; or, The poor live in a culture of poverty....

Here is one of the most familiar forms of the vicious circle of poverty. The poor get sick more than anyone else in the society. That is because they live in slums, jammed together under unhygienic conditions; they have inadequate diets, and cannot get decent medical care. When they become sick, they are sick longer than any other group in society. Because they are sick more often and longer than anyone else, they lose wages and work, and find it difficult to hold a steady job. And because of this, they cannot pay for good housing, for a nutritious diet, for doctors. At any given point in the circle, particularly when there is a major illness, their prospect is to move to an even lower level and to begin the cycle, round and round, toward even more suffering....

What shall we tell the American poor, once we have seen them? Shall we say to them that they are better off than the Indian poor, the Italian poor, the Russian poor? That is one answer, but it is heartless. I should put it another way. I want to tell every well-fed and optimistic American that it is intolerable that so many millions should be maimed in body and in spirit when it is not necessary that they should be. My standard of comparison is not how much worse things used to be. It is how much better they could be if only we were stirred....

These, then, are the strangest poor in the history of mankind.

They exist within the most powerful and rich society the world has ever known. Their misery has continued while the majority of the nation talked of itself as being "affluent" and worried about neuroses in the suburbs. In this way tens of millions of human beings became invisible. They dropped out of sight and out of mind; they were without their own political voice.

Yet this need not be. The means are at hand to fulfill the age-old dream: poverty can now be abolished. How long shall we ignore this underdeveloped nation in our midst? How long shall we look the other way while our fellow human beings suffer? How long?

2. President Johnson Declares War on Poverty (1964)*

The United States in the 1960s continued to present appalling contrasts in wealth. An official government report in 1964 declared that one-fifth of the families in the country—9.3 million in all—"enjoyed" annual incomes of less than $3,000. Under President Kennedy, Congress made a modest beginning at relieving poverty by passing several laws providing for self-help and job retraining. President Johnson threw his full weight behind the Economic Opportunity Act of 1964, which a Democratic Congress approved and implemented with an initial appropriation of $947.5 million. This legislation included provisions for a Job Corps that would provide training for unskilled young men and women, aid for education, and a domestic Peace Corps to work with Native Americans and other disadvantaged groups. In a part of his message to Congress, the president made the following plea. Was he convincing in his argument that these heavy outlays would in the long run help the taxpayer?

I have called for a national war on poverty. Our objective: total victory.

There are millions of Americans—one fifth of our people—who have not shared in the abundance which has been granted to most of us, and on whom the gates of opportunity have been closed.

What does this poverty mean to those who endure it?

It means a daily struggle to secure the necessities for even a meager existence. It means that the abundance, the comforts, the opportunities they see all around them are beyond their grasp.

Worst of all, it means hopelessness for the young.

The young man or woman who grows up without a decent education, in a broken home, in a hostile and squalid environment, in ill health or in the face of racial injustice—that young man or woman is often trapped in a life of poverty.

He does not have the skills demanded by a complex society. He does not know how to acquire those skills. He faces a mounting sense of despair which drains initiative and ambition and energy....

The war on poverty is not a struggle simply to support people, to make them dependent on the generosity of others.

It is a struggle to give people a chance.

It is an effort to allow them to develop and use their capacities, as we have been allowed to develop and use ours, so that they can share, as others share, in the promise of this nation.

Public Papers of the Presidents of the United States: Lyndon B. Johnson, 1963–1964 (Washington, DC: National Archives and Records Service, 1965), vol. 1, pp. 376–377 (March 16, 1964).

We do this, first of all, because it is right that we should.

From the establishment of public education and land grant colleges through agricultural extension and encouragement to industry, we have pursued the goal of a nation with full and increasing opportunities for all its citizens.

The war on poverty is a further step in that pursuit.

We do it also because helping some will increase the prosperity of all.

Our fight against poverty will be an investment in the most valuable of our resources—the skills and strength of our people.

And in the future, as in the past, this investment will return its cost manyfold to our entire economy.

If we can raise the annual earnings of 10 million among the poor by only $1,000 we will have added 14 billion dollars a year to our national output. In addition we can make important reductions in public assistance payments which now cost us 4 billion dollars a year, and in the large costs of fighting crime and delinquency, disease and hunger.

This is only part of the story.

Our history has proved that each time we broaden the base of abundance, giving more people the chance to produce and consume, we create new industry, higher production, increased earnings and better income for all.

Giving new opportunity to those who have little will enrich the lives of all the rest.

Because it is right, because it is wise, and because, for the first time in our history, it is possible to conquer poverty, I submit, for the consideration of the Congress and the country, the Economic Opportunity Act of 1964.

The Act does not merely expand old programs or improve what is already being done.

It charts a new course.

It strikes at the causes, not just the consequences of poverty.

It can be a milestone in our one-hundred-eighty year search for a better life for our people.

C. The Black Revolution Erupts

1. Rosa Parks Keeps Her Seat (1955)[*]

"Jim Crow," or government-enforced segregation of the races—in schools, buses, restaurants, and other public places—defined life in the South from the late nineteenth century to the end of World War II. But in the postwar era, blacks began to protest against the petty humiliations and gross inequalities of the Jim Crow regime. On December 1, 1955, Rosa Parks, an officer in the local chapter of the National Association for the Advancement of Colored People (NAACP), boarded a bus in her hometown of Montgomery, Alabama, to return home after her day's work as a seamstress. The only seat available was in the "whites only" section. She sat down, refused to move,

and was arrested for violating the city's segregation laws. Her simple gesture touched off a 381-day boycott of the Montgomery bus system by black citizens, led to a Supreme Court ruling in November 1956 that segregation in public transportation facilities was illegal, and helped to launch the civil rights career of Martin Luther King, Jr., then a charismatic young pastor in Montgomery's Dexter Avenue Baptist Church. Why did this episode prove so powerful in capturing the imagination of blacks and whites alike?

Rosa L. Parks

I had had problems with bus drivers over the years, because I didn't see fit to pay my money into the front and then go around to the back. Sometimes bus drivers wouldn't permit me to get on the bus, and I had been evicted from the bus. But as I say, there had been incidents over the years. One of the things that made this get so much publicity was the fact the police were called in and I was placed under arrest. See, if I had just been evicted from the bus and he hadn't placed me under arrest or had any charges brought against me, it probably could have been just another incident.

I had left my work at the men's alteration shop, a tailor shop in the Montgomery Fair department store, and as I left work, I crossed the street to a drugstore to pick up a few items instead of trying to go directly to the bus stop. And when I had finished this, I came across the street and looked for a Cleveland Avenue bus that apparently had some seats on it. At that time it was a little hard to get a seat on the bus. But when I did get to the entrance to the bus, I got in line with a number of other people who were getting on the same bus.

As I got up on the bus and walked to the seat I saw there was only one vacancy that was just back of where it was considered the white section. So this was the seat that I took, next to the aisle, and a man was sitting next to me. Across the aisle there were two women, and there were a few seats at this point in the very front of the bus that was called the white section. I went on to one stop and I didn't particularly notice who was getting on the bus, didn't particularly notice the other people getting on. And on the third stop there were some people getting on, and at this point all of the front seats were taken. Now in the beginning, at the very first stop I had got on the bus, the back of the bus was filled up with people standing in the aisle and I don't know why this one vacancy that I took was left, because there were quite a few people already standing toward the back of the bus. The third stop is when all the front seats were taken, and this one man was standing and when the driver looked around and saw he was standing, he asked the four of us, the man in the seat with me and the two women across the aisle, to let him have those front seats.

At his first request, didn't any of us move. Then he spoke again and said, "You'd better make it light on yourselves and let me have those seats." At this point, of course, the passenger who would have taken the seat hadn't said anything. In fact, he never did speak to my knowledge. When the three people, the man who was in the seat with me and the two women, stood up and moved into the aisle, I remained where I was. When the driver saw that I was still sitting there, he asked if I was going to stand up. I told him, no, I wasn't. He said, "Well, if you don't stand up, I'm going to have you arrested." I told him to go on and have me arrested.

He got off the bus and came back shortly. A few minutes later, two policemen got on the bus, and they approached me and asked if the driver had asked me to stand up, and I said yes, and they wanted to know why I didn't. I told them I didn't think I should have to stand up. After I had paid my fare and occupied a seat, I didn't think I should have to give it up. They placed me under arrest then and had me to get in the police car, and I was taken to jail and booked on suspicion, I believe. The questions were asked, the usual questions they ask a prisoner or somebody that's under arrest. They had to determine whether or not the driver wanted to press charges or swear out a warrant, which he did. Then they took me to jail and I was placed in a cell. In a little while I was taken from the cell, and my picture was made and fingerprints taken. I went back to the cell then, and a few minutes later I was called back again, and when this happened I found out that Mr. E. D. Nixon and Attorney and Mrs. Clifford Durr had come to make bond for me.

In the meantime before this, of course...I was given permission to make a telephone call after my picture was taken and fingerprints taken. I called my home and spoke to my mother on the telephone and told her what had happened, that I was in jail. She was quite upset and asked me had the police beaten me. I told her, no, I hadn't been physically injured, but I was being held in jail, and I wanted my husband to come and get me out....He didn't have a car at that time, so he had to get someone to bring him down. At the time when he got down, Mr. Nixon and the Durrs had just made bond for me, so we all met at the jail and we went home.

2. Students Sit In for Equality (1960)*

On February 1, 1960, four black college students sat down at the whites-only lunch counter at the Woolworth's store in Greensboro, North Carolina, and tried to order something to eat. The black waitress refused to serve them: "Fellows like you make our race look bad," she said. "That's why we can't get anyplace today, because of people like you, rabble-rousers, trouble-makers....So why don't you go on out and stop making trouble?" But the students refused to move, and sat themselves into the history books. Though the Congress of Racial Equality (CORE) had used similar tactics against segregation since its founding in 1942, the students at Greensboro had never heard of CORE's sit-ins; theirs was a spontaneous gesture, undertaken without formal leadership or preparation. Their example touched off a wave of similar protests against segregation across the South, including one in Portsmouth, Virginia, in which Edward Rodman, then a high school student, participated. What motivated him? What gave him encouragement?

Our story here begins on February 12th, Lincoln's birthday. Several girls decided to observe the occasion by staging a sit-in, in sympathy with the students of North Carolina. So, after school, the first sit-in of Portsmouth's history took place. There was no violence, but no one was served. We sat until the lunch counter at Rose's Variety Store closed.

---

*"Sit-Ins, The Students Report" by Edward Rodman, edited by James Peck, CORE, 1960, pp. 4–6. Reprinted by permission of CORE—Congress of Racial Equality.

Our group was a loosely-knit collection of high school students, each with the same ideal: "Equality for All." Frankly speaking, that is about all we had in common. We were lacking organization, leadership, and planning.

By February 15th, our numbers had increased considerably. We demonstrated at two stores at the Shopping Center. Again we met no obstruction—only a few hecklers, whose worst insults we passed off with a smile. Things were looking good. The newspaper and radio reporters were there getting our story.

Our spontaneous movement was gaining momentum quickly. We were without organization; we had no leader and no rules for conduct other than a vague understanding that we were not to fight back. We should have known the consequences, but we didn't.

I was late getting to the stores the following day, because of a meeting. It was almost 4:00 p.m. when I arrived. What I saw will stay in my memory for a long time. Instead of the peaceful, nonviolent sit-ins of the past few days, I saw before me a swelling, pushing mob of white and Negro students, news-photographers, T.V. cameras and only two policemen. Immediately, I tried to take the situation in hand. I did not know it at the time, but this day I became the sit-in leader.

I didn't waste time asking the obvious questions: "Who were these other Negro boys from the corner?" "Where did all the white hoods come from?" It was obvious. Something was going to break loose, and I wanted to stop it. First, I asked all the girls to leave, then the hoods. But before I could finish, trouble started. A white boy shoved a Negro boy. The manager then grabbed the white boy to push him out and was shoved by the white boy. The crowd followed. Outside the boy stood in the middle of the street daring any Negro to cross a certain line. He then pulled a car chain and claw hammer from his pocket and started swinging the chain in the air.

He stepped up his taunting with the encouragement of others. When we did not respond, he became so infuriated that he struck a Negro boy in the face with the chain. The boy kept walking. Then, in utter frustration, the white boy picked up a street sign and threw it at a Negro girl. It hit her and the fight began. The white boys, armed with chains, pipes and hammers, cut off an escape through the street. Negro boys grabbed the chains and beat the white boys. The hammers they threw away. The white boys went running back to their hot rods. I tried to order a retreat.

During the fight I had been talking to the store manager and to some newspaper men. I did not apologize for our sit-in—only for unwanted fighters of both races and for their conduct. Going home, I was very dejected. I felt that this outbreak had killed our movement. I was not surprised the following day when a mob of 3,000 people formed. The fire department, all of the police force, and police dogs were mobilized. The police turned the dogs loose on the Negroes—but not on the whites. Peaceful victory for us seemed distant.

Next day was rainy and I was thankful that at least no mob would form. At 10:00 a.m. I received a telephone call that was to change our whole course of action. Mr. Hamilton, director of the YMCA, urged me to bring a few students from the original sit-in group to a meeting that afternoon. I did. That meeting was with Gordon Carey, a field secretary of CORE. We had seen his picture in the paper in connection with our recent campaign for integrated library facilities and we knew he was on our side. He had just left North Carolina where he had helped the student sit-ins. He told us about CORE and what CORE had done in similar situations elsewhere. I decided along with the others, that Carey should help us organize a nonviolent, direct action group to continue our peaceful protests in Portsmouth. He suggested that an all-day workshop on nonviolence be held February 20.

Rev. Chambers organized an adult committee to support our efforts. At the workshop we first oriented ourselves to CORE and its nonviolent methods. I spoke on "Why Nonviolent Action?" exploring Gandhi's principles of passive resistance and Martin Luther King's methods in Alabama. We then staged a socio-drama acting out the right and wrong ways to handle various demonstration situations. During the lunch recess, we had a real-life demonstration downtown—the first since the fighting. With our new methods and disciplined organization, we were successful in deterring violence. The store manager closed the counter early. We returned to the workshop, evaluated the day's sit-in, and decided to continue in this manner. We established ourselves officially as the Student Movement for Racial Equality.

Since then, we have had no real trouble. Our struggle is not an easy one, but we know we are not alone and we plan to continue in accordance with our common ideal: equality for all through nonviolent action.

3. Riders for Freedom (1961)*

In December 1960, in the case of Boynton v. Virginia *(364 U.S. 454), the U.S. Supreme Court declared that segregation in waiting rooms and restaurants serving interstate bus passengers was in violation of the Interstate Commerce Act. On this narrow but firm legal base, the Congress of Racial Equality (CORE) decided to mount a dramatic protest against segregation: two racially mixed busloads of volunteers would travel from Washington, DC, through the deepest South. "Our intention," CORE director James Farmer declared, "was to provoke the southern authorities into arresting us and thereby prod the Justice Department into enforcing the law of the land." On May 4, 1961, after graphic and realistic rehearsals of the harassment and beatings they expected to receive, seven blacks and six whites set out from Washington on their fateful "Freedom Ride." The two selections below describe what happened. The first statement is by CORE director James Farmer; the second is by Hank Thomas, one of the riders. Did the Freedom Riders achieve their objectives? Were their tactics justified? What was the federal government's role at this stage of the civil rights movement? Was the attitude of whites uniform throughout the South?*

James Farmer

So we, following the Gandhian technique, wrote to Washington. We wrote to the Justice Department, to the FBI, and to the President, and wrote to Greyhound Bus Company and Trailways Bus Company and told them that on May first or May fourth—whatever the date was,[†] I forget now—we were going to have a Freedom Ride. . . .

---

*"James Farmer," "Hank Thomas," from *My Soul Is Rested: Movement Days in the Deep South Remembered* by Howell Raines, copyright © 1977 by Howell Raines. Used by permission of G. P. Putnam's Sons, a division of Penguin Group (USA), LLC and Russell & Volkening as agents for the author.
[†]May 4.

Through Virginia we had no problem. In fact they had heard we were coming, Greyhound and Trailways, and they had taken down the For Colored and For Whites signs, and we rode right through. Yep. The same was true in North Carolina. Signs had come down just the previous day, blacks told us. And so the letters in advance did something.

In South Carolina it was a different story....John Lewis* started into a white waiting room in some town in South Carolina†...and there were several young white hoodlums, leather jackets, ducktail haircuts, standing there smoking, and they blocked the door and said, "Nigger, you can't come in here." He said, "I have every right to enter this waiting room according to the Supreme Court of the United States in the Boynton case."‡

They said, "Shit on that." He tried to walk past, and they clubbed him, beat him, and knocked him down. One of the white Freedom Riders...Albert Bigelow,§ who had been a Navy captain during World War II, big, tall, strapping fellow, very impressive, from Connecticut—then stepped right between the hoodlums and John Lewis. Lewis had been absorbing more of the punishment. They then clubbed Bigelow and finally knocked him down, and that took some knocking because he was a pretty strapping fellow, and he didn't hit back at all. [They] knocked him down, and at this point police arrived and intervened. They didn't make any arrests. Intervened.

Hank Thomas

The Freedom Ride didn't really get rough until we got down in the Deep South. Needless to say, Anniston, Alabama, I'm never gonna forget that, when I was on the bus that they threw some kind of incendiary device on.

He was on the first of two buses to cross into "Bama." When it pulled into the depot at Anniston, a Klan hotbed about sixty miles from Birmingham, the bus was surrounded by white men brandishing iron bars. Anniston police held them back long enough for the bus to reach the highway again, but about six miles outside town the pursuing mob caught up.

I got real scared then. You know, I was thinking—I'm looking out the window there, and people are out there yelling and screaming. They just about broke every window out of the bus....I really thought that that was going to be the end of me.

How did the bus get stopped?

They shot the tires out, and the bus driver was forced to stop....He got off, and man, he took off like a rabbit, and might well have. I couldn't very well blame him there. And we were trapped on the bus. They tried to board. Well, we did have two FBI men aboard the bus. All they were there to do were to observe and gather facts, but the crowd apparently recognized them as FBI men, and they did not try to hurt them.

---

*Later a Congressman from Georgia.
†Rock Hill.
‡The 1960 Supreme Court case outlawing segregated facilities at bus terminals.
§Despite his military background, a Quaker pacifist. He was best known for sailing the yacht *Golden Rule* into an atomic testing area in the Pacific as a protest against nuclear warfare.

It wasn't until the thing was shot on the bus and the bus caught afire that every-thing got out of control, and...when the bus was burning, I figured...[pauses]...panic did get ahold of me. Needless to say, I couldn't survive that burning bus. There was a possibility I could have survived the mob, but I was just so afraid of the mob that I was gonna stay on that bus. I mean, I just got that much afraid. And when we got off the bus...first they closed the doors and wouldn't let us off. But then I'm pretty sure they realized, that somebody said, "Hey, the bus is gonna explode," because it had just gassed up, and so they started scattering then, and I guess that's the way we got off the bus.* Otherwise, we probably all would have been succumbed by the smoke, and not being able to get off, probably would have been burned alive or burned on there anyway. That's the only time I was really, really afraid. I got whacked over the head with a rock or I think some kind of a stick as I was coming off the bus.

What happened in Anniston after the bus was attacked?

We were taken to the hospital. The bus started exploding, and a lot of people were cut by flying glass. We were taken to the hospital, most of us, for smoke inhalation.

By whom?

I don't remember. I think I was half out of it, half dazed, as a result of the smoke, and, gosh, I can still smell that stuff down in me now. You got to the point where you started having the dry heaves. Took us to the hospital, and it was incred-ible. The people at the hospital would not do anything for us. They would not. And I was saying, "You're *doctors*, you're medical personnel." They wouldn't. Governor Patterson got on statewide radio and said, "Any rioters in this state will not receive police protection." And then the crowd started forming outside the hospital, and the hospital told us to leave. And we said, "No, we're not going out there," and there we were. A caravan from Birmingham, about a fifteen-car caravan led by the Reverend Fred Shuttlesworth, came up from Birmingham to get us out.

Without police escort, I take it?

Without police escort, but every one of those cars had a shotgun in it. And Fred Shuttlesworth had got on the radio and said—you know Fred, he's very dramatic—"I'm going to get my people." [Laughs] He said, "I'm a nonviolent man, but I'm going to get my people." And apparently a hell of a lot of people believed in him. Man, they came there and they were a welcome sight. And each one of 'em got out with their guns and everything and the state police were there, but I think they all realized that this was not a time to say anything because, I'm pretty sure, there would have been a lot of people killed.

---

*John Patterson, then governor of Alabama, maintains that he and his public safety director, Floyd Mann, were indirectly responsible for the Freedom Riders' getting off the burning bus: "Floyd recommended that we send a state plainclothes investigator to Atlanta to catch the bus and ride with the Freedom Riders, and we did. Now this has never been reported that I know of in any paper....We sent a man named E. L. Cowling....He went over to Atlanta and caught the bus, and he was on the bus when they came to Anniston....So Cowling walked up to the door of the bus and drew his pistol and backed the crowd away from the bus and told them that if anybody touched anybody he'd kill them. And he got the Freedom Riders off the burning bus. That's true."

The black drivers were openly carrying guns?

Oh, yeah. They had rifles and shotguns. And that's how we got back to Birmingham. . . . I think I was flown to New Orleans for medical treatment, because still they were afraid to let any of us go to the hospitals in Birmingham, and by that time—it was what, two days later—I was fairly all right. I had gotten most of the smoke out of my system.

No one received any attention in the hospital in Anniston?

No, No. Oh, we did have one girl, Genevieve Hughes, a white girl, who had a busted lip. I remember a nurse applying something to that, but other than that, nothing. Now that I look back on it, man, we had some vicious people down there, wouldn't even so much as *treat* you. But that's the way it was. But strangely enough, even those bad things then don't stick in my mind that much. Not that I'm full of love and goodwill for everybody in my heart, but I chalk it off to part of the things that I'm going to be able to sit on my front porch in my rocking chair and tell my young'uns about, my grandchildren about.

Postscript: That same day, Mother's Day, May 14, 1961, the second bus escaped the mob in Anniston and made it to Birmingham. At the Trailways station there, white men armed with baseball bats and chains beat the Freedom Riders at will for about fifteen minutes before the first police arrived. In 1975 a former Birmingham Klansman, who was a paid informant of the FBI at the time, told the Senate Select Committee on Intelligence that members of the Birmingham police force had promised the Klansmen that no policemen would show up to interfere with the beatings for at least fifteen minutes. In 1976 a Birmingham detective who refused to be interviewed on tape told me that account was correct—as far as it went. The detective said that word was passed in the police department that Public Safety Commissioner Eugene "Bull" Connor had watched from the window of his office in City Hall as the crowd of Klansmen, some brandishing weapons, gathered to await the Freedom Fighters. Asked later about the absence of his policemen, Connor said most of them were visiting their mothers.

4. Martin Luther King, Jr., Writes from a Birmingham Jail (1963)[*]

The year 1963 marked the one hundredth anniversary of the Emancipation Proclamation, yet millions of African Americans remained enchained by racism. Although racial prejudice was a national curse, it worked most viciously in the South, the ancient homeland of slavery. Nearly a decade after the Supreme Court's desegregation order, fewer than 10 percent of black children in the South attended classes with white children. The problem was especially acute in Birmingham, Alabama, the most segregated big city in the United States. Segregation was the rule in schools, restaurants, restrooms, ballparks, libraries, and taxicabs. Although African Americans

---

were nearly half the city's residents, they constituted fewer than 15 percent of the city's voters. More than fifty cross burnings and eighteen racial bombings between 1957 and 1963 had earned the city the nickname of "Bombingham" among blacks. Thus Birmingham was a logical choice—and a courageous one—as the site of a mass protest by the Reverend Martin Luther King, Jr., and his Southern Christian Leadership Conference. Arrested during a protest demonstration on Good Friday, 1963, King penned the following letter from jail, writing on scraps of paper smuggled to him by a prison trusty. He was responding to criticism from eight white Alabama clergymen who had deplored his tactics as "unwise and untimely"—though King throughout his life preached the wisdom of nonviolence. Why does King believe that African Americans could wait no longer for their civil rights? How does he view himself in relation to white "moderates" and black extremists?

My Dear Fellow Clergymen:

• • •

You deplore the demonstrations taking place in Birmingham. But your statement, I am sorry to say, fails to express a similar concern for the conditions that brought about the demonstrations. I am sure that none of you would want to rest content with the superficial kind of social analysis that deals merely with effects and does not grapple with underlying causes. It is unfortunate that demonstrations are taking place in Birmingham, but it is even more unfortunate that the city's white power structure left the Negro community with no alternative....

We know through painful experience that freedom is never voluntarily given by the oppressor; it must be demanded by the oppressed. Frankly, I have yet to engage in a direct-action campaign that was "well timed" in the view of those who have not suffered unduly from the disease of segregation. For years now I have heard the word "Wait!" It rings in the ear of every Negro with piercing familiarity. This "Wait" has almost always meant "Never." We must come to see, with one of our distinguished jurists, that "justice too long delayed is justice denied."

We have waited for more than 340 years for our constitutional and God-given rights. The nations of Asia and Africa are moving with jetlike speed toward gaining political independence, but we still creep at horse-and-buggy pace toward gaining a cup of coffee at a lunch counter. Perhaps it is easy for those who have never felt the stinging darts of segregation to say, "Wait." But when you have seen vicious mobs lynch your mothers and fathers at will and drown your sisters and brothers at whim; when you have seen hate-filled policemen curse, kick, and even kill your black brothers and sisters; when you see the vast majority of your twenty million Negro brothers smothering in an airtight cage of poverty in the midst of an affluent society; when you suddenly find your tongue twisted and your speech stammering as you seek to explain to your six-year-old daughter why she can't go to the public amusement park that has just been advertised on television, and see tears welling up in her eyes when she is told that Funtown is closed to colored children, and see ominous clouds of inferiority beginning to form in her little mental sky, and see her beginning to distort her personality by developing an unconscious bitterness toward white people; when you have to concoct an answer for a five-year-old son who is asking: "Daddy, why do white people treat colored people so mean?"; when you take a cross-country drive and find it necessary to sleep night after night in the uncomfortable corners of your automobile because no motel will accept you; when you are humiliated day in and day out by nagging signs reading "white" and "colored"; when your first name becomes "nigger," your middle name becomes "boy" (however old you are) and your last name becomes "John," and your wife and mother are never given the respected title "Mrs."; when you are harried by day and haunted by night by the fact that you are a Negro, living constantly at tiptoe stance, never quite knowing what to expect next, and are plagued with inner fears and outer resentments; when you are forever fighting a degenerating sense of "nobodiness"—then you will understand why we find it difficult to wait. There comes a time when the cup of endurance runs over, and men are no longer willing to be plunged into the abyss of despair. I hope, sirs, you can understand our legitimate and unavoidable impatience....

You speak of our activity in Birmingham as extreme. At first I was rather disappointed that fellow clergymen would see my nonviolent efforts as those of an extremist. I began thinking about the fact that I stand in the middle of two opposing forces in the Negro community. One is a force of complacency, made up in part of Negroes who, as a result of long years of oppression, are so drained of self-respect and a sense of "somebodiness" that they have adjusted to segregation; and in part of a few middle-class Negroes who, because of a degree of academic and economic security and because in some ways they profit by segregation, have become insensitive to the problems of the masses. The other force is one of bitterness and hatred, and it comes perilously close to advocating violence. It is expressed in the various black nationalist groups that are springing up across the nation, the largest and best-known being Elijah Muhammad's Muslim movement. Nourished by the Negro's frustration over the continued existence of racial discrimination, this movement is made up of people who have lost faith in America, who have absolutely repudiated Christianity, and who have concluded that the white man is an incorrigible "devil."

I have tried to stand between these two forces, saying that we need emulate neither the "do-nothingism" of the complacent nor the hatred and despair of the black nationalist. For there is the more excellent way of love and nonviolent protest. I am grateful to God that, through the influence of the Negro church, the way of nonviolence became an integral part of our struggle.

If this philosophy had not emerged, by now many streets of the South would, I am convinced, be flowing with blood. And I am further convinced that if our white brothers dismiss as "rabble-rousers" and "outside agitators" those of us who employ nonviolent direct action, and if they refuse to support our nonviolent efforts, millions of Negroes will, out of frustration and despair, seek solace and security in black-nationalist ideologies—a development that would inevitably lead to a frightening racial nightmare....

I wish you had commended the Negro sit-inners and demonstrators of Birmingham for their sublime courage, their willingness to suffer and their amazing discipline in the midst of great provocation. One day the South will recognize its real heroes. They will be the James Merediths,* with the noble sense of purpose

---

*Escorted by four hundred federal marshals and three thousand federal troops, James Meredith was the first black student to enroll at the historically all-white University of Mississippi in 1962. Four years later, he was wounded by gunfire while leading a voter-registration drive in Mississippi.

that enables them to face jeering and hostile mobs, and with the agonizing loneliness that characterizes the life of the pioneer. They will be old, oppressed, battered Negro women, symbolized in a seventy-two-year-old woman in Montgomery, Alabama, who rose up with a sense of dignity and with her people decided not to ride segregated buses, and who responded with ungrammatical profundity to one who inquired about her weariness: "My feets is tired, but my soul is at rest." They will be the young high school and college students, the young ministers of the gospel and a host of their elders, courageously and nonviolently sitting in at lunch counters and willingly going to jail for conscience' sake. One day the South will know that when these disinherited children of God sat down at lunch counters, they were in reality standing up for what is best in the American dream and for the most sacred values in our Judaeo-Christian heritage, thereby bringing our nation back to those great wells of democracy which were dug deep by the founding fathers in their formulation of the Constitution and the Declaration of Independence....

Yours for the cause of Peace and Brotherhood,
Martin Luther King, Jr.

5. Malcolm X Is Defiant (1964)*

The dramatic confrontation in Birmingham—marked by footage of policemen training fire hoses and attack dogs on defenseless black children—roused public support in favor of a federal civil rights bill, introduced by John F. Kennedy in June of 1963. But by spring of the following year, the bill had yet to pass, blocked by a filibuster in the Senate. While King counseled patience, black nationalist leader Malcolm X struck a less compromising tone, warning whites that civil rights would come, either by the ballot or the bullet. How does Malcolm X justify his more militant stance? How might white Americans have reacted to his message?

If we don't do something real soon, I think you'll have to agree that we're going to be forced either to use the ballot or the bullet. It's one or the other in 1964. It isn't that time is running out—time has run out! 1964 threatens to be the most explosive year America has ever witnessed. The most explosive year. Why? It's also a political year. It's the year when all of the white politicians will be back in the so-called Negro community jiving you and me for some votes. The year when all of the white political crooks will be right back in your and my community with their false promises, building up our hopes for a letdown, with their trickery and their treachery, with their false promises which they don't intend to keep. As they nourish these dissatisfactions, it can only lead to one thing, an explosion; and now we have the type of black man on the scene in America today—I'm sorry, Brother Lomax—who just doesn't intend to turn the other cheek any longer....

*George Breitman, ed., *Malcolm X Speaks: Selected Speeches and Statements,* 2nd cloth edition (New York: Pathfinder Press, 1989), pp. 37–38, 44. Copyright © 1965, 1989 by Betty Shabazz and Pathfinder Press. Reprinted by permission.

I'm not a politician, not even a student of politics; in fact, I'm not a student of much of anything. I'm not a Democrat, I'm not a Republican, and I don't even consider myself an American. If you and I were Americans, there'd be no problem. Those Hunkies that just got off the boat, they're already Americans; Polacks are already Americans; the Italian refugees are already Americans. Everything that came out of Europe, every blue-eyed thing, is already an American. And as long as you and I have been over here, we aren't Americans yet.

Well, I am one who doesn't believe in deluding myself. I'm not going to sit at your table and watch you eat, with nothing on my plate, and call myself a diner. Sitting at the table doesn't make you a diner, unless you eat some of what's on that plate. Being here in America doesn't make you an American. Being born here in America doesn't make you an American. Why, if birth made you American, you wouldn't need any legislation, you wouldn't need any amendments to the Constitution, you wouldn't be faced with civil-rights filibustering in Washington, D.C., right now. They don't have to pass civil-rights legislation to make a Polack an American.

No, I'm not an American. I'm one of the 22 million black people who are the victims of Americanism. One of the 22 million black people who are the victims of democracy, nothing but disguised hypocrisy. So, I'm not standing here speaking to you as an American, or a patriot, or a flag-saluter, or a flag-waver—no, not I. I'm speaking as a victim of this American system. And I see America through the eyes of the victim. I don't see any American dream; I see an American nightmare....

And now you're facing a situation where the young Negro's coming up. They don't want to hear that "turn-the-other-cheek" stuff, no. In Jacksonville, those were teenagers, they were throwing Molotov cocktails. Negroes have never done that before. But it shows you there's a new deal coming in. There's new thinking coming in. There's new strategy coming in. It'll be Molotov cocktails this month, hand grenades next month, and something else next month. It'll be ballots, or it'll be bullets. It'll be liberty, or it will be death. The only difference about this kind of death—it'll be reciprocal. You know what is meant by "reciprocal"? That's one of Brother Lomax's words, I stole it from him. I don't usually deal with those big words because I don't usually deal with big people. I deal with small people. I find you can get a whole lot of small people and whip hell out of a whole lot of big people. They haven't got anything to lose, and they've got everything to gain. And they'll let you know in a minute: "It takes two to tango; when I go, you go."

6. President Johnson Supports Civil Rights (1965)[*]

Prompted largely by the mass outpouring of sentiment inspired by Martin Luther King, Jr., Congress passed a major Civil Rights Act in 1964. It prohibited discrimination in most public places, forbade employers or unions to discriminate on the basis of race, and created an Equal Employment Opportunity Commission to provide enforcement. Yet King and other black leaders were determined not to rest until they had secured federal legislation protecting the right of African Americans to vote.

---

[*]*Public Papers of the Presidents of the United States: Lyndon B. Johnson, 1965*, vol. 1 (Washington, DC: National Archives and Records Service, 1966), pp. 281–287.

Once again, King chose Alabama as the stage for demonstrations designed to force the Johnson administration's hand. On March 7, 1965, demonstrators marching from Selma, Alabama, to the state capital at Montgomery were brutally beaten and dispersed by state troopers and hastily deputized "possemen." Millions of Americans witnessed the violent assault on television, and within days hundreds of clergy of all faiths had poured into Selma to aid King. One of them, a Boston Unitarian minister, died after having been clubbed by a gang of white hooligans. The pressure on Washington to act mounted to irresistible proportions, and on March 15 President Johnson addressed Congress and the nation, as follows, to plead for a voting rights bill. Although Johnson had in fact tried to discourage King from marching in Alabama, he now threw the full moral and legal weight of his office behind the cause of black voting rights. In what broader context does he try to see the civil rights movement? How do his personal feelings and experiences influence his political action?

Mr. Speaker, Mr. President, Members of the Congress:

I speak tonight for the dignity of man and the destiny of democracy.

I urge every member of both parties, Americans of all religions and of all colors, from every section of this country, to join me in that cause.

At times history and fate meet at a single time in a single place to shape a turning point in man's unending search for freedom. So it was at Lexington and Concord. So it was a century ago at Appomattox. So it was last week in Selma, Alabama.

There, long-suffering men and women peacefully protested the denial of their rights as Americans. Many were brutally assaulted. One good man, a man of God, was killed.

There is no cause for pride in what has happened in Selma. There is no cause for self-satisfaction in the long denial of equal rights of millions of Americans. But there is cause for hope and for faith in our democracy in what is happening here tonight....

...[R]arely in any time does an issue lay bare the secret heart of America itself. Rarely are we met with a challenge, not to our growth or abundance, our welfare or our security, but rather to the values and the purposes and the meaning of our beloved Nation.

The issue of equal rights for American Negroes is such an issue. And should we defeat every enemy, should we double our wealth and conquer the stars, and still be unequal to this issue, then we will have failed as a people and as a nation.

For with a country as with a person, "What is a man profited, if he shall gain the whole world, and lose his own soul?"...

This was the first nation in the history of the world to be founded with a purpose. The great phrases of that purpose still sound in every American heart, North and South: "All men are created equal"—"government by consent of the governed"—"give me liberty or give me death."....

Those words are a promise to every citizen that he shall share in the dignity of man. This dignity cannot be found in a man's possessions; it cannot be found in his power, or in his position. It really rests on his right to be treated as a man equal in opportunity to all others. It says that he shall share in freedom, he shall choose his leaders, educate his children, and provide for his family according to his ability and his merits as a human being.

To apply any other test—to deny a man his hopes because of his color or race, his religion or the place of his birth—is not only to do injustice, it is to deny America and to dishonor the dead who gave their lives for American freedom.

The Right to Vote

Our fathers believed that if this noble view of the rights of man was to flourish, it must be rooted in democracy. The most basic right of all was the right to choose your own leaders. The history of this country, in large measure, is the history of the expansion of that right to all of our people.

Many of the issues of civil rights are very complex and most difficult. But about this there can and should be no argument. Every American citizen must have an equal right to vote. There is no reason which can excuse the denial of that right. There is no duty which weighs more heavily on us than the duty we have to ensure that right.

Yet the harsh fact is that in many places in this country men and women are kept from voting simply because they are Negroes.

Every device of which human ingenuity is capable has been used to deny this right. The Negro citizen may go to register only to be told that the day is wrong, or the hour is late, or the official in charge is absent. And if he persists, and if he manages to present himself to the registrar, he may be disqualified because he did not spell out his middle name or because he abbreviated a word on the application.

And if he manages to fill out an application he is given a test. The registrar is the sole judge of whether he passes this test. He may be asked to recite the entire Constitution, or explain the most complex provisions of State law. And even a college degree cannot be used to prove that he can read and write.

For the fact is that the only way to pass these barriers is to show a white skin....

In such a case our duty must be clear to all of us. The Constitution says that no person shall be kept from voting because of his race or his color. We have all sworn an oath before God to support and to defend that Constitution. We must now act in obedience to that oath.

Guaranteeing the Right to Vote

Wednesday I will send to Congress a law designed to eliminate illegal barriers to the right to vote....

This bill will strike down restrictions to voting in all elections—Federal, State, and local—which have been used to deny Negroes the right to vote.

This bill will establish a simple, uniform standard which cannot be used, however ingenious the effort, to flout our Constitution.

It will provide for citizens to be registered by officials of the United States Government if the State officials refuse to register them.

It will eliminate tedious, unnecessary lawsuits which delay the right to vote.

Finally, this legislation will ensure that properly registered individuals are not prohibited from voting....

To those who seek to avoid action by their National Government in their own communities; who want to and who seek to maintain purely local control over elections, the answer is simple:

Open your polling places to all your people.

Allow men and women to register and vote whatever the color of their skin. Extend the rights of citizenship to every citizen of this land....

We Shall Overcome

But even if we pass this bill, the battle will not be over. What happened in Selma is part of a far larger movement which reaches into every section and State of America. It is the effort of American Negroes to secure for themselves the full blessings of American life.

Their cause must be our cause too. Because it is not just Negroes, but really it is all of us, who must overcome the crippling legacy of bigotry and injustice.

And we shall overcome.

As a man whose roots go deeply into Southern soil I know how agonizing racial feelings are. I know how difficult it is to reshape the attitudes and the structure of our society.

But a century has passed, more than a hundred years, since the Negro was freed. And he is not fully free tonight....

The time of justice has now come. I tell you that I believe sincerely that no force can hold it back. It is right in the eyes of man and God that it should come. And when it does, I think that day will brighten the lives of every American.

For Negroes are not the only victims. How many white children have gone uneducated, how many white families have lived in stark poverty, how many white lives have been scarred by fear, because we have wasted our energy and our substance to maintain the barriers of hatred and terror?

So I say to all of you here, and to all in the Nation tonight, that those who appeal to you to hold on to the past do so at the cost of denying you your future.

This great, rich, restless country can offer opportunity and education and hope to all: black and white, North and South, sharecropper and city dweller. These are the enemies: poverty, ignorance, disease. They are the enemies and not our fellow man, not our neighbor. And these enemies too, poverty, disease and ignorance, we shall overcome....

The Purpose of This Government

My first job after college was as a teacher in Cotulla, Texas, in a small Mexican-American school. Few of them could speak English, and I couldn't speak much Spanish. My students were poor and they often came to class without breakfast, hungry. They knew even in their youth the pain of prejudice. They never seemed to know why people disliked them. But they knew it was so, because I saw it in their eyes. I often walked home late in the afternoon, after the classes were finished, wishing there was more that I could do. But all I knew was to teach them the little that I knew, hoping that it might help them against the hardships that lay ahead.

Somehow you never forget what poverty and hatred can do when you see its scars on the hopeful face of a young child.

I never thought then, in 1928, that I would be standing here in 1965. It never even occurred to me in my fondest dreams that I might have the chance to help the sons and daughters of those students and to help people like them all over this country.

But now I do have that chance—and I'll let you in on a secret—I mean to use it. And I hope that you will use it with me.

D. Vietnam Troubles

1. The Joint Chiefs of Staff Propose a Wider War (1964)*

U.S. involvement in Vietnam went back at least as far as 1950, when President Truman began aiding the French in their effort to suppress a nationalist insurgency in their Indochinese colony. Despite U.S. help, the French forces collapsed in 1954. An international conference in Geneva, Switzerland, in 1954 divided Vietnam at the 17th parallel and called for elections in all of Vietnam in 1956. The elections were never held, primarily because the government in South Vietnam, encouraged by the United States, feared that the communists in the North, led by Ho Chi Minh, would score a massive victory. President Eisenhower pledged in 1954 to provide military assistance to the government of South Vietnam, and by the end of Eisenhower's term in office about seven hundred U.S. "advisers" were helping to bolster the Vietnamese military. President Kennedy thus inherited a risky but limited commitment to South Vietnam. Meanwhile, communist-led nationalist forces, abetted by the communist regime in North Vietnam, were stepping up the pressure on the shaky South Vietnamese government in Saigon. A bloody military coup in late 1963 brought a new, apparently tougher government to Saigon, setting the stage for increasing U.S. involvement. A few months later, General Maxwell D. Taylor, the chairman of the Joint Chiefs of Staff, sent the following memorandum to Secretary of Defense Robert S. McNamara, proposing intensified U.S. military actions in Vietnam. What reasons does he offer for such actions? How persuasive are his reasons?

1. National Security Action Memorandum No. 273 [NSAM 273] makes clear the resolve of the President to ensure victory over the externally directed and supported communist insurgency in South Vietnam. In order to achieve that victory, the Joint Chiefs of Staff are of the opinion that the United States must be prepared to put aside many of the self-imposed restrictions which now limit our efforts, and to undertake bolder actions which may embody greater risks.

2. The Joint Chiefs of Staff are increasingly mindful that our fortunes in South Vietnam are an accurate barometer of our fortunes in all of Southeast Asia. It is our view that if the U.S. program succeeds in South Vietnam it will go far toward stabilizing the total Southeast Asia situation. Conversely, a loss of South Vietnam to the communists will presage an early erosion of the remainder of our position in that subcontinent.

3. Laos, existing on a most fragile foundation now, would not be able to endure the establishment of a communist—or pseudo neutralist—state on its eastern flank. Thailand, less strong today than a month ago by virtue of the loss of Prime Minister Sarit would probably be unable to withstand the pressures of infiltration from the north should Laos collapse to the communists in its turn. Cambodia apparently has estimated that our prospects in South Vietnam are not promising and, encouraged by the actions of the French, appears already to be seeking an accommodation with the communists. Should we actually suffer defeat in South Vietnam, there is little reason to believe that Cambodia would maintain even a pretense of neutrality.

---

*"The Joint Chiefs of Staff Propose a Wider War," *Pentagon Papers*, 1971, pp. 274–277.

4. In a broader sense, the failure of our programs in South Vietnam would have heavy influence on the judgments of Burma, India, Indonesia, Malaysia, Japan, Taiwan, the Republic of Korea, and the Republic of the Philippines with respect to U.S. durability, resolution, and trustworthiness. Finally, this being the first real test of our determination to defeat the communist wars of national liberation formula, it is not unreasonable to conclude that there would be a corresponding unfavorable effect upon our image in Africa and in Latin America.

5. All of this underscores the pivotal position now occupied by South Vietnam in our world-wide confrontation with the communists and the essentiality that the conflict there would be brought to a favorable end as soon as possible....

6. The Joint Chiefs of Staff are convinced that, in keeping with the guidance in NSAM 273, the United States must make plain to the enemy our determination to see the Vietnam campaign through to a favorable conclusion....

7. Our considerations, furthermore, cannot be confined entirely to South Vietnam. Our experience in the war thus far leads us to conclude that, in this respect, we are not now giving sufficient attention to the broader area problems of Southeast Asia. The Joint Chiefs of Staff believe that our position in Cambodia, our attitude toward Laos, our actions in Thailand, and our great effort in South Vietnam do not comprise a compatible and integrated U.S. policy for Southeast Asia. U.S. objectives in Southeast Asia cannot be achieved by either economic, political, or military measures alone. All three fields must be integrated into a single, broad U.S. program for Southeast Asia. The measures recommended in this memorandum are a partial contribution to such a program.

8. Currently we and the South Vietnamese are fighting the war on the enemy's terms. He has determined the locale, the timing, and the tactics of the battle while our actions are essentially reactive. One reason for this is the fact that we have obliged ourselves to labor under self-imposed restrictions with respect to impeding external aid to the Viet Cong.* These restrictions include keeping the war within the boundaries of South Vietnam, avoiding the direct use of U.S. combat forces, and limiting U.S. direction of the campaign to rendering advice to the government of Vietnam. These restrictions, while they may make our international position more readily defensible, all tend to make the task in Vietnam more complex, time-consuming, and in the end, more costly. In addition to complicating our own problem, these self-imposed restrictions may well now be conveying signals of irresolution to our enemies—encouraging them to higher levels of vigor and greater risks. A reversal of attitude and the adoption of a more aggressive program would enhance greatly our ability to control the degree to which escalation will occur. It appears probable that the economic and agricultural disappointments suffered by Communist China, plus the current rift with the Soviets, could cause the communists to think twice about undertaking a large-scale military adventure in Southeast Asia.

9. ...It is our conviction that if support of the insurgency from outside South Vietnam in terms of operational direction, personnel, and material were stopped completely, the character of the war in South Vietnam would be substantially and favorably

---

*South Vietnamese guerilla force that fought alongside the North Vietnamese army against the South Vietnamese government and the United States.

altered. Because of this conviction, we are wholly in favor of executing the covert actions against North Vietnam which you have recently proposed to the President....

10. Accordingly, the Joint Chiefs of Staff consider that the United States must make ready to conduct increasingly bolder actions in Southeast Asia; specifically as to Vietnam to:

a. Assign to the U.S. military commander responsibilities for the total U.S. program in Vietnam.

b. Induce the Government of Vietnam to turn over to the United States military commander, temporarily, the actual tactical direction of the war.

c. Charge the United States military commander with complete responsibility for conduct of the program against North Vietnam.

d. Overfly Laos and Cambodia to whatever extent is necessary for acquisition of operational intelligence.

e. Induce the Government of Vietnam to conduct overt ground operations in Laos of sufficient scope to impede the flow of personnel and material southward.

f. Arm, equip, advise, and support the Government of Vietnam in its conduct of aerial bombing of critical targets in North Vietnam and in mining the sea approaches to that country.

g. Advise and support the Government of Vietnam in its conduct of large-scale commando raids against critical targets in North Vietnam.

h. Conduct aerial bombing of key North Vietnam targets, using U.S. resources under Vietnamese cover, and with the Vietnamese openly assuming responsibility for the actions.

i. Commit additional U.S. forces, as necessary, in support of the combat action within South Vietnam.

j. Commit U.S. forces as necessary in direct actions against North Vietnam.

2. President Johnson Asserts His War Aims (1965)*

On August 2–4, 1964, two U.S. destroyers in the Gulf of Tonkin were reportedly fired on by North Vietnamese torpedo boats. President Johnson, concealing the fact that the destroyers had been engaging in provocative raids on North Vietnam, used the incident to secure from Congress a sweeping mandate for U.S. military intervention (the Gulf of Tonkin Resolution). Then, in February 1965, Vietcong guerrillas attacked a U.S. base at Pleiku, South Vietnam, and Johnson seized the occasion to begin an enormous escalation of the U.S. military presence in Southeast Asia. He ordered virtually continuous bombing of North Vietnam and sharply increased the number of U.S. troops in South Vietnam (to nearly 200,000 by the end of 1965). On April 7, 1965, in a major address at Johns Hopkins University, Johnson set forth his reasons for the increasing U.S. commitment. Just two weeks earlier, the assistant secretary of defense for international security affairs had noted in a private memorandum that U.S. war aims were "70%— to avoid a humiliating U.S. defeat (to our reputation as a guarantor), 20%—to keep South Vietnam (and the adjacent) territory from Chinese hands, 10%—to permit the

*Public Papers of the Presidents of the United States: Lyndon B. Johnson (Washington, DC: National Archives and Records Service, 1966), p. 395.

people of South Vietnam to enjoy a better, freer way of life. Also—to emerge from crisis without unacceptable taint from methods used. Not—to 'help a friend.'" Was Johnson's speech consistent with that thinking?

Why are we in South Viet-Nam?

We are there because we have a promise to keep. Since 1954 every American President has offered support to the people of South Viet-Nam. We have helped to build, and we have helped to defend. Thus, over many years, we have made a national pledge to help South Viet-Nam defend its independence.

And I intend to keep that promise.

To dishonor that pledge, to abandon this small and brave nation to its enemies, and to the terror that must follow, would be an unforgivable wrong.

We are also there to strengthen world order. Around the globe from Berlin to Thailand are people whose well-being rests in part on the belief that they can count on us [to honor some forty defensive alliances] if they are attacked. To leave Viet-Nam to its fate would shake the confidence of all these people in the value of an American commitment and in the value of America's word. The result would be increased unrest and instability, and even wider war.

We are also there because there are great stakes in the balance. Let no one think for a moment that retreat from Viet-Nam would bring an end to conflict. The battle would be renewed in one country and then another. The central lesson of our time is that the appetite of aggression is never satisfied....

Our objective is the independence of South Viet-Nam and its freedom from attack. We want nothing for ourselves—only that the people of South Viet-Nam be allowed to guide their own country in their own way.

We will do everything necessary to reach that objective and we will do only what is absolutely necessary.

3. The British Prime Minister Criticizes U.S. Bombing (1965)*

Operation Rolling Thunder—large-scale bombing raids on North Vietnam—evoked worldwide criticism in 1965. Even U.S. allies grew restive. On June 3, 1965, British Prime Minister Harold Wilson sent the following cable to President Johnson, gently but firmly taking issue with U.S. policy in Vietnam. What did Wilson find most objectionable?

I was most grateful to you for asking Bob McNamara [secretary of defense] to arrange the very full briefing about the two oil targets near Hanoi and Haiphong that Col. Rogers gave me yesterday....

I know you will not feel that I am either unsympathetic or uncomprehending of the dilemma that this problem presents for you. In particular, I wholly understand the deep concern you must feel at the need to do anything possible to reduce the losses of young Americans in and over Vietnam; and Col. Rogers made it clear to us what care has been taken to plan this operation so as to keep civilian casualties to the minimum.

However,...I am bound to say that, as seen from here, the possible military benefits that may result from this bombing do not appear to outweigh the political

*Pentagon Papers, New York Times edition (1971), pp. 448–449.

disadvantages that would seem the inevitable consequence. If you and the South Vietnamese Government were conducting a declared war on the conventional pattern...this operation would clearly be necessary and right. But since you have made it abundantly clear—and you know how much we have welcomed and supported this—that your purpose is to achieve a negotiated settlement, and that you are not striving for total military victory in the field, I remain convinced that the bombing of these targets, without producing decisive military advantage, may only increase the difficulty of reaching an eventual settlement....

The last thing I wish is to add to your difficulties, but, as I warned you in my previous message, if this action is taken we shall have to dissociate ourselves from it, and in doing so I should have to say that you had given me advance warning and that I had made my position clear to you....

Nevertheless I want to repeat...that our reservations about this operation will not affect our continuing support for your policy over Vietnam, as you and your people have made it clear from your Baltimore speech onwards. But, while this will remain the Government's position, I know that the effect on public opinion in this country—and I believe throughout Western Europe—is likely to be such as to reinforce the existing disquiet and criticism that we have to deal with.

4. Secretary McNamara Opposes Further Escalation (1966)*

By the end of 1966 Vietnam was beginning to look like a bottomless pit into which the United States was dumping precious money and more precious men. Secretary of Defense McNamara, one of the original architects of U.S. involvement, was among the first high-level officials to grow disenchanted with the course of the war. In his report to the president, given here, he records his increasingly pessimistic assessment of U.S. prospects in Southeast Asia. Such views did not endear him to President Johnson, who clung to the hope that the United States could salvage some kind of victory from the Vietnam quagmire, and McNamara soon resigned. But when military men in the spring of 1968 requested an additional 200,000 troops for Vietnam, Johnson at last drew the line. He put a ceiling on U.S. troop commitments and withdrew from the 1968 presidential race so as to pursue peace more effectively. For Johnson, it was too little, too late. There was no peace in 1968 (the war dragged on five more years), and his party lost the White House in that year to the Republican candidate, Richard M. Nixon. Nixon soon announced a policy of "Vietnamization"—increasing the role of the Vietnamese in their own war, while simultaneously decreasing the U.S. role. In what ways does McNamara's 1966 report foreshadow Nixon's approach? Why was McNamara pessimistic? What was his view of the bombing operation over North Vietnam?

1. Evaluation of the situation. In the report of my last trip to Vietnam almost a year ago, I stated that the odds were about even that, even with the then-recommended deployments, we would be faced in early 1967 with a military stand-off at a much higher level of conflict and with "pacification" still stalled. I am a little less pessimistic now in one respect. We have done somewhat better militarily than I anticipated.

Pentagon Papers, New York Times edition (1971), pp. 542–551.

We have by and large blunted the communist military initiative—and military victory in South Vietnam the Viet Cong may have had in mind 18 months ago has been thwarted by our emergency deployments and actions. And our program of bombing the North has exacted a price.

My concern continues, however, in other respects. This is because I see no reasonable way to bring the war to an end soon. Enemy morale has not broken—he apparently has adjusted to our stopping his drive for military victory and has adopted a strategy of keeping us busy and waiting us out (a strategy of attriting our national will). He knows that we have not been, and he believes we probably will not be, able to translate our military successes into the "end products"—broken enemy morale and political achievements by the GVN [government of Vietnam]. . . .

Pacification is a bad disappointment. We have good grounds to be pleased by the recent elections, by [President] Ky's 16 months in power, and by the faint signs of development of national political institutions and of a legitimate civil government. But none of this has translated itself into political achievements at Province level or below. Pacification has if anything gone backward. As compared with two, or four, years ago, enemy full-time regional forces and part-time guerrilla forces are larger; attacks, terrorism and sabotage have increased in scope and intensity; more railroads are closed and highways cut; the rice crop expected to come to market is smaller; we control little, if any, more of the population; the VC [Viet Cong] political infrastructure thrives in most of the country, continuing to give the enemy his enormous intelligence advantage; full security exists nowhere (not even behind the U.S. Marines' lines and in Saigon); in the countryside, the enemy almost completely controls the night.

Nor has the Rolling Thunder program of bombing the North either significantly affected infiltration or cracked the morale of Hanoi. There is agreement in the intelligence community on these facts. . . .

In essence, we find ourselves—from the point of view of the important war (for the complicity of the people)—no better, and if anything, worse off. This important war must be fought and won by the Vietnamese themselves. We have known this from the beginning. But the discouraging truth is that, as was the case in 1961 and 1963 and 1965, we have not found the formula, the catalyst, for training and inspiring them into effective action.

2. Recommended actions. In such an unpromising state of affairs, what should we do? We must continue to press the enemy militarily; we must make demonstrable progress in pacification; at the same time, we must add a new ingredient forced on us by the facts. Specifically, we must improve our position by getting ourselves into a military posture that we credibly would maintain indefinitely—a posture that makes trying to "wait us out" less attractive. I recommend a five-pronged course of action to achieve those ends.

a. Stabilize U.S. force-levels in Vietnam. It is my judgment that, barring a dramatic change in the war, we should limit the increase in U.S. forces in SVN [South Vietnam] in 1967 to 70,000 men and we should level off at the total of 470,000 which such an increase would provide. . . .*

---

*Admiral Sharp has recommended a 12/31/67 strength of 570,000. However, I believe both he and General Westmoreland recognize that the danger of inflation will probably force an end 1967 deployment limit of about 470,000. [Footnote in the original.]

b. Install a barrier. A portion of the 470,000 troops—perhaps 10,000 to 20,000—should be devoted to the construction and maintenance of an infiltration barrier. Such a barrier would lie near the 17th parallel—would run from the sea, across the neck of South Vietnam (choking off the new infiltration routes through the DMZ [demilitarized zone] and across the trails in Laos. This interdiction system (at an approximate cost of $1 billion) would comprise to the east a ground barrier of fences, wire, sensors, artillery, aircraft and mobile troops; and to the west—mainly in Laos—an interdiction zone covered by air-laid mines and bombing attacks pinpointed by air-laid acoustic sensors....

c. Stabilize the Rolling Thunder program against the North. Attack sorties in North Vietnam have risen from about 4,000 per month at the end of last year to 6,000 per month in the first quarter of this year and 12,000 per month at present. Most of our 50 percent increase of deployed attack-capable aircraft has been absorbed in the attacks on North Vietnam. In North Vietnam, almost 84,000 attack sorties have been flown (about 25 percent against fixed targets), 45 percent during the past seven months....I recommend, as a minimum, against increasing the level of bombing of North Vietnam and against increasing the intensity of operations by changing the areas or kinds of targets struck.

Under these conditions, the bombing program would continue the pressure and would remain available as a bargaining counter to get talks started (or to trade off in talks). But, as in the case of a stabilized level of U.S. ground forces, the stabilization of Rolling Thunder would remove the prospect of ever escalating bombing as a factor complicating our political posture and distracting from the main job of pacification in South Vietnam.

At the proper time, as discussed...below, I believe we should consider terminating bombing in all of North Vietnam, or at least in the Northeast zones, for an indefinite period in connection with covert moves toward peace.

d. Pursue a vigorous pacification program....

3. The prognosis. The prognosis is bad that the war can be brought to a satisfactory conclusion within the next two years. The large-unit operations probably will not do it; negotiations probably will not do it. *While we should continue to pursue both of these routes in trying for a solution in the short run, we should recognize that success from them is a mere possibility, not a probability.* [Emphasis in original.]

The solution lies in girding, openly, for a longer war and in taking actions immediately which will in 12 to 18 months give clear evidence that the continuing costs and risks to the American people are acceptably limited, that the formula for success has been found, and that the end of the war is merely a matter of time. All of my recommendations will contribute to this strategy, but the one most difficult to implement is perhaps the most important one—enlivening the pacification program. The odds are less than even for this task, if only because we have failed consistently since 1961 to make a dent in the problem. But, because the 1967 trend of pacification will, I believe, be the main talisman of ultimate U.S. success or failure in Vietnam, extraordinary imagination and effort should go into changing the stripes of that problem.

5. Massacre at My Lai (1968)*

On the morning of March 16, 1968, the men of Charlie Company landed their helicopters on the outskirts of My Lai 4, a Vietnamese hamlet where a battalion of Vietcong were thought to be hiding. The company's orders were simple—destroy the village and clear out the Vietcong. All neutral civilians, they were told, would be away on the morning of the assault. In the previous month the war-weary soldiers had suffered a demoralizing stream of casualties, and they relished the opportunity to unleash their pent-up rage on the unsuspecting Communists. But instead of well-armed Vietcong, the soldiers found a sleepy hamlet occupied almost entirely by women, children, and old men. Acting on the orders of their superiors, the men of Charlie Company killed between 400 and 500 Vietnamese civilians. During a subsequent hearing, Herbert L. Carter, who refused to fire on the civilian population, gave the following account of the tragedy. Is Carter right to describe the killings as "murder"? Who bears the brunt of the blame for what happened at My Lai? Was Vietnam, as many came to believe, simply a "different kind of war"?

The first killing was an old man in a field outside the village who said some kind of greeting in Vietnamese and waved his arms at us. Someone—either Medina or Calley[†]—said to kill him and a big heavy-set white fellow killed the man. I do not know the name of the man who shot this Vietnamese. This was the first murder.

Just after the man killed the Vietnamese, a woman came out of the village and someone knocked her down and Medina shot her with his M16 rifle. I was 50 or 60 feet from him and saw this. There was no reason to shoot this girl....It was a pure out and out murder.

Then our squad started into the village. We were making sure no one escaped from the village. Seventy-five or a hundred yards inside the village we came to where the soldiers had collected 15 or more Vietnamese men, women, and children in a group. Medina said, "Kill everybody, leave no one standing." Wood was there with an M-60 machine gun and, at Medina's orders, he fired into the people. Sgt Mitchell was there at this time and fired into the people with his M16 rifle, also. Widmer was there and fired into the group, and after they were down on the ground, Widmer passed among them and finished them off with his M16 rifle. Medina, himself, did not fire into this group.

Just after this shooting, Medina stopped a 17 or 18 year old man with a water buffalo. Medina said for the boy to make a run for it—he tried to get him to run—but the boy wouldn't run, so Medina shot him with his M16 rifle and killed him. The command group was there. I was 75 or 80 feet away at the time and saw it plainly....Medina killed the buffalo, too....

We went on through the village. Meadlo shot a Vietnamese and asked me to help him throw the man in the well. I refused and Meadlo had Carney help him

*From James S. Olson and Randy Roberts, eds., *My Lai: A Brief History with Documents*, 1998, pp. 79–81. Published by Bedford/St. Martin's Press.
†Captain Ernest L. Medina: Commanding officer of Charlie Company, Medina planned and supervised the raid on My Lai. He faced court martial but was ultimately acquitted. Lieutenant William L. Calley: Leader of Charlie Company's 1st Platoon, Calley was the ranking officer at My Lai and the only one convicted for participating in the massacre.

throw the man in the well. I saw this murder with my own eyes and know that there was no reason to shoot the man. I also know from the wounds that the man was dead.

Also in the village the soldiers had rounded up a group of people. Meadlo was guarding them. There were some other soldiers with Meadlo. Calley came up and said that he wanted them all killed. I was right there within a few feet when he said this. There were about 25 people in this group. Calley said when I walk away, I want them all killed. Meadlo and Widmer fired into this group with his M16 on automatic fire. Cowan was there and fired into the people too, but I don't think he wanted to do it. There were others firing into this group, but I don't remember who. Calley had two Vietnamese with him at this time and he killed them, too, by shooting them with his M16 rifle on automatic fire. I didn't want to get involved and I walked away. There was no reason for this killing. These were mainly women and children and a few old men. They weren't trying to escape or attack or anything. It was murder.

A woman came out of a hut with a baby in her arms and she was crying. She was crying because her little boy had been in front of her hut and between the well and the hut and someone had killed the child by shooting it. She came out of the hut with her baby and Widmer shot her with an M16 and she fell. When she fell, she dropped the baby and then Widmer opened up on the baby with his M16 and killed the baby, too.

I also saw another woman come out of a hut and Calley grabbed her by the hair and shot her with a caliber .45 pistol. He held her by the hair for a minute and then let go and she fell to the ground. Some enlisted man standing there said, "Well, she'll be in the big rice paddy in the sky." . . .

I also saw a Vietnamese boy about 8 years old who had been wounded, I think in the leg. One of the photographers attached to the company patted the kid on the head and then Mitchell shot the kid right in front of the photographer and me. I am sure the boy died from the fire of Mitchell.

About that time I sat down by a stack of dying people and Widmer asked me if he could borrow my caliber .45 pistol and finish off the people. I gave him my pistol and he walked in among the people and would stand there and when one would move, he would shoot that person in the head with the pistol. He used three magazines of caliber .45 ammunition on these people. These were men, children, women, and babies.

6. The Soldiers' War (1966)*

Hundreds of thousands of young Americans served in Vietnam; more than fifty thousand lost their lives there during the decade-long conflict (it was the United States' longest war). Much of the fighting was not conventional warfare, with front lines and well-identified foes facing one another. Instead, the Americans faced guerrilla adversaries and their civilian supporters, who were indistinguishable from the "friendly" South Vietnamese. In the absence of a defined front, there was no "rear," and U.S. troops often felt themselves to be adrift in a hostile sea of treacherous enemies. Brutality was inevitable in this kind of environment. Two wartime letters from

---

*Glenn Munson, ed., *Letters from Viet Nam* (New York: Parallax Publishing Co., 1966), pp. 104, 118.

U.S. servicemen follow. What opinion did the writers have of the war? Of their own role in it? Of antiwar protesters at home?

Dear Mom, . . .

Yesterday I witnessed something that would make any American realize why we are in this war. At least it did me. I was on daylight patrol. We were on a hill overlooking a bridge that was out of our sector. I saw a platoon of Vietcong stopping traffic from going over the bridge. They were beating women and children over the head with rifles, clubs, and fists. They even shot one woman and her child. They were taking rice, coconuts, fish, and other assorted foods from these people. The ones that didn't give they either beat or shot. I think you know what I tried to do. I wanted to go down and kill all of those slant-eyed bastards. I started to and it took two men to stop me. Those slobs have to be stopped, even if it takes every last believer in a democracy and a free way of life to do it. I know after seeing their brave tactics I'm going to try my best. So please don't knock [President] Johnson's policy in Vietnam. There is a good reason for it. I'm not too sure what it is myself, but I'm beginning to realize, especially after yesterday. . . .

> Love,
> *Bill*

How are the people taking to the war in Portland? I've read too much . . . about the way some of those cowardly students are acting on campuses. They sure don't show me much as far as being American citizens. They have the idea that they are our future leaders. Well, I won't follow nobody if he isn't going to help fight for my freedom.

A few weeks ago, I had the chance to talk with some Marines who had come to Okinawa for four (lousy) days of leave. They were more than happy because they had been fighting for six months with no let-up. We sat in a restaurant all the time, and I wish I could have taped it on my recorder. What they had to say would have had an impact on the people back home. One showed me where he had been shot. I asked if it hurt, and he didn't feel it. Not until after he got the ———— that shot him. He was more angry than hurt. They told me of some of their patrols and how they would be talking to a buddy one minute and watch him die in the next. Or wake up in the morning and see a friend hung from a tree by hooks in his armpits with parts of his body cut and shoved into his mouth. From what they said, the Vietcong aren't the only ruthless ones. We have to be, too. *Have* to. You'd be surprised to know that a guy you went to school with is right now shooting a nine-year-old girl and her mother. He did it because if they got the chance they would kill him. Or throwing a Vietcong out of a helicopter because he wouldn't talk.

One guy (who had broke down and cried) said that his one desire is to get enough leave to go home and kick three of those demonstrators in a well-suited place and bring him back. I tell you, it's horrible to read a paper and see our own people aren't backing you up.

VIETNAM
and
SOUTHEAST
ASIA

7. The Dilemma of Vietnam (1966)

By 1966, many Americans were agonizing about their country's involvement in Southeast Asia, and a bitter argument over the Vietnam War was intensifying. In the following image, from the Chicago Sun-Times, *renowned cartoonist Bill Mauldin ridiculed both the prowar and antiwar factions. Was his criticism fair? What is the cartoonist's own view of the war? What policy choices other than escalation and withdrawal were there?*

Bill Mauldin 1966 / As published in the Chicago Sun-Times, Inc. 2005. Courtesy of The Chicago Sun-Times.

E. The Politics of Protest in the 1960s _____

1. Students for a Democratic Society Issues a Manifesto (1962)*

The civil rights struggle and the continuing Cold War inspired many young people who came of age in the 1960s to take a radically critical look at U.S. society—even before the worsening Vietnam imbroglio made radical disenchantment almost fashionable among the young. One of the earliest and most thoughtful expressions of this incipient youthful radicalism was the Port Huron Statement, drafted by Tom Hayden and adopted by the fledgling Students for a Democratic Society (SDS), then in a relatively moderate phase of development, at its national convention at Port Huron, Michigan, in 1962. This statement later proved enormously influential in shaping the political views of many young activists. What aspects of the U.S. situation does it find most deplorable? How truly "radical" are the sentiments it expresses?

We are people of this generation, bred in at least modest comfort, housed now in universities, looking uncomfortably to the world we inherit.

When we were kids the United States was the wealthiest and strongest country in the world; the only one with the atom bomb, the least scarred by modern war, an initiator of the United Nations that we thought would distribute Western influence throughout the world. Freedom and equality for each individual government of, by, and for the people—these American values we found good, principles by which we could live as men. Many of us began maturing in complacency.

As we grew, however, our comfort was penetrated by events too troubling to dismiss. First, the permeating and victimizing fact of human degradation, symbolized by the Southern struggle against racial bigotry, compelled most of us from silence to activism. Second, the enclosing fact of the Cold War, symbolized by the presence of the Bomb, brought awareness that we ourselves, and our friends, and millions of abstract "others" we knew more directly because of our common peril, might die at any time. We might deliberately ignore, or avoid, or fail to feel all other human problems, but not these two, for these were too immediate and crushing in their impact, too challenging in the demand that we as individuals take the responsibility for encounter and resolution.

While these and other problems either directly oppressed us or rankled our consciences and became our own subjective concern, we began to see complicated and disturbing paradoxes in our surrounding America. The declaration "all men are created equal..." rang hollow before the facts of Negro life in the South and the big cities of the North. The proclaimed peaceful intentions of the United States contradicted its economic and military investments in the Cold War status quo.

We witnessed, and continue to witness, other paradoxes. With nuclear energy whole cities can easily be powered, yet the dominant nation-states seem more likely to unleash destruction greater than that incurred in all wars of human history. Although our own technology is destroying old and creating new forms of social organization, men still tolerate meaningless work and idleness. While two-thirds of mankind

_____
*From the Port Huron Statement.

suffers undernourishment, our own upper classes revel amidst superfluous abundance. Although world population is expected to double in forty years, the nations still tolerate anarchy as a major principle of international conduct and uncontrolled exploitation governs the sapping of the earth's physical resources. Although mankind desperately needs revolutionary leadership, America rests in national stalemate, its goals ambiguous and tradition-bound instead of informed and clear, its democratic system apathetic and manipulated rather than "of, by, and for the people."

Not only did tarnish appear on our image of American virtue, not only did disillusion occur when the hypocrisy of American ideals was discovered, but we began to sense that what we had originally seen as the American Golden Age was actually the decline of an era. The worldwide outbreak of revolution against colonialism and imperialism, the entrenchment of totalitarian states, the menace of war, overpopulation, international disorder, supertechnology—these trends were testing the tenacity of our own commitment to democracy and freedom and our abilities to visualize their application to a world in upheaval.

Our work is guided by the sense that we may be the last generation in the experiment with living. But we are a minority—the vast majority of our people regard the temporary equilibriums of our society and world as eternally functional parts. In this is perhaps the outstanding paradox: we ourselves are imbued with urgency, yet the message of our society is that there is no viable alternative to the present. Beneath the reassuring tones of the politicians, beneath the common opinion that America will "muddle through," beneath the stagnation of those who have closed their minds to the future, is the pervading feeling that there simply are no alternatives, that our times have witnessed the exhaustion not only of Utopias, but of any new departures as well. Feeling the press of complexity upon the emptiness of life, people are fearful of the thought that at any moment things might be thrust out of control. They fear change itself, since change might smash whatever invisible framework seems to hold back chaos for them now. For most Americans, all crusades are suspect, threatening. The fact that each individual sees apathy in his fellows perpetuates the common reluctance to organize for change. The dominant institutions are complex enough to blunt the minds of their potential critics, and entrenched enough to swiftly dissipate or entirely repeal the energies of protest and reform, thus limiting human expectancies. Then, too, we are a materially improved society, and by our own improvements we seem to have weakened the case for further change.

Some would have us believe that Americans feel contentment amidst prosperity—but might it not better be called a glaze above deeply felt anxieties about their role in the new world? And if these anxieties produce a developed indifference to human affairs, do they not as well produce a yearning to believe there *is* an alternative to the present, not [that] something *can* be done to change circumstances in the school, the workplaces, the bureaucracies, the government? It is to this latter yearning, at once the spark and engine of change, that we direct our present appeal. The search for truly democratic alternatives to the present, and a commitment to social experimentation with them, is a worthy and fulfilling human enterprise, one which moves us and, we hope, others today. On such a basis do we offer this document of our convictions and analysis: as an effort in understanding and changing the conditions of humanity in the late twentieth century, an effort rooted in the ancient, still unfulfilled conception of man attaining determining influence over his circumstances of life.

2. Young Americans for Freedom Makes a Statement (1960)*

Meeting at the Sharon, Connecticut, home of conservative activist and National Review *publisher William F. Buckley, Jr., in September 1960, a group of college students drafted the following statement of principles as the founding charter of Young Americans for Freedom. YAF became a rallying point for young conservatives through the tumultuous 1960s and provided organizational support for the eventual conservative Republican resurgence that culminated in the election of Ronald Reagan in 1980. In what ways do the ideas in the following "Sharon Statement" resemble those in the manifesto of Students for a Democratic Society (see the previous document)? In what ways do they differ? How might one account for the subsequent political fates of the two ideologies and the two groups?*

The Sharon Statement

Adopted by the Young Americans for Freedom in conference at Sharon, Conn., September 9–11, 1960

In this time of moral and political crisis, it is the responsibility of the youth of America to affirm certain eternal truths.

We, as young conservatives, believe:

That foremost among the transcendent values is the individual's use of his God-given free will, whence derives his right to be free from the restrictions of arbitrary force;

That liberty is indivisible, and that political freedom cannot long exist without economic freedom;

That the purposes of government are to protect these freedoms through the preservation of internal order, the provision of national defense, and the administration of justice;

That when government ventures beyond these rightful functions, it accumulates power which tends to diminish order and liberty;

That the Constitution of the United States is the best arrangement yet devised for empowering government to fulfill its proper role, while restraining it from the concentration and abuse of power;

That the genius of the Constitution—the division of powers—is summed up in the clause which reserves primacy to the several states, or to the people, in those spheres not specifically delegated to the Federal Government;

That the market economy, allocating resources by the free play of supply and demand, is the single economic system compatible with the requirements of personal freedom and constitutional government, and that it is at the same time the most productive supplier of human needs;

That when government interferes with the work of the market economy, it tends to reduce the moral and physical strength of the nation; that when it takes

*Source: http://www.heritage.org/initiatives/first-principles/primary-sources/the-sharon-statement.

from one man to bestow on another, it diminishes the incentive of the first, the integrity of the second, and the moral autonomy of both;

That we will be free only so long as the national sovereignty of the United States is secure; that history shows periods of freedom are rare, and can exist only when free citizens concertedly defend their rights against all enemies;

That the forces of international Communism are, at present, the greatest single threat to these liberties;

That the United States should stress victory over, rather than coexistence with, this menace; and

That American foreign policy must be judged by this criterion: does it serve the just interests of the United States?

3. A War Protester Decides to Resist the Draft (1966)*

No other issue did more to breed disenchantment among young people in the 1960s than the Vietnam War. As revelations spread about the deepening U.S. involvement there, and as the government in Washington proved increasingly unable to justify the conflict to the American public, countless people, especially college youths, expressed their disaffection. For many young men of draft age, their relationship with the Selective Service System became both a political and a moral issue. One young man who decided to resist the draft was David Harris, a former Boy of the Year from Fresno, California, and, in 1966, president of the student body at Stanford University. With his friend Dennis Sweeney—who a decade and a half later would be convicted of murdering former congressman Allard K. Lowenstein, another antiwar activist— Harris helped to organize a draft resistance movement among college students. In the following passage, Harris describes his own decision to become a draft resister. (He would later spend nearly two years in a federal penitentiary as a consequence.) What were his motives? Was he justified in reaching his decision?

The more we learned about the war, the worse it seemed. Late in July, Cooley Street attended a lecture by a Canadian journalist who had just returned from North Vietnam. Dennis and the Channing Street group were at the lecture as well.†

With what amounted to only a fledgling air defense system, explained the journalist, North Vietnam had no hope of turning the American Force back. Theoretically, strategic air power destroys the enemy's industrial, logistic, and transportation systems, but North Vietnam possessed little centralized industry and only a rudimentary transportation system. Consequently, the target increasingly became the population itself. The American strategy's starting point was a calculation by Defense Department planners that it took only two Vietnamese to deal with one of their dead countrymen, but one wounded required five. Mass woundings, it was assumed, would tie the enemy's hands, and the American arsenal had developed wounding devices in great variety.

---

*Dreams Die Hard: Three Men's Journey Through the Sixties by David Harris, pp. 146–148. Copyright © 1982 by David Harris.
†Cooley and Channing are two streets in the Palo Alto, California, area where Harris and other antiwar activists lived in the 1960s.

The CBU 46 was a small explosive package stuffed with hundreds of one-inch steel darts, each shaped with fins, designed to "peel off" the outer flesh, make "enlarged wounds," and "shred body organs" before "lodging in the blood vessels." They were dropped a thousand at a time from 30,000 feet. The BLU 52 was 270 pounds of "riot control" chemical that induced vomiting, nausea, and muscle spasms, occasionally fatal to old people and children. The M-36 was an 800-pound casing containing 182 separate "incendiary bomblets," the most horrendous of which were manufactured from phosphorus, commonly lodging in the flesh and continuing to burn for as long as fifteen days, causing its victims' wounds to glow with an eerie green light.

The two antipersonnel weapons then in most common use were versions of the BLU 24/26. The "pineapple bomb" was the earliest model. A yellow cylinder, it contained 250 steel ball-bearing pellets packed around an explosive charge. On impact, its pellets fired out horizontally. A batch of a thousand pineapples would cover an area the size of four football fields, leaving anything above ground level a casualty. The "guava bomb" was the pineapple's successor. Gray and round, it doubled the number of pellets and had a fuse that let it either explode at a set altitude or on impact. Since it fired its pellets diagonally instead of on the horizontal, the Guava also fired into the holes where people might be hiding.

After the program was over, we all decided to proceed to a place we called End of the World Beach. It was the edge of a causeway supporting the eastern approach to the Dumbarton Bridge, where beer bottles, old tires, two-by-fours, tennis shoes, condoms, dead fish, and seaweed were strung out for half a mile. It captured the devastation still haunting everyone's thinking. At one point, Dennis and I stood next to each other, staring across the refuse at the blinking lights of civilization on the other side of the bay.

Without looking at Dennis, I spoke up.

"You know," I said, "those bastards have got to be stopped."

When I turned to Sweeney, he was nodding his head like he knew exactly what I meant.

Three weeks later I sat at my typewriter and wrote local Draft Board 71 in Fresno, California, a letter "To whom it may concern." I enclosed a Selective Service classification card indicating that the bearer, David Victor Harris, possessed a student deferment. The letter informed my draft board that I could no longer in good conscience carry the enclosed document or accept the deferment it signified. It was a privilege I found unwarranted for any student. It also signified tacit assent on my part for both the task the Selective Service System was performing and the power it had assumed over my life. Being even implicitly a party to the destruction of Indochina was not part of my plans. If they ordered me for induction, I warned them, I would refuse to comply.

I feel as though I have explained that act of defiance a million times in the intervening years without ever quite capturing it. The repetition eventually burdened my explanation with a shell of distance and matter-of-factness that distorts what I did. It was an act of wonderment and impulse, taken in the calmest and most practical frame of mind. I was prepared to abandon what seemed a promising future and pit myself against the war one on one, believing I would redeem my country and realize myself in the process. It seemed that to do anything else would have dishonored both. There was nothing matter-of-fact or distant about it that August. I took my life in my hands and it was the bravest I have ever been. It was also, I think, the most right. That I have never doubted. Times change and I am no longer the same person, but my past and I are still directly related.

I remember mailing that letter at the mailbox next to the neighborhood store, scuffing along in the dust at the road edge, wearing Levis, moccasins, and a brown khaki work shirt. My moustache had become a full beard and my hair covered the top of my ears. I was both frightened and exhilarated. The last barrier was down. Henceforth, I was my own soldier advancing in my own kind of war.

My adrenaline didn't diminish until long after midnight. Lying in my bed, I pictured the penitentiary as a very cold and lonely place that I planned to endure for the sake of us all.

4. The CIA Assesses "Restless Youth" (1968)*

Drawing inspiration from revolutionaries like Cuba's Che Guevara and China's Mao Zedong, students across the world—from Paris to Damascus, Mexico City to Prague—took to the streets in 1968. Though reacting to vastly different national circumstances, the youth movements shared a profound disillusionment with established authority. To U.S. President Lyndon Johnson, the escalation of student protests suggested the possibility of Communist influence, a charge he asked the CIA to investigate. What does the following report conclude about the origins and objectives of radical youth movements? How do the movements in other countries compare with the student protests in the United States?

Youthful dissidence, involving students and non-students alike, is a world-wide phenomenon. It is shaped in every instance by local conditions, but nonetheless there are striking similarities, especially in the more advanced countries. As the underdeveloped countries progress, these similarities are likely to become even more widespread.

A truly radical concept of industrial society and its institutions prompts much of the dissidence—but it, alone, does not explain the degree to which young agitators have won a wide following in such countries as France, the Federal Republic and the United States.

Some measure of dissidence is traceable to generational conflict, psychic problems, etc. But most owes its dimension to the number of students, a profusion of issues, and skillful leadership techniques.

The proximate causes are rooted in the university; they are chosen for their appeal, for the support they will engender. However, the confidence of the agitators in the likelihood of their being able to expand a limited protest rests—sometimes fragilely—on a growing base of student cynicism with respect to the relevance of social institutions and to the apparent gap between promise and performance.

Perhaps most disturbing of all is the growing belief of the militants—and many less committed young people—in the efficacy of violence as a political device....

---

*Jeremi Suri, ed., *The Global Revolutions of 1968: A Norton Casebook in History* (New York: W. W. Norton & Company, 2006), pp. 217–236.

Because of the revolution in communications, the ease of travel, and the evolution of society everywhere, student behavior never again will resemble what it was when education was reserved for the elite. The presence in the universities of thousands of lower- and lower-middle-class students has resulted in an unprecedented demand for relevant instruction. Today's students are a self-conscious group; they communicate effectively with each other outside of any institutional framework, read the same books and savor similar experiences. Increasingly, they have come to recognize what they take to be a community of interests. This view is likely to influence their future political conduct and to shape the demands they make of government....

A student in the US, France, Brazil, or Japan probably does identify with his peers in other countries and is more likely to share their values and feel that their problems are his. Because of the accessibility of foreign-language books and newspapers and the type of *avant-garde* art and films which are so popular in most university communities, there are few, if any, cultural impediments to this kind of identification....

There is no convincing evidence of control, manipulation, sponsorship, or significant financial support of student dissidents by any international Communist authority. In fact, the Russians and Chinese have received precious little for the time and money they have spent on cultivating Free World youth. The most vocal of the dissidents have been wary of being caught up in any of the international youth organizations controlled by Moscow. Self-styled Marxists and admirers of Ho Chi Minh, the dissidents are contemptuous of the neanderthal leaderships entrenched in most national Communist parties, including the CP/USA.

Thought Provokers

1. Was the Cuban missile crisis a turning point in the Cold War? Who actually "won" the confrontation over the missiles? Was President Kennedy's diplomacy in the crisis courageous or foolhardy?
2. In what ways was Lyndon Johnson an innovative political leader? What did the Great Society program owe to the New Deal? Can the United States afford the kinds of programs that Johnson dreamed of?
3. Was Martin Luther King, Jr., a "radical"? Would there have been a civil rights movement in the 1950s and 1960s without him? What motivated the sit-ins and Freedom Rides? What did they accomplish? What conditions are necessary for nonviolence to succeed as a political technique? Why did some African Americans reject King's call for nonviolence in the civil rights movement? Who deserves more credit for the civil rights advances of the 1960s, Martin Luther King or Lyndon Baines Johnson?
4. Why did the United States become involved in Vietnam? Why did it fight the war in the gradually escalating way that it did? Why did the war last so long? What distinguished the Vietnam War from previous American interventions abroad? Were events like the My Lai massacre preventable? In what ways did the Vietnam imbroglio alter the U.S. role in the world?
5. Why did a radical movement well up worldwide in the 1960s? How truly radical was it? What legacy have the 1960s movements left behind? Are the issues on which they focused dead?

38

Challenges to the Postwar Order, 1973–1980

I pledge to you the new leadership will end the war and win the peace in the Pacific.

Presidential Candidate Richard Nixon, 1968

Prologue: Richard Nixon, elected by a minority of voters in the bitterly contested election of 1968, gave his highest priority to foreign affairs, especially to ending the war in Vietnam. He sought "peace with honor"—a combination that took him nearly five years to achieve. When Nixon sent U.S. troops into Cambodia in the spring of 1970, the nation's already seething college campuses erupted. Nixon weathered the subsequent storm of unpopularity and finally succeeded in extricating the United States from Vietnam. In the process, he established diplomatic contact with the People's Republic of China and initiated a period of détente, or relaxed relations, with the Soviet Union. Nixon also had the opportunity to appoint several Supreme Court justices. He expected them to share his conservative judicial philosophy, which emphasized "law and order" and frowned on the kind of judicial activism on behalf of minorities that had characterized the Court in the 1950s and 1960s under Chief Justice Earl Warren. Nixon handily won reelection in 1972 but was soon ensnared in a controversy concerning his role in a break-in at the Democratic party offices in Washington's Watergate apartment complex. Threatened with formal impeachment and trial, Nixon resigned the presidency in August 1974. Gerald Ford, who had been appointed vice president after Nixon's original running mate, Spiro Agnew, had resigned amid scandalous accusations, became the first person ever elevated to the presidency solely by act of Congress. He speedily lost the public's confidence when he extended an unconditional pardon to the fallen Nixon. Little-known Jimmy Carter of Georgia, promising that he "would never lie," capitalized on public disgust with Nixon and Ford to win the presidency in 1976.

A. Winding Down the Vietnam War

1. Nixon's Grand Plan in Foreign Policy (1968–1969)*

Richard Nixon built his prepresidential career on a strong reputation as a hawkish cold warrior—and thus, ironically, he was in a particularly favorable position to

---

*From *RN: The Memoirs of Richard Nixon, Volume I*, by Richard M. Nixon. Copyright © 1978 by Richard Nixon.

bring some thaw to the chilly Cold War. As a certified conservative, he had a freedom of maneuver that would not have been available to a liberal Democrat, who would have been vulnerable to criticism from the very right wing that Nixon could easily control. Nixon shrewdly saw the implications of the split between China and the Soviet Union that had developed in the 1960s, and he was determined to turn that split to U.S. advantage. In the following passage from his memoirs, Nixon describes his thinking about global affairs as he embarked upon his presidency. What does he mean when he says that "the key to a Vietnam settlement lay in Moscow and Peking rather than in Hanoi"?

In the late 1940s and during the 1950s I had seen communism spread to China and other parts of Asia, and to Africa and South America, under the camouflage of parties of socialist revolution, or under the guise of wars of national liberation. And, finally, during the 1960s I had watched as Peking and Moscow became rivals for the role of leadership in the Communist world.

Never once in my career have I doubted that the Communists mean it when they say that their goal is to bring the world under Communist control. Nor have I ever forgotten Whittaker Chambers's chilling comment that when he left communism, he had the feeling he was leaving the winning side. But unlike some anticommunists who think we should refuse to recognize or deal with the Communists lest in doing so we imply or extend an ideological respectability to their philosophy and their system, I have always believed that we can and must communicate and, when possible, negotiate with Communist nations. They are too powerful to ignore. We must always remember that they will never act out of altruism, but only out of self-interest. Once this is understood, it is more sensible—and also safer—to communicate with the Communists than it is to live in icy cold-war isolation or confrontation. In fact, in January 1969 I felt the relationship between the United States and the Soviet Union would probably be the single most important factor in determining whether the world would live at peace during and after my administration.

I felt that we had allowed ourselves to get in a disadvantageous position vis-à-vis the Soviets. They had a major presence in the Arab states of the Middle East, while we had none; they had Castro in Cuba; since the mid-1960s they had supplanted the Chinese as the principal military suppliers of North Vietnam; and except for Tito's Yugoslavia they still totally controlled Eastern Europe and threatened the stability and security of Western Europe.

There were, however, a few things in our favor. The most important and interesting was the Soviet split with China. There was also some evidence of growing, albeit limited, independence in some of the satellite nations. There were indications that the Soviet leaders were becoming interested in reaching an agreement on strategic arms limitation. They also appeared to be ready to hold serious talks on the anomalous situation in Berlin, which, almost a quarter century after the war had ended, was still a divided city and a constant source of tension, not just between the Soviets and the United States, but also between the Soviets and Western Europe. We sensed that they were looking for a face-saving formula that would lessen the risk of confrontation in the Mideast. And we had some solid evidence that they were anxious for an expansion of trade.

It was often said that the key to a Vietnam settlement lay in Moscow and Peking rather than in Hanoi. Without continuous and massive aid from either or both of the Communist giants, the leaders of North Vietnam would not have been able to carry on the war for more than a few months. Thanks to the Sino-Soviet split, however, the North Vietnamese had been extremely successful in playing off the Soviets and the Chinese against each other by turning support for their war effort into a touchstone of Communist orthodoxy and a requisite for keeping North Vietnam from settling into the opposing camp in the struggle for domination within the Communist world. This situation became a strain, particularly for the Soviets. Aside from wanting to keep Hanoi from going over to Peking, Moscow had little stake in the outcome of the North Vietnamese cause, especially as it increasingly worked against Moscow's own major interests vis-à-vis the United States. While I understood that the Soviets were not entirely free agents where their support for North Vietnam was concerned, I nonetheless planned to bring maximum pressure to bear on them in this area.

I was sure that [Soviet leaders] Brezhnev and Kosygin had been no more anxious for me to win in 1968 than Khrushchev had been in 1960. The prospect of having to deal with a Republican administration—and a Nixon administration at that—undoubtedly caused anxiety in Moscow. In fact, I suspected that the Soviets might have counseled the North Vietnamese to offer to begin the Paris talks in the hope that the bombing halt would tip the balance to [Hubert] Humphrey in the election—and if that was their strategy, it had almost worked....

During the transition period Kissinger and I developed a new policy for dealing with the Soviets. Since U.S.-Soviet interests as the world's two competing nuclear superpowers were so widespread and overlapping, it was unrealistic to separate or compartmentalize areas of concern. Therefore we decided to link progress in such areas of Soviet concern as strategic arms limitation and increased trade with progress in areas that were important to us—Vietnam, the Mideast, and Berlin. This concept became known as linkage.

Lest there be any doubt of my seriousness in pursuing this policy, I purposely announced it at my first press conference when asked a question about starting SALT [Strategic Arms Limitation Talks] talks. I said, "What I want to do is to see to it that we have strategic arms talks in a way and at a time that will promote, if possible, progress on outstanding political problems at the same time—for example, on the problem of the Mideast and on other outstanding problems in which the United States and the Soviet Union acting together can serve the cause of peace."

Linkage was something uncomfortably new and different for the Soviets, and I was not surprised when they bridled at the restraints it imposed on our relationship. It would take almost two years of patient and hard-nosed determination on our part before they would accept that linkage with what we wanted from them was the price they would have to pay for getting any of the things they wanted from us.

We made our first contacts with the Soviets during the transition period. In mid-December Kissinger met with a Soviet UN diplomat who was, as we knew, actually an intelligence officer. I wanted it made clear that I was not taken in by any of the optimistic rhetoric that had characterized so much of recent Soviet-American relations. Kissinger therefore stated that while the tendency during the last few years had been to emphasize how much our two nations supposedly had in common, the Nixon administration felt that there were real and substantial differences between us and that an effort to lessen the tension created by these differences should be the central focus of our relationship. Kissinger also said that I did not want a pre-inauguration summit meeting and that if they held one with Johnson I would have to state publicly that I would not be bound by it. Nothing was heard about this summit project.

We received a prompt reply from Moscow. Our UN contact reported that the Soviet leadership was "not pessimistic" because of the election of a Republican President. He said that the Soviet leadership had expressed an interest in knowing if I desired to "open channels of communication." It was with this in mind that I said in my inaugural address, "After a period of confrontation, we are entering an era of negotiation. Let all nations know that during this administration our lines of communication will be open."

2. Nixon's Address to the Nation (1973)*

President Nixon had inherited the unwanted Vietnam War, but he kept the bloodshed going for more than four years—longer than the United States' participation in either World War I or World War II. When the North Vietnamese balked at the peace table in Paris in 1972, Nixon launched his awesome "Christmas blitz" against the North Vietnamese capital, thus prompting the so-called cease-fire that Nixon hailed as "peace with honor." By its terms, the United States retrieved some 560 prisoners of war and withdrew its remaining 27,000 troops. The South Vietnamese government of dictatorial President Thieu was permitted to receive replacements of weapons from the United States, as well as other kinds of nontroop support. Yet the North Vietnamese forces still occupied about 30 percent of South Vietnam, and they were allowed to retain there about 145,000 troops that were in a position to renew hostilities. Such was the "honorable" peace that North Vietnam immediately flouted and that vanished in about two years. To what extent does Nixon gloss over the truth in this section of his televised report to the nation on January 23, 1973?

Good evening. I have asked for this radio and television time tonight for the purpose of announcing that we today have concluded an agreement to end the war and bring peace with honor in Vietnam and in Southeast Asia....

We must recognize that ending the war is only the first step toward building the peace. All parties must now see to it that this is a peace that lasts, and also a peace that heals, and a peace that not only ends the war in Southeast Asia, but contributes to the prospects of peace in the whole world.

This will mean that the terms of the agreement must be scrupulously adhered to. We shall do everything the agreement requires of us and we shall expect the other parties to do everything it requires of them. We shall also expect other interested nations to help insure that the agreement is carried out and peace is maintained.

As this long and very difficult war ends, I would like to address a few special words to each of those who have been parties in the conflict.

Weekly Compilation of Presidential Documents 9 (1973): 43–44.

First, to the people and Government of South Vietnam: By your courage, by your sacrifice, you have won the precious right to determine your own future and you have developed the strength to defend that right. We look forward to working with you in the future, friends in peace as we have been allies in war.

To the leaders of North Vietnam: As we have ended the war through negotiations, let us now build a peace of reconciliation. For our part, we are prepared to make a major effort to help achieve that goal. But just as reciprocity was needed to end the war, so, too, will it be needed to build and strengthen the peace.

To the other major powers [China, the Soviet Union] that have been involved even indirectly: Now is the time for mutual restraint so that the peace we have achieved can last.

And finally, to all of you who are listening, the American people: Your steadfastness in supporting our insistence on peace with honor has made peace with honor possible. I know that you would not have wanted that peace jeopardized. With our secret negotiations at the sensitive stage they were in during this recent period, for me to have discussed publicly our efforts to secure peace would not only have violated our understanding with North Vietnam, it would have seriously harmed and possibly destroyed the chances for peace. Therefore, I know that you now can understand why, during these past several weeks, I have not made any public statements about those efforts.

The important thing was not to talk about peace, but to get peace and to get the right kind of peace. This we have done.

Now that we have achieved an honorable agreement, let us be proud that America did not settle for a peace that would have betrayed our allies, that would have abandoned our prisoners of war, or that would have ended the war for us but would have continued the war for the 50 million people of Indochina. Let us be proud of the 2½ million young Americans who served in Vietnam, who served with honor and distinction in one of the most selfless enterprises in the history of nations. And let us be proud of those who sacrificed, who gave their lives so that the people of South Vietnam might live in freedom and so that the world might live in peace.

3. No Peace with Honor (1973)*

The Nixon Administration touted its plan for ending the Vietnam War as "peace with honor," but many citizens saw little prospect for lasting peace and even less for honor in the legacy of the war. In the document below, what does former U.S. Foreign Service officer Zygmunt Nagorsky see as the most troublesome aspects of the conduct of the war and its messy conclusion?

To the Editor:

Somehow the tragedy of our present Vietnam involvement has not yet been fully comprehended by the American people. The President's lonely decision to bring peace with honor through massive bombings in Southeast Asia has so far brought no peace but only a good deal of dishonor for America.

---

*From Zygmunt Nagorsky, Jr., Letter to the Editor, *The New York Times*, January 14, 1973.

In Vietnam we are becoming a symbol of death and destruction. In Europe, our oldest allies are bewildered, shocked and more and more detached from their traditional cross-Atlantic ties. At home most of us feel helpless and frustrated.

It was at one time very comfortable to be on the other side of the accusing line and to look at the Germans, the Russians and the Japanese with a feeling of reassuring innocence.

Today, to be an American is to carry with it a burden of national shame. It is hard for the native-born. It seems to be even harder for someone like myself, who opted to be an American and who has lived through other types of bombing.

Can anyone within our democratic system do anything? Or should we just be silent, march, protest, write letters to editors and pray for sanity to be restored at the decision-making center of the United States?

Where are the men and women who throughout American history risked their political careers in order to stand for principles? Where are the high-placed Government officials who should be resigning in protest? Where is the cry of anguish from the Congressional benches?

How can men and women working within the body of American politics allow such erosion of the democratic process by permitting one lonely man to shield himself behind the screen of the Presidency and to make adverse decisions affecting all of us? Is there a death wish somewhere in the nation, a death wish leading toward one-man rule in a country in which the process of democratic institutions was at one time the envy and pride of foes and friends alike.

Zygmunt Nagorsky, Jr.
New York, January 9, 1973

B. The Move to Impeach Nixon

1. The First Article of Impeachment (1974)*

During the Nixon-McGovern campaign of 1972, a bungled burglary had occurred in the Democratic Watergate headquarters in Washington, DC. After Nixon's reelection, evidence turned up that the culprits, with close White House connections, had been working for the Republican Committee for the Re-election of the President (which came to be known as CREEP). A Senate investigating committee uncovered proof that the president had secretly recorded relevant White House conversations on tape. After much foot-dragging and legal obstruction by Nixon, enough of the damning tapes were surrendered to prove beyond a doubt that he had known of the attempted cover-up from an early date and had actively participated in it. After extensive hearings, the House Judiciary Committee voted three articles of impeachment, of which the following, relating to the crime of obstructing justice, was the first. This article was

---

House of Representatives Report No. 93–1305 (House Calendar No. 426; 1974), 93d Cong., 2d sess., pp. 1–2.

approved on July 27, 1974, by a committee vote of twenty-seven to eleven, with all the Democrats being joined by six Republicans. Assuming that these charges were true, did they add up to "high crimes and misdemeanors" as specified by the Constitution?

Article I

In his conduct of the office of President of the United States, Richard M. Nixon, in violation of his constitutional oath faithfully to execute the office of President of the United States and, to the best of his ability, preserve, protect, and defend the Constitution of the United States, and in violation of his constitutional duty to take care that the laws be faithfully executed, has prevented, obstructed, and impeded the administration of justice, in that:

On June 17, 1972, and prior thereto, agents of the Committee for the Re-election of the President committed unlawful entry of the headquarters of the Democratic National Committee in Washington, District of Columbia, for the purpose of securing political intelligence. Subsequent thereto, Richard M. Nixon, using the powers of his high office, engaged personally and through his subordinates and agents, in a course of conduct or plan designed to delay, impede, and obstruct the investigation of such unlawful entry; to cover up, conceal and protect those responsible; and to conceal the existence and scope of other unlawful covert activities.

The means used to implement this course of conduct or plan included one or more of the following:

1. making or causing to be made false or misleading statements to lawfully authorized investigative officers and employees of the United States;

2. withholding relevant and material evidence or information from lawfully authorized investigative officers and employees of the United States;

3. approving, condoning, acquiescing in, and counseling witnesses with respect to the giving of false or misleading statements to lawfully authorized investigative officers and employees of the United States and false or misleading testimony in duly instituted judicial and congressional proceedings;

4. interfering or endeavoring to interfere with the conduct of investigations by the Department of Justice of the United States, the Federal Bureau of Investigation, the Office of Watergate Special Prosecution Force, and Congressional Committees;

5. approving, condoning, and acquiescing in, the surreptitious payment of substantial sums of money for the purpose of obtaining the silence or influencing the testimony of witnesses, potential witnesses or individuals who participated in such unlawful entry and other illegal activities;

6. endeavoring to misuse the Central Intelligence Agency, an agency of the United States;

7. disseminating information received from officers of the Department of Justice of the United States to subjects of investigations conducted by lawfully authorized investigative officers and employees of the United States, for the purpose of aiding and assisting such subjects in their attempts to avoid criminal liability;

8. making false or misleading public statements for the purpose of deceiving the people of the United States into believing that a thorough and complete investigation had been conducted with respect to allegations of misconduct on the part of personnel of the executive branch of the United States and personnel of the Committee for the Re-election of the President, and that there was no involvement of such personnel in such misconduct; or

9. endeavoring to cause prospective defendants, and individuals duly tried and convicted, to expect favored treatment and consideration in return for their silence or false testimony, or rewarding individuals for their silence or false testimony.

In all of this, Richard M. Nixon has acted in a manner contrary to his trust as President and subversive of constitutional government, to the great prejudice of the cause of law and justice and to the manifest injury of the people of the United States.

Wherefore Richard M. Nixon, by such conduct, warrants impeachment and trial, and removal from office.

2. Impeachment as a Partisan Issue (1974)*

The second and third articles of impeachment approved by the House Judiciary Committee related to repeated abuses of presidential power and to prolonged contempt of Congress. The second article passed the committee by a tally of twenty-eight to ten; all the Democrats and seven Republicans voted yea. The third article charged Nixon with contempt of Congress for refusing to comply with eight subpoenas for the White House tapes. It was regarded as the least damaging of the three and failed to gain broad bipartisan backing, squeezing through by a narrow vote of twenty-one to seventeen. Even after his complete disgrace, Nixon had millions of supporters who believed that his removal was unjustified. Following is a part of the minority report of the House committee, signed by ten of its seventeen Republican members and dated August 20, 1974, eleven days after Nixon's formal resignation. What light does it throw on the alleged partisanship of the impeachment move?

Richard Nixon served his country in elective office for the better part of three decades and, in the main, he served it well. Each of the undersigned voted for him, worked for and with him in election campaigns, and supported the major portion of his legislative program during his tenure as President. Even at the risk of seeming paradoxical, since we were prepared to vote for his impeachment on proposed Article I had he not resigned his office, we hope that in the fullness of time it is his accomplishments—and they were many and significant—rather than the conduct to which this Report is addressed for which Richard Nixon is primarily remembered in history.

We know that it has been said, and perhaps some will continue to say, that Richard Nixon was "hounded from office" by his political opponents and media critics. We feel constrained to point out, however, that it was Richard Nixon who impeded the FBI's investigation of the Watergate affair by wrongfully attempting to implicate the Central Intelligence Agency; it was Richard Nixon, who created and preserved the evidence of that transgression and who, *knowing that it had been subpoenaed by this Committee and the Special Prosecutor*, concealed its terrible import, even from his own counsel, until he could do so no longer. And it was a unanimous Supreme Court of the United States which, in an opinion authored by the Chief Justice whom he appointed, ordered Richard Nixon to surrender that evidence to the Special Prosecutor, to further the ends of justice. [Emphasis in original.]

House of Representatives Report No. 93–1305 (House Calendar No. 426; 1974), 93d Cong., 2d sess., p. 361.

The tragedy that finally engulfed Richard Nixon had many facets. One was the very self-inflicted nature of the harm. It is striking that such an able, experienced and perceptive man, whose ability to grasp the global implications of events little noticed by others may well have been unsurpassed by any of his predecessors, should fail to comprehend the damage that accrued daily to himself, his Administration, and to the Nation, as day after day, month after month, he imprisoned the truth about his role in the Watergate cover-up so long and so tightly within the solitude of his Oval Office that it could not be unleashed without destroying his Presidency.

3. Nixon Incriminates Himself (1972)*

By August 5, 1974, much evidence of presidential misconduct and wrongdoing had been uncovered, but where was the high crime? Where was the "smoking pistol"? It finally surfaced on that day, when Nixon, forced by a unanimous decision of the Supreme Court to yield crucial tape recordings, revealed a White House conversation of June 23, 1972. In it the president was heard instructing his chief aide, H. R. Haldeman, to use the Central Intelligence Agency to quash an investigation by the Federal Bureau of Investigation. Obstruction of justice of this type was a clear-cut crime. Support for Nixon in Congress collapsed, and he was faced with the dilemma of resigning or being thrown out of office without retirement benefits amounting to more than $150,000 a year. He wisely chose to announce his resignation on August 8, 1974. How damning is the evidence in the following transcript of the conversations of June 23, 1972?

Transcript of a Recording of a Meeting Between the President and H. R. Haldeman, the Oval Office, June 23, 1972, from 10:04 to 11:39 A.M.

Haldeman. Okay—that's fine. Now, on the investigation, you know, the Democratic break-in thing, we're back to the—in the, the problem area because the FBI is not under control, because [acting director of the FBI Patrick] Gray doesn't exactly know how to control them, and they have, their investigation is now leading into some productive areas, because they've been able to trace the money.... And, and it goes in some directions we don't want it to go. Ah, also there have been some things, like an informant came in off the street to the FBI in Miami, who was a photographer or has a friend who is a photographer who developed some films through this guy, Barker, and the films had pictures of Democratic National Committee letter head documents and things. So I guess, so it's things like that are gonna, that are filtering in. [U.S. Attorney General John] Mitchell came up with yesterday, and [presidential counselor] John Dean analyzed very carefully last night and concludes, concurs now with Mitchell's recommendation that the only way to solve this, and we're set up beautifully to do it, ah, in that and that...the only network that paid any attention to it last night was NBC...they did a massive story on the Cuban...

Statement of Information, Appendix 3, *Hearings Before the Committee on the Judiciary*, House of Representatives, 93d Cong., 2d sess., pursuant to H.R. 803, p. 39.

President. That's right.

Haldeman. ...thing.

President. Right.

Haldeman. That the way to handle this is for us to have [deputy director of the CIA Vernon] Walters call Pat Gray and just say, "Stay the hell out of this...this is ah, business here we don't want you to go any further on it." That's not an unusual development,...

President. Um huh.

Haldeman. ...and, uh, that would take care of it.

President. What about Pat Gray, ah, you mean he doesn't want to?

Haldeman. Pat does want to. He doesn't know how to, and he doesn't have, he doesn't have any basis for doing it. Given this, he will then have the basis. He'll call [assistant director of the FBI] Mark Felt in, and the two of them...and Mark Felt wants to cooperate because...

President. Yeah.

Haldeman. ...he's ambitious...

President. Yeah.

Haldeman. Ah, he'll call him in and say, "We've got the signal from across the river to, to put the hold on this." And that will fit rather well because the FBI agents who are working the case, at this point, feel that's what it is. This is CIA.

President. But they've traced the money to 'em.

Haldeman. Well they have, they've traced to a name, but they haven't gotten to the guy yet.

President. Would it be somebody here?

Haldeman. [GOP fund-raiser] Ken Dahlberg.

President. Who the hell is Ken Dahlberg?

Haldeman. He's ah, he gave $25,000 in Minnesota and ah, the check went directly in to this, to this guy [Watergate burglar, Bernard L.] Barker.

President. Maybe he's a...bum....He didn't get this from the committee though, from [finance chairman for the Committee for the Re-election of the President, Maurice] Stans.

Haldeman. Yeah. It is. It's directly traceable and there's some more through some Texas people in—that went to the Mexican bank which they can also trace to the Mexican bank...they'll get their names today. And [*pause*].

President. Well, I mean, ah, there's no way...I'm just thinking if they don't cooperate, what do they say? They they, they were approached by the Cubans. That's what Dahlberg has to say, the Texans too. Is that the idea?

Haldeman. Well, if they will. But then we're relying on more and more people all the time. That's the problem. And ah, they'll stop if we could, if we take this other step.

President. All right. Fine.

Haldeman. And, and they seem to feel the thing to do is get them to stop?

President. Right, fine.

Haldeman. They say the only way to do that is from White House instructions. And it's got to be to [CIA director, Richard] Helms and, ah, what's his name...? Walters.

President. Walters.

Haldeman. And the proposal would be that Ehrlichman* [*coughs*] and I call them in...

President. All right, fine....

President. You call them in.... Good. Good deal. Play it tough. That's the way they play it and that's the way we are going to play it.

Haldeman. O.K. We'll do it.

President. Yeah, when I saw that news summary item, I of course knew it was a bunch of crap, but I thought, ah, well it's good to have them off on this wild hair thing because when they start bugging us, which they have, we'll know our little boys will not know how to handle it. I hope they will though. You never know. Maybe, you think about it. Good!...When you get in these people...when you get these people in, say: "Look, the problem is that this will open the whole, the whole Bay of Pigs thing, and the President just feels that" ah, without going into the details...don't, don't lie to them to the extent to say there is no involvement, but just say this is sort of a comedy of errors, bizarre, without getting into it, "the President believes that it is going to open the whole Bay of Pigs thing up again. And, ah because these people are plugging for, for keeps and that they should call the FBI in and say that we wish for the country, don't go any further into this case," period!

Haldeman. O.K.

President. That's the way to put it, do it straight....

Transcript of a Recording of a Meeting Between the President and H. R. Haldeman, the Oval Office, June 23, 1972, from 1:04 to 1:13 P.M.

[*Background noise, sound of writing and some unintelligible conversation*]

Haldeman. [*On the phone*] [*Unintelligible*] Where are they? Okay. I'll be up in just a minute.

[*40-second pause, with sounds of writing*]

Haldeman. I see a time way back [*unintelligible*] might find out about that report before we do anything.

President. [*Unintelligible*]

[*35-second pause*]

President. Okay [*unintelligible*] and, ah, just, just postpone the [*unintelligible, with noises*] hearings [*15-second unintelligible, with noises*] and all that garbage. Just say...this is all involved in the Cuban thing, that it's a fiasco, and it's going to make the FB, ah CIA look bad,...and it's likely to blow the whole, uh, Bay of Pigs thing which we think would be very unfortunate for CIA and for the country at this time, and for American foreign policy, and he just better tough it and lay it on them. Isn't that what you...

Haldeman. Yeah, that's, that's the basis we'll do it on and just leave it at that.

President. I don't want them to get any ideas we're doing it because our concern is political.

Haldeman. Right.

---

*John D. Ehrlichman (1925–1999), a special assistant to President Nixon.

President. And at the same time, I wouldn't tell them it is not political…

Haldeman. Right.

President. I would just say "Look, it's because of the Hunt* involvement," just say [*unintelligible, with noise*] sort of thing, the whole cover is, uh, basically this [*unintelligible*].

Haldeman. [*Unintelligible*] Well they've got some pretty good ideas on this need thing.

President. George Shultz did a good paper on that, I read it…

[*Unintelligible voices heard leaving the room*]

4. Nixon Accepts a Presidential Pardon (1974)†

To complicate the Watergate uproar, Vice President Spiro Agnew, facing unrelated criminal charges, had avoided jail by resigning in August 1973. Nixon, pursuant to the Twenty-Fifth Amendment to the Constitution, had chosen as his successor Gerald R. Ford, the House minority leader. For about a month, the nonelected president enjoyed a "honeymoon," which he abruptly ended by granting Nixon "a full, free, and absolute pardon" for "all offenses against the United States which he, Richard Nixon, has committed or may have committed or taken part in" during his presidency. Nixon promptly accepted the pardon but was careful not to confess that he had committed any crimes. Mistakes, indecision, poor judgment, yes—but crimes, no. Yet, as President Ford agreed, testifying before a House Judiciary Committee, acceptance of the pardon is "tantamount to an admission of guilt." Moreover, many of Nixon's admirers felt that he had humbled himself enough by admitting remorse for acts he had committed in the line of duty for what he regarded to be the good of the country. Is Nixon's self-justification convincing?

I have been informed that President Ford has granted me a full and absolute pardon for any charges which might be brought against me for actions taken during the time I was President of the United States.

In accepting this pardon, I hope that his compassionate act will contribute to lifting the burden of Watergate from our country.

Here in California, my perspective on Watergate is quite different than it was while I was embattled in the midst of the controversy, and while I was still subject to the unrelenting daily demands of the presidency itself.

Looking back on what is still in my mind a complex and confusing maze of events, decisions, pressures and personalities, one thing I can see clearly now is that I was wrong in not acting more decisively and more forthrightly in dealing with Watergate, particularly when it reached the stage of judicial proceedings and grew from a political scandal into a national tragedy.

No words can describe the depths of my regret and pain at the anguish my mistakes over Watergate have caused the nation and the presidency—a nation I so deeply love and an institution I so greatly respect.

---

*E. Howard Hunt, a former CIA official who had played a key role in the failed Bay of Pigs invasion in 1961, was one of the men directly implicated in the Watergate burglary.
†*San Francisco Chronicle*, September 9, 1973.

I know many fair-minded people believe that my motivations and action in the Watergate affair were intentionally self-serving and illegal. I now understand how my own mistakes and misjudgments have contributed to that belief and seemed to support it. This burden is the heaviest one of all to bear.

That the way I tried to deal with Watergate was the wrong way is a burden I shall bear for every day of the life that is left to me.

C.   The Cresting of Second-Wave Feminism

1. The National Organization for Women Proclaims the Rebirth of Feminism (1966)*

The publication of Betty Friedan's The Feminine Mystique *in 1963 (p. 731) sparked a new "second-wave" feminist revival, the first concerted effort to advance women's standing in American society since the Nineteenth Amendment had crowned the woman suffrage campaign with success in 1920. One of the main vehicles of the new feminist movement was the National Organization for Women, founded in 1966. What are the guiding assumptions of its original statement of purpose? What tactics and strategies does it advocate?*

We, men and women who hereby constitute ourselves as the National Organization for Women [NOW], believe that the time has come for a new movement toward true equality for all women in America, and toward a fully equal partnership of the sexes, as part of the world-wide revolution of human rights now taking place within and beyond our national borders.

The purpose of NOW is to take action to bring women into full participation in the mainstream of American society now, exercising all the privileges and responsibilities thereof in truly equal partnership with men....

NOW is dedicated to the proposition that women first and foremost are human beings, who, like all other people in our society, must have the chance to develop their fullest human potential....

There is no civil rights movement to speak for women, as there has been for Negroes and other victims of discrimination. The National Organization for Women must therefore begin to speak.

We believe that the power of American law, and the protection guaranteed by the U.S. Constitution to the civil rights of all individuals, must be effectively applied and enforced to isolate and remove patterns of sex discrimination, to ensure equality of opportunity in employment and education, and equality of civil and political rights and responsibilities on behalf of women, as well as for Negroes and other deprived groups....

---

*The National Organization for Women. This is a historical document (1966) and may not reflect the current language or priorities of the organization.

We do not accept the token appointment of a few women to high-level positions in government and industry as a substitute for a serious continuing effort to recruit and advance women according to their individual abilities....

We believe that this nation has a capacity at least as great as other nations, to innovate new social institutions which will enable women to enjoy true equality of opportunity and responsibility in society, without conflict with their responsibilities as mothers and homemakers. In such innovations, America does not lead the Western world, but lags by decades behind many European countries. We do not accept the traditional assumption that a woman has to choose between marriage and motherhood, on the one hand, and serious participation in industry or the professions on the other....Above all, we reject the assumption that these problems are the unique responsibility of each individual woman, rather than a basic social dilemma which society must solve. True equality of opportunity and freedom of choice for women requires such practical and possible innovations as a nationwide network of child-care centers, which will make it unnecessary for women to retire completely from society until their children are grown, and national programs to provide retraining for women who have chosen to care for their own children full time....

We believe that it is as essential for every girl to be educated to her full potential of human ability as it is for every boy—with the knowledge that such education is the key to effective participation in today's economy and that, for a girl as for a boy, education can only be serious where there is expectation that it will be used in society....

We believe that a true partnership between the sexes demands a different concept of marriage, an equitable sharing of the responsibilities of home and children and of the economic burdens of their support. We believe that proper recognition should be given to the economic and social value of homemaking and child care. To these ends, we will seek to open a reexamination of laws and mores governing marriage and divorce, for we believe that the current state of "half-equality" between the sexes discriminates against both men and women, and is the cause of much unnecessary hostility between the sexes.

We believe that women must now exercise their political rights and responsibilities as American citizens....[T]hey must demand representation according to their numbers in the regularly constituted party committees—at local, state, and national levels—and in the informal power structure, participating fully in the selection of candidates and political decision-making, and running for office themselves.

In the interests of the human dignity of women, we will protest and endeavor to change the false image of women now prevalent in the mass media, and in the texts, ceremonies, laws, and practices of our major social institutions. Such images perpetuate contempt for women by society and by women for themselves.

2. The Case for the Equal Rights Amendment (1970)*

The Equal Rights Amendment, or ERA, declared simply, "Equality of rights under the law shall not be denied or abridged by the United States or by any State on account

---

*Citizen's Advisory Council on the Status of Women, "Memorandum on the Proposed Equal Rights Amendment, March 26, 1970," *Congressional Record*, 91st Cong., 2d sess., pp. 9684–9688.

of sex." First put forth in the 1920s, the proposed ERA was ratified by a two-thirds vote of the House of Representatives in 1970 and by the same majority of the Senate in 1972. But the ERA eventually fell short of ratification by the requisite three-fourths of all the states, and it quietly disappeared from consideration in the 1980s. For a time the ERA, along with abortion rights, was a defining issue for many feminists. In the pro-ERA statement to Congress reprinted here, what arguments are brought to bear in favor of the ERA? How persuasive are they?

Numerous distinctions based on sex still exist in the law. For example:

1. State laws placing special restrictions on women with respect to hours of work and weightlifting on the job;

2. State laws prohibiting women from working in certain occupations;

3. Laws and practices operating to exclude women from State colleges and universities (including higher standards required for women applicants to institutions of higher learning and in the administration of scholarship programs);

4. Discrimination in employment by State and local governments;

5. Dual pay schedules for men and women public school teachers;

6. State laws providing for alimony to be awarded, under certain circumstances, to ex-wives but not to ex-husbands;

7. State laws placing special restrictions on the legal capacity of married women or on their right to establish a legal domicile;

8. State laws that require married women but not married men to go through a formal procedure and obtain court approval before they may engage in an independent business;

9. Social Security and other social benefits legislation which give greater benefits to one sex than to the other;

10. Discriminatory preferences, based on sex, in child custody cases;

11. State laws providing that the father is the natural guardian of the minor children;

12. Different ages for males and females in (a) child labor laws, (b) age for marriage, (c) cutoff of the right to parental support, and (d) juvenile court jurisdiction;

13. Exclusion of women from the requirements of the Military Selective Service Act of 1967;

14. Special sex-based exemptions for women in selection of State juries;

15. Heavier criminal penalties for female offenders than for male offenders committing the same crime.

Although it is possible that these and other discriminations might eventually be corrected by legislation, legislative remedies are *not* adequate substitutes for fundamental constitutional protection against discrimination. Any class of persons (i.e., women) which cannot successfully invoke the protection of the Constitution against discriminatory treatment is by definition comprised of "second class citizens" and is inferior in the eyes of law....

Following is a five-point analysis of the impact the equal rights amendment will have on the various types of Federal and State laws which distinguish on the basis of sex:

1. *Strike the Words of Sex Identification and Apply the Law to Both Sexes.* Where the law confers a benefit, privilege or obligation of citizenship, such would be extended to the other sex, i.e., the effect of the amendment would be to strike the words of sex

identification. Thus, such laws would not be rendered unconstitutional but would be extended to apply to both sexes by operation of the amendment, in the same way that laws pertaining to voting were extended to Negroes and women under the 15th and 19th amendments....

Any expression of preference in the law for the mother in child custody cases would be extended to both parents (as against claims of third parties). Children are entitled to support from *both* parents under the existing laws of most States....

2. *Laws Rendered Unconstitutional by the Amendment.* Where a law restricts or denies opportunities of women or men, as the case may be, the effect of the equal rights amendment would be to render such laws unconstitutional.

Examples are: the exclusion of women from State universities or other public schools; State laws placing special restrictions on the hours of work for women or the weights women may lift on the job; laws prohibiting women from working in certain occupations, such as bartenders; laws placing special restrictions on the legal capacity of married women, such as making contracts or establishing a legal domicile.

3. *Removal of Age Distinctions Based on Sex.* Some laws which apply to both sexes make an age distinction by sex and thereby discriminate as to persons between the ages specified for males and females. Under the foregoing analysis, the ages specified in such laws would be equalized by the amendment by extending the benefits, privileges or opportunities under the law to both sexes. This would mean that as to some such laws, the *lower* age would apply to both sexes....

4. *Laws Which Could Not Possibly Apply to Both Sexes Because of the Difference in Reproductive Capacity.* Laws which, as a practical matter, can apply to only one sex no matter how they are phrased, such as laws providing maternity benefits and laws prohibiting rape, would not be affected by the amendment. The extension of these laws to both sexes would be purely academic since such laws would not apply differently if they were phrased in terms of both sexes. In these situations, the terminology of sex identification is of no consequence.

5. *Separation of the Sexes.* Separation of the sexes by law would be forbidden under the amendment except in situations where the separation is shown to be necessary because of an overriding and compelling public interest and does not deny individual rights and liberties.

For example, in our present culture the recognition of the right to privacy would justify separate restroom facilities in public buildings.

As shown above, the amendment would not change the substance of existing laws, except that those which restrict and deny opportunities to women would be rendered unconstitutional under the standard of point two of the analysis. In all other cases, the laws presently on the books would simply be equalized, and this includes the entire body of family law.

3. The Supreme Court Upholds Abortion Rights (1973)*

In 1973 the Supreme Court reignited the abortion debate when it ruled in Roe v. Wade that state laws banning abortion were an unconstitutional infringement on

---

*Roe v. Wade, 410 U.S. 113 (1973).

a woman's right to privacy. While feminists celebrated their landmark victory, conservative religious organizations rallied for a protracted fight to reverse the Court's ruling. How did the justices use the "right to privacy" to navigate the thorny moral, medical, and societal questions surrounding the abortion debate? Does the decision leave any room for legal restrictions on abortion?

We forthwith acknowledge our awareness of the sensitive and emotional nature of the abortion controversy, of the vigorous opposing views, even among physicians, and of the deep and seemingly absolute convictions that the subject inspires. One's philosophy, one's experiences, one's exposure to the raw edges of human existence, one's religious training, one's attitudes toward life and family and their values, and the moral standards one establishes and seeks to observe, are all likely to influence and to color one's thinking and conclusions about abortion.

In addition, population growth, pollution, poverty, and racial overtones tend to complicate and not to simplify the problem.

Our task, of course, is to resolve the issue by constitutional measurement, free of emotion and of predilection. . . .

The principal thrust of appellant's attack on the Texas statutes is that they improperly invade a right, said to be possessed by the pregnant woman, to choose to terminate her pregnancy. Appellant would discover this right in the concept of personal "liberty" embodied in the Fourteenth Amendment's Due Process Clause; or in personal, marital, familial, and sexual privacy said to be protected by the Bill of Rights. . . .

The Constitution does not explicitly mention any right of privacy. In a line of decisions, however, . . . the Court has recognized that a right of personal privacy, or a guarantee of certain areas or zones of privacy, does exist under the Constitution. . . .

This right of privacy, whether it be founded in the Fourteenth Amendment's concept of personal liberty and restrictions upon state action, as we feel it is, or, as the District Court determined, in the Ninth Amendment's reservation of rights to the people, is broad enough to encompass a woman's decision whether or not to terminate her pregnancy. The detriment that the State would impose upon the pregnant woman by denying this choice altogether is apparent. Specific and direct harm medically diagnosable even in early pregnancy may be involved. Maternity, or additional offspring, may force upon the woman a distressful life and future. Psychological harm may be imminent. Mental and physical health may be taxed by child care. There is also the distress, for all concerned, associated with the unwanted child, and there is the problem of bringing a child into a family already unable, psychologically and otherwise, to care for it. In other cases, as in this one, the additional difficulties and continuing stigma of unwed motherhood may be involved. All these are factors the woman and her responsible physician necessarily will consider in consultation.

On the basis of elements such as these, appellant and some *amici* argue that the woman's right is absolute and that she is entitled to terminate her pregnancy at whatever time, in whatever way, and for whatever reason she alone chooses. With this we do not agree. Appellant's arguments that Texas either has no valid interest at all in regulating the abortion decision, or no interest strong enough to support any limitation upon the woman's sole determination, are unpersuasive. The Court's decisions recognizing a right of privacy also acknowledge that some state regulation in areas protected by that right is appropriate. As noted above, a State may properly assert important interests in safeguarding health, in maintaining medical standards, and in protecting potential life. At some point in pregnancy, these respective interests become sufficiently compelling to sustain regulation of the factors that govern the abortion decision. The privacy right involved, therefore, cannot be said to be absolute....

We, therefore, conclude that the right of personal privacy includes the abortion decision, but that this right is not unqualified, and must be considered against important state interests in regulation.

4. Phyllis Schlafly Upholds Traditional Gender Roles (1977)*

The feminist upsurge of the 1970s provoked a backlash, not all of it from men. Phyllis Schlafly, a prominent conservative, emerged as one of the most critical opponents of the new feminists' agenda, especially the ERA. In the selection that follows, what are Schlafly's principal objections to the feminist position? How does she conceive of the "Positive Woman"? What differences does she see between men and women?

The first requirement for the acquisition of power by the Positive Woman is to understand the differences between men and women. Your outlook on life, your faith, your behavior, your potential for fulfillment, all are determined by the parameters of your original premise. The Positive Woman starts with the assumption that the world is her oyster. She rejoices in the creative capability within her body and the power potential of her mind and spirit. She understands that men and women are different, and that those very differences provide the key to her success as a person and fulfillment as a woman.

The women's liberationist, on the other hand, is imprisoned by her own negative view of herself and of her place in the world around her. This view of women was most succinctly expressed in an advertisement designed by the principal women's liberationist organization, the National Organization for Women (NOW), and run in many magazines and newspapers and as spot announcements on many television stations. The advertisement showed a darling curlyheaded girl with the caption: "This healthy, normal baby has a handicap. She was born female."

This is the self-articulated dog-in-the-manger, chip-on-the-shoulder, fundamental dogma of the women's liberation movement. Someone—it is not clear who, perhaps God, perhaps the "Establishment," perhaps a conspiracy of male chauvinist pigs—dealt women a foul blow by making them female. It becomes necessary, therefore, for women to agitate and demonstrate and hurl demands on society in order to wrest from an oppressive male-dominated social structure the status that has been wrongfully denied to women through the centuries....

The second dogma of the women's liberationists is that, of all the injustices perpetuated upon women through the centuries, the most oppressive is the cruel fact that women have babies and men do not. Within the confines of the women's liberationist ideology, therefore, the abolition of this overriding inequality of women becomes the primary goal. This goal must be achieved at any and all costs—to the

---

*From Phyllis Schlafly, *The Power of the Positive Woman*, pp. 11–19. Copyright © 1977.

woman herself, to the baby, to the family, and to society. Women must be made equal to men in their ability *not* to become pregnant and *not* to be expected to care for babies they may bring into the world.

This is why women's liberationists are compulsively involved in the drive to make abortion and child-care centers for all women, regardless of religion or income, both socially acceptable and government-financed. Former Congresswoman Bella Abzug has defined the goal: "to enforce the constitutional right of females to terminate pregnancies that they do not wish to continue."

If man is targeted as the enemy, and the ultimate goal of women's liberation is independence from men and the avoidance of pregnancy and its consequences, then lesbianism is logically the highest form in the ritual of women's liberation. Many, such as [feminist author] Kate Millett, come to this conclusion, although many others do not.

The Positive Woman will never travel that dead-end road. It is self-evident to the Positive Woman that the female body with its baby-producing organs was not designed by a conspiracy of men but by the Divine Architect of the human race. Those who think it is unfair that women have babies, whereas men cannot, will have to take up their complaint with God because no other power is capable of changing that fundamental fact....

The third basic dogma of the women's liberation movement is that there is no difference between male and female except the sex organs, and that all those physical, cognitive, and emotional differences you *think* are there, are merely the result of centuries of restraints imposed by a male-dominated society and sex-stereotyped schooling. The role imposed on women is, by definition, inferior, according to the women's liberationists.

The Positive Woman knows that, while there are some physical competitions in which women are better (and can command more money) than men, including those that put a premium on grace and beauty, such as figure skating, the superior physical strength of males over females in competitions of strength, speed, and short-term endurance is beyond rational dispute....

The women's liberationists and their dupes who try to tell each other that the sexual drive of men and women is really the same, and that it is only societal restraints that inhibit women from an equal desire, and equal enjoyment, and an equal freedom from the consequences, are doomed to frustration forever. It just isn't so, and pretending cannot make it so. The differences are not a woman's weakness but her strength....

The Positive Woman recognizes the fact that, when it comes to sex, women are simply not the equal of men. The sexual drive of men is much stronger than that of women. That is how the human race was designed in order that it might perpetuate itself....

The differences between men and women are also emotional and psychological. Without woman's innate maternal instinct, the human race would have died out centuries ago. There is nothing so helpless in all earthly life as the newborn infant. It will die within hours if not cared for. Even in the most primitive, uneducated societies, women have always cared for their newborn babies. They didn't need any schooling to teach them how. They didn't need any welfare workers to tell them it is their social obligation. Even in societies to whom such concepts as "ought," "social responsibility," and "compassion for the helpless" were unknown, mothers cared for their new babies.

Why? Because caring for a baby serves the natural maternal need of a woman. Although not nearly so total as the baby's need, the woman's need is nonetheless real.

The overriding psychological need of a woman is to love something alive. A baby fulfills this need in the lives of most women. If a baby is not available to fill that need, women search for a baby-substitute. This is the reason why women have traditionally gone into teaching and nursing careers. They are doing what comes naturally to the female psyche. The schoolchild or the patient of any age provides an outlet for a woman to express her natural maternal need....

Finally, women are different from men in dealing with the fundamentals of life itself. Men are philosophers, women are practical, and 'twas ever thus. Men may philosophize about how life began and where we are heading; women are concerned about feeding the kids today. No woman would ever, as Karl Marx did, spend years reading political philosophy in the British Museum while her child starved to death. Women don't take naturally to a search for the intangible and the abstract. The Positive Woman knows who she is and where she is going, and she will reach her goal because the longest journey starts with a very practical first step.

D. Cartooning the Energy Crisis (1974)

On October 15, 1973, the Organization of Petroleum Exporting Countries (OPEC) sent shock waves through the global economy when it declared an oil embargo against the United States and its allies. Deeply unsettled by slackening oil prices, the OPEC powers saw the embargo as an opportunity to boost oil revenues while punishing the United States for its ongoing support for Israel in the Yom Kippur War. The effect on American consumers was almost immediate—widespread shortages resulted in higher prices, long lines, and eventual rationing. The following cartoons illustrate competing perspectives on the underlying causes of the energy crisis. Where does each of the cartoons place the ultimate blame?

"I blame the billions in the 3rd world, wanting
to get what we've got!"

Alfred Buescher 1974/Chicago Defender Newspaper.

Thought Provokers

1. What was the connection between détente and the end of the Vietnam War? Did Nixon's policies toward the Soviet Union and China mark a fundamental reorientation in U.S. foreign policy, or were they simply a convenient maneuver to extricate the United States from the Indochina war?

2. Why was the resolution to impeach President Nixon passed? What exactly did it name as the grounds for impeachment? Nixon later said that he gave his enemies a sword and they cut him down with it. Is that an accurate description of what happened? Should a president be forgiven for lying to the public under some circumstances?

3. How did "second-wave" feminism compare with the feminist movements of the nineteenth and early twentieth centuries? Why did abortion rights loom so large on the feminist agenda? It has been argued that women are the social group most disrupted by the demands of modernity. Comment.

4. In what ways did the energy crisis of the 1970s foreshadow the global energy issues of the following century?

39

The Resurgence of Conservatism, 1980–1992

> While [communists] preach the supremacy of the state, declare its omnipotence over individual man, and predict its eventual domination of all peoples on the Earth, they are the focus of evil in the modern world.

> *President Ronald Reagan, March 8, 1983*

Prologue: Ronald Reagan, the most conservative president in half a century, emerged victorious in the election of 1980. He set out immediately to implement a virtual revolution in U.S. politics. He attacked head-on the big government legacy of the New Deal and the Great Society. He slashed the federal budget for social programs and induced Congress to pass a sweeping tax cut. He simultaneously called for massive increases in defense spending, and federal budget deficits soared to nearly $200 billion a year in the mid-1980s. But "Reaganomics" did slay the ogre of inflation that had stalked the economy for more than a decade. Reagan took a hard line with the Soviet Union and announced a major shift in U.S. strategic doctrine in 1983, when he called for the construction of a space-based defense system against intercontinental ballistic missiles. Jolted, the Soviets made the abandonment of this so-called Star Wars scheme the precondition for any further discussion of arms control. In Central America, Reagan struggled against congressional opposition to send aid to rebels seeking to overthrow the leftist government in Nicaragua. The Reagan administration's frustrations over congressional opposition to its Central American policies led to the scandalous Iran-Contra affair. Meanwhile, new Soviet leader Mikhail Gorbachev undertook some dramatic initiatives that seemed to spell an end to the Cold War—or at least a truce. Triumphantly reelected in 1984, Reagan embraced some emotional social issues, such as prayer in the schools and the antiabortion crusade. He found support among many fundamentalist religious groups, as well as among a group of intellectuals known as neoconservatives. These same backers helped George H. W. Bush win the White House in 1988. Bush presided over the collapse of communism, won a decisive war against a menacing dictator in Iraq, and lost his bid for reelection. For those who wondered how such a thing could happen, the Democrats had a simple answer: "It's the economy, stupid."

A. A Philosophy for Neoconservatism

1. Ronald Reagan Sees "A Time for Choosing" (1964)*

In 1964, former Hollywood actor and General Electric spokesman Ronald Reagan catapulted himself to the center of the conservative movement with a nationally televised address on behalf of Republican presidential candidate Barry Goldwater. Though Goldwater lost his campaign, Reagan's rousing oratory earned him the 1966 gubernatorial nomination in California, a race he won handily. What core principles does Reagan lay out in the following passage? How do his arguments compare with those made by later conservative thinkers?

[T]his idea that government is beholden to the people, that it has no other source of power except the sovereign people, is still the newest and most unique idea in all the long history of man's relation to man. This is the issue of this election. Whether we believe in our capacity for self-government or whether we abandon the American Revolution and confess that a little intellectual elite in a far-distant capital can plan our lives for us better than we can plan them ourselves.

You and I are told increasingly that we have to choose between a left or right, but I would like to suggest that there is no such thing as a left or right. There is only an up or down—up to man's age-old dream—the ultimate in individual freedom consistent with law and order—or down to the ant heap of totalitarianism, and regardless of their sincerity, their humanitarian motives, those who would trade our freedom for security have embarked on this downward course....

For three decades we have sought to solve the problems of unemployment through government planning, and the more the plans fail, the more the planners plan. The latest is the Area Redevelopment Agency. They have just declared Rice County, Kansas, a depressed area. Rice County, Kansas, has two hundred oil wells, and the 14,000 people there have over thirty million dollars on deposit in personal savings in their banks. When the government tells you you are depressed, lie down and be depressed!

We have so many people who can't see a fat man standing beside a thin one without coming to the conclusion that the fat man got that way by taking advantage of the thin one! So they are going to solve all the problems of human misery through government and government planning. Well, now if government planning and welfare had the answer, and they've had almost thirty years of it, shouldn't we expect government to read the score to us once in a while? Shouldn't they be telling us about the decline each year in the number of people needing help?...the reduction in the need for public housing?

But the reverse is true. Each year the need grows greater, the program grows greater. We were told four years ago that seventeen million people went to bed hungry each night. Well, that was probably true. They were all on a diet! But now we are told that 9.3 million families in this country are poverty-stricken on the basis

---

*From *Speaking My Mind* by Ronald Reagan. Copyright © 1989 by Ronald Reagan.

of earning less than $3,000 a year. Welfare spending is ten times greater than in the dark depths of the Depression. We are spending 45 billion dollars on welfare. Now do a little arithmetic, and you will find that if we divided the 45 billion dollars up equally among those 9 million poor families, we would be able to give each family $4,600 a year, and this added to their present income should eliminate poverty! Direct aid to the poor, however, is running only about $600 per family. It seems that someplace there must be some overhead. . . .

Those who would trade our freedom for the soup kitchen of the welfare state have told us that they have a utopian solution of peace without victory. They call their policy "accommodation." And they say if we only avoid any direct confrontation with the enemy, he will forget his evil ways and learn to love us. All who oppose them are indicted as warmongers. They say we offer simple answers to complex problems. Well, perhaps there is a simple answer . . . not an easy one . . . but a simple one, if you and I have the courage to tell our elected officials that we want our *national* policy based upon what we know in our hearts is morally right.

We cannot buy our security, our freedom from the threat of the bomb by committing an immorality so great as saying to a billion human beings now in slavery behind the Iron Curtain, "Give up your dreams of freedom because to save our own skin, we are willing to make a deal with your slave-masters." Alexander Hamilton said, "A nation which can prefer disgrace to danger is prepared for a master, and deserves one!" Let's set the record straight. There is no argument over the choice between peace and war, but there is only one guaranteed way you can have peace . . . and you can have it in the next second . . . surrender!

2. Editor Irving Kristol Defines Neoconservatism (1983)*

Liberalism was the dominant political religion for most American intellectuals for at least a generation after the New Deal and World War II. Liberals pursued a vision of a just, equitable society, and they looked to government as the means to achieve that vision. In the 1960s, however, a reaction set in, as some intellectuals—many of them refugees from liberalism—began to express growing doubts about egalitarian "excesses" and governmental inefficiencies, as well as about the "softness" of liberal foreign policy toward the Soviet Union. One of the leading thinkers in this conservative renaissance was Irving Kristol, editor of the Public Interest, which became a prominent journal for the expression of neoconservative ideas. Kristol here defines the essence of the neoconservative outlook. What are its leading features? How does it compare to and contrast with the liberal outlook? How do its guiding foreign policy principles square with later "neocon" support for the Iraq war of 2003?

It should be clear by now that I do think there really is such a thing as neoconservatism—but it is most misleading to think of it as any kind of "movement." It holds no meetings, has no organizational form, has no specific programmatic goals, and when two neoconservatives meet they are more likely to argue with one another than to confer or conspire. But it is there, nevertheless—an impulse that

*From Irving Kristol, *Reflections of a Neoconservative: Looking Back, Looking Ahead*, pp. 75–77, 263–264. Copyright © 1983.

ripples through the intellectual world; a "persuasion," to use a nice old-fashioned term; a mode of thought (but not quite a school of thought).

What are its distinctive features? I shall list them as I see them—but to say that this listing is unofficial would be the understatement of the decade.

1. Neoconservatism is a current of thought emerging out of the academic-intellectual world and provoked by disillusionment with contemporary liberalism. Its relation to the business community—the traditional source of American conservatism—is loose and uneasy, though not necessarily unfriendly.

2. Unlike previous such currents of thought—for example, the Southern Agrarians or the Transcendentalists of the nineteenth century—neoconservatism is antiromantic in substance and temperament. Indeed, it regards political romanticism—and its twin, political utopianism—of any kind as one of the plagues of our age. This is but another way of saying it is a philosophical-political impulse rather than a literary-political impulse. Or, to put it still another way: Its approach to the world is more "rabbinic" than "prophetic."

3. The philosophical roots of neoconservatism are to be found mainly in classical—that is, premodern, preideological—political philosophy. Here the teaching and writing of the late [University of Chicago philosopher] Leo Strauss...are of importance, though many neoconservatives find him somewhat too wary of modernity. Neoconservatives are admiring of Aristotle, respectful of Locke, distrustful of Rousseau.

4. The attitude of neoconservatives to bourgeois society and the bourgeois ethos is one of detached attachment. In the spirit of Tocqueville, neoconservatives do not think that liberal-democratic capitalism is the best of all imaginable worlds—only the best, under the circumstances, of all possible worlds. This *modest* enthusiasm distinguishes neoconservatism from the Old Right and the New Right—both of which are exceedingly suspicious of it.

5. Neoconservatism is inclined to the belief that a predominantly market economy—just how "predominant" is a matter for some disagreement—is a necessary if not sufficient precondition for a liberal society. (Daniel Bell, as the theoretician for what may be called our "social-democratic wing," would presumably take issue with this judgment.) It also sees a market economy as favorable to economic growth.

6. Neoconservatives believe in the importance of economic growth, not out of any enthusiasm for the material goods of this world, but because they see economic growth as indispensable for social and political stability. It is the prospect of economic growth that has made it possible to think—against the grain of premodern political thought—of democracy as a viable and enduring sociopolitical system.

7. Neoconservatives, though respecting the market as an economic mechanism, are not libertarian in the sense, say, that [conservative economists] Milton Friedman and Friedrich A. von Hayek are. A conservative welfare state—what once was called a "social insurance" state—is perfectly consistent with the neoconservative perspective. So is a state that takes a degree of responsibility for helping to shape the preferences that the people exercise in a free market—to "elevate" them, if you will. Neoconservatives, moreover, believe that it is natural for people to want their preferences to be elevated. The current version of liberalism, which prescribes massive government intervention in the marketplace but an absolute laissez-faire attitude toward manners and morals, strikes neoconservatives as representing a bizarre inversion of priorities.

8. Neoconservatives look upon family and religion as indispensable pillars of a decent society. Indeed, they have a special fondness for all of those intermediate institutions of a liberal society which reconcile the need for community with the desire for liberty.

Karl Marx once wrote that the human race would eventually face the choice between socialism and barbarism. Well, we have seen enough of socialism in our time to realize that, in actuality as distinct from ideality, it can offer neither stability nor justice, and that in many of its versions it seems perfectly compatible with barbarism. So most neoconservatives believe that the last, best hope of humanity at this time is an intellectually and morally reinvigorated liberal capitalism....

It is the fundamental fallacy of American foreign policy to believe, in face of the evidence, that all peoples, everywhere, are immediately "entitled" to a liberal constitutional government—and a thoroughly democratic one at that. It is because of this assumption that our discussions of foreign policy, along with our policy itself, are constantly being tormented by moral dilemmas, as we find ourselves allied to nonliberal and nondemocratic regimes. These dilemmas are guilt-inducing mechanisms which cripple policy—an attitude that no nation can sustain for long—or else we take flight into sweeping crusades for "human rights," which quickly brings us up short before intractable realities.

Now, there is nothing inevitable about this state of affairs. As a matter of fact, it is only since World War I—a war fought under the Wilsonian slogans of "self-determination for all nations" and "make the world safe for democracy"—that American foreign policy began to disregard the obvious for the sake of the quixotic pursuit of impossible ideals. Before World War I, intelligent men took it for granted that not all peoples, everywhere, at all times, could be expected to replicate a Western constitutional democracy. This was a point of view, incidentally, shared more or less equally by conservatives, liberals, and socialists.

It was only with World War I and its aftermath that thinking about foreign policy lost its moorings in the real world and became utterly ideologized....

For Americans, the transition occurred via the utopian enthusiasm of Woodrow Wilson, preaching "self-determination," "human rights," "one man, one vote," "a world without war" as if these were in fact unproblematic possibilities. The consequence has been a foreign policy that is intellectually disarmed before all those cases where a government is neither totalitarian nor democratic, but authoritarian in one way or another, to one degree or another. We could, if we were sensible, calmly accept this basic reality of world politics, while using our influence to edge unenlightened despotisms toward more enlightened behavior, or enlightened despotisms toward more liberal and humane behavior. Instead, we end up in either an unstable, guilt-ridden and seemingly "immoral" alliance with them or displaying a haughty censoriousness that helps "destabilize" them.

3. Journalist Peter Steinfels Criticizes the Neoconservatives (1979)*

One of the first commentators to identify neoconservatism as a distinct body of thought was Peter Steinfels, editor of the Catholic periodical Commonweal. *In his book of 1979 about the neoconservative movement, he is sharply critical of many of*

---

its doctrines. What does he find most objectionable in neoconservative thought? What does he find most valuable?

The great virtue of neoconservatism is the serious attention it pays to the moral culture that is a fundament of our political and economic life. There is barely a serious school of liberal or even Marxist thought that holds humans to be economically determined and values, culture, and beliefs the mere reflection of socioeconomic forces. And yet in practice liberals, radicals, and socialists concentrate on questions of economic deprivation or physical pain rather than of meaning or moral capacity. They do not deny the importance of culture and values; but when they would act upon them, they almost inevitably propose to enter the chain of causes at the point of providing material support or physical well-being. Otherwise, the Left, broadly speaking, has been primarily concerned with culture by way of removing constraints—commercial pressures, government censorship, insufficient funding, traditional taboos, established conventions. The New Left did criticize liberalism in the sixties for its rendering of politics as procedure and its presentation of social science as value-free. Irving Kristol and the New Left were thus agreed on the necessity of "republican virtue" (though the New Left, unlike Kristol, would not rally to the "bourgeois ethic"). But the New Left's concern dissolved into assorted dogmatisms on the one hand, and into the cultural *laissez-faire* of "do your own thing" on the other. It was left to neoconservatism, sworn enemy of the New Left, to be the serious force reminding us that the capacity of self-government and self-direction is not a given which simply emerges once restraints are removed. It is an active power that must be fostered, nourished, and sustained; that requires supporting communities, disciplined thinking and speech, self-restraint, and accepted conventions. In a number of ways neoconservatism is not itself faithful to this insight, even contradicts it; but it has put the moral culture of society on the public agenda and no doubt will keep it there.

The second virtue of neoconservatism is its rejection of sentimentality. By sentimentality I mean the immediate emotional response that renders a reality all of a piece and "obvious." When sentimentality governs our responses to the world's ills, it clings to the visible or physical evils at hand and tends to ignore the less apparent, more diffuse, and distant dangers. It leaps to solutions and short-circuits reflection. Neoconservatism has countered this sentimentality by forcing back the discussion of many political issues to first principles and by its delight in exposing unintended consequences of well-meant measures. There is a good bit of sentimentality in neoconservatism; there is even a sentimentality of anti-sentimentality—a reflexive granting of credibility to whatever, through irony, paradox, or complexity, appears to resist the pull of sympathy, and an equally automatic suspicion of whatever appears untutored or unguarded in its registration of experience. And there is also the tendency toward that hard-headed constriction of feeling that Dickens, in *Hard Times*, fixed in the very name as well as character of Gradgrind. Nonetheless, the neoconservative presence in public controversy has certainly reduced the likelihood that the "obvious" will escape questioning. Is money what the poor need? Or better schools the solution to illiteracy? Does poverty breed crime? Should more people vote? Or campaign spending be limited? Is equality desirable? To some people, the very posing of such questions is an annoyance and a diversion. To those, however, who believe that the unexamined proposal is not worth pursuing, the neoconservative attitude appears salutary.

The third virtue of neoconservatism is related to the second: the thoroughgoing criticisms that it has made of liberal or radical programs and premises. This is less an attitude, like its anti-sentimentality, than a self-assigned agenda. Neoconservatism has taken pride in frontally challenging the excesses of the New Left and the counterculture; more important—because those excesses were probably self-liquidating and already on the wane when neoconservatism set to work—have been the detailed and often technically superior critiques of mainstream liberal notions. Despite the polemical overkill that too frequently mars such critiques, they provide a much more factually informed and sophisticated debating partner for liberal or left-wing thought than has traditional American conservatism, in any of its rugged individualist, agrarian aristocrat, or supernationalist manifestations.

To every virtue a vice. The outstanding weaknesses of neoconservatism have already been amply suggested: its formulation of an outlook largely in negative terms; its lack of internal criticism; its unwillingness to direct attention to socioeconomic structures and to the existing economic powers; its exaggeration of the adversarial forces in society; its lack of serious respect for its adversaries. If neoconservatism is to construct a convincing defense of an outlook emphasizing a stoic rationality, public restraint, and the maintenance of an ethic of achievement and excellence, it will have to confront the extent to which such an ideal challenges contemporary capitalism. If it is to defend freedom in a bureaucratic age, it will have to understand freedom in a richer sense than anti-Communism and a derived anti-statism. If it is to defend high culture and intellectual rigor, it will need to celebrate the enlarging and life-giving force of superior work and not merely issue self-satisfying strictures on the inferior or fashionable.

Neoconservatism began as an antibody on the left. Many of its leading figures originally conceived of it that way and perhaps still do: it was a reaction to what they considered the destabilizing and excessive developments of the sixties, and when these had been quelled, it would once again be indistinguishable from mainstream liberalism. Its own excesses, or at least its somewhat narrow focus of attention on one set of adversaries, would be balanced by the native strengths of the liberalism of which it was part. That, of course, has not turned out to be the case. Neoconservatism is now an independent force. To return to the biological analogy, antibodies which overreact can destroy the organism. The great danger posed by and to neoconservatism is that it will become nothing more than the legitimating and lubricating ideology of an oligarchic America where essential decisions are made by corporate elites, where great inequalities are rationalized by straitened circumstances and a system of meritocratic hierarchy, and where democracy becomes an occasional, ritualistic gesture. Whether neoconservatism will end by playing this sinister and unhappy role, or whether it will end as a permanent, creative, and constructive element in American politics, is only partially in the hands of neoconservatives themselves. It will also be determined by the vigor, intelligence, and dedication of their critics and opponents.

B. The Reagan "Revolution" in Economic Policy

1. The Supply-Side Gospel (1984)*

Since New Deal days, Keynesian economic theory had dominated federal policy. Named for the brilliant British economist John Maynard Keynes, who had developed his ideas most conspicuously in The General Theory of Employment, Interest and Money *in 1936, Keynesian theory emphasized the role of government spending, including deficit financing, in stimulating the economy. Now so-called supply-side economists argued that continual reliance on government spending sapped money and initiative from the private sector, ballooned deficits, and contained an inherently inflationary bias. The supply-siders came into their own with Ronald Reagan's election in 1980. Here one of them explains the basics of their approach. What is innovative about it? In the light of the unprecedented deficits chalked up in the Reagan years, can supply-side theory be said to have worked?*

Ronald Reagan campaigned for the presidency on a supply-side platform.... Reagan was a different kind of candidate because he emphasized the capabilities of the people and the American economy. He campaigned on a message of hope that sparked a rebirth of confidence in the people. Reagan's optimism was so unfamiliar to the Republican establishment that its candidate, George Bush, called it "voodoo economics."...

The President-elect wanted to get on with his business of using incentives to rebuild the U.S. economy. He ruled out both wage and price controls and the continuation of demand management—the economic cycle of fighting inflation with unemployment and unemployment with inflation. In place of a stop-go monetary policy ranging from too tight to too loose, there would be steady, moderate, and predictable growth in the money supply. And instead of pumping up demand to stimulate the economy, reliance would be placed on improving incentives on the supply side.

This is the policy package that became known as Reaganomics. Its controversial feature is its belief that the economy can enjoy a rise in real gross national product while inflation declines. Monetary policy would first stabilize and then gradually reduce inflation, while tax cuts would provide liquidity as well as incentives and prevent the slower money growth from causing a recession. By creating the wrong incentives and damaging the cash flow of individuals and businesses, the tax system had produced a nation of debt junkies. With the economy strung out on credit, it had to be carefully rehabilitated so as not to produce a liquidity crisis....

Keynesian theory explained the economy's performance in terms of the level of total spending. A budget deficit adds to total spending and helps keep employment high and the economy running at full capacity. Cutting the deficit, as the Republicans wanted to do, would reduce spending and throw people out of work, thereby lowering national income and raising the unemployment rate. The lower

---

income would produce less tax revenue, and the higher unemployment would require larger budget expenditures for unemployment compensation, food stamps, and other support programs. The budget deficit would thus reappear from a shrunken tax base and higher income-support payments. Patient (and impatient) Democrats, economists, columnists, and editorial writers had explained many times to the obdurate Republicans that cutting the deficit would simply reduce spending on goods and services, drive the economy down, and raise the unemployment rate. Keynesians argued that the way to balance the budget was to run a deficit. Deficit spending would lift the economy, and the government's tax revenues would rise, bringing the budget into balance. Since cutting the deficit was believed to be the surest way to throw people out of work, there were not many Republican economists. When Democrat Alice Rivlin was asked why there were no Republican economists on her "nonpartisan" Congressional Budget Committee staff, she was probably telling the truth when she said she could not find any.

The focus on the deficit had left the Republicans without a competitive political program. They were perceived by the recipients of government benefits as the party always threatening to cut back on government programs such as social security, while the taxpaying part of the electorate saw Republicans as the party that was always threatening to raise taxes in order to pay for the benefits that others were receiving. The party that takes away with both hands competes badly with the party that gives away with both hands, and that simple fact explained the decline of the Republican Party, which had come to be known as the tax collector for Democratic spending programs.

Supply-side economics brought a new perspective to fiscal policy. Instead of stressing the effects on spending, supply-siders showed that tax rates directly affect the supply of goods and services. Lower tax rates mean better incentives to work, to save, to take risks, and to invest. As people respond to the higher after-tax rewards, or greater profitability, incomes rise and the tax base grows, thus feeding back some of the lost revenues to the Treasury. The saving rate also grows, providing more financing for government and private borrowing. Since Keynesian analysis left out such effects, once supply-side economics appeared on the scene the Democrats could no longer claim that government spending stimulated the economy more effectively than tax cuts.

2. The New York Times *Attacks Reagan's Policies (1981)**

Critics of President Reagan's budget-slashing and tax-cutting policies fumed furiously but ineffectively during Reagan's first year in office. The new president appeared to be a masterful politician whose will was impossible to thwart. Some observers, however, worried about the real purposes behind Reagan's deft display of presidential leadership. In the following editorial from the New York Times, *what are alleged to be Reagan's true intentions? What does the editorial mean when it states that Reagan*

"gathers power for the purpose of denigrating its value in shaping America"? Is this assessment fair?

One thing is surely settled: the Presidency is no feeble office. Let a shrewd President single-mindedly pursue a policy broadly grounded in his election mandate, and he can put it across....

But is this President's paradoxical triumph also the nation's? He gathers power for the purpose of denigrating its value in shaping America. He does not say the nation is overextended financially. He does not say guns are momentarily more important than butter. He does not rerank the nation's needs or argue against assorted remedies. He denounces all Federal government as oppressive, as the cause of economic distress and a threat to liberty.

So Mr. Reagan has arranged to shrink annual Federal spending by 1984 by about $150 billion and cut taxes to let individuals and businesses spend that sum instead. Economically, that is mostly a transfer of purchasing power which cannot much reduce inflation or unemployment, the Federal deficit or debt. On the contrary, a big increase in military spending will enlarge the deficit unless the President finds further huge savings in civilian programs. And the pressure to find them— wherever—is what he values most about his accomplishment.

But why does the President boast that he has thus improved economic prospects? Because he holds, as a matter of faith, that a dollar spent privately creates more wealth than a dollar spent by Government.

That is surely sometimes true: a Government-run railroad that is politically beholden to its unions will tolerate more waste than a private bus company. But it surely also is sometimes untrue: a Government investment in a student or road or depressed community can stimulate more productive activity than the same sum spent by private citizens on diamonds or cameras. Government may be incompetent to achieve some of its social goals. But uncoordinated private spending is notoriously inefficient in meeting large public needs.

Take the obvious, urgent need to cool inflation. Mr. Reagan's answer is a tortuous chain of incentives: cut a family's taxes by $500 and the money goes to banks and merchants who invest in more businesses and machines which will be more efficient and hold down prices. Also: reduce a citizen's tax on the *next* earned dollar from 29 to 25 cents and he'll work harder longer and thus reduce costs.

But if it were primarily interested in economic results, Government has surer ways to achieve those results—as even Mr. Reagan's plan recognizes. For it aims large tax reductions directly at businesses that buy cost-reducing machines or job-producing plants. A still more efficient plan would have aimed more precisely at the most wanted machines and at workers who hold down wages or communities that reduce sales taxes.

The unavoidable conclusion is that Mr. Reagan wants to use his power primarily to diminish Government—even where that dilutes economic recovery and prevents efficient allocation of resources.

That the President's plan will revive the economy remains to be proved. What is no longer in doubt is that his economic remedies mask an assault on the very idea that free people can solve their collective problems through representative Government.

One day soon Americans will rediscover that their general welfare depends on national as well as parochial actions. And then they will want not just a powerful President but one who cherishes the power of Government to act for the common good.

C. The Reagan-Bush Foreign Policies

Four Views on the End of the Cold War (1994)*

At an extraordinary gathering in the summer of 1994, four of the major figures who played roles in ending the four-and-one-half-decade-long Cold War met in Colorado to assess the process by which the Cold War at last reached its finale. Margaret Thatcher was prime minister of Britain for the entire decade of the 1980s; François Mitterrand was president of France; George Bush served as Ronald Reagan's vice president and was elected president himself in 1988; and Mikhail Gorbachev was the principal architect of the enormous changes that swept through the Soviet Union in the 1980s. How do they agree, and how do they differ, in their appraisals of what happened and why in that momentous decade? Which explanation is most credible? Who should get the lion's share of the credit for ending the Cold War? Which of these leaders is most prophetic about the future?

Margaret Thatcher. There was one vital factor in the ending of the Cold War: Ronald Reagan's decision to go ahead with the Strategic Defense Initiative (SDI).

The point of SDI was to stop nuclear weapons from reaching their objective. The first nation that got it would have a tremendous advantage because the whole military balance would change. So, it was of supreme importance.

This was a completely different level of defense. It required enormous computer capability, which he knew at the time the Soviet Union could not match. And that was the end of the arms race as we had been pursuing it. I told Mr. Gorbachev when he first visited me that I was all for President Reagan going ahead with SDI and that some of our scientists would help if needed.

From that particular moment, everything was not so easy in my relationship with Mr. Gorbachev. At the same time it was clear that (with Gorbachev) we could negotiate in a different way with a different kind of person who was beginning to allow people in the Soviet Union to have freedom of worship and freedom of speech.

So the end of the Cold War had a great deal to do with Ronald Reagan and a great deal to do with Mr. Gorbachev.

Mikhail Gorbachev. I cannot agree that the SDI initiative had this much importance. SDI-type research was also done in our country. We knew that in the defense sector we could find a response. So, SDI was not decisive in our movement toward a new relationship with the West. If you accept that reforms in the Soviet Union started under the pressure from the West, particularly as a result

---

New Perspectives Quarterly: NPQ by Institute for National Strategy (U.S.); Center for the Study of Democratic Institutions. Reproduced with permission of Blackwell Publishing, Inc. in the format Republish in a book via Copyright Clearance Center.

of the implementation of SDI, that would distort the real picture and offer the wrong lesson for the future.

Of decisive importance were the changes within the Soviet Union. They necessarily preceded any change in our external relations.

We had to go a long way from a critical reassessment of the Communist model that was forcibly imposed on our country and that was sustained by repressive measures. With technological progress and the improvement of the educational and cultural level, the old system began to be rejected by people who saw that their initiative was suppressed, who saw they were not able to realize their potential.

Therefore, the first impulses for reform were in the Soviet Union itself, in our society which could no longer tolerate the lack of freedom, where no one could speak out or choose their own party or select their own creed. In the eyes of the people, especially the educated, the totalitarian system had run its course morally and politically. People were waiting for reform. Russia was pregnant.

So, the moment was mature to give possibility to the people. And we could only do it from above because initiative from below would have meant an explosion of discontent. This was the decisive factor, not SDI.

François Mitterrand. From the first moment Ronald Reagan mentioned SDI to me I made known my firm opposition. I believed this was an excessive project, and it has since been abandoned....

In the Soviet Union, the need for change went back long before Gorbachev arrived on the scene. Nikita Khrushchev and even Leonid Brezhnev were sufficiently intelligent to transform trends into habits. They made reforms; but the purpose of reform was to guarantee their power. For this reason, Soviet public opinion never trusted or believed in reform. That changed with Mr. Gorbachev. Under him reforms were carried out for the sake of reforms. That is the difference.

George Bush. I supported SDI, but you have got to remember that Ronald Reagan was very idealistic on nuclear weapons. Ronald Reagan felt SDI was a way to reduce nuclear terror. As you remember, he offered to share the technology with all countries.

At Reykjavik, he and Mikhail almost hammered out a deal to get rid of nuclear weapons altogether. And Margaret had a fit about it, as did a lot of people in the United States. I suspect François wasn't too pleased either because of the French deterrent.

I disagree with Margaret, though, about the degree to which it forced reform or accelerated change inside the Soviet Union. We had huge defense budgets at that time and they continued on through my administration. SDI was part of that, but it was nothing compared to the overall deployment of nukes all around the world....

Gorbachev. During the Chernenko* funeral, when I spoke with George Bush (then Vice President) and Margaret Thatcher, I was also talking with the leaders of the Eastern European countries. I said to all of them: "I want to assure you

---

*Konstantin Chernenko was the head of the Soviet Union from February 1984 until his death in March 1985.

that the principles that used to just be proclaimed—equality of states and non-interference in internal affairs—will now be our real policy. Therefore you bear responsibility for affairs in your own country. We need *perestroika* [restructuring] and will do it in our own country. You make your own decision." I said this was the end of the Brezhnev Doctrine.*

I must say they all took a rather skeptical attitude. They thought, "Well, Gorbachev said something about troop reductions at the UN. He is talking about reform at home. He must be in bad shape. He will improve things a little, and then the Soviet Union will go back to its old ways. This is playing the game that is usual with Soviet leaders."

During my years in power we stuck to the policy I announced. We never interfered, not militarily and not even politically. When Gustav Husak from Czechoslovakia and others came to us, we told them we would help them to the extent possible, but "your country is your responsibility."...

Mitterrand. What brought everything down was the inability to control the fantastic migration out of East Germany into Hungary and Czechoslovakia, and later to West Germany. That was the end for the Soviet empire.

If Gorbachev had chosen to use force in those countries under Soviet sway, none could have resisted. But he made it known that he considered that option an historical blunder. The very moment that Gorbachev said to the president of the GDR (East Germany) that he did not intend to use force to solve the crisis, that this was a new day and a new deal, that was the end. This was when the big shift occurred. The fault line was not in Warsaw or Prague. It was in East Berlin....

Bush. When the Berlin Wall came down, we didn't know whether there were elements inside the Soviet Union that would say "enough is enough, we are not going to lose this crown jewel, and we already have troops stationed there."

In an interview at the time in the Oval Office, I was asked why I didn't share the emotion of the American people over the fall of the Berlin Wall. Leaders of the opposition in Congress were saying that I ought to go and get up on top of the Berlin Wall with all those students to show the world how we Americans felt.

I felt very emotional, but it was my view that this was not the time to stick our fingers in the eyes of Mikhail Gorbachev or the Soviet military. We were in favor of German unity early on and felt events were moving properly.

So, we didn't want to do something stupid, showing our emotion in a way that would compel elements in the Soviet Union to rise up against Gorbachev.

Gorbachev. We were not naive about what might happen. We understood that what was underway was a process of change in the civilization. We knew that when we pursued the principle of freedom of choice and non-interference in Eastern Europe that we also deprived the West from interfering, from injecting themselves into the processes taking place there....

---

*On the occasion of the Soviet invasion of Czechoslovakia in 1968, Soviet leader Leonid Brezhnev announced the "Brezhnev Doctrine," asserting the right of the Soviet Union to intervene militarily in any Eastern European country where Communist rule was threatened.

Thatcher. Unlike George Bush, I was opposed to German unification from early on for the obvious reasons. To unify Germany would make her the dominant nation in the European community. They are powerful and they are efficient. It would become a German Europe....

Bush. To be very frank, we had our differences with Lady Thatcher and François Mitterrand. Perhaps it was because I didn't share their concerns based on the histories of the two world wars. Maybe it is because America is removed and separated.

But I felt that German unification would be in the fundamental interest of the West. I felt the time had come to trust the Germans more, given what they had done since the end of World War II....

Gorbachev. The German question was the nerve center of our European policy. You will recall that the Soviet position after World War II was that Germany should be united—but as a democratic, neutral and demilitarized country. But that did not happen....

For us the German reunification issue was the most difficult one. For President Bush and the US Administration the key issue was the future of NATO. And, today, as we see how NATO is being pushed forward instead of a European process of building common institutions, we understand why it was their concern. That is a problem.

The president of France was concerned about borders and territory. Mrs. Thatcher had geopolitical concerns about who would dominate Europe. Everyone had questions.

But I can tell you those questions cannot even be compared with the problems the Soviet leadership was facing given our enormous sacrifices during the war. So, for us, taking the decision on German unification was not easy. We had to go a very long way. We thought the process would take a long time and would be coordinated with the building of new European institutions under the umbrella not of the Americans, but of a European process....

Mitterrand. I believe that in the next century a new synthesis must be found between the two requirements stressed by President Gorbachev—the need for integration as well as the need to affirm individual personality, sovereignty and rights in different areas. And this is by no means a done deal.

The separation of the Czechs and Slovaks is a good example, but there will be other less harmonious separations in Europe. And let us hope it is not contagious and spreads to the American continent.

The aspiration for national identity is clearly understandable after what Mrs. Thatcher called the fallen empires—certainly the main feature of the 20th century. The end of empire releases ethnic and tribal groups. Each goes it alone, wanting to enjoy all the trappings of sovereignty. But that is not possible. It clashes with the other basic trend of globalization.

So, a synthesis is necessary. Though Lady Thatcher does not agree, that is what we are doing within the European community. Shall we succeed in effecting a synthesis between this need for great aggregates and this incipient need of each small community to affirm itself as such?

Absurd, would it not be, to encourage each splinter of a truth to lead an independent international life? And yet, it is injustice to prevent anyone from doing so.

So, in the next century the world must create the rule of law that protects minorities, enabling them to live freely with most of the attributes that makes it possible to meet their national aspirations. At the same time national organizations must be created so that each country can maintain its cohesiveness.

If we do not do this, we shall see a tremendous scattering and breaking away. No one will be immune. The need for decentralization in the US or Canada will prevail over a federal state. And it will be the same in Brazil, in Spain, in Belgium. There would be no end, no way out.

Will we have political leaders capable of conceiving the organization of this huge world with a few major coordination centers obeying international laws set by the international community, and at the same time making minority rules that enable each to live according to his or her yearning?

Enough said. A new generation is rising. They will have to answer this question.

D. Assessing the Reagan Presidency

1. Two Thumbs Up for Reagan (1988)

Even before Ronald Reagan's presidency came to a close, his supporters and critics alike began to judge the sources and consequences of his time in office. In the two selections that follow, from the conservative journal The National Review, *the novelist Tom Wolfe and the journalist Robert Novak enter generally favorable judgments on Reagan's political career. What do they see as the principal components of the "Reagan coalition," and what do they identify as Reagan's principal achievements?*

Head of The Class*

Tom Wolfe

Remember the "little old ladies in tennis shoes"? That was the term dreamed up in the 1960s to characterize the constituency of Barry Goldwater's version of the conservative movement. After Goldwater's rout in the 1964 election it seemed accurate enough.

It was used again two years later when another avowed conservative, Ronald Reagan, ran for governor in California. But Reagan won, a result so astounding that for the next ten years columnists spoke of the California electorate as "volatile." Reagan's popularity in California increased steadily, however. So the voter surveys began in earnest—with another astounding result. At the heart of Reagan's support were California's new, young, and very numerous working-class families.

In the 1940s, when a war economy finally hoisted the United States out of the Depression, the boom occurred earliest in California, with its aircraft plants and other

---

*From *The Reagan Legacy*, edited by Sidney Blumenthal and Thomas Byrne Edsall (New York: Pantheon, 1988).

key military industries. Wages climbed rapidly. It was in California that the term "worker" first ceased to mean someone who is defined (or enslaved) by his job. The California worker became an owner: first, of an automobile; then, soon enough, of a house (and then of a second automobile). He began to think of civic life in the same way as any new property owner. He wanted stability, including one of its major props: moral decency. He wanted freedom from government intrusion, particularly high taxes. He wanted public policy to favor people like himself, people who had earned what they possessed. He wanted to take pride in what he had accomplished; and two of pride's most popular forms were official optimism and patriotism.

How much of this had Reagan figured out analytically? Perhaps none of it, although it seems to me he has always been much more of an issue-oriented (shall I try out the adjective *intellectual?)* politician than those who call him "the great communicator" are willing to admit. In any case, his views resonated perfectly with those of the new California working class. (It might even be worth mentioning that Reagan is the only labor-union member who ever became President.)

Since the 1960s the prosperity and ethos of the California working class have spread to workers all over America—so much so that the terms *working class* and *workers* have become archaic. Today electricians, air-conditioning mechanics, burglar-alarm installers, cablevision linemen are routinely spoken of as middle-class. Many journeyman mechanics live on a scale that would have made the Sun King blink. They are a new class that has seriously altered the political make-up of this country over the past 25 years. And Ronald Reagan was their first spokesman, their first leader, their first philosopher. The existence of this class continues to baffle Democratic Party leaders. Their biggest problem in the presidential election this fall is what to do about these people whose goals they still do not understand.

The Reagan Coalition*

Robert D. Novak

Ronald Reagan not only was the first American President to begin enacting an ideological agenda from his first day in office but was more successful in achieving it than all but the wildest optimists dreamed. He has been one of the Republic's most popular Chief Magistrates. Arguably, he is the best President of the twentieth century.

Why, then, the current panic among Republicans and conservatives, who see disaster looming in the first presidential election after Reagan? Is he just another Eisenhower, warmly avuncular but lacking a legacy to steer the American Right away from oblivion? Does the apparent desire of Reagan Democrats—lower-income and ethnic—to return to their inherited party mean Reagan's political impact was ephemeral?

In truth, the Reagan legacy is strong and clear. He collapsed the folk myth that only Republicans who remind voters of liberal Democrats can be elected. He was elected on free-market principles and the promise, which he soon fulfilled, of tax-rate reduction.

---

*From *The Reagan Legacy*, edited by Sidney Blumenthal and Thomas Byrne Edsall (New York: Pantheon, 1988).

His legacy is not only the sustained prosperity of the Reagan era but a transformed political climate. Bruce Babbitt is the last presidential contender not to realize that advocacy of higher taxes is the candidate's death wish. Michael Dukakis kepi any tax-increase proposal out of the Democratic platform. Other Western leaders, even the Socialist Francois Mitterrand, publicly celebrate the glories of Reaganomics.

Other elements of the Reagan Revolution—such as the Reagan Doctrine's assertion that freedom-fighters battling to rid their countries of Communist tyranny deserve American help—have been less successfully imprinted on the national and global consciousness and less consistently pursued over the last eight years. Nevertheless, they are important bequests of the departing President.

The problem is not the legacy but the legatees. The primordial Republican mindset—a desire not to stir up controversy—was for a time strengthened by the illusion of ultimate political victory, fostered by polls indicating that Republican and Democratic sentiment was even in the country. Amid gaseous speculation about "political realignment." Republican candidates in the 1986 campaign abandoned Reaganite positions and drifted toward the mid-term election disaster.

The "realignment" chimera is an unfond memory. But it has been replaced by the notion that George Bush can be elected President by capitalizing on Reagan's modification of original principles—for example, by encouraging U.S.-Soviet Detente II and drifting to the President's left on such quintessential Democratic issues as education and the environment.

Bush does seem rock hard in his embrace of the Reaganite anti-tax position. But while the words are correct, the music is off-key. If Ronald Reagan's legacy to the nation and to the West is growth over austerity, his legacy to the Republicans is his formula for winning the allegiance of blue-collar Democrats. What the party does with it will become clearer in four months, but its use carries no statute of limitations.

2. A Skeptical View of Reagan's Legacy (2004)

The Reagan presidency is remembered as much for Reagan's personality as for his policies. In these panels, the political cartoonist Kirk Anderson explores the contrast between the undeniable appeal of Reagan's charm and the troubling specifics of some of his administration's actions. How might the two have been reconciled in the public mind?

He tripled the national debt, but he had such *CHARISMA!*

He supported apartheid, but he was *ALWAYS* personable!

He backed Saddam, but he made us feel *GOOD* about ourselves!

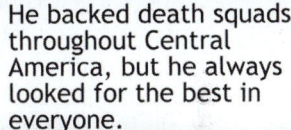

He crushed worker rights, but he was someone you could sit down and have a beer with.

Star Wars turned out to be an expensive fantasy, but he had that *INFECTIOUS OPTIMISM!*

He backed death squads throughout Central America, but he always looked for the best in everyone.

He looked the other way when Salvadoran allies raped American nuns, but he had that *SELF-DEPRECATING HUMOR!*

He confused old movies with foreign policy, but he was always *QUICK WITH A JOKE!*

He traded arms for hostages and diverted money to drug-running death squads, but he never lost his *SUNNY DISPOSITION!*

www.kirktoons.com

REMEMBERING REAGAN

KIRK ©04

Kirk Anderson/www.kirktoons.com.

3. James T. Patterson Weighs the Reagan Record (2003)*

Historian James T. Patterson analyzes the three major issues of the Reagan presidency—his impact on "Big Government," his contribution to a resurgence of conservative politics, and his effect on national morale. Patterson finds a decidedly mixed record. Judged against Reagan's own goals, should his presidency be considered a success or a disappointment?

Those who are impressed with the size of Reagan's shadow often emphasize three general points. First, that he succeeded in resisting what had appeared to be an irreversible tide of Big Government. Second, that he shoved politics and political thinking toward the right. And third, that he heightened popular faith in the nation.

The first claim is inaccurate insofar as means-tested programs for the poor are concerned. Though stemmed in 1981, they increased again after 1984, and welfare spending was higher in 1989 than it had been in 1981. In other ways, too, this claim is overstated. His own rhetoric to the contrary, Reagan was far too adept a politician to undertake any serious dismantling of large and popular social programs such as Social Security or Medicare....The number of federal employees increased more rapidly during his presidency than it had under Jimmy Carter. Federal government spending as a percentage of gross domestic product was slightly higher under Reagan than it was to become under Bill Clinton.

Reagan also failed to overturn, or even seriously to challenge, a number of highly controversial practices, such as abortion or affirmative action, that he said he would fight hard against....In coping with these matters, as with popular programs of the New Deal, a politically careful Reagan took the path of least resistance....

[H]e was careful to name conservatives to the federal courts....[But] the courts moved more slowly to the right in later years than ardent conservatives had hoped. Most of the landmark liberal decisions of the 1960s and early 1970s—concerning school prayers, criminal rights, and reproductive rights—had not been overturned as of early 2003.

The second claim, that Reagan helped move politics and political thinking to the right, seemed to be valid in the early and mid-1980s....In 1980, for instance, polls showed that there was a considerable Democratic edge—of more than 20 percent—in the expressed partisan preference of voters. After Reagan's reelection, however, Republicans were approaching parity with Democrats. The victory of George Bush in 1988 seemed to indicate that Reaganism was promoting a political realignment in the nation.

There is also little doubt that the resurgence of conservative thinking in the Reagan years placed liberal ideas on the defensive. In 1988 Bush effectively demonized the "l" word, liberalism. And Democrats, too, saw conservative handwriting on the wall. Under Bill Clinton, they moved to the right, especially in the areas of welfare and fiscal policy. The recentering of the Democratic Party under Clinton, who understood the force of Reagan's impact on political thinking, was probably a key to the revival of its fortunes in the 1990s....

It was obvious by 2003, however, that Reagan failed to accomplish what FDR had done: create a major realignment of partisan preferences. Democrats maintained firm control of the House of Representatives until 1995, recaptured the Senate between 1987 and 1995, and regained the White House in 1993....Nor is it accurate to credit Reagan alone for the resurgence of the Republican Party....As [Reagan adviser] Martin Anderson has stressed, this conservative "Revolution," as he calls it, was well on its way before 1980. Reagan gave a substantial boost to many conservative ideas, to be sure, but he was a beneficiary as well as a mover of the rise of the right.

What, then, of the final claim—that Reagan's greatest legacy was to make Americans feel good again about themselves and the future of the nation? If by this claim it is meant that Reagan—the avowed enemy of Big Government—ironically restored popular faith in the competence of Washington, that is true—to some extent....

But Reagan's tenure did not mean that the majority of Americans came to love their government. (Nor, of course, would he have wanted them to love it.) They admired the star, not the play. For one thing, Iran-Contra strengthened a host of already anguished popular doubts about the evils of federal officialdom....

The larger claim, that Reagan made Americans feel good about themselves and about their country, is in any solidly quantifiable sense unverifiable. But the claim is plausible. Like FDR, he was indeed an optimist and a booster who was fortunate politically in that he entered the White House at a somber time in United States history. Rejecting the notion that America had reached an Age of Limits, the Great Communicator told people again and again that they could still accomplish wonderful things and that the future would be better than the past. In so preaching he made effective use of the bully pulpit of the White House. Though this was often "feel good" leadership, it helped him forge a bond with many Americans. Without this leadership, the malaise of the late 1970s might have persisted.

With the limited hindsight that we now enjoy, however, it is hard to claim too much for the legacy of Reagan's presidency. Though strong as a booster, he was a frequently negligent and incurious manager. Concerning many policy areas—race relations, urban affairs, immigration and population issues, health care, action against AIDS, education, environmental concerns—he was essentially uninterested. Excepting his efforts to lower income tax rates, and—more important—his contributions to the ending of the cold war, he did little in the way of developing new or effective approaches to key problems, some of which were allowed to fester.

To speak, therefore, of a "Reagan Revolution," or of an "Age of Reagan," seems excessive. Grand phrases such as these are best reserved for twentieth-century presidents like Theodore Roosevelt, who did much to promote the activist presidency of our own times; like Franklin Roosevelt, whose New Deal inaugurated the welfare state; or like Harry Truman, whose foreign policies established America's response to the Soviet Union for forty years or more. By contrast to these formidable figures, Ronald Reagan does not seem quite so tall. Still, his legacies in the realms that he cared most about—tax rates and Soviet-American relations—have been durable as well as significant. His large shadow remains.

E. George H. W. Bush and the First Gulf War _____

1. Congressman Solarz Makes the Case for War Against Iraq (1991)*

A Democratic congressman from New York, Stephen J. Solarz was among the primary sponsors of a resolution authorizing the use of U.S. military force to remove Iraqi troops from Kuwait in 1991. In the following article, Solarz makes the case for intervention. What vision of the U.S. role in the wider world underlies the specific case made here?

The role of global policeman is one the American people do not seek and will not accept.

Yet, if being the solitary sheriff for the whole world is not a role the American people are likely to embrace with enthusiasm, they are perfectly prepared, as we saw in the Gulf, to support a policy of collective security in which our country serves as the head of an international posse attempting to bring regional bandits to justice.

Half a century ago, Franklin Roosevelt and the other leaders of the wartime alliance dreamed of a world in which the international community enforced the peace through collective action.

Now that the cold war is over, we have the opportunity to fulfill that dream.

The Gulf crisis demonstrated that it is now possible to get the Soviet Union and the other members of the Security Council to work with us instead of against us.

The United Nations wasn't paralyzed.

And the principle of collective international action against regional aggressors was dramatically strengthened.

Throughout this process, American leadership was absolutely essential. Had we not been willing to take the lead in mobilizing an international coalition against the Iraqi invasion of Kuwait, Saddam would still be in possession of what he arrogantly characterized as the 19th province of Iraq.

If, in the future, we simply walk away from our responsibilities, as we did after World War I, the very idea of collective security and international action will fall apart.

And we will pay the price.

But if we are prepared to take up the burden of leadership, as we did after World War II, it should be possible to mobilize international coalitions capable of resisting those who would wantonly invade their neighbors, thereby determining aggression in the first place.

There is one further message the Democratic party must convey to the American people if we are to convince them that we can be trusted with the responsibility of managing our foreign and national security policy.

We must demonstrate that we recognize that while force should always be a last resort, "last" is not the same as "never," and that there are times when war is not only justified but necessary.

This is, of course, a lesson we have learned from our own history.

Had it not been for the Revolutionary War, we would not have won our independence.

Had it not been for the Civil War, we would have neither preserved the Union nor freed the slaves.

_____

*137 *Congressional Record* E 2788 (July 31, 1991) (statement of Stephen Solarz).

Had it not been for the Second World War, the Third Reich might indeed have lasted for a thousand years.

And had it not been for Desert Storm, a demonic despot would have had his hands on the economic jugular of the world, and armed with chemical and biological weapons, and eventually nuclear weapons as well, he would ultimately have embarked on additional campaigns of conquest and annexation, as part of his effort to dominate the entire Middle East.

2. The Gulf War as Happy Ending or Ominous Beginning (1991)

As the first major American military effort of the post–Cold War era, Operation Desert Storm proved both encouraging and frightening: encouraging because a diverse coalition of nations, led by the United States, successfully thwarted the aggression of a dangerous dictator; frightening because it represented a new kind of global crisis, in which hot spots—particularly in the Middle East—might upset the fragile interdependence of the global community. In the following cartoon, Jim Morin cautions those who failed to see the darker realities lurking behind the conflict with Iraq. In light of subsequent history, how appropriate was his warning?

3. The Foreign Policy President Falls Short at Home (1991)

In the wake of a dramatically successful war, many commentators believed that a politically unassailable George H. W. Bush would easily win the next presidential election. They were wrong. To growing numbers of Americans, the Bush White House seemed more interested in solving international crises than in tending to pressing matters at home. That perception became all the more damaging as the American economy dipped into a prolonged recession. Mike Luckovich here captures the sentiment of those who felt that the president neglected his domestic responsibilities. What does the cartoonist's perspective suggest about the relative importance of domestic and foreign policies in the post–Cold War era?

© 1991 MIKE LUCKOVICH—ATLANTA CONSTITUTION

By permission of Mike Luckovich and Creators Syndicate, Inc.

Thought Provokers

1. Did Reagan's electoral victory in 1980 ring the death knell for the philosophy of the New Deal and the Great Society? Did the Reagan administration constitute a true revolution in U.S. politics?
2. What developments gave rise to the neoconservative philosophy? What has been the impact of neoconservatism? Are ideas important in politics?
3. Did Reagan's massive military buildup make the world a safer place? Did the prospect of a Star Wars defense stabilize or destabilize the international scene? To what degree was U.S. foreign policy responsible for the changes in Russia and Eastern Europe in the late 1980s and early 1990s? Were there any positive features of the Cold War?
4. How will the future judge Ronald Reagan, the man, as *president*? How will it judge his *presidency*?
5. What made Operation Desert Storm so successful in the field and so popular at home? Did the war against Iraq resolve or exacerbate the United States' problems in the Persian Gulf? Why did it fail to ensure George H. W. Bush's reelection?

40

America Confronts the Post–Cold War Era, 1992–2000

What's the point of having this superb military that you're always talking about if we can't use it?

UN Ambassador Madeleine Albright to Colin Powell,
Chairman of the Joint Chiefs of Staff, urging
U.S. intervention in Bosnia in 1993

Prologue: Bill Clinton was the first president elected after the fall of the Soviet Union, and the end of the Cold War raised some perplexing questions about American foreign policy: How should America exercise its now unrivaled military power? What role should it play in a world becoming ever more economically interdependent? Struggling to define a coherent foreign policy that balanced the nation's economic interests with its humanitarian ideals and strategic needs, he signed the landmark North American Trade Agreement with Canada and Mexico in 1993. An unusually gifted politician, Clinton nevertheless saw his party lose its majority in the House of Representatives in the 1994 elections, heralding a new and painful era of polarization and near-paralysis in the American political system. The feminist movement, meanwhile, continued its decades-long advance, amid new controversies about what its priorities should be. The new century opened with a bitterly contested presidential election in 2000, after which Americans waited to see what the new George W. Bush administration had in store.

A. The North American Free Trade Agreement (NAFTA)

1. Three Presidential Candidates Debate NAFTA (1992)*

Even as the European Union continued to deepen economic and political ties among the nations of the Old World, the Reagan and George H. W. Bush administrations pursued a North American free trade pact to boost commerce and facilitate cross-border investment among Canada, the United States, and Mexico. The provisional agreement became a major issue in the 1992 presidential campaign and figured especially

---

*From *The New York Times*, October 16, 1992.

823

prominently in a televised debate in October 1992 among the three principal candidates, the Republican incumbent Bush, Democratic challenger Bill Clinton, and the independent Ross W. Perot. What were the main points of contention among them?

Q: Yes, I'd like to direct my question to Mr. Perot. What will you do as President to open foreign markets to fair competition from American business, and to stop unfair competition here at home from foreign countries so that we can bring jobs back to the United States.

PEROT: We have got to stop sending jobs overseas.

To those of you in the audience who are business people, pretty simple: If you're paying $12, $13, $14 an hour for factory workers and you can move your factory south of the border, pay a dollar an hour for labor, hire young—let's assume you've been in business for a long time and you've got a mature work force—pay a dollar an hour for your labor, have no health care—that's the most expensive single element in making a car—have no environmental controls, no pollution controls and no retirement, and you don't care about anything but making money, there will be a giant sucking sound going south.

Q: Thank you Mr. Perot. I see that the President has stood up so he must have something to say about this.

BUSH: Well, Carole, the thing that saved us in this global economic slowdown is in our exports. And what I'm trying to do is increase our exports. And if, indeed, all the jobs were going to move South because of lower wages, there are lower wages now and they haven't done that. And so I have just negotiated with the President of Mexico; the North American Free Trade Agreement; and the Prime Minister of Canada, I might add, and I'm—I want to have more of these free trade agreements. Because export jobs are increasing far faster than any jobs that may have moved overseas; that's a scare tactic because it's not that many. But anyone that's here, we want to have more jobs here and the way to do that is to increase our exports.

Some believe in protection. I don't. I believe in free and fair trade and that's the thing that saved us, and so I will keep on as President trying to get a successful conclusion to the GATT round, the big Uruguay round of trade which will really open up markets for our—for our agriculture particularly—I want to continue work after we get this Nafta agreement ratified this coming year; I want to get one with Eastern Europe. I want to get one with Chile and free and fair trade is the answer, not protection. And as I say we've had tough economic times and it's exports that have saved us. Exports that have built.

Q: Governor Clinton.

CLINTON: I'd like to answer the question because I've actually been a governor for 12 years so. I've known a lot of people who've lost their jobs because of jobs moving overseas and I know a lot of people whose plants have been strengthened by increasing exports. The trick is to expand our export base and to expand trade on terms that are fair to us. It is true that our exports to Mexico for example have gone up and our trade deficit's gone down. It's also true that just today a record-high trade deficit was announced with Japan. So what is the answer?

Let me just mention three things very quickly.

No. 1, make sure that other countries are as open to our markets as our markets are to them. And if they're not, have measures on the books that don't take forever and a day to implement.

No. 2, change the tax code. There are more deductions in the tax code for shutting plants down and moving overseas than there are for modernizing plant and equipment here. Our competitors don't do that. Emphasize and subsidize modernizing plant and equipment here, not moving plants overseas.

No. 3, stop the Federal Government's program that now gives low-interest loans and job training funds to companies that will actually shut down and move to other countries but we won't do the same thing for plants that stay here. So more trade, but on fairer terms and favor investment in America.

2. Three Views of NAFTA 20 Years Later (2013)*

Two decades after its implementation, NAFTA continued to be controversial—in all three partner countries. How do the three analysts excerpted below agree and differ about NAFTA's consequences for the three societies? Have there been clear winners and losers? Whose predictions in 1992 (see the preceding document) were most accurate? In what ways do the arguments about NAFTA apply to free trade and "globalization" as a worldwide phenomenon?

Ross Perot Was Wrong

Gary Hufbauer, the Reginald Jones senior fellow at the Peterson Institute for International Economics.

Updated November 25, 2013, 10:26 A.M.

Twenty years ago, Ross Perot warned that Nafta would create a "giant sucking sound," draining millions of jobs from the American heartland. But between 1994 and 2000, the American economy created 2 million jobs annually.

Perot's fears, shared by Nafta critics, boiled down to simple mercantilism: "exports good, imports bad." In fact, for every country, both exports and imports are good. Exports create better-paying jobs, as the country specializes in producing the things it makes best. Imports give buyers more choice at lower cost, and they stimulate competing domestic firms to improve their game.

Nafta was not about the net creation or destruction of U.S. jobs; it was about better jobs and lower costs. On account of Nafta, jobs moved between sectors of the vast U.S. economy. Perhaps 60,000 U.S. workers were dislocated annually in the first decade, and they had to find new jobs in other industries. Losing a job for whatever reason is always painful, but Nafta dislocations were small compared with annual unemployment (in the 1990s) of around 8 million.

In 1993, before Nafta, the trade figures (in 2013 dollars, adjusted for inflation) were $250 billion U.S. exports of goods and services to Canada and Mexico, and $251 billion imports, for a total of $501 billion in two-way trade. In 2013, the figures

---

*"What We've Learned From Nafta," *New York Times* online, accessed March 4, 2014, http://www.nytimes.com/roomfordebate/2013/11/24/what-weve-learned-from-nafta.

are likely to be U.S. exports of $617 billion and U.S. imports of $666 billion, for a total of $1.3 trillion.

Real U.S. trade with its North American partners grew 156 percent in 20 years. Of course all three economies are larger: real North American gross domestic product grew 70 percent between 1993 and 2013 But we have calculated that real two-way trade grew faster than real gross domestic product, by a margin of 86 percentage points. Nafta can claim much of the credit, and faster trade growth raised income in all three countries.

Is Nafta also responsible for the rising U.S. trade deficit with its northern and southern neighbors, growing from $1 billion in 1993 to $49 billion in 2013? No. Trade agreements liberalize trade, but trade liberalization does not lead to trade deficits. If it did, China's trade deficit would be immense, since China has liberalized more than almost any country since 1993.

Contrary to mercantilist dogma, trade deficits reflect macroeconomic forces, like the level of private savings and investment, and the fiscal position, not the extent of protection at the border. When savings are higher, or investment is lower, or the fiscal position is stronger, the country will have a smaller trade deficit (or a larger trade surplus).

Put in proper perspective, Nafta was not about net jobs lost or gained, or changes in the trade deficit. Its goal was to increase living standards in the partner countries. With updates, Nafta has served as the model for U.S. free trade agreements with 17 other partners around the world, and currently serves as a reference for trans-Pacific and trans-Atlantic negotiations. At this pace, in another 20 years, Nafta may well be remembered as the template for U.S. commercial engagement with the world!

Mexico Suffered, and the United States Felt Its Pain

Laura Carlsen, the director of the Americas program at the Center for International Policy.

Updated November 24, 2013, 5:11 P.M.

Nafta is limping toward its 20th anniversary with a beat-up image and a bad track record. Recent polls show that the majority of the U.S. people favors "leaving" or "renegotiating" the model trade agreement.

While much has been said about its impact on U.S. job loss and eroding labor conditions, some of the most severe impacts of Nafta have been felt south of the border.

Nafta has cut a path of destruction through Mexico. Since the agreement went into force in 1994, the country's annual per capita growth flat-lined to an average of just 1.2 percent—one of the lowest in the hemisphere. Its real wage has declined and unemployment is up.

As heavily subsidized U.S. corn and other staples poured into Mexico, producer prices dropped and small farmers found themselves unable to make a living. Some two million have been forced to leave their farms since Nafta. At the same time, consumer food prices rose, notably the cost of the omnipresent tortilla.

As a result, 20 million Mexicans live in "food poverty". Twenty-five percent of the population does not have access to basic food and one-fifth of Mexican children suffer from malnutrition. Transnational industrial corridors in rural areas have contaminated rivers and sickened the population and typically, women bear the heaviest impact.

Not all of Mexico's problems can be laid at Nafta's doorstep. But many have a direct causal link. The agreement drastically restructured Mexico's economy and closed off other development paths by prohibiting protective tariffs, support for strategic sectors and financial controls.

Nafta's failure in Mexico has a direct impact on the United States. Although it has declined recently, jobless Mexicans migrated to the United States at an unprecedented rate of half a million a year after Nafta.

Workers in both countries lose when companies move, when companies threaten to move as leverage in negotiations, and when nations like Mexico lower labor rights and environmental enforcement to attract investment.

Farmers lose when transnational corporations take over the land they supported their families on for generations. Consumers lose with the imposition of a food production model heavy on chemical use, corporate concentration, genetically modified seed and processed foods. Border communities lose when lower environmental standards for investors affect shared ecosystems.

The increase in people living in poverty feeds organized crime recruitment and the breakdown of communities. Increased border activity facilitates smuggling arms and illegal substances.

After promising to renegotiate Nafta for many of these reasons, the Obama administration is now pushing the Trans-Pacific Partnership. The Pacific pact, which is a regional Nafta-style trade agreement, would grant even greater privileges to transnational corporations and would exacerbate problems for Mexico and other developing countries.

That's not good for them, and it's not good for the United States.

Mexico's Growth Has Helped the U.S.

Gerónimo Gutiérrez, the managing director of the North American Development Bank.

Updated November 24, 2013, 8:13 P.M.

Despite challenges that may sometimes seem daunting, the relationship between Mexico and the United States has shown remarkable resilience and has been by and large mutually beneficial. Nafta is largely the catalyst to the strength of this relationship.

Nafta was conceived as a way to increase trade and investment flows by setting a set of common rules to govern trade relations. Trade flows among the three countries have grown well above total output, investment flows have also increased significantly, and the vast majority of trade and investment relations among the three partners occur without disputes.

Trade between the United States and Mexico reached nearly $500 billion in 2012, which represents more than a six-fold increase since 1992 when Nafta negotiations concluded.

While an impressive figure on its face, what often astounds Americans and Mexicans alike is that Mexico buys more from the United States than the BRICs combined—Brazil, Russia, India and China. As cited by the U.S. Chamber of Commerce, 6 million U.S. jobs depend on trade with Mexico. This is a border-oriented relationship, yes, given the volume of surface trade, but states such as Ohio, Pennsylvania and New York with export goods such as transportation equipment, metals and jewelry, also benefit greatly from the growing consumer base of the U.S.'s southern neighbor. According to the Woodrow Wilson Center, 25 cents of every dollar of imported goods from Canada to the U.S. is "Made in USA" content, and the figure is 40 cents of every dollar for goods imported from Mexico. This indicates that Nafta is creating partners and not competitors among its member countries.

As for Mexico's interest in this bilateral relationship, it can be summarized in two facts: about 80 percent of Mexico's exports go to the U.S., while 50 percent of the accumulated foreign direct investment received between 2000 and 2011 comes from its northern neighbor. Moreover, Nafta has been the fundamental anchor for reforms that make Mexico a more modern economy and open society.

Nafta has been clearly successful. Yet, a difficult and complex global economic environment calls on public and private leaders to continue looking ahead. Thinking about North America, and in particular about what can be done to keep the region competitive, has never been timelier.

B. The "Gingrich Revolution" and Its Legacy

1. Bill Clinton and Newt Gingrich Debate the Role of Government (1995)*

Led by Georgia Representative Newt Gingrich, Republicans scored stunning victories in the 1994 elections, gaining substantial majorities in both chambers of Congress. As Speaker of the House in the new Republican-controlled Congress, Gingrich became a formidable political adversary to Democratic president Bill Clinton. Some observers have seen in the "Gingrich Revolution" the origins of a new era in American politics, characterized by sharp ideological differences and stubborn unwillingness to compromise. At bottom, the differences between the two parties rested on some basic disagreements not just about specific policies, but about the nature of government itself—an issue as old as the Republic. In the following exchange from 1995 between Clinton and Gingrich, what are their fundamental premises about the character of government and its relation to society at large? Which do you find more persuasive, and why?

Bill Clinton

I grew up with a sense that the absence of a strong federal government did not necessarily mean that people had more freedom and opportunity. In fact, the national government had to affirmatively step in to make sure everybody had a fair chance....

The role of government is not as simple and obvious as it was during the New Deal. At that time, the government helped working people directly by giving them jobs. The sorts of things we have to do now to create opportunity have major payoffs but you don't see them until later. Sometimes, because the connection of the policy to the job payoff is indirect, you don't see it at all. For example, I believe with all my heart that our economic plan was in the best interests of America, bringing the

---

*From *Newsweek* 125, no. 15 (1995): 20–25.

deficit down, investing more in education and giving working families with incomes under $25,000 a tax break, to encourage work over welfare. But it's hard for people to see the connection between these policies and economic growth. The same is true on trade. NAFTA opened up markets in Mexico and Canada, and the GATT treaty increased trade throughout the world. They contributed to the creation of 6.1 million new jobs and the lowest combined rate of unemployment and inflation in 25 years.

I think the American people are torn about what role government ought to play. They say they can't stand big government and they want less of it—but they have huge aspirations for it. . . .

I believe the role of government is to help create good jobs; to increase our security at home and abroad; to reform government, making it smaller and less bureaucratic; to demand more personal responsibility from all our citizens; and most important, to expand education and training so that all our citizens have the chance to make the most of their own lives.

Newt Gingrich

Because I am a conservative, people get the mistaken idea that I hate government. But one can't grow up on U.S. Army bases, attend graduate school on a National Defense Education Act Fellowship, and then go on to teach at a state college and have a hatred of government. My stepfather served in the Army for 27 years, and my dad served in the Navy and worked for the Air Force, fixing B-52s. I revere the United States government as the greatest institution of freedom in the history of the human race.

Government does some things very well. It defends the nation. It keeps the peace. It freed the slaves. It builds useful things, like the Panama Canal, and enables valuable research, like discovering the cure for polio. It can shape market forces creating the right incentives for saving or investing. Those are things government can do.

But government, as a general rule, does a very poor job at fine-grained, detailed decisions. It's too slow, too political, it just doesn't have the capacity. The idea of the government in Washington trying to decide where to put a bridge in a Georgia county is just crazy. It's insane. Government can run very small, very elite bureaucracies very well. But the longer government stays in charge of something, the more bureaucratic, the slower, the more cumbersome, the more inefficient it becomes. . . .

Our modern leaders have forgotten that government cannot substitute for private initiative, personal responsibility, or faith. . . .

Where Lyndon Johnson went wrong was that he thought government could do it all. In the 1960s, government crowded out private sector voluntarism. Secular bureaucracy crowded out spiritual commitment. . . .

Yes, there was poverty and squalor before the welfare state. The transition from a rural to an urban state in the 19th and early 20th centuries was harsh. But a tremendous effort was made to rise above that squalor, and most people did it. Huge numbers of immigrants arrived not speaking English and without any money, and a generation later they were full citizens earning a good living and moving to the suburbs. Now, under the current system, they get trapped in poverty for three generations. They get more desperate, more hopeless. They feel they have no future. That is the fruit of the 1960s when the Great Society began to destroy the spirit of America.

2. A Republican Leader Appraises the "Gingrich Revolution" (2005)*

Dick Armey was a long-serving U.S. Representative from Texas, a close political ally of Newt Gingrich, and a principal author of the "Contract with America" that constituted the Gingrich Republicans' campaign platform in 1994. In the selection below, he looks back on the consequences of the "Gingrich Revolution" from the vantage point of 10 years later. What does Armey see as its main achievements and shortcomings?

Ten years ago, Republicans staged a remarkable upset and gained control of Congress during the 1994 elections. Armed with a vision of limited government and individual freedom, Republicans won a majority in the Senate for the first time since 1986 and a majority in the House for the first time since 1954. Republican power was consolidated further in 2000, with President Bush's winning the White House....

The Contract with America was an extraordinary moment in American political history that demonstrated the importance of policy over politics. In fact, there is no better example of Armey's Axiom, "When we're like us we win; when we're like them we lose." The Contract was a defining document of limited government that garnered enough support to topple Democratic rule in Congress. Before the Republican takeover, Democrats had controlled the House for 40 years. In January 1995, when Republicans were sworn in, only one member of Congress had ever seen a Republican majority: Sid Yates, a Democrat who was over 80 years old. The only Republican who had ever seen a Republican majority was a member from Missouri who had been in Washington as a page. A major reason why it had taken so long to overcome the chronic majority status of the Democrats was that Republicans had spent much of the previous 40 years becoming more and more like the Democrats. It reached the point where one ranking Republican on a committee was described in the *Wall Street Journal* as a wholly owned subsidiary of the Democratic chairman. Even more disconcerting, nobody in the ranks of the Republican leadership was concerned or offended by the comment. Some of the young Turks (myself included) who were a constant source of embarrassment to the old guard objected, but the fact of the matter was that Republicans were content to be like Democrats and just get along in peace. That fact raises another of Armey's Axioms, "If you love peace more than freedom, you lose."...

On the strength and popularity of the Contract, Republicans won the majority. But it is important to understand that, even at that moment in 1995 when Republicans gained the majority for the first time in 40 years, it was not a majority of small-government conservatives; they were still a minority within the party. Setting party affiliations aside, the majority, composed of Democrats and moderate Republicans, still favored bigger government. For this group, it was business as usual, handing out perks and spending on pork. In fact, government would have grown were it not for the leadership's ability to exert a message of smaller government....

In retrospect, Republicans did some remarkable things in the short period after the election. One reason they were able to do so was that many Republican

*Excerpt from Dick Armey, "Reflections on the Republican Revolution," in *Republican Revolution 10 Years Later: Smaller Government or Business as Usual?*, ed. Chris Edwards (Washington DC: The Cato Institute, 2005), 5–16. Reprinted by permission of the publisher.

members were happy to be in the new majority and were much aware of the fact that the leadership had created this opportunity. Every new Republican chairman was someone who had previously been resigned to being a member of a permanent minority. Winning the majority generated an intense sense of appreciation and loyalty, and a willingness to work with the leadership that was the source of this extraordinary opportunity. Yet, as Republicans became comfortable with being in the majority, this cohesiveness began to fade, giving way to politics as usual and expanding government....

The first 100 days were remarkable. The House passed a wide range of reforms, including tax cuts, a balanced-budget amendment, and civil justice reforms....We did remarkable things in those first three or four years of a Republican majority, largely because the leadership was able to impose a standard of limited government on members who felt a debt of gratitude for the new majority status. That situation no longer exists....Current members no longer feel the same sense of loyalty to leadership as they did in 1995. The committee system has reasserted its dominance and made it much more difficult for leadership to control the agenda....Of course, the tragic events of 9/11 and the war on terrorism have fueled growth in government, and the weak economy has generated pressure for increased government intervention, such as trade protection and bailouts for specific industries. President Bush did deliver on his promise to cut taxes, but Congress has yet to muster the needed votes to make them permanent....

In the mid-1990s, the GOP took maximum advantage of the moment. We did as much as could be done and are proud of what we accomplished. The future could be even more challenging and more rewarding. Grass-roots activism will be required to break the status quo and place the nation on a more secure fiscal footing. Perhaps the most effective tactic will be mobilizing nontraditional voters who have little to lose from toppling the status quo. One key bloc of nontraditional voters who face much higher tax burdens unless Congress makes fundamental reforms is young adults. Reforming Social Security and other entitlement programs can avoid those higher tax burdens and should help mobilize the young, who should be a key outreach group for the GOP. Reforms such as Social Security personal accounts are both good politics and good policy.

C. "Third-Wave" Feminism

1. Rebecca Walker Defines the "Third Wave" (1992)*

By the final decade of the twentieth century, the "second-wave" feminist movement that had arisen in the post–World War II decades seemed to many younger women to have crested, as new concerns about workplace equity, violence against women, and balancing family and career came increasingly to the fore. In the wake of the notorious Senate confirmation hearings for Supreme Court nominee Clarence Thomas, accused by his former colleague Anita Hill of sexual harassment, then Yale student

---

*"Becoming the Third Wave," by Rebecca Walker. Reprinted by permission of *Ms. magazine*, © 1992.

Rebecca Walker, daughter of acclaimed writer Alice Walker (author, among other works, of The Color Purple*), wrote the following article in 1992 proclaiming the arrival of "third-wave" feminism." What, if anything, did she see as new in the "third wave"? In both tone and substance, how does she differ from second-wave feminist leaders like Betty Friedan (see Chapter 36, section C)?*

To me, the [Clarence Thomas Senate confirmation] hearings were not about determining whether or not Clarence Thomas did in fact harass Anita Hill. They were about checking and redefining the extent of women's credibility and power.

Can a woman's experience undermine a man's career? Can a woman's voice, a woman's sense of self-worth and injustice, challenge a structure predicated upon the subjugation of our gender? Anita Hill's testimony threatened to do that and more. If Thomas had not been confirmed, every man in the United States would be at risk. For how many senators never told a sexist joke? How many men have not used their protected male privilege to thwart in some way the influence or ideas of a woman colleague, friend, or relative? . . .

While some may laud the whole spectacle for the consciousness it raised around sexual harassment, its very real outcome is more informative. He was promoted. She was repudiated. Men were assured of the inviolability of their penis/power. Women were admonished to keep their experiences to themselves.

The backlash against U.S. women is real. As the misconception of equality between the sexes becomes more ubiquitous, so does the attempt to restrict the boundaries of women's personal and political power. Thomas' confirmation, the ultimate rally of support for the male paradigm of harassment, sends a clear message to women: "Shut up! Even if you speak, we will not listen."

I will not be silenced.

I acknowledge the fact that we live under siege. I intend to fight back. I have uncovered and unleashed more repressed anger than I thought possible. For the umpteenth time in my 22 years, I have been radicalized, politicized, shaken awake. I have come to voice again, and this time my voice is not conciliatory.

The night after Thomas's confirmation I ask the man I am intimate with what he thinks of the whole mess. His concern is primarily with Thomas' propensity to demolish civil rights and opportunities for people of color. I launch into a tirade. "When will progressive black men prioritize my rights and well-being? When will they stop talking so damn much about 'the race' as if it revolved exclusively around them?" He tells me I wear my emotions on my sleeve. I scream "I need to know, are you with me or are you going to help them try to destroy me?" . . .

I am ready to decide, as my mother decided before me, to devote much of my energy to the history, health, and healing of women. Each of my choices will have to hold to my feminist standard of justice.

To be a feminist is to integrate an ideology of equality and female empowerment into the very fiber of my life. It is to search for personal clarity in the midst of systemic destruction, to join in sisterhood with women when often we are divided, to understand power structures with the intention of challenging them.

While this may sound simple, it is exactly the kind of stand that many of my peers are unwilling to take. So I write this as a plea to all women, especially the women of my generation: Let Thomas' confirmation serve to remind you, as it did me, that the fight is far from over. Let this dismissal of a woman's experience move you to anger. Turn that outrage into political power. Do not vote for them unless they work for us. Do not have sex with them, do not break bread with them, do not nurture them if they don't prioritize our freedom to control our bodies and our lives.

I am not a postfeminism feminist. I am the Third Wave.

2. Linda Greenhouse Defends the Violence Against Women Act (2000)[*]

Linda Greenhouse, longtime Supreme Court reporter for the New York Times *here comments on the U.S. Supreme Court decision in* United States v. Morrison *that invalidated parts of the 1994 Violence Against Women Act. Her commentary is a sharp reminder that feminist aspirations, like so many others, must be pursued within a constitutional framework that can sometimes seem unjustifiably constraining. In her view, how legitimate was the Court's decision in this case?*

At first glance, the Violence Against Women Act appeared an unlikely battleground for the Supreme Court's continuing federalism wars.

This 1994 federal law neither told the states to do anything nor prohibited them from taking any action. By permitting private damage suits by victims of "gender-motivated violence" against their attackers, the law did not expose the states themselves to any new legal liability.

This was no titanic struggle among co-equal sovereigns: when the legislation was pending in Congress, the attorneys general from 38 states urged its passage, and 36 states joined a brief supporting the law before the Supreme Court. Only one, Alabama, filed a brief asking the justices to strike the law down.

Despite all that, the court invalidated a central provision of the law on Monday by a 5-to-4 vote. Developments at the court over the last five years made the law a nearly perfect target for the narrow but determined majority of justices who, through half a dozen earlier rulings, brought the court to the point at which the invalidation of the Violence Against Women Act, as an unconstitutional exercise in Congressional overreaching, was close to inevitable.

There are distinct strands to the court's new federalism jurisprudence, and in a formal sense, the decision in *United States v. Morrison*, Monday's ruling, represents only one of them: holding Congress to its limited and enumerated powers. In this sense, the ruling flowed directly from a 1995 decision that struck down, as beyond Congress's power to regulate interstate commerce, a law that made it a federal crime to carry a gun near a school. That decision, *United States v. Lopez*, was the first time since the New Deal that the court found Congress to have exceeded its authority under the commerce clause. States' rights, as such, were not directly at issue either in the *Lopez* case or in the decision on Monday.

But in a broader sense, the latest decision represents something more: a convergence between the court's focus on a Congress of limited powers and its newly found

---

solicitude for state sovereignty, the focus of other recent federalism decisions that have carved out new immunities for the states from federal court lawsuits or federal policy "commandeering." The convergence lay not so much in anything Chief Justice William H. Rehnquist's majority opinion said explicitly, but in the background music of a decision that rejected a large volume of evidence that the law's sponsors had compiled to show why a national approach to violence against women was needed.

"The court applied its own meta-test" to the legislative record, said Prof. Laurence H. Tribe of Harvard Law School: "We don't care what the findings are, if accepting them endangers our vision of state sovereignty, our view of the architecture of our system." That test applies, Professor Tribe said in an interview, "even when the states are basically willing bystanders."

Further, the decision moved the federalism counterrevolution closer than any of the other recent cases toward the core issues of civil rights for which the court for so long had given Congress wide scope. By ruling that the Violence Against Women Act was not an appropriate exercise of Congress's power to enforce the equal protection guarantee of the 14th Amendment, the court emphasized that in the area of civil rights, no less than interstate commerce, Congressional assertions of power were now to be scrutinized under a judicial microscope.

"It's the intersection of the New Deal and civil rights, coming together in a case concerning women," Prof. Judith Resnik of Yale Law School said in an interview. She said the court's rejection of the argument that violence against women was an appropriate subject for national legislation was a reminder of earlier eras, when the Supreme Court viewed labor-management issues and, even earlier, slavery, as a matter of interpersonal relations, not properly subject to federal intervention.

In the years leading up to its final passage, the Violence Against Women Act was a frequent target of criticism from federal judges, including Chief Justice Rehnquist, who singled it out in a 1998 speech as one of "the more notable examples" of laws that unduly expanded the jurisdiction of the federal courts. "Our system will look more and more like the French government, where even the most minor details are ordained by the national government in Paris," the chief justice warned in a speech to the American Law Institute.

The familiar federal civil rights laws that bar discrimination in employment and in public accommodations are not in any danger from the decision, which cast no doubt on the court"s assumption in prior cases that jobs, hotels, restaurants and the like are part of the national economy that Congress can properly regulate under its commerce power.

But when states themselves are defendants, there are strong signals that the court is looking through a different lens. Already, the court has declared states immune from suit by their employees for federal labor law violations and for age discrimination. In its next term, the justices will decide whether states can be sued under the Americans With Disabilities Act.

Beyond those particular implications, the broader fallout from the decision this week could lie outside the courtroom. Beginning with the *Lopez* decision, which invalidated a law few people had ever heard of, most of the court's federalism rulings have involved obscure statutes or obscure constitutional provisions like the 10th and 11th Amendments. As a result, a constitutional development of potentially enormous significance has been unfolding—albeit in plain sight—largely outside the realm of public discussion.

That could change, given the higher public profile of the Violence Against Women Act, the considerable attention the decision has received, and the closeness of the vote. Not too many years ago, it would hardly have seemed likely that questions about federalism might dominate a Supreme Court confirmation hearing. Now that prospect seems likely when the next vacancy occurs.

In another respect, the fallout from the decision could be surprising. Prof. Glenn H. Reynolds of the University of Tennessee Law School noted in an interview today that to regard the decision as a victory for conservatives could well be short-sighted. As recent Congressional debates on flag burning, school prayer, abortion methods and other such issues indicate, he said, much of what Congress does these days is symbolic, and much of the symbolism is conservative. But under the logic of this week's decision, Professor Reynolds added, any action in these areas would almost certainly exceed Congress's authority. "The beauty of our system is that everything bites back eventually," he said.

D. The Deadlocked Election of 2000

I. The Supreme Court Makes George W. Bush President (2000)*

The American people tried to elect a president on November 4, 2000, but one month later, after a seemingly endless series of controversies and courtroom battles over vote counting in Florida, they were still not sure who had won. On December 12, the U.S. Supreme Court overruled the Florida Supreme Court's order to conduct a manual recount and thereby made George W. Bush the next president of the United States. In Bush v. Gore, *the black-robed justices held that Florida, under pressing time constraints, could not ensure the uniform reevaluation of each vote. Without such uniformity, a recount would violate the equal protection clause of the U.S. Constitution's Fourteenth Amendment. As is apparent in the excerpt from the majority opinion provided here, the Supreme Court's decision rested heavily on the particular challenges posed by punch-card balloting. How persuasive is the Court's reasoning?*

The right to vote is protected in more than the initial allocation of the franchise. Equal protection applies as well to the manner of its exercise. Having once granted the right to vote on equal terms, the State may not, by later arbitrary and disparate treatment, value one person's vote over that of another. It must be remembered that "the right of suffrage can be denied by a debasement or dilution of the weight of a citizen's vote just as effectively as by wholly prohibiting the free exercise of the franchise."

There is no difference between the two sides of the present controversy on these basic propositions. Respondents say that the very purpose of vindicating the right to vote justifies the recount procedures now at issue. The question before us, however, is whether the recount procedures the Florida Supreme Court has adopted

---

*Bush v. Gore, 121 S. Ct. 530–533 (2000).

are consistent with its obligation to avoid arbitrary and disparate treatment of the members of its electorate.

Much of the controversy seems to revolve around ballot cards designed to be perforated by a stylus but which, either through error or deliberate omission, have not been perforated with sufficient precision for a machine to count them. In some cases a piece of the card—a chad—is hanging, say by two corners. In other cases there is no separation at all, just an indentation.

The Florida Supreme Court has ordered that the intent of the voter be discerned from such ballots....This is unobjectionable as an abstract proposition and a starting principle. The problem inheres in the absence of specific standards to ensure its equal application. The formulation of uniform rules to determine intent based on these recurring circumstances is practicable and, we conclude, necessary.

The law does not refrain from searching for the intent of the actor in a multitude of circumstances....In this instance, however, the question is not whether to believe a witness but how to interpret the marks or holes or scratches on an inanimate object, a piece of cardboard or paper which, it is said, might not have registered as a vote during the machine count. The factfinder confronts a thing, not a person. The search for intent can be confined by specific rules designed to ensure uniform treatment.

The want of those rules here has led to unequal evaluation of ballots in various respects....[T]he standards for accepting or rejecting contested ballots might vary not only from county to county but indeed within a single county from one recount team to another.

The record provides some examples. A monitor in Miami-Dade County testified at trial that he observed that three members of the county canvassing board applied different standards in defining a legal vote....Palm Beach County, for example, began the process with a 1990 guideline which precluded counting completely attached chads, switched to a rule that considered a vote to be legal if any light could be seen through a chad, changed back to the 1990 rule, and then abandoned any pretense of a *per se* rule, only to have a court order that the county consider dimpled chads legal....

...Broward County used a more forgiving standard than Palm Beach County, and uncovered almost three times as many new votes, a result markedly disproportionate to the difference in population between the counties.

...The State Supreme Court's inclusion of vote counts based on these variant standards exemplifies concerns with the remedial processes that were under way.

That brings the analysis to yet a further equal protection problem. The votes certified by the court included a partial total from one county, Miami-Dade. The Florida Supreme Court's decision thus gives no assurance that the recounts included in a final certification must be complete. Indeed, it is respondent's submission that it would be consistent with the rules for the recount procedures to include whatever partial counts are done by the time of final certification, and we interpret the Florida Supreme Court's decision to permit this. This accommodation no doubt results from the truncated contest period....[But t]he press of time does not diminish the constitutional concern. A desire for speed is not a general excuse for ignoring equal protection guarantees....

The recount process, in its features here described, is inconsistent with the minimum procedures necessary to protect the fundamental right of each voter....

The Supreme Court of Florida has said that the legislature intended the State's electors to "participate fully in the federal electoral process," as provided in 3 U.S.C. § 5. 779 So. 2d at 270....That statute, in turn, requires that any controversy or contest that is designed to lead to a conclusive selection of electors be completed by December 12. That date is upon us, and there is no recount procedure in place under the State Supreme Court's order that comports with minimal constitutional standards. Because it is evident that any recount seeking to meet the December 12 date will be unconstitutional for the reasons we have discussed, we reverse the judgment of the Supreme Court of Florida ordering a recount to proceed....

None are more conscious of the vital limits on judicial authority than are the members of this Court, and none stand more in admiration of the Constitution's design to leave the selection of the President to the people, through their legislatures, and to the political sphere. When contending parties invoke the process of the courts, however, it becomes our unsought responsibility to resolve the federal and constitutional issues the judicial system has been forced to confront.

The judgment of the Supreme Court of Florida is reversed and the case is remanded for further proceedings not inconsistent with this opinion.

2. Justice Stevens Dissents (2000)[*]

In a sharp dissent from the majority opinion in Bush v. Gore, *U.S. Supreme Court Justice John Paul Stevens contended that the Court had no grounds to meddle in the internal affairs of Florida, whose constitution and judges were fully capable of handling the matter. The obvious implication of Stevens's argument for local control was that the Florida court's decision in favor of the recount should stand—the outcome for which Al Gore's legal team had been fighting. Why do you think that Stevens's view did not prevail?*

The Constitution assigns to the States the primary responsibility for determining the manner of selecting the Presidential electors. When questions arise about the meaning of state laws, including election laws, it is our settled practice to accept the opinions of the highest courts of the States as providing the final answers. On rare occasions, however, either federal statutes or the Federal Constitution may require federal judicial intervention in state elections. This is not such an occasion.

The federal questions that ultimately emerged in this case are not substantial. Article II [of the U.S. Constitution] provides that "each *State* shall appoint, in such Manner as the Legislature *thereof* may direct, a Number of Electors."...The legislative power in Florida is subject to judicial review pursuant to Article V of the Florida Constitution, and nothing in Article II of the Federal Constitution frees the state legislature from the constraints in the state constitution that created it. Moreover, the Florida Legislature's own decision to employ a unitary code for all elections indicates that it intended the Florida Supreme Court to play the same role in Presidential

---

[*]*Bush v. Gore*, 121 S. Ct. 539–542 (2000).

elections that it has historically played in resolving electoral disputes. The Florida Supreme Court's exercise of appellate jurisdiction therefore was wholly consistent with, and indeed contemplated by, the grant of authority in Article II.

…[W]e have never before called into question the substantive standard by which a State determines that a vote has been legally cast….

Even assuming that aspects of the remedial scheme might ultimately be found to violate the Equal Protection Clause, I could not subscribe to the majority's disposition of the case. As the majority explicitly holds, once a state legislature determines to select electors through a popular vote, the right to have one's vote counted is of constitutional stature. As the majority further acknowledges, Florida law holds that all ballots that reveal the intent of the voter constitute valid votes. Recognizing these principles, the majority nonetheless orders the termination of the contest proceeding before all such votes have been tabulated. Under their own reasoning, the appropriate course of action would be to remand to allow more specific procedures for implementing the [state] legislature's uniform general standard to be established….

What must underlie petitioners' entire federal assault on the Florida election procedures is an unstated lack of confidence in the impartiality and capacity of the state judges who would make the critical decisions if the vote count were to proceed. Otherwise, their position is wholly without merit. The endorsement of that position by the majority of this Court can only lend credence to the most cynical appraisal of the work of judges throughout the land. It is confidence in the men and women who administer the judicial system that is the true backbone of the rule of law. Time will one day heal the wound to that confidence that will be inflicted by today's decision. One thing, however, is certain. Although we may never know with complete certainty the identity of the winner of this year's Presidential election, the identity of the loser is perfectly clear. It is the Nation's confidence in the judge as an impartial guardian of the rule of law.

I respectfully dissent.

3. William Safire Sees All Roads Leading to Bush (2000)[*]

A week before its historic ruling, the U.S. Supreme Court—reacting to a decision by the Florida Supreme Court to extend the legal deadline for certifying the state's vote—demanded that the Florida court "clarify" its reasoning. As the country waited to hear the Florida court's clarification, New York Times *columnist William Safire advised the state's seven justices to put an end to the turmoil by letting the machine-counted totals stand. In this excerpt, Safire argues that regardless of what the Florida court did, George W. Bush would inevitably sit in the Oval Office. Was Safire's assumption of Bush's inevitable victory justified?*

In "vacating"—nullifying—the Florida Supreme Court's decision to change election law by extending the recount deadline, the U.S. Supreme Court followed Justice Ruth Bader Ginsburg's advice to tell the state jurists to "clarify" their reasoning….

---

[*]William Safire, "Al Gore Agonistes," *New York Times*, December 7, 2000.

Despite urgent, looming deadlines—the Electoral College count this month, the inaugural next—the U.S. Supremes set no deadline for a response from the Florida court. Why? Perhaps the justices in Washington wanted to give the overreaching judges in Tallahassee time and opportunity to get out of their own trap....

...[B]y accepting the state's certification of Bush electors—the Florida Supreme Court would save itself national embarrassment. In a few seeks, it could seek to justify its earlier action that has been nullified by the U.S. Supreme Court; the justices in Washington could then choose to interpret the law for future close contests or let the matter drop as overtaken by events. All faces would be saved and roiled waters calmed.

But what if the Florida Seven rule for Gore in the latest cases and deny Bush the Florida electors? That seems unlikely, given the highest Court's strong hint in its decision to vacate the original order changing the recount deadline. But if Gore and his court supporters demand a fight to the finish, then these are among the possibilities:

1. The Florida Legislature acts to send a competing slate of electors. The House of Representatives' Republican majority selects those pledged to Bush. Result: Bush is elected president in December.

2. The U.S. Supreme Court, its ruling ignored, demands the Florida court's response by a date certain. If that reply does not satisfactorily explain the vacated decision, the Supremes rule that the state court misread the federal statute and reverse the decision to delay certification. Result: Bush is elected president in December.

3. The dispute goes to the new House of Representatives, where the Constitution calls for a state-by-state vote and Republicans control a majority of the state delegations. Result: Bush is elected president in January.

Best for the country is for the Florida Supreme Court to fill its vacated decision with a revised decision upholding the Florida secretary of state's original machine recount. Second best is a unanimous U.S. Supreme Court reversal after a convoluted Florida court "clarification." Third best is the Electoral College competition. Fourth, a divisive, embittering, party-line election in the House.

Any which way, the victor will be Bush. Gore exercised a satisfying right to protest and to contest. But to insist on political martyrdom is going a bridge too far.

Thought Provokers

1. Conventional economic theory holds that free trade is always beneficial to all parties. Is that necessarily true in practice? What other concerns—such as environmental or workplace standards—should be weighed when assessing a free trade agreement?

2. In the larger context of American history, how unusual is the so-called "polarization" that set in during the 1990s? Are the American people as polarized as their leaders?

3. What goals for women remain insufficiently realized in the twenty-first century? Are women's goals in the developing world the same as in the rich countries?

4. What did the controversies surrounding the 2000 presidential election—especially the contested results in Florida and the U.S. Supreme Court's intervention—say about the health of American democracy? Did the election's outcome hamper President George W. Bush's ability to govern effectively?

41

The American People Face a New Century, 2001–2014

If there is anyone out there who still doubts
that America is a place where all things are
possible; who still wonders if the dream of
our founders is alive in our time; who still
questions the power of our democracy; tonight
is your answer.

Barack Obama,
election night victory speech,
November 4, 2008

Prologue: On September 11, 2001, Islamic terrorists hijacked passenger planes and used them as guided missiles, killing thousands of people in New York's World Trade Center, the Pentagon, and the Pennsylvania countryside. Seeking to strike back at America's elusive enemies, President George W. Bush invaded the terrorist haven of Afghanistan in October 2001, then led the nation into a war against Iraq in 2003, alleging that Iraq was developing weapons of mass destruction that might make their way into the hands of terrorists. No weapons of mass destruction were unearthed in Iraq, and America's swift military triumph soon unraveled in the face of a fierce insurgency. By the time the last U.S. troops were withdrawn in 2011, more than 4,500 American warriors had perished. A resurgent Taliban reheated the conflict in Afghanistan, the prospect of a nuclear Iran threatened a fragile balance in the Middle East, and the "war on terror" threatened to drag on indefinitely. Meanwhile, Americans continued to grapple at home with the stubborn issues of economic justice, women's rights, immigration, and racial difference, as well as rapidly changing norms about sexual identity and especially same-sex marriage. Americans signaled a willingness to move beyond the enduring racial divide when they twice, in 2008 and 2012, elected the first African American president, Barack Obama, who in 2013 declared inequality to be "the defining challenge of our time."

A. The War Against Terror

1. President Bush Claims the Right of Preemptive War (2002)*

In a commencement address at the U.S. Military Academy at West Point on June 1, 2002, George W. Bush argued for the right of preemptive war—perhaps the most controversial element of his administration's post-9/11 foreign policy. Citing the elusiveness and unpredictability of America's new enemies, Bush declared the need to strike first and fast. In this excerpt, the president's reference to "unbalanced dictators" who might deliver weapons of mass destruction to terrorists is a thinly veiled allusion to Iraq's Saddam Hussein. Indeed Iraq was the first place Bush would test his preemption doctrine. Does he make a compelling case?

For much of the last century, America's defense relied on the cold war doctrines of deterrence and containment. In some cases, those strategies still apply, but new threats also require new thinking. Deterrence—the promise of massive retaliation against nations—means nothing against shadowy terrorist networks with no nation or citizens to defend. Containment is not possible when unbalanced dictators with weapons of mass destruction can deliver those weapons on missiles or secretly provide them to terrorist allies. We cannot defend America and our friends by hoping for the best. We cannot put our faith in the word of tyrants who solemnly sign nonproliferation treaties and then systemically break them. If we wait for threats to fully materialize, we will have waited too long.

Homeland defense and missile defense are part of stronger security; they're essential priorities for America. Yet, the war on terror will not be won on the defensive. We must take the battle to the enemy, disrupt his plans, and confront the worst threats before they emerge. In the world we have entered, the only path to safety is the path of action, and this Nation will act.

Our security will require the best intelligence to reveal threats hidden in caves and growing in laboratories. Our security will require modernizing domestic agencies such as the FBI, so they're prepared to act and act quickly against danger. Our security will require transforming the military you will lead, a military that must be ready to strike at a moment's notice in any dark corner of the world. And our security will require all Americans to be forward-looking and resolute, to be ready for preemptive action when necessary to defend our liberty and to defend our lives....

All nations that decide for aggression and terror will pay a price. We will not leave the safety of America and the peace of the planet at the mercy of a few mad terrorists and tyrants. We will lift this dark threat from our country and from the world.

Because the war on terror will require resolve and patience, it will also require firm moral purpose. In this way our struggle is similar to the cold war. Now, as then,

---

*George W. Bush, "Commencement Address at the United States Military Academy in West Point, New York," June 1, 2002; available at www.dartmouth.edu/~govdocs/docs/iraq/060102.pdf.

our enemies are totalitarians, holding a creed of power with no place for human dignity. Now, as then, they seek to impose a joyless conformity, to control every life and all of life.

America confronted imperial communism in many different ways, diplomatic, economic, and military. Yet, moral clarity was essential to our victory in the cold war....

Some worry that it is somehow undiplomatic or impolite to speak the language of right and wrong. I disagree. Different circumstances require different methods but not different moralities. Moral truth is the same in every culture, in every time, and in every place. Targeting innocent civilians for murder is always and everywhere wrong. Brutality against women is always and everywhere wrong. There can be no neutrality between justice and cruelty, between the innocent and the guilty. We are in a conflict between good and evil, and America will call evil by its name. By confronting evil and lawless regimes, we do not create a problem; we reveal a problem. And we will lead the world in opposing it....

...America stands for more than the absence of war. We have a great opportunity to extend a just peace by replacing poverty, repression, and resentment around the world with hope of a better day.... When it comes to the common rights and needs of men and women, there is no clash of civilizations. The requirements of freedom apply fully to Africa and Latin America and the entire Islamic world....

...Mothers and fathers and children across the Islamic world and all the world share the same fears and aspirations: In poverty, they struggle; in tyranny, they suffer; and as we saw in Afghanistan, in liberation, they celebrate.

America has a greater objective than controlling threats and containing resentment. We will work for a just and peaceful world beyond the war on terror.

The bicentennial class of West Point now enters this drama. With all in the United States Army, you will stand between your fellow citizens and grave danger. You will help establish a peace that allows millions around the world to live in liberty and to grow in prosperity.

2. Thomas L. Friedman Supports the War (2003)*

Much of the Bush administration's case for invading Iraq rested on the claim that Saddam Hussein was actively developing weapons of mass destruction. Yet New York Times *columnist Thomas L. Friedman believed that there was a more important reason to send in the troops. Friedman, a longtime observer of Mideast politics, insisted that by replacing Saddam's regime with a more democratic government, the United States might sow the seeds of change in that troubled region. According to Friedman, many young Arabs both resented and longed for a U.S. invasion of Iraq. Why, in Friedman's view, would Arabs desire American intervention?*

As the decision on Iraq approaches, I, like so many Americans, have had to ask myself: What do you really think? Today I explain why I think liberals under-appreciate the value of removing Saddam Hussein. And on Sunday I will explain why conservatives under-appreciate the risks of doing so—and how we should balance the two.

What liberals fail to recognize is that regime change in Iraq is not some distraction from the war on Al Qaeda. That is a bogus argument. And simply because oil is also at stake in Iraq doesn't make it illegitimate either. Some things are right to do, even if Big Oil benefits.

Although President Bush has cast the war in Iraq as being about disarmament—and that is legitimate—disarmament is not the most important prize there. Regime change is the prize. Regime transformation in Iraq could make a valuable contribution to the war on terrorism, whether Saddam is ousted or enticed into exile.

Why? Because what really threatens open, Western, liberal societies today is not Saddam and his weapons per se. He is a twisted dictator who is deterrable through conventional means. Because Saddam loves life more than he hates us. What threatens Western societies today are not the deterrables, like Saddam, but the undeterrables—the boys who did 9/11, who hate us more than they love life. It's these human missiles of mass destruction that could really destroy our open society.

So then the question is: What is the cement mixer that is churning out these undeterrables—these angry, humiliated and often unemployed Muslim youth? That cement mixer is a collection of faltering Arab states, which, as the U.N.'s Arab Human Development Report noted, have fallen so far behind the world their combined G.D.P. [Gross Domestic Product] does not equal that of Spain. And the reason they have fallen behind can be traced to their lack of three things: freedom, modern education and women's empowerment.

If we don't help transform these Arab states—which are also experiencing population explosions—to create better governance, to build more open and productive economies, to empower their women and to develop responsible media that won't blame all their ills on others, we will never begin to see the political, educational and religious reformations they need to shrink their output of undeterrables.

We have partners. Trust me, there is a part of every young Arab today that recoils at the idea of a U.S. invasion of Iraq, because of its colonial overtones. But there is a part of many young Arabs today that prays the U.S. will not only oust Saddam but all other Arab leaders as well.

It is not unreasonable to believe that if the U.S. removed Saddam and helped Iraqis build not an overnight democracy but a more accountable, progressive and democratizing regime, it would have a positive, transforming effect on the entire Arab world—a region desperately in need of a progressive model that works.

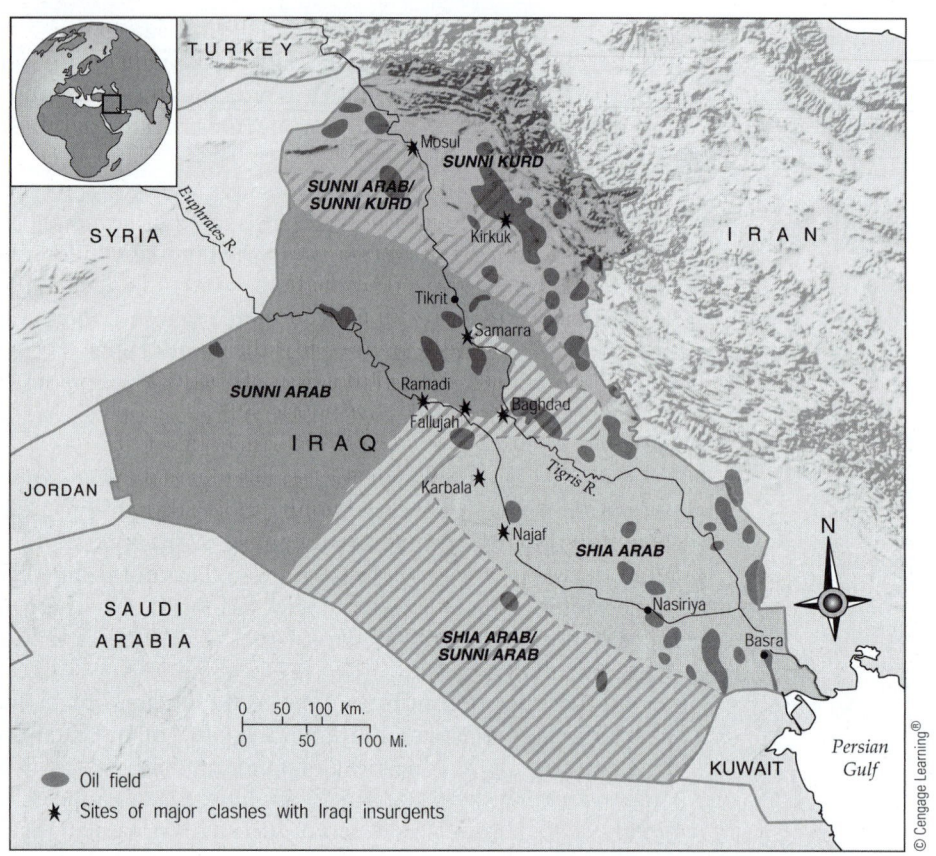

Iraq in Transition   *Carved out of the old Ottoman Empire after World War I, Iraq was long a combustible compound of rivalrous ethnic and religious groups. Saddam Hussein's dictatorial regime imposed a brutal peace on the country for twenty-four years following his ascent to power in 1979, but after the American invasion in 2003, old feuds resumed, exacerbated by stinging resentment against the occupying forces.*

Ethnic and religious groups by percent of total population (c. 25,000,000)

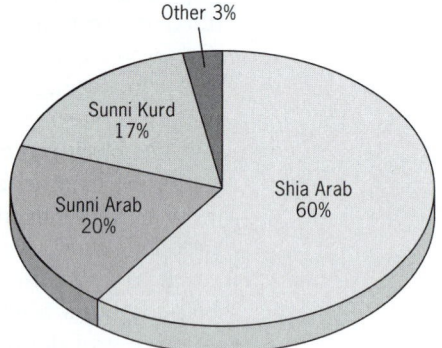

And liberals need to take heed. Just by mobilizing for war against Iraq, the U.S. has sent this region a powerful message: We will not leave you alone anymore to play with matches, because the last time you did, we got burned. Just the threat of a U.S. attack has already prompted Hezbollah to be on its best behavior in Lebanon (for fear of being next). And it has spurred Saudi Arabia's Crown Prince Abdullah to introduce a proposal to his fellow Arab leaders for an "Arab Charter" of political and economic reform.

Let me sum up my argument with two of my favorite sayings. The first is by Harvard's president, Lawrence Summers, who says: "In the history of the world, no one has ever washed a rented car." It is true of countries as well. Until the Arab peoples are given a real ownership stake in their countries—a real voice in how they are run—they will never wash them, never improve them as they should.

The second is an American Indian saying—"If we don't turn around now, we just may get where we're going." The Arab world has been digging itself into a hole for a long time. If our generation simply helps it stop digging, possibly our grandchildren and its own will reap the benefits. But if we don't help the Arabs turn around now, they just may get where they're going—a dead end where they will produce more and more undeterrables.

This is something liberals should care about—because liberating the captive peoples of the Mideast is a virtue in itself and because in today's globalized world, if you don't visit a bad neighborhood, it will visit you.

3. Dexter Filkins Finds Chaos in Iraq (2004)[*]

By 2004, American progress in Iraq had unraveled in the face of a mounting insurgency, marked by daily suicide attacks against American soldiers and Iraqi civilians. In the following passage, New York Times *reporter Dexter Filkins describes the escalating violence and the troubling prevalence of anti-American sentiments among Iraqis. What effects did suicide attacks have on Iraqi society? What might account for the attitudes of some Iraqi citizens toward the American invasion?*

Among the favorite targets of the suicide bombers were American ribbon cuttings—a pump station, for instance, or a new school—because of the crowds they brought. It got so bad that the Americans sometimes kept the unveilings of new projects a secret. Which kind of defeated the purpose. And the bombers sometimes got there anyway. Once a crowd of Iraqi children gathered around some American soldiers who were handing out candy at the unveiling of a pump station in Baghdad's Yarmouk neighborhood. A suicide bomber steered his car into the crowd of children and blew them up. And then came a second car, also filled with explosives, just to be sure. There were lots of dead children. You could never be sure about these things, but I figured the candy bombing was a target of opportunity: the suicide bombers were just loaded up and cruising, looking for targets. I'd hear that sometimes. A suicide bomber is driving around the neighborhood, looking for a target; look out.

They started to come in waves. Four a day. Ten a day. Twelve a day. Boom. Boom. Boom. Boom. Sometimes, all of them before breakfast. One morning, my colleague Ian Fisher was driving to Abu Ghraib to interview some Iraqi prisoners who were being released from American custody, when he came upon the scene of a suicide

---

[*]From Dexter Filkins, *The Forever War.* Copyright © 2008.

bombing just seconds after it had occurred. The victim had been Ezzedine Salim, the president of the Iraqi Governing Council. Ian stopped, stepped amid the bodies, did some reporting and climbed back in his car. A few more miles down the road, he came across another suicide bombing, the bomber's body in pieces on the roadside. He never made it to Abu Ghraib. "This place is crazy," he said, walking in the door.

No one wanted to stand in a crowd anymore. No one wanted to stand in line. Every morning the Iraqis who worked for the Americans in the Green Zone lined up for security checks before they were allowed inside, and the lines stretched for hundreds of yards into the streets, sometimes for hours. The same at police recruiting stations. One after the other, the car bombs flew into the lines. One after another, men wearing puffy jackets wandered into the lines, sweaty and nervous, mumbling to themselves, then exploding.

After a while, everything started to sound like a bomb. A door slamming in the house sounded like a bomb. A car backfiring sounded like a bomb. Sometimes it felt like the sounds of bombs and the call to prayer were the only sounds the country could produce, its own strange national anthem. The silence was creepy, too. One day there would be ten bombs and then the next day none. Twelve bombs and then no bombs. And I'd ask myself: Are they giving up? Or just reloading?...

I was led through the sitting area, where I spotted a woman darting out of the room on the far side—my only glimpse. I entered the dining room, and a man introduced himself. Sulaiman Abu Ibrahim, he said. He wore an ear-to-ear beard and a sheer white dishdasha through which a large stomach bulged.

The room was bare but for a television set and an acrylic mat spread wide with a Middle Eastern feast: two kinds of salad; hummus; a delicacy of crushed wheat stuffed with meat and onions called kibbeh; grilled chicken; a spinach dish, *mloukhieh;* and *mansaf,* a traditional Arab stew.

"For you, my American friend," Abu Ibrahim said, smiling and gesturing with his arms spread wide. . . .

Ibrahim had evidently figured out how little Arabic I understood, and after every couple of bites he turned to George and told him: "Look, now, the food will stick in the American's throat and he will start to choke."

We were nearing the end of the big meal.

"Would you mind if we watched a short video?" Ibrahim asked. And he popped it into a DVD player. On the TV screen appeared images of Arab fighters dressed in kafiyas, carrying Kalashnikovs and RPGs. There were scenes of Iraq. Words flashed on the screen: "The Battle for the Baghdad Airport." Ibrahim chuckled and sat back.

"Jihad is our oxygen," a voice on the video said, to the scenes of masked men firing guns. "Without jihad, we cannot breathe."

A camera panned a recently opened mass grave. Then it showed American soldiers entering Iraq.

"These are the things in Iraq the American people do not see," the voice on the DVD said. "Martyr yourself in Iraq in the name of Islam."

Ibrahim was nodding. The video flashed to a Caucasian man—the voice said he was an American—lying flat on his stomach. The screen showed a close-up of his face, and on the other side of him the legs and feet of other, unidentified men standing around him. A hand reached down, grabbed the Caucasian man's head and pulled it back. The hand produced a knife and began to cut the man's throat. The knife kept cutting, then sawing, and finally the head came free. The hand held it high.

Ibrahim was beside himself, rocking back and forth, running his finger across his throat.

"*Ameriki,*" he said, dragging the finger across his neck, "*Ameriki.*"

4. David Rothkopf Examines the Lessons of Iraq and Afghanistan (2013)*

With the conclusion of the fighting in Iraq and the winding down of the American military intervention in Afghanistan, analysts of all stripes started trying to make sense of the dozen years of war that followed the terrorist attacks of 9/11/01. David Rothkopf, an editor at Foreign Policy *magazine, focuses especially on lessons about the use of military force as an instrument of national policy. What comparisons does he draw with the Vietnam conflict and its aftermath?*

Ten years ago this March, George W. Bush launched America's invasion of Iraq. Had Twitter existed back then, #ShockandAwe would have been trending. Ground operations advanced quickly. By May, the president stood in front of a banner declaring "Mission Accomplished." Simultaneously, in a less-heralded but perhaps even more egregiously premature assessment, Defense Secretary Donald Rumsfeld declared the end of "major combat" in Afghanistan. At the time, only 8,000 U.S. troops were in Afghanistan. Today, more than eight times as many are there.

These conflicts will not only define America in the eyes of the world for many decades to come, but they will also shape the views of a generation of men and women who will decide where, when, and how the United States will flex its muscles internationally. That can be beneficial if the right lessons are drawn. But in an America that simply wants to get out and not look back, the absence to date of orderly, critical analysis of where the country went wrong has been striking.

Nothing underscores this more than this spring's other major anniversary, albeit one likely to pass largely unnoticed. On March 29, 1973, the last U.S. troops withdrew from South Vietnam, which fell into communist hands just two years later.

If Vietnam seems remote, a baby-boomer nightmare far removed from the world of drones and cyberattacks, look again. The ghost of Vietnam has been omnipresent for years in planning by senior U.S. officials and military officers—sometimes leading to successful initiatives, sometimes placing a phantom hand on the tiller of state and guiding policies into the shoals.

The officers who led U.S. forces in Iraq and Afghanistan studied the lessons of insurgency learned in Vietnam, clearly shaping their thinking. Gen. David Petraeus, who attended West Point during the last years of the Vietnam War, titled his doctoral dissertation *The American Military and the Lessons of Vietnam.* In his memoir, Stanley McChrystal, the Afghanistan war general fired by President Barack Obama, tells the

---

*Excerpt from David Rothkopf, "Lessons Learned and Not," Foreign Policy, no. 199 (2013): 86–87. Reproduced with permission of Carnegie Endowment for International Peace and National Affairs, Inc. in the format Republish in a book via Copyright Clearance Center.

story of a "memorable night in Kabul" when he and diplomat Richard Holbrooke, who served in Vietnam as a young Foreign Service officer, telephoned historian Stanley Karnow to ask about the lessons that disastrous war holds for today's Afghanistan conflict. Holbrooke spoke openly and passionately about the need to avoid that fate—an endless, costly war. But as McChrystal writes, "the lessons to be drawn were anything but incontrovertible." The same might be said about the lessons of Afghanistan and Iraq, but nonetheless we must try to identify those we can. Here are a few.

1. *The Powell Doctrine still resonates.* Shock and awe was supposed to be the ultimate manifestation of the post-Vietnam impulse not to get bogged down in another quagmire. It was the Powell Doctrine: Set clear goals, invest sufficient resources, minimize casualties, and have an exit strategy—Las Vegas-style, making the points with pyrotechnics and news releases. But you have to follow the full prescription. You have to not only set goals but set the right ones—whether it's destroying an enemy or rebuilding a society. When they get muddled, problems follow. And you must have a genuine exit strategy that stops you from wading farther into a swamp, which is different from simply announcing a victory. See the first Gulf War for an example of it working. Needless to say, things didn't pan out the second time around.

2. *Beware your past failures.* Obama's foreign-policy leadership team was all hugely influenced by Vietnam—one regional ambassador even told me that he has never had a discussion with John Kerry regarding Afghanistan in which the now secretary of state did not raise the subject. Obama's hesitance to get drawn into Libya (except in a very limited way) and Syria is emblematic of this worldview, as is the focus on "light-footprint" options, such as drones, Special Forces, and cyberattacks, that seem to offer an escape from the Vietnam syndrome.

But that syndrome can also push America into premature announcements of exits (Iraq and Afghanistan), the use of morally dubious means (drone wars), or hesitation to intervene where it might serve U.S. national interests or the global good (Syria, possibly Iran, and perhaps even places such as Mali).

3. *Know your enemy.* Consider Afghanistan. If a reasonable goal were to defeat the enemy that caused the 9/11 attacks, the United States nonetheless got into trouble when it asserted that the Taliban, by supporting al Qaeda, were part of that enemy. To defeat them, the country lurched into an alliance with Pakistani agencies that probably did as much or more to support America's terrorist adversaries as they did to help the United States. In Iraq, it took years to realize that the Sunni insurgents could be, if not brought over to America's side, at least taken off the battlefield. Sadly, in Vietnam, the United States never understood that it was fighting an indigenous nationalist insurgency, not a communist plot directed by Moscow and Beijing.

4. *Know your limitations.* The United States may be the world's most powerful country (it still is, by a lot, and will be for many decades), but that does not mean it has the power to achieve whatever it seeks to do. The country faces financial constraints. There are limits to what its allies are willing to support. There are cultural, historical, geographical, and demographic obstacles that the United States can never surmount. This means that we must test our theories relentlessly—and then retest them and then test them again. Intransigence or groupthink must not be confused with leadership or clarity of vision. Situations change. So too should policies.

5. *Beware of certainties*. Afghanistan to many—me among them—was "the good war." It was the one America should be fighting rather than Iraq. In the end, however, the likelihood of achieving any lasting positive results there is even remoter than it appears to be in Iraq, which is saying something given how volatile and worrisome conditions in Iraq are. The United States is likely to end in Afghanistan by handing considerable power or at least opportunities back to the Taliban, placing bets on a corrupt, weak regime, and leaving the people, notably the women of that country, vulnerable to new horrors. And there's nothing good about that.

6. *Beware your last success*. Bad historical analogies are common—and not just when it comes to Vietnam. The Middle East was not Eastern Europe and did not welcome Western "liberation." No flowers or sweets greeted U.S. troops along Baghdad's streets—only IEDs [improvised explosive devices]. And the surge in Iraq was not an indicator that a similar approach would work in Afghanistan, as Petraeus discovered far too late to make a difference.

7. *Wars are often won by diplomats and businessmen—not soldiers*. If history shows one thing, it is that we seldom have sufficient perspective to know what is in our long-term interest. At the end of the war, Vietnam, after all, was universally regarded as a failure. Today, however, the country has something like a market economy and is integrated into Southeast Asia—and the Soviet Union is gone, in part because it bled out economically while supporting ideological allies like the North Vietnamese.

The bottom line is simply this: America ignores these lessons at its peril. Both Iraq and Afghanistan in some way are reactions to Vietnam—but also reminders that the opposite of a policy failure is no guarantee of success.

5. A Pakistani Journalist Describes Living Under the Eye of the Drones (2012)*

In the following firsthand account, what aspects of life under the threat of drone attack are most disturbing? Are drones (also known as remotely piloted aircraft, or unmanned aerial vehicles) an acceptable and legitimate way to wage war?

American drones have changed everything for al Qaeda and its local allies in Pakistan, becoming a fact of life in a secret war that is far from over. "We don't even sit together to chat anymore," the Taliban fighter told me, his voice hoarse as he combed his beard with his fingers. We were talking in a safe house in Peshawar as the fighter and one of his comrades sketched a picture of life on the run in the borderlands of Waziristan. The deadly American drones buzzing overhead, the two men said, had changed everything for al Qaeda and its local allies.

The whitewashed two-story villa bristled with activity. Down the hall from my Taliban sources sat an aggrieved tribal elder and his son in one room and two officers from Pakistan's powerful Inter-Services Intelligence (ISI) Directorate in another. I had gathered them all there to make sense of what had become the signature

*Excerpt from Pir Zubair Shah, "My Drone War," Foreign Policy, no. 192 (2012): 1–9. Reproduced with permission of Carnegie Endowment for International Peace and National Affairs, Inc. in the format Republish in a book via Copyright Clearance Center.

incident of the war in Afghanistan and Pakistan: an American drone strike, one of the first ordered on the watch of the new U.S. president, Barack Obama. The early 2009 strike had killed a local elder, along with his son, two nephews, and a guest in the South Waziristan town of Wana. Several sources had told me the family was innocent, with no connections to the Taliban or al Qaeda. But traveling to Waziristan had become too dangerous even for me, a reporter who had grown up there. So instead I had brought Waziristan to Peshawar, renting rooms for my sources in the guesthouse. I had just one night to try to figure out what had happened.

I spent the night running from room to room, assembling the story in pieces. On the first floor sat the dead elder's brother and nephew, who told me what little they knew of the incident. On the second floor, the ISI officers, over whiskey and lamb tikka, described their work helping U.S. intelligence agents sort out targets from among the images relayed back from the drones. Then there were the two Taliban fighters, whom I had first met in Waziristan in 2007. One had been a fixer for the Haqqani network, skilled at smuggling men and materiel from Pakistan into Afghanistan. The other drew a government salary as an employee of Pakistan's agriculture department but worked across the border as an explosives expert; he had lost a finger fighting the allied forces in Afghanistan. None of the men in the house knew the others were there.

The two fighters described how the militants were adapting to this new kind of warfare. The Taliban and al Qaeda had stopped using electronic devices, they told me. They would no longer gather in huge numbers, even in mosques to pray, and spent their nights outside for safety, a life that was wearing thin. "We can't sleep in the jungle the whole of our lives," one told me. Gradually, a picture of a rare incident came into focus: a deadly strike that had mistakenly taken out a man with no connection to al Qaeda or the Taliban. . . .

Although the drone campaign has become the linchpin of the Obama administration's counterterrorism strategy in Central Asia—and one it is increasingly exporting to places such as Yemen and the Horn of Africa—we know virtually nothing about it. I spent more than half a decade tracking this most secret of wars across northern Pakistan, taking late-night calls from intelligence agents, sorting through missile fragments at attack sites, counting bodies and graves, interviewing militants and victims. I dodged bullets and, once, an improvised explosive device. At various times I found myself imprisoned by the Taliban and detained by the Pakistani military. Yet even I can say very little for certain about what has happened.

The evening of June 18, 2004, was a sweltering one in South Waziristan, and the 27-year-old local Taliban leader, Nek Muhammad Wazir, had decided to eat dinner in the courtyard of his house in the village of Kari Kot, along with his two brothers and two bodyguards. Muhammad's satellite phone rang, and he picked it up. Moments later, a missile streaked through the compound and exploded, killing all five men.

At the time, no one in the Pakistani public or media knew that it was a drone. The government would say nothing, and everyone else attributed Muhammad's killing either to a Pakistani military operation—after all, soldiers had gone looking for him without success on six occasions—or to the work of U.S. forces across the border in Afghanistan. A Taliban fighter who was within earshot of the explosion told me later that the militants were totally taken by surprise. "There was a noise in the air before, and then we heard the explosion," he recalled. The villagers, however, supplied the explanation: They collected the fragments of the missile, on which was printed in black, "Made in USA."

...[I]n reality Pakistanis are deeply torn about the drones. For every anti-American rant they inspire—the recent meteoric rise of Imran Khan, the cricketer turned politician, owes a great deal to his strong opposition to the drone strikes—there is also a recognition that these strikes from the sky have their purpose. At times, they have outright benefited the Pakistani state, as in the summer of 2009, when a drone attack killed Baitullah Mehsud, the leader of a militant alliance in Waziristan who was suspected of masterminding former Prime Minister Benazir Bhutto's 2007 assassination—Pakistan's Enemy No. 1, but a villain of less consequence to the United States.

Residents of the tribal areas are similarly conflicted. Many favor the drone strikes over the alternatives, such as military operations or less selective bombardments by Pakistani bombers and helicopter gunships. Better a few houses get vaporized than an entire village turned into refugees. Even the brother of the elder I brought to the Peshawar guesthouse said as much, allowing that "in our case, it might be faulty intelligence or mischief by someone" that had caused the strike that killed his brother. Regardless, he said, "I would always go for the drones."

Either way, they are now a fact of life in a secret war that is far from over. Once I called a source—a Taliban commander in one of the tribal areas. His brother picked up the phone and told me that the commander was asleep. It was noon, and I remarked that it was an odd time for a nap. "There are drones in the sky," the brother laughingly replied, "so he is not feeling well."

B. Rising Inequality

1. President Barack Obama Calls Inequality "The Defining Issue of Our Time" (2011)[*]

Elected as the first African American president in 2008, and reelected in 2012, Barack Obama championed an ambitious program of "progressive" reform in the face of robust Republican opposition. In this 2011 speech in Osawatomie, Kansas (where Theodore Roosevelt had laid out his "New Nationalism" program a little more than a hundred years earlier), he declared inequality and stalled social mobility to be "the defining issue of our time." What does he see as the principal dangers associated with rising inequality?

This is the defining issue of our time. This is a make-or-break moment for the middle class, and for all those who are fighting to get into the middle class. Because what's at stake is whether this will be a country where working people can earn enough to raise a family, build a modest savings, own a home, secure their retirement.

---

[*]"Remarks by the President on the Economy in Osawatomie, Kansas," http://www.whitehouse.gov/the-press-office/2011/12/06/remarks-president-economy-osawatomie-kansas, accessed March 26, 2014.

You see, this isn't the first time America has faced this choice. At the turn of the last century, when a nation of farmers was transitioning to become the world's industrial giant, we had to decide: would we settle for a country where most of the new railroads and factories were controlled by a few giant monopolies that kept prices high and wages low? Would we allow our citizens and even our children to work ungodly hours in conditions that were unsafe and unsanitary? Would we restrict education to the privileged few? Because some people thought massive inequality and exploitation was just the price of progress.

Theodore Roosevelt disagreed. He was the Republican son of a wealthy family. He praised what the titans of industry had done to create jobs and grow the economy. He believed then what we know is true today: that the free market is the greatest force for economic progress in human history. It's led to a prosperity and standard of living unmatched by the rest of the world.

But Roosevelt also knew that the free market has never been a free license to take whatever you want from whoever you can. It only works when there are rules of the road to ensure that competition is fair, open, and honest. And so he busted up monopolies, forcing those companies to compete for customers with better services and better prices. And today, they still must. He fought to make sure businesses couldn't profit by exploiting children, or selling food or medicine that wasn't safe. And today, they still can't.

In 1910, Teddy Roosevelt came here, to Osawatomie, and laid out his vision for what he called a New Nationalism. "Our country," he said, "...means nothing unless it means the triumph of a real democracy...of an economic system under which each man shall be guaranteed the opportunity to show the best that there is in him."

For this, Roosevelt was called a radical, a socialist, even a communist. But today, we are a richer nation and a stronger democracy because of what he fought for in his last campaign: an eight hour work day and a minimum wage for women; insurance for the unemployed, the elderly, and those with disabilities; political reform and a progressive income tax.

Today, over one hundred years later, our economy has gone through another transformation. Over the last few decades, huge advances in technology have allowed businesses to do more with less, and made it easier for them to set up shop and hire workers anywhere in the world. And many of you know firsthand the painful disruptions this has caused for a lot of Americans.

Factories where people thought they would retire suddenly picked up and went overseas, where the workers were cheaper. Steel mills that needed 1,000 employees are now able to do the same work with 100, so that layoffs were too often permanent, not just a temporary part of the business cycle. These changes didn't just affect blue-collar workers. If you were a bank teller or a phone operator or a travel agent, you saw many in your profession replaced by ATMs or the internet. Today, even higher-skilled jobs like accountants and middle management can be outsourced to countries like China and India. And if you're someone whose job can be done cheaper by a computer or someone in another country, you don't have a lot of leverage with your employer when it comes to asking for better wages and benefits—especially since fewer Americans today are part of a union.

Now, just as there was in Teddy Roosevelt's time, there's been a certain crowd in Washington for the last few decades who respond to this economic challenge with the same old tune. "The market will take care of everything," they tell us. If only we cut more regulations and cut more taxes—especially for the wealthy—our economy will grow stronger. Sure, there will be winners and losers. But if the winners do really well, jobs and prosperity will eventually trickle down to everyone else. And even if prosperity doesn't trickle down, they argue, that's the price of liberty.

It's a simple theory—one that speaks to our rugged individualism and healthy skepticism of too much government. It fits well on a bumper sticker. Here's the problem: It doesn't work. It's never worked. It didn't work when it was tried in the decade before the Great Depression. It's not what led to the incredible post-war boom of the 50s and 60s. And it didn't work when we tried it during the last decade.

Look at the statistics. In the last few decades, the average income of the top one percent has gone up by more than 250%, to $1.2 million per year. For the top one hundredth of one percent, the average income is now $27 million per year. The typical CEO who used to earn about 30 times more than his or her workers now earns 110 times more. And yet, over the last decade, the incomes of most Americans have actually fallen by about six percent.

This kind of inequality—a level we haven't seen since the Great Depression—hurts us all. When middle-class families can no longer afford to buy the goods and services that businesses are selling, it drags down the entire economy, from top to bottom. America was built on the idea of broad-based prosperity—that's why a CEO like Henry Ford made it his mission to pay his workers enough so that they could buy the cars they made. It's also why a recent study showed that countries with less inequality tend to have stronger and steadier economic growth over the long run.

Inequality also distorts our democracy. It gives an outsized voice to the few who can afford high-priced lobbyists and unlimited campaign contributions, and runs the risk of selling out our democracy to the highest bidder. And it leaves everyone else rightly suspicious that the system in Washington is rigged against them—that our elected representatives aren't looking out for the interests of most Americans.

More fundamentally, this kind of gaping inequality gives lie to the promise at the very heart of America: that this is the place where you can make it if you try. We tell people that in this country, even if you're born with nothing, hard work can get you into the middle class; and that your children will have the chance to do even better than you. That's why immigrants from around the world flocked to our shores.

And yet, over the last few decades, the rungs on the ladder of opportunity have grown farther and farther apart, and the middle class has shrunk. A few years after World War II, a child who was born into poverty had a slightly better than 50-50 chance of becoming middle class as an adult. By 1980, that chance fell to around 40%. And if the trend of rising inequality over the last few decades continues, it's estimated that a child born today will only have a 1 in 3 chance of making it to the middle class.

Our success has never just been about survival of the fittest. It's been about building a nation where we're all better off. We pull together, we pitch in, and we do our part, believing that hard work will pay off; that responsibility will be rewarded; and that our children will inherit a nation where those values live on.

And it is that belief that rallied thousands of Americans to Osawatomie—maybe even some of your ancestors—on a rain-soaked day more than a century ago. By train, by wagon, on buggy, bicycle, and foot, they came to hear the vision of a man who loved this country, and was determined to perfect it.

"We are all Americans," Teddy Roosevelt told them that day. "Our common interests are as broad as the continent." And we still believe, in the words of the man who called for a New Nationalism all those years ago, "The fundamental rule in our national life—the rule which underlies all others—is that, on the whole, and in the long run, we shall go up or down together."

2. Charles Murray Cites the Cultural Sources of Inequality (2012)*

Charles Murray, a controversial and conservative social scientist who has written extensively on issues concerning the welfare state and racial differences, added his voice in 2012 to the highly charged discussion of rising inequality in America. What aspects of inequality does he find most disturbing? How persuasive is his explanation for the rise of inequality?

America is coming apart. For most of our nation's history, whatever the inequality in wealth between the richest and poorest citizens, we maintained a cultural equality known nowhere else in the world—for whites, anyway. "The more opulent citizens take great care not to stand aloof from the people," wrote Alexis de Tocqueville, the great chronicler of American democracy, in the 1830s. "On the contrary, they constantly keep on easy terms with the lower classes: They listen to them, they speak to them every day."

Americans love to see themselves this way. But there's a problem: It's not true anymore, and it has been progressively less true since the 1960s.

People are starting to notice the great divide. The tea party sees the aloofness in a political elite that thinks it knows best and orders the rest of America to fall in line. The Occupy movement sees it in an economic elite that lives in mansions and flies on private jets. Each is right about an aspect of the problem, but that problem is more pervasive than either political or economic inequality. What we now face is a problem of cultural inequality.

When Americans used to brag about "the American way of life"—a phrase still in common use in 1960—they were talking about a civic culture that swept an extremely large proportion of Americans of all classes into its embrace. It was a culture encompassing shared experiences of daily life and shared assumptions about central American values involving marriage, honesty, hard work and religiosity.

Over the past 50 years, that common civic culture has unraveled. We have developed a new upper class with advanced educations, often obtained at elite schools, sharing tastes and preferences that set them apart from mainstream America. At the same time, we have developed a new lower class, characterized not by poverty but by withdrawal from America's core cultural institutions.

To illustrate just how wide the gap has grown between the new upper class and the new lower class, let me start with the broader upper-middle and working classes from which they are drawn, using two fictional neighborhoods that I hereby label Belmont (after an archetypal upper-middle-class suburb near Boston) and Fishtown (after a neighborhood in Philadelphia that has been home to the white working class since the Revolution).

To be assigned to Belmont, the people in the statistical nationwide databases on which I am drawing must have at least a bachelor's degree and work as a manager, physician, attorney, engineer, architect, scientist, college professor or content producer in the media. To be assigned to Fishtown, they must have no academic degree higher than a high-school diploma. If they work, it must be in a blue-collar job, a low-skill service job such as cashier, or a low-skill white-collar job such as mail clerk or receptionist.

People who qualify for my Belmont constitute about 20% of the white population of the U.S., ages 30 to 49. People who qualify for my Fishtown constitute about 30% of the white population of the U.S., ages 30 to 49.

I specify white, meaning non-Latino white, as a way of clarifying how broad and deep the cultural divisions in the U.S. have become. Cultural inequality is not grounded in race or ethnicity. I specify ages 30 to 49—what I call prime-age adults—to make it clear that these trends are not explained by changes in the ages of marriage or retirement.

In Belmont and Fishtown, here's what happened to America's common culture between 1960 and 2010.

Marriage: In 1960, extremely high proportions of whites in both Belmont and Fishtown were married—94% in Belmont and 84% in Fishtown. In the 1970s, those percentages declined about equally in both places. Then came the great divergence. In Belmont, marriage stabilized during the mid-1980s, standing at 83% in 2010. In Fishtown, however, marriage continued to slide; as of 2010, a minority (just 48%) were married. The gap in marriage between Belmont and Fishtown grew to 35 percentage points, from just 10.

Single parenthood: Another aspect of marriage—the percentage of children born to unmarried women—showed just as great a divergence. Though politicians and media eminences are too frightened to say so, nonmarital births are problematic. On just about any measure of development you can think of, children who are born to unmarried women fare worse than the children of divorce and far worse than children raised in intact families. This unwelcome reality persists even after controlling for the income and education of the parents.

In 1960, just 2% of all white births were nonmarital. When we first started recording the education level of mothers in 1970, 6% of births to white women with no more than a high-school education—women, that is, with a Fishtown education—were out of wedlock. By 2008, 44% were nonmarital. Among the college-educated women of Belmont, less than 6% of all births were out of wedlock as of 2008, up from 1% in 1970.

Industriousness: The norms for work and women were revolutionized after 1960, but the norm for men putatively has remained the same: Healthy men are supposed to work. In practice, though, that norm has eroded everywhere. In Fishtown, the change has been drastic. (To avoid conflating this phenomenon with the latest recession, I use data collected in March 2008 as the end point for the trends.)

The primary indicator of the erosion of industriousness in the working class is the increase of prime-age males with no more than a high school education who say they are not available for work—they are "out of the labor force." That percentage went from a low of 3% in 1968 to 12% in 2008. Twelve percent may not sound like much until you think about the men we're talking about: in the prime of their working lives, their 30s and 40s, when, according to hallowed American tradition, every American man is working or looking for work. Almost one out of eight now aren't. Meanwhile, not much has changed among males with college educations. Only 3% were out of the labor force in 2008.

There's also been a notable change in the rates of less-than-full-time work. Of the men in Fishtown who had jobs, 10% worked fewer than 40 hours a week in 1960, a figure that grew to 20% by 2008. In Belmont, the number rose from 9% in 1960 to 12% in 2008.

Crime: The surge in crime that began in the mid-1960s and continued through the 1980s left Belmont almost untouched and ravaged Fishtown. From 1960 to 1995, the violent crime rate in Fishtown more than sextupled while remaining nearly flat in Belmont. The reductions in crime since the mid-1990s that have benefited the nation as a whole have been smaller in Fishtown, leaving it today with a violent crime rate that is still 4.7 times the 1960 rate.

Religiosity: Whatever your personal religious views, you need to realize that about half of American philanthropy, volunteering and associational memberships is directly church-related, and that religious Americans also account for much more nonreligious social capital than their secular neighbors. In that context, it is worrisome for the culture that the U.S. as a whole has become markedly more secular since 1960, and especially worrisome that Fishtown has become much more secular than Belmont. It runs against the prevailing narrative of secular elites versus a working class still clinging to religion, but the evidence from the General Social Survey, the most widely used database on American attitudes and values, does not leave much room for argument.

It can be said without hyperbole that these divergences put Belmont and Fishtown into different cultures.... The members of this elite have increasingly sorted themselves into hyper-wealthy and hyper-elite ZIP Codes that I call the SuperZIPs.

[L]arge clusters of SuperZIPs can be found around New York City, Los Angeles, the San Francisco–San Jose corridor, Boston and a few of the nation's other largest cities. Because running major institutions in this country usually means living near one of these cities, it works out that the nation's power elite does in fact live in a world that is far more culturally rarefied and isolated than the world of the power elite in 1960.

And the isolation is only going to get worse. Increasingly, the people who run the country were born into that world. Unlike the typical member of the elite in 1960, they have never known anything but the new upper-class culture. We are now seeing more and more third-generation members of the elite. Not even their grandparents have been able to give them a window into life in the rest of America.

Why have these new lower and upper classes emerged? For explaining the formation of the new lower class, the easy explanations from the left don't withstand scrutiny. It's not that white working class males can no longer make a "family wage" that enables them to marry. The average male employed in a working-class occupation earned as much in 2010 as he did in 1960. It's not that a bad job market led discouraged men to drop out of the labor force. Labor-force dropout increased just as fast during the boom years of the 1980s, 1990s and 2000s as it did during bad years.

As I've argued in much of my previous work, I think that the reforms of the 1960s jump-started the deterioration. Changes in social policy during the 1960s made it economically more feasible to have a child without having a husband if you were a woman or to get along without a job if you were a man; safer to commit crimes without suffering consequences; and easier to let the government deal with problems in your community that you and your neighbors formerly had to take care of.

3. Paul Krugman Dismisses the Cultural Explanation for Inequality (2012)[*]

Paul Krugman, Nobel Prize–winning economist, Princeton professor, and New York Times *columnist, sharply criticized Charles Murray's emphasis on shifting personal values as the root explanation for growing economic inequality. What does Krugman see as the principal drivers of inequality in modern American society? Who—Krugman or Murray—makes the more persuasive case? Are there other factors, besides the ones they cite, that help to explain mounting inequality?*

Lately inequality has re-entered the national conversation. Occupy Wall Street gave the issue visibility, while the Congressional Budget Office supplied hard data on the widening income gap. And the myth of a classless society has been exposed: Among rich countries, America stands out as the place where economic and social status is most likely to be inherited.

So you knew what was going to happen next. Suddenly, conservatives are telling us that it's not really about money; it's about morals. Never mind wage stagnation and all that, the real problem is the collapse of working-class family values, which is somehow the fault of liberals.

But is it really all about morals? No, it's mainly about money.

To be fair, the new book at the heart of the conservative pushback, Charles Murray's "Coming Apart: The State of White America, 1960–2010," does highlight some striking trends. Among white Americans with a high school education or less, marriage rates and male labor force participation are down, while births out of wedlock are up. Clearly, white working-class society has changed in ways that don't sound good.

But the first question one should ask is: Are things really that bad on the values front?

Mr. Murray and other conservatives often seem to assume that the decline of the traditional family has terrible implications for society as a whole. This is, of course, a longstanding position. Reading Mr. Murray, I found myself thinking about an earlier diatribe, Gertrude Himmelfarb's 1996 book, "The De-Moralization of Society: From Victorian Virtues to Modern Values," which covered much of the same ground, claimed that our society was unraveling and predicted further unraveling as the Victorian virtues continued to erode.

Yet the truth is that some indicators of social dysfunction have improved dramatically even as traditional families continue to lose ground. As far as I can tell, Mr. Murray never mentions either the plunge in teenage pregnancies among all racial groups since 1990 or the 60 percent decline in violent crime since the mid-90s. Could it be that traditional families aren't as crucial to social cohesion as advertised?

Still, something is clearly happening to the traditional working-class family. The question is what. And it is, frankly, amazing how quickly and blithely conservatives dismiss the seemingly obvious answer: A drastic reduction in the work opportunities available to less-educated men.

Most of the numbers you see about income trends in America focus on households rather than individuals, which makes sense for some purposes. But when you see a modest rise in incomes for the lower tiers of the income distribution, you have to realize that all—yes, all—of this rise comes from the women, both because more women are in the paid labor force and because women's wages aren't as much below male wages as they used to be.

For lower-education working men, however, it has been all negative. Adjusted for inflation, entry-level wages of male high school graduates have fallen 23 percent since 1973. Meanwhile, employment benefits have collapsed. In 1980, 65 percent of recent high-school graduates working in the private sector had health benefits, but, by 2009, that was down to 29 percent.

So we have become a society in which less-educated men have great difficulty finding jobs with decent wages and good benefits. Yet somehow we're supposed to be surprised that such men have become less likely to participate in the work force or get married, and conclude that there must have been some mysterious moral collapse caused by snooty liberals. And Mr. Murray also tells us that working-class marriages, when they do happen, have become less happy; strange to say, money problems will do that.

One more thought: The real winner in this controversy is the distinguished sociologist William Julius Wilson.

Back in 1996, the same year Ms. Himmelfarb was lamenting our moral collapse, Mr. Wilson published "When Work Disappears: The New World of the Urban Poor," in which he argued that much of the social disruption among African-Americans popularly attributed to collapsing values was actually caused by a lack of blue-collar jobs in urban areas. If he was right, you would expect something similar to happen if another social group—say, working-class whites—experienced a comparable loss of economic opportunity. And so it has.

So we should reject the attempt to divert the national conversation away from soaring inequality toward the alleged moral failings of those Americans being left behind. Traditional values aren't as crucial as social conservatives would have you believe—and, in any case, the social changes taking place in America's working class are overwhelmingly the consequence of sharply rising inequality, not its cause.

C. Pluralism and Its Discontents _____

1. Justice Sandra Day O'Connor Approves Affirmative Action—for Now (2003)*

In the summer of 2003, university administrators around the nation anxiously awaited the U.S. Supreme Court's decision in the case of Grutter v. Bollinger. *The case challenged the constitutionality of admissions policies at the University of Michigan Law School, which took race into consideration when weighing the merits of applicants for admission. Twenty-five years earlier, the Court had considered a similar case in* Bakke v. Regents of the University of California. *The deciding opinion in that earlier case was penned by Justice Lewis Powell, who rejected California's version of affirmative action, but in the process signaled the Court's approval for other types of racial preferences that did not function as rigid "quotas." Within the space created by the* Bakke *decision, schools had developed creative admissions policies that held race as one among a number of relevant considerations in an applicant's profile. Drawing heavily from Powell's reasoning of a quarter-century earlier, the Court's majority opinion—written by Justice Sandra Day O'Connor—upheld the Michigan Law School's policy. What evidence supports her claim that the nation has a "compelling interest" in preserving diversity in education? What are the implications of her suggestion that twenty-five years hence such policies should no longer be necessary?*

Today, we hold that the Law School has a compelling interest in attaining a diverse student body....

...[The educational benefits of diversity] are substantial. As the District Court emphasized, the Law School's admissions policy promotes "cross-racial understanding," helps to break down racial stereotypes, and "enables [students] to better understand persons of different races." These benefits are "important and laudable," because "classroom discussion is livelier, more spirited, and simply more enlightening and interesting" when the students have "the greatest possible variety of backgrounds."

...In addition to the expert studies and reports entered into evidence at trial, numerous studies show that student body diversity promotes learning outcomes, and "better prepares students for an increasingly diverse workforce and society, and better prepares them as professionals."

These benefits are not theoretical but real, as major American businesses have made clear that the skills needed in today's increasingly global marketplace can only be developed through exposure to widely diverse people, cultures, ideas, and viewpoints. What is more, high-ranking retired officers and civilian leaders of the United States military assert that, "[b]ased on [their] decades of experience," a "highly qualified, racially diverse officer corps...is essential to the military's ability to fulfill its principle [*sic*] mission to provide national security."...We agree that "[i]t requires only a small step from this analysis to conclude that our country's other most selective institutions must remain both diverse and selective."

Grutter v. Bollinger, 123B S. CT. 2339–2341, 2346–2347 (2003).

We have repeatedly acknowledged the overriding importance of preparing students for work and citizenship, describing education as pivotal to "sustaining our political and cultural heritage" with a fundamental role in maintaining the fabric of society. This Court has long recognized that "education…is the very foundation of good citizenship." For this reason, the diffusion of knowledge and opportunity through public institutions of higher education must be accessible to all individuals regardless of race or ethnicity.…Effective participation by members of all racial and ethnic groups in the civil life of our Nation is essential if the dream of one Nation, indivisible, is to be realized.…

In order to cultivate a set of leaders with legitimacy in the eyes of the citizenry, it is necessary that the path to leadership be visibly open to talented and qualified individuals of every race and ethnicity.…Access to legal education (and thus the legal profession) must be inclusive of talented and qualified individuals of every race and ethnicity, so that all members of our heterogeneous society may participate in the educational institutions that provide the training and education necessary to succeed in America.

…Just as growing up in a particular region or having particular professional experiences is likely to affect an individual's views, so too is one's own, unique experience of being a racial minority in a society, like our own, in which race unfortunately still matters. The Law School has determined, based on its experience and expertise, that a "critical mass" of underrepresented minorities is necessary to further its compelling interest in securing the educational benefits of a diverse student body.…

We are mindful, however, that "[a] core purpose of the Fourteenth Amendment was to do away with all governmentally imposed discrimination based on race." Accordingly, race-conscious admissions policies must be limited in time. This requirement reflects that racial classifications, however compelling their goals, are potentially so dangerous that they may be employed no more broadly than the interest demands. Enshrining a permanent justification for racial preferences would offend this fundamental equal protection principle. We see no reason to exempt race-conscious admissions programs from the requirement that all governmental use of race must have a logical end point. The Law School, too, concedes that all "race-conscious programs must have reasonable durational limits."…

The requirement that all race-conscious admissions programs have a termination point "assure[s] all citizens that the deviation from the norm of equal treatment of all racial and ethnic groups is a temporary matter, a measure taken in the service of the goal of equality itself."…

We take the Law School at its word that it would "like nothing better than to find a race-neutral admissions formula" and will terminate its race-conscious admissions program as soon as practicable. It has been 25 years since [Supreme Court] Justice [Lewis] Powell first approved the use of race to further an interest in student body diversity in the context of public higher education. Since that time, the number of minority applicants with high grades and test scores has indeed increased. We expect that 25 years from now, the use of racial preferences will no longer be necessary to further the interest approved today.

2. *Justice Clarence Thomas Deems Affirmative Action Unconstitutional (2003)**

In the case of Grutter v. Bollinger, *Justice Clarence Thomas—the only African American then sitting on the nation's highest bench—dissented from the Court's majority opinion on a number of grounds. Among Thomas's arguments is the contention that racial preferences harm African Americans by removing the incentives for true achievement and stigmatizing the accomplishments of those who would have succeeded without preferential treatment. What are the merits, both psychological and political, of this argument? What are its weaknesses?*

Frederick Douglass,[†] speaking to a group of abolitionists almost 140 years ago, delivered a message lost on today's majority:

> ...The American people have always been anxious to know what they shall do with us....I have had but one answer from the beginning. Do nothing with us! Your doing with us has already played the mischief with us....And if the negro cannot stand on his own legs, let him fall also. All I ask is, give him a chance to stand on his own legs! Let him alone!...[Y]our interference is doing him positive injury.

Like Douglass, I believe blacks can achieve in every avenue of American life without the meddling of university administrators. Because I wish to see all students succeed whatever their color, I share, in some respect, the sympathies of those who sponsor the type of discrimination advanced by the University of Michigan Law School (Law School). The Constitution does not, however, tolerate institutional devotion to the status quo in admissions policies when such devotion ripens into racial discrimination....

The majority upholds the Law School's racial discrimination not by interpreting the people's Constitution, but by responding to a faddish slogan of the cognoscenti. Nevertheless, I concur in part in the Court's opinion. First, I agree with the Court insofar as its decision, which approves of only one racial classification, confirms that further use of race in admissions remains unlawful. Second, I agree with the Court's holding that racial discrimination in higher education admissions will be illegal in 25 years. I respectfully dissent from the remainder of the Court's opinion and the judgment, however, because I believe that the Law School's current use of race violates the Equal Protection Clause and that the Constitution means the same thing today as it will in 300 months....

The Constitution abhors classifications based on race, not only because those classifications can harm favored races or are based on illegitimate motives, but also because every time the government places citizens on racial registers and makes race relevant to the provision of burdens or benefits, it demeans us all....

...I believe what lies beneath the Court's decision today are the benighted notions that one can tell when racial discrimination benefits (rather than hurts) minority groups, and that racial discrimination is necessary to remedy general societal ills. This Court's precedents supposedly settled both issues, but clearly the majority still

---

Grutter v. Bollinger, 123B S. CT. 250–252, 260–262, 265 (2003).
[†]Douglass (1818–1895) was the most prominent African American of the nineteenth century. A leader of the antislavery cause, he later served as U.S. Minister to Haiti.

cannot commit to the principle that racial classifications are *per se* harmful and that almost no amount of benefit in the eye of the beholder can justify such classifications.

...I must contest the notion that the Law School's discrimination benefits those admitted as a result of it.... [N]owhere in any of the filings in this Court is any evidence that the purported "beneficiaries" of this racial discrimination prove themselves by performing at (or even near) the same level as those students who receive no preferences.

The silence in this case is deafening to those of us who view higher education's purpose as imparting knowledge and skills to students, rather than a communal, rubber-stamp, credentialing process. The Law School is not looking for those students who, despite a lower LSAT score or undergraduate grade point average, will succeed in the study of law. The Law School seeks only a facade—it is sufficient that the class looks right, even if it does not perform right.

The Law School tantalizes unprepared students with the promise of a University of Michigan degree and all of the opportunities that it offers. These overmatched students take the bait, only to find that they cannot succeed in the cauldron of competition....

It is uncontested that each year, the Law School admits a handful of blacks who would be admitted in the absence of racial discrimination. Who can differentiate between those who belong and those who do not? The majority of blacks are admitted to the Law School because of discrimination, and because of this policy all are tarred as undeserving. This problem of stigma does not depend on determinacy as to whether those stigmatized are actually the "beneficiaries" of racial discrimination. When blacks take positions in the highest places of government, industry, or academia, it is an open question today whether their skin color played a part in their advancement. The question itself is the stigma—because either racial discrimination did play a role, in which case the person may be deemed "otherwise unqualified," or it did not, in which case asking the question itself unfairly marks those blacks who would succeed without discrimination....

For the immediate future...the majority has placed its *imprimatur* on a practice that can only weaken the principle of equality embodied in the Declaration of Independence and the Equal Protection Clause. "Our Constitution is color-blind, and neither knows nor tolerates classes among citizens." It has been nearly 140 years since Frederick Douglass asked the intellectual ancestors of the Law School to "[d]o nothing with us!" and the Nation adopted the Fourteenth Amendment. Now we must wait another 25 years to see this principle of equality vindicated. I therefore respectfully dissent from the remainder of the Court's opinion and the judgment.

3. Barack Obama Reaches Across the Racial Divide (2008)*

Barack Obama's historic candidacy followed a centuries-long struggle to fulfill the egalitarian promise of the Declaration of Independence—a struggle launched by fearless abolitionists, advanced by Lincoln's Emancipation Proclamation, and accelerated by the transformative power of World War II. His political success was made possible by the grassroots protests and sit-ins of the civil rights movement,

---

*Barack Obama, "A More Perfect Union," March 18, 2008.

and by landmark federal initiatives such as the Civil Rights Act of 1964. But while his path-breaking candidacy and eventual victory signaled a decisive departure from the past, they also revealed a persistent racial divide. When furor erupted over controversial statements made by Obama's pastor and longtime mentor, the Reverend Jeremiah Wright, Obama met the issue head-on in an eloquent address that challenged Americans to confront directly the lingering resentment between whites and blacks that often went unstated but had nevertheless influenced political debates. What historical developments continue to shape the opportunities available to white and black Americans? How does Obama propose to break the stalemate over race in American society?

[R]ace is an issue that I believe this nation cannot afford to ignore right now. We would be making the same mistake that Reverend Wright made in his offending sermons about America—to simplify and stereotype and amplify the negative to the point that it distorts reality.

The fact is that the comments that have been made and the issues that have surfaced over the last few weeks reflect the complexities of race in this country that we've never really worked through—a part of our union that we have yet to perfect. And if we walk away now, if we simply retreat into our respective corners, we will never be able to come together and solve challenges like health care, or education, or the need to find good jobs for every American.

Understanding this reality requires a reminder of how we arrived at this point. As William Faulkner once wrote, "The past isn't dead and buried. In fact, it isn't even past." We do not need to recite here the history of racial injustice in this country. But we do need to remind ourselves that so many of the disparities that exist in the African-American community today can be directly traced to inequalities passed on from an earlier generation that suffered under the brutal legacy of slavery and Jim Crow.

Segregated schools were, and are, inferior schools; we still haven't fixed them, fifty years after *Brown* v. *Board of Education*, and the inferior education they provided, then and now, helps explain the pervasive achievement gap between today's black and white students.

Legalized discrimination—where blacks were prevented, often through violence, from owning property, or loans were not granted to African-American business owners, or black homeowners could not access FHA mortgages, or blacks were excluded from unions, or the police force, or fire departments—meant that black families could not amass any meaningful wealth to bequeath to future generations. That history helps explain the wealth and income gap between black and white, and the concentrated pockets of poverty that persists in so many of today's urban and rural communities.

A lack of economic opportunity among black men, and the shame and frustration that came from not being able to provide for one's family, contributed to the erosion of black families—a problem that welfare policies for many years may have worsened. And the lack of basic services in so many urban black neighborhoods—parks for kids to play in, police walking the beat, regular garbage pick-up and building code enforcement—all helped create a cycle of violence, blight and neglect that continue to haunt us....

[F]or all those who scratched and clawed their way to get a piece of the American Dream, there were many who didn't make it—those who were ultimately defeated, in one way or another, by discrimination. That legacy of defeat was passed on to future generations—those young men and increasingly young women who we see standing on street corners or languishing in our prisons, without hope or prospects for the future. Even for those blacks who did make it, questions of race, and racism, continue to define their worldview in fundamental ways. For the men and women of Reverend Wright's generation, the memories of humiliation and doubt and fear have not gone away; nor has the anger and the bitterness of those years. That anger may not get expressed in public, in front of white co-workers or white friends. But it does find voice in the barbershop or around the kitchen table. At times, that anger is exploited by politicians, to gin up votes along racial lines, or to make up for a politician's own failings....

In fact, a similar anger exists within segments of the white community. Most working- and middle-class white Americans don't feel that they have been particularly privileged by their race. Their experience is the immigrant experience—as far as they're concerned, no one's handed them anything, they've built it from scratch. They've worked hard all their lives, many times only to see their jobs shipped overseas or their pension dumped after a lifetime of labor. They are anxious about their futures, and feel their dreams slipping away; in an era of stagnant wages and global competition, opportunity comes to be seen as a zero sum game, in which your dreams come at my expense. So when they are told to bus their children to a school across town; when they hear that an African American is getting an advantage in landing a good job or a spot in a good college because of an injustice that they themselves never committed; when they're told that their fears about crime in urban neighborhoods are somehow prejudiced, resentment builds over time.

Like the anger within the black community, these resentments aren't always expressed in polite company. But they have helped shape the political landscape for at least a generation. Anger over welfare and affirmative action helped forge the Reagan Coalition. Politicians routinely exploited fears of crime for their own electoral ends. Talk show hosts and conservative commentators built entire careers unmasking bogus claims of racism while dismissing legitimate discussions of racial injustice and inequality as mere political correctness or reverse racism.

Just as black anger often proved counterproductive, so have these white resentments distracted attention from the real culprits of the middle class squeeze—a corporate culture rife with inside dealing, questionable accounting practices, and short-term greed; a Washington dominated by lobbyists and special interests; economic policies that favor the few over the many. And yet, to wish away the resentments of white Americans, to label them as misguided or even racist, without recognizing they are grounded in legitimate concerns—this too widens the racial divide, and blocks the path to understanding.

This is where we are right now. It's a racial stalemate we've been stuck in for years....

But I have asserted a firm conviction—a conviction rooted in my faith in God and my faith in the American people—that working together we can move beyond some of our old racial wounds, and that in fact we have no choice if we are to continue on the path of a more perfect union.

For the African-American community, that path means embracing the burdens of our past without becoming victims of our past. It means continuing to insist on a full measure of justice in every aspect of American life. But it also means binding our particular grievances—for better health care, and better schools, and better jobs—to the larger aspirations of all Americans—the white woman struggling to break the glass ceiling, the white man who's been laid off, the immigrant trying to feed his family. And it means taking full responsibility for our own lives—by demanding more from our fathers, and spending more time with our children, and reading to them, and teaching them that while they may face challenges and discrimination in their own lives, they must never succumb to despair or cynicism; they must always believe that they can write their own destiny....

In the white community, the path to a more perfect union means acknowledging that what ails the African-American community does not just exist in the minds of black people; that the legacy of discrimination—and current incidents of discrimination, while less overt than in the past—are real and must be addressed. Not just with words, but with deeds—by investing in our schools and our communities; by enforcing our civil rights laws and ensuring fairness in our criminal justice system; by providing this generation with ladders of opportunity that were unavailable for previous generations. It requires all Americans to realize that your dreams do not have to come at the expense of my dreams; that investing in the health, welfare, and education of black and brown and white children will ultimately help all of America prosper.

4. Changing Attitudes Toward Diversity (1937–2007)*

The unprecedented diversity of candidates in the 2008 presidential race prompted journalists and pollsters to ask if Americans were in fact ready to elect a president who did not fit the traditional mold—white, male, and with the exception of John F. Kennedy, Protestant. A 2007 poll revealed that while Americans had in fact become more tolerant of ethnic and religious diversity, certain groups continued to provoke unease. Why might some biases have proved more persistent than others? How might one explain the disparity between the figures in the two tables below?

If your party nominated a generally well-qualified person for president who happened to be ___, would you vote for that person?

Year	Black (% Yes)	Woman (% Yes)	Catholic (% Yes)	Jewish (% Yes)	Atheist (% Yes)	Homosexual (% Yes)
2007	94	88	95	92	45	55
1978	77	76	91	82	40	26
1958	38	54	67	63	18	—
1937	—	33	60	46	—	—

---

*Gallup Poll survey dates: February 9–11, 2007; July 21–24, 1978; September 10–15, 1958; January 27–February 1, 1937.

Generally speaking, do you think Americans are ready to elect a ___ as president, or not?

Year	Black (% Yes)	Woman (% Yes)	Jew (% Yes)	Atheist (% Yes)	Gay or Lesbian (% Yes)
09/2006	58	61	55	14	7

5. Cartoonists Cheer Obama's Victory (2008)

The election of Barack Obama as the nation's first African American president prompted Americans across the political spectrum to reflect on the meaning of his momentous achievement. How do the following cartoons address the historical significance of Obama's victory?

David Fitzsimmons/The Arizona Daily Star 2008/Cagle Cartoons Inc.

6. Arizona Sheriff Joe Arpaio Defends His Pursuit of Illegal Immigrants (2011)*

Joe Arpaio, the longtime sheriff in Arizona's Maricopa County, self-described as "America's toughest sheriff," began to attract national attention in 2005 with his vigorous crackdown on illegal immigrants. The United States Department of Justice eventually brought a lawsuit against him alleging racial discrimination and uncon-stitutional searches and seizures. In this document, Arpaio defends his policies in defiance of the federal action. How persuasive is he?

The following statements were made by Sheriff Joe Arpaio during a press con-ference held on 12/15/11 in response to the 22 page Department of Justice letter received 1 hour prior to DOJ press conference.

"Before we get started today, I want to say something to the citizens of Arizona and the rest of the nation.

On the surface, it may appear that today's findings and actions by our federal government are directed towards this Sheriff and the Maricopa County Sheriff's Office. The truth of the matter is that this is a sad day for America as a whole.

Today, the federal government moved to do everything it can to put this agency out of the illegal immigration enforcement business.

We are proud of the work we have done to fight illegal immigration. We have been responsible for finding and identifying 25% of the nation's illegal alien crimi-nal offenders through the 287G program. Sadly, much of that work will no longer be permitted by the Obama administration.

Today the federal government cancelled our 287 G agreement. What that means is that we are no longer able to verify the immigration status of any criminal offender brought into our jails. This was a program responsible for detecting over 44,000 illegal alien criminal offenders since 2007, many of whom we can assume were deported by ICE officials back to their country of origin.

Now with the cancellation of this agreement, illegal criminal offenders arrested and brought into my jails will go undetected and ultimately dumped back onto a street near you. For that, you can thank your federal government.

By their actions today, President Obama and his band of merry men might as well erect their very own pink neon sign at the Arizona-Mexico border saying Welcome All Illegals to your United States.... Our home is your home...."

7. Rolling Stone Magazine Interviews Sheriff Joe Arpaio (2012)†

Rolling Stone magazine profiled Sheriff Arpaio in 2012. What kind of a portrait emerges of the man and his polices? Is it fairly drawn?

---

*"Sheriff's Response to DOJ," Maricopa County Sheriff Office website, dated December 15, 2011, accessed March 20, 2014, http://www.mcso.org/MultiMedia/PressRelease/DOJ%20presser%20response%20121511.pdf.
†Excerpt from Joe Hagan, "The Long, Lawless Ride of Sheriff Joe Arpaio," *Rolling Stone*, no. 1163 (2012): 62–69. Copyright © Rolling Stone LLC 2012. All Rights Reserved. Used by Permission.

Joe Arpaio, the 80-year-old lawman who brands himself "America's toughest sheriff," is smiling like a delighted gnome. Nineteen floors above the blazing Arizona desert, the Phoenix sprawl ripples in the heat as Arpaio cues up the Rolling Stones to welcome a reporter "from that marijuana magazine."

Hey! You! Get off of my cloud!

The guided tour of Arpaio's legend has officially begun. Here, next to his desk, is the hand-painted sign of draconian rules for Tent City, the infamous jail he set up 20 years ago, in which some 2,000 inmates live under canvas tarps in the desert, forced to wear pink underwear beneath their black-and-white-striped uniforms while cracking rocks in the stifling heat. HARD LABOR, the sign reads. NO GIRLIE MAGAZINES . . . !

As Arizona has become center stage for the debate over illegal immigration and the civil rights of Latinos, Arpaio has sold himself as the symbol of nativist defiance, a modern-day Bull Connor bucking the federal government over immigration policy. As such, he's become the go-to media prop for conservative politicians, from state legislators to presidential candidates, who want to be seen as immigration hard-liners. . . .

His rhetoric and tactics have spread fear in the Latino community in Arizona. "They hate me, the Hispanic community, because they're afraid they're going to be arrested," Arpaio boasted to a TV interviewer in 2009. "And they're all leaving town, so I think we're doing something good, if they're leaving." But the all-consuming focus on immigration has come at a cost: Arpaio is so obsessed with the often illusory crimes of immigrants that he ignored more than 400 cases of sexual abuse he was responsible for investigating, including assaults on children. . . .

Yet such derelictions of duty haven't hurt Arpaio among the audience he cares about most. Since 1992, despite widespread criticism from human rights groups and local political leaders, Arpaio has been re-elected four times in Maricopa County, the most populous area of Arizona and a bastion of retirees and conservatives for whom Arpaio is a white knight, a defender of the 1950s Shangri-La they've sought to preserve in the largely white suburbs that ring Phoenix. "I'm kind of an old-fashioned guy," says Arpaio. . . .

Illegal immigration is a top concern among voters in Arizona, tied closely to fears of drugs, crime and unemployment. Maricopa, the fourth-largest county in America, is 50 miles from the Mexican border, but Phoenix, its major population center, is a destination for illegal immigrants and drug dealers alike. Thirty percent of the county's residents are Hispanic, and their numbers are soaring—up 47 percent over the past decade. But the money and political power in Maricopa still reside in the largely white and conservative suburbs around Phoenix.

It is those whites and conservatives, as it happens, who employ many of the illegal immigrants targeted by Arpaio. But the sheriff is careful to steer clear of the white owners who profit from exploiting immigrant labor. In his 20 years wearing the badge, in fact, Arpaio has busted only three businesses for hiring illegal immigrants. "You've got to prove that they knew," he says, "and it's very difficult." Instead, Arpaio goes after the undocumented workers they hire, notifying the media every time he rounds up Latino fruit pickers or factory laborers. In the process, according to the Justice Department, Arpaio has frequently arrested and detained U.S. citizens and legal residents of Latino origin, including children, for hours at a time without a charge or a warrant.

Jailing Mexicans, of course, is what sells to his base. In an influential retirement community like Sun City, where the median age is 73, Arpaio serves as an armed security cop keeping out the riffraff. And he's not alone: All of the most prominent Republican politicians in the state, including Gov. Jan Brewer, have risen to power by inflaming anti-immigrant sentiment. They blame the Obama administration for failing to crack down on illegal immigrants, even though deportation has spiked under Obama. And contrary to their overheated rhetoric, there's almost no relationship between illegal immigration and crime. "Illegal immigrants make up less than 10 percent of those arrested," says Charles Katz, a professor of criminology at Arizona State University who conducts annual studies on crime in Maricopa County. "They're involved in less criminal activity than native-born Americans." Illegal immigrants, the studies show, are twice as likely to be employed than U.S. citizens and half as likely to use illegal drugs—yet thanks to Arpaio's tactics, they're far more likely to be arrested for drug offenses.

But Arpaio doesn't care about the complicated realities of immigration. For him, the equation is simple: Fear equals votes. While I'm with him, he happily trumpets reports that Mexican drug cartels and prison gangs are offering a reward for his head—proof, in his mind, of his effectiveness, and evidence that the Latino community harbors criminals. "He's vilified Latinos in such a way that normal people, they're scared to death," says Bill Richardson, a retired police officer. Such terror, in turn, only makes it harder for the police to do their jobs. "It creates fear in the Latino community for law enforcement," he says....

The role of sheriff retains a powerful hold on the public imagination in Arizona.... Arpaio, in addition to his savvy media stunts, makes a point of calling himself a "constitutional" sheriff, emphasizing his lofty mandate to uphold the U.S. Constitution—a political dog whistle to states' rights advocates and white supremacists who have a deep-seated hatred of the federal government....

On two separate occasions, he's made a point of telling me that when he enters a Mexican restaurant, the staff runs out the back door—his idea of a joke about illegal immigrants working in kitchens. When I ask him to show me, he agrees—even insisting his deputies take us to a "dangerous" restaurant. Instead, we drive to a chain place called Garcia's, where Arpaio is greeted as a conquering hero by aging white diners with dentures and canes. A silver-haired man with Pall Malls in his pocket flags Arpaio at the entrance: "'Sup, Joe. Good to see you!"

When a Latina waitress brings Arpaio his iced tea, he eyeballs it suspiciously. "Is it safe?" he asks, tilting his head toward the kitchen. "Anybody recognize me in there?" Then he whispers out of the side of his mouth: "Don't tell the cook I'm here."

"I just know we lost half of the employees," the waitress laughs, clearly in on the staff-running-out-the-back-door joke....

Arpaio envisions himself being sheriff of Maricopa County well into his nineties, his 50-caliber pistol strapped to his wheelchair. The formula is clear: Keep stirring controversy, keep stoking the media, keep raking in the campaign contributions from far-flung donors. Just put on a show.

Hey! You! Get off of my cloud!

"After your article," promises Arpaio, "I'll probably get another $2 million."

D. The Gay Rights Revolution _____

1. The Supreme Court Invalidates the Defense of Marriage Act (DOMA) (2013)*

In a seismic cultural shift virtually unmatched for its speed and pervasiveness, many—but not all—Americans in the early twentieth century embraced tolerance of gays and lesbians, and accepted the legitimacy of same-sex marriage. In a landmark case in 2013, Supreme Court Justice Anthony Kennedy wrote the majority opinion for the Court's decision invalidating key parts of the 1996 federal Defense of Marriage Act (DOMA), opening the door to states that cared to validate same-sex marriages (which 17 had done by 2014). On what grounds does he chiefly rest his argument?

Justice Anthony Kennedy for the majority:

Two women then resident in New York were married in a lawful ceremony in Ontario, Canada, in 2007. Edith Windsor and Thea Spyer returned to their home in New York City. When Spyer died in 2009, she left her entire estate to Windsor. Windsor sought to claim the estate tax exemption for surviving spouses. She was barred from doing so, however, by a federal law, the Defense of Marriage Act, which excludes a same-sex partner from the definition of "spouse" as that term is used in federal statutes. Windsor paid the taxes but filed suit to challenge the constitutionality of this provision. The United States District Court and the Court of Appeals ruled that this portion of the statute is unconstitutional and ordered the United States to pay Windsor a refund. This Court granted certiorari and now affirms the judgment in Windsor's favor.

When at first Windsor and Spyer longed to marry, neither New York nor any other State granted them that right. After waiting some years, in 2007 they traveled to Ontario to be married there. It seems fair to conclude that, until recent years, many citizens had not even considered the possibility that two persons of the same sex might aspire to occupy the same status and dignity as that of a man and woman in lawful marriage. For marriage between a man and a woman no doubt had been thought of by most people as essential to the very definition of that term and to its role and function throughout the history of civilization. That belief, for many who long have held it, became even more urgent, more cherished when challenged. For others, however, came the beginnings of a new perspective, a new insight. Accordingly some States concluded that same-sex marriage ought to be given recognition and validity in the law for those same-sex couples who wish to define themselves by their commitment to each other. The limitation of lawful marriage to heterosexual couples, which for centuries had been deemed both necessary and fundamental, came to be seen in New York and certain other States as an unjust exclusion.

Slowly at first and then in rapid course, the laws of New York came to acknowledge the urgency of this issue for same-sex couples who wanted to affirm their commitment to one another before their children, their family, their friends, and their community. And so New York recognized same-sex marriages performed

---

*United States v. Windsor 570 U.S. ____ (2013).

elsewhere; and then it later amended its own marriage laws to permit same-sex marriage. New York, in common with, as of this writing, 11 other States and the District of Columbia, decided that same-sex couples should have the right to marry and so live with pride in themselves and their union and in a status of equality with all other married persons. After a statewide deliberative process that enabled its citizens to discuss and weigh arguments for and against same-sex marriage, New York acted to enlarge the definition of marriage to correct what its citizens and elected representatives perceived to be an injustice that they had not earlier known or understood. Against this background of lawful same-sex marriage in some States, the design, purpose, and effect of DOMA should be considered as the beginning point in deciding whether it is valid under the Constitution. By history and tradition the definition and regulation of marriage, as will be discussed in more detail, has been treated as being within the authority and realm of the separate States. Yet it is further established that Congress, in enacting discrete statutes, can make determinations that bear on marital rights and privileges....

DOMA seeks to injure the very class New York seeks to protect.... The Act's demonstrated purpose is to ensure that if any State decides to recognize same-sex marriages, those unions will be treated as second-class marriages for purposes of federal law. This raises a most serious question under the Constitution's Fifth Amendment.

DOMA's principal effect is to identify a subset of state-sanctioned marriages and make them unequal. The principal purpose is to impose inequality, not for other reasons like governmental efficiency. Responsibilities, as well as rights, enhance the dignity and integrity of the person. And DOMA contrives to deprive some couples married under the laws of their State, but not other couples, of both rights and responsibilities. By creating two contradictory marriage regimes within the same State, DOMA forces same-sex couples to live as married for the purpose of state law but unmarried for the purpose of federal law, thus diminishing the stability and predictability of basic personal relations the State has found it proper to acknowledge and protect. By this dynamic DOMA undermines both the public and private significance of state-sanctioned same-sex marriages; for it tells those couples, and all the world, that their otherwise valid marriages are unworthy of federal recognition. This places same-sex couples in an unstable position of being in a second-tier marriage. The differentiation demeans the couple, whose moral and sexual choices the Constitution protects..., and whose relationship the State has sought to dignify. And it humiliates tens of thousands of children now being raised by same-sex couples. The law in question makes it even more difficult for the children to understand the integrity and closeness of their own family and its concord with other families in their community and in their daily lives....

What has been explained to this point should more than suffice to establish that the principal purpose and the necessary effect of this law are to demean those persons who are in a lawful same-sex marriage. This requires the Court to hold, as it now does, that DOMA is unconstitutional as a deprivation of the liberty of the person protected by the Fifth Amendment of the Constitution....

The class to which DOMA directs its restrictions and restraints are those persons who are joined in same-sex marriages made lawful by the State. DOMA singles out a class of persons deemed by a State entitled to recognition and protection to enhance their own liberty. It imposes a disability on the class by refusing to acknowledge a status the State finds to be dignified and proper. DOMA instructs all federal officials, and indeed all persons with whom same-sex couples interact, including their own children, that their marriage is less worthy than the marriages of others. The federal statute is invalid, for no legitimate purpose overcomes the purpose and effect to disparage and to injure those whom the State, by its marriage laws, sought to protect in personhood and dignity. By seeking to displace this protection and treating those persons as living in marriages less respected than others, the federal statute is in violation of the Fifth Amendment. This opinion and its holding are confined to those lawful marriages.

The judgment of the Court of Appeals for the Second Circuit is affirmed.

It is so ordered.

2. Justice Antonin Scalia Dissents (2013)[*]

In a characteristically trenchant and colorful opinion, Supreme Court Justice Antonin Scalia vigorously dissented from Justice Kennedy's majority view in United States v. Windsor. *What are his most effective counterarguments?*

This case is about power in several respects. It is about the power of our people to govern themselves, and the power of this Court to pronounce the law. Today's opinion aggrandizes the latter, with the predictable consequence of diminishing the former. We have no power to decide this case. And even if we did, we have no power under the Constitution to invalidate this democratically adopted legislation. The Court's errors on both points spring forth from the same diseased root: an exalted conception of the role of this institution in America. . . .

[T]he majority says that the supporters of this Act acted with malice—with the "purpose" "to disparage and to injure" same-sex couples. It says that the motivation for DOMA was to "demean," to "impose inequality," to "impose . . . a stigma," to deny people "equal dignity," to brand gay people as "unworthy," and to "humiliat[e]" their children.

I am sure these accusations are quite untrue. To be sure (as the majority points out), the legislation is called the Defense of Marriage Act. But to defend traditional marriage is not to condemn, demean, or humiliate those who would prefer other arrangements, any more than to defend the Constitution of the United States is to condemn, demean, or humiliate other constitutions. To hurl such accusations so casually demeans this institution. In the majority's judgment, any resistance to its holding is beyond the pale of reasoned disagreement. To question its high-handed invalidation of a presumptively valid statute is to act (the majority is sure) with the purpose to "dis-parage," "injure," "degrade," "demean," and "humiliate" our fellow human beings, our fellow citizens, who are homosexual. All that, simply for supporting an Act that did no more than codify an aspect of marriage that had been unquestioned in our society for most of its existence—indeed, had been unquestioned in virtually all societies for virtually all of human history. It is one thing for a society to elect change; it is another for a court of law to impose change

[*]*United States v. Windsor* 570 U.S. (2013).

by adjudging those who oppose it *hostes humani generis*, enemies of the human race....

The penultimate sentence of the majority's opinion is a naked declaration that "[t]his opinion and its holding are confined" to those couples "joined in same-sex marriages made lawful by the State." Ante, at 26, 25. I have heard such "bald, unreasoned disclaimer[s]" before. Lawrence, 539 U. S., at 604. When the Court declared a constitutional right to homosexual sodomy, we were assured that the case had nothing, nothing at all to do with "whether the government must give formal recognition to any relationship that homosexual persons seek to enter." Id., at 578. Now we are told that DOMA is invalid because it "demeans the couple, whose moral and sexual choices the Constitution protects," ante, at 23—with an accompanying citation of Lawrence. It takes real cheek for today's majority to assure us, as it is going out the door, that a constitutional requirement to give formal recognition to same-sex marriage is not at issue here—when what has preceded that assurance is a lecture on how superior the majority's moral judgment in favor of same-sex marriage is to the Congress's hateful moral judgment against it. I promise you this: The only thing that will "confine" the Court's holding is its sense of what it can get away with.

In my opinion, however, the view that this Court will take of state prohibition of same-sex marriage is indicated beyond mistaking by today's opinion. As I have said, the real rationale of today's opinion, whatever disappearing trail of its legalistic argle-bargle one chooses to follow, is that DOMA is motivated by "bare...desire to harm" couples in same-sex marriages. Supra, at 18. How easy it is, indeed how inevitable, to reach the same conclusion with regard to state laws denying same-sex couples marital status....

In sum, that Court which finds it so horrific that Congress irrationally and hatefully robbed same-sex couples of the "personhood and dignity" which state legislatures conferred upon them, will of a certitude be similarly appalled by state legislatures' irrational and hateful failure to acknowledge that "personhood and dignity" in the first place. As far as this Court is concerned, no one should be fooled; it is just a matter of listening and waiting for the other shoe....

By formally declaring anyone opposed to same-sex marriage an enemy of human decency, the majority arms well every challenger to a state law restricting marriage to its traditional definition. Henceforth those challengers will lead with this Court's declaration that there is "no legitimate purpose" served by such a law, and will claim that the traditional definition has "the purpose and effect to disparage and to injure" the "personhood and dignity" of same-sex couples. The majority's limiting assurance will be meaningless in the face of language like that, as the majority well knows. That is why the language is there. The result will be a judicial distortion of our society's debate over marriage—a debate that can seem in need of our clumsy "help" only to a member of this institution.

As to that debate: Few public controversies touch an institution so central to the lives of so many, and few inspire such attendant passion by good people on all sides. Few public controversies will ever demonstrate so vividly the beauty of what our Framers gave us, a gift the Court pawns today to buy its stolen moment in the spotlight: a system of government that permits us to rule ourselves. Since DOMA's passage, citizens on all sides of the question have seen victories and they have seen defeats. There have been plebiscites, legislation, persuasion, and loud voices—in other words, democracy....

In the majority's telling, this story is black-and-white: Hate your neighbor or come along with us. The truth is more complicated. It is hard to admit that one's political opponents are not monsters, especially in a struggle like this one, and the challenge in the end proves more than today's Court can handle. Too bad. A reminder that disagreement over something so fundamental as marriage can still be politically legitimate would have been a fit task for what in earlier times was called the judicial temperament. We might have covered ourselves with honor today, by promising all sides of this debate that it was theirs to settle and that we would respect their resolution. We might have let the People decide.

But that the majority will not do. Some will rejoice in today's decision, and some will despair at it; that is the nature of a controversy that matters so much to so many. But the Court has cheated both sides, robbing the winners of an honest victory, and the losers of the peace that comes from a fair defeat. We owed both of them better. I dissent.

Thought Provokers

1. Was the American invasion of Iraq in 2003 justified? What impact did Saddam Hussein's removal have on the security of the United States? Did the Iraqi people benefit or suffer as a result of Hussein's fall? Did the "war against terror" strengthen or weaken America's global standing and influence?
2. What have been the principal forces driving inequality in America and elsewhere in the last several decades? Is the trend reversible? How?
3. How has America historically managed its famously broad racial, ethnic, religious, and gender diversity? How and why have attitudes about such matters changed in the last generation or two?
4. The family has often been called the basic building block of society. Do modern families fill that role in the same way that families did in the past? Do the circumstances of modern family life suggest major changes pending in the character of society at large?

Index